Orion Financial Corp. used its experience and expertise to successfully complete these transactions for the benefit of its clients.

To discuss your financial service needs with complete confidentiality, contact an experienced Orion Financial Corp. principal in our Minneapolis or Sioux Falls offices. You will receive a prompt response from one of our professionals.

WADENA SAW MILLS
Wadena, Minnesota
a division of J. Scott Industries, Inc.

has been acquired by

UNITED BUILDING CENTERS
United Building Centers
Winona, Minnesota

Orion Financial Corp.
initiated and negotiated this transaction and acted as financial advisor to J. Scott Industries, Inc.

ORION FINANCIAL CORP.
has arranged mezzanine financing for
Nevada Gold & Casinos, Inc.
Houston, Texas

The principals of Orion Financial Corp. initiated, structured, and negotiated the mezzanine financing, and participated as investors in the transaction.

BMD COMPANY, INC.
Klemme, Iowa
A Company controlled by the Principals of Orion Financial Corp.

has been acquired by

A&I Products, Inc.
Rock Valley, Iowa

Orion Financial Corp. initiated and negotiated this transaction and acted as financial advisor to BMD Company, Inc.

Food Ingredient Processor

ORION FINANCIAL CORP.
has arranged $5,000,000 in mezzanine financing to fund growth for a Midwest-based food ingredient processor

Orion Financial Corp. initiated and negotiated the mezzanine financing, and acted as financial advisor in this transaction.

MINNEAPOLIS OFFICE

Alan R. Geiwitz
Lenard D. Brinson
Joseph G. Kimmel

Orion Financial Corp.
333 South Seventh Street
Suite 2530
Minneapolis, MN 55402

Phone: (612) 339-6171
Fax: (612) 339-1419

All the right resources to get the results you want.

SIOUX FALLS OFFICE

Troy Jones

Orion Financial Corp.
3400 West 49th Street
Suite 204
Sioux Falls, SD 57106

Phone: (605) 323-1671
Fax: (605) 323-1673

For more information, visit us online at www.orionfinancial.com

FACT BOOK

2001 Edition

The directory of business in the Upper Midwest

Fact Book 2001
Published in December 2000 by CityBusiness, The Business Journal

CityBusiness
The Business Journal

527 Marquette Ave. South • Suite 300 • Minneapolis MN 55402

612.288.2100

 ISBN 0-934070-55-5

FACT BOOK

2001 EDITION

Publisher
Lisa Bormaster

Executive Editor
Beth Ewen

Editor
Tom Smith

Research
Melissa Metzler

Copy Editor
Michelle Franta

Art Director
Jonathan I. Hankin

Designer
Jorge Zegarra

Marketing Director
Maureen Tubbs

Special Events Manager
Suzanne Kessler

Circulation Manager
Kristie Hook

Associate Ad Director
Alison Simons

Account Manager
Wes Bergstrom

Advertising Sales
Sherrie Bryant
Terri C. Johnson
Alison Simons

Advertising Coordinator
Liz Goembel

Stat Man illustrations by John Bush

CONTENTS

GUIDE TO ABBREVIATIONS

Admin — Administration
Aff — Affairs
Agt — Agent
Assn — Association
Assoc — Associates
Asst — Asssistant
AVP — Assistant Vice President
BA — Bachelor of Arts
Bd — Board
BS — Bachelor of Science
Bus — Business
CEO — Chief Executive Officer
CFO — Chief Financial Officer
Chm — Chairman
CIO — Chief Information Officer
Co — Company
Coll — College
Comm — Communications
Comml — Commercial
Cont — Controller
COO — Chief Operating Officer
Corp — Corporation
Ctee — Committee
dba — doing business as
Devel — Development
Dir — Director
Dist — District
Distrib — Distribution
Dup — Duplication
DVP — Division Vice President
Ed — Editor
Engr — Engineer
Engrg — Engineering
Eqt — Equipment
est — estimated
EVP — Executive Vice President
Exec — Executive
Fdn — Foundation
Fed — Federal/Federation
Fin — Finance
FVP — First Vice President
Gen —General
GM — General Manager
Gov — Governors
GVP — Group Vice President
Hum — Human
Inc — Incorporated
Indl — Industrial
Ins — Insurance
Intl — International
JD — Juris Doctor
MBA — Master of Business Administration
Mdse — Merchandise
Mem — Member
Mfg — Manufacturing
Mgmt — Management
Mgr — Manager
Mkt — Market
Mktg — Marketing
Mng — Managing
NA — not available
Natl — National
nec — not elsewhere classified
NM — not meaningful
OEM — original-equipment manufacturer
Op — Operations
Pers — Personnel
PhD — Doctor of Philosophy
Plng — Planning
Pres — President
Prod — Production
Proj — Project
proj — projected
Ptnr — Partner
Pub — Public
Purch — Purchasing
R&D — Research and Development
Reg — Regional
Rel — Relations
Res — Resources
RVP — Regional Vice President
Sec — Secretary
Sls — Sales
Supt — Superintendent
Supv — Supervisor
Svc — Service
SVP — Senior Vice President
Svcs — Services
Syst — System(s)
U/Univ — University
VChm — Vice Chairman
VP — Vice President

EDITOR'S NOTE

Let me address the most obvious difference this year — the name. In accordance with the discontinuing of Corporate Report magazine, what was called the Corporate Report Fact Book for its first 32 editions is now simply the Fact Book.

In the November 2000 (final) issue of Corporate Report, the magazine's editor, Beth Ewen, explained why we've re-deployed our magazine resources to Ventures. "We're seeing the small-business sector of the economy exploding, while the big corporations merge and consolidate," she wrote.

Long a barometer of the large corporations residing in the Upper Midwest, the Fact Book can surely shed some light on this issue. Counts of the public companies profiled in the Fact Book, although widely reported over the years, have never been formalized.

Enter Stat Man. As he waded through 13 years of add-and-drop data, Stat kept a running total of the number of public companies in the district. The chart you see here is the result of those efforts.

When I took over the reins as Fact Book editor in 1988, the count stood at 357. By the time Stat Man arrived, three years later, the count had dropped to exactly 300. Buoyed by Stat's ministrations, not to mention a minor technology boom, the count hovered around 300 throughout most of the '90s. But in spite of his best efforts, Stat has witnessed a precipitous two-year drop in the number of public companies. You can find explanations for the current year's drops on pages 114-115.

These are the cold, hard facts that prompted the call for business unit resource re-deployment. (Look at how, after 13 years of reading press releases, I've learned to string nouns together like there's no ...)

"Tomorrow?" an agitated Stat interjected. "Will there be a tomorrow for us?"

You can't blame the little guy for feeling uneasy. With the folding of Corporate Report, Stat's venue had been snatched away from him. However, Ewen has assured him that there will be room for his pithy comments about Y2K's mergers and acquisitions in the March 2, 2001, issue of CityBusiness.

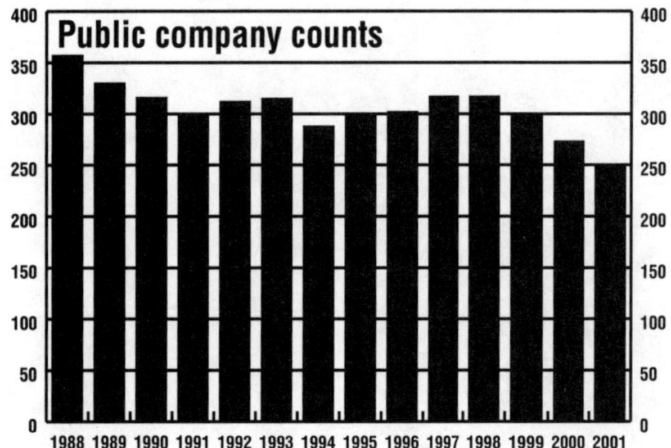

His next appearance guaranteed, a relieved Stat returned his attention to the Fact Book. "If the count is down so much," he challenged, "why hasn't our job gotten any easier?"

The short answer: more coverage of what's left. Since those days when we followed 357 companies, our public company presentation has expanded to include the following items:

- six introductory pages to help you navigate the section
- fax numbers and Web site, reflections of technological advances
- rolling eight quarters' worth of results, ending in September
- second balance sheet, for comparability
- extensive footnoting to help interpret the financial data
- background of directors (who's steering the ship)
- list of 5% shareholders (who owns the ship)
- Minnesota rankings that put each company in its place
- two-year stock chart, just like the ones in the annual reports
- recent events that have become so extensive they over-flow onto jump pages

As you can see, there's no shortage of useful information to be reported in the Fact Book. Be assured that we will continue reporting that information on an annual basis, just under a different name.

Stat Man, fluttering with anticipation, asked, "What name is that, exactly?"

The answer disappointed him. He, of course, wanted it to be called the Stat Book. Needless to say, that was one suggestion that didn't get passed along. Until now.

— Tom Smith
Fact Book editor
aka Stat Man

photograph by Diana Watters

The Ninth Federal Reserve District

Creation of the Federal Reserve System in 1914 divided what then made up the United States into 12 geographic regions. Each region was to have a Federal Reserve Bank built in its principle city to serve the commercial and banking needs of its designated "trade area." The arbitrary division was the subject of much argument. In the Ninth District, it was hotly debated whether Montana should be included or, instead, added to a West Coast district; and whether 26 northwestern Wisconsin counties and Michigan's Upper Peninsula should belong instead to the Seventh District (Chicago). Such arguments were settled by determining where most of a disputed area's checks were cleared and where wholesale trade connections were made. The Ninth District, with its Reserve Bank in Minneapolis and a branch bank in Helena, Montana, won both disputed areas.

Today the Ninth Federal Reserve District appears as shown on the map below. It was chosen as the geographic basis for the Fact Book because it closely approximates an "Upper Midwest" trade region, and because much economic information is compiled using Federal Reserve Districts as reporting entities.

NINTH DISTRICT

INTRODUCTION

This is the 33rd edition of the Fact Book, a comprehensive book of business in the Upper Midwest. The Ninth Federal Reserve District, headquartered in Minneapolis, is the geographic base for this directory. The district includes Minnesota, North Dakota, South Dakota, Montana, the 26 northwestern counties of Wisconsin and the Upper Peninsula of Michigan.

The Fact Book includes publicly owned companies in the Ninth District, private companies and non-profit organizations with 50 or more employees, and many companies that are headquartered outside the Ninth District but have operations employing 50 or more people here. The book also contains biographical sketches of top area business leaders in the Who's Who section.

Listings are prefaced by:

- **Public and private rankings by Fortune and Forbes that provide a national perspective for Ninth District companies.**
- **Business rankings from the pages of Corporate Report Magazine that sort Minnesota companies by size and performance in various categories.**
- **A five-year index to articles published in Corporate Report Magazine.**

This directory also contains a table of public company executive compensation, and indexes that sort companies by SIC code, zip code, and alphabetic order.

Data is based on information provided by the companies and individuals listed. Facts were gathered from annual reports, 10-K and 10-Q reports, prospectuses, proxy statements, shareholder letters, press releases, news items, and standard business reference publications. Those facts were then verified through several mailings, faxes and phone calls.

The Fact Book is a reference source and is not intended to be the sole basis for investment decisions. While every effort has been made to provide dependable data, the publisher cannot guarantee complete accuracy.

The Fact Book is published by CityBusiness, a subsidiary of American City Business Journals Inc., a privately held, independent publishing company not affiliated with any brokerage firm or investment sales organization. We welcome your comments and suggestions.

TOP RANK

BUSINESS RANKINGS

Later in the directory, the core listings of the companies in the Fact Book are presented alphabetically within the major groupings Public, Private, and Regional. But because some Fact Book users may wish to quickly identify the largest companies, we begin by presenting certain published lists that are ordered by company size.

With this section, users can quickly identify the largest companies in our district, by both revenue and employment, without examining each successive entry in the Fact Book.

Use it as a guide for selecting the appropriate companies for further research, or for targeting the best prospects for mailings or personal contacts.

NATIONAL RANKINGS

We have clipped all of the Ninth Federal Reserve District companies from the business rankings of two nationally recognized business magazines in order to highlight how the Upper Midwest sizes up against the rest of the United States.

CORPORATE REPORT RANKINGS

From Corporate Report Minnesota (CRM) magazine comes a compilation of research lists ranking Minnesota-based companies, organizations, and their executives in various categories.

Each list has a traditional month for its initial presentation in CRM. The lists that have been reprinted here first appeared in 2000 in the following months:

April	Public 200
May	Private 100, Cooperative/Mutual 20
June	IPO 80
July	Compensation 100
August	Employer 100
September	Foreign-owned 100
October	Performance 100
November	Nonprofit 100, 50 Highest-paid execs

SYMBOLS

•: Not on previous year's list

e: estimate

*: includes one-time gain or loss exceeding 10 percent

NA: not available

NC: no change

TOP RANK

FORBES PRIVATE 500

2000

RANK	COMPANY	REVENUE (MILLIONS)
1.	Cargill	48,000
27.	Menard	4,500
42.	Schwan's Sales Enterprises	3,350
87.	Carlson Cos.	1,950
126.	Andersen	1,500
167.	Taylor	1,300
206.	Holiday Cos.	1,100
253.	MA Mortenson	968
266.	Buffets	937
289.	Genmar Holdings	858
353.	Washington Cos.	750
389.	Lifetouch	700
391.	Rosen's Diversified	700
450.	Merrill	610
451.	Kraus-Anderson	610
487.	Johnson Brothers Wholesale Liquor	575
499.	Coborn's	561

FORTUNE 500

2000

RANK	COMPANY	REVENUE (MILLIONS)
32.	Target	33,702.0
86.	UnitedHealth Group	19,562.0
99.	Supervalu	17,420.5
110.	3M	15,659.0
125.	IBP	14,075.2
165.	Northwest Airlines	10,276.0
169.	Best Buy	10,077.9
204.	St. Paul Cos.	8641.0
212.	U.S. Bancorp	8435.4
279.	General Mills	6246.1
381.	Medtronic	4134.1
383.	Nash Finch	4123.2
458.	Hormel	3357.8

The public 200 APRIL 2000

CURRENT RANK	PRIOR RANK	COMPANY	SYMBOL	REVENUE ($000)	REVENUE CHANGE (%)	EARNINGS ($000)
1	1	**Target Corp.*** • Minneapolis • (612) 370-6948 Retail discount and department stores.	TGT	33,702,000	+9.9	1,144,000
2	3	**UnitedHealth Group** • Minnetonka • (952) 936-1300 Management of health care delivery systems and HMOs.	UNH	19,562,000	+12.7	568,000
3	2	**Supervalu Inc.** • Eden Prairie • (952) 828-4000 Wholesale foods; operating of supermarkets.	SVU	18,998,144	+8.5	225,237 *
4	4	**3M Co.** • Maplewood • (651) 733-1110 Diversified industrial and consumer products.	MMM	15,659,000	+4.2	1,763,000
5	5	**Best Buy Co. Inc.** • Eden Prairie • (952) 947-2000 Consumer electronics; major appliances; factory warranty services.	BBY	11,639,983	+22.9	294,873
6	7	**Northwest Airlines Corp.** • Eagan • (612) 726-2111 Passenger airline; international cargo carrier.	NWAC	10,276,000	+13.6	300,000
7	9	**U.S. Bancorp** • Minneapolis • (612) 973-1111 Bank holding company; diversified financial services.	USB	8,435,400	+10.1	1,506,500
8	6	**The St. Paul Cos. Inc.** • St. Paul • (651) 310-7911 Insurance and risk management; property/liability underwriting; reinsurance.	SPC	7,569,000	-2.2	834,400 *
9	10	**General Mills Inc.** • Golden Valley • (763) 764-2311 Consumer foods.	GIS	6,486,400	+5.8	598,100
10	12	**Medtronic Inc.** • Fridley • (763) 514-4000 Pacemakers, heart valves, angioplasty catheters, cardiopulmonary, neurological products, etc.	MDT	4,728,911	+16.3	936,763 *
11	11	**Nash Finch Co.** • Edina • (952) 832-0534 Wholesale and retail foods and general merchandise distribution.	NAFC	4,123,217	-0.9	19,803 *
12	13	**Hormel Foods Corp.** • Austin • (507) 437-5611 Processed and packaged meats and food products.	HRL	3,462,665	+6.7	164,906
13	14	**ReliaStar Financial Corp.** • Minneapolis • (612) 372-5432 Life and health insurance and annuities.	RLR	3,037,300	+6.6	253,600 *
14	15	**Northern States Power Co.** • Minneapolis • (612) 330-5500 Gas and electric utilities; non-regulated energy services.	NSP	2,901,229	+2.9	224,336
15	19	**Pentair Inc.** • Roseville • (651) 636-7920 Portable power tools; woodworking machinery; electrical and electronic enclosures.	PNR	2,367,752	+22.2	103,309 *
16	16	**International Multifoods Corp.** • Wayzata • (952) 594-3300 Diversified food products for foodservice, industrial, retail and agricultural customers.	IMC	2,362,916	+3.9	2,730 *
17	18	**C.H. Robinson Worldwide Inc.** • Eden Prairie • (952) 937-8500 Third-party transportation, produce distribution, financial services.	CHRW	2,261,027	+10.9	53,349
18	43	**Dura Automotive Systems Inc.** • Minneapolis • (612) 342-2311 Mechanical assemblies and integrated systems for the automotive industry.	DRRA	2,200,385	+197.6	41,220 *
19	24	**Tower Automotive Inc.** • Minneapolis • (612) 342-2310 Metal stampings and assemblies for automobile industry.	TWR	2,170,003	+18.2	117,088
20	21	**Ecolab Inc.** • St. Paul • (651) 293-2233 Chemical products and systems for cleaning, sanitation.	ECL	2,080,012	+10.2	175,786
21	25	**ADC Telecommunications Inc.** • Minnetonka • (952) 938-8080 Transmission, networking and broadband connectivity products for telecommunications networks.	ADCT	2,067,287	+24.5	153,645 *
22	22	**Bemis Co. Inc.** • Minneapolis • (612) 376-3000 Flexible packaging materials; specialty-coated and graphics products.	BMS	1,918,025	+3.8	114,775
23	23	**Musicland Stores Corp.** • Minnetonka • (952) 931-8000 Retailing of prerecorded music and video.	MLG	1,891,828	+2.4	58,380
24	20	**Deluxe Corp.** • Shoreview • (651) 483-7111 Bank checks; financial and business forms; financial services; software.	DLX	1,650,500	-14.6	203,022
25	27	**The Valspar Corp.** • Minneapolis • (612) 332-7371 Paints, coatings, stains, varnishes and specialty products.	VAL	1,445,538	+20.9	83,881

Footnotes corresponding to the asterisks in the chart are listed by company rank. All dollars are in thousands. Figures are after-tax unless otherwise indicated. NA: not available. •not on last year's list.

1 Previously known as Dayton Hudson Corp.

3 Includes pretax: nonrecurring gain, +$163,662; restructuring charge, -$103,596.

8 Includes: nonrecurring charge, -$29,900; discontinued operations, +$85,100.

10 Includes nonrecurring charges: -$97,747.

11 Includes: nonrecurring gain, +$7,045 (pretax); discontinued operations +$4,566.

13 Includes nonrecurring charges: -$23,200.

15 Includes restructuring charge: -$24,200.

16 Includes discontinued operations: -$22,100.

18 Includes nonrecurring losses: -$8,549.

21 Includes nonrecurring charges: -$70,000.

RNK

The public 200 APRIL 2000

CURRENT RANK	PRIOR RANK	COMPANY	SYMBOL	REVENUE ($000)	REVENUE CHANGE (%)	EARNINGS ($000)
26	17	**Imation Corp.** • Oakdale • (651) 704-4000 Solutions for the handling, storage, transmission and use of information.	IMN	1,412,600	+6.3	43,900 *
27	26	**H.B. Fuller Co.** • Vadnais Heights • (651) 236-5900 Adhesives, sealants, paints, waxes, coatings and specialty chemical products.	FULL	1,364,457	+1.3	43,370 *
28	29	**Ceridian Corp.** • Bloomington • (952) 853-8100 Information services.	CEN	1,342,300	+15.5	148,900
29	28	**Polaris Industries Inc.** • Plymouth • (763) 542-0500 Manufacturer of snowmobiles, ATVs, personal watercraft, motorcycles, clothing, accessories.	PII	1,321,076	+12.4	76,326
30	30	**The Toro Co.** • Bloomington • (952) 888-8801 Commercial turf-maintenance; consumer lawn-care and snow-removal equipment.	TTC	1,304,475	+13.3	35,176
31	33	**Minnesota Power Inc.** • Duluth • (218) 723-3974 Electric, water, wastewater treatment and gas utilities.	MPL	1,131,800	+8.9	68,000 *
32	35	**St. Jude Medical Inc.** • Little Canada • (651) 483-2000 Heart valves; cardiovascular products.	STJ	1,114,549	+9.7	24,227 *
33	32	**TCF Financial Corp.** • Minneapolis • (612) 661-6500 National bank holding company.	TCB	1,070,700	+2.9	166,039
34	31	**Alliant Techsystems** • Hopkins • (952) 931-6000 Aerospace and defense products for the U.S. and allied governments.	ATK	1,070,590	-0.6	73,147 *
35	40	**Regis Corp.** • Edina • (952) 947-7777 Hairstyling salons.	RGIS	1,066,601	+16.0	36,391 *
36	34	**Michael Foods Inc.** • St. Louis Park • (952) 546-1500 Wholesale foods and food ingredients.	MIKL	1,053,272	+3.2	44,056
37	41	**Dain Rauscher Corp.** • Minneapolis • (612) 371-7750 Securities brokerage and investment banking services.	DRC	1,015,138	+23.7	66,589 *
38	37	**Donaldson Co. Inc.** • Bloomington • (952) 887-3131 Filtration products worldwide.	DCI	1,004,265	+9.3	70,320
39	39	**Patterson Dental Company** • Mendota Heights • (651) 686-1600 Distribution of dental supplies and equipment.	PDCO	998,405	+16.8	60,513
40	38	**Buffets Inc.** • Eden Prairie • (952) 942-9760 Operating of buffet-style restaurants.	BOCB	936,854	+7.8	42,442
41	56	**Metris Cos. Inc.** • St. Louis Park • (952) 525-5020 Direct-marketing of consumer credit products.	MXT	857,514	+101.3	64,555 *
42	36	**Apogee Enterprises Inc.** • Bloomington • (952) 835-1874 Glass fabrication; auto glass replacement; nonresidential aluminum windows.	APOG	833,706	+9.3	20,584 *
43	47	**National Computer Systems Inc.** • Eden Prairie • (952) 829-3000 Optical-mark readers and specialized data-collection products/services.	NLCS	629,545	+24.6	42,930
44	48	**Fastenal Company** • Winona • (507) 454-5374 Threaded fasteners; construction supplies.	FAST	609,186	+21.1	65,455
45	44	**Analysts International Corp.** • Edina • (952) 835-5900 Consulting, project management, systems analysis/design, programming, software maintenance.	ANLY	596,620	-4.1	17,756
46	•	**PepsiAmericas Inc.*** • Minneapolis • (612) 661-3830 Mfrs, distributes, markets PepsiCo soft drinks in exclusive franchise territories.	PPO	575,743	+5.0	-10,531
47	51	**Hutchinson Technology Inc.** • Hutchinson • (320) 587-3797 Suspension assemblies for rigid disk drives.	HTCH	548,818	+15.8	-33,064
48	53	**Wilsons The Leather Experts** • Brooklyn Park • (763) 391-4000 Retailer of leather coats and accessories.	WLSN	543,608	+18.2	30,651
49	46	**G&K Services Inc.** • Minnetonka • (952) 912-5500 Commercial, institutional and industrial garment supply and service.	GKSRA	541,294	+5.7	37,318
50	52	**Arctic Cat Inc.** • Thief River Falls • (218) 681-8558 Snowmobiles and personal watercraft.	ACAT	490,009	+3.4	6,613 *

27 Includes restructuring charges: -$17,100 (pretax).
31 Includes nonrecurring charges: -$36,200.
32 Includes nonrecurring charges: -$119,762.
34 Includes net nonrecurring gain: +$8,936.
35 Includes nonrecurring charges: -$12,653.
37 Includes nonrecurring gain: +$9,611.
41 Includes nonrecurring loss: -$50,808.
42 Includes discontinued operations: +$14,200.
46 Headquarters moved here during 1999.
50 Includes nonrecurring charge: -$16,899.

The public 200 APRIL 2000

CURRENT RANK	PRIOR RANK	COMPANY	SYMBOL	REVENUE ($000)	REVENUE CHANGE (%)	EARNINGS ($000)
51	55	**Otter Tail Power Co.** • Fergus Falls • (218) 739-8200 Electric utility; other diversified operations.	OTTR	464,577	+7.3	44,977 *
52	49	**Norstan Inc.** • Minnetonka • (952) 352-4000 Communications services for businesses and institutions.	NRRD	454,909	-7.3	-20,094
53	54	**Graco Inc.** • Golden Valley • (763) 623-6000 Fluid-handling and bulk materials equipment.	GGG	442,474	+2.4	59,341
54	50	**Damark International Inc.** • Brooklyn Park • (763) 531-0066 Direct-mail marketing of general merchandise products.	DMRK	430,946	-11.0	1,236 *
55	57	**Tennant Co.** • Golden Valley • (763) 540-1200 Industrial, institutional, and commercial floor-maintenance equipment.	TANT	429,406	+10.3	19,693 *
56	•	**HomeServices.com Inc.*** • Edina • (952) 928-5900 Real estate-related companies Edina Realty, Edina Realty Title, and Edina Realty Mortgage.	HMSV	393,291	+40.2	7,652 *
57	61	**Mesaba Holdings Inc.** • Minneapolis • (612) 726-5151 Regional passenger airline.	MAIR	393,280	+24.0	30,673
58	59	**MTS Systems Corp.** • Eden Prairie • (952) 937-4000 Computer-based systems for product development, simulation, analysis, control.	MTSC	381,614	+1.0	2,679 *
59	60	**BMC Industries Inc.** • Minneapolis • (612) 851-6000 Precision-etched products and optical lenses.	BMC	353,854	+5.6	7,824
60	63	**Lakehead Pipe Line Partners L.P.** • Duluth • (218) 725-0100 Petroleum pipeline system.	LHP	312,600	+8.7	78,700
61	62	**Ag-Chem Equipment Co. Inc.** • Minnetonka • (952) 933-9006 Agricultural and industrial application equipment.	AGCH	297,858	-4.9	1,720
62	65	**Transport Corporation of America Inc.** • Eagan • (651) 686-2500 Truckload carriage and logistics services.	TCAM	286,885	+16.7	8,608
63	64	**Select Comfort Corp.** • Eden Prairie • (952) 551-7000 Manufacturer, retailer of adjustable-firmness sleep systems.	SCSS	273,767	+11.2	-8,204
64	71	**ValueVision International Inc.** • Eden Prairie • (952) 947-5200 TV home shopping network.	VVTV	253,535	+28.1	25,004 *
65	72	**Funco Inc.** • Eden Prairie • (952) 946-8883 Buying and reselling of used video games.	FNCO	253,463	+28.9	8,735
66	67	**Navarre Corp.** • New Hope • (763) 535-8333 Distribution of prerecorded music, PC software, interactive CD-ROM software.	NAVR	252,009	+13.8	-28,065
67	66	**Department 56 Inc.** • Eden Prairie • (952) 944-5600 Design and distribution of collectibles and specialty giftware.	DFS	245,856	+1.0	42,656
68	68	**The Rottlund Co. Inc.** • Roseville • (651) 638-0500 Designing, building, selling of single-family homes.	RH	245,354	+12.4	5,030
69	69	**Video Update Inc.** • St. Paul • (651) 222-0006 Operating, franchising of video rental superstores.	VUPDA	244,770	+13.3	-102,877
70	76	**Chronimed Inc.** • Minnetonka • (952) 979-3600 Distribution of prescription drugs, medical products, and educational materials by mail order.	CHMD	233,058	+40.7	2,072 *
71	107	**Zomax Inc.** • Plymouth • (763) 553-9300 Contract manufacturing of compact discs.	ZOMX	229,261	+275.4	25,827
72	87	**Lund International Holdings Inc.** • Anoka • (763) 576-4200 Accessory products for trucks.	LUND	194,369	+72.6	-3,832
73	•	**United Shipping & Technology Inc.** • Plymouth • (763) 941-4080 Same-day delivery system and e-commerce distributor.	USHP	193,843	+28,745.7	-14,480
74	75	**Osmonics Inc.** • Minnetonka • (952) 933-2277 Water filtration, separation, purification, and fluid-transfer products.	OSM	184,671	+3.9	964 *
75	73	**Digi International Inc.** • Minnetonka • (952) 912-3444 Hardware and software connectivity solutions for multiuser microcomputer and networked systems.	DGII	182,251	-4.9	3,735

51 Includes nonrecurring gain: -$14,469 (pretax).
54 Includes nonrecurring gain: +$297.
55 Includes restructuring charges: -$6,671 (pretax).
56 IPO 10/8/99; earnings include nonrecurring charge: -$2,200.
58 Includes nonrecurring charge: -$3,115 (pretax).
64 Includes net nonrecurring gain: +$8,250.
70 Includes nonrecurring charges: -$1,026.
73 Includes net nonrecurring charge: -$2,575.

The public 200 APRIL 2000

CURRENT RANK	PRIOR RANK	COMPANY	SYMBOL	REVENUE ($000)	REVENUE CHANGE (%)	EARNINGS ($000)
76	79	**The Sportsman's Guide Inc.** • South St. Paul • (651) 451-3030 Mail-order sporting goods.	SGDE	162,515	+13.7	12
77	85	**Rural Cellular Corp.** • Alexandria • (320) 762-2000 Cellular communication and paging services.	RCCC	156,619	+59.0	4,850
78	101	**Eagle Pacific Industries Inc.** • Minneapolis • (612) 305-0339 Manufacturer of polyvinyl chloride (PVC) pipe and polyethylene tubing products.	EPII	153,950	+108.0	12,562
79	80	**Computer Network Technology Corp.** • Plymouth • (763) 797-6000 Enterprise networking products.	CMNT	151,693	+13.6	4,655 *
80	77	**Health Risk Management Inc.** • Bloomington • (952) 829-3500 Managed health care services.	HRMI	149,793	+18.2	1,307
81	83	**Braun's Fashions Corp.** • Plymouth • (763) 551-5000 Retail women's and teens' apparel.	BFCI	129,588	+22.2	8,247
82	81	**Sheldahl Inc.** • Northfield • (507) 663-8000 Electronic materials and flexible circuitry.	SHEL	128,423	+10.2	-20,553 *
83	94	**Innovex Inc.** • Hopkins • (952) 938-4155 Precision electromagnetic products.	INVX	125,895	+47.6	-7,605
84	74	**FSI International Inc.** • Chaska • (952) 448-5440 Semiconductor surface cleaning products, resist processing eqt., chemical management systems.	FSII	120,403	-29.8	-34,180 *
85	•	**Datalink Corp.*** • Edina • (952) 944-3462 Custom design, installation of high-end data storage solutions.	DTLK	118,896	+35.2	7,309
86	82	**ITI Technologies Inc.** • North St. Paul • (651) 777-2690 Wireless security systems.	ITII	117,333	+10.9	13,710 *
87	103	**Communications Systems Inc.** • Hector • (320) 848-6231 Telecommunications equipment.	CSII	116,933	+64.3	9,014
88	84	**Thermo Sentron Inc.*** • Coon Rapids • (763) 783-2589 Precision weighing and inspection equipment.	TSR	107,786	+9.1	6,373
89	89	**National City Bancorporation** • Minneapolis • (612) 904-8500 Bank holding company.	NCBM	99,093	+4.5	16,627
90	96	**Techne Corp.** • Minneapolis • (612) 379-8854 Biotechnology products and hematology controls.	TECH	97,849	+23.7	19,957
91	90	**Hickory Tech Corp.** • Mankato • (507) 387-3355 Telecommunications holding company.	HTCO	97,069	+2.6	14,666 *
92	88	**Hawkins Chemical Inc.** • Minneapolis • (612) 331-6910 Industrial and laboratory chemicals.	HWKN	93,775	-1.7	7,912 *
93	93	**In Home Health Inc.** • Minnetonka • (952) 449-7500 Home health care services.	IHHI	84,306	-3.9	4,635
94	92	**RTW Inc.** • Bloomington • (952) 893-0403 Products, services for employers' workers' compensation programs.	RTWI	77,812	-13.7	6,167
95	109	**Paper Warehouse Inc.** • St. Louis Park • (952) 936-1000 Chain of retail stores specializing in party supplies and paper goods.	PWHS	77,318	+30.6	-1,589
96	100	**Minntech Corp.** • Plymouth • (763) 553-3300 Medical supplies and devices for hemodialysis, open-heart surgery; sterilants, water filters.	MNTX	76,272	+2.7	5,855
97	143	**Digital River Inc.** • Eden Prairie • (952) 830-9042 Electronic-commerce outsourcing solutions for software publishers, online retailers.	DRIV	75,050	+258.9	-27,653 *
98	98	**K-tel International Inc.** • Plymouth • (763) 559-6888 Entertainment products, records, and tapes	KTEL	72,367	-6.1	-5,491 *
99	113	**Verdant Brands Inc.** • Bloomington • (952) 703-3300 Environmentally oriented lawn and garden fertilizers and pesticides.	VERD	72,269	+64.0	-1,469
100	•	**Buca Inc.*** • Minneapolis • (612) 288-2382 Neighborhood restaurants that serve immigrant Southern Italian cuisine.	BUCA	71,528	+85.9	1,424 *

79 Includes net nonrecurring charge: -$901 (pretax).
82 Includes nonrecurring charge: -$8,085.
84 Includes: tax reserve, -$16,600; discontinued operations, +$10,325; R+D write-off, -$6,370 (pretax)
85 IPO 8/6/99.
86 Includes nonrecurring charge: -$2,627.
88 Majority shareholder Thermedics Inc. (Amex:TMD) is planning a cash tender offer.
91 Includes nonrecurring gain: +$9,200 (pretax).
92 Includes nonrecurring charges: -$1,112 (pretax).
97 Includes nonrecurring charges: -$6,886.
98 Includes net nonrecurring gain: +$3,700 (pretax).
100 IPO 4/20/99; earnings include nonrecurring charges: -$1,544.

The public 200 APRIL 2000

CURRENT RANK	PRIOR RANK	COMPANY	SYMBOL	REVENUE ($000)	REVENUE CHANGE (%)	EARNINGS ($000)
101	104	**Fourth Shift Corp.** • Richfield • (612) 851-1500 Client/server application software for industrial processes.	FSFT	69,249	+1.5	2,115 *
102	•	**Retek Inc.*** • Minneapolis • (612) 630-5700 Web-based business-to-business software solutions for retailers.	RETK	69,159	+25.7	-5,399 *
103	•	**iNTELEFILM Corp.** • Minneapolis • (612) 925-8840 Production of TV advertising.	FILM	67,343	+2,523.4	7,382 *
104	86	**Grow Biz International Inc.** • Golden Valley • (763) 520-8500 Franchising of retail merchandisers.	GBIZ	66,559	-30.9	-8,589 *
105	•	**Stockwalk.com Group Inc.*** • Golden Valley • (763) 542-6000 Full-service investment banker specializing in online trading.	STOK	58,230	+7.2	-2,907
106	116	**Ault Inc.** • Brooklyn Park • (763) 493-1900 External power-conversion products.	AULT	56,477	+30.9	1,575
107	•	**NetDirect Corp. International*** • Minneapolis • (612) 915-1122 Online retailer of computer hardware and software products.	VTCO	55,819	+1,064.4	-19,436
108	•	**Fargo Electronics Inc.*** • Eden Prairie • (952) 941-9470 Desktop systems, consumable supplies for plastic card personalization and data encoding.	FRGO	54,907	+15.2	4,485
109	120	**Kinnard Investments Inc.** • Minneapolis • (612) 370-2700 Securities broker.	KINN	54,868	+34.0	2,709
110	91	**Lakes Gaming Inc.** • Minnetonka • (952) 449-9092 Management of two Indian casinos in Louisiana.	LACO	54,716	-40.7	28,827
111	111	**HMN Financial Inc.** • Spring Valley • (507) 346-1100 Holding company for federal savings bank.	HMNF	51,397	-0.1	6,391
112	127	**Rehabilicare Inc.** • New Brighton • (651) 631-0590 Health care products based on electromedical technology.	REHB	50,483	+36.7	4,113 *
113	121	**Famous Dave's of America Inc.** • Eden Prairie • (952) 294-1300 American roadhouse-style barbeque restaurants.	DAVE	47,575	+16.7	-949
114	117	**PremiumWear Inc.** • Minnetonka • (952) 979-1700 Apparel wholesaler in the advertising incentive, uniform, and specialty business.	WEAR	46,952	+10.6	1,433 *
115	110	**CNS Inc.** • Bloomington • (952) 820-6696 Nonmedicinal adhesive strips to improve nasal breathing.	CNXS	46,049	-14.1	-13,756 *
116	115	**TRO Learning Inc.** • Edina • (952) 832-1000 Microcomputer-based, interactive instructional courseware and testing systems.	TUTR	45,999	+10.2	16,254 *
117	129	**Ontrack Data International Inc.** • Eden Prairie • (952) 937-1107 Services for recapturing lost or corrupted computer data.	ONDI	43,372	+21.0	4,677 *
118	119	**First Team Sports Inc.** • Anoka • (763) 576-3500 In-line roller skates.	FTSP	41,470	-0.8	-784
119	128	**CyberOptics Corp.** • Golden Valley • (763) 542-5000 Opto-electronic systems for dimensional measurement and process control.	CYBE	39,627	+8.2	-5,498 *
120	•	**ShowCase Corp.*** • Rochester • (507) 288-5922 Software developer dedicated to providing complete end-user solutions for AS/400 data access.	SHWC	38,915	+13.4	-2,667
121	123	**Nortech Systems Inc.** • Wayzata • (952) 473-4102 Wire harnesses, cable assemblies, sub-assemblies.	NSYS	38,482	+8.8	-1,988 *
122	133	**Stratasys Inc.** • Eden Prairie • (952) 937-3000 Computerized modeling systems and rapid-prototyping devices.	SSYS	37,587	+15.9	2,144
123	108	**Aetrium Inc.** • North St. Paul • (651) 704-1800 Electromechanical handling equipment for the semiconductor industry.	ATRM	37,188	-37.6	-9,013 *
124	126	**Rimage Corp.** • Edina • (952) 944-8144 Diskette and tape duplication equipment.	RIMG	36,313	+27.3	6,343
125	124	**ASV Inc.** • Grand Rapids • (218) 327-3434 Track-driven, all-season construction vehicles.	ASVI	36,168	-7.3	1,412

101 Includes discontinued operations: +$236.
102 IPO 11/18/99; earnings include nonrecurring charges: -$4,779.
103 Includes nonrecurring gain: +$16,384 (pretax).
104 Includes net restructuring charge: -$11,346 (pretax).
105 Went public 7/7/99 via a reverse merger.
107 A new symbol for the former Virtual Technology Co. is pending.
108 IPO 2/10/00.
112 Includes nonrecurring gain: +$1,076 (pretax).
114 Includes restructuring charge: -$1,200 (pretax).
115 Includes nonrecurring charge: -$6,345.
116 Includes nonrecurring tax benefit: +$10,000.
117 Includes nonrecurring charge: -$675.
119 Includes nonrecurring charges: -$7,654 (pretax).
120 IPO 6/30/99.
121 Includes discontinued operations: -$3,058.
123 Includes nonrecurring charge: -$1,600.

RNK

The public 200 APRIL 2000

CURRENT RANK	PRIOR RANK	COMPANY	SYMBOL	REVENUE ($000)	REVENUE CHANGE (%)	EARNINGS ($000)
126	136	**MEDTOX Scientific Inc.** • New Brighton • (651) 636-7466 Toxicology services, employment drug testing, occupational health testing.	TOX	35,002	+18.3	1,419 *
127	131	**FSF Financial Corp.** • Hutchinson • (320) 234-4500 Savings bank holding company.	FFHH	34,622	+4.1	2,484
128	130	**EMC Corp.** • St. Paul • (651) 290-2800 Textbook publishing; duplication services.	EMCM	34,402	+0.1	1,520
129	135	**Hector Communications Corp.** • Hector • (320) 848-6611 Owning/operating of rural local-exchange telephone companies.	HCT	34,117	+7.2	7,479 *
130	134	**Ciprico Inc.** • Plymouth • (763) 551-4000 Disk arrays and disk controller boards.	CPCI	33,132	+8.3	1,665
131	138	**Aero Systems Engineering Inc.** • St. Paul • (651) 227-7515 Jet turbine engine-testing services and products.	AERS	31,061	+14.3	-645
132	139	**Lifecore Biomedical Inc.** • Chaska • (952) 368-4300 Biocompatible implant materials.	LCBM	30,602	+15.5	2,221
133	•	**Zamba Corp.** • Edina • (952) 832-9800 Software, products, services for wireless mobile data transmission.	ZMBA	28,276	+202.2	-2,007
134	•	**Angeion Corp.*** • Vadnais Heights • (651) 484-4874 Computerized diagnostic systems for detecting heart and lung disease.	ANGN	27,400	+9.6	NA
135	198	**Global MAINTECH Inc.** • Eden Prairie • (952) 944-0400 Computer systems that monitor and control a wide range of computers in data centers.	GLBM	26,973	+401.5	-9,792
136	170	**Digital Biometrics Inc.** • Minnetonka • (952) 932-0888 Electronic fingerprint recording and identification products.	DBII	26,674	+133.6	1,737
137	132	**Health Fitness Corp.** • Bloomington • (952) 831-6830 Operating of physical therapy clinics, hospital-based fitness centers.	HFIT	26,478	+1.6	-4,333 *
138	152	**Research Inc.** • Eden Prairie • (952) 941-3300 Radiant heating devices.	RESR	25,864	+49.9	547 *
139	150	**MGI Pharma Inc.** • Bloomington • (952) 346-4700 Specialty pharmaceutical development and marketing.	MOGN	25,652	+43.7	4,731
140	146	**FieldWorks Inc.** • Eden Prairie • (952) 974-7000 Rugged laptop computers designed to withstand the rigors of field work.	FWRX	25,329	+26.6	-5,380
141	142	**HEI Inc.** • Victoria • (952) 443-2500 Ultraminiature microelectronic devices.	HEII	24,970	+9.2	-571
142	141	**Check Technology Corp.** • Minnetonka • (952) 939-9000 Computer-controlled printing systems for companies, financial-document producers.	CTCQ	23,407	-1.8	-1,415
143	140	**WSI Industries Inc.** • Long Lake • (763) 473-1271 Precision-machined and plastic injection molded components.	WSCI	23,204	-4.4	35
144	154	**ACI Telecentrics Inc.** • Minneapolis • (612) 928-4700 Outbound teleservices (telephone-based sales and marketing call centers).	ACIT	23,201	+54.3	584
145	122	**Venturian Corp.** • Hopkins • (952) 931-2500 Defense-related vehicle parts; Magic software services.	VENT	22,464	-46.1	-1,079
146	•	**Excelsior-Henderson Motorcycle Mfg. Co.*** • Belle Plaine • (763) 873-7000 Premium heavyweight cruiser and touring motorcycles.	BIGX	22,218	NM	-26,918
147	147	**Canterbury Park Holding Corp.** • Shakopee • (952) 445-7223 Pari-mutuel horse racing.	TRAK	20,271	+6.4	505
148	•	**Vicom Inc.*** • New Hope • (763) 504-3000 Sells, installs, services telecommunication systems for businesses.	VICM	20,000	+200.0	NA
149	148	**Winland Electronics Inc.** • Mankato • (507) 625-7231 Electronic and electromechanical products and assemblies.	WEX	19,864	+9.3	681
150	159	**Micro Component Technology Inc.** • Roseville • (651) 697-4000 Automatic test equipment for the semiconductor industry.	MCTI	19,816	+34.9	74

126 Includes restructuring charge: -$164.
129 Includes nonrecurring gains: +$21,149 (pretax).
134 Preliminary results, including December 1999 acquisition Medical Graphics.
137 Includes discontinued operations: -$1,425.
138 Includes restructuring charge: -$354 (pretax).
146 Currently in Chapter 11 bankruptcy; development-stage in 1998.
148 Figures are estimated (audit not yet complete).

The public 200 APRIL 2000

CURRENT RANK	PRIOR RANK	COMPANY	SYMBOL	REVENUE ($000)	REVENUE CHANGE (%)	EARNINGS ($000)
151	166	**Bio-Vascular Inc.** • St. Paul • (651) 603-3700 Cardiovascular implants and technology.	BVAS	19,457	+45.4	-331
152	155	**IntraNet Solutions Inc.** • Eden Prairie • (952) 903-2000 Integrated solutions for the management and distribution of business-critical documents.	INRS	18,916	+2.9	-577 *
153	165	**Diametrics Medical Inc.** • Roseville • (651) 639-8035 Proprietary blood-chemistry testing system.	DMED	18,687	+53.7	-10,244
154	153	**Waters Instruments Inc.** • Rochester • (507) 288-7777 Computer hardware; electric-fence controllers; medical monitors.	WTRS	18,173	+11.5	860
155	189	**Possis Medical Inc.** • Coon Rapids • (763) 780-4555 Cardiovascular and vascular medical products.	POSS	18,139	+122.3	-10,578
156	145	**Reo Plastics Inc.** • Maple Grove • (763) 425-4171 Custom injection molding and contract manufacturing.	REOP	18,089	-9.6	1,044
157	157	**MOCON Inc.** • Brooklyn Park • (763) 493-6370 High-technology testing of packaging materials and pharmaceuticals.	MOCO	17,843	+17.8	2,899
158	•	**eBenX Inc.*** • Golden Valley • (763) 525-2700 E-commerce and connectivity solutions for group health insurance benefits.	EBNX	17,526	+31.8	-5,027
159	149	**ATS Medical Inc.** • Plymouth • (763) 553-7736 Bileaflet mechanical heart valve.	ATSI	17,462	-2.8	2,638
160	156	**New Horizon Kids Quest Inc.** • Plymouth • (763) 557-1111 Hourly child care and entertainment at casinos, traditional facilities.	KIDQ	17,098	+9.6	-1,084 *
161	160	**MBC Holding Company*** • St. Paul • (651) 228-9173 Brewery for proprietary (Pig's Eye, Grain Belt Premium) and private-label beers.	MBRW	16,427	+12.5	-790
162	151	**Wells Financial Corp.** • Wells • (507) 553-3151 Savings and loan holding company.	WEFC	15,923	-7.9	1,874
163	163	**Appliance Recycling Centers Inc.** • St. Louis Park • (952) 930-9000 Recycling of major appliances and CFCs.	ARCI	15,582	+14.5	505
164	161	**Dynamic Homes Inc.** • Detroit Lakes • (218) 847-2611 Modular buildings.	DYHM	15,210	+9.4	348
165	•	**Net Perceptions Inc.*** • Eden Prairie • (952) 903-9424 Real-time relationship marketing solutions for Internet retailers.	NETP	15,129	+238.0	-12,039
166	174	**SurModics Inc.** • Eden Prairie • (952) 829-2700 Photochemical technology to improve surface characteristics of medical devices.	SRDX	15,004	+42.8	4,380
167	171	**PPT Vision Inc.** • Eden Prairie • (952) 996-9500 Vision-based automated inspection systems for manufacturing applications.	PPTV	13,697	+21.8	-7,563
168	193	**CIMA LABS Inc.** • Eden Prairie • (952) 947-8700 Drug-delivery systems, such as fast-melting tablets.	CIMA	13,392	+75.9	-1,262
169	169	**Industrial Rubber Products Inc.** • Hibbing • (218) 263-8831 Protective materials, abrasion-resistant equipment, proprietary rubber products.	INRB	12,985	+30.1	-1,619
170	•	**Ancor Communications Inc.** • Eden Prairie • (952) 932-4000 Fibre Channel communications network products.	ANCR	12,951	+194.8	-8,733
171	167	**Lectec Corp.** • Minnetonka • (952) 933-2291 Conductive, adhesive and therapeutic medical products.	LECT	12,582	+5.0	-2,268
172	199	**VideoLabs Inc.** • Golden Valley • (763) 542-0061 Electronic cameras, equipment for desktop computer video applications.	VLAB	12,538	+103.4	878
173	187	**Oakridge Holdings Inc.** • Apple Valley • (651) 895-5164 Manufacture of aviation ground support equipment; operation of cemeteries.	OKRG	11,986	+42.7	158
174	•	**PopMail.com Inc.** • Bloomington • (952) 837-9917 Permission-based marketing e-mail services to media businesses.	POPM	11,854	+121.0	-8,725 *
175	184	**XATA Corporation** • Burnsville • (952) 894-3680 Mobile information systems for the fleet trucking segment of the transportation industry.	XATA	11,758	+30.5	706

152 Includes nonrecurring charge: -$1,972.
157 IPO 12/10/99.
160 Includes nonrecurring charge: -$799.
161 Formerly known as Minnesota Brewing Co.
165 IPO 4/23/99.
174 Includes nonrecurring charge: -$2,126.

RNK

The public 200 APRIL 2000

CURRENT RANK	PRIOR RANK	COMPANY	SYMBOL	REVENUE ($000)	REVENUE CHANGE (%)	EARNINGS ($000)
176	164	**Reuter Manufacturing Inc.** • Hopkins • (952) 935-6921 Manufacturer of precision-machined products and assemblies.	RTMF	11,446	-13.0	-1,614
177	176	**New Ulm Telecom Inc.** • New Ulm • (507) 354-4111 Operation of local exchange telephone companies.	NULM	11,337	+12.1	3,545
178	168	**QCF Bancorp Inc.** • Virginia • (218) 741-2040 Holding company for federal savings bank.	QCFB	11,139	-3.9	2,150
179	179	**IPI Inc.** • Eden Prairie • (952) 975-6200 Franchisor of fast-turnaround business printers.	IDH	11,089	-3.5	1,782
180	•	**CorVu Corp.*** • Eden Prairie • (952) 944-7777 Business performance management software products and related professional services.	CRVU	10,935	+54.2	-4,393
181	•	**Great Northern Iron Ore Properties*** • St. Paul • (651) 224-2385 Owns and collects royalties on mineral and nonmineral lands on the Mesabi Iron Range.	GNI	10,926	-7.3	9,354
182	183	**ChoiceTel Communications Inc.** • Plymouth • (763) 544-1260 Independent provider of payphone services.	PHON	10,554	+18.3	-17
183	180	**Northern Technologies International Corp.** • Lino Lakes • (651) 784-1250 Corrosion-inhibiting products and electronic sensing instruments.	NTI	10,547	+10.4	2,654
184	175	**Northwest Teleproductions Inc.** • Edina • (952) 835-4455 Videotape and film production.	NWTL	10,123	+0.0	231
185	181	**The Chromaline Corp.** • Duluth • (218) 628-2217 Imaging films and chemicals for screen printing.	CMLH	9,911	+6.7	804
186	•	**Endocardial Solutions Inc.** • St. Paul • (651) 644-7890 Minimally invasive diagnostic system that diagnoses tachycardia within seconds.	ECSI	9,597	+392.2	-11,729
187	182	**First Federal Bancorporation** • Bemidji • (218) 751-5120 Savings and loan holding company.	BDJI	9,505	+2.6	815
188	177	**Photo Control Corp.** • New Hope • (763) 537-3601 Cameras, film magazines, photographic package printers and cine/video lighting.	PHOC	9,335	-6.8	301
189	185	**Insignia Systems Inc.** • Plymouth • (763) 392-6200 Sign systems for retail merchants.	ISIG	9,287	+6.7	-1,411
190	190	**MedAmicus Inc.** • Plymouth • (763) 559-2613 Medical devices for vascular access and for pressure measurement.	MEDM	9,013	+12.2	-175
191	191	**Dotronix Inc.** • New Brighton • (651) 633-1742 CRT displays and closed-circuit TV monitors.	DOTX	8,339	+8.5	-1,740
192	97	**VirtualFund.com Inc.*** • Eden Prairie • (952) 941-8687 Internet hosting of e-commerce activities.	VFND	7,151	+1,368.4	NA
193	•	**Infinite Graphics Inc.** • Minneapolis • (612) 721-6283 Precision graphics company.	INFG	7,091	+79.9	50
194	188	**Urologix Inc.** • Plymouth • (763) 475-1400 Minimally invasive medical devices for the treatment of urological disorders.	ULGX	7,083	-14.1	-8,724
195	178	**Rochester Medical Corporation** • Stewartville • (507) 533-9600 Latex-free incontinence and urological catheters and other urological devices.	ROCM	7,003	-30.0	-5,005
196	192	**RSI Systems Inc.** • Edina • (952) 896-3020 Telecommunications products for videoconferencing and other uses.	RSIS	6,992	-6.7	-2,324
197	196	**Image Systems Corporation** • Minnetonka • (952) 935-1171 High-resolution computer monitors for engineering and scientific applications.	IMSG	6,703	+2.1	63
198	•	**Vital Images Inc.** • Minneapolis • (612) 915-8000 Development and implementation of medical visualization systems and technology.	VTAL	6,624	+46.3	-3,217
199	•	**Orphan Medical Inc.** • Minnetonka • (952) 513-6900 Medical and pharmaceutical products for patients with uncommon diseases.	ORPH	6,457	+27.9	-5,221
200	195	**Coda Music Technology Inc.** • Eden Prairie • (952) 937-9611 Development, marketing of proprietary music technology products.	COMT	6,356	-0.9	-456
			COMPOSITES	209,314,937	**+4.1**	**11,342,271**

180 Went public 1/14/00 via a reverse merger.
181 Newly deemed eligible by CRM.
192 Results for ranking do not include Digital Graphics Business Unit, which is to be sold. Performance box includes all operations; earnings include tax benefit: +$14,000.

The private 100 MAY 2000

CURRENT RANK	PRIOR RANK	COMPANY	YEAR FOUNDED	REVENUE ($MIL)	REVENUE CHANGE (%)	EMPLOYEES
1	1	**Cargill Inc.** • Minnetonka • (952) 742-6000 Int'l marketer, processor, distributor of agricultural, food, financial, industrial products, services.	1865	45,714	-11.1	82,000
2	2	**Carlson Cos. Inc.*** • Minnetonka • (952) 449-1000 Travel, hospitality, relationship marketing.	1938	9,800	+25.7	63,200
3	4	**Hidden Creek Industries** • Minneapolis • (612) 332-2335 Holding company for automotive-related manufacturers.	1989	5,041	+80.0	38,665
4	3	**Schwan's Sales Enterprises Inc.** • Marshall • (507) 532-3274 Manufacture of food products such as ice cream and pizza.	1952	3,000 e	N/A	6,000
5	6	**Andersen Corp.** • Bayport • (651) 439-5150 Manufacture of windows, patio doors, roof windows.	1903	2,000 e	N/A	6,000
6	7	**Minnesota Life Insurance Co.** • St. Paul • (651) 665-3500 Insurance, pensions and investments for individuals and businesses.	1880	1,800	+28.6	4,000
7	5	**Holiday Cos.** • Bloomington • (952) 830-8700 Wholesale and retail gasoline, convenience store merchandise; retail sporting goods.	1928	1,725 e	N/A	5,500
8	8	**Taylor Corp.** • North Mankato • (507) 625-2828 Holding company for printing, stationery products and electronics operations.	1948	1,000 e	N/A	15,000
9	9	**M.A. Mortenson Co.** • Golden Valley • (763) 522-2100 Commercial and industrial construction, construction mgmt., design/build, turnkey development.	1954	968	+7.1	1,875
10	14	**Opus group of companies** • Minnetonka • (952) 936-4444 Commercial and industrial design, construction; real estate development.	1953	900	+57.9	1,552
11	•	**Jostens Inc.*** • Bloomington • (952) 830-3300 Products and services for the youth, education, sports and corporate recognition markets.	1906	782	+1.5	6,700
12	13	**Genmar Holdings Inc.** • Minneapolis • (612) 339-7900 Manufacture of recreational powerboats.	1962	705	+20.3	5,218
13	12	**Kraus-Anderson Inc.** • Minneapolis • (612) 332-7281 General contractor, real estate manager/developer.	1897	610	+3.4	1,000
14	15	**Lifetouch Inc.** • Eden Prairie • (952) 826-4000 Studio and school photography.	1936	610	+8.9	15,000
15	•	**Merrill Corp.*** • St. Paul • (651) 646-4501 Financial documents; printing, typesetting and document-management services.	1968	600 e	N/A	3,797
16	16	**Rosen's Diversified Inc.** • Fairmont • (507) 238-4201 Agribusiness holding company with interests in meat packing, chemical fertilizer, bottled water.	1946	600 e	N/A	1,500
17	11	**Lupient Automotive Group** • Golden Valley • (763) 544-6666 Auto sales and leasing at 23 locations in the Twin Cities; Rochester, Minn.; and Eau Claire, Wis.	1968	560	-20.9	1,000
18	23	**Northern Tool & Equipment Co.** • Burnsville • (952) 894-9510 Mail-order and retail hardware tools, generators, pressure washers, other light-industrial products.	1981	559	+35.7	2,250
19	17	**Johnson Brothers Wholesale Liquor** • St. Paul • (651) 649-5800 Liquor distributor.	1953	550 e	N/A	1,050
20	20	**Jerry's Enterprises Inc.** • Edina • (952) 922-8335 Retail grocery and other operations.	1947	486	+7.5	3,125
21	19	**APi Group Inc.** • Roseville • (651) 636-4320 Industrial, mechanical, electrical construction; building materials distribution.	1926	479	-1.2	3,900
22	18	**GFI America** • Minneapolis • (612) 872-6262 Processor of beef products for major restaurant chains.	1976	475	-5.9	1,125
23	22	**Coborn's Inc.** • St. Cloud • (320) 252-4222 Retail grocery operation.	1921	450 e	N/A	4,100
24	24	**Lund Food Holdings Inc.** • Edina • (952) 927-3663 Lunds and Byerly's retail grocery operations.	1939	450	+12.5	5,200
	24	**Smead Manufacturing Company** • Hastings • (651) 437-4111 Woman-owned manufacturer of office filing supplies.	1906	433	+8.3	2,900

• not on last year's list
e: estimated by Corporate Report
N/A: not available (change ratios not presented for revenue estimates)

3YG: three-year growth (the annualized growth rate since fiscal year 1996)
RPE: revenue per employee

2 Carlson: $31.4 billion under Carlson brands.
11 Jostens: public company that accepted a December 1999 bid to be taken private.
15 Merrill: former public company that was taken private in November 1999.

RNK

The private 100 MAY 2000

CURRENT RANK	PRIOR RANK	COMPANY	YEAR FOUNDED	REVENUE ($MIL)	REVENUE CHANGE (%)	EMPLOYEES
26	52	**Walser Automotive Group Inc.** • Edina • (952) 929-3535 Automobile dealership with leasing, body shop, insurance and management services.	1956	410	+9.3	720
27	27	**Marvin Lumber & Cedar Company** • Warroad • (218) 386-1430 Wood and clad wood windows, patio doors (as Marvin Windows & Doors).	1904	401	+11.3	4,000
28	65	**Pemstar Inc.** • Rochester • (507) 288-6720 Contract manufacturing, design for computer, telecommunications, medical, equipment industries.	1994	400	+116.2	3,200
	28	**Davisco Foods International Inc.** • Le Sueur • (507) 665-8861 Producer of cheese, food powders, milk proteins.	1943	380	0.0	460
	26	**Ryan Cos. US Inc.** • Minneapolis • (612) 336-1200 Design/build development firm providing full development and construction services.	1938	369	+59.1	400
31	34	**BI Performance Services** • Edina • (952) 835-4800 Performance-improvement programs (company name is a trademark of Schoeneckers Inc.).	1950	360	+12.5	1,400
32	28	**Malt-O-Meal Co.** • Minneapolis • (612) 338-8551 Production, marketing of hot, ready-to-eat cereal products.	1919	360 e	N/A	950
33	32	**Ameripride Services** • Minneapolis • (612) 331-1600 Linen supply and industrial laundering.	1890	350 e	N/A	5,500
34	33	**Little Six Inc.*** • Prior Lake • (952) 445-9000 Tribally owned gaming business.	1982	350 e	N/A	4,000
	31	**Red Wing Shoe Co. Inc.** • Red Wing • (651) 388-8211 Manufacture and distribution of footwear; leather tanning and hospitality services.	1905	342	-1.2	2,839
	34	**Ziegler Inc.** • Bloomington • (952) 888-4121 Dealer of Caterpillar construction equipment, aerial lift equipment.	1914	340 e	N/A	966
37	53	**Western Petroleum Company** • Eden Prairie • (952) 941-9090 Marketing of petroleum products.	1969	337	+53.2	52
38	38	**The Cretex Companies Inc.** • Elk River • (763) 441-2121 Concrete, metal machining and fabrication, plastic injection molding, specialty machines industries.	1917	325 e	N/A	2,000
	28	**Datacard Group** • Minnetonka • (952) 933-1223 Integrated plastic card personalization systems for financial, ID and health care applications.	1969	325	-7.1	1,900
40	34	**Luigino's Inc.** • Duluth • (218) 723-5555 Production of frozen entrees and snacks (Michelina's and Yu Sing brands).	1990	325 e	N/A	1,400
41	38	**Cardinal IG Company** • Minnetonka • (952) 935-1722 Manufacture of insulating glass units for original-equipment manufacturers.	1962	320 e	N/A	2,000
42	40	**Bremer Financial Corporation** • St. Paul • (651) 227-7621 Holding company for First American Banks in Minnesota, North Dakota, Wisconsin.	1943	317	+6.8	1,700
43	37	**Starkey Laboratories Inc.** • Eden Prairie • (952) 941-6401 Manufacture of custom-designed, in-the-ear hearing aids.	1967	312	-0.2	3,450
44	61	**McGough Cos.** • Roseville • (651) 633-5050 General construction, construction management, design/build.	1956	311	+62.0	825
45	51	**Liberty Diversified Industries Inc.** • New Hope • (763) 536-6600 Design, mfr, market products for packaging, office, industrial sectors.	1972	300	+25.0	1,400
46	49	**Young America Corp.** • Young America • (952) 467-1100 Consumer interaction processing services for Fortune 500 companies.	1972	300	+26.1	1,400
47	41	**Dart Transit Co.** • Eagan • (651) 688-2000 Motor carrier services.	1934	280	+1.1	336
48	•	**Weis Builders Inc.** • Bloomington • (952) 858-9999 General contracting, construction mgmt., pre-construction services for nonresidential buildings.	1939	280	+39.3	310
49	44	**ABC Bus Cos. Inc.** • Faribault • (507) 334-1871 Sale/lease of new and used motor coaches.	1979	275	+5.8	440
50	46	**Interplastic Corp.** • Vadnais Heights • (651) 481-6860 Resins, gelcoats, sheet molding compounds.	1959	275	+9.1	465

• not on last year's list
e: estimated by Corporate Report
N/A: not available (change ratios not presented for revenue estimates)

3YG: three-year growth (the annualized growth rate since fiscal year 1996)
RPE: revenue per employee

33 Little Six: includes Mystic Lake Casino Hotel.

The private 100 MAY 2000

CURRENT RANK	PRIOR RANK	COMPANY	YEAR FOUNDED	REVENUE ($MIL)	REVENUE CHANGE (%)	EMPLOYEES
51	49	**Lawson Software** • St. Paul • (651) 767-7000 E-business solutions for financials, human resources, procurement, distribution, analytics.	1975	268	+12.5	1,800
52	43	**Katun Corp.** • Bloomington • (952) 941-9505 Distribution, manufacture of office equipment products.	1979	256	-4.1	394
53	48	**Sun Country Airlines** • Mendota Heights • (651) 681-3900 Scheduled and charter airline company.	1983	252	-1.3	1,400
54	45	**Anderson Trucking Service Inc.** • St. Cloud • (320) 255-7400 Nationwide flatbed, heavy-haul and van carrier with 900 trucks.	1955	250	-2.0	930
55	10	**Hubbard Broadcasting Inc.*** • St. Paul • (651) 646-5555 Television and radio broadcasting, TV production, satellite news-gathering, program distribution.	1923	250 e	N/A	1,350
56	54	**Mille Lacs Band • Ojibwe Indians** • Onamia • (320) 532-4181 Operator of Indian gaming casinos in Onamia and Hinckley.	1991	250 e	N/A	3,468
57	75	**Entegris Inc.*** • Chaska • (952) 556-3131 Fluid and material-handling products for microelectronics.	1966	242	+58.1	1,500
58	60	**Slumberland Inc.** • Little Canada • (651) 482-7500 Home furnishings retailer with 66 stores in six states.	1967	238	+23.7	1,656
	55	**Adolfson & Peterson Construction** • St. Louis Park • (763) 544-1561 Commercial, industrial, institutional, design-build, general construction, construction mgmt. svcs.	1946	230	+10.0	435
60	62	**Polar Corporation** • St. Cloud • (320) 746-2255 Manufacture of liquid and dry bulk transporation equipment; national service, trailer parts business.	1946	220	+15.8	1,250
61	57	**Marquette Financial Cos.** • Minneapolis • (612) 888-8100 Bank holding company for Marquette Banks.	1992	220	+9.5	1,722
62	66	**REM Inc.** • Edina • (952) 925-5067 Health care services: senior, disability, home health care, housing, rehabilitation therapy.	1967	215	+19.4	11,500
	69	**Lyman Lumber Co.** • Excelsior • (952) 470-3600 Building-materials distribution to contractors, lumber dealers.	1897	207	+17.3	625
	68	**Dorsey & Whitney LLP** • Minneapolis • (612) 340-2600 Largest law firm in the Upper Midwest, 25th-largest in the country.	1912	202	+13.8	1,483
65	62	**Quadion Corp.** • St. Louis Park • (952) 927-1400 Manufacture of molded rubber, plastics, die castings.	1945	200 e	N/A	1,500
66	70	**Equus Computer Systems Inc.** • Minneapolis • (612) 617-6200 Custom-built PCs, primarily for computer resellers.	1989	190	+8.6	401
	62	**Gold'n Plump Poultry** • St. Cloud • (320) 251-3570 Producer, processor, marketer of premium-quality chicken.	1926	190	-5.0	1,800
68	77	**Knutson Construction Services Inc.** • Minneapolis • (612) 546-1400 General contracting, construction mgmt., design/build services for commercial, industrial clients.	1911	190	+26.7	600
69	72	**Kurt Manufacturing Co. Inc.** • Fridley • (763) 572-1500 Precision machining, precision gears, screw machining, die casting and powder coat paintings.	1946	181	+13.1	1,200
70	66	**Polka Dot Dairy • Tom Thumb Food Mkts. Inc.** • Hastings • (651) 437-9023 Dairy products distribution; and (as Tom Thumb) retail groceries, dairy, gasoline.	1957	180	0.0	1,400
71	72	**American Business Forms Inc.** • Glenwood • (320) 634-5471 Distribution of business forms.	1981	175	+9.4	220
72	87	**Bermo Inc.** • Circle Pines • (763) 786-7676 Manufacturer of metal stampings, fabricated metal assemblies and plastic-injected molded parts.	1947	175 e	N/A	675
	75	**RisComp Industries Inc.** • Plymouth • (763) 553-2220 Payroll, safety, claims, and human resource management; benefits administration.	1967	170	+11.1	5,800
74	47	**Telex Communications Inc.** • Bloomington • (952) 884-4051 Manufacture of audio, communications, audiovisual eqip. ; also products for the hearing-impaired.	1936	166	-51.2	2,928
75	86	**Technology, Engineering and Mfg. Industries Inc.** • Bagley • (218) 694-3550 Diversified mfg. company providing design, engineering, assembly and machining operations.	1967	158	+20.6	1,120

• not on last year's list
e: estimated by Corporate Report
N/A: not available (change ratios not presented for revenue estimates)

3YG: three-year growth (the annualized growth rate since fiscal year 1996)
RPE: revenue per employee

54 Hubbard Broadcasting: drop in rank due to divesting of U.S. Satellite Broadcasting.
57 Entegris: registered an initial public offering in March 2000.

RNK

The private 100 MAY 2000

CURRENT RANK	PRIOR RANK	COMPANY	YEAR FOUNDED	REVENUE ($MIL)	REVENUE CHANGE (%)	EMPLOYEES
	80	**The McCarthy Group** • Richfield • (612) 869-1414 Automobile dealers, including Wally McCarthy's: Oldsmobile, Cadillac, Chevrolet-GMC.	1949	157	+9.0	281
77	81	**Team Tires Plus** • Burnsville • (952) 894-2700 Tire retailer and wholesaler (Tires Plus Stores).	1976	156	+11.5	1,570
78	82	**Nath Cos.** • Bloomington • (952) 853-1400 Owner/manager of Burger King and Denny's restaurants, real estate and a hotel.	1990	153	+14.0	4,200
	91	**Cold Spring Granite Co.** • Cold Spring • (320) 685-3621 Quarrier and fabricator of granite building stone and memorialization products.	1898	150	+23.0	1,330
80	83	**Interstate Cos.** • Bloomington • (952) 854-5511 Distributor of diesel engines and transmissions.	1957	150	+11.1	625
81	83	**Lampert Yards Inc.** • St. Paul • (651) 695-3600 Retail lumber and building materials stores.	1887	150	+11.1	321
82	83	**Weigh-Tronix Inc.** • Fairmont • (507) 238-4461 Design, manufacture of electronic weighing equipment.	1971	150	+8.7	375
83	89	**BOR-SON Construction Inc.** • Bloomington • (952) 854-8444 Commercial, industrial, institutional, health care, multi-housing construction services.	1957	145	+13.3	350
	71	**The Miner Group International** • New Hope • (763) 504-6151 Marketer of children's promotional items; 20 printing, packaging and manufacturing facilities.	1980	141	-14.5	595
	87	**Woodcraft Industries Inc.** • St. Cloud • (320) 252-1503 Manufacturing of hardwood, engineered wood components for kitchen cabinet, furniture mfg.	1945	140	+7.7	1,500
86	98	**Fabcon Inc.** • Savage • (952) 890-4444 Precast concrete wall panels for commercial construction.	1971	132	+15.8	700
87	•	**Born Information Services Inc.** • Wayzata • (952) 404-4000 Data processing and consulting: application development, networking and communications, training	1990	130	+40.9	1,005
	92	**Walman Optical Co.** • Minneapolis • (612) 520-6000 Optical supplier.	1915	130	+8.3	683
89	90	**Scherer Bros. Lumber Co.** • Brooklyn Park • (763) 379-9633 Sale, manufacture of lumber, millwork products; land development, construction financing.	1930	127	0.0	470
90	92	**Spectro Alloys Corp.** • Rosemount • (651) 437-2815 Aluminum casting alloys.	1964	125	+4.2	120
91	97	**Welsh Cos. Inc.** • Bloomington • (952) 897-7700 Real estate services: property mgmt., leasing, design and construction, development, financing.	1978	125	+13.6	400
92	96	**Gabberts Furniture & Design Studio** • Edina • (952) 927-1500 Retail home furnishings and interior design.	1946	121	+2.5	650
	•	**Japs-Olson Co.** • St. Louis Park • (952) 932-9393 Commercial printer with computer service bureau and mailing division.	1907	120	+14.4	750
	•	**Medical Arts Press Inc.** • Brooklyn Park • (763) 493-7300 Direct-market, mfr of business forms and office supplies to health care professionals.	1929	118	N/A	600
	•	**Norcraft Co. LLC** • Eagan • (651) 234-3300 National manufacturer of cabinetry for kitchens and baths.	1975	117	+17.0	1,000
96	100	**McGlynn Bakeries Inc.** • Fridley • (763) 574-2222 Retail bakeries; wholesale frozen bakery foods, cake decorating products.	1919	116	+5.5	1,000
97	•	**Faribault Foods Inc.** • Minneapolis • (612)333-6461 Canned vegetables, soups, pastas, chili and beans.	1895	115	+21.1	500
98	•	**Ellerbe Becket** • Minneapolis • (612) 376-2000 Integrated architecture, engineering, construction services, interiors, planning.	1909	113	+7.6	685
99	•	**Thrifty White Stores** • Plymouth • (763) 513-4300 Conventional drug stores with pharmacies; outlying pharmacies; pharmacy services and support.	1957	110	N/A	1,124
100	92	**Diamond Brands Inc.** • Cloquet • (218) 879-6700 Manufacture, distribution of plastic cutlery, matches, toothpicks, clothespins.	1986	105	+6.4	680
		Composite totals		97,212	+2.3	392,341

• not on last year's list
e: estimated by Corporate Report
N/A: not available (change ratios not presented for revenue estimates)

3YG: three-year growth (the annualized growth rate since fiscal year 1996)
RPE: revenue per employee

Cooperative and mutual 20 MAY 2000

CURRENT RANK	PRIOR RANK	COMPANY	YEAR FOUNDED	REVENUE ($MIL)	REVENUE CHANGE (%)	EMPLOYEES
1	1	**Cenex Harvest States Coop.** • Inver Grove Heights • (651) 451-5151 Cooperative system that operates oil refineries/pipelines; grain marketing, food processing.	1931	6,300	-24.1	6,000
2	2	**Land O'Lakes Inc.** • Arden Hills • (651) 481-2222 Farm supply, food marketing cooperative serving customers and consumers throughout the U. S. Member	1921	5,600	+7.7	7,500
3	3	**Lutheran Brotherhood** • Minneapolis • (612) 340-7000 insurance, securities.	1917	2,950	-2.5	1,437
4	4	**AgriBank FCB** • St. Paul • (651) 282-8800 Agricultural credit institution serving 11 states in the Midwest and South.	1917	1,624	+1.1	3,132
5	5	**Associated Milk Producers Inc.** • New Ulm • (507) 354-8295 Dairy farmer cooperative processing and marketing milk products.	1969	1,100	0.0	1,700
6	6	**Federated Mutual Insurance Co.** • Owatonna • (507) 455-5200 Property, casualty, health, life, and personal lines insurance.	1904	936	+4.8	3,036
7	7	**American Crystal Sugar Co.** • Moorhead • (218) 236-4400 Processing and marketing of beet sugar, dried pulp, molasses.	1889	844	+24.7	1,800
8	8	**Minnesota Corn Processors** • Marshall • (507) 537-2676 Processor of corn-derived sweeteners, fuel ethanol, and corn co-products.	1982	599	+6.4	895
9	9	**MSI Insurance Cos.** • Arden Hills • (651) 631-7000 Multi-line and commercial agribusiness insurance; personal-lines insurance, pension plans.	1934	484	+14.5	591
10	10	**Great River Energy** • Elk River • (763) 441-3121 Wholesale electric service to 29 electric distribution cooperatives in Minnesota and Wisconsin.	1999	410	+4.9	676
11	11	**Universal Cooperatives Inc.** • Eagan • (651) 239-1000 Manufacture, purchase, and distribution of farm supplies.	1972	272	-7.5	802
12	12	**Bongards Creameries Inc.** • Bongards • (763) 466-5521 Manufacture of dairy products such as natural and process cheeses, whey powder, ice cream blends.	1908	187	-14.6	270
13	14	**First District Association** • Litchfield • (320) 693-3236 Cheese and whey products cooperative.	1921	197	+18.0	137
14	15	**Southern Minnesota Beet Sugar Coop.** • Renville • (320) 329-8305 Production of beet sugar, beet pulp pellets, molasses, betaine.	1972	167	+4.4	297
15	16	**Western National Insurance Group** • Edina • (952) 835-5350 Property and casualty insurance.	1901	166	+4.8	385
16	17	**United Hardware Distributing Co.** • Plymouth • (763) 559-1800 Distributes hardware and allied lines to Hardware Hank stores and other retailers.	1945	155	+6.9	345
17	•	**Farm Credit Leasing*** • Golden Valley • (763) 797-7400 Leases capital equipment to agricultural producers and their cooperatives, and to rural utilities.	1972	153	+5.8	160
18	18	**Meadowland Farmers Coop.** • Lamberton • (507) 752-7352 Cooperative providing grain handling; agronomy, petroleum, lumber, hardware, and feed supplies.	1905	107	-19.5	90
19	19	**Connexus Energy** • Ramsey • (763) 323-2600 Distributor of electricity to 91,500 members.	1936	106	+1.4	238
20	20	**Dakota Electric Association** • Farmington • (651) 463-7134 Cooperative electric utility.	1938	93	-6.1	230
			Composite totals	22,450	-4.3	29,721

• not on last year's list
e: estimated by Corporate Report
N/A: not available (change ratios not presented for revenue estimates)

3YG: three-year growth (the annualized growth rate since fiscal year 1996)
RPE: revenue per employee

17 Farm Credit: re-categorized from No. 78 on last year's Private 100.

Initial public offering 50 JUNE 2000

RANK	COMPANY	SYMBOL	DELIVERY DATE	NET PROCEEDS ($MIL)	IPO PRICE ($)	4-30-99 CLOSE ($)	$100 IN IPO	$100 IN S&P 500	PERFORMANCE* (%)
1	**Zomax Inc.*** • Plymouth • (763) 553-9300 Contract manufacturing of compact discs.	ZOMX	05-07-96	9.3	1.69[s]	19.50	$1,156	$220	+425.3
2	**Rural Cellular Corp.** • Alexandria • (320) 762-2000 Cellular communication and paging services.	RCCC	02-08-96	26.2	10.00	72.50	$725	$219	+231.6
3	**SurModics Inc.** • Eden Prairie • (952) 829-2700 Photochemical technology to improve surface characteristics of medical devices.	SRDX	03-09-98	15.6	7.50	24.38	$325	$136	+138.4
4	**Metris Cos. Inc.** • St. Louis Park • (952) 525-5020 Direct-marketing of consumer credit products.	MXT	10-25-96	47.4	8.00[s]	35.00	$438	$205	+113.8
5	**C.H. Robinson Worldwide** • Eden Prairie • (952) 937-8500 Third-party transportation, produce distribution, financial services.	CHRW	10-20-97	-3.0	18.00	51.88	$288	$150	+92.0
6	**Datalink Corp.** • Edina • (952) 944-3462 Custom design, installation of high-end data storage solutions.	DTLK	08-06-99	18.1	7.50	15.44	$206	$110	+86.6
7	**Digital River Inc.** • Eden Prairie • (952) 830-9042 Electronic-commerce outsourcing solutions for software publishers, online retailers.	DRIV	08-12-98	23.0	8.50	16.88	$199	$132	+50.0
8	**Wilsons The Leather Experts** • Brooklyn Park • (763) 391-4000 Retailer of leather coats and accessories.	WLSN	06-02-97	9.5	6.00[s]	15.00	$250	$169	+47.5
9	**Retek Inc.** • Minneapolis • (612) 630-5700 Web-based business-to-business software solutions for retailers.	RETK	11-18-99	76.7	15.00	22.00	$147	$101	+45.7
10	**Net Perceptions Inc.** • Eden Prairie • (952) 903-9424 Real-time relationship marketing solutions for Internet retailers.	NETP	04-23-99	47.3	14.00	20.63	$147	$106	+39.3
11	**Buca Inc.** • Minneapolis • (612) 288-2382 Neighborhood restaurants that serve immigrant Southern Italian cuisine.	BUCA	04-20-99	35.5	12.00	15.50	$129	$110	+17.6
12	**Hypertension Diagnostics Inc.** • Eagan • (651) 687-9999 Medical device for assessing risk, monitoring treatment of cardiovascular disease.	HDII	07-23-98	9.8	4.13	4.69	$114	$126	-9.7
13	**QCF Bancorp Inc.** • Virginia • (218) 741-2040 Holding company for federal savings bank.	QCFB	04-03-95	17.0	10.00	24.75	$248	$286	-13.4
14	**eBenX Inc.** • Golden Valley • (763) 525-2700 E-commerce and connectivity solutions for group health insurance benefits.	EBNX	12-10-99	93.0	20.00	15.38	$77	$101	-24.1
15	**Image Sensing Systems Inc.** • St. Paul • (651) 603-7700 Products using video image processing technology for traffic management.	ISNS	05-04-95	3.9	3.96[s]	7.00	$177	$276	-35.8
16	**HomeServices.com Inc.** • Edina • (952) 928-5900 Holding corp. for Edina Realty, Edina Realty Title, and Edina Realty Mortgage.	HMSV	10-08-99	30.5	15.00	9.75	$65	$107	-39.5
17	**Fargo Electronics Inc.** • Eden Prairie • (952) 941-9470 Systems, supplies for the plastic card personalization and data encoding industry.	FRGO	02-10-00	69.8	15.00	9.00	$60	$101	-40.7
18	**First Federal Bancorporation** • Bemidji • (218) 751-5120 Savings and loan holding company.	BDJI	04-03-95	8.0	4.44[s]	7.50	$169	$286	-41.0
19	**Medwave Inc.** • Arden Hills • (651) 639-1227 Noninvasive medical device that continually monitors blood pressure.	MDWV	11-09-95	6.3	5.00	7.00	$140	$242	-42.1
20	**ShowCase Corp.** • Rochester • (507) 288-5922 Software developer providing end-user solutions for AS/400 data access.	SHWC	06-30-99	25.1	9.00	5.38	$60	$105	-42.9
21	**Dura Automotive Sys. Inc.** • Minneapolis • (612) 342-2311 Mechanical assemblies and integrated systems for the automotive industry.	DRRA	08-14-96	51.2	14.50	16.88	$116	$217	-46.3
22	**Wells Financial Corp.** • Wells • (507) 553-3151 Savings and loan holding company.	WEFC	04-11-95	17.8	8.00	12.00	$150	$284	-47.1
23	**Endocardial Solutions Inc.** • St. Paul • (651) 644-7890 Minimally invasive diagnostic system that diagnoses tachycardia within seconds.	ECSI	03-24-97	18.4	9.00	7.88	$88	$181	-51.8
24	**Rainforest Cafe Inc.** • Hopkins • (952) 945-5400 Development, ownership, operation of combination retail/restaurant facilities.	RAIN	04-07-95	23.2	2.67[s]	2.97	$111	$283	-60.7
25	**Ontrack Data Int'l Inc.** • Eden Prairie • (952) 937-1107 Services for recapturing lost or corrupted computer data.	ONDI	10-22-96	23.9	12.00	9.19	$77	$203	-62.3

† CALCULATION: (($100 in IPO - $100 in S&P)/$100 in S&P)*100
s split-adjusted

1 Zomax: Figures have been adjusted for both August 1999 and May 2000 splits.

Initial public offering 50 JUNE 2000

RANK	COMPANY	SYMBOL	DELIVERY DATE	NET PROCEEDS ($MIL)	IPO PRICE ($)	4-30-99 CLOSE ($)	$100 IN IPO	$100 IN S&P 500	PERFORMANCE* (%)
26	**ChoiceTel Communications** • Plymouth • (763) 544-1260 Independent provider of payphone services.	PHON	11-14-97	4.5	7.00	4.00	$57	$155	-63.0
27	**Industrial Rubber Products** • Hibbing • (218) 263-8831 Protective materials, abrasion-resistant equipment, proprietary rubber products.	INRB	04-24-98	5.5	5.00	2.09	$42	$129	-67.7
28	**NetRadio Corp.** • Minneapolis • (612) 378-2211 Broadcasting of originally programmed audio entertainment over the Internet.	NETR	10-15-99	32.7	11.00	3.44	$31	$115	-72.8
29	**PopMail.com Inc.** • Bloomington • (952) 837-9917 Permission-based marketing e-mail services to media businesses.	POPM	11-07-97	11.7	5.00	2.09	$42	$155	-72.9
30	**SAC Technologies Inc.** • Eagan • (651) 687-0414 Desktop device that electronically captures fingerprints.	SACM	02-26-97	6.2	1.50[s]	0.70	$47	$178	-73.7
31	**OneLink Communications** • Eden Prairie • (952) 996-9000 Development, operation of interactive communications systems for consumers	ONEL	04-27-95	6.0	3.50	2.44	$70	$279	-75.1
32	**Coda Music Technology** • Eden Prairie • (952) 937-9611 Development, marketing of proprietary music technology products.	COMT	06-29-95	5.9	6.00	3.88	$65	$264	-75.5
33	**Famous Dave's of America** • Eden Prairie • (952) 294-1300 American roadhouse-style barbeque restaurants.	DAVE	10-21-96	15.6	6.50	2.94	$45	$202	-77.6
34	**XOX Corp.** • Bloomington • (952) 946-1191 Proprietary software for geometric computing.	XOXC	09-11-96	5.3	7.00	3.38	$48	$215	-77.6
35	**Legal Research Center** • Minneapolis • (612) 332-4950 Outsourced legal and factual research, writing services for attorneys.	LRCI	08-03-95	4.3	3.50	1.97	$56	$257	-78.1
36	**Printware Inc.** • Eagan • (651) 456-1400 "Computer-to-plate" systems for the offset printing industry.	PRTW	07-02-96	6.4	6.00	2.50	$42	$213	-80.4
37	**ACI Telecentrics Inc.** • Minneapolis • (612) 928-4700 Outbound teleservices (telephone-based sales and marketing call centers).	ACIT	10-24-96	6.5	5.00	1.88	$38	$204	-81.6
38	**RTW Inc.** • Bloomington • (952) 893-0403 Products, services for employers' workers' compensation programs.	RTWI	04-18-95	27.0	8.67[s]	4.38	$50	$284	-82.2
39	**Select Comfort Corp.** • Eden Prairie • (952) 551-7000 Manufacturer, retailer of adjustable-firmness sleep systems.	SCSS	12-03-98	43.3	17.00	3.69	$22	$125	-82.6
40	**Urologix Inc.** • Plymouth • (763) 475-1400 Minimally invasive medical devices for the treatment of urological disorders.	ULGX	06-04-96	39.6	14.00	5.06	$36	$213	-83.0
41	**Integ Inc.** • St. Paul • (651) 639-8816 Painless, bloodless hand-held glucose-monitoring product for diabetics.	NTEG	06-26-96	26.1	9.50	2.44	$26	$216	-88.1
42	**FieldWorks Inc.** • Eden Prairie • (952) 974-7000 Rugged laptop computers designed to withstand the rigors of field work.	FWRX	03-20-97	11.9	6.50	1.31	$20	$183	-89.0
43	**Mercury Waste Solutions** • Mankato • (507) 345-0522 Recycling solutions for mercury waste disposal.	MWSI	03-05-97	4.4	5.00	0.94	$19	$179	-89.5
44	**GalaGen Inc.** • Arden Hills • (651) 634-4230 Oral therapeutics that target life-threatening and infectious diseases.	GGEN	03-27-96	18.0	10.00	2.16	$22	$221	-90.2
45	**Medi-Ject Corp.** • Plymouth • (763) 475-7700 Needle-free injection systems for the self-administration of injectable drugs.	MEDJ	10-02-96	10.5	27.50[r]	5.38	$20	$207	-90.5
46	**Paper Warehouse Inc.** • St. Louis Park • (952) 936-1000 Chain of retail stores specializing in party supplies and paper goods.	PWHS	11-28-97	13.2	7.50	1.00	$13	$150	-91.1
47	**New Horizon Kids Quest** • Plymouth • (763) 557-1111 Hourly child care and entertainment at casinos, traditional facilities.	KIDQ	11-13-95	4.9	5.00	1.03	$21	$242	-91.5
48	**Optical Sensors Inc.** • Eden Prairie • (952) 944-5857 Noninvasive blood gas monitoring systems.	OPSI	02-14-96	34.3	13.00	1.38	$11	$219	-95.2
49	**RSI Systems Inc.** • Edina • (952) 896-3020 Telecommunications products for videoconferencing and other uses.	RSIS	07-25-95	7.8	6.25	0.57	$9	$256	-96.4
50	**Excelsior-Henderson*** • Belle Plaine • (763) 873-7000 Premium heavyweight cruiser and touring motorcycles.	BIGX	07-29-97	27.4	7.50	0.00	$0	$152	-100.0

† CALCULATION: (($100 in IPO - $100 in S&P)/$100 in S&P)*100
s split-adjusted
r reverse split-adjusted
50 Excelsior-Henderson: In December 1999 the company filed a voluntary petition for relief under Chapter 11 of the U.S. Bankruptcy Code.

Compensation 100 JULY 2000

RANK	CEO/COMPANY	SALARY ($)	BONUS ($)	RESTRICTED STOCK ($)	OPTIONS @ 5% ($)	OTHER ($)	TOTAL ($)
1	William W. McGuire Medtronic Inc.	1,588,461	2,978,365		53,412,807	205,342	58,184,975
2	John F. (Jack) Grundhofer * Honeywell Inc.	895,003	750,000		35,484,400	239,442	37,368,845
3	Stephen W. Sanger UnitedHealth Group	687,863	1,052,400	263,104	11,464,340	61,386	13,529,093
4	Ronald N. Zebeck * U.S. Bancorp	681,827	1,280,676	4,092,689	3,553,792 #	487,823	10,096,807
5	Robert J. Ulrich * General Mills Inc.	1,027,874	3,500,000			5,272,328	9,800,202
6	Ronald J. Peltier * ReliaStar Financial Corporation	350,000	200,000		8,958,500	140,705	9,649,205
7	Paul David Miller * Metris Companies Inc.	150,000	161,000	1,071,688	7,776,675	5,200	9,164,563
8	Allan L. Schuman Damark International Inc.	750,000	1,200,000	520,000	6,275,391	139,167	8,884,558
9	Livio D. DeSimone * Video Update Inc.	1,047,600	947,502	774,698	2,969,011 #	1,587,774	7,326,585
10	Joel W. Johnson * 3M Company	610,600	1,065,600		1,800,604	3,378,148	6,854,952
11	William W. George Dayton Hudson Corporation	800,000	329,480		5,638,049	40,530	6,808,059
12	John G. Turner * Supervalu Inc.	728,154	530,835	57,396	4,468,809 #	338,367	6,123,561
13	Richard M. Schulze Best Buy Company Inc.	1,000,000	1,550,792		3,446,000	24,890	6,021,682
14	Philip Kives * ADC Telecommunications Inc.				5,998,000		5,998,000
15	William J. Cadogan * Deluxe Corporation	683,462	412,768		4,721,315 #	63,779	5,881,324
16	John A. (Gus) Blanchard III * Musicland Stores Corporation	680,000	680,000		4,181,167	159,266	5,700,433
17	Terry L. Shepherd * Digi International Inc.	418,019	384,832		4,770,200 #	47,849	5,620,900
18	Irving Weiser * Ecolab Inc.	300,000	2,450,000		2,559,968	181,368	5,491,336
19	Douglas W. Leatherdale Pentair Inc.	940,385	2,287,500	935,812	1,231,155 #	88,770	5,483,622
20	John Buchanan * The St. Paul Companies Inc.	250,000	106,250		4,222,084		4,578,334
21	Thomas G. Hudson TCF Financial Corporation	330,000	11,880		4,134,375	36,689	4,512,944
22	James J. Howard III * Hormel Foods Corporation	730,000	233,346	335,800	2,433,187	51,250	3,783,583
23	Gene McCaffery Dura Automotive Systems Inc.	541,667	678,000		2,550,954		3,770,621
24	Winslow H. Buxton * Tennant Company	718,000	174,546		2,217,876	557,487	3,667,909
25	John H. Dasburg * National Computer Systems Inc.	500,000	1,049,750	2,002,500		98,461	3,650,711

2 Grundhofer: Option valuation doesn't include reload options.
4 Zebeck: "Other" includes supplemental executive retirement plan payments of $330,846.
5 Ulrich: "Other" includes LTIP payout of $4,756,597; and $350,972 in reportable earnings on deferred compensation.
6 Peltier: "Other" includes $136,517 credit towards payment of a promissory note.
7 Miller: Compensation is for fourth quarter (ending 3/31/99), after he succeeded Richard Schwartz.
9 DeSimone: "Other" includes LTIP payout of $1,336,500.
10 Johnson: "Other" includes LTIP payout of $3,346,155.
12 Turner: "Other" includes LTIP payout of $176,426.
14 Kives: Takes no salary; he owned 46.4% of K-tel stock at 11/15/99.
15 Cadogan: Will retire after 12- to 18-month transition to a new leader.
16 Blanchard: Will become chairman/CEO of eFunds when that division is spun off as a separate company.
17 Shepherd: Named CEO on 5/5/99; compensation is for full year.
18 Weiser: "Other" includes $168,125 in matching contributions on bonus amounts earned but deferred.
20 Buchanan: As part of Retek's spin-off from HNC Software, he received Retek option grants in exchange for HNC option grants.
22 Howard: Replaced by Wayne Brunetti in fiscal 2000; remains chairman until end of 2000.
24 Buxton: "Other" includes LTIP payout of $547,374.
25 Dasburg: Bonus includes dollar value of 20,000 phantom stock units granted in April 1999, vested immediately, and settled for $521,250 cash.

Compensation 100 JULY 2000

RANK	CEO/COMPANY	SALARY ($)	BONUS ($)	RESTRICTED STOCK ($)	OPTIONS @ 5% ($)	OTHER ($)	TOTAL ($)
26	Michael W. Wright Donaldson Company Inc.	931,505	1,583,559	801,279		116,943	3,433,286
27	James T. Anderson * ITI Technologies Inc.	400,000	2,677,416				3,077,416
28	Thomas C. Tiller * Nash Finch Company	418,273	836,545	789,063	992,474	15,769	3,052,124
29	Karl F. Storrie Jostens Inc.	500,000	800,000		1,496,769	61,220	2,857,989
30	Kendrick B. Melrose ValueVision International Inc.	597,503	1,190,530	167,845	414,190 #	478,974	2,849,042
31	Richard M. Rompala The Valspar Corporation	586,923		873,342	1,210,550	75,031	2,745,846
32	Janet M. Dolan * H.B. Fuller Company	327,500	38,415	35,000	2,011,622	203,557	2,616,094
33	John H. Roe * Northern States Power Company	700,000	874,650	24,331	836,266	13,645	2,448,892
34	Russell A. Gullotti * Tower Automotive Inc.	496,372	650,000		1,198,889	13,057	2,358,318
35	William G. Van Dyke Ceridian Corporation	539,615	678,000		984,488	29,208	2,231,311
36	Dugald K. Campbell Minnesota Power Inc.	531,690	248,400		1,392,215	18,783	2,191,088
37	Albert P.L. Stroucken St. Jude Medical Inc.	621,000	497,674		894,267	4,800	2,017,741
38	Jack W. Eugster * BMC Industries Inc.	650,000	780,000			445,234	1,875,234
39	William A. Cooper International Multifoods Corporation	700,000	1,050,000			85,818	1,835,818
40	William T. Monahan Norstan Inc.	530,040	568,823		642,600 #	53,934	1,795,397
41	Edwin L. Russell * Michael Foods Inc.	475,939	744,110		188,813 #	266,873	1,675,735
42	Paul B. Burke The Toro Company	400,000		50,000	999,000 #	217,331	1,666,331
43	Gregg A. Ostrander Polaris Industries Inc.	506,000	416,980		676,137	7,604	1,606,721
44	Susan E. Engel Merrill Corporation	543,046			976,576	69,838	1,589,460
45	Thomas L. Auth * Regis Corporation	375,000	160,000		854,314	2,400	1,391,714
46	Lawrence Perlman * Graco Inc.	795,000	564,225			4,800	1,364,025
47	Daniel J. McAthie * Alliant Techsystems	181,310			1,181,629		1,362,939
48	James A. Earnshaw * Rural Cellular Corporation	300,495	187,416		830,700 #	1,800	1,320,411
49	David R. Richard * Braun's Fashions Corporation	350,000			894,760	64,055	1,308,815
50	Gary E. Costley Apogee Enterprises Inc.	677,500	290,000	21,038	273,567	32,055	1,294,160

REV is fiscal 1999 year-over-year revenue change.
ERN is earnings change scaled by 1998 revenue.
ROE is return on average of beginning, ending equity.
TRS is calendar 1999 total return to shareholders.
Evaluated using Black-Scholes option-pricing model.

27 Anderson: Although options were granted, their valuation was not presented.
28 Tiller: Named CEO in May 1999; compensation is for full year.
32 Dolan: Named CEO in April 1999; compensation is for full year. "Other" includes LTIP payout of $185,958.
33 Roe: Replaced by Jeffrey H. Curler in fiscal 2000; remains chairman.
34 Gullotti: Will retire by 6/1/01.
38 Eugster: "Other" includes a premium of $313,998 paid on a split-dollar life insurance policy.
41 Russell: Option valuation doesn't include reload options. "Other" includes LTIP payout of $197,396.
45 Auth: Replaced by Ken Boyda in fiscal 2000; remains chairman.
46 Perlman: Replaced by Ronald L. Turner in fiscal 2000; is now retired.
47 McAthie: Was CEO for three months; compensation is for six months. Current CEO, William McLaughlin, was hired in fiscal 2000.
48 Earnshaw: Joined company as CEO 3/1/99; left 12/31/99. George Aristides was renamed CEO for fiscal 2000 on a temporary basis.
49 Richard: Replaced by Paul Baszucki in fiscal 2000.

Compensation 100 JULY 2000

RANK	CEO/COMPANY	SALARY ($)	BONUS ($)	RESTRICTED STOCK ($)	OPTIONS @ 5% ($)	OTHER ($)	TOTAL ($)
51	Mark A. Cohn Hutchinson Technology Inc.	475,000	712,500				1,187,500
52	William J. Prange * Dain Rauscher Corporation	300,000	171,133		672,131	14,736	1,158,000
53	Wayne M. Fortun MTS Systems Corporation	495,684			559,050	9,600	1,064,334
54	Russell Huffer Computer Network Technology Corporation	416,154			569,145	26,463	1,011,762
55	Thomas J. McGoldrick Arcadia Financial Ltd.	264,223	198,750		495,600	20,117	978,690
56	Maurice R. Taylor II Buffets Inc.	325,800	50,000		511,155	4,900	891,855
57	Roe H. Hatlen * Bemis Company Inc.	336,724	90,000		441,995		868,719
58	Joseph P. Micatrotto Life USA Holding Inc.	309,615	100,000		406,147		815,762
59	Richard P. Ekstrand Rainforest Cafe Inc.	362,000	274,938		165,085	5,000	807,023
60	Paul D. Finkelstein Empi Inc.	500,000	200,000			85,446	785,446
61	Sidney W. (Chip) Emery Jr. Department 56 Inc.	302,081			470,233 #	10,564	782,878
62	Daryl R. (Sid) Verdoorn RTW Inc.	182,786	345,000		237,604	8,800	774,190
63	Joel N. Waller Analysts International Corporation	410,461	340,000			20,806	771,267
64	Carl B. Lehmann * Minntech Corporation	416,000			283,003	56,789	755,792
65	Robert D. Alton Hickory Tech Corporation	241,972	223,657		198,750	84,600	748,979
66	Christopher A. Twomey Thermo Sentron Inc.	225,000	180,000		278,873 #	4,800	688,673
67	Daniel A. Potter FSI International Inc.	360,000	294,195			28,443	682,638
68	David R. Pomije Imation Corporation	270,000	40,500		352,489		662,989
69	Wolfgang von Maack * Northwest Airlines Corporation	246,668	195,000		198,099	10,220	649,987
70	Stanley Goldberg * The Sportsman's Guide Inc.	183,860				443,705	627,565
71	Eric H. Paulson Funco Inc.	293,082	125,000		81,172	77,500	576,754
72	Frederick W. Lang Wilsons The Leather Experts	362,000	189,777			6,542	558,319
73	Bryan K. Bedford * C.H. Robinson Worldwide Inc.	278,269	112,000		156,444	3,469	550,182
74	John C. MacFarlane Innovex Inc.	337,389	51,511		145,080 #	13,093	547,073
75	Ron Marshall Jr. Patterson Dental Company	498,629				46,780	545,409

REV is fiscal 1999 year-over-year revenue change.
ERN is earnings change scaled by 1998 revenue.
ROE is return on average of beginning, ending equity.

TRS is calendar 1999 total return to shareholders.
Evaluated using Black-Scholes option-pricing model.

52 Prange: February 1999 numbers; fiscal 2000 proxy was not filed by our June 5 cutoff date.
57 Hatlen: Will step down 6/30/00.
64 Lehmann: Will step down January 2001.
69 von Maack: Replaced by interim CEO C. Michael Ford in fiscal 2000. Replacement John F. Hetterick (12/1/99) was, in turn, replaced by Dean Bachelor in fiscal 2000.
70 Goldberg: "Other" includes severance payment of $235,000.
73 Bedford: Resigned; current CEO, Paul F. Foley, was hired in fiscal 2000.

Compensation 100 JULY 2000

RANK	CEO/COMPANY	SALARY ($)	BONUS ($)	RESTRICTED STOCK ($)	OPTIONS @ 5% ($)	OTHER ($)	TOTAL ($)
76	Peter L. Frechette Select Comfort Corporation	324,256	218,399			1,600	544,255
77	William H. Spell G&K Services Inc.	145,700	280,000	70,000	22,011	7,404	525,115
78	Thomas W. Haley * K-tel International Inc.	182,311			325,467	7,154	514,932
79	Joel A. Elftmann * Chronimed Inc.	315,000			90,180	91,595	496,775
80	Edward L. Lundstrom * Health Risk Management Inc.	200,176			241,731	3,687	445,594
81	Gary Olen Mesaba Holdings Inc.	270,931			165,777		436,708
82	Thomas Moberly * Osmonics Inc.	311,154			83,316	33,050	427,520
83	Dean L. Hahn * Arctic Cat Inc.	166,600	196,600			34,500	397,700
84	David H. Rotter Transport Corporation of America Inc.	250,000	122,845				372,845
85	David L. Andreas Navarre Corporation	271,656	80,736			20,450	372,842
86	James B. Aronson * Otter Tail Power Company	346,154				1,600	347,754
87	Gary T. McIlroy In Home Health Inc.	278,000			27,600	33,845	339,445
88	Joel A. Ronning Hawkins Chemical Inc.	225,000	112,500			1,000	338,500
89	Alvin E. McQuinn TSI Inc.	337,700					337,700
90	Marion Melvin Stuckey	305,000				18,333	323,333
91	D. Dean Spatz Grow Biz International Inc.	290,000			17,360 #	9,866	317,226
92	Yale T. Dolginow Ag-Chem Equipment Company Inc.	285,000				27,405	312,405
93	Curtis A. Sampson Sheldahl Inc.	202,913	50,000		31,849	13,712	298,474
94	Greg R. Meland Eagle Pacific Industries Inc.	250,000				14,000	264,000
95	Dennis W. Vollmershausen National City Bancorporation	250,000					250,000
96	Thomas E. Oland Recovery Engineering Inc.	199,500				19,258	218,758
97	John P. Schinas Lund International Holdings Inc.	204,186					204,186
98	Peter C. Lytle The Rottlund Company Inc.	100,000			62,000 #		162,000
99	Robert A. Kierlin Techne Corporation	117,000					117,000
100	Robert C. Pohlad VirtualFund.com Inc.	74,038					74,038

REV is fiscal 1999 year-over-year revenue change.
ERN is earnings change scaled by 1998 revenue.
ROE is return on average of beginning, ending equity.
TRS is calendar 1999 total return to shareholders.
Evaluated using Black-Scholes option-pricing model.

78 Haley: Replaced by William P. Murnane in fiscal 2000; remains chairman.
79 Elftmann: Replaced by Donald S. Mitchell in fiscal 2000; remains chairman.
80 Lundstrom: Named CEO in January 1999 (fiscal year end is August); compensation is for full year.
82 Moberly: Named CEO in January 1999 (fiscal year end is June); compensation is for full year.
83 Hahn: Replaced by John Hawkins in fiscal 2000; remains director.
86 Aronson (deceased): Replaced by Robert J. Meyers in December 1999.

100 largest employers AUGUST 2000

RANK 1999	RANK 1998	ORGANIZATION	MINNESOTA EMPLOYEES
1	1	State of Minnesota	55,294
2	3	Target Corp.*	35,047
3	2	United States Government	34,806
4	4	University of Minnesota	29,498
5	5	Mayo Foundation	23,376
6	6	Allina Health System	22,454
7	7	Northwest Airlines Corp.	21,301
8	9	Fairview	18,700
9	8	3M Co.	18,179
10	10	Wells Fargo & Co.*	13,938
11	12	Wal-Mart Stores Inc.	11,925
12	11	County of Hennepin	11,012
13	13	U.S. Bancorp	10,938
14	15	HealthPartners	9,634
15	16	Carlson Cos. Inc.*	9,000
16	17	Supervalu Inc.	8,600
17	20	American Express Financial Advisors	7,716
18	18	Special School District 1 — Minneapolis	7,642
19	21	IBM Corp.	7,200
20	23	Hormel Foods Corp.	7,167
21	35	ISD 625 — St. Paul	7,062
22	19	Honeywell Inc.	7,000
	24	Qwest *	7,000
24	25	HealthEast	6,918
25	22	Park Nicollet Health Services *	6,607
26	26	Taylor Corp.	6,517
27	44	Best Buy Co. Inc.	6,500
28	27	Fingerhut Cos. Inc.	6,019
29	37	Doherty Employment Group	5,800
30	28	Evangelical Lutheran Good Samaritan Soc.	5,796
31	29	Medtronic Inc.	5,696
32	14	Fleming Cos. Inc.	5,549
33	34	United Parcel Service Inc.	5,467
34	33	Northern States Power Co.	5,419
35	30	West Group	5,396
36	36	Cargill Inc.	5,111
37	39	Holiday Cos.	5,000 e
	43	REM Inc. *	5,000
39	52	CentraCare *	4,930
40	42	Andersen Corp.	4,824
41	71	ADC Telecommunications Inc.	4,781
42	38	St. Mary's/Duluth Clinic Health System	4,731
43	41	City of Minneapolis *	4,694
	40	UnitedHealth Group	4,694
45	73	Perkins Family Restaurants	4,600
46	32	ISD 11 — Anoka	4,521
47	50	Board of Social Ministry *	4,500
	60	Coborn's Inc.	4,500
	31	Kmart Corp.	4,500
50	49	Shakopee Mdewakanton Sioux*	4,461

e: estimated by Corporate Report
1YG: year-over-year growth rate
3YG: annualized three-year growth rate
FTE: full-time equivalent

2 Target Corp.: the former Dayton Hudson Corp.
10 Wells Fargo & Co.: the former Norwest Bank Minnesota N.A.
15 Carlson Cos. Inc.: companywide (does not include franchises)
22 Qwest: the former U S West, which merged with Qwest Communications International Inc. on June 30, 2000
25 Park Nicollet Health Services: the former HealthSystem Minnesota
37 REM Inc.: includes affiliates
39 CentraCare: includes St. Cloud Hospital, St. Benedicts Hospital and CentraCare Clinics
43 City of Minneapolis: city depts. 3,775; park bd. 573; library 346
47 Board of Social Ministry: the former Ebenezer Social Ministries
50 Little Six, Mystic Lake Casino

100 largest employers AUGUST 2000

RANK 1999	RANK 1998	ORGANIZATION	MINNESOTA EMPLOYEES
51	53	North Memorial Health Care	4,390
52	47	Lund Food Holdings Inc.	4,300
53	46	JCPenney Co. Inc.	4,000 [e]
	90	Marsden Bldg Maintenance Co.*	4,000
	64	Prudential Insurance Co. of America	4,000
56	51	County of Ramsey	3,925
57	73	General Mills Inc.	3,785
58	62	Hy-Vee Food Stores Inc.	3,761
59	48	Seagate Technology Inc. *	3,725
60	62	Mille Lacs Band/Ojibwe Indians	3,685
61	59	Metropolitan Council	3,674
62	57	Marathon Ashland Petroleum Inc. *	3,665
63	70	Children's Hospitals and Clinics	3,499
64	67	City of St. Paul	3,400
	64	TCF Financial Corp.	3,400
66	79	Jerry's Enterprises Inc.	3,340
67	73	Pillsbury	3,227
68	72	Sears, Roebuck & Co.	3,140
69	56	ConAgra Inc.	3,000
70	57	The St. Paul Cos. Inc.	2,958
71	69	Blue Cross and Blue Shield of Minnesota	2,916
72	64	Boston Scientific Corp. *	2,900
	78	Burlington Northern Santa Fe	2,900
74	61	ISD 279 — Osseo	2,844
75	45	ISD 196 — Rosemount	2,773
76	68	Marvin Lumber & Cedar Co.	2,750
77	76	Star Tribune	2,602
78	55	Hutchinson Technology Inc.	2,545
79	84	Guidant Corp. Cardiac Rhythm Mgmt. Group	2,500
	79	Pentair Inc.	2,500
	81	Potlatch Corp.	2,500
82	89	Apogee Enterprises Inc.	2,491
83	86	McDonald's Corp. *	2,404
84	77	Emerson Electric Co.	2,400
85	88	Minnesota Life Insurance Co.	2,392
86	87	County of St. Louis	2,288
87	96	Polaris Industries Inc.	2,235
88	93	Unisys Corp.	2,220
89	94	Benedictine Health System	2,219
90	90	ISD 281 — Robbinsdale	2,033
91	0	Snyder's Drug Stores Inc.	2,014
92	0	Land O'Lakes Inc.	2,003
93	83	Deluxe Corp.	2,000
	98	Schwan's Sales Enterprises Inc.	2,000 [e]
95	98	Ford Motor Co.	1,986
96	0	Presbyterian Homes of Minnesota Inc.	1,975
97	84	ISD 709 — Duluth	1,972
98	97	Ecolab Inc.	1,964
99	95	ISD 535 — Rochester	1,925
100	90	ISD 833 — South Washington County	1,916
		Composite total	**670,061**

e: estimated by Corporate Report
1YG: year-over-year growth rate
3YG: annualized three-year growth rate
FTE: full-time equivalent

53 Marsden/American Security: companies are under same management
59 Seagate Technology Inc.: includes Jan. 31, 2000, acquisition XIOtech Corp., Eden Prairie (70 employees)
62 Marathon Ashland Petroleum Inc.: 95.5 percent of total is from subsidiary Speedway SuperAmerica
72 Boston Scientific Corp.: announced on July 12, 2000, that it will be moving 741 of these jobs out of Minnesota in a companywide consolidation
83 McDonald's Corp.: from the 44 company-owned restaurants (does not include franchises)

RNK

100 largest foreign-owned companies SEPTEMBER 2000

RANK 00	RANK 99	COMPANY/DESCRIPTION	EMPLOYEES	PARENT NAME	COUNTRY
1	•	**National Computer Systems Inc.**† • Eden Prairie • (952) 829-3000 Optical-mark readers and specialized data-collection products/services.	5,000 *	Pearson plc (LON)	United Kingdom
2	•	**ING ReliaStar**† • Minneapolis • (612) 372-5432 Life and health insurance and annuities.	3,800 *	ING Groep N.V.	Netherlands
3	2	**Canadian Pacific Railway (Soo Line)** • Minneapolis • (612) 347-8000 Railway company.	3,000 *	Canadian Pacific Railway	Canada
	2	**McQuay International** • Plymouth • (763) 553-5330 Mfr, sales, service of HVAC equipment.	3,000 *	OYL Industries Bhd.	Malaysia
5	9	**Vincent Metal Goods** • Coon Rapids • (763) 717-9000 Distribution, processing of aluminum, stainless steel, brass, copper, carbon steel.	2,000 *	Rio Algom Ltd.	Canada
6	6	**Frigidaire Home Products Freezer** • St. Cloud • (320) 253-1212 Mfr of home freezers.	1,775	Electrolux AB	Sweden
7	9	**First Student** • St. Paul • (651) 645 5665 Twin Cities suburban school bus transportation system.	1,600	FirstGroup plc	United Kingdom
	7	**Snyder Drug Stores Inc.** • Minnetonka • (952) 935-5441 Retail pharmacy chain.	1,600	The Katz Group	Canada
9	8	**Extendicare Health Facilities Inc.** • Golden Valley • (763) 593-0887 Subacute long-term care facility with assisted living.	1,500	Extendicare Inc.	Canada
	30	**Fortis Information Technology** • Woodbury • (651) 738-4000 I/T support for the Fortis companies in the Midwest.	1,500 *	Fortis AMEV and Fortis AG	Netherlands
11	33	**Allianz Life Insurance Co. of North America**† • Minneapolis • (612) 347-6500 Individual and mass-marketed annuities, life insurance, health insurance.	1,200	Allianz AG Holding	Germany
	11	**Hubbard Feeds Inc.** • Mankato • (507) 388-9400 Mfr of animal feed.	1,200 *	Ridley Canada Ltd.	Canada
13	4	**Brown Printing Co.** • Waseca • (507) 835-2410 Printing of magazines, catalogs and inserts.	1,100	Bertelsmann AG	Germany
	13	**Marigold Foods Inc.** • Minneapolis • (612) 331-3775 Mfr, distribution of fluid-milk and cultured products, Kemps ice cream.	1,100	Koninklijke Wessanen N.V.	Netherlands
	20	**Truth Hardware** • Owatonna • (507) 451-5620 Mfr of window hardware.	1,100	FKI Industries plc	United Kingdom
16	70	**Aggregate Industries North Central Region** • Eagan • (651) 683-0600 Mfr of concrete block, sand, gravel, ready-mix concrete	1,090	Aggregate Industries plc	United Kingdom
17	16	**Blandin Paper Co.** • Grand Rapids • (218) 327-6200 Mfr of publication grades of coated printing paper.	900	UPM-Kymmene Corp.	Finland
	16	**Miracle-Ear Inc.** • Golden Valley • (763) 520-9500 Mfr, marketing of hearing instruments.	900	Amplifon SpA	Italy
	13	**Syntegra USA** • Arden Hills • (651) 415-2999 Internet and computer systems integration.	900	British Telecomm. plc	United Kingdom
20	18	**Fortis Financial Group** • Woodbury • (651) 738-4496 Mutual funds and insurance.	880	Fortis AMEV and Fortis AG	Netherlands
21	18	**Bankers Systems Inc.** • St. Cloud • (320) 251-3060 Products, services, software for the financial services industry.	850	Wolters Kluwer N.V.	Netherlands
22	21	**Syngenta Seeds Inc.** • Golden Valley • (763) 593-7333 Production, marketing of corn, soybean, alfalfa, sorghum, sunflower and wheat seed.	800 *	Syngenta AG	Switzerland
23	22	**IMI Cornelius Inc.** • Anoka • (763) 421-6120 Mfr. of beverage dispensing equipment.	770	IMI plc	United Kingdom
24	•	**Celestica Corp.**† • Rochester • (507) 536-3000 Contract manufacturer of printed circuit boards.	700	Celestica Corp.	Canada
	25	**Chemrex Inc.** • Shakopee • (952) 496-6000 Mfr. of specialty chemical products for construction.	700 *	SKW Trostberg A.G.	Germany

* more than 50 percent of the company's workers are employed out-of-state

1 National Computer Sys.(Nasdaq: NLCS): On July 31, 2000, NCS agreed to be acquired by Pearson plc in a $2.5 billion transaction expected to close in September. 2 ING ReliaStar: On May 1, 2000, ReliaStar Corp. (NYSE: RLR) agreed to be acquired by ING Group in a $6.1 billion transaction expected to close late in the 3d quarter.

11 Allianz Life Insurance Co.: Figures include sister company Life USA Holding Inc., which parent Allianz AG acquired in October 1999.

24 This IBM spin-off agreed to be sold to its new parent in January 2000.

100 largest foreign-owned companies SEPTEMBER 2000

RANK 00	RANK 99	COMPANY/DESCRIPTION	EMPLOYEES	PARENT NAME	COUNTRY
24	25	**Novartis Nutrition Corp.** • Minneapolis • (612) 925-2100 Mfr of nutritional products, food, and beverage items.	700	Novartis AG	Switzerland
27	23	**Hanson Pipe & Products Inc.—North Central** • Apple Valley • (952) 432-6050 Mfr of precast concrete products for infrastructure development.	685	Hanson plc	United Kingdom
28	•	**Fallon Worldwide**† • Minneapolis • (612) 321-2345 Full-service advertising agency.	681	Publicis Group	France
29	28	**Nilfisk-Advance Inc.** • Plymouth • (763) 473-2235 Mfr. of floor-maintenance equipment for the commercial/industrial market.	650	Nilfisk-Advance A/S	Denmark
30	•	**Champion International Corp.** • Sartell • (320) 240-7100 Manufacture of publication paper.	605	UPM-Kymmene Corp.	Finland
31	34	**Quebecor Printing Inc.**† • St. Cloud • (320) 654-2400 Commercial printing of catalogs, magazines, directories.	550	Quebecor Inc.	Canada
32	37	**McKechnie Plastic Components N. America** • St. Louis Park • (952) 929-3312 Custom injection molding of thermoplastic resins to close tolerance.	520 *	McKechnie plc	United Kingdom
33	28	**Eveleth Mines LLC**† • Eveleth • (218) 744-7805 EVTAC Mining mines and processes taconite.	480	Stelco Inc.	Canada
34	40	**Schwing America Inc.** • White Bear • (651) 429-0999 Mfr of concrete pumps, slurry pumps, transit mixers, firefighting booms.	468	Friedrich W. Schwing GmbH	Germany
35	38	**EPC Loudon** • Mora • (320) 679-3232 Custom molding of thermoplastic, injection, and structural foam.	460	Cookson Group plc	United Kingdom
36	30	**SIMS Deltec Inc.** • Arden Hills • (651) 633-2556 Implantable venous access systems; computerized drug-delivery pumps.	452	Smiths Industries plc	United Kingdom
37	15	**Cannon Equipment Co.** • Rosemount • (651) 322-6300 Mfr of point-of-purchase displays, material-handling carts, conveying systems.	450	IMI plc	United Kingdom
38	•	**Corporate Express**† • Arden Hills • (651) 636-2250 Distributor of office products, office furniture, educational products.	430	Buhrmann NV (AEX: BUHR)	Netherlands
39	45	**Champps Entertainment Inc.** • Wayzata • (952) 449-4841 Operation of casual theme restaurant/bars.	420	Compass Group plc	United Kingdom
40	43	**Siemens** • Brooklyn Park • (763) 536-4100 Provider of control systems to electric utilities worldwide.	406	Siemens AG	Germany
41	44	**Inland Ispat Mining Co.** • Virginia • (218) 749-5910 Iron ore fluxed pellets from the Minorca Mine.	372	Ispat International N.V.	United Kingdom
42	52	**Certainteed Corp.** • Shakopee • (952) 445-6450 Mfr of paper pulp, dry felt and residential roofing.	350	Saint-Gobain Corp.	France
	45	**Frontier Communications Inc. of Minnesota** • Burnsville • (952) 435-3133 Local telephone service.	350	Global Crossing Ltd.	Bermuda
44	45	**Twin City Optical Co. Inc.** • Plymouth • (763) 551-2000 Wholesale eyeglass fabricator and buying group.	340 *	Essilor International	France
45	•	**DiaSorin Inc.**† • Stillwater • (651) 439-9710 Medical test kits.	339	Snia SpA	Italy
46	49	**Turck Inc.** • Plymouth • (763) 553-9224 Mfr of proximity sensors and connector products for manufacturing.	336	Hans Turck GmbH & Co. KG	Germany
47	57	**Colle & McVoy Inc.** • Bloomington • (952) 897-7500 Marketing communications services.	312	MDC Communications Corp.	Canada
48	42	**Moore North American Publications Group** • Minneapolis • (612) 661-1000 Commercial, digital, database printing and print management.	300 * 300	Moore Corp. Ltd.	Canada
	50	**Wagner Spray Tech Corp.** • Plymouth • (763) 553-7000 Mfr of paint-spray equipment; painting and decorating products.	300 *	Wagner International AG	Switzerland
	50	**Wilson Learning Worldwide** • Eden Prairie • (952) 944-2880 Learning systems for human resource development.	285	Wilson Learning Worldwide	Japan

* more than 50 percent of the company's workers are employed out-of-state

28 Fallon McElligott: In Feb. 2000 the firm agreed to join Europe's largest agency, Publicis Group.

31 Quebecor Printing: In April 2000 Quebecor's 500-employee St. Paul plant was closed due to company realignment.

33 Eveleth Mines LLC: Other joint owners include A-K Steel Co., Middletown, Ohio, and Rouge Steel Co., Dearborn, Mich.

38 Corporate Express: Corporate Express Inc., Broomfield, Colo., was acquired by Buhrmann in October 1999.

45 Diasorin: Acquired in August 2000 from American Standard Cos., Piscataway, N.J.

100 largest foreign-owned companies SEPTEMBER 2000

RANK 00	RANK 99	COMPANY/DESCRIPTION	EMPLOYEES	PARENT NAME	COUNTRY
51	53	**Buhler Inc.** • Plymouth • (763) 847-9900 Mfr of food processing plants, die casting machines, and bulk-conveying equipment.	280	Buhler International Ltd.	Switzerland
52	•	**USFilter Control Systems** • Vadnais Heights • (651) 766-2700 Mfr of liquid-level, pressure, and flow sensors and controls.	279	Vivendi	France
53	54	**Sulzer Spine-Tech** • Edina • (952) 832-5600 Implants and surgical instruments for treatment of degenerative disc disease.	250	Sulzer Ltd.	Switzerland
54	55	**Detector Electronics Corp.** • Bloomington • (952) 941-5665 Flame, smoke, and gas detection systems for industry.	250	Williams plc	United Kingdom
	55	**Express Messenger Systems Inc.**† • Roseville • (651) 628-3200 Metro-area courier services.	250	Air Canada	Canada
	•	**Lake Superior Paper Industries**† • Duluth • (218) 628-5100 Mill for mfr of supercalendered paper.	240	Stora Enso Oyj	Sweden
57	•	**USFilter / Johnson Screens** • New Brighton • (651) 636-3900 Liquid/solid separation products, water/wastewater and surface-preparation systems.	225	Vivendi	France
58	63	**Solvay Pharmaceuticals Inc.** • Baudette • (218) 634-3500 Mfr of therapeutic products for obstetrics, gynecology, gastroenterology.	220	Solvay S.A.	Belgium
59	65	**Tetra Rex Inc.** • Minneapolis • (612) 362-8500 Carton packaging systems.	220	Tetra Laval Group	Sweden
	60	**Carl Zeiss IMT Corp.** • Brooklyn Park • (763) 533-9990 Mfr of precision measuring systems for dimensional inspection, quality control.	215	Carl Zeiss Inc.	Germany
61	90	**GN ReSound** • Minnetonka • (952) 930-0416 Mfr, distribution of custom hearing instruments.	215	GN Great Nordic Ltd.	Denmark
	61	**Gourmet Award Foods Midwest** • St. Paul • (612) 752-6300 Distribution of specialty and natural foods to grocery stores.	205	Koninklijke Wessanen N.V.	Netherlands
63	62	**Sauer-Sundstrand Electrohydraulics Division** •Plymouth •(763) 509-2000 Mfr of electrohydraulic control systems for mobile applications.	200	Sauer-Sundstrand GMBH	Germany
64	64	**CAE Vanguard Inc.** • Bloomington • (612) 896-3915 Axle supply, rebuilding, reconditioning services for railways.	200	CAE Inc.	Canada
	48	**Fiskars Inc. Power Sentry Division** • Plymouth • (763) 557-0107 Mfr of power strips, surge protectors for PCs and home entertainment equipment.	190	Fiskars Oy AB	Finland
66	65	**Wirsbo Co.** • Apple Valley • (612) 891-2000 Mfr of plastic piping for under-floor heating, plumbing systems.	185	OY Uponor AB	Finland
67	76	**Phillips & Temro Industries Inc.** • Eden Prairie • (952) 941-9700 Mfr of cold-weather starting products for vehicles, industry.	181	Thyssen Krupp	Germany
68	68	**Aero Systems Engineering Inc.**† • St. Paul • (651) 227-7515 Jet turbine engine-testing services and products.	170	Saab Aerospace	Sweden
69	74	**TL Systems Corp.** • Brooklyn Park • (763) 424-4700 Mfr of materials-handling machinery for the pharmaceutical industry.	165	Robert Bosch GmbH	Germany
70	70	**Forward Technology Industries Inc.** • Plymouth • (763) 559-1785 Mfr of plastics assembly, precision cleaning, and halogen lampmaking equipment.	165	Forward Technology plc	United Kingdom
	70	**Ritrama Duramark Cos. Inc.** • Minneapolis • (612) 378-2277 Mfr of graphic arts supplies and pressure-sensitive films.	150	Ritrama S.p.A.	Italy
72	82	**Brookfield Properties Inc.** • Minneapolis • (612) 372-1500 Development, ownership, management of commercial and retail properties.	150	Brookfield Properties Corp.	Canada
	76	**Eurest Dining / Canteen Vending / Chartwells** •St. Paul •(651) 488-0515 Retailing of dining,vending services via corporate and dining centers.	150	The Compass Group plc	United Kingdom
	69	**Smurfit Stone Container Corp.** • St. Paul • (651) 488-2551 Mfr of folding cartons.	150	Jefferson Smurfit Group plc	Ireland
	76	**Strout Plastics Division** • Bloomington • (952) 881-8673 Mfr of flexible packaging, plastic bags, construction film, tubing.	150	Jim Pattison Group	Canada

* more than 50 percent of the company's workers are employed out-of-state

54 Express Messenger Systems Inc.: Other joint owner is Citigroup Inc., New York.

54 Lake Superior Paper Industries: In February 2000 then-owner Consolidated Papers Inc. (NYSE: CDP), Wisconsin Rapids, Wis., was acquired by Stora Enso Oyj.

68 Aero Systems Engineering (Nasdaq: AERS): ASE is publicly traded.

100 largest foreign-owned companies SEPTEMBER 2000

RANK 00	RANK 99	COMPANY/DESCRIPTION	EMPLOYEES	PARENT NAME	COUNTRY
72	76	**Ventura Foods LLC** • Albert Lea • (507) 373-2431 Mfr, distribution of margarine, salad dressings, syrups, preserves, mayonnaise, olives.	148	Mitsui & Co. Ltd.	Japan
77	75	**DBL Labs Inc.** • St. Joseph • (320) 363-7211 Ophthalmic laboratory producing plastic, polycarbonate, and glass eyewear.	144	Essilor International	France
78	83	**Northwood Panelboard Co.**† • Solway • (218) 751-2023 Mfr of oriented structural board.	140	Norbord Industries Inc.	Canada
79	•	**Randstad**† • Bloomington • (952) 897-5222 Permanent and temporary office staffing, computer software training.	140	Randstad Holding nv	Netherlands
	76	**Joseph T. Ryerson & Son Inc.** • Plymouth • (763) 544-4401 Sale of steel, alloys, aluminum, and plastics.	135	Ispat International N.V.	United Kingdom
81	•	**Kewill / JobBoss Software** • Edina • (800) 777-4337 Software for job shop, batch, make-to-order, make-to-contract, discrete mfrs.	130	Kewill Systems plc	United Kingdom
82	•	**DaimlerChrysler Corp.** • Plymouth • (763) 553-2565 Automotive replacement parts; vehicle distribution, customer relations, warranty work.	130	DaimlerChrysler AG	Germany
	85	**Rexam Flexible Packaging** • Lakeville • (952) 469-5461 Mfr of food and medical packaging films, flame-retardant films, industrial packaging.	130	Rexam plc	United Kingdom
	88	**Saunatec Inc.** • Cokato • (320) 286-5584 Mfr, distribution of sauna and steambath products.	128	Saunatec plc	Finland
85	84	**Precision Optics Inc.** • St. Cloud • (320) 251-8591 Dealer in optical frames and lenses.	120	Essilor International	France
86	88	**GSI Lumonics** • Maple Grove • (763) 315-1780 Design, mfr of industrial-laser systems.	107	GSI Lumonics Inc.	Canada
87	•	**Everest Medical Corp.**† • Plymouth • (763) 473-6262 Disposable bipolar electrosurgical instruments and related medical devices.	100	Gyrus Group plc	United Kingdom
88	91	**ADT Security Services Inc.** • St. Paul • (651) 917-0000 Commercial and residential security devices, services.	100	ADT Group plc	United Kingdom
	•	**Otto Bock Health Care** • Plymouth • (612) 553-9464 Mfr of prosthetic and orthotic equipment.	100	Otto Bock Orthopadische	Germany
	91	**Pentax Vision Inc.** • Hopkins • (952) 945-2700 Supplying of anti-reflective coated lenses.	97	Asahi Optical Co. Ltd.	Japan
91	97	**Bill Communications—Human Performance** • Minneapolis • (612) 333-0471 Information products and services for training, lifelong learning.	95	VNU BV	Netherlands
92	98	**Pearl Baths Inc.** • Brooklyn Park • (763) 424-3335 Mfr of whirlpool bathtubs.	93	Maax Corp.	Canada
93	•	**Amesbury Group Inc., Plastic Profiles Div.** • Cannon Falls • (507) 263-3983 Mfr of custom profile extrusions.	90	Laird plc	United Kingdom
94	98	**Clariant Masterbatches Division** • New Hope • (763) 535-4511 Color and additive concentrates for thermoplastic applications.	90	Clariant International Ltd.	Switzerland
	100	**Disetronic Medical Systems Inc.** • Fridley • (763) 795-5200 Design, mfr, distribution of microdose pumps for medicine.	85	Disetronic Holding	Switzerland
96	•	**Corporate Express Document & Print Mgmt.**† • Bloomington • (952) 881-6676 Mfr, sale of business forms, direct mail, labels, computer supplies.	80	Buhrmann NV (AEX: BUHR)	Netherlands
97	•	**Ticona Celstran Inc.** • Winona • (507) 454-4150 Mfr of long-fiber reinforced thermoplastics for metal replacement.	80	Hoechst AG	Germany
	•	**Zero Max Inc.** • Plymouth • (763) 546-4300 Mfr of adjustable-speed drives, couplings, right-angle gear boxes, linear actuators.	75	Miki Pulley Co. Ltd.	Japan
99	•	**Bernafon-Maico Inc.** • Eden Prairie • (952) 941-4200 Mfr of custom-designed, computer programmed hearing aids.	75	Oticon Holding A/S	Denmark
	•	**Electrosonic** • Minnetonka • (952) 931-7500 Design, mfr, installation of videowalls, business communications systems for retailers.	58,173	The Mercantile Group	Finland

* more than 50 percent of the company's workers are employed out-of-state

78 Northwood Panelboard Co.: Other joint owner is Mead Panelboard Inc., Dayton, Ohio.

79 Randstad: Before being acquired, this company was known as AccuStaff.

87 Everest Medical Corp.: On April 14, 2000, Everest was acquired by a Welsh medical products maker in a cash merger valued at $51.6 million.

96 Corporate Express: Corporate Express Inc., Broomfield, Colo., was acquired by Buhrmann in October 1999.

Performance 100 OCTOBER 2000

OVER-ALL RANK	SUM OF RANKS	COMPANY	REVENUE Δ (%)	% RV RANK	REVENUE DOLLAR ($ MIL)	$ RV RANK (%)	Δ INCOME SCALED (%)	INC. RANK	EQUITY Δ (%)	EQUITY RANK	RETURN ON $100 OF STOCK ($)	TRS RANK
1	18	**NRG Energy Inc.*** • Minneapolis • (612) 373-5300 Acquisition, development, operation, maintenance of power generation facilities.	+646.7	2	+731.9	5	+45.0	3	+59.9	2	175.42[n]	6
2	35	**ADC Telecommunications Inc.** • Minnetonka•(952) 938-8080 Transmission, networking and broadband connectivity prod. for telecommunications networks.	+57.9	13	+609.0	9	+22.3[pl/cg]	7	+57.6	3	220.50[ss]	3
3	44	**PW Eagle Inc.*** • Minneapolis • (612) 305-0339 Manufacturer of polyvinyl chloride (PVC) pipe and polyethylene tubing products.	+352.7	3	+155.3	21	+40.9	4	+13.2	15	397.06	1
4	48	**Metris Cos. Inc.** • St. Louis Park • (952) 525-5020 Direct-marketing of consumer credit products.	+92.2	8	+332.5	15	+27.4[pl]	5	+32.6	6	151.14[s]	14
5	88	**FSI International Inc.** • Chaska • (952) 448-5440 Semiconductor surface cleaning products, resist processing equipment, chemical management sys.	+99.8	6	+56.7	33	+50.3[pl]	2	+6.0	36	153.26	11
6	89	**Dain Rauscher Corporation** • Minneapolis • (612) 371-2711 Securities brokerage and investment banking services.	+32.5	25	+158.6	19	+4.2	19	+12.5	19	173.45[d]	7
7	92	**Christopher & Banks Corp.** * • Plymouth • (763)551-5000 Retail women's and teen's apparel.	+44.5	19	+26.9	51	+11.0	13	+27.5	7	263.39[s]	2
8	105	**Medtronic Inc.** • Fridley • (763) 514-4000 Pacemakers, heart valves, angioplasty catheters, cardiopulmonary devices, neurological prod.,.	+20.3	34	+462.4	12	+8.7[pl]	14	+8.5	28	142.91[d]	17
9	107	**Buca Inc.** • Minneapolis • (612) 288-2382 Neighborhood restaurants that serve immigrant Southern Italian cuisine.	+88.4	9	+26.5	52	+15.8[pl]	9	+46.3	4	117.07	33
10	112	**Allete*** • Duluth • (218) 723-3974 Electric, water, wastewater-treatment, and gas utilities.	+21.0	33	+112.7	23	+13.4	12	+10.7	23	135.97[d]	21
	112	**Fastenal Co.** • Winona • (507) 454-5374 Threaded fasteners; construction supplies.	+23.9	31	+70.3	29	+2.9	25	+16.6	11	145.18[d]	16
12	115	**C.H. Robinson Worldwide Inc.** • Eden Prairie • (952) 937-8500 Third-party transportation, produce distribution, financial services.	+28.7	27	+312.4	16	+0.9	47	+17.5	10	148.02	15
13	119	**Pemstar Inc.*** • Rochester • (507) 288-6720 Contract manufacturing, design for computer, telecommunications, medical, equipment industries.	+101.9	5	+120.4	22	-0.4	70	+14.7	14	169.32[n]	8
14	124	**The St. Paul Cos. Inc.** • St. Paul • (651) 310-7911 Insurance and risk management; property/liability underwriting; reinsurance.	+13.4	46	+515.3	11	+5.2	17	+6.7	32	141.11[d]	18
15	134	**Entegris Inc.*** • Chaska • (952) 556-3131 Fluid and material-handling products for microelectronics.	+45.7	18	+55.1	36	+15.9	8	+9.0	26	100.00[n]	46
16	141	**Xcel Energy Inc.*** • Minneapolis • (612) 330-5500 Gas and electric utilities; non-regulated energy services.	+7.4	66	+101.7	24	+3.4	21	+22.1	8	135.18[d]	22
17	147	**Techne Corp.** • Minneapolis • (612) 379-8854 Biotechnology products and hematology controls.	+12.5	50	+6.0	74	+13.8	10	+17.7	9	185.02	4
18	155	**In Home Health Inc.*** • Minnetonka • (952) 449-7500 Home health care services.	+17.5	40	+7.2	70	+3.4	22	+15.8	13	155.88	10
19	162	**Pentair Inc.** • Minneapolis • (612) 338-5100 Portable power tools; woodworking machinery; electrical and electronic enclosures.	+52.8	14	+516.4	10	+4.1	20	+1.6	51	85.53[d]	67
20	169	**Stockwalk.com Group Inc.** • Golden Valley • (763) 542-6000 Full-service investment banker specializing in online trading.	+73.8	11	+20.1	56	+5.7	16	+45.7	5	70.97	81
21	172	**Northwest Airlines Corp.** • Eagan • (612) 726-2111 Passenger airline; international cargo carrier.	+12.7	48	+619.0	8	+0.6	52	+2.9	45	138.48	19
22	176	**Tower Automotive Inc.** • Minneapolis • (612) 342-2310 Metal stampings and assemblies for automobile industry.	+32.8	24	+337.1	14	+1.5	34	+10.3	24	72.47	80
23	179	**Otter Tail Power Co.** • Fergus Falls • (218) 739-8200 Electric utility; other diversified operations.	+19.9	35	+44.6	39	+1.4	36	+6.2	34	115.63[ds]	35
24	181	**U.S. Bancorp** • Minneapolis • (612) 973-1111 Bank holding company; diversified financial services.	+19.8	36	+796.3	4	+0.8	49	+5.7	38	92.97[d]	54
25	185	**UnitedHealth Group** • Minnetonka • (952) 936-1300 Management of health care delivery systems and HMOs.	+6.7	69	+652.0	6	+0.8	48	+0.3	57	176.86	5

1 NRG Energy Inc.: IPO 5/31/00
3 PW Eagle Inc.: fka Eagle Pacific Industries Inc.
7 Christopher & Banks Corp.: fka Braun's Fashions Corp.
10 Allete: fka Minnesota Power Inc.
13 Pemstar Inc.: IPO 8/8/00; asset change is three-month
15 Entegris Inc.: IPO 7/11/00
16 Xcel Energy Inc.: fka Northern States Power Co.; numbers are NSP's only
18 In Home Health Inc.: agreed 9/13/00 (after our cutoff date) to be acquired by its majority owner

Performance 100 OCTOBER 2000

OVER-ALL RANK	SUM OF RANKS	COMPANY	REVENUE Δ (%)	% RV RANK	REVENUE DOLLAR ($ MIL)	$ RV RANK (%)	Δ INCOME SCALED (%)	INC. RANK	EQUITY Δ (%)	EQUITY RANK	RETURN ON $100 OF STOCK ($)	TRS RANK
26	186	**Best Buy Co. Inc.** • Eden Prairie • (952) 947-2000 Consumer electronics; major appliances; factory warranty services.	+24.6	29	+1,436.9	2	+1.4	37	-13.5	90	127.36	28
27	187	**Innovex Inc.** • Maple Plain • (763) 479-5300 Precision electromagnetic products.	+93.1	7	+38.5	44	-11.6	88	+6.2	35	152.67[d]	13
	187	**Patterson Dental Co.** •Mendota Heights •(651) 686-1600 Distribution of dental supplies and equipment.	+11.4	52	+55.6	35	+1.1	41	+13.0	18	109.68[s]	41
29	188	**3M Co.** • Maplewood • (651) 733-1110 Diversified industrial and consumer products.	+8.3	63	+637.0	7	+1.3	38	+7.4	29	96.10[d]	51
30	190	**American Med. Systems** * • Minnetonka • (952) 933-4666 Designs, develops, manufactures, and distributes products and services for use by urologists.	+24.5	30	+9.8	63	+13.6	11	+1.4	52	117.05[n]	34
31	195	**Rural Cellular Corp.** • Alexandria • (320) 762-2000 Cellular communication and paging services.	+83.5	10	+66.6	30	-16.6	93	+243.6	1	88.54	61
32	205	**Ault Inc.** • Brooklyn Park • (763) 493-1900 External power-conversion products.	+33.8	23	+9.6	64	+1.0	43	+16.1	12	88.19	63
33	206	**Bemis Co. Inc.** • Minneapolis • (612) 376-3030 Flexible packaging materials; specialty-coated and graphics products.	+10.1	55	+94.1	25	+1.6	33	+3.6	44	97.36[d]	49
	206	**National City Bancorp.** • Minneapolis • (612) 904-8500 Bank holding company.	+18.1	38	+8.5	66	+3.1	23	+5.7	37	108.96[d]	42
35	207	**TCF Financial Corp.** • Minneapolis • (612) 661-6500 National bank holding company.	+7.8	64	+40.5	41	+1.7	31	+2.2	48	134.70[d]	23
36	208	**Regis Corp.** • Edina • (952) 947-7777 Hairstyling salons.	+14.8	43	+76.4	28	+2.6	27	+5.0	39	80.56	71
37	211	**Zomax Inc.** • Minneapolis • (763) 553-9300 Contract manufacturing of compact discs.	+16.4	41	+16.9	59	+7.1	15	+6.9	31	87.29[s]	65
38	212	**United Shipping & Technology Inc.*** • Plymouth • (763) 941-4080 Same-day delivery system and e-commerce distributor.	†	1	+277.2	17	-2,797.5	100	+11.2	22	77.88	72
39	214	**Donaldson Co. Inc.** • Bloomington • (952) 887-3131 Filtration products worldwide.	+17.7	39	+88.0	26	+0.0	67	+9.5	25	91.69[d]	57
40	215	**St. Jude Medical Inc.** • Little Canada • (651) 483-2000 Heart valves; cardiovascular products.	+7.0	67	+39.0	43	+4.4pl	18	-0.3	63	133.50	24
41	216	**Ecolab Inc.** • St. Paul • (651) 293-2233 Chemical products and systems for cleaning, sanitation.	+8.6	61	+87.3	27	+1.2	39	+3.8	42	99.70[d]	47
42	223	**HomeServices.com Inc.** • Edina • (952) 928-5900 Holding corp. for real estate-related comp. Edina Realty, Edina Realty Title, and Edina Realty Mortgage.	+35.1	22	+58.8	32	+0.1	65	+8.7	27	75.83	77
	223	**Polaris Industries Inc.** • Medina • (763) 542-0500 Mfr of snowmobiles, ATVs, personal watercraft, motorcycles, clothing, accessories.	+9.2	60	+51.7	37	+0.3	56	+13.1	17	93.87[d]	53
44	226	**Graco Inc.** • Golden Valley • (763) 623-6000 Fluid-handling and bulk materials equipment.	+14.9	42	+32.5	48	+1.9	29	+0.0	59	99.43[d]	48
45	228	**Lakes Gaming Inc.** • Minnetonka • (952) 449-9092 Management of two Indian casinos in Louisiana.	+39.0	20	+11.7	62	-21.3[cl]	94	+13.1	16	114.96	36
46	236	**Dura Automotive Systems Inc.** • Minneapolis • (612) 342-2311 Mechanical assemblies and integrated systems for the automotive industry.	+46.4	17	+440.6	13	+0.9	45	-1.8	73	61.65	88
47	237	**Supervalu Inc.** • Eden Prairie • (952) 828-4000 Wholesale foods; operating of supermarkets.	+31.7	26	+3,004.6	1	+0.2	60	-2.2	75	76.84[d]	75
48	239	**Wilsons The Leather Experts** • Brooklyn Pk. • (763) 391-4000 Retailer of leather coats and accessories.	+14.2	44	+18.2	57	+1.7	32	-24.2	97	161.69[s]	9
49	246	**Health Risk Management** • Bloomington • (952) 829-3500 Managed health care services.	+66.0	12	+45.6	38	-6.1	86	-0.9	67	107.14	43
	246	**Paper Warehouse Inc.** • St. Louis Park • (952) 936-1000 Chain of retail stores specializing in party supplies and paper goods.	+18.3	37	+6.7	72	+2.8	26	-0.5	66	104.35	45

30 American Medical Systems Holdings Inc.: IPO 8/11/00
38 United Shipping & Technology Inc.: period ended 4/1/00
49 Target Corp.: fka Dayton Hudson Corp.
† United Shipping & Technology Inc.: Revenue Δ (%)+43,996.5

p = prior period **c** = current period **l** = earnings include extraordinary LOSS exceeding 5 percent of revenue **g** = earnings include extraordinary GAIN exceeding 5 percent of revenue **d** = dividends included **n** = new issue in 2000 **s** = split-adjusted

Performance 100 OCTOBER 2000

OVERALL RANK	SUM OF RANKS	COMPANY	REVENUE Δ (%)	% RV RANK	REVENUE DOLLAR ($ MIL)	$ RV RANK (%)	Δ INCOME SCALED (%)	INC. RANK	EQUITY Δ (%)	EQUITY RANK	RETURN ON $100 OF STOCK ($)	TRS RANK
	246	**Target Corp.*** • Minneapolis • (612) 370-6948 Retail discount and department stores.	+7.8	65	+1,152	3	+0.5	53	+4.6	40	66.44[ds]	85
	246	**Tennant Co.** • Golden Valley • (763) 540-1200 Industrial, institutional, and commercial floor-maintenance equipment.	+8.4	62	+17.4	58	+1.1	42	+0.2	58	132.85[d]	26
53	252	**Computer Network Tech. Corp.** • Plymouth • (763) 268-6000 Enterprise networking products.	+21.7	32	+16.2	60	-0.8	74	+12.0	20	87.19	66
54	253	**Ceridian Corp.** • Minneapolis • (952) 853-8100 Information services.	+9.6	58	+62.0	31	-4.4	83	+3.8	43	113.91	38
55	263	**General Mills Inc.** • Golden Valley • (763) 764-2311 Consumer foods.	+6.9	68	+213.8	18	+0.5	54	-0.4	65	91.22[d]	58
56	264	**Mesaba Holdings Inc.** • Minneapolis • (612) 726-5151 Regional passenger airline.	+11.0	53	+20.9	55	-0.5	71	+6.4	33	94.46[d]	52
57	269	**Navarre Corp.** • New Hope • (763) 535-8333 Distribution of prerecorded music, PC software, interactive CD-ROM software.	+35.8	21	+30.6	49	+24.3	6	-24.1	96	39.13	97
58	270	**Communications Systems Inc.** • Hector • (320) 848-6231 Telecommunications equipment.	+11.6	51	+6.5	73	-0.6	72	+2.3	47	132.83[d]	27
59	271	**G&K Services Inc.** • Minnetonka • (952) 912-5500 Commercial, institutional, and industrial garment supply and service.	+13.7	45	+36.1	46	+0.2	62	+1.4	54	88.18[d]	64
	271	**International Multifoods Corp.** • Wayzata • (952) 594-3300 Diversified food products for foodservice, industrial, retail, and agricultural customers.	+3.7	75	+43.2	40	+0.9	46	-5.5	81	127.16[d]	29
61	284	**Hormel Foods Corp.*** • Austin • (507) 437-5611 Processed and packaged meats and food products.	+9.8	57	+157.1	20	+0.2	59	-1.9	74	77.46[ds]	74
62	289	**The Toro Co.** • Bloomington • (952) 888-8801 Commercial turf-maintenance; consumer lawn-care and snow-removal equipment.	+3.8	74	+28.5	50	+1.2	40	+1.3	55	81.43[d]	70
63	296	**Alliant Techsystems** • Hopkins • (952) 931-6000 Aerospace and defense products for the U.S. and allied governments.	+0.7	83	+4.3	76	+0.2	61	+2.6	46	125.98	30
	296	**ValueVision International** • Eden Prairie • (952) 947-5200 TV home shopping network.	+50.1	16	+55.7	34	-0.9[pg]	75	-2.7	77	54.09	94
65	299	**Chronimed Inc.** • Minnetonka • (952) 979-3600 Distribution of prescription drugs, medical products, and educational materials by mail order.	+26.5	28	+24.4	53	-1.4	76	-6.6	83	91.06	59
66	301	**The Rottlund Co. Inc.** • Roseville • (651) 638-0500 Designing, building, selling of single-family homes.	+5.7	71	+7.3	69	+0.3	58	-3.0	78	133.33	25
	301	**Sheldahl Inc.** • Northfield • (507) 663-8000 Electronic materials and flexible circuitry.	+12.5	49	+7.6	67	+3.1	24	-8.1	85	76.81	76
68	308	**Osmonics Inc.** • Minnetonka • (952) 933-2277 Water filtration, separation, purification, and fluid-transfer products.	+9.6	59	+8.7	65	-0.3	69	-0.0	60	92.52	55
69	311	**Hickory Tech Corp.** • Mankato • (507) 387-3355 Telecommunications holding company.	+6.2	70	+2.9	79	-13.3[pg]	89	+1.4	53	137.80[d]	20
70	313	**RTW Inc.** • Bloomington • (952) 893-0403 Products, services for employers' workers' compensation programs.	+10.9	54	+4.1	77	+1.8	30	-0.0	62	60.87	90
71	315	**Apogee Enterprises Inc.** • Bloomington • (952) 835-1874 Glass fabrication; auto glass replacement; nonresidential aluminum windows.	+9.9	56	+40.4	42	-2.7	79	-2.7	76	88.51[d]	62
	315	**Michael Foods Inc.** • St. Louis Park • (952) 546-1500 Wholesale foods and food ingredients.	+1.4	81	+7.1	71	+0.3	57	+0.9	56	97.06[d]	50
73	316	**The Valspar Corp.** • Minneapolis • (612) 332-7371 Paints, coatings, stains, varnishes, and specialty products.	+3.1	76	+23.1	54	+0.3	55	+1.9	49	70.09[d]	82
74	328	**BMC Industries Inc.** • Minneapolis • (952) 851-6000 Precision-etched products and optical lenses.	+2.8	77	+5.0	75	-0.2	68	-1.2	69	113.65[d]	39
75	331	**Nash Finch Co.** • Edina • (952) 832-0534 Wholesale and retail foods and general merchandise distribution.	-3.2	89	-60.4	97	+0.2	63	-1.3	70	152.80[d]	12

61 Hormel Foods Corp.: period ended 4/29/00 for assets, 7/29/00 for revenue and earnings

p = prior period **c** = current period **l** = earnings include extraordinary LOSS exceeding 5 percent of revenue **g** = earnings include extraordinary GAIN exceeding 5 percent of revenue **d** = dividends included **n** = new issue in 2000 **s** = split-adjusted

Performance 100 OCTOBER 2000

OVER-ALL RANK	SUM OF RANKS	COMPANY	REVENUE Δ (%)	% RV RANK	REVENUE DOLLAR ($ MIL)	$ RV RANK (%)	Δ INCOME SCALED (%)	INC. RANK	EQUITY Δ (%)	EQUITY RANK	RETURN ON $100 OF STOCK ($)	TRS RANK
76	332	**Deluxe Corp.** • Shoreview • (651) 483-7111 Bank checks; financial and business forms; financial services; software.	-1.3	88	-10.7	90	+1.0	44	+3.8	41	83.80[d]	69
77	333	**Hawkins Chemical Inc.** • Minneapolis • (612) 331-6910 Industrial and laboratory chemicals.	+3.9	73	+1.9	82	+0.6	51	-1.7	71	92.24[d]	56
78	336	**Datalink Corp.** • Edina • (952) 944-3462 Custom design, installation of high-end data storage solutions.	+13.3	47	+7.4	68	-4.2	82	-0.0	61	74.68	78
79	337	**Digital River Inc.** • Eden Prairie • (952) 830-9042 Electronic-commerce outsourcing solutions for software publishers, online retailers.	+131.9	4	+36.3	45	-45.8	96	-15.7	92	19.70	100
80	341	**Musicland Stores Corp.** • Minnetonka • (952) 931-8000 Retailing of prerecorded music and video.	+4.5	72	+35.5	47	+0.1	64	-26.6	98	88.89	60
81	345	**Arctic Cat Inc.** • Thief River Falls • (218) 681-8558 Snowmobiles and personal watercraft.	-4.0	90	-7.0	87	+0.7	50	-8.5	86	119.73[d]	32
82	347	**Lakehead Pipe Line Partners L.P.** • Duluth • (218) 725-0100 Petroleum pipeline system.	+1.7	80	+2.7	80	-4.9	84	-1.8	72	120.92[d]	31
83	360	**H.B. Fuller Co.** • Vadnais Heights • (651) 236-5900 Adhesives, sealants, paints, waxes, coatings, and specialty chemical products.	-1.0	87	-7.0	88	+1.5	35	-0.4	64	64.02[d]	86
84	370	**Analysts International Corp.** • Edina • (952) 835-5900 Consulting, project management, systems analysis/design, programming, software maintenance.	-12.3	92	-37.9	95	-2.6	78	+11.9	21	67.14[d]	84
	370	**INTELEFILM Corp.** • Minneapolis • (612) 925-8840 Production of TV advertising.	+50.5	15	+12.5	61	-46.2[pg]	97	-28.1	99	38.96	98
86	376	**Video Update Inc.*** • St. Paul • (651) 222-0006 Operating, franchising of video rental superstores.	-18.3	95	-23.8	93	+51.2[pl/cl]	1	-17.7	94	58.18	93
87	377	**Transport Corp. of America Inc.** • Eagan • (651) 686-2500 Truckload carriage and logistics services.	+2.4	78	+3.5	78	-2.7	80	+1.8	50	60.30	91
88	378	**Ag-Chem Equipment Co. Inc.** • Minnetonka • (952) 933-9006 Agricultural and industrial application equipment.	+0.4	84	+.8	84	-0.7	73	-16.9	93	106.63	44
	378	**Imation Corp.** • Oakdale • (651) 704-4000 Sys., product, and service solutions for the handling, storage, transmission, and use of information.	-8.3	91	-57.5	96	+2.2	28	-4.4	80	67.97	83
90	379	**Lund International Holdings Inc.** • Anoka • (763) 576-4200 Accessory products for trucks.	-0.5	86	-.5	86	+0.0	66	-1.0	68	77.66	73
91	392	**MTS Systems Corp.** • Eden Prairie • (952) 937-4000 Computer-based systems for product development, simulation, analysis, control.	+0.9	82	+1.7	83	-1.8	77	-5.9	82	84.33[d]	68
92	397	**Department 56 Inc.** • Eden Prairie • (952) 944-5600 Design and distribution of collectibles and specialty giftware.	-15.7	93	-18.3	92	-14.6	90	+7.3	30	59.67	92
93	412	**Hutchinson Technology Inc.** • Hutchinson • (320) 587-3797 Suspension assemblies for rigid disk drives.	-22.6	97	-64.0	99	-15.6	92	-7.5	84	111.76	40
94	417	**Damark International Inc.** • Brooklyn Park • (763) 531-0066 Direct-mail marketing of general merchandise products.	-42.6	100	-94.4	100	-14.7[cl]	91	-13.4	89	114.29	37
95	423	**Select Comfort Corp.** • Eden Prairie • (952) 551-7000 Manufacturer, retailer of adjustable-firmness sleep systems.	+0.4	85	+.6	85	-5.5	85	-4.1	79	61.54	89
96	446	**Digi International Inc.** • Minnetonka • (952) 912-3444 Hardware and software connectivity solutions for multiuser microcomputer and networked sys.	-38.0	99	-35.6	94	-11.5[cl]	87	-10.3	87	73.65	79
	446	**Rainforest Cafe Inc.** • Hopkins • (952) 945-5400 Development, ownership, operation of combination retail/restaurant facilities.	+2.0	79	+2.5	81	-86.2[cl]	99	-41.9	100	63.01	87
98	454	**The Sportsman's Guide Inc.** • S. St. Paul • (651) 451-3030 Mail-order sporting goods.	-20.3	96	-14.4	91	-3.3	81	-15.0	91	50.00	95
99	468	**Verdant Brands Inc.** • Bloomington • (952) 703-3300 Environmentally oriented lawn and garden fertilizers and pesticides.	-16.3	94	-8.1	89	-46.5[cl]	98	-12.7	88	21.12	99
100	482	**Norstan Inc.** • Minnetonka • (952) 352-4000 Communications services for businesses and institutions.	-25.1	98	-61.9	98	-23.2[cl]	95	-22.8	95	48.04	96

86 Video Update Inc.: period ended 4/30/00; company filed for **Chapter 11** bankruptcy protection on 9/18/00 (after our cutoff date)

p = prior period **c** = current period **l** = earnings include extraordinary LOSS exceeding 5 percent of revenue **g** = earnings include extraordinary GAIN exceeding 5 percent of revenue **d** = dividends included **n** = new issue in 2000 **s** = split-adjusted

Nonprofit 100 NOVEMBER 2000

RANK 1999	RANK 1998	ORGANIZATION	REVENUE ($)	REVENUE CHANGE (%)	CONTRIBUTIONS (% OF REVENUE)	EXPENSES ($)
1	1	**Mayo Foundation** • Rochester • (507) 284-2511	3,520,300,000	+19.0	3.0	3,414,200,000
2	3	**Blue Cross and Blue Shield of Minnesota** • Eagan • (651) 456-8000	2,883,495,000	+23.1	NA	2,906,055,000
3	2	**Allina Health System*** • Minnetonka • (952) 992-2000	2,677,769,000	+2.5	NA	2,676,522,000
4	4	**HealthPartners** • Bloomington • (952) 883-6000	1,486,377,000	+7.6	NA	NA
5	5	**Fairview*** • Minneapolis • (612) 672-6300	919,401,308	NA	0.3	917,214,952
6	6	**Park Nicollet Health Services*** • St. Louis Park • (952) 993-9900	574,287,916	+5.6	2.2	569,086,094
7	9	**Delta Dental Plan of Minnesota** • Eagan • (651) 406-5900	414,138,000	+26.7	NA	406,333,000
8	7	**HealthEast** • St. Paul • (651) 232-2300	402,842,000	+11.7	NA	395,972,000
9	8	**St. Mary's • Duluth Clinic Health System** • Duluth • (218) 726-4000	392,023,000	+16.9	NA	NA
10	10	**North Memorial Health Care** • Robbinsdale • (763) 520-5200	298,093,007	+4.6	0.2	291,950,424
11	11	**CentraCare Health System** • St. Cloud • (320) 255-5661	260,282,413	+6.0	NA	262,681,853
12	12	**Children's Hospitals and Clinics** • Minneapolis • (612) 813-6100	241,560,000	+6.3	3.4	236,360,000
13	14	**Benedictine Health System** • Duluth • (218) 720-2370	227,217,000	+27.0	0.5	213,830,651
14	17	**UCare Minnesota** • St. Paul • (651) 647-2630	189,678,141	+49.8	NA	188,868,150
15	13	**Carleton College** • Northfield • (507) 646-4000	181,316,941	-6.5	12.8	78,549,864
16	15	**University of St. Thomas** • St. Paul • (651) 962-5000	174,690,003	+1.5	15.8	156,374,086
17	18	**Billy Graham Evangelistic Association** • Minneapolis • (612) 338-0500	129,250,649	+21.8	79.2	94,617,800
18	21	**St. Luke's Hospital of Duluth** • Duluth • (218) 726-5555	117,149,546	NA	0.3	124,487,842
19	19	**Citizens' Scholarship Foundation of America** • St. Peter • (507) 931-1682	102,945,047	+4.7	87.2	88,923,545
20	16	**Aspen Medical Group** • St. Paul • (651) 641-7000	101,469,987	NA	NA	101,448,294
21	22	**National Marrow Donor Program** • Minneapolis • (612) 627-5800	95,979,520	+7.4	46.2	87,222,033
22	20	**Macalester College** • St. Paul • (651) 696-6000	91,771,667	-5.5	11.2	69,212,736
23	26	**Hennepin Faculty Associates** • Minneapolis • (612) 347-5000	85,317,970	+5.4	16.4	84,475,385
24	33	**Presbyterian Homes & Services** • Arden Hills • (651) 631-6100	84,876,186	+44.3	29.2	61,915,140
25	23	**St. Olaf College** • Northfield • (507) 646-3004	78,934,592	-11.3	22.6	66,382,790

3 Allina Health System: Prior year re-ranked on net revenue. 5 Fairview: Figures are from FY98.
6 Park Nicollet Health Services: Formerly HealthSystem Minnesota.
NA: Not Applicable/Available.

Nonprofit 100 NOVEMBER 2000

RANK 1999	RANK 1998	ORGANIZATION	REVENUE ($)	REVENUE CHANGE (%)	CONTRIBUTIONS (% OF REVENUE)	EXPENSES ($)
26	27	**Gustavus Adolphus College** • St. Peter • (507) 933-8000	77,216,943	+12.5	25.5	60,129,262
27	28	**Immanuel-St. Joseph's Hospital of Mankato** • Mankato • (507) 625-4031	76,655,751	+13.1	0.8	66,602,516
28	29	**Concordia College—Moorhead** • Moorhead • (218) 299-4000	76,026,322	+13.7	14.0	64,093,543
29	30	**Hazelden Foundation** • Center City • (651) 213-4000	68,558,493	+3.8	8.2	58,958,508
30	24	**Board of Social Ministry** • Shoreview • (651) 766-4300	64,509,291	-21.6	1.3	64,493,515
31	31	**United Way of Minneapolis Area** • Minneapolis • (612) 340-7400	62,865,416	-1.6	94.3	57,003,801
32	25	**Amherst H. Wilder Foundation** • St. Paul • (651) 642-4000	61,319,779	-25.1	21.2	55,369,320
33	32	**Walker Methodist*** • Minneapolis • (612) 827-5931	60,332,000	+1.8	0.6	60,910,000
34	36	**Bethel College & Seminary** • Arden Hills • (651) 638-6400	59,610,834	+6.6	10.8	58,182,808
35	43	**St. John's University** • Collegeville • (320) 363-2011	59,369,729	+21.2	18.1	45,831,040
36	35	**St. Joseph's Medical Center** • Brainerd • (218) 829-2861	59,368,359	+5.9	NA	52,253,979
37	52	**Albert Lea Medical Center—Mayo Health System** • Albert Lea • (507) 373-2384	58,471,865	NA	0.2	53,957,760
38	34	**Olmsted Medical Center** • Rochester • (NA)	56,454,708	NA	0.2	53,793,003
39	•	**Augsburg Fortress, Publishers** • Minneapolis • (612) 330-3300	56,183,823	-1.2	NA	NA
40	39	**Volunteers of America Care Facilities** • Golden Valley • (763) 546-3242	55,935,441	+5.8	0.1	56,681,454
41	42	**Ridgeview Medical Center** • Waconia • (952) 442-2191	55,513,299	+13.1	NA	53,045,655
42	50	**St. Olaf Hospital Association*** • Austin • (507) 437-4551	55,340,317	NA	1.5	51,204,529
43	38	**Miller-Dwan Medical Center** • Duluth • (218) 727-8762	54,366,251	+1.4	NA	54,911,249
44	41	**Hamline University** • St. Paul • (651) 523-2800	52,944,150	+7.1	16.1	51,236,285
45	75	**PreferredOne** • Golden Valley • (763) 847-4000	52,200,000	NA	NA	NA
46	40	**The College of St. Catherine** • St. Paul • (651) 690-6000	52,060,514	-0.6	9.4	49,897,081
47	•	**American Cancer Society Midwest Division** • Edina • (952) 925-2772	50,935,159	NA	91.9	47,219,018
48	46	**North Country Health Services** • Bemidji • (218) 751-5430	50,548,650	+8.3	0.5	44,054,827
49	48	**College of St. Benedict** • St. Joseph • (320) 363-5407	50,155,877	NA	11.0	46,041,805
50	45	**Lutheran Social Service of Minnesota** • St. Paul • (651) 642-5990	50,113,517	+4.2	14.9	49,340,325

32 Walker Methodist: Figures projected from 10 months due to change in year end.
41 St. Olaf Hospital Association: Formerly Austin Medical Center.
• Not on last year's list. **NA**: Not Applicable/Available.

RNK

Nonprofit 100 NOVEMBER 2000

RANK 1999	RANK 1998	ORGANIZATION	REVENUE ($)	REVENUE CHANGE (%)	CONTRIBUTIONS (% OF REVENUE)	EXPENSES ($)
51	47	**Augsburg College** • Minneapolis • (612) 330-1026	46,906,872	+1.6	14.2	43,198,363
52	49	**Saint Mary's University of Minnesota** • Winona • (507) 452-4430	44,781,468	+3.3	18.6	41,582,437
53	44	**Minneapolis Institute of Arts** • Minneapolis • (612) 870-3046	39,014,835	-20.0	50.3	27,362,879
54	37	**Minnesota Orchestral Association** • Minneapolis • (612) 371-5600	37,684,361	-32.6	51.1	27,758,759
55	51	**Gillette Children's Specialty Healthcare** • St. Paul • (651) 291-2848	37,379,125	+4.2	NA	36,133,327
56	54	**College of St. Scholastica** • Duluth • (218) 723-6000	37,269,237	+8.8	20.7	33,985,242
57	66	**YMCA of Metropolitan Minneapolis** • Minneapolis • (612) 371-8700	37,263,120	+41.2	16.3	31,178,848
58	53	**Science Museum of Minnesota** • St. Paul • (651) 221-9488	36,810,155	+5.1	59.4	22,061,284
59	57	**Northwestern College & Radio** • Roseville • (651) 631-5100	35,214,734	+11.3	26.9	33,675,919
60	55	**Augustana Care Corporation** • Minneapolis • (612) 333-1551	34,765,169	+6.7	2.3	33,312,797
61	58	**Winona Health** • Winona • (507) 454-3650	34,333,113	+9.4	0.7	32,524,184
62	56	**Lake Region Healthcare Corporation** • Fergus Falls • (218) 736-8000	33,284,614	+5.0	0.1	30,304,489
63	62	**Elim Care Inc.** • Eden Prairie • (952) 944-1164	31,328,000	+7.7	NA	NA
64	59	**Minnesota Public Radio** • St. Paul • (651) 290-1500	31,098,960	+2.5	76.6	26,319,351
65	61	**First Plan of Minnesota** • Two Harbors • (218) 834-7207	30,468,939	+5.2	NA	30,216,808
66	60	**Catholic Charities of St. Paul & Minneapolis** • Minneapolis • (612) 664-8500	30,442,615	+1.0	44.0	31,204,781
67	63	**United Way of the St. Paul Area** • St. Paul • (651) 291-8300	30,321,574	+6.9	91.7	23,966,386
68	67	**University Affiliated Family Physicians** • St. Paul • (651) 627-4301	30,087,641	+17.5	NA	29,988,658
69	65	**Sholom Community Alliance** • St. Louis Park • (952) 935-6311	28,296,000	+4.5	1.4	29,343,000
70	76	**Second Harvest St. Paul Food Bank** • Maplewood • (651) 484-5117	27,935,000	+34.1	97.0	27,049,000
71	64	**Courage Center*** • Golden Valley • (763) 588-0811	27,669,117	NA	43.3	25,133,269
72	90	**Nexus** • Plymouth • (763) 551-8640	26,617,132	+52.5	NA	25,556,780
73	69	**YMCA of Greater Saint Paul** • St. Paul • (651) 292-4100	26,599,180	+11.4	15.1	22,289,619
74	94	**Ordway Center for the Performing Arts** • St. Paul • (651) 282-3000	26,005,210	+56.2	35.8	19,814,167
75	71	**The Blake School** • Hopkins • (952) 988-3400	25,796,158	+13.4	21.4	19,986,773

71 Courage Center: Figures are from the FY98
NA: Not Applicable/Available.

Nonprofit 100 NOVEMBER 2000

RANK 1999	RANK 1998	ORGANIZATION	REVENUE ($)	REVENUE CHANGE (%)	CONTRIBUTIONS (% OF REVENUE)	EXPENSES ($)
76	68	**Regina Medical Center** • Hastings • (651) 480-4100	25,315,634	-0.9	0.4	24,566,499
77	•	**Itasca Medical Center** • Grand Rapids • (218) 326-3401	25,008,460	NA	0.1	22,628,025
78	73	**Concordia University—St. Paul** • St. Paul • (651) 641-8278	24,817,044	+11.3	17.3	24,148,429
79	•	**Theatre Live!** • Minneapolis • (612) 339-0075	24,492,085	NA	0.6	24,462,895
80	83	**Twin Cities Public Television Inc.** • St. Paul • (651) 222-1717	23,891,011	NA	84.7	23,099,607
81	70	**Minnesota Masonic Home Care Center** • Bloomington • (952) 948-7000	23,722,398	+1.6	16.7	23,824,628
82	72	**Walker Art Center** • Minneapolis • (612) 375-7600	23,240,432	NA	29.6	15,433,653
83	81	**Minneapolis Federation for Jewish Service** • St. Louis Park • (952) 593-2600	22,134,090	NA	72.8	15,647,464
84	78	**American Refugee Committee** • Minneapolis • (612) 872-7060	21,708,892	+8.4	75.3	20,661,963
85	74	**St. Gabriel's Hospital** • Little Falls • (320) 632-5441	21,640,488	-1.6	NA	21,125,029
86	89	**Accessible Space** • St. Paul • (651) 645-7271	21,496,379	+20.8	28.5	20,286,243
87	86	**Breck School** • Golden Valley • (763) 381-8100	21,051,622	+15.5	26.3	15,197,860
88	82	**Ramsey Action Programs** • St. Paul • (651) 645-6445	20,408,685	+6.9	85.7	20,757,200
89	99	**St. Paul Academy and Summit School** • St. Paul • (651) 698-2451	20,276,018	+33.2	36.2	13,232,012
90	85	**Arrowhead Economic Opportunity Agency** • Virginia • (800) 662-5711	19,764,277	+5.3	76.2	19,458,616
91	80	**Northwest Medical Center** • Thief River Falls • (218) 681-4240	19,696,982	NA	0.1	18,483,787
92	87	**Weiner Memorial Medical Center** • Marshall • (507) 532-9661	19,675,718	+8.8	0.7	18,474,539
93	79	**Public Radio International** • Minneapolis • (612) 338-5000	19,562,303	-1.8	44.2	19,434,850
94	84	**Riverview Healthcare Association** • Crookston • (218) 281-9200	19,108,882	+1.2	1.8	18,256,692
95	93	**William Mitchell College of Law** • St. Paul • (651) 227-9171	18,962,174	+12.0	12.8	17,195,182
96	•	**Parents in Community Action** • Minneapolis • (612) 377-7422	18,454,357	NA	99.4	16,804,347
97	•	**Lakewood Health System** • Staples • (NA)	18,142,907	NA	0.2	17,882,973
98	88	**St. Therese Home** • New Hope • (763) 531-5000	18,030,305	-0.2	1.1	17,536,698
99	92	**St. Joseph's Area Health Services** • Park Rapids • (218) 732-3311	18,011,794	+4.4	1.6	16,763,497
100	•	**Children's Home Society of Minnesota** • Lauderdale • (651) 646-7771	17,868,661	+27.6	24.2	16,668,041
		COMPOSITE:	18,562,076,308	+10.6	5.7	15,933,872,771

• Not on last year's list.
NA: Not Applicable/Available.

RNK

50 highest-paid nonprofit executives NOVEMBER 2000

RANK 1999	NAME	TITLE	ORGANIZATION	COMPENSATION ($)
1	**Mark Banks, M.D.**	Pres. and CEO	Blue Cross and Blue Shield of Minnesota	730,344
2	**George C. Halvorson**	Pres. and CEO	HealthPartners	727,999
3	**Gordon M. Sprenger**	Pres. and CEO	Allina Health System	646,085
4	**Michael Wood, M.D.**	Pres. and CEO	Mayo Foundation	629,678
5	**Scott R. Anderson**	Pres. and CEO	North Memorial Health Care	583,206
6	**Timothy H. Hanson**	Pres. and CEO	HealthEast	553,525
7	**David K. Wessner**	Pres. and CEO	Park Nicollet Health Services	543,083
8	**Peter E. Person, M.D.**	CEO	St. Mary's/Duluth Clinic Health System	535,264
9	**David R. Page**	Pres. and CEO	Fairview	524,209
10	**Terence R. Pladson**	Co-Pres.	CentraCare Health System	523,919
11	**Sister Kathleen Hofer**	Board Chair	St. Mary's/Duluth Clinic Health System	513,476
12	**David Strand**	Syst. VP/Market Network Pres.	Allina Health System	500,213
13	**William K. Maxwell**	EVP and COO	Fairview	480,715
14	**John R. Frobenius**	Co-president	CentraCare Health System	480,662
15	**Karen Vigil**	Operating Officer-Medica	Allina Health System	439,858
16	**Brock D. Nelson**	CEO	Children's Hospitals and Clinics	436,429
17	**Hugh C. Smith, M.D.**	Chair, Mayo Rochester Board	Mayo Foundation	426,845
18	**Robert K. Spinner**	Pres.-Allina Hosp./System VP	Allina Health System	423,661
19	**Evan M. Maurer**	Dir. and President	Minneapolis Institute of Arts	417,984
20	**Leo F. Black, M.D.**	Chair, Mayo Jacksonville Board	Mayo Foundation	417,361
21	**Mary K. Brainerd**	EVP-Care Delivery	HealthPartners	415,370
22	**Ann Schrader**	Group VP-Care Delivery Svs.	HealthEast	400,655
23	**David B. Pryor, M.D.**	SVP, Information Ofcr.	Allina Health System	397,385
24	**Eiji Oue**	Music Dir.	Minnesota Orchestral Association	377,193
25	**David W. Cress**	COO	North Memorial Health Care	370,839

* FY 1997

50 highest-paid nonprofit executives NOVEMBER 2000

RANK 1999	NAME	TITLE	ORGANIZATION	COMPENSATION ($)
26	**William Shimp, M.D.**	EVP, Chief Medical Officer	Park Nicollet Health Services	350,703
27	**Dr. Ronald A. Harmon**	Vice Chair/CEO	Albert Lea Medical Center—Mayo Health Sys.	341,842
28	**Richard M. Weinshilboum, M.D.**	VP	Mayo Foundation	340,082
29	**John Herman**	EVP, Chief Admin. Officer	Park Nicollet Health Services	336,180
30	**Richard S. Blair**	Treasurer	Allina Health System	330,462
31	**Pam Lindemoen**	SVP-Operations/Support	St. Mary's/Duluth Clinic Health System	325,675
32	**Richard Geier**	Pres., Physician	Olmsted Medical Center	319,700
33	**Margaret E. Perryman**	CEO	Gillette Children's Specialty Healthcare	318,312
34	**Gary French**	Group VP-Market Development	HealthEast	315,099
35	**Mary Johnson**	SVP-Patient Care Operations	St. Mary's/Duluth Clinic Health System	304,169
36	**Kathy Halbreich**	Dir.	Walker Art Center	297,868
37	**David J. Hyslop**	Pres.	Minnesota Orchestral Association	292,760
38	**Tom Klassen**	SVP-Corp. Services	St. Mary's/Duluth Clinic Health System	288,444
39	**Jerry W. Spicer**	Pres.	Hazelden Foundation	285,238
40	**James M. Fox**	SVP and CFO	Fairview	278,116
41	**Michael B. O'Sullivan, M.D.**	Chair, Mayo Scottsdale Board	Mayo Foundation	275,612
42	**Mark G. Mishek**	SVP-Legal, Gen. Counsel, Sec.	Allina Health System	273,490
43	**Robert Beck, M.D.**	VP-Medical Affairs	HealthEast	270,074
44	**Terril Hart, M.D.**	VP-Medical Affairs	Children's Hospitals and Clinics	266,224
45	**Melvin P. Bubrick, M.D.**	Pres.	Hennepin Faculty Associates	265,578
46	**James C. Colville**	Pres. and CEO	United Way of Minneapolis Area	265,524
47	**Kathy Cooney**	SVP-Finance and CFO	HealthPartners	261,375
48	**Phillip M. Kibort, M.D.**	VP-System Advancement	Children's Hospitals and Clinics	258,710
49	**Nancy Feldman**	CEO	UCare Minnesota	257,338
50	**Lawrence Fosbury**	SVP-Finance/Operations	Hennepin Faculty Associates	255,988

* FY 1997

Corporate Report

MAGAZINE INDEX

This section makes research easier.
The contents from the January 1996 through September 2000 issues of Corporate Report Magazine are listed.

TAP INTO FIVE YEARS OF EXCLUSIVE RESEARCH

COMPANY AND EXECUTIVE PROFILES

RANKINGS

INDUSTRY NEWS

STOCKS

ANALYSIS

STATISTICS

ENTRIES CONTAIN

ARTICLE TITLE
MAGAZINE SECTION
ISSUE DATE
PAGE NUMBER

FIND ARTICLES

CHRONOLOGICALLY

AND

BY COMPANY OR PERSON'S NAME

please note acronyms precede words
articles listed chronologically under subject heading

to order back issues, contact:
Circulation Department
527 Marquette Avenue • Suite 300 • Minneapolis, MN 55402 • 612-338-4288

CRM

C

G

J

MAGAZINE INDEX

X

PUBLIC COS.

PUBLIC COMPANIES

BASICS

contact information
250 company descriptions
1-year company history

FINANCIALS

5-year earnings history
2-year company balance sheets
2-year quarterly data
2-year stock chart

DECISION MAKERS

officers
directors
major shareholders

RECENT EVENTS

RANKINGS

SUBSIDIARIES

Information is updated annually by each company with a questionnaire.
(There was no charge for inclusion in this section.)

USES

Prospect clients
Check out the competition
Update your database

PUBLIC COMPANIES

PUB

PUBLIC COMPANIES ADDED OR RESTORED

American Medical Systems Holdings Inc.	Minnetonka, Minn.
August Technology Corp.	Bloomington, Minn.
Calendar Capital Inc.	Minneapolis
CorVu Corp.	Edina, Minn.
Credit Store Inc.	Sioux Falls, S.D.
eBenX Inc.	Plymouth, Minn.
Entegris Inc.	Chaska, Minn.
Fargo Electronics Inc.	Eden Prairie, Minn.
Founders Food & Firkins	St. Louis Park, Minn.
Jore Corp.	Ronan, Mont.
Lightning Rod Software Inc.	Minnetonka, Minn.
NRG Energy Inc.	Minneapolis
Pemstar Inc.	Rochester, Minn.
Retek Inc.	Minneapolis
Stonehaven Realty Trust	St. Paul
Vascular Solutions Inc.	Plymouth, Minn.
Voice & Wireless Corp.	St. Louis Park, Minn.
Xdogs.com Inc.	Minneapolis

PUBLIC COMPANY NAME CHANGES

Black Hawk Holdings Inc., Minneapolis, TO PW Eagle Inc.

Braun's Fashions Corp., Plymouth, Minn. TO Christopher & Banks Corp.

Coda Music Technology Inc., Eden Prairie, Minn. TO Net4Music Inc.

CyberStar Computer Corp., Eden Prairie, Minn. TO eNetpc Inc.

Dayton Hudson Corp., Minneapolis, TO Target Corp.

Minnesota Brewing Co., St. Paul, TO MBC Holding Co.

Minnesota Power Inc., Duluth, Minn. TO Allete

Montana Power Co., Butte, Mont. TO Touch America Inc.

New Ulm Telecom Inc., New Ulm, Minn. TO NU-Telecom Inc.

Northern States Power Co., Minneapolis, TO Xcel Energy Inc.

Northwest Teleproductions Inc., Edina, Minn. TO Broadview Media Inc.

TRO Learning Inc., Bloomington, Minn. TO PLATO Learning Inc.

VideoLabs Inc., Golden Valley, Minn. TO E.mergent Inc.

PUBLIC COMPANIES DROPPED OR MOVED

- Ancor Communications Inc. acquired in August 2000 by QLogic Corp. (Nasdaq: QLGC). See "QLogic" in REGIONAL section.
- Applied Biometrics Inc. reached the decision in August 2000 to terminate business operations and to dispose of all remaining corporate assets.
- Arcadia Financial Ltd. merged with a wholly owned subsidiary of Associates First Capital Corp. (NYSE: AFS) in April 2000. See "Arcadia Financial Ltd." in REGIONAL section.
- Buffets Inc. was taken private in October 2000 by Caxton-Iseman Capital Inc., a New York-based private equity firm, for a total consideration of $643 million. See "Buffets Inc." in PRIVATE section.
- Building One merged with Group Maintenance America Corp. (GroupMAC) in February 2000 and moved its headquarters to Houston.
- Carleton Corp. was acquired by Oracle Corp. in January 2000 for $8.7 million. See "Carleton Corp." in REGIONAL section.
- Cellex Biosciences Inc., following bankruptcy proceedings during 1999, is in the process of regaining SEC compliance under a new name, Unisyn Technologies Inc.
- Christian Bros., a nonreporting company, didn't provide any information.
- Dain Rauscher Corp. agreed in September 2000 to be acquired by $300 billion-asset Royal Bank of Canada (TSE, NYSE: RY). See "RBC Dain Rauscher Wessels" in REGIONAL section.
- Destron Fearing Corp. was acquired in September 2000 by Applied Digital Solutions Inc. (Nasdaq: ADSX) and merged into Digital Angel.net Inc. See "Destron Fearing Corp." in REGIONAL section.
- Dynamic Homes Inc. was acquired in September 2000 for a total of $5.7 million by an entity formed by three directors of Dynamic Homes. See "Dynamic Homes Inc." in PRIVATE section.
- Everest Medical Corp. was acquired in April 2000 by Welsh medical products maker Gyrus Group in a cash merger valued at $51.6 million. See "Everest Medical Corp." in REGIONAL section.
- Excelsior-Henderson Motorcycle Manufacturing Co. emerged from Chapter 11 bankruptcy in August 2000 as a private company after agreeing to be sold to E.H. Partners for $17.5 million. See "Excelsior-Henderson" in PRIVATE section.
- Funco Inc. was acquired in June 2000 by Babbage's Etc., a Grapevine, Texas-based unit of Barnes & Noble Inc., when its $161.5 million bid trumped Funco's existing merger agreement with Electronics Boutique.
- Global MAINTECH Inc. relocated company headquarters from Minneapolis to San Jose, Calif., in the second quarter of 2000. The corporate name was also changed, to Singlepoint Systems Inc.
- IBP Inc. agreed in October 2000 to be sold to a subsidiary of DLJ Merchant Banking Partners III L.P. for $2.4 billion in cash plus the refinancing and assumption of $1.4 billion in debt. See "IBP Inc." in PRIVATE section.

PUBLIC COMPANIES DROPPED OR MOVED

- In Home Health Inc. agreed in September 2000 to sell to Manor Care Inc. (NYSE: HCR) all the outstanding shares that it did not already own. See "In Home Health Inc." in REGIONAL section.

- Integ Inc. agreed in October 2000 to merge into a subsidiary of Inverness Medical Technology in a stock deal worth $33 million. Fewer than 50 employees.

- Jostens Inc. agreed in December 1999 to be merged into a company controlled by Investcorp (a global investment group) in a transaction valued at $950 million. See "Jostens Inc." in PRIVATE section.

- Kinnard Investments Inc. agreed in September 2000 to merge with a wholly owned subsidiary of Stockwalk.com Group Inc. (Nasdaq: STOK). See "Stockwalk.com Group Inc." in PUBLIC section.

- Lund International Holdings Inc. relocated its corporate headquarters from Anoka, Minn., to Duluth, Ga., in October 2000. See "Lund International Holdings Inc." in REGIONAL section.

- Michigan Financial Corp. agreed in November 1999 to be sold to Wells Fargo & Co. (NYSE: WFC) in a $209 million stock transaction.

- National Computer Systems was acquired in September 2000 by Pearson plc, a U.K.-based media, publishing, and education company, in a transaction valued at $2.5 billion. See "NCS Pearson" in REGIONAL section.

- Nortech Forest Technologies Inc. filed Form 15-12G, terminating its responsibility to file reports with the SEC, in October 2000.

- Northstar Computer Forms Inc. was acquired in June 2000 for $42 million by Ennis Business Forms Inc., Dallas. See "Northstar Computer Forms Inc." in REGIONAL section.

- PopMail.com Inc., according to recent documents filed with the SEC, has moved to Irving, Texas.

- PremiumWear Inc. was acquired in July 2000 by New England Business Service Inc. (NYSE: NEB) in a stock deal initially valued at $40 million. See "PremiumWear Inc." in REGIONAL section.

- PurchaseSoft Inc. announced, in June 2000, plans to move its headquarters from Edina, Minn., to Westborough, Mass.

- QCF Bancorp Inc. filed Form 15-12G, terminating its responsibility to file reports with the SEC, in August 2000.

- Rainforest Cafe Inc. was sold in October 2000 to Landry's Seafood Restaurants Inc. (NYSE: LNY) for $74.4 million in cash, despite the objections of Rainforest shareholder The State of Wisconsin Investment Board. See "Rainforest Cafe Inc." in REGIONAL section.

- ReliaStar Financial Corp. was sold to ING Group (NYSE: ING) in September 2000, for $5.1 billion plus $1 billion in assumed debt. See "ING ReliaStar" in REGIONAL section.

- Reuter Manufacturing Inc. filed for a delay of its fiscal 1999 financial information (Form NT 10-K) in March 2000. The 10-K still had not been filed by our November press date.

- Spanlink Communications Inc. was taken private in April 2000, by founders and management, for $56.7 million in cash. See "Spanlink Communications Inc." in PRIVATE section.

- Sparta Foods Inc. was acquired in April 2000 by Cenex Harvest States Cooperatives, St. Paul, in a cash deal worth $14.5 million. See "Sparta Foods Inc." in PRIVATE section.

- Sunrise International Leasing Corp.merged with The King Management Corp. in a going-private transaction in June 2000, after King acquired of all shares of Sunrise common stock it did not not already hold. See "Sunrise Int'l Leasing Corp." in PRIVATE section.

- TSI Inc. was acquired in May 2000 by JJF Acquisition, Inc., a Minneapolis-based industrial investment group, in a going-private transaction valued at $180 million. See "TSI Inc." in PRIVATE section.

- Telident Inc. voluntarily dissolved itself in May 2000, selling its assets to Teltronics Inc. (Nasdaq: TELT).

- Thermo Sentron Inc. was spun in and taken private by majority shareholder Thermedics Inc. (Amex: TMD) in April 2000. See "Thermo Sentron Inc." in REGIONAL section.

- Virtual Technology Corp., later known as NetDirect Corp. International, was negotiating a merger with online retailer BuyItNow Inc. of New Jersey at press time. See "NetDirect Corp. International" in REGIONAL section.

- WesterFed Financial Corp. agreed in September 2000 to be acquired by Glacier Bancorp Inc. (Nasdaq: GBCI), Kalispell, Mont., in a $95 million transaction expected to close in the first quarter of 2001. See "Glacier Bancorp Inc." in PUBLIC section.

- XBOX Technologies Inc., formerly Nicollet Process Engineering Inc., moved its headquarters to Coconut Grove, Fla., in June 2000.

PUBLIC COMPANIES

ACI Telecentrics Inc. 1

3100 W. Lake St., Suite 300, Minneapolis, MN 55416
Tel: 612/928-4700 Fax: 612/928-4701

ACI Telecentrics Inc. 2 ...utomated Communications Inc., is a provider of outbound telephone-based sales and marketing ... imarily to corporations in the financial services, publishing, insurance, and telecommunications ... ACI operates nine call centers throughout the Midwest.

EARNINGS HISTORY *

Year Ended Dec. 31	Operating Revenue/Sales	Net Earnings	Return on Revenue	Return on Equity	Net Earnings	Cash Dividend	Market Price Range
	(dollars in thousands)		(percent)		(dollars per share†)		
3	15,036	(906)	(6.0)	(16.3)	(0.16)	—	3.13-0.25
	15,254	(352)	(2.3)	(5.5)	(0.06)	—	6.50-3.00
	9,901	505	5.1	7.5	0.11	—	6.13-6.00
1995	5,850	162	2.8	31.0	0.04	—	
1994 ††	4,475	115	2.6	32.2	0.03	—	

†† Income figures for 1994 include pretax gain of $14,600 on sale of equipment.

BALANCE SHEET

Assets	12/31/98	12/31/97	Liabilities	12/31/98	12/31/97
	(dollars in thousands)			(dollars in thousands)	
Current (CAE 1,300 and 659)	4	4,229	Current (STD 166 and 57)	1,060	1,715
Property and equipment		3,243	Long-term debt, capital lease obligations	258	65
Goodwill	852	1,017	Deferred capital lease	473	215
Deferred taxes	137		Deferred taxes		105
Other	68	39	Stockholders' equity*	5,551	6,429
TOTAL	7,342	8,528	TOTAL	7,342	8,528

* No par common: 15,000,000 authorized; 5,731,471 and 5,708,583 issued and outstanding.

RECENT QUARTERS / **PRIOR-YEAR RESULTS**

	Quarter End	Revenue ($000)	Earnings ($000)	EPS ($)	Revenue ($000)	Earnings ($000)	EPS ($)
Q3	09/30/99	5,401	72	0.01	3,575	(172)	(0.03)
Q2	06/30/99	5,499	262	0.05	4,330	(300)	(0.05)
Q1	03/31/99	4,689	122	0.02	3,529	(244)	(0.04)
Q4	12/31/98	3,602	(190)	(0.03)	4,573	(661)	(0.12)
	SUM	19,191	266	0.05	16,007	(1,377)	(0.24)

PRIOR YEAR: Q4 earnings include $388,563/($0.07) in restructuring charges.

RECENT EVENTS

OFFICERS
Rick N. Diamond, CEO
Gary B. Cohen, President
Dana A. Olson, COO
Lois J. Dirksen, VP-Sales
Russell Jackson, CFO

DIRECTORS
Gary B. Cohen
Rick N. Diamond
Douglas W. Franchot
Phillip T. Levin
Seymour Levy
Thomas F. Madison

MAJOR SHAREHOLDERS
Rick N. Diamond, 35.7%
Gary B. Cohen, 35.7%
All officers and directors as a group (10 persons), 73.9%

SIC CODE
7389 Business services, nec

MISCELLANEOUS
TRANSFER AGENT AND REGISTAR: Norwest Bank Minnesota N.A., South St. Paul, MN
TRADED: OTC Bulletin Board
SYMBOL: ACIT
STOCKHOLDERS: 142
EMPLOYEES: 684
IN MINNESOTA: 98
GENERAL COUNSEL: Fredrikson & Byron P.A., Minneapolis
AUDITORS: Deloitte & Touche LLP, Minneapolis
INC: MN-1987
ANNUAL MEETING: May

RANKINGS
No. 154 CRM Public 200

TWO-YEAR QUARTERLY HIGH-LOW STOCK PRICES

PUB

Corporate Report FACT BOOK 2000 133

The public companies section of the 2001 *Fact Book* contains detailed information on 250 publicly held corporations headquartered in the Ninth Federal Reserve District. Public companies with common stock actively trading on Oct. 31, 2000, are eligible (regardless of size). Investment companies and public shell companies, as a rule, are excluded. No charge was made for inclusion in this publication.

Most information in the public company section was first obtained from the company's most recent annual report, 10-K, and proxy; and from financial and other news releases received throughout the year. An extensive profile was reviewed by a company representative for accuracy just prior to publication.

With reference to the sample company displayed here, the information presented in an entry can include the following:

1. BASICS

Name, address, phone, and fax.

2. DESCRIPTION

The company description explains its products, services, target markets, and/or organization. The narrative may also contain historical information or other descriptive items.

3. EARNINGS HISTORY

This chart details the company's financial results from the past five years.

Revenue consists of sales from continuing operations. Interest income is considered revenue only for financial services companies.

Net income is after taxes, extraordinary items, and effects of accounting changes. It includes any earnings from discontinued operations.

Return on (common) equity is calculated by dividing net income (less any preferred dividends) by stockholders' equity at year end. A figure greater than 75 percent (or less than a minus 75 percent) is considered *not meaningful (NM).*

Net earnings per share is calculated by dividing net income (less any preferred dividends) by basic average weighted shares outstanding during the period.

Cash dividend and *market price range* are rounded to the nearest cent.

Anomalies affecting year-to-year comparability of figures are explained case-by-case in footnotes.

While not explicitly presented, change ratios can be easily calculated from the data in the table. For example, revenue change (percent) is the following formula: ((CY REV/PY REV)-1)*100.

4. BALANCE SHEET

The balance sheets at each of the last two fiscal year ends are presented side-by-side for comparison purposes.

Current assets is the sum of those items that can be converted to cash within one year. Cash, marketable securities, inventories, accounts receivable, and prepaid expenses are common categories.

STAT MAN SAYS:

To find other companies in the area, look up ZIP code in the geographic index (beginning on p. **785**).

CAE (cash and equivalents) is a break-out of those current assets that are highly liquid: cash, of course, as well as investments with a maturity of (usually) three months or less.

Property, plant, and equipment is a net value: cost, less any accumulated depreciation.

Other categories may be net of accumulated amortization or allowance for doubtful accounts.

Current liabilities is the sum of those items that will become due within one year: notes payable, accounts payable, current portion of long-term debt, and other accrued expenses.

STD (short-term debt) is a break-out of unsecured notes, the current portion of long-term debt, and the occasional overdraft.

Long-term liabilities is also net of any current portion, accumulated depreciation, or amortization.

Shareholders' equity includes stock at par value, additional paid-in capital, and retained earnings.

5. RECENT QUARTERS

This section displays unaudited financial results, on a rolling-quarters basis, for a two-year period ending with the latest figures released by Nov. 15, 2000. Again, numbers are rounded to the nearest thousand.

STAT MAN SAYS: When compared to the top line of the earnings history (3), *SUM* for the four most-recent quarters will indicate the direction of year-in-process results.

The sum of quarterly EPS figures may disagree with a fiscal year total, due to quarterly variances in the average number of shares outstanding.

6. RECENT EVENTS

This paragraph is a chronicle of the company's year (2000). It may include comments on company performance, reports of events affecting company profitability, and news of general interest—some of which first appeared in the business pages of *Star Tribune* or the research reports of various analysts.

Items are presented in a time line, with months and quarter-end dates bold-faced to provide structure.

7. OFFICERS

An information sidebar begins with a roster of corporate officers. In most cases, the names are ranked by title, with ties broken alphabetically.

STAT MAN SAYS: Top officers may also have individual entries in the Who's Who section (beginning on p. 689).

8. DIRECTORS

Directors are listed alphabetically. The current company affiliations (past, if retired) of outside directors are included, where available, in order to give a sense of the board's makeup.

STAT MAN SAYS:

Note that while *TOTAL* assets and *TOTAL* liabilities at a certain date may not be exactly equal to the sum of their columns (due to the rounding of the numbers in those columns), they will always be equal to each other.

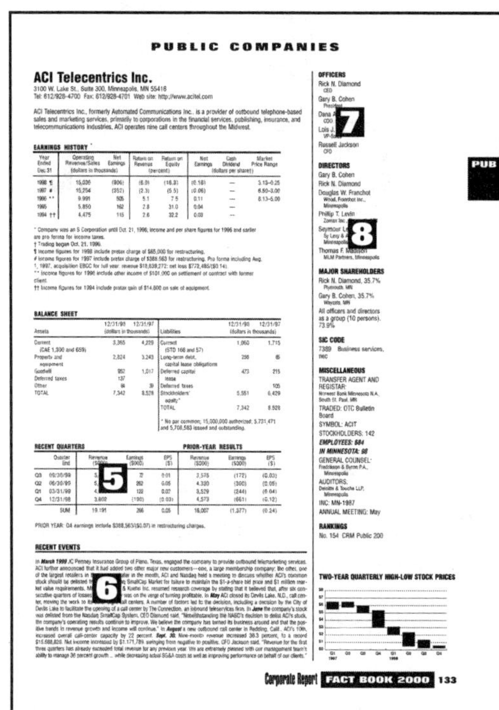

PUBLIC COMPANIES

ACI Telecentrics Inc.
3100 W. Lake St., Suite 300, Minneapolis, MN 55416
Tel: 612/928-4700 Fax: 612/928-4701 Web site: http://www.acitel.com

ACI Telecentrics Inc., formerly Automated Communications Inc., is a provider of outbound telephone-based sales and marketing services, primarily to corporations in the financial services, publishing, insurance, and telecommunications industries. ACI operates nine call centers throughout the Midwest.

EARNINGS HISTORY *

Year Ended Dec 31	Operating Revenue/Sales (dollars in thousands)	Net Earnings (dollars in thousands)	Return on Revenue (percent)	Return on Equity (percent)	Net Earnings (dollars per share)	Cash Dividend (dollars per share)	Market Price Range (dollars per share)
1998 ¶	15,036	(906)	(6.0)	(16.3)	(0.16)	—	3.13–0.25
1997 #	15,254	(352)	(2.3)	(5.5)	(0.06)	—	6.50–3.00
1996 **	9,991	505	5.1	7.5	0.11	—	8.13–5.00
1995	5,850	162	2.8	31.0	0.04	—	
1994 ††	4,475	115	2.6	32.2	0.03	—	

* Company was an S Corporation until Oct. 21, 1996; income and per share figures for 1996 and earlier are pro forma for income taxes.
† Trading began Oct. 21, 1996.
¶ Income figures for 1998 include pretax charge of $65,000 for restructuring.
# Income figures for 1997 include pretax charge of $388,563 for restructuring. Pro forma including Aug. 1, 1997, acquisition EBCC for full year: revenue $18,839,272; net loss $772,485/($0.14).
** Income figures for 1996 include other income of $101,000 on settlement of contract with former client.
†† Income figures for 1994 include pretax gain of $14,800 on sale of equipment.

BALANCE SHEET

Assets	12/31/98	12/31/97	Liabilities	12/31/98	12/31/97
	(dollars in thousands)			(dollars in thousands)	
Current (CAE 1,300 and 659)	3,365	4,229	Current (STD 168 and 57)	1,060	1,715
Property and equipment	2,824	3,243	Long-term debt, capital lease obligations	258	65
Goodwill	952	1,017	Deferred capital lease	473	215
Deferred taxes	137		Deferred taxes		105
Other	64	39	Stockholders' equity*	5,551	6,429
TOTAL	7,342	8,528	TOTAL	7,342	8,528

* No par common; 15,000,000 authorized; 5,731,471 and 5,708,583 issued and outstanding.

RECENT QUARTERS / PRIOR-YEAR RESULTS

	Quarter End	Revenue ($000)	Earnings ($000)	EPS ($)	Revenue ($000)	Earnings ($000)	EPS ($)
Q3	09/30/99	5,[illegible]	77	0.01	3,575	(172)	(0.03)
Q2	06/30/99	5,[illegible]	262	0.05	4,330	(300)	(0.05)
Q1	03/31/99	4,[illegible]	122	0.02	3,529	(244)	(0.04)
Q4	12/31/98	3,602	(190)	(0.03)	4,573	(661)	(0.12)
	SUM	19,191	266	0.05	16,007	(1,377)	(0.24)

PRIOR YEAR: Q4 earnings include $388,563/($0.07) in restructuring charges.

RECENT EVENTS

In **March 1999** JC Penney Insurance Group of Plano, Texas, engaged the company to provide outbound telemarketing services. ACI further announced that it had added two other major new customers—one, a large membership company; the other, one of the largest retailers in [illegible] [illegible] in the month, ACI and Nasdaq held a meeting to discuss whether ACI's common stock should be delisted [illegible] SmallCap Market for failure to maintain the $1-a-share bid price and $1 million market value requirements. [illegible] & Kuehn Inc. resumed research coverage by stating that it believed that, after six consecutive quarters of losses [illegible] was on the verge of turning profitable. In **May** ACI closed its Devils Lake, N.D., call center, moving the work to [illegible] call centers. A number of factors led to the decision, including a decision by the City of Devils Lake to facilitate the opening of a call center by The Connection, an inbound teleservices firm. In **June** the company's stock was delisted from the Nasdaq SmallCap System. CEO Diamond said, "Notwithstanding the NASD's decision to delist ACI's stock, the company's operating results continue to improve. We believe the company has turned its business around and that the positive trends in revenue growth and income will continue." In **August** a new outbound call center in Redding, Calif., ACI's 10th, increased overall call-center capacity by 22 percent. **Sept. 30:** Nine-month revenue increased 38.3 percent, to a record $15,688,828. Net income increased by $1,171,789, swinging from negative to positive. CFO Jackson said, "Revenue for the first three quarters has already exceeded total revenue for any previous year. We are extremely pleased with our management team's ability to manage 38 percent growth ... while decreasing actual SG&A costs as well as improving performance on behalf of our clients."

OFFICERS
Rick N. Diamond, CEO
Gary B. Cohen, President
Dana A[illegible], COO
Lois J. [illegible], VP-Sales
Russell Jackson, CFO

DIRECTORS
Gary B. Cohen
Rick N. Diamond
Douglas W. Franchot, Wood, Franchot Inc., Minneapolis
Phillip T. Levin, Zomax Inc.
Seymour L[illegible], Sy Levy & A[illegible], Minneapolis
Thomas F. Madison, MLM Partners, Minneapolis

MAJOR SHAREHOLDERS
Rick N. Diamond, 35.7%, Plymouth, MN
Gary B. Cohen, 35.7%, Wayzata, MN
All officers and directors as a group (10 persons), 73.9%

SIC CODE
7389 Business services, nec

MISCELLANEOUS
TRANSFER AGENT AND REGISTAR: Norwest Bank Minnesota N.A., South St. Paul, MN
TRADED: OTC Bulletin Board
SYMBOL: ACIT
STOCKHOLDERS: 142
EMPLOYEES: 684
IN MINNESOTA: 98
GENERAL COUNSEL: Fredrikson & Byron P.A., Minneapolis
AUDITORS: Deloitte & Touche LLP, Minneapolis
INC: MN-1987
ANNUAL MEETING: May

RANKINGS
No. 154 CRM Public 200

TWO-YEAR QUARTERLY HIGH-LOW STOCK PRICES

Corporate Report FACT BOOK 2000 133

STAT MAN SAYS:

To find a company's competitors, look up its SIC codes in the SIC index (beginning on page **811**).

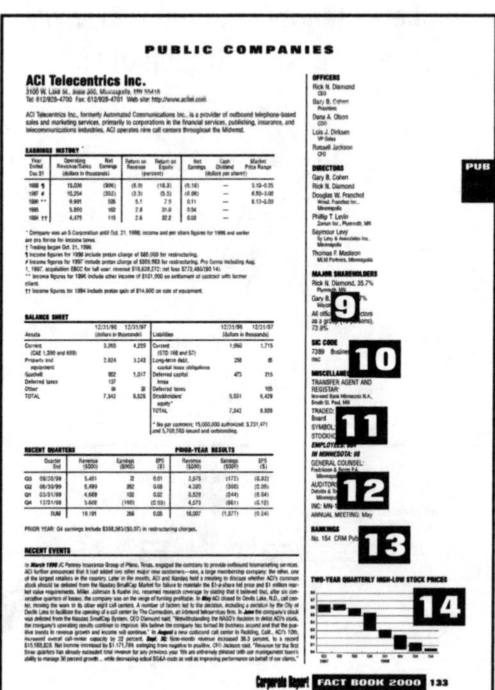

PUBLIC COMPANIES

ACI Telecentrics Inc.
3100 W. Lake St., Suite 300, Minneapolis, MN 55416
Tel: 612/928-4700 Fax: 612/928-4701 Web site: http://www.acitel.com

ACI Telecentrics Inc., formerly Automated Communications Inc., is a provider of outbound telephone-based sales and marketing services, primarily to corporations in the financial services, publishing, insurance, and telecommunications industries. ACI operates nine call centers throughout the Midwest.

EARNINGS HISTORY *

Year Ended Dec 31	Operating Revenue/Sales (dollars in thousands)	Net Earnings (dollars in thousands)	Return on Revenue (percent)	Return on Equity (percent)	Net Earnings (dollars per share†)	Cash Dividend (dollars per share†)	Market Price Range (dollars per share†)
1998 ¶	15,036	(906)	(6.0)	(18.3)	(0.16)	—	3.13-0.25
1997 #	15,254	(352)	(2.3)	(5.5)	(0.06)	—	6.50-3.00
1996 **	9,901	505	5.1	7.5	0.11	—	8.13-5.00
1995	5,850	162	2.8	31.0	0.04	—	
1994 ††	4,475	115	2.6	32.2	0.03	—	

* Company was an S Corporation until Oct. 21, 1996; income and per share figures for 1996 and earlier are pro forma for income taxes.
† Trading began Oct. 21, 1996.
¶ Income figures for 1998 include pretax charge of $85,000 for restructuring.
# Income figures for 1997 include pretax charge of $389,583 for restructuring. Pro forma including Aug. 1, 1997, acquisition EBCC for full year: revenue $18,639,272; net loss $772,485/($0.14).
** Income figures for 1996 include other income of $101,900 on settlement of contract with former client.
†† Income figures for 1994 include pretax gain of $14,600 on sale of equipment.

BALANCE SHEET

Assets	12/31/98 (dollars in thousands)	12/31/97 (dollars in thousands)	Liabilities	12/31/98 (dollars in thousands)	12/31/97 (dollars in thousands)
Current (CAE 1,300 and 689)	3,365	4,229	Current (STD 168 and 57)	1,060	1,715
Property and equipment	2,824	3,243	Long-term debt, capital lease obligations	258	65
Goodwill	952	1,017	Deferred capital lease	473	215
Deferred taxes	137		Deferred taxes		105
Other	64	39	Stockholders' equity*	5,551	6,429
TOTAL	7,342	8,528	TOTAL	7,342	8,528

* No par common; 15,000,000 authorized; 5,731,471 and 5,708,583 issued and outstanding.

RECENT QUARTERS / **PRIOR-YEAR RESULTS**

	Quarter End	Revenue ($000)	Earnings ($000)	EPS ($)	Revenue ($000)	Earnings ($000)	EPS ($)
Q3	09/30/99	5,401	72	0.01	3,575	(172)	(0.03)
Q2	06/30/99	5,499	262	0.05	4,330	(300)	(0.05)
Q1	03/31/99	4,689	132	0.02	3,529	(244)	(0.04)
Q4	12/31/98	3,602	(190)	(0.03)	4,573	(661)	(0.12)
	SUM	19,191	266	0.05	16,007	(1,377)	(0.24)

PRIOR YEAR: Q4 earnings include $388,583/($0.07) in restructuring charges.

RECENT EVENTS

In ***March 1999*** JC Penney Insurance Group of Plano, Texas, engaged the company to provide outbound telemarketing services. ACI further announced that it had added two other major new customers—one, a large membership company; the other, one of the largest retailers in the country. Later in the month, ACI and Nasdaq held a meeting to discuss whether ACI's common stock should be delisted from the Nasdaq SmallCap Market for failure to maintain the $1-a-share bid price and $1 million market value requirements. Miller, Johnson & Kuehn Inc. resumed research coverage by stating that it believed that, after six consecutive quarters of losses, the company was on the verge of turning profitable. In ***May*** ACI closed its Devils Lake, N.D., call center, moving the work to its other eight call centers. A number of factors led to the decision, including a decision by the City of Devils Lake to facilitate the opening of a call center by The Connection, an inbound teleservices firm. In ***June*** the company's stock was delisted from the Nasdaq SmallCap System. CEO Diamond said, "Notwithstanding the NASD's decision to delist ACI's stock, the company's operating results continue to improve. We believe the company has turned its business around and that the positive trends in revenue growth and income will continue." In ***August*** a new outbound call center in Redding, Calif., ACI's 10th, increased overall call-center capacity by 22 percent. ***Sept. 30*** Nine-month revenue increased 38.3 percent, to a record $15,588,828. Net income increased by $1,171,789, swinging from negative to positive. CFO Jackson said, "Revenue for the first three quarters has already exceeded total revenue for any previous year. We are extremely pleased with our management team's ability to manage 36 percent growth ... while decreasing actual SG&A costs as well as improving performance on behalf of our clients."

OFFICERS
Rick N. Diamond
CEO
Gary B. Cohen
President
Dana A. Olson
COO
Lois J. Dirksen
VP-Sales
Russell Jackson
CFO

DIRECTORS
Gary B. Cohen
Rick N. Diamond
Douglas W. Franchot
Wood, Franchot Inc., Minneapolis
Phillip T. Levin
Zomax Inc., Plymouth, MN
Seymour Levy
Sy Levy & Associates Inc., Minneapolis
Thomas F. Madison
MLM Partners, Minneapolis

MAJOR SHAREHOLDERS
Rick N. Diamond, 35.7%
Plymouth, MN
Gary B. ... 7%
Wayzata
All officers and directors as a group ... persons), 73.9%

SIC CODE
7389 Business ... nec

MISCELLANEOUS
TRANSFER AGENT AND REGISTAR:
Norwest Bank Minnesota N.A., South St. Paul, MN
TRADED: ... Board
SYMBOL: ...
STOCKHOLDERS: ...
EMPLOYEES: ...
IN MINNESOTA: 98
GENERAL COUNSEL:
Fredrikson & Byron P.A., Minneapolis
AUDITORS:
Deloitte & Touche, Minneapolis
INC: MN-...
ANNUAL MEETING: May

RANKINGS
No. 154 CRM Public ...

TWO-YEAR QUARTERLY HIGH-LOW STOCK PRICES

Corporate Report FACT BOOK 2000 133

9. MAJOR SHAREHOLDERS

This list of those who own 5 percent or more of a company's stock (or options on same) also gives the total held by insiders. The extensive footnoting that accompanies this information in the proxy statement is not presented.

10. SIC CODES

This section lists SIC codes descriptive of the company's area of business.

11. MISCELLANEOUS

Miscellaneous items, for the most part, have labels that are self-explanatory. *Stockholders* does not include beneficial holders through brokerages. Midway through the section, in bold, is the company's employee count—the full-time plus part-time total of all company operations around the globe—often with Minnesota employment broken out. The miscellaneous section often concludes with the titles and names of company officials that have extensive contact with the public.

12. RANKINGS

This is a summary of the company's positions on the regional lists of *Corporate Report (CRM)* magazine.

13. SUBSIDIARIES

The sidebar itself concludes with a list of subsidiaries, divisions, and affiliates. Addresses, phone numbers, and chief executives are also included (space permitting). A numerical notation refers to the level of reporting within the structure of the company—with *1* being a direct subsidiary, and *2* reporting to the first *1* preceding it.

14. STOCK GRAPH

The stock graph is a bar graph showing stock price ranges from each quarter of the past two fiscal years.

USES FOR THIS SECTION INCLUDE:

Learning the names and titles of company decision-makers.

Identify those who are in a specific functional area of interest to you.

Personalize your dealings with a company.

Develop mailing lists based on company size or location.

STAT MAN SAYS:

Subsidiaries are cross-referenced to their parent company in the *Fact Book* index (beginning on page **835**).

ACI Telecentrics Inc.

3100 W. Lake St., Suite 300, Minneapolis, MN 55416
Tel: 612/928-4700 Fax: 612/928-4701 Web site: http://www.acitel.com

ACI Telecentrics Inc. is a direct marketing firm providing teleservices, primarily to corporations in the financial services, publishing and telecommunications industries. ACI operates 11 call centers throughout the Midwest, California and Quebec, Canada.

EARNINGS HISTORY *

Year Ended Dec 31	Operating Revenue/Sales (dollars in thousands)	Net Earnings	Return on Revenue (percent)	Return on Equity	Net Earnings (dollars per share†)	Cash Dividend	Market Price Range
1999	22,943	527	2.3	8.6	0.09	—	2.00–0.50
1998 ¶	15,036	(906)	(6.0)	(16.3)	(0.16)	—	3.13–0.25
1997 #	15,254	(352)	(2.3)	(5.5)	(0.06)	—	6.50–3.00
1996 **	9,991	505	5.1	7.5	0.11	—	6.13–5.00
1995	5,850	162	2.8	31.0	0.04	—	

* Company was an S Corporation until Oct. 21, 1996; income and per share figures for 1996 and earlier are pro forma for income taxes.
† Trading began Oct. 21, 1996.
¶ Income figures for 1998 include pretax charge of $65,000 for restructuring.
\# Income figures for 1997 include pretax charge of $388,563 for restructuring. Pro forma including Aug. 1, 1997, acquisition EBCC for full year: revenue $18,639,272; net loss $772,485/($0.14).
** Income figures for 1996 include other income of $101,000 on settlement of contract with former client.

BALANCE SHEET

Assets	12/31/99 (dollars in thousands)	12/31/98	Liabilities	12/31/99 (dollars in thousands)	12/31/98
Current (CAE 199 and 1,300)	6,380	3,365	Current (STD 302 and 166)	2,799	1,060
Property and equipment	2,702	2,824	Long-term debt, capital lease obligations	523	258
Goodwill	882	952	Deferred capital lease	280	473
Deferred taxes		137	Deferred taxes	323	
Other	57	64	Stockholders' equity*	6,096	5,551
TOTAL	10,021	7,342	TOTAL	10,021	7,342

* No par common; 15,000,000 authorized; 5,756,267 and 5,731,471 issued and outstanding.

RECENT QUARTERS / **PRIOR-YEAR RESULTS**

	Quarter End	Revenue ($000)	Earnings ($000)	EPS ($)	Prior-Year Revenue ($000)	Prior-Year Earnings ($000)	Prior-Year EPS ($)
Q3	09/30/2000	7,000	(213)	(0.04)	5,401	72	0.01
Q2	06/30/2000	7,226	312	0.05	5,499	262	0.05
Q1	03/31/2000	7,835	303	0.05	4,689	122	0.02
Q4	12/31/99	7,354	71	0.01	3,602	(190)	(0.03)
	SUM	29,415	472	0.08	19,191	266	0.05

CURRENT: Q3 earnings include pretax impairment costs of $0.847 million.

RECENT EVENTS

In **February 2000** ACI announced an expansion of its marketing services—with the intention of becoming a leader in the front-end online customer service business. "We have always guided our strategies by keeping abreast of the manner in which our clients choose to serve their customers," said CEO Diamond. "Personal support via the Internet is the next step in customer contact in the manner most comfortable for the consumer." In **June** ACI announced a partnership with Interactive Intelligence (Nasdaq: ININ), a leading developer of multichannel interaction management software, that was to allow ACI to sell full multimedia capabilities to its current and future customers. ACI began using Interactive Intelligence's platform in its new Netcentric Center in Canada. In **September** ACI announced the signing of an Internet database company as its first Inbound Calling Client on their new EIC call processing platform. **Sept. 30**: During third quarter, the company recorded an impairment of asset charge after tax of $516,514, based on the requirements under the Statement of Accounting Standards No. 121 "Accounting for the Impairment of Long-Lived Assets," related to goodwill recorded from its Britcom acquisition of August 1997. The company concluded that an impairment charge was required based on discounted historical results and current projections of future cash flow to which the Britcom goodwill relates. Aside from that, third-quarter net income rose to $303,536 on 29.6 percent revenue growth.

OFFICERS

Rick N. Diamond
CEO

Gary B. Cohen
President

Dana A. Olson
COO

Brent J. Baskfield
VP-Client Services

Lois J. Dirksen
VP-Sales

William C. Nolte
VP-Finance, CFO

DIRECTORS

Gary B. Cohen

Rick N. Diamond

Douglas W. Franchot
Franchot, Cohen & Associates, Wayzata, MN

Phillip T. Levin
Zomax Inc., Plymouth, MN

Seymour Levy
Sy Levy & Associates Inc., Minneapolis

Thomas F. Madison
MLM Partners, Minneapolis

MAJOR SHAREHOLDERS

Rick N. Diamond, 34.7%
Plymouth, MN

Gary B. Cohen, 34.7%
Wayzata, MN

All officers and directors as a group (10 persons), 74.8%

SIC CODE

7389 Business services, nec

MISCELLANEOUS

TRANSFER AGENT AND REGISTAR:
Wells Fargo Bank Minnesota N.A.,
South St. Paul, MN

TRADED: OTC Bulletin Board

SYMBOL: ACIT

STOCKHOLDERS: 148

EMPLOYEES: 1,500

IN MINNESOTA: 110

GENERAL COUNSEL:
Fredrikson & Byron P.A., Minneapolis

AUDITORS:
Deloitte & Touche LLP, Minneapolis

INC: MN-1987

ANNUAL MEETING: May

RANKINGS

No. 144 CRM Public 200

SUBSIDIARIES, DIVISIONS, AFFILIATES

Corporation ACI Telecentrics du Quebec Inc.

PUB

ADC Telecommunications Inc.

12501 Whitewater Dr., P.O. Box 1101, Minnetonka, MN 55343
Tel: 952/938-8080 Fax: 952/946-2147 Web site: http://www.adc.com

ADC Telecommunications Inc. is a leading global supplier of voice, video, and data systems for telephone, cable television, Internet, broadcast, wireless, and private communications networks. ADC's systems enable local access and high-speed transmission of communications services from providers to consumers and businesses over fiber optic, copper, coaxial, and wireless media.

EARNINGS HISTORY *

Year Ended Oct 31	Operating Revenue/Sales (dollars in thousands)	Net Earnings	Return on Revenue (percent)	Return on Equity	Net Earnings (dollars per share†)	Cash Dividend	Market Price Range
1999	1,926,946	207,957	10.8	13.5	0.32	—	13.41–5.81
1998	1,830,483	213,278	11.7	16.1	0.33	—	10.91–3.94
1997 ¶	1,553,820	180,411	11.6	16.9	0.28	—	11.25–5.31
1996	881,929	99,032	11.2	14.9	0.17	—	8.78–3.56
1995 #	616,518	62,974	10.2	11.6	0.11	—	6.17–2.47

* All historical results have been restated to pool October 1999 acquisition Saville Systems plc. The pooling of June 2000 acquisition PairGain Technologies is reflected from fiscal year 1997 and forward only. The pooling of proposed acquisition Broadband Access Systems is not yet reflected.
† Per-share amounts restated to reflect 2-for-1 stock splits on July 17, 2000, and Feb. 15, 2000; and 2-for-1 split in October 1996.
¶ Income figures for 1997 include pretax nonrecurring charge of $22.7 million, primarily to write off R&D from the Wireless acquisition.
# Income figures for 1995 include pretax charge of $3,914,000 for personnel reduction at Fibermux.

BALANCE SHEET

Assets	07/31/00 (dollars in thousands)	10/31/99	Liabilities	07/31/00 (dollars in thousands)	10/31/99
Current (CAE 176,865 and 230,045)	2,904,131	1,319,418	Current (STD 77,758 and 35,185)	1,125,643	443,343
Property and equipment	496,426	338,588	Long-term debt	18,785	12,759
Other, principally goodwill	600,743	339,604	Stockholders' equity*	2,856,872	1,541,508
TOTAL	4,001,300	1,997,610	TOTAL	4,001,300	1,997,610

* $0.20 par common; 1,200,000,000 authorized; 709,025,000 and 662,425,000 issued and outstanding.

RECENT QUARTERS / **PRIOR-YEAR RESULTS**

	Quarter End	Revenue ($000)	Earnings ($000)	EPS ($)	Revenue ($000)	Earnings ($000)	EPS ($)
Q3	07/31/2000	891,022	18,505	0.03	534,791	6,723	0.01
Q2	04/30/2000	770,600	724,200	1.03	517,762	46,340	0.07
Q1	01/31/2000	593,900	57,200	0.08	465,190	(5,496)	(0.01)
Q4	10/31/99	634,079	42,491	0.06	501,024	59,625	0.09
	SUM	2,889,601	842,396	1.21	2,018,767	107,192	0.16

CURRENT: Q3 earnings include pretax nonrecurring charges of $85.2 million for acquisition-related expenses and $7.0 million for restructuring. Q2 and Q1 figures to the nearest thousand had not been released by press time. SUMS should be: revenue, $2,889.595 million; earnings $842.367 million. Q2 earnings include nonrecurring pretax: credit of $328.6 million on the sale of PairGain's microelectronics engineering group; gain of $722.6 million on the conversion of its investment in Siara Systems Inc.; and charge of $8.8 million for acquisition-related expenses. Q4 earnings include nonrecurring pretax charge of $30.0 million for the restructuring (consolidation) of the Broadband Access and Transport operations.

RECENT EVENTS

In **December 1999** ADC introduced its new RDS-2 two-way signal protection switch, the industry's first interactive signal protection switch for the forward path (50 MHz-1GHz) of a broadband network. ADC created the Cable Transport Systems Division, including the analog optical transport (HMX) and optical node (ISX) product lines, new digital HFC products, the Pathworx RF amplifiers, and the global portfolio of optical/RF products developed by ADC Phasor in Austria and newly acquired Comtec Electronica S.R.L. in Buenos Aires. The division's products were to be marketed under a new name: Optiworx HFC Transport Systems Platform. ADC agreed to acquire NVISION Inc.—a privately held, Grass Valley, Calif.-based provider of distribution and switching technology for television production, post-production, and broadcasting—for $20 million. In **January 2000** the Beijing province of China's PTT selected ADC's Cellworx Service Transport Node (STN) to provide voice, frame relay, and ATM transport services for the PTT's access network. ADC was chosen by ***continued on page 121***

OFFICERS

William J. Cadogan
Chairman, President, and CEO

Lynn J. Davis
SVP, Pres.-Broadband Connectivity Group

Larry J. Ford
SVP and Pres.-Integrated Solutions Group

Arun Sobti
SVP, Pres.-Broadband Access/Transport

Robert E. Switz
SVP and CFO

Mark Borman
VP-Investor Relations

Kamalesh Dwivedi
VP and Chief Information Officer

Gokul Hemmady
VP and Treasurer

Peter W. Hemp
VP-Copper Div., Broadband Connectivity

Laura N. Owen
VP-Human Resources

Jeff Pflaum
VP, General Counsel, and Secretary

Charles T. Roehrick
VP and Controller

Wayne Stewart
VP-Operations

DIRECTORS

John A. (Gus) Blanchard III
Deluxe Corp., Shoreview, MN

William J. Cadogan

James C. Castle
USCS International Inc., Rancho Cordova, CA

B. Kristine Johnson
Affinity Capital Management, Minneapolis

Alan E. Ross
Rockwell International Corp. (retired)

Jean-Pierre Rosso
Case Corp., Racine, WI

John W. Sidgmore
MCI WorldCom

John D. Wunsch
Family Financial Strategies Inc., Minneapolis

Charles D. Yost
Allegiance Telecom, Dallas

MAJOR SHAREHOLDERS

FMR Corp., 7.9%
Boston

State Farm Mutual Automobile Insurance Co., 7.8%
Bloomington, IL

Putnam Investment Management Inc., 7.7%
Boston

All officers and directors as a group (21 persons), 1.6%

SIC CODE

3661 Telephone and telegraph apparatus
3669 Communications equipment, nec
3678 Electronic connectors
3679 Electronic components, nec
3825 Instruments to measure electricity

MISCELLANEOUS

TRANSFER AGENT AND REGISTAR:
Wells Fargo Bank Minnesota N.A.,
South St. Paul, MN

TRADED: Nasdaq National Market

SYMBOL: ADCT

STOCKHOLDERS: 6,918

EMPLOYEES: 22,000

IN MINNESOTA: 5,500

GENERAL COUNSEL:
Dorsey & Whitney PLLP, Minneapolis

AUDITORS:
Arthur Andersen LLP, Minneapolis

INC: MN-1953

FOUNDED: 1935

ANNUAL MEETING: February

INVESTOR RELATIONS: Mark P. Borman

HUMAN RESOURCES: Laura Owen

RANKINGS

No. 21 CRM Public 200
No. 41 CRM Employer 100
No. 2 CRM Performance 100
No. 39 Minnesota Technology Fast 50

TWO-YEAR QUARTERLY HIGH-LOW STOCK PRICES

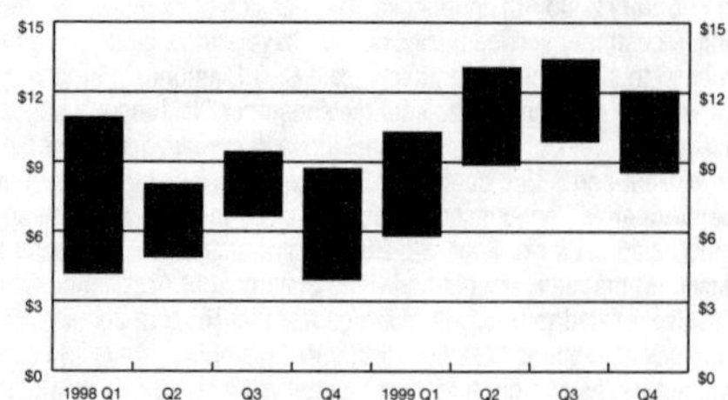

Rapid Broadcasting to supply complete transmission systems (valued at $1.3 million) for it's new stations in Sioux Falls and Rapid City, S.D. ADC released ADC D17 Tools, an advanced software package that provides tools that save time in organizing the design and construction activities of communications network facilities for buildings. ADC announced several enhancements to its award-winning Cellworx STN, including the availability of the OC-48c ring interface for network traffic. Additionally, Cellworx STN achieved Network Equipment Building Standard (NEBS) Level 3 certification, the hallmark of telecommunications network safety and reliability. ADC won two new contracts to provide its NewNet OTAserver and SMserver technologies to regional wireless network operators, in North America (Cellular One) and South America (Global Telecom, Brazil). In **February** ADC announced its Saville Interconnect Billing Platform (IBP) version 4.0, a complete inter-operator settlement solution designed to enable communications service providers to compete effectively in the increasingly complex and profitable interconnect market. ADC was named one of America's Most Admired Companies by a FORTUNE Magazine survey. ADC extended its contract with Turk Telekom of Turkey for supply of the BroadAccess Multiservice Access Platform. COMCOR, a Russian communications carrier, chose ADC's ATM Access Concentrator (AAC-3) to enable frame relay over an ATM network for delivery of permanent virtual circuit (PVC) services to businesses in Moscow. ADC announced the availability of the OMX 600 optical distribution frame (ODF), a front-facing, high-density frame designed for protecting, managing, and enhancing optical networks; and the new generation of BroadAccess, a unique multiservice access platform that enables service providers to deliver a robust mix of broadband and narrowband services to clusters of 60 to 2000 businesses, small office/home offices (SOHOs), and residential customers from a single platform. ADC and PairGain Technologies Inc. (Nasdaq: PAIR, www.pairgain.com), a leader in the design, manufacture, marketing, and sale of digital subscriber line (DSL) networking systems, reached an agreement for the acquisition of $258 million-revenue, 700-employee PairGain by ADC. Each share of PairGain's common stock was to be converted into 0.43 shares of ADC common stock with a fixed exchange ratio. Based on the closing share price of $46.81 for ADC's stock on **Feb. 22**, the pooling-of-interests transaction was valued at $1.6 billion. ADC's proposed acquisition of PairGain resulted from ADC's aggressive and determined strategy to become a leading supplier of DSL broadband access systems. [The Hart-Scott-Rodino waiting period expired on May 5; PairGain's shareholders approved the deal on June 26, and it was consummated on June 28.] MasterMind Technologies of Washington, D.C., selected ADC's NewNet Connect7 Signaling System No.7 (SS7) platform on an OEM basis. ADC announced plans to invest $46 million in a major manufacturing facility in Glenrothes, Fife (Scotland), to produce broadband connectivity products used in optical-fiber, copper, and wireless networks by the European communications industry. ADC and Alcatel announced their intent to form a worldwide business alliance to jointly offer cable telephony solutions on specific communications provider projects worldwide. ADC and LG Information and Communications, ADC's original-equipment manufacturer located in Korea, agreed to jointly develop a new high-density channelized frame relay card for ADC's established AAC ATM access concentrator product line. In **March** the company introduced ADC Ventures, a $100 million private venture capital fund focused on investing in emerging and start-up companies—in the United States, Europe, and Israel—who are engaged in developing high-performance, next-generation broadband communications technologies. ADC announced the availability of its high-powered 980nm pump laser diode and module, the company's first active optical component product line. ADC announced the worldwide availability of the Axity Broadband Wireless Access System, the first carrier-class architecture for two-way delivery of communications services over the Multichannel Multipoint Distribution Service (MMDS) wireless spectrum. ADC signed an agreement with Redback Networks that leverages each company's unique strengths to form a powerful team to provide integrated Internet/data, video, and voice solutions to the broadband multimedia market. MCI WorldCom announced plans to test cutting-edge wireless technology in Boston that was to offer customers a new, competitive alternative for high-speed, broadband service. MCI was developing this MMDS platform with technology partner ADC, which was providing full network management, design, and systems integration for the trial—including equipment for customer locations. ADC announced the availability of NewNet Distributed7, its next generation SS7 (Signaling System No.7) platform; and signed an agreement with Technology Control Services Inc. to provide its NewNet SGLite signaling gateway platform to TCS on an OEM basis. ADC bought 106 acres of land in Shakopee, Minn., where it planned to build a 450,000-square-foot manufacturing and office facility (in addition to the new corporate headquarters already under construction in Eden Prairie). The company's Minnetonka, Minn., complex, assessed at $17.5 million, was reportedly for sale. In **April** GTE agreed to use ADC's AccessPoint Universal Media Access System to deliver its VideoConnect broadcast video service to customers in California and Florida. ADC and PairGain Technologies demonstrated the next phase of HDSL2 interoperability testing between their respective Soneplex and HiGain Solitaire systems. Chunghwa Telecom Co. Ltd. (CHT), Taiwan's PTT and largest mobile telephony operator in Taiwan, selected through prime contractor Teltai (Taiwan) Ltd. ADC's Metrica/NPR for Wireless to monitor CHT's wireless (GSM/DCS and AMPS) networks, interfacing with Nortel and Ericsson infrastructure elements. ADC agreed acquire the television broadcast assets of Continental Electronics Corp. (CEC), a subsidiary of Tech-Sym Corp. (NYSE: TSY) of Houston. ADC was to acquire all designs and rights to CEC's solid-state television transmitters, digital television exciters, and other intellectual properties relating to the television broadcast portion of the business. ADC introduced the new ADC BroadWire ADSL splitter, the industry's highest-density splitter platform, which splits voice and data frequency bands so that subscribers can receive voice and high-speed data services simultaneously over a twisted pair of copper wires. ADC received orders exceeding $1.2 million from public television stations for new Digital Television (DTV) transmitter systems. "ADC will significantly exceed Wall Street's estimates for sales and earnings per share for the quarter and end of year 2000," Cadogan said. "We expect second-quarter sales will be up 45 percent to $670 million, significantly above the Wall Street consensus of $590 million." Cadogan said that second-quarter earnings per share was expected to be in the mid-20s, compared to the current consensus view of 21 cents a share. With the close of the $1.5 billion PairGain Technologies deal, ADC was expecting to see sales of $3 billion. Even without PairGain's results factored in, Cadogan said that ADC would definitely exceed the company's internal year-over-year growth targets for earnings per share and sales of 25 percent to 30 percent. "Before acquisitions, 2000 sales could exceed 40 percent annual growth," he said. "Our earnings per share could grow much higher than that." The company was seeing explosive demand in its broadband connectivity segment, with better than 70 percent year-over year growth. "Fiber optics is growing at 100 percent year-over-year," Cadogan said. He said that the company was booking more orders than it was shipping, a sign that demand should not slacken. ADC signed an alliance agreement with DSET Corp. (Nasdaq: DSET), a leading supplier of business-to-business e-commerce connectivity solutions for the telecommunications industry. ADC announced the availability of its WDM Quad Loop Extender (WQLX) module for the Soneplex system. ADC announced a contract to provide network performance management, traffic dispersion analysis tools, and expertise to Dutch wireline operator VersaTel. RTS Wireless (www.rtswireless.com), a leading developer of adaptable software systems that connect the Internet to wireless devices, entered into a strategic marketing agreement with ADC. ADC's NewNet IP CALEAserver application was selected by Telcordia Technologies. ADC launched Metrica/NPR for IP. ADC signed an OEM agreement with Mpathix Inc., Toronto, for its wireless messaging solutions, including short messaging and over-the-air service provisioning platforms. ADC signed an agreement with Symmetry Communications Systems, San Jose, Calif., to provide its NewNet Connect7 Signaling System No.7 solution to Symmetry on an OEM basis. In **May** ADC announced availability of the new ADC IPXpert platform, designed to manage IP and ATM wide-area data networks. With the IPXpert, network administrators can remotely test, restore, and control the network's physical layer using a software interface. ADC announced Singl.eView, the first integrated, scalable customer management and convergent billing solution for integrated communication providers; and Singularit.e, a new and comprehensive operational support system (OSS) framework for real-time customer contact and service management in a broadband network. ADC announced a strategic alliance with leading e-business platform provider Vitria Technology Inc. (Nasdaq: VITR) to enable integrated communications providers (ICPs) to rapidly deploy a comprehensive operational support system (OSS). Professional services powerhouse Ernst & Young LLP, one of the world's leading system integrators, was to use its Dallas Accelerated Billing and Operations Support Systems (B/OSS) Solution and Delivery Center to integrate Singl.eView into other market-leading business and operations support systems. ADC's AAC-2 ATM access concentrator was named a finalist by CMP Media Inc. for Network Computings' 2000 Well-Connected Award in the category of ATM access concentration. On May 5, ADC agreed to acquire Altitun (www.altitun.com), a leading developer and supplier of active optical components for next-generation optical networks. (Telecom providers continue to face the challenge of trying to deploy high-bandwidth networks at increasingly competitive costs. The unique technology developed by Altitun enables these carriers to meet their growing demand and enables tremendous flexibility in their networks by providing such offerings as wavelength services, dedicated optical paths, and bandwidth on demand. Altitun is the first company to deploy tunable lasers in a field environment and was the first in the world to commercially ship a tunable laser.) ADC was to issue 15,227,000 shares of its common stock to Altitun's shareholders and optionholders in this pooling-of-interests transaction. Based on ADC's closing share price of $57.25 on **May 4, 2000**, the proposed acquisition was valued at $872 million. On the same day, ADC acquired IBSEN Micro Structures (www.ibsen.dk), a photonics company focused on development and production of high-performance optical components and tools. IBSEN, based in Copenhagen, is the leading provider of Near Field Holographic phase masks—a critical component for the production of Distributed Feed Back (DFB) lasers, fiber Bragg grating, and integrated optics devices. The $80 million acquisition was to be accounted for using the purchase method. With these two acquisitions, ADC gained critical mass in key fiber-optic technologies. CEO Cadogan predicted that the deals would allow ADC to continue growing its $400 million fiber-optic business at a triple-digit pace for the next two to three years. ADC stock rose $5.88 to $63.13 on the news. ADC announced availability of the Optiworx Digital Return Transmission System (RTS), the first product in a new family of digital HFC products for cable television (CATV) operators deploying voice, data, and video for residential and business applications; and its next-generation Homeworx cable telephony system, which adds new features to the carrier-class hybrid fiber/coax (HFC) telephony platform. Network staff at Trans World Airlines Inc. (AMEX: TWA) selected ServicePoint service delivery units (SDUs) from ADC to monitor their new TWA frame relay network. A new addition to the Metrica Professional Services offering, the Business Consulting Unit, was to offer customers operational and business consulting. ADC announced the immediate availability of System Release 3.0 for the company's popular Soneplex Shelf Controller Unit (SCU). New England-based Lightship Telecom began shipping convergent bills and providing comprehensive customer care to its business customers using ADC's Saville Convergent Billing Platform (CBP). CEO Cadogan announced his intention to retire from ADC after a transition to a new leader. It was anticipated that the transition would be completed within 12 to 18 months. ADC introduced the Select Series fuse platform, the newest addition to the ADC PowerWorx power distribution and protection line. ADC announced an alliance with edocs Inc., a leading provider of Internet billing and customer management solutions, to integrate edocs' BillDirect into ADC's Singl.eView. ADC and Telcordia Technologies Inc. announced a comprehensive alliance that combined software, hardware, and consulting services for telecommunications service providers. Hekimian's (www.hekimian.com) REACT 2001 testing software began offering full interoperability with ADC's Soneplex system. ADC released an enhanced version of its software for end-to-end broadband asset management, the FiberBase 4.0 system. ADC announced the availability of the FSXpert, the first smart optical remote test access system for fiber networks. ADC launched the intelligent Access Network (iAN) platform. Research by telecom industry management consultancy Chorleywood Consulting (www.chorleywood.com) ranked ADC first among 13 billing system providers from around the world. ADC drew the highest overall customer satisfaction rating for several categories, including time-to-market. ADC announced availability of two new deep fiber nodes in the proven Optiworx ISX platform for advanced HFC networks; and the BroadWire splitter, an innovative ADSL splitter that makes the issue of line sharing a lot less complicated for broadband communications service providers. ADC and Harris Corp., a worldwide supplier of communications equipment, announced interoperability between ADC's Soneplex system and the Harris Test System, which will allow for easy metallic loop testing from a common user interface. ADC was chosen to provide its Homeworx hybrid fiber/coax (HFC) telephony platform to Black Hills FiberCom, South Dakota's largest cable telephony service provider, a $2 million award. Uniworx—a high-density, multiservice platform for cable television (CATV) operators that provides universal access and transport for delivery of voice, data, Internet, video, digital television (DTV), and high-definition television (HDTV) services for residential and business applications—debuted at SCTE's Cable-Tec Expo 2000. ADC introduced AccessPoint, for integrated IMA video capability. ADC was selected to provide its Homeworx hybrid fiber coax (HFC) telephony platform to Midcontinent Communications, which serves 200,000 subscribers in North and South Dakota, Nebraska, and Minnesota (potential value: up to $10 million over three years). Canada-based competitive local exchange carrier (CLEC) Bell Intrigna employed ADC's Singl.eView to accommodate its current explosive growth. With the support of ADC, Telinor Television S. A. de C. V., a Mexican wireless pay-TV company, began field trials of a new generation of technology focused on business

continued on page 150

PUB

APA Optics Inc.

2950 N.E. 84th Ln., Blaine, MN 55449
Tel: 763/784-4995 Fax: 763/784-2038 Web site: http://www.apaoptics.com

APA Optics Inc. develops, designs, and fabricates optical components and optical systems for laser and other industrial applications; develops and fabricates optical coatings and thin-film optical devices; researches and develops optoelectronic technology and related devices; and designs and fabricates semiconductor material layers and optoelectronic devices. APA also does research for the Department of Defense under Small Business Innovative Research (SBIR) government contracts.

EARNINGS HISTORY

Year Ended Mar 31	Operating Revenue/Sales (dollars in thousands)	Net Earnings (dollars in thousands)	Return on Revenue (percent)	Return on Equity (percent)	Net Earnings (dollars per share)	Cash Dividend (dollars per share)	Market Price Range (dollars per share)
2000	421	(3,796)	NM	(60.2)	(0.43)	—	64.00–3.50
1999	722	(2,514)	NM	(74.2)	(0.30)	—	10.00–4.00
1998	2,191	(968)	(44.2)	(16.5)	(0.12)	—	9.25–5.25
1997	2,769	(11)	(0.4)	(0.2)	0.00	—	6.75–4.25
1996	2,486	(92)	(3.7)	(2.3)	(0.01)	—	8.50–3.00

BALANCE SHEET

Assets	03/31/00 (dollars in thousands)	03/31/99 (dollars in thousands)	Liabilities	03/31/00 (dollars in thousands)	03/31/99 (dollars in thousands)
Current (CAE 5,941 and 2,812)	6,513	3,199	Current (STD 141 and 133)	396	334
Property and equipment	2,460	2,593	Long-term debt	2,908	3,082
Bond reserve funds	213	533	Stockholders' equity*	6,306	3,389
Bond placement costs	164	212	TOTAL	9,610	6,805
Other	261	269			
TOTAL	9,610	6,805			

* $0.01 par common; 15,000,000 authorized; 8,997,992 and 8,512,274 issued and outstanding.

RECENT QUARTERS / **PRIOR-YEAR RESULTS**

	Quarter End	Revenue ($000)	Earnings ($000)	EPS ($)	Revenue ($000)	Earnings ($000)	EPS ($)
Q2	09/30/2000	123	(597)	(0.05)	36	(956)	(0.11)
Q1	06/30/2000	52	(910)	(0.10)	67	(917)	(0.11)
Q4	03/31/2000	182	(935)	(0.10)	93	(758)	(0.09)
Q3	12/31/99	137	(989)	(0.11)	134	(617)	(0.07)
	SUM	493	(3,431)	(0.36)	330	(3,248)	(0.38)

RECENT EVENTS

In **January 2000** the company announced the first shipments of its new multi-mode multiplexer/demultiplexer, a component for dense wavelength division multiplexing (DWDM) systems intended for applications that use multi-mode fiber, such as local area network (LAN), campus, and metro networks. Initial quantities of the new product were supplied to a leading optical network company. APA then began actively pursuing the commercialization of its multi-mode DWDM. In **February** APA introduced a new single-mode fiber DWDM product that provides narrow channel spacing, permitting greater utilization of a given wavelength band. In **March** the company began offering a full line of advanced new DWDM MUX/DEMUX products. APA issued $5 million of 2 percent convertible preferred stock to three investors. "This transaction is the first step in our overall strategy to assure we have the resources necessary to further our goals in becoming a key supplier of DWDM components in the fast developing fiber optic telecommunications industry," said CEO Jain. **March 31:** The fourth-quarter and fiscal-year losses were expected, largely due to spending on fabrication systems, personnel, and new product marketing. "Though a loss is not welcomed, we have recognized that APA's transition to its planned role as a manufacturer and marketer of advanced technology products would only come with some costs," said Jain. "We have worked to minimize the cost, but it is being borne through the losses we have experienced." In **April** APA received an order for four of its new multimode fiber multiplexer/demultiplexer units from a U.S. systems developer and an order for one unit from a European systems developer. APA received an order for multiple units of a new 56-channel DWDM product. In **May** APA sold 118,956 shares of its common stock to one institutional investor through Ladenburg Thalmann & Co. Inc., placement agent and underwriter for the sale. The common stock was purchased at a negotiated price of $2,450,000 and net proceeds to the company were $2,341,500. In **June** Jain suggested that additional new products would be introduced in coming months, particularly in the area of gallium nitride technology. While the company's dense wavelength division multiplexing (DWDM) components were receiving considerable attention in the more visible fiber communications industry, APA's gallium nitride products, including the consumer ultraviolet light watch monitor, were expected to generate substantial coverage in the months to come. By **July** 12, APA had raised a total of $37.451 million in gross proceeds (net aggregate proceeds of $35.971 million) under an April 2000 shelf registration. The company planned to use the proceeds to expand its manufacturing capabilities, mainly at its Aberdeen, S.D., facility, and for product development and marketing activities. To take advantage of its strong cash position, APA was redeeming $5 million of convertible preferred stock issued in March 2000. In **August** APA demonstrated and shipped the initial units of its new 56-channel dense wavelength division multiplexing (DWDM) product, believed to be the only commercially available unit with both such a high channel count and low insertion loss. In **October** APA announced the receipt of more than 10 purchase orders for its DWDM products over the previous 45 days, representing $265,000 in potential sales. Later in the month, a unit of Alcatel, Paris, placed an order for 25 DWDM components. APA's board of directors adopted a shareholder rights plan seeking to offer protection for shareholders in the event of a hostile takeover action.

OFFICERS

Anil K. Jain
Chairman, President, and Treasurer

Kenneth A. Olsen
VP and Secretary

Robert M. Ringstad
CFO

DIRECTORS

William R. Franta, Ph.D.
REAL Solutions, Eden Prairie, MN

Michael A. Gort
Bravo Zulu! Interactive, Old Greenwich, CT

Anil K. Jain

Kenneth A. Olsen

Gregory J. Von Wald
Golden West Tele-tech Inc., Rapid City, SD

MAJOR SHAREHOLDERS

Anil K. Jain, 14.5%

Herman H. Lee, 6.7%
Borup, MN

Kenneth A. Olsen, 6.7%

All officers and directors as a group (6 persons), 21%

SIC CODE

3211 Flat glass

3674 Semiconductors and related devices

3827 Optical instruments and lenses

MISCELLANEOUS

TRANSFER AGENT AND REGISTAR:
Wells Fargo Bank Minnesota N.A., South St. Paul, MN

TRADED: Nasdaq National Market

SYMBOL: APAT

STOCKHOLDERS: 338

EMPLOYEES: 49

PART TIME: 1

IN MINNESOTA: 30

GENERAL COUNSEL:
Moss and Barnett P.A., Minneapolis

AUDITORS:
Ernst & Young LLP, St. Paul

INC: MN-1979

ANNUAL MEETING:
August

INVESTOR RELATIONS:
The Wallace Group

SUBSIDIARIES, DIVISIONS, AFFILIATES

Aberdeen Products Division
Aberdeen, South Dakota

TWO-YEAR QUARTERLY HIGH-LOW STOCK PRICES

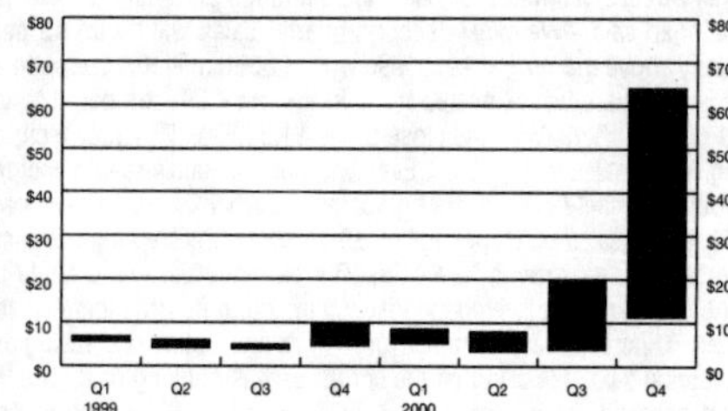

ASV Inc.

840 Lily Ln., P.O. Box 5160, Grand Rapids, MN 55744
Tel: 218/327-3434 Fax: 218/327-9122 Web site: http://www.posi-track.com

ASV (All Season Vehicles) Inc. designs, manufactures, and sells track-driven all-season vehicles. The company's two principal products, the **Posi-Track** and the **Track Truck**, use a rubber track system that takes advantage of the benefits of both traditional rubber wheels and steel tracks. Rubber track vehicles provide the traction, stability, and low ground pressure necessary for operation on soft, wet, muddy, rough, boggy, slippery, snowy, or hilly terrain. But, unlike steel track vehicles, they can be driven on groomed, landscaped, and paved surfaces without causing damage. The company introduced the Track Truck in 1985. The first Posi-Track sale occurred in October 1991.

EARNINGS HISTORY

Year Ended Dec 31	Operating Revenue/Sales (dollars in thousands)	Net Earnings	Return on Revenue (percent)	Return on Equity	Net Earnings (dollars per share*)	Cash Dividend	Market Price Range
1999	36,168	1,412	3.9	3.6	0.15	—	23.88–12.38
1998	39,019	3,366	8.6	17.2	0.43	—	26.38–14.13
1997	24,316	2,324	9.6	23.3	0.32	—	22.00–10.83
1996	12,266	922	7.5	14.7	0.13	—	12.89–2.78
1995	8,245	440	5.3	8.7	0.06	—	3.33–1.28

* Per-share amounts restated to reflect 3-for-2 stock splits effected May 14, 1998, and Jan. 17, 1997.

BALANCE SHEET

Assets	12/31/99 (dollars in thousands)	12/31/98
Current (CAE 743 and 308)	43,854	24,969
Property and equipment	4,796	4,564
TOTAL	48,650	29,533

Liabilities	12/31/99 (dollars in thousands)	12/31/98
Current (STD 254 and 219)	7,357	7,553
Capital lease obligation	2,197	2,289
Note payable		175
Stockholders' equity*	39,096	19,515
TOTAL	48,650	29,533

* $0.01 par common; 33,750,000 authorized; 9,686,457 and 8,601,835 issued and outstanding.

RECENT QUARTERS / **PRIOR-YEAR RESULTS**

	Quarter End	Revenue ($000)	Earnings ($000)	EPS ($)	Prior-Year Revenue ($000)	Prior-Year Earnings ($000)	Prior-Year EPS ($)
Q3	09/30/2000	10,533	220	0.02	8,781	21	0.00
Q2	06/30/2000	12,124	599	0.06	9,064	689	0.07
Q1	03/31/2000	11,184	417	0.04	8,463	649	0.07
Q4	12/31/99	9,860	54	0.01	8,108	525	0.07
	SUM	43,701	1,290	0.14	34,416	1,883	0.21

RECENT EVENTS

In **November 1999** the company was on the verge of entering the international market. ASV had agreed to sell some old inventory, 300 Posi-Track 2800 models, through Caterpillar dealers in Australia and South and Central America. In **February 2000** ASV was awarded the "Business-to-Business Campaign of the Year" PRWeek Award. ASV's new-concept all-terrain track vehicle was set to move into production in second quarter. Half the size of its large Posi-Track, the new offering was to be marketed to the landscaping and homeowner markets. **Sept. 30:** Nine-month net sales increased 29 percent to $33,840,722, but an unfavorable third-quarter comparison caused nine-month earnings to decline to $1,236,225 from $1,358,540. President Lemke said, "The combination of increased interest rates, rising fuel prices, and a decrease in demand for construction equipment prevented ASV's third-quarter 2000 sales and earnings from reaching the levels we had anticipated." In addition, the company's gross margin was affected during the quarter by several factors: The softening construction equipment market resulted in a decreased demand for ASV's higher margin 4810 Posi-Track; ASV began a more aggressive discount program to reduce its inventory of new 2800 series Posi-Tracks; and ASV's latest product, the RC-30, went into production during the quarter. In **October** ASV and Caterpillar Inc. added to their previous agreements when Caterpillar purchased 500,000 newly issued shares of ASV common stock for a total of $9 million, thereby increasing its ownership in ASV to about 15 percent. The two companies also announced the signing of an alliance agreement in which they planned to jointly develop and manufacture a revolutionary new product line of Caterpillar rubber track skid steer loaders called Multi-Terrain Loaders. Expected to include five new models, the product line was to feature Caterpillar's patented skid steer loader technology and ASV's patent-pending Maximum Traction Support System rubber track undercarriage.

OFFICERS

Philip C. Smaby
Chairman

Jerome T. Miner
Vice Chairman

Gary D. Lemke
President

Thomas R. Karges
CFO

Edgar E. Hetteen
VP and Secretary

DIRECTORS

Dick Benson
Caterpillar Inc., Peoria, IL

Richard A. Cooper
Caterpillar Paving Products, Brooklyn Park, MN

James Dahl
James Dahl & Co. Inc., Jacksonville, FL

Edgar E. Hetteen

Gary D. Lemke

Leland T. Lynch
Carmichael Lynch Inc., Minneapolis

Jerome T. Miner
Jerry Miner Realty Inc., Grand Rapids, MN

Philip C. Smaby

Karlin S. Symons
Kaplan, Strangis and Kaplan P.A., Minneapolis

R.E. (Teddy) Turner IV
Turner Communications Co., Atlanta

MAJOR SHAREHOLDERS

Caterpillar Inc., 14.7%
Peoria, IL

James H. Dahl, 9.8%
Jacksonville, FL

Gary D. Lemke, 8.7%

All officers and directors as a group (11 persons), 29.7%

SIC CODE

3531 Construction machinery and equipment

MISCELLANEOUS

TRANSFER AGENT AND REGISTAR:
Wells Fargo Bank Minnesota N.A.,
South St. Paul, MN

TRADED: Nasdaq National Market

SYMBOL: ASVI

STOCKHOLDERS: 262

EMPLOYEES: 112

PART TIME: 2

GENERAL COUNSEL:
Dorsey & Whitney PLLP, Minneapolis

AUDITORS:
Grant Thornton LLP, Minneapolis

INC: MN-1983

ANNUAL MEETING: June

INVESTOR RELATIONS:
Thomas R. Karges

RANKINGS

No. 125 CRM Public 200

SUBSIDIARIES, DIVISIONS, AFFILIATES

ASV Distribution Inc.
840 Lily Lane
P.O. Box 5160
Grand Rapids, MN 55744
218/327-3434

TWO-YEAR QUARTERLY HIGH-LOW STOCK PRICES

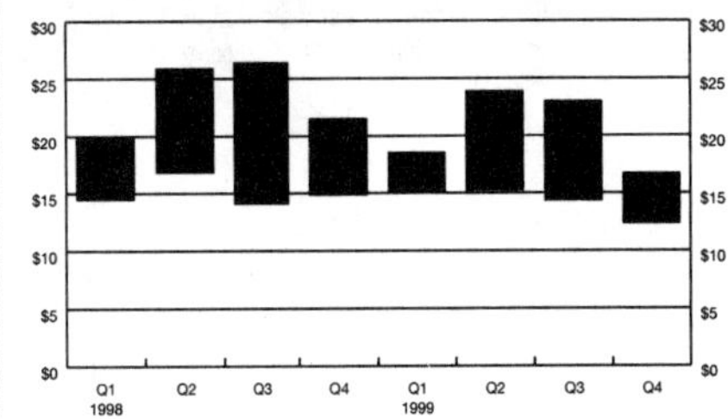

PUB

PUB

ATS Medical Inc.

3905 Annapolis Ln., Suite 105, Plymouth, MN 55447
Tel: 763/553-7736 Fax: 763/553-1492 Web site: http://www.atsmedical.com

ATS Medical Inc. manufactures and markets a new pyrolytic carbon, bileaflet mechanical heart valve. The ATS Medical Open Pivot valve is designed to improve on existing monoleaflet and bileaflet mechanical heart valves by providing improved cardiovascular performance, as well as being quieter and easier to implant and monitor. The ATS Medical valve combines a proprietary open-pivot concept and several other design features with all-pyrolytic carbon surfaces.

EARNINGS HISTORY

Year Ended Dec 31	Operating Revenue/Sales (dollars in thousands)	Net Earnings (dollars in thousands)	Return on Revenue (percent)	Return on Equity (percent)	Net Earnings (dollars per share)	Cash Dividend (dollars per share)	Market Price Range (dollars per share)
1999	17,462	2,638	15.1	4.5	0.15	—	14.94–6.00
1998	17,960	2,839	15.8	5.1	0.16	—	8.38–4.31
1997	14,516	2,103	14.5	3.9	0.12	—	8.50–4.75
1996	11,860	1,322	11.1	4.1	0.09	—	12.00–6.25
1995	9,301	715	7.7	2.5	0.05	—	9.88–3.75

BALANCE SHEET

Assets	12/31/99 (dollars in thousands)	12/31/98 (dollars in thousands)	Liabilities	12/31/99 (dollars in thousands)	12/31/98 (dollars in thousands)
Current (CAE 4,030 and 7,754)	54,912	56,841	Current	2,275	2,612
Furniture and equipment	801	1,203	Stockholders' equity*	58,842	55,820
Technology license	5,000		TOTAL	61,117	58,431
Other	403	388			
TOTAL	61,117	58,431			

* $0.01 par common; 40,000,000 authorized; 17,909,010 and 17,824,137 issued and outstanding.

RECENT QUARTERS / PRIOR-YEAR RESULTS

	Quarter End	Revenue ($000)	Earnings ($000)	EPS ($)	Prior-Year Revenue ($000)	Prior-Year Earnings ($000)	Prior-Year EPS ($)
Q3	09/30/2000	3,708	208	0.01	4,258	656	0.04
Q2	06/30/2000	2,704	(234)	(0.01)	4,722	780	0.04
Q1	03/31/2000	4,127	401	0.02	4,190	688	0.04
Q4	12/31/99	4,292	515	0.03	5,007	638	0.04
	SUM	14,831	889	0.05	18,178	2,761	0.15

RECENT EVENTS

In **January 2000** the company entered into an agreement with Sulzer Carbomedics, its sole source of pyrolytic carbon, to obtain a license to manufacture pyrolytic carbon for the ATS valve. "We have recognized for a long period of time that it would be necessary to control our destiny and make our own carbon if we are to accomplish our goal of being No. 1 in the heart valve business," said CEO Villafana. "This new agreement additionally allows for a significant reduction in our requirements to purchase valves from Carbomedics in the future and, starting with the year 2001, reduces our component costs substantially." Under the new deal, Sulzer was to help ATS build a manufacturing plant in the Twin Cities (to be online in 2003) in return for a seven-year, $41 million payment. In **February** ATS received a letter from the FDA relating to its pre-market approval (PMA) application for the ATS Medical heart valve. It asked ATS to provide additional information regarding the ATS valve. ATS Medical was expecting to submit the requested information over the next four to eight weeks, whereupon the FDA review of this additional information could take up to 180 days. Upon completion of this review, the FDA could, among other things, request additional information or schedule a meeting for presentation of clinical data to an FDA advisory panel in Washington, D.C. **June 30:** The company attributed the quarter's revenue decline to the weak Euro. Sales to non-European countries increased 5 percent while European sales declined 74 percent from prior year. "Some of our customers decided to lower their inventories in light of the record weak exchange rate incurred during the second quarter," said Villafana. "The low value of the Euro relative to the U.S. dollar, together with price cutting by some competitors, has shrunk distribution profit margins to the point that they are reluctant to take currency risk on valve inventory." In anticipation of federal approval of ATS' heart valve in fourth quarter or early 2001, the market drove the company's stock from $10 a share to $15 over the course of the summer. **Sept. 30:** The company was pleased with the increase in sales in the third quarter over the second quarter, given the fact that the Euro continued to struggle in currency exchange against the dollar. In **October** ATS received FDA approval to sell the ATS Open Pivot Bileaflet Heart Valve for the treatment of valvular heart disease in the United States.

OFFICERS

Manuel A. (Manny) Villafana
Chairman and CEO

Richard W. Kramp
President and COO

Russell W. Felkey
EVP-Regulatory Affairs

John H. Jungbauer
VP-Finance and CFO

Frank R. Santiago
VP-Sales/Marketing

RANKINGS

No. 159 CRM Public 200

DIRECTORS

David L. Boehnen
Supervalu Inc., Eden Prairie, MN

Charles F. Cuddihy Jr.
Medtronic Inc. (retired)

A. Jay Graf
CPI/Guidant Corp., Arden Hills, MN

Richard W. Kramp

Manuel A. (Manny) Villafana

MAJOR SHAREHOLDERS

Lord, Abett & Co., 11.5%
Jersey City, NJ

ITOCHU Corp., 8.7%
Tokyo

All officers and directors as a group (8 persons), 9.8%

SIC CODE

3841 Surgical and medical instruments

5047 Medical and hospital equipment, whsle

MISCELLANEOUS

TRANSFER AGENT AND REGISTAR:
Wells Fargo Bank Minnesota N.A., South St. Paul, MN

TRADED: Nasdaq National Market

SYMBOL: ATSI

STOCKHOLDERS: 509

EMPLOYEES: 86

GENERAL COUNSEL:
Dorsey & Whitney PLLP, Minneapolis
Haugen Law Firm PLLP, Minneapolis

AUDITORS:
Ernst & Young LLP, Minneapolis

INC: MN-1987

ANNUAL MEETING: April

INVESTOR RELATIONS:
John Jungbauer

TWO-YEAR QUARTERLY HIGH-LOW STOCK PRICES

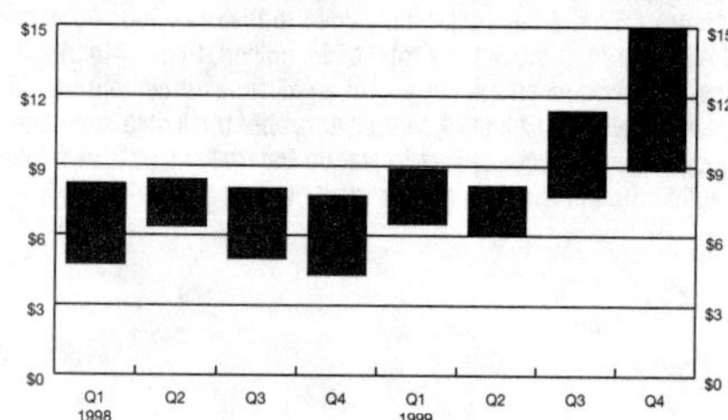

Aero Systems Engineering Inc.

358 E. Fillmore Ave., St. Paul, MN 55107
Tel: 651/227-7515 Fax: 651/227-0519 Web site: http://www.aerosysengr.com

Aero Systems Engineering Inc. (ASE) designs, equips, manufactures, and constructs electronic, mechanical, and computerized jet engine and engine accessory test equipment and jet engine test facilities, wind tunnels, and other aerodynamic test facilities. It also provides aerodynamic testing services at its own wind tunnel facility. ASE competes in the markets for wind tunnels used for testing airplanes and other forms of high-speed transportation, and in the markets for jet engine testing facilities called "test cells." Both wind tunnels and jet engine test cells require advanced capabilities in sound control and electronic test hardware and software. Test cell and wind tunnel contracts range in value from $1 million to more than $20 million. The company is an 80 percent owned subsidiary of Saab Aerospace.

EARNINGS HISTORY

Year Ended Dec 31	Operating Revenue/Sales (dollars in thousands)	Net Earnings	Return on Revenue (percent)	Return on Equity	Net Earnings (dollars per share*)	Cash Dividend	Market Price Range
1999	31,061	(645)	(2.1)	(15.1)	(0.15)	—	2.50–0.75
1998	27,181	665	2.4	13.5	0.15	—	2.61–0.80
1997	25,032	(401)	(1.6)	(9.4)	(0.09)	—	1.85–0.65
1996	20,383	(2,528)	(12.4)	(54.4)	(0.57)	—	1.34–0.55
1995	26,037	189	0.7	2.6	0.04	—	1.38–0.58

* Per-share amounts restated to reflect 15 percent stock dividend on March 10, 1999; and 3-for-2 stock split on March 6, 1998.

BALANCE SHEET

Assets	12/31/99 (dollars in thousands)	12/31/98	Liabilities	12/31/99 (dollars in thousands)	12/31/98
Current (CAE 48 and 16)	15,055	16,004	Current (STD 0 and 400)	15,621	15,850
Property, plant, and equipment	5,629	5,476	Deferred income taxes	623	480
TOTAL	20,684	21,480	Capital lease obligations	171	234
			Stockholders' equity*	4,270	4,915
			TOTAL	20,684	21,480

* $0.20 par common; 10,000,000 authorized; 4,401,625 and 4,401,625 issued and outstanding.

RECENT QUARTERS / PRIOR-YEAR RESULTS

	Quarter End	Revenue ($000)	Earnings ($000)	EPS ($)	Prior-Year Revenue ($000)	Prior-Year Earnings ($000)	Prior-Year EPS ($)
Q3	09/30/2000	8,751	340	0.08	7,841	389	0.09
Q2	06/30/2000	8,078	251	0.06	8,715	(454)	(0.10)
Q1	03/31/2000	6,760	(466)	(0.11)	6,396	(476)	(0.11)
Q4	12/31/99	8,109	(104)	(0.02)	7,650	367	0.08
	SUM	31,698	21	0.00	30,602	(174)	(0.04)

RECENT EVENTS

In **February 2000** the company was awarded three major contracts totaling $5.7 million. One, from General Electric, was for jet engine test equipment, including an ASE2000 computer system for a new test cell facility in China. The second and third contracts were both to provide new ASE2000 data acquisition systems, one to a major U.S. airline company for one of its jet engine test cells and one to Alitalia for its large test cell in Italy. In **March** Saab Aerospace acquired 80 percent ownership of the company via the acquisition of ASE's former 80 percent owner, Swedish holding company Celsius Industries AB, a corporation owned by the Swedish government. In **May** ASE was awarded two major contracts from General Electric totaling $3.5 million. The first contract was for acoustical retrofitting of a test cell facility in Brazil; the second was to provide a thrust frame adapter for a jet engine test cell in Spain. ASE received notice of a major wind tunnel contract award in the amount of $23 million from DSO National Laboratories in Singapore—for ASE to supply a refurbished Trisonic Blowdown Wind Tunnel at their location in Singapore. The contract involved the refurbishment of an existing wind tunnel and the supply of a significant amount of new equipment over a 30-month period. **Sept. 30:** Backlog at the end of the third quarter, $31.4 million, was an increase of 73% over third quarter 1999. The year-to-date orders through September were $36.3 million. The year-over-year increase in revenue was mostly attributable to a higher backlog going into the third quarter 2000 and the fact that a major wind tunnel project achieved the percentage of completion required for revenue recognition during the quarter.

OFFICERS

Christer Persson
Chairman

Charles H. Loux
President and CEO

Michael Browne
Programs

Donald Kamis
VP-Wind Tunnel/Automotive Programs

Grant Radinzel
VP-Staff Engineering, Test Cells

Richard Thomalla
VP-Test Cell Business Development

Steven R. Hedberg
CFO, Treasurer, and Secretary

HUMAN RESOURCES:
Tom Sletten

INVESTOR RELATIONS:
Steven R. Hedberg

RANKINGS

No. 131 CRM Public 200

SUBSIDIARIES, DIVISIONS, AFFILIATES

FluiDyne Aerotest Group

FluiDyne Facilities Group

Turbine Test Systems Group

DIRECTORS

Richard A. Hoel
Winthrop & Weinstine P.A., St. Paul

Charles H. Loux

A.L. Maxson
financial consultant, Edina, MN

Christer Persson
Celsius Inc., Alexandria, VA

Leon E. Ring, Ph.D.

MAJOR SHAREHOLDERS

Saab Aerospace, 80%
Stockholm

All officers and directors as a group (10 persons), 3%

SIC CODE

3559 Special industry machinery, nec

3829 Measuring and controlling devices, nec

8711 Engineering services

MISCELLANEOUS

TRANSFER AGENT AND REGISTAR:
Wells Fargo Bank Minnesota N.A., South St. Paul, MN

TRADED: Nasdaq SmallCap Market

SYMBOL: AERS

STOCKHOLDERS: 199

EMPLOYEES: 181

GENERAL COUNSEL:
Winthrop & Weinstine P.A., St. Paul

AUDITORS:
Ernst & Young LLP, Minneapolis

INC: MN-1967

ANNUAL MEETING: May

TWO-YEAR QUARTERLY HIGH-LOW STOCK PRICES

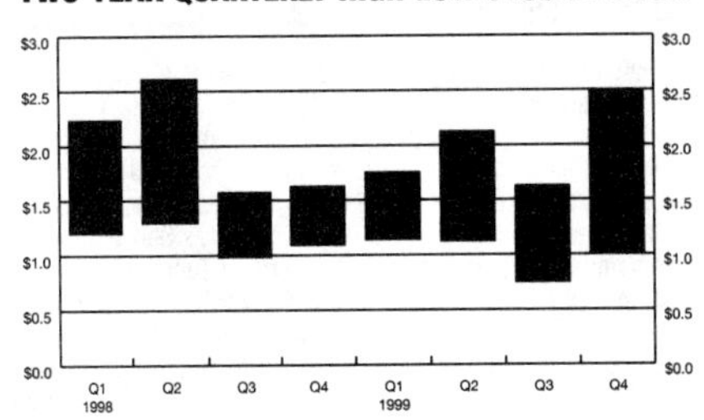

PUB

PUB

Aetrium Inc.

2350 Helen St., North St. Paul, MN 55109
Tel: 651/704-1800 Fax: 651/704-0339 Web site: http://www.aetrium.com

Aetrium Inc. designs, manufactures, and markets a variety of electromechanical equipment used in the handling and testing of semiconductor devices known as integrated circuits (ICs). The company's primary focus is on high-volume IC types and the latest package designs associated with surface-mount technology. Aetrium's products are purchased primarily by semiconductor manufacturers and are used in the "back-end" of semiconductor manufacturing processes. The company's products automate critical functions to improve manufacturing yield, increase product reliability, raise IC quality levels, and reduce manufacturing costs. Aetrium sells these products to semiconductor and equipment manufacturers worldwide.

EARNINGS HISTORY

Year Ended Dec 31	Operating Revenue/Sales (dollars in thousands)	Net Earnings (dollars in thousands)	Return on Revenue (percent)	Return on Equity (percent)	Net Earnings (dollars per share*)	Cash Dividend (dollars per share*)	Market Price Range (dollars per share*)
1999 †	37,188	(9,013)	(24.2)	(15.7)	(0.95)	—	12.44–5.13
1998 ¶	59,619	(9,450)	(15.9)	(14.1)	(1.00)	—	19.00–3.63
1997 #	67,575	1,229	1.8	2.0	0.14	—	28.25–12.50
1996	58,387	9,242	15.8	15.9	1.10	—	22.00–8.38
1995 **	47,631	3,356	7.0	6.9	0.48	—	25.25–6.67

* Per-share amounts, which include preferred stock as common stock equivalents, have been restated to reflect 3-for-2 stock split on Aug. 15, 1995.
† Income figures for 1999 include pretax nonrecurring charges totaling $1,446,083.
¶ Income figures for 1998 include pretax nonrecurring charges totaling $6,527,000.
\# Income figures for 1997 include pretax acquisition-related charge of $9,459,351.
** Income figures for 1995 include pretax acquisition-related charge of $6,338,590.

BALANCE SHEET

Assets	12/31/99 (dollars in thousands)	12/31/98 (dollars in thousands)	Liabilities	12/31/99 (dollars in thousands)	12/31/98 (dollars in thousands)
Current (CAE 13,184 and 18,132)	33,832	45,147	Current	6,174	5,659
Property and equipment	2,833	3,764	Stockholders' equity*	57,430	66,785
Deferred taxes	12,445	6,037	TOTAL	63,604	72,444
Intangible and other	14,494	17,495			
TOTAL	63,604	72,444			

* $0.001 par common; 30,000,000 authorized; 9,436,035 and 9,471,642 issued and outstanding.

RECENT QUARTERS / PRIOR-YEAR RESULTS

	Quarter End	Revenue ($000)	Earnings ($000)	EPS ($)	Prior-Year Revenue ($000)	Prior-Year Earnings ($000)	Prior-Year EPS ($)
Q3	09/30/2000	12,781	715	0.08	10,106	(1,522)	(0.16)
Q2	06/30/2000	10,855	(1,509)	(0.16)	8,013	(3,503)	(0.37)
Q1	03/31/2000	10,611	(2,819)	(0.30)	8,057	(2,294)	(0.24)
Q4	12/31/99	11,012	(1,694)	(0.18)	11,021	(1,847)	(0.19)
	SUM	45,259	(5,307)	(0.56)	37,197	(9,166)	(0.97)

CURRENT: Q3 earnings include a special pretax credit of $436,000 from the sale of royalty rights associated with the sold environmental test equipment product line. Q2 earnings include one-time charges totaling $1.370 million pretax, $1.069 million/($0.11) after-tax. Q1 earnings include special charge of $2.819 million pretax, $1.752 million/($0.19) after-tax, for restructuring and asset write-downs.
PRIOR YEAR: Q2 earnings include one-time charges totaling $2.662 million pretax, $1.600 million/($0.17) after-tax.

RECENT EVENTS

In **January 2000** the company announced plans to restructure its operations and consolidate its five current operations into three, saving more than $1 million per quarter in costs. As of April 1, 2000, Aetrium was to have operations in San Diego, North St. Paul, and Dallas, with a combined workforce of 230 people, down from 300 at year-end. As part of the restructuring, the Lawrence, Mass., operation was to close on March 31, 2000; and Aetrium's two Texas operations were to be combined. The workforce reductions were all to take place in Lawrence, Mass., and Texas. In **June** Aetrium announced plans to transfer manufacturing functions performed at the company's San Diego operation to its North St. Paul operation. The process of transferring manufacturing and certain administrative functions from San Diego to North St. Paul was to begin immediately. The San Diego operation was then to focus exclusively on engineering and marketing functions related to the continued development and deployment of Aetrium's DTX series of test handlers. In **July** Aetrium demonstrated the Aetrium Model DTX Series Dynamic Temperature IC Test Handler for the first time, at SEMICON West 2000, San Jose, Calif. The product was the first of a full line of test handlers that Aetrium was continuing to develop utilizing dynamic *continued on page 150*

OFFICERS

Joseph C. Levesque
Chairman, President, and CEO

Paul H. Askegaard
Treasurer

Gerald C. (Jerry) Clemens
VP-Reliability Test Products

Timothy G. Foley
VP-Operations, N. St. Paul Division

Douglas L. Hemer
Group VP

Daniel M. Koch
VP-Worldwide Sales

Paul H. Laufer
VP-Finance/Corporate Development

John J. Pollock
VP-Corporate Marketing

Stephen P. Weisbrod
VP-Corporate Technology

Keith E. Williams
Pres.-Aetrium Dallas Division

DIRECTORS

Darnell L. Boehm

Terrence W. Glarner
West Concord Ventures Inc., Minneapolis

Andrew J. Greenshields
Pathfinder Venture Capital Funds, Minneapolis

Douglas L. Hemer

Joseph C. Levesque

Terry Nagel
NOW Technologies Inc., Minneapolis

MAJOR SHAREHOLDERS

Woodland Partners LLC, 6%
Minneapolis

All officers and directors as a group (17 persons), 11.9%

SIC CODE

3825 Instruments to measure electricity

MISCELLANEOUS

TRANSFER AGENT AND REGISTAR:
Harris Trust and Savings Bank, Chicago

TRADED: Nasdaq National Market

SYMBOL: ATRM

STOCKHOLDERS: 200

EMPLOYEES: 235

GENERAL COUNSEL:
Oppenheimer Wolff & Donnelly LLP, Minneapolis

AUDITORS:
PricewaterhouseCoopers LLP, Minneapolis

ANNUAL MEETING: May

RANKINGS

No. 123 CRM Public 200

SUBSIDIARIES, DIVISIONS, AFFILIATES

Aetrium WEB Technology
10501 Markinson Rd.
Dallas, TX 75238
214/343-9238
Keith E. Williams

North St. Paul Division
2350 Helen St.
North St. Paul, MN 55109
651/770-2000
Timothy G. Foley

TWO-YEAR QUARTERLY HIGH-LOW STOCK PRICES

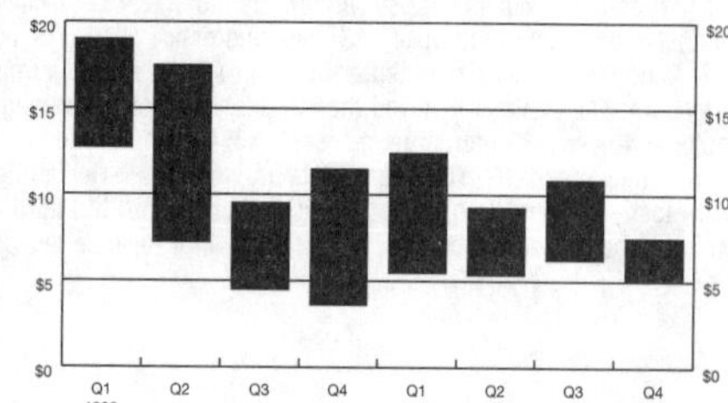

Ag-Chem Equipment Company Inc.

5720 Smetana Dr., Minnetonka, MN 55343
Tel: 952/933-9006 Fax: 952/933-8799 Web site: http://www.agchem.com

Ag-Chem Equipment Co. Inc. manufactures and markets a line of self-propelled, off-road chassis. Products include row-crop machines and high-flotation vehicles, some for industrial purposes. Usually the chassis are sold with a product application system installed and are typically used to apply liquid and dry fertilizer, crop protection products, and biosolids. The company employs a nationwide factory-direct sales force and a national parts and service network.

EARNINGS HISTORY

Year Ended Sept 30	Operating Revenue/Sales (dollars in thousands)	Net Earnings	Return on Revenue (percent)	Return on Equity	Net Earnings (dollars per share)	Cash Dividend	Market Price Range
1999	292,679	3,388	1.2	4.6	0.35	—	16.75–8.50
1998	322,122	6,848	2.1	9.7	0.71	—	22.13–12.50
1997	318,212	7,570	2.4	11.8	0.78	—	24.50–14.75
1996	280,152	9,748	3.5	17.0	1.01	—	31.75–15.75
1995 *	233,852	11,410	4.9	25.4	1.19	—	31.00–8.75

* Figures for 1995 include results of the company's largest European distributor from the Feb. 14, 1995, date it was acquired for $2.1 million plus an earnout.

BALANCE SHEET

Assets	09/30/99 (dollars in thousands)	09/30/98	Liabilities	09/30/99 (dollars in thousands)	09/30/98
Current	138,709	134,045	Current (STD 41,744 and 19,864)	72,407	57,871
Property, plant, and equipment	42,470	45,813	Long-term debt	44,299	59,903
Notes receivable	7,046	5,596	Stockholders' equity*	73,223	70,420
Intangibles and other	1,704	2,740	TOTAL	189,929	188,194
TOTAL	189,929	188,194			

* $0.01 par common; 40,000,000 authorized; 9,595,468 and 9,640,268 issued and outstanding.

RECENT QUARTERS / PRIOR-YEAR RESULTS

	Quarter End	Revenue ($000)	Earnings ($000)	EPS ($)	Prior-Year Revenue ($000)	Prior-Year Earnings ($000)	Prior-Year EPS ($)
Q3	06/30/2000	65,181	(1,384)	(0.14)	71,504	(638)	(0.07)
Q2	03/31/2000	118,074	6,883	0.72	110,995	7,505	0.78
Q1	12/31/99	58,708	(2,024)	(0.21)	53,529	(356)	(0.04)
Q4	09/30/99	56,651	(3,123)	(0.33)	66,011	487	0.05
	SUM	298,614	352	0.04	302,039	6,998	0.73

RECENT EVENTS

Dec. 31, 1999: CEO McQuinn on First-quarter results: "A 9 percent sales increase was not enough to counter a combination of cost increases that led to a bigger loss for the first quarter of fiscal 2000. We continue the positive development of both hardware and software that eventually will be the basis for our new phase of expansion and growth." In **February 2000** the Minnesota Department of Economic Security approved $228,883 in Incumbent Dislocated Worker program funds to aid 732 Ag-Chem workers in Jackson, Minn. With the slump in agriculture, the company was planning to diversify its production by training its workers to become welders. In **September** Ag-Chem issued a safety alert and undertook a majorproduct improvement program pertaining to a component in specific models of its RoGator self-propelled agricultural sprayers. The notice related only to RoGator Model Nos. 663, 664, 844, and 854 manufactured in model years 1999 and earlier and a limited number of model year 2000 RoGator 854's. A serious safety concern surrounded a vendor-supplied component; specifically the cast iron axle in the BB5 wheel motors built into such models. In light of Ag-Chem's concern for the safety of owners, operators, and bystanders, and in an effort to improve the operational dependability of those machines, Ag-Chem was planning to replace those axles. Although there had been instances of axle failures, no personal injuries had been reported to date as a result of those failures. Ag-Chem had been informed by its supplier that it would take one year to produce the replacement axles.

OFFICERS

Alvin E. McQuinn
Chairman and CEO

Donald D. Pottinger
President

Mary M. Jetland
SVP-Advanced Technology/Manufacturing

John C. Retherford
SVP and CFO

Norman A. Bauer
VP-Engineering

David A. Decklever
VP-National Accounts

Steven M. Koep
VP-Marketing Services

Greg Larson
VP-Corporate Purchasing

James M. Olson
VP-Human Resources

Barry Pace
VP-International and VP-Parts/Service

Dwight Porter
VP-Sales, North America

John Rauth
VP-Administration

John G. Trygstad
VP-Information technology

Robert L. Hoffman
Secretary

J. Joyce Lander
Asst. Secretary

DIRECTORS

G. Waddy Garrett
Alliance Agronomics Inc.

A.J. (Al) Giese
Cenex/Land O'Lakes. Agrilliance LLC., Arden Hills, MN

Robert L. Hoffman
Larkin, Hoffman, Daly & Lindgren Ltd., Bloomington, MN

Mary M. Jetland

Alvin E. McQuinn

Donald D. Pottinger

John C. Retherford

DeWalt J. Willard Jr.
Willard Agri-Services

MAJOR SHAREHOLDERS

Alvin E. McQuinn, 59.2%

All officers and directors as a group (8 persons), 61%

SIC CODE

3523 Farm machinery and equipment

MISCELLANEOUS

TRANSFER AGENT AND REGISTAR:
Chase Mellon Shareholder Services LLC, Ridgefield Park, NJ

TRADED: Nasdaq National Market

SYMBOL: AGCH

STOCKHOLDERS: 371

EMPLOYEES: 1,445

GENERAL COUNSEL:
Larkin, Hoffman, Daly & Lindgren Ltd., Bloomington, MN

AUDITORS:
KPMG LLP, Minneapolis

INC: MN-1963

ANNUAL MEETING: March

HUMAN RESOURCES: Jim Olson

PUBLIC RELATIONS: Amy Cone

RANKINGS

No. 61 CRM Public 200

SUBSIDIARIES, DIVISIONS, AFFILIATES

Lor*Al Products Inc.
2200 Hall Ave.
Benson, MN 56215
320/843-4161

Soil Teq Inc.
5720 Smetana Dr.
Minnetonka, MN 55343
612/933-9006

PUB

TWO-YEAR QUARTERLY HIGH-LOW STOCK PRICES

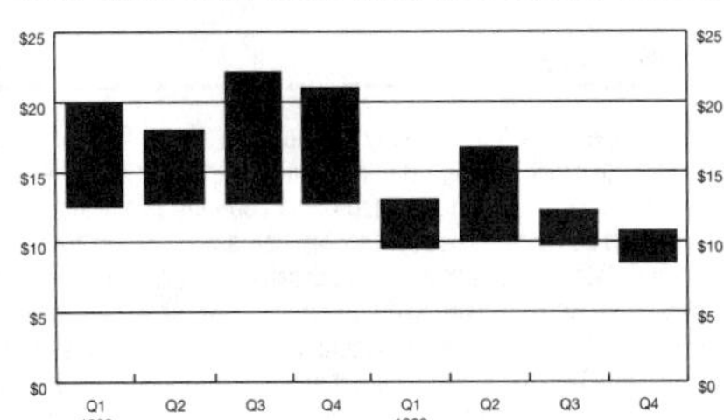

PUB

Allete

30 W. Superior St., Duluth, MN 55802
Tel: 218/723-3974 Fax: 218/720-2502 Web site: http://www.mnpower.com

Allete, formerly Minnesota Power Inc. and Minnesota Power & Light Co., has operations in four business segments: **electric** operations, which include electric and gas services, and coal mining; **water** operations, which include water and wastewater services; **automobile auctions**, which include a finance company and an auto transport company; and **investments**, which include a securities portfolio, a 21 percent equity investment in a financial guaranty reinsurance and insurance company, and real estate operations.

EARNINGS HISTORY

Year Ended Dec 31	Operating Revenue/Sales (dollars in thousands)	Net Earnings (dollars in thousands)	Return on Revenue (percent)	Return on Equity (percent)	Net Earnings (dollars per share*)	Cash Dividend (dollars per share*)	Market Price Range (dollars per share*)
1999 †	1,131,800	68,000	6.0	8.2	0.97	1.07	22.09–16.00
1998	1,039,300	88,500	8.5	11.0	1.35	1.02	23.13–19.03
1997 ¶	953,600	77,600	8.1	11.6	1.24	1.02	22.00–13.50
1996 #	846,928	69,221	8.2	10.9	1.14	1.02	14.88–13.00
1995 **	672,917	64,705	9.6	10.5	1.08	1.02	14.63–12.13

* Per-share amounts restated to reflect 2-for-1 stock split on March 2, 1999.
† Income figures for 1999 include charge of $36.2 million/($0.57) related to merger of Capital Re with ACE.
¶ Income figures for 1997 include gain of $4.7 million/$0.08 from Dec. 30, 1997, sale of Florida Water assets.
# Pro forma had the remaining 17 percent of ADESA been acquired Jan. 1 rather than in August 1996: net income $68,720,000/$1.13.
** Income figures for 1995 include gain of $2,848,000/$0.05 from discontinued operations. Pro forma had 100 percent of ADESA been acquired Jan. 1: revenue $729,674,000; net income $62,648,000.

BALANCE SHEET

Assets	12/31/99 (dollars in thousands)	12/31/98 (dollars in thousands)	Liabilities	12/31/99 (dollars in thousands)	12/31/98 (dollars in thousands)
Current (CAE 101,500 and 89,400)	564,500	487,500	Current (STD 105,600 and 90,000)	398,300	346,000
Property, plant, and equipment	1,258,800	1,178,900	Long-term debt	712,800	672,200
			Deferred taxes	139,900	153,400
Investments	197,200	263,500	Other	149,300	145,200
Goodwill	181,000	169,800	Preferred equity	106,500	106,500
Other	111,100	109,200	Common equity*	805,800	785,600
TOTAL	2,312,600	2,208,900	TOTAL	2,312,600	2,208,900

* No par common; 130,000,000 authorized; 73,500,000 and 72,300,000 issued and outstanding.

RECENT QUARTERS / PRIOR-YEAR RESULTS

	Quarter End	Revenue ($000)	Earnings ($000)	EPS ($)	Prior-Year Revenue ($000)	Prior-Year Earnings ($000)	Prior-Year EPS ($)
Q3	09/30/2000	323,500	35,000	0.50	308,000	34,500	0.50
Q2	06/30/2000	327,000	64,200	0.92	279,200	1,900	0.02
Q1	03/31/2000	322,600	30,400	0.43	257,700	20,900	0.30
Q4	12/31/99	286,900	10,700	0.15	257,400	21,400	0.31
	SUM	1,260,000	140,300	2.00	1,102,300	78,700	1.13

CURRENT: Q2 earnings include gain of $30.4 million/$0.44 from sale of investment in ACE Ltd. common stock. Q4 earnings include charge of $12.1 million/($0.17) related to merger of Capital Re with ACE.
PRIOR YEAR: Q2 earnings include charge of $24.1 million/($0.35) related to merger of Capital Re with ACE.

RECENT EVENTS

In **November 1999** the company agreed to purchase Blandin Paper Co.'s steam and electric generating facilities located at the Blandin paper mill in Grand Rapids, Minn. Minnesota Power was to operate the existing facilities, add new boiler equipment to serve Blandin's future steam needs, and continue providing supplemental retail electric service. In **December** the Minnesota Public Utilities Commission (MPUC) ended a preliminary investigation into the reasonableness of Minnesota Power's electric rates and determined that a comprehensive rate investigation was not necessary. The company exchanged 7.3 million shares of Capital Re Corp. (NYSE: KRE) common stock for 4.7 million shares of ACE Ltd. (NYSE: ACL) common stock plus $25.1 million in cash (the result of a completed merger), giving it better liquidity and the ability to pursue growth opportunities in its other businesses. **Dec. 31:** Fiscal-year net income from automotive services grew by 57 percent over prior year. The number of vehicles financed by Automotive Finance Corp. jumped 31 percent; the number of vehicles consigned at *continued on page 150*

OFFICERS

Edwin L. Russell
Chairman, President, and CEO
John A. Cirello
EVP and Pres./CEO-MP Water Resources
Donnie R. Crandell
EVP, Pres.-MP Real Estate Holding
Robert D. Edwards
EVP and Pres.-MP Electric
Branda J. Flayton
VP-Human Resources
John E. Fuller
EVP and Pres./CEO-AFC
David G. Gartzke
SVP-Finance and CFO
James P. Hallett
EVP and Pres./CEO-ADESA
Lawrence H. Fuller
VP-Corporate Development
Philip R. Halverson
VP, General Counsel, and Secretary
David Jeronimus
VP-Environmental Services
James A. Roberts
VP-Corporate Relations
Mark A. Schober
Controller
James K. Vizanko
Treasurer
Claudia Scott Welty
VP-Information Technology

DIRECTORS

Kathleen A. Brekken
Midwest of Cannon Falls Inc., Cannon Falls, MN
Merrill K. (Dutch) Cragun
Cragun Corp., Brainerd, MN
Dennis E. Evans
Hanrow Financial Group Ltd., Minneapolis
Peter J. Johnson
Hoover Construction Co., Tower, MN
George L. Mayer
Manhattan Realty Group, Larchmont, NY
Jack I. Rajala
Rajala Cos., Rajala Mill Co., Grand Rapids, MN
Edwin L. Russell
Arend J. Sandbulte
Nick Smith
Fryberger, Buchanan, Smith & Frederick P.A., Duluth, MN
Bruce W. Stender
Labovitz Enterprises, Duluth, MN
Donald C. Wegmiller
Management Compensation Group/HealthCare, Minneapolis

MAJOR SHAREHOLDERS

Mellon Bank Corp., 11.1%
Pittsburgh
All officers and directors as a group (26 persons), 1.4%

SIC CODE

4939 Combination utility services, nec

MISCELLANEOUS

TRANSFER AGENT AND REGISTAR:
Wells Fargo Bank Minnesota N.A., South St. Paul, MN
TRADED: NYSE, ALE
SYMBOL: MPL
STOCKHOLDERS: 37,000
EMPLOYEES: 8,246
GENERAL COUNSEL:
Reid & Priest LLP, New York
AUDITORS:
PricewaterhouseCoopers LLP, Minneapolis
INC: MN-1906
ANNUAL MEETING: May
INVESTOR RELATIONS:
Tim Thorp
COMMUNICATIONS:
John E. Heino

RANKINGS

No. 31 CRM Public 200
No. 10 CRM Performance 100

TWO-YEAR QUARTERLY HIGH-LOW STOCK PRICES

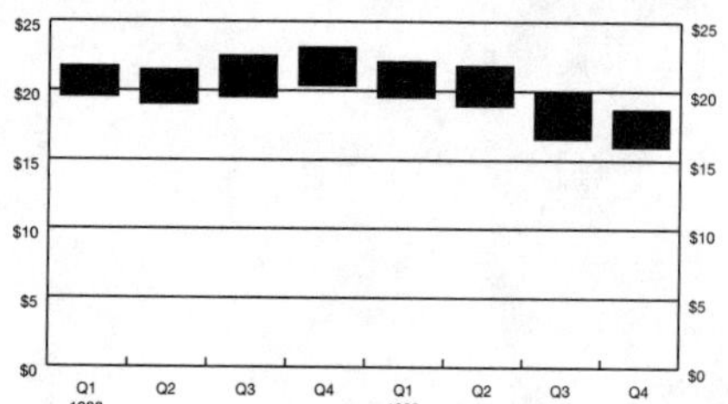

Alliant Techsystems

600 Second St. N.E., Hopkins, MN 55343
Tel: 952/931-6000 Fax: 952/931-5920 Web site: http://www.atk.com

Alliant Techsystems (ATK) has been supplying aerospace and defense products and systems to the United States and its allies for more than 50 years. Formerly the Defense and Marine Systems businesses of Honeywell Inc., ATK was launched as an independent company in September 1990. In March 1995 ATK acquired Hercules Aerospace Co.; in September 1997 Motorola's military fuze business. Today, ATK holds market leadership positions in munitions, solid propulsion, composite structures, and precision electronic fuzes. Operations, which are conducted in 12 states, are organized into three business segments. **Conventional Munitions** is the nation's largest supplier of military ammunition and one of the world's leading manufacturers of tactical missile propulsion systems, warheads, and structures. It is also a leading producer of infrared decoy flares and commercial gunpowder. **Aerospace Systems** is a global leader in the development and production of large solid-propulsion rocket motors for space and strategic applications and a provider of space launch services. It is also a leading supplier of composite structures for military and commercial aircraft, launch vehicles, and spacecraft. **Defense Systems** is a leading designer and manufacturer of electromechanical and electronic fuzes, antitank and demolition systems, precision-guided munitions, infantry weapons, secure electronics subsystems, missile warning systems, unmanned aerial vehicles, and batteries for military and aerospace applications. *continued on page 151*

EARNINGS HISTORY

Year Ended Mar 31	Operating Revenue/Sales (dollars in thousands)	Net Earnings (dollars in thousands)	Return on Revenue (percent)	Return on Equity (percent)	Net Earnings (dollars per share*)	Cash Dividend (dollars per share*)	Market Price Range (dollars per share*)
2000 †	1,077,520	73,902	6.9	64.3	4.95	—	58.17–34.00
1999 ¶	1,090,438	50,813	4.7	42.8	2.84	—	58.67–38.58
1998 #	1,075,506	68,183	6.3	25.7	3.48	—	46.00–27.00
1997 **	1,089,397	59,159	5.4	27.0	3.03	—	38.25–28.00
1996 ††	1,020,605	47,801	4.7	30.4	2.44	—	35.33–23.75

* Per-share amounts restated to reflect 3-for-2 stock split on Nov. 27, 2000.
† Income figures for 2000 include insurance gain of $9.45 million/$0.63 from disposal of discontinued operations.
¶ Income figures for 1999 include extraordinary loss of $16.802 million/($0.94) on extinguishment of debt.
\# Income figures for 1998 include gain of $0.225 million/$0.01 from disposal of discontinued operations.
** Income figures for 1997 include gain of $27.2 million/$1.39 from discontinued operations and their disposal; and loss of $17.442 million/($0.89) on change in accounting for environmental remediation liabilities.
†† Income figures for 1996 included net loss of $0.623 million/($0.03) from discontinued operations and their disposal.

BALANCE SHEET

Assets	03/31/00 (dollars in thousands)	03/31/99 (dollars in thousands)	Liabilities	03/31/00 (dollars in thousands)	03/31/99 (dollars in thousands)
Current (CAE 45,765 and 21,078)	351,050	343,108	Current (STD 55,650 and 36,500)	356,593	286,488
Property, plant, and equipment	335,628	335,751	Long-term debt	277,109	305,993
			Benefits	118,137	128,279
Goodwill	124,718	127,799	Other	39,198	54,835
Deferred charges and other	13,711	10,108	Stkhldrs' equity*	114,947	118,723
			TOTAL	905,984	894,318
Pension	80,877	77,552			
TOTAL	905,984	894,318			

* $0.01 par common; 20,000,000 authorized; 13,610,628 and 15,426,795 issued and outstanding, less 7,184,792 and 5,368,624 treasury shares.

RECENT QUARTERS / PRIOR-YEAR RESULTS

	Quarter End	Revenue ($000)	Earnings ($000)	EPS ($)	Prior-Year Revenue ($000)	Prior-Year Earnings ($000)	Prior-Year EPS ($)
Q2	10/01/2000	271,619	16,084	1.17	252,789	25,447	1.66
Q1	07/02/2000	270,084	14,965	1.10	272,721	14,601	0.95
Q4	03/31/2000	307,603	17,368	1.24	300,673	16,613	1.06
Q3	01/02/2000	244,407	16,486	1.11	274,446	16,358	0.91
	SUM	1,093,713	64,903	4.63	1,100,629	73,019	4.57

PRIOR YEAR: Q2 earnings include gain of $9.45 million/$0.61 on disposal of discontinued operations. Q4 earnings include extraordinary loss of $0.514 million/($0.03) on early extinguishment of debt. Q3 earnings include extraordinary loss of $1.661 million/($0.09) on extinguishment of debt.

OFFICERS

Paul David Miller
Chairman and CEO

Paul A. Ross
Senior Group VP-Aerospace

Robert David Shadley
Group VP-Defense Systems, VP-Army Op.

Nicholas G. Vlahakis
Group VP-Conventional Munitions

Curtis Brock
VP-Internal Audit/Shared Services

Geoffrey B. Courtright
VP-Information Technology

Charles H. Gauck
VP, Secretary, Associate General Counsel

Robert E. Gustafson
VP-Human Resources

Richard N. Jowett
VP-Public Affairs and Treasurer

Mark L. Mele
VP-Investor Relations/ Strategic Planning

Scott S. Meyers
VP and CFO

Paula J. Patineau
VP and Senior Financial Officer

John S. Picek
VP and Controller

Daryl L. Zimmer
VP and General Counsel

DIRECTORS

Frances D. Cook
U.S. ambassador (former)

Gilbert F. Decker
Walt Disney Imagineering, Glendale, CA

Thomas L. Gossage
Hercules Inc. (retired)

Jonathan G. Guss
Bogen Communications International Inc., Ramsey, NJ

David E. Jeremiah
Technology Strategies & Alliances Corp., Burke, VA

Gaynor N. Kelley
The Perkin-Elmer Corp. (retired)

Joseph F. Mazzella
Lane Altman & Owens, Boston

Paul David Miller

Robert W. RisCassi
U.S. Army (retired)

Michael T. Smith
Hughes Electronics Corp., El Segundo, CA

MAJOR SHAREHOLDERS

Neuberger Berman LLC, 10.1%
New York

All officers and directors as a group (21 persons), 2.9%

SIC CODE

3483 Ammunition, exc for small arms, nec

MISCELLANEOUS

TRANSFER AGENT AND REGISTAR:
Chase Mellon Shareholder Services LLC, New York

TRADED: NYSE

SYMBOL: ATK

STOCKHOLDERS: 10,595

EMPLOYEES: 6,500

GENERAL COUNSEL:
Daryl L. Zimmer, Minneapolis

AUDITORS:
Deloitte & Touche LLP, Minneapolis

INC: DE-1990

ANNUAL MEETING:
August

PUBLIC AFFAIRS:
Rod Bitz

INVESTOR RELATIONS:
Mark L. Mele

RANKINGS

No. 34 CRM Public 200

PUB

TWO-YEAR QUARTERLY HIGH-LOW STOCK PRICES

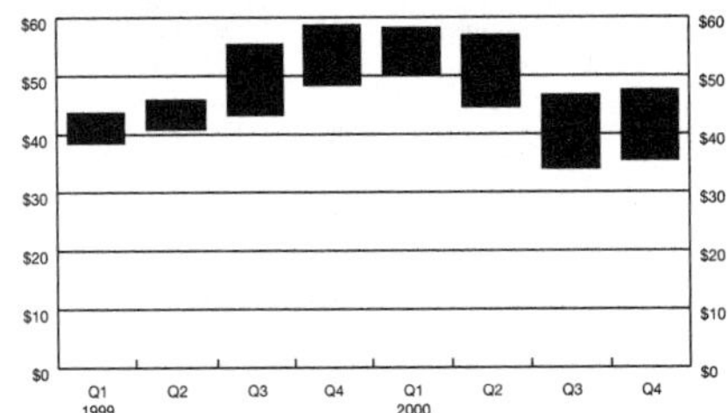

PUB

American Church Mortgage Company

10237 Yellow Circle Dr., Minnetonka, MN 55343
Tel: 952/945-9455 Fax: 952/945-9433

American Church Mortgage Co. operates as a Real Estate Investment Trust ("REIT") and is engaged in the business of making mortgage loans to churches and other nonprofit religious organizations. The company makes loans throughout the United States. The principal amount of such loans ranges from $200,000 to $1,000,000. The company may also invest up to 30 percent of its average invested assets in mortgage-secured debt securities (bonds) issued by churches and other nonprofit religious organizations. The business of the company is managed by Church Loan Advisors Inc., which provides investment advisory and administrative services. The company itself has no employees.

EARNINGS HISTORY

Year Ended Dec 31	Operating Revenue/Sales (dollars in thousands)	Net Earnings	Return on Revenue (percent)	Return on Equity	Net Earnings (dollars per share*)	Cash Dividend	Market Price Range
1999	1,109	972	NM	8.1	0.81	0.85	
1998	782	712	NM	7.2	0.86	0.90	
1997	384	361	NM	7.0	0.91	0.95	
1996	217	165	NM	5.0	0.79	—	

* At this time there is no secondary market for the company's outstanding shares.

BALANCE SHEET

Assets	12/31/99 (dollars in thousands)	12/31/98	Liabilities	12/31/99 (dollars in thousands)	12/31/98
Current (CAE 382 and 2,941)	627	3,220	Current	797	268
Loans receivable	10,190	5,995	Deferred income	165	92
Bonds receivable	2,039	1,012	Stockholders' equity*	11,953	9,906
Deferred tax	60	40	TOTAL	12,916	10,266
Organization expenses		0			
TOTAL	12,916	10,266			

* $0.01 par common; 30,000,000 authorized; 1,322,289 and 1,087,646 issued and outstanding.

OFFICERS

David G. Reinhart
President and Treasurer

DIRECTORS

Kirbyjon H. Caldwell
United Methodist Church, Houston

John M. Clarey
Miller & Schroeder Financial Inc., Minneapolis

V. James Davis

Dennis J. Doyle
Welsh Cos. Inc., Bloomington, MN

Robert O. Naegele Jr.
outdoor advertising companies, Minneapolis

David G. Reinhart

SIC CODE

6162 Mortgage bankers and correspondents
6798 Real estate investment trusts

MISCELLANEOUS

TRANSFER AGENT AND REGISTAR:
Gemisys Corp., Englewood, CO

STOCKHOLDERS: 759

EMPLOYEES: 0

GENERAL COUNSEL:
Maun & Simon PLC, Minneapolis

AUDITORS:
Boulay, Heutmaker, Zibell & Co. PLLP, Minneapolis

INC: MN-1994

ANNUAL MEETING:
August

American Medical Systems Holdings Inc.

10700 Bren Rd. W., Minnetonka, MN 55343
Tel: 952/933-4666 Fax: 952/930-6496 Web site: http://www.visitAMS.com

American Medical Systems Holdings Inc. (AMS) is a medical technology company. Key products include devices to diagnose erectile dysfunction; implantable products to treat erectile dysfunction (penile prostheses), urinary and fecal incontinence (artificial sphincters and bulking agents), urethral obstruction caused by recurrent bulbar stricture and benign prostatic hyperplasia (urethral stents); and advanced surgical products used in transurethral resection of the prostate. The company markets its products in 59 countries worldwide.

EARNINGS HISTORY

Year Ended Dec 31	Operating Revenue/Sales (dollars in thousands)	Net Earnings	Return on Revenue (percent)	Return on Equity	Net Earnings (dollars per share*)	Cash Dividend	Market Price Range
1999 †	81,353	(9,849)	(12.1)	NM	(0.69)	—	
1998 ¶	77,730	(11,359)	(14.6)	NM	—	—	
1997	91,958	10,087	11.0	8.2	—	—	
1996	97,933	17,742	18.1	15.4	—	—	
1995	89,734	11,500	12.8	11.8	—	—	

* Shares did not begin trading until Aug. 11, 2000.
† Income figures for 1999 include pretax charges of $3 million for transition and reorganization and $7.354 million for in-process research and development. Pro forma as if Dec. 16, 1999, acquisition Influence had been acquired Jan. 1: revenue $92.506 million; net loss $16.057 million/($1.12).
¶ Figures for 1998 are a combination of the predecessor (from Jan. 1, 1998, through Sept. 10, 1998) and the current company (the rest of the year).

BALANCE SHEET

Assets	06/30/00 (dollars in thousands)	12/31/99	Liabilities	06/30/00 (dollars in thousands)	12/31/99
Current (CAE 4,840 and 6,940)	46,492	45,605	Current (STD 8,000 and 6,000)	48,167	45,840
Property, plant, and equipment	26,022	26,774	Long-term notes payable	96,000	95,300
Intangibles	104,258	101,951	Minority interest	521	521
Deferred income taxes	13,163	12,533	Preferred equity		67,465
			Common equity*	45,382	(21,836)
Other	135	427	TOTAL	190,070	187,290
TOTAL	190,070	187,290			

* $0.01 par common; 95,000,000 authorized; 21,144,792 and 0 issued and outstanding.

RECENT QUARTERS / PRIOR-YEAR RESULTS

	Quarter End	Revenue ($000)	Earnings ($000)	EPS ($)	Prior-Year Revenue ($000)	Prior-Year Earnings ($000)	Prior-Year EPS ($)
Q3	09/30/2000	23,539	(348)	—	21,583	(4,769)	—
Q2	06/30/2000	25,093	(765)	—	20,065	1,389	—
Q1	03/31/2000	24,986	209	—	20,065	1,389	—
	SUM	73,618	(904)	(0.02)	61,713	(1,991)	—

CURRENT: Q2 earnings include pretax charge of $1 million for transition and reorganization.
PRIOR YEAR: Q4 earnings include pretax charge of $7.354 million for in-process research and development.

RECENT EVENTS

In **November 1999** AMS agreed to acquire Influence Inc., one of the leading manufacturers of products used for female incontinence procedures in the United States, with a direct sales force in the United States and R&D facilities in Israel. The acquisition, its third in six months, made AMS the leading provider of devices for incontinence procedures—with a sling kit, a bulking agent, and the AMS artificial urinary sphincter. [Deal completed in December.] In **February** 2000 AMS and InjecTx Inc.'s InjecTx Transurethral Injection System received a CE Mark, the labeling required to market the device for the injection of ethanol for a prostate-specific indication in many European countries. In **March** AMS filed a lawsuit against Boston Scientific Corp. in Federal District Court for the District of Minnesota—asserting that Boston Scientific was infringing or had induced the infringement of AMS-owned U.S. patent 6,039,686—a system and a method for the long-term cure of recurrent urinary female incontinence. In **April** AMS announced a new treatment option for men suffering from urinary stress incontinence. The Straight-In Male Sling System is a minimally invasive, same-day surgery procedure that resulted in a high initial success rate. (The system uses a transperineal approach to place a sling below the urethra to provide a bolstering effect. The sling is held in place with bone screws attached to the descending rami of the pubis. The procedure replicates the lost natural support and helps restore voiding function.) On **May 26**, the company filed with the SEC for an initial public offering of up to $86.25 million worth of common stock. Proceeds were to be used to repay $40 million of debt under the guaranteed portion of its

continued on page 151

OFFICERS

Douglas W. Kohrs
President and CEO

Janet L. Dick
VP-Human Resources

Martin J. Emerson
VP and Gen. Mgr.-International

Richard J. Faleschini
VP-Sales/Marketing

Lawrence W. Getlin
VP-Regulatory/Medical Affairs/Quality

Gregory J. Melsen
VP-Finance and CFO

Brian A. Millberg
VP-Manufacturing/Operations

Johann Neisz
VP-Research/Development

J. Daniel Ruys
VP-International

Eva S. Snitkin
Dir.-Business Development

DIRECTORS

Richard B. Emmitt
The Vertical Group Inc.

Douglas W. Kohrs

Christopher H. Porter, Ph.D.
Medical Genesis

David W. Stassen
Upper Lake Growth Capital LLC

James T. Treace
Medtronic/Xomed

Elizabeth H. Weatherman
E.M. Warburg, Pincus & Co. LLC

MAJOR SHAREHOLDERS

Warburg, Pincus Equity Partners L.P./Elizabeth H. Weatherman, 69.9%
New York

All officers and directors as a group (14 persons), 77.1%

SIC CODE

3842 Surgical appliances and supplies

3842 Surgical appliances and supplies

MISCELLANEOUS

TRADED: Nasdaq National Market

SYMBOL: AMMD

EMPLOYEES: 508

GENERAL COUNSEL:
Oppenheimer Wolff & Donnelly LLP, Minneapolis

AUDITORS:
Ernst & Young LLP, Minneapolis

PUBLIC AFFAIRS:
Kimberly Eggen

RANKINGS

No. 30 CRM Performance 100

Analysts International Corporation

3601 W. 76th St., Edina, MN 55435
Tel: 952/835-5900 Fax: 952/897-4555 Web site: http://www.analysts.com

Analysts International Corp. provides services and expertise in eBusiness/eCommerce, business solutions, managed services, technical staffing, and professional consulting. 4,000 information technology consultants serve clients from 45 locations in the United States, Canada and the United Kingdom. Customers include corporate and governmental clients.

EARNINGS HISTORY

Year Ended Jun 30	Operating Revenue/Sales (dollars in thousands)	Net Earnings	Return on Revenue (percent)	Return on Equity	Net Earnings (dollars per share*)	Cash Dividend	Market Price Range
2000 †	558,731	9,788	1.8	9.9	0.43	0.40	15.94–7.75
1999	620,156	22,733	3.7	23.2	1.01	0.40	31.50–9.38
1998	587,411	22,610	3.8	27.2	1.01	0.31	36.50–20.83
1997 ¶	439,546	16,381	3.7	24.8	0.74	0.24	24.50–11.67
1996	329,544	12,418	3.8	23.1	0.57	0.20	14.58–8.50

* Per-share amounts restated to reflect 3-for-2 stock split paid Dec. 3, 1997, and 2-for-1 split paid Sept. 30, 1996.
† Figures for 2000 include results of majority-owned Sequoia NET.com from its April 25, 2000, date of purchase. Pro forma for full year: revenue $608.029 million; earnings $9.938 million/$0.44.
¶ Figures for 1997 include the contributions of DPI Inc., San Jose, Calif., which was purchased July 1, 1996, for $5.6 million.

BALANCE SHEET

Assets	06/30/00 (dollars in thousands)	06/30/99	Liabilities	06/30/00 (dollars in thousands)	06/30/99
Current (CAE 2,030 and 33,870)	105,369	139,892	Current	49,607	60,668
			Long-term debt	33,913	20,000
Property and equipment	29,558	29,644	Other	7,826	7,534
			Minority interest	1,745	
Intangibles	43,997	7,029	Stockholders' equity*	99,053	98,014
Other	13,220	9,651			
TOTAL	192,144	186,216	TOTAL	192,144	186,216

* $0.10 par common; 120,000,000 authorized; 22,606,826 and 22,552,441 issued and outstanding.

RECENT QUARTERS / **PRIOR-YEAR RESULTS**

	Quarter End	Revenue ($000)	Earnings ($000)	EPS ($)	Revenue ($000)	Earnings ($000)	EPS ($)
Q1	09/30/2000	148,571	1,705	0.08	149,045	3,776	0.17
Q4	06/30/2000	138,362	1,948	0.09	154,578	5,941	0.26
Q3	03/31/2000	132,455	1,730	0.08	154,128	5,705	0.25
Q2	12/31/99	138,869	2,334	0.10	152,986	4,961	0.22
	SUM	558,257	7,717	0.34	610,737	20,383	0.90

RECENT EVENTS

In **January 2000** the company formed a new line of business centered on mobile and handheld computing. Located in the New York and New Jersey branches, the Mobile Business Computing practice was to use AiC's rapid prototyping and development methodology to provide support and service to customers throughout the United States and Canada. In **February** Managed Services Group was awarded a two-year contract from PacifiCare Health Systems of California to provide broad oversight of PacifiCare's IT services contractors. In **March** AiC opened its 49th office, in Louisville, Ky., as a result of the increased growth within its Lexington, Ky., branch office. The Canadian operations of AiC formed a strategic relationship with IntellAgent Control Corp. of Dallas. In **April** the Rochester Individual Practice Association (RIPA) and BlueCross BlueShield of the Rochester Area (BCBSRA) engaged Analysts International for a pilot project to develop and load five critical applications onto Palm hand-held computers—helping physicians to lighten their lab coats and their workload. AiC's Rapid Application Design and Development (RADD) practice gained a Capability Maturity Model (CMM) Level 2 rating. (CMM ratings have become the standard assessment and process improvement tool in the software industry. The rating defines an organization's ability to meet cost, schedule, and functionality goals.) AiC acquired 80.1 percent of $57 million-revenue Sequoia, an Auburn Hills, Mich.-based Internet professional services organization that provides strategic eBusiness solutions, for $43.5 million in cash. The acquisition represented a significant step in AiC's strategy to become the preferred partner for companies seeking to design and build effective eBusiness operations. In **May** AiC helped create new, nontraditional business opportunities for Kentucky farmers and agricultural businesses through the Web—upgrading the state of Kentucky Agriculture Department Web site (http://www.kyagr.com) with new features that enable users to build and customize their own Web sites to promote their products and services. In **June** the company's Raleigh, N.C., office established an Enterprise Consulting eBusiness team—to help customers define and implement eBusiness strategies using technology, architecture, and rapid solutions development. **June 30:** Sequential fourth-quarter revenue and net income were up 4 and 13 percent, respectively. E-business solutions revenue accounted for $35 million, or 25 percent of the total. "We came through the post-Y2K period managing our business to remain profitable and at the same time greatly expanding our e-business Internet capabilities," said CEO Lang. "We believe the IT services

continued on page 151

OFFICERS

Frederick W. Lang
Chairman and CEO

Michael J. LaVelle
President and COO

Sarah P. Spiess
EVP

John D. Bamburger
VP and CEO-Sequoia Net.com

Marti R. Charpentier
VP-Finance and Treasurer

Richard J. Chiappetta
VP-Central Region

Philip C. Colligan
VP-Eastern Region

Colleen M. Davenport
Asst. Secretary, Assoc. General Counsel

Susan Furlow
VP-North Central Region

Richard W. Gilman
VP-Southern Region

Charles E. Jones
Associate General Counsel

Alan King
VP-Western Region

Thomas R. Mahler
Secretary and General Counsel

Gary Mosley
VP-Southwest Region

Penny Quist
SVP-National Business Practices

David J. Steichen
Controller and Asst. Treasurer

DIRECTORS

Victor C. Benda
Analysts International Corp. (retired)

Willis K. Drake
Data Card Corp.(retired)

Frederick W. Lang

Michael J. LaVelle

Margaret A. Loftus
Loftus Brown-Wescott Inc.

Edward M. Mahoney
Fortis Advisers Inc. (retired)

Robb L. Prince
Jostens Inc. (retired)

MAJOR SHAREHOLDERS

T. Rowe Price Associates Inc., 7.9%
Baltimore

Richard Born, 5.8%
Orono, MN

Neuberger Berman LLC, 5.7%
New York

V.C. Benda, 5%
Minneapolis

All officers and directors as a group (10 persons), 9.7%

SIC CODE

7371 Computer programming services

MISCELLANEOUS

TRANSFER AGENT AND REGISTAR:
State Street Bank & Trust Co., Boston

TRADED: Nasdaq National Market

SYMBOL: ANLY

STOCKHOLDERS: 1,300

EMPLOYEES: 4,900

GENERAL COUNSEL:
Thomas R. Mahler, Minneapolis

AUDITORS:
Deloitte & Touche LLP, Minneapolis

INC: MN-1966

ANNUAL MEETING: October

HUMAN RESOURCES: Thomas R. Mahler

INVESTOR RELATIONS: Marti R. Charpentier

RANKINGS

No. 45 CRM Public 200

SUBSIDIARIES, DIVISIONS, AFFILIATES

AiC Analysts Ltd.
Lincoln House
The Paddocks, Cherry Hinton Rd.
Cambridge, England CB3 0AX
1223-500055

Sequoia NET.com
107 S. Squirree Rd.
Auburn Hills, MI 48326
248-299-4220
CEO John D. Bamburger

TWO-YEAR QUARTERLY HIGH-LOW STOCK PRICES

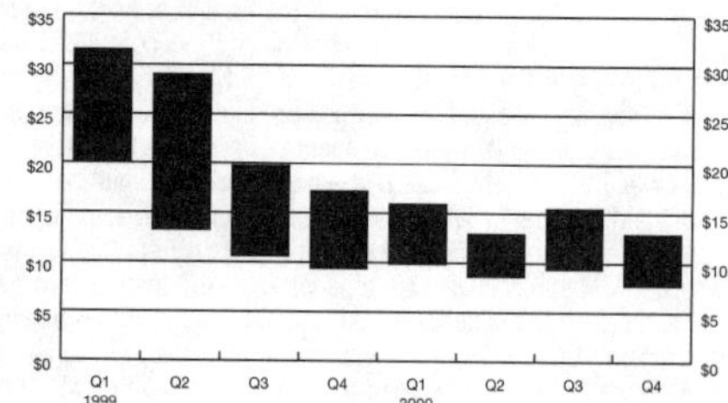

Angeion Corporation

350 Oak Grove Pkwy., Vadnais Heights, MN 55127
Tel: 651/766-3480 Fax: 651/484-4826 Web site: http://www.angeion.com

Angeion Corp., with the acquisition of Medical Graphics Corp., is in the business of developing, manufacturing, and marketing computerized, noninvasive cardiorespiratory diagnostic systems for the prevention, early detection, and cost-effective treatment of heart and lung disease. The company's proprietary software allows its systems to acquire and compute physiologic information as it is generated, display it on a video screen, and report the data in a graphic format on hard copy. The company's hardware and software technologies are protected by 19 patents, including one on a disposable pneumotach for infection control.

EARNINGS HISTORY *

Year Ended Dec 31	Operating Revenue/Sales (dollars in thousands)	Net Earnings	Return on Revenue (percent)	Return on Equity	Net Earnings (dollars per share†)	Cash Dividend	Market Price Range
1999 ¶	608	1,566	NM	21.5	0.39	—	2.75–0.72
1998	4,567	(38,838)	NM	NM	(11.23)	—	3.88–1.03
1997 #	865	(14,941)	NM	(58.0)	(4.82)	—	6.69–2.13
1997 **	4,505	(26,909)	NM	NM	(9.26)	—	7.50–2.44
1996	2,949	(15,182)	NM	(30.7)	(6.63)	—	12.00–4.88

* Revenue figures for 1999 and prior periods are restated to segregate discontinued ICD business. EPS includes these amounts from discontinued operations: ($6.72) in 1999, ($11.22) in 1998, ($4.80) in stub period, ($9.56) in 1997, and unspecified in 1996.
† Per-share amounts restated to reflect a 1-for-10 reverse stock split in May 1999.
¶ Income figures for 1999 include pretax gain of $30.79 million from settlement of lawsuits and grant of license rights. Pro forma to include Dec. 21, 1999, acquisition Medical Graphics Inc. for full year: revenue $22.188 million; earnings $2.365 million/$0.59.
# Figures are for five-month stub period from Aug. 1, 1997, through Dec. 31, 1997—due to change in year end. Calendar-year 1997: revenue $3,094,159; loss $34,114,929/($11.36).
** This and prior years ended July 31.

BALANCE SHEET

Assets	12/31/99 (dollars in thousands)	12/31/98
Current (CAE 5,263 and 1,827)	15,181	3,841
Discontinued operations	2,354	10,173
Equipment and fixtures	2,225	278
Deferred taxes	1,868	
Intangibles	10,298	
Pther	1,250	1,924
Goodwill	561	
TOTAL	33,737	16,216

Liabilities	12/31/99 (dollars in thousands)	12/31/98
Current	6,248	346
Long-term debt	20,198	22,150
Stockholders' equity*	7,291	(6,280)
TOTAL	33,737	16,216

* $0.01 par common; 7,500,000 authorized; 4,105,718 and 3,879,655 issued and outstanding.

RECENT QUARTERS / PRIOR-YEAR RESULTS

	Quarter End	Revenue ($000)	Earnings ($000)	EPS ($)	Prior-Year Revenue ($000)	Prior-Year Earnings ($000)	Prior-Year EPS ($)
Q3	09/30/2000	4,068	(1,468)	(0.42)	0	7,789	1.94
Q2	06/30/2000	3,860	(1,891)	(0.56)	0	22,903	5.72
Q1	03/31/2000	4,906	9,884	2.43	0	(8,416)	(2.12)
	SUM	12,834	6,525	1.46	0	22,276	5.54

CURRENT: Q3 earnings include gain of $22,000/$0.01 from discontinued operations. Q2 earnings include gain of $34,000/$0.01 from discontinued operations. Q1 earnings include gain of $11.029 million/$2.72 from discontinued operations.
PRIOR YEAR: Q3 earnings include loss of $7.449 million/($1.86) from discontinued operations. Q2 earnings include gain of $23.301 million/$5.82 from discontinued operations. Q1 earnings include loss of $7.621 million/($1.92) from discontinued operations.

RECENT EVENTS

In **December 1999** the company announced that a Hennepin County District Court judge had issued a memorandum and order denying the motion of U.S. Bank N.A., the trustee for the noteholders of Angeion's 7.5% Senior Convertible Notes, to obtain a temporary injunction requiring Angeion to set aside $23 million to repurchase those notes. (The trustee was alleging that certain actions recently taken by Angeion had constituted a sale or disposition of substantially all of the company's assets, in violation of the terms of the indenture.) Angeion completed its previously announced acquisition of Medical Graphics Corp. (Nasdaq: MGCC), a developer and manufacturer of cardiopulmonary products, by acquiring all of the outstanding shares of Medical Graphics for $2.15 per share, or $16.2 million. Medical Graphics was to become a wholly owned subsidiary of Angeion and continue to operate its current business. At month's end, after passing certain proposals,

continued on page 152

OFFICERS

Dennis E. Evans
Chairman

Richard E. Jahnke
President and CEO

Dale Johnson
CFO

DIRECTORS

Arnold A. Angeloni
Gateway Alliance, Minneapolis

Dennis E. Evans
Hanrow Financial Group Ltd., Minneapolis

James B. Hickey Jr.
Aequitron Medical Inc. (formerly)

Richard E. Jahnke

John C. Penn
Satellite Industries Inc., Minneapolis

Mark W. Sheffert
Manchester Cos. Inc., Minneapolis

Glen A. Taylor
Taylor Corp., North Mankato, MN

MAJOR SHAREHOLDERS

All officers and directors as a group (8 persons), 6.1%

SIC CODE

3841 Surgical and medical instruments

MISCELLANEOUS

TRANSFER AGENT AND REGISTAR:
Wells Fargo Bank Minnesota N.A., South St. Paul, MN

TRADED: Nasdaq National Market, BSE

SYMBOL: ANGN

STOCKHOLDERS: 686

EMPLOYEES: 136

GENERAL COUNSEL:
Lindquist & Vennum PLLP, Minneapolis
Faegre & Benson PLLP, Minneapolis

AUDITORS:
KPMG LLP, Minneapolis

INC: MN-1986

ANNUAL MEETING:
December

RANKINGS

No. 134 CRM Public 200

SUBSIDIARIES, DIVISIONS, AFFILIATES

Medical Graphics Corp.
350 Oak Grove Pkwy.
Vadnais Heights, MN
55127

Apogee Enterprises Inc.

7900 Xerxes Ave. S., Suite 1800, Bloomington, MN 55431
Tel: 952/835-1874 Fax: 952/835-3196 Web site: http://www.apog.com

Apogee Enterprises Inc. fabricates, distributes, coats, and installs specialized glass and aluminum products. The company is organized in two business segments. **Glass Technologies** fabricates coated high-performance architectural glass; produces optical coatings for computer anti-glare screens, laser scanners, and other optical devices; and makes custom, value-added picture framing glass and matboard products. **Glass Services** fabricates car windshields, wholesales windshields through PPG Auto Glass, a joint venture owned 34 percent by Apogee, and repairs and replaces automotive glass. The Glass Services segment also includes Harmon, Inc., a leader in building-glass services.

EARNINGS HISTORY *

Year Ended Feb	Operating Revenue/Sales (dollars in thousands)	Net Earnings	Return on Revenue (percent)	Return on Equity	Net Earnings (dollars per share†)	Cash Dividend	Market Price Range
2000 ¶	840,488	12,175	1.4	8.8	0.44	0.21	14.31–4.00
1999 #	788,062	25,233	3.2	19.3	0.91	0.21	15.50–8.13
1998 **	731,094	(51,055)	(7.0)	(46.6)	(1.84)	0.19	25.00–10.38
1997 ††	642,226	26,220	4.1	15.2	0.96	0.18	23.75–9.63
1996 ##	567,823	17,835	3.1	12.8	0.66	0.17	9.88–6.50

* Historical revenue figures restated to segregate discontinued operations.
† Per-share amounts restated to reflect 2-for-1 stock split effected Feb. 14, 1997.
¶ Income figures for 2000 include gain of $9.104 million/$0.33 from discontinued operations.
# Income figures for 1999 include gain of $5.546 million/$0.20 from discontinued operations.
** Income figures for 1998 include loss of $75.169 million/($2.70) from discontinued operations.
†† Income figures for 1997 include loss of $0.607 million/($0.02) from discontinued operations.
Income figures for 1996 include loss of $2.820 million/($0.10) from discontinued operations.

BALANCE SHEET

Assets	02/26/00 (dollars in thousands)	02/27/99	Liabilities	02/26/00 (dollars in thousands)	02/27/99
Current (CAE 7,192 and 1,318)	214,422	204,308	Current (STD 182 and 1,300)	135,397	119,796
Ppty, plant, eqt	186,039	179,996	Long-term debt	164,371	165,097
Marketable securities	24,951	27,239	Other	25,248	27,845
			Discontinued operations	18,366	22,987
Investments	418	570			
Intangibles	50,549	51,744	Stockholders' equity*	137,772	130,664
Other	4,775	2,532			
TOTAL	481,154	466,389	TOTAL	481,154	466,389

* $0.333 par common; 50,000,000 authorized; 27,743,000 and 27,623,000 issued and outstanding.

RECENT QUARTERS / **PRIOR-YEAR RESULTS**

	Quarter End	Revenue ($000)	Earnings ($000)	EPS ($)	Prior Revenue ($000)	Prior Earnings ($000)	Prior EPS ($)
Q2	09/02/2000	236,364	4,200	0.15	216,962	14,041	0.51
Q1	06/03/2000	237,253	2,020	0.07	209,663	4,570	0.17
Q4	02/26/2000	212,736	(3,458)	(0.12)	199,944	4,951	0.18
Q3	11/27/99	201,127	(2,978)	(0.11)	191,201	7,250	0.26
	SUM	887,480	(216)	(0.01)	817,770	30,812	1.11

CURRENT: Q1 consisted of 14 weeks. Q4 earnings include loss of $1.415 million/($0.05) from discontinued operations. Q3 earnings include gain of $2.31 million/$0.08 from discontinued operations.
PRIOR YEAR: Q2 earnings include gain of $8.732 million/$0.31 from discontinued operations. Q1 earnings include loss of $217,000/($0.01) from discontinued operations. Q4 earnings include gain of $2.75 million/$0.10 from discontinued operations. Q3 earnings include gain of $1.58 million/$0.06 from discontinued operations.

RECENT EVENTS

In **January 2000** Viracon was nearing completion on its work for Aurora Place, a mixed-use development on Macquarie Street in the core of Sydney's Central Business District. Meanwhile, auto glass operations had begun taking actions to reduce fixed costs, both in headcount and retail facilities. "Industry conditions in auto glass continue to be extremely weak, yet we expect to increase our unit volumes in fiscal 2000," said CEO Huffer. "To return to profitability and drive further improvement, we are reducing fixed-cost overhead and moving to a variable-cost structure that should enable us to operate profitably going forward." Forty additional retail locations were to be closed by year's end. In **February** Tru Vue added new

continued on page 152

OFFICERS

Russell Huffer
Chairman, President, and CEO

Larry D. Stordahl
EVP-Glass Technologies

Joseph T. Deckman
EVP-Glass Service

Patricia A. Beithon
General Counsel and Secretary

James S. Porter
Controller

DIRECTORS

Bernard P. Aldrich
Rimage Corp., Edina, MN

Jerome B. Cohen
Northwestern University/School of Engineering, Evanston, IL

Donald W. Goldfus
Apogee Enterprises Inc. (retired)

Barbara B. Grogan
Western Industrial Contractors Inc., Denver

Harry A. Hammerly
3M Co. (retired)

J. Patrick Horner
Condor Technology Solutions

Russell Huffer

James L. Martineau

Stephen C. Mitchell
Lester B. Knight & Associates Inc., Chicago

Laurence J. Niederhofer

Ray C. Richelsen
3M Co., Maplewood, MN

Michael E. Shannon
Ecolab Inc., St. Paul

MAJOR SHAREHOLDERS

Trust of Russell H. Baumgardner, 7.8%
Reno, NV

Putnam Investments Inc., 7.4%
Boston

All officers and directors as a group (17 persons), 7.3%

SIC CODE

1793 Glass and glazing work
3211 Flat glass
3231 Glass products
3479 Metal coating and allied services
7536 Automotive glass replacement shops

MISCELLANEOUS

TRANSFER AGENT AND REGISTAR:
American Stock Transfer Co., New York

TRADED: Nasdaq National Market

SYMBOL: APOG

STOCKHOLDERS: 2,093

EMPLOYEES: 6,900

GENERAL COUNSEL:
Dorsey & Whitney PLLP, Minneapolis

AUDITORS:
Arthur Andersen LLP, Minneapolis

INC: MN-1949

ANNUAL MEETING: June

CORPORATE COMMUNICATIONS/IR: Mary Ann Jackson

RANKINGS

No. 42 CRM Public 200
No. 82 CRM Employer 100

SUBSIDIARIES, DIVISIONS, AFFILIATES

GLASS SERVICES
Joseph T. Deckman

Curvlite

Harmon AutoGlass

Harmon Inc.

PPG Auto Glass L.L.C.

GLASS TECHNOLOGIES

Lintec

Tru Vue

Viracon

Viratec Thin Films

Wausau Window & Wall Systems

TWO-YEAR QUARTERLY HIGH-LOW STOCK PRICES

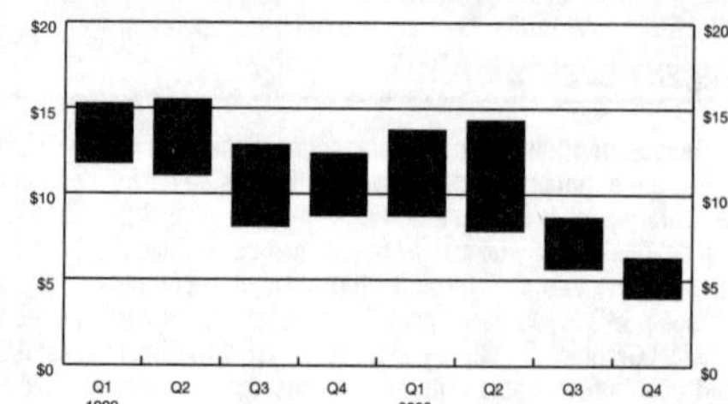

Appliance Recycling Centers of America Inc.

7400 Excelsior Blvd., St. Louis Park, MN 55426
Tel: 952/930-9000 Fax: 952/930-1800 Web site: http://www.ARCAinc.com

Appliance Recycling Centers of America Inc. (ARCA) provides comprehensive appliance-recycling services throughout the United States. The focus of the company's business is the operation of large-scale systems for collecting, reconditioning for resale, and recycling unwanted major household appliances in an environmentally sound manner. The company's customers include appliance retailers, waste-management companies, property management companies, local governments, and electric utilities. Revenue is generated from disposal fees, sale of salvaged materials, and the sale of reconditioned appliances through a chain of company-owned retail stores called Encore.

EARNINGS HISTORY

Year Ended Dec	Operating Revenue/Sales (dollars in thousands)	Net Earnings	Return on Revenue (percent)	Return on Equity	Net Earnings (dollars per share*)	Cash Dividend	Market Price Range
1999	15,582	505	3.2	27.9	0.24	—	1.50–0.50
1998 †	13,612	(3,056)	(22.5)	NM	(2.55)	—	4.00–0.50
1997	11,979	(748)	(6.2)	(22.2)	(0.66)	—	4.25–2.00
1996	14,030	(7,269)	(51.8)	NM	(6.53)	—	20.00–2.33
1995 ¶	16,241	(943)	(5.8)	(9.3)	(0.90)	—	28.50–13.50

* Per-share amounts restated to reflect 1-for-4 reverse stock split, effective Feb. 21, 1997.
† Income figures for 1998 include pretax loss of $573,000 on impaired assets.
¶ Income figures for 1995 include pretax special charge of $1,316,000 for loss on certain impaired assets and for non-recurring charges associated with the decrease in business with utility companies.

BALANCE SHEET

Assets	01/01/00 (dollars in thousands)	01/02/99
Current (CAE 220 and 14)	3,422	2,591
Property and equipment	5,723	5,781
Other	258	319
Goodwill	114	152
TOTAL	9,517	8,843

Liabilities	01/01/00 (dollars in thousands)	01/02/99
Current (STD 135 and 79)	2,877	3,062
Long-term debt	4,831	4,965
Stockholders' equity*	1,809	816
TOTAL	9,517	8,843

* No par common; 10,000,000 authorized; 2,287,000 and 1,237,000 issued and outstanding.

RECENT QUARTERS / **PRIOR-YEAR RESULTS**

	Quarter End	Revenue ($000)	Earnings ($000)	EPS ($)	Prior-Year Revenue ($000)	Prior-Year Earnings ($000)	Prior-Year EPS ($)
Q3	09/30/2000	6,188	257	0.11	4,689	532	0.23
Q2	07/01/2000	5,819	341	0.15	4,053	251	0.11
Q1	04/01/2000	4,174	291	0.13	2,818	(398)	(0.22)
Q4	01/01/2000	4,023	121	0.05	3,133	(1,370)	(1.11)
	SUM	20,204	1,010	0.44	14,693	(985)	(0.99)

RECENT EVENTS

In **April 2000** the company announced plans to open its seventh ApplianceSmart retail store on or about May 1, 2000, in the Dayton, Ohio, market. In **June** ARCA signed a two-year contract with Southern California Edison Co. to continue the company's refrigerator recycling program with Edison for the years 2000 and 2001. Under terms of the two-year agreement, refrigerator recycling volumes for each of the two years were expected to approximate the levels attained under the 1999 contract. In **August** the California Public Utilities Commission directed Southern California Edison Co. to contract with Appliance Recycling to implement a refrigerator-freezer recycling program. In **September** ARCA secured an expanded $5 million line of credit with its current lender that replaces the previous $2 million credit line. The new line of credit was to be used primarily to finance inventories of the company's ApplianceSmart retail operation. ARCA entered into a contract with Southern California Edison Co. to implement a refrigerator/freezer recycling program in the service territories of Pacific Gas & Electric (PG&E) and San Diego Gas & Electric (SDG&E). The contract resulted in a doubling of ARCA's recycling unit volume. **Sept. 30:** CEO Cameron commented, "Growth-related factors were responsible for a significant portion of our lower third-quarter earnings."

OFFICERS

Edward R. Cameron
Chairman, President, and CEO
Linda A. Koenig
Controller
Denis E. Grande
Secretary

DIRECTORS

George B. Bonniwell
Craig Hallum Inc. (retired)
Edward R. Cameron
Duane S. Carlson
business consultant, Golden Valley, MN
Marvin W. Goldstein
financial consultant
Harry W. Spell
Xcel Energy Inc. (retired)

MAJOR SHAREHOLDERS

Perkins Capital Management Inc., 28%
Wayzata, MN
Edward R. Cameron, 13.2%
Marvin Goldstein, 5%
All officers and directors as a group (6 persons), 19.6%

SIC CODE

5093 Scrap and waste materials
7623 Refrigeration service and repair

MISCELLANEOUS

TRANSFER AGENT AND REGISTAR:
Wells Fargo Bank Minnesota N.A., South St. Paul, MN
TRADED: OTC
SYMBOL: ARCI
STOCKHOLDERS: 1,009
EMPLOYEES: 130
GENERAL COUNSEL:
Mackall, Crounse & Moore PLC, Minneapolis
AUDITORS:
RSM McGladrey & Pullen Inc. LLP, Minneapolis
INC: MN-1983
FOUNDED: 1975
ANNUAL MEETING: May
INVESTOR RELATIONS:
Kent McCoy

RANKINGS

No. 163 CRM Public 200

SUBSIDIARIES, DIVISIONS, AFFILIATES

ARCA California Inc.
Oakland, CA 90220

ARCA Minnesota
Minneapolis, MN 55426

ARCA Ohio
Columbus, Ohio

ARCA of St. Louis Inc.
St. Louis, MO 63121

PUB

TWO-YEAR QUARTERLY HIGH-LOW STOCK PRICES

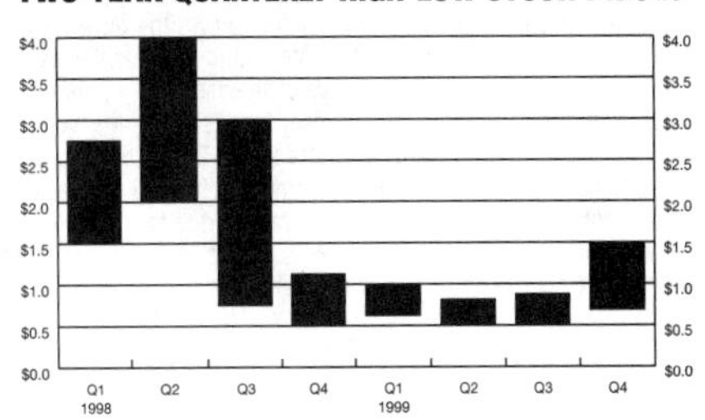

Arctic Cat Inc.

601 Brooks Ave. S., Thief River Falls, MN 56701
Tel: 218/681-8558 Fax: 218/681-3162 Web site: http://www.arctic-cat.com

Arctic Cat Inc. designs, engineers, manufactures, and markets snowmobiles and all-terrain vehicles (ATVs) under the Arctic Cat brand name, as well as related parts, garments, and accessories. The company's products are currently sold through a network of dealers in North America and distributors representing dealers in Alaska, Europe, the Middle East, Asia, and other international markets.

EARNINGS HISTORY

Year Ended Mar 31	Operating Revenue/Sales (dollars in thousands)	Net Earnings (dollars in thousands)	Return on Revenue (percent)	Return on Equity (percent)	Net Earnings (dollars per share)	Cash Dividend (dollars per share)	Market Price Range (dollars per share)
2000 *	484,011	7,621	1.6	4.7	0.30	0.24	10.50–7.75
1999	480,348	23,115	4.8	13.2	0.84	0.24	10.88–7.69
1998	504,206	25,449	5.0	14.3	0.88	0.24	12.50–8.25
1997	468,595	23,061	4.9	13.8	0.78	0.24	12.50–8.88
1996	404,996	16,646	4.1	10.7	0.56	0.24	15.88–9.50

* Income figures for 2000 include pretax charges of $15.147 million for watercraft exit costs and $3.48 million for watercraft asset impairment.

BALANCE SHEET

Assets	03/31/00 (dollars in thousands)	03/31/99 (dollars in thousands)	Liabilities	03/31/00 (dollars in thousands)	03/31/99 (dollars in thousands)
Current (CAE 60,028 and 51,413)	210,149	202,260	Current	78,077	60,221
Property, plant, and equipment	36,386	37,886	Deferred income taxes	5,900	4,446
TOTAL	246,535	240,146	Stockholders' equity*	162,558	175,479
			TOTAL	246,535	240,146

* $0.01 par common; 45,000,000 authorized; 24,887,975 and 26,388,775 issued and outstanding.

RECENT QUARTERS / PRIOR-YEAR RESULTS

	Quarter End	Revenue ($000)	Earnings ($000)	EPS ($)	Prior-Year Revenue ($000)	Prior-Year Earnings ($000)	Prior-Year EPS ($)
Q2	09/30/2000	192,854	18,606	0.77	205,507	2,172	0.08
Q1	06/30/2000	85,961	2,052	0.08	86,928	1,861	0.07
Q4	03/31/2000	82,567	(723)	(0.03)	88,565	(1,731)	(0.06)
Q3	12/31/99	109,009	4,311	0.17	109,750	4,278	0.16
	SUM	470,391	24,246	0.99	490,750	6,580	0.25

PRIOR YEAR: Q2 earnings include one-time charge of $26.2 million pretax, $16.9 million/($0.66) after-tax, for exiting PWC business.

RECENT EVENTS

In **January 2000**, three months after announcing that it was dropping its personal watercraft (PWC) line, the company was hit with a patent-infringement suit by Yamaha Motor Co. Ltd. of Japan. Yamaha alleged that Arctic Cat had infringed 17 of its PWC patents for hulls, seat latches, water-injection systems, engine parts, and switches. The company loaned two prototype four-stroke snowmobiles to the National Park Service for use in Yellowstone National Park. The National Park Service was interested in finding engine technologies that reduce emissions in the park. The next generation of an environmentally friendly, four-stroke prototype snowmobile, being tested by Arctic Cat, was equipped with Electronic Fuel Injection (EFI) and a weight-reducing aluminum block. In **April** CEO Twomey called a U.S. Department of the Interior ban on recreational snowmobiling in national parks "a premature, overreaching response that bows to politics, bypasses due process, and ignores genuine industry progress on emissions and noise reduction." The ban covered snowmobiling in Yellowstone National Park. In **July** the U.S. Court of Appeals for the 10th Circuit affirmed a previous ruling by the U.S. District Court in Colorado dismissing a lawsuit filed by Injection Research Specialists Inc. and Pacer Industries Inc. alleging misappropriation of trade secrets. Commenting on the appellate court's decision, Twomey stated: "From the outset, we believed that the claims against Arctic Cat were unfounded. In addition, the suit was brought too late and, consequently, barred by the statute of limitations." In **September** the company announced plans to manufacture five utility-class ATV models for distribution in select European agricultural markets under the Massey Ferguson brand name. (Massey Ferguson has the world's largest distribution network for agricultural equipment.) **Sept. 30:** For the six-month period, net sales were $278.815 million compared to $292.435 million for the same period in prior year. Net earnings were $20.658 million compared to adjusted net earnings of $20.932 million. Said Twomey, "As expected, Arctic Cat's second-quarter sales slightly decreased due to moderately lower dealer orders related to poor snow conditions last year. Snowmobile customer interest remains strong as evidenced by the 22 percent increase in extra-early orders that we experienced this year."

OFFICERS

William G. Ness
Chairman

Christopher A. Twomey
President and CEO

Mark E. Blackwell
VP-Marketing

Terry J. Blount
VP-Human Resources

Timothy C. Delmore
CFO and Secretary

Ronald G. Ray
VP-Manufacturing

Roger H. Skime
VP-Research/Development

Ole E. Tweet
VP-New Product Development

DIRECTORS

Robert J. Dondelinger
Northern Motors, Thief River Falls, MN

William I. Hagen
NorthStar Transport Inc., Eagan, MN

John C. Heinmiller
St. Jude Medical Inc., Little Canada, MN

Takekazu Kaito

Takeshi Natori
Suzuki Motor Corp., Hamamatsu, Japan

William G. Ness

Gregg A. Ostrander
Michael Foods Inc., St. Louis Park, MN

Kenneth J. Roering
Carlson School of Management/U. of Minnesota, Minneapolis

Christopher A. Twomey

MAJOR SHAREHOLDERS

Suzuki Motor Corp., 30.6%
Hamamatsu, Japan

Capital Group International Inc., 6.6%
Los Angeles

Artisan Partners L.P., et al., 5.3%
Milwaukee

All officers and directors as a group (13 persons), 8.8%

SIC CODE

2329 Men's and boys' clothing, nec

2339 Women's and misses' outerwear, nec

3799 Transportation equipment, nec

MISCELLANEOUS

TRANSFER AGENT AND REGISTAR:
Wells Fargo Bank Minnesota N.A., South St. Paul, MN

TRADED: Nasdaq National Market

SYMBOL: ACAT

STOCKHOLDERS: 587

EMPLOYEES: 1,400

GENERAL COUNSEL:
Lindquist & Vennum PLLP, Minneapolis
Ihle & Sparby, Thief River Falls, MN

AUDITORS:
Grant Thornton LLP, Minneapolis

INC: MN-1982

ANNUAL MEETING: August

MEDIA RELATIONS: Paul James

INVESTOR RELATIONS: Timothy C. Delmore

RANKINGS

No. 50 CRM Public 200

TWO-YEAR QUARTERLY HIGH-LOW STOCK PRICES

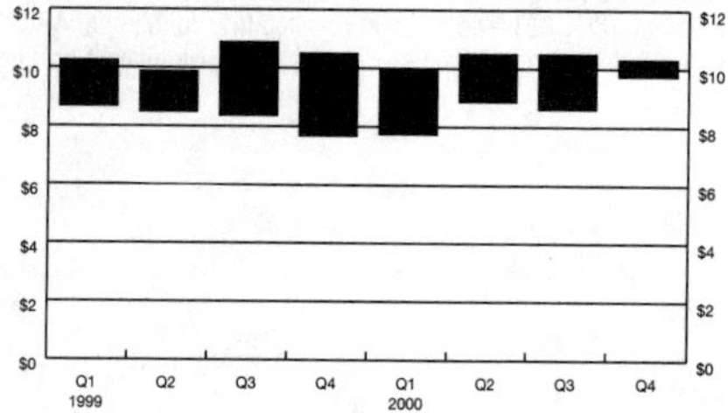

Astrocom Corporation

3500 Holly Ln., Suite 60, Plymouth, MN 55447
Tel: 763/378-7800 Fax: 763/378-1070 Web site: http://www.astrocorp.com

Astrocom Corp. designs, manufactures, and markets products tailored for high-bandwidth wide-area network (WAN) data, video, and voice applications such as Internet access, local-area network (LAN) interconnection, videoconferencing, telemedicine, and imaging. Products are purchased by private enterprise, government, and educational entities through a sales distribution channel of distributors and dealers.

EARNINGS HISTORY

Year Ended Dec 31	Operating Revenue/Sales (dollars in thousands)	Net Earnings (dollars in thousands)	Return on Revenue (percent)	Return on Equity (percent)	Net Earnings (dollars per share)	Cash Dividend (dollars per share)	Market Price Range (dollars per share)
1999	1,462	(1,107)	NM	NM	(0.07)	—	0.58–0.09
1998	2,897	(517)	(17.9)	(36.3)	(0.04)	—	0.94–0.13
1997 *	3,647	(1,891)	(51.8)	NM	(0.19)	—	3.81–0.34
1996	3,287	(1,411)	(42.9)	NM	(0.23)	—	2.00–0.25
1995 †	3,178	(1,085)	(34.1)	NM	(0.21)	—	0.88–0.13

* Fiscal 1997 auditors report contains "going concern" alert. Income figures include pretax inventory write-off of $329,430.
† Income figures for 1995 include charge of $398,000/($0.08) for write-off of inventory.

BALANCE SHEET

Assets	12/31/99 (dollars in thousands)	12/31/98	Liabilities	12/31/99 (dollars in thousands)	12/31/98
Current (CAE 557 and 549)	934	1,395	Current (STD 34 and 32)	279	217
Buildings, machinery, and equipment	123	243	Lease settlement costs	8	36
License agreements	63	66	Stockholders' equity*	843	1,458
Other	10	8			
TOTAL	1,130	1,711	TOTAL	1,130	1,711

* $0.10 par common; 50,000,000 authorized; 17,524,161 and 14,999,161 issued and outstanding.

RECENT QUARTERS / PRIOR-YEAR RESULTS

	Quarter End	Revenue ($000)	Earnings ($000)	EPS ($)	Prior-Year Revenue ($000)	Prior-Year Earnings ($000)	Prior-Year EPS ($)
Q3	09/30/2000	237	(298)	(0.01)	238	(249)	(0.02)
Q2	06/30/2000	192	(425)	(0.02)	439	(218)	(0.01)
Q1	03/31/2000	192	(409)	(0.02)	529	(235)	(0.02)
Q4	12/31/99	256	(416)	(0.03)	630	(195)	(0.01)
	SUM	877	(1,548)	(0.08)	1,836	(898)	(0.06)

RECENT EVENTS

In **March 2000** the company completed a $2.2 million private placement of its common stock to accredited investors. Net proceeds of $2.075 million were to be used for continued development of the IMUX 2000 (Inverse Multiplexer) product family, completion of the HDSL2 product, expansion of the sales and marketing program, and general working capital. "Astrocom is in the final testing phase of the company's latest product offering, the IMUX 2000," said CEO Thomas. "This financing will insure that we have the resources to market the IMUX 2000 and expand the product family into DSL and other Wide Area Network protocols." Astrocom then announced the IMUX-2000/4, the first of a family of MultiLink Access devices (inverse multiplexers) that can aggregate up to 4 serial connections (T1, E1, V.35, DSL etc.) over a singe bundled line. In **April** the company noted that it had signed six new Manufacturers' Representative Agreements over the past few months: Group IV, for coverage of the West Coast; PSA, the Southeast and Southwest; Communication Sales, Michigan, Indiana, and Kentucky; Allied Communications, New England; Strategic Associates, Ohio, Pennsylvania, Delaware, and West Virginia; and Lord & Bayer, Maryland, North Carolina, Virginia, and The District of Columbia. In **August** Astrocom announced the PowerLink DSL Bandwidth Aggregator, the first of a family of DSL Bonding Devices that can aggregate up to 16 DSL connections over a single bundled line. **Sept. 30:** Third quarter's decline in sales was the result of a continued slowdown from customers for the company's CSU/DSU products. In **October** the company signed two new Manufacturers' Representative Agreements, with Micro Plus of Boston for the New England states of Massachusetts, Connecticut, Rhode Island, New Hampshire, Vermont, and Maine; and with Unisell for New York and New Jersey. Two more agreements were pending.

OFFICERS

Ronald B. Thomas
President, CEO, Secretary, and Treasurer

Frederic H. Sweeny
SVP-Sales/Marketing

John M. Bucher
Dir.-Operations and Controller

DIRECTORS

Duane S. Carlson
business consultant, Golden Valley, MN

Gary L. Deaner

S. Albert D. Hanser

Douglas M. Pihl
Vital Images Inc., Minneapolis

Ronald B. Thomas

MAJOR SHAREHOLDERS

Ronald B. Thomas, 17.2%

Perkins Capital Management Inc., 11.1%
Wayzata, MN

S. Albert D. Hanser, 10.7%
Minneapolis

John E. Rogers, 9.2%
Minneapolis

Hanrow Capital Fund Five, 6.9%
Minneapolis

All officers and directors as a group (6 persons), 29.1%

SIC CODE

3661 Telephone and telegraph apparatus

3669 Communications equipment, nec

MISCELLANEOUS

TRANSFER AGENT AND REGISTAR:
Wells Fargo Bank Minnesota N.A., South St. Paul, MN

TRADED: OTC Bulletin Board

SYMBOL: ATCC

STOCKHOLDERS: 650

EMPLOYEES: 17

GENERAL COUNSEL:
Lommen, Nelson, Cole & Stageberg P.A., Minneapolis

AUDITORS:
Ernst & Young LLP, Minneapolis

INC: MN-1968

ANNUAL MEETING: May

TWO-YEAR QUARTERLY HIGH-LOW STOCK PRICES

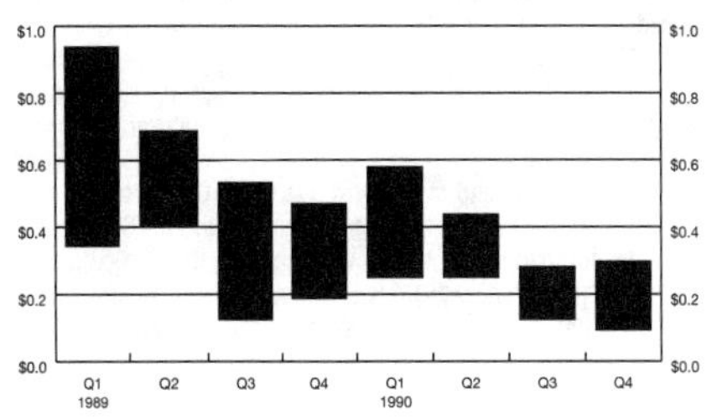

PUB

August Technology Corporation

4900 W. 78th St., Bloomington, MN 55435
Tel: 952/820-0080 Fax: 952/820-0060 Web site: http://www.augusttech.com

August Technology Corp. designs, manufactures and markets automated defect inspection solutions for the worldwide semiconductor industry, including the NSX Series for wafer, die and bump inspection.

EARNINGS HISTORY

Year Ended Dec 31	Operating Revenue/Sales (dollars in thousands)	Net Earnings	Return on Revenue (percent)	Return on Equity	Net Earnings (dollars per share*)	Cash Dividend	Market Price Range
1999	12,058	(132)	(1.1)	(3.9)	(0.02)	—	
1998	5,787	0	0.0	0.0	0.00	—	
1997	4,192	187	4.5	40.2	0.02	—	
1996	3,756	215	5.7	63.6	0.03	—	
1995	1,798	44	2.4	35.8	0.01	—	

* Trading had not begun during periods presented.

BALANCE SHEET

Assets	12/31/99 (dollars in thousands)	12/31/98	Liabilities	12/31/99 (dollars in thousands)	12/31/98
Current	5,755	2,360	Current (STD 1,478 and 284)	3,261	1,235
Property and equipment	922	325	Deferred income taxes	28	39
TOTAL	6,676	2,686	Accrued lease obligation	40	
			Stockholders' equity*	3,347	1,411
			TOTAL	6,676	2,686

* $0.01 par common; 12,000,000 authorized; 9,163,961 and 8,323,001 issued and outstanding.

RECENT QUARTERS / **PRIOR-YEAR RESULTS**

	Quarter End	Revenue ($000)	Earnings ($000)	EPS ($)	Prior-Year Revenue ($000)	Prior-Year Earnings ($000)	Prior-Year EPS ($)
Q3	09/30/2000	8,990	881	0.07	3,501	73	0.01
Q2	06/30/2000	7,696	505	0.05	3,080	184	0.02
Q1	03/31/2000	4,503	(451)	(0.05)	2,143	205	0.02
Q4	12/31/99	3,334	(594)	(0.07)	2,279	195	0.02
	SUM	24,523	340	0.00	11,002	657	0.08

RECENT EVENTS

On **June 14, 2000**, the company commenced its initial public offering of 3.3 million shares at an offering price of $12 per share (the low end of the proposed $12 to $14 range) through underwriters led by Needham & Co. Inc.; Adams, Harkness & Hill Inc.; and A.G. Edwards & Sons Inc. August Technology planned to use the proceeds from the IPO for general and corporate purposes including research and development, working capital, capital expenditures, repayment of debt, and for potential acquisitions of complementary products, technologies, or businesses. Shares opened at $15.50 and rose to $17.25 before closing at $15.19. The company raised $39.6 million, before expenses. In **July** the company introduced YieldPilot, a defect and process analysis package for wafer, die, and bump manufacturers; and the NSX-95 and NSX B-95, which provide high-speed wafer, die, and bump inspection for defects down to 0.5 micron. Also introduced at Semicon West: the Flex-Handler automation station, which increases the throughput capabilities of the NSX Series semiconductor wafer inspection systems by automatically loading and unloading wafers on film frames and die in Auer boats. August received an order from one of the world's largest IC manufacturers for a fully automated, 300mm NSX Series wafer inspection tool. In **August** the company announced shipment of multiple NSX-Series inspection systems to one of the world's largest manufacturers of disc drives (the largest single order in the company's history). August Technology announced the shipment of its 100th NSX system for wafer, die, and bump inspection. In **September** the company received an order for an NSX inspection system for semiconductor-based print heads, its first order from this market, from one of the world's largest providers of imaging solutions. August Technology was honored for the third-consecutive year as one of the 50 fastest growing companies in Minnesota. In **September** the company received an order for more than $1 million, from the one of the world's leading bump foundries, for two NSX-95 bump inspection systems. The repeat order was to be installed at the customer's facility in Taiwan, the world's fastest-growing semiconductor equipment market. **Sept. 30**: Gross margin increased to 60.9 percent during the third quarter, up from 59.2 percent in 1999. The company also experienced sequential order growth as compared to the second quarter of 2000, and achieved a record level in bookings. The book-to-bill ratio for the third quarter and first nine months, which was above industry levels, resulted in a record backlog level at the end of the third quarter. In **October** August Technology received an order valued at more than $1 million for two NSX Series bump inspection systems from Flip Chip Technologies, Phoenix, one of the world's leading bumping companies. The company expanded its headquarters to 63,000 square feet, a 50 percent increase in space. "This expansion will provide us with three new clean rooms, an engineering lab, increased production area, and additional space for our continually expanding engineering and customer service groups," said COO Klenk.

OFFICERS

Jeff L. O'Dell
President and CEO

David L. Klenk
COO

Thomas C. Velin
CFO

Thomas C. Verburgt
Chief Technical Officer

Mark R. Harless
Chief Engineer

D. Mayson Brooks
VP-Sales/Marketing

Wayne J. Hubin
VP-Manufacturing

Jim Nurse
VP-Customer Service

John Vasuta
VP-Intellectual Property, Gen. Counsel

DIRECTORS

James A. Bernards
Brightstone Capital Ltd., Minneapolis

Roger E. Gower
Micro Component Tehnology Inc., Roseville, MN

Mark R. Harless

Jeff L. O'Dell

Bradley D. Slye
Electro-Sensors Inc., Minnetonka, MN

Thomas C. Verburgt

Michael W. Wright
Entegris Inc., Chaska, MN

MAJOR SHAREHOLDERS

Mark R. Harless, 16.8%

Jeff L. O'Dell, 13.4%

Brad D. Slye/ESI Investment Co., 12.4%

Thomas C. Verburgt, 10.1%

James A. Bernards/ Brightstone Capital, 5.2%

All officers and directors as a group (11 persons), 58.8%

SIC CODE

3827 Optical instruments and lenses

MISCELLANEOUS

TRANSFER AGENT AND REGISTAR:
Wells Fargo Bank Minnesota N.A., South St. Paul, MN

TRADED: Nasdaq National Market

SYMBOL: AUGT

EMPLOYEES: 175

GENERAL COUNSEL:
Fredrikson & Byron P.A., Minneapolis

AUDITORS:
KPMG LLP, Minneapolis

INC: MN-1992

RANKINGS

No. 22 Minnesota Technology Fast 50

Ault Inc.

7105 Northland Terrace N., Brooklyn Park, MN 55428
Tel: 763/592-1900 Fax: 763/592-1911 Web site: http://www.aultinc.com

Ault Inc. is an independent manufacturer of external power supplies, battery chargers, and transformers. OEMs use Ault's products to power and/or recharge cellular mobile telephones, portable medical equipment, telephone systems, modems, local-area networks, and computer peripherals. External power devices are located outside the equipment they power, as wall plug-in or in-line components. The devices enable electronic equipment designers to remove heat and hazardous voltages from the end product, which can then function more safely and effectively.

EARNINGS HISTORY

Year Ended May	Operating Revenue/Sales (dollars in thousands)	Net Earnings	Return on Revenue (percent)	Return on Equity	Net Earnings (dollars per share)	Cash Dividend	Market Price Range
2000 *	66,123	1,864	2.8	7.2	0.42	—	8.22–6.57
1999	50,938	1,988	3.9	8.5	0.47	—	11.88–3.38
1998	41,136	1,318	3.2	6.7	0.32	—	10.13–4.63
1997	40,012	2,365	5.9	12.5	0.79	—	14.75–6.50
1996	33,774	883	2.6	15.8	0.42	—	14.38–1.75

* Income figures for 2000 include pretax gain of $1.525 million on sale of facility.

BALANCE SHEET

Assets	05/28/00 (dollars in thousands)	05/30/99	Liabilities	05/28/00 (dollars in thousands)	05/30/99
Current (CAE 2,418 and 3,303)	34,269	24,790	Current (STD 802 and 402)	16,561	8,426
Property, equipment, and leasehold improvements	10,537	6,808	Long-term debt	3,657	1,187
			Deferred rent expense		14
Intangibles	1,354	1,560	Retirement/severance	233	234
Deferred taxes	72	105	Stockholders' equity*	25,805	23,442
Other	24	41			
TOTAL	46,256	33,303	TOTAL	46,256	33,303

* No par common; 10,000,000 authorized; 4,445,432 and 4,372,789 issued and outstanding.

RECENT QUARTERS / **PRIOR-YEAR RESULTS**

	Quarter End	Revenue ($000)	Earnings ($000)	EPS ($)	Prior-Year Revenue ($000)	Prior-Year Earnings ($000)	Prior-Year EPS ($)
Q1	08/27/2000	21,642	651	0.15	13,535	212	0.05
Q4	05/28/2000	20,631	825	0.19	14,590	444	0.10
Q3	02/27/2000	17,570	514	0.12	13,965	606	0.14
Q2	11/28/99	14,387	313	0.07	11,046	463	0.11
	SUM	74,230	2,303	0.52	53,136	1,725	0.41

RECENT EVENTS

In **March 2000** the company signed a purchase agreement with Efficient Networks, Dallas, to provide inventory and Just-In-Time (JIT) service for five external power supply models that support Efficient Network's ADSL modem business. In **May** Ault announced plans to close its Gaithersberg, Md., facility and consolidate the sales and engineering functions located there into the company's Minneapolis headquarters operation. Acquired in 1998, the Gaithersberg operation was involved with the low-volume, fast-turnaround Ault Express line of external power supplies. BlueFire Research initiated coverage of Ault with an OUTPERFORM rating and a 12-month target price of $11 per share, based on a multiple of 19 times estimated earnings per share for the May 2001 fiscal year. **Aug. 27:** CEO Green commented: "Sales for the first quarter of fiscal 2001 were the highest for any three-month period in Ault's history. We are especially pleased with the company's first-quarter performance since it is usually the weakest quarter of the year. Our steadily growing sales have been paced in large measure by our expanding penetration of the high-growth broadband modem market." The positive impact of the sales growth was partly offset by a reduction in the gross margin due to growth in lower-margin linear power supplies used by Ault's XDSL customers and significantly higher air and maritime freight costs. In **September** Ault signed a manufacturing contract with Eastern Communications Co. Ltd. (EastCom) for US $1.2 million to manufacture a custom-designed Lithium Ion battery charger for EastCom's EL600 dual-frequency digital cellular telephone.

OFFICERS

Frederick M. Green
Chairman, President, and CEO
Hokung C. Choi
VP-Far East Operations
Gregory L. Harris
VP-Marketing
Donald R. Henry
VP, CFO, and Asst. Secretary
Richard A. Primuth
Secretary

DIRECTORS

James M. Duddleston
consultant
Frederick M. Green
Delbert W. Johnson
Pioneer Metal Finishing Co., Minneapolis
John G. Kassakian
Massachusetts Institute of Technology, Boston
Edward C. Lund
Eric G. Mitchell Jr.
The Pricing Advisor Inc.
Matthew A. Sutton
Honeywell Consultants Ltd.

MAJOR SHAREHOLDERS

Wellington Management Co. LLP, 9.5%
Boston
Dimensional Fund Advisors Inc., 8.6%
Santa Monica, CA
Frederick M. Green, 5.3%
All officers and directors as a group (10 persons), 10.8%

SIC CODE

3612 Transformers, except electronic
3629 Electrical industrial apparatus, nec

MISCELLANEOUS

TRANSFER AGENT AND REGISTAR:
Wells Fargo Bank Minnesota N.A.,
South St. Paul, MN
TRADED: Nasdaq National Market
SYMBOL: AULT
STOCKHOLDERS: 288
EMPLOYEES: 565
GENERAL COUNSEL:
Lindquist & Vennum PLLP, Minneapolis
AUDITORS:
RSM McGladrey & Pullen Inc. LLP, Minneapolis

INC: MN-1961
ANNUAL MEETING: September
MARKETING: Cindy Trojanowski
PURCHASING: Patrick Anderson

RANKINGS

No. 106 CRM Public 200
No. 32 CRM Performance 100

SUBSIDIARIES, DIVISIONS, AFFILIATES

Ault Korea Corporation
14-1 Pyung-Dong
Kwonseon-Ku
Suwon City, Kyungki-Do, Korea
331/293-7881
J.L. Choi

Ault (XiangHe) Electronics Co. Ltd.
XiangHe, China

TWO-YEAR QUARTERLY HIGH-LOW STOCK PRICES

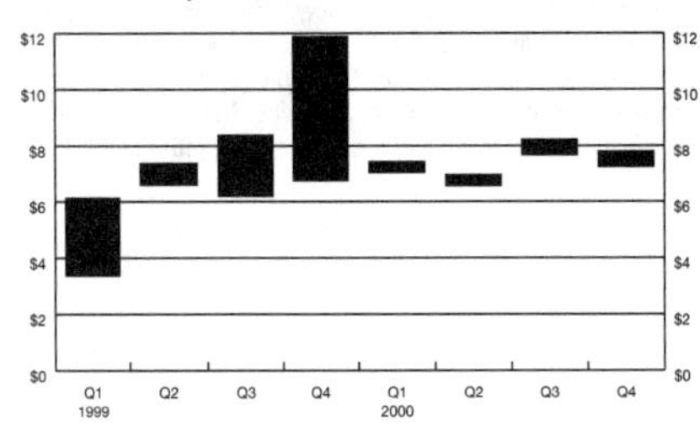

PUB

PUB

BMC Industries Inc.

One Meridian Crossing, Suite 850, Minneapolis, MN 55423
Tel: 952/851-6000 Fax: 952/851-6050 Web site: http://www.bmcind.com

BMC Industries Inc. has two primary business segments. The Buckbee-Mears Group, through its Mask Operations, is the only independent non-Asian manufacturer of aperture mask, a critical component in the picture tube of every color television and computer monitor. Buckbee-Mears is also a leading producer of precision-etched metal and electroformed parts. The Optical Products Group manufacturers and markets polycarbinate, glass and plastic multifocal and single-vision eyewear lenses under the name Vision-Ease Lens.

EARNINGS HISTORY

Year Ended Dec 31	Operating Revenue/Sales (dollars in thousands)	Net Earnings (dollars in thousands)	Return on Revenue (percent)	Return on Equity (percent)	Net Earnings (dollars per share)	Cash Dividend (dollars per share)	Market Price Range (dollars per share)
1999	353,854	7,824	2.2	5.7	0.29	0.06	13.25–4.19
1998 *	335,138	(30,635)	(9.1)	(23.0)	(1.13)	0.06	21.25–3.94
1997	312,538	35,721	11.4	20.0	1.30	0.06	35.38–15.94
1996	280,487	35,101	12.5	24.4	1.29	0.05	32.38–19.75
1995	255,355	24,547	9.6	22.6	0.91	0.04	23.63–7.69

* Income figures for 1998 include pretax charges of $42.8 million (asset impairment), $9.5 million (acquired R&D), and $11.3 million (restructuring)—after-tax total, $39.8 million/($1.48). Results of Orcolite included from May 15, 1998, date of purchase for $101 million. Pro forma for full year: revenue $349.356 million; net loss $32.253 million/($1.19).

BALANCE SHEET

Assets	12/31/99 (dollars in thousands)	12/31/98	Liabilities	12/31/99 (dollars in thousands)	12/31/98
Current (CAE 1,146 and 1,028)	149,651	151,994	Current (STD 2,303 and 1,929)	59,935	57,023
Property, plant, and equipment	151,238	162,594	Long-term debt	165,959	187,266
			Deferred taxes	2,715	3,547
Deferred income taxes	9,221	5,431	Other	18,522	18,372
			Stkhldrs' equity*	136,422	133,257
Intangibles	68,232	73,178	TOTAL	383,553	399,465
Other	5,211	6,268			
TOTAL	383,553	399,465			

* No par common; 99,000,000 authorized; 27,370,000 and 27,173,000 issued and outstanding.

RECENT QUARTERS / PRIOR-YEAR RESULTS

	Quarter End	Revenue ($000)	Earnings ($000)	EPS ($)	Prior-Year Revenue ($000)	Prior-Year Earnings ($000)	Prior-Year EPS ($)
Q3	09/30/2000	90,179	2,737	0.10	88,321	(426)	(0.02)
Q2	06/30/2000	94,237	5,475	0.20	93,339	5,007	0.18
Q1	03/31/2000	88,751	2,301	0.08	84,645	3,191	0.12
Q4	12/31/99	87,549	52	0.00	81,529	4,677	0.17
	SUM	360,716	10,565	0.39	347,834	12,449	0.46

RECENT EVENTS

In **March 2000** BMC's Vision-Ease Lens subsidiary purchased La Haute Lunette De Paris SA (HLP), an optical lens laboratory located outside Paris. HLP processes lenses in all materials, but specializes in polycarbonate eyewear lenses. The lab was to operate under the name Vision-Ease France SAS. BMC then announced the integration of its Precision Imaged Products group's two operating units, Mask Operations and Buckbee-Mears St. Paul, under the name Buckbee-Mears—to be led by COO Pouliquen. CEO Burke said, "The mask business and Buckbee-Mears St. Paul share core technologies that can be leveraged into new product opportunities. We believe that by combining the high-volume production capabilities derived from the mask business with the market access and value-added processes of Buckbee-Mears St. Paul, we can dramatically grow and diversify our revenue and profit stream. This will also allow us to more rapidly realize the benefits of the significant individual and partnership development efforts currently underway." In **July** BMC was selected by THOMSON multimedia (NYSE: TMS) as a supplier of shadow masks for its new lineup of digital high-definition television (HDTV) receivers. In **August** BMC was named "Outstanding Supplier of the Year" by American Matsushita Electronics Co. for performance excellence in 1999. **Sept. 30:** Excluding the negative impact from foreign currency translation rates during the nine-month period, revenue would have increased 5 percent from the prior period. Net earnings were $10.5 million versus $7.8 million. Said Burke, "We continue to enjoy favorable market dynamics, particularly with respect to the entertainment aperture mask side of the business."

OFFICERS

Paul B. Burke
Chairman and CEO
Benoit Pouliquen
President and COO
Kathleen P. Pepski
SVP and CFO
Jon A. Dobson
VP-Human Resources, Gen. Counsel, Sec.
Kevin E. Roe
Acting Controller
Bradley D. Carlson
Treasurer

STOCKHOLDERS: 1,100
EMPLOYEES: 3,450
AUDITORS:
Ernst & Young LLP, Minneapolis
INC: MN-1907
ANNUAL MEETING: May

RANKINGS

No. 59 CRM Public 200

DIRECTORS

Paul B. Burke
John W. Castro
Merrill Corp., St. Paul
H. Ted Davis
U. of Minnesota/Institute of Technology, Minneapolis
Joe E. Davis
National Health Enterprises, Inc. (retired)
Harry A. Hammerly
3M Co. (retired)
James M. Ramich
Corning Inc. (retired), Corning, NY

MAJOR SHAREHOLDERS

Becker Capital Management Inc., 6.5%
Portland, OR
Putnam Investments Inc., 5.9%
Boston
Dimensional Fund Advisors Inc., 5.3%
Santa Monica, CA
Oppenheimer Capital, 5%
New York
All officers and directors as a group (12 persons), 5.4%

SIC CODE

3479 Metal coating and allied services
3679 Electronic components, nec
3851 Ophthalmic goods
3999 Manufacturing industries, nec

MISCELLANEOUS

TRANSFER AGENT AND REGISTAR:
Wells Fargo Bank Minnesota N.A.,
South St. Paul, MN
TRADED: NYSE
SYMBOL: BMC

TWO-YEAR QUARTERLY HIGH-LOW STOCK PRICES

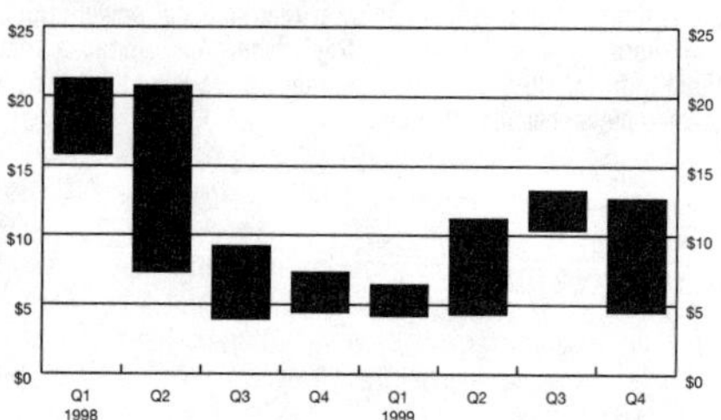

BNCCORP Inc.

322 E. Main Ave., Bismarck, ND 58501
Tel: 701/250-3040 Fax: 701/222-3653 Web site: http://www.bnccorp.com

BNCCORP Inc. is a bank holding company that provides a full range of commercial and consumer banking and financial services to small and midsize businesses, and to individuals, through 15 facilities in North Dakota (BNC National Bank) and Minnesota (BNC National Bank of Minnesota) and a non-bank commercial finance subsidiary (BNC Financial Corp.). Management believes that the company's entrepreneurial approach to banking and the introduction of new products and services will continue to attract small and midsize businesses that often aren't large enough to interest the larger banks in those market areas. *continued on page 152*

EARNINGS HISTORY *

Year Ended Dec 31	Operating Revenue/Sales (dollars in thousands)	Net Earnings	Return on Revenue (percent)	Return on Equity	Net Earnings (dollars per share†)	Cash Dividend	Market Price Range
1999 ¶	34,999	242	0.7	1.0	0.10	—	11.25–5.75
1998 #	32,644	2,267	6.9	9.0	0.95	—	23.25–9.00
1997 **	29,160	1,426	4.9	6.2	0.59	—	17.00–10.50
1996 ††	24,219	1,170	4.8	5.4	0.49	—	12.50–8.00
1995 ##	18,686	1,157	6.2	5.5	0.67	—	12.00–9.75

* Historical figures from 1996 forward have been restated to pool Jan. 1, 1998, acquisition Lips & Lahr Inc.
† Stock began trading July 17, 1995.
¶ Income figures for 1999 include gain of $867,000/$0.36 from discontinued operations and their disposal; and loss of $96,000/($0.04) cumulative effect of change in accounting principle.
# Income figures for 1998 include gain of $385,000/$0.16 from discontinued operations.
** Income figures for 1997 include gain of $127,000/$0.05 from discontinued operations.
†† Income figures for 1996 include gain of $24,000/$0.01 from discontinued operations.
Income figures for 1995 include loss of $5,000/($0.00) from discontinued operations.

BALANCE SHEET

Assets	12/31/99 (dollars in thousands)	12/31/98	Liabilities	12/31/99 (dollars in thousands)	12/31/98
Cash and due from banks	12,816	7,475	Noninterest-bearing deposits	29,798	28,475
Interest-bearing deposits with banks	5,565	2,809	Savings, NOW, money market	127,454	89,887
Federal funds sold	3,500		Time deposits $100,000+	46,779	39,162
Securities available for sale	150,992	96,601	Other time deposits	120,680	126,975
Net loans	259,179	244,327	Notes payable	103,170	58,485
Premises, leasehold improvements, equipment	12,006	8,786	Other	5,847	6,362
Interest receivable	2,613	2,356	Discontinued operation		21,731
Other	6,945	5,929	Stockholders' equity*	23,149	25,255
Deferred charges, intangibles	3,261	3,957	TOTAL	456,877	396,332
Discontinued operation		24,092			
TOTAL	456,877	396,332			

* $0.01 par common; 10,000,000 authorized; 2,442,860 and 2,433,064 issued and outstanding, less 42,880 and 42,880 treasury shares.

RECENT QUARTERS / **PRIOR-YEAR RESULTS**

	Quarter End	Revenue ($000)	Earnings ($000)	EPS ($)	Prior-Year Revenue ($000)	Prior-Year Earnings ($000)	Prior-Year EPS ($)
Q3	09/30/2000	12,933	597	0.25	8,839	190	0.08
Q2	06/30/2000	12,474	617	0.26	8,283	273	0.11
Q1	03/31/2000	10,946	555	0.23	8,260	260	0.11
Q4	12/31/99	9,616	(481)	(0.20)	8,215	467	0.20
	SUM	45,969	1,288	0.54	33,597	1,190	0.50

CURRENT: Q3 earnings include extraordinary gain of $65,000/$0.03 on early extinguishment of debt. Q2 earnings include gain of $10,000/$0.00 on disposal of asset-based lending facility; and $47,000/$0.02 on early extinguishment of debt. Q1 earnings include extraordinary gain of $122,000/$0.05 on early extinguishment of debt. Q4 earnings include gain of $438,000/$0.18 on disposal of discontinued operations.
PRIOR YEAR: Q3 earnings include gain of $186,000/$0.08 from discontinued operations. Q2 earnings include gain of $104,000/$0.04 from discontinued operations. Q1 earnings include gain of $139,000/$0.06 from discontinued operations; and loss of $96,000/($0.04) cumulative effect of accounting change. Q4 earnings include gain of $96,000/$0.04 from discontinued operations.

OFFICERS
Tracy J. Scott
Chairman and CEO
Gregory K. Cleveland
President and COO
Brad J. Scott
EVP-Finance, BNC North Dakota
James D. LaBreche
Pres.-BNC Minnesota
Brenda L. Rebel
Corporate Treasurer and CFO
David J. Sorum
Pres.-BNC National Bank, Fargo branch

DIRECTORS
Gregory K. Cleveland
John A. Hipp, M.D.
Pathology Consultants, Bismarck, ND
Richard M. Johnsen Jr.
Johnsen Trailer Sales Inc., Bismarck/Fargo, ND
James LaBreche
Mark E. Peiler
Investment Officer
Brenda L. Rebel
Brad J. Scott
Tracy J. Scott
John M. Shaffer
Atlas Inc., Bismarck, ND
David J. Sorum
Jerry R. Woodcox
Arrowhead Cleaners and Laundry Inc., Bismarck, ND

MAJOR SHAREHOLDERS
401(k) Savings Plan, 7.7%
David A. Erickson, 6.7%
Linton, ND
Tracy J. Scott, 5.6%
All officers and directors as a group (11 persons), 17.3%

SIC CODE
6021 National commercial banks

MISCELLANEOUS
TRANSFER AGENT AND REGISTAR:
American Stock Trust & Transfer, New York
TRADED: Nasdaq National Market
SYMBOL: BNCC
STOCKHOLDERS: 110
EMPLOYEES: 190

GENERAL COUNSEL:
Jones, Walker, Waechter, Poitevent, Carrere & Denegre LLP, New Orleans
AUDITORS:
Arthur Andersen LLP, Minneapolis
INC: DE-1995
FOUNDED: 1987
ANNUAL MEETING: June

SUBSIDIARIES, DIVISIONS, AFFILIATES
BNC National Bank
Bismarck, N.D.
Linton, N.D.
Ellendale, N.D.
Garrison, N.D.
Stanley, N.D.
Kenmare, N.D.
Crosby, N.D.
Watford City, N.D.

Bismarck Properties Inc.
Bismarck, N.D.

BNC National Bank of Minnesota
Minneapolis

BNC Financial Corp.
St. Cloud, Minn.

PUB

TWO-YEAR QUARTERLY HIGH-LOW STOCK PRICES

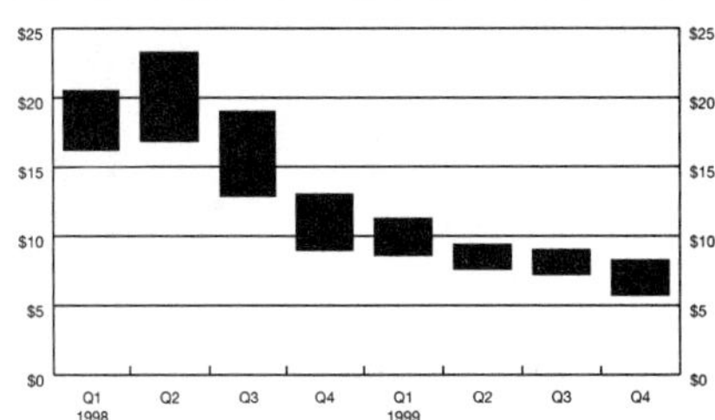

Ballistic Recovery Systems Inc.

300 Airport Rd., South St. Paul, MN 55075
Tel: 651/457-7491 Fax: 651/457-8651 Web site: http://www.airplaneparachutes.com

Ballistic Recovery Systems Inc. is engaged in the design, development, manufacture, marketing, and distribution of aviation safety products. The company is the leading supplier of ballistically deployed parachute recovery systems for use on ultralight and experimental aircraft. The parachutes, made for aircrafts of up to 1,650 pounds, are to be used in the event of a midair collision, loss of control of aircraft, engine or structural failure, or other dangerous conditions. Its 12,000 systems worldwide have saved 96 lives. BRS is developing other aviation safety products, including a parachute system for larger general-aviation aircraft and military applications that has been submitted to the FAA for certification.

EARNINGS HISTORY

Year Ended Sept 30	Operating Revenue/Sales (dollars in thousands)	Net Earnings	Return on Revenue (percent)	Return on Equity	Net Earnings (dollars per share)	Cash Dividend	Market Price Range
1999	1,798	5	0.3	0.7	0.00	—	3.00–0.44
1998	1,623	144	8.9	20.7	0.03	—	1.50–0.25
1997 *	1,855	372	20.1	68.4	0.08	—	0.81–0.31
1996 †	1,731	112	6.5	67.4	0.02	—	1.38–0.06
1995	1,137	46	4.0	NM	0.01	—	0.25–0.06

* Income figures for 1997 include gain of $198,000/$0.04 from income tax benefit.
† Income figures for 1996 include pretax charge of $34,782 for amortization of covenant not to compete that was signed by its sole U.S. competitor.

BALANCE SHEET

Assets	09/30/99 (dollars in thousands)	09/30/98	Liabilities	09/30/99 (dollars in thousands)	09/30/98
Current (CAE 181 and 20)	613	703	Current (STD 15 and 14)	298	426
Furniture and fixtures	61	79	Bank note, covenant not to compete	207	251
Patents	3	4	Stockholders' equity*	714	698
Covenant not to compete	231	269	TOTAL	1,219	1,375
Deferred tax	275	275			
Other intangibles	36	46			
TOTAL	1,219	1,375			

* $0.01 par common; 10,000,000 authorized; 5,859,449 and 5,696,927 issued and outstanding.

RECENT QUARTERS / PRIOR-YEAR RESULTS

	Quarter End	Revenue ($000)	Earnings ($000)	EPS ($)	Prior-Year Revenue ($000)	Prior-Year Earnings ($000)	Prior-Year EPS ($)
Q3	06/30/2000	755	39	0.01	548	39	0.01
Q2	03/31/2000	532	(35)	(0.01)	392	(8)	0.00
Q1	12/30/99	460	(19)	0.00	314	(95)	(0.02)
Q4	09/30/99	544	69	0.01	557	179	0.04
	SUM	2,290	54	0.01	1,811	115	0.02

RECENT EVENTS

In **October 2000** the company signed a five-year exclusive distribution deal with a Florida man who was planning to outfit used Cessnas with the BRS parachute for use in flight schools. The deal revived the company's Cessna 150 parachute program, which was once thought to have great potential until the Cessna ceased to be the industry's main training plane. In **November** BRS signed a contract with Millennium Aerospace to pursue FAA certification of a similar system for the Cessna 172. The larger, four-seat aircraft, also widely used for primary flight training, has a larger fleet than any other aircraft in general aviation.

OFFICERS

Robert L. Nelson
Chairman

Mark B. Thomas
President, CEO, and CFO

Daniel P. Johnson
VP and Secretary

DIRECTORS

Thomas H. Adams Jr.
Darrel D. Brandt
Robert L. Nelson
Wipaire Inc., South St. Paul, MN
Boris Popov
Mark B. Thomas

MAJOR SHAREHOLDERS

Darrel D. Brandt, 31.4%
Cedar Falls, IA

Boris Popov, 10%
Afton, MN

All officers and directors as a group (6 persons), 49.6%

SIC CODE

2399 Fabricated textile products, nec
3429 Hardware, nec
3728 Aircraft equipment, nec

MISCELLANEOUS

TRANSFER AGENT AND REGISTAR:
Company

TRADED: LOTC
SYMBOL: BRSI
STOCKHOLDERS: 1,100
EMPLOYEES: 13
GENERAL COUNSEL:
Maslon Edelman Borman & Brand PLLP, Minneapolis
AUDITORS:
Callahan, Johnston & Associates LLC, Minneapolis
INC: MN-1980
ANNUAL MEETING:
March
INVESTOR RELATIONS:
Boris Popov

TWO-YEAR QUARTERLY HIGH-LOW STOCK PRICES

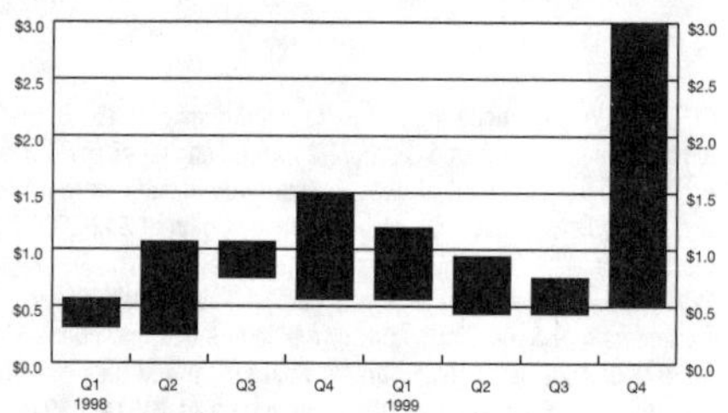

Bemis Company Inc.

222 S. Ninth St., Suite 2300, Minneapolis, MN 55402
Tel: 612/376-3030 Fax: 612/376-3180 Web site: http://www.bemis.com

Bemis Co. Inc. is a manufacturer of flexible packaging and pressure sensitive materials. Flexible packaging products and selected end uses include: high barrier films for packaging processed meat, cheese, candy, snack foods, and medical devices; polyethylene films for packaging bread, ice, frozen foods, disposable diapers and other sanitary products; multiwall and consumer sized paper bags for packaging pet products, agricultural products such as seed, feed, and fertilizer, and rice and flour. Pressure sensitive materials include printing products such as label stock used with desktop laser printers; narrow-web roll label products for labeling food, household, and personal care products; graphic films used for promotional display and signage, and a variety of specialized products.

EARNINGS HISTORY

Year Ended Dec 31	Operating Revenue/Sales (dollars in thousands)	Net Earnings	Return on Revenue (percent)	Return on Equity	Net Earnings (dollars per share)	Cash Dividend	Market Price Range
1999	1,918,025	114,775	6.0	15.8	2.19	0.92	39.94–30.44
1998	1,848,004	111,432	6.0	16.2	2.10	0.88	46.94–33.94
1997	1,877,237	107,584	5.7	16.8	2.03	0.80	47.19–35.81
1996 *	1,655,431	101,081	6.1	17.8	1.92	0.72	37.13–26.13
1995	1,523,390	85,210	5.6	16.6	1.64	0.64	29.75–23.38

* Income figures for 1996 include gain of $2.6 million/$0.05 on disposition of Hayssen unit.

BALANCE SHEET

Assets	12/31/99 (dollars in thousands)	12/31/98	Liabilities	12/31/99 (dollars in thousands)	12/31/98
Current (CAE 18,187 and 23,738)	583,581	546,911	Current (STD 1,049 and 2,946)	253,268	245,613
Property and equipment	776,241	740,101	Long-term debt	372,267	371,363
			Deferred taxes	89,635	84,679
Excess of cost over net assets acquired	150,496	160,819	Other	51,580	54,655
			Minority interest	39,498	37,862
Other	21,825	34,195	Stkhldrs' equity*	725,895	687,854
TOTAL	1,532,143	1,482,026	TOTAL	1,532,143	1,482,026

* $0.10 par common; 248,000,000 authorized; 59,098,203 and 59,056,047 issued and outstanding, less 6,909,488 and 6,786,889 treasury shares.

RECENT QUARTERS / **PRIOR-YEAR RESULTS**

	Quarter End	Revenue ($000)	Earnings ($000)	EPS ($)	Revenue ($000)	Earnings ($000)	EPS ($)
Q3	09/30/2000	529,266	32,165	0.61	492,218	31,152	0.60
Q2	06/30/2000	525,230	35,350	0.67	481,259	31,591	0.60
Q1	03/31/2000	500,748	29,643	0.55	450,607	18,738	0.36
Q4	12/31/99	493,941	33,294	0.64	460,421	25,540	0.49
	SUM	2,049,185	130,452	2.46	1,884,505	107,021	2.04

RECENT EVENTS

In **December 1999** the company agreed to purchase the remaining 13 percent minority interest in Morgan Adhesives Co. (MACtac) that it didn't own—for 1.73 million shares of common stock and a small amount of cash. In **June 2000** Morgan Stanley initiated coverage of shares of Bemis at OUTPERFORM. Bemis agreed to purchase the assets of the $33 million-revenue flexible packaging business of Arrow Industries in Dallas. CEO Curler said "The Arrow flexible packaging business will be an excellent add-on to our polyethylene packaging business and is expected to be immediately accretive to Bemis' EPS." In **July** Bemis agreed to acquire the $150 million-revenue specialty plastic films business of Viskase Cos. Inc.—which supplies a variety of shrinkable barrier bags, films, and cook-in bags to fresh beef, pork, and poultry processors—for $245 million, including $228 million in cash. "Viskase has strong and complex technologies that both complement and extend the technologies employed in our very successful high barrier flexible packaging business," said Curler. "The Viskase product line brings to Bemis immediate access to important fresh meat markets." In response to the deal, Standard & Poor's affirmed its ratings on Bemis, but revised its outlook to NEGATIVE from STABLE based on high debt levels. The affirmations were based on expectations that management would remain committed to its conservative fiscal policies and restore credit protection measures to near their preacquisition levels. [Deal completed at the end of August.] In **September** Bemis purchased Kanzaki's $78 million-revenue pressure-sensitive materials business, which supplies direct thermal pressure-sensitive products to printers for labels used for bar coding, shipping, inventory labeling, and a variety of other end uses. **Sept. 30:** Flexible Packaging sales were up 10 percent in the third quarter, while operating profit was up 4 percent from the prior year's third quarter. Nine-month operating profit, however, increased 19 percent. In Pressure Sensitive Materials, sales in the third quarter were flat with prior year levels and operating profit decreased by 26 percent. CEO Curler said, "This quarter's results are indicative of the tough challenges of the current economic and competitive environment in the marketplace. Higher raw materials costs and lower volume, reflective of a softening economy, put pressure on both sales and profit margins for the quarter. The pressure-sensitive materials business is experiencing particularly difficult market conditions in the roll *continued on page 152*

OFFICERS

John H. Roe
Chairman

Jeffrey H. Curler
President and CEO

Scott W. Johnson
SVP, General Counsel, and Secretary

Benjamin R. Field III
SVP, Treasurer, and CFO

Stanley A. Jaffy
VP-Tax and Asst. Controller

Thomas L. Sall
VP-Operations

Eugene H. Seashore Jr.
VP-Human Resources

Gene C. Wulf
VP and Controller

DIRECTORS

Dr. John G. Bollinger
U. of Wisconsin College of Engineering, Madison, WI

William J. Bolton
Supervalu Inc., Eden Prairie, MN

Winslow H. Buxton
Pentair Inc., Roseville, MN

Jeffrey H. Curler

Loring W. Knoblauch
Talon Automated Equipment Co., Detroit

Nancy P. McDonald
Hillcrest Corp., Seattle

Roger D. O'Shaughnessy
Cardinal IG Co., Minnetonka, MN

Edward N. Perry
Perkins, Smith & Cohen, Boston

John H. Roe

C. Angus Wurtele
The Valspar Corp., Minneapolis

MAJOR SHAREHOLDERS

U.S. Bancorp, 6.4%
Minneapolis

All officers and directors as a group (18 persons), 7.4%

SIC CODE

2671 Paper coated and laminated, packaging

2673 Bags: plastics, laminated, and coated

3089 Plastics products, nec

MISCELLANEOUS

TRANSFER AGENT AND REGISTAR:
Wells Fargo Bank Minnesota N.A., South St. Paul, MN

TRADED: NYSE

SYMBOL: BMS

STOCKHOLDERS: 5,316

EMPLOYEES: 9,534

GENERAL COUNSEL:
Scott W. Johnson

AUDITORS:
PricewaterhouseCoopers LLP, Minneapolis

INC: MO-1885

FOUNDED: 1858

ANNUAL MEETING: May

INVESTOR RELATIONS:
Melanie Miller

RANKINGS

No. 22 CRM Public 200

No. 33 CRM Performance 100

SUBSIDIARIES, DIVISIONS, AFFILIATES

FLEXIBLE PACKAGING

Coated and Laminated Films

Carton Sealing Tapes and Stretchfilm

Polyethylene Packaging

Multiwall and Consumer Paper Packaging

Pressure-Sensitive Materials

Metallizing and Converting

Engraving and Packaging Film Services

Pressure Sensitive Printed Products

PUB

TWO-YEAR QUARTERLY HIGH-LOW STOCK PRICES

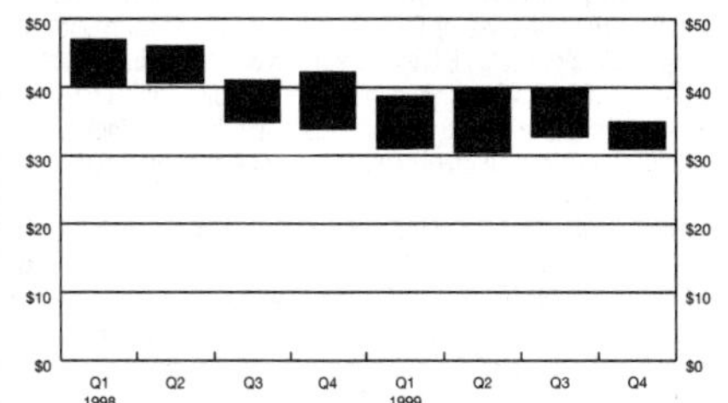

PUB

Best Buy Company Inc.

7075 Flying Cloud Dr., P.O. Box 9312 (55440), Eden Prairie, MN 55344
Tel: 952/947-2000 Fax: 952/947-2422 Web site: http://www.bestbuy.com

Best Buy Co. Inc. is the nation's leading specialty retailer, selling name-brand consumer electronics, personal computers, home office products, appliances, and entertainment software. The company has a "Concept II" strategy, a self-service, discount-style store format. The stores use noncommissioned salespeople and self-service merchandise displays to achieve a low cost structure. Its "Concept III" store format features increased product selection and extended use of interactive technology to provide customer assistance. Its "Concept IV" store format features new product categories that focus on digital technology and interactive displays.

EARNINGS HISTORY

Year Ended Feb	Operating Revenue/Sales (dollars in thousands)	Net Earnings (dollars in thousands)	Return on Revenue (percent)	Return on Equity (percent)	Net Earnings (dollars per share*)	Cash Dividend (dollars per share*)	Market Price Range (dollars per share*)
2000	12,494,023	347,070	2.8	31.7	1.70	—	80.50–40.50
1999	10,064,646	216,282	2.1	20.9	1.09	—	49.00–14.75
1998	8,337,762	81,938	1.0	14.7	0.47	—	15.30–2.16
1997 †	7,757,692	(6,177)	(0.1)	(1.4)	(0.04)	—	6.56–1.97
1996 ¶	7,214,828	46,425	0.6	10.8	0.27	—	7.41–3.19

* Per-share amounts restated to reflect 2-for-1 stock splits paid March 18, 1999, and May 26, 1998.
† Income figures for 1997 include pretax charge of $15 million to write down personal computer inventories and to narrow the office supply assortment.
¶ Fiscal 1996 contained 53 weeks.

BALANCE SHEET

Assets	02/26/00 (dollars in thousands)	02/27/99 (dollars in thousands)	Liabilities	02/26/00 (dollars in thousands)	02/27/99 (dollars in thousands)
Current (CAE 750,723 and 785,777)	2,238,460	2,071,827	Current (STD 15,790 and 30,088)	1,785,049	1,409,716
Property and equipment	698,084	423,640	Long-term liabilities	99,448	57,453
Other	58,798	36,156	Long-term debt	14,860	30,509
TOTAL	2,995,342	2,531,623	Stkhldrs' equity*	1,095,985	1,033,945
			TOTAL	2,995,342	2,531,623

* $0.10 par common; 400,000,000 authorized; 200,379,000 and 203,621,000 issued and outstanding.

RECENT QUARTERS / PRIOR-YEAR RESULTS

	Quarter End	Revenue ($000)	Earnings ($000)	EPS ($)	Prior-Year Revenue ($000)	Prior-Year Earnings ($000)	Prior-Year EPS ($)
Q2	08/26/2000	3,169,171	76,748	0.37	2,686,640	58,067	0.28
Q1	05/27/2000	2,963,718	72,158	0.35	2,385,431	46,809	0.23
Q4	02/26/2000	4,314,615	163,805	0.81	3,456,030	108,807	0.54
Q3	11/27/99	3,107,337	78,389	0.38	2,492,467	53,543	0.27
	SUM	13,554,841	391,100	1.91	11,020,568	267,226	1.32

RECENT EVENTS

In **December 1999** Best Buy and Microsoft Corp. (Nasdaq: MSFT) agreed on a comprehensive strategic alliance that encompassed broadband, narrowband, in-store, and online efforts. The parties signed a letter of intent that provided for significant joint marketing in Best Buy's retail stores, online, and through print/broadcast vehicles; profit sharing; the promotion of BestBuy.com to the 40 million users throughout Microsoft's properties; and technology assistance. Under this alliance, MSN Internet access and Microsoft's full range of connectivity solutions were to be demonstrated and sold at the more than 350 Best Buy stores in the U.S. and through BestBuy.com. In addition, Microsoft was planning to invest $200 million in Best Buy common stock. [The two companies would finalize a definitive agreement in April.] Best Buy made a $10 million strategic equity investment in etown.com (http://www.etown.com), the leading online information and shopping source for buyers of consumer electronics products. Record sales of $2.267 billion for the fiscal month of December represented a 23 percent increase over last year. Comparable-store sales increased 9.8 percent. In **January 2000**, on the year's first day of trading, Best Buy stock rose 14.5 percent to $57.50 on a Merrill Lynch analyst's prediction that the Microsoft partnership could add 10 percent to the retailer's bottom line within two years; Peter Caruso also said that the stock price could reach $100 by year's end. Having secured partnerships with substantially all name-brand consumer electronics manufacturers to include their products, the company announced plans to launch BestBuy.com, a new comprehensive Web service for consumer electronics. A new brand image campaign had Best Buy "turning on the fun"—becoming synonymous with making consumers' time more fun. BestBuy.com announced a $4 million strategic equity investment in Simplexity.com, and a strategic alliance to offer a broad range of telecommunications services online. Seven Washington, D.C.-area Best Buy locations began offering consumers one-stop shopping for high-speed Digital Subscriber Line (DSL) service from 3Com and Bell Atlantic. Best Buy stores nationwide made available Sensory Science Corp.'s (Amex: VCR) top-rated RaveMP portable Internet media player. Best Buy announced plans for a new corporate headquarters in Richfield, Minn., in a designated redevelopment area north of I-494 *continued on page 152*

OFFICERS

Richard M. Schulze
Founder, Chairman, and CEO

Bradbury H. Anderson
President and COO

Allen U. Lenzmeier
EVP and CFO

Wade R. Fenn
EVP-Marketing

Gary Arnold
SVP-Merchandising, Redline Entertainment

Scott Bauhofer
SVP

Nancy Bologna
SVP-Human Resources

Julie M. Engel
SVP-Advertising

Kevin Freeland
SVP-Inventory Management

Connie Fuhrman
SVP

Marc Gordon
SVP-Information Systems and CIO

Susan S. Hoff
SVP-Corp. Communications/ Public Affairs

Wayne R. Inouye
SVP-Merchandising, Computer Hardware

Darren Jackson
SVP-Finance and Treasurer

Joseph M. Joyce
SVP and General Counsel

Michael P. Keskey
SVP-Sales

Michael Linton
SVP-Strategic Marketing

Michael London
SVP and General Merchandise Mgr.

George Lopuch
SVP-Strategic Planning

Mike W. Marolt
SVP-Loss Prevention

David Morrish
SVP-Merchandising, Computers

Joseph Pelano Jr.
SVP-Retail Store Operations

Lowell Peters
SVP-Services

Chas Scheiderer
SVP-Logistics

Philip J. Schoonover
SVP-Digital Technology Solutions

John Walden
SVP-E-commerce

DIRECTORS

Bradbury H. Anderson

Robert T. Blanchard
Procter & Gamble Co., Cincinnati

Elliot S. Kaplan
Robins, Kaplan, Miller & Ciresi, Minneapolis

Richard M. Schulze

Mark C. Thompson
Schwab.com

Frank D. Trestman
Trestman Enterprises, Golden Valley, MN

Hatim A. Tyabji
Saraide.com

Kathy Higgins Victor
Centera Corp., Minneapolis

James Wetherbe
University of Memphis, Minneapolis

MAJOR SHAREHOLDERS

Richard M. Schulze, 18.5%

FLA Asset Management, 7.5% New York

AMVESCAP plc, 7.2%
London

FMR Corp., 6.9%
Boston

All officers and directors as a group (29 persons), 21.3%

SIC CODE

5731 Radio, TV, and electronic stores

MISCELLANEOUS

TRANSFER AGENT AND REGISTAR:
First Chicago Trust Co. NY Jersey City, NJ

TRADED: NYSE

SYMBOL: BBY

STOCKHOLDERS: 1,940

EMPLOYEES: 60,000

GENERAL COUNSEL:
Robins, Kaplan, Miller & Ciresi LLP, Minneapolis

AUDITORS:
Ernst & Young LLP, Minneapolis

INC: MN-1966

ANNUAL MEETING: June

RANKINGS

No. 5 CRM Public 200

No. 27 CRM Employer 100

No. 26 CRM Performance 100

TWO-YEAR QUARTERLY HIGH-LOW STOCK PRICES

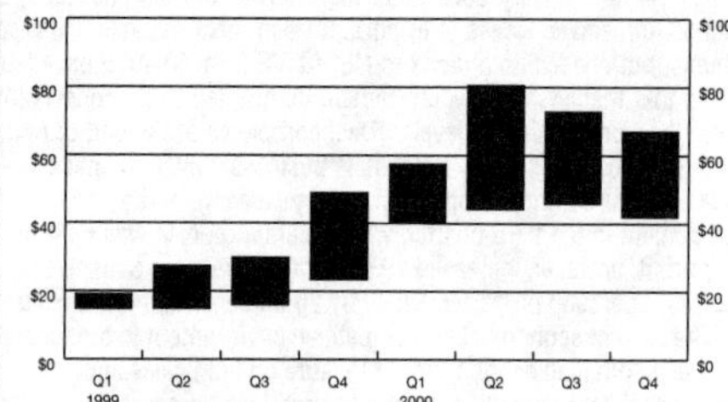

BigSky Transportation Company

1601 Aviation Place, Billings Logan International Airport, Billings, MT 59105
Tel: 406/245-9449 Fax: 406/259-8750 Web site: http://www.bigskyair.com

BigSky Transportation Co. (BigSky Transco), dba BigSky Airlines, operates as a regional air freight and passenger company serving nine Montana cities. Billings serves as the company's regional hub.

EARNINGS HISTORY

Year Ended Jun 30	Operating Revenue/Sales (dollars in thousands)	Net Earnings	Return on Revenue (percent)	Return on Equity	Net Earnings (dollars per share*)	Cash Dividend	Market Price Range
2000	21,926	(724)	(3.3)	NM	(0.58)	—	1.44–0.88
1999	15,915	(179)	(1.1)	(11.7)	(0.15)	—	2.25–1.44
1998	7,912	183	2.3	12.5	0.17	—	2.19–1.13
1997	4,871	198	4.1	18.4	0.19	—	1.31–1.06
1996	5,056	3	0.1	0.5	0.00	—	1.25–0.94

* Per-share amounts restated to reflect 1-for-5 reverse stock split effected Aug. 23, 1996.

BALANCE SHEET

Assets	06/30/00 (dollars in thousands)	06/30/99	Liabilities	06/30/00 (dollars in thousands)	06/30/99
Current (CAE 0 and 220)	3,391	2,747	Current (STD 1,435 and 1,157)	4,482	2,907
Property and equipment	3,002	2,703	Long-term debt	1,553	1,193
Deferred income taxes	365		Stockholders' equity*	804	1,527
Deposits	80	177	TOTAL	6,839	5,627
TOTAL	6,839	5,627			

* No par common; 20,000,000 authorized; 1,248,102 and 1,245,302 issued and outstanding, less 20,000 and 20,000 treasury shares.

OFFICERS

Jon Marchi
Chairman and Treasurer

Kim B. Champney
President and CEO

Craig Denney
EVP, Division Manager, and COO

Jack K. Daniels
Vice Chairman and Asst. Secretary

Stephen D. Huntington
Asst. Secretary

DIRECTORS

Jack K. Daniels
SerVair Accessories Inc. (retired)

Craig Denney

Stephen D. Huntington
Montana Technology Cos., Butte, MT

Jon Marchi
Marchi Angus Ranches, Polson, MT

Terry D. Marshall

Alan D. Nicholson
Nicholson Inc., Helena, MT

MAJOR SHAREHOLDERS

Derby West Corp. LLC, 27.7%
Sheridan, WY

Northern Rockies Venture Fund, 9.1%
Boulder, CO

H.V. Holman Ltd. Partnership, 8.7%
Las Vegas

Jon Marchi, 5.1%

All officers and directors as a group (6 persons), 15.4%

SIC CODE

4512 Air transportation, scheduled

4513 Air courier services

MISCELLANEOUS

TRANSFER AGENT AND REGISTAR:
Continental Stock Transfer & Trust Co., New York

TRADED: PSE

SYMBOL: BSA.P

STOCKHOLDERS: 1,117

EMPLOYEES: 243

PART TIME: 70

GENERAL COUNSEL:
Wright, Tolliver & Guthals P.C., Billings, MT

AUDITORS:
Eide Bailly LLP, Billings, MT

ANNUAL MEETING:
January

HUMAN RESOURCES:
Carla Tilton

PUB

Bio-Vascular Inc.

2575 University Ave., St. Paul, MN 55114
Tel: 651/603-3700 Fax: 651/642-9018 Web site: http://www.biovascular.com

Bio-Vascular Inc. develops, manufactures, and markets proprietary specialty medical products used primarily in thoracic, cardiac, neuro, vascular, and ophthalmic surgery. Bio-Vascular subsidiary Jerneen Micro Medical Technologies is a value-added manufacturer of precision components such as micro coils, wire forms, and spring components used in implantable defibrillation, intervention medicine, and other surgical applications within the medical device industry.

EARNINGS HISTORY

Year Ended Oct 31	Operating Revenue/Sales (dollars in thousands)	Net Earnings (dollars in thousands)	Return on Revenue (percent)	Return on Equity (percent)	Net Earnings (dollars per share)	Cash Dividend (dollars per share)	Market Price Range (dollars per share)
1999	18,904	(520)	(2.8)	(2.5)	(0.06)	—	4.38–2.25
1998 *	12,017	(483)	(4.0)	(2.2)	(0.05)	—	5.38–3.00
1997 †	9,694	(1,524)	(15.7)	(6.4)	(0.16)	—	7.75–3.75
1996 ¶	10,125	(1,178)	(11.6)	(3.3)	(0.12)	—	15.00–5.25
1995 #	10,426	2,186	21.0	6.2	0.27	—	18.00–4.63

* Results for 1998 include Jer-Neen Mfg. Co. from its July 31, 1998, date of purchase. Pro forma for full year: revenue $16.179 million; loss $0.561 million/($0.06).
† Income figures for 1997 include loss of $0.92 million/($0.10) on disposal of discontinued business.
¶ Revenue for 1996 was restated to segregate discontinued operations of Vital Images Inc. spin-off. Income figures include loss of $2.396 million/($0.25) on discontinued business and its disposal.
# Revenue figure for 1995 was restated and includes $1.5 million in license fees. Income figures include gain of $0.527 million/$0.06 from discontinued business.

BALANCE SHEET

Assets	10/31/99 (dollars in thousands)	10/31/98 (dollars in thousands)	Liabilities	10/31/99 (dollars in thousands)	10/31/98 (dollars in thousands)
Current (CAE 5,596 and 4,383)	12,000	13,883	Current (STD 369 and 616)	2,600	2,497
Equipment, leasehold improvements	4,936	4,354	Capital lease obligations	159	393
Intangibles	6,594	7,241	Other	527	662
Deferred income taxes	540	504	Stockholders' equity*	20,784	22,430
TOTAL	24,070	25,982	TOTAL	24,070	25,982

* $0.01 par common; 20,000,000 authorized; 8,960,633 and 9,317,183 issued and outstanding.

RECENT QUARTERS / **PRIOR-YEAR RESULTS**

	Quarter End	Revenue ($000)	Earnings ($000)	EPS ($)	Prior-Year Revenue ($000)	Prior-Year Earnings ($000)	Prior-Year EPS ($)
Q3	07/31/2000	6,354	402	0.05	5,169	42	0.00
Q2	04/30/2000	5,343	(38)	0.00	4,893	(202)	(0.02)
Q1	01/31/2000	4,382	(129)	(0.01)	3,829	(318)	(0.03)
Q4	10/31/99	5,012	(42)	0.00	4,068	(134)	(0.01)
	SUM	21,091	193	0.02	17,960	(612)	(0.07)

RECENT EVENTS

In **February 2000** the company introduced APEX Processing, a product enhancement establishing a new tissue-processing standard. APEX Processing, which had received 510(k) marketing clearance from the FDA and CE Mark registration in the European Union (EU), was to be available for the company's market-leading Tissue-Guard products, which are used to improve seals and strengthen sutures in a wide variety of surgical procedures. Bio-Vascular then received 510(k) marketing clearance from the FDA, and CE Mark registration in the European Union, for the use of Peri-Strips and Peri-Strips Dry to reinforce the gastric staple line in the bariatric surgical procedures of gastric bypass and gastric banding. In **March** Bio-Vascular gained exclusive U.S. distribution rights for a precision micro neuro dissection set manufactured by the Feather Safety Razor Co. of Japan. Study results presented at a recent Society for Clinical Vascular Surgery meeting showed that the use of Bio-Vascular's Vascu-Guard, a bovine pericardial surgical patch, in endarterectomy procedures resulted in significantly less bleeding in comparison to a Dacron patch. In **May** Bio-Vascular received favorable results from the first stage of a pre-clinical animal study for a urethral sling for use in the surgical treatment of stress urinary incontinence (SUI). In **July** Bio-Vascular completed animal studies of its urethral sling product for use in the surgical treatment of stress urinary incontinence (SUI). In the concluded studies, which compared Bio-Vascular's new remodelable tissue and a leading sling product, Bio-Vascular's remodelable tissue material demonstrated greater biocompatibility and lower levels of inflammation and fibrosis, results consistent with a lowered foreign-body reaction. Late in the month, the company submitted a 510(k) application to the FDA requesting marketing clearance for its urethral sling product. **July 31:** For the nine months, the company reported operating income of $296,000, compared to an operating loss of $709,000 for the same period in fiscal 1999. "Both business units—Branded Medical Devices and Jerneen's Contract Manufacturing and Custom Engineering unit—made strong contributions in the third quarter, with each unit achieving *continued on page 153*

OFFICERS

M. Karen Gilles
President and CEO

Fariborz Boor Boor
Pres./COO-Jerneen Micro Medical

David A. Buche
VP-Marketing/Sales

Mary L. Frick
VP-Regulatory/Quality/Clinical Affairs

Evan S. Johnston
VP-Operations

Connie L. Magnuson
VP-Finance, CFO, and Secretary

B. Nicholas Oray, Ph.D.
VP-Research/Development

James F. Pfau
Pres.-Jerneen Micro Medical

DIRECTORS

M. Karen Gilles

William Kobi
Acumen Healthcare Solutions Inc., Plymouth, MN

Richard W. Perkins
Perkins Capital Management Inc., Wayzata, MN

Anton R. Potami
William C. Norris Institute, Bloomington, MN

Timothy Scanlan
Scanlan Group of Cos., St. Paul

Edward E. Strickland
management consultant, Friday Harbor, WA

MAJOR SHAREHOLDERS

Perkins Capital Management Inc., 6.7%
Wayzata, MN

All officers and directors as a group (10 persons), 8.5%

SIC CODE

3841 Surgical and medical instruments

MISCELLANEOUS

TRANSFER AGENT AND REGISTAR:
American Stock Transfer & Trust Co., New York

TRADED: Nasdaq National Market

SYMBOL: BVAS

STOCKHOLDERS: 1,100

EMPLOYEES: 220

GENERAL COUNSEL:
Oppenheimer Wolff & Donnelly LLP, Minneapolis

AUDITORS:
PricewaterhouseCoopers LLP, Minneapolis

INC: MN-1985

ANNUAL MEETING: February

PUBLIC RELATIONS COUNSEL:
Swenson/Falker Associates Inc.

RANKINGS

No. 151 CRM Public 200

SUBSIDIARIES, DIVISIONS, AFFILIATES

Jerneen Micro Medical Technologies

TWO-YEAR QUARTERLY HIGH-LOW STOCK PRICES

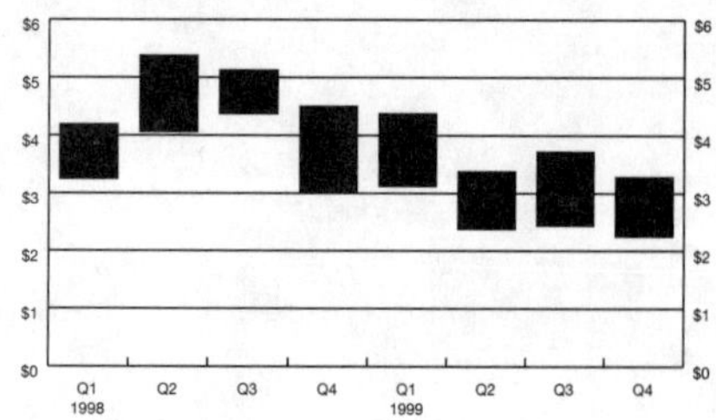

Black Hills Corporation

625 Ninth St., P.O. Box 1400, Rapid City, SD 57709
Tel: 605/721-1700 Fax: 605/721-2597 Web site: http://www.blackhillscorp.com

Black Hills Corp. is an energy and communication company that supplies regulated electric utility service to a 9,300-square-mile area in western South Dakota, northeastern Wyoming, and southeastern Montana; conducts non-regulated energy operations including 1) the mining and sale of coal from its mine located near Gillette, Wyoming; 2) the production, exploration, and operation of oil and gas interests located in the Rocky Mountain region, Texas, and California; and 3) marketing of coal, natural gas, crude oil, electricity, and related services to customers in the Rocky Mountain region, Gulf Coast, Midwest and East Coast markets; and markets communication services in the Black Hills region and develops and markets internally generated computer software.

EARNINGS HISTORY

Year Ended Dec 31	Operating Revenue/Sales (dollars in thousands)	Net Earnings	Return on Revenue (percent)	Return on Equity	Net Earnings (dollars per share*)	Cash Dividend	Market Price Range
1999	791,875	37,067	4.7	17.1	1.73	1.04	26.50–20.31
1998 †	679,254	25,808	3.8	12.5	1.19	1.00	27.94–20.69
1997 ¶	313,662	32,359	10.3	15.8	1.49	0.95	24.29–17.50
1996 #	162,588	30,252	18.6	15.7	1.40	0.92	19.17–15.17
1995	150,112	25,590	17.0	14.0	1.18	0.89	17.42–13.17

* Per-share amounts restated to reflect 3-for-2 stock split effected March 10, 1998.
† Income figures for 1998 include a noncash ceiling test write-down of $13,546,000 pretax, $8,805,000/($0.41) after-tax.
¶ Figures for 1997 include results of Black Hills Energy Resources Inc. from its July 1997 acquisition. Pro forma for full year: revenue $506,188,000; income $33,010,000/$1.52.
# Pro forma for Black Hills Energy: revenue $391,618,000; income $32,771,000/$1.51.

BALANCE SHEET

Assets	12/31/99 (dollars in thousands)	12/31/98
Current (CAE 16,482 and 14,764)	181,199	140,480
Property and equipment	464,189	389,607
Federal income taxes	11,472	12,347
Regulatory asset	3,944	3,978
Other deferred charges	14,002	13,005
TOTAL	674,806	559,417

Liabilities	12/31/99 (dollars in thousands)	12/31/98
Current (STD 98,909 and 6,420)	205,352	102,582
Federal income taxes	59,140	55,107
Investment tax credits	3,022	3,514
Reclamation costs	17,315	17,000
Regulatory liability	5,179	5,661
Other deferred credits	7,492	6,857
Long-term debt	160,700	162,030
Stockholders' equity*	216,606	206,666
TOTAL	674,806	559,417

* $1 par common; 50,000,000 authorized; 21,739,030 and 21,719,465 issued and outstanding.

RECENT QUARTERS / **PRIOR-YEAR RESULTS**

	Quarter End	Revenue ($000)	Earnings ($000)	EPS ($)	Prior-Year Revenue ($000)	Prior-Year Earnings ($000)	Prior-Year EPS ($)
Q3	09/30/2000	453,231	16,322	0.71	219,779	9,725	0.45
Q2	06/30/2000	336,978	8,061	0.38	186,195	7,763	0.36
Q1	03/31/2000	247,959	9,061	0.42	168,201	9,035	0.42
Q4	12/31/99	217,700	10,544	0.49	193,925	151	0.01
	SUM	1,255,868	43,988	2.01	768,100	26,674	1.24

PRIOR YEAR: Q4 earnings include a noncash ceiling test write-down of $8,805,000/($0.41).

RECENT EVENTS

In **January 2000** Black Hills Energy Resources sold its Pennsylvania-based natural gas marketing operations to Conectiv Energy Supply Inc. Equilon Pipeline Co. LLC, along with Black Hills Energy Resources Inc. and Black Hills Millennium Pipeline Inc., affiliates of Black Hills Corp.'s Nonregulated Energy Group, formed Millennium Pipeline Co. L.P., a joint venture, to transport crude oil from the Beaumont, Texas, area to connecting carriers in Longview, Texas. The company agreed to acquire Indeck Capital Inc., an independent power company based in Wheeling, Ill., that was formed in 1994 to own and operate independent power facilities, directly or indirectly, through independent power investment funds. And it also was to acquire an interest in Indeck North American Power Fund L.P. and Indeck North American Power Partners L.P., both independent power investment funds, in a continuing effort to expand its independent energy business unit. [Deal completed in July.] Subsidiary Black Hills FiberCom was providing bundled video entertainment services, high-speed Internet, local

continued on page 153

OFFICERS

Daniel P. Landguth
Chairman and CEO

Roxann R. Basham
VP-Finance, Secretary/Treasurer

David R. Emery
VP-Fuel Resources

Gary R. Fish
Pres./COO-Non-Regulated Business Group

Everett E. Hoyt
Pres./COO-Regulated Business Group

James M. Mattern
SVP-Administration, Asst. to the CEO

Thomas M. Ohlmacher
VP-Power Supply

Ronald D. Schnaible
SVP and Gen. Mgr.-Telecommunications

Mark T. Thies
SVP and CFO

Kyle D. White
VP-Marketing/Regulatory Affairs

DIRECTORS

Adil M. Ameer
Rapid City Regional Hospital, Rapid City, SD

Bruce B. Brundage
Brundage & Co., Denver

David C. Ebertz
Barlow Agency Inc., Gillette, WY

John R. Howard
Industrial Products Inc., Rapid City, SD

Everett E. Hoyt

Kay S. Jorgensen
Jorgensen-Thompson Creative Broadcast Services, Spearfish, SD

Daniel P. Landguth

David S. Maney
Worldbridge Broadband Services, Golden, CO

Thomas J. Zeller
RE/SPEC Inc., Rapid City, SD

MAJOR SHAREHOLDERS

All officers and directors as a group (12 persons), 1.3%

SIC CODE

1221 Bituminous coal and lignite, surface
1311 Crude petroleum and natural gas
4911 Electric services

MISCELLANEOUS

TRANSFER AGENT AND REGISTAR:
Wells Fargo Bank Minnesota N.A., South St. Paul, MN

TRADED: NYSE

SYMBOL: BKH

STOCKHOLDERS: 6,315

EMPLOYEES: 300

GENERAL COUNSEL:
Morrill Thomas Nooney & Braun LLP, Rapid City, SD

AUDITORS:
Arthur Andersen LLP, Minneapolis

INC: SD-1941

ANNUAL MEETING: May

INVESTOR RELATIONS:
Roxann Basham

PUBLIC/GOV'T RELATIONS: Barb Thirstrup

SUBSIDIARIES, DIVISIONS, AFFILIATES

Black Hills Power and Light Co.

Wyodak Resources Development Corp.

Black Hills Exploration and Production Inc.

Landrica Development Co.

Black Hills Generation Inc.

DAKSOFT Inc.

Enserco Energy Inc.

Black Hills Energy Resources Inc.

Black Hills Capital Group

Black Hills FiberCom Inc.

Black Hills Coal Network Inc.

TWO-YEAR QUARTERLY HIGH-LOW STOCK PRICES

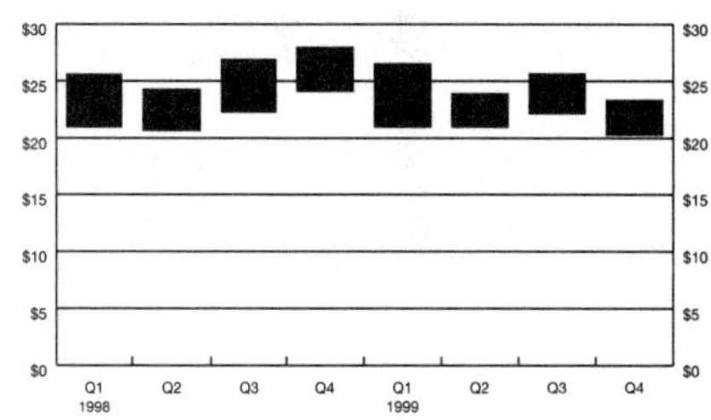

PUB

PUB

Broadview Media Inc.

4455 W. 77th St., Edina, MN 55435
Tel: 952/835-4455 Fax: 952/835-0971 Web site: http://www.broadviewmedia.com

Broadview Media Inc., formerly Northwest Teleproductions Inc., is a full-service videotape and film production company that provides and markets such services as television spot commercials, direct response commercials, and infomercials for advertisers and their agencies; cable broadcast program development and production; corporate communication for business and industry; creation and production of radio and television spot announcements for the Department of Defense; teleconferencing and telemeetings; and still and animated computer-aided graphic design. The company also provides production services to other producers for film-to-tape transfer; digital off-line and on-line editing and interformat editing; and duplication of commercials and programs in a wide variety of formats. The company owns production and postproduction facilities in Minneapolis, Dallas, and Chicago.

EARNINGS HISTORY

Year Ended Mar 31	Operating Revenue/Sales (dollars in thousands)	Net Earnings (dollars in thousands)	Return on Revenue (percent)	Return on Equity (percent)	Net Earnings (dollars per share)	Cash Dividend (dollars per share)	Market Price Range (dollars per share)
2000 *	9,942	442	4.4	29.6	0.33	—	2.28–0.25
1999	10,663	(157)	(1.5)	(14.9)	(0.12)	—	1.31–0.26
1998 †	11,192	(1,354)	(12.1)	NM	(1.00)	—	4.00–1.00
1997 ¶	11,853	(1,456)	(12.3)	(56.8)	(1.07)	—	4.50–1.38
1996 #	12,509	(2,416)	(19.3)	(60.1)	(1.73)	—	4.25–1.88

* Income figures for 2000 include pretax loss ($59,958) from severance and related charges.
† Income figures for 1998 include pretax loss ($38,000) from severance and other charges.
¶ Income figures for 1997 include pretax loss ($161,834) from severance and other charges.
# Income figures for 1996 include goodwill impairment charge ($1,060,330); cost of litigation and settlement ($100,000); and severance and other charges ($443,000).

BALANCE SHEET

Assets	03/31/00 (dollars in thousands)	03/31/99	Liabilities	03/31/00 (dollars in thousands)	03/31/99
Current (CAE 1,132 and 316)	3,131	2,970	Current (STD 397 and 670)	2,602	3,056
Property, plant, and equipment	1,965	2,877	Long-term debt and capital leases	1,053	1,882
Other	128	263	Deferred gain, building sale	78	123
TOTAL	5,225	6,110	Stockholders' equity*	1,492	1,050
			TOTAL	5,225	6,110

* $0.01 par common; 10,000,000 authorized; 1,357,759 and 1,356,425 issued and outstanding.

RECENT QUARTERS / PRIOR-YEAR RESULTS

	Quarter End	Revenue ($000)	Earnings ($000)	EPS ($)	Prior-Year Revenue ($000)	Prior-Year Earnings ($000)	Prior-Year EPS ($)
Q1	06/30/2000	2,024	76	0.06	2,693	61	0.04
Q4	03/31/2000	2,433	79	0.06	2,614	(132)	(0.10)
Q3	12/31/99	2,266	339	0.25	3,018	105	0.08
Q2	09/30/99	2,550	(37)	(0.03)	2,643	(71)	(0.05)
	SUM	9,272	457	0.34	10,968	(38)	(0.03)

RECENT EVENTS

In **April 2000** Northwest Teleproductions Inc. changed its name to Broadview Media Inc. The new name reflects the diversity of services that the company provides to the marketplace. "This new name best describes our business, our philosophy, and our marketplace. As our traditional markets have changed, we have adapted to the change by reinventing ourselves and our brand image. Our services have evolved beyond those of a video and film production company. We provide content and program development for cable and network television; we provide full service creative capabilities for our client's marketing and advertising needs; we have developed a line of educational and self help products; and we are developing an Internet initiative. Along with operating two production facilities, one in Minneapolis and one in Chicago, the company can offer clients a full service, turn key solution for their needs. These endeavors go beyond the capabilities of traditional production companies and will position us for growth," stated CEO Staden. Later in April, the company secured a new credit facility with Fidelity Bank in Edina, Minn., replacing the arrangements that the company had with Bank of America. The new agreement consisted of a term loan of $400,000 to be amortized over 48 months; a line of credit for equipment purchases of up to $400,000; and a revolving line of credit, secured by the company's accounts receivable, of up to $1,000,000—at prime-plus-1/2%. In **June** Broadview and Northwest Airlines introduced "Fearless Flying," an at-home version of Northwest's successful WINGS seminars for anxious flyers."This unique partnership with Northwest Airlines has been a great opportunity for Broadview Media," said Staden. "By creating a video version of Northwest's WINGS program, we hope to reach the estimated 30 to 50 million people in the U.S. alone who are afraid to fly."

OFFICERS

John C. McGrath
Chairman

John G. Lindell
Vice Chairman

Phillip A. Staden
President and CEO

David S. Johnson
VP

Nancy L. Reid
VP-Sales/Marketing

Michael D. Smith
VP-Programming

John Shives
Gen. Mgr.-Southwest Teleproductions

DIRECTORS

Dean Bachelor
Platinum Group

James S. Fish
University of St. Thomas, St. Paul

Charles D. Haworth
Haworth Group (retired)

Ronald V. Kelly
Pentair Inc., Roseville, MN

John G. Lindell

Steve Lose
Scitex Digital Video Inc.

John C. McGrath
Cutters Inc.

Gerald W. Simonson
Omnetics Connector Corp., Minneapolis

Philip A. Staden

MAJOR SHAREHOLDERS

John C. Lorentzen and Penney L. Fillmer, 9.9%
Wheaton, IL

McDonald & Co. Securities, 7.7%
Cleveland

Dean and Kathy L. Bachelor, 7.2%

James H. Binger Revocable Trust, 6.8%
Minneapolis

John G. Lindell, 5.5%
Green Valley, AZ

Phillip A. Staden, 5.3%
Winfield, IL

All officers and directors as a group (8 persons), 20.3%

SIC CODE

7812 Motion picture and video production

MISCELLANEOUS

TRANSFER AGENT AND REGISTAR:
American Stock Transfer & Trust Co., New York

TRADED: OTC Bulletin Board

SYMBOL: BDVM

STOCKHOLDERS: 491

EMPLOYEES: 52

GENERAL COUNSEL:
Fredrikson & Byron P.A., Minneapolis

AUDITORS:
Boulay, Heutmaker, Zibell & Co. PLLP, Minneapolis

INC: MN-1969

ANNUAL MEETING: August

INVESTOR RELATIONS: John G. Lindell

RANKINGS

No. 184 CRM Public 200

SUBSIDIARIES, DIVISIONS, AFFILIATES

Northwest Teleproductions/Chicago Inc.
142 E. Ontario St.
Chicago, IL 60611
Nancy Reid

Southwest Teleproductions Inc.
2649 Tarna Dr.
Dallas, TX 75229
John Shives

TWO-YEAR QUARTERLY HIGH-LOW STOCK PRICES

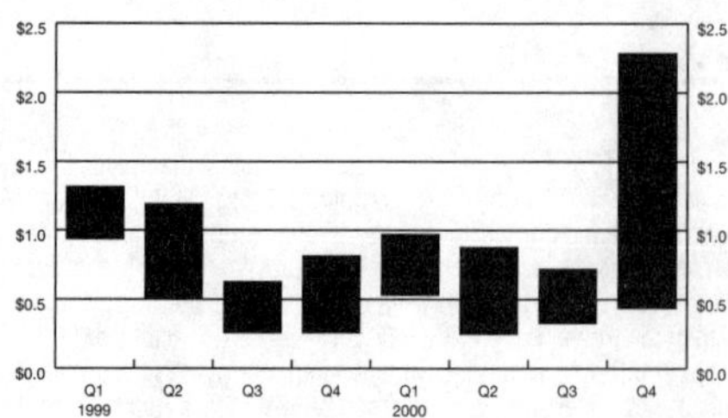

Buca Inc.

1300 Nicollet Mall, Suite 3043, Minneapolis, MN 55403
Tel: 612/288-2382 Fax: 612/827-6446

Buca Inc. owns a collection of neighborhood restaurants called Buca di Beppo that serve immigrant Southern Italian cuisine, family-style with oversized portions, in a lively atmosphere. The original Buca di Beppo opened at 12th Street and Harmon Place in downtown Minneapolis in July 1993.

EARNINGS HISTORY

Year Ended Dec	Operating Revenue/Sales (dollars in thousands)	Net Earnings	Return on Revenue (percent)	Return on Equity	Net Earnings (dollars per share*)	Cash Dividend	Market Price Range
1999 †	71,528	1,424	2.0	1.1	0.08	—	20.13–8.88
1998 ¶	38,483	(2,946)	(7.7)	NM	(2.04)	—	
1997 #	19,030	(3,319)	(17.4)	NM	(2.13)	—	
1996	11,316	(1,113)	(9.8)	NM	(1.96)	—	
1995	7,142	37	0.5	NM	0.02	—	

* Trading began April 20, 1999.
† Income figures for 1999 include pretax charge of $954,000 for subordinated debt conversion costs; and extraordinary loss of $927,000/($0.11) on extinguishment of debt.
¶ Pro forma 1998 net loss per share: ($0.42).
# Income figures for 1997 include loss of $351,000/($0.14), cumulative effect of accounting change.

BALANCE SHEET

Assets	12/26/99 (dollars in thousands)	12/27/98	Liabilities	12/26/99 (dollars in thousands)	12/27/98
Current (CAE 1,726 and 6,576)	7,573	9,256	Current (STD 50 and 205)	11,967	6,100
Property and equipment	63,763	27,697	Long-term debt	1,688	7,661
Other	4,609	607	Other	581	366
TOTAL	75,945	37,560	Redeemable stock		36,973
			Stockholders' equity*	61,709	(13,540)
			TOTAL	75,945	37,560

* $0.01 par common; 20,000,000 authorized; 10,810,295 and 1,918,056 issued and outstanding.

RECENT QUARTERS / **PRIOR-YEAR RESULTS**

	Quarter End	Revenue ($000)	Earnings ($000)	EPS ($)	Prior-Year Revenue ($000)	Prior-Year Earnings ($000)	Prior-Year EPS ($)
Q3	09/24/2000	33,438	1,682	0.12	18,641	234	0.02
Q2	06/25/2000	29,598	1,373	0.10	15,834	(1,351)	(0.18)
Q1	03/26/2000	26,924	878	0.08	14,173	(1,135)	(0.67)
Q4	12/26/99	22,880	3,676	0.34	12,133	(1,214)	(0.75)
	SUM	112,840	7,609	0.64	60,781	(3,466)	(1.58)

PRIOR YEAR: Q2 earnings include pretax subordinated-debt conversion costs of $954,000; and a loss of $231,000/($0.03) on early debt extinguishment. Q1 earnings include loss of $1,313,000/($0.52) on extinguishment of debt.

RECENT EVENTS

In **March 2000** the company announced plans to open 17 new restaurants in 2000, an increase from the previous projection of 15. The company also announced that it had executed a term sheet with its banking partners—U.S. Bank, Bank of America, and Fleet National Bank—to increase its credit facilities from $15 million to $20 million. Buca also filed a registration statement with the SEC for a secondary public offering. The 3,033,699 shares of common stock (3,000,000 by the company, the rest by certain selling shareholders) were priced at $11.625 a share. The net proceeds of about $35 million, raised during one of the worst weeks in stock market history, were to be used to fund development of new BUCA di BEPPO restaurants, to repay indebtedness, and for other general corporate purposes. In **May** Buca restructured its restaurant development function—separating the site selection and construction operations, to allow the real estate function to focus exclusively on finding optimum sites for new BUCA di BEPPO restaurants. In **August** Buca opened the company's 50th restaurant, which is located in Santa Monica, Calif., the 16th new restaurant of 2000. The 17th and final one was scheduled to open on Oct. 3 in Irvine, Calif. **Sept. 24**: CEO Micatrotto commented, "Operating margins in the quarter increased to 16.9 percent of sales from 14.8 percent in the third quarter of last year. Our ability to negotiate stronger purchasing contracts in a number of key products, including soft drinks, pasta and bulk tomatoes, has kept product costs down. Labor and direct and occupancy costs also declined as a percent of sales due to greater fixed-cost leverage at higher sales volumes, particularly at our new restaurants opened during the third quarter."

OFFICERS

Joseph P. Micatrotto
Chairman, President, and CEO

Leonard A. Ghilani
COO

Greg A. Gadel
CFO, Treasurer, and Secretary

DIRECTORS

Don W. Hays
Parasole

Joseph P. Micatrotto

Peter J. Mihajlov
Parasole

Philip A. Roberts

John P. Whaley
Norwest Equity Partners

David Yarnell
Consumer Venture Partners

Paul Zepf
Centre Partners Management LLC

MAJOR SHAREHOLDERS

Paul Zepf/Centre Capital Investors II L.P., 13.3%
New York

John P. Whaley/Norwest Equity Partners V L.P., 13.1%
Minneapolis

Philip A. Roberts, 9.5%
Minneapolis

Don W. Hays, 8.9%
Minneapolis

Peter J. Mihajlov, 8.8%
Minneapolis

Arbor Capital Management LLC, 6.6%
Minneapolis

Lord, Abett & Co., 6.5%
Jersey City, NJ

All officers and directors as a group (9 persons), 49.2%

SIC CODE

5812 Eating places

MISCELLANEOUS

TRANSFER AGENT AND REGISTAR:
Wells Fargo Bank Minnesota N.A.,
South St. Paul, MN

TRADED: Nasdaq National Market

SYMBOL: BUCA

STOCKHOLDERS: 170

EMPLOYEES: 4,000

GENERAL COUNSEL:
Faegre & Benson PLLP,
Minneapolis

AUDITORS:
Deloitte & Touche LLP,
Minneapolis

INC: MN-1994

FOUNDED: 1993

RANKINGS

No. 100 CRM Public 200

No. 9 CRM Performance 100

ADC Telecommunications Inc.

continued from page 121 data transmission services. ADC was planning to utilize Texas Instruments' TNETD4000C asymmetric digital subscriber line (ADSL) solution, the industry's first production quad-port chipset, in the company's recently announced iAN platform. ADC was named for the first time in IndustryWeek's listing of The World's 1,000 Largest Manufacturing Companies. On **June 9**, ADC and Centigram Communications Corp. (Nasdaq: CGRM, www.centigram.com), a leading global provider of unified communications, Internet-enabled call management, and wireless access protocol (WAP)-based messaging solutions for communications service providers, reached an agreement for the acquisition of $82 million-revenue Centigram, San Jose, Calif., by ADC for $199 million—$163 million in cash to Centigram stockholders, or $26.38 per share, a 19.9 percent premium; and $36 million in cash—in a purchase transaction. (Service providers worldwide incorporate an array of enhanced services such as unified messaging, paging, fax, and voicemail in order to gain additional revenue and to differentiate service offerings to their customers. In the era of the Internet and broadband communications, these voice, text, and multimedia services can be delivered over mobile phones, PCs, and other devices.) With 2,500 systems installed worldwide at more than 250 service providers, Centigram provides a readily available installed base and established customer relationships for the overlay of ADC's Singularit.e suite of OSS applications and ADC's NewNet line of enhanced services solutions. [Deal completed in July; additional payment from escrow completed Sept. 1.] ADC contracted to supply Metrica/NPR to Amena, a Spanish GSM 1800 operator. Business Week ranked ADC No. 41 on its Information Technology 100, with the comment: "This once-dull provider of jacks and plugs is now hip-deep in the fast-paced wireless and Internet markets." An alliance was established with COLO.COM (www.colo.com) to provide ADC's industry leading connectivity products to COLO.COM's carrier-neutral co-location facilities. ADC's Enterprise Category 6 connecting hardware successfully passed the full Category 6 qualification test program for electrical performance, conducted by 3P Third Party, an independent testing company based in Denmark. ADC was the only manufacturer that had been able to provide independent proof of connecting hardware compliance with the proposed Category 6 transmission standards. ADC added Metrica/Chartis, a geographic information systems (GIS)-based supervision and optimization tool, to its Singularit.e suite of OSS software solutions and consultancy services. ADC announced a new program to help emerging integrated communications providers (ICPs) with limited resources rapidly deploy Singl.eView. ADC and Spark Interactive, a leading distributor of digitally encoded content for the interactive home and business marketplace, formed a unique alliance to bundle transport infrastructure with digital content, thereby providing a turnkey opportunity for service provider customers to rapidly deploy services and reap additional revenue. In **July** ADC announced a strategic alliance with NightFire Software Inc., pioneer of e-infrastructure solutions for broadband service deployment, to provide digital subscriber line (DSL) service providers with a quick way to provision and bill for services. ADC contracted to provide its Metrica/NPR network performance solution to Chilean PCS operator Smartcom. ADC signed a global framework agreement with Compaq covering the service-assurance elements of the Singularit.e suite of OSS solutions. ADC and Austar United Communications, Australia's largest pay TV operator, announced a strategic program to develop and deploy one of the largest MMDS broadband wireless systems to date in the world. Interoperability was successfully demonstrated between ADC's recently announced iAN platform and the SpeedStream USB modem from Dallas-based Efficient Networks. An alliance was formed with North Texas Public Broadcasting Inc., Dallas, to test ADC's patent-pending Bandwidth Enhancement Technology (BET) on the organization's digital broadcast channel KERA-DT. ADC Ventures, the investment arm of ADC, announced an investment in Northstar Photonics, a start-up company focused on the development of next-generation, laser-based optical devices. ADC's NewNet CALEAserver platform was selected by Siemens Information and Communication Networks Inc., Boca Raton, Fla., as the preferred law enforcement intercept delivery solution to be introduced to its EWSD customers. PT Excelcomindo Pratama, Indonesia's third-largest and fastest-growing GSM operator, selected ADC's Interconnect Billing Platform (IBP) to manage its national and international interconnect agreements. The company said that it was in "very preliminary" talks to buy an unspecified company. **July 31**: Excluding acquisitions, ADC's third-quarter sales increased 71 percent to an all-time high of $827 million, reflecting 120 percent growth in Broadband Connectivity sales combined with 19 percent growth in Broadband Access and Transport sales and 35 percent growth in Integrated Solutions sales. International sales increased 59 percent to an all-time high of $191 million. In the seven-month period ended July 31, ADC was the fourth-best-performing stock in the S&P 500 Index, growing 131 percent to $41.94. In **August** the company's Visionary DT digital television transmitter was chosen as the best transmitter at BroadcastAsia 2000. ADC extended its contract with Turk Telekom of Turkey for supply of the BroadAccess Multiservice Access Platform (MAP). The company was planning to sell off some of its $1.5 billion stock portfolio to pay for a substantial boost in manufacturing capacity (3 million square feet worldwide) and to restore capital drained by recent spending on operations. ADC was named one of the 10 Great Places to Work in Minnesota in the August issue of Corporate Report magazine. ADC formed the Advanced Photonics Integration Center to develop customized, integrated, and fully packaged photonics solutions for ADC's customers, including original equipment manufacturers (OEMs). ADC agreed to acquire the telecommunications industry telecom systems integration business of France Electronique, a European supplier of wireless and wireline services. At month's end, Cadogan said that the company was expecting sales for the quarter ending Oct. 31 to rise by 40 percent to 50 percent from the year before, due in part to a rush by phone companies to expand their networks and cope with mounting Internet traffic. In **September** ADC said that, through its recent acquisition of IBSEN Micro Structures A/S, it had optimized a manufacturing process where very small nanometer structures can be transferred and replicated in high-volume manufacturing setups. Target application of the Near Field Holography (NFH) process was within the optical industry, especially in the telecom industry, where the need for integrated optical circuits such as distributed feedback (DFB) lasers and other grating-based integrated components was growing rapidly. ADC announced an alliance with Harris Corp.'s Network Support Division, which was to become an OEM and systems integrator for ADC's industry-leading Metrica family of network performance management products. ADC signed a new contract to allow Sonda S.A. (www.sonda.com) to distribute ADC's NewNet SMserver(TM) technology and other leading messaging and infrastructure applications to regional wireless network operators in Latin America. ADC acquired Computer Telecom Installations Ltd. (CTi), a British company offering installation, commissioning, integration, and maintenance of telecommunications networks and equipment. ADC announced the signing of a $10 million contract extension for ADC's Axity Broadband Wireless Access System in Saskatoon, Saskatchewan. InformationWeek magazine named ADC as one of the nation's most innovative users of information technology in its 12th annual InformationWeek 500 issue. ADC agreed to acquire 200-employee Broadband Access Systems (www.basystems.com), Westborough, Mass., a leading supplier of next-generation, Internet Protocol (IP) access platforms, for what was then valued at $2.25 billion in stock. Broadband Access Systems' award-winning IP access platform allows communications service providers to deliver high-performance Internet access and IP-based voice services to consumers and businesses. "The whole world is moving toward networking based on IP, and Broadband Access Systems is an early player in that market," said Cadogan. [Deal close in September; the 66 million shares, at Sept. 28 closing price of $27.81 per share, were valued at $1.84 billion.] ADC added extensive e-commerce capabilities to its Web site. The company opened its new manufacturing facility in Nanjing, China, which was to serve as the technology development and product manufacturing center for ADC's Broadband Connectivity Group, and to manufacture a range of fiber optic distribution systems, fiber optic components, and RF components and subsystems for the Chinese and Far East regional markets. ADC announced the availability of the Digivance Indoor Coverage Solution (ICS), an all-digital distributed antenna system (DAS) that transports RF signals digitally within or between buildings. ADC's NewNet OTAserver TDMA application was approved through the Nortel Networks Wireless Interoperability Testing program, gaining the Nortel Networks Compatible Product stamp of approval. U.S. Bancorp Piper Jaffray, in its monthly commentary, reiterated its STRONG BUY and raised its price target from $55 to $72. ADC unveiled a new range of Internet protocol (IP) and self-care capabilities for Singl.eView, its real-time convergent billing and integrated customer management system. ACOM Comunicacoes, Brazil's first digital broadband fixed wireless operator, purchased ADC's MMDS solution for a multicity deployment of wireless services. In **October** ADC introduced EasyAdmin Web, a suite of self-administration tools that telecommunications subscribers can use to manage their phone and Internet services via the Web. ADC unveiled a new version of its Convergent Billing Platform (CBP) that vastly improves its integration into a greater number of complex operational support systems (OSSs). ADC announced a $4.5 million contract with Companhia Riograndense de Telecomunicacoes (CRT), a leading telecommunications provider in Brazil, for the supply and installation of BroadAccess Multiservice Access Platforms. ADC agreed to provide its Metrica service assurance solution, the core element of ADC's Singularit.e suite, to Belgian operator KPN Orange. ADC agreed to provide Metrica/NPR to Philippine operator SMART. ADC signed a three-year contract with an estimated worth of $300 million to supply its complete range of Hybrid Fiber Coax (HFC) network equipment and services to Everest Connections, a St. Louis-based broadband cable network builder and alternative services provider. ADC and MEMSCAP Inc., a leading commercial provider of telecommunications MEMS (Micro-Electro-Mechanical Systems) components, agreed to jointly develop a family of MEMS-based optical communications components for a number of applications, including optical switching. Russian communications carrier COMCOR chose to deploy ADC's DV6000 digital and Optiworx analog fiber transmission systems, a $3 million purchase, in order to restore video services in the city of Moscow as quickly as possible. ADC signed a multiyear supplier agreement with MGTS (Moscow city network Public Operator), the largest operator of fixed telecom networks in Russia, for supplying the BroadAccess Multiservice Access Platform. Broadband services provider Cypress Communications (Nasdaq: CYCO), Atlanta, and Pak Telecom Mobile Ltd. (Ufone), Pakistan's newest GSM provider, both selected Singl.eView, ADC's real-time convergent billing platform. An industry-unique performance benchmark of Singl.eView—simulating a sophisticated integrated communications provider (ICP) providing service to medium-sized business customers—demonstrated Singl.eView's performance characteristics, with rating throughput in excess of 6.3 million EDRs (Event Detail Records) per hour. In a second test, simulating a high-volume, consumer wireless solution, Singl.eView supported more than 1 million subscribers, with rating throughput in excess of 15 million EDRs per hour. **Oct. 31:** Fourth-quarter sales exceeded $1 billion. In **November** ADC and The Management Network Group Inc. (Nasdaq:TMNG), a leading provider of management consulting services to the global telecommunications industry, announced a nonexclusive strategic alliance to provide leading-edge OSS solutions to ICPs (integrated communications providers) worldwide.

Aetrium Inc.

continued from page 126 conductive temperature control for high-volume production IC test handling applications. Aetrium also introduced the SC Series of Process Integrated Small Component IC Test Handlers, as well as new IC test handlers for the new generation MLF, Micro Lead Frame, SON, and QFN device packages. **Sept. 30**: "For the second consecutive quarter, bookings exceeded shipments," said CEO Levesque. "Of particular note is continued strong order rates for our newest generation reliability tester for copper technology that resulted in another record bookings quarter for our Reliability Test Products division and the addition of two more major new customers to our growing list of competitive wins."

Allete

continued from page 128 ADESA auctions climbed 13 percent. Growth through acquisitions, higher consumption, and regulatory relief helped water services boost its net income by 63 percent. "Electric operations had another solid year," CEO Russell said. "Net income, however, was down by $2.4 million due to a one-time property tax levy of $2 million on an industrial development project and regulatory denial of recovery of $2.2 million in lost margins related to conservation programs." While real estate performance was steady, net income from the investments segment decreased $2.8 million, reflecting lower portfolio returns. In **January 2000** Minnesota Power and LTV Steel Mining Co. agreed to extend until Oct. 31, 2005, their electric service and interconnection and power purchase agreements. In **February** ADESA Corp. was acquiring the Mission City Auto Auction in San Diego and nearing completion of new auction facilities in Los Angeles; Concord, Mass.; and Calgary, Alberta. Minnesota Power, Lakehead Pipe Line Partners L.P. (NYSE: LHP), and Enbridge Pipelines Inc. (Nasdaq: ENBRF) signed an agreement under which the pipeline companies could reduce electricity use during periods of high electric prices or demand, releasing energy to be marketed to other power buyers. The agreement was to run from Jan. 1, 2000, through Dec. 31, 2001. In **March** Minnesota Power announced plans to offer electric customers the opportunity to buy 100-kilowatt-hour blocks of renewable wind power by subscription. (Under terms of a 15-year agreement with Great River Energy, Minnesota Power will purchase half the output from three new wind generators to be installed at Great River Energy's existing Chandler Hills Wind Farm in southwestern Minnesota.) In **May** Minnesota Power and Potlatch Corp. (NYSE: PCH) agreed to install a 24-megawatt turbine generator at the Potlatch facility in Cloquet. Minnesota Power's nonregulated electric business was to own the turbine generator, with Potlatch operating and maintaining the unit. Through a process called cogeneration, steam used for industrial processes was to be used to produce electricity, achieving energy efficiency greater than 80 percent—more than twice the efficiency of traditional power sources. An environmentally friendly mix of wood wastes and natural gas was to fuel the process. MP Telecom announced plans to offer high-speed Digital Subscriber Line (DSL) Internet access to business customers in the Duluth area. In **June** ADESA Canada acquired the remaining 27 percent of Impact Auto Auctions, Mississauga, Ontario, Canada's largest national salvage auction chain, with 11 sites in six provinces; and $68 million-revenue Canadian Auction Group, a wholesale auto remarketing company with 13 auction sites and dealer financing operations located across Canada. The acquisitions were funded by Minnesota Power's investment portfolio and the recent sale of 4.7 million shares of ACE Ltd. (NYSE: ACL) for $127 million. ADESA then signed a letter of intent to buy eight ADT Automotive auctions and one Manheim auction from Manheim Auctions, which had collectively sold 400,000 vehicles and generated $130 million in revenue over the past 12 months. **June 30:** For the first six months of the year, the company got more earnings from its auto auction business than from its electric utility operations. In **July** the company filed to sell up to $400 million of first mortgage bonds and other debt securities, expecting to use the proceeds for acquisitions, to repay short-term debt, to redeem or repurchase long-term debt, and for general purposes. Then it called for redemption of all 113,358 outstanding shares of its 5% Preferred Stock at $102.50 per share plus accrued and unpaid dividends of 75 cents per share. In the August issue of The Wall Street Transcript, David Schanzer, vice president-Research at Janney Montgomery Scott, commented, "I actually only have one buy in my universe, and that is Minnesota Power. MPL is more of a utility conglomerate than anything else, with a water and electric play, along with the dominant automotive services business." ADESA Corp. agreed to acquire the Mid-Ark Auto Auction in Little Rock, Ark., and Central Arkansas Auto Auction in Beebe, Ark. from Kelton Keathley. Together, the Mid-Ark and Central Arkansas auctions, ADESA's 56th and 57th North American auctions, sold more than 40,000 cars last year. The company was named one of the 10 Great Places to Work in Minnesota in the August issue of Corporate Report magazine. MP Telecom announced plans to install a Cisco Powered Network of advanced ATM- and IP-based data services on its fiber-optic network linking 75 percent of Minnesota. In **September** the company began doing business under a new name, Allete (NYSE: ALE). The company's regulated electric business continued to be called Minnesota Power. "With diverse, profitable, and growing businesses operating in 39 states and six Canadian provinces, it's time for a corporate identity that better describes who we are and communicates the financial strength, diversity, and the value of our company," said Chairman Russell. Corporate Report Magazine named Allete one of the 10 great places to work in Minnesota. **Sept. 30:** Third-quarter earnings of 50 cents per share met analysts' expectations and matched prior year's strong third-quarter results. "We are on track to achieve our target of 10 percent annual earnings growth for 2000," said Russell. "Equally important, our automotive acquisitions have positioned us to grow earnings by 12 percent in 2001." Automotive Services continued its double-digit growth in net income as the number of vehicles sold at ADESA auctions increased 23 percent. Same-store EBITDA growth increased 13 percent. Third-quarter net income from Investments was lower than 1999 because of two large real estate transactions that occurred then. Net income from the company's securities portfolio and emerging technology investments posted strong increases over 1999. In Energy Services, sales to industrial, commercial, and residential customers were up 13 percent and exceeded record levels that were achieved in 1999. Net income, however, declined by $7.2 million due in large part to a lack of demand in the region's power market as a result of more moderate summer weather. Net income from Water Services was steady. In **October** ADESA completed the purchase of nine auto auctions from Manheim Auctions for $251 million: Southwest Auto Auction, Phoenix; Golden Gate Auto Auction, San Francisco; Southern States Vehicle Auction, Atlanta; Metro Auto Auction, Kansas City; Puget Sound Auto Auction, Seattle; Colorado Springs Auto Auction, Colorado Springs; and three Florida-based auctions, Bayside Auto Auction in Tampa, Clearwater Auto Auction, and Orlando-Sanford Vehicle Auction. ADESA was then operating 57 auto auctions across North America.

Alliant Techsystems

continued from page 129

RECENT EVENTS

In **December 1999** the company said that it expected sales from a new contract to supply all of the U.S. Army's requirements for small-caliber ammunition to help boost total revenue by 5 percent in fiscal year 2001. Alliant's operation of the Lake City Army Ammunition Plant in Independence, Mo., the Army's only production facility for small-caliber ammunition, was to generate total sales of $1 billion over the next 10 years. In **January 2000** ATK was selected by a European allied nation to produce 20mm training ammunition for use by its F-5E fighter aircraft. In **March** ATK received a $63 million contract to produce 120mm training ammunition for use by the U.S. Army's M1A1/A2 Abrams main battle tank. Three solid-propulsion rocket motors manufactured by Alliant Aerospace Propulsion Co., Magna, Utah, helped an Orbital Sciences Corp. Taurus rocket successfully boost the U.S. Department of Energy's Multispectral Thermal Imager satellite into its targeted orbit. Alliant put its long-time Hopkins headquarters up for sale (it was asking $13.5 million for the 550,000-square-foot facility) while searching for smaller space in the Twin Cities' western suburbs. Alliant successfully test fired a Titan IV Solid Rocket Motor Upgrade (SRMU) booster, using a new nozzle material, at Edwards Air Force Base, Calif. The hardware that ATK provides for the Sense and Destroy Armor (SADARM) precision artillery munition performed successfully during Reliability Determination/Assurance Program (RDAP) technical tests at the U.S. Army's Yuma Proving Grounds in Arizona. In **April** ATK received contracts worth $205 million for production of small- and medium-caliber ammunition and rocket system propellant and warhead components, and the transfer of medium-caliber ammunition production technology to a NATO-allied nation. Alliant Aerospace Propulsion Co., Magna, Utah, successfully completed the second of three static test firings to qualify a new solid rocket motor for The Boeing Co.'s Delta IV Medium-plus family of launch vehicles. In **May** a Lockheed Martin Titan IV B rocket powered by two Solid Rocket Motor Upgrade (SRMU) boosters designed and manufactured by Alliant Aerospace Propulsion Co. successfully launched a Defense Support Program (DSP) satellite from Cape Canaveral Air Force Station, Fla. Alliant Missile Products Co., Rocket Center, W.Va., successfully completed the first of two planned test firings of a solid rocket motor for the new Oriole suborbital launch system. In **June** ATK entered into a teaming agreement with Israel Military Industries Ltd. (IMI) under which the companies were to co-produce IMI's M971 120mm Dual-Purpose Improved Conventional Munition (DPICM) mortar cargo ammunition for sale in the United States. ATK was awarded a contract valued at $10 million to produce 120mm tactical ammunition for use by the U.S. Army's M1A1/A2 Abrams main battle tank. Alliant Integrated Defense Co., Hopkins, Minn., and Textron Systems, Wilmington, Mass., a wholly owned subsidiary of Textron Inc. (NYSE: TXT), announced an agreement to jointly develop and produce a tactical munition system that will serve as an alternative to anti-personnel landmines. Alliant Aerospace Propulsion Co., Magna, Utah, successfully completed the last of three static test firings of a new solid rocket propulsion Graphite Epoxy Motor designated as the GEM-60 for The Boeing Company's Delta IV Medium-plus family of launch vehicles. In **August** ATK was awarded a 48-month, $95 million contract (with a potential value of $103 million) from the U.S. Army Armament, Research, Development, and Engineering Center (ARDEC), Picatinny Arsenal, N.J., to continue development of the Objective Individual Combat Weapon (OICW), a next-generation military rifle system that will give American fighting troops an unprecedented capability on the 21st century battlefield. Alliant Missile Products Co., Rocket Center, W.Va., and Local 261C of the International Chemical Worker's Union Council of the United Food and Commercial Workers Union ratified a new five-year labor/management agreement. ATK produced the 100-millionth round of small-caliber ammunition at the Lake City Army Ammunition Plant in Independence, Mo., since taking over operations there on April 3, 2000. A Lockheed Martin Titan IV B rocket powered by two Solid Rocket Motor Upgrade (SRMU) boosters designed and manufactured by ATK Aerospace Propulsion Co., Magna, Utah, successfully launched a National Reconnaissance Office (NRO) satellite from Vandenberg Air Force Base, Calif. Nine of Alliant's solid propulsion rocket motors helped successfully launch a Boeing Delta III rocket from Cape Canaveral Air Force Station, Fla. In **September** ATK was awarded two contracts with a combined value of $17 million from the U.S. Army Operations Support Command, Rock Island, Ill., for production of medium-caliber target practice ammunition. **Oct. 1:** ATK completed the first half of fiscal year 2001 with solid gains in sales and earnings. Sales rose 3 percent, bolstered by a 7 percent gain in the second quarter reflecting revenue from the new contract to produce small-caliber ammunition at the Lake City Army Ammunition Plant. First-half EBITDA cash flow per share rose 20 percent to $9.48 on improved operating margins. Conventional Munitions sales for the six-month period rose 41 percent to $231 million, reflecting revenue from small-caliber ammunition production operations, which were partially offset by lower sales of medium-caliber ammunition due to production delays in the first quarter. Aerospace reported sales of $256 million versus $261 million last year, as higher sales of composite structures for space launch vehicles offset lower revenue from solid propulsion programs. Defense Systems sales declined to $73 million from $107 million, reflecting lower sales from an anti-tank munition program that was completing production, a delayed contract award for development of the Objective Individual Combat Weapon (OICW), and production delays in fuze programs. In **October** ATK signed an exclusive agreement with Hellenic Arms Industry (EBO), Athens, Greece, to transfer to EBO the technology to produce ATK's family of 120mm tactical and training tank ammunition at EBO's manufacturing facility in Greece, in support of an upcoming procurement of 246 main battle tanks by the Hellenic Ministry of Defense. ATK was awarded a $13.5 million contract from the U.S. Army Operations Support Command, Rock Island, Ill., to produce lead-free 5.56mm training ammunition as part of a U.S. Army initiative to move to "green ammunition" in the 21st century. ATK Lake City Small Caliber Ammunition Co. planned to produce the environmentally friendly ammunition at its plant in Independence, Mo. ATK and Rheinmetall DeTec AG, Ratingen, Germany, signed a teaming agreement to jointly develop next-generation large-caliber ammunition for use by future armored vehicles and current main battle tanks. The Boeing Co. awarded ATK a contract to manufacture composite aeroskirts for the new Boeing Delta IV family of space launch vehicles, with deliveries to continue through 2003.

American Medical Systems Holdings Inc.

continued from page 131 senior credit facility; to pay contingent purchase price payments relating to the acquisition of Influence; and to fund future product development and acquisitions. U.S. Bancorp Piper Jaffray, Banc of America Securities LLC, and Chase H&Q were to underwrite the offering. AMS announced an unrestricted educational grant for Healthology Inc., surrounding the first Webcast of a penile prosthesis procedure on the Internet. On **Aug. 11**, the company's IPO became effective at $11 a share, raising $68.75 million. The shares rose to $11.56 on the first day of trading. **Sept. 30**: The company's third-quarter earnings before interest, taxes, and amortization (EBITA) was $4.2 million, compared to $3.9 million in the 1999 period. Excluding the negative impact of currency exchange rate fluctuations, third-quarter sales growth was 22.1 percent. In **October** a leading urologist at Lexington Medical Center in Columbia, S.C., presented the Straight-In Male Sling System to medical professionals there.

Analysts International Corporation

continued from page 132 market is poised to grow significantly as it settles down over the next several quarters." According to President LaVelle, "One indication of the change in our business mix is the addition of approximately 420 technical consultants added by our late-April acquisition of Sequoia NET.com.z" In **July** the Minneapolis branch of AiC announced a Premier Solution Partnership with Massachusetts-based Art Technology Group (ATG) that extended Analysts International's current eBusiness offerings to provide end-to-end eBusiness solutions, from strategy to integration and implementation. In **September** AiC and ASI Associates, an e-business research and consulting firm, announced an exclusive partnership aimed at speeding eBusiness strategy development and implementation for customers. **Sept. 30:** Operating income increased 30.7 percent to $3.8 million compared to the prior quarter but decreased 35.2 percent versus the quarter ended Sept. 30, 1999. Total revenue during the quarter was comprised of $116.4 million of direct revenue and $32.2 million of sub-supplier billings that were processed through the company as specified in contracts with certain customers. The company's revenue mix was 27 percent e-business solutions and 73 percent staffing. In November AiC signed a three-year contract to serve as a strategic core supplier of information technology services to IBM Corp. (At the time, the company had several hundred full-time technology consultants working within IBM.)

Angeion Corporation

continued from page 133

Angeion adjourned its annual meeting of shareholders with respect to proposals requesting approval of previously announced transactions with ELA Medical, a wholly owned subsidiary of Sanofi-Synthelabo, a French pharmaceutical company, and Medtronic Inc. In **February 2000** shareholders approved by a two-thirds majority two previously announced transactions with ELA Medical and Medtronic. However, fewer than 25 percent of the holders of the company's 7 1/2% Senior Convertible Notes had voted. (A simple majority vote for approval from noteholders was required.) As a result, Angeion adjourned the meeting until Feb. 17 to allow noteholders to vote on the transactions. Even then, the required votes were not forthcoming. A Minneapolis District Court dismissed all claims of the plaintiff U.S. Bank with prejudice, ruling that the contested transactions by Angeion in 1999 did not constitute a sale of all or substantially all of the assets under the Indenture covering the notes, and that, therefore, note holders were not entitled to prepayment of their notes. In **March** Angeion consummated two transactions relating to its cardiac stimulation technology used in ICD devices. First, it closed an agreement with Medtronic Inc. under which Angeion granted Medtronic a one-way, nonexclusive, fully paid-up, royalty-free license for Angeion's cardiac stimulation technology. As part of the agreement, Angeion sold to Medtronic certain unfiled patent disclosures relating to cardiac stimulation devices; and both companies agreed to release each other from any patent-infringement claims for products sold or used prior to the closing date. In connection with the transaction, Medtronic made a one-time payment of $9.0 million to Angeion. Angeion also closed an agreement with ELA Medical and Sanofi-Synthelabo under which Angeion granted ELA a one-way, nonexclusive, fully paid-up, royalty-free license for Angeion's cardiac stimulation technology. As part of the agreements, Angeion sold to Sanofi-Synthelabo and ELA certain Angeion assets and liabilities related to the manufacture and sale of cardiac stimulation devices. Sanofi-Synthelabo surrendered to Angeion 745,994 shares of Angeion common stock and warrants to purchase an additional 1,897,186 shares. Medical Graphics acquired the operating assets of AeroSport Inc., a privately held Ann Arbor, Mich., corporation, and obtained an exclusive worldwide license to AeroSport's patented technology. AeroSport (http://www.aerosportinc.com) is a leading global supplier of gas-exchange metabolic analyzers for the health, fitness, and research and education markets. In **June** Angeion's Medical Graphics subsidiary discontinued distribution of the sleep disorder diagnostics product line manufactured by the Australian firm Compumedics Sleep Pty. Ltd. (Medical Graphics had been selling the products in the United States under an OEM distribution agreement since April 1997.) Compumedics USA was to assume all responsibility for service and technical support for customers who purchased systems from Medical Graphics. Many of Medical Graphics' sleep-products service and support personnel were hired by Compumedics and integrated into its support organization for other products Compumedics sells in the United States. "While we were pleased to offer the Compumedics' products as an extension of our product line to our customers over the past three years, our growth strategy is focused on other products with larger market sizes and profit potential," said CEO Jahnke. In **August** the Minnesota Court of Appeals affirmed a November 1999 decision by the Hennepin County District Court that denied the Motion of U.S. Bank N.A., the trustee for the holders of Angeion's 7.5% Senior Convertible Notes, for a temporary injunction preventing Angeion from spending its cash to pursue acquisitions or other business development initiatives. The Court of Appeals further concluded that the District Court's February 2000 decision granting summary judgment was premature, and reversed and remanded the case to the District Court for further proceedings.

Apogee Enterprises Inc.

continued from page 134

products to its Conservation Series line of picture framing glass, a high-end line used primarily by art framing professionals. In **March** Tru Vue formed a strategic alliance with Balangier Fine Art & Design to combine the pre-framed art line of Balangier with Tru Vue's picture framing glass products, which protect art against harmful ultraviolet rays. In **June** Tru Vue acquired Balangier, which currently produces about 30,000 pieces of high-end framed art annually for national retail customers. Apogee and PPG Industries of Pittsburgh (NYSE: PPG) agreed to combine their U.S. automotive replacement glass distribution businesses in a new entity, PPG Auto Glass—with PPG holding a 66 percent interest and Apogee a 34 percent interest in the new company. "Both of our firms produce auto glass parts that consumers buy at installation shops throughout the U.S.," said CEO Huffer. "The venture will increase geographic coverage, improve efficiency, and provide service benefits that will allow the new company to meet PPG's and Apogee's installer-customer needs more effectively." On June 29, Apogee and PPG were notified by the FTC of early termination of the waiting period for their filings under the Hart-Scott-Rodino Antitrust Improvements Act. The deal, which closed at the end of July, was expected to have a neutral impact on FY2001 earnings and a positive impact on FY2002 earnings. **Sept. 2:** Second-quarter earnings from continuing operations were $0.15 vs. $0.19 a year ago. The decrease was due to auto glass distribution results of two months versus three with the formation of the joint venture with PPG, as well as higher corporate and interest expense. Apogee's second-quarter sales increased 9 percent to $236.4 million, led by double-digit growth in Glass Technologies. In **November** Apogee sold the assets of its VIS'N Service Corp. subsidiary, a non-auto glass, third-party administered claims processor that had been designated for disposal earlier in the year because it did not directly support Apogee's retail auto glass repair and replacement business.

BNCCORP Inc.

continued from page 141

RECENT EVENTS

In **December 1999** the company agreed to sell its asset-based lending subsidiary, BNC Financial Corp. of St. Cloud, Minn., to Associated Banc-Corp (Nasdaq: ASBC). The sale reflected BNCCORP's emphasis on continued growth in its banking subsidiaries, including its insurance, brokerage, and financial services divisions. "This sale affords us the opportunity to substantially restructure our balance sheet," said COO Cleveland. "In addition to the sale of our asset-based loan portfolio, we will significantly reduce our outstanding long term debt, much of which was incurred for the purpose of funding the asset-based loans at BNC Financial." In **July 2000** the company established a special-purpose trust that issued $7.5 million of 12.045% trust preferred securities. The proceeds from the issuance, together with the proceeds from the issuance of $232,000 of common securities of the trust, were invested in $7.7 million of junior subordinated deferrable interest debentures of the company. Under the regulatory capital guidelines established by the Federal Reserve, the trust preferred securities qualify as Tier 1, or core capital. **Sept. 30**: Earnings for the third quarter and nine months were sharply higher than the year-ago periods. BNCCORP primarily attributed the continued upward trend in earnings to an increase in net interest income generated by its growing asset and deposit base, along with higher noninterest income from loan fees, brokerage income, insurance commissions. and fees generated by the Financial Services Division.

Bemis Company Inc.

continued from page 143

label product line with increasing raw material costs coupled with an extremely competitive pricing environment." In **October** the board authorized the repurchase of an additional 2 million shares of Bemis stock, supplementing the prevailing buyback authorization (which had 1 million shares remaining).

Best Buy Co.

continued from page 144

between I-35W and Penn Avenue. The $150 million project, expected to be complete by summer of 2002, was to include 1.5 million square feet of office space. Walser Automotive Group, one of the businesses to be displaced, was leading a group opposing the plan. Xerox Corp. (NYSE: XRX) expanded its retail presence to include Best Buy. Set to open in spring were four new stores in the Portland, Ore., area. In **February** the board of directors authorized the repurchase of an additional $400 million of the company's common stock. **Feb. 26:** Best Buy's fourth-quarter earnings of $163.8 million/$0.78 beat Wall Street estimates by 4 cents a share. Same-store sales rose 11 percent, bolstered by the popularity of large-screen televisions, personal computers, music, and videos. In **March** Best Buy and Micron Electronics Inc. (Nasdaq: MUEI) announced a groundbreaking agreement to combine the best of both the retail and direct sales models for home PC customers—using direct-to-the-manufacturer kiosks in all Best Buy retail stores. In **April** Los Angeles-based Everypath, a leading infrastructure provider for the wireless Web, agreed to develop applications to allow BestBuy.com customers to check product availability and purchase products and gift certificates from any smart phone or Palm VII over the wireless Web. Best Buy became a founding member of the WorldWide Retail Exchange, the Web-based business-to-business marketplace founded in March 2000. The open marketplace was expected to benefit all participating retailers and suppliers by offering the ability to make business decisions closer to the time of consumer demand, thereby reducing costs. (Target Corp., Minneapolis, was also a founding member.) BestBuy.com announced an alliance with RollingStone.com, the Internet's premier authority on music and popular culture. In **May** BestBuy.com selected DDB Worldwide as its advertising agency. Best Buy announced its entry into the New York City market, with 15 new stores in the New York and New Jersey areas scheduled to open in the fall. BestBuy.com inked deals with Liquid Audio Inc. (Nasdaq: LQID) and Supertracks as the initial service providers for music downloads. Best Buy and XM Satellite Radio Inc. (Nasdaq: XMSR), Washington, D.C., announced a multiyear strategic sales, marketing, and distribution agreement calling for Best Buy to sell the XM Radio service and XM-capable radios throughout its more than 350 retail stores beginning with launch of XM service in 2001. The sales effort was to initially be focused on the more than 200 million car owners in the United States. **May 27:** First-quarter earnings jumped 54 percent on sales of profitable digital products, such as digital cameras, as well as personal computers and music. On **June** 12, the company launched a revamped Web site, one with far more products than before. BestBuy.com was offering audio, video, portable electronics, photo and digital-imging products, music CDs, and DVD movies—all with the service and support of Best Buy's more than 350 retail stores. According to a new economic impact study conducted by Anton, Lubov & Associates Inc. of Minneapolis, the purchasing power of relocated Best Buy employees will mean increased sales for Richfield businesses such as restaurants, gas stations, banks, and more. The total spending was estimated at $14 million annually. In less than one year since introducing instant rebates for Internet Service Providers (ISPs), Best Buy had generated 1 million subscribers for its various Internet partners. In **August** Best Buy announced a new partnership with Whirlpool Corp. (NYSE: WHR), the world's leading manufacturer and marketer of appliances, to offer KitchenAid brand appliances at Best Buy stores nationwide beginning in September. BestBuy.com launched computers, peripherals, and accessories, as part of its ever-expanding product and content offering to online customers. **Aug. 26:** Sales for the second fiscal quarter were a record $3.169 billion. Comparable-store sales increased 5.1 percent. The company operated 373 stores at the end of the quarter as compared to 332 locations a year earlier. "Comparable-store sales were in line with company expectations," CFO Lenzmeier said. "The momentum behind the digital product cycle continues to accelerate as sales of digital cameras, camcorders, cellular communication, DVD hardware, and software continued their significant sales gains. Television sales continued strong this quarter, bolstered by increased assortment and affordability for both digital and analog products." Best Buy and Hewlett-Packard Co. (NYSE: HWP) announced an alliance to co-develop and maintain Best Buy's online photo center. In **September** Best Buy was the presenting sponsor for the 2000 Farm Aid Concert. BestBuy.com announced an alliance with E! Online, a wholly owned subsidiary of E! Networks and the No. 1 entertainment news and celebrity gossip site on the Web, that gave it access to E! Online's original up-to-the-minute entertainment news, information, gossip, reviews, games, and live premiere coverage. Verizon Wireless services were to be offered at more than 350 Best Buy stores nationwide beginning in October. On Sept. 22, Best Buy held the official grand opening its first wave of 11 stores in the New York City area. In **October** Best Buy signed an agreement to offer selected AT&T Broadband services at Best Buy retail stores. A new integrate campaign created by DDB New York and Tribal DDB heralded BestBuy.com's simple functionality by showing that even a dog can order online. Best Buy became a founding member in a new industry alliance, Internet Home Alliance, which was formed to enhance consumers' understanding, appreciation, and adoption of the Internet lifestyle. The Wall Street Journal announced a new marketing campaign to attract subscribers to The Wall Street Journal Online through point-of-purchase sales at Best Buy retail stores nationwide. In **November** Best Buy and Microsoft reached a milestone in their joint marketing and distribution alliance by signing up more than 1 million customers for MSN Internet Access online service. A new service was introduced that enables consumers to quickly and easily choose the best broadband option for them based on where they live, by comparing leading broadband alternatives at more than 400 Best Buy retail locations. On Nov. 9, Best Buy stock dropped 39 percent, to $32.06, on news that third-quarter earnings would be lower than the consensus estimate (27 cents a share vs. 44 cents a share) because of price-cutting in a slower economy.

PUB

Bio-Vascular Inc.

continued from page 146

record revenue levels," said CEO Gilles. "The successful execution of our strategies give us a considerable sense of accomplishment. Strong revenue performance and well-managed expenses led to a record quarter that offset operating and net losses in the first six months to achieve solid profitability at the nine-month mark. Further, we turned in a profitable quarter while maintaining a substantial investment in R&D, a practice we plan to continue." In **September** R.J. Steichen & Co. initiated coverage of Bio-Vascular with a BUY recommendation. Bio-Vascular signed an agreement giving it exclusive U.S. distribution and marketing rights for GLUBRAN and GLUBRAN2, surgical adhesives manufactured by GEM s.r.l. of Italy and used to seal or adhere internal or external tissues. In **October** the company received 510(k) marketing clearance from the FDA for its urethral sling product for use in the surgical treatment of stress urinary incontinence. The company was planning a tiered release of the product in the U.S. market beginning in the first quarter of its 2001 fiscal year.

Black Hills Corporation

continued from page 147

and long-distance telephone service, and a full suite of telephony products, to residential and business customers in Rapid City, S.D., and the Northern Black Hills. In **June** the Independent Energy business unit announced that both of its recently constructed electricity generation peaking facilities were complete and ready for commercial operation. Arapahoe (80 MW) and Valmont (40 MW) were to sell peaking capacity and energy to Public Service Company of Colorado under a seven-year agreement beginning in summer 2000. The South Dakota Public Utilities Commission and the Wyoming Public Service Commission approved the issuance of securities necessary to fund the Indeck Capital merger. (The only remaining regulatory approval required was from the Federal Energy Regulatory Commission.) Black Hills Energy Capital acquired an additional interest in the Indeck North American Power Fund LLP. In **September** Black Hills Energy Capital signed two 10-year contracts with Public Service of Colorado to supply electricity from the Arapahoe and Valmont facilities in the Denver and Boulder metropolitan areas. In Addition, Black Hills Energy Capital closed $60 million of nonrecourse project financing on the first phase of the Valmont and Arapahoe facilities in the Front Range of Colorado. The Independent Energy group entered the next phase of construction of Wygen #1, a nominal 80 megawatt (MW) coal-fired power plant at the company's energy complex near Gillette, Wyo. Initial construction on Wygen #1 began in the third quarter of 1999, and the company was about to name a general contractor to be responsible for completion of the engineering, design, procurement, and construction of the project. **Sept. 30:** Black Hills Exploration and Production achieved excellent success in its drilling activity during the first three quarters of 2000. Black Hills participated in the drilling and completion of 33 gross wells (5 net wells). Twenty-four of those wells were completed as producers, for a drilling success rate of 73 percent. In addition, a total of 11 wells were currently being either drilled or completed. Black Hills Corp. announced record nine-month earnings of $33.4 million (up 23 percent from 1999). "Accelerating growth of our Independent Energy business unit was fueled by increased energy prices, volumes, and strong energy marketing operations," said CEO Landguth. "In addition, our electric utility business unit continues to turn in outstanding earnings, showing increases of 23 percent and 22 percent when compared to last year, primarily due to significantly higher margins from off-system sales." Landguth also noted that the company's Communications business unit turned EBITDA positive in September after just 15 months of operation.

PUB

CNS Inc.

7615 Smetana Ln., P.O. Box 39802 (55439), Eden Prairie, MN 55344
Tel: 952/229-1500 Fax: 952/229-1700 Web site: http://www.cns.com

CNS Inc. designs, manufactures, and markets consumer health care products, including the **Breathe Right** nasal strip and FiberChoice chewable fiber tablets. CNS focuses on products that address important consumer needs within the aging well/self care market, including better breathing and digestive health.

EARNINGS HISTORY

Year Ended Dec 31	Operating Revenue/Sales (dollars in thousands)	Net Earnings	Return on Revenue (percent)	Return on Equity	Net Earnings (dollars per share*)	Cash Dividend	Market Price Range
1999 †	46,050	(13,756)	(29.9)	(25.7)	(0.89)	—	7.19–2.81
1998	53,623	2,982	5.6	3.9	0.16	—	7.75–3.38
1997	66,957	8,770	13.1	10.9	0.46	—	16.75–5.69
1996	85,867	15,522	18.1	19.5	0.83	—	25.88–13.50
1995 ¶	48,632	14,076	28.9	52.4	0.82	—	24.25–4.44

* Per-share amounts restated to reflect 2-for-1 stock split on June 22, 1995.
† Income figures for 1999 include a one-time pretax charge of $6.345 million related to termination of an international distribution agreement with 3M Co.
¶ Income figures for 1995 include net gain of 765,989/$0.04 from discontinued operations and their disposal. Due to net operating loss tax carryforwards, income figures include no income tax expense.

BALANCE SHEET

Assets	12/31/99 (dollars in thousands)	12/31/98	Liabilities	12/31/99 (dollars in thousands)	12/31/98
Current (CAE 859 and 584)	61,936	81,122	Current	11,753	9,098
Property and equipment	2,010	2,406	Stockholders' equity*	53,584	75,866
Patents and trademarks	1,391	1,435	TOTAL	65,337	84,963
TOTAL	65,337	84,963			

* $0.01 par common; 50,000,000 authorized; 19,294,570 and 19,294,570 issued and outstanding, less 4,838,098 and 2,692,144 treasury shares.

RECENT QUARTERS / PRIOR-YEAR RESULTS

	Quarter End	Revenue ($000)	Earnings ($000)	EPS ($)	Prior-Year Revenue ($000)	Prior-Year Earnings ($000)	Prior-Year EPS ($)
Q3	09/30/2000	19,221	(393)	(0.03)	10,463	(5,846)	(0.39)
Q2	06/30/2000	13,303	(709)	(0.05)	8,184	(524)	(0.03)
Q1	03/31/2000	14,633	(5,687)	(0.39)	11,934	(2,967)	(0.18)
Q4	12/31/99	15,468	(4,418)	(0.30)	14,435	1,413	0.08
	SUM	62,625	(11,207)	(0.77)	45,016	(7,924)	(0.52)

PRIOR YEAR: Q3 earnings include a one-time pretax charge of $6.345 million related to termination of an international distribution agreement with 3M Co.

RECENT EVENTS

In **March** CNS signed a license agreement with The Procter & Gamble Co. (NYSE: PG) to use the Vicks brand name on a new product introduction for the fall 2000 cough/cold season. The new Breathe Right nasal strips for colds with Vicks mentholated vapors were to be available in a range of sizes for adults and children. CNS and P&G were planning joint product promotion programs for the coming cough/cold season. CNS then introduced FiberChoice chewable fiber tablets, its new and innovative bulk fiber supplement. Said CEO Cohen, "FiberChoice tablets provide an alternative for consumers who dislike the taste, inconvenience, and gel-like consistency of existing powder products or pills that must be taken with water." In **April** CNS signed on to be anchor tenant in the new Lake Smetana Business Park in Eden Prairie, Minn., where construction had just begun. The company was planning to move its corporate headquarters from Bloomington, Minn., to a 73,000-square-foot office in the park's first building. By mid-April, 29 of the 35 states with racetracks had declared FLAIR equine nasal strips as "acceptable equipment" for use on racehorses competing at their facilities. The six states still reviewing data on the FLAIR: New Hampshire, New Jersey, New York, North Dakota, Virginia, and Wyoming. In **June** FiberChoice was introduced by CNS as the first and only bulk fiber supplement that can be safely taken without water. It was created to address consumer needs for convenience and good taste in an effective, safe, and easy-to-use product. In **July** the board of directors authorized the company to purchase up to 1 million shares (6.9 percent) of the company's common stock. **Sept. 30:** For the first nine months of 2000, net sales were $47,157,000, a 54 percent gain from the same period in 1999. The company's net loss improved to $6,789,000 compared to a net loss of $9,338,000 for the comparable period in 1999. Operating expenses rose to $38,687,000, up from $25,607,000, due chiefly to the company's higher investment in sales and marketing, including the launch of FiberChoice chewable fiber tablets. In **October** CNS announced agreements with Ceuta Healthcare Ltd., McGloin's Classic Brands, and BluFarm Distribution s.r.l. for the sale and distribution of Breathe Right nasal strips in the United Kingdom, Australia, and Italy, respectively. The company also began shipping Breathe Rights to Tokyo-based Eisai Co. Ltd. for sale in retail stores in Japan. For the upcoming cold and flu season, the company released Breathe Right nasal strips with VICKS mentholated vapors, which combat congestion by combining proven Breathe Right technology (to lift and open nasal passages) with soothing Vicks vapors.

OFFICERS

Daniel E. Cohen, M.D.
Chairman and CEO
Marti Morfitt
President and COO
Andy Anderson, Ph.D.
VP-Product Development/Regulatory
Douglas Austin
VP-Operations
David J. Byrd
VP-Finance, CFO, and Treasurer
Kirk P. Hodgdon
VP-Business Development
John J. Keppeler
VP-Worldwide Sales
Teri P. Osgood
VP-U.S. Marketing
Carol J. Watzke
VP-Consumer Strategy

DIRECTORS

Daniel E. Cohen, M.D.
Patrick Delaney
Lindquist & Vennum PLLP, Minneapolis
R. Hunt Greene
Greene Holcomb & Fisher LLC, Minneapolis
Andrew J. Greenshields
Pathfinder Venture Capital Funds, Minneapolis
H. Robert Hawthorne
Ocean Spray Cranberries Inc., Lakeville-Middleboro, MA
Marti Morfitt
Richard W. Perkins
Perkins Capital Management Inc., Wayzata, MN

MAJOR SHAREHOLDERS

Dimensional Fund Advisors Inc., 6.7%
Santa Monica, CA
Citigroup Inc., 6%
New York
Daniel E. Cohen, 5.7%
Eubel Brady & Suttman Asset Mgmt. Inc., 5.2%
Dayton, OH
All officers and directors as a group (14 persons), 13.6%

SIC CODE

3842 Surgical appliances and supplies

MISCELLANEOUS

TRANSFER AGENT AND REGISTAR:
Wells Fargo Bank Minnesota N.A.,
South St. Paul, MN

TRADED: Nasdaq National Market
SYMBOL: CNXS
STOCKHOLDERS: 800
EMPLOYEES: 76
PART TIME: 3
IN MINNESOTA: 73
GENERAL COUNSEL:
Lindquist & Vennum PLLP, Minneapolis
AUDITORS:
KPMG LLP, Minneapolis
INC: DE-1989
FOUNDED: 1982
ANNUAL MEETING: May
HUMAN RESOURCES:
Michelle Beuning
INVESTOR RELATIONS:
David Byrd

RANKINGS

No. 115 CRM Public 200

TWO-YEAR QUARTERLY HIGH-LOW STOCK PRICES

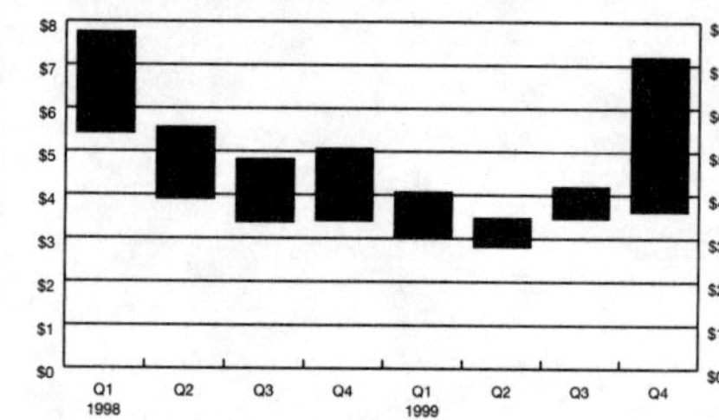

Calendar Capital Inc.

Riverplace, 43 Main St. S.E., Suite 230, Minneapolis, MN 55414
Tel: 612/362-8411 Fax: 612/362-8464 Web site: http://www.entrenaut.com

Calendar Capital Inc., *dba* **Entrenaut Inc.**, is an Internet incubator and holding company. From December 1994 until July 1, 1999, Calendar Capital was an inactive public shell company. In July 1999, a new board of directors and management assumed control of the company and proceeded to make a cash infusion to bring the company current in its filings, to have a fresh audit prepared, and to address certain liabilities. Effective Jan. 1, 2000, the company entered into a stock exchange agreement to acquire all of the outstanding common stock of Entrenaut Inc. in a reverse merger. Currently, Entrenaut operates as a wholly owned subsidiary and all of the operations of the company take place through Entrenaut. Entrenaut was formed in July 1999 to act as an incubator for early-stage, Internet-related business concepts. It provides seed capital and management oversight to Internet companies that Entrenaut believes have viable business concepts in exchange for consulting fees and equity in the companies. Entrenaut also provides strategic planning, corporate development, and market research to operating companies on a fee-for-services arrangement.

EARNINGS HISTORY *

Year Ended Mar 31	Operating Revenue/Sales (dollars in thousands)	Net Earnings (dollars in thousands)	Return on Revenue (percent)	Return on Equity (percent)	Net Earnings (dollars per share)	Cash Dividend (dollars per share)	Market Price Range (dollars per share)
2000 †	1,017	(350)	(34.4)	NM	(0.08)	—	0.81–0.01

* The historical financial statements prior to Jan. 1, 2000, are those of Entrenaut Inc.
† Figures for 2000 are for the nine-month period from July 1, 1999, through March 31, 2000. Revenue consists of management and consulting fees.

BALANCE SHEET

Assets	03/31/00 (dollars in thousands)	Liabilities	03/31/00 (dollars in thousands)
Current (CAE 22)	68	Current	1,389
Property and equipment	25	Stockholders' equity*	381
Investments	1,385	TOTAL	1,771
Goodwill	293		
TOTAL	1,771		

* $0.01 par common; 14,000,000 authorized; 12,976,418 issued and outstanding.

RECENT EVENTS

In **February 2000** the company reached an investment agreement with the Anoka/Sherburne County Capital Fund, a Coon Rapids, Minn., venture capital fund that assists promising technology-based companies. In **November** Entrenaut received approval for trading on Nasdaq's Electronic Bulletin under the name Calendar Capital (OTC Bulletin Board: CCAP). In addition Andy Johnson, former president of the E-Commerce Division at Fingerhut and currently CEO of AutoPlanet, agreed to stand for election as a new board member at the next Entrenaut board meeting in January 2001."Entrenaut is developing the kind of e-commerce businesses that I find most promising today: information-intensive, consumer-based companies that provide tangible financial benefits to people who are participating at every level of the concept," said Johnson. Entrenaut was incorporated in July 1999 by venture capitalist Paul Crawford, who also co-founded the Internet business Commission Junction, which is currently one of the preeminent affiliate services on the Web today.

OFFICERS

Paul D. Crawford
CEO and CEO-Entrenaut

Wayne Atkins
President and Pres./COO-Entrenaut

DIRECTORS

Wayne Atkins

Paul D. Crawford

Daniel C. Neisen
Neisen Brothers Partnership

MAJOR SHAREHOLDERS

All officers and directors as a group (2 persons), 2.3%

SIC CODE

8742 Management consulting services

MISCELLANEOUS

TRANSFER AGENT AND REGISTAR:
Norwest Bank Minnesota, Minneapolis

TRADED: OTC Bulletin Board

SYMBOL: CCAP

STOCKHOLDERS: 1,220

EMPLOYEES: 14

PART TIME: 2

GENERAL COUNSEL:
Messerli & Kramer, Minneapolis

AUDITORS:
Schechter Dokken Kanter Andrews & Selcer Ltd., Minneapolis

SUBSIDIARIES, DIVISIONS, AFFILIATES

Entrenaut Inc.

Canterbury Park Holding Corporation

1100 Canterbury Rd., Shakopee, MN 55379
Tel: 952/445-7223 Fax: 952/496-6486 Web site: http://www.canterburypark.com

Canterbury Park Holding Corp. conducts live thoroughbred and quarterhorse racing and pari-mutuel wagering operations at its racetrack in Shakopee, Minn. In addition to a 60-day live racing schedule in 2000, the company provides simulcast races throughout the year from Churchill Downs, Santa Anita, Gulfstream, and other top racetracks across the country. In April, the company opened a Card Club hosting unbanked card games seven days a week, 24 hours a day. The company also conducts various special events, such as craft shows and snowmobile races, at its facility.

EARNINGS HISTORY

Year Ended Dec 31	Operating Revenue/Sales (dollars in thousands)	Net Earnings	Return on Revenue (percent)	Return on Equity	Net Earnings (dollars per share)	Cash Dividend	Market Price Range
1999	20,331	437	2.2	5.2	0.14	—	7.75–3.50
1998	19,196	434	2.3	6.5	0.14	—	5.00–2.38
1997	18,202	136	0.7	2.2	0.05	—	6.50–2.00
1996	17,371	71	0.4	1.2	0.02	—	3.38–2.13
1995	17,652	(889)	(5.0)	(15.6)	(0.30)	—	3.00–1.38

BALANCE SHEET

Assets	12/31/99 (dollars in thousands)	12/31/98	Liabilities	12/31/99 (dollars in thousands)	12/31/98
Current (CAE 1,350 and 372)	1,774	819	Current	1,738	2,768
Property and equipment	8,084	8,386	Stockholders' equity*	8,451	6,650
Deferred tax	331	208	TOTAL	10,189	9,418
Intangibles		4			
TOTAL	10,189	9,418			

* $0.01 par common; 10,000,000 authorized; 3,371,999 and 3,020,167 issued and outstanding.

RECENT QUARTERS / PRIOR-YEAR RESULTS

	Quarter End	Revenue ($000)	Earnings ($000)	EPS ($)	Prior-Year Revenue ($000)	Prior-Year Earnings ($000)	Prior-Year EPS ($)
Q3	09/30/2000	11,696	480	0.14	6,925	17	0.01
Q2	06/30/2000	9,654	(252)	(0.07)	6,170	(262)	(0.08)
Q1	03/31/2000	3,759	178	0.05	3,637	527	0.17
Q4	12/31/99	3,599	155	0.05	3,539	223	0.07
	SUM	28,708	561	0.17	20,271	505	0.17

RECENT EVENTS

In **December 1999** the Minnesota Racing Commission approved 59 days of live racing for Canterbury Park (Nasdaq: TRAK) and 365 days of simulcast racing for year 2000. The Shakopee racetrack was planning to host live racing from May 20 through Labor Day, Sept. 4—slightly longer than the previous five seasons. Canterbury Park was also seeking approval for the track's card club operations plan. [In May 1999 the Minnesota Legislature had approved poker and other wagering card games at Canterbury Park.] Revenue from a card club was intended to help the Minnesota horse racing industry by providing additional sources of gaming for purses and the Minnesota Breeders' Fund. In **January 2000** the Canterbury Card Club was unanimously approved by the Minnesota Racing Commission. By **February**, construction was underway at the Shakopee racetrack—as was employee training for the card club, which was expected to bring 300 new jobs to Canterbury Park. For the first time since the racetrack opened in 1985, future book wagering on the Kentucky Derby was offered at Canterbury Park. Following approval from the Legislature during the 1999 Legislative session, on April 19 Canterbury Park opened a 24-hour legal poker card club for gamblers 18 years old and up. The Canterbury Card Club opened with 38 of its legal limit of 50 tables. Table stakes range from $2/$4 with a limit of $15/$30. The games being played initially: 7-card stud; Omaha; Texas hold 'em; 7-card hi-low; and California games such as Pai Gow Poker, Minnesota 21, and Super 9. All of the games are unbanked, with players competing against each other (not the house). The Canterbury Card Club—open seven days a week, 24 hours a day, 365 days a year—offers full food and beverage service, full card simulcasting, and bet runners for card players wishing to play horses. The 2000 live race meet at Canterbury Park began Saturday, May 20. The 59-day race meet was extended this year through Labor Day thanks to the highly successful 1999 race meet, in which Canterbury Park enjoyed its best season in attendance and wagering since purchasing the old Canterbury Downs in 1994. Overnight purses increased by 10 percent across the board at Canterbury Park even before the first race of the 2000 season was run, due to the initial success of the Canterbury Card Club. The card club's grand opening, held the weekend of June 2-4, featured a VIP party, Poker 101 Seminars presented by two of the world's top tournament poker players (Linda Johnson and Jan Fisher), a seminar by Mike Caro ("the mad genius of poker"), and a celebrity poker tournament for charity. In **July** the Canterbury Card Club added three poker tables, bringing the table total to 41. Also, for the second time this season and fourth time in the past two years, racing purses were raised at Canterbury Park, by 10 per cent across the board. **Sept. 5:** For the fourth-consecutive year, Canterbury Park enjoyed significant increases in on-track attendance and handle for its live racing meet. During the 60-day 2000 meet, 232,604 racing fans passing through the Canterbury Park turnstiles, an increase of 11.12 percent compared to the 56-day 1999 meet. The jump in attendance and increased field sizes resulted in an increase in total live-on track wagering of 12.78 percent compared to 1999. Total handle from all sources of $38,484,073 represented an increase of 4.53 percent despite a drop in out-of-state handle of 5.0 percent attributed to the loss of the Illinois market simulcasting on weekends. **Sept. 30:** The $4.8 million (68.9 percent) increase in revenue for third quarter was largely attributable to the operations of the company's Card Club. In **November** Canterbury *continued on page 187*

OFFICERS

Curtis A. Sampson
Chairman

Dale H. Schenian
Vice Chairman

Randall D. Sampson
President, General Manager, and CFO

Mark A. Erickson
VP-Facilities

Michael J. Garin
VP-Hospitality

Deborah D. Giardina
VP-Card Club Operations

John R. Harty
VP-Marketing

DIRECTORS

Brian C. Barenscheer
Boyum & Barenscheer, Minneapolis

Gibson Carothers
Gibson & Carothers, Minneapolis

Terence J. McWilliams
Autotote Systems Inc., Newark, DE

Carin Offerman
private investor, Minneapolis

Curtis A. Sampson
Communications Systems Inc., Hector, MN

Randall D. Sampson

Dale H. Schenian
City Auto Glass, South St. Paul, MN

MAJOR SHAREHOLDERS

Curtis A. Sampson, 31%

Dale H. Schenian, 13%

Brian C. Barenscheer, 6.2%

Randall D. Sampson, 5.9%

All officers and directors as a group (11 persons), 59.4%

SIC CODE

7948 Racing, including track operation

MISCELLANEOUS

TRANSFER AGENT AND REGISTAR:
Wells Fargo Bank Minnesota N.A., South St. Paul, MN

TRADED: Nasdaq SmallCap Market

SYMBOL: TRAK

STOCKHOLDERS: 404

EMPLOYEES: 703

PART TIME: 331

IN MINNESOTA: 703

GENERAL COUNSEL:
Lindquist & Vennum PLLP, Minneapolis

AUDITORS:
Deloitte & Touche LLP, Minneapolis

INC: MN-1994

ANNUAL MEETING: June

INVESTOR RELATIONS:
Judy Dahlke

HUMAN RESOURCES:
Mary Fleming

RANKINGS

No. 147 CRM Public 200

SUBSIDIARIES, DIVISIONS, AFFILIATES

Canterbury Park Concessions Inc.

TWO-YEAR QUARTERLY HIGH-LOW STOCK PRICES

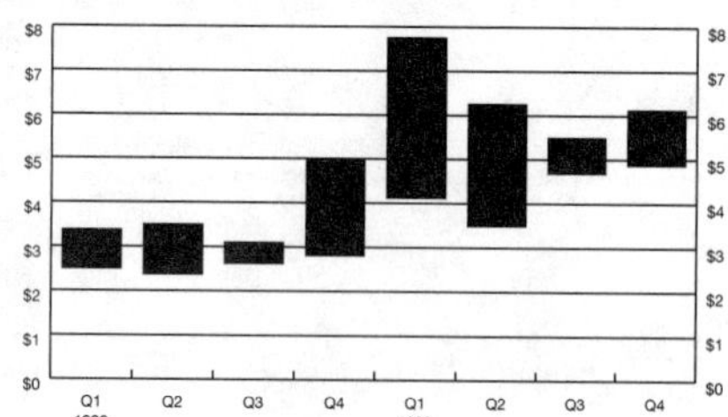

Celox Laboratories Inc.

1311 Helmo Ave. N., Oakdale, MN 55128
Tel: 651/730-1500 Fax: 651/730-8900

Celox Laboratories Inc. is a developing biotechnology company that researches, develops, manufactures, and markets cell biology products that are used in the propagation of cells derived from mammals, including humans and other species. These specialized cell growth products are used primarily in academic, pharmaceutical, and other commercial laboratories to improve the growth, productivity, and quality of cell-derived medical and other biological products such as vaccines, monoclonal antibodies, interferons, and human growth factor. The company's basal media supplements and cell-freezing medium contain no serum. Since its inception, the company has pursued a strategy of developing non-serum-based products for the growth of human and other mammalian cells, which management believes will have commercial potential.

EARNINGS HISTORY

Year Ended Aug 31	Operating Revenue/Sales (dollars in thousands)	Net Earnings	Return on Revenue (percent)	Return on Equity	Net Earnings	Cash Dividend (dollars per share)	Market Price Range
1999	198	(364)	NM	(52.6)	(0.13)	—	0.44–0.15
1998	266	(303)	NM	(30.4)	(0.11)	—	1.13–0.15
1997	221	(388)	NM	(30.0)	(0.14)	—	0.65–0.30
1996	368	(384)	NM	(22.8)	(0.14)	—	2.00–0.63
1995 *	323	(347)	NM	(16.4)	(0.13)	—	1.88–0.38

* Income figures for 1995 include investor settlement income of $133,000; and extraordinary gain of $253,621/$0.09, cumulative effect of accounting change.

BALANCE SHEET

Assets	08/31/99 (dollars in thousands)	08/31/98	Liabilities	08/31/99 (dollars in thousands)	08/31/98
Current (CAE 150 and 350)	623	886	Current	117	120
Equipment, leasehold improvements	130	172	Stockholders' equity*	692	996
Patents	55	59	TOTAL	808	1,116
TOTAL	808	1,116			

* $0.01 par common; 4,000,000 authorized; 2,909,169 and 2,744,169 issued and outstanding.

RECENT EVENTS

In **March 2000** the company announced plans to sell products online through an agreement with SciQuest.com Inc. (Nasdaq: SQST), a leading business-to-business e-marketplace for scientific products used by pharmaceutical, clinical, biotechnology, chemical, industrial, and educational organizations worldwide. CEO Polovina stated, "Strategically, this will enhance our distribution network, which already includes worldwide distributors Sigma Chemical Co. and ICN Pharmaceuticals Inc., and Japanese distributors Funakoshi Co. Ltd. and TaKaRa Shuzo Co. Ltd."

OFFICERS

Milo R. Polovina
Chairman, President, CEO, and Treasurer

Gayle R. Polovina
VP-Manufacturing

David E. Tess
VP-Finance/Administration

DIRECTORS

Milo R. Polovina

MAJOR SHAREHOLDERS

Milo R. Polovina, 24.4%

Arnold and Joy Ann Espeseth, 6.6%
Winger, MN

All officers and directors as a group (1 person), 24.4%

SIC CODE

2836 Biological products, exc diagnostic

MISCELLANEOUS

TRANSFER AGENT AND REGISTAR:
Wells Fargo Bank Minnesota N.A., South St. Paul, MN

TRADED: OTC Bulletin Board

SYMBOL: CELX

STOCKHOLDERS: 600

EMPLOYEES: 4

GENERAL COUNSEL:
Faegre & Benson PLLP, Minneapolis
Robins, Kaplan, Miller & Ciresi LLP, Minneapolis

AUDITORS:
Boulay, Heutmaker, Zibell & Co. PLLP, Minneapolis

INC: MN-1985

ANNUAL MEETING: May

SUBSIDIARIES, DIVISIONS, AFFILIATES

Protide Pharmaceuticals Inc.

PUB

Ceridian Corporation

3311 E. Old Shakopee Rd., Bloomington, MN 55425
Tel: 952/853-8100 Fax: 952/853-7272 Web site: http://www.ceridian.com

Ceridian Corp. is a leading information services company committed to helping customers improve their productivity and competitive position. The reorganized **Ceridian Human Resources** businesses focus on developing products and services to help customers improve organizational effectiveness. **Ceridian Employer Services** provides a broad range of products and services that support the employment life cycle and provide a total solutions approach to human resource management systems. **EAS Time & Attendance** is a provider of advanced, automated time and attendance software solutions. EAS serves government and commercial customers with software solutions that can be provided in conjunction with virtually any data collection hardware that customers wish to use, from electronic time cards to traditional time clock equipment. **Usertech** provides user support systems, including training and reference documentation, and expert systems to address employee and retiree questions about benefits, payroll, and human resource policies. **Ceridian Small Business Solutions** provides payroll and tax services to small businesses. **Ceridian Performance Partners** is focused on products and services that help customers improve organizational effectiveness. **Comdata Corp.** provides funds transfer and transaction processing and information services to the transportation industry. It provides funds transfer, fuel purchase, cash advance, and permit services, as well as fleet optimization and routing software for the transportation industry, and point of sale and data collection services for the truck stop industry.

continued on page 187

EARNINGS HISTORY *

Year Ended Dec 31	Operating Revenue/Sales (dollars in thousands)	Net Earnings (dollars in thousands)	Return on Revenue (percent)	Return on Equity (percent)	Net Earnings (dollars per share†)	Cash Dividend (dollars per share†)	Market Price Range (dollars per share†)
1999	1,342,300	148,900	11.1	17.7	1.03	—	40.50–16.63
1998 ¶	1,162,100	189,800	16.3	29.2	1.32	—	36.00–21.75
1997 #	1,074,800	472,400	44.0	NM	3.01	—	23.88–14.75
1996	942,600	181,900	19.3	48.8	1.20	—	27.44–18.50
1995 **	823,500	58,600	7.1	30.4	0.33	—	23.75–13.06

* Revenue figures restated for continuing operations. Income figures include the following gains from discontinued operations: $0.18; $2.79; $0.34; and $0.28—in 1998 through 1995, respectively. No adjustments have been made for the Arbitron spin-off.
† Per-share amounts restated to reflect 2-for-1 stock split effected Feb. 26, 1999.
¶ Income figures for 1998 include unusual gain of $9.2 million pretax, $5.8 million/$0.04 after-tax, from sale of land.
# Income figures for 1997 include pretax charges totaling $307.6 million, the largest portion related to an aggregate impairment loss from asset write-offs of $204.4 million.
** Income figures for 1995 include extraordinary loss of $38.9 million/($0.28) due to early retirement of debt.

BALANCE SHEET

Assets	12/31/99 (dollars in thousands)	12/31/98 (dollars in thousands)	Liabilities	12/31/99 (dollars in thousands)	12/31/98 (dollars in thousands)
Current (CAE 59,400 and 101,800)	645,300	633,700	Current (STD 200 and 300)	451,700	436,700
Property, plant, and equipment	192,800	91,300	L-t obligations	611,100	54,200
			Deferred taxes	10,300	3,600
Goodwill and other intangibles	1,047,200	377,500	Restructure reserves	26,800	29,000
			Ee benefit plans	77,700	74,100
Software and development costs	48,300	26,100	Deferred inc, other	39,600	41,500
			Stkhldrs' equity*	842,700	650,600
Prepaid pension cost	118,300	103,400	TOTAL	2,059,900	1,289,700
Deferred income taxes	4,100	53,400			
Other	3,900	4,300			
TOTAL	2,059,900	1,289,700			

* $0.50 par common; 500,000,000 authorized; 161,685,596 and 161,685,596 issued and outstanding, less 16,951,228 and 18,171,620 treasury shares.

RECENT QUARTERS / **PRIOR-YEAR RESULTS**

	Quarter End	Revenue ($000)	Earnings ($000)	EPS ($)	Prior-Year Revenue ($000)	Prior-Year Earnings ($000)	Prior-Year EPS ($)
Q3	09/30/2000	279,300	33,900	0.23	337,300	34,900	0.24
Q2	06/30/2000	283,100	32,200	0.22	322,200	35,700	0.25
Q1	03/31/2000	309,600	16,800	0.12	321,400	41,800	0.29
	SUM	872,000	82,900	0.57	980,900	112,400	0.78

CURRENT: Q3 earnings include gain of $12.0 million/$0.08 from discontinued operations. Q2 earnings include gain of $12.7 million/$0.09 from discontinued operations. Q1 earnings exclude special pretax charges of $30.5 million and include loss of $9.3 million/($0.06) from discontinued operations.

OFFICERS

Ronald L. Turner
Chairman, President, and CEO
John R. Eickhoff
EVP and CFO
Loren (Buzz) Gross
VP and Controller
Tony G. Holcombe
EVP and Pres.-Ceridian Employer Services
Shirley Hughes
SVP-Human Resources
Gary A. Krow
Pres.-Comdata
Stephen B. Morris
EVP and Pres.-Arbitron
Gary M. Nelson
VP, General Counsel, and Secretary
James J. O'Connell
VP-Gov't Relations/Hum. Res. Policy

DIRECTORS

Bruce R. Bond
William J. Cadogan
ADC Telecommunications Inc., Bloomington, MN
Nicholas D. Chabraja
General Dynamics
Dr. Ruth M. Davis
The Pymatuning Group
Robert H. Ewald
E-Stamp Corp., Mountain View, CA
Richard G. Lareau
Oppenheimer Wolff & Donnelly LLP, Minneapolis
Ronald T. LeMay
Sprint Corp., Westwood, KS
George R. Lewis
Philip Morris Cos. Inc.
Ronald L. Turner
Carole J. Uhrich
Paul S. Walsh
Pillsbury, Minneapolis

MAJOR SHAREHOLDERS

FMR Corp., 14%
Boston
AXA, 13.1%
Paris
T. Rowe Price Associates Inc., 5.4%
Baltimore
Massachusetts Financial Services Co., 5.2%
Boston
Wellington Management Co. LLP, 5%
Boston
All officers and directors as a group (15 persons), 1.9%

SIC CODE

6099 Functions related to deposit banking
7373 Computer integrated systems design
7374 Data processing and preparation
8732 Commercial nonphysical research

MISCELLANEOUS

TRANSFER AGENT AND REGISTAR:
Bank of New York
TRADED: NYSE
SYMBOL: CEN
STOCKHOLDERS: 12,600
EMPLOYEES: 11,000
PART TIME: 1,776
IN MINNESOTA: 626
GENERAL COUNSEL:
Gary M. Nelson
AUDITORS:
KPMG LLP, Minneapolis
INC: MN-1957
ANNUAL MEETING: May
INVESTOR RELATIONS:
Craig Manson

RANKINGS

No. 28 CRM Public 200

SUBSIDIARIES, DIVISIONS, AFFILIATES

Comdata Corp. (1)
5301 Maryland Way
Brentwood, TN 37027
615/370-7000
Gary A. Krow

Ceridian Employer/Employee Services (1)
Tony G. Holcombe

Centre-File (1)
75 Leman St.
London, England, E1 8EX
44-0-171-335-3000
Bruce Thew

Usertech (1)
One Selleck St.
East Norwalk, CT 06855
203/831-0300

TWO-YEAR QUARTERLY HIGH-LOW STOCK PRICES

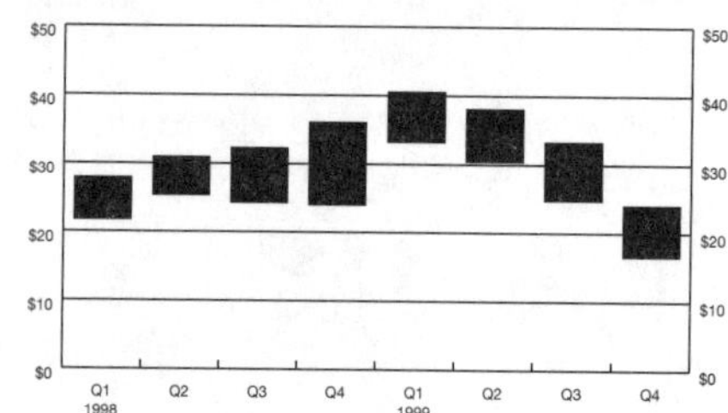

Check Technology Corporation

12500 Whitewater Dr., Minnetonka, MN 55343
Tel: 952/939-9000 Fax: 952/939-1151 Web site: http://www.ctcq3.com

Check Technology Corp. (CTC) designs, manufactures, and sells technologically advanced print production systems for financial, security, forms, and graphic arts printers worldwide. The company does business in 49 countries around the globe. This market penetration is a result of the high quality and innovative features of the company's products, and the comprehensive service and aftermarket support it provides.

EARNINGS HISTORY

Year Ended Sept 30	Operating Revenue/Sales (dollars in thousands)	Net Earnings	Return on Revenue (percent)	Return on Equity	Net Earnings (dollars per share)	Cash Dividend	Market Price Range
1999	22,308	(1,614)	(7.2)	(9.7)	(0.26)	—	3.88–1.50
1998	23,740	199	0.8	1.1	0.03	—	5.50–1.50
1997	22,867	326	1.4	1.7	0.05	—	10.88–3.88
1996	24,719	2,246	9.1	12.2	0.36	—	13.25–7.38
1995	24,361	2,053	8.4	13.1	0.34	—	7.63–4.88

BALANCE SHEET

Assets	09/30/99 (dollars in thousands)	09/30/98	Liabilities	09/30/99 (dollars in thousands)	09/30/98
Current	19,486	21,352	Current	3,750	3,717
(CAE 2,882 and 2,701)			Capital lease obligations		35
Equipment and fixtures	970	968	Stockholders' equity*	16,706	18,567
TOTAL	20,456	22,320	TOTAL	20,456	22,320

* $0.10 par common; 25,000,000 authorized; 6,154,157 and 6,178,120 issued and outstanding.

RECENT QUARTERS / **PRIOR-YEAR RESULTS**

	Quarter End	Revenue ($000)	Earnings ($000)	EPS ($)	Prior-Year Revenue ($000)	Prior-Year Earnings ($000)	Prior-Year EPS ($)
Q3	06/30/2000	7,118	131	0.02	4,220	(1,215)	(0.20)
Q2	03/31/2000	6,865	(208)	(0.03)	5,320	(510)	(0.08)
Q1	12/31/99	6,345	(120)	(0.02)	5,247	(320)	(0.05)
Q4	09/30/99	7,522	430	0.07	5,924	71	0.01
	SUM	27,849	234	0.04	20,711	(1,974)	(0.32)

RECENT EVENTS

In **December 1999** the company announced the sale of its advanced digital document production system, the Imaggia MG20, to Liberty Check printers of Roseville, Minn. Check Tech then numbered three North American check printers among its Imaggia customers—as well as commercial printers and government agencies in the United Kingdom, France, Italy, Japan, and Chile, for a total of 16 installations. In **January 2000** Check Technology and Atlanta-based John H. Harland Co. (NYSE: JH), one of the nation's biggest check printers, announced a three-year, $40 million contract for the purchase of Imaggia advanced digital document production systems—along with consumables, supplies, and a dedicated Check Technology service team to support Harland. With delivery on the contract to begin in the spring, Check Technology was expecting a significant boost in revenue and visibility. An additional 40 to 50 employees were to be hired, as well. In **March**, under a distribution agreement between Check Tech and CTC Japan (sub. Kyoto Densanshi Insatsu), of Kyoto, Japan, CTC Japan gained exclusive rights to sell the proprietary Imaggia digital imaging system to commercial printers in Japan for use in non-check business applications. In **October** Check Tech retained BlueFire Partners for investor relations and marketing communications services.

OFFICERS

Jay A. Herman
President and CEO

Rob M. Barniskis
CFO

Bruce H. Malmgren
VP-Sales/Marketing

Dieter Schilling
VP-Operations/Customer Service

Peter J. Wood
VP-Engineering

DIRECTORS

R. Stephen Armstrong
Patterson Dental Co., Mendota Heights, MN

Thomas H. Garrett III
business consultant, Minneapolis

Jay A. Herman

Gary R. Holland
Fargo Electronics Inc., Eden Prairie, MN

MAJOR SHAREHOLDERS

Annette J. and Fred H. Brenner, 7.7%
Wynnewood, PA

Perkins Capital Management Inc., 6.3%
Wayzata, MN

Dimensional Fund Advisors Inc., 5.3%
Santa Monica, CA

All officers and directors as a group (7 persons), 7.4%

SIC CODE

3555 Printing trades machinery

MISCELLANEOUS

TRANSFER AGENT AND REGISTAR:
Wells Fargo Bank Minnesota N.A.,
South St. Paul, MN

TRADED: Nasdaq National Market

SYMBOL: CTCQ

STOCKHOLDERS: 359

EMPLOYEES: 213

IN MINNESOTA: 149

GENERAL COUNSEL:
Lindquist & Vennum PLLP, Minneapolis

AUDITORS:
Ernst & Young LLP, Minneapolis

INC: MN-1981

ANNUAL MEETING:
March

RANKINGS

No. 142 CRM Public 200

SUBSIDIARIES, DIVISIONS, AFFILIATES

Check Technology France S.A.
8-10 rue du bois Sauvage
91055, Evry Cedex,
France
(33) 01 69 36 11 20
Didier Triaire

Check Technology Ltd.
3/4 Satellite Business Village, Fleming Way
Crawley, West Sussex
RH10 2NE, England
(01293) 551051
Ian Jaggard

Check Technology (Pty.) Ltd.
10/35 Leighton Place
Hornsby, N.S.W. 2077
Australia
(02) 9477 7800
Joe Der

TWO-YEAR QUARTERLY HIGH-LOW STOCK PRICES

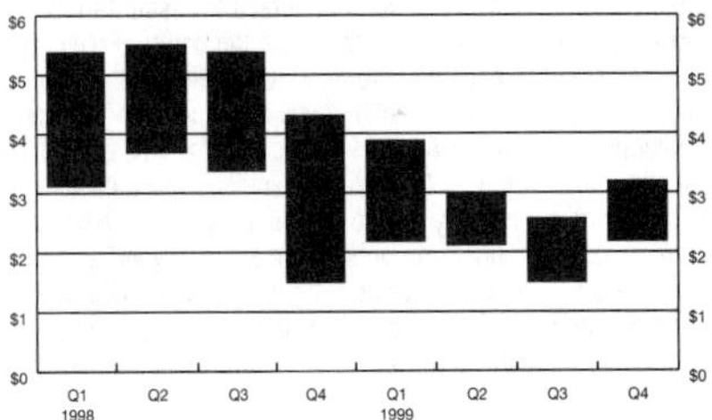

PUB

PUB

ChoiceTel Communications Inc.

9724 10th Ave. N., Plymouth, MN 55441
Tel: 763/544-1260 Fax: 763/544-1281

ChoiceTel Communications Inc. is the largest independent payphone service provider in Minnesota. The company operates in 10 states. The company believes the outlook for the pay telephone industry is favorable because of recent legislation that has led to deregulation of the rates for local pay telephone calls and an increase in the compensation for certain types of calls that previously produced little revenue for payphone service providers. The company also believes that the continued expansion in telecommunication services, including the rise in call waiting, voicemail, and pager usage, will result in increased calling volume, thus increasing the revenue generated by payphones. Deregulation is also expected to lead to reduced telephone line charges, one of the company's principal operating expenses. Since 1993, the company has completed the acquisition of four payphone routes, adding more than 2,000 telephones—1,600 in 1997 alone. The payphones operated by the company are computer-based, enabling the company to monitor phone call volume, identify malfunctioning equipment, dispatch repair service, schedule efficient coin collections, calculate commissions, print checks for location owners, rate and process long-distance calls, and generate reports that analyze and monitor the profitability of the phones. Management believes that as the company grows, the network can be expanded easily with little additional investment in infrastructure. The company was incorporated as Intelliphone Inc. and changed to its present name in April 1997.

EARNINGS HISTORY *

Year Ended Dec 31	Operating Revenue/Sales (dollars in thousands)	Net Earnings (dollars in thousands)	Return on Revenue (percent)	Return on Equity (percent)	Net Earnings (dollars per share†)	Cash Dividend (dollars per share†)	Market Price Range (dollars per share†)
1999 ¶	5	(17)	NM	(0.3)	(0.01)	—	3.63–1.50
1998 #	9,344	115	1.2	1.9	0.04	—	5.13–2.50
1997 **	7,081	(134)	(1.9)	(2.3)	(0.06)	—	6.25–4.63
1996	3,562	(605)	(17.0)	NM	(0.31)	—	
1995 ††	2,817	79	2.8	16.0	0.04	—	

* Revenue for 1998 and previous periods includes discontinued pay phone operations.
† Stock began trading Nov. 10, 1997.
¶ Income figures for 1999 include gain of $160,890/$0.05 from discontinued operations.
\# Income figures for 1998 include gain of $116,312/$0.04 from discontinued operations.
** Income figures for 1997 and prior periods include unspecified amounts from discontinued operations.
†† Income figures for 1995 are pro forma for income taxes.

BALANCE SHEET

Assets	12/31/99 (dollars in thousands)	12/31/98	Liabilities	12/31/99 (dollars in thousands)	12/31/98
Current (CAE 2,323 and 155)	4,187	1,455	Current (STD 383 and 1,297)	2,947	3,805
Property and equipment	113	38	Long-term debt	4	3,892
			Minority interest	24	
Discontinued operations	4,850	12,163	Stockholders' equity*	6,175	5,986
Deferred financing		27	TOTAL	9,150	13,683
TOTAL	9,150	13,683			

* $0.01 par common; 15,000,000 authorized; 2,926,906 and 2,915,006 issued and outstanding.

RECENT EVENTS

In **December 1999** the company called a special meeting of shareholders to consider and vote upon a proposal to approve a plan to sell certain assets of the company, including payphones located in the Midwest, Philadelphia, and Puerto Rico. Choicetel then closed the sale of 2,100 payphones located in Minnesota, Wisconsin, New York, Iowa, and North Dakota to Access Anywhere LLC, Minneapolis. These actions were taken in order to focus on the development of the public Internet access business of its subsidiary, Advants Inc. Chairman Kohler stated, "Our experience leasing, operating, and managing a network of public payphones will help us transition from a low-growth market to the dynamically growing public Internet market. We envision a future where our ADVANTS public Internet terminals are as common and essential as public payphones have been in the past." In **February 2000** Choicetel sold its route of 918 payphones located in Philadelphia to Alpha Telcom for $2 million. [Final payment received March 3.] Choicetel planned to divest the rest of its payphone network by summer. Meanwhile, in its sixth agreement of the year, Advants Inc. agreed to install terminals in all Freedom Valu Centers—the first systemwide, multistate Internet terminal installation of its kind in the nation. Freedom Valu Centers, owned by Erickson Oil Product, Inc., operates 60 petroleum/convenience retail stores in four states in the Upper Midwest. In **May** Choicetel completed a private financial placement—raising $2.2 million that, along with a portion of Choicetel's existing cash reserves, was to be used to make an additional $3 million investment in Advants Public Internet Access. Advants was to begin a pilot program to install its Internet terminal kiosks in some of the 25,000 beauty, tanning, and nail salons supplied by T.W. Enterprises. In **June** Advants installed public Internet terminals in Jerry's Food Stores. In August the board of directors authorized the company to repurchase up to 5 percent of its outstanding common stock. Advants signed an agreement to add the FreeDesk.com Virtual Office Suite, online storage, and PC Share to all Advants Internet terminals. (PC Share allows the customer to access files on any Internet-connected PC.) In **September** Advants announced a strategic alliance with New York-based InternetCash Corp. to offer the purchase of prepaid InternetCash cards to use for e-commerce purchases on Advants terminals.

OFFICERS

Gary S. Kohler
Chairman
Jeffrey R. Paletz
President
Melvin Graf
EVP and Secretary
Jack S. Kohler
VP and CFO
Dustin Elder
VP

DIRECTORS

Melvin Graf
Robert A. Hegstrom
Northwest Mortgage Services
Greg Johnson
Gary S. Kohler
Kohler Capital Management, Minneapolis
Jeffrey R. Paletz
Michael R. Wigley
Great Plains Cos. Inc.

MAJOR SHAREHOLDERS

Gary S. Kohler, 29.1%
Perkins Capital Management Inc., 12.7%
Wayzata, MN
Jeffrey R. Paletz, 9.8%
Jack S. Kohler, 9.6%
Melvin Graf, 6%
Michael Wigley, 5%
All officers and directors as a group (7 persons), 51.5%

SIC CODE

4813 Telephone communications, exc radio

MISCELLANEOUS

TRANSFER AGENT AND REGISTAR:
Wells Fargo Bank Minnesota N.A.,
South St. Paul, MN
TRADED: Nasdaq SmallCap Market
SYMBOL: PHON
STOCKHOLDERS: 300
EMPLOYEES: 28
GENERAL COUNSEL:
Robins, Kaplan, Miller & Ciresi LLP, Minneapolis
AUDITORS:
Schechter Dokken Kanter Andrews & Selcer Ltd., Minneapolis
INC: MN-1989

RANKINGS

No. 182 CRM Public 200

Christopher & Banks Corporation

2400 Xenium Ln. N., Plymouth, MN 55441
Tel: 763/551-5000 Fax: 763/551-5198 Web site: http://www.braunsfashions.com

Christopher & Banks Corp., formerly Braun's Fashions Corp., is a retailer of women's specialty apparel. The company operates a chain of 243 stores, under both the Braun's and Christopher & Banks names, in 27 states (as of July 2000) in the northern half of the United States. The company's stores offer coordinated assortments of moderately priced sportswear, sweaters, dresses, and accessories. The company's stores cater to 35- to 55-year-old women.

EARNINGS HISTORY

Year Ended Feb	Operating Revenue/Sales (dollars in thousands)	Net Earnings	Return on Revenue (percent)	Return on Equity	Net Earnings (dollars per share*)	Cash Dividend	Market Price Range
2000	143,402	11,535	8.0	30.9	1.16	—	14.67–3.36
1999 †	110,142	6,227	5.7	25.2	0.61	—	6.39–2.83
1998 ¶	99,536	4,401	4.4	21.0	0.44	—	7.17–2.83
1997 #	95,946	(621)	(0.6)	(4.0)	(0.07)	—	4.44–0.44
1996 **	97,296	(3,458)	(3.6)	(25.3)	(0.41)	—	1.56–0.67

* Per-share amounts restated to reflect 3-for-2 stock splits paid on July 11, 2000, and Dec. 14, 1999.
† Income figures for 1999 include extraordinary gain of $35,396/$0.00.
¶ Income figures for 1998 include nonrecurring pretax charge of $775,451 related to management succession plan; and extraordinary gain of $115,872/$0.01 on repurchase of senior notes.
# Income figures for 1997 include pretax charge of $7,830,000 for expenses incurred to reorganize under Chapter 11 bankruptcy, filed July 2, 1996.
** Income figures for 1996 include $1.789 million/($0.21) valuation allowance for deferred tax assets.

BALANCE SHEET

Assets	02/26/00 (dollars in thousands)	02/27/99
Current (CAE 22,685 and 12,587)	37,291	25,608
Equipment and improvements	19,781	12,955
Deferred taxes	1,630	1,468
Other	17	29
TOTAL	58,719	40,060

Liabilities	02/26/00 (dollars in thousands)	02/27/99
Current (STD 169 and 272)	15,191	9,184
Long-term debt	5,053	5,074
Accrued rent obligation	1,090	1,073
Stockholders' equity*	37,385	24,730
TOTAL	58,719	40,060

* $0.01 par common; 14,000,000 authorized; 10,122,954 and 9,786,963 issued and outstanding, less 828,000 and 828,000 treasury shares.

RECENT QUARTERS / **PRIOR-YEAR RESULTS**

	Quarter End	Revenue ($000)	Earnings ($000)	EPS ($)	Prior-Year Revenue ($000)	Prior-Year Earnings ($000)	Prior-Year EPS ($)
Q2	08/26/2000	41,548	4,194	0.41	29,207	837	0.08
Q1	05/27/2000	42,336	4,897	0.45	29,206	1,520	0.16
Q4	02/26/2000	45,185	5,258	0.52	31,371	1,969	0.20
Q3	11/27/99	39,804	3,920	0.39	30,826	2,676	0.25
	SUM	168,873	18,269	1.78	120,611	7,002	0.69

PRIOR YEAR: Q3 earnings include extraordinary gain of $35,396/$0.00.

RECENT EVENTS

In **January 2000** the company announced the fall launch of a new division catering to the women's large-size market. An extension of the company's Christopher & Banks brand, the new concept was to operate in the same geographic markets as existing Christopher & Banks stores. **March 25**: The company reported a 39 percent increase in March same-store sales for its four-week period. In April the company cautioned that such same-store increases would not continue, because it had decided not to repeat a big promotional tactic employed in April 1999. In **May** the board of directors authorized a change in the company name—from Braun's Fashions Corp. to Christopher & Banks Corp. (Nasdaq: CHBS)—which was to be presented for approval at the annual shareholder's meeting on July 26, 2000. CEO Prange commented, "Our stores exclusively feature Christopher & Banks merchandise, and part of our success is attributable to the fact that our Christopher & Banks brand has gained tremendous recognition and loyalty among our customer base. Last year, we opened 33 new Christopher & Banks stores and converted 23 existing Braun's stores to the Christopher & Banks name. In the current fiscal year, we plan to open approximately 35 new Christopher & Banks stores and we anticipate that additional remodels and name changes will enable us to operate approximately 50 percent of our stores under the Christopher & Banks name by December 2000. By December 2002, we expect to convert substantially all the remaining Braun's stores to the Christopher & Banks name." [Name change approved in July.] **May 27**: Braun's reported a 24 percent increase in May same-store sales for its four-week period. In July, even as the new name change was approaching, the company was working on yet another new name: C.J. Banks stores, targeted at larger-size women, was on track for a fall unveiling. Shareholders approved an amendment to the company's Certificate *continued on page 187*

OFFICERS

William J. Prange
Chairman and CEO

Joseph E. Pennington
President and COO

Tammy Leomazzi Boyd
Division President

Kathryn R. Gangstee
SVP-General Merchandise Manager

Lanette Menear
VP, Divisional Merchandise Mgr.

Andrew K. Moller
SVP and CFO

Ralph C. Neal
EVP-Store Operations

Nancy Scott
VP-Real Estate/Construction

Kim Westerham
VP-Merchandise Planning/Distribution

DIRECTORS

Larry C. Barenbaum
LCB Enterprises Inc., Minneapolis

Donald D. Beeler
Snyder's Drug Stores, Minnetonka, MN

Nicholas H. Cook

James J. Fuld Jr.
James J. Fuld Jr. Corp., New York

Anne L. Jones
Jones Consulting Group

Marc C. Ostrow
Pennwood Capital Corp., New York

Joseph E. Pennington

William J. Prange

MAJOR SHAREHOLDERS

Benson Associates LLC, 9.1%
Portland, OR

All officers and directors as a group (11 persons), 11.3%

SIC CODE

2331 Women's and misses' blouses and shirts

MISCELLANEOUS

TRANSFER AGENT AND REGISTAR:
Wells Fargo Bank Minnesota N.A., South St. Paul, MN

TRADED: Nasdaq National Market

SYMBOL: CHBS

STOCKHOLDERS: 73

EMPLOYEES: 1,350

GENERAL COUNSEL:
Robins, Kaplan, Miller & Ciresi LLP, Minneapolis

AUDITORS:
PricewaterhouseCoopers LLP, Minneapolis

INC: DE-1986

FOUNDED: 1956

ANNUAL MEETING: July

HUMAN RESOURCES:
Rosemary C. Wolf

INVESTOR RELATIONS:
Andrew Moller

RANKINGS

No. 81 CRM Public 200
No. 7 CRM Performance 100

PUB

TWO-YEAR QUARTERLY HIGH-LOW STOCK PRICES

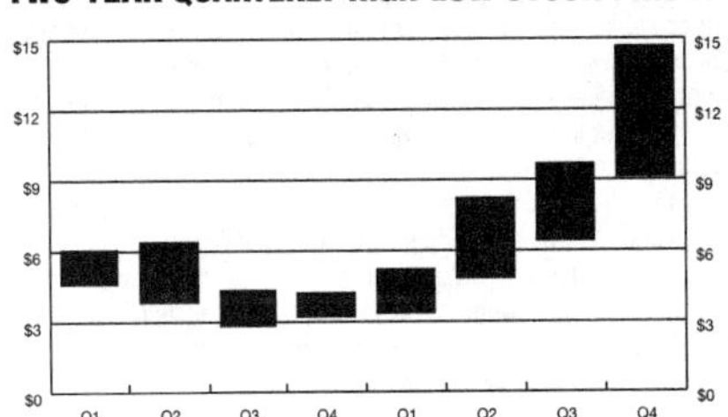

PUB

The Chromaline Corporation

4832 Grand Ave., Duluth, MN 55807
Tel: 218/628-2217 Fax: 218/628-3245 Web site: http://www.chromaline.com

The Chromaline Corp. develops, manufactures, and markets photostencil films, emulsions, screen preparation products, and photochemical imaging systems for the screen printing industry. These imaging products are sold worldwide through a network of dealers to screen printers for use in production processes. Originally known as Chroma-Glo Inc., the company started business as a screen printer of precision graphics. In 1964, to improve the printing process, it developed and patented a photochemical imaging product called the Direct/Indirect photostencil system. The company manufactured and sold this product to other screen printers as an additional business venture. In 1982 it sold the screen print business.

EARNINGS HISTORY

Year Ended Dec 31	Operating Revenue/Sales (dollars in thousands)	Net Earnings	Return on Revenue (percent)	Return on Equity	Net Earnings (dollars per share*)	Cash Dividend	Market Price Range
1999	9,911	804	8.1	14.2	0.62	—	8.41–6.14
1998	9,289	881	9.5	18.1	0.68	—	9.43–6.36
1997 †	8,900	638	7.2	16.4	0.50	—	9.24–4.55
1996 ¶	8,858	665	7.5	20.5	0.52	—	5.15–3.48
1995	7,584	500	6.6	19.3	0.39	—	3.79–3.18

* Per-share amounts restated to reflect 10 percent stock dividend paid Jan. 17, 2000; and 3-for-2 stock split effected Sept. 19, 1997.
† Income figures for 1997 include pretax charge of $445,000 for patent-litigation costs.
¶ Income figures for 1996 include pretax charge of $46,000 for patent-litigation costs.

BALANCE SHEET

Assets	12/31/99 (dollars in thousands)	12/31/98	Liabilities	12/31/99 (dollars in thousands)	12/31/98
Current (CAE 706 and 274)	4,440	3,652	Current	498	401
Property and equipment	1,556	1,424	Stockholders' equity*	5,661	4,860
Patents	95	104	TOTAL	6,159	5,261
Deferred taxes	30	43			
Other	39	39			
TOTAL	6,159	5,261			

* $0.10 par common; 4,750,000 authorized; 1,298,056 and 1,296,131 issued and outstanding.

RECENT QUARTERS / **PRIOR-YEAR RESULTS**

	Quarter End	Revenue ($000)	Earnings ($000)	EPS ($)	Revenue ($000)	Earnings ($000)	EPS ($)
Q3	09/30/2000	2,373	22	0.02	2,474	193	0.15
Q2	06/30/2000	2,740	248	0.19	2,551	258	0.20
Q1	03/31/2000	2,299	51	0.04	2,237	143	0.11
Q4	12/31/99	2,649	210	0.16	2,260	168	0.13
	SUM	10,061	530	0.41	9,523	761	0.59

RECENT EVENTS

In **December 1999**, as part of an effort to gain a Nasdaq listing for its common stock, the company announced a 10 percent stock dividend. The dividend was to provide a sufficient number of public shares to meet all Nasdaq SmallCap Market listing requirements. In **February 2000** Chromaline signed an exclusive worldwide agreement to market a new film designed by The DuPont Co. and managed by ARTech Imaging Inc. The film, RapidMask Sandblast/Etching Resist, is a photopolymer dry film for use in decorative sandblasting and etching applications. In **March** Chromaline's application for listing on the Nasdaq SmallCap Market was approved. In **May** the U.S. Federal District Court in Seattle granted Chromaline its request for a summary judgment in its patent infringement suit with the Aicello Corp.—ruling that Chromaline was not liable for infringement damages for allegedly infringing products made or sold prior to Feb. 1, 2000, the date when Aicello was issued a reexamination certificate. The ruling granted all of Chromaline's requested relief in its summary judgment pleadings and followed a re-examination of the Aicello patents by the U.S. Patent Office that Chromaline had requested. Chromaline was no longer manufacturing the allegedly infringing products, having replaced them with products based on new technology. CEO Ulland stated, "This is an important victory for our company since it essentially removes the specter of a large award for past damages." In **June** Chromaline acquired the assets and business of Nichols and Associates Inc. of Lakeville, Minn.—a manufacturer of environmentally friendly chemicals used primarily in the screen printing industry. CEO Ulland said, "This acquisition adds an excellent new product line, new distribution channels and fills out our offerings to the screen printing industry." Chromaline estimated that the acquisition would initially increase sales 5 percent to 10 percent and, once various transaction costs are absorbed, would contribute to operating income. The board of directors authorized purchases by the corporation of up to 50,000 shares (3.8 percent) of its common stock. In **August** Chromaline purchased shares and warrants amounting to less than 7 percent ownership in Apprise Technologies Inc., a Minnesota based company developing products for potential applications in photosensitive processing. In **September** European master distributor Chromaline Europe SA filed for bankruptcy under French law and was in liquidation, citing financial problems primarily caused by a weak Euro. Chromaline owned 19.5 percent of the stock of Chromaline Europe, which had accounted for 7.5 percent of Chromaline's total sales and less than 4.5 percent of its gross profit. **Sept. 30:** One-time losses associated with the bankruptcy of its ***continued on page 187***

OFFICERS

William C. Ulland
Chairman and CEO

Robert D. Banks Jr.
VP-International Sales

Toshifumi Komatsu
VP-Technology

Jeffrey A. Laabs
SFO, Treasurer, Secretary

Claude Piguet
VP-Operations

DIRECTORS

Charles H. Andresen
Magie, Andresen, Haag, Paciotti, Butterworth & McCarthy, Duluth, MN

Rondi Erickson
Apprise Technologies Inc., Duluth, MN

David O. Harris
David O. Harris Inc., Minneapolis

H. Leigh Severance
Severance Capital Management, Denver

Gerald W. Simonson
Omnetics Connector Corp., Minneapolis

William C. Ulland

MAJOR SHAREHOLDERS

William C. Ulland, 11.1%

Leigh Severance, 9.7%
Denver

All officers and directors as a group (10 persons), 22.6%

SIC CODE

3861 Photographic equipment and supplies

MISCELLANEOUS

TRANSFER AGENT AND REGISTAR:
Wells Fargo Bank Minnesota N.A.,
South St. Paul, MN

TRADED: Nasdaq SmallCap Market

SYMBOL: CMLH

STOCKHOLDERS: 450

EMPLOYEES: 75

GENERAL COUNSEL:
Hanft Fride, Duluth, MN

AUDITORS:
Deloitte & Touche LLP, Minneapolis

INC: MN-1952

FOUNDED: 1952

ANNUAL MEETING: April

HUMAN RESOURCES:
Molly Haugen

PURCHASING:
Eugene Panyan

RANKINGS

No. 185 CRM Public 200

SUBSIDIARIES, DIVISIONS, AFFILIATES

Photo Brasive Systems
4832 Grand Ave.
Duluth, MN 55807
218/628-2002
Becki Nelson

Chronimed Inc.

10900 Red Circle Dr., Minnetonka, MN 55343
Tel: 952/979-3600 Fax: 952/979-3969 Web site: http://www.chronimed.com

Chronimed Inc. is a disease-focused drug distribution company serving the prescription drug needs of people with selected chronic health conditions. The company distributes pharmaceuticals via a mail order and retail pharmacy network, providing specialized patient management services nationwide for people with long-term chronic conditions, including HIV/AIDS, organ transplants and diseases treated with biotech injectable medications.

EARNINGS HISTORY *

Year Ended June	Operating Revenue/Sales (dollars in thousands)	Net Earnings (dollars in thousands)	Return on Revenue (percent)	Return on Equity (percent)	Net Earnings (dollars per share)	Cash Dividend (dollars per share)	Market Price Range (dollars per share)
2000 †	225,887	562	0.2	0.8	0.05	—	11.00–4.94
1999 ¶	168,624	4,127	2.4	6.2	0.34	—	14.00–4.75
1998	115,614	7,151	6.2	11.5	0.60	—	15.25–7.56
1997 #	88,207	7,044	8.0	13.2	0.59	—	20.88–6.88
1996	61,536	5,459	8.9	9.6	0.45	—	25.13–10.63

* Revenue restated to segregate Diagnostic Products business (to be spun off as MEDgenesis) as discontinued operations. Income figures include the following gains from discontinued operations: $0.15, $0.28, $0.48, $0.42, and $0.38—in 2000 through 1996, respectively.
† Income figures for 2000 include pretax charge of $5.5 million for asset write-down.
¶ Income figures for 1999 include gain of $300,000/$0.02 on sale of publishing business; and one-time expenses of $800,000 pretax, $488,000/($0.04) after-tax, from search for strategic alternatives.
# Income figures for 1997 include gain of $1.7 million pretax, $1.04 million/$0.09 after-tax, on sale of Orphan Medical Inc. product marketing rights back to Orphan Medical.

BALANCE SHEET

Assets	06/30/00 (dollars in thousands)	07/02/99 (dollars in thousands)
Current (CAE 0 and 3,312)	56,396	43,527
Property and equipment	6,551	7,857
Goodwill	9,031	15,373
Deferred taxes	508	13
Discontinued operations	10,465	11,624
Other	109	148
TOTAL	83,060	78,542

Liabilities	06/30/00 (dollars in thousands)	07/02/99 (dollars in thousands)
Current (STD 2,500)	15,373	12,055
Stockholders' equity*	67,687	66,487
TOTAL	83,060	78,542

* $0.01 par common; 40,000,000 authorized; 12,147,000 and 12,088,000 issued and outstanding.

RECENT QUARTERS / **PRIOR-YEAR RESULTS**

	Quarter End	Revenue ($000)	Earnings ($000)	EPS ($)	Prior-Year Revenue ($000)	Prior-Year Earnings ($000)	Prior-Year EPS ($)
Q1	09/29/2000	64,419	1,325	0.11	50,878	328	0.03
Q4	06/30/2000	59,067	559	0.05	48,187	(288)	(0.02)
Q3	03/31/2000	57,596	(1,891)	(0.16)	44,046	466	0.04
Q2	12/31/99	58,346	1,566	0.13	41,021	2,255	0.19
	SUM	239,428	1,559	0.13	184,132	2,761	0.23

CURRENT: Q1 earnings include gain of $464,000/$0.04 from discontinued operations. Q4 earnings include charge of $530,000 pretax, $308,000/($0.03) after-tax, for spin-off costs; and gain of $122,000/$0.01 from discontinued operations and sale of securities. Q3 earnings include loss of $3,355,000/($0.28) write-off of Clinical Partners contracts line; and gain of $635,000/$0.05 from discontinued operations and sale of securities. Q2 earnings include one-time expenses of $470,000 pretax, $287,000/($0.02) after-tax, related to efforts in seeking strategic alternatives; and gain of $647,000/$0.05 from discontinued operations.
PRIOR YEAR: Q1 earnings include one-time expenses of $412,000 pretax, $251,000/($0.02) after-tax; and gain of $436,000/$0.04 from discontinued operations. Q4 earnings include one-time expenses of $800,000 pretax, $488,000/($0.04) after-tax, from search for strategic alternatives; and gain of $342,000/$0.03 from discontinued operations. Q3 earnings include gain of $683,000/$0.06 from discontinued operations. Q2 earnings include gain of $500,000 pretax, $305,000/$0.02 after-tax, on sale of publishing business; and gain of $1,171,000/$0.10 from discontinued operations.

RECENT EVENTS

In **December 1999** the company signed a contract with Mutual of Omaha for the distribution of transplant and injectable medications. The contract allowed for provision of *continued on page 187*

OFFICERS

Henry F. (Hank) Blissenbach, Pharm. D.
Chairman and CEO

Perry L. Anderson
SVP-Retail Pharmacy

Shawn L. Featherston
VP-Human Resources

Kenneth Guenthuer, Esq.
General Counsel and Secretary

Gregory H. Keane
CFO and Treasurer

Stephen T. Ritter
SVP-Mail Order Pharmacy

Patrick L. Taffe
Chief Information Officer

DIRECTORS

Henry F. Blissenbach

John Howell Bullion
Orphan Medical Inc., Minnetonka, MN

John H. Flittie
ING ReliaStar, Minneapolis

Thomas Heaney
Korn/Ferry Int'l, Minneapolis

David R. Hubers
American Express Financial Advisors Inc., Minneapolis

Charles V. Owens Jr.
Miles Laboratories Inc. (retired)

Stu Samuels
management consultant

MAJOR SHAREHOLDERS

Heartland Advisors Inc., 12.8%
Milwaukee

All officers and directors as a group (10 persons), 4.6%

SIC CODE

5912 Drug stores and proprietary stores

MISCELLANEOUS

TRANSFER AGENT AND REGISTAR:
Wells Fargo Bank Minnesota N.A., South St. Paul, MN

TRADED: Nasdaq National Market

SYMBOL: CHMD

STOCKHOLDERS: 450

EMPLOYEES: 280

GENERAL COUNSEL:
Gray, Plant, Mooty, Mooty & Bennett P.A., Minneapolis

AUDITORS:
Ernst & Young LLP, Minneapolis

INC: MN-1985

ANNUAL MEETING: November

INVESTOR RELATIONS: Paul S. Dunn

HUMAN RESOURCES: Shawn Featherston

RANKINGS

No. 70 CRM Public 200

No. 38 Minnesota Technology Fast 50

SUBSIDIARIES, DIVISIONS, AFFILIATES

StatScript Pharmacy
7400 W. 132nd St.
Suite 220
Overland Park, KS 66213
913/402-4455
Perry Anderson

PUB

TWO-YEAR QUARTERLY HIGH-LOW STOCK PRICES

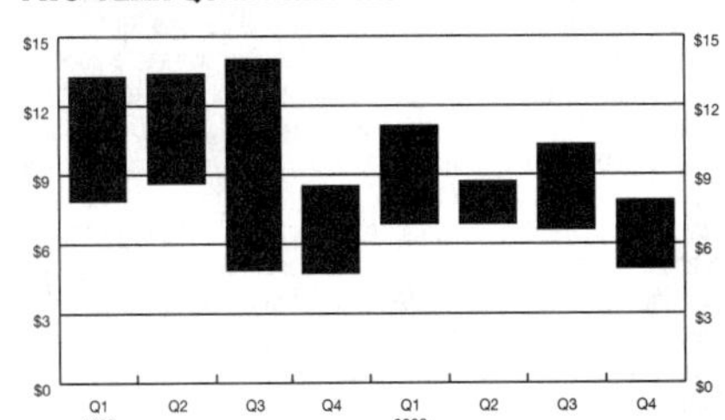

PUB

CIMA LABS Inc.

10000 Valley View Rd., Eden Prairie, MN 55344
Tel: 952/947-8700 Fax: 952/947-8770 Web site: http://www.cimalabs.com

CIMA LABS Inc. is a drug-delivery company that develops and manufactures, for its pharmaceutical partners, innovative drug-delivery systems that improve patient compliance and drug efficacy. CIMA's initial patented technologies, **OraSolv** and **DuraSolv** are oral-dosage forms that incorporate microencapsulated drug ingredients into MELTABS, fast-melting tablets that dissolve quickly in the mouth without chewing or water and effectively mask the taste of the medication. OraSolv and DuraSolv can be used for both immediate-release and sustained/controlled-release applications. The company is also developing a new buccal and sublingual system that improves the efficacy of drugs known as OraVescent. CIMA has major pharmaceutical collaborations with Novartis, Organon, Bristol-Myers Squibb, Schwarz Pharma, and Astria Zeneca.

EARNINGS HISTORY

Year Ended Dec 31	Operating Revenue/Sales	Net Earnings	Return on Revenue	Return on Equity	Net Earnings	Cash Dividend	Market Price Range
	(dollars in thousands)		(percent)		(dollars per share)		
1999	13,392	(1,262)	(9.4)	(10.9)	(0.13)	—	13.50–2.53
1998	7,612	(3,187)	(41.9)	(25.2)	(0.33)	—	4.97–2.09
1997	4,910	(5,838)	NM	(36.9)	(0.61)	—	8.25–3.88
1996	1,472	(6,346)	NM	(30.2)	(0.72)	—	11.75–4.25
1995	835	(9,107)	NM	(63.8)	(1.16)	—	10.88–3.88

BALANCE SHEET

Assets	12/31/99	12/31/98
	(dollars in thousands)	
Current (CAE 2,480 and 2,722)	8,384	4,936
Lease deposits	319	345
Patents and trademarks	207	205
Property, plant, and equipment	10,359	9,430
TOTAL	19,270	14,916

Liabilities	12/31/99	12/31/98
	(dollars in thousands)	
Current (STD 150)	4,186	2,030
Lease obligations	160	231
Long-term debt	3,350	
Common stockholders' equity*	11,574	12,656
TOTAL	19,270	14,916

* $0.01 par common; 20,000,000 authorized; 9,646,241 and 9,610,394 issued and outstanding.

RECENT QUARTERS / PRIOR-YEAR RESULTS

	Quarter End	Revenue ($000)	Earnings ($000)	EPS ($)	Prior-Year Revenue ($000)	Prior-Year Earnings ($000)	Prior-Year EPS ($)
Q3	09/30/2000	5,367	623	0.06	4,208	(181)	(0.02)
Q2	06/30/2000	5,755	383	0.04	3,228	(368)	(0.04)
Q1	03/31/2000	5,712	(240)	(0.02)	1,783	(816)	(0.08)
Q4	12/31/99	4,402	103	0.01	2,649	(415)	(0.04)
	SUM	21,236	869	0.08	11,868	(1,780)	(0.19)

CURRENT: Q1 earnings include loss of $799,000/($0.08), cumulative effect of change in accounting principle.

RECENT EVENTS

In **November 1999**, 10 European regulatory authorities agreed to mutually recognize the Swedish approval of Zomig Rapimelt, the OraSolv fast-dissolving version of the AstraZeneca antimigraine medication. Fahnestock & Co., New York, was projecting a 2 cents-per-share profit in fourth quarter, followed by 35 cents in 2000 and 80 cents in 2001. In **January 2000** Organon, a pharmaceutical business unit of Akzo Nobel, exercised an option to enter into a definitive exclusive license agreement covering an OraSolv (fast-dissolve) dosage application. CIMA was to receive a milestone payment for completion of this agreement. CIMA signed a license and development agreement with American Home Products Corp. for an undisclosed prescription product (thought to be an anti-depressant). "This is a significant event for CIMA. This illustrates the commercial viability of our second fast-dissolve technology, DuraSolv, and the continued success of all our fast-dissolve technologies," commented CEO Siebert. In **February** CIMA announced the issuance of its DuraSolv patent (U.S. Patent No. 6,024,981) from the U.S. Patent and Trademark Office. DuraSolv is a robust, oral dosage form which incorporates drug ingredients into tablets that dissolve quickly in the mouth. DuraSolv is designed to improve taste acceptance and address the difficulty of swallowing traditional tablets and capsules, while offering a convenient oral dosage form that can be taken anywhere and at anytime, therefore increasing compliance. Unlike other fast-dissolve technologies, DuraSolv can be packaged in conventional bottles or foil blisters. In **March** CIMA entered into a definitive stock purchase agreement for the sale in a private placement of 1.1 million shares at $19.00 per share, for net proceeds of $19.4 million. The company was intending to use net proceeds from this private placement to provide working capital, a capital project for expanding manufacturing capacity, and for general corporate purposes. CIMA needed to add a second production line, at a cost of $10 million to $12 million, to handle contracts for drugs scheduled to be released over the next two years. CIMA reported that the filing of a new drug application (NDA) with the FDA for a prescription pharmaceutical product incorporating the company's OraSolv technology—and an FDA regulatory filing for a prescription pharmaceutical product incorporating the company's DuraSolv technology—had both been accomplished. In **June** a new drug application (NDA) was filed by AstraZeneca (NYSE: AZN) for the OraSolv fast-dis- *continued on page 187*

OFFICERS

John M. Siebert, Ph.D.
President and CEO

John Hontz, Ph.D.
COO

David Feste
VP-Finance, CFO, and Secretary/Treasurer

Mark D. Hankins
VP-Business Development

Donald Sims, Ph.D.
VP-Quality Assurance

HUMAN RESOURCES:
Ronald Gay

RANKINGS

No. 168 CRM Public 200

No. 8 Minnesota Technology Fast 50

DIRECTORS

Terrence W. Glarner
West Concord Ventures Inc., Minneapolis

Steven B. Ratoff
Brown-Forman Corp., Louisville, KY

Joseph R. Robinson, Ph.D.
University of Wisconsin, Madison, WI

John M. Siebert, Ph.D.

MAJOR SHAREHOLDERS

President/Fellows of Harvard College, 6%
Boston

Capital Research and Management Co., 5.7%
Los Angeles

Franklin Small Cap Growth Fund, 5.5%
New York

All officers and directors as a group (5 persons), 7%

SIC CODE

2834 Pharmaceutical preparations

MISCELLANEOUS

TRANSFER AGENT AND REGISTAR:
Wells Fargo Bank Minnesota N.A.,
South St. Paul, MN

TRADED: Nasdaq National Market

SYMBOL: CIMA

STOCKHOLDERS: 75

EMPLOYEES: 120

IN MINNESOTA: 120

GENERAL COUNSEL:
Faegre & Benson PLLP, Minneapolis

AUDITORS:
Ernst & Young LLP, Minneapolis

INC: DE-1986

ANNUAL MEETING: May

TWO-YEAR QUARTERLY HIGH-LOW STOCK PRICES

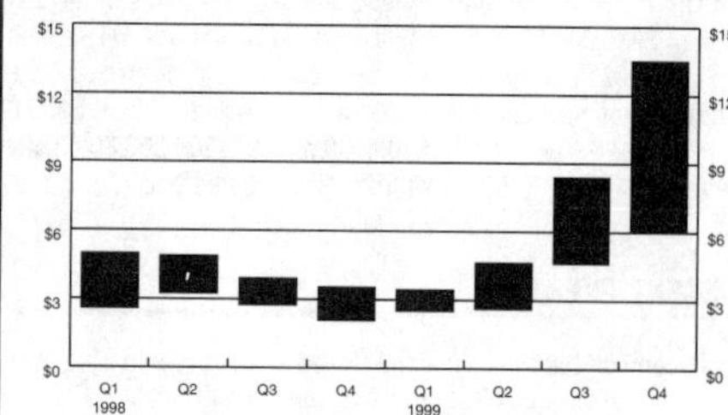

Ciprico Inc.

2800 Campus Dr., Plymouth, MN 55441
Tel: 763/551-4000 Fax: 763/551-4002 Web site: http://www.ciprico.com

Ciprico Inc. is an ISO 9000-certified company that designs, manufactures, markets, and services RAID disk arrays for high-performance data storage in imaging and digital media markets. The company's products are sold worldwide to technical, scientific, and creative professionals who require high-performance digital storage with data redundancy, large/flexible capacities and fault-tolerant features. Examples include original-equipment manufacturers (OEMs) and large end users within visual computing industries such as entertainment, medical imaging, digital prepress, satellite telemetry, and oil and gas exploration.

EARNINGS HISTORY

Year Ended Sept 30	Operating Revenue/Sales (dollars in thousands)	Net Earnings	Return on Revenue (percent)	Return on Equity	Net Earnings (dollars per share*)	Cash Dividend	Market Price Range
1999	34,059	2,056	6.0	4.3	0.42	—	14.50–6.31
1998	30,089	663	2.2	1.5	0.13	—	15.13–6.50
1997	36,390	4,249	11.7	8.8	0.84	—	20.50–11.00
1996	27,408	3,444	12.6	8.1	0.87	—	28.50–5.83
1995	15,966	396	2.5	5.1	0.12	—	7.67–2.58

* Per-share amounts restated to reflect 3-for-2 stock split on April 12, 1996.

BALANCE SHEET

Assets	09/30/99 (dollars in thousands)	09/30/98
Current (CAE 3,539 and 9,029)	40,077	39,721
Furniture and equipment	3,743	4,511
Marketable securities	9,003	5,016
Deferred income taxes	290	81
Other	125	145
TOTAL	53,238	49,473

Liabilities	09/30/99 (dollars in thousands)	09/30/98
Current	5,948	4,164
Stockholders' equity*	47,290	45,309
TOTAL	53,238	49,473

* $0.01 par common; 9,000,000 authorized; 4,954,779 and 4,916,297 issued and outstanding.

RECENT QUARTERS / **PRIOR-YEAR RESULTS**

	Quarter End	Revenue ($000)	Earnings ($000)	EPS ($)	Prior-Year Revenue ($000)	Prior-Year Earnings ($000)	Prior-Year EPS ($)
Q4	09/30/2000	8,431	(522)	(0.10)	8,562	588	0.12
Q3	06/30/2000	9,742	262	0.05	9,108	664	0.14
Q2	03/31/2000	8,191	60	0.01	8,615	522	0.11
Q1	12/31/99	6,847	(109)	(0.02)	7,774	282	0.06
	SUM	33,211	(309)	(0.06)	34,059	2,056	0.42

RECENT EVENTS

In **December 1999** the company was certified as a BROCADE Fabric Integrator, allowing Ciprico to include BROCADE switches with its SAN (storage area network) solutions. The BBC's (British Broadcasting Corp.) 28-hour New Year's broadcast, 2000 Today, relied on Ciprico Fibre Channel high-speed digital storage to support unique real-time special effects generated by SGI Onyx2 computers with InfiniteReality2 visualization subsystems. In **February 2000** Ciprico announced the availability of Seagate 73 GB drives with the 7000 Series Fibre Channel RAID disk arrays, increasing total storage capacity to 587 GB per unit. In **April** Ciprico's 6500 Series RAID disk array became the only digital storage system SGI-approved as Linux-compatible and also compatible with the IRIX and NT operating systems. Ciprico announced a partnership with SGI China to provide a full SAN (storage area network) configuration at the China Research Institute of Film Science and Technology in Beijing. The new Hayden Planetarium's centerpiece Digital Dome Projection System in the American Museum of Natural History's Rose Center for Earth and Space in New York City relies on a Ciprico high-performance Fibre Channel digital storage system to supply the imagery of literally billions of stars. Ciprico and Advanced Digital Information Corp. (Nasdaq:ADIC) announced a strategic and technical agreement to include ADIC's CentraVision Storage Area Network (SAN) file-sharing software with Ciprico's comprehensive digital SAN solution package. In **May** Ciprico showcased the new NETarray Storage System at NetWorld+Interop 2000 in Las Vegas. In **June** Ciprico announced the availability of Seagate 73 GB drives with the FibreSTORE Family Series Fibre Channel RAID disk arrays, which increase total storage capacity to 587 GB per unit. In **July** FibreSTORE RAID passed the SANMark and Fabric Build test tracks at the SAN Interoperability Plugfest in Durham, N.H. Ciprico installed a Fibre Channel SAN solution at Australia's Bond University in the campus' Non-linear Student Lab. The company launched the Ciprico Networked Storage Certification Program, designed to promote tested networked storage solutions compatible with recognized industry standards. Ciprico entered into a reseller agreement with EdgeMark Systems Inc., Silver Springs, Md. In **August** Kodak Professional was collaborating with the company to bring portrait labs a viable solution for both work-in-progress and longer-term image storage needs. In **September** the company announced that the first NETarray RAID systems had begun shipping to visual computing customers worldwide. **Sept. 30:** As expected, the company repported lower fourth-quarter results. "Although disappointed with the results this quarter," said CEO Kill, "the [$2.1 million] backlog is validation that the broadcast business opportunity is ramping up as we go into next fiscal year." In **October** the company's Ruggedized 7000 Disk Array passed the MIL-STD 901D Grade B Class III shock testing verifying the product's durability in the most rigorous and harsh environments. In **November** the 7000 Fibre Channel RAID storage solution was part of a high-speed networking demonstration in the Essential Communications booth at the Super Computing Show in Dallas.

OFFICERS

Robert H. Kill
Chairman, President, and CEO

Stephen R. Hansen
VP-Product Development/Operations

Tom Wargolet
VP-Finance and CFO

DIRECTORS

Bruce Bergman
private investor

Thomas F. Burniece
independent consultant

Gary L. Deaner
Crossworks

Robert H. Kill

Donald H. Soukup
venture capitalist

William N. Wray
private investor

MAJOR SHAREHOLDERS

Perkins Capital Management Inc., 13%
Wayzata, MN

Fidelity Research & Management Inc., 8.5%
Boston

Heartland Advisors Inc., 7.1%
Milwaukee

Dimensional Fund Advisors Inc., 5.6%
Santa Monica, CA

All officers and directors as a group (8 persons), 6%

SIC CODE

3572 Computer storage devices

3679 Electronic components, nec

MISCELLANEOUS

TRANSFER AGENT AND REGISTAR:
Wells Fargo Bank Minnesota N.A.,
South St. Paul, MN

TRADED: Nasdaq National Market

SYMBOL: CPCI

STOCKHOLDERS: 3,600

EMPLOYEES: 112

GENERAL COUNSEL:
Fredrikson & Byron P.A., Minneapolis

AUDITORS:
Grant Thornton LLP, Minneapolis

INC: DE-1978

ANNUAL MEETING:
January

HUMAN RESOURCES:
Jeanne Vencill

RANKINGS

No. 130 CRM Public 200

SUBSIDIARIES, DIVISIONS, AFFILIATES

Ciprico International Ltd.
England

Ciprico FSC Inc.
Virgin Islands

Ciprico Asia-Pacific Inc.
Japan

TWO-YEAR QUARTERLY HIGH-LOW STOCK PRICES

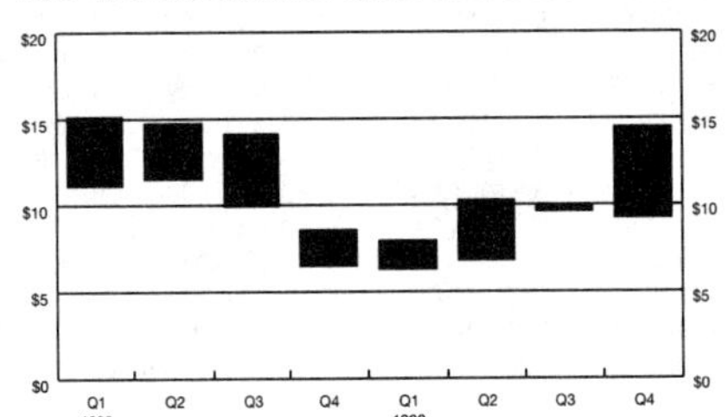

PUB

Communications Systems Inc.

213 S. Main St., Hector, MN 55342
Tel: 320/848-6231 Fax: 320/848-2702 Web site: http://www.commsystems.com

Communications Systems Inc. provides a growing package of physical connectivity infrastructure and services required for the convergence of voice, data, and video communications. Designed for open architecture environments, the company's connectivity products support the switches, hubs, and routers of major networking vendors.

EARNINGS HISTORY *

Year Ended Dec 31	Operating Revenue/Sales (dollars in thousands)	Net Earnings	Return on Revenue (percent)	Return on Equity	Net Earnings (dollars per share)	Cash Dividend	Market Price Range
1999	116,933	9,014	7.7	13.6	1.04	0.40	14.75–8.50
1998 †	71,159	7,867	11.1	12.4	0.87	0.38	19.25–10.50
1997	75,732	10,937	14.4	15.8	1.18	0.34	22.75–12.50
1996 ¶	68,705	8,233	12.0	13.9	0.89	0.30	16.50–11.25
1995 #	66,004	9,084	13.8	16.8	1.00	0.26	20.00–12.00

* Income figures include the following per-share results of discontinued contract manufacturing operations: ($0.08) and $0.02—in 1996 and 1995, respectively.
† Figures for 1998 include results of Transition Networks Inc. (acquired Dec. 1, 1998) and JDL Technologies Inc. (acquired Aug. 7, 1998) from their respective dates of purchase. Pro forma for full year: revenue $97,440,835; net income $6,473,170/$0.71.
¶ Income figures for 1996 include loss of $721,000/($0.08) from discontinued operations.
# Income figures for 1995 include gain of $160,000/$0.02 from discontinued operations.

BALANCE SHEET

Assets	12/31/99 (dollars in thousands)	12/31/98	Liabilities	12/31/99 (dollars in thousands)	12/31/98
Current (CAE 14,837 and 20,405)	59,442	57,691	Current (STD 9,043 and 9,078)	25,054	20,446
Property, plant, and equipment	10,960	11,379	Stockholders' equity*	66,422	63,454
Excess of cost over net assets acquired	8,820	8,392	TOTAL	91,476	83,900
Investments in debt securities	6,078	1,340			
Note receivable	3,365	3,765			
Deferred income taxes	2,169	548			
Other	642	784			
TOTAL	91,476	83,900			

* $0.05 par common; 30,000,000 authorized; 8,551,272 and 8,791,301 issued and outstanding.

RECENT QUARTERS / **PRIOR-YEAR RESULTS**

	Quarter End	Revenue ($000)	Earnings ($000)	EPS ($)	Revenue ($000)	Earnings ($000)	EPS ($)
Q3	09/30/2000	29,654	1,507	0.17	29,279	2,101	0.24
Q2	06/30/2000	32,074	1,588	0.18	29,807	1,748	0.20
Q1	03/31/2000	30,864	2,313	0.27	26,597	2,472	0.28
Q4	12/31/99	31,250	2,692	0.31	18,673	1,279	0.15
	SUM	123,842	8,101	0.93	104,356	7,601	0.87

RECENT EVENTS

Dec. 31, 1999: In a sign that CSI's diversification strategy was paying off, three acquisitions—JDL Technologies Inc., Transition Networks Inc., and LANart Corp.—accounted for 40 percent of the company's 1999 revenue. In **February 2000** Transition Networks announced an agreement with Hewlett-Packard, whereby the two companies were to work together to provide comprehensive networking solutions to HP's customers. In **May** Transition Networks' Conversion Center chassis received the Solaris Ready certification from Sun Microsystems Inc. for its TN-View management suite. TN announced a new, enhanced media conversion platform, The PointSystem. **June 30:** "We are very disappointed with CSI's second-quarter operating results," commented CEO Sampson. "Our primary business units posted below-plan sales and profitability due to temporary weaknesses in certain targeted markets, delays in receiving major orders, and pricing pressures. We are moving aggressively to strengthen our sales growth and return CSI's profitability to its high historic norms by refocusing sales initiatives on our best opportunities, reducing operating costs throughout the company, and enhancing CSI's competitive position in global markets." In **August** the company announced that it was engaged in discussions with a substantially larger public corporation regarding the merger of CSI into the other firm, and had retained investment banker U.S. Bancorp Piper Jaffray to assist in those discussions. Meanwhile, CSI found a new (Chinese) supplier of components needed to build the electronics filters that allow residential phones to use broadband DSL lines for regular voice calls, the company's best-performing business. In **September** CSI was still engaged in an evaluation of strategic alternatives in connection with previously reported merger discussions. To date, no formal offer had been received with respect to any extraordinary transaction. **Sept. 30:** Once again, Sampson commented: "With the exception of our Transition Networks Inc. subsidiary, all of our other business units reported below-plan sales and profitability in the third quarter. This is clearly unacceptable, and steps are being taken to strengthen the performances of our businesses."

OFFICERS

Curtis A. Sampson
Chairman and CEO

Jeffrey K. Berg
EVP and Pres.-Suttle Apparatus Corp.

Charles Braun
Controller

Paul N. Hanson
VP-Finance, CFO, and Treasurer

Thomas J. Lapping
Pres./CEO-JDL Technologies.

Lee Ludlum
Mng. Dir.-Austin Taylor Communications

Richard A. Primuth
Secretary

Michael J. Skucius
Dir.-Information Services

DIRECTORS

Paul J. Anderson
private investor, Nisswa, MN

Edwin C. Freeman
Bro-tex Inc., Tonka Bay, MN

Luella G. Goldberg
Wellesley College, Wellesley, MA

Frederick M. Green
Ault Inc., Brooklyn Park, MN

Joseph W. Parris
private investor, St. Paul

Gerald D. Pint
telecommunications consultant, Orono, MN

Curtis A. Sampson

Randall D. Sampson
Canterbury Park Holding Corp.

Wayne E. Sampson
management consultant, Stillwater, MN

Edward E. Strickland
management consultant, Friday Harbor, WA

MAJOR SHAREHOLDERS

Curtis A. Sampson, 18.7%

Putnam Investments Inc., 7.8%
Boston

John C. Ortman, 6.2%
Lawrenceville, IL

Dimensional Fund Advisors Inc., 5.1%
Santa Monica, CA

All officers and directors as a group (16 persons), 30.4%

SIC CODE

3661 Telephone and telegraph apparatus

MISCELLANEOUS

TRANSFER AGENT AND REGISTAR:
Wells Fargo Bank Minnesota N.A.,
South St. Paul, MN

TRADED: Nasdaq National Market

SYMBOL: CSII

STOCKHOLDERS: 800

EMPLOYEES: 1,000

PART TIME: 40

IN MINNESOTA: 305

GENERAL COUNSEL:
Lindquist & Vennum PLLP, Minneapolis

AUDITORS:
Deloitte & Touche LLP, Minneapolis

INC: MN-1969

ANNUAL MEETING: May

HUMAN RESOURCES: Paul Hanson

PURCHASING: Dennis Peterson

RANKINGS

No. 87 CRM Public 200

SUBSIDIARIES, DIVISIONS, AFFILIATES

Suttle Apparatus Corp.
Hector, Minn.

Suttle Caribe Inc.
Humacao, Puerto Rico

Suttle Costa Rica S.A.
San Jose, Costa Rica

Austin Taylor Communications Ltd.
Bethesda, Wales

Automatic Tool and Connector Co.
Elizabeth, N.J.

Tel Products Inc.
Indiana

JDL Technologies Inc.
Edina, Minn.

Transition Networks Inc.
6475 City West Parkway
Eden Prairie, MN 55344
612/941-7600
C.S. (Sal) Mondelli

TWO-YEAR QUARTERLY HIGH-LOW STOCK PRICES

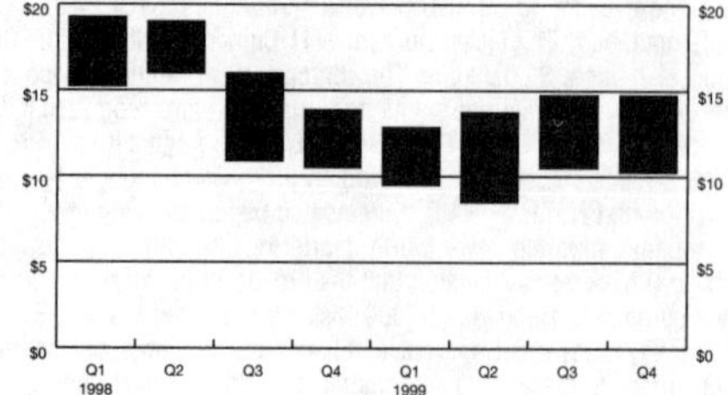

Community First Bankshares Inc.

520 Main Ave., Fargo, ND 58124
Tel: 701/298-5600 Fax: 701/271-6699 Web site: http://www.communityfirst.com

Community First Bankshares is a more than $6 billion financial services company offering a full range of financial services including banking, investments, insurance, and trust. The company serves more than 150 communities in Arizona, California, New Mexico, Colorado, Iowa, Minnesota, Nebraska, North Dakota, South Dakota, Utah, Wisconsin, and Wyoming. The company was formed through the purchase of banks in South Dakota, North Dakota, and Minnesota from First Bank System Inc. in 1987. It established its flagship bank in Fargo through the $22 million stock purchase of First Interstate Bank of North Dakota, which followed a 1991 public offering.

EARNINGS HISTORY *

Year Ended Dec 31	Operating Revenue/Sales (dollars in thousands)	Net Earnings (dollars in thousands)	Return on Revenue (percent)	Return on Equity (percent)	Net Earnings (dollars per share†)	Cash Dividend (dollars per share†)	Market Price Range (dollars per share†)
1999	537,715	74,913	13.9	18.4	1.50	0.56	24.00–13.94
1998 ¶	530,537	45,463	8.6	10.7	0.90	0.44	27.00–14.13
1997 #	392,736	60,865	15.5	15.0	1.31	0.35	27.56–13.69
1996	324,258	42,925	13.2	13.8	0.98	0.29	14.38–10.00
1995	275,910	39,093	14.2	14.8	0.94	0.24	11.88–6.63

* Historical figures restated to account for pooling-of-interests business combinations, including two separate transactions in 1999 and five in 1998.
† Per-share amounts restated to reflect 2-for-1 stock split paid May 15, 1998.
¶ Income figures for 1998 include loss of $3,908,000/($0.08) from discontinued operations and their disposal.
# Income figures for 1997 include loss of $265,000/($0.01) from early extinguishment of debt; and gain of $967,000/$0.05 from discontinued operations. Results include operations of KeyBank N.A. (Wyoming) from its July 14, 1997, purchase for $135 million.

BALANCE SHEET

Assets	12/31/99 (dollars in thousands)	12/31/98	Liabilities	12/31/99 (dollars in thousands)	12/31/98
Cash and due from banks	247,051	262,667	Nonint deposits	616,861	591,718
			Int-bearing deposits	4,293,002	4,509,347
Federal funds sold	4,775	11,990	Fed funds purchased	252,760	143,057
Int-bearing deposits	4,648	11,463	S-t borrowings	471,665	292,669
Afs securities	1,937,517	2,004,584	Long-term debt	75,622	93,524
Htm securities	74,248	92,859	Accrued interest	31,949	26,823
Net loans	3,641,475	3,485,677	Other	33,107	37,978
Bank premises, eqt	125,457	128,232	CFB Capital securities	120,000	120,000
Accrued interest	51,030	53,046			
Intangibles	126,378	133,273	Common equity*	407,269	424,656
Other	89,656	55,981	TOTAL	6,302,235	6,239,772
TOTAL	6,302,235	6,239,772			

* $0.01 par common; 80,000,000 authorized; 51,021,896 and 51,021,896 issued and outstanding, less 885,964 and 564,588 treasury shares.

RECENT QUARTERS / **PRIOR-YEAR RESULTS**

	Quarter End	Revenue ($000)	Earnings ($000)	EPS ($)	Prior-Year Revenue ($000)	Prior-Year Earnings ($000)	Prior-Year EPS ($)
Q3	09/30/2000	140,115	17,751	0.40	135,367	19,927	0.40
Q2	06/30/2000	139,162	18,261	0.38	134,947	19,203	0.38
Q1	03/31/2000	135,915	18,663	0.37	131,209	18,255	0.36
Q4	12/31/99	136,192	17,528	0.35	134,755	7,255	0.14
	SUM	551,384	72,203	1.50	536,278	64,640	1.29

CURRENT: Q4 earnings include pretax charges of $3.053 million for acquisition, integration, and conforming.

RECENT EVENTS

In **April 2000** the company announced a strategic partnership to deliver online banking services through a customized, company-branded Internet banking option. Compaq's ProLiant servers were to provide the hardware platform to support Community First's Internet banking application. The board of directors authorized the company to repurchase up to 5 million shares (10 percent) of the its common stock. Based on continued strong sales of investment products and services (1999 investment product sales of $177.6 million), CFB earned membership in INVEST Financial Corp.'s Chairman's Club. In **May** CFB purchased 400,000 shares of its common stock from Chairman Mengedoth at fair market value. Mengedoth continued to hold a beneficial interest in 280,000 shares. In **August** the board of directors authorized the company to repurchase up to 5 million shares (11 percent) of its common stock. CFB received approval from the Office of the Comptroller of the Currency to merge 11 of its existing national bank charters into one national bank charter in *continued on page 188*

OFFICERS

Donald R. Mengedoth
Chairman

Mark A. Anderson
President and CEO

Ronald K. Strand
Vice Chairman and COO

David A. Lee
Vice Chairman-Regional Banking

Thomas R. Anderson
SVP-Treasury and Treasurer

Keith A. Dickelman
East Colorado Regional President

Thomas E. Hansen
Central Region President

Bruce A. Heysse
Dir.-Mergers/Acquisitions

Thomas A. Hilt
SVP and Chief Administrative Officer

Robert W. Jorgensen
Wyoming Region Pres.

Gary A. Knutson
Pres.-Eastern Region/Utah/California

Charles A. Mausbach
Southwestern Region Pres.

Harriette S. McCaul
SVP and Mgr.-Human Resources

Brad J. Rasmus
SVP and Dir.-Financial Services

Patricia J. Staples
SVP and Dir.-Market Development

Craig A. Weiss
SVP-Finance and CFO

Dan M. Fisher
Chief Information Officer

DIRECTORS

Mark A. Anderson

Patrick E. Benedict
Benedict Farms Inc., Sabin, MN

Patrick Delaney
Lindquist & Vennum PLLP, Minneapolis

John H. Flittie
ING ReliaStar, Minneapolis

Darrell G. Knudson
Bank of Arizona

Dennis M. Mathisen
Marshall Financial Group Inc.

Donald R. Mengedoth

Marilyn R. Seymann
M ONE Inc., Phoenix

Thomas C. Wold
Wold Johnson P.C., Fargo, ND

Harvey L. Wollman
farmer/former governor, Frankfort, SD

MAJOR SHAREHOLDERS

All officers and directors as a group (28 persons), 9.8%

SIC CODE

6712 Bank holding companies

MISCELLANEOUS

TRANSFER AGENT AND REGISTAR:
Wells Fargo Bank Minnesota N.A., South St. Paul, MN

TRADED: Nasdaq National Market

SYMBOL: CFBX

STOCKHOLDERS: 2,208

EMPLOYEES: 2,667

GENERAL COUNSEL:
Lindquist & Vennum PLLP, Minneapolis

AUDITORS:
Ernst & Young LLP, Minneapolis

INC: DE-1987

ANNUAL MEETING: April

INVESTOR RELATIONS COUNSEL: Shandwick International

SUBSIDIARIES, DIVISIONS, AFFILIATES

MINNESOTA LOCATIONS

Ada, MN 56510
Benson, MN 56215
Breckenridge, MN 56520
Caledonia, MN 55921
Elbow Lake, MN 56531
Fergus Falls, MN 56538
Greenwald, MN 56335
Hokah, MN 55941
Ivanhoe, MN 56142
Lakefield, MN 56150
Little Falls, MN 56345
Mabel, MN 55954
Marshall, MN 56258
Minneota, MN 56264
Morris, MN 56267
New Munich, MN 56356
Paynesville, MN 56362
Wheaton, MN 56296
Windom, MN 56101
Worthington, MN 56187

TWO-YEAR QUARTERLY HIGH-LOW STOCK PRICES

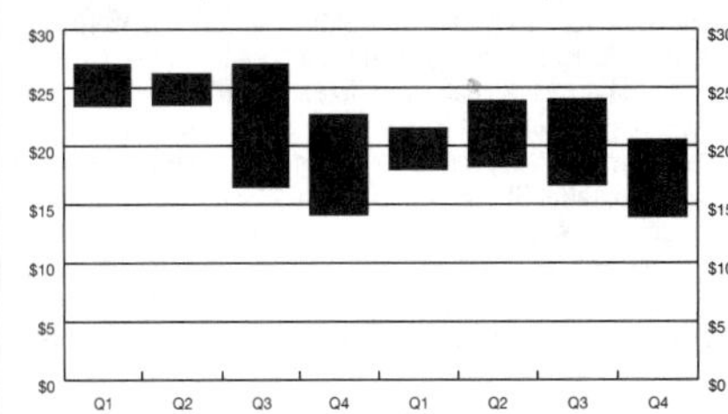

PUB

Computer Network Technology Corporation

6000 Nathan Ln. N., Plymouth, MN 55442
Tel: 763/268-6000 Fax: 763/268-6800 Web site: http://www.cnt.com

Computer Network Technology Corp. (CNT) is a global company providing high-performance Storage Area Networking solutions, Enterprise Application Integration tools, and world-class support services. The company's Channelink, FileSpeed, and UltraNet product lines offer high-speed open systems connectivity, access to legacy data, and guaranteed data integrity for applications such as remote storage, disk mirroring, and business continuance. CNT hardware, software, and services are used by organizations around the world to integrate large, business-critical applications and storage environments. The company's products are sold worldwide through a direct sales force and a network of authorized distributors.

EARNINGS HISTORY

Year Ended Dec 31	Operating Revenue/Sales (dollars in thousands)	Net Earnings	Return on Revenue (percent)	Return on Equity	Net Earnings (dollars per share)	Cash Dividend	Market Price Range
1999 *	151,693	4,655	3.1	5.9	0.20	—	30.63–7.38
1998 †	133,535	4,729	3.5	7.8	0.21	—	14.25–3.50
1997 ¶	97,841	(2,314)	(2.4)	(4.2)	(0.10)	—	7.00–3.38
1996 #	97,109	1,360	1.4	2.1	0.06	—	10.50–4.00
1995	78,837	4,022	5.1	6.6	0.18	—	12.75–4.25

* Income figures include pretax: charge of $1,331,000 for abandoned facility; and gain of $430,000 for reversal of previous integration charges.
† Income figures for 1998 include pretax charge of $927,000 for purchased R&D.
¶ Results for 1997 include operations of Internet Solutions Division since its Oct. 24, 1997, date of purchase for $11.4 million. Pro forma for full year: revenue $117,000,000; loss $9,882,000/($0.44). Income figures include pretax charges for purchased R&D ($2,750,000) and for integration ($2,184,000).
# Income figures for 1996 include pretax charge of $2,720,303 to write down purchased technology.

BALANCE SHEET

Assets	12/31/99 (dollars in thousands)	12/31/98	Liabilities	12/31/99 (dollars in thousands)	12/31/98
Current (CAE 16,184 and 11,786)	85,133	66,240	Current (STD 1,000 and 1,000)	34,418	30,653
Property and equipment	18,471	16,360	Capital lease obligations	1,780	1,816
Field-support spares	4,135	3,739	Long-term debt		1,000
Deferred tax	3,236	2,517	Stockholders' equity*	78,472	60,558
Goodwill	3,427	4,737	TOTAL	114,670	94,027
Other	268	434			
TOTAL	114,670	94,027			

* $0.01 par common; 100,000,000 authorized; 23,792,000 and 22,254,000 issued and outstanding.

RECENT QUARTERS / **PRIOR-YEAR RESULTS**

	Quarter End	Revenue ($000)	Earnings ($000)	EPS ($)	Revenue ($000)	Earnings ($000)	EPS ($)
Q2	07/31/2000	47,741	2,053	0.09	37,856	1,786	0.08
Q1	04/30/2000	43,272	1,830	0.08	36,913	2,697	0.12
Q4	12/31/99	35,855	(2,577)	(0.11)	35,893	1,691	0.08
Q3	09/30/99	41,069	2,749	0.12	33,010	1,799	0.08
	SUM	167,937	4,055	0.17	143,672	7,973	0.36

CURRENT: Q1 marks the beginning of a fiscal year that now ends in January rather than December. The month of January 2000 is not presented. Q4 earnings include net nonrecurring pretax charge of $901,000.
PRIOR YEAR: Q4 earnings include pretax charge of $927,000 for purchased R&D (Intelliframe).

RECENT EVENTS

In **January 2000**, on the first day of trading, CNT stock dropped 23 percent to $17.75 on reports that corporate insiders had sold large blocks of stock (30 percent of their holdings) in recent weeks; and that fourth-quarter earnings were expected to lag analysts' estimates (on flat sales). In **February** CNT delivered the first component in its strategy to provide storage networking applications over Internet Protocol (IP)-based networks, such as intranets and Virtual Private Networks—traditionally considered unreliable and expensive for storage applications. Specifically, CNT augmented and refined the storage transport capabilities in its UltraNet Storage Director, a high-speed switching platform, to support IP. In **April** CNT broadened the range of customer choices with the industry's first scalable support for Fibre Channel over multiple T3/E3 and ATM wide-area connections; announced two new products in its UltraNet family that enable companies to create a storage network that maximizes existing investments in SCSI and Fibre Channel technology in any environment; and delivered the UltraNet Open Systems Router, the first networking device that allows AS/400 servers to share access to storage, enabling companies to share resources and build Storage Area Network (SAN) infrastructures. CNT announced support for the new Siebel eBusiness 2000, the most comprehensive suite of eBusiness application software on the market today. CNT *continued on page 188*

OFFICERS

Thomas G. Hudson
Chairman, President, and CEO
Gregory T. Barnum
VP-Finance, CFO, and Secretary
Jeffrey Bertelsen
Controller and Treasurer
Martin F. Beyer
VP-Enterprise Solutions, Asst. Gen. Mgr.
Robert R. Beyer
VP-World Wide Quality/Customer Service
Richard E. Carlson
VP-Manufacturing
William C. Collette
VP-Advanced Technology and CTO
Peter Dixon
VP-Worldwide Business Development
Michael Ducatelli
VP-Worldwide Sales, EIS
Nick V. Ganio
VP-Worldwide Sales/Marketing/Services
Mark R. Knittel
VP-Marketing
Julie C. Quintal
VP-Quality/Business Services
Kristine E. Ochu
VP-Human Resources
Barbara Schmit
Chief Information Officer
Robert J. Williams
VP-Engineering, EIS

DIRECTORS

Patrick W. Gross
American Management Systems Inc., Fairfax, VA
Thomas G. Hudson
Erwin A. Kelen
Kelen Ventures, Minneapolis
Lawrence Perlman
Ceridian Corp., Bloomington, MN
John A. Rollwagen
St. Paul Venture Capital Inc., Bloomington, MN

MAJOR SHAREHOLDERS

Kopp Investment Advisors Inc., 19.1%
Edina, MN
Massachusetts Financial Services Co., 11.8%
Boston
All officers and directors as a group (13 persons), 7.2%

SIC CODE

3577 Computer peripheral equipment, nec

MISCELLANEOUS

TRANSFER AGENT AND REGISTAR:
Chase Mellon Shareholder Services LLC, Ridgefield Park, NJ
TRADED: Nasdaq National Market
SYMBOL: CMNT
STOCKHOLDERS: 1,000
EMPLOYEES: 691
GENERAL COUNSEL:
Leonard Street & Deinard P.A., Minneapolis
AUDITORS:
KPMG LLP, Minneapolis
INC: MN-1983
ANNUAL MEETING: May
INVESTOR RELATIONS:
Sue Nelson
HUMAN RESOURCES:
Kristin Ochu

RANKINGS

No. 79 CRM Public 200

SUBSIDIARIES, DIVISIONS, AFFILIATES

CNT International Ltd.
Langley, Slough
Berkshire SL3 6EX
United Kingdom
44-1753-792400

CNT France S.A.
92250 La Garenne Colombes
France
33-1-4130-1212

CNT Asia Pacific Pty Ltd.
North Sydney
Australia
61-2-540-5486

CNT China Limited
Hong Kong
852-2593-1121

TWO-YEAR QUARTERLY HIGH-LOW STOCK PRICES

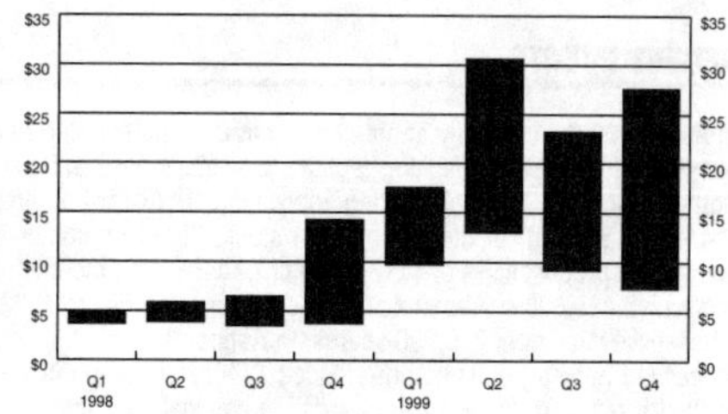

CorVu Corporation

3400 W. 66th St., Suite 445, Edina, MN 55435
Tel: 952/944-7777 Fax: 952/944-7447 Web site: http://www.corvu.com

CorVu Corp. is a holding company that develops and sells business performance management software products and related professional services through subsidiaries CorVu North America Inc., CorVu plc, and CorVu Australasia Pty. Ltd. Business performance management is a process by which an organization seeks to define its strategy, measure and analyze its performance, and ultimately manage improvements to enhance performance. One such performance management methodology is the Balanced Scorecard, which recognizes four dimensions as integral for developing an enterprise view of performance: financial, customer, internal, and innovation. CorVu is the leading global provider of Enterprise Business Performance Management software for Balanced Scorecard applications, with 20 offices worldwide and more than 2,500 customers, including such companies as Citigroup, American Express, British Airways, Prudential Insurance, and Ford Motor Co. CorVu generates revenue in three areas: (1) sale and licensing of software products; (2) consulting and training services ("professional services"); and (3) maintenance agreements entered into in connection with the sale and licensing of its products. CorVu is the survivor of the January 2000 merger between CorVu Corp. and Minnesota American Inc. (OTCBB: MNAC).

EARNINGS HISTORY *

Year Ended Jun 30	Operating Revenue/Sales (dollars in thousands)	Net Earnings	Return on Revenue (percent)	Return on Equity	Net Earnings (dollars per share)	Cash Dividend	Market Price Range
2000	12,809	(8,623)	(67.3)	NM	(0.50)	—	8.75–0.28
1999	10,588	(3,350)	(31.6)	NM	(0.35)	—	1.06–0.05
1998	6,868	(1,481)	(21.6)	NM	(0.16)	—	0.28–0.03
1997 †	2,771	217	7.8	30.4	0.05	—	
1996	2,731	83	3.0	9.7	0.01	—	

* Results from 1997 and earlier are those of predecessor company Minnesota American Inc., whose fiscal year ended Sept. 30.
† Income figures for 1997 include loss of $99,929 on impairment of assets.

BALANCE SHEET

Assets	06/30/00 (dollars in thousands)	06/30/99
Current (CAE 46 and 31)	4,494	4,221
Furniture, fixtures, and equipment	168	153
TOTAL	4,662	4,374

Liabilities	06/30/00 (dollars in thousands)	06/30/99
Current	8,640	9,264
Stockholders' equity*	(3,978)	(4,890)
TOTAL	4,662	4,374

* $0.01 par common; 25,000,000 authorized; 19,509,660 and 16,347,329 issued and outstanding.

RECENT EVENTS

In **January 2000** the company was selected by Computerworld magazine as one of the Top 100 Emerging Companies to Watch in 2000. In **March** the company successfully expanded Asia-Pacific channels activities via several strategic partnerships. CorVu and Sharp System Products (SSP) launched their Kanji version of CorVu's certified balanced scorecard solution at a press conference in Tokyo. CorVu's board of directors approved a special warrant dividend to shareholders of record April 28, 2000, a warrant entitling them to purchase an additional share of common stock for every 10 common shares they own as of the record date, at an exercise price of $8.00 per share. "The dividend will allow for the financing of our current expansion of business operations in North America, Latin America, and Europe," stated CEO MacIntosh. In addition to the warrant dividend, the company's board also approved a private placement of stock to raise an additional $2.5 million. CorVu announced an alliance partnership with Manley Group, a leading provider of e-commerce strategies, solutions and technologies, to be a certified services provider (CSP) for CorVu solutions. In **April** the Australian Defence Force Academy selected CorVu's CorManage software to be part of the Academy's business simulations. Concentra Preferred Systems, the recognized leader in health care cost-containment services, agreed to implement CorVu's CorManage. In **May** CorBusiness was chosen by HM Customs and Excise National Intelligence Division as the primary data enquiry tool for extracting and preparing data for analysis from internal and external data sources. Corvu and Skyward Inc., a leading developer of integrated school administration software and systems, announced a reseller relationship. In **June** Lutheran Brotherhood, a Minneapolis-based membership organization providing financial services to more than 1 million Lutherans, selected CorManage as its corporate Balanced Scorecard solution. A significant national defense organization chose CorBusiness as its Enterprise Business Intelligence solution. Specialist oil refiner AB Nynas Petroleum selected CorVu's CorManage business intelligence and Balanced Scorecard application to re-engineer performance measurement and management within the group. The company noted that the delays encountered in relisting on the Over-the-Counter Bulletin Board (OTCBB) were related to the volume of registrations currently being processed by the SEC. CorPortfolio was introduced to allow executives to collate disparate reporting sources together into an online enterprise information portfolio. CorVu was ranked No. 389 on the Software 500, Software Magazine's list of the world's foremost software and services providers. In **July** Dalkia Utilities Services, part of the Vivendi Group, chose the CorManage enterprise performance management solution to automate critical management functions. CorVu announced Scorecard Express, a revolutionary application and service offering that makes automated Balanced Scorecard applications available to companies of all sizes at an affordable price and in a timely manner. The SEC cleared CorVu of further comments on its amended Form 10-SB. In **August** CorVu and VantageSource LLP's Systems Reseller Group announced a global systems integration reseller agreement under which VantageSource LLP was to resell CorVu's CorManage and CorBusiness software applications. CorVu and Astea International Inc. (Nasdaq: ATEA), a leading supplier of service-centric customer relationship management (CRM) solutions, announced a reseller relationship whereby Astea was to offer CorVu's CorBusiness and CorManage products as key components of its DISPATCH-1 and ServiceAlliance CRM offering, as well as provide services and support for all CorVu products. A leading provider of financial and online broker-

continued on page 188

OFFICERS

Justin MacIntosh
Chairman, President, and CEO

David Carlson
CFO

Alan Missroon
VP-Marketing

John Stout
Secretary

DIRECTORS

David C. Carlson

Ismail Kurdi
real estate developer and investor in England

Justin M. MacIntosh

James L. Mandel
Call 4 Wireless, Minnetonka, MN

Alan Missroon

MAJOR SHAREHOLDERS

Justin M. MacIntosh/ Barleigh Wells Ltd., 47.2%

Ismail Kurdi, 6.3%

Troy Rollo/Rollosoft Pty. Ltd., 5.6%
Neutral Bay, N.S.W., Australia

All officers and directors as a group (8 persons), 59%

MISCELLANEOUS

TRADED: OTC Bulletin Board

SYMBOL: CRVU

STOCKHOLDERS: 137

EMPLOYEES: 107

IN MINNESOTA: 20

GENERAL COUNSEL:
Fredrikson & Byron P.A., Minneapolis

RANKINGS

No. 180 CRM Public 200

PUB

The Credit Store Inc.

3401 N. Louise Ave., Sioux Falls, SD 57107
Tel: 800/240-1855

The Credit Store Inc.is a technology-based financial services company that provides credit card products to consumers who may otherwise fail to qualify for a traditional unsecured bank credit card. The company reaches these consumers by acquiring portfolios of nonperforming consumer receivables and offering a new credit card to those consumers who agree to pay all or a portion of the outstanding amount due on their debt and who meet the company's underwriting guidelines. The new card is issued with an initial balance and credit line equal to the agreed repayment amount. After the consumers have made a certain number of on-time payments on their outstanding credit-card balance, the company seeks to sell or securitize the credit-card receivables generated by this business strategy. The company offers other forms of settlement to those consumers who do not accept the credit card offer.

EARNINGS HISTORY *

Year Ended May 31	Operating Revenue/Sales (dollars in thousands)	Net Earnings	Return on Revenue (percent)	Return on Equity	Net Earnings (dollars per share)	Cash Dividend	Market Price Range
2000	40,706	3,072	7.5	NM	0.03	—	5.44–2.56
1999	37,556	3,876	10.3	NM	0.06	—	3.88–1.75
1998	6,899	(29,445)	NM	NM	(0.90)	—	
1997	1,082	(14,406)	NM	NM	(0.56)	—	

* Revenue figures are net of provision for losses; EPS figures are after preferred dividends.

BALANCE SHEET

Assets	05/31/00 (dollars in thousands)	05/31/99
Cash and equivalents	1,423	3,534
Restricted cash	1,026	750
Accounts, notes receivable	2,766	1,150
Prepaid expenses	1,342	618
Due from special-purpose entities	9,333	1,231
Investments, nonperforming consumer debt	9,648	3,017
Investments, credit-card receivables	24,244	18,631
Investment in unconsolidated affiliate	1,280	1,613
Retained interest, credit-card receivables	2,143	5,130
Property and equipment	4,790	6,133
Goodwill	2,348	2,555
Deferred taxes	2,700	700
Other	1,346	719
TOTAL	64,388	45,781

Liabilities	05/31/00 (dollars in thousands)	05/31/99
Accounts payable, accrued expenses	4,499	4,313
Notes payable	23,609	6,087
Capitalized lease obligations	2,766	4,046
Subordinated notes, accrued interest related party	19,139	19,247
Preferred equity	27,000	27,000
Common equity*	(12,626)	(14,911)
TOTAL	64,388	45,781

* $0.001 par common; 65,000,000 authorized; 34,761,965 and 34,761,965 issued and outstanding.

RECENT QUARTERS / PRIOR-YEAR RESULTS

	Quarter End	Revenue ($000)	Earnings ($000)	EPS ($)	Prior-Year Revenue ($000)	Prior-Year Earnings ($000)	Prior-Year EPS ($)
Q1	08/31/2000	8,231	(2,895)	(0.10)	6,198	(2,608)	(0.09)
	SUM	8,231	(2,895)	(0.10)	6,198	(2,608)	(0.09)

RECENT EVENTS

In **November 2000** the company established a $25 million credit facility for the acquisition of nonperforming consumer debt through Varde Partners Inc. The credit facility was being made available to a wholly owned special-purpose corporation, Credit Store Services Inc. The credit facility had a three-year term and was to be secured by the portfolios acquired through the facility and by all new credit-card receivables generated by the portfolios. Varde Partners manages several partnerships that focus on the acquisition of distressed debt and is a leading financing source in this industry segment. "We are pleased to add financing from Varde to our overall acquisition program," commented President Riordan. "This facility provides the financing capacity to reach our portfolio acquisition goals for this fiscal year. Combined with our existing acquisition programs, we will continue to be positioned as one of the leading acquirers of nonperforming consumer debt."

OFFICERS

Geoffrey A. Thompson
Chairman

Kevin T. Riordan
President and COO

Michael J. Philippe
EVP, CFO, and Treasurer

DIRECTORS

Jay L. Botchman
JLB Equities Inc., Las Vegas

Barry E. Breeman
Manley-Berenson Realty & Development LLC

J. Richard Budd III
consultant

Kevin T. Riordan

Geoffrey A. Thompson
Marine Midland Bank Inc. (retired)

MAJOR SHAREHOLDERS

Jay L. Botchman/Taxter One LLC/JLB of Nevada Inc., 53.8%
Las Vegas

Michael Lauer/Lancer Partners L.P., 23.7%

All officers and directors as a group (9 persons), 57.3%

SIC CODE

6141 Personal credit institutions

MISCELLANEOUS

TRADED: AMEX
SYMBOL: CDS
STOCKHOLDERS: 260
EMPLOYEES: 305
AUDITORS:
Grant Thornton LLP, Minneapolis
INC: DE-1995
FOUNDED: 1972

CyberOptics Corporation

5900 Golden Hills Dr., Golden Valley, MN 55416
Tel: 763/542-5000 Fax: 763/542-5103 Web site: http://www.cyberoptics.com

CyberOptics Corp. designs and manufactures intelligent sensors and systems for high-precision, noncontact dimensional measurement and process control. The company's products can measure surface height to a resolution of .000015 of an inch. Its inspection systems for process control can make height, cross-sectional area, and volume computations. Industries supplied include electronics, automotive, aerospace, paper, and rubber. The company's OEM relationships, particularly in the electronics industry, offer a stable revenue base and entry into other market segments.

EARNINGS HISTORY

Year Ended Dec 31	Operating Revenue/Sales (dollars in thousands)	Net Earnings	Return on Revenue (percent)	Return on Equity	Net Earnings (dollars per share*)	Cash Dividend	Market Price Range
1999 †	39,627	(5,496)	(13.9)	(11.8)	(0.74)	—	18.71–7.00
1998	36,636	3,669	10.0	7.1	0.47	—	19.25–5.50
1997	35,120	4,597	13.1	8.6	0.58	—	25.08–8.50
1996	28,062	2,180	7.8	4.6	0.26	—	26.67–6.58
1995	30,518	4,831	15.8	9.5	0.69	—	26.50–5.00

* Per-share amounts restated to reflect 3-for-2 stock split on June 15, 2000.
† Income figures for 1999 include pretax charge of $7.301 million for acquired in-process R&D. Pro forma results, less R&D charge, had Kestra Ltd. (April 1999) and HAMA Laboratories Inc. (May 1999) been acquired Jan. 1: revenue $40,422,000; earnings $655,000/$0.09.

BALANCE SHEET

Assets	12/31/99 (dollars in thousands)	12/31/98	Liabilities	12/31/99 (dollars in thousands)	12/31/98
Current (CAE 10,196 and 4,963)	33,220	36,052	Current	4,960	3,744
Marketable securities	4,396	16,397	Stockholders' equity*	46,504	51,433
Equipment and leasehold improvements	2,705	2,571	TOTAL	51,464	55,177
Capitalized patent costs	11,143	157			
TOTAL	51,464	55,177			

* No par common; 25,000,000 authorized; 7,527,000 and 7,425,000 issued and outstanding.

RECENT QUARTERS / **PRIOR-YEAR RESULTS**

	Quarter End	Revenue ($000)	Earnings ($000)	EPS ($)	Prior-Year Revenue ($000)	Prior-Year Earnings ($000)	Prior-Year EPS ($)
Q3	09/30/2000	16,282	2,817	0.36	10,418	202	0.03
Q2	06/30/2000	14,692	1,979	0.26	8,811	(7,249)	(0.97)
Q1	03/31/2000	13,509	1,333	0.18	7,705	552	0.07
Q4	12/31/99	12,693	1,000	0.13	8,551	645	0.09
	SUM	57,176	7,129	0.92	35,485	(5,850)	(0.78)

PRIOR YEAR: Q2 earnings include pretax charges of $7.3 million for acquired in-process R&D.

RECENT EVENTS

In **November 1999** the company completed agreements with Optical Gaging Products Inc. (OGP) of Rochester, N.Y., to sell the assets and license the software of its CyberScan Cobra industrial metrology product line to OGP. (The CyberScan Cobra is a portable laser inspection system that provides two-dimensional or three-dimensional, high-resolution surface profiling.) In **March 2000** the company received the initial order for its new KS 100 post-placement inspection system, which inspects SMT circuit boards before all components are soldered to the board in the reflow oven. In **May** CyberOptics announced that the first two orders for its new-generation SE 300 solder paste inspection system were expected to ship in this year's third quarter. (The SE 300 inspects solder pads on the entire SMT circuit board and offers greater optical resolution and speed than any solder paste inspection system on the market.) CyberOptics announced plans to launch a new company to develop and market automation systems and process management tools for manufacturing high-precision fiber optic components for broadband telecommunications systems. CyberOptics was to retain a minority equity interest in the new venture, to be headed by Chairman Case. Case was to maintain many of his current responsibilities with CyberOptics, including business strategy, technology, and key customer efforts. The new company, CyberOptics Communications Corp., was not expected to have a material impact on CyberOptics Corp.'s consolidated earnings in 2000. In **June** CyberOptics said that earnings for the second quarter ending June 30 were expected to exceed 30 cents per diluted share (pre-split basis), compared to prevailing analyst estimates of 24 cents to 26 cents per share. Above-plan operating results were being driven by the across-the-board strength of its three product groups, with the SMT Sensor and Semiconductor Sensor units generating particularly strong growth. **Sept. 30:** Chairman Case commented: "CyberOptics' above-plan operating results are clearly benefiting from the strength of our two targeted markets: SMT electronic equipment and semiconductor capital equipment." Sales of SMT Sensors increased 72 percent in the third quarter of 2000 versus the year-earlier period, and were also up 13 percent from the current year's second quarter. SMT Sensor sales were paced by strong demand from major customers in Europe and Japan. Sales of SMT Systems, primarily the SE 200 (Sentry) solder paste inspection system, declined, as many prospective customers have delayed placing orders pending the October market introduction of the new-generation SE 300. In **October**

continued on page 188

OFFICERS

Steven K. Case, Ph.D.
Chairman
Steven M. Quist
President
Michael S. Willey
SVP and Gen. Mgr.-SMT Systems
Bruce E. Batten
VP-Global Sales/Customer Engineering
William J. Farmer
VP and Gen. Mgr.-OEM Sensors
Scott G. Larson
VP and CFO
Michael D. Wetle
VP and Gen. Mgr.-Semiconductor Group

DIRECTORS

Steven K. Case
Alex B. Cimochowski
Four Peaks Technologies Inc.
Kathleen P. Iverson
Rosemount Inc.
Erwin A. Kelen
Kelen Ventures, Minneapolis
Irene M. Qualters
Merck Research Laboratories
Steven M. Quist
Michael M. Selzer, Jr.
Urologix Inc.

MAJOR SHAREHOLDERS

Kopp Investment Advisors Inc., 21.3%
Edina, MN
Robert Fleming Inc., 13.1%
New York
Steven K. Case, 8.2%
Minneapolis
Dimensional Fund Advisors Inc., 6.1%
Santa Monica, CA
All officers and directors as a group (13 persons), 11.9%

SIC CODE

3823 Process control instruments

MISCELLANEOUS

TRANSFER AGENT AND REGISTAR:
Wells Fargo Bank Minnesota N.A.,
South St. Paul, MN
TRADED: Nasdaq National Market
SYMBOL: CYBE
STOCKHOLDERS: 250

EMPLOYEES: 220

GENERAL COUNSEL:
Dorsey & Whitney PLLP, Minneapolis
AUDITORS:
PricewaterhouseCoopers LLP, Minneapolis
INC: MN-1984
ANNUAL MEETING: May
INVESTOR RELATIONS:
Scott Larson

RANKINGS

No. 119 CRM Public 200

PUB

TWO-YEAR QUARTERLY HIGH-LOW STOCK PRICES

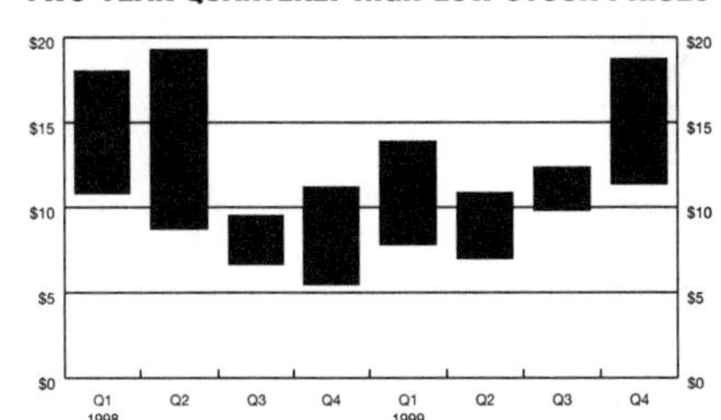

PUB

Dacotah Banks Inc.

212 Midwest Building, P.O. Box 1496, Aberdeen, SD 57402
Tel: 605/225-4850 Fax: 605/225-4929 Web site: http://www.dacotahbank.com

Dacotah Banks Inc. is a one-bank holding company. The company is the controlling shareholder of one commercial bank with 16 additional branch offices. General insurance operations are conducted in 14 of the 17 banking offices.

EARNINGS HISTORY

Year Ended Dec 31	Operating Revenue/Sales (dollars in thousands)	Net Earnings (dollars in thousands)	Return on Revenue (percent)	Return on Equity (percent)	Net Earnings (dollars per share)	Cash Dividend (dollars per share)	Market Price Range (dollars per share)
1999	45,647	6,480	14.2	10.9	6.08	0.80	
1998	43,423	6,420	14.8	11.5	6.02	0.70	
1997	38,973	5,758	14.8	11.5	5.19	0.65	
1996	35,300	4,709	13.3	9.5	3.88	0.55	
1995	32,666	4,620	14.1	10.2	3.81	0.48	

BALANCE SHEET

Assets	12/31/99 (dollars in thousands)	12/31/98 (dollars in thousands)	Liabilities	12/31/99 (dollars in thousands)	12/31/98 (dollars in thousands)
Cash and due from banks	14,706	15,324	Deposits	481,271	458,127
Interest-bearing deposits with banks	1,700	3,698	Long-term debt	12,056	8,425
Investment securities	173,493	153,309	Interest payable	4,880	5,243
Federal funds sold	9,700	26,000	Accrued expenses and other	2,528	2,300
Net loans	333,931	309,470	Stockholders' equity*	59,343	56,052
Premises and equipment	8,602	7,000	TOTAL	560,078	530,147
Foreclosed assets	33	147			
Interest receivable	9,325	9,333			
Goodwill	1,292	1,330			
Other	7,296	4,536			
TOTAL	560,078	530,147			

* $4 par common; 5,000,000 authorized; 1,428,598 and 1,428,598 issued and outstanding, less 362,262 and 361,429 treasury shares.

RECENT QUARTERS / **PRIOR-YEAR RESULTS**

	Quarter End	Revenue ($000)	Earnings ($000)	EPS ($)	Prior-Year Revenue ($000)	Prior-Year Earnings ($000)	Prior-Year EPS ($)
Q1	03/31/2000	12,850	1,803	1.69	11,061	1,609	1.51
Q4	12/31/99	11,807	1,747	1.64	11,203	1,302	1.22
Q3	09/30/99	11,436	1,607	1.51	11,305	1,943	1.82
Q2	06/30/99	11,343	1,517	1.42	10,603	1,652	1.55
	SUM	47,436	6,674	6.26	44,172	6,506	6.10

OFFICERS

Rodney W. Fouberg
Chairman and CEO

Kent E. Edson
President and CFO

Michael K. Hollan
VP

Richard O. Holland
VP

Kennith L. Gosch
Secretary

DIRECTORS

J. Douglas Austin
Austin, Hinderaker, Hopper, Strait, and Bratland, Watertown, SD

Kent E. Edson

Rodney W. Fouberg

Robert B. Lamont
private investor, Aberdeen, SD

William S. Lamont
Lamont Associates, San Francisco

Arthur R. Russo
Narregang Holding Co., Aberdeen, SD

Juletta M. Smith
retired, Aberdeen, SD

Bradford J. Wheeler
Wheeler Manufacturing, Lemmon, SD

SIC CODE

6712 Bank holding companies

MISCELLANEOUS

TRANSFER AGENT AND REGISTAR:
American Stock Transfer and Trust Co., New York

TRADED: LOTC

STOCKHOLDERS: 276

EMPLOYEES: 318

PART TIME: 51

GENERAL COUNSEL:
Dorsey & Whitney PLLP, Minneapolis
Bantz, Gosch, Cremer, Peterson & Oliver, Aberdeen, SD

AUDITORS:
Eide Bailly LLP, Aberdeen, SD

INC: SD-1964

ANNUAL MEETING: May

SUBSIDIARIES, DIVISIONS, AFFILIATES

DACOTAH BANKS

Lemmon

Bison

Clark

Bradley

Henry

Watertown

Willow Lake

Mobridge

Aberdeen

Cresbard

New Effington

Silver Valley

Sisseton

Phillips Centre

Faulkton

Webster

Roslyn

Rapid City

Aberdeen

OTHER AGENCIES

Dacotah Insurance Ltd.

Grue Abstract Co.

Huron Title Co.

Dacotah Bank

Dacotah Bank

First National Bank, Minot

Daktronics Inc.

331 32nd Ave., P.O. Box 5128, Brookings, SD 57006
Tel: 605/697-4300 Fax: 605/697-4700 Web site: http://www.daktronics.com

Daktronics designs and manufactures computer-programmable information display systems. Its installations include scoring, statistics, animation, and video displays for sports facilities; advertising and information displays for business; and data display systems for government use in transportation, legislative assembly, and other applications. Since 1968 Daktronics has provided display and scoring systems for clients in more than 70 countries. Daktronics is a three-time winner of the South Dakota ABEX Business of the Year award. Daktronics-branded products include Starburst color matrix and incandescent displays, Glow Cube reflective displays, All Sport scoreboards, ProStar video displays, and Venus control systems.

EARNINGS HISTORY

Year Ended Apr	Operating Revenue/Sales (dollars in thousands)	Net Earnings	Return on Revenue (percent)	Return on Equity	Net Earnings (dollars per share*)	Cash Dividend	Market Price Range
2000	123,350	6,224	5.0	17.2	0.71	—	18.25–4.88
1999	95,851	4,220	4.4	14.3	0.49	—	8.25–3.63
1998	69,884	3,392	4.9	13.5	0.39	—	4.44–1.81
1997	62,640	1,508	2.4	6.9	0.18	—	2.63–1.81
1996	52,507	(215)	(0.4)	(1.1)	(0.03)	—	3.63–1.63

* Per-share amounts restated to reflect 2-for-1 stock split on Jan. 7, 2000.

BALANCE SHEET

Assets	04/29/00 (dollars in thousands)	05/01/99	Liabilities	04/29/00 (dollars in thousands)	05/01/99
Current (CAE 1,217 and 1,050)	47,862	44,207	Current (STD 2,349 and 1,951)	27,199	23,615
Property and equipment	16,790	11,743	Long-term debt	7,893	8,275
Receivables	6,081	6,048	Deferred income	312	602
Advertising rights	824		Deferred income taxes	772	626
Intangibles	850	621	Stockholders' equity*	36,231	29,501
TOTAL	72,407	62,619	TOTAL	72,407	62,619

* No par common; 30,000,000 authorized; 8,873,542 and 8,749,722 issued and outstanding, less 9,840 and 9,840 treasury shares.

RECENT QUARTERS / **PRIOR-YEAR RESULTS**

	Quarter End	Revenue ($000)	Earnings ($000)	EPS ($)	Prior-Year Revenue ($000)	Prior-Year Earnings ($000)	Prior-Year EPS ($)
Q1	07/29/2000	34,536	2,122	0.23	31,467	1,767	0.20
Q4	04/29/2000	27,597	1,108	0.12	31,701	1,908	0.21
Q3	01/29/2000	27,159	1,006	0.11	17,681	356	0.04
Q2	10/30/99	37,127	2,343	0.25	24,233	843	0.09
	SUM	126,419	6,579	0.71	105,082	4,874	0.54

RECENT EVENTS

In **November 1999** the company signed a contract in excess of $7 million with Hamilton County, Ohio, to provide an integrated video and scoring system at the new Paul Brown Stadium, future home of the National Football League's Cincinnati Bengals. In **January 2000** Daktronics signed a multimillion-dollar contract to provide six additional ProStar large-screen video displays, as well as additional advertising and display equipment, at the Indianapolis 500. Daktronics reached an out-of-court settlement with entities affiliated with the Tampa Bay Buccaneers football team over a suit involving a video display system installed by Daktronics at Raymond James Stadium. Daktronics signed agreements to acquire FibreLite of Des Moines, Iowa, and Keyframe Inc. of Tampa, Fla. CEO Kurtenbach said, "FibreLite's low-cost video system is a great complement to our existing product line." Keyframe is a leading video production and video consulting company that specializes in sports events. In **March** Daktronics agreed to provide outdoor electronic LED (light emitting diode) displays for new Walgreens (NYSE: WAG) stores. The Boston Red Sox awarded Daktronics a $1.4 million contract to manufacture and install a new ProStar large-screen video display and additional display equipment in Fenway Park, the team's historic home—to be completed in time for the Red Sox home opener April 11, 2000. Daktronics agreed to manufacture and install two additional large-screen ProStar VideoPlus LED displays for the Cleveland Browns Stadium. (Daktronics provided the integrated scoring, information and video display system in the stadium for the Browns' inaugural season in 1999.) In **April** the company introduced its V-Play video server, which was developed to provide an affordable digital controller for its ProStar VideoPlus large screen LED video display system. Houston and Detroit opened their new stadiums, which featured Daktronics integrated scoring and display systems. Aelred Kurtenbach won the 2000 Minnesota and Dakotas Ernst & Young Entrepreneur of the Year Award in the Manufacturing category. In **May** the company signed a $3.4 million contract to provide 38 VMS (variable message signs) for the Hartford (Connecticut) Area Incident Management System. BlueFire Research, Minneapolis, initiated coverage of Daktronics with an OUTPERFORM rating and a 12-month target price of $18 per share, based on a multiple of 20 times estimated earnings per share for the April 2001 fiscal year. Daktronics was chosen by the New Jersey Sports & Exposition Authority to provide seven ProStar VideoPlus large screen LED video displays for Giants Stadium, Continental Airlines Arena, and Meadowlands Racetrack in East Rutherford, N.J.—an $8.8 million contract that includes responsi- *continued on page 188*

OFFICERS

Dr. Aelred J. Kurtenbach
Chairman and CEO

James B. Morgan
President and COO

Frank J. Kurtenbach
VP-Sales

Paul J. Weinand
Treasurer and CFO

Dr. Duane E. Sander
Secretary

DIRECTORS

Nancy D. Frame
U.S. Trade and Development Agency, Washington, D.C.

Roland J. Jensen
NRG Energy Inc. (retired)

Dr. Aelred J. Kurtenbach

Frank J. Kurtenbach

James B. Morgan

John L. Mulligan
Morgan Stanley Dean Witter

Charles S. Roberts
physician (retired)

Dr. Duane E. Sander
South Dakota State University

James A. Vellenga
Uptech Automation Inc.

MAJOR SHAREHOLDERS

Dr. Aelred J. Kurtenbach, 9.6%

Daktronics Inc. ESOP, 5.6%

All officers and directors as a group (10 persons), 23.8%

SIC CODE

3672 Printed circuit boards

3679 Electronic components, nec

3993 Signs and advertising displays

5046 Commercial equipment, whsle, nec

MISCELLANEOUS

TRANSFER AGENT AND REGISTAR:
Wells Fargo Bank Minnesota N.A.,
South St. Paul, MN

TRADED: Nasdaq National Market

SYMBOL: DAKT

STOCKHOLDERS: 500

EMPLOYEES: 883

PART TIME: 339

AUDITORS:
RSM McGladrey & Pullen Inc. LLP, Sioux Falls, SD

ANNUAL MEETING:
August

INVESTOR RELATIONS:
Mark Steinkamp

SUBSIDIARIES, DIVISIONS, AFFILIATES

Chrondek Inc.

Daktronics Leasing Co.

Star Circuits Inc.

TWO-YEAR QUARTERLY HIGH-LOW STOCK PRICES

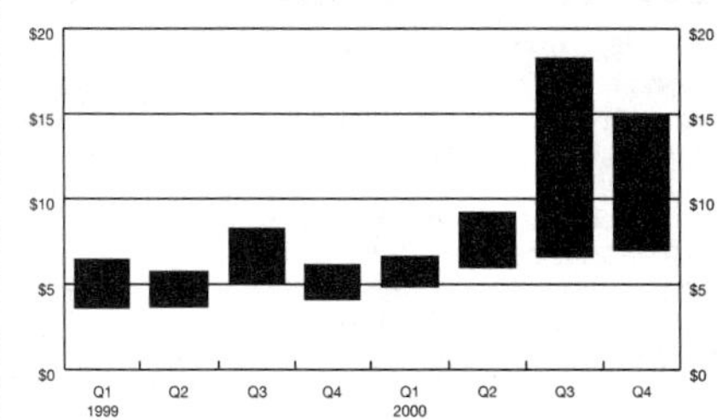

PUB

PUB

Damark International Inc.

7101 Winnetka Ave. N., Brooklyn Park, MN 55428
Tel: 763/531-0066 Fax: 763/531-0481 Web site: http://www.damark.com

Damark International Inc., operating under the Provell name, develops, markets and manages leading edge membership and customer relationship management programs. Provell's proprietary programs provide purchase price discounts and other benefits related to consumer and small business needs in the areas of shopping, travel, hospitality, entertainment, health/fitness, and finance. As of July 1, 2000, benfits were provided through nearly 2.3 million memberships. **ClickShip Direct Inc.** (CSDI) provides outsourcing of order fulfillment and customer care services to retailers, e-tailers, direct marketers, and manufacturers. These services include online and offline order capture, payment processing, inventory receipt, warehousing, merchandise shipment, after-the-sale customer service and support, and returns management. CSDI operates two 375-seat customer care centers, in Junction City, Kan., and Fayetteville, N.C., and a 720,000-square-foot fulfillment center in Brooklyn Park, Minn. CSDI, a wholly owned subsidiary of Damark International, was incorporated in January 2000.

EARNINGS HISTORY

Year Ended Dec 31	Operating Revenue/Sales (dollars in thousands)	Net Earnings	Return on Revenue (percent)	Return on Equity	Net Earnings (dollars per share)	Cash Dividend	Market Price Range
1999 *	430,946	1,236	0.3	4.2	0.21	—	16.50–6.13
1998 †	484,416	(19,615)	(4.0)	(57.6)	(2.71)	—	13.25–5.34
1997	594,627	6,305	1.1	9.2	0.78	—	18.88–9.13
1996	513,716	6,068	1.2	9.7	0.72	—	17.50–6.00
1995	500,024	(1,856)	(0.4)	(2.9)	(0.20)	—	9.00–5.50

* Income figures for 1999 include extraordinary gain of $297,000/$0.05.
† Income figures for 1998 include pretax charge of $9.8 million to write down impaired assets.

BALANCE SHEET

Assets	12/31/99 (dollars in thousands)	12/31/98
Current (CAE 3,927 and 49)	96,425	107,074
Property and equipment	25,464	30,150
Intangible and other	465	681
Deferred income taxes	2,059	2,442
Officer note receivable	1,633	
TOTAL	126,046	140,347

Liabilities	12/31/99 (dollars in thousands)	12/31/98
Current	96,629	106,285
Stockholders' equity*	29,417	34,062
TOTAL	126,046	140,347

* $0.01 par common; 20,000,000 authorized; 5,520,075 and 6,119,208 issued and outstanding.

RECENT QUARTERS / **PRIOR-YEAR RESULTS**

	Quarter End	Revenue ($000)	Earnings ($000)	EPS ($)	Prior-Year Revenue ($000)	Prior-Year Earnings ($000)	Prior-Year EPS ($)
Q3	09/30/2000	33,886	(3,263)	(0.91)	92,586	(2,393)	(0.40)
Q2	07/01/2000	51,773	(8,818)	(1.53)	112,246	(1,436)	(0.24)
Q1	04/01/2000	75,522	(26,161)	(4.64)	109,428	(906)	(0.15)
Q4	12/31/99	116,686	5,971	1.08	139,676	(9,511)	(1.50)
	SUM	277,867	(32,271)	(6.00)	453,936	(14,246)	(2.29)

CURRENT: Q3 EPS figure includes loss of ($0.34) from beneficial conversion feature attributable to preferred stock. Q1 earnings include pretax restructuring charge of $6.739 million; and loss of $14.201 million/($2.52) cumulative effect of accounting change.
PRIOR YEAR: Q2 earnings include extraordinary gain of $297,000/$0.05 on condemnation of land. Q4 earnings include pretax charge of $9.8 million to write down impaired assets.

RECENT EVENTS

In **December 1999** the company reached a settlement with Minnesota Attorney General Mike Hatch regarding certain selling practices of Damark's membership clubs. Hatch said, "Customers will get a double refund if Damark charges the consumer's card without knowing consent." Damark CFO Letak said, "Damark has addressed all of the concerns ... in the interest of avoiding expensive and protracted litigation, even though we are confident the company would have ultimately vindicated its position in court. The civil penalty ... is substantially less than our estimate for potential legal expenses." A new partnership was formed between Damark and Musicland Stores Corp. (NYSE: MLG), Minnetonka, Minn. New links between Damark's Web site and Musicland's four e-commerce sites (SamGoody.com, Suncoast.com, MediaPlay.com, and OnCue.com) improved the available selection of music, movies, software, video games, books, sheet music, and other entertainment merchandise for online shoppers. In **January 2000** Damark decided to outsource its catalog merchandising and marketing activities and to separate its membership and e-services operations. "We are winding down our internal catalog marketing and merchandising activities for financial and strategic reasons," said CEO Cohn. "First of all, we see no *continued on page 188*

OFFICERS

Mark A. Cohn
Chairman and CEO

George S. Richards
President and COO

Stephen P. Letak
EVP and CFO

Kim M. Mageau
SVP and CFO-Provell

Rodney C. Merry
SVP and CIO-Provell

Bob Adkinson
VP and CIO-ClickShip Direct

Michael T. Del Viscio
VP-Provell

Daniel Griffin
VP-Sales/Marketing, ClickShip Direct

Michael T. McGowan
VP-Provell

Michael D. Moroz
VP-Operations, ClickShip Direct

Wiley H. Sharp III
Treasurer-ClickShip Direct

Richard Thonet
VP-Provell

DIRECTORS

Mark A. Cohn

Thomas A. Cusick
TCF Financial Corp., Minneapolis

Stephen J. Hemsley
UnitedHealth Group, Minnetonka, MN

George S. Richards

Ralph Strangis
Kaplan, Strangis and Kaplan P.A., Minneapolis

MAJOR SHAREHOLDERS

Mark A. Cohn, 22.8%

SAFECO Asset Management Co., 19.8%
Seattle

Dimensional Fund Advisors Inc., 7.9%
Santa Monica, CA

All officers and directors as a group (8 persons), 32.4%

SIC CODE

7389 Business services, nec

7389 Business services, nec

MISCELLANEOUS

TRANSFER AGENT AND REGISTAR:
Wells Fargo Bank Minnesota N.A.,
South St. Paul, MN

TRADED: Nasdaq National Market

SYMBOL: DMRK

STOCKHOLDERS: 278

EMPLOYEES: 1,305

PART TIME: 580

GENERAL COUNSEL:
Kaplan Strangis & Kaplan P.A., Minneapolis

AUDITORS:
Arthur Andersen LLP, Minneapolis

INC: MN-1986

ANNUAL MEETING: April

RANKINGS

No. 54 CRM Public 200

SUBSIDIARIES, DIVISIONS, AFFILIATES

TELESERVICE FACILITIES
Junction City, Kan.
Fayetteville, N.C.

FULFILLMENT CENTER
Minneapolis

TWO-YEAR QUARTERLY HIGH-LOW STOCK PRICES

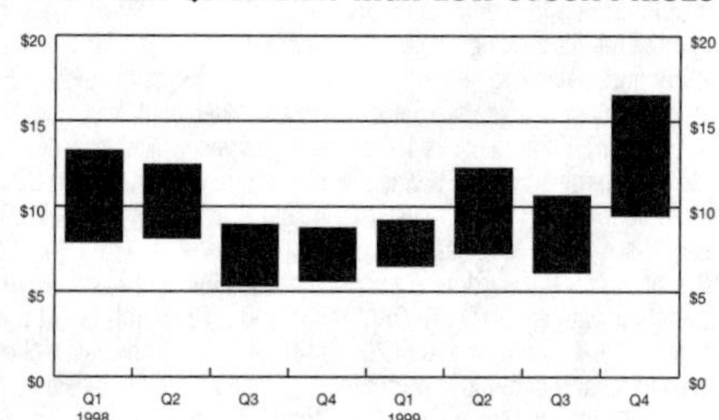

Datakey Inc.

407 W. Travelers Trail, Burnsville, MN 55337
Tel: 952/890-6850 Fax: 952/890-2726 Web site: http://www.datakey.com

Datakey Inc. is an international supplier of electronic products and services. The company provides product, subsystem and system solutions to record, store and transmit electronic information. Datakey also provides products and systems directed to the information security market that enable user identification and authentication, secure data exchange, and information validation. Other company products (proprietary memory keys, cards, and other custom-shaped tokens) make electronic information portable.

EARNINGS HISTORY

Year Ended Dec 31	Operating Revenue/Sales (dollars in thousands)	Net Earnings	Return on Revenue (percent)	Return on Equity	Net Earnings (dollars per share)	Cash Dividend	Market Price Range
1999	5,866	(2,909)	(49.6)	NM	(0.80)	—	5.63–1.00
1998	5,870	(2,289)	(39.0)	NM	(0.94)	—	7.50–1.94
1997	5,977	(4,183)	(70.0)	NM	(1.45)	—	4.88–1.88
1996 *	6,558	(1,706)	(26.0)	(20.5)	(0.60)	—	8.75–3.00
1995	7,219	176	2.4	1.7	0.06	—	8.75–2.50

* Income figures for 1996 include pretax charge of $332,000 for severance costs to be paid to the resigning CEO.

BALANCE SHEET

Assets	12/31/99 (dollars in thousands)	12/31/98
Current (CAE 344 and 853)	3,178	2,778
Equipment and leasehold improvements	752	1,084
Licenses and patents	668	674
TOTAL	4,598	4,536

Liabilities	12/31/99 (dollars in thousands)	12/31/98
Current	1,098	732
Preferred equity	375	1,702
Common equity*	3,125	2,103
TOTAL	4,598	4,536

* $0.05 par common; 10,000,000 authorized; 6,322,285 and 3,045,704 issued and outstanding.

RECENT QUARTERS / **PRIOR-YEAR RESULTS**

	Quarter End	Revenue ($000)	Earnings ($000)	EPS ($)	Prior-Year Revenue ($000)	Prior-Year Earnings ($000)	Prior-Year EPS ($)
Q3	09/30/2000	1,616	(1,346)	(0.16)	1,487	(661)	(0.18)
Q2	07/01/2000	1,837	(725)	(0.09)	1,154	(907)	(0.28)
Q1	04/01/2000	1,773	(708)	(0.10)	1,360	(726)	(0.24)
Q4	12/31/99	1,865	(614)	(0.12)	1,270	(810)	(0.44)
	SUM	7,091	(3,393)	(0.47)	5,271	(3,104)	(1.14)

RECENT EVENTS

In **December 1999** the company's smart cards were selected for the HealthKey Minnesota Project, a pilot program designed to enable secure and private health care communications over the Internet. An order of $200,000 from Datakey's Minnesota-based distributor, Key Solutions Inc., resulted from high demand for Tracker at self-serve car washes, which were integrating Tracker controllers and memory keys into their coin-based payment receptacles at their car wash bays to upgrade them to cashless vending systems. In **January 2000** Datakey was accredited with OPSEC certification by Check Point Software Technologies Ltd. (Nasdaq: CHKP). Datakey reached an agreement to enhance its Model 330 smart card with the elliptic curve cryptography of Certicom Corp., a leading provider of next-generation encryption technology. The first product delivered from a joint technology agreement between Rainbow Technologies (Nasdaq: RNBO) and Datakey was the iKey 2000 USB smart token, a compact token that can fit on a key chain. By using a computer's USB port, the iKey 2000 eliminates the need for smart card readers. Datakey's next new product was the Model 330 PKI smart card solution, the first to provide 32K of EEPROM space for the storage of multiple digital credentials, user data, and application programs and to employ up to 2048-bit RSA keys for increased information security. In **February** the company completed a $4 million private placement of 800,000 shares of common stock at $5.00 per share with accredited investors. Said CEO Boecher, "This private placement will enable us to expand our marketing and sales efforts so we can deliver our solutions to the entire business-to-business market." In **March** Datakey and CyberTrust (http://www.cybertrust.com), Needham Heights, Mass., the leading enabler of secure extranets and e-commerce for organizations, announced plans to provide their information security technologies to the Department of Defense for its Commercial PKI (public key infrastructure) Security Assessment Pilot. In **April** Datakey expanded its global presence by opening an office in Frankfurt, Germany. The company agreed to provide its Model 330 smart cards for companies doing business on the global internetwork of trust created by Identrus, the world's leading provider of identity trust for business-to-business Internet commerce. In **May** Datakey said that its Model 330 smart card was the only 32K smart card to earn FIPS 140-1 Level 2 certification from the National Institute of Standards and Technology (NIST) and the Canadian Communications Security Establishment (CSE). Datakey was a member of three teams selected as winning bidders for the General Service Administration (GSA) Smart Access Common ID Card program. The five prime contractors selected by the GSA were to integrate a variety of smart card technologies to meet individual U.S. government agency requirements. In **June** Datakey joined Phaos Technology Corporation's PKCS 11 Partner Program for the Java platform. By mid-year, OEM (original-equipment manufacturer) partners and major licensees had already placed nearly $1.2 million in new orders for Datakey's cryptographic technology. In **July** Datakey's SignaSURE Model 330 PKI smart card and interface software were used by President Clinton to digitally sign the Electronic Signatures in Global and National Commerce Act, which made *continued on page 189*

OFFICERS
Carl P. Boecher, President and CEO
Colleen Kulhanek, VP-Marketing
Tim Russell, VP, Gen. Mgr.-Integrated Sys. Solutions
Alan G. Shuler, VP and CFO
Michael L. Sorensen, VP and Gen. Mgr.-Electronic Products

DIRECTORS
Carl P. Boecher
Eugene W. Courtney, consultant
Terrence W. Glarner, West Concord Ventures Inc., Minneapolis
Gary R. Holland, Fargo Electronics Inc., Eden Prairie, MN
Thomas R. King, Fredrikson & Byron P.A., Minneapolis

MAJOR SHAREHOLDERS
Perkins Capital Management Inc., 19.6%
Raymond A. Lipkin, 8.2%
Norwest Equity Partners V, 7.8%
David B. Johnson, 5.9%
All officers and directors as a group (9 persons), 4.6%

SIC CODE
3572 Computer storage devices
3577 Computer peripheral equipment, nec

MISCELLANEOUS
TRANSFER AGENT AND REGISTAR: Wells Fargo Bank Minnesota N.A., South St. Paul, MN
TRADED: Nasdaq SmallCap Market
SYMBOL: DKEY
STOCKHOLDERS: 300
EMPLOYEES: 53
GENERAL COUNSEL: Fredrikson & Byron P.A., Minneapolis
AUDITORS: RSM McGladrey & Pullen Inc. LLP, Minneapolis
INC: MN-1976
ANNUAL MEETING: June
MARKETING/COMMUNICATIONS: Colleen Kulhanek
PUBLIC RELATIONS: Environics Communications Inc.

PUB

TWO-YEAR QUARTERLY HIGH-LOW STOCK PRICES

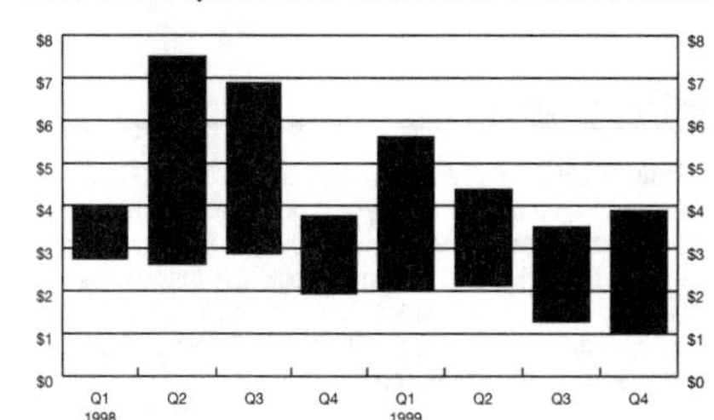

Datalink Corporation

7423 Washington Ave. S., Edina, MN 55439
Tel: 952/944-3462 Fax: 952/944-7869 Web site: http://www.datalink.com

Datalink Corp. analyzes, custom designs, integrates or assembles, installs, and supports high-end Open Systems data storage solutions for end users, value-added resellers and original-equipment manufacturers. The company has developed engineering, sales, and support capabilities to become an expert in applying the best available storage technologies to solve its customers' growing data storage needs. These technologies include hard disk, RAID, magnetic tape, CD-ROM, and optical products. Datalink also matches storage management software technologies—including backup and recovery, archive, high-availability, and near-online storage—to the specific needs of its customers.

EARNINGS HISTORY

Year Ended Dec 31	Operating Revenue/Sales (dollars in thousands)	Net Earnings	Return on Revenue (percent)	Return on Equity	Net Earnings (dollars per share*)	Cash Dividend	Market Price Range
1999	118,897	7,308	6.1	33.7	1.00	—	24.25–7.50
1998 †	87,952	6,531	7.4	NM	0.93	—	
1997	71,255	6,076	8.5	NM	0.88	—	
1996	54,652	4,872	8.9	NM	0.71	—	
1995	38,048	2,314	6.1	NM	0.34	—	

* Trading began Aug. 6, 1999.
† Income figures for 1998 include pretax costs of $0.709 million associated with a postponement of the IPO.

BALANCE SHEET

Assets	12/31/99 (dollars in thousands)	12/31/98	Liabilities	12/31/99 (dollars in thousands)	12/31/98
Current (CAE 6,515 and 2,797)	36,103	25,408	Current (STD 705)	18,296	18,731
Property and equipment	2,496	2,467	Note payable to former stockholder	1,409	
Intangibles	3,412	4,220	Capital lease obligation		13
Other	47	50	Deferred compensation		80
TOTAL	42,058	32,144	Deferred income taxes	648	602
			Stockholders' equity*	21,705	12,719
			TOTAL	42,058	32,144

* $0.001 par common; 50,000,000 authorized; 8,773,000 and 7,100,000 issued and outstanding.

RECENT QUARTERS / **PRIOR-YEAR RESULTS**

	Quarter End	Revenue ($000)	Earnings ($000)	EPS ($)	Prior-Year Revenue ($000)	Prior-Year Earnings ($000)	Prior-Year EPS ($)
Q3	09/30/2000	36,292	1,561	0.18	30,578	1,483	0.19
Q2	06/30/2000	34,911	1,406	0.16	29,844	1,966	0.31
Q1	03/31/2000	27,998	166	0.02	25,682	1,925	0.30
Q4	12/31/99	32,793	1,935	0.22	27,840	1,847	0.26
	SUM	131,994	5,068	0.58	113,944	7,221	1.07

CURRENT: Q2 earnings include pretax charge of $381,000 for costs associated with postponed IPO. Q1 earnings include loss of $0.753 million/($0.09) cumulative effect of accounting change. Q4 and earlier periods have not been restated to reflect the fiscal 2001 accounting change.
PRIOR YEAR: Q1 earnings include pretax charge of $173,000 for costs associated with postponed IPO. Pro forma earnings as if subject to income taxes: $808,000/$0.10.

RECENT EVENTS

In **January 2000** Datalink was authorized by VERITAS Software Corp. (Nasdaq: VRTS) to participate in its partner support program—and became one of only four domestic partners authorized to provide complete support for customers utilizing VERITAS Software applications. In **March** Datalink filed a registration statement with the SEC for a proposed offering of 2.5 million shares of Datalink Corp. common stock, 2.2 million shares by the company and 300,000 shares by selling stockholders. Datalink and LSI Logic Storage Systems Inc., Milpitas, Calif., formed an alliance to deliver advanced networked storage solutions. In further response to the SEC's recently issued Staff Accounting Bulletin No. 101, "Revenue recognition," Datalink agreed to prospectively modify its revenue recognition policy for hardware and software products sold to customers when Datalink provides any installation or configuration services in connection with the *continued on page 189*

OFFICERS

Robert M. Price
Chairman

Greg R. Meland
President and CEO

Daniel J. Kinsella
CFO

Stephen M. Howe
VP-Sales

Scott D. Robinson
Chief Technology Officer

Michael J. Jaeb
VP-Operations/Administration

Helen Torgerson
VP-Technical Services

DIRECTORS

Paul F. Lidsky
OneLink Communications Inc., Eden Prairie, MN

Margaret A. Loftus
Loftus Brown-Wescott Inc.

Greg R. Meland

James E. Ousley
Syntegra (USA) Inc. & Asia, Arden Hills, MN

Robert M. Price
PSV Inc., Bloomington, MN

MAJOR SHAREHOLDERS

Greg R. Meland, 39.3%
Stephen M. Howe, 8.1%
Joseph J. Kaye, 7.1%
Scott D. Robinson, 6.5%
All officers and directors as a group (9 persons), 54.5%

SIC CODE

7373 Computer integrated systems design

MISCELLANEOUS

TRANSFER AGENT AND REGISTAR:
Wells Fargo Bank Minnesota N.A., South St. Paul, MN

TRADED: Nasdaq National Market

SYMBOL: DTLK

EMPLOYEES: 156

GENERAL COUNSEL:
Messerli & Kramer P.A., Minneapolis

AUDITORS:
PricewaterhouseCoopers LLP, Minneapolis

INC: MN-1963

RANKINGS

No. 85 CRM Public 200

Deluxe Corporation

3680 Victoria St. N., P.O. Box 64235 (55164), Shoreview, MN 55126
Tel: 651/483-7111 Fax: 651/481-4477 Web site: http://www.deluxe.com

Deluxe Corp. is a holding company with four business units: Deluxe Paper Payment Systems, eFunds, iDLX Technology Partners, and Government Services. Deluxe Paper Payment Systems provides checks and related products to consumers and small businesses through multiple distribution channels. eFunds provides electronic transaction processing and integrated payment protection services to financial and retail businesses. iDLX provides information technology development and support services and business process outsourcing services to financial services companies and to all of Deluxe's businesses. Deluxe Government Services offers electronic benefits transfer services to state governments.

EARNINGS HISTORY

Year Ended Dec 31	Operating Revenue/Sales (dollars in thousands)	Net Earnings	Return on Revenue (percent)	Return on Equity	Net Earnings (dollars per share)	Cash Dividend	Market Price Range
1999 *	1,650,500	203,022	12.3	48.7	2.65	1.48	40.50–24.75
1998 †	1,933,659	145,408	7.5	24.0	1.80	1.48	37.94–26.38
1997 ¶	1,920,629	44,672	2.3	7.3	0.55	1.48	37.00–29.75
1996 #	1,980,577	65,463	3.3	9.2	0.80	1.48	39.75–27.00
1995 **	1,937,605	87,021	4.5	11.2	1.06	1.48	33.88–26.13

* Income figures for 1999 include pretax charge of $0.5 million for impairment losses.
† Income figures for 1998 include net charge of $74.8 million pretax, $46.6 million/($0.58) after-tax. Pro forma results to segregate the several businesses divested during 1998: revenue $1,683,863,000; net income $152,368,000/$1.89.
¶ Income figures for 1997 include pretax charges for impairment losses ($99 million) and for restructuring and other ($81 million).
# Income figures for 1996 include net pretax charges for impairment losses ($111.9 million) and for restructuring and other ($30.4 million).
** Income figures for 1995 include loss of $7,413,000/($0.09) from discontinued operations and their disposal.

BALANCE SHEET

Assets	12/31/99 (dollars in thousands)	12/31/98	Liabilities	12/31/99 (dollars in thousands)	12/31/98
Current (CAE 140,465 and 268,389)	418,749	608,080	Current (STD 4,357 and 7,332)	404,666	430,695
Restricted cash	28,939	3,921	Long-term debt	115,542	106,321
Long-term investments	40,846	45,208	Deferred income taxes	46,322	27,519
Property, plant, and equipment	294,785	340,077	Other	8,805	419
			Stockholders' equity*	417,308	606,565
Cost in excess of net assets acquired	51,705	42,836	TOTAL	992,643	1,171,519
Internal-use software	142,465	116,734			
Other intangibles	15,154	14,663			
TOTAL	992,643	1,171,519			

* $1 par common; 500,000,000 authorized; 72,019,898 and 80,480,526 issued and outstanding.

RECENT QUARTERS / **PRIOR-YEAR RESULTS**

	Quarter End	Revenue ($000)	Earnings ($000)	EPS ($)	Revenue ($000)	Earnings ($000)	EPS ($)
Q3	09/30/2000	404,947	49,397	0.68	417,114	49,057	0.65
Q2	06/30/2000	406,756	34,841	0.48	407,841	47,779	0.61
Q1	03/31/2000	404,426	44,322	0.61	414,077	48,033	0.60
Q4	12/31/99	411,468	58,153	0.79	498,734	57,352	0.71
	SUM	1,627,597	186,713	2.57	1,737,766	202,221	2.58

PRIOR YEAR: Q4 earnings include pretax loss of $10.5 million on sale of Social Expressions and PaperDirect Inc. businesses.

RECENT EVENTS

In **December 1999** eFunds introduced Integreat!, an Internet account-opening solution to help financial services companies successfully open more demand deposit accounts over the Internet. Deluxe Paper Payment Systems and iDLX Technology Partners rolled out Integration Services to help financial services companies integrate Deluxe's O N E (Online Network Exchange) connectivity system with their new account-opening software. Deluxe completed the sale of National Revenue Corp. (NRC), Columbus, Ohio, to Risk Management Alternatives Inc., Atlanta. NRC did not fit with Deluxe's new corporate strategy and holding company structure. eFunds achieved its highest ever transaction volume for a single day on Dec. 23 at more than 12 million transactions. In **January 2000** eFunds received the Meritorious Achievement Award for *continued on page 189*

OFFICERS

John A. (Gus) Blanchard III
Chairman, President, and CEO

Lawrence J. Mosner
Vice Chairman

Thomas W. VanHimbergen
EVP and CFO

Ronald E. Eilers
SVP and Gen. Mgr.-Paper Payment Systems

Douglas J. Treff
SVP and CFO

DIRECTORS

Calvin W. Aurand Jr.
Banta Corp., Menasha, WI

John A. (Gus) Blanchard III

Ronald E. Eilers

Daniel D. Granger
Catalina Marketing Corp., St. Petersburg, FL

Barbara B. Grogan
Western Industrial Contractors Inc., Denver

Donald R. Hollis
DRH Strategic Consulting Inc.

Cheryl E. Mayberry
Open Port Technology Inc., Chicago

Lawrence J. Mosner

Stephen P. Nachtsheim
Intel Corp., Santa Clara, CA

Robert C. Salipante
ReliaStar Financial Corp., Minneapolis

MAJOR SHAREHOLDERS

FMR Corp., 10.9%
Boston

ESL Partners L.P., 5.9%
Greenwich, CT

All officers and directors as a group (14 persons), 1.5%

SIC CODE

2761 Manifold business forms

2782 Blankbooks and looseleaf binders

6099 Functions related to deposit banking

7374 Data processing and preparation

MISCELLANEOUS

TRANSFER AGENT AND REGISTAR:
Wells Fargo Bank Minnesota N.A.,
South St. Paul, MN

TRADED: NYSE
SYMBOL: DLX
STOCKHOLDERS: 13,907
EMPLOYEES: 11,900
GENERAL COUNSEL:
Dorsey & Whitney PLLP, Minneapolis
AUDITORS:
Deloitte & Touche LLP, Minneapolis
INC: MN-1920
FOUNDED: 1915
ANNUAL MEETING: May
INVESTOR RELATIONS:
Stuart Alexander
PUBLIC RELATIONS:
Bev Bergstrom

RANKINGS

No. 24 CRM Public 200
No. 93 CRM Employer 100

SUBSIDIARIES, DIVISIONS, AFFILIATES

DELUXE PAPER PAYMENT SYSTEMS
1080 W. County Rd. F
St. Paul, MN 55126
612/483-7111
Ronald E. Eilers

DELUXE PAYMENT PROTECTION SYSTEMS
1550 E. 79th St.
Suite 700
Bloomington, MN 55425
612/854-3422
Philip J. Meyer

eFunds Corp.
400 W. Deluxe Pkwy.
Glendale, WI 53212
414/963-5000

iDLX Technology Partners Inc.
1080 West County Rd. F
St. Paul, MN 55126
612/483-7111
Nikhil Sinha

Deluxe Government Services
400 W. Deluxe Pkwy.
Glendale, WI 53212
414/963-5000
Cheryl Campbell

TWO-YEAR QUARTERLY HIGH-LOW STOCK PRICES

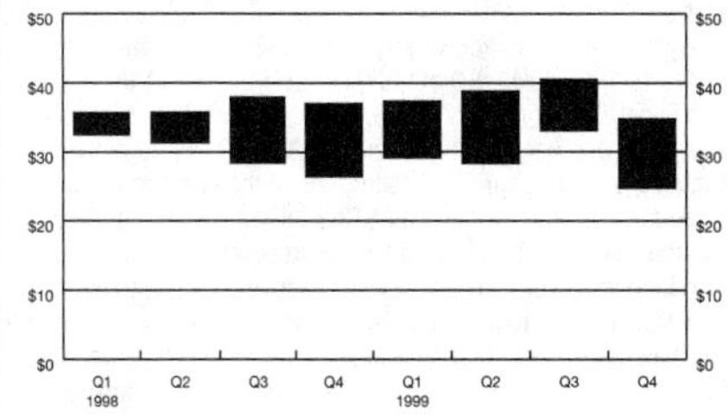

PUB

PUB

Department 56 Inc.

One Village Pl., 6436 City West Parkway, Eden Prairie, MN 55344
Tel: 952/944-5600 Fax: 952/943-4502 Web site: http://www.D56.com

Department 56 Inc. is a designer, importer, and distributor of collectibles and other specialty giftware. The company is best known for its series of collectible, handcrafted, lit ceramic, and porcelain houses, buildings, and related accessories in **The Original Snow Village Collection** and **The Heritage Village Collection**. Principal customers (accounting for 90 percent of sales) are 20,000 independent gift retailers across the United States. These retailers include 1,500 independently owned Gold Key and Showcase Dealers, who receive special recognition and qualify for improved sales terms, and who must satisfy certain requirements, such as maintaining the company's products on display in an attractive setting for at least six months. The remaining 10 percent of sales are made to department stores and mail-order houses.

EARNINGS HISTORY

Year Ended Dec	Operating Revenue/Sales (dollars in thousands)	Net Earnings	Return on Revenue (percent)	Return on Equity	Net Earnings (dollars per share)	Cash Dividend	Market Price Range
1999	245,856	42,656	17.3	27.9	2.48	—	37.88–18.31
1998	243,365	46,516	19.1	26.0	2.49	—	39.31–22.94
1997 *	219,496	42,781	19.5	22.9	2.06	—	31.75–16.88
1996	228,775	45,944	20.1	23.4	2.13	—	41.88–19.50
1995 †	252,047	48,253	19.1	32.1	2.24	—	48.00–32.63

* Income figures for 1997 include pretax gain of $2.882 million on sale of aircraft.
† Income figures for 1995 include extraordinary charge of $1.312 million/($0.06) due to refinancing of debt.

BALANCE SHEET

Assets	01/01/00 (dollars in thousands)	01/02/99	Liabilities	01/01/00 (dollars in thousands)	01/02/99
Current (CAE 3,962 and 2,783)	99,642	57,901	Current (STD 42,500)	67,353	28,625
Property and equipment	29,857	17,722	Deferred taxes	6,831	5,923
			Long-term debt	60,000	20,000
Goodwill	139,340	141,528	Stockholders' equity*	152,924	178,735
Trademarks	16,596	16,003			
Other	1,673	129	TOTAL	287,108	233,283
TOTAL	287,108	233,283			

* $0.01 par common; 100,000,000 authorized; 21,964,000 and 21,900,000 issued and outstanding.

RECENT QUARTERS / PRIOR-YEAR RESULTS

	Quarter End	Revenue ($000)	Earnings ($000)	EPS ($)	Prior-Year Revenue ($000)	Prior-Year Earnings ($000)	Prior-Year EPS ($)
Q3	09/30/2000	69,924	12,048	0.86	75,093	14,959	0.88
Q2	07/01/2000	57,746	8,278	0.58	82,721	18,738	1.06
Q1	04/01/2000	40,367	(3,158)	(0.21)	33,648	3,344	0.19
Q4	01/01/2000	54,394	5,615	0.35	52,906	6,915	0.38
	SUM	222,431	22,783	1.57	244,368	43,956	2.51

RECENT EVENTS

In **December 1999** the board of directors authorized the repurchase of $75 million worth of the company's common stock, in addition to the buyback of shares under its previous repurchase authorizations. Meanwhile, the company successfully instituted numerous changes to its business processes and systems in order to address problems encountered with the implementation of a new ERP system in January 1999. After undertaking a robust testing cycle, the company was confident that its systems were prepared to support the selling process during the critical first quarter when the majority of customer orders are received. In **February 2000** shares hit an all-time low after the report of disappointing fourth-quarter 1999 earnings (6 cents a share lower than the consensus estimate) and a prediction that 2000 results would be below 1999. Orders through Feb. 19 were down 8 percent. **April 1**: At quarter's end, accounts receivable relative to 1999 sales stood at $30.8 million. On April 27, a day after the company said that prolonged computer-related problems would reduce sales the rest of the year, Department 56 stock fell by nearly 40 percent, to a record-low $9.13. By **June** the company had made significant progress in its collection efforts related to 1999 sales. Accounts receivable relative to those sales had been reduced to $9.4 million as of June 24, 2000. Said CEO Engel, "We continue to make significant progress in resolving prior year receivables, allowing us to release customers from credit hold and begin shipping their orders. We are confident that we will have this issue fully behind us by the end of July." In **August** the board approved resumption of the company's share repurchase program and extended the expiration of the repurchase authorization, which had $72.3 million remaining. **Sept. 30**: Net income and diluted earnings per share in the first nine months were $17.2 million and $1.18, respectively, compared to $37.0 million and $2.08 in prior year. "Our mid-year product introductions across all categories are encouraging, with dealer orders for these products up strongly over last year," said Engel. "In particular, our expanded reach to new channels and consumers through our Hot Properties licensed lines will help establish the Department 56 brand name as the preferred name in terms of style, value and quality." The company's outlook for full-year diluted earnings per share was in the range of $1.40 to $1.47 on net *continued on page 189*

OFFICERS

Susan E. Engel
Chairman and CEO

David W. Dewey
EVP-Overseas Operations

Yeh-Huang Lin
VP-Asia Production

Robert S. Rose
VP-Distribution/Operations

Timothy J. Schugel
VP-Sourcing Mgmt./Production Control

Gregory G. Sorensen
VP-Technology

Alan L. Sussman
SVP, Chief Information Officer

Percy C. (Tom) Tomlinson Jr.
EVP and CFO

David H. Weiser
SVP-Legal/Hum. Res., Gen. Counsel, Sec.

Andrew E. Melville
SVP-Sales

DIRECTORS

Peter K. Barker
Goldman Sachs & Co.

Jay Chiat
screamingmedia.com, New York

Susan E. Engel

Gary Matthews
Derby Cycle Corp.

Steven G. Rothmeier
Great Northern Capital Corp., Minneapolis

Vin Weber
Clark & Weinstock Inc., Washington, D.C.

MAJOR SHAREHOLDERS

Ariel Capital Management Inc., 21.2%
Chicago

Yacktman Asset Management, 11.6%
Chicago

Firstar Corp., 7.2%
Milwaukee

All officers and directors as a group (18 persons), 8.2%

SIC CODE

3269 Pottery products, nec

5199 Nondurable goods, whsle, nec

MISCELLANEOUS

TRANSFER AGENT AND REGISTAR:
Chase Mellon Shareholder Services LLC, New York

TRADED: NYSE

SYMBOL: DFS

STOCKHOLDERS: 880

EMPLOYEES: 315

AUDITORS:
Deloitte & Touche LLP, Minneapolis

INC: DE-1992

FOUNDED: 1976

ANNUAL MEETING: May

TREASURY AND CORPORATE DEVELOPMENT:
Anthony Ishaug

HUMAN RESOURCES:
Tim Kvrey

RANKINGS

No. 67 CRM Public 200

SUBSIDIARIES, DIVISIONS, AFFILIATES

D 56 Inc.

Department 56 Sales Inc.

Department 56 Retail Inc.

TWO-YEAR QUARTERLY HIGH-LOW STOCK PRICES

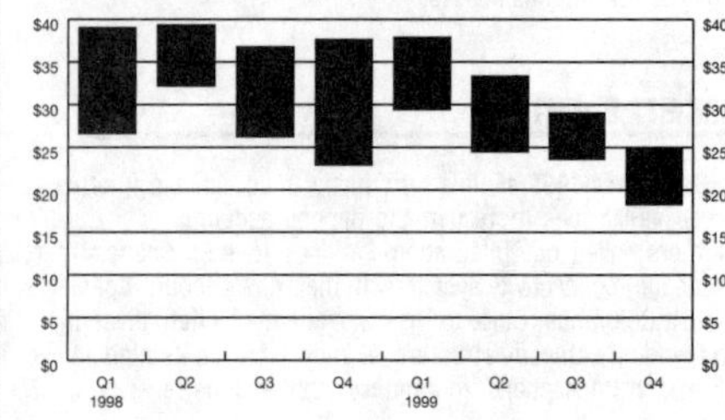

Developed Technology Resource Inc.

7300 Metro Blvd., Suite 550, Edina, MN 55439
Tel: 952/820-0022 Fax: 952/820-0011 Web site: http://www.dtr-fmi.com

Developed Technology Resource Inc. pursues investment opportunities in the food processing industry within the former Soviet Union. The company's subsidiary, FoodMaster International, owns operations that manufacture and distribute a variety of dairy products in Kazakhstan, Ukraine, and Moldova.

EARNINGS HISTORY *

Year Ended Dec 31	Operating Revenue/Sales (dollars in thousands)	Net Earnings (dollars in thousands)	Return on Revenue (percent)	Return on Equity (percent)	Net Earnings (dollars per share†)	Cash Dividend (dollars per share†)	Market Price Range (dollars per share†)
1999	1,150	(1,952)	NM	NM	(2.42)	—	3.47–0.75
1998	1,751	(186)	(10.7)	(8.8)	(0.23)	—	6.88–2.50
1997 ¶	3,310	710	21.5	43.9	0.89	—	2.00–0.88
1996 #	4,616	(157)	(3.4)	(16.8)	(0.19)	—	1.50–0.75
1995 **	1,992	(1,326)	(66.6)	NM	(1.52)	—	4.50–1.31

* Fiscal years 1997 and earlier ended Oct. 31. Results of two-month stub period Nov. 1, 1997, to Dec. 31, 1997: revenue $538,607; net income $49,763/$0.06.
† Per-share amounts restated to reflect 1-for-3 reverse stock split effected Dec. 12, 1995.
¶ Income figures for 1997 include gain of $200,000/$0.25 from discontinued operations and their disposal.
# Income figures for 1996 include loss of $30,166/($0.04) from discontinued operations.
** Revenue for 1995 does not include $1,951,989 that was reclassified to discontinued operations pursuant to a Jan. 15, 1996, agreement to sell the airport security business. Income figures include loss of $130,591/($0.15) from discontinued operations.

BALANCE SHEET

Assets	12/31/99 (dollars in thousands)	12/31/98 (dollars in thousands)
Current (CAE 193 and 5)	744	1,708
Furniture, equipment	35	44
Investment in FMI		992
TOTAL	779	2,744

Liabilities	12/31/99 (dollars in thousands)	12/31/98 (dollars in thousands)
Current	299	592
Deferred gain	15	34
Stockholders' equity*	466	2,118
TOTAL	779	2,744

* $0.01 par common; 3,333,334 authorized; 805,820 and 805,820 issued and outstanding.

RECENT QUARTERS / **PRIOR-YEAR RESULTS**

	Quarter End	Revenue ($000)	Earnings ($000)	EPS ($)	Prior-Year Revenue ($000)	Prior-Year Earnings ($000)	Prior-Year EPS ($)
Q2	06/30/2000	8	(116)	(0.12)	350	(199)	(0.25)
Q1	03/31/2000	8	(150)	(0.17)	363	(145)	(0.18)
Q4	12/31/99	164	(1,410)	(1.75)	477	(618)	(0.77)
Q3	09/30/99	273	(207)	(0.26)	380	109	0.14
	SUM	453	(1,882)	(2.30)	1,570	(853)	(1.06)

RECENT EVENTS

In **December 1999** DTR and Agribusiness Partners International announced the termination of DTR's management agreement with FoodMaster International LLC (FMI). FMI was to directly employ the managers in the country of operation.

OFFICERS

John P. Hupp
President and CEO

LeAnn H. Davis
CFO

DIRECTORS

Peter L. Hauser
Equity Securities Trading Co. Inc., Minneapolis

John P. Hupp

Roger W. Schnobrich
Hinshaw & Culbertson, Minneapolis

MAJOR SHAREHOLDERS

John P. Hupp, 13.5%

Erlan Sagadiev, 11.8%

Vladimir Drits, 6.5%
Minnetonka, MN

All officers and directors as a group (3 persons), 20.5%

SIC CODE

2026 Fluid milk

5143 Dairy products, whsle

MISCELLANEOUS

TRANSFER AGENT AND REGISTAR:
Wells Fargo Bank Minnesota N.A., South St. Paul, MN

TRADED: OTC Bulletin Board

SYMBOL: DEVT

STOCKHOLDERS: 56

EMPLOYEES: 3

GENERAL COUNSEL:
Hinshaw & Culbertson, Minneapolis

AUDITORS:
Deloitte & Touche LLP, Minneapolis

INC: MN-1991

ANNUAL MEETING: June

SUBSIDIARIES, DIVISIONS, AFFILIATES

FoodMaster International LLC
7300 Metro Blvd.
Suite 550
Edina, MN 55439

SXD Inc.
7300 Metro Blvd.
Suite 550
Edina, MN 55439

Savory Snacks LLC
Madison, Wis.

TWO-YEAR QUARTERLY HIGH-LOW STOCK PRICES

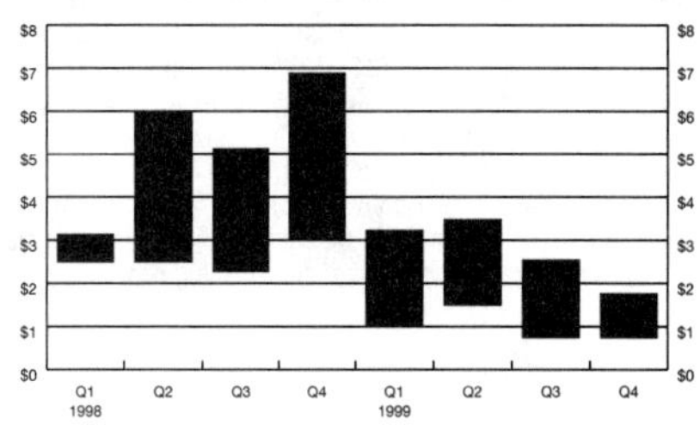

PUB

Diametrics Medical Inc.

2658 Patton Rd., Roseville, MN 55113
Tel: 651/639-8035 Fax: 651/639-8549 Web site: http://www.diametrics.com

Diametrics Medical Inc. develops, manufactures, and markets proprietary critical-care blood analysis systems that provide immediate or continuous diagnostic results at the point of patient care. The company's IRMA (Immediate Response Mobile Analysis) System consists of a portable instrument that employs single-use disposable cartridges to perform several blood chemistry tests simultaneously in a simple, two-minute procedure.

EARNINGS HISTORY

Year Ended Dec 31	Operating Revenue/Sales (dollars in thousands)	Net Earnings (dollars in thousands)	Return on Revenue (percent)	Return on Equity (percent)	Net Earnings (dollars per share)	Cash Dividend (dollars per share)	Market Price Range (dollars per share)
1999	18,687	(10,244)	(54.8)	(74.0)	(0.41)	—	8.56–3.75
1998	12,156	(17,388)	NM	NM	(0.79)	—	8.88–2.75
1997 *	10,434	(21,037)	NM	NM	(1.13)	—	10.13–3.00
1996 †	3,797	(23,575)	NM	NM	(1.56)	—	8.00–3.25
1995 ¶	1,607	(23,046)	NM	(73.9)	(1.82)	—	13.38–4.38

* Income figures for 1997 include restructuring and other charges totaling $463,816.
† Income figures for 1996 include restructuring and other charges totaling $1,334,661.
¶ Income figures for 1995 include restructuring and other charges totaling $391,834.

BALANCE SHEET

Assets	12/31/99 (dollars in thousands)	12/31/98 (dollars in thousands)	Liabilities	12/31/99 (dollars in thousands)	12/31/98 (dollars in thousands)
Current (CAE 2,786 and 3,432)	25,318	17,051	Current (STD 2,786 and 417)	10,308	5,636
Property and equipment	5,774	6,923	Long-term obligations	7,814	8,163
Other	880	1,373	Other	10	182
TOTAL	31,972	25,346	Stkhldrs' equity*	13,841	11,366
			TOTAL	31,972	25,346

* $0.01 par common; 35,000,000 authorized; 25,778,499 and 23,391,597 issued and outstanding.

RECENT QUARTERS / **PRIOR-YEAR RESULTS**

	Quarter End	Revenue ($000)	Earnings ($000)	EPS ($)	Prior-Year Revenue ($000)	Prior-Year Earnings ($000)	Prior-Year EPS ($)
Q3	09/30/2000	6,581	(487)	(0.02)	4,694	(1,981)	(0.08)
Q2	06/30/2000	6,090	(893)	(0.03)	4,640	(2,782)	(0.11)
Q1	03/31/2000	5,671	(1,143)	(0.04)	4,243	(3,908)	(0.17)
Q4	12/31/99	5,110	(1,572)	(0.06)	3,584	(3,966)	(0.17)
	SUM	23,452	(4,096)	(0.16)	17,162	(12,637)	(0.53)

RECENT EVENTS

In **December 1999** the FDA granted clearance for the marketing of the Neurotrend multiparameter monitoring system, a medical device that continuously monitors oxygen, carbon dioxide, acidity, and temperature in the brain. Monitoring of these parameters provides critical information that can guide clinicians and surgeons in treating patients with head trauma or those requiring surgical intervention in the brain. CODMAN, a Johnson & Johnson company, had exclusive rights to the global market development and distribution of the Neurotrend system. The FDA also granted Diametrics clearance to market its new stand-alone calibration system for use with both Neurotrend and Trendcare monitoring systems. In **January 2000** Sutro & Co. initiated coverage with a BUY rating and positive earnings projections. In **March** the company's new Neotrend Monitoring System was designated as one of the best life-enhancing products by Great Britain's prestigious Design Council. Neotrend was installed at the Santa Clara Valley Medical Center in San Jose, Calif., where it monitors oxygen levels in the blood of infants, especially premature babies. In **July** Diametrics was added to the Russell 2000 and Russell 3000 U.S. Equity Indexes. (The Russell 3000 is a measure of the 3,000 largest publicly traded U.S. companies in the U.S. stock market, ranked by market capitalization as of May 31. The Russell 2000 Index consists of small cap companies from the Russell 3000 Index.) **Sept. 30**: Nine-month net sales grew 35 percent to a record $18.342 million, from $13.577 million in the same period a year ago. The net loss declined, as gross profit increased 145 percent to $5.038 million. "We continue to achieve significant financial improvements as a result of our strategic partnerships with Agilent Technologies and Johnson & Johnson CODMAN. In addition, Diametrics completed several new products in the third quarter," said CEO Giddings. "These accomplishments include the release of our new H4 cartridge, completion of new software for data and information management, CE Mark of our new Neotrend-L sensor, and enhanced features for the IRMA SL blood analysis system, including availability of 26-week shelf life for our combination and blood gas cartridges, as well as bar code reading capability."

OFFICERS

David T. Giddings
Chairman, President, and CEO

Roy S. Johnson
EVP and Pres./Mng. Dir.-DML

Laurence L. Betterley
SVP-Finance and CFO

James R. Miller
SVP-Sales/Marketing/Commercial Devel.

DIRECTORS

Gerald L. Cohn
private investor/consultant

Andre de Bruin
QUIDEL Corp.

David T. Giddings

Hans-Guenter Hohmann
Agilent Technologies GmbH (Hewlett-Packard)

Roy S. Johnson

Mark B. Knudson, Ph.D.
Medical Innovation Partners, Minnetonka, MN

David V. Milligan, Ph.D.
Bay City Capital LLC

MAJOR SHAREHOLDERS

BCC Acquisition II LLC, 12.3%
San Francisco

Amarfour LLC, 6.8%
Chicago

Agilent Technologies Inc., 6.8%
Palo Alto, CA

The TCW Group Inc., 6.6%
Los Angeles

State of Wisconsin Investment Board, 5.2%
Madison, WI

All officers and directors as a group (9 persons), 6.6%

SIC CODE

3841 Surgical and medical instruments

MISCELLANEOUS

TRANSFER AGENT AND REGISTAR:
American Stock Transfer & Trust Co., New York

TRADED: Nasdaq National Market

SYMBOL: DMED

STOCKHOLDERS: 463

EMPLOYEES: 146

GENERAL COUNSEL:
Dorsey & Whitney PLLP, Minneapolis

AUDITORS:
KPMG LLP, Minneapolis

INC: MN-1990

ANNUAL MEETING: May

RANKINGS

No. 153 CRM Public 200

No. 14 Minnesota Technology Fast 50

SUBSIDIARIES, DIVISIONS, AFFILIATES

Diametrics Medical Ltd.
High Wycombe, England

TWO-YEAR QUARTERLY HIGH-LOW STOCK PRICES

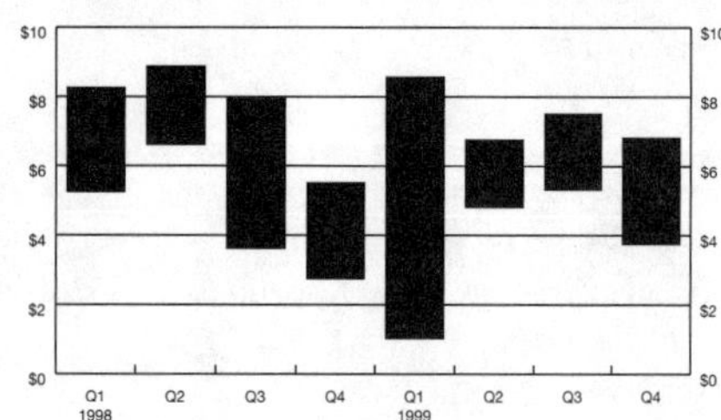

Digi International Inc.

11001 Bren Rd. E., Minnetonka, MN 55343
Tel: 952/912-3444 Fax: 952/912-4991 Web site: http://www.dgii.com

Digi International Inc. is a leading provider of data communications hardware and software that delivers seamless connectivity solutions for open systems, server-based remote access, Internet telephony, and LAN markets. The company markets its products through an international network of distributors and resellers, system integrators, and original-equipment manufacturers (OEMs).

EARNINGS HISTORY

Year Ended Sept 30	Operating Revenue/Sales (dollars in thousands)	Net Earnings (dollars in thousands)	Return on Revenue (percent)	Return on Equity (percent)	Net Earnings (dollars per share)	Cash Dividend (dollars per share)	Market Price Range (dollars per share)
1999 *	193,506	3,192	1.6	2.5	0.22	—	16.38–6.25
1998 †	182,932	(71)	0.0	(0.1)	(0.01)	—	29.50–9.63
1997 ¶	165,598	(15,791)	(9.5)	(16.5)	(1.18)	—	18.75–5.13
1996 #	193,151	9,300	4.8	8.5	0.69	—	30.75–11.88
1995	164,978	19,331	11.7	18.3	1.38	—	30.25–13.25

* Income figures for 1999 include pretax restructuring charge of $0.607 million.
† Income figures for 1998, which have been restated to reflect a change in measurement and allocations of the ITK and CDC purchase prices, include pretax charges of $16.065 million for purchased R&D and $1.02 million for restructuring; and a pretax $1.35 million gain from AetherWorks Corp.
¶ Income figures for 1997 include pretax restructuring charge of $10.471 million; and write-off, losses at AetherWorks Corp. of $11.523 million.
# Income figures for 1996 include ($0.30) adjustment for losses at AetherWorks.

BALANCE SHEET

Assets	09/30/99 (dollars in thousands)	09/30/98 (dollars in thousands)
Current (CAE 20,963 and 10,355)	96,475	90,949
Property, equipment, improvements	30,243	33,991
Intangibles	47,805	63,602
Other	1,808	2,979
TOTAL	176,330	191,521

Liabilities	09/30/99 (dollars in thousands)	09/30/98 (dollars in thousands)
Current (STD 5,089 and 10,971)	36,529	53,053
Long-term debt	9,206	11,124
Deferred income taxes	3,431	5,818
Other		275
Stockholders' equity*	127,164	121,251
TOTAL	176,330	191,521

* $0.01 par common; 60,000,000 authorized; 16,192,997 and 15,790,975 issued and outstanding, less 1,271,612 and 1,247,094 treasury shares.

RECENT QUARTERS / **PRIOR-YEAR RESULTS**

	Quarter End	Revenue ($000)	Earnings ($000)	EPS ($)	Prior-Year Revenue ($000)	Prior-Year Earnings ($000)	Prior-Year EPS ($)
Q4	09/30/2000	34,230	(7,073)	(0.47)	48,335	2,715	0.18
Q3	06/30/2000	32,354	2,513	0.17	51,145	2,253	0.15
Q2	03/31/2000	25,800	(13,282)	(0.88)	42,631	(2,251)	(0.15)
Q1	12/31/99	40,140	1,018	0.07	51,395	475	0.03
	SUM	132,525	(16,825)	(1.12)	193,506	3,192	0.21

CURRENT: Q4 earnings include pretax charges of $8.078 million for impairment loss and $1.532 million for restructuring—a total of $8.475 million/($0.56) net of taxes.
of $14.124 million/($0.94); and Aetherworks Corp. note recovery gain of $8 million/$0.53.
PRIOR YEAR: Q4 earnings include gain of $0.160 million on restructuring reversal.

RECENT EVENTS

In **December 1999** the company announced that Digi communications adapters were to be used to add enhanced remote access and fax capabilities to Hewlett-Packard Co.'s Business Communications Server (BCS) platform. In **January 2000** Digi launched "ServerPowered.com," a new Internet portal that helps resellers and integrators build and sell cost-effective, server-based systems for applications such as remote access, fax, and routing. Digi and Red Hat Inc., the leading developer and provider of open source solutions, agreed to join in marketing programs that was to enable distributors, resellers, and integrators to offer Linux-based communications servers designed specifically to suit the needs of small to medium-sized businesses. In **February** Digi implemented a broad technology and marketing initiative designed to offer industry-leading support for Microsoft's newly-launched Windows 2000 operating system. Sumisho Datacom and Internet Pro Corp. chose RAS (Remote Access Server) products from Digi International to help build Linux-based Internet point-of-presence (POP) servers for Japan's fast-growing community of Internet Service Providers (ISPs). In **March** Digi attributed the current quarter's lower-than-expected revenue to the slow pace at which its customers were placing orders following the initial slowdown industrywide following the Y2K changeover. Digi's DataFire RAS (Remote Access Server) family of products was named a *continued on page 189*

OFFICERS

Joseph T. Dunsmore
Chairman, President, and CEO
Douglas J. Glader
EVP and Gen. Mgr.-MiLAN Technology
S. (Kris) Krishnan
SVP-Finance/Admin./Accounting and CFO
Michael Bantz
VP-North American Sales
Bruce Berger
VP, Managing Dir.-European Operations
Jill Boyle
VP-Human Resources/Organizational Devel.
Donna Burke
VP-Corporate Communications
Wulf R. Halbach, Ph.D.
VP-Research/Development
Don Henry
VP-North America Sales
Michael D. Kelley
VP-Support Services
Larry McGraw
VP-International Field Operations
Burk Murray
VP-Marketing
Jon A. Nyland
VP-Manufacturing Operations
Gregory Wilkes
VP-Americas Sales
Joel Young
VP-Engineering
Mark D. Fandrich
Controller
James E. Nicholson
Secretary

DIRECTORS

Willis K. Drake
private investor, Minneapolis
Joseph T. Dunsmore
Richard E. Eichhorn
private investor
Kenneth E. Millard
Tetular Corp., Vernon Hills, IL
Robert S. Moe
Polaris Industries Inc. (retired)
Mykola Moroz
Digi International Inc. (retired)
Michael Seedman
U.S. Robotics (former)
David Stanley
Payless Cashways Inc., Kansas City, MO
James Tucker
Open Port Technology

MAJOR SHAREHOLDERS

Heartland Advisors Inc., 9.7%
Milwaukee
John P. Schinas, 9.3%
Eden Prairie, MN
All officers and directors as a group (11 persons), 13.2%

SIC CODE

3577 Computer peripheral equipment, nec
3674 Semiconductors and related devices

MISCELLANEOUS

TRANSFER AGENT AND REGISTAR:
Wells Fargo Bank Minnesota N.A.,
South St. Paul, MN
TRADED: Nasdaq National Market
SYMBOL: DGII
STOCKHOLDERS: 356
EMPLOYEES: 583
GENERAL COUNSEL:
Faegre & Benson PLLP, Minneapolis
AUDITORS:
PricewaterhouseCoopers LLP, Minneapolis
INC: DE-1985
ANNUAL MEETING: January
HUMAN RESOURCES: Tracy Roberts
PUBLIC RELATIONS: Rob Clark

RANKINGS

No. 75 CRM Public 200

SUBSIDIARIES, DIVISIONS, AFFILIATES

MFG. OPERATIONS
10000 W. 76th St.
Eden Prairie, MN 55344
612/912-4700

TWO-YEAR QUARTERLY HIGH-LOW STOCK PRICES

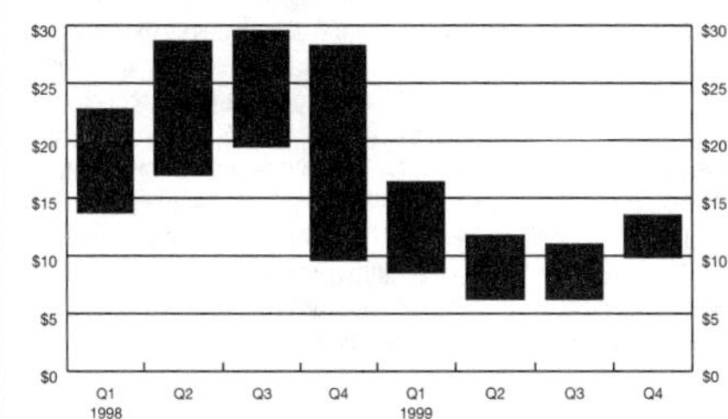

PUB

PUB

Digital Biometrics Inc.

5600 Rowland Rd., Minnetonka, MN 55343
Tel: 952/932-0888 Fax: 952/932-7181 Web site: http://www.digitalbiometrics.com

Digital Biometrics Inc., soon to be renamed Visionics Corp., develops, manufactures, and markets fingerprint recording and identification products based on electro-optical imaging technologies. The company's principal product, the TENPRINTER, is a computer-based, inkless "live scan" fingerprint system that electronically reads a fingerprint and creates a digital image. This image can either be printed on an attached printer or transmitted electronically to a central printing or storage site. The TENPRINTER is designed for use by law enforcement agencies and for commercial applications that require a high-quality fingerprint device for identification applications. In October 2000 the company agreed to acquire New Jersey-based Visionics Corp., the global face-recognition technology leader.

EARNINGS HISTORY

Year Ended Sept 30	Operating Revenue/Sales (dollars in thousands)	Net Earnings (dollars in thousands)	Return on Revenue (percent)	Return on Equity (percent)	Net Earnings (dollars per share)	Cash Dividend (dollars per share)	Market Price Range (dollars per share)
1999	22,199	99	0.4	1.4	0.01	—	3.63–0.91
1998	11,323	(4,888)	(43.2)	NM	(0.38)	—	2.66–0.97
1997 *	11,419	(6,275)	(55.0)	NM	(0.53)	—	3.88–1.50
1996	8,327	(11,687)	NM	NM	(1.24)	—	8.75–2.63
1995 †	9,098	(3,325)	(36.5)	(29.8)	(0.43)	—	12.00–6.50

* Income figures for 1997 include pretax nonrecurring charges totaling $1,859,437.
† Revenue for 1995 includes $1.8 million related to an international development project.

BALANCE SHEET

Assets	09/30/99 (dollars in thousands)	09/30/98 (dollars in thousands)	Liabilities	09/30/99 (dollars in thousands)	09/30/98 (dollars in thousands)
Current (CAE 3,175 and 840)	13,760	8,256	Current	7,375	4,472
			Debentures	148	885
Property, eqt	961	1,055	Capital lease obligations	93	113
Patents, trademarks, copyrights, licenses	17	36			
			Stkhldrs' equity*	7,130	3,948
Deferred debenture-issuance costs	8	72	TOTAL	14,747	9,418
TOTAL	14,747	9,418			

* $0.01 par common; 40,000,000 authorized; 16,017,629 and 13,661,832 issued and outstanding.

RECENT QUARTERS / PRIOR-YEAR RESULTS

	Quarter End	Revenue ($000)	Earnings ($000)	EPS ($)	Prior-Year Revenue ($000)	Prior-Year Earnings ($000)	Prior-Year EPS ($)
Q3	06/30/2000	3,901	(400)	(0.02)	6,264	423	0.03
Q2	03/31/2000	4,743	321	0.02	5,191	90	0.01
Q1	12/31/99	6,842	446	0.03	2,368	(1,192)	(0.09)
Q4	09/30/99	8,376	778	0.05	3,501	(1,162)	(0.09)
	SUM	23,863	1,145	0.07	17,324	(1,842)	(0.14)

RECENT EVENTS

In **January 2000** a large East coast financial purchasing services group selected Digital Biometrics to implement an electronic fingerprint and database reporting system to speed the process of fingerprint-based background checks on job applicants. The company established a $2 million line of credit with Riverside Bank of Minneapolis (now Associated Bank Minnesota)—replacing a prior credit facility with SPECTRUM Commercial Services. In **March** Oakland County, Mich. (suburban Detroit), selected Digi Bio to provide a system to integrate and automate police records for the County Sheriff's Office and the Michigan State Police (initial value $550,000). In **April** the company was again awarded a state contract from Rhode Island for live-scan fingerprinting equipment: additional TENPRINTER 1133S systems and central site equipment. SunTrust Equitable Securities Corp. of Nashville, Tenn., initiated research coverage on the company with a BUY recommendation. In **May** the company announced an order from NEC Technologies for 1133S TENPRINTER S-Series systems (NEC's LS21 Live Scan) and the development of customized software for the Criminal Justice Institute of Indiana—an estimated initial contract value in excess of $1 million. **June 30:** Softness in new orders and slower-than-anticipated customer readiness to receive shipments of previously ordered systems led to third-quarter revenue that was below expectations. Because the company also increased development and sales expense related to its new IBIS system to take advantage of customer interest in this leading-edge technology, it missed consensus earnings projections of 2 cents per share and reported a loss. In **August** the Philadelphia Police Department began planning for the deployment of the company's IBIS system for mobile identification. The company received a new order, valued at in excess of $3 million, from the U.S. Immigration and Naturalization Service for 100 additional live-scan fingerprint systems to be placed in 19 INS sites. Based on its revenue growth from 1995 to 1999, the company was named to Deloitte & Touche's Minnesota Technology Fast 50. In **October** the company announced an agreement enabling it to offer a range of fingerprint card scanners that capture inked fingerprint images that can be archived or transmitted to an AFIS (Automated Fingerprint Identification System). Digital Biometrics was planning to OEM DBA's ImagClear Fingerprint Card Scanner systems to small and medium-size law enforcement agencies and to commercial customers for applicant and enrollment processing throughout the United States. The company was awarded an initial order in excess of $850,000 by the Texas Department of Criminal Justice, which operates the state prisons and jails. Digital Biometrics and *continued on page 190*

OFFICERS

James C. Granger
Chairman

John J. Metil
President and interim CEO

Robert Bridigum
VP-New Product Development

Barry A. Fisher
VP-Sales/Marketing/Business Development

Robert F. Gallagher
CFO

Michel R. Halbouty
VP-Operations

RANKINGS

No. 136 CRM Public 200

No. 49 Minnesota Technology Fast 50

DIRECTORS

James C. Granger

John E. Haugo
MedServe Link Inc.

George Latimer
Macalester College, St. Paul

John E. Lawler
East/West Financial Services Inc., McLean, VA

C. McKenzie (Mac) Lewis III
Sherpa Partners LLC

John J. Metil

MAJOR SHAREHOLDERS

Perkins Capital Management Inc., 6.6%
Wayzata, MN

All officers and directors as a group (8 persons), 4.9%

SIC CODE

3695 Magnetic and optical recording media

MISCELLANEOUS

TRANSFER AGENT AND REGISTAR:
Wells Fargo Bank Minnesota N.A., South St. Paul, MN

TRADED: Nasdaq National Market

SYMBOL: DBII

STOCKHOLDERS: 7,000

EMPLOYEES: 106

GENERAL COUNSEL:
Maslon Edelman Borman & Brand PLLP, Minneapolis

AUDITORS:
KPMG LLP, Minneapolis

INC: DE-1985

ANNUAL MEETING: February

INVESTOR RELATIONS: Donald E. Berg

TWO-YEAR QUARTERLY HIGH-LOW STOCK PRICES

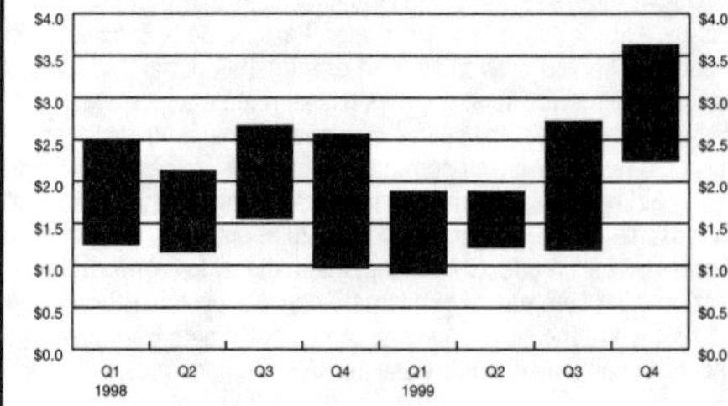

Digital River Inc.

9625 W. 76th St., Eden Prairie, MN 55344
Tel: 952/830-9042 Fax: 952/832-5709 Web site: http://www.digitalriver.com

Digital River Inc. is a leading provider of comprehensive e-commerce outsourcing solutions to software publishers and online retailers. The company has developed a technology platform that allows it to provide a suite of e-commerce services to its clients, including electronic software delivery (ESD). Digital River also provides data mining and merchandising services to assist clients in increasing Internet page-view traffic to, and sales through, their Web stores. Rather than maintaining its own branded Web store that would compete with its clients, Digital River provides an outsourcing solution that allows its clients to promote their own brands while leveraging Digital River's investment in infrastructure and technology. The company has contracts with 1,122 software publisher clients and 346 online retailer clients—including Corel Corp., Cyberian Outpost Inc., Lotus Development Corp., Micro Warehouse Inc., Network Associates Inc., and Symantec Corp.—and maintained a database of more than 123,000 software products from its various software publisher clients. Digital River's proprietary commerce network server (CNS) technology serves as the platform for its solutions. The CNS incorporates custom software applications that enable ESD, Web-store authoring, fraud prevention, export control, merchandising programs, and online registration.

EARNINGS HISTORY

Year Ended Dec 31	Operating Revenue/Sales (dollars in thousands)	Net Earnings	Return on Revenue (percent)	Return on Equity	Net Earnings (dollars per share*)	Cash Dividend	Market Price Range
1999 †	75,050	(27,653)	(36.8)	(37.8)	(1.36)	—	61.38–18.25
1998	20,911	(13,798)	(66.0)	(18.5)	(1.01)	—	44.00–5.00
1997	2,472	(3,485)	NM	NM	(0.46)	—	
1996	111	(689)	NM	NM	(0.13)	—	
1995	0	(143)	NM	(22.8)	(0.03)	—	

* Stock began trading Aug. 11, 1998.
† Pro forma figures for 1999 to include results of four separate 1999 acquisitions from Jan. 1: revenue $79.092 million; loss $31.319 million/($1.50).

BALANCE SHEET

Assets	12/31/99 (dollars in thousands)	12/31/98	Liabilities	12/31/99 (dollars in thousands)	12/31/98
Current	42,842	76,304	Current	14,065	5,741
(CAE 15,120 and 63,503)			Stockholders' equity*	73,077	74,587
Property and equipment	7,279	3,914	TOTAL	87,142	80,328
Investments	14,832				
Goodwill	22,050				
Other	139	110			
TOTAL	87,142	80,328			

* $0.01 par common; 45,000,000 authorized; 20,699,244 and 19,544,791 issued and outstanding.

RECENT QUARTERS / **PRIOR-YEAR RESULTS**

	Quarter End	Revenue ($000)	Earnings ($000)	EPS ($)	Prior-Year Revenue ($000)	Prior-Year Earnings ($000)	Prior-Year EPS ($)
Q3	09/30/2000	7,607	(8,074)	(0.37)	4,017	(8,688)	(0.42)
Q2	06/30/2000	6,635	(12,633)	(0.60)	3,065	(6,678)	(0.33)
Q1	03/31/2000	6,883	(11,991)	(0.58)	1,903	(5,344)	(0.27)
Q4	12/31/99	5,522	(6,943)	(0.33)	9,407	(4,506)	(0.26)
	SUM	26,647	(39,641)	(1.88)	18,392	(25,216)	(1.29)

PRIOR YEAR: Q4 revenue has not been reclassified for net revenue recognition.

RECENT EVENTS

In **December 1999** the company announced an agreement with two leading interactive entertainment companies, Fox Interactive and Fox Sports Interactive. As part of the agreement, Digital River was to manage online product sales and fulfillment for both www.foxinteractive.com and www.foxsports.com/videogames. Digital River agreed to provide e-commerce hosting services to Beamscope Canada Inc. (TSE: BSP)—including an e-commerce solution for Beamscope's 7,000 retailers who are interested in selling products online. An online channel agreement with Intuit Inc. (Nasdaq: INTU), the leader in e-finance, including financial software and Web-based services, added Intuit financial software solutions to Digital River's online database. The company then partnered with AHL Services Inc.(Nasdaq: AHLS), a business services company that provides outsourced e-fulfillment and customer service solutions through its Gage Marketing Services Division, to integrate business-to-business e-commerce services with Gage's ERP (enterprise resource planning) and inventory management system. In a tax-free reorganization with the liquidating company Tech Squared, Digital River received 3,000,000 shares of its own common stock that had been held by Tech Squared, plus $1,200,000 in cash, in exchange for 2,650,000 shares of Digital River common stock. In **January 2000** Digital River was selected by the USGA (United States Golf Association) to manage e-commerce for its golf store at www.usga.com; and partnered with leading game developer and publisher Red Storm Entertainment Inc. to manage e-commerce for www.redstorm.com. As part of an agreement with Fingerhut Cos. Inc., Minnetonka, Minn., one of the nation's largest direct marketing and online retailers, Digital River became the exclusive provider of more than *continued on page 190*

OFFICERS

Joel A. Ronning
CEO

Perry W. Steiner
President

Al Galgano
VP-Investor Relations

Frank Harvey
VP-E-business Services

Linda C. Ireland
VP-Direct Marketing

Draper M. Jaffray
VP-Business Development

Jay A. Kerutis
EVP-Software/Digital Commerce Services

Gregory R.L. Smith
Secretary and Controller

Robert E. Strawman
CFO and Treasurer

Terry Strom
SVP-Marketing

Gary Howorka, Ph.D.
Chief Technology Officer

Randy J. Womack
Chief Information Officer

DIRECTORS

Timothy C. Choate
FreeShop International Inc.

William J. Lansing
NBC Internet

Thomas F. Madison
MLM Partners, Minneapolis

Joel A. Ronning

Frederic M. Seegal
Wasserstein Perella Group

Christopher J. Sharples
GNI Ltd.

Perry W. Steiner

J. Paul Thorin
Fujitsu America Inc.

MAJOR SHAREHOLDERS

Fujitsu Ltd., 7.6%
Kawasaki, Japan

Joel A. Ronning, 5.4%

All officers and directors as a group (12 persons), 11.8%

SIC CODE

7389 Business services, nec

MISCELLANEOUS

TRANSFER AGENT AND REGISTAR:
Wells Fargo Bank Minnesota N.A., South St. Paul, MN

TRADED: Nasdaq National Market

SYMBOL: DRIV

STOCKHOLDERS: 332

EMPLOYEES: 317

GENERAL COUNSEL:
Cooley Godward LLP, San Francisco
Messerli & Kramer P.A., Minneapolis

AUDITORS:
Arthur Andersen LLP, Minneapolis

INC: DE-1997

FOUNDED: 1994

INVESTOR RELATIONS:
Al Galgano

RANKINGS

No. 97 CRM Public 200

PUB

Donaldson Company Inc.

1400 W. 94th St., P.O. Box 1299 (55440), Bloomington, MN 55431
Tel: 952/887-3131 Fax: 952/887-3005 Web site: http://www.donaldson.com

Donaldson Co. Inc. is a leading worldwide manufacturer of filtration systems and replacement parts. The company's product mix includes air and liquid filters and exhaust- and emission-control products for mobile equipment; in-plant air-cleaning systems; air-intake systems and exhaust products for industrial gas turbines; and specialized filters for such diverse applications as computer disk drives, aircraft passenger cabins, and semiconductor processing. Products are manufactured at 28 Donaldson plants around the world.

EARNINGS HISTORY

Year Ended Jul 31	Operating Revenue/Sales (dollars in thousands)	Net Earnings	Return on Revenue (percent)	Return on Equity	Net Earnings (dollars per share*)	Cash Dividend	Market Price Range
2000	1,092,294	70,233	6.4	25.1	1.54	0.27	24.81–19.13
1999	944,139	62,447	6.6	23.8	1.33	0.23	25.88–14.44
1998	940,351	57,051	6.1	22.3	1.16	0.19	27.19–18.56
1997	833,348	50,620	6.1	20.8	1.01	0.17	20.38–12.69
1996	758,646	43,436	5.7	19.0	0.84	0.15	14.00–11.94

* Per-share amounts restated to reflect 2-for-1 stock split on Dec. 12, 1997.

BALANCE SHEET

Assets	07/31/00 (dollars in thousands)	07/31/99	Liabilities	07/31/00 (dollars in thousands)	07/31/99
Current (CAE 24,149 and 41,944)	375,479	326,388	Current (STD 85,313 and 20,696)	235,722	142,055
Property, plant, and equipment	204,545	182,180	Long-term debt	92,645	86,691
			Other	61,125	50,605
Deferred income taxes	408		Deferred income taxes		132
Intangibles	63,885	10,984	Stockholders' equity*	280,165	262,763
Other	25,340	22,694			
TOTAL	669,657	542,246	TOTAL	669,657	542,246

* $5 par common; 80,000,000 authorized; 49,655,954 and 49,655,954 issued and outstanding, less 4,998,342 and 3,458,670 treasury shares.

RECENT QUARTERS / PRIOR-YEAR RESULTS

Quarter End	Revenue ($000)	Earnings ($000)	EPS ($)	Prior-Year Revenue ($000)	Prior-Year Earnings ($000)	Prior-Year EPS ($)
Q4 07/31/2000	301,211	18,369	0.41	254,240	18,488	0.40
Q3 04/30/2000	285,277	17,450	0.38	244,219	17,418	0.37
Q2 01/31/2000	259,256	17,406	0.38	220,249	13,172	0.28
Q1 10/31/99	246,550	17,008	0.37	225,431	13,369	0.28
SUM	1,092,294	70,233	1.54	944,139	62,447	1.33

RECENT EVENTS

In **December 1999** the company reached a definitive agreement to purchase the DCE dust control business of Invensys plc for cash consideration of $54 million. The $80 million-revenue, 640-employee DCE, headquartered in Leicester, England, is a major participant in the global industrial dust collection industry. In **January 2000** the deal was completed. In **March** the technical editors from Heavy Duty Trucking Magazine chose the Donaldson Silent Partner muffler for a Nifty Fifty award; and the Truck Writers of North America gave Silent Partner their Technical Achievement Award. In **April** Donaldson's Engine Aftermarket group upgraded its Donaldson DYNAMIC online ordering process, enabling distributors to order a variety of products more efficiently. In **July** Merrill Lynch & Co. initiated coverage of Donaldson with an intermediate accumulate and long-term buy recommendation. **July 31:** For the year, sales of $1.092 billion were up 16 percent from prior year. Businesses acquired during the fiscal year had contributed $56.6 million of revenue year-to- date. Excluding the impact of acquisitions, sales were up 10 percent from the prior year. "Crossing the $1 billion revenue mark was a significant achievement, as was delivering consistent earning growth for the 11th-consecutive year," said CEO Van Dyke. "Both the Engine and Industrial segments of our business had strong performances for the year, and we are well positioned for continued success in 2001." Gross margin was 30.0 percent, up from 29.2 percent in the prior year, reflecting both the strong Industrial product mix and the impact of the continuous focus on productivity improvements.

OFFICERS

William G. Van Dyke
Chairman, President, and CEO

William M. Cook
SVP-International

James R. Giertz
SVP-Commercial/Industrial

Nickolas Priadka
SVP-OEM Engine Systems/Parts

Lowell F. Schwab
SVP-Operations

Thomas W. VanHimbergen
SVP and CFO

Dale Couch
VP and Gen. Mgr.-Asia/Pacific

Edmund C. Craft
VP-Engine Aftermarket

Norman C. Linnell
VP, General Counsel, and Secretary

John E. Thames
VP-Human Resources/Communications

Geert Henk Touw
VP, Gen. Mgr.-Europe/Africa/Middle East

Thomas A. Windfeldt
VP, Controller, and Treasurer

DIRECTORS

F. Guillaume Bastiaens
Cargill Inc., Minnetonka, MN

Paul B. Burke
BMC Industries Inc., Bloomington, MN

Janet M. Dolan
Tennant Co., Golden Valley, MN

Jack W. Eugster
Musicland Stores Corp., Minnetonka, MN

John F. (Jack) Grundhofer
U.S. Bancorp, Minneapolis

Kendrick B. Melrose
The Toro Co., Bloomington, MN

Jeffrey Noddle
Supervalu, Inc., Eden Prairie, MN

S. Walter Richey
Meritex Inc., Minneapolis

Stephen W. Sanger
General Mills Inc., Golden Valley, MN

William G. Van Dyke

MAJOR SHAREHOLDERS

Donaldson Co. Inc. ESOP, 11.6%

Pioneering Management Corp., 10.9%
Boston

All officers and directors as a group (13 persons), 5.7%

SIC CODE

3599 Industrial machinery, nec

MISCELLANEOUS

TRANSFER AGENT AND REGISTAR:
Wells Fargo Bank Minnesota N.A., South St. Paul, MN

TRADED: NYSE

SYMBOL: DCI

STOCKHOLDERS: 1,984

EMPLOYEES: 8,478

GENERAL COUNSEL:
Dorsey & Whitney PLLP, Minneapolis
Merchant, Gould, Smith, Edell, Welter & Schmidt P.A., Minneapolis

AUDITORS:
Ernst & Young LLP, Minneapolis

INC: DE-1936

FOUNDED: 1915

ANNUAL MEETING: November

PUBLIC RELATIONS COUNSEL: Padilla Speer Beardsley Inc.

RANKINGS

No. 38 CRM Public 200

No. 39 CRM Performance 100

TWO-YEAR QUARTERLY HIGH-LOW STOCK PRICES

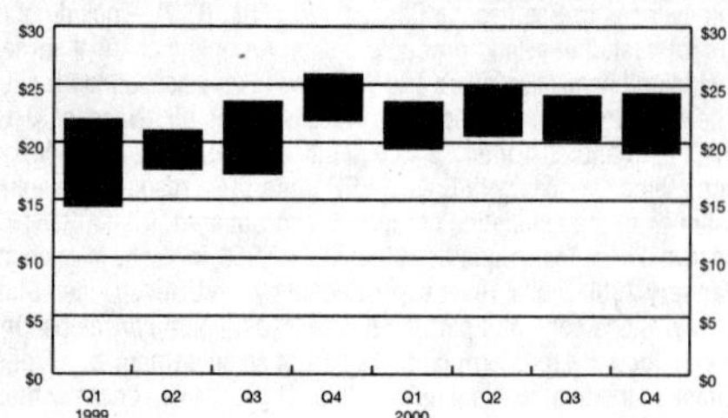

Dotronix Inc.

160 First St. S.E., New Brighton, MN 55112
Tel: 651/633-1742 Fax: 651/633-7025 Web site: http://www.dotronix.com

Dotronix Inc. designs, manufactures, and markets monochrome and color CRT displays and closed-circuit television (CCTV) monitors for a broad range of applications. **CRT displays** are used to display alphanumeric information and graphics in market quotation; word processing; computer-aided design, manufacturing, and engineering (CAD/CAM/CAE); desktop publishing; and other computer-based information systems. **CCTV monitors** are used to display video images generated by medical diagnostic imaging, closed-circuit surveillance, studio monitors, and other video-based systems.

EARNINGS HISTORY

Year Ended Jun 30	Operating Revenue/Sales (dollars in thousands)	Net Earnings	Return on Revenue (percent)	Return on Equity	Net Earnings (dollars per share)	Cash Dividend	Market Price Range
2000	7,355	(1,318)	(17.9)	(42.9)	(0.32)	—	0.94–0.20
1999	7,670	(2,040)	(26.6)	(47.3)	(0.50)	—	1.50–0.63
1998	9,258	(1,026)	(11.1)	(16.2)	(0.25)	—	2.00–0.88
1997	9,941	(1,421)	(14.3)	(19.3)	(0.34)	—	2.00–1.00
1996	14,576	841	5.8	9.3	0.20	—	2.81–1.25

BALANCE SHEET

Assets	06/30/00 (dollars in thousands)	06/30/99	Liabilities	06/30/00 (dollars in thousands)	06/30/99
Current (CAE 75 and 621)	3,433	4,386	Current (STD 453 and 398)	1,646	1,518
Property, plant, and equipment	1,158	1,306	Capital lease obligations		32
Goodwill	486	558	Deferred gain on sale of building	373	421
License agreement	15	25	Stockholders' equity*	3,074	4,313
Other	0	10	TOTAL	5,093	6,284
TOTAL	5,093	6,284			

* $0.05 par common; 12,000,000 authorized; 4,074,732 and 4,057,601 issued and outstanding.

RECENT QUARTERS / **PRIOR-YEAR RESULTS**

	Quarter End	Revenue ($000)	Earnings ($000)	EPS ($)	Revenue ($000)	Earnings ($000)	EPS ($)
Q1	09/30/2000	2,050	121	0.03	2,569	17	0.00
Q4	06/30/2000	1,726	(211)	(0.05)	2,311	(600)	(0.15)
Q3	03/31/2000	1,263	(600)	(0.15)	1,673	(637)	(0.16)
Q2	12/31/99	1,783	(519)	(0.13)	1,941	(373)	(0.09)
	SUM	6,822	(1,209)	(0.30)	8,494	(1,593)	(0.39)

CURRENT: Q3 and earlier periods do not reflect certain small revenue and earnings adjustments made at year-end.

OFFICERS

William S. Sadler
President and Treasurer

Robert J. Andrews
VP-Operations

Robert V. Kling
CFO

William R. Weissmueller
Dir.-Engineering/Sales

DIRECTORS

Ray L. Bergeson
Honeywell Inc. (retired)

L. Daniel Kuechenmeister
Honeywell Inc. (retired)

William S. Sadler

Robert J. Snow
American Artstone Co.

Edward L. Zeman
ARM Financial Group Inc.

MAJOR SHAREHOLDERS

William S. Sadler, 34.3%

All officers and directors as a group (6 persons), 35.5%

SIC CODE

3679 Electronic components, nec

MISCELLANEOUS

TRANSFER AGENT AND REGISTAR:
Northwest Shareowner Services, St. Paul, MN

TRADED: Nasdaq SmallCap Market

SYMBOL: DOTX

STOCKHOLDERS: 344

EMPLOYEES: 53

GENERAL COUNSEL:
Dorsey & Whitney PLLP, Minneapolis

AUDITORS:
Deloitte & Touche LLP, Minneapolis

INC: MN-1980

ANNUAL MEETING:
November

HUMAN RESOURCES:
Karen Kopp

RANKINGS

No. 191 CRM Public 200

TWO-YEAR QUARTERLY HIGH-LOW STOCK PRICES

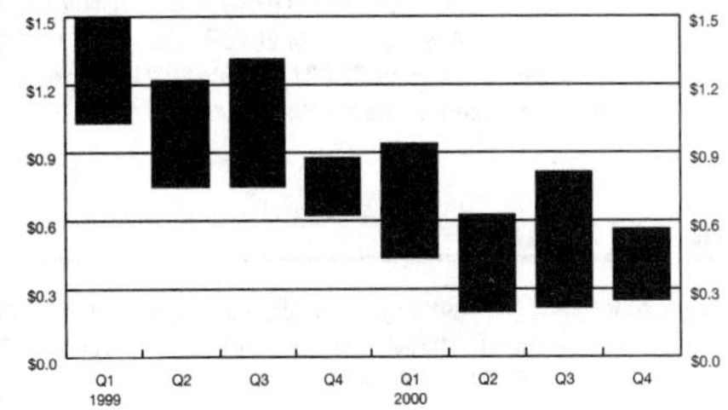

PUB

Dura Automotive Systems Inc.

4508 IDS Center, Minneapolis, MN 55402
Tel: 612/342-2311 Fax: 612/332-2012 Web site: http://www.duraauto.com

Dura Automotive Systems Inc. and its subsidiaries is the world's largest independent designer and manufacturer of driver control systems for the global automotive industry. The company is also a global supplier of window systems, door systems, and engineered mechanical components. Dura's products include: driver control products, window system products, door system products, and engineered products. Dura sells to every major North American, Japanese and European automotive Original Equipment Manufacturers (OEMs). Dura has over 80 manufacturing and product development facilities located in the United States, Australia, Brazil, Canada, the Czech Republic, France, Germany, India, Mexico, Portugal, Spain and the United Kingdom.

EARNINGS HISTORY

Year Ended Dec 31	Operating Revenue/Sales (dollars in thousands)	Net Earnings	Return on Revenue (percent)	Return on Equity	Net Earnings (dollars per share*)	Cash Dividend	Market Price Range
1999 †	2,200,385	41,220	1.9	9.6	2.53	—	34.13–15.88
1998 ¶	739,467	26,024	3.5	10.9	2.43	—	40.25–20.00
1997 #	449,111	16,642	3.7	16.4	1.89	—	35.38–22.50
1996	245,329	10,128	4.1	11.6	1.57	—	27.75–17.00
1995 **	253,726	10,126	4.0	36.6	2.04	—	

* Trading began Aug. 14, 1996.
† Income figures for 1999 include extraordinary losses of $5,402,000/($0.33) on early extinguishment of debt, and $3,147,000/($0.20) cumulative effect of change in accounting. Pro forma results giving effect to 1999 acquisitions (Adwest, Excel) as though completed at beginning of period: revenue $2,589,436,000; earnings (before ex. item) $38,138,000/$2.20.
¶ Income figures for 1998 include extraordinary loss of $643,000/($0.06) on early extinguishment of debt. Pro forma results giving effect to all 1998 acquisitions as though completed at beginning of period: revenue $886,849,000; earnings (before ex. item) $26,996,000/$2.19.
# Pro forma 1997 results giving effect to August 1997 acquisition GT Automotive as though completed at beginning of period: revenue $489,752,000; earnings $14,830,000/$1.67.
** Figures for 1995 include results of Window Regulator Business through the April 2, 1995, date it was sold to Rockwell for $18.0 million in cash, which resulted in a pretax gain of $4.2 million.

BALANCE SHEET

Assets	12/31/99 (dollars in thousands)	12/31/98	Liabilities	12/31/99 (dollars in thousands)	12/31/98
Current	793,505	275,431	Current	630,556	211,665
(CAE 23,697 and 20,544)			Long-term debt	776,750	316,417
Property, plant, and equipment	500,894	188,732	Subordinated notes	401,560	
			Other	149,755	108,014
Goodwill	1,067,937	435,960	Preferred securities	55,250	55,250
Other	82,531	29,260	Stockholders' equity*	430,996	238,037
TOTAL	2,444,867	929,383			
			TOTAL	2,444,867	929,383

* $0.01 par common; 70,000,000 authorized; 17,421,814 and 12,354,388 issued and outstanding.

RECENT QUARTERS / PRIOR-YEAR RESULTS

Quarter End	Revenue ($000)	Earnings ($000)	EPS ($)	Prior-Year Revenue ($000)	Prior-Year Earnings ($000)	Prior-Year EPS ($)
Q3 09/30/2000	587,081	10,255	0.59	580,886	11,291	0.65
Q2 06/30/2000	707,690	11,520	0.66	685,167	15,669	0.90
Q1 03/31/2000	682,769	16,460	0.94	264,701	3,492	0.27
Q4 12/31/99	669,631	10,768	0.62	241,084	10,297	0.83
SUM	2,647,171	49,003	2.81	1,771,838	40,749	2.66

CURRENT: Q2 earnings include pretax charge of $16 million for product recall.
PRIOR YEAR: Q2 earnings include loss of $2.7 million/($0.16) on early debt extinguishment. Q1 earnings include extraordinary losses of $2.702 million/($0.21) on extinguishment of debt; and $3.147 million/($0.24) cumulative effect of accounting change.

RECENT EVENTS

In **February 2000** the company was realigned around four main divisions to better serve present and future customers.
— The Engineered Products Division contains the Seat Systems, Thixotech, Plastic Products (including Engine Controls), and Mechanical Assemblies business units.

continued on page 190

OFFICERS

S.A. (Tony) Johnson
Chairman
Karl F. Storrie
President and CEO
David R. Bovee
VP
Joe A. Bubenzer
SVP
John J. Knappenberger
VP
Milton D. Kniss
VP
William F. Ohrt
VP and CFO
Michael C. Paquette
VP
Robert A. Pickering
VP
Jurgen von Heyden
VP

DIRECTORS

Robert E. Brooker Jr.
Connell Limited Partnership
J.K. (Jack) Edwards
Cummins Engine Co. Inc., Columbus, IN
James O. Futterknecht, Jr.
Excel Industries (former)
S.A. (Tony) Johnson
J. Richard Jones
John C. Jorgensen
Orscheln Management Co.
William L. Orscheln
Alkin
Eric J. Rosen
Onex Investment Corp., New York
Karl F. Storrie
Ralph R. Whitney, Jr.
Hammond, Kennedy, Whitney and Company, Inc.

MAJOR SHAREHOLDERS

American Express Co., 11.9%
New York
Onex DHC LLC, 11.3%
New York
Alkin Co., 7.8%
Moberly, MO
All officers and directors as a group (20 persons), 21%

SIC CODE

3714 Motor vehicle parts and accessories

MISCELLANEOUS

TRANSFER AGENT AND REGISTAR:
Firstar Trust Co., Milwaukee
TRADED: Nasdaq National Market
SYMBOL: DRRA
STOCKHOLDERS: 200
EMPLOYEES: 21,000
GENERAL COUNSEL:
Dickinson, Wright, Moon, Van Dusen & Freeman, Detroit
Padilla Speer Beardsley Inc., Minneapolis
AUDITORS:
Arthur Andersen LLP, Minneapolis
INC: DE-1994
ANNUAL MEETING: May
PUBLIC RELATIONS COUNSEL: Padilla Speer Beardsley Inc.
INVESTOR RELATIONS: William F. Ohrt

RANKINGS

No. 18 CRM Public 200
No. 46 CRM Performance 100

TWO-YEAR QUARTERLY HIGH-LOW STOCK PRICES

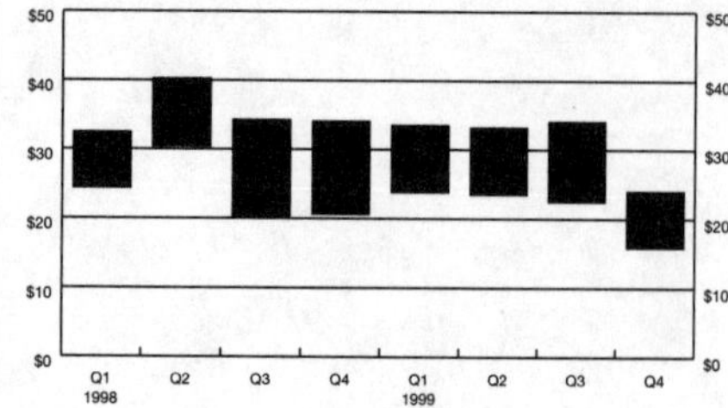

Canterbury Park Holding Corporation

continued from page 156 announced the opening of the new "Paddock Pavilion," a 17,400-square-foot enclosed, movable structure. The fully heated structure can accommodate such events as trade shows, large corporate outings, and small to mid-sized conventions.

Ceridian Corporation

continued from page 158 **RECENT EVENTS**

Dec. 31, 1999: "Most of Ceridian's businesses performed very well in 1999 and are expected to do so again in 2000," said CEO Turner. "During 2000, we have decided to undertake certain initiatives and make investments in the future of our U.S. payroll business unit; and, as a result, we are anticipating our earnings per share in 2000 will be flat to modestly up compared to 1999." In **January 2000** the company reached a proposed $5.175 million settlement of securities litigation originally brought against Ceridian and individual defendants in September 1997. In **February** Federal Express Corp. recognized Ceridian Performance Partners with a quality award. Ceridian Employer Services introduced Powerpay.com Inc., the first national, Internet-based payroll/HR services company targeted exclusively at small businesses. In **March** Ceridian Performance Partners became the first such provider of workforce-effectiveness programs to incorporate streaming audio technology in its Internet channel. In **April** Ceridian Performance Partners teamed with Consumer's Medical Resource Inc. to help people facing complex illnesses—such as cancer, AIDS, organ transplant, or Parkinson's—determine the best course of action. In **May** Comdata completed the acquisition of Stored Value Systems Inc. (SVS), a former subsidiary of National City Corp. (Comdata had acquired a majority interest in SVS in March 1999, with the option to purchase the remainder of the company at a later date.) Comdata then formed a new Retail Services division. The Arbitron Co. chose the Philadelphia market for a fourth quarter 2000 field test of its revolutionary new radio, television, and cable TV audience measurement device, the Portable People Meter—a pager-sized device that, when worn by consumers, detects inaudible codes that broadcasters embed in the audio portion of their programming. In **June** a major enhancement to Powerpay allowed Powerpay.com's payroll clients to submit payroll for processing and, within one hour, view completed payroll, download reports, and fund payroll obligations. GE Small Business Solutions, a division of GE Capital, agreed to offer Powerpay.com's payroll solutions over its Web site—http://www.GESmallBusiness.com. Powerpay.com announced plans to offer a complete suite of HR and employment compliance tools over the Internet through an agreement with HR Comply, a leading provider of compliance tools and forms library. Ceridian Performance Partners introduced two new services to help employees and employers manage the demands of caring for aging parents: LifeWorks Elder Care Assessment and LifeWorks Elder Care Facility Review. Centrefile was awarded a seven-year contract with Lloyds TSB, London, to manage, administer, and process Lloyd's payroll. In **July** Powerpay.com joined Visa Business' PartnerAdvantage, a new program that offers Visa Business cardholders ongoing benefits and savings on services and products that are key to the success of small businesses. Ceridian announced its intention to separate into two publicly traded companies, Ceridian Corp. and The Arbitron Co., through a reverse spin transaction. After the transaction, Ceridian was to consist of its Human Resources businesses and Comdata business. "We believe the separation of Arbitron and Ceridian will create two sharply focused companies well-positioned to pursue and realize their potential as independent companies in the distinctly different markets they serve," said Turner. "Both businesses are leaders in their respective industries, with strong existing businesses and attractive future prospects. As separate companies, they can better pursue attractive growth opportunities for the benefit of the employees and customers of both businesses while optimizing the value of each individual company." In **August** Ceridian announced a special meeting of shareholders on Oct. 5 to consider a proposal to approve an amendment to its certificate of incorporation to permit the company to declare a reverse stock split immediately after the previously announced proposed reverse spin-off intended to separate Ceridian into two independent, publicly traded companies. In **September** Ceridian announced an agreement to provide human resource management services to Nvest L.P. (NYSE: NEW) through Source 500 Assist, the company's application outsourcing product (ASP). Powerpay.com and the Chase Manhattan Bank (NYSE: CMB) announced a multiyear business relationship that was to offer Chase's more than 300,000 small-business customers full-service Internet and traditional payroll processing and HR services from Powerpay.com. In addition, using the global reach of the Internet, Powerpay.com was to market Chase banking services to its online customer base. Sept. 30: Ceridian met expectations by announcing diluted EPS of $0.23 and cash EPS of $0.31 for the third quarter. Revenue of $204.3 million for its Human Resources business segment was lower than expected. Comdata had a strong third quarter, with margins exceeding 29 percent. Effective this quarter, Ceridian began presenting Arbitron as a discontinued operation in its financial reports. In **October** Powerpay.com and The Principal Financial Group, the nation's largest 401(k) service provider, announced a strategic alliance to offer The Principal and Powerpay.com Power(k) Retirement Solution, an innovative, integrated new service that handles both payroll and retirement plan contributions via the Internet. Ceridian Employer/Employee Services announced its membership in HR-XML, the nonprofit consortium dedicated to standards for human resources data exchange.

Christopher & Banks Corporation

continued from page 161 of Incorporation to change the name of the company from Braun's Fashions Corp. to Christopher & Banks Corp., effective July 26. The company ranked No. 27 on Forbes' 200 Best Small Companies in America list. In **August** the company opened seven C.J. Banks stores in several Midwest locations, including the Burnsville Center and Northtown Mall in suburban Minneapolis. **Aug 26**: For the six months, net income increased to $9.1 million, from $2.4 million last year. Net sales increased 44 percent to $83.9 million, while same-store sales increased 21 percent. Prange commented, "We are extremely pleased with our record second-quarter performance, which was driven by robust sales in all merchandise categories. In addition, our gross margin increased considerably as enthusiastic customer response to our product assortments led to a dramatic improvement in full-price selling." **Oct. 28:** The company reported a 19 percent increase in October same-store sales for the five-week period. Total sales rose 47 percent to $21.4 million.

The Chromaline Corporation

continued from page 162 European master distributor reduced profits for the quarter to $21,731. The loss associated with the bankruptcy was a $54,000 write-off of Chromaline's 19 1/2 percent interest in Chromaline Europe SA and $95,000 representing the unsecured portion of a receivable from Chromaline Europe SA. Shipments to European customers had not been interrupted by the closing of the distributor.

PUB

Chronimed Inc.

continued from page 163 Chronimed's Specialty Pharmacy products and services to the roughly 1.3 million people covered by Mutual of Omaha's health insurance plans. In **March** the board of directors announced its intent to spin-off its Diagnostic Products business through a tax-free dividend to shareholders. The dividend was to provide shares in the newly formed company to shareholders of Chronimed Inc. as of a record date to be announced. Management and operations of the new Diagnostic Products company were to be independent of Chronimed. Also, it was intended that the Diagnostic Products business trade on Nasdaq's National Market System independent from the remaining Pharmacy Services business. Commenting on the decision, CEO Taylor said, "This action represents the culmination of a thorough analysis, led by Paine-Webber, of strategic alternatives available to the company. This analysis clearly demonstrated that Chronimed is really two distinct businesses in different healthcare sectors—a diagnostic products business and a specialty pharmacy services business. We learned that our integrated approach to health care was confusing to many people in the business and investment communities, and therefore the true value of the company was being discounted." In **May** Chronimed's spin-off received a favorable tax opinion from the accounting firm of Ernst & Young LLP. In the opinion of E&Y, the spinoff of the new company, MEDgenesis Inc., should be given tax-free treatment. In **June** the company was selected by Aetna U.S. Healthcare as a preferred provider of injectable medications for Aetna U.S. Healthcare members and participating physicians. In **August**, based on its revenue growth from 1995 to 1999, the company was named to Deloitte & Touche's Minnesota Technology Fast 50. In **September** Chronimed received comments from the SEC on the amended Form 10 registration statement that was filed on July 31. Commenting on the dividend status, CEO Blissenbach said, "None of the comments we received from the SEC were complicated or involved. Consequently, we anticipate being able to respond to these questions in very short order, and will file an amended registration statement in the near future." The company announced the sale of its $14.9 million-revenue Home Service Medical catalog business to Express-Med Inc. of New Albany, Ohio, for $7 million. **Sept. 29:** Revenue from the company's mail-order pharmacy segment accelerated to $34.8 million, up 30 percent, on the strength of the new Aetna U.S. Healthcare contract. The company's retail pharmacy segment was up 23 percent over last year's first quarter. Operating income was $1.4 million for the quarter, or 2.2 percent of revenue, up almost $1.6 million from last year's first quarter loss. In **October** Chronimed was engaged in negotiations to sell its MEDgenesis subsidiary while continuing to pursue a spin-off of the business. Blissenbach said, "We expect to spin off MEDgenesis unless the board of directors approves a definitive agreement to sell the subsidiary."

CIMA LABS Inc.

continued from page 164 solving version of Zomig (zolmitriptan) anti-migraine medication. In **July** CIMA its second DuraSolv agreement of the year, this one expected to add $0.8 million in product development fees and licensing revenue to the second half of 2000. The evolution of the company, from one paid for R&D to one with revenue from commercial sales as well, drove the stock price up from $20 to $40 over the summer. In **September** CIMA completed its first human bioavailability study for an active drug utilizing its OraVescent technology, and applied for several U.S. and foreign patents. (CIMA's OraVescent technology is designed to improve the transport of poorly absorbed active drugs across mucosal membranes in the oral cavity and the gastrointestinal tract, and shorten the onset of the therapeutic effect of active drugs.) An analyst attributed a late-month stock runup to independent affirmation: bullish comments made about the company during an analyst meeting held by one of CIMA's partner companies. **Sept. 30**: Product sales were $3.2 million and $9.3 million for the three-month and nine-month periods, respectively, compared to $2.0 million and $3.5 million for the comparable periods in 1999. Branded prescription product sales were $2.2 million and $2.6 million and over-the-counter product sales were $1.0 million and $6.7 million, respectively, for the three-month and nine-month periods. The company was expecting product sales in the fourth quarter to be comprised principally of branded prescription products. In October CIMA signed a second agreement with Schwarz Pharma for a controlled release formulation of its DuraSolv dosage form of an undisclosed prescription product. The agreement was expected to add $1.3 million in product development fees and licensing revenue during the product development phase, which was estimated at two years. CIMA then registered a proposed offering of 2.5 million shares of its common stock. CIMA was planning to use the net proceeds from the shares it sells for expansion of its production capabilities and facilities, drug delivery technology and product development, working capital, and other general corporate purposes, including possible acquisitions. In **November** CIMA announced the pricing of its public offering: $50 per share. At the closing of the public offering the underwriters, led by Deutsche Banc Alex. Brown, exercised their option to purchase 442,500 additional shares to cover overallotments.

Community First Bankshares Inc.

continued from page 167 order to increase efficiency and performance. **Sept. 30**: Return on average common shareholders' equity increased to 19.6 percent for the first nine months of 2000, an improvement over the 18.4 percent reported for the corresponding 1999 period. "During the course of third quarter, we continued to execute our plan to further strengthen our balance sheet," commented CEO Anderson. "We began this effort earlier this year with the decision to no longer purchase discounted lease receivables, to commence the systematic repurchase of our shares of common stock, and to reduce our reliance on short-term borrowings. This has resulted in the amortization of $86 million of discounted lease receivables during the past nine months, $37 million during the past quarter. Additionally, we have also been able to decrease short-term borrowings by $209 million during the past quarter. The decline in short-term borrowings has reduced the potential impact of further changes in borrowing rates and has provided increased capital capacity for common stock repurchases."

Computer Network Technology Corporation

continued from page 168 announced SAN over IP (storage area network over an Internet Protocol)—which enables companies to build storage infrastructures over IP-based networks, such as intranets and Virtual Private Networks (VPNs). In **May** CNT announced that its Enterprise/Access software supports IBM's MQSeries; and that its Enterprise/Access software was awarded a Customer Relationship Management (CRM) Excellence Award from Technology Marketing Corp. At NetWorld+Interop 2000 in Las Vegas, CNT demonstrated its SRDF over Internet Protocol (IP) capabilities and its SAN over Internet Protocol (IP) backup application. CNT and McDATA Corp., Broomfield, Colo., completed interoperability testing between the CNT UltraNet Open Systems Gateway and the McDATA ED-5000 Director for Fibre Channel over ATM connectivity. CNT and Gadzoox Networks Inc. (Nasdaq: ZOOX) announced certified SAN-to-WAN connectivity solutions. With a five-year OEM agreement, PTC (Nasdaq: PMTC), the leader in collaborative product commerce (CPC), licensed CNT Enterprise/Access technology for integration with PTC's Web-based collaboration solution, Windchill. CNT and Iron Mountain Inc. (NYSE: IRM), the global leader in records and information management services, created a strategic alliance to provide outsourced electronic tape vaulting services. In **June** CNT announced new, highly manageable, high-availability optical networking products for extending SAN applications. In July CNT and Nortel Networks, a leader in the development of new, high-performance optical networks and Internet Protocol (IP) infrastructures, announced plans to simplify SAN integration into enterprise IP and optical networks. CNT introduced its InVista software, a next-generation technology that sets a new standard in enabling companies to develop and deploy e-business solutions faster, more flexibly, and with less risk. In **August** Ensodex, a full-service provider of enterprise integration products and services, agreed to resell CNT's Enterprise/Access software solution. Telcel, the largest mobile telecommunications company in Mexico, chose CNT's Enterprise/Access 2000 software to integrate its Siebel Call Center application with its core legacy business systems. CNT added support for Asian languages to Enterprise/Access 2000. In **October** CNT sold 4.6 million shares of common stock, including overallotment option, in a secondary public offering. The shares were priced at $25.50 per share. The board of directors also determined to sell or spin off the company's Enterprise Integration Solutions Division in order to focus resources on SAN and storage networking products. The board set Jan. 31, 2001, as a target date for completing any sale or a decision to proceed with a spin-off. Accordingly, the financial information for this division was to be accounted for as a discontinued operation. The integration between its Enterprise/Access 2000 enterprise application integration (EAI) solution and Siebel eBusiness 2000 was successfully validated by Siebel Systems. CNT's Enterprise Integration Solutions division was awarded the Siebel Alliance Partner Award of Excellence for its outstanding customer satisfaction in the Europe, Middle East, and Africa region. EchoStar Communications/DISH Network, the fastest-growing direct broadcast satellite television products and services company, chose CNT SAN services and solutions as the cornerstone of its advanced SAN architecture.

CorVu Corporation

continued from page 169 age services chose CorManage as its Balanced Scorecard Solution. Hilton Hotels Corp. (NYSE: HLT) agreed to deploy the CorManage software application to deliver timely online, personalized, and actionable business intelligence to hotel management, field-based area vice presidents, and executives at its corporate offices. In **October** Corvy announced a reseller agreement with IBS Consulting Services., London. In **November**the city of Dayton (Ohio) chose CorVu to better understand and improve the performance of its life-saving police and fire departments. Corvu and IBM Australia agreed to jointly market and sell best-of-breed performance and data management solutions. This collaboration enabled IBM to market CorVu's Business Performance Management software in conjunction with IBM's data warehousing, analytical, and business-based intelligence solutions.

CyberOptics Corporation

continued from page 171 CyberOptics acquired $5.5 million-revenue Imagenation Corp., Portland, Ore., a leading designer and manufacturer of machine-vision components and subsystems for the semiconductor capital equipment and general-purpose machine-vision market. The all-cash transaction totaled $6 million, net of cash acquired, plus contingent considerations.

Daktronics Inc.

continued from page 173 bility for equipment installation. In **June** the company was awarded a contract in excess of $2.7 million to provide VMS (variable message signs) for the C22A2 Contract of the Central Artery Tunnel Project currently under construction in Boston. (Contractor: Honeywell Technology Solutions Inc., formerly AlliedSignal Technical Services, of Columbia, Md.; end user: the Massachusetts Highway Department/Turnpike Authority.) Daktronics agreed to design and build a spectacular, multimillion-dollar electronic display system for the front of a large new building under construction at 745 Seventh Avenue in Times Square. Daktronics agreed to design and manufacture an integrated scoring, video, information, and advertising display system for the Minnesota Wild for installation at the new Xcel Energy Center in St. Paul prior to the team's inaugural National Hockey League season in 2000. The Wild's display system was to be unlike any other, taking full advantage of recent Daktronics developments in full-color LED (light emitting diode) large-screen video displays, full-color LED digital advertising signage, and display control systems. In **July** Delta Air Lines (NYSE: DAL) selected Daktronics to provide electronic displays as part of the airline's global airport renewal project. Daktronics signed a letter of intent to purchase Sports Link, a large-screen-video rental company located in Brookings, S.D. In **October** Daktronics agreed to design and build a $6.5 million transportable display system with multiple ProStar large-screen video displays for the New York Racing Association (NYRA), to be used at Saratoga Race Course, Belmont Park, and Aqueduct Racetrack. Daktronics was named South Dakota's Business of the Year at the 2000 ABEX (Awards in Business Excellence) Program, which is administered by the South Dakota Chamber of Commerce and Industry. It was also named one of the 200 Best Small Companies in America (No. 128) by Forbes. Daktronics agreed to design and build a $1.7 million integrated video, scoring, and display system for the new Alerus Center in Grand Forks, N.D. Scheduled to open in January 2001, the city-owned Alerus Center will host University of North Dakota football and soccer games, as well as conventions, tradeshows, concerts, and many other events. Daktronics agreed to purchase an 80 percent stake in Servtrotech Inc. electronic display systems of Montreal, Quebec, thereby increasing its technological base and expanding its operations. Founded in 1983, Servtrotech is one of the leading designers, manufacturers, and system integrators of electronic displays in Canada. In **November** Daktronics agreed to design and build a $7.9 million integrated scoring and video display system for the new American Airlines Center under construction in Dallas. Scheduled to open in the summer of 2001, the arena will be home to both the NBA's Dallas Mavericks and the NHL's Dallas Stars. Daktronics agreed to provide an additional 293 LED (light emitting diode) DSUs (destination sign units) for the BART (Bay Area Rapid Transit) District to help inform and direct passengers. The value of the order for additional displays totaled $3.3 million.

Damark International Inc.

continued from page 174 compelling reason to continue funding operating losses in our retail segment of the magnitude recently experienced and expected for the foreseeable future. Secondly, we can discern no long-term competitive advantage for us as a direct retailer of discount durable goods in tomorrow's crowded marketplace. Fortunately, the order capture, product fulfillment, and customer service competencies that we have developed over the last 13 years to serve catalog customers are ideally suited for deployment in the e-services marketplace and we look forward to becoming a major participant in this growth industry. Moreover, our membership business is performing at record levels and is ready to be operated on a stand-alone basis." In **February** the board of directors approved the pursuit of a plan to separate ClickShip Direct Inc., Damark's e-services business, as an independent, publicly traded company—through a tax-free distribution of shares to Damark shareholders (likely, by the end of the year). "Access to capital will be made more efficient," said Cohn. "Although both have outstanding growth prospects and compelling economic models, each competes in a different space with its own competencies and capabilities." Analysts believed that the valuation of each business was more than the whole company's current market capitalization. In **April** Digital River (Nasdaq: DRIV) agreed to integrate its commerce system and E-Returns Management module with ClickShip Direct product fulfillment services. Damark announced that its 130-employee Membership Services operation was to to move from Brooklyn Park, Minn., to the 301 Carlson Parkway building in Minnetonka as part of its planned separation from ClickShip Direct. The company denied claims by consumer protection officials in Wisconsin that Damark telemarketers were charging some consumers' credit cards without their consent (78 complaints). The company said that the practices it agreed to in the December 1999 Minnesota settlement [see above] had been adopted nationwide. Wedgewood Golf Inc. retained ClickShip Direct as its e-commerce order fulfillment partner. ClickShip Direct hired Greer & Associates to do strategic branding and develop marketing communications programs to launch the company. ClickShip Direct was retained by XDOGS.COM (OTCBB: XDGS), a premier, destination Web site for outdoor enthusiasts, to serve as XDOGS' e-commerce order fulfillment partner. In **June** ClickShip Direct announced a partnership with Paradysz Matera to provide strategic marketing services (competitive analysis, promotion tracking, off-line and online strategy development, media research and buying, and predictive modeling) to ClickShip's client base. In **July** FIND/SVP Inc.'s (Nasdaq: FSVP) Live AnswerDesk division established a human expert question-answer service for 1to1Shopper.com, Damark's new Web-based shopping service. The Live AnswerDesk was to act as a "virtual personal shopper," providing answers in real time to members desiring gift suggestions, product information, and price comparisons. ClickShip Direct was retained by Vision Forum, a San Antonio, Texas-based catalog and conference company dedicated to strengthening families. In **July** ClickShip Direct announced the availability of eConnect, its live customer care services that enable customers to have a human interaction while still logged onto the Internet. In **August** ClickShip Direct signed an agreement with TrueSynergies Inc. to provide merchandise fulfillment services for TrueSynergies' client companies. At **September**'s end, Damark announced: the receipt of a preferred equity investment of $20 million from four institutional investors (proceeds to be used to expand Provell); a decision to delay the spin-out of ClickShip Direct while the company continued to explore opportunities to capitalize ClickShip in the prevailing unfavorable market conditions; and a unanimous jury verdict favoring the company in a four-year-old class action litigation case in New Jersey. **Sept. 30**: Provell (membership services) reported record nine-month revenue of $102 million, up 25.8 percent from the prior-year period. Record operating income of $25.6 million was up 106.5 percent. In addition, the company enrolled a record 955,000 new members during third quarter. "In our membership services unit, we continue to win new business from premier clients, confirming our ability to replace former Damark catalog memberships with new member acquisitions through client channels," said COO Richards. In **October**, Garland, Texas-based Ascendant Solutions (Nasdaq: ASDS), a provider of comprehensive system solutions for online and traditional merchants, signed an agreement to provide merchandise order management and customer care services to the Merchandise Services division of Damark and to integrate Damark's network of drop-ship vendors. ClickShip Direct was recognized by Best Buy Co. Inc. (NYSE: BBY) as a "Category Partner of the Year" for providing excellent service to BestBuy.com.

Datakey Inc.

continued from page 175 electronic signatures just as legally valid as signatures on paper. Information Resource Engineering Inc. (Nasdaq: IREG), a leading provider of Virtual Private Network (VPN) technology and solutions for secure business communications, agreed to bundle Datakey's most recent smart card technology into its SafeNet VPN client product. PKI smart cards were certified as "RSA Keon Ready" by RSA Security Inc. (Nasdaq: RSAS), ensuring RSA Keon users that Datakey smart cards will plug-and-play with their PKI architecture. In **August PKI** smart cards were granted "Entrust-Ready" status with Entrust/PKI 5.0 public key infrastructure software. Datakey received an order for 10,000 PKI smart cards from one of its partners for a new and innovative e-commerce application within the financial services industry. Datakey and InformaTech Inc., a wholly owned subsidiary of Kaneb Services Inc. (NYSE: KAB), announced that Datakey's FIPS 140-1 Level 2-certified PKI smart cards were available to all U.S. government agencies through InformaTech's GSA schedule. In **September** Digital Signature Trust Co. selected Datakey's Model 330 smart cards as meeting all of the requirements of the American Bankers Association's (ABA's) TrustID certificate program. **Sept. 30:** "Our Information Security Solutions (ISS) business unit continued its strong growth and represented more than half of our business in the third quarter," said CEO Boecher. "Our third quarter gross profit margin declined from the second quarter, reflecting the absence of licensing revenue, which carry a significantly higher profit margin." In **October** Datakey joined Digital Signature Trust Co., an affiliate of Zions Bancorp. (Nasdaq: ZION) and an issuer of universal Internet identity credentials, and E-Lock Technologies, a complete provider of Assurance Management solutions, to showcase end-to-end E-Sign technology solutions to members of the House Commerce Committee. The Federal Deposit Insurance Corp. (FDIC) deployed Datakey smart cards for 3,000 employees as complete identification smart cards, loaded with digital credentials for trusted online communications and strong user authentication (for building access).

Datalink Corporation

continued from page 176 sale. In **May** Datalink and Ancor Communications Inc. (Nasdaq: ANCR) formed a partnership to deliver data-intensive SANs. Datalink withdrew its registration statement with the SEC for a secondary offering of common shares. CEO Meland commented, "We have concluded that the current conditions in the financial markets are not conducive to completing our follow on offering at this time. We will wait for a more stable environment before returning to the equity markets for capital." Datalink was named to Business Week's list of 100 Hot Growth Companies—ranking 30th on the list, which appeared in the magazine's May 29 issue. In a separate report from leading technology trade publication NetworkWorld, Datalink placed No. 2 in revenue per employee ($880,719)—behind Apex PC Solutions, but ahead of mega-corporations like Dell, Apple, and Microsoft. In **June** the company opened new sales offices in Portland, Ore., and Raleigh, N.C. Datalink and Spectra Logic Corp. Boulder, Colo., announced a strategic partnership to provide customers with robust data protection solutions that include leading automated tape technologies for direct-attached, network-attached storage (NAS), and storage area network (SAN) environments. Crossroads Systems Inc. (Nasdaq: CRDS), the leading developer and manufacturer of storage routers for Fibre Channel SANs, named Datalink its top Solutions Provider of 1999. Datalink and EMC Corp., the world leader in information storage, signed a value-added systems integrator agreement enabling Datalink to offer the full line of EMC's CLARiiON storage systems to customers nationwide. In July Datalink opened a new sales office in San Diego. In **September** it opened two more sales offices, one in Pittsburgh and one in Austin, Texas. Datalink then had 24 offices located across the United States. **Sept. 30**: Nine-month net income before the cumulative impact of a change in accounting principle was $3.9 million, compared to $5.5 million in the same period a year ago. In **October** Datalink demonstrated a live, switched-fabric Storage Area Network (SAN) providing high-speed, high-bandwidth connections. In its most significant marketing initiative to date, aimed at capturing a larger share of the growing data storage market, Datalink launched a new branding campaign that included business and industry-trade print advertising, Web development, collateral materials, event marketing, and public relations. Meland said, "This month we introduced our new company logo, a new marketing program, and a new company themeline, Information Means the World." The campaign emphasized the company's data services side because the market puts a higher valuation on such businesses. In **November** Datalink acquired the Appliance Division of OpenSystems.com Inc., which had achieved national status as the leading independent seller of network-attached storage (NAS)."They are the No. 1 channel partner of Network Appliance Inc., the dominant NAS market leader," said Meland.

Deluxe Corporation

continued from page 177 the International Tandem Users' Group 1999 NonStop Availability Award. A licensing agreement and strategic alliance between eFunds and eConnect (OTC Bulletin Board: ECNC), a California-based developer of ATM and credit card devices and provider of Internet payment processing services, would soon enable customers to use their ATM cards with personal identification numbers (PINs) on the Internet. At month's end, Deluxe's board of directors approved a plan for a strategic realignment of Deluxe that would create two independent companies. Under the plan, Deluxe would combine its eFunds and iDLX Technology Partners businesses into a separate, independent publicly traded company, to be called eFunds Corp. Deluxe Paper Payment Systems would continue to operate under the Deluxe Corp. name and continue to trade under the ticker symbol DLX. Said CEO Blanchard, "The announcement of today's plan to split-off Deluxe's higher-growth businesses is consistent with our strategy to create strategically focused enterprises that can independently achieve their business objectives and pursue growth opportunities in their respective markets." The split-off was conditioned upon obtaining a favorable tax ruling from the Internal Revenue Service. In **February** Deluxe Paper Payment Systems acquired Designer Checks of Anniston, Ala.; then unveiled its O N E on Demand service, giving financial services companies an easy and quick way to connect with Deluxe for new-account applicant verification and check ordering services. In **March** Deluxe Paper Payment Systems enhanced its Internet personal check reordering service to offer more choices and make it easier for consumers to reorder their checks online. In **April** eFunds filed a registration statement with the SEC for an initial public offering of common stock in the proposed aggregate maximum offering amount of $100 million. [The offering was later set at 6.25 million shares at a price range of $14 to $16 a share.] Meanwhile, eFunds announced enhancements to DataNavigator that save electronic funds transfer (EFT) processors money, increase productivity, and allow them to view their settlement position instantly, helping them better manage their cash positions. In **June** Deluxe Paper Payment Systems announced that its Internet Banking Solutions program was helping nearly every online bank to date bridge the gap between virtual banking and real-world fulfillment. Q UP, a wholly owned subsidiary of S1 Corp. (Nasdaq: SONE) formed an alliance with Deluxe Paper Payment Systems to deliver customized check re-ordering via the Q UP Internet Banking Solution, allowing end-users to re-order and customize their checks while remaining in the frame of their financial institution's Web site. The 5.5 million-share eFunds IPO was priced at $13 per share. Deluxe Paper Payment Systems launched http://creditunion.deluxe.com, a Web site designed exclusively for credit unions. In **August** Deluxe outlined the company's new growth strategy at a presentation for investment analysts. Building on its experience and customized capabilities in personalization engineering, gained from producing and delivering billions of checks for millions of customers, Deluxe was planning to offer a broad range of personalized products (monogrammed shirts, stationery, and other custom products) through the Internet. **Sept. 30:** Adjusted for divestitures, Deluxe's third-quarter revenue increased 4.1 percent. Paper Payment Systems (PPS) revenue was $314.6 million, compared to $311.5 million a year ago. Designer Checks, which was acquired earlier in the year, contributed $14.6 million in revenue. Equivalent unit volume for PPS was down 5.1 percent compared to third quarter 1999; however, revenue per unit increased 6.4 percent and profit per unit was up 15.7 percent. In **October** the board of directors approved a plan to complete the separation of eFunds Corp. from Deluxe by means of a tax-free spin-off to its shareholders rather than by an exchange offer, or split-off, as previously announced. "With adverse changes in market conditions, particularly the [38 percent] decline in eFunds' stock price since the IPO, we are doubtful that the exchange would have been successful," said Blanchard. "Moreover, in contrast to what was previously expected, in today's market, the higher premium that the company anticipates would be required to be offered in eFunds stock to induce current Deluxe shareholders to participate would create an unacceptable value disparity in the treatment of exchanging and non-exchanging Deluxe shareholders." Deluxe also said that it planned to scale back its PlaidMoon e-commerce retailing initiative and reposition it within the company's existing businesses, resulting in a temporary suspension of the PlaidMoon.com Web site and a reduction in expenditures for that initiative. "Instead of being a stand-alone business as we'd planned, PlaidMoon.com will be folded into existing businesses where we have a proven track record of e-commerce success," said Vice Chairman Mosner. Deluxe Business Forms unveiled a new service allowing its small-business customers and business-forms distributors to check the status of orders using the latest wireless technology.

Department 56 Inc.

continued from page 178 revenue of $215 million, in line with current analysts' consensus estimates. In **November** Department 56 announced plans for a company-owned retail store at Downtown Disney, the retail and entertainment complex located next to the Disneyland theme park in Anaheim, Calif., to open in March of 2001.

Digi International Inc.

continued from page 181 1999 Product of the Year by Communications Solutions magazine. In **May**, at Networld + Interop, Digi announced a partnership and marketing alliance with Compaq Computer Corp. (NYSE: CPQ) through which the two companies were to jointly develop and market a family of server-based communications solutions. In **July** a partnership with Tobit Software, a developer of award-winning, network-based e-messaging software was to develop and market the FaxMail Server, a family of fax-messaging solutions for small to medium-size businesses or departments. In **August** summary judgment was entered in favor of Digi International and two of its former officers in securities lawsuits brought by a class of stock purchasers and the Louisiana State Employees Retirement System. Digi made Linux drivers available for its EtherLite line of network serial concentrators, enabling powerful serial port connectivity under the popular, versatile Linux operating system. In **September** Digi announced plans for the restructuring of its European operations, which had been losing money since their acquisition more than a year earlier. After evaluating strategic options in Europe, the company determined to refocus on its strengths in peripheral connectivity products. The restructured European organization was to be primarily sales and marketing-oriented. All product development, technical support, and manufacturing functions were to be moved to Digi's corporate headquarters. Digi agreed to acquire Inside Out Networks, a leading developer of data connection products based in Austin, Texas. The acquisition would create the most competitive and complete Universal Serial Bus (USB) product line in the industry, and bring an extensive list of satisfied corporate customers under the Digi umbrella. Digi would also benefit from Inside Out Networks' pioneering EPIC software, which provides a seamless transition between legacy software and the latest USB-attached devices. The purchase price included initial payments of $6.5 million, subject to possible post-closing adjustment, and additional payments of up to $8.5 million over three years, subject to Inside Out Networks achieving specific revenue and operating income targets. [Deal closed Oct. 2.] Digi's Educational Services unit was named an Authorized Provider of the International Association for Continuing Education and Training's (IACET) Continuing Education Unit (CEU). **Sept. 30:** Fourth-quarter income, excluding amortization of intangible assets acquired in business combinations, restructuring and asset impairment charges, and the related deferred tax benefits, was $2.4 million. CEO Dunsmore stated, "During fiscal 2000, we have aggressively refocused our business to provide a stable foundation for growth. We have rebuilt the senior management team, restructured our European operations, and reduced our inventories and channel returns to all-time lows, while aggressively growing our cash position." In **October** a Digi information technology team completed a comprehensive upgrade of its Web site (http://www.digi.com), with assistance from Wizmo, an e-business consulting, development and management services company.

Digital Biometrics Inc.

continued from page 182 New Jersey-based Visionics Corp., the global face-recognition technology leader, signed a definitive merger agreement. The merger was to combine Visionics' leadership in technology and innovation with DBI's engineering and manufacturing expertise for the development of a totally new way of delivering biometrics. The combined entity was planning to offer deployment-ready hardware components—so-called network appliances—that support facial recognition and other biometrics. On those components, developers and OEMs would be able to build large-scale applications or solutions in areas such as information security, banking, access control, law enforcement, ID solutions, and CCTV security. In the pooling-of-interests transaction, Digital Biometrics was to issue 7 million new shares (valued at $36.3 million based on the previous day's closing price) to Visionics shareholders, who would own 30 percent of the resulting outstanding shares. The merged entity was intending to adopt the Visionics name.

Digital River Inc.

continued from page 183 100,000 downloadable software titles through Fingerhut's proprietary sites, www.thehut.com and www.andysgarage.com. Digital River agreed to host and manage e-commerce for IMSI's (Nasdaq: IMSIC) online store at www.imsisoft.com. Two new e-business service offerings, E-Returns Management and E-Reseller Network System, were released—to help companies more effectively integrate e-business into their organizations. The company then announced plans to segment its business into two separate divisions—Software and Digital Commerce Services, and E-Business Services. "With the formation of E-Business Services, we are expanding our business platform to build a market leader in e-commerce outsourcing for manufacturers, distributors, and retailers," said CEO Ronning. The company planned to spend $18 million to $20 million to build the E-Business Services division. Robertson Stephens reiterated its BUY rating on Digital River after the company reported strong fourth-quarter results. Digital River agreed to manage e-commerce and product fulfillment for direct PC manufacturer Micron Electronics Inc.'s recently redesigned site, e-Additions.com. In **February** the company added four new E-Business Services clients: TDK, a manufacturer of electronics and media products; RockShox, a manufacturer of bicycle suspension systems; Plantronics, a provider of headsets and computer audio systems; and Process & Building Solutions division of Intergraph Corp. Under an an agreement with Coors Brewing Co., Digital River was to build and operate a log-in based B2B e-commerce system to automate the ordering of marketing and promotional materials for Coors' distributors and field sales partners. The company announced a new B2B software licensing commerce system and its first implementation by Symantec. The new licensing system allows software publishers to offer volume licensing to businesses via an online configurator. The company launched a German online store for Autodesk Corp., one of the largest PC software companies. In **March** it began hosting and managing e-commerce for Prosoft Engineering's online store at www.prosofteng.com. Digital River announced Enterprise Campaign Management (ECM)—providing its clients secure access to a Web interface from which they can define and execute advanced, permission-based e-mail campaigns including remote campaign control and soft and hard response tracking. Digital River's eBot product was awarded a Codie award at the SIIA (Software and Information Industry Association) Spring Symposium in San Diego. An E-Business Services agreement with Life Time Fitness was to have Digital River build and operate an online store located at http://www.lifetimefitness.com. A strategic partnership with Digital Island Inc. (Nasdaq: ISLD), a leading global e-business delivery network, combined their respective strengths to package a network infrastructure with a comprehensive e-commerce system, creating a joint e-commerce solution for application service providers (ASPs). In **April** Digital River agreed to integrate its commerce system and E-Returns Management module with the product fulfillment services of ClickShip Direct, a subsidiary of Damark International Inc. (Nasdaq: DMRK). The company announced an e-commerce agreement with Fujitsu General America Inc. to build a secure extranet site for its channel partners. Joel Ronning won the 2000 Minnesota and Dakotas Ernst & Young Entrepreneur of the Year Award in the newly formed E-Business-to-Business category. The company agreed with with BlueLight.com (http://www.bluelight.com) to provide content delivery and software products for BlueLight.com's upcoming e-commerce shopping destination. Digital River announced plans to integrate E.piphany's (Nasdaq: EPNY) analytic and real-time personalization technology into its analytics-based Enterprise Campaign Management (ECM) marketing system. The company said that it was expecting its software division to reach profitability, before depreciation and amortization, by December—and the company overall, before goodwill amortization, in the fourth quarter of 2001. In **May** Digital River agreed with AltaVista Business Solutions (http://solutions.altavista.com) to manage e-commerce, product fulfillment, and customer service for AltaVista Search Engine 3.0, the next-generation search technology designed for sophisticated e-commerce, portals, and global enterprise environments; and with CASIO Soft to host and manage their online store at http://www.casiosoft.com/consumerproductsset.html (mobile data collection and field force management solutions as well as consumer software titles). "Our business model has been extremely successful and we've built a market leadership position with our Software and Services Division, which targets profitability by year-end," said CEO Ronning at the company's annual meeting. "Now, we're committed to taking Digital River to the next level by leveraging the huge market opportunity for B2B e-commerce systems and by targeting a new sector of customers—large manufacturing, distribution, and retail companies who need to move traditional business process to the Web." Digital River announced the availability of E-Remote Control (ERC), a client administration tool-set designed to give clients access to edit and control product and pricing information within their e-commerce system. The company launched a new e-commerce site for Siemens Information and Communication Mobile at siemenscordless.com. In **June** the company implemented B2B volume licensing systems for McAfee.com (Nasdaq: MCAF), Aladdin Systems (Nasdaq: ALHI), and ScanSoft (Nasdaq: SSFT). The agreements were to allow these software publishers to sell volume software licenses online, providing a fast and easy process for small to medium-sized businesses to configure product orders and purchase multiple software licenses online. Digital River continued to expand its international operations and commerce services by opening an E-Business Services division in the United Kingdom. Digital River was selected by Nasdaq to conduct the market opening ceremonies on June 14. The company announced that it expected sales for the second quarter ending June 30 to be in the range of $30 million to $31.5 million, lower than the consensus analyst estimate, but it expected to meet or better the consensus loss per share estimate. "The expected results are related to greater than anticipated seasonality in our Software Services division," said CEO Ronning. "The second quarter is typically slower in the software market, and a lack of new product offerings from our client base compounded the situation." The market reacted harshly to these short-term revenue jitters: Shares fell 41 percent over a two-day period. By quarter's end, the company had added 20 sales professionals and six client services to its E-Business Services Divisions, expanding its team to 53. As part of the company's e-business strategy, Digital River was planning to continue to sell and implement e-commerce services for large corporations across various industries, including industrial equipment, consumer goods, sports equipment, electronics, and technology components. In **July** the company hosted a series of "Webinars," free, online seminars that focused on emerging and complex issues surrounding e-business, including product returns management, resolving channel conflict, and e-marketing. The company announced an e-commerce service agreement with the Rapala Normark Group, the leading manufacturer of fishing lures, to build its first e-commerce site. In **August** the company announced a plan to expand its B2B global e-commerce system architecture to support intra- and inter-company ordering systems, customer relationship management (CRM) and enterprise resource planning (ERP) system integration, and e-marketplaces. Digital River launched an e-commerce site for Loki Software Inc., a leading developer of Linux-based PC games. Digital River became one of the largest commerce service providers (CSPs) to complete a commerce system upgrade to Oracle 8i. Digital River completed a services integration with Net Perceptions Inc. (Nasdaq: NETP), a recognized leader in commerce analytics and personalization. For Digital River clients who choose to purchase advanced personalization capabilities such as product recommendations based on individual preferences, Digital River is offering a premium service based on Net Perceptions' Web Recommendation Channel. Based on its revenue growth from 1997 to 1999, the company was named a Deloitte & Touche's Minnesota Technology Rising Star, a new category this year. The company acquired the $1.3 million-revenue software services business of NetSales Inc., which provides outsourced business-to-business (B2B) and business-to-consumer (B2C) e-commerce services for software publishers and software retailers. In September the company announced an e-commerce agreement with Network ICE (Nasdaq: NETA) to develop, host, and manage its e-commerce site at http://www.networkice.com. Digital River announced a $2.75 million customer service center upgrade, including the integration of Siebel Call Center 2000 and Siebel eService as well as technology from other proven providers such as Blue Pumpkin and Interactive Intelligence. With the enhancements, Digital River projected that it would double response capability by the end of 2000. The company expanded its e-commerce system to build business-to-education (B2E) e-commerce solutions by adapting its commerce system features to meet the needs of the education market through volume licensing, purchase orders, customer screening and validation, and customer service. The company also broadened its e-marketing professional services. Digital River announced e-commerce agreements with three leading manufacturers of technology products including Xircom, a world leader in mobile access solutions, and S3, the manufacturer of the popular Rio MP3 player. Digital River was selected by Bloomberg Personal Finance Magazine as the 43rd-fastest-growing technology company in the United States. **Sept. 30**: Based on a consensus reached by the Emerging Issues Task Force of the Financial Accounting Standards Board regarding net versus gross revenue recognition that resulted in revised accounting standards, the company began reporting all revenue on a net basis with this quarter. Under the new standards, nine-month revenue totaled $21.1 million, a 135 percent increase from prior year. The quarterly loss was less than consensus estimates. In **October** the company announced an e-commerce agreement with Hiawatha Island Software Co. Inc., a leading developer of knowledge management, Web site promotion, and eBusiness Intelligence solutions. Under an agreement with Novell Inc. (Nasdaq: NOVL), the leading provider of Net services software, the company was to support Novell's eBusiness initiatives via an expanded e-commerce model. E-commerce agreements with ZDNet's (NYSE: ZDZ) SmartPlanet e-learning service (www.smartplanet.com), Systran Software (www.systransoft.com), and eSplice Inc., a wholly owned subsidiary of Navarre Corp. (Nasdaq: NAVR), followed. Digital River launched www.purepolaris.com, an e-commerce site for Polaris Industries (NYSE: PII), Plymouth, Minn., the world's largest snowmobile manufacturer and one of the largest U.S. manufacturers of ATVs and personal watercrafts. In **November** Nabisco Inc. signed an e-commerce agreement with Digital River, marking Nabisco's first venture into e-commerce.

Dura Automotive Systems Inc.

continued from page 186 — The Driver Controls Division contains the Shift Systems, Cables, and Brake Systems business units.

— Body and Glass Division business units include Body and Glass Europe and Body and Glass North America.

— Atwood Mobile Products Division is a leading supplier of a variety of products to the recreational vehicle, mass transit, and heavy truck markets.

In **June** Dura settled two product recall issues from the first half of 1999 involving 1998 acquisition Trident Automotive plc. Settlement of the speed control cables and a secondary hood latch issues was reached through a cost-sharing agreement. A pretax charge to operations of $16.0 million was recorded during the second quarter of 2000 to cover amounts not previously reserved. In **September** Dura announced that it was expecting earnings to drop due to continued weakness in the recreational vehicle market, production cuts related to the Firestone tire recall on the Ford Explorer and Ranger vehicles, and declines in the European currencies where Dura has 30 percent of its business. Those items were expected to reduce third-quarter 2000 earnings per share by 23 percent from the original consensus estimate of $0.75, and fourth-quarter earnings per share by 10 percent from the original consensus estimate of $1.25. Workers at Dura's plant in Talaudiere, France, went on strike. In November Dura announced plans to cease manufacturing operations at its RV-component facility in Elkhart, Ind. The decision to close the manufacturing facility reflected generally sagging RV market demand, the ability to transfer automotive business to other Dura facilities, and available RV manufacturing capacity at Dura's other Atwood Mobile Products Division facilities.

eBenX Inc.

605 N. Highway 169, Suite LL, Plymouth, MN 55441
Tel: 763/614-2000 Fax: 763/614-5127 Web site: http://www.ebenx.com

eBenX Inc. provides business-to-business e-commerce exchange for group health and welfare benefits. eBenX uses the Internet to simplify and automate the purchase, administration and payment of health care and other benefits for employers, their advisors and suppliers. eBenX has applied its proprietary technology and deep domain expertise to develop an e-commerce infrastructure that allows health and welfare benefit products to be packaged, presented and purchased electronically. The eBenX Benefit Exchange encompasses the assessment of carriers for employers, as well as a streamlined, Web-based channel for the quoting, rating and selection of new and renewal group health and welfare benefits by employers and carriers. The enrollment capabilities of the eBenX Benefit Exchange provide employees with the ability to make choices and enroll online. The eBenX Benefit Exchange includes Web-enabled, high volume rules-based interfaces that allow employers and carriers to exchange eligibility information throughout the benefit year, and to complete premium billings and payments.

EARNINGS HISTORY

Year Ended Dec 31	Operating Revenue/Sales (dollars in thousands)	Net Earnings	Return on Revenue (percent)	Return on Equity	Net Earnings (dollars per share*)	Cash Dividend	Market Price Range
1999 †	17,526	(5,027)	(28.7)	(5.0)	(1.18)	—	53.84–34.00
1998	10,122	(1,042)	(10.3)	NM	(0.30)	—	
1997	7,093	(500)	(7.0)	NM	(0.15)	—	
1996	4,360	(581)	(13.3)	NM	(0.18)	—	
1995	2,497	62	2.5	NM	0.02	—	

* Trading began Dec. 10, 1999.
† Income figures for 1999 include charge of $767,000/($0.18) for amortization of stock-based compensation.

BALANCE SHEET

Assets	12/31/99 (dollars in thousands)	12/31/98	Liabilities	12/31/99 (dollars in thousands)	12/31/98
Current (CAE 98,611 and 1,681)	103,081	3,987	Current (STD 0 and 750)	4,473	2,205
Property and equipment	2,456	1,568	Preferred equity		5,468
Deposits	62	41	Common equity*	101,126	(2,077)
TOTAL	105,599	5,596	TOTAL	105,599	5,596

* $0.01 par common; 100,000,000 authorized; 15,183,518 and 3,480,321 issued and outstanding.

RECENT QUARTERS / PRIOR-YEAR RESULTS

	Quarter End	Revenue ($000)	Earnings ($000)	EPS ($)	Prior-Year Revenue ($000)	Prior-Year Earnings ($000)	Prior-Year EPS ($)
Q3	09/30/2000	7,644	(3,650)	(0.21)	4,638	(1,590)	(0.45)
Q2	06/30/2000	6,394	(1,892)	(0.12)	3,766	(740)	(0.21)
Q1	03/31/2000	5,575	(1,785)	(0.11)	3,342	(372)	(0.11)
Q4	12/31/99	5,780	(2,325)	(0.36)	3,454	(17)	0.00
	SUM	25,393	(9,652)	(0.80)	15,200	(2,719)	(0.77)

RECENT EVENTS

In **November 1999** the company changed its name from Network Management Services Inc. to eBenX Inc. to emphasize its pioneer work to bring connectivity and e-commerce solutions to large and mid-sized employers. On Dec. 10, eBenX priced an initial public offering of 5,000,000 shares of its common stock, all by the company, at $20 per share (a price that had been raised twice). The shares are being offered through underwriters led by Robertson Stephens Inc., Warburg Dillon Read LLC, and Thomas Weisel Partners LLC. Proceeds from the offering were expected to be used for working capital, sales and marketing, development of new products and services, infrastructure, and possible acquisitions. The company's share price more than doubled during its first trading day, closing at $44.875 a share on volume of 7.7 million shares. In **January 2000** the company noted the following client relationships established during, and immediately following, its "quiet period": American Medical Response Inc.; American Red Cross; Bass Hotels & Resorts Inc.; Chevron Corp.; Dayton Hudson Corp.; Federated Department Stores Inc.; Georgia-Pacific Corp.; KPMG LLP; Nabisco Inc.; the state of Kansas; and Employer Benefit Services. eBenX was one of only 30 Internet-based businesses and service providers in the United States to be identified by EMC Corp. as having "best practices" for enterprise storage and information infrastructure. Underwriters of the eBenX IPO, led by Robertson Stephens, Warburg Dillon Read LLC and Thomas Weisel Partners LLC, exercised their option to purchase 750,000 shares of common stock for the purpose of covering overallotments, resulting in additional gross proceeds of $15 million. eBenX announced plans to relocate its national headquartersfrom St. Louis Park, Minn., to Plymouth, Minn., in April to accommodate the company's recent and future expected growth. The new facility was to provide 90,000 square feet of new office space. In **February** eBenX's first end-to-end e-commerce solution for group health insurance (for The Reader's Digest Association) included Web-enabled enrollment, eligibility administration, premium billing, and payment. In **March** the company extended its Target Corp. agreement to include HMO administrative and payment services for the Target Stores division, increasing the number of enrolled employees in the eBenX exchange by 18,000. In **April**, ahead of schedule, eBenX completed its online procurement tool, which includes Internet-based procurement and competitive vendor data. In **May** John G. Kinnard & Co. *continued on page 221*

OFFICERS

Mark W. Tierney
Chairman and Co-founder
John J. Davis
President and CEO
Michael C. Bingham
SVP and Co-founder
Sheila Bleeke
VP-Account Relations
Susan Busch
VP-Communications
Martin Freshwater
SVP-eBenX Corporate Solutions Sls./Mktg.
Ann Gjelten
VP-Health Plan Services
Scott P. Halstead
CFO and Secretary
Rich Hughes
VP-Human Resources
Jill Lammer
SVP-Group Services
Patrick McGuire
VP-Product Development
Anita Messal
VP-Corporate Partnerships
Karen Richardson
VP-Strategic Health Care Consulting
Jeff Rosenblum
Pres.-Midmarket
Randy Schmidt
VP-Mergers/Acquisitions
John Shade
Chief Information Officer

DIRECTORS

Paul V. Barber
JMI Associates III LLC, San Diego
Michael C. Bingham
James P. Bradley
Abaton.com Inc.
Daniel M. Cain
Cain Brothers LLC, New York
John J. Davis
William J. Geary
North Bridge Venture Partners L.P., Waltham, MA
John M. Nehra
Catalyst Ventures L.P., Baltimore
Mark W. Tierney

MAJOR SHAREHOLDERS

North Bridge Venture Partners L.P./William J. Geary, 13.6%
Waltham, MA
Mark W. Tierney, 12.7%
New Enterprise Associates VI L.P./John M. Nehra, 10.5%
Baltimore
JMI Equity Funds/Paul V. Barber, 8.2%
San Diego
CB Healthcare Fund L.P./Daniel M. Cain, 8.2%
New York
Michael C. Bingham, 8.1%
All officers and directors as a group (9 persons), 60.5%

SIC CODE

7372 Prepackaged software
7389 Business services, nec

MISCELLANEOUS

TRANSFER AGENT AND REGISTAR:
Continental Stock Transfer & Trust Co., New York
TRADED: Nasdaq National Market
SYMBOL: EBNX
STOCKHOLDERS: 84
EMPLOYEES: 425
GENERAL COUNSEL:
Dorsey & Whitney PLLP, Minneapolis
AUDITORS:
Ernst & Young LLP, Minneapolis

RANKINGS

No. 158 CRM Public 200
No. 19 Minnesota Technology Fast 50

SUBSIDIARIES, DIVISIONS, AFFILIATES

Arbor Associates
Constitution Place
Suite 1010
325 Chestnut St.
Philadelphia, PA 19106
215/627-3255

PUB

E.mergent Inc.

5960 Golden Hills Dr., Golden Valley, MN 55416
Tel: 763/417-4257 Fax: 763/542-0069 Web site: http://www.emergentincorporated.com

E.mergent Inc., formerly VideoLabs Inc., was incorporated to develop a hardware and software videoconferencing solution. With its merger with Acoustic Communication Systems Inc., a manufacturer of products used in videoconferencing and a provider of multimedia communication solutions, the company has evolved to become a provider of collaboration products and services. It is committed to developing tools and services for communication, education, and collaboration solutions for organizational and individual customer needs. The name change reflects the company's intent to pursue emerging technologies and services in multimedia-rich collaborative communications.

EARNINGS HISTORY

Year Ended Dec 31	Operating Revenue/Sales (dollars in thousands)	Net Earnings (dollars in thousands)	Return on Revenue (percent)	Return on Equity (percent)	Net Earnings (dollars per share)	Cash Dividend (dollars per share)	Market Price Range (dollars per share)
1999 *	12,538	878	7.0	14.8	0.18	—	3.31–0.94
1998 †	6,163	(196)	(3.2)	(4.9)	(0.05)	—	1.44–0.78
1997	6,950	753	10.8	22.8	0.24	—	2.31–0.69
1996 ¶	7,406	(2,362)	(31.9)	NM	(0.76)	—	3.75–0.56
1995 #	8,097	203	2.5	4.0	0.06	—	3.38–1.94

* Pro forma figures had the August 1999 acquisition of Acoustic Communications Systems Inc. occurred Jan. 1, 1999: revenue $18,691,462; income $1,018,991/$0.22.
† Pro forma figures had the April 1998 acquisition of Video Dynamics Inc. occurred Jan. 1, 1998: revenue $6,392,998; loss $140,384/($0.03).
¶ Income figures for 1996 include pretax charge of $1,575,000 for write-down of inventories; and net pretax gain of $213,378 on sale of assets.
# Income figures for 1995 include $198,605 gain on sale of assets.

BALANCE SHEET

Assets	12/31/99 (dollars in thousands)	12/31/98 (dollars in thousands)	Liabilities	12/31/99 (dollars in thousands)	12/31/98 (dollars in thousands)
Current (CAE 212 and 1,514)	7,286	4,136	Current (STD 36 and 22)	4,099	796
Property and equipment	834	469	Long-term debt	98	24
Patents	151	179	Unearned maintenance contracts	108	
Goodwill	1,263		Stockholders' equity*	5,951	3,964
Noncompete	724				
TOTAL	10,257	4,785	TOTAL	10,257	4,785

* $0.01 par common; 20,000,000 authorized; 5,675,440 and 4,457,471 issued and outstanding.

RECENT QUARTERS / PRIOR-YEAR RESULTS

	Quarter End	Revenue ($000)	Earnings ($000)	EPS ($)	Prior-Year Revenue ($000)	Prior-Year Earnings ($000)	Prior-Year EPS ($)
Q3	09/30/2000	5,625	317	0.06	4,277	356	0.06
Q2	06/30/2000	5,237	148	0.03	1,879	68	0.02
Q1	03/31/2000	4,661	153	0.03	1,856	72	0.02
Q4	12/31/99	4,527	382	0.07	1,573	(203)	(0.05)
	SUM	20,050	1,000	0.17	9,584	293	0.05

RECENT EVENTS

In **December 1999** the company announced an addition to its growing product line: the PTZCam high-resolution presentation camera with pan/tilt/zoom capabilities for the videoconferencing, presentations, and identification markets. In **January 2000** VideoLabs and the Visual Systems Division of 3M (NYSE: MMM) formed a strategic partnership to bring the 3M DC1000 object display camera to the market. VideoLabs designed and was to manufacture 3M's DC1000, to be sold as a valued-added product to 3M's projector line. In **February** VideoLabs unveiled a new entity called "meetingroomtools.com"—650 communication products targeted at small- to mid-sized companies and technology savvy professionals. In **March** VideoLabs' Ceiling DocCam was introduced Telecon East. In **April** the company received notification from the FDA that its new Medcam Pro Plus video camera and integrated light source had received 510(k) approval. VideoLabs MedCam Pro Plus bundle is offered in a soakable and non-soakable version for medical and industrial applications that require a low-cost, high-resolution 1/2" Sony super HAD CCD camera integrated with a powerful light source. VideoLabs partnered with its major medical distributor, MedCam Technology, in developing this product bundle. In **June** the company received the Technical Achievement Award in the document camera category for the Ceiling DocCam, introduced at Infocomm International. Effective **July** 3, the company changed its name from VideoLabs Inc. to E.mergent Inc. In **September** E.mergent's products division, VideoLabs, unveiled the FlexCam iCam, is a multipurpose video camera with VideoLabs' patented gooseneck. With the FlexCam iCam, professional users can present objects, images, or text; capture images, send video e-mail, create video portfolios, or videoconference on the Internet. **Sept. 30:** Nine-month revenue was $15.5 million vs. $8.0 million a year earlier, an increase of 94 percent. Nine-month gross profits were $5.6 million vs. $3.3 million in 1999. CEO Hansen said, "Both our prod- ***continued on page 221***

OFFICERS

James Hansen
Chairman, CEO, and Treasurer

Jill R. Larson
VP-Administration and Secretary

Robin Sheeley
CTO and Pres.-Acoustic Communication

DIRECTORS

Richard F. Craven
private investor, Minneapolis

James W. Hansen

Peter McDonnell
AdCom Videoconferencing, Canada

Robin Sheeley
Acoustic Communication Systems

MAJOR SHAREHOLDERS

Robin Sheeley, 20.1%
Plymouth, MN

Richard F. Craven, 10.5%
Edina, MN

James W. Hansen, 10.3%
Dellwood, MN

All officers and directors as a group (5 persons), 42.9%

SIC CODE

3579 Office machines, nec

3861 Photographic equipment and supplies

MISCELLANEOUS

TRANSFER AGENT AND REGISTAR:
Wells Fargo Bank Minnesota N.A., South St. Paul, MN

TRADED: Nasdaq SmallCap Market

SYMBOL: EMRT

STOCKHOLDERS: 200

EMPLOYEES: 86

GENERAL COUNSEL:
Fredrikson & Byron P.A., Minneapolis

AUDITORS:
Deloitte & Touche LLP, Minneapolis

INC: DE-1992

ANNUAL MEETING: May

RANKINGS

No. 172 CRM Public 200

TWO-YEAR QUARTERLY HIGH-LOW STOCK PRICES

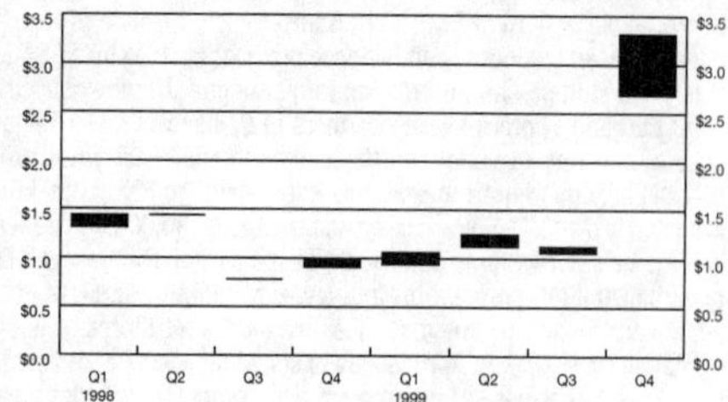

eNetpc Inc.

6825 Shady Oak Rd., Eden Prairie, MN 55344
Tel: 952/943-1598 Fax: 952/943-1599 Web site: http://www.enetpc.com

eNetpc Inc., formerly CyberStar Computer Corp., designs and manufactures a wide range of computer systems and products, including desktops, midtowers, minitowers, notebooks, workstations, and file servers. The company markets, services, and supports its products through a nationwide network of 275 authorized dealers who sell the company's products to end users, which are typically businesses purchasing multicomputer office systems.Through its VAR (value-added reseller) division, the company resells branded computers and various branded and non-branded peripheral products to end users.

EARNINGS HISTORY

Year Ended Feb	Operating Revenue/Sales (dollars in thousands)	Net Earnings	Return on Revenue (percent)	Return on Equity	Net Earnings (dollars per share*)	Cash Dividend	Market Price Range
2000	4,393	(467)	(10.6)	(38.9)	(0.12)	—	9.25–1.25
1999	4,854	(920)	(19.0)	NM	(0.24)	—	3.63–1.00
1998	5,377	(71)	(1.3)	(9.6)	(0.02)	—	

* Stock began trading June 12, 1998.

BALANCE SHEET

Assets	02/29/00 (dollars in thousands)	02/28/99	Liabilities	02/29/00 (dollars in thousands)	02/28/99
Current (CAE 496 and 73)	1,397	1,517	Current	317	957
Property and equipment	122	175	Stockholders' equity*	1,202	734
TOTAL	1,519	1,692	TOTAL	1,519	1,692

* $0.01 par common; 20,000,000 authorized; 4,333,095 and 3,928,095 issued and outstanding.

RECENT QUARTERS / **PRIOR-YEAR RESULTS**

	Quarter End	Revenue ($000)	Earnings ($000)	EPS ($)	Prior-Year Revenue ($000)	Prior-Year Earnings ($000)	Prior-Year EPS ($)
Q2	08/31/2000	3,313	(208)	(0.05)	1,005	(95)	(0.02)
Q1	05/31/2000	3,257	(184)	(0.04)	1,151	(70)	(0.02)
Q4	02/29/2000	986	(258)	(0.06)	1,349	(246)	(0.06)
Q3	11/30/99	1,251	(44)	(0.01)	1,319	(267)	(0.07)
	SUM	8,807	(694)	(0.17)	4,825	(678)	(0.17)

RECENT EVENTS

In **November 1999** the company, then known as CyberStar, retained VentureNow, Fort Lauderdale, Fla., to provide corporate finance advisory services and strategic planning support. In **December** CyberStar began offering rebates of up to $400 on selected computer systems. Microsoft's (Nasdaq: MSFT) MSN System Builder End User Mail-in Rebate Program was available to all customers purchasing a qualified CyberStar PC or Notebook. eNetpc v1.0 was made available for licensing. (eNetpc is an online configurator software package that enables any computer or office reseller to offer custom-built CyberStar PCs, notebooks, and fileservers to their customers on the Internet.) The company announced plans to support the Linux operating system on its entire line of desktop PCs and fileservers. CyberStar partnered with Tatung, Taiwan's No. 1 manufacturer of electronics, home appliances, and industrial equipment, as its OEM manufacturer for the next release of CyberStar-branded monitors. In **January 2000** CyberStar chose Intel to supply the main component platform of their new Rack mount server for Internet Service Providers. CyberStar partnered with Personal Computer Services Inc. for marketing build-to-order PC's, notebooks, and file servers on http://www.percomser.com. In **March** the company was selected as one of 200 exclusive guests from North America and Europe to attend System Builder Summit Spring 2000. Selection to participate in the event is based upon company size and growth potential, market influence and the breadth of value-added services and solutions that the company offers its customers. CyberStar completed a $1 million private placement offering of units consisting of its common stock and warrants to purchase its common stock. The proceeds of the offering were to be used to complete development of the eNetpc software, to further develop the eNetpc.com Website, and as working capital. It then launched eNetpc v1.0 B2B configurator software with Personal Computer Services Inc. (PCSI), at http://www.percomser.com. The company partnered with Computer Doctors, OIC Computers, Corporate Computing Inc., and On-Site Technology Inc. for marketing build-to-order PCs, notebooks, and file servers on the Internet. In **April** the company said that it had signed its first 25 software license agreements for eNetpc in the first month of offering the program. In **June** CyberStar acquired International Trade Center Inc., Tempe, Ariz.—a $22.5 million-revenue international distributor of computer hardware, software, and peripherals. CyberStar signed 10 more software license agreements for eNetpc Internet software. CyberStar created a new Application Service Provider (ASP) division, eNetpc ASP, to offer an array of new Web services to CyberStar's customers. In **August** the company changed its corporate name to eNetpc Inc. **Aug. 31**: The increase in sales for the second quarter of fiscal 2001 was attributed to the Virtual Distribution division, with sales of $2.7 million. In **October** the company signed a Global Solution Developer Agreement with Great Plains Software Inc. (Nasdaq: GPSI), a Fargo, N.D.-based provider of e-business solutions. In a move to reinforce the company's ASP business, eNetpc agreed to develop application software that will be deployable through Great Plains Dynamics or Great Plains eEnterpise. VP Fredrickson stated, "The new agreement with Great Plains enables us to expand our popular PC configurator software application, eSelect, by adding a fully integrated accounting module as an option. These applications will then be fully integrated on the Internet, providing a cost savings to our reseller partners by offering the software at a monthly subscription rate." In **November** eNetpc partnered with Sceptre Technologies Inc., City of Industry, Calif., to manufacture the next generation of its eNetpc-branded notebook computers; and also became a member of Allaire Corp.'s (NASDAQ: ALLR) Alliance Partner program.

OFFICERS

Jonathan Bumba
President and CEO

Brian Fredrickson
National Marketing Mgr.

Richard Palmer
Senior Buyer

DIRECTORS

James T. Greenfield
Stone Fabrics Inc.

Ed Havlik
Panasonic Multimedia

Richard A. Pomije

MAJOR SHAREHOLDERS

Richard A. Pomije, 71.7%

All officers and directors as a group (4 persons), 74.1%

SIC CODE

3575 Computer terminals

7378 Computer maintenance and repair

MISCELLANEOUS

TRANSFER AGENT AND REGISTAR:
Signature Stock Transfer Inc.

TRADED: OTC Bulletin Board

SYMBOL: ETPC

STOCKHOLDERS: 22

EMPLOYEES: 15

PART TIME: 1

AUDITORS:
Ernst & Young LLP, Minneapolis

FOUNDED: 1982

EMC Corporation

875 Montreal Way, St. Paul, MN 55102
Tel: 651/290-2800 Fax: 651/290-2828 Web site: http://www.emcp.com

EMC Corp. operates **EMC Publishing**, a St. Paul educational publisher of literature, foreign language, home economics, and business education textbooks. Wholly owned subsidiary **Digital Excellence Inc.** is a major duplicator of audiocassettes, video cartridges, compact discs, and microcomputer diskettes with packaging and fulfillment support services. **Paradigm Publishing Inc.**, another wholly owned subsidiary, is a post-secondary business education publisher. November 1997 marked the formation of a new wholly owned subsidiary, **EMC/Paradigm Custom Publishing Inc.**

EARNINGS HISTORY

Year Ended Dec 31	Operating Revenue/Sales (dollars in thousands)	Net Earnings	Return on Revenue (percent)	Return on Equity	Net Earnings (dollars per share)	Cash Dividend	Market Price Range
1999	34,402	1,520	4.4	8.6	0.70	0.15	14.00–8.25
1998	34,363	2,334	6.8	13.9	1.07	0.21	15.88–10.00
1997	33,392	2,018	6.0	13.6	0.93	0.19	14.50–11.25
1996	32,579	1,812	5.6	13.7	0.84	0.19	18.50–16.75
1995	29,575	2,262	7.6	19.3	1.05	0.19	

BALANCE SHEET

Assets	12/31/99 (dollars in thousands)	12/31/98
Current (CAE 116 and 1,468)	13,217	12,012
Property, plant, and equipment	6,148	6,582
Manuscripts and programs	7,460	6,087
Royalty advances	444	549
Cash surrender value of officers' life insurance	234	187
Notes receivable		8
TOTAL	27,503	25,426

Liabilities	12/31/99 (dollars in thousands)	12/31/98
Current (STD 286 and 79)	6,224	4,986
Long-term debt	3,307	3,392
Deferred income taxes	330	315
Stockholders' equity*	17,643	16,733
TOTAL	27,503	25,426

* $.0125 par common; 6,000,000 authorized; 2,156,960 and 2,179,360 issued and outstanding.

RECENT QUARTERS / PRIOR-YEAR RESULTS

	Quarter End	Revenue ($000)	Earnings ($000)	EPS ($)	Prior-Year Revenue ($000)	Prior-Year Earnings ($000)	Prior-Year EPS ($)
Q3	09/30/2000	16,724	2,251	1.05	15,448	2,597	1.20
Q2	06/30/2000	10,611	765	0.35	6,839	(82)	(0.04)
Q1	03/31/2000	5,443	(1,325)	(0.61)	4,469	(1,241)	(0.57)
Q4	12/31/99	7,646	246	0.11	6,581	402	0.18
	SUM	40,424	1,937	0.90	33,337	1,676	0.78

RECENT EVENTS

In **April 2000** the company cited a Nasdaq rule that requires companies to be registered under the Securities Exchange Act of 1934 in order to trade on the Nasdaq system (including its Bulletin Board). Because EMC was not so registered, its stock was scheduled for delisting—which was to move it to the so-called "pink sheets" of the National Quotations Bureau, the stocks of which many broker/dealers, including Dain Rauscher Inc., avoid. The company was deciding whether or not to go through the expensive, time-consuming registration process or to remain unregistered. EMC entered into a letter of intent to sell the assets of its wholly owned subsidiary, Digital Excellence Inc., to a private investment group for an undisclosed sum. In **June** the contemplated sale of Digital Excellence was terminated by mutual consent of the parties. In **October** EMC declared an annual dividend of $0.20 per share payable Jan. 2, 2001, to stockholders of record on Dec. 8, 2000.

OFFICERS

David E. Feinberg
Chairman and CEO
Paul R. Winter
President and Treasurer
Wolfgang S. Kraft
VP and Publisher
Robert F. O'Reilly
VP
Richard T. Stevens
VP
Honnen S. Weiss
Secretary
Carl Bratton
VP-Information Technology

DIRECTORS

David E. Feinberg
Honnen S. Weiss
Felhaber Larson Fenlon & Vogt, Minneapolis
Paul R. Winter
Robert F. Zicarelli
Norwest Venture Capital (retired)

SIC CODE

2731 Book publishing
2741 Publishing, misc
3652 Prerecorded records and tapes
7372 Prepackaged software
7379 Computer related services, nec
7812 Motion picture and video production
7819 Services allied to motion pictures

MISCELLANEOUS

TRANSFER AGENT AND REGISTAR:
Wells Fargo Bank Minnesota N.A.,
South St. Paul, MN
TRADED: LOTC
SYMBOL: EMCM
STOCKHOLDERS: 104
EMPLOYEES: 210
GENERAL COUNSEL:
Felhaber, Larson, Fenlon & Vogt, Minneapolis
AUDITORS:
PricewaterhouseCoopers LLP, Minneapolis
INC: MN-1954
ANNUAL MEETING: May
PURCHASING:
James Moreland

RANKINGS

No. 128 CRM Public 200

SUBSIDIARIES, DIVISIONS, AFFILIATES

EMC Publishing
875 Montreal Way
St. Paul, MN 55102
651/290-2800
Robert F. O'Reilly

Paradigm Publishing Inc.
875 Montreal Way
St. Paul, MN 55102
651/290-2800
Dr. Rosemary Fruehling

Digital Excellence Inc.
300 York Ave.
St. Paul, MN 55101
651/771-1555
Richard T. Stevens

EMC/Paradigm Custom Publishing Inc.

Ecolab Inc.

370 Wabasha St. N., St. Paul, MN 55102
Tel: 651/293-2233 Fax: 651/225-3123 Web site: http://www.ecolab.com

Ecolab Inc. develops and markets premium cleaning, sanitizing, and maintenance products and services for the hospitality, institutional, and industrial markets. Customers include hotels and restaurants; foodservice, health care, and educational facilities; quick-service (fast-food) units; groceries; commercial laundries; light industry; dairy plants and farms; and food and beverage processors. Ecolab operates directly in 37 countries in North America, Asia-Pacific, Latin America, and Africa. In Europe, it reaches customers through joint venture Henkel-Ecolab, which does business in 26 countries, including the Eastern European markets, and employs 4,600 associates. Ecolab serves customers in more than 100 other countries through distributors, licensees, and export operations.

EARNINGS HISTORY *

Year Ended Dec 31	Operating Revenue/Sales (dollars in thousands)	Net Earnings	Return on Revenue (percent)	Return on Equity	Net Earnings (dollars per share†)	Cash Dividend	Market Price Range
1999	2,080,012	175,786	8.5	23.1	1.36	0.44	44.44–31.69
1998 ¶	1,888,226	192,506	10.2	27.9	1.49	0.39	38.00–26.13
1997	1,640,352	133,955	8.2	24.3	1.03	0.34	28.00–18.13
1996	1,490,009	113,185	7.6	21.8	0.88	0.29	19.75–14.56
1995	1,340,881	99,189	7.4	21.7	0.75	0.26	15.88–10.00

* Revenue figures restated for continuing operations.
† Per-share amounts restated to reflect 2-for-1 stock split on Jan. 15, 1998.
¶ Income figures for 1998 include gain of $38.0 million/$0.29 from discontinued operations.

BALANCE SHEET

Assets	12/31/99 (dollars in thousands)	12/31/98
Current (CAE 47,748 and 28,425)	577,321	503,514
Property, plant, and equipment	448,116	420,205
Investment in Henkel-Ecolab	219,003	253,646
Other	341,506	293,630
TOTAL	1,585,946	1,470,995

Liabilities	12/31/99 (dollars in thousands)	12/31/98
Current (STD 112,060 and 67,991)	470,674	399,791
Long-term debt	169,014	227,041
Postretirement	97,527	85,793
Other	86,715	67,829
Stkhldrs' equity*	762,016	690,541
TOTAL	1,585,946	1,470,995

* $1 par common; 200,000,000 authorized; 145,556,459 and 144,705,783 issued and outstanding, less 16,140,244 and 15,227,043 treasury shares.

RECENT QUARTERS / **PRIOR-YEAR RESULTS**

	Quarter End	Revenue ($000)	Earnings ($000)	EPS ($)	Prior-Year Revenue ($000)	Prior-Year Earnings ($000)	Prior-Year EPS ($)
Q3	09/30/2000	600,666	60,338	0.47	554,511	55,021	0.42
Q2	06/30/2000	570,711	48,409	0.38	520,416	43,384	0.33
Q1	03/31/2000	526,260	42,612	0.33	489,304	35,038	0.27
Q4	12/31/99	515,781	42,343	0.33	483,367	39,217	0.30
	SUM	2,213,418	193,702	1.51	2,047,598	172,660	1.33

PRIOR YEAR: Q3 earnings include a nontaxable gain of $1.5 million/$0.01 on the receipt of shares from an insurance company that demutualized.

RECENT EVENTS

In **December 1999** the company purchased $5 million-revenue Metro Appliance Service Inc., a Minneapolis-based provider of commercial kitchen equipment parts and repair services. **Dec. 31:** A near doubling in profits from international operations and strong results from Henkel-Ecolab fueled the solid earnings gain in Ecolab's fourth quarter and closed out the seventh-consecutive year of double-digit earnings growth for the company. In **January 2000** the company's stock was one of three in Minnesota among the 89 stocks that Goldman Sachs & Co. listed as its analysts' favorite stock picks for 2000. The listed stocks were expected to generate a 12-month price return of 35 percent, compared with an an expected gain of only 4 percent by the S&P 500 index. Ecolab entered into a food safety partnership with Ion Beam Applications (IBA), the world's largest sterilization and ionization business, to combine Ecolab's sanitation and food-surface treatment expertise and IBA's cold-pasteurization technology and management services. In **February** Ecolab acquired Spartan de Chile Limitada and Spartan de Argentina S.A.—both licensees of Spartan Chemical Co. Inc. of Toledo, Ohio—with combined sales of $20 million; and $24 million-revenue Southwest Sanitary Distributing Co., Carrolton, Texas—a provider of cleaning and sanitizing products to quick-service restaurants. In **May** Ecolab said that it was planning to repurchase up to $200 million of its shares, about 4 percent of its stock. Ecolab formed a strategic alliance with FreshLoc Technologies, a privately held Plano, Texas, maker of wireless food-safety technology. In **June** Ecolab announced the expansion of two businesses: South Korean institutional, with the purchase of $6 million-revenue Dong Woo Deterpan Co. Ltd., Seoul; and commercial food equipment repair, with the purchase of $4 million-revenue ARR/CRS, Columbus, Ohio. Ecolab announced the filing with the FDA of a food *continued on page 221*

OFFICERS

Allan L. Schuman
Chairman, President, and CEO
Lawrence T. Bell
VP-Law and General Counsel
Alan P. Blumenfeld
VP and Chief Info. Officer
Peter D'Almada
SVP-Institutional North Amer.
John G. Forsythe
VP-Tax/Public Affairs
Steven L. Fritze
VP and Controller
Arthur E. Henningsen Jr.
SVP and Chief Planning Officer
Kenneth A. Iverson
VP and Secretary
Diana D. Lewis
VP-Human Resources
Richard L. Marcantonio
EVP-Industrial Group
William A. Mathison
SVP-Global Industrial Accounts
L. White Matthews III
EVP and CFO
James L. McCarty
Senior EVP-Institutional Group
Doug Milroy
VP, Gen. Mgr.-Food/Beverage N. America
Maurizio Nisita
SVP-Global Operations
Daniel J. Schmechel
VP and Treasurer
Mary J. Schumacher
VP and Chief Technical Officer
C. William Snedeker
VP and General Manager-Pest Elimination
John P. Spooner
EVP-International Group

DIRECTORS

Ruth S. Block
The Equitable (retired), New York
Jerry A. Grundhofer
Firstar Corp., Milwaukee
James J. Howard III
Xcel Energy Inc., Minneapolis
William L. Jews
CareFirst Inc., Ownings Mills,MD
Joel W. Johnson
Hormel Foods Corp., Austin, MN
Jerry W. Levin
Sunbeam Corp., Boca Raton, FL
Robert L. Lumpkins
Cargill Inc., Minnetonka, MN
Reuben F. Richards
Terra Industries Inc. (retired)
Richard L. Schall
consultant
Roland Schulz
Henkel KGaA, Dusseldorf, Germany
Allan L. Schuman
Hugo Uyterhoeven
Harvard University (retired)
Matthew L. White
Albrecht Woeste
Henkel KGaA, Dusseldorf, Germany

MAJOR SHAREHOLDERS

Henkel KGaA, 13.6%
Dusseldorf, Germany
HC Investments Inc., 11.3%
Wilmington, DE
Edward C. III and Abigail P. Johnson/FMR Corp., 5.2%
Boston
All officers and directors as a group (24 persons), 2.1%

SIC CODE

2841 Soap, detergents
2842 Polishes and sanitation goods
3823 Process control instruments
5169 Chemicals, allied products, nec, whsle

MISCELLANEOUS

TRANSFER AGENT AND REGISTAR:
First Chicago Trust Co. of New York, Jersey City, NJ
TRADED: NYSE, PCX
SYMBOL: ECL
STOCKHOLDERS: 5,559
EMPLOYEES: 12,870
IN MINNESOTA: 1,965
GENERAL COUNSEL:
Lawrence T. Bell, Gen. Counsel, St. Paul
AUDITORS:
PricewaterhouseCoopers LLP, Minneapolis
INC: DE-1924
FOUNDED: 1923
ANNUAL MEETING: May
EXTERNAL RELATIONS: Michael J. Monahan

RANKINGS

No. 20 CRM Public 200
No. 98 CRM Employer 100
No. 41 CRM Perform. 100

PUB

TWO-YEAR QUARTERLY HIGH-LOW STOCK PRICES

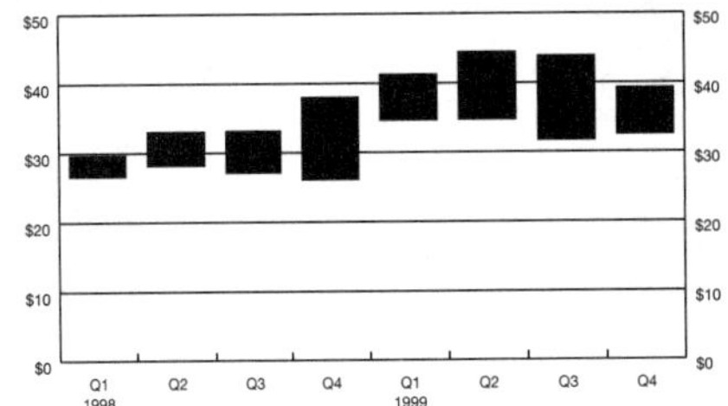

Electro-Sensors Inc.

6111 Blue Circle Dr., Minnetonka, MN 55343
Tel: 952/930-0100 Fax: 952/930-0130 Web site: http://www.electrosensors.com

Electro-Sensors Inc. operates three distinct businesses. The **Controls Division**, known as Electro-Sensors, manufactures and markets speed monitoring and motor control systems for industrial machinery. The **AutoData Systems** division designs and markets automated form-processing software and scanners used primarily for reading hand-printed characters, check marks, and bar-code information from scanned or faxed forms. The third business, **Microflame Inc.**, a wholly owned subsidiary, produces small gas torches for sale to hardware, hobby craft, and electronics retailers. In addition, the company's **ESI Investment Co.** has invested funds in other companies and businesses.

EARNINGS HISTORY

Year Ended Dec 31	Operating Revenue/Sales (dollars in thousands)	Net Earnings	Return on Revenue (percent)	Return on Equity	Net Earnings (dollars per share)	Cash Dividend	Market Price Range
1999	5,682	(22)	(0.4)	(0.3)	(0.01)	0.12	3.50–1.69
1998	6,358	230	3.6	2.8	0.12	0.12	4.25–2.72
1997	6,441	453	7.0	5.0	0.23	0.12	5.00–3.25
1996	6,143	463	7.5	5.1	0.24	0.12	7.75–3.25
1995 *	6,185	785	12.7	8.3	0.41	0.60	9.75–2.50

* Dividends for 1995 include special dividend of $0.50 per share paid on Jan. 12, 1996.

BALANCE SHEET

Assets	12/31/99 (dollars in thousands)	12/31/98	Liabilities	12/31/99 (dollars in thousands)	12/31/98
Current (CAE 2,507 and 2,313)	4,523	4,392	Current (STD 0 and 45)	642	383
Property and equipment	1,690	1,775	Deferred income taxes	297	562
Investments	2,165	2,911	Stockholders' equity*	7,440	8,133
TOTAL	8,379	9,078	TOTAL	8,379	9,078

* $0.10 par common; 10,000,000 authorized; 1,985,608 and 1,975,454 issued and outstanding.

RECENT QUARTERS / PRIOR-YEAR RESULTS

	Quarter End	Revenue ($000)	Earnings ($000)	EPS ($)	Prior-Year Revenue ($000)	Prior-Year Earnings ($000)	Prior-Year EPS ($)
Q3	09/30/2000	1,504	117	0.06	1,363	22	0.01
Q2	06/30/2000	1,374	49	0.02	1,319	(114)	(0.06)
Q1	03/31/2000	1,780	164	0.08	1,588	28	0.01
Q4	12/31/99	1,413	41	0.02	1,636	30	0.02
	SUM	6,071	371	0.19	5,905	(33)	(0.02)

RECENT EVENTS

In **March 2000** AutoData Systems began shipping AutoData Scannable Office automated data collection software. Scannable Office decreases data collection activities by up to 85 percent through unique automation technology. Integrating closely with the Microsoft Office suite, Scannable Office uses Microsoft Word to create scannable forms, and automatically maps data in Excel, Access, or any ODBC data source. By leveraging users' knowledge of Microsoft applications, a typically steep learning curve is significantly reduced. In AutoData's newest Scannable Office automated data collection software that began shipping the end of March, the unit introduced its new SmartMemory technology that learns different hand-print styles. In **June** August Technology Inc., a company for which Electro-Sensors provided seed capital, successfully completed its initial public offering. Electro-Sensors held 1.5 million shares of August Technology. In **September** AutoData Systems released AutoData Survey Plus 2000 survey-creation software, version 3, which provides users with an extremely simple way to create scannable surveys, scan and verify data, and create quick reports with the click of a button. **Sept. 30:** Sales in the production monitoring divisions continued to increase in the third quarter. Customers appeared to have worked through their Year 2000 issues and were increasing their investing in plant and equipment improvements. Sales by the AutoData division also increased, a result of the introduction of two new products in 2000.

OFFICERS
Bradley D. Slye
Chairman and President
Peter R. Peterson
Secretary

DIRECTORS
Joseph A. Marino
Cardia Inc., Burnsville, MN
Geoffrey W. Miller
Amsan MN Inc., St. Paul
Peter R. Peterson
Bradley D. Slye
John S. Strom
retired

MAJOR SHAREHOLDERS
Peter R. Peterson, 42.5%
Minnetonka, MN
Jean C. Slattery, 8.4%
Minneapolis
Electro-Sensors Inc. ESOP, 7.2%
All officers and directors as a group (6 persons), 47.7%

SIC CODE
3577 Computer peripheral equipment, nec
3625 Relays and industrial controls
3823 Process control instruments
3824 Fluid meters and counting devices

MISCELLANEOUS
TRANSFER AGENT AND REGISTAR:
Firstar Trust Co., Milwaukee
TRADED: Nasdaq SmallCap Market
SYMBOL: ELSE
STOCKHOLDERS: 550
EMPLOYEES: 42
PART TIME: 2
IN MINNESOTA: 42
GENERAL COUNSEL:
Fredrikson & Byron P.A., Minneapolis
AUDITORS:
Schweitzer Karon & Bremer, Minneapolis
INC: MN-1968
ANNUAL MEETING: April

SUBSIDIARIES, DIVISIONS, AFFILIATES
Electro-Sensors Controls Division

Drive Control Systems

AutoData Systems

Microflame Inc.
6111 Blue Circle Dr.
Minnetonka, MN 55343
612/935-3777

ESI Investment Co.

Senstar Corp.

TWO-YEAR QUARTERLY HIGH-LOW STOCK PRICES

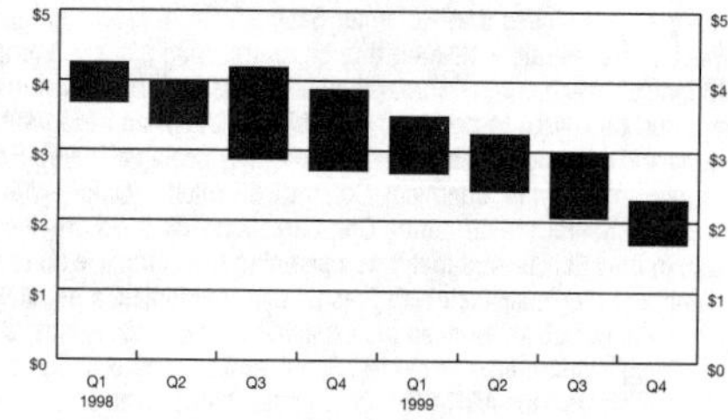

Endocardial Solutions Inc.

1350 Energy Ln., Suite 110, St. Paul, MN 55108
Tel: 651/644-7890 Fax: 651/644-7897 Web site: http://www.endocardial.com

Endocardial Solutions Inc. designs, develops, and manufactures a minimally invasive diagnostic system, the EnSite catheter and clinical workstation, that diagnoses, within the span of a few heartbeats, a potentially fatal abnormal heart rhythm called tachycardia. The company has conducted clinical trials of the EnSite System in Europe and is continuing clinical trials in the United States under an investigational device exemption from the FDA. The company is selling the EnSite System through its distributor, Medtronic Inc. The system is designed to enable electrophysiologists to rapidly and precisely locate the multiple, unpredictable points of origin of complex tachycardia. It applies proprietary mathematical algorithms to compute more than 3,000 points of electrical activity within a heart chamber and produce a high-resolution, real-time, three-dimensional color display of that activity. The company's strategy is to establish the EnSite System as the leading cardiac mapping tool for diagnosing complex tachycardia in the more than 700 electrophysiology laboratories in the United States, and others in Europe and Japan.

EARNINGS HISTORY *

Year Ended Dec 31	Operating Revenue/Sales (dollars in thousands)	Net Earnings	Return on Revenue (percent)	Return on Equity	Net Earnings (dollars per share†)	Cash Dividend	Market Price Range
1999	9,597	(11,729)	NM	NM	(1.23)	—	11.75–7.44
1998	1,950	(14,685)	NM	NM	(1.63)	—	14.75–4.13
1997	0	(8,555)	NM	(37.6)	(1.21)	—	15.00–6.88
1996 ¶	0	(6,481)	NM	NM	(6.30)	—	
1995	0	(4,734)	NM	NM	(4.63)	—	

* Prior to 1998, Endocardial Solutions was a development-stage company.
† Trading began March 19, 1997.
¶ Pro forma loss per share: ($1.12).

BALANCE SHEET

Assets	12/31/99 (dollars in thousands)	12/31/98
Current (CAE 1,770 and 654)	14,230	11,329
Furniture and equipment	2,982	2,274
Deposits	40	82
Patents	27	43
Software development costs	299	
TOTAL	17,578	13,728

Liabilities	12/31/99 (dollars in thousands)	12/31/98
Current	4,531	2,408
Long-term debt	3,500	
Capital lease obligations	1,064	812
Deferred revenue	229	43
Stockholders' equity*	8,254	10,463
TOTAL	17,578	13,728

* $0.01 par common; 40,000,000 authorized; 10,185,183 and 9,011,762 issued and outstanding.

RECENT QUARTERS / PRIOR-YEAR RESULTS

	Quarter End	Revenue ($000)	Earnings ($000)	EPS ($)	Prior-Year Revenue ($000)	Prior-Year Earnings ($000)	Prior-Year EPS ($)
Q3	09/30/2000	3,097	(2,791)	(0.23)	3,528	(2,527)	(0.25)
Q2	06/30/2000	3,737	(3,137)	(0.31)	1,719	(3,750)	(0.41)
Q1	03/31/2000	3,360	(2,502)	(0.25)	1,293	(2,913)	(0.32)
Q4	12/31/99	3,057	(2,538)	(0.25)	822	(2,746)	(0.30)
	SUM	13,251	(10,969)	(1.03)	7,362	(11,936)	(1.30)

RECENT EVENTS

In **December 1999** the FDA cleared release of an upgrade for use in the company's software product, the EnSite 3000 System for diagnostic mapping of complex arrhythmias. The upgrade was designed to enhance both performance and navigational ability. **Dec. 31**: Fourth-quarter revenue results were lower than analysts' estimates. "The selling process for U.S. hospitals has taken longer than originally expected," said CEO Bullock. In **January 2000** a fluke mechanical problem at its St. Paul plant led to a chemical leak and ventilation failure that sent nine poeple to the hospital. The company was back in production the next day. In **March** Salomon Smith Barney initiated coverage on Endocardial with a SPECULATIVE BUY rating, with a price target of $22—saying that the company's technology had a leg up on competitors, and that the number of arrythmia-mapping procedures would approach 200,000 by 2001. In **May** the Health Care Financing Administration (HCFA) assigned the company's EnSite catheter "pass-through Medicare reimbursement status" under HCFA's new outpatient reimbursement system—establishing a process for separate reimbursement of the EnSite catheter when used in outpatient procedures. In **June** the FDA cleared release of Clarity, an upgraded version of the company's software product for use in the EnSite 3000 System for diagnostic mapping of complex arrhythmias. The company also received clearance from its notified body for the European release of Clarity. The company closed a $12.7 million private placement of 2.03 million shares of common stock of the company to institutional investors through U.S. Bancorp Piper Jaffray as agent. Proceeds from the financing were to be used for general working capital, including expenses associated with U.S. market introduction, clinical trials, and ongoing research and development. **Sept. 30**: Revenue for the three-month period was $3,097,137, which fell short of market expectations.

OFFICERS

James W. Bullock
President and CEO

Frank J. Callaghan
VP-Research/Development

Richard J. Omilanowicz
VP-Manufacturing

Michael D. Dale
VP-Sales/Marketing

Graydon E. Beatty
Chief Technical Officer

DIRECTORS

Graydon E. Beatty

James W. Bullock

James E. Daverman
Marquette Venture Partners, Deerfield, IL

Robert G. Hauser, M.D.
Minneapolis Heart Institute, Minneapolis

Rick Randall
Innovasive Devices Inc. (former)

Warren S. Watson
Medtronic EP Systems

MAJOR SHAREHOLDERS

Medtronic Asset Management Inc., 20.5%
Fridley, MN

James E. Daverman, 7.7%

Marquette Venture Partners II L.P., 7.5%
Deerfield, IL

Scudder Kemper Investments Inc., 6.5%
New York

Frontier Capital Management Co. Inc., 5.9%
Boston

All officers and directors as a group (11 persons), 15.2%

SIC CODE

3845 Electromedical equipment

MISCELLANEOUS

TRANSFER AGENT AND REGISTAR:
Wells Fargo Bank Minnesota N.A.,
South St. Paul, MN

TRADED: Nasdaq National Market

SYMBOL: ECSI

STOCKHOLDERS: 97

EMPLOYEES: 152

GENERAL COUNSEL:
Dorsey & Whitney PLLP, Minneapolis

AUDITORS:
Ernst & Young LLP, Minneapolis

INC: DE-1995

FOUNDED: 1992

ANNUAL MEETING: May

INVESTOR RELATIONS:
James Bullock

HUMAN RESOURCES:
Donna Shatava

RANKINGS

No. 186 CRM Public 200

PUB

TWO-YEAR QUARTERLY HIGH-LOW STOCK PRICES

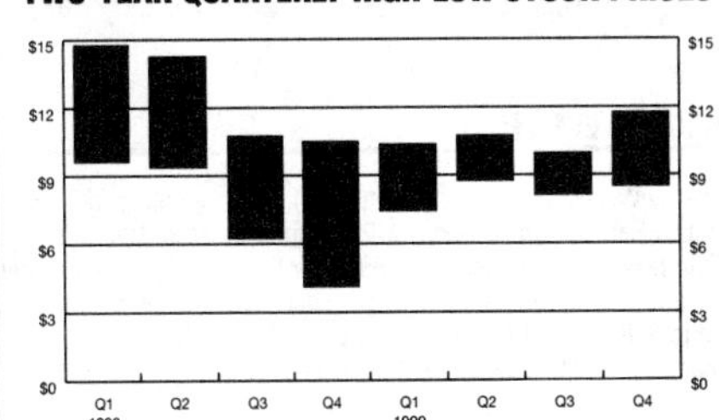

Energy West Inc.

One First Ave. S., P.O. Box 2229, Great Falls, MT 59401
Tel: 406/791-7500 Fax: 406/791-7560 Web site: http://www.ewst.com

Energy West Inc. is a regulated public utility, with certain non-utility operations conducted through its subsidiaries. The company's regulated utility operations involve the distribution and sale of natural gas to the public in the Great Falls, Mont., and Cody, Wyo., areas and sale of propane to the public through underground propane vapor systems in the Payson, Ariz., and Cascade, Mont., areas. In addition, since 1995 the company has distributed natural gas through an underground system in West Yellowstone, Mont., that is supplied by liquefied natural gas. Energy West conducts certain nonregulated nonutility operations through its three wholly owned subsidiaries, Energy West Propane Inc. (EWP), Energy West Resources Inc. (EWR), and Energy West Development Inc. (EWD). EWP is engaged in the distribution of retail and wholesale bulk propane in Wyoming, South Dakota, Nebraska, Colorado, Arizona, and Montana. EWR is involved in the marketing of gas and electricity and gas storage in Montana. EWD owns two real estate properties in Great Falls, Mont.

PUB

EARNINGS HISTORY

Year Ended Jun 30	Operating Revenue/Sales (dollars in thousands)	Net Earnings	Return on Revenue (percent)	Return on Equity	Net Earnings (dollars per share)	Cash Dividend	Market Price Range
2000	72,196	1,297	1.8	9.3	0.53	0.49	9.44–7.00
1999	53,461	1,587	3.0	11.7	0.66	0.47	10.63–8.25
1998	43,064	1,520	3.5	11.9	0.64	0.45	9.13–8.25
1997	38,215	1,293	3.4	10.8	0.55	0.43	8.75–7.88
1996	31,318	1,267	4.0	11.1	0.55	0.41	9.75–7.75

BALANCE SHEET

Assets	06/30/00 (dollars in thousands)	06/30/99
Current (CAE 112 and 225)	16,287	11,429
Property, plant, and equipment	31,804	29,372
Notes receivable	162	188
Deferred charges	3,293	3,212
TOTAL	51,547	44,201

Liabilities	06/30/00 (dollars in thousands)	06/30/99
Current (STD 5,300 and 431)	14,841	7,230
Deferred income taxes	3,699	3,565
Deferred investment tax credits	419	440
Contributions in aid of construction	994	939
Customer advances for construction	659	659
Postretirement obligation	233	647
Regulatory liability for income taxes	109	123
Deferred gain	142	165
Other	95	62
Long-term obligations	16,395	16,840
Stockholders' equity*	13,962	13,532
TOTAL	51,547	44,201

* $0.15 par common; 3,500,000 authorized; 2,475,435 and 2,433,740 issued and outstanding.

RECENT QUARTERS / **PRIOR-YEAR RESULTS**

	Quarter End	Revenue ($000)	Earnings ($000)	EPS ($)	Prior-Year Revenue ($000)	Prior-Year Earnings ($000)	Prior-Year EPS ($)
Q4	06/30/2000	16,618	22	0.01	9,536	231	0.10
Q3	03/31/2000	23,861	1,441	0.59	17,749	1,290	0.53
Q2	12/31/99	19,709	500	0.20	17,115	751	0.31
Q1	09/30/99	12,008	(666)	(0.27)	9,061	(685)	(0.28)
	SUM	72,196	1,297	0.53	53,461	1,587	0.65

RECENT EVENTS

Energy West's Montana Division(EWM) had an application for recovery of $3 million of gas costs pending before the Montana Public Service Commission (MPSC). In **December 1999** the MPSC provided interim relief in the amount of $1.5 million. In **February 2000** the Montana Consumer Counsel (MCC) intervened in this proceeding and recommended that the MPSC consider adjusting the recovery of gas costs contained in the company's application. Recommended cost disallowances amounted to $686,113 spread over three years. In **March** EWM said that it was intending to vigorously contest the recommendations made by the MCC. **June 30:** The decrease in fiscal-year 2000 earnings was primarily due to extremely warm winter conditions in Montana, Arizona, and Wyoming, affecting all of the company's operating divisions, and a *continued on page 221*

OFFICERS

Larry D. Geske
Chairman, President, and CEO

John C. Allen
VP-Human Resources, Corp. Counsel, Sec.

Sheila M. Rice
VP-Marketing/Communications

Edward J. Bernica
EVP, CFO, and COO

William J. Quast
VP, Treasurer, and Asst. Secretary

Tim A. Good
VP and Mgr.-Energy Mktg./Wholesale

Lynn F. Hardin
Asst. VP-Gas Supply/Trading

Earl L. Terwilliger Jr.
Asst. VP and Division Mgr.-Great Falls

James E. Morin
Asst. VP-Commercial/Industrial Marketing

Steven G. Powers
Asst. VP and Mgr.-Energy West Resources

Douglas R. Mann
VP and Mgr.-EnergyWest's Retail

DIRECTORS

Andrew I. Davidson
D.A. Davidson and Co. Financial Services

David A. Flitner
Flitner Ranch and Hideout Adventures Inc.

Larry D. Geske

Thomas N. McGowen Jr.
attorney, Hamilton, MT

G. Montgomery Mitchell
Stone and Webster Management Consultants

George Ruff
Qwest (retired)

Richard Schulte
Schulte Associates LLC

Dean South
Heritage Propane Corp. (retired)

MAJOR SHAREHOLDERS

Ian B. Davidson, 19.5%
Great Falls, MT

Turkey Vulture Fund XIII Ltd., 5%
Mentor, OH

All officers and directors as a group (16 persons), 27.7%

SIC CODE

1382 Oil and gas exploration services

4924 Natural gas distribution

MISCELLANEOUS

TRANSFER AGENT AND REGISTAR:
Davidson Trust Co., Great Falls, MT

TRADED: Nasdaq National Market

SYMBOL: EWST

STOCKHOLDERS: 1,600

EMPLOYEES: 131

GENERAL COUNSEL:
John C. Allen

AUDITORS:
Ernst & Young LLP, Salt Lake City

INC: MT-1909

ANNUAL MEETING:
November

SUBSIDIARIES, DIVISIONS, AFFILIATES

Energy West -Wyoming
2320 Mountain View Dr.
Cody, WY 82414
307/587-4281
Tim Good

Energy West-Montana
Bill Quast

Energy West Development Inc.
One River Park Tower
Great Falls, MT 59403
406/791-7500
Larry D. Geske

Energy West Propane Inc.

Energy West Propane Wyoming

Energy West-Arizona

Energy West Propane-Arizona

Energy West Propane-Montana

Energy West Resources Inc.

TWO-YEAR QUARTERLY HIGH-LOW STOCK PRICES

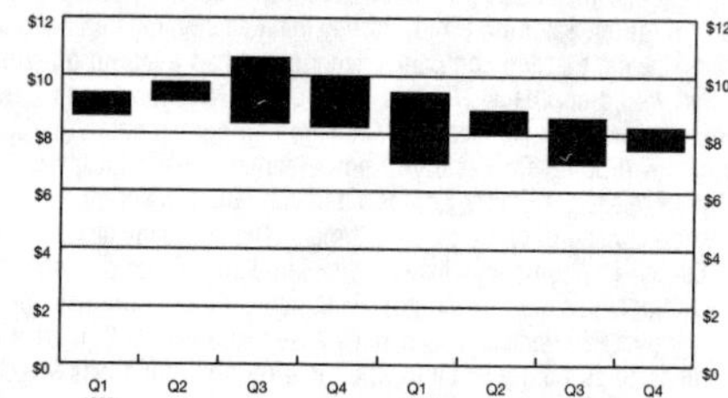

Entegris Inc.

3500 Lyman Blvd., Chaska, MN 55318
Tel: 952/556-3131 Fax: 952/556-1880 Web site: http://www.entegris.com

Entegris Inc., the result of a merger of strengths between Fluoroware Inc. and EMPAK, manufactures microelectronics materials-management, and critical fluid-management products for the data-storage, semiconductor, flat-panel, pharmaceutical, and chemical-processing industries. Its Integrated Shipping Systems business manufactures wafer and disk shipping systems for the semiconductor and disk drive industries, respectively. Entegris is an ISO 9001-registered firm with manufacturing facilities in the United States, Germany, Japan, Singapore, Malaysia, and South Korea. Through strategic alliances with Metron Technology, Marubeni, and other distributors, Entegris offers customer support on six continents.

EARNINGS HISTORY

Year Ended Aug 31	Operating Revenue/Sales (dollars in thousands)	Net Earnings	Return on Revenue (percent)	Return on Equity	Net Earnings (dollars per share*)	Cash Dividend	Market Price Range
1999	241,952	5,729	2.4	4.6	0.10	—	
1998	266,591	13,083	4.9	11.0	0.22	—	
1997	277,290	16,934	6.1	15.5	0.28	—	
1996 †	271,037	28,217	10.4	34.1	0.46	—	
1995 ¶	193,284	23,089	11.9	NM	0.36	—	

* Shares did not begin trading until July 11, 2000.
† Income figures for 1996 include gain of $455,000/$0.01 from discontinued operations.
¶ Income figures for 1995 include loss of $1,503,000/($0.02) from discontinued operations.

BALANCE SHEET

Assets	05/31/00 (dollars in thousands)	08/31/99	Liabilities	05/31/00 (dollars in thousands)	08/31/99
Current (CAE 33,247 and 16,411)	141,728	105,365	Current (STD 6,476 and 6,566)	62,868	56,505
Property, plant, and equipment	110,529	117,624	Long-term debt	44,597	48,023
Investments in affiliates	14,999	10,421	Capital lease obligations	3,489	5,807
Intangibles	8,064	6,318	Deferred taxes	8,643	6,139
Investments in marketable securities	1,148	860	Minority interest	4,265	907
Other	1,422	1,476	Stockholders' equity*	154,028	124,683
TOTAL	277,890	242,064	TOTAL	277,890	242,064

* $0.01 par common; 200,000,000 authorized; 36,808,784 and 18,354,344 issued and outstanding.

RECENT QUARTERS / PRIOR-YEAR RESULTS

	Quarter End	Revenue ($000)	Earnings ($000)	EPS ($)	Prior-Year Revenue ($000)	Prior-Year Earnings ($000)	Prior-Year EPS ($)
Q4	08/26/2000	95,812	15,143	0.24	69,777	3,197	0.05
Q3	05/31/2000	90,991	12,319	0.21	60,585	2,432	0.04
Q2	02/28/2000	84,846	11,068	0.19	60,124	1,750	0.03
Q1	11/30/99	71,816	12,045	0.20	51,467	(1,650)	(0.03)
	SUM	343,465	50,575	0.84	241,953	5,729	0.10

CURRENT: NOTE: Quarterly data is pro forma to give retroactive effect to the reclassification of redeemable common shares at the IPO. Q4 earnings include extraordinary loss of $1.149 million/($0.02) on extinguishment of debt.

RECENT EVENTS

In **December 1999** the company's Galtek SG Series valve received the 1999 Editors' Choice Best Product award from Semiconductor International magazine. One of 20 products selected, Entegris' Galtek valve—the smallest 1/4-inch orifice valve featuring all-perfluoroalkoxy (PFA) wetted surfaces—was recognized for maintaining industry flow capacity standards despite its small footprint. In **January 2000** Entegris received recognition for excellence in 300 mm front opening unified pod (FOUP) product performance and related technical support—from Semiconductor Leading Edge Technologies Inc. (SELETE). In **March** Entegris Inc. (proposed Nasdaq NMS: ENTG) filed a registration statement with the SEC for an initial public offering of 13 million shares of common stock. Entegris was offering 8.6 million shares and certain shareholders were selling 4.4 million shares. The offering price was expected to be between $15 and $17. Banc of America Securities LLC was to serve as the lead underwriter for the offering. The net proceeds to Entegris were to be used to repay indebtedness and for working capital and other general corporate purposes. In **April** Entegris introduced the industry's first reduced-pitch front-opening shipping box (FOSB) for 300 mm wafer handling. Entegris announced the development of "SpaceSaver" fluid handling components made of a revolutionary new material, DuPont Teflon PFA HP Plus. With the excellent chemical and flurorsurfactant resistance and flex life of Teflon PFA HP Plus, Entegris' new "SpaceSaver" fittings and tubing can withstand the most aggressive chemistries used in the manufacture of today's advanced semiconductors. In addition, the *continued on page 221*

OFFICERS

Daniel R. Quernemoen
Chairman

Stan Geyer
CEO

James E. Dauwalter
President and COO

John Goodman
Chief Technology Officer

John D. Villas
CFO

DIRECTORS

James A. Bernards
Brightstone Capital Ltd., Minneapolis

Robert J. Boehlke
KLA-Tencor Corporation

Mark A. Bongard
Emplast Inc.

James E. Dauwalter

Stan Geyer

Delmer M. Jensen

Gary F. Klingl
Pillsbury (retired)

Roger D. McDaniel

Daniel R. Quernemoen

MAJOR SHAREHOLDERS

WCB Holdings LLC/Mark A. Bongard, 29.3%
Chaska, MN

Entegris ESOP, 26.7%

James E. Dauwalter, 8.2%

All officers and directors as a group (9 persons), 16.7%

SIC CODE

3089 Plastics products, nec

MISCELLANEOUS

TRANSFER AGENT AND REGISTAR:
Wells Fargo Bank Minnesota N.A., South St. Paul, MN

TRADED: Nasdaq National Market

SYMBOL: ENTG

STOCKHOLDERS: 83

EMPLOYEES: 1,600

IN MINNESOTA: 900

GENERAL COUNSEL:
Dorsey & Whitney PLLP, Minneapolis

AUDITORS:
Latham & Watkins, Chicago

INVESTOR RELATIONS:
Heide Erickson

RANKINGS

No. 15 CRM Performance 100

PUB

FSF Financial Corporation

201 Main St. S., Hutchinson, MN 55350
Tel: 320/234-4500 Fax: 320/234-4542 Web site: http://www.ffhh.com

FSF Financial Corp. is the holding company for **First Federal fsb** and **Insurance Planners**. First Federal Bank offers a full line of financial services including banking, mortgage, insurance and investments. Banking products include commercial and consumer loans and deposits, offered through First Federal bank in 11 offices in the Mpls/St. Paul metro and central Minnesota areas. **Homeowners Mortgage Corp.**, a subsidiary of First Federal Bank, offers mortgage and construction products from their Vadnais Heights and Hastings offices. **Firstate Investments**, a subsidiary of First Federal Bank, offers full investment sales and services. **Insurance Planners**, a subsidiary of FSF Financial Corporation, offers a full line of insurance products and services for residential and business coverage in Hutchinson and Buffalo, servicing all banking markets.

EARNINGS HISTORY

Year Ended Sept 30	Operating Revenue/Sales (dollars in thousands)	Net Earnings	Return on Revenue (percent)	Return on Equity	Net Earnings (dollars per share)	Cash Dividend	Market Price Range
1999	34,679	2,505	7.2	5.9	0.94	0.50	15.75–11.75
1998	32,250	3,030	9.4	7.1	1.14	0.50	20.94–13.38
1997	28,825	3,124	10.8	7.2	1.06	0.50	21.00–12.75
1996 *	24,598	1,668	6.8	3.5	0.48	0.50	13.50–11.38
1995 †	20,206	2,625	13.0	4.6	0.67	0.38	13.13–7.50

* Income figures for 1996 include pretax charge of $1,030,000 for SAIF special assessment.
† Income figures for 1995 include extraordinary gain of $382,000/$0.10, cumulative effect of change in accounting for securities available for sale.

BALANCE SHEET

Assets	09/30/99 (dollars in thousands)	09/30/98	Liabilities	09/30/99 (dollars in thousands)	09/30/98
Cash, equiv	19,265	22,597	Deposits	231,651	226,542
Securities afs, eqty	19,284	19,459	FHLB borrowings	140,967	144,177
Securities afs, mort	15,979	16,574	Advances from borrowers	669	819
Securities afs, debt	12,794	3,010			
Securities htm, debt	19,937	24,412	Other	2,482	2,176
Securities htm, mort	27,587	36,418	Stockholders' equity*	42,325	42,518
Loans held for sale	5,334	2,672			
Loan receivable	278,290	280,603	TOTAL	418,094	416,232
Accrued interest	3,328	3,089			
Premises, eqt	5,314	4,111			
Foreclosed real estate	323	502			
Other	10,659	2,785			
TOTAL	418,094	416,232			

* $0.10 par common; 10,000,000 authorized; 4,501,277 and 4,501,277 issued and outstanding, less 1,695,390 and 1,603,663 treasury shares.

RECENT QUARTERS / PRIOR-YEAR RESULTS

	Quarter End	Revenue ($000)	Earnings ($000)	EPS ($)	Prior-Year Revenue ($000)	Prior-Year Earnings ($000)	Prior-Year EPS ($)
Q4	09/30/2000	10,377	872	0.39	8,734	445	0.17
Q3	06/30/2000	9,542	954	0.41	8,643	525	0.20
Q2	03/31/2000	9,053	856	0.35	8,515	693	0.26
Q1	12/31/99	8,730	821	0.32	8,787	842	0.32
	SUM	37,702	3,503	1.46	34,679	2,505	0.94

RECENT EVENTS

In **March 2000** the corporation completed the repurchase of the 260,000 shares, as had been authorized by its board of directors in September 1999. The shares were purchased at an average price of $12.31. In **April** the board authorized the repurchase of another 250,000 shares (10 percent) of the corporation's common stock. **Sept. 30:** FSF achieved record earnings for the fourth quarter and fiscal year. Net interest margin for fiscal 2000 increased to 3.21 percent from 2.74 percent for fiscal 1999. "The increase in net interest income, expense control, and our continued stock repurchases all contributed to the increase in net income for the quarter and fiscal 2000," noted CEO Glas. "The asset diversification that we began more than a year ago was the primary reason for the increase in net income, as well as our efforts to contain non-interest expense." The regular quarterly dividend of 15 cents per share of common stock to stockholders of record on Oct. 31, payable on Nov. 15, represented an increase of 2.5 cents per share over the amount paid in August 2000.

OFFICERS

Donald A. Glas
CEO

George B. Loban
President

Richard H. Burgart
CFO and Secretary

DIRECTORS

Richard H. Burgart
James J. Caturia
Jerome R. Dempsey
Donald A. Glas
Sever B. Knutson
George B. Loban
Roger R. Stearns

MAJOR SHAREHOLDERS

First Federal fsb ESOP, 12.9%

Security Bancshares Co., 7.2%
Glencoe, MN

Brandes Investment Partners L.P., 7.1%
San Diego

George B. Loban, 6.7%

Donald A. Glas, 6.6%

All officers and directors as a group (7 persons), 20.9%

SIC CODE

6712 Bank holding companies

MISCELLANEOUS

TRANSFER AGENT AND REGISTAR:
Computer Share, Denver

TRADED: Nasdaq National Market

SYMBOL: FFHH

STOCKHOLDERS: 511

EMPLOYEES: 174

PART TIME: 48

IN MINNESOTA: 126

GENERAL COUNSEL:
Mackall, Crounse & Moore PLC, Minneapolis
Malizia, Spidi, Sloane & Fisch P.C., Washington, D.C.

AUDITORS:
Bertram Cooper & Co. LLP, Waseca, MN

INC: MN-1994

ANNUAL MEETING: January

HUMAN RESOURCES: Nancy Albrecht

RANKINGS

No. 127 CRM Public 200

SUBSIDIARIES, DIVISIONS, AFFILIATES

First Federal fsb

201 Main St. S.
Hutchinson, MN 55350
320/234-4500

905 Hwy. 15
S. Frontage Rd.
Hutchinson, MN 55350
320/234-4563

305 10th Ave. S.
Buffalo, MN 55313
320/682-3035

6505 Cahill Ave. E.
Inver Grove Heights, MN 55076
612/455-1553

200 Hwy. 5
East Frontage Rd.
P.O. Box 287
Waconia, MN 55387
612/442-2141

1320 S. Frontage Rd.
Hastings, MN 55033
612/437-6169

14994 Glazier Ave.
Apple Valley, MN 55124
612/432-6840

1002 Greeley Ave.
Glencoe, MN 55336
320/864-5541

501 N. Sibley Ave.
P.O. Box 577
Litchfield, MN 55355
320/693-2861

113 Waite Ave. S.
P.O. Box 641
Waite Park, MN 56387
320/656-1133

122 E. Second St.
P.O. Box 424
Winthrop, MN 55396
507/647-5356

Firstate Services Inc.

Insurance Planners

Homeowners Mortgage Corp.

TWO-YEAR QUARTERLY HIGH-LOW STOCK PRICES

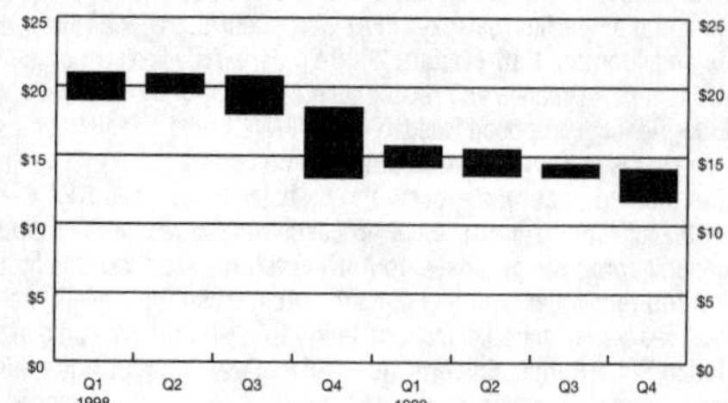

FSI International Inc.

322 Lake Hazeltine Dr., Chaska, MN 55318
Tel: 952/448-5440 Fax: 952/448-1300 Web site: http://www.fsi-intl.com

FSI International Inc. produces automated processing equipment used by microelectronics manufacturers for processing silicon wafers. The company develops, manufactures, markets, and services spray, vapor phase, and dry gas surface conditioning systems, and photoresist processing cluster tools for use in the fabrication of advanced semiconductor integrated circuits. FSI International's customers include semiconductor manufacturers located throughout North America, Europe, Japan, and the Far East.

EARNINGS HISTORY *

Year Ended Aug	Operating Revenue/Sales (dollars in thousands)	Net Earnings	Return on Revenue (percent)	Return on Equity	Net Earnings (dollars per share†)	Cash Dividend	Market Price Range
1999 ¶	113,512	(30,634)	(27.0)	(17.4)	(1.32)	—	14.31–3.50
1998	161,695	(21,952)	(13.6)	(10.7)	(0.96)	—	23.63–5.81
1997	162,888	4,640	2.8	2.1	0.21	—	20.19–10.00
1996 #	233,239	28,242	12.1	12.9	1.27	—	38.50–9.63
1995	169,891	20,533	12.1	11.0	1.18	—	35.00–8.63

* Revenue figures are restated to segregate operations of Chemical Management Division, divested in fourth quarter of fiscal 1999. Income figures include the following per-share amounts from discontinued operations: $0.41, ($0.02), $0.35, $0.31, and $0.00—in 1999 through 1995, respectively.
† Per-share amounts restated to reflect 2-for-1 stock split effected June 19, 1995.
¶ Income figures for 1999 include after-tax loss of $6.423 million/($0.28) from discontinued operations; and after-tax gain of $15.907 million/$0.69 on their disposal.
\# Income figures for 1996 include pretax charges of $1.5 million for cost-control measures.

BALANCE SHEET

Assets	08/28/99 (dollars in thousands)	08/29/98	Liabilities	08/28/99 (dollars in thousands)	08/29/98
Current	158,961	204,463	Current	66,388	47,306
(CAE 62,326 and 72,789)			(STD 30,060 and 65)		
Ppty, plant, eqt	64,091	66,139	Long-term debt	3	42,064
Investment: affiliates	14,178	15,408	Stkhldrs' equity*	176,312	204,376
			TOTAL	242,703	293,747
Deposits and other	5,473	3,440			
Deferred tax		4,296			
TOTAL	242,703	293,747			

* No par common; 50,000,000 authorized; 23,391,953 and 23,034,562 issued and outstanding.

RECENT QUARTERS / **PRIOR-YEAR RESULTS**

	Quarter End	Revenue ($000)	Earnings ($000)	EPS ($)	Prior-Year Revenue ($000)	Prior-Year Earnings ($000)	Prior-Year EPS ($)
Q4	08/26/2000	75,335	5,474	0.22	32,675	4,405	0.19
Q3	05/27/2000	67,747	3,695	0.15	37,674	(20,387)	(0.88)
Q2	02/26/2000	45,798	(3,087)	(0.12)	19,147	(7,574)	(0.33)
Q1	11/27/99	30,907	(10,624)	(0.44)	24,016	(7,078)	(0.31)
	SUM	219,787	(4,542)	(0.20)	113,512	(30,634)	(1.32)

CURRENT: Q1 earnings include pretax charge of $6.37 million for R&D write-off; and after-tax loss of $400,000/($0.01) from sale of discontinued operations.
PRIOR YEAR: Q4 earnings include net gain of $14,017,000/$0.60 from discontinued operations and their disposal. Q3 earnings include loss of $1,992,000/($0.09) from discontinued operations; and charge of $16.6 million/($0.71) for valuation reserve against deferred tax assets. Q2 earnings include loss of $1,299,000/($0.06) from discontinued operations. Q1 earnings include loss of $1,241,000/($0.05) from discontinued operations.

RECENT EVENTS

In **December 1999** company co-founder Joel Elftmann said that he was retiring as president and CEO. Donald S. Mitchell, former president of Air Products Electronic Chemicals, was named as his replacement. In **January 2000** FSI announced that SEMICONDUCTOR300, a joint venture of Infineon and Motorola, had placed an order for a POLARIS 3500 Microlithography Cluster to be used in the 300-mm pilot line at SC300's Dresden, Germany, development fab. When FSI agreed to add a two-year independent director evaluation (TIDE) provision to its share rights plan, EQSF Advisers Inc. agreed to withdraw its shareholder proposal regarding the plan. In **February** follow-on orders were received from an Asian customer for the purchase of four 200-mm ZETA Surface Conditioning Systems to be used for photoresist stripping applications in technologies at 0.18 (mu)m and below. (The ZETA System has an average selling price that ranges from $1.6 million to $2.0 million.) FSI received received a follow-on orders for five POLARIS Microlithography Clusters from a major U.S. semiconductor manufacturer, who will use the systems for resist processing applications to manufacture advanced analog devices. (The POLARIS Cluster ranges in price from $1.2 to $2.5 million depending on the model and its configuration.) **Feb. 26:** In the first half of fiscal 2000, FSI received orders for more than 20 MERCURY Surface Conditioning Systems from multiple Japanese customers—unprecedented booking activity in Japan. In **March** a Taiwan foundry customer placed orders totaling near- *continued on page 221*

OFFICERS
Joel A. Elftmann
Chairman
Donald S. Mitchell
President and CEO
Benno G. Sand
EVP-Bus. Devel./Investor Relations
Dr. Benjamin J. Sloan
EVP and Pres.-Microlithography Division
Mark A. Ahmann
VP-Administration
Arnie DeWitt
VP-Information Systems
Dean Duffy
VP-Sales
John C. Ely
Pres.-Surface Conditioning Division
Patricia Hollister
CFO
Luke R. Komarek
VP and General Counsel
Charles R. Wofford
Vice Chairman

DIRECTORS
James A. Bernards
Brightstone Capital Ltd., Minneapolis
Joel A. Elftmann
Thomas D. (Tommy) George, Ph.D.
Motorola Inc. (retired)
Terrence W. Glarner
West Concord Ventures Inc., Minneapolis
Donald S. Mitchell
Charles R. Wofford
Texas Instruments Inc. (retired)

MAJOR SHAREHOLDERS
EQSF Advisers Inc., 14.6%
New York
State of Wisconsin Investment Board, 10.8%
Madison, WI
All officers and directors as a group (14 persons), 6.8%

SIC CODE
3559 Special industry machinery, nec

MISCELLANEOUS
TRANSFER AGENT AND REGISTAR:
Harris Trust and Savings Bank, Chicago
TRADED: Nasdaq National Market

SYMBOL: FSII
STOCKHOLDERS: 1,294
EMPLOYEES: 870
GENERAL COUNSEL:
Luke Komarek, Gen. Counsel
AUDITORS:
KPMG LLP, Minneapolis
INC: MN-1973
ANNUAL MEETING:
January
INVESTOR RELATIONS:
Benno Sand

RANKINGS
No. 84 CRM Public 200
No. 5 CRM Performance 100

SUBSIDIARIES, DIVISIONS, AFFILIATES

Semiconductor Systems Inc.
47003 Mission Falls Ct.
Fremont, CA 94539
510/683-8858
Ajit Rode

Metron Technology Corp.
1350 Old Bayshore Hwy.
Suite 360
Burlingame, CA 94010
415/373-1133
Ed Segal

m*FSI Ltd.
Kyohan Kudan Building 4F
5-10, Lidabashi I-Chome
Chiyoda-Ku, Tokyo 102, Japan
(81)(3)3265-9171
Hideki Kawai

TWO-YEAR QUARTERLY HIGH-LOW STOCK PRICES

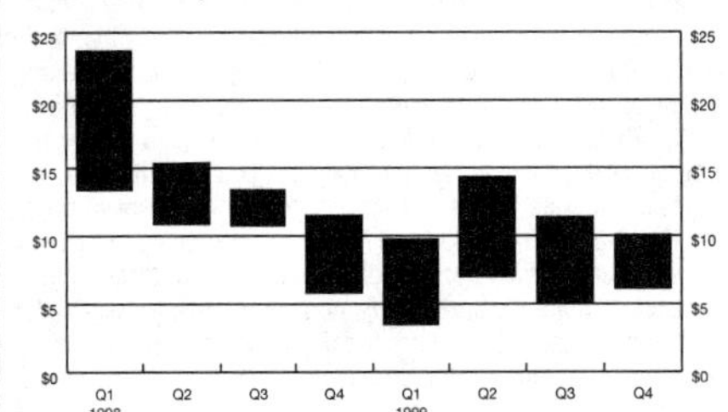

Famous Dave's of America Inc.

7657 Anagram Dr., Eden Prairie, MN 55344
Tel: 952/294-1300 Fax: 952/294-1301 Web site: http://www.famousdaves.com

Famous Dave's of America Inc. develops, owns, operates, and franchises barbecue restaurant and blues clubs. At Oct. 31, 2000, the company owned 33 locations, and franchised 7 additional units, in Minnesota, Wisconsin, Illinois, Iowa, Nebraska, Maryland, Virginia, and Utah. Famous Dave's has an additional 19 franchising development agreements to open units in Arizona, Nevada, Colorado, North Dakota, and South Dakota. Its menu features award-winning, barbecue and grilled meats, an ample selection of salads, side items, sandwiches, and unique desserts. Famous Dave's has won more than 100 regional and national awards for its barbecue meats and sauces.

EARNINGS HISTORY

Year Ended Dec	Operating Revenue/Sales	Net Earnings	Return on Revenue	Return on Equity	Net Earnings	Cash Dividend	Market Price Range
	(dollars in thousands)		(percent)		(dollars per share*)		
1999	47,575	(6,610)	(13.9)	(24.5)	(0.75)	—	3.75–1.69
1998 †	40,761	(4,829)	(11.8)	(14.6)	(0.55)	—	9.00–1.75
1997	18,202	(4,575)	(25.1)	(12.3)	(0.64)	—	21.13–6.63
1996	4,752	(707)	(14.9)	(3.7)	(0.23)	—	8.75–6.75
1995 ¶	482	(306)	(63.6)	(44.1)	(0.14)	—	

* Trading of common stock began Nov. 5, 1996.
† Fiscal 1998 was 53 weeks. Income figures include loss of $120,000/($0.01), cumulative effect of accounting change.
¶ Company began generating revenue when the Linden Hills unit opened, in June 1995.

BALANCE SHEET

Assets	01/02/00	01/03/99	Liabilities	01/02/00	01/03/99
	(dollars in thousands)			(dollars in thousands)	
Current	4,069	5,307	Current	11,239	7,096
(CAE 1,712 and 1,951)			Capital lease	577	1,000
Property, equipment, leasehold improvements	38,742	35,576	Financing lease	4,500	
			Stkhldrs' equity*	27,010	33,073
Deposits	315	286	TOTAL	43,326	41,169
Debt-issuance costs	200				
TOTAL	43,326	41,169			

* $0.01 par common; 100,000,000 authorized; 9,055,000 and 8,838,000 issued and outstanding.

RECENT QUARTERS / **PRIOR-YEAR RESULTS**

	Quarter End	Revenue ($000)	Earnings ($000)	EPS ($)	Revenue ($000)	Earnings ($000)	EPS ($)
Q3	10/01/2000	18,994	624	0.07	12,693	137	0.02
Q2	07/02/2000	18,354	1,104	0.12	12,631	(292)	(0.03)
Q1	04/02/2000	15,091	51	0.01	10,388	(316)	(0.04)
Q4	01/02/2000	11,863	(6,139)	(0.69)	11,186	(274)	(0.03)
	SUM	64,302	(4,360)	(0.50)	46,898	(745)	(0.08)

RECENT EVENTS

In **December 1999**, after completing a strategic review of all operating properties, the company was able to put in place a more focused and effective unit economics and expansion strategy. "We will build a minimum of six new restaurants during 2000," said CEO O'Dowd. "Certain locations not in core market areas are being analyzed for franchising to strategic partners." Future openings were to be concentrated in larger markets such as the Chicago market, and may include acquired restaurants as well as newly developed restaurants. In **January 2000** Famous Dave's purchased four Red River Barbeque & Grille restaurants and in the Washington, D.C. area—three in Maryland and one in Virginia. In **February** Famous Dave's completed a $3.8 million supplemental mortgage financing with Franchise Finance Corp. of America, a national real estate investment trust. The 31st Famous Dave's restaurant opened at 99 Townline Road in Vernon Hills, a northern suburb of Chicago. The Famous Dave's Bar-B-Que that opened March 30 in Addison, Ill., marked the company's fourth location in Illinois and 32nd unit overall. In **May** a new franchised location opened in East Peoria, Ill. Two additional franchised units were set to open in June in Wisconsin Dells, Wis., and at the Minneapolis-St. Paul International Airport. The company obtained a financing commitment totaling $5.1 million from Franchise Corp. of America of Scottsdale, Ariz.—the country's premier single-tenant retail property finance company. Meanwhile, the newest location in Frederick, Md., was the third opening in the company's aggressive expansion plan for the Washington, D.C., area. In **July** the company's newest location, in Columbia, Md., was the fourth opening in an aggressive expansion plan for the Washington, D.C., area this year. With a five-unit development deal, successful restaurateur William "Willy" Theisen, who built the Godfather's Pizza chain into more than 900 locations, became part of Famous Dave's expansion program in the West. Its newest location in Lombard, Ill., was the company's fifth location in the Chicago area. Its sixth, in North Riverside, Ill., was Illinois' first introduction to the Famous Dave's shack-style restaurant. Famous Dave's also announced multi-unit development commitments for 12 franchise units in seven states in its first six months of franchising. (The company had already opened seven franchised locations.) New franchise development was to expand the company's presence in Nebraska, Iowa, and Illinois, and introduce Famous Dave's into Nevada, Colorado, Arizona, North Dakota, and South Dakota. **Oct. 1**: Record sales and earnings for the third fiscal quarter included a strong comparable-sales increase of 8.5 percent from prior year. New, higher-volume units contributed to an increase in restaurant average weekly volume for the third quarter of 22 percent. Famous Dave's and Hormel Foods Corp. (NYSE: HRL), Austin, Minn., *continued on page 222*

OFFICERS
David W. Anderson
Chairman
Martin J. O'Dowd
President and CEO
Doug Anderson
VP-Marketing
Mark Bartholomay
VP-Business Development
Michael Lister
VP-Operations
Christopher O'Donnell
VP-Training/Human Resources
Howard Polski
VP-Sales
Victor Salamone
VP-Development/Purchasing
Kenneth Stanecki
CFO

INVESTOR RELATIONS:
Ken Stanecki

RANKINGS
No. 113 CRM Public 200

DIRECTORS
David W. Anderson
Thomas J. Brosig
Richard L. Monfort
private investor
Martin J. O'Dowd

MAJOR SHAREHOLDERS
David W. Anderson, 19.6%
Jundt Associates Inc., 11.1%
Minneapolis
Special Situations Fund III L.P., 8.2%
New York
All officers and directors as a group (5 persons), 23.1%

SIC CODE
5812 Eating places

MISCELLANEOUS
TRANSFER AGENT AND REGISTAR:
Firstar Trust Co., Milwaukee
TRADED: Nasdaq National Market
SYMBOL: DAVE
STOCKHOLDERS: 411
EMPLOYEES: 1,300
GENERAL COUNSEL:
Maslon Edelman Borman & Brand PLLP, Minneapolis
AUDITORS:
Lund Koehler Cox & Arkema LLP, Minnetonka, MN
INC: MN-1994
ANNUAL MEETING: June

TWO-YEAR QUARTERLY HIGH-LOW STOCK PRICES

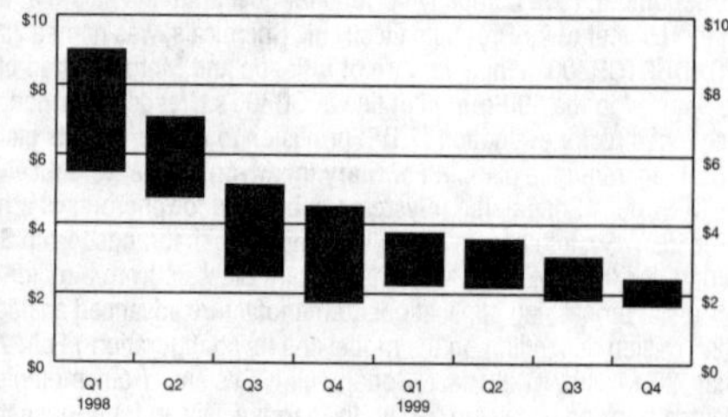

Fargo Electronics Inc.

6533 Flying Cloud Dr., Eden Prairie, MN 55344
Tel: 952/941-9470 Fax: 952/946-6890 Web site: http://www.fargo.com

Fargo Electronics Inc. is a developer, manufacture, and supplier of desktop systems and associated consumable supplies for the plastic card personalization and data encoding industry. The company has built a reputation for technological leadership in the industry by applying its engineering expertise and knowledge of printing and data encoding to incorporate state-of-the-art technologies into its card personalization systems. The ability to customize cards using these advanced technologies, coupled with the convenience of desktop systems, has created a market focused on the on-site production of high-quality, tamper-resistant, personalized identification cards that can be created quickly and economically. Fargo Electronics' customers use systems to create personalized cards for a wide variety of applications in various industries, including:

- corporate security and access;
- student identification and access;
- driver's licenses, government and military identification;
- transportation;
- recreation and gaming;
- retail loyalty and discount cards; and
- membership cards and passes.

The company distributes its products through a global network of distributors and resellers in 97 countries. Fargo Electronics has manufactured and sold more than 38,000 card personalization systems in the past five years.

EARNINGS HISTORY *

Year Ended Dec 31	Operating Revenue/Sales	Net Earnings	Return on Revenue	Return on Equity	Net Earnings	Cash Dividend	Market Price Range
	(dollars in thousands)		(percent)		(dollars per share†)		
1999 ¶	54,907	4,485	8.2	NM	(37.56)	—	
1998 #	47,647	(2,089)	(4.4)	NM	(0.98)	—	
1997	55,140	14,206	25.8	NM	0.66	—	
1996	50,317	13,301	26.4	NM	0.62	—	
1995	50,058	13,173	26.3	NM	0.61	—	

* The 1999 balance sheet is pro forma for the offering (unaudited).
† Trading began Feb. 10, 2000.
¶ EPS figure for 1999 is after $2.62 million in preferred dividends and $67 million accretion of convertible participating preferred stock.
# Income figures for 1998 include special pretax charge of $8.386 million in connection with February 1998 leveraged recapitalization. EPS is after $2.113 million in preferred dividends.

BALANCE SHEET

Assets	12/31/99	12/31/98	Liabilities	12/31/99	12/31/98
	(dollars in thousands)			(dollars in thousands)	
Current (CAE 1,508 and 1,103)	16,777	13,024	Current (STD 4,500 and 5,000)	8,503	7,840
Equipment and leasehold improvements	2,006	1,228	Notes payable, bank	21,462	48,500
			Note payable, stockholder		10,000
Deferred income taxes	29,169	31,519	Preferred equity		40,113
Deferred financing costs	331	762	Common equity*	18,353	(59,825)
			TOTAL	48,318	46,628
Other	34	96			
TOTAL	48,318	46,628			

* $0.01 par common; 12,500,000 authorized; 11,765,625 and 1,687,500 issued and outstanding.

RECENT QUARTERS / **PRIOR-YEAR RESULTS**

	Quarter End	Revenue ($000)	Earnings ($000)	EPS ($)	Revenue ($000)	Earnings ($000)	EPS ($)
Q3	09/30/2000	16,185	989	0.08	15,207	1,632	(37.40)
Q2	06/30/2000	14,060	598	0.05	13,873	1,292	0.38
Q1	03/31/2000	14,617	900	0.08	12,067	884	0.15
Q4	12/31/99	13,760	677	0.00	11,445	887	0.16
	SUM	58,622	3,164	0.21	52,592	4,695	(36.71)

CURRENT: Q3 earnings include extraordinary loss of $179,000/($0.02). Q1 earnings include extraordinary loss of $206,000/($0.03) for debt financing write-off.
PRIOR YEAR: Q3 EPS includes $67 million accretion of convertible participating preferred stock.

RECENT EVENTS

In **November 1999** the company registered an initial public offering (IPO), to be managed by BancBoston Robertson Stephens Inc., Prudential Securities, and Raymond James & Associates Inc. *continued on page 222*

OFFICERS

Gary R. Holland
President and CEO

Mark S. Andersen
VP-Sales

Gary A. Lenz
VP-Research/Development

I. Tony Haugen
VP-Mfg./Operations

Kathleen L. Phillips
VP-Marketing

Tom Platner
VP-Engineering/Mfg.

Jeffrey D. Upin
VP-Administration and General Counsel

DIRECTORS

Michael C. Child
TA Associates Inc., Boston

Everett V. Cox
St. Paul Venture Capital Inc., Eden Prairie, MN

William H. Gibbs
independent consultant/investor

Gary R. Holland

Kent O. Lillemoe
Cyberoptics Communications Corp.

Elaine A. Pullen
Trident International Inc.

MAJOR SHAREHOLDERS

TA Associates Group/Michael C. Child, 26.6%
Boston

St. Paul Venture Capital Inc./Everett Cox, 13.3%
Eden Prairie, MN

Robert P. Cummins, 9.5%
Plymouth, MN

All officers and directors as a group (7 persons), 45.6%

SIC CODE

3579 Office machines, nec

MISCELLANEOUS

TRANSFER AGENT AND REGISTAR:
Wells Fargo Bank Minnesota N.A., South St. Paul, MN

TRADED: Nasdaq National Market

SYMBOL: FRGO

STOCKHOLDERS: 11

EMPLOYEES: 178

GENERAL COUNSEL:
Oppenheimer Wolff & Donnelly LLP, Minneapolis

AUDITORS:
PricewaterhouseCoopers LLP, Minneapolis

INC: DE-1999

FOUNDED: 1974

INVESTOR RELATIONS:
Jeff Upin

PUBLIC RELATIONS:
David Schoeneck

RANKINGS

No. 108 CRM Public 200

PUB

PUB

Fastenal Company

2001 Theurer Blvd., P.O. Box 978, Winona, MN 55987
Tel: 507/454-5374 Fax: 507/453-8049 Web site: http://www.fastenal.com

Fastenal Co. sells industrial and construction supplies in eight product lines, including 51,000 different types of threaded fasteners; 21,000 different types of tools and safety supplies; 14,000 types of metal cutting tool blades; 11,000 kinds of fluid transfer components and accessories for hydraulic and pneumatic power; 4,000 kinds of material handling and storage products; 3,000 different types of janitorial and paper products; 1,000 kinds of electrical supplies; and 1,000 kinds of welding supplies. The company operates 766 store sites in 48 states, Puerto Rico, and Canada.

EARNINGS HISTORY

Year Ended Dec 31	Operating Revenue/Sales (dollars in thousands)	Net Earnings	Return on Revenue (percent)	Return on Equity	Net Earnings (dollars per share)	Cash Dividend	Market Price Range
1999	609,186	65,455	10.7	23.2	1.73	0.04	60.56–33.63
1998	503,100	52,953	10.5	24.3	1.40	0.02	56.88–20.50
1997	397,992	40,834	10.3	24.6	1.08	0.02	60.50–30.75
1996	287,691	32,539	11.3	25.8	0.86	0.02	50.00–28.75
1995	222,555	27,411	12.3	29.1	0.72	0.02	43.00–19.88

BALANCE SHEET

Assets	12/31/99 (dollars in thousands)	12/31/98
Current (CAE 27,849 and 2,086)	227,405	173,267
Marketable securities	215	265
Property and equipment	87,630	74,212
Other	3,371	3,490
TOTAL	318,621	251,234

Liabilities	12/31/99 (dollars in thousands)	12/31/98
Current (STD 0 and 4,055)	33,661	30,808
Deferred income taxes	3,000	2,780
Stockholders' equity*	281,960	217,646
TOTAL	318,621	251,234

* $0.01 par common; 50,000,000 authorized; 37,938,688 and 37,938,688 issued and outstanding.

RECENT QUARTERS / **PRIOR-YEAR RESULTS**

	Quarter End	Revenue ($000)	Earnings ($000)	EPS ($)	Prior-Year Revenue ($000)	Prior-Year Earnings ($000)	Prior-Year EPS ($)
Q3	09/30/2000	192,922	20,802	0.55	159,359	17,091	0.45
Q2	06/30/2000	188,589	20,975	0.55	153,891	17,062	0.45
Q1	03/31/2000	176,268	20,046	0.53	140,634	15,415	0.41
Q4	12/31/99	155,302	15,887	0.42	128,617	12,518	0.33
	SUM	713,081	77,710	2.05	582,501	62,086	1.64

RECENT EVENTS

In **March 2000** the company announced an online distribution agreement with EqualFooting.com, a leading B2B marketplace for industrial supplies and equipment. Fastenal product offerings were to be integrated into EqualFooting.com's online product catalogue, thus increasing Fastenal's visibility and distribution among small businesses. The latest release of Fastenal's Internet/e-commerce site (http://www.fastenal.com) focused on streamlining the purchasing process for customers by adding a collection of new tools designed to reduce ordering time and to give purchasers more control of how e-commerce is utilized within their company. **Sept. 30:** Net sales for the nine-month period totaled $557,779,000, an increase of 22.9 percent over the first nine months of 1999. Net earnings grew 24.7 percent to $61,823,000. During third quarter, Fastenal opened 20 new sites, bringing the total number of sites to 861. Management's comment on third quarter: "The sales growth [of 21.1 percent] allowed additional leverage on the infrastructure of the organization during the quarter. Consistent with the first half of 2000, the leverage was tempered somewhat by the impact of rising fuel costs. The impact was approximately $600,000 pretax (or $0.01 per share after-tax) of additional vehicle and freight costs. As we move into the final quarter of the year, we will continue our investment in additional people and store locations."

OFFICERS

Robert A. Kierlin
Chairman, President, and CEO

Timothy T. Albrecht
Information Systems Mgr.

Steven L. Applewick
Logistics Mgr.

Lisa M. Bolduan
Accounting Department Mgr.

Timothy L. Borkowski
Manufacturing Mgr.

Daniel L. Florness
Treasurer, CFO, and CAO

Nicholas Lundquist
VP-Sales

Willard D. Oberton
VP and COO

Stephen M. Slaggie
Secretary

Robert P. Strauss
Logistics Mgr.

Reyne K. Wisecup
Human Resources Development Mgr.

DIRECTORS

Michael J. Dolan
Smead Manufacturing Co., Hastings, MN

Michael M. Gostomski
Winona Heating & Ventilating Co.

Bob Hansen
Carlson School of Management/U. of Minnesota, Minneapolis

Robert A. Kierlin

Henry K. McConnon
Wise Eyes Inc., State College, PA

Willard D. Oberton

John D. Remick
Rochester Athletic Club, Rochester, MN

Stephen M. Slaggie

Reyne K. Wisecup

MAJOR SHAREHOLDERS

Robert A. Kierlin, 11.4%
Winona, MN

Albert O. Nicholas/Nicholas Co. Inc., 6.2%
Milwaukee

Stephen M. Slaggie, 5.8%
Winona, MN

Brown Capital Management Inc., 5.5%
Baltimore

All officers and directors as a group (8 persons), 24.7%

SIC CODE

5051 Metals service centers and offices

5072 Hardware, whsle

MISCELLANEOUS

TRANSFER AGENT AND REGISTAR:
Wells Fargo Bank Minnesota N.A., South St. Paul, MN

TRADED: Nasdaq National Market

SYMBOL: FAST

STOCKHOLDERS: 2,400

EMPLOYEES: 5,493

GENERAL COUNSEL:
Faegre & Benson PLLP, Minneapolis
Streater, Murphy, Gernander Forsythe & Telstad P.A., Winona, MN

AUDITORS:
KPMG LLP, Minneapolis

INC: MN-1968

FOUNDED: 1967

ANNUAL MEETING: April

INVESTOR RELATIONS: Stephen Slaggie

RANKINGS

No. 44 CRM Public 200

No. 10 CRM Performance 100

TWO-YEAR QUARTERLY HIGH-LOW STOCK PRICES

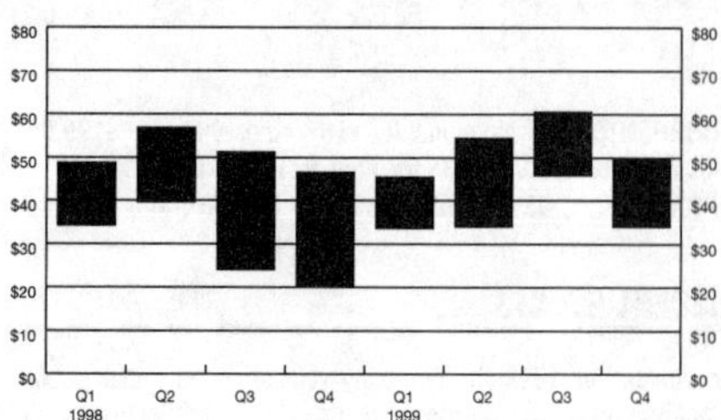

FieldWorks Inc.

7631 Anagram Dr., Eden Prairie, MN 55344
Tel: 952/974-7000 Fax: 952/974-7030 Web site: http://www.field-works.com

FieldWorks Inc. is a leader in customer-specific computing solutions for demanding field environments. Its rugged, upgradable platforms connect field forces to enterprise networks and automate remote information gathering. FieldWorks partners with customers to develop, test, and deliver total-solutions hardware, software, and service and support programs. FieldWork's quality system is ISO 9001-certified.

EARNINGS HISTORY

Year Ended Dec	Operating Revenue/Sales (dollars in thousands)	Net Earnings	Return on Revenue (percent)	Return on Equity	Net Earnings (dollars per share*)	Cash Dividend	Market Price Range
1999 †	25,329	(5,380)	(21.2)	NM	(0.61)	—	3.50–0.88
1998 ¶	20,002	(7,124)	(35.6)	NM	(0.81)	—	5.56–1.56
1997	23,815	(1,024)	(4.3)	(8.0)	(0.12)	—	7.75–3.34
1996 #	13,111	(3,296)	(25.1)	NM	(0.51)	—	
1995 **	8,242	(627)	(7.6)	(29.4)	(0.10)	—	

* Trading began in March 1997.
† Income figures for 1999 include $399,978/($0.05) in restructuring (employee severance) costs.
¶ Income figures for 1998 include $1,472,530/($0.17) in product upgrade and restructuring (employee severance) costs.
# Income figures for 1996 include loss of $376,682/($0.06) from discontinued Paragon operation.
** Income figures for 1995 include loss of $179,848/($0.03) from discontinued operation.

BALANCE SHEET

Assets	01/02/00 (dollars in thousands)	01/03/99	Liabilities	01/02/00 (dollars in thousands)	01/03/99
Current (CAE 86 and 1,690)	10,171	9,143	Current (STD 1,762 and 682)	8,342	5,066
Property and equipment	1,667	1,795	Capitalized lease obligations	40	97
Deposits and other	176	17	Notes payable	2,228	
TOTAL	12,014	10,956	Stockholders' equity*	1,403	5,793
			TOTAL	12,014	10,956

* $0.001 par common; 30,000,000 authorized; 8,894,426 and 8,823,926 issued and outstanding.

RECENT QUARTERS / **PRIOR-YEAR RESULTS**

	Quarter End	Revenue ($000)	Earnings ($000)	EPS ($)	Revenue ($000)	Earnings ($000)	EPS ($)
Q2	07/02/2000	4,050	(3,525)	(0.40)	7,119	(1,266)	(0.14)
Q1	04/02/2000	4,347	(2,280)	(0.28)	6,409	(474)	(0.05)
Q4	01/02/2000	7,016	(1,366)	(0.15)	6,370	(712)	(0.08)
Q3	10/03/99	4,784	(2,274)	(0.26)	4,412	(1,462)	(0.17)
	SUM	20,198	(9,445)	(1.09)	24,311	(3,914)	(0.44)

CURRENT: Q3 earnings include charge of $399,978/($0.04) for product upgrade and restructuring.
PRIOR YEAR: Q3 earnings include charge of $187,720/($0.02) for product upgrade and restructuring.

RECENT EVENTS

In **November 1999** the company and Glenmount International L.P., an industrial technology private equity partnership based in Irvine, Calif., signed an agreement for an equity investment of $4.25 million. Glenmount was to purchase 4.25 million shares of FieldWorks convertible preferred stock. Upon conversion, this would represent 32 percent of FieldWorks' common shares outstanding—making Glenmount the largest single shareholder. Glenmount was to be entitled to elect three members to FieldWorks' seven-member board of directors. As part of the agreement, FieldWorks was to gain strategic expertise from Glenmount through its partnership of proven entrepreneurs and its industrial links to national and international sources of technical, marketing, and production expertise; and assistance to identify, develop, and execute major strategic, acquisition, operational, and financial opportunities. [Equity investment completed in February 2000.] In **January 2000** FieldWorks was selected by two California police departments—Palm Springs and Redondo Beach—to equip their squad car fleets with the FieldWorks Series 2000 Mobile Data Server, an on-board computer and communications system that converts the cockpit of a squad car into an efficient command center as well as a comfortable and productive office environment. In **February** FieldWorks teamed up with the Minnesota Department of Transportation (Mn/DOT) to research and develop a "smart" snowplow. As part of a federally funded pilot project, a Mn/DOT snowplow was outfitted with the FieldWorks Series 2000 Mobile Data Server. The Mobile Data Server functions as the brain center in the snowplow, collecting and managing data from an array of high-tech sensors and devices. The company delivered a $1.9 million supplier order to TRW Inc. (NYSE: TRW), a major prime contractor to the U.S. Armed Forces—the largest single order for the FieldWorks 2000 Mobile Data Server (MDS) solution since its June 1999 release. In **March** the company announced the availability of the FieldWorks FW8000 Field WorkStation, designed for defense applications such as data acquisition, flightline communication,

continued on page 222

OFFICERS

David C. Malmberg
Chairman

Gary J. Beeman
Vice Chairman, VP-Info. Tech.

Thomas Sparrvik
President and CEO

Ray Meifert
VP-Sales/Marketing

Paul Penney
VP-Engineering/Operations

Warren Pillsbury
VP-Sales/Marketing

Robert C. Szymborski
VP-Business Development

RoseMary Luebke
Controller

Steve Wagner
Dir.-Human Resources

Dick Woodruff
Dir.-Professional Services

DIRECTORS

James A. Bernards
Brightstone Capital Ltd., Minneapolis

Richard Boyle
Spinnaker Industries Inc., Dallas

Robert Forbes
Glenmount International, Irvine, CA

Marvin W. Goldstein
financial consultant

Michael Johnson
lawyer

David C. Malmberg

David G. Mell

MAJOR SHAREHOLDERS

Industrial-Works Holding Co. LLC, 32.8%
Irvine, CA

Robert C. Szymborski, 6.4%
Eden Prairie, MN

All officers and directors as a group (9 persons), 14.4%

SIC CODE

3571 Electronic computers

MISCELLANEOUS

TRANSFER AGENT AND REGISTAR:
Wells Fargo Bank Minnesota N.A.,
South St. Paul, MN

TRADED: OTC Bulletin Board

SYMBOL: FWRX

STOCKHOLDERS: 156

EMPLOYEES: 114

GENERAL COUNSEL:
Dorsey & Whitney PLLP, Minneapolis

AUDITORS:
Arthur Andersen LLP, Minneapolis

ANNUAL MEETING: May

INVESTOR RELATIONS:
Karen Engebretson

COMMUNICATIONS:
Vincent Dipas

RANKINGS

No. 140 CRM Public 200

No. 40 Minnesota Technology Fast 50

PUB

TWO-YEAR QUARTERLY HIGH-LOW STOCK PRICES

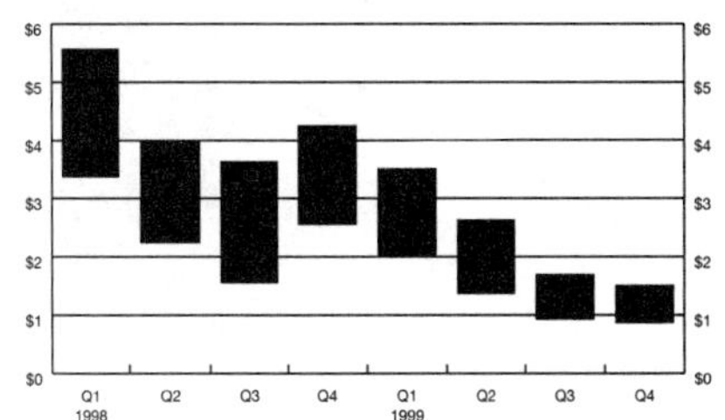

PUB

First Federal Bancorporation

214 Fifth St., P.O. Box 458, Bemidji, MN 56601
Tel: 218/751-5120 Fax: 218/751-5814

First Federal Bancorp. serves as the savings and loan holding company for First Federal Bank. The bank was originally chartered in 1910 as Beltrami County Savings and Building Association. It currently operates as a federally chartered savings bank through its main office in Bemidji, and its four branch offices in Bagley, Baudette, Bemidji, and Walker, Minn.

EARNINGS HISTORY

Year Ended Sept 30	Operating Revenue/Sales (dollars in thousands)	Net Earnings	Return on Revenue (percent)	Return on Equity	Net Earnings (dollars per share*)	Cash Dividend	Market Price Range
1999	9,323	770	8.3	5.9	0.66	—	10.50–7.25
1998	9,171	814	8.9	6.2	0.70	—	14.67–9.17
1997	8,462	708	8.4	5.9	0.58	—	9.79–7.00
1996 †	7,962	317	4.0	2.6	0.20	—	7.22–5.44
1995 ¶	7,093	682	9.6	4.5	0.38	—	6.11–4.67

* Stock began trading April 3, 1995. Per-share amounts restated to reflect 3-for-2 stock splits on May 20, 1999, and Dec. 18, 1997.
† Income figures for 1996 include $588,444 pretax SAIF assessment.
¶ EPS figure for 1995 is pro forma.

BALANCE SHEET

Assets	09/30/99 (dollars in thousands)	09/30/98
Cash	2,194	2,057
Interest-bearing deposits with banks	2,345	2,233
Securities available-for-sale	31,272	36,834
Securities held-to-maturity	33,809	23,299
Loans receivable	57,257	56,064
FHLB stock	1,248	1,148
Foreclosed real estate	188	153
Accrued interest receivable	1,075	992
Premises and equipment	2,124	2,099
Other	778	373
TOTAL	132,290	125,251

Liabilities	09/30/99 (dollars in thousands)	09/30/98
Deposits	88,111	85,866
Borrowings	29,658	24,893
Advance payments by borrowers	186	163
Accrued interest payable	578	544
Accrued expenses and other	696	702
Stockholders' equity*	13,061	13,082
TOTAL	132,290	125,251

* $0.01 par common; 4,000,000 authorized; 1,431,069 and 1,489,912 issued and outstanding, less 289,605 and 287,301 treasury shares.

RECENT QUARTERS / PRIOR-YEAR RESULTS

	Quarter End	Revenue ($000)	Earnings ($000)	EPS ($)	Prior-Year Revenue ($000)	Prior-Year Earnings ($000)	Prior-Year EPS ($)
Q3	06/30/2000	2,584	227	0.23	2,290	185	0.16
Q2	03/31/2000	2,527	169	0.15	2,282	142	0.12
Q1	12/31/99	2,514	278	0.24	2,332	233	0.20
Q4	09/30/99	2,418	210	0.18	2,395	199	0.17
	SUM	10,043	884	0.80	9,300	760	0.65

RECENT EVENTS

In **September 2000** the company announced the successful completion of an agreement with Wal-Mart Stores Inc., subject to regulatory approval, for a full-service, in-store banking facility in the new Wal-Mart Supercenter in Bemidji. The new location was tentatively scheduled to begin operations in late 2001, when the Wal-Mart Supercenter opens.

OFFICERS

Ralph T. Smith
Chairman

Martin R. Sathre
Vice Chairman

William R. Belford
President and CEO

Dennis M. Vorgert
Treasurer

Karen Jacobson
Secretary

DIRECTORS

William R. Belford
Walter R. Fankhanel
Martin R. Sathre
James R. Sharp
Ralph T. Smith
Dean J. Thompson

SIC CODE

6712 Bank holding companies

MISCELLANEOUS

TRANSFER AGENT AND REGISTAR:
Wells Fargo Bank Minnesota N.A., South St. Paul, MN

TRADED: Nasdaq SmallCap Market

SYMBOL: BDJI

STOCKHOLDERS: 219

EMPLOYEES: 48

IN MINNESOTA: 48

GENERAL COUNSEL:
Smith Law Firm, Bemidji, MN

AUDITORS:
RSM McGladrey & Pullen Inc. LLP, Duluth, MN

INC: MN-1994

FOUNDED: 1910

ANNUAL MEETING:
January

RANKINGS

No. 187 CRM Public 200

TWO-YEAR QUARTERLY HIGH-LOW STOCK PRICES

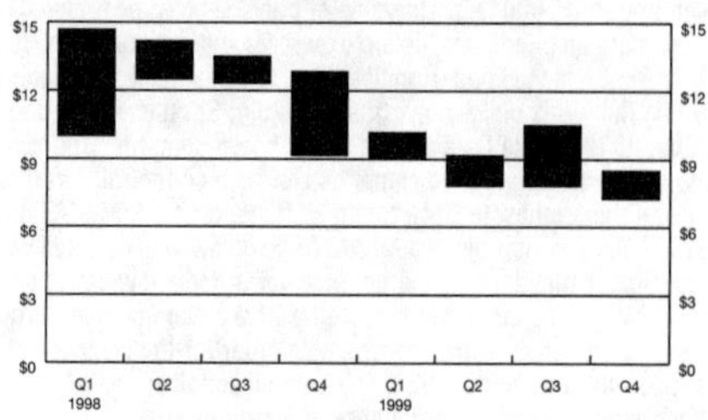

First Federal Capital Corporation

605 State St., P.O. Box 1868, La Crosse, WI 54602
Tel: 608/784-8000 Fax: 608/784-8080

First Federal Capital Corp. is a unitary thrift holding company for First Federal Savings Bank La Crosse—Madison, La Crosse, Wis. The bank was formed on June 1, 1989, with the merger of First Federal Savings Bank of La Crosse and First Federal Savings Bank of Madison, which were founded in 1934 and 1889, respectively. The bank's primary business is attracting general-public deposits through 67 retail banking and loan production offices, then using those deposits to originate loans on single-family residences.

EARNINGS HISTORY

Year Ended Dec 31	Operating Revenue/Sales (dollars in thousands)	Net Earnings	Return on Revenue (percent)	Return on Equity	Net Earnings (dollars per share*)	Cash Dividend	Market Price Range
1999	165,248	22,441	13.6	17.6	1.21	0.34	18.00–11.75
1998	150,028	19,424	12.9	15.8	1.05	0.27	18.38–12.00
1997	139,270	17,390	12.5	15.9	0.95	0.23	17.00–7.83
1996 †	123,808	10,074	8.1	10.6	0.54	0.21	8.08–6.17
1995	105,971	10,645	10.0	10.8	0.61	0.18	6.42–4.67

* Per-share amounts restated to reflect 2-for-1 stock split on June 4, 1998, and 3-for-2 stock split on June 12, 1997.
† Income figures for 1996 include pretax SAIF-recapitalization assessment of $5,941,000—after-tax $3,575,000/($0.19).

BALANCE SHEET

Assets	12/31/99 (dollars in thousands)	12/31/98	Liabilities	12/31/99 (dollars in thousands)	12/31/98
Cash, due fm banks	65,566	43,643	Deposits	1,471,259	1,460,136
Int-brng deposits	17,790	96,550	FHLB advances, other borrowings	469,580	189,778
Inv securities	873				
Mortgage-backed afs	252,165	204,109	Advance payments	5,408	1,762
Mortgage-backed hfi	103,932	102,500	Interest payable	2,516	1,948
Loans held for sale	6,346	72,002	Other	8,516	10,195
Loans hfi	1,538,595	1,177,526	Stkhldrs' equity*	127,275	122,685
FHLB stock	22,511	12,486	TOTAL	2,084,554	1,786,504
Interest receivable	15,421	13,889			
Office ppties, eqt	24,621	25,083			
Servicing rights	21,728	21,103			
Intangibles	12,463	13,485			
Other	2,543	4,129			
TOTAL	2,084,554	1,786,504			

* $0.10 par common; 100,000,000 authorized; 19,941,630 and 19,941,630 issued and outstanding, less 1,538,235 and 1,580,795 treasury shares.

RECENT QUARTERS / PRIOR-YEAR RESULTS

	Quarter End	Revenue ($000)	Earnings ($000)	EPS ($)	Prior-Year Revenue ($000)	Prior-Year Earnings ($000)	Prior-Year EPS ($)
Q3	09/30/2000	50,882	5,790	0.32	41,159	5,424	0.29
Q2	06/30/2000	47,706	5,665	0.31	40,970	6,166	0.34
Q1	03/31/2000	44,624	5,262	0.29	39,802	5,011	0.27
Q4	12/31/99	43,320	5,840	0.31	40,540	5,155	0.28
	SUM	186,532	22,557	1.23	162,471	21,756	1.18

RECENT EVENTS

In **April 2000** the company announced two actions taken at its board of directors meeting. The company declared an increased regular quarterly dividend and authorized the repurchase of up to 1,133,060 shares (6 percent) of common stock. **Sept. 30:** Nine-month net income of $16.72 million, or $0.91 per share, was a 5 percent per share increase over prior year. "Core earnings, which exclude gain on sale of loans, were up 8 percent during the quarter and 26 percent year-to-date," CEO Schini said. "The company continues to make significant strides in the quality of its earnings. Increased loan production is generating net interest income growth, while the ongoing emphasis in building noninterest income is producing solid fee income growth."

OFFICERS

Thomas W. Schini
Chairman and CEO
Bradford R. Price
EVP and Secretary
Jack C. Rusch
President and COO
Michael W. Dosland
VP and Controller
Robert P. Abell
SVP
Milne J. Duncan
SVP
Joseph M. Konradt
SVP

DIRECTORS

Marjorie A. Davenport
Gordon & Marjorie Davenport Inc., Madison, WI
Henry C. Funk
Mills Investment Corp., La Crosse, WI
John F. Leinfelder
Joseph J. Leinfelder & Sons Inc., La Crosse, WI
Richard T. Lommen
Courtesy Corp., La Crosse, WI
Patrick J. Luby
Oscar Mayer Foods Corp. (retired)
David C. Mebane
Madison Gas & Electric Co. (retired), Madison, WI
Dale A. Nordeen
First Federal Savings Bank of Madison (retired)
Phillip J. Quillin
Quillin's Inc., La Crosse, WI
Don P. Rundle
Inland Printing Co. Inc. (retired)
Jack C. Rusch
Thomas W. Schini

MAJOR SHAREHOLDERS

Gail K. Cleary, estate of Russell G. Cleary, et al., 8%
La Crosse, WI
All officers and directors as a group (16 persons), 18.7%

SIC CODE

6712 Bank holding companies

MISCELLANEOUS

TRANSFER AGENT AND REGISTAR:
Wells Fargo Bank Minnesota N.A.,
South St. Paul, MN

TRADED: Nasdaq National Market
SYMBOL: FTFC
STOCKHOLDERS: 1,474
EMPLOYEES: 950
GENERAL COUNSEL:
Michael Best & Friedrich, Milwaukee
AUDITORS:
Ernst & Young LLP, Minneapolis
INC: WI-1989
ANNUAL MEETING: April
HUMAN RESOURCES:
Milne J. Duncan
INVESTOR RELATIONS:
Jack C. Rusch

SUBSIDIARIES, DIVISIONS, AFFILIATES

First Federal Savings Bank La Crosse—Madison
La Crosse, Wis.

First Enterprises

First Cap Holdings Inc.

Turtle Creek Corp.

First Reinsurance Inc.

PUB

TWO-YEAR QUARTERLY HIGH-LOW STOCK PRICES

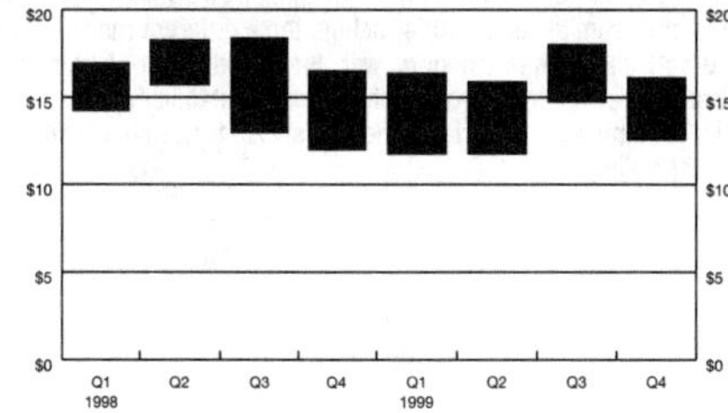

PUB

First Team Sports Inc.

1201 Lund Blvd., Anoka, MN 55303
Tel: 763/576-3500 Fax: 763/576-8000 Web site: http://www.ultrawheels.com

First Team Sports Inc. manufactures, distributes, and markets inline skates and related accessories under its UltraWheels and Skate Attack brand names; a line of backpacks and sport bags under the Crossover name brand in North America and Australia; and a premium line of ice hockey equipment through the company's subsidiary, Hespeler Hockey Company. First Team's products are manufactured and assembled to its specifications in foreign countries.

EARNINGS HISTORY

Year Ended Feb	Operating Revenue/Sales (dollars in thousands)	Net Earnings (dollars in thousands)	Return on Revenue (percent)	Return on Equity (percent)	Net Earnings (dollars per share)	Cash Dividend (dollars per share)	Market Price Range (dollars per share)
2000	45,003	18	0.0	0.1	0.00	—	3.50–0.75
1999	42,397	(5,845)	(13.8)	(24.4)	(1.01)	—	4.00–0.75
1998 *	56,337	(2,609)	(4.6)	(8.6)	(0.45)	—	9.13–2.00
1997	76,435	2,725	3.6	8.3	0.47	—	17.88–5.50
1996	97,667	7,812	8.0	26.2	1.37	—	31.75–10.75

* Income figures for 1998 include pretax charge of $974,018 for impaired-asset write-down. Pro forma as if September 1997 acquisition Hespeler Hockey had been acquired March 1, 1997: revenue $58,124,000; loss $2,487,000/($0.43).

BALANCE SHEET

Assets	02/29/00 (dollars in thousands)	02/28/99
Current (CAE 860 and 723)	31,369	26,206
Equipment and leasehold improvements	6,558	7,418
License agreements	1,331	1,680
Goodwill	1,030	1,119
Other	140	723
Deferred income taxes	1,821	1,988
TOTAL	42,249	39,134

Liabilities	02/29/00 (dollars in thousands)	02/28/99
Current (STD 851 and 1,306)	12,155	8,835
Long-term debt	5,694	5,577
Deferred income taxes	90	195
Deferred revenue	523	600
Stockholders' equity*	23,787	23,928
TOTAL	42,249	39,134

* $0.01 par common; 10,000,000 authorized; 5,860,140 and 5,803,848 issued and outstanding.

RECENT QUARTERS / **PRIOR-YEAR RESULTS**

	Quarter End	Revenue ($000)	Earnings ($000)	EPS ($)	Prior-Year Revenue ($000)	Prior-Year Earnings ($000)	Prior-Year EPS ($)
Q2	08/31/2000	8,564	(724)	(0.12)	7,265	(1,040)	(0.18)
Q1	05/31/2000	15,871	893	0.15	14,177	697	0.12
Q4	02/29/2000	14,103	814	0.14	10,477	34	0.01
Q3	11/30/99	9,575	(453)	(0.08)	7,567	(577)	(0.10)
	SUM	48,114	530	0.09	39,484	(887)	(0.15)

RECENT EVENTS

In **February 2000** the company introduced Rigged and Ready, a full line of Saddle-Cloth camouflage outdoor packs, at SHOT Show 2000 in Las Vegas. Rigged and Ready features the patented Crossover carrying system, which is ideal for many outdoor activities including shooting, bow hunting, and casting. The anatomically formed, full suspension crossover design virtually locks the pack onto the body, providing complete stability and a greater range of motion. **Aug. 31:** Second-quarter operating results improved for the eighth-consecutive quarter. Operating income for the first six months increased significantly, from $30,000 in the first half of fiscal 2000 to $834,000 in 2001. "Improved results for the quarter and first half were driven by the continued strength of both our UltraWheels inline skates and Hespeler hockey products," stated CEO Egart. "Revenues increased for the fourth quarter in a row, and have grown 15 percent through the first half of this year. Gross margins improved both during the quarter and year-to-date and, although second quarter is traditionally our lowest quarter in revenues and earnings, we are profitable through six months." In **October** the latest sales figures for the inline skates market from SportsTrend.Info, the sporting goods industry's authoritative source for product sales information, ranked First Team Sports' SQ 4 men's inline skate No. 4, behind three different models from K2, of Vashon, Wash. First Team Sports entered the hard and soft inline skate category with the introduction of its new HYBRID skate series, which combines the comfort of the UltraWheels Biofit soft boot with the visible stability and support demanded of a hard boot. In **November** First Team introduced the new 50/50 series of hockey sticks, featuring an aspen core surrounded by a fiberglass leading edge and an aircraft veneer trailing edge.

OFFICERS

Joseph Mendelsohn III
Chairman

John J. Egart
President and CEO

David G. Soderquist
Vice Chairman

Kent A. Brunner
VP-Finance and CFO

Rick Jackson
VP-Products/Product Development

Thomas R. King
Secretary

DIRECTORS

John J. Egart

Stanley E. Hubbard
Hubbard Broadcasting Inc., St. Paul

William J. McMahon

Joseph Mendelsohn III

Timothy G. Rath

David G. Soderquist

MAJOR SHAREHOLDERS

John J. Egart, 9.7%
Anoka, MN

David G. Soderquist, 7.6%
Anoka, MN

Dimensional Fund Advisors Inc., 6.4%
Santa Monica, CA

All officers and directors as a group (8 persons), 22.3%

SIC CODE

3949 Sporting and athletic goods, nec

MISCELLANEOUS

TRANSFER AGENT AND REGISTAR:
Wells Fargo Bank Minnesota N.A., South St. Paul, MN

TRADED: Nasdaq National Market

SYMBOL: FTSP

STOCKHOLDERS: 411

EMPLOYEES: 82

PART TIME: 4

IN MINNESOTA: 77

GENERAL COUNSEL:
Fredrikson & Byron P.A., Minneapolis

AUDITORS:
Ernst & Young LLP, Minneapolis

INC: MN-1986

ANNUAL MEETING: July

INVESTOR RELATIONS:
Debbie Favilla

RANKINGS

No. 118 CRM Public 200

SUBSIDIARIES, DIVISIONS, AFFILIATES

First Team Sports Exports Inc.

EUROPEAN SUBSIDIARY
First Team Sports, Inc. GMBH
Triester Strasse '391
A-8055 Graz, Austria
Lukas Piffl, Managing Director

TWO-YEAR QUARTERLY HIGH-LOW STOCK PRICES

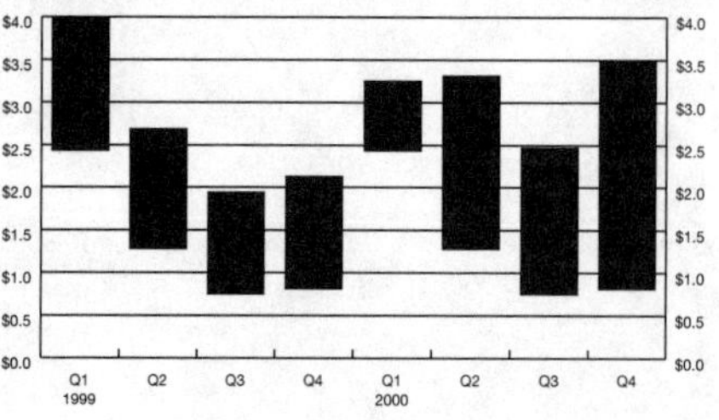

Founders Food & Firkins Ltd.

5831 Cedar Lake Rd., St. Louis Park, MN 55416
Tel: 612/525-2070

Founders Food & Firkins Ltd. operates the Granite City Food & Brewery, a full-service, casual-dining restaurant featuring an on-premise brewery. The restaurant is located in St. Cloud, Minn. The company's expansion strategy focuses on developing restaurants in smaller metropolitan and regional markets, commonly referred to as second-tier markets. Immediate targets for additional restaurants were Sioux Falls, S.D., and Fargo, N.D., markets that bear resemblance to St. Cloud in many demographic categories but have larger populations and employment bases, greater numbers of hotel rooms, and higher household incomes. Granite City's concept is to provide fresh, high-quality, made-to-order food and handcrafted beers. Granite City offers a broad menu of traditional and regional foods served in generous portions at reasonable prices, designed to offer customers an excellent value and pleasant dining experience.

EARNINGS HISTORY *

Year Ended Dec 31	Operating Revenue/Sales (dollars in thousands)	Net Earnings	Return on Revenue (percent)	Return on Equity	Net Earnings (dollars per share†)	Cash Dividend	Market Price Range
1999	1,985	(316)	(15.9)	(38.3)	(0.16)	—	
1998	0	(14)	NM	(1.3)	(0.01)	—	

* The company was a development stage company from June 26, 1997 (inception), until the first restaurant opened in June 1999.
† Trading had not begun during periods presented.

BALANCE SHEET

Assets	12/31/99 (dollars in thousands)	12/31/98
Current (CAE 107 and 1,090)	177	1,093
Property and equipment	3,277	77
License	10	
Other	16	5
Deferred offering costs	115	
Deferred tax benefit		28
TOTAL	3,595	1,204

Liabilities	12/31/99 (dollars in thousands)	12/31/98
Current	636	94
Capital lease obligations	2,133	
Stockholders' equity*	826	1,110
TOTAL	3,595	1,204

* $0.01 par common; 90,000,000 authorized; 1,969,500 and 1,969,500 issued and outstanding.

RECENT QUARTERS / **PRIOR-YEAR RESULTS**

	Quarter End	Revenue ($000)	Earnings ($000)	EPS ($)	Prior-Year Revenue ($000)	Prior-Year Earnings ($000)	Prior-Year EPS ($)
Q2	06/25/2000	964	3	0.00	0	(162)	(0.08)
Q1	03/26/2000	893	(49)	(0.03)	0	(2)	0.00
	SUM	1,857	(46)	(0.02)	0	(164)	(0.08)

RECENT EVENTS

On **June 12, 2000**, the company completed its initial public offering with the sale of 1,000,000 units. The offering was underwritten by R.J. Steichen & Co. Each unit, priced at $4.125, consisted of one share of common stock and one redeemable Class A Warrant that entitles the holder to purchase one share of common stock for $4.00 per share, commencing Aug. 5, 2001. The net proceeds from the offering were to be applied to develop restaurants in Sioux Falls, S.D., and Fargo, N.D. In **July** the company marked its first anniversary as Granite City Food & Brewery in St. Cloud, Minn., with a two-month limited run of a specialty, handcrafted beer brewed for the first time in North America: a unique Belgian-style summer beer named "Cherries Galore!" Later in the month, the company broke ground in Sioux Falls, S.D., for its second Granite City Food & Brewery restaurant and microbrewery, scheduled to open later in the year. The premier location is near major commercial retail sites such as Home Depot, a multiplex movie theater, and several hotels, and within walking distance of the Empire Mall.

OFFICERS

William E. Burdick
Chairman and Brewmaster

Steven J. Wagenheim
President and CEO

Mitchel I. Wachman
CFO and Secretary

Timothy R. Cary
VP-Operations

DIRECTORS

William E. Burdick

James G. Gilbertson
iNTELEFILM Corp., St. Louis Park, MN

Arthur E. Pew III
Champps (former)

Bruce H. Senske
Manchester Cos. Inc., Minneapolis

Mitchel I. Wachman

Steven J. Wagenheim

MAJOR SHAREHOLDERS

Brewing Ventures LLC, 44%

Bruce J. Barnett, 6.6%
Plymouth, MN

Otto G. Bonestroo, 5.3%
Lakeland Shores, MN

All officers and directors as a group (6 persons), 44.2%

SIC CODE

5812 Eating places

MISCELLANEOUS

TRANSFER AGENT AND REGISTAR:
Wells Fargo Bank Minnesota N.A., South St. Paul, MN

TRADED: Nasdaq SmallCap Market

SYMBOL: GCFBU

STOCKHOLDERS: 57

EMPLOYEES: 81

PART TIME: 64

GENERAL COUNSEL:
Briggs and Morgan P.A., Minneapolis

AUDITORS:
Schechter Dokken Kanter Andrews & Selcer Ltd., Minneapolis

INC: MN-1997

PUB

Fourth Shift Corporation

2 Meridian Crossings, Suite 800, Richfield, MN 55423
Tel: 952/851-1500 Fax: 952/851-1560 Web site: http://www.fs.com

Fourth Shift Corp. develops and markets enterprise business applications and services for midsize manufacturers. The company's revenue is derived from two major sources — software and services. Fourth Shift enables manufacturers to capitalize on e-commerce and supply-chain. Fourth Shift has a proven successful customer base on the Microsoft Windows NT environment and a growing number of Microsoft SQL Server customers. The global corporation has offices in Europe, Mexico, and Asia with a strong presence in China. Fourth Shift software is licensed by more than 3,700 customer sites in 60 countries and is translated in more than a dozen languages.

EARNINGS HISTORY

Year Ended Dec 31	Operating Revenue/Sales (dollars in thousands)	Net Earnings	Return on Revenue (percent)	Return on Equity	Net Earnings (dollars per share)	Cash Dividend	Market Price Range
1999 *	69,249	2,115	3.1	19.9	0.21	—	7.06–2.88
1998 †	68,204	2,524	3.7	35.7	0.25	—	5.56–2.25
1997 ¶	52,318	(3,790)	(7.2)	NM	(0.39)	—	6.13–2.63
1996 #	49,310	1,770	3.6	25.0	0.19	—	10.50–3.63
1995 **	37,224	(5,400)	(14.5)	NM	(0.58)	—	6.25–2.00

* Figures for 1999 include results of Computer Aided Business Solutions Inc. from June 30, 1999, date of purchase. Income figures include net gain of $236,000/$0.02 on sale of discontinued operations.
† Income figures for 1998 include net gain of $281,000/$0.03 on sale of discontinued operations.
¶ Income figures for 1997 include pretax restructuring charge of $2,566,000; and net gain of $2,311,000/$0.24 on sale of discontinued operations.
# Income figures for 1996 include net gain of $761,000/$0.08 on sale of discontinued operations.
** Income figures for 1995 include pretax $149,000 restructuring charge; and net loss of $5,605,000/($0.59) on discontinued operations and their disposal.

BALANCE SHEET

Assets	12/31/99 (dollars in thousands)	12/31/98	Liabilities	12/31/99 (dollars in thousands)	12/31/98
Current (CAE 11,784 and 10,073)	27,315	25,123	Current (STD 1,031 and 1,099)	27,029	25,487
Furniture, eqt	5,144	4,584	Long-term obligations	2,834	835
Restricted cash	490	465	Stkhldrs' equity*	10,619	7,079
Acquired software, licensing rights, goodwill	4,232		TOTAL	40,482	33,401
Software development costs	3,301	3,229	* $0.01 par common; 20,000,000 authorized; 10,532,908 and 10,201,783 issued and outstanding.		
TOTAL	40,482	33,401			

RECENT QUARTERS / **PRIOR-YEAR RESULTS**

	Quarter End	Revenue ($000)	Earnings ($000)	EPS ($)	Prior-Year Revenue ($000)	Prior-Year Earnings ($000)	Prior-Year EPS ($)
Q3	09/30/2000	14,892	(153)	(0.01)	16,525	478	0.05
Q2	06/30/2000	15,098	(3,875)	(0.37)	17,753	587	0.06
Q1	03/31/2000	16,265	(356)	(0.03)	16,977	533	0.05
Q4	12/31/99	17,994	517	0.05	19,168	1,649	0.16
	SUM	64,249	(3,867)	(0.37)	70,423	3,247	0.32

CURRENT: Q2 earnings include pretax nonrecurring charge of $849,000 associated with an expense-reduction plan. Q4 earnings include gain of $70,000/$0.01 on sale of discontinued operations.
PRIOR YEAR: Q3 earnings include gain of $86,000/$0.01 on sale of discontinued operations. Q2 earnings include net gain of $50,000/$0.00 on sale of discontinued operations. Q1 earnings include gain of $30,000/$0.00 on sale of discontinued operations. Q4 earnings include net gain of $75,000/$0.01 on sale of discontinued operations.

RECENT EVENTS

February 2000: Fourth Shift's first customer for the new millennium, ecosmetic.com, exemplified a new breed of company investing in ERP software to support their innovative e-business models. The Internet-based company serves as a fulfillment agent for board certified plastic surgeons and dermatologists. The company announced its new e-business suite of software anchored by the Fourth Shift 7 e-ERP Backbone. Fourth Shift also announced its new business approach: Complete Care by Fourth Shift. Accountants completing Fourth Shift training courses were earning continuing professional education (CPE) credits. In **March** the company released Mentor 7, an interactive training guide for Fourth Shift e-business ERP software that incorporated new techniques and java-based technologies in multimedia education. Fourth Shift announced a software and services license agreement with Crest Health Care, a Minnesota manufacturer of health care parts and equipment. Fourth Shift and Grant Thornton released BenchmarkReport.com, a new Web site providing a *continued on page 222*

OFFICERS

Marion Melvin Stuckey
Chairman and CEO

Jimmie H. Caldwell
President and COO

David G. Latzke
VP and CFO

Richard Rickenbach
VP-Business Development

Randy B. Tofteland
VP and Gen. Mgr.-Americas

Dave Gahn
Managing Dir., Asia

John Wolfenden
Managing Dir., Europe

DIRECTORS

Michael J. Adams
Adams and Cesario P.A.

Jimmie H. Caldwell

Steve J. Lair
Avalon Computer Accessories Inc.

Robert M. Price
PSV Inc., Bloomington, MN

Mark W. Sheffert
Manchester Cos. Inc., Minneapolis

Marion Melvin Stuckey

MAJOR SHAREHOLDERS

David R. Lamm, 8.2%
Burnsville, MN

Hathaway & Associates Ltd., 8.2%
Rowayton, CT

Marion Melvin Stuckey, 7.9%
Minneapolis

Oscar Capital Management, 7.3%
New York

Perkins Capital Management Inc., 7.1%
Wayzata, MN

Benson Associates LLC, 5.1%
Portland, OR

All officers and directors as a group (8 persons), 17.7%

SIC CODE

7371 Computer programming services

MISCELLANEOUS

TRANSFER AGENT AND REGISTAR:
Wells Fargo Bank Minnesota N.A.,
South St. Paul, MN

TRADED: Nasdaq National Market

SYMBOL: FSFT
STOCKHOLDERS: 287
EMPLOYEES: 522
PART TIME: 5
IN MINNESOTA: 219
GENERAL COUNSEL:
Dorsey & Whitney PLLP, Minneapolis
AUDITORS:
Arthur Andersen LLP, Minneapolis
INC: MN-1984
ANNUAL MEETING: May
COMMUNICATIONS:
Elisabeth Grant
INVESTOR RELATIONS:
David G. Latzke

RANKINGS

No. 101 CRM Public 200

SUBSIDIARIES, DIVISIONS, AFFILIATES

Fourth Shift Corporation
3000 Executive Parkway, Ste. 405
San Ramon, CA 94583
925/866-0111

Fourth Shift Europe Ltd.
Fourth Shift House
11 Worton Drive
Reading, Berkshire
England RG20LX
44-118-975-4000
John Wolfenden

Fourth Shift de Mexico S.A. de C.V.
Carr. Picacho Ajusco No. 130, Desp. 604
Col. Jardines en la Montana
Mexico, D.F.C.P. 14210
52-5-631-3725
Juan Manuel Sevilla

Fourth Shift Asia Computer Corporation Ltd.
Tianjin Finance Building
No. 123, Wei Di Road,
Hexi District
Tianjin
P.R.C. 30074
86-22-2840-1500
Dave Gahn

TWO-YEAR QUARTERLY HIGH-LOW STOCK PRICES

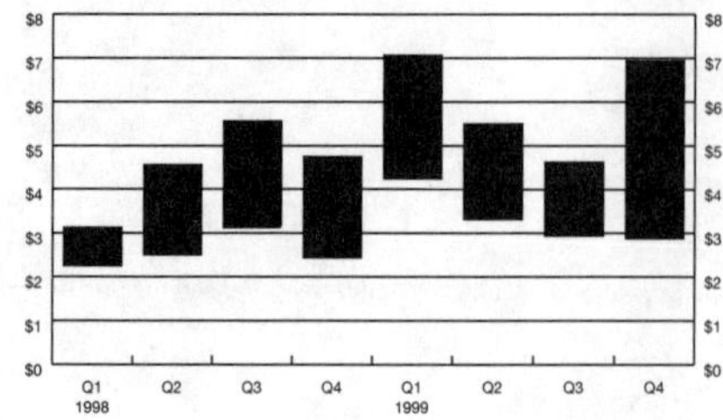

H.B. Fuller Company

1200 Willow Lake Blvd., P.O. Box 64683 (55164), Vadnais Heights, MN 55110
Tel: 651/236-5900 Web site: http://www.hbfuller.com

H.B. Fuller Co. is primarily a manufacturer of specialty chemical products. Operations include the formulation, compounding, and marketing of adhesives, sealants, coatings, paints, polymers, and other specialty chemical products. Adhesives, sealants, and coatings generate more than 91 percent of sales. The products, in thousands of formulations, are used by the automotive, packaging, nonwoven, woodworking, graphic arts, and other industries worldwide. The company operates from plants and technical service centers in the United States, Canada, Mexico, Latin America, Europe, the Caribbean, and Asia/Pacific.

EARNINGS HISTORY

Year Ended Nov	Operating Revenue/Sales (dollars in thousands)	Net Earnings	Return on Revenue (percent)	Return on Equity	Net Earnings (dollars per share)	Cash Dividend	Market Price Range
1999 *	1,364,458	43,370	3.2	11.5	3.14	0.82	72.88–38.13
1998 †	1,347,241	15,990	1.2	4.7	1.17	0.79	64.81–34.00
1997 ¶	1,306,789	36,940	2.8	10.9	2.67	0.72	60.25–44.50
1996	1,275,716	45,430	3.6	13.6	3.26	0.66	47.75–29.50
1995 #	1,243,818	28,663	2.3	9.6	2.06	0.63	39.75–27.75

* Income figures for 1999 include nonrecurring pretax restructuring charge of $17.204 million; and extraordinary charge of $0.741 million/($0.05), cumulative effect of accounting change.
† Income figures for 1998 include nonrecurring pretax restructuring charge of $26.747 million.
¶ Income figures for 1997 include extraordinary charge of $3.368 million/($0.24), cumulative effect of accounting change.
# Income figures for 1995 include loss of $2.532 million/($0.18), cumulative effect of accounting changes.

BALANCE SHEET

Assets	11/27/99 (dollars in thousands)	11/28/98	Liabilities	11/27/99 (dollars in thousands)	11/28/98
Current (CAE 5,821 and 4,605)	440,143	457,900	Current (STD 51,481 and 63,710)	265,920	285,160
Property, plant, and equipment	412,524	414,467	Long-term debt	263,714	300,074
			Accrued pensions	78,286	83,500
Deposits and miscellaneous	74,288	67,342	Other	23,801	19,833
			Minority interests	17,514	16,198
Other intangibles	28,309	34,717	Stkhldrs' equity*	376,380	341,404
Excess of cost over net assets acquired	70,351	71,743	TOTAL	1,025,615	1,046,169
TOTAL	1,025,615	1,046,169			

* $1 par common; 40,000,000 authorized; 14,040,155 and 13,982,649 issued and outstanding.

RECENT QUARTERS / PRIOR-YEAR RESULTS

	Quarter End	Revenue ($000)	Earnings ($000)	EPS ($)	Prior-Year Revenue ($000)	Prior-Year Earnings ($000)	Prior-Year EPS ($)
Q3	08/26/2000	323,109	7,394	0.53	331,916	12,068	0.87
Q2	05/27/2000	347,192	17,772	1.28	348,198	10,026	0.73
Q1	02/26/2000	321,206	9,730	0.70	327,210	7,599	0.55
Q4	11/27/99	357,134	13,677	0.99	361,097	9,038	0.66
	SUM	1,348,641	48,573	3.50	1,368,421	38,731	2.81

CURRENT: Q4 earnings include pretax charge of $6 million related to the restructuring plan; and loss of $741,000/($0.05) cumulative effect of accounting change.
PRIOR YEAR: Q3 earnings include pretax charge of $2.995 million related to the restructuring plan. Q2 earnings include pretax charge of $6.06 million related to the restructuring plan. Q1 earnings include pretax charge of $2.1 million related to the restructuring plan. Q4 earnings include pretax charge of $2.7 million related to the restructuring plan.

RECENT EVENTS

In **March 2000** the company reconfirmed its 5 percent return on sales goal from continuing operations for the full year 2000. Return on sales for fiscal year 1999 was 4.2 percent before nonrecurring charges and the recording of an accounting change. First-quarter results were expected to approximate last year's earnings of $0.67 per share, prior to last year's nonrecurring charges. Several factors were adversely affecting the first quarter results: the impact of weak currencies in Europe; lower margins due to aggressive competitive pricing, primarily in North America, coupled with higher-than-anticipated raw material and delivery costs; and recent developments in the stock market, which negatively affected the portfolio for supplemental retirement benefits (invested in the S&P 500 Index). Subsidiary Foster Products Corp. acquired the mastics, *continued on page 223*

OFFICERS

Albert P.L. Stroucken
Chairman, President, and CEO
Lars T. Carlson
SVP-Mfg. Integration
Alan R. Longstreet
SVP-Global Strategic Business Units
Raymond Tucker
CFO
Richard C. Baker
VP, General Counsel, Secretary
Evelyn M. Borsheim
Asst. Corporate Secretary
James R. Conaty
Pres./CEO-EFTEC
Matthew Critchley
Group Pres., Gen. Mgr.-Asia/Pacific
Paul Dorwart
VP, Gen. Mgr.-Linear Products
William Gacki
VP and Treasurer
Peter Koxholt
Pres./Gen. Mgr.-Europe
Stephen Large
Group Mgr.-North America
Antonio Lobo
VP, Gen. Mgr.-Latin America
James A. Metts
VP-Human Resources
Michael D. Modak
VP-Industrial Products
Walter Nussbaumer
Chief Technology Officer
Dan Piteleski
VP-Information Technology
Helmut Schweiger
VP-Europe ASC
Linda Welty
Group Pres., Gen. Mgr.-Specialty

DIRECTORS

Anthony L. Andersen
Norbert R. Berg
Edward L. Bronstien Jr.
Rybovich Spencer Inc., West Palm Beach, FL
Robert J. Carlson
Advanced Aerospace Design Corp., Scottsdale, CA
Freeman A. Ford
Fafco Inc., Menlo Park, CA
Gail D. Fosler
The Conference Board Inc., New York
Reatha Clark King
General Mills Foundation, Golden Valley, MN
Walter Kissling
John J. Mauriel Jr.
Carlson School of Management/U. of Minnesota, Minneapolis
Lee R. Mitau
U.S. Bancorp, Minneapolis
Albert P.L. Stroucken
Lorne C. Webster
Prenor Group Ltd., Montreal

MAJOR SHAREHOLDERS

Capital Guardian Trust Co., 5%
Los Angeles
All officers and directors as a group (26 persons), 4.9%

SIC CODE

2851 Paints and allied products
2891 Adhesives and sealants
2899 Chemical preparations, nec

MISCELLANEOUS

TRANSFER AGENT AND REGISTAR:
Wells Fargo Bank Minnesota N.A., South St. Paul, MN
TRADED: Nasdaq National Market
SYMBOL: FULL
STOCKHOLDERS: 4,125
EMPLOYEES: 5,400
GENERAL COUNSEL:
Dorsey & Whitney PLLP, Minneapolis
AUDITORS:
PricewaterhouseCoopers LLP, Minneapolis
INC: MN-1915
FOUNDED: 1887
ANNUAL MEETING: April
HUMAN RESOURCES:
James A. Metts
INVESTOR RELATIONS:
Richard Edwards

RANKINGS

No. 27 CRM Public 200

PUB

TWO-YEAR QUARTERLY HIGH-LOW STOCK PRICES

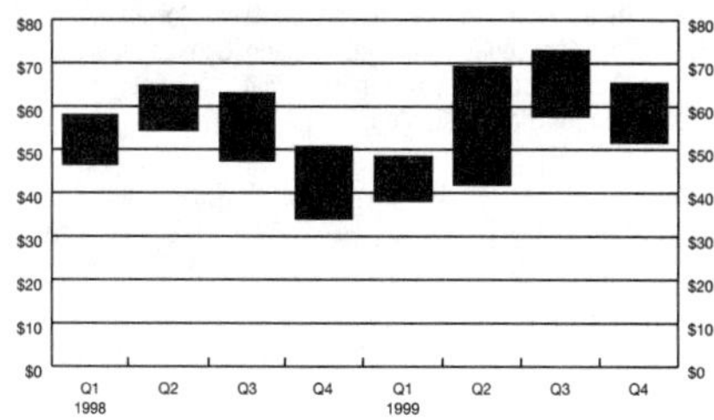

PUB

G&K Services Inc.

5995 Opus Pkwy., Suite 500, Minnetonka, MN 55343
Tel: 952/912-5500 Fax: 952/912-5999 Web site: http://www.gkservices.com

G&K Services Inc. provides and maintains commercial, institutional, and industrial garments and other textile products for a variety of businesses and institutions. The company operates in 39 U.S. states and two Canadian provinces, serving customers from 130 locations.

EARNINGS HISTORY

Year Ended June	Operating Revenue/Sales (dollars in thousands)	Net Earnings (dollars in thousands)	Return on Revenue (percent)	Return on Equity (percent)	Net Earnings (dollars per share)	Cash Dividend (dollars per share)	Market Price Range (dollars per share)
2000	577,392	37,812	6.5	13.9	1.85	0.07	54.00–14.75
1999	519,966	37,029	7.1	15.7	1.81	0.07	56.25–39.75
1998 *	502,593	32,058	6.4	16.2	1.57	0.07	47.31–33.00
1997 †	350,914	29,002	8.3	17.2	1.43	0.07	37.75–23.50
1996	305,414	22,720	7.4	16.2	1.11	0.07	32.00–18.75

* Figures for 1998 include results of National Linen Service (NLS) assets from their July 14, 1997, date of purchase for $283.4 million. Pro forma for full year: revenue $507,767,000; earnings $32,015,000/$1.57.
† Pro forma 1997 figures with NLS: revenue $472,494,000; earnings $27,010,000/$1.33.

BALANCE SHEET

Assets	07/01/00 (dollars in thousands)	06/26/99 (dollars in thousands)	Liabilities	07/01/00 (dollars in thousands)	06/26/99 (dollars in thousands)
Current (CAE 6,420 and 6,297)	176,302	162,806	Current (STD 58,355 and 28,362)	126,631	89,638
Property, plant, and equipment	216,434	198,435	Long-term debt	167,345	193,952
			Deferred income taxes	15,243	11,520
Goodwill	144,229	128,226			
Restrictive covenants/customer lists	40,911	37,805	Other	14,211	10,689
			Stockholders' equity*	271,522	235,633
Other, principally retirement plan	17,076	14,160	TOTAL	594,952	541,432
TOTAL	594,952	541,432			

* $0.50 par common; 60,000,000 authorized; 20,536,295 and 20,516,848 issued and outstanding.

RECENT QUARTERS / **PRIOR-YEAR RESULTS**

	Quarter End	Revenue ($000)	Earnings ($000)	EPS ($)	Prior-Year Revenue ($000)	Prior-Year Earnings ($000)	Prior-Year EPS ($)
Q1	09/30/2000	145,941	9,817	0.48	134,960	9,583	0.47
Q4	07/01/2000	156,644	10,437	0.51	132,832	9,683	0.47
Q3	03/25/2000	143,433	9,161	0.45	131,147	9,421	0.46
Q2	12/25/99	142,355	8,631	0.42	129,864	9,235	0.45
	SUM	588,373	38,046	1.86	528,803	37,922	1.86

RECENT EVENTS

Dec. 25, 1999: "Revenue growth rates in our core rental operations continued to improve, as expected," said Chairman Fink. "However, expenses in the direct-sale/catalog group connected with rapid expansion, continuing high costs associated with a recently expanded fulfillment center, and implementation of a new information system produced a wider operating loss than we anticipated. In addition, the company absorbed larger-than-expected expenses from ourself-insured health care plan and a non-operating charge tied to our deferred compensation plan. Absent these impacts, earnings would have been consistent with analyst earnings estimates." **Sept. 30, 2000:** First-quarter revenue from G&K's rental business increased 8.7 percent over the prior-year period to $141.9 million. "Our revenue growth initiatives are centered on accelerated internal growth through an expanded sales force, improved sales productivity, aggressively building G&K's presence in the national account market, new product introductions, and service marketing," said Fink. "Fueled by internal growth initiatives, our weekly revenue run rate during the quarter showed nice momentum," added CEO Moberly. "In particular, our focus on increasing our national account customer base is a real bright spot. Weekly revenue managed under a national account agreement was up more than 20 percent compared with last year." In November Work Wear Corporation of Canada Ltd., a subsidiary of G&K Services, has been awarded ISO 9002 certification for four of its Ontario, Canada facilities -- Cambridge, London, Hamilton and Etobicoke. This designation signifies that the Company has met international quality management and quality assurance standards set by the International Organization for Standardization.

OFFICERS

Richard M. Fink
Chairman

Thomas Moberly
President and CEO

Sally J. Bredehoft
VP-Human Resources

Timothy W. Kuck
Regional VP

Nick Maris
VP-Marketing

Bill Otto
VP-Information Systems

Richard Stutz
VP-Operations

Kathryn Trickey
VP-Sales

Robert G. Wood
EVP and Pres.-Canadian Rental Operation

Jeffrey L. Wright
CFO, Treasurer, and Secretary

DIRECTORS

Paul Baszucki
Norstan Inc., Plymouth, MN

Richard M. Fink

Wayne M. Fortun
Hutchinson Technology Inc., Hutchinson, MN

Donald W. Goldfus
Apogee Enterprises Inc. (retired)

William Hope
G&K Services Inc. (retired)

Thomas Moberly

Bernard Sweet
Republic Airlines (retired)

D.R. Verdoorn
C.H. Robinson Worldwide Inc., Eden Prairie, MN

MAJOR SHAREHOLDERS

Richard Fink, 39.7%

All officers and directors as a group (11 persons), 40.3%

SIC CODE

7218 Industrial launderers

MISCELLANEOUS

TRANSFER AGENT AND REGISTAR:
Wells Fargo Bank Minnesota N.A.,
South St. Paul, MN

TRADED: Nasdaq National Market

SYMBOL: GKSRA

STOCKHOLDERS: 600

EMPLOYEES: 7,913

GENERAL COUNSEL:
Maslon Edelman Borman & Brand PLLP, Minneapolis

AUDITORS:
Arthur Andersen LLP, Minneapolis

INC: MN-1934

FOUNDED: 1902

ANNUAL MEETING:
October

RANKINGS

No. 49 CRM Public 200

SUBSIDIARIES, DIVISIONS, AFFILIATES

G&K Services Co.

Work Wear Corp. of Canada Ltd.
Toronto

Northwest Linen Co.
Minnesota

Gross Industrial Towel & Garment Service Inc.
Minnesota

G & K Services of Canada Inc.
Ontario

912489 Ontario Limited
Ontario

La Corp. Work Wear du Quebec
Quebec

G & K Services Linen Co.

Whistle Kleen Enterprises Ltd.
Ontario

TWO-YEAR QUARTERLY HIGH-LOW STOCK PRICES

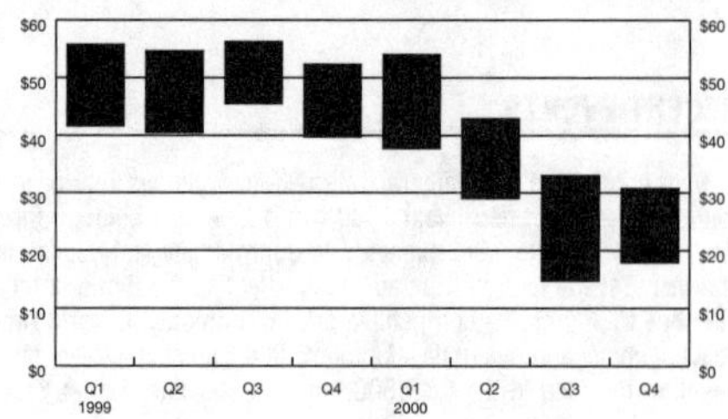

GalaGen Inc.

301 Carlson Pkwy., Suite 301, Minnetonka, MN 55305
Tel: 952/258-5500 Fax: 952/249-8221 Web site: http://www.galagen.com

GalaGen Inc. is a nutritional ingredients company that uses its proprietary science and technology to develop colostrum applications for its customers. The company is recognized for functional foods innovation and the development of industry standards for substantiating product claims. GalaGen broadens the distribution of its products through the formation of strategic alliances, which currently include companies such as Novartis, GNC, Hormel Health Labs, Estee Lauder and Wyeth-Ayerst. Its first brand, Proventra, is currently on the market as a consumer-products ingredient and as a nutritional supplement.

EARNINGS HISTORY *

Year Ended Dec 31	Operating Revenue/Sales (dollars in thousands)	Net Earnings	Return on Revenue (percent)	Return on Equity	Net Earnings (dollars per share†)	Cash Dividend	Market Price Range
1999	3,181	(2,596)	NM	(60.8)	(0.26)	—	2.75–1.38
1998	876	(4,520)	NM	NM	(0.56)	—	4.00–0.84
1997	0	(5,635)	NM	NM	(0.78)	—	4.63–1.50
1996 ¶	0	(7,487)	NM	NM	(2.24)	—	10.38–3.81
1995 #	150	(5,474)	NM	NM	(1.07)	—	

* Prior to 1998, Galagen was a development-stage company.
† Stock began trading April 1, 1996.
¶ EPS for 1996 is after payment of $7.3 million in preferred dividends.
# Income figures for 1995 include an extraordinary gain of $605,421/$0.30 on extinguishment of debt. EPS is pro forma for the offering.

BALANCE SHEET

Assets	12/31/99 (dollars in thousands)	12/31/98	Liabilities	12/31/99 (dollars in thousands)	12/31/98
Current (CAE 204 and 4,081)	3,690	4,897	Current	419	1,172
Property and equipment	287	401	Other	45	45
Deferred expenses	94	325	Stockholders' equity*	4,268	5,076
Customer list	360	450	TOTAL	4,732	6,293
Other intangibles	301	220			
TOTAL	4,732	6,293			

* $0.01 par common; 40,000,000 authorized; 10,416,462 and 8,948,446 issued and outstanding.

RECENT QUARTERS / **PRIOR-YEAR RESULTS**

	Quarter End	Revenue ($000)	Earnings ($000)	EPS ($)	Revenue ($000)	Earnings ($000)	EPS ($)
Q3	09/30/2000	105	(1,257)	(0.12)	897	(736)	(0.07)
Q2	06/30/2000	124	(1,081)	(0.10)	608	(996)	(0.10)
Q1	03/31/2000	147	(1,115)	(0.11)	584	(860)	(0.10)
Q4	12/31/99	1,092	(4)	0.00	702	(818)	(0.10)
	SUM	1,468	(3,457)	(0.33)	2,791	(3,411)	(0.36)

RECENT EVENTS

In **April 2000** the company was recognized by Nutraceuticals World magazine as one of the industry's top 10 innovators for 2000. The magazine said that GalaGen "has emerged from its pharmaceutical cocoon to hit the ground running with a combination of strong science and strategic partnerships that should secure its future in the nutraceuticals industry of tomorrow." In **July** GalaGen signed an agreement with Estee Lauder Inc. to supply Galagen's colostrum-based ingredient for use in cosmetic skin-care products. "We believe our product was selected from a group of several different colostrum products because of its purity and overall effectiveness," said CEO Cardello. "In addition, we believe this contract confirms the superiority of our patented processing technology, a technology that enables us to offer more potent ingredients that are more easily incorporated into skin care products." In **August** GalaGen was in violation of Nasdaq's minimum net tangible asset requirement. A recommendation to delist was being appealed. In **September** a Nasdaq Listing Qualifications Panel granted the company's request to transfer the listing of its securities to the Nasdaq SmallCap Market, effective Oct. 2, 2000, under a temporary exception to the net tangible assets requirement. In **October** Galagen placed $1.4 million in new equity with a group of investors led by Lombard Odier & Cie, one of the largest Swiss private banks, thereby gaining compliance with the $2 million minimum net tangible assets requirement for continued listing on Nasdaq SmallCap. GalaGen is working with Research-based Dietary ingredients Association (RDIA) to propose a third-party review system for reviewing scientific substantiation supporting structure/function claims. GalaGen's Chairman and Chief Technology Officer is RDIA's President.

OFFICERS

Robert A. Hoerr, M.D., Ph.D.
Chairman and Chief Technology Officer

Henry J. Cardello
President and CEO

Eileen F. Bostwick, Ph.D.
VP-Science/Research

Michael E. Cady
VP-Manufacturing

Frank L. Kuhar
CFO

DIRECTORS

Helmut B. Breuer
Lombard Odier Nutrition Fund

Henry J. Cardello

Austen S. Cargill II
Cargill Inc., Minnetonka, MN

Robert A. Hoerr

Ronald O. Ostby
Land O'Lakes Inc., Arden Hills, MN

Winston R. Wallin
Medtronic Inc. (chairman emeritus)

MAJOR SHAREHOLDERS

Perkins Capital Management Inc., 13.3%
Wayzata, MN

Land O'Lakes/Ronald O. Ostby, 11.6%
Arden Hills, MN

Lombard Odier & Cie, 9.7%
Geneva

All officers and directors as a group (9 persons), 18.4%

SIC CODE

2023 Dry, condensed, evaporated dairy prods

MISCELLANEOUS

TRANSFER AGENT AND REGISTAR:
Wells Fargo Bank Minnesota N.A., South St. Paul, MN

TRADED: Nasdaq SmallCap Market

SYMBOL: GGEN

STOCKHOLDERS: 150

EMPLOYEES: 18

GENERAL COUNSEL:
Faegre & Benson PLLP, Minneapolis
Merchant, Gould, Smith, Edell, Welter & Schmidt P.A., Minneapolis

AUDITORS:
Ernst & Young LLP, Minneapolis

INC: DE-1992
FOUNDED: 1987
ANNUAL MEETING: May
HUMAN RESOURCES: Sue Rehberger
INVESTOR RELATIONS: Frank Kuhar

PUB

TWO-YEAR QUARTERLY HIGH-LOW STOCK PRICES

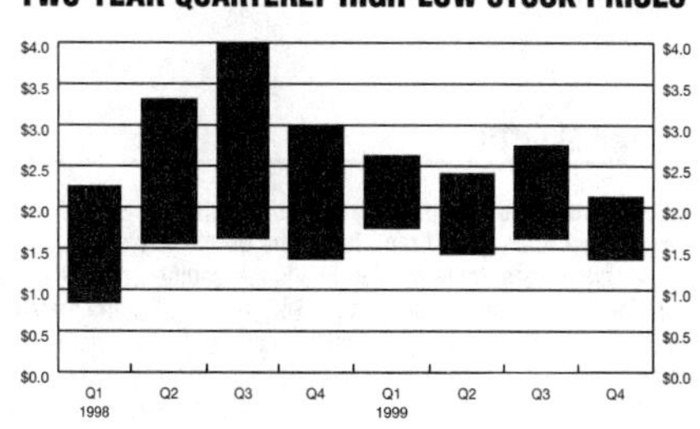

PUB

General Mills Inc.

One General Mills Blvd., P.O. Box 1113 (55440), Golden Valley, MN 55426
Tel: 763/764-2311 Fax: 763/764-4925 Web site: http://www.genmills.com

General Mills Inc. is a leading marketer of consumer foods. Its businesses include Big G cereals, Betty Crocker dessert mixes, Gold Medal flour, Bisquick baking mix, Hamburger Helper dinner mixes, Pop Secret microwave popcorn, Fruit Roll-ups and other fruit snacks, and Yoplait and Columbo yogurts. General Mills has also formed four strategic alliances that expand its international presence: CPW, a cereal joint venture with Nestle; Snack Ventures Europe (SVE), a joint venture with Pepsico Foods International; International Dessert Partners, a joint venture with CPC International, focused on Latin America; and a snack joint venture in China with WantWant Holdings.

EARNINGS HISTORY

Year Ended May	Operating Revenue/Sales (dollars in thousands)	Net Earnings	Return on Revenue (percent)	Return on Equity	Net Earnings (dollars per share*)	Cash Dividend	Market Price Range
2000	6,700,200	614,400	9.2	NM	2.05	1.10	43.94–29.38
1999 †	6,246,100	534,500	8.6	NM	1.74	1.08	42.34–29.59
1998 ¶	6,033,000	421,800	7.0	NM	1.33	1.06	39.13–30.00
1997 #	5,609,300	445,400	7.9	NM	1.41	1.02	34.38–26.00
1996	5,416,000	476,400	8.8	NM	1.50	0.96	30.25–25.00

* Per-share amounts restated to reflect 2-for-1 stock split on Nov. 8, 1999.
† Income figures for 1999 include unusual charge of $51.6 million pretax, $32.3 million/($0.11) after-tax, primarily related to streamlining manufacturing and distribution.
¶ Fiscal 1998 consisted of 53 weeks. Income figures include unusual charge of $166.4 million pretax, $100.2 million/($0.32) after-tax, primarily related to cereal line shutdowns.
# Income figures for 1997 include unusual charge of pretax $48.4 million, after-tax $29.2 million/($0.09), for adoption of SFAS 121 (accounting for impairment of long-lived assets).

BALANCE SHEET

Assets	05/28/00 (dollars in thousands)	05/30/99	Liabilities	05/28/00 (dollars in thousands)	05/30/99
Current (CAE 25,600 and 3,900)	1,190,300	1,102,500	Current (STD 413,500 and 90,500)	2,529,100	1,700,300
Land, buildings, and equipment	1,404,900	1,294,700	Long-term debt	1,760,300	1,702,400
			Deferred income taxes	297,200	288,900
Investments in and advances to affiliates	195,700	180,800	Deferred income taxes, tax leases	89,800	111,300
Marketable securities	148,100	144,600	Other liabilities	186,100	173,600
Prepaid pension	593,700	528,100	Stockholders' equity*	(288,800)	164,200
Miscellaneous	170,700	168,000			
Intangibles	870,300	722,000	TOTAL	4,573,700	4,140,700
TOTAL	4,573,700	4,140,700			

* $0.10 par common; 1,000,000,000 authorized; 408,300,000 and 408,300,000 issued and outstanding, less 122,900,000 and 104,300,000 treasury shares.

RECENT QUARTERS / PRIOR-YEAR RESULTS

	Quarter End	Revenue ($000)	Earnings ($000)	EPS ($)	Prior-Year Revenue ($000)	Prior-Year Earnings ($000)	Prior-Year EPS ($)
Q1	08/27/2000	1,674,900	158,900	0.56	1,573,600	158,500	0.52
Q4	05/28/2000	1,689,800	108,900	0.38	1,600,500	104,800	0.34
Q3	02/27/2000	1,619,600	153,300	0.51	1,495,100	141,100	0.46
Q2	11/28/99	1,817,200	193,700	0.64	1,677,400	143,600	0.47
	SUM	6,801,500	614,800	2.09	6,346,600	548,000	1.79

PRIOR YEAR: Q3 results include Lloyd's Barbecue Co. from Jan. 15, 1999; and Farmhouse Foods Co. from Feb. 10, 1999. Q2 earnings include restructuring charges: pretax $51.6 million; after-tax $32.3 million/($0.11).

RECENT EVENTS

In **December 1999** the company agreed to purchase Small Planet Foods, a leading producer of organic food products. Small Planet's Cascadian Farm brand holds the No. 1- or No. 2-share position in the markets for organic frozen fruits, vegetables, juices, and entrees. Its Muir Glen line is the leading brand of organic canned tomatoes, pasta sauces, salsa, and condiments. Combined annual sales, all brands: $60 million. [Deal completed in January.] Several analysts cut their ratings of General Mills—one citing increasing competitive pressures in cereals and disappointing sales of Hamburger Helper. General Mills was the only Minnesota company to recognized by Fortune magazine as one of the 100 "Best Companies to Work For in America." Already the nation's largest cereal maker by revenue, General Mills over- **continued on page 223**

OFFICERS

Stephen W. Sanger
Chairman and CEO

Stephen R. Demeritt
Vice Chairman

Raymond G. Viault
Vice Chairman

Marc Belton
SVP and Pres.-Big G

Peter J. Capell
Pres.-Snacks Unlimited

Randy G. Darcy
SVP-Operations

Jon L. Finley
SVP and Pres.-Global Convenience Foods

Ian R. Friendly
Pres.-Yoplait/Colombo

James A. Lawrence
EVP and CFO

Siri S. Marshall
SVP-Corporate Affairs, General Counsel

Chris O'Leary
SVP and Pres.-Betty Crocker

Michael A. Peel
SVP-Human Resources

Kendall J. Powell
SVP and CEO-Cereal Partners Worldwide

Jeffrey J. Rotsch
SVP and Pres.-Consumer Foods/Foodservice

Christina Steiner Shea
SVP and Pres.-New Ventures Division

Robert L. Stretmater
VP and Pres.-Foodservice

Danny L. Strickland
SVP-Innovation/Technology/Quality

Austin P. Sullivan Jr.
SVP-Corporate Relations

Christi L. Strauss
VP and Pres.-General Mills Canada

Kenneth L. Thome
SVP-Financial Operations

David B. VanBenschoten
VP and Treasurer

Kris Wenker
VP

DIRECTORS

Stephen R. Demeritt

Livio D. DeSimone
3M Co., Maplewood, MN

William T. Esrey
Sprint Corp., Westwood, KS

Raymond V. Gilmartin
Merck & Co. Inc., Whitehouse Station, NJ

Judith Richards Hope
Paul, Hastings, Janofsky & Walker, Washington, D.C.

Robert L. Johnson
BET Holdings Inc., Washington, D.C.

Heidi G. Miller
Priceline.com, New York

Michael D. Rose
Promus Hotel Corp., Memphis, TN

Stephen W. Sanger

A. Michael Spence
Stanford University, Stanford, CA

Dorothy A. Terrell
Natural Microsystems Corp., Chelmsford, MA

Raymond G. Viault

MAJOR SHAREHOLDERS

All officers and directors as a group (15 persons), 2.6%

SIC CODE

2026 Fluid milk
2041 Flour and other grain mill products
2043 Cereal breakfast foods
2045 Prepared flour mixes and doughs
5153 Grain and beans, whsle

MISCELLANEOUS

TRANSFER AGENT AND REGISTAR:
Wells Fargo Bank Minnesota N.A., South St. Paul, MN

TRADED: NYSE, CSE

SYMBOL: GIS

STOCKHOLDERS: 40,551

EMPLOYEES: 11,077

AUDITORS:
KPMG LLP, Minneapolis

INC: DE-1928

ANNUAL MEETING:
September

COMMUNICATIONS:
Austin Sullivan

RANKINGS

No. 9 CRM Public 200
No. 57 CRM Employer 100

TWO-YEAR QUARTERLY HIGH-LOW STOCK PRICES

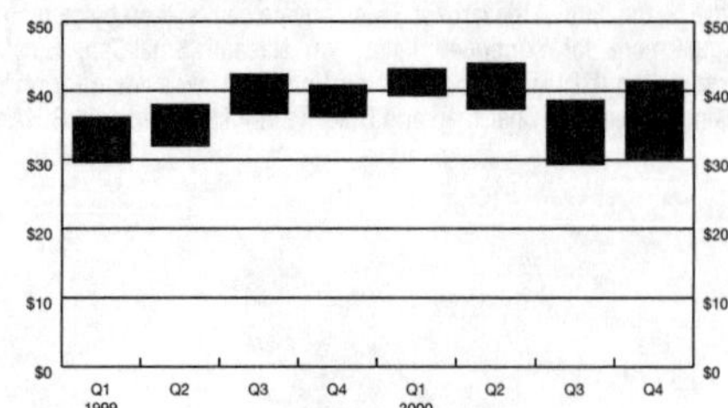

GeoResources Inc.

1407 W. Dakota Pkwy., Suite 1-B, Williston, ND 58801
Tel: 701/572-2020 Fax: 701/572-0277 Web site: http://www.dia.net/~geoi/

GeoResources Inc. is a natural resources company engaged in two primary business segments: oil and gas exploration, development, and production; and the mining of leonardite (oxidized lignite coal). GeoResources has substantial oil and gas exploration and production operations in the Williston Basin. As of Dec. 31, 1999, the company had developed oil and gas leases covering 13,765 acres in Montana and North Dakota. During 1999 it sold an average of 503 net equivalent barrels of oil per day from 134 wells located primarily in North Dakota. From leonardite, it manufactures several different specialty products, primarily for the oil well drilling mud industry in the coastal areas of the Gulf of Mexico.

EARNINGS HISTORY

Year Ended Dec 31	Operating Revenue/Sales (dollars in thousands)	Net Earnings	Return on Revenue (percent)	Return on Equity	Net Earnings (dollars per share)	Cash Dividend	Market Price Range
1999	3,340	482	14.4	10.8	0.12	—	1.44–0.56
1998 *	2,381	(1,605)	(67.4)	(39.6)	(0.39)	—	2.27–0.83
1997	4,190	766	18.3	13.5	0.19	—	3.61–2.52
1996	3,807	734	19.3	15.1	0.18	—	4.38–1.25
1995	2,874	304	10.6	7.4	0.08	—	1.75–1.00

* Income figures for 1998 include pretax charge of $1.3 million for write-down of oil and gas properties.

BALANCE SHEET

Assets	12/31/99 (dollars in thousands)	12/31/98	Liabilities	12/31/99 (dollars in thousands)	12/31/98
Current (CAE 423 and 40)	1,729	999	Current (STD 175 and 316)	1,090	888
Property, plant, and equipment	5,452	5,556	Long-term debt	1,610	1,625
Mortgage loans receivable, related party	103	103	Deferred income taxes	166	140
Other	44	47	Stockholders' equity*	4,462	4,052
TOTAL	7,329	6,705	TOTAL	7,329	6,705

* $0.01 par common; 10,000,000 authorized; 4,005,352 and 4,071,652 issued and outstanding.

RECENT QUARTERS / **PRIOR-YEAR RESULTS**

	Quarter End	Revenue ($000)	Earnings ($000)	EPS ($)	Prior-Year Revenue ($000)	Prior-Year Earnings ($000)	Prior-Year EPS ($)
Q3	09/30/2000	1,410	484	0.12	1,004	271	0.07
Q2	06/30/2000	1,203	337	0.08	759	104	0.03
Q1	03/31/2000	1,241	343	0.09	429	(133)	(0.03)
Q4	12/31/99	1,148	240	0.06	531	(1,293)	(0.32)
	SUM	5,002	1,405	0.35	2,723	(1,052)	(0.26)

PRIOR YEAR: Q4 earnings include pretax charge of $1.3 million to write down oil and gas properties.

OFFICERS

Jeffrey P. Vickers
President

Jeffrey B. Jennings
VP-Land/Finance

Thomas F. Neubauer
VP-Leonardite Operations

Connie Hial
Treasurer

Cathy Kruse
Secretary

DIRECTORS

Duane Ashley
GRACO Fishing and Rental Tools, Williston, ND

H. Dennis Hoffelt
Triangle Electric Inc., Williston, ND

Paul A. Krile
Ranco Fertiservice, Sioux Rapids, IA

Cathy Kruse

Jeffrey P. Vickers

MAJOR SHAREHOLDERS

Jeffrey P. Vickers, 9.2%

Paul A. Krile, 5.3%
Sioux Rapids, IA

All officers and directors as a group (6 persons), 16.4%

SIC CODE

1221 Bituminous coal and lignite, surface

1381 Drilling oil and gas wells

1382 Oil and gas exploration services

MISCELLANEOUS

TRANSFER AGENT AND REGISTAR:
Wells Fargo Bank Minnesota N.A., South St. Paul, MN

TRADED: Nasdaq SmallCap Market

SYMBOL: GEOI

STOCKHOLDERS: 1,300

EMPLOYEES: 17

PART TIME: 4

GENERAL COUNSEL:
Jones & Keller, Denver

AUDITORS:
Richey, May & Co. P.C., Englewood, CO

ANNUAL MEETING: June

TWO-YEAR QUARTERLY HIGH-LOW STOCK PRICES

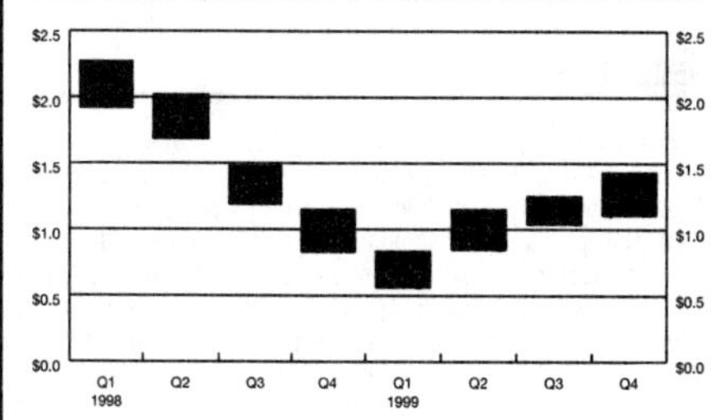

Glacier Bancorp Inc.

49 Commons Loop, Kalispell, MT 59901
Tel: 406/756-4200 Fax: 406/756-3518 Web site: http://www.glacierbank.com

Glacier Bancorp Inc. is a multibank holding company operating seven principal subsidiaries: Glacier Bank, Valley Bank of Helena, Glacier Bank of Whitefish, Big Sky Western Bank, Glacier Bank Eureka, First Security Bank of Missoula, and wholly owned subsidiary Community First Inc. which offers complete brokerage services (through an unrelated brokerage firm). Glacier Bancorp Inc. was formed in 1990 by First Federal Savings Bank of Montana to acquire all of the savings bank's stock upon its reorganization. In 1992 the company acquired Evergreen Bancorp., gaining ownership of 94 percent of First National Bank Whitefish and 93 percent of First National Bank Eureka. In 1996 it acquired Missoula Bancshares Inc., parent company of First Security Bank. Savings and checking accounts are insured by the Federal Deposit Insurance Corp. Its bank subsidiaries are members of the Federal Home Loan Bank of Seattle and Federal Reserve System.

EARNINGS HISTORY *

Year Ended Dec 31	Operating Revenue/Sales (dollars in thousands)	Net Earnings	Return on Revenue (percent)	Return on Equity	Net Earnings (dollars per share†)	Cash Dividend	Market Price Range
1999	69,985	12,179	17.4	15.5	1.16	0.58	22.16–13.52
1998	65,680	10,915	16.6	14.0	1.07	0.47	22.16–15.60
1997	61,821	10,236	16.6	15.1	1.02	0.39	18.78–11.46
1996 ¶	57,522	8,327	14.5	14.3	0.86	0.32	12.65–8.88
1995	51,218	8,840	17.3	16.8	0.90	0.28	10.02–6.83

* Historical financials restated to pool Valley Bank of Helena, acquired Aug. 31, 1998, and Big Sky Western Bank, acquired Jan. 20, 1999; but not yet Mountain West Bank of Coeur d'Alene, acquired Feb. 4, 2000, or WesterFed Financial Corp., agreed to be acquired Sept. 20, 2000.
† Per-share amounts restated to reflect 10 percent stock dividends on May 25, 2000, May 27, 1999, and Oct. 1, 1998; a 3-for-2 stock split on May 23, 1997; and annual 10 percent stock dividends in each May previous.
¶ Income figures for 1996 include pretax charges of $947,000 SAIF assessment and $563,000 merger expense.

BALANCE SHEET

Assets	12/31/99 (dollars in thousands)	12/31/98	Liabilities	12/31/99 (dollars in thousands)	12/31/98
Cash on hand	46,277	33,806	Deposits, int-brng	462,922	375,667
Fed. funds sold	64	5,883	Deposits, non	113,360	100,177
Cash deposits	1,436	2,494	FHLB advances	194,650	124,886
Investments afs	191,385	97,214	Securities sold	19,766	17,239
Investments htm		8,272	Other borrowings	6,848	1,468
Loans receivable	590,278	518,208	Accrued interest	2,646	2,278
Premises, eqt	21,394	17,382	Current taxes	46	
Real estate	550	151	Deferred taxes		1,540
FHLB stock	14,397	12,366	Minority interest	308	313
Fed. Reserve stock	1,467	1,219	Other	4,758	4,588
Accrued interest	5,112	4,348	Stkhldrs' equity*	78,813	77,810
Goodwill	7,035	2,601	TOTAL	884,117	705,966
Deferred tax asset	2,642				
Other	2,080	2,022			
TOTAL	884,117	705,966			

* $0.01 par common; 12,500,000 authorized; 10,505,488 and 9,455,185 issued and outstanding.

RECENT QUARTERS / **PRIOR-YEAR RESULTS**

	Quarter End	Revenue ($000)	Earnings ($000)	EPS ($)	Revenue ($000)	Earnings ($000)	EPS ($)
Q3	09/30/2000	23,981	3,853	0.34	20,048	3,266	0.29
Q2	06/30/2000	22,594	3,192	0.28	18,640	3,088	0.27
Q1	03/31/2000	21,461	3,228	0.28	17,787	2,969	0.27
Q4	12/31/99	21,084	3,029	0.26	16,345	2,771	0.26
	SUM	89,120	13,302	1.16	72,820	12,094	1.09

RECENT EVENTS

In **November 1999** Glacier Bank, Kalispell, Mont., entered into an agreement to sell its Hamilton branch to Ravalli County Bank, Hamilton, Mont. "Our limited presence in the Hamilton market has made growing our business at that branch a challenge," said Glacier Bancorp CEO Blodnick. In **February 2000** Glacier acquired Mountain West Bank, Coeur d'Alene, Idaho. In **May** Glacier Bank, Kalispell, Mont., entered into an agreement to sell its Thompson Falls branch to Valley Bank of Ronan located in Ronan, Mont. In **September** Glacier Bancorp acquired seven branches of Wells Fargo & Co. and First Security Corp. subsidiary banks located in Idaho and Utah that had been offered for sale in conjunction with the divestiture required by federal regulators in their approval of the merger agreement between Wells Fargo and First Security. On Sept. 20, Glacier and WesterFed Financial Corp. (Nasdaq: WSTR), Missoula, Mont., jointly announced the signing of a definitive agreement whereby Glacier Bancorp was to acquire WesterFed for a combination of cash and stock in a transaction val- *continued on page 223*

OFFICERS

John S. MacMillan
Chairman

Michael J. Blodnick
President and CEO

James H. Strosahl
EVP, CFO, and Sec./Treas.

Thomas E. Anderson
VP and Controller

William L. Bouchee
Pres.-First Security Bank

DIRECTORS

Michael J. Blodnick

William L. Bouchee

Allen J. Fetscher
Associated Agency, Missoula, MT

Fred J. Flanders
Valley Bank (retired), Helena, MT

Jon W. Hippler

L. Peter Larson
American Timber

John S. MacMillan

F. Charles Mercord
Glacier Bancorp Inc. (retired)

Everit A. Sliter
Jordahl & Sliter

Harold A. Tutvedt
Harold Tutvedt Farms

MAJOR SHAREHOLDERS

T. Rowe Price Associates Inc., 9.9%
Baltimore

All officers and directors as a group (11 persons), 15.2%

SIC CODE

6712 Bank holding companies

MISCELLANEOUS

TRANSFER AGENT AND REGISTAR:
Davidson Trust Co., Great Falls, MT

TRADED: Nasdaq National Market

SYMBOL: GBCI

STOCKHOLDERS: 2,500

EMPLOYEES: 500

GENERAL COUNSEL:
Hash & O'Brien, Kalispell, MT

AUDITORS:
KPMG LLP, Billings, MT

INC: DE-1990

ANNUAL MEETING: April

SUBSIDIARIES, DIVISIONS, AFFILIATES

Glacier Bank
Stephen J. Van Helden

Glacier Bank of Whitefish
Martin Gilman

Glacier Bank of Eureka
Don Chery

First Security Bank
Missoula, Mont.
William L. Bouchee

Valley Bank of Helena
Helena, Mont.
J. Andrew O'Neill

Community First Inc.

Big Sky Western Bank
Big Sky, Mont.
Michael F. Richards

Mountain West Bank
Coeur d'Alene, Idaho
Jon W. Hippler

TWO-YEAR QUARTERLY HIGH-LOW STOCK PRICES

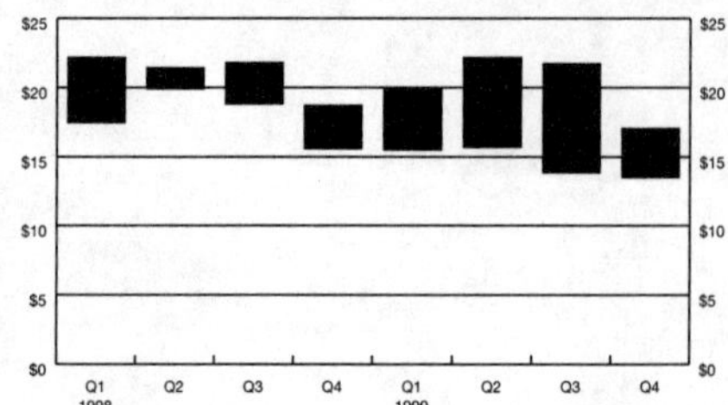

Graco Inc.

4050 Olson Memorial Hwy., P.O. Box 1441 (55440), Golden Valley, MN 55422
Tel: 763/623-6000 Fax: 763/623-6777 Web site: http://www.graco.com

Graco Inc. designs, manufactures, and markets systems and equipment to move, measure, control, dispense, and spray fluid materials in both industrial and commercial settings. Among its products are a wide array of specialized pumps, regulators, valves, atomizing devices, and accessories; an extensive line of portable painting and cleaning equipment; and sophisticated paint circulating and application technology, complete with control hardware and software.

EARNINGS HISTORY

Year Ended Dec	Operating Revenue/Sales (dollars in thousands)	Net Earnings	Return on Revenue (percent)	Return on Equity	Net Earnings (dollars per share*)	Cash Dividend	Market Price Range
1999	442,474	59,341	13.4	NM	2.93	0.44	35.88–20.00
1998 †	432,185	47,263	10.9	NM	2.06	0.44	36.50–19.88
1997	413,897	44,716	10.8	28.4	1.75	0.38	26.46–15.67
1996	391,756	36,169	9.2	28.7	1.40	0.32	17.33–11.83
1995	386,314	27,706	7.2	26.7	1.07	0.29	17.00–8.78

* Per-share amounts restated to reflect 3-for-2 stock splits paid Feb. 4, 1998, and Feb. 7, 1996.
† In 1998 the company repurchased 5.8 million shares of common stock for $190,887,000—substantially reducing shareholders' equity.

BALANCE SHEET

Assets	12/31/99 (dollars in thousands)	12/25/98	Liabilities	12/31/99 (dollars in thousands)	12/25/98
Current (CAE 6,588 and 3,555)	137,989	131,320	Current (STD 15,855 and 17,717)	78,263	82,966
Property, plant, and equipment	86,493	96,366	Long-term debt	65,695	112,582
			Retirement benefits, deferred comp	29,135	28,841
Other	11,551	6,016			
TOTAL	236,033	233,702	Stockholders' equity*	62,940	9,313
			TOTAL	236,033	233,702

* $1 par common; 33,750,000 authorized; 20,415,827 and 20,096,814 issued and outstanding.

RECENT QUARTERS / PRIOR-YEAR RESULTS

	Quarter End	Revenue ($000)	Earnings ($000)	EPS ($)	Prior-Year Revenue ($000)	Prior-Year Earnings ($000)	Prior-Year EPS ($)
Q3	09/29/2000	120,800	18,073	0.89	110,076	15,043	0.74
Q2	06/30/2000	130,168	18,331	0.91	114,703	17,961	0.89
Q1	03/31/2000	120,227	14,975	0.73	103,241	11,201	0.56
Q4	12/31/99	114,454	15,136	0.74	105,113	14,478	0.72
	SUM	485,649	66,515	3.28	433,133	58,683	2.91

CURRENT: Q4 period is 14 weeks.

RECENT EVENTS

In **December 1999** the board of directors increased Graco's quarterly divident by 27 percent, to 14 cents a share. In **February 2000** the board authorized a plan for the company to purchase up to 1.2 million shares of its outstanding common stock, to offset stock issued to satisfy stock options and for other corporate purposes. The board also approved a share rights plan to replace an existing plan set to expire on March 29, 2000. In **May** 2000 the board announced plans to move the corporate headquarters to the Russell J. Gray Technical Center on the company's northeast Minneapolis campus (88 11th Ave. N.E., near the corner of Marshall Avenue and Broadway). About 75 employees, including the executive and corporate staff, were to move from Graco's Golden Valley, Minn., headquarters building—which was being offered for sale or lease—with the move expected to be completed in July. "Locating our corporate management with our largest manufacturing and engineering locations will pay big dividends in terms of closer communication and better decision-making," said President Johnson. **Sept. 29:** Graco reported record sales, net earnings, and earnings per share for the three months. "This is our 25th-consecutive quarter of year-to-year earnings per share growth and it is our third-consecutive quarter of double-digit sales growth," said CEO Aristides. "So far this year we have reported increases in our net sales and net earnings of 13 percent and 16 percent, respectively. These figures are very good given the weakness of the dollar."

OFFICERS

David A. Koch
Chairman

George Aristides
CEO

Dale D. Johnson
President and COO

Stephen L. Bauman
VP-Human Resources

Dan A. Christian
VP and Chief Information Officer

James A. Graner
VP and Controller

D. Christian Koch
VP-Lubrication Equipment Division

Dan Little
VP-Contractor Equipment Engineering

David M. Lowe
VP and Gen. Mgr.-European Operations

Robert M. Mattison
VP, General Counsel, and Secretary

Patrick J. McHale
VP-Contractor Equipment Division

Charles L. Rescorla
VP-Manufacturing/Distribution

William C. Scherer
VP-Industrial/Automotive Engineering

Mark W. Sheahan
VP and Treasurer

Fred A. Sutter
VP-Asia Pacific/Latin America

DIRECTORS

George Aristides

Ronald O. Baukol
3M Co., Maplewood, MN

Robert G. Bohn
Oshkosh Truck Corp., Oshkosh, WI

William J. Carroll
Dana Corp., Toledo, OH

Dale D. Johnson

David A. Koch

Lee R. Mitau
U.S. Bancorp, Minneapolis

Martha A.M. Morfitt
CNS Inc., Bloomington, MN

Dale R. Olseth
SurModics Inc., Eden Prairie, MN

Mark H. Rauenhorst
Opus Corp./Opus LCC, Minneapolis

Jerald L. Scott
H.B. Fuller Co. (retired)

William G. Van Dyke
Donaldson Co. Inc., Bloomington, MN

MAJOR SHAREHOLDERS

Ariel Capital Management Inc., 14.7%
Chicago

Clarissa L. Gray Trust/David A. Koch, 7.6%

All officers and directors as a group (19 persons), 9.7%

SIC CODE

3561 Pumps and pumping equipment

3586 Measuring and dispensing pumps

3594 Fluid power pumps and motors

MISCELLANEOUS

TRANSFER AGENT AND REGISTAR:
Wells Fargo Bank Minnesota N.A.,
South St. Paul, MN

TRADED: NYSE

SYMBOL: GGG

STOCKHOLDERS: 6,416

EMPLOYEES: 1,946

GENERAL COUNSEL:
Robert M. Mattison

AUDITORS:
Deloitte & Touche LLP, Minneapolis

INC: MN-1926

ANNUAL MEETING: May

INVESTOR RELATIONS:
Mark W. Sheahan

RANKINGS

No. 53 CRM Public 200

No. 44 CRM Performance 100

SUBSIDIARIES, DIVISIONS, AFFILIATES

U.S. LOCATIONS

Graco Inc. Main, Riverside Plants/Gray Technical Center

Graco Inc.

Graco Inc.

Graco Automotive Technology Center

Graco Inc.

PUB

TWO-YEAR QUARTERLY HIGH-LOW STOCK PRICES

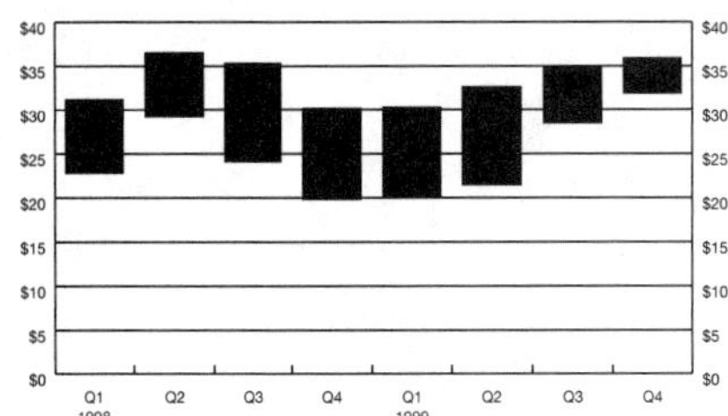

PUB

Great Northern Iron Ore Properties

W 1290 First National Bank Building, 332 Minnesota St., St. Paul, MN 55101
Tel: 651/224-2385 Fax: 651/224-2387

Great Northern Iron Ore Properties owns, in fee, mineral and nonmineral lands on the Mesabi Iron Range of Minnesota. Income is derived through royalties on iron ore minerals (principally taconite) taken from these properties by lessees. Great Northern is presently involved solely with the leasing and care of these properties. Great Northern itself has no control over the tonnage mined from its properties, but is solely involved with administering the leases on the properties. Because operating companies insist on freedom to move from property to property as mining requirements dictate, changes in production cannot be reduced to financial forecasts. Great Northern owns mineral interests in 12,033 acres on the Mesabi Iron Formation—7,443 acres that are wholly owned; 1,080 acres in which Great Northern is a tenant in common with a 91 percent interest; 3,350 acres in tenancy in common with a 50 percent interest; and 160 acres in tenancy in common with other fractional interests. Of said total, 7,152 acres are under lease and 4,881 acres are unleased.

EARNINGS HISTORY

Year Ended Dec 31	Operating Revenue/Sales (dollars in thousands)	Net Earnings	Return on Revenue (percent)	Return on Equity	Net Earnings (dollars per share)	Cash Dividend	Market Price Range
1999	10,926	9,354	NM	63.5	6.24	6.10	64.25–53.56
1998	11,783	10,152	NM	69.9	6.77	6.30	65.50–50.00
1997	10,030	8,488	NM	61.4	5.66	6.00	67.75–51.00
1996	10,530	8,988	NM	62.7	5.99	5.80	55.50–44.00
1995	9,656	8,149	NM	58.0	5.43	5.00	49.25–39.88

BALANCE SHEET

Assets	12/31/99 (dollars in thousands)	12/31/98	Liabilities	12/31/99 (dollars in thousands)	12/31/98
Current (CAE 364 and 941)	7,353	7,657	Current	2,482	2,819
U.S. Treasury Notes	4,135	4,083	Stockholders' equity*	14,725	14,522
Prepaid pension expense	433	318	TOTAL	17,207	17,341
Mineral lands	5,179	5,173			
Building and equipment	106	109			
TOTAL	17,207	17,341			

* No par common; 1,500,000 authorized; 1,500,000 and 1,500,000 issued and outstanding.

RECENT QUARTERS / PRIOR-YEAR RESULTS

	Quarter End	Revenue ($000)	Earnings ($000)	EPS ($)	Prior-Year Revenue ($000)	Prior-Year Earnings ($000)	Prior-Year EPS ($)
Q3	09/30/2000	4,660	4,267	2.84	3,169	2,785	1.86
Q2	06/30/2000	2,931	2,563	1.71	3,179	2,812	1.87
Q1	03/31/2000	1,141	700	0.47	1,594	1,168	0.78
Q4	12/31/99	2,984	2,588	1.73	2,767	2,409	1.61
	SUM	11,716	10,117	6.74	10,709	9,175	6.12

OFFICERS

Joseph S. Micallef
President, CEO, and Trustee

Thomas A. Janochoski
VP, Secretary, and CFO

Roger P. Johnson
Mgr.-Mines, Chief Engineer

DIRECTORS

Harry L. Holtz
Alliss Foundation

Joseph Micallef

Roger W. Staehle
University of Minnesota

Robert A. Stein
American Bar Association

SIC CODE

6799 Investors, nec

MISCELLANEOUS

TRANSFER AGENT AND REGISTAR:
Wells Fargo Bank Minnesota N.A., South St. Paul, MN

TRADED: NYSE

SYMBOL: GNI

STOCKHOLDERS: 2,297

EMPLOYEES: 10

GENERAL COUNSEL:
Oppenheimer Wolff & Donnelly LLP, Minneapolis

AUDITORS:
Ernst & Young LLP, Minneapolis

INC: MI-1906

RANKINGS

No. 181 CRM Public 200

TWO-YEAR QUARTERLY HIGH-LOW STOCK PRICES

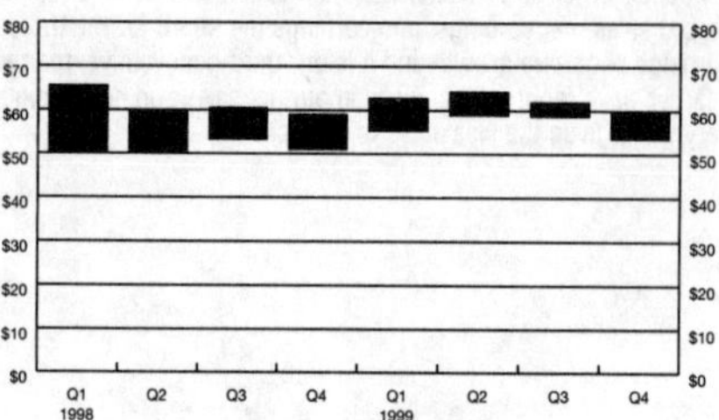

Great Plains Software Inc.

1701 S.W. 38th St., P.O. Box 9739, Fargo, ND 58103
Tel: 701/281-0555 Fax: 701/281-3752 Web site: http://www.gps.com

Great Plains Software is a developer, manufacturer, and marketer of accounting and business management software for LAN, client/server, workstation, and SQL systems. More than 3,500 VARs, consultants, and independent software vendors worldwide sell, install, and support its solutions.

EARNINGS HISTORY

Year Ended May 31	Operating Revenue/Sales (dollars in thousands)	Net Earnings	Return on Revenue (percent)	Return on Equity	Net Earnings (dollars per share*)	Cash Dividend	Market Price Range
2000 †	194,852	5,409	2.8	2.1	0.34	—	82.94–37.19
1999	134,907	12,785	9.5	9.6	0.90	—	49.00–26.75
1998 ¶	85,659	4,447	5.2	6.4	0.33	—	39.25–20.50
1997 #	57,120	3,644	6.4	29.3	0.36	—	
1996	42,271	7,461	17.7	NM	—	—	

* Trading began June 20, 1997.
† Pro forma 2000 results had the March 2000 acquisition of FRx Software Corp. occurred June 1, 1999: revenue $206,453,000; net loss $6,604,000/($0.40).
¶ Income figures for 1998 include pretax charge of $7,136,000 for acquired in-process R&D.
# ROE and EPS for 1997 are pro forma for the IPO.

BALANCE SHEET

Assets	05/31/00 (dollars in thousands)	05/31/99	Liabilities	05/31/00 (dollars in thousands)	05/31/99
Current (CAE 26,912 and 26,983)	131,394	148,904	Current (STD 1,289)	87,814	46,950
Property and equipment	46,898	19,351	Long-term debt, capital leases	3,007	
Goodwill and other intangibles	161,192	3,838	Stockholders' equity*	256,985	133,193
Deferred income taxes	1,444	2,982	TOTAL	347,806	180,143
Other	6,878	5,068			
TOTAL	347,806	180,143			

* $0.01 par common; 100,000,000 authorized; 17,375,010 and 15,362,820 issued and outstanding.

RECENT QUARTERS / **PRIOR-YEAR RESULTS**

	Quarter End	Revenue ($000)	Earnings ($000)	EPS ($)	Prior-Year Revenue ($000)	Prior-Year Earnings ($000)	Prior-Year EPS ($)
Q1	08/31/2000	67,065	(22,683)	(1.14)	39,868	3,503	0.23
Q4	05/31/2000	59,561	(2,573)	(0.15)	40,127	4,379	0.29
Q3	02/29/2000	48,057	118	0.01	35,844	3,362	0.24
Q2	11/30/99	47,366	4,361	0.28	31,807	2,860	0.21
	SUM	222,049	(20,777)	(1.00)	147,646	14,104	0.96

CURRENT: Q1 earnings include pretax items: $4.565 million restructuring charge; and $13.969 million amortization of acquired intangibles.

RECENT EVENTS

In **December 1999** Great Plains and Scala Business Solutions N.V. (AEX: SCA), Amsterdam, announced a strategic partnership to collaborate and deliver additional e-business and enterprise solutions to their global customers and clients. Scala was to expand its solution offerings to include Great Plains Enterprise Reporting and front office solutions. The two companies also planned to work together on the design and development of a new generation of Wireless Application Protocol (WAP) products to extend the e-business desktop to a variety of devices. The company expanded its international presence with the establishment of wholly owned subsidiary Great Plains Software Deutschland—after an equity investment in those operations two years earlier. Great Plains was named one of Fortune magazine's "100 Best Companies to Work for in America" for the third-consecutive year. Since joining the inaugural Fortune list at No. 53 in 1997, Great Plains had vaulted to the No. 15 position. In **January 2000** Great Plains agreed to acquire RealWorld Corp., a developer of accounting and business solutions, for 184,000 shares of Great Plains common stock and $5.5 million in cash. The deal was expected to add more than 20,000 midmarket customers and to expand channel capacity through RealWorld's partner network. The company also agreed to acquire a fixed-asset management solution for Dynamics and eEnterprise from The FORESTAR Group. Next, Great Plains expanded its European operations through the acquisition of BTK Software & Consulting AG—a developer of front office and back office solutions with offices in Germany, Austria, and Switzerland—in a cash and stock deal valued at $12.3 million. In **February** Great Plains announced immediate support for the Microsoft Windows 2000 operating system with its leading e-business product solutions, Great Plains eEnterprise, Great Plains Dynamics, and Great Plains Siebel Front Office. The company agreed to acquire FRx Software Corp., the standard for midmarket financial reporting; and PWA Group Ltd., a leading provider of upper-tier mid-market human resource and payroll solutions based in the United Kingdom. By **March** more than 200 dotcom companies were using Great Plains e-business solutions. Great Plains became a premiere e-business solutions provider for Houston-based ebaseOne Corp. (OTC Bulletin Board: EBAS), an emerging leader in the *continued on page 224*

OFFICERS

Douglas J. Burgum
Chairman, President, and CEO
Jodi A. Uecker-Rust
COO
Tami L. Reller
CFO
Jeffrey A. Young
EVP-Global Operations
Darren C. Laybourn
VP-Global Development
Lynne Stockstad
VP-E-business
Steven K. Sydness
VP-International Operations

DIRECTORS

Bradley J. Burgum
Burgum & Irby Law Firm
Douglas J. Burgum
Frederick W. Burgum
Arthur Cos. Inc.
Raymond F. Good
consultant
Sanjeev K. Mehra
Goldman, Sachs & Co., New York
J. A. Heidi Roizen
independent consultant
J. Leland Strange
Intelligent Systems Corp.
Joseph S. Tibbetts Jr.
Lightbridge Inc., Burlington, MA

MAJOR SHAREHOLDERS

Frederick W. Burgum, 12.3%
Douglas J. Bergum, 8.1%
All officers and directors as a group (11 persons), 23.7%

SIC CODE

7372 Prepackaged software

MISCELLANEOUS

TRANSFER AGENT AND REGISTAR:
Wells Fargo Bank Minnesota N.A., South St. Paul, MN
TRADED: Nasdaq National Market
SYMBOL: GPSI
STOCKHOLDERS: 284
EMPLOYEES: 1,775
GENERAL COUNSEL:
Dorsey & Whitney PLLP, Minneapolis
AUDITORS:
PricewaterhouseCoopers LLP, Minneapolis

ANNUAL MEETING:
September

SUBSIDIARIES, DIVISIONS, AFFILIATES

Great Plains Software (UK) LLC
London

Great Plains Software Australia/Asia
Sydney, Australia

PUB

TWO-YEAR QUARTERLY HIGH-LOW STOCK PRICES

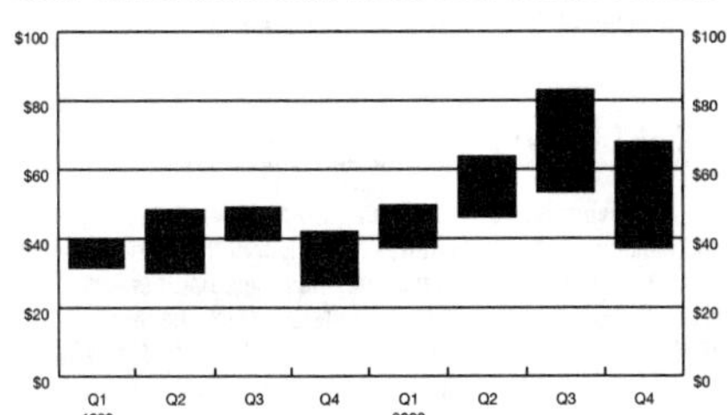

PUB

Grow Biz International Inc.

4200 Dahlberg Dr., Suite 100, Golden Valley, MN 55422
Tel: 763/520-8500 Fax: 763/520-8410 Web site: http://www.growbiz.com

Grow Biz International Inc. develops and franchises retail concepts for stores that sell, buy, and consign used and new merchandise. In 1988 the company introduced its initial store concept, **Play it Again Sports.** These stores sell and buy a broad range of used and new sporting goods, equipment, and accessories. In March 1993 Grow Biz began awarding franchises for its second store concept, **Once Upon A Child**. These stores sell and buy used and new children's clothing, toys, furniture, and accessories. The company has also introduced several newer concepts: **Music-Go-Round** provides new and used musical instruments to amateurs and professionals; and **ReTool** retail stores buy and sell used and new tools. The company acquired **Plato's Closet**, Columbus and Toledo, Ohio—a business that buys and sells used and new apparel to the teenage market. The company has 1,226 stores in operation and an additional 109 franchises awarded but not open. Of the stores in operation, there are 634 Play It Again Sports, 222 Once Upon A Child, 67 Music Go Round, and 8 ReTool stores.

EARNINGS HISTORY

Year Ended Dec	Operating Revenue/Sales (dollars in thousands)	Net Earnings	Return on Revenue (percent)	Return on Equity	Net Earnings (dollars per share)	Cash Dividend	Market Price Range
1999 *	66,558	(8,589)	(12.9)	NM	(1.65)	—	13.31–2.88
1998 †	96,351	7,244	7.5	71.3	1.28	—	15.25–9.50
1997 ¶	88,835	3,231	3.6	18.5	0.53	—	17.25–8.75
1996	91,550	2,586	2.8	14.6	0.40	—	11.25–6.84
1995	100,213	2,029	2.0	9.6	0.28	—	13.31–9.00

* Income figures for 1999 include pretax charge of $11,345,500 for restructuring related to disposal of It's About Games.
† Income figures for 1998 include pretax gain of $5,231,500 on sale of Disc Go Round.
¶ Income figures for 1997 include pretax litigation expense of $2 million. Results include Video Game Exchange from its August 1997 date of acquisition for $6,579,700. Pro forma for full year: revenue $97,230,400; earnings $3,498,000/$0.57.

BALANCE SHEET

Assets	12/25/99 (dollars in thousands)	12/26/98	Liabilities	12/25/99 (dollars in thousands)	12/26/98
Current (CAE 0 and 2,418)	21,972	30,595	Current (STD 9,288 and 14,464)	19,224	29,491
Property and equipment	4,369	5,961	Long-term debt	7,529	3,485
Receivables	1,156	1,209	Stockholders' equity*	2,889	10,165
Noncompete agreements and other	330	555	TOTAL	29,642	43,141
Goodwill	1,814	4,823			
TOTAL	29,642	43,141			

* No par common; 10,000,000 authorized; 5,346,119 and 5,079,055 issued and outstanding.

RECENT QUARTERS / **PRIOR-YEAR RESULTS**

	Quarter End	Revenue ($000)	Earnings ($000)	EPS ($)	Revenue ($000)	Earnings ($000)	EPS ($)
Q3	09/23/2000	11,542	739	0.14	16,674	(7,441)	(1.43)
Q2	06/24/2000	12,284	(1,798)	(0.33)	15,265	(121)	(0.02)
Q1	03/25/2000	12,807	25	0.00	18,535	(175)	(0.03)
Q4	12/25/99	16,085	(852)	(0.16)	24,746	837	0.16
	SUM	52,717	(1,886)	(0.35)	75,220	(6,901)	(1.32)

CURRENT: Q3 earnings include pretax gain of $0.537 million on sale of Computer Renaissance. Q2 earnings include a pretax nonrecurring charge of $3.338 million on sale of company-owned stores and write-off of certain intangible assets. Q4 earnings include pretax gain of $0.23 million on reversal of restructuring charge.
PRIOR YEAR: Q3 earnings include pretax restructuring charge of $11.575 million to discontinue operations of 60 company-owned It's About Games stores.

RECENT EVENTS

By late **November 1999**, the company had divested nearly all of its 60-store chain of It's About Games. After selling 32 stores and closing 26, only two stores remained. At the same time, Nasdaq's national market was threatening to delist the company's stock because Grow Biz's net tangible assets had declined to half the Nasdaq minimum requirement of $4 million. The listing was subsequently moved from the Nasdaq National Market to the Nasdaq SmallCap Market effective Feb. 7, 2000. In **February 2000** Computer Renaissance launched a Web site (www.compren.com) where consumers can find out what their computer equipment is worth in cash or trade. In **March** founder and CEO K. Jeffrey Dahlberg resigned. He was replaced by Winthrop Resources founder John Morgan, who also acquired 13 percent of the *continued on page 224*

OFFICERS

John Morgan
Chairman and CEO
Kirk MacKenzie
Vice Chairman
Charles V. Kanan
VP-Operations, Play it Again Sports
Mark Hooley
VP and General Counsel

DIRECTORS

William Dunlap Jr.
Campbell Mithun Esty, Minneapolis
Kirk A. MacKenzie
John Morgan
Paul C. Reyelts
Valspar Corp., Minneapolis
Mark L. Wilson
Weisman Enterprises Inc., Minneapolis

MAJOR SHAREHOLDERS

K. Jeffrey Dahlberg, 25.3%
Wayzata, MN
Ronald G. Olson, 25%
Long Lake, MN
Sheldon T. Fleck, 12.2%
Minneapolis
John L. Morgan, 10.5%
All officers and directors as a group (10 persons), 38.2%

SIC CODE

6794 Patent owners and lessors

MISCELLANEOUS

TRANSFER AGENT AND REGISTAR:
Wells Fargo Bank Minnesota N.A., South St. Paul, MN
TRADED: Nasdaq SmallCap Market
SYMBOL: GBIZ
STOCKHOLDERS: 252
EMPLOYEES: 220
PART TIME: 41
GENERAL COUNSEL:
Gray, Plant, Mooty, Mooty & Bennett P.A., Minneapolis
AUDITORS:
Arthur Andersen LLP, Minneapolis
INC: MN-1988
ANNUAL MEETING: May

RANKINGS

No. 104 CRM Public 200

SUBSIDIARIES, DIVISIONS, AFFILIATES

Play It Again Sports
Charles V. Kanan

Once Upon A Child
Becky Geyer

Music Go Round
John Paavola

ReTool
Paul Price

Plato's Closet
Becky Geyer

TWO-YEAR QUARTERLY HIGH-LOW STOCK PRICES

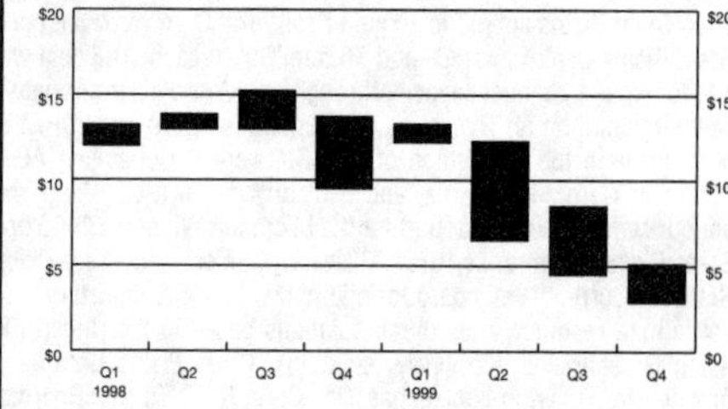

eBenX Inc.

continued from page 191 initiated coverage of eBenX with a STRONG BUY rating. Mark Tierney, the chairman and co-founder of eBenX, outlined a vision for the administration of a risk-adjusted defined contribution system that would limit health care costs, liability, and infrastructure spending for employers—and increase health plan choices for employees—through the use of an Internet-based exchange and risk-adjusted, per-employee, per-month payments to health plans. eBenX saved $4.3 million for one of its largest employer clients (Fortune top 50) on costs associated with that client's health care benefits in 1999. In **June** eBenX agreed to be a part of the PeopleSoft (Nasdaq: PSFT) MarketPlace, a business-to-business trading exchange where customers, suppliers, and employees can collaborate and do business efficiently over the Internet. The Stanton Group, Minnetonka, Minn., became a charter member of the eBenX Benefit Exchange. Raleigh, Schwarz & Powell, the largest employee-owned insurance brokerage firm in the state of Washington, became a charter member of the eBenX Benefit Exchange. In **July** five large, national employers, representing more than 80,000 employees, committed to provide eBenX Benefit Exchange services to simplify and automate the enrollment, ongoing eligibility communication, and billing and payment processes associated with the administration of health and welfare benefits. The Managed Care Organizations participating in the PlanLink Network, local and regional plans that have joined together to provide national coverage for mid-size employer groups, also joined the Exchange. eBenX shared an innovative health plan pricing model that could ultimately result in lower health care costs and more stable premium rates for employers. The model lays the groundwork for a risk-adjusted defined contribution system that would limit infrastructure spending for employers while increasing choice for employees by offering them more control over their selection of health plans. Mesirow Financial's Insurance Services Division joined the eBenX Benefit Exchange as a charter member. In **August**, based on its revenue growth from 1995 to 1999, the company was named to Deloitte & Touche's Minnesota Technology Fast 50. eBenX signed a definitive agreement to acquire Arbor Administrative Services Inc., d/b/a Arbor Associates (http://www.arborassoc.com), Philadelphia, a privately held, Web-based benefits administrator and application service provider (ASP). Arbor shareholders were to receive $17 million in cash and 2,587,500 shares of eBenX common stock, for a total value of $63.25 million based on eBenX's recent stock price of $17.88. "The acquisition of Arbor accelerates our mid-market presence," said CEO Davis. "In one shot, we add over 120,000 committed employee lives, deep domain expertise in benefits administration, great mid-market broker relationships, and a strong and satisfied mid-market customer base." [Deal completed in September.] In response to the deal, W.R. Hambrecht & Co., San Francisco, reiterated its STRONG BUY rating and $50 target price. **Sept. 30**: Excluding $1.8 million in amortization of stock-based compensation and $1.5 million in amortization of goodwill and other intangibles, the pro forma net loss for the nine months was $4.0 million/($0.24) compared with ($0.27) for the same prior-year period. Enrollment commitments had grown 53 percent, from 560,000 a year earlier to 855,000. In **October** the integration of the eBenX Benefit Exchange with PeopleSoft 7.5 HRMS benefits applications met the technical requirements to become certified by PeopleSoft's Partner Integration Team. Employers utilizing the eBenX Exchange gained the capability to check and correct their consolidated health plan bill online in order to assure accuracy. In **November** the company announced the use of eXtensible Markup Language, or XML, as a new standard for sending secured client enrollment data via the Internet. This lowered the barriers for carriers who could not yet accept a custom data interface.

E.mergent Inc.

continued from page 192 ucts and services divisions generated significant revenue growth resulting in our fifth-consecutive quarter with record revenue and continued profitability. We are entering the fourth quarter with a large backlog of orders."

Ecolab Inc.

continued from page 195 additive petition to use peroxyacetic acid as a red meat carcass antimicrobial treatment—effective against E. coli 0157: H7, Salmonella typhimurium, and Listeria monocytogenes. The company was was one of four in the Twin Cities named to Industry Week magazine's fifth annual list of the World's 100 Best-Managed Companies. It was Ecolab's second appearance on the list. In **September** Ecolab formed a joint venture with Zohar Dalia Soap & Detergent Factory of Kibbutz Dalia, Israel; and acquired Facilitec Corp., an Elgin, Ill.-based provider of rooftop grease filter products and kitchen exhaust cleaning services for restaurants. In an administrative complaint filed against Ecolab for selling and distributing several unregistered pesticides, the EPA ordered Ecolab to stop selling and distributing ChloraSorb products (used to clean up spilled bodily fluids at health care facilities) and proposed a penalty of $546,700. U.S. Bancorp Piper Jaffray, in its monthly commentary, reiterated its STRONG BUY rating and $48 price target. **Sept. 30:** Continued gains from its domestic and international businesses led Ecolab's third-quarter earnings gain of 9.7 percent, which beat analysts' forecasts by a penny. CEO Schuman said, "The third quarter was our toughest comparison of the year, and we are very pleased with these outstanding results, which yielded our 23rd-consecutive quarter of double-digit earnings per share growth. Third-quarter sales for Ecolab's U.S. Cleaning & Sanitizing operations rose 6 percent to $408 million, benefiting from new products and services as well as aggressive sales efforts and programs. Ecolab was expecting sales for both domestic and international operations to increase in the fourth quarter 2000 over the fourth quarter 1999. In **October** Ecolab purchased a 17 percent interest in start-up FreshLoc Technologies Inc., Plano, Texas, a developer of wireless food safety technology; and purchased $4 million-revenue Peterson's Parts & Service, a Salt Lake City provider of commercial equipment parts and repair services.

Energy West Inc.

continued from page 198 decrease in energy marketing income. CEO Geske said "It is highly unusual for Montana, Arizona, and Wyoming to experience warmer than normal winters all at the same time. The company's geographic diversity usually dilutes the effect of a warm winter in a single area." The company's energy marketing subsidiary, ENERGY WEST Resources (EWR), experienced a decrease in net income, from net income of $264,000 in FY1999 to a net loss of $109,000 in FY2000, as a result of startup costs in the retail energy marketing business and a reduction in gas and electricity margins caused by more competitive markets and timing associated with certain electricity supply contracts. EWR's industrial and large commercial division experienced record earnings in FY2000. EWR's focus for business development in FY2001 was expected to be mid- and large-sized commercial customers. EWR had secured a two-year, competitive electricity supply contract and had signed agreements with several Montana memberships groups, including the League of Cities and Towns, School Boards Association and other trade associations, to offer electricity supply to their members. In **July** the company completed two projects that were expected to contribute positively to earnings in FY2001: the purchase of two pipelines in northern Wyoming to be operated as natural gas gathering lines; and the opening of a propane transfer terminal, located adjacent to a rail spur and the interstate highway near Superior, Mont.

Entegris Inc.

continued from page 199 excellent melt flow of Teflon PFA HP Plus allows molding fittings in new configurations that save space in crowded equipment cabinets. In **May** DuPont Fluoroproducts presented Chairman Quernemoen with DuPont's first Bro Award for Life Achievement in Fluoropolymers. In **June** the price of the IPO's 13 million shares was revised to $13 to $15 each (from $15 to $17). In **July** the company introduced its FlareMount mounting technology, which seals the award-winning Galtek SG valves into a surface-mount manifold configuration using industry-proven Flaretek fitting technology; and the Deteq vortex flowmeter, which cobines vortex-shedding technology with Entegris' fluoropolymer molding expertise for high reliability in measuring the volumetric fluid flow. Entegris also launched its business-to-business Web site, http://www.entegris.com, providing the most-up-to-date, reliable source of materials integrity information direct from the manufacturer. On **July 10**, Entegris again revised pricing of the IPO, to $11 to $13 per share from $13 to $15. On July 11, the offering was completed at $11. Of the 13 million shares of common stock offered, 8.6 million shares were sold by Entegris and 4.4 million shares were sold by selling stockholders. Entegris granted the underwriters of the public offering the right to purchase up to an additional 1.95 million shares to cover overallotments. In **August** the company received the prestigious SEMICONDUCTOR 300 (SC300) Top Tier Supplier Award 1999 for its 300 mm front-opening unified pod (FOUP). (Entegris has been the sole supplier of 300 mm FOUPs for the pilot line at SC300—a joint venture between Infineon Technologies and Motorola in Dresden, Germany—since 1998.) Entegris won a competitive bid for its KA200 wafer carriers from Silterra Malaysia Sdn. Bhd., which planned to use these carriers in its 200 mm standard mechanical interface (SMIF) fab, the first of several such semiconductor fabs in Kulim, Malaysia, planned by the company to manufacture logic integrated circuits (ICs) with design rules of 0.25 micron, 0.18 micron, and smaller. Entegris received a volume order from a major Japanese-based semiconductor IC manufacturer for its F300 AutoPod 300 mm front-opening unified pod (FOUP) and Process One FX30 cleaning system. **Aug. 26**: Every Entegris product group had record sales for the fiscal year. Fluid Handling products experienced the highest growth, with a 77 percent sales increase from fiscal 1999 levels during the semiconductor industry expansion. Microelectronic product sales improved by 31 percent. On a pro forma basis, earnings for fiscal year 2000 were $0.79 compared to $0.09 for fiscal 1999, excluding an extraordinary charge. "Given the current industry conditions, we expect sales to increase year-over-year for fiscal 2001 by about 20 percent, and operating margins and net income to improve," President Dauwalter said. In **September** Entegris received a $1 million order for its F300 300 mm front-opening unified pods (FOUPs). The company donated $20,000 to the University of Minnesota's Department of Mechanical Engineering to enable the university to develop measurement methods for determining particle levels on plastic components, such as wafer carriers and pods. Entegris unveiled the industry's first fiber-free carrier for disk substrate polishing, which had been developed using a breakthrough, patent-pending technology recently acquired from HP Plastics in Austin, Texas.

FSI International Inc.

continued from page 201 ly $7.0 million for ZETA 200 and MERCURY Surface Conditioning Systems, to be used in photoresist stripping applications. In **April** several leading semiconductor manufacturers in the United States and Europe teamed with FSI to develop environmentally friendly wafer cleaning and resist stripping processes with ozone-based chemistries—to reduce the use of harsh and more costly chemicals, which the global semiconductor industry had employed since the 1970s. The U.S. District Court for the District of Delaware granted a motion for summary judgment in favor of FSI's subsidiary, YieldUP International Corp. (now known as SCD Mountain View), and against CFM Technologies Inc. (Nasdaq: CFMT) in patent-infringement litigation brought by CFM. The judge ruled both of CFM's patents invalid for lack of enablement. A major U.S. semiconductor manufacturer ordered a ZETA 300 Surface Conditioning System for back-end solvent strip applications on cutting-edge logic devices in the company's 300-mm pilot line. FSI was notified by a major U.S. manufacturer of semiconductors that its POLARIS 3500 Resist Processing Cluster was to be used for wafer processing in the manufacturer's new 300-mm fab. In **May** FSI received more than $60 million in orders for its POLARIS 2500 Microlithography Clusters and ZETA Surface Conditioning Systems from 1st Silicon (Malaysia) Sdn. Bhd. FSI received orders totaling $8.0 million for its POLARIS 2500 Microlithography Clusters from two major thin film head manufacturers. The systems were to perform DUV processing used in next-generation thin film head technology. When the Minnesota Job Skills Partnership presented a grant for $400,000 to Dunwoody Institute—which was to partner with FSI to develop Internet-based, on-demand training programs over the next two years—FSI matched the grant with an $800,000 in-kind contribution. In a collaborative program leveraging the benefits of a fully integrated lithography cell, FSI and ASM Lithography Holding N.V. (Nasdaq: ASML) linked one of FSI's POLARIS 2500 Microlithography Cluster tools with a PAS 5500/750 deep UV Step & Scan system from ASML. **May 27:** Sales for the third quarter of fiscal 2000 increased 80 percent to $67.7 million compared to the same period of fiscal 1999. The company also experienced sequential order growth as compared to the second quarter of fiscal 2000, with orders for the third quarter exceeding $100 million, a record level. "Our sales and record order levels reflect the strong industry conditions," commented CEO Mitchell. In **June** the ZETA® 300 Surface Conditioning System successfully completed Phase I evaluation at Selete, a technology consortium of major Japanese semiconductor manufacturers developing 300-mm wafer fabrication processes. Tower Semiconductor (Nasdaq: TSEM) upgraded its POLARIS Microlithography 1000, 2000, and 2100 Clusters with advanced process modules as a part of an ongoing capacity expansion. In **July** FSI and The Dow Chemical Co. (NYSE: DOW) signed an agreement to jointly demonstrate the use of SiLK semiconductor dielectric resins from Dow with copper circuit lines to create a fully integrated dual damascene process. FSI and Metron Technology (Nasdaq: MTCH) reached an agreement in principle with EKC Technology Inc., Hayward, Calif., to enter into a joint development project to co-develop a semiaqueous chemistry (SAC) process for back-end-of-line (BEOL) resist stripping, to meet the needs of the emerging copper/low-k markets. At month's end, FSI received an initial order for five POLARIS 3500 Microlithography Clusters from the new customer that was announced in April. In **August** a major U.S. semiconductor manufacturer ordered four ZETA 300 Surface Conditioning Systems from FSI to equip its new 300 mm semiconductor manufacturing facility. ANADIGICS Inc., a leading supplier of wireless and broadband communications solutions, placed its first order for a POLARIS 2500 Microlithography Cluster, to be used to manufacture six-inch gallium arsenide (GaAs) wafers in the company's New Jersey facility. FSI received a follow-on order of $35 million for its POLARIS 3500 Microlithography Clusters to be installed in a major U.S. semiconductor manufacturer's 300-mm fab. When installed, these systems brought this customer's installed base to 100 POLARIS Cluster units. FSI was planning to record $4.1 million in fourth-quarter charges associated with the infrastructure realignment program of its lean enterprise initiative. The company was going to close its Mountain View and Fremont, Calif., facilities and move all of their product design and manufacturing operations to Allen, Texas, or Chaska, Minn. In addition, FSI planned to discontinue production of the nickel iron-plating product that it was manufacturing for a thin-film head customer. **Aug. 26:** For fiscal year 2000, sales increased 94 percent to $219.8 million. After adjusting for special charges and a stock gain, the company's fiscal 2000 net income was $600,000, or $0.02 per share. "In fiscal 2000 the company started to recognize the benefits of its investment in infrastructure and product and process application development programs that occurred during the past few years," stated CEO Mitchell. With fiscal 2000 fourth quarter orders of more than $130 million, the company began fiscal 2001 with a record $184 million in backlog, as compared to $45 million at the beginning of fiscal 2000. In **October FSI** reported that STMicroelectronics had processed 1 million wafers since February using FSI's environmentally friendly DIO3- (ozonated water) based resist strip processing for front-end-of-line (FEOL) production, in a facility in Italy. A major U.S. semiconductor manufacturer purchased another ZETA 300 Surface Conditioning System, for back-end solvent strip applications on cutting-edge logic devices in the company's 300 mm pilot line. FSI's DIO3 Generation Module was judged by Semiconductor International magazine as a process application that demonstrates superior performance in semiconductor manufacturing.

Famous Dave's of America Inc.

continued from page 202 announced a major initiative in which Hormel Foods was to produce, market, and distribute four retail barbecue meat products (HORMEL Fully Cooked Entrees) featuring Famous Dave's award-winning "Rich and Sassy" sauce for the refrigerated meat section of grocery stores nationwide. Famous Dave's was planning to convert two existing steakhouse restaurants in the Salt Lake City suburbs to Famous Dave's units. Famous Dave's agreed to acquire four KC Masterpiece Barbecue & Grill restaurants in Kansas City and St. Louis; the royalty rights for the KC Masterpiece Barbecue & Grill Restaurant at the Kansas City International Airport; and the rights to continue expanding the brand. At month's end, the company opened in Champaign, Ill., its 40th unit overall. In **November** the company won the TOP GUN award for local store marketing excellence in the restaurant industry.

Fargo Electronics Inc.

continued from page 203 All of the 5.0 million shares were to be sold by the company at a price between $14 and $16 a share, with proceeds going toward repayment of indebtedness, redemption of preferred stock and accrued dividends, working capital, and general corporate purposes. The $15 per share IPO was declared effective Feb. 10, 2000. Smart card expert Joseph Schuler joined the company in late April as product manager for Electronic Cards. Also in April, Fargo was issued U.S. Patent No. 6,022,429 covering a plastic card lamination technique it had developed. The patent covers placement of a clear or holographic laminate patch over the surface of plastic identification cards to protect a printed image from wear or fading. In **May** Fargo announced the release of its newest robust, high-volume, high-speed Direct-To-Card (DTC) printers, the DTC700 series. In **June** the company announced the second-quarter outlook: "While we expect to post a modest profit for the second quarter, shipments of our new line of High-Definition Printer systems have not yet come up to the levels we anticipated," said CEO Holland. "We continue to operate with a backlog for the HDP product line, and had we been able to eliminate that backlog, we would have met our financial expectations for the quarter." In **September** Fargo was granted a Notice of Allowance of its patent on its High Definition Printing Series printers, which print images onto a special film that is then fused into the surface of a card through heat and pressure. Fargo introduced its Professional Series products, which include Fargo's fastest, highest-quality, and most robust printers; Persona brand printers, designed for a variety of low- to moderate-volume card printing applications; a new distribution program to recognize its channel relations with distributors and integrators worldwide; and a new series of Direct-To-Card (DTC) printers that offer high-quality, high-speed printing and an array of options that include dual card hoppers (a patent for which was recently filed) and increased security. Fargo and HID Corp. successfully completed independent lab analysis and passed standardized industry tests. Fargo established a new $30 million revolving credit facility with two Chicago-based banks: LaSalle Bank, an operating unit of ABN Amro Inc. (NYSE: ABN); and Harris Bank, an operating unit of The Bank of Montreal. **Sept. 30:** "Results in the third quarter reflect Fargo's entry into a period of transition to a totally new lineup of products," said CEO Holland. "We are very pleased with the enthusiastic response of our customers and distributors to the new product lines. However, the full benefit of this enthusiasm on Fargo's top-line growth is still approximately two quarters away, due to the sales cycle and the process of ramping up production on the new printer models."

FieldWorks Inc.

continued from page 205 on-vehicle use, and missile control. In **April** the company completed a $1.0 million equity investment by Industrial-Works Holding Co. LLC, a wholly owned subsidiary of Glenmount International LP, and also announced plans to proceed with a rights offering for shares of FieldWorks common stock. FieldWorks announced the availability of its next-generation Mobile Data Server—the FieldWorks FW2000 Series II. In **May** FieldWorks reduced its workforce by 20 positions (20 percent). CEO Mell commented, "We are taking what we believe to be the necessary actions to better align our costs as a result of the company's financial performance during the first quarter." Its stock listing was also downsized from Nasdaq National Market to Nasdaq SmallCap. In **June** the company launched the FieldWorks Strategic Alliance Reseller (STAR) Program: order referrals, sales and technical support, special marketing programs, onsite training, and preferred pricing and payment terms for qualifying value-added resellers. FieldWorks announced the signing of an agreement for a $2.5 million loan from Kontron Embedded Computers, Munich. Kontron was to provide $2.5 million for continuing operations in exchange for a subordinated note, and warrants to purchase 1.25 million shares of FieldWorks common stock at $1. As part of the agreement, FieldWorks was to grant an option to Kontron to purchase 7.75 million shares of FieldWorks common stock at a total purchase price of $7.75 million through Aug. 15, 2000. In addition, Kontron and Industrial-Works Holding Co. LLC (Glenmount) entered into an agreement that would allow Glenmount to sell to Kontron a portion of their holdings of FieldWorks convertible preferred stock in exchange for 60,000 shares of Kontron stock. Following the closing of these transactions, Kontron would own a controlling interest in FieldWorks. Stockholders reacted poorly: Fieldworks stock fell 40 percent over the week following the announcement. In **July** the company was selected by the Franklin Police Department, Franklin, Tenn., to equip the department's entire squad car fleet with the FieldWorks FW2000 Mobile Data Server. In **August** the company entered into an operating agreement with Kontron, which promised to provide FieldWorks with timely completion of existing product development programs in fourth quarter 2000 with substantial costs absorbed by Kontron. In addition, Kontron exercised an amended equity option to acquire 6 million shares of common stock of FieldWorks for a purchase price of $5.4 million. Related to Kontron's new majority position in FieldWorks, a management reorganization was announced. The 10 percent workforce reduction, primarily in management, was designed to take advantage of synergies within the two companies, reduce ongoing administrative and operating expenses, and further streamline the organization in light of Kontron's deepening involvement with FieldWorks. An additional extension until the closing of the equity transactions with Kontron, whereupon FieldWorks will satisfy the net tangible asset requirement and all other Nasdaq listing requirements, was not granted by Nasdaq. Its stock listing was delisted from Nasdaq SmallCap to the Over The Counter (OTC) Bulletin Board. The company announced the availability of the FieldWorks FW8000 Series II Field WorkStation, a next-generation version of the company's FW8000 platform and the first rugged, portable desktop of its kind to offer the performance power of the 500 MHz Intel Pentium III processor. At the end of October, FieldWorks' shareholders approved the transfer of FieldWorks stock from Industrial-Works Holding Co. LLC to Kontron Embedded Computers AG.

Fourth Shift Corporation

continued from page 210 free service that enables manufacturers to compare their financial performance against a relevant peer group, in real time, on the Web. In **April** Fourth Shift announced a strategic partnership with Abraham Technical Services Inc. to extend Complete Care to include wireless barcode data collection hardware for time and attendance management and shop floor automation. In **June** the company said that, after posting a net loss below current market expectations for the second quarter, it was going to lay off 10 percent of its workforce in an effort to trim costs. "Businesses are asking for advice on Internet strategy and looking over their shoulders for what their peers are planning, so they are holding off buying decisions," said CEO Stuckey. "This decision dam will break and the race will be on to get operational, but when is still uncertain. Fourth Shift is positioned to grow rapidly when buying decisions resume." In **July** Fourth Shift and Ultimate Software (Nasdaq: ULTI), a leading provider of Web-based payroll and employee management solutions, agreed to co-brand Fourth Shift HRMS, a "Powered by UltiPro" solution designed to deliver best-of-breed in-house payroll and human resource functionality to mid-market manufacturers. Fourth Shift and Grant Thornton LLP formed a strategic alliance to help manufacturers become more competitive and profitable using e-business solutions. Fourth Shift and SupplierMarket.com partnered to bring together enhanced e-commerce functionality for Fourth Shift users. In **August** Eastman Kodak Co., a Fourth Shift customer for 14 years, extended a global partnership agreement to include e-business solutions to enable Kodak's Fourth Shift manufacturing sites to communicate with corporate ERP systems around the world. Fourth Shift released a re-designed manufacturing analysis module for Fourth Shift 7 that helps manufacturers reduce the time and cost of producing products. For the second year in a row, Fourth Shift was among 24 companies to be recognized by start magazine as one of its "Hottest Companies of 2000," based on continuous improvement and overall product excellence. In **September** Working Family Resource Center, St, Paul, presented Fourth Shift with a Working Family Support Award. **Sept. 30**: Operating profit of $115,000 for the third quarter resulted in a 1 cent per share loss after non-operating expenses. This compared to an operating loss of $3.6 million in the previous quarter. "Third quarter results represent substantial performance improvement over last quarter, principally due to expense control," said CEO Stuckey, "but market growth has not yet resumed. In **October** Fourth Shift created Headwaters Inc., a new subsidiary dedicated to helping companies improve customer relationships. It then released Your Customer Center, a Web-based order entry and tracking system that is completely integrated with the Fourth Shift Complete Care suite of Internet-enabled enterprise resource planning applications (ERP) for manufacturers. In **November** Fourth Shift purchased Endurant Business Solutions of St. Paul. "This strategic acquisition accelerates Fourth Shift's expansion into the global e-CRM consulting arena initiated by the establishment of Headwaters Inc. earlier this fall," stated President Caldwell.

H.B. Fuller Company

continued from page 211 adhesives, sealants, and coatings business of Childers Products Co., Cleveland. **Aug. 26:** Both sales and earnings for the third quarter were below the previous year's results. CEO Stroucken remarked, "This quarter is extremely disappointing for us. Corrective measures to counteract the severe impact of rapidly escalating raw material prices did not take hold in the marketplace until late in August. Going forward, we expect raw material cost pressures and the Euro currency weakness to continue. In response, aggressive implementation of price increases is presently underway and the entire organization is focused on returning our results to levels this business is capable of producing." Fuller announced a price increase to help offset the effects of rising raw material costs on its global adhesives businesses, effective Sept. 1 for all regions. Coupled with price increases implemented earlier in the quarter, the net impact on customers was expected to be a 10 percent increase within water-based markets and an 8 percent increase within hot melt markets. In **October** Fuller announced that 27 of 33 eligible senior managers had participated to date in the company's Executive Stock Purchase Loan Program, borrowing a total of $10.6 million in personal loans to buy, cumulatively, 348,382 shares of H.B. Fuller common stock. "Our objective is to directly align key managers with shareholders' interests," said CEO Stroucken. "We expect key managers, those whom we have determined have the ability to significantly impact company results, to own a substantial amount of H.B. Fuller stock." Fuller opened Sealantsource.com, an electronic storefront with the ability to host several companies in the adhesives and sealants industry. H.B. Fuller announced the spin-off its e-business unit as a separate company named Stratyc. "As our e-business group created and clarified its mission and identified opportunities, it became apparent that a separate business structure could serve not only H.B. Fuller, but other companies as well," said Stroucken.

General Mills Inc.

continued from page 214 took Kellogg Co. as the largest cerealmaker by volume, as well—with 29.8 percent of the market (compared to Kellogg's 27.9 percent) in a recent four-week period. The gains in volume came despite recent price increases on its brands. General Mills took share from Kellogg in part by having cereals that were more difficult for private labels to copy. In **January 2000** General Mills agreed to collaborate with DuPont's Protein Technologies International (PTI) in developing and marketing soy foods. (Increased consumer awareness of soy's health benefits was already driving strong market growth for soy-based food products.) In **February** the board increased the company's stock repurchase authorization by 50 million shares, raising the treasury authorization from 120 million to 170 million shares. Believing that the incremental repurchases were to be debt-financed, Standard & Poor's downgraded General Mills' rating from STABLE to NEGATIVE. At the Consumer Analysts Group of New York's annual food, beverage, and tobacco stock conference, General Mills reaffirmed its commitment to achieving double-digit growth in earnings per share for the current fiscal year, and outlined broad growth goals for the next decade. Looking beyond 2000, CEO Sanger identified three powerful trends expected to present challenges and growth opportunities for food companies: first, consumers' increasing demand for ever-more convenient food products; second, the transformation of food retail channels, from the consolidation of traditional grocers to the emergence of Internet grocery services; and, finally, the advances of medical science and nutrition technology, which hold the promise of helping consumers choose foods they enjoy that also benefit their health. General Mills and Chumbo.com, a pioneering e-commerce company and leading online software retailer, announced a joint marketing initiative to offer consumers free popular software titles in boxes of all six Cheerios brands beginning March 1. **Feb. 27:** Third-quarter jumps in sales and earnings—fueled by new products and recent acquisitions—had the company on track for a third-consecutive year of double-digit EPS growth. In **March** General Mills and Land O'Lakes Inc., Arden Hills, Minn., formed an innovative supply chain alliance to engage in joint purchasing and refrigerated distribution activities. The alliance was expected to generate purchasing synergies and improved customer service for both companies and was to utilize new Web-based technologies from Nistevo.com. In **April** a study was published in The New England Journal of Medicine showing that people who ate a daily serving of Total breakfast cereal—with 100 percent of the daily values of folic acid and vitamin B6—significantly reduced their blood level of homocysteine, a recently identified risk factor for heart disease and stroke. General Mills announced plans to introduce a new lineup of Disney-themed fruit snacks in the summer. Targeted for kids ages 5-12, the product line was to include Winnie the Pooh Fruit Snacks, Mickey Mouse Fruity Peel-Outs, and Disney's Princess Rolls. In **May** seven of the company's cereals tied in with Dinosaur, Walt Disney Pictures' epic feature. In response to the nation's critical shortfall in calcium consumption (80 percent of adult Americans do not meet the recommended intake each day), General Mills announced that Total breakfast cereal was to be the only food in the grocery store with 100 percent fortification of calcium in a single serving. An exclusive agreement with Headbone Interactive Inc., creators of "Headbone.com," a destination Web site for kids, families, and schools, provided for two popular General Mills products—Gushers fruit snacks and Go-Gurt portable yogurt—to sponsor and promote a special summer component on Headbone.com called "Camp Headbone." **May 28:** Operating highlights for the year included the following:

— Worldwide unit volume grew 7 percent. The overall gain include incremental contributions from acquisitions, but even without that volume, shipments for General Mills' established businesses grew 4 percent.

— Big G cereals achieved record annual volume and earnings, and captured a market-leading 33 percent share of category sales.

— Yoplait and Colombo yogurts posted their fourth consecutive year of double-digit unit volume growth, and Yoplait alone captured the No. 1 market position on a dollar sales basis.

— General Mills' operating profit grew 8 percent to $1.1 billion, increasing the company's EBIT margin to 16.4 percent.

— The company's international joint ventures reached profitability, contributing $3.3 million in after-tax earnings for the year.

Sanger said, "This marks General Mills' third consecutive year of double-digit EPS growth. In 2000, our record results were driven by increased levels of consumer-focused innovation and superior topline growth." In **June** General Mills bought a stake in privately held, Sausalito, Calif.-based MarketTools Inc., the world's leading ASP (applications service provider) for research and feedback solutions, and announced a strategic partnership for conducting consumer research via the Internet. The alliance, Insight Tools, was to combine General Mills' methodologies and insights with MarketTools' pioneering software and infrastructure technology for Web-hosted research and feedback. New products for fiscal 2001 were unveiled: Harmony cereal, targeted at women's health needs; a Total retooled to include the recommended daily allowance of calcium; Big G Milk n' Cereal Bars; and Yoplait Expresse portable yogurt for adults. Cheerios and Betty Crocker become the first new primary NASCAR sponsors of the famed Petty Enterprises No. 43 Pontiac in 29 years. On **July** 17, General Mills agreed to acquire Minneapolis-based Pillsbury, Diageo plc's (LSE: DGE; NYSE: DEO) consumer foods operations, in a half-stock, half-debt deal valued at $10.5 billion, based on General Mills' stock price of $38 before a deal became widely anticipated. Up to $642 million of the transaction value will be repaid to General Mills at the first anniversary of the closing, depending on the General Mills stock price at that time. Diageo was to retain one-third ownership of General Mills, but would be barred from acquiring additional shares for 20 years. To acquire Pillsbury, General Mills had to double its debt load and issue enough new stock to push earnings per share down 20 percent for the year. The deal, expected to become final by the end of the year, was likely to result in job losses at both companies. However, the biggest source of cost efficiencies was expected to be the supply chain, not the labor force. General Mills was planning to sell Pillsbury dessert mixes, for antitrust reasons, and Green Giant canned vegetables, a low-margin commodity business, within two years. Even then, General Mills will be the third-largest food manufacturer, behind only Kraft and ConAgra. General Mills has issued an apology for a lapse in policy that resulted in CD-ROM versions of the Bible being placed in about 12 million cereal boxes. The company was was one of four in the Twin Cities named to Industry Week magazine's fifth annual list of the World's 100 Best-Managed Companies. General Mills has been on the list every year. In spite of consistently strong earnings before interest and taxes, Pillsbury experienced net losses during each of the past five years—ranging from $128 million (in fiscal 1997) to $230 million (1999)—because of significant intercompany debt as a subsidiary of Diageo, according to a preliminary proxy filing. Although Pillsbury's sales dropped slightly, from $6.14 billion in 1999 to $6.08 billion in 2000, the company narrowed its fiscal 2000 loss to $141 million. In a letter of reassurance to management and employees, General Mills explained that the $141 million loss was the result of $700 million in interest expenses that wiped out $533 million in earnings, and that those interest expenses were to be cut by nearly 50 percent as part of the acquisition agreement. At month's end, as anticipated, the Federal Trade Commission issued a request for additional information in connection with its antitrust review of the proposed acquisition. **Aug. 27:** The company reported record results for the fiscal 2001 first quarter. Earnings before interest and taxes increased 8 percent to $296 million. Interest expense in the quarter was higher, due to increased debt levels associated with prior-year acquisitions and share repurchase activity, so earnings after-tax were essentially even with last year's at $159 million. First-quarter domestic unit volume grew more than 7 percent (5 percent volume growth from the company's established businesses and 2 percentage points of incremental volume growth from the Gardetto's and Small Planet Foods businesses acquired in fiscal 2000). Domestic noncereal volume grew 12 percent in the quarter, 8 percent excluding acquisitions, led by a 20 percent unit volume increase in the convenience foods business (snacks and yogurt). Although Big G's first quarter comparison was particularly difficult, market share for Big G's top 10 established brands grew slightly, led by Cheerios, Cinnamon Toast Crunch, and Lucky Charms. Combined unit volume for the company's international operations grew 11 percent in the first quarter. Snack Ventures Europe (SVE) posted a volume gain of 13 percent, driven by good performance in SVE's core markets and the venture's continued recovery in Russia. In **September** Harvard researchers found that eating one serving of whole-grain cereal a day—cereals such as Cheerios, Wheaties, Total, and Wheat Chex—may reduce the risk of diabetes by as much as 34 percent. In **October** the Greater Minneapolis Chamber of Commerce's Minnesota Keystone Program named General Mills the year's Honored Company Award winner for its generous community giving. Consistent with the previously announced intention to sell certain assets in conjunction with the completion of the proposed acquisition of Pillsbury by General Mills, Pillsbury announced an offering to sell its Pillsbury- and Martha White-branded U.S. retail Dessert and Baking Mix business, and its Hungry Jack Potato and Hungry Jack shelf-stable breakfast businesses, which contributed more than $500 million in sales last fiscal year. In **November** General Mills and America Online agreed to implement a series of consumer marketing programs within America Online brands. In a separate effort, to better understand and meet changing consumer needs, General Mills was going to begin testing a Web site, mycereal.com, that allows visitors to create their own customized cereal based on their individual health needs and taste preferences.

Glacier Bancorp Inc.

continued from page 216 ued at $95 million. The combined company was to be the largest publicly traded bank holding company headquartered in the inland Northwest, with $2 billion in assets, $1.3 billion in loans, and $1.2 billion in deposits. WesterFed was the holding company for Montana's largest savings bank, Western Security Bank, which operates 27 offices in 14 Montana communities. **Sept. 30:** "We are very pleased to report record earnings for the quarter," said CEO Blodnick. "Strong loan growth was a significant factor in achieving this level of earnings. Prudent credit quality standards continue to be a company focus, which has resulted in nonperforming assets as a percentage of total assets to be at the lowest level in several years." Since Sept. 30, 1999, total loans, net of the reserve for loan losses, increased $103.4 million, or 17 percent. The loan growth occurred in commercial loans, which increased $67.3 million, or 26 percent, and consumer loans, which increased $21.8 million, or 15 percent. Residential real estate loans increased at a slower pace, $15.6 million or 7 percent, in accordance with management's plan to retain fewer real estate loans, which generally have lower interest rates than other types of loans.

Great Plains Software Inc.

continued from page 219 Application Service Provider (ASP) market for small and medium-sized enterprises. Great Plains added Electronic Funds Transfer (EFT) solutions for Payables Management and Receivables Management, as well as applications for electronically tracking payments and for electronic bank reconciliation. In **April** the company extended its relationship with seven of its leading partners—Aston IT Group, ATRAC, CBIZ Technologies, ePartners, InterDyn, RSM McGladrey Inc. and Scitor Corp.—who represent Great Plains solutions to large, national customers. Great Plains' eEnterprise e-business solution achieved IBM ClusterProven status. In **May** Great Plains announced plans to dramatically expand its midmarket e-business community through the acquisition of Solomon Software, a leading provider of flexible business management and e-business solutions. The combined company, Great Plains, was to have more than 130,000 customers, 2,200 team members, and a worldwide network of 2,000 channel partners. Great Plains agreed to pay 2.6 million shares of Great Plains common stock and $35 million in cash in a purchase transaction. [Deal closed in June.] The company announced the addition of Collections Management, a collections application that seamlessly integrates with Receivables Management for Dynamics and eEnterprise. **May 31**: Although at a record level, fourth-quarter revenue was below management's internal expectations, largely due to a slower post-Y2K sales recovery and lower sales results as Great Plains partners broadened their business to include Great Plains eCRM and e-business solutions. New-customer addition rates in the quarter, while higher sequentially, were below internal expectations and below pre-Y2K levels. At the **July** Microsoft's Professional Developers Conference, Great Plains announced its adoption of Microsoft .NET Framework and the C# programming language. Great Plains and Logility Inc. (Nasdaq: LGTY) announced a global strategic partnership to deliver business-to-business (B2B) collaborative commerce solutions to the midmarket that enable manufacturers, distributors, and retailers to more effectively collaborate supply chain planning and execution operations with trading partners via the Internet. Great Plains announced the availability of Great Plains eEnterprise 6.0, a seamlessly integrated global enterprise and e-business solution; Great Plains Dynamics 6.0, an enhanced package of seamlessly integrated Internet-enabled business solutions to help grow mid-market enterprises; new Web-enabled solutions Great Plains e.Timesheets and Great Plains e.Monitor; and significant enhancements to its e.Commerce and e.Order applications in conjunction with Release 6.0 of Great Plains eEnterprise and Dynamics. In **August** Great Plains signed a worldwide OEM agreement with Knosys Inc., the leading analytical tools vendor on the Microsoft SQL Server platform, to embed the analytical functionality of the ProClarity Analytical Platform into its products based on Microsoft SQL Server. **Aug. 31**: First-quarter revenue increased 68 percent over the same period last fiscal year and 13 percent sequentially over the fourth quarter of fiscal year 2000. Net income, excluding the effect of amortization of acquired intangibles and a nonrecurring restructuring charge, was $1.8 million. In **September** an expansion of its partnership with Siebel Systems Inc. (Nasdaq: SEBL) enabled Great Plains and its network of Front Office partners to offer Siebel eBusiness Applications to those midmarket customers that have enterprise-level requirements. The company also expanded its Application Service Provider (ASP) initiative. Great Plains earned the distinguished STAR Award for Electronic Support from the Software Support Professionals Association (SSPA). In **October** the company released Great Plains Siebel Front Office 6.0, a comprehensive, Web-enabled, and integrated customer relationship management (CRM) solution for midmarket customers. Great Plains entered into a collaborative educational partnership with the U.S. Small Business Administration to educate business owners on how to increase their business success with e-business solutions like Great Plains Dynamics. In **November** Great Plains was a finalist in Microsoft's 2000 Industry Solution Awards, "Best Financials Solution" category.

Grow Biz International Inc.

continued from page 220 company's stock from Dahlberg. By **May**, Morgan had completely replaced the board of directors. He also made staff changes designed to flatten out an organization that had become too pyramid-shaped. Looking to boost penetration among small-business customers, Computer Renaissance stores added a service component that was to offer consulting and network design for small-business customers. Grow Biz announced a $2.5 million charge to earnings in the second quarter—half relating to management's assessment of current information relating to notes receivable booked in connection with a sale of company-owned stores, and half to management's strategic decision to re-evaluate certain of its franchising concepts and company-owned stores that were not performing at expected levels. The company was continuing to work on financing to replace credit facilities that were to expire on July 31, 2000, and were not being renewed. In **June** the company agreed to sell its corporate headquarters facility to Koch Trucking Inc. for its headquarters, and to lease back 50 percent of the facility for itself. In **July** Grow Biz signed a nonbinding letter of intent to sell the Computer Renaissance franchise concept for $3 million to Hollis Technologies LLC of Lakeland, Fla., a franchisee that was operating five Computer Renaissance stores in the Florida market. In connection with this transaction, Grow Biz was to enter into a five-year consulting agreement to provide ongoing franchise and business consulting services. [Deal completed at the end of August.] The first Once Upon A Child children's resale store opened in Japan, in suburban Osaka. (This store is owned by The Duskin Co. Ltd., which holds master franchise rights for Once Upon A Child in Japan.) Hundreds more were planned. **Sept. 23:** During the third quarter, the company improved its balance sheet by selling its corporate headquarters for $3.5 million, the net proceeds of which were used to pay down then-existing bank debt. In addition, the company entered into a subordinated secured $7.5 million seven-year credit facility and borrowed $5.0 million under it. During the nine months ended Sept. 23, the company reduced its total debt from $16.8 million to $5.8 million. Included in the results for the third quarter was a $537,200 pretax gain on the disposition of substantially all the assets of the company's Computer Renaissance franchising and retail operations.

HEI Inc.

1495 Steiger Lake Ln., P.O. Box 5000, Victoria, MN 55386
Tel: 952/443-2500 Fax: 952/443-2668 Web site: http://www.heii.com

HEI Inc. designs and manufactures ultraminiature microelectronic devices, as well as high-technology products incorporating those devices. HEI's custom-built microelectronics, ceramic, flexible circuit, and laminate are employed in medical, hearing, telecommunications, and industrial markets. HEI sells through a company-employed sales force based at its facilities in Victoria, Minn., and Tucson, Ariz.

EARNINGS HISTORY

Year Ended Aug 31	Operating Revenue/Sales (dollars in thousands)	Net Earnings	Return on Revenue (percent)	Return on Equity	Net Earnings (dollars per share)	Cash Dividend	Market Price Range
1999 *	24,323	(223)	(0.9)	(1.6)	(0.05)	—	7.50–4.38
1998 †	20,805	(2,627)	(12.6)	(18.3)	(0.64)	—	7.38–4.25
1997 ¶	30,962	2,550	8.2	15.0	0.62	—	12.00–4.25
1996 #	20,680	2,113	10.2	15.3	0.54	—	8.00–4.75
1995	23,423	2,040	8.7	18.6	0.54	—	6.38–4.13

* Income figures for 1999 include pretax severance costs of $490,000 paid to former CEO Eugene W. Courtney.
† Income figures for 1998 include a one-time pretax charge of $5,664,000 associated with the expenses of both parties involved in the proxy contest, and related change-of-control costs.
¶ Income figures for 1997 include pretax gain of $215,000 on sale of optoelectronic switch assembly product line.
\# Income figures for 1996 include pretax net gain of $45,000 on sale of FastPoint Light Pen product line; and after-tax gain of $0.07 per share on one-time deferred-tax adjustment.

BALANCE SHEET

Assets	08/31/99 (dollars in thousands)	08/31/98	Liabilities	08/31/99 (dollars in thousands)	08/31/98
Current (CAE 1,217 and 297)	10,841	15,605	Current (STD 700 and 700)	3,333	3,741
Property and equipment	8,340	6,272	Long-term debt	3,218	3,835
			Deferred tax	246	256
Restricted cash	83		Stockholders' equity*	14,156	14,341
Investments	1,468	186			
Other	221	110	TOTAL	20,953	22,173
TOTAL	20,953	22,173			

* $0.05 par common; 10,000,000 authorized; 4,101,965 and 4,095,195 issued and outstanding.

RECENT QUARTERS / **PRIOR-YEAR RESULTS**

	Quarter End	Revenue ($000)	Earnings ($000)	EPS ($)	Revenue ($000)	Earnings ($000)	EPS ($)
Q4	08/31/2000	13,724	459	0.10	7,022	(48)	(0.01)
Q3	06/03/2000	11,589	361	0.08	6,329	131	0.03
Q2	03/04/2000	9,392	(1,656)	(0.35)	8,301	398	0.08
Q1	12/04/99	8,094	(319)	(0.07)	7,437	(88)	(0.02)
	SUM	42,799	(1,155)	(0.25)	29,089	393	0.08

PRIOR YEAR: Q1 earnings include pretax charge of $490,000—after-tax $316,000/($0.07)—severance for former CEO Courtney.

RECENT EVENTS

In **January 2000** the company's Mexico division was in receipt of orders from six new customers, with volume to ramp up in the second quarter. The orders included a $2.2 million order from a large customer within the fiberoptic communications market, and an order from a large customer in the computer peripheral market that was expected to result in more than $2 million worth of business in the next 12 months. HEI announced the opening of its new High Density Interconnect (HDI) Division, in Tempe, Ariz.—designed to provide the highest-quality flex circuits and high-performance laminate-based substrates in the world. In **February** HEI received a patent covering the innovative combination of flex circuitry with other substrates, as well as innovative uses of flexible laminates in packages with high density requirements—an advantage in many packaging applications where space and density are critical factors. HEI and Cross Technology Inc., a leader in the manufacturing and marketing of wireless Smart Cards and other ultra-miniature radio frequency (RF) applications, reached an agreement for the acquisition of Cross by HEI in a stock deal then valued at $6.4 million. The announcement caused HEI's stock to almost double, briefly, before closing Feb. 29 at $16.63 (up from $14 the previous day)—resulting in the deal being revalued at $8.4 million. [Deal completed in March.] In **August** HEI received its first production order for performing alignment of fiber optic devices. The $3 million order from a major multinational customer began immediately. (Fiber alignment is one of the key operations in the production of fiber optic assemblies used in applications such as high-speed internet routing and data communications.) Surprisingly, the announcement caused HEI's stock price to jump by 56 percent to close at $23. HEI completed a $13.5 million, three-year line of credit agreement with LaSalle Business Credit Inc., part of the Netherlands-based ABN AMRO Bank N.V. HEI planned to use this capital to fund its aggressive growth as it expands its technology and product lines worldwide. In **September** CEO Fant agreed to exchange all 1,214,300 shares of Colorado

continued on page 251

OFFICERS

Anthony J. Fant
Chairman and CEO

Donald R. Reynolds
President

William T. Goodnow
VP-Sales/Marketing

Steve E. Tondera Jr.
VP-Finance, CFO, Secretary, Treasurer

Stephen K. Petersen
Dir.-Manufacturing

Robert R. Shue
Dir.-Design/Engineering

Wray A. Wentworth
Dir.-Corporate Quality

DIRECTORS

Anthony J. Fant

Edwin W. Finch III
FHL Capital Corp.

David W. Ortlieb
consultant

Steve E. Tondera Jr.

Mack V. Traynor III
Manitou Investments

MAJOR SHAREHOLDERS

Anthony J. Fant, 29.4%

All officers and directors as a group (7 persons), 31.6%

SIC CODE

3674 Semiconductors and related devices

3679 Electronic components, nec

MISCELLANEOUS

TRANSFER AGENT AND REGISTAR:
Wells Fargo Bank Minnesota N.A., South St. Paul, MN

TRADED: Nasdaq National Market

SYMBOL: HEII

STOCKHOLDERS: 560

EMPLOYEES: 225

PART TIME: 20

IN MINNESOTA: 180

GENERAL COUNSEL:
Weil, Gotshal & Manges, New York
Gray Plant Mooty, Minneapolis

AUDITORS:
KPMG LLP, Minneapolis

INC: MN-1968

ANNUAL MEETING:
January

INVESTOR RELATIONS:
Steve Tondera

RANKINGS

No. 141 CRM Public 200

SUBSIDIARIES, DIVISIONS, AFFILIATES

Microelectronics Division
P.O. Box 5000
1495 Steiger Lake Ln.
Victoria, MN 55386
952/443-2500

Mexico Division
One Offshore Int'l
777 E. MacArthur Circle
Tucson, AZ 85714
520/618-4309
Keith (Jim) Hicks

High Density Interconnect Division
610 S. Rockford Dr.
Tempe, AZ 85281
480/968-1100
Jeffrey Flammer

Cross Technology Inc.
5201 Eden Circle
Edina, MN 55436
952/926-9440

PUB

TWO-YEAR QUARTERLY HIGH-LOW STOCK PRICES

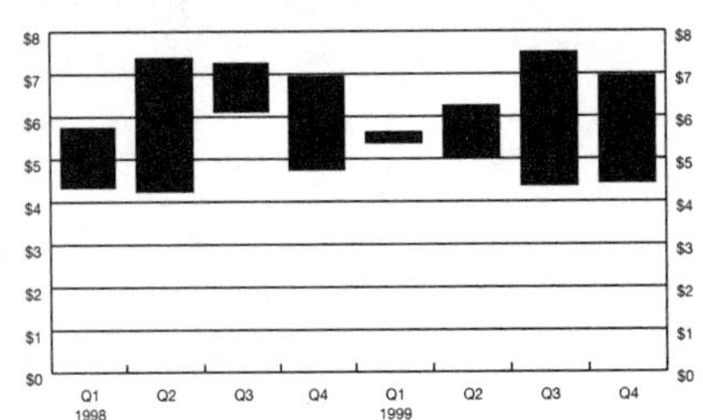

HF Financial Corporation

225 S. Main Ave., P.O. Box 5000 (57117), Sioux Falls, SD 57102
Tel: 605/333-7556 Fax: 605/333-7621 Web site: http://www.homefederal.com

HF Financial Corp. was incorporated in November 1991 for the purpose of owning all of the outstanding stock issued in the mutual-to-stock conversion of **Home Federal Savings Bank**. Home Federal and its subsidiaries offer a variety of financial services to meet the needs of families in the communities of eastern South Dakota: general banking, trust, investments, annuities, credit-life, health, life, and other insurance products and appraisal services. Originally chartered in 1929, Home Federal serves 20 cities in eastern South Dakota through its main office in Sioux Falls and its network of 27 retail banking offices located throughout eastern South Dakota and in Marshall, Minn. In 1997 Home Federal became the first bank in South Dakota to offer online banking services through the Internet.

EARNINGS HISTORY

Year Ended Jun 30	Operating Revenue/Sales (dollars in thousands)	Net Earnings (dollars in thousands)	Return on Revenue (percent)	Return on Equity (percent)	Net Earnings (dollars per share*)	Cash Dividend (dollars per share*)	Market Price Range (dollars per share*)
2000	68,401	5,267	7.7	11.2	1.36	0.40	13.94–8.00
1999	65,168	1,051	1.6	2.2	0.25	0.37	23.50–12.00
1998	59,832	6,473	10.8	11.4	1.46	0.28	24.16–14.17
1997	50,484	3,674	7.3	6.9	0.81	0.24	14.33–9.83
1996	49,113	4,722	9.6	9.2	1.03	0.22	11.25–8.83

* Per-share amounts restated to reflect 3-for-2 stock split in May 1998; and 2-for-1 stock split in January 1996.

BALANCE SHEET

Assets	06/30/00 (dollars in thousands)	06/30/99 (dollars in thousands)
Cash, equivalents	26,417	16,671
Securities afs	60,445	61,023
Mortgage-backed securities afs	53,001	41,583
Loans receivable	542,494	492,302
Loans held for sale	8,257	11,755
Accrued interest	5,346	4,831
Foreclosed r/e	1,594	1,762
Properties, eqt	13,717	14,408
Prepaid expenses	2,290	2,509
Servicing rights	2,171	1,739
Deferred taxes	4,235	5,094
Intangibles	5,030	4,945
TOTAL	724,997	658,622

Liabilities	06/30/00 (dollars in thousands)	06/30/99 (dollars in thousands)
Deposits	545,497	510,730
Advances from FHLB and other borrowings	113,020	81,613
Advances by borrowers	6,543	6,170
Accrued interest	6,844	5,870
Other	6,150	5,681
Stockholders' equity*	46,943	48,558
TOTAL	724,997	658,622

* $0.01 par common; 10,000,000 authorized; 4,769,314 and 4,755,632 issued and outstanding, less 1,105,209 and 683,572 treasury shares.

RECENT QUARTERS / **PRIOR-YEAR RESULTS**

	Quarter End	Revenue ($000)	Earnings ($000)	EPS ($)	Prior-Year Revenue ($000)	Prior-Year Earnings ($000)	Prior-Year EPS ($)
Q1	09/30/2000	17,962	1,260	0.34	17,045	1,388	0.34
Q4	06/30/2000	17,610	1,306	0.35	18,053	(1,376)	(0.34)
Q3	03/31/2000	16,669	1,317	0.35	15,258	47	0.01
Q2	12/31/99	17,077	1,256	0.32	15,896	1,087	0.25
	SUM	69,318	5,139	1.36	66,252	1,146	0.27

RECENT EVENTS

In **December 1999** subsidiary Hometown Insurors Inc. purchased Tower Insurance Associates of Sioux Falls. In **August 2000** HF agreed to acquire leasing company Mid America Capital Services Inc. for cash consideration.

OFFICERS

Curtis L. Hage
Chairman, President, and CEO

Gene F. Uher
EVP and COO

Mary F. Hitzemann
SVP-Human Resources

Brent E. Johnson
SVP, CFO, and Treasurer

Terry Kappes
SVP-Retail Banking

John B. Neuroth
SVP and Commercial Lending Officer

John E. Roers
SVP-Agricultural Lending

Mark S. Sivertson
SVP and Trust Officer

Gary L. Smith
SVP-Information Systems

Michael H. Zimmerman
SVP and Senior Retail Lending Officer

Richard H.C. Beverley
VP-Sales

Roxanne R. Bobolz
VP

Michael J. Echols
VP-Loan Service

Ted Ellinger
VP

Randall D. Fink
VP-Mortgage Loan Production Manager

Teresa L. Flamboe
VP

Anne M. Fuehrer
VP-Marketing

LaVonne R. Grassel
VP

Jack P. Hearst
VP

Diane Hovda
VP-Financial Management

Paul S. Jordahl
VP-Commercial Lending

David C. Kalil
VP

Faye A. Lee
VP

Sharon A. Manuel
VP-Electronic Banking

Gary G. Sieverding
VP-Commercial Lending

Natalie A. Solberg
VP-Retail Support

Mark Swenson
VP

Kirk L. Waugh
VP

Michael Westberg
VP

Kent Wigg
VP-Financial Management

DIRECTORS

Curtis L. Hage

Paul J. Hallem
HF Financial Corp. (retired)

Robert L. Hanson
Harold's Photo Centers

Kevin T. Kirby
Kirby Investment Corp., Sioux Falls, SD

JoEllen G. Koerner
JoEllen Koerner and Associates

Jeffrey G. Parker
Parker Transfer & Storage Inc.

Wm. G. Pederson
PAM Oil Inc.

Thomas L. Van Whye
JSI-Trane

MAJOR SHAREHOLDERS

John T. Vucurevich, 8.1%
Rapid City, SD

Jeffrey L. Gendell/Tontine Partners L.P., 7.9%
New York

HF Financial Corp. ESOP, 7%

Dimensional Fund Advisors Inc., 6.1%
Santa Monica, CA

Curtis L. Hage, 5.5%

All officers and directors as a group (18 persons), 11.6%

SIC CODE

6712 Bank holding companies

MISCELLANEOUS

TRANSFER AGENT AND REGISTAR:
Chase Mellon Shareholder Services LLC, New York

TRADED: Nasdaq National Market

SYMBOL: HFFC

STOCKHOLDERS: 583

EMPLOYEES: 320

GENERAL COUNSEL:
Gray, Plant, Mooty, Mooty & Bennett P.A., Minneapolis

AUDITORS:
RSM McGladrey & Pullen Inc. LLP, Sioux Falls, SD

INC: DE-1991

ANNUAL MEETING:
November

HUMAN RESOURCES:
Mary Hitzemann

TWO-YEAR QUARTERLY HIGH-LOW STOCK PRICES

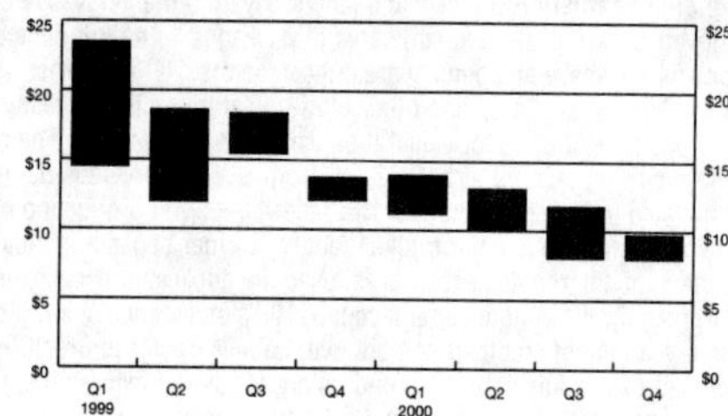

PUB

HMN Financial Inc.

101 N. Broadway, P.O. Box 231, Spring Valley, MN 55975
Tel: 507/346-1100 Fax: 507/346-1111

HMN Financial Inc. is the holding company for **Home Federal Savings Bank**, which was originally chartered in 1934. Home Federal operates seven branch offices in six southeastern Minnesota communities, three offices in Iowa, and a loan origination office in Brooklyn Park, Minn. Products and services offered by Home Federal include a full range of retail deposit and loan services, certificates of deposit, checking, retirement savings, and IRAs, along with home, auto, student, and personal loans.

EARNINGS HISTORY

Year Ended Dec 31	Operating Revenue/Sales (dollars in thousands)	Net Earnings (dollars in thousands)	Return on Revenue (percent)	Return on Equity (percent)	Net Earnings (dollars per share*)	Cash Dividend (dollars per share*)	Market Price Range (dollars per share*)
1999	51,397	6,391	12.4	9.9	1.47	—	13.50–10.50
1998	51,425	4,058	7.9	5.9	0.82	—	21.33–10.38
1997 †	43,813	5,579	12.7	6.6	1.01	—	21.67–12.00
1996 ¶	41,787	4,274	10.2	5.2	0.66	—	12.08–9.75
1995	39,326	5,620	14.3	6.1	0.73	—	10.67–8.25

* Per-share amounts restated to reflect 3-for-2 stock split on May 22, 1998.
† Pro forma 1997 results had Dec. 5, 1997, acquisition of Marshalltown Financial Corp. taken place on Jan. 1, 1997: revenue $50,860,096; earnings $4,564,781/$0.83.
¶ Income figures for 1996 include special pretax SAIF assessment of $2,351,563.

BALANCE SHEET

Assets	12/31/99 (dollars in thousands)	12/31/98 (dollars in thousands)
Cash, equivalents	9,051	20,961
Securities afs, mortgage-backed	100,777	143,146
Securities afs, other	72,700	38,479
Loans hfs	4,083	13,095
Net loans	477,896	447,455
FHLB stock	11,470	9,838
Mortgage svcg	1,124	1,006
Premises, eqt	8,530	8,382
Accrued interest	3,860	3,953
Ltd partnerships	2,975	2,437
Goodwill	4,161	4,341
Core deposit intangible	1,027	1,259
Deferred taxes	893	
Expenses, other	640	306
TOTAL	699,186	694,658

Liabilities	12/31/99 (dollars in thousands)	12/31/98 (dollars in thousands)
Deposits	400,382	433,869
FHLB advances	229,400	185,400
Accrued interest payable	1,433	1,086
Advance payments by borrowers	814	657
Accrued expenses and other	2,596	2,700
Other borrowed money		2,500
Stockholders' equity*	64,561	68,445
TOTAL	699,186	694,658

* $0.01 par common; 11,000,000 authorized; 9,128,662 and 9,128,662 issued and outstanding, less 4,370,285 and 3,835,058 treasury shares.

RECENT QUARTERS / PRIOR-YEAR RESULTS

	Quarter End	Revenue ($000)	Earnings ($000)	EPS ($)	Prior-Year Revenue ($000)	Prior-Year Earnings ($000)	Prior-Year EPS ($)
Q3	09/30/2000	14,390	1,703	0.45	12,656	1,495	0.35
Q2	06/30/2000	14,056	1,880	0.48	12,993	1,716	0.39
Q1	03/31/2000	13,274	1,530	0.38	12,790	1,602	0.35
Q4	12/31/99	12,959	1,578	0.38	13,845	2,045	0.45
	SUM	54,678	6,691	1.69	52,283	6,858	1.54

RECENT EVENTS

In **February 2000** the company's board of directors authorized the repurchase of up to 400,000 shares of HMN's common stock over the next 12-month period. HMN still had 24,800 shares remaining to be purchased in the current repurchase program, which had been authorized by the board in July 1999. In **August**, with 70,800 shares remaining to be purchased in the February repurchase program, the board authorized the repurchase of up to another 350,000 shares of HMN's common stock over the next 12-month period. **Sept. 30:** Third-quarter net interest margin increased 8 basis points over the third quarter of 1999. "The 13.9 percent increase in net income for the quarter clearly reflects the progress that management and the employees have made toward improving core earnings as outlined in our strategic plan," said President McNeil. "We will continue to focus our loan production emphasis on commercial and consumer loans and on generating new deposit account relationships that will lower our cost of funds." Commercial and consumer loans increased 55 percent during the first nine months of 2000.

OFFICERS

M.F. Schumann
Chairman
Michael McNeil
President
Timothy P. Johnson
EVP, CFO, and Treasurer
Dwain C. Jorgensen
SVP

DIRECTORS

Duane D. Benson
Minnesota Business Partnership
Allan DeBoer
RCS of Rochester Inc.
Timothy Geisler
Mayo Clinic, Rochester, MN
Timothy P. Johnson
Michael McNeil
Mahlon C. Schneider
Hormel Foods Inc.
M.F. Schumann
Schumann, Granahan, Hesse & Wilson Ltd. (retired)
Roger P. Weise
Richard Ziebell
Badger Foundry Inc.

MAJOR SHAREHOLDERS

HMN Financial Inc. ESOP, 20.1%
Pohlad Group, 9.7%
Heartland Advisors Inc., 6.3%
Milwaukee
Dimensional Fund Advisors Inc., 6.2%
Santa Monica, CA
All officers and directors as a group (12 persons), 11.4%

SIC CODE

6712 Bank holding companies

MISCELLANEOUS

TRANSFER AGENT AND REGISTAR:
Wells Fargo Bank Minnesota N.A.,
South St. Paul, MN
TRADED: Nasdaq National Market
SYMBOL: HMNF
STOCKHOLDERS: 816
EMPLOYEES: 146
GENERAL COUNSEL:
Faegre & Benson PLLP, Minneapolis
AUDITORS:
KPMG LLP, Minneapolis

INC: DE-1994
FOUNDED: 1934
ANNUAL MEETING: April
INVESTOR RELATIONS:
Timothy P. Johnson

RANKINGS

No. 111 CRM Public 200

SUBSIDIARIES, DIVISIONS, AFFILIATES

CORP./BRANCH OFFICE

Home Federal Savings Bank
101 N. Broadway
Spring Valley, MN 55975
507/346-1110

BRANCH OFFICES

715 N. Broadway
Spring Valley, MN 55975
507/346-7345

143 W. Clark St.
Albert Lea, MN 56007
507/377-3330

201 Oakland Ave. W.
Austin, MN 55912
507/433-2355

208 S. Walnut
LaCrescent, MN 55947
507/895-4090

Crossroads Shopping Center
Rochester, MN 55901
507/289-4025

1110 Sixth St. N.W.
Rochester, MN 55901
507/285-1707

175 Center St.
Winona, MN 55987
507/454-4912

Mortgage Origination
7101 Northland Circle,105
Brooklyn Park, MN 55427
612/533-2500

303 W. Main St.
Marshalltown, IA 50158
515/754-6000

29 S. Center St.
Marshalltown, IA 50158
515/754-6040

119 W. High St.
Toledo, IA 52342
515/484-5141

TWO-YEAR QUARTERLY HIGH-LOW STOCK PRICES

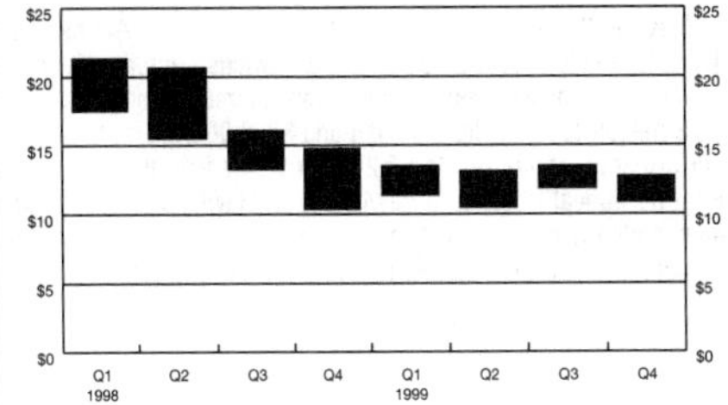

PUB

Hawkins Chemical Inc.

3100 E. Hennepin Ave., Minneapolis, MN 55413
Tel: 612/331-6910 Fax: 612/331-5304 Web site: http://www.hawkinschemical.com

Hawkins Chemical Inc. is a formulator, blender, distributor, and sales agent of more than 1,000 industrial chemicals and 800 high-grade laboratory chemicals (including reagent-grade, food-grade, and pharmaceutical-grade); and a seller and servicer of products and equipment for chemical feeding and control. Hawkins serves customers in Minnesota, Wisconsin, Iowa, North Dakota, South Dakota, Montana, Wyoming, Michigan, and Nebraska.

EARNINGS HISTORY

Year Ended Sept	Operating Revenue/Sales (dollars in thousands)	Net Earnings	Return on Revenue (percent)	Return on Equity	Net Earnings (dollars per share*)	Cash Dividend	Market Price Range
1999 †	95,460	9,699	10.2	17.5	0.87	0.25	12.00–7.50
1998	94,723	8,214	8.7	15.4	0.71	0.19	14.00–9.50
1997 ¶	87,746	7,790	8.9	15.9	0.67	0.16	10.25–5.50
1996	80,886	6,476	8.0	15.1	0.56	0.14	8.57–6.55
1995 #	83,333	5,333	6.4	14.0	0.46	0.12	7.26–5.33

* Per-share amounts restated to reflect stock dividends of: 5 percent in February 1997 and 1996, and 10 percent in February 1995.
† Income figures for 1999 include these pretax amounts: loss of $1.112 million from employee termination agreements; and gain of $2.852 million from litigation settlement.
¶ Income figures for 1997 include these pretax amounts: loss of $1.771 million from litigation and settlement costs related to 1995 fire; and gain of $1.325 million on sale of The Lynde Co.
# Revenue figures for 1995 have been restated to segregate the operations of Tessman Seed Inc., which was sold March 1, 1995. Income figures include loss of $0.391 million/($0.03) from discontinued operations.

BALANCE SHEET

Assets	10/03/99 (dollars in thousands)	09/27/98	Liabilities	10/03/99 (dollars in thousands)	09/27/98
Current (CAE 4,778 and 3,197)	44,750	42,114	Current (STD 95 and 89)	11,280	11,621
Property, plant, and equipment	18,665	18,423	Long-term debt	328	423
Intangibles	601	664	Deferred income taxes	1,030	1,012
Investments held-to-maturity	1,949	1,849	Other	786	
Notes receivable	2,844	3,303	Stockholders' equity*	55,575	53,480
Other	191	182	TOTAL	69,000	66,535
TOTAL	69,000	66,535			

* $0.05 par common; 30,000,000 authorized; 10,951,281 and 11,450,895 issued and outstanding.

RECENT QUARTERS / **PRIOR-YEAR RESULTS**

	Quarter End	Revenue ($000)	Earnings ($000)	EPS ($)	Revenue ($000)	Earnings ($000)	EPS ($)
Q3	06/30/2000	26,833	2,742	0.26	24,960	2,441	0.22
Q2	03/31/2000	22,747	1,775	0.17	22,764	1,789	0.16
Q1	12/31/99	21,626	1,640	0.15	23,311	3,426	0.30
Q4	10/03/99	24,425	2,043	0.19	24,019	2,370	0.20
	SUM	95,631	8,200	0.77	95,054	10,026	0.89

CURRENT: Q4 earnings include pretax special charges of $1,112,127.
PRIOR YEAR: Q3 earnings include pretax litigation settlement reimbursement of $97,708. Q1 earnings include pretax litigation settlement reimbursement of $2,754,000.

RECENT EVENTS

In **May 2000** the company agreed to acquire St. Mary's Chemicals Inc., also known as Universal Chemical, of St. Peter, Minn. The $4.3 million-revenue Universal, a Hawkins customer for several years, supplies pharmacies throughout the United States with the bulk pharmaceutical chemicals utilized in compounding. Terms of the acquisition called for a payment by Hawkins of $3.3 million ($2.7 million in cash and $600,000 in Hawkins Chemical stock). In addition, the agreement set forth terms for a performance bonus (up to $3,262,500) based on the five-year operating results of Universal—which was to operate as the Pharmaceutical Division of Hawkins. CEO Hawkins said, "The acquisition of Universal will create a presence for Hawkins with independently owned and operated pharmacies, which are increasingly moving to purchase bulk pharmaceutical chemicals to be compounded to customer and physician specifications."

OFFICERS

John R. Hawkins
Chairman and CEO

Kurt R. Norman
President

Marvin E. Dee
VP, CFO, Secretary, Treasurer

DIRECTORS

G. Robert Gey
Pentair Service Department Division

Dean L. Hahn
Hawkins Chemical Inc. (retired)

Howard M. Hawkins
Hawkins Chemical Inc. (retired)

John R. Hawkins

Duane Jergenson
Taylor Corp., North Mankato, MN

John S. McKeon
Golden Valley Microwave Foods Inc., Edina, MN

Donald L. Shipp
Hawkins Chemical (retired)

MAJOR SHAREHOLDERS

ESOP and Trust, 22.4%
Minneapolis

All officers and directors as a group (9 persons), 4.6%

SIC CODE

2819 Industrial inorganic chemicals, nec

MISCELLANEOUS

TRANSFER AGENT AND REGISTAR:
Wells Fargo Bank Minnesota N.A., South St. Paul, MN

TRADED: Nasdaq National Market

SYMBOL: HWKN

STOCKHOLDERS: 777

EMPLOYEES: 157

PART TIME: 2

IN MINNESOTA: 131

GENERAL COUNSEL:
Henson & Efron P.A., Minneapolis

AUDITORS:
Deloitte & Touche LLP, Minneapolis

INC: MN-1955

FOUNDED: 1938

ANNUAL MEETING: February

INVESTOR RELATIONS: Janet Lewis

RANKINGS

No. 92 CRM Public 200

SUBSIDIARIES, DIVISIONS, AFFILIATES

2026 Winter St.
Superior, WI 54880
715/392-5121

11810 N. Highway 79
Blackhawk, SD 57718
605/787-6881

Route 3, Box 152
Sioux Falls, SD 57106
605/368-5793

2001 Great Northern Dr.
Fargo, ND 58102
701/293-9618

N5642 S. Morris
Fond du Lac, WI 54935
414/923-1850

101 Greene St.
Slater, IA 50244
515/685-2250

1125 Childs Rd.
St. Paul, MN 55106
651/774-9606

Washburn, North Dakota
701/462-8588

528 Sioux Ln.
Billings, MT 59105
406/245-6246

TWO-YEAR QUARTERLY HIGH-LOW STOCK PRICES

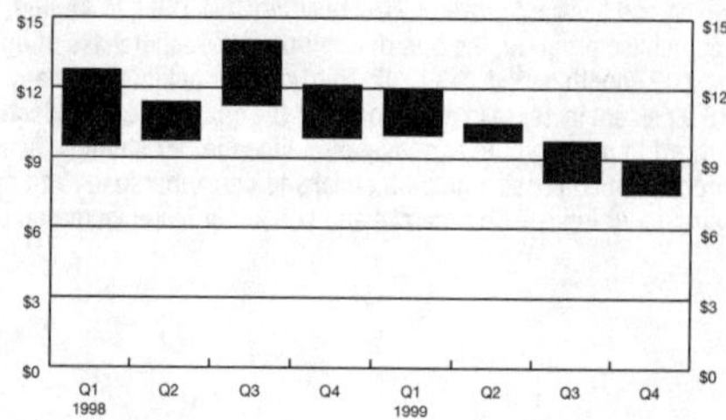

Health Fitness Corporation

3500 W. 80th St., Suite 130, Bloomington, MN 55431
Tel: 952/831-6830 Fax: 952/831-7264

Health Fitness Corp., together with its wholly owned subsidiaries, offers wellness services and products to major corporations, hospitals and insurance companies. These services include the marketing and management of corporate and hospital-based fitness centers, the maintenance and organization of a network of independent commercial fitness and health clubs, and the marketing of memberships in the network of clubs to employers and insurance companies through its International Fitness Club Network division. In addition, the company undertakes the management of on-site physical therapy clinics within certain corporate customer owned facilities. Fitness center based services include health-related programming and on-site physical therapy. Wellness services are provided to dispersed employee populations of major corporations and insurance companies.

EARNINGS HISTORY

Year Ended Dec 31	Operating Revenue/Sales	Net Earnings	Return on Revenue	Return on Equity	Net Earnings	Cash Dividend	Market Price Range
	(dollars in thousands)		(percent)		(dollars per share)		
1999 *	26,195	(2,827)	(10.8)	NM	(0.24)	—	0.75–0.28
1998 †	25,643	(8,109)	(31.6)	NM	(0.72)	—	2.44–0.25
1997 ¶	21,480	(1,047)	(4.9)	(10.3)	(0.13)	—	3.88–1.50
1996 #	16,500	1,006	6.1	10.2	0.15	—	3.75–2.00
1995 **	17,906	(212)	(1.2)	(2.9)	(0.04)	—	3.50–2.13

* Income figures for 1999 include loss of $1,425,000/($0.12) from disposal of discontinued Physical Therapy Clinic segment and Equipment segment operations.
† Income figures for 1998 include loss of $7,167,833/($0.63) from discontinued operations and their disposal.
¶ Income figures for 1997 include loss of $103,736/($0.01) from discontinued operations.
# Income figures for 1996 include gain of $859,388/$0.12 from discontinued operations.
** Figures for 1995 not restated for continuing operations.

BALANCE SHEET

Assets	12/31/99	12/31/98
	(dollars in thousands)	
Current (CAE 139 and 29)	3,866	4,462
Property, eqt	555	1,050
Goodwill	6,164	7,569
Noncompete agreements	238	592
Copyrights		584
Trade names	63	189
Contracts	17	57
Trade accounts and notes receivable	341	923
Deferred financing		585
Other	80	66
Net discontinued operations		2,558
TOTAL	11,324	18,635

Liabilities	12/31/99	12/31/98
	(dollars in thousands)	
Current (STD 421 and 479)	7,623	11,929
Long-term debt	503	862
Stockholders' equity*	3,198	5,844
TOTAL	11,324	18,635

* $0.01 par common; 25,000,000 authorized; 12,112,015 and 11,884,413 issued and outstanding.

RECENT QUARTERS / PRIOR-YEAR RESULTS

	Quarter End	Revenue ($000)	Earnings ($000)	EPS ($)	Prior-Year Revenue ($000)	Prior-Year Earnings ($000)	Prior-Year EPS ($)
Q3	09/30/2000	6,496	78	0.01	6,467	(941)	(0.08)
Q2	06/30/2000	6,285	203	0.02	6,351	(587)	(0.05)
Q1	03/31/2000	6,739	428	0.04	6,948	(1,152)	(0.10)
Q4	12/31/99	6,430	(147)	(0.01)	6,518	(5,901)	(0.52)
	SUM	25,950	561	0.05	26,283	(8,581)	(0.75)

PRIOR YEAR: Q1 earnings include loss of $1,425,000/($0.12) on disposal of discontinued operations. Q4 earnings include loss of $4,492,000/($0.40) from discontinued operations and their disposal.

RECENT EVENTS

In **April 2000** HealthSouth Corp. (NYSE: HRC) filed a lawsuit against Health Fitness and two former employees in U.S. District Court in Minnesota arising out of HealthSouth's purchase of several rehabilitation and physical therapy clinics from Health Fitness in May 1999. The lawsuit related to two of the purchased clinics. Believing the HealthSouth's claims to be groundless, the company was intending to vigorously defend the claims and to assert any counterclaims that may be appropriate. In **May** Health Fitness signed a letter of intent to merge with Healthtrax Inc., a Connecticut-based, privately held company that owns and/or manages medical fitness centers, work site fitness and rehab cen-

continued on page 251

OFFICERS

James A. Bernards
Chairman

Charles J.B. Mitchell Jr.
Acting CEO

Thomas A. Knox
Acting COO

Sean A. Kearns
VP-Finance

DIRECTORS

James A. Bernards
Brightstone Capital Ltd., Minneapolis

Charles E. Bidwell
venture capitalist

Susan H. DeNuccio
Target Stores (former)

William T. Simonet, M.D.
orthopedic surgeon

Robert K. Spinner
Abbott Northwestern Hospital

MAJOR SHAREHOLDERS

Perkins Capital Management Inc., 8.8%
Wayzata, MN

Loren S. Brink, 7.5%

George E. Kline, 7.1%
Minneapolis

Charles E. Bidwell, 6%

All officers and directors as a group (7 persons), 16.1%

SIC CODE

7991 Physical fitness facilities

MISCELLANEOUS

TRANSFER AGENT AND REGISTAR:
Wells Fargo Bank Minnesota N.A.,
South St. Paul, MN

TRADED: OTC Bulletin Board

SYMBOL: HFIT

STOCKHOLDERS: 500

EMPLOYEES: 2,277

PART TIME: 1,789

IN MINNESOTA: 102

GENERAL COUNSEL:
Fredrikson & Byron P.A.,
Minneapolis

AUDITORS:
Grant Thornton LLP, Minneapolis

INC: MN-1987

FOUNDED: 1981

ANNUAL MEETING: June

HUMAN RESOURCES:
Jeanne Crawford

TWO-YEAR QUARTERLY HIGH-LOW STOCK PRICES

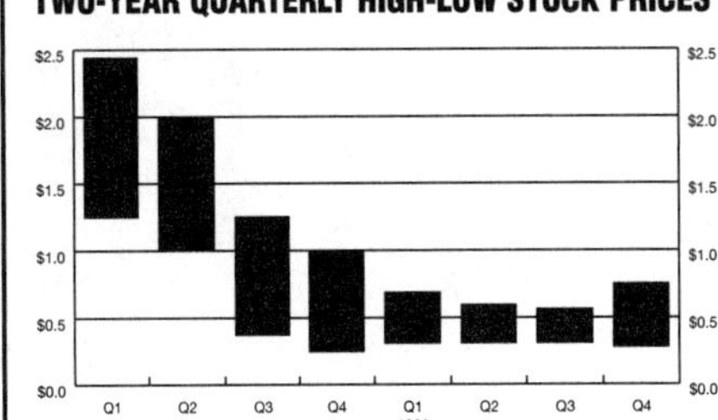

INVESTOR RELATIONS:
Sean Kearns

RANKINGS

No. 137 CRM Public 200

SUBSIDIARIES, DIVISIONS, AFFILIATES

David W. Pickering Inc.
Fitness Centers of America

Health Fitness Corporation of Canada

PUB

Health Outcomes Management Inc.

2331 University Ave. S.E., Minneapolis, MN 55414
Tel: 612/378-3053 Fax: 612/378-2930

Health Outcomes Management Inc. develops and supplies computer software and services specifically focused in the area of health care outcomes management. Health care professionals in community pharmacies, long-term care facilities, home care, and hospitals utilize the company's computerized information management software to efficiently maintain and improve patient health care. Health Outcomes' mission is to improve the quality of patient outcomes in health care cost-effectively, using modern computer software technology. The company provides the information through the following services: computer software; 24-hour-a-day, seven-day-a-week consultations via the 1-800-STAT-911 helpline; and training seminars. The company has more than 800 clients in 40 states.

EARNINGS HISTORY

Year Ended Feb	Operating Revenue/Sales (dollars in thousands)	Net Earnings	Return on Revenue (percent)	Return on Equity	Net Earnings (dollars per share)	Cash Dividend	Market Price Range
2000 *	1,278	45	3.5	NM	0.00	—	0.44–0.07
1999 †	1,378	244	17.7	NM	0.03	—	0.14–0.06
1998 ¶	1,161	(702)	(60.5)	NM	(0.08)	—	0.21–0.08
1997 #	2,302	(113)	(4.9)	NM	(0.01)	—	0.44–0.08
1996	3,183	96	3.0	NM	0.01	—	1.12–0.50

* Income figures for 2000 include gain of $8,712/$0.00 from discontinued retail pharmacy division.
† Income figures for 1999 include gain of $212,713/$0.02 from discontinued retail pharmacy division. Reported "going concern" alert.
¶ Income figures for 1998 include loss of $329,727/($0.04) from discontinued operations. Reported "going concern" alert.
# Income figures for 1997 include loss of $133,165/($0.02) from discontinued operations.

BALANCE SHEET

Assets	02/29/00 (dollars in thousands)	02/28/99
Current (CAE 47 and 30)	112	108
Property and equipment	13	26
TOTAL	125	133

Liabilities	02/29/00 (dollars in thousands)	02/28/99
Current (STD 94 and 36)	457	446
Obligation under capital leases		5
Long-term debt		71
Stockholders' equity*	(331)	(389)
TOTAL	125	133

* $0.01 par common; 15,000,000 authorized; 9,262,130 and 9,198,761 issued and outstanding.

RECENT EVENTS

In **January 2000** the company donated a patient-centered pharmaceutical care learning laboratory to the University of Utah College of Pharmacy. This software-based experiential learning tool was designed to guide students through the process of patient-centered pharmaceutical care and give them the ability to document their practices. Pharmacist developer Lary Armentrout of Health Outcomes remarked, "As the role of pharmaceutical care moves to the forefront of modern pharmacy practice, there will be a need for pharmacists who are trained in this new discipline. The University of Utah College of Pharmacy is clearly a leader in preparing its students to practice this new paradigm." In **February** the company released Critical Care Tables (CCT), its first clinical tool to be delivered to practitioners via the internet. The CCT product produces infusion rate sheets, a set of calculations that helps critical care nurses and hospital pharmacists calculate the proper pump setting for intravenous drug therapies. Health Outcomes released a Spanish language version of its Assurance Patient-Centered Pharmaceutical Care software product—to be sold in Spain through an exclusive distribution agreement with the Instituto para el Desarrollo de la Farmacia Comunitaria.

OFFICERS

Peter J. Zugschwert
Chairman and interim Pres./CEO

Michael J. Frakes, Pharm.D.
VP

Marie Cooper
Controller

DIRECTORS

Stanford M. Baratz
Matthew E. Goldberg
Jonathan R. Gordon
Peter J. Zugschwert

MAJOR SHAREHOLDERS

William A. Peter Jr., 12.8%
Bloomington, MN

Peter J. Zugschwert, 7.8%

All officers and directors as a group (6 persons), 13.1%

SIC CODE

7372 Prepackaged software

MISCELLANEOUS

TRANSFER AGENT AND REGISTAR:
Wells Fargo Bank Minnesota N.A., South St. Paul, MN

TRADED: OTC Bulletin Board

SYMBOL: HOMI

STOCKHOLDERS: 330

EMPLOYEES: 11

GENERAL COUNSEL:
Moss and Barnett P.A., Minneapolis

AUDITORS:
KPMG LLP, Minneapolis

INC: MN-1986

ANNUAL MEETING: September

SUBSIDIARIES, DIVISIONS, AFFILIATES

Pharmaceutical Care Outcomes Inc.

HO Management Inc.

Preserve Pharmacy

Health Risk Management Inc.

10900 Hampshire Ave. S., Bloomington, MN 55438
Tel: 952/829-3500 Fax: 952/829-3578 Web site: http://www.hrmi.com

Health Risk Management Inc. (HRM) delivers evidence-based solutions to the managed-care and indemnity marketplaces. Solutions for managed care organizations that are at financial risk include a suite of QualityFIRST evidence-based clinical decision support and benchmarking systems for medical risk management. HRM also provides outsourcing and risk sharing arrangements for health plans using HRM's electronically integrated health plan management services. More than 10 million health plan members benefit from QualityFIRST services. In addition, HRM provides integrated health plan solutions for more than 500,000 members of 4YourCare, a nationwide managed indemnity health plan. HRM also owns PennsylvaniaHealthMATE and OakTree Health Plan, Medicaid HMO plans in Pennsylvania.

EARNINGS HISTORY *

Year Ended Dec 31	Operating Revenue/Sales (dollars in thousands)	Net Earnings	Return on Revenue (percent)	Return on Equity	Net Earnings (dollars per share)	Cash Dividend	Market Price Range
1999 †	67,179	(1,220)	(1.8)	(3.7)	(0.26)	—	11.50–5.50
1999 ¶	163,039	371	0.2	1.1	0.08	—	16.50–5.25
1998 #	94,837	(1,043)	(1.1)	(3.1)	(0.23)	—	16.38–8.38
1997 **	62,910	2,241	3.6	6.6	0.52	—	16.75–9.38
1996	54,665	1,996	3.7	7.0	0.49	—	18.38–7.75

* Revenue figures are net of ceded premiums, but do include interest income.
† These 1999 figures are for six-month transition period beginning July 1, 1999, due to change in year end from June to December.
¶ Income figures for fiscal year ended June 1999 include pretax charge of $1.35 million for Oxford transition costs.
\# Income figures for 1998 include loss of $2,371,000/($0.52) cumulative effect of accounting change.
** Income figures for 1997 include pretax charge of $390,000 to write off costs related to terminated merger agreement.

BALANCE SHEET

Assets	12/31/99 (dollars in thousands)	06/30/99	Liabilities	12/31/99 (dollars in thousands)	06/30/99
Current (CAE 10,577 and 9,229)	32,352	36,706	Current (STD 6,825 and 7,865)	39,933	45,217
Fixed-maturity investments	6,675	8,406	Deferred income taxes	1,479	2,828
Computer software costs	26,180	26,736	Capitalized equipment leases	529	483
Property and equipment	11,078	11,825	Notes payable	3,295	3,145
			Surplus note payable	2,500	2,500
Other	4,552	4,896	Stockholders' equity*	33,101	34,396
TOTAL	80,837	88,569	TOTAL	80,837	88,569

* $0.01 par common; 20,000,000 authorized; 4,639,496 and 4,639,496 issued and outstanding.

RECENT QUARTERS / **PRIOR-YEAR RESULTS**

	Quarter End	Revenue ($000)	Earnings ($000)	EPS ($)	Revenue ($000)	Earnings ($000)	EPS ($)
Q3	09/30/2000	42,678	(8,200)	(1.76)	35,703	913	0.20
Q2	06/30/2000	57,899	(2,628)	(0.56)	35,158	636	0.14
Q1	03/31/2000	56,741	104	0.02	33,914	1,069	0.23
Q4	12/31/99	31,476	(2,133)	(0.46)	45,018	(1,311)	(0.28)
	SUM	188,794	(12,857)	(2.76)	149,793	1,307	0.28

RECENT EVENTS

In **January 2000** the company expanded its existing contract with Columbia HCA of Nashville, Tenn., by assuming the exclusive, total management of CHCA's employee self-funded health care plans. The new three-year exclusive contract was expected to total $10 million in revenue per year for HRM—an increase of more than $4 million per year over the previous contract. In **February** the board of directors approved management's business proposals to proceed with the formation of new Web-based businesses. The first Web-based, e-commerce unit to be formed was to leverage the evidence-based clinical content of the company's existing QualityFIRST medical information system unit onto the Internet for health plans and consumers. The second was to be an application service provider (ASP) using HRM's health plan management technology on the Internet. HRM Health Plans (PA) Inc. announced the completion of its acquisition of Pennsylvania HealthMATE Inc., an Integrated Delivery System that serves the Medicaid population in central Pennsylvania. In **April** Health Risk Management contracted with Landacorp Inc. (Nasdaq: LCOR), Atlanta, to implement both the maxMC medical management software and e-maxMC, Landacorp's Internet solution for providing functionality, to HRM's network of thousands of providers throughout the United States. The com- *continued on page 251*

OFFICERS

Gary T. McIlroy, M.D.
Chairman and CEO

Marlene O. Travis
President, COO, and Secretary

Thomas P. Clark
EVP-Acquisitions/Business Development

Adele M. Kimpell
EVP-Operations

Leland G. LeBlanc
SVP and CFO

Chuck Abrahamson
VP-Operations

Edward Borst
VP-Account Management/ Client Services

Michelle Jahn
VP-Sales/Account Mgmt.

Julie E. Kees
VP-Guideline Development

Michael T. McKim
VP and General Counsel

Luis A. Rosa
Pres.-Risk Business Unit

Pamela Hursh
Pres.-4YourCare Business Unit

DIRECTORS

Gary L. Damkoehler
JSA Healthcare Corp., St. Petersburg, FL

Andrew Jahelka
Chiplease Inc., Chicago

Gary T. McIlroy, M.D.

Robert L. Montgomery
Sutter Health, San Francisco

Raymond G. Schultze
Dept. of Health Services, Los Angeles

Marlene O. Travis

Vance Kenneth Travis
Triad International Ltd., Calgary, Alberta

MAJOR SHAREHOLDERS

Chiplease Inc., 14.5%
Chicago

Summit Capital Management LLC, 8.5%
Seattle

Marlene O. Travis, 8%

Gary T. McIlroy, M.D., 8%

Dimensional Fund Advisors Inc., 6.2%
Santa Monica, CA

All officers and directors as a group (13 persons), 19.7%

SIC CODE

6324 Hospital and medical service plans

MISCELLANEOUS

TRANSFER AGENT AND REGISTAR:
Wells Fargo Bank Minnesota N.A., South St. Paul, MN

TRADED: Nasdaq National Market

SYMBOL: HRMI

STOCKHOLDERS: 73

EMPLOYEES: 754

PART TIME: 20

IN MINNESOTA: 419

GENERAL COUNSEL:
Fredrikson & Byron P.A., Minneapolis

AUDITORS:
Ernst & Young LLP, Minneapolis

INC: MN-1977

ANNUAL MEETING:
January

INVESTOR RELATIONS:
George Ryan

RANKINGS

No. 80 CRM Public 200

No. 49 CRM Performance 100

SUBSIDIARIES, DIVISIONS, AFFILIATES

HRM Claim Management Inc. (1)
Trestlebridge III
5250 Lovers Ln.
Portage, MI 49002

Health Benefit Reinsurance Inc. (2)
10900 Hampshire Ave. S.
Bloomington, MN 55438
Thomas Clark

Institute for Healthcare Quality Inc. (1)
10900 Hampshire Ave. S.
Bloomington, MN 55438
Marlene O. Travis

OakTree Health Plan (1)
601 Walnut St., Suite 900
Independence Square West
Philadelphia, PA 19106
Luis Rosa

HealthMATE HealthPlan
3501 North Sixth St.
P.O. Box 5466
Harrisburg, PA 17110

TWO-YEAR QUARTERLY HIGH-LOW STOCK PRICES

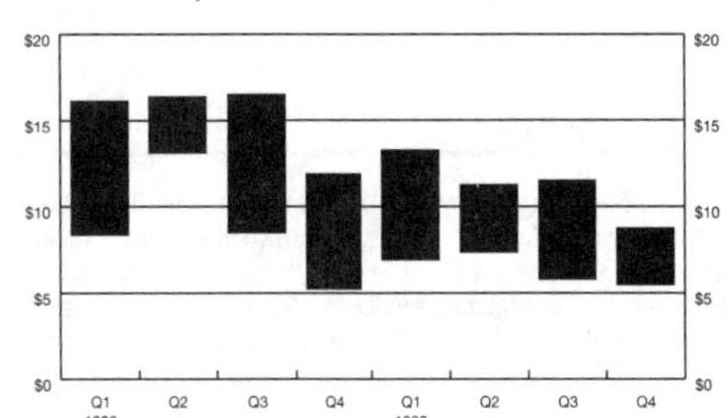

PUB

PUB

Hector Communications Corporation

211 S. Main St., Hector, MN 55342
Tel: 320/848-6611 Fax: 320/848-2323

Hector Communications Corp. owns and operates 11 independent local-exchange telephone companies, serving 37 Minnesota, South Dakota, Iowa, and Wisconsin communities. In addition, through its cable television subsidiaries, the company provided cable television services to 13,000 subscribers in Minnesota, North Dakota, South Dakota, and Wisconsin.

EARNINGS HISTORY

Year Ended Dec 31	Operating Revenue/Sales (dollars in thousands)	Net Earnings	Return on Revenue (percent)	Return on Equity	Net Earnings (dollars per share)	Cash Dividend	Market Price Range
1999 *	34,117	7,479	21.9	18.7	2.42	—	17.25–8.00
1998 †	31,839	3,910	12.3	17.2	1.63	—	12.63–7.38
1997	28,866	2,721	9.4	18.8	1.44	—	10.50–7.25
1996 ¶	20,658	1,209	5.9	12.2	0.65	—	8.75–6.00
1995	5,844	(77)	(1.3)	(0.9)	(0.04)	—	8.75–5.63

* Income figures for 1999 include pretax gain of $13.203 million on sale of marketable securities.
† Income figures for 1998 include pretax gain of $4.817 million on sale of 12.25 percent interest in Sioux Falls (S.D.) Cellular Ltd.
¶ Figures for 1996 include results of Ollig Utililties Co. from its April 25, 1996, date of purchase. Pro forma for full year: revenue $27.261 million; net income $1.098 million/$0.59.

BALANCE SHEET

Assets	12/31/99 (dollars in thousands)	12/31/98	Liabilities	12/31/99 (dollars in thousands)	12/31/98
Current (CAE 27,055 and 14,686)	32,982	19,736	Current (STD 5,607 and 6,809)	14,246	13,183
Property, plant, and equipment	51,410	50,810	Long-term debt	86,282	94,232
Excess of cost over net assets acquired	51,405	53,004	Deferred investment tax credits	140	253
Marketable securities	12,218	8,555	Deferred income taxes	9,436	8,511
Wireless telephone investments	9,689	9,483	Deferred compensation	897	990
Other investments	8,769	8,259	Minority interest (Alliance)	15,814	10,791
Deferred debenture-issue costs		371	Stockholders' equity*	39,982	22,720
Other	323	460	TOTAL	166,797	150,680
TOTAL	166,797	150,680			

* $0.01 par common; 10,000,000 authorized; 3,574,712 and 2,661,062 issued and outstanding.

RECENT QUARTERS / **PRIOR-YEAR RESULTS**

	Quarter End	Revenue ($000)	Earnings ($000)	EPS ($)	Prior-Year Revenue ($000)	Prior-Year Earnings ($000)	Prior-Year EPS ($)
Q2	06/30/2000	9,343	851	0.24	8,724	719	0.26
Q1	03/31/2000	8,488	1,205	0.33	8,320	755	0.28
Q4	12/31/99	8,140	3,773	1.07	8,539	1,824	0.69
Q3	09/30/99	8,935	2,232	0.65	8,027	874	0.34
	SUM	34,905	8,061	2.29	33,610	4,172	1.57

CURRENT: Q1 earnings include pretax gain of $1.622 million on sale of marketable securities. Q4 earnings include pretax gain of $8.749 million on sale of marketable securities. Q3 earnings include pretax gain of $3.472 million on sale of marketable securities.
PRIOR YEAR: Q2 earnings include pretax gain of $0.179 million on sale of marketable securities. Q1 earnings include pretax gain of $0.803 million on sale of marketable securities. Q1 earnings include pretax gain of $0.803 million on sale of cellular investment.

RECENT EVENTS

In **May 2000** the company's 68 percent owned subsidiary, Alliance Telecommunications Corp., signed a definitive agreement to acquire Hager TeleCom Inc. and its wholly owned subsidiary, Cannon Communications Corp. in a merger transaction for $9,124,700. The $1,448,000-revenue Hager TeleCom provides telephone service to 2,000 residential and business customers in the Hager City, Wis., area; provides Internet service to 2,500 customers, primarily in Red Wing, Minn.; and has investments in several telecommunications ventures, including Midwest Wireless LLC. Hector and Alliance agreed to use their respective cash reserves to purchase up to 325,000 shares of Hector common stock from time to time, in the open market or through privately negotiated transactions. Startup mobile phone company Wireless North, a money loser for 13.3 *continued on page 251*

OFFICERS
Curtis A. Sampson
Chairman and CEO
Steven H. Sjogren
President and COO
Paul N. Hanson
VP and Treasurer
Charles A. Braun
CFO
Richard A. Primuth
Secretary

DIRECTORS
Charles R. Dickman
private investor
James O. Ericson
consultant
Paul N. Hanson
Paul A. Hoff
Park Region Mutual Telephone Co.
Curtis A. Sampson
Wayne E. Sampson
management consultant, Stillwater, MN
Steven H. Sjogren
Edward E. Strickland
management consultant, Friday Harbor, WA

MAJOR SHAREHOLDERS
Curtis A. Sampson, 16%
Mario J. Gabelli, 9.6%
Rye, NY
Perkins Capital Management Inc., 6.7%
Wayzata, MN
All officers and directors as a group (8 persons), 23.5%

SIC CODE
4813 Telephone communications, exc radio

MISCELLANEOUS
TRANSFER AGENT AND REGISTAR:
Wells Fargo Bank Minnesota N.A.,
South St. Paul, MN
TRADED: AMEX
SYMBOL: HCT
STOCKHOLDERS: 565
EMPLOYEES: 167
PART TIME: 8
IN MINNESOTA: 140
GENERAL COUNSEL:
Lindquist & Vennum PLLP, Minneapolis
AUDITORS:
Olsen Thielen & Co. Ltd., St. Paul

INC: MN-1990
ANNUAL MEETING: May

RANKINGS
No. 129 CRM Public 200

SUBSIDIARIES, DIVISIONS, AFFILIATES

Arrowhead Communications Corp.
Cotton/Bena, Minn.

Eagle Valley Telephone Co.
Clarissa, Minn.

Hager TeleCom, Inc.
Hager City, Wisc.

Granada Telephone Co.
Granada, Minn.

Indianhead Telephone Co.
Exeland/Radisson/Weyerhaeuser, Wis.

Pine Island Telephone Co.
Pine Island/Oronoco, Minn.

North American Communications Corp.

Alliance Telecommunications Corp. (1)
(68 percent owned by Hector)
Hector, Minn.

Ollig Utilities Co.(2)
Ada, Minn.

Hastad Engineering Co. (3)
Hastad, Minn.

Loretel Systems Inc. (2)
Ada, Minn.

Hills Telephone Co. Inc. (2)

TWO-YEAR QUARTERLY HIGH-LOW STOCK PRICES

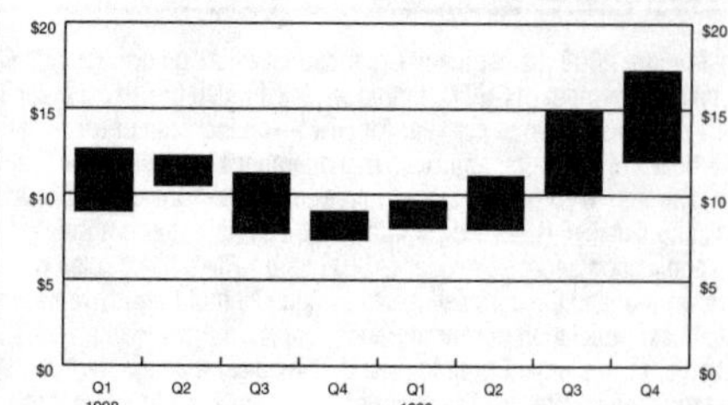

HickoryTech Corporation

221 E. Hickory St., P.O. Box 3248, Mankato, MN 56002
Tel: 507/387-3355 Fax: 507/625-9191 Web site: http://www.hickorytech.com

HickoryTech Corp., established as Mankato Citizens Telephone Co. in 1898 and reorganized as HickoryTech Corp. in 1985, has evolved into four main segments, comprising nine operating companies. The **Telephone Sector** includes two independent telephone companies in Minnesota and two independent telephone companies in Iowa. The **Billing and Data Services Sector** includes a data processing business and a billing services company for large interexchange carriers. The **Communication Product Sector** sells and services telephone apparatus. The **Communications Services Sector** includes long-distance resale and competitive local exchange telephone service (RSA 10-Cellular One brand name).

EARNINGS HISTORY

Year Ended Dec 31	Operating Revenue/Sales (dollars in thousands)	Net Earnings	Return on Revenue (percent)	Return on Equity	Net Earnings (dollars per share*)	Cash Dividend	Market Price Range
1999 †	97,069	14,666	15.1	19.7	1.07	0.44	15.31–9.88
1998 ¶	94,573	13,526	14.3	21.3	0.99	0.44	15.56–10.63
1997 #	76,462	15,479	20.2	27.9	1.12	0.40	11.92–8.92
1996 **	66,562	10,419	15.7	19.8	0.70	0.37	10.50–8.17
1995	62,847	9,900	15.8	17.1	0.64	0.33	11.92–9.33

* Per-share amounts restated to reflect 3-for-1 stock split on Aug. 17, 1998.
† Pro forma 1999 results including a full year from June 1, 1999, purchase Metro A-2 cellular property: revenue $97,228,000; net income $13,845,000/$1.01.
¶ Income figures for 1998 include net pretax gain of $1,278,000 on sale of assets.
# Income figures for 1997 include pretax gain of $6,345,000 on sale of DirecTV assets.
** Income figures for 1996 include nonrecurring $344,000/($0.02) write-down of capitalized software.

BALANCE SHEET

Assets	12/31/99 (dollars in thousands)	12/31/98
Current (CAE 2,708 and 1,133)	24,836	24,184
Property, plant, and equipment	88,186	64,464
Investments	873	4,007
Intangibles	100,231	65,337
Deposit on pending acquisition		2,812
Miscellaneous	678	625
TOTAL	214,804	161,429

Liabilities	12/31/99 (dollars in thousands)	12/31/98
Current (STD 3,764 and 680)	19,791	15,203
Long-term debt	111,149	75,362
Deferred income taxes	6,657	3,985
Deferred compensation	2,731	3,250
Stkhldrs' equity*	74,476	63,629
TOTAL	214,804	161,429

* No par common; 100,000,000 authorized; 13,787,416 and 13,662,216 issued and outstanding.

RECENT QUARTERS / **PRIOR-YEAR RESULTS**

	Quarter End	Revenue ($000)	Earnings ($000)	EPS ($)	Prior-Year Revenue ($000)	Prior-Year Earnings ($000)	Prior-Year EPS ($)
Q3	09/30/2000	25,861	2,086	0.15	24,860	2,106	0.15
Q2	06/30/2000	26,205	2,058	0.15	25,188	7,644	0.56
Q1	03/31/2000	24,075	2,083	0.15	22,159	2,799	0.20
Q4	12/31/99	24,862	2,117	0.15	25,480	3,040	0.22
	SUM	101,003	8,344	0.60	97,687	15,589	1.14

CURRENT: Q2 earnings reflect $233,000 in offsetting unusual items: a charge related to early extinguishment of debt; and a gain from final payment on sale of an Allen, Texas, business.
PRIOR YEAR: Q2 earnings include gain of $9.2 million pretax, $5.2 million/$0.38 after-tax, on sale of 6.4 percent ownership in Midwest Wireless Communications.

RECENT EVENTS

In **March 2000** subsidiary CrystalONE Wireless introduced a revolutionary new digital messaging service (Digital E-Mess@ge) that enables customers to receive text messages, news, weather, and stock quotes directly on their digital wireless phones. In **June** HickoryTech announced a partnership with the city of St. Peter, Minn., to provide competitive communications services to its residents and businesses. In **July** HickoryTech was added to the Russell 2000 and Russell 3000 U.S. Equity Indexes. (The Russell 3000 is a measure of the 3,000 largest publicly traded U.S. companies in the U.S. stock market, ranked by market capitalization as of May 31. The Russell 2000 Index consists of small cap companies from the Russell 3000 Index.) The company also announced plans for expansion into the city of Waukee, Iowa; and plans to sell its local telephone exchange in Amana, Iowa, to South Slope Cooperative Telephone Co. Inc. In **August** potential acquiror Western Wireless, Bellevue, Wash., obtained 6.78 percent of the company's outstanding common stock. CEO Alton said that he didn't foresee a merger or acquisition in the immediate future. **Sept. 30:** Third-quarter revenue grew 4 percent to *continued on page 251*

OFFICERS

Robert D. Alton
Chairman, President, and CEO
Jon L. Anderson
VP, Pres.-Communications Products Sector
David A. Christensen
VP, CFO, Treasurer, and Secretary
John Finke
VP, Pres.-Telephone Sector
Mary T. Jacobs
VP
Jay Knauf
VP and Pres.-Consumer Markets
F. Ernest Lombard
VP, Pres.-Communications Services Sector
Bruce H. Malmgren
VP, Pres.-Billing/Data Services Sector
Lane Nordquist
VP and Pres.-Information Solutions

DIRECTORS

Robert D. Alton Jr.
Lyle T. Bosacker
CEO Advisors Inc., Minneapolis
Myrita P. Craig
Cincinnati Bell Telephone, Cincinnati
Robert K. Else
El Microcircuits Inc., Mankato, MN
James H. Holdrege
Kato Engineering Division, Mankato, MN
Lyle G. Jacobson
Katolight Corp., Mankato, MN
Dr. R. Wynn Kearney Jr.
orthopedic surgeon, Mankato, MN
Starr J. Kirklin
Minnesota State University-Mankato, Mankato, MN
Robert E. Switz
ADC Telecommunications, Bloomington, MN
Brett M. Taylor Jr.
Brett's Department Stores Co., Mankato, MN

MAJOR SHAREHOLDERS

Western Wireless, 6.8%
Bellevue, WA
All officers and directors as a group (16 persons), 5.7%

SIC CODE

4813 Telephone communications, exc radio
4841 Cable and other pay TV services
7374 Data processing and preparation

MISCELLANEOUS

TRANSFER AGENT AND REGISTAR:
Wells Fargo Bank Minnesota N.A., South St. Paul, MN
TRADED: Nasdaq National Market
SYMBOL: HTCO
STOCKHOLDERS: 1,510
EMPLOYEES: 502
GENERAL COUNSEL:
Blethen, Gage, Krause, Blethen, Corcoran, Berkland & Peterson, Mankato, MN
AUDITORS:
PricewaterhouseCoopers LLP, Minneapolis
INC: MN-1985
ANNUAL MEETING: April
HUMAN RESOURCES:
Mary Jacobs

RANKINGS

No. 91 CRM Public 200

PUB

TWO-YEAR QUARTERLY HIGH-LOW STOCK PRICES

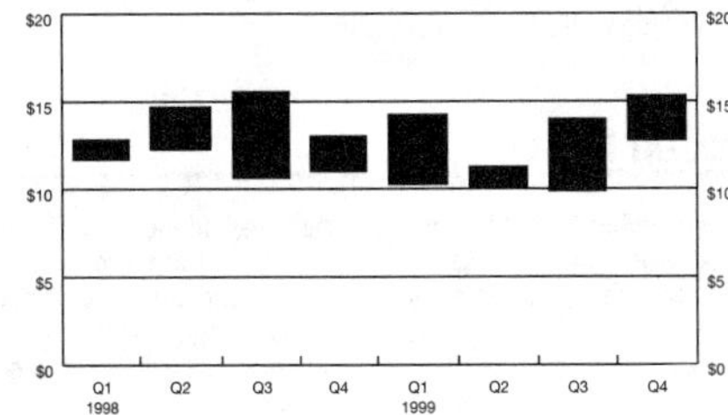

HomeServices.com Inc.

6800 France Ave. S., Suite 600, Edina, MN 55435
Tel: 952/928-5900 Fax: 952/928-5725 Web site: http://www.homeservices.com

HomeServices.com Inc. is the second-largest, full-service independent residential real estate brokerage firm in the United States based on closed transaction sides. The HomeServices.com system offers integrated real estate services, including mortgage, title and closing services, and various related e-commerce services. HomeServices.com currently operates primarily under the Edina Realty (www.edinarealty.com), Iowa Realty (www.iowarealty.com), CBSHOME Real Estate (www.cbshome.com), J.C. Nichols Residential (www.jcnichols.com), Long Realty (www.longrealty.com), Paul Semonin Realtors (www.semonin.com), Carol Jones Realty (www.caroljones.com), First Realty/GMAC (www.firstrealtyhomes.com), and Champion Realty (www.championrealty.com) brand names in 12 states: Minnesota, Iowa, Nebraska, Kansas, Missouri, Arrizona, Kentucky, Wisconsin, Indiana, North Dakota, South Dakota and Maryland. HomeServices.com ranks first or second in market share positions in each of its major markets, operates 165 branch offices, has approximately 6,400 sales associates and has an average 49-year operating history in its major markets.

EARNINGS HISTORY *

Year Ended Dec 31	Operating Revenue/Sales (dollars in thousands)	Net Earnings	Return on Revenue (percent)	Return on Equity	Net Earnings (dollars per share†)	Cash Dividend	Market Price Range
1999	393,291	7,652	1.9	9.3	0.96	—	16.50–14.50
1998	276,828	(1,481)	(0.5)	(4.2)	(0.10)	—	
1997	214,696	4,860	2.3	13.2	0.75	—	
1996	216,291	3,574	1.7	10.6	0.55	—	
1995	71,081	1,345	1.9	0.7	0.21	—	

* Results for May 27, 1998, and prior are those of predecessor Iowa Realty and subsidiaries. In 1996 Edina Realty became a subsidiary of Iowa Realty. Results of HOME Real Estate Holdings Inc. are included from July 1, 1997 (when acquired), to May 8, 1998 (when sold).
† Trading began Oct. 8, 1999.

BALANCE SHEET

Assets	12/31/99 (dollars in thousands)	12/31/98	Liabilities	12/31/99 (dollars in thousands)	12/31/98
Current (CAE 10,318 and 3,114)	31,361	34,411	Current (STD 707 and 3,436)	29,000	30,152
Office property and equipment	22,943	15,453	Long-term debt	48,110	58,009
			Agent profit-sharing	6,282	5,074
Intangibles	106,706	75,122	Other	914	91
Nonconsolidated subsidiaries	845	269	Stockholders' equity*	82,352	35,194
Held-to-maturity securities	944	651	TOTAL	166,658	128,520
Available-for-sale securities	264	297			
Restricted assets	255				
Deferred income taxes	2,679	2,148			
Other	661	169			
TOTAL	166,658	128,520			

* No par common; 38,000,000 authorized; 10,422,942 and 6,778,700 issued and outstanding.

RECENT QUARTERS / **PRIOR-YEAR RESULTS**

	Quarter End	Revenue ($000)	Earnings ($000)	EPS ($)	Prior-Year Revenue ($000)	Prior-Year Earnings ($000)	Prior-Year EPS ($)
Q3	09/30/2000	134,114	7,873	0.76	123,373	4,865	0.62
Q2	06/30/2000	138,897	7,341	0.82	103,039	6,053	0.89
Q1	03/31/2000	87,652	(2,631)	(0.28)	64,685	(1,427)	(0.21)
Q4	12/31/99	102,194	(1,839)	(0.19)	79,536	(2,018)	(0.30)
	SUM	462,857	10,744	1.11	370,633	7,473	1.00

CURRENT: Q4 earnings include one-time charge of $2.2 million/($0.22) related to options granted in connection with the company's IPO.

RECENT EVENTS

In **November 1999** the company agreed to acquire Champion Realty Inc. of Maryland—extending HomeServices' reach to the East Coast. Champion Realty completed 2,800 transaction sides in 1998 valued at $520 million. [Upon closing, in December, HomeServices was operating in 12 states.] Edina Realty continued buying brokerages, most recently the 12-agent Al Thorpe Realtors, Northfield, Minn. In 1999 Edina Realty closed 31,377 transaction sides, second-most in the metro area. (Coldwell Banker Burnet closed 32,375.) In **February 2000** HomeServices.com entered into a relationship with ImproveNet Inc. to provide its home improvement service, The Fix Up, to HomeServices.com cus- *continued on page 251*

OFFICERS

David L. Sokol
Chairman

Ronald J. Peltier
President and CEO

Chris Coile
Pres./CEO-Champion Realty

Jack W. Frost
Pres./CEO-J.C. Nichols

George E. Gans III
Pres./CEO-Paul Semonin Realtors

Doug Hedlund
VP-E-commerce

Galen Johnson
SVP and CFO

R. Michael Knapp
Pres./CEO-Iowa Realty

Greg Mason
COO-Edina Realty Title

Steven A. McArthur
SVP, General Counsel, and Secretary

Stephen E. Quinlan
Pres./CEO-Long Realty

Arne M. Rovick
Vice Chairman, Gen. Counsel-Edina Realty

Joseph J. Valenti
Pres./CEO-CBS Home

DIRECTORS

Gregory E. Abel
MidAmerican Energy Co.

Jack W. Frost

Richard R. Jaros
Level 3 Communications (retired)

R. Michael Knapp

Steven A. McArthur
MidAmerican Energy Co.

Ronald J. Peltier

W. David Scott
Magnum Resources Inc.

David L. Sokol
MidAmerican Energy Co.

MAJOR SHAREHOLDERS

MidAmerican Energy Holdings Co., 84%
Des Moines, IA

All officers and directors as a group (14 persons), 11.5%

SIC CODE

6531 Real estate agents and managers

MISCELLANEOUS

TRANSFER AGENT AND REGISTAR:
Chase Mellon Shareholder Services LLC, Dallas

TRADED: Nasdaq National Market

SYMBOL: HMSV

STOCKHOLDERS: 84

EMPLOYEES: 1,575

GENERAL COUNSEL:
Skadden, Arps, Slate, Meagher & Flom LLP, New York

AUDITORS:
PricewaterhouseCoopers LLP, Minneapolis

INC: DE-1999

INVESTOR RELATIONS:
Cindy Sattler

RANKINGS

No. 56 CRM Public 200
No. 42 CRM Performance 100

Hormel Foods Corporation

One Hormel Pl., Austin, MN 55912
Tel: 507/437-5611 Fax: 507/437-5489 Web site: http://www.hormel.com

Hormel Foods Corp. is a multinational food and consumer products company, supplying processed and packaged food products. The principal products of the company are meat and food products that are sold fresh, frozen, cured, smoked, cooked, or canned. Hormel is also a leading producer and marketer of whole and processed turkey products. Products are marketed in international areas, including the Philippines, Japan, and various European countries.

EARNINGS HISTORY

Year Ended Oct	Operating Revenue/Sales (dollars in thousands)	Net Earnings	Return on Revenue (percent)	Return on Equity	Net Earnings (dollars per share*)	Cash Dividend	Market Price Range
1999	3,357,757	163,438	4.9	19.4	1.12	0.33	22.63–14.78
1998 †	3,261,045	139,291	4.3	17.1	0.93	0.32	19.44–13.09
1997 ¶	3,256,551	109,492	3.4	13.6	0.72	0.31	16.25–11.75
1996 #	3,098,685	79,408	2.6	10.1	0.52	0.30	13.88–10.25
1995	3,046,195	120,436	4.0	16.5	0.79	0.29	13.94–11.69

* Per-share amounts restated to reflect 2-for-1 stock split paid on Feb. 15, 2000.
† Period for 1998 is 53 weeks; income figures include gain of $28.4 million pretax, $17.4 million/$0.12 after-tax, on sale of plant.
¶ Income figures for 1997 include gain of $5.2 million pretax, $3.2 million/$0.02 after-tax, from reversal of prior-year restructuring charge.
\# Income figures for 1996 include restructuring charge of $8.7 million pretax, $5.4 million/($0.04) after-tax, to exit the catfish business.

BALANCE SHEET

Assets	10/30/99 (dollars in thousands)	10/31/98	Liabilities	10/30/99 (dollars in thousands)	10/31/98
Current (CAE 188,310 and 203,934)	800,143	717,365	Current (STD 41,214 and 6,117)	385,407	267,651
Property, plant, and equipment	505,624	486,907	Long-term debt	184,723	204,874
Intangibles	98,544	105,244	Accumulated postretirement benefit obligation	252,236	248,201
Deferred income taxes	60,051	65,606	Other	22,077	21,851
Investments in affiliates	142,879	114,665	Stockholders' equity*	841,142	813,315
Other	78,344	66,105	TOTAL	1,685,585	1,555,892
TOTAL	1,685,585	1,555,892			

* $.0586 par common; 400,000,000 authorized; 142,724,870 and 147,229,092 issued and outstanding.

RECENT QUARTERS / **PRIOR-YEAR RESULTS**

	Quarter End	Revenue ($000)	Earnings ($000)	EPS ($)	Revenue ($000)	Earnings ($000)	EPS ($)
Q3	07/29/2000	886,015	29,136	0.21	816,818	29,550	0.20
Q2	04/29/2000	879,023	36,254	0.26	791,095	31,834	0.22
Q1	01/29/2000	903,913	43,848	0.31	799,005	42,380	0.29
Q4	10/30/99	950,839	59,674	0.41	912,037	45,152	0.31
	SUM	3,619,790	168,912	1.19	3,318,955	148,916	1.02

PRIOR YEAR: Q1 earnings include a one-time gain of $3,808,000/$0.03 from sale of land by minority subsidiary Campofrio Alimentacion S.A., Madrid.

RECENT EVENTS

In **November 1999** the company announced the largest profit-sharing distribution ever made to its employees. More than $9.9 million was distributed companywide—each eligible employee receiving (on average) $1,782. In **January 2000** Hormel agreed to terms with Eridania Beghin-Say, a diversified manufacturer headquartered in Paris, to form joint venture Carapelli USA LLC to introduce the Carapelli line of olive oils in retail stores throughout the United States and Puerto Rico. In **April** Hormel was named Supplier of the Year by the Meat Products Division of Wal*Mart Stores Inc., Bentonville, Ark. In **May** the Minnesota state lottery introduced a new $2 SPAM scratch-off lottery ticket. **July 29:** Operating earnings for the first nine months of the fiscal year were $109.238 million, an increase of 9.3 percent over the comparable period of fiscal 1999. Higher prices for hogs in the spot cash market placed pressure on the company's ability to obtain historical margins in its pork operations. During third quarter the Prepared Foods Group moved forward with the launch of the Carapelli olive oil line with sales and distribution ahead of plan. A three-liter tin of Carapelli olive oil was introduced in the New York and New England markets. SPAM oven-roasted turkey was rolled out nationally and was joined in 10 markets with a new Hot & Spicy SPAM luncheon meat featuring Tabasco brand pepper sauce. The Refrigerated Foods Group completed the national introduction of its Always Tender line of teriyaki and peppercorn filet of beef sirloin products. Volume, margins, and profit performance of the compa- *continued on page 251*

OFFICERS

Joel W. Johnson
Chairman, President, and CEO
Gary J. Ray
EVP-Refrigerated Foods
Michael J. McCoy
SVP-Administration and CFO
James A. Jorgenson
SVP-Corporate Staff
Mahlon C. Schneider
SVP-External Affairs and Gen. Counsel
Steven G. Binder
Group VP-Foodservice
Eric A. Brown
Group VP-Prepared Foods
David N. Dickson
Group VP-International/Corp. Development
Ronald W. Fielding
Group VP-Meat Products
Richard A. Bross
VP and Pres.-Hormel Foods Int'l
Thomas D. Day
VP-Foodservice Marketing
Forrest D. Dryden, Ph.D.
VP-Research/Development
Daniel Hartzog
VP-Sales, Meat Products
Jeffrey Ettinger
VP and Pres./CEO Jennie-O Foods
Dennis B. Goettsch
VP-Foodservice Marketing
V. Allan Krejci
VP-Public Relations
Kurt F. Mueller
VP-Fresh Pork Sales/Marketing
Gary C. Paxton
VP-Prepared Foods Operations
Larry J. Pfeil
VP-Engineering
Douglas R. Reetz
VP-Grocery Products Sales
James N. Sheehan
VP and Controller
William F. Snyder
VP-Refrigerated Foods Operations
Joe C. Swedberg
VP-Grocery Products Marketing
Larry L. Vorpahl
VP-Grocery Products Marketing

DIRECTORS

John W. Allen
Michigan State University (retired), East Lansing, MI
John R. Block
Food Distributors International, Falls Church, VA
Eric A. Brown
William S. Davila
The Vons Cos. Inc. (retired), Los Angeles
David N. Dickson
E. Peter Gillette Jr.
Piper Trust Co. (retired), Minneapolis
Luella G. Goldberg
Wellesley College, Wellesley, MA
Joel W. Johnson
Joseph T. Mallof
S.C. Johnson & Son Inc., Racine, WI
Michael J. McCoy
Gary J. Ray
Robert R. Waller, M.D.
Mayo Foundation, Rochester, MN

MAJOR SHAREHOLDERS

The Hormel Foundation, 44.9%
Austin, MN

All officers and directors as a group (26 persons), 2.7%

MISCELLANEOUS

TRANSFER AGENT AND REGISTAR:
Wells Fargo Bank Minnesota N.A., South St. Paul, MN
TRADED: NYSE
SYMBOL: HRL
STOCKHOLDERS: 11,800
EMPLOYEES: 12,100
IN MINNESOTA: 7,167
AUDITORS:
Ernst & Young LLP, Minneapolis
INC: DE-1928
FOUNDED: 1891
ANNUAL MEETING: January
PUBLIC RELATIONS: V. Allan Krejci
PURCHASING: Donald Nelson

RANKINGS

No. 12 CRM Public 200
No. 20 CRM Employer 100

TWO-YEAR QUARTERLY HIGH-LOW STOCK PRICES

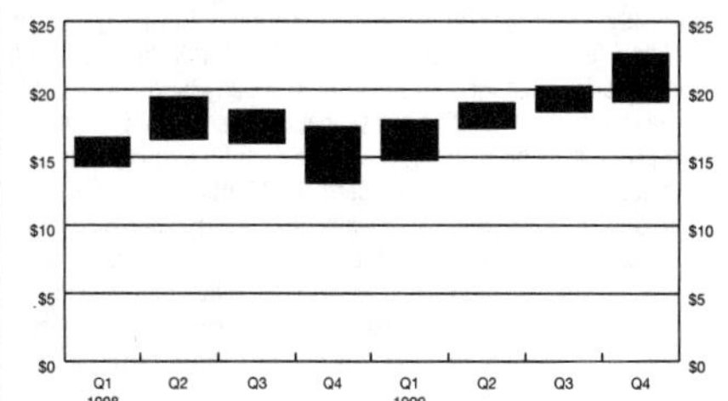

PUB

PUB

Hutchinson Technology Inc.

40 W. Highland Park, Hutchinson, MN 55350
Tel: 320/587-3797 Fax: 320/587-1810 Web site: http://www.htch.com

Hutchinson Technology Inc. develops, manufactures, and markets precision components used principally in computer rigid disk drives. It produces a majority of the worldwide supply of suspension assemblies for all sizes of disk drives produced by all of the significant disk drive manufacturers. [Suspension assemblies are very precise metal springs that hold the recording heads at microscopic distances above the disks in disk drives.] The company has benefited from two trends: the increasing sales of computer systems, especially PCs and portables; and the increasing importance of the suspension assembly in permitting better disk drive performance, including greater data storage capacity, faster access to data, and increasing reliability.

EARNINGS HISTORY

Year Ended Sept	Operating Revenue/Sales (dollars in thousands)	Net Earnings	Return on Revenue (percent)	Return on Equity	Net Earnings (dollars per share*)	Cash Dividend	Market Price Range
1999	580,270	17,638	3.0	3.8	0.77	—	51.25–11.88
1998	407,616	(48,411)	(11.9)	(20.4)	(2.46)	—	36.13–12.63
1997	453,232	41,909	9.2	14.8	2.29	—	39.00–12.58
1996 †	353,186	13,802	3.9	10.3	0.84	—	21.83–10.25
1995	299,998	21,078	7.0	17.6	1.28	—	29.67–7.67

* Per-share amounts restated to reflect 3-for-1 stock split effected Feb. 11, 1997.
† 1996 is a 53-week period. Income figures include one-time charge of ($0.23) per share to accelerate and conclude payments to IBM.

BALANCE SHEET

Assets	09/26/99 (dollars in thousands)	09/27/98
Current (CAE 98,820 and 58,942)	378,786	194,285
Property, plant, and equipment	352,936	335,289
Other	20,127	19,904
TOTAL	751,849	549,478

Liabilities	09/26/99 (dollars in thousands)	09/27/98
Current (STD 4,171 and 4,613)	69,339	93,171
Long-term debt	65,562	68,247
Other	1,989	1,230
Convertible subordinated notes	150,000	150,000
Stockholders' equity*	464,959	236,830
TOTAL	751,849	549,478

* $0.01 par common; 45,000,000 authorized; 24,744,000 and 19,780,000 issued and outstanding.

RECENT QUARTERS / **PRIOR-YEAR RESULTS**

	Quarter End	Revenue ($000)	Earnings ($000)	EPS ($)	Prior-Year Revenue ($000)	Prior-Year Earnings ($000)	Prior-Year EPS ($)
Q4	09/24/2000	116,149	1,577	0.06	141,372	(2,149)	(0.09)
Q3	06/25/2000	108,663	(22,919)	(0.92)	131,257	(5,494)	(0.22)
Q2	03/26/2000	110,937	(13,101)	(0.53)	152,366	13,748	0.61
Q1	12/26/99	123,823	(39,169)	(1.58)	155,275	11,533	0.58
	SUM	459,572	(73,612)	(2.97)	580,270	17,638	0.88

CURRENT: Q3 earnings include pretax asset-impairment and severance charges totaling $16.74 million. Q1 earnings include pretax asset-impairment and severance charges totaling $46.528 million.
PRIOR YEAR: Q4 earnings include a charge of $1.3 million/($0.04) for severance costs.

RECENT EVENTS

In **March 2000** the company reduced its workforce by 250 positions, primarily in manufacturing areas at the company's plants in Sioux Falls, S.D., and Eau Claire, Wis. CEO Fortun said that the workforce reduction was a result of continued weak demand for the company's suspension assembly products, attributed to temporary market share shifts, yield improvements at its customers, and lower disk drive component counts. Including attrition, cutbacks (this was the fourth since August 1999) had whittled Hutch Tech's work force by 18 percent. **March 26:** The resulting underutilization of manufacturing capacity contributed to second quarter's net loss. In **April** the company announced another round of layoffs—950 jobs, this time (550 of them at its Eau Claire plant)—reflecting consolidation of some operations from Eau Claire to Hutchinson and a 10 percent companywide cut in production of suspension assemblies. In **August** Hutchinson announced that, through the first nine weeks of its fiscal fourth quarter, the company had earned $0.2 million, or $0.01 a share, on net sales of $80 million. "We see signs that demand for our suspension assemblies has begun to grow after several quarters of decline," said CEO Fortun. "Our improved financial performance through the first nine weeks of our fourth quarter is a result of the cost-reduction actions we have taken over the past several quarters, combined with productivity improvements and resumption in demand growth." In **September** Hutch Tech received a Minnesota Waste Wise Smart Business Award in recognition of its waste-reduction accomplishments. **Sept. 24:** The company returned to profitability in the fourth quarter due to cost reductions and to improved productivity and yields in the production of suspension assemblies. Excluding write-downs and sev- ***continued on page 251***

OFFICERS

Jeffrey W. Green
Chairman

Wayne M. Fortun
President and CEO

Beatrice A. Graczyk
COO and VP-Operations

Rebecca A. Albrecht
VP-Human Resources

John A. Ingleman
VP, CFO, and Secretary

Richard C. Myers
VP-Administration

Richard J. Penn
VP-Sales/Marketing

R. Scott Schaefer
VP and Chief Technical Officer

Todd Bradley
Controller

Peggy J. Lietzau
Corporate Planning Director

Darlene Polzin
Investor Relations

David Radloff
Chief Information Officer

DIRECTORS

W. Thomas Brunberg
Brunberg, Thoresen & Associates, Minneapolis

Archibald Cox Jr.
Sextant Group Inc.

Wayne M. Fortun

Jeffrey W. Green

Russell Huffer
Apogee Enterprises Inc., Bloomington, MN

Steven E. Landsburg Ph.D.
U. of Rochester (NY) Dept. of Economics

William T. Monahan
Imation Corp., Oakdale, MN

Richard B. Solum

MAJOR SHAREHOLDERS

Spinnaker Technology Fund L.P./Bowman Capital Management LLC, 13.4%
San Mateo, CA

All officers and directors as a group (14 persons), 9.4%

SIC CODE

3572 Computer storage devices

3679 Electronic components, nec

MISCELLANEOUS

TRANSFER AGENT AND REGISTAR:
Wells Fargo Bank Minnesota N.A., South St. Paul, MN

TRADED: Nasdaq National Market

SYMBOL: HTCH

STOCKHOLDERS: 1,029

EMPLOYEES: 4,729

GENERAL COUNSEL:
Faegre & Benson PLLP, Minneapolis

AUDITORS:
Arthur Andersen LLP, Minneapolis

INC: MN-1965

ANNUAL MEETING:
January

HUMAN RESOURCES:
Rebecca A. Albrecht

INVESTOR RELATIONS:
Darlene Polzin

RANKINGS

No. 47 CRM Public 200

No. 78 CRM Employer 100

SUBSIDIARIES, DIVISIONS, AFFILIATES

SUBSIDIARIES

HTI Export Ltd.
P.O. Box 261
Bridgetown, Barbados

Hutchinson Technology Asia Inc.
40 W. Highland Pk.
Hutchinson, MN 55350
Richard C. Myers

MANUFACTURING LOCATIONS

Hutchinson Technology Inc.
40 W. Highland Pk.
Hutchinson, MN 55350

3401 Fourth Ave. N.
Sioux Falls, SD 57104
605/333-6000

2435 Alpine Rd.
Eau Claire, WI 54703
715/838-9800

5905 Trenton Lane N.
Plymouth, MN 55442
612/519-6200

FOREIGN OFFICES

Singapore
Leiden, Netherlands
Dong Guan, Guang Dong, PRC (China)

TWO-YEAR QUARTERLY HIGH-LOW STOCK PRICES

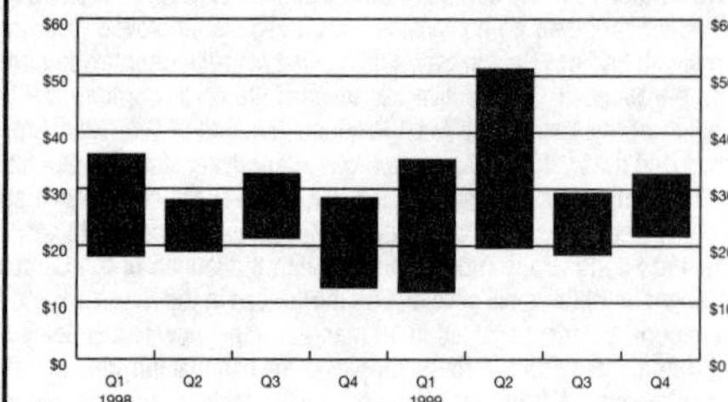

Hypertension Diagnostics Inc.

2915 Waters Rd., Suite 108, Eagan, MN 55121
Tel: 651/687-9999 Fax: 651/687-0485 Web site: http://www.hdi-pulsewave.com

Hypertension Diagnostics Inc. is engaged in the design, development, manufacturing and marketing of a proprietary medical device that it believes will non-invasively detect subtle changes in the elasticity of large and small arteries. Vascular compliance of elasticity has been investigated for many years and clinical studies suggest that a lack of arterial elasticity is an early indicator of vascular disease. The company plans to market three versions: the HDI/PulseWave CR-2000 Research CardioVascular Profiling System, the CV Profilor DO-2020 CardioVascular Profiling System and the CVProfilor MD-3000 CardioVascular Profiling System.

EARNINGS HISTORY *

Year Ended Jun 30	Operating Revenue/Sales (dollars in thousands)	Net Earnings	Return on Revenue (percent)	Return on Equity	Net Earnings (dollars per share†)	Cash Dividend	Market Price Range
2000	423	(3,324)	NM	(62.0)	(0.65)	—	7.75–2.13
1999	381	(2,214)	NM	(26.1)	(0.45)	—	4.38–2.00
1998	0	(1,142)	NM	NM	(0.51)	—	
1997	0	(872)	NM	(72.1)	(0.44)	—	
1996	0	(714)	NM	(36.1)	(0.57)	—	

* Development-stage company.
† Trading began Aug. 7, 1998.

BALANCE SHEET

Assets	06/30/00 (dollars in thousands)	06/30/99
Current (CAE 4,018 and 7,684)	5,400	8,297
Property and equipment	362	384
Patents	17	24
Other	7	7
TOTAL	5,786	8,712

Liabilities	06/30/00 (dollars in thousands)	06/30/99
Current	421	223
Stockholders' equity*	5,365	8,489
TOTAL	5,786	8,712

* $0.01 par common; 25,000,000 authorized; 5,173,697 and 5,109,235 issued and outstanding.

RECENT QUARTERS / **PRIOR-YEAR RESULTS**

	Quarter End	Revenue ($000)	Earnings ($000)	EPS ($)	Prior-Year Revenue ($000)	Prior-Year Earnings ($000)	Prior-Year EPS ($)
Q4	06/30/2000	424	(3,324)	(0.64)	248	(668)	(0.13)
Q3	03/31/2000	165	(716)	(0.14)	38	(524)	(0.10)
Q2	12/31/99	57	(959)	(0.19)	95	(541)	(0.11)
Q1	09/30/99	71	(669)	(0.13)	0	(481)	(0.11)
	SUM	718	(5,667)	(1.10)	381	(2,214)	(0.44)

RECENT EVENTS

In **November 1999** the company signed an exclusive distribution agreement with Higa Medical Systems, a division of Higa Industries, Tokyo, for distribution of HDI products throughout Japan. HDI became fully certified in accordance with ISO 9002/EN-46002 standards and the European Union Medical Device Directive. The company's non-invasive HDI/PulseWave CR-2000 Research CardioVascular Profiling Instrument was certified to carry the "CE 0123" mark. In **March 2000** HDI was issued a European patent on vascular impedance measurement and a U.S. patent covering both apparatus and method for waveform contour analysis. In **April** the company's noninvasive HDI/PulseWave CR-2000 Research CardioVascular Profiling System was selected by Alteon Inc. (OTC Bulletin Board: ALTN) for inclusion in its Phase II clinical trial of its Lead A.G.E. 'Crosslink Breaker' ALT-711. In **June** the company completed a multisite clinical trial with its CVProfilor DO-2020 CardioVascular Profiling System, and included the results in a new 510(k) Premarket Notification submission that had been forwarded to the FDA for review. In **August** a post-effective amendment to the 1998 initial public offering registration statement registering its class A redeemable warrants was declared effective by the SEC. The company had no present intention of exercising its rights to their redemption in the immediate future. Hypertension Diagnostics announced the effectiveness of its registration statement for 1,568,175 shares of its common stock (relating to placement agent's and underwriter's warrants, and options granted outside of the company's 1995 and 1998 Stock Option Plans). The company exhibited its HDI/PulseWave CR-2000 Research CardioVascular Profiling System at three key scientific meetings with a worldwide attendance: the Eighteenth Scientific Meeting of the International Society of Hypertension, an International Society of Hypertension Special Satellite Symposium, and the XXIInd Congress of the European Society of Cardiology. In **September** the company's HDI/PulseWave CR-2000 Research CardioVascular Profiling System was selected by Solvay Pharmaceuticals Inc. for use in a multicenter cardiovascular drug research trial. In **October** the same device was included in the National Institutes of Health's multiethnic study of atherosclerosis, and was selected by Pfizer Pharmaceuticals Group, New York, for use in a multicenter cardiovascular drug research trial. In **November** the company received clearance from the FDA to market the CVProfilor DO-2020 CardioVascular Profiling System for use by physicians and other health care providers to noninvasively screen patients for the presence of cardiovascular disease.

OFFICERS

Kenneth W. Brimmer
Chairman

Greg H. Guettler
President

Charles F. Chesney, D.V.M., Ph.D., R.A.C
EVP, Chief Tech. Officer, Secretary

James S. Murphy
SVP-Finance/Administration and CFO

Jay N. Cohn, M.D.
Chief Clinical Consultant

Stanley M. Finkelstein, Ph.D.
Chief Technical Consultant

DIRECTORS

Melville R. Bois
Universal Title and Financial Corp., Edina, MN

Kenneth W. Brimmer
Active IQ Technologies Inc., Minnetonka, MN

Charles F. Chesney

Jay N. Cohn
U. of Minnesota Medical School, Minneapolis

Greg H. Guettler

MAJOR SHAREHOLDERS

Jay N. Cohn, 9.3%

Charles F. Chesney, 5.9%

Stanley M. Finkelstein, 5.7%
Minneapolis

All officers and directors as a group (6 persons), 20.2%

SIC CODE

3841 Surgical and medical instruments

MISCELLANEOUS

TRANSFER AGENT AND REGISTAR:
Firstar Trust Co., Milwaukee

TRADED: Nasdaq SmallCap Market

SYMBOL: HDII

STOCKHOLDERS: 1,200

EMPLOYEES: 12

IN MINNESOTA: 12

GENERAL COUNSEL:
Lindquist & Vennum PLLP, Minneapolis

AUDITORS:
Ernst & Young LLP, Minneapolis

INC: MN-1988

ANNUAL MEETING:
December

INVESTOR RELATIONS:
James S. Murphy

PUB

TWO-YEAR QUARTERLY HIGH-LOW STOCK PRICES

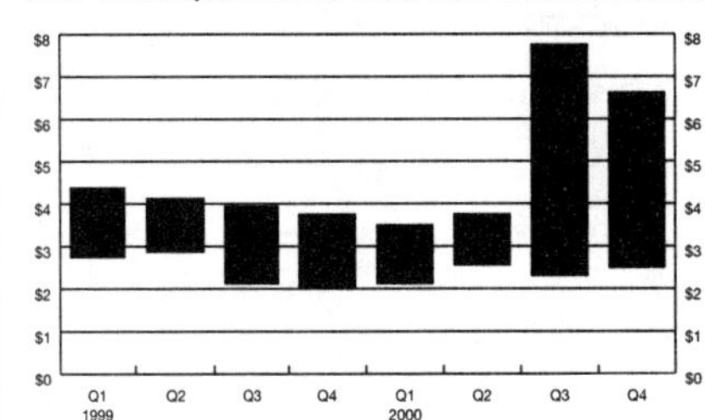

PUB

IPI Inc.

Westech Business Center, 8091 Wallace Rd., Eden Prairie, MN 55344
Tel: 952/975-6200 Fax: 952/975-6262 Web site: http://www.insty-prints.com

IPI Inc. is the parent company of **Insty-Prints Inc.**, franchisor of the Insty-Prints chain of fast-turnaround business printing centers and the parent of Dreamcatcher Franchise Corporation, Inc. Through 225 franchise locations, Insty-Prints provides full-color printing and photocopying, high-speed photocopying, bindery services, desktop publishing, and other graphic design services. As a franchisor, the company offers Insty-Prints franchise owners initial and ongoing training and support services, including advertising and marketing assistance, technical support, a direct-mail program, equipment financing, and volume purchasing. A typical Insty-Prints store is owner-operated, with four to seven employees. Dreamcatcher franchises learning centers that provide private supplemental instructive services primarily to children ages 7 to 17. This business is in its early state of development with 11 operating units and 14 under contract.

EARNINGS HISTORY

Year Ended Nov 30	Operating Revenue/Sales (dollars in thousands)	Net Earnings	Return on Revenue (percent)	Return on Equity	Net Earnings (dollars per share)	Cash Dividend	Market Price Range
1999 *	11,063	1,782	16.1	9.9	0.38	—	3.69–2.06
1998	11,497	2,032	17.7	12.5	0.43	—	5.75–3.00
1997	11,687	1,719	14.7	11.9	0.36	—	5.50–3.25
1996	11,207	1,533	13.7	12.0	0.32	—	4.38–3.25
1995	10,819	1,360	12.6	12.1	0.29	—	4.13–4.00

* Income figures for 1999 include pretax gain of $26,000 on disposal of assets.

BALANCE SHEET

Assets	11/30/99 (dollars in thousands)	11/30/98	Liabilities	11/30/99 (dollars in thousands)	11/30/98
Current (CAE 2,022 and 3,828)	14,759	13,044	Current	1,753	1,608
			Capital lease obligations	319	51
Property and equipment	1,246	561	Stockholders' equity*	17,944	16,242
Notes receivable	860	1,139			
Goodwill and other intangibles	3,151	3,157	TOTAL	20,016	17,901
TOTAL	20,016	17,901			

* $0.01 par common; 15,000,000 authorized; 4,734,000 and 4,734,000 issued and outstanding.

RECENT QUARTERS / **PRIOR-YEAR RESULTS**

	Quarter End	Revenue ($000)	Earnings ($000)	EPS ($)	Revenue ($000)	Earnings ($000)	EPS ($)
Q3	08/31/2000	2,471	151	0.03	2,755	457	0.10
Q2	05/31/2000	2,571	555	0.11	3,077	545	0.12
Q1	02/29/2000	2,398	166	0.03	2,503	374	0.08
Q4	11/30/99	2,729	406	0.09	3,047	533	0.11
	SUM	10,169	1,278	0.27	11,382	1,909	0.40

RECENT EVENTS

In December 1999 the company agreed to purchase substantially all the assets of Dreamcatcher Franchise Corp., a franchisor of learning centers, and its affiliate, Dreamcatcher Learning Centers Inc., which operates three corporate-owned locations in Colorado. Dreamcatcher Franchise Corp. has 10 operating franchised locations and 14 additional locations contracted but not opened. The acquired businesses "represent an important part of our expressed growth strategy, which is to grow IPI through acquisitions of related opportunities outside the printing industry that can take advantage of our existing business systems," said CEO Sutter. In **January 2000** the Dreamcatcher deal was completed. The company's common stock moved from the Nasdaq Small Cap Market to the American Stock Exchange. **Aug. 31:** Sutter commented, "Our results for the third quarter and nine-month period of 2000 reflect the cost of implementing our growth strategies of expanding corporate-owned Insty-Prints facilities and the development costs related to the acquisition of Dreamcatcher Franchise Corp. in January 2000. The costs associated with our growth strategies will continue to reduce earnings for the remainder of 2000. Additionally, during the nine months ended August 31, 2000, over $11 million of investments were shifted from interest/dividend-bearing to noninterest/dividend investments."

OFFICERS

Robert J. Sutter
Chairman

David C. Oswald
President and CEO

David M. Engel
VP-Finance and CFO

Thomas C. Johnson
VP-Marketing

David A. Mahler
Secretary

Robert E. Warmka
VP-Operations

DIRECTORS

Howard Grodnick
Jacobs Trading Co., Minneapolis

Irwin Jacobs
Jacobs Management Co.

Daniel T. Lindsay
Jacobs Industries Inc.

Dennis M. Mathison
Marshall Financial Group Inc.

David C. Oswald

Robert J. Sutter

MAJOR SHAREHOLDERS

Dennis M. Mathison/ Marshall Financial Group Inc., 32.8%
Minneapolis

Jacobs Industries Inc./Irwin L. Jacobs, 23%
Minneapolis

Daniel T. Lindsay, 8.2%
Minneapolis

All officers and directors as a group (12 persons), 68.3%

SIC CODE

6794 Patent owners and lessors

MISCELLANEOUS

TRANSFER AGENT AND REGISTAR:
Wells Fargo Bank Minnesota N.A., South St. Paul, MN

TRADED: AMEX

SYMBOL: IDH

STOCKHOLDERS: 270

EMPLOYEES: 54

IN MINNESOTA: 25

GENERAL COUNSEL:
Lindquist & Vennum PLLP, Minneapolis
Fredrikson & Byron P.A., Minneapolis

AUDITORS:
Arthur Andersen LLP, Minneapolis

INC: MN-1983

ANNUAL MEETING: April

COMMUNICATIONS:
Susan Selindh

HUMAN RESOURCES/ ADMINISTRATION:
Candice Hayes

RANKINGS

No. 179 CRM Public 200

SUBSIDIARIES, DIVISIONS, AFFILIATES

Insty-Prints Inc.

Dreamcatcher Franchise Corporation, Inc.

TWO-YEAR QUARTERLY HIGH-LOW STOCK PRICES

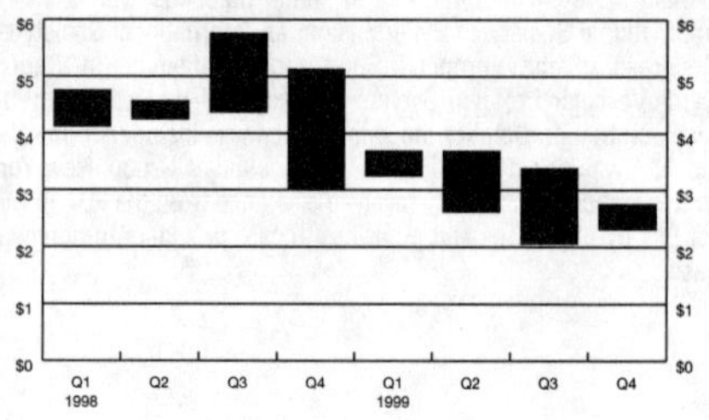

Image Sensing Systems Inc.

500 Spruce Tree Centre, 1600 University Ave. W., St. Paul, MN 55104
Tel: 651/603-7700 Fax: 651/603-7795 Web site: http://www.imagesensing.com

Image Sensing Systems Inc. (ISS) develops and markets products using video image processing technology for use in advanced traffic management systems and traffic data collection to reduce congestion and improve roadway planning. Also known as machine vision or artificial vision, video image processing uses video cameras and computers to emulate the function of the human eye. It has a variety of industrial applications. ISS has combined its proprietary machine vision technology—consisting of complex algorithms, software, and special purpose hardware—with commercially available computer hardware and video cameras to create a system that collects, processes, and analyzes video images.

EARNINGS HISTORY

Year Ended Dec 31	Operating Revenue/Sales (dollars in thousands)	Net Earnings	Return on Revenue (percent)	Return on Equity	Net Earnings (dollars per share*)	Cash Dividend	Market Price Range
1999	4,772	251	5.3	7.0	0.10	—	3.96–2.19
1998	3,368	209	6.2	6.2	0.08	—	4.17–1.30
1997	4,328	487	11.3	15.5	0.16	—	4.90–1.77
1996	3,192	(1,038)	(32.5)	(39.3)	(0.35)	—	5.00–1.67
1995	2,863	(436)	(15.2)	(11.9)	(0.17)	—	5.42–3.54

* Trading began in May 1995. Per-share amounts restated to reflect 20 percent stock dividend on April 13, 2000.

BALANCE SHEET

Assets	12/31/99 (dollars in thousands)	12/31/98	Liabilities	12/31/99 (dollars in thousands)	12/31/98
Current (CAE 1,319 and 1,326)	2,933	2,891	Current	760	818
Property and equipment	445	470	Deferred income taxes	394	366
Deferred income taxes	358	318	Minority interest	80	
Capitalized software development costs	1,014	856	Stockholders' equity*	3,602	3,351
Goodwill	86		TOTAL	4,836	4,535
TOTAL	4,836	4,535			

* $0.01 par common; 5,000,000 authorized; 2,479,200 and 2,479,200 issued and outstanding.

RECENT QUARTERS / **PRIOR-YEAR RESULTS**

	Quarter End	Revenue ($000)	Earnings ($000)	EPS ($)	Prior-Year Revenue ($000)	Prior-Year Earnings ($000)	Prior-Year EPS ($)
Q3	09/30/2000	1,495	(103)	(0.03)	895	(126)	(0.05)
Q2	06/30/2000	1,533	11	0.00	1,131	(40)	(0.02)
Q1	03/31/2000	1,095	85	0.03	1,156	55	0.02
Q4	12/31/99	1,590	483	0.19	1,144	145	0.06
	SUM	5,713	476	0.20	4,326	34	0.01

RECENT EVENTS

In **December 1999** the company's Asia subsidiary, Flow Traffic Ltd., won an order for the supply of a traffic control system for the 2-km-long Shichangling tunnel, part of National Expressway 107 running from Beijing to Guangzhou. Flow Traffic also won an order for the supply of more than 600 loop detectors to be used in major expressway projects and large cities in the People's Republic of China. New clients in December: the traffic police of Shenzhen city in Southern China; the Intelligent Transport Systems Center of the Chinese Ministry of Communication; and the Hong Kong Transport Department. In **January 2000** ISS received from ADDCO Inc. an order for the supply of the Autoscope wide-area video vehicle detection system for the Duluth Traffic Operation Communication Center project of Minnesota Department of Transportation. In **March** the Road Commission for Oakland County (RCOC), Mich., authorized the immediate delivery of an additional 24 Autoscope-2004 and four Autoscope-V8 wide-area video vehicle detection systems. The city of Cologne, Germany, authorized the purchase of the first Autoscope Solo video vehicle detection systems, part of a citywide plan to replace in-ground detection systems with Solo. Volkswagen AG in Germany purchased the first Autoscope Solo Mobile trailer for video traffic data collection and analysis along 80 km of roadway around its manufacturing facility in Wolfsburg, Germany. In **April** the Slovak Road Administration in Bratislava issued a contract for a 61-camera Autoscope system for a tunnel management project in the Slovak Republic. Autoscope Solo was selected for use as the exclusive video vehicle detection system in the Expo 2000 World's Fair in Hannover, Germany, where several Autoscope Solo systems were to be integrated into portable traffic monitoring and variable-message sign stations to control the large volume of vehicular traffic. In **May** Hong Kong and the Chinese city of Nanjing both decided to purchase Autoscope Solo for intersection control and the collection of traffic data. ISS then formalized an exclusive Autoscope distribution agreement with Golden River Traffic Ltd. for the distribution of the entire family of Autoscope products in Great Britain, Northern Ireland, and the Republic of Ireland. Orders for the supply of close to 100 loop-based Incident Detection Systems—mostly for expressways in the Chinese provinces of Xinjiang and Jiangsu—were received by Flow Traffic Limited. The Autoscope-2004-V8 system was selected for expanded implementation within NAVIGATOR, Georgia's intelligent transportation system, along Interstate 285 and 85 highways serving the Greater Atlanta area. ISS added four exclusive distributors to sell, service, and provide local support for the Autoscope Video Vehicle *continued on page 252*

OFFICERS

William L. Russell
Chairman, President, and CEO

James Murdakes
Secretary

Jeffrey F. Martin
CFO and Treasurer

DIRECTORS

Richard P. Braun

Richard C. Magnuson
BioMedix Inc.

Panos G. Michalopoulos
University of Minnesota, Minneapolis

James Murdakes

William L. Russell

C. (Dino) Xykis
Onan Corp., Fridley, MN

MAJOR SHAREHOLDERS

Panos G. Michalopoulos, 47.8%

All officers and directors as a group (6 persons), 53.6%

SIC CODE

3669 Communications equipment, nec

MISCELLANEOUS

TRANSFER AGENT AND REGISTAR:
Wells Fargo Bank Minnesota N.A., South St. Paul, MN

TRADED: Nasdaq SmallCap Market

SYMBOL: ISNS

STOCKHOLDERS: 27

EMPLOYEES: 35

GENERAL COUNSEL:
Dorsey & Whitney PLLP, Minneapolis

AUDITORS:
Ernst & Young LLP, Minneapolis

INC: MN-1984

ANNUAL MEETING: May

INVESTOR RELATIONS:
William L. Russell

TWO-YEAR QUARTERLY HIGH-LOW STOCK PRICES

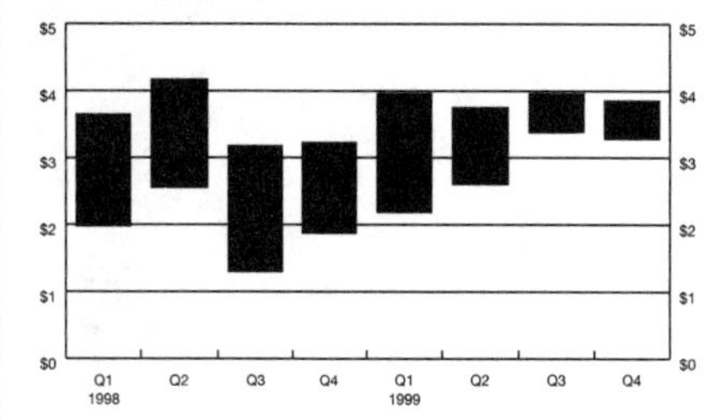

PUB

Image Systems Corporation

6103 Blue Circle Dr., Minnetonka, MN 55343
Tel: 952/935-1171 Fax: 952/935-1386 Web site: http://www.imagesystemscorp.com

Image Systems Corp. develops, assembles, and markets large, bright, high-resolution monitors for use with computers. It targets engineering and scientific applications—medical, military, and document imaging, as well as electronic and mechanical design—that are smaller, niche markets not pursued by mass-market foreign manufacturers. More than 95 percent of the company's sales come from telemarketing.

PUB

EARNINGS HISTORY

Year Ended Apr 30	Operating Revenue/Sales (dollars in thousands)	Net Earnings	Return on Revenue (percent)	Return on Equity	Net Earnings (dollars per share)	Cash Dividend	Market Price Range
2000	6,091	(105)	(1.7)	(2.9)	(0.02)	—	1.50–0.72
1999	7,215	81	1.1	2.1	0.02	—	4.00–0.63
1998	8,185	249	3.0	6.7	0.06	—	6.31–1.00
1997	8,093	827	10.2	24.0	0.19	—	4.25–3.13
1996	7,937	910	11.5	36.7	0.21	—	3.13–1.38

BALANCE SHEET

Assets	04/30/00 (dollars in thousands)	04/30/99	Liabilities	04/30/00 (dollars in thousands)	04/30/99
Current (CAE 416 and 232)	2,998	3,595	Current (STD 105 and 70)	847	989
Property and equipment	1,767	1,831	Long-term debt	248	663
TOTAL	4,764	5,426	Stockholders' equity*	3,669	3,774
			TOTAL	4,764	5,426

* No par common; 5,000,000 authorized; 4,452,597 and 4,452,597 issued and outstanding.

RECENT QUARTERS / **PRIOR-YEAR RESULTS**

	Quarter End	Revenue ($000)	Earnings ($000)	EPS ($)	Revenue ($000)	Earnings ($000)	EPS ($)
Q1	07/31/2000	1,180	(191)	(0.04)	1,365	(22)	0.00
Q4	04/30/2000	1,491	(78)	(0.02)	2,104	90	0.02
Q3	01/31/2000	1,731	(10)	0.00	2,040	7	0.00
Q2	10/31/99	1,503	5	0.00	1,607	(13)	0.00
	SUM	5,906	(274)	(0.06)	7,116	62	0.01

RECENT EVENTS

In **November 1999** the company agreed to acquire the assets of the Imaging Technologies Division of Nortech Systems (Nasdaq: NSYS), Wayzata, Minn. [In January it withdrew the letter of intent, citing a lack of agreement on how to address the existing Nortech warranty liability on previously shipped products.] In **December** Northwest Airlines began operation of its Airport Surface Management System, featuring Image Systems' AMLCD monitors, at the Detroit Airport. In **January 2000** the company introduced Display Link bundled medical imaging and workstation solutions; and a new monitor, the M21LHBMAX Stereo, for applications such as satellite imagery, vision research, motion analysis, and other scientific applications. In **February** the company said that its radiographic monitors were being purchased by customs services for use in vehicle search and cargo inspection systems. The company was found to be in compliance with the bid price requirement and all requirements necessary for continued listing on the Nasdaq SmallCap Market. A written hearing scheduled for Feb. 17 was considered moot, and the hearing file closed. Additional shipments for an April 1998 DIN-PACS (Digital Imaging Network-Picture Archiving and Communications Systems) contract were released. In **April** the company shipped the first Display Link Workstation: a fully configured high-resolution monitor, computer, and graphics card for medical-image viewing. In **May** Image Systems expanded its sales and service locations into Mainland China with the authorization of multiple companies to sell its products and the introduction of a factory-trained and -authorized service organization. In **June** the company exhibited at the 17th Symposium for Computer Applications in Radiology (SCAR 2000) in Philadelphia. In **August** Image Systems was invited to exhibit the new M21PHFMAX grayscale high-focus 21-inch portrait display at the Veterans Affairs Information Technology Conference in Austin, Texas. (The show was focused on Veteran's hospitals looking at doing their own integration of equipment.) The new product has built-in microprocessor-based calibration control for ease of setup of multiple monitors in a light box format.

OFFICERS

Dean Scheff
President

Diana Scheff
Secretary and Dir.-Marketing

Marta Scheff Volbrecht
VP-Sales

David Sorensen
VP-Operations

Laura Sorensen
Mgr.-Human Resources

Dennis Stollenwerk
VP-Technical Services

DIRECTORS

Bradley Beard
Fairview Health Services

Frederick R. Olson, M.D.
Consulting Radiologists Ltd., Minneapolis

Dean Scheff

Diana Scheff

David Sorensen

Laura Sorensen

Marta Scheff Volbrecht

Steven Volbrecht
Centex Homes, Minneapolis

MAJOR SHAREHOLDERS

Diana Scheff, 17.8%
Dean Scheff, 17%
Marta Volbrecht, 13.9%
Laura Sorensen, 13.9%
All officers and directors as a group (6 persons), 62.6%

SIC CODE

3577 Computer peripheral equipment, nec

MISCELLANEOUS

TRANSFER AGENT AND REGISTAR:
Securities Transfer Corp., Frisco

TRADED: OTC Bulletin Board

SYMBOL: IMSG

STOCKHOLDERS: 650

EMPLOYEES: 33

PART TIME: 6

GENERAL COUNSEL:
Mark Friedlander, McLean, VA

AUDITORS:
Larson, Allen, Weishair & Co. LLP, Minneapolis

INC: MN-1988

ANNUAL MEETING:
August

HUMAN RESOURCES:
Laura Sorensen

INVESTOR RELATIONS:
Diana Scheff

RANKINGS

No. 197 CRM Public 200

TWO-YEAR QUARTERLY HIGH-LOW STOCK PRICES

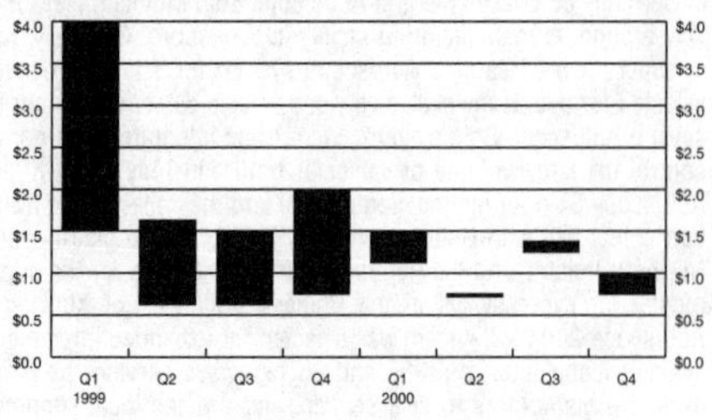

Imation Corporation

One Imation Pl., Oakdale, MN 55128
Tel: 651/704-4000 Fax: 651/704-4076 Web site: http://www.imation.com

Imation Corp. is a worldwide leader in the data storage and information management, color management, and imaging industries. The company develops, manufactures and markets a wide variety of innovative product and service solutions for data storage, color, and image management applications. Launched as an independent company on July 1, 1996, Imation is a spin-off of 3M's data storage and imaging businesses. The company has manufacturing, research, distribution, and sales facilities located in a number of countries.

EARNINGS HISTORY *

Year Ended Dec 31	Operating Revenue/Sales (dollars in thousands)	Net Earnings	Return on Revenue (percent)	Return on Equity	Net Earnings (dollars per share†)	Cash Dividend	Market Price Range
1999 ¶	1,412,600	43,900	3.1	6.1	1.18	—	34.25–15.06
1998 #	1,328,900	57,100	4.3	7.5	1.45	—	19.69–13.56
1997 **	1,502,100	(180,100)	(12.0)	(26.4)	(4.54)	—	30.38–15.56
1996 ††	1,604,900	(20,500)	(1.3)	(2.2)	(0.49)	—	33.00–20.38
1995 ##	1,637,400	(85,000)	(5.2)	(7.4)	(2.02)	—	

* Historical figures have been restated to exclude revenue from the Medical Imaging and Photo Color Systems business that was sold Aug. 2, 1999: $124.7 million, $717.6 million, $699.7 million, $673.3 million, and $608.2 million, in 1999 through 1995, respectively.
† Trading began July 1, 1996.
¶ Income figures for 1999 include net gain of $1.6 million/$0.04 from discontinued operations and their disposal.
# Income figures for 1998 include pretax gain of $16.8 million, net restructuring benefit; and after-tax gain of $69.8 million/$1.78 from discontinued operations and their disposal.
** Figures for 1997 include results of Cemax-Icon Inc. from its August 1997 date of acquisition for $51.8 million. Income figures include restructuring charge of $199.9 million pretax, $158.7 million/($4.00) after-tax—for employee separation benefits and fixed asset write-offs; and loss of $44.5 million/($1.12) from discontinued operations.
†† Income figures for 1996 include restructuring charge of $88.4 million pretax, $60.6 million/($1.46) after-tax for employee separation programs, start-up activities, and Luminous purchased R&D; and loss of $12.9 million/($0.31) from discontinued operations.
Income figures for 1995 include restructuring charge of $166.3 million pretax, $88.3 million/($2.10) after-tax; and loss of $28.4 million/($0.67) from discontinued operations.

BALANCE SHEET

Assets	12/31/99 (dollars in thousands)	12/31/98
Current (CAE 194,600 and 64,200)	771,400	919,900
Property, plant, and equipment	212,800	233,800
Other	143,400	159,600
TOTAL	1,127,600	1,313,300

Liabilities	12/31/99 (dollars in thousands)	12/31/98
Current (STD 27,300 and 25,200)	357,200	413,200
Other	44,000	106,300
Long-term debt	1,100	32,700
Stockholders' equity*	725,300	761,100
TOTAL	1,127,600	1,313,300

* $0.01 par common; 100,000,000 authorized; 42,900,000 and 42,900,000 issued and outstanding, less 5,700,000 and 1,900,000 treasury shares.

RECENT QUARTERS / **PRIOR-YEAR RESULTS**

	Quarter End	Revenue ($000)	Earnings ($000)	EPS ($)	Revenue ($000)	Earnings ($000)	EPS ($)
Q3	09/30/2000	288,500	(34,400)	(0.99)	346,000	10,800	0.30
Q2	06/30/2000	309,100	13,800	0.39	354,200	12,700	0.34
Q1	03/31/2000	328,800	20,500	0.57	341,200	6,100	0.16
Q4	12/31/99	371,200	14,300	0.39	336,300	36,900	0.93
	SUM	1,297,600	14,200	0.37	1,377,700	66,500	1.73

CURRENT: Q3 earnings include special charges totaling $61.1 million pretax ($30.1 million for restructuring, $31.0 million for capitalized software write-off), $48.5 million/($1.39) after-tax.
PRIOR YEAR: Q3 earnings include loss of $3.0 million/($0.08) on disposal of discontinued businesses. Q2 earnings include gain of $2.0 million/$0.05 from discontinued operations. Q1 earnings include gain of $2 .6 million/$0.07 from discontinued operations. Q4 earnings include pretax gain of $65 million on sale of medical imaging business; pretax loss of $2.6 million on change in credit facility; and gain of $41.7 m illion/$1.06 from discontinued operations and their disposal.

continued on page 252

OFFICERS

William T. Monahan
Chairman, President, and CEO
Bradley D. Allen
VP-Communications/Investor Relations
Karen R. Beadie
VP-Corporate Development
Barbara M. Cederberg
VP and Pres.-Color Technologies
Jacqueline A. Chase
VP-Human Resources
Robert L. Edwards
SVP, CFO, and CAO
Steven D. Ladwig
SVP and Pres.-Data Storage/Info. Mgmt.
John L. Sullivan
VP, General Counsel, and Secretary
David H. Wenck
VP-Int'l Operations Pres.-DSS
Paul R. Zeller
VP and Controller

DIRECTORS

Richard E. Belluzzo
Microsoft Corp., Redmond, WA
Lawrence E. Eaton
3M Co. (retired)
Michael S. Fields
The Fields Group, Pleasanton, CA
William W. George
Medtronic Inc., Fridley, MN
Linda W. Hart
Hart Group Inc., Dallas
Ronald T. LeMay
Sprint Corp., Westwood, KS
Marvin L. Mann
Lexmark International Inc., Lexington, KY
William T. Monahan
Glen A. Taylor
Taylor Corp., North Mankato, MN
Daryl J. White
Compaq Computer Corp. (former)

MAJOR SHAREHOLDERS

Private Capital Management Inc., 14.9%
Naples, FL
Harris Associates Inc., 10.9%
Chicago
Pioneer Investment Management Inc., 5.9%
Boston
All officers and directors as a group (19 persons), 1.6%

SIC CODE

3555 Printing trades machinery
3572 Computer storage devices
3841 Surgical and medical instruments
3861 Photographic equipment and supplies

MISCELLANEOUS

TRANSFER AGENT AND REGISTAR:
First Chicago Trust Co. of New York, Jersey City, NJ
TRADED: NYSE, CHX
SYMBOL: IMN
STOCKHOLDERS: 43,363
EMPLOYEES: 4,750
IN MINNESOTA: 1,800
AUDITORS:
PricewaterhouseCoopers LLP, Minneapolis
INC: DE-1996
ANNUAL MEETING: May
COMMUNICATIONS/ INVESTOR RELATIONS:
Brad Allen
HUMAN RESOURCES:
Jackie Chase

RANKINGS

No. 26 CRM Public 200

PUB

TWO-YEAR QUARTERLY HIGH-LOW STOCK PRICES

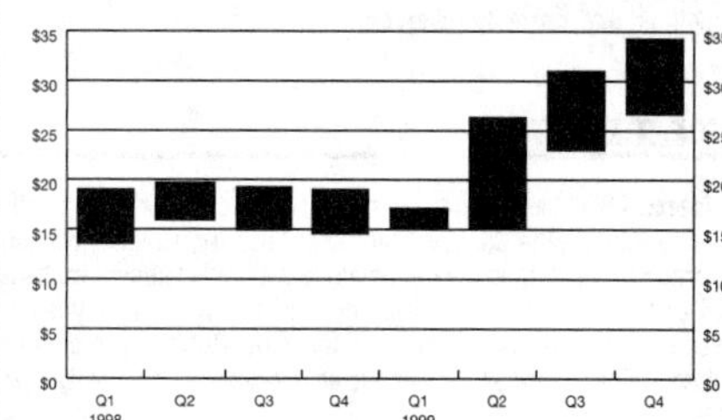

Industrial Rubber Products Inc.

3804 E. 13th Ave., Hibbing, MN 55746
Tel: 218/263-8831 Fax: 218/263-9731 Web site: http://www.irproducts.com

Industrial Rubber Products Inc. designs, produces, and supplies protective materials, abrasion-resistant products and equipment, erosion/corrosion protective linings, and proprietary rubber products. The company's first customers were low-grade iron ore (taconite) processing plants in Minnesota. Expanded operations now include sales to mineral-processing plants throughout the United States and Canada, as well as to the power, wood processing, and other heavy industries in these geographical regions. The company has three product lines. Its pipe lining and pipe products line consists of rubber-lined pipe and other pipe parts fabricated primarily for the mineral-processing industry. Its proprietary products are engineered replacement parts primarily for mineral-processing facilities. Its standard rubber products are sold, along with related services, to various industry segments. Industrial Rubber operates two production and distribution centers: a 30,000-square-foot manufacturing facility located on the Mesaba Iron Range in Minnesota; and a second facility, opened in 1996 in Clearfield, Utah, near the copper, gold, and molybdenum plants of the western United States.

EARNINGS HISTORY *

Year Ended Dec 31	Operating Revenue/Sales (dollars in thousands)	Net Earnings	Return on Revenue (percent)	Return on Equity	Net Earnings (dollars per share†)	Cash Dividend	Market Price Range
1999 ¶	12,985	(1,619)	(12.5)	(32.4)	(0.39)	—	2.13–0.25
1998 #	9,981	(168)	(1.7)	(2.5)	(0.04)	—	4.88–1.00
1997 **	14,421	1,664	11.5	NM	0.54	—	
1996	6,310	197	3.1	55.2	—	—	
1995	3,646	116	3.2	22.1	—	—	

* Income figures for years 1998 and earlier are pro forma for income taxes.
† Trading began April 24, 1998.
¶ Income figures for 1999 include pretax charge of $505,991 for restructuring.
# Income figures for 1998 include pretax charge of $209,881 for restructuring.
** Figures for 1997 are pro forma for income taxes.

BALANCE SHEET

Assets	12/31/99 (dollars in thousands)	12/31/98
Current (CAE 563 and 2,715)	4,804	6,160
Property and equipment	7,476	1,700
Deferred taxes	979	207
Cash value of life insurance	181	135
Goodwill	1,014	
Prepaid pension costs	11	
Other		24
TOTAL	14,464	8,226

Liabilities	12/31/99 (dollars in thousands)	12/31/98
Current (STD 25 and 174)	9,173	1,207
Long-term debt	291	329
Stockholders' equity*	5,000	6,690
TOTAL	14,464	8,226

* $0.001 par common; 25,000,000 authorized; 4,144,000 and 4,187,500 issued and outstanding.

RECENT QUARTERS / **PRIOR-YEAR RESULTS**

	Quarter End	Revenue ($000)	Earnings ($000)	EPS ($)	Prior-Year Revenue ($000)	Prior-Year Earnings ($000)	Prior-Year EPS ($)
Q2	06/30/2000	4,845	89	0.02	3,639	(301)	(0.07)
Q3	06/30/2000	3,840	(244)	(0.06)	4,323	50	0.01
Q1	03/31/2000	5,054	171	0.04	1,632	(226)	(0.05)
Q4	12/31/99	3,391	(1,142)	(0.28)	1,068	(608)	(0.14)
	SUM	17,130	(1,126)	(0.27)	10,662	(1,085)	(0.26)

CURRENT: Q2 earnings include net pretax charge of $53,000 for Irathane moving and Arizona closure.
PRIOR YEAR: Q4 earnings include pretax special charges totaling $689,881 for restructuring, doubtful accounts, and warranty reserves.

RECENT EVENTS

In **March 2000** the company announced the consolidating of all of its U.S. Irathane production facilities to one location in Hibbing, Minn. (The Canadian facility in Sudbury, Ontario, was not affected.) Manufacturing operations previously located in Colorado Springs, Colo., were moved to the firm's Hibbing Irathane facility. The move included all cast parts manufacturing, as well as the production of prepolymer liquids. The company leased a small facility in the Colorado Springs area to house its research and development centers. Industrial Rubber also announced an agreement to sell its vacated land and buildings in Colorado Springs for $1.7 million to an undisclosed third party—with proceeds used to reduce bank debt. CEO Burkes said, "The consolidation of our U.S. Irathane manufacturing facilities will result in *continued on page 252*

OFFICERS

Daniel O. Burkes
Chairman and CEO

Christopher M. Liesmaki
EVP and COO

James A. Skalski
Controller and Asst. Secretary

John Kokotovich
VP, CFO, and Secretary

DIRECTORS

Daniel O. Burkes

Paul F. Friesen
Friesen's Inc. (retired)

Christopher Liesmaki

James D. Mackay
Copper State Specialties, Globe, AZ

Jack R. Ryan
Ryan-Kasner-Ryan

MAJOR SHAREHOLDERS

Daniel O. and Nancy J. Burkes, 70.3%

All officers and directors as a group (7 persons), 71%

SIC CODE

3069 Fabricated rubber products, nec

3498 Fabricated pipe and fittings

MISCELLANEOUS

TRANSFER AGENT AND REGISTAR:
Wells Fargo Bank Minnesota N.A., South St. Paul, MN

TRADED: Nasdaq SmallCap Market

SYMBOL: INRB

STOCKHOLDERS: 50

EMPLOYEES: 115

GENERAL COUNSEL:
Johnson, Killen, Thibodeau & Seiler P.A., Duluth, MN
Lommen, Nelson, Cole & Stageberg P.A.

AUDITORS:
RSM McGladrey & Pullen Inc. LLP, Duluth, MN

INC: MN-1986

ANNUAL MEETING: May

INVESTOR RELATIONS:
John M. Kokotovich

RANKINGS

No. 169 CRM Public 200

Infinite Graphics Inc.

4611 E. Lake St., Minneapolis, MN 55406
Tel: 612/721-6283 Fax: 612/721-3802 Web site: http://www.igi.com

Infinite Graphics Inc. (IGI) is a precision graphics company, serving the engineering and manufacturing marketplace. The Engineering Services Division designs and produces computer-generated precision graphics, normally on a custom basis and primarily for the electronics industry. In addition, this segment produces precision glass products, designs printed circuit boards, and provides CAD/CAM services.

EARNINGS HISTORY

Year Ended Apr 30	Operating Revenue/Sales (dollars in thousands)	Net Earnings (dollars in thousands)	Return on Revenue (percent)	Return on Equity (percent)	Net Earnings (dollars per share)	Cash Dividend (dollars per share)	Market Price Range (dollars per share)
2000	8,079	(154)	(1.9)	(12.9)	(0.05)	—	3.06–1.70
1999 *	5,207	114	2.2	8.5	0.04	—	1.88–0.63
1998 †	3,612	(197)	(5.5)	(16.6)	(0.08)	—	0.88–0.56
1997 ¶	4,114	209	5.1	15.3	0.09	—	1.13–0.44
1996 #	5,150	144	2.8	12.6	0.05	—	1.25–0.50

* Pro forma 1999 figures as if January 1999 acquisition Photronics Colorado Inc. had been acquired May 1, 1998: revenue $6,647,000; net income $178,000/$0.07.
† Income figures for 1998 include loss of $223,805/($0.09) from discontinued operations.
¶ Income figures for 1997 include loss of $140,046/($0.06) from discontinued operations.
# Figures for 1996 have not been restated for discontinued operations.

BALANCE SHEET

Assets	04/30/00 (dollars in thousands)	04/30/99 (dollars in thousands)	Liabilities	04/30/00 (dollars in thousands)	04/30/99 (dollars in thousands)
Current (CAE 87)	2,068	2,236	Current (STD 322 and 112)	2,700	1,845
Property, plant, and equipment	2,916	2,716	Long-term debt	487	765
Purchased software	153	69	Capitalized lease obligations	778	1,090
Other	25	28	Stockholders' equity*	1,195	1,349
TOTAL	5,161	5,049	TOTAL	5,161	5,049

* No par common; 10,000,000 authorized; 2,802,575 and 2,802,575 issued and outstanding.

RECENT QUARTERS / PRIOR-YEAR RESULTS

	Quarter End	Revenue ($000)	Earnings ($000)	EPS ($)	Prior-Year Revenue ($000)	Prior-Year Earnings ($000)	Prior-Year EPS ($)
Q1	06/30/2000	2,584	92	0.03	1,977	35	0.01
Q4	04/30/2000	2,220	133	0.05	1,962	(128)	(0.05)
Q3	01/31/2000	1,700	(384)	(0.14)	1,098	80	0.03
Q2	10/31/99	2,157	64	0.02	1,171	126	0.05
	SUM	8,661	(95)	(0.03)	6,207	113	0.04

CURRENT: Q4: Note that summing the figures for the four quarters of FY2000 only approximates the fiscal-year totals due to company adjustments to earlier quarters that have not yet been reported discretely.

RECENT EVENTS

In **January 2000** the company agreed to acquire software operations for the printed circuit board (PCB) industry from Global MAINTECH Corp. (OTC Bulletin Board: GLBM), Eden Prairie, Minn., a worldwide leader in systems for data centers. In **March** the company retained TPL & Associates as counsel for investor relations. In **June** Infinite Graphics received a capital infusion of $500,000 from a private placement. "The capital allows Infinite Graphics to continue its aggressive strategy to capture a larger share of the dynamic worldwide LAM market," said CEO Stritch. "The capital will be used for the opening of our Singapore office, as well as accelerated marketing, research, and development." Infinite Graphics was partnering in a $1.5 million project to evaluate, research, develop, or purchase state-of-the-art systems to clean, repair, and inspect Large Area Masks (LAMs). In **August** the company announced the sale of its Irvine, Calif., facility to ARTNET Technology Inc. of San Jose, Calif. (which retained all employees from the facility).

OFFICERS

Clifford F. Stritch Jr.
Chairman, CEO, and CFO

Barry B. Onufrock
CFO and Treasurer

DIRECTORS

Michael J. Evers
Durwood Airhart
Edwin F. Snyder
Clifford F. Stritch Jr.

MAJOR SHAREHOLDERS

Clifford F. Stritch Jr., 39.2%

Robert Fink, 9.2%
Mendota Heights, MN

All officers and directors as a group (5 persons), 40.4%

SIC CODE

7336 Commercial art and graphic design

MISCELLANEOUS

TRANSFER AGENT AND REGISTAR:
Chase Mellon Shareholder Services LLC, East Hartford, CT

TRADED: LOTC

SYMBOL: INFG

STOCKHOLDERS: 205

EMPLOYEES: 74

PART TIME: 5

GENERAL COUNSEL:
Gray, Plant, Mooty, Mooty & Bennett P.A., Minneapolis

AUDITORS:
Deloitte & Touche LLP, Minneapolis

INC: MN-1969

ANNUAL MEETING:
September

HUMAN RESOURCES:
Ross Welsh

INVESTOR RELATIONS COUNSEL:
TPL & Associates

RANKINGS

No. 193 CRM Public 200

PUB

TWO-YEAR QUARTERLY HIGH-LOW STOCK PRICES

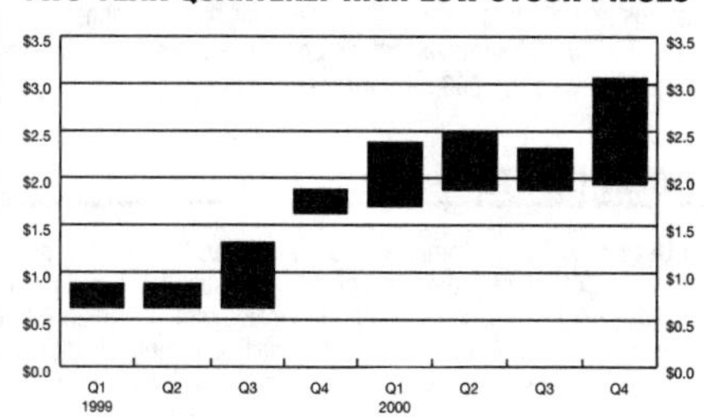

PUB

Innovex Inc.

5540 Pioneer Creek Dr., Maple Plain, MN 55359
Tel: 763/479-5300 Fax: 952/938-7718 Web site: http://www.innovexinc.com

Innovex Inc. is one of the world's leading suppliers of flexible circuit-based interconnect solutions to original-equipment manufacturers in the electronics industry. The company offers a full range of customized flexible circuit applications and services—from initial design, development, and prototype to fabrication, assembly, and test on a global basis. Innovex targets high-volume markets where miniaturization, form, and weight are driving factors and flexible circuits are an enabling technology. Applications currently addressed by the company include notebook computers, cellular telephones and pagers, data storage devices, and high-end consumer electronics such as compact-disc players. Principal customers: Acer, Alps, Compaq, Dell, Digital Equipment, IBM, Iomega, Maxtor, Motorola, Nokia, Philips, Qualcomm, ReadRite, SAE Magnetics, Samsung, Seagate, Storage Technology, Xerox Corp., and Yamaha.

EARNINGS HISTORY *

Year Ended Sept 30	Operating Revenue/Sales (dollars in thousands)	Net Earnings	Return on Revenue (percent)	Return on Equity	Net Earnings (dollars per share†)	Cash Dividend	Market Price Range
1999 ¶	103,198	6,559	6.4	6.1	0.44	0.16	19.50–8.56
1998	96,278	15,911	16.6	15.5	1.08	0.14	33.38–9.94
1997	142,004	35,094	24.7	40.4	2.43	0.11	42.88–8.94
1996 #	69,570	13,121	18.9	27.1	0.93	0.09	12.13–5.88
1995	50,194	10,029	20.0	27.8	0.73	0.08	12.38–3.00

* Revenue figures are restated for continuing operations.
† Per-share amounts restated to reflect a 2-for-1 stock split on Dec. 23, 1996; and a 3-for-2 split on May 31, 1995.
¶ Income figures for 1999 include a pretax restructuring charge of $4.461 million for discontinuation of the lead wire assembly product line and disposal of Iconovex Division. Figures include results of ADFlex Solutions from its August 1999 acquisition for $37.2 million; pro forma for full year: revenue $215.975 million; loss $6.845 million/($0.46).
\# Figures for 1996 include results of Litchfield Precision Components Inc. from its May 16, 1996, date of purchase for $9,178,000. Pro forma for Oct. 1, 1995, purchase: revenue $77,617,000; earnings $13,190,000/$0.93.

BALANCE SHEET

Assets	09/30/99 (dollars in thousands)	09/30/98
Current (CAE 6,231 and 17,021)	76,317	79,319
Property, plant, and equipment	87,158	28,501
Intangibles	4,841	1,826
Deferred income taxes	10,443	
Other	47	5
TOTAL	178,806	109,652

Liabilities	09/30/99 (dollars in thousands)	09/30/98
Current (STD 308 and 83)	45,296	6,251
Long-term debt	26,376	755
Deferred income taxes		228
Stockholders' equity*	107,134	102,418
TOTAL	178,806	109,652

* $0.04 par common; 30,000,000 authorized; 14,822,104 and 14,779,604 issued and outstanding.

RECENT QUARTERS / **PRIOR-YEAR RESULTS**

	Quarter End	Revenue ($000)	Earnings ($000)	EPS ($)	Revenue ($000)	Earnings ($000)	EPS ($)
Q4	09/30/2000	39,916	879	0.06	39,830	(485)	(0.03)
Q3	06/30/2000	38,433	393	0.03	20,636	1,510	0.10
Q2	03/31/2000	41,388	(1,157)	(0.08)	20,704	2,539	0.17
Q1	12/31/99	44,725	(11,169)	(0.75)	22,028	2,995	0.20
	SUM	164,462	(11,054)	(0.75)	103,198	6,559	0.44

CURRENT: Q3 earnings include pretax credit of $0.184 million for restructuring reversal. Q4 earnings include pretax charge of $13.785 million for restructuring.
PRIOR YEAR: Q4 earnings include pretax charge of $2.765 million for restructuring. Q3 earnings include pretax charge of $1.696 million for restructuring.

RECENT EVENTS

In **December 1999** Thomas W. Haley, founder, CEO, and largest individual shareholder of Innovex, announced his intent to resign as CEO shortly after the company's annual meeting on Jan. 19, 2000. He planned to recommend to the board of directors that COO Murnane be named to replace him. In **January 2000** Innovex discontinued its cash dividend—stating that its transformation into one of the world's leading flexible circuit manufacturers and its new strategic direction presented it with numerous high-growth opportunities, which had become the most effective use of the company's cash. In **February** Innovex successfully transferred its high-volume FSA production to its Lamphun, *continued on page 252*

OFFICERS

Thomas W. Haley
Chairman

William P. Murnane
President and CEO

Allan J. Chan
SVP-Sales/Marketing

Brian R. Dahmes
VP-Quality

Bruce R. Funk
VP-Asian Operations

Doug Keller
VP-Finance

Timothy S. McIntee
SVP-Corporate

Venkatraman B. (Ven) Rao, Ph.D.
VP-Research/Development

Srinivas Kuchipudi
VP-Operations

DIRECTORS

Gerald M. Bestler
BMC Industries Inc. (retired)

Frank L. Farrar
Performance Bankers Inc.

Thomas W. Haley

Eugene Hawk
Performance Bankers Inc., Pierre, SD

William J. Miller
Avid Technology Inc., Tewksbury, MA

William P. Murnane

Michael C. Slagle
Minnesota Benefit Planners (retired)

Bernt M. Tessem
independent consultant

MAJOR SHAREHOLDERS

Neumeier Investment Counsel LLC, 5.7%
Carmel, CA

Thomas W. Haley, 5.5%
Minnetonka, MN

All officers and directors as a group (15 persons), 7.2%

SIC CODE

3679 Electronic components, nec

MISCELLANEOUS

TRANSFER AGENT AND REGISTAR:
Wells Fargo Bank Minnesota N.A., South St. Paul, MN

TRADED: Nasdaq National Market

SYMBOL: INVX

STOCKHOLDERS: 663

EMPLOYEES: 4,800
IN MINNESOTA: 475

GENERAL COUNSEL:
Lindquist & Vennum PLLP, Minneapolis

AUDITORS:
Grant Thornton LLP, Minneapolis

INC: MN-1972

ANNUAL MEETING:
January

PURCHASING:
Bruce Johnson

HUMAN RESOURCES:
Jack Kilby

RANKINGS

No. 83 CRM Public 200
No. 27 CRM Performance 100

SUBSIDIARIES, DIVISIONS, AFFILIATES

Innovex Precision Components
530 11th Ave. S.
Hopkins, MN 55343

ADFlex Solutions Inc.
Chandler, Ariz.

TWO-YEAR QUARTERLY HIGH-LOW STOCK PRICES

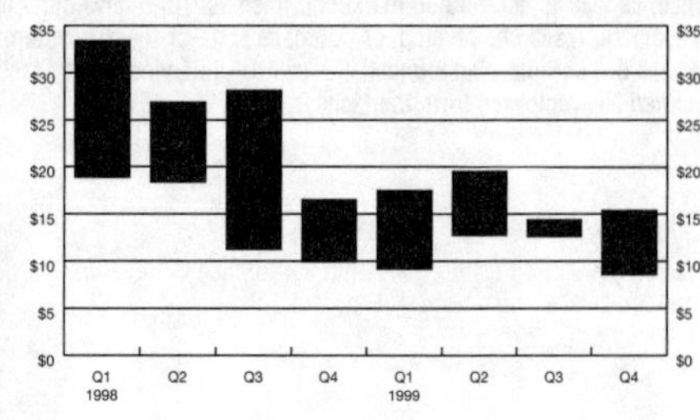

Insignia Systems Inc.

5025 Cheshire Ln. N., Plymouth, MN 55446
Tel: 763/392-6200 Fax: 763/392-6222 Web site: http://www.insigniasystems.com

Insignia Systems Inc. markets in-store promotional programs and services to retailers and manufacturers. Since its inception in 1990, the company has marketed point-of-purchase merchandising systems and resources to merchants in more than 30 classes of retail trade. The company started with simple stand-alone printers, trade-named Impulse and SIGNright, ultimately developing full-featured ODBC (open data-based connectivity) compliant software applications, trade-named Stylus. The company has evolved to market turnkey solutions that allow retailers to quickly and easily produce high-quality point-of-purchase signs, labels, and large-format promotional materials in their stores. The company continues to support the supply and service needs of its domestic clients and actively markets its products internationally through independent distributors.

EARNINGS HISTORY

Year Ended Dec 31	Operating Revenue/Sales (dollars in thousands)	Net Earnings	Return on Revenue (percent)	Return on Equity	Net Earnings (dollars per share)	Cash Dividend	Market Price Range
1999	9,287	(1,411)	(15.2)	(70.0)	(0.16)	—	4.00–0.75
1998 *	8,704	(3,416)	(39.2)	NM	(0.44)	—	3.00–1.00
1997 †	13,321	(3,380)	(25.4)	NM	(0.50)	—	4.63–1.03
1996	14,667	(999)	(6.8)	(23.9)	(0.18)	—	2.44–1.31
1995	15,547	(1,451)	(9.3)	(28.4)	(0.27)	—	2.00–0.94

* Income figures for 1998 include $545,992/($0.07) restructuring charge.
† Income figures for 1997 include $314,568/($0.05) restructuring charge.

BALANCE SHEET

Assets	12/31/99 (dollars in thousands)	12/31/98	Liabilities	12/31/99 (dollars in thousands)	12/31/98
Current (CAE 64)	3,824	3,798	Current (STD 82 and 114)	2,027	1,567
Property and equipment	219	270	Long-term debt		72
TOTAL	4,043	4,069	Stockholders' equity*	2,017	2,430
			TOTAL	4,043	4,069

* $0.01 par common; 20,000,000 authorized; 9,327,946 and 8,499,800 issued and outstanding.

RECENT QUARTERS / **PRIOR-YEAR RESULTS**

	Quarter End	Revenue ($000)	Earnings ($000)	EPS ($)	Revenue ($000)	Earnings ($000)	EPS ($)
Q3	09/30/2000	2,863	(295)	(0.03)	2,364	(390)	(0.04)
Q2	06/30/2000	3,048	(249)	(0.03)	2,300	(399)	(0.05)
Q1	03/31/2000	2,878	(254)	(0.03)	2,291	(260)	(0.03)
Q4	12/31/99	2,331	(363)	(0.04)	1,951	(996)	(0.12)
	SUM	11,121	(1,161)	(0.12)	8,907	(2,044)	(0.24)

RECENT EVENTS

In **November 1999** the company signed an initial contract with The Procter & Gamble Co. to provide in-store promotion programs for Procter & Gamble's Puffs brand through Insignia's Point-Of-Purchase-Services (POPS) program. In **December** Weis Markets Inc., Sunbury, Pa. (162 stores), and Kroger's Delta Marketing Area, Memphis, Tenn. (111 stores), increased the network of participating retailers to more than 3,000 stores. In **January 2000** the addition of Key Food Stores Co-operative Inc. (120 supermarkets in New York) and Carter's Inc. (20 supermarkets in Michigan) pushed the POPS network past 3,500 stores. In **February** the company added Smith's Food & Drug Centers Inc. and its 117 supermarkets in Arizona, Idaho, Montana, Nevada, New Mexico, Texas, Utah, and Wyoming. In **March** the company hit the million-sign mark in its POPS program. In **April** POPS added 143 Fred Meyer stores, part of The Kroger Co. (NYSE: KR). In **June** Stater Bros. Markets (155 supermarkets in southern California) and Raley's Supermarkets (135 supermarkets in northern California and Nevada) joined the POPS network. In **July** 634,000 warrants to purchase its common stock were exercised at $1.25 each, resulting in proceeds to the company of $792,500.a Initial contracts with Kellogg USA provided for in-store promotion programs for several brands during the coming 12 months. In **August** a lawsuit was started against it Insignia in New York City by News America Marketing In-Store Inc., the dominant competitor in providing in-store, shelf-mounted signs for retail stores. The complaint alleged that News America had exclusive promotional agreements with several major supermarket retailers, and that those retailers had breached the exclusivity clause of those agreements when they contracted for Insignia's POPS program. The complaint also accused Insignia of unfair competition, false advertising, and interfering with business relationships. Insignia filed suit against News America in federal district court in Minneapolis alleging that News America had engaged in anti-competitive practices and was attempting to use its dominant position in the market to stifle competition. In particular, Insignia's suit alleged that Insignia's customers had not violated their agreements with News America, and that News America's exclusive dealing clauses violated the anti-trust laws and were unenforceable. **Sept. 30:** Nine-month results featured a 26 percent increase in net sales, to $8.8 million, and a narrowed net loss, to $0.8 million. In **October** Southwest Supermarkets LLC and Minyard Food Stores Inc. signed multiyear renewals of their Insignia POPS contracts. The POPS network added Safeway

continued on page 253

OFFICERS

G.L. Hoffman
Chairman and Secretary

Scott Drill
President and CEO

Gary Vars
EVP and General Mgr.-POPS Division

John R. Whisnant
VP-Finance

DIRECTORS

Scott Drill

G.L. Hoffman

Erwin A. Kelen
Kelen Ventures, Minneapolis

W. Robert Ramsdell

Don E. Schultz
Agora Inc.

Gordon F. Stofer
Cherry Tree Investments Inc., Bloomington, MN

Frank D. Trestman
Trestman Enterprises, Golden Valley, MN

Gary L. Vars

MAJOR SHAREHOLDERS

Perkins Capital Management Inc., 17.4%
Wayzata, MN

W. Robert Ramsdell, 11.4%
Pacific Palisades, CA

G.L. Hoffman, 9.7%

Lloyd I. Miller III, 5.4%
Naples, FL

All officers and directors as a group (8 persons), 29.9%

SIC CODE

3953 Marking devices

MISCELLANEOUS

TRANSFER AGENT AND REGISTAR:
Wells Fargo Bank Minnesota N.A., South St. Paul, MN

TRADED: Nasdaq SmallCap Market

SYMBOL: ISIG

STOCKHOLDERS: 155

EMPLOYEES: 72

GENERAL COUNSEL:
Lindquist & Vennum PLLP, Minneapolis

AUDITORS:
Ernst & Young LLP, Minneapolis

INC: MN-1990

ANNUAL MEETING: May

INVESTOR RELATIONS:
John Whisnant

RANKINGS

No. 189 CRM Public 200

TWO-YEAR QUARTERLY HIGH-LOW STOCK PRICES

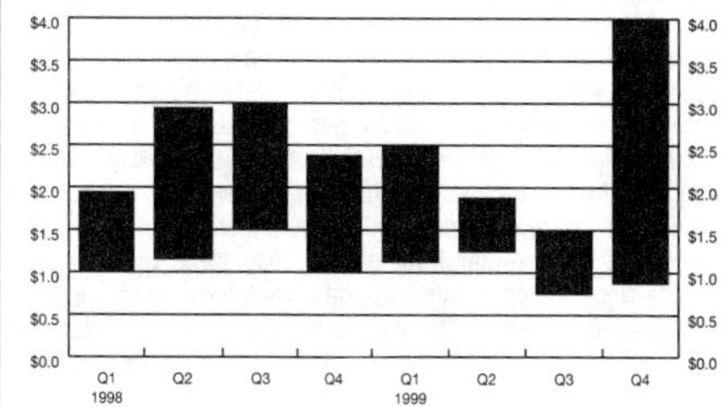

PUB

iNTELEFILM Corporation

5501 Excelsior Blvd., St. Louis Park, MN 55416
Tel: 952/925-8840 Fax: 952/926-7946 Web site: http://www.intelefilm.com

iNTELEFILM (intelligent television filmmaking) is a producer of television commercials. It formerly developed, produced, and broadcast Radio AAHS radio programming for children 12 and under, as Children's Broadcasting Corp. The company no longer distributes its programming and now owns 55 percent interests in Harmony Holdings Inc., a producer of television commercials, 100 percent of Chelsea Pictures, and 51 percent of Curious Pictures. iNTELEFILM is believed to be the largest single player in that fragmented industry.

EARNINGS HISTORY

Year Ended Dec 31	Operating Revenue/Sales (dollars in thousands)	Net Earnings	Return on Revenue (percent)	Return on Equity	Net Earnings (dollars per share*)	Cash Dividend	Market Price Range
1999 †	67,343	7,340	10.9	37.7	1.16	—	5.25–1.50
1998 ¶	2,567	7,570	NM	55.2	1.03	—	4.31–2.81
1997	5,854	(14,558)	NM	NM	(2.33)	—	6.63–3.19
1996 #	5,655	(9,868)	NM	(61.7)	(1.99)	—	13.38–3.25
1995	5,107	(6,108)	NM	NM	(2.22)	—	15.25–7.50

* Per-share amounts restated to reflect 1-for-2 reverse stock split on Jan. 23, 1996.
† Income figures for 1999 include pretax gain of $16.384 million on sale of radio station assets and subsidiary stock.
¶ Income figures for 1998 include pretax gain of $26.375 million on sale of radio station assets.
# Income figures for 1996 include charge of $1.662 million to write off deferred warrant expense.

BALANCE SHEET

Assets	12/31/99 (dollars in thousands)	12/31/98	Liabilities	12/31/99 (dollars in thousands)	12/31/98
Current (CAE 15,986 and 253)	27,191	12,537	Current (STD 192 and 10,666)	17,328	18,044
Property and equipment	2,957	120	Long-term debt	680	848
			Minority interest	139	
Investment in Harmony		5,421	Preferred stock		2,448
			Common stock*	19,471	12,481
Note receivable		15,000	TOTAL	37,618	33,822
Goodwill	6,730				
Other	739				
Deferred costs		743			
TOTAL	37,618	33,822			

* $0.02 par common; 50,000,000 authorized; 6,288,618 and 6,450,742 issued and outstanding.

RECENT QUARTERS / **PRIOR-YEAR RESULTS**

	Quarter End	Revenue ($000)	Earnings ($000)	EPS ($)	Prior-Year Revenue ($000)	Prior-Year Earnings ($000)	Prior-Year EPS ($)
Q3	09/30/2000	14,012	(2,562)	(0.40)	21,493	(331)	(0.05)
Q2	06/30/2000	15,437	(1,724)	(0.27)	23,468	(1,991)	(0.31)
Q1	03/31/2000	21,740	(1,519)	(0.24)	1,231	10,154	1.56
Q4	12/31/99	21,151	(492)	(0.09)	595	19,282	2.89
	SUM	72,340	(6,297)	(0.99)	46,787	27,114	4.09

CURRENT: Q3 earnings include $18,078 loss on sale of subsidiary.
PRIOR YEAR: Q3 earnings include $149,964 gain on sale of subsidiary. Q1 earnings include pretax gain of $16.546 million on sale of radio station assets. Q4 earnings include pretax gain of $26,374,904 on sale of radio station assets.

RECENT EVENTS

In **December 1999** iNTELEFILM announced a content-provider relationship with Los Angeles-based Hitplay Media for the delivery of short-form video content and the production of Internet video commercials on the Hitplay Targeted Video Network. iNTELEFILM's directors and animators were to develop, produce, and deliver original and archival entertainment video to Hitplay, as well as produce commercials for broadband Internet applications. In **January 2000** the company launched webADTV.com, a newly formed subsidiary combining iNTELEFILM's digital archiving and retrieval service, InteleSource.org, with additional Web-based services under development. In addition, webADTV.com was charged with applying iNTELEFILM's expertise in short-form video to new media advertising models, increasing company-wide efficiencies through the use of new Web-based technologies, and the development of a business-to-business portal. In **February** the company engaged RedChip Partners for an investor awareness program delivered on RedChip.com. "As iNTELEFILM transitions with its clients from the production of traditional media advertising models into the more interactive and permission-based environments of a broadband world, RedChip.com provides an appropriate online platform to increase investor awareness and facilitate communication with our shareholders," stated CEO Dahl. In **March** the globally recognized video compression and delivery system provider, Spot Rocket, agreed to provide digital encoding services and related video delivery expertise to inteleSource.org. The company then proposed to commence an exchange tender offer to the shareholders of Harmony Holdings Inc. to acquire all of the outstanding shares of Harmony (that is, the 45 percent stake not currently owned by it) in exchange for shares of iNTELEFILM common stock. The company was named Minnesota's sixth-fastest-growing public

continued on page 253

OFFICERS

Christopher T. Dahl
Chairman and CEO

James G. Gilbertson
Pres.-Internet Division, COO

Patrick Knisley
Pres.-Commercial Production Division

Jill J. Theis
General Counsel and Secretary

Steve Smith
CFO

DIRECTORS

William E. Cameron
Creative Digital Services

Christopher T. Dahl

Richard W. Perkins
Perkins Capital Management Inc., Wayzata, MN

William H. Spell
Spell Capital Partners, Minneapolis

Michael R. Wigley
Great Plains Cos. Inc.

MISCELLANEOUS

TRANSFER AGENT AND REGISTAR:
Wells Fargo Bank Minnesota N.A., South St. Paul, MN

TRADED: Nasdaq National Market

SYMBOL: FILM

STOCKHOLDERS: 307

EMPLOYEES: 121

PART TIME: 14

IN MINNESOTA: 25

GENERAL COUNSEL:
Briggs and Morgan P.A., Minneapolis

AUDITORS:
BDO Seidman LLP, Milwaukee

INC: MN-1990

ANNUAL MEETING: June

INVESTOR RELATIONS:
Steve Smith

RANKINGS

No. 103 CRM Public 200

TWO-YEAR QUARTERLY HIGH-LOW STOCK PRICES

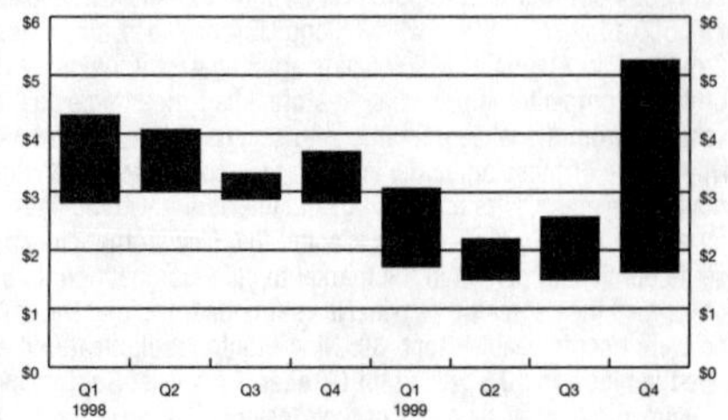

International Multifoods Corporation

110 Cheshire Ln., Suite 300, Minnetonka, MN 55305
Tel: 952/594-3300 Fax: 952/594-3304 Web site: http://www.multifoods.com

International Multifoods Corp. is strategically focused on serving the foodservice industry in North America as a distributor and manufacturer. The company also is a leading manufacturer and marketer of consumer foods in Canada. In the United States, Multifoods Distribution Group is the No. 1 distributor of food and other products to independent pizza restaurants, vending operators, and the office coffee service segment. The company manufactures and markets grain-based products, desserts, and condiments to foodservice operators and commercial customers in North America. In Canada, Robin Hood Multifoods is the leading manufacturer and marketer of branded, grain-based products and baking mixes, under the Robin Hood brand name, and of condiments under the Bick's brand name.

EARNINGS HISTORY

Year Ended Feb	Operating Revenue/Sales (dollars in thousands)	Net Earnings (dollars in thousands)	Return on Revenue (percent)	Return on Equity (percent)	Net Earnings (dollars per share)	Cash Dividend (dollars per share)	Market Price Range (dollars per share)
2000 *	2,384,715	5,135	0.2	2.0	0.27	0.80	24.19–10.75
1999 †	2,296,550	(131,870)	(5.7)	(50.7)	(7.03)	0.80	31.44–15.19
1998 ¶	2,251,096	20,024	0.9	6.5	1.09	0.80	32.44–20.00
1997 #	2,249,106	2,780	0.1	1.0	0.15	0.80	22.00–15.13
1996 **	2,194,700	24,075	1.1	7.9	1.33	0.80	23.88–17.25

* Income figures for 2000 include unusual pretax gain of $0.519 million; and loss of $19.56 million/($1.05) from disposal of discontinued Venezuela Foods operations.
† Income figures for 1999 include unusual charges of pretax $29.0 million, after-tax $18.7 million/($1.00); and loss of $138.702 million/($7.39) from discontinued Venezuela Foods operations and their disposal.
¶ Income figures for 1998 include pretax charge of $5.0 million, after-tax $3.2 million/($0.17), for certain receivables deemed not fully recoverable; and loss of $4.65 million/($0.25) from discontinued operations.
# Income figures for 1997 include unusual items resulting in pretax charges of $20.1 million, after-tax $14.8 million/($0.83); and gain of $14.154 million/$0.78 from discontinued operations.
** Income figures for 1996 include unusual items resulting in a net pretax charge of $5.7 million and after-tax gain of $0.5 million/$0.02; and gain of $9.1 million/$0.51 from discontinued operations.

BALANCE SHEET

Assets	02/29/00 (dollars in thousands)	02/28/99 (dollars in thousands)
Current (CAE 11,224 and 13,495)	353,988	340,067
Property, plant, and equipment	204,924	165,161
Goodwill	84,894	82,089
Discontinued operations		44,905
Other	92,401	64,711
TOTAL	736,207	696,933

Liabilities	02/29/00 (dollars in thousands)	02/28/99 (dollars in thousands)
Current (STD 61,521 and 35,239)	277,455	264,245
Long-term debt	147,199	121,199
Deferred taxes	23,170	17,036
Employee benefits, other	33,259	34,137
Stockholders' equity*	255,124	260,316
TOTAL	736,207	696,933

* $0.10 par common; 50,000,000 authorized; 21,844,000 and 21,844,000 issued and outstanding, less 3,106,000 and 3,068,000 treasury shares.

RECENT QUARTERS / PRIOR-YEAR RESULTS

	Quarter End	Revenue ($000)	Earnings ($000)	EPS ($)	Prior-Year Revenue ($000)	Prior-Year Earnings ($000)	Prior-Year EPS ($)
Q2	08/26/2000	585,350	5,279	0.28	568,709	(6,669)	(0.36)
Q1	05/27/2000	610,260	4,750	0.25	588,815	(3,238)	(0.17)
Q4	02/29/2000	594,999	6,913	0.37	573,200	4,508	0.24
Q3	11/30/99	632,192	8,129	0.43	611,100	2,571	0.14
	SUM	2,422,801	25,071	1.34	2,341,824	(2,828)	(0.15)

CURRENT: Q2 earnings include pretax charge of $5.275 million for unusual items.
PRIOR YEAR: Q2 earnings include loss of $11.8 million/($0.63); Q1 earnings include loss of $7.8 million/($0.41); Q4 earnings include loss of $2.5 million/($0.14); and Q3 earnings include loss of $7.2 million/($0.38)—all on discontinued operations and their disposal.

RECENT EVENTS

In **May 2000** Robin Hood Multifoods announced plans to expand its facility in Dunnville, Ontario, and consolidate condiment processing operations there over the next two years. Starting in early 2001,

continued on page 253

OFFICERS

Gary E. Costley, Ph.D., Chairman, President, and CEO
Robert S. Wright, SVP, Pres.-U.S. Foodservice/Operations
Frank W. Bonvino, VP, General Counsel, and Secretary
John E. Byom, VP-Finance and CFO
Ralph P. Hargrow, VP-Human Resources/Administration
Dennis R. Johnson, VP, Controller; CFO-Multifoods Distribution
Gregory J. Keup, VP and Treasurer
Jill W. Schmidt, VP-Communications/Investor Relations
Donald H. Twiner, VP, Pres.-Robin Hood Multifoods Inc.
David R. Berryman, Asst. Controller
Timothy J. Keenan, Senior Attorney and Asst. Secretary
Scott R. Riddle, Dir.-Business Analysis, Asst. Treasurer
Christopher S. Tangen, Pres.-U.S. Foods

DIRECTORS

Claire Arnold, Leapfrog Services Inc., Atlanta
Gary E. Costley, Ph.D.
Robert M. Price, PSV Inc., Bloomington, MN
Nicholas L. Reding, Pharmacia Corp., St. Louis
Jack D. Rehm, Meredith Corp. (retired)
Lois Dickson Rice, The Brookings Institution, Washington, D.C.
Richard K. Smucker, The J.M. Smucker Co., Orville, OH
Dolph W. von Arx, Isolux Corp., Naples, FL

MAJOR SHAREHOLDERS

T. Rowe Price Associates Inc., 9.4%, Baltimore
Archer-Daniels-Midland Co., 8.7%, Decatur, IL
Putnam Investments Inc., 5.9%, Boston
Dimensional Fund Advisors Inc., 5.6%, Santa Monica, CA
All officers and directors as a group (18 persons), 4.3%

SIC CODE

2045 Prepared flour mixes
2053 Frozen bakery products, except bread
5113 Industrial paper, whsle
5142 Frozen foods, whsle
5143 Dairy products, whsle
5145 Confectionery, whsle
5147 Meat products, whsle
5149 Groceries, nec, whsle

MISCELLANEOUS

TRANSFER AGENT AND REGISTAR: Wells Fargo Bank Minnesota N.A., South St. Paul, MN
TRADED: NYSE
SYMBOL: IMC
STOCKHOLDERS: 4,403
EMPLOYEES: 4,362
IN MINNESOTA: 350
GENERAL COUNSEL: Faegre & Benson PLLP, Minneapolis
AUDITORS: KPMG LLP, Minneapolis
INC: DE-1969
FOUNDED: 1892
ANNUAL MEETING: June
PUBLIC/INVESTOR RELATIONS: Jill Schmidt

RANKINGS

No. 16 CRM Public 200

SUBSIDIARIES, DIVISIONS, AFFILIATES

MULTIFOODS DISTRIBUTION GROUP
12650 E. Arapahoe Rd.
Englewood, CO 80112
Robert S. Wright
303/662-7100

NORTH AMERICA FOODS
U.S. Foods
111 Cheshire Ln., Ste. 100
Minnetonka, MN 55305
Christopher S. Tanger
952/404-7500

Robin Hood Multifoods Inc.
60 Columbia Way
Markham, Ontario L3R 0C9
Donald H. Twiner
905/940-960

TWO-YEAR QUARTERLY HIGH-LOW STOCK PRICES

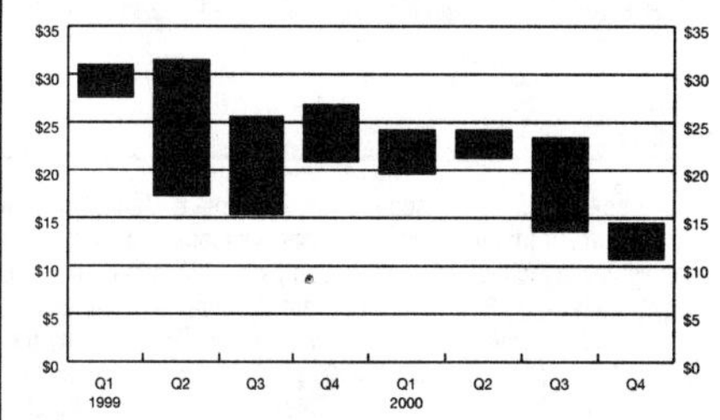

PUB

IntraNet Solutions Inc.

7777 Golden Triangle Dr., Eden Prairie, MN 55344
Tel: 952/903-2000 Fax: 952/829-5424 Web site: http://www.intranetsolutions.com

IntraNet Solutions Inc. was originally formed in 1990 as Technical Publishing Solutions Inc., a solution provider of customized document management for Fortune 1000 companies. In 1995 the company began significant work with World Wide Web technology. It is now focused on software research and development. ***Intra.doc!* Management System** allows client companies to deploy manageable libraries of shared corporate documents on dynamic Internet/intranet/extranet Web sites. The product is targeted at medium to large companies that need a cost-effective way to go beyond the basic capabilities of Web servers to build secure business libraries with check-in/check-out, revision controls, and automated publishing in Web-ready formats. In addition to its proprietary software products, the company continues to provide full-service network integration, software development, and other services.

EARNINGS HISTORY *

Year Ended Mar 31	Operating Revenue/Sales (dollars in thousands)	Net Earnings (dollars in thousands)	Return on Revenue (percent)	Return on Equity (percent)	Net Earnings (dollars per share†)	Cash Dividend (dollars per share†)	Market Price Range (dollars per share†)
2000 ¶	22,360	479	2.1	0.3	0.03	—	55.50–6.88
1999 #	17,031	(1,359)	(8.0)	(47.4)	(0.19)	—	8.75–2.75
1998 **	22,211	(4,663)	(21.0)	NM	(0.67)	—	8.38–3.38
1997 ††	20,755	(3,407)	(16.4)	NM	(0.43)	—	21.75–4.38
1996 ##	14,708	(510)	(3.5)	NM	(0.07)	—	14.75–3.00

* Financials have been restated to account for the Sept. 29, 1999, merger with InfoAccess Inc. as a pooling of interests.
† Per-share amounts restated to reflect a 1-for-4 reverse stock split on Oct. 31, 1996.
¶ Income figures for 2000 include acquisition costs of $1.972 million/($0.12).
# Income figures for 1999 include gain of $0.517 million/$0.05 on sale of hardware integration unit; and loss of $0.521 million/($0.05) from discontinued distribution group and its disposal.
** Income figures for 1998 include loss of $2.576 million/($0.27) from discontinued operations.
†† Income figures for 1997 include $0.456 million in special charges; and loss of $2.559 million/($0.20) from discontinued operations.
Income figures for 1996 include loss of $0.200 million/($0.03) from discontinued operations.

BALANCE SHEET

Assets	03/31/00 (dollars in thousands)	03/31/99	Liabilities	03/31/00 (dollars in thousands)	03/31/99
Current (CAE 8,859 and 2,177)	143,357	7,203	Current (STD 115 and 1,044)	6,245	3,490
Property and equipment	887	900	Long-term debt	11	108
			Deferred revenue	89	147
Notes receivable		106	Preferred equity		334
Other investments	832		Common equity*	140,970	4,385
Prepaid royalties	1,644		TOTAL	147,315	8,464
Software licenses	161	236			
Other	434	19			
TOTAL	147,315	8,464			

* $0.01 par common; 50,000,000 authorized; 20,665,000 and 12,450,000 issued and outstanding.

RECENT QUARTERS / PRIOR-YEAR RESULTS

Quarter End	Revenue ($000)	Earnings ($000)	EPS ($)	Prior-Year Revenue ($000)	Prior-Year Earnings ($000)	Prior-Year EPS ($)
Q2 09/30/2000	15,622	(11,014)	(0.52)	4,574	(1,484)	(0.09)
Q1 06/30/2000	9,462	2,989	0.14	4,447	317	0.02
Q4 03/31/2000	7,509	1,038	0.06	4,065	(18)	0.00
Q3 12/31/99	5,830	608	0.04	3,284	(359)	(0.04)
SUM	38,423	(6,379)	(0.28)	16,370	(1,544)	(0.11)

CURRENT: Q2 earnings include charge of $10.4 million/($0.49) for write-off of in-process R&D; and $0.59 million/($0.03) in acquisition-related costs.
PRIOR YEAR: Q2 earnings include charge of $1.972 million/($0.12) for acquisition costs.

RECENT EVENTS

In **December 1999** the company's Xpedio Content Management solution received two editor's choice awards for technology excellence, from Imaging and Document Solutions and KMWorld magazine. IntraNet made a strategic investment in activeIQ Technologies, a technology start-up company developing Internet-commerce communities and knowledge-categorization technology. In **January 2000** IntraNet became the first Web content management vendor to support the Red Hat (Nasdaq: RHAT) Linux operating system and Apache Webserver. The company then signed an exclusive OEM licensing agreement to port its Xpedio technology to the IBM AS/400 platform for e-Business Intelligence leader, ShowCase Corp. (Nasdaq: SHWC) as part of its new Enterprise Information Portal offering. The company was hon- ***continued on page 253***

OFFICERS

Robert F. Olson
Chairman and CEO

Vernon J. Hanzlik
President

Katherine Bloomfield
VP-Operations

Jim Culbertson
Pres.-InfoAccess

Tom Freeman
VP-International Sales

Michael Gadow
VP-Channels

Robin Pederson
VP-Worldwide Sales

Dan Ryan
VP-Marketing/Business Development

Gregg A. Waldon
CFO, Secretary, and Treasurer

DIRECTORS

Ronald E. Eibensteiner
Wyncrest Capital Inc., Minneapolis

Kenneth H. Holec
ShowCase Corp., Rochester, MN

Robert F. Olson

Gregg A. Waldon

Steven C. Waldron
St. Paul Software, St. Paul

MAJOR SHAREHOLDERS

Robert F. Olson, 12.7%
Eden Prairie, MN

All officers and directors as a group (6 persons), 15.9%

SIC CODE

7371 Computer programming services

7372 Prepackaged software

7373 Computer integrated systems design

MISCELLANEOUS

TRANSFER AGENT AND REGISTAR:
Wells Fargo Bank Minnesota N.A., South St. Paul, MN

TRADED: Nasdaq National Market

SYMBOL: INRS

STOCKHOLDERS: 100

EMPLOYEES: 270

GENERAL COUNSEL:
Faegre & Benson PLLP, Minneapolis

AUDITORS:
Grant Thornton LLP, Minneapolis

INC: MN-1996

FOUNDED: 1990

ANNUAL MEETING: September

HUMAN RESOURCES: Julie A. Grebin

COMMUNICATIONS: Barbara Johnson

RANKINGS

No. 152 CRM Public 200

TWO-YEAR QUARTERLY HIGH-LOW STOCK PRICES

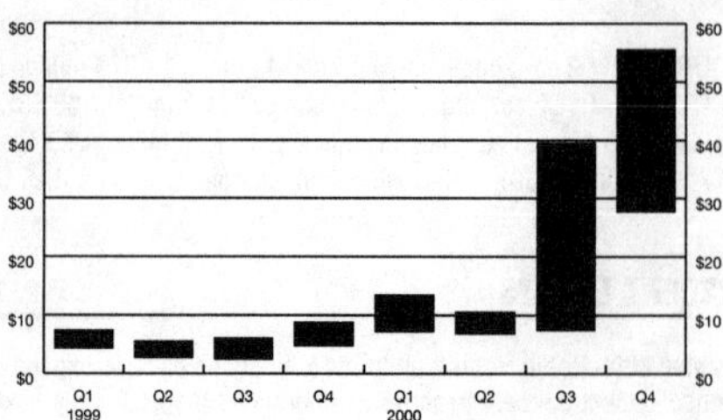

Jore Corporation

45000 Highway 93 S., Ronan, MT 59864
Tel: 406/676-4900 Web site: http://www.jorecorporation.com

Jore Corp. is a leader in the design, manufacture, and marketing of innovative power tool accessories and hand tools for the do-it-yourself and professional craftsman markets. Jore offers a comprehensive system of proprietary drilling and driving products that save users time through enhanced functionality, productivity, and ease-of-use. Jore manufactures its products using advanced technologies and equipment designs, thus achieving competitive advantages in cost, quality, and production capacity. Products are sold under private labels to the industry's largest power tool retailers and manufacturers such as Sears, Roebuck and Co., Tru*Serv Corp., Canadian Tire Corp. Ltd., Black & Decker Corp., and Makita Corp. Products also are sold under the STANLEY brand, to which Jore has an exclusive license arrangement for power tool accessories, at retailers such as The Home Depot Inc., Menard's, Ace Hardware Corp., and others.

EARNINGS HISTORY *

Year Ended Dec 31	Operating Revenue/Sales (dollars in thousands)	Net Earnings	Return on Revenue (percent)	Return on Equity	Net Earnings (dollars per share†)	Cash Dividend	Market Price Range
1999 ¶	53,872	4,930	9.2	11.0	0.46	—	12.88–7.06
1998	44,888	6,240	13.9	NM	0.66	—	
1997	23,656	2,541	10.7	NM	0.27	—	
1996	9,686	(558)	(5.8)	NM	—	—	
1995	9,416	189	2.0	24.8	—	—	

* The company was operating as an S corporation until Sept. 23, 1999. Earnings figures for periods prior to that date do not include a provision for income taxes.
† Trading began Sept. 23, 1999.
¶ Income figures for 1999 include extraordinary loss of $0.914 million/($0.09) on early retirement of debt.

BALANCE SHEET

Assets	12/31/99 (dollars in thousands)	12/31/98	Liabilities	12/31/99 (dollars in thousands)	12/31/98
Current (CAE 94 and 34)	58,683	25,111	Current (STD 3,612 and 2,254)	42,605	25,084
Property, plant, and equipment	58,561	19,816	Long-term debt	27,779	14,589
Intangibles and other	663	1,036	Deferred income taxes	2,769	
TOTAL	117,908	45,963	Stockholders' equity*	44,754	6,289
			TOTAL	117,908	45,963

* No par common; 100,000,000 authorized; 13,826,020 and 9,508,544 issued and outstanding.

RECENT QUARTERS / **PRIOR-YEAR RESULTS**

	Quarter End	Revenue ($000)	Earnings ($000)	EPS ($)	Prior-Year Revenue ($000)	Prior-Year Earnings ($000)	Prior-Year EPS ($)
Q2	09/30/2000	9,018	(1,362)	(0.10)	14,378	277	0.03
Q3	09/30/2000	15,870	253	0.02	8,259	117	0.01
Q1	03/31/2000	7,064	(523)	(0.04)	9,798	840	0.09
Q4	12/31/99	21,436	3,696	0.27	19,458	2,335	0.25
	SUM	53,387	2,064	0.15	51,894	3,568	0.38

PRIOR YEAR: Q3 earnings include extraordinary loss of $1.017 million/($0.10) on early retirement of debt.

RECENT EVENTS

In **May 2000** the company held its first annual meeting since going public. CEO Jore announced plans to build a 45,000-square-foot distribution center in Missoula. After reaching an agreement to sell its brand of handyman tools at Home Depot, the world's largest home improvement retailer, and introducing a new line of drill accessories under the familiar Stanley Works name, the company needed more space to help it keep pace with growing sales. EVP Bjornson said that the agreement with Home Depot was going to give Jore wider retail exposure and should account for 30 percent of the company's entire sales by the end of 2001. A D.A. Davidson analyst predicted that sales of Jore's quick-change drill bits and drivers from Home Depot's shelves could reach $100 million annually. **Sept. 30:** Third-quarter net revenue was $15.9 million, up 10 percent from the same period of 1999. Jore was continuing its successful strategic transition to increase sales through its direct-to-retail channels, including both sales under retailers' in-house labels and under Jore's licensed brand, Stanley. The direct-to-retail channel accounted for 76 percent of total sales in the third quarter. The focus on direct-to-retail sales and more vertically integrated production was gradually improving gross margins, which reached 32 percent in the quarter. Sales and marketing expenses nearly doubled to $1.6 million. These marketing activities, which included nationwide television advertising and promotional activities with The Home Depot and other retailers, were expected to contribute significantly to continued sales growth going forward.

OFFICERS

Matthew B. Jore
Chairman, President, and CEO

Michael W. Jore
EVP

David H. Bjornson
CFO, General Counsel, and Secretary

Kelly D. Grove
VP and Controller

Nikki M. Snyder
VP-Human Resources

Jeffery J. Eidsmoe
VP-Operations

Jeffrey M. Heutmaker
VP-Strategic Initiatives

George R. Collins
VP-Industrial Sales

DIRECTORS

David H. Bjornson
Matthew B. Jore
Michael W. Jore

MAJOR SHAREHOLDERS

Matthew B. Jore, 59.2%
Michael W. Jore, 16.5%
All officers and directors as a group (12 persons), 61.2%

SIC CODE

3423 Hand and edge tools, nec
3425 Hand saws and saw blades

MISCELLANEOUS

TRANSFER AGENT AND REGISTAR:
Chase Mellon Shareholders, Richfield Park, NJ

TRADED: Nasdaq National Market

SYMBOL: JORE

STOCKHOLDERS: 90

EMPLOYEES: 713

PART TIME: 94

GENERAL COUNSEL:
Stoel Rives LLP, Seattle

AUDITORS:
Deloitte & Touche LLP, Seattle

INC: MT-1987

ANNUAL MEETING: May

PUB

K-tel International Inc.

2605 Fernbrook Ln. N., Plymouth, MN 55447
Tel: 763/559-6000 Fax: 763/559-6822 Web site: http://www.ktel.com

K-tel International Inc. is a vertically integrated developer, marketer, and distributor of entertainment and consumer products. The company markets its product lines to retailers, wholesalers, distributors, and licensees throughout the world—or directly to the consumer via television and other forms of direct-response media, including the Internet. K-tel has active operations in the United States, Canada and the United Kingdom.

EARNINGS HISTORY

Year Ended Jun 30	Operating Revenue/Sales (dollars in thousands)	Net Earnings	Return on Revenue (percent)	Return on Equity	Net Earnings	Cash Dividend (dollars per share*)	Market Price Range
2000 †	58,604	(15,738)	(26.9)	NM	(1.58)	—	10.44–1.75
1999	77,664	(11,547)	(14.9)	NM	(1.25)	—	32.63–5.13
1998 ¶	85,626	(2,407)	(2.8)	(63.8)	(0.31)	—	39.94–3.06
1997	75,501	3,204	4.2	70.0	0.43	—	4.38–1.75
1996 #	71,987	(745)	(1.0)	(47.6)	(0.10)	—	2.56–1.63

* Per-share amounts restated to reflect 2-for-1 stock split on May 1, 1998.
† Income figures for 2000 include pretax gain of $4.341 million from the sale of its subsidiary in Finland; and a nonrecurring expense of $0.6 million from a private placement of common stock.
¶ Income figures for 1998 include a nonrecurring gain of $0.614 million.
# Income figures for 1996 include charge of $400,000 to reserve for estimated costs to complete a product replacement program.

BALANCE SHEET

Assets	06/30/00 (dollars in thousands)	06/30/99	Liabilities	06/30/00 (dollars in thousands)	06/30/99
Current (CAE 2,475 and 6,782)	18,889	30,200	Current (STD 1,945 and 1,945)	31,796	28,124
Property and equipment	939	1,549	Notes payable	4,000	4,000
			Stockholders' equity*	(12,597)	3,792
Other	3,371	4,167			
TOTAL	23,199	35,916	TOTAL	23,199	35,916

* $0.01 par common; 50,000,000 authorized; 10,320,405 and 10,241,199 issued and outstanding.

RECENT QUARTERS / **PRIOR-YEAR RESULTS**

	Quarter End	Revenue ($000)	Earnings ($000)	EPS ($)	Prior-Year Revenue ($000)	Prior-Year Earnings ($000)	Prior-Year EPS ($)
Q1	09/30/2000	9,325	(2,530)	(0.25)	18,097	2,880	0.29
Q4	06/30/2000	11,218	(11,095)	(1.01)	19,360	(1,681)	(0.17)
Q3	03/31/2000	12,885	(5,574)	(0.56)	18,506	(4,741)	(0.50)
Q2	12/31/99	16,404	(1,949)	(0.20)	21,006	(2,048)	(0.23)
	SUM	49,832	(21,148)	(2.01)	76,969	(5,590)	(0.60)

PRIOR YEAR: Q1 earnings include pretax gain of $4.341 million from the sale of its subsidiary in Finland; and a nonrecurring expense of $0.6 million from a private placement of common stock.

RECENT EVENTS

In **March 2000** K-tel hired Musicland executive Ken Onstad as its new president, replacing Lawrence Kieves. The Recording Industry Association of America certified K-tel album "Club Mix '99" as "Gold"—for more than 500,000 copies sold in the United States. Released on Cold Front, K-tel's cutting edge dance and techno imprint, the 25-track album features the hottest up-tempo songs culled from the top music charts of every possible category. Standouts include Smash Mouth's chart-topping "Walking On The Sun," Deja Vu's #1 hit "I Like The Way," Backstreet Boys' "Everybody (Backstreet's Back)," SWV's "Rain," and R. Kelly's "Thank God It's Friday." In **April** K-tel and Microsoft Corp. (Nasdaq: MSFT) announced that K-tel would soon begin selling thousands of titles from its music library as digital downloads. K-tel consolidated its two United Kingdom-based operations into one facility, reducing overhead by $500,000 per year. Effective **June** 30, K-tel closed its German subsidiary, Dominion Vertriebs GmbH, resulting in the loss of 88 positions. The subsidiary, which sold consumer goods and music products through direct marketing, had generated operating losses for the past two fiscal years. Additionally, K-tel's use of technology was allowing it to restructure its U.S. operations and lower domestic operating costs. The elimination of 35 positions on June 28 resulted in an estimated overhead reduction of $1.7 million for the coming year. On **July** 31, the U.S. District Court granted a motion dismissing a class action lawsuit brought against K-tel and certain of its executives on behalf of shareholders of the company. The granting of the motion to dismiss barred further actions by the plaintiffs. Plaintiffs' request to amend the most recent complaint in order to refile the complaint in the future was also denied. In **August** K-tel faced delisting for being out of compliance with the requirements for continued listing on the Nasdaq National Market, which include a requirement of a minimum market capitalization or total assets and total revenue of $50 million, and a market value of public float of $15 million. [In May 2000 the company had submitted a plan of compliance that wasn't accepted by the staff of Nasdaq.] K-tel

continued on page 254

OFFICERS

Philip Kives
CEO
Ken Onstad
President
A. Merrill Ayers
VP-Finance and CFO
Donald F. Bergenty
VP-Eastern Division
Mike Gleason
VP-Sales
Alan Hawley
Dir.-Operations

DIRECTORS

Herbert Davis
attorney
Lawrence Kieves
Philip Kives
Ken P. Onstad
Jay William Smalley
JWS Inc.
Dennis W. Ward
David Wolinsky
Monk Goodwin, Winnipeg, Manitoba

MAJOR SHAREHOLDERS

Philip Kives, 48.2%
Winnipeg, Manitoba
All officers and directors as a group (9 persons), 50.7%

SIC CODE

3652 Prerecorded records and tapes
5099 Durable goods, nec, whsle

MISCELLANEOUS

TRANSFER AGENT AND REGISTAR:
American Stock Transfer & Trust Co., New York
TRADED: OTC Bulletin Board
SYMBOL: KTEL
STOCKHOLDERS: 1,389
EMPLOYEES: 77
GENERAL COUNSEL:
Briggs and Morgan P.A., Minneapolis
AUDITORS:
Grant Thornton LLP, Minneapolis
INC: MN-1968
ANNUAL MEETING:
November
INVESTOR RELATIONS:
A. Merrill Ayers

RANKINGS

No. 98 CRM Public 200

SUBSIDIARIES, DIVISIONS, AFFILIATES

K-tel International (USA) Inc.
Plymouth, Minn.

Dominion Entertainment Inc.
Plymouth, Minn.

K-tel Ireland Ltd.
Dublin

K-tel Entertainment (CAN) Inc.
Winnipeg, Manitoba

K-tel Marketing Ltd.
London

K-tel Entertainment (U.K.) Ltd.
London

K-tel (Australia) Pty. Ltd.
Southport, Queensland

Seminars
Plymouth, Minn.

K-tel Consumer Products, Inc.
Plymouth, Minn.

K-tel Direct, Inc.
Plymouth, Minn.

K-tel TV, Inc.
Plymouth, Minn.

K-tel Video, Inc.
Plymouth, Minn.

K-tel Productions, Inc.
Plymouth, Minn.

K-tel Online, Inc.
Plymouth, Minn.

TWO-YEAR QUARTERLY HIGH-LOW STOCK PRICES

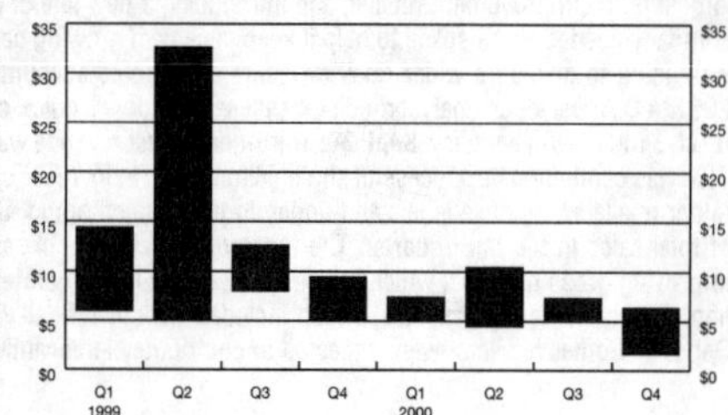

HEI Inc.

continued from page 225 MEDtech Inc. (Nasdaq: CMED), Boulder, Colo., that he had recently acquired in open market purchases for HEI common stock. The exchange ratio resulted in an immediate unrealized gain to HEI of $2 million, which was the difference in Fant's basis in the Colorado MEDtech shares and its closing price at the time of the announcement. Pursuant to that exchange, HEI made a proposal that HEI acquire Colorado MEDtech in an exchange offer and subsequent merger. Colorado MEDtech shareholders would tender each of their shares for a number of shares of HEI common stock having a value of $12, up to a maximum of an aggregate of 8.5 million HEI shares. Based on the prevailing stock price of Colorado MEDtech, this represented a 41 percent premium. In a letter to Colorado MEDtech, Fant said that HEI desired to acquire Colorado MEDtech in a negotiated transaction, but would still proceed with an exchange offer even in the absence of a negotiated agreement. HEI, as the holder of 9.9 percent of the outstanding common stock of Colorado MEDtech, then filed a complaint in the U.S. District Court for the District of Colorado against Colorado MEDtech and its directors, alleging that certain provisions of Colorado MEDtech's bylaws and "poison pill" illegally limited shareholders' statutory right to hold a special meeting to elect directors. HEI intended to demand a special meeting of shareholders to replace Colorado MEDtech's directors. Meanwhile, Colorado MEDtech hired investment banker Wasserstein Perella & Co. to evaluate HEI's acquisition proposal. In **October** Colorado MEDtech CEO Stephen K. Onody declined to meet with Fant, noting: "We believe that many of the features of a combination of our companies that you pointed out at our meeting were the type of general statements one could make about the combination of any two technology companies. At a fundamental business level, the combination of our two companies would only serve to make HEI a bigger company. We do not see this as a compelling strategic rationale." Noting that Colorado MEDtech had performed poorly over the past several years, HEI responded that its goals were: first, to acquire Colorado MEDtech by offering Colorado MEDtech shareholders HEI common stock in exchange for their Colorado MEDtech shares; and second, to increase shareholder value for all HEI shareholders, including the former Colorado MEDtech shareholders. To that end HEI was intending solicit calls of a special meeting of shareholders from other Colorado MEDtech shareholders. At that special meeting, Colorado MEDtech shareholders would be asked to vote to remove the current members of the board of directors and elect HEI's slate of nominees to replace them. In **October** the Fant exchange of Colorado MEDtech stock for HEI stock was rescinded. HEI cited negative market conditions, the announcement of legal claims that may be asserted against CMED, and the continued refusal of the CMED board to discuss a sale as factors in its decision to cease its pursuit of Colorado MEDtech. In **November** HEI successfully completed qualification testing for its new HFC Series of high-frequency chip carriers for applications in high-speed fiber-optic and wireless communications.

Health Fitness Corporation

continued from page 229 ters, and employee wellness programs. Healthtrax was to be merged into Health Fitness, with current Healthtrax shareholders receiving Health Fitness common stock representing approximately 50 percent of all Health Fitness common stock outstanding after the merger. In **August** founder Loren S. Brink resigned his position as president of sales and a director to pursue other interests. Health Fitness increased its borrowing capacity and significantly lowered its interest expenses by entering into a new $5.0 million working capital facility with Coast Business Credit. Initial proceeds of the loan were used to pay its former lender and subordinated debt holders. The letter of intent to merge with HealthTrax International was terminated, which allowed Health Fitness to engage in discussions with other interested parties and to consider other strategic options.

Health Risk Management Inc.

continued from page 231 pany announced today the issuance of an additional patent for its evidence-based QualityFIRST Medical Risk Management System—giving it two issued U.S. and three issued foreign patents. In **May** HRM resolved all outstanding issues and litigation matters pending with Chiplease Inc., Banco Panamericano Inc., Leon Greenblatt, and Leslie Jabine (a shareholder group that collectively owned 14 percent of HRM shares). The shareholders and HRM executed a standstill agreement whereby the shareholder group: was entitled to designate a person as a director on the HRM board of directors; was allowed to increase its holdings by 10 percent; was to vote its shares as may be directed by a majority of HRM's independent directors; and was to dismiss all litigation commenced by it. At the annual meeting, management confirmed that it was making contacts with investment banking firms to seek strategic advice and explore various financing structures for two Web-based businesses that the company was developing. In **August** the Institute for Healthcare Quality (IHQ) announced its most recent strategic business partnership, with Internet application service provider PBM Corp., Cleveland. HRM notified the SEC of the need to file its June quarterly earnings statement late. In **September** IHQ announced an investment banking agreement with Shattuck Hammond Partners, a division of PricewaterhouseCoopers Securities LLC, for funds to complete the development of its new Internet-based products as well as the continuing upgrades of its patented QualityFIRST clinical decision support and risk management software. The first product to be introduced, HEALTHeDECISIONS, was specifically designed to address three burgeoning trends in the health care market: (1) a shift in traditional utilization review and quality management functions from the health plan to the physician; (2) a movement toward empowerment of the health care consumer; and (3) the use of Scientific Evidence-Based Medicine systems to decrease variations in clinical decision-making. In **October** HRM announced that its new Web-based medical management system by Landacorp Inc. was scheduled to be operational January 2001. The new system was expected to significantly reduce operating costs beginning in 2001 and well into the future.

Hector Communications Corporation

continued from page 232 percent owner Hector, was to receive backing from new lead investor Touch America (NYSE: MTP), the Montana-based utility—enabling Hector to reduce its ownership to 2.7 percent by 2002. In **November** Hector announced that it was going to bring high-speed wireless broadband to rural Minnesota.

HickoryTech Corporation

continued from page 233 $25.9 million, reflecting steady growth in HickoryTech's wired telephone businesses of incumbent telephone companies and its competitive local exchange company. HickoryTech's customer base grew 17.8 percent over the same quarter one year ago, to a total of 118,500, including 5,700 customers added during the third quarter and 13,200 customers added in calendar 2000. Earnings before interest, taxes, depreciation, and amortization (EBITDA) for the quarter increased 11.5 percent to $9.6 million. In **October** HickoryTech announced plans to acquire Mankato, Minn.-based Internet service provider Internet Connections' 5,000 dial-up Internet customer accounts in south central Minnesota and the Twin Cities area. The Corporation of the City of Thunder Bay—Telephone Department signed a contract for HickoryTech's WRITE2k billing solution. The company then closed on a new $225 million senior credit facility with its syndicate of commercial bank institutions. The facility, which was to mature in nine years, replaced the company's existing $125 million credit facility. The additional $100 million in credit was to fuel a growth plan that had the company rebuilding its transmission infrastructure in several southern Minnesota communities by installing fiber optic lines to the curb and copper lines into homes that will carry phone, Internet, and cable service.

HomeServices.com Inc.

continued from page 234 tomers. In **March** the Hook Up, HomeServices.com's Web-based home connection program—which connects basic utilities and other services such as telephone, cable TV, and Internet at closing—was introduced in three markets, including the Minneapolis/St. Paul market. **March 31**: During the first quarter, closed transaction sides increased 30 percent over the same period in 1999, to 17,364; while the average home sales price increased 13.6 percent, to $151,900. (The residential real estate brokerage business is subject to seasonal fluctuations. Historically, HomeServices.com's revenue has been strongest in the second and third quarters of the year.) In **June** HomeServices.com added title services at J.C. Nichols Residential, a real estate brokerage subsidiary operating in Kansas City, Mo. In **August** HomeServices.com added a Web-based home shopping service to the menu of products and e-consumer services offered its customers. It provides online shopping for such home-related items as appliances, furniture, tools, and home-decorating accessories. A new strategic alliance with MegaMags Inc. provided an expansive Web-based home reference newsstand to HomeServices' real estate consumers. The alliance built upon HomeServices.com's existing e-consumer services, The Hook Up and The Fix Up, by offering customers hundreds of U.S. and international mass market and hard-to-find home reference magazine titles through MegaMags. HomeServices.com added title insurance services to the existing real estate products and services provided by Long Realty Co., its residential real estate brokerage subsidiary operating in Tucson, Ariz. **Sept. 30**: Nine-month revenue of $360.7 million was up 24 percent from the same period in 1999. Net income of $12.6 million was up 33 percent. EBITDA was $31.7 million, up 18 percent. Closed transaction sides were 67,778, up 18 percent, with an average home sales price of $160,700, up 7 percent. "Our ability to develop industry-leading, value-added services for our customer, such as The Hook Up, along with our expertise in cross-selling mortgage and title services, combine to deliver enhanced levels of performance," said CEO Peltier. In **October** the company purchased 1.7 million of its outstanding common shares from U.S. Bancorp Piper Jaffray in a block trade at a price of $10.50 per share. As a result of the transaction, MidAmerican Energy Holdings Co. increased its ownership to 84 percent.

Hormel Foods Corporation

continued from page 235 ny's foodservice business remained strong. Value-added segments of Jennie-O Foods also recorded gains. In **October** Hormel and Famous Dave's of America Inc. (Nasdaq: DAVE), Eden Prairie, Minn., announcde a major initiative in which Hormel was to produce, market, and distribute four retail barbecue meat products featuring Famous Dave's award-winning "Rich and Sassy" sauce. Hormel and the city of Dayton, Ohio, announced that the company was planning to open a food distribution facility in the city's Northwest Industrial Park in 2001. The 140,000-square-foot distribution facility was expected to employ 125 full-time employees and serve as a distribution center for a variety of products manufactured at Hormel Foods plants throughout the United States.

Hutchinson Technology Inc.

continued from page 236 erance costs, the company would have reported a fiscal-2000 net loss of $26.161 million. Employment at Hutchinson Technology totaled 4,729 at fiscal 2000 year end compared to 7,701 at the end of fiscal 1999. Having obtained amendments to certain financing agreements, the company was in compliance with all of its financing agreements. In **October** the company reported that suspension demand was flat to slightly up from the fiscal 2000 fourth-quarter level. "We are currently expecting to report 2001 first-quarter results that are very similar to our fiscal 2000 fourth-quarter results," said Fortun.

Image Sensing Systems Inc.

continued from page 239 Detection System product family throughout Eastern Europe and the Middle East: Danway (United Arab Emirates), Promel Projekt d.o.o. (Croatia), Eltodo Dopravni Systemy s.r.o. (Czech Republic), and ITC Inc. (Jordan). In **June** contracts were awarded to Flow Traffic Ltd. for the supply of Autoscope-2004 wide-area video vehicle detection systems and image sensors to Taiwan and to Seoul, Korea. Chairman and CEO William L. Russell accepted a new, six-year contract. In **August** ISS formed an exclusive global alliance with privately held Wireless Technology Inc. of Ventura, Calif., for the sale of products and systems that transmit wireless full-motion video, audio, and data for the ITS (intelligent transportation systems), traffic management, enforcement, and security markets. Both firms were to jointly develop an array of products complementary to the ISS Autoscope video vehicle detection system and the next generation of video detection systems. **Sept. 30**: Nine-month revenue was $4.123 million, up 30 percent from a year earlier. The increase in revenue was due primarily to more sales of Autoscope systems by Flow Traffic Ltd. CEO Russell said, "The third quarter is considerably improved over last year in spite of the rescheduling of a large domestic order to a future date. Our business development efforts internationally are contributing to revenue growth and our partnership with Wireless Technology Inc. is yielding results much faster than anticipated." In **October** the company signed an agreement with its Middle East partner, Bahrain Advanced Technology Co. (BATEC), to deliver 5,000 units of Wireless Technology's equipment, an initial order valued at US$2.43 million, over the next 12 months. In **November** ISS released Autoscope Solo Pro, which integrates a high-resolution color camera, zoom lens, and machine vision processor into a single compact unit featuring direct real-time iris and shutter-speed controls.

Imation Corporation

continued from page 241 **RECENT EVENTS**

Late in **1999**, the company was planning the rollout of a suite of Internet products and services to tap the Web's fledgling data-storage market. In **January 2000** Imation announced shipment of the one-millionth SuperDisk USB Drive for Macintosh—the high-capacity, floppy-compatible storage device designed especially for Apple's new family of iMacs. Addressing the complex, rapidly digitizing environment of engineering data management, Imation announced a strategy—including new consulting and support services, along with new technology alliances—to address customers' analog-to-digital migration requirements. The company made available a new SuperDisk drive upgrade option kit developed for corporate users of Compaq Deskpro PCs. In **February** Imation announced Imation Verifi accurate Web color, an Internet color technology that enables online shoppers to more confidently purchase products (cosmetics, apparel, home furnishings) where color accuracy is integral to the purchasing decision. For the second-consecutive year, Fortune Magazine named Imation Corp. to its America's Most Admired Companies list. Imation formed an alliance with KIP America, enabling Imation to sell, install, and service KIP large-format reprographics equipment in the engineering market. The new Extended 3590 half-inch tape cartridge (for use in IBM's new Magstar 3590E drives) was released. In **March** Imation announced a new-generation Web-based architecture for Imation Media Manager, the company's media asset management software, based on Allaire's ColdFusion; unveiled its color technologies strategy and demonstrated an array of advanced digital imaging technologies for critical color markets; announced that the Imation MatchprintTM Inkjet System was to be available as an upgrade for the Canon BJC-8500 printer beginning in June; announced next-generation digital halftone proofing colors and bases; and announced plans with Collabria Inc. to deliver a wide range of color proofing products and professional services to automate and manage the development, purchase, and production of commercially printed projects. E-commerce businesses may be losing customers when they can't assure color confidence on their Web sites, according to a BizRate.com custom report commissioned by Imation. Through the innovation of Imation Verifi accurate Web color, Imation solves the Internet color dilemma. **March 31**: Despite an atypical revenue decline, first-quarter earnings nearly quadrupled from a year ago. Data storage businesses continued to thrive, led by tape cartidges and optical media sales for networks and entire businesses. In **April** Imation launched http://www.verifi.net, for Imation Verifi Accurate Web Color technology. Imation announced plans to expand its broad portfolio of data storage and information management media, solutions, and services to include the development of data storage software. In **May** Imation and Sun Microsystems Inc. (Nasdaq: SUNW) announced plans for Imation to develop Jiro technology software for Sun's network storage products. Imation also announced plans to offer a range of Jiro technology development services for network storage vendors. Imation and Xerox established a strategic alliance to introduce printing, proofing, and imaging products to the graphic arts industry. The first planned offering from this alliance was to be a digital front end, or hardware rastor image processor (RIP), that was expected to provide network connectivity to the Xerox DocuColor 12 copier/printer engine, bringing graphic arts professionals prints/proofs that accurately and consistently simulate Imation's industry-standard Matchprint Color Proofing Systems. Imation expanded its year-old partnership with Jordan Grand Prix, one of the leading Formula One teams, for the 2000 season. Imation announced a program to provide resellers the training and tools they need to promote and sell Imation data storage media, hardware, solutions, and services. Imation and Tandberg Data ASA (OSE: TAD) announced a new addition to the award-winning Scalable Linear Recording (SLR) product group—the SLR40 tape drive and tape cartridges. In **June** Imation and AltaVista Co., the premier knowledge resource on the Internet (www.altavista.com) and a majority-owned operating company of CMGI Inc., announced a distribution agreement. People who purchase Imation data storage products at retail were to receive AltaVista's free unlimited Internet access, which was already being used by more than 2.5 million people across North America. Pursuant to the Sun Microsystems alliance, Imation demonstrated newly developed software components based on Jiro technology. Imation began offering new half-height, faster internal IDE SuperDisk Drives to resellers, integrators, and OEMs nationwide. Sun Microsystems selected Imation to provide Sun customers and partners with a range of storage validation services, including interoperability and proof-of-concept testing, utilizing Imation's SAN Solutions Lab. An alliance with Microbox enabled Imation to sell, install, and service Microbox's archival and scanning systems in the large-format document imaging market. Imation announced availability of the Imation USB Floppy Drive for Macintosh, one of the lightest and smallest drives of its kind and a stylish, portable companion for Apple Macintosh computers. In **July** Imation announced a national service alliance with KIP America, where KIP was to offer Imation's service program to provide on-site technical service to customers using KIP's reprographic and digital printing systems. An alliance with Quintek Technologies Inc. (OTCBB: QTEK) was to allow Imation to sell, install, and service Quintek's 4300 Aperture Card Imaging System under a worldwide distribution program, thereby strengthening Imation's portfolio of products and services for large-format document imaging customers. Imation unveiled its new Imation Travan FireWire 20GB Drive at Macworld Expo/New York 2000. The company cut estimates of its full-year 2000 operating income growth, from 20 percent to between 6 and 12 percent. First half's weak demand for mature and analog products, price pressure in some categories, and softer-than-expected international sales had created a shortfall that couldn't be made up in second half. The market reacted to the news by sending Imation's stock plunging by 25 percent on July 25. In **August** Imation reached an agreement with mindwrap inc. to sell, install, and service mindwrap's Optix application software. (Optix is integrated digital content management and workflow software that allows customers to scan, store, and manage any variety of documents on a network server, giving users the power to archive and retrieve any number of documents from anywhere in the world via an Internet browser.) Under a three-year agreement with XANTE Corp., manufacturer and marketer of high-performance printing solutions, Imation was to provide full life-cycle service for XANTE's entire monochrome printer series in addition to its newly launched color printer product lines. For the second-consecutive year, Imation was named one of the 10 Great Places to Work in Minnesota, in the August issue of Corporate Report magazine. Imation announced the availability of Imation Mammoth 8mm Tape Cartridge 170m 20GB, for use with the more than 1.5 million installed base of Exabyte Mammoth Tape drives, libraries, and compatible drives. Xerox Corp. (NYSE: XRX) announced plans to market a new line of professional-level digital front-ends (DFEs), also known as raster image processors (RIPs), for the Xerox DocuColor printer/copier platform. The Imation Matchprint Professional Server was to provide network connectivity to the Xerox DocuColor 12 copier/printer engine. In **September** Imation Corp. and Aprimo Inc., the fastest-growing provider of Internet-based marketing management solutions, announced a joint marketing agreement aimed at delivering the most comprehensive range of consulting and technology solutions for marketing organizations around the world. Imation was to recommend and integrate Aprimo Marketing—a comprehensive marketing management platform that facilitates strategic decision making and empowers integrated campaign and program management—as part of Imation Color Technologies professional services offerings. Imation announced its approach towards e-business initiatives and infrastructure development and previewed the gateway to its new Web site, which was in the final stages of development. "Building on a solid technology platform, we are evolving our business model and our infrastructure to deliver increased value and responsiveness to our customers while creating real business efficiencies," said Monahan. "And that's what e-business is ultimately about. What we call e-business today, will be normal business practice in the near future." Imation began consolidating its production of diskettes, a fading technology, by closing a 100-employee plant in Weatherford, Okla. Imation formed the Network Color Solutions Organization, a new group within the Imation Color Technologies business unit that was to focus specifically on color controllers and related media offerings. Imation entered into a co-marketing alliance with Western Lithotech, a Mitsubishi Chemical Co., in order to offer end users best-in-class digital halftone proofing combined with a high-quality, thermal computer-to-plate (CTP) product. **Sept. 30**: Third-quarter revenue (a decline of 16.6 percent from 1999) and operating income before restructuring charges and write-offs ($800,000 for the quarter, compared to $22.7 million in the year-earlier period) were below expectations. The company also recorded $30 million in restructuring charges (relating to previous work reductions) and a $31 million noncash software write-off. Rapid change in the computer and printing industries had resulted in sales declines for many of Imation's relatively mature product lines, especially data storage. Imation engaged the investment banking firm of Goldman, Sachs & Co. to explore strategic alternatives such as financial restructuring, stock repurchases, spin-offs, joint ventures, and business combinations. "With more than $200 million in cash and very low debt, Imation has a solid financial position despite recent disappointing revenue performance," said Monahan, who was frustrated that the company's long-term value was not being recognized by the market. In **October** Imation's Wahpeton, N.D., plant was selected by INDUSTRYWEEK, the leading manufacturing management magazine, as a winning facility in the publication's 11th annual Best Plants competition. Imation introduced a new version of its popular USB Floppy Drive, one of the lightest and smallest available; a new line of high-performance CD-ReWritable drives, including the Imation CD Burn-R 12X10X32 and the Imation CD Burn-R 8X4X32; and Imation Black Watch T9940 half-inch tape cartridges for use in StorageTek's (NYSE: STK) T9940 tape drives.

Industrial Rubber Products Inc.

continued from page 242 operating efficiencies, better service for our customers, decreased transportation costs, and reduced interest expense." Industrial Rubber and Nordberg Sales Corp. signed a Strategic Alliance Purchasing Agreement with Cleveland-Cliffs Inc.'s six managed mines to supply Nordberg crusher castings. Cliffs was to purchase from Industrial Rubber/Nordberg 90 percent of Cliffs' crusher casting requirements for five years, beginning **May 1, 2000** (indicated annual purchases of $7.0 million).

Innovex Inc.

continued from page 244 Thailand, facility. In **March** Innovex moved to its new world headquarters in Maple Plain, Minn. The state-of-the-art, 80,000-square-foot facility was specifically designed for manufacturing advanced flexible circuit materials used for high-density interconnect applications. In addition, the facility was to house Innovex's corporate offices and research and development laboratory, along with the development and prototype production of Innovex's flexible suspension assembly (FSA). In **April** analysts were saying that the transfer of manufacturing facilities from Mexico to Thailand was likely to keep earnings flat for the current quarter, as the uncertainty was keeping some clients away. In **June** Innovex said that the results for its third fiscal 2000 quarter were going to be better than previously anticipated—a net loss per share of $0.02 or less, compared to a street consensus of a net loss of $0.08 per share. "The Innovex team is executing well on the transfer of our Mexico operations to Thailand and we have been able to reduce redundant operating costs faster than originally expected," commented CEO Murnane. "In addition, we continue to rationalize our product line and eliminate non-profitable products. Since the ADFlex acquisition nine months ago, we have substantially reduced our breakeven point so that we can now leverage the revenue growth that is expected later this year into considerable earnings growth." In **July** Innovex announced the qualification and shipment of preproduction volumes of its Flexible Suspension Assembly (FSA) to Seagate Technology Inc. (NYSE: SEG), the world's leading disk drive supplier. The FSA preproduction units were slated for multiple Seagate drive programs. In **September** Innovex introduced its Flex Gimbal Suspension Assembly (FgSA) product line, which provides significant improvement in suspension performance for disk drives. This innovative product eliminated the suspension assembly stainless steel gimbal component that had been used almost exclusively since the early days of disk drive technology. The conventional stainless steel gimbal was replaced by a proprietary flexible circuit gimbal with superior performance. (To date, however, there had been no independent validation of this next-generation technology.) Innovex licensed its proprietary Flex Suspension Assembly (FSA) attachment technology to Magnecomp and Optimal Technology Ltd., Hong Kong, a joint venture of Magnecomp and SAE Magnetics (HK) Ltd., a wholly owned subsidiary of TDK Corp. of Japan. **Sept. 30:** Excluding a charge related to the restructuring of its manufacturing network in November 1999, the company's fiscal-year loss would have been $1.4 million/($0.09). The company attributed its fourth-quarter earnings improvement to cost reductions resulting from the closing of its factory in Agua Prieta, Mexico, and lower operating costs related to a more mature product mix. During the quarter, the company successfully transferred its finishing operations from Mexico to Lamphun, Thailand.

Insignia Systems Inc.

continued from page 245 Inc., which operates 1,467 supermarkets in the United States, principally under the Safeway, Vons, Randalls, Dominick's, and Carrs banners. In **November** Insignia POPS rolled out in 181 Alpha 1 Marketing-serviced supermarkets operating under the C-Town, Bravo, and AIM trading names; and in 139 Met Foodmarkets and Pioneer Food Stores—mostly in New York, with a few located in New Jersey and Pennsylvania—part of New Jersey-based White Rose Food.

iNTELEFILM Corporation

continued from page 246 company in Corporate Report magazine's April issue. Delivering on its strategy to provide content for winning companies in the online, TV, and feature film worlds, several of the company's subsidiaries created original content for Oxygen Media, Cartoon Network, and AtomFilms. Adding to its roster of award-winning animated television shows, iNTELEFILM subsidiary Curious Pictures created an animated series entitled "Avenue Amy" for Oxygen Media's new cable television network. The animated series is also streamed online at www.oxygen.com. Continuing its long-time relationship with the Cartoon Network, Curious Pictures created a new animated series, "Sheep in the Big City." In **May** the company formed DCODE, a creative service company. DCODE, which combines the creativity of advertising minds with the technical proficiency of production companies, provides a fresh approach to the traditional advertising services provided by many advertising agencies. In **June** iNTELEFILM completed its previously authorized stock repurchase program. Subsidiary WebADTV.com Inc. agreed to acquire Cosmic Inventions, creators of Spot Rocket and Digiexpress products which was consummated on September 1, 2000. In **August** webADTV announced an agreement with Excalibur Technologies Corp. (Nasdaq: EXCA) to receive a three-year, paid up license for the Excalibur Screening Room and Excalibur RetrievalWare products in exchange for cash and stock in webADTV. Under an exclusive licensing agreement with CDXC Corp., a leading digital asset management company, webADTV agreed to market the CDXC Solution, an Internet-based digital asset management service, to the top 100 U.S. advertising agencies. WebADTV.com made Jim Bergeson, CEO of of Colle and McVoy, a member of its board of advisors. In **September** webADTV.com Inc. announced that iNTELESource.org, the premiere digital video archiving and retrieval service designed specifically for global advertising agencies, had entered into an agreement with Colle & McVoy Inc., Bloomington, Minn., one of the top 100 advertising agencies in the world. In **October** the company announced the rollout of Virtual Movie Studio, a kid-sized studio complete with a color video camera that can be linked to a TV or VCR, movie sets, and plastic actors ($200 retail).

International Multifoods Corporation

continued from page 247 processing handled at a plant in Scarborough, Ontario, was to be gradually shifted to Dunnville, which was undergoing a 65,000-square-foot expansion. "Americans are eating out or taking out more and more every year," said CEO Costley at the **June** annual meeting. "In fact, within a few years, more money will be spent on food prepared away from home than home-cooked food. With our strategic focus on businesses that manufacture for and distribute to the foodservice industry, we're well positioned to grow along with that trend. What's more, a tight labor market is forcing foodservice providers to look to companies like us for creative ways to save labor during food preparation." Multifoods agreed to move its headquarters for the second time in three years when TCF National Bank offered $12 million to buy the Wayzata lakefront building that Multifoods had acquired for $5.8 million. **Aug. 26:** Second-quarter operating earnings, excluding unusual items, were $11.7 million, up 7 percent from $10.9 million in the year-earlier quarter, and the company generated a $2 million improvement in Economic Value Added. "We had a record second quarter in North America Foods, driven by continued improvement in our business mix and better asset utilization," said CEO Costley. "In our distribution business, we benefited in last year's second quarter from inflation in cheese prices, which resulted in a $1.5 million unfavorable year-over-year comparison. Profitability this year also was affected by regional pricing pressures. These factors masked the headway we are making in reducing costs and improving productivity." In **September** the board of directors approved a share rights plan to replace an existing plan adopted in 1990 and expiring Oct. 4, 2000.

IntraNet Solutions Inc.

continued from page 248 ored by KMWorld Magazine, a leading computer trade magazine for buyers of enterprise knowledge management and business intelligence products, for providing one of the most outstanding products of 1999, the Xpedio Content Management System. In **February** the company introduced Xpedio WAM for securely managing Web site assets. In **March** IntraNet priced an offering of 4,300,000 shares of IntraNet Solutions' common stock—2,305,000 shares by the company and 1,995,000 shares by selling shareholders—at $46 a share. (The majority of the selling shareholders represented shares related to the acquisition of InfoAccess Inc. in September 1999.) The company planned to use the net proceeds of the offering for working capital and general corporate purposes. Meanwhile, Merrill Lynch (NYSE: MER) was planning to use Xpedio on its B2B e-commerce site for institutional clients. The Lambeth Council Website (www.lambeth.gov.uk), powered by Xpedio Content Management System, won Revolution Magazine's "Best User of New Media in Customer Service" award. In **April** the Xpedio Content Management System was upgraded to support HDML (Handheld Device Markup Language), WAP, and WML (Wireless Markup Language) standards—in addition to XML, HTML, and PDF standards, allowing native content from desktops to be automatically converted and formatted for wireless handheld devices such as palm computers, cellular phones, and pagers. CEO Olson was named a finalist in the 2000 Entrepreneur of the Year Awards by Ernst & Young. The underwriters of IntraNet's public offering exercised their option to acquire an additional 520,000 shares at a price of $46.00 per share—giving the company a current cash position in excess of $150 million. The comapny made a number of worldwide sales management appointments and nearly doubled its direct sales force from last quarter—to 33 direct representatives. In **May** the Redmond Police Department in Redmond, Wash. (home to some of the country's major high-tech firms, such as Microsoft and Nintendo of America), chose the Xpedio Content Publisher for rapid Web publishing and access to critical information. As an add-on to Xpedio Content Management System, newly released Xpedio Merge features a component-based publishing module for assembling complex publications from a variety of managed source content. CEO Olson was selected as a finalist for the Ernst and Young 2000 Entrepreneur of the Year Award, which recognizes outstanding business leadership for eBusiness and eProducts in Minnesota and the Dakotas. In **June** pericom, a U.K. software and IT services company, was granted exclusive European rights to resell the departmental project version of Intra.doc! IntraNet confirmed that it was engaged in discussions and negotiations concerning a potential acquisition of the Information Exchange Division (IED) of Inso Corp. (Nasdaq: INSO). Inso's IED develops dynamic Web content publishing and conversion technology for XML, WML, and HTML, as well as wireless and mobile device viewing applications. In July the company announced the availability of Xpedio Report Parser, a new product that enables the secure Web delivery of business-critical information; and the acquisition of Inso's Information Exchange Division (IED). IED's products and technologies were to be integrated with IntraNet's Xpedio Web Content Management product line, strengthening its position as the leading content management solution for business-to-business and business-to-employee Web sites. Chicago-based IED has 350 OEM customers, including Compaq Computer Corp., Novel,l and SUN Microsystems; and 450 corporate customers, including Hewlett-Packard, Agilent Technologies, Merrill Lynch, KPMG, and Shell Oil. In **July** the company announced a strategic acquisition of InfoAgent Solutions BV, an authorized integrator of IntraNet's software products for Continental Europe. At month's end, IntraNet moved its corporate headquarters in Eden Prairie to 7777 Golden Triangle Drive from 8091 Wallace Road to accommodate rapid growth and expansion. (Since November 1999, the company's total headcount had tripled from 85 to more than 275 employees, and the number of employees in the Eden Prairie office had doubled to more than 100.) The new headquarters facility has more than 30,000 square feet. It features a state-of-the-art multimedia room for customer visits and presentations, a large training facility, a back-up power supply, and extensive video, audio, and data connectivity to the remote field offices. The facility also features a new data center (four times larger than the data center at the previous site) designed for 24-hour reliability and security for both IntraNet Solutions' and customer applications. Employee perks include an exercise/recreation room and an outdoor picnic area with barbecue pits. In August IntraNet announced its support of the Scalable Vector Graphics Specification (SVG) released as a candidate recommendation by the World Wide Web Consortium (W3C). In **August** the company announced an agreement with Yahoo! Inc. (Nasdaq: YHOO) to provide the millions of users of Yahoo!Mail (http://mail.yahoo.com) with a new e-mail file attachment viewing feature. Through IntraNet Solutions' Outside In Server integration, Yahoo! Mail now delivers comprehensive Web-based attachment viewing. A strategic marketing and integration partnership with Netegrit Inc. (Nasdaq: NETE), the leading provider of e-commerce infrastructure solutions for secure portal management, provided for Xpedio Content Management System to integrate with Netegrity's SiteMinder secure portal management solution to provide a secure Web content management solution for net marketplaces and B2B or B2E portals. The company released Xpedio 4.0, a new version of the Xpedio Content Management system with enhanced security and business personalization features. IntraNet Solutions announced the integration of its Outside In viewing technology with Compaq's iPAQ Home Internet Appliance, allowing iPAQ customers to view native files on Web sites or e-mail attachments on their iPAQ Web terminal without running the native application. IKON Office Solutions (NYSE: IKN), a leading provider of products and services that help businesses communicate, formed a strategic relationship with IntraNet. Through the deal, which has multimillion-dollar potential, IntraNet Solutions agreed to license its Web-based content management products, including its Intra.doc! software products, to IKON as the core architecture for IKON's Digital Express 2000, a document repository system with hosted document and customized order management capabilities. In **September** IntraNet announced an expanded relationship with Hewlett-Packard Co., a leading provider of computing and imaging solutions and services, to include its Quick View Plus viewing application on the new HP Jornada 720 Handheld PC. Customer Driven Machining, a precision component and assembly manufacturing company, selected Xpedio to power its Web-based manufacturing operations. The company joined OASIS (Organization for Structured Information Standards), the world's largest Extensible Markup Language (XML) interoperability consortium. Scott County, one of the fastest-growing counties in Minnesota, selected Xpedio as the core system behind its e-government technology initiative. IntraNet announced the availability of Outside In Version 6.1. (The Outside In family of developer technologies leads the industry in viewing, conversion, and access of unstructured business content by all types of clients and applications, including wireless.) **Sept. 30**: License revenue represented 82 percent and service revenue 18 percent of the $15.6 million in revenue for second quarter. Pro forma net income, before the effect of acquisition-related expenses, was $3.4 million. Olson said, "We significantly exceeded consensus analyst estimates in terms of revenue, net income, and earnings per share, and had a number of key wins and vendor displacements due to the continued broad acceptance of our Web content management products in the business-to-business and business-to-employee markets." In **October** the company formed a strategic relationship with Synetics, a leading systems integrator of content management, knowledge management, and systems engineering Web-based solutions, to bring Web content management to the government sector. The company formed a strategic relationship with RESoft Inc., a leading Web-based document management company serving the commercial real estate industry, to integrate Xpedio Content Management system into RESoft's new document management suite of products, REDocs. REDocs enables real estate owners and operators to easily manage property and portfolio information in a secure Web-based environment. The company expanded its base of systems integrators by partnering with Lighthouse Solutions, a leading integrator of multilingual, XML-based content management solutions, and Fortuna Technologies, a leading e-business consulting and services company. A **November** agreement with Wireless Ronin Technologies (WRT), a leading provider of tools enabling Internet access through wireless devices, allowed WRT to include IntraNet's Quick View Plus (QVP) viewing technology on the new freedomPORT advanced wireless portal device, allowing its users to view more than 70 file formats created in standard business applications on their handheld devices without having access to the native application. Quick View Plus viewing technology was released for the Symbian software platform for next-generation mobile phones.

K-tel International Inc.

continued from page 250 appealed the staff's decision and, simultaneously, applied to list its common stock on The Nasdaq SmallCap Market. K-tel stock fell 75 cents to $1.06 on the news. CEO Kives offered to support the company's cash and equity position by converting into equity $1.945 million of indebtedness of K-tel to K-5 Leisure Products, whose principal owner is Kives. Offering further support of the company, Kives was leaving in place an $8 million subordinated line of credit by K-5 Leisure Products that was the source of the above indebtedness. "It is my personal belief that our company is undervalued. We are currently developing opportunities to further leverage our growing music library through both traditional and new media formats and channels," stated Kives. K-tel became an Amazon.com Associate to outsource K-tel's consumer order and fulfillment services on its www.ktel.com site. In **September**, in a move to further leverage its content library and wholesale distribution channels, K-tel launched a DVD product line. It had acquired the rights to more than 125 DVD releases, 100 of which represented music titles that fit K-tel's traditional market niche. As a result of K-tel's failure to meet Nasdaq's continued listing requirements, its stock was delisted from the Nasdaq National Market on Sept. 27. In **October** K-tel announced that its music publishing and recorded music catalogs were going to be represented by Spirit Music Group, a leading music publisher. Spirit Music is a market leader in the licensing of music into feature films, network television programs, and national advertisement campaigns.

LaCrosse Footwear Inc.

1319 Saint Andrew St., La Crosse, WI 54603
Tel: 608/782-3020 Fax: 608/782-3025 Web site: http://www.lacrosse-outdoors.com

LaCrosse Footwear Inc. designs, develops, markets, and manufactures protective footwear and rainwear for the sporting/outdoor, farm/general utility, occupational, and children's markets. The company markets its products through an employee sales force, selected distributors, and independent representatives. In March 1994 the company acquired Danner Shoe Manufacturing Co., a producer of premium-quality leather footwear for the sporting/outdoor and occupational markets. The company offers 250 styles of footwear under the LaCrosse and Danner brand names. In May 1996 the company acquired the assets of Red Ball Inc., including the trade name. Besides its La Crosse plant, the company has manufacturing operations in Hillsboro, Racine, and Clintonville, Wis.; Claremont, N.H.; and Portland, Ore.

EARNINGS HISTORY

Year Ended Dec 31	Operating Revenue/Sales (dollars in thousands)	Net Earnings	Return on Revenue (percent)	Return on Equity	Net Earnings (dollars per share)	Cash Dividend	Market Price Range
1999	124,328	(2,637)	(2.1)	(4.7)	(0.41)	0.13	9.50–4.25
1998	133,405	2,260	1.7	3.6	0.34	0.13	14.13–7.75
1997 *	145,503	6,779	4.7	11.0	1.02	0.13	17.25–10.75
1996	121,997	5,386	4.4	9.6	0.80	0.11	12.25–8.75
1995	98,571	3,328	3.4	6.3	0.48	0.09	12.00–8.00

* Results for 1997 include Pro-Trak Corp. from its July 1997 date of acquisition. Pro forma had it been acquired Jan. 1: revenue $149,282,000; earnings $6,918,000/$1.03.

BALANCE SHEET

Assets	12/31/99 (dollars in thousands)	12/31/98	Liabilities	12/31/99 (dollars in thousands)	12/31/98
Current (CAE 2,022 and 364)	68,529	67,502	Current (STD 15,800 and 12,169)	27,737	22,701
Property and equipment	12,811	14,002	L-t obligations	10,702	9,827
			Comp, benefits	3,193	3,052
Goodwill	13,446	14,125	Stockholders' equity*	56,388	63,035
Deferred taxes and other	3,234	2,986	TOTAL	98,020	98,615
TOTAL	98,020	98,615			

* $0.01 par common; 50,000,000 authorized; 6,717,627 and 6,717,627 issued and outstanding, less 343,178 and 73,200 treasury shares.

RECENT QUARTERS / PRIOR-YEAR RESULTS

	Quarter End	Revenue ($000)	Earnings ($000)	EPS ($)	Prior-Year Revenue ($000)	Prior-Year Earnings ($000)	Prior-Year EPS ($)
Q3	09/30/2000	37,239	(837)	(0.14)	37,024	813	0.13
Q2	07/01/2000	31,385	(461)	(0.08)	26,788	(320)	(0.05)
Q1	04/01/2000	31,030	(323)	(0.05)	27,946	(150)	(0.02)
Q4	12/31/99	32,570	(2,980)	(0.47)	36,502	738	0.11
	SUM	132,224	(4,601)	(0.74)	128,260	1,081	0.17

CURRENT: Q4 earnings include pretax charge of $1.844 million for restructuring.

RECENT EVENTS

Dec. 31, 1999: The warm temperatures and drought conditions that prevailed across most of the country negatively affected sales for the quarter. According to CEO Gantert, "The soft consumer demand for protective footwear during the past three years has resulted in the strategic decision to refocus our attention and resources on building our core LaCrosse and Danner footwear brands. Accordingly, we have decided to discontinue our Lake of the Woods product line and significantly reduce our Red Ball line." In **May 2000** LaCrosse Footwear introduced Leathernecks, its newest line of all-leather work boots. This natural extension into leather footwear was a demonstration of the company's customer-driven business strategy and a signal of its intentions for growth. **Sept. 30**: The nine-month net loss ($1.62 million) prompted the company to notify employees at its La Crosse, Wis., manufacturing facility that it would be reducing manufacturing employment by 200 employees before the end of the year in a move driven by the need to substantially reduce product costs in order to remain competitive.

OFFICERS

George W. Schneider
Chairman

Richard A. Rosenthal
Vice Chairman

Mark E. Leopold
EVP and COO

Joseph P. Schneider
EVP, interim Pres./CEO-Danner

David F. Flaschberger
VP-Human Resources

Robert J. Sullivan
VP-Finance/Administration and CFO

DIRECTORS

Patrick K. Gantert

Craig L. Leipold
Rainfair Inc.

Richard A. Rosenthal
University of Notre Dame (retired)

George W. Schneider

Joseph P. Schneider

Luke E. Sims
Foley & Lardner, Milwaukee

Frank J. Uhler Jr.

John Whitcombe
Burkley, Greenburg, Fields & Whitcombe

MAJOR SHAREHOLDERS

Schneider Family Voting Trust, 52.5%
La Crosse, WI

George W. and Virginia F. Schneider, 23.4%
La Crosse, WI

Firstar Corp., 10.5%
Milwaukee

Shufro, Rose & Co. LLC, 5.6%
New York

All officers and directors as a group (11 persons), 32%

SIC CODE

3021 Rubber and plastics footwear

3143 Men's footwear, except athletic

3144 Women's footwear, except athletic

3149 Footwear, except rubber, nec

MISCELLANEOUS

TRANSFER AGENT AND REGISTAR:
Firstar Trust Co., Milwaukee

TRADED: Nasdaq National Market

SYMBOL: BOOT

STOCKHOLDERS: 300

EMPLOYEES: 950

PART TIME: 10

GENERAL COUNSEL:
Foley & Lardner, Milwaukee

AUDITORS:
RSM McGladrey & Pullen Inc. LLP, La Crosse, WI

INC: WI-1982

FOUNDED: 1897

ANNUAL MEETING: May

HUMAN RESOURCES:
David Flaschberger

INVESTOR RELATIONS:
Robert J. Sullivan

SUBSIDIARIES, DIVISIONS, AFFILIATES

Danner Shoe Manufacturing Co.
Portland, Ore.

PUB

TWO-YEAR QUARTERLY HIGH-LOW STOCK PRICES

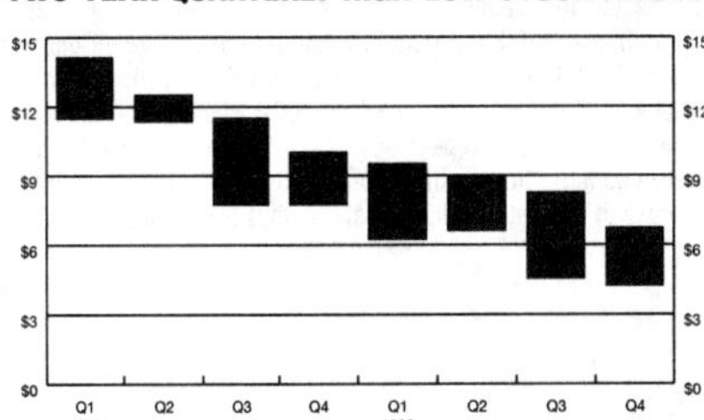

Lakehead Pipe Line Partners L.P.

Lake Superior Place, 21 W. Superior St., Duluth, MN 55802
Tel: 403/231-5949 Fax: 403/231-5989 Web site: http://www.lakehead.com

Lakehead Pipe Line Partners L.P., a publicly held master limited partnership, owns the U.S. portion of the world's longest liquid petroleum pipeline. The pipeline, spanning 3,200 miles of North America, has been in operation since 1950. The partnership was formed in December 1991, when it acquired the U.S. pipeline business of Lakehead Pipe Line Co. Inc. The Canadian portion of the pipeline system continues to be owned and operated by Lakehead's parent, Interprovincial Pipe Line Inc. of Edmonton, Alberta, a business unit of IPL Energy Inc., Calgary, Alberta. Lakehead Pipe Line Co. Inc., the general partner for the partnership, holds 16 percent interest in the partnership. The remaining 84 percent is owned by 35,000 registered or beneficial owners.

PUB

EARNINGS HISTORY

Year Ended Dec 31	Operating Revenue/Sales (dollars in thousands)	Net Earnings (dollars in thousands)	Return on Revenue (percent)	Return on Equity (percent)	Net Earnings (dollars per share*)	Cash Dividend (dollars per share*)	Market Price Range (dollars per share*)
1999	312,600	78,700	25.2	12.0	2.48	3.49	48.75–32.25
1998	287,700	88,500	30.8	16.4	3.07	3.36	54.00–43.00
1997	282,100	78,300	27.8	14.8	3.02	2.92	47.88–33.00
1996 †	274,500	52,400	19.1	12.8	2.11	2.60	34.88–21.63
1995 ¶	268,500	39,600	14.7	9.4	1.60	2.56	30.63–22.00

* The general partner's allocation of net income has been deducted before calculating net income per unit.
† Income figures for 1996 include $20.1 million pretax provision for prior years' rate refunds.
¶ Income figures for 1995 include $22.9 million pretax provision for prior years' rate refunds.

BALANCE SHEET

Assets	12/31/99 (dollars in thousands)	12/31/98 (dollars in thousands)	Liabilities	12/31/99 (dollars in thousands)	12/31/98 (dollars in thousands)
Current (CAE 40,000 and 47,000)	86,400	111,300	Current	39,500	102,300
			Long-term debt	784,500	814,500
Property, plant, and equipment	1,321,300	1,296,200	Minority interest	3,600	2,600
			Partners' capital*	586,100	495,000
Deferred charges and other	6,000	6,900	TOTAL	1,413,700	1,414,400
TOTAL	1,413,700	1,414,400			

* No par common; 28,902,750 authorized; 28,902,750 and 26,202,750 issued and outstanding.

RECENT QUARTERS / PRIOR-YEAR RESULTS

	Quarter End	Revenue ($000)	Earnings ($000)	EPS ($)	Prior-Year Revenue ($000)	Prior-Year Earnings ($000)	Prior-Year EPS ($)
Q3	09/30/2000	74,900	14,200	0.42	79,600	19,800	0.60
Q2	06/30/2000	78,300	16,500	0.49	80,400	22,500	0.71
Q1	03/31/2000	78,800	20,100	0.62	74,000	21,700	0.75
Q4	12/31/99	78,600	14,700	0.43	70,200	18,800	0.64
	SUM	310,600	65,500	1.96	304,200	82,800	2.71

RECENT EVENTS

In **February 2000** Lakehead Pipe Line Partners, Minnesota Power Inc. (NYSE: MPL), and Enbridge Pipelines Inc. (Nasdaq: ENBRF) signed an agreement under which the pipeline companies could reduce electricity use during periods of high electric prices or demand, releasing energy to be marketed to other power buyers. The agreement was to run from Jan. 1, 2000, through Dec. 31, 2001. **Sept. 30**: Nine-month net income of $50.8 million or $1.53 per unit, compared to $64.0 million, or $2.06 per unit for the same period in 1999. Cash provided from operating activities increased 13 percent to $98.1 million, providing adequate cash flow coverage of the current cash distribution to unit holders. Year-to-date deliveries on the Lakehead System averaged 1.331 million barrels per day, compared to 1.371 million barrels per day for the same period in 1999. Volumes transported in the third quarter were lower than anticipated, primarily because supply from a producer's oil sands plant was reduced by an unexpected maintenance turnaround and because poor weather conditions throughout the spring and summer impaired oil exploration and development in western Canada. The partnership was expecting annual 2000 net income of approximately $65 million. In **October** Lakehead welcomed the announcement by its affiliate Enbridge Inc. that the second phase of the Terrace Expansion Program will proceed in 2001. Phase II includes construction of facilities to increase capacity on the Canadian portion of the integrated pipeline system that links western Canada with U.S. and eastern Canadian markets. While Phase II did not involve construction on the Lakehead System, the partnership was expecting to benefit directly from the 40,000-barrel-per-day increase in capacity as additional volumes from the Alberta Oil Sands come on stream.

OFFICERS

Steven J. Wuori
Pres. of General Partner
Jody L. Balko
Chief Accountant
Lawrence H. DeBriyn
VP of General Partner
Susan D. Lenczewski
Corporate Secretary of General Partner
Michael J. Miller
Asst. Chief Accountant of General Ptnr.
J.K. Whelen
Treasurer
S. Mark Curwin
Asst. Secretary of General Partner

DIRECTORS

Patrick D. Daniel
Lawrence H. DeBriyn
F. William Fitzpatrick
Ernest C. Hambrook
Hambrook Resources Inc., Columbine Valley, CO
Charles A. Russell
Derek P. Truswell
Steven J. Wuori

SIC CODE

4612 Crude petroleum pipe lines

MISCELLANEOUS

TRANSFER AGENT AND REGISTAR:
Chase Mellon Shareholder Services LLC, Ridgefield Park, NJ
TRADED: NYSE
SYMBOL: LHP
STOCKHOLDERS: 2,900
EMPLOYEES: 370
GENERAL COUNSEL:
Fredrikson & Byron P.A., Minneapolis
Andrews & Kurth, Houston
AUDITORS:
PricewaterhouseCoopers LLP, Minneapolis
INC: DE-1991
FOUNDED: 1949
HUMAN RESOURCES:
Don Hoag
INVESTOR RELATIONS:
Tracy Barker

RANKINGS

No. 60 CRM Public 200

SUBSIDIARIES, DIVISIONS, AFFILIATES

Lakehead Pipe Line Co. Inc.
Lake Superior Place
21 W. Superior St.
Duluth, MN 55802

TWO-YEAR QUARTERLY HIGH-LOW STOCK PRICES

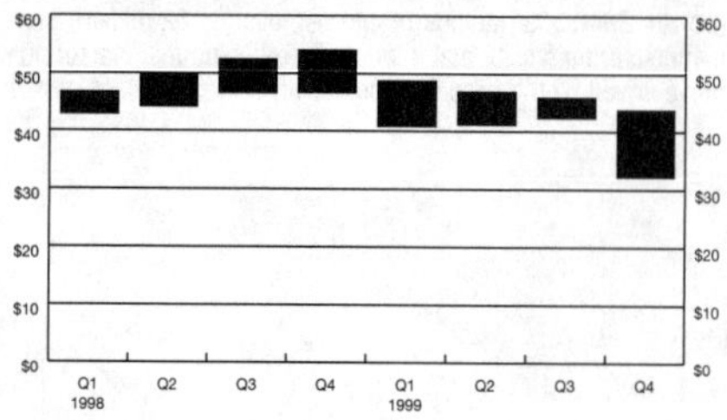

Lakes Gaming Inc.

130 Cheshire Ln., Minnetonka, MN 55305
Tel: 952/449-9092 Fax: 952/449-9353 Web site: http://www.lakesgaming.com

Lakes operates in the Indian casino management business, deriving revenue almost exclusively from management fees. Lakes manages one land-based, Indian-owned casino in Louisiana: Grand Casino Coushatta, in Kinder, La., owned by the Coushatta Tribe of Louisiana, and has entered into development management agreements with three separate tribes for three new casino operations. Lakes' strategy is to develop and manage Indian-owned casino properties that offer the opportunity for long-term development of related entertainment amenities—including hotels, theaters, recreational vehicle parks, and other complementary amenities designed to enhance the customers' total entertainment experience and to differentiate facilities managed by Lakes from its competitors.

EARNINGS HISTORY

Year Ended Dec	Operating Revenue/Sales (dollars in thousands)	Net Earnings	Return on Revenue (percent)	Return on Equity	Net Earnings (dollars per share*)	Cash Dividend	Market Price Range
1999 †	54,716	28,827	52.7	18.0	2.72	—	13.25–6.84
1998 ¶	92,347	61,180	66.3	46.5	5.80	—	
1997	78,515	45,203	57.6	38.1	4.32	—	
1996 #	77,273	(108,737)	NM	NM	(10.46)	—	

* Stock did not begin trading until Jan. 4, 1999.
† Income figures for 1999 include $1.264 million pretax gain on sale of securities.
¶ Revenue figures for 1998 include $36.8 million from management contracts for Grand Casino Mille Lacs and Grand Casino Hinckley that concluded during the year and will not contribute to results going forward. Income figures include $4.473 million pretax loss on sale of securities.
# Income figures for 1996 include pretax $160.9 million Stratosphere write-down.

BALANCE SHEET

Assets	01/02/00 (dollars in thousands)	01/03/99
Current (CAE 24,392 and 56,774)	80,224	88,678
Property and equipment	1,888	1,265
Land held for development	54,812	26,647
Notes receivable	20,022	25,118
Restricted cash	12,149	4,992
Unconsolidated affiliates	8,446	8,590
Other	5,997	6,079
TOTAL	183,538	161,369

Liabilities	01/02/00 (dollars in thousands)	01/03/99
Current	21,391	25,990
Long-term debt	1,500	975
Deferred income taxes	786	2,733
Stockholders' equity*	159,861	131,671
TOTAL	183,538	161,369

* $0.01 par common; 100,000,000 authorized; 10,629,000 and 10,576,000 issued and outstanding.

RECENT QUARTERS / PRIOR-YEAR RESULTS

	Quarter End	Revenue ($000)	Earnings ($000)	EPS ($)	Prior-Year Revenue ($000)	Prior-Year Earnings ($000)	Prior-Year EPS ($)
Q3	10/01/2000	10,684	4,976	0.47	14,440	7,440	0.70
Q2	07/02/2000	10,655	(5,311)	(0.50)	14,892	8,622	0.81
Q1	04/02/2000	31,053	16,115	1.52	15,109	8,562	0.81
Q4	01/02/2000	10,275	4,203	0.40	28,017	11,875	1.12
	SUM	62,667	19,983	1.88	72,458	36,499	3.45

CURRENT: Q2 earnings include pretax charge of $18 million, provision for litigation loss.

RECENT EVENTS

In **February 2000** Lakes Gaming and the Coushatta Tribe of Louisiana agreed to a new five-year management contract for the Tribe's Grand Casino Coushatta operation. The new contract was to become effective in January 2002, when the current contract term expires, and continue until January 2007. "Grand Casino Coushatta has exceeded both our and the Tribe's expectations since the day it opened in January 1995," stated Berman. "Although the calculation of Lakes' management fee is significantly less under the new agreement, we feel the new formula is fair to both parties." In **March** voters in California overwhelmingly approved a state constitutional amendment permitting California tribes to operate Nevada-style casinos on Indian lands. (Lakes, in partnership with Kean Argovitz Resorts, had agreements in place for the development and management of casino resort operations with the Jamul Indian Village near San Diego and with the Shingle Springs Band of Miwok Indians near Sacramento.) The company reached an agreement with the Tunica-Biloxi Tribe of Louisiana for the early buyout of the management contract for Grand Casino Avoyelles. The $23 million buyout left Lakes with only one casino resort under management. With the three casino properties under development on behalf of Indian tribes not likely to produce any revenue until the first quarter of 2002, the company was heading for a potential cash flow crunch. In **May** the board adopted a Shareholder Rights Plan designed to ensure the fair *continued on page 284*

OFFICERS

Lyle Berman
Chairman and CEO

Timothy J. Cope
EVP, CFO, and Secretary

Joseph Galvin
Chief Administrative Officer

DIRECTORS

Lyle Berman

Timothy J. Cope

Morris Goldfarb
G-III Apparel Group Ltd., New York

Ronald Kramer
Dresdner, Kleinwort, Wasserstein, New York

Neil I. Sell
Maslon Edelman Borman & Brand PLLP, Minneapolis

Joel N. Waller
Wilsons The Leather Experts, Brooklyn Park, MN

MAJOR SHAREHOLDERS

Lyle Berman, 13.5%

FMR Corp., 10%
Boston

Trust for Lyle Berman's children, 7.5%

Highfields Associates LLC, 5.4%
Boston

Dimensional Fund Advisors Inc., 5.1%
Santa Monica, CA

All officers and directors as a group (6 persons), 17.8%

SIC CODE

7011 Hotels and motels

7993 Coin-operated amusement devices

7999 Amusement and recreation, nec

MISCELLANEOUS

TRANSFER AGENT AND REGISTAR:
Wells Fargo Bank Minnesota N.A.,
South St. Paul, MN

TRADED: Nasdaq National Market

SYMBOL: LACO

STOCKHOLDERS: 10,630,453

EMPLOYEES: 25

GENERAL COUNSEL:
Maslon Edelman Borman & Brand PLLP, Minneapolis

AUDITORS:
Arthur Andersen LLP, Minneapolis

INC: MN-1998

ANNUAL MEETING: August

INVESTOR RELATIONS: Timothy J. Cope

RANKINGS

No. 110 CRM Public 200

No. 45 CRM Performance 100

PUB

PUB

Lectec Corporation

10701 Red Circle Dr., Minnetonka, MN 55343
Tel: 952/933-2291 Fax: 952/933-4808 Web site: http://www.therapatch.com

Lectec is a health and consumer products company that develops, manufactures and markets products based on its advanced skin-interface technologies. Primary products include over-the-counter therapeutic patches, diagnostic electrodes, and hydrogens for electrocardiography and related applications.

EARNINGS HISTORY

Year Ended Jun 30	Operating Revenue/Sales (dollars in thousands)	Net Earnings (dollars in thousands)	Return on Revenue (percent)	Return on Equity (percent)	Net Earnings (dollars per share)	Cash Dividend (dollars per share)	Market Price Range (dollars per share)
2000 *	14,596	(2,859)	(19.6)	(60.6)	(0.74)	—	5.00–1.19
1999	12,279	(1,683)	(13.7)	(22.4)	(0.43)	—	4.75–1.25
1998	12,922	(404)	(3.1)	(4.2)	(0.10)	—	9.75–3.25
1997 †	12,256	(2,267)	(18.5)	(25.8)	(0.59)	—	13.50–4.88
1996	13,101	(632)	(4.8)	(5.8)	(0.17)	—	16.00–8.50

* Income figures for 2000 include pretax expense of $0.645 million for medical tape asset impairment.
† Income figures for 1997 include restructuring charge of $2,180,353.

BALANCE SHEET

Assets	06/30/00 (dollars in thousands)	06/30/99	Liabilities	06/30/00 (dollars in thousands)	06/30/99
Current (CAE 100 and 1,022)	5,236	5,904	Current (STD 23 and 11)	3,724	2,406
Property, plant, and equipment	3,039	4,028	Deferred income taxes		197
Patents and trademarks	199	200	Long-term obligations	31	21
TOTAL	8,475	10,133	Stockholders' equity*	4,720	7,509
			TOTAL	8,475	10,133

* $0.01 par common; 15,000,000 authorized; 3,904,465 and 3,876,476 issued and outstanding.

RECENT QUARTERS / PRIOR-YEAR RESULTS

	Quarter End	Revenue ($000)	Earnings ($000)	EPS ($)	Prior-Year Revenue ($000)	Prior-Year Earnings ($000)	Prior-Year EPS ($)
Q1	09/30/2000	4,189	(598)	(0.15)	3,008	(604)	(0.16)
Q4	06/30/2000	4,353	(816)	(0.21)	3,077	(521)	(0.13)
Q3	03/31/2000	3,935	(643)	(0.17)	3,196	(349)	(0.09)
Q2	12/31/99	3,300	(795)	(0.20)	3,103	(661)	(0.17)
	SUM	15,777	(2,852)	(0.73)	12,384	(2,135)	(0.55)

CURRENT: Q4 earnings include pretax expense of $0.645 million for medical tape asset impairment.

RECENT EVENTS

In **November 1999** the Company established a new $2 million line of credit with Wells Fargo Business Credit Inc. **Dec. 31:** The 5.0 percent increase in net sales for the six-month period reflected a tripling of TheraPatch sales, which more than offset a reduction of 16.1 percent in conductive and medical tape sales. In **April 2000** Lectec announced the signing of a multiyear supply agreement with Neutrogena Corp., a wholly owned subsidiary of Johnson & Johnson (NYSE: JNJ), to manufacture an acne care product utilizing Lectec's proprietary skin interface technologies. The topical patch product was developed by Lectec, and was to be manufactured in Minnetonka. Neutrogena had exclusive rights to distribute the product throughout the world. Products supplied under this agreement were expected to generate more than $1 million in sales annually for Lectec. Initial shipments of product to Neutrogena were made during LecTec's third quarter. **June 30:** Net sales for the fiscal year increased 18.9 percent to $14.596 million. Net sales for the fourth quarter were up 41.5 percent. In the fourth quarter, the company recorded a $730,000 charge related to the plan to divest LecTec's medical tape product line. Due primarily to this charge and to the investment spending in the company's Consumer Products Division, LecTec reported a net loss for the year. CEO Young stated, "In fiscal 2000 we re-invented ourselves, transforming from an R&D technology-based company to an integrated company with true sales and marketing strength with our innovative topical OTC (over-the-counter) drug delivery technology as our strategic platform. In summary, in fiscal year 2000 we exceeded our distribution network goals, launched three new TheraPatch products, and signed a multiyear supply agreement with Johnson & Johnson Consumer Products Co. worldwide, one of the largest consumer products companies in the world." In **July** Lectec began shipping a second product covered under the multiyear supply agreement with Johnson & Johnson Consumer Products Co.—a CLEAN & CLEAR-brand acne care product utilizing LecTec's proprietary skin-interface technologies. In **September** LecTec signed a multiyear supply agreement with Novartis Consumer Health Inc. to manufacture two vapor patch products under the cough/cold brand Triaminic. **Sept. 30:** First-quarter net sales of $4.189 million increased 39.5 percent from prior year. *continued on page 284*

OFFICERS

Rodney A. Young
Chairman, President, and CEO
Tim Fitzgerald
VP-Operations
John D. LeGray
VP-Quality Assurance/ Regulatory Affairs
Daniel M. McWhorter
VP-Research/Development
Doug Nesbit
CFO and Secretary
Jane M. Nichols
VP-Marketing/New Business Development
Tim Quinn
VP-Consumer Products

DIRECTORS

Lee M. Berlin
Lectec Corp. (retired)
Allan C. Hymes, M.D.
Lectec Corp. (founder)
Paul O. Johnson
private investor
Bert J. McKasy
Lindquist & Vennum PLLP, Minneapolis
Marilyn K. Speedie
U. of Minnesota College of Pharmacy, Minneapolis
Donald C. Wegmiller
Management Compensation Group/HealthCare, Minneapolis
Rodney A. Young
Sheldon L. Zimbler
Procter & Gamble (former)

MAJOR SHAREHOLDERS

Lee M. Berlin, 14.4%
Alan C. Hymes, M.D., 10.7%
All officers and directors as a group (12 persons), 36.6%

SIC CODE

3842 Surgical appliances and supplies

MISCELLANEOUS

TRANSFER AGENT AND REGISTAR:
Wells Fargo Bank Minnesota N.A., South St. Paul, MN
TRADED: Nasdaq National Market
SYMBOL: LECT
STOCKHOLDERS: 337
EMPLOYEES: 93
IN MINNESOTA: 90

GENERAL COUNSEL:
Dorsey & Whitney PLLP, Minneapolis
AUDITORS:
Grant Thornton LLP, Minneapolis
INC: MN-1977
ANNUAL MEETING:
November
HUMAN RESOURCES:
Alice Ong

RANKINGS

No. 171 CRM Public 200

SUBSIDIARIES, DIVISIONS, AFFILIATES

Lectec International Corp. (SFSC)
City of Amalie
St. Thomas, U.S. Virgin Islands

TWO-YEAR QUARTERLY HIGH-LOW STOCK PRICES

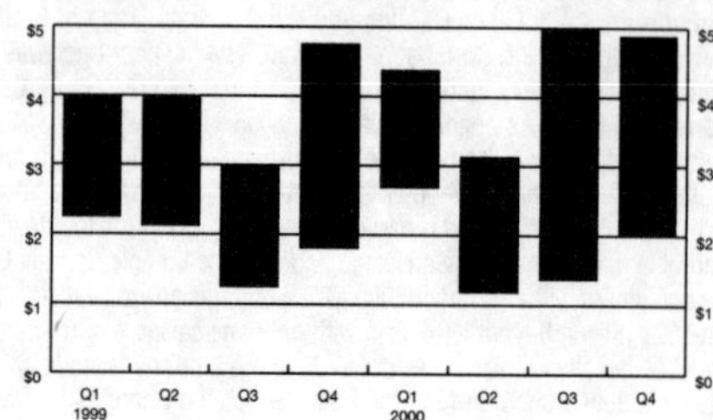

Legal Research Center Inc.

700 Midland Square Building, 331 Second Ave. S., Minneapolis, MN 55401
Tel: 612/332-4950 Fax: 612/332-7454 Web site: http://www.lrci.com

Legal Research Center Inc. (LRC) offers services responding to three major trends in the marketplace: outsourcing, electronic lawyering, and alternative dispute resolution (ADR). LRC's staff of research attorneys and information specialists, operating on a project or contract basis, deliver outsourced legal and nonlegal research and writing services to corporate counsel and attorneys in private practice across North America. The company is developing the Center for Alternative Dispute Resolution Enterprises, a proprietary ADR training program for corporate and legal use.

EARNINGS HISTORY

Year Ended Dec 31	Operating Revenue/Sales (dollars in thousands)	Net Earnings	Return on Revenue (percent)	Return on Equity	Net Earnings (dollars per share*)	Cash Dividend	Market Price Range
1999	4,394	716	16.3	38.0	0.30	—	3.00–0.20
1998	2,403	55	2.3	5.9	0.02	—	0.50–0.19
1997 †	1,779	(2,065)	NM	NM	(0.91)	—	1.88–0.13
1996 ¶	2,736	(1,657)	(60.6)	(58.3)	(0.75)	—	4.38–1.25
1995	1,404	(393)	(28.0)	(9.3)	(0.33)	—	4.25–2.50

* Trading began Aug. 3, 1995.
† Income figures for 1997 include loss of $1,124,525/($0.49) from discontinued operations and their disposal.
¶ Income figures for 1996 include loss of $563,913/($0.25) from discontinued operations.

BALANCE SHEET

Assets	12/31/99 (dollars in thousands)	12/31/98
Current (CAE 1,347 and 436)	1,915	958
Furniture and equipment	21	44
Notes receivable		50
Development costs	129	233
TOTAL	2,066	1,284

Liabilities	12/31/99 (dollars in thousands)	12/31/98
Current	183	146
Notes payable		200
Stockholders' equity*	1,883	938
TOTAL	2,066	1,284

* $0.01 par common; 20,000,000 authorized; 3,602,454 and 3,327,633 issued and outstanding.

RECENT QUARTERS / PRIOR-YEAR RESULTS

	Quarter End	Revenue ($000)	Earnings ($000)	EPS ($)	Prior-Year Revenue ($000)	Prior-Year Earnings ($000)	Prior-Year EPS ($)
Q3	09/30/2000	1,221	196	0.08	1,214	258	0.11
Q2	06/30/2000	13,117	239	0.10	1,108	244	0.10
Q1	03/31/2000	1,222	233	0.10	820	79	0.03
Q4	12/31/99	1,253	135	0.06	824	123	0.05
	SUM	16,813	802	0.34	3,965	704	0.30

RECENT EVENTS

In **May 2000** Heller Financial Inc. (NYSE: HF) selected LRC as its preferred provider of outsourced legal research, writing, and knowledge management services—because of its passion for excellence and its commitment to customer service, technological innovation, and strategic partnering. In **June** a strategic business alliance was struck with Integrity Interactive Corp. (IIC) to offer industry-leading, Web-based legal compliance training. In **July** a "Legal Environment Scan" study was conducted for the National Association of Realtors by Legal Research Center. It was to provide realtors with a wealth of information about the many emerging areas of agent/broker liability in real estate transactions, employment relations, fair housing, and property management. In August the company completed a transaction to acquire an equity stake in partner Integrity Interactive Corp. **Sept. 30:** Third-quarter earnings declined slightly from the same period a year ago because of LRC's investments in its strategic alliance with Integrity Interactive, including capital outlays for additional sales staff, new technology, and marketing. In **October** Legal Research Center prepared the "State-by-State Guide to Employee Leave and Disability," a new book released by Aspen Publishers to help in-house counsel make sure that their organizations comply with federal and state employee leave laws. (Legal definitions of "disability" and "family medical leave" are evolving rapidly, and outdated employment leave practices are exposing organizations to civil and criminal sanctions.)

OFFICERS

Christopher R. Ljungkull
Co-chairman, CEO, and CFO

Arun K. Dube
Co-chairman

James R. Seidl
President

Kevin Campana
COO

DIRECTORS

Bruce Aho
Arun K. Dube
Christopher R. Ljungkull
James R. Seidl

MAJOR SHAREHOLDERS

Christopher R. Ljungkull, 30%

James R. Seidl, 25%

Robin A. Moles, 5.4%

All officers and directors as a group (4 persons), 53.4%

SIC CODE

8732 Commercial nonphysical research

MISCELLANEOUS

TRANSFER AGENT AND REGISTAR:
Wells Fargo Bank Minnesota N.A., South St. Paul, MN

TRADED: Nasdaq SmallCap Market

SYMBOL: LRCI

STOCKHOLDERS: 56

EMPLOYEES: 23

GENERAL COUNSEL:
Parsinen Kaplan Levy Rosberg & Gotlieb P.A., Minneapolis

AUDITORS:
Lurie, Besikof, Lapidus & Co. LLP, Minneapolis

INC: MN-1991

FOUNDED: 1978

ANNUAL MEETING: June

INVESTOR RELATIONS:
Frank G. Hallowell

PUB

TWO-YEAR QUARTERLY HIGH-LOW STOCK PRICES

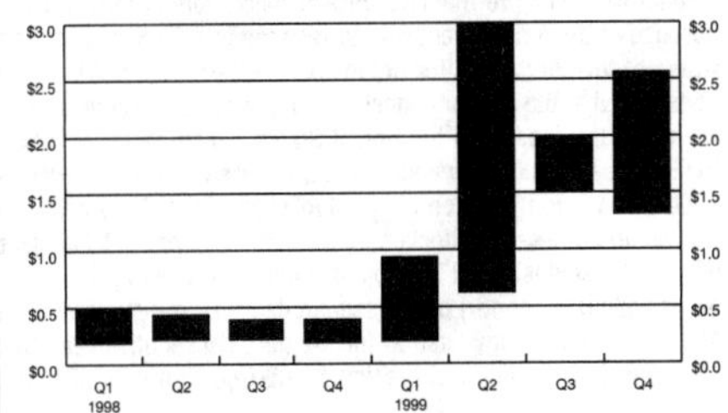

Lifecore Biomedical Inc.

3515 Lyman Blvd., Chaska, MN 55318
Tel: 952/368-4300 Fax: 952/368-3411 Web site: http://www.lifecore.com

Lifecore Biomedical Inc. develops, manufactures, and markets medical and surgical devices for applications in dentistry, drug delivery, general surgery, ophthalmology, veterinary, and wound-care management. The company's products are distributed internationally through direct sales, OEM, and contract manufacturing alliances. Lifecore operates through two business units: Hyaluronate Division and Oral Restorative Division. The company is FDA-compliant, and ISO 9001- and EN 46001-certified.

PUB

EARNINGS HISTORY

Year Ended Jun 30	Operating Revenue/Sales (dollars in thousands)	Net Earnings	Return on Revenue (percent)	Return on Equity	Net Earnings (dollars per share)	Cash Dividend	Market Price Range
2000	32,823	(1,599)	(4.9)	(2.9)	(0.13)	—	23.75–5.63
1999	27,321	1,576	5.8	2.8	0.13	—	17.00–5.75
1998	25,570	233	0.9	0.4	0.02	—	26.25–12.50
1997	18,913	(1,033)	(5.5)	(2.0)	(0.08)	—	22.13–11.50
1996 *	14,063	(4,000)	(28.4)	(7.7)	(0.40)	—	21.25–7.38

* Income figures for 1996 include pretax gain of $754,000 from insurance proceeds.

BALANCE SHEET

Assets	06/30/00 (dollars in thousands)	06/30/99	Liabilities	06/30/00 (dollars in thousands)	06/30/99
Current (CAE 1,101 and 544)	19,420	23,255	Current (STD 243 and 1,458)	3,890	6,606
Property, plant, and equipment	30,352	31,983	Long-term obligations	6,477	6,720
Intangibles	5,286	5,951	Stockholders' equity*	55,421	55,471
Security deposits	847	841	TOTAL	65,788	68,797
Inventories	9,368	6,321			
Other	515	446			
TOTAL	65,788	68,797			

* $0.01 par common; 50,000,000 authorized; 12,606,124 and 12,416,729 issued and outstanding.

RECENT QUARTERS / PRIOR-YEAR RESULTS

	Quarter End	Revenue ($000)	Earnings ($000)	EPS ($)	Prior-Year Revenue ($000)	Prior-Year Earnings ($000)	Prior-Year EPS ($)
Q1	09/30/2000	7,896	(606)	(0.05)	7,140	114	0.01
Q4	06/30/2000	8,951	(1,174)	(0.09)	8,086	1,149	0.09
Q3	03/31/2000	8,205	(927)	(0.07)	6,849	570	0.05
Q2	12/31/99	8,527	388	0.03	6,881	450	0.04
	SUM	33,579	(2,319)	(0.18)	28,956	2,283	0.18

RECENT EVENTS

In **December 1999** the FDA reported that it had scheduled a review of the company's premarket approval (PMA) application for its ferric hyaluronate product, INTERGEL Adhesion Prevention Solution, at a Jan. 12, 2000, meeting of the General and Plastic Surgery Devices Advisory Panel. The company received a $5 million advance from its largest customer, Alcon Laboratories Inc., to be repaid through future ophthalmic sodium hyaluronate shipments to Alcon. In **January 2000** the FDA panel voted not to approve Lifecore's PMA for INTERGEL, on the grounds that test data was unconvincing. After characterizing the advisory panel vote as "a tremendous travesty," CEO Bracke stated, "We are actively discussing follow-up options with the FDA." Lifecore stock fell 57 percent the next day. A week later the company said that it still expected to obtain approval for this product, but that the idling of hyaluronate manufacturing necessitated by the approval delay would result in an estimated 9-cent per-share loss in each of the third and fourth fiscal quarters. In **February** INTERGEL Adhesion Prevention Solution was chosen as a finalist in the Medical Design Excellence Awards (MDEA) 2000 competition sponsored by Medical Device & Diagnostic Industry magazine—one of five surgical product finalists. In **April** Lifecore began direct-marketing of the company's oral restorative products in Germany through a new subsidiary, Lifecore Biomedical GmbH, based in Bonn. (The German dental implant market, estimated at $120 million, is the world's second-largest dental implant market after the United States.) In **June** the company filed an amendment to its pre-market approval application for INTERGEL with the FDA's Center for Devices and Radiological Health. The purpose of the amendment was to respond to a General and Plastic Surgery Devices Advisory Panel Meeting held in January where panel members voted not to approve the product. While the company believed that it had satisfactorily answered all questions raised at the January panel meeting, it could make no assurances that its response would be adequate to obtain approval to market the product in the United States. Lifecore's ferric hyaluronan adhesion prevention product, marketed as GYNECARE INTERGEL Adhesion Prevention Solution, received a Silver Award in the finals of the Medical Design Excellence Awards (MDEA) 2000 competition. The company established a joint venture for its oral restorative business in Scandinavia. Lifecore Biomedical AB was to be based in Stockholm, the birthplace of dental implantology. In **July** a strategic marketing and distribution alliance with the Musculoskeletal Transplant Foundation, Edison, N.J., resulted in Lifecore's Oral Restorative Division representing MTF's human allograft (donor) bone tissue to dental surgery professionals. In **August** the company was named to Deloitte & Touche's Minnesota Technology Fast 50 for the third-consecutive year. **Sept. 30:** Hyaluronan Division revenue increased 21 percent to $3,415,000. Operating income was $1,000, compared to $305,000 for the same period of last year.

continued on page 284

OFFICERS

James W. Bracke, Ph.D.
President and CEO

Dennis J. Allingham
EVP and CFO

Brian J. Kane
VP-Marketing/New Business Development

Colleen M. Olson
VP-Administrative Operations

DIRECTORS

James W. Bracke, Ph.D.

Orwin L. Carter, Ph.D.
business consultant, Stillwater, MN

Joan L. Gardner
community volunteer, White Bear Lake, MN

Thomas H. Garrett III
business consultant, Minneapolis

John C. Heinmiller
St. Jude Medical Inc., Little Canada, MN

Richard W. Perkins
Perkins Capital Management Inc., Wayzata, MN

MAJOR SHAREHOLDERS

Heartland Advisors Inc., 10.6%
Milwaukee

The Vertical Group, 7.9%
Summitt, NJ

Putnam Investments Inc., 6.2%
Boston

Johnson & Johnson, 6%
New Brunswick, NJ

All officers and directors as a group (9 persons), 8.1%

SIC CODE

2833 Medicinals and botanicals

3842 Surgical appliances and supplies

MISCELLANEOUS

TRANSFER AGENT AND REGISTAR:
Wells Fargo Bank Minnesota N.A.,
South St. Paul, MN

TRADED: Nasdaq National Market

SYMBOL: LCBM

STOCKHOLDERS: 675

EMPLOYEES: 180

PART TIME: 5

IN MINNESOTA: 175

GENERAL COUNSEL:
Dorsey & Whitney PLLP, Minneapolis
Vidas, Arrett & Steinkraus, Minnetonka, MN

AUDITORS:
Grant Thornton LLP, Minneapolis

INC: MN-1965

ANNUAL MEETING:
November

ADMINISTRATION:
Colleen Olson

HUMAN RESOURCES:
Julia Jensen

RANKINGS

No. 132 CRM Public 200

No. 46 Minnesota Technology Fast 50

SUBSIDIARIES, DIVISIONS, AFFILIATES

Oral Restorative Division
3515 Lyman Blvd.
Chaska, MN 55318
612/368-4300
Dennis J. Allingham

Hyaluronate Division
3515 Lyman Blvd.
Chaska, MN 55318
612/368-4300
Dennis J. Allingham

Lifecore Biomedical S.p.A.
Verona, Italy

Lifecore Biomedical
Bonn, Germany

TWO-YEAR QUARTERLY HIGH-LOW STOCK PRICES

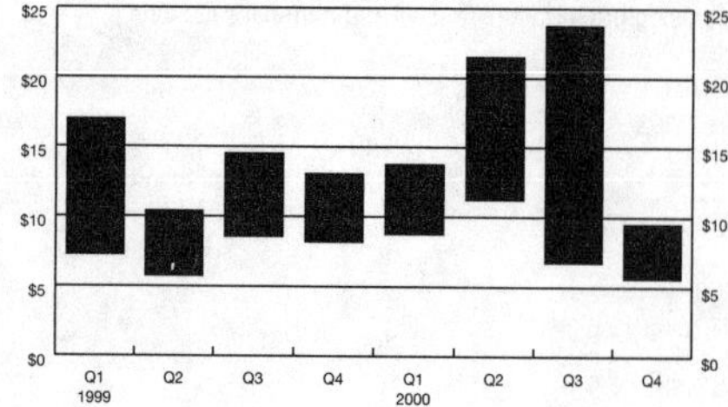

Lightning Rod Software Inc.

5900 Green Oak Dr., Minnetonka, MN 55343
Tel: 952/837-4000 Fax: 952/837-4020 Web site: http://www.lightrodsoft.com

Lightning Rod Software Inc. enables e-businesses to improve customer communications and build customer loyalty. Lightning Rod Interaction Manager allows online prospects and customers to receive fast, accurate assistance from contact center agents via a wide range of communication tools: Web chat and collaboration, Web callback, e-mail, interactive voice response (IVR), phone, and fax. The software offers real-time sales and service capability, integrated queuing, and reporting. Lightning Rod clients include such e-tail sites as www.babystyle.com and www.boo.com, and online trading site www.stockwalk.com. CE Software Holdings Inc. completed the acquisition of Lightning Rod Software Inc. (formerly known as ATIO Corporation USA Inc.) on April 28, 2000, through the merger of Lightning Rod with and into CE Software. For accounting purposes, the merger was treated as a reverse acquisition of CE Software by Lightning Rod.

EARNINGS HISTORY *

Year Ended Dec 31	Operating Revenue/Sales (dollars in thousands)	Net Earnings	Return on Revenue (percent)	Return on Equity	Net Earnings (dollars per share†)	Cash Dividend	Market Price Range
1999	2,095	(4,780)	NM	NM	(0.62)	—	
1998	697	(4,169)	NM	NM	(0.55)	—	

* Historical figures are those of ATIO Corp. USA Inc.
† Stock began trading on May 2, 2000.

BALANCE SHEET

Assets	12/31/99 (dollars in thousands)	12/31/98	Liabilities	12/31/99 (dollars in thousands)	12/31/98
Current (CAE 121 and 0)	408	207	Current	6,703	2,514
Property and equipment	344	452	Redeemable common stock	500	500
TOTAL	752	659	Stockholders' equity*	(6,450)	(2,354)
			TOTAL	752	659

* $0.01 par common; 50,000,000 authorized; 8,700,000 and 7,600,000 issued and outstanding.

RECENT QUARTERS / **PRIOR-YEAR RESULTS**

	Quarter End	Revenue ($000)	Earnings ($000)	EPS ($)	Prior-Year Revenue ($000)	Prior-Year Earnings ($000)	Prior-Year EPS ($)
Q3	09/30/2000	340	(1,958)	(0.60)	490	(1,245)	(0.78)
Q2	06/30/2000	144	(1,740)	—	737	(1,274)	(0.78)
Q1	03/31/2000	155	(1,801)	—	632	(685)	(0.78)
	SUM	639	(5,499)	(0.60)	1,859	(3,204)	(0.78)

RECENT EVENTS

On **May 2, 2000**, the company began trading as a public company as the result of a merger finalized the week before with CE Software Holdings (Nasdaq: CESH). Terms of the merger were approved at the CE Software annual shareholders meeting. As part of the merger agreement, operating subsidiary CE Software Inc., based in West Des Moines, Iowa, was spun off to its shareholders as a separate company. In **July** LROD signed a business alliance agreement giving ATIO Corp. Pty Ltd. the exclusive right to sell, upgrade, and support Lightning Rod Interaction Manager in sub-Saharan Africa, including South Africa. Lightning Rod and Norstan Inc. (Nasdaq: NRRD) partnered to develop and implement a multichannel customer interaction solution to support customer voice interactions for Metamail Inc., developer of the world's first visual messaging system. LROD announced plans to augment its traditional sales model with an Application Service Provider (ASP) rental model. In partnership with Integris, a world-class provider of mission-critical e-infrastructure management services, LROD planned the launch an Internet Protocol-based product suite that was to flow across the Internet and utilize a browser to access and run the applications. LROD became a new member of the CT Media Value Network from Dialogic, an Intel company. LROD signed a beta agreement with State Capitol Credit Union to test the Lightning Rod Interaction Manager 4 product suite. In **August** LROD and Syntegra, the e-business consulting and systems integration arm of British Telecommunications plc (NYSE: BTY), announced a strategic global alliance allowing Syntegra to sell Lightning Rod Software's Interaction Manager product suite to its customers. Based on its revenue growth from 1995 to 1999, the company was named to Deloitte & Touche's Minnesota Technology Fast 50. CEO Ellis credited the company's focus on building superior products and ensuring customer satisfaction as key factors in its 177 percent revenue growth over the past five years. **Sept. 30:** For the nine-month period, revenue was $639,000, a decrease of 66 percent from the comparable period in 1999. The net loss year-to-date increased to $5,499,000. "Changing market conditions in the third quarter, including a much more difficult financing environment, negatively impacted our target markets and made it extremely difficult for us to ramp up our sales at the rate that we originally expected," stated CEO Ellis. In **October** the company announced a strategic business alliance with Agiliti, which was to add the Lightning Rod Interaction Manager to its portfolio of rentable, Web-based applications. It also announced support for Shoreline Communications' Distributed Internet Voice Architecture (DIVA) IP voice platform, allowing small to medium-sized contact centers and branch offices to deliver cost-effective voice-enabled customer care capabilities. MiTech AMS Ltd, a division of MiTech Group plc, and the NextClick Network of global personalization technology organizations both signed agreements to integrate LROD's Interaction Manager.

OFFICERS

Willem J. Ellis
President and CEO

Jeffrey D. Skie
CFO

Bouwe Hamersma
Chief Technical Officer

Elizabeth S. Fischer
EVP-Sales

Lori Cocking
VP-Human Resources

Ian Thomsen
VP-Marketing

Thomas Patin
General Counsel

DIRECTORS

Willem J. Ellis

Thomas F. Madison
MLM Partners, Minneapolis

James E. Ousley
Syntegra (USA) Inc. & Asia, Arden Hills, MN

Thomas Patin

Sven A. Wehrwein
Center for Diagnostic Imaging, Golden Valley, MN

SIC CODE

7372 Prepackaged software

MISCELLANEOUS

TRADED: Nasdaq SmallCap Market

SYMBOL: LROD

EMPLOYEES: 59

GENERAL COUNSEL: Fredrikson & Byron P.A., Minneapolis

AUDITORS: PricewaterhouseCoopers LLP, Minneapolis

MARKETING/COMMUNICATIONS: Amy Eggen

RANKINGS

No. 43 Minnesota Technology Fast 50

PUB

LodgeNet Entertainment Corporation

3900 W. Innovation St., Sioux Falls, SD 57107
Tel: 605/330-1330 Fax: 605/988-1532 Web site: http://www.lodgenet.com

LodgeNet Entertainment Corp. is a specialized communications company that assembles, installs, and operates guest pay movie systems; and provides satellite-delivered, free-to-guest programming, interactive games, multimedia entertainment, and guest information services to hotels, motels, and resorts. The company serves 750,287 rooms in hotels throughout the United States, Canada, and selected international markets. The company's patented b-LAN system technology enables the delivery of video-on-demand, network-based video games, PRIMESTAR digital basic and premium cable programming, and other interactive multimedia entertainment and information services geared to the needs of travelers. ResNet Communications, a LodgeNet subsidiary, provides similar services in multifamily residential complexes nationwide, including DBS programming provided by ResNet equity investor TCI Satellite Inc.

EARNINGS HISTORY

Year Ended Dec 31	Operating Revenue/Sales (dollars in thousands)	Net Earnings	Return on Revenue (percent)	Return on Equity	Net Earnings (dollars per share)	Cash Dividend	Market Price Range
1999 *	181,272	(36,428)	(20.1)	NM	(3.05)	—	25.13–5.75
1998 †	166,351	(39,912)	(24.0)	NM	(3.45)	—	12.50–5.13
1997 ¶	135,710	(25,619)	(18.9)	(51.7)	(2.27)	—	17.38–8.00
1996 #	97,721	(16,610)	(17.0)	(22.0)	(1.74)	—	18.00–9.00
1995	63,213	(7,026)	(11.1)	(16.4)	(0.96)	—	13.00–6.63

* Income figures for 1999 include pretax gain of $14.739 million on sale of investments.
† Income figures for 1998 include restructuring charge of $3.3 million/($0.28).
¶ Income figures for 1997 include extraordinary loss of $210,000/($0.02), cumulative effect of change in accounting principle.
# Income figures for 1996 include extraordinary loss of $3,253,000/($0.34) on early redemption of debt.

BALANCE SHEET

Assets	12/31/99 (dollars in thousands)	12/31/98	Liabilities	12/31/99 (dollars in thousands)	12/31/98
Current (CAE 1,644 and 5,240)	66,689	38,912	Current (STD 5,915 and 5,718)	33,704	31,151
Property and equipment	204,334	209,437	Long-term debt	277,075	262,375
			Minority interest		730
Unconsolidated affiliates	11,434	32,701	Common stockholders' equity*	(5,504)	11,774
Debt-issuance costs	8,710	6,637	TOTAL	305,275	306,030
Other	14,108	18,343			
TOTAL	305,275	306,030			

* $0.01 par common; 20,000,000 authorized; 11,970,852 and 11,942,387 issued and outstanding.

RECENT QUARTERS / **PRIOR-YEAR RESULTS**

	Quarter End	Revenue ($000)	Earnings ($000)	EPS ($)	Prior-Year Revenue ($000)	Prior-Year Earnings ($000)	Prior-Year EPS ($)
Q3	09/30/2000	52,894	(4,144)	(0.34)	49,640	2,309	0.19
Q2	06/30/2000	48,129	(6,539)	(0.54)	44,269	(24,826)	(2.08)
Q1	03/31/2000	47,733	(7,682)	(0.64)	41,965	(11,027)	(0.92)
Q4	12/31/99	45,398	(2,884)	(0.24)	43,330	(18,272)	(1.54)
	SUM	194,154	(21,249)	(1.76)	179,204	(51,816)	(4.35)

CURRENT: Q4 earnings include pretax gain of $7.644 million on sale of investment.
PRIOR YEAR: Q3 earnings include pretax gain of $7.095 million on sale of investment. Q4 earnings include pretax restructuring charge of $3.3 million related to ResNet merger.

RECENT EVENTS

In **December 1999** the company introduced a traveler-oriented portal to its OnLine by LodgeNet high-speed Internet access service. The popular Pokemon Snap, a Nintendo 64 video game, was made available on LodgeNet in-room game systems. In **January 2000** LodgeNet became the first in its industry to equip 100 percent of its (more than 660,000) installed guest pay interactive rooms with on-demand capability. LodgeNet entered into a multiyear agreement with DIRECTV Inc. that was to bring DIRECTV programming to the more than 3,700 hotels and 400,000 rooms currently subscribing to LodgeNet cable television service. LodgeNet and Wayport Inc., Austin, Texas, announced a strategic alliance through which the two companies were to bundle their respective television and connectivity services. In **February** LodgeNet installed Nintendo 64 (N64) video games in its 100,000th guest room. A leading hospitality newsmagazine chose the high-speed Internet alliance between LodgeNet and Wingate Inns International Inc. as a highlight of one of the industry's most newsworthy trends for 1999. Carlson Hospitality Worldwide designated LodgeNet as the sole preferred provider of television-based interactive entertainment and information services for all Radisson and Regent corporate-owned, managed, and franchised properties in the *continued on page 284*

OFFICERS

Scott C. Petersen
Chairman, President, and CEO
David M. Bankers
SVP and Chief Technology Officer
John M. O'Haugherty
SVP and COO
Jeffrey T. Weisner
SVP and CFO
Daniel P. Johnson
VP and General Counsel
Michael J. Kanyetzny
VP-Information Systems
Peter F. Klebanoff
VP-Industry Relations
Roger McAulay
VP-Internet Technologies
Steve McCarty
VP-Sales
Steven M. Pofahl
VP-Technical Operations
Ronald W. Pierce
VP, Controller
Steven D. Truckenmiller
VP-Guest Pay Services
Darla J. Werner
VP-Corporate Technologies

DIRECTORS

R. Douglas Bradbury
Level 3 Communications Inc.
Lawrence Flinn Jr.
United Video Satellite Group, Stamford, CT
Richard R. Hylland
NorthWestern Corp., Huron, SD
Rodney F. Leyendecker
NorCom Advanced Technologies Inc.
Scott C. Petersen

MAJOR SHAREHOLDERS

Red Coat Capital Management LLC, 16.7%
New York
Alex Brown Investment Management, 8.1%
Baltimore
Tim C. Flynn, 5.9%
Wellington Management Co. LLP, 5.8%
Boston
All officers and directors as a group (17 persons), 16.1%

SIC CODE

7999 Amusement and recreation, nec

MISCELLANEOUS

TRANSFER AGENT AND REGISTAR:
Harris Trust and Savings Bank, Chicago
TRADED: Nasdaq National Market
SYMBOL: LNET
STOCKHOLDERS: 164
EMPLOYEES: 702
GENERAL COUNSEL:
Pillsbury, Madison & Sutro, San Francisco
AUDITORS:
Arthur Andersen LLP, Minneapolis
INC: DE-1980
ANNUAL MEETING: May
COMMUNICATIONS:
Ann Parker

SUBSIDIARIES, DIVISIONS, AFFILIATES

ResNet Communications

TWO-YEAR QUARTERLY HIGH-LOW STOCK PRICES

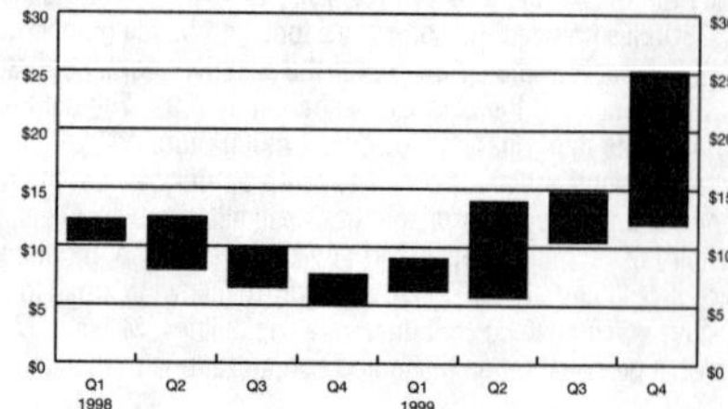

MBC Holding Company

882 W. Seventh St., St. Paul, MN 55102
Tel: 651/228-9173 Fax: 651/290-8211

MBC Holding Co., formerly Minnesota Brewing Co., operates the former Jacob Schmidt Brewery in St. Paul, which it acquired from G. Heileman Brewing Co. in October 1991. The fifth-largest U.S. regional brewer, Minnesota Brewing's proprietary products include **Pig's Eye**, **Premium**, and **Grain Belt** beers. Its full product line includes regular, light, nonalcoholic, malt liquor, ice beers, and micro-style brews. The company also produces a number of private-label and contract brands of beer and water. MBC has a minority interest in Gopher State Ethanol, which is currently operating an ethanol facility in St. Paul. MBC is also a joint-venture partner in an entity that will manufacture and market liquid carbon dioxide.

EARNINGS HISTORY *

Year Ended Dec 31	Operating Revenue/Sales (dollars in thousands)	Net Earnings (dollars in thousands)	Return on Revenue (percent)	Return on Equity (percent)	Net Earnings (dollars per share)	Cash Dividend (dollars per share)	Market Price Range (dollars per share)
1999 †	17,748	(865)	(4.9)	(43.3)	(0.29)	—	3.00–1.50
1998	14,763	(1,380)	(9.3)	(47.0)	(0.40)	—	3.56–1.25
1997	18,101	(4,310)	(23.8)	NM	(1.27)	—	5.38–1.38
1996	24,875	(1,862)	(7.5)	(26.2)	(0.55)	—	8.75–3.00
1995 ¶	31,384	26	0.1	0.3	0.01	—	5.88–4.00

* Sales figures are net of excise taxes.
† Income figures for 1999 include pretax charge of $272,270 as provision for discontinued product lines.
¶ Income figures for 1995 include pretax gain of $1 million per transition agreement with Pete's Brewing Co.

BALANCE SHEET

Assets	12/31/99 (dollars in thousands)	12/31/98
Current (CAE 26 and 67)	4,678	4,483
Property and equipment	827	3,482
Investments: unconsolidated subsidiary	1,672	
Investments: U.S. Treasury Note	500	
Investments: joint venture, other	120	
Other	422	484
TOTAL	8,218	8,449

Liabilities	12/31/99 (dollars in thousands)	12/31/98
Current	4,113	4,252
Long-term debt	1,603	1,262
Deferred gain	198	
Stockholders' equity*	2,305	2,934
TOTAL	8,218	8,449

* $0.01 par common; 10,000,000 authorized; 3,506,860 and 3,462,711 issued and outstanding.

RECENT QUARTERS / **PRIOR-YEAR RESULTS**

	Quarter End	Revenue ($000)	Earnings ($000)	EPS ($)	Prior-Year Revenue ($000)	Prior-Year Earnings ($000)	Prior-Year EPS ($)
Q3	09/30/2000	7,648	505	0.13	5,150	71	0.01
Q2	06/30/2000	8,509	514	0.14	4,333	131	0.03
Q1	03/31/2000	5,435	75	0.01	3,295	(392)	(0.12)
Q4	12/31/99	4,971	(676)	(0.20)	3,650	(601)	(0.18)
	SUM	26,562	418	0.08	16,427	(790)	(0.26)

CURRENT: Q4 earnings include write-off related to discontinuance of certain labels.

RECENT EVENTS

In **January 2000** the company changed its name. It felt that the name Minnesota Brewing no longer accurately reflected all of its operations and interests. The new name was expected to benefit the company's efforts to diversify its operations through the formation of subsidiaries and participation in joint ventures. The name Minnesota Brewing was preserved as the name of its brewing operations subsidiary. In **May** Gopher State Ethanol LLC, which had constructed a facility to produce ethanol, distilled grains, and raw carbon dioxide gas, began initial production. (The company has a 28 percent ownership interest in Gopher State, an unconsolidated subsidiary.) **Sept. 30**: Nine-month net sales of $21.6 million represented an increase of 69.0 percent from the same period in 1999. Net income was $1.1 million versus a net loss in prior year. Net sales increased due to the addition of contract customers and a continuing increase in export sales. The increase in net income was a result of several factors, including the increased utilization of bottling capacity, the continued cost-cutting measures implemented by the company, and the sharing of costs pursuant to several agreements entered into with Gopher State.

OFFICERS

Bruce E. Hendry
Chairman

John J. (Jack) Lee
President and CEO

Michael Hime
VP-Finance, CFO, and Treasurer

Jeff Crawford
Sales Manager

Phil Gagne
Brewmaster

DIRECTORS

Robert A. Awsumb
Attorney at Law

John T. Elliot
Elliott Contracting Corp.

James Freeman
Wacofilters, Norristown, PA

Bruce E. Hendry

Thomas Houts
Gryphics, Inc., Plymouth, MN

John J. (Jack) Lee

Dick Perrine
The Hays Group

MAJOR SHAREHOLDERS

Minnesota Brewing Management Co./Bruce E. Hendry, 52.2%

John J. Lee, 7.2%
St. Paul

Perkins Opportunity Fund, 6.1%
Wayzata, MN

All officers and directors as a group (7 persons), 60.1%

SIC CODE

2082 Malt beverages

MISCELLANEOUS

TRANSFER AGENT AND REGISTAR:
Wells Fargo Bank Minnesota N.A., South St. Paul, MN

TRADED: Nasdaq SmallCap Market

SYMBOL: MBRW

STOCKHOLDERS: 287

EMPLOYEES: 143

GENERAL COUNSEL:
Lindquist & Vennum PLLP, Minneapolis

AUDITORS:
RSM McGladrey & Pullen Inc. LLP, Minneapolis

INC: MN-1991

ANNUAL MEETING: May

RANKINGS

No. 161 CRM Public 200

SUBSIDIARIES, DIVISIONS, AFFILIATES

Minnesota Brewing Co.

PUB

TWO-YEAR QUARTERLY HIGH-LOW STOCK PRICES

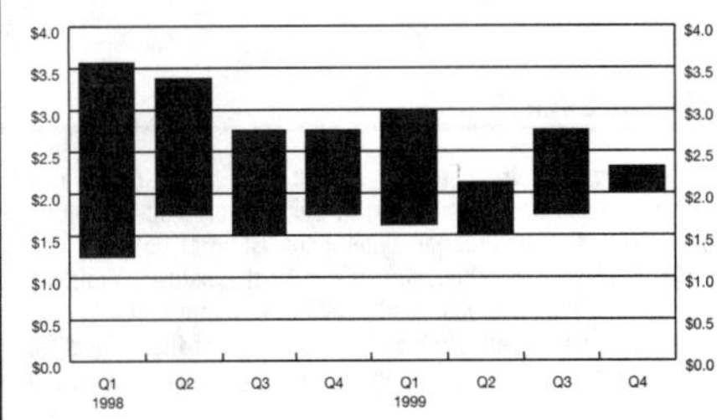

PUB

MDU Resources Group Inc.

918 E. Divide Ave., P.O. Box 5650, Bismarck, ND 58506
Tel: 701/222-7900 Fax: 701/222-7607 Web site: http://www.mduresources.com

MDU Resources Group Inc. is a multidimensional natural resources company. Its public utility division, **Montana-Dakota Utilities Co.** and Great Plains Natural Gas Co., the public utility divisions of the company, generate, transmit and distribute electricity, distribute natural gas and provide related value-added products and services in the Northern Great Plains. The company, through its wholly owned subsidiary, Centennial Energy Holdings Inc., owns WBI Holdings Inc., Knife River Corp., and Utility Services Inc. WBI Holdings provides natural gas transportation, underground storage and gathering services through a pipeline systems and provides energy marketing and management services throughout the United States. WBI Holdings is also engaged in oil and natural gas acquisition, exploration and production throughout the United States and in the Gulf of Mexico. Knife River mines and markets aggregates and related value-added construction materials products and services in the western United States, including Alaska and Hawaii. Utility Services is a full service engineering, design and build company specializing in construction and maintenance of power and natural gas distribution and transmission systems as well as communication and fiber optic facilities.

EARNINGS HISTORY

Year Ended Dec 31	Operating Revenue/Sales (dollars in thousands)	Net Earnings (dollars in thousands)	Return on Revenue (percent)	Return on Equity (percent)	Net Earnings (dollars per share*)	Cash Dividend (dollars per share*)	Market Price Range (dollars per share*)
1999	1,279,809	84,080	6.6	12.4	1.53	0.82	27.19–18.81
1998 †	896,627	34,107	3.8	6.1	0.66	0.78	28.88–18.83
1997	607,674	54,617	9.0	13.9	1.24	0.75	22.33–14.00
1996 ¶	514,701	45,470	8.8	12.7	1.05	0.73	15.67–13.25
1995	464,246	41,633	9.0	12.1	0.96	0.72	15.39–11.44

* Per-share amounts restated to reflect 3-for-2 stock splits on July 13, 1998, and Oct. 13, 1995.
† Income figures for 1998 include pretax charge of $66 million for write-downs of oil and natural gas properties.
¶ Income figures for 1996 include pretax charge of $26,753,000 for costs on natural gas repurchase commitment.

BALANCE SHEET

Assets	12/31/99 (dollars in thousands)	12/31/98 (dollars in thousands)	Liabilities	12/31/99 (dollars in thousands)	12/31/98 (dollars in thousands)
Current (CAE 77,504 and 39,216)	351,696	240,649	Current (STD 19,121 and 18,292)	187,327	169,469
Property, plant, and equipment	1,248,176	1,084,677	Deferred taxes	213,771	173,094
			Other	115,627	129,506
Investments	43,128	43,029	Long-term debt	563,545	413,264
Deferred charges and other	123,303	84,420	Preferred equity	16,500	16,600
			Common equity*	669,533	550,842
TOTAL	1,766,303	1,452,775	TOTAL	1,766,303	1,452,775

* $1 par common; 150,000,000 authorized; 57,277,915 and 53,272,951 issued and outstanding, less 239,521 and 239,521 treasury shares.

RECENT QUARTERS / PRIOR-YEAR RESULTS

	Quarter End	Revenue ($000)	Earnings ($000)	EPS ($)	Prior-Year Revenue ($000)	Prior-Year Earnings ($000)	Prior-Year EPS ($)
Q3	09/30/2000	530,800	40,000	0.63	375,591	29,098	0.53
Q2	06/30/2000	362,979	21,126	0.35	290,267	17,796	0.33
Q1	03/31/2000	371,989	13,364	0.23	259,046	12,721	0.24
Q4	12/31/99	354,905	24,465	0.43	276,812	(439)	(0.01)
	SUM	1,620,673	98,955	1.64	1,201,716	59,176	1.08

CURRENT: Q3 figures are rounded.

RECENT EVENTS

In **January 2000** the company agreed to acquire Great Plains Natural Gas Co., distributing to 19 communities in western Minnesota and southeastern North Dakota, in a stock-for-stock exchange. The 70-employee, Fergus Falls, Minn.-based company operates a natural gas system consisting of 65 miles of high-pressure transmission lines and 435 miles of distribution mains that serve 22,000 customers. In **April** subsidiary Prairielands Energy Technology acquired 100 percent of Houston-based Innovatum Inc., a global leader in the development of submerged pipeline and cable tracking and locating technology. Innovatum had recently unveiled a new product that allows for the artificial magnetization of submerged pipeline and cable. Knife River added $8 million-revenue D'Agostino Cos., a provider of concrete ready-mix and related *continued on page 284*

MDU RESOURCES GROUP, INC.

OFFICERS

Martin A. White
President and CEO

Cathleen M. Christopherson
VP-Corporate Communications

Richard A. Espeland
VP-Human Resources

Douglas C. Kane
EVP, CAO, Chief Devel. Officer

Lester H. Loble II
VP, General Counsel, and Secretary

Douglass A. Mahowald
Asst. Treasurer and Asst. Secretary

Vernon A. Raile
VP, Controller, Chief Accounting Officer

Warren L. Robinson
EVP, Treasurer, and CFO

Ronald D. Tipton
CEO-Montana-Dakota Utilities Co.

Robert E. Wood
VP-Public Affairs/Environmental Policy

DIRECTORS

Thomas S. Everist
L.G. Everist Inc., Sioux Falls, SD

David M. Heskett

Douglas C. Kane

Richard L. Muus
Midwest Federal Savings Bank (retired)

Robert L. Nance
Nance Petroleum Corp., Billings, MT

John L. Olson
Blue Rock Products Co., Sidney, MT

San W. Orr Jr.
attorney, Wausau, WI

Harry J. Pearce
General Motors Corp.

Homer A. Scott Jr.
First Interstate Bank, Sheridan, WY

Dr. Joseph T. Simmons
University of South Dakota, Vermillion, SD

Sister Thomas Welder
U. of Mary, Bismarck, ND

Martin A. White

MAJOR SHAREHOLDERS

All officers and directors as a group (18 persons), 1.4%

SIC CODE

1221 Bituminous coal and lignite, surface
1311 Crude petroleum and natural gas
1442 Construction sand and gravel
1611 Highway and street construction
1623 Water, sewer, and utility lines
1629 Heavy construction, nec
1794 Excavating and foundation work
2951 Asphalt paving mixtures and blocks
3241 Cement, hydraulic
3271 Concrete block and brick
3273 Ready-mixed concrete
4911 Electric services
4922 Natural gas transmission
4924 Natural gas distribution
4932 Gas and other services combined
5051 Metals service centers and offices
5063 Electrical apparatus and eqp, whsle
5211 Lumber and bldg mtls, retail

MISCELLANEOUS

TRANSFER AGENT AND REGISTAR:
Wells Fargo Bank Minnesota N.A., South St. Paul, MN

TRADED: NYSE, PSE

SYMBOL: MDU

STOCKHOLDERS: 14,652

EMPLOYEES: 3,791

GENERAL COUNSEL:
Thelen Reid & Priest LLP, New York

AUDITORS:
Arthur Andersen LLP, Minneapolis

INC: DE-1924

ANNUAL MEETING: April

HUMAN RESOURCES:
Richard A. Espeland

INVESTOR RELATIONS:
Warren L. Robinson

TWO-YEAR QUARTERLY HIGH-LOW STOCK PRICES

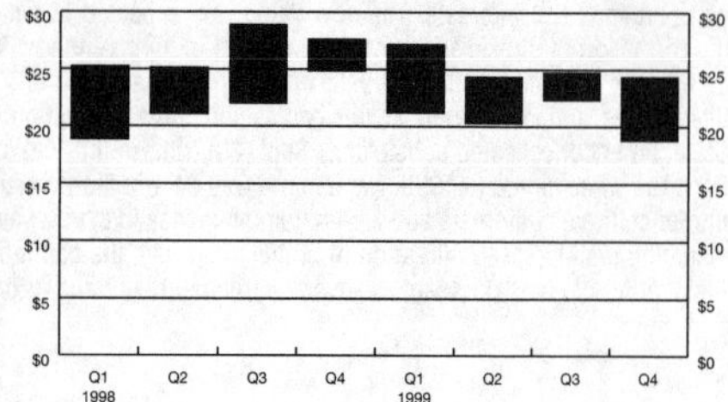

MGI Pharma Inc.

6300 W. Old Shakopee Rd., Suite 110, Bloomington, MN 55438
Tel: 952/346-4700 Fax: 952/346-4800 Web site: http://www.mgipharma.com

MGI Pharma Inc. acquires, develops, and markets differentiated specialty pharmaceutical products for therapeutic markets of unmet need. MGI's current product portfolio is made up of products that address special needs in oncology and rheumatology; however, the company plans to expand its scope as it grows its business. The company markets its products to physicians throughout the United States, with sales made to pharmaceutical wholesalers for distribution to the ultimate consumers. Sales of Salagen Tablets account for the majority of MGI's sales. The company is commercializing its products outside the United States through various alliances. Product development efforts are primarily directed toward MGI 114, the lead compound in a family of promising anti-cancer analogs known as the acylfulvenes. MGI is currently sponsoring three phase two human clinical studies and a phase one drug combination study with MGI 114. To augment MGI's development efforts with MGI 114, the National Cancer Institute is conducting seven phase two and two phase one clinical studies. MGI expects to announce an approval strategy for MGI 114 in the first half of 2000.

EARNINGS HISTORY *

Year Ended Dec 31	Operating Revenue/Sales (dollars in thousands)	Net Earnings	Return on Revenue (percent)	Return on Equity	Net Earnings (dollars per share)	Cash Dividend	Market Price Range
1999	25,652	4,731	18.4	19.2	0.32	—	14.06–7.63
1998	17,849	414	2.3	2.4	0.03	—	12.81–3.88
1997	13,496	(1,785)	(13.2)	(11.9)	(0.13)	—	5.56–3.19
1996	9,745	(6,622)	(68.0)	(40.5)	(0.50)	—	6.63–3.63
1995	13,323	(2,614)	(19.6)	(15.6)	(0.21)	—	6.75–3.63

* Revenue categories include sales, promotion, licensing, and interest and other.

BALANCE SHEET

Assets	12/31/99 (dollars in thousands)	12/31/98	Liabilities	12/31/99 (dollars in thousands)	12/31/98
Current (CAE 8,249 and 6,513)	27,569	20,107	Current	4,329	4,011
Equipment and furniture	1,027	540	Stockholders' equity*	24,644	17,111
Other	377	475	TOTAL	28,974	21,122
TOTAL	28,974	21,122			

* $0.01 par common; 30,000,000 authorized; 14,979,640 and 14,542,472 issued and outstanding.

RECENT QUARTERS / PRIOR-YEAR RESULTS

	Quarter End	Revenue ($000)	Earnings ($000)	EPS ($)	Prior-Year Revenue ($000)	Prior-Year Earnings ($000)	Prior-Year EPS ($)
Q3	09/30/2000	6,753	(5,985)	(0.36)	5,812	953	0.06
Q2	06/30/2000	7,978	1,224	0.08	6,041	611	0.04
Q1	03/31/2000	5,570	253	0.02	5,500	683	0.05
	SUM	20,301	(4,508)	(0.27)	17,353	2,247	0.15

RECENT EVENTS

In **December 1999** the company initiated a phase I human safety study of its novel anti-cancer compound irofulven (also referred to as MGI 114) on a weekly dosing schedule that was designed for more convenient use with other anti-cancer drugs. The study was expected to determine the maximum tolerated dose of irofulven when administered on this schedule to patients with advanced solid tumors. By **February 2000**, with 49 patients already enrolled, full enrollment was imminent in MGI's 50-patient Phase 2 clinical study to test the safety and efficacy of irofulven in the treatment of pancreatic cancer patients who have failed gemcitabine (Gemzar) therapy. The primary clinical endpoint for this study was six-month survival, with secondary endpoints for objective tumor shrinkage, time to tumor progression, and quality of life measures. An expansion of MGI's field sales organization, targeted for completion early in the second quarter of 2000, was to result in 41 sales representatives in the U.S. covering most potential prescribers of MGI products. In **March** MGI filed a registration statement with the SEC to sell 2.5 million shares of its common stock. The company intended to use net proceeds to fund research and development, product commercialization, potential product acquisitions, product development opportunities, working capital, and other general corporate purposes. In **May** CIBA Vision, the eye care unit of Novartis AG, signed an exclusive licensing agreement for Salagen Tablets in Europe. Under the agreement, CIBA Vision was to market Salagen to ophthalmologists, rheumatologists, and oncologists in European countries. Results from a clinical trial of irofulven, a novel anti-cancer agent being developed by MGI, demonstrated anti-tumor activity in patients with advanced pancreatic cancer for which gemcitabine had failed. MGI closed on the sale of 1 million newly issued shares of its common stock at $18 per share in a registered direct placement to selected institutional investors. Net proceeds of $16.5 million were to be used to fund expanded development activities for irofulven, its promising anti-cancer product candidate; product commercialization; potential product acquisitions; product development opportunities; working capital, and other general corporate purposes. In **August** MGI and MethylGene Inc. entered

continued on page 285

OFFICERS

Hugh E. Miller
Chairman

Charles N. Blitzer
President and CEO

Leon O. (Lonnie) Moulder Jr.
EVP

Michael T. Cullen Jr., M.D.
VP-Clinical Affairs, Chief Medical Ofcr.

William C. Brown
CFO and Secretary

HUMAN RESOURCES:
Shirley Anderson

DIRECTORS

Charles N. Blitzer

Andrew J. Ferrara
Boston Healthcare

Joseph S. Frelinghuysen
J.S. Frelinghuysen & Co.

Michael E. Hanson
Eli Lilly and Co. (retired)

Hugh E. Miller
ICI Americas Inc. (retired)

Timothy G. Rothwell
Pharmacia & Upjohn Inc.

Lee J. Schroeder
Lee Schroeder & Associates

Arthur L. Weaver, M.D.
Arthritis Center of Nebraska

MAJOR SHAREHOLDERS

Avenir Corp., 6%
Washington, D.C.

All officers and directors as a group (11 persons), 3.7%

SIC CODE

2834 Pharmaceutical preparations

MISCELLANEOUS

TRANSFER AGENT AND REGISTAR:
Wells Fargo Bank Minnesota N.A.,
South St. Paul, MN

TRADED: Nasdaq National Market

SYMBOL: MOGN

STOCKHOLDERS: 810

EMPLOYEES: 102

GENERAL COUNSEL:
Dorsey & Whitney PLLP, Minneapolis

AUDITORS:
KPMG LLP, Minneapolis

INC: MN-1979

ANNUAL MEETING: May

INVESTOR/PUBLIC RELATIONS: Bill Brown

RANKINGS

No. 139 CRM Public 200

PUB

TWO-YEAR QUARTERLY HIGH-LOW STOCK PRICES

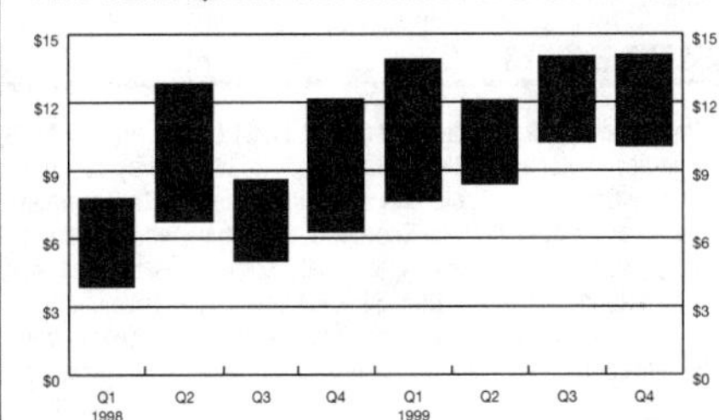

MTS Systems Corporation

14000 Technology Dr., Eden Prairie, MN 55344
Tel: 952/937-4000 Fax: 952/937-4515 Web site: http://www.mts.com

MTS Systems Corp. provides hardware and software products and services that its worldwide customers can use to improve product quality, stimulate innovation, and increase machine and worker productivity. The company currently operates in two market sectors. **Mechanical Testing and Simulation**: MTS products and services are used for evaluating the performance characteristics (e.g., durability and fatigue) of materials, vehicles, components, and structures. **Factory Automation**: MTS instrumentation products monitor and automate industrial processes and equipment.

PUB

EARNINGS HISTORY *

Year Ended Sept 30	Operating Revenue/Sales (dollars in thousands)	Net Earnings	Return on Revenue (percent)	Return on Equity	Net Earnings (dollars per share†)	Cash Dividend	Market Price Range
1999 ¶	390,542	12,445	3.2	7.6	0.60	0.24	15.44–9.63
1998	362,163	21,539	5.9	14.1	1.05	0.24	20.00–11.56
1997 #	323,424	21,891	6.8	16.4	1.08	0.20	19.63–9.63
1996	278,170	15,170	5.5	13.4	0.74	0.16	11.25–6.94
1995 **	234,131	10,461	4.5	9.8	0.57	0.14	7.25–5.13

* Historical figures have been restated to account for the May 28, 1999, merger with DSP Technology Inc. as a pooling of interests.
† Per-share amounts restated to reflect 2-for-1 stock splits on Feb. 2, 1998, and April 1, 1996.
¶ Income figures for 1999 include pretax charges for restructuring ($5.711 million) and DSP acquisition ($1.391 million).
# Income figures for 1997 include pretax gain of $4.3 million on sale of land.
** Figures for 1995 include the results of Power-Tek Inc. (now known as MTS-PowerTek Inc.), Farmington Hills, Michigan, from its November 1994 date of purchase.

BALANCE SHEET

Assets	09/30/99 (dollars in thousands)	09/30/98	Liabilities	09/30/99 (dollars in thousands)	09/30/98
Current (CAE 18,083 and 12,589)	223,651	204,311	Current (STD 11,379 and 29,423)	104,713	110,223
Property and equipment	73,633	69,942	Deferred income taxes	5,517	4,851
Other	36,063	38,769	Long-term debt	60,258	45,259
TOTAL	333,347	313,022	Stockholders' equity*	162,859	152,689
			TOTAL	333,347	313,022

* $0.25 par common; 64,000,000 authorized; 20,883,639 and 20,657,186 issued and outstanding.

RECENT QUARTERS / **PRIOR-YEAR RESULTS**

	Quarter End	Revenue ($000)	Earnings ($000)	EPS ($)	Revenue ($000)	Earnings ($000)	EPS ($)
Q3	06/30/2000	94,989	3,697	0.18	95,363	5,293	0.25
Q2	03/31/2000	95,291	1,371	0.07	93,262	3,146	0.15
Q1	12/31/99	87,214	(6,040)	(0.29)	96,142	3,726	0.18
Q4	09/30/99	105,775	280	0.01	102,766	5,759	0.28
	SUM	383,269	(692)	(0.03)	387,533	17,924	0.87

CURRENT: Q4 earnings include $3.115 million pretax acquisition expense.
PRIOR YEAR: Q3 earnings include pretax acquisition-related charge of $1.391 million. Q1 earnings include $2.596 million pretax restructuring expense.

RECENT EVENTS

In **November 1999** the company received a $1.8 million order for Spinning Wheel Integrated Force Transducers (SWIFT) from a Detroit-based global vehicle manufacturer—to be used by its product development group for data acquisition and laboratory simulation testing of light trucks and sport utility vehicles. In **December** MTS said that it had provided critical design and engineering services for the breakthrough Scout robot prototype recently demonstrated at the University of Minnesota. (Scout robots are small, lightweight, highly maneuverable surveillance devices that are expected to eventually play a crucial role in military and civilian reconnaissance activities.) **Dec. 31:** CEO Emery said, "We had three issues that hurt our first-quarter results. The first were revenue shortfalls in two of our business units that precluded us from realizing anticipated margins during the quarter. The second was notification late in December and early January that we had technical and schedule difficulties on two large projects that required us to re-evaluate the project costs. For both projects, we recorded what *continued on page 285*

OFFICERS

Sidney W. (Chip) Emery Jr., Ph.D.
Chairman, President, and CEO

Keith D. Zell
EVP

William G. Anderson
VP-Automation Division

Steven M. Cohoon
VP-Vehicle Dynamics Group

Kelly H. Donaldson Jr.
VP-Strategic Planning/Product Management

James M. Egerdahl
VP-Service/Support Division

Laura B. Hamilton
VP-Material Testing/Aerospace Division

David E. Hoffman
VP and CFO

Donald G. Krantz
VP-Advanced Engineering Systems Division

Kathleen M. Staby
VP-Human Resources

Mauro G. Togneri
VP-Sensors Division

DIRECTORS

Charles A. Brickman
Pinnacle Capital Corp., Chicago

Jean-Lou Chameau, Ph.D.
Georgia Institute of Technology, Atlanta

Sidney W. (Chip) Emery

Bobby I. Griffin
Medtronic Inc. (retired)

Russell A. Gullotti
NCS Pearson, Eden Prairie, MN

Brendan C. Hegarty, Ph.D.
consultant, Minneapolis

Thomas E. Holloran
University of St. Thomas, St. Paul

Linda Hall Whitman
Ceridian Corp., Bloomington, MN

MAJOR SHAREHOLDERS

Mairs and Power Growth Fund Inc., 7.7%
St. Paul

E. Thomas Binger, 5.5%
St. Louis Park, MN

All officers and directors as a group (18 persons), 4.8%

SIC CODE

3823 Process control instruments

3829 Measuring and controlling devices, nec

7372 Prepackaged software

MISCELLANEOUS

TRANSFER AGENT AND REGISTAR:
Wells Fargo Bank Minnesota N.A., South St. Paul, MN

TRADED: Nasdaq National Market

SYMBOL: MTSC

STOCKHOLDERS: 2,055

EMPLOYEES: 2,436

IN MINNESOTA: 1,200

GENERAL COUNSEL:
Robins, Kaplan, Miller & Ciresi LLP, Minneapolis
Westman, Champlin & Kelly, Minneapolis

AUDITORS:
Arthur Andersen LLP, Minneapolis

INC: MN-1966

ANNUAL MEETING:
January

INVESTOR RELATIONS:
Thomas J. Minneman

HUMAN RESOURCES:
Genny Lubbers

RANKINGS

No. 58 CRM Public 200

SUBSIDIARIES, DIVISIONS, AFFILIATES

AeroMet Corp.
Dr. Frank Arcella

Automation Division
2121 Bridge St.
New Ulm, MN 56073

MTS International Ltd.
Barbados, West Indies

MTS (Japan) Ltd.
Izumikan Gobancho
12-11 Gobancho,
Chiyoda-Ku
Tokyo 102
Japan

MTS Korea Inc.
Sungdam Bldg, 3 floor, 142-35
Samsung-Dong, Gangnam-Ku
Seoul, Korea 135-090

MTS Sensor Technologie GmbH and Co. KG
Postfach 8130
D-5880 Ludenscheid, Germany

TWO-YEAR QUARTERLY HIGH-LOW STOCK PRICES

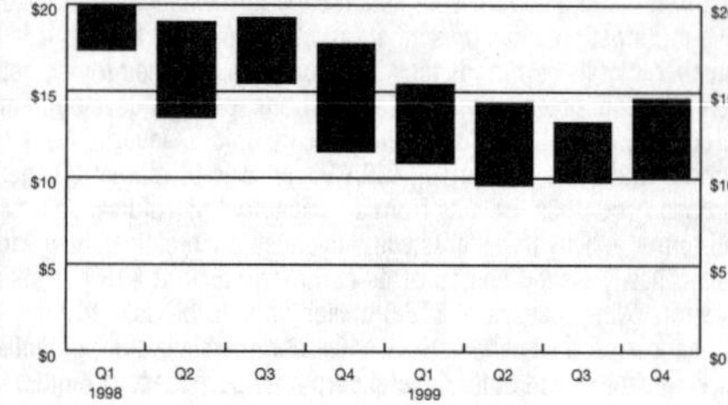

Marten Transport Ltd.

129 Marten St., Mondovi, WI 54755
Tel: 715/926-4216 Fax: 715/926-4530 Web site: http://www.marten.com

Marten Transport Ltd. provides time- and temperature-sensitive truckload motor carrier services to customers nationwide. The company serves customers with more demanding delivery deadlines, or those who ship products requiring modern temperature-controlled trailers. As of Sept. 30, 2000, the company operated a fleet of 1,850 tractors and 2,606 (all 53-foot) trailers. The company was founded in 1946. Marten Transport was reorganized under Wisconsin law in 1970, taken public in 1986, and reincorporated under Delaware law in 1988.

EARNINGS HISTORY

Year Ended Dec 31	Operating Revenue/Sales (dollars in thousands)	Net Earnings	Return on Revenue (percent)	Return on Equity	Net Earnings (dollars per share*)	Cash Dividend	Market Price Range
1999	219,200	8,457	3.9	14.2	1.93	—	14.63–9.50
1998	193,648	7,574	3.9	14.2	1.69	—	19.25–12.38
1997	172,412	5,307	3.1	11.6	1.19	—	17.17–8.00
1996	146,151	1,630	1.1	4.1	0.37	—	12.33–7.83
1995	137,704	5,009	3.6	13.1	1.14	—	14.00–10.00

* Per-share amounts restated to reflect a 3-for-2 stock split on Jan. 5, 1998.

BALANCE SHEET

Assets	12/31/99 (dollars in thousands)	12/31/98	Liabilities	12/31/99 (dollars in thousands)	12/31/98
Current (CAE 0 and 1,116)	39,310	31,985	Current (STD 5,659 and 8,899)	32,814	31,205
Property and equipment	145,720	123,757	Long-term debt	63,599	47,232
Other	889	967	Deferred income taxes	29,901	24,994
TOTAL	185,919	156,709	Stockholders' equity*	59,605	53,278
			TOTAL	185,919	156,709

* $0.01 par common; 10,000,000 authorized; 4,300,145 and 4,477,645 issued and outstanding.

RECENT QUARTERS / PRIOR-YEAR RESULTS

	Quarter End	Revenue ($000)	Earnings ($000)	EPS ($)	Prior-Year Revenue ($000)	Prior-Year Earnings ($000)	Prior-Year EPS ($)
Q3	09/30/2000	65,267	1,706	0.41	55,873	2,001	0.47
Q2	06/30/2000	64,811	2,470	0.58	54,558	2,198	0.49
Q1	03/31/2000	60,293	1,624	0.38	48,731	1,422	0.32
Q4	12/31/99	60,038	2,836	0.66	49,035	1,626	0.36
	SUM	250,409	8,636	2.03	208,197	7,247	1.64

RECENT EVENTS

In **January 2000** the company announced that its board of directors had authorized management to purchase, from time to time, up to 300,000 shares (7 percent) of Marten's common stock. In **September** Marten said that it expected net income for its third quarter ending Sept. 30 to be in a range of 41 to 46 cents per diluted share, or below previous expectations. [It came in at 41 cents.] Chairman Marten said, "The recent additional rise in diesel fuel prices, along with a lower-than-expected equipment utilization level, will result in a higher operating ratio in the third quarter than we previously anticipated." Marten also said that the industry-wide problem of recruiting and retaining sufficient numbers of qualified drivers was a key factor in the company's lower equipment-utilization rate.

OFFICERS

Randolph L. Marten
Chairman and President

Darrell D. Rubel
EVP, CFO, Treasurer, and Asst. Secretary

Robert G. Smith
COO and VP-Operations

Timothy P. Nash
VP-Sales

Franklin J. Foster
VP-Finance

DIRECTORS

Jerry M. Bauer
Bauer Built Inc., Durand, WI

Larry B. Hagness
Durand Builders Service Inc., Durand, WI

Thomas A. Letscher
Oppenheimer Wolff & Donnelly LLP, Minneapolis

Christine K. Marten
Northwest Airlines Corp., Eagan, MN

Randolph L. Marten

Darrell D. Rubel

Thomas J. Winkel
management consultant, Pewaukee, WI

MAJOR SHAREHOLDERS

Randolph L. Marten, 44.1%
Mondovi, WI

Christine K. Marten, 13.5%
Mondovi, WI

FMR Corp., 10.4%
Boston

Heartland Advisors Inc., 9.5%
Milwaukee

All officers and directors as a group (9 persons), 59.9%

SIC CODE

4213 Trucking, except local

MISCELLANEOUS

TRANSFER AGENT AND REGISTAR:
Chase Mellon Shareholder Services LLC, Ridgefield Park, NJ

TRADED: Nasdaq National Market

SYMBOL: MRTN

STOCKHOLDERS: 283

EMPLOYEES: 1,492

GENERAL COUNSEL:
Oppenheimer Wolff & Donnelly LLP, Minneapolis

AUDITORS:
Arthur Andersen LLP, Minneapolis

INC: DE-1988

FOUNDED: 1946

ANNUAL MEETING: May

PUB

TWO-YEAR QUARTERLY HIGH-LOW STOCK PRICES

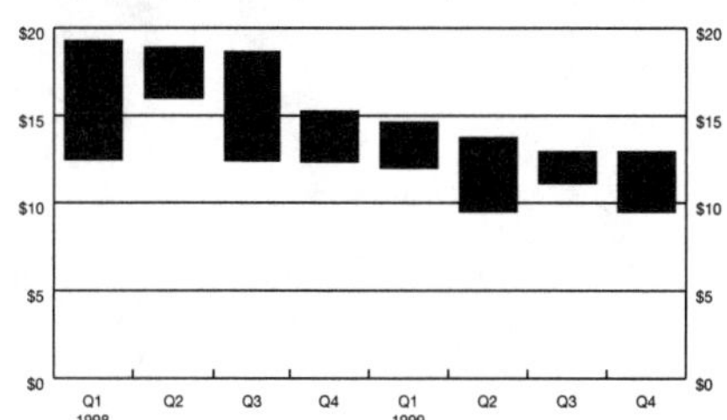

PUB

MedAmicus Inc.

15301 Highway 55 W., Plymouth, MN 55447
Tel: 763/559-2613 Fax: 763/559-7548 Web site: http://www.medamicus.com

MedAmicus Inc. designs, manufactures, and markets proprietary medical devices, including a percutaneous vessel introducer and related vascular access products; designs, manufactures, and markets a pressure-measurement system utilizing a proprietary fiber-optic transducer for measuring and monitoring physiological pressures in the human body; and manufactures medical devices and components for other medical product companies as a contract manufacturer.

EARNINGS HISTORY

Year Ended Dec 31	Operating Revenue/Sales (dollars in thousands)	Net Earnings (dollars in thousands)	Return on Revenue (percent)	Return on Equity (percent)	Net Earnings (dollars per share)	Cash Dividend (dollars per share)	Market Price Range (dollars per share)
1999	9,013	(175)	(1.9)	(7.3)	(0.04)	—	2.25–0.97
1998	8,032	(144)	(1.8)	(5.6)	(0.03)	—	3.13–0.81
1997	7,173	(146)	(2.0)	(5.4)	(0.04)	—	3.63–1.88
1996	5,660	(1,071)	(18.9)	(38.3)	(0.28)	—	4.75–2.13
1995	5,295	(359)	(6.8)	(16.2)	(0.11)	—	4.00–1.88

BALANCE SHEET

Assets	12/31/99 (dollars in thousands)	12/31/98	Liabilities	12/31/99 (dollars in thousands)	12/31/98
Current (CAE 1,006 and 1,022)	3,716	3,532	Current	1,992	1,642
Property and equipment	691	678	Capital lease obligations	47	4
Patent rights	31	10	Stockholders' equity*	2,399	2,574
TOTAL	4,438	4,220	TOTAL	4,438	4,220

* $0.01 par common; 9,000,000 authorized; 4,114,774 and 4,112,274 issued and outstanding.

RECENT QUARTERS / PRIOR-YEAR RESULTS

	Quarter End	Revenue ($000)	Earnings ($000)	EPS ($)	Prior-Year Revenue ($000)	Prior-Year Earnings ($000)	Prior-Year EPS ($)
Q3	09/30/2000	2,578	110	0.03	2,276	(89)	(0.02)
Q2	06/30/2000	2,805	161	0.04	2,199	11	0.00
Q1	03/31/2000	2,611	(75)	(0.02)	2,287	26	0.01
Q4	12/31/99	2,251	(123)	(0.03)	2,231	71	0.02
	SUM	10,245	73	0.02	8,994	19	0.00

RECENT EVENTS

In **March 2000** the company received FDA regulatory clearance to market a new epidural introducer, a kit used to introduce neurostimulation leads into the epidural space. MedAmicus then announced the market release of its Lumax pro Cystometry System for use in diagnosing the causes of incontinence and other urological disorders. In **April** MedAmicus announced plans to increase by 45 percent the size of its current headquarters and manufacturing facility to accommodate business growth. The company signed a new five-year lease with its existing landlord to add space adjacent to its current leasehold. In **July** Martin McLees, an analyst with Miller, Johnson and Kuehn, was predicting the company's first profitable year since it went public in 1991. In **August** MedAmicus signed an agreement with Med-Design Corp. (Nasdaq: MEDC) for the right to manufacture and distribute Med-Design's center-line retractable Safety Seldinger Introducer Needle. **Sept. 30:** For the nine months, MedAmicus reported revenue of $7,994,000, an 18 percent increase from the same period in 1999, and net income of $196,000, compared to a net loss of $52,000 last year. "Our Percutaneous Delivery Solutions business unit sales grew 27 percent during the quarter, reflecting orders from several new customers plus the continued growth in orders from our core customer base," said CEO Hartman. "Our introducer customer base now totals 12 customers, compared to three at the beginning of 1999." In **October** MedAmicus and Med-Design began development of a new retractable Safety Seldinger Introducer Needle, tentatively scheduled to launch in the United States during early summer 2001. Michael Simpson, COO and EVP of Med-Design, stated, "This new needle will bring a new level of safety to percutaneous (through the skin) delivery techniques at a time when the demand for these minimally invasive procedures is growing exponentially." The companies also announced development activities on a second product, a next-generation cardiovascular device.

OFFICERS

James D. Hartman
President and CEO

Christina M. Temperante
VP, Gen. Mgr.-Fiber Optic Division

David Liebl
VP-Operations/Technology/Fiber Optics

Mark Kraus
VP, Gen. Mgr.-Vascular Delivery Systems

Dennis S. Madison
VP-Quality/Regulatory Affairs

Michael D. Erdmann
Controller

DIRECTORS

Thomas L. Auth
ITI Technologies Inc., North St. Paul, MN

James D. Hartman

Richard L. Little
MedAmicus Inc. (retired)

Richard F. Sauter
University of St. Thomas, St. Paul

Michael M. Selzer Jr.
Urologix Inc., Plymouth, MN

MAJOR SHAREHOLDERS

Richard L. Little, 9.6%
Orono, MN

Pyramid Trading L.P., 8.4%
Chicago

All officers and directors as a group (8 persons), 19.7%

SIC CODE

3841 Surgical and medical instruments

MISCELLANEOUS

TRANSFER AGENT AND REGISTAR:
Wells Fargo Bank Minnesota N.A., South St. Paul, MN

TRADED: Nasdaq SmallCap Market

SYMBOL: MEDM

STOCKHOLDERS: 156

EMPLOYEES: 84

GENERAL COUNSEL:
Leonard Street & Deinard P.A., Minneapolis

AUDITORS:
RSM McGladrey & Pullen Inc. LLP, Minneapolis

INC: MN-1981

ANNUAL MEETING: April

INVESTOR RELATIONS:
Mike Erdmann

HUMAN RESOURCES:
Deb Schuneman

RANKINGS

No. 190 CRM Public 200

TWO-YEAR QUARTERLY HIGH-LOW STOCK PRICES

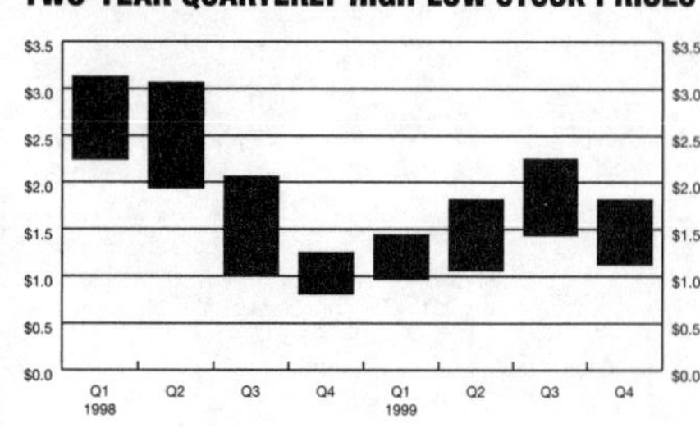

Medi-Ject Corporation

161 Cheshire Ln. N., Suite 100, Plymouth, MN 55441
Tel: 763/475-7700 Fax: 763/476-1009 Web site: http://www.mediject.com

Medi-Ject Corp. is a drug delivery company focused on developing, manufacturing, and marketing needle-free injection systems for the self-administration of a wide range of injectable drugs. The company's product, the Medi-Jector system, is a hand-held, spring-powered device that injects drugs from a needle-free syringe through the skin as a narrow, high-pressure stream of liquid .007" in diameter. Medi-Ject has entered into licensing and development agreements with multinational pharmaceutical and medical device companies covering the design and manufacture of customized injection systems for specific drug therapies. In addition, Medi-Ject and Becton Dickinson and Co. have a strategic alliance to develop and commercialize less-expensive, more user-friendly injectors with proprietary, advanced technology.

EARNINGS HISTORY

Year Ended Dec 31	Operating Revenue/Sales (dollars in thousands)	Net Earnings	Return on Revenue (percent)	Return on Equity	Net Earnings (dollars per share*)	Cash Dividend	Market Price Range
1999	3,482	(3,703)	NM	NM	(2.70)	—	7.00–1.28
1998	2,699	(5,769)	NM	NM	(4.07)	—	14.38–1.56
1997	3,717	(2,972)	NM	(31.8)	(2.12)	—	31.88–9.38
1996	3,692	(2,239)	(60.6)	(18.5)	(1.93)	—	30.00–15.63
1995 †	2,575	(1,882)	(73.1)	NM	(2.30)	—	

* Per-share amounts restated to reflect 1-for-5 reverse stock split effected Jan. 28, 1999. Stock began trading Oct. 2, 1996.
† EPS figure for 1995 is pro forma for the initial public offering.

BALANCE SHEET

Assets	12/31/99 (dollars in thousands)	12/31/98	Liabilities	12/31/99 (dollars in thousands)	12/31/98
Current (CAE 85 and 2,852)	705	3,772	Current (STD 14)	903	704
Equipment, furniture, and fixtures	1,003	1,278	Note payable	54	
			Stockholders' equity*	1,053	4,630
Patent rights	302	284			
TOTAL	2,010	5,334	TOTAL	2,010	5,334

* $0.01 par common; 3,400,000 authorized; 1,424,729 and 1,424,752 issued and outstanding.

RECENT QUARTERS / **PRIOR-YEAR RESULTS**

	Quarter End	Revenue ($000)	Earnings ($000)	EPS ($)	Revenue ($000)	Earnings ($000)	EPS ($)
Q3	09/30/2000	455	(1,125)	(0.82)	509	(1,129)	(0.84)
Q2	06/30/2000	767	(917)	(0.66)	577	(998)	(0.72)
Q1	03/31/2000	484	(842)	(0.62)	1,592	(265)	(0.20)
Q4	12/31/99	804	(1,311)	(0.95)	343	(2,587)	(1.83)
	SUM	2,510	(4,196)	(3.03)	3,021	(4,979)	(3.58)

PRIOR YEAR: Q1 licensing revenue includes one-time settlement fee.

RECENT EVENTS

In **January 2000** the company agreed to acquire Permatec Holding A.G., a privately held drug delivery company in Basel, Switzerland. The merger was expected to be completed by year end. In **February** Medi-Ject entered into an agreement with Chronimed (Nasdaq: CHMD), Minnetonka, Minn., for distribution of its needle-free injection devices and supplies in the U.S. diabetes market. Medi-Ject was honored with an Award of Distinction by The Communicator Awards, an international video competition, in the Medical Product Overview category—for its Medi-Jector Vision marketing video, produced for Medi-Ject Corp. by Minneapolis-based Take 1 Productions. In **March** the company entered into an agreement with Infusiones Gove S.A. DE C.V. for the exclusive distribution of the Medi-Jector Vision needle-free insulin delivery system in the Mexican insulin diabetes market. In **April** Medi-Ject signed a Note Purchase Agreement and received $500,000 from Permatec Holding AG in exchange for the a promissory note relating to their intent to form a business combination. Under the new Note Purchase Agreement, Permatec agreed to loan the company up to $4 million subject to certain conditions, including satisfactory progress on the proposed business combination. The company entered into a research agreement with Organon, a pharmaceutical company noted for its core expertise in hormonal therapy products, to explore the development of a new needle-free syringe for use with the Medi-Jector Vision injector. In **May** the Australian Therapeutic Goods Administration granted regulatory approval to market in Australia a Medi-Ject needle-free injector, the SciTojet, for use with human growth hormone. An exclusive agreement with Comar Cardio Technology srl provided for the distribution of the Medi-Jector Vision needle-free insulin injection system in Italy. In **July** Medi-Ject signed a Stock Purchase Agreement with Permatec Holding AG, a privately held drug delivery company located in Basel, Switzerland, and three of Permatec's subsidiaries. Medi-Ject was to acquire all of the outstanding stock of Permatec Pharma AG (a Switzerland company), PermatecTechnologie AG (a Switzerland company), and Permatec NV (a Netherlands Antilles company) in exchange for 2.9 million shares of Medi-Ject common stock. Upon closing of the transaction, Medi-Ject was to be renamed Antares Pharma Inc. Permatec would emerge as the majority shareholder of Antares, resulting in a change of control. Several product development agreements were to remain in place, including an ***continued on page 285***

OFFICERS

Franklin Pass, M.D.
Chairman, President, and CEO

Peter Sadowski, Ph.D.
EVP and Chief Technical Officer

Lawrence M. Christian
VP-Finance/Administration and CFO

Michael Kasprick
VP-Sales/Marketing

Julius Sund
VP-Manufacturing

DIRECTORS

Kenneth L. Evenstad
Upsher-Smith Laboratories

Stanley Goldberg
Goldmark Advisors

Karl Groth
First Circle Medical Inc.

Geoffrey Guy
GW Pharmaceuticals Ltd.

Franklin Pass, M.D.

Fred L. Shapiro, M.D.
Hennepin Faculty Associates, Minneapolis

MAJOR SHAREHOLDERS

Becton Dickinson and Co., 32.4%
Franklin Lakes, NJ

Franklin Pass, M.D., 7.4%

All officers and directors as a group (8 persons), 11.4%

SIC CODE

3841 Surgical and medical instruments

MISCELLANEOUS

TRANSFER AGENT AND REGISTAR:
Wells Fargo Bank Minnesota N.A., South St. Paul, MN

TRADED: Nasdaq SmallCap Market

SYMBOL: MEDJ

STOCKHOLDERS: 2,022

EMPLOYEES: 38

IN MINNESOTA: 38

GENERAL COUNSEL:
Leonard Street & Deinard P.A., Minneapolis

AUDITORS:
KPMG LLP, Minneapolis

INC: MN-1979

ANNUAL MEETING: May

INVESTOR RELATIONS:
Lawrence M. Christian

TWO-YEAR QUARTERLY HIGH-LOW STOCK PRICES

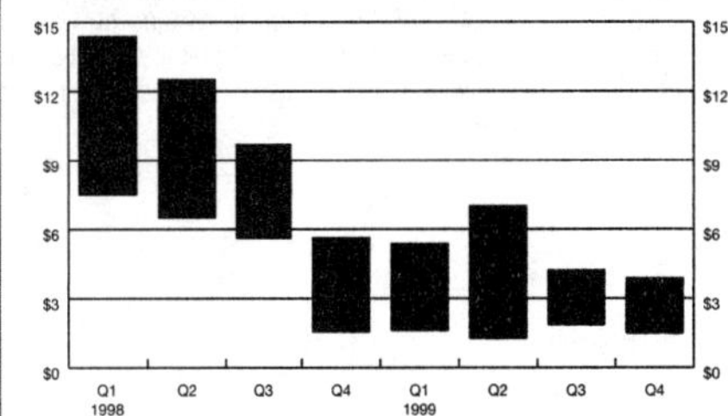

PUB

PUB

MEDTOX Scientific Inc.

402 W. County Rd. D, New Brighton, MN 55112
Tel: 651/636-7466 Fax: 651/628-6121 Web site: http://www.medtox.com

MEDTOX Scientific Inc., through its MEDTOX Laboratories subsidiary, is the leader in providing esoteric toxicology services to hospitals, pharmaceutical companies, and laboratories nationwide. This subsidiary also provides employment drug testing and occupational health testing, including biological monitoring for exposure to industrial chemicals, heavy metals, and solvents. Its MEDTOX Diagnostics subsidiary develops and manufactures diagnostic devices for quick and economical on-site analysis for drugs of abuse and agricultural toxins. Additionally, its diagnostics subsidiary provides contract manufacturing using its patented technology and proprietary manufacturing processes.

EARNINGS HISTORY

Year Ended Dec 31	Operating Revenue/Sales (dollars in thousands)	Net Earnings	Return on Revenue (percent)	Return on Equity	Net Earnings (dollars per share*)	Cash Dividend	Market Price Range
1999	35,003	1,419	4.1	11.1	0.49	—	10.06–2.56
1998	29,576	(2,297)	(7.8)	(20.3)	(0.79)	—	8.75–3.75
1997	28,600	25	0.1	0.2	0.01	—	12.50–5.00
1996	26,726	(12,809)	(47.9)	NM	(11.71)	—	73.75–8.75
1995	7,526	(7,285)	NM	NM	(15.42)	—	

* Per-share amounts restated to reflect 1-for-20 reverse stock split in February 1999.

BALANCE SHEET

Assets	12/31/99 (dollars in thousands)	12/31/98	Liabilities	12/31/99 (dollars in thousands)	12/31/98
Current (CAE 576)	10,294	7,618	Current (STD 1,236 and 1,140)	11,250	10,897
Equipment and improvements	2,816	2,975	Restructuring accrual	85	76
Goodwill	13,161	14,007	Capital leases	409	516
TOTAL	26,271	24,600	Long-term debt	1,737	1,785
			Stockholders' equity*	12,790	11,326
			TOTAL	26,271	24,600

* $0.15 par common; 7,400,000 authorized; 2,904,410 and 2,899,669 issued and outstanding.

RECENT QUARTERS / **PRIOR-YEAR RESULTS**

	Quarter End	Revenue ($000)	Earnings ($000)	EPS ($)	Prior-Year Revenue ($000)	Prior-Year Earnings ($000)	Prior-Year EPS ($)
Q2	06/30/2000	11,316	481	0.17	9,152	741	0.26
Q1	03/31/2000	9,676	297	0.10	7,835	160	0.06
Q4	12/31/99	8,942	169	0.06	6,982	(2,466)	(0.85)
Q3	09/30/99	9,073	349	0.12	7,609	(192)	(0.07)
	SUM	39,007	1,296	0.45	31,578	(1,757)	(0.61)

PRIOR YEAR: Q2 earnings include restructuring costs of $164,000/($0.06).

RECENT EVENTS

In **January 2000** Dougherty and Co. LLC, Minneapolis, initiated coverage of MEDTOX with a BUY recommendation. In May Miller, Johnson & Kuehn initiated coverage of MEDTOX with a STRONG BUY recommendation. In **July** the company signed a definitive agreement to provide private-label diagnostic drug screening devices for Drugtest.com Inc., a Houston-based provider of innovative drug testing and data management services. At July's end, MEDTOX Diagnostics submitted its newly developed PROFILE-ER product to the FDA for 510(k) premarket clearance. In **August** MEDTOX Scientific completed a private equity financing with accredited investors, raising proceeds of $4.5 million before expenses. MEDTOX Laboratory Inc. acquired the client list of a competitor for drugs of abuse sample collection services. The acquisition was expected to double collection volume at Medtox' Bloomington, Minn., collection site. Additionally, Medtox entered into agreements to provide sample collection services for two Fortune 500 companies. Medtox estimated that annual revenue from the client list acquisition and the new clients would exceed $500,000. Based on its revenue growth from 1995 to 1999, the company was named to Deloitte & Touche's Minnesota Technology Fast 50. In September the company expanded its July private equity financing to include an additional $1.0 million investment from a single institutional investor, bringing the total raised in the private placement to $5.5 million before expenses.

OFFICERS

Harry G. McCoy, Pharm.D.
Chairman and President

Richard J. Braun
CEO

James B. Lockhart
CFO

DIRECTORS

Richard J. Braun

Miles E. Efron
North Star Universal Inc., St. Louis Park, MN

James W. Hansen
E.mergent Inc., Golden Valley, MN

Brian P. Johnson
Touchstone Venture Partners

Harry G. McCoy

Samuel C. Powell, Ph.D.
Powell Enterprises, Burlington, NC

MAJOR SHAREHOLDERS

Harry G. McCoy, 7.3%

All Officers and Directors as a group (6 persons), 14.5%

SIC CODE

8071 Medical laboratories

MISCELLANEOUS

TRANSFER AGENT AND REGISTAR:
American Stock Transfer & Trust Co., New York

TRADED: AMEX

SYMBOL: TOX

STOCKHOLDERS: 3,033

EMPLOYEES: 340

GENERAL COUNSEL:
Hinshaw & Culbertson, Minneapolis

AUDITORS:
Deloitte & Touche LLP, Minneapolis

INC: DE-1983

ANNUAL MEETING:
September

RANKINGS

No. 126 CRM Public 200

No. 25 Minnesota Technology Fast 50

TWO-YEAR QUARTERLY HIGH-LOW STOCK PRICES

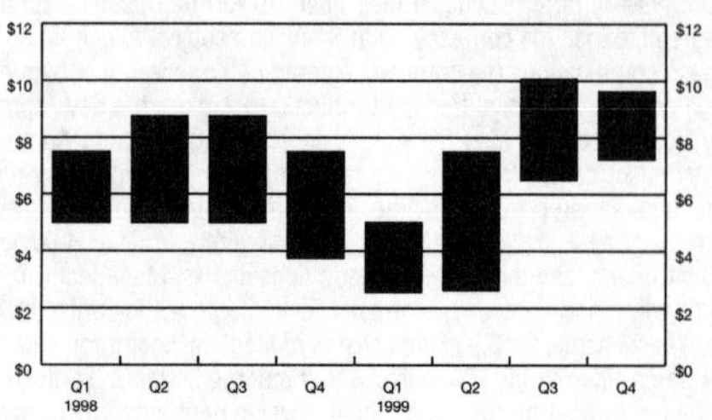

PUB

Medtronic Inc.

7000 Central Ave. N.E., Fridley, MN 55432
Tel: 763/514-4000 Fax: 763/514-3464 Web site: http://www.medtronic.com

Medtronic Inc. is the world's leading medical technology company, pioneering device-based therapies that alleviate pain, restore health, and extend life. The company serves customers and patients in 120 countries, with operations organized into three global areas: Americas, Europe/Middle East/Africa, and Asia/Pacific. The company concentrates its efforts in the areas of Cardiac Rhythm Management (Bradycardia Pacing, Tachyarrhythmia Management, Heart Failure Management, and Atrial Fibrillation Management); Vascular (Coronary Vascular and Peripheral Vascular); Cardiac Surgery (Cardiopulmonary, Heart Valves, DLP Cannulae, and Blood Management); and Neurological and Spinal (Neurostimulation, Drug Delivery, Neurosurgery, and Diagnostic Systems).

EARNINGS HISTORY *

Year Ended Apr 30	Operating Revenue/Sales (dollars in thousands)	Net Earnings	Return on Revenue (percent)	Return on Equity	Net Earnings (dollars per share†)	Cash Dividend	Market Price Range
2000 ¶	5,014,600	1,098,500	21.9	24.5	0.92	0.16	57.19–31.31
1999 #	4,232,400	476,300	11.3	12.6	0.40	0.13	44.06–24.44
1998 **	3,423,100	594,600	17.4	21.7	0.52	0.11	28.88–16.56
1997 ††	3,010,300	582,000	19.3	26.9	0.50	0.10	17.84–11.84
1996	2,570,000	488,000	19.0	24.1	0.47	0.07	15.44–8.97

* Historical figures are restated to pool fiscal 2000 acquisition Xomed and fiscal 1999 acquisitions AVE, Sofamor Danek, and Physio-Control.
† Per-share amounts restated to reflect 2-for-1 stock splits effected on Sept. 24, 1999; and in August 1997, and September 1995.
¶ Income figures for 2000 include pretax nonrecurring charges totaling $13.8 million (net of changes in estimates).
\# Income figures for 1999 include pretax nonrecurring charges totaling $554.1 million.
** Income figures for 1998 include pretax nonrecurring charges totaling $205.3 million.
†† Income figures for 1997 include pretax nonrecurring charges totaling $49.8 million.

BALANCE SHEET

Assets	04/30/00 (dollars in thousands)	04/30/99	Liabilities	04/30/00 (dollars in thousands)	04/30/99
Current (CAE 448,400 and 228,500)	3,013,400	2,444,800	Current (STD 316,300 and 239,200)	991,500	1,006,200
Property, plant, and equipment	946,500	772,300	Long-term debt	14,100	23,400
Goodwill, other intangibles	1,361,400	1,374,200	Deferred income taxes	15,200	30,800
Investments	210,100	212,700	Other	157,100	177,200
Other	138,000	204,400	Stockholders' equity*	4,491,500	3,770,800
TOTAL	5,669,400	5,008,400	TOTAL	5,669,400	5,008,400

* $0.10 par common; 1,600,000,000 authorized; 1,197,698,035 and 1,191,896,614 issued and outstanding.

RECENT QUARTERS / **PRIOR-YEAR RESULTS**

	Quarter End	Revenue ($000)	Earnings ($000)	EPS ($)	Prior-Year Revenue ($000)	Earnings ($000)	EPS ($)
Q1	07/28/2000	1,309,900	289,000	0.24	1,133,200	252,400	0.21
Q4	04/30/2000	1,432,300	322,300	0.27	1,146,597	160,578	0.13
Q3	01/28/2000	1,258,800	263,200	0.22	1,064,842	(34,117)	(0.03)
Q2	10/29/99	1,190,300	260,600	0.22	1,006,388	119,168	0.10
	SUM	5,191,300	1,135,100	0.95	4,351,027	498,029	0.42

CURRENT: Q1 earnings include charge of $16.9 million pretax, $11.4 million/($0.01) after-tax, for litigation judgment. Q4 earnings include pretax special credit of $24.9 million and litigation settlement expense of $24.0 million--for a net after-tax gain of $0.6 million/$0.00. Q3 earnings include nonrecurring charge of $14.7 million pretax, $12.1 million/($0.01) after-tax, for Xomed merger. PRIOR YEAR: Q4 earnings include special charges of $124,611,000 pretax, $85,647,000/($0.07) after-tax. Q3 earnings include nonrecurring charges of $302.2 million pretax, $248.2 million/($0.21) after-tax, for AVE and Sofamor Danek mergers. Q2 earnings include special charge of $116.4 million pretax, $97.9 million/($0.09) after-tax.

RECENT EVENTS

In **November 1999** the company's Synergy Neurostimulation System, the first and only totally implantable dual-channel therapy designed to aid in the management of chronic intractable pain of the trunk or limbs, was approved

continued on page 272

OFFICERS

William W. George
Chairman and CEO

Arthur D. Collins Jr.
President and COO

Glen D. Nelson, M.D.
Vice Chairman

Janet S. Fiola
SVP-Human Resources

Bob Guezuraga
SVP and Pres.-Cardiac Surgery

Steven B. Kelmar
SVP-e-Business/External Relations

Stephen H. Mahle
SVP and Pres.-Cardiac Rhythm Mgmt.

Andy Rasdal
SVP and Pres.-Vascular

Robert L. Ryan
SVP and CFO

David J. Scott
SVP and General Counsel

Scott Solano
SVP-Corporate Technology

Keith E. Williams
SVP, Pres.-Neurologic/Spinal/ENT

Barry W. Wilson
SVP and Pres.-Europe/Middle East/Africa

Robert H. Blankmeyer
VP and Pres.-Medtronic Xomed

Chuck Brynelsen
VP and Pres.-Asia Pacific

Michael F. DeMane
VP and Pres.-Spinal

Gary L. Ellis
VP, Corp. Cont, and Treas.

Laurance Fairey
VP and Pres.-Neurologic Technologies

Jodi L. Harpstead
VP, Pres.-Arrhythmia Mgmt. Global Mktg.

Richard Martin
VP and Pres.-Medtronic Physio-Control

William V. Murray
VP and Pres.-Pacing

Jon T. Tremmel
VP and Pres.-Tachyarrhythmia Management

Scott R.. Ward
VP and Pres.-Neurological

DIRECTORS

Michael R. Bonsignore
Honeywell Int'l Inc.

William R. Brody
The Johns Hopkins University

Paul W. Chellgren
Ashland Inc.

Arthur D. Collins Jr.

Frank Douglas, M.D.
Aventis Pharma AG, Frankfurt

William W. George

Antonio M. Gotto Jr., M.D.
Cornell U. Medical Center

Bernadine P. Healy
Ohio State University

Thomas E. Holloran
U. of St. Thomas, St. Paul

Glen D. Nelson, M.D.

Denise M. O'Leary
venture capitalist, San Mateo, CA

Jean-Pierre Rosso
Case Corp., Racine, WI

Richard L. Schall
consultant

Jack W. Schuler
Stericycle Inc.

Gerald W. Simonson
Omnetics Connector Corp., Minneapolis

Gordon M. Sprenger
Allina Health Systems Inc., Minneapolis

Richard A. Swalin, Ph.D.
U. of Arizona, Tucson, AZ

MAJOR SHAREHOLDERS

All officers, directors as a group (23 persons), 0.9%

MISCELLANEOUS

TRANSFER AGENT AND REGISTAR:
Wells Fargo Bank Minnesota
South St. Paul, MN
TRADED: NYSE
SYMBOL: MDT
STOCKHOLDERS: 42,500
EMPLOYEES: 21,498
IN MINNESOTA: 5,968
GENERAL COUNSEL:
Faegre & Benson PLLP
Fredrikson & Byron P.A.
AUDITORS:
PricewaterhouseCoopers LLP
INC: MN-1957
FOUNDED: 1949
ANNUAL MEETING:
August
INVESTOR RELATIONS:
Rachael Scherer
COMMUNICATIONS:
Jessica Stoltenberg

RANKINGS

No. 10 CRM Public 200
No.31 CRM Employer 100
No. 8 CRM Perform. 100

TWO-YEAR QUARTERLY HIGH-LOW STOCK PRICES

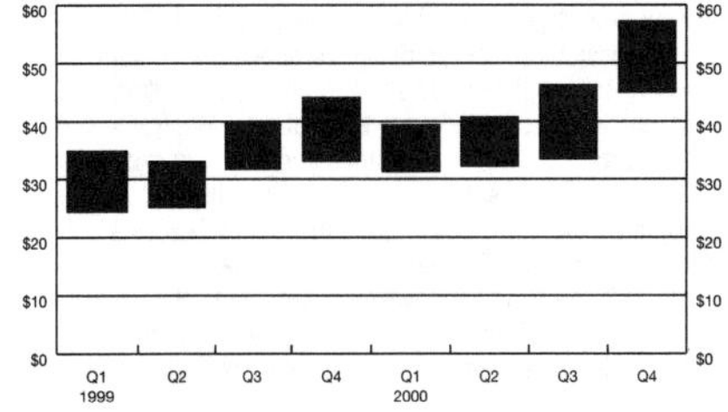

by the FDA. PMA approval of a single-operator exchange version of its recently-released S670 coronary stent system was also received. In **December** Medtronic announced clearance by the Japanese Ministry of Health and Welfare to market its S670 with Discrete Technology Coronary Stent System, which incorporates the most advanced stent design and delivery system technologies available on the market. Then the company announced the first implant and the start of worldwide human clinical trials for its ADVANTAGE bileaflet mechanical heart valve. Medtronic AVE, Santa Rosa, Calif., sued Johnson & Johnson's Cordis Corp., Miami Lakes, Fla., for allegedly infringing a patent for a method of inserting a catheter to repair blood vessels of heart patients. Medtronic completed its previously announced business transaction to acquire a substantial portion of the assets of the Image Guided Surgery business of Elekta AB, Norcross, Ga., for $11.75 million, plus the assumption of certain liabilities. Medtronic announced the worldwide release of Today's Kappa, the next-generation software package for its Medtronic Kappa family of pacemakers, the world's No. 1-selling pacing series. In **January 2000** the company's stock was one of three in Minnesota among the 89 stocks that Goldman Sachs & Co. listed as its analysts' favorite stock picks for 2000. The listed stocks were expected to generate a 12-month price return of 35 percent, compared with an an expected gain of only 4 percent by the S&P 500 index. Medtronic spent $9.2 million to acquire an 18 percent stake in VidaMed Inc., Fremont, Calif., which makes a device to treat noncancerous enlargements of the prostate. Medtronic formed "Medtronic.com" to launch a new patient-management business involving collaborations with information technology leaders Microsoft Corp. and International Business Machines Corp. (IBM). Within 18 months, patients linked to the new systems were to have direct connectivity to specialty care teams of physicians anywhere in the world, at any time, via an Internet-based program. Medtronic committed to an initial investment of $228 million over four years. For the second stage of its Internet strategy, Medtronic agreed to form an exclusive, four-year, $100 million global partnership with Healtheon/WebMD (Nasdaq: HLTH) to provide health care information on the Internet and other communications media to consumers and physicians. Medtronic then established a Corporate E-Business Center to unify all aspects of its Internet strategy. FDA clearance was received for the Reveal Plus Insertable Loop Recorder (ILR), the world's first and only implantable heart monitor with new auto-activation capabilities. Medtronic announced plans for a $31 million expansion of its European headquarters and production facilities located in Tolochenaz, Switzerland, near Lausanne—an initiative that will create 200 additional jobs by 2006. **Jan. 28:** A turnaround in the vascular business, coupled with continued strong sales of defibrillators, helped produce a 28 percent third-quarter earnings increase (exluding merger charges) that was in line with expectations. In **February** Medtronic Physio-Control announced new additions to the LIFEPAK 12 defibrillator/monitor series making the popular device even more functional for a wider variety of users. An electroluminescent (EL) display manufactured by Planar Systems Inc.—slightly larger than the alternate LCD screen and with a wider viewing angle—is ideal for use in the hospital emergency department and coronary care unit, as well as on portable crash carts. Another enhancement is the lead-select keypad. As part of establishing its presence in the emerging market of radiation therapies to prevent restenosis, Medtronic acquired XRT Corp., a privately owned, St. Paul company that develops minimally invasive, intravascular radiation therapies. In **March** Medtronic Physio-Control joined the the National Golf Course Owners Association's Smart Buy Network, a group purchasing program, and began offer LIFEPAK 500 AEDs to NGCOA members. (Golf courses are among the most common places where cardiac arrest occurs.) Medtronic obtained the right to affix CE (Conformite Europeenne) marking to its Reveal Plus Insertable Loop Recorder (ILR), which was to be sold in all countries of the European Union and the European Free Trade Area. Smith & Nephew Inc. and Medtronic Surgical Navigation Technologies (part of Sofamor Danek) agreed to form a strategic alliance to jointly develop, market, and sell image-guided surgical applications for orthopaedic procedures. ETEX Corp., an advanced biomaterials company headquartered in Cambridge, Mass., signed a major agreement with the Sofamor Danek Division of Medtronic—setting up a long-term relationship to jointly develop products for spinal applications. Medtronic joined Johnson & Johnson, GE Medical Systems, Baxter International Inc., and Abbott Laboratories to form an Internet-based buying exchange designed to speed customer transactions and make them more cost-efficient. The new company was to be based in Chicago and begin operating in fall 2000. Boston Scientific Corp., Natick, Mass., filed a patent-infringement suit alleging that a coronary stent system sold by Medtronic was violating one of its patents. Medtronic's Activa Parkinson's Control Therapy, which uses bilateral brain stimulation to treat the symptoms of advanced, levodopa-responsive Parkinson's disease, received a unanimous conditional approval for marketing clearance by the Neurological Device Panel Advisory Committee to the FDA. Conditions included: a three-year, long-term clinical follow-up, including cognitive and neuropsychological factors; physician instruction on selecting electrodes and programming; and several recommended label changes. In **April**, after the FDA cautioned Medtronic that its Internet site included a number of representations regarding its Activa product that went beyond uses approved in the United States, the disputed information was removed from the site. Medtronic announced humanitarian device exemption (HDE) FDA approval for an implantable therapy using electrical stimulation of the stomach to treat patients with a severe, often life-threatening, form of gastroparesis. Medtronic purchased NetForce Inc.'s E-Gate clinical data acquisition and migration tool, which is used by pharmaceutical, biotechnology, and medical device companies to assist in clinical and safety data management. The FDA released a letter warning Medtronic of a regulatory problem with some of its external defibrillators (Physio-Control's Life Pak 500) that had not been properly remedied. Medtronic launched an additional version, and new enhancements, for Its market-leading AneuRx Stent Graft System. Cephalon Inc., West Chester, Pa., agreed to co-promote Medtronic Intrathecal Baclofen Therapy for the treatment of severe spasticity—to neurologists and neurosurgeons in the United Kingdom, France, and Austria. **April 30:** With broad-based strength and momentum across all of the company's major businesses, Medtronic achieved record revenue of $5.015 billion for fiscal 2000, a 19 percent increase (on a constant currency basis)—despite difficult comparable numbers and competition. Foreign exchange reduced the annual revenue increase by $33.5 million and the growth rate to 18.5 percent. Company officials credited three key factors in Medtronic's major businesses that contributed to fourth quarter's strong performance and balanced growth: (1) continued physician preference for Medtronic's market-leading technology in its implantable and external defibrillators, as well as strong performance in its pacemaker lines; (2) accelerating sales momentum in the Vascular business (sales rose 70 percent in the quarter to $253 million) from the S670 coronary stent system and the AneuRx endovascular graft for treatment of abdominal aortic aneurysms; and (3) strong growth from the broadened Neurological, Spinal and Ear, Nose and Throat (ENT) product portfolio, which was generating 25 percent of total Medtronic revenue and grew at more than 25 percent. In a survey released in May, a majority of elderly patients who had received Medtronic InterStim Therapy for Urinary Control for relief from the bladder control problems of urge incontinence, significant symptoms of urgency-frequency, and non-obstructive retention expressed satisfaction with the therapy. The Vitatron organization of Medtronic announced commercial release outside the United States of three new products designed to advance and refine therapies for atrial fibrillation (AF). Medtronic made a significant investment in Itamar Medical Ltd. Inc., Caesaria, Israel, to enable Itamar to accelerate and broaden its research, development, and initial commercialization efforts involving peripheral arterial tonometry (PAT), a unique physiological signal that can be measured by the company's proprietary products noninvasively and can provide substantial medical information. CE Mark approval and market introduction in select international geographies of the Medtronic BeStent2 With Discrete Technology Rapid Exchange Coronary Stent Delivery System was announced. Medtronic's latest-generation small vessel stent, the S660 With Discrete Technology Coronary Stent System, received marketing clearance from the FDA. Midway over the Atlantic Ocean, a British Airways flight crew tested the newest addition to its inflight medical kit—a tiny portable heart monitor—and used it to transmit diagnostic data via cutting-edge satellite communications technology. A scientific study demonstrated that a unique implantable heart monitor called the Reveal Insertable Loop Recorder (ILR) provides an earlier answer for unexplained, recurrent "blackouts," or fainting, compared with conventional cardiovascular testing. Medtronic announced the worldwide launch of four new products to further the adoption of beating heart bypass surgery: the Octopus3 Tissue Stabilization System, combined with the ClearView Intracoronary Shunt, the QuickFlow DPS Distal Perfusion System, and the ClearView Blower/Mister System. Medtronic Physio-Control (NYSE: MDT), the world's largest manufacturer of external defibrillators, and Data Critical Corporation (Nasdaq: DCCA), a leader in cutting-edge wireless capabilities for healthcare, today announced that Medtronic Physio-Control, will handle sales, service and distribution of Data Critical's wireless communication technology products in Europe. In **June** Data Critical Corp. (Nasdaq: DCCA), a leader in cutting-edge wireless capabilities for health care, announced that Medtronic Physio-Control had agreed to handle sales, service, and distribution of Data Critical's wireless communication technology products in Europe. An FDA warning letter to Medtronic noted that some of the adverse incidents in the clinical trials of the AneuRx stent graft were not reported within the prescribed time. Medtronic announced CE Mark approval and the introduction of its next-generation renal stent system, the Medtronic Bridge X3 Renal Stent System, in major markets outside the United States. Offering one solution for patients with two high-risk heart cond tions—heart failure and sudden cardiac death—Medtronic announced commercial release outside the United States of its Medtronic InSync ICD cardiac resynchronization system. Medtronic announced approval by the FDA to market its new Jewel AF ICD—the world's first and only ICD to offer new therapeutic capabilities for detecting and treating arrhythmias of the atria (upper chambers), in addition to the ventricles (lower chambers). Cardiac Science Inc (OTC: DFIB) signed an agreement to license its proprietary technology to Medtronic Physio-Control for integration into LIFEPAK products for the hospital market. The board of directors approved a first-quarter dividend of 5 cents per share, reflecting its intention to increase the annual dividend for fiscal 2001 by 4 cents to 20 cents, which is consistent with the company's objective of distributing 20 percent of the prior year's earnings per share as dividends. At month's end, Edwards Lifesciences Corp., Irvine, Calif., accused Medtronic of infringing two patents it holds for devices used in coronary surgery. Medtronic brands involved: Hancock II and Mosaic valves, Duran surgical devices. A study reported in the June issue of The Journal of Urology indicated that sacral nerve stimulation (such as Medtronic InterStim Therapy for Urinary Control) is a safe and effective therapy for people who suffer from significant symptoms of urinary urgency-frequency and who have not responded favorably to more traditional treatment options, such as pelvic muscle exercises, biofeedback, medications, and surgeries. The IsoMed Constant-Flow Infusion System, a new implantable drug pump from Medtronic, received approval from the FDA for use in a promising colorectal liver cancer treatment that delivers cancer-fighting medication directly to the liver, the most common place for colon cancer to spread. On July 25, the U.S. District Court for the Western District of Tennessee entered an Order finding that Surgical Dynamics Inc.'s procedure for implanting the Ray TFC spinal fusion cage device literally infringes Medtronic Sofamor Danek's U.S. Patent No. 5,741,253 ("the '253 patent"). The companies were to proceed to trial in September on the issue of damages and on Surgical Dynamic's allegation that the patent is invalid. Medtronic Sofamor Danek was also asserting the '253 patent against Osteotech Inc. in a separate suit pending in the same court. **July 28:** Medtronic met expectations with its first-quarter earnings increase of 19 percent (excluding one-time charges), but disappointed analysts with its revenue number. The implantable defibrillator business, which lost a couple of points of market share to Guidant Corp., didn't grow as strongly as expected. In **August** Medtronic received approval from the FDA for its Mosaic porcine bioprosthetic heart valve. The company was was one of four in the Twin Cities named to Industry Week magazine's fifth annual list of the World's 100 Best-Managed Companies. It was Medtronic's third appearance on the list. For the second-consecutive year, Medtronic was named one of the 10 Great Places to Work in Minnesota, in the August issue of Corporate Report magazine. Implementing an established succession plan, the board of directors announced at the annual meeting of shareholders that Arthur D. Collins Jr. will succeed William W. George as chief executive officer on May 1, 2001, and as chairman on April 30, 2002. Under George's watch, since 1991, annual sales had quintupled to $5 billion and the stock price had increased at five times the rate of the S&P 500. George noted that Collins had held responsibility for Medtronic's operating organizations during a period when revenue quadrupled and the company evolved from a specialized developer and manufacturer of implantable devices to a broad-line medical technology supplier with expanding product lines serving neurological, surgical, vascular, otolaryngology, and spinal markets, as well as the company's traditional cardiac rhythm management customers. In a move to provide physicians with new therapy options to optimize atrial tachyarrhythmia management, Medtronic announced the European and Canadian release of its new Medtronic AT500 DDDRP Pacing System, the world's first to offer an exclusive trio of atrial therapy management capabilities that include monitoring, prevention, and termination. In **September** European physicians implanted Medtronic GEM III DR ICD (Dual Chamber Model 7275), the first of a new generation of ICDs with advances in detection, device longevity, and diagnostic capabilities designed to treat potentially lethal heart rhythms such as sudden cardiac arrest. Medtronic confirmed that it had made a proposal in July to acquire $47.9 million-revenue Cyberonics Inc. (Nasdaq: CYBX), a Houston-based market leader in medical devices for the treatment of epilepsy, for $26 per share in Medtronic stock (a total value, in September, of $483 million, or 62 percent higher than prevailing market value). When Cyberonics rejected the offer, Medtronic hired the proxy con-

continued on page 285

Medwave Inc.

4382 Round Lake Rd. W., Arden Hills, MN 55112
Tel: 651/639-1227 Fax: 651/639-1338

Medwave Inc. is engaged exclusively in the development, manufacturing, and marketing of a proprietary, noninvasive system that continually monitors arterial blood pressure of adults, and in the development of related technology and products. Utilizing the company's proprietary technology, the VASOTRAC System monitors blood pressure continually, providing new readings every 15 heartbeats. The company also developed a hand-held blood pressure measurement device, the Vasotrax.

EARNINGS HISTORY *

Year Ended Apr 30	Operating Revenue/Sales (dollars in thousands)	Net Earnings	Return on Revenue (percent)	Return on Equity	Net Earnings (dollars per share†)	Cash Dividend	Market Price Range
2000	486	(2,553)	NM	(72.9)	(0.47)	—	10.00–6.38
1999 ¶	510	(720)	NM	(12.2)	(0.13)	—	14.50–8.50
1998	593	(2,337)	NM	(35.6)	(0.48)	—	15.00–8.00
1997	73	(1,610)	NM	(29.7)	(0.34)	—	12.88–7.75
1996	0	(672)	NM	(10.0)	(0.17)	—	8.00–5.00

* Development-stage company.
† Stock began trading in November 1995.
¶ Income figures for 1999 include "stand-still" payment of $1.5 million.

BALANCE SHEET

Assets	04/30/00 (dollars in thousands)	04/30/99	Liabilities	04/30/00 (dollars in thousands)	04/30/99
Current (CAE 1,155 and 1,175)	3,274	4,206	Current	267	241
Property and equipment	82	70	Stockholders' equity*	3,500	5,903
Patents	10	28	TOTAL	3,767	6,143
Investments	400	1,839			
TOTAL	3,767	6,143			

* No par common; 50,000,000 authorized; 5,499,596 and 5,436,596 issued and outstanding.

RECENT QUARTERS / **PRIOR-YEAR RESULTS**

	Quarter End	Revenue ($000)	Earnings ($000)	EPS ($)	Revenue ($000)	Earnings ($000)	EPS ($)
Q1	07/31/2000	84	(669)	(0.12)	40	(580)	(0.11)
Q4	04/30/2000	115	(734)	(0.13)	52	843	0.16
Q3	01/31/2000	251	(619)	(0.11)	95	(553)	(0.10)
Q2	10/31/99	80	(620)	(0.11)	162	(525)	(0.10)
	SUM	530	(2,642)	(0.48)	349	(815)	(0.15)

PRIOR YEAR: Q4 earnings include "stand-still" payment of $1.5 million.

RECENT EVENTS

In **December 1999** the company reached an agreement with Critical Care Concepts (3Ci) for distribution of Medwave's Vasotrac APM 205A product in the hospital market. This new method for noninvasively monitoring blood pressure offered frequency of measurement, speed to the first reading, waveform analysis, and patient comfort, many of the features previously found only in highly invasive methods. At its **January 2000** shareholders meeting, Medwave introduced and demonstrated a new model of its Handheld Spot Check Blood Pressure Unit—an earlier generation of which had been submitted to the FDA. In **February** Medwave entered into an agreement with E-Wha International of Seoul, South Korea, to become the exclusive distribution company for Medwave's Vasotrac APM 205A in South Korea. In March the company entered into an agreement with Biotronic Instrument Enterprise Ltd. of Taichung, Taiwan, to be the exclusive distributor for Medwave's Vasotrac APM 205A product in Taiwan. In **May** Medwave entered into an agreement making MOVI S.p.a. of Milano, Italy, the exclusive distribution company for Medwave's Vasotrac APM205A in Italy. In June Nihon Kohden of Tokyo agreed to become the exclusive distribution company in Japan for Medwave's Vasotrac APM 205A. Medwave formally submitted its Handheld Blood Pressure Monitoring Unit, the Vasotrax, to the FDA for 510(k) review. Having completed marketing focus groups on the Vasotrax, as well as clinical studies of the performance, Medwave had a high degree of confidence in both product performance and market acceptance. In **July** the company entered into an agreement with Mammendorf Institute for Physics and Medicine (MIPM) of Munich for MIPM to become a distribution company for Medwave's Vasotrac APM 205A in Germany, Austria, and Switzerland. In **August** Medwave received the CE mark, allowing the company to sell the Vasotrac APM 205A noninvasive blood pressure device in European Union countries. Medwave entered into a research agreement with Arkansas Children's Hospital Research Institute of Little Rock, Ark., that was to provide clinical testing and ultimately validate Medwave's Vasotrac APM 205A Non Invasive Blood Pressure Monitor for use in pediatrics. Medwave introduced its Vasotrax product to nurse anesthetists at their annual convention in Chicago. In **September** Medwave received 510(k) approval from the FDA for the Vasotrax, which then became available for sale in the United States. Medwave immediately reached an agreement with Critical Care Concepts (3Ci) for distribution of Vasotrax in the U.S. hospital market. Medwave reached an OEM supplier agreement with Nihon Kohden of Tokyo, under which Medwave was to become an OEM supplier for Nihon Kohden regarding noninvasive blood pressure technology. In **October** a study reported that volunteers found the Vasotrac significantly more comfortable than the upper arm cuff methods of blood pressure measurement; surgical patients with deliberately induced hypotension could be monitored with negligible bias; and Vasotrac may be used for continual noninvasive BP monitoring in children over 4 years of age.

OFFICERS

Timothy O'Malley
President and CEO

Mark T. Bakko
CFO

DIRECTORS

G. Kent Archibald

William D. Corneliuson
B.C. Holdings Inc.

Norman Dann
Pathfinder Ventures Inc. (retired)

Jeffrey W. Green
Hutchinson Technology Inc., Hutchinson, MN

Timothy O'Malley

MAJOR SHAREHOLDERS

G. Kent Archibald, 10.3%

David B. Johnson, 8.9%
Golden Valley, MN

John R. Albers, 8.2%
Dallas

Aaron Boxer Revocable Trust, 7.2%
St. Louis Park, MN

William D. Corneliuson, 6.6%
Milwaukee

All officers and directors as a group (6 persons), 18.1%

SIC CODE

3841 Surgical and medical instruments

MISCELLANEOUS

TRANSFER AGENT AND REGISTAR:
Wells Fargo Bank Minnesota N.A.,
South St. Paul, MN

TRADED: Nasdaq SmallCap Market

SYMBOL: MDWV

STOCKHOLDERS: 150

EMPLOYEES: 18

PART TIME: 1

GENERAL COUNSEL:
Fredrikson & Byron P.A., Minneapolis

AUDITORS:
Ernst & Young LLP, Minneapolis

INC: MN-1984

ANNUAL MEETING:
November

INVESTOR RELATIONS:
Mark Bakko

TWO-YEAR QUARTERLY HIGH-LOW STOCK PRICES

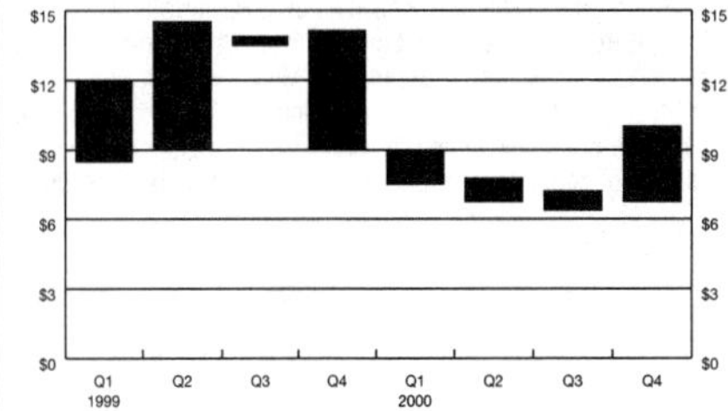

PUB

Mercury Waste Solutions Inc.

302 N. Riverfront Dr., Mankato, MN 56001
Tel: 507/345-0522 Fax: 507/345-1483 Web site: http://www.mercurywastesolutions.com

Mercury Waste Solutions Inc. provides services to mercury waste generators to reduce the risk of liability associated with mercury waste disposal. The company currently operates a mercury waste retorting facility in Union Grove, Wisconsin; a facility for recycling and storing fluorescent and other mercury-containing lamps in Roseville, Minn.; and mercury waste storage and collection facilities in Indianapolis; Atlanta; and Albany, N.Y.

EARNINGS HISTORY

Year Ended Dec 31	Operating Revenue/Sales (dollars in thousands)	Net Earnings	Return on Revenue (percent)	Return on Equity	Net Earnings (dollars per share*)	Cash Dividend	Market Price Range
1999 †	5,538	(1,499)	(27.1)	(57.0)	(0.43)	—	4.25–0.50
1998 ¶	6,299	392	6.2	9.5	0.11	—	5.00–2.25
1997 #	2,862	(1,173)	(41.0)	(32.0)	(0.34)	—	5.25–2.09
1996	1,335	(985)	(73.8)	NM	(0.40)	—	
1995 **	1,549	40	2.6	NM	—	—	

* Stock began trading March 5, 1997.
† Income figures for 1999 include net business interruption claim recovery of $328,940.
¶ Figures for 1998 include Mercury Refining Co. Inc. from May 1998 date acquired. Pro forma from Jan. 1, 1998: revenue $6,922,996; net income $453,469/$0.11. Income figures include net business interruption claims recovery of $445,006.
# Figures for 1997 include Ballast & Lamp Recycling Inc. from September 1997 date acquired. Income figures include business interruption claim expenses of $110,719.
** Results for 1995 are those of predecessor USE. USE earned a substantial portion of its income from sales of the Model 2000, a source from which the company earned no income or revenue in 1996. Income for 1995 is pro forma for income taxes.

BALANCE SHEET

Assets	12/31/99 (dollars in thousands)	12/31/98	Liabilities	12/31/99 (dollars in thousands)	12/31/98
Current (CAE 26 and 75)	1,380	1,800	Current (STD 1,058 and 462)	2,984	1,522
Property, eqt	1,929	2,145	Long-term debt	19	1,073
Restricted cash	95	91	Closure funds	30	30
Intangibles	2,261	2,712	Stockholders' equity*	2,631	4,123
TOTAL	5,665	6,749	TOTAL	5,665	6,749

* $0.01 par common; 10,000,000 authorized; 3,480,097 and 3,480,097 issued and outstanding.

RECENT QUARTERS / **PRIOR-YEAR RESULTS**

	Quarter End	Revenue ($000)	Earnings ($000)	EPS ($)	Prior-Year Revenue ($000)	Earnings ($000)	EPS ($)
Q3	09/30/2000	2,197	181	0.03	1,330	(506)	(0.15)
Q2	06/30/2000	1,616	(173)	(0.05)	1,478	(425)	(0.12)
Q1	03/31/2000	1,533	(123)	(0.04)	1,281	(153)	(0.04)
Q4	12/31/99	1,450	(415)	(0.12)	1,500	(310)	(0.09)
	SUM	6,796	(530)	(0.17)	5,588	(1,395)	(0.40)

RECENT EVENTS

In **June 2000** the company reached a settlement with the state of Wisconsin regarding alleged violations related primarily to an incident at its Union Grove, Wis., facility in October of 1998. The company conducted an extensive internal investigation and modified its material inspection procedures, satisfying all of the state's concerns. Mercury Waste also agreed to pay the state $25,000 a year for the next three years to settle the state's claims and recover its costs. The company's Union Grove, Wis., processing facility was issued a Part B Hazardous Waste Treatment and Storage Permit from the Wisconsin Department of Natural Resources and the Environmental Protection Agency, to allow the company to store up to 696 drums of material at the Wisconsin Facility. In **November** Mercury Waste received a letter from Nasdaq Amex stating that the company's common stock had failed to maintain a minimum bid price of $1 per share over the previous 30 consecutive trading days as required for continued listing. Its stock was in danger of being delisted from trading on Feb. 2, 2001, shoould the minimum bid price not equal or exceed $1 for a minimum of 10 consecutive trading days.

OFFICERS

Bradley J. Buscher
Chairman and CEO

Mark G. Edlund
President

Donald J. Wodek
EVP-Operations/Legal/Regulatory Affairs

Todd J. Anderson
EVP and CFO

DIRECTORS

Bradley J. Buscher

Mark G. Edlund

Robert L. Etter
Wolf, Etter and Co., CPAs

Frank L. Farrar
Beresford Bancorp. Inc.

Alan R. Geiwitz
Orion Financial Corp.

Joel H. Gottesman
Conseco Finance Corp., St. Paul

MAJOR SHAREHOLDERS

Bradley J. Buscher, 37.3%
Mark G. Edlund, 19.5%
Alan R. Geiwitz, 7.5%
Joel H. Gottesman, 6.1%
All officers and directors as a group (10 persons), 70%

SIC CODE

4955 Hazardous waste management

MISCELLANEOUS

TRANSFER AGENT AND REGISTAR:
Wells Fargo Bank Minnesota N.A., South St. Paul, MN

TRADED: Nasdaq SmallCap Market

SYMBOL: MWSI

STOCKHOLDERS: 450

EMPLOYEES: 43

GENERAL COUNSEL:
Maslon Edelman Borman & Brand PLLP, Minneapolis

AUDITORS:
RSM McGladrey & Pullen Inc. LLP, Minneapolis

INC: MN-1996

FOUNDED: 1992

ANNUAL MEETING: May

INVESTOR RELATIONS:
Todd J. Anderson

SUBSIDIARIES, DIVISIONS, AFFILIATES

Roseville Facility
2007 W. County Rd. C-2
Roseville, MN 55113
612/628-9370

Union Grove Facility
21211 Durand Ave.
Union Grove, WI 53182
414/878-2599

Indianapolis Facility
1002 West Troy Ave.
Indianapolis, IN 46225
317/782-3228

Atlanta Facility
2112 Northwest Parkway S.E.
Marietta, GA 30067
770/953-8000

Albany Facility
26 Railroad Ave.
Albany, NY 12205

TWO-YEAR QUARTERLY HIGH-LOW STOCK PRICES

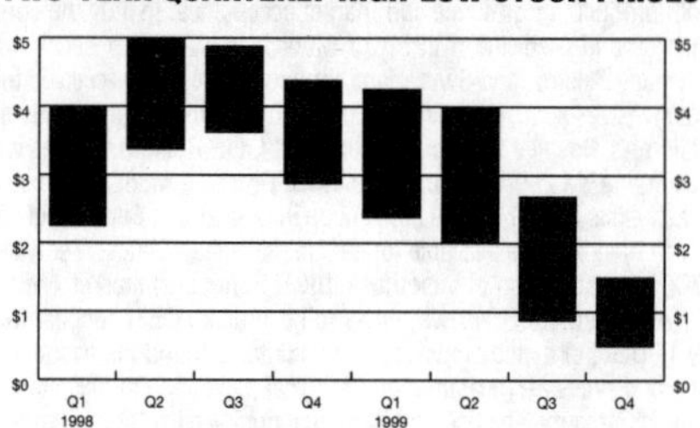

Mesaba Holdings Inc.

7501 26th Ave. S., MSP International Airport, Minneapolis, MN 55450
Tel: 612/726-5151 Fax: 612/726-1568 Web site: http://www.mesaba.com

Mesaba Holdings Inc. is the parent company of Mesaba Airlines, a domestic air carrier operating as a Northwest Airlink affiliate under a code-sharing agreement with Northwest Airlines. Mesaba Airlines serves 103 U.S. and Canadian Cities from Northwest Airlines three major hubs in Minneapolis/St. Paul, Detroit, and Memphis. Mesaba operates a fleet of 109 jet-prop and pure jet aircraft including the 30-34 passenger Saab 340 and the 69 passenger Avro RJ85. Mesaba receives ticketing and certain check-in, baggage, freight, and aircraft handling services from Northwest at certain airports. In addition, Mesaba receives its computerized reservations services from Northwest. Northwest also performs all marketing schedules and yield management and pricing services for Mesaba's flights. Mesaba believes that its competitive position is enhanced as a result of its marketing and other agreements with Northwest, particularly through the ability of Mesaba to offer its passengers coordinated flight schedules to the destinations served by Northwest.

EARNINGS HISTORY

Year Ended Mar 31	Operating Revenue/Sales (dollars in thousands)	Net Earnings	Return on Revenue (percent)	Return on Equity	Net Earnings (dollars per share*)	Cash Dividend	Market Price Range
2000	406,199	31,061	7.6	21.5	1.54	—	17.00–8.88
1999 †	331,753	21,271	6.4	19.5	1.07	—	28.75–9.75
1998	277,225	19,804	7.1	26.2	1.03	—	21.00–7.50
1997	185,701	11,986	6.5	24.1	0.63	—	10.75–5.92
1996 ¶	170,455	56,275	33.0	NM	3.21	0.04	10.75–3.25

* Per-share amounts restated to reflect 3-for-2 stock split on April 30, 1998.
† Income figures for 1999 include write-off of $800,000/(0.04) from accounting change.
¶ Income figures for 1996 include pretax gain of $49,303,000 on tax-free distribution of subsidiary Airways to Mesaba shareholders.

BALANCE SHEET

Assets	03/31/00 (dollars in thousands)	03/31/99	Liabilities	03/31/00 (dollars in thousands)	03/31/99
Current	139,952	116,369	Current	44,686	48,674
(CAE 100,172 and 83,152)			Capital lease obligations	3,866	4,359
Property and equipment	54,109	47,195			
			Other	14,454	16,951
Other	13,663	15,659	Stockholders' equity*	144,718	109,239
TOTAL	207,724	179,223			
			TOTAL	207,724	179,223

* $0.01 par common; 60,000,000 authorized; 20,267,141 and 19,863,829 issued and outstanding.

RECENT QUARTERS / PRIOR-YEAR RESULTS

	Quarter End	Revenue ($000)	Earnings ($000)	EPS ($)	Prior-Year Revenue ($000)	Prior-Year Earnings ($000)	Prior-Year EPS ($)
Q2	09/30/2000	115,070	8,800	0.43	102,503	7,318	0.36
Q1	06/30/2000	107,826	7,718	0.38	99,815	9,076	0.45
Q4	03/31/2000	102,873	6,816	0.34	89,954	6,428	0.32
Q3	12/31/99	101,008	7,851	0.39	89,641	6,730	0.34
	SUM	426,777	31,185	1.54	381,913	29,552	1.48

RECENT EVENTS

On **Dec. 3, 1999**, the company received a level-one rating for Y2K readiness from the Federal Aviation Administration. **March 31, 2000:** Mesaba generated a record 148.1 million Revenue Passenger Miles (RPMs) in March, an increase of 27.7 percent over 1999. Monthly records were also set for ASMs and number of passengers. In **May** Mesaba stock was rated NEUTRAL in new coverage at PaineWebber Inc. In **June** employees rejected an effort by the International Association of Machinists (IAM) to represent the customer service and ramp service agents. The vote, which covered 924 Mesaba Airlines associates, resulted in 606 votes for no union representation. In **July**, faced with the dilemma of having all of its business on a fixed contract with Northwest Airlines, the board announced that it had appointed a special committee to evaluate strategic growth options that would enhance Mesaba's stock price. One part of the new stretegy: to purchase leases of Saab 340 aircraft, convert some of them into cargo-only planes, and use them to capture some of the demand for just-in-time and overnight deliveries created by e-commerce by flying high-yielding small packages to small cities. **Sept. 30:** Mesaba reported record earnings for the second fiscal quarter. Unit costs remained flat at 13.4 cents per ASM compared to the prior year, and improved by 2.7 percent to 13.2 cents for the six-month period. "Mesaba maintained its focus on cost control during the quarter," stated CFO Weil. "Unlike our competitors, we have no exposure to rising fuel costs due to our contracts with Northwest Airlines." In October Mesaba generated 150.1 million Revenue Passenger Miles (RPMs), an increase of 10.9 percent over the October 1999 results. Available Seat Miles (ASMs) increased 10.2 percent to 254.4 million from 230.9 million in the prior year. Systemwide Passenger Load Factor (PLF) increased 0.4 points year-over-year to 59.0 percent. The airline carried 549,300 passengers, an 11.6 percent increase over the same period last year. In **November** Mesaba confirmed that it had received a proposal from Northwest Airlines to acquire the entire public interest in Mesaba at a price of $13 per share. Its board of directors appointed a special committee of independent directors to deal with the Northwest proposal on behalf of Mesaba and its public shareholders.

OFFICERS

Carl R. Pohlad
Chairman

Paul F. Foley
President and CEO

Scott R. Bussell
VP-Technical Operations

Scott L. Durgin
VP-Customer Service

John S. Fredericksen
VP-Administration and General Counsel

John G. Spanjers
VP-Operations Support

Robert E. Weil
VP-Finance and CFO

DIRECTORS

Richard H. Anderson
Northwest Airlines Corp., Eagan, MN

Donald E. Benson
Marquette Bancshares Inc., Minneapolis

Paul F. Foley

Pierson M. (Sandy) Grieve
Palladium Equity Partners LLC

Carl R. Pohlad
Pohlad Cos., Minneapolis

Robert C. Pohlad
Pohlad Cos., Minneapolis

Douglas M. Steenland
Northwest Airlines Corp., Eagan, MN

Raymond Zehr Jr.
Pohlad Cos., Minneapolis

MAJOR SHAREHOLDERS

Northwest Airlines Corp., 40.2%
Eagan, MN

Wellington Management Co. LLP, 10%
Boston

Carl R. Pohlad, 9.5%
Minneapolis

All officers and directors as a group (12 persons), 11.1%

SIC CODE

4512 Air transportation, scheduled

4513 Air courier services

MISCELLANEOUS

TRANSFER AGENT AND REGISTAR:
Wells Fargo Bank Minnesota N.A.,
South St. Paul, MN

TRADED: Nasdaq National Market

SYMBOL: MAIR
STOCKHOLDERS: 863
EMPLOYEES: 3,372
PART TIME: 840
GENERAL COUNSEL:
Briggs and Morgan P.A., Minneapolis
AUDITORS:
Arthur Andersen LLP, Minneapolis
INC: MN-1983
ANNUAL MEETING: August
MARKETING/COMMUNICATIONS: Warren R. Wilkinson

PUB

RANKINGS

No. 57 CRM Public 200

SUBSIDIARIES, DIVISIONS, AFFILIATES

Mesaba Aviation Inc.
7501 26th Ave. S.
Minneapolis, MN 55450
612/726-5151
Bryan Bedford

TWO-YEAR QUARTERLY HIGH-LOW STOCK PRICES

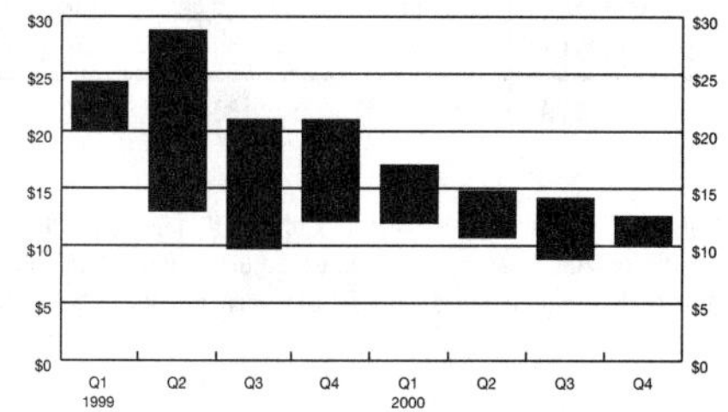

PUB

Metris Companies Inc.

10900 Wayzata Blvd., Minnetonka, MN 55305
Tel: 952/525-5020 Fax: 952/358-4428 Web site: http://www.metriscompanies.com

Metris Cos. Inc. is an information-based direct marketer of consumer credit products and fee-based services primarily to moderate income consumers. Consumer credit products currently include primarily unsecured credit cards issued by a subsidiary, Direct Merchants Credit Card Bank, National Association. Consumer credit products are marketed to individuals for whom credit bureau information is available and to existing customers of a former affiliate, Fingerhut Corp. Fee-based services include debt waiver programs, membership clubs, extended service plans, and third-party insurance. Fee-based services are marketed to our credit card customers and to customers of third parties.

continued on page 285

EARNINGS HISTORY

Year Ended Dec 31	Operating Revenue/Sales (dollars in thousands)	Net Earnings (dollars in thousands)	Return on Revenue (percent)	Return on Equity (percent)	Net Earnings (dollars per share*)	Cash Dividend (dollars per share*)	Market Price Range (dollars per share*)
1999 †	859,941	64,555	7.5	(21.0)	(1.07)	0.02	30.75–12.67
1998	428,691	57,348	13.4	24.3	0.97	0.01	26.71–5.92
1997	256,990	38,058	14.8	21.6	0.66	0.01	15.94–7.33
1996	156,416	20,016	12.8	14.4	0.40	—	8.58–6.71
1995	58,699	4,581	7.8	6.4	0.10	—	

* Per-share amounts restated to reflect 3-for-2 stock split on June 15, 2000; and 2-for-1 stock split on June 15, 1999. Shares began trading Oct. 25, 1996.
† Income figures for 1999 include extraordinary loss of $50.808 million/($0.88) on early extinguishment of debt; EPS was reduced by a $101.615 million adjustment for the retirement of Series B Preferred Stock , as well as by $24.586 million in preferred dividends.

BALANCE SHEET

Assets	12/31/99 (dollars in thousands)	12/31/98
Cash and due from banks	28,505	22,114
Federal funds sold	118,962	15,060
Short-term investments	46,966	173
Net retained interests in loans securit ized	1,010,373	360,186
Loans held for securitization	2,570	3,430
Property and equipment	56,914	21,982
Accrued interest and fees receivable	17,704	6,009
Prepaid expenses and deferred charges	57,371	59,104
Deferred income taxes	185,613	153,021
Customer base intangible	83,809	81,892
Other receivables due from securitizations	243,978	185,935
Credit card loans	131,038	
Other	61,279	36,813
TOTAL	2,045,082	945,719

Liabilities	12/31/99 (dollars in thousands)	12/31/98
Debt	345,012	310,896
Deposits	775,381	
Accounts payable	45,850	19,091
Current income taxes payable	22,969	31,783
Deferred income	171,666	124,892
Accrued expenses and other	60,403	26,075
Preferred equity	329,729	201,100
Common equity*	294,072	231,882
TOTAL	2,045,082	945,719

* $0.01 par common; 100,000,000 authorized; 57,919,432 and 57,779,250 issued and outstanding.

RECENT QUARTERS / **PRIOR-YEAR RESULTS**

	Quarter End	Revenue ($000)	Earnings ($000)	EPS ($)	Prior-Year Revenue ($000)	Prior-Year Earnings ($000)	Prior-Year EPS ($)
Q3	09/30/2000	374,469	48,360	0.66	240,016	31,183	0.41
Q2	06/30/2000	353,782	48,280	0.69	181,688	(22,306)	(2.24)
Q1	03/31/2000	339,273	49,958	0.73	178,864	21,640	0.30
Q4	12/31/99	259,373	34,038	0.46	123,004	16,728	0.27
	SUM	1,326,897	180,636	2.54	723,572	47,245	(1.25)

CURRENT: Q1 earnings include loss of $3.438 million/($0.06) cumulative effect of accounting change.
PRIOR YEAR: Q2 earnings include extraordinary loss of $50.808 million/($0.88) on early extinguishment of debt; EPS was reduced by $101.615 million adjustment for the retirement of Series B Preferred Stock.

OFFICERS

Ronald N. Zebeck
Chairman and CEO

David D. Wesselink
Vice Chairman

Patrick J. Fox
EVP-Business Development

Joseph A. Hoffman
EVP-Consumer Credit Cd. Mktg./Operations

Jon Mendel
EVP-Human Resources

David R. Reak
EVP-Risk Management/ Recovery/Collections

Douglas L. Scaliti
Pres./COO-Enhancement Services

Adolph T. Barclift
EVP-Information Services

Jean C. Benson
EVP-Finance and Controller

Matt Melius
EVP-e-commerce

Ralph A. Than
SVP and Treasurer

Lorraine Waller
SVP and General Counsel

Benson Woo
CFO

DIRECTORS

Lee R. Anderson
APi Group Inc., Golden Valley, MN

C. Hunter Boll
Thomas H. Lee Co.

John A. Cleary
John Cleary Enterprises, Stamford, CT

Thomas M. Hagerty
Thomas H. Lee Co.

David V. Harkins
Thomas H. Lee Co.

Walter M. Hoff
NDC Health Information Services

Thomas H. Lee
Thomas H. Lee Co.

Derek V. Smith
ChoicePoint Inc., Alpharetta, GA

Edward B. Speno
Credit Card Services Corp.

Frank D. Trestman
Trestman Enterprises, Golden Valley, MN

Ronald N. Zebeck

MAJOR SHAREHOLDERS

Thomas H. Lee/Thomas H. Lee Co., 32.9%
Boston

NewSouth Capital Management Inc., 7.8%
Memphis, TN

All officers and directors as a group (21 persons), 39.3%

SIC CODE

6141 Personal credit institutions

MISCELLANEOUS

TRANSFER AGENT AND REGISTAR:
Computershare Investor Services, Chicago

TRADED: NYSE

SYMBOL: MXT

STOCKHOLDERS: 533

EMPLOYEES: 3,100

GENERAL COUNSEL:
Dorsey & Whitney PLLP, Minneapolis

AUDITORS:
KPMG LLP, Minneapolis

INC: DE-1996

ANNUAL MEETING: May

INVESTOR RELATIONS:
David Wesselink

INVESTOR RELATIONS:
Mark Van Ert

RANKINGS

No. 41 CRM Public 200

No. 4 CRM Performance 100

SUBSIDIARIES, DIVISIONS, AFFILIATES

Direct Merchants Credit Card Bank N.A.
6909 E. Greenway Pkwy.
Scottsdale, AZ 85254

Metris Receivables Inc.
600 S. Highway 169
St. Louis Park, MN
55426

Metris Direct Inc.
Interchange Tower
Suite 1800
600 S. Highway 169
St. Louis Park, MN
55426

TWO-YEAR QUARTERLY HIGH-LOW STOCK PRICES

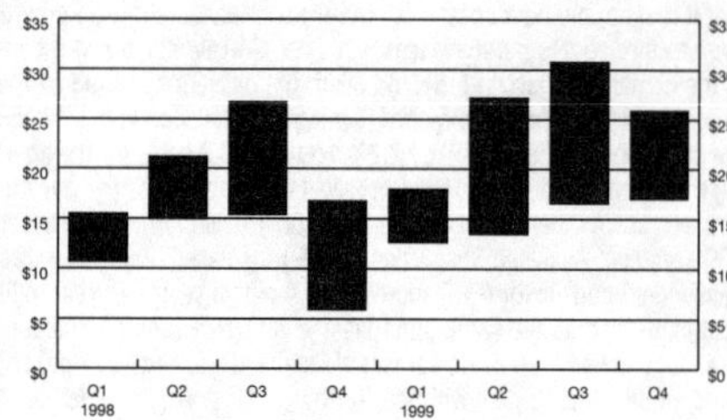

Michael Foods Inc.

324 Park National Bank Bldg., 5353 Wayzata Blvd., St. Louis Park, MN 55416
Tel: 952/546-1500 Fax: 952/546-3711 Web site: http://www.michaelfoods.com

Michael Foods Inc. is a holding company that, through its operating subsidiaries, is engaged in the food processing and distribution business primarily throughout the United States. Principal products are egg products, refrigerated grocery products, refrigerated potato products, and specialty dairy products.

EARNINGS HISTORY

Year Ended Dec 31	Operating Revenue/Sales (dollars in thousands)	Net Earnings (dollars in thousands)	Return on Revenue (percent)	Return on Equity (percent)	Net Earnings (dollars per share)	Cash Dividend (dollars per share)	Market Price Range (dollars per share)
1999	1,053,272	44,056	4.2	16.7	2.15	0.27	28.75–16.69
1998	1,020,484	40,257	3.9	16.5	1.86	0.23	31.13–20.25
1997 *	956,223	32,439	3.4	14.2	1.53	0.20	28.38–10.00
1996 †	616,395	(3,073)	(0.5)	(1.8)	(0.16)	0.20	13.50–9.50
1995	536,627	17,591	3.3	9.8	0.91	0.20	14.50–9.00

* Figures for 1997 include results of Papetti's from its Feb. 26, 1997, date of acquisition for $106 million. Pro forma for full year: revenue $1,004,818,000; earnings $32,992,000/$1.54.
† Income figures for 1996 reflect pretax charges of $10,472,000 for asset impairment losses; and $12,225,000 for frozen french fry product line inventory mark-down. Pro forma results assuming that the Feb. 26, 1997, acquisition of Papetti's had occurred at beginning of period: revenue $982,532,000; net loss $1,146,000/($0.06).

BALANCE SHEET

Assets	12/31/99 (dollars in thousands)	12/31/98 (dollars in thousands)	Liabilities	12/31/99 (dollars in thousands)	12/31/98 (dollars in thousands)
Current (CAE 4,961 and 2,047)	173,255	177,820	Current (STD 3,130 and 10,663)	121,491	116,523
Property, plant, and equipment	286,799	250,211	Long-term debt	175,404	155,444
Goodwill	116,729	120,172	Deferred income taxes	36,423	35,400
Joint ventures, other	21,134	3,313	Stockholders' equity*	264,599	244,149
TOTAL	597,917	551,516	TOTAL	597,917	551,516

* $0.01 par common; 40,000,000 authorized; 20,301,624 and 21,095,067 issued and outstanding.

RECENT QUARTERS / **PRIOR-YEAR RESULTS**

	Quarter End	Revenue ($000)	Earnings ($000)	EPS ($)	Prior-Year Revenue ($000)	Prior-Year Earnings ($000)	Prior-Year EPS ($)
Q3	09/30/2000	276,568	11,818	0.65	269,911	10,713	0.53
Q2	06/30/2000	266,616	12,275	0.64	258,031	11,746	0.57
Q1	03/31/2000	251,926	9,489	0.47	253,378	8,417	0.40
Q4	12/31/99	271,952	13,180	0.65	277,420	10,170	0.48
	SUM	1,067,062	46,762	2.41	1,058,740	41,046	1.98

RECENT EVENTS

In **January 2000** the company announced that its board of directors had concluded the formal strategic alternatives review process begun in August 1999. After an extensive review of several strategic alternatives, as well as a number of preliminary exploratory discussions with third parties regarding possible business combinations, none of the transactions investigated satisfied the board's criteria for enhancing shareholder value. Michael Foods shares fell 15 percent on the news—closing Jan. 21 at $21.81. In **February** the board authorized the purchase of an additional 2 million shares (9.9 percent) of the company's common stock—citing its excellent value as a prudent use of the company's rising free cash flow. By **May**, the company had exhausted that share repurchase authorization. Given the valuation level of the stock, the highly accretive earnings per share impact of repurchases at such levels, and the company's continuing strong cash flow, the board authorized a new 500,000-share (2.7 percent) repurchase program. In **August** the U.S. Patent and Trademark Office issued a Notice of Allowability regarding the reissuance of the fourth of four egg-processing patents that Michael Foods exclusively licenses from North Carolina State University. Based upon significantly enhanced product patent protection covering extended shelf-life liquid eggs with an extended refrigerated shelf-life, management was expecting to aggressively pursue parties who had infringed the four licensed patents, or may do so in the future. Michael Foods settled its egg product patent infringement litigation against Nulaid Foods Inc. Michael Foods was to realize royalty payments from Nulaid's sales of extended shelf-life liquid whole eggs for the duration of the patents' lives; and was to receive a one-time payment from Nulaid to pay for all its past production of the products covered by the patents. In **September** U.S. Bancorp Piper Jaffray, in its monthly commentary, noted that the company was trading at nearly a 25 percent discount to the P/E multiple of its peer group (small-cap food stocks) and projected a 12-month target price of $33. **Sept. 30:** Commenting on record third-quarter results, CEO Ostrander said, "Outstanding results from our Refrigerated Distribution Division, coupled with an on-going earnings improvement at our Dairy Products Division, led to higher corporate earnings for the third quarter. Excellent distributed products unit sales growth of 9 percent, along with tight expense controls and normal raw material costs, drove strong Refrigerated Distribution earnings growth. While Dairy Products sales were flat, the sales mix improved, with excellent growth seen in creamer sales. This, along with a *continued on page 286*

OFFICERS

Gregg A. Ostrander
Chairman, President, and CEO

Jeffrey J. Michael
Vice Chairman, Lead Director

John D. Reedy
EVP, CFO, and Treasurer

Jeffrey M. Shapiro
EVP and Secretary

Dean Sprinkle
EVP-Sales

Mark D. Witmer
Asst. Treasurer

J.D. Clarkson
Pres.-Northern Star Co. /Kohler Mix

Bill L. Goucher
Pres.-M.G. Waldbaum Co.

Norman A. Rodriguez
Pres.-Crystal Farms

DIRECTORS

Richard A. Coonrod
Coonrod Agriproduction Corp., Minneapolis

Daniel P. Dillon
Welch Foods Inc., Concord, MA

Jerome J. Jenko
Jenko & Associates, Santa Fe, NM

Arvid C. Knudtson
consultant, St. Paul

Joseph D. Marshburn
consultant, Lakeland, FL

Jeffrey J. Michael
Corstar Holdings Inc.

Margaret (Peggy) Moore
PepsiCo Inc., Purchase, NY

Gregg A. Ostrander

Arthur J. Papetti
Papetti's Hygrade Egg Products Inc., Elizabeth, NJ

Stephen T. Papetti
Papetti's Hygrade Egg Products Inc., Elizabeth, NJ

MAJOR SHAREHOLDERS

Jeffrey J. Michael, 15.5%

4J2R1C Ltd. Partnership, 7.7%
Eden Prairie, MN

3J2R Ltd. Partnership, 7.1%
Eden Prairie, MN

Sanford C. Bernstein & Co. Inc., 5%
New York

All officers and directors as a group (18 persons), 24.4%

SIC CODE

5143 Dairy products, whsle

5144 Poultry products, whsle

MISCELLANEOUS

TRANSFER AGENT AND REGISTAR:
Wells Fargo Bank Minnesota N.A.,
South St. Paul, MN

TRADED: Nasdaq National Market

SYMBOL: MIKL

STOCKHOLDERS: 388

EMPLOYEES: 4,530

GENERAL COUNSEL:
Maun & Simon PLC, Minneapolis

AUDITORS:
Grant Thornton LLP, Minneapolis

INC: MN-1928

ANNUAL MEETING: April

INVESTOR RELATIONS:
Mark D. Witmer

RANKINGS

No. 36 CRM Public 200

SUBSIDIARIES, DIVISIONS, AFFILIATES

Crystal Farms Refrigerated Distribution Co.
Park Place W., Suite 200
6465 Wayzata Blvd.
St. Louis Park, MN 55426

Farm Fresh Foods Inc.
6602 Clara St.
Bell Gardens, CA 90201

Kohler Mix Specialties Inc.
4041 Highway 61
White Bear Lake, MN
55110

M.G. Waldbaum Co.
500 Park National Bank Building
5353 Wayzata Blvd.
St. Louis Park, MN 55416

Northern Star Co.
3171 Fifth St. S.E.
Minneapolis, MN 55414

Wisco Farm Cooperative
450 N. CP Ave.
Lake Mills, WI 53551

Papetti's Hygrade Egg Products Inc.
One Papetti Plaza
Elizabeth, NJ 07206

PUB

TWO-YEAR QUARTERLY HIGH-LOW STOCK PRICES

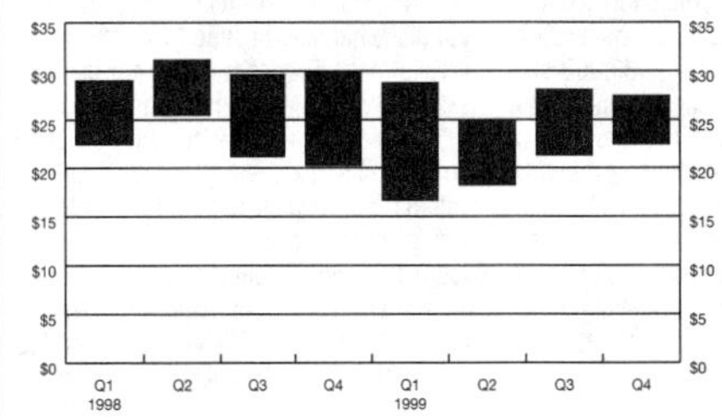

Micro Component Technology Inc.

2340 W. County Rd. C, Roseville, MN 55113
Tel: 651/697-4000 Fax: 651/697-4200 Web site: http://www.mct.com

Micro Component Technology Inc. manufactures test handling and automation solutions satisfying the complete range of handling requirements of the global semiconductor industry. MCT has recently introduced several new products under its Smart Solutions line of automation products, including Tapestry, SmartMark, and SmartSort, designed to automate the back-end of the semiconductor manufacturing process. MCT has the largest installed IC test handler base of any manufacturer, with over 11,000 units worldwide. The Company has sales and support offices worldwide, and its Aseco Corporation subsidiary is located in Marlborough, Mass.

PUB

EARNINGS HISTORY

Year Ended Dec 31	Operating Revenue/Sales (dollars in thousands)	Net Earnings	Return on Revenue (percent)	Return on Equity	Net Earnings (dollars per share)	Cash Dividend	Market Price Range
1999 *	11,356	121	1.1	1.7	0.02	—	5.56–2.13
1999 †	15,171	(1,466)	(9.7)	(21.1)	(0.20)	—	2.69–0.44
1998	16,975	(3,879)	(22.9)	(46.2)	(0.54)	—	5.63–1.00
1997	16,129	(1,563)	(9.7)	(12.8)	(0.22)	—	3.88–1.75
1996 ¶	22,318	3,220	14.4	23.5	0.44	—	8.00–3.00

* These 1999 figures are for six-month stub period from june 27, 1999, to Dec. 31, 1999, due to change in year end.
† Figures for this 1999 and all prior periods are for fiscal years ended in June.
¶ Income figures for 1996 include pretax gain of $1.524 million; as well as gain of $0.652 million/$0.09 on reserve reversal.

BALANCE SHEET

Assets	12/31/99 (dollars in thousands)	06/26/99	Liabilities	12/31/99 (dollars in thousands)	06/26/99
Current (CAE 1,045 and 1,927)	9,384	9,270	Current (STD 51 and 51)	2,998	3,005
Property, plant, and equipment	865	673	Long-term debt	70	33
			Stkhldrs' equity*	7,256	6,952
Other	75	47	TOTAL	10,324	9,990
TOTAL	10,324	9,990			

* $0.01 par common; 20,000,000 authorized; 7,540,647 and 7,416,922 issued and outstanding.

RECENT QUARTERS / **PRIOR-YEAR RESULTS**

	Quarter End	Revenue ($000)	Earnings ($000)	EPS ($)	Revenue ($000)	Earnings ($000)	EPS ($)
Q3	09/30/2000	16,617	(383)	(0.03)	5,745	130	0.02
Q2	07/01/2000	14,806	(961)	(0.09)	4,455	54	0.01
Q1	04/01/2000	12,161	(266)	(0.03)	4,028	(125)	(0.02)
Q4	12/25/99	5,611	(9)	0.00	3,020	(576)	(0.08)
	SUM	49,195	(1,619)	(0.15)	17,248	(517)	(0.07)

CURRENT: Q1 includes results of Aseco Corp. from Feb. 1, 2000, date of acquisition.

RECENT EVENTS

In **February 2000** MCT announced its new MCT 5115 integrated handler and, simultaneously, the receipt of an order for multiple units. The system is targeted at new Chip Scale and near Chip Scale packages such as those being manufactured by semiconductor producers and major assembly and test subcontractors. The company also completed its previously announced acquisition of Aseco Corp. (Nasdaq: ASEC). In **March** MCT received multiple orders for its Tapestry Series of device strip and wafer level handling systems, totaling more than $2.0 million. In **April** Aseco received orders for multiple units of S-170 and S-130 Handlers totaling in excess of $2.5 million. In **May** the company introduced a revolutionary new automation product for semiconductor manufacturing: the SmartSort system, a high-speed, intelligent singulation and sorting system for offloading semiconductor packages. Micro Component Technology announced the receipt of an order of $1.6 million for multiple units of its 7632 multisite pick and place handler. In **June** MCT registered a public offering of 3 million shares of common stock, along with a 450,000-share overallotment. Proceeds to the company were to be used for working capital and general corporate purposes, including new product development, repayment of bank debt, purchase of manufacturing equipment, and sales and marketing expansion. In **July** MCT received an order for multiple Tapestry strip based test handlers with integrated SmartMark laser marking systems from Amkor Technology Inc. (Nasdaq: AMKR), an industry leader in strip testing; and two first-time orders for Tapestry test handling systems from two customers (orders totaling $900,000). MCT introduced the S-900 "RoadRunner" SOIC, tri-temperature, asynchronous, quad-site gravity handler, based upon the successful S-170 platform from its Aseco subsidiary. In **August** MCT's Infinity Systems Division received an order for multiple Tapestry strip test handling and SmartSort high-speed singulation and sort systems with electronic strip mapping for integration into an assembly and test line at a large integrated device manufacturer. In conjunction with its Infinity Systems Division, MCT received an $0.8 million order for a new Isocut isolation saw and SmartSort high-speed singulation and sorting system; and a separate order for multiple S-170

continued on page 286

OFFICERS

Roger E. Gower
Chairman, President, CEO, and Secretary

Dennis L. Nelson
EVP-Sales/Marketing

Jeffrey S. Mathiesen
VP and CFO

Lawrence J. Brezinski
VP-Engineering

DIRECTORS

Dr. Sheldon Buckler

Roger E. Gower

D. James Guzy
Arbor Co.

Donald Kramer
private investor, Boston

Sebastian Silari

David Sugishita
Synopsis, Sunnyvale, CA

Donald VanLuvanee
Electro Scientific Industries Inc., Portland, OR

Patrick Verderico
IPAC, San Jose, CA

MAJOR SHAREHOLDERS

All officers and directors as a group (11 persons), 6%

SIC CODE

3674 Semiconductors and related devices

3825 Instruments to measure electricity

MISCELLANEOUS

TRANSFER AGENT AND REGISTAR:
Wells Fargo Bank Minnesota N.A., South St. Paul, MN

TRADED: Nasdaq National Market

SYMBOL: MCTI

STOCKHOLDERS: 244

EMPLOYEES: 180

GENERAL COUNSEL:
Best & Flanagan, Minneapolis

AUDITORS:
Deloitte & Touche LLP, Minneapolis

INC: MN-1972

ANNUAL MEETING:
March/Apr

RANKINGS

No. 150 CRM Public 200

SUBSIDIARIES, DIVISIONS, AFFILIATES

MCT ASIA
Samuel Johnston

Micro Component Technology Asia Pte. Ltd.
6 New Industrial Rd.
#05-01/02
Hoe Huat Industrial Bldg.
Singapore 536199
65-280-1855

Infinity Systems
7755 S. Research Dr.
Suite 120
Tempe, AZ 85284
480/456-3500

Aseco Corp.
500 Donald Lynch Blvd.
Marlboro, MA 01752
508/481-8896

TWO-YEAR QUARTERLY HIGH-LOW STOCK PRICES

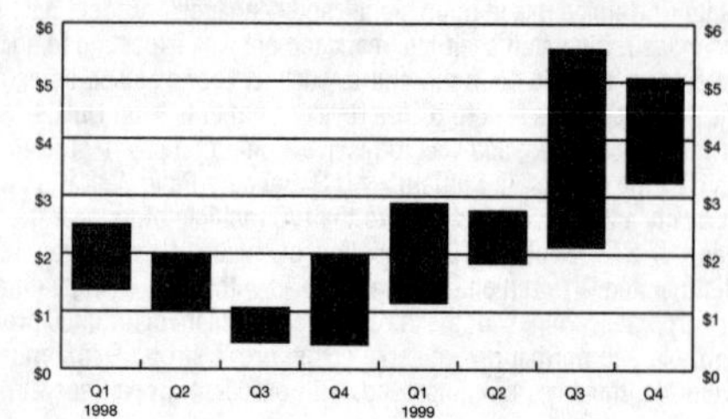

3M Company

3M Center, 225-15-15, Maplewood, MN 55144
Tel: 651/733-1110 Fax: 651/736-2133 Web site: http://www.3m.com

3M Co. (Minnesota Mining & Manufacturing) markets worldwide a diversified group of products ranging from coated abrasives and pressure-sensitive tapes to chemical, reflective, health care, electrical, consumer, and office products. Operations are organized into six segments: Consumer and Office Markets; Electro and Communications Markets; Industrial Markets; Health Care Markets; Specialty Material Markets; and Transportation, Graphics and Safety Markets. 3M products are manufactured and marketed by 35 divisions and by foreign subsidiary companies that serve all principal overseas markets in more than 60 countries.

EARNINGS HISTORY

Year Ended Dec 31	Operating Revenue/Sales (dollars in thousands)	Net Earnings	Return on Revenue (percent)	Return on Equity	Net Earnings (dollars per share)	Cash Dividend	Market Price Range
1999 *	15,659,000	1,763,000	11.3	28.0	4.39	2.24	103.38–69.31
1998 †	15,021,000	1,175,000	7.8	19.8	2.91	2.20	97.88–65.63
1997 ¶	15,070,000	2,121,000	14.1	35.8	5.14	2.12	105.50–80.00
1996 #	14,236,000	1,526,000	10.7	24.3	3.65	1.92	85.88–61.25
1995 **	13,460,000	976,000	7.3	14.2	2.32	1.88	69.88–50.75

* Income figures for 1999 include pretax gain of $28 million on reversal of restructuring charge.
† Income figures for 1998 include charge of $493 million pretax, $313 million/($0.78) after-tax, for restructuring; and extraordinary loss of $38 million/($0.10) from early extinguishment of debt.
¶ Income figures for 1997 include gain of $803 million pretax, $495 million/$1.20 after-tax, on divestiture of National Advertising Co.
# Income figures for 1996 include gain of $10 million/$0.02 on disposal of discontinued businesses.
** Income figures for 1995 include pretax $79 million restructuring charge; and net loss of $330 million/($0.79) on discontinued operations and their disposal.

BALANCE SHEET

Assets	12/31/99 (dollars in thousands)	12/31/98	Liabilities	12/31/99 (dollars in thousands)	12/31/98
Current (CAE 387,000 and 211,000)	6,066,000	6,219,000	Current (STD 1,130,000 and 1,492,000)	3,819,000	4,222,000
Property, plant, and equipment	5,656,000	5,566,000	Long-term debt	1,480,000	1,614,000
			Other	2,308,000	2,381,000
Investments	487,000	623,000	Stockholders' equity*	6,289,000	5,936,000
Other	1,687,000	1,745,000			
TOTAL	13,896,000	14,153,000	TOTAL	13,896,000	14,153,000

* $0.01 par common; 1,500,000,000 authorized; 472,016,528 and 472,016,528 issued and outstanding, less 73,305,711 and 70,092,280 treasury shares.

RECENT QUARTERS / PRIOR-YEAR RESULTS

	Quarter End	Revenue ($000)	Earnings ($000)	EPS ($)	Prior-Year Revenue ($000)	Prior-Year Earnings ($000)	Prior-Year EPS ($)
Q3	09/30/2000	4,252,000	499,000	1.26	3,997,000	459,000	1.14
Q2	06/30/2000	4,224,000	470,000	1.19	3,863,000	476,000	1.18
Q1	03/31/2000	4,052,000	487,000	1.22	3,776,000	384,000	0.95
Q4	12/31/99	4,023,000	444,000	1.11	3,785,000	211,000	0.52
	SUM	16,551,000	1,900,000	4.78	15,421,000	1,530,000	3.80

CURRENT: Q3 earnings include nonrecurring costs of $118 million, primarily related to the company's decision to phase out its perfluorooctanyl chemistry; and nonrecurring gains of $119 million related to asset sales. Q1 earnings include one-time gain of $50 million pretax, $31 million/$0.08 after-tax, as a breakup fee to end an inhaler marketing agreement with Hoechst AG.
PRIOR YEAR: Q3 earnings include pretax litigation charge of $73 million, gain of $43 million on divestitures, and gain of $26 million on restructuring reversal—a net after-tax loss on one-time items of $3 million/($0.01). Q2 earnings include gain of $104 million pretax, $55 million/$0.14 after tax, from gains on divestitures, net of an investment valuation adjustment. Q4 earnings include pretax charge of $161 million for restructuring; and extraordinary loss of $38 million/($0.10) from early extinguishment of debt.

RECENT EVENTS

In **November 1999** Polaroid Corp. (NYSE: PRD) announced that 3M's Optical Systems Division had purchased Polaroid's computer monitor anti-glare filter business. In **December** 3M Drug Delivery Systems Division announced a partnership agreement with Forest Laboratories for the long-term supply and manufacture of hydrofluroalkane (HFA) flunisolide metered-dose inhalers (MDIs), which do not use chloroflurocarbons (CFCs) as a propellant. *continued on page 280*

OFFICERS

Livio D. DeSimone
Chairman and CEO
Harry C. Andrews
EVP-Electro/Communications Markets
Ronald O. Baukol
EVP-International Operations
John W. Benson
EVP-Health Care Markets
Harry W. Borrelli
VP-Latin America/Africa
Robert J. Burgstahler
VP-Finance/Administrative Services
David P. Drew
VP-Information Technology
Joseph Giordano
VP-Asia Pacific
M. Kay Grenz
VP-Human Resources
Paul F. Guehler
VP-Research/Development
Charles E. Kiester
SVP-Engineering/Manufacturing/Logistics
Ronald G. Nelson
VP and Controller
Moe S. Nozari
EVP-Consumer/Office Markets
Edoardo Pieruzzi
VP-Europe/Middle East
David W. Powell
VP-Marketing
Charles Reich
EVP-Specialty Material Markets
Roger P. Smith
VP and Secretary
John J. Ursu
SVP-Legal Affairs/General Counsel
Ronald A. Weber
EVP-Transp./Graphics/Safety Markets
Harold J. Wiens
EVP-Industrial Markets
Janet L. Yeomans
VP and Treasurer
Carolyn A. Bates
Asst. Secretary
Thomas A. Boardman
General Counsel and Asst. Secretary
Gregg M. Larson
Asst. Secretary
Stephen J. Rowley
Asst. Secretary

DIRECTORS

Ronald O. Baukol
Edward A. Brennen
Sears, Roebuck and Co. (retired)
Livio D. DeSimone
Edward M. Liddy
The Allstate Corp.
Edward R. McCracken
The Prasad Project
Aulana L. Peters
Gibson, Dunn & Crutcher
Rozanne L. Ridgway
Asst. Secretary of State for Europe/Canada (former)
Frank Shrontz
Boeing Co. (retired)
F. Alan Smith
Advanced Accessory Systems
Louis W. Sullivan
Morehouse School of Medicine

MAJOR SHAREHOLDERS

All officers and directors as a group (25 persons), 0.5%

SIC CODE

2672 Paper coated and laminated, nec
2834 Pharmaceutical preparations
2891 Adhesives and sealants
2899 Chemical preparations, nec
3089 Plastics products, nec
3291 Abrasive products
3643 Current-carrying wiring devices
3679 Electronic components, nec
3842 Surgical appliances and supplies

MISCELLANEOUS

TRANSFER AGENT AND REGISTAR:
Wells Fargo Bank Minnesota N.A., South St. Paul, MN
TRADED: NYSE, PSE
SYMBOL: MMM
STOCKHOLDERS: 138,066
EMPLOYEES: 70,549
IN MINNESOTA: 20,000
GENERAL COUNSEL:
John J. Ursu, company
AUDITORS:
PricewaterhouseCoopers LLP, Minneapolis
INC: DE-1929
FOUNDED: 1902
ANNUAL MEETING: May

TWO-YEAR QUARTERLY HIGH-LOW STOCK PRICES

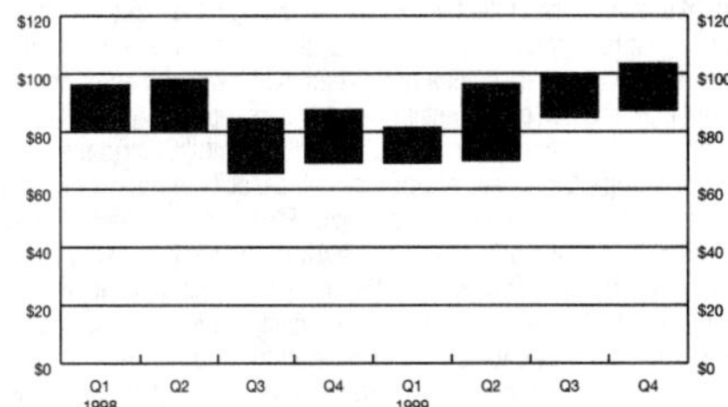

PUB

INVESTOR RELATIONS:
Jon A. Greer

RANKINGS

No. 4 CRM Public 200

No. 9 CRM Employer 100

No. 29 CRM Performance 100

SUBSIDIARIES, DIVISIONS, AFFILIATES

Applies to all sectors, groups, and divisions listed.
3M Center
Maplewood, MN 55144
612/733-1110

Consumer and Office Markets Research and Development

Automotive Innovation Center

Advertising, Public Relations and Design Services, Consumer and Office Markets

Industrial Tape and Specialties

Health Information Systems

Traffic Control Materials

Commercial Care

Business Development and Market Services

Abrasive Systems

Home Care

Drug Delivery Systems

Medical-Surgical

Office Supplies

Electronic Products

Dyneon LLC

Research and Development, Corporate Technology

Occupational Health and Environmental Safety

Protective Materials

Personal Care and Related Products

Pharmaceuticals

Performance Materials

Construction and Home Improvement Markets

Telecom Systems

Automotive

Research and Development, Corp. Technology, Industrial Markets

Automotive Aftermarket

R&D Corporate Technology, Electro/Comm Markets

Bonding Systems

Skin Health

Visual Systems

Electrical Products

Research & Development, Corp. Technology, Specialty Material Market

Commercial Graphics

Packaging Systems

Industrial Mineral Products

Dental Products

Specialty Materials Manufacturing

Industrial Markets

Stationery Products

Safety and Security Systems

Tape Manufacturing

Adhesives

Global Consumer Key Accounts

R&D, Corp. Tech., Health Care Markets

Optical Systems

Electronic Handling and Protection

Superabrasives and Microfinishing Systems

Sumitomo 3M Limited

Health Care Markets, Europe

UK/Ireland

Canada

Mexico

France

Telecom Markets, Europe and Middle East

Consumer and Office Markets, Europe

Western Europe Marketing Subsidiaries

Consumer and Office Markets, Europe and Middle East

Germany

Brazil

3M Italy

Industrial Markets, Europe

Traffic and Personal Safety Markets, Europe

Electro-Telecom Markets, Europe

The previously announced acquisition of the unowned 46 percent portion of joint venture Dyneon was completed. **Dec. 31:** 3M finished off 1999 with great momentum, as its fourth-quarter earnings increase of 28 percent (to $1.10 per share) easily beat analysts' expectations ($1.02). Sales in the Asia-Pacific region were up 25 percent. Cost-cutting benefits were represented by a year-end workforce of 70,500—3M's lowest in many years. **January 2000:** 3M's new U-clamp interconnect system, primarily for connecting sensors or probes to programmable logic controllers, provides an easy and efficient way to connect electrical wiring in industrial control systems. On Jan. 6, 3M stock climbed 8 percent, to $100.75, as investors fled flashy Web stocks for blue chips. It was the largest single-day increase in 12 years. 3M and Applied Materials Inc. (Nasdaq: AMAT) announced a strategic agreement to jointly develop a slurry-free, fixed abrasive chemical mechanical planarization (CMP) process for manufacturing the copper and low-k dielectric interconnect structures in high-performance, next-generation semiconductors. 3M Electronic Products Division introduced a new interconnect system for interconnecting printed circuit boards in high-end applications. 3M was granted a semi-exclusive license for Presstek Inc.'s (Nasdaq: PRST) intellectual property relating to vacuum-deposited polymer multilayer technology (VDPML). 3M Insulation Products unveiled its latest innovations in apparel technology: the first 3M garments designed to incorporate a variety of Thinsulate Insulation products with specific body zones in mind. In **February** 3M agreed to acquire German company Quante AG, a leading supplier to the telecommunications equipment market, for $300 million. [In October, although it was expanding in some places in Europe, Quante was forced to make 400 job cuts at other locations to lower costs amid price pressures.] 3M Drug Delivery Systems Division was actively seeking development and marketing partners for new pain-management programs utilizing transdermal and transbuccal delivery technologies. 3M Promotional Markets launched an Internet affiliate marketing program for Post-it Personalized Notes On-Line that promised to increase the number of visitors to its Post-it Personalized Notes Print Shop. 3M Health Information Systems was awarded an enterprise license (valued at $33 million over six years) from the Department of Defense Military Health System for 3M Care Innovation. 3M Pharmaceuticals and Aventis Pharmaceuticals (formerly Hoechst Marion Roussel) terminated an agreement to co-promote 3M's CFC-free metered-dose inhalers due to a subsequent merger. 3M announced the formation of 3M Network Solutions Inc., a separate, wholly owned telecommunications services company to be based in Austin, Texas, that was to offer a suite of service solutions to build, maintain, and rehabilitate communications networks worldwide. In addition, the current Electronic Products Division in Austin was to be separated into two divisions, reflecting the differences in market focus and technologies of two longstanding operating units. The new Interconnect Solutions Division became a stand alone division. A Ramsey County District Court jury ordered a group of insurance companies to pay 3M $150 million for uncovered costs related to breast-implant litigation. 3M Unitek Corp. was granted injunctive relief in its lawsuit against California-based Ormco Corp. to halt sale of Ormco's "inspire!" ceramic orthodontic brackets until trial. In **March** 3M Commercial Graphics Division and Scitex Wide Format Printing Ltd., a fully owned subsidiary of Scitex Corp. Ltd. (Nasdaq: SCIX), announced the latest advancement in large-format digital printing technology: the Scitex Pressjet Digital Press, which uses 3M inks, graphic films, and software optimized for the equipment. Several new technologies—including high-performance broad-bandwidth dispersion compensation fiber Bragg gratings for gigabit and terabit communications systems—positioned 3M to expand its business in the global market for optical communications equipment. In response to increased customer demand for fiber gratings, 3M tripled manufacturing capacity of polarization maintaining (PM) fiber and fiber Bragg gratings. The new 3M Low Skew Pleated Foil Cable (PFC) from 3M Interconnect Solutions systems added the benefits of low skew cabling to a growing list of completed assemblies, compatible cables, and connectors. 3M Visual Systems Division announced the availability of the new 3M Personal Projector MP7630 for traveling professionals. The $68.4 million verdict against 3M in the LePage case, which was delivered in October 1999, was upheld by a federal judge. ican Inc. and 3M announced a sponsorship agreement linking 3M Health Care with information about how health professionals can reduce the risks of surgical site infections (http://www.icanprevent.com). In **April** 3M's Optical Systems Division purchased Polaroid's Technical Polarizer and Display Films business and patented technologies—including Polaroid's polarizer (circular, h-type, and k-type), plastic display, and certain display-viewing-enhancement film technologies. U.S. Environmental Protection Agency (EPA) Region 5 filed civil administrative complaints against 3M facilities in Hutchinson, St. Paul, and Cottage Grove, Minn., for violation of Federal rules on hazardous waste. Fines totaling $109,855 were proposed. 3M reported a strong first-quarter earnings increase of 27 percent (19 percent excluding a one-time gain), which beat analysts' expectations by 5 cents a share. However, there were "whisper expectations" that the company's estimate for the year would increase by a similar amount. When it was raised by only 2 cents, the stock price actually fell. 3M Library Systems and the National University of Singapore Library announced plans to introduce an integrated system of digital identification technology to the university's six libraries (2 million books), making it the largest library site radio frequency identification (RFID) project in the world. In **May** 3M said that 14 Taiwanese networking manufacturers had selected its breakthrough fiber optic technology as part of an initiative to lead the world's adoption of fiber optic LANs. 3M products that serve the "new economy" were driving faster growth and high-quality returns, said CEO DeSimone at the annual meeting. Some of 3M's fastest-growing products included flexible electronic circuits, fiber optic components for telecommunications, and optical films for flat panel displays. Traditional product lines providing solutions to fast-growing markets include microstructured abrasives for silicon wafer finishing, adhesives that conduct electricity, and custom tapes used in electronic devices. DeSimone noted that 3M's "largest single opportunity" was a new family of immune response modifiers. The first product based on this technology, Aldara (imiquimod) Cream 5%, had become a leading treatment for genital warts. Clinical trials on three new indications were under way. "This family of drugs represents an enormous potential breakthrough in medicine and a multibillion dollar opportunity for 3M over the next five to 10 years," he said. 3M announced plans to phase out of the perfluorooctanyl chemistry used to produce certain repellents and surface-disinfectant products. The affected product lines, representing about 2 percent of 3M's nearly $16 billion in annual sales, included many Scotchgard products: soil, oil, and water repellent products; coatings used for oil and grease resistance on paper packaging; fire-fighting foams; and specialty components for other products. "Our decision anticipates increasing attention to the appropriate use and management of persistent materials," said EVP Reich. In **June** 3M increased an earlier offer for the preferred shares of Quante AG, a Wuppertal, Germany-based maker of telecommunications systems and services, to $40.7 million (a 7.7 percent premium). 3M agreed to serve as title sponsor of Randy MacDonald's No. 72 Chevrolet through the remaining 11 races of the 2000 NASCAR Craftsman Truck Series season. **June 30:** Strong second-quarter results in electronic and telecommunications businesses fueled an 11.6 percent earnings increase (exclusive of one-time gains) that surpassed analysts' estimates. In **July** 3M purchased 275-employee, Vancouver, British Columbia-based Dynapro Technologies Inc., a touch-screen company, to augment its fast-growing optical systems division. BreezeCom Ltd. agreed to provide its entire suite of wireless products and systems to be sold under the 3M brand name. 3M Interconnect Solutions Division announced the MTP/MTO Multi-Mode Fiber Optic Cable Assemblies as its first offering in a family of Parallel Optic Interconnect solutions. Consumers fighting increased tarnish caused by summer's higher humidity were able to get a free package of $5.99 3M Anti-Tarnish Strips at new Internet web site http://www.marshawhitney.com. In **August** scientists from 3M Drug Delivery Systems (DDS) reported an exciting new technology to be used in pulmonary therapeutic: a novel excipient, using oligolactic acid, which increases formulation options for a variety of drugs in hydrofluoroalkane-based metered dose inhalers, and additionally may provide for the sustained release of pharmaceuticals within the lungs. A California resident was pressing a suit seeking damages for customers overcharged during 3M's monopoly of the tape market. The company was was one of four in the Twin Cities named to Industry Week magazine's fifth annual list of the World's 100 Best-Managed Companies. 3M has been on

continued on page 286

Minntech Corporation

14605 28th Ave. N., Plymouth, MN 55447
Tel: 763/553-3300 Fax: 763/553-3387 Web site: http://www.minntech.com

Minntech Corp. develops, manufactures, and markets medical devices, sterilants, and water filtration products. Minntech is expanding into new businesses based on its internally developed technologies in hollow-fiber membrane devices, chemical sterilants, dialysis solutions, and electronic products. The company's products are used in kidney dialysis, open-heart surgery, and the preparation of pure water for medical, industrial, and laboratory use.

EARNINGS HISTORY

Year Ended Mar 31	Operating Revenue/Sales (dollars in thousands)	Net Earnings (dollars in thousands)	Return on Revenue (percent)	Return on Equity (percent)	Net Earnings (dollars per share)	Cash Dividend (dollars per share)	Market Price Range (dollars per share)
2000	74,357	5,941	8.0	11.4	0.87	0.10	16.75–7.50
1999	76,264	7,160	9.4	14.8	1.05	0.10	17.13–9.00
1998	69,381	4,685	6.8	11.2	0.69	0.10	14.25–9.00
1997 *	65,907	(3,372)	(5.1)	(9.0)	(0.50)	0.10	21.50–9.50
1996 †	64,769	4,308	6.7	10.5	0.66	0.10	23.63–11.50

* Income figures for 1997 include pretax charge of $9,569,000 for restructuring and other items.
† Income figures for 1996 include pretax charge of $936,000 for fiber production scale-up losses.

BALANCE SHEET

Assets	03/31/00 (dollars in thousands)	03/31/99	Liabilities	03/31/00 (dollars in thousands)	03/31/99
Current (CAE 10,687 and 9,171)	41,102	41,275	Current (STD 0 and 252)	8,419	9,371
Property and equipment	15,359	15,021	Deferred income taxes		82
Patent costs	544	524	Deferred compensation	866	755
Goodwill	541	960	Stockholders' equity*	52,308	48,518
Other	4,047	946	TOTAL	61,593	58,726
TOTAL	61,593	58,726			

* $0.05 par common; 20,000,000 authorized; 6,686,714 and 6,778,617 issued and outstanding.

RECENT QUARTERS / **PRIOR-YEAR RESULTS**

	Quarter End	Revenue ($000)	Earnings ($000)	EPS ($)	Prior-Year Revenue ($000)	Prior-Year Earnings ($000)	Prior-Year EPS ($)
Q2	09/30/2000	18,048	1,290	0.19	18,880	1,238	0.18
Q1	07/01/2000	17,033	(21)	0.00	18,828	1,168	0.17
Q4	03/31/2000	17,923	1,844	0.27	19,838	1,758	0.26
Q3	12/31/99	18,726	1,691	0.25	19,743	2,486	0.37
	SUM	71,730	4,804	0.71	77,289	6,650	0.98

RECENT EVENTS

In **November 1999** the company opened its first dialyzer reprocessing center in Orlando, Fla. [A second and third, in Boston and Atlanta, were scheduled by the end of August 2000.] In **December** the company's board of directors extended the company's stock repurchase program, which started in August 1998, by authorizing purchases by the corporation of up to an additional 300,000 shares (4.4 percent) of its common stock. **Dec. 31:** Third-quarter results were below forecast, although the revenue shortfall was partially offset by reduced operating expenses. The lower-than-expected purchases from LifeStream, Minntech's OEM partner, were expected to improve over the next two quarters as LifeStream worked through existing inventory and started ordering new product. On the horizon: Clinical trials for a new dialyzer reprocessing sterilant, for which Minntech had secured an exclusive option to license the rights, were to begin in Germany in spring 2000. Also expected in spring was a 510(k) filing with the FDA for the Automatic Endoscope Reprocessing System (AERS), the development of which was nearing completion. In **March 2000** Minntech completed the repurchase of 300,000 shares of its common stock authorized in August 1998, and was continuing to repurchase shares under the December extension. In **April** the company introduced the Renapak 2 Concentrate Manufacturing System, which provides dialysis clinics with an innovative, quality-conscious method of producing their own hemodialysis concentrates. Minntech submitted a 510(k) filing to the FDA for its next-generation endoscope reprocessing products—an automated endoscope reprocessor and companion sterilant. In **May** the company signed a letter of intent to acquire substantially all of the assets of Di-Chem Concentrate Inc., an OEM manufacturer of hemodialysis concentrates located in Lewisberry, Pa. The deal was to establish a manufacturing presence to strengthen Minntech's existing eastern distribution hub, established in fiscal 1999 in Harrisburg, Pa. [The deal was canceled in November in favor of expanding on the existing supply relationship with Di-Chem..] **June 30:** First-quarter earnings were lower than analysts had expected. The company attributed the earnings shortfall to a decline in revenue, largely related to the recent product divestiture and ongoing transition of its cardiosurgery business, as well as start-up costs for two major distribution centers, sales force expansion, and severance costs *continued on page 286*

OFFICERS

William Hope
Chairman and interim Pres./CEO

Barbara A. Wrigley
EVP-Corp. Development, General Counsel

Paul E. Helms
SVP-Operations

Andrew Cambell
VP-Sales

Jules L. Fisher
VP and CFO

Robert W. Johnson
VP-Quality Assurance/Regulatory Affairs

Michael Petersen
VP-Research/Development

Kevin Finkle
Controller

DIRECTORS

Norman Dann
Pathfinder Ventures Inc. (retired)

George Heenan
University of St. Thomas, St. Paul

Amos Heilicher
Advance-Carter Co., Golden Valley, MN

William Hope
G&K Services Inc. (retired)

Malcolm W. McDonald
Space Center Inc., Minneapolis

Fred L. Shapiro, M.D., F.A.C.P.
Hennepin Faculty Associates, Minneapolis

Donald H. Soukup
venture capitalist

MAJOR SHAREHOLDERS

Heartland Advisors Inc., 19.7%
Milwaukee

AMVESCAP plc, 10.7%
London

T. Rowe Price Associates Inc., 10.1%
Baltimore

Wellington Management Co. LLP, 7%
Boston

Fleet Boston Corp., 5.8%
Boston

Putnam Investments Inc., 5.3%
Boston

All officers and directors as a group (14 persons), 18%

SIC CODE

3589 Service industry machinery, nec

3841 Surgical and medical instruments

MISCELLANEOUS

TRANSFER AGENT AND REGISTAR:
Wells Fargo Bank Minnesota N.A., South St. Paul, MN

TRADED: Nasdaq National Market

SYMBOL: MNTX

STOCKHOLDERS: 464

EMPLOYEES: 425

PART TIME: 9

GENERAL COUNSEL:
Faegre & Benson PLLP, Minneapolis

AUDITORS:
PricewaterhouseCoopers LLP, Minneapolis

INC: MN-1974

ANNUAL MEETING: August

RANKINGS

No. 96 CRM Public 200

SUBSIDIARIES, DIVISIONS, AFFILIATES

EUROPEAN OFFICE

Minntech B.V.
Sourethweg 11
6422 PC Heerlen
The Netherlands

JAPANESE OFFICE

Minntech Japan Corp.
Sumitomo Seimei Bldg., 4F
10-10 Yocho-machi
Shinjuku-ku, Tokyo 162
Japan

PUB

TWO-YEAR QUARTERLY HIGH-LOW STOCK PRICES

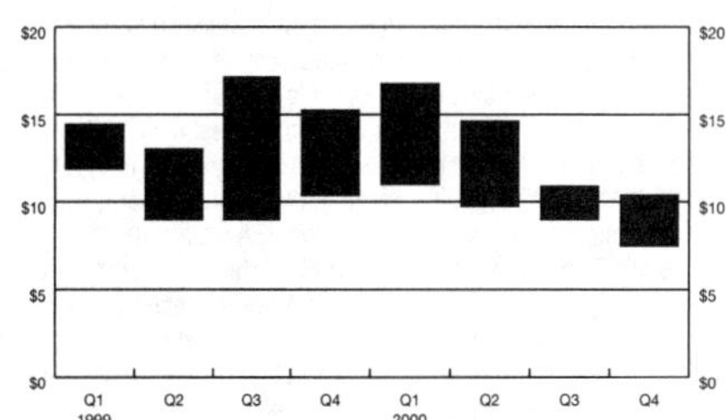

PUB

MOCON Inc.

7500 Boone Ave. N., Brooklyn Park, MN 55428
Tel: 763/493-6370 Fax: 763/493-6358 Web site: http://www.mocon.com

MOCON Inc., formerly Modern Controls Inc., is a leading provider of systems and services designed to assess materials and processes. The company develops, manufactures, and markets high-tech instrumentation designed to test packages and packaging materials, films, and pharmaceutical products. The company performs Consulting and Developmental Services (CDS) for a variety of companies in development and manufacturing. MOCON markets products used in research laboratories, production environments, and quality-control applications in the food, plastics, electronics, paints and coatings, medical, and pharmaceutical industries.

EARNINGS HISTORY

Year Ended Dec 31	Operating Revenue/Sales (dollars in thousands)	Net Earnings	Return on Revenue (percent)	Return on Equity	Net Earnings (dollars per share*)	Cash Dividend	Market Price Range
1999	17,843	2,899	16.2	19.0	0.46	0.20	8.50–4.38
1998	15,146	2,328	15.4	15.4	0.37	0.20	11.63–4.06
1997	17,017	3,728	21.9	24.8	0.58	0.18	15.00–6.33
1996	14,768	3,082	20.9	24.5	0.48	0.16	8.00–6.42
1995	12,844	2,570	20.0	20.6	0.38	0.14	7.42–4.13

* Per-share amounts restated to reflect a 3-for-2 stock split paid on Sept. 12, 1997.

BALANCE SHEET

Assets	12/31/99 (dollars in thousands)	12/31/98
Current (CAE 1,275 and 1,352)	10,872	11,403
Marketable securities	4,259	3,063
Property and equipment	1,182	1,147
Goodwill	965	1,070
Technology rights, other intangibles	540	600
Other	385	392
TOTAL	18,204	17,675

Liabilities	12/31/99 (dollars in thousands)	12/31/98
Current	2,837	2,471
Deferred income taxes	112	98
Stockholders' equity*	15,255	15,106
TOTAL	18,204	17,675

* $0.10 par common; 22,000,000 authorized; 6,073,097 and 6,287,960 issued and outstanding.

RECENT QUARTERS / PRIOR-YEAR RESULTS

	Quarter End	Revenue ($000)	Earnings ($000)	EPS ($)	Prior-Year Revenue ($000)	Prior-Year Earnings ($000)	Prior-Year EPS ($)
Q3	09/30/2000	4,591	827	0.14	4,465	753	0.12
Q2	06/30/2000	4,550	810	0.13	4,432	716	0.11
Q1	03/31/2000	4,515	794	0.13	4,454	694	0.11
Q4	12/31/99	4,492	736	0.12	3,942	715	0.11
	SUM	18,148	3,167	0.52	17,293	2,878	0.46

RECENT EVENTS

In **January 2000** MOCON subsidiary Microanalytics successfully introduced the OXY.TRAX, a unique new test system for use in the petrochemical industry. The OXY.TRAX system is able to measure trace levels of oxygenated hydrocarbons in a variety of hydrocarbon products and process streams, such as liquefied petroleum gases. In **February** MOCON, which operates the largest permeation testing laboratory in the world, began a laboratory expansion effort that was to double the capacity of its main testing laboratory located at company headquarters. The board declared a 10 percent increase in the dividend and also authorized stock repurchases. In **March** MOCON scientist Michelle Stevens presented a technical paper on a new method for fuel permeation analysis at the Society of Automotive Engineers World Congress in Detroit. A new version of the Aromatrax system produced by Microanalytics enabled the company to rapidly screen multiple test samples for off-odors. MOCON received an order from a major pharmaceutical company for a system—using the LC-Transform technology developed by MOCON subsidiary Lab Connections—to aid in the identification of impurities in drugs under development. In **July** MOCON acquired intellectual property that provides a unique method for detecting leaks in the Tyvek packaging widely used by the medical industry. In **August** MOCON introduced its new Enhanced Windows Line of permeation instruments. In **September** the company completed its new "cGMP-certified" testing laboratory for the medical device and pharmaceutical industries. "Medical device and drug makers are required to validate the current and future shelf-life of their packaged products," EVP Mayer said. "MOCON's new cGMP laboratory will be a high-quality, verifiable outside source for this important research and quality control test data." MOCON received the largest single order in the company's history, a more than $400,000 order from a domestic laboratory for an integrated, state-of-the-art MOCON permeation test system. MOCON sold its first VERICAP 4000 capsule weighing and sorting system, which features the fastest weight sensor in the world, designed to help pharmaceutical companies meet exacting FDA requirements for prescription drugs in capsule form. **Sept. 30:** Nine-month sales were $13,656,000 compared to $13,350,000 for the first nine months of 1999. Net income and net income per share increased 12 percent and 18 percent to $2,431,000 and 40 cents, respectively. In **October** MOCON announced the development of a new high-sensitivity water vapor measurement capability for use in its permeation laboratory. This new technology, AQUATRAN, is able to measure the transmission of water vapor through packaging and other materials at rates lower than ever before. In **November** MOCON exhibited the newest addition to its permeation product line, the OX-TRAN 2/61, at Pack Expo 2000 in Chicago.

OFFICERS

Robert L. Demorest
Chairman and CEO

Daniel W. Mayer
EVP

Dane D. Anderson
CFO, Secretary, and Treasurer

DIRECTORS

Dean B. Chenoweth
Advantek Inc., Minnetonka, MN

Robert L. Demorest

J. Leonard Frame
Phoenix Solutions Co., Minneapolis

Daniel W. Mayer

Ronald A. Meyer

Richard A. Proulx
independent consultant

Paul L. Sjoquist
Palmatier, Sjoquist, Voight & Christensen, P.A., Minneapolis

Thomas C. Thomas
Oppenheimer Wolff & Donnelly LLP, San Jose, CA

MAJOR SHAREHOLDERS

Fenimore Asset Management Inc., 15%
Cobleskill, NY

William N. Mayer, 5%

Royce & Associates Inc., 5%
New York

All officers and directors as a group (9 persons), 11.3%

SIC CODE

3829 Measuring and controlling devices, nec

MISCELLANEOUS

TRANSFER AGENT AND REGISTAR:
Wells Fargo Bank Minnesota N.A.,
South St. Paul, MN

TRADED: Nasdaq National Market

SYMBOL: MOCO

STOCKHOLDERS: 511

EMPLOYEES: 88

PART TIME: 1

IN MINNESOTA: 69

GENERAL COUNSEL:
Oppenheimer Wolff & Donnelly LLP, Minneapolis

AUDITORS:
KPMG LLP, Minneapolis

INC: MN-1966

ANNUAL MEETING: May

RANKINGS

No. 157 CRM Public 200

SUBSIDIARIES, DIVISIONS, AFFILIATES

MOCON FSC Inc.

Microanalytics Instrumenataion Corp.
2713 Sam Bass Rd.
Round Rock, TX 78681

Lab Connections, Inc.
10 Bearfoot Rd.
Suite 2000
Northborough, MA 01532

TWO-YEAR QUARTERLY HIGH-LOW STOCK PRICES

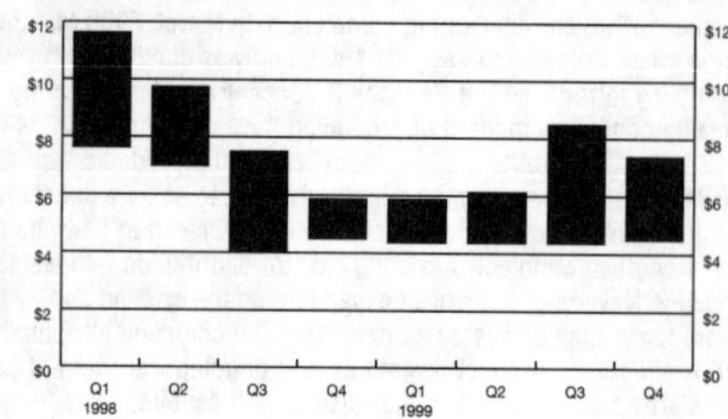

Musicland Stores Corporation

10400 Yellow Circle Dr., Minnetonka, MN 55343
Tel: 952/931-8000 Fax: 952/931-8300 Web site: http://www.musicland.com

Musicland Stores Corp. is the leading specialty retailer of home-entertainment software products in the United States. The company sells compact discs, prerecorded audio cassettes, prerecorded video cassettes, books, computer software, and related accessories. As of June 30, 2000 the company operated 1,328 stores (including 659 Sam Goody stores, 406 Suncoast stores, 77 Media Play stores, and 186 On Cue stores) in 49 states, Puerto Rico, and the Virgin Islands. The company also publishes an independent music magazine, Request.

EARNINGS HISTORY

Year Ended Dec 31	Operating Revenue/Sales (dollars in thousands)	Net Earnings	Return on Revenue (percent)	Return on Equity	Net Earnings (dollars per share)	Cash Dividend	Market Price Range
1999	1,891,828	58,380	3.1	53.4	1.65	—	15.25–6.75
1998	1,846,882	38,033	2.1	59.4	1.10	—	18.00–6.50
1997	1,768,312	13,971	0.8	74.4	0.42	—	8.50–0.69
1996 *	1,821,594	(193,738)	(10.6)	NM	(5.80)	—	5.25–1.25
1995 †	1,722,572	(135,750)	(7.9)	(69.3)	(4.00)	—	11.00–3.75

* Income figures for 1996 include pretax charge of $95.253 million for remaining goodwill write-down in the music division; and restructuring charges totaling $75 million to close underperforming stores.
† Income figures for 1995 include pretax charge of $138.0 million for goodwill write-down in the music division.

BALANCE SHEET

Assets	12/31/99 (dollars in thousands)	12/31/98	Liabilities	12/31/99 (dollars in thousands)	12/31/98
Current	816,947	730,123	Current	655,362	607,153
(CAE 335,693 and 257,218)			Long-term debt	258,950	258,871
Property	236,550	233,424	Other	39,904	43,634
Other	10,077	10,093	Stkhldrs' equity*	109,358	63,982
TOTAL	1,063,574	973,640	TOTAL	1,063,574	973,640

* $0.01 par common; 75,000,000 authorized; 36,187,454 and 36,041,934 issued and outstanding, less 2,015,700 treasury shares.

RECENT QUARTERS / **PRIOR-YEAR RESULTS**

	Quarter End	Revenue ($000)	Earnings ($000)	EPS ($)	Prior-Year Revenue ($000)	Prior-Year Earnings ($000)	Prior-Year EPS ($)
Q3	09/30/2000	389,393	62	0.00	386,337	728	0.02
Q2	06/30/2000	402,486	1,714	0.05	381,059	1,499	0.04
Q1	03/31/2000	415,821	2,044	0.06	401,797	1,374	0.04
Q4	12/31/99	722,635	54,779	1.58	699,906	50,025	1.42
	SUM	1,930,335	58,599	1.70	1,869,099	53,626	1.52

RECENT EVENTS

In **December 1999** a new partnership was formed between Musicland Stores and Damark International Inc. (Nasdaq: DMRK), Brooklyn Park, Minn. New links between Musicland's four e-commerce sites (SamGoody.com, Suncoast.com, MediaPlay.com, and OnCue.com) and Damark's Web site improved the available selection of music, movies, software, video games, books, sheet music, and other entertainment merchandise for online shoppers. Musicland took an equity position in Supersoni.com (http://www.supersoni.com), a new Web-based entertainment destination that promotes new music by featuring downloadable, digital video clips of popular music. **Dec. 31**: A strong holiday season capped off a 53 percent earnings increase for fiscal 1999. Other achievements in the year included opening 39 stores, developing an e-commerce strategy, and reducing debt. In **January 2000** Musicland's board authorized an increase in the company's stock buyback program from 3 million shares to 4 million. The company also announced plans to open 70 stores in 2000, funding the expansion from operations. In **February** Musicland announced an agreement with RealNetworks Inc. aimed at getting more people to sample and purchase music online by using a customized version of RealJukebox. In **March** the board of directors authorized an increase in the company's stock buyback program from 4 million to 6 million shares. In **April**, hoping to drive more traffic to its e-commerce sites and its traditional stores, Musicland formed a marketing alliance with AltaVista Co., Palo Alto, Calif., the Internet's premier media and commerce network. **April 29**: Comparable-store sales increased 17.0 percent for the four weeks. In **May** the customer loyalty program REPLAY reached 1 million members, fueled by the program's rollout to its Media Play stores earlier in the month. **May 27**: Comparable-store sales increased 4.7 percent for the four weeks. Said CFO Benson, "Strong music releases by Britney Spears and Eminem, combined with healthy gains in our electronics and DVD categories, contributed to the increases this month." In **June** Musicland's in-house advertising department earned seven 21st Annual Telly Awards for TV, commercial, and video advertising. Musicland won four silver and three bronze awards for its outstanding television commercials in 1999. In **August** Request Magazine earned Print Magazine's Regional Design Annual 2000, an award honoring graphic design in magazines. During Pepsi-Cola Co.'s (NYSE: PEP) "PepsiStuff.com" promotion—a joint online effort between Pepsi and Yahoo!, a leading global Internet communications, commerce, and media company—more than 1.5 billion bottles of Pepsi product promoted Sam Goody (www.SamGoody.com). **Aug. 26**: Comparable-store sales decreased 1.7 percent for the four-week period. "Healthy gains in VHS, DVD, books and electronics mostly offset the continued weak *continued on page 286*

OFFICERS

Jack W. Eugster
Chairman, President, and CEO

Keith A. Benson
Vice Chairman and CFO

Gilbert L. Wachsman
Vice Chairman

Jonathan T.M. Reckford
Pres.-Stores

Richard J. Odette
SVP-Music Merchandising

Douglas M. Tracey
SVP-E-commerce/Logistics

Randy L. Abbott
Division VP-Stores, Media Play

Archie Benike
VP-Marketing

Scott C. Burtness
VP-Hardlines Merchandising

Peter J. Busch
VP-Video Merchandising

Richard C. Casari
VP-Inventory Management

Michael J. Colon
Division VP-Stores, Sam Goody

Paula M. Connerney
Division SVP-Store Operations

Steven J. Danker
VP and Chief Information Officer

Jon Estes
Division VP-Stores, On Cue

Robert A. Faulkner
VP and Controller

Heidi M. Hoard
VP, General Counsel, and Secretary

Cynthia Holland
VP-Book Merchandising

Merry Beth Hovey
VP-Advertising

Tamara A. Kozikowski
VP-Real Estate

Larry Kurzeka
Division VP-Stores, Suncoast

Jay Landauer
VP-Human Resources

Jim Nermyr
VP and Treasurer

Karl A. Sowa
VP-Electronic Commerce

O. Keith Wanke
VP-Loss Prevention

DIRECTORS

Keith A. Benson

Jack W. Eugster

Kenneth F. Gorman
Apollo Partners LCC

William A. Hodder
Donaldson Co. Inc. (retired)

Josiah O. Low III
Donaldson, Lufkin & Jenrette

Terry T. Saario, Ph.D.
Bravo LLC

Gilbert L. Wachsman

Tom F. Weyl
Martin/Williams Advertising

Michael W. Wright
Supervalu Inc., Eden Prairie, MN

MAJOR SHAREHOLDERS

Alfred and Annie Teo, 16.9%
Lyndhurst, NJ

MAAA Trust, Teo children, 9.6%
Upper Montclair, NJ

Mellon Financial Corp., 8%
Pittsburgh

Barclays Global Investors N.A., 6.6%
San Francisco

Jack W. Eugster, 5.1%

All officers and directors as a group (14 persons), 10.1%

SIC CODE

5735 Record and prerecorded tape stores

MISCELLANEOUS

TRANSFER AGENT AND REGISTAR:
Wells Fargo Bank Minnesota N.A., South St. Paul, MN

TRADED: NYSE

SYMBOL: MLG

STOCKHOLDERS: 489

EMPLOYEES: 15,900

PART TIME: 10,000

GENERAL COUNSEL:
Heidi Hoard

AUDITORS:
Arthur Andersen LLP, Minneapolis

INC: DE-1988

FOUNDED: 1956

ANNUAL MEETING: July

COMMUNICATIONS:
Brant K. Skogrand

RANKINGS

No. 23 CRM Public 200

TWO-YEAR QUARTERLY HIGH-LOW STOCK PRICES

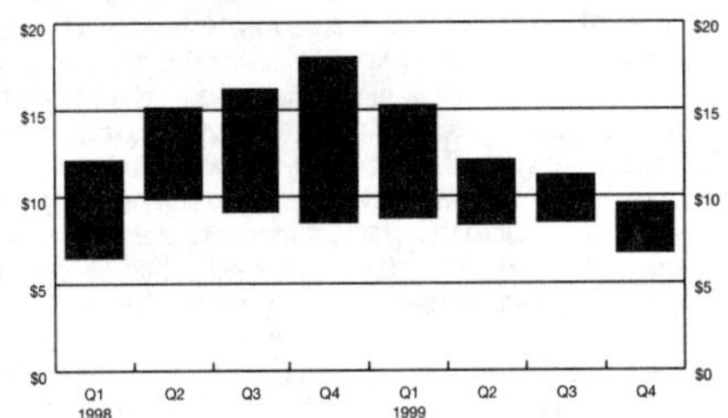

PUB

Lakes Gaming Inc.

continued from page 257 treatment of shareholders in connection with any potential takeover of the company and to guard against partial tender offers, open market accumulations, and other abusive tactics to gain control of the company. In **June** a settlement agreement was reached regarding both the Stratosphere shareholders' litigation and the Grand Casinos Inc. shareholders' litigation, both of which were filed in 1996. The agreement called for Lakes to pay $9 million dollars to the Grand Casino shareholders and $9 million dollars to the Stratosphere shareholders for full and final settlement for all federal- and state-related actions. CEO Berman stated, "We feel it is in the best interest of Lakes and its shareholders to resolve these lawsuits. Settlement of these two complaints removes one of the major uncertainties that has been associated with our company." In **July** Lakes Gaming formed a joint venture, Metroplex-Lakes LLC, with Metroplex LLC to develop Las Vegas real estate controlled by Lakes. Metroplex-Lakes LLC was planning to develop an upscale retail, commercial, hotel, and entertainment complex on 16 acres surrounding the corner of Harmon Avenue and Las Vegas Boulevard (the "Strip"). In **August** Lakes Gaming agreed to form a joint venture for the purpose of developing two new gaming facilities on Indian-owned land in California. Under the agreement, Lakes was to form two separate limited liability companies with MRD Gaming, a limited liability company based in Las Vegas that successfully developed two other Indian casinos, one in Arizona and one in Kansas. The partnership between Lakes and MRD was to hold contracts to develop and open two casino resort facilities with two separate American Indian Tribes in California. Development at each casino resort location was to start as soon as various regulatory approvals were obtained by each applicable Tribe. Lakes Gaming also announced that it was actively negotiating agreements with prospective partners that would result in two new business ventures. One potential area of new business involved the life settlement industry. Lakes already agreed to provide up to $3 million in bridge loans to a participant in the industry. Lakes' commitment to proceed with a further term loan was subject to the borrower's securing a $150 million revolving warehouse credit facility to enable the borrower to purchase existing life insurance policies from persons 65 years or older, which provides liquidity to the holder of the policy during their lifetime. Another business opportunity involved international Internet gaming. Lakes was considering establishing one or more Web sites to conduct online gaming in a regulated country, taking wagers placed from only outside the United States. Lakes had identified an experienced provider of online gaming technology and was negotiating a contract under which Lakes would license the provider's technology for the new gaming Web sites. **Oct. 1:** Revenue for third quarter was derived solely from fees related to the management of Grand Casino Coushatta. Operating results at Grand Casino Coushatta continued to improve in all areas compared to the same quarter last year including total revenue, gaming revenue, and hotel occupancy. Revenue and earnings for the quarter are less than the same period last year due to the fact that the company's management contract for Grand Casino Avoyelles was bought out by the Tunica-Biloxi Tribe of Louisiana at the end of the first quarter of 2000.

Lectec Corporation

continued from page 258 LecTec's net loss was primarily due to an increase in sales and marketing expenditures made to fund growth of the company's consumer products business. "Sales of our over-the-counter (OTC) topical drug delivery therapeutic consumer products increased 186 percent over the same period a year ago, representing 59 percent of total first-quarter sales compared to 29 percent last year," commented Young.

Legal Research Center Inc.

continued from page 260 Improvements in revenue were primarily due to increased ophthalmic and contract aseptic sales. Reduced income continued to reflect increased unabsorbed overhead costs associated with decreased hyaluronan production, slowed due to a setback in the company's attempt to obtain FDA approval of GYNECARE INTERGEL Adhesion Prevention Solution for U.S. distribution. Oral Restorative Division revenue increased 4 percent to $4,481,000, but lost $400,000 thanks to increased overhead charges due to international expansion and associated increased sales and marketing promotions, as well as new product development activity. In **October** BlueFire Research initiated coverage of Lifecore Biomedical with an OUTPERFORM rating and a 12-month target price of $15 per share.

LodgeNet Entertainment Corporation

continued from page 262 United States and Canada. In **April** LodgeNet launched a new direct-response advertising service to capitalize on the marketing and advertising value of the more than 200 million travelers who pass through the company's installed North American guest rooms each year. (LodgeNet inserts banner ads on the interactive television menus that guests use to browse and order on-demand movies, Nintendo video games, Internet on TV, and other LodgeNet services. Viewers are able to respond to promotional opportunities by entering their e-mail address.) In **May**, through a licensing agreement with GuestVision, LodgeNet agreed to provide on-demand movies, Nintendo 64 video games, and Internet-on-TV service to the 300-room Carlton Hotel in Tel Aviv, Israel. At HITEC 2000, in **June**, LodgeNet premiered an all-new interactive digital system—featuring independently produced Web films ("Web Cinema") and on-demand, digital-quality music. The company agreed to provide its comprehensive bundle of customized, interactive television and high-speed Internet connectivity services to The Inn at Spanish Bay, The Lodge at Pebble Beach, and Casa Palmero, all properties of the prestigious Pebble Beach Co. LodgeNet and Wayport Inc., a leading provider of high-speed Internet solutions for people on the move, signed their first joint Internet services agreement encompassing an entire lodging group (Kinseth Hospitality Cos.). By the end of **July**, LodgeNet had installed 4,000 hotels with its interactive systems and services. In **August** LodgeNet and SurfControl Inc., Scotts Valley, Calif., joined forces to provide hotel guests with the ability to customize the content that they access through LodgeNet's Internet-on-TV service. By this time, the company was delivering one or more interactive guest pay services to more than 700,000 guest rooms in the United States and Canada. Thanks to an exclusive agreement between LodgeNet and Nintendo of America Inc., video game fans in more than 162,000 hotel rooms were able to enjoy Mario Tennis the same week it hit shelves at consumer retail outlets. **Sept. 30:** LodgeNet reported its 28th-consecutive increase in comparative quarterly revenue and EBITDA (earnings before interest, taxes, depreciation, and amortization). EBITDA increased 13.6 percent to $19.3 million. The company's operating income increased 58.8 percent to $2.8 million. "LodgeNet continued to deliver solid results across all key growth metrics, as we executed on both a strategic and operational level," said CEO Petersen. "Our industry-leading room growth, combined with a focus on financial discipline, resulted in record EBITDA and EBITDA margin. In addition, we continued to decrease our long-term debt and are on track to report positive operating income for the full year, the first time in our public history." In **October** LodgeNet and Hilton Hotels Corp. (NYSE: HLT), Beverly Hills, Calif., one of the world's leading hotel companies, announced an agreement by which LodgeNet's interactive television services were to be phased into Hilton's owned, leased, and joint venture hotels in the United States (more than 220 properties with 70,000 rooms). This deployment was to begin in the fourth quarter of 2000 and continue as existing contracts expire. LodgeNet expected the Hilton agreement to lead to incremental room growth of between 40,000 to 60,000 hotel rooms in each of the next five years on top of the company's existing growth plans. As a result, LodgeNet will become the largest provider of interactive television services to the hotel room industry. CEO Petersen commented, "LodgeNet's outlook for 2001 is strong, as we expect double-digit revenue and EBITDA growth while continuing to improve our operating and financial ratios." In **November** LodgeNet premiered The Legend of Zelda: Majora's Mask on its N64-equipped, interactive television systems in 180,000 hotel rooms; and announced that, beginning in January, it will offer guests access to first-season episodes of HBO's critically-acclaimed, original series "The Sopranos" and "Sex and the City."

MDU Resources Group Inc.

continued from page 264 services in the Bozeman, Mont., area. Preston, Reynolds & Co. Inc., one of the Rocky Mountain region's leading producers of coal-bed methane, sold substantially all of its assets to WBI Holdings Inc., the pipeline, energy services, and oil and gas production subsidiary of MDU, for a combination of cash and stock. In **May** MDU completed the acquisition of $35 million-revenue Connolly-Pacific Co., a southern California aggregate mining and marine construction company, from L.G. Everist Inc. Indirect subsidiary Morse Bros. Inc. acquired the operating assets of three Oregon-based construction materials companies with aggregate revenue of $26 million. In **June** WBI Holdings agreed to purchase certain natural gas gathering system assets from Kinder Morgan Inc., including more than 1,000 miles of gathering lines, 14,000 horsepower of compression, and a natural gas processing facility. Knife River acquired Empire Sand & Gravel Co. Inc., a Billings, Mont., construction company. MDU acquired Hamlin Electric Co., Fort Morgan, Colo., a full-service contractor primarily to the electric utility industry. MDU acquired The Wagner-Smith Co., Dayton, Ohio, a diversified electrical contractor in the industrial, utility, institutional, and government markets with operations in traffic signal systems; street lighting; equipment manufacturing, rental and sales; industrial pump distribution and repair; and mechanical construction services. **June 30:** As a result of its acquisition and drilling program, Fidelity Exploration & Production Co. increased its reserve holdings from 357 billion cubic-feet-equivalent (Bcfe) of oil and natural gas reserves to 390 Bcfe. In addition to those proven reserves, newly acquired leasehold positions held unproven reserves of natural gas with the potential to exceed 1 trillion cubic feet. In **August** MDU acquired four Oregon corporations, collectively known as Beaver State, that produce aggregate materials, asphalt, ready-mixed concrete, and construction materials in the southern Oregon County of Douglas. In **September** Westmoreland Coal Co. (Amex: WLB), Colorado Springs, Colo., agreed to acquire Knife River's coal operations for $28.8 million in cash, excluding final settlement cost adjustments and other consideration. Closing of the transaction was expected to occur by year-end, subject to board approval and other contingencies. Included in the sale were active coal mines in North Dakota and Montana, coal sales agreements, reserves, mining equipment, and certain rights to the inactive Gascoyne Mine in North Dakota. The operations produce 3 million tons of coal annually. Knife River coal mining management and employees at the Beulah, N.D., and Savage, Mont., locations were to join Westmoreland. **Sept. 30:** Year-to-date earnings for the nine months totaled $73.9 million, compared to $59.0 million for the comparable period last year. "Significantly higher earnings at both our oil and natural gas production segment and our construction materials and mining segment boosted our consolidated earnings," said CEO White. "In addition, I am delighted that our stock price ... has appreciated approximately 50 percent since the beginning of the year." Third-quarter earnings at the oil and natural gas production segment more than doubled to $10 million. Oil and natural gas production increased a combined 25 percent from a year ago, reflecting production from oil and gas properties acquired late last year and new production from the coal bed natural gas properties. In addition, strong oil and natural gas prices also contributed to the boost in earnings. Realized oil prices averaged 36 percent higher, while natural gas prices averaged 32 percent higher for the quarter. At the construction materials and mining segment, quarterly earnings reached $19.2 million in 2000 as compared to $13.6 million for the same period last year. The earnings increase resulted from acquisitions made during the prior 12 months and higher ready-mixed concrete, aggregate, and cement volumes at existing operations, partially offset by higher energy costs. At the utility, third quarter electric earnings increased 25 percent to $5.9 million due to higher retail and wholesale electric sales and lower operation and maintenance expenses. These increases were partially offset by higher purchased power costs because an electric generating station was down for repairs during July and part of August. In **October** Knife River acquired A-1 Paving Inc., a construction company headquartered in Kalispell, Mont., that produces aggregate materials and asphalt and provides construction services in the Flathead Valley region of northwestern Montana.

MGI Pharma Inc.

continued from page 265

into a license, research, and development agreement for MG98 and novel small molecule inhibitors of DNA methyltransferase (DNA MeTase) for North America. In **September** the company initiated a Phase 2 liver cancer trial with its novel anti-cancer compound, irofulven, to evaluate the safety and efficacy of irofulven in those patients. U.S. Bancorp Piper Jaffray, in its monthly commentary, reiterated its STRONG BUY rating for MGI stock, as well as its one-year price target of $51. **Sept. 30:** Total costs and expenses more than doubled to $13.4 million in the 2000 third quarter from $5.1 million in the 1999 third quarter, primarily due to an increase in research and development expense related to in-licensing of MG98, an anticancer compound soon to enter Phase 2 clinical trials, and the related small molecule DNA methyltransferase inhibitor program acquired from MethylGene. In **October** MGI announced the selection of pancreatic cancer as the first tumor target in its registration strategy for irofulven, its novel anti-cancer compound. In a multicenter, international trial, irofulven was to be tested in advanced pancreatic cancer patients whose disease had progressed after treatment with gemcitabine (Gemzar), the prevailing standard-of-care treatment for pancreatic cancer. The pivotal Phase 3 trial was expected to begin enrolling patients near the end of 2000.

MTS Systems Corporation

continued from page 266

we believe are prudent reserves to complete our obligations. The third was the strengthening of the dollar to the euro that caused a currency loss on the unhedged portion of certain contracts. These issues exacerbated what was already expected to be a slow start to the fiscal year. Unfortunately, most of this projected loss for the quarter will not be made up over the balance of our fiscal year. Consequently, we are revising our earnings outlook for fiscal 2000 to be 70 cents to 75 cents, still heavily weighted toward the second half of the year." AeroMet Corp. received orders totaling more than $600,000 during the first quarter—a significant portion for pre-production components for military aircraft. In **January 2000** Volvo Car Corp., Gothenburg, Sweden, placed a $6 million order for new software and hardware technology for evaluating car designs. In **February** MTS received a $4 million order for a new version of its patented Flat-Trac dynamic tire test system. MTS released its new Jury Evaluation Software, the most comprehensive software on the market for recording and analyzing human responses to sound characteristics in products and components. In **March** MTS received a $5 million, three-year contract from a major global automotive manufacturer to provide a broad range of technical services in North America, Great Britain, and continental Europe. AeroMet received orders in its second fiscal quarter of $1,000,000 from The Boeing Co. to provide full-scale wing test articles for its F/A-18 E/F Navy aircraft program. In **April** MTS discontinued manufacturing operations in Paris and moved them to its Raleigh, N.C., facility. In **May** MTS signed a $1.2 million Dual Use Science and Technology agreement with the Office of Naval Research to design and build the world's most advanced friction stir welding process development system—to be used to explore and develop applications of friction stir welding for high-strength structural alloys. In **June** MTS received a contract for the first phase of what was expected to be a $37 million contract from the U.S. Army—for the design, development, manufacture, and installation of an advanced roadway simulator at the U.S. Army's Aberdeen Test Center (ATC) at the Aberdeen Proving Ground in Maryland. MTS announced the first sales of Component Empirical Dynamics Models (EDM), a revolutionary tool for use in new vehicle development. Coupled with ADAMS virtual prototyping software, vehicle design engineers could accurately assess vehicle performance and durability much earlier in the design process. MTS received two contracts from the Lockheed-Martin Corp. to supply full-scale fatigue test control systems for the P-3 Orion and S-3 Viking aircraft. In **July** Nissan Technical Center, Atsugi, Japan, named MTS as partner in its new initiative for long-range strategic testing innovation. Simultaneously, Nissan placed a $2.3 million order with MTS for advanced software and hardware for evaluating car designs. In **September** AeroMet successfully completed component article tests by all three major U.S. military aircraft suppliers: The Boeing Co., Lockheed Martin Corp., and Northrop Grumman Corp. In all full-scale component tests performed, the laser-formed titanium alloy articles exceeded both the fatigue and static strengths required for the replacement of conventionally manufactured parts. Dr. Frank Arcella, AeroMet's president, said that the test results were an important milestone in the acceptance of the laser-forming process for the manufacture of titanium alloy components in military and commercial aircraft and engines. MTS received its largest single order for SWIFT sensors, an order exceeding $3 million dollars. In **October** MTS was awarded contracts totaling more than $20 million for physical testing systems, modeling software, virtual testing tools, and consulting services by Mazda Motor Co., Hiroshima, Japan.

Medi-Ject Corporation

continued from page 269

agreement with BioSante Pharmaceuticals Inc. (OTC Bulletin Board: BTPH; CDNX: BAI) for the commercialization of testosterone and estrogen gels and patches, and an agreement with Solvay Pharmaceuticals of Belgium to provide a transdermal gel containing a combination of estrogen and progestigen. The combined entities also agreed to continue testing of a new needle-free injector design for the Organon division of Akzo Nobel. The Antares research team, believing that new injector designs containing sustained release drugs could provide a market advantage and add life cycle management for injected drug formulations, were planning to look at such products. "By combining skills in device engineering and pharmaceutical formulation chemistry, diversifying our product portfolio, and broadening our geographic presence, Antares will provide an important new service to our customers, pharmaceutical manufacturers," said Pass. In **August** Medi-Ject announced successful initial preclinical results from its collaboration with BioSante Pharmaceuticals to develop improved drug delivery systems for DNA vaccines that combine Medi-Ject's needle-free, pressure-assisted injection system and BioSante's novel vaccine adjuvant technology.

Medtronic Inc.

continued from page 272

sulting firm of MacKenzie Partners Inc., New York, to continue pursuing a deal. But, later in the month, Medtronic withdrew its proposal, citing the unwillingness of Cyberonics' management to negotiate a sale and the amount of resources that a protracted hostile takeover attempt would take. Medtronic announced the first use of a new patient management system designed to capture critical physiologic information from a heart-failure patient's implanted medical device in the comfort of home and deliver it to the attending physician via the Internet. The Vitatron organization of Medtronic announced the commercial release of its Vitatron Selection AFm (Model 902), the first pacing system available in the United States with new monitoring capabilities designed to help physicians more effectively manage and treat atrial fibrillation. Medtronic announced the full U.S. launch of its Z2 family of coronary guide catheters, currently the No. 1 family in Europe and Japan. Medtronic's R1 Rapid Exchange Balloon Dilatation Catheter with Perfusion Technology received clearance from the FDA. Signaling a new frontier in the use of stents, Medtronic received CE Mark approval for its INX Neurovascular Stent, the first of its kind in the industry and the only stent designed specifically for use in the brain. Medtronic received permission to expand the medical indications for its Medtronic Jewel(R) AF implantable cardioverter defibrillator (ICD) to serve European patients who have only atrial fibrillation. Medtronic announced the beginning of a European clinical study of the new Medtronic InSync III cardiac resynchronization system. (Cardiac resynchronization therapy is used in an effort to improve the pumping capability of a failing heart.) When BeStent2 With Discrete Technology Coronary Stent Delivery System, available in both over-the-wire and rapid exchange versions, received approval from the FDA, Medtronic became the only company to provide physicians worldwide with a choice of laser cut and modular coronary stents to best suit their individual preferences. Medtronic announced the first European implants of the GEM III AT ICD. In a move to further enhance its interventional vascular product offerings and add innovations designed to reduce complications in the treatment of vascular disease, Medtronic agreed to acquire 110-employee PercuSurge Inc., Sunnyvale, Calif., a privately held company founded in 1995. PercuSurge makes products that capture debris dislodged during artery-clearing procedures. The stock transaction, valued at $225 million, was to be accounted for as a pooling of interests. Medtronic expected the deal to be neutral to earnings in the first year after the acquisition is closed and accretive thereafter. The Medical and Surgical Procedures Panel of the Health Care Financing Administration's Medicare Coverage Advisory Committee unanimously affirmed the effectiveness of Medtronic's InterStim Therapy for Urinary Control, which uses sacral nerve stimulation to treat patients with refractory urinary urge incontinence and urgency-frequency. The decision was likely to result in a national Medicare coverage policy. The board declared a dividend rights distribution. George stated: "Like the rights plan that we adopted in 1991, the new plan is designed to assure that all Medtronic shareholders receive fair and equal treatment in the event of any proposed takeover of the company and to guard against abusive tactics to gain control of Medtronic without paying all shareholders a premium for that control. The rights are not being adopted in response to any specific takeover threat, but are a response to the general takeover environment." In **November** the Medtronic Microelectronics Center announced its third major expansion and enhancement project in six years, in order to regain the necessary manufacturing capacity to support the significant growth of the Cardiac Rhythm and Neurological businesses. European physicians implanted another model in a new generation of ICDs, the Medtronic GEM III VR ICD (Single Chamber Model 7231). Medtronic agreed to supply its full line of cardiovascular products to Consorta Catholic Resource Partners health care facilities, which comprise more than half of all Catholic hospitals in the United States.

Metris Companies Inc.

continued from page 276

RECENT EVENTS

In **December 1999** Metris and Prodigy Communications Corp. (NASDAQ: PRGY), White Plains, N.Y., one of the nation's largest Internet service providers, signed a contract under which they will offer the Prodigy MasterCard and Metris' fee-based products to Prodigy's members. Under the terms of the five-year contract, valued at up to $58 million if expected thresholds are achieved, Prodigy and Metris were to promote and distribute the Prodigy MasterCard to Prodigy's 2 million members (based on the completion of Prodigy's proposed alliance with SBC) beginning in the spring of 2000. A **January 2000** co-brand credit card alliance with ADIR Financial Services Inc.—whose affiliate, La Curacao, is a leading southern California Hispanic-focused retailer—gave Metris an entry into the Hispanic market. In **March** Metris increased its earnings guidance for full-year 2000 from $2.80 to $2.85 per share, driven in part by stronger revenue (from both the credit card and fee-based businesses), stronger margins, and improved credit quality. Metris celebrated the grand opening of its new Tulsa, Okla., facility. Metris Receivables Inc. issued $600 million of five-year credit-card-asset-backed securities. In May Metris signed an agreement with WebMiles—the first customer loyalty company to offer a global, unrstricted mileage reward program—to issue the WebMiles MasterCard. A consumer protection lawsuit was filed against Direct Merchants Credit Card Bank and its parent, Metris Cos., for allegedly engaging in widespread deceptive and unlawful business practices. Among the misconduct the plaintiff alleged was that Direct Merchants Bank: routinely assesses fees for the purchase of fee-based services, such as its PurchaseShield program, that cardholders did not authorize; repeatedly charges late payment fees and interest for cardholder payments that are not in fact late or delayed; makes solicitations in connection with checks issued to cardholders that are misleading and do not disclose the true value of the checks issued to cardholders; and regularly promises a lower interest rate in connection with balance transfers, convenience checks, and cash advances than the interest rate that the cardholder receives. Meanwhile, Direct Merchants Credit Card Bank contracted to offer The Sportsman's Guide MasterCard and Metris' enhancement services to The Sportsman's Guide (Nasdaq: SGDE) customers. In **June** the company granted stock options to all Metris employees. Under the Ownership Bonus Program 2000, once the options vest, eligible employees can purchase 100 shares of Metris stock at $37 per share, the stock's closing market price as of June 1, 2000. The stock options vest on June 1, 2003, or when Metris stock closes at or above $75 per share, whichever happens first. Direct Merchants Credit Card Bank initiated the direct offering of

Jumbo Certificates of Deposits directly to deposit customers. In **July** Metris Receivables Inc. issued $600 million of three-year credit card asset-backed securities. Direct Merchants Credit Card Bank and Popular Inc., parent company of Banco Popular North America, the country's leading Hispanic-owned bank, announced that Direct Merchants Bank had agreed to purchase Banco Popular's U.S. Bankcard Program, with $180 million in receivables. [Deal closed in August.] In August Metris and The Sportsman's Guide Inc. (Nasdaq: SGDE), a catalog retailer and Internet e-tailer of outdoor and general merchandise, officially launched The Sportsman's Guide MasterCard. In **September** Fortune ranked Metris No. 41 on its list of America's Fastest-Growing Companies. U.S. Bancorp Piper Jaffray, in its monthly commentary, rated Metris a BUY, with a 12-month price target of $39. **Sept. 30**: The managed credit card loan portfolio increased by $661.7 million during the third quarter, resulting in a portfolio of more than $8.5 billion. The managed net interest margin remained constant at 13.2 percent. Zebeck commented, "We're excited that through three quarters of this year we have surpassed the total earnings and revenue from 1999. As a result of the strong performance and the company's momentum, we are raising our earnings guidance for full year 2000 to $2.09 to $2.10 per share. We are also establishing earnings guidance for full year 2001 of $2.50 to $2.55 per share." In **October** Metris invited country atists Brooks & Dunn to perform for its employees at a party to celebrate the opening of the company's new headquarters in Minnetonka (at the northeast corner of I-394 and County Road 73). To reinforce the company's commitment to helping employees balance work and family issues, Metris dedicated a portion of the new building for Metris KIDS, an on-site child care facility for employees' children. The facility also features a company-subsidized cafe and employee fitness center. Metris Receivables announced plans to issue $500 million of five-year credit card asset-backed securities. "We are very pleased with this deal," said Zebeck. "This transaction is a nice enhancement of our liquidity position and is consistent with our diversification of funding strategy for the business." In **November** Metris designated its Orlando, Fla., facility as its Hispanic operations center.

Michael Foods Inc.

continued from page 277 steady improvement in plant operating costs, pushed Dairy Products operating earnings well ahead of depressed prior year levels. Our largest division, Egg Products, had a challenging third quarter, but still showed solid results." In **November** Crystal Farms initiated a recall of two Marble-Jack cheese stick products to safeguard against a possible contamination of Listeria monocytogenes.

Micro Component Technology Inc.

continued from page 278 series test handlers valued at more than $2.3 million. MCT announced the public offering of 3 million shares of its common stock at $6.50 per share, all by the company. Proceeds were earmarked for working capital, new product development, general corporate purposes—including repayment of bank debt—and potential acquisitions of complementary products, technology, and businesses. The underwriters exercised their overallotment option to purchase 290,000 shares, generating $1.8 million more in net proceeds to the company. **Sept. 30**: For the nine-month period, earnings before goodwill, which represents earnings per share on a fully diluted basis excluding amortization of intangible assets, were $1,523,000/$0.13 compared to $64,000/$0.01 in the prior year. "We continue to be cautiously optimistic about today's semiconductor capital equipment market," said CEO Gower. "We also believe that some of this strength evolves from our ability to supply automated strip-based processes, which not only meet new capacity requirements, but also provide our customers with significant device cost reduction opportunities."

3M Company

continued from page 280 the list every year. 3M Visual Systems Division announced the availability of two new personal projectors, weighing only five pounds but with a full set of features. Drug Delivery Systems Division (DDS) announced the capability to provide its drug development partners with an in-house, two-dimensional and three-dimensional (SPECT) fast-scanning gamma scintigraphy service. 3M's medical divisions joined Global Healthcare Exchange LLC, the Internet-based health care trading exchange launched in March of 2000. 3M said that it was planning to make three acquisitions by October that would add $400 million in sales a year by 2003. Of the three companies, makers of electronics and telecommunications products, two were said to be publicly traded. 3M's Optical Systems Division purchased the aftermarket accessory computer monitor antiglare filters business known as GlareGuard and GlareDefender from Optical Coating Laboratory Inc., including related trademarks and patents. 3M made available samples of the 3M Pulse Compressor dispersion compensation module, a passive optical component that can be used to correct for chromatic dispersion in giga and terabit communications systems, and maintain optimal broadband performance. In its first major title sponsorship in sports since the Barcelona Olympics in 1992, 3M agreed to become the title sponsor for the former Coldwell Banker Burnet Classic, Minnesota's Senior PGA Tour event. In **September** 3M Electronic Products Division acquired the Eau Claire, Wis.-based single chip module substrate business—also known as the high-density, multilayer integrated circuit packaging business—of Delaware-headquartered W.L. Gore & Associates. [Deal closed Oct. 2.] 3M Pharmaceuticals announced that the FDA had granted approval for QVAR (beclomethasone dipropionate HFA) Inhalation Aerosol for the treatment of asthma. QVAR, a unique aerosol metered dose inhaler (MDI) that contains beclomethasone dipropionate (BDP) in a solution and no chlorofluorocarbon (CFC) propellant, is the first inhaler designed to deliver smaller-particle-sized medication to the large, intermediate, and small airways, which allows QVAR to control asthma at a lower dose than conventional CFC-containing BDP inhalers. 3M Interconnect Solutions Division announced the 3M High Speed Digital Data Transmission System Based on Mini Delta Ribbon (MDR) Technology, a high-bandwidth system that addresses both the performance and reliability requirements of the current communications equipment market. 3M announced at its biennial security analyst meeting that it expected annual sales growth of about 11 percent and per-share earnings growth of about 13 percent over the next three years. It also announced plans to aggressively expand the scope of its Scotchgard brand, including reformulations of products discontinued because of health concerns, by year's end. The 3M Enterprise Network Business Unit was formed to manage the company's ongoing growth in the enterprise market, and to position 3M to expand the breadth of its enterprise solutions beyond fiber to the desk into both active and passive equipment for copper, fiber, and wireless networks. 3M also entered the routing switch market, with the introduction of a Gigabit Ethernet routing switch. **Sept. 30:** Net income reached $499 million, up from $462 million in the year-earlier quarter. The quality of 3M earnings continued to be high, with operating income 19.2 percent of sales, net income 11.7 percent of sales, and return on invested capital 20.3 percent. "3M continues to deliver solid, top-line-driven earnings growth," said DeSimone. "We're growing through a strong flow of innovative products, close relationships with customers, and our strong international presence. These platforms provide us with many avenues for growth, while cushioning us from disruptions in any single market or region of the world." Sales totaled $4.252 billion, an increase of 6.4 percent. Unit sales increased 11 percent. Sales growth was particularly strong in the Asia-Pacific area. In **October** 3M Interconnect Solutions Division released a 3M High Speed Mini Delta Ribbon (MDR) Digital Data Transmission System to support the new digital I/O interface Camera Link Standard. 3M entered into a definitive merger agreement to acquire $92.8 million-revenue Robinson Nugent Inc. (Nasdaq: RNIC), a New Albany, Ind.-based manufacturer of electronic interconnect products, for $115 million in 3M stock, including the assumption of $12 million in debt. John K. Woodworth, general manager, 3M Interconnect Solutions Division, said, "Robinson Nugent is an innovative company with talented people and fast-growing, quality products. This acquisition broadens our product base by giving us higher-speed copper interconnects, complements our customer relationships, and fits into our strategy to expand further in the telecommunications sector." The deal was 3M's eighth acquisition of the year. 3M and Cogent Light Technologies announced plans to work together to bring the new 3M HL High Luminance Light Fiber with Cogent Light's SolarTec CL light source to market. The American Chiropractic Association endorsed a sixth ergonomic product manufactured by 3M's Office Supply Division, the Renaissance Mouse. 3M Pharmaceuticals and McNeil Consumer Healthcare, a Johnson & Johnson (NYSE: JNJ) company, joined forces to co-market 3M's new asthma drug, QVAR inhalation aerosol (beclomethasone diproprionate HFA) (BDP), which was approved by the FDA in September for the maintenance treatment of asthma. At month's end, 3M submitted a shelf filing to sell up to $1.5 billion of sales securities. In **November** 3M Pharmaceuticals said that it had presented phase II clinical trial results for resiquimod in the treatment of recurrent genital herpes (at the 40th Interscience Conference on Antimicrobial Agents and Chemotherapy in Toronto) and had initiated phase III clinical trials for recurrent genital herpes in both the United States and in Europe. Phase II results showed that the total number of recurrences was significantly decreased for patients on active study medication compared to a placebo gel. 3M Drug Delivery Systems expanded its outsourcing capabilities to provide contract tablet manufacturing at its Northridge, Calif., pharmaceutical production plant. 3M, Anoto, and Ericsson announced a collaborative agreement to produce wireless digital Post-it Notes. 3M agreed to acquire MicroTouch Systems Inc., a Methuen, Mass.-based manufacturer of touch-screen products, for $160 million.

Minntech Corporation

continued from page 281 related to recent management changes. In **August** R.J. Steichen & Co. reduced its rating on Minntech stock to NEUTRAL from BUY. Minntech opened a 3,200-square-foot dialyzer reprocessing center in Atlanta. The company's second reprocessing center (there's one in Orlando, Fla.), it has the capacity to perform 125,000 reprocessing cycles per year. **Sept. 30:** CEO Hope attributed the second-quarter earnings increase (as compared to the first quarter) to a 6 percent sales gain and cost-control initiatives.

Musicland Stores Corporation

continued from page 283 summer music release schedule," said Benson. **Sept. 30**: Store per share earnings were $0.07, compared to $0.05 during the third quarter of 1999. E-commerce generated a per share loss of $0.07 for the quarter versus a loss of $0.03 for the same period last year. As a result, consolidated net earnings per share were flat, versus $0.02 per share in last year's third quarter. "I am pleased that we continued the earnings growth momentum of our store operations in the face of lower than expected sales due to the quarter's weak new music release schedule," said CEO Eugster. In **October** Musicland invested in Golf Galaxy, a rapidly growing retail store chain based in Minneapolis, by obtaining a minority stake of just under 20 percent ownership. "We have been interested in investing in promising retail strategies where our expertise in product management and distribution could add value," said Eugster. Through a first-of-its-kind alliance, Sam Goody and Mall of America branded the Mall's main rotunda "Sam Goody Central," a showcase for live events and concerts at the Mall. Request magazine reached the 1 million-subscriber milestone beginning with the November/December issue. **Oct. 28:** Comparable-store sales decreased 1.4 percent for the four weeks. In **November** Musicland opened its 200th On Cue store, in Tahlequah, Okla.; as well as its third Media Play in Cincinnati.

NRG Energy Inc.

901 Marquette Ave., Suite 2300, Minneapolis, MN 55402
Tel: 612/373-5300 Web site: http://www.nrgenergy.com

NRG Energy Inc. is a leading global energy company primarily engaged in the acquisition, development, ownership, and operation of power generation facilities and the sale of energy, capacity, and related products. Majority-owned by Xcel Energy Inc. (formerly Northern States Power Co., or NSP), NRG is one of the three largest independent power generation companies in the United States and the fifth-largest independent power generation company in the world, measured by our net ownership interest in power generation facilities. As of Sept. 1, 2000, NRG owned all, or a portion, of 60 generation projects that had a total generating capacity of 23,611 megawatts (MW); its net ownership interest in those projects was 13,672 MW, of which 10,910 MW were located in the United States. NRG intends to continue to grow, through a combination of acquisitions and development of power generation facilities and related assets in the United States and abroad. NRG believes that its facility operations and engineering expertise, fuel and environmental strategies, labor and government relations expertise, and legal and financial skills give it a competitive advantage in the independent power market. The company also believes that its experience in meeting or exceeding applicable environmental regulatory standards and our environmental compliance record will give us an advantage as regulators continue to impose increasingly stringent environmental requirements on the operation of power generation facilities.

EARNINGS HISTORY

Year Ended Dec 31	Operating Revenue/Sales (dollars in thousands)	Net Earnings (dollars in thousands)	Return on Revenue (percent)	Return on Equity (percent)	Net Earnings (dollars per share*)	Cash Dividend (dollars per share*)	Market Price Range (dollars per share*)
1999	500,018	57,195	11.4	6.4	—	—	
1998	182,130	41,732	22.9	7.2	—	—	
1997	118,252	21,982	18.6	4.9	—	—	

* Trading commenced on May 31, 2000.

BALANCE SHEET

Assets	12/31/99 (dollars in thousands)	12/31/98
Current (CAE 31,483 and 6,381)	323,970	91,958
Property, plant, and equipment	1,919,323	204,729
Investments in projects	988,671	800,924
Capitalized project costs	2,592	13,685
Notes receivable, affiliates	65,494	101,887
Notes receivable	5,787	3,744
Intangibles	55,586	22,507
Debt-issuance costs	20,081	7,276
Other	50,180	46,716
TOTAL	3,431,684	1,293,426

Liabilities	12/31/99 (dollars in thousands)	12/31/98
Current	524,355	42,368
Minority interest	14,373	13,516
Consolidated project-level nonrecourse debt	1,026,398	113,437
Corporate-level long-term debt	915,000	504,781
Deferred income taxes	16,940	19,841
Deferred investment tax credits	1,088	1,343
Postretirement, other benefit obligations	24,613	11,060
Other and deferred income	15,263	7,748
Stockholders' equity*	893,654	579,332
TOTAL	3,431,684	1,293,426

* $1 par common; 1,000 authorized; 1,000 and 1,000 issued and outstanding.

RECENT QUARTERS / **PRIOR-YEAR RESULTS**

	Quarter End	Revenue ($000)	Earnings ($000)	EPS ($)	Prior-Year Revenue ($000)	Prior-Year Earnings ($000)	Prior-Year EPS ($)
Q3	09/30/2000	624,798	88,604	0.49	170,408	27,607	0.19
Q2	06/30/2000	522,009	43,581	0.28	66,659	2,341	0.02
Q1	03/31/2000	323,027	8,746	0.06	46,514	(940)	(0.01)
	SUM	1,469,834	140,931	0.83	283,581	29,008	0.20

RECENT EVENTS

In **January 2000** NRG agreed to acquire 1,875 megawatts (MW) of fossil-fueled electric generating capacity and other assets from Conectiv (NYSE: CIV) of Wilmington, Del., for $800 million—boosting its already-substantial holdings in the Northeast. In **February** NRG executed a memorandum of understanding with GE Power Systems, a division of General Electric Co., to purchase 11 gas turbine generators and five steam turbine generators over the next five years for $500 million. In **March** NRG completed the purchase from National Power plc of the 680-megawatt gas-fired Killingholme A combined-cycle, gas-turbine power station in North Lincolnshire, England. The purchase price of 390 million pounds sterling (U.S. $620 million) was to be funded through a combination of equity and nonrecourse project financing. Also completed: the purchase of 1,708 megawatts of fossil fuel generating assets from Cajun Electric Power Cooperative Inc., for *continued on page 310*

OFFICERS

David H. Peterson
Chairman, President, and CEO

Leonard A. Bluhm
EVP and CFO

Keith G. Hilless
SVP-Asia Pacific

Craig A. Mataczynski
SVP-North America

John A. Noer
SVP

Ronald J. Will
SVP-Europe

James J. Bender
VP, General Counsel, Secretary

Brian B. Bird
VP and Treasurer

Roy R Hewitt
VP-Administrative Services

Valorie A. Knudsen
VP-Corp. Strategy/Portfolio Assessment

Louis P. Matis
VP-Corporate Operating Services

David E. Ripka
VP and Controller

DIRECTORS

Wayne H. Brunetti
Xcel Energy Inc., Minneapolis

Luella G. Goldberg
Wellesley College, Wellesley, MA

Pierson M. (Sandy) Grieve
Palladium Equity Partners LLC

William A. Hodder
Donaldson Co. Inc. (retired)

James J. Howard III
Xcel Energy Inc., Minneapolis

Gary R. Johnson
Xcel Energy Inc., Minneapolis

Richard C. Kelly
New Century Energies, Denver

Cynthia L. Lesher
Xcel Energy Inc., Minneapolis

Edward J. McIntyre
Xcel Energy Inc., Minneapolis

David H. Peterson

MAJOR SHAREHOLDERS

Xcel Energy Inc., 82%
Minneapolis

SIC CODE

4931 Electric and other services combined

MISCELLANEOUS

TRADED: NYSE
SYMBOL: NRG
EMPLOYEES: 1,809
AUDITORS:
PricewaterhouseCoopers LLP, Minneapolis

RANKINGS

No. 1 CRM Performance 100

PUB

NU-Telecom Inc.

400 Second St. N., P.O. Box 697, New Ulm, MN 56073
Tel: 507/354-4111 Fax: 507/354-1982 Web site: http://www.newulmtel.net

NU-Telecom Inc., formerly New Ulm Telecom, has as its principal line of business the operation of local exchange telephone companies. **New Ulm Telecom Inc.**, **Western Telephone Co.**, and **Peoples Telephone Co.** are independent telephone companies that are regulated by the state utilities commissions. The company serves 16,686 access lines. **New Ulm Phonery Inc.** is a nonregulated telecommunications business that sells and services telephone apparatus on a retail level. **New Ulm Cellular #9 Inc.** owns an interest in a limited liability corporation that provides cellular phone service in southern Minnesota. New Ulm Telecom provides telephone service to the cities of New Ulm, Courtland, Klossner, and Searles, and to adjacent rural areas. Western Telephone Co. provides telephone service to the cities of Springfield and Sanborn and adjacent rural areas. Peoples Telephone Co. provides telephone service to Aurelia, Iowa, and adjacent rural areas. Peoples Telephone Co. operates a cable television system in the city of Aurelia, Iowa, serving 380 customers. Western Telephone Co. operates three cable television systems in Minnesota (cities of Sandborn, Jeffers, and Wabasso). New Ulm Telecom Inc., Western Telephone Co., and Peoples Telephone Co. derive their principal revenue from local service charges to their subscribers and access charges to interexchange carriers for providing access to the long-distance network. Revenue is also received from long-distance carriers for providing the billing and collection of long-distance toll calls to subscribers.

EARNINGS HISTORY

Year Ended Dec 31	Operating Revenue/Sales (dollars in thousands)	Net Earnings (dollars in thousands)	Return on Revenue (percent)	Return on Equity (percent)	Net Earnings (dollars per share*)	Cash Dividend (dollars per share*)	Market Price Range (dollars per share*)
1999	11,757	3,329	28.3	16.2	1.92	0.95	
1998	10,479	3,239	30.9	17.2	1.87	1.07	
1997	9,667	2,813	29.1	16.1	1.62	0.99	
1996	9,346	2,404	25.7	14.7	1.39	0.65	
1995	8,975	2,255	25.1	14.9	1.30	0.58	

* The company's common stock is not traded on an exchange or in the OTC market. Per-share amounts restated to reflect a 3-for-1 stock split effected April 1, 1996.

BALANCE SHEET

Assets	12/31/99 (dollars in thousands)	12/31/98 (dollars in thousands)	Liabilities	12/31/99 (dollars in thousands)	12/31/98 (dollars in thousands)
Current (CAE 1,533 and 2,551)	4,236	5,223	Current (STD 367 and 367)	2,013	2,332
Property, plant, and equipment	12,397	11,532	Long-term debt	2,933	3,300
			Deferred credits	1,528	1,542
Excess of cost over net assets acquired	3,446	3,560	Stockholders' equity*	20,553	18,869
Notes receivable	977	783	TOTAL	27,027	26,043
Cellular investments	5,282	4,507			
Other	689	437			
TOTAL	27,027	26,043			

* $5.00 par common; 6,400,000 authorized; 1,732,455 and 1,732,455 issued and outstanding.

RECENT QUARTERS / **PRIOR-YEAR RESULTS**

	Quarter End	Revenue ($000)	Earnings ($000)	EPS ($)	Prior-Year Revenue ($000)	Prior-Year Earnings ($000)	Prior-Year EPS ($)
Q2	06/30/2000	3,156	688	0.40	2,984	930	0.54
Q1	03/31/2000	2,924	782	0.45	2,742	826	0.48
Q4	12/31/99	3,104	745	0.43	2,684	960	0.55
Q3	09/30/99	2,927	829	0.48	2,611	761	0.44
	SUM	12,111	3,044	1.76	11,021	3,477	2.01

RECENT EVENTS

In **October 2000** Preferred Voice Inc. (OTC Bulletin Board: PFVI) announced an agreement to install its Voice Integrated Platform System (VIPS) in the central switching office of New Ulm Telecom, extending the company's voice dialing coverage throughout Minnesota. Voice applications to be made available to New Ulm customers included Local Connect (an alternative to directory assistance), voice-activated navigation through any voice mailbox, standard personal voice dialing directories, and Speech2Content (up-to-date information on news, sports, stock updates, weather, business, and entertainment). Later in the month, the company decided to give its home office and subsidiaries one common name. With this change, New Ulm Telecom, Western Telephone, and Peoples Telephone became unified as NU-Telecom.

OFFICERS

James P. Jensen
Chairman

Bill Otis
President

Mark W. Retzlaff
VP

Lavern J. Biebl
Treasurer

Gary L. Nelson
Secretary

Barbara A. Bornhoft
Asst. General Manager, Asst. Secretary

Christopher Hopp
Asst. Treasurer

DIRECTORS

Lavern J. Biebl

Rosemary Dittrich
D&A Trucking Inc.

Mary Ellen Domeier
State Bank & Trust Co.

James P. Jensen

Duane Lambrecht
Shelter Products

Perry Meyer
farmer

Gary L. Nelson

Robert Ranweiler
Biebl, Ranweiler & Co.

Mark W. Retzlaff

MAJOR SHAREHOLDERS

Ruth B. Wines, 5.3%
Corona Del Mar, CA

All officers and directors as a group (12 persons), 7.9%

SIC CODE

4813 Telephone communications, exc radio

MISCELLANEOUS

TRADED: LOTC
SYMBOL: NULM
STOCKHOLDERS: 950
EMPLOYEES: 47
AUDITORS:
Olsen Thielen & Co. Ltd., St. Paul
INC: MN-1905
ANNUAL MEETING: May

RANKINGS

No. 177 CRM Public 200

SUBSIDIARIES, DIVISIONS, AFFILIATES

Western Telephone Co.

Peoples Telephone Co.

New Ulm Phonery Inc.

New Ulm Cellular #7 Inc.

New Ulm Cellular #8 Inc.

New Ulm Cellular #9 Inc.

New Ulm Cellular #10 Inc.

Nash Finch Company

7600 France Ave. S., P.O. Box 355 (55440), Edina, MN 55440
Tel: 952/832-0534 Fax: 952/844-1234

Nash Finch Co. (NFC), the third-largest public food wholesaler in the United States, is a wholesale and retail distributor of a broad line of food and general merchandise products. The company operates 128 supermarkets, principally under the Econofoods, Sun Mart, and Family Thrift Center trade names. The company has two business segments. Wholesale operations, which include 15 distribution centers serving 2,000 affiliated and independent supermarkets, U.S. military commissaries, and other customers in 30 states.

EARNINGS HISTORY *

Year Ended Dec	Operating Revenue/Sales (dollars in thousands)	Net Earnings	Return on Revenue (percent)	Return on Equity	Net Earnings (dollars per share)	Cash Dividend	Market Price Range
1999 †	4,123,213	19,803	0.5	11.5	1.75	0.36	14.50–5.88
1998 ¶	4,160,011	(61,637)	(1.5)	(39.4)	(5.45)	0.72	20.00–13.13
1997 #	4,341,095	(1,228)	0.0	(0.5)	(0.11)	0.72	24.88–17.50
1996 **	3,323,970	20,032	0.6	8.6	1.83	0.75	21.75–15.50
1995 ††	2,839,628	17,414	0.6	8.1	1.60	0.74	20.50–15.25

* Historical revenue figures have been restated to segregate Nash DeCamp Co. as a discontinued operation. EPS includes these amounts from Nash DeCamp and its 1998 disposal: $0.40, ($1.46), ($0.01), $0.06, and $0.07—in 1999 through 1995, respectively.
† Figures for 1999 include results of Erickson's Diversified Corp. from its June 10, 1999, date of acquisition. Pro forma with full-year results: revenue $4,169,621,000; earnings $14,914,000/$1.32.
¶ Income figures for 1998 include pretax special charges of $68,471,000 for restructuring; and extraordinary charge of $5,569,000/($0.49) from early extinguishment of debt.
# Fiscal 1997 is 53 weeks. Income figures include pretax special charges totaling $30,034,000.
** Figures for 1996 include results of three acquisitions from their respective purchase dates. Pro forma had they been acquired at beginning of period: revenue $4,507,600,000; net income $13,761,000/$1.26.
†† Pro forma 1995 for 1996 acquisitions: revenue $4,589,362,000; net income $19,060,000/$1.70.

BALANCE SHEET

Assets	01/01/00 (dollars in thousands)	01/02/99
Current (CAE 16,389 and 848)	465,563	467,108
Investments in affiliates	508	4,805
Notes receivable	20,712	12,936
Property, plant, eqt	235,626	222,378
Goodwill	101,751	62,914
Other intangibles	13,652	14,891
Direct financing leases	15,444	16,155
Deferred tax	9,187	31,908
TOTAL	862,443	833,095

Liabilities	01/01/00 (dollars in thousands)	01/02/99
Current (STD 58,091 and 41,417)	327,327	331,473
Long-term debt	314,091	293,280
Capitalized lease	33,718	34,667
Deferred comp	4,545	6,450
Other	10,088	10,752
Stkhldrs' equity*	172,674	156,473
TOTAL	862,443	833,095

* $1.667 par common; 25,000,000 authorized; 11,641,000 and 11,575,000 issued and outstanding, less 231,000 and 234,000 treasury shares.

RECENT QUARTERS / **PRIOR-YEAR RESULTS**

	Quarter End	Revenue ($000)	Earnings ($000)	EPS ($)	Prior-Year Revenue ($000)	Prior-Year Earnings ($000)	Prior-Year EPS ($)
Q3	10/07/2000	1,220,468	4,014	0.35	1,289,156	8,043	0.71
Q2	06/17/2000	917,662	4,359	0.38	935,951	2,272	0.20
Q1	03/25/2000	892,673	2,252	0.20	934,797	1,192	0.11
Q4	01/01/2000	963,309	8,296	0.73	971,443	(65,709)	(5.80)
	SUM	3,994,112	18,921	1.66	4,131,347	(54,202)	(4.78)

CURRENT: Q3 consists of 16 weeks. Q4 earnings include pretax gain of $7.045 million on reversal of prior-year special charges.
PRIOR YEAR: Q3 period is 16 weeks. Earnings include gain of $4.566 million/$0.40 from discontinued operations and their disposal. Q4 earnings include pretax special charges of $69,733,000; and net loss of $16,311,000/($1.44) from discontinued operations and their disposal.

RECENT EVENTS

In **December 1999** the company terminated a previously announced agreement in principle to acquire Fairway Foods of Michigan Inc., a Menominee, Mich.-based wholesale division of Fairway Foods Inc. (sub. Holiday Cos., Bloomington, Minn.). **Jan. 1, 2000:** The company returned to profitability for the fourth quarter and the year. "We completed the company's restructuring within one year—well ahead of plan," said CEO Marshall. "This closes the door on restructuring and we are now well-positioned to aggressively grow our retail and wholesale operations." In **January** Nash Finch acquired Hinky Dinky Supermarkets Inc. through a cash purchase of Hinky Dinky stock. ***continued on page 310***

OFFICERS

Allister P. Graham
Chairman
Ron Marshall Jr.
President and CEO
Christopher A. Brown
EVP-Merchandising
Jerry L. Nelson
EVP and Pres.-Food Distribution
Bruce A. Cross
SVP-Business Transformation
Robert B. Dimond
SVP and CFO
Arthur L. Keeney
SVP-Corporate Retail Stores
John M. McCurry
SVP-Wholesale Operations
William A. Merrigan
SVP-Distribution/Logistics
Norman R. Soland
SVP, General Counsel, and Secretary
Larry C. Adams
VP-Southeast Wholesale
Michael A. Baker
VP-Perishables
Deborah A. Carlson
VP-Store Development
James R. Dorcy
VP-Marketing/Advertising
John Hulsey
VP-Central Wholesale
LeAnne M. Stewart
VP and Controller
Philip E. Bortscheller
Asst. Treasurer

DIRECTORS

Carole F. Bitter
Harold Friedman Inc., Butler, PA
James L. Donald
Pathmark Stores Inc.
Richard A. Fisher
Network Systems Corp. (retired)
Jerry L. Ford
Jetways Inc.
Allister P. Graham
The Oshawa Group Ltd. (retired)
John H. (Jack) Grunewald
Polaris Industries Inc. (retired)
Richard G. Lareau
Oppenheimer Wolff & Donnelly LLP, Minneapolis
Ron Marshall
Robert F. Nash
Nash Finch (retired)
Jerome O. Rodysill
Nash Finch (retired)
John E. Stokely
Richfood Holdings Inc. (former)
William R. Voss
Natural Nutrition Group Inc., Chicago

MAJOR SHAREHOLDERS

Franklin Resources Inc., 8.1%
San Mateo, CA
Dimensional Fund Advisors Inc., 5.8%
Santa Monica, CA
All officers and directors as a group (24 persons), 4.1%

SIC CODE

5142 Frozen foods, whlse
5147 Meat products, whlse
5148 Fruits and vegetables, whlse
5411 Grocery stores

MISCELLANEOUS

TRANSFER AGENT AND REGISTAR:
Wells Fargo Bank Minnesota N.A., South St. Paul, MN
TRADED: Nasdaq National Market
SYMBOL: NAFC
STOCKHOLDERS: 2,348
EMPLOYEES: 13,500
GENERAL COUNSEL:
Norman R. Soland
AUDITORS:
Ernst & Young LLP, Minneapolis
INC: DE-1921
FOUNDED: 1885
ANNUAL MEETING: May
FINANCE:
LeAnne M. Stewart

RANKINGS

No. 11 CRM Public 200

PUB

TWO-YEAR QUARTERLY HIGH-LOW STOCK PRICES

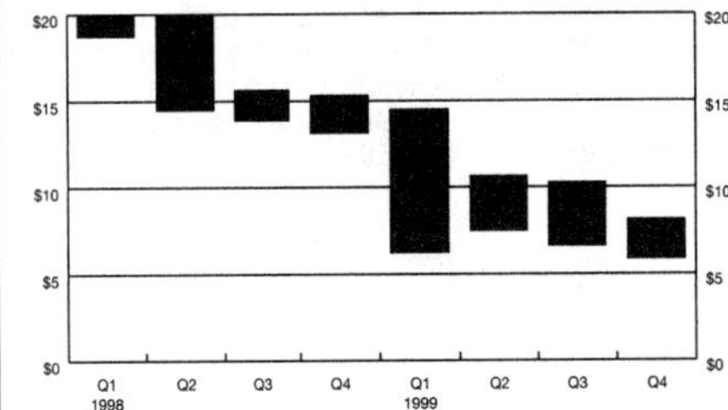

National City Bancorporation

Sixth on the Mall, 651 Nicollet Mall, Minneapolis, MN 55402
Tel: 612/904-8500 Fax: 612/904-8016 Web site: http://www.nationalcitybank.com

National City Bancorp. (NCBC), a bank holding company, owns National City Bank of Minneapolis, which has two offices in the metropolitan Minneapolis area. It also owns Diversified Business Credit Inc., a commercial finance company. NCBC provides its subsidiaries with advice and specialized services in various fields of financial and banking policy.

EARNINGS HISTORY

Year Ended Dec 31	Operating Revenue/Sales (dollars in thousands)	Net Earnings (dollars in thousands)	Return on Revenue (percent)	Return on Equity (percent)	Net Earnings (dollars per share*)	Cash Dividend (dollars per share*)	Market Price Range (dollars per share*)
1999	99,093	16,627	16.8	10.9	1.90	—	27.50–16.00
1998	94,817	15,664	16.5	10.6	1.77	—	35.25–23.38
1997 †	91,190	13,722	15.0	10.3	1.54	—	27.27–16.59
1996	80,281	12,686	15.8	10.7	1.42	—	18.39–14.46
1995	75,566	12,696	16.8	12.0	1.42	—	17.84–9.58

* Per-share amounts restated to reflect annual 10 percent stock dividends.
† Income figures for 1997 include gain from state income tax refund of $1.369 million pretax; $850,000/$0.09 after-tax.

BALANCE SHEET

Assets	12/31/99 (dollars in thousands)	12/31/98 (dollars in thousands)
Cash and due from banks	36,997	52,271
Available-for-sale securities	135,340	133,897
Held-to-maturity securities	46,572	41,255
Federal funds sold and resale agreements	55,655	6,100
Net loans	824,702	752,324
Bank premises and equipment	8,921	10,399
Accrued income receivable	7,600	7,499
Customer acceptance liability	1,424	824
Other	22,969	21,113
TOTAL	1,140,180	1,025,682

Liabilities	12/31/99 (dollars in thousands)	12/31/98 (dollars in thousands)
Deposits	614,308	517,494
Federal funds purchased and repurchase agreements	89,950	98,702
Commercial paper	38,777	99,396
Other short-term borrowed funds	45,053	12,663
Acceptances outstanding	1,424	824
Other	22,719	10,315
Long-term debt	176,000	139,000
Stockholders' equity*	151,949	147,288
TOTAL	1,140,180	1,025,682

* $1.25 par common; 40,000,000 authorized; 8,861,944 and 8,861,944 issued and outstanding, less 125,222 and 45,030 treasury shares.

RECENT QUARTERS / PRIOR-YEAR RESULTS

	Quarter End	Revenue ($000)	Earnings ($000)	EPS ($)	Prior-Year Revenue ($000)	Prior-Year Earnings ($000)	Prior-Year EPS ($)
Q3	09/30/2000	29,504	4,552	0.54	26,607	5,023	0.57
Q2	06/30/2000	28,594	4,723	0.56	23,882	3,914	0.45
Q1	03/31/2000	26,701	4,270	0.49	22,944	3,605	0.41
Q4	12/31/99	25,660	4,085	0.47	24,113	3,430	0.39
	SUM	110,459	17,630	2.05	97,546	15,972	1.82

PRIOR YEAR: Q3 earnings include a state income tax refund of $1,233,000, for an after-tax gain of $769,000/$0.09.

RECENT EVENTS

In **March 2000** David Nash, Bloomington, Minn., senior vice president of business development for National City Bank of Minneapolis and a top-ranked 55+ Minnesota tennis player, won both his singles and doubles matches to lead the United States to a 2-1 victory over France in the Austria Cup in Pietermaritzburg, South Africa. In **September** the company introduced the "Image Automated Lockbox" system, a new check image retrieval system that provides Internet access to not just checks but also images of invoices and other supporting documents that accompany customer payments, allowing businesses to make more immediate cash flow decisions like whether to keep shipping to a customer who has been slow in paying. **Sept. 30:** Without regard for the 1999 state income tax refund of $1,233,000, third-quarter net income increased $298,000, or 7.0 percent, for the quarter and $1,772,000, or 15.1 percent, for the nine-month period.

OFFICERS

David L. Andreas
President and CEO

Thomas J. Freed
Secretary and CFO

Robert L. Olson
Pres./CEO-Diversified Business Credit

DIRECTORS

Wendell R. Anderson
Larkin, Hoffman, Daly & Lindgren Ltd., Bloomington, MN

David L. Andreas

Terry L. Andreas
School for Field Studies, Beverly, MA

Michael J. Boris
consultant, Plymouth, MN

Sharon N. Bredeson
Staff-Plus Inc., Minneapolis

John H. Daniels Jr.
Willeke and Daniels, Minneapolis

James B. Goetz Sr.
Goetz Cos., La Crosse, WI

Esperanza Guerrero-Anderson
Milestone Growth Fund Inc., Minneapolis

C. Bernard Jacobs

David C. Malmberg
Fieldworks Inc., Eden Prairie, MN

Walter E. Meadley Jr.

Robert L. Olson
Diversified Business Credit Inc., Minneapolis

Roger H. Scherer
Scherer Bros. Lumber Co., Brooklyn Park, MN

MAJOR SHAREHOLDERS

Dorothy Inez Andreas, 19.6%
Mankato, MN

Lowell W. Andreas, 9.8%
Mankato, MN

Dwayne O. Andreas, 7%
Mankato, MN

David L. Andreas, 7%
Minneapolis

All officers and directors as a group (17 persons), 12.3%

SIC CODE

6021 National commercial banks

6712 Bank holding companies

MISCELLANEOUS

TRANSFER AGENT AND REGISTAR:
National City Bank of Minneapolis

TRADED: Nasdaq National Market

SYMBOL: NCBM

STOCKHOLDERS: 2,300

EMPLOYEES: 282

GENERAL COUNSEL:
Maslon Edelman Borman & Brand PLLP, Minneapolis

AUDITORS:
Ernst & Young LLP, Minneapolis

INC: IA-1937

ANNUAL MEETING: April

RANKINGS

No. 89 CRM Public 200

No. 33 CRM Performance 100

SUBSIDIARIES, DIVISIONS, AFFILIATES

Diversified Business Credit Inc.
Dain Rauscher Plaza
60 S. Sixth St.
Minneapolis, MN 55402
612/667-8700
Robert L. Olson

National City Bank of Minneapolis
651 Nicollet Mall
Minneapolis, MN 55402
612/904-8000
David L. Andreas

TWO-YEAR QUARTERLY HIGH-LOW STOCK PRICES

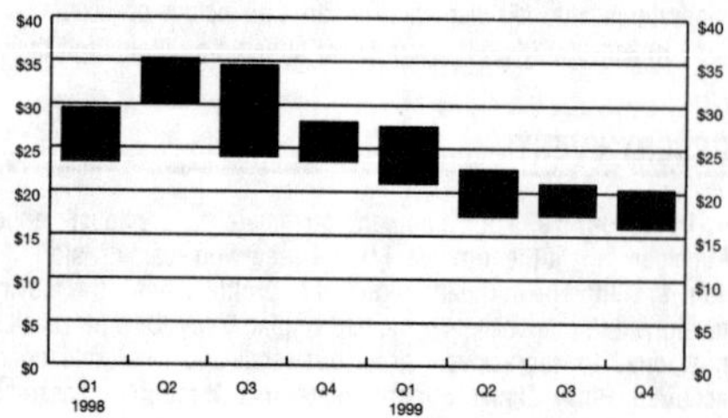

National Presto Industries Inc.

3925 N. Hastings Way, Eau Claire, WI 54703
Tel: 715/839-2121 Fax: 715/839-2148 Web site: http://www.presto-net.com

National Presto Industries Inc. manufactures and distributes small electrical appliances and housewares, including private-label and premium sales products. For the year ended Dec. 31, 1999: 61 percent of consolidated revenue was provided by **cast products** (fry pans, griddles, deep fryers, and multi-cookers); 9 percent by **motorized nonthermal appliances** (can openers, slicer/shredders, knife sharpeners, electric knives, and bread slicing systems); and 26 percent by **noncast/thermal appliances** (stamped cookers and canners, stainless steel cookers, hot-air and microwave corn poppers, microwave bacon cookers, coffemakers, tea kettles, and heaters). Wal-Mart Stores Inc. accounted for 46 percent of sales.

EARNINGS HISTORY *

Year Ended Dec 31	Operating Revenue/Sales	Net Earnings	Return on Revenue	Return on Equity	Net Earnings	Cash Dividend	Market Price Range
	(dollars in thousands)		(percent)		(dollars per share†)		
1999	114,697	20,822	18.2	8.2	2.84	2.00	42.88–34.13
1998	107,073	19,733	18.4	7.8	2.68	2.00	43.50–36.06
1997	109,540	16,982	15.5	6.8	2.31	2.00	44.19–35.88
1996	106,008	14,720	13.9	6.0	2.00	2.00	44.00–36.25
1995 ¶	120,172	18,969	15.8	7.8	2.61	2.15	48.00–38.75

* Revenue is net of freight, discounts, etc.
† Certain of these dividend amounts were paid prior to applicable period.
¶ Income figures for 1995 include pretax gain of $2.316 million, principally from a litigation judgment.

BALANCE SHEET

Assets	12/31/99	12/31/98
	(dollars in thousands)	
Current	275,945	273,301
(CAE 88,075 and 114,565)		
Property, plant, and equipment	12,309	10,564
Other	11,139	10,897
TOTAL	299,393	294,762

Liabilities	12/31/99	12/31/98
	(dollars in thousands)	
Current	44,061	40,357
Stockholders' equity*	255,332	254,405
TOTAL	299,393	294,762

* $1 par common; 12,000,000 authorized; 7,440,518 and 7,440,518 issued and outstanding, less 230,912 and 81,040 treasury shares.

RECENT QUARTERS / **PRIOR-YEAR RESULTS**

	Quarter End	Revenue ($000)	Earnings ($000)	EPS ($)	Revenue ($000)	Earnings ($000)	EPS ($)
Q2	07/02/2000	20,399	2,848	0.40	18,762	3,133	0.43
Q1	04/02/2000	18,507	3,018	0.42	21,610	3,280	0.45
Q4	12/31/99	49,254	10,665	1.46	47,508	10,428	1.42
Q3	09/30/99	25,071	3,744	0.51	24,306	3,735	0.51
	SUM	113,231	20,275	2.79	112,186	20,576	2.80

OFFICERS

Melvin S. Cohen
Chairman

Maryjo Cohen
President and CEO

James F. Bartl
EVP, Secretary, Resident Counsel

Richard F. Anderl
VP-Engineering

Neil L. Brown
VP-Manufacturing

Donald E. Hoeschen
VP-Sales

Larry R. Hoepner
VP-Purchasing

Randy F. Lieble
CFO and Treasurer

DIRECTORS

James F. Bartl

Richard Cardozo
University of Minnesota, Minneapolis

Maryjo Cohen

Melvin S. Cohen

Michael J. O'Meara
People's National Bank, Eau Claire, WI

John M. Sirianni
U.S. Bancorp Piper Jaffray Inc., Minneapolis

MAJOR SHAREHOLDERS

Maryjo Cohen, 28.6%

Dimensional Fund Advisors Inc., 7.2%
Santa Monica, CA

Melvin S. Cohen, 6.5%

American Century Investment Management Inc., 6%
Kansas City, MO

All officers and directors as a group (8 persons), 29.7%

SIC CODE

3634 Electric housewares and fans

MISCELLANEOUS

TRANSFER AGENT AND REGISTAR:
Harris Trust and Savings Bank, Chicago

TRADED: NYSE

SYMBOL: NPK

STOCKHOLDERS: 814

EMPLOYEES: 711

GENERAL COUNSEL:
Robins, Kaplan, Miller & Ciresi LLP, Minneapolis

AUDITORS:
Grant Thornton LLP, Minneapolis

INC: WI-1906

FOUNDED: 1906

ANNUAL MEETING: May

SUBSIDIARIES, DIVISIONS, AFFILIATES

National Holding Investment Co. (1)
200 W. Ninth St. Plaza
Wilmington, DE 19801
302/428-7000

Presto Manufacturing Co. (2)
Presto Lane
Jackson, MS 39206
601/366-3481

Presto Products Manufacturing Co. (3)
1301 LaVelle Rd.
Alamogordo, NM 88310
505/437-7660

Jackson Sales & Storage Co. (2)
Presto Lane
Jackson, MS 39206
601/366-3481

Canton Sales & Storage Co. (2)
555 Mathews Dr.
Canton, MS 39046
601/859-1013

National Defense Corp. (1)
3925 N. Hastings Way
Eau Claire, WI 54703
715/839-2121

Presto Export Ltd. (1)
Christiansted, St. Croix
U.S. Virgin Islands

TWO-YEAR QUARTERLY HIGH-LOW STOCK PRICES

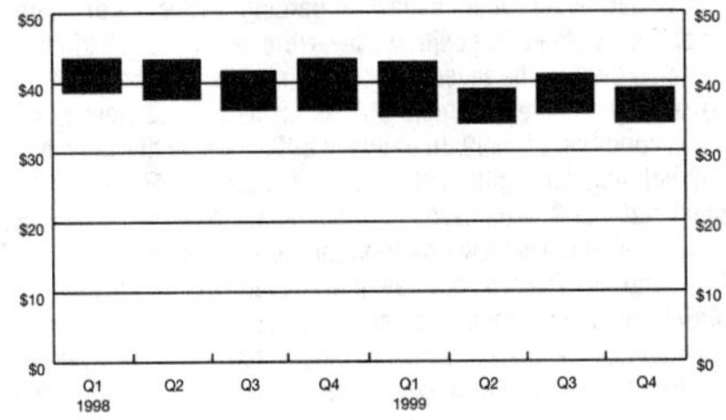

PUB

Navarre Corporation

7400 49th Ave. N., New Hope, MN 55428
Tel: 763/535-8333 Fax: 763/504-1107 Web site: http://www.navarre.com

Navarre Corp. distributes home entertainment products including recorded music, personal computer software, and interactive CD-ROM software. The company's products are sold to more than 500 wholesale and retail customers with more than 10,000 locations. The company's primary customers include music and computer specialty chains; membership wholesale clubs; mass merchandisers and discount retailers; and wholesalers and rack jobbers.

EARNINGS HISTORY *

Year Ended Mar 31	Operating Revenue/Sales (dollars in thousands)	Net Earnings	Return on Revenue (percent)	Return on Equity	Net Earnings (dollars per share†)	Cash Dividend	Market Price Range
2000	285,165	(7,785)	(2.7)	(23.3)	(0.33)	—	18.63–3.53
1999 ¶	210,386	(27,670)	(13.2)	NM	(4.41)	—	27.00–2.19
1998	196,648	(974)	(0.5)	(22.5)	(0.14)	—	5.25–2.00
1997	200,697	(6,189)	(3.1)	NM	(0.92)	—	18.31–2.38
1996	158,354	1,319	0.8	13.7	0.22	—	5.69–2.25

* With the spin-off of majority-owned subsidiary NetRadio Corp. in an initial public offering, Navarre's ownership decreased to less than 50 percent. Since Nov. 5, 1999, the interest has been reported on the equity method.
† Per-share amounts restated to reflect 2-for-1 stock split on June 21, 1996.
¶ EPS for 1999 includes a $34.229 million charge associated with the nondetachable conversion feature included in the preferred stock and accompanying warrants issued in May 1998.

BALANCE SHEET

Assets	03/31/00 (dollars in thousands)	03/31/99	Liabilities	03/31/00 (dollars in thousands)	03/31/99
Current (CAE 15,739 and 92)	95,234	74,522	Current (STD 0 and 93)	68,288	54,202
Property and equipment	2,469	3,361	Long-term debt		114
NetRadio note receivable	9,597		Preferred equity	8,010	
Investments	1,941		Common equity*	33,413	25,164
Goodwill	391	853	TOTAL	109,711	79,480
Other	79	744			
TOTAL	109,711	79,480			

* No par common; 100,000,000 authorized; 23,534,435 and 23,344,046 issued and outstanding.

RECENT QUARTERS / **PRIOR-YEAR RESULTS**

	Quarter End	Revenue ($000)	Earnings ($000)	EPS ($)	Revenue ($000)	Earnings ($000)	EPS ($)
Q1	09/30/2000	78,378	(8,448)	(0.33)	67,398	(3,184)	(0.14)
Q1	06/30/2000	55,166	(2,121)	(0.09)	57,751	(2,604)	(0.11)
Q4	03/31/2000	60,879	(2,007)	(0.09)	27,704	(22,282)	(0.97)
Q3	12/31/99	99,137	10	0.00	74,740	(4,082)	(0.26)
	SUM	293,560	(12,566)	(0.50)	227,593	(32,152)	(1.48)

CURRENT: Q1 earnings include one-time charge of $9.597 million/($0.37) for write-off of NetRadio's equity and loan.
PRIOR YEAR: Q2 earnings include $4,338,000/($0.18) operating loss from NetRadio.com. Q1 earnings include $2,234,000/($0.10) operating loss from NetRadio.com.

RECENT EVENTS

In **December 1999** two class-action complaints were filed in the U.S. District Court for the District of Minnesota on behalf of persons who purchased common stock issued by Navarre at artificially inflated prices during the period Nov. 25, 1998, through Dec. 9, 1998. The cases allegedly involve the making of false and misleading statements that the company was spinning off a majority-owned subsidiary and taking the newly formed company public by the end of the 1998 year. The company believed it had abided by all securities laws regarding disclosure of information and that the lawsuits were without merit. It intended to vigorously defend its position. Navarre entered into distribution agreements with Loki Entertainment Software and Cybernet Systems Corp.—the seventh and eighth publisher agreements for the Linux operating system and its related products. **Dec. 31:** Navarre's computer products division achieved a 33 percent market share in the distribution of Linux-related software during the second half of 1999. In **January 2000** Digital Entertainment agreed to license Preview Systems' (Nasdaq: PRVW) technology solution for digital distribution of music. In **February** Digital Entertainment announced a strategic alliance with I-Jam Multimedia LLC, a pioneer in the digital audio arena, to provide a virtual online mega store component on I-Jam's Web site. Navarre signed exclusive distribution agreements with Lil' Joe Records and with new joint venture between Kenny Rogers' Dreamcatcher Records and talent impresario Lou Pearlman's Trans Continental Records, for the United States and Canada. In **March** Digital Entertainment, renamed eSplice, appointed Sonic Foundry Inc. (AMEX: SFO) as vendor of choice to facilitate the encoding of the digital online audio CD catalog. In **May** Navarre selected Los Angeles-based Sutro & Co. Inc. as its exclusive financial advisor and investment banker. CEO Paulson and superstar enter- *continued on page 310*

OFFICERS

Eric H. Paulson
Chairman, President, and CEO

Charles E. Cheney
Vice Chairman, CFO, and Chm./CEO-D.E.

Brian Burke
VP-Computer Products Divison

James S. Chiado Jr.
VP, Gen. Mgr.-Music Distribution Div.

Kathleen A. Conlin
VP and Controller

Joyce Fleck
VP-Marketing

Tom Lenaghan
VP, Gen. Mgr.-Alternative Retail Mktg.

Margot McManus
VP-Human Resources

Donavan W. Pederson
EVP and COO-NetRadio Corp.

John Turner
VP-Operations

Ian Warfield
Pres./COO-Digital Entertainment

DIRECTORS

Charles E. Cheney

Eric H. Paulson

James G. Sippl
Sipple & Associates, Eden Prairie, MN

Michael L. Snow
Maslon Edleman Borman & Brand PLLP, Minneapolis

Alfred Teo
Hillman Eye Care/Sigma Group

Dickinson G. Wiltz
business consultant

MAJOR SHAREHOLDERS

Eric H. Paulson, 9.4%

Fletcher International Ltd., 5.6%
New York

All officers and directors as a group (6 persons), 15.4%

SIC CODE

5045 Computers, peripherals, and software, whsle

5065 Electronic parts and eqp, whsle

MISCELLANEOUS

TRANSFER AGENT AND REGISTAR:
Wells Fargo Bank Minnesota N.A., South St. Paul, MN

TRADED: Nasdaq National Market

SYMBOL: NAVR

STOCKHOLDERS: 23,500

EMPLOYEES: 303

GENERAL COUNSEL:
Lindquist & Vennum PLLP, Minneapolis
Winthrop & Weinstine P.A.

AUDITORS:
Ernst & Young LLP, Minneapolis

INC: MN-1983

ANNUAL MEETING:
September

INVESTOR RELATIONS:
Carol Felber

HUMAN RESOURCES:
Margot McManus

RANKINGS

No. 66 CRM Public 200

SUBSIDIARIES, DIVISIONS, AFFILIATES

eSplice
Ian Warfield

Net Radio Corp.
Edward Tomechko

TWO-YEAR QUARTERLY HIGH-LOW STOCK PRICES

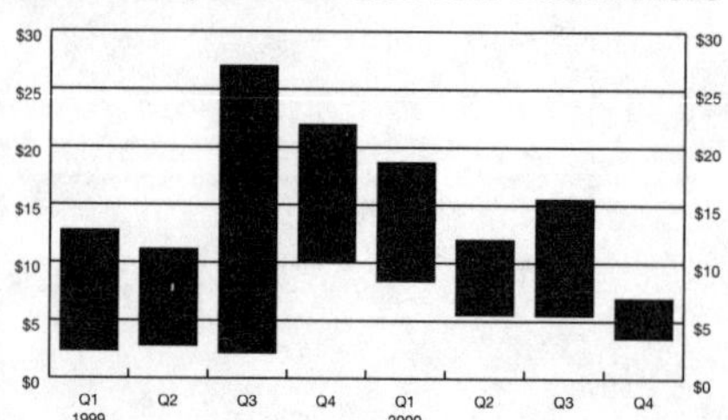

Net4Music Inc.

6210 Bury Dr., Eden Prairie, MN 55346
Tel: 952/937-9611 Fax: 952/937-9760 Web site: http://www.codamusic.com

Net4Music Inc. was created in October 2000 by the merger of Coda Music Technology Inc., Eden Prairie, and Net4Music S.A., Paris. Coda develops and markets proprietary music notation software for publishers, composers, arrangers, copyists, music educators, students, and church musicians. Since 1988 the company has marketed Finale music notation software products. Since 1994 it has marketed the Smart Music (previously known as Vivace) system, a musical accompaniment system that responds to tempo changes by musicians. Net4Music has revolutionized the distribution of sheet music by licensing digital distribution rights to create the world's largest catalog of digital sheet music titles from all music genres and offering secure downloads of this sheet music. Net4Music's innovative services empower the music end-user by providing musicians and composers with immediate access to one of the largest collections of musical scores along with copyright protection for music publishing. Through Net4Music's website, musicians can reference and download sheet music for faster, easier and safer distribution than was previously possible.

EARNINGS HISTORY

Year Ended Dec 31	Operating Revenue/Sales (dollars in thousands)	Net Earnings (dollars in thousands)	Return on Revenue (percent)	Return on Equity (percent)	Net Earnings (dollars per share*)	Cash Dividend (dollars per share*)	Market Price Range (dollars per share*)
1999	6,356	(456)	(7.2)	(18.1)	(0.07)	—	6.00–1.19
1998 †	6,413	(804)	(12.5)	(27.2)	(0.13)	—	2.00–0.50
1997	5,563	(1,512)	(27.2)	(40.4)	(0.28)	—	2.50–0.75
1996	5,500	(1,771)	(32.2)	(59.1)	(0.41)	—	5.50–1.50
1995	4,934	(1,650)	(33.4)	(35.4)	(0.44)	—	6.88–4.38

* Stock began trading June 29, 1995.
† Income figures for 1998 include pretax charege of $856,000 for product repositioning.

BALANCE SHEET

Assets	12/31/99 (dollars in thousands)	12/31/98 (dollars in thousands)
Current (CAE 1,345 and 563)	2,758	2,776
Equipment, furniture, and fixtures	250	273
Repertoire development costs	487	643
Prepaid royalties	192	185
Software deposit	200	
Other	100	88
TOTAL	3,987	3,965

Liabilities	12/31/99 (dollars in thousands)	12/31/98 (dollars in thousands)
Current	1,469	1,011
Stockholders' equity*	2,518	2,955
TOTAL	3,987	3,965

* No par common; 15,000,000 authorized; 6,216,319 and 6,194,732 issued and outstanding.

RECENT QUARTERS / **PRIOR-YEAR RESULTS**

	Quarter End	Revenue ($000)	Earnings ($000)	EPS ($)	Prior-Year Revenue ($000)	Prior-Year Earnings ($000)	Prior-Year EPS ($)
Q3	09/30/2000	2,640	744	0.12	2,464	218	0.04
Q2	06/30/2000	1,057	(345)	(0.05)	956	(531)	(0.09)
Q1	03/31/2000	1,804	60	0.01	1,216	(275)	(0.04)
Q4	12/31/99	1,720	133	0.02	1,550	205	0.03
	SUM	7,221	592	0.09	6,187	(384)	(0.06)

RECENT EVENTS

In **January 2000** Coda Music Technology released a teaching tool that helps students hear and see when they are playing in tune: Intonation Trainer. The sophisticated, yet simple-to-use, software product helps students be more aware of pitch, know what to listen for, and anticipate pitch problems before they play a note. In **March** Coda released Allegro 2000, the latest upgrade to its mid-level notation product, which was designed specifically for performing musicians that need their music to look as great as it sounds. In **June** Coda announced SmartMusic Studio Online on the Internet. In **August** Coda and Net4Music S.A. signed an agreement under which Coda would acquire all the shares of Net4Music in consideration for shares of Coda common stock. Under the terms of the proposed transaction, Coda's existing shareholders would own, on a fully diluted basis, one-third of the combined company. Following the transaction, the combined company would be called Net4Music Inc. and would have more than $15 million in cash. "The goal of this transaction," stated Net4Music CEO Francois Duliege, who would be CEO of the combined company, "is to match the leader in digital print rights with the leader in music notation and music education technologies. In doing so, we intend to create the leading global Internet company providing proprietary products, services, and technologies to a full range of music makers—including students, teachers, professionals, and hobbyists. We also intend to offer our services to print music publishers and music dealers so that they can grow their businesses via the Internet." In September pending acquisition Net4Music announced that it had secured digital distribution rights to the entire catalog of German publisher Schott Musik International. The deal covered a wide range of classical and contemporary music, including important works by Beethoven, Wagner, Stravinsky, Orff, Rodrigo, Ligeti, Henze, Penderecki, Takemitsu, and others. In October Net4Music and Coda introduced Finale NotePad, a free downloadable version of Coda's world-renowned music notation software, alsoavailable on CD-ROM for $19.95. In **October** Coda shareholders approved the Net4Music transaction.

OFFICERS

John W. Paulson
Chairman and CEO

Barbara Sima Remley
CFO, Secretary, and Treasurer

Mark E. Dunn
SVP-Product Development

Glenna A. Dibrell
VP-Marketing/Sales

DIRECTORS

Tim Bajarin
Creative Strategies Inc.

Tim Heaney
Techne Corp., Minneapolis

Larry A. Pape
private investor

John W. Paulson

Gordon F. Stofer
Cherry Tree Investments Inc., Bloomington, MN

Benson K. Whitney
Gideon Hixon Ventures, Minneapolis

MAJOR SHAREHOLDERS

Benson K. Whitney, 19.7%
Minnetonka, MN

J.M. Hixon Partners LLC, 18%
Minneapolis

Gordon F. Stofer/Cherry Tree Ventures IV, 10.7%
Minnetonka, MN

John W. Paulson, 7.6%

All officers and directors as a group (10 persons), 41.5%

SIC CODE

3931 Musical instruments

7371 Computer programming services

MISCELLANEOUS

TRANSFER AGENT AND REGISTAR:
Wells Fargo Bank Minnesota N.A.,
South St. Paul, MN

TRADED: Nasdaq SmallCap Market

SYMBOL: NMUS

STOCKHOLDERS: 150

EMPLOYEES: 55

IN MINNESOTA: 55

GENERAL COUNSEL:
Fredrikson & Byron P.A., Minneapolis

AUDITORS:
RSM McGladrey & Pullen Inc. LLP, Minneapolis

INC: MN-1990

FOUNDED: 1988

ANNUAL MEETING: April

INVESTOR RELATIONS:
Barbara S. Remley

RANKINGS

No. 200 CRM Public 200

PUB

PUB

Net Perceptions Inc.

7901 Flying Cloud Dr., Eden Prairie, MN 55344
Tel: 952/842-5000 Fax: 952/842-5005 Web site: http://www.netperceptions.com

Net Perceptions Inc. is a leading supplier of real-time relationship marketing solutions that enable Internet retailers to market to customers on a personalized, one-to-one basis. Net Perceptions solutions can increase new and repeat business by recording more about each customer's individual needs, tastes, and preferences with every interaction, then making increasingly personalized product and service recommendations. Net Perceptions operates offices in New York and San Francisco, as well as overseas. The company provides its personalization technology and support to Internet retailers including Art.com; Audio Book Club; Bertlesmann; Billboard TalentNet; CDnow; iVillage; Let's Eat Out; and Ticketmaster Online.

EARNINGS HISTORY

Year Ended Dec 31	Operating Revenue/Sales (dollars in thousands)	Net Earnings	Return on Revenue (percent)	Return on Equity	Net Earnings (dollars per share*)	Cash Dividend	Market Price Range
1999	15,129	(12,039)	NM	(24.9)	(0.78)	—	43.13–9.75
1998	4,477	(4,968)	NM	NM	(1.40)	—	
1997	317	(4,722)	NM	NM	(3.01)	—	
1996 †	4	(1,027)	NM	(34.8)	(3.40)	—	

* Trading began April 23, 1999.
† Period from July 3, 1996 (inception), to Dec. 31, 1996.

BALANCE SHEET

Assets	12/31/99 (dollars in thousands)	12/31/98	Liabilities	12/31/99 (dollars in thousands)	12/31/98
Current (CAE 17,457 and 972)	47,025	4,496	Current	9,653	4,028
Marketable securities	6,317		Long-term liabilities	707	538
Investment in joint venture	197		Preferred equity		650
Property and equipment	4,749	1,019	Common equity*	48,388	421
Other	460	122	TOTAL	58,748	5,637
TOTAL	58,748	5,637			

* $.0001 par common; 50,000,000 authorized; 22,025,716 and 6,633,308 issued and outstanding.

RECENT QUARTERS / PRIOR-YEAR RESULTS

	Quarter End	Revenue ($000)	Earnings ($000)	EPS ($)	Prior-Year Revenue ($000)	Prior-Year Earnings ($000)	Prior-Year EPS ($)
Q3	09/30/2000	7,725	(15,769)	(0.60)	4,114	(3,018)	(0.15)
Q2	06/30/2000	12,402	(11,730)	(0.46)	2,814	(3,123)	(0.17)
Q1	03/31/2000	9,492	(3,787)	(0.17)	1,895	(2,876)	(0.19)
Q4	12/31/99	6,306	(3,022)	(0.14)	1,662	(1,897)	(0.13)
	SUM	35,925	(34,308)	(1.37)	10,485	(10,914)	(0.63)

CURRENT: Q2 earnings include charge of $800,000/($0.03) for lease abandonment.
PRIOR YEAR: Q2 EPS is pro forma. Q1 EPS is pro forma. Q4 EPS is pro forma.

RECENT EVENTS

In **December 1999** the company formed a strategic partnership with MicroStrategy Inc. (Nasdaq: MSTR), a leading worldwide provider of e-business software, to enable organizations to more effectively analyze their online customers. MicroStrategy's Intelligent E-Business Platform was to be embedded in the new version of Net Perceptions for e-commerce 5.0. Then efollett.com, the world's first and largest online college bookstore, became the latest company to 0link with Net Perceptions' personalization solutions. The company certified Omnikron Systems Inc., Calabasas, Calif., as the first Premier Partner to successfully implement Net Perceptions latest product release, e-Commerce 5.0. In **January 2000** ZDNet (NYSE: ZDZ), the leading Web destination for people who buy, use, and learn about technology, agreed to license the Net Perceptions for Ad Targeting solution. Net Perceptions agreed to acquire privately held, 60-employee KD1 Inc. (Knowledge Discovery One, http://www.kd1.com), a leader in building advanced data analysis solutions for multi-channel and dot.com retailers. Net Perceptions was to issue 2.24 million shares of its common stock (then valued at $126 million) in the purchase transaction—giving it more tools for its online customers, as well as products that it can take to offline (bricks-and-mortar) retailers. [Deal completed in February.] Fingerhut Cos. Inc., one of the world's largest direct marketing and online retailers and a division of Federated Department Stores Inc. (NYSE: FD), selected Net Perceptions as its preferred technology partner for advanced e-commerce solutions. The company agreed to help Home Box Office (HBO) establish the network's online properties as destinations of choice for people seeking personalized entertainment recommendations and information. At month's end, the company signed partner agreements with three Asian resellers for distribution and support of Net Perceptions' technology throughout China, Hong Kong, Korea, Singapore, and Taiwan. In **February** wine.com, the leading global wine portal, deployed Net Perceptions for E-Commerce for wine purchasing, as well as Net Perceptions' award-winning real-time one-to-one recommendation solution, to help its customers make wine selections that both broaden their current knowledge and fit their personal tastes. Net Perceptions for Marketing Campaigns 2.0 allows marketers to create and execute individually targeted outbound e-mails designed to increase profits and improve customer loyalty. The *continued on page 310*

OFFICERS

Steven J. Snyder
President and CEO

Nanci Andersen
VP-Customer Solutions

Paul Bieganski
Chief Technical Officer

Thomas M. Donnelly
CFO and Secretary

David J. Govan III
VP-Sales, Eastern U.S./Latin America/Canada

Rike Harrison
SVP-Customer Solutions

Steve Jacob
SVP-Field Operations

Bradley N. Miller
VP-Product Development

John T. Riedl
Chief Scientist

DIRECTORS

Douglas J. Burgum
Great Plains Software Inc., Fargo, ND

William Lansing
Fingerhut Cos. Inc.

John T. Riedl

Steven J. Snyder

Ann L. Winblad
Hummer Winblad Venture Partners, San Francisco

MAJOR SHAREHOLDERS

London Pacific Life & Annuity Co., 9.9%
Raleigh, NC

Wells Fargo & Co., 9.5%
Minneapolis

Steven J. Snyder, 6.5%

All officers and directors as a group (9 persons), 19.5%

SIC CODE

7372 Prepackaged software

MISCELLANEOUS

TRANSFER AGENT AND REGISTAR:
Wells Fargo Bank Minnesota N.A.,
South St. Paul, MN

TRADED: Nasdaq National Market

SYMBOL: NETP

STOCKHOLDERS: 318

EMPLOYEES: 369

GENERAL COUNSEL:
Gunderson Dettmer Stough Villeneuve Franklin & Hachigian LLP,
Menlo Park, CA

AUDITORS:
PricewaterhouseCoopers LLP, Minneapolis

INC: DE-1996

RANKINGS

No. 165 CRM Public 200

NetRadio Corporation

10025 Valley View Rd., Suite 190, Eden Prairie, MN 55344
Tel: 952/259-6702 Fax: 952/259-6785 Web site: http://www.netradio.com

NetRadio Corp. is a broadcaster of originally programmed audio entertainment over the Internet. Netradio.com uses content to attract a large, diverse audience and retain its customers for extended periods of time. Every month more than 1 million unique listeners access NetRadio.com's 120 channels of music- and information-on-demand, 24 hours a day, seven days a week. The site connects with music enthusiasts through 15 interactive music communities ranging from Jazz, Modern Rock, and New Age to Vintage Rock and Classical. The company uses audio content to generate revenue from sales of audio merchandise through its online music store, CDPoint; and from Internet advertising, including advertisements placed within its audio broadcasts. The company's interactive display, NetCompanion, encourages impulse purchases by providing information about the music being played or the products being advertised, and by linking the listener directly to CDPoint or to its advertisers' Web sites.

EARNINGS HISTORY *

Year Ended Dec 31	Operating Revenue/Sales (dollars in thousands)	Net Earnings	Return on Revenue (percent)	Return on Equity	Net Earnings (dollars per share†)	Cash Dividend	Market Price Range
1999	1,449	(14,998)	NM	NM	(2.21)	—	14.00–6.63
1998	255	(3,977)	NM	NM	(0.67)	—	
1997	331	(2,741)	NM	NM	—	—	
1996	321	(2,254)	NM	NM	—	—	

* Results prior to March 21, 1997, are those of predecessor company Net Radio Nevada.
† Trading began Oct. 15, 1999.

BALANCE SHEET

Assets	12/31/99 (dollars in thousands)	12/31/98	Liabilities	12/31/99 (dollars in thousands)	12/31/98
Current (CAE 11,721 and 50)	30,987	1,030	Current	4,126	1,206
			Note payable	9,597	5,235
Property and equipment	2,626	881	Capital lease obligations	90	129
Note receivable, officer	62	63	Stockholders' equity*	19,968	(3,830)
Deferred offering costs		240	TOTAL	33,781	2,740
Goodwill	106	526			
TOTAL	33,781	2,740			

* No par common; 50,000,000 authorized; 10,007,900 and 5,922,500 issued and outstanding.

RECENT QUARTERS / **PRIOR-YEAR RESULTS**

	Quarter End	Revenue ($000)	Earnings ($000)	EPS ($)	Revenue ($000)	Earnings ($000)	EPS ($)
Q3	09/30/2000	456	(4,384)	(0.44)	374	(4,217)	(0.71)
Q2	06/30/2000	616	(4,143)	(0.41)	234	(2,568)	(0.43)
Q1	03/31/2000	565	(4,296)	(0.43)	172	(2,640)	(0.45)
	SUM	1,637	(12,823)	(1.28)	780	(9,425)	(1.59)

RECENT EVENTS

In **November 1999** the company announced that Michael Florin and Alan Gould, CFA, Gerard Klauer Mattison & Co., had initiated coverage of NetRadio with a BUY recommendation and a 12-month price target of $25 per share. In **December** a broad technology and marketing agreement with Microsoft Corp. (Nasdaq: MSFT) enabled NetRadio to offer its 120 originally programmed channels of music and information in the Windows Media format. [By mid-January NetRadio.com had already converted nearly half of their 120 stations to the Windows Media format.] In **January 2000** NetRadio.com and INTERVU Inc. (Nasdaq: ITVU), the leading service provider for Internet audio and video delivery solutions, announced an alliance to distribute NetRadio.com's music content to NetRadio's broad base of online music fans. In **February** the company unveiled a strategic relationship with Kerbango, creator of the world's first stand-alone Internet radio. Forbes' "Best of the Web" edition rated NetRadio.com a "Best of the Web" site. **Feb. 29**: The company claimed five out of the six leading slots in Arbitron's February 2000 InfoStream Webcast report, including the top two rankings. **March 31**: 2.9 million unique users accessed at least one of NetRadio.com's online offerings during March, including its Web site content, listening page, and Windows Media Player or RealPlayer content streams. In **April** NetRadio formed a content distribution and marketing alliance with Australia's leading Webcaster, DigitalOne. "This relationship, which will help strengthen and extend our brand overseas, is Netradio.com's first big step in implementing a global strategy," said CEO Tomechko. "Currently, 20 percent of our traffic comes from outside the United States, and that will continue to grow as we develop partnerships around the world." In **May** the company engaged Fleishman-Hillard Inc. as its worldwide public relations agency of record. NetRadio and the Arbitron Co., a division of Ceridian Corp. (NYSE: CEN), announced an alliance that was to lead to full inclusion of all NetRadio.com channels in Arbitron's InfoStream reporting service. In **June** NetRadio signed on as an official co-sponsor of Warner Brothers recording artist Don Henley's Inside Job Tour for summer 2000. In **July** the company announced an alliance with Microsoft WebTV Networks Inc., a leading provider of enhanced TV services using Internet and digital technologies, for the inclusion of selected NetRadio content in Windows Media Format in the audio/video streaming section of WebTV. A partnership with Road Runner, the nation's pre-eminent broadband service provider, made selected NetRadio streaming media available to the more than 912,000 Road Runner subscribers in the United States. In **August** NetRadio and AudioBasket, a premier provider of

continued on page 311

OFFICERS

Eric H. Paulson
Chairman and interim Pres./CEO

Mark Bauer
VP-Audio Content

Richard W. Hailey
Chief Technology Officer

Stephen Holderman
EVP-Marketing/Sales/Business Development

Becky Waller
Managing Editor and Creative Director

Michael P. Wise
VP, CFO, and Secretary

DIRECTORS

James Caparro
Island/Mercury/Def Jam Music Group, New York

Charles E. Cheney
Navarre Corp., New Hope, MN

Marc H. Kalman
Chancellor Media Inc., Minneapolis

Gene McCaffery
ValueVision International Inc., Eden Prairie, MN

Eric H. Paulson
Navarre Corp., New Hope, MN

MAJOR SHAREHOLDERS

Navarre Corp., 50%
New Hope, MN

ValueVision International Inc., 14.3%
Eden Prairie, MN

All officers and directors as a group (11 persons), 3.6%

SIC CODE

7379 Computer related services, nec

MISCELLANEOUS

TRADED: Nasdaq National Market

SYMBOL: NETR

STOCKHOLDERS: 23

EMPLOYEES: 50

PART TIME: 6

IN MINNESOTA: 48

GENERAL COUNSEL:
Dorsey & Whitney PLLP, Minneapolis

AUDITORS:
Ernst & Young LLP, Minneapolis

INVESTOR RELATIONS COUNSEL:
BlueFire Partners

PUBLIC RELATIONS COUNSEL:
Fleishman-Hillard Inc.

New Horizon Kids Quest Inc.

16355 36th Ave. N., Suite 700, Plymouth, MN 55446
Tel: 763/557-1111 Fax: 763/383-6101

New Horizon Kids Quest provides hourly child care and entertainment for children aged six weeks to 12 years. Kids Quest is a "drop in" center that operates primarily in casinos. As of Sept. 30, 2000, the company operated 21 Kids Quest centers in 10 states, including three with supervised nonviolent video entertainment centers. The company also provides traditional child care at 10 New Horizon Child Care locations in Boise, Idaho, and has added traditional care at its Mall of America location. The company also operates employee child care centers in Joliet, Ill., for Empress Casino and the Mobil Oil Co.; in Las Vegas, at the Venetian Resort-Casino-Hotel; and in Morton, Minn., at Jackpot Junction Casino Hotel. Additionally, the company is scheduled to add employee child care at its location in Marksville, La., at Grand Casino Avoyelles.

EARNINGS HISTORY

Year Ended Dec 31	Operating Revenue/Sales (dollars in thousands)	Net Earnings	Return on Revenue (percent)	Return on Equity	Net Earnings (dollars per share*)	Cash Dividend	Market Price Range
1999 †	17,098	(1,084)	(6.3)	(27.8)	(0.33)	—	2.63–0.38
1998	15,600	22	0.1	0.4	0.01	—	4.13–1.50
1997	13,856	3	0.0	0.1	0.00	—	5.25–1.56
1996 ¶	9,888	(1,601)	(16.2)	(32.5)	(0.49)	—	12.25–4.13
1995	5,639	(369)	(6.5)	(5.7)	(0.16)	—	8.50–6.50

* Trading commenced Nov. 14, 1995.
† Income figures for 1999 include pretax charges of $367,272 for write-down of fixed assets; and $431,441 for write-down of goodwill.
¶ Income figures for 1996 include charges totaling $1,275,347 for write-down of fixed assets and goodwill.

BALANCE SHEET

Assets	12/31/99 (dollars in thousands)	12/31/98	Liabilities	12/31/99 (dollars in thousands)	12/31/98
Current (CAE 155 and 208)	1,275	1,397	Current (STD 1,425 and 1,489)	2,969	2,857
Property and equipment	5,361	5,938	Long-term debt	1,382	1,720
Goodwill	494	992	Stockholders' equity*	3,899	4,982
Notes receivable	951	1,050	TOTAL	8,250	9,559
Other	168	181			
TOTAL	8,250	9,559			

* $0.01 par common; 20,000,000 authorized; 3,293,300 and 3,293,300 issued and outstanding.

RECENT QUARTERS / PRIOR-YEAR RESULTS

	Quarter End	Revenue ($000)	Earnings ($000)	EPS ($)	Prior-Year Revenue ($000)	Prior-Year Earnings ($000)	Prior-Year EPS ($)
Q3	09/30/2000	4,846	163	0.05	4,864	(773)	(0.23)
Q2	06/30/2000	4,382	96	0.03	4,387	(100)	(0.03)
Q1	03/31/2000	4,203	14	0.00	4,009	(176)	(0.05)
Q4	12/31/99	3,839	(35)	(0.01)	3,591	(295)	(0.09)
	SUM	17,269	237	0.07	16,851	(1,344)	(0.41)

PRIOR YEAR: Q3 earnings include a charge to operations for asset write-downs (including goodwill) and lease-termination costs of $798,713/($0.24).

RECENT EVENTS

In **December 1999** a Kids Quest hourly child care center opened at the Cliff Castle Casino in Camp Verde, Ariz., as part of a new 115,000-square-foot casino and entertainment center. In **April 2000** New Horizon Kids Quest opened its newest employee child care facility at The Venetian Resort Hotel Casino, the first on-site employee child care facility on the Las Vegas strip. Exclusive to the employees of The Venetian, the facility was to offer educational-based child development programs for close to 200 children, six weeks to 12 years of age. In **May** Park Place Entertainment extended the contract term for the Kids Quest facilities at Grand Casino Gulfport and Grand Casino Biloxi on the Mississippi Gulf Coast until May of 2004. In **July** New Horizon opened a Kids Quest hourly child care center and a nonviolent video entertainment center for Ho-Chunk Casino and Bingo located in the Wisconsin Dells. In **August** a 10,000-square-foot Kids Quest hourly and employee child care center was opened at the Jackpot Junction Casino Hotel in Morton, Minn., as part of a hotel expansion at the resort. **Sept. 30**: Net income for the three-month period was $162,630/$0.05, the best third-quarter performance in the company's history, primarily due to improvements in center operating income from existing Kids Quest locations (those centers open during both periods) combined with the contribution from new Kids Quest centers opened since the second quarter of 1999. Year-to-date center operating income from the company's Idaho operations increased to $83,733 from a loss of $92,067 for the same period in 1999.

OFFICERS

William M. Dunkley
Chairman and CEO

Susan K. Dunkley
President

Patrick R. Cruzen
CFO

DIRECTORS

Lyle Berman
Lakes Gaming Inc., Plymouth, MN

Kenneth W. Brimmer
Active IQ Technologies Inc., Minnetonka, MN

Patrick R. Cruzen

Susan K. Dunkley

William M. Dunkley

MAJOR SHAREHOLDERS

Lakes Gaming Inc., 26.6%
Plymouth, MN

William M. Dunkley, 14%

Susan K. Dunkley, 14%

All officers and directors as a group (6 persons), 56.8%

SIC CODE

8351 Child day care services

MISCELLANEOUS

TRANSFER AGENT AND REGISTAR:
Wells Fargo Bank Minnesota N.A., South St. Paul, MN

TRADED: Nasdaq SmallCap Market

SYMBOL: KIDQ

STOCKHOLDERS: 42

EMPLOYEES: 536

GENERAL COUNSEL:
Dunkley, Bennett & Christensen P.A., Minneapolis
Maslon, Edelman, Borman & Brand, Minneapolis

AUDITORS:
Arthur Andersen LLP, Minneapolis

INC: MN-1992

ANNUAL MEETING: June

MARKETING: Troy Dunkley

RANKINGS

No. 160 CRM Public 200

SUBSIDIARIES, DIVISIONS, AFFILIATES

Kids Quest Centers

New Horizon Centers

TWO-YEAR QUARTERLY HIGH-LOW STOCK PRICES

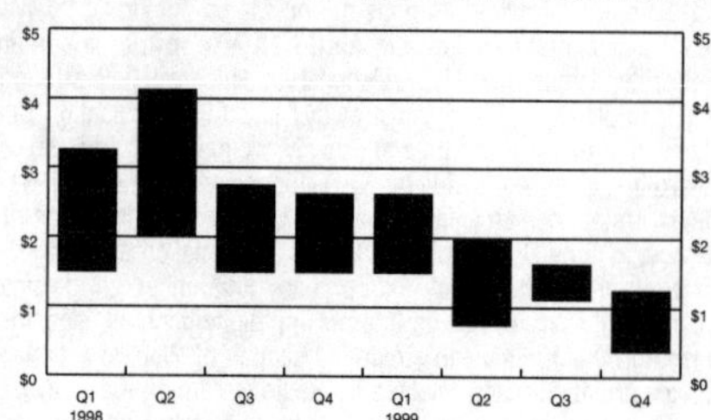

Norstan Inc.

5101 Shady Oak Rd., Minnetonka, MN 55344
Tel: 952/352-4000 Fax: 952/352-4461 Web site: http://www.norstan.com

Norstan is a global leader in technology services providing information technology and communication systems solutions to business clients worldwide. Headquartered in the Twin Cities, Norstan has sales, consulting, and service offices in 68 locations in 58 cities throughout the United States and Canada. Through its three operating units—Communication Solutions, Global Services, and Financial Services—Norstan offers leading-edge technology products, world-class technology services, and competitive financial offerings as a single-source solution provider.

EARNINGS HISTORY

Year Ended Apr 30	Operating Revenue/Sales (dollars in thousands)	Net Earnings (dollars in thousands)	Return on Revenue (percent)	Return on Equity (percent)	Net Earnings (dollars per share*)	Cash Dividend (dollars per share*)	Market Price Range (dollars per share*)
2000 †	418,521	(68,949)	(16.5)	NM	(6.37)	—	14.25–5.13
1999 ¶	482,709	5,890	1.2	5.4	0.56	—	26.19–8.00
1998 #	456,365	3,855	0.8	3.9	0.40	—	29.00–14.00
1997 **	398,075	10,217	2.6	12.1	1.12	—	20.25–13.13
1996	321,364	8,489	2.6	12.6	1.00	—	13.88–10.88

* Per-share amounts restated to reflect 2-for-1 stock split on July 31, 1996.
† Income figures for 2000 include pretax charges of $1.969 million for restructuring and $32.244 million for write-down of goodwill.
¶ Income figures for 1999 include pretax charge of $1.522 million for restructuring.
\# Income figures for 1998 include pretax charge of $14.667 million for restructuring.
** Figures for 1997 include results of Connect Computer Co. from its June 4, 1996, date of acquisition for $15.0 million.

BALANCE SHEET

Assets	04/30/00 (dollars in thousands)	04/30/99 (dollars in thousands)	Liabilities	04/30/00 (dollars in thousands)	04/30/99 (dollars in thousands)
Current (CAE 29 and 867)	147,332	175,863	Current (STD 21,744 and 24,554)	107,510	97,624
Property and equipment	42,184	49,729	Long-term debt	67,445	61,411
Lease receivables	41,874	39,736	Discounted lease rentals	24,285	32,604
Goodwill	4,462	39,994	Deferred income taxes		7,542
Deferred income taxes	3,320		Other	1,864	
Other	4,421	3,194	Stockholders' equity*	42,489	109,335
TOTAL	243,593	308,516	TOTAL	243,593	308,516

* $0.10 par common; 40,000,000 authorized; 11,239,113 and 10,763,726 issued and outstanding.

RECENT QUARTERS / PRIOR-YEAR RESULTS

	Quarter End	Revenue ($000)	Earnings ($000)	EPS ($)	Prior-Year Revenue ($000)	Prior-Year Earnings ($000)	Prior-Year EPS ($)
Q1	07/29/2000	90,647	(7,540)	(0.69)	116,204	882	0.08
Q4	04/30/2000	93,909	(45,843)	(4.19)	130,297	3,011	0.28
Q3	01/29/2000	92,164	(11,772)	(1.08)	111,509	(3,478)	(0.33)
Q2	10/30/99	116,244	(12,215)	(1.13)	125,053	3,691	0.35
	SUM	392,964	(77,370)	(7.10)	483,063	4,106	0.39

CURRENT: Q4 earnings include pretax charge of $32.244 million for write-down of goodwill.
PRIOR YEAR: Q3 earnings include pretax charge of $1,522,000 for restructuring.

RECENT EVENTS

In **November 1999** the company's president and CEO, David R. Richard, resigned, as did EVP and CFO Kenneth S. MacKenzie. Richard said: "While I believe that the strategy Norstan has embarked on is correct, I am disappointed in the progress we have made in executing that strategy during my watch." Norstan was also nearing the end of its review of strategic alternatives with Donaldson, Lufkin & Jenrette Securities Corp. New CEO Baszucki said: "The board has decided that it is in the best interest of our shareholders for Norstan management to focus on restructuring our business, enhancing the operations of our business, controlling our costs, and reinvigorating top-line growth. Therefore, we are announcing today that Norstan will run as two operating units: Communications and IT Consulting Services. The IT business will focus on transforming from a staff augmentation business to a practice-based, high-value consulting services company. The communications business will accelerate its emphasis on bundling products and services to create comprehensive, single-source solutions for our customers." Norstan also sold its Web-based consumer education services business to TechSkills.com for $2.6 million. In **January 2000** a new $4 million Norstan solution dramatically upgraded communications at the city ***continued on page 311***

OFFICERS

Paul Baszucki
Chairman
James C. Granger
President and CEO
Richard Cohen
Vice Chairman and CFO
Richard Camuso
VP-Finance/Planning/Administration
Pat Fischer
VP, Gen. Mgr.-Multi-Media Distribution
Kim Keller
VP-Integrated Technologies Group
Michael E. Laughlin
EVP-Communication Services
Jerry P. Lehrman
VP and General Counsel
Jeffrey A. Lusenhop
Pres.-Norstan Consulting
Jeffrey A. Mattson
VP, Gen. Mgr.-Norstan Resale Services
Winston E. Munson
Secretary
Kevin Paulsen
EVP-Global Services
Alan Perry
VP-Human Resources
Mary Lynne Perushek
VP-Information Services
Larry J. Schmidt
VP-Advanced Solutions Group
Neil Sell
Secretary
Peter E. Stilson
EVP-Communication Solutions
Michael J. Theisen
EVP-Convergent Services
Roger D. Van Beusekom
EVP-Financial Services
Robert J. Vold
VP, Gen. Mgr.-Norstan Financial Services
Jack White
VP-Sales, Western U.S.
Kenneth R. Roken
VP-Corporate Communications
David Hegre
VP-Sales, Central Market
Ted Stine
VP-Sales, Eastern Market
Keith Matthews
Exec. Managing Ptnr., Norstan Consulting
Neil Miller
VP and Gen. Mgr. Multimedia Distribution

DIRECTORS

Paul Baszucki
Richard Cohen
James C. Granger
Connie M. Levi
Gerald D. Pint
telecommunications consultant, Orono, MN
David R. Richard
Jagdish N. Sheth, Ph.D.
Emory University, Atlanta
Herbert F. Trader
consultant
Mercedes Walton
AT&T (former)

MAJOR SHAREHOLDERS

Heartland Advisors Inc., 17.1%
Milwaukee
Dimensional Fund Advisors Inc., 8.7%
Santa Monica, CA
David L. Babson & Co. Inc., 5%
Cambridge, MA
All officers and directors as a group (13 persons), 11.6%

SIC CODE

4899 Communication services, nec
7371 Computer programming services

MISCELLANEOUS

TRANSFER AGENT AND REGISTAR:
Wells Fargo Bank Minnesota N.A., South St. Paul, MN
TRADED: Nasdaq National Market
SYMBOL: NRRD
STOCKHOLDERS: 2,979
EMPLOYEES: 2,247
GENERAL COUNSEL:
Maslon Edelman Borman & Brand PLLP, Minneapolis
AUDITORS:
Arthur Andersen LLP, Minneapolis
INC: MN-1960
ANNUAL MEETING: September
PUBLIC RELATIONS: Kenneth R. Croken
COMMUNICATIONS: Carol Weler

RANKINGS

No. 52 CRM Public 200

TWO-YEAR QUARTERLY HIGH-LOW STOCK PRICES

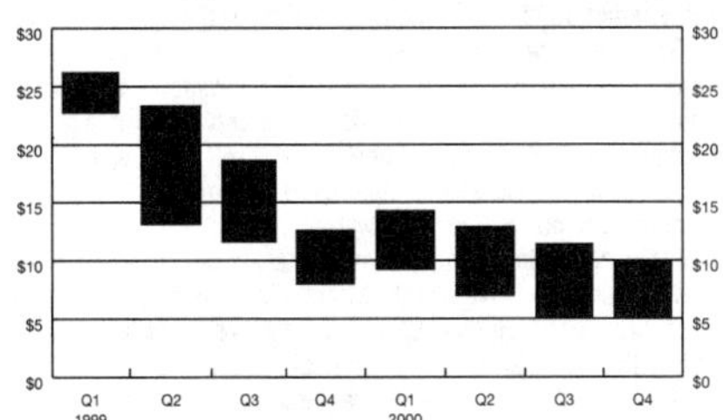

PUB

Nortech Systems Inc.

1120 Wayzata Blvd., Wayzata, MN 55391
Tel: 952/473-4102 Fax: 952/449-0442 Web site: http://www.nortechsys.com

Nortech Systems Inc.—based in Wayzata, Minn., with facilities in Aitkin, Bemidji, Merrifield, Plymouth, and Fairmont, Minn., and Augusta, Wis.—is a manufacturer of wire harnesses, cable assemblies, and electromechanical assemblies for commercial and defense industries. Nortech's Imaging Technologies Division designs, manufactures, and markets high-performance display monitors for medical imaging, document imaging, radar, and industry applications.

EARNINGS HISTORY *

Year Ended Dec 31	Operating Revenue/Sales (dollars in thousands)	Net Earnings	Return on Revenue (percent)	Return on Equity	Net Earnings (dollars per share†)	Cash Dividend	Market Price Range
1999	38,482	(1,988)	(5.2)	(32.4)	(0.85)	—	4.25–1.31
1998	35,357	330	0.9	4.1	0.14	—	6.63–3.44
1997	32,907	678	2.1	9.0	0.29	—	6.00–4.50
1996 ¶	23,608	446	1.9	6.5	0.19	—	9.00–5.00
1995 #	15,933	1,332	8.4	23.0	0.55	—	8.50–3.00

* Revenue figures have been restated for continuing operations. Income figures include these losses from the discontinued operations of the Display Products and Medical Management segments: $3,058,465/($1.30), including loss on disposal; $496,142/($0.21); $396,232/($0.17); $407,005/($0.17); and $54,361/($0.02)—in 1999 through 1995, respectively.
† EPS figures are after preferred dividends.
¶ Figures for 1996 include results of Zercom Corp. from its Nov. 4, 1996, date of purchase for $6.4 million. Pro forma for Jan. 1 purchase: revenue $39,702,215; net income $230,045/$0.10.
# Income figures for 1995 include pretax research and development costs of $124,919.

BALANCE SHEET

Assets	12/31/99 (dollars in thousands)	12/31/98	Liabilities	12/31/99 (dollars in thousands)	12/31/98
Current (CAE 453 and 375)	16,670	15,649	Current (STD 0 and 811)	6,978	4,665
Property and equipment	6,442	6,304	Notes payable	10,247	11,147
			Preferred equity	250	250
Goodwill and other intangibles	116	131	Common equity*	6,128	8,115
			TOTAL	23,604	24,176
Deferred taxes	300	475			
Other		57			
Discontinued operations	76	1,560			
TOTAL	23,604	24,176			

* $0.01 par common; 9,000,000 authorized; 2,351,907 and 2,351,377 issued and outstanding.

RECENT QUARTERS / **PRIOR-YEAR RESULTS**

	Quarter End	Revenue ($000)	Earnings ($000)	EPS ($)	Prior-Year Revenue ($000)	Prior-Year Earnings ($000)	Prior-Year EPS ($)
Q3	09/30/2000	13,724	547	0.23	9,334	(1,452)	(0.62)
Q2	06/30/2000	13,200	448	0.19	9,422	(1,159)	(0.49)
Q1	03/31/2000	12,569	410	0.17	9,467	249	0.11
Q4	12/31/99	10,259	375	0.16	9,430	(231)	(0.10)
	SUM	49,752	1,780	0.76	37,653	(2,594)	(1.10)

CURRENT: Q4 earnings include gain of $68,008/$0.03 from discontinued operations.
PRIOR YEAR: Q3 earnings include net loss of $1,678,516/($0.71) from discontinued operations and their disposal. Q2 earnings include loss of $1,447,957/($0.62) from discontinued operations. Q4 earnings include loss of $516,275/($0.22) from discontinued operations.

RECENT EVENTS

In **November 1999** the company agreed to sell the assets of its Imaging Technologies Division to Image Systems Corp. (Nasdaq: IMSG), Minnetonka, Minn. "Given the changing complexion of the monitor industry, we came to realize that a full-time focus and commitment was required," said CEO Finkelson. "We chose to divest ourselves of this business to concentrate on our core contract manufacturing operations. In **January 2000** Image Systems withdrew its letter of intent. Nortech was continuing to negotiate with other parties about the sale of this division. "Negotiations with Image Systems stalled over warranty-related issues," said CEO Finkelson. Meanwhile, the Intercon 1 division of Nortech Systems achieved certification under ISO 9002. In **February** Computron Display Systems, Mount Prospect, Ill., acquired the assets of the Imaging Technologies Division for $300,000. "Completing this transaction enables us to focus exclusively on our contract manufacturing business, which remains strong," said CEO Finkelson. In **March** the Medical Services subsidiary signed a one-year contract to provide claims-processing services for the Hughes Clinic, St. Paul. In **May** Aerospace Systems achieved certification under two prestigious quality standards—ISO 9001, an international quality system for design and manufacturing; and AS9000, which contains specific quality criteria required by the aerospace/defense industry. **Sept. 30**: Nine-month *continued on page 312*

OFFICERS

Quentin E. Finkelson
Chairman, President, and CEO
Patrick Gilligan
EVP-Technology/Corporate Development
Gregory D. Tweed
EVP and COO
Garry M. Anderly
SVP-Finance, Treasurer
Donald E. Horne
VP-Corporate Procurement
Peter L. Kucera
VP-Corporate Quality

DIRECTORS

Michael J. Degen
The Toro Co., Bloomington, MN
Quentin E. Finkelson
Myron D. Kunin
Regis Corp., Edina, MN
Richard W. Perkins
Perkins Capital Management Inc., Wayzata, MN

MAJOR SHAREHOLDERS

Myron Kunin, 40.1%
Edina, MN
Quentin E. Finkelson, 7.9%
All officers and directors as a group (9 persons), 51.3%

SIC CODE

3496 Fabricated wire products, misc
3577 Computer peripheral equipment, nec
3672 Printed circuit boards
3679 Electronic components, nec
3812 Search and navigation equipment
3841 Surgical and medical instruments
3844 X-ray apparatus and tubes
3845 Electromedical equipment
7374 Data processing and preparation

MISCELLANEOUS

TRANSFER AGENT AND REGISTAR:
Wells Fargo Shareowner Services, South St. Paul, MN
TRADED: Nasdaq National Market

SYMBOL: NSYS
STOCKHOLDERS: 1,274
EMPLOYEES: 736
PART TIME: 107
IN MINNESOTA: 662
GENERAL COUNSEL:
Bert M. Gross, Minneapolis
AUDITORS:
Larson, Allen, Weishair & Co. LLP, Minneapolis
INC: MN-1990
FOUNDED: 1979
ANNUAL MEETING: May
INVESTOR RELATIONS:
Sue Kesler
INVESTOR RELATIONS:
Warren Djerf

RANKINGS

No. 121 CRM Public 200

SUBSIDIARIES, DIVISIONS, AFFILIATES

Aerospace Systems Division
1007 E. 10th St.
P.O. Box 998
Fairmont, MN 56031
507/235-3355
Mike Wasnard

Nortech Systems/ Merrifield Operations
Merrifield, Minn.
218/765-3151
William Hannah

Nortech Systems
Intercon 1 Division
HC7 Airport Rd.
Aitkin, MN 56431
218/765-3329
Bud Brown

Nortech Systems Inc.
Bemidji Operations
4050 Norris Ct.
Bemidji, MN 56601
Gary Nedstrom

TWO-YEAR QUARTERLY HIGH-LOW STOCK PRICES

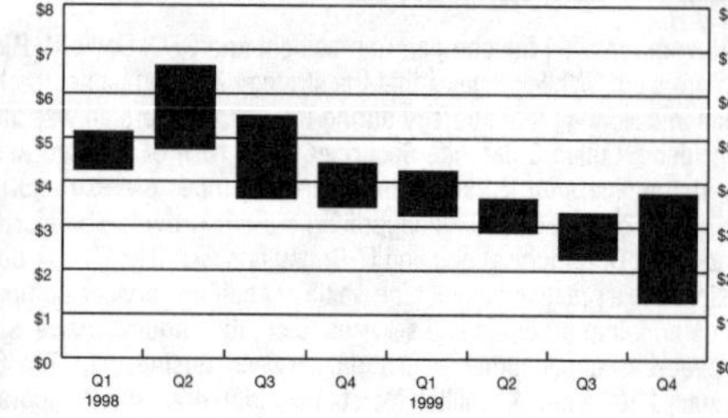

Northern Technologies International Corporation

6680 N. Highway 49, Lino Lakes, MN 55014
Tel: 651/784-1250 Fax: 651/784-2902 Web site: http://www.ntic.com

Northern Technologies International Corp. develops, manufactures, and markets proprietary corrosion-inhibiting products and electronic sensing instruments. The company's corrosion-inhibiting products, marketed under the name **Zerust**, are used in protective packaging by a wide variety of companies, in industries such as transportation, nuclear power, electronics, aerospace, power generation, on- and off-road automotive equipment, agriculture, and metal processing. The Zerust product line includes corrosion-inhibiting packaging films, chipboard, fiberboard, corregated cartons, dunnage trays and bins, bubble cushioning and foamsheet, pellets, tablets, and capsules—all of which emit vapors that protect metal surfaces. The company's electronic sensing instruments include portable oil-quality analyzers for on-site evaluation of oils and fluids; and instruments that provide for on- and off-line measurement of fiber denier and critical tubing measurements.

EARNINGS HISTORY

Year Ended Aug 31	Operating Revenue/Sales (dollars in thousands)	Net Earnings	Return on Revenue (percent)	Return on Equity	Net Earnings (dollars per share)	Cash Dividend	Market Price Range
1999	9,871	2,538	25.7	23.7	0.65	0.16	8.38–5.00
1998	10,077	2,619	26.0	29.5	0.64	0.15	12.75–6.44
1997	8,729	2,616	30.0	25.9	0.62	0.12	12.50–4.75
1996	6,869	2,088	30.4	25.2	0.49	0.10	7.63–4.63
1995	6,214	1,843	29.7	29.7	0.42	0.08	8.75–2.94

BALANCE SHEET

Assets	08/31/99 (dollars in thousands)	08/31/98	Liabilities	08/31/99 (dollars in thousands)	08/31/98
Current (CAE 2,750 and 2,200)	6,149	4,913	Current	677	346
Property, eqt	1,115	955	Deferred gross profit	60	120
Investment in joint ventures	3,425	2,754	Stockholders' equity*	10,724	8,881
Investment in European holding company	247	248	TOTAL	11,462	9,347
Deferred taxes	210	120			
Other	316	357			
TOTAL	11,462	9,347			

* $0.02 par common; 10,000,000 authorized; 3,865,103 and 3,847,452 issued and outstanding.

RECENT QUARTERS / **PRIOR-YEAR RESULTS**

	Quarter End	Revenue ($000)	Earnings ($000)	EPS ($)	Prior-Year Revenue ($000)	Prior-Year Earnings ($000)	Prior-Year EPS ($)
Q3	05/31/2000	2,813	763	0.20	2,442	662	0.17
Q2	02/29/2000	2,694	474	0.12	2,006	375	0.10
Q1	11/30/99	2,832	674	0.17	2,155	558	0.14
Q4	08/31/99	3,267	943	0.24	2,255	824	0.21
	SUM	11,605	2,854	0.73	8,859	2,419	0.61

RECENT EVENTS

In **December 1999** the company's board of directors authorized the repurchase from time to time of up to 200,000 shares (5.2 percent) of its common stock in open-market or privately negotiated transactions, based on market conditions. In **July 2000** the company ranked No. 113 on Forbes' 200 Best Small Companies in America list.

OFFICERS

Philip M. Lynch
Chairman and Co-CEO

G. Patrick Lynch
President and Co-CEO

Constance M. Fason
VP-Domestic Marketing/Sales

Elsie F. Gilles
Controller and Asst. Secretary

Matjaz Korosec
VP-Financial Planning and Treasurer

Donald A. Kubik
VP and Chief Technology Officer

DIRECTORS

Sidney Dworkin
Advanced Modular Systems

Vincent J. Graziano

Gerhard Hahn
Excor

Donald A. Kubik

Richard G. Lareau
Oppenheimer Wolff & Donnelly LLP, Minneapolis

Philip M. Lynch

Haruhiko Rikuta
Taiyo Petroleum Gas Co., Japan

Milan R. Vukcevich
Bicron/Saint-Gobain, Ohio

MAJOR SHAREHOLDERS

Inter Alia Holding Co., 23.6%
Shaker Heights, OH

All officers and directors as a group (13 persons), 32.9%

SIC CODE

2899 Chemical preparations, nec

3089 Plastics products, nec

3823 Process control instruments

MISCELLANEOUS

TRANSFER AGENT AND REGISTAR:
Wells Fargo Bank Minnesota N.A.,
South St. Paul, MN

TRADED: AMEX

SYMBOL: NTI

STOCKHOLDERS: 500

EMPLOYEES: 27

GENERAL COUNSEL:
Oppenheimer Wolff & Donnelly LLP, Minneapolis

AUDITORS:
Deloitte & Touche LLP, Minneapolis

INC: DE-1978

FOUNDED: 1970

ANNUAL MEETING:
January

RANKINGS

No. 183 CRM Public 200

TWO-YEAR QUARTERLY HIGH-LOW STOCK PRICES

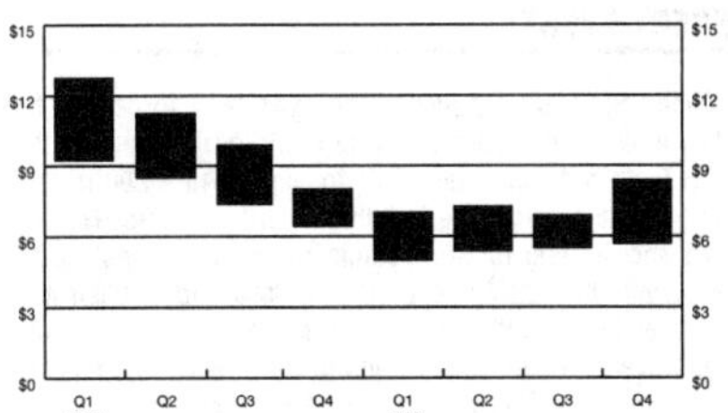

PUB

Northwest Airlines Corporation

5101 Northwest Dr., Eagan, MN 55111
Tel: 612/726-2111 Fax: 612/726-3942 Web site: http://www.nwa.com

Northwest Airlines Corp. (NWA Corp.) is the indirect parent of Northwest Airlines Inc. (Northwest). Northwest is the world's fourth-largest passenger airline (by revenue passenger miles), operating through three domestic hubs, in Detroit; Memphis, Tenn.; and Minneapolis/St. Paul; and Asian hubs in Tokyo and Osaka, Japan. Northwest is also a major international cargo carrier.

EARNINGS HISTORY

Year Ended Dec 31	Operating Revenue/Sales (dollars in thousands)	Net Earnings	Return on Revenue (percent)	Return on Equity	Net Earnings (dollars per share*)	Cash Dividend	Market Price Range
1999 †	10,276,000	300,000	2.9	NM	3.69	—	35.50–21.50
1998 ¶	9,044,800	(285,500)	(3.2)	NM	(3.48)	—	65.31–18.63
1997 #	10,225,800	596,500	5.8	NM	5.79	—	49.13–33.13
1996 **	9,880,500	536,100	5.4	NM	5.80	—	55.13–30.50
1995 ††	9,084,900	392,000	4.3	NM	4.30	—	52.50–15.88

* EPS figures are after preferred dividends of $0.5 million, $0.8 million, $13.5 million, $37.5 million, and $57.8 million—in 1999 through 1995, respectively; and preferred stock transaction gains of $74.5 million in 1996 and $58.9 million in 1995.
† Income figures for 1999 include gain of $28 million pretax, $18 million/$0.23 after-tax, from the sale of a portion of its investment in Equant N.V.; net nonrecurring credit of $27 million pretax, $17 million/$0.21 after-tax, related primarily to outside maintenance costs; and one-time, pretax charge of $19 million for aircraft write-downs.
¶ Income figures for 1998 include pretax charges: $66 million related to the retirement of seven Boeing 747 aircraft; and $103 million for retroactive payments related to collective bargaining agreements.
# Income figures for 1997 include loss of $9.3 million/($0.10) on extinguishment of debt.
** Income figures for 1996 include gain of $74.5 million/$0.75 from preferred stock transactions.
†† Income figures for 1995 include gain of $49.9 million/$0.55 on extinguishment of debt; and gain of $58.9 million/$0.64 from preferred stock transactions.

BALANCE SHEET

Assets	12/31/99 (dollars in thousands)	12/31/98	Liabilities	12/31/99 (dollars in thousands)	12/31/98
Current (CAE 749,000 and 480,000)	2,063,000	1,870,100	Current (STD 312,000 and 319,000)	3,577,000	3,461,700
Property and equipment	5,748,000	5,658,500	Long-term debt	3,354,000	3,681,500
			Capital leases	537,000	597,300
Flight equipment under capital leases	588,000	610,000	Deferred tax	1,222,000	1,112,700
			Benefits	542,000	500,100
Investments in affiliated companies	690,000	675,900	Other	535,000	579,400
			Preferred security of subsidiary	626,000	564,100
International routes	681,000	704,300			
Other	814,000	762,000	Redeemable stock	243,000	260,700
TOTAL	10,584,000	10,280,800	Common stock*	(52,000)	(476,700)
			TOTAL	10,584,000	10,280,800

* $0.01 par common; 315,000,000 authorized; 109,576,810 and 108,953,764 issued and outstanding, less 27,497,612 and 28,978,351 treasury shares.

RECENT QUARTERS / PRIOR-YEAR RESULTS

	Quarter End	Revenue ($000)	Earnings ($000)	EPS ($)	Prior-Year Revenue ($000)	Prior-Year Earnings ($000)	Prior-Year EPS ($)
Q3	09/30/2000	3,178,000	207,000	2.49	2,843,000	180,000	2.21
Q2	06/30/2000	2,927,000	115,000	1.40	2,597,000	120,000	1.47
Q1	03/31/2000	2,570,000	3,000	0.04	2,281,000	(29,000)	(0.36)
Q4	12/31/99	2,555,000	29,000	0.35	2,212,200	(181,300)	(2.31)
	SUM	11,230,000	354,000	4.29	9,933,200	89,700	1.00

RECENT EVENTS

In **December 1999**, pursuant to an open-skies agreement between the United States and Italy, Northwest Airlines and Alitalia Italian Airlines, in cooperation with KLM Royal Dutch Airlines, announced daily nonstop Detroit-Rome and Detroit-Milan, Italy, flights (with code-share benefits), to begin in **April 2000**. In an effort to restart bargaining, union flight attendants and Northwest held a meeting before the National Mediation Board. However, the union's proposal for industry-leading wages was deemed unrealistic, leading to an indefinite recess. Northwest named Skies America International Publishing and Communications, along with Nishitetsu Agency Co. of Japan, to publish its inflight magazine, WorldTraveler. Northwest introduced its new Customer Guide (both print and online versions), which outlines Northwest's Customers First service commitments and provides travel tips and explanations of Northwest's operations and policies for each step of a typical travel experience. The airline invested $60 million to build a new hangar and cargo facility at Sea-Tac

continued on page 312

OFFICERS

John H. Dasburg
President and CEO

Richard H. Anderson
EVP and COO

Mickey P. Foret
EVP-Finance, CFO, Pres.-Northwest Cargo

J. Timothy Griffin
EVP-Marketing/Distribution

Phil Haan
EVP-International/Sales/Info. Services

Douglas M. Steenland
EVP and Chief Corporate Officer

Ray Vecci
EVP-Customer Service, Pres.-Michigan Op.

Bob Brodin
SVP-Labor Relations

Hiram Cox
SVP and Controller

Stephen E. Gorman
SVP-Technical Operations

Mary Carroll Linder
SVP-Corporate Communications

Daniel B. Matthews
SVP and Treasurer

Dirk McMahon
SVP-Ground Operations

Thomas Momchilov
SVP-Human Resources

Bernhardt Wruble
SVP-Legal Affairs

Gene Peterson
VP-Regulatory, Chief Safety Officer

DIRECTORS

Ray W. Benning Jr.
International Brotherhood of Teamsters

Richard C. Blum
Blum & Associates Inc.

Elaine L. Chao
The Heritage Foundation

Alfred A. Checchi

James G. Coulter
Texas Pacific Group

John H. Dasburg

Doris Kearns Goodwin
author and historian, Concord, MA

Marvin L. Griswold
International Brotherhood of Teamsters (retired)

Dennis F. Hightower
Harvard University, Boston

Thomas L. Kempner
Loeb Partners Corp.

George J. Kourpias
International Association of Machinists & Aerospace Workers (retired)

Melvin R. Laird
director emeritus

Frederic V. Malek
Thayer Capital Partners

Walter F. Mondale
Dorsey & Whitney LLP, Minneapolis

V.A. Ravindran
Paracor Finance Inc.

Michael Ristow
Air Line Pilots Assn.

Leo Van Wijk
KLM Royal Dutch Airlines

Gary L. Wilson

MAJOR SHAREHOLDERS

AXA Financial Inc., 23.8%
New York

Gary L. Wilson, 20.3%
Washington, D.C.

Alfred A. Checchi, 13.5%

Trusts for ALPA employees/State Street Bank & Trust Co., 9.3%
North Quincy, MA

Richard C. Blum/BLUM Capital Partners L.P., 6.2%, San Francisco

Institutional Capital Corp., 5.1%, Chicago

All officers and directors as a group (22 persons), 35.8%

MISCELLANEOUS

TRANSFER AGENT AND REGISTAR:
Wells Fargo Bank Minnesota N.A., South St. Paul, MN

TRADED: Nasdaq National Market

SYMBOL: NWAC

STOCKHOLDERS: 1,321

EMPLOYEES: 56,000

GENERAL COUNSEL:
Simpson Thacher & Bartlett, New York

AUDITORS:
Ernst & Young LLP, Minneapolis

INC: DE-1989

FOUNDED: 1934

ANNUAL MEETING: April

INVESTOR RELATIONS:
Mark S. Long

RANKINGS

No. 6 CRM Public 200
No. 7 CRM Employer 100
No. 21 CRM Performance 100

TWO-YEAR QUARTERLY HIGH-LOW STOCK PRICES

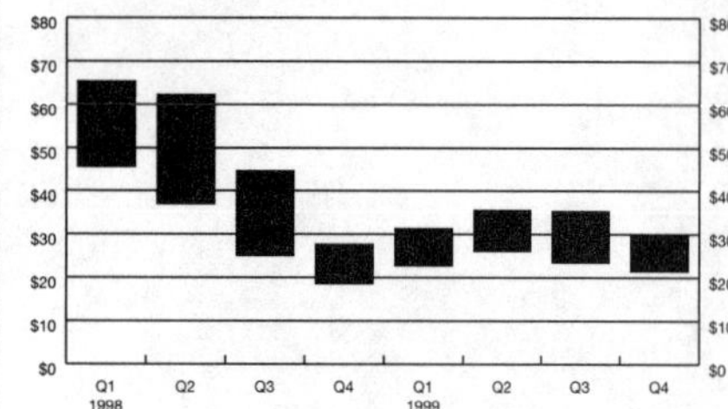

NorthWestern Corporation

125 S. Dakota Ave., Suite 1100, Sioux Falls, SD 57104
Tel: 605/978-2908 Fax: 605/978-2910 Web site: http://www.northwestern.com

NorthWestern Corp. is a $5 billion diversified services and solutions company. NorthWestern serves more than 2 million energy and communications customers nationwide. The company's revenues have risen from $200 million to $5 billion over the past five years. NorthWestern's partner entities include Expanets, the largest U.S. mid-market provider of networked communications solutions and services; Blue Dot, a national provider of air conditioning, heating, plumbing and related services; CornerStone Propane Partners, L.P., the nation's fifth largest retail propane distribution entity; and NorthWestern Public Service, a provider of electric, natural gas and communication services to Midwestern customers.

EARNINGS HISTORY

Year Ended Dec 31	Operating Revenue/Sales (dollars in thousands)	Net Earnings	Return on Revenue (percent)	Return on Equity	Net Earnings (dollars per share*)	Cash Dividend	Market Price Range
1999	3,004,340	44,663	1.5	12.6	1.64	1.05	27.13–20.63
1998	1,187,187	30,391	2.6	9.6	1.45	0.99	27.38–20.25
1997	918,070	26,264	2.9	14.1	1.31	0.93	23.50–16.94
1996	344,009	26,054	7.6	14.0	1.28	0.89	18.25–13.38
1995 †	204,970	19,306	9.4	11.8	1.11	0.87	14.19–12.13

* Per-share amounts restated to reflect 2-for-1 stock split in 1997.
† Figures for 1995 include results of Synergy Group Inc. from its Aug. 15, 1995, date of acquisition for a net purchase price of $104.9 million.

BALANCE SHEET

Assets	12/31/99 (dollars in thousands)	12/31/98	Liabilities	12/31/99 (dollars in thousands)	12/31/98
Current (CAE 29,677 and 30,865)	383,598	267,168	Current (STD 49,870 and 31,614)	269,047	209,429
Property	681,663	629,278	Long-term debt	309,350	256,350
Investments and other	149,490	213,777	Subsidiaries debt	473,757	332,525
Goodwill, other intangibles	742,010	618,251	Deferred income taxes	64,855	74,072
TOTAL	1,956,761	1,728,474	Other	86,797	94,795
			Minority interests	361,549	387,952
			Preferred equity	91,250	91,250
			Common equity*	300,156	282,101
			TOTAL	1,956,761	1,728,474

* $1.75 par common; 50,000,000 authorized; 23,109,000 and 23,017,000 issued and outstanding.

RECENT QUARTERS / **PRIOR-YEAR RESULTS**

	Quarter End	Revenue ($000)	Earnings ($000)	EPS ($)	Revenue ($000)	Earnings ($000)	EPS ($)
Q3	09/30/2000	1,613,573	9,947	0.36	753,443	8,838	0.31
Q2	06/30/2000	1,596,399	7,702	0.26	595,850	6,837	0.22
Q1	03/31/2000	1,330,944	16,239	0.63	509,354	14,880	0.57
Q4	12/31/99	1,145,693	14,108	0.54	378,182	11,450	0.49
	SUM	5,686,609	47,996	1.78	2,236,829	42,005	1.59

CURRENT: Q3 earnings include loss of $1.046 million/($0.05) on cumulative effect of change in accounting principle.

RECENT EVENTS

In **April 2000** Expanets, one of NorthWestern's partner entities, purchased the U.S. small and mid-sized business sales organization from Lucent Technologies' (NYSE: LU) Enterprise Networks Group. This transaction and the resulting strategic alliance positioned Expanets as the largest integrated solutions provider for small and mid-sized businesses in the United States. **Sept. 30:** Third-quarter earnings were enhanced by increased preferred stock investments in the communications sector, as well as strong revenue from late-summer energy sales. "For the sixth-consecutive quarter, we have generated double-digit earnings growth," said CEO Lewis. In **October** NorthWestern agreed to acquire The Montana Power Co.'s (NYSE: MTP) energy distribution and transmission business for $1.1 billion in cash, including $488 million in existing Montana Power debt. The transaction was to be accounted for as a purchase and was expected to be accretive to NorthWestern's earnings per share upon its completion, anticipated in the first half of 2001. The Montana Power assets included regulated electric and natural gas distribution and transmission operations, along with certain unregulated, energy-related businesses that provide products and services to industrial, institutional, and commercial customers. In **November** the board of directors announced a new annual dividend rate of $1.19, a 7.2 percent increase over the previous rate. With this dividend, NorthWestern had increased dividends for 17 consecutive years and paid dividends for 54 consecutive years.

OFFICERS

Merle D. Lewis
Chairman and CEO
Richard R. Hylland
President and COO
Michael J. Hanson
Pres./CEO-Northwestern Public Service
Walter A. (Trey) Bradley III
VP and Chief Information Officer
Michael L. Childers
VP-Customer Strategies
Alan D. Dietrich
VP-Legal Administration
Eric R. Jacobsen
VP, General Counsel, Chief Legal Officer
David A. Monaghan
Controller and Treasurer
Daniel K. Newell
SVP-Finance and CFO
Kipp D. Orme
VP-Finance
Rogene A. Thaden
VP-Communications
John R. Van Camp
VP-Human Resources
Paul Wyche
VP and Chief Communications Officer

DIRECTORS

John C. Charters
Qwest Cyber.Solutions LLC, Denver
Randy G. Darcy
General Mills Inc., Golden Valley, MN
Gary G. Drook
AFFINA, Peoria, IL
Richard R. Hylland
Jerry W. Johnson
U. of South Dakota School of Business, Vermillion, SD
Merle D. Lewis
Larry F. Ness
First Dakota Financial Corp., Yankton, SD
Marilyn R. Seymann
M ONE Inc., Phoenix
Bruce J. Smith
Luebs Beltzer Leininger Smith & Busick, Grand Island, NE

MAJOR SHAREHOLDERS

Franklin Fund, 7.8%
San Mateo, CA
NorthWestern ESOP, 6.2%
All officers and directors as a group (14 persons), 1%

SIC CODE

4813 Telephone communications, exc radio
4899 Communication services, nec
4924 Natural gas distribution
4931 Electric and other services combined
4931 Electric and other services combined
4932 Gas and other services combined

MISCELLANEOUS

TRANSFER AGENT AND REGISTAR:
Wells Fargo Bank Minnesota N.A., South St. Paul, MN
TRADED: NYSE
SYMBOL: NOR
STOCKHOLDERS: 10,475
EMPLOYEES: 10,000
GENERAL COUNSEL:
Alan D. Dietrich, Sioux Falls, ND
AUDITORS:
Arthur Andersen LLP, Minneapolis
INC: DE-1923
ANNUAL MEETING: May
PUBLIC AFFAIRS: Warren K. Lotsberg
COMMUNICATIONS: Paul H. Wyche

SUBSIDIARIES, DIVISIONS, AFFILIATES

NorthWestern Corp.

NorthWestern Growth

Blue Dot

CornerStone Propane

Expanets

TWO-YEAR QUARTERLY HIGH-LOW STOCK PRICES

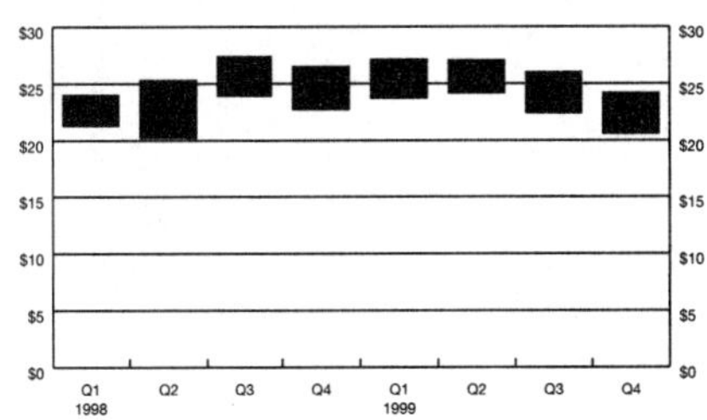

PUB

Oakridge Holdings Inc.

4810 120th St. W., Apple Valley, MN 55124
Tel: 651/895-5164 Fax: 651/454-5143 Web site: http://www.stinar.com

Oakridge Holdings Inc. operates two adjacent cemeteries near Hillside, Ill., used for the interment of human remains. The combined cemeteries have 176.7 total acres, of which 12.8 are used for interior roads and other improvements—leaving 163.9 net acres with 137,000 burial plots, of which 39,068 remain in inventory. The cemeteries have two mausoleums with 975 niches and 3,190 crypts of which 152 niches and 359 crypts remain in inventory. The company also holds deeds to 188 unsold crypts located in Forest Home Cemetery in Forest Park, Ill. Cook and Dupage counties in Illinois serve as the principal market for the company's services. The company estimates that it has an inventory of cemetery and mausoleum spaces representing a 26- to 35-year supply, based on the maintenance of current sale levels. Principal products of Stinar include truck-mounted stairways for use on aircraft, fuel and water trucks, foodservice and catering vehicles, vehicles used in transporting and loading luggage and cargo, sanitary services vehicles, and other custom-built ground support vehicles used by airports, commercial airlines, and the military. Stinar also provides limited service and repairs on vehicles it sells.

EARNINGS HISTORY *

Year Ended Jun 30	Operating Revenue/Sales (dollars in thousands)	Net Earnings (dollars in thousands)	Return on Revenue (percent)	Return on Equity (percent)	Net Earnings (dollars per share)	Cash Dividend (dollars per share)	Market Price Range (dollars per share)
2000	13,393	274	2.0	13.4	0.20	—	7.00–0.75
1999	12,409	488	3.9	27.6	0.36	—	4.50–1.59
1998	2,767	130	4.7	10.8	0.10	—	4.00–0.56
1997	2,585	214	8.3	21.4	0.16	—	1.19–0.38
1996	2,615	174	6.7	22.1	0.13	—	1.32–0.25

* Pro forma results including Stinar operations: revenue $15,483,743 and $12,473,303; earnings $220,299/$0.17 and $153,371/$0.12—in 1998 and 1997, respectively.

BALANCE SHEET

Assets	09/30/00 (dollars in thousands)	06/30/99	Liabilities	09/30/00 (dollars in thousands)	06/30/99
Current (CAE 902 and 950)	11,406	5,320	Current (STD 319 and 76)	9,302	3,417
Property and equipment	3,156	2,848	Long-term debt	3,407	3,044
Investment in land	140		Stockholders' equity*	2,046	1,771
Othr	53	65	TOTAL	14,755	8,232
TOTAL	14,755	8,232			

* $0.10 par common; 5,000,000 authorized; 1,391,503 and 1,388,003 issued and outstanding.

RECENT QUARTERS / PRIOR-YEAR RESULTS

	Quarter End	Revenue ($000)	Earnings ($000)	EPS ($)	Prior-Year Revenue ($000)	Prior-Year Earnings ($000)	Prior-Year EPS ($)
Q4	06/30/2000	4,076	(114)	(0.08)	2,578	(184)	(0.14)
Q3	03/31/2000	2,750	121	0.09	2,842	74	0.05
Q2	12/31/99	3,530	121	0.09	3,422	257	0.19
Q1	09/30/99	3,037	147	0.11	3,567	341	0.25
	SUM	13,393	274	0.20	12,409	488	0.36

PRIOR YEAR: Q1 is the first period to reflect operations of Stinar Corp. acquisition.

RECENT EVENTS

In **December 1999** Stinar Corp. was awarded a $6.8 million contract to provide 204 Flightline Tow Tractors to the U.S. Department of Defense.

OFFICERS

Robert C. Harvey
Chairman and CEO

Robert B. Gregor
VP and Secretary

Marie Leshyn
CEO-Cemetery

DIRECTORS

Robert B. Gregor

Robert C. Harvey

Hugh McDaniel
real estate broker, San Diego

MAJOR SHAREHOLDERS

Robert C. Harvey, 24.9%

Jerry R. and Linda L. Kenline, 13.6%
Shorewood, MN

Robert B. Gregor, 12%

All officers and directors as a group (3 persons), 37.2%

SIC CODE

3537 Industrial trucks and tractors

6553 Cemetery subdividers and developers

MISCELLANEOUS

TRANSFER AGENT AND REGISTAR:
Chemical Mellon Shareholder Services LLC, Ridgefield Park, NJ

TRADED: OTC Bulletin Board

SYMBOL: OKRG

STOCKHOLDERS: 2,109

EMPLOYEES: 148

PART TIME: 11

GENERAL COUNSEL:
Oppenheimer Wolff & Donnelly LLP, Minneapolis
Fagel & Haber, Chicago

AUDITORS:
Stirtz Bernards Boyden Surdel & Larter P.A., Edina, MN

INC: MN-1961

ANNUAL MEETING: February

ADMINISTRATION: Paul Balli

RANKINGS

No. 173 CRM Public 200

SUBSIDIARIES, DIVISIONS, AFFILIATES

Oakridge Cemetery (Hillside) Inc.

Glen Oak Cemetery Co.

Stinar HG Inc.
3255 Sibley Memorial Hwy.
Eagan, MN 55121
651/454-5112

TWO-YEAR QUARTERLY HIGH-LOW STOCK PRICES

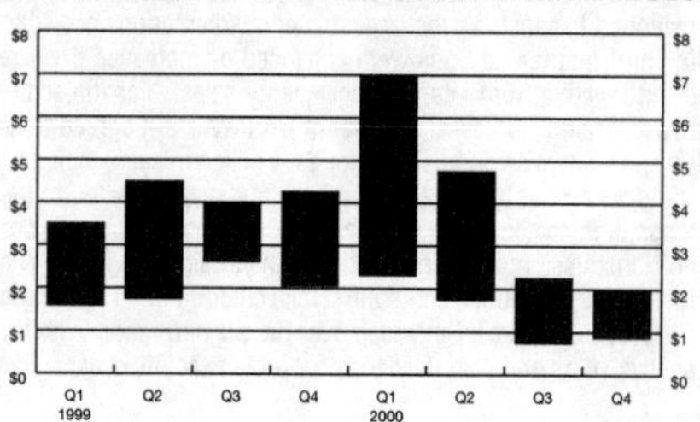

OneLink Communications Inc.

Southwest Crossing Tech Center, 10340 Viking Dr., Suite 150, Eden Prairie, MN 55344
Tel: 952/996-9000 Fax: 952/942-9424 Web site: http://www.onelink.com

OneLink Communications Inc., based in Minneapolis, specializes in transforming telecommunications data into visual business intelligence that enables business leaders to make more-informed decisions. The company markets its TeleSmart Data Services solution to telecommunications network providers, who use the service to build and/or enhance business customer relationships and increase customer satisfaction, loyalty, and retention.

EARNINGS HISTORY *

Year Ended Dec 31	Operating Revenue/Sales (dollars in thousands)	Net Earnings (dollars in thousands)	Return on Revenue (percent)	Return on Equity (percent)	Net Earnings (dollars per share†)	Cash Dividend (dollars per share†)	Market Price Range (dollars per share†)
1999	1,850	(1,528)	NM	(36.1)	(0.23)	—	3.63–1.13
1998 ¶	1,417	(924)	(65.2)	NM	(0.18)	—	2.88–0.16
1997 #	976	(2,507)	NM	NM	(0.71)	—	2.75–1.00
1996 **	1,099	(1,897)	NM	NM	(0.65)	—	4.13–1.38
1995 ††	704	(1,055)	NM	(32.4)	(0.46)	—	5.25–3.25

* Revenue figures have been restated for continuing operations.
† Trading began April 28, 1995.
¶ Income figures for 1998 include gain of $216,878/$0.04 from discontinued operations and their disposal.
\# Income figures for 1997 include loss of $1,140,667/($0.32) from discontinued operations and their disposal.
** Figures for 1996 have not been restated for continuing operations.
†† Figures for 1995 have not been restated for continuing operations.

BALANCE SHEET

Assets	12/31/99 (dollars in thousands)	12/31/98 (dollars in thousands)	Liabilities	12/31/99 (dollars in thousands)	12/31/98 (dollars in thousands)
Current (CAE 3,729 and 420)	4,170	651	Current (STD 0 and 3)	1,068	577
Property and equipment	1,115	269	Stockholders' equity*	4,229	358
Deposits	11	15	TOTAL	5,297	935
TOTAL	5,297	935			

* $0.01 par common; 50,000,000 authorized; 9,254,018 and 5,015,607 issued and outstanding.

RECENT QUARTERS / **PRIOR-YEAR RESULTS**

	Quarter End	Revenue ($000)	Earnings ($000)	EPS ($)	Prior-Year Revenue ($000)	Prior-Year Earnings ($000)	Prior-Year EPS ($)
Q3	09/30/2000	583	(839)	(0.09)	501	(222)	(0.03)
Q2	06/30/2000	549	(854)	(0.09)	409	(281)	(0.04)
Q1	03/31/2000	520	(861)	(0.09)	478	(253)	(0.05)
Q4	12/31/99	462	(772)	(0.10)	332	(145)	(0.03)
	SUM	2,115	(3,325)	(0.37)	1,720	(902)	(0.15)

PRIOR YEAR: Q3 earnings include gain of $78,206/$0.02 from discontinued operations.

RECENT EVENTS

In **January 2000** the company announced the completion of a private placement of 2 million shares of its common stock resulting in proceeds of $3,500,000. The placement was targeted at new investors, specifically to investor groups in California. The company was planning to use the proceeds to develop and implement enhancements to its TeleSmart Web product, as well as for designing additional Internet products to complement TeleSmart Web. In **February** OneLink executed a five-year extension of its contract with U S WEST (NYSE: USW). Under the new terms of the agreement, U S WEST was to continue to provide TeleSmart services to its business customers under its Call Reports brand. In addition, U S WEST took a minority equity stake in OneLink. In **March** the company signed a consulting contract to implement its TeleSmart Web business intelligence service for Bell Atlantic—the fourth incumbent local exchange carrier (ILEC) to offer TeleSmart as a value-added service to business customers—as well as another unidentified local exchange carrier. In **May** the company announced a new service called TeleFlash—a weekly e-mail to business customers that contains summary reports about the number of calls received on their telephone lines from the previous week, including how many calls were answered, busy, or unanswered along with additional analysis of their weekly call activity. **Sept. 30:** Year-to-date revenue grew 19 percent over the first nine months of 1999. During third quarter, OneLink's technical development team completed nearly 90 percent of the systems integration work needed to enable Verizon to launch the TeleSmart Web product in its territories subject to testing and negotiation of a definitive service agreement. Unfortunately, August labor difficulties at Verizon delayed their ability to launch the product. TeleSmart Web continued to be available to business customers of Qwest, under the "Call Reports OnLine" brand, and Cincinnati Bell, under the "Call Analysis Online" brand. The company was designing aggressive marketing programs to build awareness and promote trial of the product, among businesses that use the phone as their primary revenue generator, through appointments, reservations, and orders.

OFFICERS

Ronald E. Eibensteiner
Chairman

Paul F. Lidsky
President and CEO

Kirk C. Danzl
Chief Technology Officer

Gregory H. Mohn
VP-Business Development

Kaye R. O'Leary
CFO

INVESTOR RELATIONS: Paul Lidsky
BUSINESS DEVELOPMENT: Gregory H. Mohn

DIRECTORS

Ronald E. Eibensteiner
Wyncrest Capital Inc., Minneapolis

Tom Kieffer

Paul F. Lidsky

John F. Stapleton
Advanced BioSurfaces Inc.

Vin Weber
Clark & Weinstock Inc., Washington, D.C.

MAJOR SHAREHOLDERS

Perkins Capital Management Inc., 23.4%
Wayzata, MN

Ronald E. Eibensteiner, 13.5%

Fargo Investments L.P., 9.5%
Los Angeles

Wyncrest Capital, 8.6%
Minneapolis

Wayne W. Mills, 6.7%

All officers and directors as a group (7 persons), 23.1%

SIC CODE

5065 Electronic parts and eqp, whsle

MISCELLANEOUS

TRANSFER AGENT AND REGISTAR:
American Stock Transfer & Trust Co., New York

TRADED: OTC

SYMBOL: ONEL

STOCKHOLDERS: 1,200

EMPLOYEES: 20

GENERAL COUNSEL:
Maslon Edelman Borman & Brand PLLP, Minneapolis

AUDITORS:
Lund Koehler Cox & Arkema LLP, Minnetonka, MN

INC: MN-1990

ANNUAL MEETING: May

TWO-YEAR QUARTERLY HIGH-LOW STOCK PRICES

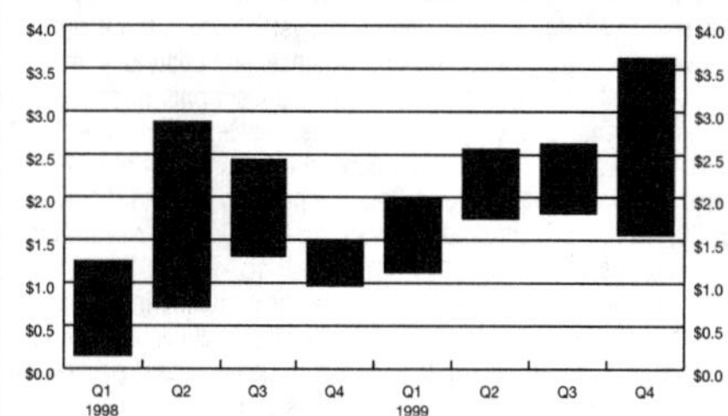

PUB

PUB

Ontrack Data International Inc.

9023 Columbine Rd., Eden Prairie, MN 55347
Tel: 952/937-1107 Fax: 952/937-5815 Web site: http://www.ontrack.com

Ontrack Data International Inc., a leading provider of data availability software and service solutions, helps companies and individuals protect, back up, and recover their valuable data. Using hundreds of proprietary tools and techniques, Ontrack can recover lost or corrupted data from all operating systems and types of storage devices through do-it-yourself, remote, and in-lab capabilities. Ontrack provides award-winning software tools to help prevent critical data loss through a broad line of problem solving, file management, and productivity utilities. Ontrack recently introduced its RapidRecall line of backup and restore software and services for remote users.

EARNINGS HISTORY

Year Ended Dec 31	Operating Revenue/Sales (dollars in thousands)	Net Earnings	Return on Revenue (percent)	Return on Equity	Net Earnings (dollars per share*)	Cash Dividend	Market Price Range
1999 †	43,372	4,677	10.8	9.5	0.48	—	13.25–3.56
1998	35,841	5,198	14.5	12.2	0.53	—	24.38–6.38
1997	35,249	5,656	16.0	14.4	0.58	—	27.75–13.13
1996	26,763	3,124	11.7	9.6	0.46	—	15.33–10.88
1995	17,145	2,205	12.9	NM	0.37	—	

* Shares began trading Oct. 21, 1996.
† Figures for 1999 include results of Mijenix Corp. from July 15, 1999, date of acquisition. Pro forma for full year: revenue $46,925,000; net income $4,328,000/$0.44. Income figures include pretax charge of $675,000 for Legato Systems Inc. terminated-merger costs.

BALANCE SHEET

Assets	12/31/99 (dollars in thousands)	12/31/98	Liabilities	12/31/99 (dollars in thousands)	12/31/98
Current	38,049	39,583	Current	6,810	3,669
(CAE 14,992 and 14,724)			Common equity*	49,031	42,780
Furniture and equipment	6,002	4,019	TOTAL	55,841	46,449
Intangibles	8,467	2,131	* $0.01 par common; 25,000,000 authorized;		
Marketable securities	3,323	716	10,023,000 and 9,697,234 issued and outstanding.		
TOTAL	55,841	46,449			

RECENT QUARTERS / **PRIOR-YEAR RESULTS**

	Quarter End	Revenue ($000)	Earnings ($000)	EPS ($)	Prior-Year Revenue ($000)	Prior-Year Earnings ($000)	Prior-Year EPS ($)
Q3	09/30/2000	13,325	930	0.09	12,047	1,588	0.16
Q2	06/30/2000	12,929	1,413	0.14	9,065	1,077	0.11
Q1	03/31/2000	11,784	1,290	0.12	8,410	900	0.09
Q4	12/31/99	13,850	1,112	0.11	8,797	845	0.09
	SUM	51,888	4,745	0.46	38,319	4,410	0.45

CURRENT: Q4 earnings include pretax charge of $675,000 for terminated-merger costs.

RECENT EVENTS

In **December 1999** the company announced plans to ship EasyUninstall 2000, an easy-to-use software utility program that safely removes unwanted personal computer files and programs. Also available: Fix-It Utilities 2000—the only system-repair utility to support all Microsoft Windows platforms, including Windows 95, 98, NT, and 2000 operating systems. In **January 2000** Ontrack and Legato Systems Inc. (Nasdaq: LGTO), Palo Alto, Calif., terminated a November 1999 agreement that would have merged Ontrack with a wholly owned subsidiary of Legato. The breakup came in the wake of the steep decline in Legato's stock price that followed news of a third-quarter earnings restatement, a slow fourth quarter, and analyst downgrades. In **February** Ontrack released DataEraser V2.0, a data-scrubbing software program designed to completely erase a personal computer's hard disk of all data. The company launched the Ontrack Server Recovery Program, a members-only program for IT professionals offering special data recovery support and services tailored to their needs. The company announced plans for support of the Microsoft Windows 2000 operating system on Ontrack products and data recovery services. In **March** Ontrack released PowerDesk 4, a powerful desktop enhancement utility designed to ease file management in Microsoft Windows 95, 98, NT, and 2000 operating systems. Ontrack formed Electronic Information Management Business Unit to help companies recover electronic information for regulatory proceedings and compliance. In **April** John G. Kinnard & Co. initiated coverage of Ontrack with a BUY rating. The company announced the availability of its Remote Data Recovery service over the Internet for computer systems running under the Sun Solaris operating system. PC Magazine honored software utility program, Ontrack SystemSuite 2000, with its Editors' Choice Award. In **May** Ontrack released the first "do-it-yourself" data recovery solution for data lost as a result of the VBS.LoveLetter worm. EasyRecovery for VBS.LoveLetter Worm software restores MP2, MP3, JPG, and JPEGs to their original usable condition. In **June** the company introduced CaptureIt, a new product that allows organizations engaged in electronic legal discovery to capture electronic evidence without costly hardware downtime; and Internet Cleanup, an Internet data privacy software solution that automatically and permanently removes Internet tracking data such as cookies, history files, cache files, ActiveX controls, and plug-ins. PC World honored Ontrack *continued on page 313*

OFFICERS

Michael W. Rogers
Chairman and CEO

Gary S. Stevens
SVP-Engineering

John M. Bujan
VP, General Counsel, and Secretary

Tony Cueva
VP-North American Sales

Andrea Johnson
VP-Marketing

Jeffery J. May
VP-Product Management

Thomas P. Skiba
VP and CFO

Pierre-Michel Kronenberg
Chief Technology Officer

DIRECTORS

John E. Pence

Michael W. Rogers

Roger D. Shober
Control Data Systems Inc. (retired)

Gary S. Stevens

Robert M. White, Ph.D.
Carnegie Mellon University

MAJOR SHAREHOLDERS

Gary S. Stevens, 18.3%

Michael W. Rogers, 17.6%

John E. Pence, 13.9%
Hot Springs, SD

All officers and directors as a group (10 persons), 51%

SIC CODE

7372 Prepackaged software

MISCELLANEOUS

TRANSFER AGENT AND REGISTAR:
Wells Fargo Bank Minnesota N.A.,
South St. Paul, MN

TRADED: Nasdaq National Market

SYMBOL: ONDI

STOCKHOLDERS: 91

EMPLOYEES: 400

IN MINNESOTA: 230

GENERAL COUNSEL:
Robins, Kaplan, Miller & Ciresi LLP, Minneapolis

AUDITORS:
Grant Thornton LLP, Minneapolis

INC: MN-1985

ANNUAL MEETING: May

FINANCE AND INVESTOR RELATIONS:
Thomas Skiba

RANKINGS

No. 117 CRM Public 200

No. 48 Minnesota Technology Fast 50

SUBSIDIARIES, DIVISIONS, AFFILIATES

CALIFORNIA
940 South Coast Dr.
Suite 225
Costa Mesa, CA 92626

COLORADO
3030 Sterling Circle
Boulder, CO 80301

WASHINGTON, D.C.
1922 Isaac Newton Square
Reston, VA 20190

NEW JERSEY
Gateway Plaza Building
One Harmon Meadow Blvd.
Suite 225
Secaucus, NJ 07094

UNITED KINGDOM
The Pavilions
One Weston Rd.
Kiln Lane
Epsom, Surrey
KT17 1JG
44-1372-741999

GERMANY
Hans-Klemm-Strasse 5
71034 Boeblingen
49-7031-644-00

JAPAN
182 Shinkoh
Iruma, Saitama 358-0055
81-429-32-6365

FRANCE
2, impasse de la Noisette
91371 Verrieres-le-Buisson Ceder 413
France
33-0-1-49-19-22-63

TWO-YEAR QUARTERLY HIGH-LOW STOCK PRICES

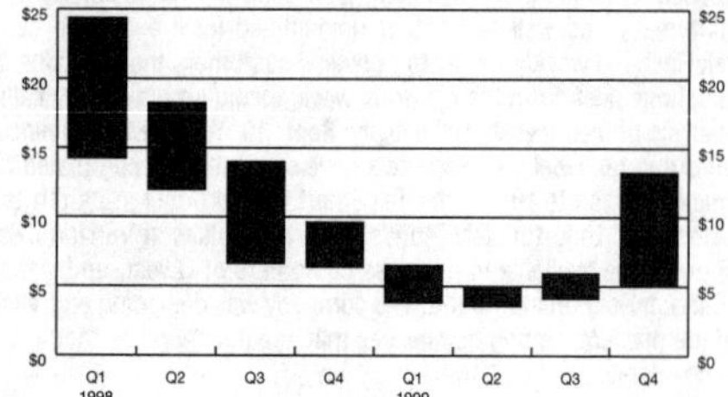

Optical Sensors Inc.

7615 Golden Triangle Dr., Suite A, Eden Prairie, MN 55344
Tel: 952/944-5857 Fax: 952/944-6022 Web site: http://www.opsi.com

Optical Sensors Inc., previously known as Optical Sensors for Medicine, manufactures fiber-optic blood gas sensors that provide a noninvasive method for monitoring a critically ill patient's blood gases. The SensiCath system, a patient-attached, on-demand arterial blood gas monitoring system, provides accurate results within 60 seconds, without drawing blood from the patient.

EARNINGS HISTORY *

Year Ended Dec 31	Operating Revenue/Sales (dollars in thousands)	Net Earnings	Return on Revenue (percent)	Return on Equity	Net Earnings (dollars per share†)	Cash Dividend	Market Price Range
1999	134	(7,785)	NM	NM	(0.88)	—	1.81–0.50
1998	1,019	(11,817)	NM	NM	(1.34)	—	6.00–0.91
1997	141	(11,333)	NM	(56.2)	(1.35)	—	11.50–4.50
1996	163	(9,385)	NM	(30.2)	(1.30)	—	14.88–5.25
1995 ¶	0	(8,131)	NM	NM	(2.70)	—	

* Development-stage company prior to 1998.
† Stock began trading on Feb. 14, 1996.
¶ Pro forma EPS figure for 1995, assuming IPO completed at beginning of period: ($1.05).

BALANCE SHEET

Assets	12/31/99 (dollars in thousands)	12/31/98	Liabilities	12/31/99 (dollars in thousands)	12/31/98
Current (CAE 1,450 and 8,079)	2,838	10,189	Current	837	1,086
Property and equipment	911	1,846	Capital lease obligations	104	495
Patents	530	514	Stockholders' equity*	3,355	10,984
Other	16	17	TOTAL	4,296	12,565
TOTAL	4,296	12,565			

* $0.01 par common; 30,000,000 authorized; 8,935,304 and 8,829,401 issued and outstanding.

RECENT QUARTERS / PRIOR-YEAR RESULTS

	Quarter End	Revenue ($000)	Earnings ($000)	EPS ($)	Prior-Year Revenue ($000)	Prior-Year Earnings ($000)	Prior-Year EPS ($)
Q3	09/30/2000	0	(921)	(0.10)	29	(1,533)	(0.17)
Q2	06/30/2000	0	(1,032)	(0.11)	2	(1,660)	(0.19)
Q1	03/31/2000	0	(2,725)	(0.30)	60	(2,965)	(0.34)
Q4	12/31/99	44	(1,627)	(0.18)	220	(2,923)	(0.33)
	SUM	44	(6,306)	(0.70)	311	(9,081)	(1.03)

RECENT EVENTS

In **December 1999** the company began mass deployment of FiberPath Release 1.5. In **February 2000** Optical Sensors signed a non-binding letter of intent with a major supplier of medical products and services (a confidentiality understanding precludes identifying the company) to negotiate a definitive agreement for Optical Sensors' CapnoProbe product and technology. CEO LaPlante said, "This potential partner would add exceptional strength and significant resources to the planned commercialization of our product, which incorporates the power of our fiber optic platform into a new hand-held instrument to measure tissue hypoxia." [Agreement discontinued in May.] In **March** the company received a commitment for $3 million in new financing from a group of private investors. LaPlante said, "With these additional funds, we will be continuing with our ongoing studies comparing CapnoProbe data to various critical care parameters including arterial-venous gap, cardiac output, lactate and other tissue CO2 devices." In **April** another patent was issued in the Institute of Critical Care Medicine patent portfolio relating to Optical Sensors' CapnoProbe product. U.S. Patent No. 6,055,447 provides broad coverage and protection of the method and apparatus for using CO2 sensors anywhere in the mouth, nose, or pharynx to assess impairment of a patient's blood circulation. In **May** Optical Sensors discontinued negotiations regarding distribution rights for CapnoProbe technology with the company that had signed a nonbinding letter of intent in February. Optical Sensors was continuing to discuss with other companies a potential transaction that would recognize the value of its technology, and was still planning to prepare the CapnoProbe product for FDA clearance and subsequent commercialization. In **August** the company received $500,000 in proceeds from the sale of 1 million shares of newly created Series A Preferred Stock to a private investment organization. Optical Sensors also received a commitment whereby it may request the purchase by the investment organization of up to 3,333,334 additional shares of Series A Preferred Stock for an aggregate additional purchase price of $1 million. In **November** Optical Sensors announced that, following the end of the third quarter, it had received $500,000 in proceeds from the sale of 1,333,334 shares of additional Series A Preferred Stock to that same private investment organization.

OFFICERS

Paulita M. LaPlante
President and CEO

Victor Kimball
VP-Strategic Planning/Product Devel.

Wesley G. Peterson
VP-Finance, CFO, and Secretary

DIRECTORS

Richard B. Egen
NephRx Corp., Chicago

Samuel B. Humphries
American Medical Systems, Minneapolis

Paulita LaPlante

Richard J. Meelia
The Kendall Co., Mansfield, MA

Demetre M. Nicoloff, M.D.
Cardiac Surgical Associates, Minneapolis

Gary A. Peterson
Baton Development Inc.

MAJOR SHAREHOLDERS

Special Situations Funds, 18.6%
New York

Circle F Ventures LLC/Hayden R. Fleming, 17.4%
Scottsdale, AZ

Norwest Venture Capital, 9.1%
Minneapolis

All officers and directors as a group (8 persons), 6%

SIC CODE

3841 Surgical and medical instruments

MISCELLANEOUS

TRANSFER AGENT AND REGISTAR:
Wells Fargo Bank Minnesota N.A., South St. Paul, MN

TRADED: Nasdaq National Market

SYMBOL: OPSI

STOCKHOLDERS: 209

EMPLOYEES: 23

GENERAL COUNSEL:
Oppenheimer Wolff & Donnelly LLP, Minneapolis

AUDITORS:
Ernst & Young LLP, Minneapolis

INC: DE-1996

FOUNDED: 1989

ANNUAL MEETING: May

TWO-YEAR QUARTERLY HIGH-LOW STOCK PRICES

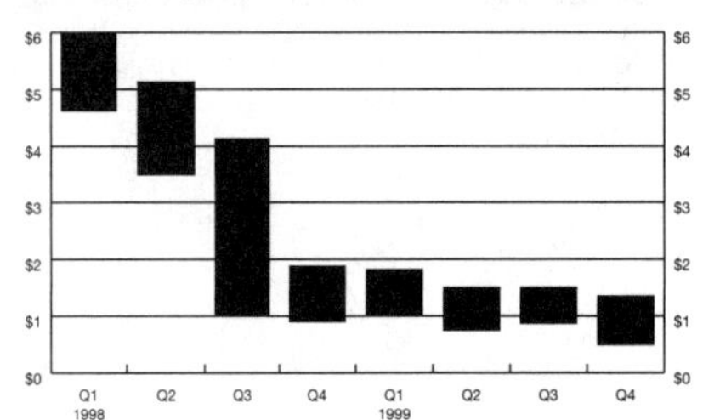

Orphan Medical Inc.

13911 Ridgedale Dr., Suite 475, Minnetonka, MN 55305
Tel: 952/513-6900 Fax: 952/541-9209 Web site: http://www.orphan.com

Orphan Medical Inc. is dedicated to serving people with inadequately treated or uncommon diseases. The company acquires, develops, and markets products of high medical value to well-defined patient populations treated by health care professionals.

EARNINGS HISTORY

Year Ended Dec 31	Operating Revenue/Sales (dollars in thousands)	Net Earnings (dollars in thousands)	Return on Revenue (percent)	Return on Equity (percent)	Net Earnings (dollars per share)	Cash Dividend (dollars per share)	Market Price Range (dollars per share)
1999	6,457	(5,221)	NM	NM	(0.90)	—	10.00–4.75
1998	5,048	(8,237)	NM	NM	(1.36)	—	13.88–4.75
1997	655	(11,388)	NM	NM	(1.87)	—	9.63–3.50
1996 *	37	(7,617)	NM	(51.5)	(1.43)	—	11.13–5.38
1995 †	0	(2,998)	NM	(40.0)	(0.80)	—	8.50–4.88

* Prior-period comparison: net loss $5,157,947/($1.89) for the 12 months ended Dec. 31, 1995.
† Figures are for six-month stub period from July 1, 1995, through Dec. 31, 1995.

BALANCE SHEET

Assets	12/31/99 (dollars in thousands)	12/31/98 (dollars in thousands)	Liabilities	12/31/99 (dollars in thousands)	12/31/98 (dollars in thousands)
Current (CAE 205 and 2,980)	5,841	8,746	Current	2,680	3,471
Property and equipment	353	301	Stockholders' equity*	3,561	5,576
Other	47		TOTAL	6,241	9,047
TOTAL	6,241	9,047			

* $0.01 par common; 25,000,000 authorized; 6,606,207 and 6,560,096 issued and outstanding.

RECENT QUARTERS / **PRIOR-YEAR RESULTS**

	Quarter End	Revenue ($000)	Earnings ($000)	EPS ($)	Prior-Year Revenue ($000)	Prior-Year Earnings ($000)	Prior-Year EPS ($)
Q3	09/30/2000	2,611	(1,724)	(0.23)	1,428	(1,229)	(0.21)
Q2	06/30/2000	3,025	(1,005)	(0.15)	1,524	(1,504)	(0.25)
Q1	03/31/2000	2,742	(898)	(0.15)	1,402	(1,521)	(0.25)
Q4	12/31/99	2,103	(967)	(0.18)	1,505	(1,926)	(0.32)
	SUM	10,481	(4,594)	(0.71)	5,859	(6,180)	(1.04)

RECENT EVENTS

In **November 1999** the U.S. Senate approved legislation (S 1561) directing the Attorney General to make illicitly manufactured gamma hydroxybutyrate (GHB) an illegal substance, while making the company's medically formulated GHB product, Xyrem (sodium oxybate) oral solution, available to treat patients with the sleeping disorder narcolepsy. In **January 2000** results of two clinical trials showed measurable benefits from Xyrem in the treatment of two primary symptoms of narcolepsy: cataplexy, the sudden loss of muscle control precipitated by emotion; and EDS, excessive daytime sleepiness. In **February** President Clinton signed federal legislation directing the U.S. Attorney General to use her emergency scheduling authority to make gamma hydroxybutyrate (GHB) a Schedule I substance within 60 days. (Schedule I is the designation by which illegal drugs are controlled.) The bill further directed the Attorney General to treat GHB products being studied under FDA-approved protocols (such as Xyrem) as Schedule III substances. The company entered into a definitive purchase agreement for the sale of 1.265 million shares of newly issued common stock to OrbiMed Advisors LLC for $10.1 million ($8 per share). It then obtained $1 million in additional financing through a private placement of 100,000 shares to the DG Lux Lacuna Apo BioTech Fund, which is managed by Medical Strategy. Proceeds of the investments were intended to fund working capital and the ongoing development of Xyrem (sodium oxybate) oral solution. In **March** Israel's Ministry of Health approved Busulfex (busulfan) Injection for marketing in that country. Orphan signed an international distribution agreement with IDIS World Medicines, United Kingdom, to distribute all of Orphan Medical's approved products in countries where the company was not currently represented. In **August** the FDA accepted Orphan's supplemental new drug application (NDA) for Antizol (fomepizole) Injection for the treatment of methanol poisoning and granted the application priority review status, which obligates the FDA to a goal of acting on the NDA within six months from the date of submission. **Sept. 30:** Nine-month revenue of $8.4 million represented a 92 percent increase from prior year. "Our revenue through nine months of this year significantly exceeds revenue from all of 1999," commented CEO Bullion. Sales of Antizol (fomepizole) Injection again exceeded expectations. In **October** Orphan Medical submitted a new drug application (NDA) to the FDA for Xyrem (sodium oxybate) oral solution as a treatment for the symptoms of narcolepsy. The FDA also granted that NDA priority review status.

OFFICERS

John Howell Bullion
Chairman and CEO

William Houghton, M.D.
COO

Timothy McGrath
CFO

Patti A. Engel
VP-Marketing/Sales

Dayton T. Reardan, Ph.D.
VP-Regulatory Affairs

DIRECTORS

John Howell Bullion

Michael Greene
UBS Capital LLC

W. Leigh Thompson, M.D., Ph.D.
Profound Quality Resources Ltd., South Carolina

Julius Vida, Ph.D.
Vida International Pharmaceutical Consultants

William M. Wardell, M.D., Ph.D.
Covance

Lawrence C. Weaver, Ph.D.
College of Pharmacy, Univ. of Minnesota (retired)

MAJOR SHAREHOLDERS

UBS Capital II LLC, 15.4%
New York

OrbiMed Advisors Inc., 15.3%
New York

John Howell Bullion, 5.5%

All officers and directors as a group (10 persons), 9.1%

SIC CODE

2834 Pharmaceutical preparations

MISCELLANEOUS

TRANSFER AGENT AND REGISTAR:
Wells Fargo Bank Minnesota N.A.,
South St. Paul, MN

TRADED: Nasdaq National Market

SYMBOL: ORPH

STOCKHOLDERS: 275

EMPLOYEES: 53

PART TIME: 6

AUDITORS:
Ernst & Young LLP, Minneapolis

INC: MN-1994

ANNUAL MEETING: May

RANKINGS

No. 199 CRM Public 200

TWO-YEAR QUARTERLY HIGH-LOW STOCK PRICES

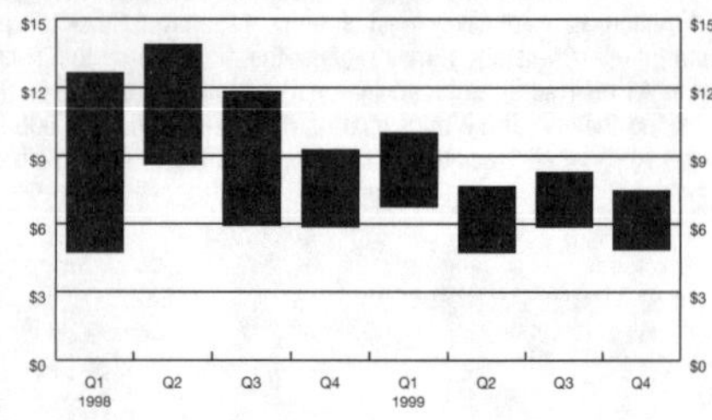

Osmonics Inc.

5951 Clearwater Dr., Minnetonka, MN 55343
Tel: 952/933-2277 Fax: 952/298-8611 Web site: http://www.osmonics.com

Osmonics Inc. is a manufacturer of high technology equipment, controls and components that purify water, separate and handle fluids, remove impurities, concentrate wastes and enable clean water to be recycled or discharged to the environment. Core products serve applications in three markets: specialty filtration and separations, process water treatment and household water treatment. Founded in 1969, Osmonics is the world's largest vertically integrated manufacturer of crossflow membranes and equipment. The company supplies a broad line of water treatment and purification products and sells its products through a global network of distributors, original equipment manufacturers and system integrators.

EARNINGS HISTORY

Year Ended Dec 31	Operating Revenue/Sales (dollars in thousands)	Net Earnings	Return on Revenue (percent)	Return on Equity	Net Earnings (dollars per share)	Cash Dividend	Market Price Range
1999 *	184,671	964	0.5	0.9	0.07	—	12.25–7.50
1998 †	177,819	(1,053)	(0.6)	(1.0)	(0.08)	—	17.50–7.75
1997 ¶	164,905	9,793	5.9	9.6	0.70	—	22.50–13.63
1996	155,946	13,467	8.6	13.7	0.95	—	24.88–18.25
1995	130,783	11,879	9.1	NM	0.84	—	21.25–13.25

* Pro forma figures for 1999 to include results of July 1, 1999, acquisition ZyzaTech Water Systems Inc. from Jan. 1: revenue $190.497 million; earnings $1.021 million/$0.07.
† Income figures for 1998 include special charges of $9,988,000 pretax, $7,569,000/($0.54) after-tax.
¶ Income figures for 1997 include special charges of $1,448,000 pretax, ($0.07) after-tax; and gain of $1,330,000/$0.09—recovery on discontinued operations.

BALANCE SHEET

Assets	12/31/99 (dollars in thousands)	12/31/98	Liabilities	12/31/99 (dollars in thousands)	12/31/98
Current (CAE 1,807 and 576)	83,512	89,381	Current (STD 21,312 and 28,177)	51,351	55,405
Property and equipment	58,330	56,813	Long-term debt	32,201	31,665
			Deferred taxes	6,256	4,806
Restricted cash	325	560	Other	16	18
Goodwill	48,826	43,927	Stkhldrs' equity*	104,542	102,155
Investments	1,008	1,016	TOTAL	194,366	194,049
Other	2,365	2,352			
TOTAL	194,366	194,049			

* $0.01 par common; 50,000,000 authorized; 14,262,130 and 13,991,291 issued and outstanding.

RECENT QUARTERS / PRIOR-YEAR RESULTS

	Quarter End	Revenue ($000)	Earnings ($000)	EPS ($)	Prior-Year Revenue ($000)	Prior-Year Earnings ($000)	Prior-Year EPS ($)
Q3	09/30/2000	47,592	1,019	0.07	46,898	1,458	0.10
Q2	06/30/2000	49,399	1,848	0.13	46,457	2,139	0.15
Q1	03/31/2000	50,285	1,592	0.11	44,521	1,582	0.11
Q4	12/31/99	46,795	(4,215)	(0.30)	43,710	1,089	0.08
	SUM	194,071	244	0.02	181,586	6,268	0.44

CURRENT: Q1 earnings include pretax special charge of $0.25 million. Q4 earnings include special charge of $3.655 million pretax/($0.27) after-tax, for in-process R&D and other.
PRIOR YEAR: Q3 earnings include credit of $1.080 million pretax/$0.01 after-tax, net gain on sale of operation, special charges, and restructuring.

RECENT EVENTS

In **December 1999** Osmonics sold two product lines to ResinTech Inc. of Cherry Hill, N.J. The two product lines, the Aries DI Loop and the associated disposable cartridges, were manufactured at the company's Rockland, Mass., facility. In **January 2000** Osmonics announced plans to close its Phoenix facility by the end of the third quarter 2000—part of a continuing effort to rationalize product lines and reduce excess manufacturing capacity. In **June** Osmonics was issued a warning letter by the FDA related to Osmonics' Millenium Portable Reverse Osmosis System manufactured in its Kent, Wash., facility. These units produce pure water for kidney dialysis. The company was addressing the issues, and planned to file a response outlining the appropriate corrective actions within the FDA's timeline. "We take the FDA's letter very seriously," said CEO Spatz. "We are taking immediate actions to resolve the issues identified in their audit and to improve our operation. We certainly do not want to minimize the findings, but we want the public to know that at no time have the pure water aspects of our medical systems been compromised or has any patient been put at risk." The Osmonics medical dialysis line was expanded in mid-1999 by the acquisition of ZyzaTech, a leader in pure water systems for dialysis. The Millenium Portable Reverse Osmosis System product line, part of the ZyzaTech acquisition, represented less than 1 percent of total Osmonics revenue. In **August** the FDA said that efforts taken by the company to resolve quality reporting errors appeared to be acceptable. The Orec Test Chamber business was sold to CCS Instruments Inc. as part of Osmonics' ongoing business ratio-

continued on page 313

OFFICERS

D. Dean Spatz
Chairman and CEO

Edward J. Fierko
President and COO

Roger S. Miller
SVP-Corporate Sales/Marketing

Keith B. Robinson
CFO and SVP-Finance/Administration

Phil Rolchigo
VP-Research/Development

Ruth Carol Spatz
Corporate Secretary

DIRECTORS

Ralph E. Crump
Crump Industrial Group, Trumbull, CT

William Eykamp
membrane consultant, Medford, MA

Charles W. Palmer
private investor

Verity C. Smith
Veritec Consultants

Michael L. Snow
Maslon Edelman Borman & Brand PLLP, Minneapolis

D. Dean Spatz

Ruth Carol Spatz

MAJOR SHAREHOLDERS

Heartland Advisors Inc., 9.5%
Milwaukee

State Farm Mutual Automobile Insurance Co., 9.5%
Bloomington, IL

Charles W. Palmer, 9.2%

D. Dean Spatz, 7.6%

Ruth Carol Spatz, 7.4%

Dimensional Fund Advisors Inc., 5.4%
Santa Monica, CA

All officers and directors as a group (15 persons), 27.7%

SIC CODE

3556 Food products machinery

3559 Special industry machinery, nec

3569 General industrial machinery, nec

3589 Service industry machinery, nec

MISCELLANEOUS

TRANSFER AGENT AND REGISTAR:
Wells Fargo Bank Minnesota N.A., South St. Paul, MN

TRADED: NYSE

SYMBOL: OSM

STOCKHOLDERS: 1,862

EMPLOYEES: 1,436

GENERAL COUNSEL:
Maslon Edelman Borman & Brand PLLP, Minneapolis

AUDITORS:
Deloitte & Touche LLP, Minneapolis

INC: MN-1969

ANNUAL MEETING: May

INVESTOR RELATIONS: Keith B. Robinson

CORPORATE COMMUNICATIONS: Kristi A. Schmitz

RANKINGS

No. 74 CRM Public 200

SUBSIDIARIES, DIVISIONS, AFFILIATES

DOMESTIC LOCATIONS

Rockford, Ill.
815/964-9421

Vista, Calif.
760/598-1800

Milwaukee, Wisc.
262/238-4400

Escondido, Calif.
760/735-6224

Minnetonka, Minn.
612/933-2277

Westborough, Mass.
508/366-8212

Fairfield, N.J.
973/575-8388

Liverpool, N.Y.
315/453-6100

FOREIGN LOCATIONS

Le Mee sur Seine, France

Tokoyo, Japan

Singapore

Aarau, Switzerland

Bangkok 10110, Thailand

Tsimshatsui, Kowloon, Hong Kong

Shanghai, China

TWO-YEAR QUARTERLY HIGH-LOW STOCK PRICES

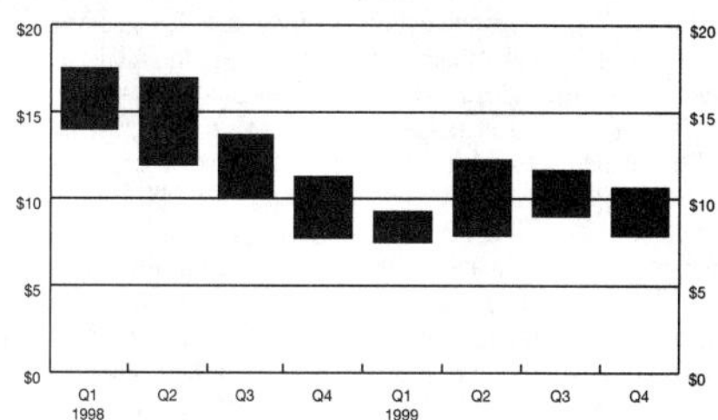

PUB

PUB

Otter Tail Power Company

215 S. Cascade St., P.O. Box 496, Fergus Falls, MN 56537
Tel: 218/739-8200 Fax: 218/739-8218 Web site: http://www.otpco.com

Otter Tail Power Co. is a diversified corporation that provides electricity and energy services to nearly a quarter million people in Minnesota, North Dakota, and South Dakota. Otter Tail's subsidiary Varistar Corporation, operates plastics, health services, manufacturing, construction, telecommunications, and transportation businesses with customers across the United States.

EARNINGS HISTORY

Year Ended Dec 31	Operating Revenue/Sales (dollars in thousands)	Net Earnings (dollars in thousands)	Return on Revenue (percent)	Return on Equity (percent)	Net Earnings (dollars per share*)	Cash Dividend (dollars per share*)	Market Price Range (dollars per share*)
1999 †	464,577	44,977	9.7	17.4	1.79	0.99	22.78–17.00
1998 ¶	433,152	34,520	8.0	14.3	1.36	0.96	21.38–15.06
1997	399,327	32,346	8.1	14.3	1.29	0.93	19.19–15.00
1996	370,933	30,624	8.3	14.4	1.23	0.90	19.31–15.88
1995	326,329	28,945	8.9	14.4	1.19	0.88	18.88–15.38

* Per-share amounts restated to reflect 2-for1 stock split distributed March 15, 2000.
† Income figures for 1999 include pretax gain of $14.469 million on sale of radio station assets.
¶ Income figures for 1998 include special charge of $9.522 million (pretax); and gain of $3.819 million/$0.16, cumulative effect of accounting change.

BALANCE SHEET

Assets	12/31/99 (dollars in thousands)	12/31/98 (dollars in thousands)	Liabilities	12/31/99 (dollars in thousands)	12/31/98 (dollars in thousands)
Current (CAE 24,762 and 3,919)	119,936	98,788	Current (STD 5,948 and 6,618)	77,314	63,232
Plant	502,956	500,186	Noncurrent	26,514	22,842
Deferred debits	8,942	10,882	Deferred credits	121,330	124,585
Investments	19,502	20,612	Long-term debt	176,437	181,046
Intangibles	23,311	21,176	Preferred stockholders' equity	33,500	38,831
Other	6,141	3,968	Common stockholders' equity*	245,693	225,076
TOTAL	680,788	655,612	TOTAL	680,788	655,612

* $5 par common; 50,000,000 authorized; 23,849,974 and 23,759,008 issued and outstanding.

RECENT QUARTERS / **PRIOR-YEAR RESULTS**

	Quarter End	Revenue ($000)	Earnings ($000)	EPS ($)	Prior-Year Revenue ($000)	Prior-Year Earnings ($000)	Prior-Year EPS ($)
Q3	09/30/2000	143,634	10,602	0.42	123,619	10,380	0.41
Q2	06/30/2000	133,729	9,160	0.36	112,397	7,146	0.27
Q1	03/31/2000	134,755	10,417	0.42	111,485	9,249	0.36
Q4	12/31/99	117,076	18,202	0.74	115,708	10,870	0.43
	SUM	529,194	48,381	1.95	463,209	37,645	1.48

CURRENT: Q4 earnings include pretax gain of $14,469,000 from sale of radio station assets.

RECENT EVENTS

Dec. 31, 1999: The company set records in 1999 for earnings per share and for both electric utility and diversified operating revenue. Strong power pool sales during the summer months offset reductions in retail electric revenue. Diversified operating revenue represented almost 50 percent of total operating revenue. As a group, these diversified operations continued to show growth in operating income, with strong performance from manufacturing and selling PVC pipe, stamping and fabricating metal parts, electrical construction contracting, transportation, and telecommunications. **March 31, 2000:** Electric operating income declined in the first quarter, primarily because of increased purchased power costs. The 20.9 percent revenue increase, as well as the 6-cent EPS increase, were attributed to strong demand within the PVC pipe industry and the January acquisition of an additional PVC pipe manufacturer. In **June** Otter Tail sold its model for an Internet-based software technology designed to facilitate and ensure full, robust customer choice in the retail electric market to Retx.com, an Atlanta-based e-business provider to the retail energy industry. **Sept. 30:** Third-quarter operating income increased to $19.2 million from last year's $18.9 million, while total revenue increased 16.2 percent to $143.6 million. Operating income for the electric utility increased $811,000, reflecting increased retail revenue and continued strong power pool margins. The plastic segment remained consistent with the quarter of 1999. Manufacturing increased $413,000 because of increased sales at the metal-parts stamping and automotive frame-straightening subsidiaries. Operating income increased $1.2 million for the health services segment because of increased margins and more imaging scans performed. Third-quarter operating income from the other business operation segment was $2 million less than in 1999 due, in part, to last year's sale of telecommunication company investments and less contracted work at the construction companies during 2000. In **October** Otter Tail and UtiliCorp, an international energy an services company headquartered in Kansas City, Mo., told the Federal Energy Regulatory Commission that they were intending to join the Midwest Independent Transmission System Operator. Otter Tail said in its *continued on page 313*

OFFICERS

John C. MacFarlane
Chairman, President, and CEO

John D. Erickson
EVP, CEO and Treas.

Marlowe E. Johnson
VP-Delivery Customer Service

Douglas L. Kjellerup
VP and COO-Energy Delivery

Lauris N. Molbert
VP and COO-Varistar

Rodney C.H. Scheel
VP-Delivery Systems

Ward L. Uggerud
VP, COO-Energy Supply

George Koeck
Corporate Secretary and General Counsel

Jeffrey J. Legge
Controller-Utility

Charles E. Brunko
Asst. Secretary, Asst. Treasurer

DIRECTORS

Thomas M. Brown
Dorsey & Whitney LLP (retired)

Dayle Dietz
North Dakota State College of Science (retired)

Dennis R. Emmen
Otter Tail Power Co. (retired)

Maynard D. Helgaas
Midwest Agri-Development Corp., Jamestown, ND

Arvid R. Liebe
Liebe Drug Inc., Milbank, SD

John C. MacFarlane

Kenneth L. Nelson
Kenny's Candy Co. Inc., Perham, MN

Nathan I. Partain
Duff & Phelps Investment Management Co., Chicago

Robert N. Spolum
Melroe Co. (retired)

MAJOR SHAREHOLDERS

Otter Tail Power Co. ESOP c/o Mellon Bank N.A., 7.4%
Pittsburgh

Cascade Investment LLC, 5%
Kirkland, WA

All officers and directors as a group (13 persons), 0.5%

SIC CODE

4911 Electric services
6719 Holding companies, nec

MISCELLANEOUS

TRANSFER AGENT AND REGISTAR:
Wells Fargo Bank Minnesota N.A., South St. Paul, MN

TRADED: Nasdaq National Market

SYMBOL: OTTR

STOCKHOLDERS: 13,438

EMPLOYEES: 1,973

GENERAL COUNSEL:
Dorsey & Whitney PLLP, Minneapolis
Hoff, Svingen, Athens & Russell, Fergus Falls, MN

AUDITORS:
Deloitte & Touche LLP, Minneapolis

INC: MN-1907

ANNUAL MEETING: April

COMMUNICATIONS: Cris Anderson

HUMAN RESOURCES: Tom Brause

RANKINGS

No. 51 CRM Public 200
No. 23 CRM Performance 100

TWO-YEAR QUARTERLY HIGH-LOW STOCK PRICES

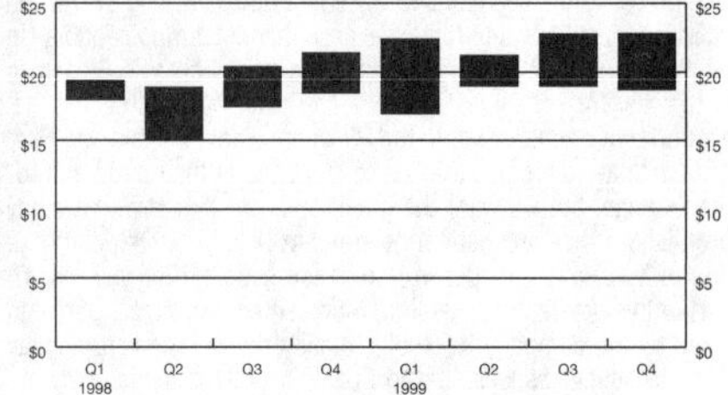

Oxboro Medical International Inc.

13828 Lincoln St. N.E., Ham Lake, MN 55304
Tel: 763/755-9516 Fax: 763/755-9466 Web site: http://www.oxboromedical.com

Oxboro Medical International Inc. develops, manufactures, and markets medical and surgical products. Some of Oxboro Medical's products are silicone loops, color-coding identification roll and sheet tape, radiopaque clamp covers (silicone and fabric), suture aid booties, instrument guards (for protecting instruments during sterilization), pin covers (for Steinmann Pins/K-wires), bulldog occluders, endoscope guards, catheter/tube holders, syringe recap pads, and guards for minimally invasive surgical instruments.

EARNINGS HISTORY *

Year Ended Sept 30	Operating Revenue/Sales (dollars in thousands)	Net Earnings	Return on Revenue (percent)	Return on Equity	Net Earnings (dollars per share†)	Cash Dividend	Market Price Range
1999 ¶	4,513	(948)	(21.0)	(44.4)	(2.09)	—	9.38–2.38
1998 #	4,451	(1,454)	(32.7)	(51.2)	(2.61)	—	11.25–4.69
1997	4,802	(88)	(1.8)	(2.1)	(0.16)	—	7.50–4.38
1996	4,150	98	2.4	2.3	0.18	—	8.75–5.31
1995	3,877	213	5.5	5.2	0.40	—	8.44–6.25

* On June 30, 1999, the company sold its Oxboro Outdoors subsidiary. Figures for 1999 and 1998 (only) have been restated accordingly.
† Per-share amounts restated to reflect 1-for-5 reverse stock split effected Aug. 13, 1999.
¶ Income figures for 1999 include net loss of $1.022 million/($2.26) from discontinued operations and gain on their disposal.
# Income figures for 1998 include loss of $1.372 million/($2.46) from discontinued operations.

BALANCE SHEET

Assets	09/30/99 (dollars in thousands)	09/30/98	Liabilities	09/30/99 (dollars in thousands)	09/30/98
Current (CAE 303 and 71)	2,415	2,920	Current (STD 45 and 8)	899	1,259
Property, plant, and equipment	1,041	1,243	Long-term obligation	428	379
Cash surrender value of life insurance	100	287	Deferred income taxes	94	103
Other		128	Stockholders' equity*	2,135	2,837
TOTAL	3,556	4,578	TOTAL	3,556	4,578

* $0.01 par common; 2,000,000 authorized; 742,468 and 487,716 issued and outstanding.

RECENT QUARTERS / **PRIOR-YEAR RESULTS**

	Quarter End	Revenue ($000)	Earnings ($000)	EPS ($)	Revenue ($000)	Earnings ($000)	EPS ($)
Q4	09/30/2000	1,140	178	0.13	1,118	262	0.59
Q3	06/30/2000	1,184	241	0.18	1,155	(148)	(0.34)
Q2	03/31/2000	1,109	223	0.17	1,199	(1,014)	(2.35)
Q1	12/31/99	1,154	263	0.27	1,041	(47)	(0.10)
	SUM	4,587	905	0.74	4,513	(948)	(2.19)

PRIOR YEAR: Q4 earnings include gain of $105,000/$0.24 from disposal of discontinued operations. Q3 earnings include loss of $193,446/($0.44) from discontinued operations. Q2 earnings include loss of $826,706/($1.91) from discontinued operations. Q1 earnings include loss of $106,615/($0.22) from discontinued operations.

RECENT EVENTS

In **August 2000** the company filed a registration statement with the SEC in connection with its proposed offering of warrants enabling holders to purchase up to 417,794 shares of the company's $.01 par value common stock ("incentive warrants"), which it was planning to offer to holders of the common stock purchase warrants issued in connection with the Sept. 1, 1999, rights offering. **Sept. 30:** For the fiscal year, the company earned record income from continuing operations of $904,670. *** In **October** the company said that gross proceeds from the sale of Oxboro Common Stock in the Incentive Warrant offering were $1.1 million. Chairman Brimmer noted, "We're proud of our record performance for 2000, which reflected $1,071,295 EBITDA compared to $334,185 for 1999, an increase of 221 percent for the year, representing the fruition of a major turnaround effort. This excellent performance, combined with our current base of over $3 million in cash and investments, provides an excellent base for growth.

OFFICERS

Kenneth W. Brimmer
Chairman

J. David Berkley
President

Linda Erickson
CFO

DIRECTORS

Kenneth W. Brimmer
Active IQ Technologies Inc., Minnetonka, MN

Gary Copperud
CMM Properties LLC

Robert Garin
consultant, Plymouth, MN

MAJOR SHAREHOLDERS

CMM Properties LLC/Gary W. Copperud, 30.6%
Fort Collins, CO

Kenneth W. Brimmer, 18.1%
Hopkins, MN

All officers and directors as a group (5 persons), 47.7%

SIC CODE

5047 Medical and hospital equipment, whsle

MISCELLANEOUS

TRANSFER AGENT AND REGISTAR:
Wells Fargo Bank Minnesota N.A.,
South St. Paul, MN

TRADED: Nasdaq SmallCap Market

SYMBOL: OMED

STOCKHOLDERS: 515

EMPLOYEES: 47

IN MINNESOTA: 47

GENERAL COUNSEL:
Lindquist & Vennum PLLP, Minneapolis

AUDITORS:
Grant Thornton LLP, Minneapolis

INC: MN-1978

ANNUAL MEETING:
March

SUBSIDIARIES, DIVISIONS, AFFILIATES

Oxboro Medical Inc.

TWO-YEAR QUARTERLY HIGH-LOW STOCK PRICES

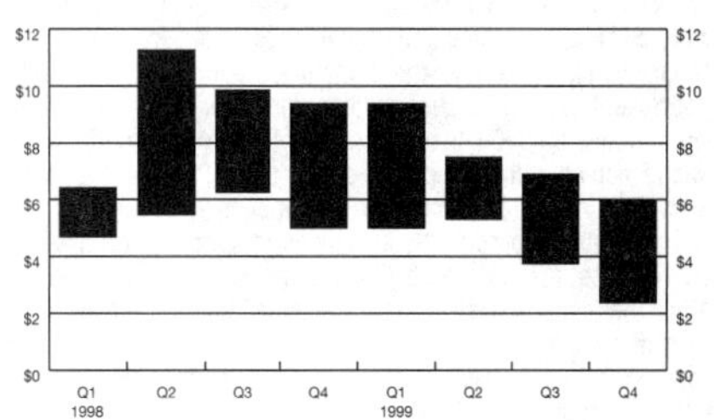

NRG Energy Inc.

continued from page 287 $1.026 billion. The Northern States Power Co. board of directors approved the potential sale in a public offering of up to 18 percent interest in the common stock of subsidiary NRG Energy. The uncertainty prevailing in the stock market during mid-April did not prevent NRG Energy from filing for a $600 million IPO (18 percent of its common stock). All proceeds from the offering were to remain with NRG Energy. NRG Thermal Corp., a wholly owned subsidiary of NRG Energy, signed an agreement with Statoil Energy Inc. to acquire Harrisburg Steam Works and Statoil Energy Power/Paxton L.P., both in Harrisburg, Pa. [Deal completed in July.] On **May 30**, the successful IPO of 28.17 million shares of common stock was priced at $15 per share. The $422.55 million in gross proceeds was the largest-ever IPO by a Minnesota company. [Closed June 5.] NRG Energy planned to repay a $300 million loan from Citicorp USA Inc. and devote the balance to general corporate purposes. "The pricing of the IPO reflects the shareholder value that NRG and NSP have been creating since NRG was formed in 1989," said NSP CEO Jim Howard. The common stock began trading on the New York Stock Exchange on May 31, opening at $15.88 and rising to $16.63. Said NRG CEO Peterson, "We are very pleased with the value placed on the offering, especially during such a turbulent market period." NRG granted the underwriters an overallotment option to purchase up to an additional 4,225,500 shares—which they did, increasing the total offering from 16 percent to 18 percent of NRG's common stock. The balance was retained by NSP. In **June** its shares were rated BUY in new coverage at both Salomon Smith Barney and ABN Amro. NRG was in discussions to buy the Hennepin County garbage-to-energy plant in Minneapolis. The Estonian Cabinet approved the terms under which NRG may proceed to purchase a 49 percent interest in Narva Power, which owns 3,000 megawatts of oil shale-fired generation plants. The newly acquired, 87-megawatt, gas-fired Bulo Bulo power generation facility, located in Carrasco, Bolivia, entered into commercial operation. In **July** NRG and Dynegy Inc. (NYSE: DYN) jointly completed a 100-megawatt (MW) expansion of the Rocky Road Power Plant, a natural gas-fired, simple-cycle peaking facility in East Dundee, Ill. NRG Thermal Corp. reached stock purchase agreements with Statoil Energy Inc. to acquire First State Power Management Inc., Dover, Del. [deal closed in August], and Statoil's Distributed Generation and Engineering Services Group, Chester, Pa. In **August** NRG was the successful bidder in the South Australian Government's electricity privatization auction for Flinders Power, South Australia's final generation company to be privatized. NRG agreed to pay (Aus.) $313 million ($180 million U.S.) cash for a 100-year lease of the Flinders Power assets. Flinders Power includes two power stations totaling 760 megawatts (MW), the Leigh Creek coal mine 175 miles north of the power stations, a dedicated rail line between the two, and Leigh Creek township. NRG South Central Generating LLC acquired the Koch Power Louisiana Sterlington (La.) Project from Koch Power Inc. At month's end NRG said that it was forming a group with Germany's HEW AG and Sweden's Vattenfall AB that might bid for Veag AG, a utility in eastern Germany. In **September** the company priced a $350 million offering of 8.25 percent senior notes due 2010. The 10-year note offering was priced at 99.703 to yield 8.294 percent. NRG finalized the purchase of 24.4 percent of the common shares of Itiquira Energetica S.A.—owner of a 156-megawatt (MW) hydroelectric power generation facility located in the State of Mato Grosso in southwestern Brazil—for 14.5 million Brazilian reals (US $7.9 million). NRG revised its expected earnings for the third quarter to 45 cents per share, five cents above the First Call consensus estimate, primarily due to the ability of NRG's generating facilities to satisfy the increased, weather-related demand for electricity in various regions of the United States, particularly in the West. **Sept. 30**: "Our quarterly and year-to-date financial results validate our strategy of establishing a top-three position in our core markets, while maintaining fuel and dispatch level diversity," said Peterson. "Our baseload and intermediate dispatch facilities provide a foundation for consistent earnings, while our peaking facilities enable us to benefit from markets in which weather and local market conditions contribute to stronger demand for electricity." Management remained comfortable with the First Call consensus earnings estimates of 19 cents per share for the fourth quarter. In **October** NRG and EnBW Energie Baden-Wurttemberg AG joined together to bid on the outstanding majority of stock up for sale in the Vereinigte Energiewerke AG (VEAG). "We want to maintain VEAG as an independent company and develop it to become a leading competitive power in the German electricity market," explained NRG CEO Peterson and EnBW board member Dr. Klaus J. Kasper. NRG signed an asset purchase agreement as the successful bidder in Sierra Pacific Resources' (NYSE: SRP) auction of its 50 percent interest in the 522-MW coal-fired North Valmy Generating Station and 100 percent interest in 25 MW of peaking units near Valmy Station. In **November** NRG and Avista-STEAG LLC formed a partnership to build, operate, and manage a 633 MW (maximum ISO rating) natural gas-fired merchant power plant, the Brazos Valley project, in Fort Bend County, Texas, 30 miles southwest of Houston. NRG announced plans to acquire a 5,961 MW portfolio of operating projects and projects in construction and advanced development from LS Power LLC, New Brunswick, N.J., for $658 million.

Nash Finch Company

continued from page 289 Headquartered in Omaha, Neb., Hinky Dinky is the majority owner of 12 Nebraska supermarkets operated under the names Hinky Dinky and Econofoods. In **May** Nash Finch announced the opening of a new 60,000-square-foot Econofoods store in Marshalltown, Iowa, which replaced an older store. In addition, NFC completed the remodeling of three additional Econofoods stores, in Dubuque, Iowa; Peru, Ill.; and Waterloo, Iowa. The Marshalltown Econofoods is a "Fresh Place" concept store that includes high-quality fresh produce, expanded deli and bakery offerings, Kids Korner (free in-store child care), natural and organic foods, full-service meat and seafood, specialty and ethnic departments, pharmacy, and signature products available only at NFC stores. In **June** John Haedicke, former CFO, sued the company over his dismissal. Nash Finch held the grand opening of a new 65,000-square-foot Econofoods replacement store in Cedar Rapids, Iowa. In **July** Nash Finch announced a partnership with the Priceline WebHouse Club that allowed customers to use the Internet to name their own price for groceries and then shop for them at NFC-owned and -operated supermarkets at savings of up to half-off average store prices. The initial stores offering the Priceline WebHouse Club were two Econofoods stores in Rochester, Minn. Additional supermarkets were to be added throughout the year. The company said that it had earned the business of several significant new customers—conventional supermarkets, discount stores, and military business—representing more than $120 million annualized. A newly formed partnership with the Catalina Marketing Corp. (NYSE: POS) extended the value of the Catalina Marketing Network to NFC's independent retail customers. (The Catalina Marketing Network includes individually customized communications and promotions, printed at checkout, that include programs such as sampling, in-store instant-win games, pre-paid calling cards, rebate programs, couponing and advertising, as well as the Catalina Loyalty Marketing program, for retailers using or implementing a card-based frequent shopper program.) In **August** Nash Finch and Aon Consulting received the APEX 2000 Grand Award, recognizing excellence in the design and illustration of publications by professional communicators, for an innovative employee benefits communication publication, "Benefits: Food for Thought." The company gained the food distribution business of Food Farm Inc. (a group of independent retailers based in Kinston, N.C. that operate 63 stores under the Piggly Wiggly banner), representing more than $200 million in annualized sales. **Oct. 7:** Net earnings were $4.0 million in the 16-week third quarter, compared to $1.7 million in prior year. In **October** the company earned the business of several more customers, amounting to more than $40 million in sales on an annual basis.

Navarre Corporation

continued from page 292 tainer Kenny Rogers, founder of Dreamcatcher Entertainment, appeared together on CNN-fn "Morning Market Watch" to discuss Navarre's fiscal year-end earnings report, the evolution of the music industry, and Rogers' No. 1 single, "Buy Me a Rose," from his CD, "She Rides Wild Horses." (Rogers is the first artist from an independent label to have a No.1 single on the Billboard Country Music charts in more than 15 years. Navarre is the exclusive distributor for Dreamcatcher Entertainment Inc. music and CDs.) eSplice and Web developer is.com developed an e-commerce solution that allows for the integration of digital and physical goods in a single virtual shopping cart. Navarre's computer products division increased its market share position in the distribution of PC entertainment software to 60 percent for both April and May, and its market share in the education and reference categories to 30.2 percent (as reported by PC Data). In **August** the company signed the following exclusive distribution agreements: renowned singer-songwriter Judy Collins' new Wildflower Records; Strictly Hype Recordings Inc. (all full-length CDs); Scarlet Moon Records Inc. (Paul Overstreet), and Grapeshot Media. Navarre's computer products division signed a distribution agreement with Symantec Corp. (Nasdaq: SYMC), a world leader in Internet security. In **September** eSplice and Liquid Audio Inc. (Nasdaq: LQID), a leading provider of software and services for the Internet delivery of music, teamed up to offer affiliate customers a selection of promotional and for-sale digital music downloads. The music division signed an exclusive distribution agreement with multi-platinum singer/songwriter/producer Richard Marx of Signal 21 Music. eSplice signed an agreement with Servistream, a provider of online customer service and electronic customer relationship management services. eSplice debuted its first online superstore, with TheWest.com, which specializes in a variety of content, packaged goods, and services with a western flair. Navarre announced plans to take a one-time, noncash charge of $9.6 million for the write-off of its loan to NetRadio Corp. Navarre announced an agreement to acquire two operating divisions from Toronto-based Beamscope Canada Inc. (BSP.TO) that generate revenue of $116 million Canadian. [In October Navarre terminated the deal, saying that certain closing conditions could not be satisfied and that certain material adverse information about the business had not been disclosed to Navarre.] The computer products division signed a distribution agreement with Canon Software Publishing. **Sept. 30:** Net sales for the home entertainment business segment for the fiscal second quarter increased by 17.0 percent from the same period last year, to $78,375,000. Operating income of $1,512,000 was a 31.6 percent increase over last year. In **October** Navarre entered into a Securities Redemption Agreement with Fletcher International Ltd. to repurchase $3.4 million of Class B Convertible Preferred Stockheld by Fletcher. [Deal was done later in the month.] The board of directors then authorized the company to repurchase up to 5 million shares of Navarre (20 percent of its outstanding common stock) in market or private transactions. Navarre signed an agreement with H.B. Halicki Productions for the exclusive distribution on VHS and DVD video of "Gone in 60 Seconds."

Net Perceptions Inc.

continued from page 294 GreenLight Go! Web site analysis and reporting tool represented the first time marketers could get complete answers to business-critical questions from a single source—without additional analysis or number crunching. The company registered a proposed offering of up to 2,850,000 shares of common stock—2,000,000 by the company and up to 850,000 by selling stockholders. [Later, what had become 2,625,471 shares of the common stock were priced at $45.25 per share and released March 24—just in time, as NETP proceeded to lose 82 percent of its value during the April tech stock slide.] In March Net Perceptions and Art Technology Group completed the integration of ATG's Dynamo Product Suite of E-commerce and personalization applications with the Net Perceptions for E-commerce recommendation engine. Forbes ASAP, a regular supplement of Forbes Magazine, rated Net Perceptions No. 12 among the 100 fastest-growing tech companies in the United States—citing its market-leading position and the growth possibilities as the number of online shoppers grows. Upside Magazine also chose Net Perceptions as an "E-Business Winner" in the Platform & Tools category of its "E-Business 150" list. The company entered into an agreement with SBC Communications (NYSE: SBC) to install Net Perceptions 1:1 real-time personalization technology in areas of SBC's call center operations. Dain Rauscher Wessels Internet infrastructure analyst Stephen Sigmond initiated coverage of Net Perceptions, $36.56, with a BUY-SPECULATIVE rating and a 12-month price target of $75. In April Steven Snyder was named a finalist in the 2000 Entrepreneur of the Year Awards by Ernst & Young. The company introduced Net Perceptions Intelligence for Advertising, the first data analysis solution proven to maximize revenue return for print promotional campaigns. Leading global financial services firm J.P. Morgan & Co. Inc. (NYSE: JPM) licensed Net Perceptions for Knowledge Management software and associated consulting. Documentum (Nasdaq: DCTM), the leading provider of Internet-scale content management solutions for powering e-business applications, announced an agreement to seamlessly integrate its 4i eBusiness Edition with Net Perceptions' personalization solution. The company signed an agreement with Ernst & Young, one of the world's largest and most respected business solutions consultancies, to serve as a systems integrator of Net Perceptions' personalization technology. The Children's Place (Nasdaq: PLCE), a specialty retailer of apparel and accessories for children from newborn to 12 years of age, with 344 retail outlets and an expanding e-commerce presence, was able to demonstrate dramatic click-through and conversion rates in a targeted e-mail campaign using Net Perceptions' one-to-one personalized e-mail application. In **May** the company entered into a reseller agreement with Hewlett-Packard Co. (NYSE: HWP) that was to allow HP to offer the Net Perceptions' realtime personalization technology with HP's worldwide e-services offerings. In **June** Net Perceptions announced the availability of Net Perceptions for Knowledge Management 2.0—featuring a people-centric approach that enables large organizations to slash costly search time, drastically reduce reinvented wheels, and bring together the right employees at the right time. Net Perceptions and Exchange Applications Inc. (Nasdaq: EXAP), now doing business as Xchange Inc., announced an agreement to co-market each other's products, providing the first ASP-enabled e-mail marketing solution that combines Net Perceptions' individually personalized recommendations with Xchange's targeted e-mail delivery system. In **July** the company announced a long-term agreement allowing Interelate, the leading customer intelligence application service provider (ASP), to host and deploy Net Perceptions' real-time personalization and data analysis software. The company launched the most comprehensive ASP-delivered business intelligence and personalized marketing service to date, Net Perceptions Personalization Network. A reseller agreement with Angara, a leading provider of online marketing services, called for the incorporation of Angara Converter into Net Perceptions Personalization Network. National specialty retailer Williams-Sonoma Inc. (NYSE: WSM) signed an agreement licensing both Net Perceptions for E-commerce and the Personalization Network's Intelligence Channel. An agreement with ACTV Inc. (Nasdaq: IATV), a leading digital media company commercializing proprietary technologies for interactive digital TV and Enhanced TV, was to bring Net Perceptions' 1:1 personalization capabilities to the television landscape. Organic Inc. (Nasdaq: OGNC), a leading Internet professional services firm targeting the customer-to-business market, signed an agreement to resell Net Perceptions' Intelligence Channel. In August Digital River Inc. (Nasdaq: DRIV), the world's largest commerce service provider (CSP), completed a services integration with Net Perceptions. Based on its revenue growth from 1997 to 1999, the company was named a Deloitte & Touche's Minnesota Technology Fast 50 Rising Star, a new category this year. In **September** Kmart Corp. (NYSE:KM) selected the company's Commerce Solutions advertising and merchandising analytic solution, used by retailers to deliver detailed insights into product sales performance and forecast the profitability of advertising and promotions. Net Perceptions confirmed that it was working closely with Intel Corp. to optimize Net Perceptions solutions for Intel Pentium III Xeon processor so that businesses could more quickly and easily deploy Net Perceptions' array of e-commerce personalization solutions on their Intel-based systems. The company introduced E-commerce Analyst, a new product that does two important things: it looks deeply into customer behaviors and reveals distinct segments according to what products they buy and when (such as people who always get the latest DVDs as soon as they are released, or those who want only infant clothes and accessories); and it reveals unexpected relationships between products (a yard and garden merchandiser might discover that buyers of aquatic gardening supplies show surprising interest in yard furniture as well). The company said that it expected to report a loss ranging from ($0.22) to ($0.32) per share before the amortization of intangibles and stock compensation expense—analysts were expecting ($0.13)—compared to ($0.15) on the same basis in the prior-year period. In spite of its attempts to diversify its revenue, its financial results remained closely tied to the electronic retailing industry, which was in a down cycle. The next day, as analysts questioned the company's business model itself, investors slashed 62 percent ($200 million) from Net Perception's market cap. **Sept. 30**: The third-quarter loss came in at $8.0 million/($0.30) before the amortization of intangibles and stock compensation expense. In **October** 24k Gold Points, the leading clicks-and-mortar loyalty company backed by travel, hospitality, and loyalty-marketing giant Carlson Cos. Inc., brought together three industry leaders in the areas of e-commerce and personalization—Net Perceptions, BroadVision Inc. (Nasdaq: BVSN), and OrderTrust Inc.—in a first-ever partnership to develop the company's integrated e-commerce solution. the company announced a reduction in its workforce of 17 percent, or 65 people, and a fourth-quarter charge of $1 million. As part of the re-alignment, the company combined its Network Solutions and Commerce Solutions business units to more effectively focus its sales strategy. The company announced internal sales goals for the quarter beginning Oct. 1, 2000, that ranged from $8 million to $9 million, and for the full year 2001 from $45 million to $60 million, reflecting compound quarterly growth of 15 percent to 20 percent on a sequential basis. For profitability, the company was targeting the fourth quarter of 2001. In **November** Net Perceptions and Integra (IEA NM or INTG NM), Europe's leading provider of managed Web hosting and e-business solutions, announced a strategic alliance for Integra to operate and distribute Net Perceptions' real-time personalization and data analytics software throughout Europe.

NetRadio Corporation

continued from page 295 customized audio news and information on demand, signed a licensing agreement involving delivery of NetRadio.com Music News content to users of AudioBasket's service. **Aug. 31**: NetRadio's "80's Hits" channel claimed the top slot in Arbitron's August Webcasting report. NetRadio also claimed seven of the top 10 slots, and 34 of the top 75 slots measured in the report. In **September** Playboy.com began providing a link on its Web site to an online player highlighting 10 NetRadio streaming audio channels. NetRadio and COMEDY CENTRAL, the only all-comedy network, announced a partnership to launch a 24/7 all-comedy Internet radio station. The COMEDY CENTRAL partnership also marked NetRadio's first co-branded agreement as part of its strategy to develop similar agreements with a number of leading content providers. **Sept. 30**: Third-quarter revenue was $456,000, an increase of 22 percent from $374,000 in the third quarter of 1999, but down 26 percent sequentially from the second quarter of 2000. Monthly average unique guests were 2.1 million, a 110 percent increase from 1.0 million for the same period last year, but a 22 percent sequential decrease from 2.7 million for the previous quarter, a factor of the summer season impact on its primarily in-office listener base. In **October**, with the company trading at a 52-week low of $1.38, President and CEO Edward Tomechko resigned. Akoo.com, a leading Internet entertainment network, signed a nonexclusive agreement with NetRadio to distribute Kima, a newly introduced wireless Internet audio device. Candy Cintron, former head of sales and marketing for Caliente/Atlantic records, agreed to program five Latin music channels for NetRadio.com. In **November** six new NetRadio.com LiveStations were added to the preset menu on RealPlayer 8 from RealNetworks Inc. (Nasdaq: RNWK), bringing the total number to 20.

Norstan Inc.

continued from page 297 of Scottsdale, Ariz., for internal operations and the quality of services delivered to citizens. Charles Schwab Canada Co. awarded Norstan a contract to install industry-leading communication systems solutions in its Toronto and Montreal central locations and associated branch offices. Norstan created a new marketing and sales organization, the Advanced Solutions Group, to focus on the growing demand for the company's bundled convergence product and service business solutions. In **February** TriHealth, a community partnership encompassing the strengths of two of Cincinnati's finest health care organizations, installed a Norstan-designed wireless phone system in the Neonatal Intensive Care Unit of its Good Samaritan Hospital. TransLink, the Regional Transportation Network of Greater Vancouver, awarded Norstan Canada Ltd. a $1.1 million contract to design and install an integrated voice response system to serve customers traveling on public transit in the region. Norstan expanded its portfolio of Internet-based conferencing and collaboration services through an alliance with leading application service provider Envoyglobal.com. In **March** Norstan's information technology business unit, Norstan Consulting, announced plans to reduce costs, eliminate jobs, and focus its information technology (IT) consulting practice on e-business and customer relationship management, exclusively—actions taken in response to significant losses recently posted by the IT consulting business unit. As a result, 25 percent of total Norstan Consulting workforce, 180 consulting and sales jobs, were to be eliminated—including 30 jobs in the Twin Cities. A new Norstan-designed voice, video, and data communication system was being deployed at Paul Brown Stadium—the new home field of the Cincinnati Bengals (completion date August 2000)—to ensure effective communication both on the field and throughout the organization. The $500,000 system was to interconnect coaches, trainers, players, the media, restaurants, other concessions, and the Bengals management and administrative staff anywhere in the stadium. Norstan entered into an agreement with IBM's Lotus Development Corp. and AVT Corp. to offer unified messaging solutions to customers. In **April** Nebraska Public Power District selected Norstan's Advanced Services Group to help build a state-of-the-art Customer Care Center serving NPPD's customers throughout Nebraska. Norstan developed a conferencing and collaboration solution valued at $1.1 million to meet the demanding communication requirements of Musicland Stores Corp. Norstan was named an IP/Telephony Specialized Channel Partner by Cisco Systems Inc. Otterbein Retirement Living Communities awarded Norstan Inc. a contract to install a collaboration and conferencing system to link staff at all six of its retirement communities in Ohio. Norstan announced a new growth strategy to achieve a significant increase in new revenue in fiscal 2001 (which was to start on May 1). Company officials projected that incremental revenue resulting from this strategy would reach an annual "run rate" of $100 million by year-end fiscal 2001. Specifically, Norstan planned to market its industry-leading professional, consulting, and traditional support services through a broad spectrum of enterprise solution providers in addition to the company's current direct enterprise marketing activities. Such enterprise solution providers include Competitive Local Exchange Carriers (CLECs), Incumbent Local Exchange Carriers (ILECs), Internet Service Providers (ISPs), and Applications Services Providers (ASPs) as well as other channel partners, such as Value-Added Resellers (VARs), Systems Integrators, and Manufacturer Direct channels. **April 30:** Problems in its computer consulting business caused a $45.8 million fourth-quarter loss and 230 job cuts. In **May** Lasik Vision Corp., North America's fastest growing provider of laser vision eye correction, installed a Norstan Canada Ltd. call centre solution. In **June** Norstan Resale Services became Vibes Technologies Inc. as part of Norstan's strategy to become the first e-commerce provider of quality refurbished communication equipment and services. As the successor to Norstan Resale Services, Vibes already was a leading service provider and distributor of refurbished equipment through traditional marketing channels. However, the new Vibes organization was preparing to open for business on the Internet in October 2000 at www.vibestech.com. Wilsons The Leather Experts (Nasdaq: WLSN), the leading specialty retailer of leather outerwear, awarded Norstan Communications and Norstan Consulting a contract to link its retail stores via Cisco routing equipment to the home office In Brooklyn Park, Minn. In **July** Norstan and Lightning Rod Software Inc., (Nasdaq: LROD) partnered to develop and implement a multichannel customer interaction solution to support customer voice interactions for Metamail Inc., developer of the world's first visual messaging system. Norstan and Rockwell Electronic Commerce, a global supplier of industry-leading customer contact management technology, announced a long-term strategic agreement calling for Norstan to resell Rockwell's portfolio of industry-leading multimedia customer contact management technology through its network of North American sales and consulting offices. **July 29:** First quarter's net loss of $7.5 million was in line with company expectations. In **August** Norstan and Rockwell reached a bilateral agreement to provide advanced call center technology solutions and services for today's rapidly evolving North American customer contact marketplace. Norstan was ranked No. 76 on the 2000 VARBusiness 500, the industry's definitive ranking of the top 500 Solutions Providers (Internet services companies, consultants, and integrators) in North America. Norstan agreed to provide support center, technical, distribution, and professional services support to Science Applications International Corp.—a Fortune 500 research and engineering firm providing information technology, systems integration, and e-business products and services to commercial and government customers—in conjunction with SAIC's customer-focused Next Generation Solutions technology initiative. In **September** Norstan and Ericsson Enterprise Systems, a leader in voice, data, and mobility solutions for converging networks, announced a landmark partnership to ensure their customers access to the most advanced communications support and system integration capabilities in the marketplace. Norstan was to acquire and service Ericsson's MD 110 PABX direct sales accounts in North America to create a new organization, Norstan Large Systems and Services, dedicated to ensuring that Ericsson Enterprise customers maximize the return on their telecom investments. The deal was expected to boost Norstan's 2001 annual revenue by $150 million and be accretive to earnings. According to Baszucki, "It gives us nationwide coverage, puts us into new markets, and gives us a whole new revenue stream in the services area." Riverstone Inc., a leading provider of outsource customer contact and fulfillment services to e-commerce enterprises, awarded Norstan's Advanced Services Group a $1.4 million contract to expand services to current and new customers. In **October** Norstan entered into an agreement with PlaceWare Inc. to extend its service offering in the burgeoning business-to-business Web conferencing market. Norstan and Dialogic Communications Corp., the leader in interactive voice response (IVR) technology for the cable television (CATV) industry, partnered to provide the most comprehensive CATV call center solution available. In **November** a large, international health and personal care company awarded Norstan Conferencing Solutions Group a three-year, $2.7 million managed services contract to design, install, and maintain a worldwide conferencing and collaboration system.

Nortech Systems Inc.

continued from page 298 net sales from continuing operations of $39,492,921 increased 40 percent from prior year. Net income from continuing operations increased 84 percent to $1,404,845. "This marks our fifth consecutive record-setting quarter for both revenue and net income," said Finkelson about third-quarter results. "The outlook remains very positive across our key markets." In **October** the company announced plans to reapply for listing on the Nasdaq Stock Market's National Market System in early 2001, after year-end financial results become available.

Northwest Airlines Corporation

continued from page 300 International Airport, Seattle. **Dec. 31**: Despite a 25 percent increase in fuel costs, fourth-quarter profits of $29 million/$0.31 easily beat analysts' expectations. On a "fuel-neutral" basis, Northwest lowered costs by 3.3 percent, mainly in ticketing and maintenance. Airline passenger service declined in 1999 by most measures, but Northwest was among three of the 10 major carriers with improved performance. Consequently, it jumped from ninth in 1998 to fourth in the overall rankings (which were led by Southwest). An alleged "sickout" (an illegal job action) by flight attendants, which forced the carrier to cancel 300 flights, prompted Northwest to seek a restraining order against the attendants' union. In the latest in a series of awards received by nwa.com, ZDNet's usability review of airline Web sites rated Northwest's No. 1. Northwest's WorldPerks frequent-flyer program was the highest rated U.S.-based program reviewed by InsideFlyer Magazine, the leading authority on airline free-travel programs. A Northwest Airlines computerized system to help pilots plot and fly around relatively localized areas of turbulence received special recognition by Air Transport World magazine. In **February 2000** Northwest was named "On-Time Airline of the Decade" among the seven U.S. network airlines, based on statistics released by the Department of Transportation. Northwest announced plans to operate a new, fourth bank of flights from Memphis-Shelby County International Airport, a 25 percent expansion in service that was to provide Memphis-area passengers and travelers throughout the South with more convenient connections to Northwest destinations around the world. Northwest and Continental (Airlines) Connection carrier Gulfstream International Airlines, Fort Lauderdale, Fla., announced a code-share agreement to increase convenience and enhance travel benefits to and from Florida and the Bahamas. Northwest announced plans to begin new daily non-stop service between Minneapolis/St. Paul and New York's John F. Kennedy International Airport on May 1. The airline introduced a weekday night special discount coach fare that doesn't require a Saturday night stay on the road. Northwest agreed to put its sickout lawsuit, pursuant to which it had begun court-authorized searchers of flight attendants' home computers, on hold in order to further labor negotiations. The airline signed a code-share agreement in which American Eagle Airlines was to provide service between Los Angeles and seven destinations in California for Northwest passengers. Northwest, Alitalia, and KLM Royal Dutch Airlines implemented reciprocal frequent-flyer programs, as well as code-sharing, to 42 cities in Europe, the Middle East, Africa, and the United States. In **March** CEO Dasburg said that Northwest Airlines and other big carriers could report losses this year if fuel prices remain at current levels (85 cents a gallon vs. expected average of 67 cents). Relatively unhedged for fuel until the fourth quarter, Northwest was going to take a hit of $600 million in higher fuel costs unless prices moderated. Rising fuel costs had already caused the airline to delay buying new aircraft. Northwest and Sabre Holdings Corp. settled a dispute over Internet site Travelocity.com's use of real-time flight data provided by Northwest. Northwest was to receive financial consideration and credit as the source. After thwarting a price increase advanced by its competitor, Northwest raised fares a weel later. Northwest announced new nonstop jet service between its hub in Minneapolis/St. Paul and San Antonio. In response to the steep, continued climb in jet fuel prices, Northwest Airlines Cargo announced plans to implement an increase in its fuel surcharge—from $0.10/kg to $0.15/kg on all North American-origin transpacific and transatlantic shipments. Northwest and Continental announced initiatives to enhance their seamless service: shared self-service kiosks for customer check-in; and Interline E-Ticket, to allow customers to use one e-ticket when flying Northwest and Continental within the same itinerary. Data systems serving the Northwest Airlines operations center in Minneapolis/St. Paul were restored following a cable cut that disrupted Northwest flights for several hours. Northwest's plan to increase its hauling capacity to Atlanta by 40 percent beginning June 1—the same day that low-fare AirTran Airways had set for launching its own service on the route—was seen by two Congressmen and a local airport official as possible evidence of anti-competitive practices. Northwest was planning to implement several new procedures in how it processes reservations—in order to improve customer satisfaction by increasing the availability of seats for sale on full flights and reducing the number of denied boardings, and to prevent agents from booking multiple flights for a passenger while intending to pay for only one. The company's proxy revealed pay raises of 12 percent to 82 percent for top executives—sure to become an issue in current contract negotiations with union-represented flight attendants and mechanics. The Web site nwa.com received several more top rankings from some of the most prestigious and knowledgeable Internet researchers and surveyors. It was selected as one of ActivMedia Research's top 100 consumer e-commerce Web sites; it was ranked one of the top 25 one-to-one Web sites by Peppers and Rogers Group; it received the award for "Best redesign of a Web site" by Internet World magazine; and it received the No. 1 spot in customer confidence and finished second overall in the Spring 2000 Airline Scorecard rankings from the Gomez Advisors. **March 31**: In spite of high fuel prices, which took $110 million ($1.20 a share) away from earnings, and excluding a one-time gain, Northwest outperformed Wall Street's projected 73-cent loss by 22 cents a share—thanks to help on the revenue side from the late Easter. In addition, the airline topped all major airlines in on-time performance during March—for the first time in 11 months. In April Northwest flight attendants were given another chance to vote on a tentative agreement between their union and the airline. This one offered increased pension benefits and pay, as well as full benefits for domestic partners. A new marketing partnership was announced between Northwest and The Independent Film Channel (IFC). Jack Bavis, a senior mediator at the National Mediation Board, joined Northwest to head its labor relations with unions representing ground employees. **April 30**: For the second-consecutive month, Northwest led the nation's 10 largest carriers in on-time performance. In **May** Tokyo NWA workers staged a one-day walkout to protest their own unsettled contract negotiations. At month's end, Teamster flight attendants ratified a new contract with Northwest Airlines, ending the lengthy and often bitter dispute between the union and management. According to Teamsters President James P. Hoffa, "This contract provides tremendous wage gains, industry-leading pension rates, and the best scope protections in the industry." On May 31, Northwest shares rose 20 percent on speculation that the proposed takeover by United Airlines (the No. 1 U.S. carrier) of US Airways (No. 6) had put Northwest (No. 4) in play. A June 1 broadcast report had Northwest beginning talks about a possible merger with American Airlines (No. 2). Northwest announced plans to expand Asia/Pacific code-share service significantly with Continental Airlines and to introduce new North America-Japan code-share service with Japan Air System in the summer. Northwest became the first airline to implement a luggage service recovery program that provides inconvenienced customers with a recovery packet when a lost bag is returned to them. The packet contains a dollars-off voucher (at least $25) for future travel, along with a comment card and a letter of apology. Northwest Airlines Cargo and JAL (Japan Airlines) Cargo reached a long-term agreement for a cargo alliance. Northwest announced plans to hire 100 additional reservations sales agents at its Iron Range Reservations Center in Chisholm, Minn., beginning in mid-July. The new jobs would bring total employment at the Chisholm center to 650, surpassing job-creation criteria set in 1996 when Northwest used government economic assistance in opening the centers. Northwest was backing a new online ticketing service, Hotwire.com, that would sell cheap seats that might otherwise be left empty. At June's close, Northwest's board formed a three-member committee, to be led by Pulitzer Prize-winning historian Doris Kearns Goodwin, to address the long-standing problem with employee relations. **June 30**: Northwest's industry-leading June passenger load factor of 82.8 percent, a gain of 3.1 points over the previous year, was the highest in company history. Second-quarter cargo division revenue set an all-time high of $210 million. If not for a year-over-year fuel price increase of 61.5 percent, Northwest would have set a company profits record. With the industry struggling with flight delays and cancellations, Northwest's 75.0 percent on-time performance in June was the best among the nation's 10 largest airlines. In **July** Northwest Airlines Cargo acquired two Boeing 747-200 series wide-body aircraft to be used as all-cargo freighters, which brought the number of main-deck 747-200 freighters to 12. The Summer 2000 Internet Airlines Scorecard, released by Gomez, a leading authority on the Internet and e-commerce, rated Northwest the No. 1 overall Web site. The Washington Post reported that American Airlines had made a $44 a share ($3.7 billion) buyout offer, well short of Northwest's initial asking price, thought to be in excess of $100. Other than price, there appeared to be no sticking point to an agreement. Northwest assigned more than 100 additional staff to assist with luggage delays developing on its trans-Atlantic service due to heavy summer volume through Amsterdam's Schiphol Airport. Northwest and partner KLM were losing about 1,000 bags per day in their under-powered luggage system. Northwest became the first major network carrier to offer an Internet check-in program for all passengers when it instituted the practice on outbound flights in Memphis, Tenn. A new Priority Pet Center Information Line, 888-NWA-4PET, was set up to assist passengers planning travel with their pets. America West Airlines Inc. (NYSE: AWA), Federal Express Corp. (NYSE: FDX), and Northwest announced the creation of an airline industry business-to-business e-commerce exchange with 10 of the world's major airlines. The exchange, to be officially launched in the next few months as Aeroxchange (http://www.aeroxchange.com), planned to offer the most comprehensive selection of aircraft technical parts and services, as well as general business supplies, to airlines on the Web. Northwest reached agreements with The Boeing Co. and Airbus Industrie to accelerate deliveries of five Boeing 757-200 aircraft from 2004 to 2001 and deliveries of five Airbus A320/A319-family aircraft from 2002 to 2001. Northwest was honored by the National Association of the Deaf for the carrier's inclusion of people with disabilities on its Customers with Disabilities Advisory Board. Alliance partners Northwest and KLM Royal Dutch Airlines announced plans to increase service and improve connections between North America and India in the fall. **July 31**: For the second-consecutive month, Northwest had a record number of passengers. The airline's 81.6 percent load factor for July was only slightly less than June's all-time record of 82.8 percent. In **August** a government report that Northwest employees didn't understand or properly address the dangers of a luggage compartment chemical spill led to a tightening of the airline's procedures. Northwest received the 2000 CIO-100 award from IDG's CIO magazine. The award—which focused this time on excellence, innovation, and improved business performance through the use of customer-oriented practices—recognizes organizations around the world that exemplify the highest level of operational and strategic excellence. COO Anderson agreed to serve as the first chairman of the Minnesota Business Leadership Network, which was joining 22 other state BLNs as an employer-led endeavor to enhance employment opportunities for qualified individuals with disabilities. Northwest confirmed that it had joined five other airlines in a new online venture, Minneapolis start-up MilePoint.com, to allow travelers to cash in mileage awards for discounts on goods and services from more than 100 online merchants. **Aug. 31**: Northwest reclaimed the No. 1 spot among the 10 largest airlines in on-time performance, with 79.2 percent of its flights deemed on-time during the month. In **September** union mechanics reached a tentative agreement with Northwest management on the lengthy noneconomic portion of a new contract, setting up a second phase of talks on wages, pension, and other financial matters. On **Sept. 8**, Northwest joined the nation' s other major airlines in raising domestic fares, adding a surcharge of $20 per round trip to cover the higher cost of jet fuel. In response to recent moves by competitors to improve amenities, Northwest and KLM Royal Dutch Airlines launched an improved international business class service that provides business class customers with more than 50 percent additional leg room, improved recline, and a host of other enhancements. In view of a possible merger between British Airways (BA) and KLM, Northwest and BA were discussing possible ties. A new brand-advertising campaign—themed "clearing the way," as in providing a hassle-free travel experience—was launched in domestic and international newspapers and in the electronic media. By mid-month, customers were able to view their flight reservations from hand-held wireless connections such as Web-enabled wireless phones and Palm Pilots. Negotiators for Northwest's mechanics union made an aggressive contract proposal that would effectively double wages for the average veteran technician. Northwest was recognized as one of the most innovative users of information technology, ranked No. 96 out of 500 companies in InformationWeek magazine's 12th annual InformationWeek 500. **Sept. 30**: Northwest posted the highest September load factor in the company's history, flying 6.50 billion revenue passenger miles—an increase of 5.1 percent from the previous year—with only a 0.5 percent increase in available seat miles. Quarterly net income of $207 million was achieved in the face of higher fuel prices (which had increased 58.7 percent, or $200 million pre-tax, year-over-year). Excluding nonrecurring gains, the company's third quarter earnings per diluted share of $2.06 exceeded the First Call consensus estimate of $1.98. In **October** Northwest announced plans to increase service between Nagoya, Japan, and Manila, the Philippines, from four weekly flights to daily service; and nonstop Minneapolis/St. Paul-Tokyo service from 10 weekly flights to twice-daily service, all beginning April 1, 2001. Northwest and Continental Airlines launched the world's largest interline e-ticket network. This technology allows customers to use electronic tickets when their itineraries include travel on both carriers; and it also allows the two airlines to accept e-ticketed customers traveling on changed itineraries involving the other carrier, without the need for conversion to a paper ticket. Northwest also began allowing passengers in the Twin Cities to print their boarding passes off the Internet, as an alternative to standing in line at airport ticket counters. Northwest earned a second Gold Award from the National Business and Disability Council. For the second-consecutive time, Northwest was the No. 1 Web site overall among airlines according to the Internet Airlines Scorecard. Posting the highest October load factor in company history, Northwest flew 6.49 billion revenue passenger miles (RPM) in October, an increase of 3.2 percent from the 6.29 billion RPM in the previous year. Available seat miles (ASM) increased 2.4 percent from 8.42 billion ASM in October 1999 to 8.62 billion ASM in 2000, producing a 0.5 point increase in load factor. Cargo ton miles (CTM) systemwide were up 0.2 percent from 1999's 232.2 million CTM to 232.7 million CTM in October 2000. In **November** an antitrust trial in which the Justice Department was challenging Northwest's voting control of Continental Airlines began in Detroit. Both the government and Continental were alleging that Northwest was in the midst of a power play, but Northwest was claiming it had no intention of taking control of its alliance partner. [The two airlines reached an agreement in principle on Nov. 6 regarding the sale to Continental of its common stock held by Northwest.] Meanwhile, Northwest proposed to Mesaba Holdings Inc. (Nasdaq: MAIR) that Northwest acquire for $13 per share all of the shares of Mesaba that Northwest did not already own. (Northwest owned 28 percent, plus warrants to acquire an additional 12 percent.) The $190 million offer was prompted by Mesaba's sluggish stock price and by recent interest shown by Phoenix-based Mesa Air Group, a 3 percent stockholder in Mesaba. When the National Mediation Board halted contract talks indefinitely, officials of the mechanics union filed a suit accusing Northwest of failing to negotiate in good faith. The airline denied any truth to the allegations, calling the lawsuit a negotiating strategy.

Ontrack Data International Inc.

continued from page 304 SystemSuite 2000 with its 2000 World Class Award for best utility. The company introduced Ontrack SystemSuite for ASP, a Web-enabled version of its PC "mega-utility" suite. Ontrack's PC utility programs received two more awards from leading industry publications. ZDNet honored Ontrack ZipMagic 2000 in the file utilities category on behalf of PC Magazine, Computer Gaming World, FamilyPC, ZDTV, and ZDNet Downloads; and Ontrack PowerDesk 4 Pro received Winmag.com's annual Win100 Award, which honors the top software products in a variety of categories. End-of-month upgrades to EasyRecovery "do-it-yourself" data recovery software addressed customer and market demands for an easier and more powerful product. The company ranked No. 101 on Forbes' 200 Best Small Companies in America list. In **August** the company released ZipMagic 4.0 file compression utility, which includes unique time-saving features that automate the zipping of e-mail attachments, improve basic zip handling, and create Internet-secure encrypted zip files. In **September** the company introduced Fix-It Utilities 3.0, a problem-solving utility designed to optimize, protect, and tune up any Windows 95, 98, 2000, NT, and now the new Me operating system. **Sept. 30**: Third-quarter net income decreased to $0.9 million from $1.6 million in the same period a year earlier. Ontrack attributed the disappointing results to a combination of higher-than-expected investments in its Electric Information Management business and Application Service Provider delivery model as the company prepared those business lines for future growth; and to lower-than-expected revenue and earnings as a result of a recently recognized seasonality in the EIM business, an extended sales cycle for its Rapid Recall product line, and unfavorable foreign currency fluctuations. The news precipitated a 40 percent stock drop on Oct. 12. The new Ontrack SystemSuite 3.0, designed to keep PC operating systems at peak performance, included new and improved tools to recover lost data, optimize hard drive performance, warn against hard drive failure, and diagnose system resources. A partnership agreement with McAfee.com (Nasdaq: MCAF), the leading global Internet Application Service Provider (ASP) of online PC security and management services, united Ontrack data recovery products and services with McAfee.com's ASP model. The company introduced Fix-It Utilities 3.0, to fix and tune up Windows 95,98, Me, NT and 2000 systems. In **October** the company released Ontrack SystemSuite 3.0, the newest version of its multi-award winning PC mega-utility suite. New and improved features included a new defragmenting tool, a do-it-yourself data recovery option, improved diagnostics tools, a new hard drive failure early warning system, as well as a multimedia tutorial and bootable rescue CD. In **November** ZipMagic 4.0 and EasyRecovery 5.0 were named to WinMag.com's WinList. The company was granted a patent (U.S. 6,145,088) for its Remote Data Recovery service. Also in the month, the company introduced RapidRecall 5.0, an Internet-based eSupport system that provides users constant access to their critical data by automatically and efficiently backing up all user data stored on a PC; announced an alliance with McAfee.com (Nasdaq: MCAF), the leading global Internet Application Service Provider (ASP) of online PC security and management services; and announced enhanced and expanded support of its Remote Data Recovery service over the Internet.

Osmonics Inc.

continued from page 307 nalization related to the Phoenix facility closure. In **September** Osmonics reached an agreement with Corning Inc., Corning, N.Y., to initially source and eventually manufacture and market the parallel plate bioreactor currently sold by Corning under the trademark CellCube. (The CellCube module features a patented design that promotes faster, more productive cell growth in bio-pharmaceutical applications.) The product was not expected to have much impact on company revenue.

Nortech Systems Inc.

continued from page 308 Order 2000 compliance filing that it planned to transfer operational control of its transmission facilities to the Midwest ISO by the end of the year. **June 30, 2000**: second quarter earnings per share increased 29 percent due to strong results of its electric and plastics segments.

PUB

PUB

PPT Vision Inc.

12988 Valley View Rd., Eden Prairie, MN 55344
Tel: 952/996-9500 Fax: 952/996-9501 Web site: http://www.pptvision.com

PPT Vision Inc., formerly Pattern Processing Technologies Inc., designs, manufactures, markets, and integrates machine vision-based automated inspection systems for manufacturing applications such as electronic and mechanical assembly verification, verification of printed characters, packaging integrity, surface-flaw detection, and measurement tasks. The company's vision systems are sold throughout North America, Europe, and Asia to a broad range of industry categories, including manufacturers of automotive and electronic components, consumer goods, pharmaceuticals, and plastics.

EARNINGS HISTORY

Year Ended Oct 31	Operating Revenue/Sales (dollars in thousands)	Net Earnings (dollars in thousands)	Return on Revenue (percent)	Return on Equity (percent)	Net Earnings (dollars per share*)	Cash Dividend (dollars per share*)	Market Price Range (dollars per share*)
1999	11,325	(7,734)	(68.3)	(40.3)	(1.43)	—	6.88–3.13
1998	13,512	103	0.8	0.4	0.02	—	10.38–5.56
1997	12,055	660	5.5	2.4	0.12	—	10.38–5.56
1996	12,693	3,711	29.2	13.8	0.88	—	19.25–6.88
1995 †	9,750	1,347	13.8	26.2	0.37	—	8.67–1.67

* Per-share amounts restated to reflect 3-for-2 stock split on April 5, 1996.
† Income figures for 1995 include fourth-quarter income tax benefit of $407,000/$0.11.

BALANCE SHEET

Assets	10/31/99 (dollars in thousands)	10/31/98 (dollars in thousands)	Liabilities	10/31/99 (dollars in thousands)	10/31/98 (dollars in thousands)
Current (CAE 2,135 and 1,986)	16,118	22,097	Current	2,674	1,602
Fixed assets	2,400	2,254	Deferred rent		102
Other	3,327	3,536	Stockholders' equity*	19,171	27,871
Deferred income tax benefit		1,688	TOTAL	21,845	29,575
TOTAL	21,845	29,575			

* $0.10 par common; 10,000,000 authorized; 5,256,275 and 5,440,583 issued and outstanding.

RECENT QUARTERS / **PRIOR-YEAR RESULTS**

	Quarter End	Revenue ($000)	Earnings ($000)	EPS ($)	Prior-Year Revenue ($000)	Prior-Year Earnings ($000)	Prior-Year EPS ($)
Q3	07/31/2000	4,714	(1,648)	(0.31)	2,915	(1,044)	(0.19)
Q2	04/30/2000	4,125	(705)	(0.13)	3,247	(406)	(0.08)
Q1	01/31/2000	4,107	(541)	(0.10)	1,735	(711)	(0.13)
Q4	10/31/99	3,428	(5,572)	(1.04)	3,145	(39)	(0.01)
	SUM	16,374	(8,466)	(1.59)	11,042	(2,200)	(0.41)

RECENT EVENTS

In **February 2000** R.J. Steichen & Co., impressed with first-quarter results, upgraded its rating on PPT to VALUE BUY from NEUTRAL. In **March** the company was preparing to ship the initial orders of its SpeedScan 3-D Sensor, a scanning device using PPT's patented SMI technology. The new technology, in development for three years, was supposedly faster and more detailed than laser scanning. Executives were predicting that SpeedScan would soon be PPT's core product. In **June** PPT received follow-on orders for three PPT861 3-D inspection systems from a leading manufacturer of precision components for hard disk drives. PPT and National Instruments Corp. (Nasdaq: NATI) ended a lawsuit brought by NIC alleging patent infringement. PPT agreed to make a minor modification to new releases of its Vision Program Manager software to eliminate certain similarities to patented features of NIC's LabVIEW, and to make a one-time payment of $1 million to NIC. Director Peterson purchased 170,000 shares of PPT common stock directly from the company at a price of $6 per share, thereby enabling PPT to maintain its current level of working capital strength in view of the settlement. In **August** PPT received an order exceeding US $3.7 million as part of its long-term OEM supply agreement with Tokyo Weld Co. Ltd., a world leader in developing and manufacturing a broad range of high-speed passive component assembly and test equipment. In **September** PPT received an order for a PPT861 3D inspection system from a world leading supplier of microelectronics, semiconductors, and communications products. Equipped with PPT's patented Scanning Moire Interferometry (SMI) 3D technology, this PPT861 was to be used to perform high-speed coplanarity inspection of both leaded and bumped (BGA) components.

OFFICERS

Joseph C. Christenson
President and CEO
David L. Friske
VP-Manufacturing
Arye Malek
VP-Marketing
Thomas R. Northenscold
Gen. Mgr.-Vision Systems Division
Larry G. Paulson
Chief Technology Officer
Richard R. Peterson
CFO
Thomas G. Lovett IV
Secretary

DIRECTORS

Joseph C. Christenson
Robert W. Heller
Heller Capital Inc.
Bruce C. Huber
U.S. Bancorp Piper Jaffray Inc., Minneapolis
David C. Malmberg
Fieldworks Inc., Eden Prairie, MN
Larry G. Paulson
Peter R. Peterson
Electro-Sensors Inc., Eden Prairie, MN

MAJOR SHAREHOLDERS

Peter R. Peterson/ESI Investment Co., 20.1%
Minnetonka, MN
Dimensional Fund Advisors Inc., 7.4%
Santa Monica, CA
All officers and directors as a group (9 persons), 30.8%

SIC CODE

3823 Process control instruments

MISCELLANEOUS

TRANSFER AGENT AND REGISTAR:
Wells Fargo Bank Minnesota N.A.,
South St. Paul, MN
TRADED: Nasdaq National Market
SYMBOL: PPTV
STOCKHOLDERS: 562
EMPLOYEES: 109
GENERAL COUNSEL:
Lindquist & Vennum PLLP, Minneapolis
Schwegman, Lundberg & Woessner, Minneapolis

AUDITORS:
PricewaterhouseCoopers LLP, Minneapolis
INC: MN-1981
ANNUAL MEETING:
March
INVESTOR RELATIONS:
Thomas R. Northenscold

RANKINGS

No. 167 CRM Public 200

TWO-YEAR QUARTERLY HIGH-LOW STOCK PRICES

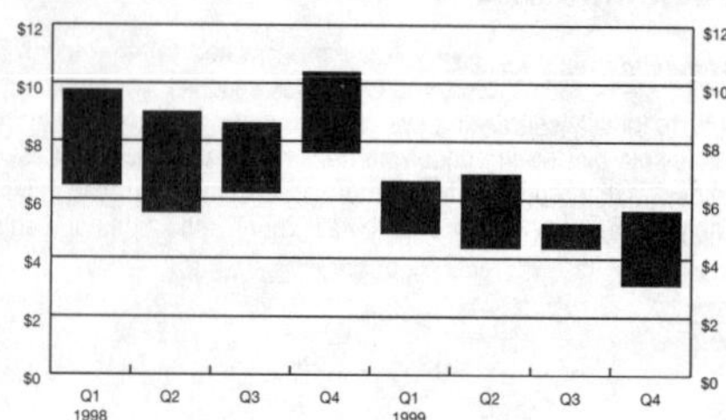

PW Eagle Inc.

222 S. Ninth St., Suite 2880, Minneapolis, MN 55402
Tel: 612/305-0339 Fax: 612/371-9651 Web site: http://www.pweagleinc.com

PW Eagle Inc., formerly known as Eagle Pacific Industries Inc. (Nasdaq: PWEI), is a leading extruder of polyvinyl chloride (PVC) pipe and polyethylene (PE) pipe and tubing products. The company is the second-largest pipe producer in the United States, the largest in the western United States, and the nation's largest buyer of PVC resin. Its products serve the following industries: turf irrigation, commercial and industrial plumbing, natural gas, water well, agriculture, and telecommunications.

EARNINGS HISTORY

Year Ended Dec 31	Operating Revenue/Sales (dollars in thousands)	Net Earnings	Return on Revenue (percent)	Return on Equity	Net Earnings (dollars per share)	Cash Dividend	Market Price Range
1999 *	153,950	14,562	9.5	59.8	1.88	—	5.00–1.25
1998 †	74,007	1,131	1.5	4.2	0.05	—	2.50–1.50
1997	71,685	931	1.3	5.4	0.06	—	4.00–2.25
1996 ¶	65,280	1,751	2.7	20.8	0.30	—	4.00–1.25
1995 #	51,330	(865)	(1.7)	(23.1)	(0.27)	—	3.50–1.38

* Income figures for 1999 include pretax nonrecurring expenses of $3.788 million. Results of PWPipe included from Sept. 16, 1999, date of purchase for $73.8 million. Pro forma for full year: revenue $303.249 million; net income $17.756 million/$2.43.
† Income figures for 1998 include extraordinary loss of $0.656 million/($0.10) on debt prepayments.
¶ Income figures for 1996 include extraordinary loss of $1.728 million/($0.32) on debt prepayments.
# Figures for 1995 include Pacific Plastics Inc. results from its July 10, 1995, date of acquisition for $6.75 million. Pro forma for Jan. 1 acquisition: revenue $69.495 million; net loss $0.505 million/($0.18).

BALANCE SHEET

Assets	12/31/99 (dollars in thousands)	12/31/98	Liabilities	12/31/99 (dollars in thousands)	12/31/98
Current (CAE 2,669)	77,325	19,129	Current (STD 10,441 and 1,850)	75,590	21,093
Property, eqt	74,895	22,635	Long-term debt	37,500	10,583
Deferred financing costs	5,300	96	Subordinated debt	26,752	
			Preferred equity	5,887	10,000
Land held for sale	1,346	2,491	Common equity*	22,058	7,803
Goodwill	3,874	3,986	TOTAL	167,787	49,479
Deferred income taxes	4,901	825			
Other	146	317			
TOTAL	167,787	49,479			

* $0.01 par common; 33,500,000 authorized; 7,721,214 and 6,635,035 issued and outstanding.

RECENT QUARTERS / **PRIOR-YEAR RESULTS**

	Quarter End	Revenue ($000)	Earnings ($000)	EPS ($)	Prior-Year Revenue ($000)	Prior-Year Earnings ($000)	Prior-Year EPS ($)
Q3	09/30/2000	85,618	4,559	0.58	36,162	3,924	0.42
Q2	06/30/2000	106,748	13,199	1.70	24,448	4,005	0.54
Q1	03/31/2000	92,599	9,166	1.21	19,586	330	0.02
Q4	12/31/99	73,754	6,304	0.87	14,343	(59)	(0.04)
	SUM	358,719	33,228	4.35	94,538	8,199	0.94

RECENT EVENTS

In **April 2000** the company agreed to acquire a 41,000-square-foot PVC pipe manufacturing facility in Phoenix, and certain production equipment located in the facility, from Uponor ETI. BlueFire Research initiated coverage with an OUTPERFORM rating and a 12-month target price of $24.50 per share, based on an enterprise valuation of five times EBITDA for the fiscal year that ends in December 2000. "In our view, Spell Capital Partners, the equity buyout group that controls the company, has created both a low-cost producer as well as an industry leader that can continue to take market share through consolidation,"said BlueFire Research Managing Director Lee Schafer. "The company is operating in a very favorable industry environment and, unless the economy goes into a sharp recession, these conditions should last into 2001. We also take comfort in the fact that Eagle Pacific is a growth company that will generate real cash earnings in 2000 of more than $3 per share." At the **May** annual meeting, shareholders approved the name change from Eagle Pacific Industries Inc. to PW Eagle. In **August** PW Eagle completed the acquisition, from Uponor ETI, of a 41,000-square-foot PVC pipe manufacturing facility in Phoenix and certain production equipment located in the facility. **Sept. 30:** Absent nonrecurring charges, pro forma basic EPS would be $1.10 and $2.00 for the three-month and nine-month periods, respectively. "During the third quarter, we experienced a general slowing of the economy and a reduction of both resin and pipe prices, which resulted in a decrease in demand and our gross margins compared to the first half of this year," commented CEO Spell. However, we continue to experience the positive effects of the significant capacity and process improvement investments that we have made over the last several years, and the synergies that we are recognizing from the integration of the Eagle Pacific and PWPipe businesses."

OFFICERS

Harry W. Spell
Chairman
Bruce A. Richard
Vice Chairman
William H. Spell
CEO
James K. Rash
President
John R. Cobb
SVP-Operations
Larry I. Fleming
SVP
Neil R. Chinn
VP-Human Resources
Roger Robb
CFO
Keith H. Steinbruk
VP-Technical Director
Dobson West
Secretary and General Counsel

DIRECTORS

George R. Long
Mayfield Corp., Plymouth, MN
Richard W. Perkins
Perkins Capital Management Inc., Wayzata, MN
Bruce A. Richard
Harry W. Spell
Xcel Energy Inc. (retired)
William H. Spell

MAJOR SHAREHOLDERS

CB Capital Investors L.P., 14.7%
New York
William H. Spell, 8.1%
Massachusetts Mutual Group, 7.1%
Springfield, MA
Perkins Capital Management Inc., 6.2%
Wayzata, MN
Harry W. Spell, 5.5%
All officers and directors as a group (12 persons), 25.9%

SIC CODE

3084 Plastics pipe
3089 Plastics products, nec

MISCELLANEOUS

TRANSFER AGENT AND REGISTAR:
Wells Fargo Bank Minnesota N.A.,
South St. Paul, MN
TRADED: Nasdaq National Market

SYMBOL: PWEI
STOCKHOLDERS: 1,893
EMPLOYEES: 840
IN MINNESOTA: 3
GENERAL COUNSEL:
Fredrikson & Byron P.A., Minneapolis
AUDITORS:
PricewaterhouseCoopers LLP, Minneapolis
INC: MN-1985
ANNUAL MEETING: May

RANKINGS

No. 78 CRM Public 200
No. 3 CRM Performance 100

SUBSIDIARIES, DIVISIONS, AFFILIATES

MANUFACTURING FACILITIES

Phoenix, Ariz.
Perris, Calif.
Cameron Park, Calif.
Visalia, Calif.
Tacoma, Wash.
Sunnyside, Wash.
Eugene, Ore.
Hastings, Neb.
Hillsboro, Ore.
Midvale, Utah
Baker City, Ore.

PUB

TWO-YEAR QUARTERLY HIGH-LOW STOCK PRICES

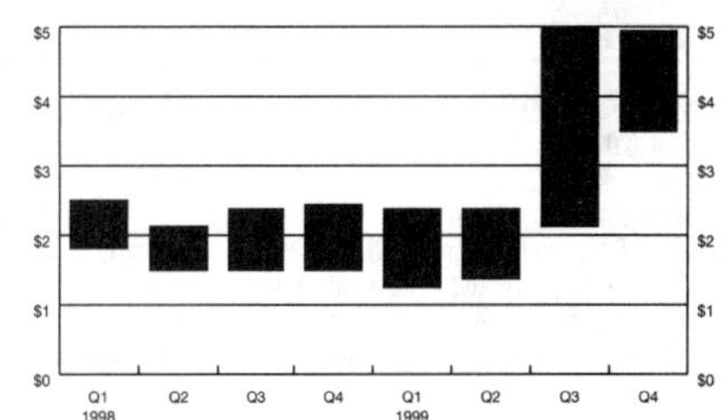

PUB

Paper Warehouse Inc.

7630 Excelsior Blvd., St. Louis Park, MN 55426
Tel: 952/936-1000 Fax: 952/936-9800 Web site: http://www.partysmart.com

Paper Warehouse Inc. is a growing chain of stores specializing in party supplies and paper goods. The company's eight principal markets are Minneapolis/St. Paul; Kansas City, Mo.; Denver; Seattle; Omaha, Neb.; Oklahoma City; Des Moines, Iowa; and Tucson, Arizona. Paper Warehouse stores offer an extensive assortment of special occasion, seasonal, and everyday paper products—including party supplies, gift wrap, greeting cards, and catering supplies—at everyday low prices. At July 28, 2000, the company had 146 stores (99 company-owned and 47 franchised stores) in 24 states under the names Paper Warehouse and Party Universe.

EARNINGS HISTORY *

Year Ended Jan	Operating Revenue/Sales (dollars in thousands)	Net Earnings (dollars in thousands)	Return on Revenue (percent)	Return on Equity (percent)	Net Earnings (dollars per share†)	Cash Dividend (dollars per share†)	Market Price Range (dollars per share†)
2000 ¶	82,371	(4,449)	(5.4)	(46.1)	(0.96)	—	3.06–1.38
1999	63,491	(521)	(0.8)	(3.7)	(0.11)	—	7.00–1.69
1998 #	52,949	(207)	(0.4)	(1.4)	(0.08)	—	8.63–5.63
1997	43,002	808	1.9	45.1	0.37	—	
1996	33,478	797	2.4	25.5	0.36	—	

* Earnings figures for 1998 and prior periods are pro forma for income taxes.
† Stock began trading Nov. 24, 1997.
¶ Income figures for 2000 include repositioning charge of $3.962 million pretax, ($0.51) per share after-tax; and extraordinary loss of $108,506/($0.02), cumulative effect of accounting change.
# Income figures for 1998 include pretax expenses of $260,852 for canceled acquisition; and extraordinary charge of $109,765/($0.04) for extinguishment of debt.

BALANCE SHEET

Assets	01/28/00 (dollars in thousands)	01/29/99	Liabilities	01/28/00 (dollars in thousands)	01/29/99
Current (CAE 469 and 988)	22,510	19,166	Current (STD 716 and 461)	17,810	13,797
Property and equipment	10,007	9,976	Convertible subordinated debt	4,000	
Deferred taxes	3,177	239	Other long-term debt	2,448	1,497
Other	1,695	1,071	Reserve for store closings	2,188	
TOTAL	37,389	30,453	Deferred rent credits	1,302	1,068
			Stockholders' equity*	9,641	14,090
			TOTAL	37,389	30,453

* $0.01 par common; 40,000,000 authorized; 4,627,936 and 4,627,936 issued and outstanding.

RECENT QUARTERS / **PRIOR-YEAR RESULTS**

	Quarter End	Revenue ($000)	Earnings ($000)	EPS ($)	Prior-Year Revenue ($000)	Prior-Year Earnings ($000)	Prior-Year EPS ($)
Q2	07/28/2000	23,592	879	0.19	19,922	101	0.02
Q1	04/28/2000	19,738	(985)	(0.21)	16,692	(1,217)	(0.26)
Q4	01/28/2000	23,974	(2,914)	(0.63)	18,921	(55)	(0.01)
Q3	10/29/99	21,783	(418)	(0.09)	17,001	(157)	(0.03)
	SUM	89,087	(3,439)	(0.74)	72,536	(1,328)	(0.29)

CURRENT: Q2 earnings include pretax credit of $0.53 million for reversal of repositioning charge. Q4 earnings include pretax charge of $3.962 million for repositioning.
PRIOR YEAR: Q1 earnings include charge of $108,056/($0.02) for cumulative effect of accounting change.

RECENT EVENTS

In **December 1999** the company announced plans to open up to 10 new or remodeled company-owned stores in fiscal 2000. **Jan. 28, 2000**: For the fourth quarter, sales for company-owned stores increased 27 percent to $23.6 million, while full-year sales increased 30 percent to $81.1 million. The company also said same-store sales increased 16 percent for the quarter and 10 percent for the 12-month period. "New Years' sales, heavily boosted by the millennium event, were better than expected, said CEO Dolginow. "Although Christmas sales were strong, we did realize some margin pressure during fourth quarter due to a more heavily promoted Christmas season.... We are disappointed that our Web site has not performed up to our expectations." In **February** the company received notification from Nasdaq that it was not in compliance with the Nasdaq National Market's maintenance standard requiring that the company maintain at least $5 million of public float. In order to comply, Paper Warehouse's common stock had to trade above $1.85 for 10 consecutive *continued on page 341*

OFFICERS

Yale T. Dolginow
Chairman, President, and CEO

Michael A. Anderson
VP-Franchising

Steven R. Anderson
VP and Chief Information Officer

Steven P. Durst
VP-Merchandising

Kristen Lenn
VP-Human Resources

Willard V. Lewis
VP-Store Development

Carol A. Nelson
VP-Stores

Cheryl W. Newell
VP and CFO

Diana Purcel
Controller

DIRECTORS

Arthur H. Cobb
Cobb & Associates Ltd.

Diane C. Dolginow

Yale T. Dolginow

Marvin W. Goldstein
financial consultant

Jeffrey S. Halpern
Southwest Casino and Hotel Corp.

Martin A. Mayer
financial consultant

Richard W. Perkins
Perkins Capital Management Inc., Wayzata, MN

MAJOR SHAREHOLDERS

Perkins Capital Management Inc., 17%
Wayzata, MN

All officers and directors as a group (9 persons), 44.2%

SIC CODE

5943 Stationery stores
5947 Gift, novelty, and souvenir shops

MISCELLANEOUS

TRANSFER AGENT AND REGISTAR:
Wells Fargo Bank Minnesota N.A., South St. Paul, MN

TRADED: Nasdaq SmallCap Market

SYMBOL: PWHS

STOCKHOLDERS: 160

EMPLOYEES: 1,344

PART TIME: 990

IN MINNESOTA: 469

GENERAL COUNSEL:
Oppenheimer Wolff & Donnelly LLP, Minneapolis

AUDITORS:
Grant Thornton LLP, Minneapolis

INC: MN-1987

FOUNDED: 1983

ANNUAL MEETING: June

FRANCHISING:
Michael Anderson

HUMAN RESOURCES:
Kristen Lenn

RANKINGS

No. 95 CRM Public 200
No. 49 CRM Performance 100

TWO-YEAR QUARTERLY HIGH-LOW STOCK PRICES

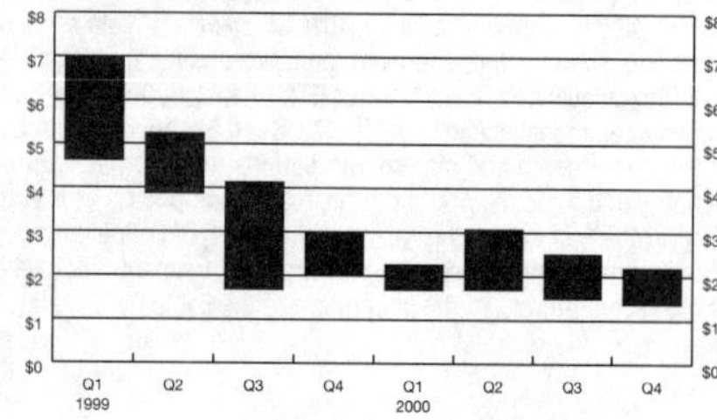

Patterson Dental Company

1031 Mendota Heights Rd., Mendota Heights, MN 55120
Tel: 651/686-1600 Fax: 651/686-9331 Web site: http://www.pattersondental.com

Patterson Dental Co. is one of the two largest distributors of dental products in North America. The company, a full-service, value-added supplier to dentists, dental laboratories, institutions, physicians, and other healthcare professionals, provides: consumable products (including x-ray film, restorative materials, hand instruments and sterilization products); advanced technology dental equipment, practice management software; and office forms and stationery. The company offers its customers a broad selection of dental products including more than 82,500 stock keeping units of which approximately 2,800 are private-label products sold under the Patterson name. Patterson also offers customers a full range of related services including dental equipment installation, maintenance and repair, dental office design and equipment financing. The company markets its dental products and services through over 1,000 direct sales representatives and equipment specialists, operating from 94 sales offices in the United states and Canada. The company processes nearly 12,000 customer orders each business day using a computerized order processing network that links the company's sales offices and 11 distribution centers. Patterson publishes a catalog, Patterson Today, containing approximately 15,000 dental products.

EARNINGS HISTORY *

Year Ended Apr	Operating Revenue/Sales (dollars in thousands)	Net Earnings (dollars in thousands)	Return on Revenue (percent)	Return on Equity (percent)	Net Earnings (dollars per share†)	Cash Dividend (dollars per share†)	Market Price Range (dollars per share†)
2000	1,040,348	64,472	6.2	19.5	0.96	—	25.06–16.25
1999	878,773	49,896	5.7	18.8	0.75	—	23.19–14.50
1998	778,169	40,769	5.2	19.4	0.61	—	16.33–10.29
1997 ¶	687,895	32,617	4.7	19.9	0.50	—	12.29–6.67
1996	606,983	28,648	4.7	21.9	0.43	—	10.58–7.25

* Historical results restated to pool Canadian Dental Supply Ltd., acquired Aug. 26, 1997.
† Per-share amounts restated to reflect 2-for-1 stock split on July 21, 2000; and 3-for-2 split on Feb. 17, 1998.
¶ Figures for 1997 include the results of Colwell division from its Oct. 1, 1996, date of acquisition from Deluxe Corp.

BALANCE SHEET

Assets	04/29/00 (dollars in thousands)	04/24/99 (dollars in thousands)	Liabilities	04/29/00 (dollars in thousands)	04/24/99 (dollars in thousands)
Current (CAE 113,453 and 78,746)	351,408	286,644	Current	112,906	98,692
Property and equipment	46,022	37,018	Noncurrent	3,458	3,332
Intangibles	50,730	46,867	Deferred credits	5,142	6,027
Other	3,816	2,721	Common stockholders' equity*	330,470	265,199
TOTAL	451,976	373,250	TOTAL	451,976	373,250

* $0.01 par common; 100,000,000 authorized; 67,363,446 and 67,298,626 issued and outstanding.

RECENT QUARTERS / **PRIOR-YEAR RESULTS**

	Quarter End	Revenue ($000)	Earnings ($000)	EPS ($)	Prior-Year Revenue ($000)	Prior-Year Earnings ($000)	Prior-Year EPS ($)
Q1	07/29/2000	268,294	16,094	0.24	254,599	14,489	0.21
Q4	04/29/2000	277,142	17,980	0.27	235,199	14,022	0.21
Q3	01/29/2000	260,172	17,192	0.25	230,176	13,748	0.21
Q2	10/30/99	248,435	14,811	0.22	213,325	11,897	0.18
	SUM	1,054,043	66,077	0.98	933,299	54,156	0.81

PRIOR YEAR: Q1 consisted of 14 weeks.

RECENT EVENTS

In **March 2000** the company acquired Guggenheim Bros. Dental Supply Co., Hawthorne, Calif., a full-service dental products distributor with 1999 sales of $20 million. The acquisition significantly increased Patterson's market share and coverage in California. **July 29**: First-quarter sales for fiscal 2001 increased 13.4 percent on a comparable basis (excluding the impact of the extra week in the first quarter of fiscal 2000). "Patterson's top line growth continued to outpace what we estimate to be the 7 percent to 9 percent growth of the dental supply market by a substantial margin," said CEO Frechette. The company's modestly below-consensus first-quarter earnings resulted primarily from softness in sales of higher-margin practice management software and dental office forms and stationery. In **August** Patterson acquired $3.1 million-revenue Micheli Dental Supply Inc., doing business as ABE Dental, a Belmont, Calif.-based distributor of consumable dental products. In **September** the company acquired eCheck-Up.com, a newly developed Internet service that was to provide online payroll, human resources, and payables processing, as well as benchmarking capabilities to subscribing dental customers through its Web site.

OFFICERS

Peter L. Frechette
Chairman, President, and CEO
R. Stephen Armstrong
EVP, CFO, and Treasurer
Scott Kabbes
Pres.-EagleSoft
R. Reed Saunders
Pres.-Colwell Systems
Normand Senecal
Pres.-Patterson Dental Canada
Lynn Askew
VP-Management Information Systems
Mary Baglien
VP-Human Resources
Gary D. Johnson
VP-Sales
Rich Kochmann
VP-Marketing
James W. Wiltz
VP, Pres.-Patterson Dental Supply, Inc.
Matthew L. Levitt
Secretary and General Counsel

DIRECTORS

David K. Beecken
Beecken Petty & Co., Lisle, IL
Ronald E. Ezerski
retired, Bonita Springs, FL
Peter L. Frechette
Andre B. Lacy
LDI Management Inc., Indianapolis
Burt E. Swanson
Briggs and Morgan P.A., St. Paul

MAJOR SHAREHOLDERS

First American Asset Mgmt. as ESOP Trustee, 10.6%
Minneapolis
Ronald E. Ezerski, 7.5%
Peter L. Frechette, 7.1%
FMR Corp., 5.1%
Boston
Fidelity Research & Management Inc., 5.1%
Boston
All officers and directors as a group (12 persons), 17%

SIC CODE

5047 Medical and hospital equipment, whsle
5961 Catalog and mail-order houses

MISCELLANEOUS

TRANSFER AGENT AND REGISTAR:
Wells Fargo Bank Minnesota N.A., South St. Paul, MN
TRADED: Nasdaq National Market
SYMBOL: PDCO
STOCKHOLDERS: 2,573
EMPLOYEES: 3,796
PART TIME: 88
IN MINNESOTA: 307
GENERAL COUNSEL:
Briggs and Morgan P.A., Minneapolis
AUDITORS:
Ernst & Young LLP, Minneapolis
INC: MN-1992
FOUNDED: 1877
ANNUAL MEETING: September
INVESTOR RELATIONS: R. Stephen Armstrong
EQUITY MARKET PARTNERS: Richard Cinquina

RANKINGS

No. 39 CRM Public 200
No. 27 CRM Performance 100

SUBSIDIARIES, DIVISIONS, AFFILIATES

Direct Dental Supply Co.

Patterson Dental Canada Inc.
(formerly Healthco Canada Inc.)

Patterson Dental Supply Inc.

PUB

TWO-YEAR QUARTERLY HIGH-LOW STOCK PRICES

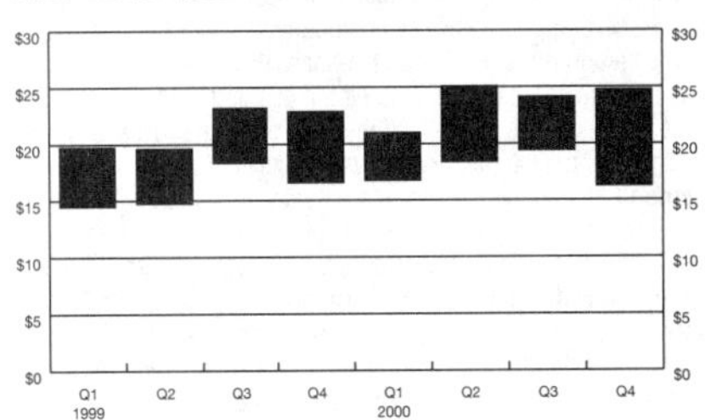

PUB

Pemstar Inc.

3535 Technology Dr. N.W., Rochester, MN 55901
Tel: 507/288-6720 Fax: 507/280-0838 Web site: http://www.pemstar.com

Pemstar is a contract manufacturing and engineering company that produces precision electromechanical and electronic products and assemblies for a blue-chip list of more than 100 large and medium-sized companies in the computer, computer storage device, telecommunications, medical, automotive, and industrial equipment industries. Pemstar's founding team of former IBM executives specializes in solving a customer's problems through early intervention and intensive engineering. After low-volume production has perfected the manufacturing process, Pemstar moves the customer's operations to an appropriate international facility, to take advantage of low labor costs.

EARNINGS HISTORY

Year Ended Mar 31	Operating Revenue/Sales (dollars in thousands)	Net Earnings	Return on Revenue (percent)	Return on Equity	Net Earnings (dollars per share*)	Cash Dividend	Market Price Range
2000 †	393,842	2,651	0.7	11.7	0.23	—	
1999	187,381	1,666	0.9	10.1	0.15	—	
1998	165,049	5,317	3.2	48.4	0.55	—	
1997	31,895	950	3.0	31.6	0.12	—	
1996	22,021	631	2.9	NM	0.08	—	

* Shares did not begin trading until Aug. 8, 2000.
† Pro forma had the acquisitions of Quadrus Mfg. (June 7, 1999) and Turtle Mountain (Aug. 1, 2000) occurred April 1, 1999: revenue $436.891 million; earnings $1.302 million/$0.11.

BALANCE SHEET

Assets	03/31/00 (dollars in thousands)	03/31/99	Liabilities	03/31/00 (dollars in thousands)	03/31/99
Current (CAE 2,727 and 827)	133,443	41,899	Current (STD 23,143 and 6,115)	83,794	29,116
Property and equipment	34,933	17,561	Long-term debt	51,114	7,000
Goodwill	20,691	3,794	Capital lease obligations	4,067	90
Other	1,384	1,336	Deferred grant income	1,713	1,808
Deferred income taxes		393	Deferred revenue	350	1,017
TOTAL	190,451	64,983	Deferred income taxes	17	
			Minority interest	174	848
			Preferred equity	26,549	8,549
			Common equity*	22,673	16,555
			TOTAL	190,451	64,983

* $0.01 par common; 150,000,000 authorized; 13,819,000 and 11,270,000 issued and outstanding.

RECENT QUARTERS / **PRIOR-YEAR RESULTS**

	Quarter End	Revenue ($000)	Earnings ($000)	EPS ($)	Prior-Year Revenue ($000)	Prior-Year Earnings ($000)	Prior-Year EPS ($)
Q2	09/30/2000	143,902	1,106	0.05	97,560	388	0.03
Q1	06/30/2000	122,604	149	0.01	68,598	915	0.08
Q4	03/31/2000	115,939	357	0.03	49,512	114	0.01
Q3	12/31/99	111,745	991	0.09	50,677	445	0.04
	SUM	494,190	2,603	0.18	266,347	1,862	0.17

RECENT EVENTS

In **November 1999** CEO Al Berning was named the 1999 National Ernst & Young Entrepreneur of the Year in the Emerging Entrepreneur category. In **June 2000** Pemstar, hoping to raise $92.4 million, filed a registration statement with the SEC for an initial public offering of 8.4 million shares of stock to be offered by an underwriting group lead managed by Lehman Brothers and Robertson Stephens. The company signed a definitive agreement to acquire Turtle Mountain Corp. of Dunseith, N.D. [Deal completed in August.] The $11-a-share IPO, effective Aug. 8, grossed $92.4 million. Shares rose 23 percent on their first trading day. The company announced the opening of the ProCenter (Product Realization and Optimization Center) located at its San Jose, Calif., facility. The ProCenter was designed to provide Pemstar's customers with leading-edge product and equipment design and prototype services, with specific focus on the optical networking and wireless telecommunications industries. In **September** Needham & Co. Inc. initiated coverage with a BUY rating (at $18.31) and a six- to 12-month price target of $24, given that the company was strategically positioned to experience double the 20 percent annual growth rate of the $88 billion EMS market. Lehman Brothers initiated coverage with a 1 BUY rating and a 12-month price target of $25. Robertson Stephens chimed in with a BUY for long-term investors. **Sept. 30**: Cash earnings (net income plus tax effected amortization expense) for second quarter, which totaled $0.06 per share versus $0.04 per share in the prior-year period, exceeded analysts' estimates. "During the September quarter we saw deeper sales penetration sequentially in existing accounts from the first fiscal quarter, including wireless companies interWAVE and Western Multiplex, as well ***continued on page 341***

OFFICERS

Allen J. Berning
Chairman and CEO

Robert D. Ahmann
EVP-Manufacturing Systems

William B. Leary
EVP-Rochester Site Operations

Gary L. Lingbeck
EVP-North American Sales, Secretary

Robert R. Murphy
EVP-Corporate Operations, Treasurer

Steve V. Petracca
EVP-Business Development

Karl D. Shurson
EVP-Quality

Hargopal (Paul) Singh
EVP-International Operations

David L. Sippel
EVP-Engineering Services and CTO

William J. Kullback
VP-Finance and CFO

Robert J. Legendre
VP-Worldwide Materials

DIRECTORS

Robert D. Ahmann
Allen J. Berning
Thomas A. Burton
independent consultant
Bruce M. Jaffe
private investor
William B. Leary
Gary L. Lingbeck
Robert R. Murphy
Michael J. Odrich
Lehman Brothers' Venture Capital Fund
Steve V. Petracca
Karl D. Shurson
Hargopal (Paul) Singh
David L. Sippel

MAJOR SHAREHOLDERS

Lehman Brothers Inc./Michael J. Odrich, 18.4%
New York

All officers and directors as a group (13 persons), 41.2%

SIC CODE

3571 Electronic computers

3699 Electrical equipment and supplies, nec

3999 Manufacturing industries, nec

8711 Engineering services

MISCELLANEOUS

TRADED: Nasdaq National Market

SYMBOL: PMTR

EMPLOYEES: 3,500

GENERAL COUNSEL:
Dorsey & Whitney PLLP, Minneapolis

AUDITORS:
Ernst & Young LLP, Minneapolis

INVESTOR RELATIONS:
William J. Kullback

RANKINGS

No. 13 CRM Performance 100

No. 4 Minnesota Technology Fast 50

Pentair Inc.

Wells Fargo Center, 90 S. Seventh St., 36th Floor, Minneapolis, MN 55402
Tel: 612/338-5100 Web site: http://www.pentair.com

Pentair Inc. is a diversified manufacturer operating in three principal markets: professional tools and equipment, water and fluid technologies, and electrical and electronic enclosures. Pentair brands include Delta woodworking machinery; Porter-Cable power tools; Myers, Fairbanks Morse, Aurora, and Hydromatic pumps; Fleck water conditioning control valves; WellMate composite pressure vessels; Pac-Fab pool and spa equipment; Century, Solar, and Lincoln service equipment; Lincoln Industrial lubrication systems; and Hoffman and Schroff enclosures. Pentair operates in more than 50 locations around the world.

EARNINGS HISTORY *

Year Ended Dec 31	Operating Revenue/Sales (dollars in thousands)	Net Earnings	Return on Revenue (percent)	Return on Equity	Net Earnings (dollars per share†)	Cash Dividend	Market Price Range
1999 ¶	2,367,753	103,309	4.4	10.4	2.36	0.64	48.88–30.94
1998	1,937,578	106,840	5.5	15.6	2.67	0.60	45.75–27.88
1997 #	1,839,056	91,600	5.0	15.0	2.28	0.54	39.63–27.50
1996	1,567,065	74,509	4.8	13.5	1.86	0.50	32.25–23.06
1995 **	1,402,871	77,200	5.5	15.7	1.96	0.40	26.25–19.88

* Historical revenue figures were restated in 1995 to segregate results of disposed paper businesses.
† EPS is primary. Per-share amounts restated to reflect 2-for-1 stock split on Feb. 16, 1996.
¶ Figures for 1999 include results of WEB Tool & Mfg. Inc., Essef Corp., and DeVilbiss Air Power Co. from their respective dates of acquisition (April 2, Aug. 10, and Sept. 3, 1999). Pro forma with full-year results: revenue $2.927 billion; earnings $106 million/$2.42.
# Income figures for 1997 include pretax gain of $10,313,000 on sale of Federal Cartridge business.
** Income figures for 1995 include gain of $16.7 million/$0.45 from discontinued operations (paper products and joint venture segments) and their disposal. Figures include results of Fleck Controls Inc. from its November 1 date of purchase for $133.9 million. Pro forma for Jan. 1 purchase: revenue $1.46 billion; net income 78.5 million/$1.97.

BALANCE SHEET

Assets	12/31/99 (dollars in thousands)	12/31/98	Liabilities	12/31/99 (dollars in thousands)	12/31/98
Current (CAE 66,228 and 32,039)	1,150,478	748,569	Current (STD 177,788 and 52,874)	760,947	394,793
Property, plant, and equipment	403,807	308,258	Long-term debt	857,296	288,026
			Pensions	67,182	60,564
Goodwill	1,187,525	474,488	Benefits	44,043	41,868
Deferred income taxes			Reserves	22,885	29,441
			Other	50,563	30,162
Other	61,156	23,351	Deferred taxes	6,845	447
TOTAL	2,802,966	1,554,666	Preferred equity		53,638
			Common equity*	993,205	655,727
			TOTAL	2,802,966	1,554,666

* $.1667 par common; 250,000,000 authorized; 48,317,068 and 38,503,587 issued and outstanding.

RECENT QUARTERS / **PRIOR-YEAR RESULTS**

	Quarter End	Revenue ($000)	Earnings ($000)	EPS ($)	Revenue ($000)	Earnings ($000)	EPS ($)
Q3	09/30/2000	715,926	12,673	0.26	604,918	29,809	0.70
Q2	07/01/2000	781,886	36,559	0.75	507,225	28,285	0.66
Q1	04/01/2000	712,278	33,899	0.70	470,493	2,240	0.05
Q4	12/31/99	785,117	42,975	0.90	524,043	32,921	0.84
	SUM	2,995,207	126,106	2.62	2,106,679	93,255	2.25

PRIOR YEAR: Q1 earnings include charge of $38.0 million pretax, $24.2 million/($0.57) after-tax, for restructuring.

RECENT EVENTS

In **February 2000** Pentair Electronic Packaging unit received a $12 million order from the Motorola Communications Enterprise group for the supply of telecommunications cabinets. The editors of Consumers Digest selected two Water Ace-brand pumps (the Water Ace Model RS2A, a submersible sump pump, and the Water Ace Model R6S, a utility pump) as "Best Buys," saying that they offer today's consumer outstanding value. In **March** Pentair's equipment businesses—DeVilbiss Air Power Co. of Jackson, Tenn., and Century Manufacturing of Bloomington, Minn.—again received the Sears 1999 Partners in Progress Award; and the editors of four national publications recognized eight Porter-Cable and Delta tools for their superior performance, features, and value. In **May** the company moved its corporate headquarters from suburban Roseville, Minn., to Minneapolis' Norwest Center—to consolidate strategic leadership close to other business leaders in town, and to consolidate infrastructure support operations in one place. Sales and earnings of Pentair will grow at *continued on page 341*

OFFICERS

Winslow H. Buxton
Chairman

Joseph R. Collins
Vice Chairman

Randall J. Hogan
President and CEO

Louis L. Ainsworth
SVP and General Counsel

John S. Abbott
VP, Pres.-Pentair Electronic Packaging

Richard J. Cathcart
EVP, Pres.-Water/Fluid Technologies

George M. Danko
SVP-Corp. Devel./Central Operating Svs.

Peter B. Dessing
Pres.-Equipment

Karen A. Durant
VP and Controller

David D. Harrison
EVP and CFO

Deb S. Knutson
VP-Human Resources

Frederick A. Leers
VP-Water Technologies, Asia

Roy T. Rueb
VP, Secretary, and Treasurer

H. Eugene Swacker
Pres.-DeVilbiss Air Power Co.

DIRECTORS

George N. Butzow
MTS Systems Corp. (retired)

Winslow H. Buxton

William J. Cadogan
ADC Telecommunications Inc., Bloomington, MN

Joseph R. Collins

Barbara B. Grogan
Western Industrial Contractors Inc., Denver

Charles A. Haggerty
Western Digital, Irvine, CA

Harold V. Haverty
Deluxe Corp. (retired)

Quentin J. Hietpas
University of St. Thomas, St. Paul

Randall J. Hogan

Walter Kissling
H.B. Fuller Co., Vadnais Heights, MN

Stuart Maitland
Ford Motor Company

Augusto Meozzi
German Isola Group

Richard M. Schulze
Best Buy Co., Eden Prairie, MN

Karen E. Welke
3M Co., Maplewood, MN

MAJOR SHAREHOLDERS

Brinson Partners Inc., 6.7%
Chicago

All officers and directors as a group (14 persons), 2.7%

SIC CODE

3546 Power-driven handtools
3553 Woodworking machinery
3561 Pumps and pumping equipment
3586 Measuring and dispensing pumps
3629 Electrical industrial apparatus, nec
3644 Noncurrent-carrying wiring devices

MISCELLANEOUS

TRANSFER AGENT AND REGISTAR:
Wells Fargo Bank Minnesota N.A., South St. Paul, MN

TRADED: NYSE

SYMBOL: PNR

STOCKHOLDERS: 4,395

EMPLOYEES: 13,900

GENERAL COUNSEL:
Henson & Efron P.A., Minneapolis

AUDITORS:
Deloitte & Touche LLP, Minneapolis

INC: MN-1966

ANNUAL MEETING: April

COMMUNICATIONS/PUB. AFFAIRS: Mark J. Cain

RANKINGS

No. 15 CRM Public 200
No. 79 CRM Employer 100
No. 19 CRM Performance 100

TWO-YEAR QUARTERLY HIGH-LOW STOCK PRICES

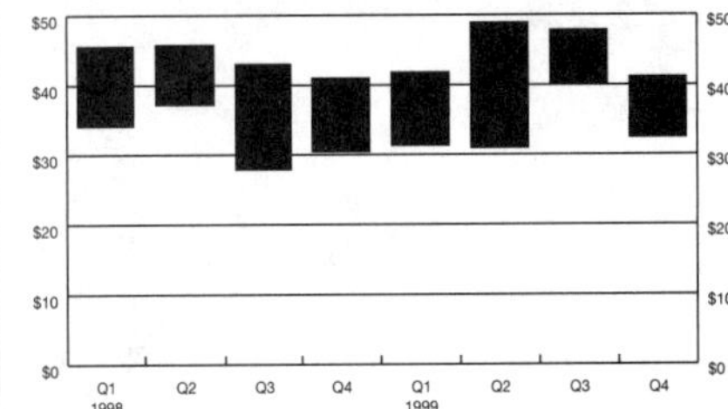

PUB

Photo Control Corporation

4800 Quebec Ave. N., New Hope, MN 55428
Tel: 763/537-3601 Fax: 763/537-2852

Photo Control Corp. designs, manufactures, and markets professional cameras, long-roll film magazines, package printers, photographic accessories, and electronic flash equipment. The principal market for the camera and magazine equipment is the subsegment of the professional photography market that requires high-volume equipment, such as school photographers. Package printers are sold to photographic processing labs that specialize in producing color-print packages, such as wedding and school photography. The market for the electronic flash equipment extends to all professional and experienced amateur photographers. All equipment is marketed throughout the United States and in some foreign countries.

EARNINGS HISTORY

Year Ended Dec 31	Operating Revenue/Sales (dollars in thousands)	Net Earnings	Return on Revenue (percent)	Return on Equity	Net Earnings (dollars per share)	Cash Dividend	Market Price Range
1999	9,335	301	3.2	4.8	0.19	—	4.63–1.19
1998	10,015	(1,017)	(10.2)	(17.1)	(0.63)	—	3.75–1.00
1997 *	10,423	(2,259)	(21.7)	(32.4)	(1.41)	—	4.38–2.25
1996	14,212	68	0.5	0.7	0.04	—	5.50–3.13
1995	14,699	(582)	(4.0)	(6.3)	(0.37)	—	6.25–3.50

* Income figures for 1997 include these pretax items: $1.26 million provision for inventory losses, and $99,589 moving cost; partially offset by $645,671 gain on sale of building.

BALANCE SHEET

Assets	12/31/99 (dollars in thousands)	12/31/98	Liabilities	12/31/99 (dollars in thousands)	12/31/98
Current (CAE 819 and 731)	6,020	5,251	Current	1,173	886
Plant and equipment	1,622	1,757	Other accrued expense	685	616
Cash value of life insurance	308	285	Stockholders' equity*	6,251	5,951
Deferred income taxes	160	160	TOTAL	8,110	7,453
TOTAL	8,110	7,453			

* $0.08 par common; 5,000,000 authorized; 1,604,163 and 1,604,163 issued and outstanding.

RECENT QUARTERS / **PRIOR-YEAR RESULTS**

	Quarter End	Revenue ($000)	Earnings ($000)	EPS ($)	Prior-Year Revenue ($000)	Prior-Year Earnings ($000)	Prior-Year EPS ($)
Q3	09/30/2000	3,721	599	0.38	2,963	264	0.17
Q2	06/30/2000	3,719	505	0.32	2,744	283	0.18
Q1	03/31/2000	2,109	(84)	(0.05)	1,830	(200)	(0.12)
Q4	12/31/99	1,798	(47)	(0.03)	1,367	(622)	(0.39)
	SUM	11,346	974	0.61	8,904	(274)	(0.17)

RECENT EVENTS

In **October 2000** the company announced the acquisition of the operating assets of Lindahl Specialties of Elkhart, Ind., which manufactures and sells the Lindahl product line of photographic accessories for portrait, wedding, commercial, and industrial photographers, including lens shades, filters, flash brackets, and private-label/OEM items. Bob Lindahl, principal owner of Lindahl Specialties, was retained as a consultant. Manufacturing of Lindahl products was moved to Photo Control's own plant in November 2000. Photo Control then entered into an agreement to license and purchase the assets and rights for BookEndz Docking Stations from Pilot Technologies Inc. of Minneapolis.

OFFICERS

Leslie A. Willig
Chairman

John R. (Jack) Helmen
President and CEO

Curtis R. Jackels
VP-Finance

Mark J. Simonett
VP, Secretary

DIRECTORS

Thomas J. Cassady
Merrill Lynch Pierce Fenner & Smith, Woodstock, VT

John Helmen

James R. Loomis
Magnavox Electronic System Co., Fort Wayne, IN

Leslie A. Willig

MAJOR SHAREHOLDERS

Leslie A. Willig, 12.2%
Fremont, IN

Richard P. Kiphart, 8.6%
Chicago

Patrick J. Bruggeman, 6.2%
Fort Wayne, IN

All officers and directors as a group (9 persons), 23.8%

SIC CODE

3861 Photographic equipment and supplies

MISCELLANEOUS

TRANSFER AGENT AND REGISTAR:
Signature Stock Transfer Inc. Dallas

TRADED: Nasdaq SmallCap Market

SYMBOL: PHOC

STOCKHOLDERS: 348

EMPLOYEES: 78

PART TIME: 4

IN MINNESOTA: 77

GENERAL COUNSEL:
Gray, Plant, Mooty, Mooty & Bennett P.A., Minneapolis

AUDITORS:
Virchow, Krause & Co., Minneapolis

INC: MN-1959

ANNUAL MEETING: May

HUMAN RESOURCES:
Curt Jackels

RANKINGS

No. 188 CRM Public 200

SUBSIDIARIES, DIVISIONS, AFFILIATES

Camerz Photo Products Division
4800 Quebec Ave. N.
New Hope, MN 55428
612/537-3601
John Helmen

Nord Photo Engineering Division
4800 Quebec Ave. N.
New Hope, MN 55428
612/537-3601
John Helmen

Norman Enterprises Division
4800 Quebec Ave. N.
New Hope, MN 55428
612/537-3601
John Helmen

TWO-YEAR QUARTERLY HIGH-LOW STOCK PRICES

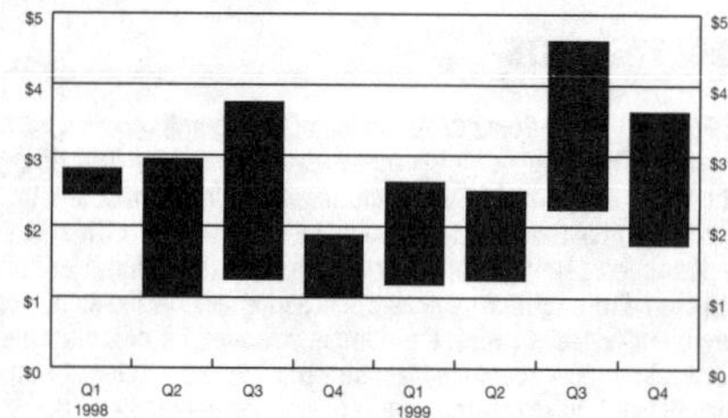

PLATO Learning Inc.

10801 Nesbitt Ave. S., Bloomington, MN 55437
Tel: 952/832-1000 Fax: 952/832-1200 Web site: http://www.plato.com

PLATO Learning Inc. and its subsidiaries provide computer-based and e-learning instruction and related services, offering basic to advanced level courseware in reading, writing, math, science, and life and job skills. The Company's PLATO Learning System and PLATO Web Learning Network provide more than 2,000 hours of objective-based, problem solving courseware and include assessment, alignment, and management tools to facilitate the learning process. PLATO courseware is delivered via networks, CD-ROM, private intranets, and the Internet. Single topic PLATO courseware is available through the company's e-commerce Web site and a growing number of distributors. PLATO courseware is marketed to middle and high schools, colleges, job training programs, correctional institutions, military education programs, corporations and consumers.

EARNINGS HISTORY

Year Ended Oct 31	Operating Revenue/Sales (dollars in thousands)	Net Earnings	Return on Revenue (percent)	Return on Equity	Net Earnings (dollars per share)	Cash Dividend	Market Price Range
1999	44,135	15,031	34.1	73.4	2.18	—	10.06–5.31
1998	43,278	3,068	7.1	NM	0.48	—	11.38–4.88
1997	36,959	(20,217)	(54.7)	NM	(3.24)	—	21.88–7.00
1996	41,405	982	2.4	4.7	0.16	—	19.75–5.94
1995	37,337	3,752	10.0	19.2	0.60	—	10.50–3.75

BALANCE SHEET

Assets	10/31/99 (dollars in thousands)	10/31/98
Current (CAE 63 and 466)	21,243	18,662
Equipment and leasehold improvements	1,269	1,073
Product development costs	6,843	6,380
Deferred taxes	10,357	
Other	1,476	1,292
TOTAL	41,188	27,407

Liabilities	10/31/99 (dollars in thousands)	10/31/98
Current	14,204	20,283
Long-term debt	3,050	3,050
Deferred revenue	420	405
Other	133	
Preferred stock	2,006	
Redeemable common stock	1,799	
Stkhldrs' equity*	19,576	3,669
TOTAL	41,188	27,407

* $0.01 par common; 25,000,000 authorized; 6,560,000 and 6,535,000 issued and outstanding, less 122,000 and 120,000 treasury shares.

RECENT QUARTERS / PRIOR-YEAR RESULTS

	Quarter End	Revenue ($000)	Earnings ($000)	EPS ($)	Prior-Year Revenue ($000)	Prior-Year Earnings ($000)	Prior-Year EPS ($)
Q3	07/31/2000	16,138	2,323	0.31	12,624	2,523	0.38
Q2	04/30/2000	12,240	356	0.03	9,545	(54)	(0.11)
Q1	01/31/2000	7,525	(1,623)	(0.23)	5,661	(2,846)	(0.44)
Q4	10/31/99	16,305	15,408	2.23	14,397	4,899	0.76
	SUM	52,208	16,464	2.33	42,227	4,522	0.59

CURRENT: Q4 earnings include a nonrecurring tax benefit of $10 million for the elimination of the company's federal income tax valuation allowance, related to its net operating loss carryforward, due to significantly improved current and predicted future profitability.

RECENT EVENTS

In **January 2000** TRO Learning announced its intent to change its company name to PLATO Learning to capitalize on the strength of the PLATO brand name in the markets it serves. The required legal review and formal name search had commenced, and the final name was to be determined at the March annual meeting based on the results of those initiatives. CEO Roach explained, "With the increased focus we have placed on our PLATO brand, it has become quite apparent that our current clients and potential customers readily recognize the PLATO name." In **February** TRO formed a strategic partnership with Sunburst Communications, a Houghton Mifflin Co., to market PLATO mathematics software titles to teachers nationwide through Sunburst's catalog distribution network. TRO received a contract valued in excess of $450,000 from the Mississippi Department of Education to provide PLATO courseware to 80 vocational schools involved in the Partners in Education Construction Initiative. In **March** nschool.com—a free, Web-based, teacher-driven education system providing a new level of communication among administrators, teachers, and families—began offering software titles from the PLATO Educators' Choice catalog to its member community. By the end of March, the 540 preferred shares issued under the January 1999 convertible preferred stock transaction were fully converted into 1,060,921 common shares. The total number of shares issued and outstanding was more than 7.5 million. Conversion had also begun on the 1997 subordinated convertible debenture, which began to reduce the company's long term debt. Presidetn Murray commented, "The addition of almost 1.1 million shares to our float appears to be one of the reasons behind the recent increase in daily trading volume. Now that we are out from under this preferred stock overhang I expect to see more institutional holdings of TUTR. I also anticipate a reduction in the TUTR short position." In **April** Proviso Township HSD in Maywood, Ill., agreed tol implement PLATO in high continued on page 341

OFFICERS

William R. Roach
Chairman and CEO

John Murray
President, COO, and acting CFO

G. Thomas Ahern
SVP-PLATO Education Sales/Marketing

Wellesley R. (Rob) Foshay, Ph.D.
VP-Instructional Dsgn./Cognitive Lrng.

David H. LePage
VP-PLATO Support Services/Distribution

Mary Jo Murphy
VP, Chief Acctg. Officer, and Controller

Frank Preese
VP-Product Development

James Riesterer
VP-Marketing

Steven R. Schuster
VP, Secretary, and Treasurer

DIRECTORS

Jack R. Borsting, Ph.D.
University of Southern California, Los Angeles

Hurdis M. Griffith, Ph.D.
Rutgers U./College of Nursing, Newark, NJ

John L. Krakauer
private investor/consultant, Silverthorne, CO

Maj. Gen. Vernon B. Lewis Jr.
Military Professional Resources Inc. (USA retired), Alexandria, VA

John Murray

Dennis J. Reimer
General, U.S. Army (retired)

William R. Roach

Arthur W. Stellar, Ph.D.
Kingston (N.Y.) School District

MAJOR SHAREHOLDERS

William R. Roach, 17%
Hoffman Estates, IL

Cherry Tree & Co. LLC, 8.1%
Edina, MN

KA Investments LDC, 7.2%
Minnetonka, MN

All officers and directors as a group (14 persons), 32.7%

SIC CODE

8299 Schools and educational services, nec

MISCELLANEOUS

TRANSFER AGENT AND REGISTAR:
Wells Fargo Bank Minnesota N.A., South St. Paul, MN

TRADED: Nasdaq National Market

SYMBOL: TUTR

STOCKHOLDERS: 407

EMPLOYEES: 350

GENERAL COUNSEL:
Winston & Strawn, Chicago

AUDITORS:
PricewaterhouseCoopers LLP, Minneapolis

INC: DE-1989

ANNUAL MEETING: April

INVESTOR RELATIONS:
Swenson NHB, www.nhbpr.com

HUMAN RESOURCES:
Patricia Hawver

RANKINGS

No. 116 CRM Public 200

SUBSIDIARIES, DIVISIONS, AFFILIATES

PLATO, Inc.

CyberEd, Inc.

TWO-YEAR QUARTERLY HIGH-LOW STOCK PRICES

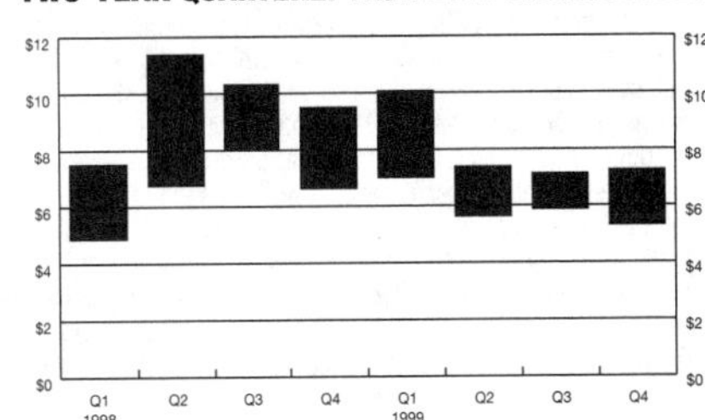

PUB

Polaris Industries Inc.

2100 Highway 55, Medina, MN 55340
Tel: 763/542-0500 Fax: 763/542-0599 Web site: http://www.polarisindustries.com

Polaris Industries Inc. designs, engineers, and manufactures snowmobiles, all-terrain vehicles (ATVs), motorcycles, personal watercraft, and the Polaris Ranger for recreational and utility use. The company markets them—together with related accessories, clothing, and replacement parts—through dealers and distributors worldwide.

EARNINGS HISTORY

Year Ended Dec 31	Operating Revenue/Sales (dollars in thousands)	Net Earnings (dollars in thousands)	Return on Revenue (percent)	Return on Equity (percent)	Net Earnings (dollars per share*)	Cash Dividend (dollars per share*)	Market Price Range (dollars per share*)
1999	1,321,076	76,326	5.8	45.4	3.09	0.80	45.63–27.00
1998 †	1,175,520	31,015	2.6	20.2	1.20	0.72	39.19–24.75
1997	1,048,296	65,383	6.2	38.6	2.45	0.64	33.25–22.25
1996	1,191,901	62,293	5.2	40.1	2.24	0.60	35.75–19.13
1995	1,113,852	60,776	5.5	51.3	2.19	4.27	33.25–25.08

* Per-share amounts restated to reflect 3-for-2 stock split on Oct. 17, 1995. Cash dividend in 1995 includes special dividend of $3.84 per share.
† Income figures for 1998 include charge of $61.4 million pretax, $39.6 million/($1.53) after-tax, provision for litigation loss.

BALANCE SHEET

Assets	12/31/99 (dollars in thousands)	12/31/98 (dollars in thousands)	Liabilities	12/31/99 (dollars in thousands)	12/31/98 (dollars in thousands)
Current (CAE 6,184 and 1,466)	214,714	183,840	Current	233,800	204,964
Property and equipment	150,922	124,254	Borrowings under credit agreement	40,000	20,500
Deferred taxes	16,000	21,000	Stockholders' equity*	168,227	153,233
Intangibles	22,081	22,967	TOTAL	442,027	378,697
Investments in affiliates	38,310	26,636			
TOTAL	442,027	378,697			

* $0.01 par common; 80,000,000 authorized; 24,226,000 and 25,355,000 issued and outstanding.

RECENT QUARTERS / **PRIOR-YEAR RESULTS**

	Quarter End	Revenue ($000)	Earnings ($000)	EPS ($)	Prior-Year Revenue ($000)	Prior-Year Earnings ($000)	Prior-Year EPS ($)
Q3	09/30/2000	396,962	29,266	1.25	388,883	27,249	1.11
Q2	06/30/2000	342,785	16,188	0.69	324,308	15,106	0.60
Q1	03/31/2000	270,991	9,749	0.41	237,769	9,067	0.36
Q4	12/31/99	370,116	24,904	1.03	330,947	22,674	0.89
	SUM	1,380,854	80,107	3.38	1,281,907	74,096	2.96

RECENT EVENTS

In **February 2000** Polaris and Karts International Inc. (OTCBB:KINT) signed an exclusive, three-year licensing agreement to design and distribute Polaris go-karts and mini-bikes—manufactured by Karts International and sold through Polaris dealers nationwide. In addition, Karts International was to design and manufacture variations of the Polaris go-kart line and market them to its existing customers. Beginning in **March**, one unique signature NASCAR item was to be auctioned off each week throughout the 2000 NASCAR season on the Polaris Web site, www.polarisindustries.com. In **April** Polaris launched its new branding strategy "The Way Out." Geared toward the working world, "The Way Out" targets individuals who need to escape from everyday pressures and get away from the cell phones and fax machines that run their lives. The new positioning suggests heading for open terrain on Polaris snowmobiles, all-terrain vehicles, personal watercraft, or Victory motorcycles. In **May** the board of directors adopted ashareholder rights plan. "The rights are not being distributed in response to any specific effort to acquire the company," stated CEO Tiller. In **July** Polaris launched two models of the Victory motorcycle in the United Kingdom. In **August** Victory Motorcycles introduced its newest cruiser model at the 60th Annual Sturgis (S.D.) Rally. Polaris voluntarily recalled 13,600 ATVs because of sticky throttles that can prevent the vehicle from slowing down. Polaris announced a new loyalty marketing program for kids, PRO Club Go!, designed to retain riders of kid-sized Polaris recreational vehicles. Polaris became a corporate partner of the Minnesota Wild by signing a three-year deal. The sponsorship included shared marketing rights, fan interactive promotions, product displays, television advertising, participation in Minnesota Wild events, and other in-arena activities. Polaris and BubbaJunk.com, an online lifestyle portal and classified ads site, hosted an ATV event in Texarkana, Texas, over Labor Day weekend. Filmed and televised nationally by The Nashville Network (TNN), it was the first-ever nationally televised ATV event. Also in **September**, Victory Motorcycles announced its sponsorship of the Minnesota Vikings. Polaris and Dodge announced a first-of-its-kind partnership encompassing co-promotions and shared vehicle placement in advertising, dealerships, and special events. The Polaris Indy 800 RMK mountain model was named 2001 Sled of the Year by SnoWest magazine for the second year in a row; and the Indy 600 XC SP, featuring the new EDGE chassis, was named 2001 Snowmobile of the Year by Snow Goer magazine. **Sept. 30:** "Year-to-date, our financial performance has benefited from continuing strength in the all-terrain vehicle business as well as sales and income contributions from growth areas such as parts, garments, and accessories; international sales; andfinancial services," said Tiller. In **October** Polaris launched its first e-commerce venture, purepolaris.com, where customers can purchase items from Polaris' high-margin line of apparel and vehicle accessories. The company agreed to share online commissions with its dealers.

OFFICERS

W. Hall Wendel Jr.
Chairman

Thomas C. Tiller
President and CEO

Jeffrey A. Bjorkman
VP-Operations

John B. Corness
VP-Human Resources

Michael W. Malone
VP-Finance, CFO, and Secretary

Richard R. (Dick) Pollick
VP-International

Thomas H. Ruschhaupt
VP-Sales/Service

DIRECTORS

Andris A. Baltins
Kaplan, Strangis and Kaplan P.A., Minneapolis

Raymond J. Biggs
Huntington Bancshares of Michigan

Beverly F. Dolan
Textron Inc. (retired)

William E. Fruhan Jr.
Harvard Business School, Boston

Robert S. Moe
Polaris Industries Inc. (retired)

Gregory R. Palen
Spectro Alloys Corp., Rosemount, MN

R.M. (Mark) Schreck
RMS Engineering

J. Richard (Dick) Stonesifer
General Electric (retired)

Bruce A. Thomson
Tomsten Inc.

Thomas C. Tiller

W. Hall Wendel Jr.

MAJOR SHAREHOLDERS

Capital Guardian Trust Co. and Capital Group International Inc., 8.2%
Los Angeles

Trimark Financial Corp. Inc., 7.2%
Toronto

All officers and directors as a group (16 persons), 8.7%

SIC CODE

2329 Men's and boys' clothing, nec

2339 Women's and misses' outerwear, nec

3799 Transportation equipment, nec

MISCELLANEOUS

TRANSFER AGENT AND REGISTAR:
Wells Fargo Bank Minnesota N.A., South St. Paul, MN

TRADED: NYSE, PSE

SYMBOL: PII

STOCKHOLDERS: 2,928

EMPLOYEES: 3,500

GENERAL COUNSEL:
Bowman & Brooke, Minneapolis

AUDITORS:
Arthur Andersen LLP, Minneapolis

INC: MN-1994

FOUNDED: 1954

ANNUAL MEETING: May

HUMAN RESOURCES:
John Corness

INVESTOR RELATIONS:
Cela Sandin

RANKINGS

No. 29 CRM Public 200

No. 87 CRM Employer 100

No. 42 CRM Performance 100

SUBSIDIARIES, DIVISIONS, AFFILIATES

Applies to all divisions listed:
2100 Highway 55
Medina, MN 55340
763/542-0500

ATV Unit
Mitchell Johnson

Snowmobile Unit
Bob Nygaard

PWC Unit
Ron Bills

Motorcycle Unit
Mark Blackwell

TWO-YEAR QUARTERLY HIGH-LOW STOCK PRICES

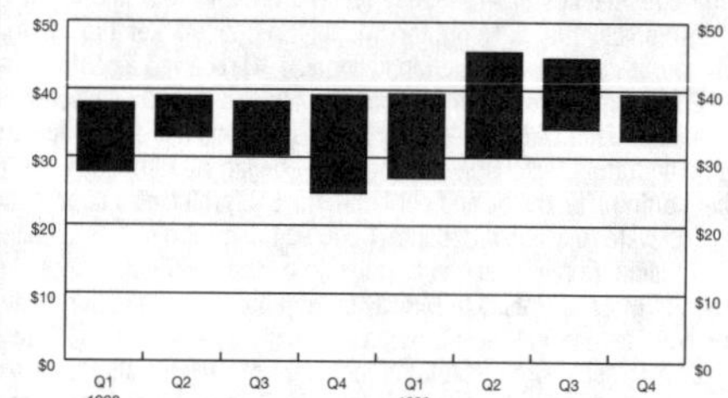

Possis Medical Inc.

9055 Evergreen Blvd. N.W., Coon Rapids, MN 55433
Tel: 763/780-4555 Fax: 763/780-2227 Web site: http://www.possis.com

Possis Medical Inc. is a medical device company whose mission is to provide physicians and patients with innovative, medically effective and cost-efficient devices to treat some of the most serious cardiovascular conditions, such as heart attack, stroke, pulmonary embolism, and clogged peripheral vessels that can lead to leg loss. The company has a portfolio of FDA-approved products—the AngioJet System for removing blood clots, the Perma-Flow Coronary Bypass Graft, and the Perma-Seal Dialysis Access Graft—which are highly differentiated, next generation medical devices with the potential to become preferred treatments.

EARNINGS HISTORY *

Year Ended Jul 31	Operating Revenue/Sales (dollars in thousands)	Net Earnings (dollars in thousands)	Return on Revenue (percent)	Return on Equity (percent)	Net Earnings (dollars per share)	Cash Dividend (dollars per share)	Market Price Range (dollars per share)
2000	20,428	(10,590)	(51.8)	(51.7)	(0.67)	—	14.13–6.00
1999	13,123	(12,021)	NM	(73.7)	(0.90)	—	14.88–4.31
1998	6,118	(11,969)	NM	NM	(0.98)	—	17.00–9.25
1997	4,834	(8,496)	NM	(42.9)	(0.70)	—	22.00–11.50
1996	1,606	(8,173)	NM	(29.6)	(0.70)	—	21.75–12.25

* Revenue has been restated for continuing operations. Income figures include per-share gains from discontinued operations of $0.01, $0.04, and $0.04—in 1997-95, respectively.

BALANCE SHEET

Assets	07/31/00 (dollars in thousands)	07/31/99	Liabilities	07/31/00 (dollars in thousands)	07/31/99
Current	21,290	16,834	Current	4,502	3,304
(CAE 4,053 and 9,151)			(STD 180 and 92)		
Property	3,714	2,789	Long-term debt	7	100
Goodwill		198	Other		102
TOTAL	25,004	19,821	Stkhldrs' equity*	20,495	16,315
			TOTAL	25,004	19,821

* $0.40 par common; 100,000,000 authorized; 16,700,942 and 14,998,360 issued and outstanding.

RECENT QUARTERS / **PRIOR-YEAR RESULTS**

	Quarter End	Revenue ($000)	Earnings ($000)	EPS ($)	Prior-Year Revenue ($000)	Prior-Year Earnings ($000)	Prior-Year EPS ($)
Q4	07/31/2000	6,317	(2,742)	(0.16)	4,762	(2,411)	(0.16)
Q3	04/30/2000	4,472	(2,906)	(0.18)	3,739	(3,225)	(0.23)
Q2	01/31/2000	5,155	(2,350)	(0.16)	2,763	(3,153)	(0.25)
Q1	10/31/99	4,483	(2,592)	(0.17)	1,860	(3,232)	(0.26)
	SUM	20,428	(10,590)	(0.67)	13,123	(12,021)	(0.91)

RECENT EVENTS

In **November 1999** the company began its fourth round of private placements to raise capital. In **January 2000** Possis Medical received Medicare Part B approval in the state of Georgia for use of its AngioJet Rheolytic Thrombectomy System to remove blood clots from coronary arteries and grafts when used in conjunction with coronary balloon angioplasty. In **February** Possis signed. AngioJet Rheolytic Thrombectomy System contracts with AmeriNet, the largest membership-based health care group purchasing organization in the United States, and with the Department of Veterans Affairs National Acquisition Center. In **March** Possis secured gross proceeds of $15 million in a new financing through a private placement of Possis common stock and warrants with a group of investors led by The Tail Wind Fund Ltd., a worldwide investor in emerging growth companies. Shares of Possis were downgraded from BUY to NEUTRAL by George K. Baum & Co. In **April** the FDA gave 510(k) clearance for use of the AngioJet Rheolytic Thrombectomy System's LF140 catheter to treat thrombus in leg (peripheral) arteries. This clearance makes the AngioJet System the first and only new-generation thrombectomy device with FDA-approved labeling for this important indication. In **May** the FDA gave 510(k) clearance for use of the AngioJet Rheolytic Thrombectomy System's new Xpeedior 60 catheter for removing clots from dialysis access grafts. At month's end, Possis reported enrollment of the first stroke patient in the Thrombectomy in Middle Cerebral Artery Embolism (TIME 1) trial using the company's AngioJet Rheolytic Thrombectomy System in the treatment of ischemic stroke. The TIME 1 feasibility trial, being conducted at six sites in the United States, was to enroll up to 30 patients. The TIME 1 trial, expected to be completed in 12 months, was to be followed by a TIME 2 trial to provide definitive evidence of device safety and effectiveness for ischemic stroke. In **July** Possis released the Xpeedior 100 catheter for removing clots in the arteries of the leg. **July 31:** U.S. AngioJet System revenue for the fourth fiscal quarter and the fiscal year was $6.04 million and $19.029 million, respectively. U.S. AngioJet System revenue increased by 36 percent for the fourth quarter and by 59 percent for the fiscal year (when compared to the prior-year periods). U.S. AngioJet System revenue was driven primarily by robust growth in the coronary business and by strong market response to two new products introduced in the fourth quarter: the Xpeedior 60 catheter for dialysis access grafts and the Xpeedior 100 catheter for peripheral arteries. The catheter utilization rate for the AngioJet System, a measure of recurring demand, increased to 11.0 in the fourth quarter, compared to 8.3 in the third quarter, and 10.8 in the same period a year ago. In **August**, based on its revenue growth from 1995 to 1999, the company was named to Deloitte & Touche's Minnesota Technology Fast 50.

OFFICERS

Donald C. Wegmiller
Chairman

Robert G. Dutcher
President and CEO

Irving R. Colacci
VP-Legal/Human Res., Gen. Counsel, Sec.

T.V. Rao
VP and Gen. Mgr.-AngioJet

Robert J. Scott
VP-Manufacturing Operations

James D. Gustafson
VP-Quality Systems, Reg./Clin. Affairs

Eapen Chacko
VP-Finance and CFO

DIRECTORS

Dean Belbas
General Mills Inc. (retired)

Robert G. Dutcher

Seymour J. Mansfield
Mansfield, Tanick & Cohen P.A., Minneapolis

William C. Mattison Jr.
Gerard Klauer Mattison & Co., New York

Whitney A. McFarlin
Angeion Corp., Plymouth, MN

Donald C. Wegmiller
Management Compensation Group/HealthCare, Minneapolis

Rodney A. Young
Lectec Corp., Minnetonka, MN

MAJOR SHAREHOLDERS

All officers and directors as a group (13 persons), 7.6%

SIC CODE

3841 Surgical and medical instruments

MISCELLANEOUS

TRANSFER AGENT AND REGISTAR:
Wells Fargo Bank Minnesota N.A.,
South St. Paul, MN

TRADED: Nasdaq National Market

SYMBOL: POSS

STOCKHOLDERS: 1,680

EMPLOYEES: 228

GENERAL COUNSEL:
Dorsey & Whitney PLLP, Minneapolis

AUDITORS:
Deloitte & Touche LLP, Minneapolis

INC: MN-1956

FOUNDED: 1952

ANNUAL MEETING: December

PUBLIC/INVESTOR RELATIONS: Eapen Chacko

HUMAN RESOURCES: Irving R. Colacci

RANKINGS

No. 155 CRM Public 200

No. 33 Minnesota Technology Fast 50

SUBSIDIARIES, DIVISIONS, AFFILIATES

Possis Medical Europe B.V.
Nieuwegein, Netherlands

TWO-YEAR QUARTERLY HIGH-LOW STOCK PRICES

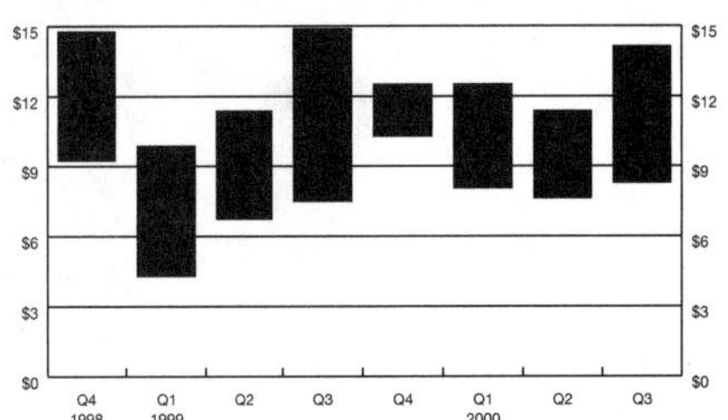

Prevent Products Inc.

1167 Ottawa Ave., West St. Paul, MN 55118
Tel: 651/457-4385 Fax: 651/457-4385 Web site: http://www.preventproducts.com

Prevent Products Inc. was incorporated for the purpose of developing new health care products. The company develops and sells rehabilitative and protective products to nursing home residents. It also develops certain other types of medical products, such as the phlebopump.

EARNINGS HISTORY

Year Ended Oct 31	Operating Revenue/Sales (dollars in thousands)	Net Earnings	Return on Revenue (percent)	Return on Equity	Net Earnings (dollars per share)	Cash Dividend	Market Price Range
1999	688	(9)	(1.2)	(2.0)	0.00	—	
1998	678	(100)	(14.7)	(22.9)	(0.05)	—	
1997	666	69	10.4	18.4	0.04	—	
1996	590	(2)	(0.3)	(0.7)	0.00	—	
1995	579	32	5.5	12.1	0.02	—	

BALANCE SHEET

Assets	10/31/99 (dollars in thousands)	10/31/98	Liabilities	10/31/99 (dollars in thousands)	10/31/98
Current (CAE 78 and 90)	358	385	Current	30	38
Property and equipment	23	14	Stockholders' equity*	428	437
Intangibles	28	30	TOTAL	458	475
Deferred income taxes	50	47			
TOTAL	458	475			

* $0.01 par common; 5,000,000 authorized; 1,865,000 and 1,865,000 issued and outstanding.

RECENT QUARTERS / **PRIOR-YEAR RESULTS**

	Quarter End	Revenue ($000)	Earnings ($000)	EPS ($)	Prior-Year Revenue ($000)	Prior-Year Earnings ($000)	Prior-Year EPS ($)
Q3	07/31/2000	170	20	0.01	184	7	0.00
Q2	04/30/2000	137	20	0.01	150	21	0.01
Q1	01/31/2000	146	14	0.01	166	(13)	(0.01)
Q4	10/31/99	188	(23)	(0.01)	199	1	0.00
	SUM	642	31	0.02	698	16	0.01

OFFICERS

Carol McKay Garcia
President

SIC CODE

3842 Surgical appliances and supplies

MISCELLANEOUS

AUDITORS:
Samuel T. Kantos & Associates, Shoreview, MN

INC: MN-1986

Printware Inc.

1270 Eagan Industrial Rd., Eagan, MN 55121
Tel: 651/456-1400 Fax: 651/454-3684 Web site: http://www.printwareinc.com

Printware Inc. designs, builds, and markets "computer-to-plate" systems that are used by the offset printing industry to create printing plates directly from computer data. These systems replace the traditional process of typesetting, paste-up, camera work, and processing film to produce a printing plate. Computer-to-plate technology provides one-step platemaking (including text, graphics, and photographic halftones) directly from computer data, much as a laser printer makes printed pages directly from computer data. The key benefits of computer-to-plate technology are lower costs, faster turnaround, less equipment, and fewer environmental limits on disposal of by-products. The company sells Platesetters (the key hardware element), Platesetter supplies, and raster image processors for connecting the Platesetter to the customer's computer network.

EARNINGS HISTORY

Year Ended Dec 31	Operating Revenue/Sales (dollars in thousands)	Net Earnings (dollars in thousands)	Return on Revenue (percent)	Return on Equity (percent)	Net Earnings (dollars per share*)	Cash Dividend (dollars per share*)	Market Price Range (dollars per share*)
1999	4,623	275	6.0	1.9	0.07	—	3.94–1.88
1998	6,997	1,934	27.6	11.1	0.39	—	4.25–2.63
1997	6,986	2,159	30.9	13.8	0.44	—	5.50–3.13
1996	7,416	2,383	32.1	18.0	0.56	—	6.63–4.50
1995 †	8,388	1,793	21.4	41.5	0.49	—	

* Stock began trading on July 2, 1996.
† Income figures for 1995 include pretax gain of $192,335 on arbitration award from a dispute with former customer A.B. Dick Co.

BALANCE SHEET

Assets	12/31/99 (dollars in thousands)	12/31/98 (dollars in thousands)
Current (CAE 56 and 653)	11,374	15,810
Property and equipment	186	217
Intangibles	22	25
Deferred income taxes	2,057	1,461
Lease receivables	1,717	1,003
TOTAL	15,356	18,515

Liabilities	12/31/99 (dollars in thousands)	12/31/98 (dollars in thousands)
Current	834	1,100
Stockholders' equity*	14,521	17,415
TOTAL	15,356	18,515

* No par common; 15,000,000 authorized; 3,269,494 and 4,834,516 issued and outstanding.

RECENT QUARTERS / PRIOR-YEAR RESULTS

	Quarter End	Revenue ($000)	Earnings ($000)	EPS ($)	Prior-Year Revenue ($000)	Prior-Year Earnings ($000)	Prior-Year EPS ($)
Q3	09/30/2000	1,095	(79)	(0.02)	1,355	21	0.01
Q2	07/01/2000	1,605	(34)	(0.01)	1,266	101	0.02
Q1	04/01/2000	1,264	92	0.03	920	(97)	(0.02)
Q4	12/31/99	1,082	250	0.08	1,834	832	0.17
	SUM	5,046	229	0.07	5,375	857	0.18

RECENT EVENTS

In **November 1999** the company introduced a RIP-based control panel applet for Platestream Platesetter. The new application uses a graphical interface to provide up-to-the-instant plate status, platesetter diagnostics, and interactive help menus. In **February 2000** Printware reached a distribution agreement with PrintNation.com, the world's largest supplier of printing equipment and supplies. In **March** the company received an order from California-based Mission Announcement Co. for a complete web-to-press system. On **March 31**, dissident shareholders filed a preliminary proxy statement with the SEC in connection with the annual meeting. Company performance over the past few years had some shareholders eager to replace the board of directors. The company convened its annual meeting as scheduled on **April 13**, then immediately adjourned until June 7, 2000—to allow the dissidents and the company additional time. In **May** the company completed a multiple-unit platesetter system sale to Wisconsin-based Liturgical Publications Inc. The sale, valued at between $200,000 and $250,000, included the installation of four PlateStream computer-to-plate systems at two LPi plants. In **June**, based on preliminary figures, shareholders voted to elect all nominees of the opposition Shareholders' Committee to Improve Printware Shareholder Value to the board of directors of Printware. Gary S. Kohler, a spokesperson for the opposition slate, stated: "I am gratified by Printware's shareholders' strong statement of support by voting to elect our new board. It is difficult to unseat an incumbent board. Our message to shareholders has been a message of realism—that change is needed—and shareholders have agreed with us." Printware opened new sales offices in the San Francisco Bay area and in Ohio. In **September** Printware introduced PlateStream-SC, a low-cost computer-to-plate system targeted at small commercial printers.

OFFICERS

Daniel A. Baker, Ph.D.
President and CEO

Thomas W. Petschauer
EVP and CFO

Timothy S. Murphy
VP-Marketing/Sales

INVESTOR RELATIONS:
Thomas Petschauer

DIRECTORS

Daniel A. Baker, Ph.D.

Charlie Bolger
Bolger Printing

Stanley Goldberg
Goldmark Advisors

Gary S. Kohler
Whitebox Advisors, Minneapolis

Roger C. Lucas, Ph.D.

Douglas M. Pihl
Vital Images Inc., Vadnais Heights, MN

Andrew Redleaf

MAJOR SHAREHOLDERS

Pyramid Trading L.P., 13.7%
Chicago

Pyramid Trading L.P., 10.4%
Chicago

Allen L. Taylor, 10.2%

Daniel A. Baker, 9.8%

R.J. Steichen & Co., 7.7%
Bloomington, MN

Thomas W. Petschauer, 6.3%

SIC CODE

3577 Computer peripheral equipment, nec

MISCELLANEOUS

TRANSFER AGENT AND REGISTAR:
ComputerShare, Lakewood, CO.

TRADED: Nasdaq National Market

SYMBOL: PRTW

STOCKHOLDERS: 1,200

EMPLOYEES: 40

PART TIME: 1

IN MINNESOTA: 33

GENERAL COUNSEL:
Robins, Kaplan, Miller & Ciresi LLP, Minneapolis

AUDITORS:
Deloitte & Touche LLP, Minneapolis

INC: MN-1985

ANNUAL MEETING: April

TWO-YEAR QUARTERLY HIGH-LOW STOCK PRICES

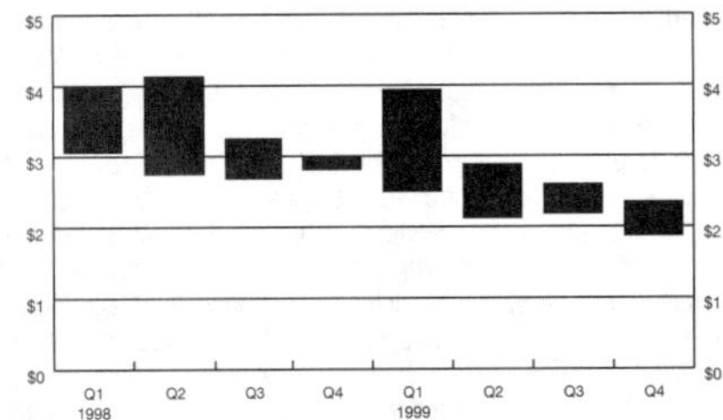

PUB

Quantech Ltd.

815 Northwest Pkwy., Suite 100, Eagan, MN 55121
Tel: 651/647-6370 Fax: 651/647-6369 Web site: http://www.quantechltd.com

Quantech Ltd. is completing development of its FasTraQ system for the hospital emergency department. This system consists of a countertop instrument and disposable cartridges that are expected to run tests for a number of different medical conditions using Quantach's proprietary surface plasmon resonance technology. Test information would be delivered by wireless communication devices to the emergency department staff treating a patient. Quantech's system is intended to streamline the way patients are diagnosed in the hospital emergency department by economically providing STAT test results faster than current methods can. Quantech expects its system to include an initial menu of more than 20 STAT tests grouped in patient diagnosis-related panels such as cardiac enzymes (heart attack), pregnancy, red and white blood cell counts, blood coagulation, kidney function and pancreas function. Tests for liver functions, electrolytes, drugs of abuse, therapeutic drugs, and additional STAT tests will also be made available on the system.

EARNINGS HISTORY *

Year Ended Jun 30	Operating Revenue/Sales (dollars in thousands)	Net Earnings	Return on Revenue (percent)	Return on Equity	Net Earnings (dollars per share†)	Cash Dividend	Market Price Range
2000	150	(6,023)	NM	NM	(2.12)	—	5.00–0.88
1999	0	(4,290)	NM	NM	(1.75)	—	3.88–0.53
1998	0	(3,649)	NM	NM	(1.45)	—	7.00–2.20
1997	0	(3,925)	NM	NM	(1.66)	—	21.88–4.06
1996	0	(2,397)	NM	(45.4)	(1.50)	—	32.50–3.74

* Development-stage company.
† Per-share amounts restated to reflect 1-for-20 reverse stock split effected June 1, 1998.

BALANCE SHEET

Assets	06/30/00 (dollars in thousands)	06/30/99	Liabilities	06/30/00 (dollars in thousands)	06/30/99
Current (CAE 1,328 and 436)	1,514	530	Current (STD 58)	1,565	1,056
Property and equipment	944	166	Long-term debt	46	
			Minority interest	340	
License agreement	2,083	2,409	Preferred equity	14,636	5,113
Deposits	79		Common equity*	(11,940)	(3,051)
Patents	26	13	TOTAL	4,646	3,118
TOTAL	4,646	3,118			

* No par common; 51,538,740 authorized; 6,204,416 and 2,741,534 issued and outstanding.

RECENT QUARTERS / **PRIOR-YEAR RESULTS**

	Quarter End	Revenue ($000)	Earnings ($000)	EPS ($)	Prior-Year Revenue ($000)	Prior-Year Earnings ($000)	Prior-Year EPS ($)
Q1	09/30/2000	40	(2,070)	(0.64)	0	(1,239)	(0.47)
Q4	06/30/2000	150	(2,039)	(0.34)	0	(1,102)	(0.40)
Q3	03/31/2000	0	(1,330)	(0.78)	0	(493)	(0.24)
Q2	12/31/99	0	(1,416)	(0.56)	0	(1,152)	(0.47)
	SUM	190	(6,854)	(2.32)	0	(3,985)	(1.57)

RECENT EVENTS

In **January 2000** the company received FDA clearance to market a quantitative hCG pregnancy test. The Quantech test measures levels of hCG in a woman to determine whether or not she is pregnant. The pregnancy test is part of the test menu that was to be available on Quantech's FasTraQ Patient Treatment Information Platform for the hospital emergency department. Quantech made its final minimum royalty payment on its license for its surface plasmon resonance (SPR) technology. The ability of Quantech to maintain its exclusive worldwide rights to the technology was then no longer subject to minimum payments, but royalties only upon the sale of product. "The minimum royalties have been a financial burden to Quantech during its development stage," said CEO Case. "This last minimum payment comes at a very important time as the company moves toward the introduction of a commercial product this year." Quantech then announced the formation of a new, 80 percent Quantech-owned corporation called HTS BioSystems Inc. HTS was formed to develop and market systems using advanced SPR technology for fields outside of the regulated medical markets. By **May**, HTS Biosystems Inc., had begun operations to pursue accelerated development of high-throughput, cost-effective molecular detection systems for the rapidly growing pharmaceutical and genomics research markets. The new company had rights to proven technology and a prototype system from its majority shareholder, Quantech, that were to enable it to commercialize its FLEX CHIP Kinetic Analysis System in 2001. Meanwhile, Quantech signed a six-year lease for a new headquarters facility in Eagan, Minn., because company expansion required additional space. Quantech entered into a System Technology Evaluation Agreement with the Diagnostic Systems Department of Mitsubishi Chemical Corp. of Japan, which was to conduct an evaluation of Quantech's FasTraQ Emergency Department Patient Testing System and underlying SPR technology. In **June** Quantech filed a new patent application to further expand its intellectual property base beyond its already-existing eight worldwide patents. This filed patent application related to further improvements to Quantech's SPR technology. **June 30**: "The increased loss [in fiscal 2000] was in line with our forecasts, and resulted from higher expenses for Quantech operations as well as HTS BioSystems *continued on page 341*

OFFICERS

Robert Case
CEO

Gregory G. Freitag
COO and CFO

Thomas R. Witty, Ph.D.
EVP-Research/Development

DIRECTORS

Robert Case
Case + Associates, Chicago

Gregory G. Freitag

Robert W. Gaines, M.D.
orthopedic surgeon, Columbia, MO

James F. Lyons

Richard W. Perkins
Perkins Capital Management Inc., Wayzata, MN

Edward E. Strickland
management consultant, Friday Harbor, WA

MAJOR SHAREHOLDERS

Perkins Capital Management Inc., 7.7%
Minneapolis

Special Situations Private Equity Fund, 5.4%
New York

All officers and directors as a group (7 persons), 26.5%

SIC CODE

3841 Surgical and medical instruments

MISCELLANEOUS

TRANSFER AGENT AND REGISTAR:
StockTrans Inc., Ardmore, PA

TRADED: OTC Bulletin Board, LOTC

SYMBOL: QQQQ

STOCKHOLDERS: 500

EMPLOYEES: 38

IN MINNESOTA: 38

GENERAL COUNSEL:
Fredrikson & Byron P.A., Minneapolis

AUDITORS:
RSM McGladrey & Pullen Inc. LLP, Minneapolis

INC: MN-1992

FOUNDED: 1989

ANNUAL MEETING: December

INVESTOR RELATIONS: George Dodge

INVESTOR RELATIONS: Gregory G. Freitag

TWO-YEAR QUARTERLY HIGH-LOW STOCK PRICES

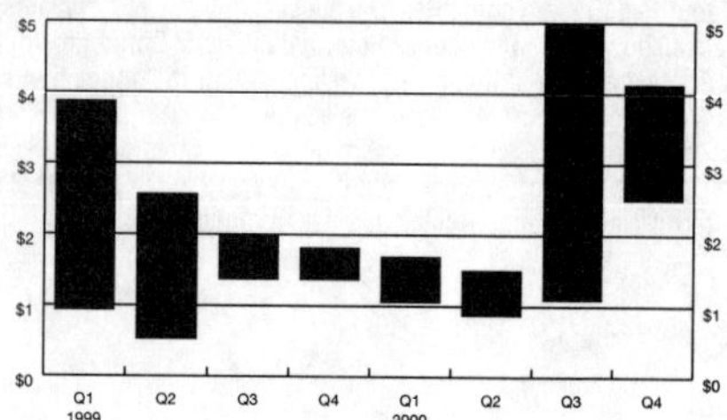

RDO Equipment Company

2829 S. University Dr., P.O. Box 7160, Fargo, ND 58106
Tel: 701/237-7363 Fax: 701/271-6328 Web site: http://www.rdoequipment.com

RDO Equipment Co. is one of the leading and fastest-growing companies engaged in the restructuring and consolidation of the equipment and truck retail industries in the United States. It operates more than 60 retail stores in 11 states, specializing in the distribution, sale, service, rental, and finance of equipment and trucks to the agricultural, construction, manufacturing, transportation, and warehousing industries, as well as to public service entities, government agencies, and utilities.

EARNINGS HISTORY *

Year Ended Jan 31	Operating Revenue/Sales (dollars in thousands)	Net Earnings	Return on Revenue (percent)	Return on Equity	Net Earnings (dollars per share†)	Cash Dividend	Market Price Range
2000 ¶	688,970	6,537	0.9	6.0	0.50	—	10.38–5.50
1999 #	578,624	1,668	0.3	1.6	0.13	—	19.38–7.13
1998 **	429,403	13,251	3.1	13.1	1.01	—	25.25–14.88
1997 ††	302,413	6,483	2.1	7.4	0.69	—	19.00–17.13
1996	223,557	4,841	2.2	14.1	0.51	—	

* Historical figures are pro forma for income taxes and the IPO.
† Stock began trading Jan. 24, 1997.
¶ Income figures for 2000 include pretax gain of $0.786 million on sale of RDO Rental Co. Pro forma to include full-year results of all fiscal 2000 acquisitions: revenue $717.183 million; net income $6.312 million/$0.48.
# Income figures for 1999 include pretax charge of $2.2 million for restructuring. Pro forma to include full-year results of all fiscal 1999 and fiscal 2000 acquisitions: revenue $702.137 million; net income $1.935 million/$0.15.
** Pro forma to include full-year results of all fiscal 1998 acquisitions: revenue $453,661,000; net income $13,594,000/$1.02.
†† Pro forma to include full-year results of all fiscal 1997 acquisitions: revenue $406,860,000; net income $8,107,000/$0.96.

BALANCE SHEET

Assets	01/31/00 (dollars in thousands)	01/31/99	Liabilities	01/31/00 (dollars in thousands)	01/31/99
Current (CAE 4,207 and 51)	302,813	278,117	Current (STD 15,121 and 27,478)	238,588	241,378
Property and equipment	21,944	63,702	Long-term debt	11,483	28,055
Deposits	1,035	1,075	Deferred income taxes	1,460	5,210
Goodwill and other	36,205	36,326	Minority interest	1,191	1,839
TOTAL	361,997	379,220	Stockholders' equity*	109,275	102,738
			TOTAL	361,997	379,220

* $0.01 par common; 27,500,000 authorized; 13,181,500 and 13,181,500 issued and outstanding.

RECENT QUARTERS / **PRIOR-YEAR RESULTS**

	Quarter End	Revenue ($000)	Earnings ($000)	EPS ($)	Revenue ($000)	Earnings ($000)	EPS ($)
Q2	07/31/2000	183,452	(1,297)	(0.10)	177,211	3,842	0.29
Q1	04/30/2000	185,935	871	0.07	180,542	2,130	0.16
Q4	01/31/2000	165,695	(1,748)	(0.13)	149,578	1,957	0.15
Q3	10/31/99	165,522	2,313	0.18	150,764	(7,264)	(0.55)
	SUM	700,604	139	0.01	658,095	665	0.05

PRIOR YEAR: Q3 earnings include pretax charges of $15 million (inventory) and $2.2 million (restructuring).

RECENT EVENTS

In **February 2000** United Rentals Inc. (NYSE: URI) acquired all of the shares of RDO Rental Co., a construction equipment rental operation located in the Southwest. In **July** RDO filed suit in Minnesota state court against John Deere Construction Equipment Co. and related parties alleging that those companies had violated the Minnesota Heavy and Utility Equipment Manufacturers and Dealers Act and had intentionally and inappropriately interfered and conspired to interfere with RDO Equipment's John Deere construction equipment dealership agreements. The suit sought unspecified monetary damages and a ruling that John Deere Construction Equipment does not have the right to terminate RDO Equipment's dealership agreements. In **August** RDO announced that results for the quarter ended July 31 would be below current analysts' estimates and would likely result in a net loss of $1.2 million to $1.8 million. While revenue would show an increase, largely due to agricultural operations, the increase would not be sufficient to offset continuing equipment and truck margin pressures and higher-than-anticipated expenses related to the consolidation and integration of acquired truck dealerships.

OFFICERS

Ronald D. Offutt
Office of the Chairman and CEO
Paul T. Horn
Office of the Chairman and President
Allan F. Knoll
Office of the Chairman and Secretary
Gary L. Weihs
COO
Thomas K. Espel
CFO
Randall C. Amerine
VP-Product Support/Strategic Development
Sonna L. Bakken
VP-Human Resources
Charles Calhoun
EVP-Used Equipment Division
Stephen R. Decker
SVP-Southwest Construction
Steven B. Dewald
SVP-RDO Financial Services Co.
Mark A. Doda
SVP and Controller
John H. Hastings
SVP-Central Construction
Myrna F. Hoekstra
VP-Training/Communications
Kenneth J. Horner Jr.
EVP-Construction Equipment Division
Larry B. Kerkhoff
EVP-West Agriculture
Christi J. Offutt
SVP-Midwest Agriculture
Larry E. Scott
SVP-Southwest Construction Equipment
Jack Summerville
SVP-South Central Construction Equipment
Randall D. Taylor
SVP-Northwest Agriculture
Terry W. Tolbert
SVP-Southwest Agriculture
Alan L. Wiley
SVP-Minnesota Construction

DIRECTORS

Bradford M. Freeman
Freeman Spogli & Co. Inc., Los Angeles
Ray A. Goldberg
Harvard Business School, Boston
Paul T. Horn
Norman M. Jones
LB Community Bank & Trust, Minneapolis
Allan F. Knoll
Ronald D. Offutt
James D. Watkins
J.D. Watkins Enterprises Inc., Ocala, FL

MAJOR SHAREHOLDERS

Ronald D. Offutt (Class A and Class B), 58.8%
Fargo, ND
State of Wisconsin Investment Board, 13.9%
Madison, WI
Tweedy, Browne Co. LLC/TBK Partners L.P., 11%
New York
Allan F. Knoll, 10.3%
Fargo, ND
Paul T. Horn, 7.1%
Fargo, ND
Dimensional Fund Advisors Inc., 6.5%
Santa Monica, CA
Wellington Management Co. LLP, 5.2%
Boston
All officers and directors as a group (24 persons, Class A and Class B), 64.2%

SIC CODE

5082 Construction eqp, whsle
5083 Farm eqp, whsle
5084 Industrial eqp, whsle
7353 Heavy construction equipment rental

MISCELLANEOUS

TRANSFER AGENT AND REGISTAR:
Wells Fargo Bank Minnesota N.A., South St. Paul, MN
TRADED: NYSE
SYMBOL: RDO
STOCKHOLDERS: 233
EMPLOYEES: 1,602
GENERAL COUNSEL:
Oppenheimer Wolff & Donnelly LLP, Minneapolis
AUDITORS:
Arthur Andersen LLP, Minneapolis
INC: DE-1997
FOUNDED: 1968
ANNUAL MEETING: May
INVESTOR RELATIONS:
Richard J. Moen, 612/519-3670
HUMAN RESOURCES:
Sonna Bakken
701/237-7363

TWO-YEAR QUARTERLY HIGH-LOW STOCK PRICES

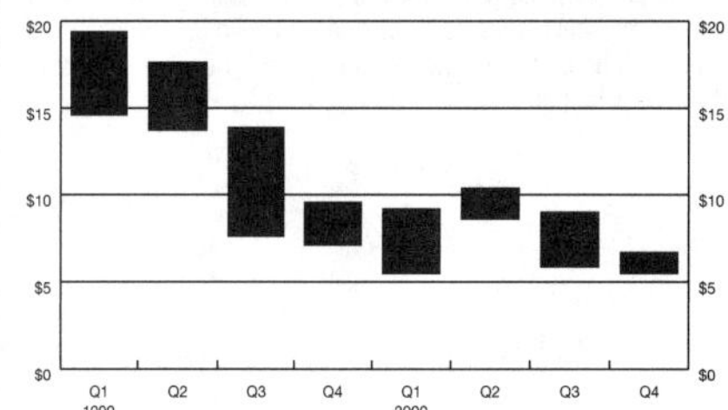

PUB

PUB

RSI Systems Inc.

5555 W. 78th St., Suite F, Edina, MN 55439
Tel: 952/896-3020 Fax: 952/896-3030 Web site: http://www.rsivideo.com

RSI Systems Inc. designs, manufactures, and distributes a family of high-performance, cross-platform H.320 and H.323-ready affordable videoconferencing engines. These compact, component-based systems can be installed in a variety of general or customized videoconferencing applications. RSI introduced the industry's first cross-platform, computer-free component-based videoconferencing appliance for attachment to televisions and other nonintelligent devices. The company makes the MediaPro 384 series of multimedia videoconferencing engines. Operating at 384, 256, and 128 Kbps, these systems can be attached to laptop computers, PCs, and nonintelligent display systems such as television, projectors, etc. The MediaPro 384 products offer full interoperability among all popular-brand H.320 videoconferencing engines. Their self-contained component design internalizes all required electric components (inverse multiplexer and network terminal adapters), making them small, lightweight portable appliances.

EARNINGS HISTORY

Year Ended Jun 30	Operating Revenue/Sales (dollars in thousands)	Net Earnings	Return on Revenue (percent)	Return on Equity	Net Earnings (dollars per share*)	Cash Dividend	Market Price Range
2000 †	4,576	(2,482)	(54.2)	NM	(0.33)	—	2.38–0.38
1999	9,199	(879)	(9.6)	(59.1)	(0.13)	—	4.00–1.50
1998	4,663	(1,960)	(42.0)	NM	(0.34)	—	4.00–1.25
1997 ¶	2,571	(5,685)	NM	NM	(1.30)	—	8.00–1.00
1996	1,626	(4,879)	NM	NM	(1.56)	—	9.25–7.75

* Trading began on July 25, 1995.
† Income figures for 2000 include inventory write-downs totaling $0.342 million/($0.05).
¶ Income figures for 1997 include pretax charge of $1,422,427 for inventory write-downs.

BALANCE SHEET

Assets	06/30/00 (dollars in thousands)	06/30/99	Liabilities	06/30/00 (dollars in thousands)	06/30/99
Current	1,756	4,050	Current	1,845	2,947
Furniture and equipment	462	523	Capital lease obligations	72	140
TOTAL	2,218	4,573	Stockholders' equity*	300	1,486
			TOTAL	2,218	4,573

* $0.01 par common; 10,000,000 authorized; 7,775,258 and 6,837,281 issued and outstanding.

RECENT QUARTERS / PRIOR-YEAR RESULTS

	Quarter End	Revenue ($000)	Earnings ($000)	EPS ($)	Prior-Year Revenue ($000)	Prior-Year Earnings ($000)	Prior-Year EPS ($)
Q1	09/30/2000	888	(290)	(0.03)	1,624	(756)	(0.11)
Q4	06/30/2000	1,086	(354)	(0.05)	1,454	(933)	(0.14)
Q3	03/31/2000	741	(690)	(0.09)	2,790	47	0.01
Q2	12/31/99	1,125	(682)	(0.09)	2,593	(39)	(0.01)
	SUM	3,840	(2,016)	(0.26)	8,460	(1,682)	(0.25)

RECENT EVENTS

In **December 1999** the board of directors approved repurchase of up to 600,000 shares of RSI common stock over the next 12 months. "The board has given management the discretion to buy back RSI stock from time to time, to help counteract the dilutive impact of option grants and equity financing," stated CFO Hanzlik. In **March 2000** RSI announced the MediaPro 384 MP Multipoint System, which allows multiple users to participate in video conferences. In **May** RSI received an equipment order for what was anticipated to become the world's largest telemedical implementation of videoconferencing. Pahth Telecommunications, the company's distributor in Australia, was notified by the Western Australia Health Department that RSI equipment had been selected as a result of a public tender there. Videoconferencing was to be employed in the province to reduce the cost and time involved in diagnosis and treatment, as well as for training, occupational therapy, and other applications of medical resources. A leading national consortium, MiCTA, selected MediaPro 384 video conferencing equipment to offer to its members. In **August**, based on its revenue growth from 1995 to 1999, the company was named to Deloitte & Touche's Minnesota Technology Fast 50.

OFFICERS

Richard F. Craven
Chairman

Eugene W. Courtney
CEO

James D. Hanzlik
CFO

Greg Craven
VP-Sales/Marketing

Roger Berg
Dir.-Operations

Marti D. Miller
VP-Engineering

DIRECTORS

Richard F. Craven
private investor, Minneapolis

S. Albert D. Hanser
private investor, Minneapolis

Byron G. Shaffer
private investor, Minneapolis

MAJOR SHAREHOLDERS

Richard F. Craven, 22.4%
Edina, MN

Alan C. and Delores V. Phillips Rev. Trust, 9.4%

Byron G. Shaffer, 5.3%

All officers and directors as a group (6 persons), 30.2%

SIC CODE

3577 Computer peripheral equipment, nec

7373 Computer integrated systems design

MISCELLANEOUS

TRANSFER AGENT AND REGISTAR:
Wells Fargo Bank Minnesota N.A., South St. Paul, MN

TRADED: OTC Bulletin Board

SYMBOL: RSIS

STOCKHOLDERS: 125

EMPLOYEES: 21

IN MINNESOTA: 16

GENERAL COUNSEL:
Fredrikson & Byron, Minneapolis

AUDITORS:
Lund, Kohler, Cox & Arkema LLP, Minneapolis

INC: MN-1993

ANNUAL MEETING:
January

INVESTOR RELATIONS:
James Hanzlik

RANKINGS

No. 196 CRM Public 200

No. 2 Minnesota Technology Fast 50

TWO-YEAR QUARTERLY HIGH-LOW STOCK PRICES

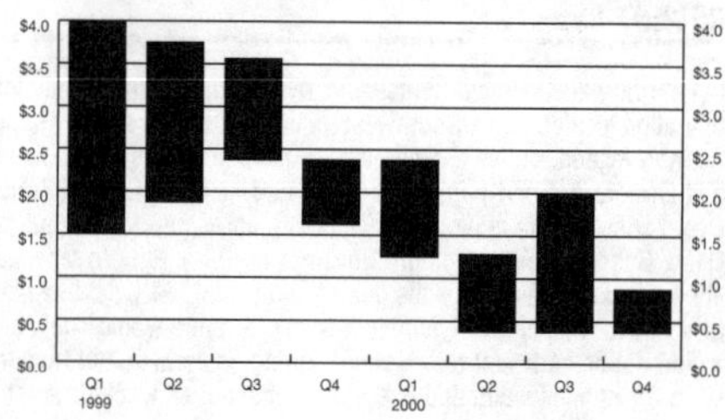

RTW Inc.

8500 Normandale Lake Blvd., Suite 1400, Bloomington, MN 55437
Tel: 952/893-0403 Fax: 952/893-3700 Web site: http://www.rtwi.com

RTW Inc. manages disability products for employers. Its primary product is a workers' compensation management system designed to lower employers' costs and return injured employees to work as soon as possible. RTW combines its proprietary management system, the RTW SOLUTION, with insurance products underwritten by subsidiary American Compensation Insurance Co. RTW serves employers in Minnesota, Colorado, Missouri, Michigan, Massachusetts, Kansas, Illinois, Wisconsin, South Dakota, Indiana, Connecticut, Rhode Island, and New Hampshire. Clients come from many industries, including manufacturing, health care, hospitality, and wholesale/retail.

EARNINGS HISTORY

Year Ended Dec 31	Operating Revenue/Sales (dollars in thousands)	Net Earnings	Return on Revenue (percent)	Return on Equity	Net Earnings (dollars per share*)	Cash Dividend	Market Price Range
1999	77,812	6,167	7.9	11.1	0.50	—	7.88–4.06
1998	90,152	(7,081)	(7.9)	(13.5)	(0.59)	—	10.38–3.81
1997	88,263	5,799	6.6	9.9	0.49	—	19.25–5.25
1996	68,725	8,982	13.1	17.5	0.76	—	33.50–14.75
1995	49,433	7,058	14.3	17.0	0.67	—	20.33–9.00

* Trading began in April 1995. Per-share amounts restated to reflect 3-for-2 stock split on May 17, 1996.

BALANCE SHEET

Assets	12/31/99 (dollars in thousands)	12/31/98
Investments	108,064	126,631
Cash and cash equivalents	302	700
Accrued investment income	1,475	1,761
Premiums receivable	9,435	6,554
Reinsurance recoverables, unpaid claims	41,179	21,403
Reinsurance recoverables, paid claims	2,323	867
Deferred policy-acquisition costs	1,487	1,501
Furniture and equipment	3,881	4,565
Other	8,365	8,952
TOTAL	176,511	172,934

Liabilities	12/31/99 (dollars in thousands)	12/31/98
Unpaid claim and claim-settlement expenses	99,831	97,269
Unearned premiums	12,766	13,027
Accrued expenses and other	8,349	7,559
Notes payable		2,461
Stockholders' equity*	55,565	52,618
TOTAL	176,511	172,934

* No par common; 25,000,000 authorized; 12,312,000 and 11,935,000 issued and outstanding.

RECENT QUARTERS / **PRIOR-YEAR RESULTS**

Quarter End	Revenue ($000)	Earnings ($000)	EPS ($)	Prior-Year Revenue ($000)	Prior-Year Earnings ($000)	Prior-Year EPS ($)
Q3 09/30/2000	19,622	1,879	0.18	19,142	1,611	0.13
Q2 06/30/2000	21,730	1,791	0.17	18,894	1,487	0.12
Q1 03/31/2000	20,158	1,597	0.13	18,877	1,233	0.10
Q4 12/31/99	20,899	1,836	0.15	17,609	(6,317)	(0.53)
SUM	82,409	7,103	0.63	74,522	(1,986)	(0.18)

RECENT EVENTS

In **March 2000** RTW repurchased 1,419,000 shares from a group consisting of David C. Prosser(RTW's founder and a director), certain members of his family, and J. Alexander Fjelstad (an RTW director and former RTW executive). The company paid $5.19 per share, or $7.36 million. After completing the transaction, the combined ownership of Mr. Prosser, members of his family, and Mr. Fjelstad was reduced from 52 percent to 45 percent. In connection with the repurchase, Mr. Prosser retired from the company, resigned as chairman and was paid $225,000 as a termination benefit. He was expected to remain as a member of the board. Each member of the selling group entered into a two-year standstill and voting agreement under which each agreed, among other things, not to acquire additional securities of RTW and not to initiate or support certain initiatives designed to effect fundamental changes in RTW policy or structure. RTW borrowed $8.0 million under to a term loan agreement to fund the repurchase. In **April** CEO Lehmann notified the board of directors that he was intending to step down as CEO in January 2001. The transition plan: During 2000, in addition to serving as chairman and CEO, Lehmann was to actively participate in recruiting a new president and CEO. In **May** RTW resumed purchases of its common stock under its share repurchase program, repurchasing 635,000 shares at $4 per share. **Sept. 30**: For the nine months, the company reported gross premiums earned of $70.9 million versus $65.4 million for the comparable period in 1999. Premiums in force were $88.9 million, compared with $85.7 million a year earlier and $87.2 million at Dec. 31, 1999.

OFFICERS

Debora S. Allen
Chief Information Officer

Vina L. Marquart
VP-Human Resources

Carl B. Lehmann
Chairman, President, and CEO

Jeffrey B. Murphy
CFO, Secretary, and Treasurer

Anthony J. Rotondi
COO

David J. LeBlanc
Chief Underwriting Officer

DIRECTORS

Mark E. Hegman
Peninsula Investments

David R. Hubers
American Express Financial Advisors Inc., Minneapolis

Carl B. Lehmann
RTW Inc., Bloomington, MN

David C. Prosser

Steven M. Rothschild
Twin Cities RISE!, Minneapolis

MAJOR SHAREHOLDERS

Resource Trust Co., 13.5%
Bloomington, MN

The Kaufman Fund Inc., 10.7%
New York

David C. Prosser, 9.8%

John W. Prosser, 8%
Chanhassen, MN

Polly J. Wolner, 6.9%
Rice Lake, WI

Woodland Partners LLC, 5.7%
Minneapolis

Dimensional Fund Advisors Inc., 5.6%
Santa Monica, CA

Thomas C. Prosser, 5.6%
Eden Prairie, MN

Wasatch Advisors Inc., 5%
Salt Lake City

All officers and directors as a group (11 persons), 16.1%

SIC CODE

6331 Fire, marine, and casualty insurance

MISCELLANEOUS

TRANSFER AGENT AND REGISTAR:
Wells Fargo Bank Minnesota N.A.,
South St. Paul, MN

TRADED: Nasdaq National Market

SYMBOL: RTWI

STOCKHOLDERS: 2,000

EMPLOYEES: 249

GENERAL COUNSEL:
Lindquist & Vennum PLLP, Minneapolis

AUDITORS:
Deloitte & Touche LLP, Minneapolis

ANNUAL MEETING: May

HUMAN RESOURCES:
Vina L. Marquart

INVESTOR RELATIONS:
Jeffrey B. Murphy

RANKINGS

No. 94 CRM Public 200

SUBSIDIARIES, DIVISIONS, AFFILIATES

American Compensation Insurance Co.

TWO-YEAR QUARTERLY HIGH-LOW STOCK PRICES

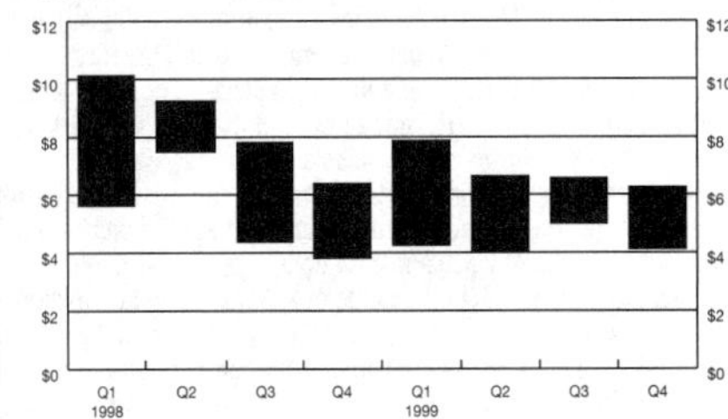

PUB

PUB

Raven Industries Inc.

205 E. Sixth St., P.O. Box 5107, Sioux Falls, SD 57117
Tel: 605/336-2750 Fax: 605/335-0268 Web site: http://www.ravenind.com

Raven Industries Inc. is a diversified manufacturer of specialized plastics, electronics, and apparel. Raven operates in three segments. The **sewn products** group manufactures outerwear, ski pants, cleanroom suits, and inflatable advertising balloons. The **electronics** group manufactures flow control hardware for the agriculture industry; communication modules for the defense industry; and systems for automating commercial baking plants and feed mills. The **plastics** group produces co-extruded plastic films, in thicknesses from 0.25 mm to 30.0 mm, for the commercial construction, oil-pit lining, and hazardous-storage industries; plastic storage tanks for agricultural chemical application; and pickup-truck toppers.

EARNINGS HISTORY

Year Ended Jan 31	Operating Revenue/Sales (dollars in thousands)	Net Earnings	Return on Revenue (percent)	Return on Equity	Net Earnings (dollars per share)	Cash Dividend	Market Price Range
2000 *	147,906	6,762	4.6	12.4	1.55	0.66	18.25–13.50
1999	152,798	6,182	4.0	9.9	1.30	0.62	22.75–15.25
1998 †	149,619	8,062	5.4	13.1	1.66	0.56	25.75–19.63
1997	139,441	7,688	5.5	13.6	1.62	0.50	23.50–16.00
1996	120,444	6,197	5.1	12.6	1.31	0.45	20.75–15.50

* Income figures for 2000 include pretax gain of $1.186 million on sale of Glasstite.
† Income figures for 1998 include pretax gain of $1.794 million on sale of investment in affiliate.

BALANCE SHEET

Assets	01/31/00 (dollars in thousands)	01/31/99	Liabilities	01/31/00 (dollars in thousands)	01/31/99
Current (CAE 5,707 and 5,335)	55,371	60,279	Current (STD 1,044 and 1,060)	14,702	15,128
Property, plant, and equipment	15,068	19,563	Long-term debt	3,024	4,572
			Other	1,802	1,664
Other	3,608	3,815	Stockholders' equity*	54,519	62,293
TOTAL	74,047	83,657	TOTAL	74,047	83,657

* $1 par common; 100,000,000 authorized; 5,218,114 and 5,215,489 issued and outstanding, less 1,302,007 and 521,403 treasury shares.

RECENT QUARTERS / **PRIOR-YEAR RESULTS**

	Quarter End	Revenue ($000)	Earnings ($000)	EPS ($)	Revenue ($000)	Earnings ($000)	EPS ($)
Q2	07/31/2000	32,386	1,173	0.34	36,965	1,816	0.40
Q1	04/30/2000	31,544	1,677	0.44	34,495	1,439	0.31
Q4	01/31/2000	31,475	1,253	0.31	39,641	1,603	0.34
Q3	10/31/99	44,971	2,254	0.52	44,787	2,053	0.44
	SUM	140,376	6,357	1.61	155,888	6,911	1.49

RECENT EVENTS

In **March 2000** the company's board of directors authorized the repurchase of an additional 500,000 shares of common stock, raising the total current authorization to 650,000 shares. The company already had repurchased 780,000 shares of stock in fiscal year 2000, and an additional 61,000 shares in the current fiscal year, under previous authorizations. In **April** Raven reported that both sales and earnings were running ahead of expectations due to strong performance in its Electronics Segment. Sales of flow control devices used for precision-farming applications were up sharply despite a depressed agricultural market. In **June**, working closely with NASA, the company launched the second flight of a new super-pressure Ultra Long Duration Balloon (ULDB). The ULDB prototype, which is only one-tenth the size of the actual research balloon, remained aloft a full 27 hours. "The advanced design of the ULDB will allow balloon payloads to be carried around the world several times and, unlike most satellite missions, return the instrument for refurbishment and reflight," said Raven Balloon Engineer Mike Smith. Raven announced plans to sell its plastic tank division during the third quarter ending Oct. 31, 2000. In connection with that decision, it signed a letter of intent to sell certain operating assets of its fiberglass and polyethylene plastic tank operations to Norwesco Inc., St. Bonifacius, Minn. [Deal completed in August.] At month's end, the board of directors authorized the repurchase of an additional 500,000 shares of common stock, raising the total current authorization to 665,000 shares. **July 31:** Noting a decline in its Electronics Segment—due in part to start-up costs of a new plant that was opened in the quarter and a falloff in orders from a major customer—Raven announced that net income for its second quarter was down 35 percent to $1.2 million. The leading positive factor in overall sales and earnings was engineered film sales, which continued strong, up 11 percent for the second quarter and 14 percent for the first six months. In **September** Raven signed a five-year strategic supplier agreement to build secure telephony and network encryption equipment for Motorola Inc. (NYSE: MOT). Raven planned to produce two systems that secure both voice and data transmissions. Although dependent on customer demand, the estimated total value of the five-year agreement was in the range of $50 million to $80 million. Production of the first product, a compact lightweight desktop device, was to begin in October 2000, and the second product, used to secure computer networks, in the spring of 2001. Meanwhile, continued cost pressures from competition were forcing customers to reduce the volume of business they do with Raven and to switch to offshore suppliers. Because of this reduction

continued on page 341

OFFICERS

Conrad J. Hoigaard
Chairman

Ronald M. Moquist
President and CEO

Gary L. Conradi
VP-Administrative Services

Thomas Iacarella
VP-Finance, Secretary/Treasurer

DIRECTORS

Anthony W. Bour
Showplace Wood Products, Sioux Falls, SD

David A. Christensen
Raven Industries Inc. (retired)

Thomas S. Everist
L.G. Everist Inc., Sioux Falls, SD

Mark E. Griffin
Lewis Drugs Inc., Sioux Falls, SD

Conrad J. Hoigaard
Hoigaards Inc., Minneapolis

Kevin T. Kirby
Kirby Investment Corp., Sioux Falls, SD

Ronald M. Moquist

MAJOR SHAREHOLDERS

Fenimore Asset Management Inc., 15.4%
Cobleskill, NY

T. Rowe Price Associates Inc., 11%
Baltimore

Dimensional Fund Advisors Inc., 8.6%
Santa Monica, CA

David A. Christensen, 5.8%

All officers and directors as a group (9 persons), 15%

SIC CODE

2329 Men's and boys' clothing, nec

2339 Women's and misses' outerwear, nec

3089 Plastics products, nec

3523 Farm machinery and equipment

3672 Printed circuit boards

MISCELLANEOUS

TRANSFER AGENT AND REGISTAR:
Wells Fargo Bank Minnesota N.A., South St. Paul, MN

TRADED: Nasdaq National Market

SYMBOL: RAVN

STOCKHOLDERS: 3,221

EMPLOYEES: 1,000

GENERAL COUNSEL:
Davenport, Evans, Hurwitz & Smith, Sioux Falls, SD

AUDITORS:
PricewaterhouseCoopers LLP, Minneapolis

INC: SD-1956

ANNUAL MEETING: May

HUMAN RESOURCES:
Barbara K. Ohme

INVESTOR RELATIONS:
Karen M. Iversen

SUBSIDIARIES, DIVISIONS, AFFILIATES

Aerostar International Inc.
1813 E Ave.
Sioux Falls, SD 57103
605/331-3500
Mark West

Beta Raven Inc.
4372 Green Ash Dr.
Earth City, MO 63044
314/291-4504
Ron Moquist

Glasstite Inc.
RR 1, Box 1A
Dunnell, MN 56127
507/695-2378
Ron Moquist

Raven Industries Inc.
205 E. Sixth St.
Sioux Falls, SD 57104
605/336-2750
David A. Christensen

TWO-YEAR QUARTERLY HIGH-LOW STOCK PRICES

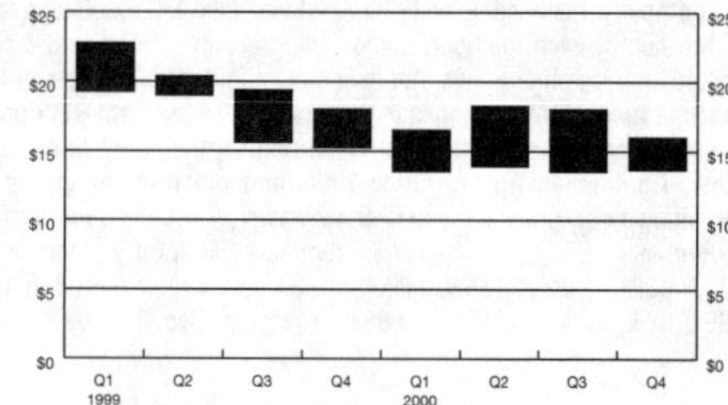

Regis Corporation

7201 Metro Blvd., Edina, MN 55439
Tel: 952/947-7777 Fax: 952/947-7900 Web site: http://www.regiscorp.com

Regis Corp. owns, operates, and franchises hairstyling salons located in major enclosed shopping malls and strip centers throughout the United States and Canada, as well as in major department stores in the United Kingdom. The Regis worldwide operations included 5,807 hairstyling salons (3,948 of them company-owned) at Sept. 30, 2000, operating through six divisions: **Regis Salons**, moderate-to-upscale services appealing primarily to women; **MasterCuts Salons**, discount haircutters and hairstylists appealing to the entire family; **Trade Secret Salons**, hair-care services with emphasis on the sale of professional hair care and beauty products; **International Salons**, shopping center and department store salons in the United Kingdom; **Wal-Mart Salons**, discount family-oriented salons located in Wal-Mart stores; and strip center salons, primarily **Supercuts** and **Cost Cutters**, affordable hair salons in strip centers.

EARNINGS HISTORY *

Year Ended Jun 30	Operating Revenue/Sales (dollars in thousands)	Net Earnings	Return on Revenue (percent)	Return on Equity	Net Earnings (dollars per share†)	Cash Dividend	Market Price Range
2000 ¶	1,142,993	49,654	4.3	17.8	1.22	0.12	22.94–10.81
1999 #	991,900	32,205	3.2	13.7	0.80	0.10	28.44–15.17
1998 **	860,620	33,894	3.9	17.2	0.86	0.06	20.00–15.29
1997 ††	765,170	9,377	1.2	6.0	0.26	0.05	22.67–10.17
1996 ##	661,383	11,690	1.8	8.8	0.32	0.05	22.00–8.33

* Financials have been restated to pool the following acquisitions: Oct. 31, 1999, Supercuts U.K.; May 20, 1999, The Barbers; March 15, 1999, Heidi's; and Oct. 25, 1996, Supercuts.
† Per-share amounts restated to reflect 3-for-2 stock splits on March 1, 1999, and June 4, 1996.
¶ Income figures for 2000 include net pretax charges of $2.94 million for nonrecurring items, mainly merger transaction costs.
# Income figures for 1999 include pretax charges of $16.133 million for restructuring, merger transaction costs, Year 2000 remediation.
** Income figures for 1998 include pretax loss of $1.979 million on divestiture of Anasazi.
†† Income figures for 1997 include pretax charges of $18.731 million for merger transaction costs, restructuring, Supercuts officer litigation.
Income figures for 1996 include pretax charges of $12.823 million for restructuring, Supercuts litigation.

BALANCE SHEET

Assets	06/30/00 (dollars in thousands)	06/30/99	Liabilities	06/30/00 (dollars in thousands)	06/30/99
Current (CAE 14,888 and 10,353)	143,804	117,383	Current (STD 9,983 and 23,945)	103,044	106,640
Property and equipment	260,532	215,952	Long-term debt	224,618	143,041
			Other	21,552	16,682
Goodwill	208,724	153,956	Stkhldrs' equity*	279,141	234,219
Other	15,295	13,291	TOTAL	628,355	500,582
TOTAL	628,355	500,582			

* $0.05 par common; 50,000,000 authorized; 40,702,707 and 40,419,122 issued and outstanding.

RECENT QUARTERS / **PRIOR-YEAR RESULTS**

	Quarter End	Revenue ($000)	Earnings ($000)	EPS ($)	Prior-Year Revenue ($000)	Prior-Year Earnings ($000)	Prior-Year EPS ($)
Q1	09/30/2000	310,754	12,715	0.31	266,108	12,638	0.31
Q4	06/30/2000	302,968	14,592	0.36	264,978	5,007	0.12
Q3	03/31/2000	288,062	11,617	0.29	249,660	7,939	0.20
Q2	12/31/99	285,855	10,807	0.27	245,265	10,127	0.25
	SUM	1,187,639	49,731	1.22	1,026,011	35,711	0.89

CURRENT: Q3 earnings include nonrecurring charge of $2.851 million/($0.07).
PRIOR YEAR: Q1 and all prior periods restated to pool October 1999 Supercuts (Holdings) Ltd. acquisition. Q4 earnings include nonrecurring charge of $8.231 million/($0.20). Q3 earnings include nonrecurring charge of $1.571 million/($0.04). Q2 earnings include pretax charge of $1.532 million for Y2K remediation.

RECENT EVENTS

In **December 1999** the company announced the acquisition of 112 salons—with $28 million in annualized revenue—in eight transactions. In **March 2000** Yellowave Corp. (OTCBB: YWAV), Los Angeles, sold its Cutco Salons Inc. subsidiary (146 franchised salons across the United States and Canada) to Regis for $3.6 million in cash. Regis acquired 184 more salons ($9 million in annualized revenue) in 11 March transactions. Of the acquired salons, 146 were franchised units operating primarily under the Haircrafters and Great Expectations names. **June 30**: Revenue for

continued on page 342

OFFICERS

Myron D. Kunin
Chairman

Paul D. Finkelstein
President and CEO

Mary F. Andert
EVP-Merchandising/Marketing

Kris Bergly
COO-Strip Center Division

John Briggs
COO-Wal-Mart Salons Division

Raymond Duke
SVP and COO-International

Christopher A. Fox
EVP-Real Estate

Bert M. Gross
SVP, General Counsel, and Secretary

Bruce D. Johnson
SVP-Design/Construction

Mark Kartarik
SVP and Pres./COO-Supercuts

Sharon Kiker
COO-Regis Hairstylists

Norma Knutson
COO-Trade Secret

Gordon B. Nelson
SVP-Fashion/Education

Randy L. Pearce
EVP and Chief Administrative Officer

Robert Ribnick
COO-MasterCuts

DIRECTORS

Rolf F. Bjelland
Lutheran Brotherhood, Minneapolis

Paul D. Finkelstein

Christopher A. Fox

Tom Gregory
TLG Associates, Solvang, CA

Van Zandt Hawn
Goldner Hawn Johnson & Morrison Inc.

Susan S. Hoyt
Staples Inc., Westborough, MA

David Kunin
Anasazi Exclusive Salon Products Inc., Dubuque, IA

Myron D. Kunin

MAJOR SHAREHOLDERS

Curtis Squire Inc./Myron Kunin, 9.8%

Fidelity Research & Management Inc., 5.4%
Boston

All officers and directors as a group (14 persons), 12.4%

SIC CODE

7231 Beauty shops

MISCELLANEOUS

TRANSFER AGENT AND REGISTAR:
Wells Fargo Bank Minnesota N.A., South St. Paul, MN

TRADED: Nasdaq National Market

SYMBOL: RGIS

STOCKHOLDERS: 13,000

EMPLOYEES: 35,000

GENERAL COUNSEL:
Bert M. Gross, Minneapolis

AUDITORS:
PricewaterhouseCoopers LLP, Minneapolis

INC: MN-1922

ANNUAL MEETING: November

INVESTOR RELATIONS: Randy L. Pearce

RANKINGS

No. 35 CRM Public 200

No. 36 CRM Performance 100

SUBSIDIARIES, DIVISIONS, AFFILIATES

Regis Salons

MasterCuts Salons

Trade Secret Salons

International Salons

Wal-Mart Salons Smart Style

Supercuts

Cost Cutters

Style America

Hair Masters

PUB

TWO-YEAR QUARTERLY HIGH-LOW STOCK PRICES

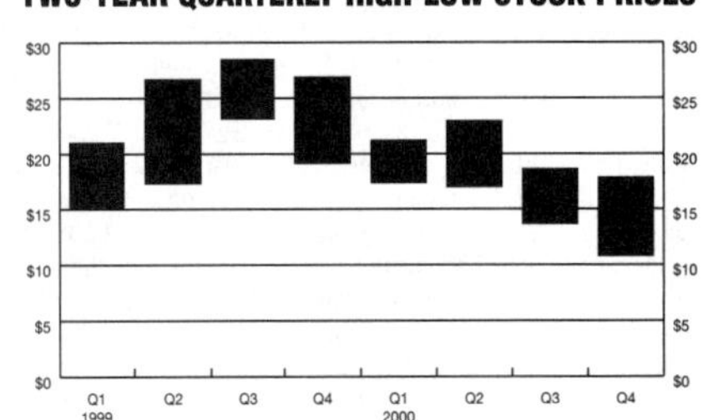

PUB

Rehabilicare Inc.

1811 Old Highway 8, New Brighton, MN 55112
Tel: 651/631-0590 Fax: 651/638-0476 Web site: http://www.rehabilicare.com

Rehabilicare Inc. designs, manufactures, and distributes electrotherapy products used for rehabilitation and pain management in clinics and at home. The products help patients regain or improve physical capabilities impaired by injury or illness. The devices are lightweight, battery-powered electric pulse generators, available in a variety of treatment modalities. To deliver treatment, they are connected with wires to electrodes placed on the skin. The company is a leader in miniaturizing bulky tabletop technology. All of its products are portable and are designed to be equally effective in the clinic and at home. The company offers what it believes to be the widest range of portable electrotherapy products available from any one supplier. Sales representatives from the company's direct-sales division market the company's full line of products directly to clinics. Clinicians use the products in the clinic and refer those products to patients for in-home use. Rehabilicare's wholesale division supplies products to its domestic and international network of electrotherapy and home health care dealers.

EARNINGS HISTORY *

Year Ended Jun 30	Operating Revenue/Sales (dollars in thousands)	Net Earnings	Return on Revenue (percent)	Return on Equity	Net Earnings (dollars per share)	Cash Dividend	Market Price Range
2000 †	58,815	2,203	3.7	8.7	0.21	—	4.47–2.00
1999	41,795	2,860	6.8	12.4	0.27	—	4.38–1.81
1998 ¶	33,812	(1,009)	(3.0)	(5.0)	(0.10)	—	4.56–2.50
1997	32,134	1,793	5.6	8.4	0.17	—	4.31–2.38
1996	8,703	282	3.2	3.9	0.06	—	5.25–2.25

* Figures for 1998 and 1997 (only) were restated to pool the March 17, 1998, Staodyn Inc. merger.
† Income figures for 2000 include pretax charge of $2.094 million for Medicare lawsuit expenses; and pretax gain of $1.076 million on sale of building.
¶ Income figures for 1998 include pretax merger-related expenses of $4.421 million.

BALANCE SHEET

Assets	06/30/00 (dollars in thousands)	06/30/99
Current (CAE 2,227 and 561)	34,689	29,879
Property and equipment	5,596	4,618
Intangibles	12,152	1,150
Deferred taxes	224	40
Other	47	12
TOTAL	52,708	35,700

Liabilities	06/30/00 (dollars in thousands)	06/30/99
Current (STD 2,170 and 1,241)	13,192	8,332
Long-term debt	13,663	4,067
Deferred taxes	584	247
Stockholders' equity*	25,270	23,053
TOTAL	52,708	35,700

* $0.10 par common; 25,000,000 authorized; 10,558,710 and 10,494,908 issued and outstanding.

RECENT QUARTERS / **PRIOR-YEAR RESULTS**

	Quarter End	Revenue ($000)	Earnings ($000)	EPS ($)	Prior-Year Revenue ($000)	Prior-Year Earnings ($000)	Prior-Year EPS ($)
Q1	09/30/2000	15,068	1,122	0.10	13,876	1,434	0.14
Q4	06/30/2000	16,211	(1,133)	(0.11)	10,909	760	0.07
Q3	03/31/2000	13,950	669	0.06	10,920	687	0.07
Q2	12/31/99	14,778	1,232	0.12	10,882	774	0.07
	SUM	60,006	1,891	0.18	46,587	3,655	0.35

CURRENT: Q4 earnings include pretax charge of $1.776 million for Medicare settlement expenses.
PRIOR YEAR: Q1 earnings include pretax gain of $1.076 million on sale of building.

RECENT EVENTS

March 31, 2000: The company blamed a 5 percent revenue slide on the lawsuit (explained below), citing its impact on morale and productivity. On the other hand, Swiss subsidiary Compex reported a 34 percent increase in revenue for the quarter, the result of a push into Spanish and German markets. (Plans were to introduce Compex electrotherapy products in the United States by the end of 2000.) In **June** Rehabilicare announced receipt from the U.S. Patent and Trademark Office of patent number 6,064,911, entitled "Device Using Both HVPC and NMS Electrotherapy." The technology addressed by this patent is used in the company's Ortho Dx portable, dual-purpose neuromuscular stimulator device. In **September** Rehabilicare reached an agreement with the U.S. Government to settle allegations of improper Medicare billing that were asserted in a lawsuit filed by a former employee. The company agreed to pay a total of $1,588,510 to settle the lawsuit. The company denied allegations that it engaged in fraudulent Medicare billing practices. Although the terms of the settlement, including the amount to be paid by the company, were agreed to in principle with the United States, the settlement remained subject to final agency approvals, including review and approval by the U.S. Department of Health and Human Services Office of Counsel to the Inspector General with respect to necessary compliance provisions. [The lawsuit was originally brought by a former employee, Elizabeth Mies, on Dec. 31, 1998, and filed under seal as required by the Civil False Claims Act. *continued on page 342*

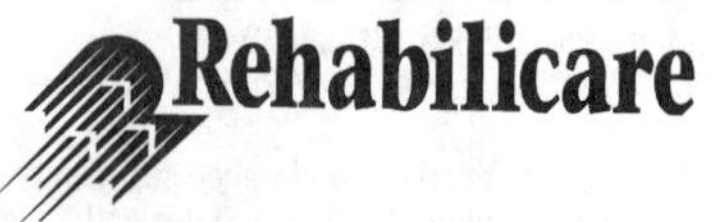

OFFICERS

Robert C. Wingrove
Chairman and Chief Technical Officer
David B. Kaysen
President and CEO
Wayne K. Chrystal
VP-Operations
William J. Sweeney
VP-Sales/Marketing
W. Glen Winchell
VP-Finance and CFO

DIRECTORS

Frederick H. Ayers
F.H. Ayers Inc., Boulder, CO
W. Bayne Gibson
Bayne Gibson & Assoc., Longmont, CO
Richard E. Jahnke
Angeion Corp., Vadnais Heights, MN
David B. Kaysen
John H.P. Maley
Magister Corp., Chattanooga, TN
Robert C. Wingrove
Rehabilicare Inc.

MAJOR SHAREHOLDERS

Beverly Enterprises Inc., 9.2%
Fort Smith, AK
All officers and directors as a group (9 persons), 5.6%

SIC CODE

3845 Electromedical equipment

MISCELLANEOUS

TRANSFER AGENT AND REGISTAR:
Wells Fargo Bank Minnesota N.A., South St. Paul, MN
TRADED: Nasdaq National Market
SYMBOL: REHB
STOCKHOLDERS: 800
EMPLOYEES: 252
IN MINNESOTA: 93
GENERAL COUNSEL:
Dorsey & Whitney PLLP, Minneapolis

AUDITORS:
Ernst & Young LLP, Minneapolis
INC: MN-1972
ANNUAL MEETING:
December
PUBLIC RELATIONS COUNSEL:
Lippert/Heilshorn & Associates
HUMAN RESOURCES:
Alla Byrne

RANKINGS

No. 112 CRM Public 200
No. 26 Minnesota Technology Fast 50

SUBSIDIARIES, DIVISIONS, AFFILIATES

Rehabilicare (U.K.) Ltd.
Fairview Estate
Reading Road, Henley-on-Thames
Oxfordshire, RG9 1HE
England

Compex S.A.
Z.I. Larges Pieces
Chemin du Devent
CH-1024 Ecublens
Switzerland

TWO-YEAR QUARTERLY HIGH-LOW STOCK PRICES

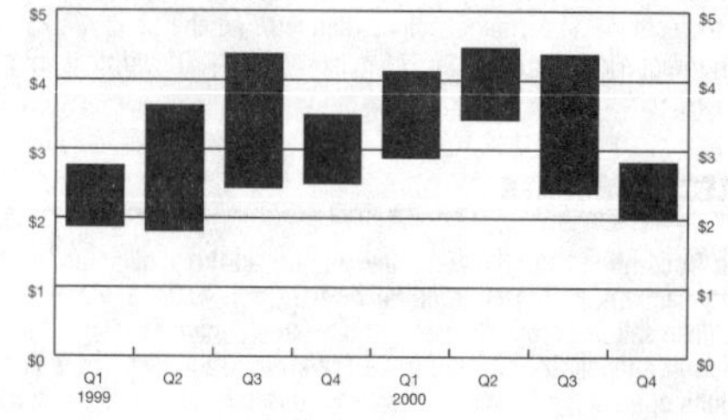

Reo Plastics Inc.

11850 93rd Ave. N., Maple Grove, MN 55369
Tel: 763/425-4171 Fax: 763/425-0735

Reo Plastics Inc. designs tools and manufactures custom injection-molded plastic parts for all types of industries. While specializing in high-tolerance precision parts, the company can accommodate larger parts and longer production runs. The company maintains a second operations department to perform hot stamping, machining, painting, sonic welding inserts, cementing, and total assembly. The company also offers new-product design and metal-to-plastic conversion.

EARNINGS HISTORY

Year Ended Apr 30	Operating Revenue/Sales (dollars in thousands)	Net Earnings	Return on Revenue (percent)	Return on Equity	Net Earnings (dollars per share)	Cash Dividend	Market Price Range
2000	19,861	1,306	6.6	10.0	2.51	—	
1999	17,606	858	4.9	7.2	1.62	—	
1998	22,724	2,221	9.8	19.9	4.17	—	
1997	20,113	1,240	6.2	13.8	2.33	—	
1996	17,358	735	4.2	9.5	1.38	—	

BALANCE SHEET

Assets	04/30/00 (dollars in thousands)	04/30/99	Liabilities	04/30/00 (dollars in thousands)	04/30/99
Current (CAE 680 and 3,066)	8,792	8,724	Current (STD 532 and 521)	2,201	1,861
Property and equipment	6,571	5,594	Deferred taxes	336	322
Investment in held-to-maturity securities	228		Long-term debt		200
			Stockholders' equity*	13,055	11,934
TOTAL	15,592	14,317	TOTAL	15,592	14,317

* $0.10 par common; 1,000,000 authorized; 516,410 and 527,500 issued and outstanding.

RECENT QUARTERS / **PRIOR-YEAR RESULTS**

	Quarter End	Revenue ($000)	Earnings ($000)	EPS ($)	Revenue ($000)	Earnings ($000)	EPS ($)
Q2	10/31/99	9,498	700	1.34	9,015	515	0.97
	SUM	9,498	700	1.34	9,015	515	0.97

CURRENT: Q2 figures are for six months.
PRIOR YEAR: Q2 figures are for six months.

OFFICERS

Earl A. Patch
President and Treasurer

Elmer R. Douglas
VP, Plant Mgr.

James L. Swenson
VP-Sales/Marketing

James G. Wolf
VP

Roland S. Curtis
VP and Controller

DIRECTORS

Roland S. Curtis
Elmer R. Douglas
Ernest A. Lindstrom
Earl A. Patch
Carolyn P. Sample
James L. Swenson
James G. Wolf

SIC CODE

3089 Plastics products, nec

3544 Special dies, tools, jigs, and fixtures

MISCELLANEOUS

TRANSFER AGENT AND REGISTAR:
Wells Fargo Bank Minnesota N.A.,
South St. Paul, MN

TRADED: LOTC

SYMBOL: REOP

STOCKHOLDERS: 100

EMPLOYEES: 200

GENERAL COUNSEL:
Lindstrom Law Offices,
Edina, MN

AUDITORS:
RSM McGladrey & Pullen Inc. LLP, Minneapolis

INC: MN-1962

ANNUAL MEETING:
August

RANKINGS

No. 156 CRM Public 200

PUB

Research Inc.

6425 Flying Cloud Dr., P.O. Box 24064 (55424), Eden Prairie, MN 55344
Tel: 952/941-3300 Fax: 952/941-3628 Web site: http://www.researchinc.com

Research Inc. designs, manufactures, and sells control instrumentation and heating devices that solve heating and control problems. The company operates as one business segment through three operating divisions: Thermal Solutions, Drying, and Research International. Applications for the products include assembly of surface-mount printed circuit boards, and specialized heating systems for material testing, printing, solar simulation, and curing/finishing. The company's products are sold throughout the United States and in Canada, Europe, the Far East, Australia, and South America. Sales are through independent sales representatives and distributors.

EARNINGS HISTORY

Year Ended Sept 30	Operating Revenue/Sales (dollars in thousands)	Net Earnings	Return on Revenue (percent)	Return on Equity	Net Earnings (dollars per share*)	Cash Dividend	Market Price Range
1999 †	24,410	380	1.6	10.5	0.30	—	8.44–2.00
1998 ¶	16,731	(3,518)	(21.0)	NM	(2.82)	0.12	9.60–1.69
1997 #	22,843	1,117	4.9	17.1	0.80	0.38	8.00–3.80
1996 **	19,661	290	1.5	4.0	0.20	0.21	7.60–4.80
1995	20,923	627	3.0	8.7	0.44	0.18	9.60–3.60

* Per-share amounts restated to reflect 5-for-4 stock split paid Dec. 31, 1997.
† Income figures for 1999 include pretax restructuring charge of $354,000 to close U.K. facility.
¶ Income figures for 1998 include pretax restructuring charge of $1,676,000.
# Income figures for 1997 include pretax gain of $1,147,094 on sale of land.
** Income figures for 1996 include pretax gain of $344,400 on sale of Dimension product line.

BALANCE SHEET

Assets	09/30/99 (dollars in thousands)	09/30/98	Liabilities	09/30/99 (dollars in thousands)	09/30/98
Current (CAE 350 and 108)	10,316	8,195	Current (STD 682 and 4,100)	5,967	8,154
Property and equipment	821	2,392	Long-term debt	377	
			Deferred gain	1,891	
Deferred income taxes	733	786	Stockholders' equity*	3,635	3,218
TOTAL	11,870	11,373	TOTAL	11,870	11,373

* $0.50 par common; 5,000,000 authorized; 1,290,144 and 1,266,337 issued and outstanding.

RECENT QUARTERS / PRIOR-YEAR RESULTS

	Quarter End	Revenue ($000)	Earnings ($000)	EPS ($)	Prior-Year Revenue ($000)	Prior-Year Earnings ($000)	Prior-Year EPS ($)
Q4	09/30/2000	8,009	362	0.27	8,007	167	0.13
Q3	06/30/2000	6,442	219	0.17	5,464	26	0.02
Q2	03/31/2000	7,505	275	0.21	5,545	106	0.08
Q1	12/31/99	6,848	249	0.19	5,394	82	0.06
	SUM	28,804	1,104	0.85	24,410	380	0.30

PRIOR YEAR: Q4 earnings include pretax charge of $354,000 for restructuring.

RECENT EVENTS

In **February 2000** the company terminated a formal strategic alternative search process undertaken the previous June with the assistance of John G. Kinnard & Co. The company said that during the process several alternatives were explored, but ultimately none met the company's objectives. Management said that, because of operating improvements and a stronger working capital position, its best course of action was to continue to execute the plans management had developed and pursued during the previous 18 months. **Sept. 30:** Record sales for the fourth quarter and fiscal year produced major gains in profitability over the same periods in prior year. Sales gains reflected continued strong sales of the company's reflow oven product lines to the PC board assembly and semiconductor industries. Net income nearly tripled, while expenses as a percentage of revenue declined from 35 percent (excluding restructuring charge) in fiscal 1999, to 31 percent in 2000.

OFFICERS

Claude C. Johnson
President and CEO

Bruce E. Bailey
VP-Drying Division

David G. Brady
VP-Assembly Automation Division

N.R. Cox
VP

Richard L. Grose
VP-Research International

Karen M. O'Rourke
VP

Brad Yopp
Treasurer

Margaret R. Clyne
Operations Mgr.

DIRECTORS

John Colwell Jr.
Colwell Industries Inc., Minneapolis

Claude C. Johnson

Edward L. Lundstrom
Sheldahl Inc., Northfield, MN

Gerald E. Magnuson
Lindquist & Vennum PLLP (retired)

Charles G. Schiefelbein
Capital Growth Services

MAJOR SHAREHOLDERS

Kenneth G. Anderson, 8.3%
Minneapolis

Dimensional Fund Advisors Inc., 7.1%
Santa Monica, CA

Charles G. Schiefelbein, 5.1%

All officers and directors as a group (10 persons), 15.5%

SIC CODE

3567 Industrial process furnaces and ovens

3625 Relays and industrial controls

3823 Process control instruments

5065 Electronic parts and eqp, whsle

MISCELLANEOUS

TRANSFER AGENT AND REGISTAR:
Wells Fargo Bank Minnesota N.A., South St. Paul, MN

TRADED: Nasdaq SmallCap Market

SYMBOL: RESR

STOCKHOLDERS: 566

EMPLOYEES: 130

GENERAL COUNSEL:
Lindquist & Vennum PLLP, Minneapolis

AUDITORS:
Arthur Andersen LLP, Minneapolis

INC: MN-1966

FOUNDED: 1952

ANNUAL MEETING:
February

RANKINGS

No. 138 CRM Public 200

SUBSIDIARIES, DIVISIONS, AFFILIATES

Research International Division

Drying Division

Thermal Solutions Division

TWO-YEAR QUARTERLY HIGH-LOW STOCK PRICES

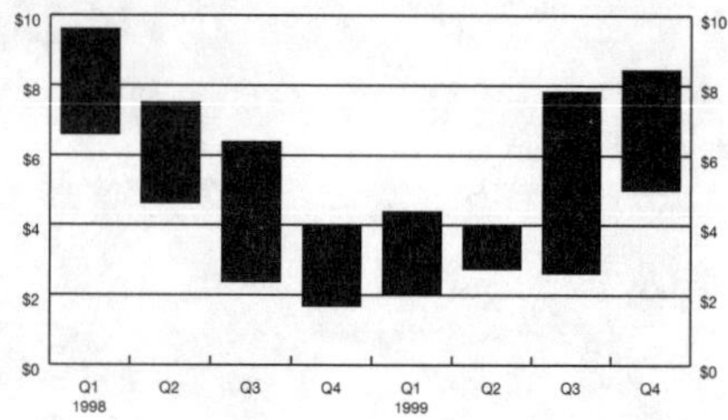

Retek Inc.

801 Nicollet Mall, Minneapolis, MN 55402
Tel: 612/630-5700 Web site: http://www.retek.com

Retek is a provider of Web-based business-to-business software solutions for retailers and their trading partners. The company's software solutions enable retailers to use the Internet to communicate and collaborate efficiently with the suppliers, distributors, wholesalers, logistics providers, brokers, transportation companies, consolidators, and manufacturers that make up the global retail supply chain. Its solutions are rapidly deployable, highly scalable, and retail-industry focused. They incorporate technology that predicts customer demand and behavior. Retek believes that Retail.com is the first electronic-commerce network providing collaborative business-to-business software solutions to the retail industry. Retek's more than 100 retailer customers include Brooks Brothers, Ann Taylor, and Gander Mountain. Retek is majority-owned by HNC Software Inc. (Nasdaq: HNCS), San Diego.

EARNINGS HISTORY *

Year Ended Dec 31	Operating Revenue/Sales (dollars in thousands)	Net Earnings	Return on Revenue (percent)	Return on Equity	Net Earnings (dollars per share†)	Cash Dividend	Market Price Range
1999	69,159	(5,369)	(7.8)	(4.3)	(0.13)	—	93.94–32.56
1998 ¶	55,033	3,878	7.0	10.8	0.10	—	
1997	30,923	3,476	11.2	14.1	—	—	
1996	13,433	2,233	16.6	10.9	—	—	
1995	3,836	(244)	(6.4)	NM	—	—	

* EPS prior to 1999 is pro forma.
† Trading began Nov. 18, 1999.
¶ Income figures for 1998 include pretax acquisition-related charges totaling $2.18 million.

BALANCE SHEET

Assets	12/31/99 (dollars in thousands)	12/31/98
Current (CAE 83,680 and 415)	124,800	28,143
Deferred income taxes	12,151	13,960
Property and equipment	8,291	4,887
Intangibles	8,958	4,010
Other	33	283
TOTAL	154,233	51,283

Liabilities	12/31/99 (dollars in thousands)	12/31/98
Current	30,258	15,267
Stockholders' equity*	123,975	36,016
TOTAL	154,233	51,283

* $0.01 par common; 150,000,000 authorized; 46,502,778 and 1,000 issued and outstanding.

RECENT QUARTERS / **PRIOR-YEAR RESULTS**

	Quarter End	Revenue ($000)	Earnings ($000)	EPS ($)	Prior-Year Revenue ($000)	Prior-Year Earnings ($000)	Prior-Year EPS ($)
Q3	09/30/2000	26,362	(9,507)	(0.20)	20,069	1,633	0.04
Q2	06/30/2000	19,589	(15,214)	(0.32)	21,043	1,772	0.04
Q1	03/31/2000	13,964	(11,286)	(0.24)	16,647	1,688	0.04
Q4	12/31/99	11,400	(10,462)	(0.24)	15,204	1,707	0.04
	SUM	71,315	(46,469)	(1.01)	72,963	6,800	0.17

CURRENT: Q3 earnings include pretax noncash charge of $5,235,000.
charge of $8,557,000.
pretax noncash charge of $3,999,000.
PRIOR YEAR: Q3 earnings include pretax noncash charge of $264,000. Q2 earnings include pretax noncash charge of $258,000. Q1 earnings include pretax noncash charge of $258,000. Q4 earnings include pretax noncash charge of $143,000.

RECENT EVENTS

On **Nov. 18, 1999**, the company commenced the initial public offering of 5.5 million shares of its common stock at a price of $15 per share. All of the shares were offered by the company. The shares were sold through an underwriting syndicate managed by Credit Suisse First Boston Corp., BancBoston Robertson Stephens Inc., and U.S. Bancorp Piper Jaffray Inc. The firm's stock more than doubled on the first day of trading to close at $32.69—giving Retek a market value of $1.49 billion. In **December** it was reported that Retek was to be anchor tenant in the 420,000-square-foot office tower being built by Ryan Cos. as part of its Target store project on Nicollet Mall. When the 11-story tower opens in October 2001, as many as 400 Retek employees are expected to fill half of its space. Credit Suisse First Boston initiated coverage with a STRONG BUY. In **January 2000** Retek announced retail.com Design, the industry's first e-service created to manage the retail apparel design process. Another new service from retail.com, Private Label Exchange, was developed to eenable private-label retailers to use the Internet to post product specifications and invite bids from manufacturers. Furthermore, through a new partnership with Celarix Inc., a provider of Web-based, transportation procurement and global logistics services, retail.com began offering logistics-based data for analysis, trending, and alerting—including a state-of-the art solution enabling supply chain professionals to oversee the entire supply chain process, from sourcing to shipment to delivery, in real *continued on page 342*

OFFICERS
John Buchanan
Chairman and CEO
Gordon Masson
President
Jeremy P.M. Thomas
Pres.-Retail.com
John L. Goedert
SVP-Research/Development
Jim Mattecheck
SVP
Duncan B. Angove
VP-E-business
David A.J. Bagley
VP-Product Strategy/Marketing
Peter Baskin
VP-Online Publishing
Gregory A. Effertz
VP-Finance/Admin., CFO, Treas., and Sec.
Art Hawkins
VP-VSP Business Development
Victor Holysh
VP-Services
Thomas Redd
VP-Global Marketing

DIRECTORS
John Buchanan
N. Ross Buckenham
PageMart Wireless Inc.
Ward Carey
HNC Software Inc., San Diego
Charles H. Gaylord
technology investor
Alex Way Hart
financial consultant
Glen A. Terbeek
Breakaway Strategies Inc.
Stephen E. Watson
Gander Mountain LLC

MAJOR SHAREHOLDERS
HNC Software Inc., 86%
San Diego
All officers and directors as a group (15 persons), 0.005%

SIC CODE
7372 Prepackaged software

MISCELLANEOUS
TRANSFER AGENT AND REGISTAR:
ChaseMellon Shareholder Services, Ridgefield Park, NJ
TRADED: Nasdaq National Market
SYMBOL: RETK
STOCKHOLDERS: 1,025
EMPLOYEES: 461
GENERAL COUNSEL:
Shearman & Sterling, Menlo Park, CA
AUDITORS:
PricewaterhouseCoopers LLP, San Diego
INC: DE-1999
FOUNDED: 1985

CORPORATE COMMUNICATIONS: George Beard

RANKINGS
No. 102 CRM Public 200

PUB

PUB

Rimage Corporation

7725 Washington Ave. S., Edina, MN 55439
Tel: 952/944-8144 Fax: 952/944-7808 Web site: http://www.rimage.com

Rimage Corp. designs, manufactures, and sells on demand CD-R and diskette publishing systems. The company is in the electronics industry segment that deals with the movement of images with microprocessor technology. Rimage is also using its technical, manufacturing, and marketing capabilities to broaden into other microprocessor-based products.

EARNINGS HISTORY *

Year Ended Dec 31	Operating Revenue/Sales (dollars in thousands)	Net Earnings	Return on Revenue (percent)	Return on Equity	Net Earnings (dollars per share†)	Cash Dividend	Market Price Range
1999	36,313	6,343	17.5	34.7	0.84	—	12.83–7.67
1998 ¶	28,530	5,053	17.7	41.5	0.72	—	9.67–2.44
1997	21,012	1,925	9.2	32.4	0.28	—	3.67–1.06
1996	23,237	(5,179)	(22.3)	NM	(0.75)	—	4.56–1.22
1995 #	17,359	(1,383)	(8.0)	(15.0)	(0.20)	—	3.72–1.78

* Historical revenue figures have been restated for continuing operations, but not yet to pool acquisition Cedar Technologies. EPS figures include these amounts from discontinued operations: $0.06, ($0.08), ($0.19), ($0.23), and $0.49—in 1999 through 1995, respectively.
† Per-share amounts restated to reflect 3-for-2 stock splits on April 7, 2000, and Nov. 27, 1998.
¶ Income figures for 1998 include pretax gain of $361,098 on lease restructure.
# Income figures for 1995 include $230,504 in merger expense.

BALANCE SHEET

Assets	12/31/99 (dollars in thousands)	12/31/98	Liabilities	12/31/99 (dollars in thousands)	12/31/98
Current	22,016	16,037	Current	4,708	4,502
(CAE 13,441 and 7,349)			Stkhldrs' equity*	18,255	12,168
Property, eqt	817	566	TOTAL	22,963	16,670
Other	130	67			
TOTAL	22,963	16,670			

* $0.01 par common; 10,000,000 authorized; 7,657,221 and 7,404,132 issued and outstanding.

RECENT QUARTERS / **PRIOR-YEAR RESULTS**

	Quarter End	Revenue ($000)	Earnings ($000)	EPS ($)	Prior-Year Revenue ($000)	Prior-Year Earnings ($000)	Prior-Year EPS ($)
Q3	09/30/2000	9,989	1,195	0.14	11,115	2,069	0.26
Q2	06/30/2000	13,377	2,481	0.30	9,893	1,416	0.18
Q1	03/31/2000	13,156	2,154	0.26	8,641	1,095	0.14
Q4	12/31/99	10,245	1,645	0.21	8,507	1,329	0.18
	SUM	46,767	7,475	0.92	38,156	5,909	0.76

CURRENT: Q4 figures do not reflect operations of Cedar Technologies.
PRIOR YEAR: Q2 earnings include gain of $379,000/$0.05 from discontinued operations and disposal of same. Q1 earnings include gain of $111,000/$0.01 from discontinued operations and disposal of same. Q4 figures do not reflect Cedar Technologies; earnings include gain of $208,000/$0.03 from discontinued operations.

RECENT EVENTS

In **November 1999** the company began shipping its new single-drive CD-Recordable (CD-R) publishing system, Producer 2000 Amigo. Rimage had received orders from distributors totaling $1 million for the new system, which had been unveiled in September. In **February 2000** Rimage agreed to provide the CD-Recordable (CD-R) technology for Liquid Audio Inc.'s (Nasdaq: LQID) on-demand audio CD kiosks at the Arcadia Group's TopShop/TopMan stores in the United Kingdom. Rimage entered the DVD market by offering an exclusive feature that provides surface printing on DVD-R media. Rimage agreed to acquire Cedar Technologies Inc., a manufacturer of CD-R desktop publishing and duplication equipment, for stock in a pooling-of-interests transaction. [Deal completed in March.] Microboards Technology Inc., Chanhassen, Minn., agreed to continue distributing the Cedar Technologies product line. In **March** a strategic partnership allowed musicmaker.com to install more than $1 million of Rimage's CD-R equipment in musicmaker.com's new state-of-the-art custom CD production and fulfillment facility in Reston, Va. In **April** Rimage announced the broad availability of the industry's first DVD-R publishing system, Producer 2000 Protege DVD-R, which allows users to easily and efficiently record and print on-demand DVD-Rs. Available through Rimage's distributor channel, the system retails for $45,000. Rimage and Mitsui Advanced Media Inc. showcased a new DVD-R media, the first to allow full-surface printing on the face of the disc. In **May** Imaging & Document Solutions Magazine selected the company's new Producer 2000 Protege DVD-R Automated Publishing System as one of 21 "Best of AIIM 2000" award winners. Rimage's existing distribution channels—Optical Laser, Inc., NewWave Technologies, Consan, and Brooke Distributors Inc.—unanimously adopted the Cedar Technologies line. Rimage agreed to provide the CD-R technology for Tribeka Ltd.'s Burn Your Own software production systems. The partnership dramatically expanded software availability to consumers while enabling bricks and mortar retailers to compete effectively with virtual e-tailers. In June the Perfect Image Producer Family of Products began featuring DVD-R and CD-R recording in the same systems, as a result of software upgrades that included a number of other features in addition to the toggle functionality. The Rimage Producer *continued on page 342*

OFFICERS

Richard McNamara
Chairman

Bernard P. Aldrich
President and CEO

David J. Suden
Chief Technology Officer

Kenneth J. Klinck
VP-Sales/Marketing

Robert M. Wolf
Principal Accounting Officer

DIRECTORS

Bernard P. Aldrich

Ronald R. Fletcher
Developers Service Corp.

Richard F. (Pinky) McNamara
Activar Inc., Minneapolis

Steven M. Quist
CyberOptics Corp., Golden Valley, MN

James L. Reissner
Activar Inc., Minneapolis

David J. Suden

MAJOR SHAREHOLDERS

Richard F. McNamara, 11.8%
Bloomington, MN

George E. Kline, 9.4%
Minneapolis

Ronald R. Fletcher, 5.3%
Washington, D.C.

All officers and directors as a group (8 persons), 32.2%

SIC CODE

3572 Computer storage devices

MISCELLANEOUS

TRANSFER AGENT AND REGISTAR:
Wells Fargo Bank Minnesota N.A.,
South St. Paul, MN

TRADED: Nasdaq National Market

SYMBOL: RIMG

STOCKHOLDERS: 142

EMPLOYEES: 120

GENERAL COUNSEL:
Dorsey & Whitney PLLP, Minneapolis

AUDITORS:
KPMG LLP, Minneapolis

ANNUAL MEETING: May

RANKINGS

No. 124 CRM Public 200

SUBSIDIARIES, DIVISIONS, AFFILIATES

Rimage Europe Gmbh
Germany
Konrad Rottermund

Rimage Development
750 Camden Ave.
Suite B
Campbell, CA 95008

TWO-YEAR QUARTERLY HIGH-LOW STOCK PRICES

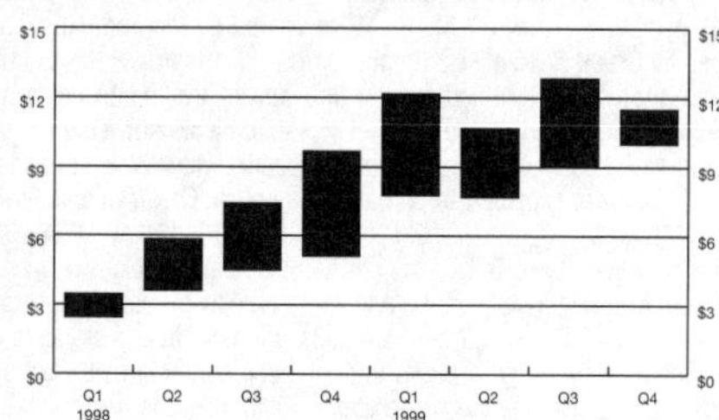

C.H. Robinson Worldwide Inc.

8100 Mitchell Rd., Suite 1700, Eden Prairie, MN 55344
Tel: 952/937-8500 Fax: 952/937-7809 Web site: http://www.chrobinson.com

C.H. Robinson Worldwide Inc., the largest third-party logistics company in North America, is a global provider of multimodal transportation services and logistics solutions through a network of 134 branch offices in 40 states, along with offices in Canada, Mexico, Argentina, Brazil, Venezuela, Belgium, the United Kingdom, France, Germany, Poland, Spain, Italy, and South Africa. Through contracts with more than 17,000 motor carriers, the company maintains the largest network of motor-carrier capacity in North America. C.H. Robinson provides a wide range of value-added logistics services, such as raw materials sourcing, freight consolidation, cross-docking, and contract warehousing. Much of the company's logistics expertise can be traced to its significant experience in handling perishable commodities.

EARNINGS HISTORY *

Year Ended Dec 31	Operating Revenue/Sales (dollars in thousands)	Net Earnings	Return on Revenue (percent)	Return on Equity	Net Earnings (dollars per share†)	Cash Dividend	Market Price Range
1999 ¶	2,261,027	53,349	2.4	21.6	0.65	0.15	21.03–12.00
1998	2,038,139	43,015	2.1	25.4	0.52	0.13	13.50–7.19
1997 #	1,790,785	27,587	1.5	19.8	0.33	1.27	13.25–9.88
1996	1,605,905	34,600	2.2	22.4	0.41	0.09	
1995	1,445,975	31,541	2.2	23.7	0.36	0.07	

* Net revenue, which factors out what the company pays the transportation company and the produce grower (in millions): $293.283, $245.666; $206.020; $179.069; and $160.094—in 1999 through 1995, respectively. Income figures include the following per-share gains from discontinued operations and their disposal: $0.19, $0.03, and $0.02—in 1997 through 1995, respectively.
† Trading began Oct. 15, 1997. Per-share amounts restated to reflect 2-for-1 stock split on Dec. 1, 2000.
¶ Pro forma figures for 1999 to include results of Dec. 16, 1999, acquisition American Backhaulers Inc. from Jan. 1: net revenue $345.706 million; earnings $55.032 million/$0.65.
# Income figures for 1997 include pretax charge of $24,656,000 related to IPO. Dividend includes $1.16 related to IPO.

BALANCE SHEET

Assets	12/31/99 (dollars in thousands)	12/31/98	Liabilities	12/31/99 (dollars in thousands)	12/31/98
Current (CAE 49,637 and 99,341)	343,052	374,843	Current	275,894	239,598
Property and equipment	24,747	19,484	Stockholders' equity*	246,767	169,518
Goodwill	144,625	8,485	TOTAL	522,661	409,116
Other intangibles	8,951	4,128			
Other	1,286	2,176			
TOTAL	522,661	409,116			

* $0.10 par common; 130,000,000 authorized; 84,772,000 and 84,772,000 issued and outstanding, less 204,000 and 2,392,000 treasury shares.

RECENT QUARTERS / **PRIOR-YEAR RESULTS**

	Quarter End	Revenue ($000)	Earnings ($000)	EPS ($)	Revenue ($000)	Earnings ($000)	EPS ($)
Q3	09/30/2000	747,615	18,460	0.22	593,354	14,042	0.17
Q2	06/30/2000	750,994	18,944	0.22	579,423	13,982	0.17
Q1	03/31/2000	650,091	15,209	0.18	509,275	10,772	0.13
Q4	12/31/99	578,975	14,553	0.18	507,097	11,118	0.13
	SUM	2,727,675	67,166	0.80	2,189,149	49,914	0.61

RECENT EVENTS

In **December 1999** the company finalized its acquisition of all of the ongoing operations and certain assets of American Backhaulers Inc. for $100 million in cash and 1,120,715 shares of newly issued C.H. Robinson stock. For the second-consecutive year, C.H. Robinson was named one of the 10 Great Places to Work in Minnesota, in the **August 2000** issue of Corporate Report magazine. At month's end, the company acquired $24 million-revenue, 38-employee Trans-Consolidated Inc., a Brooklyn Center, Minn.-based third-party logistics company specializing in refrigerated less-than-truckload (LTL) services for perishable food manufacturers. **Sept. 30**: While net revenue increased 42.9 percent oer 1999 to $107.2 million, income from operations increased 35.9 percent to $30.2 million. "This was a solid quarter for us, even as certain segments of the economy appear to be slowing. This again supports our belief that we can perform well through economic cycles," said CEO Verdoorn. "Our transportation results were strong in all modes. Surface-based North America continues to be our core competency, but we are particularly pleased about increasing success in our international air and ocean business."

OFFICERS

Daryl R. (Sid) Verdoorn
Chairman and CEO
John P. Wiehoff
President
Barry W. Butzow
SVP
Gregory D. Goven
SVP
Owen P. Gleason
VP, General Counsel, and Secretary
James V. Larsen
VP-Transportation
Chad M. Lindbloom
VP and CFO
Thomas K. Mahlke
Controller
Timothy P. Manning
VP-Branch Operations
Joseph J. Mulvehill
VP-International
Michael T. Rempe
VP-Produce
Troy A. Renner
Treasurer
J.J. Singh
Pres., T-Chek Systems
Mark Walker
VP and Chief Information Officer

DIRECTORS

Looe Baker III
Brisan Ingredients Inc.
Barry W. Butzow
Robert Ezrilov
Metacom Inc.
Greg Gaven
Owen P. Gleason
Dale S. Hanson
Gerald A. Schwalbach
Superior Storage LLC
Daryl R. (Sid) Verdoorn

MAJOR SHAREHOLDERS

Daryl R. (Sid) Verdoorn, 7.2%
FMR Corp., 7%
Boston
All officers and directors as a group (17 persons), 18.2%

SIC CODE

4731 Freight transportation arrangement
5148 Fruits and vegetables, whsle

MISCELLANEOUS

TRANSFER AGENT AND REGISTAR:
Wells Fargo Bank Minnesota N.A.,
South St. Paul, MN
TRADED: Nasdaq National Market
SYMBOL: CHRW
STOCKHOLDERS: 1,400
EMPLOYEES: 3,125
GENERAL COUNSEL:
Dorsey & Whitney PLLP,
Minneapolis
AUDITORS:
Arthur Andersen LLP,
Minneapolis
INC: MN-1997
FOUNDED: 1905
ANNUAL MEETING: May
INVESTOR RELATIONS:
Angela Freeman
HUMAN RESOURCES:
Colleen Zwach

RANKINGS

No. 17 CRM Public 200
No. 12 CRM Performance 100

PUB

TWO-YEAR QUARTERLY HIGH-LOW STOCK PRICES

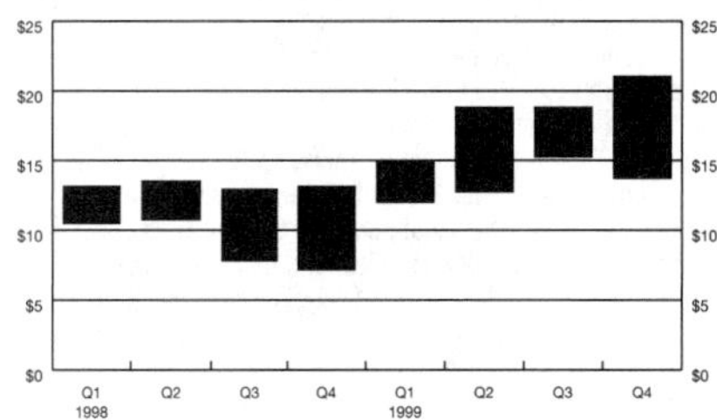

PUB

Rochester Medical Corporation

One Rochester Medical Dr. N.W., Stewartville, MN 55976
Tel: 507/533-9600 Fax: 507/533-9725 Web site: http://www.rocm.com

Rochester Medical Corp. develops, manufactures, and markets innovative urinary continence care products for urinary dysfunction and urine drainage management. The company currently manufactures and markets a broad line of functionally and technologically enhanced latex-free versions of standard continence care products, including male external catheters, Foley catheters, and intermittent catheters. The company markets its products under its own Rochester Medical brand and through private-label arrangements.

EARNINGS HISTORY

Year Ended Sept 30	Operating Revenue/Sales (dollars in thousands)	Net Earnings	Return on Revenue (percent)	Return on Equity	Net Earnings (dollars per share)	Cash Dividend	Market Price Range
1999	7,341	(4,401)	(59.9)	(16.2)	(0.83)	—	15.50–8.38
1998	9,518	(2,258)	(23.7)	(7.3)	(0.44)	—	17.88–8.00
1997	7,615	(2,099)	(27.6)	(12.2)	(0.51)	—	21.00–12.25
1996	5,540	(1,360)	(24.5)	(7.1)	(0.35)	—	22.25–12.88
1995	3,131	(1,311)	(41.9)	(35.7)	(0.49)	—	21.00–8.50

BALANCE SHEET

Assets	09/30/99 (dollars in thousands)	09/30/98	Liabilities	09/30/99 (dollars in thousands)	09/30/98
Current (CAE 4,216 and 2,864)	17,011	21,064	Current	1,525	1,818
Property, plant, and equipment	11,472	11,420	Stockholders' equity*	27,177	30,918
Patents	219	252	TOTAL	28,702	32,736
TOTAL	28,702	32,736			

* No par common; 20,000,000 authorized; 5,349,500 and 5,269,500 issued and outstanding.

RECENT QUARTERS / **PRIOR-YEAR RESULTS**

	Quarter End	Revenue ($000)	Earnings ($000)	EPS ($)	Prior-Year Revenue ($000)	Prior-Year Earnings ($000)	Prior-Year EPS ($)
Q4	09/30/2000	1,695	(1,579)	(0.30)	1,880	(1,438)	(0.27)
Q3	06/30/2000	2,111	(1,352)	(0.25)	1,733	(1,233)	(0.23)
Q2	03/31/2000	2,047	(1,266)	(0.24)	1,381	(999)	(0.19)
Q1	12/31/99	2,008	(1,334)	(0.25)	2,346	(730)	(0.14)
	SUM	7,860	(5,531)	(1.04)	7,341	(4,401)	(0.82)

RECENT EVENTS

In **December 1999** the company formed a distribution and customer service program for the FemSoft Insert to be administered by McKesson Pharmaceutical Partners Group (MPPG), a business unit of McKesson HBOC Inc. MPPG's Healthcare Delivery Systems unit has provided design consultation and development support for the program through their expertise in similar managed-distribution programs. The board of directors authorized a stock repurchase program under which up to 1 million shares (18.7 percent) of the company's outstanding common stock may be repurchased. No time limit was placed on the duration of the program. In study results published in the December issue of Antimicrobial Agents and Chemotherapy, investigators concluded that the in vitro antibacterial activity of Rochester Medical Corp.'s Release-NF Antibacterial Foley Catheter is markedly superior in several respects to that of C.R. Bard's Infection Control Foley Catheter. The study found that, except for vancomycin resistant E. faecium, Rochester Medical's Release-NF catheter was active against all the bacterial isolates tested, and it showed broad inhibition of the Multi Drug Resistant strains as well as the susceptible strains of bacteria. In contrast, the C.R. Bard I.C. catheter did not inhibit any of the bacteria, except for certain staphylococci—and those were more actively inhibited by Release-NF and for a longer period of time. In **January 2000** Rochester Medical's new FemSoft Insert became commercially available for the first time. In **March** Medline Industries Inc. began marketing, selling, and distributing the company's RELEASE-NF Foley Catheter in the United States. In **June** the company received 510K clearance from the FDA to market its newly developed hydrophilic silicone catheters—hydrophilic intermittent catheters, Foley catheters, and suprapubic urine drainage catheters. (The hydrophilic surface of these catheters becomes very slippery when wetted, providing an extremely low-friction surface.) To free up manufacturing capacity for its new, higher-margin products, Rochester Medical wanted to sell its basic Foley catheter business to Maersk Medical of Denmark. However, as CEO Conway reported in **July**, "The companies have been unable to reach a definitive agreement on the contemplated transaction. We will continue to manufacture and sell Foley catheters, and in the future we expect to introduce our new hydrophilic Foley that was recently cleared by the FDA." The company signed an agreement with Rusch S.R.L, Italy, for marketing and distribution of the FemSoft Insert in the Italian market. The company received FDA clearance to market its new Antibacterial Personal Catheter, designed for intermittent catheterization for patients with incontinence and other voiding dysfunction as well as for surgical and sampling procedures. In **August** Prudential Securities lowered its rating on Rochester Medical from ACCUMULATE to HOLD after lowering revenue estimates. In **September** Rochester Medical began television commercials for the FEMSOFT Insert in the Detroit area, the company's primary test market. "The initial response to the ads has been remarkable," said CEO Conway. "We have certainly confirmed that there is tremendous interest in learning more about this new approach to dryness." **Sept. 30:** The company reported a fiscal-year net loss of $5.531million/($1.04). The increase in the loss, compared to last fiscal year, was primarily attributable to costs associated with market introduction of the FemSoft insert and nonrecurring transaction and staff restructuring costs. "We are now emerging from a several year period of intensive product and technology development, extensive clinical research and testing, and significant development of market introduction materials for *continued on page 343*

OFFICERS

Anthony J. Conway
Chairman, President, and CEO

Brian J. Wierzbinski
EVP, CFO, and Treasurer

Philip J. Conway
VP-Operations

Dara Lynn Horner
VP-Marketing

Richard D. Fryar
VP-Research/Developement

DIRECTORS

Darnell L. Boehm
Aetrium Inc., North St. Paul, MN

Anthony J. Conway

Peter R. Conway
Halcon Corp., Stewartville, MN

Philip J. Conway

Richard D. Fryar

Roger W. Schnobrich
Hinshaw & Culbertson, Minneapolis

Brian J. Wierzbinski

MAJOR SHAREHOLDERS

Zesiger Capital Group LLC, 10.1%
New York

Anthony J. Conway, 8.4%
Chatfield, MN

Woodland Partners LLC, 6.5%
Minneapolis

Vector Securities International Inc., 5.2%
Deerfield, IL

All officers and directors as a group (15 persons), 22.8%

SIC CODE

3841 Surgical and medical instruments

MISCELLANEOUS

TRANSFER AGENT AND REGISTAR:
Wells Fargo Bank Minnesota N.A., South St. Paul, MN

TRADED: Nasdaq National Market

SYMBOL: ROCM

STOCKHOLDERS: 121

EMPLOYEES: 135

GENERAL COUNSEL:
Dorsey & Whitney PLLP, Minneapolis

AUDITORS:
Ernst & Young LLP, Minneapolis

INC: MN-1988

ANNUAL MEETING: February

INVESTOR RELATIONS: Brian J. Wierzbinski

RANKINGS

No. 195 CRM Public 200

TWO-YEAR QUARTERLY HIGH-LOW STOCK PRICES

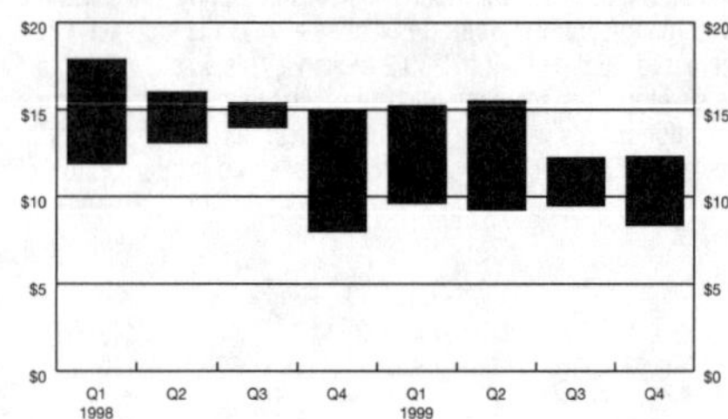

The Rottlund Company Inc.

2681 Long Lake Rd., Roseville, MN 55113
Tel: 651/638-0500 Fax: 651/638-0501

The Rottlund Co. Inc. designs, constructs, markets, and sells detached single-family homes and attached townhomes and villas in the metropolitan areas of Minneapolis/St. Paul; Des Moines, Iowa; southern New Jersey; Naples-Ft. Myers, Orlando, and Tampa, Fla.; and Indianapolis. The company owns, or controls through options, more than 2,300 home sites in communities under development, and land for the development of more than 3,500 additional planned home sites in proposed communities. A subsidiary, North Coast Mortgage Inc., was formed to support the residential home construction business and to create an additional revenue source for the company.

EARNINGS HISTORY

Year Ended Mar 31	Operating Revenue/Sales (dollars in thousands)	Net Earnings	Return on Revenue (percent)	Return on Equity	Net Earnings (dollars per share)	Cash Dividend	Market Price Range
2000	260,834	5,459	2.1	14.7	0.94	—	5.75–2.31
1999	252,675	5,177	2.0	16.4	0.90	—	5.75–3.00
1998	160,830	(598)	(0.4)	(2.3)	(0.10)	—	5.25–3.00
1997 *	180,457	1,236	0.7	4.6	0.22	—	8.50–4.50
1996 †	131,583	4,242	3.2	16.7	0.75	—	9.50–5.50

* income figures for 1997 include pretax write-down of $1.5 million for land valuation adjustment.
† Figures for 1996 include results of Kevin Scarborough Inc. from its Feb. 20, 1996, date of purchase for $9.8 million. Pro forma for April 1, 1995, purchase: revenue $147,467,000; net income $3,405,000/$0.59.

BALANCE SHEET

Assets	03/31/00 (dollars in thousands)	03/31/99	Liabilities	03/31/00 (dollars in thousands)	03/31/99
Cash and equivalents	8,087	6,558	Senior notes payable	21,845	26,731
Escrow, other receivables	2,447	2,607	Mortgage notes payable	1,224	1,451
Land, development costs, finished lots	47,224	46,315	Accounts payable	10,785	8,905
			Accrued liabilities	6,459	6,132
Residential housing completed, under construction	30,231	23,727	Income taxes payable	158	4,263
			Revolving credit facility	21,135	10,285
Property, equipment	867	941	Stockholders' equity*	37,160	31,598
Deferred income taxes	1,796	1,605	TOTAL	98,766	89,365
Other	8,114	7,612			
TOTAL	98,766	89,365			

* $0.10 par common; 40,000,000 authorized; 5,804,000 and 5,773,000 issued and outstanding.

RECENT QUARTERS / PRIOR-YEAR RESULTS

	Quarter End	Revenue ($000)	Earnings ($000)	EPS ($)	Prior-Year Revenue ($000)	Prior-Year Earnings ($000)	Prior-Year EPS ($)
Q2	09/30/2000	75,766	3,037	0.52	62,813	1,148	0.20
Q1	06/30/2000	49,605	253	0.04	49,587	316	0.05
Q4	03/31/2000	87,657	2,917	0.50	78,752	2,489	0.43
Q3	12/31/99	60,777	1,078	0.19	58,786	1,023	0.18
	SUM	273,805	7,285	1.26	249,938	4,976	0.86

CURRENT: Q1 earnings include extraordinary loss of $612,000/($0.11) from debt extinguishment.

RECENT EVENTS

In **March 2000** the company was making plans for a 1,020-unit residential development on a 125-acre site in northeast Plymouth, Minn. **Sept. 30:** Rottlund achieved the highest second-quarter sales and net income in the company's history. Backlog consisted of 580 homes with a sales value of $120.2 million, 4 percent less than the sales value of $125.0 million for 712 homes at Sept. 30, 1999, due to the company's exit from the Orlando, Ft. Myers, and Indianapolis markets. Sales value of backlog on a comparable market basis increased 15 percent. New orders for 356 homes with a sales value of $69.2 million were received for the quarter, compared to 390 homes with a sales value of $67.6 million for the same period in 1999. Said CEO Rotter, "These results include the sale of the majority of the land and inventory positions in the Indianapolis market, and we expect to be completely out of the Indianapolis market by the end of the fiscal year so that we may continue to focus on markets where we can generate higher returns."

OFFICERS

David H. Rotter
President

Bernard J. Rotter
VP

Todd M. Stutz
EVP

John J. Dierbeck III
EVP

Steven A. Kahn
CFO

DIRECTORS

John J. Dierbeck III

Dennis J. Doyle
Welsh Cos. Inc., Bloomington, MN

Bernard J. Rotter

David H. Rotter

Scott D. Rued
Hidden Creek Industries, Minneapolis

Lawrence B. Shapiro

Todd M. Stutz

MAJOR SHAREHOLDERS

David H. Rotter, 37.5%
Bernard J. Rotter, 36.4%
Shirley A. Rotter, 13.5%
Heartland Advisors Inc., 10.2%
Milwaukee
All officers and directors as a group (7 persons), 80.8%

SIC CODE

1521 Single-family housing construction
1522 Residential construction, nec

MISCELLANEOUS

TRANSFER AGENT AND REGISTAR:
Wells Fargo Bank Minnesota N.A.,
South St. Paul, MN
TRADED: AMEX
SYMBOL: RH
STOCKHOLDERS: 150
EMPLOYEES: 233
GENERAL COUNSEL:
Gray, Plant, Mooty, Mooty & Bennett P.A., Minneapolis
AUDITORS:
Arthur Andersen LLP, Minneapolis
INC: MN-1973
ANNUAL MEETING:
September

PUBLIC RELATIONS:
Lawrence B. Shapiro

RANKINGS

No. 68 CRM Public 200

SUBSIDIARIES, DIVISIONS, AFFILIATES

Rottlund Homes of Indiana L.P. (1)
5519 E. 82nd St., Suite F
Indianapolis, IN 46250
Pat Duggan

Rottlund Homes of Iowa Inc. (1)
2928 104th St.
Urbandale, IA 50322
Lynn James

Rottlund Homes of Florida Inc. (1)
8695 College Parkway, Suite 239
Ft. Myers, FL 33919
Robert Gleason

Tampa Division (2)
3023 Eastland Blvd., Suite 106
Clearwater, FL 34621

Rottlund Homes of New Jersey Inc. (1)
10 Foster Ave., Suite A1
Gibbsboro, NJ 08026
Kevin Scarborough

PUB

TWO-YEAR QUARTERLY HIGH-LOW STOCK PRICES

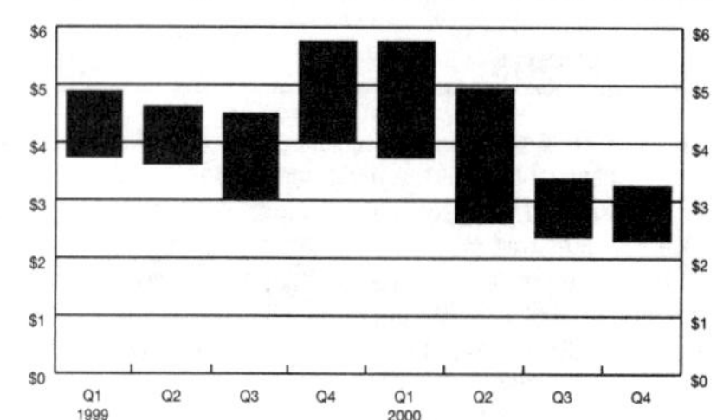

PUB

Rural Cellular Corporation

3905 Dakota St. S.W., P.O. Box 2000, Alexandria, MN 56308
Tel: 320/762-2000 Fax: 320/808-2181 Web site: http://www.rccwireless.com

Rural Cellular Corp. provides wireless communications services, offering cellular, long-distance, PCS, and paging services to Midwest, East Coast, South and Northwest markets located in 14 states. RCC Minnesota is the company's core operation and the largest provider of cellular and paging services in northern Minnesota. Wireless Alliance is a joint venture formed in 1996 by RCC and an affiliate of Aerial Communications Inc. It primarily markets pcs digital wireless services under the Unicel trade name in selected markets of Minnesota, Wisconsin, North Dakota, and South Dakota.

EARNINGS HISTORY *

Year Ended Dec 31	Operating Revenue/Sales (dollars in thousands)	Net Earnings (dollars in thousands)	Return on Revenue (percent)	Return on Equity (percent)	Net Earnings (dollars per share†)	Cash Dividend (dollars per share†)	Market Price Range (dollars per share†)
1999	156,619	4,850	3.1	NM	(1.22)	—	99.00–11.50
1998 ¶	98,532	(6,624)	(6.7)	NM	(1.76)	—	18.25–10.13
1997 #	53,903	(1,266)	(2.3)	(3.8)	(0.14)	—	13.25–8.63
1996	30,460	3,477	11.4	9.9	0.41	—	13.50–8.75
1995	20,327	790	3.9	14.5	0.13	—	

* Historical revnue figures have not yet been adjusted to include incollect revenue as service revenue (per RCC policy adopted in April 2000).
† Trading began on Feb. 8, 1996.
¶ Income figures for 1998 include extraordinary loss of $1.042 million/($0.12) on early extinguishment of debt. Results include Atlantic Cellular Co. and Western Maine Cellular operations from their respective dates of acquisition. Pro forma for full year: revenue $122.198 million; loss $25.151 million/($2.82).
# Results for 1997 include Unicel operations from their May 1, 1997, date of acquisition. Pro forma for full year: revenue $58.721 million; loss $3.861 million/($0.44).

BALANCE SHEET

Assets	12/31/99 (dollars in thousands)	12/31/98 (dollars in thousands)
Current (CAE 1,285 and 2,062)	23,373	18,992
Property and equipment	130,651	131,714
Licenses, other intangibles	318,632	309,672
Deferred debt-issuance costs	11,099	11,761
Restricted funds in escrow	35,000	
Other	7,523	8,385
TOTAL	526,278	480,524

Liabilities	12/31/99 (dollars in thousands)	12/31/98 (dollars in thousands)
Current	29,260	28,530
Long-term debt	339,742	298,851
Minority interest		1,663
Exchangeable preferred stock	147,849	132,201
Stockholders' equity*	9,427	19,279
TOTAL	526,278	480,524

* $0.01 par common; 20,000,000 authorized; 9,122,000 and 8,983,000 issued and outstanding.

RECENT QUARTERS / **PRIOR-YEAR RESULTS**

	Quarter End	Revenue ($000)	Earnings ($000)	EPS ($)	Prior-Year Revenue ($000)	Prior-Year Earnings ($000)	Prior-Year EPS ($)
Q3	09/30/2000	110,145	(6,972)	(1.63)	52,208	7,554	0.39
Q2	06/30/2000	99,757	(14,360)	(2.24)	43,162	1,290	(0.29)
Q1	03/31/2000	46,629	867	(0.57)	36,613	(1,555)	(0.60)
Q4	12/31/99	39,342	(2,439)	(0.72)	32,108	(2,783)	(0.72)
	SUM	295,873	(22,904)	(5.16)	164,091	4,506	(1.22)

CURRENT: Q2 earnings include extraordinary loss of $925,000/($0.08). Q1 preferred stock dividend of $6.887 million exceeded net income, causing negative EPS. Q4 revenue has not been restated.
PRIOR YEAR: Q2 preferred stock dividend of $3.92 million exceeded net income, causing negative EPS. Q4 revenue has not been restated.

RECENT EVENTS

In **January 2000** the company registered a public offering of 2.4 million shares of Class A common stock,110,000 shares of junior exchangeable preferred stock, and an additional 25,000 shares of its already existing senior exchangeable preferred stock. The combined net proceeds of the offerings were to be used, together with a new $1.2 billion credit facility and the issuance of convertible preferred stock, to finance the pending acquisition of the licenses, operations, and related assets of Triton Cellular Partners L.P. [completed April 3]; to repay amounts owing under the existing credit facility; and to fund capital expenditures and operating expenses. In **February** the SEC declared effective RCC's registration statement for a follow-on offering of 2,390,000 shares of its Class A common stock at $61 7/8 per share. The underwriters included Donaldson, Lufkin & Jenrette, Merrill Lynch & Co., Banc of America Securities LLC, First Union Securities Inc., The Robinson-Humphrey Co., and DLJdirect Inc. Combined with two preferred stock issues, the combined net proceeds from the offer- *continued on page 343*

OFFICERS

Richard P. Ekstrand
President and CEO

Ann K. Newhall
EVP and COO

Wesley E. Schultz
EVP and CFO

Rick O'Connor
SVP-Northeast Region

Regan Anderson
VP-South Region

Michael H. Brown
VP-Business Integration

David J. DelZoppo
VP-Finance/Accounting

Scott G. Donlea
VP-Market Development

Karen Henrikson
VP-Human Resources

Frederick (Fritz) Hibbler, Ph.D.
VP and Chief Information Officer

Thomas F. McLaughlin
VP-Atlantic Region

Robert L. Moore
VP-Midwest Region

Ken Robblee
VP-Northwest Region

W.A. (Lex) Wilkinson Jr.
VP-Inter-Carrier Relations

DIRECTORS

Richard P. Ekstrand

Paul Finnegan
Madison Dearborn Partners

Jeffrey S. Gilbert
Paul Bunyan Rural Telephone Cooperative

John Hunt
Boston Ventures Management Inc.

Ann K. Newhall

Marvin C. Nicolai
Consolidated Telephone Co.

George M. Revering
Midwest Information Systems

Wesley E. Schultz

Don C. Swenson
Arvig Communications Systems

George W. Wikstrom Jr.
Wikstrom Telephone Company

MAJOR SHAREHOLDERS

Telephone & Data Systems Inc., 9.1%
Chicago

Don C. Swenson/Arvig Enterprises, 6.7%
Perham, MN

Baron Capital Group Inc., 5.7%
New York

Marvin C. Nicolai/ Consolidated Telephone Co., 5%
Brainerd, MN

All officers and directors as a group (12 persons), 21.9%

SIC CODE

4812 Radiotelephone communications

MISCELLANEOUS

TRANSFER AGENT AND REGISTAR:
Wells Fargo Bank Minnesota N.A.,
South St. Paul, MN

TRADED: Nasdaq National Market

SYMBOL: RCCC

STOCKHOLDERS: 143

EMPLOYEES: 1,062

GENERAL COUNSEL:
Moss and Barnett P.A.,
Minneapolis

AUDITORS:
Arthur Andersen LLP,
Minneapolis

INC: MN-1990

ANNUAL MEETING: May

INVESTOR RELATIONS:
Chris Boraas

PUBLIC RELATIONS:
Barb Ostrandor

RANKINGS

No. 77 CRM Public 200

No. 31 CRM Performance 100

TWO-YEAR QUARTERLY HIGH-LOW STOCK PRICES

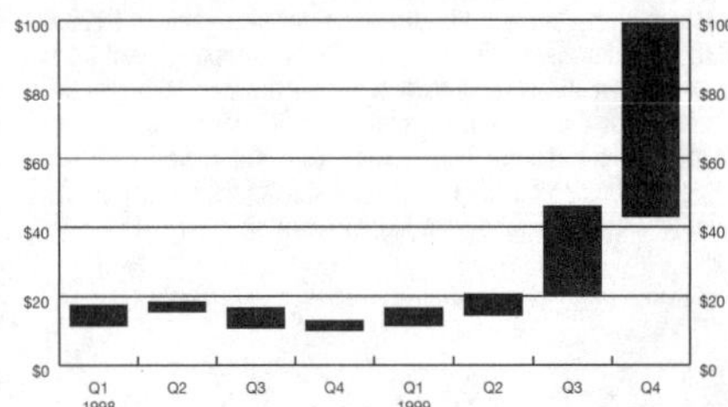

Paper Warehouse Inc.

continued from page 316 trading days prior to May 1, 2000. In **March** Dolginow said, "In response to operating losses and to strengthen our competitive position, during the fourth quarter we adopted a plan to close four underperforming stores. We also re-evaluated our prior estimate regarding the expected recovery of rent on previously closed stores. In addition, in response to a significant change in the e-commerce advertising environment, and to current and projected operating losses in our e-commerce business, we reviewed the assets associated with our Internet investment for impairment. As a result of this review and, based upon the results of an outside appraisal, we recorded an impairment charge in the fourth quarter to reflect these assets at their fair market value." **April 28**: Comparable-store sales increased a strong 12 percent for the quarter. In **May**, expressing optimism for the current fiscal year, Dolginow noted, "We plan to open only one new company-owned store in 2000, relocate three stores, and remodel two existing stores. By limiting new store initiatives our attention is concentrated on maximizing the performance of our existing store base and insuring that our large class of 1998 and 1999 stores to mature fully." The company signed a multistore franchise agreement to develop stores under its Party Universe trademark in Calgary, Alberta, the company's first international franchise location. The first store was expected to open in the fall of 2000. In **June** the company closed on an agreement with a subtenant for the sublease of the previous Maple Grove, Minn., location, which was relocated in March 2000. **July 28**: For the six-month period, total revenue of $43.3 million grew 18.3 percent over the prior-year period. Comparable-store sales increased 13.4 percent, up substantially from 6.3 percent for the prior-year period. In **August** the Nasdaq Listing Qualifications Panel moved the company's stock listing to the Nasdaq SmallCap Market from the Nasdaq National Market because it was not able to regain compliance with the maintenance standard requiring at least $5 million of "public float." The board of directors approved a rights offering to its existing shareholders of record: 0.323 rights for each share of common stock held, with each whole right entitling its holder to purchase one share of the company's $.01 par value common stock at a subscription price of $1.25, for a total subscription of up to 1.5 million shares. A registration statement on Form S-3 to that effect was filed on Aug. 31. [The company raised $1.2 million.] In **October** Paper Warehouse's shareholder rights offering was declared effective by the SEC. The company was intending to use the proceeds from the rights offering for working capital and general corporate purposes. In **October** Paper Warehouse relaunched its Web site, PartySmart.com, after correcting certain navigational and other functional problems. The company formed a strategic partnership with Hallmark Cards Inc., signing a multiyear agreement allowing Hallmark to be the exclusive supplier for greeting cards for Paper Warehouse's corporate and franchise stores.

Pemstar Inc.

continued from page 318 as optical companies QLogic and ONI Systems," said Berning. In **October** Brix Networks, Billerica, Mass., chose Pemstar as its international contract manufacturer—to build, configure, test, and ship the Brix 100 and Brix 1000 verifiers (hardware-based platforms). The company was named one of the fastest-growing private companies in the country by Inc. magazine: No. 136 on the Inc. 500. (Pemstar is no longer private.) Management said that it expected to meet or exceed the consensus analysts' earnings estimate for the company's 2001 fiscal third quarter, ending Dec. 31, 2000.

Pentair Inc.

continued from page 319 strong double-digit rates at least through the next five years, CEO Buxton told a group of financial executives. "We are retaining the solid Old Economy principles on which Pentair was built, but we are accelerating our migration into the realm of New Economy capabilities," he said. The editors of Consumers Digest selected an Ex-Cell-brand pressure washer as a "Best Buy." The pressure washer is a 3,200 pounds-per-square-inch, four gallons-per-minute Model EXWGC3240 powered by a 11-horsepower Honda engine and manufactured by DeVilbiss Air Power Co. in its Decatur, Ark., facility. In **June** Pentair signed a joint agreement with a Brazilian enclosure manufacturer giving Pentair an immediate, major presence in the fast-growing South American telecom enclosures market and helping support Pentair's key global customers including Lucent, Motorola, Nortel, and Rockwell. Under the mutual exclusive agreement, Metalurgica Taunus Ltda. (Taunus), Boituva, Brazil, was to provide local support and manufacturing for Pentair's worldwide enclosure businesses. In **July** Pentair warned that sustained strong performances by its water and enclosures businesses were expected to be largely offset by near-term delays in achieving the benefits of cost initiatives in its tool and service equipment businesses, causing the company to miss second-quarter earnings estimates by 15 cents. Pentair also reported that it was establishing a reserve to cover the deterioration in credit quality of a significant customer. In **August** Water Technologies Group launched an e-commerce Web site, e-watershop India http://www.e-watershop.com), to increase its already-substantial water purification business in the rapidly growing economies of Asia. In **September** Pentair said that the turnaround of its tools and equipment business was not expected to be resolved until early in 2001. To compound the difficulties, the tools and equipment group's president resigned. **Sept. 30:** Revenue for the third quarter increased 18 percent, while EPS of $.26 was in line with revised expectations. In Water Technologies, a sales gain of 30 percent and an operating income improvement of 42 percent reflected solid organic performance gains, as well as the contributions of Essef, acquired in early August of 1999. In the Enclosures Group, revenue grew 18 percent and operating income improved by 51 percent. Pentair's enclosure businesses saw tremendous growth in the telecom and datacom markets, and with industrial original-equipment manufacturers. Lincoln Industrial contributed strong profits to the Equipment Group, but losses in Service Equipment (SE) continued to hurt results. Third-quarter revenue grew 27 percent in the Tools Group, but operating income declined 63 percent as a result of resulted from a chain of events linked to difficulties encountered during the first-quarter start-up of a new tools distribution center in Tennessee. In **October** Popular Mechanics named Porter-Cable's new handheld oscillating spindle sander (model 121) the winner of the 2001 Design & Engineering Award. Selected among thousands of new products introduced during 2000, the spindle sander was the only power tool selected in the competition. Under a new brand strategy for Pentair's businesses serving the pool and spa equipment industry, eight pool and spa equipment brands were being aligned under the new name "Pentair Pool Products." Porter-Cable and Delta renewed their commitment to co-sponsor The New Yankee Workshop, public television's step-by-step woodworking show hosted by Master Carpenter Norm Abram. In **November** Pentair announced that COO Hogan, 45, who was recruited to the company after successful executive careers at McKinsey & Co., General Electric, and United Technologies Corp., was to succeed Winslow H. Buxton as CEO, effective Jan. 1, 2001. Record sales to new, high-growth markets prompted the Enclosures Group to expand aluminum enclosure manufacturing capabilities in its Anoka and Brooklyn Center, Minn., facilities.

PLATO Learning Inc.

continued from page 321 schools and alternative schools district-wide in a contract valued in excess of $375,000. PLATO was to be used in a variety of programs, with focus on raising student test scores in reading and math on the Illinois Learning Standards accountability exam. The company was included in dbusiness.com's "50 to Watch," a list of the 50 most dynamic private and public small to medium-sized companies in the Twin Cities. In **May** BlueFire Research initiated coverage of PLATO Learning with an OUTPERFORM rating and a 12-month target price of $19.75 per share, based on a multiple of 25 times estimated earnings per share for the October 2001 fiscal year. In **June** national reseller CCV Software began distributing more than 65 PLATO Educational Titles in math, reading, writing, vocabulary, and science as part of its product offerings to K-12 schools, colleges, and universities. The Mississippi Library Commission agreed to offer the company's new PLATO browser-based Internet courseware to every public library throughout the state in a three-year subscription agreement. The Davis County School District in Farmington, Utah, which serves more than 50,000 students, agreed to expand its use of PLATO in a contract valued at $500,000. PLATO's library of more than 65 individual PLATO Educational Titles in math, reading, writing, vocabulary, and science was to be distributed by Learning Services Inc., via catalog and the Internet (at www.learnserv.com). In **July** PLATO announced plans to integrate more than 25 science courses from the Discovery Channel School into the PLATO Learning System. PLATO completed a $5 million private placement of common stock with an institutional investor. The acquisition of CyberEd Inc., a provider of multimedia science courseware for high schools, for $4.8 million in cash, enabled PLATO to integrate the CyberEd science courseware with the PLATO Learning system and add 44 titles to PLATO's existing individual titles product line. Edudex, a leading distributor of video and software in the high school and higher education markets, agreed to distribute more than 65 PLATO educational titles as part of its more than 50,000 products marketed to educators and librarians. SchoolSoft, an innovative value-add reseller of educational software, agreed to distribute the entire library of PLATO educational titles via its online software catalog at www.school-soft.com. In **August** PLATO announced the PLATO Simulated Test System, the first Web-based assessment tool to fully integrate state-standards practice tests and skill assessments to help students prepare for state-mandated tests. In **October** PLATO notified holders of its 10% Subordinated Convertible Debentures, issued in 1997, of its intent to redeem the debt certificates at a cash redemption price of $25,250 plus accrued interest for each $25,000 face value. Alternatively, the holders of the Debentures could convert the debt into common shares of TUTR at a ratio of $9.01 for each common share. (PLATO Learning common stock closed at $19.438 on Oct. 12.)

Quantech Ltd.

continued from page 326 startup costs that are consolidated with Quantech's financial statements," said CEO Case. "Quantech made significant progress during the last fiscal year, and is poised to achieve its next major milestone of placing clinical units in hospitals." In **July** subsidiary HTS Biosystems Inc. completed its initial round of financing in the aggregate amount of $1.9 million. In **September** Quantech filed to raise $5 million—the largest single capital addition in the company's history—in a private placement of its equity securities. The securities were sold at $10 per unit, with each unit consisting of four shares of stock and one five-year warrant to purchase stock at $3.50 per share. "This funding fuels the necessary growth of our organization and triggers the initiation of our product commercialization effort," said CEO Case. The private placement was oversubscribed by $2.5 million, bringing the total amount raised in this offering to $7.5 million. In **October** HTS Biosystems received a combined license from Boston Probes Inc. and Applied Biosystems (NYSE: PEB) for the use of Boston Probes' peptide nucleic acid (PNA) technology in the field of proteomics.

Raven Industries Inc.

continued from page 330 in sales volume, Raven was forced to discontinue operations at its Sportswear facilities in Salem and Beresford, S.D., two of its five sportswear-manufacturing facilities. (Sportswear Division sales were down 23 percent, or $7 million, in fiscal 2000.) Product lines were to be shifted to other facilities in South Dakota, affecting some 80-85 employees, or 25 percent of the Sportswear Division employees. In **October** Raven Industries received a $2 million order for chemical injection systems. This new Raven product will be used in conjunction with an insecticide for in-furrow rootworm control in newly planted corn. CEO Moquist commented, "Our new chemical injection system provides effective pesticide control and minimizes overapplying costly chemicals. This means savings for the grower and a safer, sounder environment."

Regis Corporation

the fiscal year rose 15.2 percent from prior year, to a record $1.1 billion. Systemwide sales grew to $1.7 billion, a 12.1 percent increase from fiscal 1999. Net income grew to a record $52.4 million, up 19.7 percent from the $43.8 million reported last year, excluding nonrecurring items. Same-store sales for domestic company-owned salons increased 4.3 percent for the year. "The successful execution of our growth strategy resulted in the expansion of our salon base by 715 salons, said CEO Finkelstein. "At the same time, we benefited from solid internal revenue growth in our higher-margin divisions. Wal-Mart, our fastest-growing division, increased from 544 to 695 salons. We are also pleased to have strengthened our international operations by acquiring 68 Supercuts stores in the United Kingdom, giving us control over the Supercuts brand name in Europe." In **July** Regis announced the recent acquisition of 125 salons ($30 million in annualized revenue) in 15 transactions, the majority of which were acquired from franchisees. **Sept. 30**: Revenue for the first quarter of fiscal 2001 grew to a record $310.8 million, a 17 percent increase over the same quarter last year. Systemwide sales grew 15 percent to $455.5 million. Same-store sales for domestic company-owned salons increased 5 percent. "The real story for our first quarter was once again our ability to meet our full-year acquisition growth target in just the first three months of our fiscal year," said Finkelstein. "To date, we have closed or contracted to close deals in excess of 500 salons." In **October** Regis announced the acquisition of 322 salons, 190 of which were franchised units and 250 of which were located in Canada, in one transaction. The acquired salons, operating under the First Choice Haircutters name, generate $26 million in annualized revenue, including $1.6 million in royalty income. Total consolidated revenue increased 13 percent in the month of October to $101 million. In addition, sales at its domestic salons open at least one year rose 4.4 percent for the same period, which was generally in line with the company's expectations.

Rehabilicare Inc.

continued from page 332 The employee alleged that the company improperly submitted approximately 500,000 Medicare claims and received more than $120 million in overpayments from the Medicare program. The U.S. Government intervened in the action on Nov. 8, 1999. The complaint was not unsealed until Jan. 21, 2000, and the company did not obtain a copy of the complaint until Feb. 7, 2000.] Under the terms of the settlement, Rehabilicare was also required to enter into a Corporate Integrity Agreement (CIA). The specific terms of the CIA had not yet been finalized. The CIA was to have a duration of five years and provide for an independent audit of claims submitted to federal health care programs to ensure, among other things, proper filing of future Medicare claims. The company had previously hired a corporate compliance officer and implemented a corporate compliance program to ensure that the company would be in compliance with all applicable laws and regulations. On another subject, professional athletes who use Compex products were out in force at the 2000 Summer Olympic Games held in Sydney. "We are particularly proud of Heike Drechler of Germany, who won a Gold medal in the long jump,": said CEO Kaysen. "Heike is a veritable living legend of this sport and Compex is using her likeness extensively in European advertising and she is making promotional appearances on our behalf." **Sept. 30:** First-quarter gross margin was 68.5 percent compared to 71.5 percent (before a one-time charge) in the prior year. The reduction resulted primarily from increased focus on sales of Compex sport products through retail store outlets, rather than direct to consumers, in order to expand market penetration. In **November** the company announced the initiation of clinical studies at two Southern California locations utilizing its OrthoDx. One study was focused on patellofemoral pain and the other on improved rehabilitation after ACL surgical repair.

Retek Inc.

continued from page 335 time through the Internet. Another new service, retail.com Assort, was designed to facilitate and optimize the process by which retailers plan merchandise assortments. Finally, the new retail.com Intelligence Center was developed to help retailers make informed decisions more quickly by providing market trends, performance management, and real-time monitoring of external and internal events—right to their desktop. Retek established a strategic reselling partnership with HighTouch Technologies (www.hightouch.net), a leading provider of customer direct commerce technology. Retek joined the National Retail Federation's Internet Commerce Council (iCC) and Association for Retail Technology Standards (ARTS) in an effort to improve education and resources available in the retail community, and to help implement standards that reduce technology costs for retailers. February's new customers included the largest automotive parts retailer in Germany, ATU, and WHSmith, the U.K.'s largest book and media store chain. In **March** the Great Atlantic & Pacific Tea Co. (A&P), one of the nation's largest supermarket chains, chose Retek and IBM (NYSE: IBM) to help support phase II of a massive overhaul of the company's supply chain and business management infrastructure. Retail.com and Celarix Inc. teamed up to provide ShopKo with e-logistics solutions. HomeBase Inc. (NYSE: HBI), an Irvine, Calif., home improvement chain, reported a successful implementation of Retek's Internet retail systems, completed on time and under budget. In **April** Leading U.S. fashion retailer Nordstrom Inc. selected Retek to provide retail software to enhance the company's retail supply chain processes and speed response time to its customers. John Buchanan was named a finalist in the 2000 Entrepreneur of the Year Awards by Ernst & Young. The latest e-service available on retail.com was retail.com Top Plan. Retek signed an agreement to acquire HighTouch Technologies, an innovative specialist in multichannel customer relationship solutions, for $18 million in cash and $9 million of Retek common stock. SPS Commerce, a St. Paul-based leader in retail and manufacturing B2B exchanges, entered into a joint business relationship with Retek. Retek and Syncra Systems Inc., a leading provider of B2B supply chain collaboration solutions, announced a new strategic alliance in the consumer packaged goods market. In **May** Retek and the Return Exchange, an Internet-based product return solution provider, announced a new strategic partnership to market The Return Exchange's Verify-1 online product return authorization service. In **June** Tommy Hilfiger Europe BV joined U.K. department store Selfridges in a collaborative brand-management initiative developed with Retek's retail community network, retail.com. Retek added the jewelry/accessories and footwear markets to its apparel marketplace on retail.com. In **July** Retek announced the immediate availability of the Retek Retail Server, a complete retail exchange framework designed specifically for the multidimensional, dynamic needs of retail exchanges. Tesco, Britain's largest retailer, selected Retek as a strategic partner to support its expanding nonfood business. Tesco planned to use Retek's Trade Management System to support its worldwide sourcing activities. Retek was invited by the WorldWide Retail Exchange to provide its Retek Retail Server and design collaborative solution as part of the solution for the Exchange's new technology platform. Best Buy Inc. (NYSE: BBY), the nation's No. 1 specialty retailer of consumer electronics, personal computers, entertainment software, and appliances, selected Retek to deliver the systems infrastructure that will support Best Buy's business through its next stage of rapid growth. Retek unveiled its newest http://retail.com marketplace, designed to serve the grocery and consumer packaged goods industries. Connecticut-based Ames Department Stores selected Retek Data Warehouse (RDW) software to manage its rapidly growing retailing and merchandising operations. In **August** retail.com, advertising agency Fallon Worldwide, and noted trend expert Tom Julian joined forces to provide the latest research, demographics, and trend information to retail.com members. HNC Software Inc. (Nasdaq: HNCS) declared a dividend on HNC common stock of all the shares of Retek Inc. common stock owned by HNC. (HNC currently owned 40 million shares of Retek, representing 84.5 percent of Retek's outstanding common stock.) The Retek shares were to be distributed on or about Sept. 29, 2000, to HNC shareholders. A partnership with RetailExchange.com, a leading online business-to-business global marketplace for excess retail goods, brought RetailExchange.com's off-price consumer goods marketplace to Retek's retail.com community. In **September** IBM (NYSE: IBM) and Retek expanded their strategic alliance, which was then to generate revenue of more than $1 billion by 2003 for the two companies. The new elements of the alliance called for both companies to jointly market, sell, and service a comprehensive retail e-business solution consisting of Retek applications and IBM software and hardware technologies, including DB2* Universal Database. IBM was to promote Retek's products worldwide as the foundation for its retail e-market solution. The announcement of this deal, seen as a stamp of approval, sent Retek's stock surging (up 29 percent for the day, to close at $41.38). Other new partners: Fasturn, a leading provider of sourcing solutions to the apparel industry; and Fairchild Publications Inc., publisher of Womenswear Daily, Executive Technology, and the Daily News Record. Retek and MultiAsia Inc. announced the first customers for their newly formed electronic exchange that serves Asian retailers: department store operator Beijing Sanhe Commercial Affairs Develop Co. Ltd. and auto parts provider Beijing Cexin Investment Consulting Co. Ltd. **Sept. 30**: In another quarter of record growth in software license bookings, third-quarter bookings rose 192 percent, to $33.0 million, compared with the third quarter of 1999. The quarterly operating loss, excluding noncash items and including other income, was $5.8 million, or $0.12 per share. In **October** EDS (NYSE: EDS) agreed to provide its clients with Retek's real-time, online order management systems and Web-enabled product fulfillment tools as part of a new digital Customer Relationship Management (CRM) offering. ILOG (Nasdaq: ILOG; EURO.NM) agreed to combine its ILOG optimization software with Retek's predictive technology to help provide millions in savings for Retek customers. The 130-store Speeds Shoes, Melbourne, Australia, became the first retailer to activate the Retek Merchandising System solutions through a mid-market Service model. Retek announced its position as one of the founding partners behind newly planned venture PerformanceRetail Inc. The Houston-based company was to provide online applications and services specifically tailored to simplify and automate the $230 billion convenience-store industry. Retek Integrator version 2.0, a new collaborative retail exchange solution, delivers the real-time messaging architecture for cross-firewall communication between a retailer's in-house systems and exchanges powered by Retek Retail Server. Retek was selected to provide the information infrastructure for RadioShack, a $4.1 billion retailer of consumer electronics with more than 7,100 locations worldwide. In **November** leading fashion retailer The Wet Seal Inc. (Nasdaq: WTSLA) went live on Retek's complete business infrastructure solution. J.C. Penney Co. Inc. selected Retek to provide key components of its business systems infrastructure designed to dramatically enhance supply/demand chain execution, improve its logistics capabilities, and increase customer satisfaction.

Rimage Corporation

continued from page 336 Prostar, which allows users to create up to 35 unique CDs every 10 minutes in an unattended environment, was showcased at Replitech in Miami Beach, Fla. In **August** Rimage and imix.com announced a strategic partnership through which imix.com was to use Rimage equipment to offer its customers the world's first customizable DVD-Rs. In **September** Rimage announced the release of the Biz-Card Feature that enables all Perfect Image Producer Systems to record and print on card-size CD-R media. Rimage also released the Cedar Desktop Publisher 8000 (DPT 8000), a plug-and-play complete duplication system that fits on a desktop and supports high-volume unattended CD-R duplication. An alternative to CD-ROM replication, this system enables service bureaus and office environments to record and print large quantities of CDs without the capital expense and lead times usually associated with CD-ROM production. Rimage announced a strategic partnership with Amplified Holdings Inc., the leading online business-to-business fulfillment service for the world's largest online retailers, to integrate Rimage's CD-Recordable (CD-R) equipment into its business-to-business online custom CD and just-in-time CD manufacturing. MARCAN, leading DVD/CD solutions provider, began offering the Rimage Family of Perfect Image Products. **Sept. 30**: Rimage was expecting revenue and net earnings for the quarter to be lower than the expectations of the analysts who follow the company's stock. The company expected $10 million in revenue [that would prove correct] and an EPS range of 10 cents to 15 cents [EPS would come in at12 cents], compared to analysts' prevailing EPS expectations ranging from 26 cents to 27 cents on estimated revenue between $13 million and $14 million. The company attributed the lower results to lower-than-anticipated orders from certain of its strategic partners and weakness in European currencies. In **October** Rimage began shipping Cedar Network Publisher products, network-ready products that are small enough to fit on a desktop but powerful enough to handle CD production for an entire company.

these products," said Conway. "These developmental efforts have been highly productive, but they have also been very expensive, time consuming, and highly demanding on the creative energies of key personnel throughout the company." In **October** a major regional insurer in Iowa, after completion of its review process, confirmed coverage for the FEMSOFT Insert.

Rural Cellular Corporation

continued from page 340 ings of $299.5 million were to be used, together with a new $1.2 billion credit facility and the issuance of $110.0 million in convertible preferred stock, to finance the pending acquisition of Triton Cellular Partners L.P., to repay amounts owing under RCC's existing credit facility, to fund capital expenditures, and for general corporate purposes. In **June** AirCell Inc., a Colorado-based company that offers air-to-ground communications systems for the aviation market using 800 MHz cellular technologies, named Rural Cellular its Provider of the Year for 1999. RCC entered into a definitive agreement to acquire all of the outstanding shares of the Saco River Telegraph and Telephone Co. Saco River provides wireless and ILEC telecommunication services to southern Maine and eastern New Hampshire, including: Portsmouth, Manchester, and Nashua, N.H.; and Portland, Maine. In **September** RCC successfully installed and integrated the Preferred Voice Inc. (OTCBB: PFVI) Voice Integrated Platform System (VIPS) at RCC's corporate office in Alexandria. RCC planned to market the voice-activated dialing feature under the name "Voice Dial" in all of its operating regions, beginning with the Midwest Region on Oct. 1. National Telemanagement Corp. (NTC) signed an agreement with Rural Cellular for NTC's unique iRoam service, offering seamless nationwide roaming and other key benefits to RCC's Smartpay Wireless prepaid subscribers in 14 states. **Sept. 30:** RCC Cellular net customer additions increased to 20,631 in the third quarter of 2000 as compared to net additions of 9,524 in the third quarter of 1999, resulting in cellular penetration increasing to 10.8 percent. EBITDA rose 104 percent to $48.9 million. Total revenue increased 111 percent to a third-quarter record $110.1 million. Operating income increased 58 percent to $22.2 million. CEO Ekstrand commented: "Our business fundamentals remain strong, highlighted by our industry-leading retention together with solid customer growth. Our revenue base continues to benefit from solid local customer-service revenue."

PUB

SAC Technologies Inc.

1285 Corporate Center Dr., Suite 175, Eagan, MN 55121
Tel: 651/687-0414 Fax: 651/687-0515 Web site: http://www.sacman.com

SAC Technologies Inc., dba BIO-key International, is a biometrics identification technology development, licensing, and integration company, providing tested and certified biometrics technology for security and access control applications for the commercial, industrial, and consumer markets. SAC Technologies has pioneered the development of high-performance one-to-many fingerprint identification technology that can be used without the aide of a personal identification number, password, or smartcard. This unique BIO-key identification technology has been packaged into a Web-based Biometric Identification Server Architecture for e-commerce and Web-based transaction applications. The company offers its products through OEMs, master distributors, value-added resellers, and system integrators.

EARNINGS HISTORY *

Year Ended Dec 31	Operating Revenue/Sales (dollars in thousands)	Net Earnings	Return on Revenue (percent)	Return on Equity	Net Earnings (dollars per share†)	Cash Dividend	Market Price Range
1999	464	(2,594)	NM	NM	(0.37)	—	3.13–0.50
1998	385	(5,951)	NM	NM	(0.79)	—	10.75–1.50
1997	464	(2,594)	NM	(71.2)	(0.37)	—	20.75–4.75
1996	32	(823)	NM	NM	(0.18)	—	
1995	229	(86)	(37.7)	NM	(0.02)	—	

* Development-stage enterprise.
† Trading began Feb. 26, 1997. Per-share amounts restated to reflect a 2-for-1 stock split on July 11, 1997.

BALANCE SHEET

Assets	12/31/99 (dollars in thousands)	12/31/98	Liabilities	12/31/99 (dollars in thousands)	12/31/98
Current (CAE 101 and 1,063)	190	1,640	Current (STD 150)	933	2,716
Equipment, furniture, and fixtures	79	135	Convertible debentures	1,112	
Other	91	384	Stockholders' equity*	(1,684)	(557)
TOTAL	361	2,160	TOTAL	361	2,160

* $0.01 par common; 20,000,000 authorized; 9,106,257 and 7,510,867 issued and outstanding.

RECENT QUARTERS / **PRIOR-YEAR RESULTS**

	Quarter End	Revenue ($000)	Earnings ($000)	EPS ($)	Prior-Year Revenue ($000)	Prior-Year Earnings ($000)	Prior-Year EPS ($)
Q2	06/30/2000	0	(948)	(0.10)	15	(932)	(0.12)
Q1	03/31/2000	0	(559)	(0.06)	125	(738)	(0.10)
Q4	12/31/99	16	(657)	(0.08)	22	(1,408)	(0.19)
Q3	09/30/99	2	(1,101)	(0.17)	63	(1,450)	(0.19)
	SUM	18	(3,265)	(0.40)	225	(4,528)	(0.59)

CURRENT: Q3 EPS includes loss of ($0.04) on convertible preferred stock dividend and accretion.

RECENT EVENTS

In an **April 2000** SEC filing, the company said that it only had enough cash to last through June 30, but it was seeking to raise $1.25 million in a private placement. In **August** SAC Technologies closed on a definitive agreement with Jasper Consulting Inc. that vested SAC with sole ownership of its proprietary biometric technology. (The company had entered into an agreement with Jasper and certain current and former of principals of SAC who were involved in the invention of certain biometric technologies.) It also permitted the company to sell or license its products and technologies in any market without payment of any fees or royalties to Jasper. As a result, management believed that SAC was significantly better positioned to commence the commercial distribution of its products and technologies and the execution of its business plan. On **Aug. 16**, SAC received bridge financing in the amount of $200,000 from the Shaar Fund Ltd., the company's principal institutional investor. In **September** SAC announced plans to do business as BIO-key International and to focus its marketing efforts on Internet and intranet security through licensing of its BIO-key Identification technology.

OFFICERS

Barry M. Wendt
Chairman and CEO

Gary E. Wendt
CFO

Ronald A. Burgmeier
VP-Finance

Brent J. Crego
VP-Business Development

Benedict A. Wittig
Secretary and Dir.-Systems Software

DIRECTORS

Jeffry R. Brown
Chancellor Marketing Group

Richard T. Fiskum

Barry M. Wendt

Gary E. Wendt

Benedict A. Wittig

MAJOR SHAREHOLDERS

Barry M. Wendt, 12.8%

Richard T. Fiskum, 12.8%

Benedict A. Wittig, 12.8%

The Shaar Fund Ltd., 10%
Curacao, Netherlands Antilles

Gary E. Wendt, 5.1%
Las Vegas

All officers and directors as a group (5 persons), 30.8%

SIC CODE

3576 Computer communications equipment

MISCELLANEOUS

TRANSFER AGENT AND REGISTAR:
Firstar Trust Co., Milwaukee

TRADED: OTC Bulletin Board, BSE

SYMBOL: SACM

STOCKHOLDERS: 86

EMPLOYEES: 6

GENERAL COUNSEL:
Doherty, Rumble & Butler P.A., Minneapolis

AUDITORS:
Divine, Scherzer & Brody Ltd., Minneapolis

INC: MN-1993

ANNUAL MEETING:
November

COMMUNICATIONS:
Joseph A. Girouand

SUBSIDIARIES, DIVISIONS, AFFILIATES

LAS VEGAS OFFICE

4620 S. Valley View Blvd.
Suite A
Las Vegas, NV 89103
702/798-9777

TWO-YEAR QUARTERLY HIGH-LOW STOCK PRICES

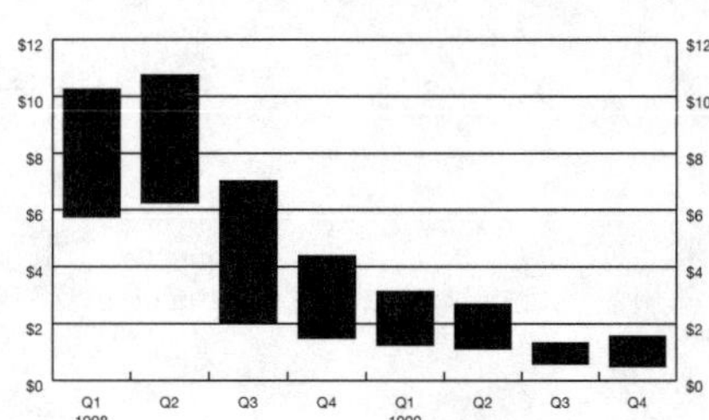

St. Jude Medical Inc.

One Lillehei Plaza, Little Canada, MN 55117
Tel: 651/483-2000 Fax: 651/490-4333 Web site: http://www.sjm.com

St. Jude Medical Inc. develops, manufactures, and markets medical devices for cardiovascular applications. The company manufactures the world's most frequently implanted mechanical heart valve, as well as two types of tissue heart valves; plus annuloplasty rings, cardiac rhythm management products, diagnostic EP (electrophysiology) catheters, and specialty introducer products. The company began manufacturing and marketing its bileaflet pyrolytic carbon-coated prosthetic heart valve in 1977.

EARNINGS HISTORY *

Year Ended Dec 31	Operating Revenue/Sales (dollars in thousands)	Net Earnings	Return on Revenue (percent)	Return on Equity	Net Earnings (dollars per share†)	Cash Dividend	Market Price Range
1999 ¶	1,114,549	24,227	2.2	3.1	0.29	—	40.75–22.94
1998	1,015,994	129,082	12.7	16.0	1.51	—	39.69–19.19
1997 #	994,396	53,140	5.3	5.4	0.58	—	42.88–27.06
1996 **	876,747	60,637	6.9	6.6	0.67	—	46.00–29.63
1995	848,078	117,116	13.8	13.7	1.30	—	43.25–23.67

* Historical figures restated to pool results of Ventitrex, acquired in second quarter 1997; and Daig Corporation, acquired in second quarter 1996.
† Per-share amounts restated to reflect a 3-for-2 stock split on Nov. 16, 1995.
¶ Income figures for 1999 include pretax charge of $115.228 million for purchased R&D; and pretax special charge of $9.754 million. All figures include results of acquisitions Vascular Science Inc. from Sept. 27, 1999, and Angio-Seal from March 16, 1999.
# Income figures for 1997 include pretax special charge of $58.669 million; and extraordinary charge of $1.566 million/($0.02), cumulative effect of an accounting change.
** Income figures for 1996 include pretax charge of $40.35 million for purchased R&D; and pretax special charge of $52.926 million.

BALANCE SHEET

Assets	12/31/99 (dollars in thousands)	12/31/98	Liabilities	12/31/99 (dollars in thousands)	12/31/98
Current (CAE 9,655 and 3,775)	690,299	682,464	Current	282,522	203,397
			Long-term debt	477,495	374,995
Property and equipment	342,780	328,259	Stockholders' equity*	794,021	806,220
Goodwill, other intangibles	452,519	322,434	TOTAL	1,554,038	1,384,612
Deferred income taxes	51,838	44,667			
Other	16,602	6,788			
TOTAL	1,554,038	1,384,612			

* $0.10 par common; 250,000,000 authorized; 83,780,585 and 84,174,699 issued and outstanding.

RECENT QUARTERS / **PRIOR-YEAR RESULTS**

	Quarter End	Revenue ($000)	Earnings ($000)	EPS ($)	Revenue ($000)	Earnings ($000)	EPS ($)
Q3	09/30/2000	286,969	37,999	0.45	275,814	(36,994)	(0.44)
Q2	06/30/2000	300,939	34,119	0.41	290,659	37,205	0.44
Q1	03/31/2000	295,499	15,828	0.19	266,734	(12,057)	(0.14)
Q4	12/31/99	281,342	36,073	0.43	248,452	30,423	0.36
	SUM	1,164,749	124,019	1.48	1,081,659	18,577	0.22

CURRENT: Q2 earnings include charge of $5 million/($0.06) for purchased R&D. Q1 earnings include charge of $26.101 million pretax, $22.213 million/($0.27) after-tax, for costs related to the voluntary recall of Silzone-coated products.
PRIOR YEAR: Q3 earnings include after-tax charge of $73.898 million/($0.87) for purchased R&D expense and special charges. Q1 earnings include charge of $47.775 million pretax, $45.864 million/($0.54) after-tax, for Angio-Seal purchased R&D.

RECENT EVENTS

In **December 1999** the company received FDA approval for U.S. market release of its Livewire TC ablation catheters with Universal Temperature Monitoring (manufactured by St. Jude Medical's Daig division). St. Jude Medical introduced a unique therapy for atrial fibrillation, a cardiac arrhythmia affecting millions of patients worldwide that accounts for enormous health care expenditures. This proprietary therapy, known as Dynamic Atrial Overdrive (DAO), was being incorporated into advanced St. Jude Medical pacemakers. It allows the patient to maintain normal variability in heart rates over the course of the day. St. Jude Medical announced the first implants, in Germany, of the Photon DR implantable cardioverter-defibrillator (ICD) with dual-chamber pacing capabilities. Prudential Vector Healthcare Group reiterated its STRONG BUY, with a 12-month price target of $56 a share. In **January 2000** St. Jude Medical launched a new cardiac pac- *continued on page 369*

OFFICERS

Ronald A. Matricaria
Chairman
Terry L. Shepherd
President and CEO
Robert Cohen
VP-Business/Technology Development
Frieda J. Falk
VP-Administration
Peter L. Gove
VP-Corporate Relations
John C. Heinmiller
VP-Finance, CFO
Jeri Jones
VP and Chief Information Officer
Kevin T. O'Malley
VP and General Counsel
Michael J. Coyle
Pres.-Daig
George J. Fazio
Pres.-Health Care Services
Steven J. Healy
Pres.-Heart Valve Division
Daniel J. Starks
Pres.-CRMD

DIRECTORS

Lowell C. Anderson
Allianz Life Insurance Co. of North America, Minneapolis
Stuart M. Essig
Integra Life Sciences, Plainsboro, NJ
Thomas H. Garrett III
business consultant, Minneapolis
Ronald A. Matricaria
Walter L. Sembrowich, Ph.D.
Aviex Inc., Minneapolis
Terry L. Shepherd
Daniel J. Starks
Roger G. Stoll
Fresenius Medical Care, Lexington, MA
David A. Thompson
Abbott Laboratories, North Chicago, IL
Gail R. Wilensky
Project Hope, Washington, D.C.

MAJOR SHAREHOLDERS

Iridian Asset Management LLC, 7%
West Westport, CT
All officers and directors as a group (21 persons), 5.4%

SIC CODE

3842 Surgical appliances and supplies
3845 Electromedical equipment

MISCELLANEOUS

TRANSFER AGENT AND REGISTAR:
First Chicago Trust Co. of New York, Jersey City, NJ
TRADED: NYSE, Chicago Board Options Exchange
SYMBOL: STJ
STOCKHOLDERS: 4,443
EMPLOYEES: 4,379
GENERAL COUNSEL:
Lindquist & Vennum PLLP, Minneapolis
AUDITORS:
Ernst & Young LLP, Minneapolis
INC: MN-1976
ANNUAL MEETING: May
INVESTOR RELATIONS:
Laura C. Merriam

RANKINGS

No. 32 CRM Public 200
No. 40 CRM Performance 100

SUBSIDIARIES, DIVISIONS, AFFILIATES

Daig, a St. Jude Medical company
14901 DeVeau Pl.
Minnetonka, MN 55345
612/933-4700
Michael J. Coyle

St. Jude Medical Heart Value Division
One Lillehei Plaza
St. Paul, MN 55117
Steven J. Healy

St. Jude Medical International Division
Avenue Arianelaan 5
Brussels, Belgium 1200
011-32-2-774-6811

St. Jude Medical-Cardiac Rhythm Management Division
15900 Valley View Ct.
P.O. Box 9221
Sylmar, CA 91392
Daniel J. Starks

TWO-YEAR QUARTERLY HIGH-LOW STOCK PRICES

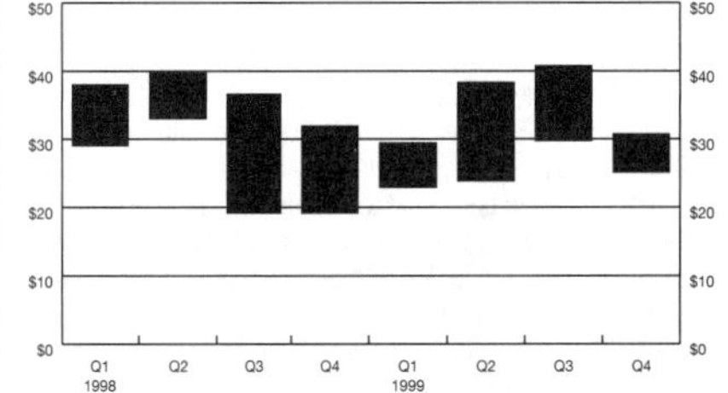

PUB

PUB

The St. Paul Companies Inc.

385 Washington St., St. Paul, MN 55102
Tel: 651/310-7911 Fax: 651/310-8294 Web site: http://www.stpaul.com

continued on page 369

EARNINGS HISTORY *

Year Ended Dec 31	Operating Revenue/Sales (dollars in thousands)	Net Earnings	Return on Revenue (percent)	Return on Equity	Net Earnings	Cash Dividend (dollars per share†)	Market Price Range
1999 ¶	7,569,000	834,000	11.0	12.7	3.61	1.04	37.06–25.38
1998 #	7,708,000	89,348	1.2	1.2	0.33	1.00	47.19–28.06
1997	8,308,000	929,292	11.2	13.9	3.97	0.94	42.66–28.94
1996	7,893,000	732,702	9.3	12.5	3.01	0.88	30.00–25.31
1995	7,273,000	768,000	10.6	14.2	2.96	0.80	29.63–21.81

* Historical figures have been restated to pool the results of USF&G, acquired in April 1998; and to eliminate the revenue of the operations sold to MetLife on Sept. 30, 1999, and to Aon Corp. in May 1997 (Minet); and to segregate the nonstandard auto business, slated to be sold to Prudential. Per-share figures include the following amounts from discontinued operations: $0.37, ($0.46), ($0.58), ($2.53), and ($0.98)—in 1999 through 1995, respectively.
† Per-share amounts restated to reflect 2-for-1 stock split in May 1998.
¶ Income figures for 1999 include extraordinary loss of $30 million/($0.13), cumulative effect of accounting change.
# Income figures for 1998 include merger charge of $434.0 million/($1.85) and after-tax restructuring charge of $22.3 million/(0.09).

BALANCE SHEET

Assets	12/31/99 (dollars in thousands)	12/31/98
Investments	26,207,000	26,498,000
Cash	165,000	146,000
Management securities hfs	45,000	107,000
Reinsurance: unpaid losses	4,426,000	3,974,000
Reinsurance: paid losses	195,000	157,000
Ceded unearned premiums	641,000	288,000
Receivables: underwriting premiums	2,334,000	2,085,000
Receivables: interest, dividends	358,000	354,000
Receivables: other	230,000	52,000
Deferred policy acquisition costs	959,000	878,000
Deferred income taxes	1,271,000	1,193,000
Properties, equipment	507,000	510,000
Goodwill	509,000	592,000
Other	1,026,000	1,030,000
TOTAL	38,873,000	37,864,000

Liabilities	12/31/99 (dollars in thousands)	12/31/98
Insurance reserves: losses. loss adjustment	17,934,000	18,186,000
Insurance reserves: future policy benefits	4,885,000	4,142,000
Insurance reserves: unearned premiums	3,118,000	3,092,000
Debt	1,466,000	1,260,000
Payables: reinsurance premiums	654,000	291,000
Payables: income taxes	319,000	221,000
Payables: accrued expenses, other	1,156,000	1,225,000
Securities lending	1,216,000	1,368,000
Other	1,228,000	940,000
Preferred equity	449,000	518,000
Common equity*	6,448,000	6,621,000
TOTAL	38,873,000	37,864,000

* No par common; 480,000,000 authorized; 224,830,894 and 233,749,778 issued and outstanding.

RECENT QUARTERS / **PRIOR-YEAR RESULTS**

	Quarter End	Revenue ($000)	Earnings ($000)	EPS ($)	Prior-Year Revenue ($000)	Prior-Year Earnings ($000)	Prior-Year EPS ($)
Q3	09/30/2000	2,031,200	231,000	1.04	1,784,700	326,800	1.43
Q2	06/30/2000	2,104,500	211,600	0.98	1,933,400	203,800	0.89
Q1	03/31/2000	2,252,800	357,400	1.60	1,908,900	164,900	0.70
Q4	12/31/99	1,942,000	138,900	0.60	1,842,000	100,800	0.41
	SUM	8,330,500	938,900	4.22	7,469,000	796,300	3.43

CURRENT: Q3 earnings include gain of $0.6 million/$0.00 from discontinued operations. Q2 earnings include loss of $7.2 million/($0.03) from discontinued operations. Q1 earnings include loss of $4.6 million/($0.02) from discontinued operations. Q4 earnings include loss of $87.7 million/($0.38) from discontinued operations sold to MetLife in October 1999.
PRIOR YEAR: Q3 earnings include gain of $190.1 million/$0.84 from discontinued operations. Q2 earnings include loss of $15.3 million/($0.07) from discontinued operations. Q1 earnings include extraordinary charge of $29.9 million/($0.13) cumulative effect of accounting change; and loss of $2.0 million/($0.01) from discontinued operations. Q4 earnings include after-tax restructuring charge of $22.3 million/(0.09); and gain of $5.3 million/$0.02 from discontinued operations.

OFFICERS

Douglas W. Leatherdale
Chairman and CEO

James F. Duffy
Chm./CEO-St. Paul Re

Steven W. Lilienthal
Pres.-U.S. Operations

Michael J. Conroy
EVP and CAO-St. Paul Fire and Marine

Paul J. Liska
EVP and CFO

John A. MacColl
EVP-Baltimore Operations

Bruce A. Backberg
SVP and Chief Legal Counsel

James L. Boudreau
SVP and Treasurer

Tom Bradley
SVP and Controller

Karen L. Himle
SVP-Corporate Affairs

Wayne L. Hoeschen
SVP-Information Systems

James Hom
SVP-Strategic Planning/Development

James R. Lewis
SVP-Commercial Lines Group

David Nachbar
SVP-Human Resources

Kevin M. Nish
SVP-Catastrophe Risk

Kent Urness
SVP-Global Specialty Practices

Marita Zuraitis
SVP-Commercial Lines Group

Thomas E. Bergmann
VP-Treasurer

Laura C. Gagnon
VP-Finance/Investor Relations

Sandra Ulsaker Wiese
Corporate Counsel, Secretary

DIRECTORS

H. Furlong Baldwin
Mercantile Bancshares Corp.

Norman P. Blake Jr.
Promus Hotel Corp.

Michael R. Bonsignore
Honeywell Inc.

John H. Dasburg
Northwest Airlines Corp., Eagan, MN

W. John Driscoll
Rock Island Co. (retired)

Kenneth M. Duberstein
The Duberstein Group

Pierson M. (Sandy) Grieve
Palladium Equity Partners LLC

Thomas R. Hodgson
Abbott Laboratories, North Chicago, IL

David John
The BOC Group, Windlesham, England

William H. Kling
Minnesota Public Radio, St. Paul

Douglas W. Leatherdale

Bruce K. MacLaury
The Brookings Institution, Washington, D.C.

Glen D. Nelson, M.D.
Medtronic Inc., Fridley, MN

Dr. Anita M. Pampusch
Bush Foundation, St. Paul

Gordon M. Sprenger
Allina Health Systems Inc., Minneapolis

MAJOR SHAREHOLDERS

Sanford C. Bernstein & Co. Inc., 8.6%
New York

All officers and directors as a group (31 persons), 1.8%

SIC CODE

6331 Fire, marine, and casualty insurance

MISCELLANEOUS

TRANSFER AGENT AND REGISTAR:
Wells Fargo Bank Minnesota N.A.,
South St. Paul, MN

TRADED: NYSE

SYMBOL: SPC

STOCKHOLDERS: 22,603

EMPLOYEES: 12,000

GENERAL COUNSEL:
Oppenheimer Wolff & Donnelly LLP, Minneapolis

AUDITORS:
KPMG LLP, Minneapolis

INC: MN-1853

ANNUAL MEETING: May

COMMUNICATIONS:
David Monfried

INVESTOR RELATIONS:
James Boudreau

RANKINGS

No. 8 CRM Public 200
No. 70 CRM Employer 100
No. 14 CRM Performance 100

TWO-YEAR QUARTERLY HIGH-LOW STOCK PRICES

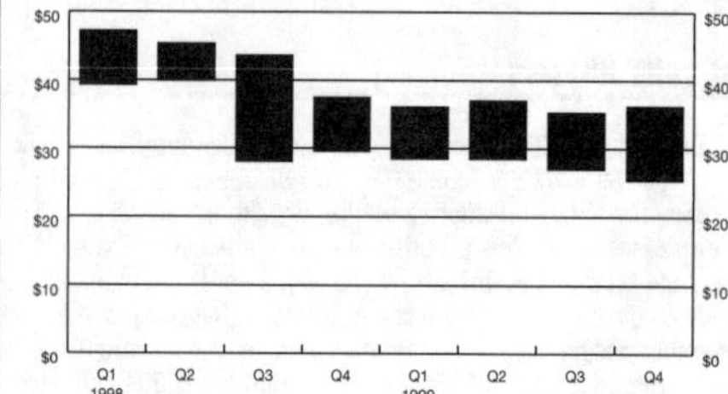

Select Comfort Corporation

10400 Viking Dr., Eden Prairie, MN 55344
Tel: 952/551-7000 Fax: 952/551-7826 Web site: http://www.selectcomfort.com

Select Comfort Corp. is the leading vertically integrated manufacturer, specialty retailer, and direct marketer of premium-quality, premium-priced innovative air beds and sleep-related products. Select Comfort believes it is revolutionizing the mattress industry by offering a differentiated product through a variety of service-oriented distribution channels. Select Comfort's products have been clinically proven to address broad-based consumer sleep problems through the company's proprietary air bed technology and the ability to customize the firmness on each side of the mattress at the touch of a button. The company offers its air beds under the Select Comfort brand through 324 Select Comfort retail stores, direct-marketing operations, and road show events.

EARNINGS HISTORY

Year Ended Dec	Operating Revenue/Sales (dollars in thousands)	Net Earnings	Return on Revenue (percent)	Return on Equity	Net Earnings (dollars per share*)	Cash Dividend	Market Price Range
1999 †	273,767	(8,204)	(3.0)	(15.4)	(0.45)	—	35.25–3.63
1998 ¶	246,269	5,195	2.1	4.3	0.74	—	29.19–19.63
1997 #	184,430	(2,846)	(1.5)	NM	(1.59)	—	
1996	102,028	(3,685)	(3.6)	NM	(2.62)	—	
1995	68,629	(4,560)	(6.6)	NM	(3.16)	—	

* Stock began trading on Dec. 3, 1998.
† Income figures for 1999 include pretax charge of $1.404 million associated with plans to close 22 stores.
¶ Income figures for 1998 include extraordinary charge of $1.441 million/($0.35) on early extinguishment of debt.
# Income figures for 1997, pro forma for the offering: $1.583 million/$0.08.

BALANCE SHEET

Assets	01/01/00 (dollars in thousands)	01/02/99	Liabilities	01/01/00 (dollars in thousands)	01/02/99
Current (CAE 7,441 and 45,561)	54,116	75,817	Current (STD 51 and 930)	39,646	33,568
Property and equipment	34,823	29,125	Long-term debt	36	29
			Other	2,809	1,946
Deferred taxes	4,248	440	Common stock*	53,374	70,691
Other	2,678	852	TOTAL	95,865	106,234
TOTAL	95,865	106,234			

* $0.01 par common; 95,000,000 authorized; 17,713,247 and 18,435,687 issued and outstanding.

RECENT QUARTERS / PRIOR-YEAR RESULTS

	Quarter End	Revenue ($000)	Earnings ($000)	EPS ($)	Prior-Year Revenue ($000)	Prior-Year Earnings ($000)	Prior-Year EPS ($)
Q3	09/30/2000	68,056	(5,443)	(0.30)	68,281	(3,698)	(0.20)
Q2	07/01/2000	61,787	(3,184)	(0.19)	65,750	348	0.02
Q1	04/01/2000	76,159	(2,782)	(0.16)	71,632	1,188	0.06
Q4	01/01/2000	68,104	(6,042)	(0.33)	67,434	5,606	0.31
	SUM	274,106	(17,451)	(0.99)	273,097	3,444	0.19

PRIOR YEAR: Q4 earnings include loss of $1,441,000/($0.08) from early extinguishment of debt.

RECENT EVENTS

In **November 1999** the company filed a patent infringement complaint against Simmons Co. and Price Manufacturing Inc. in U.S. District Court in Minneapolis. The complaint asserted that Simmons, an Atlanta innerspring mattress company, was infringing on three Select Comfort patents by selling Simmons-branded air beds with a hand-held remote control to adjust the firmness of the bed. Price, a Canadian manufacturer, was manufacturing the beds for Simmons. [A settlement was reached with Simmons in February 2000 under which Simmons discontinued the infringing practice.] Based in part on several studies by outside consulting firms, the company was planning strategic changes in its business operations and marketing plans in 2000, including a change in stock symbol from AIRB to SCSS (for Select Comfort sleep solutions). It planned to promote the profitable growth of its retail operations by: incorporating its new store design, which was shown to increase store traffic and sales, into more existing stores through remodels and relocations; slowing down retail store growth by opening only 15 mall-based stores in 2000, with the goal of increasing store density in some existing markets; and by developing detailed market-by-market and store-by-store plans to invest in winning stores and address underperforming stores. Additional strategic priorities: Marketing was being integrated across the company's selling channels—for consistency of message and efficiency in advertising spending; to drive consumers to their preferred sales channel; and to downplay the air-filled feature, the benefits of which weren't well-understood. Select Comfort planned to provide in-home delivery and set-up of its beds in major metropolitan areas, along with removal of old mattresses, by the end of the second quarter 2000—as well as delivery within 72 hours. Early results from a 16-store test were promising for the company's sofa sleeper line, introduced earlier in the year. Finally, Select Comfort planned to test distribution of its products through select wholesale *continued on page 370*

OFFICERS

Patrick A. Hopf
Chairman

William McLaughlin
President and CEO

Ted Atkinson
SVP-Marketing

Tracey T. Breazeale
SVP-Strategic Planning/Branding

Renee Christensen
SVP-E-commerce

Mark A. Kimball
SVP, CAO, Gen. Counsel, and Secretary

Gregory T. Kliner
SVP-Operations

Ronald E. Mayle
SVP-Retail

Noel Schenker
SVP-Marketing/New Business Development

James D. Gaboury
VP-Direct Sales

James C. Raabe
CFO

Michael Thyken
VP and Chief Information Officer

DIRECTORS

Thomas J. Albani
Electrolux Corp. (former)

Patrick A. Hopf
St. Paul Venture Capital Inc., Bloomington, MN

Christopher P. Kirchen
Brand Equity Ventures

David T. Kollat
22 Inc.

William Lansing
Fingerhut Cos. Inc.

William R. McLaughlin

Ervin R. Shames
independent mgmt consultant

Jean-Michel Valette
Franciscan Estates Inc., California

MAJOR SHAREHOLDERS

St. Paul Venture Capital Inc./Patrick A. Hopf, 31%
Bloomington, MN

Consumer Venture Partners/Christopher P. Kirchen, 11.3%
Greenwich, CT

General Electric Capital Corp., 5.7%
Stamford, CT

All officers and directors as a group (15 persons), 46.5%

SIC CODE

2515 Mattresses and bedsprings

MISCELLANEOUS

TRANSFER AGENT AND REGISTAR:
Wells Fargo Bank Minnesota N.A., South St. Paul, MN

TRADED: Nasdaq National Market

SYMBOL: SCSS

STOCKHOLDERS: 157

EMPLOYEES: 1,979

GENERAL COUNSEL:
Oppenheimer Wolff & Donnelly LLP, Minneapolis

AUDITORS:
KPMG LLP, Minneapolis

INC: MN-1987

RANKINGS

No. 63 CRM Public 200

PUB

PUB

Semitool Inc.

655 W. Reserve Dr., Kalispell, MT 59901
Tel: 406/752-2107 Fax: 406/752-5522 Web site: http://www.semitool.com

Semitool Inc. designs, manufactures, markets, and services equipment used in the fabrication of semiconductors. The company's products include spray and immersion chemical processing tools, thermal processing equipment, process control workstations, and carrier cleaning systems. The company's products are also used in the manufacture of materials and devices fabricated with similar processes—including thin film heads, compact disc masters, flat panel displays, hard disk media, and inkjet print heads.

EARNINGS HISTORY *

Year Ended Sept 30	Operating Revenue/Sales (dollars in thousands)	Net Earnings	Return on Revenue (percent)	Return on Equity	Net Earnings (dollars per share†)	Cash Dividend	Market Price Range
1999	122,528	(6,745)	(5.5)	(8.3)	(0.49)	—	6.94–2.13
1998	180,501	4,805	2.7	5.5	0.17	—	13.13–2.56
1997	193,952	12,523	6.5	15.4	0.45	—	13.44–4.19
1996	174,204	15,136	8.7	22.3	0.55	—	12.25–5.13
1995 ¶	128,326	14,403	11.2	27.3	0.57	—	18.38–4.33

* Historical figures represent a pooling of interests between the company and February 1996 acquisition Semy Engineering Inc.
† Stock began trading in February 1995. Per-share amounts restated to reflect 2-for-1 stock split in March 2000; and 3-for-2 stock split in August 1995.
¶ 1995 income figures are pro forma.

BALANCE SHEET

Assets	09/30/99 (dollars in thousands)	09/30/98	Liabilities	09/30/99 (dollars in thousands)	09/30/98
Current (CAE 4,789 and 7,287)	97,301	87,008	Current (STD 0 and 3,596)	44,993	34,600
Property, plant, and equipment	30,336	36,302	Long-term debt	3,911	3,836
Intangibles	3,406	3,965	Deferred income taxes	1,955	2,860
Other	841	715	Stockholders' equity*	81,025	86,694
TOTAL	131,884	127,990	TOTAL	131,884	127,990

* No par common; 30,000,000 authorized; 27,628,000 and 27,584,000 issued and outstanding.

RECENT QUARTERS / **PRIOR-YEAR RESULTS**

	Quarter End	Revenue ($000)	Earnings ($000)	EPS ($)	Revenue ($000)	Earnings ($000)	EPS ($)
Q4	09/30/2000	70,674	8,579	0.30	29,838	(2,735)	(0.10)
Q2	03/31/2000	54,308	5,188	0.18	25,816	(2,967)	(0.11)
Q1	12/31/99	49,555	3,731	0.14	30,422	(1,141)	(0.04)
Q4	09/30/99	36,452	98	0.00	41,686	(703)	(0.03)
	SUM	210,989	17,596	0.63	127,762	(7,546)	(0.27)

RECENT EVENTS

Dec. 31, 1999: The company reported substantially improved results for the first quarter of fiscal 2000. "During the first quarter we experienced strong demand for our products, particularly our electrochemical deposition products," commented then-CEO Gualandris. "We are pleased to have won multiple and repeat orders from customers, and it is clear that customers are now moving our electrochemical deposition products and Spectrum, the most recent addition to our advanced surface preparation product line, into high-volume production applications." In **January 2000** Semitool announced the resignation of Gualandris, who was leaving to join a global chip manufacturer. In **February** the company received an order for multiple LT210c ECD tools from one of North America's leading semiconductor manufacturers for use in applying copper interconnects in high-volume production of semiconductor devices. In **April** subsidiary SEMY Engineering announced the initial phases of a multi-phase, multimillion-dollar project with Cypress Semiconductor Corp.'s Bloomington, Minn., fab. In **June** SEMY Engineering received an initial order from ATMEL Corp. to provide productivity improvements to its factory in France, with the expectation of follow-on orders for installations in the United States and Asia. Semitool registered a public offering of an aggregate amount of 4,100,000 shares of common stock—3,036,000 to be offered by Semitool and 1,064,000 by certain shareholders of Semitool. In **July** Semitool announced a licensing agreement allowing Shipley Co. LLC, Marlborough, Mass., a leading supplier of material and process technologies to the microelectronics and printed wiring board industries, to manufacture and distribute a patent-pending electrochemical deposition (ECD) chemistry developed by Semitool. The company introduced the Paragon, a new class of copper ECD tools for high-volume processing. In **August** Semitool announced, in light of market conditions, its intent to amend its June registration statement by converting it into a shelf registration statement registering $75 million of its securities. **Sept. 30**: Fiscal-year 2000 net income was a record $24.4 million, compared with a net loss of $6.7 million for the prior year. Net sales nearly doubled, to $239.4 million, which was 23 percent higher than the previous record of $194.0 million set in fiscal year 1997. "But, more significant for our future positioning in the industry, our most notable achievements for the year surrounded the growth in new orders for our proprietary technologies and products necessary for the manufacture of advanced semiconductor devices," said CEO Thompson. In *continued on page 370*

OFFICERS

Raymon F. Thompson
Chairman

Fabio Gualandris
President and CEO

Timothy C. Dodkin
SVP, Managing Dir.-Semitool Europe

William A. Freeman
SVP-Finance and CFO

Kazi Heinink
VP-Marketing

Jurek Koziol, Ph.D.
VP, Gen. Mgr.-Electrochemical Technology

Gregory L. Perkins
VP-Operations

Gary Spray
VP-Sales

Larry A. Viano
Treasurer and Controller

Calvin S. Robinson
Secretary

DIRECTORS

Howard E. Bateman
Entech Inc. (former owner)

Richard A. Dasen
independent businessman

Tim Dodkin

Daniel J. Eigeman
Junkermier, Clark CPAs, Kalispell, MT

John Osborne
LAM Research Corp.

Calvin S. Robinson
Crowley, Haughey, Hanson, Toole & Dietrich PLLP, Kalispell, MT

Raymon F. Thompson

MAJOR SHAREHOLDERS

Raymon F. and Ladeine A. Thompson, 45.7%

All officers and directors as a group (12 persons), 46.6%

SIC CODE

3559 Special industry machinery, nec

MISCELLANEOUS

TRANSFER AGENT AND REGISTAR:
BankBoston, Boston, MA.

TRADED: Nasdaq National Market

SYMBOL: SMTL

STOCKHOLDERS: 208

EMPLOYEES: 1,071

PART TIME: 93

GENERAL COUNSEL:
Morrison & Foerster, Palo Alto, CA
Crowly, Haughy, Hanson Toole & Dietrick PLLP, Kalispell, MT

AUDITORS:
PricewaterhouseCoopers LLP, Boise, ID

INC: MT-1979

ANNUAL MEETING:
February

TWO-YEAR QUARTERLY HIGH-LOW STOCK PRICES

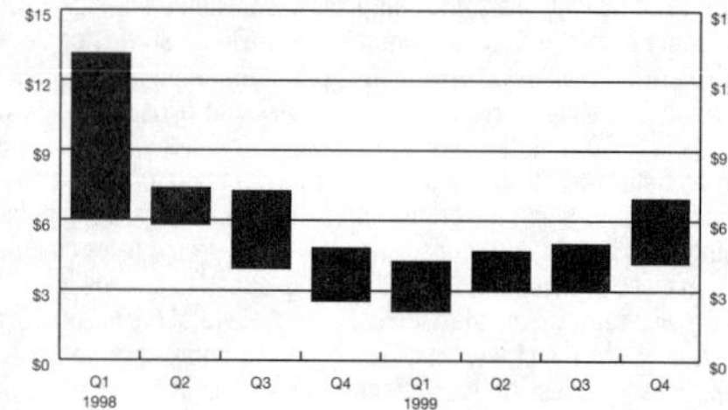

Sheldahl Inc.

1150 Sheldahl Rd., Northfield, MN 55057
Tel: 507/663-8000 Fax: 507/663-8435 Web site: http://www.sheldahl.com

Sheldahl Inc. uses proprietary vacuum deposition, laminating and coating technology, and high-volume roll-to-roll manufacturing processes to produce high-quality laminates, printed circuitry, and high-density substrates, primarily for sale to the automotive electronics and data communications markets. Half of Sheldahl's laminates are sold in roll form to other manufacturers; the company uses the balance in the production of printed circuitry and interconnect systems.

EARNINGS HISTORY

Year Ended Aug	Operating Revenue/Sales (dollars in thousands)	Net Earnings	Return on Revenue (percent)	Return on Equity	Net Earnings (dollars per share)	Cash Dividend	Market Price Range
1999 *	122,086	(21,488)	(17.6)	(36.1)	(2.15)	—	8.63–4.56
1998 †	117,045	(36,497)	(31.2)	(47.2)	(3.97)	—	24.63–4.94
1997	105,266	(7,969)	(7.6)	(9.6)	(0.89)	—	26.75–14.88
1996	114,120	4,772	4.2	6.3	0.55	—	31.13–14.75
1995	95,216	3,134	3.3	7.7	0.45	—	19.25–10.25

* Income figures for 1999 include pretax charges totaling $10.685 million, for restructuring and impairment.
† Income figures for 1998 include pretax charges totaling $11.8 million, for restructuring and impairment; and loss of $5,206,000/($0.56), cumulative effect of accounting change.

BALANCE SHEET

Assets	08/27/99 (dollars in thousands)	08/28/98	Liabilities	08/27/99 (dollars in thousands)	08/28/98
Current (CAE 1,043 and 1,005)	40,290	32,847	Current (STD 4,142 and 4,296)	23,353	23,628
Plant and equipment	82,845	102,257	Long-term debt	29,284	27,829
Other	795	1,202	Other	3,477	3,961
TOTAL	123,930	136,306	Restructuring reserves	2,484	2,131
			Stkhldrs' equity*	65,332	78,757
			TOTAL	123,930	136,306

* $0.25 par common; 50,000,000 authorized; 11,610,356 and 9,660,614 issued and outstanding.

RECENT QUARTERS / **PRIOR-YEAR RESULTS**

	Quarter End	Revenue ($000)	Earnings ($000)	EPS ($)	Prior-Year Revenue ($000)	Prior-Year Earnings ($000)	Prior-Year EPS ($)
Q4	09/01/2000	33,747	(6,231)	(0.57)	32,995	(12,023)	(1.10)
Q3	05/26/2000	36,152	(3,667)	(0.36)	32,575	(1,435)	(0.18)
Q2	02/25/2000	32,030	(1,594)	(0.18)	28,042	(5,693)	(0.55)
Q1	11/26/99	34,811	(1,402)	(0.16)	28,474	(2,337)	(0.29)
	SUM	136,740	(12,894)	(1.27)	122,086	(21,488)	(2.12)

PRIOR YEAR: Q4 earnings include charge of $8,085,000/($0.71), primarily to write off impaired assets. Q3 earnings include gain of $500,000/$0.04 from reversal of previous restructuring costs. Q2 earnings include pretax restructuring costs of $3.1 million.

RECENT EVENTS

In **December 1999** the company told the SEC that it planned to make a late filing of its annual report for the year ended Aug. 27, 1999. With auditors concerned about low cash flow, Sheldahl was making efforts to loosen debt-contract terms and to raise money with a private stock placement. Director Dennis Mathisen, frustrated that the board was focusing only on the possibility of developing a joint venture for the micro-products division, resigned. The Mathisen investor group, which included associate Irwin Jacobs, then proceeded to increase its Sheldahl stake to 11 percent—with designs to replace the board, sell the company, or take other action to move the stock. The group said that it would withhold its vote for management's slate of directors at the scheduled Jan. 12 meeting of Sheldahl shareholders. In **January** Sheldahl received an infusion of $1.8 million in exchange for new preferred equity from two of its current shareholders, including Molex Inc. (Nasdaq: MOLX). In **February** Sheldahl introduced new large-format panels for ComClad HF, its proprietary family of high-frequency laminates for circuits used in wireless communications. Sheldahl announced that it was engaged in discussions with Molex regarding a potential acquisition by Molex. Molex, Sheldahl's largest shareholder, had discussed a proposal under which Molex would pay $7.75 per share of common stock in cash (a 15 percent premium) for all outstanding equity interests in Sheldahl not currently owned by Molex. Molex and Sheldahl had not reached an agreement in principle, nor entered into a definitive agreement, and no assurances were given as to whether an agreement will be signed or a transaction consummated. However, Sheldahl and Molex had entered into an agreement pursuant to which Sheldahl was to deal exclusively with Molex through March 10, 2000. A Minnesota state court complaint was filed against the company, its directors, and Molex claiming that the consideration to be paid in the proposed transaction was unfair and inadequate for the company's shareholders. The Irwin Jacobs Investor Group sent Sheldahl an acquisition offer letter with an indicated offer price of $8.50 per share to acquire Sheldahl. "We will not sit by and watch the company be sold to an insider for a fire-sale price," Jacobs wrote. Analysts spec- *continued on page 370*

OFFICERS
James E. Donaghy
Chairman
Kenneth J. Roering
Vice Chairman
Edward L. Lundstrom
President and CEO
Jill D. Burchill
VP and CFO
Gregory D. Closser
VP-Materials/Flexible Interconnect
Michele Edwards
VP-Supply Chain Operations
James Havener
VP-Micro Products Business Unit
Sidney J. Roberts
VP-Research/Development

DIRECTORS
James E. Donaghy
John G. Kassakian
Massachusetts Institute of Technology, Boston
Edward L. Lundstrom
Gerald E. Magnuson
Lindquist & Vennum PLLP (retired)
William B. Miller
Miller and Co., Scotland
Kenneth J. Roering
Carlson School of Management/U. of Minnesota, Minneapolis
Ray Wieser
Molex Inc.

MAJOR SHAREHOLDERS
Molex Inc., 18.3%
Lisle, IL
Marshall Financial Group (Irwin L. Jacobs et al.), 9.8%
Minneapolis
All officers and directors as a group (14 persons), 12.2%

SIC CODE
3643 Current-carrying wiring devices

MISCELLANEOUS
TRANSFER AGENT AND REGISTAR:
Wells Fargo Bank Minnesota N.A.,
South St. Paul, MN
TRADED: Nasdaq National Market
SYMBOL: SHEL
STOCKHOLDERS: 2,000
EMPLOYEES: 847

GENERAL COUNSEL:
Lindquist & Vennum PLLP, Minneapolis
AUDITORS:
Arthur Andersen LLP, Minneapolis
INC: MN-1955
ANNUAL MEETING:
January

RANKINGS
No. 82 CRM Public 200

PUB

SUBSIDIARIES, DIVISIONS, AFFILIATES

Automotive Technology Center
6060 Dixie Hwy.
Suite E
Clarkston, MI 48346
810/623-2111

Britton Operation
East Highway 10
Britton, SD 57430
605/448-5104

Micro Products Operation
1285 S. Fordham St.
Longmont, CO 80503
303/651-2880
Keith L. Casson

Northfield East Operation
805 N. Highway 3
Northfield, MN 55057
507/663-8000

Northfield West Operation
1150 Sheldahl Rd.
Northfield, MN 55057
507/663-8000

TWO-YEAR QUARTERLY HIGH-LOW STOCK PRICES

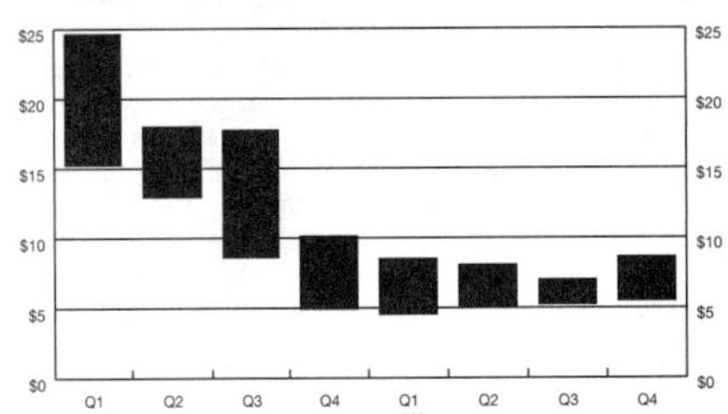

PUB

ShowCase Corporation

4115 Highway 52 N., Suite 300, Rochester, MN 55901
Tel: 507/288-5922 Fax: 507/287-2803 Web site: http://www.showcasecorp.com

ShowCase Corp. is an AS/400 client/server software developer dedicated to providing complete end-user solutions for AS/400 data access. This total solution includes query, reporting, and EIS tools; middleware; database administration tools and support; and training services—all dedicated to facilitating end-user data access.

EARNINGS HISTORY

Year Ended Mar 31	Operating Revenue/Sales (dollars in thousands)	Net Earnings	Return on Revenue (percent)	Return on Equity	Net Earnings (dollars per share*)	Cash Dividend	Market Price Range
2000	39,523	(4,094)	(10.4)	(17.5)	(0.46)	—	14.38–2.94
1999	35,519	(616)	(1.7)	(27.1)	(0.14)	—	
1998	23,756	(3,234)	(13.6)	NM	(0.82)	—	
1997	18,027	50	0.3	1.9	0.01	—	
1996	13,278	814	6.1	32.3	0.21	—	

* Stock began trading on June 29, 1999.

BALANCE SHEET

Assets	03/31/00 (dollars in thousands)	03/31/99	Liabilities	03/31/00 (dollars in thousands)	03/31/99
Current (CAE 11,677 and 8,900)	40,643	17,718	Current (STD 2 and 5)	18,514	16,721
Property and equipment	2,088	2,092	Long-term debt		2
Goodwill	56	116	Capital lease obligations		85
TOTAL	42,787	19,926	Deferred revenue	914	846
			Stockholders' equity*	23,359	2,272
			TOTAL	42,787	19,926

* $0.01 par common; 50,000,000 authorized; 10,522,113 and 4,502,867 issued and outstanding.

RECENT QUARTERS / **PRIOR-YEAR RESULTS**

	Quarter End	Revenue ($000)	Earnings ($000)	EPS ($)	Revenue ($000)	Earnings ($000)	EPS ($)
Q2	09/30/2000	12,522	391	0.04	8,506	(1,565)	(0.15)
Q1	06/30/2000	11,412	(591)	(0.06)	10,505	185	0.04
Q4	03/31/2000	10,865	(1,210)	(0.12)	10,257	218	0.05
Q3	12/31/99	9,647	(1,505)	(0.15)	9,543	125	0.03
	SUM	44,446	(2,915)	(0.28)	38,811	(1,037)	(0.04)

RECENT EVENTS

In **January 2000** the company announced its Enterprise Intelligence Initiative—a comprehensive, Web-based solution that extends the ShowCase data warehousing and business intelligence product line to the growing Enterprise Information Portal (EIP) market. ShowCase also announced a licensing agreement with IntraNet Solutions Inc. (Nasdaq: INRS), Eden Prairie, Minn., giving ShowCase exclusive rights to sell the Xpedio product line on the AS/400. In **March** ShowCase teamed up with IBM to develop the new IBM DB2 OLAP (On-Line Analytical Processing) Server for the AS/400—a more robust server platform by which to store multidimensional data and more quickly build and deploy Web-based analytical applications. One year after signing a reseller agreement with IBM, ShowCase reported that the alliance was delivering excellent results across Europe, the Middle East, Africa, and Latin America. In **April** the company announced its commitment to bring its STRATEGY integrated data warehousing and business intelligence suite to the Windows NT platform. In **June** Showcase announced an OEM contract with IBM under which ShowCase was responsible for joint development of the IBM DB2 OLAP (On-Line Analytical Processing) Server for the AS/400, to be available June 23, and IBM gained access to the Essbase technology for the AS/400 for sale under its own brand name. ShowCase significantly extended its offerings to thousands of AS/400 organizations with the launch of the new IBM DB2 OLAP (On-Line Analytical Processing) Server for the AS/400, a joint development effort between IBM and ShowCase. In **August** the company announced a new release of the ShowCase Enterprise Information Portal (EIP) that integrates Version 4.0 of IntraNet Solutions Inc.'s (Nasdaq: INRS) Xpedio Web content management system with ShowCase's STRATEGY data warehousing and business intelligence suite. **Sept. 30**: Revenue for the period totaled a record $12.5 million, up 47 percent from the year-ago period. The company posted net income of $391,000, compared to a net loss of $1.6 million. These results exceeded the consensus analysts' estimates. "We are pleased with both our return to profitability and strong growth in license revenue," said CEO Holec. "The quarter benefited from a greater number of customer deployments and the sale of new products. These results demonstrate the market's growing acceptance of our Enterprise Intelligence solution and the desire to use the Web to easily disseminate corporate information.") In **November** $141.9 million-revenue SPSS Inc. (statistical analysis software), Chicago, agreed to buy ShowCase, in a $94 million stock deal (a 50 percent premium), in order to gain Showcase's customer base.

OFFICERS

Kenneth H. Holec
President and CEO

Craig W. Allen
CFO

Jonathan P. Otterstatter
EVP-Technology

Theresa Z. O'Neil
VP-Marketing

Patrick Dauga
EVP-Worldwide Field Operations

Paul Hesser
VP-Global Client Services

Freddie Masse
VP-Org'l Development/Human Resources

Kevin R. Potrzeba
VP-Sales

DIRECTORS

William B. Binch
Hyperion Solutions (former)

Dr. Promod Haque
Norwest Venture Partners

Kenneth H. Holec

C. McKenzie (Mac) Lewis III
Sherpa Partners LLC

Jack Noonan
SPSS Inc.

MAJOR SHAREHOLDERS

Promod Haque/Norwest Equity Partners, 26.6%
Palo Alto, CA

David G. Wenz, 8.6%
Rochester, MN

Dennis Semerad, 8.1%
Rochester, MN

Kenneth H. Holec, 7.8%

All officers and directors as a group (11 persons), 37%

SIC CODE

3577 Computer peripheral equipment, nec

MISCELLANEOUS

TRANSFER AGENT AND REGISTAR:
Wells Fargo Bank Minnesota N.A., South St. Paul, MN

TRADED: Nasdaq National Market

SYMBOL: SHWC

STOCKHOLDERS: 109

EMPLOYEES: 283

IN MINNESOTA: 131

GENERAL COUNSEL:
Dorsey & Whitney PLLP, Minneapolis

AUDITORS:
KPMG LLP, Minneapolis

INC: MN-1989

RANKINGS

No. 120 CRM Public 200

No. 34 Minnesota Technology Fast 50

Solid Controls Inc.

820 S. Fifth St., Hopkins, MN 55343
Tel: 952/933-9053 Fax: 952/933-8961

Solid Controls Inc. designs and manufactures a diversified line of integrated machine controls that are sold primarily to manufacturers of plastic parts for the automotive, household products, and electronics industries throughout the world. Compatible with both new and used injection-molding machines, the company's products optimize machine set-up time and cycle times while minimizing material and power usage. Controls utilize touch-screen panels in dual-language capability for users throughout the world.

EARNINGS HISTORY

Year Ended Mar 31	Operating Revenue/Sales (dollars in thousands)	Net Earnings	Return on Revenue (percent)	Return on Equity	Net Earnings (dollars per share)	Cash Dividend	Market Price Range
2000	2,315	64	2.8	4.1	0.07	0.06	
1999	1,761	(185)	(10.5)	(11.3)	(0.19)	0.10	
1998	2,116	(38)	(1.8)	(2.0)	(0.04)	0.13	
1997	2,054	9	0.4	0.4	0.01	0.13	
1996 *	2,500	48	1.9	2.2	0.05	0.13	

* Income figures for 1996 include gain of $177,356 on life insurance proceeds from policies held on the late Edward A. Cashin.

BALANCE SHEET

Assets	03/31/00 (dollars in thousands)	03/31/99
Current (CAE 25 and 148)	1,220	1,040
Marketable equity securities	154	201
Software development costs	346	330
Property and equipment	61	29
Cash surrender value of life insurance	226	183
Deferred income taxes	29	31
TOTAL	2,036	1,814

Liabilities	03/31/00 (dollars in thousands)	03/31/99
Current	446	182
Stockholders' equity*	1,590	1,632
TOTAL	2,036	1,814

* $0.05 par common; 1,500,000 authorized; 967,404 and 979,404 issued and outstanding.

OFFICERS

Ronald A. Kokesh
President

A. Larry Katz
Secretary

Kevin R. Kokesh
VP-Sales/Marketing

DIRECTORS

A. Larry Katz
Katz & Manka Ltd., Minneapolis

Kevin R. Kokesh

Ronald A. Kokesh

SIC CODE

3674 Semiconductors and related devices

MISCELLANEOUS

TRANSFER AGENT AND REGISTAR:
Firstar Trust Co., Milwaukee

TRADED: LOTC

SYMBOL: SLDC

STOCKHOLDERS: 262

EMPLOYEES: 20

IN MINNESOTA: 20

GENERAL COUNSEL:
Katz & Manka Ltd., Minneapolis

AUDITORS:
Larson, Allen, Weishair & Co. LLP, Minneapolis

INC: MN-1968

ANNUAL MEETING: July

INVESTOR RELATIONS:
Kevin R. Kokesh

PUB

PUB

SpectraSCIENCE Inc.

14405 21st Ave. N, Suite 111, Plymouth, MN 55447
Tel: 763/745-4120 Fax: 763/745-4126 Web site: http://www.spectrascience.com

SpectraSCIENCE Inc. develops minimally invasive medical delivery systems to facilitate the diagnosis and treatment of a broad range of human diseases by using advanced spectroscopy, fiber optics, and computer hardware and software. The company's current product is the Virtual Biopsy System (VBS), which is targeted for the detection and differentiation of cancerous, precancerous, and healthy tissues of the colon.

EARNINGS HISTORY

Year Ended Dec 31	Operating Revenue/Sales	Net Earnings	Return on Revenue	Return on Equity	Net Earnings	Cash Dividend	Market Price Range
	(dollars in thousands)		(percent)		(dollars per share)		
1999	0	(2,180)	NM	(57.9)	(0.41)	—	8.50–3.06
1998	0	(2,414)	NM	NM	(0.52)	—	8.00–2.88
1997	0	(1,644)	NM	NM	(0.37)	—	9.13–2.44
1996	0	(1,546)	NM	(49.0)	(0.47)	—	10.63–4.25
1995	135	(1,346)	NM	(30.7)	(0.47)	—	7.88–2.00

BALANCE SHEET

Assets	12/31/99	12/31/98	Liabilities	12/31/99	12/31/98
	(dollars in thousands)			(dollars in thousands)	
Current (CAE 4,362 and 301)	4,634	573	Current (STD 600)	1,116	601
Fixed assets	294	248	Lease commitment	46	
TOTAL	4,928	820	Stockholders' equity*	3,766	220
			TOTAL	4,928	820

* $0.25 par common; 10,000,000 authorized; 6,420,705 and 4,737,804 issued and outstanding.

RECENT EVENTS

In **November 1999** the Gastroenterology and Urology Devices Panel of the Medical Devices Advisory Committee for the FDA voted to recommend FDA clearance for the Company to market its Virtual Biopsy System for use in colonoscopy and flexible-sigmoidoscopy. In **January 2000** SpectraSCIENCE announced that it had raised $4,525,000 in financing since early November—$3,528,998 through a private placement of its common stock, $396,804 from stock option exercises, and $600,000 from a transaction convertible into equity securities of the company. Net proceeds to the company after commissions and expenses were $4,187,002. "This additional financing, combined with our recent move into an expanded manufacturing facility and the positive recommendation by the FDA Medical Device Panel of our pre-market application for the Virtual Biopsy System, well positions us for the future," said CEO Sievert. In **February** the FDA's Office of Device Evaluation (ODE) requested that SpectraSCIENCE address queries raised by the FDA's advisory panel and the ODE's reviewing staff regarding the previously submitted pre-market application (PMA) for the Virtual Biopsy System. Sievert stated, "The FDA has not rejected or disapproved our PMA submission. However, before a final decision can be made, the FDA is asking us to re-analyze the statistical results to ensure the VBS can be appropriately labeled." In **July**, after an extensive audit of SpectraSCIENCE's manufacturing facilities, and review of the internal quality systems used in the production of the SpectraSCIENCE Virtual Biopsy System, the company received ISO 9001 Certification from its European Notified Body. In **October** SpectraSCIENCE received CE Mark authorization from its Notified Body in Munich, allowing commercial distribution of the Virtual Biopsy System in the European Union.

OFFICERS

Chester E. Sievert Jr.
Chairman, President, and CEO

Scott G. Anderson
VP-Marketing/Sales

DIRECTORS

Johan de Hond, M.D.
Hospital Diaconesse, Meppel, The Netherlands

Terrence W. Glarner
West Concord Ventures Inc., Minneapolis

Henry Holterman
Reggeborgh Beheer BV, Rijseen, Netherlands

Delwin K. Ohrt, M.D.
health/technology consultant, Minneapolis

Chester E. Sievert Jr.
SpectraScience Inc., Plymouth, MN

MAJOR SHAREHOLDERS

Reggeborgh Beheer BV, 11.7%
Rijssen, Netherlands

Perkins Capital Management Inc., 9%
Wayzata, MN

Nathanial S. Thayer, 6.6%
Pawtucket, RI

All officers and directors as a group (4 persons), 10.4%

SIC CODE

3841 Surgical and medical instruments

3845 Electromedical equipment

MISCELLANEOUS

TRANSFER AGENT AND REGISTAR:
Wells Fargo Bank Minnesota N.A., South St. Paul, MN

TRADED: OTC Bulletin Board

SYMBOL: SPSI

STOCKHOLDERS: 1,025

EMPLOYEES: 13

IN MINNESOTA: 13

GENERAL COUNSEL:
Dorsey & Whitney PLLP, Minneapolis

AUDITORS:
Ernst & Young LLP, Minneapolis

INC: MN-1983

ANNUAL MEETING: May

The Sportsman's Guide Inc.

411 Farwell Ave., South St. Paul, MN 55075
Tel: 651/451-3030 Fax: 651/450-6130 Web site: http://www.sportsmansguide.com

The Sportsman's Guide Inc., engaged in the retail mail-order catalog business, features value-priced outdoor gear and general merchandise, with a special emphasis on hunting, shooting, camping and hiking. The company's products are marketed both on the Internet and through monthly and specialty issues of The portsman's Guide Catalog, which the company distributes throughout the United States. The merchandise includes hunting, shooting, fishing, camping, military surplus, and boating equipment and accessories; outdoor recreational apparel and imprinted apparel; binoculars, boots, and knives; off-road vehicle accessories; and a variety of gift items. The company also has two small retail stores from which it sells discontinued and overstocked merchandise.

EARNINGS HISTORY

Year Ended Dec	Operating Revenue/Sales (dollars in thousands)	Net Earnings	Return on Revenue (percent)	Return on Equity	Net Earnings (dollars per share*)	Cash Dividend	Market Price Range
1999	162,515	12	0.0	0.1	0.00	—	7.75–2.19
1998	142,876	1,416	1.0	8.3	0.32	—	10.25–2.88
1997	128,113	2,475	1.9	38.9	1.06	—	7.38–2.19
1996	112,270	2,327	2.1	60.1	1.00	—	2.50–0.31
1995	101,832	(1,744)	(1.7)	NM	(0.75)	—	10.00–0.94

* Per-share amounts restated to reflect 1-for-10 reverse stock split in March 1997.

BALANCE SHEET

Assets	01/02/00 (dollars in thousands)	01/03/99	Liabilities	01/02/00 (dollars in thousands)	01/03/99
Current (CAE 0 and 2,303)	47,541	38,914	Current (STD 2,455 and 30)	36,272	26,423
Property and equipment	5,764	4,798	Long-term debt	40	78
Other	191	191	Deferred income taxes	170	407
TOTAL	53,496	43,903	Stockholders' equity*	17,014	16,995
			TOTAL	53,496	43,903

* $0.01 par common; 36,800,000 authorized; 4,747,810 and 4,746,560 issued and outstanding.

RECENT QUARTERS / PRIOR-YEAR RESULTS

	Quarter End	Revenue ($000)	Earnings ($000)	EPS ($)	Prior-Year Revenue ($000)	Prior-Year Earnings ($000)	Prior-Year EPS ($)
Q3	09/30/2000	29,640	(692)	(0.15)	34,659	(1,146)	(0.24)
Q2	06/30/2000	25,938	(876)	(0.18)	32,683	133	0.03
Q1	03/31/2000	30,733	(922)	(0.19)	38,384	428	0.09
Q4	12/31/99	56,789	597	0.13	52,483	469	0.10
	SUM	143,100	(1,893)	(0.40)	158,209	(116)	(0.02)

CURRENT: Q3 revenue figure represents an accounting change that has not yet been reported discretely.
PRIOR YEAR: Q4 consists of 14 weeks.

RECENT EVENTS

Dec. 31, 1999: Total Internet gross sales for 1999 were $13.4 million, nearly $1.0 million above the $12.5 million that management had projected and well above last year's total of $1.2 million. The company also noted that, during the fourth quarter of 1999, its e-commerce Web sites, http://www.sportsmansguide.com and http://www.bargainoutfitters.com, reported a total of 1.3 million total user sessions, averaging 15,000 per day, with an average length of user session of nearly 16 minutes. CEO Olen stated, "The results of our Internet operations more than validate that ours is an Internet model that will succeed." In **March 2000** the company signed a binding letter of intent with E Com Ventures Inc. (Nasdaq: ECMV), which was to become a significant minority shareholder in SGDE. ECOMV has the ability to direct Internet traffic and visibility to its portfolio of member companies along with the management skills to enable an existing B2C the opportunity to evolve into a B2B company. Anything Internet Corp. (OTCBB: ANYI), a Colorado Springs, Colo.-based e-service company, entered into a joint marketing agreement with The Sportsman's Guide. The agreement was expected to be mutually beneficial as the cross-marketing undertaken by the two companies increased the number of Internet customers and corresponding revenue. In **April** GuideOutdoors.com entered into a marketing agreement with Gage Outdoor Expeditions LLC giving Guide Outdoors visitors access to the expedition travel planning services offered through GageOutdoor.com (http://www.gageoutdoor.com). Gary Roach, a famed master fisherman, was to be featured on GuideOutdoors.com, as was Bill Jordan, a nationally known hunting expert. Sally O'Neal Coates, a celebrated outdoor travel writer, and Lisa Price, a well-known outdoors columnist, were to be featured in the women's section on GuideOutdoors.com. Direct Merchants Credit Card Bank, a subsidiary of Metris Cos. Inc. (NYSE: MXT), contracted to offer The Sportsman's Guide MasterCard and Metris' enhancement services to The Sportsman's Guide customers. GuideOutdoors went live **June** 1 with its new Web site. Jim Moynagh, a nationally known bass fisherman, agreed to be featured on GuideOutdoors.com sharing anecdotes about his fishing tournament experiences and tips on how to make a bass outing a successful adventure. The GuideOutdoors.com launch not only generated sig- *continued on page 370*

OFFICERS

Gary Olen
Chairman

Gregory R. Binkley
Pres., CEO, Pres./CEO-GuideOutdoors.com

Charles B. Lingen
SVP-Finance, CFO, and Treasurer

John M. Casler
SVP

Barry W. Benecke
SVP-Creative Services

Bernie Bauhof
SVP-Information Systems/Tech. and CIO

Janine Shovein
VP-Sales/Customer Service

DIRECTORS

Gregory Binkley
Mark F. Kroger
Charles B. Lingen
Gary Olen
Leonard Paletz
William T. Sena
Sena Weller Rohs Williams
Vincent W. Shiel
Outdoor Consulting Inc.

MAJOR SHAREHOLDERS

Dr. Vincent W. Shiel, 11%
Hobe Sound, FL

Ralph E. Heyman (individually and as trustee), 8.1%
Dayton, OH

Dimensional Fund Advisors Inc., 6.9%
Santa Monica, CA

E Com Ventures Inc./Ilia Lekach, 6.3%

Kalmar Investments Inc., 6.3%
Greenville, DE

Gary Olen, 5.4%

All officers and directors as a group (10 persons), 27.9%

SIC CODE

5961 Catalog and mail-order houses

MISCELLANEOUS

TRANSFER AGENT AND REGISTAR:
Corporate Stock Transfer, Denver,CO

TRADED: Nasdaq National Market

SYMBOL: SGDE

STOCKHOLDERS: 330

EMPLOYEES: 875

GENERAL COUNSEL:
Chernesky, Heyman & Kress, Dayton, OH

AUDITORS:
Grant Thornton LLP, Minneapolis

INC: MN-1977

ANNUAL MEETING: July

HUMAN RESOURCES:
Berghetta Schmidt

INVESTOR RELATIONS:
Charles B. Lingen

RANKINGS

No. 76 CRM Public 200

PUB

TWO-YEAR QUARTERLY HIGH-LOW STOCK PRICES

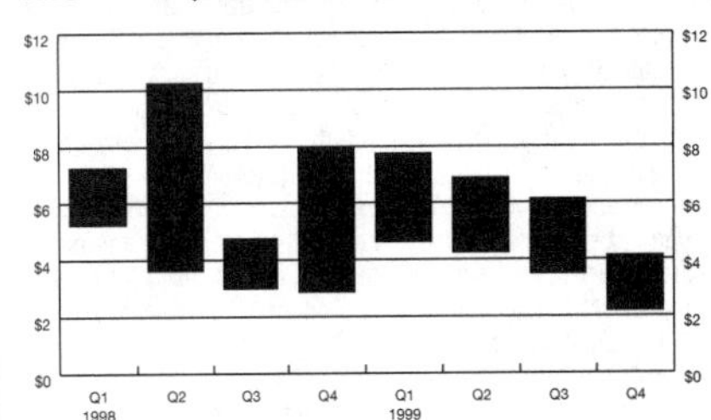

PUB

Stockwalk.com Group Inc.

5500 Wayzata Blvd., Suite 800, Golden Valley, MN 55416
Tel: 763/542-6000 Fax: 763/542-3585

Stockwalk.com Group Inc., formerly the privately held Miller, Johnson & Kuehn Inc., is a broker-dealer specializing in retail and institutional brokerage services, investment banking, municipal bonds, CDs, early-stage corporate finance, and clearing services. The company is a member of Securities Investor Protection Corp. and the Chicago Stock Exchange. Other offices: St. Paul; Minneapolis; Scottsdale, Ariz.; La Jolla, Calif.; Clearwater, Fla.; and Houston.

EARNINGS HISTORY *

Year Ended Mar 31	Operating Revenue/Sales (dollars in thousands)	Net Earnings	Return on Revenue (percent)	Return on Equity	Net Earnings (dollars per share)	Cash Dividend	Market Price Range
2000	70,970	(1,700)	(2.4)	(6.9)	(0.09)	—	18.38–7.25
1999	55,590	1,273	2.3	18.2	0.08	—	9.63–0.63
1998	47,093	(1,224)	(2.6)	NM	(0.08)	—	
1997	32,607	190	0.6	7.4	0.01	—	
1996	26,944	525	1.9	21.9	0.03	—	

* Results for 1999 and prior years are those of MJK Holdings Inc., the accounting acquiror.

BALANCE SHEET

Assets	03/31/00 (dollars in thousands)	03/31/99	Liabilities	03/31/00 (dollars in thousands)	03/31/99
Cash	5,534	3,201	Short-term borrowings	29,500	33,900
Cash and equivalents, segregated	83,009	73,131	Payable to customers	280,364	203,314
Receivable from customers	216,216	139,911	Payable to brokers, dealers	160,153	53,364
Receivable from brokers, dealers	160,230	70,350	Trading securities sold, not yet purchased	1,339	812
Deposits at clearing organizations	26,235	8,492	Notes payable	7,544	4,538
Trading securities owned	8,320	9,274	Subordinated liabilities	18,575	9,675
Secured demand notes receivable	18,575	9,675	Other	16,747	9,739
Goodwill	10,285	1,380	Stockholders' equity*	24,652	7,011
Other	10,471	6,939	TOTAL	538,875	322,353
TOTAL	538,875	322,353			

* $0.04 par common; 50,000,000 authorized; 21,575,313 and 4,255,971 issued and outstanding.

RECENT QUARTERS / **PRIOR-YEAR RESULTS**

	Quarter End	Revenue ($000)	Earnings ($000)	EPS ($)	Revenue ($000)	Earnings ($000)	EPS ($)
Q2	09/30/2000	33,406	(1,861)	(0.07)	13,891	(1,259)	(0.07)
Q1	06/30/2000	20,797	(1,161)	(0.05)	13,205	(1,044)	(0.07)
Q4	03/31/2000	26,656	1,600	0.08	14,105	(62)	0.00
Q3	12/31/99	17,218	(996)	(0.05)	13,990	500	0.03
	SUM	98,076	(2,419)	(0.09)	55,191	(1,866)	(0.10)

RECENT EVENTS

In **December 1999** the company commenced a cash tender offer for all shares of Kinnard Investments Inc. (Nasdaq: KINN), Minneapolis, at a price of $7.50 per share. (Kinnard Investments owns John G. Kinnard & Co. Inc., a regional broker-dealer.) CEO Miller stated that the offer to Kinnard shareholders represented a significant premium over the trading range of Kinnard stock during the past several years and afforded Kinnard shareholders an opportunity to sell at a price that was unlikely to be achieved in the foreseeable future. "The combination of our two firms will nearly double the size of our company and provide more full-service resources to our respective clients," Miller stated. Kinnard responded by immediately forming a special committee of its board of directors to review the offer. The Kinnard committee then unanimously rejected the tender offer. Meanwhile, Digital Insight Corp. (Nasdaq: DGIN) agreed to market a private-label version of Stockwalk.com's online brokerage services to client financial institutions. In **January 2000** Stockwalk.com increased its offer to $8 per share; extended the offer until Jan. 31, 2000; and withdrew the condition in its original offer that the purchase of stock pursuant to the offer be approved by Kinnard in accordance with the Minnesota Business Combination Act (a necessary step in obtaining absolute control of Kinnard). The increased bid reflected recent developments that had boosted Kinnard's value: an exercise of warrants that raised $4 million; and a $16 million judgement against Dain Rauscher (although that award could still be overturned on appeal). Still, the special committee of the board of directors of Kinnard unanimously rejected the revised tender offer—saying that it continued to be financially inadequate, highly contingent, and not in the best interests of Kinnard and its shareholders—and urged shareholders not to tender their shares in response to Stockwalk's offer. "Kinnard's opinion in no way terminates this bid from going forward," said Miller, who called the $8 per-share offer a "premium price." Later in the month, Stockwalk.com announced that it would become a participant in the process undertaken by Kinnard and its financial advisor, U.S. Bancorp Piper Jaffray, to explore strategic alternatives to enhance shareholder value—and consequently was dropping its hostile tender offer. Stockwalk.com contracted with ATIO Corp. (http://www.atio.com) to extend the *continued on page 370*

OFFICERS

Eldon C. Miller
Chairman and CEO

Paul R. Kuehn
President

Philip T. Colton
SVP, General Counsel, and Secretary

John C. Feltl
SVP

John E. Feltl
Pres./CEO-R.J. Steichen

Jeffrey L. Houdek
CFO

David B. Johnson
EVP

Matthew L. Kyler
VP-Marketing

Frank H. Lallos
Pres.-Stockwalk.com

Todd W. Miller
COO

Randy Nitzsche
CEO-Stockwalk.com Inc.

Stanley D. Rahm
SVP

Robert J. Vosburgh
CEO-Online Brokerage Solutions

DIRECTORS

John E. Feltl
David B. Johnson
Paul R. Kuehn
Eldon C. Miller
Richard J. Nigon
Stanley D. Rahm
N. Lee Wesley
private investor

MAJOR SHAREHOLDERS

David B. Johnson, 16.7%
Golden Valley, MN
Eldon C. Miller, 16.3%
Paul R. Kuehn, 16.3%
John E. Feltl, 9.2%
Stanley D. Rahm, 6.9%
All officers and directors as a group (15 persons), 75.1%

SIC CODE

6211 Security brokers and dealers

MISCELLANEOUS

TRANSFER AGENT AND REGISTAR:
Wells Fargo Bank Minnesota N.A.,
South St. Paul, MN

TRADED: Nasdaq National Market

SYMBOL: STOK
STOCKHOLDERS: 124
EMPLOYEES: 82
GENERAL COUNSEL:
Maun & Simon PLC, Minneapolis
AUDITORS:
Ernst & Young LLP, Minneapolis
FOUNDED: 1981
INVESTOR RELATIONS:
Matthew Kyler
HUMAN RESOURCES:
Kathleen Munger

RANKINGS

No. 105 CRM Public 200
No. 20 CRM Performance 100

SUBSIDIARIES, DIVISIONS, AFFILIATES

R.J. Steichen & Co.
120 S Sixth St.
Suite 100
Minneapolis, MN 55402
612/341-6200
John E. Feltl

Kinnard Investments Inc.
Kinnard Financial Center
920 Second Ave. S.
Minneapolis, MN 55402
612/370-2700
William F. Farley

TWO-YEAR QUARTERLY HIGH-LOW STOCK PRICES

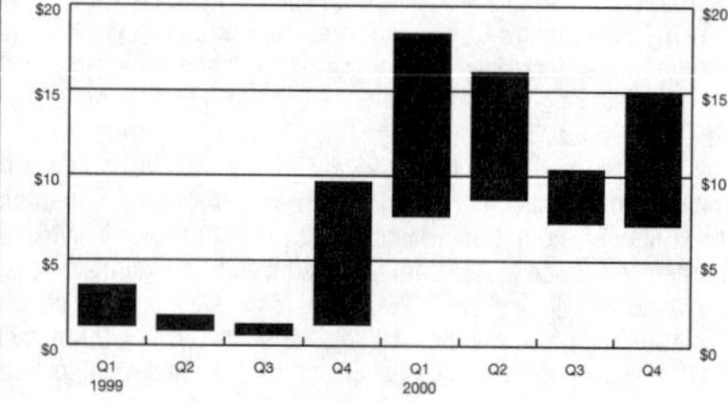

Stonehaven Realty Trust

2550 University Ave. W., Suite 240 N, St. Paul, MN 55114
Tel: 651/917-5536 Fax: 651/645-0615

Stonehaven Realty Trust, formerly Wellington Properties Trust, is a self-administered real estate investment trust (REIT). In November 1998 the company became an umbrella partnership REIT and formed an operating partnership, Wellington Properties Investments L.P., of which the company is the sole general partner. Through the operating partnership and wholly owned subsidiaries, the company acquires, develops, owns, and operates investment properties. As of December 31, 1999, the company owned four properties: a 119,722-square-foot office building in Minneapolis; a 77,533-square-foot office building in St. Cloud, Minn.; a 50,291-square-foot light industrial facility in Burnsville, Minn.; and a 72-unit apartment community in Schofield, Wis. Management believes that the company is organized and operates in a manner that satisfies the requirements for taxation as a REIT under the Internal Revenue Code of 1986 and expects to continue to operate in such a manner. Under such provisions, the company must distribute at least 95 percent of its taxable income to its shareholders and meet certain other organizational, asset, and income tests. As a REIT, the company generally is not subject to federal income tax on taxable income that is distributed to the company's shareholders.

EARNINGS HISTORY

Year Ended Dec 31	Operating Revenue/Sales (dollars in thousands)	Net Earnings	Return on Revenue (percent)	Return on Equity	Net Earnings (dollars per share*)	Cash Dividend	Market Price Range
1999 †	6,897	(1,387)	(20.1)	(9.5)	(1.02)	0.44	6.33–2.25
1998	3,509	(941)	(26.8)	(19.8)	(0.80)	0.44	10.58–3.79

* Per-share amounts restated to reflect a 4.75-for-3 stock split on March 24, 1999.
† Income figures for 1999 include loss of $35,565/($0.03) cumulative effect of change in accounting principle; extraordinary loss of $482,272/($0.35); and gain of $686,716/$0.50 on sale of investment in real estate.

BALANCE SHEET

Assets	12/31/99 (dollars in thousands)	Liabilities	12/31/99 (dollars in thousands)
Investments in real estate	33,787	Mortgage loans and notes payable	19,291
Cash and cash equivalents	2,893	Accounts payable and accrued expenses	478
Marketable securities	5,188	Related-party payable	9
Restricted cash	681	Rents received in advance, securitiy deposits	72
Accounts receivable, trade and other	3	Dividends/distributi ons payable	862
Investment in unconsolidated subsidiary	100	Minority interest in unconsolidated subsidiary	7,836
Deferred rent receivable	56	Preferred equity	11
Deferred financing costs	327	Common equity*	14,528
Prepaid and other	51	TOTAL	43,086
TOTAL	43,086		

* $0.01 par common; 100,000,000 authorized; 1,388,080 issued and outstanding.

RECENT QUARTERS / **PRIOR-YEAR RESULTS**

	Quarter End	Revenue ($000)	Earnings ($000)	EPS ($)	Prior-Year Revenue ($000)	Prior-Year Earnings ($000)	Prior-Year EPS ($)
Q3	09/30/2000	1,951	(1,502)	(0.36)	1,814	(28)	(0.02)
Q2	06/30/2000	2,120	(1,322)	(0.27)	1,772	(1,435)	(1.06)
Q1	03/31/2000	1,744	(137)	(0.16)	1,673	(102)	(0.08)
	SUM	5,814	(2,961)	(0.79)	5,259	(1,565)	(1.16)

PRIOR YEAR: Q2 earnings include extraordinary loss of $377,647/($0.28). Q1 earnings include loss of $35,565/($0.03) cumulative effect of change in accounting principle.

RECENT EVENTS

In **February 2000** Stonehaven acquired RESoft Inc. (then known as NETLink International Inc.) to capitalize on the growing online real estate services sector. **June 30:** RESoft successfully launched three real estate technology products during the second quarter: RERFP, an online vendor bidding and auction service; REDocs, an online document management system; and REBuild, a customized version of RERFP designed specifically for general contractors and developers. In **July** Stonehaven announced a strategic operating plan designed to accelerate the growth of its technology division and position the company to expand its national reach in the rapidly growing online real estate services sector. The plan created two operating divisions, RESoft Inc., to provide technology real estate solutions, and Stonehaven Realty, to provide traditional real estate solutions. To date, Stonehaven had executed strategic partnerships with 29 major real *continued on page 371*

OFFICERS

Arnold K. Leas
Chairman

Duane H. Lund
CEO

Odeh Muhawesh
President

Ann K. Wessels
CFO

Robert F. Rice
Secretary

DIRECTORS

Steven B. Hoyt
Hoyt Properties Inc.

Paul T. Lambert
The Shidler Group (former)

Arnold K. Leas
Company (former)

Duane H. Lund

Robert F. Rice

Robert D. Salmen
Equity Financial Services

Mark S. Whiting
TriNet Corporate Realty Trust Inc. (former)

MAJOR SHAREHOLDERS

Steven B. Hoyt/American Real Estate Equities LLC, 29.9%

Duane H. Lund/American Real Estate Equities LLC, 19.4%

Paul T. Lambert/American Real Estate Equities LLC, 14%

Ann K. Wessels, 12%

Odeh Muhawesh, 12%

Arnold K. Leas, 6.9%

Wellington Management Corp., 6.3%
Brookfield, WI

All officers and directors as a group (9 persons), 57.1%

SIC CODE

6519 Real property lessors, nec

MISCELLANEOUS

TRADED: AMEX
SYMBOL: RPP
STOCKHOLDERS: 310
EMPLOYEES: 2
AUDITORS:
PricewaterhouseCoopers LLP, Chicago
INC: MD-1994

SUBSIDIARIES, DIVISIONS, AFFILIATES

RESoft Inc.

PUB

Stratasys Inc.

14950 Martin Dr., Eden Prairie, MN 55344
Tel: 952/937-3000 Fax: 952/937-0070 Web site: http://www.stratasys.com

Stratasys Inc. develops, manufactures, and markets a variety of rapid-prototyping devices that permit engineers and designers to create physical models and prototypes out of plastic and other materials directly from computer-aided-design (CAD) workstations. The company's computerized modeling system uses its proprietary technology to make models and protypes directly from a designer's three-dimensional CAD design. These systems can be used in office environments, which makes them appealing to the design-intensive automotive, aerospace, consumer products, and medical products industries.

EARNINGS HISTORY

Year Ended Dec 31	Operating Revenue/Sales (dollars in thousands)	Net Earnings	Return on Revenue (percent)	Return on Equity	Net Earnings (dollars per share)	Cash Dividend	Market Price Range
1999	37,587	2,144	5.7	7.4	0.37	—	9.25–3.31
1998 *	32,437	(3,318)	(10.2)	(11.8)	(0.55)	—	13.50–4.50
1997	29,636	515	1.7	1.6	0.09	—	25.75–10.25
1996	22,920	3,503	15.3	13.3	0.67	—	24.50–14.13
1995	10,275	371	3.6	2.1	0.09	—	20.25–5.25

* Income figures for 1998 include pretax charge of $6,512,665 for purchased in-process R&D.

BALANCE SHEET

Assets	12/31/99 (dollars in thousands)	12/31/98
Current (CAE 2,532 and 11,243)	27,580	31,549
Property and equipment	3,235	3,602
Intangibles	3,410	2,789
Deferred income taxes	2,507	3,072
Other	382	179
TOTAL	37,113	41,190

Liabilities	12/31/99 (dollars in thousands)	12/31/98
Current	8,012	12,894
Obligations under capital leases	318	193
Deferred taxes		
Stockholders' equity*	28,783	28,103
TOTAL	37,113	41,190

* $0.01 par common; 15,000,000 authorized; 6,101,961 and 6,100,524 issued and outstanding.

RECENT QUARTERS / **PRIOR-YEAR RESULTS**

	Quarter End	Revenue ($000)	Earnings ($000)	EPS ($)	Prior-Year Revenue ($000)	Prior-Year Earnings ($000)	Prior-Year EPS ($)
Q3	09/30/2000	9,002	171	0.03	10,359	965	0.17
Q2	06/30/2000	9,023	327	0.06	8,864	213	0.04
Q1	03/31/2000	9,298	376	0.07	7,603	(193)	(0.03)
Q4	12/31/99	10,760	1,159	0.21	9,336	(3,814)	(0.63)
	SUM	38,083	2,033	0.37	36,163	(2,830)	(0.46)

PRIOR YEAR: Q4 earnings include one-time charge of $6,512,665 pretax, ($0.64) after-tax, on acquisition of in-process engineering.

RECENT EVENTS

In **July 2000** the company introduced Prodigy, the first low cost office-modeling system that produces tough, durable ABS parts for functional testing of prototype designs. The first system to address the office-modeling sector of the rapid prototyping industry, the new product incorporated innovative technology acquired in 1999. **Sept. 30:** Third-quarter revenue and profits were below the company's previous expectations and analyst estimates due in part to continued revenue weakness in Europe. However, sales of the recently introduced Prodigy had exceeded the company's expectations and order backlog for the company's systems remained high by historical standards. In **October** Stratasys announced that its rapid prototyping system had been used by Brandeis University scientists when they programmed a computer to follow the laws of evolution and design a basic robot. After the program allowed the robot design to evolve through 600 design generations, the computer sent the fittest design to the Stratasys Genisys 3D Printer, a rapid prototyping system, which built the three-dimensional structure from the computer's design file, requiring no tooling or human intervention. The successful automated evolution and construction project was a giant leap for artificial intelligence. In **November** Stratasys introduced its fastest machine yet, the Maxum. The new system can operate 50 percent faster than previous systems by Stratasys, helping manufacturers get their products to market sooner.

OFFICERS

S. Scott Crump
Chairman and CEO

Thomas W. Stenoien
CFO and Secretary

DIRECTORS

Ralph E. Crump
Crump Industrial Group, Trumbull, CT

S. Scott Crump

Clifford H. Schwieter
C.H. Schwieter & Associates, Cincinnati

Cameron Truesdell
private investor

Arnold J. Wasserman
P&A Associates, Jersey City, NJ

Gregory L. Wilson
Mity-Lite Inc., Orem, UT

MAJOR SHAREHOLDERS

S. Scott Crump, 12.2%
Wayzata, MN

Cameron Truesdell, 9%
Preston, WA

Ralph E. Crump, 5.1%
Trumbull, CT

All officers and directors as a group (7 persons), 28.9%

SIC CODE

7373 Computer integrated systems design

MISCELLANEOUS

TRANSFER AGENT AND REGISTAR:
North American Stock Transfer Co., Freeport, NY

TRADED: Nasdaq National Market, PSE

SYMBOL: SSYS

STOCKHOLDERS: 153

EMPLOYEES: 218

PART TIME: 6

IN MINNESOTA: 174

GENERAL COUNSEL:
Snow Becker Krauss P.C., New York
Best & Flanagan, Minneapolis

AUDITORS:
Rothstein, Kass & Co. P.C., Roseland, NJ

INC: DE-1989

ANNUAL MEETING: May

HUMAN RESOURCES:
Cary Feik, Mgr.

INVESTOR RELATIONS:
Tom Stenoien

RANKINGS

No. 122 CRM Public 200

No. 31 Minnesota Technology Fast 50

TWO-YEAR QUARTERLY HIGH-LOW STOCK PRICES

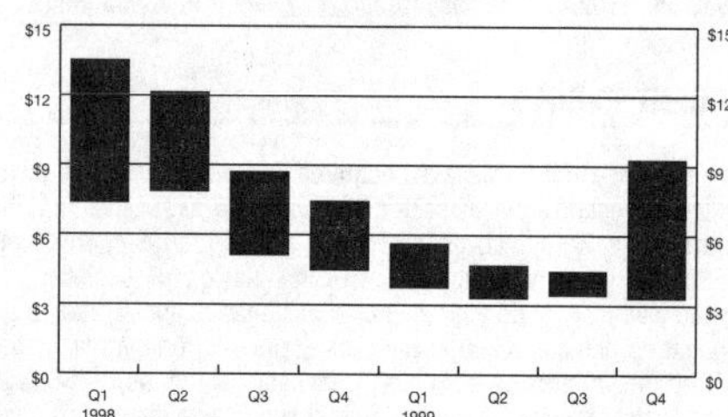

Supervalu Inc.

11840 Valley View Rd., P.O. Box 990 (55440), Eden Prairie, MN 55344
Tel: 952/828-4000 Fax: 952/828-8955 Web site: http://www.supervalu.com

Supervalu Inc., the nation's leading food distribution and 10th largest retailer company, supplies 6,100 supermarkets in 48 states. At fiscal year 2000 end, the company owned or licensed 1,117 stores. In fiscal 2000, the company's food distribution business provided 71 percent of sales; food retailing, 29 percent. Corporate-owned stores operate principally under the names Cub Foods, Shop 'n Save, Shoppers Food Warehouse, Metro; Bigg's, Save-A-Lot, Farm Fresh, Scott's Foods, Laneco, and Hornbachers.

EARNINGS HISTORY *

Year Ended Feb	Operating Revenue/Sales (dollars in thousands)	Net Earnings (dollars in thousands)	Return on Revenue (percent)	Return on Equity (percent)	Net Earnings (dollars per share†)	Cash Dividend (dollars per share†)	Market Price Range (dollars per share†)
2000 ¶	20,339,079	242,941	1.2	13.3	1.88	0.54	26.31–15.75
1999	17,420,507	191,338	1.1	14.7	1.59	0.53	28.75–20.31
1998 #	17,201,378	230,757	1.3	19.2	1.84	0.52	24.28–14.31
1997	16,551,902	175,044	1.1	13.4	1.30	0.50	16.31–13.63
1996	16,486,321	166,433	1.0	13.7	1.22	0.49	16.38–12.81

* In 1997 and earlier years, the company had a 46 percent ownership in ShopKo, a mass merchandise discount retailer, which was accounted for under the equity method.
† Per-share amounts restated to reflect 2-for-1 stock split distributed on Aug. 18, 1998.
¶ Income figures for 2000 include pretax charge of $103.596 million for restructuring and other; and pretax gain of $163.662 million on sale of Hazelwood Farms Bakeries. Pro forma had Aug. 31, 1999, acquisition Richfood Holdings Inc. been acquired Feb. 28, 1999: revenue $22,309.061 million; earnings $261.406 million/$1.88.
\# Fiscal 1998 consists of 53 weeks.

BALANCE SHEET

Assets	02/26/00 (dollars in thousands)	02/27/99 (dollars in thousands)	Liabilities	02/26/00 (dollars in thousands)	02/27/99 (dollars in thousands)
Current (CAE 10,920 and 7,608)	2,177,639	1,582,527	Current (STD 170,381 and 208,913)	2,509,620	1,521,907
Property, plant, and equipment	2,168,210	1,699,024	Long-term debt	1,408,858	835,485
Notes receivable	86,914	48,697	Obligations under capital leases	544,883	410,784
Investment in direct-financing leases	92,310	112,576	Deferred income taxes	3,306	54,096
Goodwill	1,608,580	567,890	Other	207,207	138,038
Other	361,700	255,235	Stockholders' equity*	1,821,479	1,305,639
TOTAL	6,495,353	4,265,949	TOTAL	6,495,353	4,265,949

* $1 par common; 400,000,000 authorized; 150,670,000 and 150,670,000 issued and outstanding, less 16,008,000 and 30,561,000 treasury shares.

RECENT QUARTERS / PRIOR-YEAR RESULTS

	Quarter End	Revenue ($000)	Earnings ($000)	EPS ($)	Prior-Year Revenue ($000)	Prior-Year Earnings ($000)	Prior-Year EPS ($)
Q2	09/09/2000	5,333,823	57,296	0.43	4,145,775	45,482	0.37
Q1	06/17/2000	6,953,393	69,965	0.53	5,289,720	66,721	0.56
Q4	02/26/2000	5,541,852	72,084	0.52	4,200,917	54,380	0.45
Q3	12/04/99	5,361,732	58,654	0.42	4,079,696	45,260	0.38
	SUM	23,190,800	257,999	1.91	17,716,108	211,843	1.76

CURRENT: Period is 12 weeks unless otherwise noted. Q1 period is 16 weeks.
PRIOR YEAR: Q1 period is 16 weeks. Earnings include pretax: gain of $163.662 million on sale; and charge of $103.596 million for restructuring.

RECENT EVENTS

In **December 1999** the board of directors authorized a stock repurchase program under which Supervalu could acquire up to 5 percent, or 7 million shares, of its currently outstanding stock. In **January 2000** the company entered into a national supply agreement with Foster City, Calif.-based Webvan Group Inc. to supply all of Webvan's markets within geographic reach of Supervalu's national distribution network. **Feb. 26:** Aided by the acquisition Richfood Holdings, Supervalu's fiscal 2000 revenue jumped 16.8 percent to pass the $20 billion mark. The acquisition also helped the company turn in a third consecutive year of double-digit EPS growth by adding 4 cents to earnings. In **April** the board adopted a Shareholder Rights Plan under which Supervalu was to distribute one preferred stock purchase right for each outstanding share of common stock held by stockholders of record on April 24, 2000. The plan was not adopted in response to any specific effort to acquire control of the company. In **May** Supervalu broadened its reach to consumers in the Greater

continued on page 371

OFFICERS

Michael W. Wright
Chairman and CEO

Jeffrey Noddle
Pres./COO, interim Pres./COO-Retail Food

David L. Boehnen
EVP

Alec C. Covington
EVP and Pres./COO-Food Distribution

Pamela K. Knous
EVP and CFO

Robert W. Borlik
SVP and Chief Information Officer

Kim M. Erickson
SVP-Strategic Planning and Treasurer

J. Andrew Herring
SVP-Corp. Development/External Relations

Gregory C. Heying
SVP-Distribution

Mike Jackson
SVP-Operations, Retail Food Cos.

W. O'Neill McDonald
SVP-Wholesale Food Cos.

Ronald C. Tortelli
SVP-Human Resources

Leland Dake
VP-Wholesale Merchandising

Stephen Kilgriff
VP-Legal Services

Sherry Smith
VP and Controller

Karen Borman
Asst. Controller

John Breedlove
Secretary

Frank J. O'Keefe
Asst. Treasurer-Tax

Warren E. Simpson
Senior Counsel and Asst. Secretary

DIRECTORS

Lawrence A. Del Santo
The Vons Cos. Inc. (retired)

Susan E. Engel
Department 56 Inc., Eden Prairie, MN

Edwin C. (Skip) Gage
Gage Marketing Group LLC, Plymouth, MN

William A. Hodder
Donaldson Co. Inc. (retired)

Garnett L. Keith Jr.
SeaBridge Investment Advisors LLC

Richard L. Knowlton
Hormel Foundation, Austin, MN

Charles M. Lillis
Lone Tree Capital Mgmt., Englewood, CO

Jeffrey Noddle

Harriet K. Perlmutter
Papermill Playhouse, Short Hills, NJ

Steven Rogers
Northwestern University, Evanston, IL

Carole F. St. Mark
Growth Management LLC, Morris, CT

Michael W. Wright

MAJOR SHAREHOLDERS

AMVESCAP plc, 7.4%
London

Sanford C. Bernstein & Co. Inc., 7.3%
New York

All officers and directors as a group (27 persons), 3.2%

SIC CODE

5141 Groceries whsle, general line

MISCELLANEOUS

TRANSFER AGENT AND REGISTAR:
Wells Fargo Bank Minnesota N.A.,
South St. Paul, MN

TRADED: NYSE

SYMBOL: SVU

STOCKHOLDERS: 7,600

EMPLOYEES: 67,000

GENERAL COUNSEL:
Dorsey & Whitney PLLP, Minneapolis

AUDITORS:
KPMG LLP, Minneapolis

INC: DE-1925

FOUNDED: 1870

ANNUAL MEETING: July

COMMUNICATIONS: Rita Simmer

RANKINGS

No. 3 CRM Public 200

No. 16 CRM Employer 100

No. 47 CRM Performance 100

PUB

TWO-YEAR QUARTERLY HIGH-LOW STOCK PRICES

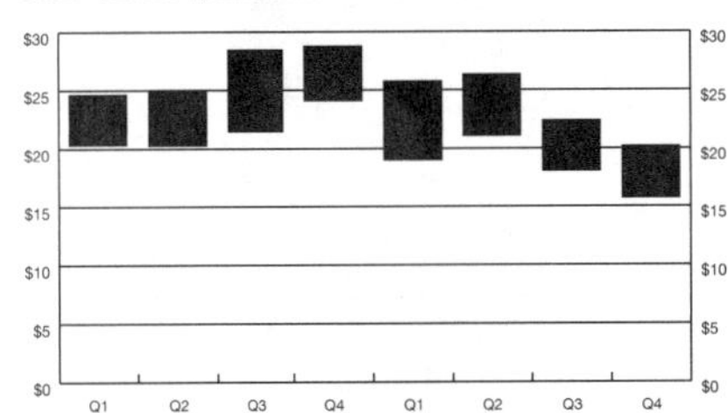

Surgidyne Inc.

9909 South Shore Dr., Plymouth, MN 55441
Tel: 763/595-0665 Fax: 763/595-0667

Surgidyne Inc. designs, develops, manufactures, and markets specialty medical and surgical wound drainage products. The company's products are composed of VariDyne microelectronic battery-powered suction systems for postoperative wound drainage and autotransfusion, disposable SABER and SCEPTRE bulb evacuators for closed wound suction, and disposable products for use with the above systems. The company began contract manufacturing, packaging services, and limited component sales for original-equipment manufacturers in 1994.

EARNINGS HISTORY

Year Ended Dec 31	Operating Revenue/Sales (dollars in thousands)	Net Earnings (dollars in thousands)	Return on Revenue (percent)	Return on Equity (percent)	Net Earnings (dollars per share)	Cash Dividend (dollars per share)	Market Price Range (dollars per share)
1999	634	44	6.9	13.2	0.00	—	0.50–0.07
1998	573	2	0.3	0.5	0.00	—	0.10–0.03
1997	487	(70)	(14.4)	(43.0)	(0.01)	—	0.28–0.03
1996	635	(18)	(2.9)	(7.8)	0.00	—	0.19–0.03
1995	691	1	0.1	0.4	0.00	—	0.25–0.05

BALANCE SHEET

Assets	12/31/99 (dollars in thousands)	12/31/98 (dollars in thousands)	Liabilities	12/31/99 (dollars in thousands)	12/31/98 (dollars in thousands)
Current (CAE 70 and 11)	329	279	Current (STD 46 and 46)	158	135
Furniture and equipment	10	12	Preferred stock	400	400
			Common stock*	(212)	(237)
Patents, trademarks, other	4	5	TOTAL	346	298
Deposits	4	4			
TOTAL	346	298			

* No par common; 18,400,000 authorized; 7,017,085 and 7,017,085 issued and outstanding.

RECENT EVENTS

In **July 2000** the company signed an investment banking agreement with Equity Securities Investment Corp., Minneapolis, to assist and advise Surgidyne in the identification and evaluation of new business opportunities, which may include the sale of the company.

OFFICERS

Theodore A. Johnson
Chairman and CEO

Vance D. Fiegel
President

Charles B. McNeil
EVP and Treasurer

William F. Gearhart
Secretary

DIRECTORS

Vance D. Fiegel
EMBRO, St. Louis Park, MN

William F. Gearhart
Interventional Technologies

Theodore A. Johnson
Minnesota Cooperation Office for Small Business

David B. Kaysen
Rehabilicare Inc., New Brighton, MN

David R. Knighton, M.D.
Institute for Reparative Medicine, St. Louis Park, MN

Charles B. McNeil

Arthur W. Schwalm
Cardiac Pacemakers Inc. (retired)

MAJOR SHAREHOLDERS

Charity Inc., 12.5%
Fridley, MN

Theodore A. Johnson, 9.1%

Charles B. McNeil, 7.3%

All officers and directors as a group (7 persons), 23.2%

SIC CODE

3842 Surgical appliances and supplies

MISCELLANEOUS

TRANSFER AGENT AND REGISTAR:
Wells Fargo Bank Minnesota N.A.,
South St. Paul, MN

TRADED: LOTC

STOCKHOLDERS: 396

EMPLOYEES: 5

AUDITORS:
RSM McGladrey & Pullen Inc. LLP, Minneapolis

INC: MN-1984

INVESTOR RELATIONS:
Larry Hanson

SurModics Inc.

9924 W. 74th St., Eden Prairie, MN 55344
Tel: 952/829-2700 Fax: 952/829-2743 Web site: http://www.surmodics.com

SurModics Inc., formerly BSI Corp., focuses on the use of covalently bonded coatings to modify material surfaces. This surface modification, marketed under the trademark PhotoLink, is a technology based on a photochemical process that improves the surface characteristics of medical devices without changing mechanical properties or dimensions. PhotoLink offers capabilities to make a surface more lubricious or wettable, or more able to resist blood clotting, reduce infection rates, and even deliver drugs over time. SurModics also provides a line of immunoassay and conjugate stabilizers for diagnostic kit manufacturers. The company commercializes its PhotoLink technology through licensing relationships with medical device and diagnostic companies around the world—currently holding licenses with 47 companies covering more than 100 different products, most of which are in the medical device field.

EARNINGS HISTORY *

Year Ended Sept 30	Operating Revenue/Sales (dollars in thousands)	Net Earnings	Return on Revenue (percent)	Return on Equity	Net Earnings (dollars per share†)	Cash Dividend	Market Price Range
1999	13,494	4,360	32.3	14.7	0.30	—	9.38–3.25
1998	9,779	1,637	16.7	7.2	0.13	—	7.06–3.59
1997	7,582	236	3.1	4.6	0.02	—	
1996	6,183	(194)	(3.1)	(4.1)	(0.02)	—	
1995	5,956	(322)	(5.4)	(6.9)	(0.03)	—	

* EPS figures for 1997 and earlier periods are pro forma for the offering.
† Stock began trading March 4, 1998. Per-share amounts restated to reflect 2-for-1 stock split on Dec. 6, 2000.

BALANCE SHEET

Assets	09/30/99 (dollars in thousands)	09/30/98	Liabilities	09/30/99 (dollars in thousands)	09/30/98
Current (CAE 1,975 and 1,343)	8,074	6,562	Current	2,239	1,483
			Deferred revenue		124
Property and equipment	5,275	1,240	Common stockholders' equity*	29,719	22,698
Investments	15,917	16,249	TOTAL	31,958	24,305
Deferred tax	2,465				
Other	228	254			
TOTAL	31,958	24,305			

* $0.05 par common; 15,000,000 authorized; 7,701,921 and 7,214,085 issued and outstanding.

RECENT QUARTERS / PRIOR-YEAR RESULTS

	Quarter End	Revenue ($000)	Earnings ($000)	EPS ($)	Prior-Year Revenue ($000)	Prior-Year Earnings ($000)	Prior-Year EPS ($)
Q4	09/30/2000	5,524	1,531	0.09	3,862	1,117	0.07
Q3	06/30/2000	4,165	861	0.06	3,685	1,214	0.08
Q2	03/31/2000	4,441	904	0.06	3,308	1,105	0.08
Q1	12/31/99	4,149	944	0.06	2,639	925	0.06
	SUM	18,279	4,240	0.27	13,494	4,361	0.30

RECENT EVENTS

In **December 1999** coverage of the company was initiated by Miller Johnson & Kuehn, with a STRONG BUY recommendation; and by Dain Rauscher Wessels, with a BUY-AGGRESSIVE rating. In **January 2000** SurModics announced that its PhotoLink surface modification technology was being used to coat a portion of a coronary stent system from Medtronic Inc. (NYSE: MDT), the S670 with Discrete Technology Rapid Exchange Coronary Stent System, that had recently been approved by the FDA. In **April** SurModics introduced the most recent addition to its PhotoLink coating technology: an advanced lubricious coating for stainless steel and nitinol guidewires that are used to introduce and position catheters within arteries and veins during medical procedures. In **July** SurModics and Motorola Inc.'s (NYSE: MOT) BioChip Systems unit entered into a licensing and development agreement granting Motorola exclusive rights to SurModics' proprietary PhotoLink technology for use in Motorola's biochips. As part of the agreement, Motorola and SurModics were forming a joint development committee, comprising personnel from both companies, to oversee the collaborative research effort. Additionally, SurModics was to develop and supply various chemical reagents to be used by Motorola in its bioarray production. The value of the agreement was expected to exceed $25 million over four years, and "could prove to be a much bigger agreement over time," according to CEO Olseth. The announcement caused SurModics stock to surge 32 percent to $43.75. SurModics was added to the Russell 2000 and Russell 3000 U.S. Equity Indexes. (The Russell 3000 is a measure of the 3,000 largest publicly traded U.S. companies in the U.S. stock market, ranked by market capitalization as of May 31. The Russell 2000 Index consists of small cap companies from the Russell 3000 Index.) The company ranked No. 145 on Forbes' 200 Best Small Companies in America list. **Sept. 30:** Fiscal-year revenue increased 35 percent to $18.3 million. Double-digit growth occurred across all PhotoLink revenue categories, as each established new annual records. In total, PhotoLink revenue increased 60 percent for the year. Income from operations increased 120 percent to $5.3 million. In **November** the company granted DIARECT AG of Freiburg, Germany, exclusive rights to distribute SurModics' stabilization product line in Western and Central Europe.

OFFICERS

Dale R. Olseth
Chairman and CEO

James C. Powell
President and COO

Stephen C. Hathaway
VP and CFO

Patrick E. Guire, Ph.D.
SVP and Chief Scientific Officer

Richard C. Carlson
VP-Marketing/Sales

Walter H. Diers Jr.
VP-Corporate Development

Lise Duran, Ph.D.
VP-Product Development

Marie J. Versen
VP-Quality Mgmt./Regulatory Compliance

DIRECTORS

Donald S. Fredrickson, M.D.
D.S. Fredrickson Associates

James J. Grierson
Honeywell Inc. (retired)

Patrick E. Guire, Ph.D.

Kenneth H. Keller, Ph.D.
Hubert H. Humphrey Institute, Minneapolis

David A. Koch
Graco Inc., Golden Valley, MN

Kendrick B. Melrose
The Toro Co., Bloomington, MN

John A. Meslow
Medtronic, Inc. (retired)

Dale R. Olseth

MAJOR SHAREHOLDERS

Arbor Capital Management, 7.4%
Minneapolis

Dale R. Olseth, 7.4%
Minneapolis

David A. Koch, 6.2%
Minneapolis

SIC CODE

2869 Industrial organic chemicals, nec

8731 Commercial physical research

MISCELLANEOUS

TRANSFER AGENT AND REGISTAR:
Firstar Trust Co., Milwaukee

TRADED: Nasdaq National Market

SYMBOL: SRDX

STOCKHOLDERS: 227

EMPLOYEES: 119

IN MINNESOTA: 119

GENERAL COUNSEL:
Fredrikson & Byron P.A., Minneapolis

AUDITORS:
Arthur Andersen LLP, Minneapolis

INC: MN-1979

ANNUAL MEETING: January

INVESTOR RELATIONS: Stephen Hathaway

RANKINGS

No. 166 CRM Public 200

TCF Financial Corporation

801 Marquette Ave., Mail Code 100-01-A, Minneapolis, MN 55402
Tel: 612/661-6500 Fax: 612/745-2773 Web site: http://www.tcfbank.com

TCF Financial Corp. is an $11 billion national bank holding company based in Minneapolis with banking offices in Minnesota, Illinois, Michigan, Wisconsin, and Colorado. Other TCF affiliates provide leasing, mortgage banking, and annuity and mutual fund sales. Established as a mutual institution in 1938, TCF converted to stock ownership in 1986. In 1987 it reorganized into a holding company. In 1997 the company received approval from the Office of the Comptroller of the Currency to convert its federal subsidiaries into national banks.

EARNINGS HISTORY *

Year Ended Dec 31	Operating Revenue/Sales (dollars in thousands)	Net Earnings	Return on Revenue (percent)	Return on Equity	Net Earnings (dollars per share†)	Cash Dividend	Market Price Range
1999	1,070,700	166,039	15.5	20.5	2.01	0.73	30.69–21.69
1998	1,040,389	156,179	15.0	18.5	1.77	0.61	37.25–15.81
1997 ¶	909,282	145,061	16.0	15.2	1.72	0.47	34.38–18.75
1996 #	794,496	100,377	12.6	15.9	1.23	0.36	22.69–14.81
1995 **	763,751	72,244	9.5	12.3	0.88	0.30	16.69–9.28

* Historical periods pool results of Winthrop Resources Corp. (acquired June 1997).
† Per-share amounts restated to reflect 2-for-1 stock splits effected Nov. 28, 1997, and Nov. 30, 1995.
¶ Figures include results of Standard Financial Inc. from its Sept. 4, 1997, date of purchase for $423.7 million. Pro forma for Jan. 1, 1997, purchase: revenue $1,018.204 million; earnings $145.829 million/$1.63.
# Income figures for 1996 include pretax FDIC special assessment of $34.803 million.
** Income figures for 1995 include $0.963 million/($0.01) penalty on early repayment of FHLB advances; and one-time merger-related charges totaling $32.8 million/($0.40).

BALANCE SHEET

Assets	12/31/99 (dollars in thousands)	12/31/98	Liabilities	12/31/99 (dollars in thousands)	12/31/98
Cash, due fm banks	429,262	420,477	Deposits	6,584,835	6,715,146
Investments	148,154	277,715	Securities sold to repurchase	1,010,000	367,280
Securities afs	1,521,661	1,677,919	FHLB advances	1,759,787	1,804,208
Loans hfs	198,928	213,073	Lease rentals	178,369	183,684
Net loans	7,839,988	7,061,165	Other borrowings	135,732	105,874
Goodwill	158,468	166,645	Accrued interest payable	40,352	27,601
Deposit base intangibles	13,262	16,238	Accrued expenses and other	143,659	115,299
Other	351,993	331,362	Stockholders' equity*	808,982	845,502
TOTAL	10,661,716	10,164,594	TOTAL	10,661,716	10,164,594

* $0.01 par common; 280,000,000 authorized; 92,804,205 and 92,912,246 issued and outstanding, less 10,863,017 and 7,343,117 treasury shares.

RECENT QUARTERS / **PRIOR-YEAR RESULTS**

	Quarter End	Revenue ($000)	Earnings ($000)	EPS ($)	Revenue ($000)	Earnings ($000)	EPS ($)
Q3	09/30/2000	295,985	46,697	0.60	271,175	42,760	0.52
Q2	06/30/2000	290,711	46,662	0.60	262,376	40,989	0.50
Q1	03/31/2000	270,110	40,721	0.51	257,960	37,340	0.45
Q4	12/31/99	279,189	44,950	0.55	267,403	39,504	0.47
	SUM	1,135,995	179,030	2.25	1,058,914	160,593	1.93

CURRENT: Q4 earnings include pretax gain of $5.5 million on sales of subsidiaries.
PRIOR YEAR: Q1 earnings include pretax gains from sales of securities/loan servicing and from revenue from discontinued operations: $9.998 million.

RECENT EVENTS

Dec. 31, 1999: For the fiscal year, TCF reported the following.
— Record net income of $166 million
— Record diluted earnings per share of $2.00, up 14 percent
— Increased Power Assets(R) by $826.4 million
— Increased retail checking accounts to 1,044,000, up 14 percent
— Opened 35 new bank branches
— Grew fee income 12 percent

continued on page 371

OFFICERS

William A. Cooper
Chairman and CEO

Thomas A. Cusick
Vice Chairman and COO

Gregory J. Pulles
Vice Chairman, Gen. Counsel, Secretary

Lynn A. Nagorske
President

Mark L. Jeter
Pres./CEO-TCF Bank Minnesota

Neil W. Brown
EVP, CFO, and Treasurer

Craig Dahl
EVP-Leasing/Equipment Financing

William E. Dove
EVP

Ronald J. Palmer
EVP

Mary E. Sipe
EVP

Earl D. Stratton
EVP

Paul B. Brawner
SVP

Philip M. Broom
SVP

Timothy G. Doyle
SVP

Daniel R. Edward
SVP

Daniel P. Engel
SVP

Kevin J. Fink
SVP

Wallace A. Fudold
SVP

Antoinette M. Jelinek
SVP

Jason E. Korstrange
SVP

Mark R. Lund
SVP

Norman G. Morrisson
SVP

Patricia L. Quaal
SVP

R. Craig Woods
SVP

Barbara E. Shaw
SVP

David Stautz
SVP, Asst. Treasurer, and Controller

Diane O. Stockman
VP-Corporate Affairs, General Counsel

DIRECTORS

William F. Bieber
Acrometal Management Corp.

Rudy Boschwitz
Home Valu Inc., former U.S. Senator, Fridley, MN

William A. Cooper

Thomas A. Cusick

John M. Eggemeyer III
Castle Creek Capital LLC

Robert E. Evans

Luella G. Goldberg
Wellesley College, Wellesley, MA

George G. Johnson
George Johnson & Co. CPAs, Detroit

Thomas J. McGough
McGough Construction Co. Inc., Roseville, MN

Lynn A. Nagorske

Gerald A. Schwalbach
Superior Storage LLC

Ralph Strangis
Kaplan, Strangis and Kaplan P.A., Minneapolis

MAJOR SHAREHOLDERS

Putnam Investments Inc., 9%
Boston

Advisory Committee of TCF ESOP, 5.6%
Minneapolis

All officers and directors as a group (28 persons), 8.1%

MISCELLANEOUS

TRANSFER AGENT AND REGISTAR:
BankBoston, NA, Boston

TRADED: NYSE

SYMBOL: TCB

STOCKHOLDERS: 10,900

EMPLOYEES: 7,200

GENERAL COUNSEL:
Gregory J. Pulles

AUDITORS:
KPMG LLP, Minneapolis

INC: DE-1987

FOUNDED: 1923

ANNUAL MEETING: May

COMMUNICATIONS:
Jason Korstange

INVESTOR RELATIONS:
Ann M. Storberg

RANKINGS

No. 33 CRM Public 200

No. 64 CRM Employer 100

No. 35 CRM Performance 100

TWO-YEAR QUARTERLY HIGH-LOW STOCK PRICES

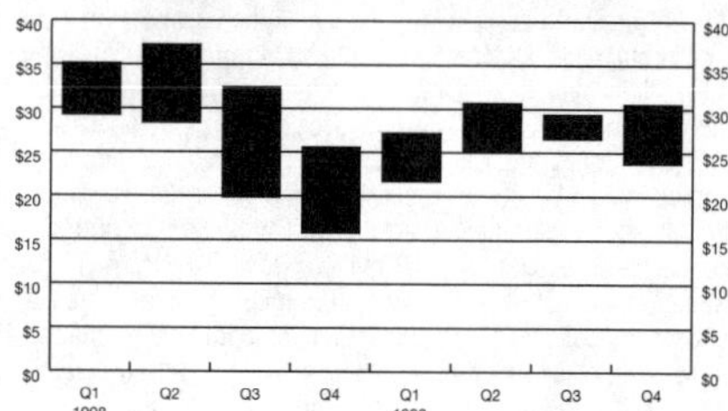

Target Corporation

777 Nicollet Mall, Minneapolis, MN 55402
Tel: 612/370-6948 Fax: 612/370-6565 Web site: http://www.target.com

Target Corp., formerly Dayton Hudson Corp., is a general merchandise retailer with multiple large-scale retail formats. As of September 2000, the corporation operated 1,273 stores in 45 states. Its three operating divisions include **Target** (942 stores in 44 states, 78 percent of fiscal 1999 revenue); **Mervyn's** (267 stores in 14 states, 12 percent of revenue); and the Department Store Division (9 percent of revenue) composed of **Dayton's** stores (19 stores in four states), **Hudson's** stores (21 stores in one state), and **Marshall Field's** (24 stores in four states).

EARNINGS HISTORY *

Year Ended Jan	Operating Revenue/Sales (dollars in thousands)	Net Earnings	Return on Revenue (percent)	Return on Equity	Net Earnings (dollars per share†)	Cash Dividend	Market Price Range
2000 ¶	33,702,000	1,144,000	3.4	19.2	1.28	0.20	37.88–27.63
1999 #	30,662,000	935,000	3.0	18.1	1.04	0.18	31.88–16.88
1998 **	27,487,000	751,000	2.7	17.4	0.84	0.17	18.42–9.47
1997 ††	25,092,000	463,000	1.8	12.4	0.51	0.16	9.97–6.13
1996 ##	23,234,000	311,000	1.3	9.0	0.34	0.15	6.64–5.38

* Historical revenue figures were restated in February 2000 to reclassify leased sales amounts in accordance with new revenue-recognition accounting guidelines.
† Per-share amounts restated to reflect 2-for-1 stock splits on July 19, 2000, and April 30, 1998; and a 3-for-1 split on July 17, 1996.
¶ Income figures for 2000 include one-time pretax charge of $5 million for mainframe outsourcing; and extraordinary charge of $41 million/($0.05) from purchase and redemption of debt.
# Income figures for 1999 include pretax charge of $25 million, net of unusual items; and extraordinary charge of $27 million/($0.03) from purchase and redemption of debt.
** Income figures for 1998 include pretax securitization gain of $27 million; and extraordinary charge of $51 million/($0.06) from purchase and redemption of debt.
†† Income figures for 1997 include pretax charge of $134 million for real estate repositioning; and extraordinary charge of $11 million/($0.01) from purchase and redemption of debt.
Fiscal 1996 consisted of 53 weeks.

BALANCE SHEET

Assets	01/29/00 (dollars in thousands)	01/30/99	Liabilities	01/29/00 (dollars in thousands)	01/30/99
Current (CAE 220,000 and 255,000)	6,483,000	6,005,000	Current (STD 498,000 and 256,000)	5,850,000	5,057,000
Property and equipment	9,899,000	8,969,000	Long-term debt	4,521,000	4,452,000
			Deferred taxes	910,000	822,000
Other	761,000	692,000	Preferred stock		24,000
TOTAL	17,143,000	15,666,000	Preferred equity		268,000
			Common equity*	5,862,000	5,043,000
			TOTAL	17,143,000	15,666,000

* $.1667 par common; 3,000,000,000 authorized; 911,682,776 and 883,619,612 issued and outstanding.

RECENT QUARTERS / **PRIOR-YEAR RESULTS**

	Quarter End	Revenue ($000)	Earnings ($000)	EPS ($)	Revenue ($000)	Earnings ($000)	EPS ($)
Q3	10/28/2000	8,582,000	215,000	0.24	7,927,000	232,000	0.26
Q2	07/29/2000	8,251,000	258,000	0.28	7,687,000	224,000	0.25
Q1	04/29/2000	7,746,000	239,000	0.26	7,158,000	194,000	0.21
Q4	01/29/2000	10,930,000	494,000	0.55	10,055,000	423,000	0.47
	SUM	35,509,000	1,206,000	1.33	32,827,000	1,073,000	1.20

CURRENT: Q2 earnings include extraordinary charge of $1 million/($0.00) from purchase/redemption of debt. Q2 earnings include extraordinary gain of $1 million/$0.00 from purchase/redemption of debt. Q4 earnings include charge of $28 million/($0.03) related to purchase/redemption of debt.
PRIOR YEAR: Q3 earnings include charge of $9 million/($0.01), purchase/redemption of debt. Q2 earnings include extraordinary charge of $4 million/($0.00), purchase/redemption of debt. Q4 earnings include net pretax charge of $22 million (tax gain less mainframe outsourcing); and charge of $24 million/($0.03) related to purchase/redemption of debt.

RECENT EVENTS

In **December 1999** Target Stores sponsored four television specials during CBS' holiday kickoff, "12 Days of Christmas," which featured 12 nights of programming to celebrate the holidays. Dayton's *continued on page 371*

TARGET CORPORATION

OFFICERS
Robert J. Ulrich
Chairman and CEO, Chm./CEO-Target Stores
Linda L. Ahlers
Pres.-Daytons, Marshall Fields, Hudson's
Bart Butzer
Pres.-Mervyn's
Richard J. Kuzmich
Pres./CEO-Associated Merchandising Corp.
Dale Nitschke
Pres.-Target Direct
Gregg W. Steinhafel
Pres.-Target Stores
Gerald L. Storch
Pres.-Target Financial Services/New Bus.
Erica C. Street
Pres.-Target Brands
Ertugrul Tuzcu
EVP-Daytons, Marshall Fields, Hudson's
Todd V. Blackwell
SVP-Human Resources
John D. Griffith
SVP-Property Devel., Target
James T. Hale
EVP, General Counsel and Secretary
Maureen W. Kyer
SVP-Mervyns
Douglas A. Scovanner
EVP and CFO
Paul L. Singer
SVP, Chief Information Officer
Gail J. Dorn
VP-Community Relations
Nate K. Garvis
VP-Government Affairs
Susan D. Kahn
VP-Investor Relations
Stephen C. Kowalke
VP and Treasurer
Jane P. Windmeier
SVP-Finance
Jack N. Reif
Asst. Treasurer
Sara J. Ross
Asst. Treasurer

DIRECTORS
Livio D. DeSimone
3M Co., Maplewood, MN
Roger A. Enrico
PepsiCo Inc., Dallas
William W. George
Medtronic Inc., Fridley, MN
Michele J. Hooper
James A. Johnson
Johnson Capital Partners, Washington, D.C.
Richard M. Kovacevich
Wells Fargo & Co., San Francisco
Susan A. McLaughlin
BellSouth Telecommunications
Anne M. Mulcahy
Xerox Corp., Bloomington, MN
Stephen W. Sanger
General Mills Inc., Golden Valley, MN
George W. Tamke
Emerson Electric Co., St. Louis
Solomon D. Trujillo
Qwest, Englewood, CO
Robert J. Ulrich

MAJOR SHAREHOLDERS
FMR Corp., 9%
Boston
State Street Bank and Trust Co., 8.9%
Boston
AMVESCAP plc, 7.1%
London
All officers and directors as a group (26 persons), 1%

MISCELLANEOUS
TRANSFER AGENT AND REGISTAR:
First Chicago Trust Co. of N.Y., Jersey City, NJ
TRADED: NYSE, PSE
SYMBOL: TGT
STOCKHOLDERS: 13,883
EMPLOYEES: 280,000
IN MINNESOTA: 35,000
GENERAL COUNSEL:
James T. Hale, Minneapolis
AUDITORS:
Ernst & Young LLP, Minneapolis
INC: MN-1902
ANNUAL MEETING: May
INVESTOR RELATIONS:
Susan D. Kahn
COMMUNICATIONS:
Carolyn Brookter

RANKINGS
No. 1 CRM Public 200
No. 2 CRM Employer 100
No. 49 CRM Perform.100

TWO-YEAR QUARTERLY HIGH-LOW STOCK PRICES

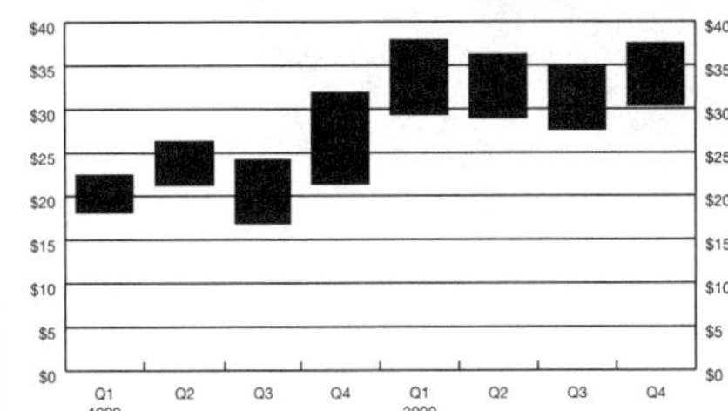

PUB

PUB

Techne Corporation

614 McKinley Place N.E., Minneapolis, MN 55413
Tel: 612/379-8854 Fax: 612/379-6580 Web site: http://www.rndsystems.com

Techne Corp. is a holding company with two subsidiaries—Research and Diagnostic Systems Inc. (R&D Systems) and R&D Systems Europe Ltd. (R&D Europe). **R&D Systems** is divided into biotechnology and hematology divisions. Biotechnology Division manufactures purified cytokines (proteins), antibodies, and assay kits that are sold to biomedical researchers and clinical research laboratories. Hematology Division develops and manufactures whole-blood hematology controls and calibrators, which are sold to hospital and clinical laboratories to ensure accurate test results from hematology instruments. **R&D Europe** distributes R&D Systems biotechnology products in Europe.

EARNINGS HISTORY

Year Ended Jun 30	Operating Revenue/Sales (dollars in thousands)	Net Earnings	Return on Revenue (percent)	Return on Equity	Net Earnings (dollars per share*)	Cash Dividend	Market Price Range
2000	103,838	26,583	25.6	18.8	0.65	—	70.00–12.38
1999	90,901	16,656	18.3	17.2	0.41	—	14.75–6.13
1998 †	67,291	15,183	22.6	23.8	0.40	—	10.00–6.72
1997	60,924	10,882	17.9	22.6	0.29	—	7.63–5.06
1996	54,589	8,638	15.8	22.2	0.23	—	8.25–3.31

* Per-share amounts restated to reflect 2-for-1 stock splits on Dec. 1, 2000, and Nov. 17, 1997.
† Pro forma figures for 1998 as if July 1998 acquisition of research products business of Genzyme Corp. had occurred July 1, 1997: revenue $81.527 million; net income $5.538 million/$0.14.

BALANCE SHEET

Assets	06/30/00 (dollars in thousands)	06/30/99	Liabilities	06/30/00 (dollars in thousands)	06/30/99
Current (CAE 17,356 and 12,769)	86,301	50,850	Current (STD 824)	12,561	13,463
Property and equipment	46,266	15,065	Log-term debt	18,935	
			Deferred rent		1,964
Intangibles	36,336	45,565	Royalty payable	7,768	11,536
Deferred income taxes	3,938	3,137	Stockholders' equity*	141,145	96,838
Other	7,569	9,183	TOTAL	180,410	123,801
TOTAL	180,410	123,801			

* $0.01 par common; 50,000,000 authorized; 41,381,998 and 40,265,310 issued and outstanding.

RECENT QUARTERS / **PRIOR-YEAR RESULTS**

	Quarter End	Revenue ($000)	Earnings ($000)	EPS ($)	Prior-Year Revenue ($000)	Prior-Year Earnings ($000)	Prior-Year EPS ($)
Q1	09/30/2000	27,722	7,503	0.18	24,621	4,848	0.12
Q4	06/30/2000	27,313	8,521	0.21	24,312	5,007	0.12
Q3	03/31/2000	26,777	7,650	0.19	23,789	4,537	0.11
Q2	12/31/99	25,127	5,564	0.14	21,464	3,587	0.09
	SUM	106,939	29,238	0.71	94,187	17,979	0.45

RECENT EVENTS

In **May 2000** Merrill Lynch initiated coverage of Techne shares at NEAR-TERM ACCUMULATE and LONG-TERM BUY. On **Sept. 1**, Techne stock, which had been trading around $30 a year before, closed at $101.88. The price was being driven by investor interest in biotechnology in general and gene-mapping in particular. At the time, Techne was estimated to have a 50 percent share of the market for research proteins (cytokines) and related materials used in drug research. Later in the month, Techne filed a lawsuit in the U.S. District Court for the District of Minnesota to dispute a $31.9 million invoice received from Amgen Inc. relating to the delivery of biological materials under a supply agreement. Recently, Amgen had sent an invoice to Techne saying that it had mistakenly failed to invoice Techne for Erythropoietin (EPO) that had been supplied from time to time during the course of their nine-year relationship and that $31.9 million was due. "By not invoicing Techne in a timely and commercially reasonable manner or in a manner contemplated by our agreements," stated CEO Oland, "Amgen deprived Techne of the opportunity to address this issue with Amgen in a timely fashion." **Sept. 30:** First-quarter consolidated sales were a record $27.7 million, an increase of 13 percent from the first quarter of 1999. R&D Systems' Biotechnology Division net sales increased 19 percent to $17.9 million, and R&D Systems' Hematology Division net sales increased 11 percent to $3.5 million. Consolidated net income increased 55 percent to $7.5 million. Gross margins as a percent of sales also increased, from 72 percent to 75 percent.

OFFICERS

Thomas E. Oland
Chairman, President, CEO, and Treasurer

Thomas C. Detwiler, Ph.D.
VP-Scientific/Regulatory Affairs

Monica Tsang, Ph.D.
VP-Research

Marcel Veronneau
VP-Hematology Operations

James A. Weatherbee, Ph.D.
VP and Chief Scientific Officer

Timothy M. Heaney
VP, Secretary, General Counsel

DIRECTORS

Christopher Henney, Ph.D., D.Sc.
Dendreon Corp., Mountain View, CA

G. Arthur Herbert
CEO Advisors Inc., Maitland, FL

Roger C. Lucas, Ph.D.

Howard O'Connell
Kinnard Investments Inc., Minneapolis

Thomas E. Oland

Lowell E. Sears
Sears Capital Management, Portola Valley, CA

Dr. Randolph C. Steer
pharmaceutical consultant, Rancho Mirage, CA

MAJOR SHAREHOLDERS

Kopp Investment Advisors Inc., 12.2%
Edina, MN

D.F. Dent & Co., 5.9%
Baltimore

All officers and directors as a group (11 persons), 9.2%

SIC CODE

2835 Diagnostic substances

2836 Biological products, exc diagnostic

MISCELLANEOUS

TRANSFER AGENT AND REGISTAR:
Chase Mellon Shareholder Services LLC, Ridgefield Park, NJ

TRADED: Nasdaq National Market

SYMBOL: TECH

STOCKHOLDERS: 350

EMPLOYEES: 486

PART TIME: 57

GENERAL COUNSEL:
Fredrikson & Byron P.A., Minneapolis

AUDITORS:
Deloitte & Touche LLP, Minneapolis

INC: MN-1981

ANNUAL MEETING:
October

HUMAN RESOURCES:
Lea Simoane

INVESTOR RELATIONS:
Kathy Backes

RANKINGS

No. 90 CRM Public 200

No. 17 CRM Performance 100

SUBSIDIARIES, DIVISIONS, AFFILIATES

Research and Diagnostic Systems Inc.
614 McKinley Place N.E.
Minneapolis, MN 55413
612/379-8854

R&D Systems Europe Ltd.
4-10 The Quadrant
Barton Lane
Abingdon, Oxon, OX14 3YS
United Kingdom
(1235) 529449

R&D Systems GmbH
Borisigstrasse 7
65205 Wiesbaden-Nordenstadt
Germany
(6122) 90980

TWO-YEAR QUARTERLY HIGH-LOW STOCK PRICES

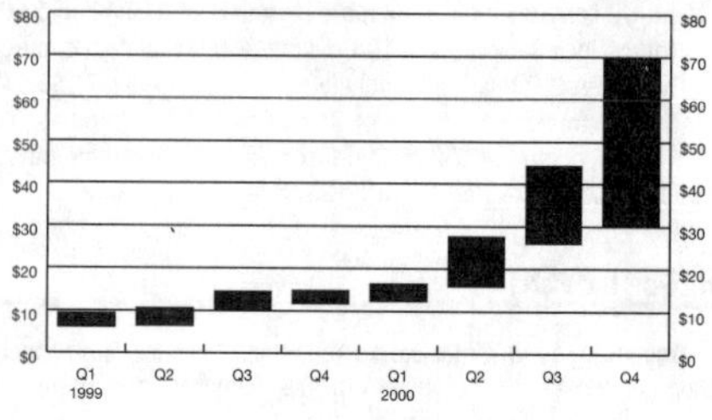

Tennant Company

701 N. Lilac Dr., P.O. Box 1452, Golden Valley, MN 55440
Tel: 763/540-1200 Fax: 763/540-1437 Web site: http://www.tennantco.com

Tennant Co. is a manufacturer of nonresidential floor-maintenance and outdoor cleaning equipment, floor coatings and related offerings. The company's products—which include sweepers, scrubbers, extractors, buffers and other specialized floor cleaning and supplies, plus industrial floor coatings—are used to clean and protect floor surfaces in factories, warehouses, shopping malls, supermarkets, and other areas with heavy vehicle or foot traffic. Tennant has an extensive manufacturing and distribution network, with facilities located throughout North America, Europe, Japan, and Australia.

EARNINGS HISTORY

Year Ended Dec 31	Operating Revenue/Sales (dollars in thousands)	Net Earnings	Return on Revenue (percent)	Return on Equity	Net Earnings (dollars per share*)	Cash Dividend	Market Price Range
1999 †	429,407	19,693	4.6	14.5	2.16	0.76	45.00–31.44
1998	389,388	25,325	6.5	19.3	2.67	0.74	44.81–33.00
1997	372,428	24,205	6.5	18.1	2.43	0.72	39.63–26.13
1996	344,433	21,027	6.1	16.3	2.09	0.69	27.50–21.25
1995	325,368	19,662	6.0	17.2	1.98	0.68	29.00–22.25

* Per-share amounts restated to reflect 2-for-1 stock split on April 26, 1995.
† Income figures for 1999 include pretax restructuring charges of $6.671 million.

BALANCE SHEET

Assets	12/31/99 (dollars in thousands)	12/31/98	Liabilities	12/31/99 (dollars in thousands)	12/31/98
Current (CAE 14,928 and 17,693)	165,093	150,868	Current (STD 12,902 and 7,302)	74,999	56,991
Property, plant, and equipment	66,306	66,640	Long-term debt	16,003	23,038
			Employee-related benefits	30,616	27,802
Installment accounts receivable	967	2,843	Stockholders' equity*	135,915	131,267
Deferred income taxes	6,061	2,657	TOTAL	257,533	239,098
Intangibles	18,486	15,631			
Other	620	459			
TOTAL	257,533	239,098			

* $0.375 par common; 30,000,000 authorized; 8,989,480 and 9,122,960 issued and outstanding.

RECENT QUARTERS / **PRIOR-YEAR RESULTS**

	Quarter End	Revenue ($000)	Earnings ($000)	EPS ($)	Revenue ($000)	Earnings ($000)	EPS ($)
Q3	09/30/2000	115,100	7,200	0.79	104,300	3,200	0.35
Q2	06/30/2000	115,100	7,600	0.84	106,400	6,000	0.66
Q1	03/31/2000	108,400	5,500	0.60	99,700	4,900	0.53
Q4	12/31/99	119,000	5,700	0.63	105,300	7,100	0.76
	SUM	457,600	26,000	2.86	415,700	21,200	2.30

CURRENT: Q4 earnings include pretax charge of $3.6 million for restructuring.
PRIOR YEAR: Q3 earnings include pretax charge of $3.1 million for restructuring.

RECENT EVENTS

June 30, 2000: Second-quarter results improved across all product lines and geographic areas. Operating margins rose from 8.8 percent in the prior-year period to 10.5 percent, evidence that 1999's restructuring efforts were still working their way through the business. The news boosted Tennant stock to a 52-week high of $38.44 on July 25. The city of Washington, D.C., placed an order for Tennant outdoor cleaning equipment and parts (20 Model 830-II sweepers and 20 ATLV litter vacuums) valued at more than $2.5 million. **Sept. 30:** Third quarter was the fourth consecutive quarter of record sales, net earnings, and earnings per share (before restructuring charges) for the company. Net earnings of $7.2 million compared with $6.3 million adjusted for items affecting comparability in the 1999 third quarter. Negative foreign currency exchange effects, resulting primarily from the weakness of the Euro against the U.S. dollar, reduced Tennant's net sales by $2.7 million and reduced earnings per share by 7 cents. "The expansion of our commercial cleaning and outdoor equipment businesses, along with growth in our aftermarket parts and service revenues and in sales to other international markets are beginning to reduce the historical cyclicality in our business," said CEO Dolan. In **October** Tennant's common shares began trading on the New York Stock Exchange. The move was expected to increase Tennant's visibility in the investment community while providing greater liquidity, narrower bid-ask spreads, and reduced volatility in the trading of the company's shares.

OFFICERS

Janet M. Dolan
President and CEO

James H. Moar
COO

Thomas J. Vander Bie
SVP-N.A. Commercial Sales

Richard M. Adams
VP

Anthony T. Brausen
VP and CFO

Thomas J. Dybsky
VP

Anthony Lenders
VP and Managing Dir.-Europe

John T. Pain III
VP and Treasurer

Keith D. Payden
VP and Chief Information Officer

James J. Seifert
VP, General Counsel, Secretary

Steven K. Weeks
VP

Dean A. Niehus
Controller

DIRECTORS

Arthur D. Collins Jr.
Medtronic Inc., Fridley, MN

David C. Cox
Cowles Media Co. (former)

Andrew P. Czajkowski
Blue Cross and Blue Shield of Minnesota, Eagan, MN

Janet M. Dolan

Pamela K. Knous
Supervalu Inc., Eden Prairie, MN

William I. Miller
Irwin Financial Corp., Columbus, IN

Edwin L. Russell
Allete, Duluth, MN

Stephen G. Shank
Capella University

Frank L. Sims
Cargill Inc., Minnetonka, MN

MAJOR SHAREHOLDERS

U.S. Bank N.A., 9.5%
Minneapolis

Trimark Financial Corp., 9.3%
Toronto

Mackenzie Financial Corp., 7%
Toronto

U.S. Bank N.A. (held in trust for the Pennock family), 6.3%
Minneapolis

Roger L. Hale, 5.2%

All officers and directors as a group (17 persons), 5.2%

SIC CODE

3589 Service industry machinery, nec

MISCELLANEOUS

TRANSFER AGENT AND REGISTAR:
Wells Fargo Bank Minnesota N.A., South St. Paul, MN

TRADED: NYSE

SYMBOL: TNC

STOCKHOLDERS: 3,500

EMPLOYEES: 2,241

PART TIME: 47

IN MINNESOTA: 1,465

GENERAL COUNSEL:
James Seifert, Minneapolis

AUDITORS:
KPMG LLP, Minneapolis

INC: MN-1909

FOUNDED: 1870

ANNUAL MEETING: May

PURCHASING:
Donald Carlton

RANKINGS

No. 55 CRM Public 200

No. 49 CRM Performance 100

SUBSIDIARIES, DIVISIONS, AFFILIATES

Tennant Holding B.V.
Industrielaan 6
P.O. Box 6
Uden, Noord Brabant, Netherlands
04132-63955
Anthony Lenders

Tennant-Commercial
Holland, Mich.
616/786-2330
Thomas J. Vander Bie

PUB

TWO-YEAR QUARTERLY HIGH-LOW STOCK PRICES

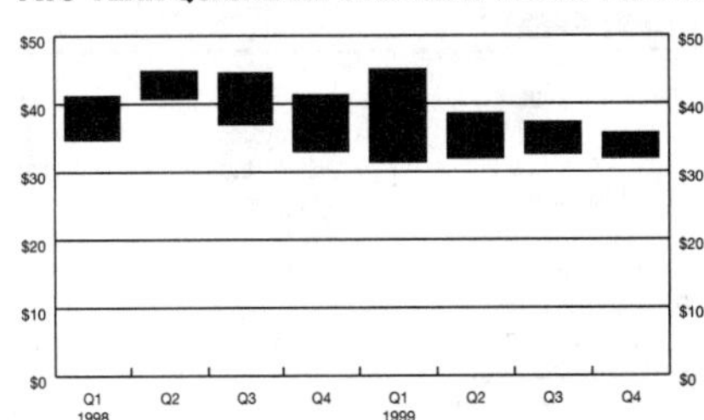

PUB

The Toro Company

8111 Lyndale Ave. S., Bloomington, MN 55420
Tel: 952/888-8801 Fax: 952/887-8258 Web site: http://www.toro.com

The Toro Co. manufactures and markets a variety of products worldwide, including gas-powered walk-behind mowers, riding and reel mowers, and lawn and garden tractors; gas and electric snowthrowers, trimmers, and turf-refuse management equipment; outdoor low-voltage lighting systems; composters; and organic fertilizers. Other products include riding and reel mowing equipment; debris-management equipment; aerating equipment for golf courses, parks, municipalities, landscape contractors, and schools; water-management systems for large turf areas (sports fields, golf courses) and residential lawns; and water-quality improvement systems. Toro plants are located in Bloomington, Shakopee, Mound, and Windom, Minn.; Tomah and Plymouth, Wis.; Riverside, Calif.; Oxford and Sardis, Miss.; and in Belgium. The company was originally incorporated in Minnesota in 1935.

EARNINGS HISTORY *

Year Ended Oct 31	Operating Revenue/Sales (dollars in thousands)	Net Earnings	Return on Revenue (percent)	Return on Equity	Net Earnings (dollars per share)	Cash Dividend	Market Price Range
1999 †	1,274,997	35,059	2.7	12.5	2.72	0.48	39.50–22.19
1998 ¶	1,110,434	4,090	0.4	1.6	0.32	0.48	46.31–16.50
1997 #	1,051,204	34,845	3.3	14.4	2.88	0.48	43.75–31.50
1996 **	930,909	36,409	3.9	17.0	3.00	0.48	36.25–28.38
1995 ††	932,853	36,667	3.9	19.8	2.92	0.48	30.38–21.63

* In 1996 Toro changed its year end from July 31 to Oct. 31. Results of stub period Aug. 1, 1996, through Oct. 31, 1996: revenue $192,278,000; earnings $3,997,000/$0.32.
† Income figures for 1999 include $1.732 million restructuring charge (pretax).
¶ Income figures for 1998 include pretax charge of $15,042,000 for restructuring, impairment loss, and special marketing programs.
# Income figures for 1997 include $2.6 million restructuring charge (pretax); and extraordinary loss of $1.663 million/($0.14) on early debt retirement.
** Income figures for 1996 include nonrecurring gain of $0.10 per share from lawsuit settlement.
†† Figures for 1995 and years prior are for year ended July 31.

BALANCE SHEET

Assets	10/31/99 (dollars in thousands)	10/31/98
Current (CAE 11,960 and 90)	531,742	479,437
Property, plant, and equipment	124,172	127,137
Deferred income taxes	8,876	3,763
Goodwill and other	122,388	113,654
TOTAL	787,178	723,991

Liabilities	10/31/99 (dollars in thousands)	10/31/98
Current (STD 57,098 and 31,580)	305,805	258,210
Long-term debt	195,600	196,844
Other	6,110	5,538
Stkhldrs' equity*	279,663	263,399
TOTAL	787,178	723,991

* $1 par common; 35,000,000 authorized; 13,508,055 and 13,508,055 issued and outstanding, less 938,746 and 738,495 treasury shares.

RECENT QUARTERS / **PRIOR-YEAR RESULTS**

	Quarter End	Revenue ($000)	Earnings ($000)	EPS ($)	Prior-Year Revenue ($000)	Prior-Year Earnings ($000)	Prior-Year EPS ($)
Q3	07/28/2000	345,166	16,442	1.29	325,317	10,323	0.80
Q2	04/28/2000	441,799	26,920	2.11	433,108	24,090	1.86
Q1	01/28/2000	280,239	913	0.07	250,761	796	0.06
Q4	10/31/99	265,811	(150)	(0.01)	229,696	(12,349)	(0.96)
	SUM	1,333,015	44,125	3.46	1,238,882	22,860	1.77

PRIOR YEAR: Q3 earnings include pretax restructuring charge of $722,000 related to Australian operation. Q4 earnings include pretax restructuring charge of $4,590,000 related to profit-improvement initiative.

RECENT EVENTS

In **February 2000** the company reached a multiyear agreement with the PGA European Tour to be its official supplier of turf-maintenance equipment and irrigation systems. The board of directors authorized the purchase of up to 1 million shares (7.9 percent) of Toro's outstanding stock. In **March** Toro subsidiary Exmark Manufacturing Co. Inc. settled patent-infringement claims it had alleged against Ransomes Inc., a subsidiary of Textron Inc., for $125,600. In **May** Toro agreed to become the turf-maintenance and irrigation equipment provider for the Indianapolis Motor Speedway. The Toro-brand badge was to appear atop the main straightaway scoring tower. Toro was also to supply its Toro Wheel Horse 5xi garden tractors for use by the race teams throughout the event. **July 28:** Profits for the third quarter increased substantially over the same period last year, exceeding analyst expectations for the quarter. "We're very pleased with our overall earnings performance for the quarter, particularly since the weather did not favor sales of some turf products," said CEO Melrose. "Despite the weather, we still recorded a modest sales increase. We also received an early boost from '5 by Five' reengi- *continued on page 372*

OFFICERS

Kendrick B. Melrose
Chairman and CEO

J. David McIntosh
EVP-Professional Business/International

Michael Drazan
VP-Information Services

Dennis P. Himan
VP, Gen. Mgr.-Landscape Business

Michael J. Hoffman
VP, Gen. Mgr.-Commercial Business

William D. Hughes
VP and General Manager-Consumer Business

Randy B. James
VP and Controller

Stephen D. Keating
Asst. Treasurer

Ram N. Kumar
VP-Distributor Development/New Business

J. Lawrence McIntyre
VP, Secretary, and General Counsel

Karen M. Meyer
VP-Administration

Richard W. Parod
VP and Gen. Mgr.-Irrigation Business

N. Jeanne Ryan
Asst. Secretary

Stephen P. Wolfe
VP-Finance, Treasurer, and CFO

DIRECTORS

Ronald O. Baukol
3M Co., Maplewood, MN

Robert C. Buhrmaster
Jostens Inc., Bloomington, MN

Winslow H. Buxton
Pentair Inc., Roseville, MN

Janet K. Cooper
U.S. West, Denver

Katherine J. Harless
GTE Airfone Inc., Oak Brook, IL

Kendrick B. Melrose

Robert H. Nassau
St. Raymond Wood Products Holding Ltd., Boston

Dale R. Olseth
SurModics Inc., Eden Prairie, MN

Gregg W. Steinhafel
Target Stores

Christopher A. Twomey
Arctic Cat Inc., Thief River Falls, MN

Edwin H. Wingate
Target Corp. (retired)

MAJOR SHAREHOLDERS

Franklin Resources Inc., 6.5%
San Mateo, CA

All officers and directors as a group (20 persons), 8.1%

MISCELLANEOUS

TRANSFER AGENT AND REGISTAR:
Wells Fargo Bank Minnesota N.A., South St. Paul, MN

TRADED: NYSE

SYMBOL: TTC

STOCKHOLDERS: 6,073

EMPLOYEES: 4,673

GENERAL COUNSEL:
Doherty, Rumble & Butler P.A., Minneapolis

AUDITORS:
KPMG LLP, Minneapolis

INC: DE-1984

FOUNDED: 1914

ANNUAL MEETING:
March

INVESTOR RELATIONS:
Stephen D. Keating

PUBLIC RELATIONS:
Don St. Dennis

RANKINGS

No. 30 CRM Public 200

SUBSIDIARIES, DIVISIONS, AFFILIATES

U.S. locations

Abilene, Texas
Baraboo, Wis.
Beatrice, Neb.
Bloomington, Minn.
Dallas
El Cajon, Calif.
El Paso, Texas
Evansville, Ind.
Houston
Itaska, Ill.
Laguna, Calif.
Lakeville, Minn.
Lincoln, Neb.
Madera, Calif.
Mountaintop, Pa.
Oxford, Miss.
Plymouth, Minn.
Plymouth, Wis.
Riverside, Calif.
San Antonio, Texas
Sanford, Fla.
Shakopee, Minn.
Tomah, Wis.
Windom, Minn.

TWO-YEAR QUARTERLY HIGH-LOW STOCK PRICES

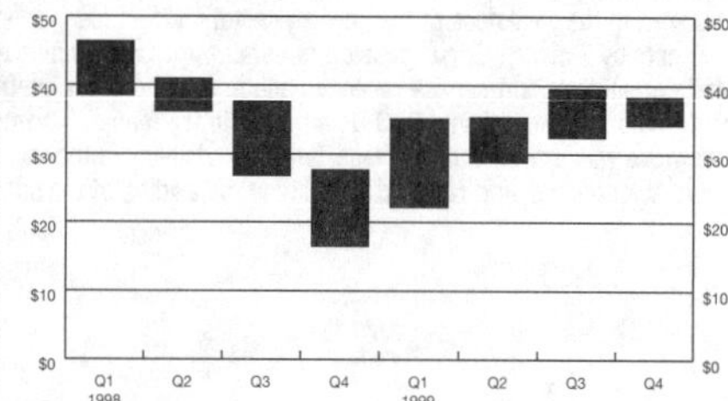

Touch America Inc.

40 E. Broadway, Butte, MT 59701
Tel: 406/723-5421 Fax: 406/497-3018 Web site: http://www.mtpower.com

Touch America Inc., formerly The Montana Power Co., provides telecommunications services. (The former company's utility business— nonutility oil and natural gas businesses—were discontinued in late 2000.) Touch America has a 12,000-mile fiber-optic network that is expected to reach 18,000 miles by year-end 2000 and 26,000 miles by year-end 2001. The network is used for wholesale long-haul voice, data and image transmission as a carrier's carrier, as well as for Touch America's own direct connections to individuals and businesses through its wireless services, metropolitan fiber offerings, and private-line, long-distance, and Internet applications.

EARNINGS HISTORY *

Year Ended Dec 31	Operating Revenue/Sales (dollars in thousands)	Net Earnings	Return on Revenue (percent)	Return on Equity	Net Earnings (dollars per share†)	Cash Dividend	Market Price Range
1999	1,342,309	150,346	11.2	14.5	1.34	0.80	42.63–24.56
1998	1,267,271	165,620	13.1	14.9	1.47	0.80	28.56–14.53
1997	1,023,597	128,632	12.6	12.4	1.14	0.80	16.13–10.50
1996	973,208	119,386	12.3	11.4	1.02	0.80	11.50–10.31
1995 ¶	953,224	56,937	6.0	5.3	0.46	0.80	12.06–10.56

* Historical revenue figures have not yet been restated for continuing operations.
† Per-share amounts restated to reflect 2-for-1 stock split on July 16, 1999.
¶ Income figures for 1995 include pretax charge of $74,297,000 to write down long-lived Entech assets.

BALANCE SHEET

Assets	12/31/99 (dollars in thousands)	12/31/98
Current (CAE 554,407 and 10,116)	887,036	328,235
Plant and property	1,705,026	2,081,510
Independent power investments	23,460	24,268
Reclamation fund	43,460	41,542
Other investments	93,231	84,256
Advanced coal royalties	12,506	14,312
Regulatory assets related to income taxes	60,538	121,735
Regulatory assets, other	150,486	154,193
Other deferred charges	73,000	78,044
TOTAL	3,048,743	2,928,095

Liabilities	12/31/99 (dollars in thousands)	12/31/98
Current (STD 58,955 and 166,112)	508,598	415,951
Deferred income taxes	8,847	323,906
Investment tax credit	13,330	33,819
Accrued mining reclamation costs	135,075	129,558
Deferred revenue	311,751	19,950
Net proceeds from generation sale	219,726	
Other deferred credits	101,434	95,123
Long-term debt	618,512	698,329
Preferred stock, securities	122,654	122,654
Common stockholders' equity*	1,008,816	1,088,805
TOTAL	3,048,743	2,928,095

* No par common; 240,000,000 authorized; 110,218,973 and 110,121,040 issued and outstanding.

RECENT QUARTERS / **PRIOR-YEAR RESULTS**

	Quarter End	Revenue ($000)	Earnings ($000)	EPS ($)	Revenue ($000)	Earnings ($000)	EPS ($)
Q3	09/30/2000	264,605	25,227	0.23	335,977	29,212	0.26
Q2	06/30/2000	333,773	36,417	0.34	309,500	25,249	0.22
Q1	03/31/2000	364,864	31,279	0.29	321,768	33,824	0.30
Q4	12/31/99	375,353	62,060	0.56	397,692	70,399	0.63
	SUM	1,338,595	154,983	1.42	1,364,937	158,684	1.41

CURRENT: Q3 revenue is for continuing operations only. Q2 and all earlier periods include revenue from discontinued operations.

RECENT EVENTS

In **December 1999** PPL Global, a subsidiary of PPL Corporation (NYSE: PPL) of Allentown, Pa., acquired 11 hydroelectric power plants, one storage reservoir, and interests in four coal-fired power plants and other related assets, totaling 1,315 megawatts—for a purchase price of $759 million. The Los Angeles Department of Water and Power (LADWP) and Montana Power completed a three-way transaction to terminate the remaining 11 years of an existing power sales agreement between LADWP and Montana Power; establish a new agreement between the two firms; and immediately assign the power available and the obligation to purchase the power under a new agreement to an undisclosed

continued on page 372

OFFICERS

Robert P. Gannon
Chairman, President, and CEO

Jerrold P. Pederson
Vice Chairman and CFO

Richard F. Cromer
EVP and COO-Energy Supply

John D. Haffey
EVP and COO-Energy Services Division

Michael J. Meldahl
EVP and COO-Technology

Perry J. Cole
VP-Corp. Business Development

David A. Johnson
VP-Distribution Services

Pamela K. Merrell
VP-Human Resources and Secretary

William A. Pascoe
VP-Transmission Services

Michael E. Zimmerman
VP and General Counsel

Susan D. Breining
Asst. Secretary

Harry Freebourn
Asst. Treasurer

Ernie Kindt
Asst. Controller

Rose Marie Ralph
Asst. Secretary

Ellen M. Senechal
Treasurer

David S. Smith
Controller

Daniel J. Sullivan
Chief Information Officer

DIRECTORS

Tucker Hart Adams
The Adams Group Inc., Colorado Springs

Alan F. Cain
Blue Cross and Blue Shield of Montana (retired)

John G. Connors
Microsoft Corp., Redmond, WA

R.D. Corette
Corette Pohlman & Kebe, Butte, MT

Kay Foster
Planteriors Unlimited, Billings, MT

Robert P. Gannon

John R. Jester
Bargain Street, Tacoma, WA

Carl Lehrkind III
Lehrkind's Inc., Bozeman, MT

Deborah McWhinney
Internet Profiles Corp., San Francisco

Jerrold P. Pederson

N.E. Vosburg
Pacific Steel & Recycling, Great Falls, MT

MAJOR SHAREHOLDERS

All officers and directors as a group (22 persons), 0.6%

SIC CODE

1221 Bituminous coal and lignite, surface
1311 Crude petroleum and natural gas
4931 Electric and other services combined

MISCELLANEOUS

TRANSFER AGENT AND REGISTAR:
First Chicago Trust Co. of New York, Jersey City, NJ
TRADED: NYSE, PSE
SYMBOL: MTP
STOCKHOLDERS: 33,000
EMPLOYEES: 2,416
GENERAL COUNSEL:
Michael E. Zimmerman
AUDITORS:
PricewaterhouseCoopers LLP, Portland, OR
INC: MT-1961
FOUNDED: 1912
ANNUAL MEETING: May
COMMUNICATIONS: Cort Freeman
INVESTOR RELATIONS: Linda McGillen

PUB

TWO-YEAR QUARTERLY HIGH-LOW STOCK PRICES

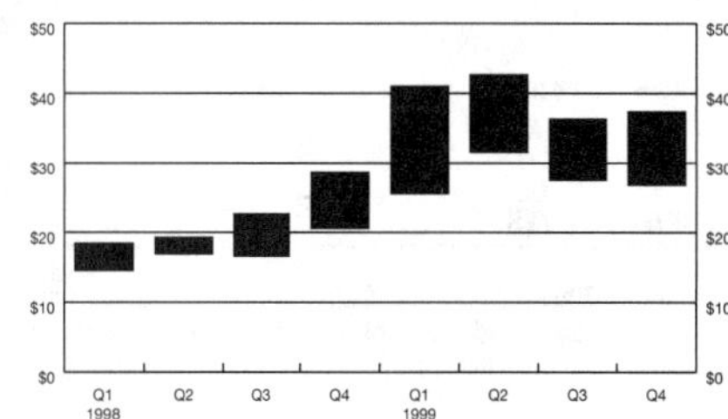

Tower Automotive Inc.

4508 IDS Center, Minneapolis, MN 55402
Tel: 612/342-2310 Fax: 612/332-2012 Web site: http://www.towerautomotive.com

Tower Automotive Inc. produces a broad range of assemblies and modules for vehicle structures and suspension systems for automotive manufacturers—including Ford, DaimlerChrysler, General Motors, Honda, Toyota, Nissan, Auto Alliance, BMW, Volkswagen, Mercedes, and Fiat. Products include body structural assemblies (such as pillars and package trays), control arms, suspension links, engine cradles, and full-frame assemblies. The company has its operating headquarters in Grand Rapids, Mich.

EARNINGS HISTORY

Year Ended Dec 31	Operating Revenue/Sales	Net Earnings	Return on Revenue	Return on Equity	Net Earnings	Cash Dividend	Market Price Range
	(dollars in thousands)		(percent)		(dollars per share*)		
1999 †	2,170,003	117,088	5.4	16.1	2.50	—	28.25–13.50
1998 ¶	1,836,479	88,040	4.8	14.5	1.91	—	27.13–15.81
1997 #	1,235,829	46,244	3.7	9.0	1.14	—	24.28–14.88
1996 **	399,925	20,637	5.2	11.3	0.81	—	16.06–7.06
1995	222,801	12,071	5.4	14.1	0.56	—	8.75–3.75

* Per-share amounts restated to reflect 2-for-1 stock split on July 15, 1998.
† Pro forma figures for 1999 had the July 29, 1999, acquisition of Active Tool Corp. and Active Products Corp. (for $315 million), and the Oct. 29, 1999, equity investment in Seojin Industrial Co. Ltd. (of $21 million) occurred at the beginning of this period: revenue $2,363.925 million; net income $126.039 million/$2.69.
¶ Pro forma figures for 1998 had the July 1, 1998, acquisition of IMAR s.r.l. and ASLAMT S.p.A. (for $49.5 million plus earnout) occurred at the beginning of this period: revenue $1,867.543 million; net income $84.582 million/$1.83.
# Pro forma figures for 1997 had all acquisitions occurred at the beginning of this period: revenue $1,520.803 million; net income $29.389 million/$1.29. Income figures include extraordinary loss of $2.434 million/($0.06) on early extinguishment of debt.
** Results for 1996 include MascoTech Stamping Technologies Inc. from May 31, 1996; and Trylon Corp. from Jan. 16, 1996.

BALANCE SHEET

Assets	12/31/99	12/31/98
	(dollars in thousands)	
Current (CAE 3,617 and 3,434)	558,056	436,094
Property, plant, and equipment	1,075,861	821,873
Restricted cash		2,677
Joint ventures	290,705	209,625
Goodwill	585,109	421,700
Other	42,819	44,198
TOTAL	2,552,550	1,936,167

Liabilities	12/31/99	12/31/98
	(dollars in thousands)	
Current (STD 13,876 and 18,191)	431,116	329,158
Long-term debt	699,678	316,579
Capital leases	21,543	25,770
Convertible subordinated notes	200,000	200,000
Deferred income taxes	50,736	20,376
Other	163,592	178,738
Preferred securities	258,750	258,750
Stockholders' equity*	727,135	606,796
TOTAL	2,552,550	1,936,167

* $0.01 par common; 200,000,000 authorized; 46,879,454 and 46,281,880 issued and outstanding.

RECENT QUARTERS / **PRIOR-YEAR RESULTS**

	Quarter End	Revenue ($000)	Earnings ($000)	EPS ($)	Revenue ($000)	Earnings ($000)	EPS ($)
Q3	09/30/2000	536,210	6,965	0.15	536,152	23,741	0.50
Q2	06/30/2000	681,020	39,293	0.83	530,680	32,628	0.69
Q1	03/31/2000	685,364	37,123	0.79	498,572	28,076	0.60
Q4	12/31/99	604,599	32,643	0.70	468,625	27,208	0.59
	SUM	2,507,193	116,024	2.46	2,034,029	111,653	2.39

CURRENT: Q3 earnings include extraordinary loss of $2.988 million/($0.06) on early extinguishment of debt.

RECENT EVENTS

In **February 2000** the company acquired all of the outstanding common stock of $120 million-revenue Dr. Meleghy GmbH & Co. KG for total consideration of $110 million. Dr. Meleghy is a producer of structural components and assemblies for the European automotive industry. Tower and Defiance Testing & Engineering Services Inc., a subsidiary of GenTek Inc. (NYSE: GK), formed a product technology and development joint venture, DTA *continued on page 372*

OFFICERS

S.A. (Tony) Johnson
Chairman
Dugald K. Campbell
President and CEO
Jim Arnold
VP
Anthony A. Barone
VP and CFO
Richard S. Burgess
VP
Tom G. Pitser
VP
Scott D. Rued
VP

DIRECTORS

Dugald K. Campbell
Kim B. Clark
Harvard Business School, Boston
Jurgen Geissinger
INA Holding
S.A. (Tony) Johnson
F.J. (Joe) Loughrey
Cummins Engine Co. Inc., Columbus, IN
James R. Lozelle
Scott D. Rued
Enrique Zambrano
Proeza S.A. de C.V., Mexico

MAJOR SHAREHOLDERS

American Express Co., 8.3%
New York
Capital Research and Management Co., 7.9%
Los Angeles
Morgan Stanley Dean Witter, 6%
New York
Lazard Freres & Co. LLC, 5.7%
New York

SIC CODE

3714 Motor vehicle parts and accessories

MISCELLANEOUS

TRANSFER AGENT AND REGISTAR:
First Chicago Trust Co. of New York, Jersey City, NJ
TRADED: NYSE
SYMBOL: TWR
STOCKHOLDERS: 2,351
EMPLOYEES: 12,000
GENERAL COUNSEL:
Varnum, Riddering, Schmidt & Howlett, Grand Rapids, MI

AUDITORS:
Arthur Andersen LLP, Minneapolis
INC: DE-1993
FOUNDED: 1955
ANNUAL MEETING: May
PUBLIC RELATIONS COUNSEL: Padilla Speer Beardsley Inc.
INVESTOR RELATIONS: Judy Vijums

RANKINGS

No. 19 CRM Public 200
No. 22 CRM Performance 100

TWO-YEAR QUARTERLY HIGH-LOW STOCK PRICES

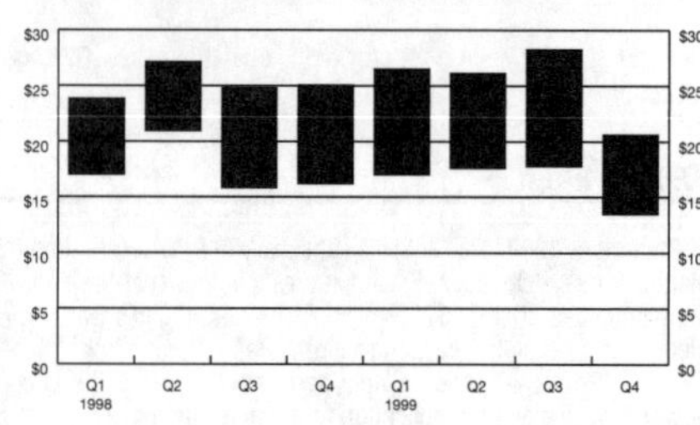

Transport Corporation of America Inc.

1715 Yankee Doodle Rd., Eagan, MN 55121
Tel: 651/686-2500 Fax: 651/686-2551 Web site: http://www.transportamerica.com

Transport Corp. of America Inc. provides truckload carriage and logistics services in various lengths of haul. The company primarily serves the midwestern and eastern half of the United States and parts of Canada. To both its employee drivers and its independent contractors, the company offers more at-home time, higher rates of pay, and driver-friendly freight. Its fleet includes 2,000 tractors and 5,000 trailers. In November 1994 the company completed an initial public offering that raised $14.5 million.

EARNINGS HISTORY

Year Ended Dec 31	Operating Revenue/Sales (dollars in thousands)	Net Earnings	Return on Revenue (percent)	Return on Equity	Net Earnings (dollars per share)	Cash Dividend	Market Price Range
1999 *	285,585	8,276	2.9	11.0	1.02	—	16.25–9.75
1998 †	245,913	10,656	4.3	17.3	1.46	—	18.25–10.00
1997	186,392	7,752	4.2	15.3	1.18	—	17.25–10.25
1996 ¶	164,666	6,294	3.8	14.6	0.98	—	14.13–8.88
1995	144,254	6,106	4.2	16.8	0.91	—	14.25–9.50

* Pro forma figures for 1999 to include results of May 1, 1999, acquisition Robert Hansen Trucking Inc. from Jan. 1: revenue $295.074 million; earnings $7.965 million/$0.97.
† Pro forma figures for 1998 to include results of July 1, 1998, acquisition North Star Transport Inc. from Jan. 1: revenue $283.275 million; earnings $10.934 million/$1.38.
¶ Income figures for 1996 include a loss of $202,000/($0.03) on the start-up costs and launch expense of Transport International Express.

BALANCE SHEET

Assets	12/31/99 (dollars in thousands)	12/31/98	Liabilities	12/31/99 (dollars in thousands)	12/31/98
Current (CAE 745 and 448)	39,838	38,477	Current (STD 14,899 and 13,717)	39,242	35,271
Property and equipment	205,821	160,760	Long-term debt	106,106	79,531
Other	26,482	25,315	Deferred income taxes	31,396	27,749
TOTAL	272,141	224,552	Put option common stock	20,268	20,268
			Stockholders' equity*	75,129	61,733
			TOTAL	272,141	224,552

* $0.01 par common; 15,000,000 authorized; 7,114,490 and 6,687,873 issued and outstanding.

RECENT QUARTERS / **PRIOR-YEAR RESULTS**

	Quarter End	Revenue ($000)	Earnings ($000)	EPS ($)	Revenue ($000)	Earnings ($000)	EPS ($)
Q3	09/30/2000	73,549	1,647	0.20	70,722	2,644	0.32
Q2	06/30/2000	73,431	1,263	0.15	75,034	3,959	0.49
Q1	03/31/2000	72,200	914	0.11	67,145	2,079	0.26
Q4	12/31/99	72,684	(406)	(0.05)	69,263	3,202	0.41
	SUM	291,864	3,418	0.41	282,164	11,884	1.48

RECENT EVENTS

In **January 2000** the company entered into an agreement providing for its merger with a wholly owned subsidiary of USFreightways Corp. in a stock-for-stock transaction valued at $149 million. In **February**, by mutual agreement of the boards of directors of both companies, the agreement between USF and Transport was terminated. In **April** Transport America announced plans to begin repurchasing shares of its common stock again under an existing share repurchase plan. **Sept. 30:** CEO Meyers had this comment on third-quarter results: "Despite an increasingly challenging environment in the transportation industry during the quarter, we were able to achieve an operating ratio of 93 percent. We experienced record high fuel costs, which were mostly offset by recoveries from our existing fuel surcharge program, and we continue to work on the industry issue of driver retention. In addition, our network balance was stressed when one of our major customers temporarily shut down part of their operation for almost half of the quarter. Even with these challenges, we were able to improve tractor productivity and reduce deadhead when compared to both last quarter and last year."

OFFICERS

Robert J. Meyers
President, CEO, COO, and CIO
David L. Carter
VP-Risk Management
Keith R. Klein
CFO
Larry E. Johnson
VP-Marketing
Robert C. Stone
VP-Fleet Management
Jeffrey P. Vandercook
VP-Operations

DIRECTORS

Anton J. Christianson
Cherry Tree Investments Inc., Bloomington, MN
Robert J. Meyers
Michael J. Paxton
Sunbeam Health & Safety Co., Chicago
Kenneth J. Roering
Carlson School of Management/U. of Minnesota, Minneapolis
William Slattery
Shamrock Business Group Inc., Minneapolis

MAJOR SHAREHOLDERS

T. Rowe Price Associates Inc., 7.9%
Baltimore
Wellington Management Co. LLP, 7.7%
Boston
Estate of James B. Aronson, 6.8%
Eagan, MN
Anton J. Christianson/ Cherry Tree Ventures, 6.6%
Bloomington, MN
Central Securities Corp., 6.4%
New York
William I. Hagen, 6.4%
Roseau, MN
All officers and directors as a group (12 persons), 10.6%

SIC CODE

4213 Trucking, except local

MISCELLANEOUS

TRANSFER AGENT AND REGISTAR:
Wells Fargo Bank Minnesota N.A.,
South St. Paul, MN
TRADED: Nasdaq National Market

SYMBOL: TCAM
STOCKHOLDERS: 384
EMPLOYEES: 1,815
IN MINNESOTA: 1,020
GENERAL COUNSEL:
Robins, Kaplan, Miller & Ciresi LLP, Minneapolis
AUDITORS:
KPMG LLP, Minneapolis
INC: MN-1980
ANNUAL MEETING: May

RANKINGS

No. 62 CRM Public 200

SUBSIDIARIES, DIVISIONS, AFFILIATES

Transport International Express Inc.

North Star Transport Inc.

TWO-YEAR QUARTERLY HIGH-LOW STOCK PRICES

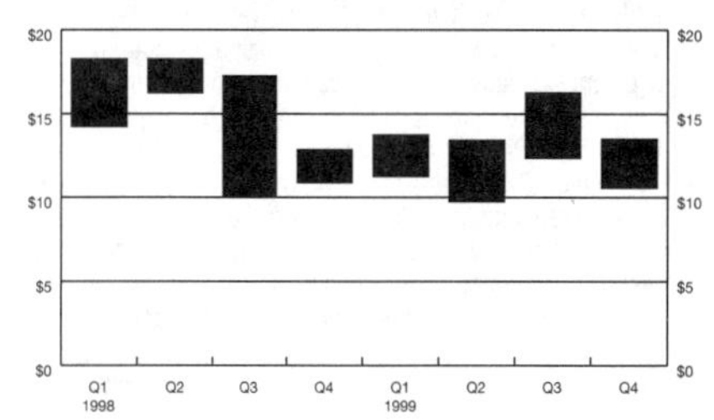

PUB

Tricord Systems Inc.

2905 Northwest Blvd., Suite 20, Plymouth, MN 55441
Tel: 763/557-9005 Fax: 763/557-8403 Web site: http://www.tricord.com

Tricord Systems Inc. designs, develops and markets a line of innovative server appliances that enable critical business services ranging from data storage and content management to e-Commerce. Based on distributed file system technology, these intelligent, single purpose devices feature seamless aggregation with unprecedented ease of management. Offices in Colorado, California, and Georgia.

EARNINGS HISTORY

Year Ended Dec 31	Operating Revenue/Sales (dollars in thousands)	Net Earnings	Return on Revenue (percent)	Return on Equity	Net Earnings (dollars per share)	Cash Dividend	Market Price Range
1999 *	0	(7,637)	NM	NM	(0.39)	—	7.00–1.75
1998 †	0	(2,111)	NM	(36.1)	(0.14)	—	2.97–0.44
1997 ¶	0	(10,931)	NM	NM	(0.81)	—	2.03–0.50
1996 #	0	(15,204)	NM	NM	(1.14)	—	7.25–1.36
1995 **	0	(37,153)	NM	NM	(2.81)	—	6.38–2.56

* Income figures for 1999 include net gain of $0.07 million/$0.00 from discontinued operations and their disposal.
† Income figures for 1998 include gain of $1.743 million/$0.12 from discontinued operations.
¶ Income figures for 1997 include loss of $6.435 million/($0.48) from discontinued operations.
# Income figures for 1996 include loss of $11.948 million/($0.90) from discontinued operations.
** Income figures for 1995 include loss of $32.875 million/($2.49) from discontinued operations.

BALANCE SHEET

Assets	12/31/99 (dollars in thousands)	12/31/98	Liabilities	12/31/99 (dollars in thousands)	12/31/98
Current (CAE 3,082 and 6,215)	3,155	7,110	Current	530	1,511
Equipment and improvements	277	243	Stkhldrs' equity*	2,902	5,842
TOTAL	3,432	7,353	TOTAL	3,432	7,353

* $0.01 par common; 75,000,000 authorized; 20,169,000 and 18,961,000 issued and outstanding.

RECENT QUARTERS / **PRIOR-YEAR RESULTS**

	Quarter End	Revenue ($000)	Earnings ($000)	EPS ($)	Revenue ($000)	Earnings ($000)	EPS ($)
Q3	09/30/2000	0	(3,363)	(0.14)	0	(2,073)	(0.11)
Q2	06/30/2000	0	(3,106)	(0.13)	0	(1,699)	(0.09)
Q1	03/31/2000	0	(2,193)	(0.11)	0	(1,838)	(0.10)
Q4	12/31/99	0	(2,027)	(0.10)	0	(630)	(0.04)
	SUM	0	(10,689)	(0.48)	0	(6,240)	(0.33)

CURRENT: Q2 earnings include gain of $40,000/$0.00 on disposal of discontinued operations. Q1 earnings include gain of $44,000/$0.00 on disposal of discontinued operations. Q4 earnings include gain of $49,000/$0.00 on disposal of discontinued operations.
PRIOR YEAR: Q3 earnings include loss of $453,000/($0.02) on discontinued operations and their disposal. Q2 earnings include gain of $152,000/$0.01; Q1 earnings include gain of $322,000/$0.02; and Q4 earnings include gain of $202,000/$0.01—all from discontinued operations.

RECENT EVENTS

In **April 2000** the company closed a $26 million capital investment through a private placement of 3,250,000 shares of common stock. Managed by Wit SoundView, institutions participating in the financing included Oppenheimer Funds and The Abernathy Group. This equity infusion was to be used to launch a new line of server appliances. "We are very pleased to have additional capital from such a prominent group of investors," said co-CEO Mitcham. Added co-CEO Canion, "Tricord is now poised to bring to market storage-based products that enable an unprecedented level of scalability to meet the demands of Internet and e-commerce companies." In **June** Tricord was awarded U.S. Patent No. 6,029,168 for a key technology that balances files across multiple distributed server appliances. "This patent is the result of years of effort building a flexible, distributed file system that will enable us to deliver a revolutionary line of server appliances," said President Wrabetz. "The awarding of this patent validates the unique benefits of our technology and will help to solidify our technology leadership position in this dynamic, emerging marketplace." (According to International Data Corp., the server appliance market is projected to grow to $12 billion by 2004.) Tricord opened a facility in Westminster, Colo. In **July** Tricord chose JWT Specialized Communications (sub. J. Walter Thompson) as its partner for branding, marketing communications, and public relations efforts. In **August** Tricord was preparing to implement a comprehensive e-business strategy that included enterprise resource planning (ERP) software and systems integration and the design and implementation of e-commerce processes and services. BORN, a leading e-business and technology consulting firm, was helping Tricord design and implement e-commerce strategies designed around its customers and its highly specialized technology solutions. J.D. Edwards' comprehensive OneWorld solution was selected as the back-office platform for enterprise resource planning and management. "The primary goal of this effort is to make it easy for customers to do business with Tricord," said President Wrabetz. "We are *continued on page 373*

OFFICERS

Yuval Almog
Chairman

Joan Wrabetz
President and CEO

Dennis Cindrich
VP-Sales

Greg Dahl
Pres.-Marketing/Business Development

Alexander H. Frey, Dr.
SVP and Chief Technical Officer

Steven E. Opdahl
CFO

Charles E. (Ed) Pearsall
VP-Engineering

DIRECTORS

Yuval Almog
Coral Group Inc.

Tom R. Dillon
NetFlix.com Inc.

Donald L. Lucas
private investor

John J. Mitcham

Fred G. Moore
Horison Inc., Boulder, CO

Joan Wrabetz

MAJOR SHAREHOLDERS

Joseph R. (Rod) Canion, 30.2%

John Mitcham, 6.6%
Plymouth, MN

All officers and directors as a group (10 persons), 30.2%

SIC CODE

3571 Electronic computers

MISCELLANEOUS

TRANSFER AGENT AND REGISTAR:
Wells Fargo Bank Minnesota N.A.,
South St. Paul, MN

TRADED: Nasdaq SmallCap Market

SYMBOL: TRCD

STOCKHOLDERS: 336

EMPLOYEES: 80

IN MINNESOTA: 55

GENERAL COUNSEL:
Oppenheimer Wolff & Donnelly LLP, Minneapolis

AUDITORS:
PricewaterhouseCoopers LLP, Minneapolis

INC: DE-1992

FOUNDED: 1987

ANNUAL MEETING: May

COMMUNICATIONS:
Liz Hersey

TWO-YEAR QUARTERLY HIGH-LOW STOCK PRICES

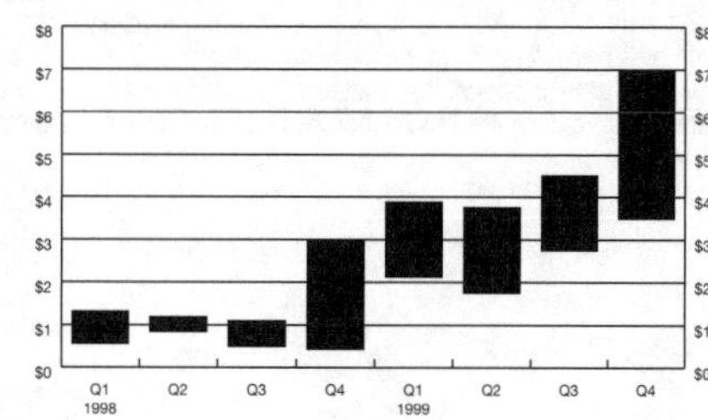

St. Jude Medical Inc.

continued from page 345 ing lead in the European market that is the thinnest of its type in the world. The Tendril SDX lead employs an extendable-retractable helix for active fixation in either the atrium or the ventricle. The company then initiated a worldwide voluntary recall of all field inventory of heart valve replacement and repair products incorporating its proprietary Silzone coating on the sewing cuff fabric—but stopped short of recommending explants of its products with Silzone coating unless routine patient monitoring should detect complications—specifically, a postoperative complication known as paravalvular leak. The company announced the full commercial release of Entity, its newest AutoCapture Pacing System, in the United States. In **February** St. Jude Medical announced that it had received an investigational device exemption (IDE) from the FDA for its new dual-chamber ICD, Photon DR, and that U.S. clinical trials were underway. Also announced: the first implants of the Genesis system, an innovative new device-based ventricular resynchronization system for the treatment of congestive heart failure (CHF) and suppression of atrial fibrillation (AF), two significant and often linked global health care challenges. In **March** St. Jude Medical released a new cardiac defibrillation lead in the United States for use with ICDs: the TVL-ADX lead, based on the company's proven Tendril DX cardiac pacing lead technology. FDA approval for U.S. market release was received for the 6F (French) Angio-Seal vascular closure device. The company completed an initial clinical study in Germany of the Aortic Connector System, a new approach to the treatment of coronary artery disease. The company notified physicians of a microprocessor anomaly that could lead to a malfunction in a very small number of its Trilogy family of pacemakers. (There had been no reported patient injuries associated with the situation; however, a Pennsylvania recipient would sue the company in April—claiming negligence, fraud, and willful misconduct.) The company received FDA approval of the Tendril SDX steroid-eluting active fixation pacing lead; and the right to affix CE marking to its Photon DR dual-chamber ICD. **March 31:** Better-than-expected first-quarter earnings reflected a sales increase for the heart valve business—even after the January product recall. In **April** St. Jude Medical announced the one-millionth implant of its "gold standard" mechanical heart valve, a landmark achievement far surpassing any other heart valve company. (St. Jude Medical devices are used in nearly 50 percent of all heart valve procedures worldwide.) St. Jude Medical announced the global market release of its new line of 4F Supreme catheters, in decapolar and quadripolar electrode spacings and various curve configurations. In **May** the company announced the first implants of its new Integrity AFx pacemaker system. The company's most sophisticated pacemaker family, the Affinity AutoCapture pacing system, was launched in Japan, based on recent regulatory and reimbursement approvals; the Affinity VDR AutoCapture Pacing System was released globally. A Massachusetts woman became the second to sue the company regarding the recalled Silzone product. The U.S. market release of the Integrity AFx AutoCapture Pacing System was announced. St. Jude Medical announced the initial implementation of the Housecall transtelephonic monitoring system, the only system available that can use a telephone to download a complete set of diagnostic data and programmed parameters from a patient's implanted cardioverter-defibrillator (ICD). The first U.S. implant of the Integrity AFx (model 5346) AutoCapture Pacing System was done based on an investigational device exemption (IDE) from the FDA. Conformite Europeene (CE) Mark approval was granted the Frontier 3x2 three-port, multi-chamber stimulation device, an innovative new approach for treating congestive heart failure (CHF) and suppressing atrial fibrillation (AF); and the Aortic Clip, designed to facilitate rapid, simple, and reproducible anastomoses for use in coronary artery bypass graft (CABG) surgery. St. Jude Medical and Cambridge Heart Inc. (Nasdaq: CAMH) announced the Alternans Before Cardioverter-Defibrillator (ABCD) trial, a cooperative study on the accuracy of Microvolt T-wave Alternans to identify certain candidates for ICD therapy. In **June** shares of St. Jude Medical were rated BUY in new coverage at Donaldson Lufkin & Jenrette Securities. The company announced U.S. market release of the St. Jude Medical Fast-Cath Duo line of Swartz Guiding Introducers, which provide access into the left atrium of the heart through the intra-atrial septum, facilitating the simultaneous deployment of multiple diagnostic electrophysiology (EP) catheters. The company was alerting doctors that a small number of Tempo and Meta pacemakers (less than 1 percent of the 15,000 in use worldwide) were affected by a circuitry problem that might cause them to malfunction. The company launched in Europe its advanced TVL-ADX lead, designed to be used with ICDs. The company submitted a pre-market approval application to the FDA for its Photon DR dual-chamber implantable bradycardia cardioverter defibrillator, the fifth-generation ICD from St. Jude Medical, merging state-of-the-art bradycardia capabilities with advanced and powerful tachycardia therapy. In **July** the company announced the global market release of its new 6 French (F) Spyglass angiography catheters, which are used in coronary angiography procedures to obtain images of coronary arteries to identify structural cardiac diseases. St. Jude filed a lawsuit alleging that the Duett sealing device from its newest competitor, Vascular Solutions, infringed certain patents assigned to St. Jude Medical. (The premarket approval application for Duett had been approved by the FDA on June 22, 2000, allowing Vascular Solutions to commence sales of the device in the United States.) St. Jude Medical initiated the LV3P-CHF* study, a multi-center European clinical study designed to evaluate left ventricular-based stimulation versus right ventricular pacing for the treatment of pacemaker patients with heart failure. In **August** St. Jude Medical lost an arbitration with Guidant Corp. over four patents licensed by Guidant to Telectronics, whose heart rhythm assets were subsequently acquired by St. Jude. According to the arbitrator, St. Jude did not buy enough assets from Telectronics to transfer the licenses. The ruling allowed Guidant to reinstate a patent-infringement lawsuit that had been on hold. The company received an Investigational Device Exemption (IDE) from the FDA to begin its Post AV Node Ablation Evaluation (PAVE) clinical study. (PAVE is a multicenter study designed to evaluate treatment options for patients with chronic atrial fibrillation (AF) who receive an "ablate and pace" procedure.) In **September** results from a European study evaluating DDD pacing based on ventricular AutoCapture in children, presented at the XXII Congress of the European Society of Cardiology (ESC), Amsterdam,confirmed the effectiveness of the St. Jude Medical AutoCapture technology in children requiring DDD/R pacing. **Sept. 30:** None-month net sales of $883.4 million were $50.2 million, or 6 percent, higher than the comparable period of 1999. The stronger U.S. dollar reduced year-to-date 2000 sales by $22.0 million compared to the first nine months of 1999. Exclusive of nonrecurring charges, nine-month net earnings were $115.2 million; on the same basis, 1999 net earnings were $107.9 million. In **October** St. Jude Medical received an investigational device exemption (IDE) from the FDA for the Dual Chamber And VVI Implantable Defibrillator (DAVID) clinical trial. The company announced the global market release of the St. Jude Medical 8F Angio-Seal Millennium Platform, incorporating several advanced features compared to current 8F Angio-Seal products. The company received an IDE from the FDA to begin its Ventricular Resynchronization Therapy Randomized (VecToR) clinical trial. Cordis Corp. and Biosense Webster Inc., two Johnson & Johnson (NYSE: JNJ) companies, joined St. Jude Medical to introduce Alliance OneSource, a new cooperative sourcing venture related to the supply of key medical device products to major hospital centers across the country. St. Jude Medical received premarket approval (PMA) from the FDA for market release of the Photon DR dual-chamber ICD, which offers powerful tachycardia therapy, precise arrhythmia sensing, and supra-ventricular tachycardia (SVT) discrimination. In **November** the company released a new electrophysiology catheter to assist clinicians in the diagnosis and treatment of supraventricular tachycardias. The Livewire Duo-Decapolar catheter, with special electrode spacing, allows physicians to simultaneously map in both the right atrium and coronary sinus with a single steerable catheter. St. Jude Medical announced a three-year purchasing agreement with Consorta, a leading health care resource management and group purchasing organization.

The St. Paul Companies Inc.

continued from page 346 The St. Paul Cos. Inc. is a worldwide insurance organization whose subsidiaries provide a full range of property-liability insurance, life insurance, and reinsurance products and services. **St. Paul Fire and Marine** is the nation's eighth-largest property-liability underwriter. The company not only is the largest U.S. underwriter of medical liability and surety insurance, but also ranks among the largest underwriters of reinsurance, ocean-marine, and excess- and surplus-lines insurance. It also holds a majority position in **The John Nuveen Co.**, an asset management and investment banking firm. Minnesota's oldest corporation, The St. Paul Cos. Inc. was established in 1853 as St. Paul Fire and Marine Insurance Co. It became a management company in 1968.

RECENT EVENTS

In **December 1999** more than 1,000 members of the safety group Independent Community Bankers of America (ICBA) shared a $1.257 million dividend because of their participation in the ICBA/St. Paul Insurance Program. St. Paul Syndicate Management Ltd., the company's operation at Lloyd's, acquired a marine portfolio from Norwich Union. The company obtained approval from the Australian government to incorporate a property-casualty insurer there. The St. Paul Cos. announced a definitive agreement to acquire 900-employee MMI Cos. Inc. (NYSE: MMI), a Deerfield, Ill.-based provider of insurance products and consulting services, for $10 per share in cash, or $200 million—plus the assumption of $120 million of current MMI debt. The combination was to create the largest global integrated provider of insurance and risk management services for the health care industry— generating $1 billion annually in premiums and fees from health care customers. Analysts said that the deal was a nice fit and came at a reasonable price. [Deal completed in April 2000.] The St. Paul also agreed to pay $37 million to acquire Pacific Select Insurance Holdings Inc. and its wholly owned subsidiary, Pacific Select Property Insurance Co.—a Walnut Creek, Calif., insurer that sells earthquake coverage to California homeowners. **Dec. 31:** The company's intense restructuring efforts led to a 31 percent increase in fiscal-year operating earnings, to $636.3 million. In **January 2000** The St. Paul agreed to sell its nonstandard auto insurance business, a 900-employee USF&G unit that serves hard-to-insure drivers, to The Prudential Insurance Co. of America for $200 million in cash—with proceeds from the sale earmarked for general corporate purposes, which may include strategic acquisitions, expansion of specialty product offerings, and continuation of the company's share repurchase program. The sale reflected The St. Paul's continuing strategy of focusing its property-liability insurance operations on its business and professional insurance lines. [Deal completed in May 2000.] Subsidiary St. Paul International Insurance Co. Ltd. was appointed by the Law Society of England and Wales as its professional indemnity insurance provider. In **February** The St. Paul introduced a new interactive, educational Web site designed for high-tech companies. The site, www.stpaul.com/technology, features the intelligent "coverage calculator" that can take company information and provide the user with a no-obligation recommendation of insurance products that match the company's needs. The St. Paul joined 14 other insurance companies in a unified effort to combat the growing problem of insurance fraud. The Coalition Against Insurance Fraud (CAIF) is a national organization dedicated exclusively to fighting insurance fraud through public advocacy and education. In **March**, in a continuing effort to make construction sites as safe as possible, The St. Paul introduced Construction Safety Services (CSS)—a fee-based service program that provides companies with the expertise of a wide range of consulting, training, and job site safety professionals for short- to long-term projects. **March 31:** Although first-quarter operating earnings increased only 3 percent (the 63 cents a share was 3 cents short of analysts' expectations), the company reported price and business-retention increases that exceeded expectations. In **April** The St. Paul received certification for commercial lines download with AMS Services Inc., and commercial lines auto download with Applied Systems. The St. Paul introduced digital marine cargo certificates that can be issued from the company's Web site, www.stpaul.com, giving U.S. and Canadian customers immediate access to documents essential for insuring marine cargo; and a new Marine Property insurance policy that combines marine property and marine general liability coverages in a single package. The St. Paul issued a total of $500 million of senior notes to pay down commercial paper and for general corporate purposes. "This offering, despite volatile financial market conditions, attracted substantial investor interest. In addition, we significantly broadened our investor base to include many first-time buyers of St. Paul securities," said CFO Liska. Standard & Poor's assigned the offering its single A-plus rating—reflecting The St. Paul's current financial leverage and management's intended use of proceeds. At the **May** annual meeting, CEO Leatherdale pointed out (in light of the recent acquisition of Minneapolis-based ReliaStar Financial Corp.) that his strategy of streamlining the company into more of a specialty insurer had not only made it more profitable, but had also helped to stave off takeover attempts. Backing up this commitment to independence, the board of directors announced a new $300 million share repurchase program. Lee Bennett, SVP and general counsel of Claim Services, was appointed chairman of the Insurance Executive Committee of the International Association of Defense Counsel (IADC). The St. Paul introduced SPCQuote, a Web-based tool that gives agents the ability to access current pricing information on more than 3,500 small commercial businesses such as retail establishments, manufacturers, and contractors. In **June** the company took the lead in endorsing the recommended case handling guidelines for U.S.-based insurers and law firms—published by the Defense Research Institute (DRI) of Chicago—that were designed to improve the quality and effectiveness of case handling for clients. The St. Paul was named the endorsed carrier of the Louisiana Independent Oil and Gas Association. Subsidiary F&G Life signed a 10-year lease for 56,000 square feet of new office space in downtown Baltimore. The company was planning to trim the number of independent agents who sell its commercial insurance, from 5,200 to 4,100 by the end of 2000. In **July** The St. Paul began using Alta Analytics' NetMap for Claims, a software product to detect fraud rings, attorney schemes, and medical provider fraud perpetrated against U.S.-based policyholders and their businesses. The report of strong second-quarter earnings boosted the company's stock to a 52-week high of $44.63 on July 27. Lee Bennett, senior vice president and general counsel of The St. Paul Cos. Claim Services, was elected vice president of the International Association of Defense Counsel (IADC). In **August** COO James E. Gustafson, once thought to be a possible successor to Leatherdale, decided to leave the company. "It has become apparent to the board and me that there was not a fit between The St. Paul and Jim's considerable skills," said Leatherdale of the mutual decision. St. Paul International Insurance Co. Ltd. announced its intent to acquire the Australia Pacific Professional Indemnity Insurance Co. Ltd. (APPIIL), Brisbane, from GIO Holdings Ltd., adding 2,000 solicitors as St. Paul policyholders in Queensland, Australia, where indemnity insurance is mandatory. [Deal completed in October.] In **September** Fidelity & Guaranty Life Insurance Co. introduced a new equity-indexed annuity linked to multiple stock market indices. PowerSelect offers four interest-crediting options and the ability to transfer account values among options annually, a feature the company refers to as Account Value Reallocation. For the ninth time, The St. Paul Cos. was named to Working Mother magazine's list of the 100 best companies for working mothers. The company booked 50 million pounds in gross written premiums of solicitors' business in England and Wales, a 20 percent to 30 percent market share for that niche. The technology Web site designed by Bolger Concept to Print for The St. Paul Cos. received an award of excellence from the Insurance Marketing Communications Association. A new report from The St. Paul, based on 14 years of medical professional liability claims data, pinpointed key factors that reduce patient injury and medical liability costs. The company's model for health care systems improvement, based on the findings, focused on reducing the frequency of diagnostic error and improving overall patient care and safety. By following the model, health care organizations can reduce the cost of each closed claim by $36,500 on average. The company decided to cease the underwriting operations of Unionamerica, a London-based reinsurance underwriting subsidiary of the recently acquired MMI Cos. The St. Paul established a risk management grant program for 25 members of the International City/County Management Association (ICMA) to provide an on-site evaluation of a city or county's current loss-control practices. **Sept. 30:** The St. Paul reported third-quarter after-tax operating earnings from continuing operations of $171.9 million, or $0.73 per share, 1 cent higher than the consensus analyst estimate. Third-quarter 1999 earnings were $151.4 million, or $0.62 per share. "Our work over the last two years is delivering results. Our underwriting, pricing, and expense actions, along with our focus on commercial and specialty business and global specialty expertise, continue to position us to take advantage of improving market conditions," said Leatherdale. "The most exciting development in the third quarter was the acceleration of growth in our property-liability insurance operations. The biggest drivers of our growth were price increases and improving retention levels." Third-quarter 2000 property-liability net written premiums, at $1.49 billion, were up 22 percent over third-quarter 1999 premiums. Property-liability pretax operating earnings rose to $240.9 million, compared with $185.8 million a year ago. In **October** the company was named the endorsed carrier of the Missouri Independent Community Bankers Association. Expanding its operations to New Zealand, the company opened an office in Auckland as St. Paul International Insurance Co. Ltd.

Select Comfort Corporation

continued from page 347 channels. In **January 2000** Minnesota Vikings wide receiver Cris Carter formalized his relationship with Select Comfort by signing an official endorsement agreement to participate in print, radio, television, advertisements, and public relations activities. In **March**, after an eight-month search, Select Comfort hired its fourth CEO in a little more than a year—William McLaughlin, a former Pillsbury executive, who had been based in London as president of Frito Lay Europe, Middle East, and Africa. As part of its cost-cutting efforts, the company abolished its Roadshow distribution channel. In **May**, in addition to a 50-person layoff earlier in the year, the company laid off 77 of the 442 employees at its manufacturing plant in Plymouth, Minn., as it shifted some air bed production to Salt Lake City. In **June** the company returned to its partnership with New York-based advertising agency Messner Vetere Berger McNamee Schmetterer/EURO RSCG. A new catalog featured more than 150 product offerings designed to provide solutions for sleep, relaxation, and well-being. The first wave of catalog mailings was to current Select Comfort bed owners—nearly 725,000 households. In **August** the company said that plans to relaunch its new-look Web site had been postponed until fall. [It would later say November.] The company signed a two-year sponsorship agreement with NFL Properties, the marketing and licensing arm of the NFL. (The company worked with NFL teams throughout the 1999-2000 season, providing beds to players during training camp to help improve their quality of sleep as a critical step in enhancing their overall performance.) As an official sponsor through the 2002 season, Select Comfort will incorporate the NFL into its marketing, advertising, and communications efforts. In **September** the company announced a new relationship with Gabberts Inc. under which Gabberts Furniture and Design Studio, located in the Galleria Shopping Center, Edina, Minn., was to be the first traditional furniture retailer to offer the Select Comfort bed. **Sept. 30**: CEO McLaughlin said, "Third-quarter sales improved by 10 percent over the second quarter, but not to the level we feel is necessary or attainable. The target we set earlier in the year was to attain profitability in the fourth quarter. While this remains our goal, we need to progress more quickly to meet that challenge." Comparable-store sales for the third quarter increased by 4 percent. In **October** the company agreed to acquire SleepTec, the supplier of Select Comfort's new sofa sleeper, a revolutionary product that provides consumers a solution to the problem of uncomfortable sofa sleepers. An initial engagement on the QVC shopping channel had company officials contemplating more appearances. The company said that it was planning to exit its Eden Prairie corporate offices, returning 100-plus employees to the manufacturing site in Plymouth; and to consolidate call-center operations in Plymouth, closing a 19-employee center in South Carolina. Thirteen underperforming stores were slated for closure (none in the Twin Cities), reducing nationwide outlets to 324.

Semitool Inc.

continued from page 348 **October** the company announced delivery of another of its advanced, high-volume single-wafer processing tools, the Millennium, to a leading semiconductor company in Japan, to be used in advanced development of polymer removal for device structures utilizing low-K dielectric and copper. The company received an order for two of its high-volume Millennium single wafer processing systems from a major foundry in Taiwan. The small-footprint Millennium, equipped with Semitool's Capsule process system, was to be used for side-selectable cleaning. Semitool introduced the Scepter Solvent 50-wafer, single-chamber, semi-automated batch processing tool, which doubles the productivity of earlier models, offering a 50-wafer single-chamber capacity. In **November** Semitool announced the Storm 300, a 300 mm version of its production-proven family of container cleaning products.

Sheldahl Inc.

continued from page 349 ulated that Jacobs' bid might be aimed at getting Molex to raise its bid for Sheldahl—which could be worth $11 a share if sold in pieces. In **March** Sheldahl introduced the Density Patch, an innovative extension of its flexible circuitry line that makes it possible to incorporate lower-density circuits into larger assemblies at minimal cost. The new solution was designed for specialized functions such as automotive instrumentation, electrical control units, and consoles. The exclusivity period with Molex expired on March 10. Later in the month, Molex notified Sheldahl that it would not make an acquisition proposal after all. Molex did agree, however, to waive a $750,000 exclusivity fee in the event that the Jacobs group definitively agree to acquire Sheldahl. In **April** the Jacobs group abandoned its bid for Sheldahl, saying that it had overlooked a Minnesota anti-takeover law that prevents someone with an ownership stake as high as Jacobs' from acquiring a company without preapproval from that company's board. Some analysts were now viewing Jacobs' $8.50-a-share bid as a bluff meant to solicit higher bids than the $7.75 per share offered by Molex. However, Jacobs said that his group was ready to complete the deal if Sheldahl could get a court ruling that would permit it to proceed. In **May** it was reported that several companies were interested—either in Sheldahl itself (International Flex Technologies Inc.) or in its Longmont, Colo., microproducts unit (3M Co., Molex). In **June** Sheldahl began exclusive negotiations with International Flex Technologies Inc. (IFT), a privately held company in Endicott, N.Y., that had recently spun off from IBM. The proposal: Sheldahl would acquire IFT in exchange for shares of Sheldahl's common stock. In addition Morgenthaler Partners, the majority owner of IFT, and other potential investors would infuse $40 million in new capital into Sheldahl in exchange for shares of a new series of convertible preferred stock—representing beneficial ownership, in all, of 43 percent of Sheldahl. [A definitive merger agreement for a price of 7.6 million Sheldahl shares was signed in November.] Sheldahl received production purchase orders from a major DSP and ASIC semiconductor company for significant volume of Micro Products' ViaThin tape ball grid array substrates over the next 12 months. Sheldahl and IFT agreed to extend to Aug. 21, 2000, an exclusivity agreement that was originally scheduled to terminate Aug. 7, 2000. In mid-**August**, Morgenthaler Venture Partners invested $2 million in the company through a debt instrument that was convertible into common stock. In mid-**October** (accurate) reports that the IFT deal was reportedly nearing conclusion prompted a revival in Sheldahl's flagging stock price.

The Sportsman's Guide Inc.

continued from page 353 nificant online and traditional media attention but also contributed to growth in Internet sales, to nearly 15 percent of total sales for the first six months of 2000. In **July** the company announced at its annual meeting a plan to reduce expenses and return the company's catalog to profitability. Certain organizational changes, including reductions in headcount, were to reduce expenses by more than $1 million on an annual basis. In addition, the catalog strategy was refocused. In **August** The Sportsman's Guide and Metris Cos. Inc. (NYSE: MXT), one of the fastest-growing direct marketing companies in the United States, officially launched The Sportsman's Guide MasterCard.

Stockwalk.com Group Inc.

continued from page 354 online trading company's existing CyberCall functionality to Stockwalk.com's private-labeling customers. In **February** Stockwalk.com announced plans to provide Stockwalk.com investment trading terminals in Northwest Airlines (Nasdaq: NWAC) WorldClubs. The company signed an agreement with Virtual Communications Inc., Monroeville, Pa. to have Virtual Communications market a private-label version of Stockwalk.com's online brokerage services to its financial institution clients. Stockwalk.com signed an agreement with Regency Systems Inc. allowing Regency to offer the private-label version of Stockwalk.com's online brokerage services to its client base of more than 1,500 community banks. In **March** Telescan Inc. (Nasdaq: TSCN), Houston, agreed to combine its online financial analytics with Stockwalk.com's online brokerage services for small and mid-sized regional banks. Still hoping to acquire Kinnard, Stockwalk raised $12.3 million in a private placement of 1,645,841 shares of common stock at $7.50 per share with accredited investors. Private-label versions of Stockwalk.com's online brokerage services were to be offered through separate agreements with The Forms Group, Open Solutions Inc., and Pearse EFT Inc. **March 31**: The company turned a profit in its fiscal fourth quarter despite spending heavily on its fledgling online brokerage business. An **April** agreement allowed Member Emporium, the e-commerce division of cavion.com (Nasdaq: CAVN), to offer cavion.com's 116 credit union customers in 24 states the private-label version of Stockwalk.com's online brokerage services. MJK purchased the brokerage assets of clearing client Concord Services LLC of Chicago. Stockwalk.com signed an agreement with Life Time Fitness Inc. of Minneapolis to provide a private-labeled online trading site for the fitness club's Web site. Eldon Miller won the 2000 Minnesota and Dakotas Ernst & Young Entrepreneur of the Year Award in the e-Finance category. Stockwalk.com and Minnesota Life Insurance Co., St. Paul, agreed to provide privately labeled online securities trading to financial institutions. The company filed to take on as much as $34.5 million in a convertible debt offering—perhaps to build up its war chest for another run at Kinnard, or for another acquisition. In **May** the company agreed to offer privately labeled Internet trading to the clients of Orlando, Fla.-based Phoenix International Ltd. Inc., a leading global provider of client/server-based core banking products and services to the financial services industry; and to the Internet banking clients of SLMsoft.com's EC-street e-commerce network. The company began offering bonds (proprietary municipal, corporate, and government bonds offering attractive yields and a variety of maturities) and certificates of deposit (a nationwide inventory) on its Web site. In **June** the company agreed to provide a private-label version of Stockwalk.com's online brokerage services for NWA Federal Credit Union, Bloomington, Minn. Stockwalk.com, Kinnard Investments Inc. (Nasdaq: KINN), and privately owned R.J. Steichen & Co. announced plans to combine their securities brokerage and investment banking firms under the Stockwalk.com Group holding company. In the Kinnard agreement, Kinnard shareholders were to receive $6.00 cash and one-half share of Stockwalk common stock for each share of outstanding Kinnard common stock. In the Steichen merger agreement, John E. (Jack) Feltl, the sole shareholder of Steichen, was to receive 4.3 million shares of restricted Stockwalk common stock in exchange for the outstanding common stock of Steichen, and up to an additional 2 million shares based upon Steichen's operations during the next two years. Together, the deals were valued at $90 million. The big winner: Steichen CEO Jack Feltl, who received a one-time cash dividend of $21 million. Steichen and Kinnard were to continue to be operated as independent subsidiaries of Stockwalk.com Group Inc. Stockwalk, Kinnard, and Steichen had combined revenue in excess of $180 million for the 12 months ended March 31, 2000. The three firms employ more than 850 people, including more than 400 registered representatives. Outside of Minneapolis, the three firms also operate 34 branch offices in eight states. [Steichen merger completed Aug. 1; Kinnard, Sept. 8.] By the end of June, Stockwalk.com, through its Telescan alliance, had fully integrated new Web site content for its investors. Among the new features added to the site: customizable alerts, where clients enter personal stock favorites and then view a scrolling ticker comprised of those selections; in-depth stock and mutual fund screening tools; expanded analysis of earnings reports and technical charting capabilities; financial calculator/planning tools, and access to discussion groups and investment newsletters. In **July** the company announced an agreement to allow CyFi (Cyberspace Financial Services, a division of Farin & Associates Inc.) to offer its more than 200 financial services clients a private-label version of the Stockwalk.com online brokerage technology. Life Time Fitness also signed an agreement with Stockwalk.com, to offer online brokerage services on its Web site. In **August** Stockwalk.com completed a $20 million public offering of subordinated convertible notes, and a $1.42 million overallotment option, led by Southwest Securities Inc., Dallas. The proceeds were to be used to complete the acquisition of Kinnard Investments and to provide working capital for the Online Brokerage Solutions subsidiary. Online Brokerage Solutions signed an agreement with Yodlee.com, the pioneer and leading provider of account aggregation services, to include Yodlee technology in its private-label packages. Stockwalk enabled Denver police to invest online from the Denver Police Federal Credit Union's home page. Online Brokerage Solutions agreed to privately label its online investing platform for ESL Federal Credit Union of Rochester, N.Y., the 16th-largest federally insured credit union. Online Brokerage Solutions signed an agreement with Strategy.com, a Personal Information Network and wholly owned subsidiary of MicroStrategy Inc. (Nasdaq: MSTR) to offer Strategy.com services as part of Online Brokerage's private-label packages. In **September** Online Brokerage Solutions privatized the online investing platform of ParaMas Internet Inc., a free ISP serving the Hispanic community. Stockwalk.com and Dain Rauscher Corp. (NYSE: DRC) settled the NASD arbitration case filed against Dain Rauscher by John G. Kinnard and Co. As part of the settlement, Dain Rauscher paid Stockwalk.com $13.3 million. [In December 1999, an NASD arbitration panel awarded Kinnard $16.6 million; with interest, the award had grown to $17.2 million.] **Sept. 30**: Second-quarter financial results reflected only partial contributions from the Steichen and Kinnard subsidiaries. Stockwalk.com completed the Steichen merger on Aug. 1 and the Kinnard merger on Sept. 8. The combined revenue of all entities would have been $46.2 million had the mergers occurred on July 1. The operating results do not reflect the $13.3 million collected in connection with the settlement of a Kinnard arbitration ruling. The tax-adjusted value of the award, which was reflected in the purchase of Kinnard, will result in a reduction of future amortization expense to the combined entity. Losses for the quarter were attributed to the continued investment of capital into Online Brokerage Solutions and to miscellaneous expenditures related to merger and acquisition activities. Overall revenue, excluding the impact of the Steichen and Kinnard transactions, increased 63.4 percent for the quarter. Interest income from Stockwalk.com operations increased $5.8 million as a result of an increase in customer margin accounts. In **October** subsidiary Online Brokerage Solutions Inc., formerly the private-label services division of Stockwalk.com, announced its name change; the establishment of its own broker-dealer; and an agreement to private-label its online brokerage platform for The Trust Co. of New Jersey (Nasdaq: TCNJ). The company combined the equity research staffs of its Miller, Johnson & Kuehn (MJK), John G. Kinnard, and R.J. Steichen full-service broker subsidiaries and named Clinton H. Morrison, a Kinnard analyst, director of research and head of the 16-person department. Stockwalk.com completed an agreement with Al Frank Asset Management Inc. to become the exclusive selling broker of the Al Frank Fund (VALUX), a small- to midcap value fund that mainly invests in undervalued and out-of-favor common stocks to be held in a broadly diversified portfolio for their long-term (three- to five-year) potential. The fund is associated with the long-running The Prudent Speculator investment newsletter.

Stonehaven Realty Trust

continued from page 355 estate operators and professionals throughout the country to facilitate the national expansion of its technology solutions. Stonehaven Realty's properties in the Twin Cities were 99.5 percent occupied, providing a steady and predictable positive cash flow to the company. Stonehaven engaged Colliers Towle Real Estate to explore valuation and capital appreciation opportunities, which may include a sale of some or all of Stonehaven's assets or a refinance of existing mortgages. "We are pleased about the rate at which we have introduced new products to the growing online real estate sector and the continued strong performance of our real estate portfolio," said CEO Lund. "Our new strategic plan will allow us to better capture a sizable portion of the emerging online real estate industry." To ensure greater operational and capital flexibility, Stonehaven was initiating a stock repurchase program in lieu of its historical common stock dividend plan, having authorized the purchase of up to 150,000 shares of common stock per quarter instead of a quarterly common stock dividend distribution. Said Lund, "The new dividend policy is consistent with our prevailing business plan, which focuses on the rapid growth and expansion of our online real estate services division."

Supervalu Inc.

continued from page 357 Atlanta market, commencing distribution of grocery items to Internet grocer Webvan.com. In **June** Wright said that he was planning to step down as CEO in June 2001, and announced Jeff Noddle as president, COO, and heir-apparent. In **July** the company joined the WorldWide Retail Exchange (WWRE), a retail-focused business-to-business exchange designed to enable transactions between business partners operating in the food, non-food, drugstore, and textiles sectors. In **August** five middle managers who were replaced after the 1998 installation of a new technology system sued the company over alleged age discrimination. Supervalu filed to raise as much as $707 million from the sale of debt securities. **Sept. 9:** Second-quarter results marked the company's 14th-consecutive quarter of record sales and earnings per share. Excluding the benefit of one-time items in last year's first quarter, net earnings for the first half of fiscal 2001 increased 25.7 percent to $127.3 million. The retail food business delivered a sales increase of 25.6 percent to $2.1 billion in the second quarter. Sales growth in the quarter reflected the addition of 102 retail stores from last year's acquisition of Richfood and 132 new store openings, including 103 limited-assortment stores. At quarter's end, there were 1,144 stores, representing 6 percent square footage growth over the prior year. Same-store sales for the second quarter were negative 3 percent. In addition to the continued self-cannibalization which began in the first quarter as a result of an acceleration of store openings in existing markets, competitive activities intensified in the second quarter in several key markets. The food distribution business achieved a sales increase of 30.8 percent to $3.2 billion. These results continued to be driven primarily by last year's addition of nearly 800 distribution customers from the Richfood acquisition and incremental volume, principally Kmart. Versus one year ago, SUPERVALU was distributing to an additional 1,100 Kmart and eight SuperTARGET locations. In **October**, on the heels of its affiliation of D&W Food Centers, a 26-store chain in Grand Rapids, Mich., Supervalu added two highly successful Mid-Atlantic accounts—Graul's Markets and McCaffrey's Markets—to the company's Richfood region, based in Richmond, Va.

TCF Financial Corporation

continued from page 360 Said CEO Cooper, "Our traditional branch banking, and consumer and commercial lending businesses all operated at record levels. Our emerging de novo businesses (supermarket banking, leasing and equipment finance, etc.) have started to make significant contributions and will be an engine of growth in future years." In **February 2000** TCF launched the TCF Express Phone Card, a loyalty and reward program exclusively for users of the free TCF Check Card. In **March** the board of directors authorized a new program for the company to acquire up to 4.1 million shares (5 percent) of TCF common stock. At a **June** investors conference, CEO Cooper said that the company's new products—an online discount brokerage, credit life insurance, and an expense-management debit card—were aimed at upscale customers, a departure from its past focus on middle-income customers. Intending to consolidate workers currently at three Wayzata locations, TCF National Bank acquired the Wayzata lakefront building that was serving as headquarters for International Multifoods Corp. **June 30:** The company impressed analysts by reporting blockbuster second-quarter earnings that beat estimates by 5 cents a share. In **September** TCF's 212 supermarket branches topped $1 billion in retail deposits. (TCF had opened 162 supermarket branches over the previous three years, creating the fourth-largest supermarket branch network in the United States.) **Sept. 30:** TCF increased Power Assets by $586.6 million, or 15 percent from year-end 1999, and increased checking account deposits by $203.1 million, or 11 percent, over the same period. Top-line revenue increased 10 percent and fee income by 18 percent from the 1999 third quarter. "Our unique strategy of growing the TCF franchise through de novo expansion continued to pay off," said Cooper. In **October** TCF opened a new branch in Elk River, Minn.

Target Corporation

continued from page 361 said it was planning a store in a proposed mall in Maple Grove, Minn. for (at the earliest) fall 2003. In **January 2000** Target Stores was awarded the 1999 Corporate Volunteerism Council (CVC) Leadership Award, in recognition of its leadership in anticipating and responding to the changing needs of Twin Cities communities. Target Corp. discontinued four catalogs and cut 30 jobs at its 420-employee mail-order subsidiary, Rivertown Trading Co. Its three largest catalogs—Season, Signals, and Wireless—remain, as does its burgeoning e-commerce business. In an unrelated move, Donna Avery, president of Rivertown, resigned. **Jan. 29:** Net retail sales for the four weeks increased 11.4 percent to $2.052 billion, from $1.843 billion a year ago. Comparable-store sales increased 5.7 percent. Fourth-quarter earnings surged 15 percent, outpacing industry leader Wal-Mart, on the strength of a strong holiday season and the higher mark-ups on Target's innovative upscale brand names. Comparable-sales increases by division: 5.6 percent for Target Stores; a 4.8 percent decrease for Mervyn's; and a 1.6 percent decrease for the Department Stores. In **February** the company formed a new business unit called "Target Direct," which was to be responsible for all the company's electronic retailing and direct marketing efforts. The business united the current e-commerce team at the company with its Rivertown Trading direct marketing unit into one integrated organization. For an unprecedented sixth time, Target Stores captured the Best of Show trophy at the Retail Advertising Conference for its multimedia campaign, "Sign of the Times," which encompassed broadcast, print, point-of-purchase materials, and in-store signage. Target Stores announced its intent to open 24 stores in 16 states—including its first store in Connecticut—on July 23. **Feb. 26**: Net retail sales for the four weeks increased 8.7 percent to $2.194 billion; comparable-store sales increased 3.8 percent from the same period a year ago. In **March** Target Corp. announced plans to repurchase an additional $1 billion of its common stock. Target Stores placed an initial $6 million order with Tefron Ltd. (NYSE: TFR), one of the world's leading producers of seamless intimate apparel. Target Stores announced a partnership with top fashion designer Mossimo Giannulli (Mossimo Inc.) to create an exclusive line of contemporary apparel for the family. The deal was to take effect in February 2001. [Whether Mossimo Inc. could stay afloat that long, through cash-flow problems, was in doubt as early as May.] In **April** Target Corp. received an Environmental Initiative Award for environmental management from the Minnesota Environmental Initiative—in recognition of Target's environmental services initiatives, including comprehensive waste-prevention, materials use-management, environmental education, and recycling efforts. **April 29:** Net retail sales for the four weeks increased 17.0 percent from a year ago to $2.460 billion. Comparable-store sales increased 11.1 percent. However, taking into account the timing of the Easter holiday, these results were slightly below plan. Beginning **May** 1, Target added stainless steel cookware to its exclusive Kitchen Essentials from Calphalon collection. Target Stores entered into a strategic multichannel marketing alliance with E*TRADE Group Inc. (Nasdaq: EGRP), a global leader in online personal financial services. Pursuant to that agreement, Target announced plans to open a 400-square-foot, experimental E-Trade financial services center at the SuperTarget in Roswell, Ga. In **June** Target Stores and America Online Inc. (NYSE: AOL), the world's leading interactive services company, announced a broad strategic alliance that contained expansive cross-marketing arrangements combining significant off-line co-branding campaigns and in-store offerings with extensive online initiatives. Target and Ryan Cos. U.S. Inc. broke ground on the first phase of a 1.3 million-square-foot Target North Office Campus in Brooklyn Park, Minn. Four disabled California women filed a lawsuit over alleged denial of basic access at Mervyn's. In **July** Target Stores began offering Club Wedd and Lullaby Club gift registry services on target.com to help save time and simplify planning for a wedding or a baby. Target announced the March 11, 2001, scheduled opening of 24 new stores in 16 states, from California to Delaware. The launch was to include the first North Dakota SuperTarget store, in Grand Forks, and additional SuperTarget stores in Florida, Georgia, Nebraska, and Texas. Target.com instituted a new technology platform to increase the functionality and scalability of its Web site. **July 29:** Second-quarter profits rose 13 percent, led by sales of private-label products at Target Stores. In **August** Standard & Poor's raised its ratings on several types of Target Corp. debt and called the outlook for Target stable. Target then announced plans to issue $500 million in debt, which was rated A2 by Moody's and A by Standard & Poor's, for general corporate purposes. Target.com significantly expanded its online merchandise selection, adding thousands of new products for the whole family. The new apparel collection, for instance, enabled guests to get the most-wanted fashions in all of the Target-owned brands, including Cherokee and Merona, and more unique, trendier items like toggle cargo pants and denim jackets. Dayton's Commercial Interiors purchased Rowley-Schlimgen Inc., a provider of office furnishings, products, and services in central Wisconsin and northern Illinois. Target Stores and America Online Inc. (NYSE: AOL), the world's leading interactive services company, the rolled out a joint marketing and promotion initiatives. CD-ROMs featuring a special edition of the AOL service, with co-branded features and packaging, were made available at more than 900 Target stores nationwide. Target launched http://www.target.etrade.com, a co-branded financial services Web site between Target Stores and E*TRADE Group Inc. "We know through our popular registry services, Club Wedd and Lullaby Club, that Target guests trust our products to support them in major life events," said Jerry Storch, president of financial services and new businesses for Target Corp. "We also want to support our guests as they prepare financially for those life events." **Aug. 26:** Net retail sales for the four weeks increased 7.5 percent to $2.742 billion. Comparable-store sales increased 2.5 percent. "Sales for the corporation were slightly below plan in the month of August," said CEO Ulrich. "In light of current business trends and the strength of last year's results, we now expect earnings per share to decline somewhat in the third quarter. We expect our growth in earnings per share to resume in the fourth quarter and we remain confident in our ability to deliver average annual earnings per share growth of 15 percent over time, despite our outlook for lower double-digit growth in fiscal 2000." In **September** target.com significantly expanded its online merchandise selection to include Target exclusives Michael Graves electronics, Philips appliances, and Sonia Kashuk beauty products. In **October** a report was circulating that French company Carrefour, the world's No. 2 retailer behind Wal-Mart, was interested in acquiring Target as its entry into the U.S. market. Target was to begin selling Visor handheld computers, accessories, and Springboard expansion modules under a distribution agreement with Handspring Inc. (Nasdaq: HAND). At month's end, Target launched a brand-reinforcing redesign of its flagship Web site, target.com. **Oct. 28:** Net retail sales for the four weeks increased 9.1 percent from a year ago, to $2.639 billion. Comparable-store sales increased 3.5 percent. "Sales for the corporation were slightly better than plan during October, driven by stronger-than-expected sales at Mervyn's," said Ulrich. "Sales at Target were essentially on plan for the month, while sales at our Department Stores were below plan in October."

The Toro Company

continued from page 364 neering efforts as our divisions and departments began to refocus on process improvement and expense management." In **August** Toro's restructuring of its problem-plagued irrigation division resulted in a reduction in staff. In **September** Toro announced a multiyear agreement with Hazeltine National Golf Club, site of the 2002 PGA Championship, establishing Toro as the official supplier of turf-maintenance equipment and irrigation systems. In **October** subsidiary Lawn-Boy Inc. recalled some power mowers because of safety problems. There were reports that wear caused by the mulch fan could cause the mowers' blades to crack, break off, and fly out from the machine.Toro obtained a settlement of a 1999 patent lawsuit against Ariens Co., Stens Co., and Rotary Corp. over replacement mower blades.

Touch America Inc.

continued from page 365 third party. In **March 2000**, after careful review of options and strategies, The Montana Power Co. announced plans to divest the company's multiple energy businesses—separating them from Montana Power's telecommunications unit, Touch America. The energy businesses included Montana Power's electricity and natural gas transmission and distribution utilities; coal mining; oil and natural gas production, processing, and marketing; and independent power production. Touch America is the surviving company, with its shares held directly by Montana Power shareholders. The board's decision was based on the following conclusions: — Because energy and telecommunications are very different businesses, the company's present structure cannot meet the demands of both and ensure the full success of each one. — The complete attention of the management team is needed in order to continue to aggressively grow Touch America's national fiber-optic and wireless networks, including increasing traffic and revenue and building brand awareness. — In this fast-paced and rapidly-changing business climate, opportunities must be acted upon with urgency, requiring organizational structures that are focused and less complicated than Montana Power's present structure. — Finally, the realities of size and scale in energy and telecom cannot be ignored. As time goes on, without separation, the whole will be less than the sum of the parts, adversely affecting employees, customers, communities, and shareholders. In **May** Sierra Pacific Communications (SPC), a subsidiary of Sierra Pacific Resources (NYSE: SRP), and Touch America formed a partnership called Sierra Touch America LLC to construct a new 750-mile fiber-optic network between Sacramento, Calif., and Salt Lake City. Touch America and Williams Communications (NYSE: WCG) executed a definitive agreement to exchange dark fiber on high-speed, long-haul fiber-optic routes connecting key cities in the central part of the country. In **June** the FCC approved Touch America's acquisition of Qwest Communications' long-distance and related telephone business within the 14-state U S West region. (This action completed formal FCC review of Qwest's merger with U S West.) On June 30, Touch America's president Mike Meldahl said, "The transaction has been completed and what was Qwest's long-distance voice and data traffic in the U S West region now is flowing on Touch America's network." In **July** Touch America's Personal Communication Services (PCS) joint venture with Qwest Wireless began operations in Spokane, Wash., and Boise, Idaho. In **August** the company filed with the Public Service Commission (PSC) a combined electric and natural gas utility rate increase request to account for higher transmission and distribution costs to serve customers, and to maintain the financial stability of the energy-delivery systems. The company agreed to sell for US $475 million its nonregulated oil and gas business unit to PanCanadian Petroleum Ltd. of Calgary (Toronto: PCP), one of Canada's largest producers and marketers of crude oil, natural gas, and gas liquids. [Deal completed at the end of October.] In **September** privately held BBI Power Corp. agreed to acquire Montana Power's independent power business for $84.5 million in cash. **Sept. 30:** An 80 percent increase in Touch America's telecommunication income from operations in the third quarter helped consolidated earnings, but higher energy costs and related adverse impacts due to drought, plant outages, and wildfires resulted in third-quarter earnings of $0.23 per share, compared to $0.26 per share in prior year. In **October** NorthWestern Corp. (NYSE: NOR), a $5 billion-revenue energy and communications company, finalized a definitive agreement to acquire Montana Power's electric and natural gas utility business for $1.1 billion, which included $488 million in existing Montana Power debt. "In evaluating potential bidders, we said we would examine a broad range of factors, including, but not limited to, financial strength, operating experience to preserve reliable electricity and natural gas service, reputation for fair dealing with customers and employees, and the ability to finalize any transactions," Gannon said. "NorthWestern's stellar track record and reputation clearly meets our objectives." Gannon added that Montana Power had in place agreements to sell not only its utility business, but also its nonregulated businesses in oil and natural gas, coal, and independent power production. "The cash proceeds from these sales, totaling some $1.3 billion, will be reinvested in Touch America, our telecommunications subsidiary, which is a national long-haul broadband data, voice and video transport company," Gannon said. "This is our future and focus." In **November** Touch America announced that it was building a fiber-optic network along the Illinois State Toll Highway Authority's rights-of-way in northern Illinois and the tunnels and tracks of the Chicago Transit Authority to enhance its ability to provide high-speed, broadband fiber-optic service connectivity for five distinct network routes into Chicago.

Tower Automotive Inc.

continued from page 366 Development (Westland, Mich.), to provide product testing services, primarily to Tower. In **May** Tower acquired all of the outstanding common stock of $53 million-revenue Algoods Inc. for $33 million. Algoods manufactures aluminum heat shields and impact discs for the North American automotive industry from aluminum mini-mill and manufacturing operations located in Toronto. Its primary customer is DaimlerChrysler. Tower told 400 Milwaukee employees at a plant that makes truck frames for the Ford Ranger that it planned to move production to the Twin Cities to be closer to Ford's Ranger assembly plant in St. Paul. The board of directors approved the purchase of up to $100 million of shares of the company's common stock from time to time, if authorized by the executive committee of the board. In **July** Tower acquired the remaining 60 percent equity interest in Metalurgica Caterina S.A., a supplier of structural stampings and assemblies to the Brazilian automotive market, for $42 million. (Tower had acquired the initial 40 percent equity interest in March 1998.) Subsidiary R.J. Tower Corp. completed an offering of Euro 150 million of senior notes in a private placement. The company replaced its existing credit facility with a new six-year $1.15 billion senior unsecured agreement. In **August** the announced Ford Explorer and Ranger production cuts and the further weakening of the heavy-truck market were expected to reduce third-quarter earnings by $0.03 to $0.05 per share. Tower agreed to pay $38 million to acquire a 17 percent equity interest in Yorozu Corp., a supplier of suspension modules and structural parts to the Japan, Thailand, Mexico, and United States automotive markets, from Nissan Motor Co. Ltd. The $643 million-revenue Yorozu, based in Japan, is publicly traded on the first tier of the Tokyo Stock Exchange. Its principle customers include Nissan, Auto Alliance,

General Motors, Ford, and Honda. Yorozu employs more than 3,300 and operates from six manufacturing facilities located in close proximity to its major customers. **Sept. 30:** For both the third quarter of 2000 and 1999, revenue was $536 million. However, operating income declined 42 percent to $28 million from the $48 million reported in prior year. "Our third-quarter results were impacted by volume declines associated with the Ranger and Explorer programs, heavy-truck sales declines, new product launches, and schedule disruptions created by irregular releases from our customers," explained Campbell. "These conditions have offset a portion of the gains made during the first six months to bring our nine-month results for 2000 to approximately the same level as the results of the comparable 1999 period." In **October** Tower agreed to sell its Roanoke, Va., heavy truck rail manufacturing business to its joint venture partner, Metalsa S. de R.L., for $55 million in cash plus an earnout to Tower of up to $30 million based upon Metalsa heavy truck achieving certain profit levels over the next three years. (Tower Automotive has a 40 percent ownership position in Metalsa S. de R.L., a privately owned company headquartered in Monterrey, Mexico.) In addition, Tower announced plans to phase out its heavy truck rail manufacturing and related activities in Milwaukee by March 2001; and to reduce its stamping capacity and consolidating related support activities. "The decision to exit the heavy truck rail business reflects our intent to focus our investments and efforts on growing our light vehicle structures and modules business around the world," said CEO Campbell. "The consolidation of stamping production reflects our efforts to more effectively utilize our capacity."

Tricord Systems Inc.

continued from page 368 in a unique position to build a true click-and-mortar infrastructure for the 21st century, to match the way we do business to our technological leadership." **Sept. 30**: The nine-month loss from continuing operations was $8.762 million, compared to a loss of $5.631 million for the same period in 1999. The losses reflected the ongoing development of the company's revolutionary new server appliances and the related building of infrastructure. In **October** a new strategic relationship with Linuxcare, a leader in providing comprehensive professional services and solutions for Linux and open-source software, had Linuxcare providing Linux consulting, testing, integration, and development services for Tricord's line of revolutionary server appliances and for Samba, an open-source network file system protocol.

U.S. Bancorp

U.S. Bank Place, 601 Second Ave. S., P.O. Box 522 (55480), Minneapolis, MN 55402
Tel: 612/973-1111 Fax: 612/973-2446 Web site: http://www.usbank.com

U.S. Bancorp, the ninth-largest bank holding company in the nation, operates approximately 1,000 banking offices in the Midwest and West. The company provides comprehensive banking, trust, investment and payment systems products and services to consumers, businesses, and institutions. It operates a network of 5,000 ATMs and provides 24-hour, seven-day-a-week telephone customer service. The company offers full-service brokerage services at approximately 100 offices in the West and Midwest through U.S. Bancorp Piper Jaffray. The company is the largest provider of Visa corporate and purchasing cards in the world, and one of the largest providers of corporate trust services in the nation. *continued on page 375*

EARNINGS HISTORY *

Year Ended Dec 31	Operating Revenue/Sales (dollars in thousands)	Net Earnings	Return on Revenue (percent)	Return on Equity	Net Earnings (dollars per share†)	Cash Dividend	Market Price Range
1999 ¶	8,435,400	1,506,500	17.9	19.7	2.07	0.78	38.06–21.88
1998 #	7,664,000	1,327,400	17.3	22.2	1.81	0.70	47.31–25.63
1997 **	6,908,800	838,500	12.1	14.1	1.13	0.62	38.88–22.50
1996 ††	6,891,500	1,218,700	17.7	20.8	1.60	0.55	24.67–15.33
1995 ##	6,234,100	897,100	14.4	16.4	1.19	0.48	17.92–10.88

* Figures (exc. dividends) restated for poolings, including U.S. Bancorp of Portland, Ore. No adjustments have yet been made to account for proposed merger with Firstar Corp.
† Per-share amounts restated to reflect 3-for-1 stock split paid May 18, 1998.
¶ Income figures for 1999 include pretax charge of $62.4 million for merger, integration, and resizing.
# Income figures for 1998 include pretax charge of $216.5 million for merger, integration, and resizing.
** Income figures for 1997 include pretax charge of $511.6 million for merger, integration, and resizing.
†† Figures for 1996 include results of FirsTier Financial Inc., Omaha, Neb., from its Feb. 16, 1996, date of purchase. Revenue figure includes $190 million termination fee and $65 million state income tax refund. Income figures include pretax SAIF special assessment of $61.3 million and pretax charge of $88.1 million for merger, integration, and resizing.
Income figures for 1995 include pretax charge of $98.9 million for merger, integration, and resizing.

BALANCE SHEET

Assets	12/31/99 (dollars in thousands)	12/31/98
Cash, due fm banks	4,036,000	4,772,000
Federal funds sold	713,000	83,000
Securities purchased to resell	324,000	461,000
Trading securities	617,000	537,000
Available-for-sale securities	4,871,000	5,577,000
Net loans	61,890,000	58,121,000
Bank premises, eqt	862,000	879,000
Interest receivable	433,000	456,000
Customers' liability	152,000	166,000
Goodwill, intangibles	3,066,000	1,975,000
Other	4,566,000	3,411,000
TOTAL	81,530,000	76,438,000

Liabilities	12/31/99 (dollars in thousands)	12/31/98
Non-brng deposits	16,050,000	16,377,000
Int-brng deposits	35,480,000	33,657,000
Fed funds purchased	297,000	1,255,000
Securities sold to repurchase	1,235,000	1,427,000
Other borrowings	724,000	683,000
Long-term debt	16,563,000	13,781,000
Company-obligated securities	950,000	950,000
Acceptances	152,000	166,000
Other	2,441,000	2,172,000
Stkhldrs' equity*	7,638,000	5,970,000
TOTAL	81,530,000	76,438,000

* $1.25 par common; 1,500,000,000 authorized; 754,368,668 and 744,797,857 issued and outstanding, less 1,038,456 and 19,036,139 treasury shares.

RECENT QUARTERS / **PRIOR-YEAR RESULTS**

	Quarter End	Revenue ($000)	Earnings ($000)	EPS ($)	Revenue ($000)	Earnings ($000)	EPS ($)
Q3	09/30/2000	2,547,300	401,300	0.54	2,164,400	396,400	0.55
Q2	06/30/2000	2,456,400	393,100	0.53	2,040,800	374,300	0.52
Q1	03/31/2000	2,359,000	379,000	0.51	1,978,300	366,800	0.51
Q4	12/31/99	2,251,900	369,000	0.50	1,983,000	349,200	0.48
	SUM	9,614,600	1,542,400	2.08	8,166,500	1,486,700	2.05

CURRENT: Q1 earnings include nonrecurring charge of $8.6 million/($0.01). Q4 earnings include nonrecurring charge of $16.1 million/($0.02).
PRIOR YEAR: Q3 earnings include nonrecurring charge of $10.5 million/($0.01). Q2 earnings include nonrecurring charge of $9.5 million/($0.01). Q1 earnings include nonrecurring charge of $1.8 million/($0.00). Q4 earnings include nonrecurring charge of $28.1 million/($0.04).

OFFICERS

John F. (Jack) Grundhofer
Chairman, President, and CEO

Gary T. Duim
Vice Chairman

Richard A. Zona
Vice Chairman

John M. Murphy Jr.
EVP and Chm.-U.S. Bank for Minnesota

Andrew Cecere
Vice Chairman and CFO

Andrew S. Duff
VChair-Wealth Mmgt.; Pres.-Piper Jaffray

J. Robert Hoffmann
EVP and Chief Credit Officer

Lee R. Mitau
Corporate Development and Gen. Counsel

Daniel C. Rohr
VChair-Corporate Banking

Robert H. Sayre
EVP-Human Resources

Daniel W. Yohannes
VChair-Consumer Banking

Daniel J. Frate
VChair-Payment Systems

Peter G. Michielutti
EVP Information Services

Kent V. Stone
Branch Channel

R. Todd Firebaugh
EVP-Corporate Management Office

James L. Chosy
VP, Associate Gen. Counsel, Secretary

Christian R. Rasmussen
Business Banking

Daniel M. Quinn
VChair-Commercial Banking/Real Estate

DIRECTORS

Linda L. Ahlers
Target Corp., Minneapolis

Harry L. Bettis
rancher, Payette, ID

Arthur D. Collins Jr.
Medtronic Inc., Fridley, MN

Peter H. Coors
Coors Brewing Co., Golden, CO

Robert L. Dryden
The Boeing Co., Seattle

Joshua Green III
Joshua Green Corp., Seattle

John F. (Jack) Grundhofer

Delbert W. Johnson
Pioneer Metal Finishing Co., Minneapolis

Joel W. Johnson
Hormel Foods Corp., Austin, MN

Jerry W. Levin
Sunbeam Corp., Boca Raton, FL

Edward Jay Phillips
Phillips Beverage Co., Minneapolis

Paul A. Redmond
Avista Corp. (retired)

Richard G. Reiten
Northwest Natural Gas Co., Portland, OR

S. Walter Richey
Meritex Inc., Minneapolis

Warren R. Staley
Cargill Inc., Minnetonka, MN

MAJOR SHAREHOLDERS

All officers and directors as a group (31 persons), 4.2%

SIC CODE

6022 State commercial banks
6111 Federal and fed-sponsored credit agencies
6162 Mortgage bankers and correspondents
6411 Insurance agents, brokers, and service
6712 Bank holding companies

MISCELLANEOUS

TRANSFER AGENT AND REGISTAR:
First Chicago Trust Co. of New York, Jersey City, NJ
TRADED: NYSE
SYMBOL: USB
STOCKHOLDERS: 38,104
EMPLOYEES: 26,891
GENERAL COUNSEL:
Dorsey & Whitney PLLP, Minneapolis
AUDITORS:
Ernst & Young LLP, Minneapolis
INC: DE-1929
ANNUAL MEETING: April
INVESTOR RELATIONS:
John R. Danielson
HUMAN RESOURCES:
Robert H. Sayre

RANKINGS

No. 7 CRM Public 200
No. 13 CRM Employer 100
No. 24 CRM Performance 100

TWO-YEAR QUARTERLY HIGH-LOW STOCK PRICES

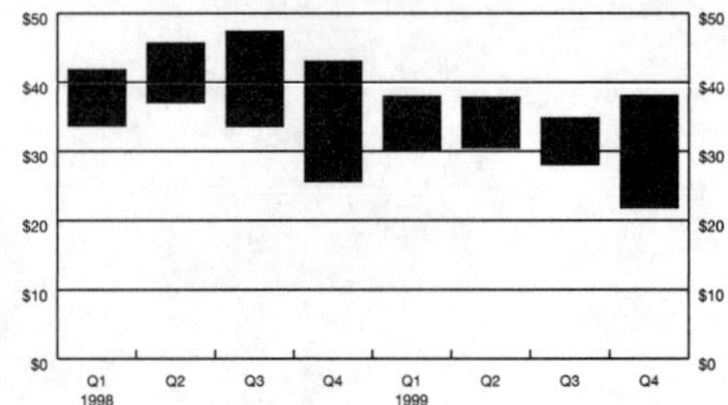

SELECT SUBSIDIARIES, DIVISIONS, AFFILIATES

U.S. Bancorp Piper Jaffray Inc. (1)
800 Nicollet Mall, S. 800
Minneapolis, MN 55402
612/303-6000
Andrew Duff

U.S. Bank N.A. (1)
First Bank Wrigley Bldg.
410 N. Michigan Ave.
Chicago, IL 60611
Larry Lewton

U.S. Bank (1)
1515 Arapahoe St.
Denver, CO 80202
303/820-5301
Robert Malone

U.S. Bank Aspen (1)
420 E. Main St.
Aspen, CO 81611
303/925-1450
Jaylene Park

FBS Card Services Inc. (1)
601 Second Ave. S.
Minneapolis, MN 55402
612/973-2059
David Ingraham

U.S. Bancorp Information Services Inc. (1)
1200 Energy Park Dr.
St. Paul, MN 55108
612/973-1111

U.S. Bank N.A. (1)
U.S. Bank Place
601 Second Ave. S.
Minneapolis, MN 55402
612/973-1111

U.S. Bancorp Investments (2)
Opus Building, 14th Floor
100 S. Fifth St.
Minneapolis, MN 55402
612/973-3600

Republic Acceptance Corp. (2)
2338 Central Ave. N.E.
Minneapolis, MN 55418
612/782-1828

U.S. Bank (N.A.) (1)
U.S. Bank Milwaukee
201 W. Wisconsin Ave.
Milwaukee, WI 53259
414/227-6000

U.S. Bank Montana N.A. (1)
U.S. Bank Billings
303 N. Broadway
Billings, MT 59101
406/657-8000
Phil Woodend

U.S. Bank fsb (1)
U.S. Bank Bismarck
200 N. Third St.
Bismarck, ND 58501
701/222-6300

U.S. Bank of South Dakota (N.A.) (1)
Sioux Falls, SD 57117
605/339-8600

U.S. Bank (1)
303 Third St. N.W.
East Grand Forks, MN
56721
218/733-1166

First System Agencies (1)

FBS Life Insurance Co. (2)
16 Ninth Ave. N.
Hopkins, MN 55343
612/936-5820

U.S. Bank Trust N.A. (1)
180 E. Fifth St.
St. Paul, MN 55101
612/244-6000

PUB

RECENT EVENTS

In **December 1999** U.S. Bancorp announced that strategic investments, combined with lower-than-expected fourth quarter revenue, would result in reduced earnings growth. For the quarter, EPS was expected to be 10 percent below current consensus estimates; for fiscal year 2000, 5 percent below. (On the news, USB stock dropped 27 percent to $25.625, its sharpest fall in five years.) Revenue growth for the fourth quarter was being affected by flat net interest income, as a result of higher loan-funding costs and lower-than-expected growth in higher-spread consumer loans. Higher expenses—reflecting investments in the areas of sales and service, technology, and marketing—were also a factor. "Investments to accelerate growth have also tempered our year 2000 expectations," said CEO Grundhofer. "This past August we named a new management team drawn from an internal pool of talented executives who have the charter to make us an increasingly customer-centered company." To achieve that, it would be necessary to fund such improvements as increasing the number of tellers, telephone bank representatives, small-business bankers, and branches, and installing new branch technology—hurting short-term results. In addition, the company was taking deliberate steps to change its business mix to achieve higher-growth revenue streams. Over the next five years, investments in the higher-growth Payment Systems and Wealth Management businesses are expected to increase their contribution to 45 percent of company earnings—from the current 30 percent. On succeeding days, USB stock continued its decline as analysts downgraded earnings estimates and some ratings. U.S. Bank agreed to pay $3.8 million in back wages to 2,815 employees at its 786 branches in 17 states in an agreement with the U.S. Department of Labor regarding overtime pay for employees classified as personal bankers. U.S. Bancorp Insurance Services, in partnership with Great-West Life & Annuity Insurance Co., launched a new online insurance product allowing instant life insurance coverage. **Dec. 31:** Record fourth-quarter operating earnings of $385.1 million/$0.52, up 2 percent from prior year, were still at the low end of revised estimates. U.S. Bancorp Piper Jaffray led the nation in 1999 in the number of bond issues senior managed (537) and, for the first time, ranked among the top 10 investment banks in the country for total par value of issues ($5.2 billion, an increase of 33 percent from 1998). In **January 2000** USB and Harley-Davidson Inc. (NYSE: HDI) announced a strategic alliance under which U.S. Bank was to acquire and manage Harley-Davidson Financial Services' affinity card program, the Harley-Davidson Chrome Visa. U.S. Bancorp Piper Jaffray was set to begin offering online trading on March 1. In **February** Staples Inc. (Nasdaq: SPLS), in partnership with U.S. Bancorp (NYSE: USB), launched a Visa Business Card, the first such credit card offered by an office supplies retailer and one of the only business cards to offer rewards with no annual fee. The board of directors authorized the repurchase of up to $2.5 billion (17 percent) of the company's common stock over a two-year period ending March 31, 2002. George K. Baum & Co. raised its rating on shares of USB to STRONG BUY from BUY, with a 12-month price target of $30. In **March** USB agreed to acquire Oliver-Allen Corp., a Larkspur, Calif.-based, privately held information technology leasing company. By the end of the month, USB had notified its 6.5 million customers about the most comprehensive privacy policy of any major bank in the nation. U.S. Bancorp was the first major financial services firm to have completed this mailing, well in advance of when all banks were required to make such disclosures under the recently-enacted federal Gramm-Leach-Bliley Act. "This puts us at the forefront of protecting the privacy of customers' financial information," said CEO Grundhofer. "While many other banks and financial services companies are still reviewing and updating their privacy policies, we've already given all of our customers clear written notice of what our policy is, how we protect their private information, and how they can opt out of direct marketing programs." **March 31:** Unlike its last report, the company's first-quarter results came in about as expected—with a 5 percent increase in operating earnings, to 52 cents a share. U.S. Bancorp Piper Jaffray grew its equity underwriting business exponentially, increasing its number of equity offerings by 254 percent over first quarter 1999 (vs. 76 percent for the investment banking industry as a whole)—and ranking third for number of IPOs and ninth in number of equity offerings among the nation's 110 investment banks. In **April** U.S. Bancorp Piper Jaffray formed a new "fund of funds" to provide institutional and high-net-worth investors the opportunity to invest in a diversified mix of private equity funds and direct investments. The new $200 million fund, U.S. Bancorp Piper Jaffray Private Equity Partners I L.P., was to provide investors access to 15 to 20 premiere venture capital funds, as well as established private equity buyout funds, most of which are only available to their existing investor group and select institutional investors. A new collaboration between U.S. Bank and AMA Solutions, a subsidiary of the American Medical Association, made U.S. Bank CreditLines and Home Equity Lines available to AMA members at special prices and with features designed for the specific needs of physicians. U.S. Bancorp received permission to bid on $809 million of Los Angeles municipal-bond business after bank officials agreed to open inner-city branches and maje other investments in low-income neighborhoods. A shareholder proposal—that the board change its directors' terms from three years to one—garnered 49.7 percent of the votes, narrowly failing to pass. U.S. Bancorp Piper Jaffray won a $360,000 arbitration award from rival Dain Rauscher Inc. over the 1998 departure of top stockbrokers from Piper's Duluth office. U.S. Bancorp Piper Jaffray launched www.gotoanalysts.com—giving investors free access to its institutional-quality and insightful industry research from all of its senior equity research analysts covering the technology, health care, consumer, financial institutions, and industrial growth sectors. The 2000 Reuters Survey named four U.S. Bancorp Piper Jaffray equity research analysts among the top 10 in the nation for the quality of their coverage in their respective industries: Senior Analyst Allan Hickok in the restaurant industry, Senior Analysts Rebecca Yarchover and Brent Rystrom in the retail industry and Senior Analyst Michael Grondahl in the electrical equipment industry. The U.S. Bank Kroger Visa card was named one of the three best rebate Visa credit card in the country by Kiplinger's Personal Finance magazine. Remedy Corp. (Nasdaq: RMDY), the world's leading provider of eCRM and eBusiness Infrastructure solutions announced an alliance to integrate U.S. Bank's payment products and processes with Remedy's eProcurement solution. LiveCapital.com, the leading business-to-business e-marketplace for small-business financing, announced an agreement with U.S. Bank to offer business credit cards over the Internet. U.S. Bancorp and Albertson's Inc., Boise, Idaho, launched the Albertson's Sav-on Visa, a new co-branded credit card, to Albertson's Northern California retail food and drug store customers. Royal Bank (NYSE: RY; TSE), Toronto, was to join forces with USB to offer co-branded commercial charge cards to businesses and multinational corporations based in Canada and the United States. In **May** U.S. Bancorp and U.S. Bancorp Piper Jaffray hosted the Grand Opening of the nation's most technologically advanced equities trading floor—surpassing even Wall Street in communications technology—at the new U.S. Bancorp Center. Representatives from the building's architectural firm, Ellerbe Becket, and its construction company, Ryan Cos., were also on hand. U.S. Bancorp Piper Jaffray and Harris Interactive (Nasdaq: HPOL), a leading Internet-based market research firm, joined forces to provide investors with valuable information on consumer e-commerce trends. Two former Piper brokers and a current one brought a sex-discrimination suit against the firm in federal court in San Francisco alleging that Piper's male-dominated workplace systematicaly denies woman brokers equal opportunities and pay. Piper, which has no-tolerance policies in place, denied the allegations. The U.S. Postal Service awarded Payment Systems a two-year task order, with two one-year options, to provide a comprehensive national fleet card program for its fleet of 170,000 vehicles. New services from U.S. Bancorp Piper Jaffray—Prime Account and the Premier investment program—allow investors to make deposits and withdrawals in their brokerage accounts at U.S. Bank branches and ATMs; permit unlimited online stock trades; and come with a debit card, checks, and automatic sweeps of spare cash into a money market fund. In **June** U.S. Bank announced the launch of U.S. Bank Image Check Web, an Internet-based check image retrieval service for businesses that provides daily access to images of paid checks via the Internet. The company agreed to acquire $650 million-asset Scripps Financial Corp., San Diego, for $155 million in stock. [Deal completed in October.] At month's end, USB and Pitney Bowes Inc. (NYSE: PBI), through its subsidiary Pitney Bowes Credit Corp., announced a strategic alliance under which U.S. Bank was to acquire and service the PitneyWorks Business Rewards Visa and Business Visa card portfolios. **June 30:** U.S. Bancorp Piper Jaffray's Equity Capital Markets Division significantly increased its equity offering volume, ending the second quarter with an 85 percent increase year-over-year (72 vs. 39) in the number of equity offerings completed. Capital raised from equity offerings increased from $3.363 billion in 1999 through second quarter to $12.138 billion year-to-date. Initial public offerings (IPOs) were up 42.3 percent year over year. In **July** U.S. Bancorp Piper Jaffray advised Churchill Capital, Minneapolis, in the sale of Lindsay, Calif.-based National Diversified Sales Inc., a leading manufacturer of high-quality, proprietary irrigation and drainage products, to an investor group led by Graham Partners. By signing a nonbinding letter of intent with project developer Opus Corp., U.S. Bancorp began a process that could result in the construction of a $55 million client service center in the West Side River Flats area of St. Paul, between Wabasha and Robert streets. The city was expected to work with the bank to create a mixed-use "urban village," with offices, townhouses, and stores. About 750 bank jobs and 750 housing units were expected there. The company revised its profit forecast downward for the second time in seven months, saying that higher EPS growth was going to take longer to achieve than previously expected. The new earnings estimate: between $2.18 and $2.23 per share. U.S. Bancorp Piper Jaffray moved up six spots in the 2000 Wall Street Journal All-Star Analysts Survey, which ranked 472 analysts from 82 securities firms. In **August** the company appointed a chief privacy officer, Patricia Bauer, making her one of only a handful of executives in the nation to be charged specifically with guarding customer privacy. U.S. Bancorp became the first bank in the country to join the Privacy Leadership Initiative, a coalition of more than 20 corporate CEOs working to address consumers' concerns about privacy. U.S. Bancorp Piper Jaffray's online investment sites ranked in the top five on Gomez's first-ever Internet Full-Service Broker Scorecard. (Gomez, a leading e-commerce authority for both consumers and e-businesses, rated investor Web sites across the country based 100 or more objective criteria.) New: U.S. Bank Visa Buxx, a parent-authorized, re-loadable, prepaid payment card that helps teach teens financial responsibility while providing a safe alternative to cash. U.S. Bank's Student Banking Division launched two new online loans—the U.S. Bank Gap Education Loan and the U.S. Bank Graduate Education Loan—for financing college and graduate education. U.S. Bank installed Minnesota's first voice-

PUB

United Financial Corporation

120 First Ave. N., P.O. Box 2779, Great Falls, MT 59403
Tel: 406/727-6106 Fax: 406/761-5798 Web site: http://www.heritagemontana.com

United Financial Corp. is a bank holding company headquartered in Great Falls, Mont., with operations in 11 other Montana communities. Substantially all of United's banking business is conducted through its wholly owned subsidiaries Heritage Bank F.S.B. and Heritage State Bank, a banking subsidiary. United had assets of approximately $349.8 million, deposits of $242.8 million, and shareholders' equity of $29.3 million at June 30, 2000. United is now the majority shareholder of Valley Bancorp Inc.

EARNINGS HISTORY *

Year Ended Dec 31	Operating Revenue/Sales (dollars in thousands)	Net Earnings	Return on Revenue (percent)	Return on Equity	Net Earnings (dollars per share)	Cash Dividend	Market Price Range
1999	20,871	2,469	11.8	8.4	1.47	—	24.13–16.75
1998	17,541	2,267	12.9	7.4	1.43	—	31.50–19.00
1997 †	7,988	1,352	16.9	5.5	1.10	0.97	27.00–18.75
1996	8,087	1,103	13.6	4.5	0.90	0.89	19.75–17.50
1995	7,988	1,722	21.6	7.0	1.41	0.81	18.25–15.50

* On Feb. 3, 1998, the company completed a merger with Heritage Bancorp., which was the accounting acquiror. However, historical information displayed here is still that of the former United Financial.
† Pro forma 1997 figures for combined companies: revenue $14,729,000; earnings $1,892,000/$1.11; total assets $184,168,000.

BALANCE SHEET

Assets	12/31/99 (dollars in thousands)	12/31/98	Liabilities	12/31/99 (dollars in thousands)	12/31/98
Cash and equivalents	11,457	19,256	Deposits: interest-bearing	161,131	148,725
Securities available-for-sale	53,044	51,900	Deposits: noninterest-bearing	18,751	18,895
Net loans receivable	186,348	143,359	FHLB advances	46,425	22,175
Loans held for sale	1,191	5,717	Securities sold to repuchase	11,546	9,451
Stock in FHLB of Seattle	3,046	1,232	Advance payments by borrowers	408	343
Accrued interest receivable	2,259	1,918	Income taxes payable	476	116
Premises and equipment	4,873	3,482	Accrued interest payable	1,528	1,267
Real estate owned	14	304	Accrued expenses and other	602	1,062
Deferred income taxes	740	102	Stockholders' equity*	29,359	30,528
Investment in Valley Bancorp Inc.	4,549	2,684	TOTAL	270,226	232,561
Goodwill	1,289	1,400			
Intangibles	537	607			
Other	879	600			
TOTAL	270,226	232,561			

* No par common; 8,000,000 authorized; 1,698,312 and 1,698,312 issued and outstanding, less 46,000 treasury shares.

RECENT QUARTERS / **PRIOR-YEAR RESULTS**

	Quarter End	Revenue ($000)	Earnings ($000)	EPS ($)	Revenue ($000)	Earnings ($000)	EPS ($)
Q3	09/30/2000	7,721	633	0.38	5,423	644	0.38
Q2	06/30/2000	7,253	607	0.37	5,131	624	0.37
Q1	03/31/2000	6,673	559	0.34	4,760	573	0.34
Q4	12/31/99	5,557	628	0.38	5,034	604	0.36
	SUM	27,204	2,427	1.47	20,348	2,445	1.44

RECENT EVENTS

In **June 2000** the company filed with the Federal Deposit Insurance Corp. and the Montana Division of Banking and Financial Institutions to merge its thrift subsidiary, Heritage Bank fsb, into Heritage State Bank, its state charter commercial bank. Survivor Heritage State Bank was then to change its name to Heritage Bank. Also, the board of directors of United approved a stock repurchase program of up to 100,000 shares (6 percent of the outstanding stock). **Sept. 30:** For the first nine months of 2000, United earned $1,798,932 before special one-time charges, compared to $1,841,350 in 1999. In addition to expenses relating to the forthcoming merger of subsidiary banks Heritage Bank and Heritage State Bank, third-quarter earnings included a special one-time addition to the loan loss reserve primarily related to the deterioration of a single loan. CEO Weise, stated, "Notwithstanding the increased loan loss provision, our earnings trend at the present time is positive."

OFFICERS

John M. Morrison
Chairman

Kurt R. Weise
President and CEO

Kevin P. Clark
SVP and Secretary

Steve L. Feurt
SVP and Chief Credit Officer

DIRECTORS

Larry D. Albert
Central Bank, Stillwater, MN

J. William Bloemendaal
Great Falls Orthopaedic Associates

Kevin P. Clark

Elliott L. Dybdal
Talcott Building Co.

Steve Feurt

Jerome H. Hentges
Central Bank, Stillwater, MN

William L. Madison
Johnson Madison Lumber Co.

John M. Morrison

Kurt R. Weise

MAJOR SHAREHOLDERS

John M. Morrison, 29.8%

Eighteen Seventy Financial Inc., 7.3%
Purchase, NY

All officers and directors as a group (10 persons), 39.3%

SIC CODE

6035 Federal savings institutions

MISCELLANEOUS

TRANSFER AGENT AND REGISTAR:
Davidson Trust Co., Great Falls, MT

TRADED: Nasdaq National Market

SYMBOL: UBMT

STOCKHOLDERS: 233

EMPLOYEES: 104

AUDITORS:
KPMG LLP, Billings, MT

ANNUAL MEETING: April

HUMAN RESOURCES:
Pat Compson

INVESTOR RELATIONS:
Kurt Weise

SUBSIDIARIES, DIVISIONS, AFFILIATES

Heritage Bank

Heritage State Bank

Community Service Corp.

TWO-YEAR QUARTERLY HIGH-LOW STOCK PRICES

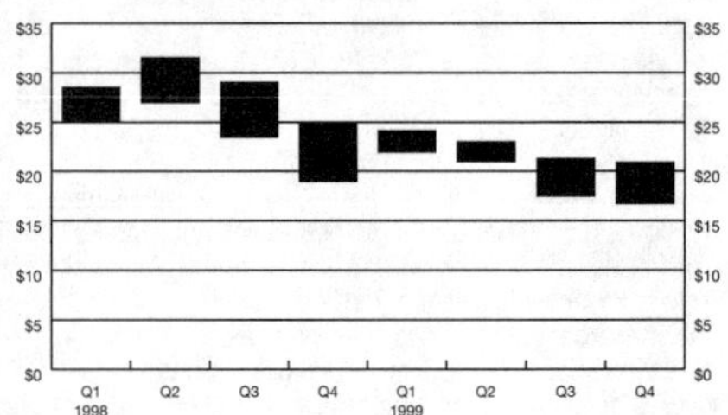

UnitedHealth Group

300 Opus Center, 9900 Bren Rd. E., P.O. Box 1459 (55440), Minnetonka, MN 55343
Tel: 952/936-1300 Fax: 952/936-5918 Web site: http://www.unitedhealthgroup.com

UnitedHealth Group is the nation's largest health care management services company, serving 40 million Americans through its operations in all 50 states and Puerto Rico. The company's services include HMOs, PPOs, point-of-service and health insurance products, managed mental health and substance abuse services, utilization management, workers' compensation and disability management services, specialized provider networks, employee-assistance services, Medicare and managed-care programs for the aged, third-party administration (TPA) services, health care evaluation services, information systems, and administrative services.

EARNINGS HISTORY

Year Ended Dec 31	Operating Revenue/Sales (dollars in thousands)	Net Earnings	Return on Revenue (percent)	Return on Equity	Net Earnings (dollars per share*)	Cash Dividend	Market Price Range
1999	19,562,000	568,000	2.9	14.7	1.63	0.02	35.00–19.69
1998 †	17,355,000	(166,000)	(1.0)	(5.3)	(0.56)	0.02	36.97–14.78
1997	11,794,000	460,000	3.9	9.5	1.15	0.02	30.06–21.22
1996 ¶	10,073,790	355,637	3.5	8.6	0.88	0.02	34.50–15.00
1995 #	5,670,878	285,964	5.0	8.7	0.79	0.02	32.81–17.06

* Per-share amounts restated to reflect 2-for-1 stock split on Dec. 22, 2000.
† Income figures for 1998 include charge of $900 million pretax, $704 million/($1.83) after-tax, for operational realignment and other special items.
¶ Income figures for 1996 include pretax merger costs of $14.968 million.
\# Income figures for 1995 include pretax restructuring charges of $153.796 milion. ROE, EPS are after preferred dividends.

BALANCE SHEET

Assets	12/31/99 (dollars in thousands)	12/31/98	Liabilities	12/31/99 (dollars in thousands)	12/31/98
Current (CAE 1,605,000 and 1,644,000)	4,568,000	4,254,000	Current (STD 591,000 and 459,000)	5,892,000	5,316,000
Long-term investments	2,568,000	2,610,000	Long-term debt	400,000	249,000
Property and equipment	278,000	294,000	Deferred income taxes and other	118,000	72,000
Goodwill and other intangibles	2,859,000	2,517,000	Stockholders' equity*	3,863,000	4,038,000
TOTAL	10,273,000	9,675,000	TOTAL	10,273,000	9,675,000

* $0.01 par common; 500,000,000 authorized; 334,940,000 and 367,860,000 issued and outstanding.

RECENT QUARTERS / PRIOR-YEAR RESULTS

	Quarter End	Revenue ($000)	Earnings ($000)	EPS ($)	Prior-Year Revenue ($000)	Prior-Year Earnings ($000)	Prior-Year EPS ($)
Q3	09/30/2000	5,369,000	182,000	0.56	4,903,000	144,000	0.41
Q2	06/30/2000	5,220,000	170,000	0.52	4,858,000	135,000	0.39
Q1	03/31/2000	5,099,000	174,000	0.53	4,809,000	132,000	0.36
Q4	12/31/99	4,992,000	157,000	0.46	4,645,000	132,000	0.28
	SUM	20,680,000	683,000	2.08	19,215,000	543,000	1.45

CURRENT: Q1 earnings include a net permanent tax benefit of $14 million/$0.04 related to the contribution of Healtheon Corp. common stock to the UnitedHealth Foundation. Q4 earnings include one-time tax benefit of $5 million/$0.01.
PRIOR YEAR: Q4 EPS includes charge of $20 million/($0.05) for preferred stock redemption premium.

RECENT EVENTS

In **January 2000** the company's stock was one of three in Minnesota among the 89 stocks that Goldman Sachs & Co. listed as its analysts' favorite stock picks for 2000. The listed stocks were expected to generate a 12-month price return of 35 percent, compared with an an expected gain of only 4 percent by the S&P 500 index. In **March** the American Medical Association filed a class-action suit against UnitedHealth subsidiary United Healthcare—alleging that it reduced payments to thousands of New York doctors (forcing patients to pay higher bills) by using invalid data to determine reimbursement rates. In **April** Ingenix released Clinical Care Groups, advanced episode-of-care grouping technology that included the industry's most comprehensive accounting of pharmaceutical data available. This tool creates episodes-of-care from health care claims data as a framework to evaluate the quality, outcomes, and cost-effectiveness of health care services. In **May** UnitedHealth Group, together with Cole Managed Vision, the managed care division of Cole Corp., introduced new services for AARP mem- *continued on page 404*

OFFICERS

William W. McGuire, M.D.
Chairman and CEO
Stephen J. Hemsley
President and COO
Robert J. Backes
SVP-Human Resources
Ronald B. Colby
CEO-Specialized Care Services
James B. Hudak
EVP and CEO-UnitedHealth Technologies
Arnold H. Kaplan
CFO
Paul F. LeFort
Chief Information Officer
David J. Lubben
Secretary and General Counsel
Kevin W. Pearson
CEO-Ingenix Health Information
John S. Penshorn
Dir.-Capital Markets
Lois Quam
CEO-Ovations
Jeannine M. Rivet
CEO-United HealthCare
Kevin H. Roche
CEO-Ingenix International
R. Channing Wheeler
CEO-Uniprise

DIRECTORS

William C. Ballard Jr.
Greenebaum, Doll & McDonald, Louisville, KY
Richard T. Burke
Phoenix Coyotes, Phoenix
Stephen J. Hemsley
James A. Johnson
Federal National Mortgage Association, Washington, D.C.
Thomas H. Kean
Drew University/State of New Jersey
Douglas W. Leatherdale
The St. Paul Cos. Inc., St. Paul
William W. McGuire, M.D.
Walter F. Mondale
Dorsey & Whitney LLP, Minneapolis
Mary O'Neil Mundinger, Dr.P.H.
Columbia University, New York
Robert L. Ryan
Medtronic Inc., Fridley, MN
William G. Spears
Spears, Benzak, Salomon & Farrell Inc., New York
Gail R. Wilensky
Project Hope, Washington, D.C.

MAJOR SHAREHOLDERS

Massachusetts Financial Services Co., 7.8%
Boston
FMR Corp., 7.2%
Boston
All officers and directors as a group (17 persons), 5.5%

SIC CODE

6324 Hospital and medical service plans
8099 Health and allied services, nec

MISCELLANEOUS

TRANSFER AGENT AND REGISTAR:
Wells Fargo Bank Minnesota N.A.,
South St. Paul, MN
TRADED: NYSE
SYMBOL: UNH
STOCKHOLDERS: 11,271
EMPLOYEES: 29,000
GENERAL COUNSEL:
Dorsey & Whitney PLLP, Minneapolis
AUDITORS:
Arthur Andersen LLP, Minneapolis
INC: MN-1977
FOUNDED: 1974
ANNUAL MEETING: May
HUMAN RESOURCES:
Robert Backes
INVESTOR RELATIONS:
John Penshorn

RANKINGS

No. 2 CRM Public 200
No. 43 CRM Employer 100
No. 25 CRM Performance 100

TWO-YEAR QUARTERLY HIGH-LOW STOCK PRICES

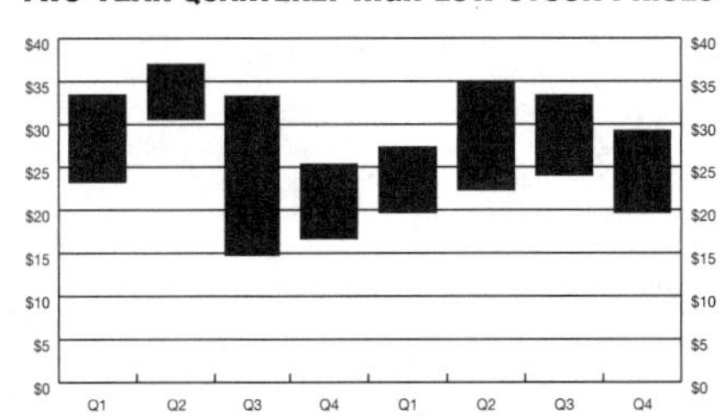

United Shipping & Technology Inc.

9850 51st Ave. N., Plymouth, MN 55442
Tel: 952/941-4080 Fax: 952/941-6440 Web site: http://www.u-ship.com

United Shipping & Technology Inc. (US&T), formerly U-Ship Inc., manufactures, markets, and operates self-service, automated shipping systems for use by consumers and small-business shippers who ship packages and priority letters through major carriers in the air express and package delivery market. The company's Automated Shipping Center (ASC) is a customer-operated, self-service, automated package shipping center located in selected 24-hour retail environments. The ASC features voice-prompted instructions, an interactive graphic interface, a variety of shipping options, and automatic package weighing. In September, when the company acquired Corporate Express Delivery Systems Inc. (renamed Velocity Express), US&T became the largest same-day delivery system and e-commerce distributor in the United States.

EARNINGS HISTORY

Year Ended Jun 30	Operating Revenue/Sales (dollars in thousands)	Net Earnings	Return on Revenue (percent)	Return on Equity	Net Earnings (dollars per share*)	Cash Dividend	Market Price Range
2000 †	471,152	(28,212)	(6.0)	NM	(2.27)	—	17.69–2.63
1999 ¶	1,483	(2,894)	NM	NM	(0.42)	—	4.25–0.63
1998	953	(1,901)	NM	(59.4)	(0.38)	—	2.38–0.16
1997	918	(2,528)	NM	NM	(0.61)	—	3.63–1.00
1996	713	(2,184)	NM	(67.4)	(1.13)	—	5.50–1.00

* Per-share amounts restated to reflect 1-for-4 reverse stock split effected Feb. 29, 1996.
† EPS figure for 2000 includes loss of ($0.25) on beneficial conversion feature. Pro forma had Aug. 28, 1999, acquisition Corporate Express Delivery Systems (CEDS) been acquired July 1, 1999: revenue $558.428 million; loss $37.553 million/($2.69).
¶ Pro forma figures for 1999 had Jan. 13, 1999, acquisition Twin City Transportation Inc. and Aug. 28, 1999, acquisition CEDS been acquired July 1, 1998: revenue $607.612 million; loss $42.357 million/($6.15).

BALANCE SHEET

Assets	07/01/00 (dollars in thousands)	06/30/99	Liabilities	07/01/00 (dollars in thousands)	06/30/99
Current (CAE 3,993 and 252)	76,136	1,976	Current (STD 7,167 and 40)	118,078	825
Property and equipment	12,796	858	Long-term debt	39,495	617
Goodwill	89,220	1,426	Other	12	
Notes receivable from related party	1,354		Preferred equity	25,261	
Other	2,217	128	Common equity*	(1,123)	2,946
TOTAL	181,723	4,388	TOTAL	181,723	4,388

* $0.004 par common; 75,000,000 authorized; 16,400,000 and 10,611,000 issued and outstanding.

RECENT QUARTERS / PRIOR-YEAR RESULTS

	Quarter End	Revenue ($000)	Earnings ($000)	EPS ($)	Prior-Year Revenue ($000)	Prior-Year Earnings ($000)	Prior-Year EPS ($)
Q1	09/30/2000	133,091	(7,185)	(0.58)	53,724	(1,617)	(0.15)
Q4	07/01/2000	139,620	(7,518)	(0.76)	728	(837)	(0.06)
Q3	04/01/2000	138,900	(7,847)	(0.50)	483	(797)	(0.11)
Q2	01/01/2000	138,908	(11,230)	(0.86)	148	(656)	(0.13)
	SUM	550,519	(33,780)	(2.70)	55,082	(3,907)	(0.45)

CURRENT: Q4 EPS includes further loss of $3.508 million/($0.24) for impact of beneficial conversion feature of Series B Preferred issued in May.

RECENT EVENTS

In **December 1999**, following its acquisition of Corporate Express Delivery Systems of Houston, the company formed a new business development group under the direction of SVP Bane. In **January 2000** the company rolled out a beta version of the industry's most advanced, browser-based, real-time delivery tracking system to same-day shipping customers. US&T raised a total of $9.0 million through an equity private placement. A portion of the proceeds were to be used to fund additional investments in the company's technology applications and e-commerce business expansion; the remainder, to enhance its working capital position. In **February** US&T announced the formation of a new division within its Corporate Express Delivery Systems subsidiary that was to focus exclusively on e-commerce distribution in the B2B and B2C market segments. This action reflected US&T's objective to become the premier "backbone" transportation/logistics solutions supplier to the burgeoning number of e-commerce businesses across the United States. In **March** the company said that it was expanding its operations in the Northeast by opening five e-commerce support centers in four different states. These centers, to be run by US&T's subsidiary, Corporate Express Delivery Systems (CEDS), were to support the company's position as a leading provider of e-commerce logistics services. In **April** Corporate Express Delivery Systems agreed to *continued on page 404*

OFFICERS

Peter C. Lytle
Chairman and CEO
Marshall T. Masko
Vice Chairman
Timothy G. Becker
CFO
Charles Garrett
Pres.-Intelligent Kiosk Co.
Steven Hanousek
Pres.-Advanced Courier Services
Jeffry J. Parell
Pres./CEO-Velocity Express Inc.
Mark E. Ties
VP-Finance

DIRECTORS

James A. Bartholomew
financial consultant
Timothy G. Becker
Jim Brown
TH Lee.Putnam Internet Partners L.P.
Peter C. Lytle
Marshall T. Masko
NordicTrack (former)
Ronald G. Olson
Grow Biz International Inc., Golden Valley, MN
Marlin Rudebusch
Minntech Corp., Plymouth, MN
Tim L. Traff
USFilter (former)

MAJOR SHAREHOLDERS

TH Lee.Putnam Internet Partners L.P., 23.7%
New York
Richard and Mabeth Neslund, 11.7%
Wayzata, MN
Bayview Capital Partners L.P., 8.3%
Wayzata, MN
RS Investment Management Co. LLC, 6.4%
San Francisco
Peter C. Lytle, 6.1%
Brahman Management Corp., 5.9%
New York
Tudor Investment Corp., 5.9%
Greenwich, CT
All officers and directors as a group (10 persons), 15%

SIC CODE

4731 Freight transportation arrangement

MISCELLANEOUS

TRANSFER AGENT AND REGISTAR:
American Stock Transfer & Trust Co., New York
TRADED: Nasdaq SmallCap Market
SYMBOL: USHP
STOCKHOLDERS: 427
EMPLOYEES: 7,073
GENERAL COUNSEL:
Briggs and Morgan P.A., Minneapolis
AUDITORS:
Lurie, Besikof, Lapidus & Co. LLP, Minneapolis
INC: UT-1979
ANNUAL MEETING: May
INVESTOR RELATIONS:
Tana DeBore

RANKINGS

No. 73 CRM Public 200
No. 38 CRM Performance 100

SUBSIDIARIES, DIVISIONS, AFFILIATES

U-Ship International Ltd.

U-Ship America Inc.

IQ(K)
Charles Garrett

Velocity Express

TWO-YEAR QUARTERLY HIGH-LOW STOCK PRICES

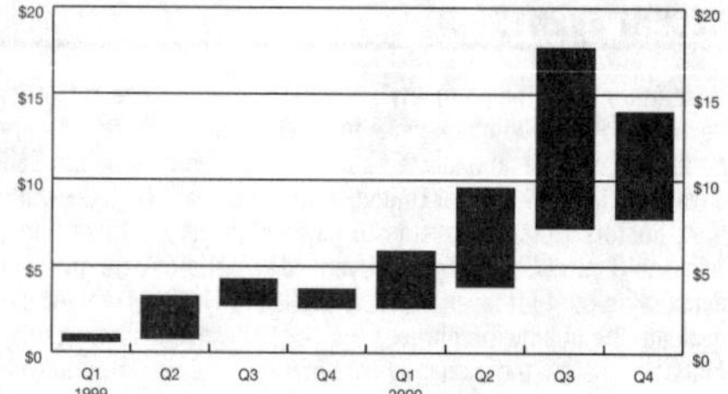

Urologix Inc.

14405 21st Ave. N., Plymouth, MN 55447
Tel: 763/475-1400 Fax: 763/475-1443 Web site: http://www.urologix.com

Urologix Inc. manufacturers its proprietary Targis system to treat patients with benign prostatic hyperplasia (BPH). The Targis System's nonsurgical, targeted, high-energy design improves the quality of life for patients while minimizing risks, complications, and costs. The treatment can be done in a physician's office, without anesthesia.

EARNINGS HISTORY

Year Ended Jun 30	Operating Revenue/Sales (dollars in thousands)	Net Earnings (dollars in thousands)	Return on Revenue (percent)	Return on Equity (percent)	Net Earnings (dollars per share*)	Cash Dividend (dollars per share*)	Market Price Range (dollars per share*)
2000	8,163	(7,098)	NM	(24.7)	(0.62)	—	10.44–2.38
1999	6,110	(14,016)	NM	(39.5)	(1.24)	—	8.94–2.25
1998 †	11,194	(15,013)	NM	(30.4)	(1.44)	—	25.25–8.25
1997	5,504	(8,234)	NM	(25.4)	(0.90)	—	19.88–10.38
1996	362	(7,593)	NM	(18.7)	(1.22)	—	17.00–10.00

* Stock began trading on May 30, 1996.
† Income figures for 1998 include litigation settlement expense of $3,376,144/($0.32).

BALANCE SHEET

Assets	06/30/00 (dollars in thousands)	06/30/99	Liabilities	06/30/00 (dollars in thousands)	06/30/99
Current (CAE 458 and 657)	26,317	32,322	Current	3,185	3,519
Property and equipment	1,679	2,251	Capitalized lease obligations		3
Other	3,960	4,415	Stockholders' equity*	28,770	35,467
TOTAL	31,956	38,988	TOTAL	31,956	38,988

* $0.01 par common; 25,000,000 authorized; 11,607,624 and 11,428,937 issued and outstanding.

RECENT QUARTERS / **PRIOR-YEAR RESULTS**

	Quarter End	Revenue ($000)	Earnings ($000)	EPS ($)	Prior-Year Revenue ($000)	Prior-Year Earnings ($000)	Prior-Year EPS ($)
Q1	09/30/2000	1,935	(1,460)	(0.13)	1,910	(2,031)	(0.18)
Q4	06/30/2000	2,005	(1,631)	(0.14)	1,909	(2,520)	(0.22)
Q3	03/31/2000	2,327	(1,623)	(0.14)	1,342	(2,361)	(0.21)
Q2	12/31/99	1,921	(1,813)	(0.16)	1,234	(2,937)	(0.26)
	SUM	8,188	(6,526)	(0.57)	6,396	(9,848)	(0.86)

RECENT EVENTS

In **December 1999** the FDA lifted key contraindications for the company's Targis System. Specifically, any patient with a hip implant or penile implant located at least 1.5 inches away from the prostatic urethra can now be treated with the Targis treatment. Urologix submitted a PMA supplement to the FDA requesting approval of shortened treatment time, known as the Express Protocol, for the Targis System. **Dec. 31**: Targis procedure kit sales for the second quarterexceeded 1,300 kits, a 21 percent increase from the previous quarter and an 80 percent increase from the second quarter of fiscal 1999. In **February 2000** the company amended its international distribution agreement with Boston Scientific Corp. (NYSE: BSX). Under the amended agreement, which runs through June 2001, Urologix was to maintain responsibility for the sales and marketing of the Targis System in Europe, with Boston Scientific continuing to pay Urologix an agreed-upon amount for Urologix' sales and marketing efforts. In **March** the FDA approved a software enhancement to the current Targis Cruise Control, giving physicians the ability to perform a fully automated treatment, and incorporating a unique dual-sensor feedback system (patent pending). In **April** the Health Care Financing Administration (HCFA) officially released in the Federal Register its new Hospital Outpatient Prospective Payment System establishing fixed rates for hospital outpatient services to Medicare beneficiaries. Targis, a Level XI new technology, was assigned to a new Ambulatory Payment Classification (APC) number 0980. (Targis was one of only a few new devices selected for designation as a reimbursed new technology.) This APC was assigned a national fixed payment rate of $1,875 that was to be adjusted locally by a wage index. This fixed rate included a "minimum unadjusted coinsurance," or patient co-pay, of $375. The company had been hoping for a rate closer to $2,000 without the co-pay. In **May** details of a five-year study, which were presented this week at the American Urological Association (AUA) meeting in Atlanta, demonstrated that the Targis Treatment is an effective and safe alternative for treating BPH and provides positive long-term results. In **June** Urologix received FDA approval for use of its Express Protocol, an enhancement to Targis treatment that significantly reduces treatment time of benign prostate hyperplasia (BPH), or enlarged prostate disease, from 60 minutes to less than 30 minutes. Meanwhile, in order to build a market for its device, the company was offering a rental option. According to analysts following the company, the program was seeing a solid 30 percent renter-to-buyer conversion rate. In **July**, based on clinical outcomes from randomized prospective trials, the World Health Organization recommended the Targis treatment from Urologix for the treatment of benign prostatic hyperplasia. HCFA's proposed payment rates and a schedule for implementing minimally invasive thermotherapy treatments for Benign Prostatic Hyperplasia (BPH) in the urologist's office included coverage of the Targis procedure. However, certain cost factors were inadvertently omitted in the calculation of the office reimbursement rate for transurethral microwave thermotherapy. In **August** HCFA published a recalculated rate. The combi-

continued on page 405

OFFICERS

Mitchell Dann
Chairman

Michael M. Selzer Jr.
President and CEO

Ronald A. Blasewitz
SVP and COO

Kirsten Doerfert
VP-Marketing

Christopher R. Geyen
VP and CFO

David Monteculvo
VP-Product Development/Operations

David J. Talen
VP-Urologix International

DIRECTORS

Mitchell Dann
Sapient Capital, Jackson, WY

Susan Bartlett Foote
Division of Health, Minneapolis

Bobby I. Griffin
Medtronic Inc. (retired)

Paul A. LaViolette
Boston Scientific Corp., Natick, MA

Richard D. Randall
Innovasive Devices Inc. (former)

Michael M. Selzer Jr.

Eric Simon
EDAP Technomed

David C. Utz, M.D.
consultant (urology)

MAJOR SHAREHOLDERS

Dimensional Fund Advisors Inc., 6.9%
Santa Monica, CA

John Reid, 5.1%
NewMarket, NH

Boston Scientific Corp., 5%
Natick, MA

All officers and directors as a group (12 persons), 13.2%

SIC CODE

3841 Surgical and medical instruments

MISCELLANEOUS

TRANSFER AGENT AND REGISTAR:
Wells Fargo Bank Minnesota N.A.,
South St. Paul, MN

TRADED: Nasdaq National Market

SYMBOL: ULGX

STOCKHOLDERS: 348

EMPLOYEES: 76
PART TIME: 2
IN MINNESOTA: 58

GENERAL COUNSEL:
Lindquist & Vennum PLLP, Minneapolis

AUDITORS:
Arthur Andersen LLP, Minneapolis

INC: MN-1991

ANNUAL MEETING: November

HUMAN RESOURCES/INVESTOR RELATIONS:
Christopher Geyen

RANKINGS

No. 194 CRM Public 200
No. 11 Minnesota Technology Fast 50

SUBSIDIARIES, DIVISIONS, AFFILIATES

Urologix Europe
Gaetano Martinolaan 95
6229 GS Maastricht, The Netherlands
+31 (0)43.3566.345

PUB

TWO-YEAR QUARTERLY HIGH-LOW STOCK PRICES

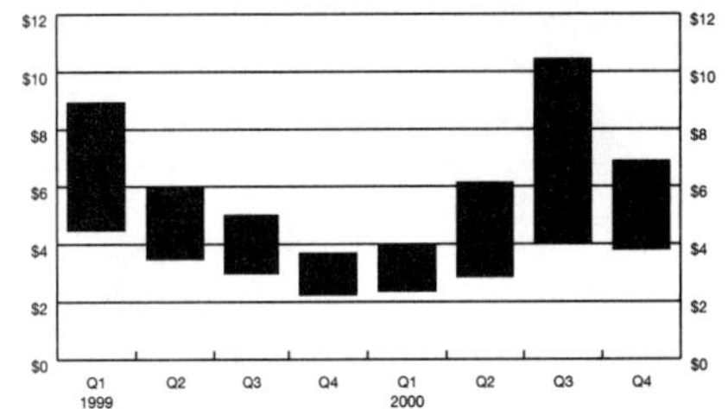

PUB

Uroplasty Inc.

2718 Summer St. N.E., Minneapolis, MN 55413
Tel: 612/378-1180 Fax: 612/378-2027 Web site: http://www.uroplasty.com

Uroplasty Inc. is a manufacturer and distributor of urological and plastic surgery implantable medical devices. The primary focus of the company's business is the marketing of an implantable device called Macroplastique, a solid silicone injectable suspension that has application in the minimally invasive treatment of stress incontinence and vesicoureteral reflux. Currently, all sales of Uroplasty's products are to customers outside the United States.

EARNINGS HISTORY

Year Ended Mar 31	Operating Revenue/Sales (dollars in thousands)	Net Earnings (dollars in thousands)	Return on Revenue (percent)	Return on Equity (percent)	Net Earnings (dollars per share*)	Cash Dividend (dollars per share*)	Market Price Range (dollars per share*)
2000	5,560	(1,349)	(24.3)	(31.8)	(0.23)	—	3.63–2.00
1999 †	5,309	332	6.3	5.8	0.06	—	7.00–1.50
1998	4,336	408	9.4	19.9	0.10	—	3.50–0.50
1997	3,335	218	6.5	17.7	0.06	—	
1996 ¶	2,297	(287)	(12.5)	(39.2)	(0.10)	—	

* Share prices reported for periods beginning in July 1997.
† Income figures for 1999 include pretax gain of $39,565 on liquidation of foreign subsidiary.
¶ Income figures for 1996 include gain of $496,119/$0.17 on sale of intangible asset.

BALANCE SHEET

Assets	03/31/00 (dollars in thousands)	03/31/99 (dollars in thousands)	Liabilities	03/31/00 (dollars in thousands)	03/31/99 (dollars in thousands)
Current (CAE 1,553 and 1,588)	4,394	4,964	Current (STD 49 and 46)	826	717
Property, plant, and equipment	1,097	1,228	Capital lease obligations	25	26
Marketable securities		761	Note payable	504	605
			Stockholders' equity*	4,245	5,717
Intangibles	109	112			
TOTAL	5,600	7,066	TOTAL	5,600	7,066

* $0.01 par common; 20,000,000 authorized; 5,975,271 and 5,923,371 issued and outstanding.

RECENT QUARTERS / PRIOR-YEAR RESULTS

	Quarter End	Revenue ($000)	Earnings ($000)	EPS ($)	Prior-Year Revenue ($000)	Prior-Year Earnings ($000)	Prior-Year EPS ($)
Q2	09/30/2000	1,211	(608)	(0.10)	1,101	(348)	(0.06)
Q1	06/30/2000	1,479	(176)	(0.03)	1,470	(154)	(0.03)
Q4	03/31/2000	1,464	(436)	(0.07)	1,433	144	0.02
Q3	12/31/99	1,525	(410)	(0.07)	1,366	(160)	(0.03)
	SUM	5,679	(1,631)	(0.27)	5,369	(519)	(0.09)

RECENT EVENTS

In **February 2000** Uroplasty and its European subsidiaries received notification that they had successfully demonstrated compliance with the Medical Devices Directive 93/42/EEC for a newly developed set of instruments for the non-endoscopic delivery of Macroplastique: the Macroplastique Implantation System (MIS). Uroplasty was therefore authorized to use the CE mark on the MIS. In August the U.S. Patent and Trademark Office granted the company a patent covering its Macroplastique Implantation Device. Uroplasty entered into a distribution agreement with PORGES S.A. to act as the exclusive distributor of Uroplasty's urology products in Belgium and Luxembourg. **Sept. 30**: Second-quarter unit sales of Macroplastique Implants increased 22 percent compared to prior year. Increases in sales dollars were lower than the increase in units sold primarily as a result of a strengthening of the U.S. dollar during the periods compared to the currencies in counties where the company sells it products. CEO Holman stated, "The strength of our increasing unit sales amid increasing competition for stress urinary incontinence dollars demonstrates the widespread acceptance the Macroplastique product line has achieved, as well as the relentless work of our sales team and distributors."

OFFICERS

Daniel G. Holman
President and CEO

Chris Harris
VP-Corporate Development

Susan Hartjes-Holman
VP-Operations/Regulatory Affairs, Sec.

Larry Heinemann
VP-Sales/Marketing

Donald A. Major
CFO

Arie J. Koole
Controller

DIRECTORS

Daniel G. Holman

Thomas E. Jamison
attorney

R. Patrick Maxwell
consultant/entrepreneur

Joel R. Pitlor
Joel R. Pitlor Inc.

MAJOR SHAREHOLDERS

Mindich Family LLC/Bruce P. Mindich, 10.9%
Tarrytown, NY

Paddington Management Corp./Bruce P. Mindich, 7.5%
Paramus, NJ

All officers and directors as a group (9 persons), 14.5%

SIC CODE

3841 Surgical and medical instruments

MISCELLANEOUS

TRANSFER AGENT AND REGISTAR:
StockTrans Inc., Ardmore, PA

TRADED: NASD

SYMBOL: UROP.OB

STOCKHOLDERS: 630

EMPLOYEES: 63

PART TIME: 6

GENERAL COUNSEL:
Richard P. Keller, Esq., St. Paul

AUDITORS:
KPMG LLP, Minneapolis

INC: MN-1992

ANNUAL MEETING:
August

INVESTOR RELATIONS:
Christie Reeves

SUBSIDIARIES, DIVISIONS, AFFILIATES

Uroplasty BV
Hofkamp 2
6161 DC Geleen
Netherlands

Uroplasty Ltd.
Unit 3, Woodside Business Park
Whitley Wood Lane
Reading
Berkshire RG2 8LW
United Kingdom

TWO-YEAR QUARTERLY HIGH-LOW STOCK PRICES

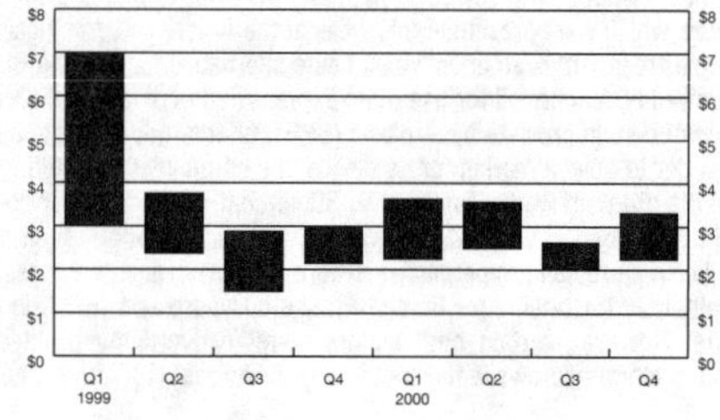

The Valspar Corporation

1101 Third St. S., Minneapolis, MN 55415
Tel: 612/332-7371 Fax: 612/375-7723 Web site: http://www.valspar.com

The Valspar Corp., the manufacturer of America's first varnish, is one of the largest domestic manufacturers of paints and related coatings. Valspar's operating groups are organized into four classes: CONSUMER COATINGS manufactures and distributes latex- and oil-based paints for the do-it-yourself market; PACKAGING COATINGS supplies coatings for the food and beveage industries; INDUSTRIAL COATINGS supplies metal, wood, and plastic finishes for OEM markets; and SPECIAL PRODUCTS produces resins, colorants, floor coatings, and industrial maintenance and marine coatings. Valspar has 24 manufacturing plants throughout North America, three plants in Europe, and two plants in Australia. It also licenses its technology worldwide.

EARNINGS HISTORY

Year Ended Oct	Operating Revenue/Sales (dollars in thousands)	Net Earnings	Return on Revenue (percent)	Return on Equity	Net Earnings (dollars per share*)	Cash Dividend	Market Price Range
1999 †	1,387,677	82,142	5.9	20.9	1.90	0.46	39.69–28.00
1998	1,155,134	72,130	6.2	21.2	1.66	0.42	42.13–25.75
1997 ¶	1,017,271	65,877	6.5	22.3	1.51	0.36	32.94–24.00
1996	859,799	55,893	6.5	22.0	1.28	0.33	25.50–19.13
1995	790,175	47,520	6.0	22.4	1.09	0.30	20.94–15.25

* Per-share amounts restated to reflect 2-for-1 stock split on March 21, 1997.
† Income figures for 1999 include pretax restructuring charge of $8.346 million.
¶ Fiscal year 1997 consisted of 53 weeks.

BALANCE SHEET

Assets	10/29/99 (dollars in thousands)	10/30/98
Current (CAE 33,189 and 14,990)	514,928	426,069
Property, plant, and equipment	312,133	233,482
Goodwill	218,668	92,872
Other	64,991	49,257
TOTAL	1,110,720	801,680

Liabilities	10/29/99 (dollars in thousands)	10/30/98
Current (STD 53,899 and 24,340)	374,712	267,984
Long-term debt	298,874	164,768
Deferred income taxes	11,148	8,910
Deferred liabilities	32,230	19,830
Stockholders' equity*	393,756	340,188
TOTAL	1,110,720	801,680

* $0.50 par common; 120,000,000 authorized; 53,321,312 and 53,321,312 issued and outstanding, less 10,337,999 and 9,902,827 treasury shares.

RECENT QUARTERS / PRIOR-YEAR RESULTS

	Quarter End	Revenue ($000)	Earnings ($000)	EPS ($)	Prior-Year Revenue ($000)	Prior-Year Earnings ($000)	Prior-Year EPS ($)
Q3	07/28/2000	385,070	25,466	0.60	398,076	25,833	0.60
Q2	04/28/2000	392,780	25,371	0.59	356,702	22,444	0.52
Q1	01/28/2000	323,671	11,455	0.27	265,810	9,716	0.22
Q4	10/29/99	367,089	24,148	0.56	309,629	21,038	0.49
	SUM	1,468,610	86,440	2.02	1,330,217	79,031	1.82

RECENT EVENTS

In **April 2000** the company's board of directors adopted a Shareholder Rights Plan, to further the long-term interests of Valspar shareholders by protecting the company against hostile takeovers. Under the plan, Valspar shareholders were to receive rights to acquire additional Valspar common shares in the event a person or group acquires 15 percent or more of the Valspar common shares. The adoption of the Shareholder Rights Plan was not taken in response to or in anticipation of any specific or proposed change in control of Valspar. In **June** Valspar and $656.2 million-revenue, 2,500-employee Lilly Industries Inc. (NYSE: LI), Indianapolis, approved a definitive merger agreement under which Valspar would acquire all outstanding shares of Lilly Industries common stock for $31.75 per share in cash, a 146.6 percent premium over Lilly's prevailing $12.88 price. The total value of the transaction: $975 million, including the assumption of $213 million in debt. (Pricey, but reasonable, most analysts agreed.) "These two companies are an extraordinarily good business fit, with their complementary technologies and global technical, manufacturing, and customer support capabilities," said CEO Rompala. "Lilly has an excellent reputation for innovative technology, quality products, and outstanding customer service." In **July** Valspar announced that earnings for the third quarter ending July 28, 2000, were expected to be flat with last year's third quarter (59 cents per share). The company had experienced soft sales in its architectural coatings and coating intermediates product lines, and rising raw material costs had not been fully offset by price increases. In addition, the stronger U.S. dollar had reduced reported packaging coatings revenue in Europe and Australia. Valspar and Lilly received requests for additional information and other documentary materials from the FTC. The requests extended the waiting period under the Hart-Scott-Rodino Antitrust Improvements Act during which the parties may not complete the transaction. In **October** the board of directors authorized the company to repurchase, over a period of 12 months, up to 2 million shares, or 4.7 percent of its outstanding common stock.

OFFICERS

Richard M. Rompala
Chairman, President, and CEO
John M. Ballbach
SVP-Operations
Stephen M. Briggs
SVP-E-commerce
Rolf Engh
SVP, General Counsel, and Secretary
Steven L. Erdahl
SVP-Operations
William L. Mansfield
SVP-Packaging/Industrial Coatings
Paul C. Reyelts
SVP and CFO
Kenneth H. Arthur
Group VP-Architectural
Joel C. Hart
Group VP-Automotive/International
Robert T. Smith
Group VP-Industrial
Larry B. Brandenburger
VP-Research/Development
Gary E. Gardner
VP-Human Resources/Public Affairs
Steven C. Lindberg
VP-Engineered Polymer Solutions
Kathleen P. Pepski
VP and Controller
Deborah D. Weiss
VP and Treasurer
Thomas A. White
VP-Manufacturing
Thomas L. Wood
VP-Purchasing/Logistics

DIRECTORS

Susan S. Boren
SpencerStuart, Minneapolis
Jeffrey H. Curler
Bemis Co. Inc., Oshkosh, WI
Charles W. Gaillard
General Mills Inc., Golden Valley, MN
Thomas R. McBurney
McBurney Management Advisors, Minneapolis
Kendrick B. Melrose
The Toro Co., Bloomington, MN
Gregory R. Palen
Spectro Alloys Corp., Rosemount, MN
Lawrence Perlman
Ceridian Corp., Bloomington, MN
Edward B. Pollak
Witco Corp., Stamford, CT
Richard M. Rompala
Michael P. Sullivan
International Dairy Queen Inc., Bloomington, MN
Richard L. White, Ph.D.
Bayer Corp. (retired)
C. Angus Wurtele

MAJOR SHAREHOLDERS

C. Angus Wurtele, 9%
Capital Research and Management Co., 8.8%
Los Angeles
Resource Trust Co., 8%
Minneapolis
Nicholas Co. Inc., 5.2%
Milwaukee
All officers and directors as a group (15 persons), 13%

SIC CODE

2851 Paints and allied products

MISCELLANEOUS

TRANSFER AGENT AND REGISTAR:
ChaseMellon Shareholder Services LLC, Ridgefield Park, NJ
TRADED: NYSE
SYMBOL: VAL
STOCKHOLDERS: 1,818
EMPLOYEES: 4,500
GENERAL COUNSEL:
Lindquist & Vennum PLLP, Minneapolis
AUDITORS:
Ernst & Young LLP, Minneapolis
INC: DE-1934
FOUNDED: 1806
ANNUAL MEETING: February
HUMAN RESOURCES/PUBLIC AFFAIRS: Gary E. Gardner
INVESTOR RELATIONS: Paul C. Reyelts

RANKINGS

No. 25 CRM Public 200

TWO-YEAR QUARTERLY HIGH-LOW STOCK PRICES

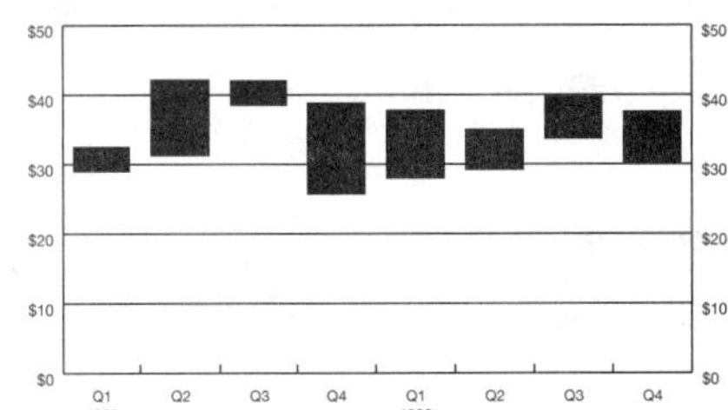

PUB

PUB

ValueVision International Inc.

6740 Shady Oak Rd., Eden Prairie, MN 55344
Tel: 952/947-5200 Fax: 952/947-0188 Web site: http://www.vvtv.com

ValueVision International Inc. is an integrated electronic direct marketing company that markets its products directly to consumers primarily through its television home shopping network, which uses recognized on-air television home shopping personalities to market brand-name merchandise and proprietary and private-label consumer products at competitive or discount prices. The company's 24-hour-per-day television home shopping programming is distributed primarily through long-term cable affiliation agreements and the purchase of month-to-month full- and part-time block lease agreements of cable and broadcast television time. In addition, the company distributes its programming through company-owned or affiliated, low-power television stations, and satellite dishes. The company also complements its television home shopping business by the sale of merchandise through its Internet shopping Web site (www.vvtv.com). ValueVision is undertaking strategic commerce initiatives under a new rebranding strategy. ValueVision's home shopping television network will be re-branded and its companion Internet shopping service will be launched together with a wide-ranging direct e-commerce strategy.

EARNINGS HISTORY

Year Ended Jan 31	Operating Revenue/Sales (dollars in thousands)	Net Earnings	Return on Revenue (percent)	Return on Equity	Net Earnings (dollars per share)	Cash Dividend	Market Price Range
2000 *	274,927	29,330	10.7	7.8	0.89	—	62.00–8.13
1999 †	203,728	4,639	2.3	4.3	0.18	—	15.25–3.00
1998 ¶	217,982	18,104	8.3	17.3	0.57	—	5.44–3.13
1997 #	159,478	18,090	11.3	14.3	0.57	—	8.56–4.63
1996 **	88,910	11,020	12.4	10.7	0.38	—	7.31–3.88

* Income figures for 2000 include these net pretax nonoperating amounts: gains of $33.23 million on sale of broadcast stations and $2.347 million on sale of property and investments; and charge of $1.991 million for write-down of investments.
† Income figures for 1999 include these net pretax nonoperating amounts: gains of $19.75 million on sale of broadcast stations and $8.1 million on sale of property and investments; and charges of $7.1 million for Time Warner litigation settlement, $6.11 million for write-down of investment in CML Group, and $2.35 million in National Media Corp. terminated acquisition costs.
¶ Income figures for 1998 include one-time net pretax gain of $38.85 million.
# Income figures for 1997 include one-time net pretax gain of $27,858,449.
** Income figures for 1996 include one-time net pretax gain of $7,863,453.

BALANCE SHEET

Assets	01/31/00 (dollars in thousands)	01/31/99	Liabilities	01/31/00 (dollars in thousands)	01/31/99
Current (CAE 138,221 and 44,264)	382,854	98,320	Current (STD 0 and 393)	51,587	32,684
Property, eqt	14,350	14,069	Long-term obligations		675
FCC licenses	124	2,019			
Cable agreement	6,394		Deferred income taxes	6,725	
Montgomery Ward	1,679	1,876			
Paxson Comm.	3,911	9,713	Preferred stock	41,622	
Goodwill	64	5,962	Common stock*	371,921	108,411
Investments, other	62,479	9,160	TOTAL	471,855	141,770
Deferred taxes		651			
TOTAL	471,855	141,770			

* $0.01 par common; 100,000,000 authorized; 38,192,164 and 25,865,466 issued and outstanding.

RECENT QUARTERS / PRIOR-YEAR RESULTS

	Quarter End	Revenue ($000)	Earnings ($000)	EPS ($)	Prior-Year Revenue ($000)	Prior-Year Earnings ($000)	Prior-Year EPS ($)
Q2	07/31/2000	85,677	3,236	0.08	57,875	1,048	0.03
Q1	04/30/2000	81,001	3,180	0.08	53,142	6,368	0.24
Q4	01/31/2000	87,335	4,679	0.12	65,943	422	0.02
Q3	10/31/99	76,575	17,235	0.46	50,027	(6,341)	(0.25)
	SUM	330,588	28,330	0.75	226,987	1,497	0.05

PRIOR YEAR: Q1 earnings include one-time pretax gain of $9.980 million. Q4 earnings include one-time net pretax loss of $1.73 million. Q3 earnings include one-time pretax charges of $8.68 million.

RECENT EVENTS

In **December 1999** the company retained Banc of America Securities LLC to assist in exploring investment opportunities as part of aggressive growth plans for the future. Virtually debt free, ValueVision has said that an integral part of its business plan includes utilizing a large portion of its $300 million in available cash for strategic investments. "We are currently making major changes in both the entertainment values and products offered in our *continued on page 405*

OFFICERS

Gene McCaffery
Chairman and CEO

Steve Jackel
Pres.-ValueVision, TV Home Shopping

Richard D. Barnes
SVP and CFO

Nathan E. Fagre
SVP and General Counsel

DIRECTORS

Mark W. Begor

John Flannery
GE Equity

Marshall S. Geller
Geller & Friends Inc.

Robert J. Korkowski
private investor

Gene McCaffery

Paul D. Tosetti
Latham & Watkins

MAJOR SHAREHOLDERS

NBC/GE Capital Equity Investments Inc., 37%
Stamford, CT

All officers and directors as a group (11 persons), 39.8%

SIC CODE

5999 Retail stores miscellaneous

MISCELLANEOUS

TRANSFER AGENT AND REGISTAR:
Wells Fargo Bank Minnesota N.A.,
South St. Paul, MN

TRADED: Nasdaq National Market

SYMBOL: VVTV

STOCKHOLDERS: 350

EMPLOYEES: 520

GENERAL COUNSEL:
Faegre & Benson PLLP, Minneapolis

AUDITORS:
Arthur Andersen LLP, Minneapolis

INC: MN-1990

ANNUAL MEETING: June

INVESTOR RELATIONS:
Richard Barnes

RANKINGS

No. 64 CRM Public 200

TWO-YEAR QUARTERLY HIGH-LOW STOCK PRICES

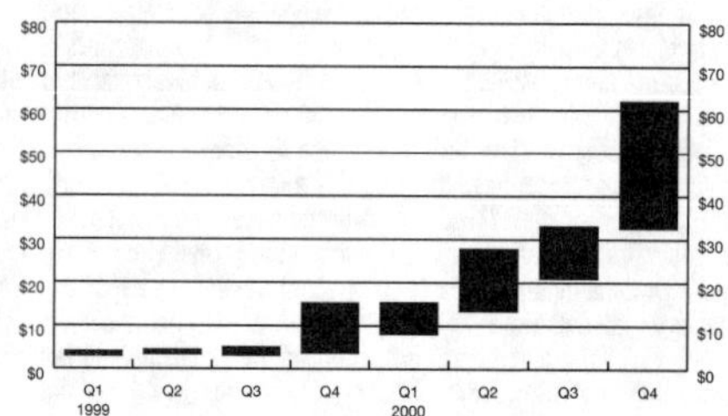

Vascular Solutions Inc.

2495 Xenium Ln. N., Plymouth, MN 55441
Tel: 763/553-2970 Fax: 763/553-2089 Web site: http://www.vascularsolutions.com

Vascular Solutions manufactures, markets, and sells the Vascular Solutions Duett sealing device, which enables cardiologists and radiologists to rapidly seal the puncture site following catheterization procedures such as angiography, angioplasty, and stenting. The product combines a simple balloon-catheter delivery mechanism with a powerful, proprietary procoagulant, or blood-clotting mixture. The company believes that its product offers advantages over both manual compression and the three existing FDA-approved devices used to seal the puncture site following the catheterization procedure. Vascular Solutions began selling its product in Europe in February 1998. More than 7,500 deployments of the device have been performed worldwide. A 2.675 million-share initial public offering (IPO) of stock was postponed due to continuing difficulties in bringing medical device stocks to market.

EARNINGS HISTORY

Year Ended Dec 31	Operating Revenue/Sales (dollars in thousands)	Net Earnings	Return on Revenue (percent)	Return on Equity	Net Earnings (dollars per share*)	Cash Dividend	Market Price Range
1999 †	1,429	(7,862)	NM	(70.4)	(1.95)	—	
1998	494	(5,141)	NM	(48.8)	(1.40)	—	
1997	0	(1,652)	NM	(22.9)	(0.62)	—	

* Trading had not begun during periods presented.
† Pro forma 1999 loss per share: ($1.01).

BALANCE SHEET

Assets	12/31/99 (dollars in thousands)	12/31/98	Liabilities	12/31/99 (dollars in thousands)	12/31/98
Current	11,610	10,394	Current	1,123	461
(CAE 10,529 and 9,897)			Preferred stock	38	38
Property and equipment	685	613	Common stock*	11,134	10,508
TOTAL	12,295	11,007	TOTAL	12,295	11,007

* $0.01 par common; 16,222,223 authorized; 5,250,291 and 3,699,617 issued and outstanding.

RECENT QUARTERS / PRIOR-YEAR RESULTS

	Quarter End	Revenue ($000)	Earnings ($000)	EPS ($)	Prior-Year Revenue ($000)	Prior-Year Earnings ($000)	Prior-Year EPS ($)
Q3	09/30/2000	2,037	(2,100)	(0.19)	405	(1,735)	(0.40)
Q2	06/30/2000	708	(2,819)	(0.53)	308	(1,819)	(0.49)
Q1	03/31/2000	643	(1,931)	(0.37)	207	(1,714)	(0.46)
	SUM	3,388	(6,850)	(1.09)	919	(5,268)	(1.35)

RECENT EVENTS

In **March 2000** the company's motion for summary judgment against Datascope Corp. was granted, thereby dismissing all counts of the patent infringement complaint brought by Datascope in July 1999 in U.S. District Court. Datascope's complaint alleged that the clinical studies of the Duett sealing device infringed and, upon receipt of FDA approval, sales of the device would infringe, patents held by Datascope. In **June** the FDA approved the premarket approval application of the Vascular Solutions Duett sealing device. The approval allowed Vascular Solutions to commence Duett sales in the United States. In **July** Vascular Solutions was named as a defendant in a lawsuit initiated by St. Jude Medical Inc. (NYSE: STJ) in the U.S. District Court for the District of Minnesota. The lawsuit alleged that the Vascular Solutions Duett device infringed certain patents assigned to St. Jude Medical. The ongoing U.S. market launch of the Duett sealing device was unaffected by this litigation. The company launched its initial public offering on July 20, selling 3.5 million shares at $12 each. Proceeds were to be used for hiring and training a direct U.S. sales force and for general corporate purposes. The IPO was warmly received, with the price climbing to $16.19 at the close of trading. In **August** the underwriters exercised their overallotment option to purchase an additional 525,000 shares of common stock at a price of $12 per share from the company. **Sept. 30**: The reduction in the net loss compared with the second quarter of 2000 was achieved by the effects of the beginning of U.S. sales, where it grabbed 4 percent of the maket, combined with increased interest income and reduced litigation expenses. Profitability forecasts were projecting positive earnings for as early as the second quarter of 2001. In **October** the Vascular Solutions Duett sealing device was approved by the Health Care Finance Administration for pass-through reimbursement under the Outpatient Prospective Payment System of Medicare. "We believe that this separate reimbursement for the Duett device will continue the shift of the standard of care toward sealing devices and away from manual compression, which is still being used in over 80 percent of the catheterizations in the United States," commented CEO Root.

OFFICERS

Howard Root
CEO

Gary Gershony, M.D.
Medical Director

Deborah L. Jensen
VP-Regulatory/Quality/Clinical Research

Jerry Johnson
CFO and Secretary

Michael Nagel
VP-Sales/Marketing

James Quackenbush
VP-Manufacturing

Charmaine Sutton
VP-Regulatory Affairs

Will Sutton
VP-Research/Development

DIRECTORS

Steven Brandt
XRT Corp. (former)

Gary Gershony, M.D.

James Jacoby Jr.
Stephens Inc., Little Rock, AR

Gerard Langeler
Olympic Venture Partners, Kirkland, WA

Howard Root

MAJOR SHAREHOLDERS

Stephens Investment Partners III LLC/James Jacoby Jr., 21.6%
Little Rock, AR

Olympic Venture Partners/Gerard Langeler, 14.4%
Kirkland, WA

TGI Fund II LC, 7.2%
Seattle

Gary Gershony, M.D., 6.1%

All officers and directors as a group (10 persons), 45.4%

SIC CODE

3841 Surgical and medical instruments

MISCELLANEOUS

TRANSFER AGENT AND REGISTAR:
Wells Fargo Bank Minnesota N.A.,
South St. Paul, MN

TRADED: Nasdaq National Market

SYMBOL: VASC

EMPLOYEES: 86

GENERAL COUNSEL:
Dorsey & Whitney PLLP, Minneapolis

AUDITORS:
Ernst & Young LLP, Minneapolis

INC: MN-1996

PUB

Venturian Corporation

11111 Excelsior Blvd., Hopkins, MN 55343
Tel: 952/931-2500 Fax: 952/931-2402

Venturian Corp. is an investment and management company. Subsidiary **Napco International**, formerly Napco Industries, founded in 1918, is a distribution, manufacturing, and service business that sells a broad line of defense-related products. It designs and markets replacement parts and upgrade kits for U.S.-made military wheeled and tracked vehicles, helicopters, and planes; and markets a broad range of electronic security, communications equipment, and engineering services.

EARNINGS HISTORY *

Year Ended Dec 31	Operating Revenue/Sales (dollars in thousands)	Net Earnings	Return on Revenue (percent)	Return on Equity	Net Earnings (dollars per share†)	Cash Dividend	Market Price Range
1999 ¶	22,464	(1,079)	(4.8)	(10.2)	(0.81)	—	8.64–4.55
1998 #	41,713	1,831	4.4	15.7	1.43	—	9.32–5.30
1997 **	27,579	(2,325)	(8.4)	(24.8)	(1.87)	—	8.03–4.92
1996	28,398	84	0.3	0.8	0.07	—	8.64–3.03
1995 ††	24,845	(158)	(0.6)	(1.5)	(0.13)	—	5.61–2.42

* Revenue restated for continuing operations.
† Per-share amounts restated to reflect 11-for-10 stock split on Oct. 15, 1999; and 3-for-2 stock split on April 15, 1998.
¶ Income figures for 1999 include gain of $817,000 from demutualization.
\# Income figures for 1998 include gain of $218,000 from life insurance proceeds.
** Income figures for 1997 include gain of $306,000 on sale of property and equipment.
†† Income figures for 1995 include net loss of $1,095,000/($0.89) from discontinued operations and write-off of liabilities.

BALANCE SHEET

Assets	12/31/99 (dollars in thousands)	12/31/98	Liabilities	12/31/99 (dollars in thousands)	12/31/98
Current (CAE 1,249 and 3,009)	13,617	13,188	Current (STD 578 and 372)	6,179	4,179
Property and equipment	2,373	2,551	Long-term debt	4,179	4,424
Cash surrender value of life insurance	3,740	3,445	Deferred compensation, postretirement benefits	1,961	2,180
Rental real estate	2,781	2,891	Stockholders' equity*	10,527	11,697
Other	335	405			
TOTAL	22,846	22,480	TOTAL	22,846	22,480

* $1 par common; 30,000,000 authorized; 1,340,589 and 1,333,715 issued and outstanding.

RECENT QUARTERS / **PRIOR-YEAR RESULTS**

	Quarter End	Revenue ($000)	Earnings ($000)	EPS ($)	Revenue ($000)	Earnings ($000)	EPS ($)
Q3	09/30/2000	6,649	(32)	(0.02)	5,164	440	0.33
Q2	06/30/2000	8,260	549	0.42	5,664	(377)	(0.28)
Q1	03/31/2000	7,044	31	0.02	7,074	18	0.01
Q4	12/31/99	4,562	(1,160)	(0.87)	9,429	521	0.36
	SUM	26,515	(612)	(0.46)	27,331	602	0.42

RECENT EVENTS

In **December 1999** the terms of a recently announced agreement under which ATIO Corp. USA Inc. was to merge with CE Software Holdings Inc. (Nasdaq: CESH) were to result in Venturian's having an ongoing ownership of 15 percent of the merged company's outstanding shares of publicly traded stock. CEO Rappaport stated, "[CE Software's] CyberCall product has been lauded by industry analysts and trade journals as e-commerce's most comprehensive customer interaction solution. Venturian and its shareholders are now positioned to benefit from the expanding role of e-commerce in the growing Internet economy." In **February 2000** the board of directors authorized the purchase of up to 5 percent of current outstanding shares in the open market—and also suspended the company's quarterly cash dividend, believing periodic purchases of stock and reinvestment in business opportunities to be better uses of cash toward the goal of enhancing shareholder value than paying dividends. In **May** the company was notified by the Nasdaq Listing Qualifications Panel that its common stock was to be transferred to and trade on the Nasdaq SmallCap market effective with the opening of business on May 5. The panel's notification was based on the company's noncompliance with the Nasdaq National Market System's market value of public float requirement. **Sept. 30:** CEO Rappaport commented, "Operating results for both the quarter and year-to-date show improvement over the prior periods, reflecting better results at Napco International due to higher order backlogs."

OFFICERS

Gary B. Rappaport
Chairman and CEO

Don M. House Jr.
President and COO

Charles B. Langevin
Pres.-Napco International

Mary F. Jensen
CFO and Treasurer

Reinhild D. Hinze
VP-Operations and Treas.-Napco

DIRECTORS

Anthony S. Cleberg
Morris Knudsen Corp., Boise, ID

Jon B. Kutler
quarterback Investment Partners Inc.

Charles B. Langevin

Gary B. Rappaport

Melissa E. Rappaport
America West Airlines

J. Stephen Schmidt
TNB Holdings Inc.

Morris M. Sherman
Leonard, Street and Deinard P.A., Minneapolis

Morris M. Sherman
Leonard, Street and Deinard P.A., Minneapolis

MAJOR SHAREHOLDERS

Gary B. Rappaport, 24.6%
Hopkins, MN

Quarterdeck Equity Partners Inc./Jon B. Kutler, 13.1%
Washington, D.C.

Oppenheimer Group Inc., 6.1%
New York

The Charles Schwab Co./Venturian Group Profit Sharing, 5.5%
San Francisco

Hesperus Partners Ltd., 5.3%
Chicago

All officers and directors as a group (10 persons), 51.3%

SIC CODE

5012 Motor vehicles, whsle
5013 Automotive parts, whsle
5014 Tires and tubes, whsle
5065 Electronic parts and eqp, whsle
5088 Transportation eqp, whsle

MISCELLANEOUS

TRANSFER AGENT AND REGISTAR:
American Stock Transfer & Trust Co., New York
TRADED: Nasdaq
SYMBOL: VENT
STOCKHOLDERS: 426
EMPLOYEES: 118
GENERAL COUNSEL:
Leonard Street & Deinard P.A., Minneapolis
AUDITORS:
Grant Thornton LLP, Minneapolis
INC: MN-1983
FOUNDED: 1918
ANNUAL MEETING: May

RANKINGS

No. 145 CRM Public 200

SUBSIDIARIES, DIVISIONS, AFFILIATES

Napco International Inc.
11111 Excelsior Blvd.
Hopkins, MN 55343
612/931-2400
Charles B. Langevin

Napco International Foreign Sales Corp.
U.S. Virgin Islands

TWO-YEAR QUARTERLY HIGH-LOW STOCK PRICES

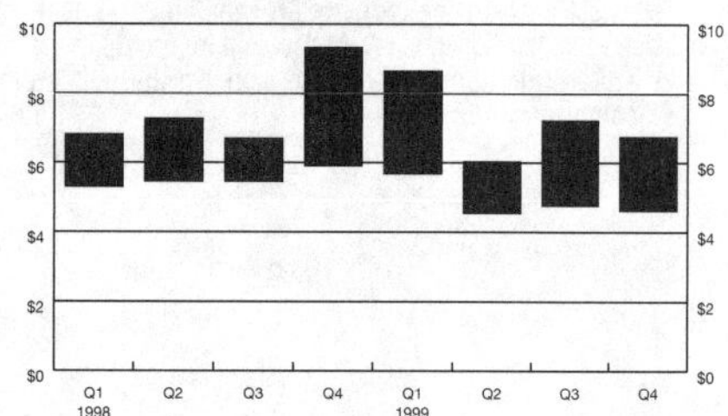

Verdant Brands Inc.

9555 James Ave. S., Suite 200, Bloomington, MN 55431
Tel: 952/703-3300 Fax: 952/887-1300 Web site: http://www.verdantbrands.com

Verdant Brands Inc. develops, manufactures, and markets a variety of pest control products on a national basis under Safer, Black Leaf, All Pro Check Mate, and Dexol brand names.

EARNINGS HISTORY *

Year Ended Dec 31	Operating Revenue/Sales (dollars in thousands)	Net Earnings	Return on Revenue (percent)	Return on Equity	Net Earnings (dollars per share†)	Cash Dividend	Market Price Range
1999	74,720	(10,901)	(14.6)	NM	(2.12)	—	6.88–1.50
1998 ¶	48,152	(2,320)	(4.8)	(10.1)	(0.67)	—	14.69–5.00
1997 #	18,821	(546)	(2.9)	(5.1)	(0.24)	—	10.63–5.00
1996 **	14,673	(568)	(3.9)	(5.7)	(0.26)	—	13.75–6.88
1995	14,194	(2,173)	(15.3)	(20.7)	(1.00)	—	12.50–6.25

* Figures for 1997 and earlier are for years ended Sept. 30. Stub quarter from Oct. 1, 1997, through Dec. 31, 1997 (due to change in year end): revenue $4,767,000; loss $1,197,000/($0.45).
† Per-share amounts restated to reflect 1-for-5 reverse stock split effected Aug. 23, 1999.
¶ Figures for 1998 include the results of Consep Inc. from its December 1998 date of acquisition for $11,511,237. Pro forma if acquired Jan. 1, 1998: revenue $84,804,000; loss $8,793,000/($0.34).
# Figures for 1997 include the results of Dexol Industries Inc. from its March 1997 date of acquisition for $3,012,790. Pro forma if acquired Oct. 1, 1996: revenue $21,793,000; loss $1,128,000/($0.45).
** Income figures for 1996 include charge of $312,771/($0.14) for costs related to the abandoned Chas. H. Lilly Co. acquisition attempt.

BALANCE SHEET

Assets	12/31/99 (dollars in thousands)	12/31/98	Liabilities	12/31/99 (dollars in thousands)	12/31/98
Current (CAE 122 and 1,783)	34,560	32,958	Current (STD 3,006 and 653)	24,943	19,079
Property and equipment	6,902	6,636	Long-term debt	14,966	16,958
Intangibles	10,308	19,124	Stockholders' equity*	12,094	22,891
Other	233	210	TOTAL	52,003	58,928
TOTAL	52,003	58,928			

* $0.01 par common; 10,000,000 authorized; 5,112,850 and 5,182,850 issued and outstanding.

RECENT QUARTERS / **PRIOR-YEAR RESULTS**

	Quarter End	Revenue ($000)	Earnings ($000)	EPS ($)	Prior-Year Revenue ($000)	Prior-Year Earnings ($000)	Prior-Year EPS ($)
Q3	09/30/2000	10,266	(9,040)	(1.77)	13,837	(2,458)	(0.48)
Q2	06/30/2000	19,995	(20,622)	(4.03)	27,560	1,284	0.25
Q1	03/31/2000	21,524	50	0.01	22,030	1,219	0.24
Q4	12/31/99	11,293	(10,946)	(2.12)	8,842	(1,514)	(0.40)
	SUM	63,078	(40,558)	(7.92)	72,269	(1,469)	(0.39)

CURRENT: Q2 earnings include special charges of $8,719,000 for impairment of intangible assets, $2,576,000 for obsolete and excess inventory, $1,705,000 for restructuring expenses, $1,690,000 for doubtful accounts, and $1,680,000 for valuation adjustments to property and equipment for sale.

RECENT EVENTS

March 31, 2000: The company blamed a shortfall in first-quarter earnings (compared to prior year) on its private-label business, where several key accounts reduced inventories. In addition, Verdant's California agricultural distribution business had gotten off to a slow start. In **May** Verdant engaged AgriCapital Corp. to assist in the divestiture of part of its Commercial Dealers business unit. The $25.7 million-revenue Commercial Dealers unit operates distribution businesses that market the products of a wide range of suppliers to the agribusiness market. In **June** John Hetterick, president and CEO and a director since 1993, resigned. (Verdant had pursued a strategy of growth through merger and acquisition since 1996, joining four businesses together and increasing sales revenue from $15 million to $85 million on a pro forma basis. While successful in building the revenue base, the complexity of the businesses acquired, combined with decreased demand for some product lines because of industry changes and unfavorable weather patterns, led to ongoing losses and cash flow problems.) Verdant then engaged the services of The Platinum Group, a Minneapolis-based turnaround management company, which installed its own slate of officers. Those officers, in turn, retained the services of the investment banking firm of Goldsmith, Agio, Helms, & Lynner Ltd. to assist in pursuing the sale of Verdant Brand's retail business. "Despite the operational difficulties we have experienced, our retail brands are strong in the marketplace," said President Mallory. "In particular, the Safer brand is in its second consecutive season of double-digit growth. Because the company currently has inadequate capital to invest in the brand-building activities and infrastructure that this business requires to operate successfully, a sale of the retail portion of Verdant's business is being explored as a way of maximizing shareholder value." The company also received a default notice from GE Capital Credit, as a result of loan covenant violations under its credit facility. In **August**, in response to cash flow prob- *continued on page 405*

OFFICERS

Dean Bachelor
Chairman and CEO

Bruce Mallory
President and COO

Volker G. Oakey
EVP and Chief Technology Officer

Paul J. DiCicco
SVP-Operations

Mike Blair
CFO

Pat Brennan
VP-Finance

Scott A. Glatstein
VP and Gen. Mgr.-Retail Brands Division

Paul D. Goodspeed
VP-Safer Ltd.

Steve Hartmeier
VP-Commercial Products Division

DIRECTORS

Dean Bachelor
The Platinum Group

Robert W. Fischer
Robert W. Fischer & Co. Inc., Minneapolis

Stanley Goldberg
Goldmark Advisors

Donald E. Lovness

Richard Mayo
Richard Mayo & Associates

Franklin Pass, M.D.
Medi-Ject Corp., Plymouth, MN

Gordon F. Stofer
Cherry Tree Investments Inc., Bloomington, MN

Frederick F. Yanni Jr.
Health Services Medical Corp. of Central New York Inc.

MAJOR SHAREHOLDERS

Ray Lipkin, 6.4%
Wayzata, MN

GE Capital Corp., 6.1%
Chicago

All officers and directors as a group (12 persons), 5.7%

SIC CODE

2879 Agricultural chemicals, nec

MISCELLANEOUS

TRANSFER AGENT AND REGISTAR:
Wells Fargo Bank Minnesota N.A., South St. Paul, MN

TRADED: Nasdaq National Market

SYMBOL: VERD
STOCKHOLDERS: 325
EMPLOYEES: 188
PART TIME: 3
GENERAL COUNSEL:
Dorsey & Whitney PLLP, Minneapolis
AUDITORS:
Deloitte & Touche LLP, Minneapolis
INC: MN-1961
ANNUAL MEETING: April
INVESTOR RELATIONS:
Mark Eisenschenk

RANKINGS

No. 99 CRM Public 200

SUBSIDIARIES, DIVISIONS, AFFILIATES

Safer Ltd.
3 Pullman Court
Scarborough, Ontario
M1X1E4
416/291-8150

Safer Inc.
9555 James Ave. S.
Suite 200
Bloomington, MN 55431
612/703-3300

Southern Resources Inc.
310 Hwy. 341 S.
Fort Valley, GA 31030

Dexol
1450 W. 228th St.
Torrance, CA 90501

PUB

TWO-YEAR QUARTERLY HIGH-LOW STOCK PRICES

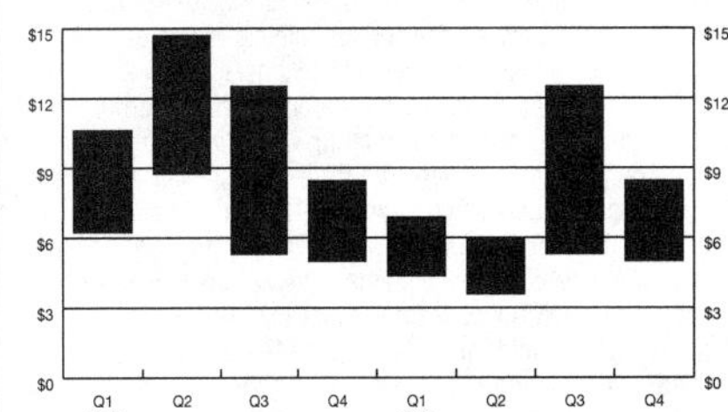

PUB

Vicom Inc.

9449 Science Center Dr., New Hope, MN 55428
Tel: 763/504-3000 Fax: 763/504-3060

Vicom Inc. is a business telecommunications company that sells, installs, and services private telephone and interconnect systems, voicemail systems, and other related communication systems for commercial, professional, and institutional users in Minnesota, Nebraska, and Ohio. The company has programs to allow end users to either rent, lease-purchase, or outright purchase the systems. Vicom currently provides telephone equipment and service to more than 2,000 customers, with 20,000 lines (furnished to users by U S West and other line providers) and 40,000 telephones in service. Telecommunication systems distributed by the company are intended to provide users with flexible, cost-effective alternatives to systems available from major telephone companies such as those formerly comprising the Bell System and from other interconnect telephone companies. The systems include equipment and components manufactured or supplied by other companies. Service of systems provides a significant portion of Vicom's revenue. The company has separate divisions that offer data networking, voicemail, and line analysis services, and a wholly owned subsidiary, Vicom Midwest Telecommunication Systems Inc., which sells, installs, and services telecommunication equipment in Nebraska and Ohio.

EARNINGS HISTORY

Year Ended Dec 31	Operating Revenue/Sales (dollars in thousands)	Net Earnings	Return on Revenue (percent)	Return on Equity	Net Earnings (dollars per share)	Cash Dividend	Market Price Range
1999 *	20,389	(2,064)	(10.1)	NM	(0.54)	—	4.13–1.56
1998 †	6,458	(1,444)	(22.4)	NM	(0.68)	—	1.50–0.31
1997	6,639	56	0.8	5.8	0.03	—	
1996	5,515	(1,141)	(20.7)	NM	(0.55)	—	
1995 ¶	6,379	136	2.1	6.7	0.06	—	

* Pro forma figures for 1999 as if Nov. 1, 1999, acquisition of Ekman Inc. had occurred Jan. 1, 1999: revenue $44.942 million; loss $2.296 million/($0.48).

† Pro forma figures for 1998 as if year-end acquisition of the Midwest region of Enstar Networking Corp. had occurred Jan. 1, 1998: revenue $16.930 million; loss $1.340 million/($0.29).

¶ Income figures for 1995 include pretax gain of $0.52 million from proceeds of a life insurance policy on Douglas Sause, former director.

BALANCE SHEET

Assets	12/31/99 (dollars in thousands)	12/31/98	Liabilities	12/31/99 (dollars in thousands)	12/31/98
Current (CAE 204)	7,763	5,071	Current (STD 4,373 and 1,220)	10,646	5,115
Property and equipment	1,324	647	Notes and installment obligations payable	927	826
Goodwill	3,249	549			
Deferred income taxes		249	Preferred equity	384	337
			Common equity*	643	353
Other	263	114	TOTAL	12,599	6,631
TOTAL	12,599	6,631			

* No par common; 50,000,000 authorized; 4,984,845 and 3,612,995 issued and outstanding, less 199,939 and 106,759 treasury shares.

RECENT QUARTERS / **PRIOR-YEAR RESULTS**

	Quarter End	Revenue ($000)	Earnings ($000)	EPS ($)	Prior-Year Revenue ($000)	Prior-Year Earnings ($000)	Prior-Year EPS ($)
Q3	09/30/2000	10,219	(115)	(0.01)	3,189	(460)	(0.13)
Q2	06/30/2000	8,688	(855)	(0.12)	4,563	(294)	(0.09)
Q1	03/31/2000	9,718	(1,187)	(0.23)	4,646	6	0.00
	SUM	28,625	(2,157)	(0.36)	12,398	(749)	(0.22)

RECENT EVENTS

In **December 1999** the company agreed to acquire Corporate Technologies, Fargo, N.D., in a cash and stock deal, thereby forming a $50 million-revenue telecommunications company serving private and public sector customers throughout the Upper Midwest. The 18-year-old Corporate Technologies ranks as one of the nation's 50 largest network value-added resellers. [Deal completed in January.] CEO Mandel commented, "Corporate Technologies brings valuable vendor relationships and additional technological expertise to our offerings. These synergies place us at the forefront of information technology offerings for our customers." Vicom was named 11th in Teleconnect magazine's list of the nation's 50 largest telecommunication companies. The ranking far exceeded company and industry expectations, which generally held that Vicom would grow to be about the 20th-largest. In **January 2000** Corporate Technologies USA won a $2.4 million contract to install data networking service solutions and telecommunications systems and to provide ongoing service to those systems within the Fargo Public School's Metropolitan Area Network throughout the greater Fargo, N.D., area. In **March** Vicom began offering a new integrated broadband service for multi-unit dwellings. Marketed through a new division, Multiband Inc., the service allowed subscribers to receive local and long-distance telephone service, satellite television service, and high-speed digital Internet access. Vicom's 1999 merger and acquisition activity, combined with forecasted internal *continued on page 405*

OFFICERS

James L. Mandel
CEO

Steven M. Bell
President

Craig Palmer
VP-Operations

DIRECTORS

Steven M. Bell

Jonathan B. Dodge
Dodge & Fox (CPAs)

David Ekman
Corporate Technologies

Marvin Frieman

Paul Knapp
Space CenterVentures Inc.

Pierce A. McNally
Minnesota American Inc., Minnetonka, MN

Mark K. Mekler
Piper Jaffray Inc., Minneapolis

Manuel A. (Manny) Villafana
ATS Medical Inc., Plymouth, MN

MAJOR SHAREHOLDERS

David Ekman, 25.3%
Fargo, ND

Americable Inc., 22.1%
Eden Prairie, MN

Steven M. Bell, 8.4%

Marvin Frieman, 8.4%

All officers and directors as a group (9 persons), 67.1%

SIC CODE

4813 Telephone communications, exc radio

MISCELLANEOUS

TRANSFER AGENT AND REGISTAR:
Corporate Stock Transfer, Minneapolis

TRADED: OTC Bulletin Board

SYMBOL: VICM

STOCKHOLDERS: 349

EMPLOYEES: 184

GENERAL COUNSEL:
Winthrop & Weinstine P.A., Minneapolis

AUDITORS:
Lurie, Besikof, Lapidus & Co. LLP, Minneapolis

INC: MN-1975

ANNUAL MEETING: June

INVESTOR RELATIONS COUNSEL: Swenson NHB

RANKINGS

No. 148 CRM Public 200

SUBSIDIARIES, DIVISIONS, AFFILIATES

Vicom Midwest Telecommunication Systems Inc.

Multiband Inc.
Corporate Technologies
VSA Inc.

Video Update Inc.

3100 World Trade Center, 30 E. Seventh St., St. Paul, MN 55101
Tel: 651/222-0006 Fax: 651/312-2644 Web site: http://www.videoupdate.com

Video Update Inc. owns, operates, and franchises video rental superstores—retail video stores that carry more than 7,500 rental units (videocassettes, video games, or audio books). The company operates company-owned video superstores in the Twin Cities area, and also franchises them, primarily in the Midwest and Northeast. Video Update opened its first franchised video store in 1983, its first company-owned superstore in 1989. The company owns and operates 652 stores located in 31 states and five provinces in Canada, and franchised 55 additional video specialty stores predominantly in the United States.

EARNINGS HISTORY

Year Ended Apr 30	Operating Revenue/Sales (dollars in thousands)	Net Earnings (dollars in thousands)	Return on Revenue (percent)	Return on Equity (percent)	Net Earnings (dollars per share)	Cash Dividend (dollars per share)	Market Price Range (dollars per share)
2000 *	220,962	(36,149)	(16.4)	NM	(1.23)	—	1.16–0.23
1999 †	254,096	(110,371)	(43.4)	NM	(3.77)	—	2.97–0.50
1998 ¶	156,154	(14,480)	(9.3)	(13.2)	(0.71)	—	5.31–1.69
1997	91,799	4,620	5.0	5.1	0.29	—	9.75–3.50
1996	50,504	1,628	3.2	2.6	0.17	—	13.00–4.25

* Income figures for 2000 include pretax charges for goodwill valuation ($7.354 million) and fixed asset valuation ($4.314 million), less store closing charge reversal of $5.42 million.
† Income figures for 1999 include pretax charges for inventory valuation ($50.629 million), fixed asset valuation ($6.6 million), and store closings ($8.198 million).
¶ Income figures for 1998 include pretax charge for store closings ($5.082 million). Figures include results of Moovies Inc. (267 retail stores) from its March 1998 acquisition for $83.459 million. Pro forma if acquired May 1, 1997: revenue $248.134 million; loss $28.562 million/($0.98).

BALANCE SHEET

Assets	04/30/00 (dollars in thousands)	04/30/99 (dollars in thousands)
Cash and cash equivalents	1,763	1,235
Accounts receivable	1,823	3,826
Mdse inventory	2,116	6,393
Video/game rental inventory	38,976	45,040
Property and equipment	42,801	59,395
Prepaid expenses	1,015	6,419
Goodwill	66,223	77,715
Other	5,311	7,185
TOTAL	160,028	207,208

Liabilities	04/30/00 (dollars in thousands)	04/30/99 (dollars in thousands)
Notes payable	138,440	117,124
Accounts payable	27,703	54,945
Accrued expenses	17,492	23,054
Accrued compensation	5,520	8,062
Accrued rent	6,671	7,118
Stockholders' equity*	(35,798)	(3,095)
TOTAL	160,028	207,208

* $0.01 par common; 60,000,000 authorized; 29,278,457 and 29,278,457 issued and outstanding.

RECENT QUARTERS / **PRIOR-YEAR RESULTS**

	Quarter End	Revenue ($000)	Earnings ($000)	EPS ($)	Prior-Year Revenue ($000)	Prior-Year Earnings ($000)	Prior-Year EPS ($)
Q4	04/30/2000	48,943	(25,594)	(0.87)	59,527	(89,141)	(3.04)
Q3	01/31/2000	57,468	1,058	0.04	70,692	(2,123)	(0.07)
Q2	10/31/99	54,487	(9,749)	(0.33)	62,184	(12,629)	(0.43)
Q1	07/31/99	60,064	(1,864)	(0.06)	61,693	(6,478)	(0.22)
	SUM	220,962	(36,149)	(1.23)	254,096	(110,371)	(3.77)

CURRENT: Q4 earnings include pretax charges of $7.354 million related to goodwill impairment and $4.314 million related to fixed-asset impairment.
PRIOR YEAR: Q4 earnings include pretax charges of $16.135 million related to store closings and $50.629 million related to change in inventory amortization method, a total of $43.607/($1.49) after-tax.

RECENT EVENTS

In **November 1999** a group of local investors that had recently acquired a 5.3 percent stake in the company was urging Video Update management to explore a number of options to boost the lagging stock price. At the end of August, Video Update, Millennium Internet Corp. (owner-operator of popular online movie destination MovieWeb.com), and Unique Business Systems Inc. (UBS), the leading provider of video retail point-of-sale (POS) software, teamed up to launch the MovieWeb Video Retail Network. Set for a fourth-quarter national rollout, the MovieWeb Video Retail Network is a one-stop marketing and business services solution created expressly for video retailers and their members. By leveraging the combined resources of local video retail affiliates and the popular MovieWeb.com online consumer movie destination, the MovieWeb Video Retail Network empowers its video retailer members with an extensive array of online and offline e-commerce capabilities, consumer marketing programs, and other business services designed to increase their local market share against the major chains. In **September** the company's Form 10-K for the fiscal year ended April 30, 2000, was finally filed. It disclosed that the *continued on page 406*

OFFICERS

Daniel A. Potter
Chairman and CEO
John M. Bedard
President
Daniel C. Howard
COO
Michael P. Gebauer
CFO
Richard Bedard
EVP
Michael G. Schifsky
SVP

DIRECTORS

John M. Bedard
Teodore Coburn
Brown, Coburn & Co.
Daniel C. Howard
Paul Kelnberger
Johnson, West & Co. PLC, St. Paul
Bernard R. Patriacca
Errands Etc. Inc.
Daniel A. Potter

MAJOR SHAREHOLDERS

Daniel A. Potter, 6.1%
All officers and directors as a group (9 persons), 12.2%

SIC CODE

5735 Record and prerecorded tape stores

MISCELLANEOUS

TRANSFER AGENT AND REGISTAR:
American Stock Transfer & Trust Co., New York
TRADED: OTC Bulletin Board
SYMBOL: VUPDA
STOCKHOLDERS: 352
EMPLOYEES: 5,274
GENERAL COUNSEL:
O'Connor, Broude & Aronson, Waltham, MA
AUDITORS:
Ernst & Young LLP, Minneapolis
INC: DE-1994
FOUNDED: 1983
ANNUAL MEETING:
December

RANKINGS

No. 69 CRM Public 200

TWO-YEAR QUARTERLY HIGH-LOW STOCK PRICES

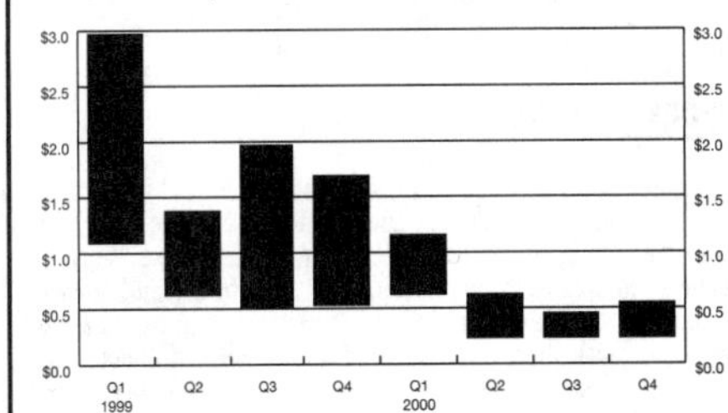

PUB

VirtualFund.com Inc.

7156 Shady Oak Rd., Eden Prairie, MN 55344
Tel: 952/941-8687 Fax: 952/941-8652 Web site: http://www.virtualfund.com

VirtualFund.com Inc., formerly LaserMaster Technologies Inc., is an Internet venture resources and investment company. Its primary expansion initiative is represented by the Internet Services Business Unit (ISBU) that is currently funding investment and development-stage companies with highly viral growth potential. The ISBU is architecting venture-stage growth opportunities in the Internet marketplace that encompass Internet commerce, content, and collaboration—all aimed at increasing the annuities available from Internet hosting of these activities.

EARNINGS HISTORY *

Year Ended Jun 30	Operating Revenue/Sales (dollars in thousands)	Net Earnings	Return on Revenue (percent)	Return on Equity	Net Earnings (dollars per share)	Cash Dividend	Market Price Range
2000 †	6,901	19,081	NM	57.7	1.16	—	11.50–1.14
1999 ¶	4,138	(7,823)	NM	NM	(0.50)	—	5.25–1.19
1998 #	0	1,841	NM	13.3	0.12	—	5.25–1.69
1997 **	0	(17,200)	NM	NM	(1.20)	—	6.25–1.63
1996 ††	0	(10,462)	NM	(66.9)	(0.93)	—	7.63–3.63

* Revenue restated for continuing operations.
† Income figures for 2000 include nonrecurring and start-up expenses totaling $14.3 million/($0.87); and gain of $40.802 million/$2.48 from discontinued operations and their disposal.
¶ Figures for 1999 include TEAM Technologies from Dec. 18, 1998, date of acquisition; income figures include gain of $2.555 million/$0.16 from discontinued operations.
# Income figures for 1998 include gain of $3.599 million/$0.23 from discontinued operations.
** Income figures for 1997 include loss of $12.836 million/($0.90) from discontinued operations.
†† Income figures for 1996 include loss of $8.214 million/($0.73) from discontinued operations.

BALANCE SHEET

Assets	06/30/00 (dollars in thousands)	06/30/99	Liabilities	06/30/00 (dollars in thousands)	06/30/99
Current (CAE 39,641 and 250)	42,098	8,627	Current (STD 476 and 702)	11,288	6,353
Property and equipment	1,697	1,491	Long-term debt	92	570
			Preferred stock		7,500
Goodwill		10,132	Common stock*	33,074	5,944
Other	659	116	TOTAL	44,454	20,367
TOTAL	44,454	20,367			

* $0.01 par common; 50,000,000 authorized; 17,577,002 and 15,803,866 issued and outstanding.

RECENT QUARTERS / **PRIOR-YEAR RESULTS**

	Quarter End	Revenue ($000)	Earnings ($000)	EPS ($)	Prior-Year Revenue ($000)	Prior-Year Earnings ($000)	Prior-Year EPS ($)
Q4	06/30/2000	1,766	10,563	0.60	1,631	(3,195)	(0.20)
Q3	04/02/2000	1,636	(1,934)	(0.12)	2,020	(1,348)	(0.09)
Q2	01/02/2000	1,598	11,875	0.75	487	(2,611)	(0.17)
Q1	10/03/99	1,901	(1,422)	(0.09)	0	(669)	(0.04)
	SUM	6,901	19,082	1.14	4,138	(7,823)	(0.50)

CURRENT: Q4 earnings include pretax charge of $7.838 million to write off goodwill; and after-tax gain of $23.4 million/$1.33 from discontinued operations and their disposal. Q3 earnings include gain of $1.109 million/$0.07 from discontinued operations. Q2 earnings include $14.555 million/$0.92 income tax benefit and $0.946 million/$0.06 gain from discontinued operations. Q1 earnings include gain of $0.792 million/$0.05 from discontinued operations.
PRIOR YEAR: Q4 earnings include gain of $2.508 million/$0.16 from discontinued operations. Q3 earnings include gain of $0.41 million/$0.03 from discontinued operations. Q2 earnings include loss of $0.627 million/($0.04) from discontinued operations. Q1 earnings include gain of $0.264 million/$0.02 from discontinued operations.

RECENT EVENTS

In **December 1999** the company received the results from its Nasdaq Listing Qualifications Panel hearing on Nov. 18. The company was allowed to resume trading as VFND, with the fifth character "E" removed. In addition, Nasdaq requested further documentation supporting compliance with Nasdaq Listing Requirements. In **January 2000** management completed its review of its deferred tax assets after its decision to sell the Digital Graphics Business Unit, which was announced Oct. 21, 1999. The sale of the DGBU was expected to provide proceeds that would allow the company to use all of its deferred tax assets of $14 million. This revaluation of the deferred taxes increased the company's net tangible assets, bringing it into compliance with Nasdaq requirements. B2BXchange chose Onvoy, Plymouth, Minn., to provide *continued on page 406*

OFFICERS

Melvin L. Masters
Chairman, President, and CEO

Robert J. Wenzel
COO

David Alexander
Secretary

Sandra J. Ferrian
General Counsel

Stephen Fisher, `
Senior Strategist-B2BXchange Inc.

James H. Horstman
CFO

Lawrence J. Lukis
Chief Engineer

Thomas D. Ryan
EVP

Timothy N. Thurn
Treasurer

Danny J. Vatland
Chief Technical Officer

DIRECTORS

Edward S. Adams
U. of Minnesota School of Law, Minneapolis

Rohan Champion
Federal Express Corp.

Timothy R. Duoos
Lyndale Garden Center Inc., Richfield, MN

Steve Fisher

Jean-Louis Gassee
Be Inc., Menlo Park, CA

Melvin L. Masters

Ralph D. Rolen
First Tennessee National Bank, Memphis, TN

Roger Wikner
Miller & Schroeder Financial Inc. (former)

MAJOR SHAREHOLDERS

Melvin L. Masters, 17.2%

Sihl-Zurich Paper Mill on Sihl AG, 14.4%
Zurich

All officers and directors as a group (9 persons), 23.8%

SIC CODE

3577 Computer peripheral equipment, nec

MISCELLANEOUS

TRANSFER AGENT AND REGISTAR:
Wells Fargo Bank Minnesota N.A.,
South St. Paul, MN

TRADED: Nasdaq National Market

SYMBOL: VFND
STOCKHOLDERS: 216
EMPLOYEES: 186
GENERAL COUNSEL:
Dorsey & Whitney PLLP, Minneapolis
AUDITORS:
Deloitte & Touche LLP, Minneapolis
INC: MN-1988
FOUNDED: 1985
ANNUAL MEETING: April
INVESTOR RELATIONS:
Michael Dreis

RANKINGS

No. 192 CRM Public 200

SUBSIDIARIES, DIVISIONS, AFFILIATES

B2BX Corp.

RSPnet.com

TWO-YEAR QUARTERLY HIGH-LOW STOCK PRICES

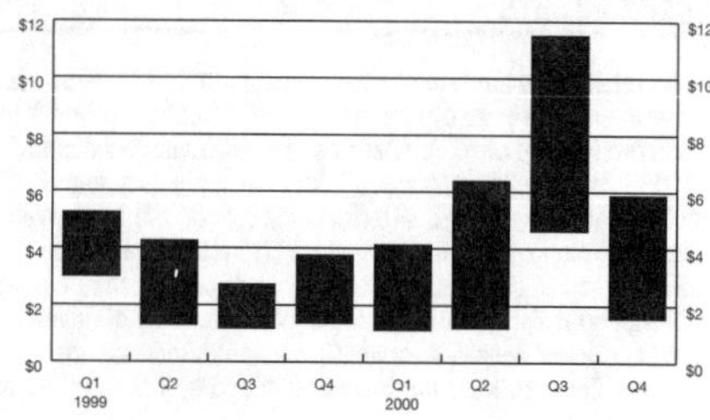

Vital Images Inc.

3300 Fernbrook Ln. N., Suite 200, Plymouth, MN 55447
Tel: 612/915-8000 Fax: 612/915-8010 Web site: http://www.vitalimages.com

Vital Images Inc., is a provider of 3D imaging software for use in clinical diagnosis, surgical planning and screening applications. The Company's technology utilizes high-speed volume visualization and analysis, as well as network communications based on DICOM and Internet protocols. Vital Images cost-effectively brings 3D visualization and analysis into the day-to-day practice of medicine. The company markets its products to healthcare providers and to manufacturers of diagnostic imaging equipment through a direct sales force in the United States and independent resellers in international markets.

EARNINGS HISTORY *

Year Ended Dec 31	Operating Revenue/Sales (dollars in thousands)	Net Earnings	Return on Revenue (percent)	Return on Equity	Net Earnings (dollars per share†)	Cash Dividend	Market Price Range
1999	6,623	(3,218)	(48.6)	(52.8)	(0.64)	—	8.38–1.50
1998	4,527	(3,209)	(70.9)	NM	(0.66)	—	3.25–1.00
1997	1,218	(4,774)	NM	(65.8)	(1.00)	—	2.50–1.19
1996	882	(2,546)	NM	NM	(0.54)	—	
1995	2,894	253	8.7	NM	0.07	—	

* Fiscal years 1995 and 1996 ended Oct. 31. In 1997 the company changed its fiscal year end to Dec. 31. Results from two-month stub period ended Dec. 31, 1996: revenue $64,966; loss $520,703/($0.11).
† Shares began independently trading on May 14, 1997.

BALANCE SHEET

Assets	12/31/99 (dollars in thousands)	12/31/98	Liabilities	12/31/99 (dollars in thousands)	12/31/98
Current (CAE 5,332 and 1,751)	7,801	5,021	Current	2,392	1,662
			Deferred revenue	175	142
Property and equipment	864	916	Stockholders' equity*	6,098	4,134
TOTAL	8,666	5,938	TOTAL	8,666	5,938

* $0.01 par common; 20,000,000 authorized; 6,695,867 and 4,870,497 issued and outstanding.

RECENT QUARTERS / **PRIOR-YEAR RESULTS**

	Quarter End	Revenue ($000)	Earnings ($000)	EPS ($)	Prior-Year Revenue ($000)	Prior-Year Earnings ($000)	Prior-Year EPS ($)
Q3	09/30/2000	2,828	(525)	(0.08)	1,719	(447)	(0.09)
Q2	06/30/2000	2,513	(802)	(0.12)	1,120	(1,308)	(0.27)
Q1	03/31/2000	2,270	(665)	(0.10)	1,740	(765)	(0.16)
Q4	12/31/99	2,045	(697)	(0.13)	1,526	(732)	(0.15)
	SUM	9,656	(2,689)	(0.43)	6,105	(3,252)	(0.66)

RECENT EVENTS

In **December 1999** Vital Images and ALI Technologies Inc. (TSE: ALT) announced an agreement to cooperatively market Vital Images' diagnostic 2D and 3D visualization and analysis software with ALI's image management and networking products. Vital Images completed a private placement of its common stock of $5.4 million for expansion of its sales staff, additional research and development, increased marketing and promotional expenses, and general working capital. At year's end, the company announced the release for shipment of Vitrea 2, a Microsoft Windows NT-compatible version of its Vitrea software. In **January 2000**, the company was issued U.S. Patent No. 5,986,662 entitled "Advanced Diagnostic Viewer Employing Automated Protocol Selection for Volume-Rendered Imaging," which covers the mechanism for automated protocol selection utilized in Vitrea 2. In **August** the company received 510(k) clearance from the FDA for a new option to VScore, its coronary artery calcium scoring software. The newly approved option, called VScore with EKG Gate, utilizes an alternative measurement process that exposes Vital Images' calcium scoring technology to a much larger potential market. In **September**, the company the company received approval from Nasdaq to list its common stock on the Nasdaq SmallCap Market. **Sept. 30**: Nine-month revenue rose 66 percent to $7,612,000 compared with $4,578,000 in the year-ago period. Software license fee revenue increased 85 percent to $5,221,000. The net loss for the period narrowed to $1,992,000. Under an **October** marketing and distribution agreement with Toshiba America Medical Systems Inc., Toshiba was to offer Vital Images' Vitrea software and systems to its customers and prospects as its 2D/3D visualization product of choice.

OFFICERS

Douglas M. Pihl
Chairman

Albert Emola
President and CEO

Vincent J. Argiro, Ph.D.
Chief Technology Officer and Founder

Gregory S. Furness
VP-Finance, CFO, Treasurer, Secretary

Jay D. Miller
VP-Business Development and Gen. Mgr.

Steven P. Canakes
VP-Sales

David M. Frazee
VP-Engineering

Robert C. Samec
VP-Regulatory/Quality Affairs

Cindy J. Edwards
Dir.-Human Resources

DIRECTORS

Vincent Argiro, Ph.D.

Albert Emola

James B. Hickey Jr.
Aequitron Medical Inc. (formerly)

Richard W. Perkins
Perkins Capital Management Inc., Wayzata, MN

Douglas M. Pihl

Michael W. Vannier, M.D.
U. of Iowa College of Medicine, Iowa City, IA

Sven A. Wehrwein
financial consultant/writer, Golden Valley, MN

MAJOR SHAREHOLDERS

Jess S. Morgan & Co. Inc., 13.9%
Los Angeles

Perkins Capital Management Inc., 13%
Wayzata, MN

Vincent J. Argiro, 5.9%

All officers and directors as a group (12 persons), 14.1%

SIC CODE

7373 Computer integrated systems design

MISCELLANEOUS

TRANSFER AGENT AND REGISTAR:
American Stock Transfer & Trust Co., New York

TRADED: Nasdaq SmallCap Market

SYMBOL: VTAL

STOCKHOLDERS: 1,200

EMPLOYEES: 67

IN MINNESOTA: 52

GENERAL COUNSEL:
Winthrop & Weinstine P.A., St. Paul

AUDITORS:
PricewaterhouseCoopers LLP, Minneapolis

INC: MN-1997

FOUNDED: 1988

ANNUAL MEETING: May

INVESTOR RELATIONS:
Gregory S. Furness

RANKINGS

No. 198 CRM Public 200

SUBSIDIARIES, DIVISIONS, AFFILIATES

TECHNICAL OPERATIONS:
505 N. Fourth St.
Fairfield, IA 52556
515/472-7726

TWO-YEAR QUARTERLY HIGH-LOW STOCK PRICES

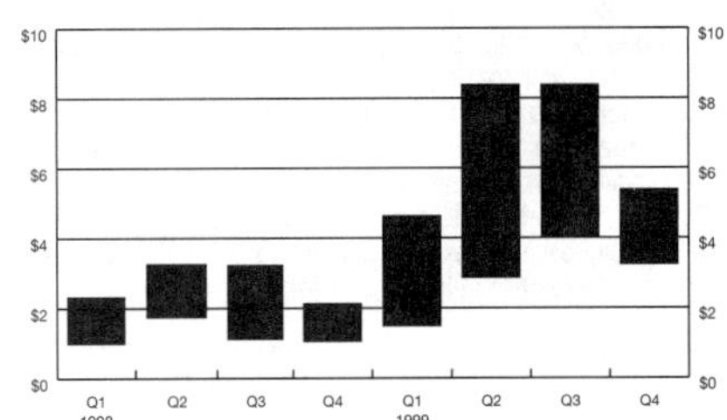

PUB

Voice & Wireless Corporation

600 S. Highway 169, Suite 654, St. Louis Park, MN 55426
Tel: 952/546-2075 Web site: http://www.knscintl.com

Voice & Wireless Corp., formerly Kensington International Holding Corp., is a holding company with ownership interests in multiple industries and segments ranging from traditional brick and mortar businesses to Internet/technology services and products. During 1999, the company mapped out a new strategy to reposition itself to grow in the business-to-business Internet and communications environment by emphasizing advanced Internet-related communications services and products. The company owns 85 percent of Florida corporation Mail Call Inc., the creator of a convenient and easy-to-use method of accessing and managing e-mail from any telephone in the world. Mail Call's customers dial a toll-free number, connect to Mail Call's automated system, and hear their e-mail as Mail Call reads their messages to them. Without keyboard or computer, the customer may respond verbally (leaving a voice response as though sending a voicemail) to the e-mail. Mail Call delivers the "voice" e-mail as a return message to the sender. Mail Call has a Web Site at www.mailcall.net. The company also owns Ives Design Inc., a 26-employee manufacturer of store display fixtures; and different percentage interests in 28 operating oil and gas wells in Oklahoma, Texas, and Arkansas.

EARNINGS HISTORY

Year Ended Dec 31	Operating Revenue/Sales (dollars in thousands)	Net Earnings (dollars in thousands)	Return on Revenue (percent)	Return on Equity (percent)	Net Earnings (dollars per share)	Cash Dividend (dollars per share)	Market Price Range (dollars per share)
1999	3,622	103	2.8	22.4	0.03	—	4.25–0.06
1998	3,935	201	5.1	NM	0.06	—	

BALANCE SHEET

Assets	12/31/99 (dollars in thousands)	12/31/98 (dollars in thousands)
Current (CAE 1,026 and 72)	1,823	854
Property and equipment	276	296
Investment in oil and gas properties	65	68
Investments in unconsolidated corporations	40	
Investments in unconsolidated oil/gas partnership		10
Notes receivable	11	17
Loan costs	27	33
Intangibles	5	
TOTAL	2,247	1,277

Liabilities	12/31/99 (dollars in thousands)	12/31/98 (dollars in thousands)
Current (STD 437 and 156)	873	765
Long-term debt	448	816
Capital lease obligations		6
Minority interest in consolidated subsidiary	467	
Stockholders' equity*	459	(309)
TOTAL	2,247	1,277

* No par common; 50,000,000 authorized; 5,239,150 and 3,238,750 issued and outstanding.

RECENT QUARTERS / PRIOR-YEAR RESULTS

	Quarter End	Revenue ($000)	Earnings ($000)	EPS ($)	Prior-Year Revenue ($000)	Prior-Year Earnings ($000)	Prior-Year EPS ($)
Q2	06/30/2000	859	(191)	(0.02)	1,153	74	0.02
Q1	03/31/2000	1,099	(154)	(0.02)	862	15	0.00
	SUM	1,958	(345)	(0.04)	2,015	89	0.03

RECENT EVENTS

Dec. 31, 1999: Fiscal-year net income of $102,942 was a decrease from 1998 due to increased operating costs and legal and accounting fees incurred for the acquisition of Mail Call. In addition, Ives Design's largest customer delayed orders into the year 2000 due to Y2K fears. This produced the largest revenue month in the history of the company in **January 2000**. In **April** the company acquired the rights, title, and interest to a patent-pending, digital wireless earpiece from Micro Talk Technologies Inc. The digital wireless earpiece allows the user to listen and speak on their cellular phone hands-free and without wires. The wireless earpiece works with phones, multimedia computers, stereos, and most televisions on the market today. The company hoped to start marketing the device during fall 2000. Also in April, the company loaned Stroke of Fortune Inc. $175,000 to complete the installations of four to five wide-angle, wireless electronic monitoring systems. The first commercial application is for golf courses. By the end of **July**, systems had been installed on a course in Palm Springs, Calif., another in Myrtle Beach, N.C., and two in the Orlando, Fla., area using the proceeds of the loan. A wireless camera is used to monitor and record a golfer's tee shot, the golf ball's flight to the green, and the place where the ball lands on the green. The golfer receives a gift certificate for the pro shop if the ball lands within 10 feet of the pin or a cash prize for a hole-in-one. In addition to Stroke of Fortune paying the loan back, it is responsible for paying to the company 7 percent of all future gross revenue generated under this program. In **October**, in its efforts to expand communications activities and increase investor relations activities, the company retained New York City-based investor relations firm DeMonte Associates, which specializes in micro-cap emerging growth companies with areas of expertise in high-technology.

OFFICERS

Mike Nakonechny
Chairman

Mark Haggerty
CEO

Holly Callen Hamilton
VP and Secretary

Jeff Etten
CFO

DIRECTORS

Keith Bernhardt
American Gas (former)

Mark Haggerty

Holly Callen Hamilton

Mike Nakonechny
NAK Associates Corp., Elverson, PA

Keith A. Witter
Askar Corp., Rochester, MN

MAJOR SHAREHOLDERS

Keith Bernhardt, 6%
W. Hartford, CT

All officers and directors as a group (9 persons), 27.3%

SIC CODE

1381 Drilling oil and gas wells

1751 Carpentering

2541 Wood partitions and fixtures

7371 Computer programming services

MISCELLANEOUS

TRADED: OTC Bulletin Board

SYMBOL: KNSC

STOCKHOLDERS: 850

WSI Industries Inc.

15250 Wayzata Blvd., Wayzata, MN 55391
Tel: 952/473-1271 Fax: 952/473-2945 Web site: http://www.wsiindustries.com

WSI Industries Inc., formerly Washington Scientific Industries Inc., provides contract machining services to customers from a variety of industries, including agriculture, construction, avionics/aerospace, defense, recreational vehicles, computers, and engines. Programs specialize in the machining of complex, close-tolerance parts requiring unique and specialized processes. Partnerships and long-term relationships are established to respond to the customer's need for multiyear programs. WSI's total manufacturing solution extends from design engineering and materials purchasing to manufacturing and shipping.

EARNINGS HISTORY

Year Ended Aug	Operating Revenue/Sales (dollars in thousands)	Net Earnings	Return on Revenue (percent)	Return on Equity	Net Earnings (dollars per share)	Cash Dividend	Market Price Range
1999 *	21,550	261	1.2	3.2	0.11	—	6.69–2.75
1998	23,948	1,874	7.8	23.4	0.77	—	8.00–4.56
1997 †	24,153	1,584	6.6	26.2	0.65	—	6.00–2.08
1996	20,174	(367)	(1.8)	(8.2)	(0.15)	—	4.75–3.00
1995 ¶	30,409	945	3.1	20.1	0.39	—	4.38–2.75

* Pro forma figures for 1999 had Taurus and Bowman acquisitions occurred at beginning of period: revenue $33,802,000; earnings $2,105,000/$0.83.
† Fiscal year 1997 consisted of 53 weeks. Income figures include a one-time gain of $410,000 from the sale of excess equipment.
¶ Income figures for 1995 include pretax gains of $254,419 for pension curtailment; and $889,911 for real estate sale.

BALANCE SHEET

Assets	08/29/99 (dollars in thousands)	08/30/98	Liabilities	08/29/99 (dollars in thousands)	08/30/98
Current (CAE 131 and 2,697)	6,658	6,676	Current (STD 1,722 and 709)	5,247	3,438
Property, plant, and equipment	12,182	6,939	Long-term debt	10,666	1,802
			Pension liability	347	380
Intangibles	5,685		Stockholders' equity*	8,264	7,995
TOTAL	24,525	13,615	TOTAL	24,525	13,615

* $0.10 par common; 10,000,000 authorized; 2,453,425 and 2,448,800 issued and outstanding.

RECENT QUARTERS / PRIOR-YEAR RESULTS

	Quarter End	Revenue ($000)	Earnings ($000)	EPS ($)	Prior-Year Revenue ($000)	Prior-Year Earnings ($000)	Prior-Year EPS ($)
Q4	08/27/2000	8,066	209	0.08	6,191	348	0.14
Q3	05/28/2000	9,086	603	0.24	5,989	57	0.02
Q2	02/27/2000	7,711	(223)	(0.09)	3,729	(421)	(0.17)
Q1	11/28/99	7,295	51	0.02	5,641	277	0.11
	SUM	32,158	640	0.26	21,550	261	0.11

CURRENT: Q3 earnings include gain of $121,000 on pension curtailment. Q2 earnings include gain of $126,000 on sale of equipment. Q1 earnings include gains of $232,000 on pension curtailment and $269,000 on sale of equipment; and loss of $249,000 in severance costs.

RECENT EVENTS

In **January 2000** the company said that the plant consolidation initiative announced in fall 1999 was proceeding as planned. WSI was closing its Long Lake facility and consolidating all manufacturing at two other plants. In the first quarter of fiscal 2000, severance, relocation, and other expenses related to the consolidation were partially offset by one-time gains on the termination of the Long Lake defined benefit pension plan and on the sale of excess manufacturing equipment. All manufacturing was being consolidated into facilities in Rochester, Minn. (Bowman Tool and Machining), and Osseo, Minn. (Taurus Numeric Tool), plants that were in closer proximity to WSI's customers. Proceeds from the pending sale of the 176,000-square-foot Long Lake facility were to be used to reduce the long-term debt supporting the Taurus and Bowman acquisitions. **Aug. 27:** Consolidated fiscal-year net sales of $32.157 million were up 49 percent from fiscal 1999. Consolidated net income was up 145 percent. "WSI has completed a very important transitional year," said CEO Pudil. "Having completed a lengthy and costly manufacturing consolidation initiative, WSI is now in a better position to operate from an efficient, low-cost platform that will enable us to compete aggressively on a global basis going forward. We are also benefiting from the two acquisitions transacted over the past 18 months that have provided us with a stronger, more diversified and more balanced customer base."

OFFICERS

George J. Martin
Chairman

Michael J. Pudil
President and CEO

Paul D. Sheely
VP-Finance and CFO

Gerald E. Magnuson
Secretary

DIRECTORS

Paul Baszucki
Norstan Inc., Plymouth, MN

Melvin L. Katten
Katten, Muchin & Zavis, Chicago

Gerald E. Magnuson
Lindquist & Vennum PLLP (retired)

George J. Martin
Pow Con Inc. (retired)

Eugene J. Mora
Amserv Healthcare Inc. (retired)

Michael J. Pudil

MAJOR SHAREHOLDERS

Michael J. Pudil, 6.8%

All officers and directors as a group (7 persons), 11.8%

SIC CODE

3449 Miscellaneous structural metalwork

3499 Fabricated metal products, nec

MISCELLANEOUS

TRANSFER AGENT AND REGISTAR:
Wells Fargo Bank Minnesota N.A.,
South St. Paul, MN

TRADED: Nasdaq SmallCap Market

SYMBOL: WSCI

STOCKHOLDERS: 615

EMPLOYEES: 111

IN MINNESOTA: 111

GENERAL COUNSEL:
Lindquist & Vennum PLLP, Minneapolis

AUDITORS:
Ernst & Young LLP, Minneapolis

INC: MN-1950

ANNUAL MEETING:
January

INVESTOR RELATIONS COUNSEL: Equity Market Partners

RANKINGS

No. 143 CRM Public 200

SUBSIDIARIES, DIVISIONS, AFFILIATES

Taurus Numeric Tool Inc.
Osseo, Minn.

Bowman Tool & Machine, Inc.
Rochester, MN

TWO-YEAR QUARTERLY HIGH-LOW STOCK PRICES

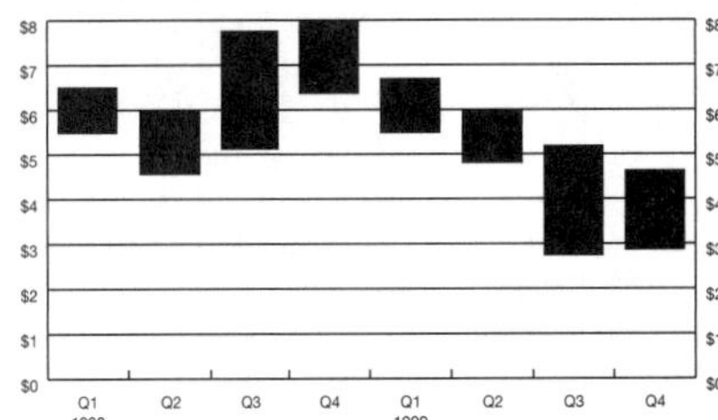

PUB

WTC Industries Inc.

150 Marie Ave. E., West St. Paul, MN 55118
Tel: 651/554-3140 Fax: 651/450-5182 Web site: http://www.pentapure.com

WTC Industries Inc., formerly Water Technologies Corp., develops, manufactures, and markets water filtration and purification products for commercial and personal use. The company's products include devices suitable for personal travel, camping, and emergency use; point-of-use systems for the home; and water purification systems for light industrial and commercial applications.

EARNINGS HISTORY

Year Ended Dec 31	Operating Revenue/Sales (dollars in thousands)	Net Earnings	Return on Revenue (percent)	Return on Equity	Net Earnings (dollars per share*)	Cash Dividend	Market Price Range
1999	5,142	(142)	(2.8)	NM	(0.12)	—	9.94–1.06
1998 †	3,786	(3,042)	NM	NM	(2.69)	—	11.88–1.88
1997	3,285	(1,513)	(46.1)	NM	(1.39)	—	19.38–2.50
1996	2,937	(3,039)	NM	NM	(2.99)	—	32.50–12.50
1995	2,883	(3,221)	NM	NM	(4.59)	—	50.00–17.50

* Per-share amounts restated to reflect 1-for-10 reverse stock split effected Jan. 6, 1999.
† Income figures for 1998 include expenses—$350,000 loss on royalty agreement and $463,500 loss on minimum-purchase contract—totaling ($0.72) per share.

BALANCE SHEET

Assets	12/31/99 (dollars in thousands)	12/31/98	Liabilities	12/31/99 (dollars in thousands)	12/31/98
Current (CAE 11 and 25)	944	677	Current (STD 139 and 862)	1,160	1,657
Property and equipment	325	194	Long-term debt	5,405	4,398
			Accrued minimum purchase commitments	292	345
Other	5	12	Stockholders' equity*	(5,583)	(5,518)
TOTAL	1,275	882	TOTAL	1,275	882

* $0.10 par common; 15,000,000 authorized; 1,169,364 and 1,146,031 issued and outstanding.

RECENT QUARTERS / **PRIOR-YEAR RESULTS**

	Quarter End	Revenue ($000)	Earnings ($000)	EPS ($)	Revenue ($000)	Earnings ($000)	EPS ($)
Q3	09/30/2000	2,286	(230)	(0.16)	1,463	27	0.02
Q3	09/30/2000	2,286	(230)	(0.16)	1,013	(169)	(0.14)
Q2	06/30/2000	1,958	(195)	(0.13)	1,484	83	0.07
Q1	03/31/2000	1,186	(317)	(0.25)	1,182	(83)	(0.07)
	SUM	7,715	(973)	(0.69)	5,142	(142)	(0.12)

RECENT EVENTS

In **March 2000** subsidiary PentaPure Inc. was selected as the exclusive supplier of water filtration systems for the General Electric Appliance Division's (GEA) 2001 model-year refrigerator program. The company was awarded the business for water filtration systems to be used in all refrigerators containing Smart Water and Smart Water Plus water filtration systems—an order valued at $10 million annually. **Sept. 30:** Regarding third-quarter results, which featured record revenue, CEO Carbonari said, "The increase in sales was driven by increased sales of proprietary water systems to the domestic OEM market. Earnings continue to be lower primarily due to considerable investments to increase production capacity and new product development for the OEM market."

OFFICERS

Robert C. Klas Sr.
Chairman and CEO

Greg Jensen
CFO, Treasurer, and Secretary

Andrew Rensink
VP-Operations

DIRECTORS

John A. Clymer
Resource Companies, Inc., Minneapolis

Robert C. Klas Jr.
TapeMark Co., West St. Paul, MN

Robert C. Klas Sr.
TapeMark Co., West St. Paul, MN

Dr. Ronald A. Mitsch
3M Co. (former)

Biloine W. Young
writer, St. Paul

MAJOR SHAREHOLDERS

Robert C. Klas Sr., 80.3%
West St. Paul, MN

Jan H. Magnusson, 11.8%
Shoreview, MN

All officers and directors as a group (8 persons), 81.3%

SIC CODE

3589 Service industry machinery, nec

MISCELLANEOUS

TRANSFER AGENT AND REGISTAR:
Wells Fargo Bank Minnesota N.A.,
South St. Paul, MN

TRADED: OTC Bulletin Board

SYMBOL: WTCO

STOCKHOLDERS: 850

EMPLOYEES: 46

PART TIME: 4

IN MINNESOTA: 46

GENERAL COUNSEL:
Lindquist & Vennum PLLP, Minneapolis

AUDITORS:
RSM McGladrey & Pullen Inc. LLP, Minneapolis

INC: DE-1978

ANNUAL MEETING: May

INVESTOR RELATIONS:
Greg Jensen

SUBSIDIARIES, DIVISIONS, AFFILIATES

PentaPure Inc.
James J. Carbonari

TWO-YEAR QUARTERLY HIGH-LOW STOCK PRICES

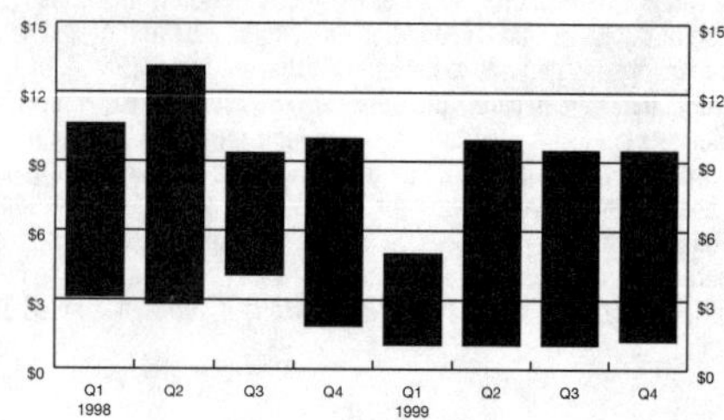

Waters Instruments Inc.

2950 Xenium Ln., Suite 108, Plymouth, MN 55441
Tel: 763/551-1125 Fax: 763/509-7450 Web site: http://www.wtrs.com

Waters Instruments Inc. operates four principal business groups: Waters Network Systems, Waters Technical Systems, Zareba Systems, and Waters Medical Systems. All four business groups sell principally within the United States. **Waters Network Systems** provides local-area-network connectivity solutions for the K-12 educational market. **Waters Technical Systems** subcontract manufactures product assemblies and cable harness assemblies for the communications and computer industries. **Zareba Systems** manufactures and distributes monitoring products and electrical fence controllers for animal management and pet containment. **Waters Medical Systems** produces medical instrumentation for cardiac catheterization labs and organ preservation.

EARNINGS HISTORY

Year Ended Jun 30	Operating Revenue/Sales (dollars in thousands)	Net Earnings	Return on Revenue (percent)	Return on Equity	Net Earnings (dollars per share)	Cash Dividend	Market Price Range
2000	19,807	837	4.2	10.2	0.57	0.04	34.00–4.00
1999	17,585	1,006	5.7	13.6	0.68	0.04	6.38–3.63
1998	15,785	685	4.3	10.7	0.47	0.04	7.75–4.63
1997	14,466	663	4.6	11.5	0.45	0.04	5.88–3.75
1996	13,952	548	3.9	10.6	0.37	0.04	6.75–2.13

BALANCE SHEET

Assets	06/30/00 (dollars in thousands)	06/30/99	Liabilities	06/30/00 (dollars in thousands)	06/30/99
Current (CAE 1,563 and 3,618)	9,413	8,707	Current	2,612	2,879
Property, plant, and equipment	1,414	1,559	Deferred income taxes	61	59
Excess of cost over net assets of business acquired	28	45	Stockholders' equity*	8,185	7,376
Investments	3	3	TOTAL	10,858	10,314
TOTAL	10,858	10,314			

* $0.10 par common; 5,000,000 authorized; 1,479,948 and 1,471,279 issued and outstanding.

RECENT QUARTERS / **PRIOR-YEAR RESULTS**

	Quarter End	Revenue ($000)	Earnings ($000)	EPS ($)	Revenue ($000)	Earnings ($000)	EPS ($)
Q1	09/30/2000	4,701	289	0.20	4,789	360	0.24
Q4	06/30/2000	6,826	841	0.57	5,796	366	0.25
Q3	03/31/2000	4,946	(229)	(0.16)	4,342	269	0.18
Q2	12/31/99	3,246	(135)	(0.09)	2,986	(41)	(0.03)
	SUM	19,719	766	0.52	17,913	954	0.65

RECENT EVENTS

In **February 2000** the company agreed to acquire $9.1 million-revenue Garrett Communications Inc., Fremont, Calif., producer of the Magnum line of Ethernet LAN products, for 375,000 shares of Waters common stock and $2.25 million in cash. At month's end, however, Waters received a communication that Garrett's board of directors had voted not to proceed with the proposed merger transaction. **Sept. 30:** "While our Medical Systems division increased sales by 30 percent over the first quarter of the prior year, the overall corporate sales were flat as a result of our network and farm divisions," said CEO Grabowski. "We continue to wait for the K-12 education E-rate fund disbursement situation to be resolved for our Waters Network Systems division, and a major customer from our American FarmWorks division experienced business and inventory-control problems." In **October** the company changed the name of its American FarmWorks division to Zareba Systems, and launched an innovative new Web site, www.zarebasystems.com, to enable buyers to configure their own fence control system. "We felt the name American FarmWorks no longer reflects the direction we envision for our business and markets," said CEO Grabowski. "As we target customers who are not on the farm, we needed a name that would not be confusing to our growing variety of end users, including those located outside of the United States."

OFFICERS

Jerry W. Grabowski
President and CEO

Gregg J. Anshus
CFO and Treasurer

Gary E. Carlson
Gen. Mgr.-Waters Network Systems

Donald G. Dalland
VP-Mfg. and Gen. Mgr.-Waters Technical

John A. Grimstad
Secretary and General Counsel

Roni E. Henry
Dir.-Human Resources/Administration

Kathy Hult
Dir.-Marketing

Ron W. Oblizajek
Dir.-MIS

Walter D. (Dave) Schollman
Gen. Mgr.-Waters Medical

DIRECTORS

William R. Franta
REAL Solutions, Eden Prairie, MN

Jerry W. Grabowski

John A. Grimstad
Fredrikson & Byron P.A., Minneapolis

Charles G. Schiefelbein
Capital Growth Services

MAJOR SHAREHOLDERS

Charles G. Schiefelbein, 13.7%
Minneapolis

Woodland Investment Co./Kohl Gift Trust, 11.6%
Irving, TX

All officers and directors as a group (5 persons), 19.6%

SIC CODE

3577 Computer peripheral equipment, nec

3679 Electronic components, nec

3699 Electrical equipment and supplies, nec

3845 Electromedical equipment

MISCELLANEOUS

TRANSFER AGENT AND REGISTAR:
Wells Fargo Bank Minnesota N.A., South St. Paul, MN

TRADED: Nasdaq National Market

SYMBOL: WTRS

STOCKHOLDERS: 618

EMPLOYEES: 172

GENERAL COUNSEL:
Fredrikson & Byron P.A., Minneapolis

AUDITORS:
RSM McGladrey & Pullen Inc. LLP, Rochester, MN

INC: MN-1960

ANNUAL MEETING: October

HUMAN RESOURCES/ INVESTOR RELATIONS: Gregg Anshus

RANKINGS

No. 154 CRM Public 200

SUBSIDIARIES, DIVISIONS, AFFILIATES

Zareba Systems
P.O. Box 6117
Rochester, MN 55903
800/962-2880
Jerry Grabowski

Waters Medical Systems
P.O. Box 6117
Rochester, MN 55903
800/426-9877
Dave Schollman

Waters Technical Systems
P.O. Box 6117
Rochester, MN 55903
877/426-9678
Don Dalland

Waters Network Systems
2950 Xenium Ln. N.
Suite 108
Minneapolis, MN 55441
800/328-2275
Gary E. Carlson

PUB

TWO-YEAR QUARTERLY HIGH-LOW STOCK PRICES

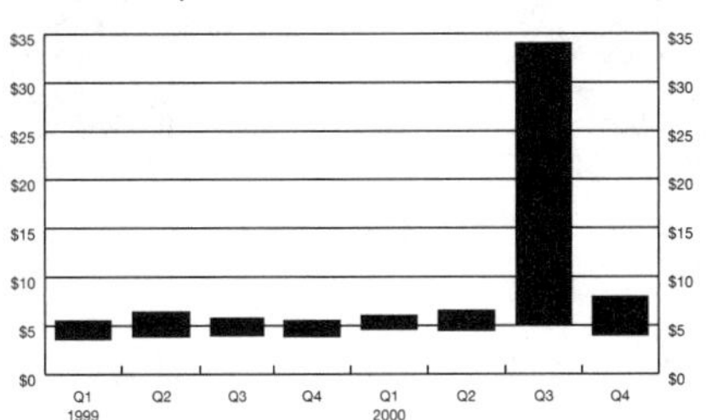

PUB

Wells Financial Corporation

53 First St. S.W., P.O. Box 310, Wells, MN 56097
Tel: 507/553-3151 Fax: 507/553-6295

Wells Financial Corp. is a bank holding company for Wells Federal Bank fsb. Wells Federal is a federally chartered stock savings bank with eight full-service offices in Faribault, Martin, Blue Earth, Nicollet, Steele, and Freeborn counties in Minnesota. The bank obtained its current name in 1991.

EARNINGS HISTORY

Year Ended Dec 31	Operating Revenue/Sales (dollars in thousands)	Net Earnings	Return on Revenue (percent)	Return on Equity	Net Earnings (dollars per share*)	Cash Dividend	Market Price Range
1999	15,923	1,874	11.8	8.0	1.26	—	16.25–9.94
1998	17,295	2,476	14.3	9.6	1.42	—	21.94–15.25
1997	16,434	2,220	13.5	7.5	1.18	—	19.00–12.88
1996 †	15,683	1,200	7.7	4.3	0.61	—	13.25–9.88
1995 ¶	14,298	1,270	8.9	4.4	0.50	—	11.38–8.50

* Stock began trading April 11, 1995.
† Income figures for 1996 include special pretax SAIF assessment of $1,085,000.
¶ EPS for 1995 is from April 11, 1995, date of conversion.

BALANCE SHEET

Assets	12/31/99 (dollars in thousands)	12/31/98
Cash and cash equivalents	4,200	19,446
Certificates of deposit	400	500
Securities available for sale	2,551	2,968
Securities held to maturity	15,559	5,539
Loans held for sale	521	6,097
Loans receivable	172,713	154,305
Accrued interest receivable	1,350	843
Premises and equipment	1,558	1,249
Foreclosed real estate	55	
Income taxes receivable	16	
Other	913	929
TOTAL	199,836	191,876

Liabilities	12/31/99 (dollars in thousands)	12/31/98
Deposits	156,984	158,441
Borrowed funds	17,000	5,000
Advances from borrowers (taxes, insurance)	1,262	1,220
Income taxes: Current		128
Income taxes: Deferred	763	885
Accrued interest payable	116	100
Accrued expenses and other	254	210
Stockholders' equity*	23,457	25,892
TOTAL	199,836	191,876

* $0.10 par common; 7,000,000 authorized; 2,187,500 and 2,187,500 issued and outstanding, less 758,343 and 535,340 treasury shares.

RECENT QUARTERS / **PRIOR-YEAR RESULTS**

	Quarter End	Revenue ($000)	Earnings ($000)	EPS ($)	Revenue ($000)	Earnings ($000)	EPS ($)
Q3	09/30/2000	4,531	426	0.36	3,934	444	0.30
Q2	06/30/2000	4,253	399	0.32	3,937	473	0.31
Q1	03/31/2000	4,032	410	0.30	4,019	541	0.34
Q4	12/31/99	4,033	416	0.30	4,350	620	0.39
	SUM	16,849	1,651	1.28	16,240	2,078	1.35

RECENT EVENTS

In **May 2000** the board of directors approved the repurchase of up to 70,000 shares of Wells' outstanding stock. The repurchases were expected to be made in open-market transactions, subject to the availability of stock, market conditions, the trading price of the stock and the company's financial performance. **Sept. 30**: Total assets increased by from $199.8 million at Dec. 31, 1999, to $217.5 million, due to a $19.5 million increase in the company's loan portfolio. President Kruse was pleased, not only with the growth in the loan portfolio but also that much of the growth occurred in home equity and farm real estate loans, which generally have shorter terms and higher rates than loans on single-family dwellings. Kruse went on to state that the company planned to continue to aggressively originate residential real estate loans for sale to the secondary market in order to expand customer base and increase servicing and other fee income.

OFFICERS

Lawrence H. Kruse
President and CEO

Gerald D. Bastian
VP

James D. Moll
Treasurer, Principal Fin./Acctg. Officer

Richard Mueller
Secretary

DIRECTORS

Gerald D. Bastian

Randel I. Bichler
Bichler Law Office

David Buesing
Wells Concrete Products Inc.

Lawrence H. Kruse

Richard Mueller
Wells Drug Co. Inc.

Dale E. Stallkamp

MAJOR SHAREHOLDERS

Thomson Horstmann & Bryant Inc., 11.4%
Saddle Brook, NJ

Wells Federal Bank fsb ESOP, 9.8%
Wells, MN

Hovde Capital LLC, 9.5%

John Hancock Advisors Inc., 8.8%
Boston

All officers and directors as a group (7 persons), 9.9%

SIC CODE

6712 Bank holding companies

MISCELLANEOUS

TRANSFER AGENT AND REGISTAR:
Registrar and Transfer Co., Cranford, NJ

TRADED: Nasdaq National Market

SYMBOL: WEFC

STOCKHOLDERS: 547

EMPLOYEES: 66

PART TIME: 2

GENERAL COUNSEL:
Malizia, Spidi, Sloane & Fisch P.C., Washington, D.C.
Randel I. Bichler, Esq., Wells, MN

AUDITORS:
RSM McGladrey & Pullen Inc. LLP, Rochester, MN

INC: MN-1994

FOUNDED: 1934

ANNUAL MEETING: April

RANKINGS

No. 162 CRM Public 200

SUBSIDIARIES, DIVISIONS, AFFILIATES

Main office:
53 First St. S.W.
Wells, MN 56097

Branch offices:
1300 S. Riverfront Dr.
Mankato, MN 56001

1400 Madison Ave.
Mankato, MN 56001

300 S. State St.
Fairmont, MN 56031

120 S. Minnesota Ave.
St. Peter, MN 56082

303 S. Main St.
Blue Earth, MN 56082

1710 W. Main St.
Albert Lea, MN 56007

108 West Park Sq.
Owatonna, MN 55060

TWO-YEAR QUARTERLY HIGH-LOW STOCK PRICES

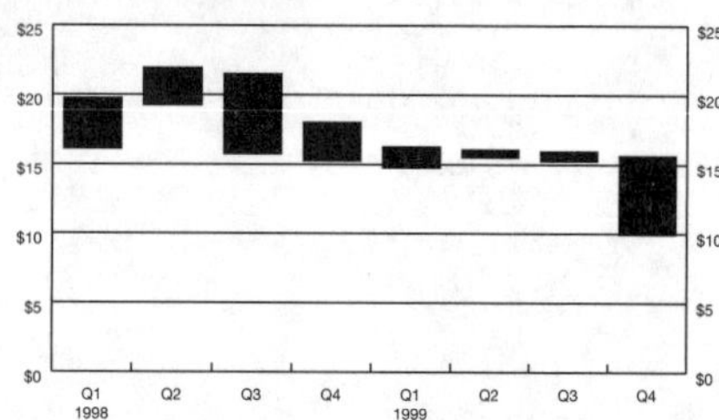

Wilsons The Leather Experts

7401 Boone Ave. N., Brooklyn Park, MN 55428
Tel: 763/391-4000 Fax: 763/391-4137 Web site: http://www.wilsonsleather.com

Wilsons The Leather Experts is the country's largest retailer of men's and women's leather outerwear, apparel, and accessories. It operates 461 retail leather stores—in 45 states, the District of Columbia, and England—under the names Wilsons The Leather Experts, Tannery West, and Georgetown Leather Design. Unlike most other retailers, which buy finished goods, Wilsons buys leather, then contracts with overseas manufacturers to sew most of its products.

EARNINGS HISTORY *

Year Ended Jan	Operating Revenue/Sales (dollars in thousands)	Net Earnings (dollars in thousands)	Return on Revenue (percent)	Return on Equity (percent)	Net Earnings (dollars per share†)	Cash Dividend (dollars per share†)	Market Price Range (dollars per share†)
2000 ¶	543,608	30,651	5.6	23.4	1.87	—	13.42–6.00
1999	459,372	18,177	4.0	18.5	1.17	—	11.17–5.67
1998 #	418,140	10,838	2.6	14.9	0.81	—	7.75–5.67
1997 **	454,761	12,765	2.8	NM	2.08	—	
1995 ††	462,394	(173,415)	(37.5)	NM	—	—	

* Historical figures have been restated to reflect a new accounting method for layaway sales adopted in fourth quarter 2000.
† Trading began May 27, 1997. Per-share amounts restated to reflect 3-for-2 stock split on March 15, 2000.
¶ Income figures for 2000 include two extraordinary losses: $0.958 million/($0.06) on early extinguishment of debt; and $1.449 million/($0.09), cumulative effect of change in accounting principle.
# Income figures for 1997 include extraordinary gain of $3,763,000/$0.28 on early extinguishment of debt.
** Figures for 1997 are 13-month sums of: predecessor companies for five months ended May 25, 1996 (revenue $109.6 million, loss $11.1 million); and current company for eight months ended Feb. 1, 1997 (revenue $345.1 million, earnings $23.9 million/$2.08).
†† Income figures for 1995 include $182.2 million restructuring charge. Pro forma results excluding closed stores: revenue $409.7 million; earnings $13.9 million.

BALANCE SHEET

Assets	01/29/00 (dollars in thousands)	01/30/99 (dollars in thousands)	Liabilities	01/29/00 (dollars in thousands)	01/30/99 (dollars in thousands)
Current (CAE 124,926 and 108,235)	220,834	205,664	Current	93,979	74,115
			Long-term debt	43,890	70,000
Property and equipment	49,587	36,195	Other	3,478	3,099
			Stockholders' equity*	131,207	98,177
Other	2,133	3,532			
TOTAL	272,554	245,391	TOTAL	272,554	245,391

* $0.01 par common; 150,000,000 authorized; 16,585,234 and 16,250,136 issued and outstanding.

RECENT QUARTERS / **PRIOR-YEAR RESULTS**

	Quarter End	Revenue ($000)	Earnings ($000)	EPS ($)	Prior-Year Revenue ($000)	Prior-Year Earnings ($000)	Prior-Year EPS ($)
Q3	10/28/2000	108,592	(2,364)	(0.14)	97,663	(2,135)	(0.13)
Q2	07/29/2000	56,551	(15,403)	(0.92)	47,267	(14,834)	(0.91)
Q1	04/29/2000	90,308	(1,377)	(0.08)	81,343	(4,178)	(0.26)
Q4	01/29/2000	317,335	51,798	3.13	269,185	40,259	2.48
	SUM	572,786	32,654	1.98	495,458	19,112	1.18

CURRENT: Q1 earnings include extraordinary loss of $623,000/($0.04) on early extinguishment of debt. Q4 earnings include loss of $1.449 million/($0.09) cumulative effect on prior years of change in accounting principle.
PRIOR YEAR: Q3 earnings include extraordinary loss of $119,000/($0.01) on early extinguishment of debt. Q2 earnings include extraordinary loss of $839,000/($0.05) on early extinguishment of debt. Q1 earnings include loss of $1.449 million/($0.09) on cumulative effect of accounting change.

RECENT EVENTS

In **December 1999** Wilsons announced the launch of www.wilsonsleather.com, the company's new online retail store. In **March 2000** Wilsons entered into a joint-venture agreement with National Basketball Association superstar Kevin Garnett to design and produce a premium line of leather apparel and accessories. The new product line, trademarked as "OBF (Official Block Family) by Kevin Garnett," was to feature a selection of fashionable premium men's apparel, as well as complementary leather accessories. In **April** the company repurchased and canceled an additional $13.3 million of its 11.25% Senior Notes. **Aug. 26**: Year-to-date sales increased 14.9 percent to $167.9 million from $146.1 mil- *continued on page 406*

OFFICERS

Joel N. Waller
Chairman and CEO
David L. Rogers
President and COO
John Serino
EVP-Store Sales
John Fowler
SVP and General Merchandise Mgr.
W. Michael Bode
VP-Manufacturing
Betty Goff
VP-Human Resources
Linda Ireland
VP and Gen. Mgr.-E-commerce
Jed Jaffe
VP-Store Sales
Jeffrey W. Orton
VP-Information Systems
David B. Sharp
VP-Marketing
Lisa Stanley
VP-Marketing
David Tidmarsh
VP-Information Systems
Daniel R. Thorson
Treasurer
Thomas R. Wildenberg
Chief Accounting Officer and Controller

DIRECTORS

Lyle Berman
Lakes Gaming Inc., Plymouth, MN
Thomas J. Brosig
Gary Crittenden
Monsanto Co., St. Louis
Morris Goldfarb
G-III Apparel Group Ltd., New York
Marvin W. Goldstein
financial consultant
David L. Rogers
Joel N. Waller

MAJOR SHAREHOLDERS

Neil I. Sell (trustee), 19.5%
Minneapolis
Morris Goldfarb/G-III Apparel Group Ltd., 15.3%
New York
Joel N. Waller, 9.5%
Brooklyn Park, MN
David L. Rogers, 9.1%
Wellington Management Co. LLP, 6.9%
Boston

All officers and directors as a group (16 persons), 40.7%

SIC CODE

5651 Family clothing stores
5651 Family clothing stores
5948 Luggage and leather goods stores
5948 Luggage and leather goods stores

MISCELLANEOUS

TRANSFER AGENT AND REGISTAR:
Wells Fargo Bank Minnesota N.A.,
South St. Paul, MN
TRADED: Nasdaq National Market
SYMBOL: WLSN
STOCKHOLDERS: 45
EMPLOYEES: 4,200
GENERAL COUNSEL:
Faegre & Benson PLLP, Minneapolis
AUDITORS:
Arthur Andersen LLP, Minneapolis
ANNUAL MEETING: June

RANKINGS

No. 48 CRM Public 200
No. 48 CRM Performance 100

TWO-YEAR QUARTERLY HIGH-LOW STOCK PRICES

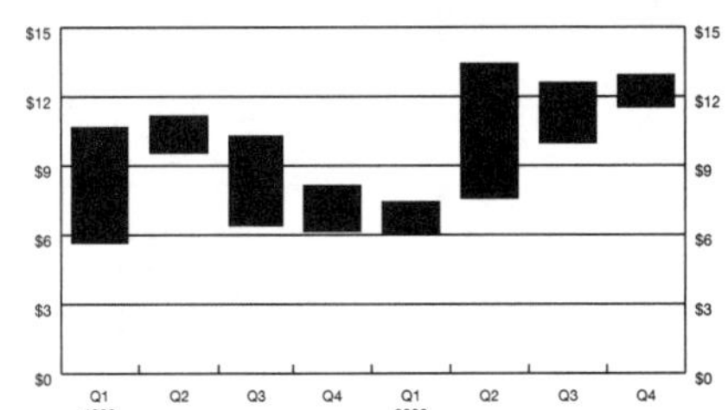

Winland Electronics Inc.

1950 Excel Dr., Mankato, MN 56001
Tel: 507/625-7231 Fax: 507/387-2488 Web site: http://www.winland.com

Winland Electronics Inc., an ISO 9001-registered firm, is a leading full-service provider of electronic manufacturing services (EMS) to original-equipment manufacturers (OEMs). The company responds to customer needs by providing a mix of value-added services that go beyond traditional contract manufacturing. The full range of services provided by Winland includes product design, value engineering, manufacturing engineering, testing, warranty repair, shipping, and warehousing.

EARNINGS HISTORY

Year Ended Dec 31	Operating Revenue/Sales (dollars in thousands)	Net Earnings	Return on Revenue (percent)	Return on Equity	Net Earnings (dollars per share)	Cash Dividend	Market Price Range
1999	19,864	681	3.4	15.0	0.24	—	4.00–1.88
1998	18,176	856	4.7	22.4	0.30	—	3.50–1.63
1997	12,383	567	4.6	19.5	0.20	—	4.25–1.78
1996	8,361	264	3.2	11.4	0.10	—	4.50–2.00
1995	5,851	(150)	(2.6)	(7.8)	(0.06)	—	3.50–1.88

BALANCE SHEET

Assets	12/31/99 (dollars in thousands)	12/31/98	Liabilities	12/31/99 (dollars in thousands)	12/31/98
Current (CAE 40 and 20)	6,216	6,501	Current (STD 657 and 573)	3,715	4,052
Property and equipment	5,639	5,124	Deferred revenue	202	209
			Long-term debt	3,239	3,430
Patents and trademarks	4	6	Deferred taxes	166	111
TOTAL	11,859	11,631	Stockholders' equity*	4,537	3,828
			TOTAL	11,859	11,631

* $0.01 par common; 20,000,000 authorized; 2,886,786 and 2,886,786 issued and outstanding.

RECENT QUARTERS / PRIOR-YEAR RESULTS

	Quarter End	Revenue ($000)	Earnings ($000)	EPS ($)	Prior-Year Revenue ($000)	Prior-Year Earnings ($000)	Prior-Year EPS ($)
Q3	09/30/2000	4,659	(213)	(0.07)	4,177	47	0.02
Q2	06/30/2000	5,105	66	0.02	4,654	121	0.04
Q1	03/31/2000	4,218	16	0.01	6,615	443	0.15
Q4	12/31/99	4,418	70	0.02	5,365	329	0.11
	SUM	18,399	(61)	(0.02)	20,810	941	0.33

RECENT EVENTS

In **January 2000** the company's common stock moved from Nasdaq's Small Cap market system to the American Stock Exchange (AMEX). CEO Hankins stated, "We believe Winland's accomplishments can receive better visibility under Amex and its specialist system, and thereby gain broader recognition within the financial community." In **February** Winland was on the verge of launching the largest marketing and sales campaign in the company's history. The primary purpose of the campaign was to promote the new line of DC Motor Controllers and a second new line of proprietary products scheduled for introduction in March of 2000. In **August**, based on its revenue growth from 1995 to 1999, the company was named to Deloitte & Touche's Minnesota Technology Fast 50. **Sept. 30:** The decline in nine-month net sales was the result of the softer sales experienced by some of Winland's largest OEM customers. As a consequence, the company was expecting to record a net loss for the year. CEO Hankins stated, "Although current sales levels are disappointing, Winland is optimistic about the long-term sales potential for the OEM customer base, the new proprietary products, and the prospects of the marketing department securing new OEM customers." In **October** Winland released for sale and production a new proprietary product, the SEK Series Motor Shaft Encoder Kit.

OFFICERS

W. Kirk Hankins
Chairman and CEO

Lorin E. Krueger
President and COO

Kirk P. Hankins
VP-Sales/Marketing

Kimberly E. Kleinow
VP-Procurement/Materials

Jennifer A. Thompson
VP-Financial Operations

Terry E. Treanor
VP-Manufacturing

Steve Vogel
VP-Engineering

DIRECTORS

Thomas J. DePetra
International Concept Development Inc.

S. Robert Dessalet
management consultant

David L. Ewert
Jones Metal Products Inc., Mankato, MN

Kirk P. Hankins

W. Kirk Hankins

Lorin E. Krueger

James P. Legus
CommonLine Inc.

MAJOR SHAREHOLDERS

W. Kirk Hankins, 10.3%

Lorin E. Krueger, 8.7%

Dyna Technology, 5.1%
LeCenter, MN

All officers and directors as a group (9 persons), 26.5%

SIC CODE

3585 Refrigeration and heating equipment

3625 Relays and industrial controls

3679 Electronic components, nec

3812 Search and navigation equipment

3822 Environmental controls

3829 Measuring and controlling devices, nec

3999 Manufacturing industries, nec

5063 Electrical apparatus and eqp, whsle

MISCELLANEOUS

TRANSFER AGENT AND REGISTAR:
Wells Fargo Bank Minnesota N.A.,
South St. Paul, MN

TRADED: AMEX

SYMBOL: WEX

STOCKHOLDERS: 492

EMPLOYEES: 127

GENERAL COUNSEL:
Fredrikson & Byron P.A., Minneapolis

AUDITORS:
RSM McGladrey & Pullen Inc. LLP, Minneapolis

INC: MN-1973

ANNUAL MEETING: May

ADMINISTRATION:
Linda Annis

RANKINGS

No. 149 CRM Public 200

No. 35 Minnesota Technology Fast 50

TWO-YEAR QUARTERLY HIGH-LOW STOCK PRICES

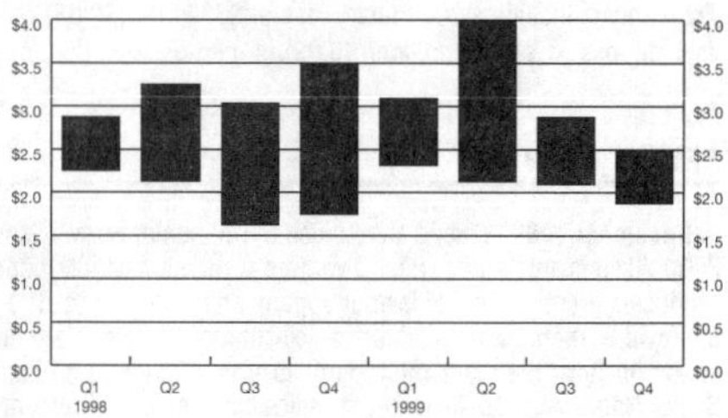

Winter Sports Inc.

P.O. Box 1400, Whitefish, MT 59937
Tel: 406/862-1900 Fax: 406/862-2955

Winter Sports Inc., *dba* The Big Mountain Ski and Summer Resort, is the operator of Montana's largest ski resort, which is located eight miles north of Whitefish, Montana. It includes hotels, motels, restaurants, bars, chairlifts, summer programs, hiking trails, meeting facilities, and entertainment programs. In fiscal 1993 real estate sales became a significant business segment.

EARNINGS HISTORY

Year Ended May 31	Operating Revenue/Sales (dollars in thousands)	Net Earnings	Return on Revenue (percent)	Return on Equity	Net Earnings (dollars per share*)	Cash Dividend	Market Price Range
2000	15,173	1,498	9.9	15.7	1.49	—	9.38–6.00
1999	12,588	(437)	(3.5)	(5.4)	(0.43)	—	12.00–7.50
1998	9,257	(317)	(3.4)	(3.8)	(0.32)	—	17.88–10.00
1997	10,151	231	2.3	2.6	0.23	—	14.25–10.50
1996	9,510	113	1.2	1.3	0.11	—	15.14–13.46

* Per-share amounts restated to reflect 4 percent stock dividends in December 1996 and November 1995.

BALANCE SHEET

Assets	05/31/00 (dollars in thousands)	05/31/99	Liabilities	05/31/00 (dollars in thousands)	05/31/99
Current (CAE 297 and 236)	1,249	1,196	Current (STD 0 and 24)	3,095	1,724
Property and equipment	14,621	16,211	Long-term debt	1,996	6,589
Other	210	420	Deferred income taxes	1,447	1,471
TOTAL	16,079	17,827	Stockholders' equity*	9,541	8,043
			TOTAL	16,079	17,827

* No par common; 5,000,000 authorized; 1,008,368 and 1,008,368 issued and outstanding.

RECENT QUARTERS / **PRIOR-YEAR RESULTS**

	Quarter End	Revenue ($000)	Earnings ($000)	EPS ($)	Revenue ($000)	Earnings ($000)	EPS ($)
Q1	09/10/2000	2,006	(102)	(0.10)	1,817	(418)	(0.41)
Q4	05/31/2000	3,839	72	0.07	4,349	50	0.05
Q3	02/27/2000	8,126	2,242	2.22	6,911	735	0.73
Q2	12/05/99	1,392	(398)	(0.39)	451	(672)	(0.67)
	SUM	15,363	1,814	1.80	13,528	(306)	(0.30)

OFFICERS

Michael J. Collins
President and CEO

Jami M. Phillips
CFO and Treasurer

Michele Reese
VP

Sandra K. Unger
Corporate Secretary

DIRECTORS

Charles R. Abell
Whitefish Credit Union, Whitefish, MT

Jerome T. Broussard

Brian T. Grattan

Dennis L. Green
Dasen Co., Flathead County Title Co.

Charles P. Grenier

Jerry J. James

Michael T. Jenson
Whitefish Gallery and Jenson Studio, Whitefish, MT

Darrel R. (Bill) Martin

Michael Muldown
Allstate Insurance Co.

MAJOR SHAREHOLDERS

Dennis L. Green, 22.5%
Kalispell, MT

Richard A. and Susan D. Dasen, 22.3%
Kalispell, MT

Budget Finance, 22.3%
Kalispell, MT

Jerome T. Broussard, 8.8%
Whitefish, MT

Mary Jane Street, 7.2%
Whitefish, MT

Michael J. Collins, 5%
Whitefish, MT

All officers and directors as a group (10 persons), 46.4%

SIC CODE

6531 Real estate agents and managers

7999 Amusement and recreation, nec

MISCELLANEOUS

TRANSFER AGENT AND REGISTAR:
Company

TRADED: OTC Bulletin Board

SYMBOL: WSKI

STOCKHOLDERS: 741

EMPLOYEES: 450

PART TIME: 400

AUDITORS:
Jordahl & Sliter PLLC, Kalispell, MT

INC: MT-1947

ANNUAL MEETING:
October

ADMINISTRATION:
Sandi Unger

HUMAN RESOURCES:
Warren Dobler

SUBSIDIARIES, DIVISIONS, AFFILIATES

Big Mountain Water Co.

Big Mountain Development Corp.

Big Mountain Resort Reservations

PUB

TWO-YEAR QUARTERLY HIGH-LOW STOCK PRICES

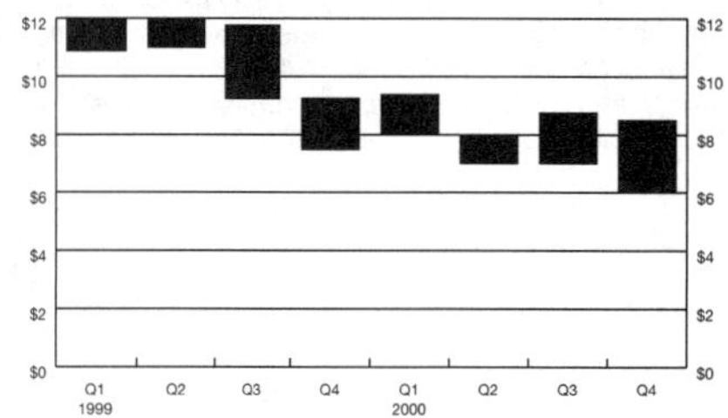

PUB

XATA Corporation

151 E. Cliff Rd., Suite 10, Burnsville, MN 55337
Tel: 952/894-3680 Fax: 952/894-2463 Web site: http://www.xata.com

XATA Corp. develops, markets, and services fully integrated mobile information systems for the fleet trucking segment of the transportation industry. XATA systems utilize proprietary software, onboard touch-screen computers, and related hardware components and accessories to capture and communicate operating information that assists fleet management in improving productivity and profitability. The **Distribution Information System** includes an onboard computer designed for easy use by the professional driver and software designed for adaptability to the customer's management information needs. XATA is the surviving entity of the Dec. 5, 1991, merger of Northwest Acquisition Inc., a public company formed in May 1989 to acquire an operating company, and XATA Corp., a privately held Minnesota company.

EARNINGS HISTORY

Year Ended Sept 30	Operating Revenue/Sales (dollars in thousands)	Net Earnings	Return on Revenue (percent)	Return on Equity	Net Earnings (dollars per share)	Cash Dividend	Market Price Range
1999	11,182	493	4.4	12.0	0.11	—	4.75–0.91
1998	9,215	(4,249)	(46.1)	NM	(0.97)	—	7.25–2.00
1997 *	10,404	(2,421)	(23.3)	(33.9)	(0.55)	—	10.50–3.38
1996 †	10,313	1,554	15.1	16.9	0.36	—	11.50–6.63
1995	7,130	787	11.0	36.0	0.22	—	9.38–3.38

* Income figures for 1997 include pretax loss of $1,806,860 to write down goodwill and acquired software of Payne & Associates.
† Figures for 1996 include results of Payne & Associates from its Aug. 23, 1996, date of acquisition for $2.9 million. Pro forma with Payne for the full year: revenue $11,153,148; earnings $1,008,810/$0.24.

BALANCE SHEET

Assets	09/30/99 (dollars in thousands)	09/30/98	Liabilities	09/30/99 (dollars in thousands)	09/30/98
Current (CAE 122)	2,624	2,565	Current (STD 486 and 310)	3,741	3,557
Equipment and leasehold improvements	540	1,229	Long-term debt		461
Capitalized software development costs	4,465	2,685	Stockholders' equity*	4,107	2,968
Acquired software	67	265	TOTAL	7,848	6,986
Goodwill	117	145			
Other	36	97			
TOTAL	7,848	6,986			

* $0.01 par common; 8,333,333 authorized; 4,435,633 and 4,430,633 issued and outstanding.

RECENT QUARTERS / **PRIOR-YEAR RESULTS**

	Quarter End	Revenue ($000)	Earnings ($000)	EPS ($)	Revenue ($000)	Earnings ($000)	EPS ($)
Q3	06/30/2000	3,255	302	0.07	2,929	177	0.04
Q2	03/31/2000	3,163	394	0.09	3,367	338	0.08
Q1	12/31/99	2,929	135	0.03	2,352	(78)	(0.02)
Q4	09/30/99	2,534	56	0.01	2,200	(1,709)	(0.39)
	SUM	11,880	887	0.20	10,848	(1,272)	(0.29)

RECENT EVENTS

In **January 2000** Foster Farms chose XATA to provide the onboard computers and other key hardware and software components for its next-generation fleet management system; as did the TDL Group, best known for the operation of the Tim Hortons chain of coffee and donut shops in Canada and the United States, and Somerset Food Service, a member of UniPro Foodservice, the largest broadline and systems cooperative distribution group in the world. In **February** XATA granted Cancom the distribution rights to resell XATA Fleet Management Solutions throughout Canada. In **May** Instinct Trucking Ltd., Edmonton, Alberta, and Brookshire Grocery Co., Tyler, Texas, chose XATA's next-generation fleet management system. A contract was finalized with Toys R Us Inc. for a nationwide implementation of onboard computers system with GPS and other key hardware and software components for its next-generation fleet management system. In **August** Deere & Co.'s John Deere Special Technologies Group agreed to make an equity investment in XATA. The $3.1 million investment was to result in a 14 percent ownership stake in XATA. "This partnership will allow us to effectively launch our next generation of mobile solutions and to penetrate new markets with our industry-leading applications," said Bill Flies, chief technical officer of XATA.

OFFICERS

Stephen A. Lawrence
Chairman

Edward T. Michalek
President and CEO

William P. Flies
Chief Technical Officer

Tom Flies
VP-Product Development

Joel Jorgenson
VP-Sales/Marketing/Support Services

Gary C. Thomas
VP-Administration and CFO

Donald E. Horst
VP-Logistics Services

Dennis A. Quy
VP-Hardware Engineering

DIRECTORS

Barry Batcheller
Phoenix International Corp.

Richard L. Bogen
Cook Associates, Atlanta

William P. Flies

Carl M. Fredericks
Fredericks, Shields & Co. LLC, San Diego

Roger W. Kleppe
Blue Cross and Blue Shield of Minnesota, Eagan, MN

Stephen A. Lawrence
Lawrence Transportation Co.

Charles Ray Stamp Jr.
Deere & Co.

MAJOR SHAREHOLDERS

William and Linda Flies, 24%

Deere & Co., 14%
Moline, IL

All officers and directors as a group (9 persons), 33.9%

SIC CODE

3571 Electronic computers

7373 Computer integrated systems design

MISCELLANEOUS

TRANSFER AGENT AND REGISTAR:
Wells Fargo Bank Minnesota N.A., South St. Paul, MN

TRADED: Nasdaq SmallCap Market

SYMBOL: XATA

STOCKHOLDERS: 90

EMPLOYEES: 52

GENERAL COUNSEL:
Moss and Barnett P.A., Minneapolis

AUDITORS:
Grant Thornton LLP, Minneapolis

INC: MN-1989

FOUNDED: 1985

ANNUAL MEETING:
February

INVESTOR RELATIONS:
Gary C. Thomas

RANKINGS

No. 175 CRM Public 200

TWO-YEAR QUARTERLY HIGH-LOW STOCK PRICES

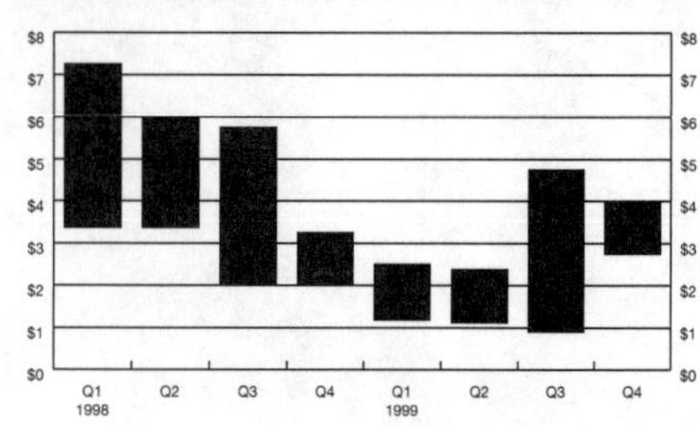

Xcel Energy Inc.

414 Nicollet Mall, Minneapolis, MN 55401
Tel: 612/330-5500 Fax: 612/330-6297 Web site: http://www.nspco.com

Xcel Energy Inc.—created by the August 2000 merger of Northern States Power Co. (NSP) and new Century Energies—is a utility company that generates, transmits, and distributes electricity and distributes natural gas. Xcel operates in 12 states, where it provides a comprehensive portfolio of energy-related products to 3 million electric customers and 2 million electricity customers internationally. NSP-Minnesota serves parts of Minnesota, North Dakota, South Dakota, and Arizona. NSP-Wisconsin serves parts of Wisconsin and the Upper Peninsula of Michigan. Major operating companies include Public Service of Colorado headquartered in Denver and Southwest service in Amarillo. NRG Energy Inc., an NSP subsidiary, is the fifth-largest independent power producer. Viking Gas Transmission Co., a wholly owned subsidiary, engages in natural gas transportation services in the Upper Midwest. Energy Masters International Inc., also a wholly owned subsidiary, provides comprehensive energy services. Seren, a wholly owned subsidiary, provides broadband communication and information services.

EARNINGS HISTORY *

Year Ended Dec 31	Operating Revenue/Sales (dollars in thousands)	Net Earnings (dollars in thousands)	Return on Revenue (percent)	Return on Equity (percent)	Net Earnings (dollars per share†)	Cash Dividend (dollars per share†)	Market Price Range (dollars per share†)
1999	2,869,011	224,336	7.8	8.6	1.43	1.45	27.94–19.31
1998	2,819,174	282,373	10.0	11.2	1.84	1.43	30.81–25.69
1997	2,733,746	237,320	8.7	9.5	1.61	1.40	29.44–22.25
1996	2,654,206	274,539	10.3	12.3	1.91	1.37	26.69–22.25
1995	2,568,584	275,795	10.7	13.0	1.96	1.34	24.75–21.25

* Historical figures have not yet been restated for the August 2000 merger with NCE. Pro forma results for 1999 for the combined company: revenue $6.869 billion; net income $571 million/$1.70.
† Per-share amounts restated to reflect a 2-for-1 stock split effected June 1, 1998.

BALANCE SHEET

Assets	12/31/99 (dollars in thousands)	12/31/98 (dollars in thousands)	Liabilities	12/31/99 (dollars in thousands)	12/31/98 (dollars in thousands)
Current (CAE 0 and 42,364)	1,033,806	754,065	Current (STD 294,831 and 369,200)	1,826,136	1,232,262
Utility plant	4,451,451	4,395,234	Deferred taxes	811,638	814,983
Regulatory assets	248,127	331,940	Deferred credits	118,582	128,444
External decomm. fund, other investments	561,682	479,402	Regulatory	461,569	372,239
			Benefit obligations	143,905	129,514
Nonregulated property	2,086,476	282,524	Other	89,667	81,123
			Long-term debt	3,453,364	1,851,146
Nonregulated investments	1,047,248	862,596	Preferred equity	305,340	305,340
			Common equity*	2,557,530	2,481,246
Nonregulated notes receivable	66,876	106,427	TOTAL	9,767,731	7,396,297
Prepayments, deferred charges, receivables	158,096	88,194			
Intangibles	113,969	95,915			
TOTAL	9,767,731	7,396,297			

* $2.50 par common; 350,000,000 authorized; 155,729,663 and 152,696,971 issued and outstanding, less 392,325 and 641,884 treasury shares.

RECENT QUARTERS / **PRIOR-YEAR RESULTS**

	Quarter End	Revenue ($000)	Earnings ($000)	EPS ($)	Prior-Year Revenue ($000)	Prior-Year Earnings ($000)	Prior-Year EPS ($)
Q3	09/30/2000	6,606,253	389,027	1.14	5,043,773	423,244	1.26
	SUM	6,606,253	389,027	1.14	5,043,773	423,244	1.26

CURRENT: Q3 figures are for nine months; EPS includes merger-related special charges ($0.43) and extraordinary loss ($0.06).

RECENT EVENTS

In **November 1999** Energy Masters International was awarded eight federal energy efficiency contracts with a total value of $10 million, for project construction at seven federal installations. In **December** Energy Masters was competitively selected by the U.S. Coast Guard Support Center in Elizabeth City, N.C., and the Department of Energy to act as the Coast Guard's strategic energy partner. **Dec. 31:** NSP blamed lower earnings for fourth quarter and year end on an adverse regulatory ruling by the Minnesota Public Utilities Commission to disallow NSP's recovery of conservation incentives. The decision resulted in a decrease of 27 cents per share. Other setbacks included investment write-downs and unfavorable weather conditions. "While we are disappointed with 1999 results, we move into 2000 with a clean balance sheet, an operating utility with strong ongoing earnings potential, and increased earnings from NRG, the world's seventh-largest independent power producer," said CEO Howard. "With a return to normal weather, continued earnings growth from NRG, and by meeting *continued on page 406*

OFFICERS

James J. Howard III
Chairman

Wayne Brunetti
President and CEO

Paul E. Anders Jr.
VP and Chief Information Officer

Paul Bonavia
Pres.-Energy Markets

Grady P. Butts
VP-Subsidiary Services

Cathy Hart
VP and Secretary

Gary R. Johnson
VP and General Counsel

Richard D. Kelly
President Enterprises

Cynthia L. Lesher
Pres.-NSP Gas

John McAfee
VP-Engineering

Edward J. McIntyre
VP and CFO

Paul E. Pender
VP and Treasurer

James T. Petillo
Pres.-Retail

Dave Ripka
VP and Controller

David Sparby
VP-Regulatory/Gov't Affairs

Marilyn Taylor
VP-Human Resources

Patricia K. Vincent
VP-Marketing/Sales

Keith Wietecki
Pres./CEO-Seren Innovations

David M. Wilks
Pres.-Energy Supply

DIRECTORS

Wayne H. Brunetti

C. Coney Burgess
Burgess-Herring Ranch Co.

David A. Christensen
Raven Industries Inc. (retired)

Giannantonio Ferrari
Honeywell Inc.

Roger R. Hemminghaus
Ultramar Diamond Shamrock Corp.

A. Barry Hirschfeld
A B Hirschfeld Press Inc.

James J. Howard III

Douglas W. Leatherdale
The St. Paul Cos. Inc., St. Paul

Albert F. Moreno
Levi Strauss & Co.

Dr. Margaret R. Preska
Minnesota State Colleges & Universities

A. Patricia Sampson
Dr. Sanders and Associates; The Sampson Group

Allan L. Schuman
Ecolab Inc., St. Paul

Rodney E. Slifer
Slifer, Smith & Frampton

W. Thomas Stephens
MacMillan Bloedel Ltd. (retired)

MAJOR SHAREHOLDERS

U.S. Bank, Xcel Energy ESOP trustee, 7.6%
St. Paul

Sanford C. Bernstein & Co. Inc., 5.9%
New York

All officers and directors as a group (18 persons), 0.9%

SIC CODE

4931 Electric and other services combined

MISCELLANEOUS

TRANSFER AGENT AND REGISTAR:
Wells Fargo Bank Minnesota N.A., South St. Paul, MN

TRADED: NYSE, PSE

SYMBOL: XEL

STOCKHOLDERS: 81,569

EMPLOYEES: 12,000

GENERAL COUNSEL:
Gary R. Johnson

AUDITORS:
PricewaterhouseCoopers LLP, Minneapolis

INC: MN-2000

FOUNDED: 1909

ANNUAL MEETING: April

HUMAN RESOURCES:
Marilyn Taylor

INVESTOR RELATIONS:
Richard J. Kolkmann

RANKINGS

No. 14 CRM Public 200

No. 34 CRM Employer 100

No. 16 CRM Performance 100

PUB

TWO-YEAR QUARTERLY HIGH-LOW STOCK PRICES

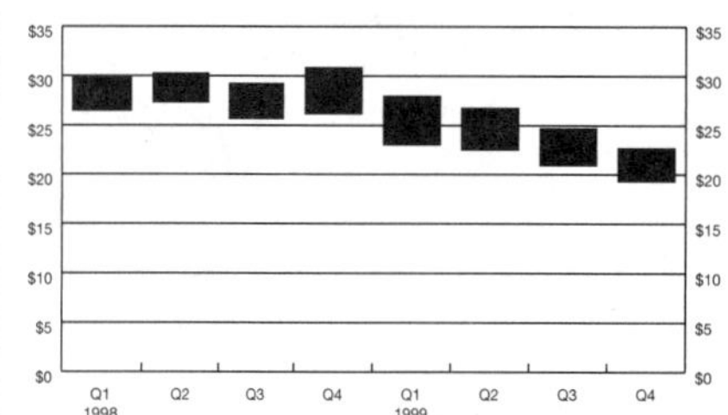

PUB

Xdogs.com Inc.

527 Marquette Ave. S., Suite 2100, Minneapolis, MN 55402
Tel: 612/359-9020 Web site: http://www.xdogs.com

Xdogs.com Inc. provides the North American market with access to a unique portfolio of products not otherwise available. The company's distribution relationships are with European manufacturers of best-in-class outdoor sports and lifestyle clothing and equipment that are new to the North American market but have dominant market share in their respective markets. Offering exclusive and unique product lines that differentiate the company from its competitors is a key to its competitive advantage. Xdogs' innovative approach of offering these products through a combination of online and traditional retail channels is unique to the outdoor industry. Xdogs.com also operates and maintains a dynamic, content-rich Web site that supports a community of outdoor adventurers and enthusiasts. The Sled Dogs Co., its name prior to May 1999, emerged from Chapter 11 bankruptcy on Sept. 10, 1998.

EARNINGS HISTORY

Year Ended Mar 31	Operating Revenue/Sales (dollars in thousands)	Net Earnings	Return on Revenue (percent)	Return on Equity	Net Earnings (dollars per share)	Cash Dividend	Market Price Range
2000	2	(6,739)	NM	NM	(0.71)	—	6.25–2.06
1999 *	46	1,476	NM	NM	0.63	—	3.25–0.04
1998	233	(2,510)	NM	NM	(10.03)	—	0.34–0.02
1997 †	1,463	(4,370)	NM	NM	(0.33)	—	1.19–0.19
1996 ¶	877	(3,750)	NM	NM	(0.41)	—	2.94–0.44

* Figures for 1999 combine predecessor company (first quarter) and reorganized company (second through fourth quarters). Income figures include reorganization fees (loss of $0.897 million) and extraordinary items (gain of $2.967 million).
† Figures for 1997 are for the nine-month transition period from July 1, 1996, through March 31, 1997, due to change in year end.
¶ Figures for 1996 are for 12-month period ended June 30.

BALANCE SHEET

Assets	03/31/00 (dollars in thousands)	03/31/99
Current (CAE 282 and 86)	325	104
Office equipment	99	
Intangibles	183	
TOTAL	608	104

Liabilities	03/31/00 (dollars in thousands)	03/31/99
Current	822	50
Stockholders' equity*	(215)	55
TOTAL	608	104

* $0.01 par common; 20,000,000 authorized; 9,685,104 and 6,604,625 issued and outstanding.

RECENT QUARTERS / PRIOR-YEAR RESULTS

	Quarter End	Revenue ($000)	Earnings ($000)	EPS ($)	Prior-Year Revenue ($000)	Prior-Year Earnings ($000)	Prior-Year EPS ($)
Q1	06/30/2000	97	(610)	(0.06)	0	(208)	(0.02)
	SUM	97	(610)	(0.06)	0	(208)	(0.02)

RECENT EVENTS

In **January 2000** the company executed a distribution agreement with Oxbow S.A. to become its exclusive North American distributor (excluding the Caribbean basin). Oxbow manufactures outdoor sportswear including footwear, luggage, business bags, and pouches. In **February** Xdogs executed a distribution agreement with Metzler Design Brillenvertrieb GmbH to become its exclusive North American distributor. Metzler manufactures eyewear under the Lumen trademark. In **June** xdogs announced a four-year exclusive North American Distribution Rights Agreement with Gaastra International Sportswear B.V., the Dutch sailing company. Gaastra is a century-old company with an outstanding reputation for innovative and durable sailing gear and sailing-inspired apparel. The Gaastra line of foul weather gear competes with top lines such as Gill, Helly Hansen, Musto, and Henri Lloyd. The more casual sportswear line compares favorably with Tommy Hilfiger (NYSE: TOM); Polo Ralph Lauren (NYSE: RL), and Nautica (Nasdaq: NAUT).

OFFICERS

Kent Rodriguez
Chairman and CEO

Craig C. Avery
Secretary

Hans Figi
VP-Sales

DIRECTORS

Craig C. Avery
Craig C. Avery Co., Minneapolis

Douglas Barton
Douglas Communications Inc.

Robert Corliss
Infinity Sports and Leisure Group, Lebanon, NJ

Kent Rodriguez
investment banker

MAJOR SHAREHOLDERS

Kent Rodriguez, 34.8%
Minneapolis

All officers and directors as a group (4 persons), 38.9%

SIC CODE

5091 Sporting and recreational goods, whsle

5941 Sporting goods and bicycle shops

MISCELLANEOUS

TRANSFER AGENT AND REGISTAR:
Wells Fargo Bank Minnesota N.A., South St. Paul, MN

TRADED: OTC Bulletin Board

SYMBOL: XDOG

STOCKHOLDERS: 1,000

EMPLOYEES: 14

GENERAL COUNSEL:
Leonard Street & Deinard P.A., Minneapolis

AUDITORS:
Cordovano and Harvey, Denver

INC: NV-1999

FOUNDED: 1991

INVESTOR RELATIONS:
Alliance Corporate Service

XOX Corporation

7640 W. 78th St., Suite 120, Bloomington, MN 55439
Tel: 952/946-1191 Fax: 952/946-1195 Web site: http://www.xox.com

XOX Corp. is recognized as a leader in the field of commercial geometric computing systems. The company designs, develops, and markets proprietary software for creating virtual mock-ups or models within the computer that capture the complete geometry of objects or spatial areas of interest.

EARNINGS HISTORY

Year Ended Dec 31	Operating Revenue/Sales (dollars in thousands)	Net Earnings (dollars in thousands)	Return on Revenue (percent)	Return on Equity (percent)	Net Earnings (dollars per share*)	Cash Dividend (dollars per share*)	Market Price Range (dollars per share*)
1999 †	2,621	928	35.4	62.9	0.30	—	2.88–0.88
1998	2,241	378	16.8	73.7	0.12	—	3.50–1.00
1997	914	(2,471)	NM	NM	(0.83)	—	3.50–1.00
1996	807	(1,667)	NM	NM	(0.88)	—	7.75–5.00
1995	421	(1,601)	NM	NM	(1.21)	—	

* Trading began Sept. 11, 1996.
† Income figures for 1999 include extraordinary gain of $110,245/$0.03 on extinguishment of debt.

BALANCE SHEET

Assets	12/31/99 (dollars in thousands)	12/31/98 (dollars in thousands)
Current (CAE 1,390 and 1,194)	1,598	1,367
Property and equipment	59	63
TOTAL	1,657	1,430

Liabilities	12/31/99 (dollars in thousands)	12/31/98 (dollars in thousands)
Current	182	404
Long-term obligations		496
Accrued payroll taxes		18
Stockholders' equity*	1,475	512
TOTAL	1,657	1,430

* $0.025 par common; 20,000,000 authorized; 3,096,378 and 3,072,901 issued and outstanding.

RECENT QUARTERS / PRIOR-YEAR RESULTS

	Quarter End	Revenue ($000)	Earnings ($000)	EPS ($)	Prior-Year Revenue ($000)	Prior-Year Earnings ($000)	Prior-Year EPS ($)
Q2	06/30/2000	591	54	0.02	596	130	0.04
Q1	03/31/2000	684	201	0.07	559	151	0.05
Q4	12/31/99	813	395	0.13	622	71	0.02
Q3	09/30/99	654	252	0.08	563	157	0.05
	SUM	2,742	902	0.29	2,340	508	0.17

RECENT EVENTS

In **January 2000** the company reported that its first end-user product, ShapesProspector, was exceeding internal sales projections. During the fourth quarter, XOX had sold more than 10 of its PC-based geometric earth-modeling tool kits for oil and gas exploration. ShapesProspector customers included Belco, Chesapeake, Chevron, Cross Timbers, Los Alamos, Marathon, Mitchell Energy, PennzEnergy, Phillips, and Ranger. In **April** the company introduced a new cost-effective approach for salt dome mapping through ShapesProspector. With this enhancement, ShapesProspector became the only PC-based product capable of handling multiple Z values in salt dome mapping. In **October** XOX unveiled ShapesPlanner, a 2-D/3-D planning tool for wellbore trajectory design and quality assurance that eliminates costly mistakes and reduces cycle time, because wells are viewed in the context of a full 3-D geologic model. ShapesPlanner supports standard interpolation schemes; generates minimum length path subject to constraints such as pre- and post-hold, minimum radius, and dog-leg severity; and computes intersection angles with surfaces and faults in fully linked 3-D, map, and cross-section views.

OFFICERS

Steven B. Liefschultz
Chairman
John R. Sutton
CEO
Mark Senn
President and COO
William F. Fuller
EVP-Business Development

DIRECTORS

Peter Dahl
Bank Windsor
Craig Gagnon
Oppenheimer Wolff & Donnelly LLP, Minneapolis
Layton Kinney
MIN-CORP
Steven B. Liefschultz
Remada Co.
Bernard J. Reeck
Group Services Corp./The Cellars Wines & Spirits Inc.
Brian D. Zelickson, M.D.
dermatologist

MAJOR SHAREHOLDERS

Robert J. Fink, 6.1%
Mendota Heights, MN
Minnesota Investment Network Corp., 5%
Minneapolis
All officers and directors as a group (6 persons), 36%

SIC CODE

7372 Prepackaged software

MISCELLANEOUS

TRANSFER AGENT AND REGISTAR:
Wells Fargo Bank Minnesota N.A., South St. Paul, MN
TRADED: OTC Bulletin Board
SYMBOL: XOXC
STOCKHOLDERS: 182
EMPLOYEES: 16
GENERAL COUNSEL:
Gray, Plant, Mooty, Mooty & Bennett P.A., Minneapolis
AUDITORS:
Grant Thornton LLP, Minneapolis
INC: DE-1985
ANNUAL MEETING: June
INVESTOR RELATIONS:
Mark Senn
ADMINISTRATION:
Elaine Hallen

RANKINGS

No. 23 Minnesota Technology Fast 50

SUBSIDIARIES, DIVISIONS, AFFILIATES

XOX Technologies
Bangalore, India
T.K. Srikanth

PUB

TWO-YEAR QUARTERLY HIGH-LOW STOCK PRICES

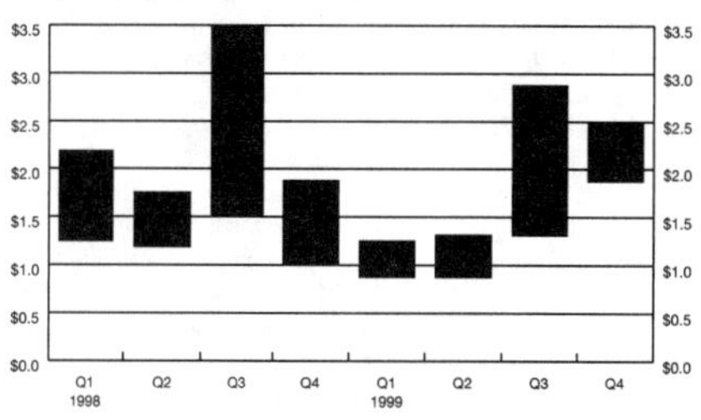

PUB

Zamba Corporation

7301 Ohms Ln., Suite 200, Edina, MN 55439
Tel: 952/893-3923 Fax: 952/832-9383 Web site: http://www.gozamba.com

Zamba Corp., is the nation's largest consulting and systems integrator dedicated exclusively to customer care. Customer care encompasses traditional front office applications such as customer support, field services, and marketing automation. The market for customer care software is projected by Gartner Group to grow at an average annual rate of 54 percent through 2002. Zamba's mission is to set an entirely new standard in customer care by designing and implementing integrated solutions that dramatically improve its customers' ability to care for their clients—from prospect to partner. Zamba's dedication exclusively to customer care differentiates the company from other broadly focused industry players such as Cambridge Technology Partners, AnswerThink, Sapient, and Technology Solutions Co.

EARNINGS HISTORY *

Year Ended Dec 31	Operating Revenue/Sales (dollars in thousands)	Net Earnings (dollars in thousands)	Return on Revenue (percent)	Return on Equity (percent)	Net Earnings (dollars per share)	Cash Dividend (dollars per share)	Market Price Range (dollars per share)
1999	28,276	(2,007)	(7.1)	(19.4)	(0.07)	—	18.94–1.50
1998 †	9,358	(2,785)	(29.8)	(24.9)	(0.10)	—	4.06–1.31
1997	6,363	(9,271)	NM	NM	(0.36)	—	4.88–1.00
1996	7,199	(10,232)	NM	(66.5)	(0.40)	—	7.00–3.50
1995	6,173	(12,358)	NM	(48.7)	(0.50)	—	7.88–3.13

* Historical figures for 1999 and earlier periods have been restated to pool Dec. 29, 1999, acquisition Camworks Inc.

† Pro forma 1998 figures including results of the Sept. 22, 1998, purchase Quicksilver Group Inc. from Jan. 1: revenue $11,229,000; loss $7,669,000/($0.29).

BALANCE SHEET

Assets	12/31/99 (dollars in thousands)	12/31/98	Liabilities	12/31/99 (dollars in thousands)	12/31/98
Current (CAE 7,969 and 3,054)	11,845	6,015	Current (STD 573 and 320)	4,998	1,843
Property and equipment	1,036	1,275	Long-term debt	816	1,333
Restricted cash	110	210	Stockholders' equity*	10,350	11,195
Identifiable intangibles	3,044	6,768	TOTAL	16,164	14,371
Goodwill	67	38			
Other	62	65			
TOTAL	16,164	14,371			

* $0.01 par common; 55,000,000 authorized; 31,029,517 and 30,014,203 issued and outstanding.

RECENT QUARTERS / **PRIOR-YEAR RESULTS**

	Quarter End	Revenue ($000)	Earnings ($000)	EPS ($)	Prior-Year Revenue ($000)	Prior-Year Earnings ($000)	Prior-Year EPS ($)
Q2	06/30/2000	9,715	(523)	(0.02)	7,007	(727)	(0.02)
Q1	03/31/2000	8,217	(886)	(0.03)	5,350	(1,055)	(0.04)
Q4	12/31/99	7,961	(505)	(0.02)	4,069	(1,592)	(0.06)
Q3	09/30/99	7,958	280	0.01	1,633	(258)	(0.01)
	SUM	33,851	(1,634)	(0.05)	18,059	(3,632)	(0.12)

CURRENT: Q4 and prior figures have been restated for 12/99 Camworks and 1/00 Fusion acquisitions.

RECENT EVENTS

In **November 1999** the company said that it was making a major push to establish a higher standard for customer care on the Web. "E-business service problems are creating nightmares for consumers, especially during this record e-shopping holiday season," said CEO Edelhertz. "E-shoppers deserve a new standard that puts their needs first." In **December** Zamba completed the wireless communications portion of an integrated Customer Care solution for BellSouth (NYSE: BLS) that provides BellSouth's 15,000 service technicians real-time access to customer and network information from the field. The company acquired $3 million-revenue, 37-employee Camworks, a leading e-business solutions provider based in St. Paul, for $15 million. The thought that e-commerce consulting might be the company's missing link fueled a 25.7 percent jump in Zamba's stock price. In **January 2000** Zamba acquired Fusion Consulting Inc., a Colorado Springs, Colo.-based consulting firm specializing in front office and contact center customer care solutions, for $1.3 million. Zamba then entered into an extended business alliance with Aspect Communications Corp. (Nasdaq: ASPT) that was to allow ZAMBA Solutions to augment its list of customer care technology offerings with the Aspect Customer Relationship Portal. Zamba released a "company soundtrack" of original music designed to build its brand image. The company, which is named after a highly-skilled, agile form of South American dance, was planning to distribute the CD to clients, prospects, partners, employees, investors, and Web site visitors. The company formed a new support services group aimed at providing continuing support and engineering services for its customer-care solutions. later in the month, Zamba announced the launch of its Siebel (Nasdaq: SEBL) practice. That announcement also included a disclosure that Zamba had recently been chosen by Personnel *continued on page 407*

OFFICERS

Paul D. Edelhertz
Chairman

Joseph B. Costello
Vice Chairman

Doug Holden
President and CEO

Peter D. Marton
EVP and COO

Karen Woodson
SVP and Chief People Officer

David Bayliss
VP-Marketing

Michael H. Carrel
VP and CFO

Todd X. Fitzwater
VP

BUSINESS DEVELOPMENT: Melissa Olson

RANKINGS

No. 133 CRM Public 200

DIRECTORS

Joseph B. Costello
think3, Santa Clara, CA

Paul D. Edelhertz

Michael Fabaischi
LPA Software

John Olsen
Cadence Design Systems Inc. (previous)

Sven A. Wehrwein
Center for Diagnostic Imaging, Golden Valley, MN

MAJOR SHAREHOLDERS

Coral Partners, 12.8%
Minneapolis

Joseph B. Costello, 7.5%

Motorola Inc., 7.1%
Schaumberg, IL

All officers and directors as a group (9 persons), 16.8%

SIC CODE

7373 Computer integrated systems design

MISCELLANEOUS

TRANSFER AGENT AND REGISTAR:
Wells Fargo Bank Minnesota N.A., South St. Paul, MN

TRADED: Nasdaq National Market

SYMBOL: ZMBA

STOCKHOLDERS: 4,000

EMPLOYEES: 185

GENERAL COUNSEL:
Cooley Godward LLP, Palo Alto, CA

AUDITORS:
KPMG LLP, Minneapolis

INC: DE-1990

ANNUAL MEETING: May

TWO-YEAR QUARTERLY HIGH-LOW STOCK PRICES

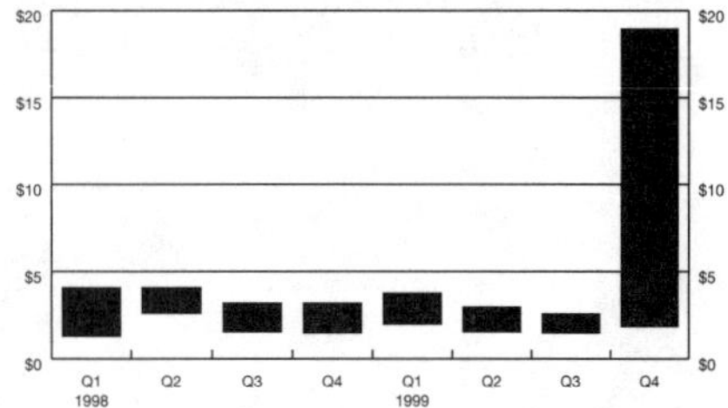

Zomax Inc.

5353 Nathan Ln., Plymouth, MN 55442
Tel: 763/553-9300 Fax: 763/519-3710 Web site: http://www.zomax.com

Zomax Inc. is an international outsource provider of process management services. The company's fully integrated services include "front-end" E-commerce support, call center and customer support solutions; DVD authoring services; CD and DVD mastering; CD and DVD replication; supply chain and inventory management; graphic design; print management; assembly; packaging; warehousing; distribution and fulfillment; and RMA processing.

EARNINGS HISTORY *

Year Ended Dec	Operating Revenue/Sales (dollars in thousands)	Net Earnings	Return on Revenue (percent)	Return on Equity	Net Earnings (dollars per share†)	Cash Dividend	Market Price Range
1999 ¶	229,261	25,827	11.3	31.3	0.87	—	27.78–6.16
1998	61,074	3,561	5.8	7.1	0.14	—	5.00–0.97
1997	47,877	3,128	6.5	19.0	0.15	—	3.75–1.03
1996	26,867	2,152	8.0	14.7	0.12	—	2.16–1.25
1995	16,858	2,141	12.7	41.4	0.15	—	

* Historical income figures are pro forma as though all consolidated companies were taxable entities for all periods presented.
† Trading began May 7, 1996. Per-share amounts restated to reflect 2-for-1 stock splits on May 8, 2000, and Aug. 12, 1999.
¶ Income figures for 1999 include pretax gain of $3.685 million on unconsolidated entity stock sale.

BALANCE SHEET

Assets	12/31/99 (dollars in thousands)	12/25/98	Liabilities	12/31/99 (dollars in thousands)	12/25/98
Current (CAE 51,128 and 25,621)	94,104	39,549	Current (STD 3,990 and 1,380)	46,638	12,580
Property and equipment	40,642	18,925	Notes payable	10,603	1,746
			Deferred taxes	2,633	1,010
Goodwill, other	1,111	2,287	Stkhldrs' equity*	82,430	50,087
Investment in unconsolidated entity	6,447	4,662	TOTAL	142,304	65,423
TOTAL	142,304	65,423			

* No par common; 40,000,000 authorized; 30,966,000 and 28,756,000 issued and outstanding.

RECENT QUARTERS / **PRIOR-YEAR RESULTS**

	Quarter End	Revenue ($000)	Earnings ($000)	EPS ($)	Revenue ($000)	Earnings ($000)	EPS ($)
Q3	09/29/2000	58,824	5,457	0.17	61,603	7,453	0.25
Q2	06/30/2000	62,940	7,797	0.24	55,140	4,918	0.17
Q1	03/31/2000	57,359	6,394	0.20	48,235	1,968	0.07
Q4	12/31/99	64,283	11,488	0.37	17,463	1,062	0.04
	SUM	243,406	31,136	0.99	182,441	15,401	0.52

CURRENT: Q4 EPS includes a gain of $0.065 from an increase in the value of the company's Chumbo holdings.

RECENT EVENTS

Dec. 31, 1999: Fourth-quarter earnings of 69 cents a share came in well ahead of analysts' estimates of 46 cents. The company continued to benefit from the growth of the DVD market. (DVDs are more profitable for Zomax to make than CDs.) In addition, the company benefited 13 cents a share from an increase in the value of its holdings in Chumbo. In **February 2000** Pacific Crest Securities raised its rating on company shares from BUY to STRONG BUY, with a 12-month price target of $70. In **May** Zomax announced plans to increase its replication capacity by 20 percent in the second half of the yea—reflecting continued strong demand for both CDs and DVDs. In **September** Zomax was ranked No. 6 overall on Fortune magazine's "100 Fastest Growing Companies" for 2000. (Zomax reported 115 percent average revenue growth, 88 percent EPS growth, and 92 percent average total return growth over the past three years.) Zomax announced that its third-quarter financial results were expected to be lower than current consensus estimates. The shortfall was primarily the result of general market softness, in particular the European market; a major customer modifying a third-quarter program that the company was unable to replace with other business; an increase in polycarbonate prices due to increasing crude oil prices; and further weakening of European currencies. The announcement cost Zomax half its market value, as shares closed **Sept. 22** at $8.34, down from the previous day's close of $17.37. In **October** Zomax was again named one of Forbes "200 Best Small Companies in America." No. 11 overall, Zomax has reported 115 percent average revenue growth and 88 percent EPS growth over the past three years. The board of directors authorized a common stock repurchase program of up to 2 million shares.

OFFICERS

James T. Anderson
Chairman and CEO

Anthony Angelini
President and COO

Michelle S. (Mikki) Bedard
EVP-Sales/Marketing

James E. Flaherty
CFO and Secretary

Steve Gunning
VP-North American Sales

INVESTOR RELATIONS:
James E. Flaherty

HUMAN RESOURCES:
Tom Duenow

RANKINGS

No. 71 CRM Public 200
No. 37 CRM Performance 100

PUB

DIRECTORS

James T. Anderson
Qwest (retired

Anthony Angelini

Robert Ezrilov
Metacom Inc.

Phillip T. Levin

Howard P. Liszt
Campbell Mithun Esty, Minneapolis

Janice Ozzello Wilcox
Marquette Bancshares Inc., Minneapolis

MAJOR SHAREHOLDERS

Pilgram Baxter & Associates Ltd., 12.9%
Wayne, PA

Phillip T. Levin, 8.4%
Brooklyn Park, MN

All officers and directors as a group (8 persons), 11.3%

SIC CODE

7379 Computer related services, nec

MISCELLANEOUS

TRANSFER AGENT AND REGISTAR:
Wells Fargo Bank Minnesota N.A., South St. Paul, MN

TRADED: Nasdaq National Market

SYMBOL: ZOMX

STOCKHOLDERS: 455

EMPLOYEES: 2,000

PART TIME: 150

IN MINNESOTA: 300

GENERAL COUNSEL:
Fredrikson & Byron P.A., Minneapolis

AUDITORS:
Arthur Andersen LLP, Minneapolis

INC: MN-1996

FOUNDED: 1993

ANNUAL MEETING: April

TWO-YEAR QUARTERLY HIGH-LOW STOCK PRICES

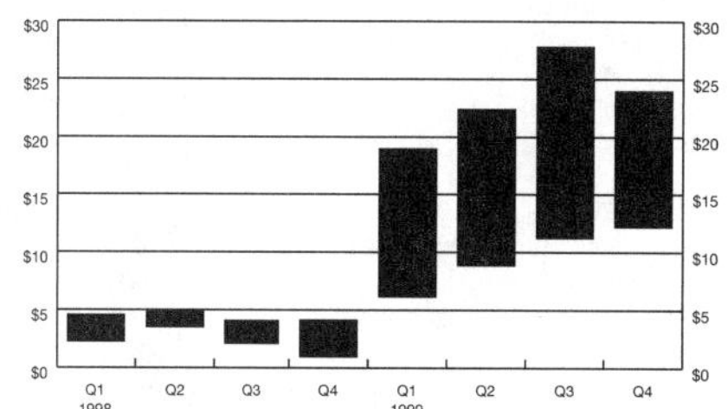

U.S. Bancorp

continued from page 375 guided ATM machines in the new U.S. Bancorp Center, at 800 Nicollet Mall in downtown Minneapolis. The machines allow visually impaired persons to use ATMs by plugging in a headset and privately listening to voice prompts that guide them through the transaction. Philip G. Heasley, president and COO, decided not to renew his employment contract with the company. "I'm at a point in my career when I want to run a company as a CEO," Heasley explained, "and I've decided to look outside U.S. Bancorp." He agreed to stay on through late fall in a transition role, and to continue to serve as U.S. Bancorp's representative on the Visa board. At month's end, U.S. Bancorp agreed to acquire Lyon Financial Services Inc., a wholly owned subsidiary of privately held Schwan's Sales Enterprises Inc., Marshall, Minn. The $1.1 billion-asset Lyon Financial specializes in small-ticket lease transactions: office technology such as copiers, computers, and telephone systems; as well as medical, construction, and other types of equipment. Lyon Financial was to become a division of U.S. Bancorp Leasing & Financial. All 423 employees were offered employment. In **September** U.S. Bancorp concluded two legal matters from 1999 relating to privacy, including the settlement of a consolidated class action suit ($3.5 million) and an agreement with a multistate task force of attorneys general ($4 million). The company introduced the U.S. Bank Visa eProcurement Card, to help large corporate customers process payments for large-ticket items online. **Sept. 30:** Operating earnings were $410.9 million for the third quarter of 2000, compared with $409.0 million for the third quarter of 1999. Consumer banking earnings dropped, but commercial loan growth, payment systems, and capital markets took up the slack. Total revenue on a taxable-equivalent basis, before available-for-sale securities transactions, grew by $148.0 million, or 9.5 percent, driven by core loan growth, credit card fee revenue, investment banking and brokerage activity, and acquisitions. U.S. Bank was the nation's leading Small Business Administration (SBA) lender for 2000 based on dollar volume. U.S. Bank provided $406.5 million in SBA-guaranteed loans to 845 small businesses nationwide. In **October** U.S. Bank said that it was opening three new full-service branches in Minnesota—in Roseville, Maplewood, and Lakeville—in response to a growing customer base in that region. (It is uncommon for a bank to open newly constructed branches, since most acquire established banks or build branches within stores such as supermarkets. These are the first newly constructed branches opened by U.S. Bank in 2000, and the first to open in Minnesota since 1997.) On **Oct. 4**, Firstar Corp. (NYSE: FSR) announced that it had signed a definitive agreement to merge with U.S. Bancorp in a pooling-of-interests transaction valued at $21.2 billion. The Firstar/U.S. Bancorp combination would become the eighth-largest bank holding company in the United States, with assets of more than $160 billion, deposits of $107 billion, assets under management of $145 billion, and a pro forma market capitalization of $40 billion. The franchise will span 24 Midwestern and Western states with 2,200 branches. Firstar agreed to exchange 1.265 shares of Firstar common stock for each share of U.S. Bancorp common stock in a tax-free exchange agreement. Based on Firstar's closing stock price of $22.38 on Sept. 29, this represented a price of $28.30 for each U.S. Bancorp share, a premium of 24.4 percent over U.S. Bancorp's closing price that date and a multiple of 11.7 times U.S. Bancorp's estimated 2001 earnings per share. The transaction was expected to close in the first quarter of 2001. After the closing, the combined companies were to operate under the U.S. Bancorp name from corporate headquarters in Minneapolis. Jerry Grundhofer, president and CEO of Firstar, was to continue in those positions in the combined company. Jack Grundhofer was to serve as chairman of the board until his planned retirement on Dec. 31, 2002. (The two Grundhofers are brothers.) The board of directors was to be composed of 14 members from Firstar and 11 members from U.S. Bancorp. Jack Grundhofer remarked, "Our geographies fit together, our business lines complement each other, we are both devoted to high standards of customer service, and we have a lot of other strengths to offer each other in areas ranging from sales culture to information technology. By any standard, we've built a tremendous institution at U.S. Bancorp. But as we considered how best to convert our potential into real value for our shareholders and our customers, it became clear that combining with Firstar was far and away the best course to follow. " Firstar Bank of Minnesota, with 29 Twin Cities-area offices, was currently the fourth-largest bank in Minnesota. The combined bank's $15.32 billion in Minnesota deposits (before the required divestment of $500 million) represents a 35.8 percent market share, moving it ahead of Wells Fargo as the largest bank in the state. In addition to Jerry Grundhofer and Jack Grundhofer, the senior management team of the new U.S. Bancorp was to include: David Moffett, currently vice chairman of Firstar, as chief financial officer; Andrew Duff, currently vice chairman of U.S. Bank, as head of wealth management, trusts and investments, and capital markets; Richard Davis, currently vice chairman of Firstar, as head of consumer banking; Daniel Frate, currently vice chairman of U.S. Bank, as head of payment systems; Joseph Hasten, currently vice chairman of Firstar, as head of large corporate banking; Daniel Quinn, currently vice chairman of U.S. Bank, as head of middle market corporate banking; William Chenevich, currently vice chairman of Firstar, as head of information technology and operations; Robert Hoffman, currently EVP of U.S. Bancorp, as chief credit officer; Steve Smith, currently EVP of Firstar, as head of human resources: and Lee Mitau, currently EVP of U.S. Bancorp, as general counsel. Fitch, the international rating agency, affirmed its ratings of Firstar (senior rating A+) and U.S. Bancorp (senior rating A+') following their proposed merger announcement. "The pooling-of-interests accounting treatment will temporarily create a robust capital position due to restrictions in treasury share repurchases. While most of the estimated $800 million pretax restructuring charge will be incurred at the inception of the merger, capital levels will still remain above what we believe to be normal operating targets. Asset quality trends have been stable and the risk profile will be strengthened based on enhanced regional and sector diversity." Although tempered somewhat by the rapid consolidation and transformation of the Firstar franchise over the past few years, Fitch nevertheless assigned a Positive Outlook to the ratings. Shares of Firstar slumped to $20 the day of the deal, trimming some $2.2 billion from the price. Meanwhile, U.S. Bancorp Piper Jaffray advised Linsalata Capital Partners, the owners of CMS Hartzell, on the sale of CMS Hartzell to SCI Systems Inc. Firstar reported that its third-quarter profits rose 18 percent as the bank exceeded cost-cutting targets. U.S. Bancorp Piper Jaffray opened a new brokerage office in Newport Beach, Calif., its 143rd nationwide and ninth in California. Corporate VAT Management, The Seattle-based creator of autoVAT software, entered into a co-marketing partnership with U.S. Bank to enable corporate customers to increase recovery of foreign value-added taxes. U.S. Bancorp Piper Jaffray's Nasdaq trading department ranked No. 1 in the regional trading category for 2000 in the 14th annual survey in Equities Magazine. In **November** U.S. Bancorp Piper Jaffray introduced a comprehensive array of financial calculators to help people learn what they need to know to get the most from their retirement nest egg.

UnitedHealth Group

continued from page 377 bers that provide significant savings and personalized information regarding eye exams and eyewear options. In **June** UnitedHealth Foundation began distributing a new international source of information, Clinical Evidence, to 400,000 doctors in the United States. Clinical Evidence provides doctors with the latest scientific evidence on what works in medicine so that doctors and patients can make the most informed decisions possible regarding treatment options. UnitedHealthcare announced that it will not renew its Medicare+Choice contracts in 21 counties across the United States, effective Dec. 31, 2000. The company reaffirmed that its Medicare Supplement Insurance plans offered to AARP members provide an excellent and long-established alternative to Medicare+Choice HMO products. UnitedHealth doubled its land holdings in Eden Prairie, Minn., by buying a contiguous 35-acre parcel from Honeywell International Inc. for $8 million. In the long run, the land may be used for a corporate headquarters campus. In **July** UnitedHealth Group launched Ingenix Pharmaceutical Services, a global drug development and marketing resource company. Ingenix offers pharmaceutical and biotechnology companies access to a comprehensive suite of drug development and marketing services, combined with a host of unique data and analytic capabilities. Ingenix clients have access to more than 340,000 practicing physicians and their patients to accelerate the clinical trials process and facilitate product awareness and appropriate use. In **August** U.S. Bancorp Piper Jaffray initiated coverage of UnitedHealth Group with a STRONG BUY rating. "We believe UnitedHealth is the leading market maker and coordinator of health services in the industry," said Senior Healthcare Analyst Daren Marhula. "UnitedHealth creates and manages vast amounts of transaction-related information, which enables the company to deliver as its primary service, fundamental health care and market level knowledge to employers, consumer, providers, and other payors." In **September** Symmetry Health Data Systems Inc. announced a patent infringement lawsuit against Ingenix Inc. The initial claims were for patent infringement, violation of the Federal Trade Commission Act, breach of contract, and breach of the duty of good faith and fair dealing. At issue was Symmetry's patented Episode Treatment Groups (ETG) methodology, an illness classification and episode chronology software product used by more than 300 managed health care plans and their providers across the United States. U.S. Bancorp Piper Jaffray, in its monthly commentary, initiated coverage with a STRONG BUY-AGGRESSIVE rating and a $135 price target. **Sept. 30:** The company achieved record revenue and earnings in the third quarter. The 9.6 percent revenue increase over prior year reflected strong and balanced growth across the company despite targeted pullbacks in certain geographic and Medicare market segments in the UnitedHealthcare business unit. Earnings from operations increased to $309 million, up $70 million over the prior year and $21 million sequentially. Consolidated operating margin improved 90 basis points year-over-year, reaching 5.8 percent. Said CEO McGuire, "The strength and consistency of results across our business segments reflect accelerating growth as the marketplace responds to our segments' broad-based product offerings, our effective and practical application of information technology, and our focus on excellence in consumer and provider service." As an example of the company's robust growth, in the commercial health benefit arena the UnitedHealthcare and Uniprise business units increased the number of people served in continuing market segments by an aggregate of 1.2 million in the past 12 months—with no acquisitions in these market segments during this time frame. In **October** Lifemark Corp. (Nasdaq: LMRK) announced plans to merge with EverCare, an operating unit of Ovations, which is a subsidiary of UnitedHealth Group. The merger was to create a national leader in serving the health and well-being needs of America's elderly across the full continuum of care settings. The combined company was to operate as EverCare, with EverCare's Marcia Smith continuing as CEO. The UnitedHealth Group board of directors renewed a stock repurchase program under which up to 16 million shares (10 percent) of the company's common stock may be repurchased.

United Shipping & Technology Inc.

continued from page 378 provide scheduled delivery service, inventory control and local stocking for SwapIt, the first consumer-focused product exchange marketplace on the Web for previously owned CDs, DVDs, and games. In **May** the company signed a definitive agreement for an infusion of equity in the amount of $25.2 million from Internet investment giant TH Lee.Putnam Internet Partners L.P. and TH Lee.Putnam Internet Parallel Partners L.P. (collectively, "THLi"), a leading investment firm focused on Internet-related businesses with high-growth strategies. The company announced that Corporate Express Delivery Systems had been awarded $5 million in projected annualized new and renewal business from customers like Carrier Corp., Nortel/BellSouth, evineyard.com, Charles Levy, Bergen Brunswig, Southdown (formerly Florida Mining), Amway, and McKesson. In **June** the company renamed its service Velocity Express (http://www.velocityexp.com). Its delivery vehicles were repainted with the new logo, and drivers began wearing company uniforms (like delivery people for FedEx and United Parcel Services). The company completed the sale of one of its operating units, Midnite Express, to the original owner of Midnite Express. The main thrust of Midnite Express' business was providing same-day delivery needs for the entertainment industry—a niche that was not a key fit within the core capabilities of Velocity Express. **July 1**: "The positive trend in EBITDA improvement continued in the fourth quarter and, as a result, our operating loss for the quarter improved by over $1 million," said CFO Becker. "Meanwhile, our net loss attributable to common shareholders for the quarter was impacted by a one-time, noncash charge. We believe that last year's spending on unifying a national footprint should allow us to achieve our goals, and we believe that we are on track to be EBITDA positive on a consistent basis and to achieve profitability by the end of fiscal 2001." In **July** one of the nation's largest computer software companies began using the company's same-day delivery business, Velocity Express, to transport more than 275 items per day. Velocity Express also agreed to provide scheduled delivery service for Father Orsini's Italian Specialties Inc. (http://www.orsinifoods.com), the most-original tomato sauce company in the country. In **August** Velocity Express provided a logistics solution to enable one of the country's largest oil companies to continue operating at full capacity while undergoing a major reinstallation of its entire stock of desktop computers at corporate headquarters. In **September** the company signed a definitive agreement for an additional private placement of equity in the amount of $12 million from funds managed by TH Lee.Putnam Internet Partners L.P. [completed Sept. 25]. The company announced its intent to launch initiatives to become the leader in "Green Shipping." The initiatives, to be executed by US&T's Velocity Express subsidiary over the span of several years, included the development of systems and technologies focused on three specific areas:

1) reducing the mileage associated with the delivery of ground and air packages;

2) reducing the amount of reshipping materials required for individual B2B and B2C deliveries;

3) reducing the company's dependence on traditional fossil-fueled vehicles.

Velocity Express gained a number of new health care customers, adding $8 million to the company's projected annual revenue. Velocity Express upgraded the company's electronic tracking and package management system to include expanded bar code scanning, signature capture, and remote transmission features that were to provide the company's national and regional customer base with timely tracking and billing management information beyond what was then available on the Velocity Express Web site, www.velocityexp.com. Velocity Express was awarded significant new business by one of the country's leading B2B retail chains, extending Velocity Express' work with this chain to an expanded number of cities across the country. In **October** Velocity Express began offering the first nationwide same-day transport program to pick, ship, and deliver rush and emergency shipments during the busy holiday season. In October the company relocated its same-day delivery operations from Chicagoy's northwest side to new quarters in Hodgkins, Ill., to enhance operating efficiencies and improve customer service. The 35,000-square-foot facility was large enough to accommodate the docking and loading of the company's fleet of vans and trucks, inbound and outbound freight staging, and secure warehousing of customers' time-sensitive products and materials. In **November** the company sold one of its two air courier operating units, Tricor America Inc., based in San Francisco, to Tricor's former owners. Said CEO Lytle, "Given the divergence between Velocity Express' and Tricor's core competencies, it makes sense from both strategic and financial perspectives that Tricor operate independently."

Urologix Inc.

continued from page 379 nation of higher rates and shorter treatments drove the stock price from $4 to $8 over a two-month period. In **September** Urologix announced the release of Cruise II software (which features a unique dual-temperature feedback system that achieves an optimal targeted heating pattern in the diseased prostate and customizes treatment for each individual patient) and the issuance of the U.S. patent for its dual-temperature feedback system. The company also said that it planned to increase its sales staff from 12 people to 18 in the next few months. **Sept. 30**: During the first quarter, increased treatment revenue and record procedure kit sales were offset by a decrease in equipment sales as hospitals and urologists prepare to transition to an office-based procedure. Gross profit, as a percent of sales, improved to 57 percent from 40 percent in the same quarter a year ago, while the net loss for the quarter decreased 28 percent to $1.5 million. "The response to office-based microwave procedures has been overwhelmingly positive," said CEO Selzer. "We achieved record sales of disposable Targis procedure kits and generated significant interest and excitement for our treatment." In **October** Urologix acquired main competitor EDAP Technomed's (Nasdaq: EDAPY) Transurethral Microwave Thermotherapy (TUMT) product line, related patents, and technologies. Urologix paid total consideration of $7,988,000 in cash, issued 1,365,000 shares of Urologix common stock and 327,466 warrants to purchase common stock, and agreed to assume certain obligations in connection with the acquisition. (After issuance of the shares to EDAP, Urologix had 13 million shares outstanding.) EDAP's main microwave thermotherapy offering, Prostatron, is the pioneer of cooled microwave thermotherapy, a technological advancement that provides a superior treatment for men with BPH. The acquisition of Prostatron, combined with Urologix' Targis treatment, positioned Urologix as a premiere provider of minimally invasive BPH solutions. An FDA notice, written in collabration with Urologix, was sent to health care providers to reinforce the importance of following the manufacturer's instructions when performing microwave thermotherapy procedures. Since 1996, the FDA had received 16 reports of "thermal injuries" related to microwave thermotherapy systems. As a result, the FDA recommended that physicians properly select patients suitable for this procedure and that they follow the manufacturer's treatment protocols. In **November** HCFA published final rates for office-based reimbursement for cooled microwave thermotherapy scheduled to become effective beginning Jan. 1, 2001. The change was a significant milestone for Urologix, and the urology field, as it marked the first time that patients would be covered directly by Medicare for in-office cooled thermotherapy treatment of enlarged prostate.

ValueVision International Inc.

continued from page 382 core television shopping business," said CEO McCaffery. Vice Chairman Goldfarb added, "ValueVision is currently pursuing a number of strategic investments with leading e-commerce companies." ValueVision began broadcasting TV programming live on the Web using Microsoft Windows Media, following finalization of an agreement with Microsoft Corp. An agreement with Atlanta-based Cox Communications Inc. expanded carriage of ValueVision. The company made a $10 million equity investment in BigStar Entertainment Inc. (Nasdaq: BGST), which operates bigstar.com, a leading Shop-A-Tainment destination and online movie store. ValueVision achieved a pre-Christmas December sales increase of 84 percent over the same prior-year period. In addition, sales from ValueVision's e-commerce subsidiary also continued to achieve substantially greater percentage gains than television sales. In **January 2000** ValueVision and NBCi took minority equity stakes in ROXY.com, the fastest growing online consumer electronics retailer, and agreed to spotlight ROXY on the SnapTV home shopping television and Internet service as well as on NBCi's Web properties and in select NBCi television and radio advertisements. The multifaceted agreement was valued in excess of $20 million. NBC and ValueVision entered into a strategic alliance with Petopia.com, the "Internet Pet Paradise" and leading online pet store. Included were agreements related to cable programming on ValueVision's SnapTV. ValueVision signed a strategic marketing agreement with redtagoutlet.com Inc., an online close-out merchandiser, to co-produce live programming for SnapTV. In **February** NBC and ValueVision, announced multiple-year strategic alliances with SelfCare.com, a leading health and wellness e-commerce site targeting women and their families. Actress Meredith Baxter appeared on ValueVision's SnapTV offering her "Signature Collection" of personal skin-care products. In new coverage, Gerard Klauer Mattison & Co. rated company shares BUY, with a 12-month price target of $50. In **April** the company co-produced and began airing The Petopia.com Show—a live, one-hour show featuring pet-related education, entertainment, and shopping. ValueVision and ROXY.com, the fastest growing online consumer electronics retailer, premiered "Electronics Without the Static," the nation's first show merging live TV network and Internet channels to provide consumer electronics information, entertainment, and shopping. ValueVision and wine.com, the award-winning global wine destination, launched "The Best of Wine Show," a monthly wine show series, on the SnapTV network. In **May** the company acquired state-of-the-art customer support call center facilities that will expand its capability to provide commerce services for the polo.com launch planned for later this year. The facilities, previously operated by Damark International Inc., were located in a 25,000-square-foot building in Brooklyn Center, Minn. A long-term agreement with Time Warner Cable called for expanded carriage of ValueVision's television network in an additional 5 million cable households. In **June** Manhattan Associates Inc. (Nasdaq: MANH), the leading provider of technology-based supply chain execution solutions, teamed up with ValueVision to provide third-party e-fulfillment services for Ralph Lauren Media's polo.com initiative planned to launch later in the year. ValueVision parnered with, and invested in, IdeaForest.com, a newly formed online arts and crafts business. Meanwhile, the company released assurances that the name and branding issue being dealt with by NBC Internet—which planned to integrate all of its consumer properties under the single NBCi.com brand (including folding the Snap.com and Xoom.com names into one property)—was not a strategic issue for ValueVision. In **July** ValueVision and Transmedia Network Inc. (NYSE: TMN) jointly announced a strategic marketing alliance under which Transmedia's iDine-branded dining rewards memberships were to be offered to the 34.2 million households on ValueVision's home shopping network. ValueVision also made a minority equity investment in Transmedia. **July 31:** Sales and earnings showed substantial, continuing improvements in television home shopping and Internet operations during the fiscal second quarter. In **October** ValueVision announced an agreement with Paxson Communications Corp. (Amex: PAX), owner and operator of the nation's largest broadcast television station group and PAX TV, the newest broadcast television network, for carriage of ValueVision's television network in the Boston area on WPXB Channel 60. The board of directors reached an agreement with Gene McCaffery to extend his contract through April 1, 2004, as chairman and CEO of ValueVision. In **November** ValueVision expanded its television network distribution in the Dallas area on KTAQ-TV Channel 47, a full-power broadcast television station that reaches 560,000 cable households.

Verdant Brands Inc.

continued from page 385 lems, the company placed a moratorium on the payment of $16 million in trade accounts payable, causing many vendors, some critical to operations, to withhold credit and otherwise restrict the company's ability to acquire materials and services. Verdant's senior secured creditor was continuing to fund operations on a restricted basis; however, funding was inadequate for normal operations and the its continuation was uncertain. Also, Verdant Brands was notified by Nasdaq that it had failed to maintain the minimum market value of public float and the minimum bid price required for continued listing on the Nasdaq National Market. Verdant had until Oct. 30 to demonstrate compliance and avoid delisting, but in it determined to delist the company at the opening of business on Sept. 11. In **September** Verdant signed a letter of intent with Woodstream Corp. for the purchase by Woodstream of the operating assets associated with the environmentally sensitive, insecticide, pest control, and fertilizer products sold through retail distribution (the Safer, Chemfree, Blocker, Surefire, Insectigone, and Ringer brand names). Through this transaction, Verdant Brands was completing the first step of its strategic plan to focus its future marketing efforts in areas other than the retail division.

Vicom Inc.

continued from page 386 growth, was expected to result in revenue for the year 2000 of approximately $50 million. The board of directors approved a special warrant dividend under which each shareholder received a warrant entitling them to purchase an additional share of common stock, for each common share they owned, at an exercise price of $8.75 per share (the closing price of the company's common stock on March 10). The warrants will expire on April 11, 2002. Newly formed subsidiary Multiband Inc. signed contracts with property management companies. Vicom officials stated that the company undertakes a survey before the execution of these contracts to determine the likely penetration of subscriptions, and requires a minimum level of anticipated penetration. Vicom took a step toward meeting its goal of becoming a reporting company under the Securities Exchange Act of 1934 by filing its Form 10 with the SEC. The document had to be declared effective by May 17, 2000, in order for the company's common stock to continue to trade on the over-the-counter Bulletin Board. (If not, Vicom's common stock would be traded on the "pink sheets.") The company's ultimate goal was a Nasdaq listing. Vicom then said that it had undertaken and completed a number of strategic cost savings initiatives, following its merger with Corporate Technologies, that were expected to realize annualized cost savings in the range of $500,000 to $700,000. In **May** Multiband Inc. affirmed contracts for 3,000 homes, having started service to 215 of them over the last weekend in April. Vicom received comments from the SEC with respect to the Form 10 filed in early April. When Vicom's Form 10 was not declared effective by May 17, 2000, its common stock was delisted from the over-the-counter Bulletin Board to the "pink sheets." Meanwhile, the company hung NASDAQ 2000 banners throughout its headquarters building as a constant reminder of its primary goal: to shift from a nonreporting firm to a Nasdaq SmallCap Market company by year's end. In **June** Vicom responded to its second round of comments from the SEC with respect to the Form 10. In **July** Minot (N.D.) Public Schools purchased a complete Cisco network system from Corporate Technologies USA. Corporate Technologies also was awarded a contract for the state of North Dakota's new broadband telecommunication network connecting 552 locations in 194 cities throughout North Dakota. The multimillion-dollar three-year award targets the customer premises equipment portion of the contract, including providing routers and other equipment statewide to connect endpoints to the new broadband network. Another new $480,000 contract, for the Moorhead, Minn., Public School District, included data networking service solutions, telecommunications systems, and ongoing service to 10 Moorhead Public School District locations. Vicom's Registration Statement on Form 10 was declared effective by the SEC, making Vicom a reporting company under the Securities Exchange Act of 1934. CEO Mandel commented, "This clears the way for trading in our stock to now take place on the Nasdaq Over-the-Counter Bulletin Board as soon as Monday, July 17, 2000. This is also another step in the process of becoming a Nasdaq-listed company." With the Form 10 having been declared effective, the company was able to begin a variety of corporate initiatives designed to enhance shareholder value and raise capital for growth and expansion of broadband and other business initiatives. Capital available to the company subject to the exercise of outstanding warrants was $70 million. By the end of July, Multiband Inc. had affirmed multiple contracts with property management companies to supply its integrated broadband service to 4,000 homes, largely through Twin Cities-area multiunit dwellings. in **August** Vicom, saying that it believed it had met the requirements, filed the forms necessary to seek a listing on the Nasdaq stock exchange. The company's S-1 Registration Statement was declared effective by the SEC. As a result, a majority of the company's outstanding shares and warrants were now registered and no longer subject to trading restrictions. Vicom expected its shares to resume trading on the Nasdaq Bulletin Board in the near future. Additionally, Vicom had begun the process of making its warrants tradable. Vicom received a STRONG BUY rating from Equity Securities Investments Inc., with a six-month target price of $20 per share. Equity Research cited a number of factors in its rating, including extraordinary industry growth for Integrated Telecommunications Providers (ICPs), Vicom's well-documented recent efforts toward Nasdaq SmallCap status, experienced management aggressive at growing the business, and the company's impending infusion of up to $70 million in capital made available through the exercise of its warrants. On Sept. 25, the SEC declared effective the company's S-1 Registration Statement for the sale of debentures up to $50 million. In **October** newly formed subsidiary Multiband Inc. signed a letter of intent with BH Equities/Management obtaining the right to market its integrated broadband service to 21,000 apartment units in eight states.

Video Update Inc.

continued from page 387 company had defaulted on $6 million in principal and interest due a major lender, and had tapped out its supply of credit. Outside auditors Deloitte & Touche concluded that there were substantial doubts about Video Update's ability to continue as a going concern. On Sept. 19, Video Update filed for protection under Chapter 11 of the U.S. Bankruptcy Code, listing $129.4 million in assets and $210.3 million in debts. The largest unsecured creditor, Ingram Entertainment Inc. of Tennessee, was owed $16.2 million. During its attempt to restructure its operations for the benefit of creditors and shareholders, the company intended to continue to operate normally and expected no interruption of service to its customers. The court authorized Video Update to finance its post-petition operations through an interim "cash collateral" order and to pay any and all outstanding wages and related benefits to its employees. In **October** the company said that it had hired Keen Realty LLC to organize a bankruptcy aution of the leaseholds on up to one-fifth of its 586 stores, most of them in the Southeast, as part of its way out of bankruptcy court.

VirtualFund.com Inc.

continued from page 388 co-location services for its growing Internet hosting capabilities. VirtualFund was in the process of organizing 12 wholly owned subsidiaries for B2BXchange, which were to have responsibility for designated geographic regions: Singapore, Japan, Korea, Vietnam, Australia, China, India, European Union, Russian Federation, Middle East region, Latin America, and Africa and surrounding regions. In **February** all 1,499,998 shares of outstanding Series A convertible preferred stock were automatically converted into shares of common stock in VirtualFund on a one-to-one basis. The Series A preferred shares, issued as part of the acquisition of TEAM Technologies in December 1998, carried a $5 per share guaranteed value on their maturity date of Dec. 17, 2000. In **April** General Electric Capital Corp. extended its financing relationship with the company through the end of fiscal 2000 (June 30, 2000). B2BXchange launched more than 1,600 industry-specific VerticalXchange trading communities; and the second phase of B2BXchange, a comprehensive suite of Internet tools and services (http://www.b2bxchange.net). Prior to the launch of B2BXchange Phase II, the company created the FastStart 8 program by targeting eight specific VerticalXchange markets that would be quickly populated after the launch. The FastStart 8 included:

http://www.myPrintingXchange.com
http://www.myAgriculturalXchange.com
http://www.myManufacturingXchange.com
http://www.myPublishingXchange.com
http://www.MinorityVendorXchange.com
http://www.myRestaurantXchange.com
http://www.myHotelXchange.com
http://www.myTradeshowXchange.com

Each market represented by the FastStart 8 was assigned a Vertical Marketing Manager charged with identifying and selecting (a) content providers, (b) application partners, (c) anchor tenants, and (d) subscribers. Each of these VerticalXchange trading communities was to provide business-to-business (B2B) customers with access to industry-specific content, tools, and services. Details of the sale of the Digital Graphics Business Unit (DGBU) to MacDermid Graphic Arts Inc., a division of MacDermid Inc. (NYSE: MRD): sale price $50 million, subject to certain post-closing adjustments as agreed upon between the companies; includes ColorSpan Corp., Kilborn Photo Products Inc., and SuppliesByAir. In **May** the company received "early termination of the HSR [Hart-Scott-Rodino] waiting period" for the sale of DGBU to MacDermid Graphic Arts. [Deal closed in July.] In **June** VirtualFund's board of directors authorized the repurchase, from time to time, of up to 2 million shares of its common stock on the open market or in privately negotiated transactions. In **September** the company commenced suit against Jaffray Communications Inc., doing business as Vitesse Networks Inc., and its president and COO, Mark Kittrell. The lawsuit alleged that Kittrell had violated his agreement not to compete against VirtualFund and its subsidiaries and had recruited away RSPN employees to Vitesse. The suit also alleged certain securities law violations and misrepresentations by Kittrell in connection with the conversion of VirtualFund preferred stock to common stock. In **October** VirtualFund selected Metiom, a leader in global business-to-business e-commerce, to partner in the joint creation of the B2BXchange Marketplace solution. The Metiom ConnectTrade software was to be integrated into VirtualFund's Commerce Environment Operating System (CEOS). When VirtualFund completed its June share-repurchase program, the board of directors authorized the company to repurchase another 2 million shares, or 13.2 percent of its outstanding common stock. In October VirtualFund's RSPNetwork was preparing to introduce its new StorageVault product line, a secure Internet-based file storage service that provides online storage capabilities for small-office/home-office workers, mobile professionals, and SMEs (Small or Medium-sized businesses and Enterprise workgroups). StorageVault enables users to save their files to a RSPNetwork data center, which provides off-site, secure access for their data.

Wilsons The Leather Experts

continued from page 395 lion one year ago. Year-to-date comparable store sales increased 6.8 percent on top of an 8.5 percent increase for the same period in 1999. CEO Waller commented, "We are pleased with the strength of our fashion apparel and accessories businesses, and believe this upcoming fall season will be strong for leather. We are looking forward to beginning our first major outerwear promotion of the season in September, and remain optimistic about our prospects for the balance of the year." In **September** Wilsons signed a definitive purchase agreement to acquire $75 million-revenue El Portal Group Inc., Las Vegas, a privately held upscale retailer of premium travel products and accessories, for cash. El Portal retails a variety of premier brands such as Tumi, Coach, Bally, Hartmann, and Kenneth Cole, as well as their own El Portal brands, in 38 stores in three western states, Hawaii, and Guam. El Portal has historically been profitable during all four quarters of the year, whereas Wilsons' business is skewed toward the Christmas season. The terms of the transaction included a $15.4 million payment to the El Portal Group in addition to the assumption of $13.8 million in debt. The acquisition was expected to increase EPS by 15 cents to 20 cents. El Portal's current management team was to continue to lead its operations from its Las Vegas facility. [The deal was completed in November.] **Oct. 28:** Sales for the four weeks increased 7.3 percent from prior year, to $49.8 million. Comparable-store sales decreased 1.1 percent compared to a 17.3 percent increase the year before.

Xcel Energy Inc.

continued from page 399 our business plan for the year, we expect to achieve earnings of approximately $1.95 per share in 2000." In **January 2000** the California Public Utilities Commission approved Seren Innovations' application to provide local telephone service—as well as long-distance telephone service for Astound customers—in the East Bay area of San Francisco. NSP acquired Natrogas Inc. in a stock transaction. NSP and New Century Energy's merger plans were boosted when they received approval from the Federal Energy Regulatory Commission (FERC)—no strings attached. Said Howard, "It puts us on schedule to complete the merger in the second quarter." Energy Masters International was selected by the city of Glendale, Calif., to act as the municipal utility's strategic energy partner in delivering energy demand management solutions to the city's largest business customers. NSP and the Minnesota Department of Commerce signed an agreement that insulated customers from up to $60 million in merger costs. In **March** the Xcel Energy merger moved forward on three fronts: Minnesota Administrative Law Judge Steven Mihalchick released a finding of fact document in which he concluded that the merger was in the public interest, and recommended that the Minnesota Public Utilities Commission approve it; the state of Arizona gave its final approval to the merger; and the waiting period under the Hart-Scott-Rodino Act expired, completing the Justice Department review of the merger. The Minneapolis Public Housing Authority won three prestigious national awards for its energy management and conservation program undertaken in partnership with Energy Masters International. The NSP board of directors approved the potential sale in a public offering of up to 18 percent interest in the common stock of NRG Energy. The purpose of the offering: to raise capital to fund a portion of NRG Energy's project investments and other capital requirements for 2000. A possible precursor to other spin-offs that could occur after the merger, this move was hailed as an opportunity for NSP shareholders to realize some of the heretofore hidden value of NRG. In **April** NSP named Northern Alternative Energy Inc. (NAE) a winner among 1999 proposals for new electric generating resources. NAE, a Minneapolis-based developer of renewable energy projects, submitted a bid for building a hybrid wind and natural gas power plant to optimize seasonal fluctuations in mid-western wind resources and natural gas supply costs—thereby delivering the best "green-blended" electricity to NSP's grid. North Dakota approved the Xcel Energy merger. NSP said that it may invest up to $250 million over the next five years to expand Seren Innovations—and that it was seeking private equity investors to that end. NSP signed a lease for the top two floors of the new U.S. Bancorp center in downtown Minneapolis to house its top executives—and the finance, investor relations, and legal departments—after the creation of Xcel Energy. NSP said that it may invest up to $250 million over the next five years to expand its Seren Innovations subsidiary, and was seeking private equity investors for the growing business. At month's end, the Minnesota PUC unanimously approved the New Century Energies merger. (Minnesota was the seventh of nine states to sign off on the deal.) In **May** DemandVideo, the instant entertainment and information source on TV, signed a multiyear contract with Seren Innovations to be the exclusive provider of video on demand (VOD) services to Seren's Astound subscribers in St. Cloud, Minn., California's Contra Costa County, and other franchise areas. The Public Utility Commission of Texas approved the proposed Xcel Energy merger, wrapping up the last of nine required state approvals. Instrument Manufacturing Co. Inc., Storrs, Conn., agreed to acquire the cable diagnostic assets of NSP subsidiary Ultra Power Technologies Inc., Brooklyn Park, Minn. The Nuclear Regulatory Commission approved applications from NSP, one Iowa-, and two Wisconsin-based utilities to transfer operating authority of five nuclear power plants to a new nuclear management company that was to start business in the summer. On May 30, NSP announced the successful IPO by its wholly owned subsidiary NRG Energy. The initial public offering of 28,170,000 shares of common stock was priced at $15 per share. (NSP retained the balance of NRG's equity, which amounted to 82 percent after overallotments were exercised.) The common stock began trading on the New York Stock Exchange on May 31 under the symbol "NRG." [See separate entry in PUBLIC section.] In **June** CheckFree (Nasdaq: CKFR), the leading provider of electronic billing and payment (EBP) services, made electronic billing and payment available to any residential customer who receives an NSP bill for electric or natural gas services. Seren began a challenge to MediaOne by announcing plans to offer cable in a dozen northwest suburbs of the Twin Cities. The Palo Alto, Calif., City Council selected Energy Masters International as strategic energy partner to the city's municipal utility in delivering energy demand management solutions to Palo Alto's largest business customers. Information packets were sent by NSP and merger partner New Century Energies telling 1,500 employees that they will have to reapply for their jobs. About 800 job cuts (6 percent) were planned. Negotiators may have broken a yearlong stalemate NSP, government regulators, and environmental groups over a proposed transmission line over the St. Croix River near Taylors Falls, Minn. A tentative agreement called for a scaled-back, lower-power version. In **August** Energy Masters International was competitively selected by the Housing Authority of the city of Austin (HACA) to develop and implement an energy management program for the authority's 1,928 public housing units and related facilities. On Aug. 17, just 17 months after the announcement of merger plans, NSP and New Century Energies cleared the last hurdle when the SEC approved their combination under the new name Xcel Energy Inc. The merger created one of the 10 largest electricity and natural gas companies in the United States. Stock began trading on the New York Stock Exchange on Aug. 21 under the symbol XEL. New Century Energies shareholders received 1.55 shares of Xcel Energy stock for each share of NCE they held. NSP shareholders, which got one-for-one, weren't required to exchange their existing NSP stock. Xcel Energy officials said this was the perfect time to launch the new company, considering that the utility stocks sector had gained 39 percent since March. "But our own performance has been even more phenomenal," said Chairman Howard. "NSP shares have risen 50 percent since March and NCE shares are up 56 percent. Shares in NRG, our subsidiary that completed an initial public offering in May, are up a whopping 75 percent." At month's end, Xcel Energy and the National Hockey League's Minnesota Wild announced a three-year partnership agreement to promote and develop the sport of hockey in Minnesota. Energy Masters International received a delivery order from Beale Air Force Base in California for a $6.6 million energy conservation measure. In **September** the U.S. Court of Appeals revived a 1998 suit in which the company tried to recover $1.6 billion in damages stemming from the U.S. Department of Energy's failure to accept and dispose of spent fuel from two of the company's nuclear power plants. Xcel and IBM announced an 11-year strategic relationship aimed at building Xcel's technology infrastructure into an engine that can support and foster corporate re-engineering and future business growth. The new contract, valued at $440 million, built on an existing agreement signed in 1999 between IBM and New Century Energies and increased the total value of the relationship to more than $1.2 billion. The board of directors declared Xcel Energy's first common stock dividend at a quarterly rate of 37.5 cents per share, or $1.50 per share on an annualized basis. **Sept. 30:** Excluding special charges and extraordinary items, Xcel Energy's third-quarter operating earnings rose 14 percent from a year ago. The company's 82 percent stake in NRG Energy contributed 23 cents per share in the third quarter of 2000, compared with 8 cents per share on a 100 percent ownership basis in 1999.

Zamba Corporation

continued from page 402 Decisions International, an international human resources consulting and services company, for a multiyear project to implement a customer care solution with Siebel's sales, marketing, and customer service software. In **February** Zamba announced a long-term business and delivery relationship with Best Buy Co. Inc. (NYSE: BBY), the nation's leading consumer electronics retailer. Zamba was to help Best Buy develop a leading-edge system for Best Buy's customers with performance service plans to get their electronics repaired easily and efficiently. The system was to augment Best Buy's current service offerings, managing the entire lifecycle of repairs for customers from initial contact to fulfillment. Zamba completed design and implementation of an enhanced customer care system for Hertz Corp. (NYSE: HRZ). The second-generation GEM (Gold Electronic Manifest) system uses a sophisticated combination of wireless and Web-based technologies to help Hertz make the rental process easier and more efficient for its #1 Club Gold customers renting from airport locations. In **March** Zamba was retained to work with the highly skilled Quixtar IT team to design, develop, and implement a customer care system for Quixtar.com, whose Website offers exclusive health, beauty, and home products, plus thousands of brand-name products. Zamba was selected by Symbol Technologies Inc. (NYSE: SBL) to assist with the Symbol Service Division's implementation of contract and call-handling applications. In **April** Zamba completed a new-employee training program for Asera, a provider of Internet solutions for the business-to-business demand chain. The new program was designed to prepare Asera employees for effective customer contact. In **May** Zamba deployed a pilot customer-care system for Viking Freight Inc. , the next-day, less-than-truckload freight transportation subsidiary of FedEx Corp. (NYSE: FDX). Headquartered in San Jose, Calif., Viking Freight serves customers throughout western United States. Zamba joined the Siebel Alliance Program as a Siebel Consulting Partner, to deploy solutions based on Siebel eBusiness Applications. Zamba completed a front-office customer care solution for Enbridge Services that was to help the company better understand and serve its customers. The complex system was planned and integrated in an impressively short time frame and while Enbridge Services, a new subsidiary of Enbridge Inc., was concurrently defining its business processes. In **June** Zamba announced an initiative to expand its Mobile and Wireless Technology competency, to deliver leading-edge solutions in the rapidly-growing CRM and e-commerce marketplace. In **July** Zamba formed a partnership with Primus (Nasdaq: PKSI) to deliver solutions to rapidly transform the enterprise, leveraging the Primus Internet-based eCRM software suite with Zamba's proven consulting and systems integration expertise in the eCRM space. Zamba expanded its roster of blue-chip clients with new customer wins United HealthCare, General Mills, and Hewlett-Packard Co. In **August** Zamba agreed to develop and implement an extensive, customer-centric solution for Quantum|ATL. ATL, an element of Quantum's DLT and Storage Systems Group (NYSE: DSS), is a leading provider of DLTtape libraries. As a partner to e-comeleon limited, Zamba provided an integrated buyer-centric "e-frastructure" (electronic infrastructure) of digital business strategy, experience modeling, technology services, and training to rapidly deliver the site on-time and on-budget. In **September** Zamba announced an alliance with E.piphany Inc. (Nasdaq: EPNY), the leading provider of intelligent customer interaction software, whereby Zamba was to provide consulting and systems integration services to implement E.piphany software for clients that require advanced, Web-based customer-centric solutions. Zamba also announced a MobileEnterprise partner agreement with Aether Systems Inc. (Nasdaq: AETH), a leading provider of wireless data services and systems whose industry-standard ScoutWare product suite was to help Zamba extend business from the desktop to wireless devices for companies wishing to initiate mobile and wireless business capabilities.

NOTES

NOTES

NOTES

NOTES

NOTES

NOTES

NOTES

NOTES

NOTES

PRIVATE COMPANIES

Includes 1,552 companies with at least 50 employees in the Ninth Federal Reserve District

CONTACT INFORMATION

DESCRIPTION

EXECUTIVES

REVENUE

STOCKHOLDERS

TOTAL EMPLOYEES

YEAR FOUNDED

RECENT EVENTS

SIC CODES

RANKINGS FROM CITYBUSINESS

Information is updated annually by each company with a questionnaire
Note: financial information is proprietary and may not be disclosed

(There was no charge for inclusion)

A Demonstrations Inc. 970 Raymond Ave., G50, St. Paul, MN 55114. Tel: 651/645-1358; Fax: 651/659-0324. Judi Koch, Pres. A-Plus Demonstrations employs independent contractors to do in-store promotional work, merchandising, trade shows, couponing, grand openings, and customer surveys. 950 employees. Founded in 1975. SIC 8743.

A Plus Industries Inc. 13375 Commerce Blvd., Rogers, MN 55374. Tel: 763/428-8280; Fax: 763/428-4914. B. Iwarsson, Pres. A Plus Industries is a high-tech precision sheet metal manufacturer. 90 employees (all in Minnesota). Founded in 1993. SIC 3444.

ABC Bus Companies Inc. 1506 30th St. N.W., Faribault, MN 55021. Tel: 507/334-1871; Fax: 507/334-0246; Web site: http://www.abc-bus.com. Clarence C. Cornell, Chm.; Dane Cornell, EVP; Ron Cornell, Pres. and CEO; Robert Foley, COO. Annual revenue $275 million. ABC Bus Cos. sells and leases new and used motor coaches to tour and charter services, colleges, churches, and businesses nationwide. It also sells parts (International Coach Parts Inc.); operates six body and repair shops; and does interior and exterior refurbishing. The company has regional divisions in Texas, New Jersey, Florida, Minnesota, Illinois, and California. Two subsidiaries are located in Faribault, Minn.: ABC Bus Inc. (Duane Geiger); and ABC Bus Leasing Inc. (Tim Wayland). 450 employees (115 in Minnesota; 30 part-time). Founded in 1979. SIC 5012. No. 49 CRM Private 100.

AEC Engineering Inc. 400 First Ave. N., Suite 400, Minneapolis, MN 55401. Tel: 612/332-8905; Fax: 612/334-3101. John R. Buzek, Pres.; Jenangir Rudina, VP; Patricia Altendorfer, Hum. Res. Dir.; Gordon Warner, VP; Tom Lorentz, Engrg. Mgr. AEC Engineering is an engineering firm providing complete engineering and inspection services to industrial and municipal clients. It has offices in Birmingham, Ala., and Richmond, Va. 86 employees. Founded in 1980. SIC 8711.

AJ Manufacturing Inc. 1217 Oak St., Bloomer, WI 54724. Tel: 800/328-9448; Fax: 715/568-3099; Web site: http://www.ajdoor.com. Steve Larson, Pres.; Sheldon Gough, VP-Mktg.; Dale Hanson, VP and Treas. Annual revenue $12 million. AJ Manufacturing makes metal entry doors and windows for commercial applications in new and remodel construction. AJ also manufactures a line of access doors for the HVAC Industry. 120 employees (3 in Minnesota). Founded in 1991. Patents applied for access door construction. SIC 3442.

AME Group P.O. Box 307, Elk River, MN 55330. Tel: 763/441-2800; Fax: 763/441-2827. Peter W. Fischer, Pres.; Steve Linegar, Gen. Mgr. AME Group makes and distributes ready-mix concrete. Owned by AVR Inc., Apple Valley, Minn. 60 employees. Founded in 1967. SIC 3273.

APi Group Inc. 2366 Rose Place, Roseville, MN 55113. Tel: 651/636-4320; Fax: 651/636-0312. Lee R. Anderson, Chm. and CEO; Loren Rachey, CFO; Jeff Jessen, Pres. and COO. Annual revenue $479 million. APi and its subsidiaries are engaged in industrial, mechanical, electrical, fire-protection, insulation, and roofing construction, as well as building-materials distribution, equipment sales and rental, and steel fabrication. The 16 members of the APi Group operate 79 offices internationally. Minnesota members include The Jamar Co., Viking Automatic Sprinkler Co., and LeJeune Steel Co. (all with separate entries in this section); as well as APi Supply Inc., Lakehead Electric Co., Twin City Garage Door Co., and ASDCO. 4,500 employees (850 in Minnesota). Founded in 1926. SIC 1711, 1731, 1799, 3444, 5039. No. 21 CRM Private 100.

ASAP Inc. 3000 France Ave. S., St. Louis Park, MN 55416. Tel: 952/926-4735. Ted Politis, Pres. ASAP performs comprehensive graphics reproduction services. 150 employees. Founded in 1984. SIC 7336.

AVR Inc. 14698 Galaxie Ave., Apple Valley, MN 55124. Tel: 952/432-7132; Fax: 952/432-7530. Peter W. Fischer, VP; Stephen Linegar, VP; Liza F. Robson, VP. AVR Inc. (formerly Apple Valley Red-E-Mix) makes concrete ready-mix. AVR has one division, Minnesota State Curb & Gutter; and owns AME Group, Elk River, Minn. 400 employees (all in Minnesota). Founded in 1966. SIC 3273.

Aaladin Industries Inc. R.R. 1, Box 2B, Elk Point, SD 57025. Tel: 605/356-3325; Fax: 605/356-2330. Pat Wingen, Chm., Pres., and CEO; Bruce Kelly, Gen. Mgr.-Rugged Gear; Lee Schaefer, Gen. Mgr.-Steel Engrg.; Randy Wheelock, Sls. Mgr. Annual revenue $12 million. Aaladin Industries manufactures hot and cold high-pressure washers, steam cleaners, parts washers, waste oil furnaces, hose reels, concrete cleaners, and gun racks. 90 employees (1 part-time). Founded in 1981. SIC 3569.

Abdallah Candies Inc. 3501 W. County Rd. 42, Burnsville, MN 55306. Tel: 952/890-4770. Stephen R. Hegedus, Pres.; Stephen A. Hegedus, VP. Abdallah Candies is a manufacturer and wholesaler of caramel, as well as boxed and bulk chocolates. 80 employees. Founded in 1917. SIC 2064, 2066.

AbelConn 9210 Science Center Dr., New Hope, MN 55428. Tel: 763/533-3533; Fax: 763/536-0349; Web site: http://www.abelconn.com. Cliff Olson, CEO; Ronald Natzel, VP-Sls.; Wallace Olson, Pres. AbelConn manufactures connector products, and assembles printed circuit boards. Formerly known as Fabri-Tek Inc. and, more recently, as CTS/Interconnect. 110 employees (all in Minnesota). Founded in 1959. SIC 3672, 3678.

Abhe & Svoboda Inc. 17066 Revere Way, P.O. Box 251, Prior Lake, MN 55372. Tel: 952/447-6025; Fax: 952/447-1000. Gail Svoboda, Chm., Pres., CEO, and Treas.; Don Holle, VP; Roxane Svoboda, Sec. Abhe & Svoboda is a construction contractor, primarily for infrastructure repair work on dams, bridges, and tanks. 170 employees (24 in Minnesota). Founded in 1969. SIC 1521, 1761.

Able Care Home Services 11801 Xeon Blvd. N.W., Coon Rapids, MN 55448. Tel: 763/754-6706; Fax: 763/755-3631. Patricia Crocker, Dir.-Clinical Op. Able Care Home Services, a sister company to Mary T Inc., provides Medicare-certified home health care. 164 employees. SIC 8082.

ABRA Auto Body and Glass Inc. 6601 Shingle Creek Pkwy., Suite 200, Brooklyn Center, MN 55430. Tel: 763/561-7220; Fax: 763/561-7433; Web site: http://www.abraauto.com. Roland Benjamin, Pres. and CEO; Duane Rouse, SVP and CFO; Tim Adelmann, EVP and COO; Jerry Harn, VP-Industry Rel.; Jay W. Trumbower, VP-Corp. Devel./Acquisitions. Annual revenue $120 million. ABRA Auto Body and Glass is one of the country's fastest-growing collision repair companies, with 50 company-owned stores and 18 franchises in 10 states (including 28 Minnesota locations). The facilities provide full-service collision repair, paintless dent removal, and auto glass replacement and repair. ABRA's plans for accelerated national growth over the next several years include acquiring existing facilities and building new locations. Principal stockholders: Benjamin, Adelmann, GE Capital Services. 900 employees (350 in Minnesota). Founded in 1984. In December 1999 ABRA received the 1999 Collision Business of the Year (Category 3-Chain Operations) award. In January 2000 ABRA's Kenosha, Wis., repair center was selected to paint the Super Bowl XXXIV "WilsonFootball on Wheels" car. In July Mark Wahlin, director of franchising, was elected to serve a one-year term as the collision division director for the Alliance of Automotive Service Providers-Minnesota. In August ABRA was named one of the 10 Great Places to Work in Minnesota by Corporate Report magazine. ABRA acquired a repair center in West Allis (Milwaukee), Wis., that was previously owned by Cara Collision & Glass. ABRA's Georgia Repair facilities received the Consumer Choice Award for 2000. In October CEO Roland Benjamin was awarded the Torch of Truth Award by the Better Business Bureau in recognition of his leadership and commitment to advancing the principle of truth in advertising. SIC 7532, 7536. No. 6 CityBusiness Fastest-growing Private Companies.

Accelerated Payments Inc. 421 W. Travelers Trail, Burnsville, MN 55337. Tel: 952/937-0787; Fax: 952/937-0123; Web site: http://www.acceleratedpayments.com. Gary Halleen, Pres. and CEO; Jonathan E. Blood, VP-Sls. Accelerated Payments Inc. (API) is an application solutions provider (ASP) providing turnkey solutions for working 360-degree e-service to support critical back office operations for companies. This includes general ledger, accounts payable/receivable and customer care applications, managing the capture and distribution of management reports, statements, invoices, paper, fax, e-mail mesages, e-billing, and all other computer-generated information. API offers a unique approach to the marketplace with pay-by-the-transaction billing to these services without expensive software, hardware, or other capital investments. API's state-of-the-art service centers are fully equipped with the latest document and data archival technologies for the capturing, scanning, indexing, storing, rapid access, and distribution of data worldwide. 50 employees. SIC 7372.

Access Cash International 20 Yorkton Ct., St. Paul, MN 55117. Tel: 651/490-0413; Fax: 651/490-0545; Web site: http://www.accesscash.com. Frank Capan, CEO; Jon Thomas, EVP and COO; Charles Hayssen, EVP and CFO; Bryan Gray, SVP and Sls. Mgr. Annual revenue $54.4 million. Access Cash International provides ATMs and related services to retailers and financial institutions in the United States and Canada. 127 employees (72 in Minnesota; 2 part-time). Founded in 1994. SIC 6099. No. 44 CityBusiness Fastest-growing Private Companies.

Achieve Healthcare Information Systems 7690 Golden Triangle Dr., Eden Prairie, MN 55344. Tel: 952/995-9800; Fax: 952/995-9735. Lawrence Garatoni, Chm. and CEO; Richard Giddings, Pres.; Chris Hawver, Chief Mktg. Officer; Chris McPartland, CFO. Achieve Healthcare Information Systems provides financial and clinical software, services, and consulting to the post-acute care industries, including nursing homes, assisted living, home health, adult day care, and retirement communities. 180 employees (160 in Minnesota). Founded in 1973. SIC 7372.

The Ackerberg Group 3100 W. Lake St., Suite 100, Minneapolis, MN 55416. Tel: 612/824-2100; Fax: 612/924-6499. Norman J. Ackerberg, Chm.; Stuart I. Ackerberg, Pres.; Larry H. Gertgen, SVP; Mary L. Armstrong, VP. The Ackerberg Group is a full-service real estate company specializing in property management, leasing, brokerage, asset management, development, construction, consultation, and related services for commercial and multifamily properties. 120 employees (35 in Minnesota; 50 part-time). Founded in 1964. SIC 6531.

Acrometal P.O. Box 408, Brainerd, MN 56401. Tel: 218/829-4719; Fax: 218/828-6620. William F. Bieber, Chm.; Paul M. Lindbloom, Pres. and CEO; James Beckmann, Dir.-Purch.; James T. Voiss, VP-Fin. Acrometal's products include tape reels and wire packaging equipment and rifle manufacture/assembly. Owned by Acrometal Management Corp., Plymouth, Minn. 75 employees (all in Minnesota). Founded in 1946. SIC 3499.

Acrotech Midwest P.O. Box 220, Crosby, MN 56441. Tel: 218/546-5115; Fax: 218/546-1200. Jorg Freyer, Pres.; Don Miller, Sls. Mgr. Acrotech Midwest makes custom blow-molded plastic products for consumers nationwide. 140 employees (all in Minnesota). Founded in 1965. SIC 3089.

Action Communication 4875 White Bear Pkwy., White Bear Lake, MN 55110. Tel: 651/653-9799; Fax: 651/541-6309. Deanna Karstens, Pres. Action Communication manufactures copier and designer paper. 65 employees. SIC 2678.

Adaytum Software Inc. 2051 Killebrew Dr., Suite 400, Bloomington, MN 55425. Tel: 952/858-8585; Web site: http://www.adaytum.com. John David Guy (Guy) Haddleton, CEO; Tim Bradley, EVP-Sls. Op.; Susan Strother, EVP-Mktg.; Daniel Mayleben, CFO. Annual revenue $23 million. Adaytum Software provides integrated business planning applications for planning, budgeting, forecasting, modeling, reporting, and performance analysis. 350 employees (130 in Minnesota). Founded in 1990. In 1999 the company launched Adaytum e.Planning, its new flagship Web-based solution product that delivers business planning power throughout the enterprise. In December the company secured a $6.1 million second-round venture capital financing investment led by St. Paul Venture Capital with additional participation from Hambrecht & Quist. In January 2000 the company established wholly owned subsidiaries in Sydney, Australia, and in Toronto—giving it stronger sales and support operations in those regions. Adaytum and Deloitte & Touche LLP, one of the nation's leading professional services firms, announced an alliance to extend Web-based business planning to e-businesses. In February 2000 the company released "Adaytum e.Planning Reporter," a fourth module for the company's flagship business-planning system. The product transforms the standard, zero-maintenance Web browser into a powerful management reporting and analysis client that enables users to slice-and-dice business planning information, view plans from multiple perspectives and dimensions, generate business statistics, analyze results over time, and drill down for further details and analysis. Aberdeen Group released a new profile white paper—"e.Planning: Fixing the Broken Planning Process"—that voiced strong support for Adaytum's new Web-based solution for collaborative business planning (calling it "a revolution in financial software"). In May Adaytum secured a global Adaytum e.Planning licensing agreement with ABN AMRO Bank N.V., the world's sixth-largest bank. The US $1 million contract was Adaytum's largest-ever sale to date. Adaytum and Andersen Consulting, a leading global management and technology consultancy, formed an alliance to market and co-develop business planning solutions to organizations throughout the world. In August the company filed to raise between $45 million and $63.25 million in an initial public offering of stock (5 million shares plus a 750,000-share overallotment to be priced between $9 and $11). In September Adaytum secured a $24 million cash-and-services investment from a group of investors led by AC Ventures, the venture capital unit of Andersen Consulting, with additional participation from St. Paul Venture Capital, 3i, and Chase H&Q. Proceeds from the financing were to be used by the company to continue its growth in worldwide sales, marketing, and product development. In October Adaytum secured a $10 million Series E preferred stock investment by American Express Financial Corp. The proceeds were earmarked for general corporate purposes, including expansion of its sales force, consulting practices, and market branding initiatives. SIC 7372. No. 15 Minnesota Technology Fast 50.

Addco Inc. 240 Arlington Ave. E., St. Paul, MN 55117. Tel: 651/488-8600; Fax: 651/558-3600. Tim Nicholson, Pres.; John Nicholson, EVP-Engrg.; Jeffrey Nicholson, EVP-Sls./Mktg.; Lisa Risser Dumke, VP-Bus. Devel. Addco manufactures electronic and mechanical control devices, traffic control products including portable changeable message signs, the cone wheel, the portable traffic signal, and rubber latches. 85 employees. Founded in 1956. In March 2000 the company announced a large contract with URS Greiner Woodward Clyde for installation of an intelligent transportation system in Albuquerque, N.M. The $1.4 million contract called for a comprehensive system designed to optimize traffic flow and maximize safety during major road reconstruction at the intersection of highways I-40 and I-25, known as the "Big I" project. SIC 3714, 3993.

Adolfson & Peterson Construction 6701 W. 23rd St., P.O. Box 9377 (55440), St. Louis Park, MN 55426. Tel: 763/544-1561; Fax: 763/525-2333; Web site: http://www.a-p.com. David G. Adolfson, Chm.; Michael Peterson, Pres.; Scott Weicht, EVP; Brook Adolfson, SVP; Harlan Hallquist, VP; David Molda, VP; Michael Michelsen, VP and Treas.; John Palmquist, VP; Clyde Terwey, VP. Annual revenue $280 million. Adolfson & Peterson provides general contracting, construction management, and design/build services for commercial, industrial, institutional, and clean room facilities. 490 employees. Founded in 1946. SIC 1542. No. 59 CRM Private 100.

Advance Shoring & Equipment Company 1400 Jackson St., St. Paul, MN 55117. Tel: 651/489-8881; Fax: 651/489-9416. O.A. Haug, Owner; Terry Haug, Pres.; Karen Haug, VP. Advance Shoring & Equipment is a construction equipment distributor. The company leases and sells cranes, hoists, shoring systems, and scaffolding to general contractors. 50 employees (all in Minnesota). Founded in 1960. SIC 7353.

Advanced Flex Inc. 15115 Minnetonka Industrial Rd., Minnetonka, MN 55345. Tel: 952/930-4800; Fax: 952/935-4236. Larry G. Bergman, Pres. and CEO; Craig Bergman, VP and Gen. Mgr.; Tab Erickson, Nat'l Sls. Mgr.; Herb Girtz, VP-Quality/Tech. Advanced Flex is a service-oriented supplier and manufacturer of printed circuit boards, predominantly multilayer boards. The company also offers quick-turn deliveries of multilayer rigid circuit boards, and builds some flexible and rigid-flex circuits. 162 employees (all in Minnesota). Founded in 1972. SIC 3672.

Advanced Web Solutions 1011 First St. S., Suite 203, Hopkins, MN 55343. Tel: 952/939-2500; Web site: http://www.advancedwebsolutions.com. Satya P. Garg, Chm., Pres., CEO, and CFO; Rakesh Verma, CTO; Scott A. Schwefel, VP-Mktg. Advanced Web Solutions is one of the largest providers of Web site design and hosting services to small businesses in the United States. The company offers effective, affordable Internet solutions for millions of small businesses that might otherwise be intimidated by the cost, time, or technology involved in establishing a Web presence. Advanced Web's current business solution consists of Web site design and hosting, unlimited Internet access, a virtual domain name, and up to five e-mail accounts—all for $24.95 per month. The company designs and hosts Web sites for a diverse group of more than 50,000 clients. Management believes that Advanced Web's focused marketing efforts, low-cost design and development capabilities, and affordable Internet solutions represent significant competitive advantages. In July 1999 the company's plans for an initial public offering that would have raised $34.5 million were scrapped amid charges of fraud. FTC regulators alleged that the company, then known as WebValley, had systematically charged customers more than $9 million since 1997 for services that they hadn't ordered. 80 employees (15 in Minnesota; 3 part-time). Founded in 1996. SIC 7379.

Advantage Sales & Marketing 7825 Telegraph Rd., Bloomington, MN 55438. Tel: 952/829-0833; Fax: 952/829-0942. Jay Wallace, CEO. Advantage Sales & Marketing is a distributor of a variety of food brands to wholesale and retail outlets. Other location: Fargo, N.D. Formerly known as L.S. Sorem & Associates Inc. 100 employees (84 in Minnesota; 4 part-time). Founded in 1948. SIC 5141.

Advantek Inc. 5801 Clearwater Dr., Minnetonka, MN 55343. Tel: 952/938-6800; Fax: 952/938-1800. Timothy L. Cowen, Pres.; Howard Marschel, VP and CFO; Dean B. Chenoweth, VP-Engrg. Advantek manufactures surface-mount taping equipment and materials, embossed carrier tape, cover tape, and reels. 700 employees. Founded in 1978. SIC 2672.

Aeration Industries International Inc. 4100 Peavey Rd., P.O. Box 59144 (55459), Chaska, MN 55318. Tel: 952/448-6789; Fax: 952/448-7293. Daniel Durda, Pres. and CEO; Paul Karpinko, VP-Sls.; William Randall, VP-Admin. Aeration Industries builds and distributes patented aspirator aerators used in wastewater treatment and aquaculture—as well as other wastewater pollution control equipment, including a mechanical surface aerator licensed exclusively from a European company; package plant systems; and a microfloat unit for pretreatment of fats, oils, and grease. Aeration for golf course ponds, golf course lakes, and recreational water. 75 employees (45 in Minnesota). Founded in 1974. SIC 3589.

Affco LLC 1015 E. Sixth St., Anaconda, MT 59711. Tel: 406/563-8494; Fax: 406/563-3368. Jim Liebetrau, Pres. and Gen. Mgr.; Robert Mackey, VP and Op. Mgr.; Ron Tuohimaa, Mgr.-Acctg./Admin. Affco's current business activities include a foundry, fabrication shop, machine shop, mining construction and equipment installation crews, and an industrial supply store. Owned by three partners, all of Anaconda, its office, manufacturing plant, foundry, forge, and store are all located at the former site of the Anaconda Mining and Smelting Co. 100 employees. Founded in 1980. SIC 1796, 3325, 3441, 3462, 5085.

The Affiliated Group 316 First Ave. S.W., Rochester, MN 55902. Tel: 800/223-0290; Fax: 507/280-7068; Web site: http://www.theaffiliatedgroup.com. Mark Neeb, Pres. and CEO; Paul Skovbroten, VP-Op. The Affiliated Group provides services that creatively maximize client revenue and profits through superior customer communications. 95 employees. SIC 8742.

Agiliti Inc. 4300 MarketPointe Dr., Suite 100, Bloomington, MN 55435. Tel: 952/918-2000; Fax: 952/918-2100; Web site: http://www.agiliti.com. Tom Kieffer, Chm. and CEO; Steve Giese, COO; Mark Payne, CFO. Annual revenue $2.7 million. Agiliti is the leading provider of best-of-class, rentable Web-based applications and services. The company is creating the market by building an extensive portfolio of these services and delivering them in collaboration with a nationwide channel of independent consulting and integration partners. Agiliti's proprietary ASP management technology enables these services to be hosted anywhere, and combines secure, reliable delivery with unified sign-on, administration, billing, and reporting. Agiliti serves more than 600 customers. 150 employees (140 in Minnesota). Founded in 1999. Sm@rt Reseller Magazine named the company in its "Sm@rt 100" list in 2000, recognizing it as "one of the most successful and dynamic businesses" in the industry. In October the company announced a strategic business alliance with Lightning Rod Software Inc. (Nasdaq: LROD), a leading provider of real-time customer interaction and loyalty solutions for e-businesses, to add the award-winning Lightning Rod Interaction Manager to its portfolio of rentable, Web-based applications. The company also began offering businesses a full portfolio of rentable e-commerce services through agreements with applications developers and service providers Intershop Communications, Vignette Corp., and InfoSpace. SIC 7371.

AgriBank FCB 375 Jackson St., P.O. Box 64949 (55164), St. Paul, MN 55164. Tel: 651/282-8800; Fax: 651/282-8353; Web site: http://www.farmcredit.com. Meredith Yarick, Chm.; William J. Collins, CEO. Annual revenue $1.49 billion. AgriBank is an agricultural credit institution providing wholesale credit and support services. The $21.4 billion-asset regional bank serves 21 Farm Credit Services organizations in the 11 states of the Seventh Farm Credit District: Arkansas, Illinois, Michigan, Minnesota,

Missouri, North Dakota, Wisconsin, Indiana, Kentucky, Ohio, and Tennessee. Merger of former Farm Credit Banks of: St. Paul (founded in 1917); St. Louis (added in May 1992); and Louisville, Ky. (added in January 1994). 3,108 employees. Founded in 1917. SIC 6111. No. 4 CRM Cooperatives/Mutuals 20.

Agsco Inc. 1160 12th St. N.E., P.O. Box 13458, Grand Forks, ND 58201. Tel: 701/775-5325; Fax: 701/775-9587. Randy Brown, Pres. and CEO; Dave Glessner, CFO and Sec. Agsco formulates and distributes agricultural chemicals and manufactures assemblies for the handling of liquid chemicals and other liquids in closed systems. Agsco's Precision Farming Division utilizes global positioning system and variable-rate fertilizer application to custom-apply fertilizer for farmers. 130 employees (15 in Minnesota; 30 part-time). Founded in 1935. SIC 2879, 5169, 5191.

Air Gas 1007 Monitor St., La Crosse, WI 54601. Tel: 608/784-6228; Fax: 608/784-8277. R.B. Graw, CEO; Lee Fosser, Pres. Air Gas is a distributor of industrial machinery and equipment, welding supplies, gasses, industrial tools, abrasives, high-speed cutting tools, and carbides. The company also operates Arrow Safety, a division engaged in direct mail of safety supplies. 65 employees (14 in Minnesota). Founded in 1946. SIC 5084, 5085.

Alamco Wood Products Inc. 1410 Ninth St. W., Albert Lea, MN 56007. Tel: 507/373-1401; Fax: 507/373-8116. C.I. Vermedahl, CEO; J.L. Forman, VP-Sls. Annual revenue $11 million. Alamco Wood Products makes structural laminated wood beams and arches, wood bridges, sound barriers, panels, and electric utility poles. 85 employees (all in Minnesota). Founded in 1982. SIC 2439.

Albers Sheetmetal & Ventilating Inc. 200 W. Plato Blvd., St. Paul, MN 55107. Tel: 651/224-5428; Fax: 651/224-1742. George C. Albers, Pres. Albers Sheetmetal & Ventilating is engaged in sheet-metal fabrication, heating, contracting, plumbing, and mechanical services. 50 employees. Founded in 1966. SIC 3444.

Albinson Reprographics LLC 1401 Glenwood Ave., Minneapolis, MN 55405. Tel: 612/374-1120; Fax: 612/374-1129; Web site: http://www.albinson.com. Terrill K. Albinson, Pres.; Tracy Albinson, EVP, Gen. Mgr. With four metro locations and a St. Cloud facility, Albinson Reprographics provides reprographic services, products, supplies, and media for the Upper Midwest. Reprographic services include: digital color and black/white output in large and small format, high-speed copying, electronic storage, archiving, scanning, large format plotting, laminating, and mounting. Additional offerings are facility management, engineering, and wide-format copiers and printers, scanners, software, and equipment repair. 90 employees (all in Minnesota). Founded in 1946. SIC 2752, 2759, 3861, 7334.

Alexandria Extrusion Company 401 County Rd. 22 N.W., Alexandria, MN 56308. Tel: 320/763-6537; Fax: 320/762-0312; Web site: http://www.alex-extrusion.com. Thomas Schabel, Pres.; Brian Bloedorn, VP-Sls./Mktg.; Alan Sholts, VP-Mfg.; Timothy D. Froemming, Treas. Annual revenue $43 million. Alexandria Extrusion manufactures aluminum extrusion products. In 1997 the company was acquired in a management buyout. 300 employees. Founded in 1966. SIC 3499.

Alexandria Peterson Company 2612 S. Broadway St., Alexandria, MN 56308. Tel: 320/762-1158; Fax: 320/762-0486. M.M. Peterson, Owner; Neil Peterson, Gen. Mgr. Alexandria Peterson Co. operates two retail grocery stores: Pete's County Market, Alexandria; and Donny's Warehouse Foods, Long Prairie, Minn. 170 employees. Founded in 1944. SIC 5411.

Alkota Cleaning Systems Inc. P.O. Box 288, Alcester, SD 57001. Tel: 605/934-2222; Fax: 605/934-1808. Joe Bjorkman, Pres.; Gene Bowling, VP-Mktg.; Gary L. Scott, VP, Sec., and Treas.. Alkota Cleaning Systems manufactures steam cleaners, high-pressure washers, and space heaters. 68 employees. Founded in 1983. SIC 3549.

All American Manufacturing 205 East St., Boyceville, WI 54725. Tel: 715/643-2222; Fax: 715/643-2266; Web site: http://www.better-line.com. Mark Kinney, CEO. All American is a manufacturer of advertising specialties and screen-printing on textiles, a distributor of golf and beach towels, and an importer of headwear. 160 employees. Founded in 1982. SIC 2393, 2396, 2399.

Allen Interactions Inc. 8000 W. 78th St., Suite 450, Edina, MN 55439. Tel: 952/947-4055. Michael Allen, CEO. Annual revenue $5 million. Allen Interactions assists organizations in developing engaging interactive multimedia learning applications by providing training, custom development services, and general expertise. 60 employees. Founded in 1993. SIC 8299. No. 46 CityBusiness Fastest-growing Private Companies.

Alliance Health Services Inc. 2204 E. 117th St., Burnsville, MN 55337. Tel: 952/882-1030; Fax: 952/882-1477; Web site: http://www.alliancehealthcare.com. Alana Fiala, Admin.; Judy Ophus, R.N., Dir.-Nursing; Gayle C. Ericksen, Dir.-Network Devel. Alliance Health Services is a home health agency, supported-living provider, medical supplier, and personal-care provider organization. 2,000 employees (all in Minnesota). Founded in 1989. SIC 8082.

Allied Interstate Inc. 435 Ford Rd., St. Louis Park, MN 55426. Tel: 952/546-6600; Fax: 952/595-2127. Douglas Lewis, Pres.; Dennis Lewis, VP; Dawn Mueller-Lehtinen, VP. Allied Interstate is a collection agency. 370 employees (50 part-time). Founded in 1954. SIC 7322.

Allied Professionals 3209 W. 76th St., Suite 201, Edina, MN 55435. Tel: 952/832-5101; Fax: 952/832-0656. Patricia Mulligan, Pres.; Sharon Stadnik, Admin.; Greg Mulligan, Legal Counsel; Diane Tracy, Dir.-Mktg. Allied Professionals is a medical and dental temporary health care staffing service. 300 employees. Founded in 1989. SIC 7363.

Allstate Peterbilt Utility 558 E. Villaume Ave., South St. Paul, MN 55075. Tel: 651/455-6500; Fax: 651/450-8161. Glenn D. Evans, Pres.; Jeff Pengra, Gen. Mgr.; Glenn Meuwissen, Sls. Mgr.; John Meuwissen, Parts Mgr.; Don Peterson, Svc. Mgr. Allstate Peterbilt Utility is a truck and trailer dealership. 107 employees. Founded in 1971. SIC 5012.

Alltool Manufacturing Company Inc. 19188 Industrial Blvd., Elk River, MN 55330. Tel: 763/441-6150; Fax: 763/441-6563. Brian J. Moran, Dir.; Robert E. Silkett, Dir.; Kenneth L. Isaacson, Dir.; Randall P. Krenz, Pres. and CEO. Annual revenue $12.5 million. Alltool Manufacturing's operations include metal stamping and fabrication, tube bending, and tool and die fabrication. 164 employees (all in Minnesota). Founded in 1974. SIC 3469, 3542, 3569, 7692.

Allweather Roof Inc. 3023 Snelling Ave., Minneapolis, MN 55406. Tel: 612/721-2545; Fax: 612/721-4236; Web site: http://www.allweatherroof.com. George Heriot, Pres.; Loren Butterfield, VP; Ken Sorensen, Sec. Annual revenue $5.6 million. Allweather Roof (AWR) is a commercial roofing contractor. 57 employees (46 in Minnesota). Founded in 1925. SIC 1761.

Almco Inc. 507 Front St., Albert Lea, MN 56007. Tel: 507/377-2102; Fax: 507/377-0451; Web site: http://www.almcoinc.com. Keith A. Kligge, Pres. and Dir.-Sls.; Kent R. Olsen, Chm. and Dir.-Engrg. Almco manufactures metalworking equipment for metal finishing and parts cleaning, and related repair parts and supplies. 66 employees (57 in Minnesota). Founded in 1945. SIC 3549.

Rocco Altobelli Inc. 14301 Burnsville Pkwy. W., Burnsville, MN 55337. Tel: 952/707-1900; Fax: 952/707-9907. Dianne Altobelli, Pres.; Rocco Altobelli, CEO. Rocco Altobelli Inc. operates beauty shops. The company's subsidiary, Altobelli Hair Products International, also operates out of company headquarters. 400 employees. Founded in 1972. SIC 7231.

Altron Inc. 6700 Industry Ave. N.W., Anoka, MN 55303. Tel: 763/427-7735; Fax: 763/427-3980. Alan C. Phillips, Pres., Sls./Mktg. Annual revenue $36 million. Altron is engaged in printed circuit board assembly, surface-mounted assembly, light mechanical assembly, harness and cable assembly, turnkey electronic subcontract service, and in-circuit and functional testing. 200 employees. Founded in 1974. SIC 3672, 3679.

Alumacraft Boat Company 315 W. Saint Julien, St. Peter, MN 56082. Tel: 507/931-1050; Fax: 507/931-9056. David Benbow, Pres.; Ken Zimmerman, EVP. Alumacraft manufactures aluminum boats and canoes. 200 employees. Founded in 1946. SIC 3732.

Ambassador Press 1400 Washington Ave. N., Minneapolis, MN 55411. Tel: 612/521-0123; Fax: 612/521-4587; Web site: http://www.amb-press.com. Barry Engle, Pres. and CEO; Ed Engle, EVP. Ambassador Press prints annual reports, brochures, catalogs, and other commercial material. 70 employees. Founded in 1960. SIC 2752.

Amcon Construction Company LLC 200 W. Highway 13, Burnsville, MN 55337. Tel: 952/890-1217; Fax: 952/890-0064. Todd Christopherson, Pres.; Dennis Cornelius, VP; Gordon Schmitz, VP, Treas., and Sec.; James Winkels, VP. Amcon Construction is a general contracting company specializing in the construction of industrial, commercial, and office buildings; shopping centers; warehouses; churches, and schools. 50 employees (all in Minnesota; 6 part-time). Founded in 1971. In June 2000 the company was awarded the Minnesota Construction Management Association Project of the Year 2000 for the Living Word Christian Center, Phase V—Maranatha Academy, Brooklyn Park. SIC 1541, 1542.

Amerect Inc. 1110 Seventh Ave., Newport, MN 55055. Tel: 651/459-9909; Fax: 651/459-5258. Peter Taubenberger, Pres. Amerect erects structural, reinforcing, and miscellaneous steel, and engages in plant maintenance, crane service, and machinery moving and installation. 126 employees (1 part-time). Founded in 1982. SIC 1791.

American Agco 545 Hardman Ave., South St. Paul, MN 55075. Tel: 651/451-1349; Fax: 651/451-0708. Gary Duclos, Pres.; Tony Duclos, VP; Jim Sowers, Dir.-Nutrition; Tim Ehde, Dir.-Fin.; Jon Duclos, Sls. Mgr.; Frank Ahern, Op. Mgr. American Agco manufactures and distributes products for livestock. Its Drover Division manufactures and distributes a variety of products for other domestic animals. 120 employees (119 in Minnesota). Founded in 1936. SIC 5191.

American Amusement Arcades 850 Decatur Ave. N., Golden Valley, MN 55427. Tel: 763/645-6810. Amos Heilicher, Board Mem.; Daniel Heilicher, Board Mem.; Norman Pink, Board Mem.; David Lieberman, Board Mem.; Stephen E. Lieberman, Board Mem.; Harold Okinow, Board Mem. American Amusement Arcades, formerly known as Advance Carter and Twin City Novelty Co., is in the amusement and coin-operated vending business. It owns and operates six Circus Pizza restaurants and several Piccadilly Circus amusement arcades. It also handles coin-operated amusement, cigarette, and music machines in Minnesota, Wisconsin, North Dakota, South Dakota, and parts of Michigan. 180 employees. Founded in 1933. SIC 5812, 5962.

American Business Forms Inc. 31 E. Minnesota Ave., P.O. Box 218, Glenwood, MN 56334. Tel: 320/634-5471; Fax: 320/634-5265; Web site: http://www.americanbus.com. Larry Zavadil, Pres. and CEO; Craig McLain, VP; Dion Harste, VP; Mike Stai, VP-Op.; Blake Wold, VP; Sandra Triplett, Hum. Res. Annual revenue $171 million. American Business Forms distributes business forms in 35 states. 255 employees (175 in Minnesota; 37 part-time). Founded in 1981. SIC 5112. No. 71 CRM Private 100.

American Converters Inc. 5360 Main St. N.E., Fridley, MN 55421. Tel: 763/574-1044; Fax: 763/574-1015. Curt Pohl, CEO; Steve Pasell, Pres.; Scott Nelson, VP-Sls.; Vince Brytowski, VP-Mfg.; Jeff Tobias, Pres.-Web Label. American Converters is a fabricator of flexible foams. Its Value Added Services Division is an assembly and distribution operation. The company's subsidiary, Web Label Ltd., manufactures pressure-sensitive labels. 150 employees. Founded in 1976. SIC 2759, 3086.

American Crystal Sugar Company 101 N. Third St., Moorhead, MN 56560. Tel: 218/236-4400; Fax: 218/236-4422. Wayne Langen, Chm.; James J. Horvath, Pres. and CEO; Jim Dudley, VP-Ag.; Dan Mott, Sec. and Gen. Counsel; Joe Talley, VP-Fin.; David Berg, VP-Admin.; Dave Walden, VP-Op.; Sam Wai, Corp. Cont. Annual revenue $731 million. American Crystal Sugar, a cooperative, processes and markets beet sugar under the Crystal Sugar brand name. Affiliated with United Sugars Corp., Minneapolis (Tom McKenna, Pres.). Also affiliated with Midwest Agri-Commodities, Corte Madera, Calif., which markets dried pulp and molasses. 1,800 employees. Founded in 1889. In July 2000 four sugar representatives, including American Crystal CEO Horvath, testified before the Senate Agriculture Committee that prices American sugar farmers were receiving for their crop had plunged 34 percent since the start of the 1996 Farm Bill; and that, unless flaws in existing trade agreements are fixed and loopholes that permit companies to circumvent import quotas are closed, the crisis in the domestic sugar industry would only get worse. SIC 2063. No. 7 CRM Cooperatives/Mutuals 20.

American Engineering Testing Inc. 550 Cleveland Ave. N., St. Paul, MN 55114. Tel: 651/659-9001; Fax: 651/659-1379; Web site: http://www.amengtest.com. Terry E. Swor, Pres.; Richard D. Stehly, SVP; Robert Kaiser, VP; Daniel J. Larson, VP; Michael R. Schmidt, VP; Jeffrey K. Voyen, VP; Robert W. Krogsgaard, Cont. Annual revenue $15 million. American Engineering Testing Inc. is an independent laboratory specializing in geotechnical, environmental, materials testing and engineering services, property transfer site assessments, and forensics. The company has branch offices in Mankato, Marshall, Duluth, and Rochester, Minn.; Wausau, Wis.; Rapid City and Pierre, S.D. It also has two affiliated companies in St. Paul: American Petrographic Services Inc. (Scott Wolter, Pres.) and American Consulting Services Inc. (Richard Stehly, Pres.). 200 employees (165 in Minnesota; 6 part-time). Founded in 1971. SIC 8711, 8734.

American Federal Bank 215 N. Fifth St., Fargo, ND 58108. Tel: 701/235-4248; Fax: 701/461-5972. Steven P. Worwa, Pres. and CEO; Robert W. Watkins, SVP-Accounting and CFO; Marlene S. Daniels, VP-Hum. Res./Mktg.; Ross L. Olson, COO and EVP. American Federal Bank is an independent community savings bank with eight retail offices and assets of $206.8 million. American Federal Investments Inc. (East Grand Forks, N.D.; Ryland Syverson, Managing Director) is a finance subsidiary that offers investment products, including insurance and annuity products. American Federal Bank's parent company is AFS Financial Corp., East Grand Forks. 145 employees. Founded in 1891. SIC 6035.

American Guidance Service Inc. 4201 Woodland Rd., Circle Pines, MN 55014. Tel: 763/786-4343; Fax: 763/783-5505; Web site: http://www.agsnet.com. Linda Hein, EVP-Sls./Mktg.; Gerald G. (Jerry) Adams, EVP/ CFO; Larry Rutkowski, Pres. and CEO. Annual revenue $55 million. American Guidance Service (AGS) develops and publishes (in the United States and other major English-speaking countries) educational tests, textbooks, and other instructional programs for special education, students-at-risk, early childhood education, guidance, parent education, test prep, and teacher training. 186 employees (155 in Minnesota; 8 part-time). Founded in 1957. SIC 2731, 2741.

The American Hardware Insurance Group 5995 Opus Pkwy., P.O. Box 435 (55440), Minnetonka, MN 55343. Tel: 952/935-1400; Fax: 952/939-4566. David W. Lemon, EVP. The American Hardware Insurance Group is a direct-writing property and casualty insurance company operating in 35 states. The business began by selling insurance to hardware stores, then extended service to other related businesses. In May 1993 it affiliated with Motorists Mutual, Columbus, Ohio. 288 employees. Founded in 1899. SIC 6331.

American Iron 2800 Pacific St. N., Minneapolis, MN 55411. Tel: 612/529-9221; Fax: 612/529-2548. Fred Isaacs, Chm.; John D. Isaacs, Pres. and CEO; Daryl Parks, VP and Gen. Mgr.; Mark Newberry, Environment. American Iron & Supply Co., the leading Minnesota metal-recycling company, processes ferrous and nonferrous scrap metal. With the September 1997 acquisition of American Steel and Industrial Supply, Minneapolis, the company also became a distributor of new steel. 80 employees (all in Minnesota). Founded in 1885. SIC 5093.

American Materials Corporation 717 Short St., P.O. Box 388, Eau Claire, WI 54701. Tel: 715/835-2251; Fax: 715/835-3324. Paul T. Ayres, Pres. American Materials is a manufacturer of ready-mix concrete, industrial sand and gravel, and packaged concrete and mortar mixes. It is also a general contractor and road builder. 225 employees. Founded in 1917. SIC 3273.

American Security Corporation 1717 University Ave. W., St. Paul, MN 55104. Tel: 651/644-1155; Fax: 651/641-0523. Adrian Marsden, Chm. and CEO; Mark Shields, Pres.; Lawrence C. May, VP; Mary Marsden, Sec. American Security offers private security, armored vehicles, vault services, and investigative services. 1,000 employees. Founded in 1959. SIC 7381, 7389.

American Spirit Graphics Corporation 801 S.E. Ninth St., Minneapolis, MN 55414. Tel: 612/623-3333; Fax: 612/623-9314. A. Oscar Carlson, Chm. and CEO; Myron D. Angel, EVP and Gen. Mgr.; Brad Bloss, VP-Nat'l Accts.; Lauren Drevlow, VP-Sls.; Suzanne L. Miller, VP-Fin./Admin. Annual revenue $45 million. American Spirit Graphics is a high-quality, four-color commercial web printer. It specializes in press-pasted-and-trimmed, digest-sized products from 16 through 36 pages in four-page increments. Its double gate-folds or stacked 4's, developed in 1990, are well accepted in the market. The company also produces free-standing inserts with computerized multiple destination shipping expertise. It acquired Wright Printing in Des Moines, Iowa, in November 1996. Wright will operate half and full web presses as American Spirit Graphics/Des Moines. 320 employees. Founded in 1985. In January 2000 the company agreed to acquire the 55-employee, $7 million-revenue Carlson Print Group, Bloomington, Minn.—from A. Oscar Carlson's son and nephew. SIC 2759.

American Timber Company/American Stud Company P.O. Box 128, 155 Goodcreek Rd., Olney, MT 59927. Tel: 406/881-2311; Fax: 406/881-2323. L. Peter Larson, Pres.; David R. Larson, Sls./Credit Mgr. American Timber operates a sawmill, logging operation, and compost plant. The company also produces wood chips. 165 employees. Founded in 1927. SIC 2421.

Ameripride Services 700 Industrial Blvd. N.E., Minneapolis, MN 55413. Tel: 612/371-4200; Fax: 612/331-2507; Web site: http://www.ameripride.com. Larry Steiner, Pres. Annual revenue $350 million (estimated by Fact Book). Ameripride is a professional uniform rental service company supplying 300,000 companies in the United States through its rental division, Ameripride Uniform Service. Subsidiary Canadian Linen is the No. 1 rental company in Canada. The former American Linen also has garment manufacturing facilities in the United States, the Caribbean, and Canada. 5,500 employees (708 in Minnesota). Founded in 1890. SIC 7218. No. 33 CRM Private 100.

Ames Construction Inc. 2000 Ames Dr., Burnsville, MN 55306. Tel: 952/435-7106; Fax: 952/435-7142. Richard J. Ames, Pres. and Sec.; Raymond Ames, VP and Treas.; Dennis McGill, Fin. Mgr. Ames Construction is a heavy, civil, and mining general contractor, with division offices in Salt Lake City, Phoenix, and Denver. 700 employees. Founded in 1960. SIC 1629.

Amsoil Inc. 925 Tower Ave., Amsoil Building, Superior, WI 54880. Tel: 715/392-7101; Fax: 715/392-5225. A.J. Amatuzio, Pres. and CEO; Dean Alexander, VP and Gen. Mgr.; Alan Amatuzio, VP-Mfg.; Dennis Sailor, VP-Fin. Amsoil is a manufacturer of synthetic lubricants, oil filters, air filters, water filters, and automotive appearance products. 130 employees (50 in Minnesota; 10 part-time). Founded in 1972. SIC 2992, 3589.

Anchor Bancorp Inc. 1055 E. Wayzata Blvd., Wayzata, MN 55391. Tel: 952/476-5244; Fax: 952/476-5243. Winton Jones, Chm.; Carl W. Jones, Pres. and COO; David R. Marks, SVP-Info. Svs.; Jeff Bussey, VP-Op./Appl.; Vickie Edman, VP-Admin. Svs.; Bryan D. Enquist, VP-Network Operations; Christopher W. Jones, VP-Info. Svs.; Marianne Meyer, VP and Sec.; Julie Betts, Mktg. Svs. Ofcr.; Marsha M. Drake, Dir.-Internal Audit; Thomas H. Erickson, Chief Credit Review Officer; Fred K. Holzapfel, Mgr.-Computer Op.; Jack Jolley, Dir.-Info. Svs.; Edward M. Kennedy, Dir.-Corp. Fin.; Roberta L. Klein, Dir.-Mktg.; Deborah Koutek, Bank Appli. Support Officer; Kathie A. Leary, Bank Appli. Support Officer; Karen Lewis, Dir.-Trust Svs. Anchor Bancorp is a $525 million-asset bank holding company for the following Minnesota banks: Anchor Bank N.A., Wayzata; Anchor Bank West St. Paul N.A.; Anchor Bank Saint Paul; Heritage National Bank, North St. Paul; and Anchor Bank Farmington, N.A. Each community bank is independently managed, with local authority to provide decisions within its market. 253 employees (245 in Minnesota; 51 part-time). Founded in 1981. SIC 6712.

Anchor Block Company 2300 McKnight Rd., North St. Paul, MN 55109. Tel: 651/777-8321; Fax: 651/777-0169; Web site: http://www.anchorblock.com. Glenn Bolles, Pres.; John Hogan, VP and Gen. Mgr. Anchor Block Co. (originally Oscar Roberts Concrete Products Co.) manufactures concrete blocks and various products for architectural, commercial, institutional, and residential markets. Products include concrete landscape retaining wall units, burnished blocks, and astra-glaze units. Anchor has two sister companies: Anchor Wall Systems, Minnetonka, Minn., which licenses the manufacture of concrete retaining walls; and Zenith Products Co., Maple Grove, Minn., which manufactures burnished concrete masonry products. 120 employees (100 in Minnesota). Founded in 1982. SIC 3271, 3273.

Anchor Paper Company 480 Broadway, P.O. Box 65648 (55165), St. Paul, MN 55101. Tel: 651/298-1311; Fax: 651/298-0060; Web site: http://www.anchorpaper.com. Paul Kulemkamp, Pres.; Linda Hartinger, Sls. Mgr.; Terry Anderson, Packaging Div. Anchor Paper Co. is an employee-owned distributor of printing and writing paper, with retail stores in Plymouth and New Brighton, Minn. An industrial division produces packaging materials, packaging equipment, and janitorial supplies. 128 employees (125 in Minnesota; 10 part-time). Founded in 1923. SIC 2671, 3565, 5087, 5111.

Anderberg-Lund Printing Company 6999 Oxford St., St. Louis Park, MN 55426. Tel: 952/920-9720; Fax: 952/920-1103. Jack B. Anderberg, CEO; Paul Anderberg, VP-Sls./Mktg.; Greg Anderberg, VP-Admin. Annual revenue $10.2 million. Anderberg-Lund, a commercial printer and envelope manufacturer, also does foil stamping, die cutting, silkscreen printing, fully digital integrated to CTP. 74 employees (5 part-time). Founded in 1971. SIC 2759.

Andersen Corporation 100 Fourth Ave. N., Bayport, MN 55003. Tel: 651/264-5150. Sarah Andersen, Chm.; Donald L. Garofalo, Pres. and CEO; Michael O. Johnson, SVP-Corp. Bus. Svs. and CFO; Patrick Riley, SVP-Corp. Op.; Charles W. Schmid, EVP-Window/Patio Door Business Group; Kurt E. Heikkilas, VP-Tech./Bus. Devel. Annual revenue $2 billion (estimated by Forbes). Andersen manufactures a complete line of vinyl-clad wood windows and patio doors. Andersen products are sold to wholesale distributors that supply dealer and retail outlets nationally. With sales worldwide, Andersen markets products throughout the United Kingdom, Japan, Mexico, Canada, Korea, Portugal, Spain, Kuwait, Brazil, Argentina, and Israel. Andersen is one of the nation's 100 largest employee-owned companies. 6,000 employees. Founded in 1903. In November 1999 Andersen and Builders FirstSource Inc., Dallas, signed a letter of intent for Builders to acquire Tennessee Building Products (TBP) from Andersen. The $50 million-revenue TBP, acquired by Andersen in the Morgan Products deal in July, is a leading manufacturer and distributor of millwork products, including doors, windows, and interior trim products. EVP Schmid said, "We do not intend to operate builder-direct businesses, so TBP does not fit with our distribution strategy of selling to dealers. We have therefore decided to sell this part of the business." In January 2000 Andersen agreed to sell its millwork distribution business in Sioux Falls, S.D., to Fargo Glass & Paint Co., Fargo, N.D. In June the company agreed to explore the purchase of the St. Croix Mall and adjacent strip center in Oak Park Heights, Minn., from Northwestern Mutual Life Insurance Co. [Deal completed in November.] In September Andersen announced that it will no longer source wood from endangered forests and it will give preference to Forest StewardshipCouncil (FSC) or equivalent certified wood supplies in the manufacture of its products. SIC 2431. No. 5 CRM Private 100; No. 40 CRM Employer 100.

Anderson Automatics 6401 Welcome Ave. N., Brooklyn Park, MN 55429. Tel: 763/533-2206; Fax: 763/533-0320. Douglas P. Anderson, Pres.; Michael Anderson, COO; Randy Dillon, Dir.-Quality Assurance; Harvey Hoek, Dir.-Sls.; James Swanson, Mfg./Engrg. Annual revenue $8 million. Anderson Automatics performs manufacturing of automatic screw machine products; CNC machining; mechanical sub-assembly. Offering statistical process control, pull system, and JIT delivery, Anderson serves the aircraft/aerospace, electronics, hydraulics, automotive, defense, and medical industries. 70 employees (66 in Minnesota). Founded in 1914. ISO 9002 registered. SIC 3451.

Anderson Bros. Construction Company of Brainerd P.O. Box 668, Brainerd, MN 56401. Tel: 218/829-1768; Fax: 218/829-7607. Dave Johnson, Pres.; Terrence M. Johnson, Treas.; Linnea M. Anderson, Exec. Sec.; Alan Jensen, VP; Douglas C. Olson, VP. Anderson Bros. Construction manufactures hot-mix bituminous mixture. 150 employees. Founded in 1940. SIC 2951.

Anderson Cadillac 7400 Wayzata Blvd., Golden Valley, MN 55426. Tel: 763/544-3501; Fax: 763/544-7666. C.W. Briggs, Chm.; C.W. York, Pres. Anderson Cadillac is a motor vehicle dealership specializing in Cadillacs. 61 employees. Founded in 1953. SIC 5511.

Anderson Chemical Company P.O. Box 1041, Litchfield, MN 55355. Tel: 320/693-2477; Fax: 320/693-8238; Web site: http://www.andersonchemco.com. J. Terry Anderson, Pres.; Leif E. Anderson, EVP; Bruce R. Anderson, EVP. Annual revenue $16 million. Anderson Chemical is a compounder of detergent, sanitation, and water-treatment chemicals for food processing, institutional, and industrial markets. 63 employees (49 in Minnesota; 3 part-time). Founded in 1910. SIC 5169.

Anderson Fabrics Inc. P.O. Box 311, Lake Road, Blackduck, MN 56630. Tel: 218/835-6677; Fax: 218/835-4666. Ron Anderson, Pres.; D'Ann Anderson, VP. Anderson Fabrics manufactures custom drapes and bedspreads, makes residential and contract interior products, wholesales fabrics, distributes hardware, and fabricates Graber window hardware fashions. 283 employees. Founded in 1980. SIC 2221.

Anderson Trucking Service Inc. 203 Cooper Ave. N., St. Cloud, MN 56303. Tel: 320/255-7400; Fax: 320/650-2320. Harold E. Anderson, Pres.; Rollie H. Anderson, EVP; Scott Fuller, Cont. Annual revenue $250 million. Anderson Trucking is a nationwide flatbed, heavy-haul, and van carrier operating more than 900 trucks. Besides general commodities, Anderson also transports specific ones such as granite, iron and steel, machinery, size-and-weight items, lumber, pipe, building materials, and construction equipment. 930 employees. Founded in 1955. SIC 4213. No. 54 CRM Private 100.

Walter G. Anderson Inc. 4535 Willow Dr., Hamel, MN 55340. Tel: 763/427-5575; Fax: 763/478-6572. R.G. Anderson, CEO; Walter E. Gervais, Pres.; Greg Till, COO; Mark Pederson, VP and Gen. Mgr.; Marc Anderson, VP-Mfg.; Darrel Johnson, VP-Sls.; Greg Prescher, VP-Fin./Admin. Walter G. Anderson produces folding cartons at facilities in Hamel and Mound, Minnesota. 148 employees (all in Minnesota). Founded in 1950. SIC 2657.

Andex Industries Inc. 1911 Fourth Ave. N., P.O. Box 887, Escanaba, MI 49829. Tel: 906/786-6070; Fax: 906/786-3133. John T. Anthony, Pres. Andex Industries manufactures miscellaneous plastic products. 140 employees. Founded in 1962. SIC 3089.

Angus-Palm Industries Inc. P.O. Box 610, Watertown, SD 57201. Tel: 605/886-5681; Fax: 605/886-6179. Robert A. Kluver, Pres.; Marty Comes, VP-Sls.; Clifford O. Glembin, VP-Admin.; William Knese, VP-Fin.; Gary E. Stone, VP-Mfg.; Darrin Hofmeister, Dir.-Engrg. Annual revenue $55 million. Angus-Palm Industries manufactures roll bars, roll bar cabs, and steel specialties fabrication. 700 employees. Founded in 1969. SIC 3443, 3537.

Apothecary Products Inc. 11750 12th Ave. S., Burnsville, MN 55337. Tel: 952/890-1940; Fax: 952/890-0418. Terry Noble, CEO; John Creel, Pres.; M. Ellen Davis, SVP; Don Shaffer, Cont.; David Polfliet, VP-Sls. Annual revenue $35 million. Apothecary Products provides over-the-counter patient compliance aids (dosage containers with the trade name Ezy-Dose) and private-label pharmaceuticals—as well as printing services, equipment, and supplies—for the pharmacy and medical communities internationally. 208 employees (all in Minnesota). Founded in 1975. SIC 3829.

The Araz Group 8500 Normandale Lake Blvd., Suite 2050, Bloomington, MN 55437. Tel: 952/896-1200; Fax: 952/896-4888; Web site: http://www.araz.com. Nazie Eftekhari, Chm. and CEO. The Araz Group is a full-service managed-care company offering utilization, case management, maternity, claim, disability and workers' compensation, and pharmaceutical management; managed-care consulting; and a range of preferred-provider network options to 250,000 people through networks in Minnesota, North Dakota, South Dakota, and Iowa. Subsidiary Medtor, an IME company, is also located in Bloomington. Previously known as Ethix Midwest, the company was Minnesota's first PPO. 85 employees (84 in Minnesota). Founded in 1982. In January 2000 HealthSystem Minnesota, St. Louis Park, Minn., entered into an agreement to become a participating provider in the Araz Group health insurance network—a move expected to increase clinic volume by 2,000 to 4,000 patients annually. SIC 6324.

Architectural Alliance 400 Clifton Ave. S., Minneapolis, MN 55403. Tel: 612/871-5703; Fax: 612/871-7212; Web site: http://www.archalliance.com. Thomas J. DeAngelo, AIA and Pres.; Bruce Albinson, AIA; Carey Brendalen, AIA; Sharry L. Cooper, IIDA; Cliff Dunham, AIA; Cynthia L.S. Ellsworth, Ofcr.; Tom Hysell, AIA; Dennis W. LaFrance, AIA; Eric Peterson, AIA; Peter Vesterholt, AIA. Annual revenue $14 million. Architectural Alliance provides architectural, planning, interior design, and construction observation services for public and private companies. The company has designed new facilities, renovations, and additions to existing facilities, as well as restorations of historic structures. Project types include aviation, corporate, institutional, and retail. Major projects include Minnesota Children's Museum, St. Paul Companies, Minnesota Life corporate office building, Blue Cross and Blue Shield of Minnesota office building, H.B. Fuller Willow Lake Research & Development Laboratory Facility, United States Courthouse and Federal Office Building (interior architecture), Hennepin County Public Works Facility, University of Minnesota Jackson Hall, and the Minneapolis/St. Paul International Airport (MSP) Green Concourse Expansion. The firm's work on Northstar Crossing, the award-winning retail area area at MSP, helped it build a national reputation that is winning jobs around the country. 85 employees. Founded in 1970. SIC 7389, 8712.

Architectural Sales of Minnesota Inc. 4550 Quebec Ave. N., New Hope, MN 55428. Tel: 763/533-1595; Fax: 763/533-7852. Charles J. Tambornino, Pres.; Tom Dean, VP; John Dean, VP. Annual revenue $8 million. Architectural Sales of Minnesota is an acoustical and ceiling tile and wall contractor, flooring contractor including carpet, raised floors. 80 employees (all in Minnesota). Founded in 1959. SIC 1752, 5039.

Argosy Electronics Inc. 10300 W. 70th St., Eden Prairie, MN 55344. Tel: 952/942-9232; Fax: 952/942-0503. Gary Maas, Pres. Argosy Electronics manufactures custom in-the-ear, canal, and completely-in-the-canal hearing aids and sells BTE's. 215 employees (209 in Minnesota). Founded in 1979. Merged with Lori-Unitron in March 2000. SIC 3842.

Armstrong, Torseth, Skold and Rydeen Inc. 8501 Golden Valley Rd., Suite 300, Golden Valley, MN 55422. Tel: 763/545-3731; Fax: 763/525-3289. Paul Erickson, Pres. Armstrong, Torseth, Skold and Rydeen does architectural, mechanical, and electrical engineering; interior design; and landscape architecture. 130 employees. Founded in 1944. SIC 8711, 8712.

Arrow Tank & Engineering Company 650 N. Emerson, Cambridge, MN 55008. Tel: 763/689-3360; Fax: 763/689-1263. John Haskins, Chm., Pres., and CEO; Milt Swenson, Sls. Mgr.-LPG Related Products; Dennie DeWall, Sls. Mgr. Annual revenue $36 million. Arrow Tank and Engineering Co. makes fire-fighting bladder vessels, propane trucks and tanks, ASME vessels, and fabricated stainless and carbon steel weldments. It also does non-code carbon and stainless plate fabrication. 226 employees. Founded in 1958. SIC 3443, 3498, 3795.

Art Resources Gallery 494 Jackson St., St. Paul, MN 55101. Tel: 651/636-6367; Fax: 651/292-8475. Thomas W. Swanson, Pres. Art Resources Gallery provides specialized picture framing services. The company also offers the Upper Midwest's largest supply of artwork and framing materials. Affiliated with Twin City Picture Framing Company Inc., Roseville, Minn. 100 employees. Founded in 1898. SIC 5999.

Ashley Furniture Industries Inc. One Ashley Way, Arcadia, WI 54612. Tel: 608/323-3377; Fax: 608/323-7857. Ron Wanek, Chm. and CEO; Charles Vogel, VChm. and CSO; Todd Wanek, Pres. and COO; Benjamin Vogel, EVP. Ashley Furniture Industries manufactures bedroom, occasional, dining room, and upholstered furniture. 2,600 employees (54 in Minnesota). Founded in 1945. SIC 2511.

Asset Marketing Services Inc. 14101 W. Southcross Dr., Burnsville, MN 55337. Tel: 952/707-7000; Fax: 952/707-7505. Nicholas J. Bruyer, CEO. Asset Marketing deals in coin and sports memorbilia/collectibles. 200 employees. SIC 5999.

Associated Finishing 320 Mallard Ln., Mankato, MN 56001. Tel: 507/345-5861; Fax: 507/345-5828. Chuck Klammer Jr., Pres. Associated Engineering of Mankato is engaged in industrial metal finishing, powder coating, RFI shielding, silkscreening, pad printing, metal stripping, chromate conversion coat, deburring, and glass etching. 90 employees. Founded in 1965. SIC 2752, 3479.

Associated Milk Producers Inc. 315 N. Broadway, P.O. Box 455, New Ulm, MN 56073. Tel: 507/354-8295; Fax: 507/359-8651. Mark Furth, CEO. Annual revenue $1.1 billion. Associated Milk Producers is a dairy farmer cooperative, processing and marketing milk and milk products. Operations are located in Rochester, Paynesville, New Ulm, Dawson, and Duluth, Minn.; Arlington, Mason City, Sibley, and Sanborn, Iowa; Blair, Jim Falls, and Portage, Wis.; and Freeman, S.D. AMPI is owned by more than 6,000 Upper Midwest milk producers. 1,700 employees. Founded in 1969. SIC 2023. No. 5 CRM Cooperatives/Mutuals 20.

Associated Potato Growers Inc. 2001 N. Sixth St., Grand Forks, ND 58203. Tel: 701/775-4614; Fax: 701/746-5767. Darren Damers, VP; Joel Sannes, Pres. Annual revenue $15 million. Associated Potato Growers is a shipper, packer, and marketer of fresh potatoes. 100 employees (80 part-time). Founded in 1948. SIC 0161, 0179, 5148.

Astrup Drugs Inc. 905 N. Main, Austin, MN 55912. Tel: 507/433-7447; Fax: 507/433-7447. L.B. Astrup, Pres. Astrup Drugs operates a chain of nine Sterling Drug Stores. 230 employees. Founded in 1950. SIC 5912.

Atrium Catering 275 Market St., Suite C25, Minneapolis, MN 55405. Tel: 612/339-8322; Fax: 612/339-7601. Ken Cole, Dir.-Sls./Mktg.; Michael Colosimo, Gen. Mgr. Atrium Catering offers food preparation, pre-

PVT

sentation, and service, catered on-site at International Market Square and off-site throughout the Twin Cities. The Atrium at International Market Square is a dramatic special-event facility that accommodates up to 2,200 for dinners and 5,000 for receptions. The building also contains 20,000 square feet of carpeted exhibit space, and additional spaces designed for smaller events. 170 employees (120 in Minnesota; 50 part-time). Founded in 1984. SIC 5812.

Atscott Manufacturing Company Inc. 1300 Holstein Dr., Pine City, MN 55063. Tel: 320/629-2501; Fax: 320/629-7129. John Norris, Pres. Atscott is a complete machine and fabrication shop involved in painting and anodizing. It has complete electromechanical product lines. 100 employees (96 in Minnesota). Founded in 1963. SIC 3544, 3599.

Audio Research Corporation 5740 Green Circle Dr., Minnetonka, MN 55343. Tel: 963/577-9700; Fax: 952/939-0604. William Z. Johnson, Pres. and CEO; Gerald L. Oxborough, EVP and Gen. Mgr. Audio Research Corp. manufactures amplifiers and pre-amps. 70 employees. Founded in 1970. SIC 3651.

Audubon Engineering & Manufacturing P.O. Box 277, Audubon, MN 56511. Tel: 218/439-6186; Fax: 218/439-3391. Donald W. Ricke, Chm.; David W. Ricke, Pres.; Jay Meacham, Sec. and Treas.; Tony Passanante, Dir.-Sls. Audubon Engineering & Manufacturing is a general machine shop, specializing in CNC milling, turning, hobbing, broaching, and spline rolling. Audubon manufactures and assembles subassemblies for OEMs, and is also involved in the design, manufacture, and assembly of transmissions and gear boxes. Held by Technology, Engineering and Manufacturing Industries Inc. (TEAM Industries), Bagley, Minn. 265 employees (all in Minnesota). Founded in 1984. SIC 3599.

Augies Inc. 1900 W. County Rd. C, Roseville, MN 55113. Tel: 651/633-5308; Fax: 651/633-5308. Raymond C. Augustine, Pres.; Leroy Augustine, VP; Albert Augustine, Sec. and Treas. Augies makes pre-cooked, individually wrapped food—mostly sandwiches. 50 employees (all in Minnesota; 15 part-time). Founded in 1956. SIC 2099.

Augustine Medical Inc. 10393 W. 70th St., Eden Prairie, MN 55344. Tel: 952/947-1200; Fax: 952/947-1400; Web site: http://www.augustinemedical.com. Scott D. Augustine, M.D., Founder, Chm., and CEO; Marie Humbert, CFO. Annual revenue $53.5 million. Augustine Medical manufactures the Bair Hugger Patient Warming System for the control of hypothermia during and after surgery. The company is pursuing development of other products serving the acute and critical care segments of the health care market. 174 employees. Founded in 1987. In January 2000 the company named Minneapolis-based advertising and marketing communications agency Whitney Morse its agency of record. In June the U.S. District Court in Minneapolis awarded Mallinckrodt Inc. (NYSE: MKG) the costs of litigation incurred during a lengthy legal battle with Augustine Medical over its right to manufacture and market its WarmTouch blankets. SIC 3841.

The Austad Golf Stores 2801 E. 10th St., Sioux Falls, SD 57103. Tel: 605/336-3135; Fax: 605/336-7221; Web site: http://www.golfunderground.com. David B. Austad, Pres. and CEO; Pat Penney, VP and CFO; Jeff Caraway, VP and Gen. Mgr. Annual revenue $20 million. Austad Golf Stores is a retailer of golf equipment and apparel. 150 employees (60 in Minnesota; 70 part-time). Founded in 1963. SIC 5961.

Austin Packaging Company 1118 N. Main St., Austin, MN 55912. Tel: 507/433-6623; Fax: 507/433-9717. Bob Thatcher, CEO; Jim Heimark, Pres.; Jeff Thatcher, EVP. Austin Packaging Co. is a manufacturer of liquid USDA refrigerated or frozen flexible portion packaged food products. 170 employees. SIC 7379.

Awardcraft Inc. 10900 Nesbitt Ave. S., Bloomington, MN 55437. Tel: 952/948-0400; Fax: 952/948-0220. William DeGonda, Chm.; Steve DeGonda, Pres. and CEO; Mike Schuffenhauer, EVP-Fin.; Sue Tobias, VP-Sls./Mktg. Awardcraft manufactures corporate recognition awards using chemical etching, laser engraving, glass etching, silkscreening, vacuum forming, and foil stamping. 100 employees (all in Minnesota). Founded in 1977. SIC 3231, 3914.

Ayres Associates 3433 Oakwood Hills Pkwy., Eau Claire, WI 54701. Tel: 715/834-3161; Fax: 715/831-7500; Web site: http://www.primenet.com/~ayres. Patrick Quinn, Pres.; Dean Schultz, EVP; Siamak Kusha, EVP; Richard Mauch, EVP. Annual revenue $34 million. Ayres Associates specializes in civil, structural, transportation, water resources, and river engineering; architecture; environmental science; surveying; photogrammetry; and automated mapping. Ayres Associates' offices are located in Sacramento, Calif.; Denver and Fort Collins, Colo.; Jacksonville and Tampa, Fla.; Midland, Mich.; Duluth, Minn.; and Eau Claire, Green Bay, Madison, and Milwaukee, Wis. 428 employees (3 in Minnesota; 62 part-time). Founded in 1959. SIC 8711.

BH Electronics Inc. 12219 Wood Lake Dr., Burnsville, MN 55337. Tel: 952/894-9590; Fax: 952/894-9380. Richard Jackson, Pres. and CEO. Annual revenue $15 million. BH Electronics designs and manufactures transformers, inductors, magnetic components, electromechanical assemblies, and computer interface devices. 125 employees (all in Minnesota). Founded in 1969. SIC 3677.

BI Performance Services 7630 E. Bush Lake Rd., Edina, MN 55439. Tel: 952/835-4800; Fax: 952/844-4033. Guy Schoenecker, Pres. and CEO; Lanny Schoenecker, EVP. Annual revenue $360 million. BI Performance Services (formerly Business Incentives), a trade name for Schoeneckers Inc., sells communications, training, measurement, and reward systems for performance improvement. 1,400 employees. Founded in 1950. In November 1999 BI won the prestigious Malcolm Baldrige National Quality Award—one of only four winners in the nation and two in Minnesota (the other being Sunny Fresh Foods, Monticello, Minn., the egg further-processing business of Cargill). In December BI acquired Total Training Network LLC and Peak Performers International Inc., both of Golden Valley, Minn., with a combined 50 employees. The former markets CD-based training libraries for businesses; the latter provides management seminars. In April 2000 BI acquired UserView Inc.—a 14-year-old Twin Cities company that designs and develops interactive media solutions (Web-based and CD-interactive learning) that positively affect performance—and renamed it e-Learning Solutions. SIC 4729. No. 31 CRM Private 100.

BWBR Architects Inc. 400 Sibley St., Suite 500, St. Paul, MN 55101. Tel: 651/222-3701; Fax: 651/222-8961; Web site: http://www.bwbr.com. C. Jay Sleiter, Pres. and CEO; Terry L. Anderson, SVP; Wilford F. Johnson, SVP; Stephen P. Patrick, SVP. BWBR Architects provides professional design services for a wide range of building types, including health care, financial, office, correction/detention, education, recreational, religious, manufacturing and transit. Services include project feasibility, programming, architectural and interior design, construction documentation, and observation. 100 employees (all in Minnesota). Founded in 1922. SIC 8712.

Bachman's Inc. 6010 Lyndale Ave. S., Minneapolis, MN 55419. Tel: 612/861-7600; Fax: 612/861-7745; Web site: http://www.bachmans.com. Todd L. Bachman, Chm. and CEO; Dale L. Bachman, Pres.; Dick Herberg, COO; Lee W. Bachman, CFO and Treas.; Alan B. Bachman, Sec.; Paul G. Bachman, VP; Donald Swenson, VP-Prod. Annual revenue $79 million. Bachman's Inc., a horticultural-based firm, markets products and services for home and business. Bachman's has 22 stores in the Twin Cities metropolitan area, including six full-service floral, gift, and garden centers. Bachman's also operates indoor and outdoor landscaping divisions; a nursery wholesale division; seven acres of greenhouses; and a 513-acre growing range near Lakeville, Minnesota, which produces many of the plants, flowers, and landscaping products sold and leased through Bachman's locations. 1,100 employees (all in Minnesota; 500 part-time). Founded in 1885. SIC 5261.

Bad River Lodge & Casino P.O. Box 8, Highway 2, Odanah, WI 54861. Tel: 715/682-7121. Bad River Lodge & Casino offers high-stakes pull tabs, entertainment and restaurants. 225 employees. Founded in 1990. SIC 7011.

Badger Foundry Company P.O. Box 1306, Winona, MN 55987. Tel: 507/452-5760; Fax: 507/452-6469. A.R. Callender, Pres.; Dan Motl, VP and CFO; Charles Will, VP-Sls. Annual revenue $15 million. Badger operates a gray-iron jobbing foundry. 165 employees (all in Minnesota). Founded in 1910. SIC 3321.

Bailey Nurseries Inc. 1325 Bailey Rd., St. Paul, MN 55119. Tel: 651/459-9744; Fax: 651/459-5100. G.J. Bailey, Chm.; Rodney Bailey, Pres.; Patrick Bailey, VP-Sls./Mktg.; Dan Bailey, Purch. Bailey Nurseries is a wholesale grower of nursery stock. 700 employees (200 in Minnesota; 500 part-time). Founded in 1905. SIC 0181.

Balzer Inc. P.O. Box 458, Mountain Lake, MN 56159. Tel: 507/427-3133; Fax: 507/427-3640. Wayne E. Powell, Pres. Balzer Inc., also known as Balzer Manufacturing Corp., makes flail shredders and liquid-waste wagons. 61 employees. Founded in 1946. SIC 3523.

Ban-Koe Systems Inc. 9100 W. Bloomington Freeway, Bloomington, MN 55431. Tel: 952/888-6688; Fax: 952/888-3344. William L. Bangtson, Pres.; Loren K. Adams, CFO. Annual revenue $17.7 million. Ban-Koe specializes in frontline labor management systems, including time clocks, data collection, labor reporting, and shop floor control as well as in commercial building systems such as fire alarms, communication systems, sound reinforcements, and wall clocks. 168 employees (126 in Minnesota; 2 part-time). Founded in 1981. For the second year in a row, Kronos Incorporated presented Ban-Koe Systems with the Curt Gerber Award of Recognition, given to the largest, most prestigious Kronos dealers generating the highest sales and providing superior customer service during the year. SIC 5044, 5063, 5065, 7373, 7374.

Bang Printing Highways 18 and 25, P.O. Box 587, Brainerd, MN 56401. Tel: 218/829-2877; Fax: 218/829-7145. John E. Kurtzman, Chm.; Christopher Kurtzman, Pres. Bang Printing is engaged in book and catalog manufacturing, including design, typesetting, digital prepress, booklet stitching, perfect bindery, spiral bindery, and distribution/fullfillment. The company also provides mailing services. 150 employees. Founded in 1899. SIC 2759, 2789.

Bank of North Dakota P.O. Box 5509, Bismarck, ND 58502. Tel: 701/328-5600; Fax: 701/328-5632; Web site: http://www.banknd.com. Eric Hardmeyer, SVP-Lending and interim Pres.; Edward B. Sather, SVP-Investment/Trust; Dale Eberle, SVP-Retail/Bank Op.; Julie Kubisiak, Dir.-Student Loans. Annual revenue $30.5 million. The Bank of North Dakota is the only state-owned and -operated bank in the nation. 181 employees (9 part-time). Founded in 1919. SIC 6022.

Banner Engineering Corporation 9714 10th Ave. N., Plymouth, MN 55441. Tel: 763/544-3164; Fax: 763/544-3213; Web site: http://www.baneng.com. Robert W. Fayfield, Chm., Pres., and CEO; Larry B. Evans, COO. Annual revenue $100 million. Banner Engineering is the nation's largest manufacturer of optoelectronic sensing devices—including lasers, fiber optics, and photoelectric controls—for the factory automation and robotics industries. The company has five manufacturing plants in the Midwest, plus sales offices in 44 countries. 600 employees. Founded in 1966. SIC 3625.

Barbarossa & Sons Inc. P.O. Box 367, Osseo, MN 55369. Tel: 763/425-4146; Fax: 763/425-0797. Gordon F. Barbarossa, Chm.; Robert R. Barbarossa, Pres.; Paul C. Flykt, EVP; James H. Thompson, Sec. and Treas. Barbarossa constructs pumping stations, and installs sewer, water, and storm lines. Barbarossa Blasting—a division of Barbarossa & Sons—is engaged in specialty blasting. 102 employees (92 in Minnesota). Founded in 1946. SIC 1623.

Barr Engineering Company 4700 W. 77th St., Edina, MN 55435. Tel: 952/832-2600; Fax: 952/832-2601; Web site: http://www.barr.com. Douglas E. Connell, Chm. and VP; Lawrence Molsather, Pres.; Douglas Barr, VP; John Borovsky, VP; Larry Dalen, VP; John D. Dickson, VP; Alan Fandrey, VP; Dale W. Finnesgaard, VP; William J. Forsmark, VP; Allan Gebhard, VP; Ken Haberman, VP; Beth Havlik, VP; James P. Herbert, VP; Mark Hibbs, VP; Nancy Johnson Dent, VP; Gregory D. Keil, VP; Steve Klein, VP; Leonard J. Kremer, VP; Jim Langseth, VP; John Larson, VP; Harry F. Larson, VP; John Lee, VP; Bradley J. Lindaman, VP; John L. Lund, VP; Dean Malotky, VP; Nels Nelson, VP; Robert Obermeyer, VP; Dennis E. Palmer, VP; George Pruchnofski, VP; John Quist, VP; Tom Radue, VP; Cliff Rasch, VP; Mike Relf, VP; Dave Rian, VP; Henry Runke, VP; Tim Russell, VP; Michael R. Shoberg, VP; Timothy W. Skoglund, VP; Philip B. Solseng, VP; Lori Stegink, VP; Brian E. Toevs, VP; Daniel E. Umfleet, VP; Dale L. Wikre, VP; Ray Wuolo, VP. Annual revenue $30 million. Barr Engineering offers consulting services in engineering environmental sciences, and information technology to clients in industry and government in the areas of air, water, site remediation, environmental management, process and facility design, materials handling, and information technology such as database design and implementation, Internet/intranet, and environmental management software. Barr has additional offices in Hibbing and Duluth, Minn.; Jefferson City, Mo.; and Ann Arbor, Mich. 319 employees (302 in Minnesota; 31 part-time). Founded in 1966. SIC 8711.

Barrel O'Fun Snack Foods 800 Fourth St. N.W., P.O. Box 230, Perham, MN 56573. Tel: 218/346-7000; Fax: 218/346-7003. Ken Nelson, Pres. and CEO; Mike Holper, VP and COO; Kurt Nelson, Gen Mgr.; Wayne Caughey, CFO; Nancy Belka, Dir.-Hum. Res.; Bob Colling, Dir.-Proc. Control; Randy Johnson, Dir.-Sls. Barrel O'Fun is a manufacturer of potato chips, popcorn, cheese corn, caramel corn, extruded corn snacks, taco/tortilla chips, and pretzels. 345 employees. Founded in 1973. SIC 2096.

Barrett Moving & Storage Company 7100 Washington Ave. S., Eden Prairie, MN 55344. Tel: 952/944-6550; Fax:

952/828-7110. Joe Langer, Chm.; R.H. Eidsvold Jr., Pres.; Randy Koepsell, Gen. Mgr. Barrett Moving & Storage provides worldwide moving and storage of household goods, computers, and displays. 224 employees (165 in Minnesota; 17 part-time). Founded in 1900. In June 2000 Barrett acquired two United Van Lines agencies, in Kenosha, Wis., and Gurnee, Ill. Said President Eidsvold, "This increased capacity will serve our customers well at a time when demand for all moving services is up dramatically throughout the country." SIC 4214, 4226.

Basin Electric Power Cooperative 1717 E. Interstate Ave., Bismarck, ND 58501. Tel: 701/223-0441; Fax: 701/224-5336; Web site: http://www.basinelectric.com. Wayne Child, Pres.; Robert L. McPhail, Gen. Mgr.; Richard Weber, Asst. Gen. Mgr. Basin Electric is a consumer-owned regional cooperative, responsible for supplying wholesale electric power to 117 rural electric systems and 1.5 million people in eight states. Basin Electric is a diversified energy group that not only generates electricity but also markets coal and produces natural gas (from coal and byproducts of the coal gasification process). Basin Electric has two major subsidiaries: Dakota Gasification Co. and Dakota Coal Co. 1,790 employees. Founded in 1961. SIC 4911.

Bauer Built Inc. Highway 25 S., P.O. Box 248, Durand, WI 54736. Tel: 715/672-4295; Fax: 715/672-4675. Jerry M. Bauer, Pres. Bauer Built is a wholesale and retail distributor of tires, batteries, automotive accessories, petroleum products, and related services. 500 employees (100 in Minnesota; 90 part-time). Founded in 1944. SIC 5013, 5014, 5531.

Bauer Welding & Metal Fabricators Inc. 2159 Mustang Dr., Mounds View, MN 55112. Tel: 763/786-6025; Fax: 763/786-7447; Web site: http://www.bauerweld.com. Douglas K. Bauer, Pres. and CEO; Stan Nymeyer, VP and Gen. Mgr.; Don Bancroft, Cont.; Mike Thume, Engrg. Mgr.; Joe Tucci, Materials Mgr. Annual revenue $10 million. Bauer Welding & Metal Fabricators manufactures weldments, custom-fabricated tanks, OEM tubular parts, and assemblies. The company also engages in metal-tube fabricating, CNC Tubebending and Robotic Welding. 100 employees. Founded in 1946. SIC 3498.

Bay West Inc. 5 Empire Dr., St. Paul, MN 55103. Tel: 651/291-0456; Fax: 651/291-0099; Web site: http://www.baywest.com. Don Erickson, Pres. and CEO; Marty Wangensteen, Dir.-Op.; Lon Larson, CFO. Bay West Inc. is an environmental services firm offering industrial, environmental, marine, and emergency services including industrial cleaning and maintenance, remediation/environmental cleanup, investigation/engineering, safety/industrial hygiene, waste management/permitting and marine construction and commercial diving including industrial and contaminated sediment dredging. Bay West also has offices in Kansas City, Mo. 80 employees (74 in Minnesota). Founded in 1974. In January 2000 the company received a hazardous waste transporter license—one element of Bay West's expansion of its turnkey hazardous and special industrial waste management services. The company had also expanded its truck fleet and added staff. In February the Navy awarded Bay West a contract for up to five years for operation and maintenance services at the Naval Industrial Reserve Ordnance Plant (NIROP) in Fridley, Minn. In April the Minneapolis Community Development Agency awarded the company a two-year contract to provide environmental and geotechnical services at sites in Minneapolis. The company initiated remediation work at the Twin Cities Army Ammunition Plant, Arden Hills, Minn. In May the St. Paul Port Authority awarded Bay West a contract to perform the reconstruction of a barge terminal on the Mississippi River in St. Paul. In June the company was awarded a delivery order by the Minnesota Pollution Control Agency to assist in the cleanup of the Pig's Eye Dump, St. Paul, the state's largest unpermitted landfill. In July Bay West was awarded a $1.1 million order to construct, operate, and maintain a Superfund landfill in Kellogg, Idaho. SIC 1629, 8744.

Beall Trailers of Montana Inc. 1430 Highway 87 E., Billings, MT 59101. Tel: 406/252-7163; Fax: 406/256-6159. Jerry E. Beall, Pres.; David W. Shannon, VP and Gen. Mgr.; Scott Koch, Sec. Beall manufactures and repairs pneumatic trailers for the coal and petroleum industries. 97 employees. SIC 3537.

Bec-Lin Foods Inc. 354 Water St., Excelsior, MN 55331. Tel: 952/470-1619; Fax: 952/470-5010. William Schoeneberger, Pres. and Co-owner; Jim Bixler, VP and Co-owner; Miles Nelson, Sls. Mgr.; Chris Bixler, Sls. Mgr.; Bob Colling, Plant Mgr. Bec-Lin Foods produces Mexican (tortillas, tacos, taco shells, tortilla chips) and Scandinavian (lefse, potato dumplings) specialty foods. It has a plant in Perham, Minn. 85 employees (all in Minnesota). Founded in 1982. SIC 2041.

Becker Brothers Inc. 825 First St. N.W., New Brighton, MN 55112. Tel: 651/633-8604; Fax: 651/633-2122. Harold Becker, CEO; William Becker, Sec. and Treas. Becker Brothers is a full floor-covering installation service. 100 employees (all in Minnesota). Founded in 1960. SIC 1752.

Becklund Home Health Care Inc. 8421 Wayzata Blvd., Golden Valley, MN 55426. Tel: 763/544-0315; Fax: 763/544-9406. Rhoda Becklund, Pres.; J. Robert Becklund, VP; Thomas Becklund, Treas. Becklund Home Health Care is a Medicare-certified, Class A-licensed home health agency. Becklund provides personal health care assistance that enables its clients to stay at home. Other locations: St. Peter, Minn.; Austin, Texas. 1,600 employees. Founded in 1984. SIC 8082.

Beco Helman Inc. 801 Washington Ave. N., Minneapolis, MN 55401. Tel: 612/338-5634. Frank Thomas, Pres. Beco Helman manufactures women's and men's apparel for retail markets and nursing homes. 55 employees. Founded in 1952. SIC 2331.

Bedford Industries Inc. 1659 Rowe Ave., P.O. Box 39, Worthington, MN 56187. Tel: 507/376-4136; Fax: 507/376-6742; Web site: http://www.bedfordind.com. Robert B. Ludlow, Pres.; Robert Boushek, VP-Op.; Norma Cook, Mktg./Admin. Mgr.; David Groff, Regional Sls. Dir.; Linda Hill, Mgr.-Hum. Res.; Patricia S. Ludlow, Sec. and Treas.; Mike Pederson, Engrg. Mgr.; David Reker, Cont.; Bill Shoup, Info. Sys. Mgr.; Bob Tims, Purch./Quality Mgr.; John Van Ede, Prod. Mgr. Annual revenue $20 million. Bedford Industries are innovators in plastic and paper twist-tie bag closures, identification ties and tags, labels, bag closing machinery, packaging solutions, and other packaging closures. 170 employees (155 in Minnesota; 2 part-time). Founded in 1966. SIC 3089, 3565.

The Bedroom Inc. dba HOM Furniture 10301 Woodcrest Dr. N.W., Coon Rapids, MN 55433. Tel: 763/767-3600. Wayne Johansen, CEO. Annual revenue $87 million. The Bedroom Inc. dba HOM Furniture, is a retailer of home furnishings and accessories. 600 employees. Founded in 1981. SIC 5712. No. 28 CityBusiness Fastest-growing Private Companies.

Behrens Inc. 471 W. Third St., P.O. Box 187, Winona, MN 55987. Tel: 507/454-4664; Fax: 507/452-2106. Steven Moen, VP-Sls./Mktg.; Keith Schmidt, Pres. Behrens manufactures galvanized garbage cans, hot galvanized pails, and other sheet metal products. 85 employees (all in Minnesota). Founded in 1911. SIC 3411.

Bell Lumber & Pole Company P.O. Box 120786, New Brighton, MN 55112. Tel: 651/633-4334; Fax: 651/633-8852. M.J. Bell III,

Pres.; Scott Kirk, VP; Tom Brix, Treas. Bell manufactures utility poles. 50 employees. Founded in 1909. SIC 2491.

Beltmann North American Company Inc. 2480 Long Lake Rd., Roseville, MN 55113. Tel: 651/639-2800; Fax: 651/639-2938. Dann W. Battina, Pres.; Paul Zagaria, CFO. Beltmann is engaged in the domestic and international relocation and transportation of household goods and high-value products. It is also an agent for North American Van Lines. It has offices in Minneapolis/St. Paul; Milwaukee; Chicago; Des Moines, Iowa; Kansas City, Mo.; Orlando, Jacksonville, and Pompano Beach, Fla.; Westchester County, N.Y.; Long Beach, Calif.; Raleigh, N.C.; and Ontario. 700 employees. Founded in 1955. SIC 4214.

Beltrami Electric Cooperative Inc. 2025 Paul Bunyan Dr. N.W., Bemidji, MN 56601. Tel: 218/751-2540; Fax: 218/444-3676. Roger A. Spiry, Mgr. Beltrami Electric Cooperative provides electrical services to Beltrami and Itasca counties, and parts of three others. 62 employees (all in Minnesota; 1 part-time). Founded in 1940. SIC 4911.

Jeff Belzer's Todd Chevrolet 21111 Cedar Ave., Lakeville, MN 55044. Tel: 952/469-4444. Jeffery A. Belzer, Pres. and CEO; Jeffrey A. Krapu, VP and Sec. Jeff Belzer's Todd Chevrolet is a franchised Chevrolet automobile dealership and a franchised Dodge automobile dealership. 206 employees. Founded in 1980. SIC 5511.

Benchmark Computer Learning 4510 W. 77th St., Suite 210, Edina, MN 55435. Tel: 952/896-6800; Fax: 952/896-9728; Web site: http://www.benchmarklearning.com. Scott Schwefel, CEO; Phil Hinderaker, Pres. Annual revenue $8 million. Benchmark is Minnesota's first and largest authorized technical education center for Microsoft, Novell, Lotus, igeneration, and A+. It offers classes, performance consulting, mentoring, and software migration planning. 50 employees. SIC 8243.

Alvin E. Benike Inc. 2960 Highway 14 W., Rochester, MN 55901. Tel: 507/288-6575; Fax: 507/288-0116; Web site: http://www.benike.com. John Benike, CEO; Jim Benike, Treas. Alvin E. Benike Inc. is a general building contractor for commercial, industrial, and institutional construction. The company specializes in medical, high-tech, and dairy processing in southeastern Minnesota. 160 employees (all in Minnesota). Founded in 1937. SIC 1541.

Berg Grain and Produce 2202 Fifth Ave., Fargo, ND 58102. Tel: 701/293-3434; Fax: 701/235-4584. Arnold Berg Jr., Pres. Berg Grain and Produce is a dry-van and refrigerated-trailer transportation company. 125 employees. SIC 4213.

Bergen's Greenhouses Inc. 801 W. Willow St., Detroit Lakes, MN 56501. Tel: 218/847-2138; Fax: 218/847-3515. Robert J. Bergen, Pres., CEO, and Owner. Bergen's grows year-round flowering, foliage, and holiday plants, plugs, and bedding plants. Currently run by the third and fourth generations of the family. 120 employees (100 in Minnesota). Founded in 1921. SIC 5193, 5992.

Berger Transfer & Storage Inc. 2950 Long Lake Rd., Roseville, MN 55113. Tel: 651/639-2260; Fax: 651/639-2277; Web site: http://www.alliedagent.com/berger. William R. Dircks, CEO; Duane Johnson, Pres. Annual revenue $68 million. Berger Transfer is a transportation company that hauls household goods, computers, high-value machines, and office and store fixtures nationwide. It also does local office moving, data-record storage and retrievals, warehousing, and five-state distribution. The company's terminals are located in Los Angeles; Dallas and Austin, Texas; Grand Rapids, Mich.; Addison, Ill.; Minneapolis, and St. Paul. 425 employees. Founded in 1910. SIC 4213.

Bergin Fruit & Nut Company 740 Kasota Circle, Minneapolis, MN 55414. Tel: 612/378-1234; Fax: 612/378-1808. Ray W. Bergin Jr., Pres.; John Bergin, VP; Tom R. Bergin, VP. Annual revenue $11.5 million. Bergin Fruit & Nut is engaged in wholesale distribution of a complete line (including European) of fresh fruit and vegetables, and a complete line of all nut meats. The company also processes more than 100 food items. 84 employees. Founded in 1951. SIC 5145, 5148.

The Bergquist Company 18930 W. 78th, Edina, MN 55439. Tel: 952/835-2322; Fax: 952/835-0430; Web site: http://www.bergquistcompany.com. Carl R. Bergquist, Chm., Pres., Mgr.-Membrane Switch; James Plewacki, Cont.; LeRoy Morgan, CFO; Mark Green, VP-Res./Devel.; Mike Frederick, VP and Gen. Mgr.-Thermal Products; Duane Dungey, VP-Distribution; Bob Savage, VP-Sls., Thermal Products; Sarah Black, Sls. Mgr.-Touch Controls; Tom Coey, Coordinator-Sls./Distrib.; Don Conroy, Op. Mgr.-Membrane Switch; Bob Kranz, Op. Mgr.-Thermal Products; Steve Taylor, Op. Dir.-IMC Boards; Jeff Fishbein, Res./Devel. Mgr. The Bergquist Co. manufactures electronic components, insulation materials, and membrane switches for the electronics and automotive industries. 500 employees. Founded in 1964. In May 2000 the company bought the former Redmond Products building, a 130,000-square-foot headquarters and manufacturing facility in Chanhassen, Minn. In August the company announced TIC-7500 Thermal Interface Compound, a next-generation material that provides the low thermal resistance mandatory for increasingly faster and hotter microprocessors. SIC 3679, 5065.

Bermo Inc. 4501 Ball Rd. N.E., Circle Pines, MN 55014. Tel: 763/786-7676; Fax: 763/785-2159. Fred P. Berdass, Chm.; Daniel M. Berdass, Pres.; Jerry Atherton, VP-Sls./Engrg.; Robert J. Mycka, VP-Op.; Margo Berdass, Sec. and Treas. Annual revenue $175 million (estimated by Fact Book). Bermo manufactures metal stampings, fabricated metal assemblies, and plastic-injected molded parts. 675 employees. Founded in 1947. SIC 3465, 3469, 3599. No. 71 CRM Private 100.

Bernatello's Pizza P.O. Box 729, Maple Lake, MN 55358. Tel: 320/963-6191; Fax: 320/963-6447. Bill Ramsay, Pres.; Joe Casselius, Purch. Agent; Jim Cousin, Cont. and Purch. Agent; Clayton Lecy, Sls. Mgr. Bernatello's Pizza makes frozen pizza and deli items. 50 employees (all in Minnesota; 6 part-time). Founded in 1982. SIC 2038.

Chas. A. Bernick Inc. P.O. Box 7008, St. Cloud, MN 56302. Tel: 320/252-6441; Fax: 320/656-2121. Michael A. Heinen, Pres.; John Torgerson, Cont. Chas. A. Bernick Inc. is a Pepsi Cola bottler and beer distributor. 250 employees (all in Minnesota). Founded in 1935. SIC 2082.

Berwald Roofing Inc. 2440 Charles St. N., North St. Paul, MN 55109. Tel: 651/777-7411; Fax: 651/777-1371. Eugene Berwald, Pres.; Kenneth Berwald, VP. Berwald Roofing is in the roofing and sheet metal business. 100 employees. Founded in 1950. SIC 1761.

Best Brands Inc. 1765 Yankee Doodle Rd., Eagan, MN 55121. Tel: 651/454-5850; Fax: 651/454-0062. Ken Malecha, Pres.; Wayne Mosey, VP; Brad Wadsten, VP; Mike Schultz, VP. Best Brands makes and distributes bakery products and a complete line of packaging supplies and equipment, ingredients, frozen doughs for the baking industry. Local management purchased the company from Swiss food company Hero AG in June 1997. 340 employees (210 in Minnesota). Founded in 1971. SIC 2033, 2041, 5149.

Best Care Inc. 3014 University Ave. S.E., Minneapolis, MN 55414. Tel: 612/378-1040. Nazneen Khatoon, Pres. Best Care provides skilled nursing, home health aides, physical and occupational therapy, homemaking, live-ins, case management, and insurance assessment to 600 metro-area patients. 225 employees. Founded in 1990. SIC 8082.

Billings Truck Center Box 30236, Billings, MT 59107. Tel: 406/252-5121; Fax: 406/252-5910. Cliff Hanson, Pres. and CEO. Billings Truck Center is a truck dealership. 59 employees. Founded in 1957. SIC 5511.

Birchwood Laboratories Inc. 7900 Fuller Rd., Eden Prairie, MN 55344. Tel: 952/937-7900; Fax: 952/937-7979. Norman Villwock, Pres. and CEO; Daniel Brooks, VP; Mark Ruhland, VP; Stephen Souder, VP; Mike Shelton, VP; William Shannon, VP; Michael Wenner, VP. Birchwood Laboratories manufactures disposable medical dressings and supplies; gun-care products, accessories, and targets; and industrial metal-finishing chemicals. It also does contract packaging for other businesses. 94 employees. Founded in 1979. SIC 2842, 2899, 3842, 7389.

Birchwood Lumber & Veneer Company Inc. P.O. Box 68, Birchwood, WI 54817. Tel: 715/354-3441; Fax: 715/354-3786. B.G. Kennen, Chm. and Pres.; Ronald C. Hipp, EVP. Birchwood Lumber & Veneer is a manufacturer of door skins. 200 employees. Founded in 1959. SIC 2435.

Birdsall Sand & Gravel Company 2900 W. Chicago St., P.O. Box 767, Rapid City, SD 57709. Tel: 605/342-9250; Fax: 605/394-7246. Charles H. Lien, Chm.; Mike Vidal, Pres. Birdsall Sand & Gravel produces ready-mixed concrete, and sand and gravel. 78 employees (16 part-time). Founded in 1948. SIC 1442, 3273.

Bishop Fixture & Millwork Inc. 26611 Fallbrook Ave. N., Wyoming, MN 55092. Tel: 651/222-1859; Fax: 651/462-4210. Hub Nelson, Pres. Bishop Fixture & Millwork manufactures custom architectural millwork and fixtures—including hand rails and chair rails—for stores, hospitals, and banks. 120 employees. Founded in 1983. SIC 2431.

Blachowske Truck Line Inc. P.O. Box 530, Fairmont, MN 56031. Tel: 507/235-6621; Fax: 507/235-9163. Dwane K. Blachowske, Pres. Blachowske Truck Line is a common carrier shipping company specializing in dry bulk. It serves the 48 contiguous states and has a branch office in Brandon, South Dakota. 50 employees. Founded in 1959. SIC 4213.

Black Bear Casino & Hotel 1785 Highway 210, P.O. Box 777, Carlton, MN 55718. Tel: 218/878-2327. Michael Himango, Casino Mgr. Black Bear Casino & Hotel includes high-stakes bingo, the Black Bear Grill, the Skywalk Cafe, an arcade, live entertainment, pull tabs, casino perk parking, child care in the hotel, two gift shops, a convention center, a pool, and Jacuzzi rooms. 625 employees. Founded in 1993. SIC 7011.

Black Hills Gold by Coleman 5125 Highway 16 S., P.O. Box 6400, Rapid City, SD 57709. Tel: 605/394-3700; Fax: 605/394-3719. Dwight Sobczak Sr., Pres. and CEO; Dwight Sobczak Jr., VP-Sls./Mktg. Black Hills Gold by Coleman manufactures a complete line of Black Hills gold jewelry for men and women. 350 employees. Founded in 1983. SIC 3911.

Black Hills Jewelry Manufacturing Company 405 Canal St., P.O. Box 3100 (57709), Rapid City, SD 57701. Tel: 605/343-0157; Fax: 605/343-4683. Jack Malehorn, Pres. and CEO; Laurie Blomstrom, SVP-Op.; Charles G. Hull, VP-Fin. and CFO; Jan Myers, VP-Sls./Mktg.; Ruby Fender, VP-Hum. Res./CIO. Black Hills Jewelry manufactures tri-color gold jewelry under the trade name Landstrom's Original Black Hills Gold Creations. 201 employees. Founded in 1919. SIC 3911.

D.H. Blattner & Sons Inc. 400 County Rd. 50, Avon, MN 56310. Tel: 320/356-7351; Fax: 320/356-7392; Web site: http://www.dhblattner.com. Scott Blattner, Pres.; Roland I. Wiek, EVP; Stephen C. Blattner, CFO; Jim Potter, EVP-Op.; John Blattner, VP-Admin. Svs.; David Blattner Jr., VP; Chris Blattner, VP-Eqt. D.H. Blattner & Sons engages in highway heavy construction and contract mining. 450 employees (60 in Minnesota). Founded in 1907. SIC 1041, 1446, 1611, 1622.

Blue Rock Products Company P.O. Box 1708, Sidney, MT 59270. Tel: 406/482-3403. John L. Olson, Pres. and Owner; Tim Feeley, VP and Gen. Mgr.; Lance R. Averett, VP and Gen. Sls. Mgr.; Karen M. Olson Beeken, VP-Hum. Res. Blue Rock Products Co. bottles and distributes soft drinks and fruit juices. 100 employees. Founded in 1918. SIC 2086.

Bluewater 811 E. Maple, Mora, MN 55051. Tel: 320/679-3811; Fax: 320/679-3820. Al Hagen, SVP; Connie Nordlander, Dir.-Mktg. Bluewater (formerly Boatel Industries Inc.) manufactures luxury fiberglass motor yachts, yachts, and cruisers. 70 employees (all in Minnesota). Founded in 1954. SIC 3732.

Boelter Industries Inc. 202 Galewski Dr., P.O. Box 916, Winona, MN 55987. Tel: 507/452-2315; Fax: 507/452-2649. L.B. Boelter, Pres. and CEO; Dennis L. Boelter, VP and Gen. Mgr. Boelter designs and manufactures folding cartons and special paper products. 125 employees (110 in Minnesota). Founded in 1934. SIC 2657.

Boker's Inc. 3104 Snelling Ave., Minneapolis, MN 55406. Tel: 612/729-9365; Fax: 612/729-8910; Web site: http://www.bokers.com. W.C. Tedlund, Chm. and CEO; Amy Kersey, Pres.; Mark Kersey, VP; Barry Tedlund, VP; Linda Demma, Cont. and Treas.; Matthew J. Kisch Jr., Dir.-Admin. Annual revenue $15 million. Boker's manufactures metal stampings and non-standard flat washers. 141 employees (138 in Minnesota). Founded in 1919. SIC 3452, 3469.

Carl Bolander & Sons Company 251 Starkey St., P.O. Box 7216, St. Paul, MN 55107. Tel: 651/224-6299; Fax: 651/223-8197. David C. Bolander, Chm. and CEO; Bruce D. Bolander, Pres. and COO; Dorothy Bolander, EVP; Richard O'Gara, SVP; Dominique Najjar, Sec. and CFO; Timothy E. Gillen, Cont. and Treas. Bolander is engaged in excavating, grading, landfill construction and landfill remediation/closure, demolition, and pile driving. Subsidiary SKB Environmental, founded in 1983, is involved in demolition waste disposal, waste disposal, yard waste processing, and wood recycling. 275 employees (220 in Minnesota). Founded in 1924. SIC 1611.

Bolands Manufacturing Company 2300 Main St., Lino Lakes, MN 55038. Tel: 651/429-0273; Fax: 651/426-8691. Lee Marvin, Gen. Mgr.; Cindy Puent, Sls. Mgr. Bolands manufactures vinyl products, such as stadium cushions and raingear. 100 employees. Founded in 1979. SIC 3069.

Bolger Concept to Print 3301 Como Ave. S.E., Minneapolis, MN 55414. Tel: 651/645-6311; Fax: 651/645-1750; Web site: http://www.bolgerinc.com. Charles Bolger, Exec. Officer; Dik Bolger, Exec. Officer; Bill Dusek, Cont.; Mike Oslund, Sls. Mgr.; Julie Sullivan, Mktg. Dir. Annual revenue $18 million. Bolger provides solutions for marketing communications needs. Services include: graphic design, Web site design, multimedia, printing, mailing and fulfillment. 145 employees. Founded in 1936. In September 2000 the technology Web site designed by Bolger Concept to Print for The St. Paul Cos. received an award of excellence from the Insurance Marketing Communications Association. SIC 2732, 2752, 2791.

Bolton & Menk Inc. 515 N. Riverfront Dr., Mankato, MN 56001. Tel: 507/625-4171; Fax: 507/625-4177; Web site: http://www.boltonmenk.com. William Sayre, Chm.; Jon Rippke, Pres.; Robert Brown, VP; Bruce Firkins, VP; Nancy Thorkelson, Mktg. Coordinator; Robert Butterfield, Bus. Mgr. Annual revenue $13.8 million. Bolton & Menk is an engineering and surveying firm specializing in civil and environmental engineering and surveying services. Branch offices in Sleepy Eye, Burnsville, Fairmont, and Willmar, Minn.; Ames, Iowa; and Liberty, Mo. 200 employees (193 in Minnesota; 42 part-time). Founded in 1949. SIC 8711, 8713.

Bondhus Corporation 1400 E. Broadway, Monticello, MN 55362. Tel: 763/295-2162; Fax: 763/295-4440. John Bondhus, Pres. and CEO. Bondhus manufactures and markets (worldwide) standard and Balldriver hex tools in various styles. The company has sales offices in Germany and Japan, and a production facility in Barbados. 138 employees (94 in Minnesota). Founded in 1965. SIC 3423.

Bonestroo Rosene Anderlik Associates Inc. 2335 W. Highway 36, Roseville, MN 55113. Tel: 651/636-4600; Fax: 651/636-1311. Otto Bonestroo, Chm. and CEO; Marvin Sorvala, Pres.; Joseph Anderlik, EVP; Jerry Bourdon, COO; Glenn Cook, VP; Robert Schunicht, VP. Bonestroo Rosene Anderlik Associates is an engineering and architectural firm offering civil, environmental, and municipal design services. The firm also provides electrical, structural, transportation, hydraulics, and water resources engineering. In addition to its corporate headquarters, the firm has three office locations in Minnesota: Rochester, managed by Dale Grove; Willmar, managed by Dale Swanson; and St. Cloud (Bonestroo Williamson Kotsmith), managed by Sid Williamson. It also has an office in Mequon, Wis., managed by Rick Schmidt. 245 employees (212 in Minnesota; 15 part-time). Founded in 1956. SIC 8711, 8712.

Bongards Creameries Inc. 13200 County Rd. 51, Bongards, MN 55368. Tel: 763/466-5521; Fax: 763/466-5556. Roger Engelmann, Pres.; Tom Otto, Gen. Mgr.; Allen Lingen, VP; Kevin Sons, Sec. and Treas. Annual revenue $186 million. Bongards Creameries manufactures cheese, processed cheese, whey powder, ice cream blends, and bakery blends. 270 employees (all in Minnesota). Founded in 1908. SIC 2022. No. 12 CRM Cooperatives/Mutuals 20.

Border States Industries 105 25th St. N., P.O. Box 2767, Fargo, ND 58108. Tel: 701/293-5834; Fax: 701/237-9811. Paul Madson, CEO; Brad Thrall, Pres.; Greg Hoffelt, SVP-Info. Tech; Tammy Miller, SVP-Fin. Annual revenue $290 million. Border States Industries is a 21-branch wholesale electrical distributor serving the industrial MRO, industrial OEM, contractor, communications, commercial, and utility markets in 10 states. Border States Electric Supply, Plymouth (Roger Labahn, NE Regional Mgr.), is the Minnesota division. 630 employees (100 in Minnesota). Founded in 1952. SIC 5063.

Border States Paving Inc. Cass County Road 20, P.O. Box 2586, Fargo, ND 58108. Tel: 701/237-4860; Fax: 701/237-0233. Lloyd O. Thompson, Chm.; Dan Thompson, Pres.; Nancy Slotten, EVP and Treas.; Thomas Lee, Sec.; Donald Carlson, VP. Border States Paving is engaged in highway, airport, and municipal construction. 175 employees (25 in Minnesota; 140 part-time). Founded in 1967. SIC 1611.

BORN 294 E. Grove Ln., Suite 100, Wayzata, MN 55391. Tel: 952/404-4000; Fax: 952/404-4444; Web site: http://www.born.com. Richard Born, CEO; Dale Holmgren, Pres.; Ron Froehling, VP-Sls./Mktg.; Jim Mohs, VP-Op. Nat'l; Donald E. Berg, CFO; Robert E. Woods, Gen. Counsel. Annual revenue $155 million. BORN, formerly Born Information Services, is an e-business and information technology consulting company. The company offers a broad portfolio of e-business and technology solutions from its offices throughout North America. BORN is differentiated by its tradition of unsurpassed technology expertise; its strong track record of delivery; and its experienced, enthusiastic people. An industry leader in employee and customer satisfaction, the company has been ranked on the Inc. 500 list of the fastest-growing U.S. private companies for four of the past five years. 1,000 employees. Founded in 1990. In February 2000 BORN's Dallas office joined with Data General, a Division of EMC Corp. (NYSE: EMC) and Microsoft Corp. to launch a new Business Solutions Center, designed to deliver comprehensive business intelligence and knowledge management solutions to a variety of customers. James M. Prebil, formerly of Gelco Information Network, joined the company as its e-business managing director. (At the time, more than 60 percent of BORN's business was focused on providing e-business solutions for customers.) In April BORN was contracted by E-CityDesk.com Inc. to provide complete system integration and business process development services for its online procurement site. E-CityDesk.com is an independent trading exchange specializing in the distribution of products and services for the HVAC, plumbing, and electrical products industries. BORN achieved Premier certified partner with Cisco Systems Inc. In May BORN representatives were appointed to three strategic Microsoft Certified Solution Provider Partner (MCSP) Advisory Councils—the Microsoft Infrastructure Advisory Council (Joel Roetzer, Infrastructure Technology Solution Manager, Minneapolis); the Microsoft Business Intelligence Advisory Council (Dave Williams, Business Unit Leader for Business Intelligence, Dallas); and the Microsoft Windows DNA Advisory Council (Nick Zimmer, Technical Solutions Leader, Microsoft e-Commerce Practice, Milwaukee). In June BORN announced an innovative new suite of solution services to empower businesses to get the most from their J.D. Edwards enterprise software.

In July BORN announced a collaboration with ReliaStar Life Insurance Co. to develop an e-business solution for the firm's worksite business, as well as train ReliaStar's information technology staff on cutting-edge Internet technologies for bringing the company's new offerings to market. BORN was selected by Trek Bicycle Corp., a leading bicycle and accessory manufacturer and distributor, to integrate its U.S. and European financial, distribution, inventory management, pricing, and sales order management systems through a customized installation of J.D. Edwards OneWorld software. BORN announced a strategic alliance with Manugistics Group Inc. (Nasdaq: MANU), a leading global provider of intelligent supply chain solutions for enterprises and evolving e-business trading networks; and an agreement to work with FreightWise Inc. to help the company launch a new business-to-business (B2B) Internet marketplace for transportation services. Full-page ads appeared in September issues of Fast Company, BusinessWeek, Fortune, Fortune Small Business, Entrepreneur, Kiplinger's Personal Finance, Money, and Mutual Funds, launching a new national print and radio advertising campaign focused on communicating BORN's brand as a high-tech consultancy that has a long track record of delivering innovative e-business and technology solutions. An alliance agreement was to provide Nistevo Corp.'s growing network members a wide range of BORN's supply chain consulting services. In October BORN announced plans to move its headquarters from the Boatworks on Lake Minnetonka in March 2001 in order to consolidate its local operations at the Carlson Center. Later in the month, BORN underwent its first-ever round of job cuts, laying off 70 employees (35 in the Twin Cities), or 6.5 percent of its workforce. SIC 7371. No. 87 CRM Private 100. No. 15 CityBusiness Fastest-growing Private Companies.

BOR-SON Construction Inc. 2001 Killebrew Dr., Suite 141, P.O. Box 1611, Bloomington, MN 55440. Tel: 952/854-8444; Fax: 952/854-8910. Wm. Arthur Young, Pres.; James Mrozek, Sec. and Treas.; Raymond Schwartz, VP-Estimating; Roger Raaum, VP-Field Op.; Frank Delmont, Dir.-Sls./Mktg.; James Slinger, Senior Proj. Mgr.; James Williams, Dir.-Risk Mgmt. Annual revenue $150 million. As one of the Midwest's largest and most diversified construction firms, BOR-SON provides preconstruction planning, design/build, construction management, and general construction services. The employee-owned company specializes in commercial, industrial, institutional, healthcare and multihousing projects. 350 employees (all in Minnesota). Founded in 1957. SIC 1522, 1541, 1542, 8741. No. 83 CRM Private 100.

Boulay, Heutmaker, Zibell & Company PLLP 5151 Edina Industrial Blvd., Suite 500, Edina, MN 55439. Tel: 952/893-9320; Fax: 952/835-7296; Web site: http://www.bhz.com. Rick Burrock, Managing Ptnr. Annual revenue $11.9 million. Boulay, Heutmaker, Zibell & Co. (BHZ) is one of the Midwest's leading independent accounting firms. Our clients range in size from sole proprietorships to larger companies. In addition to traditional tax, audit and accounting services, BHZ services include mergers and acquisitions, litigation support, business valuations, computers and technology, management consulting, securities and exchange commission services, small-business services, employee benefits and personal financial planning. 130 employees (12 part-time). Founded in 1934. SIC 8721.

Bouquet Enterprises Inc. 233 Glasgow Ave. S.W., Kellogg, MN 55945. Tel: 507/767-4994; Fax: 507/767-4766. Thomas Bouquet, Pres.; Carol J. Bouquet, VP and Sec.; Julie Brugermeirer, Sls. Mgr.; Angela Dodge, Mktg. Dir.; Kirk Lineweaver, Cont. Annual revenue $7 million. Bouquet Enterprises is a manufacturer/importer of giftware and decorative accessories. It wholesales to gift stores, department stores and catalog companies throughout the United States, Canada, and Europe. 80 employees (65 in Minnesota; 6 part-time). SIC 3269, 5199.

Bowman and Brooke LLP 150 S. Fifth St., Suite 2600, Minneapolis, MN 55402. Tel: 612/339-8682; Fax: 612/672-3200; Web site: http://www.bowman-brooke.com. Richard A. Bowman, Managing Ptnr.; Michelle M. Bailey, Chief of Op. Annual revenue $29 million. Bowman and Brooke LLP is a law firm, with a focus on litigation. Other offices: Detroit; San Jose, Calif.; Phoenix; Los Angeles; and Richmond, Virginia. 212 employees (80 in Minnesota; 18 part-time). Founded in 1985. SIC 8111.

Brandtjen & Kluge Inc. 539 Blanding Woods Rd., St. Croix Falls, WI 54024. Tel: 715/483-3265; Fax: 715/483-1640. Hank Brandtjen III, Pres.; Mark A. Maegaard, CFO. Brandtjen & Kluge manufactures graphic arts equipment, including foil-stamping presses, short-run continuous-form presses, die-cutting presses, and related equipment. 90 employees. Founded in 1919. SIC 3555.

Branick Industries Inc. 4245 Main Ave., Fargo, ND 58102. Tel: 701/281-8888; Fax: 701/281-5900. Duane E. Brasch, Pres. and CEO. Branick Industries manufactures retreading equipment and automotive specialty tools. 70 employees. Founded in 1923. SIC 3559.

Braun Intertec Corporation 6875 Washington Ave. S., Eden Prairie, MN 55439. Tel: 952/941-5600; Fax: 952/833-4701; Web site: http://www.brauncorp.com. J.S. (Jack) Braun, Founder and Chm. Emeritus; George D. Kluempke, Pres. and CEO; Cameron G. Kruse, SVP and Chief Tech. Officer; Charles Brenner, VP; Michael Heuer, VP and Corp. Compliance Ofcr.; Richard Ross, VP, Dir.-Hum. Res.; Scott Barnard, Treas.; Jodi Norman, Corp. Sec. Annual revenue $35 million. Braun Intertec is an engineering, consulting and testing firm providing solutions for property development, redevelopment, facilities management and infrastructure related issues. It provides services to clients during each stage of development from the pre-project geotechnical and environmental evaluations through materials evaluation during construction and property management issues. Services are provided on a national and international basis from 12 office locations. 400 employees. Founded in 1957. In February 2000 the company sold its energy and industrial groups to Omaha, Neb.-based HDR Engineering Inc. The business groups represented only 5 percent of Braun's total revenue and workforce. SIC 8711, 8734.

Brede Exposition Services 2211 Broadway St. N.E., Minneapolis, MN 55413. Tel: 612/331-4540; Fax: 612/331-8380. William Casey Sr., CEO; William Casey III, Pres.; James McNeill, EVP; Harlan Sandberg, Treas. and Cont. Brede is a convention-services contractor. 100 employees. Founded in 1898. SIC 3993, 7389.

Bremer Financial Corporation 445 Minnesota St., Suite 2000, St. Paul, MN 55101. Tel: 651/227-7621; Fax: 651/312-3550; Web site: http://www.bremer.com. Terry M. Cummings, Chm.; Stan K. Dardis, Pres. and CEO; Charlotte S. Johnson, VP; William H. Lipschultz, VP; Daniel C. Reardon, VP; Kenneth P. Nelson, EVP and Group Pres.; John Wosepka, EVP and Community Banking Dir.; Robert Buck, SVP and CFO; Ann Hengel, SVP and Risk Mgmt. Dir.; Ernest W. (Bud) Jensen, SVP and Chief Credit Officer; Carla Paulsen, SVP and Dir.-Hum. Res.; Todd Sipe, SVP and Retail Banking Svs. Dir.; Stuart F. Bradt, Cont.; Janice A. Aus, Sec.; Steven Meads, Pres./CEO-Bremer Bank Twin Cities. Annual revenue $316.9 million (earnings $40.1 million; assets $4.09 billion). Bremer Financial Corp. has 97 banking locations—in Minnesota (50), North Dakota (31), and Wisconsin (16). The company provides a broad range of financial services to individuals, businesses, and agriculture. Ninety-two percent of the company is owned by the Otto Bremer Foundation, a charitable trust that returns earnings to communities via grants supportive of childhood education, opportunities for youth, and rural issues. The other 8 percent is owned by employees. 1,700 employees. Founded in 1943. Dec. 31, 1999: Fiscal-year net interest income was $139.1 million, an increase of 12 percent from 1998, as a result of continued strong loan growth and an increase in the net interest margin. Revenue was up 6.8 percent. The drop of 3.4 percent in net earnings was due to additional operating costs related to acquired entities; an increase in the provision for credit losses; and the absence of last year's one-time state tax refund of $4.5 million. In January 2000 Bremer gained federal approval to acquire Northwest Equity Corp., Amery, Wis., and its subsidiary, $100 million-asset Northwest Savings Bank. [Deal completed in March.] Sept. 30: Bremer reported nine-month net income of $33.8 million, an increase of 16.5 percent over the same period a year ago. Year-to-date average assets increased by 13.1 percent. CEO Dardis believed Bremer's local decision-making philosophy, which empowers employees to manage the relationship at the client level, to be critical to the organization's ability to continue that growth trend. SIC 6712. No. 42 CRM Private 100.

C.G. Bretting Manufacturing Company 3401 Lake Park Rd., Ashland, WI 54806. Tel: 715/682-5231; Fax: 715/682-4138. Tad Bretting, Chm. and Pres.; David Bretting, COO. C.G. Bretting designs and manufactures contract machining and paper-converting equipment: napkin folders, printers, and towel folders. 475 employees. Founded in 1890. SIC 3554.

Bridgeman's Ice Cream Shoppe 5700 Smetana Dr., Minnetonka, MN 55343. Tel: 952/931-3099; Fax: 952/931-3199; Web site: http://www.bridgemans.com. Steve Lampi, Pres.; Patrick Janisch, Op. Mgr. Bridgeman's is a chain of 31 franchised restaurants in Minnesota, Wisconsin, and Iowa. 500 employees (300 part-time). Founded in 1936. SIC 5812.

Bridon Cordage Inc. 909 E. 16th St., P.O. Box 449, Albert Lea, MN 56007. Tel: 507/377-1601; Fax: 507/377-7221. William J. Adams, Pres. Bridon manufactures polypropylene baling twine for the agricultural industry. Formerly a subsidiary of Bridon plc; now owned locally. 100 employees. Founded in 1975. SIC 2298.

Briggs and Morgan P.A. 2200 First National Bank Building, St. Paul, MN 55101. Tel: 651/223-6600; Fax: 651/223-6450; Web site: http://www.briggs.com. Jeffrey F. Shaw, Pres.; Richard G. Mark, VP; Michael J. Grimes, Treas.; Brian Wenger, Sec. Briggs and Morgan is a 155-attorney regional law firm. Practice areas include business law and commercial litigation, antitrust, appellate, construction, e-commerce, employee benefits, entrepreneurial services, environmental, banking and financial services, franchise, health care, intellectual property and technology, labor and employment, mergers and acquisitions, probate and trust, public finance, real estate, securities and securities litigation, tax, transportation, trade regulation, telecommunications, and utilities. Its practice is evenly divided between its two Twin Cities offices. Its Minneapolis office is located at 2400 IDS Center, Minneapolis, MN, 55402; telephone: 612-334-8400; fax: 612-334-8650. 350 employees (all in Minnesota). Founded in 1882. SIC 8111.

Brin-Northwestern Glass Company 2300 N. Second St., Minneapolis, MN 55411. Tel: 612/529-9671; Fax: 612/529-9670. Douglas M. Nelson, CEO; Patrick Rome, Pres. Brin-Northwestern Glass distributes and installs glass and aluminum framing. Subsidiaries include Hentges Glass, Rochester, Minn.; Heartland Glass, St. Cloud, Minn.; Moose Lake Paint & Glass, Moose Lake, Minn.; A&C Johnson Paint Co., La Crosse, Wis.; Piltz Glass & Mirror Inc., Eau Claire, Wis.; and St. Germain Glass Co., St. Germain Cabinet Co., and St. Germain Paint Co., Duluth, Minn. 180 employees (175 in Minnesota; 10 part-time). Founded in 1912. SIC 1793, 1799, 3211, 3231, 5231.

Brink Electric Construction Company 2950 N. Plaza Dr., Rapid City, SD 57702. Tel: 605/342-6966; Fax: 605/342-5905. Douglas Brink, Pres. Brink Electric performs electrical construction work. 100 employees. Founded in 1946. SIC 1731.

Brissman-Kennedy Inc. 295 Pennsylvania Ave. E., St. Paul, MN 55101. Tel: 651/646-7933; Fax: 651/645-6395; Web site: http://www.brissman-kennedy.com. Chris Norgren, Chm., Pres., and CEO; Stewart Erck, VP-Sls.; Geoff Miller, VP-Fin. Brissman-Kennedy is a wholesaler and retailer of janitorial cleaning supplies and equipment. 78 employees (55 in Minnesota). Founded in 1947. SIC 2842.

Brock-White Company 2575 Kasota Ave., St. Paul, MN 55108. Tel: 651/647-0950; Fax: 651/647-0403. W. Brock, Chm.; Richard Garland, Pres.; Dale Williamson, EVP; G. White, VP; N. O'Leary, Sec. Brock-White is a wholesaler of construction specialty products and material. It has 12 offices throughout the Upper Midwest and prairie Canada. 170 employees. Founded in 1954. SIC 5039.

Broncho Company Inc. 522 W. 27th St., Hibbing, MN 55746. Tel: 218/263-8366; Fax: 218/262-6478. James Rhude, Pres.; Pat Garrity, Cont.; Michael P. Riley, Sec. and Treas.; Cary Rhude, Mgr. Broncho Co., dba Electric Power Door Co., designs and manufactures customized, heavy-industrial metal doors for companies nationwide. 50 employees (all in Minnesota). Founded in 1987. SIC 3442.

Brookdale Plastics Inc. 9909 South Shore Dr., Plymouth, MN 55441. Tel: 763/797-1000; Fax: 763/797-5252; Web site: http://www.brookdaleplastics.com. Robert Kramer, Pres.; Steve Eichten, CFO; Joe Meirell, Plant Mgr.; Lynn Weiss, Sls./Mktg. Mgr. Annual revenue $7 million. Brookdale Plastics is widely regarded as a major innovator in the plastic thermoforming industry. The company forms plastic packaging and components for a wide variety of industries including electronic/components devices, OEM's medical, point-of-purchase, and consumer product manufacturers. 60 employees (all in Minnesota). Founded in 1963. SIC 3089.

Bro-Tex Co. Inc. 800 Hampden Ave., St. Paul, MN 55114. Tel: 651/645-5721; Fax: 651/646-1876; Web site: http://www.brotex.com. Roger H. Greenberg, Chm. and Pres.; Edwin C. Freeman, VP and Gen. Mgr. Bro-Tex is a full-service converter and manufacturer of disposable and cloth wipers (BX 100-brand wipers) and sorbent products. Bro-Tex recycles textile waste into a sound-deadening material for use in the automotive industry, bedding, and carpet underlayment. 100 employees (95 in Minnesota). Founded in 1923. SIC 2211, 2299, 2679.

Brown & Bigelow Inc. 345 Plato Blvd. E., St. Paul, MN 55107. Tel: 651/293-7000; Fax: 651/293-7277. William D. Smith, Pres. and Owner; William D. Smith Jr., EVP; Philip R. Jungwirth, SVP-Admin. Brown & Bigelow manufactures and markets calendars, playing cards, and other advertising and promotional products. 1,000 employees. Founded in 1896. SIC 2752, 5199.

Brown-Wilbert Inc. 2280 N. Hamline Ave., Roseville, MN 55113. Tel: 651/631-1234; Fax: 651/631-1428. Christopher C. Brown, Pres.; Jerry J. Brown, CEO; Don Vomhof, CFO. Brown-Wilbert manufactures precast concrete products, principally burial vaults. The company has 14 manufacturing locations in Minnesota, Wisconsin, and North Dakota. 150 employees. Founded in 1922. SIC 3272.

Bruegger's Bagel Bakery 1433 E. Franklin Ave., Suite 3B, P.O. Box 13257 (55414), Minneapolis, MN 55404. Tel: 612/871-8483; Fax: 612/871-1697. J. Kurt Schreck, Co-owner; Kari Schreck, Co-owner; Thomas Alf, Cont. Bruegger's Bagel Bakery operates 32 stores that serve bagels, bagel sandwiches, and soups. 750 employees. Founded in 1984. SIC 5461.

Buerkle Buick-Honda Company 3350 Highway 61 N., Vadnais Heights, MN 55110. Tel: 651/484-0231; Fax: 651/484-9463; Web site: http://www.buerkle.com. W.W. Buerkle, Pres. Annual revenue $68 million. Buerkle Buick-Honda is a motor vehicle dealer. 130 employees (all in Minnesota; 5 part-time). Founded in 1953. SIC 5511.

Buff 'N Shine Center 10820 W. Bush Lake Rd., Bloomington, MN 55438. Tel: 952/944-9033; Fax: 952/253-1921. Harry Schleeter, Owner and Pres. Buff 'N Shine is a chain of full-service car wash and detailing businesses in the Minneapolis metro area. Holding company: Auto Butler Inc. 220 employees. SIC 7542.

Buffalo Wings Inc. 1919 Interchange Tower, 600 S. Highway 169, Minneapolis, MN 55426. Tel: 612/593-9943; Fax: 612/593-9787; Web site: http://www.buffalowings.com. Sally J. Smith, Pres. and CEO; Stephen E. David, COO and EVP; Mary J. Twinem, CFO, Sec., and Treas. Annual revenue $50 million, an increase of 50 percent ($150 million systemwide revenue). The company operates and franchises Buffalo Wild Wings Grill and Bar restaurants. As of Nov. 10, 2000, there were 128 restaurants in 20 states. The company planned to open seven more by year's end. 1,500 employees (200 in Minnesota; 1,200 part-time). SIC 5812.

Buffets Inc. 1460 Buffet Way, Eagan, MN 55121. Tel: 651/994-8608; Fax: 651/365-2356; Web site: http://www.buffet.com. Roe H. Hatlen, Chm. and Exec. Ofcr.-Devel.; C. Dennis Scott, VChm.; Kerry A. Kramp, Pres. and CEO; David Goronkin, COO; R. Michael Andrews Jr., EVP and CFO; Glenn D. Drasher, EVP-Marketing; Harold T. Mitchell III, EVP, Gen. Counsel, Sec., CAO; Jean C. Rostollan, EVP-Purchasing; Michael C. Shrader, EVP-Human

Resources/Training; Clark C. Grant, SVP-Fin. and Treasurer; Neal L. Wichard, SVP-Real Estate; David T. Crowley, VP-Devel./Construction; Brent P. DeMesquita, VP-Hum. Res. Planning/Org'l Development; Brad J. McNaught, VP-Real Estate; Marguerite C. Nesset, VP-Acctg. and Controller; Ken W. Smith, VP-Field Training; David A. Wagner, VP-Info. Sys. Annual revenue $936.9 million (earnings $42.4 million). Buffets operates a chain of buffet-style restaurants. The company's restaurants, operating under the names Old Country Buffet and Hometown Buffet, offer a wide variety of soups, salads, entrees, vegetables, nonalcoholic beverages, and desserts presented in a self-service buffet format. The company uses a "scatter system" of eight buffet islands (instead of a traditional straight-line system) in most of its stores. On Dec. 29, 1999, Buffets was operating 126 Hometown Buffets, 254 Old Country Buffets, 11 Original Roadhouse Grills, three Country Roadhouse Buffet & Grills, six Granny's Buffets, one Soup'n Salad Unlimited, and two Tahoe Joe's Famous Steakhouses—a total of 403 restaurants in 37 states. In addition, the company had 24 franchised restaurants in 10 states. Formerly a publicly traded company, Buffets was taken private in October 2000 by an affiliate of Caxton-Iseman Capital Inc., a New York-based private equity firm, and Buffets management. 25,000 employees. Founded in 1983. In December 1999 the company acquired six Granny's Buffet Restaurants in Washington, Idaho, and Montana through a cash-based asset purchase. In June 2000 Buffets and Caxton-Iseman Capital Inc. announced a definitive agreement under which an affiliate of Caxton-Iseman Capital was to acquire Buffets for $13.85 in cash for each common share—a 14 percent premium over the market price before the deal was announced—for a total consideration of $665 million. Following completion of the transaction, Buffets was to continue to be headquartered in Eagan and to be operated as a private company under the leadership of Kerry A. Kramp. Existing Buffets senior managers were expected to own 16 percent of the common stock of the company. A commitment for senior debt financing for the transaction had been received from Lehman Brothers Inc. and FleetBoston Robertson Stephens Inc. Committed mezzanine financing had been arranged by Credit Suisse First Boston. Management's frustration with the company's stagnant stock price was an element driving the sale. July 12: Restaurant sales for the 28-week period were $542.9 million, up 8.4 percent from prior year. Net earnings of $27.4 million were up 22.8 percent. After a special meeting of shareholders had comfortably approved the going-private merger, which was then valued at $643 million, the deal was consummated on Oct. 2. A week later, W.P. Carey & Co. LLC (NYSE: WPC), a leader in the ownership and net leasing of corporate properties, closed on the acquisition of Buffets' headquarters facility. The sale-leaseback transaction was done as part of the financing of the management buyout. SIC 5812. No. 40 CRM Public 200.

Bureau of Engraving Inc. 3400 Technology Dr., Minneapolis, MN 55418. Tel: 612/362-5100; Fax: 612/788-7792. Thomas R. Stuart, Chm. and CEO; Arnold Stull, CFO. Bureau of Engraving engages in web and sheetfed offset printing. It also operates a complete bindery facility. The company specializes in the fields of graphic arts, home-study education, and the manufacture of printed circuit boards. 750 employees (700 in Minnesota; 25 part-time). Founded in 1898. SIC 2752, 2759, 2789, 3679.

Burgess International Group Inc. 7110 Ohms Ln., Edina, MN 55439. Tel: 952/924-2495; Fax: 952/831-3167. Bernard J. Brey, Pres. Burgess International Group does textbook publishing, book printing and binding, commercial printing, and desktop publishing. 150 employees. Founded in 1918. SIC 2731, 2759.

Butterfield Foods Company 225 Hubbard Ave., P.O. Box 229, Butterfield, MN 56120. Tel: 507/956-5103; Fax: 507/956-5751. Richard A. Downs, Pres. Butterfield Foods manufactures frozen specialties and chicken products. 140 employees. Founded in 1947. SIC 2015.

Bystrom Brothers Inc. 2200 Snelling Ave. S., Minneapolis, MN 55404. Tel: 612/721-7511; Fax: 612/721-6745. Mikeal Bystrom Sr., Pres. Bystrom Brothers custom-manufactures steel and brass products, specializing in components for factories and manufacturers. 150 employees (all in Minnesota). Founded in 1954. SIC 3451.

CBR Inc. 2040 St. Clair Ave., St. Paul, MN 55105. Tel: 651/690-1050; Fax: 651/690-0440. Carole Howe, CEO; Jim Steton, COO; David Barthold, EVP. Annual revenue $12 million. CBR is a specialty retailer in airports. 165 employees (55 in Minnesota; 110 part-time). Founded in 1974. SIC 5999.

CBSA 10159 Wayzata Blvd., Minnetonka, MN 55305. Tel: 952/541-0444; Fax: 952/545-6235. Clifford Koltes, Pres.; James McMahil, EVP; Peter Royse, VP-Self-funded Sls.; Craig Nelson, VP-Group Op. Annual revenue $38 million. CBSA (formerly Corporate Benefit Services of America) provides employee benefits and third-party administrative services. 550 employees (400 in Minnesota; 25 part-time). Founded in 1971. SIC 6411.

CES International 3140 Harbor Ln. N., Plymouth, MN 55447. Tel: 612/553-7912; Fax: 612/553-7706; Web site: http://www.ces.com. Kenneth I. Geisler, Pres. and CEO. CES International is the global leader in Internet-based, real-time infrastructure reliability solutions. The CES Centricity operations resource management system helps companies in the deregulating utility, transportation, and telecommunications markets meet mission-critical, customer service, and infrastructure reliability imperatives through the deployment of e-business solutions. 100 employees. Founded in 1990. SIC 7372.

The Companies of CHB & Hennepin Home Health 6200 Shingle Creek Pkwy., Suite 350, Brooklyn Center, MN 55430. Tel: 763/521-0072; Fax: 763/560-9560. Claudette L. Heywood, Pres. CHB & Hennepin Home Health is a home-care company performing a variety of services in clients' homes. 525 employees. Founded in 1974. SIC 8361.

CPS Technology Solutions 10205 51st Ave. N., Plymouth, MN 55442. Tel: 763/553-1514; Fax: 763/553-9058; Web site: http://www.cpsmn.com. Robert B. Kennedy, Pres.; Michael L. Jensen, VP. CPS Technology Solutions sells and repairs IBM midrange computers, PC equipment, and peripherals. 73 employees. Founded in 1983. SIC 5045, 7378.

CSM Corporation 2575 University Ave. W., Suite 150, St. Paul, MN 55114. Tel: 651/646-1717; Fax: 651/646-2404; Web site: http://www.csmcorp.net. Gary S. Holmes, Pres.; David Carland, VP; Steve Dubbs, VP-Lodging; James Ottenstein, CFO. CSM Corp. is involved in real estate acquisition, leasing, development, investment, and property management. 400 employees. Founded in 1973. In December 1999 the company fully leased a 367,000-square-foot industrial campus in Chanhassen, Minn., that was still under development. In March 2000 CSM said it was planning to build a water park in the Marriott Hotels (Milwaukee Road Depot renovation project) in order to attract weekend family visitors. In May CSM Lodging LLC, a division of CSMCorp., announced the formation of a $100 million dollar fund for the acquisition of existing hotels, as a continuation of its aggressive growth strategy. "With our ability to finance all projects internally, we plan to capitalize on a marketplace that was saturated with new hotels over the past few years," said VP Dubbs. "At a time when lenders are less likely to finance hotel projects, we see a tremendous opportunity to grow our business through acquisitions." In June CSM and Lutheran Brotherhood, Minneapolis, were reportedly in negotiations to jointly purchase the ADC

Telecommunications Inc. headquarters in Minnetonka, Minn. (assessed value $17.5 million). In July, seeing a demand for space in the area, CSM proposed to build a 110,000-square-foot, two-story office building with some industrial space in Eden Prairie, Minn. The 131-suite Towne Place Suites by Marriott opened in October in the Warehouse District. CSM was also developing an $8 million, 120-room Courtyard by Marriott in the Centre Pointe Business Park in Roseville, Minn. SIC 6512.

Calhoun Beach Club—Minneapolis Inc. 2925 Dean Pkwy., Minneapolis, MN 55416. Tel: 612/927-9951; Fax: 612/925-8307. Gary Benson, Owner. Calhoun Beach Club is a private athletic and social club complete with multipurpose athletic facility, private dining room, public grill, and catering service. 110 employees. Founded in 1977. SIC 7997.

Cambridge Metal & Plastics 200 S. Cleveland St., Cambridge, MN 55008. Tel: 763/689-4800; Fax: 763/689-3339. Curtis Hough, Pres.; JoAnn Peterson, Cont.; George Yacevich, Gen. Mgr. Cambridge Metal & Plastics manufactures snowmobile, motorcycle, RV, and ATV accessories; does sheet metal fabrication and contract manufacturing; and makes metal stampings. 230 employees. Founded in 1937. SIC 3444, 3469, 3544, 3599, 3799.

Capella Education Company 330 Second Ave. S., Suite 550, Minneapolis, MN 55402. Tel: 612/339-7665; Web site: http://www.capellauniversity.edu. Stephen Shank, CEO; Stephen Weiss, Pres. and COO. Annual revenue $8.4 million. Capella Education Co., formerly Learning Ventures, provides distance learning for higher education and training markets. Capella Education Co. is the for-profit parent of Capella University, an accredited, fully online university located in Minneapolis. Through its Web-based campus, Capella University offers a wide variety of courses and degree programs that are created especially for working adults. Capella University currently has enrollment of more than 1,600 students in 20 countries and all 50 states. 128 employees. Founded in 1993. In June 2000 Capella University's Harold Abel School of Psychology became the first fully online psychology program to receive approval from the American Psychological Association (APA) for its continuing professional education courses. Capella University launched an undergraduate IT program designed specifically to produce technology experts who can meet the needs of American employers. In July the rapidly growing company was planning to lease three floors (57,000 square feet) of the Piper Jaffray Tower in downtown Minneapolis to house up to 265 employees by 2001. A national survey of working adults revealed that 54 percent believed that college courses offered via the Internet are the future of higher education. In October the company was named one of the fastest-growing privately held companies in the country by Inc. magazine. SIC 8299. No. 5 CityBusiness Fastest-growing Private Companies.

Cardinal IG Company 12301 Whitewater Dr., Suite 250, Minnetonka, MN 55343. Tel: 952/935-1722; Fax: 952/935-5538. Adelyn Luther, Chm.; Roger O'Shaughnessy, Pres. Annual revenue $320 million (estimated by Fact Book). Cardinal manufactures insulating glass units for original equipment manufacturers. 2,000 employees. Founded in 1962. SIC 3229, 3231. No. 41 CRM Private 100.

Cardinal Industries Inc. 724 Commerce St., Aberdeen, SD 57401. Tel: 605/225-7862; Fax: 605/225-7929. R.A. Proudfit, Chm., Pres., and CEO. Cardinal Industries does custom moldings of plastic and rubber, and custom products assembly. It has a branch plant located in Aberdeen, S.D. 125 employees. Founded in 1964. SIC 3061, 3089.

Cargill Inc. 15407 McGinty Rd. W., Minnetonka, MN 55391. Tel: 952/742-6000; Fax: 952/742-7393; Web site: http://www.cargill.com. Warren R. Staley, Chm. and CEO; Gregory R. Page, Pres. and COO; Robert L. Lumpkins, VChm. and CFO; F. Guillaume Bastiaens, VChm.; David W. Raisbeck, VChm.; Fredric W. Corrigan, EVP; David M. Larson, EVP; Hubertus P. Spierings, EVP. Annual revenue $47.6 billion (earnings $480 million; earnings include certain asset write-downs). Cargill is an international marketer, processor and distributor of agricultural, food, financial and industrial products and services with operations in 60 countries. The company provides supply chain management, food applications and health and nutrition. The company's major businesses include the trading and processing of grains and oilseeds, fruits and fruit juices, tropical commodities and fibers, meats and eggs, salt, and petroleum; the production and sale of feeds and fertilizers; the manufacture and sale of steel; transportation; financial trading and futures brokerage; and agricultural consulting services. Cargill operations are located in 60 countries worldwide. Directors: Marianne Leibmann, William B. MacMillan, John H. MacMillan IV, Greg M. Stitzer, Susan M. Cargill, Gregory R. Page, Robert L. Lumpkins, Warren R. Staley, F. Guillaume Bastiaens, David W. Raisbeck, Arthur D. Collins Jr. (Medtronic Inc.), Livio D. DeSimone (3M Co.), Richard M. Kovacevich (Wells Fargo & Co.), Michael H. Armacost (The Brookings Institution), Michael W. Wright (Supervalu Inc.), S. Curtis Johnson (S.C. Johnson & Son Inc.), and John C. MacMillan. 85,000 employees. Founded in 1865. In November 1999 Sunny Fresh Foods, Monticello, Minn., the egg further-processing business of Cargill, won the prestigious Malcolm Baldrige National Quality Award—one of only four winners in the nation and two in Minnesota (the other being BI Performance Services, Edina), as well as the first-ever food manufacturer to win the award. The nation's second-largest egg processor, next to St. Louis Park, Minn.-based Michael Foods (Nasdaq: MIKL), 380-employee Sunny Fresh supplies the egg patty inside McDonald's Corp.'s breakfast sandwiches. Nov. 30: Cargill reported a much-improved $295 million in earnings for the first half of the 2000 fiscal year. "Cargill's results were led by our financial businesses, which continued their strong recovery from a year ago, and our beef processing business," said Vice Chairman Lumpkins. "Other top performers included poultry processing, animal nutrition and cattle feeding, cocoa, and energy and sugar trading." Slow recovery in Asian demand, combined with a fourth year of good global harvests and excess industry capacity, contributed to disappointing results for Cargill's grain and oilseeds businesses. In December Cargill told customers that its facilities would begin accepting crops modified through "modern biotechnology."

In January 2000 Cargill and The Dow Chemical Co., Midland Mich., finalized an agreement to fund Cargill Dow Polymers' construction of the first world-scale facility in Blair, Neb., to develop commercial polymers from annually renewable resources, such as corn. Cargill and Dow were to invest more than $300 million in NatureWorks, producer of "natural plastic." Feb. 29: Cargill reported $191 million in earnings for the third quarter, compared with $192 million a year ago. That brought earnings for the first nine months of fiscal 2000 to $486 million, compared with last year's $779 million, which included a one-time gain from the sale of the company's international seed business. For the third straight year, Cargill's grain and oilseeds businesses suffered from depressed demand stemming from the 1997 Asian economic crisis that, coupled with large global supplies and ongoing industry overcapacity, had taken a toll on the agriculture and food industry. In March Cargill, Dupont, and Cenex Harvest States Cooperatives agreed to develop, by May 1, an agricultural mall on the Internet called Rooster.com—where farmers can shop for seed and fertilizer and market their grain. Cargill and Ariba Inc. (Nasdaq: ARBA) announced Novopoint.com—an open, Internet business-to-business (B2B) exchange powered by the Ariba B2B Commerce platform—for food and beverage manufacturers and their suppliers. In April the world's leading meat and poultry processors—Cargill and its redmeat business (Excel Corp.), IBP Inc. (NYSE: IBP), Smithfield Foods Inc. (NYSE: SFD), Tyson Foods Inc. (NYSE: TSN), Gold Kist Inc., and Farmland Industries Inc.'s red meat businesses (Farmland National Beef and Farmland Foods)—signed a letter of intent to create an online, business-to-business marketplace for meat and poultry products, service, and information. [Prompted by Minnesota lawmakers, the FTC launched an investigation of the alliance's effect on competition.] In May Cargill and Pioneer Hi-Bred International Inc. settled a lawsuit filed in October 1998 by Pioneer alleging that Cargill's corn seed business had misappropriated some Pioneer genetic material. Under the settlement, Cargill agreed to destroy improperly obtained material in its corn breeding program; not to engage in the practice of isolating parent seed from bags of Pioneer's hybrid seed corn, a process known as "chasing selfs"; and to pay Pioneer $100 million for past damages and to resolve rights to use genetic material that was in dispute. With the settlement in place, Cargill proceeded with plans to sell its North American seed business.

Cargill and three other large steel producing and trading companies (South Korea's Samsung, Luxembourg's Trade Arbed S.A., and Switzerland's Duferco) formed an Internet B2B steel exchange to be based in New York. Cargill and Hayashibara Co. Ltd. of Japan signed a letter of intent to evaluate the trehalose market in the Americas to determine the feasibility of Cargill establishing a manufacturing and marketing business for the multifunctional sweetener.

May 31: Cargill reported $480 million in net earnings for fiscal 2000, compared with $597 million a year ago. Operating earnings, before charges for a write-down of assets in a number of businesses and a small loss from discontinued operations, were $659 million, a 200 percent increase from the previous year. Revenue in fiscal 2000 was $48 billion, up 4 percent from the previous year. "Strong performances from several businesses, most notably in our financial markets family and beef processing, contributed to this significant improvement in operating earnings over last year's depressed results," said CEO Staley. "We also made good progress in restructuring our organization and portfolio around our new corporate strategy to take our basic expertise in food and agriculture to new levels of value and customer service." The global capital markets and value investing groups helped pace the financial businesses to a strong year. Cargill's North Star Steel staged a solid recovery. Despite a slowly recovering Asian economy, earnings among the company's grain trading and processing businesses remained depressed. In June Cargill exited, for the first time, a major global commodities market, announcing plans to sell its 400-employee, London-based coffee business to Ecom Agroindustrial Corp. of Geneva. Cargill also indicated that it was looking for an exit strategy for its profitable rubber business. Cargill also agreed to transfer its Petfood Operation, the leading Argentine petfood business, to Nestle Argentina S.A. after a review of the prospects in the local market. Cargill began the first phase of a $24 million expansion in Cedar Rapids, Iowa. In July Cargill, Sysco Corp., Tyson Foods Inc., and McDonald's Corp. created Electronic Foodservice Network, a Chicago-based online marketplace for the foodservice industry. In August Cargill restructured AgHorizons' individual Farm Service Centers into Farm Service Groups, realigning responsibilities in order to better serve farmers' needs for solutions in such areas as grain marketing, crop management, and cash management. A joint venture between Cargill and The Hudson Cos., Troy, Ala., acquired Fontina Foods Inc., a Port St. Lucie, Fla., producer of herb blends and custom sauces for the foodservice industry. Aug. 31: Cargill's $172 million in first-quarter earnings were up from $150 million in the same period a year ago, led by Cargill's beef processing and financial businesses. Good supplies of cattle coupled with strong domestic and export demand boosted results in beef processing. In the capital markets, the company's earnings growth reflected a balanced mix of financial trading and investing activities. Agile trading and risk management in the global petroleum and sugar markets also contributed to the earnings improvement. Despite signs of slowly recovering demand, the global grain and oilseeds markets remained under a supply overhang that continued to dampen earnings in those businesses.

PVT

In September The Dow Chemical Co.'s (NYSE: DOW) wholly owned subsidiary, Mycogen Seeds, agreed to acquire the assets of Cargill Hybrid Seeds. The purchase included all seed research, production, and distribution assets of Cargill Hybrid Seeds in the United States and Canada except Cargill's InterMountain Canola, Goertzen Seed Research, and the Western Canadian seed distribution business. [Deal completed in November.] Cargill and Florida-based SunPure agreed to form a joint venture to combine their 400-employee North American citrus processing businesses. In October the company acquired a majority interest in Fertiza, which has 5 percent of the Brazilian fertilizer market, bringing Cargill's total share of that market to 15 percent. Cargill, ADM, Cenex Harvest States, DuPont, and Louis Dreyfus announced the formation of Pradium, a separate company that was planning to operate an online business-to-business marketplace and information resource—and to trade cash grains, oilseeds, and commodity by-product exchanges—at www.pradium.com. In November Cargill AgHorizons launched ProPricing, a grain-marketing contract that allows producers to shift the burden of hedging futures contracts into the hands of futures-hedging professionals. SIC 2011, 2015, 2076, 4449, 6221. No. 1 CRM Private 100. No. 36 CRM Employer 100.

Caribou Coffee Company 615 N. Third St., Minneapolis, MN 55401. Tel: 612/359-2700; Fax: 612/359-2730; Web site: http://www.caribou-coffee.com. Don Dempsey, Chm. and CEO; Jay Willoughby, Pres.; Kim Puckett, Founder; John Puckett, Founder; Ed Finn, CFO. Annual revenue $77.2 million. Caribou Coffee serves gourmet coffee, teas, and baked goods and pastries at 145 stores in Minnesota, Georgia, North Carolina, Michigan, Ohio, and Illinois. 2,200 employees. Founded in 1992. In January 2000 the company discontinued its discount punch cards, which were cutting into its margins. Instead, Caribou was planning to fund efforts to attract and keep workers. In a court case over a canceled contract with Franklin Street Bakery, Minneapolis, Caribou was found to have breached its contract by moving pastry production to a Chicago bakery in 1999. A Hennepin County jury awarded $900,000 in damages. In April the company said that it was shelving plans for an IPO—in favor of private financing, perhaps from Carl Pohlad and his family. SIC 5812. No. 35 CityBusiness Fastest-growing Private Companies.

Carisch Inc. 641 E. Lake St., Suite 226, Wayzata, MN 55391. Tel: 952/473-4291; Fax: 952/476-7293. George Carisch, Chm.; Gerald Carisch, Pres. Carisch is a chain of Arby's restaurants, and commercial office and retail facilities. 390 employees. Founded in 1965. SIC 5812.

Carley Foundry Inc. 8301 Coral Sea St. N.E., Blaine, MN 55449. Tel: 763/780-5123; Fax: 763/780-9426. Mike Carley, Pres. Carley Foundry manufactures premium-quality sand, aluminum casting, and permanent mold castings. 50 employees. Founded in 1957. SIC 3365.

Carlson Companies Inc. 1405 Xenium Ln., Plymouth, MN 55441. Tel: 763/212-5000; Fax: 763/212-2219; Web site: http://www.carlson.com. Marilyn C. Nelson, Chm., Pres., and CEO; Michael Batt, Pres./CEO-Carlson Leisure Group; Steve Brown, SVP and Chief Information Ofcr.; Doug Cody, VP-Public Rel./Communications; John M. Diracles Jr., VP and Treas.; Barbara C. Gage, Pres.-Carlson Family Fdn.; Herve Gourio, Pres./CEO-Carlson Wagonlit Travel; Richard F. Hamm Jr., VP-Strategic Devel./Acquisitions; Rosalyn Mallet, SVP-Hum. Res.; Curtis C. Nelson, Pres./CEO-Carlson Hospitality Worldwide; Anita Phillips, VP-Corp. Fin. Svs./Bus. Risk Mgmt.; Martyn R. Redgrave, EVP and CFO; Dean A. Riesen, Pres./CEO-Tonkawa Inc.; James J. Ryan, VP and Pres./CEO-Carlson Mktg. Group; Donna Snyder, Exec. Dir.-Carlson Family Fdn.; Bill Van Brunt, SVP and Gen. Counsel. Annual revenue $9.8 billion ($31.4 billion under Carlson brands). Carlson Cos. encompasses a diversified, worldwide group of service companies operating primarily in the businesses of travel, marketing, and hospitality, employing more than 188,000 people under the brands worldwide. The groups are: Carlson Wagonlit Travel (business travel agency, co-owned with Accor Group, Paris); Carlson Leisure Group (leisure travel agencies and tour operations, including Nieman Marcus Travel Services); Carlson Marketing Group (incentive and loyalty marketing); Carlson Hospitality Worldwide (Regent International Hotels), Radisson Hotels & Resorts, (Radisson Seven Seas Cruises, Country Inns, Suites By Carlson, Italianni's, and T.G.I. Friday's) and 24K Gold Points. Parent company is Carlson Holdings Inc. of Minneapolis. 63,200 employees (9,000 in Minnesota). Founded in 1938.

In November 1999 Carlson Marketing Group (CMG) was honored with the 1999 Franklin Covey Organization of Excellence Award, for sustaining a strong work culture while striving to achieve long-term performance results. [CMG would win the 2000 Franklin Covey Team Recognition for Synergy & Impact Award the following year.] Dec. 31: The year was marked by solid growth of Carlson's corporate and consumer businesses; record-breaking sales generated by its brands systemwide; and bold expansion into the burgeoning dot-com arena. The company announced that 1999 gross systemwide sales under Carlson-related brands reached a record-breaking $31.4 billion, compared with $22 billion in 1998. The 1999 merger of Carlson's leisure travel business in the United Kingdom with Thomas Cook operations there accounted for a majority of the increase. Carlson's gross company-owned sales totaled $9.8 billion, compared with $7.8 billion in 1998. Five years ago, less than 5 percent of the company's systemwide sales came from outside the United States. Today, well over 50 percent of systemwide sales are delivered by operations outside the United States. The company was continuing to enhance technology to redefine its market position as a business-to-business and business-to-consumer leader worldwide. In January 2000 Twin Cities Internet start-up company Surtsey Inc.'s staff and proprietary technical expertise were incorporated into the Carlson Shared Services Technology organization. Radisson Hotels Worldwide unveiled a striking, contemporary new brand identity and new company name (Radisson Hotels & Resorts), reflecting its 21st-century strategy for leadership in the world's travel industry. The hotel group also said it was planning to open 55 new hotels in 2000. Carlson Marketing Group acquired Organizational Studies Inc., Toronto, which specializes in providing research-validated measurement tools such as employee opinion and customer loyalty surveys and linkage research programs. The company began an organizational restructuring that was to more closely align its Gold Points Plus program with its Internet commerce operations. In February Carlson Hospitality Worldwide's Regent International Hotels expanded into the new business area of luxury vacation ownership—with the first "Club Regent" at the exclusive The Canyons alpine resort in Park City, Utah. Carlson Restaurants Worldwide opened a T.G.I. Friday's in Ireland, the 50th country to welcome the Friday's brand. In May the company said that it was pursuing the purchase of the 78 percent of Thomas Cook Group that it did not already own. Carlson Marketing Group was named the largest U.S. provider of marketing services ($271.5 million in revenue) by trade journal Advertising Age. In June Carlson was ranked third on Working Woman magazine's Top 500 Women-Owned Businesses list—up from fourth the year before. In June two Carlson Hospitality Worldwide affiliates announced strategic alliances: Carlson Hotels Worldwide, with Olympus Hospitality Group to grow the Radisson Hotels & Resorts, Regent International Hotels, Park Plaza, and Park Inn brands under both companies through a focused franchise development and acquisition program; and Carlson Lifestyle Living Inc., with Ryan Cos. U.S. Inc. to spur growth of new Carlson Park lifestyle communities across the western United States. In July Radisson Hotels & Resorts added its first hotel in Venezuela—a new, five-star hotel in Caracas. Carlson Cos. was named one of the 10 Great Places to Work in Minnesota in the August issue of Corporate Report magazine. As part of a plan to better integrate its hospitality, travel, and marketing services, the company started a multimillion-dollar online loyalty plan called 24k Gold Points (www.24k.com). Sept. 30: During third quarter, Radisson Hotels & Resorts welcomed 11 hotels (2,784 guest rooms) to the brand, including its first hotels in Bahrain and Venezuela. Country Inns & Suites by Carlson, which had grown systemwide revenue by 32 percent year-to-date, opened nine new hotels and signed 13 license agreements during the quarter. In November a German travel company agreed to acquire Thomas Cook. Consequently, Carlson was expected to divest its 22 percent stake.

SIC 4724, 5812, 6719, 7011, 7389. No. 15 CRM Employer 100. No. 2 CRM Private 100.

Henry Carlson Company 1105 W. Russell, Sioux Falls, SD 57104. Tel: 605/336-2410; Fax: 605/332-1314. H. Carlson Jr., CEO; Iola Brendtro, Sec.; Henry (Chip) Carlson III, VP; Dave Derry, VP. Annual revenue $36 million. Henry Carlson Co. specializes in general contracting of industrial and commercial buildings. 115 employees (50 part-time). Founded in 1918. SIC 1541.

Carousel Automobiles 8989 Wayzata Blvd., Golden Valley, MN 55426. Tel: 763/544-9591; Fax: 763/513-9309. Laurence F. LeJeune, Chm. and Sec.; Jon C. Hansen, Pres.; Thomas W. Studer, VP-Fin. Carousel Automobiles is an Audi and Porsche dealership. Carousel is owned by LeJeune Investment Inc., same address. 70 employees. Founded in 1978. SIC 5511.

Carsus Corporation 3771 N. Dunlap St., Arden Hills, MN 55112. Tel: 651/490-1066; Fax: 651/490-1071. David R. Mitchell, Pres. Carsus Corp. is engaged in retail sales and distribution. 101 employees (40 in Minnesota; 84 part-time). Founded in 1976. SIC 5947.

Carter Day International Inc. 500 73rd Ave. N.E., Fridley, MN 55432. Tel: 763/571-1000; Fax: 763/571-3012. Paul W. Ernst, Pres. and CEO. Carter Day International designs, manufactures, and sells equipment used to size and separate processed material ranging from grain to recycled plastics. 120 employees (114 in Minnesota). Founded in 1881. SIC 3523, 3556, 3569.

Cass-Clay Creamery Inc. P.O. Box 2947, Fargo, ND 58108. Tel: 701/232-1566; Fax: 701/232-9234; Web site: http://www.cassclay.com. Alan Qual, Chm.; Keith Pagel, Pres. and Gen. Mgr. Cass-Clay Creamery processes a full line of dairy products. 300 employees. Founded in 1934. SIC 2021, 2022, 2023, 2024, 2026.

CAT PUMPS 1681 94th Ln. N.E., Blaine, MN 55449. Tel: 763/780-5440; Fax: 763/780-2958; Web site: http://www.catpumps.com. William Bruggeman, CEO; Steve Bruggeman, Pres.; Thomas (Kelly) Shultis, Product Devel. Mgr.; Scott Stelzner, New Products Mgr.; Darla Jean Thompson, Dir.-Mktg. CAT Pumps manufactures high-pressure positive displacement, triplex pumps up to 660 GPM/18,000 PSI, in brass, duplex-alloy and hastelloy. With belt, direct-drive, gearbox, clutch, gas, electric, diesel drive, and custom designed Power Units from 1 HP to 1100 HP. 125 employees. Founded in 1969. SIC 3561.

Catalog Marketing Service 300 Second St. N.W., New Brighton, MN 55112. Tel: 651/636-6265; Fax: 651/636-0879. R. Kenmore Johnson, Pres.; Elouise Johnson, VP; Steve Neseth, VP. Catalog Marketing Service, formerly Computerized Mailing Systems Inc., provides computerized mail and direct-marketing services for large catalog mailers nationwide. 225 employees (10 in Minnesota). Founded in 1982. SIC 7331.

Catco Parts & Service 2785 Long Lake Rd., Roseville, MN 55113. Tel: 651/636-4311; Fax: 651/636-5420. Harvey Peterson, Chm. and CEO; Tom Peterson, Pres. and COO; Bill McEnery, VP-Op.; Manuel Barreiro, Inventory Mgr.; Dave Gerdes, VP-Sls./Mktg.; Dave Goldner, VP-Fin. Catco specializes in medium- and heavy-duty vehicle parts service and mobile fluid-power service. Branches in Fargo, N.D.; Eau Claire, Green Bay, and Fond du Lac, Wis.; and Burnsville, Mankato, St. Cloud, Rochester, Owatonna, Willmar, and Bemidji, Minn. 256 employees. Founded in 1949. SIC 5012.

Ceco Concrete Construction Corporation 15924 Lincoln St. N.E., Ham Lake, MN 55304. Tel: 763/434-4637; Fax: 763/434-8716. James D. Paquin, District Mgr. Annual revenue $140 million. Ceco Concrete Construction is a concrete-formwork subcontractor specializing in commercial construction. 1,200 employees (100 in Minnesota). Founded in 1912. SIC 1771.

Cedar River Lumber Company Inc. U.S. 2, P.O. Box 340, Powers, MI 49874. Tel: 906/497-5365; Fax: 906/497-5512. Donald LeBoeuf, Pres.; Jeff LeBoeuf, Plant Mgr.; David LeBoeuf, Gen. Mgr.; Eleanor LeBoeuf, CFO, Sec., and Treas.; Gregory LeBoeuf, Plant Mgr. Cedar River Lumber Co. manufactures lumber (all types of timbers, including landscape), and cedar and pine log homes. 76 employees (all in Minnesota; 1 part-time). Founded in 1979. SIC 2439, 2452.

Cemstone Products Company 2025 Centerpoint Blvd., Mendota Heights, MN 55120. Tel: 651/688-9292; Fax: 651/688-0124. H.T. Becken, CEO; T.W. Becken, Pres. Cemstone produces sand, gravel, and ready-mix concrete. 150 employees. Founded in 1927. SIC 3273.

Cenex Harvest States Cooperatives 5500 Cenex Dr., Inver Grove Heights, MN 55077. Tel: 651/451-5151; Fax: 651/451-4310; Web site: http://www.cenexharveststates.com. Steven Burnet, Chm.; John D. Johnson, Pres. and CEO; Allen Anderson, VP-Gov't Affairs; Jim Bareksten, VP-Country Svs.; Michael Bergeland, EVP-Grain/Ag. Svs.; Gaylon Bratland, VP-Risk Mgmt.; Al Giese, Co-pres., Agriliance LLC; Jodi Heller, VP-Corp. Acctg.; Tom Larson, EVP-Member Svs./Pub. Affairs; Patrick Kluempke, EVP-Corp. Planning; Lee Morin, VP-Refined Fuels; Jay Debertin, VP-Refining/Terminals; Mark Palmquist, EVP-Grain/Food; Tom Medd, VP-Wheat Milling; John Schmitz, EVP-Fin./Admin.; David Swenson, VP-County Op.; Debra Thornton, SVP-Legal/Admin.; James D. Tibbetts, SVP-Foods; Leon Westbrock, EVP-Energy/Crop Inputs. Cenex Harvest States is a producer-to-consumer cooperative system owned by farmers, ranchers, and their local co-ops—from the Great Lakes to the Pacific Northwest, and from the Canadian border to Texas. This fully integrated agricultural foods cooperative operates oil refineries/pipelines, and provides a wide variety of products and services ranging from grain marketing to food processing. Through a broad range of working parternships, Cenex Harvest States also markets and distributes petroleum products, agronomic inputs, and feed to rural America—as well as grain and processed food products to customers around the world. The unification of Cenex Inc. and Harvest States Cooperatives took effect on June 1, 1998. 6,500 employees (1,900 in Minnesota). Founded in 1931. Aug. 31, 1999: Near-record-low commodity prices contributed to a 51 percent decline in earnings from the $177.3 million recorded in 1998. Economic distress on the farm, along with a wet spring, reduced sales of crop inputs, including plant food and energy products. Consolidated net sales for the 12-month period were $6.3 billion, down 24 percent from the $8.3 billion reported for fiscal 1998. In November members narrowly rejected a proposed merger with Farmland Industries, Kansas City, Mo. Nov. 30: First-quarter earnings of $9.1 million were up 10 percent from the previous year; consolidated net sales of $2 billion were up from $1.8 billion. Grain operations posted solid returns, as the volume of grain handled increased slightly to nearly 330 million bushels for the quarter, 5 percent more than a year ago. Wheat milling operations posted a strong recovery. In December, in spite of the failure of the unification plan, Land O'Lakes, Cenex Harvest States Cooperatives, and Farmland Industries decided to proceed with the establishment of an agronomy marketing joint venture company, Agriliance LLC, and a closely associated seed marketing structure to become effective early in the new year. In December Cenex agreed to acquire New Brighton, Minn.-based Sparta Foods Inc. (Nasdaq SmallCap: SPFO), a $15.7 million-revenue supplier of Mexican-style packaged foods, for $14.5 million in cash—a 10 percent premium over its stock price.

In February 2000 Cenex Harvest States agreed to acquire Dakota Valley Mills, Fairmount, N.D., a state-of-the-art mill that processes primarily spring wheat for bakery flour customers in the Midwest. [Deal closed in April.] Feb. 29: Earnings of $5.0 million for the first half of the fiscal year declined from $16.9 million for the same period the previous year. Consolidated net sales for the six-month period of $3.9 billion were up 19 percent. Ongoing global market conditions, including weakness in plant food manufacturing businesses, and high crude oil prices affected earnings and sales through the second quarter. The volume of grain handled increased to 605 million bushels from 564 million bushels a year ago. In March Cenex, Dupont, and Cargill Inc. agreed to develop, by May 1, an agricultural mall on the Internet called Rooster.com—where farmers can shop for seed and fertilizer and market their grain. Cenex announced that it was piloting a program (MVP for "More Value Produced"), uniquely designed to meet highly specialized grain buyer specifications, with a guaranteed production protocol from seed selection through delivery. In April, citing concerns about the worsening farm economy, Cenex and Farmland postponed a second membership vote on their proposed merger that had been set for late summer. In May the board of directors named John D. Johnson as president and CEO to succeed Noel K. Estenson, who was to retire June 1. May 31: Third-quarter net income was $51.2 million, an increase of 32 percent from 1999. Favorable spring planting conditions in much of the cooperative's trade area contributed to strong volume movement of agricultural inputs despite continued market turmoil in the petroleum and crop nutrient industries. In June Cenex acquired the tortilla and lefse business of Bec-Lin of Perham Inc., a privately owned, Minnesota-based company. In July Cenex noted that it remained committed to the construction of a new soybean crushing facility in Fairmont, Minn., but that a recent tightening of crushing margins had made it imprudent to move too quickly. In October Cenex, ADM, Cargill, Cenex Harvest States, DuPont, and Louis Dreyfus announced the formation of Pradium, a separate company that was planning to operate an online business-to-business marketplace and information resource—and to trade cash grains, oilseeds, and commodity by-product exchanges—at www.pradium.com. SIC 1311, 2875, 2911, 4922, 5153, 5191. No. 1 CRM Cooperatives/Mutuals 20.

Central Container Corporation 3901 N. 85th Ave., P.O. Box 43310, Brooklyn Park, MN 55443. Tel: 763/425-7444; Fax: 763/425-7917; Web site: http://www.centralcontainer.com. James E. Haglund, Chm. and Pres.; Jerry Condon, COO; Steve Braun, VP-Sls./Mktg.; David Quam, CFO. Annual revenue $21 million. Central Container manufactures and distributes corrugated packaging, foam packaging, chip boxes, and static control products. 95 employees (all in Minnesota). Founded in 1959. SIC 2653.

Central Livestock Association Inc. 310 Market Ln., South St. Paul, MN 55075. Tel: 651/451-1844; Fax: 651/451-1774. Donald G. Kampmeier, Pres. and Gen. Mgr.; Doug Appleby, EVP; Curt Zimmerman, VP-Mktg.; Mark Esch, CFO. Central Livestock Association is a cooperative agency for buying and selling livestock. 130 employees. Founded in 1921. SIC 5154.

Century Tool 21495 147th Ave N., Rogers, MN 55374. Tel: 763/428-2168; Fax: 763/428-4079. Don Lundgren, Chm.; Jerry Korpela, Pres. Century Tool manufactures precision machine parts used in the military, robotics, and food industries. 60 employees (all in Minnesota). Founded in 1968. SIC 3444.

Ceramic Industrial Coatings 325 Highway 81, Osseo, MN 55369. Tel: 763/424-2044; Fax: 763/424-1014. Lyle Sommers, Pres.; Dan Manion, Gen. Mgr. Ceramic Industrial Coatings manufactures paints, epoxy, and other coatings for distribution nationwide. 50 employees (all in Minnesota). Founded in 1976. SIC 2851, 2891.

Challenge Printing Inc. 7500 Golden Triangle Dr., Eden Prairie, MN 55344. Tel: 952/942-7086; Fax: 952/942-0973; Web site: http://www.challengeprinting.com. Robert Lothenbach, Pres. and CEO; Jay Carroll, VP-Sls./Mktg. Challenge Printing is a color sheet-fed printing company specializing in advertising pamphlets and brochures. 315 employees. Founded in 1988. SIC 2752.

Champion Air 8009 34th Ave. S., Suite 700, Bloomington, MN 55425. Tel: 952/814-8700; Fax: 952/814-8718. Michael J. Gerend, Pres. and CEO; Stephen M. Spellman, EVP and CFO. Champion Air is a charter airline. 400 employees (275 in Minnesota; 35 part-time). Founded in 1993. SIC 4522.

Champion Auto Stores Midwest Autoparts Distribution Ctr., 2565 Kasota Ave., St. Paul, MN 55108. Tel: 651/644-6448; Web site: http://www.championauto.com. Gary D. Bebeau, Pres.; Dene E. Billbe, Pres. Champion Auto Stores is a dealer organization of 154 stores (39 corporate, 115 franchised) that supply parts and accessories for the do-it-yourself automotive enthusiast. Crown Auto Service Centers provide service and installation at more than 70 locations. 750 employees. Founded in 1956. SIC 5013.

Chaska Building Center 350 E. Highway 212, Chaska, MN 55318. Tel: 952/448-3330; Fax: 952/448-3496. John D. Klingelhutz, Owner and Pres. Chaska Building Center is a lumberyard and a retailer of building supplies. 160 employees (all in Minnesota). Founded in 1964. SIC 5031, 5211.

Cheapo 80 N. Snelling, St. Paul, MN 55104. Tel: 651/644-8775; Fax: 651/644-8566. Al Brown, Owner and Pres.; Mary Hesch, Gen. Mgr. Cheapo sells new and used music titles at seven stores in the Twin Cities area: Minneapolis, St. Paul, Minnetonka, and Fridley. The company changed its name from Applause in early 1995. 65 employees (all in Minnesota). Founded in 1972. SIC 5735.

Checker Machine Inc. 2701 Nevada Ave. N., New Hope, MN 55427. Tel: 763/544-5000; Fax: 763/544-1272. Margaret Lipinski, Pres.; Steve Lipinski, VP; Warren White, Cont. Checker Machine provides large-capacity machining, grinding, and metal fabrication (welding operations). 85 employees (all in Minnesota). Founded in 1976. SIC 3599, 3629, 7692.

Chesley Truck Sales Inc. 2845 Long Lake Rd., P.O. Box 130370, Roseville, MN 55113. Tel: 651/636-3400; Fax: 651/636-8456. George Chesley, Pres.; Steve Chesley, Gen. Mgr. Chesley Truck Sales Inc. is a freightliner truck dealership. 90 employees (all in Minnesota). Founded in 1984. SIC 5012.

Church Mutual Insurance 3000 Schuster Ln., Merrill, WI 54452. Tel: 715/536-5577; Fax: 715/539-4451. Dieter H. Nickel, Chm. and CEO. Annual revenue $247.7 million. Church is a mutual insurance company that provides property and liability insurance for churches and church-related institutions. 677 employees (10 in Minnesota; 44 part-time). Founded in 1897. SIC 6331.

Cimpls Inc./Cimpl Meats P.O. Box 80, Yankton, SD 57078. Tel: 605/665-1665; Fax: 605/665-8908. Dave Frankforter, Plant Mgr. Cimpls is involved in meat packing, beef slaughtering, and boneless beef and sausage manufacturing. 170 employees. Founded in 1949. SIC 2011, 2013.

Circuit Check Inc. 6550 Wedgewood Rd., Suite 120, Maple Grove, MN 55311. Tel: 763/694-4100; Fax: 763/694-4150; Web site: http://www.circuitcheck.com. H. Victor Nelson III, Pres.; Greg Michalko, VP and Sls. Mgr.; Todd Fossum, Engrg. Mgr.; Ron Trok, VP and CFO. Annual revenue $22 million. Circuit Check manufactures electrical test equipment and test fixtures for the electronics industry. 190 employees. Founded in 1978. SIC 3825.

Circuit Science Inc. 15831 Highway 55, Plymouth, MN 55447. Tel: 763/559-9515; Fax: 763/559-2569. Terry Lutts, Pres.; Earl Monchamp, VP-Mfg.; Jeff Johnson, VP-Sls. Circuit Science manufactures double-sided, multilayered printed circuit boards for the computer industry. 166 employees (all in Minnesota; 3 part-time). Founded in 1977. SIC 3672.

Cirrus Design Corporation 4515 Taylor Circle, Duluth, MN 55811. Tel: 218/727-2737; Fax: 218/727-2148; Web site: http://www.cirrus-design.com. Alan Klapmeier, Pres.; Dale Klapmeier, EVP; Peter McDermott, EVP and CFO; R. Thomas Shea, VP-Sls./Mktg.; William King, VP-Bus. Admin.; Judi Northey, VP-Hum. Res. Cirrus Design Corp. is an aircraft manufacturer. Its first plane, the SR20 four-seater, is the first new general-aviation aircraft in years. It is made of composite materials rather than metal, and includes numerous amenities (leather seats, built-in parachutes, cell phones, CD player, cup holders) designed to attract newcomers to flying. The Cirrus Airframe Parachute System, manufactured by Ballistic Recovery Systems Inc. (OTC Bulletin Board: BRSI), South St. Paul, Minn., is designed to safely lower the aircraft to the ground in an emergency. The company has a 111,000-square-foot production plant at the Duluth airport; and a plant in Grand Forks, N.D., that makes wings and other equipment to be shipped to Duluth for final assembly. 500 employees (408 in Minnesota). Between late July 1999, when the first SR20 came off the assembly line, and late November 1999, orders rose by 100, to 420. By November, the company was close to achieving the goal of completing one plane every five days. By February 2000, orders had exceeded 500. By the end of May, the completion rate had improved to one every 4.4 days (the new goal was one a day), and 37 planes had been made. On June 1, Cirrus announced plans to move fuselage production to Grand Forks by summer's end—for reasons of efficiency. The company still expected to have 600 Duluth employees, along with 150 more in Grand Forks, at full production. Cirrus received a production certificate allowing it to inspect its planes on the production line without direct FAA oversight. In October the public got its first look at the SR22, which is powered by a 310-horsepower engine (compared to the SR20's 200-horsepower model). The FAA was still testing the SR22, but approvals may be received in time for mass production to begin in January 2001. SIC 3721.

Citizens Independent Bank 5050 Excelsior Blvd., St. Louis Park, MN 55416. Tel: 952/926-6561; Fax: 952/926-7544; Web site: http://www.bankcib.com. Brad Bakken, Pres. and CEO; Constance Bakken, Chm. Annual revenue $13.1 million. Citizens Independent Bank is a full-service commercial bank. 94 employees (76 in Minnesota; 18 part-time). Founded in 1949. SIC 6021.

City Motor Company Inc. 3900 10th Ave. S., Great Falls, MT 59405. Tel: 406/761-4900; Fax: 406/455-8318. R.H. Oakland, CEO. City Motor Co. is a motor vehicle dealership specializing in the Chevrolet, Cadillac, and Toyota lines. 86 employees. Founded in 1954. SIC 5511.

Clarity Coverdale Fury Advertising Inc. One Financial Plaza, Suite 1300, 120 S. Sixth St., Minneapolis, MN 55402. Tel: 612/339-3902; Fax: 612/359-4392; Web site: http://www.ccf-ideas.com. Tim Clarity, Pres. and CEO; Jac Coverdale, VP and Exec. Creative Dir.; Jerry Fury, VP-Creative Dir.; Gary Hellmer, VP and Group Brand Dir.; Diane Kraner, VP and Dir.-Media; Chris Bearg, VP and Dir.-Brand Planning. Annual revenue $10.4 million ($70 million in capitalized billings.). Clarity Coverdale Fury Advertising is a full-service advertising agency. The firm builds brands through strategic and creative marketing. Major clients: Johnsonville Sausage, Pillsbury Bakeries & Foodservice, Malt-O-Meal, and Belvedere Vodka. Parachute Design Inc., a division of Clarity Coverdale, specializes in strategic, non-mass media brand-building tools such as packaging, corporate identity, point-of-sale, sales support systems, and collateral. 74 employees. Founded in 1979. In March 2000 a company television spot for Johnsonville Breakfast Sausage (the one featuring a deaf boy) was named one of Adweek magazine's Best Spots of the 1990s. In October the firm won seven awards at The Show 2000 in Minneapolis. SIC 7311.

Clarklift of Minnesota Inc. 501 W. 78th St., P.O. Box 20028, Bloomington, MN 55420. Tel: 952/887-5400; Fax: 952/881-3030; Web site: http://www.clarkliftofmn.com. Clayton Schubert, Pres.; Jeffrey Schubert, VP. Annual revenue $29 million. Clarklift of Minnesota is engaged in the sale and service of forklift trucks, personnel carriers, racks, shelving, and industrial batteries. The company has a branch office in West Fargo, N.D., and a divisional office, Quality Storage Products, in Bloomington. 140 employees (125 in Minnesota; 2 part-time). Founded in 1949. SIC 3537, 5084.

Classic Manufacturing Inc. 2980 Granada Ln. N., Oakdale, MN 55128. Tel: 651/770-1212; Fax: 651/770-2077; Web site: http://www.classic-mfg.com. James W. Jackson, Pres. and CEO; Jeffrey P. Jackson, VP and Gen. Mgr.; Roger J. Jackson, VP-Sls. Mgr. Annual revenue $16 million. Classic Manufacturing Inc. is a full-service machining and machine building company, emphasizing quality, technology, delivery, and competitive pricing. Capabilities include designing, building, and assembling special machines, jigs, gauges, and fixtures; wiring of industrial electronics; and prototype production. 100 employees (90 in Minnesota). Founded in 1987. SIC 3599.

Clearr Corporation 3750 Williston Rd., Minnetonka, MN 55345. Tel: 952/931-2100; Fax: 952/931-2259; Web site: http://www.clearrcorp.com. Andy Steinfeldt, Pres.; Pete Nelson, VP and Gen. Mgr.; Dan Gourde, CFO. Clearr Corp. manufactures a comprehensive range of backlit, edgelit, nonlit, and sequential-image graphic display products and signs. 85 employees. Founded in 1959. SIC 7319.

Clement Chevrolet Cadillac 1000 12th St. S.W., Rochester, MN 55902. Tel: 507/289-0491; Fax: 507/289-6820. G.A. Bridwell, Pres.; Joe Beavers, VP and Gen. Mgr. Clement Chevrolet Cadillac and Subaru Geo is a motor vehicle dealer and car rental company. 130 employees. Founded in 1924. SIC 5511.

Cloverdale Foods Company P.O. Box 667, Mandan, ND 58554. Tel: 701/663-9511; Fax: 701/663-8736. Don L. Russell, Dir.; Steve Russell, Chm.; Jim Miller, EVP; T.J. Russell, Pres. and CEO; Kirk Olson, Cont. Annual revenue $53 million. Cloverdale Foods Co. is a meat processor. 267 employees (3 in Minnesota; 74 part-time). Founded in 1914. SIC 2013.

PVT

Clow Stamping Company Box 23C, Star Route, Merrifield, MN 56465. Tel: 218/765-3111; Fax: 218/765-3904. Reg Clow, Pres.; Pat Paumen, VP-Customer Svc.; Rusty Laney, Estimating Mgr. Annual revenue $28 million. Clow Stamping does ISO 9002-certified metal stamping of short to medium volume, with value-added services of welding machinery and other assemblies. 310 employees (all in Minnesota). Founded in 1970. SIC 3443, 3469.

Clyde Machines Inc. North Highway 55, P.O. Box 194, Glenwood, MN 56334. Tel: 320/634-4504; Fax: 320/634-4506. Sallie DeBoer, CEO. Clyde Machines manufactures airline ground-support equipment. 50 employees (10 part-time). Founded in 1961. SIC 3537.

Coborn's Inc. 1445 E. Highway 23, St. Cloud, MN 56304. Tel: 320/252-4222; Fax: 320/252-0014. Dan Coborn, Chm.; Don Wetter, CEO; Bill Coborn, Sec.; Chris Coborn, Pres.; Bob Thueringer, COO; Mark Coborn, EVP. Annual revenue $450 million (estimated by Fact Book). Coborn's Inc. operates a regional supermarket chain in central Minnesota; Fargo and Bismarck, N.D.; and Mason City, Iowa. Its 58 stores include Coborn's supermarkets, Little Dukes convenience stores, Cash Wise warehouse food stores, off-sale liquor stores, and pharmacies. Coborn's headquarters supports facilities for central administration, bakery, foods, and floral operations. 4,100 employees. Founded in 1921. SIC 5411. No. 23 CRM Private 100. No. 47 CRM Employer 100.

Cold Spring Granite Company 202 S. Third Ave., Cold Spring, MN 56320. Tel: 320/685-3621; Fax: 320/685-8490; Web site: http://www.coldspringgranite.com. Patrick D. Alexander, Chm. and CEO; Patrick Mitchell, Pres. and COO; George Schnepf, VP-Fin. and CFO; John Maile, VP-Commercial Svs.; Mike Baklarz, VP-Memorialization Sls. Annual revenue $150 million. Cold Spring Granite is the world's leading quarrier and fabricator of granite products, with seven locations in six states and Canada; the largest of its facilities is in Cold Spring. Product lines include architectural and monumental granites with interior, landscape, and industrial applications; architectural bronze and bronze memorials., and DiamondWright diamond tools. 1,350 employees. Founded in 1898. SIC 1411, 3281. No. 79 CRM Private 100.

Colder Products Company 1001 Westgate Dr., St. Paul, MN 55114. Tel: 651/645-0091; Fax: 651/645-5404. Michael Lyon, Chm.; Ronald Toensing, Pres. Colder Products Co. manufactures quick-disconnect couplings for flexible tubing. 160 employees (152 in Minnesota; 10 part-time). Founded in 1978. SIC 3498.

Cole Papers Inc. and Cole Wholesale Floors 1300 38th St. N., P.O. Box 2967, Fargo, ND 58102. Tel: 701/282-5311; Fax: 701/282-5513. Chuck Perkins, Pres. and CEO; James P. Critelli, SVP. Cole distributes industrial and printing papers, janitorial supplies, wholesale floor coverings, and cabinets from 10 stocking locations. From these locations, 26 trucks offer local delivery service in Minnesota, North Dakota, central and eastern South Dakota, eastern Montana, northwest Iowa, northeast Nebraska, and western Wisconsin. The original Fargo Paper Co. was founded by Robert Cole as a locally owned paper distribution company. Cole Papers Inc. became the name in 1987 in honor of the Cole family. 160 employees (40 in Minnesota). Founded in 1918. SIC 5023, 5087, 5111, 5112, 5113.

Colliers Towle Real Estate 330 Second Ave. S., Suite 800, Minneapolis, MN 55401. Tel: 612/341-4444; Fax: 612/347-9389; Web site: http://www.colliers.com. Mark W. Reiling, Pres.; Kathleen Nye-Reiling, Principal; Dawn Grant, VP; Mark Kolsrud, SVP; Dennis McClinton, SVP; Rodger Skare, VP. Colliers Towle Real Estate is a full-service commercial real estate firm providing services in sales and leasing, facility and property management, appraisal and consultation, investments, land, and corporate services. In February 1999 Towle Real Estate Co. changed its name to better reflect its ownership and partnership with Colliers International Property Consultants. 123 employees (all in Minnesota). Founded in 1909. In April 2000 the company launched a new Internet strategy utilizing SPACElink technology from Stonehaven (AMEX: RPP) to integrate its building operations online and to provide property owners with real-time access to critical information about their properties. "We wanted to be one of the first property managers to embrace this new online technology," said President Reiling. "SPACElink gives us a centralized online system that links all of our services, so clients can retrieve their property information over the Internet, whenever they choose. This program ultimately allows us to better service our clients and help them save time and money." Colliers Towle's Jon Peterson was named Minnesota Commercial Realtor of the Year by the Organization of Commercial Realtors. SIC 6162, 6531.

Collins Electrical Systems Inc. dba ColliSys 4990 N. Highway 169, New Hope, MN 55428. Tel: 763/535-6000; Fax: 763/535-6961. Richard W. Boe, Pres. and CEO; Robert Gorg, VP and Treas.; Gregg A. LaBonne, VP and Sec. Annual revenue $25 million. ColliSys performs electrical construction and engineering for commercial, industrial, and communication systems. The company also maintains a Special Serivces Division and an Outdoor Division. 125 employees. Founded in 1933. SIC 1731.

Colonial Craft 2772 Fairview Ave. N., Roseville, MN 55113. Tel: 651/631-3110; Fax: 651/631-2925; Web site: http://www.colonialcraft.com. Eric Bloomquist, CEO; Jeff Howe, Pres. Colonial Craft manufactures hardwood door and window grilles, custom mouldings, and standard architectural mouldings. Its Moulding Division is located in Luck, Wis. 250 employees (150 in Minnesota; 25 part-time). Founded in 1965. In April 2000 the company imported its first FSC-certified hardwood (i.e., from sustainably managed forests) from Bolivia—to be used for Char-Broil wood components, including grill handles and shelves. The National Safety Council and the Minnesota Safety Council honored Colonial Craft with safety awards—for improvements achieved even though the company had added a third shift, several new employees, and a new finishing system. Eric Bloomquist was named a finalist in the 2000 Entrepreneur of the Year Awards by Ernst & Young. SIC 2431.

Colonnade Properties LLC 4900 Viking Dr., Edina, MN 55435. Tel: 952/820-1600; Fax: 952/820-1620; Web site: http://www.north-co.com. Paul Taylor III, CEO; Joseph Sambuco, Pres.; Michael H. Maney, EVP-Prop. Op.; Eva B. Stevens, SVP-Reg. Asset Mgmt.; Dawn Driessen, VP-

Cont. Prop. Op.; Lee Willhite, VP-Hum. Res. Colonnade Properties LLC is an integrated real estate company in the areas of real estate investment, development, asset and property management. It currently manages an 11 million square foot portfolio. 134 employees (52 in Minnesota). Founded in 1979. In February 2000 Northco Real Estate's affiliate, Northco Management Services, merged with Taylor Simpson in New York and formed Colonnade Properties LLC. SIC 6531.

Colorbrite Inc. 1001 Plymouth Ave. N., Minneapolis, MN 55411. Tel: 612/522-6711; Fax: 612/522-9263. David Baudhuin, Pres.; Anthony Waldera, CEO. Annual revenue $18 million. Colorbrite is a lithographic trade shop creating high-quality color separations and plates for offset and flexo printing. 100 employees. Founded in 1967. SIC 2752.

Columbia Falls Aluminum Company 2000 Aluminum Dr., Columbia Falls, MT 59912. Tel: 406/892-8400; Fax: 406/892-8201. Larry E. Tate, VP and Gen. Mgr. CFAC is a tolling operation, reducing customers' alumina to primary aluminum. 600 employees. Founded in 1955. SIC 3334.

Colwell Industries Inc. 123 N. Third St., Minneapolis, MN 55401. Tel: 612/340-0365; Fax: 612/340-0132. Thomas G. Colwell, Chm.; John G. Colwell Jr., Pres.; Felton T. Colwell, Pres.-Technical Finishing Svs.; Daniel C. Nicklay, EVP and Treas.; Carolyn C. Dahl, Sec. Annual revenue $58 million. Colwell Industries is a holding company with two operating divisions: Colwell/General Inc. (sampling aids for the paint and decorative-products industries); and Colwell Merchandising (contract assembly of window treatments). 750 employees (30 in Minnesota). Founded in 1951. SIC 3999.

Command Tooling Systems LLC 13931 Sunfish Lake Blvd. N.W., P.O. Box 9, Ramsey, MN 55303. Tel: 763/576-6910. David D. Koentopf, Chm.; Joseph A. Norwood, Pres. and CEO. Annual revenue $18.7 million. Command Tooling Systems LLC, formerly Command Corp., is a manufacturer of tool cutting holders that are used to create precision parts on computer-automated machines. 98 employees (90 in Minnesota). Founded in 1981. SIC 3545, 5084.

Commercial Trucking and Leasing 1145 Homer St., St. Paul, MN 55116. Tel: 651/690-4704. Commercial Trucking operates 75 power units and 240 dry-van trailers of all sizes, providing local and over-the-road truck-load services 105 employees. Founded in 1964. SIC 4731.

Commonwealth Electric of Minnesota Inc. 554 Broadway St., St. Paul, MN 55101. Tel: 651/697-8300; Fax: 651/224-1760. Tracy Donovan, Chm. and CEO; Dick Bromstad, Pres.-Systems Group; Terry Towey, Pres.-Electrical Group; Rick Donovan, COO; Jim Johnson, CFO. Commonwealth Electric is an electrical contractor and a systems integrator. It also manufactures custom electrical control panels, power panels, and electrical enclosures. Electrical and control projects previously designed, produced, installed, and serviced include the Metrodome, the Mall of America, and the Target Center. 300 employees. Founded in 1987. SIC 1731, 3613.

Community Channel.com 605 Highway 169 N., Suite 200, Plymouth, MN 55441. Tel: 763/542-3032; Fax: 763/545-9906; Web site: http://www.communitychannel.com. Community Channel.com is a Web design firm that specializes in assigning and marketing for small and large firms. 50 employees. Founded in 1995. SIC 7379.

Como Oil Company 2716 W. Superior, Duluth, MN 55806. Tel: 218/722-6666; Fax: 218/722-3701. Robert Hall, Pres. and Owner; Mark Oestreich, VP-Fin., Sec., Treas. Como Oil is a wholesaler and retailer of petroleum products, propane, and lube oils. 75 employees. Founded in 1946. SIC 5172.

Component Manufacturing Company 4101 N. Fourth Ave., Sioux Falls, SD 57104. Tel: 605/339-3647; Fax: 605/339-2651. Lloyd L. Reaves, Chm.; Tom Reaves, Pres. Component Manufacturing Co. manufactures commercial buildings, roof and floor trusses, farm buildings, and grain-storage bulkheads. 75 employees. SIC 2439.

Computech Resources Inc. 6600 City West Pkwy., Eden Prairie, MN 55344. Tel: 952/833-0930; Fax: 952/833-0931; Web site: http://www.compures.com. Bill Larsen, Pres. and CEO; Susan Behnke, VP-Technical; Ed Konopasek, VP-Sls.; Gary Morgan, VP-Minnesota. Annual revenue $26 million. Computech Resources is an e-business solution provider. IBM and Lotus are its premier business partners. 68 employees (16 in Minnesota; 3 part-time). The company was No. 10 on the Inc. 500 list of fastest-growing private companies in 1999. SIC 7372.

Computer Chrome 803 Transfer Rd., St. Paul, MN 55114. Tel: 651/646-2442; Fax: 651/646-1461. Jim Kronschnabel, Pres.; Kristin Sperry, Cont. Computer Chrome produces presentation graphics, including slides, overheads, color copies, color prints, large posters, and multimedia screen presentations, print design, Web design, large format printing and video production. 70 employees (all in Minnesota). Founded in 1975. SIC 7336.

Computer System Products Inc. 14305 21st Ave. N., Plymouth, MN 55447. Tel: 763/475-8326; Fax: 952/475-8457; Web site: http://www.csp.com. Duncan Lee, CEO; Michael Kelley, Pres.; David Peters, SVP. Computer System Products is an ISO 9001-certified manufacturer and distributor of custom and traditional computer cabling, LAN hardware, and on-site cabling systems and components for the communications and computer industries. It has two locations in Plymouth. 200 employees. Founded in 1982. SIC 3669, 3678, 3679.

Com-Tal Machine and Engineering Inc. 5000 Township Pkwy., White Bear Township, MN 55110. Tel: 651/483-2611; Fax: 651/483-0308; Web site: http://www.comtal.com. John Melquist, Pres. Annual revenue $22 million. Com-Tal designs and manufactures automated assembly and process machines, Com-Tal also designs, builds and installs full production lines. 150 employees (155 in Minnesota; 5 part-time). Founded in 1967. SIC 3559, 3569, 3599, 3841.

Comtrol Corporation 900 Long Lake Rd., New Brighton, MN 55112. Tel: 651/631-7654; Fax: 651/631-8117; Web site: http://www.comtrol.com. Robert Beale, CEO; Lee Stagni, COO; Paul Hammar, SVP-Hospitality; David Hopmann, VP-Engrg./Mfg.; Robert Kemmis, VP-Res./Devel. Annual revenue $32 million. Comtrol Corp., inventor of the multiport serial controller for personal computers, is a global provider of data communications and enterprise integration solutions. Comtrol is a manufacturer of high-speed data communications products for multiple peripheral device control, remote user-to-LAN access, wide-area networking, and Internet access. The company operates facilities in North America and Europe and distributes its products through value-added distributors and resellers worldwide. 80 employees. Founded in 1982. Dec. 31, 1999: For the year, the company reported a 53 percent increase in sales and triple-digit growth in profits. By revenue, Comtrol had become the second-largest provider of data communications products behind market-leader Digi International (Nasdaq: DGII), Minnetonka, Minn. Company officials credited the sales increase to an increasing demand for its products through e-commerce distribution, and to strong demand for its new "thin server" platforms that provide serial device connectivity over local-area networks and the Internet. In March Comtrol launched an industrial automation group called the IA-TEAM, dedicated to Internet-enabling the industry with highly reliable custom "device-control" and "application" thin servers—segments of the thin server market projected to grow from $508 million in 1997 to more than $4 billion in 2003. Comtrol's April 2000 market share figures revealed a leadership position in the U.S. distribution market and marked an all-time market share high for the company. Exceptional sales of its Ethernet-attached and new USB-connected serial device hubs has stimulated the company's strong performance. Company officials indicated that it was sustaining its leading position for the month of May as well, ranking Comtrol at the top in the U.S. distribution market for the first time ever. In May Comtrol joined forces with Massachusetts-based Intellution Inc., one of the world's leading developers of industrial automation software, to provide solutions for the industrial automation marketplace. In June Comtrol and Menusoft, a leading provider of PC-based restaurant management systems, formed a strategic business alliance encompassing their joint solution for the food service industry. Comtrol's enterprise integration technology was submitted to Hospitality Industry Technology Integration Standards (HITIS) as the basis for developing an interface standard for legacy systems in hotels and motels. In July Comtrol announced the availability of its latest innovation, the RocketPort USB Modem Hub. In September Comtrol released the Property Link Planner, an Internet-based tool for planning systems integration projects within hotels and motels. In October Comtrol expanded its family of RocketPort Serial Hubs with a two-port model. SIC 3577.

Concrete Design Specialties Inc. 1156 Homer St., St. Paul, MN 55116. Tel: 651/699-1345; Fax: 651/699-1830; Web site: http://www.custom-rock.com. Paul Mooty, Pres.; Tony Nasvik, Dir.-Mktg.; Wayne Goldade, Fin. Annual revenue $12 million. Concrete Design Specialties, dba Custom Rock International, specializes in coloring and texturing concrete in the use of decorative paving and simulated stone wall services, primarily for resort hotels, theme parks, casino gaming facilities, and zoos. It also does commercial and residential projects and custom rock paving, formations, and simulations with custom form liners. It has an office in Las Vegas. 120 employees (18 in Minnesota; 102 part-time). Founded in 1971. SIC 1741, 1771, 3272.

Concrete Inc. 5000 Demers Ave., Grand Forks, ND 58201. Tel: 701/772-6687; Fax: 701/772-4315. David Buesing, Pres.; Jeffrey P. Stumpf, VP and Sec.; Robert A. Sween, VP and Treas.; James A. Glick, VP. Concrete Inc. is a manufacturer of prestress, precast concrete products; ready-mix concrete; and sand and gravel. 150 employees (10 in Minnesota). Founded in 1891. SIC 3271.

Condux International Inc. 145 Kingswood Rd., P.O. Box 247, Mankato, MN 56002. Tel: 507/387-6576; Fax: 507/387-1124; Web site: http://www.condux.com. Brad Radichel, Pres.; Earl Elster, VP; John Haugum, VP and Gen. Mgr. Condux International is a manufacturer of tools and equipment used to install power, telephone, and fiber-optic cable. 150 employees. Founded in 1888. SIC 3531.

Conklin Company Inc. 551 Valley Park Dr., P.O. Box 155, Shakopee, MN 55379. Tel: 952/445-6010; Fax: 952/496-4292. Charles W. Herbster, Chm., Pres., and CEO; Judy Herbster, EVP. Conklin Co. manufactures and distributes chemical and biological products in the building and construction, agricultural, industrial, and consumer markets. Product lines are roofing, specialty coatings, fertilizer, animal feed, lubricants, human health, and nutrition. The company has a direct sales force of more than 20,000 in the United States. 128 employees (116 in Minnesota). Founded in 1969. SIC 2843, 2851, 2891, 2992, 3479.

The Conlin Companies 4900 IDS Center, Minneapolis, MN 55402. Tel: 612/375-0084; Fax: 612/332-2116. Paul Gunville, Pres.; E. Joseph Conlin, Chm. Annual revenue $38 million. Conlin Cos. owns and operates retail furniture stores in 17 cities in North Dakota, South Dakota, Montana, and Wyoming. The company also operates a residential interior design company, Conlin-Rudd Interior Design, in Minneapolis. 300 employees. Founded in 1937. SIC 5712.

Connexus Energy 14601 Ramsey Blvd., Ramsey, MN 55303. Tel: 763/323-2600; Fax: 763/323-4275. Peter Wojciechowski, Chm.; Richard D. Newland, Pres. and CEO; Michael Bash, VP-Bus. Resources and CFO; Tamara Ferguson, Acting VP-Hum. Res.; John Gasal, VP-Power Supply; Larry Peterson, Corp. Svs.; Michael Rajala, VP-Corp. Devel.; Judy Stephenson, VP-Mktg.; Matthew Yseth, VP-Electric Op. Annual revenue $118 million. Connexus Energy is a 91,000-member cooperative that distributes electricity. The largest customer-owned utility in Minnesota, Connexus Energy provides electricity to homes and businesses in portions of Anoka, Chisago, Hennepin, Isanti, Ramsey, Sherburne, and Washington counties. Known until September 1998 as AEC (Anoka Electric Cooperative). 238 employees. Founded in 1936. In October 2000 Connexus signed an agreement with Malvern, Pa.-based SCT (Nasdaq: SCTC), a leading global provider of e-business solutions for the energy, utility, and communications markets, to offer SCT's Banner customer management solution (CMS), as part of SCT's SinglePoint Application Service Provider (ASP) program, on a subscription basis to utility companies. SIC 4911. No. 19 CRM Cooperatives/Mutuals 20.

Connor Sports Flooring Corporation P.O. Box 246, Amasa, MI 49903. Tel: 906/822-7311; Fax: 906/822-7800. John Olson, CEO; Paul Bujold, VP. Connor Sports Flooring Corp. is a manufacturer of hardwood flooring. 105 employees. SIC 2435.

Consolidated Lumber Company 808 N. Fourth St., Stillwater, MN 55082. Tel: 651/439-3138; Fax: 651/439-9756. Dale H. Remus, Chm.; David L. Majeski, Pres. and CEO; Patricia J. Ogborn, Sec. and Treas.; Michael T. Zgodava, VP. Annual revenue $53.4 million. Consolidated Lumber deals in building supplies and lumber products. 196 employees (90 in Minnesota). Founded in 1903. SIC 5211.

Consortium Book Sales & Distribution Inc. 1045 Westgate Dr., Suite 90, St. Paul, MN 55114. Tel: 651/221-9035. Randall Beek, CEO; Peter Heege, CFO. Consortium is a book distribution company serving the Upper Midwest. 120 employees (37 in Minnesota). Founded in 1903. SIC 5192.

Continental Data Inc. 279 N. Medina St., Loretto, MN 55357. Tel: 763/479-1400; Fax: 763/479-1210. Dennis Bergquist, Pres.; Lee Welch, VP. Continental Data is a computer service bureau featuring high-volume data entry, fulfillment services, inbound telemarketing, and a letter shop. 120 employees (20 part-time). Founded in 1978. SIC 7374.

Continental Machines Inc. 5505 W. 123rd St., Savage, MN 55378. Tel: 952/890-3300; Fax: 952/895-6450. Michael L. Wilkie, Chm.; Mike Johnson, Pres.; Gary A. Heist, Treas. and Cont.; David Wall, Sec. Continental Machines manufactures DoAll-brand band saws, power saws, grinders, and hydraulic components. 360 employees. Founded in 1928. SIC 3541, 3545, 3553, 3561, 3569.

Control Assemblies Company 15400 Medina Rd., Plymouth, MN 55447. Tel: 763/557-9711; Fax: 763/557-9646. David Fox, CEO; Mark Skinner, Pres.; Roger Jaros, VP; Gregg Phelps, VP. Control Assemblies Co. has been serving the industrial automation market by designing and building control systems for the process and material handling industries. The company also has extensive experience with food processing, filtration, motor control, and project management. Control Assemblies is a systems integrator with personnel who have developed wide experience in electrical, programmable logic controller, computer, bar coding, data collection, pneumatic and electromechanical technologies. 75 employees (55 in Minnesota). Founded in 1966. SIC 3823.

Control Products Inc. 1724 Lake Dr. W., Chanhassen, MN 55317. Tel: 952/448-2217; Fax: 952/448-1606. Chris Berghoff, Pres.; Jim Helgerson, Regional Bus. Mgr.; Mark Bjornstad, Regional Bus. Mgr. Control Products manufactures both standard and custom electric controls for food service, HVAC, industrial, and medical industries. 100 employees. Founded in 1985. In August 2000 President Berghoff was among 10 American CEOs selected for a national delegation aimed at promoting business relationships between the United States and Malaysia. SIC 3822.

Convertinns Inc. 333 Main St., Wabasha, MN 55981. Tel: 952/565-4524; Fax: 952/565-4003. John Hall, Pres.; John Hall Jr., VP, Sec., and Treas.. Annual revenue $3.5 million. Convertinns operates Anderson House Hotel, which has complete dining and banquet facilities and a bar; and Anderson House Tour Co., a travel service. 70 employees (50 in Minnesota). Founded in 1975. SIC 4724, 7011.

Cool Air Mechanical Inc. 1441 Rice St., St. Paul, MN 55117. Tel: 651/489-8821; Fax: 651/489-6763. Vern J. Worms, Pres.; Charles L. Worms, VP; Chris J. Worms, VP; Jeffrey J. Worms, Sec. and Treas. Annual revenue $10.5 million. Cool Air Mechanical is a mechanical contractor operating in Minnesota, Wisconsin, Iowa, North Dakota, and South Dakota. 65 employees (all in Minnesota). Founded in 1966. SIC 1711.

Coordinated Business Systems Ltd. Gateway Business Park, 511 W. Travelers Trail, Burnsville, MN 55337. Tel: 952/894-9460; Fax: 952/894-9238; Web site: http://www.coordinated.com. James Oricchio, Pres.; Donna Oricchio, VP and Treas. Coordinated Business Systems provides sales of and service for digital duplications, document management systems, color copiers, laser printers, facsimile systems, multifunctional network printers, and digital copier/printers systems. It is Minnesota's largest authorized dealer for Kyocera Mita copiers and facsimiles. Other locations: Rochester and Red Wing, Minn. Coordinated Business Systems is an authorized dealer of Mita, Kyocera Hitachi, and Doc Star. 85 employees (78 in Minnesota; 2 part-time). Founded in 1983. SIC 5044, 5065.

Copeland Truc-King 5400 Main St., Suite 201, Fridley, MN 55421. Tel: 763/572-0505. Copeland specializes in moving and storage, freight hauling, and warehousing. 70 employees (12 part-time). Founded in 1957. SIC 4731.

Copper Sales Inc. 1001 Lund Blvd., Anoka, MN 55303. Tel: 763/576-9595; Fax: 763/576-9596; Web site: http://www.unaclad.com. Copper Sales Inc. (CSI) is an architectural-metal service center. Its flat sheet, slit coils, and other architectural metal products include standing seam roof panels, soffit panels, vertical wall plate, and composite and honeycomb panels. Owned and directed by six partners. 208 employees (200 in Minnesota). Founded in 1973. SIC 5051.

Corchran Inc. 1340 S. State St., Waseca, MN 56093. Tel: 507/835-3910; Fax: 507/835-1382; Web site: http://www.corchran.com. Jerry N. Brandt, Pres.; Joel D. Matheson, Cont. Corchran is engaged in metal fabrication and assembly for industrial, commercial, and agricultural customers. 86 employees (all in Minnesota). Founded in 1949. SIC 3400, 3441.

Core Products International Inc. 808 Prospect Ave., Osceola, WI 54020. Tel: 715/294-2050; Fax: 715/294-2622. Philip H. Mattison, Pres.; Royce A. Keehr, Treas. Annual revenue $5 million. Core Products International manufactures and distributes orthopaedic soft goods, including cervical pillows and backrests, and ankle, knee, wrist, elbow, lumbosacral, rib, abdominal, trochanter, industrial, and sacroiliac supports. 50 employees. Founded in 1988. SIC 3842.

Corporate Graphics 1750 Northway Dr., North Mankato, MN 56003. Tel: 507/388-3300; Fax: 507/386-6303. Joe Keenan, Pres. Corporate Graphics performs complete graphics service—from business cards to books—through Corporate Graphics Commercial businesses. Owned by Taylor Corp., North Mankato, Minn. 120 employees. Founded in 1976. SIC 2752, 2759.

Corporate Travel Services 2 Appletree Square, Suite 100, Bloomington, MN 55425. Tel: 952/798-8900; Fax: 952/861-2522. Deborah Callahan, Owner, Pres., and CEO; Patricia A. Kleinman, COO; Mike Diffley, CIO. Corporate Travel Services, Minnesota's fifth-largest travel management company, serves the travel management needs of corporations worldwide. In addition to business travel management, the company has well-established clients in meeting, incentive, and infinity groups. As a combined entity, the knowledge and experience of the three divisions bring expertise to business travel management (both domestic and international), infinity groups, meeting and incentives planning, and leisure and student travel. 86 employees (83 in Minnesota; 3 part-time). Founded in 1974. SIC 4724.

Cortec Advanced Film Division 410 E. First Ave., Cambridge, MN 55008. Tel: 763/689-4100; Fax: 763/689-5833; Web site: http://www.springlakepackaging.com. Boris A. Miksic, Pres. and CEO; Victor M. Jarnegan, Plant Mgr.; Maggie Norstrom, Op. Mgr. Cortec Advanced Film Division manufactures polyethylene bags and film, plain or printed. Miksic, owner of Cortec Corp., purchased Spring Lake Packaging in February 1997. 70 employees (7 part-time). Founded in 1974. SIC 3081.

Coulee Region Enterprises Inc. P.O. Box 319, Bangor, WI 54614. Tel: 608/486-2882; Fax: 608/486-4235; Web site: http://members.aol.com/couleereg/conlee.html. Edward Solberg, Pres.; Lawrence Rayner Jr., Treas. and Sec.; Peter Solberg, VP. Coulee Region Enterprises manufactures hardwood dimension. Includes kitchen cabinet parts, furniture parts, and specialty items. 85 employees. Founded in 1968. SIC 2426.

Country Classic Dairies Inc. 1001 N. Seventh Ave., P.O. Box 968, Bozeman, MT 59771. Tel: 406/586-5426; Fax: 406/586-5110. Keith Nye, CEO; Dick Flikkema, Pres.; Stan Dyk, VP; Jerry Leep, Sec. and Treas. Country Classic Dairies, also known as Darigold Farms of Montana, manufactures and distributes dairy products in Montana and Wyoming. 52 employees. Founded in 1932. SIC 2026, 5143.

Cramer Building Services Company 5916 Pleasant Ave. S., Minneapolis, MN 55419. Tel: 612/861-7232; Fax: 612/861-7827. Richard D. Cramer, Pres. Annual revenue $20 million. Cramer Building Services provides HVAC sales and service for Trane-brand products. 87 employees (all in Minnesota). Founded in 1973. SIC 5075.

Crane Creek Construction Inc. P.O. Box 246, Owatonna, MN 55060. Tel: 507/451-8950; Fax: 507/451-0575. Donald Redman, Pres. Crane Creek Construction manufactures asphalt and gravel products. 90 employees. Founded in 1970. SIC 2951.

Creative Carton 8600 Wyoming Ave. N., Brooklyn Park, MN 55445. Tel: 763/493-5521; Fax: 763/493-6511; Web site: http://www.creative-carton.com. Michael Sime, CEO; Robert Peterson, CFO; Jim Graven, Gen. Mgr. Annual revenue $23.5 million. Creative Carton provides standard/custom corrugated cartons, packaging supplies, and machines. It has grown through taking on the extreme-rush, last-minute projects that other box makers shun. Same-day orders ("911" service) make up 30 percent of the company's business. 130 employees (all in Minnesota). Founded in 1976. Aug. 31, 2000: For the fiscal year, the company produced and shipped 747 same-day orders, all on time. SIC 2653, 5199.

Creative Garments Inc. 316 Lake St. W., Chisholm, MN 55719. Tel: 218/254-5721; Fax: 218/254-4339. Sharon Klotzbach, Owner, Pres., and Sec.; Linda Lee, Owner, VP, and Treas. Creative Garments is a garment manufacturer that specializes in winter outerwear, fleece, and embroidery. 110 employees. Founded in 1991. SIC 2329, 2339.

Creative Publishing International 5900 Green Oak Dr., Suite 300, Minnetonka, MN 55343. Tel: 952/936-4700; Fax: 952/933-1456; Web site: http://www.howtobookstore.com. David D. Murphy, Pres. and CEO; John M. Hudgens, SVP and CFO. Creative Publishing International publishes books in 120 countries and 28 languages on popular topics ranging from home improvement, home decorating, and creative sewing, to cooking, nature, and outdoor hunting and fishing. The books are published under national consumer brand names including Black & Decker, Singer, Coats & Clark, Today's Homeowner, Field & Stream, and Outdoor Life. 120 employees. Founded in 1969. SIC 2732.

Crescent Printing Company Inc. 1001 Commercial Ct., P.O. Box 127, Onalaska, WI 54650. Tel: 608/781-1050; Fax: 608/781-6158. Roger C. Bjorge, Pres.; Dennis Krumenaur, Gen. Mgr.; James O. Lund, VP and Art Dir.; Ben Rudert, Mgr.-Acct. Svs. Crescent Printing Co. provides complete art and typesetting, heatset and cold web offset printing, and four-color sheet-fed printing. 63 employees (8 in Minnesota; 1 part-time). Founded in 1949. SIC 2752, 2759.

Crest Electronics P.O. Box 727, Dassel, MN 55325. Tel: 320/275-3382; Fax: 320/275-2306. Warren T. Anderson, Pres. and CEO. Crest Electronics is a catalog marketer specializing in nurse-call equipment and other product categories critical to the maintenance of operations at health care facilities, including lighting fixtures, signage, cubicle curtains and accessories, bed maintenance items, wheelchair parts, and repair services. 80 employees (all in Minnesota; 4 part-time). Founded in 1967. SIC 3669.

Crestliner Inc. 609 13th Ave. N.E., Little Falls, MN 56345. Tel: 320/632-6686; Fax: 320/632-2127. Al Kubelbeck, Pres. Crestliner manufactures aluminum fishing and pontoon boats. Division of Genmar Holdings Inc., Minneapolis. 243 employees (1 part-time). Founded in 1945. SIC 3732.

The Cretex Companies Inc. 311 Lowell Ave., Elk River, MN 55330. Tel: 763/441-2121; Fax: 763/441-7385; Web site: http://www.cretexinc.com. John H. Bailey, Chm.; Albert H. Bailey, VChm.; Thomas C. Bender, Pres. and CEO; Donald A. Schumacher, EVP; John M. Bailey, VP. Annual revenue $325 million (estimated by Fact Book). Cretex is a holding company involved in the concrete, metal machining and fabrication, precision machining, plastic injection molding, and specialty machines industries. Its 18 divisions and subsidiaries throughout the country include these Minnesota locations: Elk River Concrete Products, Maple Grove; Elk River Machine Co., Elk River; RMS Co., Coon Rapids; Juno Inc., Plymouth; and Com-Tal Machine and Engineering Inc., St. Paul. 2,000 employees. Founded in 1917. In March 2000 Jim Adams, manager of manufacturing services, was elected chairman of the National Precast Concrete Association. SIC 3089, 3272, 3441, 3451, 3599. No. 38 CRM Private 100.

Crow Wing Power Highway 371 N., P.O. Box 507, Brainerd, MN 56401. Tel: 218/829-2827; Fax: 218/825-2209. Bette Mazzenga, Pres.; Gordon Martin, Treas. Crow Wing Power is a rural electric cooperative serving 33,000 customers in Cass, Crow Wing, and Morrison counties. 78 employees. Founded in 1936. SIC 4911.

Crown Holdings Inc. 2500 W. County Rd. C, Roseville, MN 55113. Tel: 651/639-8900; Fax: 651/639-8051. Clifford I. Anderson, Chm. and Pres.; George E. Anderson, EVP; Ralph A. Romano, VP-Fin. Crown Holdings owns two subsidiaries: Crown Iron Works Co., which builds vegetable-oil production equipment, and Crown Auger Manufacturing Inc., a job shop. The company also has offices in Malaysia and Honduras. Europa Crown Ltd. in Hull, England, is a jointly owned affiliate. The company builds products under the brand names Crown and Wurster & Sanger. 85 employees (all in Minnesota). Founded in 1878. In April 2000 Crown Iron Works, Europa Crown, and Alfa Laval Oil & Protein Technology A/S agreed to align their global networks to coordinate international sales, marketing, fabrication, and supply of vegetable oil processing systems. Crown Iron Works agreed to build what was to be one of the Middle East's largest oilseed extraction and vegetable oil refineries, in Port of Damietta, Egypt. SIC 3443, 3535, 3556, 3559.

Crystal Cabinet Works Inc. 1100 Crystal Dr., Princeton, MN 55371. Tel: 763/389-4187; Fax: 763/389-3825. Jeffrey R. Hammer, Chm. and Pres.; Mark Walsh, Nat'l Sls. Mgr. Annual revenue $46 million. Crystal Cabinet manufactures several complete cabinet lines, including custom wood cabinetry with an optional wood interior, quality stock cabinetry, internationally styled laminate, and architectural casework cabinetry. 625 employees. Founded in 1947. SIC 2434, 2499.

Crysteel Manufacturing Inc. P.O. Box 178, Lake Crystal, MN 56055. Tel: 507/726-2728; Fax: 507/726-2559. Peter D. Jones, Pres.; James E. Mehrman, Cont.; Terry Chesney, VP-Op.; Bob Miller, Sls./Mktg. Mgr. Crysteel Manufacturing produces (truck) dump bodies and hoists. 250 employees (200 in Minnesota). Founded in 1968. SIC 3713, 3714.

Culligan Water Conditioning 6030 Culligan Way, Minnetonka, MN 55345. Tel: 952/933-7200; Fax: 952/933-5049; Web site: http://www.culliganwater.com. F. Wayne Packard, Chm. and CEO; John Packard, Pres.; Mark Forsberg, Cont.; Dave Recker, Gen. Mgr. Culligan Water Conditioning provides sales and service of water treatment equipment and products. 300 employees (89 in Minnesota). Founded in 1946. SIC 5074.

Cummins North Central Inc. 2690 Cleveland Ave. N., Roseville, MN 55113. Tel: 651/636-1000; Fax: 651/638-2442. Jim Andrews, Owner and Pres.; Russell W. Sheaffer, VP-Sls./Mktg.; J.R. Boelsen, VP-Fin. and CFO; Tom Patterson, VP-Op.; Bob Shockman, VP-Power Generation. Annual revenue $70 million. Cummins North Central sells and services diesel and natural gas engines, parts, generator sets, power units, and transport refrigeration equipment. 200 employees (140 in Minnesota). Founded in 1954. SIC 5013.

Cuningham Group 201 Main St. S.E., Suite 325, Minneapolis, MN 55414. Tel: 612/379-3400; Fax: 612/379-4400; Web site: http://www.cuningham.com. John W. Cuningham, Chm.; John E. Quiter, Pres.; John Hamilton, VP; Thomas L. Hoskens, VP; Doug Lowe, VP; Rick Solberg, VP; Victor Caliandro, AIA-Owner/Principal; Roger Kipp, Owner/Principal; Kenneth Powell, AIA-Owner/Principal; James S. Scheidel, AIA-Owner/Principal; Mark Sopko, AIA-Owner/Principal; Jeffrey P. Stebbins, Owner/Principal; Jonathan Watts, AIA-Owner/Principal. Annual revenue $21.2 million. Cuningham Group provides architectural, interior design, planning, and construction services in a variety of practice areas through offices in Minneapolis, Phoenix, and Los Angeles. Market segments served include education, entertainment, worship/nonprofit, resort, hospitality, corporate, retail, restaurant, urban, and civic. 160 employees (105 in Minnesota; 5 part-time). Founded in 1968. The past year proved critical for the firm as Cuningham Group expanded into international markets. SIC 8712.

Custom Business Forms 210 Edge Place N.E., Minneapolis, MN 55418. Tel: 612/789-0002; Fax: 612/789-6321. Frank A. Miske Jr., Pres. Custom Business Forms is a full-service printing company that specializes in snap-apart, continuous, and word processing forms for industry. 101 employees (1 part-time). Founded in 1969. SIC 2677, 2761.

Custom Products of Litchfield Inc. 1715 Sibley Ave. S., P.O. Box 718, Litchfield, MN 55355. Tel: 320/693-3221; Fax: 320/693-7252; Web site: http://www.800cabline.com. Arvid Reinke, Pres. and Treas.; Randy Reinke, VP and Sec. Annual revenue $11.5 million. Custom Products manufactures rollover protective structures (ROPS) and cab enclosures for all types of off-highway vehicles. The company does custom sheet metal fabrication and light-to-medium plate work, including laser and plasma cutting, forming, bending, hydraulic tube bending to 6-inch round and 4-inch squares, conveyerized wash and paint line. It also does robotic welding. 105 employees (all in Minnesota; 5 part-time). Founded in 1959. SIC 3444, 3523, 3531, 3537.

Custom Research Inc. 8401 Golden Valley Rd., P.O. Box 27900, St. Louis Park, MN 55427. Tel: 952/542-0800; Fax: 952/542-0864; Web site: http://www.customresearch.com. Judith S. Corson, Pres. Annual revenue $30 million. Custom Research is a Malcolm Baldrige National Quality Award-winning company engaged in marketing research, customer-satisfaction measurement, and database marketing. Clients include multinational consumer, medical, service, and industrial products companies. 120 employees. Founded in 1974. SIC 8742.

Cutler-Magner Company 12th Avenue West and Waterfront, P.O. Box 16807, Duluth, MN 55816. Tel: 218/722-3981; Fax: 218/722-2667. Clarence La Liberte, Pres.; Robert Kanuit, VP and CFO; Dana Stone, VP-Op.; David La Liberte, VP-Hum. Res. Cutler-Magner manufactures chemical lime, hydrated lime, and fine-ground limestone at its wholly owned subsidiary, CLM Corp., in Superior, Wis., using rotary kilns for calcining the limestone; a hydrator and air separator for producing hydrated lime; and a high-side roller mill and air separator for producing fine-ground limestone. The salt plant in Duluth, Minn., processes rock and evaporated salt (using drying, screening, crushing, blending, and briqueting equipment) to make products for the industrial and agricultural trade. 76 employees (36 in Minnesota). Founded in 1880. SIC 3274, 3299.

D.C. Group Inc. 1977 West River Rd. N., Minneapolis, MN 55411. Tel: 612/529-9516. H. Stephen Frank, CEO. Annual revenue $5.5 million. D.C. Group provides electrical filtering and backup systems maintenance for corporations nationwide. As the only independent service provider that is ISO-certified (9002), the company has been instrumental in certifying Uninterruptible Power Supply (UPS) and related power systems as Y2K-compliant for dozens of companies in the Fortune 500 and 25 of the Forbes World Super 50. 104 employees. Founded in 1992. In October 2000 the company was named to the Inc. 500 as one of the fastest-growing companies in the country. “We had an extraordinary year fueled by the seemingly limitless Y2K compliance issues,” said CEO Frank. SIC 1731. No. 25 CityBusiness Fastest-growing Private Companies.

DCI Inc. 600 54th Ave. N., P.O. Box 1227, St. Cloud, MN 56302. Tel: 320/252-8200; Fax: 320/252-0866. Larry Korf, Pres.; David Dixon, Dir.-Engrg.; Chuck Leonard, Dir.-Sls.; Wayne Brinkman, VP-Materials Mgmt.; Jeff Keller, VP-Fin.; Dennis McCarty, VP-Mfg. DCI is a manufacturer of stainless steel storage tanks and process vessels for the dairy, food, beverage, pharmaceutical, biotechnology, and chemical industries. In August 1994 the company opened a division in Cedar City, Utah. 280 employees (240 in Minnesota). Founded in 1955. SIC 3443, 3556.

DFG Inc. 258 Hennepin Ave., Minneapolis, MN 55401. Tel: 612/338-7581; Fax: 612/371-7488; Web site: http://www.dolphinstaffing.com. Dorothy Dolphin, Chm.; Kathleen A. Dolphin, Pres. Annual revenue $30 million. DFG Inc. is the managing company for Dolphin Staffing and Industrial Staffing. Dolphin Staffing specializes in providing qualified professional, technical and clerical temporary employees to businesses, government and non-profit entities across the Twin Cities. Industrial Staffing, serving the metro area since 1976, provides light industrial temporary employees. 20,075 employees (20,000 part-time). Founded in 1969. SIC 7363.

D&J Transfer Company P.O. Box 455, Highway 4 North, Sherburne, MN 56171. Tel: 507/764-4252; Fax: 507/764-4172. B.R. Hartke, Pres.; D.P. Hartke, VP; J.L. Hartke, Treas. D&J Transfer Co. is an interstate motor carrier dealing in long-distance trucking with refrigerated trailers. Its fleet of 102 tractors and 165 trailers hauls frozen food, general commodities, meat, and produce. 155 employees (40 in Minnesota). Founded in 1962. SIC 4213.

DPRA Environmental E. 1500 First National Bank, 322 Minnesota St., St. Paul, MN 55101. Tel: 651/227-6500; Fax: 651/227-5522; Web site: http://www.dpra.com. Richard Seltzer, Chm. and CEO; Chris Lough, SVP; Marty Bonnell, VP; Steven Heikkila, Principal; Carol Sarnat, Principal; Robert Wahlstrom, Principal. Annual revenue $21 million. DPRA offers environmental and engineering consulting services to business and government. It provides environmental site assessments, engineering studies, site investigation and remediation services, policy and economics analysis, and information services. DPRA has nine offices nationwide, including: Dallas; Denver; Washington, D.C.; Milwaukee; Princeton, N.J.; Manhattan, Kan; Oak Ridge, Tenn; and Toronto. 160 employees (25 in Minnesota). Founded in 1979. SIC 8711.

DRS Ahead Technology 520 Blanding Woods Rd., St. Croix Falls, WI 54024. Tel: 763/519-9129; Fax: 763/519-9138. DRS uses advanced magnetic technology to design and manufacture magnetic heads. 85 employees (all in Minnesota). Founded in 1954. SIC 3679.

DS Manufacturing Inc. 67 Fifth St. N.E., P.O. Box 999, Pine Island, MN 55963. Tel: 507/356-8322; Fax: 507/356-8436. Jim Preisler, Pres.; John Happe, VP-Fin./Admin. DS Manufacturing (formerly Pine Plating Co. Inc.) manufactures and finishes steel parts; and designs and manufactures aftermarket motorcycle accessories. 160 employees. Founded in 1961. SIC 3444, 3471, 3499.

Dacon Engineering and Service Company 4725 Highway 7, St. Louis Park, MN 55416. Tel: 952/920-8040; Fax: 952/920-7619. Rolland R. Davis, CEO and Owner; Perry Domaas, Gen. Mgr.; Marjorie A. Brown, VP-Admin. Annual revenue $11 million. Dacon provides contract engineering services with emphasis on engineers, designers, drafters, and technicians. 275 employees (all in Minnesota). Founded in 1965. SIC 8711.

Dacotah Paper Company 3940 15th N.W., Fargo, ND 58108. Tel: 701/281-1730; Fax: 701/281-0446. Matthew D. Mohr, Chm. and Pres.; Eric W. Mohr, VP; G.M. Pederson, Treas. Dacotah Paper is a wholesaler of industrial and personal service paper. 110 employees (12 in Minnesota; 3 part-time). Founded in 1906. SIC 5113.

Dadco Food Products 2715 Hogarth St., P.O. Box 1107, Eau Claire, WI 54702. Tel: 715/834-3418; Fax: 715/834-0151. Mark D. Donnelly, Pres.; Richard McHugh, VP-Sls./Mktg.; Ronald L. Dervetsky, CFO. Dadco Food Products manufactures frozen pizza. Owned by Dadco Diversified Inc. 100 employees. Founded in 1947. SIC 2038.

Daggett Truck Line Inc. County Road 10, Frazee, MN 56544. Tel: 218/334-3711; Fax: 218/334-2566. Delta Daggett, Pres.; Fred Daggett, VP; Robert Daggett, VP; David Daggett, Sec. and Treas. Daggett Truck Line is a shipping company serving the continental United States. It offers vans, refrigerated trucks, drop-deck trucks, and livestock trucks. 110 employees. Founded in 1930. SIC 4213.

Dahl Motor La Crosse Inc. 711 S. Third St., La Crosse, WI 54601. Tel: 608/784-9600; Fax: 608/784-9630. Harry Dahl, Pres. Dahl Ford La Crosse is a motor vehicle dealer. 110 employees. Founded in 1911. SIC 5511.

Dahlen Transport Inc. 1680 Fourth Ave., Newport, MN 55055. Tel: 651/459-3344; Fax: 651/458-4400. Richard Steeley, Pres. Dahlen is a common and contract carrier of petroleum, propane, acids, chemicals, hazardous waste, sugar, flour, and general freight, with terminals in Wisconsin and Iowa. 170 employees. Founded in 1943. SIC 4212, 4213.

Dahlgren & Company Inc. 1220 Sunflower St., Crookston, MN 56716. Tel: 218/281-2985; Fax: 218/281-6218; Web site: http://www.sunflowerseed.com. Kelly Engelstad, Pres.; Charles Considine, VP-Domestic Sls.; Tim Egeland, CFO; Thomas J. Miller, VP-Int'l Sls. Annual revenue $60 million. Dahlgren processes and sells edible sunflowers. In November 1997 company management, assisted by GE Capital Commercial Finance Inc., Bloomington, Minn., led a buyout of 79 percent of the company. 180 employees (150 in Minnesota). Founded in 1955. SIC 5145, 5159.

Daily Printing Inc. 2333 Niagara Ln., Plymouth, MN 55447. Tel: 763/475-2333; Fax: 763/449-6320; Web site: http://www.dailyprinting.com. Robert Manuel, Chm.; R. Peter Jacobson, Pres. and CEO; Don Bergeron, VP-Op.; Russ Horbal, VP-Mfg.; Jack Patterson, VP-Sls.; Dan Sandvik, VP-Prod.; Ken Rein, Treas. Annual revenue $18 million. Daily Printing is engaged in full-service, sheetfed commercial printing. 106 employees (all in Minnesota). Founded in 1950. SIC 2759.

Daily Telegram Company 1226 Ogden Ave., Superior, WI 54880. Tel: 715/394-4411; Fax: 715/394-9404. John B. Murphy, Chm. and CEO; Elizabeth M. Burns, VP; George A. Nelson, VP; Lois L. Wessman, Sec.; Robert J. Wallace, Treas. Daily Telegram is a newspaper publisher. 60 employees (15 part-time). Founded in 1890. SIC 2711.

Dairyland Power Cooperative 3200 East Ave. S., P.O. Box 817, La Crosse, WI 54602. Tel: 608/788-4000; Fax: 608/787-1420; Web site: http://www.dairynet.com. Dennis Engel, Chm.; George Webb, VChm.; William L. Berg, Pres. and CEO; Robert C. Mueller, VP-Fin./Admin.; Dale Pohlman, VP-Strategic Planning; Charles Sans Crainte, VP-Generation; Bruce Staples, VP-Transmission. Annual revenue $173.8 million. Dairyland Power is a generation and transmission cooperative supplying power to 25 electric cooperatives and 18 municipal utilities (including those served by GEN~SYS Energy) throughout a 44,500-square-mile area. The Dairyland system serves 230,000 consumer-members in four states via 3,134 miles of transmission power lines from four Dairyland Power generating plants (with a total capacity of 985 megawatts). 548 employees (15 part-time). SIC 4931.

Dakota Electric Association 4300 220th St. W., Farmington, MN 55024. Tel: 651/463-7134; Fax: 651/463-6359; Web site: http://www.dakotaelectric.com. Eldon Johnson, Pres. and CEO; Margaret D. Schreiner, Chm.; Jerry Pittman, VChm.; Janet Lekson, Treas.; Bill Holton, Sec. Annual revenue $96 million. Dakota Electric Association is a cooperative electric utility. 230 employees. Founded in 1938. SIC 4911. No. 20 CRM Cooperatives/Mutuals 20.

Dakota Gasification Company 1100 E. Interstate Ave., Bismarck, ND 58501. Tel: 701/221-4400; Fax: 701/221-4450. Robert L. McPhail, Pres. and CEO; Kent E. Janssen, VP and COO. Dakota Gasification Co. produces synthetic natural gas and associated byproducts. The company owns and operates the $2.1 billion Great Plains Synfuels energy plant, the nation's only commercial-scale coal gasification facility that manufactures natural gas. Built as part of America's effort to reduce reliance on foreign oil, the synfuels plant continues produces natural gas from lignite and makes fertilizers and other valuable products from the gasification process. Formerly ANG Coal Gasification Co. Owned by Basin Electric Power Cooperative, Bismarck. 633 employees (48 part-time). Founded in 1984. In October 2000 Dakota Gasification Co. and PanCanadian Petroleum Ltd. launched one of the continent's largest carbon dioxide miscible flood projects, at Weyburn, Saskatchewan. The $1.1 billion project will inject 95 million cubic feet per day of CO(2) into a 46-year-old oil field, one of Canada's largest and most prolific reservoirs, which will boost oil production by more than 50 percent to 30,000 barrels a day over the next decade. The CO(2) is being supplied by Dakota Gasification, which built a 325-kilometer pipeline from the Great Plains Synfuels Plant at Beulah to the Weyburn oil field. SIC 1311.

Dakota Granite Company P.O. Box 1351, Milbank, SD 57252. Tel: 605/432-5580; Fax: 605/432-6155; Web site: http://www.dakgran.com. C.D. Monson, Chm. and CEO; J.J. Stengel, Pres.; N. Fosheim, Sec. and Treas. Dakota Granite manufactures granite monuments, tiles, countertops, and slabs, and quarries granite blocks. 99 employees. Founded in 1925. SIC 1411, 3281.

Dakota Growers Pasta Company One Pasta Ave., P.O. Box 21, Carrington, ND 58421. Tel: 701/652-2855; Fax: 701/652-1009. Timothy J. Dodd, Pres., CEO, and Gen. Mgr.; Thomas P. Friezen, VP-Fin. and Principal-Fin./Accounting Officer. Dakota Growers Pasta is an agricultural cooperative that owns and operates state-of-the-art integrated facilities at which durum wheat provided by the company's members is milled into high-quality semolina. This semolina is processed through advanced Italian pasta processing equipment utilizing ultra-high temperature drying for consistent quality. In addition to marketing its pasta products, the company distributes excess semolina production and byproducts of the milling process. In February 1998 Primo Piatto Inc. (the former manufacturing facilities of The Creamette Co.), New Hope, Minn., became a wholly owned subsidiary, creating the nation's second-largest pasta company (to Hershey Foods Corp./American Beauty brand), with 500 million pounds of annual production. The company has a total of 1,085 members, whose operations are located in North Dakota, Minnesota, and Montana. 470 employees (180 in Minnesota). Founded in 1991. SIC 2098.

Dakota Industries Inc. P.O. Box 932, Sioux Falls, SD 57101. Tel: 605/332-5930; Fax: 605/334-8521. Donald P. Mackintosh, Chm. and Pres.; Richard Flugge, CFO. Dakota Industries manufactures outerwear pants, running suits, parkas, and jackets. 50 employees. Founded in 1968. SIC 2329, 2339, 2399.

Dakota Manufacturing Company Inc. 1909 S. Rowley, Mitchell, SD 57301. Tel: 605/996-5571; Fax: 605/996-5572. A. Dean Oehlerking, Pres. Dakota Manufacturing makes low-boy and specialty trailers for construction, oil-field heavy machinery, and over-the-road haulers. 170 employees (5 part-time). Founded in 1963. SIC 3715.

Dakota, Minnesota & Eastern Railroad Corporation 337 22nd Ave. S., P.O. Box 178, Brookings, SD 57006. Tel: 605/697-2400; Fax: 605/697-2499. Kevin V. Schieffer, Pres. and CEO; Lynn A. Anderson, VP-Mktg.; Kurt V. Feaster, VP-Fin.; John L. Waltman, VP-Energy. Dakota, Minnesota & Eastern is a closely held regional railroad. 350 employees. SIC 4011.

Dakota Supply Group P.O. Box 2886, Fargo, ND 58108. Tel: 701/237-9440; Fax: 701/237-6504; Web site: http://www.dakotasupply-group.com. Ben Herr, Pres. and CEO; Warren Lundberg, EVP; Steve Carlson, VP; Tom Rosendahl, VP; Todd Kumm, VP and CFO. Annual revenue $90 million. Dakota Supply Group distributes contractor, utility, and telecommunications equipment to contractors and resellers in North Dakota, South Dakota, and Minnesota. It also supplies products to more than 150 telcos in seven states. Twelve branches throughout the Dakotas offer innovative distribution services and quick delivery from Dakota Electric Supply's fleet of trucks. The company also supplies waterworks, plumbing and mechanical products. 230 employees (10 in Minnesota; 8 part-time). Founded in 1898. SIC 5063.

Dakota Tribal Industries P.O. Box 308, Fort Totten, ND 58335. Tel: 701/766-4251; Fax: 701/766-4723. Phillip Longie, Pres. DTI is primarily a textile/sewing business, specializing in general-purpose and military tents. The company has the capabilities to perform all manufacturing operations, from the delivery of rolled textile goods to the material layout, cutting, sewing, stenciling, and packaging of the finished product. 90 employees. Founded in 1985. SIC 2329, 2339, 2394, 2399, 3089.

Dakota Tube 221 Airport Dr., Watertown, SD 57201. Tel: 605/882-2156; Fax: 605/882-4815. Jack Steinbauer, Owner; Patty Flemming, Purch. Agent. Dakota Tube (formerly Edina Engineering Co.) fabricates hydraulic steel lines. 175 employees. SIC 3492.

Dalco Enterprises Inc. 3010 Broadway N.E., Minneapolis, MN 55413. Tel: 612/331-8940; Fax: 612/331-3842. Ted Stark, Owner and CEO; Rod Dummer, VP-Mktg./Sls.; Audrey Petersen, Pres.; Ted Stark III, VP-Fin./Admin.; Larry Tranberg, VP-Op.; Chuck Panzer, VP-Nat'l Accounts. Dalco Enterprises is a distributor of janitorial supplies and equipment. 102 employees. Founded in 1959. SIC 5087.

Dalton Gear Company 212 Colfax Ave. N., Minneapolis, MN 55405. Tel: 612/374-2150; Fax: 612/374-2467; Web site: http://www.daltongear.com. E.R. Wood, Chm.; Tim Wood, Pres. and CEO; Joan M. Wood, Sec. Dalton Gear manufactures gears, sprockets, and other power transmission equipment. 68 employees. Founded in 1955. SIC 3566, 3568.

D'Amico and Partners Inc. 221 N. First St., Minneapolis, MN 55401. Tel: 612/374-1776; Fax: 612/374-1869. Richard D'Amico, Pres.; Richard K. Horn, COO; Larry D'Amico, VP; Steve Davidson, VP; Paul Smith, CFO. Annual revenue $31.6 million. D'Amico and Partners is a restaurateur that owns and operates 14 Twin Cities-area restaurants under the names D'Amico Cucina, Campiello, D'Amico and Sons, Linguini and Bob, and the Metropolitan Ballroom and Clubroom. Since its introduction, the concept has been honored with numerous local, regional, and national awards for its food, ambiance, and high standard of service quality. The company also does catering. 900 employees. Founded in 1983. In August 2000 D'Amico & Partners announced that Campiello Ristorante was to open its second location in Southwest Florida at the upscale shopping area The Promenade in Bonita Springs. SIC 5812.

Dart Transit Company 800 Lone Oak Rd., P.O. Box 64110 (55164), Eagan, MN 55121. Tel: 651/688-2000; Fax: 651/683-1826. Donald G. Oren, Pres. and CEO; Terry Hoitink, CFO. Annual revenue $280 million. Dart Transit is a truckload motor carrier serving 48 states and various Canadian provinces. Along with its Dallas subsidiary, Fleetline Inc., the company operates 2,400 trucks and 6,500 trailers. 336 employees. Founded in 1934. In April 2000 Oren and his wife filed a petition asking the courts to overturn an IRS order denying deductions for $15.3 million in Dart Transit Co. losses and ordering them to pay additional taxes for the years 1993-95. SIC 4213. No. 47 CRM Private 100.

Data Base Ideas Inc. 6200 Shingle Creek Pkwy., Suite 400, Brooklyn Center, MN 55430. Tel: 763/561-4990; Fax: 763/561-9022; Web site: http://www.dbii.com. Sophie Bell Kelley, Pres. and CEO; Scott Lien, Senior Ptnr. and Founder; Dick Salvatore, Senior Ptnr. and Founder; Michelle Hayden, Cont. Data Base Ideas provides information technology consulting services to the large corporate market, including many Twin Cities Fortune 1000 companies. Services include analysis, design, programming, testing, and implementation; project management; database design, data, and process modeling; and full client/server and object-oriented technologies at both the application and relational database level. Application areas: financial systems, purchasing, human resources, government, manufacturing, and many others. 85 employees (all in Minnesota). Founded in 1988. SIC 7371.

Datacard Group 11111 Bren Rd. W., Minnetonka, MN 55343. Tel: 952/933-1223; Fax: 952/931-0418; Web site: http://www.datacard.com. Jerry E. Johnson, Pres. and CEO; Michael Carey, VP-Hum. Res.; Jeffrey J. Hattara, CFO; Paul A. Schroeder, Gen. Mgr.-Secure Issuance Division. Annual revenue $325 million. DataCard Group is a privately owned holding company for three core business units. DataCard Worldwide manufactures card personalization systems and transaction terminals. Credentia offers identity systems based on digital imaging, biometrics, and smart cards. MedAssure provides hospitals with patient ID systems. Major markets include financial institutions, retailers, health care providers, insurers, colleges and universities, and government agencies. Owned by the Quandt family of Bad Homburg, Germany. 1,900 employees. Founded in 1969. In January 2000 the company launched the Datacard ImageCard HiFX—a new desktop card printer that offers true "edge-to-edge" printing, as well as color saturation and image resolution that is comparable to offset printing. In March Datacard Group acquired Platform Seven—a leading independent provider of smart card and e-commerce security products, solutions, and services—from NatWest Bank, part of the Royal Bank of Scotland Group. The company joined GlobalPlatform, a worldwide organization dedicated to the development of smart card standards and the advancement of multi-application smart cards. In May, at CardTech/SecurTech 2000, Datacard: a) was chosen as the exclusive sales and service provider of Otto Kuennecke mail processing systems in the United States and Canada; b) unveiled a laser engraving module for its high-volume card issuance systems that engraves secure, high-resolution images below the surface of a plastic card; c) announced that its laser engraving systems were to be used to issue Dutch passports and national ID cards beginning January 2001; d) introduced ViaNet Reporting Software, the next introduction in the company's ViaNet portfolio of Internet-based identity information software; and e) unveiled version 1.1 of its Preface ID software, which directly addresses the card design and production needs of startup programs. In July the company was selected as a solutions partner to the prime contractors participating in the U.S. General Service Administration (GSA) Smart Access Common ID Card program. In August ScanSource Inc., Greenville, S.C., agreed to become an authorized distributor of Datacard card printers and integrated photo ID systems. In September Datacard Group

PVT

unveiled two new software-driven cameras for its integrated photo ID solutions portfolio, the Datacard 860 camera for low-volume and the Datacard MRAC-1500 for mid-range image capture; Version 2.0 of the Datacard ID Works photo ID software family; and Version 4.0 of its Data Retrieval, Image Capture, and Card Issuance modules in the Internet-based Datacard ViaNet identity information software family. Maple Roll Leaf and Coding Products—two divisions of Illinois Tool Works Inc (ITW)—agreed to be the exclusive manufacturer of topping foils, UltraGrafix print ribbons, indent ribbons, cleaning tapes, clear topcoats, and card stickers for Datacard Group under a strategic alliance. Datacard was to continue to exclusively sell, distribute, and support its complete portfolio of card personalization supply products on a worldwide basis. In October Datacard announced a software-driven process for application loading and personalization of Visa Smart Debit/Credit (VSDC) cards that use the Open Platform specification, and the shipment of the company's 600th smart card personalization module. Datacard Group and Cybernetix Group signed an agreement that called for Datacard to provide sales and service for the new Cybernetix HPX card-issuance system. SIC 3579. No. 38 CRM Private 100.

Data Input Services Corporation 9555 James Ave. S., Suite 270, Bloomington, MN 55431. Tel: 952/881-7000; Fax: 952/881-5303. Rita Miller Daugherty, CEO; Jan Runyan, VP. Data Input Services provides data entry services to the business community. The company also provides online data capture, facilities management, off-shore data capture, large-volume name-and-address conversions, conversions for computer media, clerical services, and processing services. DISC also provides backfile conversion and image services to its clients. 130 employees. Founded in 1980. SIC 7379.

Data Recognition Corporation 5900 Baker Rd., Minnetonka, MN 55345. Tel: 952/935-5900; Fax: 952/945-7301; Web site: http://www.drc-mn. Russ Hagen, CEO; Susan Engeleiter, Pres. and COO; David Chayer, VP-Res./Test Develop.-Educ.; Majeana Hallstrom, VP-Mktg. and Acct. Mgr.-Educ.; Steve Larson, CFO; Russ Spencer, VP-Surveys; Susan Trent, VP-Perform. Assess./Educ. Annual revenue $50 million. Data Recognition Corp. (DRC) provides full-service information management for education, government, and business providing the highest-quality technology and services available. Information management projects include educational testing and assessment processing; survey design, administration, processing and analyses; and high-speed laser-printing and mailing services. 275 employees (all in Minnesota). Founded in 1974. SIC 7374.

Data Sciences International Inc. 4211 Lexington Ave. N., Arden Hills, MN 55126. Tel: 651/481-7410; Fax: 651/481-7417. Brian Brockway, Pres. Data Sciences International is a manufacturer of implantable radio-telemetry devices to monitor vital signs. 95 employees (92 in Minnesota; 3 part-time). Founded in 1983. SIC 3823, 3825.

DataSource Hagen 5051 Highway 7, St. Louis Park, MN 55416. Tel: 952/836-2000; Fax: 952/836-2150; Web site: http://www.datasource.net. Roar Lund, Pres.; Steve Sherritt, VP and Gen. Mgr.; Steve Hoffman, Dir.-Sls./Mktg.; Shannon Vander Giessen, Mgr.-PSO. DataSource Hagen provides professional services to design, install, and maintain local- and wide-area networks. The company offers professional services consulting in Internet/intranet Web development, UNIX, Novell, Microsoft (Solution Provider Partner), IBM AIX, and HP-UX systems for business and government institutions. A National Service Provider, the company does hardware configuration, technical staffing, help desk, custom/classroom training, and warranty repair—with a strong focus on services and outsourcing. DataSource/Connecting Point acquired Hagen Computing Solutions, Richfield, Minn., in 1997. 110 employees (all in Minnesota). Founded in 1982. SIC 7373.

Davidson Companies Davidson Building, Great Falls, MT 59401. Tel: 406/727-4200; Fax: 406/268-3007; Web site: http://www.dadco.com. Ian B. Davidson, Chm.; Vincent M. Purpura, Pres. and CEO; William Johnstone, Pres.-D.A. Davidson & Co.; John H. Davant, Pres./COO-Davidson Investment Advisors; Michael Morrison, Pres.-Davidson Travel; Joe Heffernan, Pres.-Davidson Trust. Annual revenue $111.3 million. Davidson Companies is a holding company that controls D.A. Davidson & Co., a full-service investment firm; Davidson Trust Co., a full-service multistate trust company; Davidson Investment Advisors, a money management company; and Davidson Travel, a comprehensive travel agency. 650 employees. Founded in 1935. SIC 6211.

Davidson Printing Company 4444 Haines Rd., P.O. Box 16990 (55816), Duluth, MN 55811. Tel: 218/733-2590; Fax: 218/733-2603. William Abene, Owner and CEO; Chris Stern, Plant Mgr.; Richard Sienkiewicz, EVP-Op.; Roger Turner, VP-Fin.; Jeff Elliott, Mktg. Dir. Davidson Printing is a sheetfed offset publication printer specializing in monthly business, consumer, association, and trade magazines. 90 employees (all in Minnesota). Founded in 1958. SIC 2721.

Davis-Frost Inc. 1209 Tyler St. N.E., Minneapolis, MN 55413. Tel: 612/789-8871; Fax: 612/789-0308. Calvin C. Henning, Pres.; David E. Boie, EVP; Gerhart Baker, VP-Mfg.; Denise R. Henning, VP-Tech.; Catherine A. Salin, VP-Fin./Systems/Hum. Res. Annual revenue $32 million. Davis-Frost (formerly Frost Paint & Oil Corp.) manufactures environmentally safe industrial paints and coatings. 180 employees (40 in Minnesota). Founded in 1915. SIC 2851.

Davisco Foods International Inc. 620 N. Main St., Le Sueur, MN 56058. Tel: 507/665-8861; Fax: 507/665-8869; Web site: http://www.daviscofoods.com. Mark E. Davis, Pres.; Jon Davis, VP; Martin E. Davis, VP and Sec.; Mitch Davis, VP; James T. Ward, VP and Treas. Annual revenue $380 million. Davisco Foods International produces cheese and manufactures various food powders and milk proteins. Among its products: whey protein hydrolyzates for use as ingredients in nutritional supplements, infant formulas, sports drinks, and meal substitutes for weight-reduction programs. Originally known as St. Peter Creamery. 460 employees. Founded in 1943. In September 2000 Davisco and Land O'Lakes, Arden Hills, Minn., announced the initiation of a feasibility study to consider the formation of an operating partnership that would lead to the construction of a world-class cheese manufacturing facility in South Dakota. (Davisco operates a whey manufacturing facility in Lake Norden, S.D., and Land O'Lakes operates a cheese manufacturing plant in Volga, S.D.) "Davisco and Land O'Lakes believe that South Dakota and the surrounding region have the potential to achieve and sustain a competitive position in the dairy marketplace, in terms of both production and processing," President Davis said. "The development of a large-scale, world-class cheese manufacturing facility in the region would clearly enhance that potential." SIC 2022, 2023. No. 29 CRM Private 100.

Dayton Rogers Manufacturing Company 8401 W. I-35W Service Dr., Minneapolis, MN 55440. Tel: 612/784-7714; Fax: 612/784-8209. John W. Seeger Sr., Chm. and CEO; John Seeger Jr., Pres.; Steve Wennes, CFO; John Moylan, VP-Hum. Res.; Rick Steer, VP and Gen. Mgr.-Minneapolis Div.; Dave Hewitt, Purch. Mgr.. Dayton Rogers manufactures short- and medium-run metal stampings and precision metal fabrications. 450 employees (119 in Minnesota). Founded in 1929. SIC 3469.

Dealers Manufacturing Company 7120 Northland Terrace, Brooklyn Park, MN 55428. Tel: 763/535-8900; Fax: 763/971-6250. David W. Goodwin, CEO; John Mathiesen, Pres.; Jerry Kelly, VP and Gen. Mgr.-Distribution; Larry Schmidt, VP-Mfg. Sls.; Jim Tucker, VP-Fin.; Duane Wanner, VP-Corp. Devel. Annual revenue $56.7 million. Dealers Manufacturing remanufactures and distributes gasoline and diesel engines; and component parts for automotive, marine, commercial, and agricultural applications. The company sells directly to automobile dealerships in a five-state area in the Upper Midwest and indirectly throughout the United States. 286 employees. Founded in 1944. SIC 3714.

Decathlon Hotel & Athletic Club 1700 E. 79th St., Bloomington, MN 55425. Tel: 952/854-7777; Fax: 952/854-3792. John F. Swaney, VP and Gen. Mgr. Decathlon Hotel & Athletic Club is a private business, social, and athletic club specializing in business meeting space, fine dining, banquets, hotel accommodations, and full athletic facilities. The Decathlon Club is the home of the Hobey Baker Memorial Award, a national award given annually to the top collegiate hockey player. 140 employees (all in Minnesota; 50 part-time). Founded in 1968. SIC 7997.

Dedicated Logistics Inc. 2896 Centre Pointe Dr., St. Paul, MN 55175. Tel: 651/631-5918; Fax: 651/631-5958; Web site: http://www.dl-inc.com. Thomas Wintz, Pres.; Dennis Bierschnach, SVP and CFO; Gary Eikas, EVP. Annual revenue $40 million. Dedicated Logistics is a common and private-contract carrier engaged in all fields of transportation—local cartage, pool distribution, warehousing, and leasing. 250 employees. Founded in 1976. SIC 4214, 7513.

Dee Inc. 1302 Foskett St., P.O. Box 627, Crookston, MN 56716. Tel: 218/281-5811; Fax: 218/281-7321. Jim Ellinger, CEO; Marc Sorensen, COO; Nick Nicholas, CFO. Annual revenue $14 million. Dee manufactures sandcast and permanent mold aluminum castings, and provides CNC machining. 140 employees. Founded in 1973. SIC 3365.

DeLite Outdoor Advertising Inc. 3435 Washington Dr., Eagan, MN 55122. Tel: 651/905-3904; Fax: 651/905-3907. Jeff Eurard, CEO; Lonny Binder, CFO. DeLite Outdoor is an oudoor advertising and billboards company. 50 employees. SIC 7312.

Dell-Comm, Inc. 4860 Mustang Circle, Mounds View, MN 55112. Tel: 763/783-0035; Fax: 763/783-0896; Web site: http://www.dell-comm.com. Del Freichels, CEO; Karen Aho, VP; Jim Freichels, Pres. Annual revenue $14.2 million. Dell-Com designs and installs voice and data communications. Other locations: Fargo, Bismark, and Grand Forks, N.D.; Sioux Falls, S.D.; and Rapid City, S.D. 142 employees (100 in Minnesota; 2 part-time). Founded in 1990. Selected to wire the 32-story Target Corp. headquarters in Minneapolis. SIC 1731.

Delta Environmental Consultants Inc. 2770 Cleveland Ave. N., Roseville, MN 55113. Tel: 651/639-9449; Fax: 651/639-9497. Jerry R. Rick, Pres. and CEO. Delta Environmental Consultants provides a variety of environmental consulting and contracting services for private clients throughout the United States and United Kingdom. Services include development and implementation of strategic environmental plans, hazardous waste remediation, environmental assessment/compliance services, industrial hygiene and safety, air quality management, and wastewater treatment process and design. The company has 18 offices in the United States and one in the United Kingdom. 480 employees. Founded in 1986. SIC 8731.

Denning Consulting Services Inc. 9400 Golden Valley Rd., Golden Valley, MN 55427. Tel: 763/595-9490. Raymond Denning, CEO. Annual revenue $8.7 million. Denning provides full life-cycle software consulting and training (user-end and technical) services to a primarily Fortune 1000 base of customers. 57 employees. Founded in 1984. SIC 7371.

Dental Services Group, Sentage Corporation 5775 Wayzata Blvd., Suite 670, Golden Valley, MN 55416. Tel: 763/541-9622; Fax: 763/541-1358. George J. Obst, CEO; Ojars A. Papedis, CFO; Robert A. Ditta, VP; Joseph C. Gerace, VP. Sentage Corp. has 35 corporate-owned dental laboratories and 62 laboratory affiliates—in the United States, Canada, and Mexico—that manufacture oral appliances. The company's proprietary products include snoring/sleep apnea appliances, oral appliances to treat TMJ disorders, and a number of other oral appliances. The local laboratory in Minneapolis, Boos Dental Laboratory, was founded in 1902. 1,030 employees (70 in Minnesota; 275 part-time). Founded in 1989. SIC 3843, 8072.

Desmond's Formal Wear 2338 Commerce St., P.O. Box 1447, La Crosse, WI 54602. Tel: 608/781-7770; Fax: 608/781-5125. John G. Desmond, Pres.; Steven Sheely, VP; John W. Desmond, Sec. and Treas.; Michael J. McArdle, Asst. Sec. and Cont. Desmond's Formal Wear is engaged in nationwide rental and sale of men's formal wear. Desmond's operates 55 retail outlets in 10 states and 11 metro locations, and also serves more than 1,300 wholesale clients. 326 employees. Founded in 1948. SIC 5611, 7219.

Despatch Industries Inc. 63 St. Anthony Pkwy., P.O. Box 1320 (55440), Minneapolis, MN 55418. Tel: 612/781-5363; Fax: 612/781-5353; Web site: http://www.despatch.com. Patrick J. Peyton, Chm. and CEO; Anthony Fabiano, Pres. and COO; Hans Melgaard, VP-Res./Devel.; Geri Ronningen, Sec. Despatch Industries designs and manufactures standard industrial ovens and custom thermal processing systems for the electronics, pharmaceutical, metals, and other general materials markets. 300 employees (all in Minnesota). Founded in 1902. In April 2000 the company announced expanded test capabilities at the Despatch Innovation Center. A new high-temperature, high-capacity batch oven was able to simulate virtually any thermal process—such as sterilizing vials, burning in electronic components, or heat treating aluminum parts. SIC 3567, 3569, 3821.

Determan Brownie Inc. 1241 72nd Ave. N.E., Fridley, MN 55432. Tel: 763/571-8110; Fax: 763/571-1789; Web site: http://www.determan.com. James R. Determan, Pres. and CEO; Tom Determan, Pres.; Gary Quam, VP-Mfg.; Thomas Grzechowiak, VP-Sls./Mktg.; John LaFontsee, VP-Op.; Gerrie Summerville, Sec.; Thomas Valcheck, CFO. Determan manufactures truck tanks and aviation fueling equipment. The company also distributes and installs petroleum equipment, meters, pumps, and related items to industrial and petroleum-handling customers. 180 employees (182 in Minnesota; 2 part-time). Founded in 1964. SIC 3443.

Diamond Brands Inc. 1800 Cloquet Ave., Cloquet, MN 55720. Tel: 218/879-6700; Fax: 218/879-6369. Naresh K. Nakra, Pres. and CEO; Frank J. Chalk, VP-Fin. and CFO; James Lincoln, VP-Sls.; Peter Lynn, VP-Bus. Devel.; Christopher A. Mathews, VP-Mfg.; Kenneth Towney, VP-Mktg. Annual revenue $104.7 million (loss $15.9 million; includes loss of $16.1 million from discontinued operations). Diamond Brands is a leading manufacturer and marketer of a broad range of branded consumer products, including wooden lights, cutlery, and woodenware. Products are marketed primarily under the Diamond, Forster, and Empire brand names. The company believes it has the leading domestic retail market share in the wooden match, plastic cutlery, toothpick, clothespin, and wooden craft product categories. The company's products are sold in substantially all major grocery stores, drug stores, mass merchandisers, and warehouse clubs in the United States. In order to strengthen relationships with its customers, the company employs a category management strategy, including a corporate rebate program that provides incentives to grocery retailers to buy multiple products from the company. Diamond Brands produces its products at four automated manufacturing facilities located in Cloquet; East Wilton and Strong, Maine; and Kansas City, Kan. In the United States, Diamond Brands believes it is the sole manufacturer of wooden matches and the largest manufacturer of toothpicks and clothespins. The company's predecessor, Diamond Match, was formed in 1881 following the consolidation of 12 match companies. An

April 1998 recapitalization made Diamond Brands a reporting company under SEC rules. 680 employees. Founded in 1986. In December 1999 Diamond Brands sold its candle division to an investor group that planned to operate under the name Empire Candle Manufacturing LLC. As a result, Diamond recorded a one-time, noncash write-off of $16.1 million. Dec. 31: Net sales for the year (continuing operations) increased 6.4 percent to $104.7 million—due primarily to a 15.2 percent increase in plastic cutlery/straws and a 12.4 percent increase in wooden matches. EBITDA totaled $29.1 million, or 27.8 percent of net sales, compared with $25.9 million or 26.3 percent of net sales. March 31, 2000: During the quarter, investment funds controlled by Seaver Kent & Co. LLC and Texas Pacific Group made a $9.425 million 12 7/8 percent Bridge Loan investment in Diamond Brands, which used the proceeds to retire $45 million par value of its Senior Discount Debentures. As of March 31, the bonds had accreted to $30.8 million (68 percent of their par value). June 30: Net sales for the six-month period totaled $50.7 million, a 2.3 percent decrease from the corresponding period in 1999. Net sales for plastic cutlery/straws increased 8.1 percent; however, this was offset by a 9.0 percent decrease in all other product lines. EBITDA was $6.5 million, or 23.7 percent of net sales, compared to $8.3 million, or 28.0 percent of net sales. "Our second-quarter results reflect the negative impact of raw material prices," commented CEO Nakra. SIC 2499, 3999. No. 100 CRM Private 100.

Dietrich & Sons Inc. P.O. Box 777, Valley City, ND 58072. Tel: 701/845-1590; Fax: 701/845-2276. Richard J. Dietrich, Chm. and Pres. Dietrich & Sons is a school-bus distributor that also offers bus contract services. 125 employees. Founded in 1964. SIC 3714.

Discount Farm Center P.O. Box 84, Watertown, SD 57201. Tel: 605/888-5888; Fax: 605/888-3610. Robb B. Sexauer, Chm. and Pres.; L.A. Friezen, Sec. and Cont.; Larry G. Landmark, VP-Seed Div. Discount Farm Center's operations include country elevators, subterminal elevators, fertilizer plants, feed plants, and seed-conditioning plants across the Midwest. 88 employees (8 part-time). Founded in 1891. SIC 5191.

Dittrich Specialties 2110 N. Broadway St., New Ulm, MN 56073. Tel: 507/359-2650; Fax: 507/359-5413. Robert Dittrich, Pres. Dittrich Specialties manufactures small mechanical assemblies, printed circuit boards, and blister packaging. It is a subcontractor for 3M Company. 110 employees (all in Minnesota). Founded in 1982. SIC 3672.

Diversified Adjustment Service Inc. 600 Coon Rapids Blvd., Coon Rapids, MN 55433. Tel: 763/783-2301; Fax: 763/783-2390; Web site: http://www.diversifiedadjustment.com. Kathleen J. Zurek, Pres.; Sally Gallagher, EVP. Diversified Adjustment Service is a collection agency. 110 employees. SIC 7322.

Diversified Graphics Inc. 1700 N.E. Broadway St., Minneapolis, MN 55413. Tel: 612/331-1111; Fax: 612/331-4079. Jeffrey Gacek, CEO; W. Scott Morrow, Pres. Annual revenue $33 million. Diversified Graphics is in the communications service business, specializing in high-quality sheetfed print productions. 200 employees (210 in Minnesota; 10 part-time). Founded in 1949. SIC 2759.

Diversified Plastics Inc. 8617 Xylon Court, Brooklyn Park, MN 55445. Tel: 763/424-2525; Fax: 763/424-3673. James Dow, Pres.; Annette Lund, Sec. Annual revenue $5 million. Diversified Plastics does custom injection molding of thermoplastics, as well as assembly work such as silkscreening, pad printing, hot stamping, and ultrasonic welding. To guarantee quality molds, tooling division Design Tool & Engineering, a wholly owned subsidiary, builds and maintains all of the company's molds. One of the first injection molders of its size in the United States to become ISO 9002-certified, Diversified is currently preparing for QS9000 automotive certification. 70 employees (2 part-time). Founded in 1977. In September the company moved to its new location on Xylon Court. SIC 3089.

Divine, Scherzer & Brody 222 S. Ninth St., Suite 3000, Minneapolis, MN 55402. Tel: 612/359-9630; Fax: 612/359-0572. Laurence E. Gamst, Managing Ptnr.; Barry Divine, Ofcr.; Thomas A. Manning, Ofcr.; Paul D. Maves, Ofcr.; Marvin K. Mirsky, Ofcr.; Arnold Segal, Ofcr.; Jack VanderWaal, Ofcr.; Nate Wayne, Ofcr. Annual revenue $5.5 million. Divine, Scherzer & Brody is an accounting firm serving individuals, institutions, corporations, and partnerships in a growing range of industries. Services include: accounting and business consulting, audit, tax, financial and estate planning, management consulting, systems analysis and implementation, and employee benefits. Member BKR International. 55 employees (54 in Minnesota; 3 part-time). Founded in 1950. SIC 8721.

Doherty Employment Group 7625 Parklawn Ave., Edina, MN 55435. Tel: 952/832-8383; Fax: 952/832-8355; Web site: http://www.dohertyeg.com. Timothy E. Doherty, CEO; Valerie K. Doherty, COO; Jim Haubrich, CFO; Becky Woods, VP-Hum. Res. Annual revenue $102 million. Doherty Employment Group is a staffing specialist that operates three specialized temporary staffing services, an employee payroll service, and a professional employer organization. Its 50 offices, spread throughout Minnesota and Wisconsin, feature a completely computerized system and extended office hours. Doherty's fastest growing division is Doherty Employer Services, an accredited professional employer organization, providing outsourcing programs to manage human resources, workers' compensation, payroll and employee benefits. 155 employees (150 in Minnesota). Founded in 1980. SIC 7361. No. 29 CRM Employer 100.

Dola International 501 Royalston Ave., Minneapolis, MN 55405. Tel: 612/339-7521; Fax: 612/339-0963. Thomas L. Hoffelder, Pres. and Treas.; John E. Allen, VP and Sec. Annual revenue $16 million. Dola International (also known as Northwest Automatic Products Inc.) is in the business of high-volume, close-tolerance machining with screw machine base. Broad secondary capabilities include chrome plating of hydraulic spools. 130 employees (all in Minnesota). Founded in 1920. SIC 3451.

Dolan Media Company 650 3rd Ave. S., Minneapolis, MN 55402. Tel: 612/317-9420; Fax: 612/321-0563; Web site: http://www.dolanmedia.com. James P. Dolan, Chm., Pres., and CEO; Scott J. Pollei, EVP and CFO; Brian Long, Pres.-National Group; Samuel B. Spencer, Pres.-Regional Group. Dolan Media is a closely held specialized business information company that publishes business/court newspapers, commercial newspapers, and other print and electronic media products serving the law, credit, finance, construction, and commercial real estate markets. Its electronic information companies include Banko, a nationwide bankruptcy-data company; U.S. Corporate Services, which sells Uniform Commercial Code and tax lien information to law, credit, and finance customers; Bankruptcy Document Retrieval Inc., which gathers court records on demand for law and credit customers; and Probate Finders LLC which gathers probate information nationwide. Dolan Media's newspapers serve as platforms for aggressive development of local and regional business information services—in Minneapolis-St. Paul; Portland, Ore.; Milwaukee; Baltimore; Oklahoma City; St. Louis; Norfolk, Va.; Rochester, N.Y.; Colorado Springs; Ronkonkoma, N.Y. (Long Island); Vancouver, Wash.; Boise, Idaho; Madison, Wis.; Kansas City, Mo.; New Orleans. 1,100 employees (190 in Minnesota). Founded in 1993. In January 2000 Dolan acquired Oklahoma City-based Hogan Information Services Co., the nation's largest public records gatherer, from First Data Corp. (NYSE: FDC). Hogan Information gathers public records across the country on a daily basis, adds them to its very large historical databases, and sells the information to large credit-granting customers (banks, credit bureaus, and credit card issuers) and to marketing companies. Dolan and infoUSA (NASDAQ: IUSA), the leading provider of business and consumer information products, database marketing services, data processing services, and Internet marketing solutions, signed a definitive long-term data licensing agreement. Dolan then acquired e-commerce and Web developer clickdata.com from Marketing Solutions Ltd. (http://www.clickdata.com and http://www.TopList.com). Clickdata.com specializes in integrating large volumes of data into its proprietary databases and distributing it electronically to customers. In April James Dolan was named a finalist in the 2000 Entrepreneur of the Year Awards by Ernst & Young. In May Dolan acquired a controlling interest in Wade Systems LLC, Oklahoma City, which is automating federal district and bankruptcy courts nationwide and provides e-filing services to attorneys. In August Dolan acquired Henry M. Greene & Associates Inc., a specialist in telephone-based business-to-business sales, marketing, and research. The 300-employee Greene & Associates handles outsourced teleservices work for national and international customers—many of whom are professional publishers serving law, finance. and credit industries—from call centers in Lake Forest, Ill. (a Chicago suburb), and Manchester, Iowa. Dolan's Probate Finder LLC and E-Debt.com, a Web site for the trading of portfolios of debt, established a strategic partnership to provide a numerical rating, or a ProScore, for portfolios of deceased accounts, indicating the collectability and fair market value to debt buyers. In September Dolan acquired the Phoenix-based Acollaid product line from Acxiom Corp. (Nasdaq: ACXM). Acollaid (a contraction of the term A COLLection AID) provides database and screening services to the credit industry. Dolan also entered into a long-term data licensing agreement with Acxiom. SIC 2711, 2741.

Domain Inc. 201 N. Knowles Ave., New Richmond, WI 54017. Tel: 715/246-6525; Fax: 715/243-7686. William L. Buell, Pres. and CEO. Domain manufactures animal nutrition products and provides related services. 50 employees. Founded in 1899. SIC 2048.

Dominium Management Services Inc. 2355 Polaris Ln. N., Suite 100, Plymouth, MN 55447. Tel: 763/354-5500; Fax: 763/354-5520. Dean A. Clark, Pres. and CEO; Stuart Zook, COO; Lorelei Koester, VP-Property Mgmt.; Paul L. Vogel, VP and CFO. Dominium Management Services manages multifamily properties—whether luxury, affordable, low-income, or subsidized. It serves more than 14,000 units across the Midwest and South. 60 employees. SIC 6531.

Donnelly Custom Manufacturing Co. 105 Donovan Dr., Alexandria, MN 56308. Tel: 320/762-2396; Fax: 320/762-1770. Stan Donnelly, CEO; Ron Kirscht, Pres.; Jim McCarthy, Dir.-Engrg. Svs.; Jerry Bienias, VP-Fin./Tech. Op. Annual revenue $24 million. Donnelly Custom Manufacturing Co. is a custom molder of plastic components. In addition, it provides customers with assembly and engineering services. 214 employees (213 in Minnesota; 8 part-time). Founded in 1984. SIC 3089.

Dorsey & Whitney LLP Pillsbury Center South, 220 S. Sixth St., Minneapolis, MN 55402. Tel: 612/340-2600; Fax: 612/340-2868; Web site: http://www.dorseylaw.com. Thomas O. Moe, Chm.; Peter S. Hendrixson, Managing Ptnr.; Eugene Holderness, COO; Curtis Meltzer, CIO; Scott Cotie, CFO; Joan Oyaas, Dir.-Hum. Res.; Carol Poulson, Mktg. Dir. Annual revenue $209 million. Dorsey & Whitney is the 25th largest law firm in the United States. The firm has 19 offices around the world (14 U.S. cities and five foreign countries), more than 650 lawyers and 1000 support staff. The firm focuses on corporate law and litigation. Clients include public and private companies, non-profits, cooperatives, Indian tribes, governmental bodies and individuals. Other areas of practice include emerging companies, intellectual property, corporate finance, securitizations and asset-backed financing, public finance, and project finance. Included among the firm's partners is former Vice President of the United States Walter F. Mondale. 1,565 employees (935 in Minnesota; 118 part-time). Founded in 1912. In 1999 Dorsey's Mergers & Acquisitions Group, for the fourth-consecutive year, ranked first in the nation among legal advisers for the number of domestic mergers, sales, and purchases of businesses completed—a record 223 deals. In February 2000 David Aaron, Under Secretary of Commerce for International Trade, left his post to join the firm as a senior international trade adviser. June 30: The firm continued to rank first in the nation among legal advisers for the number of deals completed in the first half of 2000, with 105 deals. "Buy-side deals continue to be active," said William B. Payne, head of Dorsey & Whitney's Mergers & Acquisitions Group. "During this year, we have continued to represent major players. Our client ADC has announced four major deals this year, aggregating $2.7 billion, including the $1.5 billion PairGain transaction. Other deals included Valspar's $1 billion acquisition of Lilly Industries and the acquisition of The Jim Henson Co. (the Muppets) by our client EM.TV & Merchandising AG. We also were involved in major sell-side assignments," he added. In August Managing Partner William Johnstone resigned, after just 15 months with the firm, to head a securities firm in his home state of Montana. SIC 8111. No. 64 CRM Private 100.

The Dotson Company Inc. 200 W. Rock St., Mankato, MN 56001. Tel: 507/345-5018; Fax: 507/345-1270. Dennis Dotson, Pres. The Dotson Co. operates a foundry working with gray and ductile iron. 100 employees. Founded in 1876. SIC 3321.

Dougherty & Company LLC 90 S. Seventh St., Suite 4400, Minneapolis, MN 55402. Tel: 612/376-4000; Fax: 612/376-4192; Web site: http://www.doughertymarkgts.com. Michael E. Dougherty, Chm.; Gerald A. Kraut, Pres. and CEO; Sean Faeth, CFO; Mark Landreville, EVP-Investment Banking; Stuart H. Mason, EVP-Equity Capital Mkts.; Steven D. McWhirter, Pres.-Dougherty Funding; Frank Tonnemaker, Pres./CEO-Voyageur Asset Mgmt. Annual revenue $24 million. Dougherty & Company LLC's 20 investment banking professionals and 50 equity and fixed income sales professionals specialize in corporate finance services (debt and equity offerings, valuations, fairness opinions, and M&A advisory services); origination and distribution of tax free and taxable fixed income securities; and investment advice for individual and institutional investors. Holding company Dougherty Financial Group also controls Voyageur Asset Management, an institutional money manager, and Dougherty Funding originates structures, which negotiates secured & unsecured loans to fund corporate growth, recapitalizations, strategic acquisitions and fixed asset financing. The company was created in September 1997 through the merger of two 20-year-old firms: Dougherty Dawkins LLC and Summit Investment Corp. Inc. 111 employees (108 in Minnesota). Founded in 1997. In October 2000 the firm's holding company Dougherty Financial Group, which also controls $6 billion-asset institutional money manager Voyageur Asset Management, was in the final stages of negotiations to sell Voyageur to Dain Rauscher Inc., Minneapolis. SIC 6211.

Douglas Corporation 9650 Valley View Rd., Eden Prairie, MN 55344. Tel: 952/941-2944; Fax: 952/942-3125; Web site: http://www.douglascorp.com. Douglas Skanse, Pres.; Joseph Hamelin, VP, Corp. Sec.; James Rinck, VP-Sls./Mktg. Annual revenue $56 million. Douglas Corp. manufactures product-identification items, including nameplates, decorative emblems, graphic overlays, membrane switches, and plastic enclosures. 650 employees (all in Minnesota). Founded in 1933. SIC 3089.

Douglas Machine 3404 Iowa St., Alexandria, MN 56308. Tel: 320/763-6587; Fax: 320/763-4614. Vernon J. Anderson, Pres.; Fred Higgenbottom, COO; Paul L. Anderson, EVP; Jack Anderson, VP-Op.; Rick Paulsen, VP-Fin./Admin.; Dale Haug, VP-Engrg.; James Bice, VP-Sls./Mktg. Annual revenue $49 million. Douglas Machine designs and manufactures packaging machinery. Subsidiaries include AccuLift, Blanchester, Ohio, palletizers and depalletizers; Davis Engineering, Deerwood, Minn., a dedicated aftermarket group; and Dimension Industries, Maple Grove, Minn., paperboard packaging, web handling, and specialized machinery design (robotic technology). Management reacquired the company from APV plc in December 1993. 540 employees (550 in Minnesota; 10 part-time). Founded in 1964. SIC 3565.

Tony Downs Foods Company 400 Armstrong Blvd. N., St. James, MN 56081. Tel: 507/375-3111; Fax: 507/375-3048. Richard A. Downs, CEO. Downs Foods produces prepared meat products, boneless chicken, and frozen and canned specialties at plants in St. James and Madelia, Minn., under the names DownsFare and Infra-Red. 420 employees. Founded in 1947. SIC 2013, 2038.

Dri-Steem Humidifier Company 14949 Technology Dr., Eden Prairie, MN 55344. Tel: 952/949-2415; Fax: 952/949-2933; Web site: http://www.dristeem.com. Bernard Morton, Pres.; Julie Samuelson, Dir.-Admin.; Chris Morton, Mfg. Mgr. Dri-Steem Humidifier manufactures industrial and commercial humidification systems, specializing in custom engineering of these products. 140 employees. Founded in 1965. SIC 3585.

C.J. Duffey Paper Company 528 Washington Ave. N., Minneapolis, MN 55401. Tel: 612/338-8701; Fax: 612/338-1320. John W. Duffey, Pres. and Treas.; David E. Hewes, VP and Gen. Mgr. C.J. Duffey Paper Co. is a wholesale distributor of printing paper. 120 employees. SIC 5111.

Duininck Companies 408 Sixth St., P.O. Box 208, Prinsburg, MN 56281. Tel: 320/978-6011; Fax: 320/978-4978. Norman Duininck, Ofcr.; Harris Duininck, Ofcr. Duininck Cos. is a holding company for four divisions: Duininck Brothers Inc., a paving contractor for highway and street construction; Prinsco Inc., a manufacturer of polyethylene pipe; Hart Ranch (Rapid City, S.D.), a vacation resort; and Indian Harvest Specialtifoods Inc. (Bemidji, Minn.), a packager and distributor of wild rice. Other location: a grain-processing plant in Polusa, Calif. 700 employees (300 in Minnesota; 450 part-time). Founded in 1926. SIC 1611, 2099, 6719, 7011.

Dundee Nursery & Landscaping 16800 Highway 55, Plymouth, MN 55446. Tel: 763/559-4004; Fax: 763/559-8483. Gerald W. Theis, CEO; Kenneth Theis, VP-Landscape Installation; Elaine Theis, Sec.; Dave Hoyt, VP-Landscape Sls.; Richard Mulhollam, VP-Nursery Prod.; Larry Goetzinger, VP-Fin./Admin. Annual revenue $8.5 million. Dundee Nursery and Landscaping is a multilocation retail garden center, landscape design, wholesale nursery and florist. 69 employees (all in Minnesota; 14 part-time). Founded in 1946. SIC 0781.

Dunham Associates Inc. 8200 Normandale Blvd., Suite 500, Bloomington, MN 55437. Tel: 952/820-1400; Fax: 952/820-2760. Dunham Associates is an engineering firm specializing in lighting design, CFD modeling and code review. SIC 8712.

Dunn Brothers Coffee 1569 Grand Ave., St. Paul, MN 55105. Tel: 651/698-0618. Ed Dunn, Pres.; Scott Kee, Op. Mgr. Dunn Brothers operates coffee cafes throughout the Twin Cities. 115 employees. Founded in 1987. SIC 5461, 5812.

Duo Plastics Inc. 5119 212th St. W., Farmington, MN 55024. Tel: 651/463-4800; Fax: 651/463-4804; Web site: http://www.duoplastics.com. Paul Silvernagel, Pres.; Dave Hawkins, Op. Dir. Duo Plastics is a custom plastic injection molder performing molding, blow molding, and assembly operations. Duo has 34 presses in a 77,000-square-foot manufacturing facility. 105 employees. Founded in 1979. SIC 3089.

Duplication Factory Inc. 4275 Norex Dr., Chaska, MN 55318. Tel: 952/448-9912; Fax: 952/448-3983. Barry Johnson, Pres. Duplication Factory is a video marketing company that duplicates, packages, and distributes video advertising by direct mail. 100 employees. Founded in 1986. SIC 7331, 7819.

Dura-Process Company 4000 Winnetka Ave. N., New Hope, MN 55427. Tel: 763/544-3381; Fax: 763/544-0704. James W. Fahlgren, Pres.; Don Heil, CFO; Betty Jeppesen, Dir.-Op. Dura-Process Co. is a manufacturer of plastic decorative trim, nameplates, appliques, and membrane switches—for sale to the appliance and automotive industries. The company owns Graphic Metals Inc., Bay City, Mich., which is a manufacturer of decorated aluminum trim; and Twin Cities Industries Inc., New Hope, which designs signs, numbers, and letters, and distributes them to hardware and sports outlets. 144 employees (50 in Minnesota; 2 part-time). Founded in 1958. SIC 3469, 3613.

Dura Supreme Inc. 300 Dura Dr., Howard Lake, MN 55349. Tel: 320/543-3872; Fax: 320/543-3310. Keith P. Stotts, Pres.; Roy A. Scherer, VP; Dick Schwartz, CFO; Glen O. Peterson, VP-Sls./Mktg. Dura Supreme manufactures prefinished (custom and stock) kitchen, bath, and light commercial casework for distribution to dealers in all states. 300 employees (all in Minnesota). Founded in 1963. SIC 2434.

Dura-Tech Inc. 3216 Commerce St., La Crosse, WI 54603. Tel: 608/781-2570; Fax: 608/781-1730. Peter J. Bentz, Pres.; Peter L. Johnson, VP-Op. Annual revenue $17 million. Dura-Tech manufactures nameplates, labels, overlays, panels, and decorative products for the OEM, automotive, appliance, and electronic marketplace. 250 employees (10 in Minnesota; 8 part-time). Founded in 1978. SIC 2759.

Duratech Industries International Inc. P.O. Box 1940, Jamestown, ND 58401. Tel: 701/252-4601; Fax: 701/252-0502; Web site: http://www.dura-ind.com. Dennis Mecklenburg, Pres. and CEO; Ron Siwa, CFO. Duratech Industries manufactures farm machinery and industrial grinding equipment for compost and waste recycling. 130 employees. Founded in 1966. SIC 3523.

Durex Products Inc. P.O. Box 354, Luck, WI 54853. Tel: 715/472-2111; Fax: 715/472-2115. Ronald G. Martin, Pres. and CEO; D.A. Kelly, Treas. and VP-Fin.; J.J. Schommer, VP-Hum. Res. and Sec. Annual revenue $17.5 million. Durex Products is a manufacturer of woven-wire screen cloth used in the sizing of materials ranging from cranberries to taconite, coal, and phosphate. Durex also manufactures polyurethane and rubber screens, molded urethane parts, and custom-designed or OEM parts. These products are marketed through the company's sales force and a nationwide dealer network. 159 employees (4 in Minnesota; 7 part-time). Founded in 1965. SIC 3089, 3496.

Dyna-Graphics Corporation 4080 Norex Dr., Chaska, MN 55318. Tel: 952/368-3344; Fax: 952/368-3388; Web site: http://www.dyna-graphics.com. W.L. Bury, Chm., Pres., and CEO; Ed Wulff, EVP and Gen. Mgr.; A.M. Bury, Sec. and Treas.; Mike Kenneo, Sls.; Scott Nelson, Cont. Dyna-Graphics Corp. manufactures flexible membrane switches, graphic control panels, and silkscreen decals. 85 employees (all in Minnesota; 1 part-time). Founded in 1972. SIC 7336.

Dynamic Air Inc. 1125 Wolters Blvd., Vadnais Heights, MN 55110. Tel: 651/484-2900; Fax: 651/484-7015. James Robert Steele, Chm., Pres., and CEO; Donald Johannsen, EVP. Annual revenue $39.6 million. Dynamic Air manufactures pneumatic conveying systems, dust collectors, weighing systems, and mixers. The company has a subsidiary, Dynamic Air Ltd., in Milton Keynes, U.K. 175 employees (183 in Minnesota; 10 part-time). Founded in 1969. SIC 3535.

Dynamic Homes Inc. 525 Roosevelt Ave., Detroit Lakes, MN 56501. Tel: 218/847-2611; Fax: 218/847-2617; Web site: http://www.dynamichomes.com. Israel Mirviss, Chm.; Scott Lindemann, Pres. and CEO; Clyde R. Lund Jr., Sec.; Eldon R. Matz, Cont. and Treas. Annual revenue $15.2 million (earnings $0.3 million). Dynamic Homes manufactures and markets modular, preconstructed single-family and multifamily dwellings and light commercial buildings. The company's single-family homes are offered in 60 basic designs. Every Dynamic structure is built in a controlled plant environment and then shipped to the on-site location for erection or completion. The company's products are marketed through a network of 70 builder-dealers in Minnesota, Iowa, North Dakota, South Dakota, Wyoming, Nebraska, and Wisconsin. 116 employees (all in Minnesota; 3 part-time). Founded in 1970. In March 2000 Dynamic agreed to sell the assets of its Shagawa Resort property in northern Minnesota, which was not a strategic fit with Dynamic's core competency in home construction. Grand Ely Lodge LLC was to pay $2.3 million and assume various obligations of the resort, which had been operating under the license of a Holiday Inn SunSpree Resort since its inception in 1996. [Deal completed in May.] In June the company signed a letter of intent to be acquired by an entity to be formed by three directors of Dynamic Homes. The letter of intent was approved by a special committee of three persons who are independent of Dynamic Homes and its directors. The pending all-cash transaction was valued at $2.55 per share (for a total of $5.7 million), compared to the closing market price of $1.94 per share at the close of trading on June 20. The acquisition of the company was subject to a definitive agreement, which was completed in September, and stockholder approval, set for late November. It was anticipated that the company's manufacturing facility would remain in Detroit Lakes. SIC 2452. No. 164 CRM Public 200.

E-Tech Inc. 2310 Snelling Ave. S., Minneapolis, MN 55404. Tel: 612/722-1366; Fax: 612/722-4709. Beverly Ekola, CEO; Lee Ekola, Pres.; David Harrington, Gen. Mgr. E-Tech (formerly Ekola Engineering) designs, manufactures, and installs computerized overhead monorail systems for industrial use in the United States, Canada, and the Far East. 50 employees (all in Minnesota). Founded in 1970. SIC 3536.

ECM Publishers Inc. 4095 Coon Rapids Blvd., Coon Rapids, MN 55433. Tel: 763/712-2400; Fax: 763/712-2480. Julian L. Andersen, Chm. and CEO; Jeffrey Athmann, Pres. and COO; Robert Cole, Mktg. Dir.; Maxine Gift, Treas. and Dir.-Accounting; Gene Merriam, VP-Fin. and CFO. Annual revenue $29 million. ECM Publishers Inc. publishes various weekly community newspapers and shoppers. It also performs commercial printing services and distributes publications and printed advertising media through its alternate delivery system. The company operates from 15 Minnesota and Wisconsin locations under 33 different tradestyles, including ABC Newspapers, Anoka County Union, Coon Rapids Herald, Elk River Star News, Isanti County News, Princeton Union Eagle, Caledonia Argus, and The Scotsman. 510 employees (496 in Minnesota; 168 part-time). Founded in 1976. In November 2000 the firm landed a 10-year contract to print the national edition of the New York Times for its 15,000 Twin Cities subscribers. To meet the needs of its first daily newspaper, the company planned to borrow $6 million to buy equipment, expand its 60,000-square-foot Princeton facility by 20 percent, and add 17 employees.SIC 2711, 2759.

El Microcircuits 1651 Pohl Rd., Mankato, MN 56001. Tel: 507/345-5786; Fax: 507/345-7559; Web site: http://www.eimicro.com. Robert K. Else, Pres.; Perry Eimers, Sls. Mgr.; Lenore Else, Mgr.-Corp. Devel.; Rob Else, Engrg. Mgr.; Tim Kloss, Materials Mgr. Annual revenue $36 million. El Microcircuits manufactures surface-mount turnkey electronic printed circuit assemblies for the medical and telecom industries. 175 employees (all in Minnesota). Founded in 1984. SIC 3679.

E&O Tool & Plastics Inc. 19178 Industrial Blvd., Elk River, MN 55330. Tel: 763/441-6100; Fax: 763/441-6452; Web site: http://www.eoplastics.com. Don Erdman, Co-pres.; Jim Osterman, Co-pres.; Jay Caswell, CFO. Annual revenue $10 million. E&O Tool & Plastics does custom plastic injection molding. 110 employees (all in Minnesota; 6 part-time). Founded in 1985. SIC 3089.

Earl's Distributing Inc. P.O. Box 16047, Missoula, MT 59806. Tel: 406/721-3900; Fax: 406/721-7374. Earl Sherron Jr., Pres.; Donna Sherron, Sec. and Treas. Earl's Distributing sells beer, wine, and soft drinks. 72 employees. Founded in 1969. SIC 5149, 5181, 5182.

East Central Energy 412 N. Main St., Braham, MN 55006. Tel: 320/396-3351; Fax: 320/396-4114. J. Londgren, Chm.; G. Bye, Pres. and CEO; D. Severson, VP-Planning; P. Gelhorn, Engrg. Mgr.; Gwen Thomas, VP-Admin. Cust. Svc.; N. Warnberg, Info. Sys. Mgr.; LeRoy Thurn, VP-Op./Engrg.; Dennis Korpi, Fin./Hum. Res. Mgr.; Henry Fischer, Bus./Community Devel. Mgr.; Ted Dimberio, Product Devel./Mktg. Mgr. Annual revenue $44.4 million. East Central Energy is a rural electric cooperative. 153 employees (162 in Minnesota; 9 part-time). Founded in 1936. SIC 4911.

East River Electric Power Cooperative 121 S.E. First St., P.O. Box E, Madison, SD 57042. Tel: 605/256-4536; Fax: 605/256-8058; Web site: http://www.erepc.com. Wayne Wright, Pres.; Jeffrey L. Nelson, CEO and Gen. Mgr.; Wallace Johnson, VP; James Ryken, Sec.; Robert Ching, Treas. Annual revenue $62.4 million. East River Electric Power Cooperative transmits wholesale electric power to 22 rural electric and municipal systems in eastern South Dakota and western Minnesota. 94 employees (2 in Minnesota; 4 part-time). Founded in 1951. SIC 4911.

Easy Systems Inc. 102 Mill St., P.O. Box 416, Welcome, MN 56181. Tel: 507/728-8214; Fax: 507/728-8215. Mark Gaalswyk, Pres. and CEO; Dave Thompson, CFO; Joel Dekkers, Dir.-Sls./Mktg.; Larry Swanson, Dir.-Op. Easy Systems provides software and equipment to automate the mixing of livestock feed to provide optimum nutrition levels at every stage of an animal's growth. 70 employees (55 in Minnesota). Founded in 1986. SIC 3523, 7372.

Eau Claire Press Company 701 S. Farwell St., P.O. Box 570, Eau Claire, WI 54702. Tel: 715/833-9200; Fax: 715/833-9244. Charles Graaskamp, Chm. and Pres.; Pieter Graaskamp, Gen. Mgr. Eau Claire Press is the publisher of the Leader Telegram (daily newspaper) and The Country Today (weekly). The company is also engaged in printing of newspaper supplements, and in high-quality sheetfed commercial printing. It also hosts an Internet service in Northwest Wisconsin. 295 employees. Founded in 1912. SIC 2711.

The Egan Companies 7100 Medicine Lake Rd., New Hope, MN 55427. Tel: 763/544-4131; Fax: 763/591-5595; Web site: http://www.eganco.com. Craig Sulentic, Pres. and CEO; Joe Egan, VP-Mktg.; James Malecha Jr., CFO; Bill John, Pres. (Interchad); Don Swanson, Pres. (Egan-McKay); Ted Von Bank, Pres. (Egan Automation). Annual revenue $103 million. Egan Cos. is a mechanical/electrical contractor specializing in commercial and industrial construction. 700 employees. Founded in 1948. SIC 1711, 1731.

Egger Steel Company P.O. Box E, Sioux Falls, SD 57101. Tel: 605/336-2490; Fax: 605/332-3023; Web site: http://www.eggersteel.com. Albert E. Egger, Chm.; Stephen E. Egger, Pres.; Doug Johnson, EVP and Gen. Mgr. Annual revenue $23.4 million. Egger fabricates structural and reinforcing steel for buildings and bridges, distributes metal specialty products, and operates a steel service center. 164 employees. Founded in 1946. SIC 3441.

Elder Jones Inc. 1120 E. 80th St., Suite 211, Bloomington, MN 55420. Tel: 952/854-2854; Fax: 952/854-2703. John Elder, Pres.; David Goodermont, VP; Robert Kanne, VP. Elder Jones Inc. is a general contractor engaged in the construction of retail stores, restaurants, and office/light industrial improvements throughout the United States and Canada. 120 employees (45 in Minnesota; 20 part-time). Founded in 1971. SIC 1542.

Electric Cords Inc. 5350 Highway 61, White Bear Township, MN 55110. Tel: 651/426-7958; Fax: 651/426-7943. Richard F. Tschida, Pres. Electric Cords manufactures electric cords for industrial use in the United States and Canada. 100 employees. Founded in 1964. SIC 3643.

Electric Wire Products Corporation 130 N.E. Second St., Minneapolis, MN 55413. Tel: 612/379-2926; Fax: 612/379-3249. William J. McLellan Sr., Chm., Pres., and CEO; Laura Benson, VP; Kathryn J. McLellan, VP; W.J. McLellan III, VP; James R. McLellan, VP; Mike Chaffee, Engr.; Duane Dormanen, Prod.; Marion Drahos, Customer Svc.; Jason Hanks, Engr.; Margaret M. McLellan, Sec. and Treas.; Gerald Neuman, Purch. Electric Wire Products Corp. manufactures wiring harnesses and electrical plug and cord sets. 160 employees. Founded in 1952. SIC 3699.

Electronic Systems Inc. 600 E. 50th St. N., P.O. Box 5013, Sioux Falls, SD 57117. Tel: 605/338-6868; Fax: 605/338-5061; Web site: http://www.electronicsi.com. Leo Reynolds, Pres. and CEO; David Stewart, Treas.; Darrel Rupp, Chief-Engrg.; Earl Cook, VP-Op. Electronic Systems provides electronics contract manufacturing services that include surface mount technology and full engineering support. The company produces printed circuit board assemblies, and system level and finished electronic products for OEMs in the industrial, medical, electrical power, and business equipment sectors. 250 employees. Founded in 1980. SIC 3679.

Electro-Plating Engineering Company Inc. 55 W. Ivy Ave., St. Paul, MN 55117. Tel: 651/488-6621; Fax: 651/488-1964. Daniel M. Shiely, Pres. Annual revenue $7.8 million. Electro-Plating Engineering Co. does electroplating on metal. 65 employees (75 in Minnesota; 10 part-time). Founded in 1946. In June 2000 the IRS filed tax liens totaling $510,885 against the company, which had run into cash flow problems after starting a new business unit in 1995. In July the company filed for Chapter 11 to restructure bank debt of $500,000. SIC 3471.

Ellerbe Becket 800 LaSalle Ave., Minneapolis, MN 55402. Tel: 612/376-2000; Fax: 612/376-2271; Web site: http://www.ellerbebecket.com. Robert A. Degenhardt, CEO; Richard Lincicome, Pres.-Architecture; Randy Wood, Pres.-Engrg.; Rick Miller, CFO; Karen Homan, CIO; Scott Berry, Principal; Geoff Glueckstein, Principal; Janice Linster, Principal; David Loehr, Principal. Annual revenue $113 million. Ellerbe Becket provides integrated architectural, engineering, and construction services from 11 locations worldwide. The firm has clients in corporate, developer, government, health care, higher education, sports, and entertainment industries. Services range from strategic facilities planning through post-construction. 736 employees (389 in Minnesota; 6 part-time). Founded in 1909. SIC 1542, 8711, 8712. No. 98 CRM Private 100.

Embers America 1664 University Ave., St. Paul, MN 55104. Tel: 651/645-6473; Fax: 651/645-6866; Web site: http://www.embersamerica.com. David Kristal, CEO; Jon Otto, CFO; Henry Kristal, Co-chair; Brad Birnberg, COO. Embers America is a restaurant franchise and operating company with 53 franchised, independently owned restaurants and company-owned stores in five Midwest states. 150 employees. Founded in 1956. In May 2000, fueled in part by start-up financing from Lyle Berman, the company launched FoodStreet plus—an Internet-based purchasing service for the restaurant industry, particularly independent owners and operators seeking to improve costs through volume purchasing. In June the company added seven locations—five in Minnesota and one each in Wisconsin and Iowa—bringing its total to 53. In August Embers scaled back its projections for restaurant openings for the next four years from 1,300 to 500 in an effort to maintain quality. It still planned to sign agreements for 20 additional locations before the end of 2000. SIC 5812.

Emerald First Financial Ltd. 6462 City West Pkwy., Eden Prairie, MN 55344. Tel: 952/837-0073; Fax: 952/837-0074; Web site: http://www.emeraldfirstfinancial.com. Jeffrey C. Mack, Chm., Pres., and CEO; Jeffrey Z. Hillrgoss, EVP and CFO; Lawrence R. Filiberto, EVP-Credit Admin. Emerald First Financial Ltd. is a Minneapolis-based consumer financial services company specializing in originating, purchasing, selling, and servicing retail installment contracts for new and used marine, motorcycle, RV, and recreational sport vehicle products. The company is licensed to purchase contracts that are originated through indirect methods using a dealership network in 47 states and through direct methods in 38 of those states via the www.leisureloans.com Web site. Market coverage encompasses five regions that are centered in New York, California, Florida, Texas, and Minnesota. The company also provides a full range of finance and insurance products to both individuals and dealers, which include insurance and extended service contracts (warranties). 88 employees. Founded in 1997. SIC 6141.

Empi Inc. 599 Cardigan Rd., Shoreview, MN 55126. Tel: 651/415-9000; Fax: 651/415-7305; Web site: http://www.empi.com. Joseph E. Laptewicz Jr., Chm. and CEO; Patrick D. Spangler, EVP and CFO; H. Philip Vierling, VP-Sls./Mktg.; Robert W. Clapp, VP-Mfg.; Barbara C. Hutto, VP-Hum. Res./Facilities; Robert N. Hamlin, VP-Res./Devel. Empi serves the rehabilitation, orthapedic, and incontinence-treatment medical markets through the development, manufacturing, and marketing of innovative, cost-effective biomedical products and services to continually improve the quality of life for patients with functional disabilities. Empi has become a leader in the rehabilitation medical device market through its electrotherapy rehabilitation products: TENS (transcutaneous electrical nerve stimulation) and NMS (neuromuscular stimulation) devices and their accessories. In addition, the company has developed a proprietary iontophoretic drug delivery system to deliver local anethesia and anti-inflammatory medications noninvasively; a line of dynamic splinting orthoses for use in range-of-motion rehabilitation; and proprietary systems for the treatment of urinary incontinence. In May 1999 Empi, then a publicly traded company, agreed to be acquired by global investment firm The Carlyle Group, Washington, D.C., for $164 million. 500 employees (250 in Minnesota). Founded in 1977. In July 2000 Empi acquired Ormed GmbH, formerly a division of G. Hug GmbH. Ormed, founded in 1968, is a leading European manufacturer and marketer of products serving the orthapedic rehabilitation market. It markets such products as continuous passive motion devices, knee braces, electrotherapy, and a wide range of orthapedic soft goods. Ormed, headquartered in Freiburg, Germany, with operations in India, the United States, and other European locations, employs 120 people worldwide. Sales of the combined companies were expected to exceed $100 million in calendar year 2000. In October Empi turned the tide in a nine-year battle with Medicare over reimbursement for Innova, a female urinary incontinence device already covered by more than 300 private health plans. Medicare agreed to pay, but only if the user hadn't been helped by conventional exercises. SIC 3841, 3845.

Empire Sand & Gravel Company Inc. 2817 Second Ave. N., Suite 300, Billings, MT 59101. Tel: 406/252-8465; Fax: 406/252-0506. Meredith L. Reiter, Pres.; Gregory Reiter, EVP; Sandra Reiter, CFO. Empire Sand & Gravel Co. constructs highways, streets, and airports. 200 employees. Founded in 1955. SIC 1611.

Empire Screen Printing Inc. N5206 Marco Rd., Onalaska, WI 54650. Tel: 608/783-3301; Fax: 608/783-3306. James Brush, Pres.; James Schwinefus, VP; Kathleen Cuellar, VP-Sls.; Lori Taube, Purch. Annual revenue $22.1 million. Empire Screen Printing manufactures pressure-sensitive decals and overlays, and does doming, lasercutting, hard tool, four-color process, point-of-purchase display, static cling, embossing, and serializing. 320 employees (12 in Minnesota; 10 part-time). Founded in 1960. SIC 2759.

Emplast Inc. 950 Lake Dr., Chanhassen, MN 55317. Tel: 952/975-3500; Fax: 952/975-3501; Web site: http://www.emplast.com. Mark Bongard, CEO; Gene Booker, Op. Mgr.; Leon Korkowski, CFO; Pete Thompson, Nat'l Sls./Mktg. Mgr. Emplast Inc. converts plastic resin into products using injection and blow molding processes for the semiconductor, computer, and memory disk industries as well as other custom molding applications. On-site facilities include tooling; applications, packaging, and materials laboratories; cleanroom facilities; and plastics recycling facilities. Its Custom Molding and Memory Products divisions are located at 1501 Park Rd., Chanhassen. The company was formerly Bush Lake Industries Inc., then Empak Inc., until spun off from Empak in 1998. 186 employees. Founded in 1980. SIC 3089.

Enderes Tool Company Inc. 14925 Energy Way, Apple Valley, MN 55124. Tel: 952/891-1200; Fax: 952/891-1202. Mark Bothum, Pres. and CEO; Todd Dahl, CFO. Enderes Tool Co. manufactures mechanics' handtools—chisels, punches, screwdrivers, stone drills, ripping bars, masons tools, carrier tools—for retail sale nationwide. 80 employees (all in Minnesota). Founded in 1912. SIC 3423.

Enercept Inc. 3100 Ninth Ave. S.E., Watertown, SD 57201. Tel: 605/882-2222; Fax: 605/882-2753. John P. Devine, Pres. and CEO; Barbara Hartley, Gen Mgr.; Neal Mack, Sls. Mgr.; Bob Williamson, Prod. Mgr. Annual revenue $5 million. Enercept manufactures panels for residential and commercial super-insulated building systems. 50 employees (4 part-time). Founded in 1982. SIC 2452.

Energy Economics Inc. 109 South St. S.E., Dodge Center, MN 55927. Tel: 507/374-2557; Fax: 507/374-2646. J. Kenneth Berry, Pres.; James T. Hulsebus, Treas.; Merwin Lindahl, Sec. Energy Economics designs, manufactures, and sells gas meters of all sizes for commercial and industrial use. The company also specializes in the rustproofing and reinforcing of underground gas tanks, pipes, and electrical lines. 70 employees. Founded in 1975. SIC 1623, 3824.

Energy Masters International Inc. 1385 Mendota Heights Rd., Mendota Heights, MN 55120. Tel: 651/686-4000; Fax: 651/686-4050. John Tastad, Pres.; Jim Becker, VP-Op.; Richard Bromstad, VP-Engrg./Sls.; Mike Chase, VP-Construction; John Tripp, VP-Mktg.; Mark Tastad, Dir.-Mfg. Energy Masters International is an energy-management company that replaces or retrofits building systems—lighting, air conditioning, drives and motors, industrial process controls, and energy-management systems—to save energy and update technology. ESI is one of nine 3M-licensed manufacturers of Silverlux, a component used in lighting upgrades. Offices: Atlanta; San Diego; Oklahoma City; Kansas City, Mo.; Chicago; and Omaha, Neb. 350 employees (100 in Minnesota). Founded in 1992. SIC 1711, 1731.

ENStar Inc. 7450 Flying Cloud Dr., Eden Prairie, MN 55344. Tel: 952/941-3200; Fax: 952/947-8660. Miles E. Efron, Chm.; Jeffrey J. Michael, Pres. and CEO; Peter E. Flynn, EVP and Pres.-Americable; Thomas S. Wargolet, CFO and Sec.; Ronald D. Newman, Pres.-Enstar Networking. ENStar Inc. is a holding company whose principal subsidiaries are Americable Inc. and Enstar Networking Corp. Americable is a provider of networking and connectivity products, cable assemblies, and custom OEM manufacturing solutions. Enstar Networking is a network integrator providing services that build, maintain, and secure network infrastructures. ENStar also owns 25 percent of the common stock of CorVel Corp. (Nasdaq: CRVL). CorVel is an independent, nationwide provider of managed care services to employers and insurers. 298 employees (255 in Minnesota; 12 part-time). Founded in 1995. On Dec. 1, 1999, ENStar Inc. (Nasdaq: ENSR) announced the completion of its going-private transaction—through a merger of ENStar Acquisition Inc., a corporation formed by James Michael and Jeffrey Michael and certain related entities, with and into ENStar, with ENStar as the surviving corporation. SIC 6719.

Enstrom Helicopter Corporation Twin County Airport, P.O. Box 490, Menominee, MI 49858. Tel: 906/863-1200; Fax: 906/863-6821; Web site: http://www.enstromhelicopter.com. Robert M. Tuttle, Pres.; Robert Jenny, VP; Robert Cleland, VP; Charles Schumacher, VP. Enstrom Helicopter manufactures three-place piston-powered helicopters and five-place turbine-powered helicopters. 100 employees. Founded in 1959. SIC 3721.

Entolo 7125 Sandburg Rd., Golden Valley, MN 55427. Tel: 763/593-9660; Fax: 763/593-0848; Web site: http://www.haasmultiples.com. Tom Van Hercke, Pres. and CEO; Michael Maher, VP-Fin./Admin. and CFO; Ronda Anderson, VP-Prod. Entolo, formerly HaasMultiples, provides strategic planning, design, fabrication, installation, and project management services to the retail, corporate event, themed destination, and entertainment markets. 130 employees. Founded in 1955. SIC 3993.

Entronix International Inc. 9600 54th Ave. N., Plymouth, MN 55442. Tel: 763/559-9654; Fax: 763/559-9652; Web site: http://www.entronix.com. Martin Lehman, CEO; Michael Johnson, Pres. Annual revenue $20 million. Entronix International Inc. provides contract electronic manufacturing and personal communication and electronic control remanufacturing. 335 employees (all in Minnesota). Founded in 1966. SIC 5731, 7622.

EnviroBate 3301 E. 26th St., Minneapolis, MN 55406. Tel: 612/729-1080; Web site: http://www.envirobate.com. Jerry Larson, Pres. Envirobate provides commercial, industrial, and residential hazardous materials handling, specializing in asbestos and lead remediation. 215 employees. Founded in 1991. SIC 4953.

Environments Inc. 5700 Baker Rd., Minnetonka, MN 55345. Tel: 952/933-9981; Fax: 952/933-6048. Roger Wothe, Pres.; Dave Schoenberger, Dir.-Op.; Jim Goeman, Field Op. Annual revenue $22 million. Environments manufactures custom store fixtures and casework, as well as stock market trading room furniture. Customers include Williams-Sonoma and its Pottery Barn division, National Car Rental, Brooks Brothers, Alamo Car Rental, and Wolf Camera. 93 employees (all in Minnesota; 2 part-time). Founded in 1969. SIC 2541.

Equus Computer Systems Inc. 719 Kasota Ave., Minneapolis, MN 55414. Tel: 612/617-6200; Fax: 612/617-6298; Web site: http://www.equuscs.com. Andy S. Juang, Pres. and CEO; Don Woessner, CFO. Annual revenue $176 million. Equus Computer Systems is a national manufacturer delivering built-to-order desktop PCs and servers to value-added resellers, specializing in small- and medium-business users. Equus sells, builds and services custom-made Nobilis-brand or private-label systems from customer configuration centers in Minneapolis/St. Paul, Chicago, Detroit, Cleveland, Dallas, St. Louis, Kansas City, Denver, and Seattle. The company is the largest minority-owned business in the Twin Cities. 375 employees (100 in Minnesota). Founded in 1989. SIC 3571. No. 66 CRM Private 100.

Ergotron Inc. 1181 Trapp Rd., Eagan, MN 55121. Tel: 651/452-8135; Fax: 651/681-7717; Web site: http://www.ergotron.com. Harry C. Sweere, Owner and CEO; Mike Bristow, Pres., CFO, and COO; David Swendson, VP-Sls.; Janet Ahern, Dir.-Hum. Res.; Mark Ellson, Dir.-Op.; Jim Fischer, Dir.-Info. Svs.; Robert Fluhrer, Dir.-Engrg.; Kim Kuhn, Dir.-Prod. Mgmt.; Greg Mohwinkel, Dir.-Acctg.; Sheila Veschusio, Dir.-Mktg. Annual revenue $42 million. Ergotron manufactures a broad line of ergonomic computer work-center equipment used in engineering, design, manufacturing, desktop publishing, and networking applications. Under development is a product line for medical, engineering, educational, manufacturing, and office environments that uses vertical lift systems and various suspension technologies. 150 employees (135 in Minnesota). Founded in 1982. SIC 3577.

Erickson Oil Products Inc. 1231 Industrial Rd., Hudson, WI 54016. Tel: 715/386-8241; Fax: 715/386-2022; Web site: http://www.freedomvalu.com. Claire L. Erickson, Chm.; David Erickson, Pres.; Gary Vander Vorst, EVP and CFO; Johnny Gill, SVP; Darren Forbes, VP and Dir.-Merch. Annual revenue $135 million. Erickson Oil Products operates a gasoline convenience store chain. 725 employees (375 in Minnesota; 400 part-time). Founded in 1950. Celebrated 50th Anniversary in 2000. SIC 5411, 5541.

PVT

Eschelon Telecom Inc. 6160 Golden Hills Dr., Golden Valley, MN 55416. Tel: 763/553-1001; Fax: 763/553-2724; Web site: http://www.eschelon.com. Cliff Williams, Chm. and CEO; Rick Smith, Pres. and COO; Geoff Boyd, CFO; James L. Lawrence, EVP-Central Region. Annual revenue $41.7 million. Eschelon Telecom is a rapidly growing, integrated communications provider offering broadband voice and data services to small and medium-sized business customers in select markets within the Midwest and West. Eschelon offers local telephone, long-distance, data services, DSL, Internet services, and business telephone systems to provide a complete telecommunications solution. Eschelon Telecom was formerly Advanced Telecommunications Inc. 850 employees (400 in Minnesota). Founded in 1996. In January 2000 the company completed an additional round of $10 million of private equity capital with Bain Capital, J. P. Morgan, and Stolberg Equity Partners—bringing the total financing package completed since October 1999 to $150 million. This financing was to allow Eschelon to fund its integrated voice and data services network build-out, and to expand to reach a total of 10 key markets in Minnesota, Washington, Oregon, Utah, Arizona, Nevada, and Colorado. The company then purchased interconnection gateway (Mantiss' CLECware) and middle-ware (Vitria's BusinessWare) software to add to the foundation of its Operations Support Systems (OSS) for the future. In April the company launched its full range of telecommunications services in Phoenix. In May Eschelon announced plans to deploy Nortel Networks' Enterprise Edge 1000, an Internet protocol (IP)-enabled communications system, providing Eschelon's customers with a single platform for voice, data, and IP services. The company completed a $135 million senior secured debt facility that was to assist in funding its market expansion activities. Specifically, the proceeds of the financing were to be used to help expand the company's integrated voice and data services network build-out in its planned 26-market footprint in Minnesota, Washington, Oregon, Utah, Arizona, Nevada, Idaho, Colorado, Montana, New Mexico, Nebraska, and North Dakota. The financing was led by GE Capital Corp., FleetBoston Financial, and Firstar Bank. In July, having placed its own equipment in 17 Qwest central offices, the company began offering DSL service in the Twin Cities, focusing on small and midsize businesses. The new high-speed service promised "always on" access to the Internet. At month's end, Eschelon added another $35 million in venture capital, from Wind Point Partners and Bain Capital. In August the company completed the installation of its network facilities in the Portland, Ore., area; in September, in the Seattle area. SIC 4813.

Etoc Company Inc. 10179 Crosstown Circle, Eden Prairie, MN 55344. Tel: 952/925-0280; Fax: 952/922-7149. S.A. Cote, Pres.; Jim Olson, CFO; Mark Ronnei, Sec. Annual revenue $15.5 million. Etoc operates Camp Lincoln and Camp Lake Hubert children's camps in Nisswa, Minn. (with clients from all over the world); Grand View Lodge, an American Plan Resort on Gull Lake in Nisswa, Minn.; and three championship 18-hole golf courses, the Pines, the Preserve, and Deacon Lodge. 425 employees (all in Minnesota; 325 part-time). Founded in 1926. SIC 7699.

Evergreen Industries 4921 Babcock Trail E., Inver Grove Heights, MN 55077. Tel: 651/457-4441; Fax: 651/457-0676. Joseph E. Ahern, Pres. Evergreen Industries produces natural Christmas decorations. 120 employees. Founded in 1964. SIC 3999.

L.G. Everist Inc. P.O. Box 5829, Sioux Falls, SD 57117. Tel: 605/334-5000; Fax: 605/334-3656. Thomas Everist, Pres.; Jay Van Den Top, Sec. and Treas. L.G. Everist is an aggregate producer (crushed rock, sand and gravel) that is involved in railroad operation and marine construction. 200 employees (20 in Minnesota). Founded in 1914. SIC 1429, 1442, 1629.

Excelsior-Henderson Motorcycle Manufacturing Company 805 Hanlon Dr., Belle Plaine, MN 56011. Tel: 763/873-7000; Fax: 763/873-7030; Web site: http://www.excelsior-henderson.com. Daniel L. Hanlon, Co-founder; David P. Hanlon, Co-founder; John Hetterick, Acting CEO; Jon Carlson, Acting COO; Jennie L. Hanlon, Co-founder, Spiritual Road Crew Leader; Jack Thornton, Pres. and COO; Terrance Adams, CFO; Allan C. Hurd, SVP-Engrg./Mfg.; Gary (Jet) Johnson, SVP-Sls./Mktg. Excelsior-Henderson manufactures, markets, and sells premium heavyweight cruiser and touring motorcycles that evoke an authentic American motorcycling heritage and lifestyle. Production initially began in the fourth quarter of 1998. The company's motorcycles feature current technology, but reflect distinctive designs, styling, and names reminiscent of the motorcycles produced in the early part of this century by Excelsior Supply Co. (one of the "Big Three" motorcycle manufacturers, along with Harley-Davidson and Indian) under the brand names Excelsior and Henderson. 119 employees. Founded in 1993. In December 1999 the company filed a voluntary petition for relief under Chapter 11 of the U.S. Bankruptcy Code, made necessary by a lack of obtaining additional financing. In related actions, the company also temporarily ceased manufacturing operations and, as a result, had been forced to lay off 101 employees of its 116-person workforce. "This is a severe step that we would have preferred not to take," said Michael Meyer of the law firm Ravich, Meyer, Kirkman, McGrath & Nauman, bankruptcy counsel to the company. "However, it does provide the necessary breathing room for the company to continue to seek the financing or a strategic transaction that is felt to be in the best interest of customers, dealers, shareholders, and employees." In March 2000 the company unveiled a new, restyled model (hand-built) at the country's largest motorcycle rally, in Daytona Beach, Fla. The creditor-endorsed move was an indication that new financing was close. At the end of the month, the company reached an agreement with E.H. Partners, a West Palm Beach, Fla., investment firm headed by Norm Taplin, regarding a proposed plan of reorganization. The company tentatively agreed to be sold for $17.5 million. The plan proposed a new board for the firm that would include Deborah Dentry, president of a West Palm Beach accounting firm; Palm Beach-area lawyers Taplin and Fred Cohen; and Excelsior-Henderson co-founders Dave and Dan Hanlon. In May the bankruptcy court approved the disclosure statement to be distributed to creditors in connection with a proposed plan of reorganization. The proposed plan described how the various secured and unsecured creditors were to be paid. The principal amount of the loan from the state of Minnesota would be paid off in nine years, with interest deferred until the end of the term. In August Excelsior-Henderson announced that it had emerged from bankruptcy and that its modified plan of reorganization under Chapter 11 of the U.S. Bankruptcy Code had been confirmed. The company's public stockholders and its co-founders did not retain an equity interest. In October, after a two-month review of the business by both new management and consultants, E.H. Partners announced that restructuring and relaunching the company was going to require a more extended period of time than originally anticipated to execute a successful, high-impact re-entry of the brand. Given that conclusion, management decided to plan new-model market entry for 2002 to allow the company the time needed to properly restaff the organization, reestablish its dealer network, perfect the design of its original market entry motorcycles, and develop a broader line of both motorcycles and accessories. In the interim, expenses were to be minimized and focused on preparation for re-entry. The company did not anticipate adding significant numbers of employees in the immediate future. SIC 3751. No. 146 CRM Public 200.

ExpressPoint Technology Services Inc. 1109 Zane Ave. N., Golden Valley, MN 55422. Tel: 763/543-6000; Fax: 763/543-5900; Web site: http://www.expresspoint.com. Mike Cibulka, Chm. and Founder; John Schaaf, Pres. and CEO; Mike Dudley, VP-Hum. Res.; Frank Hallowell, VP and CFO; Pat Harrison, VP-Op.; Mac Humphrey, CIO; Bob McClure, VP-Sls./Mktg. Annual revenue $67 million. From product introduction through end-of-life, ExpressPoint supports sales, marketing, and field service commitments in the computer industry. The company specializes in inventory management, parts sourcing, procurement & stocking, product & component level repair, system sales, returned goods management, process planning and engineering services. 600 employees (400 in Minnesota). Founded in 1983. SIC 5045, 7378.

Eye Kraft Optical Inc. P.O. Box 400, St. Cloud, MN 56302. Tel: 888/455-2022; Fax: 800/950-7070; Web site: http://www.eyekraft.com. James T. Negaard, Pres.; Lawrence Lahr, VP; Michael Moeller, Sec. Eye Kraft Optical manufactures ophthalmic products. 100 employees (all in Minnesota; 10 part-time). Founded in 1954. SIC 3851.

F-M Asphalt Inc. P.O. Box 697, Moorhead, MN 56561. Tel: 218/287-2319; Fax: 218/287-2515. M. Hayes, CEO; Bill Pieterick, Gen. Mgr. F-M Asphalt manufactures asphalt paving compounds and other concrete-related products. 100 employees. Founded in 1961. SIC 2951, 3272.

FMS Corporation 8635 Harriet Ave. S., Bloomington, MN 55420. Tel: 952/888-7976; Fax: 952/888-7978; Web site: http://www.fmscorporation.com. Greg Sweet, CEO; Mike Sweet, Pres.-Sign Products Div.; John Sweet, Pres.-Powder Metal Div. FMS Corp. manufactures precision powder metal parts for a wide variety of applications. 85 employees (all in Minnesota). Founded in 1946. SIC 3399, 3469, 3499.

FRS Industries Inc. 64 N. Fourth St., Fargo, ND 58102. Tel: 701/235-5347; Fax: 701/235-0753. Gary Westerholm, Pres.; Dan Cullen, VP; Timothy Dockter, CFO, Sec., and Treas. FRS Industries manufactures rubber stamps, awards, ribbons and buttons, trophies, advertising specialties, engraved signage, screen printing, and commercial printing. 70 employees. Founded in 1885. SIC 3069, 3499, 3914, 3993.

Fabcon Inc. 6111 W. Highway 13, Savage, MN 55378. Tel: 952/890-4444; Fax: 952/890-6657. Michael Le Jeune, Pres. and CEO; Dianne Cutter, VP-Quality/Admin.; James O. Hasse, SVP-Op.; Thomas J. Mahoney, VP, Treas.; Paul Nicolai, Cont.; Mark Hansen, VP-Project Mgmt./Engrg.; Jim Houtman, VP-Mktg./Sls. Fabcon manufactures insulated concrete wall panels. In 1995 Fabcon celebrated its 3,600th project; in 24 years it has produced more than 70 million square feet of precast concrete panels. In 1995 Fabcon acquired two former licensees, one in Columbus, Ohio, and one in Westfield, Indiana, which are now organized as Fabcon LLC. 700 employees. Founded in 1971. SIC 3272. No. 86 CRM Private 100.

Fabyanske, Westra & Hart P.A. 920 Second Ave. S., Suite 1100, Minneapolis, MN 55402. Tel: 612/338-0115; Fax: 612/338-3857. Scott L. Anderson, Pres.; Gary C. Eidson, VP; Marvin T. Fabyanske, VP; Kyle E. Hart, VP; Jeremiah J. Kearney, VP; Paul L. Ratelle, VP; Gregory T. Spalj, VP; Dean B. Thomson, VP; Dennis J. Trooien, VP; Thomas J. Tucci, VP; Mark W. Westra, VP. Fabyanske, Westra & Hart is a law firm concentrating on construction, commercial litigation, commercial finance, commercial real estate, and tax and business planning. 60 employees (all in Minnesota; 4 part-time). Founded in 1981. SIC 8111.

Faegre & Benson LLP 90 S. Seventh St., Minneapolis, MN 55402. Tel: 612/336-3000; Fax: 612/336-3026; Web site: http://www.faegre.com. Philip S. Garon, Chm.-Mgmt. Ctee. Faegre & Benson is a legal services firm. Its 330 lawyers practice in all areas of civil law, with emphasis on litigation, securities, mergers and acquisitions, banking, bankruptcy, construction, environmental, employee benefits, ERISA, intellectual property, health, labor and employment, nonprofit, public finance, real estate, tax, and trusts/estate planning. In March Mary Stumo of the firm's labor and employment group was elected to Faegre's eight-member management committee. Other Faegre & Benson offices are located in Denver; Des Moines; London; and Frankfurt. 776 employees (647 in Minnesota; 63 part-time). Founded in 1886. SIC 8111.

Fagen Inc. 501 W. Highway 212, P.O. Box 159, Granite Falls, MN 56241. Tel: 320/564-3324; Fax: 320/564-3278. Roland Fagen, CEO; Daryl Gillund, Pres.; Jennifer A. Johnson, CFO; Mike Ellgen, SVP; Milt Willman, SVP; Randy Shelsta, EVP; Frank Marquette, VP; Diane Fagen, Sec. and Treas. Fagen Inc. is a civil, mechanical, and electrical contractor specializing in heavy industrial construction. 700 employees (200 in Minnesota). Founded in 1988. SIC 1541, 1711, 1731.

Fairmont Foods of Minnesota Inc. 905 E. Fourth St., Fairmont, MN 56031. Tel: 507/238-9001; Fax: 507/238-9560. Larry McGuire, CEO and COO. Fairmont Foods of Minnesota processes and packages frozen foods. 310 employees. Founded in 1987. SIC 2038.

Falcon Plastics Inc. 1313 Western Ave., P.O. Box 788, Brookings, SD 57006. Tel: 605/692-7354; Fax: 605/692-7204. Don Bender, CEO; Carol Bender, Treas. and Sec.; Jay Bender, COO; Guy Bender, COO; Shaun Riedesel, VP. Annual revenue $20 million. Falcon Plastics makes custom injection-molded plastics; performs sonic welding, assembly, and decoration of plastics; and constructs injection-molding tools. 265 employees (12 part-time). Founded in 1975. SIC 3089.

Fargo Assembly Company 3300 Seventh Ave. N., P.O. Box 2340, Fargo, ND 58108. Tel: 701/298-3803; Fax: 701/298-3806. Ron Bergan, CEO; Mary Alice Bergan, Treas. Fargo Assembly manufactures wire harnesses. 350 employees (50 part-time). Founded in 1975. SIC 3643, 3714.

Fargo Glass & Paint Company 1801 Seventh Ave. N., Fargo, ND 58102. Tel: 701/235-4441; Fax: 701/235-3435. Gerald Lovell, Pres.; Dan Mattison, VP and Sec. Fargo Glass & Paint wholesales glass products, paints, varnishes, hard- and soft-surface floor coverings, residential and commercial (Andersen) windows, and in-house millwork. 150 employees. Founded in 1917. In January 2000 Andersen Corp., Bayport, Minn., agreed to sell its millwork distribution business in Sioux Falls, S.D., to Fargo Glass & Paint. SIC 5023.

Fargo Tank Company 4401 W. Main, Fargo, ND 58102. Tel: 701/282-2345; Fax: 701/282-5516. Kolbjorn Rommesmo, Pres.; Ole Rommesmo Jr., VP. Fargo Tank Co. builds steel tanks, does structural steel fabrication, and distributes building materials to wholesalers. 150 employees. Founded in 1945. SIC 3441, 3443, 5211.

Faribault County Register 125 N. Main St., Blue Earth, MN 56013. Tel: 507/526-7324; Fax: 507/526-4080. Kelly Anderson, Bus. Mgr. Faribault County Register, formerly Shopper Enterprises Inc., publishes the Faribault and Freeborn County Registers; five shoppers in southern Minnesota; and one shopper in northern Iowa. 150 employees. Founded in 1977. SIC 2711, 2759.

Faribault Foods Inc. 1000 Baker Building, Minneapolis, MN 55402. Tel: 612/333-6461; Fax: 612/342-2908. Edmund B. MacDonald, Chm.; Reid V. MacDonald, Pres. and CEO; Darrell Charboneau, CFO; Michael S. Peroutka, EVP-Sls./Mktg.; W. Michael Cureton, VP-Op.; Michael Gilbertson, VP-Private-label Sls.; Bruce Macdonald, VP-Acctg.; Andrew Murray, VP-Purch.; Jim Nelson, VP-Engrg.; Marcia Richter, VP-Res./Devel. (Faribault office). Annual revenue $120 million. Faribault Foods is a processor of canned vegetables, baked, refried, and miscellaneous beans and pasta products, marketing to national private-label accounts and to its own Butter Kernel, Kuner's, Pride, Finest, and Mrs. Grimes regional brands. The company also operates facilities in Faribault and Cokato, Minn.; Mondovi, Wis.; Grimes, Iowa; and Brighton, Colo. 500 employees (420 in Minnesota). Founded in 1895. SIC 2033. No. 97 CRM Private 100.

Farm Credit Leasing 5500 Wayzata Blvd., Suite 1600, Golden Valley, MN 55416. Tel: 763/797-7400; Fax: 763/797-3555; Web site: http://www.fcleasing.com. Doug Sims, Chm.; Philip J. Martini, Pres. and CEO; Bradley R. Brolsma, SVP-Commercial Unit; Brian Legried, SVP-LeasExpress Unit; Thomas H. Vicker, SVP, Sec., and Gen. Counsel. Annual revenue $152.6 million (earnings $10.1 million). Farm Credit Leasing (FCL), the seventh-largest independent leasing company in the nation, serves agricultural producers and their cooperatives, rural utilities, and Farm Credit System entities. FCL provides equipment leasing for all types of equipment used in the agriculture and rural utility industries—including fleets of automobiles and trucks, ag production and processing equipment, material-handling equipment, storage facilities, office equipment and computers, utility equipment, and switching and communication equipment. The company also provides leasing-related services (fleet, licensing, purchasing) and lease syndication. Besides its corporate headquarters, the company maintains 10 sales offices throughout the country. FCL is part of the 84-year-old, $88 billion Farm Credit System, one of the largest and oldest cooperatives in the nation. CoBank—the system's $24 billion, Denver-based cooperative bank specializing in agribusiness, ag export, and rural utility financing—is FCL's majority owner. AgFirst Farm Credit Bank of Columbia, S.C., owns the balance of FCL's common stock. The five other Farm Credit Banks own preferred stock in the company. 160 employees (135 in Minnesota). Founded in 1972.

Sept. 30, 1999: FCL reported a 6 percent increase in its fiscal 1999 revenue and a 7 percent increase in net earnings. In addition, FCL had record new lease placements totaling $546 million, up 21 percent. At fiscal year end, FCL had total assets of $792 million, up 3 percent from fiscal 1998. The company also manages lease portfolios for Farm Credit System lease investors. With those assets, FCL had total assets under management of $1.6 billion, up from $1.2 billion. In May 2000 CEO Martini noted, "LeaseManager, our new portfolio management product, has allowed us to keep our new business performance consistent this year even with a sluggish ag economy. It has kept new lease volume and revenue steady while other segments of our business have remained soft." June 30: Year-to-date (six months), FCL had new lease placements totaling $272.3 million, down 1.6 percent. Portfolio and fee income increased to $40.0 million, up 6 percent. After-tax net income was also ahead of last year at $5.2 million, up from $4.7 million. "Many of our larger customers appear to be taking a cautious approach to their capital expenditures because of current economic conditions," said CEO Martini. "However, even with new lease placements slightly behind last year's pace, we have been able to maintain our profitability. We've accomplished that through business growth in areas such as our LeaseManager product as well as independently originated leases through brokers and vendor programs." In July Farm Credit Leasing reorganized into two business lines: LeasExpress, to serve the needs of small and midsize agricultural producers; and the Commercial line, to serve cooperative, commercial producer, and agribusiness customers. SIC 5083, 6159, 7513, 7514. No. 17 CRM Cooperatives/Mutuals 20.

Farmers Home Group 1550 E. 78th St., Richfield, MN 55423. Tel: 612/861-4511; Fax: 612/861-2147. Roger R. Frank, Chm.; Donald H. Preusser, Pres. and CEO; Charles Chasney, VP-Info. Sys.; Jonathan Farris, VP-Underwriting; Richard S. Folsom, VP-Compliance; Steven R. Good, Treas.; Donald Grimm, VP-Claims. Annual revenue $62 million. Farmers Home Group (FHG) provides property and casualty insurance for personal lines markets. Its three subsidiaries—Farmers Home Mutual Insurance Co., Western Home Insurance Co., and Pioneer Insurance Co.—write personal lines of insurance, amounting to $65 million in annual direct written premium, in Arizona, California, Idaho, Minnesota, Nevada, North Dakota, Oregon, Utah, and Washington. Branch offices: Seattle; Salt Lake City; Phoenix; and Burbank, Calif. 100 employees (95 in Minnesota). Founded in 1898. In February 2000 Standard & Poor's raised its financial strength rating on Farmers Home Mutual Insurance Co. to double-'Bpi' from single-'Bpi'. SIC 6331.

Farmers Union Marketing & Processing Association P.O. Box 319, Redwood Falls, MN 56283. Tel: 507/637-2938; Fax: 507/637-5409. Don W. Davis, Pres. and CEO; David D. Morman, Treas.; Dan Hildebrandt, Op. Mgr.; Larry Risty, Sls. Mgr. Annual revenue $48.9 million. Farmers Union Marketing & Processing (also doing business as Central Bi-Products Inc.) is in the rendering business—processing blood, feathers, bones, and grease from packing houses, eviscerating plants, and dead stock. The company also processes pet food ingredients and handles insurance. 236 employees (232 in Minnesota; 1 part-time). Founded in 1929. SIC 2048, 2077.

Darrel A. Farr Development Corporation 3025 Harbor Ln. N., Suite 317, Plymouth, MN 55447. Tel: 763/553-9972; Fax: 763/553-9983. Darrel A. Farr, Pres.; Lucinda A. Gardner, VP. Darrel A. Farr Development Corp. is a real estate developer. 75 employees. Founded in 1965. SIC 6552.

Featherlite Exhibits 7300 32nd Ave. N., Crystal, MN 55427. Tel: 763/537-5533; Fax: 763/537-0084. L.O. Nelson, Owner and CEO; Graeme Nelson, Pres. Featherlite Exhibits manufactures trade show exhibits. 100 employees (all in Minnesota). Founded in 1964. SIC 3993.

Federated Cooperatives of East Central Minnesota 211 Cleveland St. S., Cambridge, MN 55008. Tel: 763/689-1751; Fax: 763/689-0114. DeLane Johnson, Gen. Mgr. Federated Cooperatives of East Central Minnesota supplies liquefied petroleum gas to members in nine east central Minnesota communities. 80 employees. Founded in 1942. SIC 5984.

Federated Mutual Insurance Company 121 E. Park Square, Owatonna, MN 55060. Tel: 507/455-5200; Fax: 507/455-5452. A.T. Annexstad, Chm., Pres., and CEO; Peggy J. Birk, SVP and General Counsel.; Sarah L. Buxton, EVP-Insurance Op.; Paul F. Droher, EVP-Insurance Op.; Steven W. Judd, SVP-Actuarial Svs.; David W. Ramsey, SVP-Federated Mutual Agency; Raymond R. Stawarz, SVP-Acctg.; Gregory J. Stroik, SVP-Investments/Tax; Jock Kinnett, EVP-Insurance Op.; A. Daniel Lewis, EVP-Insurance Op.; Mark D. Scharmer, EVP-Insurance Op. Annual revenue $936 million. Federated Mutual is a $3.1 billion-asset company that handles property, casualty, health, and life insurance—both personal and commercial lines—specializing in total-lines insurance to selected commercial markets. 3,036 employees. Founded in 1904. SIC 6311, 6321, 6331. No. 6 CRM Cooperatives/Mutuals 20.

Feed-Rite Inc. 305 E. Sixth St., P.O. Box 5500, Sioux Falls, SD 57117. Tel: 605/336-3330; Fax: 605/336-9246. Ed Moloney, Chm. and Pres.; John Richardson, CFO; Werner Braun, Gen. Mgr.; Larry Larson, Fin. Mgr. Feed-Rite, dba Zip Feed Mills, is a manufacturer of livestock feed. It also does private-label manufacturing. 86 employees (7 part-time). Founded in 1937. SIC 2048.

Fey Industries Inc. 200 Fourth Ave. W., Edgerton, MN 56128. Tel: 507/442-4311; Fax: 507/442-3686. Norman E. Fey, Pres.; Anton E. Haga, VP-Sls.; Scott Mundt, VP-Mfg.; Michael R. Fey, Nat'l Sls. Mgr.; Michelle D. Mitchell, Mktg. Mgr. Annual revenue $21 million. Fey Industries manufactures vinyl ring binders, pocket secretaries, calendars, desk & clip folders. A full line of thermoformed media packaging including audio, video & CD/DVD. Recent additions to the line include custom designed retail packaging including clamshells, blisters and flexible packaging. Fey also offers complete contract packaging and fulfillment services. 260 employees (285 in Minnesota; 25 part-time). Founded in 1965. SIC 2759, 2782.

Final Touch Services Inc. 1759 Selby Ave., St. Paul, MN 55104. Tel: 651/641-1018; Fax: 651/641-0502. Michael Lange, Chm.; David Trumble, Pres.; Mahmoud Shirif, Ph.D., CAO and CFO. Final Touch Services specializes in high-rise window washing. Other services include high-angle safety system consulting, building inspection, robotic window cleaning, pressure washing, and new-construction cleanup. It sells and leases high-rise lifts from Denmark, and also operates robotic window-washing systems. 70 employees (all in Minnesota; 50 part-time). Founded in 1986. SIC 7349.

Firefly Creek Casino R.R. 2, P.O. Box 96, Granite Falls, MN 56241. Tel: 320/564-2121; Fax: 320/564-2547. Mitch Corbine, Gen. Mgr.; Barbara J. Anderson, Asst. Mgr.; Deb Kvam, Customer Svc. Dir.; Phyllis Littlecreek, Mktg. Dir. Firefly Creek Casino is a casino gaming enterprise owned and operated by the Upper Sioux Community. 190 employees. Founded in 1990. SIC 7999.

FirePond Inc. 1983 Premier Dr., P.O. Box 4459, Mankato, MN 56002. Tel: 507/388-0500; Fax: 507/345-6579; Web site: http://www.cwcinc.com. Jerry Johnson, Chm. and Founder; Klaus Besier, Pres. and CEO; Al Bennett, Pres.-Product Div.; Joe Fuca, VP; Lee Ginsburg, SVP-Organizational Growth; Ilya Gorelik, SVP-Product Strategy/Devel.; James Iglesias, Pres.-Industry Solutions Div.; Paul Lavallee, EVP-Sls.; Paul McDermott, CFO; Scott Schwartzman, VP-Professional Svs.; Sosaburo Shinzo, Pres.-FirePond Japan; Cary Tripp, VP-Transportation Bus. Sls., N.A. FirePond designs and sells electronic sales and training software, primarily for Fortune 500 companies, through offices worldwide: Minneapolis, Detroit, Dallas, Moscow, Amsterdam, and Lyon, France. Its systems, which help salespeople make more professional presentations and proposals to customers, include a powerful configurator for complex products that are customized to some degree. Its customers include General Motors, Compaq, Renault, Freightliner, Volvo, DAF, Ingersoll-Rand, Hitachi, and Carrier. Formerly CWC (Clear With Computers), it was acquired in 1997 by investment company General Atlantic Partners. 300 employees. Founded in 1983. SIC 7371.

First District Association 216 W. Commercial St., P.O. Box 842, Litchfield, MN 55355. Tel: 320/693-3236; Fax: 320/693-6243; Bill Dropik, Chm.; Clinton Fall, Pres. Annual revenue $198 million. First District is a processor of various cheeses, cream, whey blends, whey protein concentrate, lactose, and dairy calcium. 137 employees (all in Minnesota). Founded in 1921. SIC 2022, 2023. No. 13 CRM Cooperatives/Mutuals 20.

The First National Bank Bemidji 502 Minnesota Ave., Bemidji, MN 56601. Tel: 218/751-2430; Fax: 218/759-4355. Joseph Welle, Chm.; Tom Welle, Pres.-First Natl. Bank Bemidji; Paul Welle, Pres.-First Bemidji Holding Co. The First National Bank Bemidji, which is held by First Bemidji Holding Company, is a full-service commercial bank. 89 employees. Founded in 1897. SIC 6021.

First Supply Group 106 Cameron Ave., La Crosse, WI 54601. Tel: 608/784-3839; Fax: 608/791-3621. Edward J. Felten, Chm.; Joseph S. Poehling, VChm. and Pres.; Tom Golden, SVP and CFO; Elliot Collier, VP-Contractor Sls.; Tim Landreman, VP-Industrial Sls.; Timothy J. Haggerty, VP; Mike Hickok, VP-Purch.; James M. Poehling, VP; David S. Prahler, VP and Sec.; Bob Beranek, MN Regional Mgr.; Phil Dunst, Central Regional Mgr.; Jerry Stahl, Western Region Mgr. First Supply Group distributes flooring; plumbing, heating, and building products; waterworks; well supplies; refrigeration supplies; and spas—from locations in La Crosse, Madison, Eau Claire, Appleton, Green Bay, Wisconsin Rapids, Rhinelander, and Milwaukee, Wis.; Rochester, Mankato, and Minneapolis, Minn.; Dubuque, Iowa; and Rockford, Ill. Subsidiary names: Rochester Supply Co., Eau Claire Plumbing Supply Co., Rockford Supply Co., Wisconsin Supply Corp., First Supply Milwaukee, First Supply Dubuque, Mankato Supply, and Minnesota Pump & Supply Corp. 650 employees (80 in Minnesota). Founded in 1898. SIC 5072, 5074.

Fisher Industries P.O. Box 1034, Dickinson, ND 58601. Tel: 701/225-9184; Fax: 701/227-4456. Tom Fisher, Chm.; Mike Fisher, VP; Rob Rebel, Gen. Mgr.; Florian Friedt, Gen. Mgr.-General Steel & Supply; Clyde Frank, Cont. Fisher Industries provides construction sand and gravel, and steel fabrication. Through subsidiary General Steel & Supply, the company provides steel design and fabrication, machining, and OEM crushing. The company also handles industrial supplies and materials-handling equipment. 300 employees. Founded in 1940. SIC 1442, 3441, 3531, 5084.

Lloyd Flanders Industries Inc. 3010 10th St., Menominee, MI 49858. Tel: 906/863-4491; Fax: 906/863-6700. Dudley Flanders, Pres.; Gene Davenport, EVP; Lou Rosebrook, VP-Sls./Mktg. Lloyd Flanders Industries has two plants. One, in Menominee, Mich., manufactures indoor/outdoor wicker furniture. The other, in Fort Smith, Ark., manufactures the furniture's aluminum, sling, cushion, and strap lines. 490 employees. SIC 2519.

Flo-Pac Corporation 700 N. Washington Ave., Suite 400, Minneapolis, MN 55401. Tel: 612/332-6240; Fax: 612/344-1663. Jeffrey A. Bowen, Chm. and Pres.; Everett E. Madsen, EVP; Timothy J. Taveggia, CFO. Annual revenue $35.5 million. Flo-Pac manufactures industrial maintenance brushes for hand operations, and replacement brushes for power buffers, scrubbers, and sweeping machines. The company operates three brush-manufacturing facilities: Flour City Brush Co., Minneapolis; Pacific Coast Brush Co., Fontana, Calif.; and South Eastern Brush Co., East Point, Ga. 216 employees (92 in Minnesota). Founded in 1913. SIC 3991.

Flour City Packaging Corporation 500 Stinson Blvd., Minneapolis, MN 55413. Tel: 612/378-2100; Fax: 612/378-9441. J.T. Van de Water, Pres. and CEO; Gerald McCullen, COO. Flour City produces custom packaging, designs and manufactures rigid boxes and folding cartons, and provides contract packaging and printing. 150 employees (all in Minnesota). Founded in 1903. SIC 2652, 2657.

Floyd Total Security 9036 Grand Ave. S., Bloomington, MN 55420. Tel: 952/881-5625; Fax: 952/881-6524; Web site: http://www.floydtotalsecurity.com. Michael S. Karch, CEO; Robert C. Bossert Jr., Pres.; Robert A. Gibson, VP. Floyd Total Security is full-service security provider. Floyd provides complete sales, installation, and 24-hour service of the following products and services: high security locksmithing hardware, security and fire alarm systems, card access control systems, and closed-circuit television surveillance systems. Floyd operates its own U.L. listed 24 -hour Central Station monitoring facility located in Bloomington, MN. 110 employees (102 in Minnesota). Founded in 1945. SIC 7382.

FoldCraft Company 615 Centennial Dr., Kenyon, MN 55946. Tel: 507/789-5111; Fax: 507/789-8315. Charles Mayhew, Pres.; Steve C. Sheppard, CEO; Doug Westra, Treas. Annual revenue $35 million. FoldCraft manufactures restaurant seating. 280 employees (250 in Minnesota). Founded in 1955. SIC 2511, 2514.

Foley Company 5354 Parkdale Dr., Suite 300, St. Louis Park, MN 55416. Tel: 952/595-7500. Walter M. Ringer Jr., Chm. and CEO; Walter M. Ringer III, VChm.; John M. Ringer, VChm.; Richard Hentges, Pres. and COO. Annual revenue $32 million. Foley operates as a holding company for three operating divisions: Foley-Belsaw Institute, Kansas City, Mo. (correspondence course sold through direct mail, replacement equipment for graduates); Foley-Martin, Kingsford, Mich., and Minneapolis (kitchen woodwork and furniture); Foley-United, River Falls, Wis. (turf-maintenance and sharpening equipment). 200 employees (15 in Minnesota; 5 part-time). Founded in 1926. SIC 3559.

Fond du Luth 129 E. Superior St., Duluth, MN 55802. Tel: 218/722-0280; Fax: 218/722-7505. Maurice Ojibway, Casino Mgr. Fond du Luth is a casino owned and operated by the Fond du Lac Band of Lake Superior Chippewa. It offers slots, blackjack, and bingo. 320 employees. SIC 7999.

Food Engineering Corporation 2765 Niagara Ln., Plymouth, MN 55447. Tel: 763/559-5200; Fax: 763/559-4657. Ralph D. Burgess Jr., Chm. and CEO; Peter Davis, Pres.; John Bloomgren, VP-Mktg./Sls.; Suzanne B. Jackson, VP and Dir.-Fin.; Donald E. Lyman, VP-Sls. Tech. Annual revenue $18 million. Food Engineering Corp. designs and manufactures processing machinery and equipment for the food, chemical, pharmaceutical, and tobacco industries. In July 1992 it broke ground on a project to double the size of its manufacturing and office facilities in Plymouth. 150 employees (147 in Minnesota). Founded in 1965. SIC 3535.

Food-N-Fuel Inc. 4366 Round Lake Rd. W., Arden Hills, MN 55112. Tel: 651/633-7863; Fax: 651/633-0015. Fred Curtis, Chm.; George Thelen, Pres.; Edward Bird, VP; Richard Kary, Sec. and CFO. Food-N-Fuel operates convenience stores with gasoline facilities. 90 employees. Founded in 1978. SIC 5411.

S.B. Foot Tanning Company Bench St., Red Wing, MN 55066. Tel: 651/388-4731; Fax: 651/388-8054. Silas B. Foot III, Pres. and CEO; Karen Meier, Sec.; Jerome Dietzman, VP-Hum. Res.; Don Eddlemon, VP-Op.; Peter Hendrickson, VP-Sls.; William Foot, VP-MIS; Tom Yoemans, Treas. S.B. Foot Tanning manufactures finished leather from cattle hides for use in footwear, belts, bags, upholstery, and accessories. The company became a subsidiary of Red Wing Shoe Co. in 1986. 400 employees (300 in Minnesota). Founded in 1872. In June 2000 Genesco Inc. (NYSE: GCO), Nashville, Tenn., sold its leather finishing business to S.B. Foot. SIC 3111.

FORCE America Inc. 501 E. Cliff Rd., Suite 100, Burnsville, MN 55337. Tel: 952/707-1300; Fax: 952/707-1330; Web site: http://www.forceamerica.com. Kenneth J. Slipka, Chm. and CEO; Steven Loeffler, Pres. and COO; Gregory S. Jude, CFO and Treas. Force America Inc., formerly Mid-America Power Drives, is a leading specialist in hydraulic and mechanical drive systems. Products are marketed nationally through 10 regional service centers. Typical applications include agricultural, logging, mining, utility, and highway-maintenance equipment. Effective Oct. 1, 1997, Mid-America Power Drives Manufacturing & Distributing Inc., Burnsville, and Pederson-Bells Equipment Co. Inc., Fort Dodge, Iowa, merged to form Force America. 152 employees (48 in Minnesota). Founded in 1953. SIC 5013, 5084, 5085.

Fortune Bay Resort Casino Chippewa Reservation, 1430 Bois Forte Rd., Tower, MN 55790. Tel: 218/753-6400; Fax: 218/753-6404. Fortune Bay is located on Lake Vermillion and includes a 10,000 square foot banquet space, full-service restaurant, on-site daycare, bingo, blackjack, pull tabs, video slots, RV lot, full service marina, and nature trails. 420 employees. Founded in 1986. SIC 7011.

Forum Communications Company 101 N. Fifth, P.O. Box 2020, Fargo, ND 58102. Tel: 701/235-7311; Fax: 701/241-5406. William C. Marcil, Pres. and Publisher; Charles Bohnet, VP and Gen. Mgr.; Lloyd Case, VP, CFO, and Cont. Forum Communications is a publisher of weekly, daily, and Sunday newspapers. The company owns newspapers in Fargo and Dickinson, N.D.; Mitchell, S.D.; and Worthington, Willmar, Detroit Lakes, Wadena, Alexandria, Bemidji, Blackduck, and Park Rapids, Minn. Other interests include commercial printing plants in Detroit Lakes and Wadena.; broadcast properties in Fargo, Grand Forks, Bismarck, and Minot, N.D.; Sign Pro, a commercial sign company; and Dakota Photographics, Fargo. 1,000 employees. Founded in 1917. SIC 2711, 4832, 4833.

Foster Klima & Company 6400 Flying Cloud Dr., Eden Prairie, MN 55344. Tel: 952/903-2200; Fax: 952/903-2399; Web site: http://www.fosterk.com. Doug Flink, Ptnr.; Tim Foster, Ptnr.; George Klima, Ptnr.; Bill Plante, Ptnr. Annual revenue $9 million. Foster Klima is a provider of insurance, investments, and employee benefits. It is also a general agent for Guardian Life Insurance Co. of America. 115 employees (112 in Minnesota; 4 part-time). Founded in 1924. SIC 6411.

Fountain Industries Company 922 14th St., Albert Lea, MN 56007. Tel: 507/373-2351; Fax: 507/373-7404. Mark Olchefske, Pres.; Stan Axsmith, VP. Fountain Industries manufactures food service equipment and products, automotive repair equipment, parts washers and metal fabrication. Part of the Sundet Group of Cos., Minneapolis. 65 employees. Founded in 1966. SIC 2034, 3581.

Foursome Inc. 841 E. Lake, Wayzata, MN 55391. Tel: 952/473-4667; Fax: 952/473-9731. G. Engel, Pres.; G. Isensee, Sec. and Treas. Foursome is a retailer of clothing and shoes for the family. 70 employees (all in Minnesota; 30 part-time). Founded in 1936. SIC 5651.

Fox Point Sportswear Inc. 1905 E. 14th St., P.O. Box 507, Merrill, WI 54452. Tel: 715/536-9461; Fax: 715/536-6971. John J. Bocke, Pres.; Dennis Baacke, VP. Fox Point Sportswear manufactures winterwear apparel, bicycle clothing, contract sewing, premium programs, hunting apparel, nylon products, and fleece apparel. 150 employees. Founded in 1971. SIC 2329.

The Frandsen Corporation 20 N. Lake St., Forest Lake, MN 55025. Tel: 651/407-5700; Fax: 651/407-5650. Dennis K. Frandsen, Chm. and CEO; Tom Pesek, Pres.; Phil Arneson, EVP; Marcia Wegleitner, Corp. Cont. Annual revenue $155 million. The Frandsen Corp. is a holding company for several businesses. Plastech Corp., the largest of its four manufacturing companies, manufactures and assembles highly engineered, ISO 9000-certified, custom injection molding products at plants in Minnesota and in Amery, Wis. Its customers include Donaldson, Toro, and 3M. Other Frandsen companies include Allied Plastics Inc., a Coon Rapids, Minn., custom plastics fabricator that serves nationwide markets; Miller Manufacturing Inc., Eagan, Minn., which serves farm, ranch, and pet supply markets throughout the United States (Little Giant-brand); Internet Inc., a New Hope, Minn.-based converter of extruded plastic netting; and 200-employee Frandsen Financial Corp., now consisting of 22 community banks in Minnesota and Wisconsin. 1,100 employees. Founded in 1960. SIC 3089, 6712.

Franklin Foods 1925 W. First St., Duluth, MN 55806. Tel: 218/727-6651; Fax: 218/727-4427. David Holcombe, VP and Gen. Mgr.; Ben Loukes, Cont. Franklin Foods produces fluid-milk products, and handles many other dairy products, juices and drinks. 89 employees (all in Minnesota; 4 part-time). Founded in 1923. SIC 2026.

Fredrikson & Byron 1100 International Centre, 900 Second Ave. S., Minneapolis, MN 55402. Tel: 612/347-7000; Fax: 612/347-7077; Web site: http://www.fredlaw.com. John A. Satorius, Pres.; John Schenk, Exec. Dir.; Konrad J. Friedemann, SVP, Chair-Corp. Div.; John M. Koneck, SVP, Chair-Litigation Div.; Clare Borovac, Dir.-Mktg.; Darlene Gonyer, Admin. Svs. Mgr. Fredrikson & Byron, a 150-attorney firm, offers a full range of legal and business services in 31 practice areas. It serves a broad range of clients, including multinational corporations, public companies, privately held businesses, entrepreneurs, government agencies, family businesses, and private individuals. One of the Upper Midwest's largest business and trial law firms, Fredrikson & Byron also has offices in London and Washington, D.C.; and affiliated offices in Mexico City, Warsaw, Montreal, Toronto, and Vancouver. 330 employees (328 in Minnesota). Founded in 1948. In December 1999 the Fredrikson & Byron Pro Bono Housing team was presented with the 1999 Housing Team of the Year Award by the Volunteer Lawyer's Network—for having the highest participation rate and for taking more pro bono cases than any other participating law firm. SIC 8111.

Freedom Oil 19 S. First St., Suite 2003/B, Minneapolis, MN 55401. Tel: 612/341-3736; Fax: 612/340-9412. Robert A. Williams, Chm. and CEO. Annual revenue $34 million. Freedom Oil specializes in oil distribution, service stations, real estate, and farms. 220 employees (all in Minnesota; 75 part-time). Founded in 1963. SIC 5541.

Fremont Industries Inc. 4700 Industrial Blvd., Shakopee, MN 55379. Tel: 952/445-4121; Fax: 952/496-3027. Mark L. Gruss, Pres.; Edward H. Chang, EVP; Paul Spekman, VP and COO; Greg Smith, VP and CFO. Annual revenue $29 million. Fremont Industries manufactures specialty industrial and water-treatment chemicals. 121 employees. Founded in 1954. SIC 2819, 2842, 2899.

Fritz Company Inc. 1912 Hastings Ave., Newport, MN 55055. Tel: 651/459-9751; Fax: 651/459-7381. James P. Fritz, Chm. and CEO; Edwin P. Lindborg, Pres.; Terry Waldoch, VP-Sls./Mktg. Fritz Co. wholesales confections and tobacco. 130 employees. Founded in 1940. SIC 5145.

Fujikura Richard Manufacturing 6250 Bury Dr., Eden Prairie, MN 55346. Tel: 952/934-3000; Fax: 952/934-4928. Matthew Broms, Chm.; Richard A. Broms, Pres.; Thomas Breslin, VP. Fujikura Richard Manufacturing does job shop high-volume precision machining for computer peripherals, aerospace, and other industries using close-tolerance machining. 175 employees. Founded in 1956. SIC 3599.

Fusion Coatings Inc. 1101 E. Eighth St., Winona, MN 55987. Tel: 507/452-1112; Fax: 507/452-9099. Russell K. Glover III, Pres. and Owner; David A. Stark, Purch. Fusion Coatings specializes in the application of plastic coatings used in agricultural flooring and recreation equipment, such as decks, tables, benches, and chairs. Its parent company is National Can Retinning Co. of Minnesota. 135 employees (all in Minnesota). Founded in 1967. SIC 1799.

GFI Primary Foods 2815 Blaisdell Ave. S., Minneapolis, MN 55408. Tel: 612/872-6262; Fax: 612/870-4955. Robert D. Goldberger, Pres. and CEO; Howard Goldberger, VP and COO. Annual revenue $475 million. GFI Primary Foods is a vertically integrated company slaughtering, deboning, and further processing beef products (hamburgers, steaks, and related products). Finished products are sold to major restaurant chains nationally. Plants are located in Minneapolis; Fargo, N.D.; and Rapid City, S.D. 1,125 employees. Founded in 1976. SIC 2011. No. 22 CRM Private 100.

GML Inc. 500 Oak Grove Pkwy., Vadnais Heights, MN 55127. Tel: 651/490-0000; Fax: 651/490-1651. John Ledy, Pres.; Dave Jessen, VP-Sls./Mktg. GML manufactures custom graphics for use on plastic and paper products. 160 employees. Founded in 1959. SIC 2754.

GPK Products 1601 43rd St. N.W., Fargo, ND 58102. Tel: 701/277-3225; Fax: 701/277-9286. Mick Pflugrath, Chm.; Spencer Hildre, Pres. GPK Products manufactures plastic pipe fittings for sewer, drainage, and Schedule 40 markets. 153 employees. Founded in 1972. SIC 3084.

Gabberts Furniture & Design Studio 3501 Galleria, Edina, MN 55435. Tel: 952/927-1500; Fax: 952/927-1555. James D. Gabbert, Chm. and CEO; Gary Pedersen, EVP and Chief Admin. Ofcr.; Richard Brozic, VP-Distribution Center Op. (Minnesota); Paula King, SVP-Sls./Store Op. Gabberts is an upscale retailer whose operations include retail home furnishings and an interior design studio. The company's signature store is located in the Galleria in Edina. Other stores are located in Dallas and Fort Worth, Texas. 650 employees (272 in Minnesota; 86 part-time). Founded in 1946. In September 2000 Select Comfort Corporation (Nasdaq: SCSS), the Eden Prairie, Minn.-based home furnishings manufacturer, announced a newly established relationship with Gabberts. The Galleria store was to be the first traditional furniture retailer to offer the Select Comfort bed (which until then had only been available at company-owned stores and leased departments, through direct marketing, and on the Internet). SIC 5712. No. 92 CRM Private 100.

Gage Brothers Concrete Products Inc. 4301 W. 12th St., Sioux Falls, SD 57106. Tel: 605/336-1180; Fax: 605/330-0560. A.C. Gage, Chm.; A.C. Gage Jr., Pres.; R.T. Devaney, CFO. Gage Brothers manufactures various concrete products—including precast fascia panels, precast and prestressed structural units, concrete block, and ready-mix concrete. 150 employees. Founded in 1945. SIC 3271, 3272, 3273.

Gage Marketing Group LLC 10000 Highway 55, Bassett Creek Office Bldg., Plymouth, MN 55441. Tel: 763/595-3800; Fax: 763/595-3871; Web site: http://www.gage.com. Edwin C. (Skip) Gage, Chm. and CEO; Tom Belle, COO; John Kalenberg, EVP; Bob Borman, VP and Gen. Mgr.-Sweeps/Games/Contests; Carol Mack, VP and Creative Dir.; Lester Morrow, Pres.-In Store Mktg.; Doug Reeves, VP and Gen. Mgr.; Tom Wilkolak, VP, Gen. Mgr., and Promotional Mktg. Annual revenue $80 million. Gage Marketing Group is a results-driven direct-sales, promotion, and point-of-purchase display agency that integrates market planning, development, and execution—using information as the platform—to drive the consumer and business-to-business behaviors its clients are seeking. GMG also partners with AHL Services Inc. (Nasdaq: AHLS), Atlanta, to provide executional services including fulfillment, teleservices, and lettershop through Gage Marketing Support Services. Clients include: Alcoa, American Express, Anheuser Busch, Century Manufacturing, Energizer, Ford Motor Co., Gatorade, Goodyear, Kaiser Permanente, Lawry's Food, Miller Brewing Co., Nissan, Wal-Mart, and Target. Other offices: New Hope and Wayzata, Minn., and Irvine, Calif. In 1998 Gage sold its $80 million-revenue marketing fulfillment businesses to AHL Services for $81.1 million. 300 employees (250 in Minnesota). Founded in 1991. In April 2000 the Sweepstakes & Contests Division announced www.sweepsWork.com—a self-contained online sweepstakes application designed to increase e-commerce transactions and sales, heighten brand visibility, and drive traffic to Internet sites. In May the company made three investments and signed one letter of intent to expand its integrated marketing services offering. The investments included the acquisition of Kuester Partners Inc. and The Wilshire Group Inc., as well as a substantial equity stake in Marketing Bridge. Gage has also signed a Letter of Intent to purchase 50 percent of Bitstream Underground. In July Gage and Leede Research, Manitowoc, Wis., formed a new marketing research firm called The Leede Group, a Gage Marketing Group Partner, which was to provide both qualitative and quantitative marketing research support to Gage's clients, as well as to its own clients. Now located in Gage's headquarters, Leede has state-of-the-art focus group facilities as well as usability laboratories for Internet and Web design testing. SIC 4724, 8742.

Gaines & Hanson Printing Company Inc. 5121 Winnetka Ave. N., New Hope, MN 55428. Tel: 763/533-1000; Fax: 763/533-5432. Frank J. Wind, Pres. and CEO; Paul J. Fix, EVP; Bruce A. Leve, VP-Sls./Mktg.; Russell Massucci, VP-Prod. Annual revenue $24.9 million. Gaines & Hanson is in the printing business, exclusively serving the advertising insert market. 165 employees (all in Minnesota). Founded in 1977. SIC 2752.

Galaxy Computer Services Inc. 171 Cheshire Ln., Suite 100, Plymouth, MN 55441. Tel: 763/475-9111; Fax: 763/404-3960; Web site: http://www.galaxycomputer.com. Dan Tims, Pres.; Peter Schoon, VP. Galaxy Computer Services provides computer sales, support, and maintenance. 50 employees (35 in Minnesota). Founded in 1984. SIC 5734.

Gandy Company Inc. 528 Gandrud Rd., Owatonna, MN 55060. Tel: 507/451-5430; Fax: 507/451-2857. D.E. Gandrud, Pres.; D.R. Thomas, VP and COO. Gandy Co. is a manufacturer of granular-chemical and fertilizer applicators, and a custom manufacturer of sheet metal parts and assemblies—with its CAD/CAM system, CNC laser cutting, CNC turret press, CNC press brake, welding, and powder painting facilities. 100 employees. Founded in 1936. SIC 3499, 3523, 3524.

Garelick Manufacturing Company 644 Second St., St. Paul Park, MN 55071. Tel: 651/459-9795; Fax: 651/459-8269. Saul S. Garelick, Chm.; Kenneth D. Garelick, Pres.; H.J. Garelick, Dir.; Lewis H. Coronis, VP-Op.; Richard J. Garelick, SVP. Garelick manufactures products and accessories for the recreational boating market. 125 employees. Founded in 1952. SIC 3429.

Garlock Equipment Company 2601 Niagara Ln., Plymouth, MN 55447. Tel: 763/553-1935; Fax: 763/553-7765. Larry Hines, Chm.; David L. Nelson, Pres.; David Evans, VP-Sls./Mktg. Garlock Equipment Co. is a manufacturer of roofing and construction equipment. 70 employees (all in Minnesota). Founded in 1959. SIC 3531, 3535, 3536.

The Gaughan Companies 199 N.W. Coon Rapids Blvd., Suite 314, Coon Rapids, MN 55433. Tel: 763/786-6320; Fax: 763/786-9320. Alan J. Hamel, Pres.; Patrick McGaughlan, VP. Annual revenue $11 million. The Gaughan Cos. are primarily engaged in commercial development, property management, and real estate sales. 60 employees (all in Minnesota; 30 part-time). Founded in 1969. SIC 6531.

Gauthier Industries Inc. 3105 22nd St. N.W., P.O. Box 6700, Rochester, MN 55903. Tel: 507/289-0731; Fax: 507/289-6883; Web site: http://www.gauthind.com. David Kocer, Pres. and CEO; Dave Purcell, Purch.; Sue Gintz, Customer Svc./Sls.; Bob McDermott, Cont. Annual revenue $12 million. Gauthier Industries produces metal stampings (including precision sheet fabrications) and manufactures electrical enclosures, special products, powder coating, contract assembly and packaging. 130 employees (all in Minnesota). Founded in 1946. ISO 9002 Certified. SIC 3469, 3499, 3629.

M.A. Gedney Company P.O. Box 8, Chaska, MN 55318. Tel: 952/448-2612; Fax: 952/448-1790; Web site: http://www.gedneypickle.com. Gedney Tuttle, Chm.; Jeffrey Tuttle, Pres. and CEO; J.R. Cook, VP-Tech. Svs.; Michael R. Custer, VP-Retail Sls.; Edward Forbes, VP-Sls./Mktg.; T.E. Hitch, VP-Op.; Carl Tuttle, VP-MIS/Engrg.; David Watling, Treas. and CFO. Annual revenue $50 million. Gedney manufactures pickles, salad dressing, vinegar, sauerkraut, mustard, syrup, salsa, sauces, and preserves. The company controls about 60 percent of the retail pickle trade in the Midwest. 115 employees (all in Minnesota). Founded in 1881. In July 2000 Gedney agreed to acquire the pickle and related products business from Cains Foods L.P., of Ayer, Mass., including the Cains plant located in South Deerfield, Mass., which manufactures pickles, peppers, relish, and sauces for sale under the Cains and Oxford brands. The Cains business is of equal size to Gedney. Gedney's plans were to continue operating the South Deerfield plant with its existing workforce, and some additional management talent from Gedney. [The transfer of ownership was completed in September.] SIC 2035, 2099.

Gelco Information Network Inc. 10700 Prairie Lakes Dr., Eden Prairie, MN 55344. Tel: 952/947-1500; Fax: 952/947-1525; Web site: http://www.gelco.com. Neil J. Vill, Pres. and CEO; William C. Shively, EVP-Sls.; Charles Buckner, SVP-Sls.; Conrad Honeycutt, SVP-Sls.; Jonathan Klem, SVP and Gen. Mgr.-Gelco Gov't Network; Jim Prebil, SVP-Strategic Initiatives; Ted Valleau, SVP-Sls.; Adam Brown, CFO; Nezih Cahir, VP-Tech.; Ken Davison, VP-Product Mgmt./Mktg.; Craig Peterson, VP-Admin.; Leo Smith, VP-Client Svs.; Patricia Becker, Dir.-Mktg. Communications. Gelco Information Network is a leading worldwide supplier of cost-effective, outsourced solutions for the payment processing and management of corporate travel expense and consumer packaged goods trade promotion spending. Gelco's comprehensive solutions are built around such Gelco products as ExpenseLike, TIPS, Traveletter Direct, Traveletter, Branchpay, Rapidraft, Rapidpay, and Rapideal. 325 employees (200 in Minnesota). Founded in 1894. In December 1999 Gelco and the Association of Sales & Marketing Cos. partnered to create a convenience-store-specific, Web-based training program designed for sales and marketing agency employees and new hires. Developed with funding from The Quaker Oats Co., the training tool was made available on the Internet starting Jan. 1, 2000. Dec. 31: Gelco helped its customers manage $3.5 billion in total travel and entertainment-related transactions in 1999. An estimated $5 billion in trade funds were transacted using Gelco commerce and trade management solutions. In March 2000 Gelco agreed to provide ExpenseLink/Web to The Toro Co. (NYSE: TTC), Bloomington, Minn. Gelco was working working with KPMG LLC to develop business-to-business e-commerce solutions that will streamline interaction between manufacturers, wholesalers, retailers, and brokers in the United States and Canada. Both solutions were scheduled for release during the third quarter of 2000. Coors Brewing Co., the third-largest brewer in the United States, became the latest major corporation to use Gelco's suite of e-commerce business expense management tools. The Boeing Co., Seattle (NYSE: BA), chose Gelco to provide automated e-business travel solutions using Gelco Travel Manager software. On May 1, Gelco released ExpenseLink/Direct—its newest Web-based expense management solution. Gelco announced plans to use Wells Fargo & Co. (NYSE: WFC) to implement the electronic funds transfer transaction processing portion of Gelco's new business-to-business e-commerce solution. Gelco announced an agreement with BellSouth to process an estimated 450,000 expense reports annually for the telecommunications leader; and a partnership with Trancentrix, a leading bank-independent, business-to-business payment intermediary, to enable direct reimbursement to clients' employees located in more than 75 countries, in the local currency. Gelco's Help Desk service was exceeding industry customer satisfaction in all categories measured by Service 800 Inc., an independent customer satisfaction service measurement organization.

In June Gelco chose KPMG Consulting to assist in the development phase of Gelco's new business-to-business e-commerce solutions. Gelco announced ExpenseLink/Web 4.3. In July five additional health care corporations—Elan Pharmaceutical, Arjo Inc., Curon Medical Inc., Medimmune Inc., and Radionics—selected Gelco's ExpenseLink travel expense management service. In August Gelco Information Network and eLabor.com formed a partnership to provide customers with a complete Web-based solution for labor resource planning and travel and expense management. Aberdeen Group, an IT consulting and market strategy firm, defined Gelco as a front runner in travel expense management, with the broadest product functionality in the market combined with a unique ability to support multidivisional organizations operating different systems environments. In September Gelco announced ExpenseLink/Direct 4.0. Later in the month, it was decided that the company's two operational groups, Trade Management and Expense Management, were to be operated as separate companies: Trade Management Group for trade promotion management and commerce management solutions to the consumer packaged goods industry; Expense Management Group for eBusiness travel management and reimbursement applications through an array of delivery options leveraging a 100 percent Web-enabled infrastructure. In October Gelco was awarded a contract by the General Accounting Office to host its travel management application via a government portal. The Army and Air Force Exchange System (AAFES), Dallas, and the NASA Jet Propulsion Laboratory (JPL), near Pasadena, Calif., agreed to implement Gelco Travel Manager v7.1C to handle the agencies' end-to-end Internet business travel management. Gelco formed an alliance with American Management Systems Inc. (AMS) to integrate Gelco Travel Manager with AMS Momentum financial systems. Gelco Information Network and Garber Travel partnered to provide business expense management and reimbursement for Garber's business travel clients.SIC 7374.

General Litho Services Inc. 6845 Winnetka Circle, Brooklyn Park, MN 55428. Tel: 763/535-7277; Fax: 763/535-7322; Web site: http://www.genlithco.com. Gary Garner, Pres.; Jim Benedict, VP-Mktg.; Mike Farr, VP-Mfg.; Jeanne Haro, VP-Sls. Support; Beth Ann Swedberg, VP-Admin.; Alan Fischer, Treas.; Al Golder, Cont. Annual revenue $18 million. General Litho Services is a full-service provider of printing, data processing, and lettershop services to the Upper Midwest and nationwide. It supplies sheetfed printing and mailing services tailored to businesses of all sizes, and offers integrated solutions to the direct-response industry. A new, 55,000-square-foot facility completed in early 2000 nearly doubled the size of its headquarters. 161 employees. Founded in 1984. In March 2000 the company completed its first acquisition—the purchase of Heartland Graphics Inc., Roseville, Minn. SIC 2752, 2759.

General Office Products Company 4521 Highway 7, St. Louis Park, MN 55416. Tel: 952/925-7500; Fax: 952/925-7531; Web site: http://www.gopco.com. John E. Boss, Chm.; John E. Boss Jr., Pres.; David J. Boss, Treas. and Sec.; Edward Pisarski, VP-Sls.; Trent G. Bernstein, VP and CFO; Rodney M. Skoge, VP-Op. Annual revenue $56.5 million. General Office Products markets contract furniture, design, and related services. 98 employees (all in Minnesota). Founded in 1963. SIC 5399, 5712, 7389.

General Security Services Corporation 9110 Meadowview Rd., Bloomington, MN 55425. Tel: 952/858-5000; Fax: 952/858-5050. Whitney W. Miller, Pres.; Andrew C. Pierucki, VP. General Security Services Corp. provides security products and services for residential, commercial, and government clients nationwide. Products include alarm systems, card access, closed-circuit TV, metal detectors, X-ray machines, and personal security devices. Services include smoke, fire, security, monitoring, patrol, and transport. 2,800 employees (600 in Minnesota). Founded in 1946. In February 2000 the company launched its Security Training Services Division—to bring professional, customized training to Minnesota businesses. SIC 3669, 7381.

Genmar Holdings Inc. 100 S. Fifth St., Suite 2400, Minneapolis, MN 55402. Tel: 612/339-7900; Fax: 612/337-1930; Web site: http://www.genmar.com. Irwin L. Jacobs, Chm.; Grant E. Oppegaard, Pres. and CEO; Roger R. Cloutier II, EVP and CFO; Steven J. Kubisen, SVP-Tech./Corp. Devel.; Mary P. McConnell, SVP, Gen. Counsel, and Sec.; John S. Rosendahl, SVP-Bus. Devel.; George E. Sullivan, SVP-Mktg.; David H. Vigdal, SVP-Op.; Mark W. Peters, VP and Cont.; Ronald V. Purgiel, VP-Purch.; Daniel W. Schuette, VP-Info. Sys. Annual revenue $858 million. Genmar Holdings' operating companies manufacture recreational powerboats under the brand names Aquasports, Carver, Crestliner, Glastron, Hatteras, Larson, Logic, Lund, Nova, Ranger, Scarab, Trojan and Wellcraft. Genmar markets and sells its products through a network of 1,300 independent authorized dealers in all 50 states and in 30 foreign countries. 6,426 employees (1,705 in Minnesota). Founded in 1962. Documents were filed in late September 1999 that called for the raising of up to $84.5 million through the sale of 6.5 million shares (22 percent of the company) in an initial public offering (IPO). In December 1999 the company officially withdrew its IPO because of "discussions with certain parties that could result in transactions that would have a material impact on the company." Proceeds were supposed to help construct a plant for the recently developed closed-mold fiberglass manufacturing technology, using virtual engineered composites (VEC), that Genmar was hoping would establish new standards in the recreational boat industry. (The company had received a Governor's Award for Excellence in Waste and Pollution Prevention because the process reduces air emissions and solid waste.) Chairman Jacobs explained that "the interest in this [technology] is way more than I had anticipated." An agreement was expected that would result in a significant equity investment by a corporate partner outside of the industry. June 30: Genmar achieved record revenue and profits for fiscal year 2000. Revenue increased 22 percent; operating profit rose 65 percent, to $61 million. In July the company launched its VEC manufacturing technology into the marketplace with a recently completed production plant in Little Falls, Minn., and a major marketing effort. The Minneapolis office of Rapp Collins Worldwide was to spearhead a million-dollar marketing campaign touting VEC's benefits, not only to boats but also to such disparate applications as bathtubs and automotive parts. Said Jacobs, "VEC allows for the first significantly enhanced automotive-like manufacturing factory for the boating industry. Roplene technology has progressed to a new level that will allow us to develop another industry-changing product offering. These two new technologies, along with the progress being made in the aluminum research and development group, has positioned Genmar as the technology leader in the marine industry." SIC 3732. No. 12 CRM Private 100.

Robert Gibb & Sons Inc. 205 S.W. 40th St., Fargo, ND 58103. Tel: 701/282-5900; Fax: 701/281-0819. Robert Gibb Jr., Pres. Annual revenue $25 million. Gibb & Sons is a contractor for heating, ventilating, air conditioning, plumbing, fire sprinkler, concrete paving, and sewer and water utilities. Its subsidiary is Urban Contracting Co., Fargo (Jon Chose). 195 employees (30 in Minnesota; 30 part-time). Founded in 1915. SIC 1611, 1623, 1711, 1731.

Gilleland Chevrolet 3019 W. Division St., St. Cloud, MN 56301. Tel: 320/251-4943; Fax: 320/255-7007. Duane Gilleland, Pres. Gilleland Chevrolet (formerly Baston Chevrolet) is a Chevrolet car and truck dealership serving central Minnesota. 135 employees. Founded in 1939. SIC 5511.

Glencoe Butter & Produce Association P.O. Box 100, Glencoe, MN 55366. Tel: 320/864-5577; Fax: 320/864-6490. Dale Schauer, Chm.; Michael Matousek, VChm.; David Lenzmeier, Gen. Mgr.; Charles Jensen, Treas. and Sec. Glencoe Butter & Produce is a cooperative for cheese and whey powder. 58 employees. Founded in 1894. SIC 2021, 2022, 2023, 4222, 5191.

Glen's Food Center Inc. 210 E. Lincoln, Luverne, MN 56156. Tel: 507/283-4429; Fax: 507/283-4570. Glen Gust, Pres.; Douglas Gust, Ptnr. Glen's Food Center operates two full-service grocery supermarkets in Minnesota: Glen's Food Center, Luverne; and Canby Food Center, Canby. It also has one in Forest City, Iowa. 100 employees (all in Minnesota; 60 part-time). Founded in 1976. SIC 5411.

Global Computronics Inc. 4575 Chatsworth St., Shoreview, MN 55126. Tel: 651/604-5700; Fax: 651/604-5757; Web site: http://www.gcisystems.com. Kay Kuba, Pres. and CEO; Sanjay Kuba, VP and Chief Tech. Ofcr.; Vaneeta Varma, CFO; Anita Kuba, Dir.-Op.; Ramesh Kuba, Trustee. Annual revenue $60 million. Golbal Computronics Inc., dba GCI Systems, provides information technology consulting services to corporate and government accounts in the Twin Cities. GCI's technology products and service solutions include network, enterprise, outsourcing, and mobile office. In addition, GCI Systems offers professional IT staffing services. In 2000 Kuba was named one of the 25 top businesswomen in Minnesota (No. 7) by CityBusiness. 83 employees (79 in Minnesota; 3 part-time). Founded in 1988. SIC 7371.

Globe Tool & Manufacturing Company Inc. 730 24th Ave. S.E., Minneapolis, MN 55414. Tel: 612/331-6750; Fax: 612/331-4742; Web site: http://www.globetool.com. Tim Knapp, Pres.; Edward St. Clair, VP; Carolyn Stark, CFO. Globe Tool & Manufacturing Co. manufactures cases for implantable medical devices. It specializes in deep drawing, battery cases, pacemaker cases, and defibrillator cases. 190 employees (185 in Minnesota). Founded in 1954. SIC 3469, 3544.

Goebel Fixture Company 528 Dale St. S.W., Hutchinson, MN 55350. Tel: 320/587-2112; Fax: 320/587-2378. Virgil E. Goebel, Chm.; Robert Croatt, Pres. Annual revenue $20.2 million. Goebel manufactures custom wood store fixtures, architectural millwork, and wood products. 125 employees (all in Minnesota). Founded in 1935. SIC 2431, 2541.

Gold'n Plump Poultry 4150 S. Second St., Suite 200, St. Cloud, MN 56301. Tel: 320/251-3570; Fax: 320/240-6250; Web site: http://www.goldnplump.com. Donald P. Helgeson, Chm.; Michael J. Helgeson, CEO; Steve Jurek, EVP-Prod./Admin. and CFO; Tim Wensman, EVP-Sls./Mktg. Annual revenue $190 million. Gold'n Plump Poultry is a provider of value-added poultry products and related services with operations in St. Cloud, Luverne, and Cold Spring, Minn.; and Arcadia, Wis. It contracts with about 300 poultry growers. 1,612 employees (1,170 in Minnesota; 71 part-time). Founded in 1926. In June 2000 the company announced plans to close a plant in Chippewa Falls, Wis., that it had opened in 1998 to debone dark meat from chicken thighs. Decreased demand for dark poultry meat and record low poultry prices were cited. In July Gold'n Plump announced plans to sell its 180-employee processing plant in Sauk Rapids, Minn., enabling the company to more fully utilize the capabilities of its expanded Cold Spring facility and the recently acquired Luverne plant. In September Huisken Meats of Chandler, Minn., agreed to buy it. SIC 0251, 2015. No. 66 CRM Private 100.

Goodin Company 2700 N. Second St., Minneapolis, MN 55411. Tel: 612/588-7811; Fax: 612/588-7820. B.D. Reisberg, Chm.; Gerard Melgood, Pres.; Steven Kelly, VP-Sls.; Brian Sand, Treas.; G.D. Skagerberg, VP-Op. Annual revenue $75 million. Goodin Co. wholesales plumbing and heating equipment, pipe valves, fittings, and water well supplies. 225 employees (all in Minnesota). Founded in 1937. SIC 5074.

Gopher Motor Rebuilding Inc. 6401 Cambridge St., St. Louis Park, MN 55426. Tel: 952/929-0441; Fax: 952/929-6733. William G. Smith, Pres. Gopher Motor Rebuilding rebuilds engines for vehicles. 72 employees. Founded in 1948. SIC 3714.

Gopher Resource Corporation 3385 Highway 149, Eagan, MN 55121. Tel: 651/454-3310; Fax: 651/454-7926. Irving Kutoff, Pres.; John Tapper, Gen. Mgr. Gopher Resource Corp. is a metal recycling facility. 170 employees (all in Minnesota). Founded in 1948. SIC 3339.

Gopher State Litho Corporation 3232 E. 40th St., Minneapolis, MN 55406. Tel: 612/724-3600; Fax: 800/451-9195; Web site: http://www.gopherstatelitho.com. Bill Ketz, Pres.; Steven Ketz, VP. Gopher State Litho prints books, brochures, fliers, and weekly publications. The company also has mailing capabilities. 78 employees (all in Minnesota; 10 part-time). Founded in 1970. SIC 2752.

Gordy's Inc. 1131 Oxford St., Worthington, MN 56187. Tel: 507/376-4121. Gordon B. Anderson, CEO; Tom Anderson, Pres.; Bruce Anderson, VP and Sec. Gordy's owns and operates five grocery stores in Minnesota and Iowa; and jointly owns and operates eight stores in South Dakota. 1,500 employees. Founded in 1963. SIC 5411.

Graf/X 3000 Second St. N., Minneapolis, MN 55411. Tel: 612/588-7571; Fax: 612/588-8783. Scott Bachman, CEO; Don Giacchatti, Pres.; Jim Thompson, General Mgr.-Print; Dieter Slezak, Gen. Mgr.-Graphic. Annual revenue $9.1 million. Graf/X, founded by Scott Bachman and The Publishing Group of Minneapolis, performs graphic design, commercial printing, publishing and digital media (signs). 59 employees (64 in Minnesota; 5 part-time). Founded in 1990. SIC 2752, 2791, 2796, 7336.

Grand Portage Lodge & Casino Box 234, Grand Portage, MN 55605. Tel: 800/543-1384; Fax: 218/475-2309; Web site: http://www.grandportagemn.com. Debbie Corcoran, Gen. Mgr.-Lodge Op.; Mary Ann Gagnon, Gen. Mgr.-Casino Op. Grand Portage Lodge & Casino is an Indian gaming casino controlled by the Grand Portage Band of Chippewa Indians. The facilities include a 100-room lodge, a marina, RV sites, and an indoor pool and sauna. 200 employees. Founded in 1975. SIC 7011, 7999.

Grandma's Saloon & Deli 522 Lake Ave. S., Duluth, MN 55802. Tel: 218/727-4192; Fax: 218/723-1986. Don Bleau, Pres.; Doug Dalager, Gen. Mgr.; Joe Bennett, VP-Op.; Brian Daugherty, VP-Mktg. Annual revenue $5 million. Grandma's restaurants offer a blend of antiques, American food, and a neighborhood-bar atmosphere. The company has locations in Canal Park, and Miller Hill, Duluth; the West Bank, Minneapolis; Bloomington, Plymouth, and Virginia, Minn.; and Fargo, N.D. It annually sponsors Grandma's Marathon on the third Saturday in June; and Grandma's German Oktoberfest during the last full week of September. 250 employees. Founded in 1976. SIC 5812.

Granite City Ready Mix P.O. Box 1305, St. Cloud, MN 56302. Tel: 320/252-4322; Fax: 320/259-1792. Robert C. Bogard Sr., Chm. and CEO; Robert C. Bogard Jr., Pres.; Jeffery J. Tschida, VP-Op.; Wayne Schmitz, Sec. and Treas. Granite City Ready Mix operates eight ready-mix concrete plants and three aggregate washing plants in central Minnesota. 105 employees. Founded in 1959. SIC 3273.

Max Gray Construction Inc. 2501 Fifth Ave. W., P.O. Box 689, Hibbing, MN 55746. Tel: 218/262-6622; Fax: 218/262-2109. James M. Erickson, Pres. Annual revenue $17 million. Max Gray Construction is a general building contractor serving northern Minnesota and northwest Wisconsin. It specializes in commercial, industrial, institutional, and multifamily buildings; designing and building; and Varco-Pruden pre-engineered metal building systems. 55 employees (50 in Minnesota; 1 part-time). Founded in 1983. SIC 1521, 1522, 1541, 1542.

Gray, Plant, Mooty, Mooty & Bennett P.A. 3400 City Center, 33 S. Sixth St., Minneapolis, MN 55402. Tel: 612/343-2800; Fax: 612/333-0066; Web site: http://www.gpmlaw.com. Bruce Mooty, Managing Ptnr.; Catherine M. Godlewski, Exec. Dir.; Dave Bahls, Treas.; Michael Flom, Sec. Gray, Plant, Mooty, Mooty & Bennett is a full-service law firm, with 130 attorneys representing clients across the country. The firm maintains practice groups in the following areas: litigation, business law, employee benefits, franchising, intellectual property, entrepreneurial services, tax-exempt organizations, health and human services, international, corporate finance/securities, environmental, employment, tax, real estate, trusts and estate planning, government relations, reorganization and bankruptcy, public law, and finance. 300 employees. Founded in 1866. In July 2000 Gray, Plant attorney Clinton A. Schroeder (of the Financial and Estate Planning Group and the Tax Department) was elected president of the American Council on Gift Annuities. SIC 8111.

Great Clips Inc. 3800 80th St. W., Suite 400, Bloomington, MN 55431. Tel: 952/893-9088; Fax: 952/844-3444; Web site: http://www.greatclips.com. Ray Barton, Chm. and CEO; Rhoda Olsen, Pres. and COO; Terri Miller, VP-Mktg.; Steve Hockett, VP-Op.; Steve Overholser, CFO; Charles Simpson, VP-Franchise Devel.; Dean Wieber, SVP-Real Estate. Great Clips is a franchisor of low-cost hair-care salons. With its total of 1300 salons in 65 cities in 30 states and two western Canada provinces—including 102 locations in the Twin Cities—the company has become the third-largest chain in its industry. The salons, all but 18 of which are franchised, are located primarily in neighborhood strip malls and open seven days a week. Their discount prices range from $9 to $11 for a haircut; $4 to $6 for styling. 230 employees (74 in Minnesota; 80 part-time). Founded in 1982. SIC 7231.

Great Northern Cabinetry Inc. P.O. Box 207, Rib Lake, WI 54470. Tel: 715/427-5255; Fax: 715/427-5227. Phil Staat, Pres.; George Brower, VP; Jim Lally, MIS. Great Northern Cabinetry Inc. is a manufacturer of fine cabinetry, including kitchen, bath, and specialty cabinetry. 60 employees (4 in Minnesota). Founded in 1972. SIC 2434, 2511.

Great River Energy 17845 E. Highway 10, P.O. Box 800, Elk River, MN 55330. Tel: 763/441-3121; Fax: 763/241-2366; Web site: http://www.greatriverenergy.com. Henry Hanson, Board Chair; James Van Epps, Pres. and CEO; Winnie Klick, VP-Employee Res.; Gordon Westerlind, VP-Generation; Ron Larson, VP-Fin.; William R. Kaul, VP-Transmission; Rick Lancaster, VP-Public Affairs; Kandace Olsen, Mgr.-Communications; David Saggau, VP and Gen. Counsel; Louy Theeuwen, Coordinator-Exec./Strategic Svs. Annual revenue $410.5 million (loss $9.7 million; total assets $1.37 billion). Great River Energy (GRE) is the second-largest electric utility in Minnesota, based on generating capacity, and the fourth-largest generation and transmission cooperative in the country, in terms of assets. It was formed Jan. 1, 1999, by the merger of United Power Association, Elk River (founded in 1937), and Cooperative Power, Eden Prairie, Minn. (founded in 1949). GRE provides wholesale electric service to 29 electric distribution cooperatives in Minnesota and Wisconsin. Those member cooperatives serve nearly half a million member/consumers, or about 1.5 million people. GRE and its member cooperatives are not-for-profit companies owned by the consumers they serve. Great River's 1,600-megawatt generation system is composed of an effective mix of base load and peaking power plants, including coal-fired, refuse-derived fuel, oil-fired plants, and wind generation. GRE's 4,300-mile electric transmission system is consistently ranked among the most reliable in the United States. 676 employees (376 in Minnesota). Founded in 1999. In March 2000 Great River Energy and Lakefield Junction L.P. announced an agreement for Great River to purchase Lakefield's 550-megawatt simple-cycle, combustion turbine peaking plant project, located in southwestern Minnesota. Completion is scheduled for June 2001. In April Great River Energy entered into an alliance, called Split Rock Energy, with Minnesota Power to pool generation resources and jointly serve their customers. In May Great River Energy began construction of the Pleasant Valley Station peaking plant, a 434 megwatt simple-cycle, gas-fired combustion turbine plant located in southeastern Minnesota, slated for completion June 2001. At the September annual meeting, Chairman Hanson noted that the volatile wholesale electric market during the summer of 1999 served as the driver for many of the changes Great River Energy made in the past year. Great River Energy's subsequent financial losses caused the company to raise its wholesale rate, implement a power cost adjustment, and enter into projects and alliances to help mitigate its risk in the future. The company had also created an LLC with Minnesota Power in Duluth (Split Rock Energy) to pool generation resources and jointly serve customers, as well as buy and sell energy on the wholesale power market. With Stanton Station undergoing a scheduled maintenance outage, employees conducted a "black start" drill on procedures necessary to bring the electric system back on-line after a total, regional blackout. SIC 4911. No. 10 CRM Cooperatives/Mutuals 20.

Howard R. Green Co. 1326 Energy Park Dr., St. Paul, MN 55108. Tel: 651/644-4389. Howard R. Green Co. is an engineering firm specializing in surveying, exterior renovation, and waste management. SIC 8711.

Greenspring Company 444 Cedar St., Suite 1900, St. Paul, MN 55101. Tel: 651/290-1552; Fax: 651/290-1188. William H. Kling, Pres.; Conley Brooks Jr., Chm.; Thomas J. Kigin, EVP, Sec., and Treas.; Deborah Chernick, CFO; Steven R. Fox, Pres.-Minnesota Monthly Publications; Timothy B. Shears, Pres.-The MNN Radio Networks. Annual revenue $9.6 million. Greenspring Co. is a taxable for-profit subsidiary of Minnesota Communications Group, the nonprofit parent support organization of Minnesota Public Radio. Greenspring operates subsidiaries Minnesota Monthly Publications, a commercial print media group; and The MNN Radio Networks (WMNN 1330 AM and KLBB 1400 AM in the Twin Cities). During 1998, Greenspring's main subsidiary, Rivertown Trading Co., was sold to Target Corp. (NYSE: TGT), Minneapolis, for an estimated $123 million. 94 employees (all in Minnesota; 6 part-time). Founded in 1987. SIC 2721, 2741, 7922.

Greenway Co-op Service 3520 E. River Rd., P.O. Box 6878, Rochester, MN 55903. Tel: 507/289-4086; Fax: 507/289-7653. John King, Chm.; Robert Clowes, VChm.; Dan Wodrich, Gen. Mgr. Greenway Co-op Service does petroleum retailing and fertilizer mixing/application. 140 employees. Founded in 1930. SIC 5171.

Gresser Concrete/Masonry 1771 Yankee Doodle Rd., Eagan, MN 55121. Tel: 651/454-5976; Fax: 651/454-4850. M.C. Gresser, Chm.; M.J. Gresser, Pres. and CEO; George Polusny, VP-Info.; David Vogt, VP-Sls.; Chuck Bertrand, VP-Admin.; Mark Jersted, VP-Field Op. Annual revenue $40 million. Gresser Concrete/Masonry is a commercial and industrial concrete and masonry contractor. 220 employees (210 in Minnesota; 5 part-time). Founded in 1969. SIC 1741, 1771.

Griffin Companies 510 Marquette Ave., Suite 300, Minneapolis, MN 55402. Tel: 612/338-2828; Fax: 612/338-5288; Web site: http://www.griffincos.com. Robert S. Dunbar, Pres.; Robert Fransen, Pres.-Prop. Mgmt.; Steve Chirhart, VP-Sls./Leasing, Office; Craig Kirkpatrick, VP-Sls./Leasing, Office; Mark Moore, VP-Sls./Leasing, Industrial; William M. Ostlund, VP-Sls./Leasing; Jim Wenthold, VP-Sls./Leasing, Industrial. Griffin Cos. is a full-service real estate company offering property management, leasing, brokerage, and asset management services. 60 employees. Founded in 1969. In September 2000 Griffin and Shaferichardson merged their property management divisions to form 87-employee GriffinSR, with 3 million square feet under management. SIC 6531.

Griffiths Corporation 2717 Niagara Ln., Plymouth, MN 55447. Tel: 763/557-8935; Fax: 763/559-5290. Arthur A. Hahn, VP-Fin./Admin.; H.F. Griffiths, Chm. and CEO; Kenneth H. Griffiths, Pres.; Henry J. Robinson, Sec.

Griffiths Corp. is a holding company with eight plants, seven of which are out of state. Trade names are Wrico Stamping Company and K-Tek. The company produces short- and long-run stampings and assemblies, and sheet metal. 700 employees. Founded in 1966. SIC 3469.

Gross-Given Manufacturing Company 75 W. Plato Blvd., St. Paul, MN 55107. Tel: 651/224-4391; Fax: 651/224-3609. John Edgerton Jr., Chm.; Alan J. Suitor, Pres. and CEO; Colin Garner, SVP-Sls./Mktg.; Scott Edgerton, SVP-Op.; Richard Gross, SVP-Total Quality Mgmt.; Paul Ihn, SVP-Engrg.; Randy Wourms, Materials Mgr.; Mark Schmidt, VP-Fin.; Jack Flynn, VP-Mktg. Gross-Given manufactures vending machines. 600 employees (400 in Minnesota; 10 part-time). Founded in 1935. SIC 3581.

H-S Precision Inc. 1301 Turbine Dr., Rapid City, SD 57701. Tel: 605/341-3006; Fax: 605/342-8964; Web site: http://www.hsprecision.com. Thomas Houghton, Pres.; Patricia Hoeke, VP; Janet Thompson, Sls. Mgr.; Vivian Houghton, Sec. H-S Precision is a manufacturer of firearms, rifle stocks, rifle barrels, ammunition test barrels, and related equipment. 75 employees. Founded in 1920. SIC 3484.

The Hadley Companies 11300 Hampshire Ave. S., Bloomington, MN 55438. Tel: 952/943-8474; Fax: 952/943-8098. Ray Johnson, Chm.; Gary Schmidt, Pres.; Bradford Shinkle IV, VP and Gen. Mgr.; William C. Gaddis, VP and Gen. Mgr.-Wholesale; Michael Amundson, SVP-Fin./Op. The Hadley Cos. carves, paints, and markets decorative decoys; publishes limited-edition representational art; and operates retail art galleries. 250 employees. Founded in 1975. SIC 3949, 8412.

Hairstylists Management Systems Inc. 12700 Industrial Park Blvd., Plymouth, MN 55441. Tel: 763/550-1332; Fax: 763/550-1307. Elliot Cohen, CEO; Michael Kunin, Pres. and COO; Michael Brooks, VP-Fin.; Wayne Williams, Dir.-Purch. Hairstylists Management Systems owns and operates hairstyling salons. Founded by former Maxim's executives, who reacquired 220 salons from now-defunct MEI Diversified. 1,250 employees (55 in Minnesota). Founded in 1993. SIC 7231.

Halcon Corporation 1811 Second Ave. N.W., P.O. Box 96, Stewartville, MN 55976. Tel: 507/533-4235; Fax: 507/533-9349. Peter R. Conway, Pres.; William M. Gludt, CFO; Carl Luedtke, VP-Sls.; Al Snyder, Purch. Halcon manufactures and sells wood office furniture to businesses nationwide. 250 employees. Founded in 1977. SIC 2521.

Haldeman-Homme Inc. 430 Industrial Blvd., Minneapolis, MN 55413. Tel: 612/331-4880; Fax: 612/378-2236; Web site: http://www.haldemanhomme.com. E.R. Stalock, Chm.; M.D. Propp, Pres.; D.C. Turnock, VP; K.C. Gunther, Treas. and Sec.; P.A. Fedje, VP. Annual revenue $29 million. Haldeman-Homme is a wholesaler of institutional and industrial laboratory casework, materials-handling equipment, and storage equipment. The Anderson-Ladd division sells and installs residential and commercial hardwood flooring and athletic flooring. 130 employees (129 in Minnesota). Founded in 1924. SIC 5049.

Mathew Hall Lumber Company 127 Sixth Ave. N., St. Cloud, MN 56302. Tel: 320/252-1920; Fax: 320/252-0743. James A. Hall, Pres.; Loran Hall, VP and Gen. Mgr.; John Hall, Sec.; Dan Hall, Mgr.-Component Div.; Pauline M. Hall, Treas. Mathew Hall Lumber Co. is a full-service retail building material supplier to the construction industry. It has a truss and component plant in St. Joseph, Minn. 110 employees. Founded in 1889. SIC 5211.

Hallett Wire Products Company P.O. Box 16447, 307 S. 37th Ave. W. (55807), Duluth, MN 55816. Tel: 218/628-2281; Fax: 218/628-2284; Web site: http://www.hallettwier.com. J.W. McGiffert, Pres.; Steve Grindy, VP-Mktg.; William Haugen, VP-Fin.; Lee Olson, Cont.; Craig Studley, VP-Op. Hallett Wire Products manufactures low-carbon wire and welded wire fabric, and engages in sales representation for other construction and concrete-related accessories. The company has a manufacturing plant in St. Joseph, Mo., and Kingman, Ariz. 155 employees. Founded in 1974. SIC 3496.

Hammel Green and Abrahamson Inc. 1201 Harmon Place, Minneapolis, MN 55403. Tel: 612/337-4100; Fax: 612/332-9013; Web site: http://www.hga.com. Daniel Avchen, CEO; Stephen A. Fiskum, COO; Gary Nyberg, VP and Dir.-HGA Healthcare Architecture; Anita Barnett, VP and Dir.-HGA Corp.; Gary Reetz, VP and Dir.-HGA Cultural Group. Annual revenue $56.1 million. Hammel Green and Abrahamson is a provider of architectural, engineering, interior design, and landscape architectural services. The company focuses on health care, higher educational, cultural and religious, and corporate/government clients. A nationwide practice is served from offices in Minneapolis and Rochester, Minn.; Milwaukee; and Sacramento, Calif. 574 employees (425 in Minnesota; 46 part-time). Founded in 1953. In February 2000 the firm extended its reach into western U.S. markets by acquiring Stephen J. Short & Associates Inc., a Sacramento, Calif.-based architecture and planning firm known for its health care facilities. In July Minnesota Public Radio, St. Paul, chose Hammel Green and Abrahamson to design its new home. SIC 8711, 8712.

Hancock Concrete Products Company Inc. 17 Atlantic Ave., Hancock, MN 56244. Tel: 320/392-5207; Fax: 320/392-5155. Gene D. Schmidgall, Pres.; Richard R. Schmidgall, VP; Robert Schmidgall, VP. Annual revenue $13 million. Hancock Concrete Products manufactures concrete pipe. 150 employees (all in Minnesota). Founded in 1916. SIC 3272.

Hanefeld Brothers Inc. P.O. Box 646, South St. Paul, MN 55075. Tel: 651/451-6863; Fax: 651/451-1659. David Hanefeld, Pres. Hanefeld Brothers is a local and long-distance livestock transportation company. 100 employees. Founded in 1986. SIC 4213.

Hanson Silo Company 11587 County Rd. 8 S.E., Lake Lillian, MN 56253. Tel: 320/664-4171; Fax: 320/664-4140. Gregg Hanson, Chm. and Pres.; Peter Gillen, Dir.-Fin. Hanson Silo manufactures and distributes—nationwide and in Canada—concrete stave silos and hardware for silos; silo unloaders and related equipment; and contract manufacturing and powder coating of metal products. 95 employees (94 in Minnesota; 5 part-time). Founded in 1916. SIC 3272, 3523.

Happy Chef Systems Inc. 500 S. Front St., P.O. Box 3328, Mankato, MN 56002. Tel: 507/345-4571; Fax: 507/345-4585. Thomas P. Frederick Sr., Pres.; Thomas Frederick Jr., VP; Larry Johnson, Dir.-Op. Happy Chef Systems operates Four Happy Chef family restaurants, Ruttles 50's Grills, and Stoney's Restaurant—in Minnesota, South Dakota, Iowa, and Wisconsin. 1,650 employees (750 in Minnesota; 1,200 part-time). Founded in 1963. SIC 5812.

Hardrives Inc. 14475 Quiram Dr., Rogers, MN 55374. Tel: 763/428-8886; Fax: 763/428-8868. Steven K. Hall, Pres. and CEO; Kevin Gannon, VP; Ron Hall, VP; Don Hall, VP; Sig Langerud, Div. Gen. Mgr. Hardrives produces hot-mix blacktop, Redi Mixed concrete, and precast concrete products. 350 employees. Founded in 1963. SIC 2951, 3272.

Harmony Engineering Corporation 460 Hoover St. N.E., Minneapolis, MN 55413. Tel: 612/623-0510; Fax: 612/623-4364. James Nemec, Pres. Harmony Engineering produces precision machining and sheet metal for the aerospace, dairy, computer, and defense industries. 200 employees (all in Minnesota). Founded in 1970. SIC 3444, 3599.

Harmony Enterprises Inc. 704 Main Ave. N., P.O. Box 479, Harmony, MN 55939. Tel: 507/886-6666; Fax: 507/886-6706; Web site: http://www.harmony1.com. Donald C. Cremer, CEO; Steve Cremer, Pres. Harmony Enterprises manufactures roof-lift systems for the recreational vehicle industry. A separate unit, GPI Division, manufactures hydraulic balers for the recycling of wastepaper and cardboard, and stationary compactors for the compacting of waste materials. The company manufactures products under the brand names Heco and GPI. 65 employees (all in Minnesota). Founded in 1962. SIC 2394, 3559.

Harris Contracting Company 909 Montreal Circle, St. Paul, MN 55102. Tel: 651/602-6500; Fax: 651/602-6699. Robert F. Hosch, Chm. and CEO; Paul Thornton, Pres.; Rawley Brodeen, VP; Jerry Crane, CFO; Jerry Dalton, VP; Rob Latta, VP; Jerry Mullenbach, Pres.-Quality Plumbing/Heating; Kerby Olson, VP; Dean Osland, EVP-Commercial Div.; Randy Stewart, VP-Harris Air Systems Co. Harris Contracting, formerly Harris Mechanical Contracting, provides sheet metal, heating, cooling, industrial piping, maintenance, plumbing, temperature control, and ventilation services for business and industry throughout the continental United States. The company has two subsidiaries: Harris Air Systems Co., St. Paul; and Quality Plumbing & Heating Co., Rochester, Minn. 382 employees (370 in Minnesota). Founded in 1954. SIC 1711.

Hartzell Manufacturing 2516 Wabash Ave., P.O. Box 64529 (55164), St. Paul, MN 55114. Tel: 651/646-9456; Fax: 651/643-2300; Web site: http://www.hartzell.com. J. David O'Halloran, Pres.; James Santelli, VP and CFO. Hartzell Manufacturing is a leader in custom engineering, plastic injection molding, and metal die-casting. Other Hartzell facilities are located in Turtle Lake and St. Croix Falls, Wis.; Denton, Texas; and Pompano Beach, Fla. Hartzell was acquired in 1993 by Goldner Hawn Johnson & Morrison and members of management. In 1997 Goldner Hawn sold its controlling interest to Linsalata Capital Partners, a Cleveland investment firm. 824 employees. Founded in 1958. SIC 3363, 3364.

Harvest Ventures Inc. P.O. Box 309, 8602 Highway 7, St. Bonafacius, MN 55375. Tel: 952/446-9616; Fax: 952/446-1716; Web site: http://www.harvestventures.com. Daniel M. Schlueter, CEO; Russ Schlueter, Co-owner. Harvest Ventures develops innovative and alternative pet products that enhance the lives of consumers and their pets. 60 employees (20 in Minnesota). Founded in 1996. Introduced in 1998, Crystal Clear Litter Pearls is the fastest-growing litter in the market today. SIC 2048.

Hastings Bus Company 425 E. 31st St., Hastings, MN 55033. Tel: 651/437-1888; Fax: 651/438-3319. Pat Regan, Pres. Hastings Bus Co. is a school bus contractor and a local charter school bus service. 100 employees (90 part-time). Founded in 1978. SIC 4141, 4151.

Hauenstein & Burmeister Inc. 2629 30th Ave. S., Minneapolis, MN 55406. Tel: 612/721-5031; Fax: 612/728-2792. Robert Johnston, Pres.; Martin J. Beckman, VP and Treas.; Mark D. Johnson, VP; Jack T. Hammang, VP; Bruce W. Engelsma, Sec. H&B is engaged in manufacturing and construction. H&B Elevators manufactures passenger elevator cabs and entrances for new and modernization projects. A specialist in interior construction for commercial, industrial, office, and retail businesses, H&B Interiors is a general contractor. H&B Hollow Metal distributes commercial metal doors and frames, and customized wood doors. H&B Specialized Products distributes and installs specialty seating, folding doors, floors, and casework for schools and labs. 200 employees (all in Minnesota). Founded in 1923. SIC 1542, 1752, 3446, 3534.

Hauser Art Glass Company Inc. P.O. Box 587, Winona, MN 55987. Tel: 507/457-3500; Fax: 507/457-3500. Michael F. Hauser, Pres.; James A. Hauser, EVP. Annual revenue $6.2 million. Hauser Art Glass Co. restores, designs, and fabricates stained glass windows for churches, and installs protective storm windows for churches. Subsidiary: The Willet Studios of Stained Glass, Philadelphia (founded in 1898). 70 employees (35 in Minnesota). Founded in 1946. SIC 3231.

Hayden & Associates Inc. 7825 Washington Ave. S., Suite 120, Bloomington, MN 55439. Tel: 952/941-6300; Fax: 952/941-9602; Web site: http://www.haydenassoc.com. Lowell Singerman, Co-CEO; Steve Benedict, Co-CEO. Annual revenue $11.7 million. Hayden & Associates is a professional recruiting firm specializing in the placement of sales, marketing, and information services professionals. 110 employees (all in Minnesota). Founded in 1970. SIC 7361.

Hayfield Window and Door Company P.O. Box 25, Hayfield, MN 55940. Tel: 507/477-3224; Fax: 507/477-3605. Richard Rouhoff, Pres.; Brian Rouhoff, VP. Hayfield Window and Door manufactures a variety of oak clad, vinyl, and aluminum windows and patio doors. Entry doors are also available. 160 employees (157 in Minnesota; 5 part-time). Founded in 1951. SIC 2431, 5031.

Hays Group IDS Center Suite 1650, 80 S. Eighth St., Minneapolis, MN 55402. Tel: 612/333-3323; Fax: 612/373-7270; Web site: http://www.haysgroup.com. James Hays, Pres. and CEO; William Mershon, Exec. VP; Stephen Lerum, CFO. Annual revenue $20 million. The Hays Group offers a full array of risk management, property and casualty insurance, claims, loss control, employee benefits and retirement planning services. Offices in Minneapolis, Chicago, Milwaukee, Kansas City, and Boston provide customized products and services. 180 employees (110 in Minnesota). Founded in 1994. SIC 6411.

Health Delivery Systems Inc. 2161 University Ave. W., Suite 117, St. Paul, MN 55114. Tel: 651/917-9653; Fax: 651/917-9664. Michael Fishbein, Pres. and CEO; Brian Gaudreau, Dir.-Mktg. Health Delivery Systems Inc., dba Northstar Home Care Services, is a health care provider operating in the 11-county metro area of Minneapolis/St. Paul. Its staff of RNs, LPN/LVNs, PTs, OTs, MSWs, psychiatric RNs, home health aides, homemakers, and live-ins provide disease management services for AIDS, Alzheimer's, asthma, behavioral health care, COPD, diabetes, maternity, neonatal, pediatric, oncology, terminal care, transplants, and ventilator use. Other services provided: apnea monitoring, medical case management, DME, home dialysis, IV therapy, nutritional counseling, phototherapy, PICC insertion, post-partum care, rehab home care. Monthly summary reports are provided to case managers and third-party administrator accounts. The company is licensed by the State of Minnesota and is certified for Medicare and Medicaid Services. 78 employees. Founded in 1992. SIC 8082.

Hedahls Inc. 100 E. Broadway, P.O. Box 1038, Bismarck, ND 58502. Tel: 701/223-8393; Fax: 701/221-4251. Dick Hedahl, Pres.; Larry

Lysengen, CEO. Hedahls sells automotive parts and equipment. 175 employees. Founded in 1916. SIC 5013.

Hedstrom Lumber Company Inc. 1504 Gunflint Trail, Grand Marais, MN 55604. Tel: 218/387-2995; Fax: 218/387-2204. Howard Hedstrom, Pres.; John Hedstrom, VP; Chris Hegg, VP-Fin. Hedstrom Lumber operates a sawmill in Grand Marais and Two Harbors, Minn. It sells lumber wholesale. 125 employees. Founded in 1914. SIC 5211.

Heinrich Envelope Corporation 925 Zane Ave. N., Golden Valley, MN 55422. Tel: 763/544-3571; Fax: 763/544-6287. Anthony A. Popp, Pres. Heinrich Envelope manufactures plain and printed envelopes. Owned by Taylor Corp., North Mankato, Minn. 90 employees. Founded in 1976. SIC 2677.

Help/Systems Inc. 6101 Baker Rd., Suite 210, Minnetonka, MN 55345. Tel: 952/933-0609; Fax: 952/933-8153. Richard Jacobson, CEO; Janet Dryer, Pres. Help/Systems is a software developer whose products include the Robot Automated Operations Solution. 135 employees. Founded in 1982. SIC 7372.

Hennepin Home Health Care 6200 Shingle Creek Pkwy., Suite 350, Brooklyn Center, MN 55430. Tel: 763/521-0072. Claudette Heywood, Pres. Hennepin Home Health Care provides home health care services. 200 employees. Founded in 1974. SIC 8082.

Herc-U-Lift 5655 Highway 12 W., Maple Plain, MN 55359. Tel: 763/479-2501; Fax: 763/479-2296. Les Nielsen, Pres.; June Nielsen, Sec.; Eugene Ellingson, EVP; Jack Piche, VP; Brad Ellingson, Treas. Annual revenue $35 million. Herc-U-Lift sells, rents, and services materials-handling equipment. 127 employees (105 in Minnesota; 2 part-time). Founded in 1968. SIC 5084.

Hiawatha Rubber Company 1700 67th Ave. N., Brooklyn Center, MN 55430. Tel: 763/566-0900; Fax: 763/566-9537; Web site: http://www.hiawatharubber.com. Arthur J. Popehn, Chm.; Thomas J. Popehn, SVP; James C. Popehn, Pres. Hiawatha is engaged in custom rubber molding, rubber-to-metal bonding, and precision grinding of rolls for business machines, printers, and paper handling devices. 95 employees. Founded in 1955. SIC 3069.

Hidden Creek Industries 4508 IDS Center, Minneapolis, MN 55402. Tel: 612/332-2335; Fax: 612/332-2012. S.A. (Tony) Johnson, Pres. and CEO; Scott D. Rued, EVP and CFO; Carl E. Nelson, VP and Cont. Annual revenue $5.04 billion. Hidden Creek Industries acquires and builds automotive-related industrial manufacturing companies. Hidden Creek currently has significant interests in several platform companies. Dura Automotive Systems Inc., Rochester Hills, Mich., taken public in August 1996, designs and manufactures mechanical assemblies and integrated systems for the automotive industry. Tower Automotive Inc., Grand Rapids, Mich., taken public in 1994, manufactures structural steel components for the automotive industry. [See separate entries in the public companies section]. Trim Systems Inc., a joint venture with ASC Inc., is the market leader in heavy truck interior trim systems. Hidden Creek, itself, is a partnership between J2R Corp. and Onex Corp., Toronto. 38,665 employees (10 in Minnesota). Founded in 1989. In December 1999 Hidden Creek acquired Hadley Auto Transport Inc., a leading automotive transport company based in Santa Ana, Calif. The $100 million-revenue Hadley, which was to continue under the direction of the current management team, provides transport services to automotive manufacturers, including Ford and Chrysler. In March 2000 Hidden Creek acquired a 580-employee, $104 million-revenue unit of Dana Corp. The commercial vehicle cab system group makes mirrors, windshield-wiper motors, and heating controls (Moto Mirror and Sprague) for beverage trucks, car haulers, and other medium- to heavy-duty trucks. SIC 3711, 3714. No. 3 CRM Private 100.

HighJump Software 7555 Market Place Dr., Eden Prairie, MN 55344. Tel: 952/947-4088; Fax: 952/947-0440; Web site: http://www.highjumpsoftware.com. Chris Heim, CEO; Duff Davidson, VP-Sls.; Steve Kickert, VP-Product Devel.; Jeff Laurel, VP-Strategic Alliances; Craig Levinsohn, VP-Mktg.; Joel Schlachenhaufsen, VP-Op.; Greg Twedt, VP-D.C. Bus. Annual revenue $18.5 million. HighJump Software, formerly Data Collection Systems, is a developer of software and complete bar code solutions for data collection and warehouse management. Early in 2000, with a new offering called e-Fulfillment Advantage, the company moved into the promising field of product distribution software keyed to the e-commerce market. 140 employees (all in Minnesota). Founded in 1983. In July 2000 HighJump was given a Top 100 software vendor award from Manufacturing Systems. In August The company announced an $8.5 million capital infusion from St. Paul Venture Capital Inc. and Upper Lake Growth Capital, Eden Prairie; and a name change, from Data Collection Systems to HighJump Software. The company released e-Fulfillment Advantage version 2.0 which added two new modules, Advantage Source and Advantage Dashboard, to the company's existing Warehouse Advantage, Advantage Link, and Web-based Customer Service Advantage components. In October HighJump chose Exodus Communications Inc. (Nasdaq: EXDS), a leader in complex Internet hosting and managed services, to provide Web-hosting infrastructure for HighJump's customers. HighJump Software and Symbol Technologies, a global leader in wireless and Internet-based mobile data transaction systems, announced a strategic partnership that involves integrating Symbol's handheld RF terminals with HighJump Software's bar code data collection and supply chain execution software. SIC 7372. No. 40 CityBusiness Fastest-growing Private Companies.

Highland Manufacturing Company P.O. Box 427, Worthington, MN 56187. Tel: 507/376-9460; Fax: 507/376-5915. Dave Bennett, Chm.; Greg DeGroot, Pres. Highland Manufacturing makes mobile homes that are 14, 16, and 28 feet wide and triple wide. 150 employees. Founded in 1986. SIC 2451.

Hill Wood Products Inc. P.O. Box 398, Cook, MN 55723. Tel: 218/666-5933; Fax: 218/666-5726; Web site: http://www.hillwoodproducts.com. Raymond J. Hill, Chm.; Steven A. Hill, Pres.; Donald T. Hill, VP; Tim Johnson, CFO. Hill Wood Products manufactures wood products: birch and ash dowels, furniture dimension parts, and precut pallet lumber; wood biomass fuel; wood-joining biscuits; and mouldings. The company also operates a sawmill; dry kilns; and sawing, planing, gluing, painting, varnishing and sanding machinery. 70 employees (all in Minnesota). Founded in 1957. SIC 2429, 2431, 2499, 2511.

Hills Materials Company 1311 W. Main, P.O. Box 2320, Rapid City, SD 57709. Tel: 605/394-3300; Fax: 605/341-3446. Lynn R. Kading, Pres. Annual revenue $40 million. Hills Materials deals in asphalt and ready-mix concrete, crushed stone, calcium feed additive, mineral filler, ready-bag concrete. 400 employees. Founded in 1963. SIC 1442, 2951, 3531.

Himec Inc. 1400 N.W. Seventh St., Rochester, MN 55901. Tel: 507/281-4000; Fax: 218/281-5206; Web site: http://www.himec.com. Charles Hiley Jr., CEO; Dennis Tarpenning, Pres.; Greg Donley, CFO; Joe Beckel, First VP. Annual revenue $35 million. Himec is a plumbing, heating, air-conditioning, and fire protection contracting company. Himec also has 24-hour on-call service and preventive maintenance, specialty sheet metal fabrication, and mobile crane service. 250 employees (all in Minnesota). Founded in 1975. SIC 1711.

Hirshfield's Inc. 725 Second Ave. N., Minneapolis, MN 55405. Tel: 612/377-3910; Fax: 612/377-2734. Hans Hirshfield, CEO. Annual revenue $45 million. Hirshfield's is a wholesaler/retailer of paints, wallcoverings, carpet, and window fashions. The company also manufactures paints and coatings. 400 employees. Founded in 1894. SIC 5198.

Hitchcock Industries Inc. 8701 Harriet Ave. S., Bloomington, MN 55420. Tel: 952/881-1000; Fax: 952/887-7858. Gregory T. Hitchcock, Chm., Pres., and CEO; Thomas G. Murphy, VP-Fin. and CFO; John C. Church, VP-Mktg./Planning; Gene A. Johnson, VP-Personnel. Hitchcock Industries is a non-ferrous foundry producing aluminum magnesium castings, machining and related services. 500 employees (all in Minnesota). Founded in 1916. SIC 3365, 3369, 3544.

W. Hodgman & Sons Inc. 1100 Marcus St., Fairmont, MN 56031. Tel: 507/235-3321; Fax: 507/235-3160. Lyle Maschoff, Pres. W. Hodgman & Sons is engaged in highway and street construction involving bituminous paving, gravel crushing, hauling, concrete breaking, and recycling. The company's quarry operation produced concrete and bituminous aggregate, riprap, and seal coat aggregate. The company has a quarry operation, Sioux Rock Products, in Jeffers, Minn. 150 employees. Founded in 1930. SIC 2951, 3281.

Hoigaards Inc. 3550 S. Highway 100, St. Louis Park, MN 55416. Tel: 952/929-1351; Fax: 952/929-2669. Conrad J. Hoigaard, CEO; Brien O'Brien, Sec. and Treas.. Hoigaards retails sporting goods and casual furniture. 75 employees. Founded in 1895. SIC 5712, 5941.

Holaday Circuits Inc. 11126 Bren Rd. W., Minnetonka, MN 55343. Tel: 952/933-3303; Fax: 952/933-4787. Marshall V. Lewis, Chm. and Pres.; John Erickson, VP-Fin. Holaday Circuits produces circuit boards. 320 employees. Founded in 1976. SIC 3679.

Holden Graphic Services 607 Washington Ave. N., Minneapolis, MN 55401. Tel: 612/339-0241; Fax: 612/349-0433. Harold L. Holden, Chm. Emeritus; George T. Holden, Chm. and CEO; Harold L. Holden Jr., VChm. Annual revenue $59.6 million. Holden Graphic Services manufactures custom continuous data processing, snap-a-part, and word processing business forms; printed roll products; pressure sensitive labels; and direct-mail promotional printing, personalization, and mailing services and teleservices. Holden also specializes in computerized documents management, distribution management, fulfillment, and pic-n-pak programs involving systems/forms design; reorder, inventory, and security control; warehousing; and traffic coordination/distribution. 510 employees (70 in Minnesota). Founded in 1940. SIC 2761, 7331.

Hole-In-The-Wall Casino & Hotel P.O. Box 98, Highways 77 and 35, Danbury, WI 54830. Tel: 715/656-3444. Don Alexander, Gen. Mgr.. Hole-In-The-Wall offers a 35-site RV park, live music, and a restaurant. 220 employees. Founded in 1991. SIC 7011.

Holiday Companies 4567 W. 80th St., P.O. Box 1224 (55440), Bloomington, MN 55437. Tel: 952/830-8700; Fax: 952/830-8864; Web site: http://www.holidaystationstores.com. Ronald A. Erickson, Chm. and CEO; Donovan Erickson, Pres.; Gerald Erickson, VP; Dennis Lindahl, VP; Stephen E. Watson, Pres./CEO-Gander Mountain. Annual revenue $1 billion. Holiday Cos. is a diversified holding company engaged in wholesale and retail sale of gasoline. Holiday Stationstores is a recognizedleader in the petroleum and convenience store industry, with more than 300 corporately owned stores located throughout 11 states in the northern tier region of the United States: Minnesota, Wisconsin, Michigan, Iowa, North Dakota, South Dakota, Nebraska, Montana, Wyoming, Idaho, and Washington. For more than 60 years, Holiday Stationstores has been committed to serving customers with high-quality gasoline products, along with a wide selection of prepared food, groceries, and general merchandise items. Holiday Cos.' other businesses include Erickson Petroleum Corp. (World Wide Inc.); and Lyndale Terminal Co. An affiliated company owns and operates 38 Gander Mountain stores in Minnesota, Wisconsin, Michigan, Ohio, Iowa, Pennsylvania, and Indiana. 5,500 employees. Founded in 1928. In December 1999 Nash Finch Co. (Nasdaq: NAFC), an Edina, Minn.-based food wholesaler and retailer, terminated a previously announced agreement in principle to acquire Holiday subsidiary Fairway Foods of Michigan Inc., Menominee, Mich. In January 2000 Gander Mountain announced plans to open new 31,000-square-foot stores in Kalamazoo, Turner City and Lansing, Mich., in the spring; and to close its store in Plymouth, Minn. In February Fairway put its 41-acre, 557,000-square-foot Northfield (Minn.) Distribution Center on the selling block. Asking price: $14.95 million. In March Gander Mountain announced that seven more new stores in five Midwestern states were to be opened in August and September: 31,000-square-foot locations in Canton, Ohio; Green Bay, Wis.; Madison, Wis.; Erie, Pa.; Cedar Rapids, Iowa; and a 20,760-square-foot location in Sheboygan, Wis. SIC 5172, 5499, 5941, 6719. No. 37 CRM Employer 100. No. 7 CRM Private 100.

Hollstadt & Associates Inc. 14300 Nicollet Ct., Suite 301, Burnsville, MN 55306. Tel: 952/892-3660; Fax: 952/892-5044; Web site: http://www.hollstadt.com. Rachel Hollstadt, CEO. Annual revenue $17 million. Hollstadt & Associates (H&A) is a project management and information technology (IT) consulting firm. The company provides professional services and solutions in project management, strategic e-business initiatives, and CRM with a focus on customer contact centers. 100 employees. Founded in 1990. SIC 7371, 7373. No. 29 CityBusiness Fastest-growing Private Companies.

The Homark Company Inc. 100 Third St., P.O. Box 309, Red Lake Falls, MN 56750. Tel: 218/253-2777; Fax: 218/253-2116. Don Schnyder, Chm.; Gerald W. Bjorgan, Sec. and Treas. Homark manufactures HUD approved manufactured homes. 130 employees. Founded in 1986. SIC 3448.

Home of Economy Inc. P.O. Box 13430, Grand Forks, ND 58208. Tel: 701/772-6611; Fax: 701/772-6521. Jean G. Kiesau, Chm. and Pres.; A.P. Raymond, EVP; D.N. Johnson, Sec. and Treas. Home of Economy owns five general merchandise stores across North Dakota, which are operated as one-stop shopping centers. 300 employees. Founded in 1946. SIC 5251.

Home Valu 5401 East River Rd., Fridley, MN 55421. Tel: 763/571-2636; Fax: 763/571-3411. Rudy E. Boschwitz, Chm.; Gerry E. Boschwitz, Pres. and CEO; Ken Boschwitz, VP; Dan Boschwitz, VP; Ellen Boschwitz, VP; Tom Boschwitz, VP. Home Valu, previously known as Plywood Minnesota, retails home-remodeling products for the do-it-yourselfer, and offers installation on all items it sells. Its 11-store network consists of four stores in the Twin Cities; two in Des Moines, Iowa; one in Madison, Wis.; three in Milwaukee; and one in Indianapolis. 450 employees. Founded in 1963. SIC 5211, 5713.

Homecrest Industries Inc. P.O. Box 350, Wadena, MN 56482. Tel: 218/631-1000; Fax: 218/631-2609. Donald L. Bottemiller, Pres.; Lawrence Calhoun, VP-Fin.; Clayton White, VP-Hum. Res.; Phil Powell, VP-Op.; Jan Trinkley, VP-Sls. Homecrest manufactures steel and aluminum patio and casual furniture. 466 employees (464 in Minnesota). Founded in 1954. SIC 2514.

Honeymead Products Company 2020 S. Riverfront Dr., P.O. Box 3247, Mankato, MN 56002. Tel: 507/625-7911; Fax: 507/345-2254. James Tibbetts, Pres.; Albert Ambrose, SVP-Processing; Mark Hingiss, SVP-Oilseed Refining; Larry M. Salzwedel, VP-Admin.; Pamela Schubbe, VP-Flour Sls. Honeymead Products—a division of Cenex Harvest States Cooperatives, Inver Grove Heights, Minn.—processes and refines soybeans. 200 employees. Founded in 1947. SIC 2075.

Horner Flooring Company P.O. Box 380, Dollar Bay, MI 49922. Tel: 906/482-1180; Fax: 906/482-6115; Web site: http://www.info@hornerflooring.com. Douglas Hamar, Pres.; Mark Young, VP-Mfg. Horner Flooring manufactures maple and oak flooring, portable basketball and dance floors, and flooring for racquetball courts, roller rinks, and aerobics studios. 75 employees. Founded in 1891. SIC 2426.

Horton Inc. 1170 15th Ave. S.E., Minneapolis, MN 55414. Tel: 612/331-5931; Fax: 612/627-5709; Web site: http://www.hortoninc.com. Hugh K. Schilling Sr., Chm. and CEO; Randy Nord, Pres. and COO; Mike Ramsay, CFO; Jim O'Rourke, VP-Sls./Mktg.; Tom Nelson, VP-Mfg.; Dale Bloomstrand, VP-MIS; Chuck Rectenwal, VP-Hum. Res.; Ron Losee, VP-Engrg.; Gene Stanchfield, VP-Mfg. Horton is a leading manufacturer of engine cooling system solutions for diesel engine applications worldwide. Horton has manufacturing facilities located in the United States, Canada, Mexico, and Australia. In June 1999 Horton Inc. split its two divisions into separate companies: Horton Inc. and Nexen Group Inc. 275 employees (75 in Minnesota). Founded in 1951. In June 2000 the company broke ground on a 41,000-square-foot corporate headquarters in Roseville, Minn., which was to include expanded R&D areas plus a specialized vehicle test cell equipped with a dynomometer and ram air capabilities to help product diversification, development, and testing. SIC 3568.

Hubbard Broadcasting Inc. 3415 University Ave., St. Paul, MN 55114. Tel: 651/646-5555; Fax: 651/642-4103. Stanley S. Hubbard, Chm., Pres., and CEO; Gerald D. Deeney, SVP; Stanley E. Hubbard, VP and Pres.-Hubbard Media Group; Ginny Hubbard Morris, VP and Pres.-Hubbard Radio; Robert W. Hubbard, VP and Pres.-Hubbard Television; Suzanne J. Cook, VP-Hum. Res.; Harold C. Crump, VP-Corp. Affairs; Ronald L. Lindwall, CFO; Kathryn Hubbard Rominski, Sec.; David A. Jones, Gen. Counsel; C. Thomas Newberry, VP and Cont.; Bruce Hagerty, Building Svs. Annual revenue $250 million (estimated by Fact Book). Hubbard Broadcasting Inc. operates two radio stations, 11 television stations—six in Minnesota, the largest being the Twin Cities' KSTP-TV Channel 5; two in New York state; and three in New Mexico—and three television production companies. HBI is also managing general partner and majority shareholder of Conus communications, a multifaceted media partnership providing television production and transmission services to local, national, and international broadcasters and corporate clients. In December 1998 Hubbard sold subsidiary U.S. Satellite Broadcasting Co. Inc. to Hughes Electronics Corp. for $1.25 billion in cash and stock. 1,350 employees (800 in Minnesota; 250 part-time). Founded in 1923. In March 2000 KSTP-TV's Channel 5 Eyewitness News Investigative Unit was awarded the National Headliner Silver Medallion for "Blood Priority," a three-part investigation of problems with military helicopters that aired in November 1999. In April the company took over the operations of KVBM-TV Channel 45, a UHF television station. In June KSTP named Susan Anderson station manager of KSTC. In September KSTC-TV, the former KVBM, made its debut as the only fully independent television station in the Twin Cities. Along with KSTP-TV Channel 5, it also represented the first "duopoly," where a broadcasting company owns more than one station in a designated market area. In October Hubbard agreed to purchase its seventh Minnesota television station, ABC affiliate KAAL-TV, which serves the Austin, Minn./Rochester, Minn./Mason City, Iowa market. Hubbard Broadcasting gave $10 million to the University of Minnesota's School of Journalism and Mass Communication. KSTP-TV took away 20 golden Emmy statues—the most of any Minnesota television station—at the inaugural awards banquet of the new Minneapolis/St. Paul Chapter of the National Academy of Television Arts and Sciences. Additionally, two HBI icons were inducted into NATAS' Silver Circle: founder Stanley E. Hubbard and Channel 5 Eyewitness News reporter Jason Davis. SIC 4833. No. 54 CRM Private 100.

Huckle Publishing Inc. 514 Central Ave., P.O. Box 249, Faribault, MN 55021. Tel: 507/334-1853; Fax: 507/334-8569; Web site: http://www.faribault.com. James Huckle, Pres.; David Balcom, Publisher and VP; Ronald Ensley, Publisher. Huckle publishes the Faribault Daily News, the Faribault Area Shopper, the Owatonna People's Press, and the Owatonna Area Shopper. 110 employees. Founded in 1914. SIC 2711.

Hunt Electric Corporation 2300 Territorial Rd., St. Paul, MN 55114. Tel: 651/646-2911; Fax: 651/643-6575. Robert F. Tipler, CEO; Michael Hanson, Pres.; Duane Grundhoefer, EVP; Jim Basara, VP; Jack Galvin, VP; Lamont Herman, VP; Tim Holmberg, VP; Curtis Southward, VP-Nat'l Div. Annual revenue $72 million. Hunt Electric Corp. is engaged in electrical contracting for business and industry in California, Colorado, Georgia, Florida, Kansas, Michigan, Ohio, Indiana, New Mexico, Louisiana, Minnesota, Wisconsin, South Dakota, North Dakota, Oklahoma, and Virgina. 650 employees (475 in Minnesota; 6 part-time). Founded in 1965. SIC 1731.

Hunt Technologies Inc. 6436 County Rd. 11, Pequot Lakes, MN 56472. Tel: 218/562-4877; Fax: 218/562-5133; Web site: http://www.turtletech.com. Bruce Kraemer, Chm. and CEO; Paul Hunt, Chief Tech. Officer; Kevin Hummel, Sls. Mgr. Annual revenue $31 million. Hunt Technologies, Inc. is an electronics design firm. The company's flagship product is the Turtle automated meter reading system that remotely reads residential electric meters. Using a patented ultra-narrow bandwith technology, the Turtle System offers a wide range of energy management capabilities. The system includes a substation receiver that continuously reads up to 3,000 transmitters at great distances through power lines. Data from the system is relayed to the utility to be used for billing services, distribution system maintenance, customer services, and line-loss prevention. 106 employees (99 in Minnesota). Founded in 1986. SIC 3824.

Hutchinson Manufacturing 720 Highway 7 W., P.O. Box 487, Hutchinson, MN 55350. Tel: 320/587-4653; Fax: 320/587-3620; Web site: http://www.hutchmfg.com. Tom Daggett, Pres.; Farid Currimbhoy, VP; Wanda Bryant, Dir.-Mktg.; Kathy Hombach, Cont. Annual revenue $14.5 million. Hutchinson Manufacturing is a custom metal fabricator—producing metal products requiring design engineering, fabrication, welding, painting, and assembly. 136 employees (all in Minnesota; 10 part-time). Founded in 1953. SIC 3443.

Hydra Mac International 1110 Pennington Ave., Thief River Falls, MN 56701. Tel: 218/681-7130; Fax: 218/681-7134. John Luoma, CEO; Harlan Altepeter, Sls. Mgr. Hydra Mac International manufactures gear-drive skid-steer loaders, crawler-loaders, and related attachments. Owned by Magnum Inc., Rapid City, S.D. 76 employees. Founded in 1970. SIC 3537.

IBP Inc. 800 Stevens Port Dr., Dakota Dunes, SD 57049. Tel: 605/235-2061; Fax: 605/235-2404; Web site: http://www.ibpinc.com. Robert L. Peterson, Chm. and CEO; Richard L. Bond, Pres. and COO; Kenneth W. Browning Jr., EVP; R. Randolph Devening, Pres./CEO-Foodbrands America; Craig J. Hart, VP and Cont.; David C. Layhee, Pres.-Value-Added Ground Meats; Eugene D. Leman, Pres.-Fresh Meats; James V. Lochner, EVP; Charles F. Mostek, EVP; Kenneth L. Rose, EVP; Jerry S. Scott, EVP; Larry Shipley, Pres.-IBP Enterprises. Annual revenue $14.08 billion (earnings $313.3 million). IBP is a leading producer of high-quality fresh beef and pork, and supplies premium, fully prepared meats and other consumer-ready foods for the retail and foodservice industries. The company has two business segments, Fresh Meats and Enterprises. Fresh Meats produces fresh beef and processed beef and pork products. Fresh Meats' primary products include boxed beef and fresh pork, which are marketed mainly in the United States to grocery chains, meat distributors, wholesalers, retailers, restaurant and hotel chains, and processors who produce cured and smoked products (bacon, ham, luncheon meats, sausage). Fresh Meats also produces inedible allied products, such as hides and other items used to manufacture leather, animal feed, and pharmaceuticals; and edible allied products, which include a variety of meat items. Enterprises produces frozen and refrigerated food products for the foodservice industry. DLJ Merchant Banking Partners III is slated to be the majority owner some time early in 2001. 45,000 employees. Founded in 1960. In December 1999 the company expanded its presence in Eastern Europe by acquiring part ownership of a meat processing plant in Tushinsky, a suburb of Moscow. IBP agreed to acquire $800 million-revenue Corporate Brand Foods America (CBFA), Houston, a leading privately held processor and marketer of meat and poultry products for the retail and foodservice markets. The transaction would make IBP one of the world's leading producers of high-margin, value-added processed meat, poultry, and other food products. In February 2000 the CBFA deal was completed. Based on IBP's prevailing stock price of $14.313 per share, the value of the transaction was $550 million, including the redemption of $28 million in preferred stock and the refinancing of $316 million of CBFA debt. March 31: Continued strong results by IBP's fresh meat operations, including increased export sales, helped deliver solid first-quarter earnings. "Our fresh meat operations flourished in the first quarter, particularly in the international marketplace," CEO Peterson said. "Despite some growing pains within Foodbrands related to the former Thorn Apple Valley facilities, we experienced strong fundamentals in our processed foods operations." In April the world's leading meat and poultry processors—IBP, Cargill Inc. and its red meat business (Excel Corp.), Smithfield Foods Inc. (NYSE: SFD), Tyson Foods Inc. (NYSE: TSN), Gold Kist Inc., and Farmland Industries Inc.'s red meat businesses (Farmland National Beef and Farmland Foods)—signed a letter of intent to create an online, business-to-business marketplace for meat and poultry products, service, and information. IBP then took a major step in its mission to create the most recognized label in the retail meat case. It unveiled Thomas E. Wilson as the name of its new consumer brand, which was to cover a variety of fresh, frozen, and cooked meat items, and also include marinated and seasoned cuts. "This is an exciting time for IBP as we realize the fulfillment of our strategy to produce and market brand-name cuts of beef and pork," according to Peterson. "Building on a heritage of quality, Thomas E. Wilson is a strong foundation for establishing IBP's branded products effort." As the president of Wilson & Co., Thomas E. Wilson worked to develop many of today's popular value-added beef and pork products, and well-known brands such as Wilson Certified Hams.

In June IBP voluntarily recalled 265,927 pounds of ground beef produced on May 13 at its Geneseo, Ill., plant. A product sample analyzed in distribution by USDA was found to contain E. coli 0157:H7. June 24: Strong product demand and solid export sales were major factors behind positive second-quarter earnings. In July the company chose Sherman, Texas, as the site for one of its new case-ready meats operations that was to employ up to 1,400 people. IBP was expecting to spend $40 million to $60 million to renovate Sherman's former Oscar Mayer plant, which closed in 1998. A second major case-ready meats plant of similar size was to be operated in a renovated manufacturing plant in Goodlettsville, Tenn. Sept. 23: Continued strength in consumer demand for proteins, along with record export sales, contributed to earnings of $78.4 million in the quarter, $198 million year-to-date (before nonrecurring items). "The success story for IBP this year continues to be strong demand for our finished products both in the U.S. and internationally," CEO Peterson said. "Our fresh pork operations and Foodbrands America contributed to that success, despite facing higher raw material costs than a year ago." In October IBP and Donaldson, Lufkin & Jenrette Inc. (NYSE: DLJ) jointly announced that Rawhide Holdings Corp., a wholly owned subsidiary of DLJ Merchant Banking Partners III L.P., a private equity fund affiliated with Donaldson, Lufkin & Jenrette, had reached an agreement to acquire the stock of IBP for $2.4 billion in cash plus the refinancing and assumption of $1.4 billion in debt, for total consideration of $3.8 billion. If the purchase is completed, in early 2001, DLJ Merchant Banking Partners III and affiliated funds will become the majority owner of IBP. Other investors include Archer Daniels Midland Co. (NYSE: ADM), Booth Creek Partners, and certain IBP management employees. CEO Peterson stated, "This transaction allows stockholders to receive cash for all their shares at a very attractive price. Another advantage is that DLJ Merchant Banking Partners III will be an excellent source of capital for IBP to implement our long-term business plan." IBP management was to remain in place following the merger. No changes in operations or staffing were expected. Later in the month, Smithfield Foods submitted an unsolicited bid of $2.7 billion in stock. Government officials were reviewing the antitrust implications. SIC 2013.

I.C. System Inc. 444 E. Highway 96, P.O. Box 64444 (55164), Vadnais Heights, MN 55110. Tel: 651/483-8201; Fax: 651/481-6303; Web site: http://www.icsystem.com. John A. Erickson, Chm.; Barbara Erickson, CEO; Kenneth Rapp, Pres.; Sandra Bainbridge, SVP-Sls.; Kurt Heinbigner, CFO; Louise Jensen, VP-Mktg.; Margaret Porcher, VP-Data Mgmt. Svs.; Phil Trovato, SVP-Op. I.C. System is a privately owned company helping businesses acquire, develop, and manage their customer relationships. Founded in 1938, I.C. System is a nationwide provider of customized business solutions providing lead generation, database management, telemarketing, call center, and accounts receivable management services. I.C. System specializes in service to the medical, retail, financial services, utility, telecommunications, publishing, and manufacturing industries. Offices in Mason City, Iowa; Fargo, N.D.; and Boca Raton, Fla. 700 employees (500 in Minnesota; 64 part-time). Founded in 1938. In April 2000 the company was awarded a National Business Solution Award from the U.S. Postal Service for entering into business venture to process significant volumes of new, pre-canceled ad mail for a consumer lending products company. The company launched Medical Insurance Recovery Service, a method of encouraging insurance carriers to respond to health care providers and resolve claims quickly; and DentistWorld.com, an Internet service that gives dentists an effective and affordable way to communicate with patients and build their practices. I.C. System was the first company to utilize MinnesotaJobs.com, a video employment advertising Web site, to better reach persons seeking jobs in Minnesota. In August the company received approval to automate FASTforward certification for its combined mail facility. SIC 7322, 7374, 7379.

ICES Ltd. 5354 Parkdale Dr., Suite 375, St. Louis Park, MN 55416. Tel: 952/542-0028; Fax: 952/542-0030; Web site: http://www.icesltd.com. Albert Coleman, CEO. Annual revenue $14 million. ICES (International Computer Engineering Services) performs computer, systems integration, and multimedia services: information systems development, contract data processing, network consulting, video teleconferencing systems, multimedia productions, computer systems maintenance, and contract and permanent placement of computer professionals. Clients include the U.S. Air Force, Dept. of Agriculture, Environmental Protection Agency, and Veterans Administration (government sector); 3M Co., Diageo plc, Deluxe Corp., and Imation Corp. (private sector). 105 employees (25 in Minnesota). Founded in 1986. SIC 7371.

IRC (Interstate Reporting Company) 817 Vandalia St., St. Paul, MN 55102. Tel: 651/649-0146; Fax: 651/649-0180. Jon E. DeVary, Pres. and CEO; Amy L.E. Westgaard, Field Op. Mgr. IRC provides investigative services—including surveillance, background checks, and activities checks—mainly to the insurance industry. Offices: Des Moines, Iowa; Denver; and Kansas City, Mo. 54 employees (32 in Minnesota). Founded in 1989. SIC 7381.

IRC Industries Inc. 204 Mississippi Ave., Red Wing, MN 55066. Tel: 651/388-7108; Fax: 651/388-9223. Kris Webster, Chm.; David E. Leiseth, Exec. Dir.; Paul Kramp, Treas. IRC Industries does subcontract work for business and industry. It also provides a supported-work program and work-crew program that integrates clients into the community. IRC Industries has another location at 224 Main St., Zumbrota, Minn. 320 employees (240 in Minnesota; 12 part-time). Founded in 1969. SIC 2499, 3172, 3699, 3999.

Ibberson Inc. 828 Fifth St. S., Hopkins, MN 55343. Tel: 952/938-7007; Fax: 952/939-0451; Web site: http://www.ibberson.com. Walter D. Hanson, CEO; Dunnley L. Mattke, Pres. and COO; Raymond Dahle, CFO;

Steve Kimes, EVP and Gen. Mgr.; Glenn Higgins, SVP-Construction Op.; Gerry Leukam, SVP-Tech. Op.; Chandler Thomas, VP; Bryant Berg, VP-Project Mgmt.; Mark Geitzenauer, EVP and Managing Dir.; Steve Frankosky, EVP-Engrg. Op.; Darryl V. Wernimont, VP-Bus. Devel. Ibberson is a design/engineering/construction services firm specializing in both conventional and prebuilt-modular processing facilities for the food, feed and grain, pet food, and mineral industries. Types of projects include new construction, renovation, expansion, repair, and feasibility studies. Ibberson has expanded in the past two decades to include Ibberson International Inc. (Mark Geitzenauer, Mgr.) and Ibberson Engineering Inc. (Stephen Frankosky, Mgr.). 242 employees (78 in Minnesota). Founded in 1881. SIC 1541, 8711.

Ican Inc. 12982 Valley View Rd., Eden Prairie, MN 55344. Tel: 952/946-7420; Fax: 952/996-0235; Web site: http://www.icaninc.net. Dr. Michael T. Osterholm, Chm.; Michael E. Moen, Pres. and CEO; James V. Adam, CFO. Ican is a provider of Internet-based expert knowledge and decision-support resources for health professionals. Its initial focus is the prevention, control, diagnosis, and treatment of infectious diseases, which are the leading cause of death worldwide. Its products are developed by internationally recognized experts. Ican's revenue models are built around the concept of connecting health professionals with corporate customers—medical/surgical and pharmaceutical product manufacturers, group purchasing organizations, health plans, and professional associations—and providing both with valuable information and services. 51 employees (49 in Minnesota; 3 part-time). Founded in 1998. IcanPREVENT(www.icanprevent.com), launched in March 2000 and updated daily, is a comprehensive yet easy-to-navigate source of in-depth information and breaking news on infectious diseases, infection control measures, and infection control-related medical products. In icanPREVENT's first seven months, ican secured more than 7,000 paid subscriptions and developed partnership agreements with Premier Inc., 3M Health Care, Neoforma.com, BJC Health System, and Lippincott Williams and Wilkins. SIC 8099.

PVT

IDeaS Inc. 3500 Yankee Dr., Suite 350, Eagan, MN 55121. Tel: 651/905-3200; Fax: 651/905-3299; Web site: http://www.e-yield.com. Ed Booth, Pres. and CEO; Mark Robinow, CFO; Sanjay Nagalia, Co-founder; Ravi Mehrotra, Co-founder; Subhash Gupta, Co-founder. IDeaS Inc. offers an innovative technology and support solution, branded e-yield, to the world's leading hotels and resorts. 120 employees. SIC 7372.

Illbruck Inc. 3800 Washington Ave. N., Minneapolis, MN 55412. Tel: 612/521-3555; Fax: 612/521-5639; Web site: http://www.illbruck.com. Robert J. Huebsch, Pres. Illbruck is a manufacturer and supplier of plastic foam products. Manufacturing plants: Detroit; Rochester, N.Y. 280 employees (150 in Minnesota). Founded in 1974. SIC 3086.

Imaginet LLC 1300 Nicollet Ave., Suite 500, Minneapolis, MN 55403. Tel: 651/704-6300; Web site: http://www.imaginet.com. Scott Litman, Pres. and CEO; Dan Mallin, COO; John Doyle, Gen. Mgr. Annual revenue $14.5 million. Imaginet is a Web design firm specializing in convergence for e-business, e-commerce, content, and relationship management. Clients include Dain Rauscher, DirectAg.com, Goodyear, The St. Paul Cos., and Select Comfort. The company was bought back from Imation Corp. by its management team, in partnership with Gage Marketing Group, in March 1999. 110 employees. Founded in 1991. In May 2000 the company secured a $2.5 million credit line from Century Bank to fuel growth, expand infrastructure, and increase capacity. In August the company was named one of the Great Places to Work among small to medium-size employers by CityBusiness newspaper. In September the company said that it was planning to open offices in several central U.S. cities beginning in 2001 and could double staff over the next year. SIC 7379.

Imperial Custom Molding Inc. 20600 County Rd. 81, Rogers, MN 55374. Tel: 763/428-8310; Fax: 763/428-8359; Web site: http://www.icmplastics. William H. Hassell, Pres.; Steve Jenkins, VP-New Bus. Devel.; Robert King, CFO. Annual revenue $28.5 million. Imperial Custom Molding is a contract manufacturer of subassemblies and full assemblies using plastic injection molding, thermoset compression molding, blowmolding, and tooling. Major Minnesota clients include 3M Co., Maplewood, and Hoffman Engineering, Anoka. 385 employees (all in Minnesota). Founded in 1975. In January 2000 the company was planning a $1 million expansion of its thermoset molding business—to meet demand from a new customer and expand business with an existing one. The addition of eight molding presses could boost annual revenue by $18 million. SIC 3089.

Imperial Developers Inc. 21980 Kenrick Ave., Suite 100, Lakeville, MN 55044. Tel: 952/469-6004; Fax: 952/469-6419. Allen Schefers, Pres. Imperial Developers is a firm specializing in foundation and excavation contracting; airport, highway, sewer, and water construction; and demolition, grading, and land clearing. 50 employees (all in Minnesota). Founded in 1977. SIC 1611, 1623, 1794, 1795.

Import Specialties Inc. dba Heartland America 8085 Century Blvd., Chaska, MN 55318. Tel: 952/943-9080; Fax: 952/943-9081. Bruce Bekke, CEO; Mark Platt, Pres. and COO; Thomas Bulver, VP-Op. Import Specialties does business as Heartland America, a mail-order marketer of electronics, housewares, phones, furniture, and lighting. 95 employees (all in Minnesota). Founded in 1986. SIC 5961.

Impressions Inc. 1050 Westgate Dr., St. Paul, MN 55114. Tel: 651/646-1050; Fax: 651/646-7228; Web site: http://www.i-i.com. Mark G. Jorgensen, Chm.; Mark A. Jorgensen, Pres.; Evelyn Jorgensen, EVP; Steve Holupchinski, CFO; Mike Jorgensen, Treas.; Mitch Jorgensen, VP; David Bade, VP; Tim Hewitt, Sls. Mgr. Impressions provides integrated print communications services from electronic imaging and desktop publishing to multicolor sheetfed printing, binding, specialty finishing, and distribution. The Consumer Packaging Division serves the graphic and structural design, manufacturing, and inventory control needs of the company's packaging customers. 295 employees (45 part-time). Founded in 1967. SIC 2759.

Independent Delivery Service 440 Minnehaha Ave. W., St. Paul, MN 55103. Tel: 651/487-1050; Fax: 651/487-1807; Web site: http://www.independentdel.com. Michael Depe, CEO. Independent Delivery Service does alternative delivery of advertising materials, newspapers, directories, and product samples. 70 employees (all in Minnesota; 20 part-time). Founded in 1973. SIC 7331.

Independent Machine Service of Minnesota Inc. 2020 E. Greenwood St., P.O. Box 26, Thief River Falls, MN 56701. Tel: 800/522-3531; Fax: 800/441-3509; Web site: http://www.imslabels.com. Darrell Magner, Pres.; Kathy Magner, Office Mgr.; John Rogers, Sls./Mktg. Mgr.; Todd Bottem, Prod. Mgr.; Julie Borchardt, Pre-press Mgr. Independent Machine Service of Minnesota manufactures price-marking and barcode labels and tags. 80 employees. Founded in 1984. SIC 2759, 3577.

Indianhead Truck Line Inc. 1947 W. County Rd. C, Roseville, MN 55113. Tel: 651/633-2661; Fax: 651/633-1349. Lester A. Wilsey III, Pres.; Roger D. Wilsey Sr., CFO; Robin A. Wilsey, VP. Indianhead Truck Line is a motor truck common carrier of bulk commodities. 90 employees. Founded in 1931. SIC 4213.

Industrial Custom Products 2801 37th Ave. N.E., St. Anthony, MN 55421. Tel: 763/781-2255; Fax: 763/781-1144; Web site: http://www.industrialcustom.com. Herb Houndt, Pres. Industrial Custom

Products forms heavy gauge plastics for OEM and material handling applications. It specializes in custom components. It also offers die-cutting and fabricating for a broad range of nonmetallic materials. 130 employees (80 in Minnesota; 8 part-time). Founded in 1956. SIC 2675, 3053, 3069.

Industrial Hardfacing Inc. 18489 Twin Lake Rd., Elk River, MN 55330. Tel: 763/441-2733; Fax: 763/441-4050. Don E. Millslagle Jr., Pres.; Ken Warneke, CFO. Annual revenue $6.1 million. Industrial Hardfacing has one plant that does tool grinding and repair. Two other plants are involved in the manufacturing and remanufacturing of extraction equipment and wear parts for the vegetable oil, rendering, pet food, and cereal industries. 98 employees (27 in Minnesota; 2 part-time). Founded in 1964. SIC 3556, 3599.

Industrial Louvers Inc. 511 S. Seventh St., Delano, MN 55328. Tel: 763/972-2981; Fax: 763/972-2911; Web site: http://www.industriallouvers.com. Jo Reinhardt, Pres. and COO. Industrial Louvers Inc. manufactures architectural metal products for the nonresidential construction market. 70 employees. Founded in 1971. SIC 3446.

Industrial Molded Rubber Products Inc. 15600 Medina Rd., Suite 100, Plymouth, MN 55447. Tel: 763/559-9500; Fax: 763/559-1894. For 30 years, Industrial Molded Rubber Products, Inc. has provided custom-molded rubber components and rubber-covered rollers used in a variety of industrial and commercial applications. Molded products are fabricated using injection, transfer, compression and rubber-to-metal bond molding techniques. The company fabricates new rollers and recovers existing rollers in sizes up to 36 inches in diameter and 240 inches in length. Expertise in material formulation and tool engineering along with a broad range of molding and roll building processes combine to offer customers a full range of services to cost-effectively satisfy their elastomer needs. Founded in 1970.

Inland Printing Company 20009 West Ave. S., La Crosse, WI 54601. Tel: 608/788-5800; Fax: 608/787-5870. Jack Glendenning, Chm. and CEO; Mark Glendenning, Pres. and COO; Greg Prairie, VP and CFO; John Gates, VP-Op.; Dan Pretasky, VP-Sls. Annual revenue $40.1 million. Inland Printing Co. is engaged in commercial printing and label printing. 220 employees. SIC 2752.

Innsbruck Investments Inc. 1605 County Rd. 101, Plymouth, MN 55447. Tel: 763/473-1387; Fax: 763/473-3424. Steve Erickson, Pres.; Greg Erickson, VP; Mike Erickson, Sec. and Treas. Innsbruck Investments, dba Erickson's NewMarket, is a franchised food store of Supervalu. Innsbruck Investments also owns the Cub Store in Plymouth; and Erickson's NewMarket in New Brighton, Minn. 490 employees (all in Minnesota; 365 part-time). Founded in 1969. SIC 5411.

Inspec Inc. 5801 Duluth St., Golden Valley, MN 55422. Tel: 763/546-3434; Fax: 763/546-8669. Richard W. Phillips, Pres.; Robert W. Singewald, VP. Inspec Inc. is an engineering and architectural firm specializing in the design and testing of roofs, pavements, other exterior systems. 67 employees. Founded in 1973. In June 2000 the company received the 1999-2000 Firm of the Year Award from the Consulting Engineers Council of Minnesota. SIC 8712.

The Instant Web Companies 7951 Powers Blvd., Chanhassen, MN 55317. Tel: 952/474-0961; Fax: 952/474-6467. Frank Beddor Jr., Chm.; James Andersen, Pres. and CEO; Pete Karle, EVP and CFO; Don Brady, EVP-Op.; James M. Cartwright, EVP-Sls.; Beverly Lohs, VP-Hum. Res. Instant Web is a campus of graphic arts companies providing total package services to large direct-mail marketers. Under private, common ownership, Instant Web, United Mailing and Victory Envelope work as one company to provide computer forms, letters, brochures, plastic cards, order forms, envelopes, mail file preparation, laser and impact personalization, embossing and card match/affixing, inserting, and mailing. 1,000 employees (all in Minnesota). Founded in 1969. SIC 2657, 2677, 2759.

Institute for Environmental Assessment 9201 W. Northland Circle, Brooklyn Park, MN 55445. Tel: 763/535-7721; Fax: 763/535-9177. Bruce Bomier, Pres.; Joan Nephew, CEO; Joe Schwartzbauer, COO; Dale Dufault, CFO. Institute for Environmental Assessment is an environmental services company that offers asbestos control/air monitoring and project design, Phase I environmental assessments, indoor air quality investigations, underground storage tank remediation, training, and environmental mangement services. 65 employees (56 in Minnesota; 5 part-time). Founded in 1983. SIC 8711.

Integra Telecom of Minnesota Inc. 7760 France Ave. S., Suite 1200, Edina, MN 55435. Tel: 952/746-7051. Carol Wirsbinski, Local; Dudley Slater, Long-distance. Integra Telecom of Minnesota is a local and long-distance carrier that provides facilities-based local telephone service, switched toll-free and 1-plus dedicated toll-free, DSL and dial-up Internet service, and T-1. Area served: full metro, Scott and Rice counties, St. Cloud, Fergus Falls, and Brainerd. 207 employees. Founded in 1997. Acquired Info Tel Communications, Baxter, Minn. SIC 4813.

Integrated Health Systems-Dairyland 625 S. Lakeshore Dr., Glenwood, MN 56334. Tel: 320/634-5331; Fax: 320/634-5316; Web site: http://www.dairyland-hosp.com. Stephen R. Klick, Pres.; Margaret Klick, Sec. and Treas.; Robert Moore, CFO; Alan Grundei, COO. Annual revenue $25 million. Integrated Health Systems-Dairyland (IHS-D), formerly Dairyland Computer & Consulting Co., sells computer systems and support services to hospitals nationwide. 160 employees (87 in Minnesota). Founded in 1980. SIC 5045, 7373.

Intek Plastics Inc. 800 E. 10th St., Hastings, MN 55033. Tel: 651/437-7700; Fax: 651/437-3805; Web site: http://www.intekplastics.com. Franz R. Altpeter, Pres. and CEO; Ken Kimmes, VP-Bus. Devel.; Craig Wallin, CFO; Dale Harbath, VP-Op. Annual revenue $46 million. Intek Plastics Inc. (formerly Profile Extrusions Co.) develops and manufactures thermoplastic weatherstrips and sealing systems for window and door manufacturers. The company also manufactures extruded thermoplastic composite components for OEM manufacturers in various industries. Formerly Profile Extrusions Co., Intek Weatherseal Products. In April 2000 Intek opened a 51,000-square-foot, 50-employee manufacturing plant in Eau Claire, Wis. 380 employees (340 in Minnesota). Founded in 1961. SIC 3089.

Inter City Oil Company Inc. 1921 South St., Duluth, MN 55812. Tel: 218/728-3641; Fax: 218/728-5140. Judy L. Weber, Pres. and CEO; D.K. Flesher, CFO, Sec., and Treas. Inter City Oil is an independent petroleum marketer, distributing products and operating convenience stores in four states and more than 70 cities. 400 employees. Founded in 1953. SIC 5172.

Interelate 9855 W. 79th St., Eden Prairie, MN 55344. Tel: 952/908-8000; Fax: 952/908-8001; Web site: http://www.interelate.com. Wade Myers, CEO; Mike Gaard, SVP; Jeff McCandless, CFO. Interelate is a customer intelligence ASP (application service provider) that rapidly delivers to decision-makers a unified view of relevant customer information and analysis. This innovative solution empowers clients to grow sales and profits through data mining, campaign management, personalization, and real-time recommendation. Interelate combines deep expertise in data analysis, CRM (customer relationship management), database marketing, and industry verticals with leading analytics software, proven methodologies, and third-party data through a secure, Web-delivered service. 230 employees. SIC 7372.

International Research & Evaluation 21098 IRE Control Center, Eagan, MN 55121. Tel: 952/888-9635; Fax: 952/888-9124; Web site: http://www.ire-ittn.com. Randall L. Voight, Chm., Pres., and CEO; Valentina Voight, CFO; George Franklin Jr., VP-Strategic Op.; Julie Swanson, Sec.; Sharon King, Treas.; James Kovin, Sls. Mgr.; Al Munday, Advertising Dir.; Karen Jorgenson, Hum. Res.; Carl Rein, Prod. Mgr.; Richard E. Danford, Pub. Rel. Dir.; Rick Kenrick, Communications Dir. Annual revenue $118.7 million. International Research & Evaluation is engaged in a variety of business and automation services through four operating divisions. Research Publications Division does electronic, optical disk, and micrographic publishing; Design Concepts Division offers office automation, database development, records management, and seminar services; ITTD Network facilitates technology transfer and remote computing services; and Think Tank Division undertakes market research and feasibility studies. 133 employees (67 in Minnesota; 31 part-time). Founded in 1972. SIC 2522, 5021, 7311, 7331, 7372, 7373, 8231.

PVT

Interplastic Corporation 1225 Willow Lake Blvd., Vadnais Heights, MN 55110. Tel: 651/481-6860; Fax: 651/481-9834. James D. Wallenfelsz, Chm. and Pres.; Robert A. DeRoma, SVP; Mark J. Brost, VP-Fin./Admin.; Ivan M. Levy, VP, Sec., and Chief Legal Officer. Annual revenue $275 million. Interplastic has four operating divisions: The Commercial Resins Division and Silmar Resins Division manufacture and sell polyester resins to the composite industry. Commercial Resins also manufactures and sells gel coats. North American Composites distributes resins and nonresin products to the reinforced fiberglass industry. The Molding Products Division makes and sells sheet molding compound. 465 employees. Founded in 1959. SIC 2821, 3089, 5162. No. 49 CRM Private 100.

Interstate Companies 2601 E. 80th St., Bloomington, MN 55420. Tel: 952/854-5511; Fax: 952/854-2999. G. Galarneau Jr., Chm. and CEO; J. Caswell, Pres. and Gen. Mgr.; Larry Schwartz, VP-Fin. and Sec./Treas. Annual revenue $155 million. Interstate Cos. Inc. (ICI) provides financial and administrative assistance to each of its four operating divisions, Interstate Detroit Diesel (IDD), Interstate Power Product & Services (IPPS), Interstate Bearing Technologies (IBT), and Interstate Transport Refrigeration (ITR) and entities under common control of its parent. 635 employees. Founded in 1957. SIC 5084. No. 79 CRM Private 100.

Interstate Meat Service Inc. 2309 Myers Rd., Albert Lea, MN 56007. Tel: 507/377-2228; Fax: 507/377-3905; Web site: http://www.interstatemeats.com. Donald Falk, Pres.; R.A. Andersen, Fin. Mgr.; Mark Falk, Op. Mgr.; Steve Falk, Sls. Mgr.; Tom Falk, Office Mgr. Annual revenue $50 million. Interstate Meat Service is a wholesale meat distributor serving the five-state area. Also offers LTC freight and fresh and frozen storage. 60 employees (35 part-time). Founded in 1978. SIC 5147.

Intrepid Companies Inc. 6750 France Ave. S, Suite 275, Edina, MN 55435. Tel: 952/920-1958; Fax: 952/928-9795. Todd J. Garamella, Pres.; Greg Vonarx, CFO. Intrepid provides home health care and medical supplemental staffing services. 7,800 employees (950 in Minnesota). Founded in 1994. SIC 7361.

Investment Advisers Inc. 3600 U.S. Bank Place, P.O. Box 357, Minneapolis, MN 55440. Tel: 612/376-2700; Fax: 612/376-2616; Web site: http://www.iaifunds.com. Keith Wirtz, Pres. and Chief Investment Ofcr.; Lindsay Johnston, COO; John Adam Alexander, EVP and Dir.-Bus. Devel. Investment Advisers Inc. (IAI) performs investment management and related services for various pension funds, institutions, and individuals. 75 employees. Founded in 1947. In December 1999 the company lost 60 percent of its institutional bond business when the State of Minnesota pulled its $658 million account. The State Board of Investment cited the weak performance of an IAI-managed bond account and IAI's dwindling asset base. By the end of 1999 IAI had reduced the portion of high-risk venture capital investments to 6.2 percent or less of each of its funds. In February 2000 IAI closed its fixed-income investment business to focus on domestic and international equities. In June Federated Investors Inc. (NYSE: FII), Pittsburgh, reached a definitive agreement to purchase IAI's mutual fund assets: 11 funds totaling $400 million in assets, 92 percent of which were equity assets. IAI continued to manage money for institutional clients, including pension and profit sharing funds, multi-employer funds, foundations, and endowments. IAI also reached a preliminary agreement for a management buyout from its British owners by year's end. SIC 6722.

Investment Rarities Inc. 7850 Metro Pkwy., Bloomington, MN 55425. Tel: 952/853-0700; Fax: 952/851-8732; Web site: http://www.investmentrarities.com. James R. Cook, Pres.; Diane Cook, VP. Investment Rarities deals in precious metals and rare coins—specializing in gold. The company has sold and delivered over $2.3 billion of gold, silver, and platinum since its inception. 100 employees. Founded in 1973. SIC 6221.

Isle Vista Casino P.O. Box 1167, Highway 13 N., Bayfield, WI 54814. Tel: 715/779-3712. Gary Rifue, Gen. Mgr. Isle Vista offers restaurants, entertainment, a campground, marina, bingo, music festivals, and cultural events. 112 employees (34 part-time). Founded in 1992. SIC 7999.

Iten Chevrolet 670 Brooklyn Blvd., Brooklyn Center, MN 55429. Tel: 763/561-9220; Fax: 763/561-2188. Joseph Iten, Owner and Pres.; Peter Iten, Sec. and Treas.; Martin J. Iten, VP. Annual revenue $96.8 million. Iten Chevrolet deals in automobiles, trucks, recreational vehicles, and commercial trucks—including sales, service, and parts. 148 employees (all in Minnesota; 4 part-time). Founded in 1926. SIC 5511.

J&B Wholesale Distributing Inc. 13200 43rd St. N.E., St. Michael, MN 55376. Tel: 763/497-3913; Fax: 763/547-6208. Robert Hageman, Chm. and Pres. J&B Wholesale Distributing is a wholesale processor, supplier, and distributor of meat, poultry, seafood, and frozen food products. 350 employees. Founded in 1979. SIC 2011, 2015, 2038, 2092.

Jackpot Junction Casino Hotel P.O. Box 420, 39375 County Highway 24, Morton, MN 56270. Tel: 507/644-3000; Fax: 507/644-2529; Web site: http://www.jackpotjunction.com. Brian Pendleton, Gen. Mgr.; Travis O'Neil, Asst. Gen. Mgr. Jackpot Junction Casino Hotel, an enterprise of the Lower Sioux Indian Community, offers 300,000 square feet of live casino action. Jackpot has 1,650 video slots, 36 blackjack tables, bingo, pulltabs, three restaurants, four full-service bars, a 40-unit RV park, live entertainment every weekend, headline acts, and an outdoor entertainment facility. Hotel accommodations include 276 deluxe rooms at the Lower Sioux Lodge and 120 rooms at the Dakota Inn. There is also an 18-hole championship golf course and New Horizon Kids Quest hourly childcare. 950 employees (all in Minnesota). SIC 7011, 7993, 7999.

Jacobson LLC 2765 Niagara Ln., Plymouth, MN 55447. Tel: 763/544-8781; Fax: 763/557-5557; Web site: http://www.jacobsonmn.com. Ralph Burgess, Chm.; Frank J. Palcher, Pres. and COO; Sue Jackson, CFO. Annual revenue $9 million. Jacobson manufactures size-reduction machinery and process systems. 60 employees (all in Minnesota). Founded in 1910. SIC 3559.

The Jamar Company Inc. 4701 Mike Colalillo Dr., Duluth, MN 55807. Tel: 218/628-1027; Fax: 218/628-1174. Joseph R. Link, Pres. The Jamar Co. is a general contractor specializing in plumbing, heating, air conditioning, ventilation, sheet metal, and ductwork. It also does boiler maintenance and roofing. Jamar serves businesses and individuals in the northern parts of Minnesota, Wisconsin, and Michigan. Owned since 1985 by the APi Group, Roseville, Minn. 100 employees (all in Minnesota). Founded in 1913. SIC 1711, 1761.

Japs-Olson Company 7500 Excelsior Blvd., St. Louis Park, MN 55426. Tel: 952/932-9393; Fax: 952/912-1900. Robert E. Murphy, Chm. and CEO; Michael R. Murphy, COO; Michael Beddor, Pres.; Ed O'Connor, CFO. Annual revenue $132 million. Japs-Olson, a commercial printer, operates a computer service bureau and a mailing division. The company offers computerized laser addressing and flexographic printing. 750 employees. Founded in 1907. SIC 2752, 2759. No. 93 CRM Private 100.

Jasc Software Inc. P.O. Box 44997, Eden Prairie, MN 55344. Tel: 952/930-9800; Web site: http://www.jasc.com. Kris Tufto, CEO; Robert Voit, Pres. and COO; David Hawkins, CFO; Craig Letourneau, VP-Sls./Mktg.; Jon Ort, CTO; John Krenz, Dir.-Prod. Devel. Annual revenue $31 million. Jasc Software provides Web designers and advanced consumers with Windows-based digital imaging and management solutions that are powerful, easy-to-use, and affordable. 119 employees (118 in Minnesota; 2 part-time). Founded in 1991. In January 2000 the company released Jasc Media Center Plus, a new tool that gives Web developers, digital image enthusiasts, and home hobbyists the power to organize, publish, and share multimedia files. In June Paint Shop Pro Version 6 was honored by PC World with a 2000 World Class Award for Best Image Editing Software—the second year it had received this award. In August the company released Jasc Quick View Plus 6.0, the new version of the industry-leading file viewer that opens almost any file and e-mail attachment. In September Jasc released Jasc Paint Shop Pro 7.0, the complete graphics and photo editor for digital photographers, home and business users, and Web designers. In October Jasc's flagship digital imaging program, Jasc Paint Shop Pro, was selected by ConsumerREVIEW.com as the recipient of a 2000 CHOICE Award. For the third year in a row, Jasc Software was named one of the fastest-growing companies in the country by Inc. magazine. SIC 7371. No. 13 Minnesota Technology Fast 50.

Javelin Solutions Inc. 100 N. Sixth St., Minneapolis, MN 55403. Tel: 612/752-1560. Dale Klein, CEO; Chad Johnson, VP-Bus. Devel. Annual revenue $6.6 million. Javelin Solutions is a single-source provider of Internet strategy, creative identity, technology, and managed services. 100 employees. Founded in 1996. As 2000 drew to a close, Javelin was operating at an annual run rate of $18 million. Planning to extend its operations to other states, the company was in talks with venture capital firms to obtain an outside investment, likely in the range of $5 million. SIC 7379. No. 11 CityBusiness Fastest-growing Private Companies.

Jefferson Partners L.P. 2100 E. 26th St., Minneapolis, MN 55404. Tel: 612/332-8745; Fax: 612/332-5532. Charles A. Zelle, Pres. and CEO; Jeffery D. Kruger, CFO, Sec., and Treas. Annual revenue $17.3 million. Jefferson Partners L.P. is an inter-city bus transporter. It also offers charters, domestic and international tours, package express, bus-maintenance services, and daily scheduled bus service from Minnesota to Texas. 221 employees (94 in Minnesota; 96 part-time). Founded in 1919. SIC 4131.

Norman G. Jensen Inc. 3050 Metro Dr., Suite 300, Bloomington, MN 55425. Tel: 952/854-7363; Fax: 952/854-8302; Web site: http://www.ngjensen.com. Dennis Jensen, VP. Annual revenue $21 million. Norman G. Jensen Inc. is a U.S. customs broker and international freight forwarder, with locations in California, Idaho, Michigan, Montana, North Dakota, New York, Utah, Washington, Maine, and Vermont. Other locations in Minnesota: Ranier and Grand Portage. 400 employees (65 in Minnesota). Founded in 1937. SIC 4226.

Jerry's Enterprises Inc. 5101 Vernon Ave., Edina, MN 55436. Tel: 952/922-8335; Fax: 952/929-9281. Gerald A. Paulsen, CEO; Robert N. Shadduck, Pres.; George St. Germain, VP-Op.; Kent D. Dixon, VP-Fin.; David Gerdes, VP-Hum. Res. Annual revenue $578 million. Jerry's Enterprises consists of 14 retail supermarkets in the Minneapolis/St. Paul area and four in Fla.; plus two Jerry's True Valu Hardware, Lucile's Fashions, Animal Crackers, Jerry's Complete Printing, Minnesota Meat Masters, and Sweet William's Flowers. 3,350 employees. Founded in 1947. SIC 5411. No. 20 CRM Private 100. No. 66 CRM Employer 100.

Johanneson's Inc. P.O. Box 608, Bemidji, MN 56601. Tel: 218/751-9644; Fax: 218/751-8442. Keith Johanneson, Pres.; Richard Johanneson, Sec. and Treas. Johanneson's owns and operates five Food 4 Less and Marketplace Foods grocery stores in northern Minnesota and North Dakota. 600 employees. Founded in 1955. SIC 5411.

The John Roberts Company 9687 E. River Rd., Coon Rapids, MN 55433. Tel: 763/755-5500; Fax: 763/755-0394. Robert A. Keene, Chm.; Michael R. Keene, CEO; Bob Winping, VP; Michael V. Thews, VP; William Culbert, VP; John Foster, VP. Annual revenue $66.4 million. The John Roberts Co. is a commercial printer involved in advertising and packaging. The company specializes in four-, five-, and six-color process printing. 400 employees (all in Minnesota). Founded in 1951. SIC 2759.

Al Johnson Construction Company 2626 E. 82nd St., Suite 300, Bloomington, MN 55425. Tel: 952/854-5097; Fax: 952/854-5791. Tom R. Gessner, Chm. and CEO; R.T. Taylor, VP and CFO; A.R. Ruud, VP-Eqt.; W.F. Cealfoss, VP; P.T. Kocourek, Treas. and Asst. Sec.; K.J. Gessner, VP and Sec. Al Johnson Construction is a general contractor specializing in heavy construction, including locks, dams, powerhouses, major bridges, and marine and underground construction. Subsidiaries include Red Devil Equipment Co., Brooklyn Park, Minn., and Jesco Co., Bloomington, Minn. 250 employees (80 in Minnesota). Founded in 1928. SIC 1622, 1629.

Johnson Bros. Corporation 23577 Minnesota Highway 22, Litchfield, MN 55355. Tel: 320/693-2871; Fax: 320/693-4112. Walter D. Johnson, Pres.; Ken O. Hafner, SVP; Jack V. McCreery, SVP; Philip R. Johnson, EVP; Bradley A. Eilerston, VP; James R. Florey, VP; Kevin A. Johnson, VP; Steven Jackson, VP; Merlyn D. Lokken, VP; Joseph H. Michels, VP; Paul Scharmer, VP; Michael Swanson, VP; Kathy A. Aamot, Sec.; Barry J. Konsor, Treas. Johnson Bros. is a heavy-construction contractor and a civil design firm specializing in power plants, materials-handling facilities, hydro facilities, underground utilities, sitework, bridges, highways, and environmental and waste-management services. 800 employees. Founded in 1929. SIC 1622, 1629, 8711.

Johnson Brothers Wholesale Liquor 2341 University Ave. W., St. Paul, MN 55114. Tel: 651/649-5800; Fax: 651/649-5894. Lynn Johnson, CEO. Annual revenue $550 million (estimated by Forbes). Johnson Brothers is a liquor wholesaler. 1,050 employees. Founded in 1953. SIC 5182. No. 19 CRM Private 100.

Johnson (J.R.) Supply Inc. 2582 Long Lake Rd., Roseville, MN 55113. Tel: 651/636-1330; Fax: 651/636-5708. J.R. Johnson, Owner and CEO; Brad Johnson, Pres. J.R. Johnson Supply is a wholesale horticultural supply distributer and an injection plastic molding company specializing in horticultural containers. Besides its main plant in Roseville, the company has a branch facility in Sun City, Fla. The greenhouse growing operations and the wholesale florist operation were spun off in January 1997 to form Johnson Wholesale Florist Inc. 70 employees (all in Minnesota). Founded in 1916. SIC 3089, 5193.

Johnson Litho Graphics of Eau Claire Ltd. 2219 Galloway St., Eau Claire, WI 54703. Tel: 715/832-3211; Fax: 715/832-5120. Everett Jon Papke, Pres. Johnson Litho Graphics operates as a commercial printer in the lithography field. 70 employees. Founded in 1978. SIC 2759.

Johnson Printing & Packaging Corporation 40 77th Ave. N.E., Fridley, MN 55432. Tel: 763/574-1700; Fax: 763/574-0191. Stuart Weitzman, Co-owner; Charles Silverman, Co-owner. Johnson Printing & Packaging does commercial printing and manufactures folding cartons. 95 employees. Founded in 1912. SIC 2759.

R.M. Johnson Company 890 Norway Dr., P.O. Box J, Annandale, MN 55302. Tel: 320/274-3594; Fax: 320/274-3859; Web site: http://www.primenet.com/~dccfunds/rmj.html. Robert Johnson, Pres. and CEO; Ralph Johnson, Sls. Mgr. R.M. Johnson Co. manufactures the E-Z Car Crusher. Other location: Kimball, Minn. 75 employees (81 in Minnesota; 6 part-time). Founded in 1972. SIC 3542.

Johnstech International Corporation 1210 New Brighton Blvd., Minneapolis, MN 55413. Tel: 612/378-2020; Fax: 612/378-2030; Web site: http://www.johnstech.com. David A. Johnson, Pres.; Julie Simonett, CFO; Kent Ferris, Engrg. Dir.; Phil Musgrove`, Dir.-Sls.; Jeff Rynberk, Dir.-Op. Johnstech International designs, manufactures, and distributes high-performance test contractor and test solutions for the semiconductor industry. 100 employees (90 in Minnesota). Founded in 1991. In August 2000, based on its revenue growth from 1995 to 1999, the company was named to Deloitte & Touche's Minnesota Technology Fast 50. SIC 3825. No. 50 Minnesota Technology Fast 50.

J.R. Jones Fixture Company 3216 Winnetka Ave. N., Crystal, MN 55427. Tel: 763/544-4239; Fax: 763/544-3106. Douglas Jones, Pres.; Robert Jones, VP. J.R. Jones Fixture manufactures custom woodwork fixtures used in store displays. 60 employees (all in Minnesota). Founded in 1942. SIC 2431.

John T. Jones Construction Company 2213 Seventh Ave. N., Fargo, ND 58102. Tel: 701/232-3358; Fax: 701/232-7040. John B. Jones, Pres.; Jeffrey T. Jones, CEO, Sec., and Treas.. Jones Construction is a general contractor specializing in water and wastewater treatment plants. 100 employees. Founded in 1952. SIC 1541.

Jones Metal Products Inc. 3201 Third Ave., Mankato, MN 56001. Tel: 507/625-4436; Fax: 507/625-2994. Thomas Richards, Chm.; David L. Ewert, Pres. and COO; Lynn Paul Schwarz, VP and Treas.; Marcia Richards, Sec. Annual revenue $11.8 million. Jones Metal Products is a metal fabrication job shop. 127 employees. Founded in 1942. SIC 3499.

Jostens Inc. 5501 Norman Center Dr., Bloomington, MN 55437. Tel: 952/830-3300; Fax: 952/897-4116; Web site: http://www.jostens.com. Robert C. Buhrmaster, Chm., Pres., and CEO; Carl H. Blowers, SVP-Manufacturing; William N. Priesmeyer, SVP and CFO; Andrew Black, VP and CIO; Mike Bailey, VP, Gen. Mgr.-Jostens School Solutions; William J. George, VP, General Counsel, Secretary; Steven Tighs, VP-Hum. Res.; Brian K. Beutner, Sec.; Greg S. Lea, VP and Gen. Mgr.-Colleges/Universities; Lee McGrath, VP and Treas.; Lynda Nordeen, Dir.-Corp. Communications. Annual revenue $782.4 million (earnings $43.2 million; includes pretax special charge of $20.2 million). Jostens is a leading provider of products and services that recognize achievement and affiliation, primarily for the youth, education, sports-award, and corporate markets. Jostens' operations are classified into two business segments: school-based recognition products and services (School Products), and corporate recognition and performance incentive products and services (Recognition). The School Products segment manufactures and sells yearbooks, class rings, graduation products, and student photography packages, as well as customized products for alumni. The Recognition segment manufactures and sells customized sales, service, and performance awards for companies of all sizes. 6,700 employees. Founded in 1906. The company made two important year-end 1999 announcements. First, it planned to align its organization to spur growth in its school-based business segment, following a period of internally focused infrastructure improvement. A nonrecurring charge of $20 million pretaxwas to include costs to eliminate 100 full-time positions, from all levels of employment, primarily in corporate staff functions. Second, Jostens agreed to be merged into a company controlled by Investcorp (a global investment group) and certain other international co-investors in a transaction valued at $950 million, including the assumption of $100 million in debt. Jostens shareholders were to receive $25.25 per share in cash. Following the merger, Jostens would be 94 percent owned by: Investcorp (a group of Middle East investors that specializes in buying companies that it thinks are undervalued) and other international co-investors; DB Capital Partners, an affiliate of Deutsche Bank; and Jostens senior management. In response, shares rose $5.31 to $24.25. In spite of a fairness opinion issued by outside investment bank C.S. First Boston, two shareholder lawsuits were filed claiming that the price agreed on was unfair.

In January 2000 Jostens invested $2.5 million to obtain a minority equity position in privately held Planet Alumni Inc., which created and owns planetalumni.com, a fast-growing online community that helps former classmates and alumni stay in touch. In February Jostens Recognition Division received the Quasar Award for Customer Service from Federal Express Corp.'s FedEx Employee Benefits Department. In April the company announced plans to sell $240 million of subordinated debt to help finance the buyout. It was also securing a $635 million bank loan. Jostens was chosen by the St. Louis Rams to create and manufacture the team's Super Bowl XXXIV championship rings. Jostens would also produce the conference championship rings for the 1999 AFC Champion Tennessee Titans. Meanwhile, the Jostens-crafted 1999 National League Baseball Championship rings were presented to the Atlanta Braves. On May 9, shareholders approved the company's pending merger. A day later, Investcorp, a global investment group, and certain other co-investors completed their acquisition of Jostens through a merger of Jostens witha company controlled by Investcorp. The transaction was valued at $920 million, including the assumption of $70 million in debt. July 1: Jostens reported six-month net income of $52.7 million, excluding transaction costs of $45.7 million associated with the Investcorp merger, an increase of 11.9 percent over the the year-earlier period. Six-month sales were $476.4 million, compared with $469.5 million in the same period last year. In July an appeals panel affirmed that Jostens did not have to pay a $25.2 million 1998 jury award to rival Taylor Publishing Co. because there wasn't enough evidence to prove it had engaged in monopolistic practices in the yearbook market. SIC 2732, 2752, 3911, 7384. No. 11 CRM Private 100.

Joyner's Die Casting & Plating Co. Inc. 7801 Xylon Ave. N., Brooklyn Park, MN 55445. Tel: 763/425-2104; Fax: 763/425-1640; Web site: http://www.thomasregister.com/joyners. Orlyn D. Joyner, Pres.; Dwight Joyner, VP. Joyner's operates a zinc die casting and metal finishing/plating facility as well as manufacturing and marketing elevator braille signage. 95 employees. Founded in 1944. SIC 3364, 3471.

Juno Inc. 14755 27th Ave. N., Suite C-1, Plymouth, MN 55447. Tel: 763/553-1312; Fax: 763/553-1360. Archie Olson, Pres. Annual revenue $33.4 million. Juno Inc., formerly Juno Tool and Plastic Corp., supplies precision-molded plastic parts and components to the medical health care industry and to the consumer and commercial electronics markets. 250 employees (190 in Minnesota). Founded in 1954. SIC 3089.

Juntunen Media Group 708 N First St., Minneapolis, MN 55401. Tel: 612/341-3348; Fax: 612/341-0242; Web site: http://www.juntunen.com. William Juntunen, CEO; Patti Albrecht, CFO, Pres.-Juntunen Mobile Television; Brad Stokes, VP and Gen. Mgr.-Post Production; Tan Mayhall, Dir.-Internet Strategies. Juntunen Media Group is a communications company that specializes in strategy, production, and distribution of high-impact media for corporations, agencies, sports and entertainment companies. Media includes video and live television, webcasting, video streaming, DVD, CD-ROM. The company also provides production support to producers. 54 employees. Founded in 1984. In 1999 Juntunen formed Juntunen Mobile Television to serve major clients with large-scale (53-foot) mobile television control centers. In May 2000 the company sold its division which specialized in interactive applications to a subsidiary of True North Communications Inc. (NYSE: TNO). SIC 8743.

KFYR-TV 1738 N. Fourth St., P.O. Box 1738, Bismarck, ND 58502. Tel: 701/255-5757; Fax: 701/255-8159. Judith Ekberg Johnson, Chm., Pres., and CEO; Edward J. Kautzman, Treas.; Bruce Johnson, Sec. KFYR-TV operates one AM radio station, one FM station, and five television stations in Fargo, Bismarck, Minot, Dickinson, and Williston, N.D. 244 employees (13 in Minnesota; 46 part-time). Founded in 1925. SIC 4832, 4833.

K&G Manufacturing Company P.O. Box 187, Faribault, MN 55021. Tel: 507/334-5501; Fax: 507/334-3627; Web site: http://www.kgmfg.com. Thomas S. Gerbig, Chm. and CEO; Gary J. Noble, Pres.; Eugene W. Tatge, EVP; James Arndt, CFO. K&G Manufacturing specializes in the application of CAD/CAM software to the manufacturing environment, specifically offering services in all phases of the manufacture of precision-machined components for the medical, computer, aircraft, and hydraulic industries. 70 employees (all in Minnesota; 5 part-time). Founded in 1937. SIC 3544, 3599.

KKE Architects 300 First Ave. N., Minneapolis, MN 55401. Tel: 612/339-4200. Ronald Krank, Chm.; Ronald C. Erickson, CEO; Gregory G. Hollenkamp, Pres.; Robert C. Mayeron, Treas.; Thomas E. Gerster, Dir. Annual revenue $22.3 million. KKE is a broad-based firm specializing in architecture, planning, and interior design. Areas of concentration include: commercial development, government, education (K-12), corporate retail, designs for aging, hospitality/entertainment, mixed-use, office interiors, and housing. 175 employees. Founded in 1968. SIC 8712. No. 45 CityBusiness Fastest-growing Private Companies.

KRS Computer and Business School 8332 Highway 7, St. Louis Park, MN 55426. Tel: 952/938-8823. Ken Schnitker, CEO. Annual revenue $7.7 million. KRS Computer and Business School is a provider of post-secondary education. 102 employees. Founded in 1990. SIC 8244. No. 2 CityBusiness Fastest-growing Private Companies.

Kath Fuel Oil Service 3096 Rice St., Roseville, MN 55113. Tel: 651/484-3325; Fax: 651/484-6743. Bruce Kath, Pres.; Steve Dahl, VP; Jeff Larson, Sec. and Treas. Annual revenue $90 million. Kath Fuel Oil Service is a fuel oil and auto parts dealer, and machine shop. It also does heating, air conditioning, and electrical work. It has branded gas programs for Phillips, Ashland, and Conoco gas stations. 300 employees. Founded in 1945. SIC 1711, 1731, 3449, 5983.

Katolight Corporation 3201 Third Ave., Mankato, MN 56001. Tel: 507/625-7973; Fax: 507/625-2968; Web site: http://www.katolight.com. Lyle G. Jacobson, Pres. and CEO; Thomas Ferris, Industrial Sls. Mgr.; Keith Burg, Agricultural Sls. Mgr.; John Griebel, Purch. Mgr.; Bruce Prange, Dir.-Mfg./Materials. Annual revenue $60 million. Katolight manufactures electrical generator sets and controls for standby and continuous power. 155 employees (152 in Minnesota; 4 part-time). Founded in 1952. SIC 3621.

Katun Corporation 10951 Bush Lake Rd., Bloomington, MN 55438. Tel: 952/941-9505; Fax: 952/941-4307. Larry J. Stroup, Pres. and CEO. Katun is the world's leading aftermarket distributor of toners and developers, photoreceptors, and parts—as well as a manufacturer of fuser rollers and other select products for office equipment. More than 60 percent of sales is to international customers. 394 employees (342 in Minnesota; 53 part-time). Founded in 1979. In March 2000 rising sales prompted Katun to increase the size of its operations facility in Aguascalientes, Mexico. The expansion, to be final in the fall, would quadruple warehouse and office space to 60,000 square feet. Katun also has a Mexico City unit. In May Katun partnered with a Hong Kong distribution company to supply its products through local warehouse/showroom facilities in major cities in China. Sharp Corp. filed a suit charging Katun with infringing on two patents for photocopying technology. In June COO Stroup assumed the role of CEO, replacing T. Michael Clarke. The company launched the user-friendly Katun On-Line Catalogue, allowing office equipment and printer dealers worldwide to assemble and submit orders via the Internet. SIC 5044. No. 52 CRM Private 100.

Kaye's Printing P.O. Box 2065, Fargo, ND 58107. Tel: 701/237-4525; Fax: 701/234-9782. Darrell Veavick, Gen. Mgr.; Gary Bendewald, Plant Mgr.; Jay Johnson, Cont. Kaye's Printing does commercial printing on sheetfed presses and on heatset web, and offers lithograph and mailing services. 140 employees. Founded in 1948. SIC 2752.

Kell Container Corporation 421 Palmer St., P.O. Box 28, Chippewa Falls, WI 54729. Tel: 715/723-1801; Fax: 715/723-7744. John D. Kell, CEO; Tom Kell, Pres.; Joe Fesenmaier, Comptroller; Ralph Follendorf, VP-Sls.; Rick Gates, VP-Mfg.; Charles Kell, Treas. and Sec.; Mike Schleismann, VP-Kell Specialty Products. Kell Container manufactures corrugated containers, POP, POS, and high-quality graphics. 200 employees (2 in Minnesota). Founded in 1964. SIC 2653.

Kempf Paper Corporation 3145 Columbia Ave. N.E., Minneapolis, MN 55418. Tel: 612/781-9225; Fax: 612/781-9249. Gus Kempf, Owner and Pres. Kempf Paper Corp. is a wholesale distributor of roll paper for printing companies. 60 employees (all in Minnesota). Founded in 1976. SIC 2621.

Kenny's Candy Company Inc. 609 Pinewood Ln., P.O. Box 269, Perham, MN 56573. Tel: 218/346-2340; Fax: 218/346-2343. Kenneth L. Nelson, Pres.; Denny Sullivan, Gen. Mgr. Kenny's Candy Co. is a licorice manufacturer specializing in private labels. It has two facilities in Perham, as well as a plant in Parkers Prairie, Minn. 290 employees (all in Minnesota; 35 part-time). Founded in 1987. SIC 2064.

Kerker 7701 France Ave. S., Suite 600, Edina, MN 55435. Tel: 952/835-7922; Fax: 952/835-2232; Web site: http://www.kerker.com. Charles Kelly, Pres.; Philip Wendorf, EVP and CFO; Laurin Leih, EVP and Media Dir.; Chris Preston, EVP and Creative Dir.; Christine Fruechte, SVP and Dir.-Client Svc.; Mike Gray, VP, Mktg. Dir.; Diane Norman, VP and Dir.-Bus. Devel.; Liz Warren, VP and Dir.-Prod. Svs.; Gary Young, VP and Dir.-Pub. Rel. Annual revenue $6.1 million. Kerker is a full-service, integrated marketing communications agency that offers advertising, public relations, direct marketing, promotion, interactive, design and account planning to a broad range of local, national and global, consumer and business clients. Clients include: 3M, American Medical Systems, Baldwin, Boomerang Marketing, Buca di Beppo, Definity Health, EcoWater, HighJump Software, Sub-Zero, Thermo King, United Sugars, Wolf Gourmet. Kerker is a member of Worldwide Partners, the world's largest network of independent marketing communications firms. 51 employees (all in Minnesota). Founded in 1950. In 2000 the agency celebrated its 50th anniversary. Kerker won five Midwest Direct Marketing Association ARC Awards, two International Association of Business Communicators Silver Quill Awards, and two Retail Advertising Conference Awards. In September, Kerker landed three new accounts totaling $10 million in collective billings, the largest one-month account gain in agency history. New business partnerships with Barrett Moving and Storage, Boomerang Marketing, Buca di Beppo, Definity Health, HighJump Software, and Wolf Gourmet pushed annualized billings from $36 million to $50 million. In October the firm won nine awards at The Show 2000 in Minneapolis. SIC 7311.

Kewadin Casino 2186 Shunk Rd., Sault Ste. Marie, MI 49783. Tel: 906/632-0530; Fax: 906/635-4959; Web site: http://www.kewadin.com. Bernard Bouchor, Tribal Chm./CEO; Rick McDowell, CFO; Steve Sprecker, Casino Mgr. Kewadin Casino provides entertainment through Vegas-style gaming, performances, hotel accommodations, and restaurants. Its five locations—in Sault Ste. Marie, St. Ignace, Manistique, Christmas, and Hessel, Mich.—are owned and operated by the Sault Tribe of Chippewa Indians. After a $30 million expansion completed in 1997, the Sault Ste. Marie location has 39,009 square feet of gaming space for $100,000 live keno, slots (more than 1,088 machines), blackjack (33 tables), poker, roulette, and craps; nightly entertainment in the new 1,500 seat Dreammaker Theater; and a new 365-room hotel. 1,700 employees (250 part-time). Founded in 1985. SIC 7999.

Key Cadillac Inc. 6825 York Ave. S., Edina, MN 55435. Tel: 952/920-4300; Fax: 952/920-4821. Adam Stanzak, Pres.; Dennis Burg, VP; Michael Stanzak, VP; Pam Thompson, Sec. Key Cadillac is a motor vehicle dealer. 76 employees (all in Minnesota; 2 part-time). Founded in 1973. SIC 5511.

Khoury Inc. 1011 N. Stephenson Ave., P. O. Box 729, Iron Mountain, MI 49801. Tel: 906/774-6333; Fax: 906/774-8211. James Khoury, Chm.; Dan Khoury, CEO; Stephen Kerr, Pres. Khoury manufactures unfinished ready-to-assemble and assembled furniture. Khoury also owns and operates two sawmills. 250 employees. Founded in 1945. SIC 2511.

Kleespie Tank and Petroleum Equipment Inc. 3 Development Dr., P.O. Box 600, Morris, MN 56267. Tel: 320/589-2100; Fax: 320/589-2206. Robert Kleespie, Owner; Jon Boutain, CFO; Tim Esterling, Sls. Mgr. Kleespie Tank and Petroleum Equipment manufactures equipment used in the petroleum industry—for service stations, truck tanks, LP bobtails, LP & anhydrous transports, tank pressure vessels, and anhydrous tanks. Other locations: Newport, Minn.; Portage, Wis.; and Mandan, N.D. 210 employees (155 in Minnesota; 10 part-time). Founded in 1972. SIC 3443, 3586, 3713.

Klein Financial Inc. 105 Third St. W., Chaska, MN 55318. Tel: 952/448-2484; Fax: 952/448-7788. Daniel Klein, Pres.; Alan Klein, EVP; James Klein, EVP; Gene Weber, SVP and Treas.; Robert Peroutka, SVP; James Renckens, SVP. Annual revenue $72.7 million. Klein Financial Inc., formerly Klein Bancorporation Inc., is an $940 million-asset bank holding company with nine commercial banks in Minnesota. 373 employees (all in Minnesota; 75 part-time). Founded in 1975. In January 2000 the company entered into two acquisition agreements: Preferred Bancshares, a $34 million bank holding company in Big Lake, Minn.; and Home Town Mortgage Inc., a mortgage broker organization based in Chaska, Minn. SIC 6712.

Knitcraft Corporation 4020 W. Sixth St., Winona, MN 55987. Tel: 507/454-1163; Fax: 507/454-1589. Bernhard J. Brenner, Pres.; Wilfried Hahn, VP; Samuel Shea, VP. Knitcraft, under the brand name St. Croix, produces handcrafted sweaters and men's sweater-shirts. 300 employees. Founded in 1961. SIC 2253.

Knowlan's Super Markets Inc. 111 E. County Rd. F, Vadnais Heights, MN 55127. Tel: 651/483-9242; Fax: 651/483-0622. Marie K. Aarthun, Pres. and CEO. Knowlan's owns seven retail supermarkets in the St. Paul area: three Knowlan's Super Markets (22,000 to 25,000 square feet); and Festival Foods franchises in White Bear Lake, Vadnais Heights, Circle Pines, and Brooklyn Park, Minn. (50,000 to 55,000 square feet). 658 employees (511 part-time). Founded in 1920. In June 2000 Knowlan's sold one of its four Knowlan's Super Markets—the Randolph Avenue store in St. Paul. The small neighborhood store did not fit with plans to expand the large-supermarket Festival Foods chain. SIC 5411.

Knutson Construction Services Inc. 5500 Wayzata Blvd., Suite 300, Golden Valley, MN 55416. Tel: 763/546-1400; Fax: 763/546-2226; Web site: http://www.knutsonconstruction.com. John A. Curry, Chm.; Steven O. Curry, Pres. and CEO; Chad Lewis, EVP and Gen. Mgr.; Edward B. Curtiss, VP; Richard H. Peper, VP; Lawrence A. Trom, VP; Mike Wolf, CFO. Knutson Construction Services provides general construction, construction management, and design/build services for commercial and industrial building projects. Representative projects include hospitals, schools, retail facilities, parking garages, and industrial/manufacturing plants. Owned by Michael/Curry Cos. Inc., Minneapolis. 600 employees (350 in Minnesota). Founded in 1911. SIC 1541, 1542. No. 66 CRM Private 100.

Kolstad Company Inc. 8501 Naples St. N.E., Blaine, MN 55449. Tel: 763/792-1033; Fax: 763/379-8980. Paul O'Brien, Pres.; Dave McNeill, VP-Purch.; Dave Becker, VP-Svc.; Don Dass, VP-Mfg. Kolstad manufactures beverage truck and trailer bodies, aluminum tool boxes, service bodies, recycling bodies, and platforms. The company also distributes truck bodies, truck equipment, and heavy-duty parts; and performs trailer service (repairing, painting, sandblasting, lettering, and wreck rebuilding). 85 employees. Founded in 1947. SIC 3537, 3713, 3715.

Komo Machine Inc. 11 Industrial Blvd., Sauk Rapids, MN 56379. Tel: 320/252-0580; Fax: 320/656-2470; Web site: http://www.komo.com. Robert Kindt, Pres.; Allan Beyer, VP-Fin. Komo Machine manufactures computerized machine tools for the metalworking, woodworking, and automotive industries. 300 employees. Founded in 1966. SIC 3559.

D.J. Kranz Company Inc. 725 Highway 169 N., Plymouth, MN 55441. Tel: 763/525-0100; Fax: 763/525-1261. Herman Elsen, CEO; Lawrence D. Elsen, Pres.; Donald Schroden, VP; Bruce Quam, VP. Annual revenue $46 million. D.J. Kranz Co. constructs commercial, institutional, and industrial buildings. 60 employees (all in Minnesota). Founded in 1928. SIC 1541.

Kraus-Anderson Incorporated 523 S. Eighth St., Minneapolis, MN 55404. Tel: 612/332-7281; Fax: 612/332-0217; Web site: http://www.krausanderson.com. Bruce W. Engelsma, Chm. and CEO; Burton F. Dahlberg, Pres. and COO; Daniel W. Engelsma, EVP; Carl E. Carlson, VP; Thomas L. Dunleavy, CFO; Janice R. Goebel, Sec.; Mary Jo Walter, Asst. Sec. Annual revenue $610 million. Kraus-Anderson is a general contracting and real estate holding and management company. Its operations include Kraus-Anderson Construction Company (Minneapolis, St. Paul, Midwest, North, and Building Company divisions), Kraus-Anderson Realty Company, Kraus-Anderson Insurance Agency, Kraus-Anderson Mortgage Company, Kraus-Anderson Development Finance Company, Key Group Advertising Inc., and Kraus-Anderson Capital. 900 employees. Founded in 1897. SIC 1541, 1542, 6411, 6512. No. 13 CRM Private 100.

Krofam Inc. 180 E. Highway 14, P.O. Box 850, Philip, SD 57567. Tel: 605/859-2542; Fax: 605/859-2499. Arthur A. Kroetch, Chm. and Pres.; Gerald Carley, VP and COO; Karen Kroetch, VP, Sec., and Treas.; Jerry Kroetch, VP-Sls./Mktg. Annual revenue $20 million. Krofam is a holding company for Scotchman Industries Inc., which manufactures hydraulic ironworkers; and circular cold saws; Dakota Case Inc., which manufactures boxes for displaying individual pieces of jewelry; and Scotchman Credit Corp., a leasing company. Scotchman Industries, Krofam's oldest company, was founded in 1967. 125 employees (2 part-time). Founded in 1993. SIC 3542.

A.W. Kuettel & Sons Inc. 1225 Port Terminal Rd., Duluth, MN 55802. Tel: 218/722-3901; Fax: 218/722-6113. Charles Kuettel, Pres.; William Kuettel, VP; Thomas Kuettel, Treas. and Sec. A.W. Kuettel & Sons provides pipe and boiler insulation, pipe fabrication, roofing, plumbing, heating and ventilation, sheet metal work, and metal fabrication. 60 employees. Founded in 1924. SIC 1711, 1761, 3498.

Kurt Manufacturing Company Inc. 5280 Main St. N.E., Fridley, MN 55421. Tel: 763/572-1500; Fax: 763/541-8466; Web site: http://www.kurt.com. William G. Kuban, Pres.; Roger DeLacey, CFO; Steve Carlsen, EVP; Kern Walker, VP-Hum. Res. Annual revenue $185 million. Kurt Manufacturing specializes in high-precision machining, precision gears, screw machining, die casting, fabrication, and powder coat paintings for the computer, aerospace, defense, automotive, and commercial industries. The company designs and builds special machines, fixtures, and dedicated work cells to suit any production requirements. It also manufactures the Kurt Anglock Vise; statistical gauging systems, Kurt Check, and MagNum i; and a full line of manual and power wheelchairs through the Theradyne Division. 1,200 employees (1,000 in Minnesota). Founded in 1946. SIC 3363, 3451, 3499, 3545, 3566.

Kwik Trip Inc. P.O. Box 2107, 1626 Oak St., La Crosse, WI 54602. Tel: 608/781-8988; Fax: 608/781-8950. John Hansen, Pres.; Donald Zietlow, Chm. Kwik Trip Inc. owns more than 260 retail gasoline and grocery stores. 3,000 employees. Founded in 1965. SIC 5411, 5541.

LCO Casino, Lodge & Convention Center 13767 W. County Rd. B, Hayward, WI 54843. Tel: 800/526-2274. LCO offers a 288-seat bingo hall, buffet, restaurant, convention center, sauna and exercise room. 350 employees. Founded in 1994. SIC 7011.

LHB Engineers & Architects 21 W. Superior Place, Suite 500, Duluth, MN 55802. Tel: 218/727-8446; Fax: 218/727-8456; Web site: http://www.lhbcorp.com. Harvey H. Harvala, Pres. and CEO; William D. Bennett, VP; Richard A. Carter, VP; Steven H. McNeill, VP; Susan K. Quam, CFO; David M. Sheedy, VP. LHB is an architectural and engineering firm. It has a regional office at 250 Third Ave. N., Suite 450, Minneapolis, MN 55401 (Tel: 612/338-2029; Fax: 612/338-2088). 110 employees. Founded in 1965. In May 2000 LHB was awarded two of the American Institute of Architects' Earth Day 2000 "Top 10 List" awards for the following architectural design solutions that protect and enhance the environment: the Green Institute's Phillips Eco-Enterprise Center (PEEC) in Minneapolis; and the Wendy and Malcolm McLean Environmental Living and Learning Center (ELLC) at Northland College in Ashland, Wis. In June LHB opened an office in Chicago, to better serve its pipeline and fiber optic clients in the area. In July LHB received the Construction Specifications Institute Minneapolis/St. Paul chapter's Environmental Sensitivity Award. SIC 8712.

L&M Radiator Inc. 1414 E. 37th St., Hibbing, MN 55746. Tel: 218/263-8993; Fax: 218/262-6606. Alex Chisholm, Chm.; Dan Chisholm, Pres.; Mary Ellen Chisholm, Treas. L&M Radiator Inc. makes engine cooling radiator cores, oil coolers, radiator shutters, and full radiator systems for OEM and aftermarkets. The company maintains four plants in three countries—the United States, Mexico, and Australia. 237 employees (136 in Minnesota; 6 part-time). Founded in 1957. SIC 3714.

LSI Corporation of America Inc. 2100 Xenium Ln. N., Plymouth, MN 55441. Tel: 763/559-4664; Fax: 763/559-4395. Gerald A. Wellik, Chm. and Pres.; Keith Wrobel, VP-Mktg.; Mike Disblowe, VP-Op.; Dan Brown, VP and Cont.; Bill Bowman, VP-Engrg.; Jamie Wellik, VP. LSI manufactures plastic laminate casework for health care and educational facilities. 225 employees. Founded in 1968. SIC 2541.

La Crosse Division/L.B. White Company W6636 L.B. White Rd., Onalaska, WI 54650. Tel: 608/783-2800; Fax: 608/783-6115. Anthony V. Wilson, Pres. The La Crosse Division of L.B. White is a manufacturer of under-bar equipment. 91 employees. Founded in 1952. SIC 2542, 2599, 3469, 3581, 3585.

La Crosse Graphics Inc. 3025 East Ave. S., P.O. Box 249, La Crosse, WI 54601. Tel: 608/788-2500; Fax: 608/788-2660. Heath T. Schumper, Treas.; Timothy J. Morgan, Pres.; Dave Villeneuve, VP, Sec. Annual revenue $5 million. La Crosse Graphics is engaged in the printing business, specifically process lithography and hot-stamp embossing. 56 employees (3 part-time). Founded in 1987. SIC 2752.

La Crosse Milling Company Highway 35, P.O. Box 86, Cochrane, WI 54622. Tel: 608/248-2222; Fax: 608/248-2221; Web site: http://www.lacrossemilling.com. Rick L. Schwein, Pres.; Jim Backus, VP. La Crosse Milling, operating two plants, processes oats for food products; and oats, corn, and barley for animal feed ingredients. 55 employees (10 part-time). Founded in 1945. SIC 2041, 2048.

Lake Air Metal Products Inc. 385 90th Ave. N.W., Coon Rapids, MN 55433. Tel: 763/785-2429. Bradley Severson, CEO. Lake Air Metal provides design engineering services, precision, production sheet metal fabrication, and electrical/mechanical assembly services for high-technology industries. 135 employees. Founded in 1972. SIC 3444, 8711.

Lake Country Power 2810 Elida Dr., Grand Rapids, MN 55744. Tel: 800/421-9959. Jerry Ketola, Board Pres.; Tim Reilley, Gen. Mgr.. Lake Country Power is an electric distribution cooperative that also offers

Internet services, economic development and business financing programs. 126 employees (all in Minnesota). Founded in 1997. SIC 4911.

Lake Region Electric Cooperative 1401 S Broadway, P.O. Box W, Pelican Rapids, MN 56572. Tel: 218/863-1171. David Weaklend, Gen. Mgr.. Annual revenue $19.1 million. Lake Region Electric Cooperative is an electric distributor that also offers satellite television and UHF wireless. 85 employees (all in Minnesota). Founded in 1937. SIC 4911.

Lake Region Manufacturing Company Inc. 340 Lake Hazeltine Dr., Chaska, MN 55318. Tel: 952/448-5111; Fax: 952/448-3441. Mark Fleischhacker, Pres.; J.F. Fleischhacker Jr., CEO; Gary E. Melton, CFO; Kathy Roehl, EVP. Annual revenue $69 million. Lake Region Manufacturing Co. manufactures diagnostic, therapeutic, and implantable medical devices. The company has two subsidiaries: Lake Region Medical Inc., Pittsburgh; and Lake Region Manufacturing Co. Ltd., New Ross, Ireland. 1,100 employees (660 in Minnesota). Founded in 1947. SIC 3841.

Lake of the Torches Resort Casino 510 Old Abe Rd., P.O. Box 550, Lac du Flambeau, WI 54538. Tel: 715/588-7070. Lake of the Torches Resort Casino offers 500-seat bingo, two restaurants, entertainment, resort amenities, 8,500-square-foot convention center, RV and campground, a pool, arcade, full service bar and lounge, Jacuzzi, and patio suites. 450 employees. Founded in 1991. SIC 7011.

Lakeland Envelope Company 717 Prior Ave. N., St. Paul, MN 55104. Tel: 651/644-2748; Fax: 651/644-5428. Sheila Godes, CEO; Thomas Godes, COO. Lakeland Envelope Co. manufactures envelopes. 70 employees (all in Minnesota). Founded in 1973. SIC 2677.

Lakeland Tool & Engineering Inc. 2939 Sixth Ave., Anoka, MN 55303. Tel: 763/422-8866; Fax: 763/422-8867. Donald R. Gross, Pres.; Martin C. Sweerin, Treas. and Sec. Lakeland Tool & Engineering is a manufacturer of plastic custom molding, light-assembly plastic parts, and injection molds. 140 employees. Founded in 1973. SIC 3544.

Lakeside Machine Inc. Industrial Park, P.O. Box 151, Gladstone, MI 49837. Tel: 906/428-2333; Fax: 906/428-4343. Gregory Hansen, Pres. and CEO; Francis M. Magnuson, EVP and Gen. Mgr.; H.J. Goodyear, VP and Sec.; Paul Paulson, Cont. and Treas. Lakeside Machine is a subcontract machining source serving the construction equipment and automotive industries. 170 employees (4 part-time). Founded in 1974. SIC 3599.

Lampert Yards Inc. 1850 Como Ave., P.O. Box 64076 (55164), St. Paul, MN 55108. Tel: 651/695-3600; Fax: 651/695-3601; Web site: http://www.lampertyards.com. Robert Eagan, VP-Sls./Op.; Daniel L. Fesler, Chm, Pres. and CEO; Donald G. Bratton, VP-Purch.; Federick L. Chown, VP; Barb Hojer, VP-Hum. Res.; Pam Leier, VP-Mktg.; Rick E. Lingen, CFO. Lampert Yards operates retail lumber and building materials stores at 37 locations in Iowa, Minnesota, South Dakota, and Wisconsin. 600 employees (320 in Minnesota; 200 part-time). Founded in 1887. SIC 5211.

Land O'Lakes Inc. 4001 Lexington Ave. N., Arden Hills, MN 55112. Tel: 651/481-2222; Fax: 651/481-2022; Web site: http://www.landolakes.com. Stan Zylstra, Chm.; John E. (Jack) Gherty, Pres.; Duane Halverson, EVP and COO-Agricultural; Chris Policinski, EVP and COO-Dairy Foods (consumer); Jack Prince, EVP and COO-Dairy Foods (milk mfg.); Dan Knutson, SVP and CFO; Don Berg, VP-Public Affairs. Annual revenue $5.6 billion (earnings $21.4 million; includes $54.2 million gain on sale of Alex Fries flavoring business). Land O'Lakes is a food processing/marketing and farm supply cooperative owned by 300,000 farmers in 30+ states in the Midwest, West Coast, and East Coast. It distributes farm supplies to its members, while processing and marketing their farm commodities. Land O'Lakes-brand food products are distributed nationwide. 7,500 employees. Founded in 1921. In December 1999 Land O'Lakes, Cenex Harvest States Cooperatives, and Farmland Industries announced the establishment of an agronomy marketing joint venture company, Agriliance LLC, and a closely associated seed marketing structure to become effective early in the new year. Dec. 31: Although the company had doubled in size in four years (sales were up 8 percent this year), its earnings of $21.4 million had slipped to the lowest levels in more than a decade (and down from $68.6 million in 1998). Problems with declining butter and cheese prices, with pigs placed on members' farms, and with fertilizer prices all hurt results. Still, the company increased its patronage distribution, to $48.7 million. In January 2000 Land O'Lakes and Cooperative Business International Inc. formed Specialty Grains LLC, a partnership to integrate seed contracting and the marketing and delivery of specialty grains to overseas customers. In February Land O'Lakes agreed to purchase the assets of Madison (Wis.) Dairy Produce Co. and begin operating the Midwest's largest butter production facility. Land O'Lakes and Alto Dairy Cooperative announced plans to enter into a feasibility study to consider the construction of a jointly owned cheese plant in Wisconsin. In March Land O'Lakes and General Mills Inc. (NYSE: GIS) formed an innovative supply chain alliance to engage in joint purchasing and refrigerated distribution activities. The alliance was expected to generate purchasing synergies and improved customer service for both companies and was to utilize new Web-based technologies from Nistevo.com. In May Dean Foods Co. (NYSE: DF) agreed to purchase Land O'Lakes' Upper Midwest fluid milk operations. [Deal completed in July.] The two organizations also announced their agreement to form a joint venture to market and license certain value-added fluid and cultured dairy products to further expand and leverage the Land O'Lakes brand name nationwide. In June Land O'Lakes voluntarily recalled a limited quantity of Land O'Lakes Margarine in stick form that could contain pieces of metal.

In July Land O'Lakes and Farmland Industries agreed to establish Land O'Lakes Farmland Feed LLC, a joint venture company that was to consolidate all aspects of the feed businesses of Land O'Lakes and Farmland. North America's largest feed company, with initial sales of $1.6 billion, Land O'Lakes Farmland Feed was to be governed by a management committee with an equal number of representatives from the two parent companies. Ownership was to reflect the economic interest contributed by each party. Land O'Lakes was to manage the operations of the new company under a management contract. The new company, headquartered in Arden Hills, Minn., was to be led by Bob DeGregorio, vice president of the Land O'Lakes Feed Division. Key feed employees from Land O'Lakes and Farmland were to round out the management team. In August Land O'Lakes acquired a cheese plant from Beatrice Group, a division of ConAgra Inc. The 169-employee, 70,000-square-foot facility, located in Gustine, Calif., produces mozzarella and cream cheese. In September 2000 Land O'Lakes and Davisco Foods International Inc., Le Sueur, Minn., announced the initiation of a feasibility study to consider the formation of an operating partnership that would lead to the construction of a world-class cheese manufacturing facility in South Dakota. (Davisco operates a whey manufacturing facility in Lake Norden, S.D., and Land O'Lakes operates a cheese manufacturing plant in Volga, S.D.) SIC 5191. No. 92 CRM Employer 100. No. 2 CRM Cooperatives/Mutuals 20.

Landscape Structures Inc. 601 Seventh St. S., Delano, MN 55328. Tel: 763/972-3391; Fax: 763/972-3185. Steven King, Chm.; Barbara A. King, Pres. Annual revenue $85 million. Landscape Structures is a manufacturer of park and play equipment and early-childhood play equipment for schools, parks, child-care centers, hospitals, and fast-food restaurants. 375 employees (all in Minnesota). Founded in 1971. SIC 3944, 3949.

Larkin, Hoffman, Daly & Lindgren Ltd. 1500 Wells Fargo Plaza, 7900 Xerxes Ave. S., Bloomington, MN 55431. Tel: 952/835-3800; Fax: 952/896-3333; Web site: http://www.lhdl.com. Thomas

P. Stoltman, Pres.; Richard A. Knutson, COO; Jon S. Swierzewski, Counsel; Todd I. Freeman, CFO; Larry D. Martin, Co-chair, Mktg. Ctee.; Andrew F. Perrin, Co-chair, Mktg. Ctee. Larkin, Hoffman, Daly & Lindgren Ltd. is a law firm specializing in land use and development; governmental relations; financial institutions; business, corporate, securities, and financing; employment and labor law; environmental; real estate; family law; health law; estate planning; international business transactions; franchising; tax, trusts, and estates; and all aspects of litigation and trial law. 186 employees (all in Minnesota; 11 part-time). Founded in 1958. In July 2000 Larkin, Hoffman and Internet business-to-business services company netbriefings.com announced that popular demand had induced them to make their high-tech-law seminar, "E-commerce—the Net Effect," available free through the Internet. SIC 8111.

Larkin Industries Inc. 2020 Energy Park Dr., St. Paul, MN 55108. Tel: 651/645-6000; Fax: 651/645-6082. Michael Larkin, CEO; Lynnette Larkin, Pres. Larkin Industries does foil stamping, embossing, die cutting, laminating, folding, gluing, and industrial parts manufacturing. 58 employees (50 in Minnesota; 1 part-time). Founded in 1976. SIC 3554.

Larsen Design + Interactive 7101 York Ave. S, Suite 120, Edina, MN 55435. Tel: 952/835-2271; Fax: 952/921-3368; Web site: http://www.larsen.com. Tim Larsen, Pres.; Catherine Gillis, VP-Mktg.; Lisa Helminiak, VP-Interactive; Richelle J. Huff, VP-Branding; Gayle Jorgens, VP-Creative; Eric Simon, VP-Interactive; Paul Wharton, VP-Creative; Nancy Whittlesey, VP-Creative. Annual revenue $11.1 million. Larsen Design + Interactive, is a strategic marketing and communications design firm specializing in branding, identity, graphic design, and interactive media. The firm is headquartered in Minneapolis and has an office in Silicon Valley. 80 employees (71 in Minnesota). Founded in 1975. SIC 7379. No. 42 CityBusiness Fastest-growing Private Companies.

Larson Allen Weishair & Company 220 S. Sixth St., Suite 1000, Minneapolis, MN 55402. Tel: 612/376-4500; Fax: 612/376-4850; Web site: http://www.larsonallen.com. Gordon A. Viere, CEO. Larson Allen Weishair & Co. LLP, one of the 20 largest accounting and business consulting firms in the United States, helps clients successfully manage business ventures and finance. The firm provides assurance and tax services; business consulting; financial services and technology to middle-market enterprises. Larson Allen is composed of certified public accountants as well as service and industry consultants. 650 employees. Founded in 1953. In May 2000 senior accountant Martha Vogel was elected president of Skyway Business and Professional Women. SIC 8721.

Larson Boats 700 Paul Larson Memorial Dr., Little Falls, MN 56345. Tel: 320/632-5481; Fax: 320/632-1439; Web site: http://www.larsonboats.com. Jeffrey C. Olson, Pres. Larson Boats manufactures 15-foot to 33-foot powerboats. A division of Genmar Holdings Inc., Minneapolis. 750 employees. Founded in 1913. SIC 3732.

J.H. Larson Electrical Company 700 Colorado Ave. S., Golden Valley, MN 55416. Tel: 763/545-1717; Fax: 763/545-1909; Web site: http://www.jhlarson.com. C.E. (Chuck) Pahl, CEO; Greg A. Pahl, Pres.; Edward Chesen, VP and Gen. Mgr.; Joy L. Pahl, Treas. Larson Electrical is a wholesaler of electrical, plumbing, and heating equipment, with branch locations in Fairmont, Golden Valley, St. Paul and Minneapolis, Minn.; Sioux Falls and Watertown, S.D.; and Hudson and Eau Claire, Wis. The company markets a variety of construction-related products to more than 3,000 customers in a five-state area. 220 employees (140 in Minnesota). Founded in 1930. SIC 5063.

Larson Manufacturing Company Inc. 2333 Eastbrook Dr., Brookings, SD 57006. Tel: 605/692-6115; Fax: 605/696-6222. O. Dale Larson, Pres.; Bill R. Hay, VP; Ben Remer, Cont. Larson Manufacturing Co. makes life-core doors, patio storm doors, and related aluminum windows. 1,100 employees. Founded in 1964. SIC 3442.

Laser Engineering 1200 Lakeview Dr., Chaska, MN 55318. Tel: 952/448-7722; Fax: 952/448-7876. Kenneth E. Carney, Pres. Laser Engineering manufactures acrylic point-of-purchase displays and store fixtures. The company also does laser machining, silk screening, and forming. 50 employees. Founded in 1976. SIC 7336.

Laser Machining Inc. 500 Laser Dr., Somerset, WI 54025. Tel: 715/247-3285; Fax: 715/247-5650. William E. Lawson, Tech. Dir.; Noel Biebl, Pres.; Rita M. Lawson, VP; Dave Plourde, Sls. Mgr. Laser Machining is a laser systems manufacturer and laser job shop for industrial cutting, welding, drilling, and engraving. The company also has a complete line of engraving and cutting systems, and has custom systems available. 170 employees. Founded in 1978. SIC 3699.

Lawson Software 380 Saint Peter St., St. Paul, MN 55102. Tel: 651/767-7000; Fax: 651/767-7141; Web site: http://www.lawson.com. William Lawson Sr., Chm.; Richard Lawson, CEO; Jay Coughlan, Pres. and COO; Robert G. Barbieri, EVP and CFO; Michael A. Bevilacqua, VP and Treas.; Jim DeSocio, VP and Gen. Mgr.-Professional Services Business Unit; William Lawson Jr., EVP-Advanced Tech.; Tony Marzulli, VP-Product/Industry Mktg.; Michael Milbrandt, EVP-Op.; Eric Morgan, VP and Gen. Mgr.-Healthcare Business Unit; Peter C. Patton, SVP-Int'l Op./Business Devel.; Richard Patton, EVP-Res./Devel.; Robert Toatley, EVP and Gen. Mgr.-Retail Business Unit; Nancy Lynch Harrower, Dir.-Corp. Communications. Annual revenue $313 million. Lawson Software is a full-service provider of Web-deployable, enterprise-wide client/server business solutions. Lawson's systems assist companies in the management financial and capital resources, personnel-related information, and materials distribution and inventory, incorporating leading-edge technologies to provide true open solutions. The LAWSON INSIGHT Business Management System is composed of six complete, fully integrated process suites for financials, human resources, procurement, supply chain, collaborative commerce, and enterprise budgeting. The LAWSON INSIGHT II Value Management Solutions include products for financial and operational performance analysis. Typical customers are multisite, multinational companies. Lawson has offices in 15 countries with more than 20 distributors worldwide. The company is headquartered in Minneapolis and London. 1,800 employees (1,075 in Minnesota). Founded in 1975.

In January 2000 Lawson won a major contract with Belk Inc., the largest privately held department store chain in the United States. The company said it had won 30 contracts for its Lotus Domino-powered solutions in their first 60 days of general availability. Lawson won the Best in Showcase Beacon Award from Lotus Development Corp. for its Information Office Enterprise Portal solution. In February Lawson was ranked first among health care financials software vendors in a KLAS Enterprises Healthcare I.T. (Information Technology) Performance Report—placing first in 11 of 18 performance categories. Lawson released six new e-commerce solutions within the Lawson Collaborative Commerce Suite: Lawson Trade Communications Services, Payment Server Integrator, Site Builder, Auction System, Mail Server, and e-Resource Management. New ijob customers in March included McLeodUSA Inc., Cedar Rapids, Iowa; Dain Rauscher Corp., Minneapolis; and Boeing Employees' Credit Union, Tukwila, Wash. Lawson also announced seven more agreements with key government consultants and contractors to provide Lawson e-business enterprise applications for front-to back-office information management. A partnership with Novient Inc. was established to further extend the capabilities of the latter product by allowing for seamless data integration and transfer between the Lawson and Novient products. Lawson formed a new enterprise consulting agreement with PricewaterhouseCoopers LLP. Lawson announced commercial availability of lawson.insight, its next-generation flagship e-business software product line. Lawson announced a $3.6 million contract with ClientLogic for an array of Lawson products powering e-business. In April Lawson announced a global distribution agreement to integrate and sell its new line of enterprise applications with the comprehensive suite of eBusiness applications for sales, marketing, and customer service of Siebel Systems Inc. (Nasdaq: SEBL), the world's leading supplier of eBusiness application software. Lawson completed an independent audit validating its preparations for compliance with the Health Insurance Portability and Accountability Act (HIPAA). Lawson announced the following major contract wins that extended its lead in delivering integrated e-business solutions to top retail chains: Andronico's Markets; Family Christian Stores; Friendly Ice Cream Corp.; Holiday Cos.; Interbond Corp. of America; Miner's Inc.; Taco Cabana Inc.; Value City Department Stores Inc.; and The Yankee Candle Co. Inc. In May Lawson released ijob version 4.0; and named Ann Wyatt Browneto the position of industry marketing director for the company's professional services business unit. May 31: The company reported fiscal-year revenue of $313 million, an overall revenue growth rate of 18 percent. Lawson's international revenue increased 41.5 percent. Lawson experienced 36.6 percent growth in contracting activity for target vertical markets, including health care, retail, professional services, financial services, public sector, and telecommunications. In June Lawson and Hewlett-Packard Co. announced a strategic alliance to offer seamless, personalized e-service solutions forthe enterprise end-user: Lawson's ijob e-recruitment solution with its HPInfrastructure-on-Tap computing backbone. Lawson announced a technology partnership with James E. Van Ella and Associates, a premier provider of pre-employment background investigations, to integrate its real-time background checking technology with Lawson's ijob electronic recruitment service. Lawson's largest human resources and payroll installation in the world was launched for the Civil Service Department of the Government of Tanzania to manage payroll distribution for more than 300,000 civil servants. Lawson announced a half-million-dollar contract win with Rural Cellular Corp., Alexandria, Minn., in the rapidly growing telecommunications field, an area of increasing interest and growth to Lawson. Lawson announced a $2.7 million contract with Mott MacDonald, a leading global engineering consulting firm.

In July Lawson announced a major e-business contract with Clark Retail Enterprises Inc., a $1.8 billion owner and operator of convenience food stores and gasoline retail locations; 20 new customer wins for ijob, including Borden Foods Corp., Kwik Trip Inc., and Wilsons The Leather Experts; the signing of 15 new LawsonTone application service provider (ASP) partners; and the delivery of 30 new performance indicators in its Workforce Analytics e-service, bringing the total number of indicators offered to 70. In August Lawson announced the largest single contract in its history, an e-business contract with HCA, the nation's leading health care provider. Lawson announced beta availability of the Lawson Digital Depot e-procurement service for the health care market. Lawson announced an e-business software contract with Kemper Insurance Cos. valued at $1.3 million. Lawson was named one of the 10 Great Places to Work in Minnesota in the August issue of Corporate Report magazine. Based on its revenue growth from 1995 to 1999, the company was named to Deloitte & Touche's Minnesota Technology Fast 50. Lawson partnered with AIRS, the global leader in e-recruitment information services, to integrate the AIRS SearchStation Web-based passive candidate finder with its ijob Internet recruitment e-service. Aug. 31: In the best quarter of contracting activity in the company's 25-year history, Lawson reported total revenue of $84.2 million in the first quarter of fiscal year 2001, up 15.3 percent from the same quarter last year. License fee revenue grew 36 percent in its key target markets of health care, retail, professional services, financial services, public sector, and telecommunications. In September Lawson and EYT, formerly Ernst & Young Technologies, announced GoEYT powered by Lawson Application Service Provider (ASP). EYT and Lawson also announced delivery of GoFinancials, the first ASP offering available in the GoEYT suite. Houston-based MIRUS Information Technologies, the leader in the multiunit restaurant Enterprise Application Services Provider (ASP) market, joined the LawsonTone ASP Partner Program. ijob version 5.0 enhancements included new search engine technology, a new resume management system, and additions to relationship management functionality. Lawson was named "Best Supplier of Software Solutions or Products" in the NCI (health care supply chain consulting firm) 2000 Supplier Quality Awards. In October Lawson Software announced the formation of a new vertical market initiative for the telecommunications industry, its sixth and newest vertical market. Lawson announced general availability of the Pay to Bill component of its industry-leading lawson.insight Financials. The solution addresses the unique needs of professional employer organizations (PEOs), which have unique and complex billing processes that differ significantly from other types of organizations. Analysts International Corp. (Nasdaq: ANLY), Edina, Minn., licensed lawson.insight Human Resources, Employee-based Self-Evident Applications (SEA), Analytics, and e-Broadcasting to optimize human resources processes for its more than 5,000 employees. Lawson appointed Tornado-IS, a London-based professional services firm specializing in new technology business solutions, to provide implementation consulting services as a member of Lawson's Global Alliance Integrated Network (GAIN) program.At month's end, Lawson announced the signing of 20 new LawsonTone application service provider (ASP) partners. SIC 7372. No. 27 Minnesota Technology Fast 50. No. 50 CityBusiness Fastest-growing Private Companies.

Lawyer Wholesale Nursery 950 State Highway 200 W., Plains, MT 59859. Tel: 406/826-3883; Fax: 406/826-5700; Web site: http://www.lawyernsy.com. John N. Lawyer, Pres. Lawyer is a wholesale nursery and seed operation. It sells bare-root seedlings and transplants of evergreen/deciduous broad-leafs and conifers to customers in all 50 states and abroad. Its seeds are also traded internationally. 110 employees (75 part-time). Founded in 1959. SIC 5193.

Leaders Manufacturing Inc. 800 S.W. 19th Ave., P.O. Box 1183, Willmar, MN 56201. Tel: 320/231-3897; Fax: 320/231-3863. Bruce Ferrel, Owner; Craig Nelson, Plant Mgr. Leaders Manufacturing cuts and packages abrasives for 3M Co. 107 employees (all in Minnesota; 17 part-time). Founded in 1989. SIC 3291.

Leaf Industries Inc. 13310 Industrial Park Blvd., Plymouth, MN 55441. Tel: 763/559-4470; Fax: 763/559-0633. Ronald S. Leafblad, Chm. and CEO; Frank Brantman, Pres.; Jim Schollett, CFO. Annual revenue $13.1 million. Leaf Industries is engaged in precision metal fabrication and finishing, and manufactures metal parts and cabinets for computers and related components. 142 employees (all in Minnesota). Founded in 1979. SIC 3469, 3496, 3499.

LearningByte International 300 S. Highway 169, Suite 350, Golden Valley, MN 55426. Tel: 952/543-3500; Fax: 952/546-6698; Web site: http://www.learningbyte.com. Rajiv Tandon, Pres. and CEO; Keith Thorndyke, EVP and COO; Deborah Moore, CFO. LearningByte International is the leading developer of custom e-learning solutions for Global 2000 companies. LearningByte uses open-standards technology that enables nonprogrammers to quickly revise, upgrade, and maintain e-learning solutions. Based on the concept of the learning object, the company provides unmatched instructional and interactive flexibility, allowing adults to learn in digestible portions targeted to their specific needs. Originally a unit of Control Data Corp., LearningByte has 35 years of experience in worldwide technical information and instruction. 200 employees. Founded in 1992. In October 2000 LearningByte International announced a merger with privately held Image Dynamics Inc., a San Diego-based performance consulting and custom training development firm. "Image Dynamics brings extensive consulting experience along with a successful track record of delivering creative, blended training solutions," said CEO Tandon. "Add LearningByte International's long history of adult learning and a Web-born technology that enables scalable production, and now you have an industry-leading player with unmatched eLearning experience and a very focused mission: improve our clients' employee performance at lowest total cost." The current Image Dynamics office was to remain in San Diego as a West Coast division of the company. LearningByte and VSI Holdings (Amex: VIS), Bloomfirld Hills, Mich., a leading provider of organizational development and training using technology-based and traditional delivery processes for corporate users, entered into a three-year alliance to design and develop eLearning courses. VSIH was to commit resources to generate an estimated $30 million in revenue to be sourced to LearningByte. SIC 7371, 7372, 7379, 8299, 8331.

K.O. Lee Company 200 S. Harrison St., Aberdeen, SD 57401. Tel: 605/225-5820; Fax: 605/225-7267. Krestie Utech, Chm.; Richard

Hickman, Pres. and CEO; Karl Lee, VP. Annual revenue $5.9 million. Lee manufactures machine tools—including tool grinders, surface grinders, cylindrical and universal O.D./I.D. grinders, and automotive engine head maintenance equipment. 59 employees (2 part-time). Founded in 1888. SIC 3541.

Leeann Chin Inc. 3600 W. 80th St., Suite 210, Bloomington, MN 55431. Tel: 952/896-3606; Fax: 952/896-3615. Leeann Chin, Chm. and Founder; Steve Finn, CEO; Keith D. Kersten, Pres.-Leeann Chin Food Holdings Division. Leeann Chin Inc. owns and operates 50 Twin Cities area locations and fine-dining buffets serving contemporary Chinese cuisine at affordable prices. Its buffet restaurants, carryout locations, and supermarket express locations have been ranked in local Diner's Choice Award competitions for 20 years. A major Midwest expansion program—in the Twin Cities and St. Cloud, Minn.; Kansas City, Mo.; and Detroit—was expected to increase the company's total square footage by 60 percent. 1,000 employees (950 in Minnesota; 886 part-time). Founded in 1980. In December 1999 the company opened a new restaurant in Maple Grove, Minn.—its 56th quick-service restaurant. In February 2000 the company established a new unit, Leeann Chin Food Holdings Division, to focus on developing Leeann Chin ready-to-heat prepared entrees and signature sauces distributed to supermarkets, colleges, airlines, and other commercial accounts. In August the company opened its latest restaurant, in Brooklyn Center, Minn., in the Brookdale Corner Shopping Center at the intersection of Xerxes Avenue and Bass Lake Road. New menu items created by company founder Leeann Chin, such as "orange-peel chicken" (breaded chicken tossed in a sesame glaze with Sichuan chilis and candied orange peels) were being offered exclusively at the new location. In October Ms. Chin kicked off a series of events to celebrate the publication of her new book, Everyday Chinese Cooking. SIC 5812.

Leef Bros. Inc. 212 James Ave. N., Minneapolis, MN 55405. Tel: 612/374-3880; Fax: 612/374-1827. Jeffrey D. Leef, Pres.; L.A. Carlson Jr., VP. Leef Bros. is a textile supply company that provides uniform rental and sales, shop and wiping towels, rental floor mats, treated dust mops, linens, and continuous-cloth toweling to a variety of customers in Minnesota, western Wisconsin, South Dakota, and North Dakota. 250 employees (150 in Minnesota; 10 part-time). Founded in 1908. SIC 7218.

Legacy Management & Development 7151 York Ave. S., Edina, MN 55435. Tel: 952/831-1448. Roxanne Givens, Owner. Legacy is a full-service multifamily real estate developer and manager. 74 employees. Founded in 1972. SIC 6531.

LeJeune Steel Company 118 W. 60th St., Minneapolis, MN 55419. Tel: 612/861-3321; Fax: 612/861-2724. Bob Oberaigner, VP. LeJeune Steel Co. fabricates structural steel for use in industrial, commercial, and large-scale residential construction projects. Its one subsidiary, Wisconsin Structural Steel, is located in Barronett, Wis. (John Peterson, VP). LeJeune has been owned since 1989 by the APi Group, Roseville, Minn. 175 employees (120 in Minnesota). Founded in 1944. SIC 3312.

Lenz Inc. 1180 State Highway 7 E., Hutchinson, MN 55350. Tel: 320/587-4030; Fax: 320/587-8791. Craig Lenz, Pres. and Treas.; Roger Mumm, CFO; Paul Lenz, VP and Sec. Annual revenue $23 million. Lenz manufactures fertilizer equipment and parts, makes pickup truck bumper hitches, and distributes Case/Tyler agricultural equipment. Also known as Ag Systems Inc. 70 employees (62 in Minnesota; 20 part-time). Founded in 1963. SIC 3523, 5083.

Hal Leonard Corporation 960 E. Mark St., Winona, MN 55987. Tel: 507/454-2920; Fax: 507/454-4042. Keith Mardak, Chm., CEO, and Treas.; Larry Morton, Pres.; John Cerullo, EVP; Daniel Bauer, SVP and Sec. Annual revenue $90 million. Hal Leonard Corp. publishes music. 340 employees (190 in Minnesota). Founded in 1947. SIC 2741.

Leonard, Street and Deinard 150 S. Fifth St., Suite 2300, Minneapolis, MN 55402. Tel: 612/335-1500; Fax: 612/335-1657; Web site: http://www.leonard.com. Lowell Noteboom, Pres.; Ted Soto, COO; Ivy S. Berndardson, Dir.-Mergers/Acquisitions. Leonard, Street and Deinard's (LS&D) 160 attorneys provide a full range of legal services with practices that include business and commercial litigation; banking; business planning and counseling; computer and information technology; corporate; capital markets; employment law; employee benefits; environmental law; governmental relations and lobbying; intellectual property; construction; public law; bankruptcy; municipal finance; products liability and tort litigation; real estate development and finance; corporate finance and securities law; tax and estate planning; family law; health law; insurance; Indian law; labor relations; mergers and acquisitions; sports and entertainment law; trademarks and copyrights; white-collar crime; and probate. St. Paul office: 2270 Minnesota World Trade Center, 30 E. Seventh St., St. Paul, MN 55101; Tel 651/222-7455, Fax 651/222-7644. Mankato office: 121 E. Walnut St., P.O. Box 967, Mankato, MN 56001; Tel 507/345-1179, Fax 507/345-1182. 350 employees (all in Minnesota). Founded in 1922. In May 2000 LS&D was in exploratory talks with Fredrikson & Byron, Minneapolis, about the potential merger of the two firms to create the Twin Cities' second-largest law firm (next to Dorsey & Whitney). In June the two firms agreed to call off those talks. In November the firm moved its St. Paul satellite office to Lawson Commons from the World Trade Center. SIC 8111.

Lerner Publications Company 241 First Ave. N., Minneapolis, MN 55401. Tel: 612/332-3344; Fax: 612/332-7615. Harry J. Lerner, CEO; Adam Lerner, Publisher. Annual revenue $14.5 million. Lerner Publications Co. is the nation's leading independent, nonfiction, school and library book publisher—publishing more than 200 books a year for young readers in grades K-12. 115 employees (all in Minnesota). Founded in 1959. In April 2000 the company was preparing to go beyond the library to the classroom, with LernerClassroom—a teaching curriculum division that was to pair teaching guides with several of Lerner's nonfiction books. In June Lerner launched the Lerner Classroom division producing and promoting classroom curriculum products linked to Lerner and Carolrhoda books. SIC 2731.

LeRoy Products Corporation P.O. Box 479, LeRoy, MN 55951. Tel: 507/324-5836; Fax: 507/324-5171. Larry Erickson, Pres.; Kent Meyers, VP. LeRoy Products Corp. is an electromechanical assembly job shop. 120 employees (81 in Minnesota). Founded in 1956. SIC 3672, 3679.

Le Sueur Inc. 1409 Vine St., P.O. Box 149, Le Sueur, MN 56058. Tel: 507/665-6204; Fax: 507/665-6083. Ervin A. Mueller, Chm.; Mark Mueller, Pres.; Henry Prevot, VP and COO. Le Sueur Inc. produces aluminum alloys in sand-cast, permanent-mold, die-cast processes, and thermoplastic injection molding. 475 employees (all in Minnesota). Founded in 1946. SIC 3089, 3365.

Lewis Drugs Inc. 2701 S. Minnesota Ave., Suite 1, Sioux Falls, SD 57105. Tel: 605/367-2800; Fax: 605/367-2876. Mark E. Griffin, Pres. and CEO; Doug Gravning, Gen. Mdse. Mgr.; Scott Cross, CFO. Annual revenue $85 million. Lewis Drugs operates drug stores and proprietary stores. 800 employees (50 in Minnesota; 500 part-time). Founded in 1943. SIC 5912.

Lexington Manufacturing & Construction Inc. 1330 115th Ave. N.W., Coon Rapids, MN 55448. Tel: 763/754-9055; Fax: 763/754-9605. Robert Dimke, Pres.; John Dimke, VP. Annual revenue $21 million. Lexington Manufacturing makes architectural woodwork, precision-machined wood and composite components, and mouldings. It also offers CNC routing service and profile wrapping. 150 employees (all in Minnesota; 8 part-time). Founded in 1958. SIC 2431.

Liberty Diversified Industries Inc. 5600 N. Highway 169, New Hope, MN 55428. Tel: 763/536-6600; Fax: 763/536-6685; Web site: http://www.libertydiversified.com. Ben Fiterman, Chm.; Michael B. Fiterman, Pres. and CEO; David Lenzen, EVP; Bill Kovack, Group VP-Packaging/Related Products; Dick Seidenstricker, Group VP-National Markets. Annual revenue $285 million. Liberty Diversified Industries (LDI) is a family of companies that design, manufacture, and market products and creative solutions for the packaging, office, and industrial business sectors. LDI companies include Liberty Carton Co., Safco, Valley Craft, Presentation Packaging, Protecta-Pack Systems, Northern Package, Liberty Paper Inc., LDI Fibres, Diversi-Plast, and Bicknell and Fuller. 1,525 employees. Founded in 1918. In July 2000 LDI agreed to acquire the assets of the Corrugated Packaging Division of Bicknell & Fuller, Peabody, Mass. LDI also formed a joint venture with The Standard Group, Jackson Heights, N.Y., to purchase the assets and operate what was previously Bicknell & Fuller's Folding Carton Division. SIC 2653, 3089, 3441, 5112.

PVT

Liberty Enterprises 5267 Program Ave., Mounds View, MN 55112. Tel: 651/604-5300; Fax: 651/604-5289; Web site: http://www.libertysite.com. David Copham, Chm.; Robert Anderson, Pres. and CEO; Michael Provenzano, EVP-Tech./Op.; Paul Annett, EVP-Admin.; Harry Merickel, EVP-Sls./Mktg.; Leon Steinberg, EVP-Corp. Devel.; Paul Malone, VP-Planning/Res.; Claudia Zweber, VP-Strategic/Venture Fin. Annual revenue $120 million. The credit union movement's leading provider of payment systems and marketing services, Liberty partners with nearly 5,500 credit unions in all 50 states, Guam, and Puerto Rico. Liberty's core product remains the check. Liberty's growing list of credit union-focused products, services and technologies are checks, database marketing, data processing, direct marketing, creative services, Web site design and hosting, card services, financial supplies, outsource marketing and market research. The company serves credit unions from check production plants throughout the country: Madison, WI; Knoxville, TN; Harrisburg, PA; Simi Valley, CA; and Dallas, TX. Liberty also has established marketing centers in Los Angeles, St. Louis and Hartford, CT. 900 employees (450 in Minnesota). Founded in 1985. In June 2000 Liberty acquired the Connecticut Credit Union Association's marketing services unit, creating a Liberty Marketing Center for Connecticut and other East Coast credit unions. In August Liberty acquired the credit union date processing division of FiTECH Systems, Atlanta. SIC 2761.

Pete Lien & Sons Inc. P.O. Box 440, Rapid City, SD 57709. Tel: 605/342-7224; Fax: 605/342-6979. Bruce H. Lien, Chm.; Charles H. Lien, VP and Treas.; Robert J. Schurger, EVP; Pete C. Lien, Pres, Sec., and COO. Pete Lien & Sons is a regional limestone quarrier, aggregate producer, and lime manufacturer with divisions providing concrete ready mix, concrete block, silica sand, and fabricated steel. The company has three subsidiaries in Rapid City—Dakota Steel, Dakota Block, and Birdall Sand & Gravel; and one, Colorado Lien, in Fort Collins, Colo. 360 employees. Founded in 1944. SIC 3274, 3281.

B.A. Liesch Associates Inc. 13400 15th Ave. N., Plymouth, MN 55441. Tel: 763/559-1423; Fax: 763/559-2202. Brian B. Liesch, CEO and COO; Kenneth P. Olson, VP; Harry L. Summit, P.E., VP; John C. Lichter, P.E., VP; Jim de Lambert, VP. B.A. Liesch Associates specializes in groundwater hydrogeology, underground storage tank remediation programs, wastewater treatment systems, air-quality control, agricultural-chemical services, OSHA/health and safety services, waste, and environmental management. 80 employees. Founded in 1968. SIC 8731.

Life Time Fitness 6442 City West Pkwy., Eden Prairie, MN 55344. Tel: 952/947-0000; Fax: 952/947-0077; Web site: http://www.lifetimefitness.com. Bahram Akradi, CEO; Shaun Nugent, CFO. Annual revenue $63 million. Life Time Fitness is a sports, health, and fitness provider with more than 225,000 members nationwide. The company owns and operates 22 family fitness and recreation centers in Illinois, Indiana, Michigan, Minnesota, Ohio, and Virginia. 150 employees. Founded in 1992. SIC 7991.

Lifetouch Inc. 11000 Viking Dr., Eden Prairie, MN 55344. Tel: 952/826-4000; Fax: 952/826-4557; Web site: http://www.lifetouch.com. Richard P. Erickson, Chm. ; Paul Harmel, Pres. and CEO. Annual revenue $700 million. Lifetouch, the largest school-photography business in the country, produces photographs of 20 million children and family groups in department stores, studios, and schools throughout the United States. Operations include yearbooks and related services. Lifetouch is one of the nation's 100 largest employee-owned companies. 16,000 employees. Founded in 1936. In September 2000 the company was chosen by Indigo N.V. as the North American test site for its recently launched Indigo Publisher 8000, an ultra-high-speed Series 2 digital color press. SIC 7221.

Lillie Suburban Newspapers 2515 Seventh Ave. E., North St. Paul, MN 55109. Tel: 651/777-8800; Fax: 651/777-8288. N. Ted Lillie, Publisher; Jeffery R. Enright, Publisher and Circ./Distribution Dir.; Bruce Anderson, Cont.; Ted H. Lillie, Advertising Dir. Lillie Suburban Newspapers is a printer of 11 suburban weekly newspapers, and is also a commercial printer. 120 employees. Founded in 1938. SIC 2711, 2741.

Lincoln Stores Inc. 517 E. Fourth St., Duluth, MN 55805. Tel: 218/722-3925; Fax: 218/722-9419. James S. Lundberg, Pres.; Robert F. Lundberg, VP; Terry Lundberg, Treas.; Anthony Walzcak, Sec. Lincoln Stores owns and operates Daugherty Hardware Co., Duluth; Daugherty Appliance Co., Superior, Wis.; and Poplar Hardware Co., Poplar, Wis. 120 employees (40 in Minnesota). Founded in 1946. SIC 5251, 5722.

Lincoln Wood Products Inc. 701 N. State St., P.O. Box 375, Merrill, WI 54452. Tel: 715/536-2461; Fax: 715/536-9783. Carl A. Bierman, Chm. ; J.C. Bierman, Pres. and Treas.; Rick Bliese, Sec.; Roger Emanuel, Gen. Mgr. Lincoln Wood manufactures a complete line of wood window units, clad wood windows, wood patio doors, clad patio doors, and insulated glass. 522 employees (4 part-time). Founded in 1947. SIC 2431.

Lind Shoe Company 501 Laser Dr., Somerset, WI 54025. Tel: 715/247-5463; Fax: 715/247-5440. Jeffrey R. Lind, Pres. Lind Shoe Co. manufactures—and distributes worldwide—upper-end bowling and golf shoes. 73 employees. Founded in 1919. SIC 3149.

Lindquist & Vennum PLLP 4200 IDS Center, 80 S. Eighth St., Minneapolis, MN 55402. Tel: 612/371-3211; Fax: 612/371-3207; Web site: http://www.lindquist.com. Daryle Uphoff, Managing Ptnr.; Jill LaMere, Exec. Dir. Lindquist & Vennum is a commercial law firm based in Minneapolis, with additional offices in Saint Paul and Denver. With over 140 lawyers, Lindquist & Vennum provides a wide range of business and litigation services. The firm's corporate practice-known for M&A, securities and private finance transactions-has a client base comprised of venture stage and emerging market companies, as well as publicly held companies. Industry expertise includes medical device manufacturers, high tech, financial institutions, agribusiness/cooperatives, health care, investment banking and communications. The litigation practice addresses a broad scope of commercial and civil matters, including class actions and disputes related to securities, intellectual property, shareholder, employment, products liability, franchise and premises negligence. Other significant practices include employee benefits, labor and employment, public law, trusts and estates, tax planning and defense, bankruptcy and creditors' remedies, white collar crime, environmental, and commercial real estate. 270 employees (250 in Minnesota; 22 part-time). Founded in 1968. In March 2000 Timothy Keller, former Silicon

Graphics Cray Division general counsel, joined the firm as a partner. SIC 8111.

Lintex Corporation 2609 Territorial Rd., St. Paul, MN 55114. Tel: 651/646-6600; Fax: 651/646-3210. John Sleizer, Pres. Lintex Corp. is a wholesale distributor of textiles and interiors to acute-care and long-term health care facilities nationwide. Products include linens, apparel, surgical textiles, furnishings, and interior design. 80 employees (75 in Minnesota). Founded in 1954. SIC 5023.

Litho Inc. 1280 Energy Park Dr., St. Paul, MN 55108. Tel: 651/644-3000; Fax: 651/644-4839. Duane Pogue, Pres.; Brian Johnson, VP-Sls.; Ron Boekermann, VP-Mfg.; Jim Hannon, COO. Annual revenue $26.2 million. Litho Inc. (formerly Litho Specialties Inc.) is a commercial sheetfed and web printer, producing catalogs, magazine inserts, annual reports, and marketing support materials for the agency, design, and corporate marketplace. 158 employees (161 in Minnesota; 3 part-time). Founded in 1947. SIC 2752.

Litho Technical Services 1600 W. 92nd St., Bloomington, MN 55431. Tel: 952/888-7945; Fax: 952/888-9014; Web site: http://www.lithotechusa.com. Gary R. Heimer, Pres.; Bob Johnson, VP-Sls./Mktg.; Ron Anderson, Plant Foreman. Litho Technical Services is a commercial printer that handles a wide range of jobs—from electronic prepress to final bindery finishing and packaging. Acquired in 1993 by Taylor Corp., North Mankato, Minn. 120 employees (all in Minnesota; 3 part-time). Founded in 1960. SIC 2752.

Littfin Lumber Co. Inc. 555 Baker Ave. W., P.O. Box 666, Winsted, MN 55395. Tel: 320/485-3861; Fax: 952/473-1245. John A. Littfin, Chm., Pres., and CFO; Steve Laxen, VP. Littfin Lumber Co. is a manufacturer and wholesaler of floor and roof trusses. 280 employees (all in Minnesota; 30 part-time). Founded in 1962. SIC 2439.

Llewellyn Worldwide Ltd. 84 S. Wabasha St., P.O. Box 64383 (55164), St. Paul, MN 55107. Tel: 651/291-1970; Fax: 651/291-1908; Web site: http://www.llewellyn.com. Carl L. Weschke, Pres.; Sandra K. Weschke, Sec. and Treas.; Robert Van Moorlehem, Cont.; Greg Sundem, MIS Mgr.; Nanette Peterson, Prod. Mgr. Annual revenue $18 million. Llewellyn Worldwide, doing business as Llewellyn Publications, publishes quality trade books and a monthly consumer magazine specializing in astrology, New Age, and parapsychology. It also publishes tarot decks and various "occult" kits in English and Spanish titles. Llewellyn Espanol has a full line of Spanish books. 109 employees (117 in Minnesota; 9 part-time). Founded in 1901. SIC 2731.

Local Oil Distribution Inc. 2015 Seventh Ave. N., Anoka, MN 55303. Tel: 763/421-4923; Fax: 763/421-0304. Gary Dehn, CFO; Greg Dehn, VP; Harry Blair, CEO. Local Oil Distribution is a heating oil distributor, a fuel oil dealer, and an operator of three SuperAmerica stores. 90 employees (all in Minnesota; 70 part-time). Founded in 1951. SIC 5983.

Lockridge Grindal Nauen PLLP 100 Washington Ave. S., Suite 2200, Minneapolis, MN 55401. Tel: 612/339-6900; Fax: 612/339-0981; Web site: http://www.locklaw.com. Richard A. Lockridge, Ptnr.; H. Theodore Grindal, Ptnr.; Charles N. Nauen, Ptnr. Lockridge Grindal Nauen PLLP (formerly Schatz Paquin Lockridge Grindal & Holstein) is a law firm specializing in: class action, employment, commercial, and environmental litigation in federal and state courts; corporate and commercial law; state and government relations; and health care-related corporate and commercial matters and Indian law. Additional office: Washington, D.C. 68 employees (65 in Minnesota; 6 part-time). Founded in 1978. In December 1999 the firm filed a class-action complaint in the U.S. District Court for the District of Minnesota on behalf of persons who purchased common stock issued by Navarre Corp. (Nasdaq: NAVR) at artificially inflated prices during the period Nov. 25, 1998, through Dec. 9, 1998. The case allegedly involves the making of false and misleading statements that the company was spinning off a majority-owned subsidiary and taking the newly formed company public by the end of the 1998 year. In September 2000, the firm added three new partners: Hugh V. Plunkett, J. Michael Schwartz and Robert K. Shelquist, all formerly of Plunkett, Schwartz, Peterson P.A. All three practice commercial litigation in the state and federal courts. SIC 8111.

Lodal Inc. P.O. Box 2315, Kingsford, MI 49802. Tel: 906/779-1700; Fax: 906/779-1160. John Giuliani, Sec. and Treas. Lodal manufactures garbage trucks, refuse-handling equipment, recycling vehicles, and recycling-system bins. 80 employees. Founded in 1946. SIC 3711.

Loffler Business Systems Inc. 5707 Excelsior Blvd., St. Louis Park, MN 55416. Tel: 952/925-6800; Fax: 952/925-5781; Web site: http://www.loffler.com. James Loffler, Pres.; Gordon Running, VP, Gen Mgr.; Mark Stokes, VP-Sls. Annual revenue $13.3 million. Loffler sells copiers, fax machines, dictation, voice loggers, network, multi-functional printers and copiers. 90 employees (all in Minnesota). Founded in 1986. In January 2000 the company was named the exclusive Twin Cities dealer for Minolta Corp.'s MicroPress Cluster Printing System. In June Loffler acquired Mattson Business Products, Brooklyn Center, Minn. SIC 5044. No. 36 CityBusiness Fastest-growing Private Companies.

Lofton Label Inc. 6290 Claude Way E., Inver Grove Heights, MN 55076. Tel: 651/457-8118; Fax: 651/457-3709. Richard Gajewski, Pres. Lofton Label manufactures pressure-sensitive customized labels for individuals and businesses. 100 employees. Founded in 1981. SIC 2672.

Logicbay 7900 International Dr., Suite 750, Bloomington, MN 55425. Tel: 952/854-3413; Web site: http://www.tej.com. Paul Tobin, CEO. Logicbay is a Web design firm specializing in Internet, intranet and extranet applications as well as Web and computer training. 55 employees. Founded in 1995. SIC 7379.

Lommen, Nelson, Cole & Stageberg P.A. 1800 IDS Center, 80 S. Eighth St., Minneapolis, MN 55402. Tel: 612/339-8131; Fax: 612/339-8064; Web site: http://www.lommen.com. Phillip A. Cole, Pres.; Margie R. Bodas, Practice Mgr.; Glenn R. Kessel, Sec.; John R. McBride, VP; Roger V. Stageberg, Treas.; Bradley G. Wicklund, Admin. Lommen, Nelson, Cole & Stageberg P.A. offers legal services in the areas of litigation, workers' compensation, professional malpractice, municipal, appellate, securities, mergers and acquisitions, estate planning and probate, real estate, corporate and commercial, employment, and family practice. The law firm has an additional office in Hudson, Wis. 71 employees (66 in Minnesota; 6 part-time). Founded in 1953. SIC 8111.

Loram Maintenance of Way Inc. 3900 Arrowhead Dr., P.O. Box 188, Hamel, MN 55340. Tel: 763/478-6014; Fax: 763/478-6916. P.V. Wilson, Pres. and CEO; D.D. Cherrey, VP-Fin.; D.H. Isdahl, VP-Op.; W.R. Malmo, VP, Sec., and Gen. Counsel; H. Vanaki, VP-Engrg./Mfg.; P.J. Homan, Dir.-Mktg. Loram Maintenance of Way manufactures, leases, and sells sophisticated equipment for maintaining and repairing railway roadbeds and rails. The equipment, complete with operating crew, is generally leased to railroads on a short-term or multiyear basis. 500 employees. Founded in 1954. SIC 3441, 3531, 3743, 7359.

August Lotz Co. Inc. 146 N. Center St., P.O. Box 39, Boyd, WI 54726. Tel: 715/667-5121; Fax: 715/667-5101. Mark Schlichter, Pres.; Mark Barton, VP. August Lotz Co. manufactures futon furniture, industrial benchtops, and table tops. 100 employees. Founded in 1897. SIC 2499.

Lou-Rich Inc. 505 W. Front St., Albert Lea, MN 56007. Tel: 507/377-8910; Fax: 507/373-7110. James A. Anderson, Chm., Pres., and CEO; Rod Uher, Purch. Mgr.; Randy Eggum, VP-Op.; Terry Anderson, Dir.-Personnel; Mike Larson, Dir.-Engrg.; Steve Tufte, Dir.-Fin.. Lou-Rich is an ISO 9001-certified contract manufacturer performing the following: tooling, short- and long-term run stampings, CNC machining, painting, and prototype building. It serves the agricultural equipment, food processing, medical, commercial transportation, and automated sawing industries from manufacturing operations in Albert Lea and Hayward, Minn.; Brandon, S.D.; and Lake Mills, Iowa. 255 employees (230 in Minnesota). Founded in 1972. SIC 3544.

H.R. Loveall Construction Company 120 Sixth Ave. S.E., Winnebago, MN 56098. Tel: 507/893-3127; Fax: 507/893-3618. Don Weerts, CEO; Tom Loveall, VP. Loveall Construction provides bituminous paving and gravel. 67 employees. Founded in 1924. SIC 1442.

Lowell Inc. 9425 83rd Ave. N., Brooklyn Park, MN 55445. Tel: 763/425-3355; Fax: 763/425-8510. Patrick Lilja, Pres.; Mahlow Femrite, Mktg. Dir. Lowell Inc. provides full-service, ultra-precision machining of small complex components, and assemblies. Lowell has expertise in a number of areas, including milling, turning, EDM'ing, lapping, grinding, and metal finishing. Lowell has developed many strategic alliances with manufacturing support service industries. 60 employees. Founded in 1964. SIC 3499.

Lowry-Marprint Inc. 1607 Ninth St., White Bear Lake, MN 55110. Tel: 651/429-7722; Fax: 651/429-6006. Michael Klawitter, Sls. Mgr. Lowry-Marprint manufactures labels, data collection systems, label applicators, and inkjet-coding and bar-coding systems. Service center: Des Moines, Iowa. 85 employees (84 in Minnesota). Founded in 1974. SIC 3577, 3579, 5084.

Lube Tech 900 Mendelssohn Ave. N., Roseville, MN 55427. Tel: 651/636-7990; Fax: 651/636-2519. Christian N. Bame, Pres.; Paul J. Martin, COO. Lube Tech is a multibrand distributor of lubricating oils, commercial fuels, home heating oil, and chemicals in Minnesota, Wisconsin, and North Dakota. 83 employees. SIC 5172.

Luigino's Inc. 525 Lake Ave. S., Duluth, MN 55802. Tel: 218/723-5555; Fax: 218/723-5409. Luigino F. (Jeno) Paulucci, Chm.; Ronald O. Bubar, Pres. and CEO. Annual revenue $325 million (estimated by Fact Book). Luigino's produces Frozen Pasta and Sauce Entrees and Snacks under the Michelina's brand; and frozen Chinese Entrees, Dinners, and Egg Roll Snacks under the Michelina's Yu Sing brand. The company has sales and administration offices, plus a manufacturing plant, in Duluth; and additional plants in Jackson, Ohio. 1,400 employees. Founded in 1990. In June 2000 Paulucci stepped down as CEO in favor of President Bubar in order to spend more time developing his newest venture, Self Serve Centers Inc.—premium frozen meals from vending machines that accept credit cards. SIC 2038. No. 38 CRM Private 100.

Lund Boat Company P.O. Box 248, New York Mills, MN 56567. Tel: 218/385-2235; Fax: 218/385-2227. Larry Lovold, Pres.; George Cecrle, VP-Sls.; Keith Boyne, VP-Mktg. Lund Boat Co. is one of the world's largest manufacturers of aluminum fishing boats. Division of Genmar Holdings Inc., Minneapolis. 510 employees (493 in Minnesota; 10 part-time). Founded in 1948. SIC 3732.

Lund Food Holdings Inc. 4100 W. 50th St., Suite 2100, Edina, MN 55424. Tel: 952/927-3663; Fax: 952/915-2600. Russell T. (Tres) Lund III, Pres. and CEO; Von Martin, SVP and CAO; James Geisler, VP-Op.; Tamra Laska, VP-Hum. Res.; Frederick Miller, VP-Fin.; John Pazahanick, VP-Store Devel./Real Estate; Steve Vuolo, VP-Mktg. Annual revenue $450 million. Lund Food Holdings Inc. is the holding company for two Minnesota retail grocery store chains. Lunds operates seven stores in the Twin Cities communities of Bloomington, Edina, Minneapolis, Minnetonka, Richfield, St. Paul, and Wayzata. Byerly's operates 12 stores—in Bloomington, Burnsville, Chanhassen, Eagan, Edina, Golden Valley, Maple Grove, Minnetonka, Roseville, St. Louis Park, St. Paul, and St. Cloud. 5,200 employees (4,982 in Minnesota; 3,967 part-time). Founded in 1939. In December 1999 the company signed a letter of intent with local juice company Sola Squeeze to bring juice bars to several Lunds and Byerly's stores in 2000. SIC 5411. No. 23 CRM Private 100. No. 52 CRM Employer 100.

Lundell Manufacturing Corporation 2700 Ranchview Ln., Plymouth, MN 55447. Tel: 763/559-4114; Fax: 763/557-4118; Web site: http://www.lundellmfg.com. LeRoy Lundell, CEO; Tom Lundell, Pres.; P. Lundell, Sec. and Treas.; Steven Wittwer, VP-Sls./Mktg. Annual revenue $14.8 million. Lundell Manufacturing Corp. is a custom designer/fabricator of flexible materials. It also provides laminating, die cutting, full engineering and materials-selection assistance. In addition, it conducts in-house laboratory testing of materials and adhesives. The company's client list includes 3M, Monsanto, and UniRoyal. 74 employees (72 in Minnesota). Founded in 1978. SIC 3069.

Lupient Automotive Group 750 Pennsylvania Ave., Suite 1500, Golden Valley, MN 55426. Tel: 763/544-6666; Fax: 763/513-5517. James W. Lupient, Pres. Annual revenue $560 million. Lupient Automotive Group sells and leases automobiles. The company has 23 franchises in Minneapolis/St. Paul and Rochester, Minn.; and Eau Claire, Wis. 1,000 employees. Founded in 1968. SIC 5511. No. 17 CRM Private 100.

Lurie, Besikof, Lapidus & Co. LLP 2501 Wayzata Blvd., Minneapolis, MN 55405. Tel: 612/377-4404; Fax: 612/377-1325; Web site: http://www.lblco.com. Farley S. Kaufmann, Managing Ptnr. Annual revenue $16.2 million. Lurie, Besikof, Lapidus & Co. LLP is an accounting and consulting firm. Experience includes: manufacturing, wholesale, retail, medical services, construction, real estate, automobile dealers, banking, professional associations, high tech, international corporations and sole proprietorships. Clients include public and private businesses. 140 employees (all in Minnesota; 8 part-time). Founded in 1941. SIC 8721.

Lutheran Brotherhood 625 Fourth Ave. S., Minneapolis, MN 55415. Tel: 612/340-7000; Fax: 612/340-8389; Web site: http://www.luthbro.com. Richard C. Kessler, Chm.; Bruce J. Nicholson, Pres. and CEO; Michael Loken, SVP-Info. Technology Resources; Jennifer Martin, SVP-Corp./Hum. Svs.; Jerald Sourdiff, SVP and CFO; Daniel G. Walseth, SVP, Sec., and Gen. Counsel; David Angstadt, EVP and Chief Mktg. Ofcr.; Randall L. Boushek, SVP-Investments; James R. Olson, SVP-Membership Svs. Annual revenue $2.95 billion. Lutheran Brotherhood is a member-owned fraternal benefit society of 1.2 million Lutherans joined together for financial security, benevolent outreach and volunteer service. Lutheran Brotherhood's mission is to improve the quality of life for its members, to strengthen communities, and to aid Lutheran congregations and institutions. The organization offers a broad range of financial products and services to Lutherans nationwide. 1,501 employees. Founded in 1917. In December 1999 LB Community Bank & Trust fsb—a bank subsidiary of Lutheran Brotherhood—received approval from the Office of Thrift Supervision to offer personal trust services. The approval effectively launched LB Personal Trust Services, the bank's trust department, headed by William Kuhlmann. Dec. 31: Total assets under management grew 14.6 percent in 1999 to $26.5 billion, including $5.1 billion in mutual funds and $9.1 billion in variable insurance products (separate accounts). Life insurance in force rose 3.2 percent to $48.8 billion. Fraternal allocations also reached record levels, hitting $76.6 million, up 16.1

percent. LB also reported that it provided more than $1.6 billion in dividends and benefits (such as life insurance claims and surrenders, matured contracts, annuity payments, etc.) to members, up 8.3 percent. Revenue dipped slightly to $2.95 billion, compared to $3.03 billion the previous year. In April 2000 Duff & Phelps Credit Rating Co. reaffirmed the AA+ (its second-highest rating) claims-paying ability of LB and its variable insurance products subsidiary. In May A.M. Best Co. affirmed LB's AA++ (Superior) financial strength, A.M. Best's highest rating. In June LB and CSM Corp., St. Paul, were reportedly in negotiations to jointly purchase the ADC Telecommunications Inc. headquarters in Minnetonka, Minn. (assessed value $17.5 million). LB already owned two single-story building on an adjacent site. Kessler was named chairman-elect in June, and Nicholson became the 5th CEO in Lutheran Brotherhood history. SIC 6311, 6321. No. 3 CRM Cooperatives/Mutuals 20.

Luverne Truck Equipment Inc. 1200 Birch St., Brandon, SD 57005. Tel: 605/582-7200; Fax: 605/582-7434. A. Russell Melgaard, Chm. and CEO; Charles E. Madison, EVP; John Schulzentenberg, Pres.; Dale Kille, VP; Bernie Stoltenberg, Sec. Luverne Truck Equipment designs, manufactures, and markets truck accessories—primarily for the pickup truck aftermarket. 240 employees. Founded in 1963. SIC 3714.

Lydon-Bricher Manufacturing Company 455 Hayward Ave. N, Oakdale, MN 55128. Tel: 651/714-5700; Fax: 651/501-9246. Steven McKay, Pres. Lydon-Bricher Manufacturing makes custom table pads used to protect table tops and similar surfaces. 75 employees (25 in Minnesota). Founded in 1911. SIC 2392.

Lyle Signs Inc. 6294 Bury Dr., Eden Prairie, MN 55346. Tel: 952/934-7653; Fax: 952/934-0406. Buzz Pierce, Pres.; Jeff Edson, VP-Admin.; Jim Boser, VP-Mfg.; Mike Russell, Sls. Mgr. Lyle Signs manufactures traffic-control and street signs. 100 employees (11 in Minnesota). Founded in 1912. SIC 3993.

Lyman Lumber Company 300 Morse Ave., P.O. Box 40, Excelsior, MN 55331. Tel: 952/470-3600; Fax: 952/470-3666. James Hurd, Pres.; John Gilpin, SVP and CFO. Annual revenue $206.5 million. Lyman Lumber distributes materials to building contractors. An affiliate company, Automated Building Components, distributes to large contractors and lumber concerns. A subsidiary, Mid America Cedar, distributes building material to lumber dealers in the Midwest and Southeast. 625 employees. Founded in 1897. SIC 2431, 5211. No. 63 CRM Private 100.

Lyndale Garden Center Inc. 6412 Lyndale Ave. S., Richfield, MN 55423. Tel: 612/861-2221; Fax: 612/866-8540. Chad Ruth, Pres. and CEO. Lyndale Garden Center is a nationally recognized retailer of lawn and garden products. The company owns and operates three lawn and garden superstores in the Twin Cities that offer the area's widest selection of annuals, perennials, fertilizer, trees and shrubs, pottery, patio furniture, and gardening gifts. The company also owns and operates a growing range and a commercial interior plant leasing operation. 500 employees. Founded in 1948. SIC 5261.

MCG Inc. 14700 Martin Dr., Eden Prairie, MN 55344. Tel: 952/975-1680; Fax: 952/975-1682; Web site: http://www.mcg-net.com. Brett D. Reese, CEO; Emil Lonardo, Pres.; Bob Reese, CFO. MCG designs, manufactures, sells, and repairs high-performance servomotors and controls, including: synchros, resolvers, encoders, brakes, and other related components. The acronym "MCG" stands for "Motion Control Group." 140 employees (all in Minnesota). Founded in 1961. SIC 3621.

MJ Electric Inc. P.O. Box 686, Iron Mountain, MI 49801. Tel: 906/774-8000; Fax: 906/779-4217. W.J. Brule, Chm.; D.J. Brule, Pres.; J.O. McCash, Treas. and Sec.; R.W. Biallas, VP; R. Tachich, VP; S. Pontbrind, VP. MJ Electric Inc. is one of the largest electrical contractors in the United States. 542 employees. Founded in 1960. SIC 1731.

MJR Industries Inc. 5600 N. 13th, Menominee, MI 49858. Tel: 906/863-4401; Fax: 906/863-5889; Web site: http://www.nu-vu.com. Jay Jabas, Pres.; John Olson, Sec. and Treas. Annual revenue $10 million. MJR Industries Inc. produces food service equipment, filter systems, liquid handling and reclamation systems, and conveyor systems and industrial parts washing. 80 employees (3 part-time). Founded in 1974. SIC 3499, 3535, 3556, 3569, 3589, 3599, 3714.

MKH Decorative Packaging Inc. 3240 Winpark Dr., Crystal, MN 55427. Tel: 763/593-0001; Fax: 763/593-1361. M.K. Hole, Pres. MKH Decorative Packaging specializes in printing on bottles, jars, and tubes used in the hair-care industry. 65 employees (all in Minnesota). Founded in 1979. SIC 2752.

MPM Inc. 509 S. Wisconsin Ave., Frederic, WI 54837. Tel: 715/327-4276; Fax: 715/327-4280. Gary E. Edling, Gen. Mgr.; L. Kemp, Sec.; B. Wicklund, Customer Svc.; S. Hinrichs, Personnel Mgr. MPM manufactures custom-molded plastic components. 80 employees. Founded in 1932. SIC 3089.

MSI Insurance Companies 2 Pine Tree Dr., P.O. Box 64035 (55164), Arden Hills, MN 55112. Tel: 651/631-7000; Fax: 651/639-5400; Web site: http://www.msi-insurance.com. Gasper Kovach Jr., Chm.; James F. Van Houten, Pres. and CEO; Richard V. Atkinson, VP and Chief Casualty Actuary; Alan Blackwell, VP and Chief Life Actuary; Robert L. Gaecke, VP and Gen. Mgr.-Personal Ins./Risk Mgmt.; Y. John Lee, VP-Commercial Op.; Joseph J. Pingatore, VP, Gen. Counsel, and Sec.; Charles W. Quandt, VP and Gen. Mgr.-Commercial Ins./Risk Mgmt.; Alan T. Reiss, VP-Devel.; Stephen L. Rohde, VP-Fin., CFO, Gen. Mgr.-Pension Solutions Inc.; Mark Schmiel, VP-Pension Sls. (Pension Solutions Inc.); Gil Wenzel, VP-Hum. Res. Annual revenue $483.7 million (earnings $14.7 million). MSI consists of four insurance companies: Mutual Service Casualty Insurance Co., Mutual Service Life Insurance Co., Modern Service Insurance Co., and MSI Insurance Co.; a defined contribution pension plan provider, Pension Solutions Inc.; an agribusiness specialty broker, Cornwall & Stevens Co. Inc.; and its fiscal agent, Mutual Service Cooperative. It offers multiple-line, commercial, and personal-lines insurance; plus pension plan services. The $857 million-asset MSI Cos. is the nation's only group of insurance companies governed as a cooperative. MSI Insurance is licensed in 46 states and the District of Columbia. 591 employees. Founded in 1934. Dec. 31, 1999: The combined companies' 1999 sales revenue of $483.7 million was up 14.5 percent over 1998. On a statutory basis, combined assets (including assets held in trust for Pension Solutions Inc.) increased by 10.8 percent to $1.3

billion. Statutory operating surplus increased by 10.3 percent to $136.5 million. In March 2000 MSI elected Gasper Kovach Jr., the CEO of Highland-Exchange Service Corp., Waverly, Fla., as its board chairman. In June MSI and the Country Cos. insurance group of Bloomington,Ill., finalized a strategic alliance (not a merger) designed to providegeographic diversification and improved financial strength for both organizations. SIC 6411. No. 9 CRM Cooperatives/Mutuals 20.

MSP Communications 220 S. Sixth St., Suite 500, Minneapolis, MN 55402. Tel: 612/339-7571; Fax: 612/339-5806. Burton D. Cohen, CEO and Publsher.; Brian Anderson, VP and Editor; Gary Johnson, VP and COO; Tom E. Benson, Group Publisher. MSP Communications owns and publishes a variety of magazines and other publications, including Mpls.St.Paul Magazine, U.S. Art, ComputerUser, and Twin Cities Business Monthly. In addition, MSP does custom publishing for dozens of organizations, including the Minnesota Twins (Twins magazine), the Sons of Norway (Viking magazine), Twin Cities Public Television (TV2), Dayton Hudson, PYA Monarch, Control Data, and 3M. Owned by Key Investment Inc. (Vance Opperman). 100 employees. Founded in 1978. SIC 2721.

MTI Distributing Company 14900 21st Ave. N., Plymouth, MN 55447. Tel: 763/475-2200; Fax: 763/475-0351. Michael E. Anderson, Pres. and Owner. Annual revenue $45 million. MTI Distributing Co. is a distributor of Toro- and Echo-brand and other allied lines of turf-care products. Branch warehouses: Burnsville and Fridley, Minn.; Fargo, N.D. 104 employees (98 in Minnesota; 6 part-time). Founded in 1968. SIC 5083.

MacArthur Company 2400 Wycliff St., St. Paul, MN 55114. Tel: 651/646-2773; Fax: 651/642-9630. Richard C. Lockwood, Pres.; Clyde A. Rhodes, VP. MacArthur Co. is a distributor of industrial and commercial insulations, specialty products, and roofing materials. 150 employees (46 in Minnesota). Founded in 1913. SIC 5031, 5039.

Machine Tool Supply Inc. 3150 Mike Collins Dr., Eagan, MN 55121. Tel: 651/452-4400; Fax: 651/452-3219. Roy Otto, Chm.; Wayne Lund, SVP; Gary Sukopp, Pres. Machine Tool Supply distributes machine tools. 60 employees. Founded in 1953. SIC 5085.

Mackall, Crounse & Moore PLC 1400 AT&T Tower, 901 Marquette Ave., Minneapolis, MN 55402. Tel: 612/305-1400; Fax: 612/305-1414; Web site: http://www.mcmlaw.com. Shane H. Anderson, Chief Mgr.; Joseph Mule, CEO. Mackall, Crounse & Moore PLC is a full-service, 40-attorney law firm practicing in administrative law; alternative dispute resolution; banking; commercial transactions and creditor rights; construction law; corporate law and securities; employee benefits; estate and business planning; family law; franchise and distribution law; immigration law; international law; intellectual property; labor and employment law; litigation; personal injury; real estate; software protection and computer law; and tax law. 85 employees (all in Minnesota). Founded in 1918. SIC 8111.

Mackay Envelope Corporation 2100 Elm St. S.E., Minneapolis, MN 55414. Tel: 612/331-9311; Fax: 612/331-8229; Web site: http://www.mackay.com. T. Scott Mitchell, Pres. and COO; Douglas Mahoney, CFO. Annual revenue $85 million. Mackay manufactures envelopes for consumer, direct-mail, and photofinishing markets. The company produces 17 million envelopes a day for clients such as U.S. Bank, General Mills, and Fingerhut. 450 employees (261 in Minnesota). Founded in 1959. In September 2000 founder and owner Harvey Mackay sold the company to its president, Scott Mitchell, along with Private Capital Management Inc., Eagan, Minn. There were no plans to close or move Mackay Envelope's Minneapolis operations. SIC 2677.

Madsen-Johnson Corporation 901 Industrial Rd., Hudson, WI 54016. Tel: 715/386-8201; Fax: 715/386-5950. Craig Johnson, CEO; Mark Morse, EVP; Paul Kujak, VP. Annual revenue $13.2 million. Madsen-Johnson Corp. is a general contractor specializing in commercial and industrial construction. 60 employees (all in Minnesota). Founded in 1985. SIC 1541.

Magenic Technologies Inc. 600 S. Highway 169, Suite 701, St. Louis Park, MN 55426. Tel: 952/512-7800; Fax: 952/512-7801; Web site: http://www.magenic.com. Greg Frankenfield, CEO; Paul Fridman, Chief Bus. Devel. Ofcr. Annual revenue $22 million. Magenic Technologies is a technology consulting company specializing in architecture and applications development. Clients include Honeywell, Novartis, and 3M. 200 employees (115 in Minnesota; 2 part-time). Founded in 1995. In August 2000 the company was named one of the Great Places to Work among small to medium-size employers by CityBusiness newspaper. In October, the company was named on the Twin Cities 50 Fastest Growing Private Companies. SIC 7379. No. 13 CityBusiness Fastest-growing Private Companies.

Mail Handling Services Inc. 7550 Corporate Way, Eden Prairie, MN 55344. Tel: 952/975-5000; Fax: 952/975-5080. Wayne G. Cummings, Pres.; Thomas C. Silver, VP; Joel Bahr, Mgr. Mail Handling Services is a letter shop that does printing, data processing, lasering, inkjetting, labeling, inserting, and hand assembly. 262 employees. Founded in 1978. SIC 7331.

Malco Products Inc. 14080 State Highway 55 N.W., P.O. Box 400, Annandale, MN 55302. Tel: 320/274-8246; Fax: 320/274-2269. Paul Hansen, Pres.; Don Schmidt, EVP; Bruce Berhow, VP. Malco Products manufactures hand and edge tools for the heating, air-conditioning, sheet metal, roofing, siding, gutter, and downspout trades. They also manufacture lawn and garden, landscape, and irrigation tools for professionals. 213 employees (172 in Minnesota). Founded in 1950. SIC 3423.

Malt-O-Meal Company 2600 IDS Center, 80 S. Eighth St., Minneapolis, MN 55402. Tel: 612/338-8551; Fax: 612/339-5710. John W. Lettmann, Pres. and CEO; John Stull, VP-Mfg.; Gordon Robertson, Cont.; Diane Dietz, VP-Logistics; Tom Tebbenkamp, VP-Op. Annual revenue $360 million (estimated by Fact Book). Malt-O-Meal produces and markets Malt-O-Meal label and private-label hot and ready-to-eat breakfast cereals. The company is the nation's leading producer of cereals sold in plastic bags. Familiar brands include Toasty O's, Corn Bursts, Colossal Crunch, Tootie Fruities, Golden Puffs, and Frosted Mini-Spooners. 950 employees. Founded in 1919. SIC 2043. No. 31 CRM Private 100.

Mamac Systems Inc. 7400 Flying Cloud Dr., Eden Prairie, MN 55344. Tel: 952/835-1626; Fax: 952/829-5331; Web site: http://www.mamac-sys.com. S. Asim Gul, Pres. and CEO; Renee Paul, Dir.-Bus./Fin.; Helmut Schildknecht, Dir.-Global Sls./Mktg. Annual revenue $15 million. Mamac Systems Inc. manufactures sensors, transducers, and control peripherals for industrial/commercial automation systems, HVAC, and energy management. The company operates wholly owned subsidiaries Mamac Systems Pty. Ltd., Australia; Mamac Systems U.K. Ltd., United Kingdom; Mamac Systems Canada Ltd., Markham (Toronto), Canada; and Mamac Systems Asia Pte. Ltd., Singapore. 100 employees (79 in Minnesota). Founded in 1981. SIC 3822, 3823.

Management Resource Solutions Inc. 7600 Wayzata Blvd., Suite 100, Golden Valley, MN 55426. Tel: 763/253-6500; Fax: 763/253-6565. Robert Arvold, Pres. Management Resource Solutions (MRS), formerly Beckwith Inc., does xerographic copying/duplicating. It operates copy centers and on-site facilities-management programs for legal, health care, and corporate organizations. Its 18 centers are located primarily in the Twin Cities. 70 employees. Founded in 1984. SIC 7334.

Maple Island Inc. 2497 Seventh Ave. E., Suite 105, North St. Paul, MN 55109. Tel: 651/773-1000; Fax: 651/773-2155. Daniel W. O'Brien, Chm.; Greg Johnson, Pres. and CEO; R.D. Zirbel, VP. Maple Island manufactures and packages dried dairy-based products. It has production facilities in Wanamingo, Minn.; and Medford, Wis. Affiliated with F.H. Stoltze Land & Lumber. 110 employees (40 in Minnesota). Founded in 1935. SIC 2023, 2024.

Maracom Corporation 508 Industrial Dr. S.W., P.O. Box 737, Willmar, MN 56201. Tel: 320/235-3300; Fax: 320/235-2233; Web site: http://www.maracom.com. Evert Peterson, Chm.; Gary Peterson, Pres.; Dalen Caspers, VP-Sls.; Michael Gustafson, Office Mgr. Maracom Corp. is in the commercial printing business, specializing in color card products. 75 employees. Founded in 1951. SIC 2759.

Mark VII Distributors Inc. 475 N. Prior Ave., St. Paul, MN 55104. Tel: 651/646-6063; Fax: 651/646-6036. W. Rockwell Wirtz, Pres.; Kevin P. Ryan, VP and Gen. Mgr.; Phyllis Otis, Cont. Mark VII Distributors is a beer distributor. 125 employees. Founded in 1984. SIC 5181.

Market & Johnson Inc. P.O. Box 630, Eau Claire, WI 54702. Tel: 715/834-1213; Fax: 715/834-2331. Marvin Market, Pres.; Dan Market, VP; Steve Breitenfeldt, Treas. and Sec. Market & Johnson is in the nonresidential construction business. 380 employees (40 in Minnesota; 100 part-time). Founded in 1948. SIC 1542.

Marquette Financial Companies 3900 Dain Rauscher Plaza, 60 S. Sixth St., Minneapolis, MN 55402. Tel: 612/888-8100; Fax: 612/948-5890. Carl R. Pohlad, Pres.; James O. Pohlad, EVP; Thomas A. Herbst, EVP; Albert J. Colianni Jr., EVP and COO; Jann Ozzello Wilcox, CFO; Jeffrey Arnold, SVP, Comm'l Banking Mgr.-Marquette Capital Bank N.A.; Doug Hile, Pres.-Marquette Bank N.A.; Lisa Meyer, SVP-Mktg./Admin.; Randy Mueller, Pres.-marquette.com; Margaret S. Murphy, COO-marquette.com; Edward Padilla, Pres./CEO-Northland Marquette Capital Group; Jerry Schwallier, Pres.-Private Financial Services Group; Duane E. White, SVP and Dir.-Specialty Finance Group. Marquette Financial Cos. is one of the nation's largest privately owned financial services organizations. It consists of banks and non-bank companies, in 16 states, with more than $5.5 billion in assets. Its four business lines include Super Community Banking (120-plus offices), Marquette Capital banking (private and middle-market capital banking), marquette.com (e-commercee financial services), and diversified businesses (non-bank). It takes pride in an entrepreneurial approach and a commitment to technological innovation. 1,722 employees (1,184 in Minnesota; 431 part-time). Founded in 1992. In a December 1999 move that reflected its strategic importance to the company, Marquette upped its investment and dedicated a senior management team to head up its e-commerce strategies. In September 2000 the company formed Marquette Private Financial Services Group, headed up by banking industry veteran Jerry Schwallier, to focus on the unique financial needs of privately owned businesses and their executives and professionals. SIC 6712. No. 61 CRM Private 100.

W.P. & R.S. Mars Company 4319 W. First St., Duluth, MN 55807. Tel: 218/628-0303; Fax: 218/628-3594. Robert S. Mars Jr., Chm. and CEO; Robert S. Mars III, Pres.; B.G. Mars, VP; R.E. Palmer, VP. Annual revenue $21.3 million. W.P. & R.S. Mars Co. is an equipment distributor, specializing in industrial supplies and machinery. Its subsidiary—Conveyor Belt Service Inc. located in Virginia, Minn.—repairs, rebuilds, and installs conveyor belting. 92 employees (91 in Minnesota; 1 part-time). Founded in 1923. In April 2000 the company donated $10,000 to assist in the efforts Manufacturing Technology of Minnesota and the Minnesota Precision Manufacturing Association to make people aware of the quality careers available in the industry. In May Mars was one of 16 manufacturers and distributors to win an American Eagle Award for company programs that promote the principles of the American free-enterprise system. SIC 5084.

Marsden Bldg Maintenance Co. 1717 University Ave. W., St. Paul, MN 55104. Tel: 651/641-1717; Fax: 651/641-0523; Web site: http://www.marsden.com. Adrian (Skip) Marsden, Owner, Chm., and CEO; Dan McCarthy, CFO-Marsden, American; Guy Mingo, Pres./COO-Marsden Co. Marsden provides cleaning, engineering services, and other building-maintenance activities. 4,000 employees (3,000 in Minnesota; 1,000 part-time). Founded in 1952. SIC 7349. No. 53 CRM Employer 100.

Marvin Lumber & Cedar Company Highway 11, P.O. Box 100, Warroad, MN 56763. Tel: 218/386-1430; Fax: 218/386-2925. William S. Marvin, Chm.; Frank R. Marvin, VChm.-Corp. Centers; John W. (Jake) Marvin, CEO; Susan I. Marvin, Pres.; Elliot Larson, CFO; Dean Ekman, VP-Planning; Judy Lendin, VP-Admin.; George G. Marvin, Group VP; Robert Marvin, VP-Transportation; Duff Marshall, VP-Sls.; Rick Trontret, Dir.-Hum. Res. Annual revenue $450 million. Marvin Lumber & Cedar manufactures wood and clad wood window and patio door units. Operating units include Marvin Windows, Warroad; Marvin Doors, Ripley, Tenn.; and Integrity Windows, Fargo, N.D. 4,500 employees (2,900 in Minnesota). Founded in 1904. In 1999 the company resumed its long tradition of paying annual profit-sharing bonuses after missing one year. Employees shared $6.9 million, an average of $2,200 each. Marvin's new line of Ultimate-brand double-hung windows—which are tighter, more energy-efficient, and easier to maintain—was a major contributor to record annual revenue of $400 million. (There were even plans to add a second production line a couple of years ahead of schedule.) In August 2000 the U.S. Court of Appeals for the Eighth Circuit reversed a key claim in a 1999 U.S. District Court ruling, allowing Marvin to pursue a jury trial in its suit against PPG Industries for breach of warranty. (In a six and a half-year-old suit, Marvin claimed that, because PPG's wood preservative had not performed as promised, some of Marvin's windows and doors manufactured during the late 1980s had begun to rot prematurely.) Most of Marvin's claims for breach of contract, breach of warranty, and fraud were barred by the four-year statute of limitations, but one of the 13 counts, a warranty issue, was allowed to proceed. In October a Pennsylvania couple sued the company in Hennepin County District Court—seeking class-action status—to recover replacement costs for their defective windows. (In 1999 Marvin had stopped paying full replacement cost, instead offering a discount on new windows.) SIC 2431. No. 27 CRM Private 100. No. 76 CRM Employer 100.

Mary T Inc. 1555 118th Ln. N.W., Coon Rapids, MN 55448. Tel: 763/754-2505; Fax: 763/754-0332; Web site: http://www.martytinc.com. Mary M. Tjosvold, CEO; Ardis Anderberg, Dir.-HHA; Sarah Deeny, Dir.-Program Svs.; Suganda Kamalapuri, CFO; Ed Miller, Dir.-Hum. Res.; Margaret Tjosvold, Sec. and Treas. Annual revenue $20 million. The Mary T Inc. organization provides customized services and living options for seniors and people with specialized needs. 760 employees (all in Minnesota; 265 part-time). Founded in 1976. SIC 8361.

Maslon Edelman Borman & Brand 3300 Wells Fargo Center, 90 S. Seventh St., Minneapolis, MN 55402. Tel: 612/672-8200; Fax: 612/672-8397; Web site: http://www.maslon.com. Howard Tarkow, Chm. and Governance Committee; Gary Haugen, Governance Ctee.; Clark Whitmore, Governance Ctee.; Sandy Callen, Dir.-Hum. Res./Office Admin.; Kelly Griffith, Dir.-Mktg.; Sarah Taylor, Dir.-Fin. Maslon Edelman Borman & Brand represents businesses and individuals worldwide in the areas of commercial law, litigation, and government relations. Areas of specialty include mergers and acquisitions, securities, real estate, tax law, employment and labor law, intellectual property law, financial services law, construction law, insurance law, estate planning and probate, gaming, nonprofits, professional and products liability, and family law. As a member of Commercial Law Affiliates, it is one of 200 medium-sized business law firms worldwide committed to quality,

PVT

cost-effective representation. 150 employees (all in Minnesota). Founded in 1956. SIC 8111.

Master Mark Plastic Products/Avon Plastics Inc. P.O. Box 662, Albany, MN 56307. Tel: 320/845-2111; Fax: 320/845-7093; Web site: http://www.mastermark.com. Donald J. Reum Sr., Dir.; Mark T. Reum, CEO; Nick Demuth, Pres.; Tom Weber, VP; Brenda Tschida, Treas. and Sec.; Donald J. Reum Jr., VP. Master Mark Plastics is a custom plastics-extrusion manufacturer. 110 employees. Founded in 1967. SIC 3089.

Mastercraft Industries 120 W. Allen St., Rice Lake, WI 54868. Tel: 715/234-8111; Fax: 715/234-6370. D.W. Ringwelski, Pres.; E.V. Johnston, Chm. and VP; M. Lauerman, VP. Annual revenue $22 million. Mastercraft Industries is a manufacturer of custom kitchen cabinets, custom and stock interior shutters and doors, and drawers for the cabinet-front replacement market. 310 employees. Founded in 1946. SIC 2431, 2434, 2511.

PVT

Mate Precision Tooling 1295 Lund Blvd., Anoka, MN 55303. Tel: 763/421-0230; Fax: 763/421-0285. Dean A. Sundquist, Chm. and CEO; Jack Schneider, Pres. Mate Precision Tooling designs and manufactures precision computer numerical-controlled punch-press tooling systems, which are used to crimp, flute, ripple, mark, and punch holes into sheet metal. Industries served by Mate's 50,000 products include electronics, telecommunications, vending equipment, and heating and air-conditioning. Besides the Anoka plant, which operates on a 24-7 basis, Mate does some manufacturing at smaller plants in Germany, England, Sweden, Malaysia, and Argentina. 500 employees. Founded in 1962. In June 2000 the company opened a 300,000-square-foot facility in Anoka housing headquarters, design, manufacturing, and distribution operations (its sixth major expansion). "We hope to be able to double our output in this building," said CEO Sundquist. By October, output per employee had already increased by one-third. SIC 3544.

Mathiowetz Construction Company 30676 County Rd. 24, Sleepy Eye, MN 56085. Tel: 507/794-6953; Fax: 507/794-3514. Brian J. Mathiowetz, Pres.; Julie Anderson, VP-Admin.; David W. Domm, VP; Robert Sharp, VP-Eqt. Maintenance; Ronda Mathiowetz, Sec. and Treas. Annual revenue $12 million. Mathiowetz Construction Co. does highway/heavy contractor, private grading, site work, and soil conservation work. 160 employees (all in Minnesota). Founded in 1924. SIC 1629.

Matrix Communications Inc. 171 Cheshire Ln., Suite 700, Plymouth, MN 55441. Tel: 763/475-5500; Fax: 763/475-5599; Web site: http://www.matrixcomm.com. Matrix Communications sells and installs NEC, Lucent Technologies, Active Voice and Centigram. The company is also a strategic agent for U S West, does voice and data cabling, TSON networking, wireless service and call centers. 96 employees. Founded in 1985. SIC 5065.

Mat's Inc. 940 Aldrin Dr., Eagan, MN 55121. Tel: 651/406-8300. John Dawson, CEO; Don Kloster, VP. Mat's Inc. offers trucking services without storage, within a five-state area. 65 employees. Founded in 1975. SIC 4212.

Mattox Enterprises 4900 Highway 52 N., Rochester, MN 55901. Tel: 507/288-7564; Fax: 507/252-2532. Gary Mattox, Owner; Greg Groves, Gen. Mgr. Mattox Enterprises owns and operates three stores: Universal Ford Toyota, Rochester (new and used cars); Universal Power, Marine and RV, Rochester (lawn and garden equipment, watercraft, and RVs); and Universal Chevrolet Geo, Winona (new and used cars). 200 employees (all in Minnesota; 10 part-time). Founded in 1975. SIC 5261, 5511, 5551, 5561.

Maun & Simon PLC 2000 Midwest Plaza Blvd. W., 801 Nicollet Mall, Minneapolis, MN 55402. Tel: 612/904-7400; Fax: 612/907-7424; Web site: http://info@maunlaw.com. Barry A. Gersick, Managing Ptnr.; David A. Aune, COO. Maun & Simon PLC provides legal services in the areas of real estate, corporate and business organizations, litigation, estate planning, probate, banking, taxation, bankruptcy, securities, employment, and environmental and utility regulations. 62 employees (all in Minnesota; 5 part-time). Founded in 1961. SIC 8111.

Mavo Systems 4300 Main St. N.E., Fridley, MN 55421. Tel: 763/788-7713; Fax: 763/788-9560; Web site: http://www.mavo.com. Cynthia Meuwissen, Pres.; Larry Reese, VP; Dana Krakeski, Dir.-Sls./Mktg.; Jay Robertson, Const. Mgr.; Dana Sawrey, Op. Mgr.; Chuck Tatton, Proj. Mgr./Estimator. Mavo Systems is a full service Specialty Contractor specializing in Asbestos, Lead, Microbial Abatement, HVAC/Duct Cleaning and Decontamination, Interior Demolition, Mechanical Insulation and Firestopping for Commercial, Industrial and Institutional Buildings. 100 employees (all in Minnesota). Founded in 1982. SIC 8711.

Wally McCarthy's 1900 W. 78th St., Richfield, MN 55423. Tel: 612/869-1414; Fax: 612/869-7962. Wally McCarthy, Owner and CEO; Jason W. McCarthy, Pres.-McCarthy's Oldsmobile-GMC Trucks Inc. Annual revenue $157 million. Wally McCarthy's is an automobile dealer. Its dealerships include Wally McCarthy's Cadillac Inc. and McCarthy's Oldsmobile-GMC Inc. 281 employees. Founded in 1949. In August 2000 McCarthy decided to sell his Wally McCarthy's Oldsmobile Inc. dealership in Richfield, Minn., to Key Cadillac, Edina, Minn., after agreeing to sell the Richfield land to Best Buy for the new corporate headquarters it was building in the area. McCarthy was looking to buy another dealership in town for his 100 displaced employees. Otherwise, they would be offered jobs at either Key Cadillac or one of McCarthy's remaining dealerships. SIC 5511. No. 76 CRM Private 100.

McCombs Frank Roos Associates 15050 23rd Ave. N., Plymouth, MN 55447. Tel: 763/476-6010; Fax: 763/476-8532; Web site: http://www.mfra.com. McCombs Frank Roos is an environmental services company. 65 employees (60 in Minnesota; 5 part-time). Founded in 1965. SIC 8711.

C.S. McCrossan Inc. 7865 Jefferson Hwy., Maple Grove, MN 55311. Tel: 763/425-4167; Fax: 763/425-1255. Charles S. McCrossan, Pres. C.S. McCrossan is a highway, tunnel, and heavy road construction company. The I-394/Highway 100 interchange in Golden Valley, Minn., was one of its projects. 550 employees. Founded in 1956. SIC 1611, 1622.

McDowall Company 2720 S. 1 1/2 St., P.O. Box 1244, St. Cloud, MN 56302. Tel: 320/251-8640; Fax: 320/251-9317. John McDowall, Pres. and CEO; Lawrence McDowall, Treas.; Peter McDowall, Sec. Annual revenue $12 million. McDowall is a commercial heating, air-conditioning, ventilating, energy management, and roofing and architectural sheet metal contractor. Founded in Illinois, McDowall has been in St. Cloud since 1948. 94 employees (all in Minnesota). Founded in 1895. SIC 1711, 1761, 7623.

McGlynn Bakeries Inc. 7350 Commerce Ln., Fridley, MN 55432. Tel: 763/574-2222; Fax: 763/574-2210; Web site: http://www.mcglynn.com. Burton J. McGlynn, Chm.; Michael J. McGlynn, CEO; John R. Prichard, COO; Daniel J. McGlynn, CEO-Bakery Div.; Robert Kulpinski, Pres.-Bakery Div.; Mike Cannon, VP-Bakery Div.; Doug Hale, VP-Bakery Div.; Tammy Kampsula, VP-Bakery Div.; Christine McKenna, Pres.-DecoPac Div.; Jane Alston, VP-DecoPac Div.; John Anderson, VP-DecoPac Div. McGlynn Bakeries owns and operates retail bakeries in major department stores, discount stores, grocery stores, and shopping centers in Minnesota and Wisconsin. The company distributes bakery products wholesale to grocery stores, convenience stores, department stores and commercial bakeries in the Twin Cities. The company also wholesales cake-decorating supplies internationally through its DecoPac division and wholesales frozen bakery products nationally through its Concept 2 Baker's (C2B) division. 1,000 employees. Founded in 1919. SIC 2051. No. 96 CRM Private 100.

McGough Companies 2737 N. Fairview Ave., Roseville, MN 55113. Tel: 651/633-5050; Fax: 651/633-5673; Web site: http://www.mcgough.com. Lawrence J. McGough, Chm.; Thomas J. McGough, Pres. and CEO; Thomas J. McGough Jr., COO. Annual revenue $258 million. McGough Cos. offer strategic facility planning, turnkey development, construction and facilities management services. 850 employees (6 in Minnesota). Founded in 1956. SIC 1541. No. 44 CRM Private 100. No. 31 CityBusiness Fastest-growing Private Companies.

McKie Ford Inc. P.O. Box 740, Rapid City, SD 57709. Tel: 605/348-1400; Fax: 605/348-5906. R. McKie, Pres. McKie Ford is a motor vehicle dealer. 100 employees. Founded in 1979. SIC 5511.

McLaughlin Gormley King Company 8810 10th Ave. N., Golden Valley, MN 55427. Tel: 763/544-0341; Fax: 763/544-6437. W.D. Gullickson Jr., Pres.; Thomas Major, Treas.; Daniel Untiedt, Mktg. Dir.; Brad Ward, Purch. Mgr.; Fred Preiss, Dir.-Corp. Res.; Christopher Riley, Gen. Counsel and Sec. McLaughlin Gormley King Co. manufactures natural and synthetic pyrethroid (halogenated and non-halogenated) insecticides and insect repellents; insect-growth regulators; and dog, cat, and deer repellents. A subsidiary, Insect Control & Research, is located in Baltimore. Sumitomo Chemical Co. and Sumitomo Corp. of Japan hold a combined 32.9 percent stake. 60 employees. Founded in 1902. SIC 2879.

McNally Industries Inc. Broadway and Pine Street, P.O. Box 129, Grantsburg, WI 54840. Tel: 715/463-5311; Fax: 715/463-5261; Albert Scheideler, Chm. and Pres.; D. Erickson, VP; Paul Lombardi, VP; Lori Lien, Mgr.-Acctg./Admin. McNally Industries produces precision mechanical systems and components for aerospace, military, and industrial applications; and the Northern line of specialty gear pumps. 90 employees (10 in Minnesota). Founded in 1939. SIC 3499, 3599.

Meadowland Farmers Co-op 101 First Ave. E., Lamberton, MN 56152. Tel: 507/752-7352; Fax: 507/752-7106. John Valentin, Gen. Mgr. Annual revenue $107 million. Meadowland Farmers Co-op provides full-service grain handling, plus agronomy, petroleum, lumber, hardware, and feed supplies. 90 employees. Founded in 1905. SIC 2048, 5153, 5172. No. 18 CRM Cooperatives/Mutuals 20.

Meagher & Geer PLLP 4200 Multifoods Tower, 33 S. Sixth St., Minneapolis, MN 55402. Tel: 612/338-0661; Fax: 612/338-8384. Steven C. Eggimann, Managing Ptnr.; D.J. Steinhauser, Dir.-Admin. Meagher & Geer's practice encompasses all aspects of insurance law, civil and commercial litigation, and business and commercial law and appellate. 175 employees. Founded in 1929. SIC 8111.

Mebco Industries Inc. 6031 Culligan Way, Minnetonka, MN 55345. Tel: 952/930-1970; Fax: 952/930-1971. Wendy Ostlund, Pres. and CEO; John Tomlinson, Cont.; Mike Lalim, Int'l Sls. Mgr. Mebco Industries is a manufacturer and international distributor of hairbrushes and combs. 50 employees (all in Minnesota). Founded in 1985. SIC 3089.

Meca Sportswear Inc. 1752 Terrace Dr., Roseville, MN 55113. Tel: 651/638-3800; Fax: 651/638-3899. T.A. Bramwell, Pres.; R.J. Schuster, VP-Fin./Admin., Treas., and Sec.; T.D. Bramwell, VP-Op; D.A. Bramwell, VP-Sls.; D. York, VP-Sls. Incentives/Promotions. Annual revenue $13.5 million. Meca Sportswear manufactures athletic- and academic-award jackets, emblems, banners, screening, and industrial clothing. The company is also involved in business promotions and sales incentives. 180 employees (40 in Minnesota). Founded in 1968. SIC 2399.

Medical Arts Press Inc. 8500 Wyoming Ave. N., Brooklyn Park, MN 55445. Tel: 763/493-7300; Fax: 763/493-7305; Web site: http://www.medicalartspress.com. Steven Wexler, CEO; Edward C. Winthrop, Pres.; Terri Abraham, Gen Mgr.-Hayes Mktg.; Joseph Everhart, Gen. Mgr.-Smile Makers Inc.; James Hoffman, VP-Sls./Mktg.; Michael T. Kasner, CFO; Steven Spark, VP-Op. Annual revenue $138 million. Medical Arts Press and its wholly owned subsidiaries direct-market and manufacture customized and standardized business forms and office- and practice-related supplies to health care professionals and businesses. Products include business forms, labels, filing supplies, marketing ideas, stationery products, books, furniture, apparel, software, and clinical supplies. The company markets its products through catalogs, telemarketing, and the Internet for specific segments of the health care industry—including physicians, dentists, chiropractors, podiatrists, and eyecare professionals. The company conducts operations from multi-use facilities in three locations in the United States and one in Canada. Products are sold primarily in North America. 625 employees (525 in Minnesota; 60 part-time). Founded in 1929. In December 1999 investment firm Freeman Spogli & Co., Los Angeles, agreed to pay $277 million for a 70 percent interest in the company. Management retained the remaining 30 percent. SIC 5961. No. 94 CRM Private 100.

Medical Concepts Development Inc. 2500 Ventura Dr., Woodbury, MN 55125. Tel: 651/735-0498; Fax: 651/735-7197. Lee Annett, Pres.; Dave Padget, VP; Mark St. Michael, Op. Dir.-Fin.; Stephen W. Hannes, Op. Dir.-Sls./Mktg. Medical Concepts Development manufactures ISO 9001- and EN 46001-certified disposable surgical drape products, custom adhesive coating, and other custom components for the hospital and OEM market. Its worldwide sales reach 32 countries. 85 employees (15 part-time). Founded in 1984. SIC 3842.

MedSource Technologies Inc. 110 Cheshire Ln., Suite 100, Minnetonka, MN 55305. Tel: 952/807-1234; Fax: 952/807-1235; Web site: http://www.medsourcetech.com. Richard Effress, Chm. and CEO; Fred Burditt, CFO; Jim Drill, VP-Sls./Mktg. Annual revenue $100 million. MedSource Technologies is the world's largest and best-resourced supplier of precision components and finished devices to medical device and equipment manufacturers. MedSource serves customers locally and around the world, providing complete and cost-effective chain management solutions. Each of the MedSource companies, known as Centers of Excellence, contributes a different core competency and manufacturing capability. As a single integrated company, MedSource offers customers a comprehensive scope of services: collaborative product development, functional design and analysis, complete project management, precision machining, precision metal stamping and wire forming, precision metal injection manufacturing, high-precision plastic injection molding and mold-making, grinding and coiling, laser processing, and assembly, including cleanroom manufacturing, packaging, and sterilization. Since its inception, the company has bought 10 component suppliers, including Kelco Industries, Brooklyn Park, Minn, which does precision machining of microcomponents used in devices such as pacemakers. 1,000 employees. Founded in 1998. By the end of October 2000, when MedSource completed a $40 million private placement of equity, it had raised $140 million in its continuing march toward an initial public offering. The largest current stockholder: Kidd & Co., a Greenwich, Conn., investment firm. SIC 3672, 8711.

Menard Inc. 4777 Menard Dr., Eau Claire, WI 54703. Tel: 715/876-5911; Fax: 715/876-5901. John Menard, Pres. Menard operates a chain of retail home centers. The company has a total of 146 stores in the Upper

Midwest, including 15 stores in Minnesota. 5,000 employees. Founded in 1960. SIC 5211.

Denny Menholt Frontier Chevrolet 1617 First Ave. N., Billings, MT 59101. Tel: 406/259-5575; Fax: 406/259-4531. Dennis Menholt, Pres.; Don G. Knudson, VP. Denny Menholt Frontier Chevrolet is a motor vehicle dealer. 190 employees (10 part-time). Founded in 1930. SIC 5511.

Merchandising Inc. 2701 Fourth Ave. S.W., Willmar, MN 56201. Tel: 320/235-2454; Fax: 320/235-1361. Michael M. Stulberg, Chm. and CEO; John Somody, VP and Sec.; Sandra Somody, VP; Margie Haust, CFO; Donna Gertgen, Treas. Merchandising Inc. is a wholesaler of health and beauty supplies and general merchandise in an eight-state area. 225 employees. Founded in 1946. SIC 5122.

PVT

Merchant & Gould P.C. 3200 IDS Center, 80 S. Eighth St., Minneapolis, MN 55402. Tel: 612/332-5300; Fax: 612/332-9081; Web site: http://www.merchant-gould.com. D. Randall King, Chm., CEO, and Managing Dir.; Jeffrey Sjobeck, COO and CFO; Mark J. DiPietro, Sec. Merchant & Gould (M&G, formerly known as Merchant, Gould, Smith, Edell, Welter & Schmidt) is a law firm practicing intellectual property law, including patent, trademark, copyright, unfair competition, trade secret, Internet and computer law, and litigation. Other offices: Denver, Seattle, Atlanta. 320 employees (271 in Minnesota; 25 part-time). Founded in 1900. M&G celebrated its 100-year anniversary in 2000. The firm opened its Seattle office in February and an Atlanta office in June. In May it signed a four-story (94,000 square feet) lease at the IDS center, filling space that American Express Financial Advisors was vacating to move to a new corporate headquarters. In October Managing Intellectual Property, a London-based trade magazine, reported that M&G had moved to No. 1 in the central United States in both patent litigation and prosecution. (It was No. 2 and No. 1, respectively, in 1999.) SIC 8111.

Mereen-Johnson Machine Company Inc. 4401 Lyndale Ave. N., Minneapolis, MN 55412. Tel: 612/529-7791; Fax: 612/529-0120. Charles R. Johnson, Chm.; Russell D. McBroom, Pres., CEO, and CFO; Max Green, VP-Engrg.; Marvin West, VP-Sls. Mereen-Johnson produces industrial woodworking machines, materials-handling equipment, and gray iron castings. 185 employees (100 in Minnesota). Founded in 1905. SIC 3321, 3553.

Merit Chevrolet Inc. 2695 Brookview Dr., I-94 and Century Ave., St. Paul, MN 55119. Tel: 651/739-4400; Fax: 651/702-9230. Bruce Rinkel, CEO. Merit Chevrolet sells Chevrolet new and used cars and trucks and Chevrolet commercial vehicles. It also provides service, parts, body repair (night service available), and complete leasing services. 96 employees. Founded in 1949. SIC 5511, 7513, 7515, 7539.

Meritcare Medical Center 737 Broadway, Fargo, ND 58123. Tel: 701/234-2000; Fax: 701/234-2345. Gregory J. Post, M.D., Pres. Meritcare Medical Center is a group medical practice. 3,548 employees. Founded in 1919. SIC 8011.

Merrill Corporation One Merrill Circle, Energy Park, St. Paul, MN 55108. Tel: 651/646-4501; Fax: 651/649-1348; Web site: http://www.merrillcorp.com. Paul G. Miller, Chm.; John W. Castro, Pres. and CEO; Rick R. Atterbury, EVP and Chief Tech. Ofcr.; Kathleen A. Larkin, VP-Hum. Res.; Steven J. Machov, VP, Gen. Counsel, and Sec.; Robert Nazarian, CFO; B. Michael James, Pres.-Financial Document Svs.; Joseph P. Pettirossi, Pres.-Managed Communications Program; Raymond J. Goodwin, Pres.-Merrill Print Group; Mark A. Rossi, Pres.-Investment Company Svs.; Allen J. McNee, Pres.-Document Management Svs. Annual revenue $587.7 million (loss $17.6 million; includes $42.6 million of merger costs). Merrill Corp. is a diversified document- and information-management company that provides financial, legal, corporate, and investment-company clients worldwide with an expanding and innovative range of document services, both paper and electronic. Services include on-demand, 24-hour-per-day typesetting, printing, document reproduction, distribution, and fulfillment. In June 1999 Merrill, then a publicly traded company, agreed to be taken private in a transaction valued at $520 million. 3,797 employees. Founded in 1968. Oct. 31, 1999: Revenue for the nine months was a record at $442.4 million, an increase of 12.9 percent. Net income decreased 21.1 percent, to $18.3 million, due to increased selling, general, and administration expenses of $6.6 million and merger costs of $1.2 million. On Nov. 23, Merrill completed its going-private transaction. Approved by Merrill's shareholders that morning, the transaction was accomplished through a merger of Viking Merger Sub Inc., an affiliate of DLJ Merchant Banking Partners II L.P., with and into Merrill, with Merrill as the surviving corporation. Said CEO Castro, "This enables us to continue our focus on innovative products and services that enable our clients to better communicate with their clients." In December the company announced a joint marketing venture between Merrill IR Edge, a strategic initiative of Merrill's Financial Document Services business unit, and StreetFusion, the network for financial events. The venture combined the Merrill Web Edge product, a customized Web page authoring and information management tool, with Street Fusion's investor relations event planning, management, and Webcasting services. In January 2000 Merrill announced a new business-to-business Web site, http://www.MerrillDirect.com, whose secure self-serve modules were to serve as an Internet-based service for the development and preparation of financial documents by corporations, law firms, investment banks, and accounting firms. Merrill opened new client service centres in the heart of the financial districts of both London and Paris. Merrill announced a new technology-based, litigation support service alliance between its Document Management Services business and INTEGREX, a service-based subsidiary of Owens Corning. In February Merrill announced a new Web-based, litigation support system and litigation repository service, UR-Law. In March Merrill signed a joint marketing agreement with StreetFusion—a financial information network linking more than 5,000 public companies, nearly 1,500 of the nation's leading buyside and sellside firms, and millions of individual investors—to combine Merrill IR Edge's WebEdge, an integrated suite of services for investor relations communications, with StreetFusion's event planning, event management, and event Webcasting services to create StreetFusion WebEdge. In April Investment Company Services subsidiary Merrill Communications LLC purchased substantially all the assets of the financial services and training documentation business of Ames On-Demand, Somerville, Mass.—a full-service digital print and fulfillment operation. In May Merrill acquired substantially all of the assets of NTEXT Corp. (www.ntext.com), a legal and financial translation company, for Merrill's Financial Document Services business. "This acquisition is a great fit for Merrill," said CEO Castro. "Many of our existing clients currently use document-translation services. By adding this capability to our portfolio we strengthen Merrill's ability to fully meet our customers' needs." A strategic alliance between Document Management Services and RESoft Inc., a Minneapolis-based real estate technology company, was to deliver expanded scanning services for commercial real estate owners and operators. In July Merrill held its second initial public offering (IPO) seminar, in Dallas. The seminars are aimed at CEOs and CFOs of emerging companies who are expecting to take their companies public within 24 months. July 31: Revenue for the six months was $350.9 million, an increase of 18 percent from the first half of last year. EBITDA, exclusive of merger costs and start-up and transition costs related to European operations, increased 9 percent to $42.8 million. In August Merrill's Financial Document Services (FDS) business opened an office in Frankfurt. In November Document Management Services launched the Merrill Electronic Discovery Group, created through an alliance with Computer Forensics Inc., the leading consulting and forensic analysis service for electronic data in the United States. SIC 2759. No. 15 CRM Private 100.

Merrill Distributing Inc. 1301 Memorial Dr., Merrill, WI 54452. Tel: 715/536-4551; Fax: 715/536-5757. Ralph A. Schewe, Chm., VP, and Sec.; John T. Schewe, Pres. and Treas. Merrill Distributing Inc. is a wholesale distributor of candies, confections, chips and snacks, fountain supplies, cigars, cigarettes, tobaccos, retail groceries, paper, and food (dry, refrigerated, and frozen); as well as bar, restaurant, and janitorial supplies. 70 employees. Founded in 1912. SIC 5145.

Merrill Manufacturing Corporation 236 S. Genesee St., P.O. Box 566, Merrill, WI 54452. Tel: 715/536-5533; Fax: 715/536-5590; Web site: http://www.merrill-mfg.com. Richard L. Taylor, Pres., CEO, and Treas.; James A. Stiles, VP-Sls./Mktg.; Patrick Taylor, Dir.-Mfg.; Richard L. Taylor Jr., Dir.-Mktg. Merrill Manufacturing makes custom wire products (wireforms, welded wire assemblies) and metal stampings. 150 employees. Founded in 1916. SIC 3496.

Messerli & Kramer P.A. 1800 Fifth Street Towers, 150 S. Fifth St., Minneapolis, MN 55402. Tel: 612/672-3600; Fax: 612/672-3777; Web site: http://www.messerlikramer.com. Jerome J. Simons Jr., Pres. Messerli & Kramer is a law firm with offices in Minneapolis, St. Paul, and Plymouth, Minn. The firm serves the business community in a variety of ways. Its practice consists of eight departments that serve the needs of small to midsize businesses (General Business and Banking, Business Litigation, Corporate Finance and Securities, Credit and Collections, Employment and Labor, Government Relations, Real Property Services, Business Succession Planning); and two departments that provide services for individuals (Estate Planning and Probate, Family Law). 140 employees. Founded in 1965. SIC 8111.

Metacom Inc. 7303 Boone Ave. N., Brooklyn Park, MN 55428. Tel: 763/391-0300; Fax: 763/391-0474. Phillip T. Levin, CEO; Robert Ezrilov, Pres.; DeeDee Drays, EVP and Gen. Counsel; Jere Clune, VP-Sls.; Kathy Brown Zerwas, VP-Op.; Chuck Martin, CFO. Metacom markets and distributes audio products. 75 employees (all in Minnesota). Founded in 1970. SIC 3652.

Metafile Information Systems Inc. 2900 43rd St. N.W., Rochester, MN 55901. Tel: 507/286-9232; Fax: 507/286-9065. Allan C. Sprau, Pres. and CEO. Metafile Information Systems manufactures software for document image processing under the brand name Metaview Folders. 50 employees. Founded in 1979. SIC 7372.

Metal Craft Machine & Engineering 12797 Meadowvale Rd. N.W., Elk River, MN 55330. Tel: 763/441-1855; Fax: 763/441-0798. Jack Mowry, Pres.; Kathy Eckert, Cont.; Sean Mowry, VP; Trisha Mowry, VP. Metal Craft Machine & Engineering is a precision machine job shop that manufactures parts to customer specifications. 106 employees (53 in Minnesota; 2 part-time). Founded in 1973. ISO 9002 certified. SIC 3499.

Metallics Inc. 7274 W. County Highway 2, P.O. Box 99, Onalaska, WI 54650. Tel: 608/781-5200; Fax: 608/781-2254. Doug Dale, Pres.; Todd Dale, EVP. Metallics manufactures nameplates and industrial decorative trim. 242 employees. Founded in 1947. SIC 3993.

Metal-Matic Inc. 629 S.E. Second St., Minneapolis, MN 55414. Tel: 612/378-0411; Fax: 612/392-3399. G.J. Bliss Sr., Chm., Pres., and CEO; Robert J. Van Krevelen, EVP; G.J. Bliss Jr., VP; T.J. Bliss, VP. Metal-Matic manufactures welded steel tubing. 515 employees. Founded in 1951. SIC 3317.

A.A. Metcalf Moving and Storage 1255 Highway 36 E., Maplewood, MN 55109. Tel: 651/484-0211; Fax: 651/484-0134. Allen Metcalf, Pres. and CEO; Jon Archbold, VP; Cindy Borup, VP. Metcalf Moving and Storage is engaged in the moving and storage of household goods, office and industrial complexes, and electronics—locally, nationally, and worldwide. It has offices in Minneapolis, St. Paul, and Rochester. It also acts as agent for Mayflower Transit, Indianapolis. 100 employees. Founded in 1919. SIC 4214.

Metro Legal Services Inc. The Towle Building, 330 Second Ave. S., Suite 150, Minneapolis, MN 55401. Tel: 612/332-0202; Fax: 612/332-5215; Web site: http://www.metrolegal.com. Jeff Budde, Pres.; Scott Gray, VP. Metro Legal Services offers support services for the legal community. Other office: St. Paul. 100 employees (35 in Minnesota; 65 part-time). Founded in 1969. SIC 7363.

Metro Machine & Engineering Corporation 8001 Wallace Rd., Eden Prairie, MN 55344. Tel: 952/937-2800; Fax: 952/937-2374. Robert Midness, Chm., Pres., and CEO; Mike Huss, Dir.-Engrg.; Todd Lewis, Sls. Metro Machine & Engineering manufactures special machines, hydraulic components, and performs contract machining. 60 employees (all in Minnesota). Founded in 1952. SIC 3523, 3569, 3599.

Metro Sales Inc. 1640 E. 78th St., Richfield, MN 55423. Tel: 612/861-4000; Fax: 612/866-8069. Jerry Mathwig, Pres. Metro Sales sells and services office copiers, facsimile equipment, typewriters, and shredders. 200 employees. Founded in 1969. SIC 5044.

Metro Systems Furniture 6775 Shady Oak Rd., Eden Prairie, MN 55344. Tel: 952/933-5050; Fax: 952/944-1449; Web site: http://www.metrosystems-inc.com. Jim W. Harmon, Owner; Nathan Oliver, VP-Sls./Mktg. Annual revenue $33 million. Metro Systems is a full-service office furniture dealership that sells and leases new and used furnishings. It owns and maintains a fleet of 10 air-ride semitrailer trucks for nationwide delivery. The company also offers refurbishing, painting, and CADD/space-planning services. 95 employees. Founded in 1968. SIC 5021, 5932.

Metropolitan Corporation 7625 Metro Blvd., Suite 300, Edina, MN 55439. Tel: 952/893-1277; Fax: 952/893-1428. Tom Grossman, Pres.; Dave Norton, Cont. Metropolitan Corp. is a holding company for several auto dealerships and a leasing company. Divisions include Metro Financial Services (Edina), Freeway Ford, Suburban Chevrolet, Rosedale Chevrolet, and Prestige Lincoln/Mercury. It is also affiliated with Brookdale Ford, Brooklyn Center, Minn.; and Phoenix Management Inc., Edina. 470 employees. Founded in 1983. SIC 6719.

The Meyer Companies 14 Seventh Ave. N., St. Cloud, MN 56303. Tel: 320/259-4000; Fax: 320/259-4044. Lawrence Meyer, CEO; Roger Eckstrand, COO and CFO; Peg Meyer, Pres.-Meyer Marketing Ltd.; Tom Caprio, Pres.-Meyer Telemarketing. Annual revenue $7.6 million. The Meyer Cos. offers advertising, telemarketing, and computer data management services. Other office location: Brainerd, Minn. 270 employees. Founded in 1976. SIC 7389.

Meyers Printing Company 7277 Boone Ave. N., Brooklyn Park, MN 55428. Tel: 763/533-9730; Fax: 763/531-5771; Web site: http://www.meyers.com. David G. Dillon, CEO; Chris Dillon, Pres.-Display/Label Div.; Karen L. Hagedorn, CFO; Russ Blondin, VP-Display Div.; Gregg Temple, VP-Sls., Label Div.; Ken Smith, VP-Label Mfg.; Dave Youngquist, Pres.-Meyers Communication Svs. Annual revenue $65 million. Meyers has two operating divisions: Meyers Display, a point of purchase printing company, creating signs, displays, and plastic printed materials for merchandising; Meyers Label, a pressure-sensitive label printer, producing multicolor primary labels for package decoration, multi-ply coupons and related label products. 325 employees (330 in Minnesota; 5 part-time). Founded in 1949. SIC 2752.

Michaels Restaurant 15 S. Broadway, Rochester, MN 55904. Tel: 507/288-2020; Fax: 507/288-5553. Michael J. Pappas, Pres.; Charles W. Pappas, Sec. and Treas.; George M. Pappas, VP; James E. Pappas, VP. Annual revenue $4.1 million. Michaels Restaurant is a full-service dining establishment. 160 employees. Founded in 1951. SIC 5812.

Michaud Cooley Erickson 1200 Metropolitan Centre, 333 S. Seventh St., Minneapolis, MN 55402. Tel: 612/339-4941; Fax: 612/339-8354. Dean Rafferty, Pres.; Monty Talbert, VP; Douglas Cooley, VP; Joe Tennyson, VP-Fin./Admin. Annual revenue $13 million. Michaud Cooley Erickson (MCE) provides mechanical, electrical, fire-protection, lighting, security, commissioning and facilities management engineering solutions for buildings. 112 employees (all in Minnesota). Founded in 1946. SIC 8711.

Mico Foods Inc. 1011 Hoffman Dr., P.O. Box 630, Owatonna, MN 55060. Tel: 507/451-2585; Fax: 507/451-0315. Mark Michels, Pres.; Bob Michels, VP; Tom Michels, VP; Brad Olson, Sec. and Treas. Mico Foods owns and operates Kernel Restaurants in Owatonna and in Menomonie, Wis. 100 employees. Founded in 1974. SIC 5812.

MICO Inc. 1911 Lee Blvd., North Mankato, MN 56003. Tel: 507/625-6426; Fax: 507/625-3212. Gordon J. McGrath, Pres.; V.J. Tillman, VP-OEM Design; Daniel S. McGrath, VP-Sls.; Brent McGrath, Sec. and Treas.; David Ewel, Dir.-Engrg.; Greg Rogers, Supply Chain Mgr. MICO Inc. designs and manufactures portable transfer pumps, hydraulic brake systems (including brake cylinders, disc brakes, multiple disc brakes, valves, and actuators), and hydraulic clutches and steering units. 405 employees (301 in Minnesota; 12 part-time). Founded in 1946. SIC 3714.

Micom Corporation 475 Eighth Ave. N.W., New Brighton, MN 55112. Tel: 651/636-5616; Fax: 651/636-1352. E. Walhof, CEO; M. Walhof, Cont. Micom manufactures printed circuit boards. 175 employees. Founded in 1965. SIC 3672.

Micro Control Company 7956 Main St. N.E., Fridley, MN 55432. Tel: 763/786-8750; Fax: 763/786-6543; Web site: http://www.micro-control.com. Harold E. Hamilton, Pres.; Phil Bailey, VP-Res./Devel.; Mike O'Donnell, VP-Op.; Eleanor Hamilton, Treas. Annual revenue $31 million. Micro Control Co. manufactures automatic test systems for the electronics industry. It also does contract manufacturing as a service. 200 employees (195 in Minnesota). Founded in 1972. SIC 3823.

Micro Dynamics Corporation 7550 Market Place Dr., Eden Prairie, MN 55344. Tel: 952/941-8041; Fax: 952/941-8065. Michael C. Brown, CEO; Jeff Tomassoni, VP-Bus. Devel.; Win Wood, VP-Tech. Annual revenue $24 million. Employee-owned Micro Dynamics Corp. is an electronic manufacturing services provider with customers in medical, telecom, computer, military and industrial industries. Capabilities include ISO 9001, three facilities, six SMT lines, three pin-in-hole lines, test services, design (materials procurement & mgmt.), engineering, BGA intensive PCA's, x-ray, BGA Repair, system integration. 190 employees (180 in Minnesota; 10 part-time). Founded in 1981. SIC 3679.

Microboards Technology Inc. 1721 Lake Dr. W., Chanhassen, MN 55317. Tel: 952/556-1600; Fax: 952/556-1620; Web site: http://www.microboards.com. Mitch Ackmann, Pres.; Chuck Alcon, VP-Sls./New Product Devel. Microboards Technology is an owner/manufacturer/distributer of CD-R and DVD-R products, specializing in authoring/mastering duplication, storage, and pro-audio markets. Subsidiary offices are located in Japan, the United Kingdom, India, and Miami. 50 employees. In October 2000 the company formed Microboards Manufacturing LLC with the acquisition of Champion Duplicators Inc., which has traditionally been known for the engineering and manufacturing of automated stand-alone duplication systems. SIC 7389.

Microvena Corporation 1861 Buerkle Rd., White Bear Lake, MN 55110. Tel: 651/777-6700; Fax: 651/773-3776; Web site: http://www.microvena.com. Joe Katzenstein, VP-Sls./Mktg.; Dave Schwantes, Dir.-Fin.; Daniel Bulver, VP-Op.; Ann Quinlan-Smith, Dir.-RA/QA. Annual revenue $22.4 million. Microvena Corp. is a manufacturer of interventional medical devices (guidewires, snares, microsnares), mechanical thrombectomy devices, transcatheter closure devices for congenital heart defects, and (through its Neurovena division) neurovascular devices. Subsidiary of Phillips Plastics Corp., Phillips, Wis. 189 employees. Founded in 1989. In March 2000 a Hennepin County District Court judge ordered the company to pay $5.9 million to local real estate developer Continental Distribution Center—for violating a 15-year lease agreement. SIC 3841.

MicroVoice Applications Inc. 5100 Gamble Dr., Suite 400, St. Louis Park, MN 55416. Tel: 952/373-9300; Fax: 952/373-9779. Wayne Miller, Pres.; Steve Lazar, VP; Bret Busse, Mktg. Dir.; Mike James, VP-Sls.; Catherine Clary, VP-Op. MicroVoice Applications is a provider of custom-designed audiotext software and systems for the publishing industry worldwide. Applications are designed using interactive voice response and voicemail technology. Products include classified programs, circulation applications, information lines, contests, and polling programs. Among its 300 newspaper clients: Boston Globe, Detroit News/Free Press, Philadelphia News/Inquirer, San Francisco Chronicle/Examiner, Washington Post, and New York Times, and Phoenix Gazette. 200 employees. Founded in 1989. In December 1999 the company settled a patent-infringement lawsuit brought against it by Ronald A. Katz Technology Licensing L.P., Los Angeles. MicroVoice agreed to pay for a license to use certain computer-telephony technology covered by a broad-based patent portfolio held by Katz. The license covers the "Electronic Personal Classifieds" field of use. The settlement included payments for past infringement, ongoing royalties, and a consent judgment admitting validity and infringement of the Katz patents. According to CEO Miller, "We have reached the conclusion that these are core patents in the Electronic Classifieds industry [and] we are convinced that obtaining this license is necessary to protect our own company and our customers." SIC 7371.

Mid America Steel Inc. 92 Northern Pacific Ave., P.O. Box 2807, Fargo, ND 58108. Tel: 701/232-8831; Fax: 701/280-0103. Don Clark, Pres. and CEO; G.R. Cook Jr., Treas.; R.R. Hentges, VP; James Simonson, VP-Purch.; John Simonson, Personnel. Annual revenue $25.1 million. Mid America Steel fabricates structural steel, plate, and reinforcing bars; and manufactures storage tanks and pressure vessels. There is a branch facility in Bismarck, N.D. 160 employees. Founded in 1905. SIC 3441, 3443, 3446, 3449.

Mid-City Cleaning Contractors 7276 Commerce Circle E., Fridley, MN 55432. Tel: 763/571-9056; Fax: 763/571-5838. Greg Weiers, CFO; Chad Weiers, Pres. Annual revenue $6 million. Mid-City Cleaning Contractors operates a janitorial and contract cleaning service. 440 employees. Founded in 1967. SIC 7349.

Midcom Inc. 121 Airport Dr., P.O. Box 1330, Watertown, SD 57201. Tel: 605/886-4385; Fax: 605/886-4486. Dennis Holien, CEO; J. Hill, Pres. Midcom designs and manufactures telecommunication and ion power transformers. Its Huron, S.D., plant, which opened in September 1992, employs 200. Two new divisions opened since 1994: one in Aberdeen, S.D., and the other in Waverly, Iowa. 2,500 employees. Founded in 1973. SIC 3677.

Mid Continent Engineering Inc. 405 35th Ave. N.E., Minneapolis, MN 55418. Tel: 612/781-0260; Fax: 612/782-1320. Charles N. Marvin, Chm. and Pres.; John Rahja, Gen. Mgr. and Cont. Annual revenue $18.5 million. Mid Continent does precision machining and custom sheet metal fabrication. Primary customers are the computer industry, aerospace divisions of large companies, and some commercial accounts. 145 employees (all in Minnesota; 15 part-time). Founded in 1949. SIC 3599.

Midcontinent Media Inc. 7900 Xerxes Ave. S., Suite 1100, Bloomington, MN 55431. Tel: 952/844-2600; Fax: 952/844-2660. N.L. Bentson, Chm.; Joe H. Floyd, Pres.; Mark Niblick, EVP. Midcontinent Media is actively involved in cable television, radio broadcasting, specialized computer software for imaging technology, business telephone service, and long-distance service. It operates radio stations in Sioux Falls, S.D., and cable TV companies throughout the Upper Midwest. Midcontinent Cable Co. is a wholly owned subsidiary that commenced cable television operations with the construction of its first system in South Dakota in 1968. Midcontinent formed a partnership with AT&T, formally known as TCI, in 1972 that now serves 164 communities and 134,000 subscribers in South Dakota, North Dakota, northern Nebraska, and western Minnesota. The majority of the Midcontinent systems are now interconnected by a newly constructed fiber network extending from southeastern South Dakota into central North Dakota. Midcontinent Media's origins were in the motion picture theater business in the 1930s. 870 employees (29 in Minnesota; 197 part-time). Founded in 1933. SIC 4832, 4841.

Mid-Rivers Telephone Co-Op Inc. 106 Second Ave. S., P.O. Box 280, Circle, MT 59215. Tel: 406/485-3301; Fax: 406/485-2924. Rob Reukauf, Pres.; Mark Robbins, VP; Gene Engen, Sec. and Treas.; Gerry Anderson, Gen. Mgr. Mid-Rivers Telephone Co-Op is in telephone communications. 87 employees (2 part-time). Founded in 1952. SIC 4813.

Midway National Bank of St. Paul 1578 University Ave. W., St. Paul, MN 55104. Tel: 651/628-2661; Fax: 651/643-8518. John A. Ritt, Chm., Pres., and CEO. Midway National Bank of St. Paul is a $336.8 million-asset, nationally chartered commercial bank offering traditional retail and commercial banking, investments, and trusts. 211 employees (208 in Minnesota; 15 part-time). Founded in 1927. SIC 6021.

Midwest Asphalt Corporation P.O. Box 5477, Hopkins, MN 55343. Tel: 952/937-8033; Fax: 952/937-6910. Blaine M. Johnson, Pres.; Blair B. Bury, VP; Maynard Schuldt, Sec. and Treas. Midwest Asphalt Corp. makes asphalt paving mixtures and crushed rock and gravel products. It also performs contract construction, asphalt milling, custom recycling, aggregate crushing, and asphalt paving. 120 employees. Founded in 1968. SIC 2951.

Midwest Bottle Gas Company 3600 Highway 157, La Crosse, WI 54601. Tel: 608/781-1010. James A. Senty, Pres. and CEO; John Senty, VP. Midwest Bottle Gas Co. handles retail and wholesale bottle gas, natural gas, and appliances. The company has propane retail operations in Florida, Georgia, Minnesota, and Wisconsin. 220 employees. Founded in 1947. SIC 5541, 5722, 5983, 5984.

Midwest of Cannon Falls 32057 64th Ave., P.O. Box 20, Cannon Falls, MN 55009. Tel: 507/263-4261; Fax: 507/263-7752. Kathleen Brekken, Pres. and CEO; Timothy McCord, CFO; Jeffrey Haynes, Pres.-American Specialty Confections; Tom Durkin, VP-Sls./Dsgn./Asian Op. Midwest of Cannon Falls is a wholesale designer and distributor of giftware and home decor. It offers more than 5,000 items, 90 percent of which is only available through the company. Customers include nearly 20,000 specialty retail stores, catalog dealers, and national department stores and chains. 469 employees (335 in Minnesota; 200 part-time). Founded in 1955. SIC 5199.

Midwest Editions Inc. 1060 33rd Ave. S.E., Minneapolis, MN 55414. Tel: 612/378-2620; Fax: 612/378-9616. Lance Johnson, Owner and Pres. Midwest Editions specializes in trade binding, including hard-bound and perfect-bound books. 55 employees. Founded in 1970. SIC 2789.

Midwest Graphics and Response Systems Inc. 9600 Fallon Ave. N.E., P.O. Box 307, Monticello, MN 55362. Tel: 763/295-3000; Fax: 763/295-3008. Steve Krenz, Pres. and CEO; Michael Vikesland, VP. Midwest Graphics and Response Systems provides turnkey communication and response systems. Data services include database development and maintenance, profiling, postal optimization, and response analysis. Production capabilities include litho and digital print, mailing, and fulfillment services. Response services include: inbound and outbound 800 phone service, reply mail processing, Internet response capture, inbound and outbound fax service, and e-mail distribution. 130 employees (all in Minnesota). Founded in 1994. SIC 7331.

Midwest Medical Insurance Holding Company 7650 Edinborough Way, Edina, MN 55435. Tel: 952/838-6700; Fax: 952/838-6808; Web site: http://www.midmedical.com. David P. Bounk, Pres./CEO-MMIHC; Jack Kleven, Pres.-MMIC. The MMIC group of companies offers an array of insurance, employees benefits, health care and technology consulting, and Internet-based products and services to physicians and group practices in the Upper Midwest. Member companies include Midwest Medical Insurance Co., MMIC Benefits, Midwest Medical Solutions, and MedPower Information Resources. 90 employees. Founded in 1980. SIC 6411.

Midwest Motor Express Inc. 5015 E. Main, P.O. Box 1058, Bismarck, ND 58502. Tel: 701/223-1880; Fax: 701/224-1405; Web site: http://www.mmeinc.com. John T. Roswick, Pres.; Joe Greenstein, VP; Tony Holtberg, VP-Op.; Tony Mieldazis, VP-Sls.; Jodi Heflin Kary, Treas.; Marlin Kling, EVP and Sec. Annual revenue $28.9 million. Midwest Motor Express is a trucking company that transports general commodities (except household goods, commodities in bulk, and class A and B explosives) in North Dakota, Minnesota, Montana, South Dakota, Colorado, Washington, Oregon, Wyoming, Iowa, Nebraska, Illinois, and Wisconsin. 400 employees. Founded in 1938. SIC 4213.

Midwest Tire & Muffler Inc. P.O. Box 3149, Rapid City, SD 57709. Tel: 605/348-2160; Fax: 605/348-2313. Russell J. Haley, Chm. and Pres.; Earl Moe, Sec.; Bill Hinzman, Treas.; Lawrence W. Haley, VP and Gen. Mgr. Midwest Tire & Muffler is a distributor of tires, wheels, and accessories. It also operates 11 retail stores (Tire/Muffler/Alignment Centers), and three wholesale warehouses. 130 employees. Founded in 1969. SIC 5013, 5014, 5531.

Mikara Corp. 3109 Louisiana Ave. N., New Hope, MN 55427. Tel: 763/546-9500; Fax: 763/546-5212. Barbara Mitchell Christie, CEO; Michael P. Hicks, Pres. Mikara sells professional beauty products in Minnesota, Iowa, Wisconsin, North Dakota, South Dakota, and Nebraska. National Salon Resources division wholesales professional salon products; Beauty Mart division is a cash-and-carry distributor of professional and retail beauty products. The former publicly traded National Beauty Inc. was taken private in July 1992. 240 employees. Founded in 1970. SIC 5199.

Mikros Engineering Inc. 8755 Wyoming Ave. N., Brooklyn Park, MN 55445. Tel: 763/424-4642; Fax: 763/424-3913. James Talmage, Chm. and Pres.; John Mitlyng, VP and COO; Bill Talmage, VP and CFO. Annual revenue $15 million. Mikros Engineering is engaged in custom injection molding. 80 employees. Founded in 1963. SIC 3089.

Mille Lacs Band/Ojibwe Indians HCR 67, Box 194, Onamia, MN 56359. Tel: 320/532-4181; Fax: 320/532-4209; Web site: http://www.millelacsojibwe.org. Melanie Benjamin, CEO; Ken Mimmack, Commissioner-Corp. Affairs. Annual revenue $250 million (estimated by Fact Book). The Mille Lacs Band of Ojibwe Indians owns and operates entertainment complexes in Onamia (Grand Casino Mille Lacs) and Hinckley (Grand Casino Hinckley), Minn. The Band also owns a bank, a bakery, convenience stores, gas stations, fast-food restaurants, three hotels, and equity in a bottled water company. 3,468 employees (all in Minnesota). Founded in 1991. In April 2000 Grand Casino Hinckley opened a new restaurant, The Winds Steakhouse, featuring casual elegance and gourmet food. The Tribe announced plans to open a 67-acre language and cultural immersion center—offering a unique opportunity for people to experience sugar bushing and wild rice harvesting, and to learn the Ojibwe language and culture. In August the Band's Small Business Development Program was selected as a finalist for Harvard Universoty's prestigious Honoring Nations Award. The Band was one of 11 tribes across the nation that agreed to commit $1 million each to found the nation's largest intertribal bank, to be located in Denver. SIC 7999. No. 54 CRM Private 100. No. 60 CRM Employer 100.

Miller Auto Center 2930 Second St., St. Cloud, MN 56301. Tel: 320/251-1363; Fax: 320/251-1939. Thomas Miller, Owner; Mike Miller, Gen. Mgr.-Rogers; Steve Ritchard, Gen. Mgr.-Cambridge; Dan Dunn, Gen. Mgr.-St. Cloud. Miller Auto Center provides sales and service for a variety of makes of new and used cars—Lincoln-Mercury, Ford, Pontiac, Chevrolet/Geo, Chrysler-Plymouth, Dodge, Jeep, Jeep/Eagle, and Nissan—through car dealerships in St. Cloud, Rogers, and Cambridge, Minn. It also operates Miller Auto Leasing, a leasing company; and Miller Marine, a boat dealer. 200 employees (all in Minnesota; 6 part-time). Founded in 1956. SIC 5511, 5551.

Miller Bag Company 861 E. Hennepin Ave., Minneapolis, MN 55414. Tel: 612/378-3200; Fax: 612/378-2247. Mike Miller, Pres.; Gene Filapek, Sls. Mgr. Miller Bag is an original equipment manufacturer of quality packaging, cases, and bags from concept to design to production. 100 employees (25 in Minnesota). Founded in 1918. SIC 2393.

Miller Meester Advertising 17 N. Washington, Minneapolis, MN 55401. Tel: 612/337-6600; Fax: 612/337-9100; Web site: http://www.millermeester.com. Robert V. Miller, Chm. and CEO; Greg Leaf, COO and Dir.-Pub. Rel. Miller Meester Advertising is a full-service advertising agency offering in-house media, research, public relations, product publicity, sales promotion, direct marketing, and audiovisual services and Web site development to agricultural, business-to-business, and consumer clients worldwide. Major clients: American Cyanamid, Cargill Seeds, Larson Manufacturing, Pulte Homes of Minnesota, Vision-Ease Lens, and Delta Dental Plans Association. 75 employees. Founded in 1975. In February 2000 the firm announced three new clients: ARAG, Des Moines, Iowa; Genetiporc, Canada; and Pet Care Systems, Detroit Lakes, Minn. Former creative director Patricia Ray won $711,000 in damages from the firm over alleged sex discrimination leading to her 1998 termination. In September the firm boosted billings by nearly $30 million when it won major assignments from BASF Corp., the new owner of American Cyanamid. SIC 7311.

Miller & Schroeder Financial Inc. 220 S. Sixth St., Suite 300, P.O. Box 789 (55440), Minneapolis, MN 55402. Tel: 612/376-1500; Fax: 612/376-1410; Web site: http://www.millerschroeder.com. James F. Dlugosch, Chm. and CEO; John Clarey, EVP; David Borden, SVP and Investment Banker; Steven W. Erickson, SVP-Managing Dir.; Kenneth Halloran, SVP and Mng. Dir.-Sls./Trading; Christopher J. Mason, SVP and Dir.-Fixed Income Banking; Jerome Tabolich, SVP and Pres.-Miller & Schroeder Investments Corp. Annual revenue $33 million. Miller & Schroeder Financial is one of the nation's leading investment firms. Other locations: St. Paul; Seattle; Solana Beach, Calif.; Atlanta; Milwaukee; Chicago; and Sacramento, Calif. In August 1999 a proposed merger with Kinnard Investments Inc. (Nasdaq: KINN), Minneapolis, was terminated. 190 employees (130 in Minnesota). Founded in 1963. Late in 1999, the firm surpassed two important milestones: As of Dec. 1, Miller & Schroeder had underwritten more than $1 billion in debt issued by participants in the U.S. gaming industry; and the commercial loan portfolio serviced by Miller & Schroeder had exceeded $1 billion in value. In May 2000 subsidiary Miller & Schroeder Capital Corp. acquired American Investors Group Inc., Minnetonka, Minn. In June 2000 the firm was accused of breaking federal regulations by paying for overseas trips taken by County of San Bernardino (Calif.) officials, who then awarded the firm their municipal bond underwriting business ($1 million in fees over six years). Charges included breach of fiduciary duty and unjust enrichment. The firm said that it would vigorously defend itself with respect to all of the allegations contained in the complaint, of which the specific allegations against Miller & Schroeder constituted a very small portion. Meanwhile, Miller & Schroeder and the Tachi Yokut Tribe of the Santa Rosa Rancheria closed a $57,525,000 syndicated, debt-financing deal that was to be used to complete and open the tribe's Palace Casino. In September the firm closed a $70 million debt financing transaction to support the completion and opening of a new casino to be operated by the Agua Caliente Band in Rancho Mirage, Calif. In October the firm filed suit against the American Indian owners and the management company of an upstate New York casino to recover a $12 million loan from February 1999. SIC 6211.

Millerbernd Manufacturing Company P.O. Box 98, Winsted, MN 55395. Tel: 320/485-2111; Fax: 320/485-4420. David Millerbernd, Pres.; Stephen Millerbernd, VP and Treas.; Magdalen Schlagel, Office Mgr./Accountant. Millerbernd manufactures welded steel rings and cylinders, and lighting poles. 100 employees. Founded in 1933. SIC 3443, 3646.

Milltronics Manufacturing Company 1400 Mill Ln., Waconia, MN 55387. Tel: 952/442-1410; Fax: 952/442-6457; Web site: http://www.milltronics.net. Tim Rashleger, Pres. Annual revenue $30 million. Milltronics Manufacturing manufactures automated milling machines and lathes. 150 employees (147 in Minnesota; 3 part-time). Founded in 1973. Tim Rashleger became sole owner 8/31/2000. SIC 2431.

Minar Ford Inc. 1100 Silver Lake Rd., New Brighton, MN 55112. Tel: 651/633-9010; Fax: 651/633-6521. Cushman K.D. Minar Jr., Owner and Pres.; Bob Lewis, Gen. Mgr. Minar Ford is an automobile and heavy-duty truck dealer. 135 employees (6 part-time). Founded in 1929. SIC 5511.

Minco Products Inc. 7300 Commerce Ln., Fridley, MN 55432. Tel: 763/571-3121; Fax: 763/571-9142; Web site: http://www.minco.com. Karl Schurr, Pres. Minco Products makes flexible circuits, flexible blanket heaters, and temperature detectors and controls. 715 employees. Founded in 1956. SIC 3679, 3699, 3823, 3829.

The Miner Group International 5100 Highway 169 N., New Hope, MN 55428. Tel: 763/504-6151; Fax: 763/504-5483. Jonathan S. Miner, Head Coach and Gen. Mgr. Annual revenue $157 million. The Miner Group International is a marketer and manufacturer of children's promotional and educational items. It has vertically integrated printing, packaging, manufacturing data storage, and marketing facilities in Minnesota (where it is the state's fifth-largest printing company) and branches in Mexico, China, Taiwan, and Indonesia. 650 employees (552 in Minnesota). Founded in 1980. In August 2000 the School Division-Mission Nutrition-announced bookmarks and meal bags featuring Pikachu and his Pokemon friends this Fall to help children learn about good nutrition. The Retail division is working actively with Digiman and Powderpuff Girls, as weil as other licensors, to introduce new Seasonal and Everyday products-including Deluxe Valentine Kits for 2001. The Kidcentive's Division continues its work with key companies in the restaurant market with innovative kid's meal promotions. The printing and manufacturing facilities continue to support Mello Smello's innovative products as well as working with Fortune 500 companies across the country with their specialty printing, packaging and distribution capabilities as an ISO 9002 and world class supplier. SIC 2675, 2759, 5091, 5092, 5112, 5162, 5199. No. 84 CRM Private 100.

Miner's Inc. 5065 Miller Trunk Hwy., Hermantown, MN 55811. Tel: 218/729-5882; Fax: 218/729-5893. James Miner, Pres.; Mike Miner, VP and Treas.; James Miner Jr., VP and Sec. Miner's owns and operates 16 Super One Supermarkets in Minnesota, Wisconsin, and Michigan; and owns Miner's Enterprises, a trucking business serving Super One stores. 1,800 employees (900 in Minnesota). Founded in 1957. SIC 4212, 5411.

Minn-Dak Farmers Cooperative 7525 Red River Rd., Wahpeton, ND 58075. Tel: 701/642-8411; Fax: 701/642-6814. Victor Krabbenhoft, Chm.; Mike Hasbargen, VChm.; Steven M. Caspers, EVP and Interim President; Patricia J. Keough-Wilson, Dir.-Corp./Public Relations; John Nyquist, Purch. Mgr.; Jeff Carlson, Dir.-Tech. Svs. Annual revenue $152.7 million. Minn-Dak is a manufacturer of beet sugar and related by-products (beet molasses and beet pulp pellets). 329 employees (210 in Minnesota; 84 part-time). Founded in 1974. SIC 2063.

Minneapolis Grain Exchange 130 Grain Exchange Building, 400 S. Fourth St., Minneapolis, MN 55415. Tel: 612/321-7101; Fax: 612/321-7121; Web site: http://www.mgex.com. John Miller, Chm.; Kent Horsager, Pres. and CEO; Gary B. Wollan, VP-Op.; Mark Bagan, VP-Market Regulations; Beth Hanson, VP-Fin.; Teri Huffaker, VP-Mktg./Public Rel. The Minneapolis Grain Exchange (MGE) is a not-for-profit cash, futures, and options exchange of 402 members representing most of the major companies in the grain industry. It is the only futures market for hard red spring wheat, white wheat, black tiger and white shrimp, and Twin Cities electricity. 73 employees. Founded in 1881. In April 2000 CEO James H. Lindau announced plans for a May 31 retirement. MGE ownership approved a proposal to list cottonseed futures and options contracts, which began trading May 11, 2000. The MGE was the first futures exchange to offer cottonseed trading. SIC 6221.

Minnesota Bearing Company 1104 Glenwood Ave., Minneapolis, MN 55405. Tel: 612/374-2100; Fax: 612/377-8143. Robert D. Weiser, Chm. and CEO; William S. Mayer, Pres.; Raymond L. Olson, Treas.; Billie Jo Schons, Sec. Minnesota Bearing Co. distributes bearings, chains, conveyor systems, power transmissions, and welding supplies through 14 sites—including Air-Hydraulic Systems Inc. and Iowa Bearing Co. Inc. 175 employees. Founded in 1936. SIC 5084, 5085.

Minnesota Corn Processors 901 N. Highway 59, Marshall, MN 56258. Tel: 507/537-2676; Fax: 507/537-2655. Dan Thompson, Pres. and CEO; Roger F. Evert, VP-Hum. Res./Admin.; Mike Mote, Chief Info. Ofcr.; Brad Schultz, VP-Commodities; Lawrence J. Schiavo Jr., VP-Op./Bus. Devel.; Stanley L. Sitton, SVP-Sls./Mktg.; Daniel H. Stacken, VP and CFO; Roger L. Untiedt, VP-Tech. Annual revenue $584 million. Cooperatively owned Minnesota Corn Processors (MCP) operates two corn wetmilling plants, one in Marshall, MN and one in Columbus, NE as well as its distribution stations throughout the United States. 925 employees (400 in Minnesota). Founded in 1982. In April 2000 MCP selected a hosted solution from Manugistics Group Inc., Rockville, Md., to power a trading network with its key customers. MCP was expecting the Manugistics solution, b-networks.com, to help propel the company into the technological forefront of the food and agriculture industry by creating a trading network for the customers of its many corn products. In June Minnesota Corn Processors converted from business to a limited liability company (LLC). In addition, Liquid Sugars Inc. was merged into MCP and no longer exists as a subsidiary. SIC 2046. No. 8 CRM Cooperatives/Mutuals 20.

Minnesota Diversified Products 9091 County Rd. 50, Rockford, MN 55373. Tel: 763/477-5854; Fax: 763/477-5863; Web site: http://www.diversifoam.com. Benjamin G. Sachs, Pres.; Carl Mura, EVP. Minnesota Diversified Products manufactures extruded and expanded polystyrene products for insulation, protective packaging, roofing, lumberyard, garage doors, and packaging markets. An operating unit does business as Diversifoam Products Inc. 140 employees. Founded in 1969. SIC 3086.

Minnesota Electrical Supply Company P.O. Box 997, 1209 E. Highway 12, Willmar, MN 56201. Tel: 320/214-4229; Fax: 320/214-4242; Web site: http://www.mnelectric.com. Steve Peterson, Pres. and CEO; Dennis Anfinson, VP-Procurement; Roy Stoel, VP-Sls.; Dave Stuhr, VP-Tech Svs.; Renee Cool, Mktg./Communications; Connie Stahnke, Dir.-Employee Rel.; John Klaers, Cont. Annual revenue $60 million. Minnesota Electrical Supply is an eight-store wholesaler of electrical apparatus and equipment. The company features full customer-service departments at each location; drop-shipping from off-site to customer site; overnight shipping; electronic data interchange transactions; and remote real-time computer system access for orders, pricing, and inventory. Besides Willmar, Minnesota locations include Alexandria, St. Cloud, Marshall, Faribault, Mankato, Bemidji, and its newest location Coon Rapids. 140 employees (all in Minnesota; 3 part-time). Founded in 1945. SIC 5063.

PVT

Minnesota Fabricators 7166 Fourth St. N., Oakdale, MN 55128. Tel: 651/738-9000; Fax: 651/738-9009. Gerhard Schmidt, Pres.; Dave Krebsbach, VP-Mfg.; Deborah Morken, VP-Admin. Annual revenue $5 million. Minnesota Fabricators specializes in metal tubing bending, precision machining, sheet metal, assembly, and welding. 50 employees. Founded in 1976. SIC 3317, 3444.

Minnesota Hardwoods Inc. 313 Fourth St., P.O. Box 148, Courtland, MN 56021. Tel: 507/359-2705; Fax: 507/354-8199. Frank S. Kilibarda Sr., Owner and Pres.; Frank S. Kilibarda Jr., VP and Gen. Mgr.; Douglas J. Kilibarda, VP-Mktg. Minnesota Hardwoods operates two log processing facilities, one in Courtland, Minn., and one in Fort Dodge, Iowa. It also operates a hardwood lumber manufacturing plant and a pallet manufacturing plant in Courtland. The company sells to wholesalers and end-users nationwide, 50 percent of its sales are exported to Europe and Asia. 103 employees. Founded in 1976. SIC 5031.

Minnesota Historical Society 345 W. Kellogg Blvd., St. Paul, MN 55101. Tel: 651/296-6126; Fax: 651/296-1004. Nina Archabal, Exec. Dir. The Minnesota Historical Society nurtures knowledge of, and respect for, the history of Minnesota. It does this by collecting, preserving, and recounting Minnesota's past—through 24 historic sites, extensive libraries and collections, innovative exhibits, educational programs, and book publishing. 725 employees (400 part-time). Founded in 1849. SIC 8621.

Minnesota Knitting Mills Inc. 1450 Mendota Heights Rd., Mendota Heights, MN 55120. Tel: 651/452-2240; Fax: 651/452-8915; Web site: http://www.mnknit.com. Ted Kuller, Chm.; Harold Kuller, CEO; Stuart Marofsky, Pres. Minnesota Knitting Mills manufactures knit trimming (waistbands, collars, cuffs) for outerwear, athletic wear, and sportswear. 80 employees. Founded in 1908. SIC 2259.

Minnesota Life Insurance Company 400 Robert St. N., St. Paul, MN 55101. Tel: 651/665-3500; Fax: 651/665-4488; Web site: http://www.minnesotamutual.com. Robert L. Senkler, Chm., Pres., and CEO; Robert E. Hunstad, EVP; John F. Bruder, SVP-Fin. Svs.; James E. Johnson, SVP-Group Ins.; Dennis E. Prohofsky, SVP, Gen. Counsel, and Sec.; Terrence M. Sullivan, SVP-Individual Insurance; Randy F. Wallake, SVP-Pensions; William N. Westhoff, SVP-Asset Mgmt.; Keith M. Campbell, SVP-Hum. Res. Corp. Svs.; Gregory S. Strong, SVP and CFO. Annual revenue $1.8 billion. Minnesota Life Insurance Co. (Minnesota Life) provides financial security for individuals and businesses in the form of insurance, pensions, and investments. Minnesota Life is one of the 15 most highly rated insurance company groups in the nation, including AA+ from Fitch, A++ from A.M. Best, AA+ from Standard & Poor's, and Aa2 from Moody's Investors Services. The company has more than $200 billion of life insurance in force and $20 billion in assets under management. Minnesota Life and its wholly owned subsidiaries, Northstar Life Insurance Co. and The Ministers Life Insurance Co., serve more than 7 million people across America. Ascend Financial Services is a broker-dealer subsidiary. 4,400 employees (2,300 in Minnesota). Founded in 1880. In December 1999 Minnesota Life enabled employees of General Mills Inc. (NYSE: GIS) to enroll for group life insurance by using both Internet and voice-response technologies. The ability to simplify enrollment with this leading-edge, outsourced system was one of the reasons General Mills selected Minnesota Life as its new group life insurance carrier. Dec. 31: 1999 net operating earnings of $122.5 million were up 34 percent from the previous year. Among the reasons for the increase were higher sales, positive investment margins, the sale of the company's reinsurance operations, and the tax savings and expense reductions from restructuring to a stock company. Net income climbed 7 percent to $175 million; assets under management rose 12 percent to $20.6 billion; and insurance in force increased 13 percent to $200 billion. In March 2000 Fitch lowered the claims paying ability ratings of Minnesota Life to 'AA'+ (Double-A-Plus) from 'AAA' (Triple-A), outlook stable. The ratings continued to reflect Minnesota Life's very strong capital base and high-quality investment portfolio. Additionally, the company possesses diversified revenue and profitability streams, excellent persistence throughout all of its business units, and a high-quality individual life insurance franchise. Finally, the company's strong management team has a conservative philosophy aimed at preserving the company's very high levels of financial strength and claims paying ability. This rating action was based on a general deteriorating credit trend within the life insurance industry and the fact that Minnesota Life's evolving business mix was exposing the company to industry-related challenges—and did not reflect any material change in Minnesota Life's near-term performance, solvency characteristics, or liquidity. To cope with the tight labor market, Minnesota Life teamed with Lifeworks Services, Mendota Heights, Minn., to hire 13 developmentally disabled adults for entry-level jobs. March 31: Net earnings increased 81 percent in first quarter, to $72.1 million, largely on investment gains. Sales also increased sharply, up 90 percent to $671.5 million, led by the company's investment products. In April Ascend Financial Services and the company's Individual Life business unit agreed to combine forces with Stockwalk.com, Golden Valley, Minn., to provide privately labeled online securities trading to financial institutions. In June Minnesota Life made Computerworld's 100 Best Places to Work in IT list for the fifth-straight year, ranking 26th. June 30: Net operating income increased to $30.4 million from $20.5 million in the second quarter of 1999. Net income, which includes after-tax realized investment gains and losses, increased to $47.5 million from $33.0 million. Sales of Minnesota Life products totaled $960.6 million in the first half of 2000, 30 percent higher than the first half of 1999. "We continue to enjoy strong operating performance from each of our businesses this year. In addition, despite volatile markets, we realized significant capital gains from our investment portfolio," said CEO Senkler. "Sales results were very good, and, coupled with the recent roll-out of several new life insurance and investment products and expansion of our Internet-servicing capabilities, we anticipate continued strong performance in the second half of the year." In July Standard & Poor's affirmed its double-'A'-plus counterparty credit and financial strength ratings and its double-'A'-minus surplus note rating on the company. The outlook was stable. The ratings reflected the insurer's extremely strong capital base, diverse product lines, excellent liquidity, and very strong asset quality. Offsetting the positive factors to some extent were the company's continuing reliance on its individual insurance product line as a source of earnings and its need to generate greater overall earnings if it is to realize the full potential of the mutual holding company form of ownership. In September Minnesota Life introduced VAL (variable adjustable life) Horizon. VAL Horizon complements existing products that have a strong focus on building death benefit by providing additional opportunities to use living benefits by focusing on cash value accumulation. SIC 6311. No. 6 CRM Private 100. No. 85 CRM Employer 100.

Minnesota Tile 4825 France Ave. N., Brooklyn Center, MN 55429. Tel: 763/531-4170; Fax: 763/531-4155. William J. Dale, Chm.; Alan Dale, Pres. and CEO. Minnesota Tile distributes and installs ceramic tile, marble, and granite products. 100 employees. Founded in 1930. SIC 1743.

Minnesota Timberwolves Target Center, 600 First Ave. N., Minneapolis, MN 55403. Tel: 612/337-3865; Fax: 612/673-1699. Rob Moor, Pres.; Roger Griffith, CFO; Chris Wright, VP-Sls./Mktg.; Kevin McHale, Gen. Mgr.; Flip Saunders, Head Coach. Minnesota Timberwolves is a professional basketball team that began play in the National Basketball Association (NBA) in 1989. The team was acquired in March 1995 by investors led by Glen Taylor of Taylor Corp., North Mankato, Minn. Marquee players include Kevin Garnett, Joe Smith, Terrell Brandon, Wally Szczerbiak, and Sam Mitchell. 70 employees (all in Minnesota). Founded in 1987. The 2000 offseason was marred by the death of starting shooting guard Malik Sealy in a Twin Cities traffic accident. SIC 7941.

Minnesota Twins Baseball Club Inc. 34 Kirby Puckett Place, Minneapolis, MN 55415. Tel: 612/375-1366; Fax: 612/375-7480; Web site: http://www.twinsbaseball.com. Christopher E. Clouser, CEO; T. Geron (Jerry) Bell, Pres. and COO; Terry Ryan, Gen. Mgr.; Kirby Puckett, EVP; Dave St. Peter, SVP-Bus. Affairs; Tom Kelly, Field Mgr.; Kip Elliott, CFO; Eric Curry, VP-Corp. Partnerships; Patrick Klinger, VP-Mktg. Minnesota Twins is a professional baseball club competing in the American League's Central Division. Veteran players include Brad Radke, Eric Milton, Matt Lawton, and Ron Coomer. The former Washington Senators baseball club moved to Minnesota in 1961. The Twins won world championships in 1987 and 1991. To keep the team in Minnesota, majority owner Carl R. Pohlad is seeking public financing for a new stadium and/or qualified local buyers. 800 employees (450 in Minnesota). Founded in 1961. In June 2000 the Twins announced the creation of a broad-based citizen committee to help address the challenge of keeping the franchise permanently in Minnesota. CEO Clouser said that "Minnesotans For Major League Baseball" would be asked to gather information, analyze alternatives, and ultimately recommend appropriate steps to ensure the long-term viability of the team in Minnesota. The committee was to consist of 120 representatives of business and community interests statewide. SIC 7941.

The Minnesota Valley Electric Cooperative 125 Minnesota Valley Electric Dr., Jordan, MN 55352. Tel: 952/492-2313; Fax: 952/492-3137. Minnesota Valley Electric Cooperative is an electric distribution cooperative that also offers wireless services, water heaters, and emergency medical response. 84 employees (18 part-time). Founded in 1937. SIC 4911.

Minnesota Valley Testing Laboratories 1126 N. Front, New Ulm, MN 56073. Tel: 507/354-8517; Fax: 507/359-2890. Thomas R. Berg, Pres. and CEO. Minnesota Valley Testing Laboratories provides analytical testing services in chemistry and microbiology to the food, environmental, energy, and agricultural industries. Laboratories are located in New Ulm and Mankato, Minn; Grand Forks and Bismarck, N.D.; and Nevada, Iowa. 130 employees (90 in Minnesota). Founded in 1951. SIC 8734.

Minnesota Vikings Football Club 9520 Viking Dr., Eden Prairie, MN 55344. Tel: 952/828-6500; Fax: 952/828-6540; Web site: http://www.vikings.com. Red McCombs, Owner; Gary Wood, Pres.; Dennis Green, Head Coach; Mike Kelly, VP-Bus. Op.; Steve Poppen, VP-Fin.; Bob Hagan, Dir.-Pub. Rel.; Phil Huebner, Dir.-Ticket Sls. Annual revenue $46.4 million. Minnesota Vikings Football Club is a professional football team that competes in the National Football League (NFL). The organization also owns the 500-employee, $35 million-revenue Minnesota Vikings Food Service Inc., an Edina, Minn.-based vending machine and cafeteria management company. 108 employees (112 in Minnesota; 4 part-time). Founded in 1960. From the 1998 season to the 2000 season, the Vikings' annual payroll increased at 15.8 percent, the fifth-lowest rate among the 31 NFL teams, dropping it from the fifth-highest payroll in the league ($50.3 million) to No. 25 ($58.2 million). SIC 7941.

Minnesota Wire & Cable Company 1835 Energy Park Dr., St. Paul, MN 55108. Tel: 651/642-1800; Fax: 651/642-9286. Fred N. Wagner, Chm. and CEO; Paul J. Wagner, Pres. and CEO; Joan C. Thompson, EVP and CFO. Annual revenue $13 million. Minnesota Wire & Cable Co. (first known as Wagner Consultants Corp., then MWCC) is a vertically integrated manufacturer of wire and cable products for manufacturers of medical, communication, and industrial equipment. Minnesota Wire introduced a new process for producing carbon fiber for conducting electricity and has become the leading supplier of these fibers to the med-tech industries. Minnesota Med-Equip, a subsidiary formed in 1995, distributes music products internationally. A second subsidiary, started in 1999, Minnesota Bramstedt Surgical, repairs surgical instruments. Its facilities are located in St. Paul and in Eau Claire, Wis. 160 employees (100 in Minnesota; 25 part-time). Founded in 1968. SIC 3643.

Minnetonka Moccasin Company Inc. 1113 E. Hennepin, P.O. Box 529, Minneapolis, WI 55440. Tel: 612/331-8493; Fax: 612/331-3721. David Miller, Pres. Minnetonka Moccasin Co. makes leather moccasins, slippers, and casual shoes. 50 employees. Founded in 1946. SIC 3142, 3149.

Minnkota Power Cooperative Inc. P.O. Box 13200, Grand Forks, ND 58208. Tel: 701/795-4000; Fax: 701/795-4214. Harvey Tallackson, Pres.; David W. Loer, Pres. and CEO; Wally Lang, VP-Engrg.; Luther Kvernen, VP-Generation/Transmission; Don Zeman, VP-Fin./Admin.; David Sogard, VP-Legal/Gov't Affairs; Al Tschepen, VP-Planning/Sys. Op. Annual revenue $110 million. Minnkota generates and transmits electric energy to 12 associated electric cooperatives, which, in turn, retail to 98,339 consumers. Minnkota owns and operates 544 megawatts of generating capacity. Total power-supply capacity is 672 megawatts. Length of transmission line owned is 2,861 miles. 320 employees. Founded in 1940. SIC 4911.

MinnPar Inc. 900 Sixth Ave. S.E., Minneapolis, MN 55414. Tel: 612/379-0606; Fax: 612/378-3741; Web site: http://www.minnpar.com. Emil Kucera, Pres.; John Ackelson, VP-Op.; Don Neudauer, VP-Fin.; Zeke Yargici, VP-Sls./Mktg. MinnPar is a supplier/manufacturer of OEM construction equipment parts. 50 employees. Founded in 1983. SIC 3531.

Minn/Serv Inc. 6300 Penn Ave. S., Richfield, MN 55423. Tel: 612/866-0041; Fax: 612/866-0048. Lee A. Johnson Jr., Chm., Pres., and CEO; Don Jackson, VP. Annual revenue $21.5 million. Minn/Serv, dba Signature Dining (formerly known as Canteen Co. of Minnesota Inc.), is a franchised retailer of vending and food services via concessions and workplace cafeterias. 475 employees (all in Minnesota). Founded in 1942. SIC 5962.

Minuti-Ogle Co. Inc. 7030 Sixth St. N, Oakdale, MN 55128. Tel: 651/735-5800; Fax: 651/735-7053; Web site: http://www.minuti-ogle.com. Thomas G. Panek, Pres. and CEO; Randy Stevens, CFO; Scott Panek, VP. Annual revenue $40 million. Minuti-Ogle is a plaster, stucco, drywall, steel stud, insulation, and spray-fireproofing contractor. 360 employees (all in Minnesota). Founded in 1902. SIC 1742.

Mister Car Wash 8280 Flying Cloud Dr., Eden Prairie, MN 55344. Tel: 952/835-6868; Fax: 952/835-1946; Web site: http://www.mistercar-wash.com. Ronald Peterson, CEO and Asst. Sec.; William Martin, Pres.; Lawrence Minich, CFO, Sec., and Treas. Annual revenue $7 million. Mister Car Wash is a wash company with eight locations in the Twin Cities metro area: Edina, St. Louis Park, Roseville, and Brooklyn Park are full service locations. Anoka, Eden Prairie, Stillwater and West St. Paul are express locations. 125 employees (all in Minnesota). Founded in 1998. SIC 7542.

Mitchell Metal Products Inc. 905 S. State St., P.O. Box 207, Merrill, WI 54452. Tel: 715/536-7176; Fax: 715/536-1163. Dale Mitchell, Pres.; Arlette J. Mitchell, Sec.; Daniel Frick, Asst. VP and Plant Mgr.; Shirley Mitchell, Treas. Mitchell Metal Products manufactures metal stampings, as well as hardware for manufacturers of furniture, windows, office equipment, original equipment, and seasonal wreath rings. 70 employees (2 part-time). Founded in 1954. SIC 3429, 3469.

Modern Tool Inc. 1200 Northdale Blvd., Coon Rapids, MN 55448. Tel: 763/754-7337; Fax: 763/754-7557. Barry Larson, Pres. and CEO; Richard Arens, VP; John Brose, Sls. Mgr.; Paul Schultz, Purch. Mgr. Modern Tool is engaged in precision sheet metal fabrication; short- and long-run stamping; and the manufacture of tool-and-die jigs, complex weldments, assemblies, and fixtures. 180 employees. Founded in 1962. SIC 3544.

Modernistic 169 Jenks Ave., St. Paul, MN 55117. Tel: 651/291-7650; Fax: 651/291-2571; Web site: http://www.modernisticinc.com. Jim Schulte, CEO; Keith Wilson, Pres. and COO; Scott Schulte, VP; Deb Olson, Mktg. Dir.; Mike McGuire, Cont. Annual revenue $14 million. Modernistic is a full-service graphic communications and print finishing firm (foil stamping, embossing, folding/gluing, UV-coating). Markets covered are point-of-purchase displays, fleet decals, industrial converting, and finishing. 135 employees. Founded in 1938. SIC 2675, 2759.

Molin Concrete Products 415 Lilac St., Lino Lakes, MN 55014. Tel: 651/786-7722; Fax: 651/786-0229. Thomas Molin, Pres.; John Saccoman, VP-Sls./Mktg.; Paul Kourajian, Dir.-Engrg.; Mark Groff, Fin. Mgr. Molin Concrete manufactures precast concrete floor, roof slabs, wall panels, beams, and columns for construction applications. 100 employees. Founded in 1897. SIC 3272.

Moline Machinery Ltd. 114 S. Central Ave., Duluth, MN 55807. Tel: 218/624-5734; Fax: 218/628-3853; Web site: http://www.moline.com. Gary Moline, Pres. and CEO; Kevin Boreen, CFO. Moline Machinery manufactures dough cutters and sheeters, food processing conveyors, and donut process systems. 120 employees (118 in Minnesota). Founded in 1947. SIC 3556.

Monson Trucking Inc. 5102 S. Cant Rd., Duluth, MN 55804. Tel: 218/525-6681; Fax: 218/525-7310. Robert Monson, Pres. and CEO; Mark Monson, VP; Michael Monson, VP; Mary Monson, Sec.; Carrie Monson France, Asst. Sec. Monson Trucking specializes in dry freight truck loads. The company serves the north-central United States and central Canada from Duluth and from terminals in Red Wing and Virginia, Minn. 280 employees (15 part-time). Founded in 1915. SIC 4213.

Montana Energy Research & Development Institute 220 N. Alaska, P.O. Box 3809, Butte, MT 59702. Tel: 406/782-0463; Fax: 406/723-8328. Donald R. Peoples, Pres.; John Cote, Chm. Montana Energy Research & Development Institute is a research and development management firm. Its subsidiary, MSE Technical Applications, is engaged in project management and facility operations that include compliance activities, hazardous-waste engineering, and high-temperature materials testing. 367 employees. Founded in 1974. SIC 8734, 8741, 8744.

Morey Fish Company LLC 742 Decatur Ave. N., Golden Valley, MN 55427. Tel: 763/541-0129; Fax: 763/541-0518. Dieter Pape, Pres. and CEO; Loren A. Morey, EVP and COO; Gregory Frank, SVP; William J. Frank, VP-Bus. Devel.; Tim Lundstrom, Corp. Cont.; Michelle Pape, VP-Mktg.; James Walstrom, VP-Sls. Morey Fish Co. processes, wholesales, and distributes fresh, smoked, and fresh-frozen fish. 125 employees (all in Minnesota). Founded in 1937. SIC 2091.

Morgan Printing 402 Hill Ave., P.O. Box 471, Grafton, ND 58237. Tel: 701/352-0640; Fax: 701/352-1502; Web site: http://www.morganprinting.com. John D. Morgan Jr., Pres.; Jackie Thompson, VP. Annual revenue $2.6 million. Morgan Printing, a third-generation family business, is in the printing and newspaper business. It specializes in black-and-white comic books. The company maintains a sales office in Grand Forks, N.D. 48 employees. Founded in 1959. SIC 2711, 2752.

Morgen Manufacturing Company 117 W. Third St., P.O. Box 160, Yankton, SD 57078. Tel: 605/665-9654; Fax: 605/665-7017. Jim Cope, Pres. Morgen Manufacturing makes pumps and conveyors to place ready-mix concrete. It also makes adjustable masonry scaffolding. 100 employees. Founded in 1950. SIC 3531, 3535.

Morrison-Maierle Inc. 910 Helena Ave., P.O. Box 6147 (59604), Helena, MT 59601. Tel: 406/442-3050; Fax: 406/442-7862. J.H. Morrison Jr., Chm.; J.A. Maierle, Pres.; Robert Morrison, VP; Ken Salo, VP; Jack Schunke, VP. Morrison-Maierle is a civil engineering design and environmental services firm that offers a broad range of services throughout the western United States and internationally. 165 employees. Founded in 1945. SIC 8711.

Morrissey Inc. 9304 Bryant Ave. S., Bloomington, MN 55420. Tel: 952/888-4675; Fax: 952/888-3915; Web site: http://www.morrissey.com. Dave Mealman, Pres. and CEO. Morrissey is a custom manufacturer of prototypes, stampings (both short- and long-run) and mechanical assemblies. In-house tooling and design functions are available. The company also has laser and turret press capabilities. 103 employees (all in Minnesota; 3 part-time). Founded in 1946. SIC 3469.

M.A. Mortenson Company 700 N. Meadow Ln., Golden Valley, MN 55422. Tel: 763/522-2100; Fax: 763/522-2278; Web site: http://www.mortenson.com. Mauritz A. Mortenson Jr., Chm. and CEO; Thomas R. McCune, Pres. and COO; Tom Gunkel, EVP; Paul Campbell, SVP; Peter Conzemius, SVP and CFO; Paul Cossette, SVP; Brad Funk, SVP; Dan Johnson, SVP; Bob Nartonis, SVP; John V. Wood, SVP; Greg Clark, VP; Ken Sorenson, VP. Annual revenue $968 million. Mortenson Co. is a total facility services organization. According to ENR, it is the 39th largest general contractor in the U.S. and has nine operating groups with six offices and seven service centers located throughout the U.S. It also operates in international markets. Mortenson customizes development, design, construction and operation services to meet each customer's need. The organization provides programming and feasibility analysis, real estate services, design, design-build, design-build-operate, general contracting, construction management, and facility management/operation services. 2,000 employees (250 in Minnesota). Founded in 1954. The Design-Build Institute of America selected Mortenson for two design-build awards in its Y2000 national competition: the East Grand Forks School for best project in the public sector under $15 million and the University of Minnesota Jackson Hall for best design-build renovation/restoration project. Significant recent projects include the Xcel Energy Center, University of Minnesota-Molecular and Cellular Biology Project, 50 South Sixth Street 30-story office building in downtown Minneapolis, Marquette Plaza renovation, Minneapolis Convention Center Expansion, Regions Hospital, St. Paul, and the University of Minnesota Gateway Building. SIC 1541. No. 9 CRM Private 100.

Moss & Barnett Professional Association 4800 Wells Fargo Center, 90 S. Seventh St., Minneapolis, MN 55402. Tel: 612/347-0300; Fax: 612/339-6686; Web site: http://www.moss-barnett.com. Thomas J. Shroyer, CEO; Richard Johnson, CFO; Dave F. Senger, Chm. Moss & Barnett is a full-service, 72-attorney law firm. Today, it is best known for its work with small to medium-sized entrepreneurial firms—frequently family-owned businesses—assisting them with corporate, estate planning, tax, and other issues. 166 employees. Founded in 1896. In January 2000 a number of the attorneys and staff of Hessian & McKasy joined Moss & Barnett—increasing the number of attorneys at Moss & Barnett from 57 to 67. SIC 8111.

MotivAction Inc. 16355 36th Ave. N, Suite 100, Plymouth, MN 55446. Tel: 763/544-7200; Fax: 763/525-5302; Web site: http://www.motivaction.com. William Bryson, Pres.; Jeff Beegle, VP-Sls./Mktg.; Marlyn Sjaarda, VP and CFO. MotivAction provides interactive online applications full-service performance management services such as recognition, incentives, measurement, promotion, administration, and meetings. Other locations: Atlanta; Cincinnati; Houston; Philadelphia; and Irvine, Calif. 85 employees (80 in Minnesota; 2 part-time). Founded in 1976. SIC 8741.

Mrs. Gerry's Kitchen Inc. 2110 Y.H. Hanson Ave., Albert Lea, MN 56007. Tel: 507/373-6384; Fax: 507/373-5617; Web site: http://www.mrsgerrys.com. Geraldine (Gerry) Vogt, Pres. and CEO; Gerald R. Vogt, Sec. and Treas.; Alan Oliver, COO; Dawn Smith, Sls. Mgr.-Food Svc.; Tom Riemann, Sls. Mgr.-Retail Sls.; Chad Vogt, Purch. Agent; Leean Dulitz, Office Mgr. Annual revenue $12 million. Mrs. Gerry's Kitchen Inc. makes prepared salads—potato salads, macaroni salad, cole slaws, pasta, three-bean salad, gelatins, dips and spreads (vegetable and fruit), and other seasonal items—with a total line of 100 products. The company's one brand name is Mrs. Gerry's. Founded by Geraldine (Gerry) Vogt. 110 employees (103 in Minnesota). Founded in 1973. SIC 5141.

Multi-Tech Systems Inc. 2205 Woodale Dr., Mounds View, MN 55112. Tel: 651/785-3500; Fax: 651/785-9874; Web site: http://www.multitech.com. Raghu Sharma, Chm. and Pres.; Warren Mesenbring, VP; Chip Harleman, VP-Sls./Mktg.; Gene Schweiss, Cont. Annual revenue $87 million. Multi-Tech Systems is an ISO 9002-certified manufacturer of its state-of-the-art MultiModem line of dial-up communications products. Other products include ISP/intranet communications servers, data/fax modems, MultiMux voice/data/fax statistical multiplexers, FRADs, Routers, DSUs, multi-user serial interface systems and telecommuting communications systems. The company also offers the MultiModem PCS, a voice/data/fax personal communications system with patented simultaneous voice/data transmission (DSVD) capability. Multi-Tech's products are available in 80 countries through a diverse network of distributors, manufacturers, representatives, system integrators, value-added resellers (VARs), and retailers. 350 employees. Founded in 1970. In February 2000 Multi-Tech filed separate lawsuits against three multinational PC manufacturers—Compaq, Dell, and Gateway—alleging infringement of six of the company's U.S. patents. In lawsuits filed in U.S. District Court for the District of Minnesota, Multi-Tech was claiming that the three computer defendants were in violation of patented technology involving the simultaneous transmission of voice, data, and video over a communications line. In April the company was granted a patent for the upgrading of a reprogrammable modem with code being downloaded from a remote computer via a communications line. U.S. patent number 6,031,867 covers these "flash memory" upgrades, commonly used in modems that require updates and are connected to a computer. In June the company announced MultiModemDSL, a full-featured ADSL external modem with USB support. On June 28, Multi-Tech filed a countersuit against Microsoft's declaratory judgment regarding Multi-Tech's patents for simultaneous voice, data, and video communications. (Microsoft had previously filed an action against Multi-Tech seeking a declaration from the court that it did not infringe certain Multi-Tech patents and/or that the patents are invalid. Multi-Tech responded with this suit against Microsoft charging them with infringing five of the company's U.S patents. This was all part of a continuing series of legal actions by Multi-Tech started earlier in the year.) In August the company announced that its MultiVOIP line of voice and Fax over IP gateways were being marketed as remote location solutions for larger Cisco VOIP networks. The Santa Cruz Operation Inc. (SCO) certified selected Multi-Tech WAN server cards as the first such devices to receive SCO's highest certification level. In September the company announced a T1 VOIP gateway in a desktop box about the size of an answering machine. SIC 3661.

Murnane Conlin White & Brandt P.A. 1800 Piper Jaffray Plaza, 444 Cedar St., St. Paul, MN 55101. Tel: 651/227-9411; Fax: 651/223-5199; Web site: http://www.murnane.com. Michael S. Ryan, Pres. and CEO; Robert W. Murnane, Shareholder; John E. Brandt, VP; Daniel A. Haws, Shareholder; John D. Hirte, Shareholder; Steven J. Kirsch, Shareholder; C. Todd Koebele, Shareholder; William L. Moran, Shareholder; Andrew T. Shern, Sec.; Michael P. Tierney, Shareholder; Thomas A. Gilligan, Shareholder. Murnane Conlin is a general and civil law firm specializing in insurance, workers' compensation, product liability, real estate, banking, corporate, and probate. 62 employees (all in Minnesota; 9 part-time). Founded in 1940. SIC 8111.

Murphy McGinnis Media 625 U.S. Bank Place, 130 W. Superior St., Duluth, MN 55802. Tel: 218/723-8000; Fax: 218/723-8980. John Murphy, Chm. and Co-owner; Jim McGinnis, Pres. and Co-owner; Steven J. Gall, VP-Sls./Mktg.; Charles R. Johnson, Exec. VP and Co-owner. Murphy McGinnis Media operates the Up North Newspaper Network, an award-winning group of 14 newspapers located within 120 miles of Duluth—the Duluth Budgeteer, Superior (Wis.) Daily Telegram, the Mesabi Daily News (Virginia, Minn.), and other daily and weekly newspapers and shoppers. The company also owns Murphy McGinnis Interactive, an Internet company specializing in Web site development, electronic commerce, and residential Internet access; Manney's Shopper, a regional free-distribution weekly shopper network (150,000 homes); and Northland Delivery, which delivers publications, product samples, and other items to households. 600 employees. Founded in 1996. SIC 2711.

Murphy Warehouse Company 701 24th Ave. S.E., Minneapolis, MN 55414. Tel: 612/623-1200; Fax: 612/623-9108; Web site: http://www.murphywarehouse.com. Richard T. Murphy Sr., Chm.; Richard T. Murphy Jr., Pres.; Richard F. Miller, VP-Fin.; Michael J. Butchert, VP; Laurie M. Murphy, VP and Sec.; Paul Welna, VP-Op. Murphy Warehouse is a logistics services company providing distribution, transportation, warehousing, order fulfillment, and value-added services for domestic and international clients. It also operates the Midwest International Logistics Center—incorporating Foreign Trade Zone #119, a U.S. Customs Centralized Examination Station (CES), a Container Freight Station (CFS), and a U.S. Customs General Order Facility. 195 employees (all in Minnesota). Founded in 1956. Winner of CityBusiness "Best in Real Estate-New Industrial Development 1999" for the 406,000 square foot Cummins Power Supplier D.C. and Park in Fridley, Minnesota. SIC 4214, 4222, 4225.

Muscle Bound Bindery 701 Plymouth Ave. N., Minneapolis, MN 55411. Tel: 612/522-4406; Fax: 612/522-0927. Gerald L. Hanson, Pres. Annual revenue $7.5 million. Muscle Bound Bindery does hard-bound, case-bound, and perfect-bound books; book covers; and drilling, folding, laminating, and cutting. 100 employees (all in Minnesota). Founded in 1967. SIC 2789.

Muska Electric Company 1985 Oakcrest Ave., Roseville, MN 55113. Tel: 651/636-5820; Fax: 651/636-0916. Mahlon Christensen, Pres.; Gary Nelson, VP; Randolph Luhrs, Treas. and Sec. Muska is a commercial and industrial electrical contractor. 160 employees (10 part-time). Founded in 1919. SIC 1731.

Nagel Lumber Company Inc. 5135 Highway B, P.O. Box 209, Land O'Lakes, WI 54540. Tel: 715/547-3361; Fax: 715/547-3715. Edwin Nagel, Pres.; Cathy Nordine, VP and Sec. Nagel Lumber is a manufacturer of lumber for pallets, furniture, landscape timbers, and studs. The company can dry-kiln and plane lumber. A division, Aspen Valley Lumber Co., produces T&G paneling and performs edge-glued panel-door care. 110 employees. Founded in 1950. SIC 2421, 2499.

Nahan Printing Inc. 7000 Saukview Dr., P.O. Box 697, St. Cloud, MN 56302. Tel: 320/251-7611; Fax: 320/259-1378. Michael J. Nahan, Pres.; Linda M. Linn, VP. Nahan Printing does commercial and direct-mail printing. 550 employees. Founded in 1962. SIC 2752.

Wayne Nasi Construction Inc. Highway 77 W., Hurley, WI 54534. Tel: 715/561-5153; Fax: 715/561-3065; Web site: http://www.wnasi.com. Wayne Nasi, Pres. Nasi Construction operates a construction company. 120 employees. Founded in 1976. SIC 1521.

Nath Companies 900 E. 79th St., Bloomington, MN 55420. Tel: 952/853-1400; Fax: 952/853-1410; Web: http://www.nathcompanies.com. Mahendra Nath, Pres. and CEO; Ashok Mehta, SVP-Op.; Patty Porteous, CFO; Asha Nath, VP, Treas., and Sec. Annual revenue $153 million. Nath Companies is a family-owned business that owns and manages 133 Burger King restaurants (the fourth-largest Burger King franchisee in the country); 11 Denny's restaurants; four commercial office buildings; six apartment buildings; a Quality Inn & Suites; and a Ramada Inn. 4,200 employees. Founded in 1990. In July 2000 the company purchased its second hotel, the 256-room Ramada Inn Minneapolis/St. Paul in Roseville, Minn., for $5.9 million. SIC 5812, 6512, 6513, 7011. No. 47 CityBusiness Fastest-growing Private Companies. No. 78 CRM Private 100.

National Business Systems 2905 W. Service Rd., Eagan, MN 55121. Tel: 651/854-4664; Fax: 651/854-4557. David Ihle, CEO; Ted Naegeli, Pres.; Brad Buchanan, VP; Joe Tafs, VP. Annual revenue $77 million. National Business Systems performs data entry, computer output, microfilm source and laser printing services, and sells a full line of data processing and microfilm supplies in seven states. 300 employees (150 in Minnesota; 100 part-time). Founded in 1972. SIC 7374, 7389.

National Checking Company Inc. 899 Montreal Circle, P.O. Box 64534 (55164), St. Paul, MN 55102. Tel: 651/251-1500; Fax: 651/251-1501; Web site: http://www.nationalchecking.com. Ben Olk, Pres. and CEO; Tom Minea, VP-Prod.; Mark Hotinger, CFO and Treas.; Ben A. Olk, VP; Matt Olk, VP. National Checking is a manufacturer of restaurant guest checks and cash register rolls. The company also manufactures business forms through Midwest Business Forms Division and general printing through the Focus Business Graphics Division. All sales are through a distributor network. 105 employees (97 in Minnesota). Founded in 1905. SIC 2759, 2761.

National Lodging Companies Inc. 11800 Singletree Ln., Eden Prairie, MN 55344. Tel: 952/944-5700; Fax: 952/943-5666. John H. Klinkhammer, Chm. and CEO; Terrance P. DeRoche, Pres.; Jerry Easley, CFO; Steven W. Sherf, VP-Devel. National Lodging Cos. is a developer, owner, and

PVT

manager of hotel/motel properties. 650 employees. Founded in 1986. SIC 7011.

National Mower Company 700 Raymond Ave., St. Paul, MN 55114. Tel: 651/646-4079; Fax: 651/646-2887. Robert S. Kinkead Jr., Pres.; John Kinkead, VP. National Mower manufactures lawn and tractor mowers, primarily for golf courses. 55 employees (all in Minnesota). Founded in 1919. SIC 3524.

National Polymers Inc. 7920 W. 215th St., P.O. Box 770, Lakeville, MN 55044. Tel: 952/469-4977; Fax: 952/469-2051. Dennis Anderson, CEO. National Polymers manufactures miscellaneous plastics products. 82 employees (75 in Minnesota; 37 part-time). Founded in 1972. SIC 3089.

Natural Resource Group Inc. 900 Second Ave. S., Suite 1800, Minneapolis, MN 55402. Tel: 612/347-6789; Fax: 612/347-6780. William Regan, Pres. Natural Resource Group is an environmental services company that offers consulting services to pipeline companies in the areas of environmental management, permitting, and regulatory compliance. 50 employees. Founded in 1992. SIC 8711.

B.F. Nelson Folding Cartons Inc. 752 30th Ave. S.E., Minneapolis, MN 55414. Tel: 612/331-1193; Fax: 612/331-1598. Larry Ross, Pres. and CEO; Gary Sotebeer, EVP; Ron Anderson, VP-Sls.; Brian Bosma, VP. B.F. Nelson Folding Cartons manufactures folding paper cartons. It specializes in "microflute corrugated" box operations: bonding a sturdy corrugated-cardboard bottom layer to a top layer that can accept high-quality graphics. SIC 2657.

New Horizon Shamrock 2717 Highway 14 W., Rochester, MN 55901. Tel: 612/920-1958; Fax: 612/920-3316. Patricia Jump, R.N., M.A., CEO; Becky Smith, R.N., M.A., VP-Clinical Svs. New Horizon Shamrock is a Medicare/Medicaid-certified, full-service home health care agency—with six offices serving the southern two-thirds of Minnesota. 329 employees. Founded in 1980. SIC 8082.

New Richmond Industries Inc. 905 N. Knowles Ave., New Richmond, WI 54017. Tel: 715/246-6571; Fax: 715/246-6574. Dick Simma, Pres.; Steve Swanson, Gen. Mgr. New Richmond Industries' operations include filling, wire harness assembly, parts assembly, and packaging. 95 employees. Founded in 1972. SIC 2499, 3599, 3643.

Newman Signs P.O. Box 1728, Jamestown, ND 58402. Tel: 701/252-1970; Fax: 701/252-7325. Harold Newman, Pres.; Dean Anderson, Gen. Mgr.; Russell J. Newman, VP. Newman Signs manufactures and installs traffic signs and outdoor advertising. 150 employees. Founded in 1955. SIC 3993.

NewMech Companies Inc. 1633 Eustis, St. Paul, MN 55108. Tel: 651/645-0451; Fax: 651/642-5591; Web site: http://www.newmech.com. Ronald A. Pearson, CEO; Jerry Poser, EVP; Larry Jordan, EVP; L. Raymond, VP; Tim Mielke, VP; W. Henquinet, Sec. and Treas.; Troy A. Pearson, VP; Richard K. Poser, VP; Steven G. Poser, VP; Paul C. Jordan, VP. NewMech Cos. offers complete mechanical contracting services provided by its divisions: Heating, Plumbing, Sheet Metal, Sprinkler, Industrial, Millwright, and Spiro Pipe & Service. 450 employees (all in Minnesota). Founded in 1921. In February 2000 CEO Pearson was installed as president of the Mechanical Contractors Association of America during the organization's convention in San Diego. SIC 1711.

NextNet Wireless Inc. 9555 James Ave. S., Bloomington, MN 55431. Tel: 952/929-4008; Fax: 952/929-4080; Web site: http://www.nextnetwireless.com. Ralph Muse, CEO; Vladimir Kelman, VP-Devel.; Merv Grindahl, VP and Chief Architect. NextNet Wireless is a start-up company developing the industry's first MMDS broadband wireless access systems for rapid deployment of high-speed, two-way voice and data services over the "last mile" of the communications network. The company's Expedience system is built around an economic business model that enables MMDS service providers to deliver low-cost, converged services to all of their residential and small business subscribers. NextNet Wireless, a spin-off of Zamba Corp. (Nasdaq: ZMBA), is funded by an investment group led by JAFCO Ventures, DCM-Doll Capital Management, and Cabletron Systems Inc. 55 employees. Founded in 1998. SIC 3669.

Nico Plating 2929 First Ave., Minneapolis, MN 55408. Tel: 612/822-2185; Fax: 612/822-4580. Denny Donaldson, Pres. Nico Plating is engaged in metal finishing. In July 1994 the company received preliminary approval for $6.5 million in tax-exempt revenue bonds and a $75,000 development loan from the city of Minneapolis for an expansion that will double employment. 119 employees. Founded in 1971. SIC 3471.

The Nicollet Island Inn & Restaurant 95 Merriam St., Minneapolis, MN 55401. Tel: 612/331-1800; Fax: 612/331-6528. Patrick Boyum, Gen. Mgr.; Regina Charboneaw, Exec. Chef. The Nicollet Island Inn is a full-service hotel and restaurant in the historic St. Anthony Falls/Main Street district of Minneapolis. 85 employees. Founded in 1988. SIC 5812, 7011.

Nobles Manufacturing 1105 E. Pine St., P.O. Box 866, St. Croix Falls, WI 54024. Tel: 715/483-3079; Fax: 715/483-1884. Ted Priem, Chm. and Owner; Jerry Lee, Treas. Nobles Industries manufactures washing and cleaning equipment. 60 employees. Founded in 1944. SIC 3589.

Nodak Electric Cooperative Inc. 4000 32nd Ave. S., P.O. Box 13000, Grand Forks, ND 58208. Tel: 701/746-4461; Fax: 701/795-6701. George Berg, Pres. and CEO; David W. Kent, Chairman; Lee McLaughlin, VP; Carol Niemeier, Sec. and Treas. Annual revenue $27.2 million. Nodak Electric Cooperative is an electric utility. 70 employees (9 in Minnesota; 11 part-time). Founded in 1940. SIC 4911.

Nodak Mutual Insurance Company 1101 First Ave. N., P.O. Box 2502, Fargo, ND 58108. Tel: 701/298-4200; Fax: 701/652-2770. John P. Czerwonke, EVP and CEO; Jim Harmon, Pres.; Scott Martin, VP-Mktg.; Kirk Holmes, VP-Claims; Dave Johnston, VP-Op./Corp. Communications; William Pietsch, Sec.; Gary Duncan, Treas. and CFO. Nodak Mutual Insurance is a property and casualty insurance company. 104 employees (4 part-time). Founded in 1946. SIC 6331.

Nonin Medical Inc. 2605 Fernbrook Ln. N., Plymouth, MN 55447. Tel: 763/553-9968; Fax: 763/553-7807; Web site: http://www.nonin.com. Jerry Zweigbaum, CEO. Nonin Medical manufactures medical monitors. Products include pulse oximetry monitors, OEM modules for pulse oximetry, and accessories and testing equipment for pulse oximeters. 81 employees. SIC 3841.

Nonvolatile Electronics Inc. 11409 Valley View Rd., Eden Prairie, MN 55344. Tel: 952/829-9217; Fax: 952/996-1600; Web site: http://www.nve.com. James M. Daughton, Pres.; Dick George, CFO. Nonvolatile Electronics (NVE) is an ISO 9001-certified company that designs, develops, and produces magnetic sensors, switches, and isolators. In addition, NVE provides custom R&D on a variety of magnetic topics, including MRAM, a totally nonvolatile semiconductor memory using proprietary Giant Magnetoresistive Ratio (GMR) and Spin-Dependent Tunneling (SDT) materials. 60 employees (58 in Minnesota). Founded in 1989. SIC 3674, 8731.

Norcostco Inc. 3203 N. Highway 100, Crystal, MN 55422. Tel: 763/533-2791; Fax: 763/533-3718. James T. Scott, Chm., CEO, and Treas.; Roger E. Deters, Pres. Norcostco is a dealer in theatrical supplies and men's formalwear. 180 employees. Founded in 1884. SIC 5699.

Norcraft Companies LLC 3020 Denmark Ave., Suite 100, Eagan, MN 55121. Tel: 651/234-3300; Fax: 651/234-3398; Web site: http://www.norcraftcompanies.com. Thomas W. Klein, Pres.; Dave Aasen, VP-Fin./Admin.; David B. Van Horne, VP-Sls./Mktg.; Fran Ploetz, VP-Mfg.; Carl Bohn, VP-Sls. Annual revenue $120 million. Norcraft manufactures kitchen cabinetry, and bathroom vanities. The company sells two separate brands: Mid Continent Cabinetry, for the builder/remodeler market; and Norcraft Cabinetry, for the retail home center market. Manufacturing facilities are located in Cottonwood, Minn., and Newton, Kan. and Mohave, AZ—with regional service centers in California, Nevada, Arizona, and Florida. In June 1998 Norcraft Cos. Inc. was acquired by private equity firm Pfingsten Partners LLC, Deerfield, Ill. 1,200 employees (400 in Minnesota). Founded in 1975. In June 2000 the company acquired UltraCraft of Liberty, N.C. The acquisition made Norcraft one of the top 10 U.S. kitchen and bath cabinet firms; added semi-custom and frameless cabinets to its product mix; increased its offerings to the important remodeling segment of the industry; and gave the company its first manufacturing facility on the East Coast, as well as an expanded customer base in the East Coast market. SIC 2434. No. 95 CRM Private 100.

Nordic Fiberglass Inc. P.O. Box 27, Warren, MN 56762. Tel: 218/745-5095; Fax: 218/745-4990. Susan Haugen, Pres.; Nancy Haugen, VP; Wayne Spidahl, Gen. Mgr.; Linda Conely, Sec. and Treas. Nordic Fiberglass manufactures fiberglass products for the electric utility industry. 122 employees (67 in Minnesota; 2 part-time). Founded in 1970. SIC 3089.

Nordic Press Inc. 8501 54th Ave. N., New Hope, MN 55428. Tel: 763/535-6440; Fax: 763/535-1821. Olaf A. Bjorkedal, Pres.; John C. Jacobson, VP; Al Vander Plaats, CFO and Gen. Mgr. Nordic Press is engaged in commercial printing and, as Nordic Packaging Inc., in folding-carton manufacturing. 180 employees (all in Minnesota). Founded in 1968. SIC 2631, 2752.

Nor-Lake Inc. Second and Elm Street, P.O. Box 248, Hudson, WI 54016. Tel: 715/386-2323; Fax: 715/386-6149. DuWayne A. Bakke, Pres. and CEO; Barbara A. Richardson, Chm. and Sec. Annual revenue $33 million. Nor-Lake is a manufacturer of commercial refrigeration equipment. 233 employees (20 in Minnesota; 3 part-time). Founded in 1947. SIC 3585.

NorStar Products International Inc. 1255 Port Terminal Dr., P.O. Box 16150, Duluth, MN 55802. Tel: 218/722-9200; Fax: 218/722-6443; Web site: http://www.norstarproducts.com. Gerald R. DeMeo, Pres. and CEO; Kelvin R. Herstad, VP and CFO; Gary Werkhoven, P.E., VP-Engrg. NorStar Products International manufactures and distributes truck-mounted, hydraulically powered equipment for use by electric utilities, municipalities, government agencies, and industry. Sales are both domestic and international. 54 employees (all in Minnesota). Founded in 1995. SIC 3569.

North American Outdoor Group Inc. 12301 Whitewater Dr., Suite 260, Minnetonka, MN 55343. Tel: 952/936-9333; Fax: 952/988-0974. Nancy Evensen, Pres. and CEO; Mark LaBarbera, SVP-Media; Kate Pope, SVP-Fin./Op.; Greg Carey, VP-Home Media; Tony DeFrance, VP-Mktg.; LouAnne Drenchahn, VP-Hum. Res.; Bill Miller, VP-Editorial/Production; Russ Nolan, VP and Group Publisher; Mike Vail, VP-New Product Devel. Annual revenue $200 million. North American Outdoor Group (NAOG) is the world's largest lifestyle affinity membership organization, with more than 3.6 million members. It is the only company of its kind that combines membership, publishing, and continuity marketing. It operates six special-interest clubs: PGA TOUR Partners Club, North American Hunting Club, North American Fishing Club, Handyman Club of America, National Home Gardening Club, and Cooking Club of America. 400 employees. Founded in 1978. SIC 2721, 2721.

North Country Ford 3401 Coon Rapids Blvd., Coon Rapids, MN 55433. Tel: 763/427-1120; Fax: 763/427-9373. David Luther, Pres. North Country Ford (formerly Art Goebel Ford) is a Ford car and truck dealership. 87 employees (84 in Minnesota). Founded in 1954. SIC 5511.

North Country Lumber Company Inc. P.O. Box 499, Mellen, WI 54546. Tel: 715/274-4311; Fax: 715/274-2304. Thomas Jokinen, Pres.; Debra Delegan, Treas. and Sec.; Jean Stilin, VP. North Country Lumber Co. performs sawmill, planing, sliced hardwood veneer, dimension, and dry kiln services. 60 employees. Founded in 1978. SIC 2421.

North Shore Bank of Commerce 131 W. Superior St., Duluth, MN 55802. Tel: 218/722-4784; Fax: 218/722-7904. Larry D. Johnson, Pres. and CEO. North Shore Bank of Commerce is a full-service commercial bank with five Duluth locations and more than $100 million in assets. Owned by North Shore Financial Holdings Inc., Duluth. 92 employees (all in Minnesota). Founded in 1915. SIC 6022.

North Star Companies 269 Barstead Rd. S., Cottonwood, MN 56229. Tel: 507/423-6262; Fax: 507/423-6323. Clifford Hanson, Pres.; Jeff Mauland, EVP; Al Anderson, SVP; Joe Hoff, SVP; Terry Timm, SVP. Annual revenue $75 million. North Star Cos. is made up of two insurance companies: North Star Mutual Insurance Co., which provides farm and home property and casualty insurance; and North Star General Insurance Co., which provides auto insurance. 144 employees (135 in Minnesota; 4 part-time). Founded in 1920. SIC 6331.

North Star Foods Inc. 1279 St. Charles Ave., P.O. Box 587, St. Charles, MN 55972. Tel: 507/932-4831; Fax: 507/932-5624. Robert L. Hartzell, Pres. North Star Foods processes fresh and frozen prepared foods and cooked roast beef, turkey, chicken, and pork products for institutional trade. 150 employees. Founded in 1971. SIC 2015, 2038.

North Star International Trucks Inc. 3000 Broadway St. N.E., Minneapolis, MN 55413. Tel: 612/378-1660; Fax: 612/378-2646. M.T. Gleeson, Pres.; D.W. Williams, EVP; D.L. Montgomery, VP; D. Olson, VP-Sls.; L. Waters, VP-Fin. Annual revenue $48 million. North Star International Trucks sells commercial trucks and has parts and service available. It also rents and leases trucks through its subsidiary, North Star Truck Rental & Leasing Inc. 114 employees (109 in Minnesota). Founded in 1982. SIC 5012, 7538.

North Star Plating and Finishing Company Inc. 2110 10th St. S., P.O. Box 204, Brainerd, MN 56401. Tel: 218/829-6324; Fax: 218/829-9664. Ronald G. Brown, Pres.; Kim Wood, VP. North Star Plating & Finishing manufactures stamped metal automotive body parts and various other automotive parts and supplies. The company has a warehouse in Minneapolis and 12 other locations in Iowa, Missouri, Wisconsin, and Illinois. 215 employees. Founded in 1968. SIC 3465, 5013.

North Star Resource Group 2701 University Ave., Minneapolis, MN 55414. Tel: 612/872-1300; Fax: 612/872-3869. Phillip C. Richards, Chm.; Nick Stevens, Pres.; David Vasos, VP-CRI Securities; Ann Elliott, VP-Marathon Advisors. North Star Resource Group is an association of professionals who work to help clients accumulate wealth, solve business-succession problems, and evaluate estate-planning options. The company provides its services through three divisions: North Star Consultants, Marathon Advisors Inc., and CRI Securities Inc. Offices: Minneapolis, Grand Rapids, Bloomington, Eden Prairie, and Rochester, Minn.; Phoenix and Tuscon, Ariz.; Iowa City, Iowa; Madison, Wis.; Fargo, N.D.; and Billings, Mont. 74 employees (54 in Minnesota). Founded in 1969. SIC 6282, 6289.

North States Industries Inc. 1200 Mendelssohn Ave., Suite 210, Golden Valley, MN 55427. Tel: 763/541-9101; Fax: 763/541-9026. Peter M. Runyon, Pres. and CEO; Dean Weisbeck, CFO. Annual revenue $19 million. North States Industries is a manufacturer of plastic juvenile furniture, and bird feeders. 140 employees (55 in Minnesota). Founded in 1952. SIC 2499, 3999.

Northeast Bank of Minneapolis 77 Broadway St. N.E., Minneapolis, MN 55413. Tel: 612/379-8811; Fax: 612/362-3262. Belva H. Rasmussen, Chm. and CEO; Thomas M. Beck, Pres.; Gail Mikolich, EVP and Cashier; Michael Collins, EVP; Larry Crane, EVP and Branch Mgr.; Larry Pietrzak, EVP and Branch Mgr. Annual revenue $14.5 million. Northeast Bank of Minneapolis is an independent, full-service community bank with $180 million in assets, $113 million in loans, and locations in Minneapolis, Coon Rapids, and Columbia Heights, Minn. 84 employees (all in Minnesota; 19 part-time). Founded in 1947. SIC 6022.

Northern Cap Manufacturing Company 2633 Minnehaha Ave. S., Minneapolis, MN 55406. Tel: 612/729-3000; Fax: 612/729-1976. Sam Rafowitz, Chm.; Ken Rafowitz, CEO; Ivan Rafowitz, Pres. Northern Cap Manufacturing Co. makes caps and hats. 150 employees (all in Minnesota). Founded in 1950. SIC 5136.

Northern Engine & Supply Company Inc. 2929 W. Superior St., Duluth, MN 55806. Tel: 218/624-1443; Fax: 218/628-2314. Gordon W. Seitz, Pres.; Robert Seitz, VP; Thomas Seitz, VP; Nancy Dodd, Treas.; Jim Hellman, Branch Mgr.-Fargo, N.D.; George Opoien, Purch. Agent; Elizabeth Seitz, Sec.; Bob Van Guilder, Branch Mgr. Annual revenue $9.5 million. Northern Engine & Supply is a wholesale store selling general construction, mining, and industrial machinery and equipment. Additional stores located in Fargo, N.D.; Gillette, Wyo.; and Proctor and Virginia, Minn. 48 employees (36 in Minnesota; 5 part-time). Founded in 1957. SIC 5082, 5084.

Northern Improvement Company P.O. Box 2846, Fargo, ND 58108. Tel: 701/277-1225; Fax: 701/277-1516. J.L. McCormick, Chm.; Thomas McCormick, Pres.; Steve McCormick, EVP; W.D. Berg, Sec.; Brad Ballweber, VP and Treas. Northern Improvement Co. is engaged in heavy highway construction. 600 employees (25 in Minnesota). Founded in 1935. SIC 1611.

Northern Lights Casino Box 1003, HCR 73, Walker, MN 56484. Tel: 800/252-7529. Rooney White, Gen. Mgr. Northern Lights Casino offers a restaurant and full-service bar. 350 employees. Founded in 1990. SIC 7993.

Northern Michigan Veneers Inc. P.O. Box 352, Gladstone, MI 49837. Tel: 906/428-3113; Fax: 906/428-1525. John D. Besse, Pres.; Gregory Besse, Sec. Northern Michigan Veneers operates a veneer-splicing facility and manufactures face veneer. 125 employees. Founded in 1966. SIC 2435.

Northern Pride Inc. P.O. Box 598, Thief River Falls, MN 56701. Tel: 218/681-1201; Fax: 218/681-7183. Russel W. Christianson, Gen. Mgr. Annual revenue $22 million. Northern Pride is a turkey processing plant. 210 employees (all in Minnesota). Founded in 1989. SIC 2015.

Northern Tool & Equipment Company 2800 Southcross Dr. W., P.O. Box 1219, Burnsville, MN 55306. Tel: 952/894-9510; Fax: 952/894-1020. Donald L. Kotula, CEO; Charles Albrecht, Pres. and COO; Bradley J. Beckman, CFO. Annual revenue $559 million. Northern Tool sells hardware tools, generators, pressure washers, and do-it-yourself items. It also operates 40 retail stores in Minnesota, Wisconsin, Iowa, Texas, and the Southeast. 1,800 employees. Founded in 1981. In August 2000 the company announced a staffing adjustment that resulted in the layoff of 3 percent of its workforce. SIC 3423, 3599, 3714, 5251. No. 18 CRM Private 100.

Northern Wire LLC 1100 Taylor St., P.O. Box 545, Merrill, WI 54452. Tel: 715/536-9551; Fax: 715/536-5389; Web site: http://www.northernwire.com. Ara A. Cherchian, Pres. Annual revenue $16 million. Northern Wire LLC is a custom-wire-forming operation. 210 employees (3 part-time). Founded in 1973. SIC 3479, 3496.

Northern Wire Products Inc. P.O. Box 70, St. Cloud, MN 56302. Tel: 320/252-3442; Fax: 320/252-2832; Web site: http://www.cloudnet.com/~nwire/. Ronald Carlson, Pres. and CEO. Northern Wire Products is a manufacturer of fabricated wire forms for OEM; a designer and fabricator of point-of-purchase displays; and an applicator of custom powder coating. 200 employees. Founded in 1959. SIC 3479, 3496.

Northland Aluminum Products Inc. Highways 7 and 100, 5005 County Rd. 25, St. Louis Park, MN 55416. Tel: 952/920-2888; Fax: 952/924-9668. H. David Dalquist, Chm.; H. David Dalquist III, Pres. and CEO. Northland Aluminum's subsidiary, Nordic Ware, manufactures and distributes metal cookware and bakeware, microwave cookware, and kitchenware accessories. Other subsidiaries include Industrial Coatings (Minneapolis), which manufactures nonstick and protective coatings for all applications. 350 employees (150 part-time). Founded in 1946. SIC 3089.

Northland Electric Supply Company P.O. Box 1275, Minneapolis, MN 55440. Tel: 612/676-2800; Fax: 612/676-2564. Jack M. Vilett, Pres.; Marv Spartz, VP-Op. and Fin.; Margie Basney, VP-Mktg./Planning; Ron Penberthy, VP-Sls. Northland Electric Supply is a third-generation electrical wholesaler serving Minnesota, western Wisconsin, and border areas of North and South Dakota and Iowa. The largest independent electrical distributor in the Upper Midwest, Northland distributes electrical and industrial-systems supplies through branches in Minneapolis, Mankato, Rochester, St. Cloud, and Owatonna, Minn.; and Hudson and Eau Claire, Wis. 177 employees. Founded in 1920. SIC 5063.

Northland Stainless 1119-A Bridge St., P.O. Box 100, Tomahawk, WI 54487. Tel: 715/453-5326; Fax: 715/453-5357; Web site: http://www.northlandstainless.com. Ara A. Cherchian, Pres., CEO, and Treas.; Tim Keyes, Gen Mgr.; Walter Dieter, Sls. Mgr. Annual revenue $8.6 million. Northland Stainless manufactures stainless steel reactors, pressure vessels, and tanks for the food, beverage, chemical, paper, and pharmaceutical industries. The company also fabricates other equipment and products using cast-alloy, titanium, and aluminum. 85 employees (3 part-time). Founded in 1973. SIC 3443, 3444, 3554, 3795.

Northwest Packaging Inc. 1996 University Ave., St. Paul, MN 55104. Tel: 651/649-1040; Fax: 651/649-1540. Arthur Durand, Pres.; Thomas Klinger, VP. Northwest Packaging manufactures corrugated packaging and displays. Warehouse/sales offices in Mankato and Duluth, Minn. 60 employees. Founded in 1987. SIC 2653.

Northwest Swiss-Matic Inc. 7600 32nd Ave. N., Crystal, MN 55427. Tel: 763/544-4222; Fax: 763/544-6873; Web site: http://www.nwswissmatic.com. G. Lee Martin, CEO; John G. Graeber, Pres.; E. Terry Haubruch, VP and Prod. Mgr. Annual revenue $12 million. Northwest Swiss-Matic is engaged in automatic screw machine work and precision mechanical assembly. 125 employees (all in Minnesota). Founded in 1962. SIC 3451, 3599.

Northwestern Products Inc. 3255 Spring St. N.E., Minneapolis, MN 55413. Tel: 612/331-9384; Fax: 612/331-6721. Robert Cutshell, Owner; Briant Cutshell, Pres.; David A. Fryer, Sls. Mgr. Northwestern Products manufactures and distributes Christian inspirational gift products worldwide. The company owns 10 Northwestern Bookstores. Locations: Twin Cities area (7); Waterloo, Iowa; Cedar Rapids, Iowa; and Boynton Beach, Florida. 250 employees (200 in Minnesota; 45 part-time). Founded in 1954. SIC 5942, 5947.

Northwestern Travel LP 7250 Metro Blvd., Edina, MN 55439. Tel: 952/921-3700; Fax: 952/832-2080; Web site: http://www.nwtm.com. John C. Noble, Chm. and CEO; Arthur Dahl, Pres. and COO; Lorri Anderson, VP-Hum. Res.; Richard Eller, SVP-Corp. Devel.; Sue Kerby, Div. Pres.-Dayton's Travel Service/Mainline Cruise; Jeff Langfeldt, VP-Info. Svs.; Lisa Miller, VP-Customer Rel.; Evelyn Molzhan, VP-Onsite Op.; Roger Przytarski, CFO; Andrea Ritchie, Div. Pres.-Northwestern Travel Mgmt.; Tim Shaughnessy, VP-Employee Recruitment/Retention Programs; Wever Weed, Dir.-Communications; Claudia Wilson, Div. Pres.-Northwestern Incentive Svs. Annual revenue $38.5 million ($480 million in volume). Northwestern Travel, a global partner of Woodside Travel Trust, is among the 12 largest travel management companies in the United States. Its 168 locations in 26 states serve travelers through four divisions: Northwestern Travel Management and Northwestern Incentive Services (business); Mainline Cruise & Travel; and Dayton's Travel Services. 808 employees (641 in Minnesota; 195 part-time). Founded in 1969. In January 2000 the company acquired Racine, Wis.-based Veltra Corp., Wisconsin's seventh-largest travel agency. The deal increased Northwestern's presence in eastern Wisconsin, where it already had a corporate travel office in Milwaukee, by extending its reach southward and by adding leisure travel to its offerings. SIC 4724.

Norval Industries Inc. P.O. Box 862, Wayzata, MN 55391. Tel: 952/476-4400; Fax: 952/476-8445. John Valene, Pres. Norval Industries Inc. manufactures lead plate, nuclear shielding products, and X-ray shielding products. 50 employees. Founded in 1936. SIC 3356, 3842.

Nott Company 4480 Round Lake Rd. W., Arden Hills, MN 55112. Tel: 651/415-3400; Fax: 651/415-3444. R.A. Rosa, CEO; E.L. Davis, COO; D.R. Babcock, CFO. Nott Co. distributes and services power transmission, mechanical, and rubber products; custom-fabricates and distributes synthetic and rubber products; distributes, leases, and services mobile materials-handling equipment; and distributes fluid power components and systems. The company has operations in Minneapolis, Bloomington, Duluth, and Hibbing, Minn.; and Des Moines, Iowa. 194 employees (190 in Minnesota). Founded in 1879. SIC 5085.

Nova Consulting Group Inc. 1107 Hazeltine Blvd., Suite 400, Chaska, MN 55318. Tel: 952/448-9393; Fax: 952/448-9572. Steven B. Cummings, Pres. Annual revenue $10 million. Nova Consulting performs environmental, engineering and architectural services. 119 employees (89 in Minnesota; 22 part-time). Founded in 1987. SIC 8731.

NuAire Inc. 2100 Fernbrook Ln. N., Plymouth, MN 55447. Tel: 763/553-1270; Fax: 763/553-0459; Web site: http://www.nuaire.com. Richard Peters, Pres.; William Peters, VP; Gerald Peters, VP; James Peters, VP; James Sande, VP; Buck Richerson, VP. NuAire manufactures products for life-science research. 200 employees. Founded in 1971. SIC 3821.

Nybo Manufacturing Inc. 4500 Valley Industrial Blvd., Shakopee, MN 55379. Tel: 952/445-4500; Fax: 952/445-0771; Web site: http://www.nybo.com. Dennis Nybo, CEO; Kelly Schwab, Pres. Annual revenue $7 million. Nybo Manufacturing performs contract manufacturing of metal components, products, and special machinery. 50 employees (all in Minnesota). Founded in 1959. SIC 3444, 3449, 3499, 3599.

Nystrom Inc. 1701 Madison St. N.E., Minneapolis, MN 55413. Tel: 612/781-3491; Fax: 612/425-0870. Jim Nystrom, Owner and Pres.; Sue Thomas, CFO; Scott Sustacek, COO. Annual revenue $15.9 million. Nystrom Inc. is an integrated manufacturer and distributor of commercial construction products. The company markets direct to contractors under the Nystrom Building Products brand name and to distributors under the Cierra Products brand name. 80 employees (82 in Minnesota; 2 part-time). Founded in 1948. In August 2000 the company acquired Airline Products Co., Hagerstown, Md., a privately held provider of louvers to the commercial construction market. SIC 3444.

ObjectFX Corp 2515 Wabash Ave., Suite 200, St. Paul, MN 55114. Tel: 651/644-6064; Fax: 651/644-0366; Web site: http://www.objectfx.com. Mark Tudor, Pres. and CEO; Bruce Gilmore, EVP; William Alldredge, VP-Fin. and CFO. Annual revenue $3.7 million. ObjectFX develops and markets software that enables the interactive visualization and analysis of information through interactive maps, schematics, network diagrams, and logical views via the Web. The company's two software suites, SpatialFX and C-it Software, are designed specifically for the Web. Combining lightweight clients with highly scalable back-end application servers, they allow users in many different industries to view and interact with multiple sources of real-time business information, thereby enabling faster, more effective business decisions. ObjectFX's products can be installed at customer sites or accessed through Web-based service providers. They serve a wide range of applications such as transportation and logistics management, telecommunications network monitoring, and supply chain optimization. In addition, they provide new kinds of mangement applications for markets such as high-tech consumer electronics, retail, and the public sector. ObjectFX software is installed at such leading organizations as BellSouth, Eaton Trucking Information Systems Division, Motorola, Boeing, FedEx Custom Critical, J. B. Hunt, Lucent Technologies, Sprint, TRW, Qwest, and the U.S. Postal Service. In October 2000 Locate Networks Inc., a provider of wireless location-based services that manage and locate valued assets and people, selected ObjectFX's SpatialFX location/mapping services engine to translate real-time geographic coordinates into addresses that can be displayed as map or text format on multiple communications devices, including pagers, handheld devices, and computers.50 employees (1 part-time). SIC 7372.

Ochs Brick Company Box 106, Springfield, MN 56087. Tel: 507/723-4221; Fax: 507/723-4223; Web site: http://www.ochsbrick.com. Matt Van Hoomissen, Pres. and CEO; Don Herweyer, VP-Sls.; Phil Weller, VP-Prod.; Sharon Pieschel, VP-Admin.; Helen Lamote, Cont. Annual revenue $15 million. Ochs manufactures face brick products and distributes and sells brick and related masonry products such as glass block; retaining wall systems, pavers, and synthetic stone. The company has sales offices in North St. Paul and Edina, Minn. 90 employees (89 in Minnesota; 3 part-time). Founded in 1891. SIC 3251, 5032.

O'Day Equipment Inc. 1301 N.W. 40, P.O. Box 2706, Fargo, ND 58108. Tel: 701/282-9260; Fax: 701/281-9770. Jim O'Day, Pres.; Al Peach, VP; Lee Holschuh, Sec. and Treas. O'Day Equipment manufactures steel storage tanks. It also designs and installs fueling equipment systems. 90 employees (16 in Minnesota; 2 part-time). Founded in 1935. SIC 3443.

R.D. Offutt Company 2829 S. University, Fargo, ND 58109. Tel: 701/237-6062; Fax: 701/239-8750. Ronald D. Offutt, Pres.; Allan F. Knoll, Treas. and Sec.; Paul T. Horn, VP. R.D. Offutt is a potato grower and processor in nine states. 1,500 employees (1,200 in Minnesota). Founded in 1964. SIC 0134.

Old Dutch Foods Inc. 2375 Terminal Rd., Roseville, MN 55113. Tel: 651/633-8810; Fax: 651/633-8894. Steven Aanenson, Pres. and CEO; Eric Aanenson, VP-Op. and COO; Trace Benson, Cont.; Jay Buckingham, Sls. Mgr.; Matt Colford, Mktg. Mgr. Old Dutch manufactures potato chips, popcorn, and corn snacks, and distributes a variety of packaged snack foods. Brand names include Old Dutch, Rip L, Dutch Crunch, and Northern Lites. Old Dutch's Upper Midwest market share for potato chips is 32 percent. 515 employees (395 in Minnesota). Founded in 1934. In January 2000 the company completed a $10 million upgrade of its Calgary, Alberta, plant that added 50,000 square feet (tripling its size) and brought in state-of-the-art equipment for the manufacture of corn-based snacks (cheese puffs, corn curls, and "Restaurante Style" tortilla chips). SIC 2096.

Old Home Foods Inc. 370 University Ave., St. Paul, MN 55103. Tel: 651/228-9035; Fax: 651/228-1820. Richard G. Hanson, CEO; John Bonifaci, CFO; June C. Woolley, Sec. and Treas.; Geoff Murphy, VP-Op.; David Holdsworth, Dir.-Mktg. Old Home Foods produces cottage cheese, yogurt, sour cream, dips, and specialty food products. 104 employees. Founded in 1925. In 1999 the company changed the packaging of some of its dairy products from their familiar, old-fashioned waxy paper tubs to plastic. The new program included talking directly to the consumer to avoid any backlash. SIC 5143.

Old Peoria Company Inc. 7900 Chicago Ave. S., Bloomington, MN 55420. Tel: 952/854-8600; Fax: 952/851-0501. Kalman Goldenberg, Chm.; Arnold Lifson, Pres.; Paul Curley, VP and CFO. Annual revenue $90 million. Old Peoria Co. Inc., dba Quality Wine & Spirits Co., is a wholesale liquor distributor. Other location: Des Moines, Iowa. 159 employees (113 in Minnesota). Founded in 1934. SIC 5182.

Olsen Thielen & Co. Ltd. 223 Little Canada Rd., Little Canada, MN 55117. Tel: 651/483-4521; Fax: 651/483-2467; Web site: http://www.olsen-thielen.com. Kenneth H. Vohs, Chm.; Thomas R. Farm, Pres.; Michael L. Bromelkamp, VP; Dennis R. Carson, VP; John W. Coleman, VP; Lisa K. Dunnigan, VP; Rick H. Ehrich, VP; Nancy J. Fuhr, VP; Patrick M. Hall, VP; Jeffrey L. Hanson, VP; Andrew K. Janneke, VP; Steven J. Johnson, VP; Gregory I. Nelson, VP; Patrick D. Powers, VP; Kelly M. Salwei, VP; Stephen N. Sarracco, VP; Eric P. Sheehan, VP; Deborah L. Stambaugh, VP; McClelland Troost, VP. Olsen Thielen is a full-service accounting firm that specializes in auditing and accounting; income tax planning and preparation; business and personal financial planning; employee benefits plan design and administration; business management and administrative services consulting; and computer systems and network consulting, installation, and training. The firm has offices in Little Canada and Eden Prairie, Minn. 155 employees. Founded in 1921. In November 1999 the firm acquired Troost & Co. P.A., CPAs, of Minnetonka, Minn. SIC 8721.

Onvoy 10405 Sixth Ave. N., Third floor, Plymouth, MN 55441. Tel: 763/230-4100; Fax: 763/230-4200; Web site: http://www.onvoy.com. Paul Hoff, Chm.; Janice Aune, Pres. and CEO; Raymond E. Winkler, Pres.-Network Technologies; Mary Lang, VP-Strategic Bus. Devel.; Kathy Duff, Dir.-Op.; Robert Gannon, Dir.-Customer Care; Joy Gullikson, Dir.-External Rel.; Gary Kosin, Dir.-Customer Engrg.; Kathryn Lovik, Dir.-Corp./Mktg. Communications; Phillip Swiler, Dir.-Retail Sls.; Dave Walters, Dir.-Core Engrg. Annual revenue $75 million. Onvoy is a provider of integrated voice, data, and Internet services composed of former companies MEANS Telcom, MEANS Communications, and MRNet. Onvoy is Minnesota's largest Internet service provider and operates one of the largest networks in Minnesota. Through this network the company provides a full spectrum of telecommunications and Internet services including 1+ and 800/888 long-distance, calling cards, operator services, videoconferencing, frame relay, DSL, OCN connectivity, ATM, e-commerce, Web hosting, and consulting and design services. 250 employees. Founded in 1988. In January 2000 B2BXchange Inc., a leading provider of business-to-business Internet hosting, tools, and solutions—sub. VirtualFund (Nasdaq: VFND)—chose Onvoy to provide co-location services for its growing Internet hosting capabilities. Covad Communications (Nasdaq: COVD) and Onvoy installed the first U.S. CLEC-shared line, with U S West in Minnesota. In February Onvoy completed the first phase of a massive network upgrade. In March Onvoy introduced a digital subscriber line (DSL) service built over its own network. In May Onvoy completed a 10-fold expansion of its Minneapolis Data Center to meet the explosive demand for secure data storage. A strategic partnership with Genesis Innovations Inc. of St. Paul made Onvoy's ultra-reliable high-speed Internet and hosting services available to Genesis customers. In June Onvoy completed the first phase of a two-phase network expansion and protection project: Onvoy's expanded network can carry more than 1 million phone calls simultaneously on a single strand of fiber; the "self-healing" network automatically re-routes traffic in less than 50 milliseconds in the event of physical damage to the network. In September Onvoy announced the completion of phase two. A strategic partnership with The Computer Connection of Lake City, Minn., was to make Onvoy's Internet and hosting services available to The Computer Connection's customers. In August Onvoy completed a major investment to collocate in facilities around its Duluth office. This positioned Onvoy to be among the first companies in the Duluth area able to offer high-speed DSL service over its own facilities. (Other providers, with the exception of U S WEST, must use other company networks and equipment to bring this super-fast Internet service to customers.) SIC 4813, 4822. No. 21 CityBusiness Fastest-growing Private Companies.

Open Systems Holdings Corp. 1157 Valley Park Dr., Shakopee, MN 55379. Tel: 952/403-5700; Fax: 952/496-2495; Web site: http://www.osas.com. Michael M. Bertini, CEO; Steve Beckey, Devel. Mgr.; Dave Link, Devel. Mgr.; Paul Lundquist, VP-Sls.; Craig Faulds, VP-Op.; Amy Reynolds, Mktg. Mgr. Open Systems develops, publishes, and markets business, accounting, distribution, and manufacturing software for businesses in the mid-size market. Products are sold through value-added resellers in North America, Europe, and Asia. Products include TRAVERSE Accounting Business Software for Windows, OPEN SYSTEMS Accounting Software, and TRAVERSE Client/Server. 140 employees. Founded in 1976. SIC 7372.

Oppenheimer Wolff & Donnelly LLP 45 S. Seventh St., Suite 3400, Minneapolis, MN 55402. Tel: 612/607-7000; Fax: 612/607-7100; Web site: http://www.oppenheimer.com. Michael J. Bleck, Chm. and CEO; Howard S. Booth, COO; Katherine A. Wilson, Dir.-Mktg. Annual revenue $97 million. Oppenheimer Wolff & Donnelly is an international law firm of more than 300 lawyers. The firm represents a wide variety of business, financial, and institutional clients in a wide range of matters. Clients include major publicly held national and international companies, as well as partnerships and emerging businesses. 800 employees (400 in Minnesota; 70 part-time). Founded in 1886. In August 2000 the firm expanded its Internet focus teams to meet the need for leading-edge, Internet-focused counsel. Oppenheimer's Internet & e-Commerce team has formed four new Internet focus teams to add to the two it established in 1999. Each team features an online form, leveraging the Internet's unique capabilities to deliver timely and trustworthy legal guidance. SIC 8111.

Opus Group 10350 Bren Rd. W., Minnetonka, MN 55343. Tel: 952/656-4444; Fax: 952/656-4529. Keith Bednarowski, Chm.-Opus Corp.; Mark Rauenhorst, Pres./CEO-Opus Corp.; John Albers, VP-Architecture, Opus Architecture/Engineers; Luz Campa, SVP-Tax, Opus Corp.; Jack Crocker, Pres./COO-Opus North; Pat Dady, VP-Opus National LLC; Andrew Deckas, EVP-Opus National LLC; Mike Dwyer, VP-Opus Northwest Mgmt. LLC; Becky Finnigan, VP-Sls./Investments, Opus Northwest; Jim Heller, VP and Gen. Mgr.-Opus Northwest LLC; Julie Kimble, VP-Nat'l Acct. Mgmt.; Wade Lan, VP-Asset Mgmt., Opus Properties; Lori Larson, VP-Sls., Opus Northwest LLC; Wade Lau, VP-Asset Mgmt., Opus Properties; Jan Maistrovich, VP-Hum. Res., Opus Corp.; John McKenzie, VP-Opus Northwest Construction Corp.; Tim Murnane, VP-Opus Northwest LLC; Jim Murrey, VP-Nat'l Mktg., Opus; Dennis Neu, VP-Op., Opus Architects/Engineers; Dan Nichol, VP and Gen. Counsel, Opus Corp.; Joe Rauenhorst, Pres./CEO-Opus East; Neil Rauenhorst, Pres./CEO-Opus South; Tom Roberts, Pres./CEO-Opus West; Ron Schiferl, SVP and CFO-Opus Corp.; John Solberg, Pres.-Opus Northwest LLC. Annual revenue $1.2 billion. Opus Group is a design, construction, and development firm offering services including real estate development, architecture, engineering, construction, property management, financing and leasing. Opus has offices in 27 locations throughout the United States: Allentown, Atlanta, Austin, Chicago, Columbus, Dallas, Denver, Fort Lauderdale, Houston, Indianapolis, Kansas City, Los Angeles, Miami, Milwaukee, Minneapolis, Orange County, Orlando, Pensacola, Philadelphia, Phoenix, Portland, Sacramento, San Francisco, San Jose, Seattle, Tampa, and Washington, D.C. Several additional entities comprise the Opus Group: Opus National, L.L.C. supports the Opus companies with sales, finance and national tenant marketing activities; Opus Architects & Engineers, Inc. provides design services; Opus Properties, L.L.C. provides asset management; and Opus management companies provide property management services. 1,352 employees (449 in Minnesota; 11 part-time). Founded in 1953. In April 2000 Opus completed construction on the 30-story, 1 million-square-foot Class "A" office tower for American Express Financial Advisors in downtown Minneapolis. Bolstered by development opportunities and the growth of Northern California, Opus West Corp. opened a regional office in San Jose—the company's fourth office in the state. SIC 1541. No. 10 CRM Private 100.

Orion Consulting Inc. 3800 W. 80th St., Suite 1050, Bloomington, MN 55431. Tel: 952/857-1600; Fax: 952/857-1699; Web site: http://www.orionconsulting.com. David P. Wicker, CEO; Mark A. Downey, Pres.; Thomas J. Brown, VP-Business Devel.; Mark Besser, VP-Delivery; Danette Bucsko, CFO. Annual revenue $17.4 million. Orion provides information technology consulting services in mainframe, client/server, Internet/intranet, and software package implementation and integration. Clients include American Express, Northwest Airlines, Cargill, ValueVision, Donaldson, and Gateway. 195 employees. Founded in 1983. SIC 7371. No. 32 CityBusiness Fastest-growing Private Companies.

Owens Companies Inc. 930 E. 80th St., Bloomington, MN 55420. Tel: 952/854-3800; Fax: 952/854-3769; Web site: http://www.owensco.com. Robert Owens, Chm. ; John Owens, Pres. and CEO; John Finley, EVP; James Owens, VP-Mktg.; Charlie McLauchlan, VP-Automation; A. William Hooke, VP-Water Treatment; Mandy L. Beech, VP-Hum. Res.; Jerry Kalin, VP-Home Comfort; Gene Sieve, VP-Engineering. Six divisions—Building Services, Automation, Engineering, Water Treatment, Home Comfort, and Mechanical Contracting—that serve the commercial, residential, and industrial HVAC and refrigeration industries. Named National Contractor of the Year in 1996. Owens Engineering, a member of the Consulting Engineers Council of Minnesota, offers a full range of engineering analysis and design services. Owens Building Services has the largest commercial/industrial service fleet in the state, and a 24-hour dispatcher. Owens Mechanical Contracting operates both sheet metal and piping crews and a NEBB-Certified test and balance staff. Owens Water Treatment is supported by an ISO 9001-certified laboratory. Owens Automation installs and monitors Windows-based, "open protocol" DDC control systems. Annual revenue $15 million. 150 employees. Founded in 1957. In April 2000 Owens acquired Service One Cos. Inc., Plymouth, Minn., and moved into the residential market. It became the core of Owens Home Comfort division. SIC 1711, 8711.

Owens Forest Products Company Inc. 2320 E. First St., Duluth, MN 55812. Tel: 218/723-1151; Fax: 218/724-9486. Robert M. Owens, Pres.; Keith Richmond, VP; Mary Ellen Owens, VP and Sec.; E.J. Anderson, Treas. and Asst. Sec.; Scott Ruhman, Asst. Sec.; Gregg Blodgett, Dir.; John Hosler, Dir.; Phil Stocker, Hum. Res. Mgr.; Eric Canton, Dir. Owens Forest Products Co. Inc. is a hardwood lumber wholesaler selling to manufacturers and distributors worldwide. Owens also operates a hardwood concentration yard with dry kilns at Marathon, Wis. Division Heritage Veneered Products operates a door manufacturing facility producing interior residential doors under the brand names Woodport, Stallion, and Mastercraft. 175 employees (15 in Minnesota). Founded in 1974. SIC 5031.

PGI Mailers 2009 N. Broadway St., New Ulm, MN 56073. Tel: 507/354-1849; Fax: 507/354-1851. Jeff Brower, CEO; Jeff Woll, VP; Lee Kastman, Plant Mgr. PGI Mailers is a bindery and letter shop. 152 employees (95 part-time). Founded in 1986. SIC 2789.

Pace Analytical Services Inc. 1700 Elm St., Suite 200, Minneapolis, MN 55414. Tel: 612/607-1700; Fax: 612/607-6444; Web site: http://www.pacelabs.com. Steve A. Vanderboom, Pres. and CEO; Mike Prasch, Cont.; Jack Dullaghan, VP-Sls./Mktg.; Rolf Krogstad, Info. Sys. Dir. Annual revenue $38 million. Pace Analytical is one of the five largest environmental laboratory firms in the country. It offers sampling and analytical services to industrial companies, engineering and consulting firms, and governmental agencies through a nationwide system of eight laboratories. Analytical testing services identify contaminants in the soil, water, and air—which assists entities in their compliance with environmental regulations. Services include standard organic and inorganic compounds analysis; air toxics analysis, dioxin analysis; and water, groundwater, and air sampling. Pace Analytical also offers mobile laboratories for on-site analysis. 520 employees (220 in Minnesota). Founded in 1995. I SIC 8734.

Pace Manufacturing Inc. P.O. Box 800, 600 S. Sioux Blvd., Brandon, SD 57005. Tel: 605/582-7221; Fax: 605/582-7222. Dan Apland, Cont.; Leroy Stumpe, Dir.-Engrg. Pace Manufacturing produces hydraulic fittings, hose assemblies, and pressure washers. 75 employees (1 in Minnesota; 1 part-time). Founded in 1967. SIC 3451.

Pacific Steel & Recycling 1401 Third St. N.W., Great Falls, MT 59403. Tel: 406/727-6222; Fax: 406/727-9833; Web site: http://www.pacific-steel.com. N.E. (Tuck) Vosburg, Pres. and CEO; Bill Knick, VP-Op.; Ed Leppien, VP-Steel Div.; Bob Short, Sec. and Hum. Res. Mgr.; Dick Langley, Senior Purch. Agent. Pacific Steel & Recycling (previously Pacific Hide & Fur Depot) has one line of business that sells steel products (plate, sheet, bars, angles) with some preprocessing; and also sells agricultural products (gates, feeders, pens, fencing). Another business line recycles scrap iron, nonferrous metals, and fibers; and also purchases and sells wild raw furs, cattle hides, and deer/elk skins and antlers. The company has 37 branch locations in Idaho, Montana, Utah, Washington, and Wyoming. 550 employees. Founded in 1890. SIC 5051, 5083, 5093, 5159.

Pack-It Bindery Inc. 811 Pine St., St. Croix Falls, WI 54024. Tel: 715/483-1807; Fax: 715/483-1810. Paul Christensen, CEO. Pack-It Bindery is engaged in bookbinding: spiral, wire loop, plastic comb, and perfect binding. 75 employees. Founded in 1974. SIC 2789.

Package Technology 700 Xenia Ave. S., Golden Valley, MN 55416. Tel: 763/504-6151; Fax: 763/504-5493. Jonathan S. Miner, CEO. Package Technology, formerly Olympic, is a full-service general commercial sheetfed printer specializing in conventional printing, as well as litho UV inks and coatings. Part of IDI Print Group, Minneapolis, and a subsidiary of The Miner Group International. 108 employees (all in Minnesota; 15 part-time). Founded in 1962. SIC 2752.

Packaging Inc. 11580 K-tel Dr., P.O. Box 538, Minnetonka, MN 55343. Tel: 952/935-3421; Fax: 952/935-0978. George J. Gardner, Chm.; Steve Heath, Pres.; Rex Nelson, VP; Jim Davis, VP; Barb Illies, Sec. and Treas.; David Glaeser, VP; Edward Konar, Asst. VP; Jackie Brown, Asst. VP; Elizabeth Gleaser, Asst. Sec. and Treas. Packaging Inc. is a distributor of strapping systems, pneumatic nailing and stapling products, packaging film, and automated machinery. 101 employees (50 in Minnesota; 24 part-time). Founded in 1957. SIC 5085.

Padco Inc. 2220 Elm St. S.E., Minneapolis, MN 55414. Tel: 612/378-7270; Fax: 612/378-9388. Robert I. Janssen, Senior Pres. and CEO; Ed Goldstein, Pres.; Chandra Meka, VP; Dean Cowdry, VP; David Bergeson, VP. Padco is an international company offering a full line of painting, wallcovering, and do-it-yourself home improvement products. Padco affiliates include: Padco Companies Inc., Minneapolis; Padco Ltd., Toronto; Padco Gmbh, Fulda, Germany; Padco S.A., San Jose, Costa Rica; and Padco S.A., Mexico City. 100 employees (75 in Minnesota). Founded in 1959. SIC 3991.

Paddock Laboratories Inc. 3940 Quebec Ave. N., New Hope, MN 55427. Tel: 763/546-4676; Fax: 763/546-4842; Web site: http://www.paddocklabs.com. Bruce Paddock, Pres.; Allan Slizewski, Dir.-Sls./Mktg.; Ed Maloney, Dir.-Op.; David Slettum, Dir.-Fin./Admin. Paddock Laboratories Inc. manufactures and markets specialty and generic pharmacuticals for niche markets of the health care industry. 140 employees (all in Minnesota; 10 part-time). Founded in 1977. SIC 2834.

Padilla Speer Beardsley Inc. 224 Franklin Ave. W., Minneapolis, MN 55404. Tel: 612/871-8877; Fax: 612/871-7792; Web site: http://www.psbpr.com. John R. Beardsley, Chm. and CEO; Lynn Casey, SVP and COO; Marian Briggs, SVP; Anthony P. (Tony) Carideo, SVP; David Hakensen, SVP; Thomas Jollie, SVP; David Kistle, SVP; John Mackay, SVP; Jerry Erickson, CFO; Michael N. Greece, VP and Mng. Dir.-New York. Annual revenue $8.1 million. Padilla Speer Beardsley (PSB) is the largest independently owned counseling firm in the Upper Midwest. The employee-owned firm is recognized for its award-winning public relations programs developed on behalf of clients from a wide variety of industries. The firm offers expertise in investor relations, consumer and business-to-business marketing communications, public affairs, media relations, crisis communication, employee communications, research, and special events. 99 employees (92 in Minnesota; 9 part-time). Founded in 1961. In March PSB partnered with Walker Information to market and sell four of Walker's proprietary measurement products—a corporate reputation report, an employee relationship report, a customer feedback report, and a supplier relationship report. SIC 8743.

Palace Bingo-Casino-Hotel R.R. 3, P.O. Box 221, Cass Lake, MN 56633. Tel: 218/335-7500; Fax: 218/335-7527. Palace Bingo includes restaurants, entertainment, and resort amenities. 493 employees. Founded in 1990. SIC 7011.

Palen/Kimball Company 550 Vandalia St., St. Paul, MN 55114. Tel: 651/646-2800; Fax: 651/642-2564. G. Richard Palen, Chm.; Gregory Palen, CEO; Chris Markert, Pres. Palen/Kimball Co. designs, constructs, and installs heating, ventilation, and air-conditioning systems. 50 employees (all in Minnesota). Founded in 1932. SIC 3585.

Palm Beach Beauty Companies 2700 E. 28th St., Minneapolis, MN 55406. Tel: 612/724-0471; Fax: 612/728-5591; Web site: http://www.palmbeachbeauty.com. Ben B. Kaitz, Pres. and Treas.; Richard Kaitz, EVP; Miriam Collins Kaitz, VP and Sec. Palm Beach Beauty Cos., formerly Miriam Collins Palm Beach Laboratories, formulates health and beauty aids, cosmetics, lotions and conditioners, shampoos, permanent-waving products, and related items. 72 employees. Founded in 1938. SIC 2844.

Pam Oil Inc. 200 S. Petro Ave., Sioux Falls, SD 57107. Tel: 605/336-1788; Fax: 605/339-9969; Web site: http://www.pam-companies.com. William G. Pederson, Pres. and CEO; Dennis Schulte, CFO. Pam Oil is a wholesale distributor of auto parts, lubricants and accessories, and chemicals. 450 employees. SIC 5013, 5172.

Pan-O-Gold Country Hearth Baking Company 444 E. Saint Germain St., St. Cloud, MN 56304. Tel: 612/340-9696; Fax: 320/251-3759. Howard R. Alton III, CEO; James K. Akervik, VChm.; Dan Cotton, VP; Verlyn Owen, SVP. Pan-O-Gold is a custom wholesale baker for supermarkets and restaurants in Minnesota, North Dakota, South Dakota, parts of Wisconsin, Michigan, Iowa, Nebraska, Montana, and Wyoming. Major brands include Country Hearth, Holsum, Village Health, and Hillbilly breads. Related companies deal in real estate and leasing operations. 800 employees (350 in Minnesota). Founded in 1911. SIC 2051.

Paper, Calmenson & Co. Highways 280 and 36, P.O. Box 64432 (55164), Roseville, MN 55113. Tel: 651/631-1111; Fax: 651/631-9076. Ervin F. Kamm Jr., Pres. and CEO; J. James Collova, Corp. Sec. and CFO; Penny Helberg, VP-Hum. Rel.; Francis J. Zimny, VP and Gen. Mgr.-Pacal Industries; Bert Rivers, VP-Op., Pacal Blades; John Arvig, VP and Gen. Mgr.-Pacal Business Center. Annual revenue $48 million. Paper, Calmenson & Co. (PCAL) fabricates industrial steel parts and subassemblies. PCAL Blades manufactures and distributes blades and accessories for earth-moving and snow-removal equipment. PCAL Business Center leases manufacturing, storage, and office space at its St. Paul location. Branch plants are located in Bucyrus, Ohio; La Crosse, Wis.; and West Jordan, Utah. 340 employees (all in Minnesota). Founded in 1891. SIC 3443, 3531.

PaR Systems Inc. 899 W. Highway 96, Shoreview, MN 55126. Tel: 651/484-7261; Fax: 651/483-2689; Web site: http://www.par.com. Mark Wrightsman, Pres. and CEO. Annual revenue $32 million. PaR Systems designs, manufactures, and services automated robotic processing systems and special remote handling equipment for the nuclear and manufacturing industries. 164 employees (159 in Minnesota; 23 part-time). Founded in 1961. SIC 3569.

Pareo Inc. 120 S. Sixth St., Suite 2250, Minneapolis, MN 55402. Tel: 612/371-0400. Ray Kuntz, CEO. Annual revenue $9.3 million. Pareo, an information technology consulting company, is a developer of large-scale computer applications and a source for the selection and implementation of specific-application solutions. 90 employees. Founded in 1994. SIC 7379. No. 34 CityBusiness Fastest-growing Private Companies.

Park Construction Company 7900 Beech St. N.E., Fridley, MN 55432. Tel: 763/786-9800; Fax: 763/786-2952. Bruce R. Carlson, Pres.; Jeff Carlson, VP and Sec.; John Hedquist, CFO. Annual revenue $53.7

million. Park Construction specializes in bridge, tunnel, and highway construction; excavations; and golf courses. Its golf division provides winter construction work in warm-weather states. 250 employees (200 in Minnesota). Founded in 1916. SIC 1622.

Park Industries 6600 Saukview Dr., P.O. Box 188, St. Cloud, MN 56303. Tel: 320/251-5077; Fax: 320/251-8126; Web site: http://www.parkind.com. Thomas L. Schlough, Pres. and CEO; Gary Stroeing, VP and Sec.; Roger Barthelemy, CFO. Annual revenue $20 million. Park Industries manufactures stone-fabricating and equipment, sold throughout the United States and Canada, with limited exports to 14 countries. 115 employees (112 in Minnesota). Founded in 1952. SIC 3559.

Park Printing Inc. 2801 California St. N.E., Minneapolis, MN 55418. Tel: 612/789-4333; Fax: 612/789-6636; Web site: http://www.parkprint.com. Ralph Koloski, CEO; Timothy Koloski, Pres.; Michael Koloski, VP; Cheryl Mariner, CFO. Annual revenue $14 million. Park Printing is a multicolor, commercial, sheetfed printing company. It has a full range of electronic prepress capabilities and press capacity ranging from 19-inch/one-color to 64-inch/six-color. A fulfillment division with complete FedEx and UPS computer systems for shipping rounds out Park's start-to-finish approach to print projects. 76 employees (all in Minnesota). Founded in 1963. SIC 2759.

Parsons Electric Company 5960 N.E. Main St., Fridley, MN 55432. Tel: 763/571-8000; Fax: 763/571-7210; Web site: http://www.parsons-electric.com. Joel Moryn, Pres.; Jack Claeson, VP; Michael Northquest, Cont. Annual revenue $88 million. Parsons Electric Co. performs electrical construction and service—including design, power quality, motor repair, tele/data and industrial and commercial wiring. Parsons' parent company is Bracknell Corp. Toronto, Canada. 600 employees (3 part-time). Founded in 1927. SIC 1731.

Pearson Candy Company 2140 W. Seventh St., St. Paul, MN 55116. Tel: 651/698-0356; Fax: 651/696-2222. Pearson Candy Co. manufactures confectionery products. 175 employees. Founded in 1909. SIC 2064.

The Pedro Companies 106 E. 10th St., St. Paul, MN 55101. Tel: 651/224-9491; Fax: 651/224-8674. Eugene Pedro, CEO; Carl Pedro Jr., Pres. The Pedro Cos. sells and manufactures business and catalog cases, leather goods, luggage, and briefcases. 90 employees. Founded in 1914. SIC 3161, 3199.

Peerless Chain Company 1416 E. Sanborn St., Winona, MN 55987. Tel: 507/457-9100; Fax: 507/457-9187; Web site: http://www.peerlesschain.com. Harrington Bischof, Chm.; Tom Wynn, VP-Sls./Mktg.; Greg Klein, CFO; Gerald L. Faurote, Pres. and CEO; John McCauley, VP-Op. Annual revenue $46.2 million. Peerless Chain is a manufacturer of tire chains, substantially all types of commercial and industrial chain, and wire-form products in various lengths and diameters. 354 employees (305 in Minnesota). Founded in 1917. SIC 3496.

Peerless Plastics Inc. 510 Willow, Farmington, MN 55024. Tel: 651/463-7147; Fax: 651/463-8074. Kurt Kuno, Pres. Peerless Plastics manufactures kindermats, mortuary supplies, office machine covers, and custom vinyl products. 90 employees. Founded in 1954. SIC 3081, 3089.

Pelican Technology Partners 8500 Normandale Lake Blvd., Suite 1770, Bloomington, MN 55437. Tel: 952/921-8872; Fax: 952/921-8988; Web site: http://www.pelicangroup.com. Kojo Benjamin Taylor, Pres. Pelican Technology Partners is a consulting firm that provides personnel and services to corporate accounts for contract, project, and permanent information system employees; also computer training, staffing, and systems integration. 300 employees. Founded in 1983. SIC 7371, 7379.

Pella Windows & Doors 15300 25th Ave. N., Plymouth, MN 55447. Tel: 763/745-1400; Fax: 612/745-1406. Randy Linn, Pres.; Brenda Smith, Treas. Pella Windows & Doors, formerly Pella Products Inc., is a wholesale and retail distributor of Pella-brand windows and doors. 78 employees (74 in Minnesota; 5 part-time). Founded in 1943. SIC 5031.

Peoples Electrical Contractors 277 E. Fillmore Ave., St. Paul, MN 55107. Tel: 651/227-7711; Fax: 651/227-9684. N. R. Lindberg, Chm.; Steven E. DeWald, Pres.; Dennis R. Sorheim, CFO, Sec., and Treas. Peoples Electrical Contractors is a commercial and industrial electrical-construction contractor, including communications and temperature control systems. 203 employees (all in Minnesota; 2 part-time). Founded in 1922. SIC 1731.

Pepsi-Cola Bottling Company P.O. Box 1335, Huron, SD 57350. Tel: 605/352-8543; Fax: 605/352-8545. Earl D. Nordby, Pres. Pepsi-Cola Bottling Co. manufactures and sells soft drinks and spring water. 54 employees. Founded in 1931. SIC 2086.

Pepsi-Cola of Mankato Inc. P.O. Box 3226, Mankato, MN 56002. Tel: 507/625-7777; Fax: 507/345-4176. David Meade, Gen. Mgr. Pepsi-Cola of Mankato is a distributor of soft drinks. Owned by the Gillette Group, La Crosse, Wis. 100 employees. Founded in 1946. SIC 5149.

Performark Inc. 10701 Hampshire Ave. S., Bloomington, MN 55438. Tel: 952/946-7300; Fax: 952/942-6940. A. Joseph Lethert, Founder; Edward Herzog, Pres. and COO; Roberta L. Dircks, CFO; Marshall Gage, VP-Sls. Devel.; Jack Brown, VP-Op.; Mary Schneider, VP-New Bus. Devel.; Brennan Baas, VP-ATD; John Pierce, VP-ATD; Joanne Sullivan, VP-ATD; Dave Sandum, Dir.-Tech. Performark provides sales and marketing support services that offer performance improvement programs, lead management services, and tactical administrative services. 160 employees (all in Minnesota; 40 part-time). Founded in 1984. SIC 8741, 8742.

Periscope Marketing Communications 921 Washington Ave. S., Minneapolis, MN 55415. Tel: 612/339-2100; Fax: 612/339-1700; Web site: http://www.periscope.com. Bill Simpson, Chm. and CEO ; Greg Kurowski, Pres.; Mark Haumersen, Exec. Creative Dir.; George Creel, VP-Acct. Planning/Res. Annual revenue $14 million (estimated by Fact Book; $87.3 million in capitalized billings, up 7.6 percent). Periscope Marketing Communications specializes in strengthening brands through award-winning creative work. The agency manages clients' brands across a wide range of deliverables, including print, broadcast, and outdoor advertising, commercial Web sites, intranets, corporate identity, sales literature, direct mail, and catalogs. Clients include 3M, ADC Telecommunications, Arctic Cat, Digi International, Evangelical Lutheran Church in America, Metro Transit, Minnegasco, Born Information Services, the Peace Corps, Target Stores, and Treasure Island Resort and Casino. New since last year: Chicago-based Access Global, an online wholesale financial services firm; Golf Galaxy, a golf equipment retailer; Washington, D.C.-based American Public Transportation Association's inaugural industry promotion effort; Time Warner's RoadRunner high-speed Internet access service; Quack.com's voice-activated Internet access business; Mastercraft Boat Co., Venore, Tenn.; Lawson Software, St. Paul; and Life Fitness, Franklin Park, Ill. Periscope has been recognized by the American Association of Advertising

Agencies as one of the top eight midsize creative agencies in the country. 130 employees. Founded in 1960. In October 2000 the firm won 11 awards at The Show 2000 in Minneapolis. SIC 2759, 7311.

Personnel Decisions International 2000 Plaza VII Tower, 45 S. Seventh St., Minneapolis, MN 55402. Tel: 800/633-4410; Fax: 612/904-7120; Web site: http://www.personneldecisions.com. Marvin D. Dunnette, Chm.; Lowell Hellervik, CEO; Ken Hedberg, Pres. and COO; Peter Ramstad, EVP; LeRoy Martin, CFO. Personnel Decisions International (PDI) is a global consulting firm based in organizational psychology. It provides employee testing and development services. 850 employees. Founded in 1967. In July 2000 PDI and HRSoft formed a strategic alliance under which HRSoft's human resource planning software was to be joined with PDI's consulting experience and research to enable organizations to more effectively resolve their most pressing talent-management challenges, including workforce planning, succession management, and leadership development. In September ePredix Inc., a San Francisco-based developer of online assessment, acquired PDI's selection products division in exchange for an ownership stake and an ePredix products distribution agreement. In October the company and the city of St. Paul were reportedly discussing the consolidation of PDI's Twin Cities operations in downtown St. Paul. SIC 8742.

The Petters Companies 7585 Equitable Dr., Eden Prairie, MN 55344. Tel: 952/934-9918; Fax: 952/975-2295; Web site: http://www.redtagoutlet.com. Rod Elofson, Pres. The Petters Cos. is a liquidation and close-out merchant with retail, online, and wholesale businesses. Its five retail stores, operating as Petters Warehouse Direct, are located in Fridley, St. Paul, Edina, St. Cloud, and Eden Prairie, Minn. Other Petters operations include Internet business redtagoutlet.com Inc. Founded in 1993. In January 2000 founder Tom Petters sold the Petters Warehouse District business to management in order to focus on his Internet business, redtagoutlet.com Inc. SIC 5099, 5199.

Pew Construction Company Inc. P.O. Box 2100, Missoula, MT 59806. Tel: 406/721-2001; Fax: 406/721-0000. Thomas R. Pew, Pres. Pew Construction Co. does nonresidential and residential construction, and produces ready-mix concrete and aggregate. 50 employees. Founded in 1913. SIC 8741.

Phillips Plastics Corporation 7 Long Lake Dr., Phillips, WI 54555. Tel: 715/339-3005; Fax: 715/339-3092. Robert F. Cervenka, CEO; James Solinsky, VP-Fin.; Larry Smith, COO; Dick Stoltz, CEO-Svs. Group. Annual revenue $217 million. Phillips Plastics manufactures injection-molded thermoplastics, with complete in-house decorating and tooling, for OEMs in the automotive, medical, appliance, communications, electronics, industrial, and lawn and garden markets. Phillips' 16 business units throughout the state of Wisconsin have grown at an average annual rate exceeding 20 percent since the company's inception. Phillips also has design centers in Santa Clara, Calif., and Framingham, Mass., and a manufacturing facility in Coeur d'Alene, Idaho. 1,500 employees. Founded in 1964. In February 2000 the company formed a strategic alliance with injection molder AMS Plastics, San Diego. SIC 3089.

Phillips Plating Corporation 984 N. Lake Ave., Phillips, WI 54555. Tel: 715/339-3031; Fax: 715/339-3033. William Baratka, Pres.; Dave Baratka, EVP; Robert Baratka, CFO. Annual revenue $4.4 million. Phillips Plating does electroplating of copper, nickel, and chrome on plastic parts, and of nickel and chrome on steel, EMI and RFI shielding. 85 employees (10 part-time). Founded in 1970. SIC 3471.

Phymetrics 6509 Flying Cloud Dr., Eden Prairie, MN 55344. Tel: 952/828-6100; Fax: 952/828-6322; Web site: http://www.phymetrics.com. David Chalmers, Pres. and CEO; John Haddock, Pres. and CEO; James Burkstrand, Dr., VP-Mktg./Sls.; Dr. James Burkstrand, VP-Mktg./Sls. Phymetrics—consisting of Physical Electronics Inc., Evans AnalyticalGroup, and High Voltage Engineering Europa B.V. (HVEE), is the world's leading provider of integrated surface analysis and materials characterization solutions. Manufacturing companies across a broad range of industries, from semiconductor to biomedical and electronics, rely on Phymetrics instruments and services to develop new materials, improve product performance, and increase product yield. Phymetrics' total solutions approach offers customers market-leading surface analysis instruments and particle accelerator systems through its Physical Electronics and HVEE divisions. Global analytical lab services are offered through its Evans Analytical Group division. Phymetrics instrumentation and lab services offer its customers unparalleled expertise in a broad range of analytical techniques including Auger, ESCA, SIMS, TOF-SIMS and many others. Phymetrics and its divisions also have offices in California, New Jersey, Texas, the United Kingdom, Europe, Japan, and Asia. The local operations were acquired in May 1994 from Perkin-Elmer Corp. by management and Chemical Ventures Partners, which sold them to Massachusetts-based High Voltage Engineering in August 1997. The corporate name and headquarters were changed in October 2000. 360 employees (280 in Minnesota). Founded in 1969. The company is in the process of expanding its service offerings to include online consulting, on-site lab management, and advanced training. In October 2000 Physical Electronics introduced its new TRIFT III Time-of-Flight Secondary Ion Mass Spectrometer (TOF-SIMS) at the American Vacuum Society Conference in Boston. The TRIFT III TOF-SIMS is a surface analysis instrument that provides organic and inorganic characterization of solid surfaces, such as semiconductors, hard disks, polymers, and paint and other surface coatings. SIC 3821, 3821, 3826, 3826.

Pier Foundry & Pattern Shop Inc. 51 State St., St. Paul, MN 55107. Tel: 651/222-4461; Fax: 651/222-4185. Randall Grilz, Pres.; Don Grilz Jr., VP. Pier is a jobbing foundry that offers complete pattern shop services. 60 employees (all in Minnesota). Founded in 1889. SIC 3325.

Pierce Company 1019 First Ave. N., P.O. Box 2887, Fargo, ND 58108. Tel: 701/235-5586; Fax: 701/232-5121. Rick Graalum, Pres.; Colin Kelly, VP-Prod.; Mark McGuigan, VP-Fin. Pierce Co. is a printer and lithographer, a handler of office products, Konica copier, and Standard duplicator distributor. 62 employees (15 part-time). Founded in 1904. SIC 2752, 5943.

Pioneer Metal Finishing 1717 W. River Rd. N., Minneapolis, MN 55411. Tel: 612/588-0855; Fax: 612/588-0892. Delbert W. Johnson, Chm. and CEO; Rich Dudkiewicz, Pres. and COO. Pioneer Metal Finishing is an aluminum and magnesium anodizer. In 1997 the company was sold to Pioneer management by previous owner Safeguard Scientifics Inc., Wayne, Pa. 500 employees (170 in Minnesota). Founded in 1946. SIC 3471, 3479.

Pioneer Mutual Life Insurance Company 203 10th St. N., Fargo, ND 58102. Tel: 701/277-2300; Fax: 701/277-2234; Web site: http://www.pmlife.com. Douglas Oksendahl, Pres. and CEO; Duane Engebretson, EVP-Mktg. Annual revenue $68.2 million. Pioneer Mutual Life Insurance Co. provides life insurance and annuities. The company is licensed in 40 states and markets products through 700 independent insurance agents. 75 employees. Founded in 1868. SIC 6311.

Plastic Products Company Inc. 30355 Akerson St., Lindstrom, MN 55045. Tel: 651/257-5980; Fax: 651/257-9774. Marlene A. Messin, Owner and Pres.; Frank E. Messin, EVP; Alton Berg, Treas.; Lori Johnson, Sec. Annual revenue $97 million. Plastic Products does custom plastic injection molding. Secondary operations include decorating, assembly, packaging, thermoforming, pad printing, sonic welding, hot-stamping, shrink-wrapping, and silkscreening. Other plants are located in Princeton, Minn.; Lebanon and Greenville, Ky.; Greenfield, Tenn.; Oklahoma City; and Moline, Ill. 795 employees (260 in Minnesota). Founded in 1962. SIC 3089.

Plexus 1700 93rd Ln. N.E., Blaine, MN 55449. Tel: 920/722-3451. Sean Nguyen, Pres. and CEO; Duc Lam, CFO; John Pham, Dir.-Quality; Candi Oulette, Purch. Mgr. Plexus assembles and tests printed circuit boards on a consignment and turnkey basis. Majority owner Sean Nguyen started the former Nguyen Electronics Inc. (NEI) in his basement. 66 employees. Founded in 1986. SIC 3672.

Pohlig Manufacturing Inc. dba Continental Bridge 8301 State Highway 29 N., Alexandria, MN 56308. Tel: 320/852-7500; Fax: 320/852-7067; Web site: http://www.continentalbridge.com. Bruce R. Pohlig, Pres. and CEO; Gordy Vipond, VP-Sls.; Tony Schneider, Cont.; Craig Thorstad, VP-Engrg.; Gary Westphal, Purch./Production. Annual revenue $10.9 million. Continental Bridge designs and manufactures prefab steel bridges for pedestrian, vehicular, and material-handling uses. 70 employees (all in Minnesota). Founded in 1972. SIC 3441.

Polar Corporation 1015 W. Saint Germain St., Suite 420, St. Cloud, MN 56301. Tel: 320/746-2255; Fax: 320/656-5638; Web site: http://www.polarcorp.com. James W. Jungels, Chm., Pres., and CEO; Donald Stover, CFO. Annual revenue $220 million. Polar Corp. manufactures liquid and dry bulk transportation equipment (tank trailers) with 29 locations in 15 states for service and trailer parts distribution. Equipment and parts are sold internationally. 1,250 employees (400 in Minnesota). Founded in 1946. SIC 3715, 7699. No. 60 CRM Private 100.

Polar Plastics Inc. 6959 N. 55th St., Oakdale, MN 55128. Tel: 651/770-2925; Fax: 651/770-7578. Andrew Ave'Lallemant, Pres. Annual revenue $77 million. Polar Plastics manufactures pallet stretch wrap, construction film, custom bags, and automotive flashings. 80 employees (74 in Minnesota; 2 part-time). Founded in 1967. SIC 3089.

PolarFab 2800 E. Old Shakopee Rd., Bloomington, MN 55425. Tel: 952/876-3000; Fax: 952/876-2350; Web site: http://www.vtc.com. Larry E. Jodsaas, Chm. and CEO; Gregory Peterson, Pres., COO, and CFO. Annual revenue $70 million. PolarFab, formerly VTC Inc., provides an analog foundry service for the semiconductor industry. PolarFab's wafer fabrication business, which has been in operation for more than 30 years, has leading technology in BiPolar, BiCMOS, and Power BiCMOS processes that have been fine-tuned to the analog and mixed-signal markets. The company also offers a full quality and reliability service, failure analysis capability, production wafer and package testing, and in-house, quick-turn prototype assembly. Customers include industry giants Lucent Technologies and Maxim Integrated Circuits. PolarFab is ISO9002 certified, with a plan in place to be QS9000 registered. VTC was a subsidiary of Control Data Corp. until sold to private investors in October 1990. Ten years later, part of the company was sold to Lucent Technologies, and the remaining operations were renamed PolarFab. 480 employees. Founded in 1984. In February 2000 Lucent Technologies (NYSE: LU) Microelectronics Group agreed to acquire the products and the design, marketing, and sales teams of VTC Inc. for about $100 million in cash plus up to an additional $50 million over two years based on certain performance-based manufacturing goals. In March the company shared $16 million of the proceeds with the 690-plus employees in Bloomington; Longmont, Colo.; and Irvine, Calif., in keeping with the theme over the past 10 years of its "ship coming in." SIC 3674.

Polka Dot Dairy/Tom Thumb Food Markets Inc. 110 17th St. E., Hastings, MN 55033. Tel: 651/437-9023; Fax: 651/438-2638. Wallace R. Pettit, Pres. Polka Dot Dairy is a dairy products distributor. The company's wholly owned subsidiary, Tom Thumb, is a retail grocery chain consisting of 131 stores in Minnesota and Wisconsin. 1,400 employees. Founded in 1957. SIC 5143. No. 70 CRM Private 100.

Polman Transfer Inc. Highway10 W., P.O. Box 470, Wadena, MN 56842. Tel: 218/631-1753; Fax: 218/631-3969. Nick Polman, Pres.; D.J. Polman, VP. Annual revenue $9.5 million. Polman Transfer is a truck transport company. Other shop: Cass Lake, Minn. 90 employees. Founded in 1953. SIC 4213.

Poly Foam Inc. 116 Pine St. S., Lester Prairie, MN 55354. Tel: 320/395-2551; Fax: 320/395-2702. R.E. Humboldt, Pres.; W. Rogers, CFO. Annual revenue $8.6 million. Poly Foam manufactures expanded polystyrene foam for packaging, insulation, and flotation. 77 employees (76 in Minnesota). Founded in 1960. SIC 3086.

Popp Communications 620 Mendelssohn Ave. N., Golden Valley, MN 55427. Tel: 763/546-9707; Fax: 763/544-9798; Web site: http://www.popp.com. William J. Popp, Pres. and CEO; Paula Popp Mertews, Ofcr.; Sarah Padula, Treas. Annual revenue $15 million. Popp Communications provides local phone service, worldwide long distance, toll-free numbers, business phone systems, Internet service, worldwide audio teleconferencing, international calling to 224 countries, WATS access services, and calling cards. 75 employees (80 in Minnesota; 5 part-time). Founded in 1981. Expanded product line to include local phone service, telephone and voicemail systems and Internet service offerings. SIC 4813.

Power/mation Division Inc. 1310 Energy Ln., P.O. Box 8198, St. Paul, MN 55108. Tel: 651/605-3300; Fax: 651/605-4400; Web site: http://www.powermation.com. Doug Lowe, Pres. and CEO; David E. Dummer, VP-Fin. and CFO. Power/mation Division Inc., a center for automation technology, distributes automation and motion-control hardware. Other offices are located in Waukesha and Green Bay, Wis.; Cedar Rapids, Iowa; Mountain Iron, Minn.; Omaha, Neb.; Chicago and Rockford, Ill.; Kansas City and St. Louis, Mo.; and Des Moines, Iowa. 205 employees (120 in Minnesota). Founded in 1961. SIC 5063, 5065.

Pragmatek Consulting Group Ltd. One Main St. S.E., Suite 400, Minneapolis, MN 55414. Tel: 612/333-3164; Web site: http://www.pragmatek.com. Steve Bloom, CEO. Annual revenue $22.1 million. Pragmatek is an e-business and management consulting firm. Core services include management consulting, software selection and implementation, and a broad range of technology deployment services. Seasoned consultants deliver results that improve an organization's business systems, supply chains, business intelligence, and customer relationship management. The firm works with fast-growth companies in manufacturing, distribution, retail, and packaged goods industries. 88 employees (78 in Minnesota). Founded in 1989. In April 2000 the company was selected as a national consulting partner by SAP America Inc. Selection criteria included the firm's experience in: employing best practices across an industry to effectively redesign business process; and making implementations faster and more efficient for clients. Pragmatek also introduced its new Customer Relationship Management (CRM) services—entering a burgeoning market predicted to reach $16.8 billion by 2003. Steven Bloom was named a finalist in the 2000 Entrepreneur of the Year Awards by Ernst & Young. In June Pragmatek announced expanded client relationship management and e-business services that help companies improve speed, efficiency, and profitability by conducting business on the Internet. The new offering was supported by cutting-edge partnerships, including the firm's new alliance with San Mateo, Calif.-based Siebel Systems Inc. (Nasdaq: SEBL), a leading provider of eBusiness application software. In July the company announce a strategic partnership with Digital River Inc. for delivering Web-enabled enterprise systems. The partnership's first joint engagement was a contract with the U.S. headquarters of Rapala Normark Corp., the world's leading manufacturer of fishing lures. In August the company opened a Dallas/Fort Worth office to serve manufacturers, distributors, and retailers in Texas that are experiencing fast growth and need business systems to grow with them. SIC 7379. No. 9 CityBusiness Fastest-growing Private Companies.

Precision Associates Inc. 740 Washington Ave. N., Minneapolis, MN 55401. Tel: 612/333-7464; Fax: 612/342-2417; Web site: http://www.precisionassoc.com. Arnold E. Kadue, Chm. and CEO; Paul A. Kadue, Pres. and CFO. Annual revenue $10.4 million. Precision manufactures synthetic rubber products and custom molded products. 170 employees (all in Minnesota; 8 part-time). Founded in 1955. SIC 3069, 3089.

Precision Diversified Industries Inc. 14755 27th Ave. N., Plymouth, MN 55447. Tel: 763/553-9838; Fax: 763/553-9732. Ron Jecha, Chm. and Pres.; David McGraw, VP and Gen. Mgr. Precision Diversified Industries designs and manufactures prototype printed circuit boards. It also designs and assembles electrical test fixtures. 150 employees (149 in Minnesota). Founded in 1975. SIC 3577, 3672, 3679.

Precision Inc. 1800 Freeway Blvd., Brooklyn Center, MN 55430. Tel: 763/561-6880; Fax: 763/561-9050. David Anderson, Pres.; Lyle Shaw, EVP. Annual revenue $9 million. Precision Inc. designs and manufactures transformers and inductors for the electronics industry. The company specializes in application. 118 employees (96 in Minnesota). Founded in 1964. SIC 3677.

Precision Powerhouse 911 Second St. S., Minneapolis, MN 55415. Tel: 612/333-9111; Fax: 612/332-9200; Web site: http://www.powerhouse.com. Dan Piepho, Pres. and CEO; Warren Shore, Mgr.-Customer Relations; Brynn Moen, Audio Engrg.; Buddy Cohen, VP-Mktg. Precision Powerhouse, formerly known as Precision Tapes Inc., is a fully integrated media production, duplication, and manufacturing center that creates, manufactures, edits, and ships video, audio, and multimedia products. 80 employees. Founded in 1983. SIC 3652.

Premera Foods 72241 250th Ave., Hayfield, MN 55940. Tel: 507/365-8463; Fax: 507/365-8288. Eugene Sander, CEO. Premera Foods, formerly IFP Inc., provides custom food processing and packaging. 185 employees. Founded in 1981. In October 2000 the company paid $130,000 to settle national-origin discrimination claims brought by a group of Hispanic employees who said that they were subject to disciplinary action for speaking Spanish, even when not working. SIC 2099.

Premier Salons International 5421 Selpl Rd., Suite 110, Minnetonka, MN 55343. Tel: 952/564-7200. Brian Luborsky, Chm. and CEO. Premier operates over 1,000 full-service hair-care salons within department and specialty stores in the United States and Canada. 7,000 employees (250 in Minnesota). Founded in 1994. SIC 7231.

Premium Waters Inc. 2125 N.E. Broadway, Minneapolis, MN 55413. Tel: 612/379-4141; Fax: 612/379-3543. Greg Nemec, Pres. Premium Waters bottles and distributes spring water and drinking water. It operates plants in Willmar, Minn., and Chippewa Falls, Wis. 200 employees (100 in Minnesota). Founded in 1836. SIC 5149.

Presque Isle Power Plant 2701 Lakeshore Blvd. N., Marquette, MI 49855. Tel: 906/228-4500; Fax: 906/226-5760. Les Kowalski, Plant Mgr. Presque Isle Power Plant is an electric generation facility owned and operated by Wisconsin Electric Power Company (Milwaukee). 196 employees. Founded in 1955. SIC 4911.

Print Craft Inc. 315 Fifth Ave. N.W., New Brighton, MN 55112. Tel: 651/633-8122; Fax: 651/633-1862; Web site: http://www.printcraftinc.com. Tommy Merickel, Pres. Print Craft provides multicolor commercial printing to manufacturers, advertising agencies, and promotional groups across the United States. Products include brochures, manuals, catalogs, annual reports, books, and packaging. Owned by Taylor Corp., North Mankato, Minn. 155 employees (all in Minnesota). Founded in 1964. SIC 2759.

Printing Arts Inc. 8801 Wyoming Ave. N., Brooklyn Park, MN 55445. Tel: 763/425-4251; Fax: 763/425-4616. Raymond F. Becker, Chm.; Tim Becker, Pres.; Dan Becker, VP-Mfg.; Tom Lundberg, VP and Sec. Printing Arts is a commercial printer offering one- to six-color printing on brochures and saddle-stitched booklets, from desktop to addressing and mailing. 51 employees (50 in Minnesota). Founded in 1973. SIC 2752.

Printing Partners of America 15020 27th Ave. N., Plymouth, MN 55447. Tel: 763/553-1617; Fax: 763/553-0956; Web site: http://www.wattpeterson.com. Dennis E. Watt, Chm. and CEO; Bruce Schulz, Pres.; Howard Dicke, CFO; Lou Claude, VP-Finishing; Amy Blake, Hum. Res. Mgr.; David B. Peterson, VP-Sls.; Paul Pyzdrowski, VP-Prod.; Tina Feauto, Mktg. Mgr. Annual revenue $32 million. Printing Partners of America is an ISO 9002-compliant commercial printer providing full-color sheetfed and web printing for clients nationwide. The company offers state-of-the-art equipment in prepress, press, bindery, finishing, mailing and packaging services. Company divisions include Watt/Peterson, Plymouth and Brainerd, Minn.; and Cimarron Printing, Marshall, Minn. 250 employees (all in Minnesota). Founded in 1963. In June 2000 marketplace pressures led to the merger of Watt/Peterson Inc. and Cimarron Printing. CEO Watt was looking for other companies to join in, as the printing industry continues its decade-long consolidation. SIC 2752.

Priority Envelope Inc. 2920 Northwest Blvd., Suite 160, Plymouth, MN 55441. Tel: 763/519-9190; Fax: 763/519-9199; Web site: http://www.priorityenv.com. Ryan Wenning, Pres.; Paul Siegle, VP; Gene Muilenburg, CFO. Priority Envelope litho prints one- to four-color envelopes and converts all types of business and specialty envelopes. It offers full prepress and post-press services. 75 employees (all in Minnesota). Founded in 1996. SIC 2677.

Process Displays Company 7108 31st Ave. N., New Hope, MN 55427. Tel: 763/546-1133; Fax: 763/546-0821. Jack Bernie, Pres.; Arline Bernie, VP; Gordon Bredenberg, Sec.; Rick Anderson, VP. Annual revenue $27 million. Process Displays Co. does screen printing, offset lithography, die cutting, and related graphic arts services. 130 employees (all in Minnesota). Founded in 1937. SIC 2752, 2759.

Proco Wood Products Inc. 11885 Brockton Ave. N., Osseo, MN 55369. Tel: 763/428-4356; Fax: 763/428-7010. Shawn Weinand, Pres.; Al Mogensen, Sls. Mgr. Proco Wood Products manufactures and installs custom store fixtures for retail display, nationwide. 60 employees. Founded in 1976. SIC 2431.

Product Fabricators Inc. 6675 Ash Street, North Branch, MN 55056. Tel: 651/674-4322; Fax: 651/674-8957. Michael P. Murphy Sr., CEO; Carol M. Murphy, CFO. Annual revenue $9 million. Product Fabricators is a subcontractor for sheet metal fabrication, painting, and machining. 138 employees (132 in Minnesota). Founded in 1973. SIC 3444.

Production Engineering Corporation 3515 Marshall St. N.E., Minneapolis, MN 55418. Tel: 612/788-9123; Fax: 612/788-0472. Mike Albers, Pres.; Richard Castle, VP. Production Engineering does precision CNC machining, horizontal and vertical to 30-inch by 80-inch; precision sheet metal fabrication; certified welding; and assembly, bonding, and metal finishing. Its one subsidiary is Excel Metal Finishing in Minneapolis. 85 employees. Founded in 1957. SIC 3444.

Professional Alternatives 15600 Wayzata Blvd., Suite 300, Wayzata, MN 55391. Tel: 952/404-2600; Fax: 952/404-2602; Web site: http://www.pro-alt.com. David Dodge, Pres. and CEO. Annual revenue $3.3 million. Professional Alternatives is a professional placement agency specializing in the placement of human resources and information technology professionals on a contract, contract-to-hire and direct hire basis. 54 employees (all in Minnesota; 20 part-time). Founded in 1992. May 2000 Created IT Alternatives which focuses on the placement of IT professionals. SIC 7361. No. 10 CityBusiness Fastest-growing Private Companies.

Professional Litho Inc. 807 13th Ave. S., Minneapolis, MN 55404. Tel: 612/338-0400; Fax: 612/338-8055; Web site: http://www.pro-litho.com. Craig L. Hanson, Pres.; David T. Lee, EVP-Sls./Mktg.; Gary N. Larson, Dir.-Mfg. Professional Litho is a high-quality prepress company providing a full range of system, desktop, and conventional services. Specialties include drum scanning, high-end retouching, page makeup, film outputting, digital photography, interactive CD-ROM production, design services, and digital asset management. 70 employees (all in Minnesota). Founded in 1974. SIC 2752, 2759.

Progress Casting Group Inc. 2600 Niagara Ln., Plymouth, MN 55441. Tel: 763/557-1000; Fax: 763/557-0320. Bill Bieber, Owner; Robert Silhacek, Pres. and CEO; Mark Alexander, VP-Fin.; Kevin Coleman, VP-Op., Albert Lea Div.; Gary Johnson, VP-Tech.; Gary Obele, VP-Admin./Org. Devel.; Randy Ruegg, VP-Op., Twin Cities Div.; Victor Phillips, Dir.-Info. Tech. Annual revenue $65 million. Progress Casting Group Inc. operates divisions in Plymouth and Albert Lea, Minn. The company makes sand, permanent mold, and low-pressure permanent mold aluminum castings. Industries served include commerical aerospace, food equipment, and recreational vehicle. 520 employees (all in Minnesota). Founded in 1935. SIC 3365.

Progressive Contractors Inc. 14123 42nd St. N.E., St. Michael, MN 55376. Tel: 763/497-6100; Fax: 763/497-6101. M.S. McGray, Pres.; Gerald L. Ingman, VP and Sec.; Ted Durkee, CFO and Treas. Annual revenue $87 million. Progressive is a heavy highway construction contractor. 400 employees (300 in Minnesota). Founded in 1971. SIC 1611.

Progressive Technologies Inc. 10525 Hampshire Ave. S, Suite 600, Bloomington, MN 55438. Tel: 952/942-7200; Fax: 952/942-7300; Web site: http://www.progressive-tech.com. Progressive Technologies sells and installs Lucent Technologies equipment and is a strategic agent for U S West. 55 employees. Founded in 1990. In December 1999 the company was named Employer of the Year by the Minnesota State Council on Disability—for its support of eight disabled workers who clean phones and computers. SIC 1731.

Promotion Mailing Center Inc. 31205 Falcon Ave., P.O. Box 245, Stacy, MN 55079. Tel: 651/462-1213; Fax: 651/462-4118; Web site: http://www.promotion-mailing.com. DeVere L. Monson, CEO; DeAnn O. Montague, Pres.; Mark J. Urich, VP-Op. Promotion Mailing Center handles consumer responses to rebates and coupons, administers contests and sweepstakes, and processes inbound 1-800 telephone orders. It also does collating and assembly. 90 employees (88 in Minnesota; 20 part-time). Founded in 1983. SIC 7389.

Pro-Tech Inc. 711 S. Pine St., P.O. Box 46, Waconia, MN 55387. Tel: 952/442-2189; Fax: 952/442-2472. Gerald Maas, Pres. Pro-Tech manufactures printed circuit boards that are components on transistor dials—for commercial and military markets. 75 employees (all in Minnesota). Founded in 1968. SIC 3672.

QC Inspection Services Inc. 11975 Portland Ave. S., Suite 102, Burnsville, MN 55337. Tel: 952/895-1150; Fax: 952/895-1152. Dan Medford, Pres.; Gary Lane, VP. QC Inspection Services is a management consulting firm with four divisions: Dimensional Inspection Services, which provides reverse engineering, source inspection, overload inspection, first-article inspection, mold evaluation, sorting operations, R&D dimensional evaluation, and capability studies; QC Placement Services, which provides temporary technical specialists for employment needs; Training and Consultation, which offers quality-control training and consulting services on location; and Subcontract Services, which provides outsourcing operations. Other office: Chicago. 120 employees (80 in Minnesota). Founded in 1986. SIC 8742.

Quadion Corporation 3630 Wooddale Ave. S., P.O. Box 1236 (55440), St. Louis Park, MN 55416. Tel: 952/927-1400; Fax: 952/927-1422. Robert W. Carlson Jr., Chm.; James R. Lande, CEO. Annual revenue $130 million. Through its two divisions, Minnesota Rubber (St. Louis Park), and QMR Plastics, Quadion manufactures custom-molded rubber and plastic products. The company has six plants in North America, one in western Europe, and one in Singapore. 1,300 employees (550 in Minnesota). Founded in 1945. SIC 3069, 3544. No. 65 CRM Private 100.

Quali-Tech Inc. 318 Lake Hazeltine Dr., Chaska, MN 55318. Tel: 952/448-5151; Fax: 952/448-3603; Web site: http://www.qualitechco.com. Delbert L. Ploen, Chm., Pres., and CEO; Cory S. Ploen, EVP; Bill Gunter, VP-Op.; Kye Ploen, VP-Foods Div.; Dewey Klaustermeier, VP-Ag Div. Quali-Tech manufactures premixes and specialty ingredients for the animal feed industry. The company also manufactures flavor particulates for the industrial foods industry. 75 employees (all in Minnesota; 10 part-time). Founded in 1967. SIC 2048, 2833.

Quality Boneless Beef Company P.O. Box 337, West Fargo, ND 58078. Tel: 701/282-0202; Fax: 701/282-0583; Web site: http://www.qualitymeats.com. Kenneth Scherber, Pres.; Dan Richard, Sec. Annual revenue $20 million. Quality Boneless Beef Co. distributes portion-cut meats, fish, and seafood, as well as smoked meats and sausage. 90 employees (4 part-time). Founded in 1967. SIC 2011, 5146.

Quality Circuits Inc. 1102 Progress Dr., Fergus Falls, MN 56537. Tel: 218/739-9707; Fax: 218/739-9705. Wayne B. Dirkman, Pres.; Robert Perry, VP; Brad W. Dirkman, Engrg. Mgr. Annual revenue $24 million. Quality Circuits manufactures printed wiring boards. 120 employees (all in Minnesota). Founded in 1988. SIC 3672.

Quicksilver Express Courier Inc. 203 Little Canada Rd. E., Little Canada, MN 55117. Tel: 651/484-1111; Fax: 651/484-3192; Web site: http://www.qec.com. Michael Crary, CEO; Rebecca Wagner, Treas.; Curtis Sloan, Sec. Annual revenue $34 million. Quicksilver Express Courier is an on-call courier with operations in Denver, Colo.; Minneapolis/St. Paul; and Milwaukee, Wis. as well as Kansas City, Mo. The company provides same-day interstate and intracity service in all vehicle sizes. 800 employees (375 in Minnesota; 65 part-time). Founded in 1982. SIC 4215.

Quillins Inc. 1515 West Ave. S., La Crosse, WI 54601. Tel: 608/785-1424; Fax: 608/785-7175. Phillip J. Quillin, Pres.; Lyle Quillin, VP. Quillins operates supermarkets and pharmacies. 800 employees (94 in Minnesota; 450 part-time). Founded in 1945. SIC 5411, 5912.

RAO Manufacturing Company 200 Mississippi St. N.E., Fridley, MN 55432. Tel: 763/566-9080; Fax: 763/571-3666; Web site: http://www.raomfg.com. Robert A. Olsen, CEO; Richard A. Olsen, VP; Richard J. Guimont, Sec. and Treas. Annual revenue $9.8 million. RAO Manufacturing is a manufacturer of metal stampings and fabrication. 85 employees (all in Minnesota). Founded in 1927. SIC 3469.

RBE Electronics Inc. 714 Corporation St., Aberdeen, SD 57401. Tel: 605/226-2448; Fax: 605/226-0710. Roger R. Ernst, Pres.; John Malsom, Sls. Mgr.; Troy Anderson, MN Plant Mgr.; Jerry Feickert, S.D. Plant Mgr. RBE Electronics manufactures electronic industrial controls. 80 employees (30 in Minnesota). Founded in 1982. SIC 3625, 3629, 3647, 3679, 3694.

RESoft Inc. 4150 Olson Memorial Hwy., Suite 400, Golden Valley, MN 55422. Tel: 763/398-1100; Fax: 763/398-1101; Web site: http://www.resoftinc.com. Duane H. Lund, CEO; Mary S. Henschel, Pres.; Odeh A. Muhawesh, Cf. Knowledge Ofcr.; Randy W. Strobel, CFO; Garrett D. Farmer, VP-Corp. Devel. RESoft is a real estate document management company that initiates a paperless office environment for property owners and managers. Additional products include procurement, build, and wireless applications. The company is a subsidiary of Stonehaven Realty Trust, Golden Valley, Minn. 50 employees. SIC 7372.

REM Inc. 6921 York Ave. S., Edina, MN 55435. Tel: 952/925-5067; Fax: 952/925-0739; Web site: http://www.reminc.com. Tom Miller, Pres.; Craig Miller, VP; Doug Miller, VP; Peg DuBord, Regional Admin.; Shelly Calkins, Devel. Ofcr.; Jim Hokanson, Real Estate Svs. Annual revenue $215 million. REM Inc. is a national provider of health care services including senior services, disability services, home health care, housing services, and rehabilitation therapy. 12,000 employees. Founded in 1967. In October 2000 REM acquired RESA Inc., a six-person Intermediate Care Facility for Persons with Developmental Disabilities (ICF/DD) located in Minnetonka, Minn.; and Thomas J. Apartments, which did business under the name Wilson Apartments, a 15-person ICF/DD located in St. Paul. SIC 8361. No. 37 CRM Employer 100. No. 62 CRM Private 100.

RFA—Minnesota Engineering 11495 Valley View Rd., Eden Prairie, MN 55344. Tel: 952/941-2250; Fax: 952/941-2991. Jim Rother, Pres. RFA (previously Rogers, Freels & Associates) provides mechanical engineering and design services for product development, cost reduction, and manufacturing. 65 employees (64 in Minnesota; 3 part-time). Founded in 1943. SIC 8711.

RJF Agencies Inc. 14601 27th Ave. N., Suite 109, Plymouth, MN 55447. Tel: 763/746-8000. Bill Jeatran, CEO. Annual revenue $6.5 million. RJF Agencies is an independent insurer that offers all types of insurance, as well as many other products and services. 103 employees. Founded in 1986. SIC 6411. No. 19 CityBusiness Fastest-growing Private Companies.

R&M Manufacturing Company 4838 W. 35th St., St. Louis Park, MN 55416. Tel: 952/929-0468; Fax: 952/929-9589. Jerome Bofferding, Pres. R&M Manufacturing Co. runs a sheet metal job shop. 150 employees. Founded in 1969. SIC 3444.

RMS Company 8600 Evergreen Blvd., Coon Rapids, MN 55433. Tel: 763/786-1520; Fax: 763/783-5073. Arthur A. Mouyard, Pres.; Lee Zachman, Cont. RMS Co. provides precision machining for the medical device industry and MIL-C-26500 Aerospace connectors. Owned by The Cretex Cos. Inc., Elk River, Minn. 400 employees (395 in Minnesota). Founded in 1967. SIC 3599.

R&O Elevator Company Inc. 6310 Pillsbury Ave. S., Bloomington, MN 55420. Tel: 952/888-9255; Fax: 952/948-3800. Lee C. Arnold, Pres. R&O Elevator Co. installs and maintains elevator, escalator, and dumbwaiter equipment. 60 employees. Founded in 1925. SIC 1796.

ROI Systems Inc. 435 Ford Rd., Suite 700, St. Louis Park, MN 55426. Tel: 952/595-0500; Fax: 952/595-9450; Web site: http://www.roito-day.com. Paul C. Merlo, Pres. and CEO; Mike Carnahan, Chm. and EVP-Res./Devel.; Chris Holm, EVP; Bill Pisarra, EVP-Channel Sls./Mktg.; Robert A. Garbutt, VP-Direct Sls. Annual revenue $23 million. ROI Systems Inc. is a leading developer of extended Enterprise Resource Planning (ERP) software solutions and cost-effective implementations for mid-sized discrete manufacturers. The company's Internet-enabled ERP system, MANAGE 2000, effectively automates and manages business critical operations across the supply chain. The easy-to-implement system ties the front and back office together by integrating over 40 applications for production, planning, engineering, finance, and customer relationship management. The extended suite offers seamless interfaces to business intelligence, advanced planning and scheduling, and e-business technologies. MANAGE 2000 runs on Windows NT, UNIX, and AS/400 platforms. 179 employees. Founded in 1978. In April 2000 ROI became an Agile Application Adapter, establishing an alliance with Agile Software Corp., a leading provider of collaborative manufacturing commerce solutions. Also this year ROI introduced a quick response manufacturing (QRM) information technology blueprint designed to help manufacturers improve product quality, speed their time-to-market, and reduce product expenses. In September ROI announced its offering of XML-based EDI through its alliance with TIE Commerce, a complete B2B e-commerce solution provider. Sept. 30: ROI reported year-to-date profitability through the third quarter. In the fourth quarter of the year, ROI introduced a major new release of MANAGE 2000 that contained new functionality across the system and new e-business capabilities. It was validated as IBM ServerProven. SIC 7371.

RSP Architects Ltd. 120 First Ave. N., Minneapolis, MN 55401. Tel: 612/339-0313; Fax: 612/339-6760; Web site: http://www.rsparch.com. Michael J. Plautz, Senior Principal; Jim Fitzhugh, Principal-Govt./Military; Robert Lucius, Principal-Retail; David C. Norback, Principal-Corporate; Stephen J. Fautsch, Principal; Michael R. Lyner, Principal; Terry Wobken, Senior Associate-Industrial/High Tech; Jeremy P. Mayberg, Principal; Pat Parrish, Principal; Richard Varda, Principal. RSP Architects maintains a diverse practice with particualr emphasis in corporate and interior architecture, retail, industrial, and institutional projects. With more than 230 employees, the firm has eight locations across the United States. With over $4 billion (construction value) of projects, RSP has developed a record and reputation for delivering design solutions that are creative, innovative, and technically effective; all while meeting established programs, budgets, and schedules. RSP provides planning, architecture, interior design, facility management/corporate services, and accessibility consulting. Clients include American Express Co., Andersen Corp., Best Buy Co. Inc., Ryan Cos., Target Corp., UnitedHealth Group, U.S. Army Corps of Engineers, and the University of Minnesota. 240 employees. Founded in 1978. In June 2000 the MCDA received approval from the Minneapolis City Council to sell the Grain Belt Brew House to Ryan Cos. U.S. Inc., Minneapolis, for redevelopment as an office complex. RSP was to be the project's architect as well as its only tenant. SIC 7389, 8712.

RTC Inc. 1777 Oakdale Ave., West St. Paul, MN 55118. Tel: 651/450-7400; Fax: 651/450-7555. Mark Nelson, Pres. and Owner; Marc Jaker, VP; Bob Lynch, Cont.; Mark Duppong, Dir.-Engrg.; Greg Radke, Prod. Mgr.; Peter Shannon, Quality Mgr.; Joyce Wallach, Office Mgr. Annual revenue $6.4 million. RTC is a precision CAD/CAM tool shop and a custom injection molder, also offering manual, automatic and robotic assembly, product design, and engineering; and a manufacturer of several proprietary products. Products include switches, telephone electronic parts, threaded closures, overcaps, computer accessories, specialty optical lenses, oval deodorant sticks, catheters, medical components, and devices. RTC is ISO 9002 certified. The company has two facilities: a 30,000-square-foot plant in St. Paul and a 93,000-square-foot plant in West St. Paul. 127 employees (all in Minnesota). Founded in 1964. SIC 3089, 3544, 3841.

RTD Company 440 N. Emerson, Cambridge, MN 55008. Tel: 763/689-4870; Fax: 763/689-5033. Carroll Johnson, CEO; Tom Johnson, Pres. RTD Co. manufactures resistance temperature detectors. 55 employees (all in Minnesota). Founded in 1976. SIC 3822.

RTP Company 580 E. Front St., Winona, MN 55987. Tel: 507/454-6900; Fax: 507/454-2041. H.L. Miller, CEO; B.A. Miller, Pres. RTP is a custom producer of specialty thermoplastic compounds for all major markets. 850 employees (250 in Minnesota). Founded in 1982. SIC 3087.

RZ Solutions 8011 34th Ave., Suite 424, Bloomington, MN 55425. Tel: 952/814-5555. Tom Hymanson, CEO. Annual revenue $4.4 million. RZ Solutions captures corporate data and transforms it into actionable information. 47 employees. Founded in 1993. SIC 7379. No. 26 CityBusiness Fastest-growing Private Companies.

Rahr Malting Company 301 Fourth Ave. S, Suite 567, Minneapolis, MN 55415. Tel: 612/332-5161; Fax: 612/332-6841. Guido R. Rahr Jr., Chm.; T.C. Haffenreffer Jr., VChm.; John F. Alsip III, Pres. and CEO; W.B. Otteson, VP-Sls.; James C. Olsen, VP-Fin., Sec., and Treas.; Robert S. Micheletti, VP-Op. Rahr Malting manufactures barley malt, malt sprouts, and barley byproducts. 100 employees. Founded in 1847. SIC 2083.

Rainbow Signs Inc. 3500 Thurston Ave., Anoka, MN 55303. Tel: 763/576-6700; Fax: 763/576-6701. Michael E. Holmberg, Pres. Rainbow Signs designs, manufactures, and distributes signs and displays. 190 employees (all in Minnesota). Founded in 1954. SIC 2752, 3993.

Rainier Technology Inc. 1660 S. Highway 100, Suite 228, St. Louis Park, MN 55416. Tel: 952/595-8895; Fax: 952/595-8797; Web site: http://www.rainier.com. Dave Eaton, Chm. and Founder; Terry Palmberg, Pres. and CEO; Ellen Hoeg, VP-Mktg.; Tim Blanski, Dir.-Sls. Annual revenue $17 million. Rainier Technology is a computer consulting firm that specializes in the innovation and integration of Web solutions for e-commerce and knowledge management at Global 2000 and high-potential start-up companies. Rainier, a member of the Microsoft e-Commerce Partner Advisor Council, has one of the largest groups of Microsoft-certified solution professionals in the world, and the largest in the central United States. The company has other offices in the United States and Europe. 205 employees. Founded in 1994. In October 2000 Rainier announced the successful deployments of Microsoft Exchange 2000 for Coldwell Banker Burnet and West TeleServices Corp., and the worldwide public launch of Exchange 2000. SIC 7371, 7373. No. 6 Minnesota Technology Fast 50. No. 17 CityBusiness Fastest-growing Private Companies.

Rajala Companies 216 Fourth St. S.E., P.O. Box 578, Deer River, MN 56636. Tel: 218/246-8149; Fax: 218/246-2822. John I. Rajala, Pres. and Treas.; John A. Rajala, VP; Randolph B. Rajala, VP. Rajala Cos. has three operating divisions that produce wholesale lumber: Rajala Mill Co., Big Fork, Minn.; and Rajala Timber Co. and Rajala Lumber Co., Deer River. It also has a small sawmill in Grand Rapids, Minn. (Liila Forest Products). 155 employees (all in Minnesota). Founded in 1969. SIC 2421.

Ramaley Printing Company/Northwestern Printcrafters 120 W. Plato Blvd., St. Paul, MN 55101. Tel: 651/224-7631; Fax: 651/223-5609. Robert A. Crepeau Jr., Chm. and Pres.; Michael H. Crepeau, VP; Jill Wagner, Accounting Mgr. Ramaley Printing/NWPC specializes in commercial lithographic printing and typesetting. Owned by the Crepeau Co., St. Paul. 70 employees (all in Minnesota). Founded in 1863. SIC 2752.

Randy's Sanitation Inc. 4351 U.S. Highway 12 S.E., P.O. Box 169, Delano, MN 55328. Tel: 763/479-3335; Fax: 763/972-6042. Randy Roskowiak, Owner; Sandra Roskowiak, Owner; Mark Stoltman, Gen. Mgr. Randy's Sanitation provides garbage and recycling services. 114 employees. Founded in 1979. SIC 4953.

Rapid Chevrolet Company Inc. 2090 Deadwood Ave., Rapid City, SD 57702. Tel: 605/343-1282; Fax: 605/343-5458. Victor Toscana, CEO. Rapid Chevrolet Co. is a new and used motor vehicle dealership that sells Chevrolet and Toyota. 116 employees. Founded in 1932. SIC 5511.

Rapid Serv Inc. 709 E. Minnehaha Ave., Suite 2, St. Paul, MN 55106. Tel: 651/793-9335; Fax: 651/793-9345. Ronald Juelfs, Owner; Sandin Grasdalen, VP and Gen. Mgr.; David Hoffman, VP-Op. Annual revenue $3.1 million. Rapid Serv is an on-call and scheduled courier (state route). Rapid Serv supplies expedited courier and freight service to Minnesota and the surrounding four states. 55 employees (all in Minnesota). Founded in 1979. SIC 4215.

Rapit Printing 1415 First Ave. N.W., New Brighton, MN 55112. Tel: 651/633-4600; Fax: 651/633-9512. Ray Halloway, Owner and CEO. Rapit Printing Specializes in instant and commercial printing. 130 employees (all in Minnesota). Founded in 1975. SIC 2752.

Rayven Inc. 431 Griggs St. N., St. Paul, MN 55104. Tel: 651/642-1112; Fax: 651/642-9497; Web site: http://www.rayven.com. Gerry Ingalls, Pres.; Joe Heinemann, EVP. Rayven manufactures coated and laminated films and tapes for industrial and retail markets. Reprofilm—the company's brand-name, self-adhesive film—is used by draftsmen and architects worldwide. 60 employees. Founded in 1954. SIC 2672.

Red Lake Gaming Enterprises Inc. P.O. Box 543, Red Lake, MN 56671. Tel: 218/679-2111; Fax: 218/679-2191. Marvin Hanson, COO. Red Lake Gaming Enterprises Inc. operates three Minnesota casinos: Lake of the Woods Casino, Warroad; River Road Casino, Thief River Falls; and Red Lake Casino, Red Lake. The company is owned by the Red

Lake Band of the Chippewa. 550 employees (all in Minnesota; 125 part-time). Founded in 1992. SIC 7999.

Red River Valley & Western Railroad Company P.O. Box 608, Wahpeton, ND 58074. Tel: 701/642-8257; Fax: 701/642-3534. William Drusch, Pres.; David E. Thompson, SVP-Mktg.; J. Victor Sargent, VP-Field Op. The Red River Valley & Western (RRVW) is a 740-mile regional railroad providing transportation services. The railroad began operations July 19, 1987, over track in central and southeastern North Dakota acquired from the Burlington Northern, now Burlington Northern and Santa Fe Railway Co. 73 employees. Founded in 1987. SIC 4011.

Red Wing Publishing Company 2760 N. Service Dr., P.O. Box 82, Red Wing, MN 55066. Tel: 651/388-8235; Fax: 651/388-8912. Arlin Albrecht, Chm., Pres., and CFO. Red Wing is a publishing company—a group of 15 affiliated newspapers (two of which are published daily) in Minnesota and Wisconsin, with related ventures in commercial printing and free-distribution publications. Included are the following suburban Twin Cities papers: Prior Lake American, Eden Prairie News, Chanhassen Villager, Jordan Independent, Chaska Herald, Savage Pacer, and Shakopee Valley News. 350 employees. Founded in 1857. SIC 2711.

Red Wing Shoe Company Inc. 314 Main St., Red Wing, MN 55066. Tel: 651/388-8211; Fax: 651/388-7415; Web site: http://www.redwingshoe.com. William J. Sweasy, COO; David A. Baker, EVP, Gen. Counsel, Sec.; Rick Bawek, EVP-Fin. and CFO; Roger Bunn, VP-Retail Op.; Lorrie Tongen, Treas. and Cont. Annual revenue $342 million. Red Wing Shoe Co. manufactures shoes. It offers more than 200 styles in a wide variety of sizes. Many of the styles—including rugged work, steel toe, casual/service shoes, and outdoor—are specifically designed to perform in certain work environments. The company's organizational structure is based on its four branded product lines: Red Wing, Vasque, Irish Setter, and WORX-brand footwear. There are 400 Red Wing Shoe Stores (170 company-owned) and a total of 4,200 multibranded dealers across the United States. Active in the international marketplace since 1960, Red Wing Shoe has distributors in many other countries. The company owns a tanning operation, as well as Red Wing's historic St. James Hotel. 2,839 employees. Founded in 1905. In April 2000 the company agreed to acquire the two remaining plants of 93-year-old Kaufman Footwear, the Canadian company that makes Sorel- and Black Diamond-brand products, and thereby add Kaufman's rubber footwear to Red Wing's mostly leather products. In June those talks broke down, causing Red Wing to call off the deal. One reason given was the timing of the deal, which would not have allowed product to be produced and delivered in time for fall. SIC 3143, 3144, 3149. No. 35 CRM Private 100.

redtagoutlet.com 7585 Equitable Dr., Eden Prairie, MN 55344. Tel: 952/934-9918. Thomas Petters, Pres. Annual revenue $19.4 million. redtagoutlet.com operates redtagbiz.com, a leading B2B Internet wholesale exchange for buyers and sellers of consumer merchandise. The company is focused on creating the first efficient worldwide business-to-business Internet marketplace for buying and selling consumer goods. redtagbiz.com offers its participants a cost-effective, highly serviced online source for consumer electronics, sporting goods, apparel, housewares, and other merchandise. redtagoutlet.com was founded by its chairman, Thomas J. Petters, in August 1998. Petters has more than 20 years experience in the business-to-business wholesale industry. 62 employees. Founded in 1998. In October 2000 the company launched a Sports Marketing/Special Markets Division that was to provide promotions to sports franchises and brand-name products to special markets. The new division enabled redtagbiz.com to provide an additional product source and new distribution channel to retailers and manufacturers to these special markets. SIC 7372.

Reell Precision Manufacturing Corporation (RPM) 1259 Willow Lake Blvd., Vadnais Heights, MN 55110. Tel: 651/484-2447; Fax: 651/484-3867; Web site: http://www.reell.com. Robert L. Wahlstedt, Chm.; Robert H. Carlson, Co-CEO; Steven A. Wikstrom, Co-CEO; Linda A. Hamlin, CFO. Annual revenue $28 million. RPM designs and manufactures wrap spring clutches and positioning hinges. 210 employees (all in Minnesota). Founded in 1970. SIC 3568.

Reese Enterprises Inc. 16350 Asher Ave., P.O. Box 459, Rosemount, MN 55068. Tel: 651/423-1126; Fax: 651/423-2662. Chester W. Ellingson III, Chm./Pres.-Reese Enterprises; Robert T. Ellingson, Pres.-Astro Plastic Div. Reese Enterprises manufactures weather strips, extruded plastic profiles, and dirt-control foot gratings. 114 employees. Founded in 1925. SIC 3089.

Regent Aviation St. Paul Downtown Airport, 515 Eaton St., St. Paul, MN 55107. Tel: 651/224-1100; Fax: 651/224-1982. Michael F. Cleary, Pres.; Christy Bieber Orris, VP and Gen. Mgr. Air Regent Investors (dba Regent Aviation) provides hangar, fuel, and maintenance for general and corporate aviation. Regent also provides corporate aircraft management and executive aircraft charter in a variety of five- to nine-passenger aircraft. Owned by Acrometal Management Corp., Plymouth, Minn. 70 employees (all in Minnesota; 10 part-time). Founded in 1988. SIC 4522, 4581.

Larry Reid's White Bear Dodge 3430 Highway 61, White Bear Lake, MN 55110. Tel: 651/482-6100; Fax: 651/481-1677. Larry Reid, Owner. Larry Reid's White Bear Dodge is a Dodge automobile dealership. The company has both a service department and a body and paint repair shop for each line. 100 employees. Founded in 1986. SIC 5511.

Reinhart 1500 Saint James St., P.O. Box 2859, La Crosse, WI 54602. Tel: 608/782-2660; Fax: 608/782-5084. Marjorie A. Reinhart, Chm.; Gerry Connolly, VP and Sec.; Mark Drazkowski, VP; Robert Reinhart, VP; Edward J. Hengel Jr., VP and Asst. Sec. Reinhart is a wholesale institutional food supplier. 550 employees. Founded in 1972. SIC 5141.

Reliable Bronze & Manufacturing Inc. 340 Rush Point Dr., Stanchfield, MN 55080. Tel: 763/689-4143. Charles Olson, Pres. Reliable Bronze & Manufacturing makes bronze bushing bearings for various contractors. 60 employees (all in Minnesota). Founded in 1968. SIC 3364.

Remmele Engineering Inc. 10 Old Highway 8 S.W., New Brighton, MN 55112. Tel: 651/635-4100; Fax: 651/635-4168; Web site: http://www.remmele.com. William J. Saul, Chm.; Thomas R. Moore, Pres.; Ken Wilson, VP-Mktg.; William Iacoe, VP-Automation; Philip Foster, VP-Fin.; Tom Dolezal, VP and Gen. Mgr.; Scott Furey, VP-Hum. Res.; Scott Fisher, Dir.-Info. Svs.; John Bowden, VP and Gen. Mgr.; Richard Heitkamp, Dir.-Advanced Mfg.; Kent Paul, VP and Gen. Mgr.; Charles Jungmann, Dir.-Capital Eqt. Remmele, with its six plants in Minnesota, designs, develops, manufactures, and services special factory automation machinery for manufacturers worldwide. Remmele typically builds computer-controlled automation systems and one-of-a-kind special machines for companies in automotive, computer, medical device, electric motor, and other high-tech industries. Systems are generally used for assembly, testing, metal removal, metal fabrication, special packaging, or web-handling applications. Remmele also designs and builds special tooling for the aircraft and aerospace industries and makes complex component parts to customer designs. Tooling and parts range in size from miniature machining to parts as large as 75 tons. Tolerances can be as close as a few microns. Remmele also manufactures large quantities of close-tolerance parts for the computer, defense, aircraft, medical, and automotive industries. 528 employees. Founded in 1949. SIC 3544, 3559, 3569, 3579, 3669.

Response Inc. 120 First St. N.E., Rochester, MN 55906. Tel: 507/281-5005; Fax: 507/281-5474; Web site: http://www.response.net. Beverly Rowland, Pres. Response Inc. is an industry remarketer of IBM midrange computers, pharmacy software, printers, displays, CD-ROMs, and other midrange peripherals. It also has an ownership interest in Rural Connections, the region's largest Internet service provider. 120 employees. Founded in 1978. SIC 5734.

Retail Merchandising Services Inc. 12935 16th Ave. N., Plymouth, MN 55441. Tel: 763/553-7732; Fax: 763/519-1606. Annette Lamers, Pres. Retail Merchandising Services provides retail merchandising services for manufacturers—through service representatives in 36 states. 360 employees. Founded in 1984. SIC 7389.

F.T. Reynolds Company P.O. Box 968, Glendive, MT 59330. Tel: 406/365-2114; Fax: 406/365-3137. John K. Reynolds, Pres. and CEO; Ronald Barone, VP; Charles D. Marman, Sec. and Treas. F.T. Reynolds Co. operates five grocery stores in eastern Montana, and one small wholesale warehouse in Glendive. 160 employees. Founded in 1925. SIC 5411.

Rice Lake Weighing Systems 230 W. Coleman, Rice Lake, WI 54868. Tel: 715/234-9171; Fax: 715/234-6967; Web site: http://www.rlws.com. Mark O. Johnson, Pres. and CEO. Rice Lake Weighing Systems is a manufacturer of electronic scales and weighing components. 325 employees. Founded in 1947. SIC 3596.

Richfield State Agency Inc. 6625 Lyndale Ave. S., Richfield, MN 55423. Tel: 612/798-3342; Fax: 612/798-3191. Martin V. Chorzempa, Chm. and CEO; Lynn R. Evans, Pres. and COO; Dawn Gast, SVP and CCO; Katie Kelley, SVP and CLO; Steven L. Kirchner, VChm.; John Gill, SVP and CFO; Hank Donatell, VP and Cont.; Tim Melin, SVP-Trust; Dave Stavenger, SVP-Retail Banking. Annual revenue $8.3 million. Richfield State Agency, a holding company, owns $620 million-asset Richfield Bank & Trust Co., a commercial bank as well as many Real Estate Holdings. 285 employees (all in Minnesota; 51 part-time). Founded in 1947. In January 2000 Richfield Bank, one of the top 10 banks in the state in terms of the number of SBA loans generated, was awarded "preferred lender status" by the Small Business Administration. SIC 6022.

Rider Bennett Egan & Arundel LLP 333 S. Seventh St., Suite 2000, Minneapolis, MN 55402. Tel: 612/340-7951; Fax: 612/340-7900; Web site: http://www.riderlaw.com. Eric J. Magnuson, Managing Ptnr.; Joseph R. Finnegan, Firm Admin. Rider Bennett Egan & Arundel is a law firm practicing in all areas of litigation, business/corporate, and trusts and estates, with an emphasis on agribusiness and co-op law: alternative dispute resolution; appellate practice; aviation; banking and institutional finance; bankruptcy; commercial real estate; computer/Internet law; conservatorships and guardianships; copyright law; creditor rights litigation; dram shop/liquor liability; education law; employment law; entrepreneurial services; environmental law; family law; fraud litigation; immigration law; intellectual property; life, health, and disability; mechanic's lien; mergers and acquisitions; nonprofit law; products liability; railroad law; shareholder-dispute litigation; trademarks, copyrights, and patents; transportation law; white collar criminal law, and workers' compensation. Along with the Minnesota Department of Trade and Economic Development, the firm publishes "Incorporating and Operating a Minnesota Business Corporation" and "An Employer's Guide to Employee Handbooks in Minnesota." 252 employees (all in Minnesota). Founded in 1960. In March 2000 Rider Bennett attorney Eric Magnuson received the William Mitchell School of Law Distinguished Alumni Award. In May the firm established a white-collar practice with the addition of veteran criminal defense attorney Bruce Hanley. In September 2000 Jan M. Gunderson received a Distinguished Alumni Award from Hamline University School of Law. In October 2000 Robert B. Jaskowiak received an Outstanding Service Award from the Minnesota Justice Foundation. SIC 8111.

Riedell Shoes Inc. 122 Cannon River Ave., Red Wing, MN 55066. Tel: 651/388-8251; Fax: 651/388-8616. Robert Riegelman, Pres. and CFO; Scott Riegelman, EVP; Dan Riegelman, EVP. Riedell Shoes manufactures ice skating boots, roller skating boots, and hockey skates; and markets in-line skates. 125 employees. Founded in 1945. SIC 3149, 3949.

Right Now Technologies 111 S. Grand Ave., Bozeman, MT 59715. Tel: 888/322-3566; Fax: 406/522-4227; Web site: http://www.rightnowtech.com. Greg Gianforte, CEO; Jeff Honeycomb, Pres.; Susan Carstonson, CFO. Right Now Technologies develops and sells Web-based customer service software. 92 employees. SIC 7379.

Rihm Motor Company 2108 University Ave., St. Paul, MN 55114. Tel: 651/646-7833; Fax: 651/646-0630. John Rihm, Pres. and CEO; Mark Shide, Cont. Rihm Motor Co. is a wholesale and retail truck dealer. 75 employees. Founded in 1934. SIC 5012, 5013.

Rimrock Pontiac Cadillac GMC 2540 Phyllis Ln., Billings, MT 59102. Tel: 406/651-5000; Fax: 406/655-8590; Web site: http://www.rimrockauto.com. Stephen A. Zabawa, VP, Sec., and Treas.; John E. Soares, Pres. Annual revenue $43.2 million. Rimrock Pontiac Cadillac GMC sells and services new and used vehicles. 77 employees (4 part-time). Founded in 1987. SIC 5511.

RisComp Industries Inc. 2905 Northwest Blvd., Suite 30, Plymouth, MN 55441. Tel: 763/553-2220; Fax: 763/557-2198. Robert J. Wood, Pres.; Kurt R. Wood, VP; David R. Nelson, CFO. RisComp Industries Inc., dba RJ Associates, is a professional employer organization that provides solutions to employee administration problems. Services include total payroll management, complete safety and claims management, human resource management, and benefits administration. Its slogan: "A better way to run your business." 5,800 employees (4,200 in Minnesota; 1,000 part-time). Founded in 1967. SIC 7389. No. 73 CRM Private 100.

Risdall Linnihan Advertising 2475 15th St. N.W., New Brighton, MN 55112. Tel: 651/631-1098; Web site: http://www.risdall.com. John Risdall, Chm. and CEO; Neal Linnihan, Pres.; Kevin O'Cauaghan, EVP, Chief Creative Officer. Annual revenue $15.8 million. Risdall Linnihan Advertising (RLA) is a locally owned, independent ad agency. Major clients include Smith System Manufacturing Co., U.S. Filter, 3M Co., and Honeywell Inc. Trade journal Advertising Age ranks RLA as the No. 4 business-to-business ad agency in the nation. 61 employees (all in Minnesota). RLA's 1999 billings were 52.7 percent higher than previous year's—the greatest increase at any large Twin Cities agency. SIC 7311.

River Road Casino & Bingo R.R. 3, P.O. Box 168A, Thief River Falls, MN 56701. Tel: 218/679-2111; Fax: 218/679-2191. River Road Casino & Bingo includes a bingo hall and restaurant. 235 employees. Founded in 1992. SIC 7999.

Riverside Color 3000 84th Ln. N.E., Blaine, MN 55449. Tel: 763/784-5808; Fax: 763/784-0749. Stan R. Hildestad, Pres. and Treas.; Bob Lilledahl, VP; Jerry Marquis, VP and Sec. Riverside Color specializes in color separation and prepress services including complete Macintosh-based systems and Postscript output. 53 employees (1 part-time). Founded in 1975. SIC 2796.

Riverside Electronics One Riverside Dr., Lewiston, MN 55952. Tel: 507/523-3220; Fax: 507/523-2831. Stephen H. Craney, Pres. and CEO; Ali Shafiei, Mgr.-Sls./Mktg.; Rodney Allen, Mgr.-Special Projects; John Keane, Gen. Mgr. Annual revenue $42 million. Riverside Electronics is a custom electronics assembler (pin-through and surface-mount), specializing in custom electronic and electromechanical devices for the OEM market. 440 employees (all in Minnesota). Founded in 1984. SIC 3672.

Riverway Company 6889 Rowland Rd., Suite 200, Eden Prairie, MN 55344. Tel: 952/833-1300; Fax: 952/833-1357. Terry Becker, Pres. and COO; W.D. Peltonen, VP-Acctg. Annual revenue $61.8 million. Riverway offers water transportation, such as towboat and barge services. 72 employees (19 in Minnesota). Founded in 1937. SIC 4492.

Riverwood Inn and Conference Center 10990 95th St. N.E., Monticello, MN 55362. Tel: 763/441-6833; Fax: 763/441-3186; Web site: http://www.riverwoodinn.com. Arlene M. DeCandia, CEO; Jeff Wermager, Gen. Mgr.-Regency Mgmt. Co.; Mary Loahr-Wright, Dir.-Sls. Riverwood offers a unique meeting environment overlooking the Mississippi River bluff. Located 35 minutes northwest of downtown Minneapolis, the facilities accommodate groups of two to 150, 59 guest rooms and suites. Regency Management Co. from Sioux Falls, S.D. was hired to manage the facilities in February 1996. 85 employees (all in Minnesota). Founded in 1978. SIC 7389.

Road Machinery & Supplies Company 5633 W. Highway 13, Savage, MN 55378. Tel: 952/895-9595; Fax: 952/895-9564. Michael R. Sill, Chm.; Michael M. Sill II, Pres. and CEO; William T. Holte, CFO; David Johnson, VP-Sls.; Glenn Karr, VP-Southern Op.; John Ruud, VP-Northern Op.; Chuck Petter, VP. Annual revenue $100 million. Road Machinery is a distributor of construction, mining, and forestry equipment. It has four offices in Minnesota, one in Michigan, five in Iowa, and one in Illinois. 210 employees (134 in Minnesota; 4 part-time). Founded in 1926. SIC 5082, 7353.

Ro-Banks Tool & Manufacturing Company 909 S. Fourth Ave., Wahpeton, ND 58075. Tel: 701/642-2671; Fax: 701/642-6198. Robert T. Banks, Pres. Ro-Banks Tool & Manufacturing is engaged in metal stamping, metal fabrication, and tool and die making. 102 employees (5 part-time). Founded in 1963. SIC 3544.

Roberts Automatic Products Inc. 880 Lake Dr., Chanhassen, MN 55317. Tel: 952/949-1000; Fax: 952/949-9240; Web site: http://www.robertsautomatic.com. Walter G. Roberts, Chm.; Ted Roberts, Pres.; James C. Roberts, EVP; Robert H. Nickson, VP-Admin.; Ronald Olberg, VP-Engrg.; Dave Sjolund, VP-Mfg.; Katie Roberts Saindon, Sls. Mgr.; Doug Campbell, Quality Mgr. Annual revenue $14 million. Roberts Automatic Products Inc. is a precision production machine shop specializing in close tolerance and complex screw machine parts and CNC machining with and without secondary operations. Materials run include brass, steel, stainless steel, alloy steel, aluminum. and Hastellog. 100 employees (all in Minnesota). Founded in 1947. SIC 3451.

Roberts-Hamilton Company 7300 Northland Dr., Brooklyn Park, MN 55428. Tel: 612/315-0100; Fax: 763/315-0199. Patrick Finn, Pres. and CEO. Roberts-Hamilton is a wholesaler of plumbing, heating, and cooling supplies, and is the license holder for The Plumbery Showrooms, Top Line, and Plumbing and Heating by Professionals. 70 employees (69 in Minnesota). Founded in 1898. SIC 5074.

Robins, Kaplan, Miller & Ciresi LLP 2800 LaSalle Plaza, 800 LaSalle Ave., Minneapolis, MN 55402. Tel: 612/349-8500; Fax: 612/339-4181; Web site: http://www.rkmc.com. Michael V. Ciresi, Exec. Chm.; Steven A. Schumeister, Managing Ptnr.; Patrick Mandile, COO; Richard Nigon, CFO. Robins, Kaplan, Miller & Ciresi LLP is a national law firm with offices in Atlanta; Boston; Chicago; Los Angeles, Minneapolis; Orange County; and Washington, D.C. The firm's litigation and dispute resolution practice represents individuals, insurance companies, and businesses as both plaintiffs and defendants. The firm's business practice assists clients in addressing the challenging legal issues arising in the conduct of business. The firm represents clients ranging from startup businesses to established firms, private to public companies. Litigation and business practices include antitrust and trade regulation; bankruptcy and insolvency; base closure and privatization; business; catastrophe; commercial law and finance; communications, corporate finance and securities; corporate products liability; distributors and dealerships/franchising; emerging growth companies; employment; environmental; estate planning, probate, trust and estate administration; government relations; insurance, intellectual property; licensing and protection of intellectual property; maritime; mass tort; mergers, acquisitions, and consolidations; personal injury/medical malpractice; real estate, finance and development; science and technology; surety, fidelity and construction; science and technology; and tax and employee benefits. 610 employees. Founded in 1938. In 2000 a federal appeals court upheld a $69 patent-infringement verdict returned in 1997 on behalf of Robins, Kaplan client Unocal Corp., a California oil refiner with a patent for making cleaner-burning gasoline. In May the firm filed the first personal injury lawsuit involving defective Silzone heart valves from St. Jude Medical Inc. (NYSE: STJ), Little Canada, Minn. Susan Richard Nelson, who joined Robins, Kaplan in 1984 and became a partner in 1988, was appointed to the position of U.S. Magistrate Judge for the District of Minnesota. In June Executive Board Chairman Ciresi was named to the National Law Journal's "100 most influential lawyers." In July the firm hired K. Craig Wildfang and Christopher W. Madel, antitrust attorneys who have handled numerous high-profile antitrust investigations for the U.S. Department of Justice (DOJ). In 2000, the firm represented Best Buy in its negotiations of a strategic alliance with Microsoft pursuant to which Best Buy receives prominent promotion, revenue sharing for alliance subscribers, marketing funds and technology assistance. In 1998, the firm achieved a historic result in one of its biggest cases to date, by leading the state of Minnesota and Blue Cross and Blue Shield to a $6.6 billion settlement against the tobacco industry. SIC 8111.

Robinson Rubber Products Company Inc. 4600 Quebec Ave. N., New Hope, MN 55428. Tel: 763/535-6798; Fax: 763/535-0828. Bradley Robinson, Pres.; Jay Beck, VP and Gen. Mgr.; Steve Millhouse, VP-Sls. Robinson Rubber Products manufactures molded items, rollers, and extrusions. 57 employees. Founded in 1949. SIC 3069.

Robot Aided Manufacturing Center Inc. 5140 Moundview Dr., Red Wing, MN 55066. Tel: 651/388-1821; Fax: 651/385-2279. Larry Lautt, Pres. and CEO. RAM Center provides consulting; feasibility studies; and application design, development, and turnkey installations—on an international scope. Its principal business is light-industrial robotic automation/integration and computer interface development. 100 employees. Founded in 1986. SIC 3599, 8731.

Rockler Companies Inc. 4365 Willow Dr., Medina, MN 55340. Tel: 763/478-8201; Fax: 763/478-8393; Web site: http://www.woodworkersstore.com. Ann Rockler Jackson, CEO; David LaPorte, Pres. Annual revenue $60 million. Rockler Cos., dba Rockler Woodworking and Hardware (formerly The Woodworkers' Store), is a retailer of woodworking supplies. It operates through 21 retail stores (from San Diego to Boston) and through mail order (6 million catalogs mailed annually). Rockler also publishes Woodworker's Journal magazine for 205,000 subscribers. 340 employees. Founded in 1954. SIC 2721, 5251, 5961.

Rollins Container Inc. 9661 Newton Ave. S., Bloomington, MN 55431. Tel: 952/888-7550; Fax: 952/888-1435. John R. Burwell, Pres.; Tom Hogan, Gen. Mgr. Rollins Container is a manufacturer of corrugated paper products. 66 employees. Founded in 1971. SIC 2653.

Ronning Enterprises/Home Manufacturing & Supply Co. Inc. 4401 E. Sixth St., Sioux Falls, SD 57103. Tel: 605/336-6000; Fax: 605/336-7879. D. Wayne Ronning, Chm.; Slate Ronning, Pres.; Scott Huber, VP; Harriet Ronning, Sec.; Chuck Point, VP; Kathy Kroening, Asst. Sec.; Marty Hefner, Purch. Agent; Carey Schave, Estimator. Ronning Enterprises, dba Ronning Homes and Neighborhoods, develops residential property into single-family and multifamily lots. It has also built over 4,000 homes. A separate company under same ownership at same location, Home Manufacturing and Supply Co. Inc., dba Home Supply Co., sells building materials and manufactures components for wood buildings. 50 employees. Founded in 1956. SIC 1521, 5211.

Ron's Foods 708 Main St., Suite 2, Elk River, MN 55330. Tel: 763/441-8994; Fax: 763/441-8995. Ronald Dargis, Owner. Ron's Foods operates four Minnesota supermarkets: Ron's Foods, Elk River; Festival Foods, Alexandria and Park Rapids; and No-Frills, St. Peter. 550 employees (all in Minnesota). Founded in 1972. SIC 5411.

Ron-Vik Inc. 800 Colorado Ave. S., Golden Valley, MN 55416. Tel: 763/545-0276; Fax: 763/545-0142. Jack N. Vikre, Pres. and CEO; James Greupner, COO; Norm Olafson, CFO; Geoff McNair, Quality Mgr.; Scott Rische, Sls. Mgr.; Ken Weyandt, Op. Mgr. Annual revenue $10.4 million. Ron-Vik manufactures wire cloth filters, in-line strainers, filter washers, suction line strainers, and other custom wire cloth products. 109 employees (110 in Minnesota; 1 part-time). Founded in 1948. SIC 3569.

W.A. Roosevelt Company 2727 Commerce St., La Crosse, WI 54601. Tel: 608/781-2000; Fax: 608/781-8364. J.M. Brindley, Chm.; S.W. Reiman, Pres.; T.M. Brindley, EVP; R.W. Spencer, VP-Fin. W.A. Roosevelt Co. wholesales electrical, plumbing, heating, air conditioning, and refrigeration supplies. It operates branches in Plover and Rice Lake, Wis. 105 employees (6 part-time). Founded in 1868. SIC 5063, 5074, 5078.

Rosco Manufacturing Company 311 S. Union, P.O. Box B, Madison, SD 57042. Tel: 605/256-6942; Fax: 605/256-0240; Web site: http://www.roscomfg.com. Jon Knuths, Pres.; Don Weber, VP; Shelly Knuths, Sec.; Leroy Knuths, CEO. Rosco Manufacturing is a maker of small compactors, liquid-asphalt applicators, street flushers, and power brooms. It also manufactures pothole patchers and chip spreaders for asphalt applications. 125 employees (1 in Minnesota; 5 part-time). Founded in 1928. SIC 3531.

Rosemount Office Systems Inc. 21785 Hamburg Ave., Lakeville, MN 55044. Tel: 952/469-4416; Fax: 952/469-5981. Vernon H. Heath, Chm.; Barry R. Mumm, Pres. and CEO; Lloyd C. Mollenkopf, EVP; Mary E. Rolf, VP and CFO. Rosemount Office Systems manufactures and markets office furniture, specializing in panel-based furniture. The company has a showroom in Minneapolis. 150 employees (all in Minnesota). Founded in 1966. SIC 2522.

Rosen's Diversified Inc. 1120 Lake Ave., Fairmont, MN 56031. Tel: 507/238-4201; Fax: 507/238-9966. Thomas J. Rosen, Pres. and CEO; Robert A. Hovde, CFO; Elmer H. Rosen, VChm. Annual revenue $750 million. Rosen's Diversified Inc. is an agribusiness holding company with interests in meat packing, chemicals, fertilizer, and technology. Subsidiaries include Long Prairie Co., Rosen's Inc., and Skylark Meats. 1,800 employees. Founded in 1946. SIC 2011, 2819, 2873, 2874. No. 15 CRM Private 100.

Ross Sportswear Inc. 9909 South Shore Dr., Plymouth, MN 55441. Tel: 763/545-9544; Fax: 763/542-9237. Michael Ross, Owner and Pres.; Pam Hoover, Mdse. Mgr.; Jonathon Gilbert, Dir.-Sls./Mktg.; Dan Mosow, Fin. Ofcr. Ross Sportswear manufactures and markets men's and women's active sportswear and licensed products. Showroom: New York. 60 employees (all in Minnesota; 50 part-time). Founded in 1980. SIC 2329, 2339.

Rough Rider Industries P.O. Box 5521, Bismarck, ND 58502. Tel: 701/328-6161; Fax: 701/328-6164. Dennis Fracassi, Dir.; Thomas Haan, Mktg. Mgr. Rough Rider Industries manufactures hardwood office furniture. 140 employees. Founded in 1974. SIC 2521.

Roverud Construction Inc. 601 Highway 44 E., Spring Grove, MN 55974. Tel: 507/498-3377; Fax: 507/498-5835. Jeff Roverud, Pres.; Curt Roverud, Sec. Roverud Construction quarries limestone, produces aggregate, and resurfaces roads. 74 employees (36 in Minnesota). Founded in 1929. SIC 1422.

Royal Concrete Pipe Inc. 30630 Forest Blvd., Stacy, MN 55079. Tel: 651/462-2130; Fax: 651/462-5772. Bill Makens, Pres.; Julian Trangsrud, VP and Gen. Mgr. Royal Concrete Pipe manufactures pipe, septic tanks, manholes, and concrete products for municipalities. 100 employees (all in Minnesota). Founded in 1985. SIC 3272.

Rubber Industries Inc. 200 Cavanaugh Dr., P.O. Box 128, Shakopee, MN 55379. Tel: 952/445-1320; Fax: 952/445-7934. Arthur J. Hatch, Pres. and CFO; Sandy Thangaraj, VP-Tech.; Cameron Morningstar, VP-Op.; John Engler, Quality Assurance Mgr.; Bruce Nelson, VP-Sls./Mktg.; Pat Fischer, Customer Svc. Mgr.; Cindy Bahmiller, New Project Mgr. Rubber Industries, a custom molder of engineered rubber component parts, also offers parts-design consultation and prototype services. 75 employees. Founded in 1969. SIC 3069.

Rupp Industries Inc. One Rupp Plaza, 3700 W. Preserve, Burnsville, MN 55337. Tel: 952/894-3000; Fax: 952/707-5104. Ruth E. Rupp, Chm.; Eric D. Estergren, Pres. and CEO; Roger D. Johnson, VP; Richard L. Brown, VP; William R. Bush Jr., Sec. Annual revenue $18.5 million. Rupp Industries operates through two divisions: Rupp Air Management manufactures direct-fired and indirect-fired heaters (gas, electric, steam, and heat-recovery) designed for the commercial and industrial market; Temp-Air rents and leases temporary heating and cooling equipment to commercial, industrial, and special events industries. Regional offices are located in Ohio, Illinois, Wisconsin, Colorado, Pennsylvania, Michigan, Massachusetts, and Delaware. 163 employees (116 in Minnesota). Founded in 1965. SIC 3433, 3585.

Russell & Herder 315 E. River Rd., P.O. Box 605, Brainerd, MN 56401. Tel: 218/829-3055; Fax: 218/829-2182; Web site: http://www.russellherder.com. Carol Russell, Principal; Brian Herder, Principal; John Bement, Gen. Mgr.-St. Paul; Jim Engel, Gen. Mgr.-Brainerd; Steve Greenfield, Gen. Mgr.-Duluth. Russell & Herder is a full-service, integrated marketing firm that works in the areas of creative development, advertising, public relations, strategic planning, media placement, event planning, interactive media, and market research. With offices in Brainerd, St. Cloud, Duluth, and St. Paul, Russell & Herder is the only marketing firm in Greater Minnesota to be elected into the American Association of

Advertising Agencies. The firm serves clients throughout the United States and Canada in many industries: health care, tourism, telecommunications, forest products, marine, recreation, financial services, higher education manufacturing, and building products. 85 employees (all in Minnesota; 10 part-time). Founded in 1984. In January 2000 the firm formed an official alliance with St. Paul-based Digital Boundaries, an interactive media software development company, that created a new 16-employee entity called Ruckus Interactive. In March the firm claimed Best of Show at the American Advertising Awards in both St. Cloud and Duluth, Minn. (for a series of Clow Stamping print ads). In May its unconventional creative work made it a finalist, for the second year in a row, for the American Association of Advertising Agencies' prestigious O'Toole Agency Award. In August Russell & Herder, which offers small- and large-scale events planning on a local and national level, started a new division dedicated solely to marketing and coordinating special events, and added a specialist to manage that service: Patricia Stoll. SIC 7311, 8743.

Ryan Companies U.S. Inc. 700 International Centre, 900 Second Ave. S., Minneapolis, MN 55402. Tel: 612/336-1200; Fax: 612/337-5552. Francis J. Ryan, Chm.; James R. Ryan, CEO; Patrick G. Ryan, Pres.; Russell J. Ryan, VChm.; Michael R. McElroy, EVP-Properties; William J. McHale, EVP-Retail Devel.; Richard Collins, VP; Elizabeth (Betty) Goodman, VP and Chief Gen. Counsel; Timothy M. Gray, CFO. Annual revenue $422 million. Ryan is a designer, developer, and builder of industrial, retail, commercial, environment, and housing projects. Other services Ryan offers include financing, ownership, leasing, and property management. In addition to Minneapolis, Ryan has offices in Hibbing, Minn.; Cedar Rapids, Iowa; Phoenix, Arizona; Chicago, Illinois; and DesMoines, Iowa. 400 employees. Founded in 1938. In February 2000 Ryan was awarded the 1999 NAIOP Award of Excellence for the "best office build-to-suit over 100,000 square feet": the Minnesota Department of Revenue building at 600 N. Robert St., St. Paul. In May Ryan broke ground for Veritas Software Corp.'s 143,157-square-foot facility in Roseville, Minn. (Centre Point Business Campus). Cornerstone Properties Inc. (NYSE: CPP) purchased U.S. Bancorp Center (800 Nicollet Mall, between Eighth and Ninth streets in downtown Minneapolis) from developer Ryan Cos. U.S. for $135 million. In June Ryan and Carlson Lifestyle Living Inc., an emerging business entity of Carlson Hospitality Worldwide, announced a joint-venture agreement to develop 25 Carlson Park lifestyle communities across the western United States over the next 15 years. The MCDA received approval from the Minneapolis City Council to sell the Grain Belt Brew House to Ryan for redevelopment as an office complex. RSP Architects Ltd., Minneapolis, was to be the project's architect as well as its only tenant. Ryan broke ground on the first phase of the 1.3 million-square-foot Target North Office Campus, Brooklyn Park, Minn. In July Ryan acquired a 250,000-square-foot distribution center in Carol Stream, Ill., which was leased to Saturn Freight Systems Distribution. SIC 1541. No. 30 CRM Private 100.

PVT

Jim Ryan Chevrolet Inc. P.O. Box 1366, Minot, ND 58701. Tel: 701/852-3571; Fax: 701/852-4891; Web site: http://www.ryanchebrolet.com. J.M. Ryan, Pres.; Kathleen Gaddie, Dealer. Jim Ryan Chevrolet is a Chevrolet motor vehicle dealership owned by J.R. Holding Co., Minot. 81 employees (2 part-time). Founded in 1973. SIC 5511.

Ryt-way Industries Inc. 21850 Grenada Ave., Lakeville, MN 55066. Tel: 952/469-1417; Fax: 952/469-9580. Glenn W. Hasse Jr., Pres. and CEO; Gerald G. Hasse, VP. Annual revenue $35 million. Ryt-way Industries provides custom food blending and packaging. It also manufactures and sells food service products. 500 employees. Founded in 1965. SIC 2023, 2034, 2099.

SJ Electro Systems Inc. P.O. Box 1619, Detroit Lakes, MN 56502. Tel: 218/847-1317; Fax: 218/847-4617; Web site: http://www.sjerhombus.com. Lois Solheim, Chm.; Laurie Lewandowski, Pres. and CEO. SJ Electro Systems manufactures liquid-level control devices. 180 employees (all in Minnesota). Founded in 1975. SIC 3823.

SPS Commerce Inc. 1450 Energy Park Dr., St. Paul, MN 55108. Tel: 651/603-4400; Fax: 651/603-4403; Web site: http://www.spscommerce.com. Steve Waldron, Pres. and CEO; Bernardo Sotomayor, EVP and Chief Tech. Ofcr.; Jim Radabaugh, SVP and COO; Archie Black, CFO; Roger Anderson, VP-Tech. Support; Tom Boutin, VP-Int'l Sls.; Raymond Brons, VP-Major Accounts; Joe Dalman, VP-Professional Svs.; Marshall Erickson, VP-Bus. Devel.; Craig Evans, VP-Mktg.; Jim Frome, VP-Mktg.; Michael Harrington, VP-Client Svs.; Rolf Holman, VP-Sls.; Carla Underwood, VP-SPS Commerce. SPS Commerce, formerly St. Paul Software, offers electronic data interchange (EDI) software translators and mapping products, as well as complementary professional services, for the e-commerce industry. Its products support multiple hardware platforms and operating systems. The company also provides options for task management, scheduling, and fax processing—and an EDI service bureau. 198 employees (191 in Minnesota; 2 part-time). Founded in 1981. In January 2000 SPS added a new browser-based business intelligence service to its offerings. Developed by SPS, it enables organizations to derive real value by accessing and analyzing their e-commerce transaction data online. In February the company secured $15 million in financing from new investors including Brinson Partners, as well as certain current investors: St. Paul Venture Capital, Damac Al Baraka Investment Co., Granite Private Equity, and Axiom Venture Partners. SPS was planning to use the proceeds from the offering for working capital to fuel the growth of business-to-business e-commerce services for its online trading community. Walgreen Co. (NYSE: WAG) contracted with SPS Commerce to assist in electronically automating vendors' transactions for both its warehouse and direct store delivery trading community. In March the company acquired RNetEC, Sacramento, Calif.—the leading provider of Universal Product Code (UPC) solutions for retailers and vendors. In April SPS sold its $9 million-revenue SPS Solutions software business to Hoofddorp, Netherlands-based TIE Holding, developers of Internet software. The sale was to enable SPS Commerce to focus solely on its Internet-based retail and manufacturing B2B exchanges. SPS and Retek (Nasdaq: RETK), a leading provider of retail solutions for the new economy, entered into a joint business relationship to provide retailers and their trading partners with a complete, Internet-based services and software solution. In June Netmarket Group Inc. contracted with SPS Commerce to provide Web-based exchange services for its online sites. In July DFS Group Ltd., San Francisco, which operates a global supply chain to more than 150 stores worldwide, selected SPS Commerce to provide Web-based exchange services to streamline the company's trading processes. Outdoor retailers Gander Mountain LLC and Recreational Equipment Inc. also contracted with SPS to provide end-to-end, Web-based exchange services. In August the company launched its Yellow Pages directory, a comprehensive, online directory of thousands of exchange participants. In September SPS Commerce and SVI (Amex: SVI), a leading global supplier of enterprise software solutions for the retail industry, formed a joint marketing and development partnership. In October sporting goods retailer Galyan's Trading Co. became the 50th retail customer to contract with SPS for its supply chain enablement and optimization services. SIC 7373.

SPS Companies 6363 Highway 7, St. Louis Park, MN 55416. Tel: 952/929-1377; Fax: 952/929-1862. Ralph E. Gross, Pres. SPS Cos. wholesales plumbing, heating, and air-conditioning supplies. 280 employees. Founded in 1951. SIC 5074, 5075.

SRF Consulting Group Inc. One Carlson Pkwy. N., Suite 150, Plymouth, MN 55447. Tel: 763/475-0010; Fax: 763/475-2429; Web site: http://www.srfconsulting.com. Robert B. Roscoe, Pres.; Peter A. Fausch, EVP; Randall F. Geerdes, SVP; Ferrol O. Robinson, SVP; Barry J. Warner, SVP. SRF Consulting is a full service consulting firm with a broad base of planning and design services, including: structural engineering, transportation planning, environmental services, community planning, landscape architecture and urban design, civil engineering, highway engineering, traffic engineering, intelligent transportation systems, land surveying, in-construction services. 165 employees (all in Minnesota). Founded in 1961. SIC 0781.

S-T Industries Inc. 301 Armstrong Blvd. N., St. James, MN 56081. Tel: 507/375-3211; Fax: 507/375-4503; Web site: http://www.thomasregister.com/stind. Margaret A. Smith, Pres. and CFO; Grant M. Lillevold, VP-Engrg.; Robert J. Friesen, VP-Mktg.; Khalil A. Gharbi, VP-Mfg. S-T Industries manufactures and markets precision measuring tools, optical comparators, and video inspection equipment. 122 employees (120 in Minnesota; 5 part-time). Founded in 1942. SIC 3545.

S&T Office Products Inc. 1000 Kristen Ct., Vadnais Heights, MN 55110. Tel: 651/483-4411; Fax: 651/483-0550; Web site: http://www.stofficeproducts.com. Frank Tschida, Pres. and CEO; Gary Sirek, VP; Pat Crowley, VP. S&T Office Products is a distributor of commercial office products, specializing in stationery, furniture, and printing. 155 employees. Founded in 1971. SIC 5943.

S&W Plastics LLC 10206 Crosstown Circle, Eden Prairie, MN 55344. Tel: 952/942-7760; Fax: 952/942-7686; Web site: http://www.swplastics.com. C. Scott Thiss, CEO; Russ Jones, VP-Sls./Engrg.; Dare Presler, VP-Mfg. Annual revenue $16.5 million. S&W Plastics is an ISO 9002-certified, midsize manufacturer specializing in plastic injection molding, tool production, and plastic parts assembly for the computer, electronics, medical, and industrial markets. S&W's specific plastic technology expertise includes large tonnage molding, stack mold manufacturing, clean controlled environment molding, and creative strategic customer alliances. 115 employees (all in Minnesota). Founded in 1970. SIC 3089.

SafeNet Consulting Inc. 5850 Opus Pkwy., Suite 290, Minnetonka, MN 55343. Tel: 952/930-3636; Fax: 952/930-3737; Web site: http://www.safenetconsulting.com. Martin Miller, Owner and Managing Ptnr.; Jay Nelson, Owner and Managing Ptnr.; Robert Purdy, Owner and Managing Ptnr. Annual revenue $19.1 million. SafeNet Consulting Inc., Minnesota's fastest-growing IT consulting services company ever, is an e-business and technology consulting services company. It provides end-to-end solutions, project delivery, and strategic staffing to commercial and government clients. Current specialty Practice Areas include Application Development/Web Enablement, Date Management, Healthcare Industry Solutions, Project Management, Quality Assurance & Testing, and Web Technologies. SafeNet Consulting currently has additional offices in Milwaukee and Denver. 165 employees (120 in Minnesota). Founded in 1994. In April 2000 Martin Miller, Jay Nelson, and Bob Purdy were all named finalists in the 2000 Entrepreneur of the Year Awards by Ernst & Young for the second time. SafeNet Consulting was ranked ninth on the 1999 Inc. 500, the highest ranking ever for a Minnesota IT services company. The company created an advanced Internet architecture that is being used by numerous dot-com companies as their trading engine or interface. SIC 7371, 7379. No. 18 CityBusiness Fastest-growing Private Companies.

Sagebrush Corporation 12219 Nicollet Ave. S., Burnsville, MN 55337. Tel: 952/890-5484; Web site: http://www.sagebrushcorp.com. Jay Stead, Pres. and CEO; Al Bennett, SVP; Eric Johnson, SVP; Suzy Riesterer, SVP and CFO. Annual revenue $70 million. Sagebrush Corp. is the largest, fastest-growing firm dedicated to the market for K-12 information solutions, a category that includes library automation systems, quality-bound books, cataloging services, Internet solutions, and other educational resources. 580 employees (210 in Minnesota; 20 part-time). Founded in 1982. In January 2000 Sagebrush Corp. and Winnebago Software Co., two leaders in K-12 information solutions, completed a merger of their privately held firms. In April the company released Athena v8.1, an upgrade to its award-winning library automation program. The 32-bit application provides additional features, better performance, and greater flexibility. In August, based on its revenue growth from 1995 to 1999, the company was named to Deloitte & Touche's Minnesota Technology Fast 50. SIC 7372, 7374. No. 10 Minnesota Technology Fast 50.

Sailboats Inc. 250 Marina Dr., Superior, WI 54880. Tel: 715/392-7131; Fax: 715/392-7133. Jack Culley, Pres.; Joe Radtke, VP-Barkers Island Marina; Karen Bertie, Cont. Sailboats Inc., dba Barkers Island Marina, is a marina that also offers sailing instruction, charters, and boat sales. Sailboats also operates Manitowoc Marina in Manitowoc, Wis.; a sailboat charter operation in Lake Superior and Lake Michigan; and an air charter service out of Superior, Wis. 65 employees. Founded in 1970. SIC 4493.

St. Croix Casino & Hotel 777 U.S. Highway 8, Turtle Lake, WI 54889. Tel: 715/986-4777; Fax: 715/986-2877. Ben Bock, COO; LeRoy Buck, CFO; JoAnn Downs, Gen Mgr.; Vivian Mitchell, Hum. Res. Dir. St. Croix Casino & Hotel offers over 1,000 slots and blackjack, a buffet, restaurant, entertainment, bingo, high-stakes pull tabs, and a snack bar. 1,000 employees. Founded in 1992. SIC 7011.

St. Croix Meadows Greyhound Racing Park 2200 Carmichael, Hudson, WI 54016. Tel: 715/386-6800; Fax: 715/386-4851. Ron Geier, Pres.; Bonnie Romano, Mktg. Dir. St. Croix Meadows provides pari-mutuel greyhound racing and simulcasting. 110 employees (14 in Minnesota). Founded in 1991. SIC 7948.

St. Croix Press Inc. 1185 S. Knowles Ave., New Richmond, WI 54017. Tel: 715/246-5811; Fax: 715/243-7551. Ed A. Monette, Chm. and Pres.; Chuck Williams, CFO and Sec.; Dean O. Lindquist, Sls. Mgr.; Mike Monette, Gen. Mgr. St. Croix Press is a short-run magazine and catalog printer. 195 employees (3 part-time). Founded in 1971. SIC 2752, 2759.

St. Croix Rods 856 Fourth Ave. N., P.O. Box 279, Park Falls, WI 54552. Tel: 715/762-3226; Fax: 715/762-3293; Web site: http://www.stcroixrods.com. Paul Schluter, Pres. and Gen. Mgr.; Jeff Schluter, VP-Sls./Mktg.; David Schluter, VP-Mfg. St. Croix Rods manufactures and markets St. Croix fiberglass and graphite fishing rods; and private-brand fishing rods for other companies. 110 employees (1 in Minnesota). Founded in 1948. SIC 3949.

St. Marie's Gopher News Company 9000 10th Ave. N., Golden Valley, MN 55427. Tel: 763/546-5300; Fax: 763/525-3100. R. Gary St. Marie, Chm.; Donald O. Weber, Pres.; Scott Andrus, Dir.-Sls.; Craig Travis, Mktg. Mgr. St. Marie's Gopher News is a wholesale distributor of periodicals (primarily magazines and books); specialty products (including baseball, football, and all sports trading cards); and children's books and products. 126 employees (7 part-time). Founded in 1905. SIC 5994.

St. Paul Linoleum & Carpet Company 2956 Center Ct., Eagan, MN 55121. Tel: 651/686-7770; Fax: 651/686-6660; Web site: http://www.stpaullinocpt.com. Clement J. Commers, Pres. and CFO; Michael J. Commers, VP; Lynn Hansch, VP; Mark Schmidt, VP; Robert Good, Sec. and Treas. Annual revenue $21 million. St. Paul Linoleum & Carpet is a commercial floor covering contractor. 90 employees (all in Minnesota). Founded in 1938. SIC 1752, 1799.

Satellite Industries Inc. 2530 Xenium Ln. N., Plymouth, MN 55441. Tel: 763/553-1900; Fax: 763/553-1905; Web site: http://www.satelliteco.com. Al Hilde Jr., Chm.; John Pran, CEO; Todd Hilde, Pres.; Tim Hilde, EVP-Satellite Shelters; Thomas Vickman, VP-Fin. Satellite Industries Inc. manufactures portable toilets, sinks, deodorizers, and service trucks, serving customers in over 70 countries around the world. Satellite Industries is part of a group of family-owned businesses. Satellite Shelters Inc. supplies mobile offices and relocatable modular buildings in a variety of floor plans. Satellite Shelters also serves as a general contractor and can complete turnkey building projects for clients. Jackson Hole Aviation LLC, Jackson, Wyo., is a fixed-based operation serving commercial and private aircraft and offering charter flights with its own fleet in Wyoming. Western Aircraft Inc., Boise, Idaho, is a $29.5 million-revenue aircraft services company. 150 employees (100 in Minnesota). Founded in 1957. SIC 2452, 2842, 3715.

Saturn of St. Paul Inc. 3400 Highway 61 N., White Bear Lake, MN 55110. Tel: 651/483-9106; Fax: 651/483-8649. Wes Rydell, Pres.; Dave Roen, Gen. Mgr; .Lee Olderbak, Svc. Mgr.; Doug Johnson, Parts Mgr.; Tom Weed, Cont. Annual revenue $95 million. Saturn of St. Paul sells new and used vehicles. It also provides service and maintenance, including quick lubes and oil changes, for all makes and models. Other Minnesota locations: Inver Grove Heights, Mounds View, St. Paul. 240 employees (all in Minnesota; 35 part-time). Founded in 1990. SIC 5511, 7549.

Ron Saxon Ford Inc. 225 University Ave., St. Paul, MN 55103. Tel: 651/222-0511; Fax: 651/222-2851. Michael Saxon, Gen. Mgr.. Ron Saxon Ford is a motor vehicle dealer. 90 employees (85 in Minnesota; 5 part-time). Founded in 1957. SIC 5511.

Schechter Dokken Kanter Andrews & Selcer CPAs Ltd. 100 Washington Ave. S., Suite 1600, Minneapolis, MN 55401. Tel: 612/332-5500; Fax: 612/332-1529. Russell Andrews, Pres.; Herbert Schechter, VP and Dir.-Trust Mgmt. Group; Martin Kanter, VP; Joseph Kenyon, VP; Charles Selcer, VP; Eric Wille, VP; James Reasoner, Treas.; Richard Ledin, Sec. Schechter Dokken Kanter Andrews & Selcer CPAs Ltd. is a certified public accounting firm performing accounting, audit, tax, and advisory services, as well as litigation consulting. It serves clients in retailing, manufacturing, not-for-profit, real estate, gaming, wholesale distribution, hospitality, entertainment, and high-net-worth/high-income individuals. The firm's trust management group administers family trusts, estates, charitable foundations, and employee benefits plans. Associates are in 132 U.S. cities and 47 countries. 55 employees. Founded in 1990. SIC 8721.

Scherer Bros. Lumber Company 9110 83rd Ave. N., Brooklyn Park, MN 55445. Tel: 612/379-9633; Fax: 612/627-0679. Peter Scherer, Pres. and CEO; Bill Clemen, VP-Retail; Bob Heurung, CFO; Ray Roeder, VP-Mfg.; Gregory Scherer, VP-Mktg.; Kris Scherer, Treas.; Linda Scott, Dir.-Hum. Res. Annual revenue $149 million. Scherer Bros. Lumber Co. is a supplier of lumber, windows, trusses and building materials to professional builders and remodelers. It is also involved in land development and construction financing. Far North Windows and Doors is a window and door manufacturing division. 520 employees. Founded in 1930. In June 2000 Far North Windows and Doors announced plans to consolidate its northeast Minneapolis operations in a new 133,000-square-foot building in Champlin, Minn., in January 2001. SIC 5211. No. 89 CRM Private 100.

Schlagel Inc. 491 Emerson St. N., Cambridge, MN 55008. Tel: 763/689-5991; Fax: 763/689-5310. Christopher Schlagel, Pres.; William Schlagel, VP. Schlagel is a manufacturer of grain-, feed-, and fertilizer-handling equipment, with worldwide sales. 80 employees (77 in Minnesota). Founded in 1957. SIC 3523.

Schmidt 1101 N.W. Frontage Rd., Byron, MN 55920. Tel: 507/775-6400; Fax: 507/775-6655. Tom Foegen, Pres. Schmidt is engaged in heatset and non-heatset web printing. Owned by Taylor Corp., Mankato, Minn. 390 employees. Founded in 1912. SIC 2752.

Schmidt Laboratories Inc. 4605 Rusan St., P.O. Box 1264, St. Cloud, MN 56302. Tel: 320/255-9787; Fax: 320/255-9982; Web site: http://www.schmidtlabs.com. Chris Foley, Pres.; Denise Schmidt, VP-Mktg. Schmidt Laboratories is a manufacturer of prescription eyeglasses. 175 employees (all in Minnesota). Founded in 1982. SIC 3851.

Paul A. Schmitt Music Company 88 S. 10th St., Minneapolis, MN 55403. Tel: 612/339-4811; Fax: 612/339-3574. Thomas M. Schmitt, Chm., Pres., and CEO; Jerry Hovey, VP; Wayne Reinhardt, VP; Jill Rivard, VP; Doug Schmitt, VP; Paul Seppala, VP, CFO, and Treas. Annual revenue $65 million. Paul A. Schmitt Music Co. is in the music retailing business. It operates 24 music stores in North Dakota, South Dakota, Minnesota, Nebraska, and Wisconsin, Colorado, Kansas, Missouri, and California. 355 employees. Founded in 1896. After 60 years at the 88 South 10th building, distinctive for its "wall of music" mural, Schmitt was making plans to centralize its administrative, distribution, and warehouse functions in Brooklyn Center in a May 2001 move. SIC 5736.

Schneiderman's Furniture 8198 Elmer Rd., Meadowlands, MN 55765. Tel: 218/427-2131; Fax: 218/427-2223. Larry Schneiderman, CEO. Annual revenue $37 million. Schneiderman's is a furniture store chain with locations in Meadowlands, Chaska, Bloomington, Duluth, Lakeville, Minnetonka, Roseville, and Woodbury, Minn. 210 employees (228 in Minnesota; 18 part-time). Founded in 1948. SIC 5712.

Schoeneman Bros. Company 305 E. Eighth St., Sioux Falls, SD 57102. Tel: 605/336-2440; Fax: 605/336-2529. H.M. Schoeneman, Pres.; Alvin Schoeneman, VP and Treas.; A. Cecil Schoeneman, Sec. Schoeneman Bros. is a lumber and materials dealer with eight lumberyards. 65 employees. Founded in 1888. SIC 5211.

Scholl's Inc. 4440 W. Round Lake Rd., Arden Hills, MN 55112. Tel: 651/636-0892; Fax: 651/636-8532. Thomas Scholl, CEO; Dan Scholl, Pres. and COO; Patrick Lang, VP and Treas.; Al Monita, VP-Purch. Scholl's Inc. distributes health and beauty aids, school supplies, party goods, cosmetics, and hair-care products. 180 employees. Founded in 1935. SIC 5122.

Schott Corporation 1000 Parker Lake Rd., Wayzata, MN 55391. Tel: 952/475-1173; Fax: 952/475-1786. O.W. Schott, Chm. and CEO; W.A. Schott, VP; Paul Larkin, CFO. Schott custom-designs and manufactures transformers, inductors, magnetic components, and high-current power supplies. 450 employees (445 in Minnesota). Founded in 1951. SIC 3612, 3677, 3679.

Schroeder Milk Company 2080 Rice St., Roseville, MN 55113. Tel: 651/487-1471; Fax: 651/487-1476; Web site: http://www.schroedermilk.com. Ernie Schroeder, Pres.; Frank Neises, COO. Schroeder Milk Co. produces fluid dairy products, and distributes them to food-service wholesalers, grocery stores, and convenience stores. It also does contract packaging of juice, dairy, and other fluid products. 160 employees. Founded in 1884. SIC 2024, 2026.

J&R Schugel Trucking Inc. 2026 N. Broadway St., New Ulm, MN 56073. Tel: 507/359-2900; Fax: 507/354-4366. Jerry Schugel,

Pres.; Richard Schugel, VP; James F. Guldan, Sec. and Treas. Annual revenue $61 million. Schugel Trucking specializes in temperature-controlled dry & flatbed freight. The company has regional offices in Columbus, Ohio; Champaign, Ill.; and Norcross, Ga. 460 employees (160 in Minnesota; 15 part-time). Founded in 1974. SIC 4213.

Terry Schulte Automotive Inc. 4200 W. 12th St., Sioux Falls, SD 57107. Tel: 605/336-1700; Fax: 605/335-8184. T. Schulte, Pres. and CEO; Lee Andersen, Cont.; Bill Termaat, Gen. Mgr. Terry Schulte Automotive is a new and used motor vehicle dealership that sells Chevrolet, Jeep, Mitsubishi, and Subaru. 150 employees. Founded in 1975. SIC 5511.

Schwan's Sales Enterprises Inc. 115 W. College Dr., Marshall, MN 56258. Tel: 507/532-3274; Fax: 507/537-8450. Alfred Schwan, Chm.; M. Lenny Pippin, Pres. and CEO; Dan Herrmann, Cont.; Donald Miller, CFO. Annual revenue $3 billion (estimated by Forbes). Schwan's manufactures food products, including ice cream and pizza (Tony's, Red Baron, Freschetta), and is an international distributor of frozen foods. 6,000 employees (2,000 in Minnesota). Founded in 1952. In May 2000 Schwan's debuted a new ground beef product line that uses Titan Corp.'s (NYSE: TTN) revolutionary SureBeam technology to eliminate the threat of harmful food-borne bacteria. In August Schwan's sold $1.1 billion-asset, 423-employee Lyon Financial Services Inc., a wholly owned subsidiary, to U.S. Bancorp (NYSE: USB). In September the company said that it was looking to buy a third plant in order to expand production for Tony's Pizza Service. Under consideration: a 330,000-square-foot plant in New Hampton, Iowa, that had been shut down by Sara Lee Corp. In November the company announced plans to open a $9.5 million centralized R&D facility in Marshall in 2001 to create new products. The 75,000-square-foot, 50-employee center will bring R&D for dough technology, hand-held foods, and ice cream under one roof. Regarding expansion of pizza production: In addition to the Sara Lee plant in Iowa, the company was seriously considering a site in Missouri. SIC 2024, 2038. No. 4 CRM Private 100. No. 93 CRM Employer 100.

Schwickert's of Mankato Inc. 221 Minnesota St., P.O. Box 487, Mankato, MN 56001. Tel: 507/387-3106; Fax: 507/387-4688; Web site: http://www.schwickerts.com. Kim Schwickert, Pres.; Steven L. Hanson, CFO; Kent T. Schwickert, VP; Jill S. Johnson, Sec. and Treas. Annual revenue $21.6 million. Schwickert's of Mankato is a holding company for the mechanical and roofing contractor companies Schwickert Inc., Schwickert Co., and Schwickert's in Rochester Inc. 210 employees (200 in Minnesota; 10 part-time). Founded in 1906. SIC 1711, 1761.

Scicom Data Services Ltd. 10101 Bren Rd. E., Minnetonka, MN 55343. Tel: 952/933-4200; Fax: 952/936-4132. Richard A. Walter, Chm. and CEO; Steven B. Dille, Pres. and COO; Dale Carlson, EVP; Sam LeCount, SVP; John J. Honzl, VP and CFO; Tom King, Sec.; Eileen A. Davenport, Cont. and Asst. Sec. Annual revenue $26 million. Scicom Data Services provides computing digital document and mail processing services to commercial customers nationwide. The company was publicly traded until February 1989, when management took it private via an ESOP. 200 employees (210 in Minnesota; 10 part-time). Founded in 1959. SIC 7374.

Scoville Press Inc. 14505 27th Ave. N., Plymouth, MN 55447. Tel: 763/553-1400; Fax: 763/553-0042. Donald C. Wildman, Chm.; Rick Gulbrand, Pres.; Bill Arendt, VP-Fin. Annual revenue $24 million. Scoville Press prints subscription and reader service cards for publications. The company specializes in loose-deck, direct-response card packs and customized direct-mail products. 195 employees (all in Minnesota). Founded in 1974. SIC 2752, 2759.

Sebastian Joe's 4301 Nicollet Ave. S., Minneapolis, MN 55409. Tel: 612/824-3461; Fax: 612/824-0657. Michael Pellizer, Co-owner; Ken Pellizer, Co-owner; Todd Pellizer, Co-owner. Sebastian Joe's is a chain of ice cream/coffee cafes in the Twin Cities. 90 employees. Founded in 1984. SIC 5812.

Sebesta Blomberg & Associates Inc. 2381 Rosegate, P.O. Box 131750, Roseville, MN 55113. Tel: 651/634-0775; Fax: 651/634-7400; Web site: http://www.sebesta.com. James Sebesta, CEO; James J. Blomberg, Principal; Oleksa P. Breslawec, Principal; John A. Carlson, Principal; Rebecca T. Ellis, Principal; Dean R. Sharpe, Principal. Annual revenue $16.8 million. Sebesta Blomberg provides professional facility services including engineering, facilities management, program management, and construction services for industrial, institutional, educational, governmental, and utility customers nationally and internationally. 180 employees (135 in Minnesota; 5 part-time). Founded in 1994. SIC 8711, 8742, 8744. No. 37 CityBusiness Fastest-growing Private Companies.

Security American Financial Enterprises Inc. 10901 Red Circle Dr., Minnetonka, MN 55343. Tel: 952/544-2121; Fax: 952/945-3419. Orem O. Robbins, Chm.; Susan Albrecht, Pres. and CEO; Kevin J. Stangler, EVP and CFO. SAFE is the parent of Security Life and Health Insurance Co. of America and Congress Life Insurance Co., which offer life and health insurance and annuities—individual and group—in 43 states. Security Life concentrates on special markets, such as pre-plan and pre-fund funeral arrangements. Once a publicly traded company, it was taken private in November 1989. 68 employees (all in Minnesota). Founded in 1972. In August 2000 Weiss Ratings Inc., a national financial-safety ratings firm known for its conservative ratings, gave its lowest grade (E) to Security Life and Health Insurance Co. of America, based on information from the first quarter. Among other analysts, A.M. Best was rating the company a B. SIC 6311, 6399.

Seelye Plastics Inc. 9700 Newton Ave. S., Bloomington, MN 55431. Tel: 952/881-2658; Fax: 952/881-6203. Richard F. (Pinky) McNamara, CEO; Jim Ressner, Pres.; Joe Petrich, VP and Gen. Mgr. Seelye Plastics is a wholesaler, fabricator, and machine shop that specializes in sheet plastic, plastic pipes and valves, plastic welding equipment, and plastic tanks for original-equipment manufacturers. It has branches offices in Fargo, N.D.; Cedar Rapids, Iowa; Duluth, Minn.; and Omaha, Neb. Seelye is owned by Activar Inc., Edina, Minn. 136 employees (123 in Minnesota; 6 part-time). Founded in 1968. SIC 3084, 3089.

Select Communications 111 Cheshire Ln., Suite 700, Minnetonka, MN 55305. Tel: 952/595-0010; Fax: 952/595-9780. Rob Alexander, CEO. Select Communications is the nation's sixth-largest wireless provider. 60 employees. Founded in 1995. SIC 4813.

Semling-Menke Company Inc. South Nast Street, P.O. Box 378, Merrill, WI 54452. Tel: 715/536-9411; Fax: 715/536-3067. John P. Semling, Pres. and CEO; Alan Malm, VP-Special Proj.; Wilburn J. Weber, Treas.; Linda Semling Peterson, EVP. Annual revenue $72 million. Semling-Menke Co. manufactures doors, wood and aluminum clad wood window units, and patio doors. Subsidiaries include Semling-Menke Co. of Utah Inc. (Patrick Semling, VP and Gen. Mgr.); Northern Specialty Co. Inc. (John P. Semling, Pres.); and Semco Transport Co. (John P. Semling, Pres.). 675 employees. Founded in 1941. SIC 2431, 3442.

Sencore Inc. 3200 Sencore Dr., Sioux Falls, SD 57107. Tel: 605/339-0100; Fax: 605/335-6379. Alan Bowden, Pres. and CEO; Doug Bowden, EVP. Sencore designs, manufactures, and sells electronic test equipment, including frequency counters, audio and video analyzers, CRT testers, transistor testers, digital capacitance and inductance meters, computer monitor service instruments, and associated equipment. 175 employees. Founded in 1951. SIC 3825.

Servall Uniform & Linen Supply 410 Fourth St., Rapid City, SD 57701. Tel: 605/343-0680; Fax: 605/348-9463. Brad D. Dudley, Pres. Servall Uniform & Linen Supply rents commercial linen and garments, serves as a commercial laundry, and supplies dust-control items, paper, and janitorial supplies. 60 employees. Founded in 1938. SIC 7218.

Setter Leach & Lindstrom Inc. 1100 Peavey Bldg., 730 Second Ave. S., Minneapolis, MN 55402. Tel: 612/338-8741; Fax: 612/338-4840; Web site: http://www.setterleach.com. George Theodore, P.E., Pres. and CEO; Howard Goltz, AIA, Principal-Service/Technology Team; Daniel J. Gormley, Dir.-Bus. Devel.; Robert Egge, AIA, Principal-Govt. Team; Nancy Simonson, Dir.-Hum. Res.; Jon Trumbull, Principal. Annual revenue $18.2 million. Setter Leach & Lindstrom provides architecture, engineering, and interior design services to corporate and public clients. It specializes in the design and management of large public assembly projects (Minneapolis Convention Center, Hennepin County Adult Detention Center, Ellsworth AFB Rushmore Center), manufacturing and distribution facilities (US Foodservice/Carolinas Distribution Center and Corporate Headquarters, McLane/Carolina Distribution Center), and service and technology projects (Qwest, Inflow, Carlson Center East). 170 employees (all in Minnesota). Founded in 1917. SIC 8711, 8712.

Seven Clans 1201 E. Lake St., Warroad, MN 56763. Tel: 218/386-3381. Seven Clans offers a restaurant, free parking, and shuttle service. 158 employees. Founded in 1991. SIC 7011.

7-Sigma Inc. 2843 26th Ave. S., Minneapolis, MN 55406. Tel: 612/722-5358; Fax: 612/252-6292. Kris Wyrobek, Pres.; Tom Schwartz, VP-Sls./Mktg.; Tom Linn, VP-Op.; Matt Haws, VP-Fin. 7-Sigma is an innovative manufacturer of precision polymer components including fuser and pressure rollers for printers and copiers. 100 employees (all in Minnesota; 5 part-time). Founded in 1973. SIC 3069, 3577, 5045, 5734.

Sew What Corporation 1818 St. Clair Ave., St. Paul, MN 55105. Tel: 651/647-0478; Fax: 651/644-3463. Theodore A. Kvasnik, Pres. and CEO; Elaine K. Kvasnik, Sec. and Treas. Sew What Corp. is engaged in alterations, tailoring, dry cleaning, laundry, and embroidery. It also sells and repairs wicker furniture. The company runs four divisions under four names—a total of 24 stores, both wholesale and retail. It also leases space and property to others. 100 employees. Founded in 1973. SIC 5699, 7219.

Sewall Gear Manufacturing Company 705 Raymond Ave., St. Paul, MN 55114. Tel: 651/645-7721; Fax: 651/645-1823. David O. Sewall, Owner, Chm., and CEO; Jack Bataglia, Pres. Sewall Gear is a manufacturer of custom-made gears, gear racks, and related products. 80 employees. Founded in 1939. SIC 3566.

Sexton Printing Inc. 250 E. Lothenbach Ave., West St. Paul, MN 55118. Tel: 651/457-9255; Fax: 651/457-7040. Tim Sexton, Pres.; Gerald Sexton, Chm.; James Sexton, EVP; Scott Wosje, Dir.-Sls./Mktg.; Thomas P. Sexton, VP-Admin./Personnel; Bill Sexton, Treas., VP-Prod./Purch.; Jeff Stoks, VP-Digital Prod./ Info. Svs.; Sheila Stai, Sec.; Manuel Melendez, Hum. Res. Annual revenue $9.6 million. Sexton Printing is engaged in full-service commercial printing featuring electronic prepress, one- to five-color Heidelberg printing, full bindery, and mailing services. The company specializes in magazines, newsletters, booklets, catalogs, directories, and similar multipage products. 78 employees (all in Minnesota; 3 part-time). Founded in 1949. SIC 2752.

Shafer Electronics Company 30410 Regal Ave., Shafer, MN 55074. Tel: 651/257-5332; Fax: 651/257-1041. Richard Cohoes, Pres.; Bob Hartley, Sls. Mgr.; Kris Ewert, Op. Mgr.; Curtis Cohoes, Mfg. Mgr.; Jeff Chartrand, Materials Mgr. Shafer Electronics builds turnkey products for other companies. 200 employees. Founded in 1973. SIC 3559, 3679.

Shakopee Mdewakanton Sioux Community/Little Six Inc. 2400 Mystic Lake Blvd., Prior Lake, MN 55372. Tel: 952/445-9000; Fax: 952/496-7280; Web site: http://www.mysticlake.com. Edward Stevenson, CEO; Rick Atchison, VP-Mktg.; Ann Beinert, VP-Admin.; Ken Davie, VP-Casino; Kyle Kossol, VP-Fin.; Rich Langelius, VP-Prop. Op.; Tom Neukom, VP-Hospitality; Tom Polushy, VP-Little Six Casino. Annual revenue $350 million (estimated by Fact Book). Shakopee Mdewakanton Sioux Community/Little Six is a tribally owned and operated gaming corporation that owns one of the Upper Midwest's largest gaming facilities, which attracts millions of visitors a year. Mystic Lake Casino Hotel and Little Six Casino, located 20 minutes south of Minneapolis/St. Paul, are enterprises of the Shakopee Mdewakanton Sioux Community (SMSC). Other ventures include Dakotah Sport & Fitness, Playworks, Dakotah Meadows RV Park, and the Dakotah Convenience Store and Mall. SMSC is the largest employer in Scott County. 4,000 employees (all in Minnesota). Founded in 1982. SIC 5084, 7999, 8742. No. 33 CRM Private 100. No. 50 CRM Employer 100.

Shapco Printing Inc. 524 N. Fifth St., Minneapolis, MN 55401. Tel: 612/375-1150; Fax: 612/334-5879. Joel Shapiro, Pres.; Alan Shapiro, VP; Robert Shapiro, VP. Annual revenue $23 million. Shapco is a sheetfed printing company specializing in color printing with a waterless press. 120 employees (all in Minnesota; 10 part-time). Founded in 1976. SIC 2752.

Shari Candies Inc. 1804 N. Second St., Mankato, MN 56001. Tel: 507/387-1181; Fax: 507/387-4463. Arlen T. Kitsis, Pres.; Rick Williams, Warehouse Mgr.; Sue Caven, Cont.; Wally Schilf, Nat'l Sls. Mgr.; Steve Kitsis, VP; Mike Parker, Dir.-Op.; James Oslund, Prod. Mgr. Shari Candies packages candies, confectioneries, snacks, baking nuts, glazed fruits, and almond bark under Shari Candies and other private labels. Manufacturing facilities are located at 1804 N. Second St., Mankato, MN 56001. 106 employees. Founded in 1944. SIC 2064, 5145.

Shaw Lumber Company 217 Como Ave., St. Paul, MN 55103. Tel: 651/488-2525; Fax: 651/488-9779. Jim Schuetze, Pres. and CEO; Del Drusenstjerna, VP-Sls./Mktg.; Rick Kukowski, Dir.-Op.; Bruce Furness, Cont. Shaw Lumber operates as a retail lumber and building-materials dealer. It also manufactures architectural millwork. 96 employees (all in Minnesota). Founded in 1886. SIC 2431.

Shaw-Lundquist Associates 2757 W. Service Rd., Eagan, MN 55121. Tel: 651/454-0670; Fax: 651/454-7982; Web site: http://www.shawlundquist.com. Fred Shaw, Pres.; Thomas J. Meyers, VP; Hoyt Hsiao, VP. Annual revenue $64.2 million. Shaw-Lundquist Associates is a general contractor, construction manager, and design-build contractor for commercial, industrial, institutional, and multi-unit residential clients. It is the second-largest minority-owned business in the Twin Cities. 70 employees (40 part-time). Founded in 1974. SIC 1522, 1541, 1542.

Shingobee Builders 669 Medina St. N., P.O. Box 8, Loretto, MN 55357. Tel: 763/479-1300; Fax: 763/479-3267. Gae Veit, CEO; Keith McDonald, Pres.; Steve Schultz, EVP; Loren Kjersten, VP; Stacy Mero, Sec. Shingobee Builders is a general contractor serving corporations, government agencies, reservations, and private owners. Clients include Mille Lacs Band/Ojibwe, Shakopee Mdewakanton Sioux Community, McDonald's Corp., Target, Holiday Stores, U S West, Northern States Power Co., and Sears. The company is both the third-largest minority-owned business in the Twin Cities and the sixth-largest woman-owned business. 105 employees. Founded in 1980. SIC 1541.

Shooting Star Casino 777 Casino Rd., P.O. Box 418, Mahnomen, MN 56557. Tel: 218/935-2711. Raymond Brenny, Gen. Mgr.; Steve Drewes, CFO; Jack Fabre, Dir.-Gaming; Jeff Murray, Dir.-Food/Beverage; Greg Pavek, Dir.-Nongaming; LeAnn Person, Dir.-Hotel/Event Center Op. Annual revenue $55 million. Shooting Star Casino, Hotel offers live entertainment, an indoor pool, a gift shop, an RV park, pull-tabs, child care, bingo, and a meeting, banquets and event center. 1,000 employees (120 part-time). Founded in 1991. SIC 7011.

Shopforschool.com 5051 Highway 7, Suite 100, St. Louis Park, MN 55416. Tel: 877/425-2292; Fax: 952/922-1869; Web site: http://www.shopforschool.com. Gary Blackford, CEO and Founder; Tim Walsh, Pres. and Founder. Shopforschool is a school support company for K-12 schools. 100 employees (30 in Minnesota). Founded in 1999. The company launched Shop for School MasterCard in fall 2000. SIC 5943.

Shoremaster Inc. One Shoremaster Dr., P.O. Box 358, Fergus Falls, MN 56537. Tel: 218/739-4641; Fax: 218/739-4008. Dennis Tuel Sr., CEO; Dennis Tuel Jr., SVP; Loren Tungseth, VP; Erik Ahlgren, Pres.; Marsha Tuel, Treas.; Kirstin Tuel, Sec. Annual revenue $18 million. Shoremaster is a manufacturer of commercial marinas, residential waterfront equipment, marine fabric products and plastic rotational products. 100 employees (95 in Minnesota). Founded in 1972. SIC 2394, 2821, 3536.

Short Elliot Hendrickson Inc. (SEH) 3535 Vadnais Center Dr., Vadnais Heights, MN 55110. Tel: 651/490-2000; Fax: 651/490-2150; Web site: http://www.sehinc.com. Gary R. Gray, Pres. and CEO; Gary Lidgerding, CFO; Joan Johnson, Mgr.-Hum. Res.; Chris Shaw, Corp. Communications Mgr.; Steven Wagener, Automation Mgr. Annual revenue $48 million. SEH is a consulting firm of engineers, architects, planners, and scientists offering services in architecture, engineering, environmental, and transportation to government, business, and education. Other offices: Minnetonka, St. Cloud, Gaylord, Duluth, and Grand Rapids, Minn.; Chippewa Falls, Madison, and the Fox River Valley, in Wis.; Lake County, Ind.; and Chicago. 565 employees (424 in Minnesota; 75 part-time). Founded in 1927. In March 2000 SEH opened a new office, in Houghton, Mich., serving the Upper Peninsula and northeast Wisconsin. In May the firm added electrical engineering to its list of multidisciplined service offerings. SIC 8711, 8712, 8713.

Shur-Co 2309 Shurlok St., P.O. Box 713, Yankton, SD 57078. Tel: 605/665-6000; Fax: 605/665-0501. William Shorma, Pres. Shur-Co manufactures tarping systems for trucks and trailers, as well as other truck equipment accessories. 300 employees (15 part-time). Founded in 1953. SIC 2394.

Sico America Inc. 7525 Cahill Rd., Edina, MN 55439. Tel: 952/941-1700; Fax: 952/941-6737; Web site: http://www.sicoinc.com. Kermit Wilson, Chm.; Harold K. (Hal) Wilson, Pres. and CEO; Andrew J. Shea, EVP; Keith T. Dahlen, VP-Fin.; Jerry Danielson, VP-Sls.; Doug Jensen, VP-Engrg.; Harry Levey, VP-Purch. Annual revenue $51.5 million. Sico America manufactures and distributes equipment for the effective and efficient utilization of space: mobile folding tables and stages, portable dance floors, wallbeds, wall cabinet systems, and food service equipment. The company has manufacturing facilities in Edina, Minn.; Belleville, Wis.; and Conway, Ark. 353 employees (170 in Minnesota; 5 part-time). Founded in 1951. SIC 2531.

Sieff Holding Company 6616 Lyndale Ave. S., Richfield, MN 55423. Tel: 612/866-9398; Fax: 612/869-7636. John P. Sieff, Chm., Pres., and Treas.; Ron Herington, Gen. Mgr.; Peter Sieff, VP; Jane Sieff, Sec. Annual revenue $4 million. Sieff Holding Co. owns and operates Lyndale Hardware Co. (6616 Lyndale Ave., Richfield, MN 55423); and owns and leases properties. Formerly publicly traded as The S&M Co., which was bought out by management in 1994. 70 employees (all in Minnesota). Founded in 1921. SIC 5251.

Signal Financial Corporation 1395 Commerce Dr., Suite 100, Eagan, MN 55120. Tel: 651/905-3100; Fax: 651/905-3131. R. Scott Jones, Chm.; Galen T. Pate, Pres.; Marcia O'Brien, CFO; Alishia Horning, VP and Mktg. Dir. Signal Financial Corp., formerly United Community Bancshares, is an $875 million-asset bank holding company combining the strengths of three of Minnesota's strongest independently owned and locally run community banks. Signal Banks have offices in West St. Paul, Eagan, Savage, St. Louis Park, New Hope, Red Wing, Lanesboro, and Rushford, Minn. Other operations include a trust company, a consumer finance company and a data processing and technology solutions company. 420 employees. The December 1999 name change, from United Community Bancshares to Signal Financial Corp., also signaled the merger of two bank charters (Signal and Park National banks), which was expected to add efficiency and save costs. SIC 6712.

Simons Engineering 800 Marquette Ave., Suite 200, Minneapolis, MN 55402. Tel: 612/332-8326. Rick Sivula, VP and Gen. Mgr. Simons Engineering is a project management and consulting engineering group. 130 employees. Founded in 1956. SIC 8711.

Sioux Falls Construction Company 800 S. Seventh Ave., P.O. Box F, Sioux Falls, SD 57101. Tel: 605/336-1640; Fax: 605/334-9342; Web site: http://www.sfconst.com. Frank L. Boyce, Chm.; John C. Marshman, Pres.; Eugene Moser, Sec.; Marvin Peterson, VP; David Fleck, VP; Tom Wilson, Asst. VP; Darrel Hoyer, Asst. VP; Brad Goldstine, Asst. VP; Randy Knecht, Treas.; Marlyn Bergeson, Asst. VP. Sioux Falls Construction is a general contractor engaged in the construction of buildings, bridges, treatment plants, and asphalt paving. 100 employees. Founded in 1910. SIC 1542.

Sioux Falls Shopping News Inc. 4005 S. Western Ave., Sioux Falls, SD 57105. Tel: 605/339-3633; Fax: 605/335-6873. K.A. Lesnar, Pres. and CEO; Jeff Weiland, Mgr.-Western Commercial Printing. Sioux Falls Shopping News provides advertising, commercial printing, typesetting, and layout services. As Western Commercial Printing, the company is a full four-color printer of brochures, newsletters, catalogs, and fliers. Its facilities include a full-service bindery, design, typesetting, and mailing. 90 employees. Founded in 1939. SIC 2711, 2759, 2791.

Sioux Manufacturing Corporation P.O. Box 400, Fort Totten, ND 58335. Tel: 701/766-4211; Fax: 701/766-4228. C.R. McKay, Pres.; Lori Brown, Asst. Cont.; Jan Martin, Asst. Cont. Annual revenue $9 million. Sioux Mfg. Corp. manufactures composite ballistic panels, and camouflage netting. The company also does compression molding, autoclave processing, wet-jet cutting, metal fabrication, and assembly operations. 63 employees. Founded in 1973. SIC 3089, 3444, 3499, 3795.

Sioux Valley Southwestern Electric Company P.O. Box 216, Colman, SD 57017. Tel: 605/534-3535; Fax: 605/256-1693. Don Marker, Gen. Mgr.; Joel Brick, Dir.-Telecommunications; Elaine Garry, Dir.-Customer/Employee Relations; Carl Kreun, Dir.-Fin.; Martin McGrane, Dir.-Communications; John Miller, Dir.-Engrg./Op.; Edie Larsen, Exec. Asst. Annual revenue $24.9 million. Sioux Valley Southwestern is engaged in the distribution of electric power, electrical wiring services, high speed wireless Internet, and wireless television. 95 employees (12 in Minnesota; 4 part-time). Founded in 1938. SIC 4911.

Sit Investment Associates Inc. 90 S. Seventh St., Suite 4600, Minneapolis, MN 55402. Tel: 612/332-3223; Fax: 612/342-2018; Web site: http://www.sitinvest.com. Eugene Sit, CEO; Peter L. Mitchelson, Pres.; Roger J. Sit, EVP. Sit Investment Associates is a money management group, offering mutual funds and corporate pension plans to institutions, endowments, foundation, and high net worth individuals. 66 employees (all in Minnesota; 4 part-time). Founded in 1981. SIC 6722.

SkipperLiner Industries 621 Park Plaza Dr., La Crosse, WI 54601. Tel: 608/784-5110; Fax: 608/784-7778. Noel Jordan, Chm.; Jim Reider, VP-Fin.; John Cushman, VP-Op.; Dan Nelson, VP-Sls./Mktg. SkipperLiner Industries designs and builds houseboats, excursion vessels, work boats, and motor yachts. 100 employees. Founded in 1971. SIC 3732.

Skogen's Festival Support Center 237 Second Ave. S., Onalaska, WI 54650. Tel: 608/783-5500; Fax: 608/783-6065. David Skogen, Pres.; Barb Skogen, VP; Terry Lee, Hum. Res. Mgr.; Marlin Greenfield, Gen. Mgr. Skogen's IGA Stores operates retail grocery stores. 850 employees. Founded in 1946. SIC 5411.

Skyline Builders Inc. 3647 McKinley St. N.E., Minneapolis, MN 55418. Tel: 612/781-3184; Fax: 612/781-3670. R.A. Stinski, Pres. Skyline is a building contractor, real estate agency, and property management company. 130 employees. Founded in 1961. SIC 6513, 6531.

Skyline Displays Inc. 3355 Discovery Rd., Eagan, MN 55121. Tel: 651/234-6000; Fax: 651/234-6571; Web site: http://www.skylinedisplay.com. Gordon P. Savoie, Chm. and Owner; Reed Edstrom, VP-Sls./Mktg.; Ken Haglind, VP-Fin.; Robert L. (Lanny) Moline, VP-Op. Skyline Displays builds and distributes portable trade show exhibits. The displays it specializes in are portable, easy to set up and dismantle, and range in size from a 10-foot blackwall board to a $250,000 custom display bigger than a house. The company also has manufacturing operations in Toronto and in Guadalajara, Mexico; and branch offices in Beijing, London, and Bogota. Local customers include Northwest Airlines and Jostens Inc. 500 employees. Founded in 1980. SIC 3993.

Slidell Inc. 2355 LeMoud Rd., Owatonna, MN 55060. Tel: 507/451-0365; Fax: 507/451-2405; Web site: http://www.slidellinc.com. Dale Nelson, Sls. Coordinator. Slidell Inc. is a manufacturer and supplier of turnkey packaging systems, including net-weigh and gross-weigh scales; net-weigh and gross-weigh bag filling systems with multiwall paper and polybag capabilities; closing equipment; and semi-automatic entry-level bagging equipment for fully automatic high-speed systems. Slidell offers a full line of bag-filling equipment, extensive application experience, and worldwide technical service and support. 130 employees. Founded in 1975. SIC 5084.

Slumberland Inc. 3060 Centerville Rd., Little Canada, MN 55117. Tel: 651/482-7500; Fax: 651/490-0479. Kenneth R. Larson, Pres. and CEO; Paul Kaufman, VP-Op. and Treas.; Wayne Deilke, Dir.-Twin Cities Sales; Clay Diggins, Dir.-Regional Sls.; Keith Freeburg, Dir.-Franchising; Kenny Larson, Dir.-Mdsg.; John Newstrand, Dir.-Advertising; Kim Salo, Dir.-Hum. Res. Annual revenue $238.2 million. Slumberland Inc. is a service-oriented home furnishings retailer emphasizing a broad selection of brand-name mattresses and sofas. Its 68 stores in seven states (Minnesota, Iowa, Nebraska, North Dakota, South Dakota, Illinois, and Wisconsin) include 14 stores in the Minneapolis/St. Paul area. The company is the Upper Midwest's largest retailer of La-Z-Boy recliners and sofas. 1,656 employees. Founded in 1967. In September 2000 the company was honored by the Better Business Bureau (BBB) of Minnesota and North Dakota with an Integrity Award, for business practices that uniquely exemplify the BBB's mission and principles. SIC 5712. No. 58 CRM Private 100.

Smarte Carte Inc. 4455 White Bear Pkwy., White Bear Lake, MN 55110. Tel: 651/429-3614; Fax: 651/426-0927. Ed Rudis, Pres. and COO; Garret Roosma, EVP and CFO; Tom Rock, VP and Gen. Counsel. Annual revenue $70 million. Smarte Carte is the leading global marketer of baggage cart, stroller, and locker services for airport and shopping center use. Its airport carts, which are available from easy-to-use dispensers, have a stainless steel, tubular frame that holds luggage of any shape or size. Smarte Carte services are used by 40 million travelers annually at 200 airports worldwide. Owned by Blum Capital Partners, L.P. 1,200 employees (120 in Minnesota). Founded in 1970. In June 2000 the company received its third patent on the Alliance cart management system. This one protects the operational methods for managing cart flow within a cart management system, as well as the ability to audit revenue and prevent fraud by identifying each cart individually. SIC 7359.

Smead Manufacturing Company 600 Smead Blvd., Hastings, MN 55033. Tel: 651/437-4111; Fax: 651/437-9134; Web site: http://www.smead.com. Sharon Lee Avent, Pres. and CEO; Michael Dolan, EVP and COO; David Fasbender, SVP-Sls./Mktg.; Wally Glashan, VP-Op.; Joseph Vossen, VP-Info. Sys.; Al Arends, VP-Mktg.; Dean Schwanke, VP-Hum. Res.; Dale Olson, VP-Fin.; Tom Sullivan, VP-Sls.; Ken Linde, Mktg. Communications Mgr. Annual revenue $433 million. Smead manufactures office filing supplies for wholesalers, dealers, and office superstore chains. With more than 2,000 SKUs, Smead product offerings include standard file folders, Flex-I-Vision hanging folders and related products, color-coded filing supplies, Alpha-Z self-adhesive label products, filing accessories, expanding files and wallets, shelving products, made-to-order products, and state-of-the-art Smead Link document management software. Most products include post-consumer recycled materials. Its six manufacturing plants are located in Hastings; Logan, Ohio; Locust Grove, Ga.; McGregor, Texas; Cedar City, Utah; and River Falls, Wis. One of the industry's most recognized symbols of quality is the Smead red-and-maroon-plaid packaging. Smead is one of the largest metro-area woman-owned businesses. 2,900 employees (850 in Minnesota). Founded in 1906. In 2000 the company launched a line of InnDura plastic folders and filing products made of polypropylene, the first product in Smead's history to be made from anything other than paper. In August Smead announced the company's underwriting of the new PBS program, "Organizing from the Inside Out," with Julie Morgenstern. In September Smead's European subsidiary Atlanta Group BV acquired certain assets of Geographics Europe, Ltd.—a subsidiary of Geographics Inc. (OTCBB: GGIT), a Blaine, Wash.-based manufacturer of value-added and designer stationery paper and office products—including inventory, customer files, customer records, sales history, sales orders, supply contracts, designs, goodwill, and know-how. Geographics retained ownership of its copyrights and trademarks, but licensed them to Smead/Atlanta Group. SIC 2675, 2678. No. 25 CRM Private 100.

Smith Foundry Company 1855 E. 28th St., Minneapolis, MN 55407. Tel: 612/729-9395; Fax: 612/729-2519. Neil C. Ahlstrom, Pres. and CEO. Smith Foundry manufactures gray and ductile iron castings. It does both long- and short-run jobbing work for Upper Midwest manufacturers. 77 employees (all in Minnesota; 2 part-time). Founded in 1923. SIC 3321.

Smyth Companies Inc. 1085 N. Snelling Ave., P.O. Box 64669 (55164), St. Paul, MN 55108. Tel: 651/646-4544; Fax: 651/646-8949. Bill Hickey, Pres. and COO; Greg Arko, EVP; Craig Curran, EVP; John Giuliani, EVP; Dave Baumgardner, CEO; Jack Briggs, VP-Display Div.; Ken Rush, VP-Mfg.; Dan Hickey, EVP-Sls./Mktg.; John Hickey, Ofcr. Annual revenue $100 million. Smyth Co. is a manufacturer of labels, commercial printing, creative art, dimensional displays, and pressure-sensitive labels, coupons, and label-application machinery. 630 employees (500 in Minnesota). Founded in 1877. SIC 2752, 2759.

Soderberg Inc. 230 Eva St., St. Paul, MN 55107. Tel: 651/291-1400; Fax: 651/291-7402. Aloys Willenbring, Chm. and Pres.; Craig Giles,

VP-Sls./Mktg.; Robert Grundtner, Treas. Annual revenue $42 million. Soderberg manufactures and wholesales eyewear, contact lenses, and refracting equipment. 355 employees (110 in Minnesota; 16 part-time). Founded in 1945. SIC 3841, 3851.

Solonis One Meridian Crossing, Suite 810, Richfield, MN 55423. Tel: 612/798-2100; Web site: http://www.solonis.com. William Cavanaugh, CEO. Annual revenue $8.6 million. Solonis is a full-service IT consulting firm that specializes in e-commerce, systems development, design, implementation, and project management. 100 employees (90 in Minnesota). Founded in 1991. SIC 7379. No. 33 CityBusiness Fastest-growing Private Companies.

Solutran 3600 Holly Ln., Suite 60, Plymouth, MN 55447. Tel: 763/559-2225; Fax: 763/559-8872; Web site: http://www.solutran.com. E. Lloyd Hauser, CEO; Joseph F. Keller, Pres. Solutran, formerly United Check Clearing Corp. (UCCC), provides accurate and rapid processing of high-volume financial transactions. Offering convenient and easy-to-use products and services, Solutran gives its clients customized solutions that improve the bottom line. 80 employees (all in Minnesota). Founded in 1984. SIC 6099.

Sonar Hotel Corporation 1630 S. Broadway, Rochester, MN 55904. Tel: 507/288-1844. Mark S. Anderson, CEO and Owner; Georgianne Johnson, Gen. Mgr. Annual revenue $5.8 million. Sonar Hotel Corp. is in the full-service hotel business. 150 employees. Founded in 1963. SIC 7011.

Sons Tool Inc. 460 Thompson Rd., Woodville, WI 54028. Tel: 715/698-2471; Fax: 715/698-2335. Wesley G. Swanson, Pres.; Kurt W. Swanson, VP. Annual revenue $13.5 million. Sons Tool produces metal stampings, tools and dies, and subassemblies. 95 employees (10 part-time). Founded in 1963. SIC 3469.

Sonstegard Foods Company 707 E. 41st St., Suite 222, Sioux Falls, SD 57105. Tel: 605/338-4642; Fax: 605/338-9765. P.O. Sonstegard, Pres. Sonstegard Foods Co. processes egg products. 250 employees. Founded in 1972. SIC 0252.

Soo Plastics Inc. 1351 Industrial Park Dr., Sault Ste. Marie, MI 49783. Tel: 906/635-5220; Fax: 906/635-2917. Ken Cross, Purch. Mgr.; Wayne E. Olsen, Cont. Soo Plastics manufactures both industrial and consumer plastic products at plants in Salina, Kan; and Sault Ste. Marie, Mich. 252 employees. Founded in 1979. SIC 3089.

Source Inc. 2000 Energy Park Dr., St. Paul, MN 55108. Tel: 651/646-4422; Fax: 651/646-3480. Stephen D. Rial, Pres.; Chuck Nickolay, CFO. Source Inc. is in the commercial printing business. 110 employees. Founded in 1960. SIC 2759.

South Dakota Wheat Growers Association 110 Sixth Ave. S.E., P.O. Box 1460, Aberdeen, SD 57401. Tel: 605/225-5500; Fax: 605/225-0859. Jake Boomshia, Pres.; Verland Losinger, Gen. Mgr. South Dakota Wheat Growers is a cooperative association involved in grain marketing and farm supply. 350 employees (50 part-time). Founded in 1923. SIC 2048, 2875, 5153.

Southern Minnesota Beet Sugar Co-op P.O. Box 500, Renville, MN 56284. Tel: 320/329-8305; Fax: 320/327-3252. Steve Kramer, Chm.; Alan Ritacco, Pres. and CEO. Southern Minnesota Beet Sugar Co-op produces beet sugar, beet pulp pellets, molasses, separator molasses, and betaine. 297 employees (all in Minnesota; 9 part-time). Founded in 1972. SIC 2063. No. 14 CRM Cooperatives/Mutuals 20.

Southside Lumber Company Inc. 21901 Industrial Blvd., B-178, Rogers, MN 55374. Tel: 763/428-4112; Fax: 763/428-2971. E.C. Day, Pres.; A.H. Tatur, VP-Op.; Franklin Morris, EVP; Richard Hughes, VP-Fin. Southside Lumber Co. is a supplier of lumber, building materials, and floor and roof trusses. 70 employees (all in Minnesota). Founded in 1907. SIC 5211.

Sowles Company Inc. 2813 Bryant Ave. S., Minneapolis, MN 55408. Tel: 612/872-4656; Fax: 612/872-6824. L.H. Sowles, CEO; Gary Lewherer, VP; Dan Sowles, Pres.; S. Berg, Sec. and Office Mgr.; Sheila Stenseth, Cont. Annual revenue $40 million. Sowles Co. erects structural steel; installs materials-handling equipment; does plant maintenance; and sells, services, and leases tower cranes. 400 employees. Founded in 1961. SIC 1791.

Spanlink Communications Inc. 7125 Northland Terrace, Brooklyn Park, MN 55428. Tel: 763/971-2000; Fax: 763/971-2300; Web site: http://www.spanlink.com. Mark Francis, Pres. and CEO; Stephen H. Bostwick, VP-Sls.; Timothy E. Briggs, VP-Fin. and CFO; Jonathan M. Silverman, VP-Res./Devel., Chief Tech Officer; Bryan Willborg, VP-Customer Solutions; Loren A. Singer Jr., Sec. Annual revenue $11.1 million (earnings $0.3 million). Spanlink Communications Inc. designs, develops, and markets interactive computer telecommunications software and services that link business computer systems, telecommunications systems, and the Internet. Using the company's products, a business can allow its customers to interact with its computer system via the telephone, a fax machine, or an Internet Web browser. 95 employees (4 part-time). Founded in 1988. In late November 1999 rumors of a buyout sent publicly traded Spanlink stock to a high of $8 a share. One of the likely suitors: marketing partner Lucent Technologies, Murray Hill, N.J. In December four of Spanlink's CTI software products successfully completed testing in Siemens Information and Communication Networks' Siemens Ready developers support program: CTI Server for Microsoft Windows NT; FastCall Agent for Windows 95, 98, NT, and 2000; FastCall Enterprise Server; and Extra Agent version 7.1. In January 2000 Spanlink signed a staged contract valued at $1 million with U S WEST. The contract called for Spanlink to develop a new call steering system that was to provide state-of-the-art customer service for the telecommunications leader. The company's FastCall Agent CTI solution was named the TELECONNECT Magazine Product of the Year for 1999. In February two Spanlink products were named Product of the Year by leading telecommunications industry publications. The FastCall Enterprise Server was named as a Product of the Year by Communications Solutions magazine, formerly CTI Magazine. Additionally, FastCall.commerce, a business-to-business application of Spanlink's FastCall Enterprise products, was named as a product of the year by CaLL CENTER CRM Solutions magazine. Spanlink announced its intent to take the company private and cash out public shareholders—and that Cisco Systems Inc. was to be investing in the newly private company through the purchase of convertible preferred shares. Spanlink Acquisition Corp. (SA Corp.) was formed by founders and management who currently own more that 50 percent of Spanlink Communications to commence a tender offer for all outstanding shares of the Spanlink Communications common stock not owned by SA Corp. for $10.50 per share in cash. In March Stephen M. Russell, a holder of 2,000 shares of Spanlink's common stock, commenced a legal action against Spanlink and others with respect to Spanlink's proposed going-private transaction. At month's end, SA Corp. extended the expiration date of its tender offer until April 12—to allow it to mail to all shareholders of Spanlink Communications an amendment to the offer, and to allow shareholders an opportunity to review the amendment. On April 13, SA Corp.'s holdings reached 98 percent, allowing it to merge with Spanlink without seeking a vote by Spanlink shareholders. After the company was taken private, and was off the Nasdaq market, New York law firm Rabin & Peckel filed a class-action suit arguing that the tender offer failed to disclose the new relationship with Cisco Systems, which might have gained shareholders a more favorable offer.

In May, building upon Cisco Systems' recent investment in Spanlink, the two companies announced an extended relationship to include consulting initiatives focused on the Cisco Internet Communications Software Group (ICSG). Spanlink was expecting to hire up to 200 skilled workers as it expanded its work for Cisco. In August Spanlink announced the development of an integration module making it easier for contact centers to integrate Cisco Systems' Intelligent Contact Management software, a key component of Cisco's customer contact software platform, and Lucent Technologies' CONVERSANT Voice Information System. President and CEO Brett Shockley resigned to join Cisco Systems, one of Spanlink's investors. Mark Francis, vice president of business development, was immediately named to Shockley's positions. At year's end, Spanlink was on the verge of a major expansion planned to take the company beyond the $100 million-revenue mark by mid-2002. SIC 7371.

Sparta Foods Inc. 1565 First Ave. N.W., New Brighton, MN 55112. Tel: 651/697-5500; Fax: 651/697-0600; Web site: http://www.spartafoods.com. Michael J. Kozlak, Chm.; Joel P. Bachul, Pres. and CEO; Craig S. Cram, EVP-Sls./Op.; A. Merrill Ayers, SVP-Fin./Admin. and CFO; Eric J. Stack, VP and Cont. Annual revenue $15.7 million. Sparta Foods Inc. manufactures, markets, and distributes corn and flour tortillas, tortilla chips, and Mexican-style salsas. Sparta products are sold at retail through supermarkets under its La Canasta, Cruz, Mexitos, Paradiso, and Chapala proprietary labels; or under private label for others, including Crystal Farms Refrigerated Distribution Co. Sparta products are also sold to food service establishments through distributors such as Alliant Foodservice Inc., U.S. Food Service Inc., and Sysco Corp. Sparta Foods was formed in January 1991 through a reverse merger with a blind pool, whereby Sparta Corp. acquired the operating business of La Canasta of Minnesota Inc. Sparta was subsequently acquired in April 2000 by Cenex Harvest States Cooperatives, St. Paul. 220 employees (150 in Minnesota). Founded in 1988. In November 1999 the company received initial purchase orders from Minneapolis-based Target Stores for value-sized bags of La Canasta tortilla chips. On Dec. 31, Sparta Foods signed a definitive agreement with Cenex Harvest States Cooperatives, St. Paul, for the acquisition of Sparta Foods in a transaction in which Sparta was to receive consideration of $1.41 per share in cash ($14.5 million) and $5 million in debt assumption. Chairman Kozlak said, "We are pleased that this agreement has been reached with Cenex Harvest States and feel that our shareholders are receiving excellent value for their investment at this price. Through a talented management team and a strong market growth for tortilla products, Sparta Foods has progressed from a very troubled company a few years ago to a growth platform for a rapidly consolidating industry, as evidenced by its recent acquisition of the Phoenix-based Food Products Corp." [Deal was completed in June 2000.] SIC 2033, 2096, 2099.

Specialty Engineering Inc. 1766 E. Highway 36, Maplewood, MN 55109. Tel: 651/777-8311; Fax: 651/748-3256. Dave G. Pennock, CEO; David Myhr, Pres.; Gene Castle, Dir.-Op.; Kathleen Langton, Dir.-Fin.; Jerry McKenzie, Purch. Mgr. Specialty Engineering is engaged in precision sheet metal fabrication and engineering services for original equipment manufacturers. 95 employees. Founded in 1958. SIC 3499.

Specialty Manufacturing Company 5858 Centerville Rd., White Bear Township, MN 55127. Tel: 651/653-0599; Fax: 651/653-0989. Bruce A. Lawin, Pres.; Mark Nosbush, VP; Dan McKeown, Pres. Specialty Manufacturing makes hose reels, brass and plastic flow-control valves, and lawn and garden accessories. 200 employees. Founded in 1900. SIC 3429, 3469, 3494, 3524.

Spectro Alloys Corporation 13220 Doyle Path, Rosemount, MN 55068. Tel: 651/437-2815; Fax: 651/438-3714. Gregory R. Palen, Pres. and CEO; Timothy Woldt, CFO. Annual revenue $125 million. Spectro Alloys is a manufacturer and recycler of secondary aluminum casting alloys. 120 employees. Founded in 1964. SIC 3365. No. 90 CRM Private 100.

Spectrum Community Health Inc. 2021 E. Hennepin Ave., Suite 300, Minneapolis, MN 55413. Tel: 612/627-9177. Cathy Berg, Pres. Annual revenue $17 million. Spectrum Community Health provides nursing care, home health aids, homemakers, PCA, physical therapy, occupational therapy, and speech therapy to 1,100 metro-area patients. The organization is co-owned by Cathy Berg and Merle Sampson. 282 employees. Founded in 1982. SIC 8082.

Spectrum Industries Inc. 1600 Johnson St., Chippewa Falls, WI 54729. Tel: 715/723-6750; Fax: 715/723-9002. D. Hancock, Pres.; Dean White, VP; E. Mower, Treas. and Sec. Spectrum Industries manufactures custom fabricated products, including computer furniture for office and schools and display fixtures for retail stores. Spectrum manufactures its products under the brand names Class, Career 2000, and Oak Valley Wood Craft. 195 employees (1 in Minnesota; 20 part-time). Founded in 1968. SIC 2521, 2531.

Sports Restaurants Inc. 8078 Brooklyn Blvd., Brooklyn Park, MN 55445. Tel: 763/493-2979; Fax: 763/493-4897. Nicholas Grammas, Pres.; Dean Paschke, Gen. Mgr.-Brooklyn Park; Bob Paul, Gen. Mgr.-Burnsville. Sports Restaurants Inc. owns and operates Benchwarmer Bob's Sports Cafe, a family sports restaurant known for its huge portions of food, its children's menu, and an array of televisions for customers to watch. Second location: Burnsville, Minn. 200 employees (all in Minnesota). Founded in 1990. SIC 5812.

Stamper Black Hills Gold Jewelry P.O. Box 3210, Rapid City, SD 57709. Tel: 605/342-0751; Fax: 605/343-9783; Web site: http://www.stamperbhg.com. Rodney E. Stamper, Pres. and CEO; Bradley G. Benham, VP-Fin.; Jerry Magstadt, VP-Sls. Annual revenue $10 million. Stamper Black Hills Gold manufactures gold and sterling silver jewelry. 98 employees. Founded in 1959. SIC 3911.

Stampings of Minnesota Inc. 21980 Hamburg Ave., Lakeville, MN 55044. Tel: 952/469-4911; Fax: 952/469-5934. Walter M. Schmitt, Pres. Stampings of Minnesota performs metal fabrication and tool and die. 90 employees. Founded in 1955. SIC 3469.

Standard Iron & Wire Works Company 207 Dundas Rd., Monticello, MN 55369. Tel: 763/295-8700; Fax: 763/295-8701. L.T. Demeules, Chm.; R.T. Demeules, CEO; Harold Ramsey, VP; Bill Demeules, VP; Joe Demeules, VP; Don Hunter, Cont. Standard Iron & Wire Works, a contract manufacturer of metal fabrications, performs bending, laser cutting, punching, burning, welding, machining, and finishing of steel and aluminum. 260 employees (275 in Minnesota; 15 part-time). Founded in 1930. SIC 3441, 3444, 3499.

Stanton Group 3405 Annapolis Ln. N., Suite 100, Plymouth, MN 55447. Tel: 763/278-4000; Fax: 763/278-4007; Web site: http://www.stanton-group.com. Jeffrey R. Nevin, CEO; Tom Singsank, VP and Treas.; Tom Campbell, Dir.-Retirement Svs.; Paul Chapman, Dir.-Benefits Admin.; John Moynihan, Dir.-Client Svs.; Renee Olmschenk, Dir.-Mktg.; Ward Ring, Dir.-Natl. Sls. Annual revenue $13 million. Stanton Group, formerly DCA, is an employee-benefits administration and consulting firm. Traditional areas of specialty include direct compensation consulting and salary/benefits surveying; actuarial services; profit-sharing, 401(k), and defined benefit record-keeping and consulting; COBRA/continuation services; and flexible spending account and transportation reimbursement administration. Recent service additions include executive benefit design and administrative; integrated, "turnkey" retirement plan solutions; corporate insurance plan solutions; and automated benefit enrollment services. Owned by the Pohlad family through holding company Searchcorporation, Inc. 170 employees (all in Minnesota; 15 part-time). Founded in 1953. On June 1, 2000, the company changed its name. The new name stems from Stanton Consulting Services, whose compensation specialists had been producing surveys and consulting under the DCA name since 1976. SIC 6371, 8742.

Star Exhibits 6820 Shingle Creek Pkwy., Brooklyn Center, MN 55430. Tel: 763/561-4655; Fax: 763/561-4688; Web site: http://www.starexhibits.com. Mark Johnson, Pres. and CEO; Bruce Dreblow, VP and Gen. Mgr. Annual revenue $12.6 million. Star Exhibits is a full-service exhibit house that provides three-dimensional marketing solutions, including trade show exhibits, POP displays, and lobby design/construction. 85 employees (89 in Minnesota; 4 part-time). Founded in 1993. SIC 3993. No. 30 CityBusiness Fastest-growing Private Companies.

Starkey Laboratories Inc. 6700 Washington Ave. S., Eden Prairie, MN 55344. Tel: 952/941-6401; Fax: 952/828-9262. William F. Austin, Chm. and CEO; Jerry Ruzicka, Pres. and COO; Jim Bremer, VP-Credit; Bob Erickson, SVP-Fin.; Keith Guggenberger, VP-Info. Svs.; Dale Thorstad, SVP-Corp. Devel.; Jeff Sticha, VP-Mfg.; Tom Victorian, VP-Engrg. Annual revenue $309 million. Starkey Laboratories manufactures custom-designed, in-the-ear hearing aids. Starkey owns Qualitone, St. Louis Park, Minn., and Micro Tech, Plymouth, Minn. 3,450 employees. Founded in 1967. SIC 3841, 3842. No. 43 CRM Private 100.

State Fund Mutual Companies 3500 W. 80th St., Suite 700, Bloomington, MN 55431. Tel: 952/838-4200; Fax: 952/838-2000; Web site: http://www.sfmic.com. Patricia R. Johnson, Pres. and CEO; Terrence L. Miller, VP and Treas.; Frances M. Kaitala, VP-Insurance Op.; Robert T. Lund, Sec. and Gen. Counsel; Margaret L. Kasting, VP-Claims; Andrew W. Lynn, VP and Chief Defense Counsel. Annual revenue $51.7 million. State Fund Mutual Cos. (SFM), a full-service enterprise specializing in workers' compensation coverage and services, works with thousands of Minnesota employers and employees to prevent injuries, administer claims, manage costs, and help injured employees return to work. SFM operates three subsidiaries: CompCost Inc. provides medical bill review, case management, and third-party administration services; CompRehab Inc. provides vocational rehabilitation and ergonomic services; and SFM Systems Inc. offers specialized workers' compensation software. SFM Companies works through independent insurance agencies. 180 employees. Founded in 1983. SIC 6321.

Stearns Cooperative Electric Association 900 E. Kraft Dr., P.O. Box 40, Melrose, MN 56352. Tel: 320/256-4241; Fax: 320/256-3618. Stearns is an electric distribution cooperative that also offers security systems, rural TV, cellular phones, surge protection, and water distillers. 56 employees. Founded in 1937. SIC 4911.

Steiger Lumber Company Sellar Street, P.O. Box 200, Bessemer, MI 49911. Tel: 906/667-0266; Fax: 906/667-0545. Paul Steiger, Chm.; Pat Steiger, Pres.; Tom Steiger, VP; Dick Steiger, Sec. and Treas. Steiger Lumber is a sawmill and logging operation engaged in lumber manufacturing, custom kiln-drying, and planing. 51 employees. Founded in 1945. SIC 2411.

Steinwall Inc. 1759 116th Ave. N.W., Coon Rapids, MN 55448. Tel: 763/767-7060; Fax: 763/767-7061; Web site: http://www.steinwall.com. Maureen Steinwall, Pres.; Don Blue, VP-Engrg.; Leigh Burlingame, VP-Op.; Bill O'Connell, Quality. Steinwall is engaged in precision custom thermoplastic injection molding and mold making. 58 employees (3 part-time). Founded in 1965. SIC 3089.

Stenerson Brothers Lumber Company 2700 12th Ave. S., Moorhead, MN 56560. Tel: 218/233-3437; Fax: 218/233-2819. Leslie G. Stenerson, Pres.; John G. Stenerson, Sec., Treas., and Gen. Mgr. Annual revenue $18 million. Stenerson Lumber operates five retail stores that offer lumber and building products to contractors and consumers. Other stores: Detroit Lakes, and Fergus Falls Minn.; Grand Forks and Wahpeton, N.D. 75 employees. Founded in 1889. SIC 5211.

Stern Rubber Company Airport Industrial Park, Staples, MN 56479. Tel: 218/894-3898; Fax: 218/894-3124. Terrel L. Stern, Chm.; Allan Northquest, VP; Bob Jackson, Dir.-Mfg.; Dennis Page, Dir.-Quality/IS; Bob Wise, Customer Svc. Mgr.; Bonnie Gastecki, Cont.; Fred Eiesland, Hum. Res. Coord. Stern Rubber, formerly American Rubber Co., is a custom molder of rubber mechanical parts that operates on-site tooling facilities. 165 employees (all in Minnesota). Founded in 1969. SIC 3069.

Steven Fabrics Company 1400 Van Buren St. N.E., Minneapolis, MN 55413. Tel: 612/781-6671; Fax: 612/781-2135. Richard Schommer, Pres. and Owner; Jere DeRocker, VP and Gen. Mgr.; Ed Lavery, Dir.-Sls./Mktg.; Dick Merhar, Cont. Steven Fabrics is a manufacturer, wholesaler, and distributor of vertical blinds, duette shades, silhouette shades, aluminum and vinyl horizontal blinds, wood blinds, pleated shades, custom draperies and fabrics, bedspreads, linings, trims, and other custom window treatments. 210 employees (206 in Minnesota). Founded in 1946. SIC 2391, 2591.

Stevens Lee Company 1600 Xenium Ln. N., Plymouth, MN 55441. Tel: 763/553-1881; Fax: 763/553-1209. Harold R. Rubin, Chm.; Stuart A. Rubin, Pres.; Raymond R. Bishop, VP-Mktg.; Michael E. Rodich, VP-Mktg.; Paul Benenson, VP-Purch.; Benjamin H. Rubin, EVP, Sec., and Treas. Stevens Lee Co. manufactures commercial food service equipment, including refrigerators, freezers, milk dispensers, refrigerated display cases and sandwich/salad units, and lettuce-preparation equipment. 131 employees (5 part-time). Founded in 1950. SIC 3585, 3589.

Stewart Lumber Company 421 Johnson N.E., Minneapolis, MN 55413. Tel: 612/378-1520; Fax: 612/378-1484. Mark E. Lindgren, Pres.; W. Nelson, Sls./Gen. Mgr. Stewart Lumber Co. is a supplier of lumber, plywood products, and all other building materials. Owned by Shaw Lumber Co., St. Paul. 70 employees (5 part-time). Founded in 1919. SIC 5211.

Stillwater Motor Company 5900 Stillwater Blvd. N., P.O. Box 337, Stillwater, MN 55082. Tel: 651/439-4333; Fax: 651/439-4425; Web site: http://www.stillwatermotors.com. Daniel Raduenz, Pres.; Patricia Raduenz, VP. Annual revenue $53.2 million. Stillwater Motor Co. is an automobile dealership for Chevrolet, Buick, and Jeep. 95 employees (all in Minnesota; 10 part-time). Founded in 1922. SIC 5511.

F.H. Stoltze Land & Lumber 2497 Seventh Ave. E., Suite 105, North St. Paul, MN 55109. Tel: 651/773-1000; Fax: 651/773-2155. Daniel W. O'Brien, Chm. and Pres.; Greg Johnson, Treas. and Sec.; Michael Lyngholm, EVP. F.H. Stoltze Land & Lumber operates sawmills and planing businesses in Columbia Falls, Mont.; and Sigurd, Utah. Affiliated with Maple Island Inc. 150 employees. Founded in 1914. SIC 2421.

Strata Corporation 1625 N. 36th, P.O. Box 13500, Grand Forks, ND 58208. Tel: 701/746-7491; Fax: 701/775-8144. James R. Bradshaw, Chm. and Pres.; Mark Johnson, CFO; Gerald Brorby, Sec. Strata Corp. produces wholesale sand and gravel, manufactures concrete products, and performs road construction. 300 employees. Founded in 1962. SIC 1442, 1611, 3272.

Streater Store Fixtures 411 S. First Ave., Albert Lea, MN 56007. Tel: 507/373-0611; Fax: 507/373-7630; Web site: http://www.streater.com. Tom Stensrude, VP and Gen. Mgr.; Robert Cote, SVP-Sls.; Dan Juntunen, Cont. Streater manufactures store fixtures and permanent point-of-purchase display fixtures. Streater is an affiliate of L.A. Darling Company, a member of the Marmon Group of companies. 650 employees. Founded in 1917. SIC 2542, 2599, 8711.

Stremel Manufacturing Company 260 Plymouth Ave. N., Minneapolis, MN 55411. Tel: 612/339-8261; Fax: 612/339-2661. Holly Andries, Chm.; James Andries, Pres.; Al LineBerry, VP; Ed Shelleny, Cont.; Tracy Brown, Sls. Mgr. Stremel Manufacturing is a job shop engaged in precision metal fabrication and machining. 92 employees (all in Minnesota). Founded in 1894. SIC 3444, 3499, 3599.

Stringer Business Systems Inc. 960 Blue Gentian Rd., Eagan, MN 55121. Tel: 651/994-7700; Fax: 651/637-2202; Web site: http://www.stringerbusiness.com. Stringer sells copiers, fax machines, color copiers, imaging systems, duplicators, and printers. 220 employees. SIC 5044.

PVT

Stuart Corporation 1050 W. 80th St., Bloomington, MN 55420. Tel: 952/948-9500; Fax: 952/948-9570. Stuart H. Nolan, Chm. and CEO; Gail Williams, Treas. Stuart Corp. is a development and property management firm active in multifamily and commercial development in the Upper Midwest area. 225 employees. Founded in 1970. SIC 6531.

Stylmark Inc. 6536 Main St. N.E., P.O. Box 32008, Fridley, MN 55432. Tel: 763/574-7474; Fax: 763/574-1415; Web site: http://www.stylmark.com. David Brink, Chm.; Daryl Walsh, Pres.; Steve Huston, VP and CFO; Ernie Otto, VP; Jerry Otto, VP. Stylmark manufactures showcase components, decor trim, and hardware for the glass industry, all from aluminum extrusions. It also manufactures a line of stainless steel showcases. Founded as Designware Industries Inc. 150 employees (145 in Minnesota; 2 part-time). Founded in 1954. SIC 3429.

Summit Packaging 828 Kasota Ave., Minneapolis, MN 55414. Tel: 612/378-2500; Fax: 612/378-9659. William Schroeder, Chm.; Donald Schroeder, Pres. Schroeder Group is a manufacturer and distributor of corrugated shipping and packaging products, a manufacturer of displays and specialty products, and an assembly packaging contractor. The company has offices in Nebraska, Iowa, and Minnesota, with manufacturing facilities in Nebraska and Minnesota. Formerly Summit Packaging Inc.; before that, the John Halper Box Co. 175 employees. Founded in 1932. SIC 2679, 5113.

Sun Country Airlines 2520 Pilot Knob Rd., Suite 250, Mendota Heights, MN 55120. Tel: 651/681-3900; Fax: 651/681-3970; Web site: http://www.suncountry.com. William La Macchia Sr., Chm.; William La Macchia Jr., Pres. and CEO; Gordon Graves, VP-Maintenance/Engrg.; Tammy Lee, VP-Corp. Affairs; Dan Madsen, VP-Info. Svs.; Mark Christiano, Dir.-Info. Svs. Annual revenue $260 million. Sun Country is the third-largest charter airline company in the United States. Its fleet of four DC-10 and 12 Boeing 727 airplanes—flying to 26 destinations in North America, Mexico, and the Caribbean—provided charter service to 2.6 million vacationers in 1998. Until 1999, its strategy was to focus tightly on these vacation-package charters rather than to compete with scheduled airlines. In January 1999, in a major shift in marketing and operating strategy, Sun Country announced plans to become a competitive, scheduled air carrier—a low-fare alternative to Northwest Airlines in the Twin Cities—effective June 1, 1999. 1,400 employees. Founded in 1983. In December 1999 the FAA reported that Sun Country Airlines had achieved a level-one rating for Y2K readiness, the highest rating available. The airline applauded the major airlines for implementing a plan to treat customers with respect, procedures that Sun Country had in place when it began scheduled service in June. The airline reached an agreement to become a signatory carrier at Detroit's Wayne County International airport. Dec. 31: The company had anticipated an annual loss of between $12 million and $14 million in its first year as a scheduled airline. However, with unhedged fuel costs $8.5 million over budget and passengers more difficult to attract than expected, the loss widened to $16.8 million. Sun Country was contracted to charter the University of St. Thomas baseball team for a historic flight to Havana, Cuba, on Jan. 22, 2000, and the return on Jan. 29. In February the airline, which had already earned the business of nearly 40 Minneapolis/St. Paul companies, announced a new "onefare" program, an Internet travel program dedicated to serving small, medium, and large businesses by providing the most competitive rates. In March Sun Country received approval from the U.S. Department of Transportation to begin scheduled service to several locations in Mexico. In April Sun Country announced that it planned to expand its service to include new connecting service to San Diego beginning Sept. 6. The airline received approval from the Mexican government to begin scheduled service to several locations in Mexico. In May CEO La Macchia told a U.S. Senate panel that Northwest, "arguably the most predatory and anticompetitive" of all the major carriers, was seeking to crush his low-fare airline. Sun Country Airlines received approval from the U.S. Department of Transportation for three daily round-trips into Chicago O'Hare International Airport beginning Sept. 3. The award gives Sun Country a decisive competitive edge over other carriers who are flying into Chicago's Midway airport. Eight new, custom-ordered 737-800 planes—to be delivered starting in 2001—will feature a new look for Sun Country (blue trimmed with orange). Sun Country was the first commercial airline to install MedAire's Emergency Services Kits, first-aid kits designed specifically for the needs of the traveling public. At the end of June, Sun Country finally succumbed to high fuel prices, adding a $20 surcharge to its round-trip fares. The airline was in discussions with Spirit Airlines and National Airlines about sharing ground services and terminal space at Chicago's O'Hare International Airport to reduce costs. June 30: Although second-quarter sales of $74.1 million were up 27.5 percent, the company lost money again, this time $4.1 million. In the year and a half of competing with Northwest, the airline had lost $27.9 million. "No one expected Sun Country to be profitable at this point," said spokeswoman Tammy Lee.

In July La Macchia launched an around-the-clock telephone reservations center in Bloomington, Minn., to streamline direct ticket sales. After its own low fares increased passenger traffic to Milwaukee by more than 75 percent, Sun Country accused Northwest of using abusive fare tactics to capture much of that growth for itself. In August Sun Country unveiled phase one of its loyalty program, a co-branded "Smile Awards" credit card that gives customers a faster, easier way to earn free travel, with fewer restrictions and no black-out dates. Families and friends can pool points and more quickly accumulate free travel. Sun Country Airlines was planning to inaugurate its new scheduled service to Chicago's O'Hare International airport for departures starting Oct. 9, 2000, allowing business and leisure travelers a more affordable choice for air travel to O'Hare. In an attempt to capitalize on the retreat of Vanguard Airlines from the route, Sun Country rolled out a $59 one-way fare (14-day advance), which Northwest was expected to match. In addition to its twice-daily scheduled departures to and from O'Hare, Sun Country was planning to offer new connecting service to and from Chicago starting Oct. 11. Seasonal service to Honolulu was to begin Dec. 26, 2000. In October Sun Country, after discovering excessive corrosion in a DC-10, decided to replace it with a Boeing 727. On Oct. 28, Sun Country implemented a new, more customerfriendly measurement procedure for carry-on luggage that gives customers more flexibility in their carry on choices. Passengers now have their carry-on luggage measured to ensure that it meets a new linear size requirement of 48 inches, rather than adhering to the standard system of measurement. Example: An item measuring 9" x 15.5" x 23.5" meets the new standard. SIC 4512, 4522. No. 53 CRM Private 100.

Sunrise International Leasing Corporation 5500 Wayzata Blvd., Suite 725, Golden Valley, MN 55416. Tel: 763/593-1904; Fax: 763/513-3299. Peter J. King, Chm. and CEO; Jeffrey G. Jacobsen, EVP; R. Bradley Pike, VP and Gen. Mgr.-Direct Leasing. Annual revenue $86.1 million (earnings $2.9 million). Sunrise International Leasing Corp., formerly Sunrise Resources Inc., buys, sells, and leases data processing and other high-technology equipment. The company also leases, through its vendor division, a wide range of capital equipment through close relationships with the manufacturers of such equipment. In addition to its leasing activities, the company sells equipment, including used equipment sold at the end of the lease term. 53 employees. Founded in 1989. In January 2000 the company signed a definitive merger agreement with The King Management Corp. for the acquisition of all of the outstanding shares of Sunrise common stock not held by 57 percent shareholder King Management and its affiliates. Under the terms of the merger agreement, which was unanimously approved by the board of directors, Sunrise was to merge into King Management, and Sunrise shareholders not affiliated with King Management were to receive consideration of $5.25 per share in cash. In February a stockholder filed a complaint as a class action in the Court of Chancery for the State of Delaware against Sunrise and its directors. The complaint alleged breach of fiduciary duty in connection with the King merger. March 31: Fiscal-year revenue increased 67 percent from prior year, to $86.1 million; net income shrank to $2,883,000 from $3,438,000. Fiscal year 2000 leasing margins were lower than the previous year. Depreciation expenses increased 97 percent due to the increased volume of leases and to accelerated rates of depreciation used to more closely match future book values to the projected market values at the end of the lease term. Interest expenses increased 87 percent due to increased borrowing levels and rate increases on variable rate debt. Provisions for losses increased 146 percent to cover exposures on known problems and to maintain reserves, per company formula, to cover anticipated future portfolio losses. In addition, operating results for the year were impacted by merger related expenses totaling $1 million. The company predicted that recent interest rate increases will have an adverse effect on profitability for the foreseeable future because the costs of the company's borrowings will be increased, only a portion of which can be passed on to customers. Reports of loan defaults, bankruptcies, and performance problems with a number of independent leasing companies led banks and other funding sources to substantially reduce or slow down their commitments to fund the leasing industry. As a result, Sunrise had been forced to significantly reduce the amount of equipment it purchased, adversely affecting future revenue and profits. In May two stockholder class action lawsuits were settled—with Sunrise agreeing, among other things, to amend the merger agreement to require that the merger to be approved by a majority of the outstanding shares of Sunrise common stock not held by King Management. On June 28, Sunrise's stockholders voted overwhelmingly to approve the going-private transaction, which was immediately completed. SIC 5046, 6159.

Super Radiator Coils 104 Peavey Rd., Chaska, MN 55318. Tel: 952/556-3330; Fax: 952/920-4650. Jon Holt, Pres.; Keith Michelson, VP-Engrg.; Jim Bast, EVP and CFO; Ken Klatt, Dir.-Materials. Super Radiator Coils manufactures heat transfer coils. The company has locations in Chaska, Minn.; Richmond, Va.; and Phoenix, Ariz. 214 employees (78 in Minnesota). Founded in 1928. SIC 3498.

Superior Plating Inc. 315 First Ave. N.E., Minneapolis, MN 55413. Tel: 612/379-2121; Fax: 612/379-8933. E.J. McMonagle, Chm.; M.P. McMonagle, Pres.; David Hopkins, Dir.-Fin. Superior Plating does electroplating on metals. 130 employees. Founded in 1919. SIC 3471.

Superpumper Inc. P.O. Box 1847, Minot, ND 58702. Tel: 701/852-0867; Fax: 701/852-8462. Terry Domres, VP and COO; Bruce Hest, Sec. and Treas. Annual revenue $43 million. Superpumper operates convenience stores. 220 employees (30 in Minnesota; 58 part-time). Founded in 1983. SIC 5541.

SuperSolutions Corp. 10100 Viking Dr., Eden Prairie, MN 55344. Tel: 952/942-6297; Fax: 952/942-6451; Web site: http://www.supersolutions.com. Darshan Karki, CEO; Bill Brummond, Pres. and COO; Jeff Brown, VP; Paul Mattiacci, VP-Implementation/Client Svs. SuperSolutions develops and services its software application Daybreak-The Big Picture. Daybreak is a loan portfolio management software that automates the lending process for providers of consumer and commercial loans. Daybreak, which operates in client-server and Internet-based environments, includes modules for loan origination, servicing, and collection. Daybreak is designed for companies that provide home improvement loans, home equity lines of credit, second mortgages, and loans for automobiles, recreational vehicles, boats, motorcycles, and manufactured housing. 68 employees. Founded in 1989. In November 2000 Mitsubishi Motors Credit of America Inc. selected SuperSolutions' Daybreak Lending Software as its credit processing solution. SIC 7372.

Surdyk's 303 E. Hennepin Ave., Minneapolis, MN 55414. Tel: 612/379-3232. Jim Surdyk, Pres. Surdyk's is a liquor retailer. 60 employees. Founded in 1933. In December 1999 Surdyk's filed a lawsuit against competitor MGM Liquor Warehouse alleging false and deceptive advertising. The contention was that, in copying Surdyk's annual fall wine event, MGM featured wines that were unavailable from distributors in a bait-and-switch promotion. SIC 5921.

Survivalink Corporation 5420 Feltl Rd., Minnetonka, MN 55343. Tel: 952/939-4181; Fax: 952/939-4191; Web site: http://www.survivalink.com. Mark T. Wagner, Chm. and CEO; John R. Brintnall, Pres. and COO; Kenneth F. Olson, VP-Engrg.; John F. Nealon, VP-Mktg.; Sew-Wah Tay, VP-RA/QA; Michael J. Musich, VP-Op. Survivalink develops, manufactures, and markets automated external defibrillators (AEDs) for the first-responder market to treat victims of sudden cardiac arrest, one of the leading causes of death in the United States. The product's trade name is FirstSave. 60 employees (41 in Minnesota; 1 part-time). Founded in 1992. In April 2000 Survivalink and its U.K. distributor LifeTec Medical Ltd. were awarded a bid valued at 750,000 pounds ($1.2 million) from the Department of Health in England to provide AEDs. A new text screen feature for the FirstSave AED was able to provide users with a visual display of comprehensive instructions to guide them through a sudden cardiac arrest emergency rescue in loud environments, such as those around machinery or large crowds, where it can be difficult to hear the audible prompts provided by the FirstSave AED. In May Survivalink announced a strategic partnership with Softspikes Inc. to sell its FirstSave AED and complementary products to golf clubs and resorts (golf courses have been identified as one of the top five places people suffer sudden cardiac arrest outside the home); announced a partnership with Moore Medical Corp. to distribute its FirstSave AED and complementary products to the occupational health market; and donated 10 FirstSave AEDs to the General Services Administration of the federal government. In September Survivalink placed its FirstSave AEDs in public facilities throughout Vancouver, British Columbia, as part of the North American Public Access Defibrillation (PAD) trial. The purpose of the PAD trial was to evaluate the effectiveness of AEDs on cardiac arrest survival rates when the devices are readily accessible to lay rescuers. Korean Airlines purchased 40 FirstSave AEDs to equip all long-haul aircraft in its international fleet. On Oct. 27, Congress passed the Cardiac Arrest Survival Act (HR 2498). The bill recommends placement of AEDs in federal buildings and provides nationwide Good Samaritan protection that exempts from liability anyone who renders emergency treatment with a defibrillator to save someone's life. SIC 3845.

Swanson & Youngdale Inc. 6565 W. 23rd St., P.O. Box 26070, St. Louis Park, MN 55426. Tel: 952/545-2541; Fax: 952/545-4435; Web site: http://www.swansonyoungdale.com. Robert Swanson, Pres.; Dennis Prindle, EVP; Doug Rynda, VP; Clark Anderson, Sec. and Treas.; Tim Kavanaugh, VP. Annual revenue $29.2 million. Swanson & Youngdale is a commercial and industrial painting contractor with division offices in Duluth and Rochester, Minn., and a satellite facility in Beulah, N.D. 300 employees (250 in Minnesota). Founded in 1946. SIC 1721.

E.A. Sween Company 16101 W. 78th St., Eden Prairie, MN 55344. Tel: 952/937-9440; Fax: 952/937-0186; Web site: http://www.deliexpress.com. Thomas E. Sween, Chm., Pres., and CEO; Robert Linner, SVP-Direct Store Delivery; Bill Bastian, SVP-Deli Express Branded Sandwiches; Stephen Hoese, SVP-Fin./Admin.; Bill Lewis, SVP-Combined Distribution Centers; Monica Green, VP-Op.; Lavonne Kucera, VP-Food Safety; Ron Myshka, VP-MIS. E.A. Sween Co., dba Deli Express, delivers fast-food pro-

PVT

grams primarily to convenience stores in 26 states. 750 employees. Founded in 1956. SIC 5149, 5962.

Sweetman Construction Concrete Materials 1201 W. Russell, P.O. Box 84140 (57118), Sioux Falls, SD 57104. Tel: 605/357-6000; Fax: 605/334-6221. G.P. Sweetman, Pres.; Kevin Moore, Treas. Sweetman Construction Concrete Materials manufactures ready-mix concrete, crushed quartzite, asphalt, concrete, and washed sand-and-gravel products. 200 employees. Founded in 1952. SIC 1429, 1442, 2951, 3273.

Swingen Construction Company Highway 2 W., P.O. Box 13456, Grand Forks, ND 58208. Tel: 701/775-5359; Fax: 701/775-7631. Walter I. Swingen, Chm.; Daniel Swingen, Pres. and CEO; Ronald Ellingson, VP-Engrg.; Richard Lian, VP-Construction; Laurie Christianson, Treas. and Sec. Swingen Construction Co. is engaged in highway and municipal construction. 120 employees (30 in Minnesota). Founded in 1948. SIC 1622.

PVT

Dave Syverson Ford Lincoln 2310 E. Main, Albert Lea, MN 56007. Tel: 507/373-1438; Fax: 507/373-3063. D.B. Syverson, Pres.; Lowell T. Bruns, Treas. and Op. Mgr.; Robert Syverson, Sec. Dave Syverson Ford Lincoln is a motor vehicle dealer. 90 employees (10 part-time). Founded in 1968. SIC 5511.

T

TC/American Monorail Inc. 3839 County Rd. 116, Hamel, MN 55340. Tel: 763/478-6565; Fax: 763/478-6051. Jerry Lague, Owner; Paul Lague, Pres.; Dan Scalf, VP; John Magnotti, Nat'l Sls. Mgr.; William Swanson, Sls. Admin. Mgr. TC/American Monorail manufactures and markets overhead electric cranes, and monorail systems. Its Jet Edge division builds and sells high-pressure water machines for industrial and construction uses. 178 employees. Founded in 1955. SIC 3536.

TC Molding 1880 Oak Crest Ave., Roseville, MN 55113. Tel: 651/636-6367; Fax: 651/636-8153. Thomas W. Swanson, Pres. TC Molding, fromerly Twin City Picture Framing Company Inc., is the oldest picture framing establishment in the Twin Cities. The company also carries art, posters, and fine art. Affiliated with Art Resources Gallery, St. Paul. 120 employees (100 in Minnesota). Founded in 1898. SIC 5999.

TLC Polyform Inc. 13055 15th Ave. N., Plymouth, MN 55441. Tel: 763/542-2240; Fax: 763/542-1709; Web site: http://www.tlcpolyform.com. John F. Lau Jr., CEO; John Galvin, Pres. and CFO; David C. Lau, EVP; Michael V. Vallafskey, VP and COO; Susan Aspelund, Cont. TLC Polyform is a manufacturer of thermoformed growing containers for horticulture and agriculture. Manufacturing facilities are located in Minnesota, Georgia, Michigan and Arizona. Products are sold for domestic and international distribution. 145 employees (22 in Minnesota). Founded in 1980. Acquired TFI Plastics/Cyberplast Industries of Michigan in September 2000. SIC 3089.

TMI Coatings Inc. 2805 Dodd Rd., Eagan, MN 55121. Tel: 651/452-6100; Fax: 651/452-0598; Web site: http://www.tmicoatings.com. Tracy Gliori, Pres.; Mary Imre, CEO; Neil Klein, Cont. TMI Coatings is an industrial painting contractor that installs protective coatings and linings—including tank linings, containment dike linings, flooring, and protective coatings—for industry. 73 employees (46 in Minnesota; 1 part-time). Founded in 1967. SIC 1721, 1799, 3479.

TMI Systems Design Corporation 50 S. Third Ave. W., Dickinson, ND 58601. Tel: 701/225-6716; Fax: 701/225-6719. Dennis W. Johnson, Chm. and CEO; Dean G. Rummel, Pres. and COO; Cal Kolling, VP; Kevin Kovash, VP; George Unruh, VP; Jeff Swank, VP; Ron Hartl, VP. Annual revenue $40 million. TMI Systems Design Corp. is a furniture manufacturing company. The company manufactures its products under the brand names Trimline and Trimrail. 417 employees (46 part-time). Founded in 1969. SIC 2521, 2531.

TO Plastics Inc. 2901 E. 78th St., Bloomington, MN 55425. Tel: 952/854-2131; Fax: 952/854-2154. Charles Goers, Pres., COO, and Gen. Mgr. TO Plastics manufactures plastics products. 200 employees. SIC 3089.

T&R Electric Supply Company Inc. P.O. Box 180, Colman, SD 57017. Tel: 605/534-3555; Fax: 605/534-3861. James R. Thompson, Pres.; Kenneth E. Ross, VP. T&R Electric Supply Co. remanufactures electrical transformers. 130 employees. SIC 3612.

TSI Inc. 500 Cardigan Rd., P.O. Box 64394 (55164), Shoreview, MN 55126. Tel: 651/483-0900; Fax: 651/490-2748; Web site: http://www.tsi.com. John J. Fauth, Chm.; James E. Doubles, Pres. and CEO; Lowell D. Nystrom, SVP; Jugal A. Agarwal, VP-Bus. Devel.; Laura J. Cochrane, Sec. and Counsel; Mark J. Schwirtz, Cont. Annual revenue $111 million. TSI develops, manufactures, and markets measuring and control instruments for a variety of applications. The company's products can best be divided into two market segments. The Safety, Comfort, and Health segment consists of instruments that monitor and control the environments in which people work and live. These include analytical and research instruments used to characterize very small particles, products that monitor indoor air quality, and products that help protect people from toxic airborne substances. The Productivity and Quality Improvement segment produces instruments that help customers enhance their industrial processes and improve their products. These include flow-related measuring instruments, noncontact measuring devices for manufacturers of metals and wire, filter testers, and instruments for measuring the speed and concentration of droplets in industrial sprays. 672 employees (344 in Minnesota; 22 part-time). Founded in 1961. In December 1999 the U.S. Army exercised a previously negotiated $5.1 million option for 908 units of the military version of TSI's PORTACOUNT Respirator Fit Tester. Delivery wais scheduled to begin in April 2000 and continue through May 2001 at a rate of 70 units per month. In January 2000 TSI's board of directors unanimously approved a $15.25-per-share cash transaction in which TSI was to be acquired by JJF Acquisition Inc., a Minneapolis-based industrial investment group headed by John J. Fauth. The transaction, which was valued at $180 million, was to result in TSI becoming privately held. On May 3, shareholders approved the merger. "Our primary goal will be to help the company grow and become an even stronger force in the markets it serves," said Fauth. "This region is home to many good, solid companies whose growth has been hobbled by Wall Street's disinterest in smaller, non-Internet-based enterprises," Fauth said. "We believe that by recapitalizing through a combination of private equity and debt, many of these companies can realize their full potential as more nimble operations. JJF Group and other investment firms will continue to be active in 'liberating' high-quality companies such as TSI." The merger was to be financed through a combination of equity provided by JJF Group and debt secured by JJF Group from a syndicate of lenders led by U.S. Bank. SIC 3822, 3823, 3824, 3826, 3829.

Taber Bushnell Inc. 7709 Winpark Dr., New Hope, MN 55427. Tel: 763/546-0994; Fax: 763/546-4469; Web site: http://www.taberbushnell.com. Jerry Hetland, Owner and CEO; Paul Schulz, VP-Fin.; Gary Hartmann, VP-Op.; Charles Remillard, VP-Sls. Taber Bushnell manufactures tool-and-die and metal stampings for the automotive and computer industry. 112 employees. Founded in 1958. SIC 3469.

Tafco Equipment Company 1304 W. First, P.O. Box 339, Blue Earth, MN 56013. Tel: 507/526-3247; Fax: 507/526-7346. T.M. Ankeny, Pres. and COO; C.J. Ankeny, Sec. and Treas.; Ronald P. Liggett, Cont.; S.L. Ankeny, VP. Tafco Equipment manufactures truck equipment and accessories, agricultural truck bodies, and hoists, plus industrial/agricultural ventilating fans. 65 employees (all in Minnesota). Founded in 1962. SIC 3564, 3713, 3714, 5013.

TAJ Technologies Inc. 1168 Northland Dr., Mendota Heights, MN 55120. Tel: 651/688-2801; Fax: 651/688-8321; Web site: http://www.tajtech.com. K.C. Sukumar, Pres. Annual revenue $10.3 million. TAJ specializes in implementing Web Solution-Information Portals, Business Intelligence, e-commerce solutions and business logic components, and client server solutions. TAJ implements its solutions utilizing industry standard tools and methodologies. 115 employees (104 in Minnesota). Founded in 1987. SIC 7371.

Tapemark Company 150 E. Marie Ave., West St. Paul, MN 55118. Tel: 651/455-1611; Fax: 651/450-8498; Web site: http://www.tapemark.com. Robert C. Klas Sr., Chm.; Robert C. Klas Jr., Pres.; James Burmeister, SVP and CFO; David Plum, SVP-Bus. Op. Annual revenue $70 million. Tapemark is a pressure-sensitive label converter. Its Label Division prints custom labels for food and personal-care products; tamper-evident and warning labels; and direct-mail action devices. The Medical Products and Industrial Fabricating Divisions produce disposable medical devices and die-cut, pressure-sensitive parts for joining, bonding, and sealing industrial applications. 350 employees. Founded in 1952. SIC 2672, 2759, 3842, 5084.

Taylor Corporation 1725 Roe Crest Dr., North Mankato, MN 56003. Tel: 507/625-2828; Fax: 507/625-2988. Glen A. Taylor, Chm. and CEO; Brad J. Schreier, Pres. and COO; Al Fallenstein, EVP; Bill Kozita, EVP and CFO; Jean Taylor, EVP; Ed Alvarez, Pres.-Comm. Group; Paul Schleich, Pres.-Direct Mktg. Group; John Schmitt, Pres.-Imprinting Group. Annual revenue $1 billion (estimated by Fact Book). Taylor Corp. is a holding company. Its operating divisions and affiliates are involved in the printing and electronics industries. Minnesota companies are: Ad Graphics, Carlson Craft, Corporate Graphics International, Corporate Graphics Commercial, Fine Impressions, Heinrich Envelope, James Tower, LTS Print Systems, Litho Tech, Masterpiece Studios, Micro-Trak Systems, National Recognition Products, Precision Press, Print Craft, Schmidt Printing, Taymark, Taytronics, Thayer Publishing, Travel Tags, Web Graphics Midwest. 15,000 employees (6,500 in Minnesota). Founded in 1948. In March 2000 Taylor signed a letter of intent with American Pad & Paper Co. (OTCBB: AMPP) to purchase of AP&P's Creative Card Division, located in Chicago. "Creative Card and its Century Greetings brand are well-known in their respective distribution channels, and their products are highly regarded by consumers," said John Schmitt, president of the Taylor Corp. Imprinting Group. [Definitive agreement signed in April.] SIC 2759, 3679. No. 8 CRM Private 100. No. 26 CRM Employer 100.

Teaching Temps Inc. 5353 Wayzata Blvd., Suite 606, Golden Valley, MN 55416. Tel: 952/844-9000; Fax: 952/844-0235. Joseph Noonan, Pres. Teaching Temps provides professional/para professional substitute teachers, assistant teachers, and child-care aides for public, private, parochial schools and learning centers throughout the seven-county metro area. Celebrating its 20th year. 100 employees (all in Minnesota; 40 part-time). Founded in 1981. SIC 7363.

TEAM Industries Inc. 105 Park Ave., Bagley, MN 56621. Tel: 218/694-3550; Fax: 218/694-3552; Web site: http://www.team-ind.com. David W. Ricke, Pres. and CEO; Robert Skawski, VP; Beatrice Ricke, Sec. and Treas.. Annual revenue $174 million. TEAM Industries Inc. is a holding company providing design, engineering, precision machining, and die-casting products. Subsidiaries include Motek Engineering & Manufacturing, Cambridge, Minn.; Product Research & Development, Bagley, Minn.; Audubon Engrg. & Mfg., Audubon, Minn.; Straight River Engrg. & Mfg., Park Rapids, Minn.; and DL Manufacturing in Detroit Lakes, Minn. 1,150 employees. Founded in 1967. In April 2000 Motek achieved QS-9000 quality registration. SIC 3599. No. 75 CRM Private 100.

Team Vantage Molding 22455 Everton Ave. N., Forest Lake, MN 55025. Tel: 651/464-3900; Fax: 651/982-1299. Raymond NewKirk, Pres.; Don Emerson, Op. Mgr. Annual revenue $12 million. Team Vantage Molding, formerly known as Regal Plastic Products, specializes in custom injection molding for the automotive, commercial, and medical industries. Engineering services are also provided as needed. 98 employees (all in Minnesota). Founded in 1976. SIC 3089.

Tech Central Inc. 3300 Edinborough Way, Suite 204, Edina, MN 55435. Tel: 952/837-8000; Fax: 952/837-8001; Web site: http://www.tech-central.com. John Jay, Pres.; Kathryn Hammond, Senior Ptnr. and VP. Annual revenue $6.1 million. Tech Central is a technical consulting firm specializing in contract engineering and information technology consulting. Tech Central Inc. is a licensed permanent search firm. 230 employees. Founded in 1990. Named one of 50 fastest growing privately held companies by CityBusiness. SIC 7361, 7363, 7371, 8711.

Tech-Pro Inc. 3000 Centre Pointe Dr., Roseville, MN 55113. Tel: 651/634-1400; Fax: 651/634-1499; Web site: http://www.tech-pro.com. Dave Vadis, Pres.; Keith Horland, Ptnr.; Dennis Van Ravenhorst, Staffing; Doug Larson, Op. Annual revenue $41.8 million. Tech-Pro is a national information technology consulting services company headquartered in the Twin Cities. Services provided include project management, application maintenance and development, business analysis, and network administration. Technical areas include mainframe, midrange, client/server, network, and e-business applications. Branch offices are located in Denver, Phoenix, and Indianapolis. 300 employees (250 in Minnesota). Founded in 1989. SIC 7371. No. 39 CityBusiness Fastest-growing Private Companies.

techies.com Inc. 7101 Metro Blvd., Edina, MN 55439. Tel: 612/944-1020; Web site: http://www.techies.com. Dan Frawley, Pres. and CEO; Doug Berg, Chief Techie; Tony Abena, EVP and COO; John Barrow, VP-Client Mktg.; Lisa Shough, VP-Sls.; Larry Stranghoener, CFO; Peter Brasket, VP-Bus. Devel.; George Johnson, VP-Mktg.; Dan Meiusi, VP-Op.; Cynthia Morgan, VP-Content and Exec. Producer. techies.com is a full-service career resource for technology professionals throughout the United States. The company is a leading online destination for technology professionals and for businesses that want to recruit, market to, and interact with these professionals. The company allows technology professionals who become its members to maximize their career options, develop proactive relationships with potential employers, and obtain relevant content on technology-related issues. The company offers large and small companies access to an extensive pool of technology professionals, customized recruiting solutions, access to market intelligence, and a marketplace to sell technology-related products and services. The company currently generates revenue primarily from the sale of online recruiting solutions to more than 1,100 client companies. The company is also expanding its revenue opportunities from advertising, sponsorships, and e-commerce activities. As of Oct. 23, 2000, the company had 620,000 members across the United States, up from 210,000 on Dec. 31, 1999, and 26,600 a year earlier than that. 525 employees. Founded in 1994. In May 2000 the company withdrew an initial public offering of 6 million shares due to prevailing market conditions. (It had been hoping to raise $60 million by selling a 20 percent stake in the company.) The company acquired tecHound.com, a Washington, D.C.-based regional source for technology careers. techies and Brainpower, the Net market maker for IT contractor services, partnered to develop a co-branded career exchange site.

In June, 60 people were laid off. The company's "Twin Cities TECHFORCE 2000 Report" ranked the area No. 7 in the nation in average salary of technology professionals. When it comes to skills, area experts in C++, SQL Server, and JD Edwards were among the most in-demand. The company developed the report using data collected from its 480,000 members nationwide (including 50,000 on twincities.techies.com), as well as 1,600 client companies nationwide who post jobs on the site. In October the company launched a new site for its client companies that improved their ability to find qualified candidates. New product "techies eXpress" was designed for recruiters at companies with limited hiring requirements. techies.com and Chimes Inc., the largest ASP for resource acquisition and Centralized Vendor Management services, formed a strategic alliance that was to allow techies.com to provide its corporate clients access to Chimes' Human Capital Management Solutions. In November a company study showed that, in addition to standard health care and retirement programs, technologists preferred the following fringe benefits: discounted or free home PCs and equipment (36%); discounted or free home Internet access (23%); spa/health club memberships (21%); company automobile (17%); mobile/wireless phone (17%). The company began giving its members the option to "go public" with their career profiles, allowing techies.com's client companies direct access to thousands of active job seekers who register on the site. SIC 7361.

Technical Die Castings Inc. Highway 14 W., P.O. Box 349, Stockton, MN 55988. Tel: 507/689-2194; Fax: 507/689-2197. Dick Green, Pres.; Greg King, VP. Technical Die Castings manufactures tools, dies, and zinc and aluminum die castings. 110 employees. Founded in 1974. SIC 3363, 3364, 3544.

Technical Ordnance Inc. 9200 Nike Rd., P.O. Box 800, St. Bonifacius, MN 55375. Tel: 952/446-1526; Fax: 952/446-1990. Norman H. Hoffman, Chm., Pres., and CEO; Ronald L. Augsburger, VP and Gen. Mgr.; Gerald R. Storms, Treas. Technical Ordnance manufactures explosive and actuated devices for the defense and aerospace industries. Corporate offices are located in St. Bonifacius, with a production loading plant in Clear Lake, S.D. 150 employees (25 in Minnesota). Founded in 1964. SIC 2892, 2899.

Technical Services for Electronics Inc. 108 Fifth Ave. N.W., P.O. Box 616, Arlington, MN 55307. Tel: 507/964-2237; Fax: 507/964-2465. Paul Kamba, CEO; Lyle C. Fahning, Pres.; Bob C. Cosgrove, CFO. Annual revenue $16 million. Technical Services for Electronics is a manufacturer of custom cable assemblies (subcontract electronic assemblies, wire cable assemblies, and molded cable assemblies) for the computer, communications, medical, and instrumentation industries. Plants are located in Arlington and Jackson, Minn. 185 employees (all in Minnesota). Founded in 1972. SIC 3679.

Technigraph Corporation 850 W. Third St., Winona, MN 55987. Tel: 507/454-3830; Fax: 507/454-6470. John R. Eddy, Pres.; Charles W. Eddy, VP-Sls./Mktg. Technigraph Corp. does container decorating by printing on plastic bottles and 3-D parts. It primarily serves the cosmetic, personal care, and chemical-trade markets. 100 employees (95 in Minnesota; 10 part-time). Founded in 1953. SIC 2759.

Telex Communications Inc. 12000 Portland Ave. S., Burnsville, MN 55337. Tel: 952/884-4051; Fax: 952/884-0043; Web site: http://www.telex.com. Edgar S. Woolard Jr., Chm.; Ned C. Jackson, CEO; Glen Cavanaugh, Pres.-Multimedia/RF Communications. Annual revenue $343.6 million. Telex Communications is a leader in the design, manufacture, and marketing of sophisticated audio, wireless, and multimedia communications devices to commercial, professional, and industrial markets; as well as one of the largest manufacturers and marketers of high-quality, high-performance sound systems products for the professional audio market. Telex's broad-based product line includes computer audio microphones, LCD projectors, digital matrix intercoms, headsets, hearing aids, wireless microphones, wireless LAN antennas, and other radio frequency transmission devices. Brand names include Telex, Electro-Voice, Altec Lansing, Klark Teknik, Vega, Dynacord, RTS, ProStar, University Sound, and Midas. The company operates manufacturing plants in Blue Earth, Glencoe, and Rochester, Minn.; Lincoln, Neb.; and Saguaro, Mexico. It distributes its products in more than 70 countries throughout the world, with international offices in London, Paris, Amsterdam, Singapore, Prague, and Toronto. Acquired in 1997 by Greenwich Street Capital Partners Inc., a New York private equity investment fund. 3,156 employees (1,010 in Minnesota; 38 part-time). Founded in 1936. In January 2000 the company announced that its Computer Audio Products group had developed and launched the world's smallest and lightest wireless telephone headsets, targeted at telephone and computer users who need hands-free, cordless communications; had released two new headsets for telephone and computer professionals who work in call centers; had released the Telex H-51 Stereo Computer Headset, for computer voice applications; and had entered into a distribution agreement with Ingram Micro for an assortment of Telex products, including 16 items for computer and telephony use. The company's M-560 Super-Directional USB Digital Microphone received an Innovations 2000 award at the 2000 International CES (Consumer Electronics Show). In April Telex announced the availability of the industry's first Universal Serial Bus (USB) microphones for Apple iBook and iMac products. Telex purchased the former Arrow Automotive factory in Morrilton, Ark.—planning to create a state-of-the-art production facility designed to optimize Telex's manufacturing capacities, realize the benefits of the latest production technologies, improve customer satisfaction, and fully support the continued growth of its Electro-Voice speaker business. In May Telex was planning to double its space by moving from Bloomington, Minn., to a new 114,000-square-foot corporate headquarters in Burnsville by July. Telex received a preliminary arbitration ruling entitling it to a payment of $7.7 million in connection with a dispute arising out of Telex's purchase of Mark IV Industries' Audio Products Group in December 1996. Payment of the arbitration award, together with interest of $2 million, remained subject to finalization of the arbitration decision under the terms of the parties' binding arbitration agreement. Telex also received a $9.6 million cash payment for all previously disclosed outstanding receivables related to Altec Lansing royalty fees and the sale of the trademark. In June the company announced the opening of its new manufacturing facility in Morrilton, Ark. Existing manufacturing facilities in Austin, Texas, and Newport, Tenn., were to be closed and operations relocated to Morrilton. Three full-duplex products were added to its line of USB digital audio equipment: the H-551 USB Digital Stereo Headset, the H-541 USB Digital Computer Headset, and the P-500 USB Digital Audio Converter. SIC 3651, 3679, 3695. No. 74 CRM Private 100.

Tempco Manufacturing Company Inc. 2475 Highway 55, Mendota Heights, MN 55120. Tel: 651/452-1441; Fax: 651/452-1125. T.A. Cronen, Chm. and CFO; P.J. Cronen, Pres. Tempco manufactures short- to medium-run metal stampings and small assemblies. 225 employees. Founded in 1945. SIC 3469.

Temroc Metals Inc. 4375 Willow Dr., Hamel, MN 55340. Tel: 763/478-6360; Fax: 763/478-6905; Web site: http://www.temroc.com. Elmer Schumer, Pres.; Elmer Schumer, Pres.; Carmen Goff, VP-Prod.; Carmen Goff, VP-Prod.; Doug Martin, VP-Sls.; Doug Martin, VP-Sls. Temroc Metals is a leading producer of customized aluminum extrusions and fabricated metal products for outdoor recreational products, architectural products, electronics, and other markets. Its products are used in a variety of engineered applications. 150 employees. Founded in 1963. In March 2000 the privately held Temroc, along with its subsidiary, AaCron Inc., an anodizing company based in Plymouth, Minn., agreed to be acquired by Quanex Corp. (NYSE: NX), Houston. As of October, the deal had not yet been finalized. SIC 3354, 3354.

Tenere Inc. 10860 N. 60th St., P.O. Box 210, Stillwater, MN 55082. Tel: 651/439-7202; Fax: 651/439-1668. Ben Prescott, Owner. Tenere, formerly known as Hansman Industries Inc., fabricates precision sheet metal and stampings for business machines. 140 employees. Founded in 1946. SIC 3444, 3469, 3569.

Ternes Register System Inc. 4851 White Bear Pkwy., White Bear Township, MN 55110. Tel: 651/407-4800; Fax: 651/487-4801. James N. Ternes, Owner; Eric Ternes, Owner; Larry Lundgren, Pres. Ternes Register System is an international supplier and manufacturer of register control systems used in the printing industry. 95 employees (89 in Minnesota). Founded in 1961. SIC 3555, 3577.

Tescom Corporation 12616 Industrial Blvd., Elk River, MN 55330. Tel: 763/441-6330; Fax: 763/241-3224. Donald E. Glesmann, Chm. and CEO; Edward Cunnington, Pres. and COO; James Tomczak, CFO and Treas. Annual revenue $30 million. Tescom manufactures high-pressure regulators and valves for industrial fluid control in the specialty gas, semiconductor, commercial diving, and aerospace markets. Operating divisions: High Purity Controls, Industrial Controls, and Electronic Controls. 270 employees (272 in Minnesota; 2 part-time). Founded in 1917. SIC 3494, 3541.

Tessier's 218 E. First Ave., P.O. Box 188, Mitchell, SD 57301. Tel: 605/996-7548; Fax: 605/996-3131. Mark R. Buche, Pres.; Gopal Vyas, VP. Annual revenue $23.4 million. Tessier's is a heating, ventilation, and air-conditioning contractor. Other locations are in Sioux Falls and Rapid City, S.D.; and Rochester, Minn. 195 employees (14 in Minnesota; 3 part-time). Founded in 1919. SIC 1761.

TestQuest Inc. 5929 Baker Rd., Suite 475, Minnetonka, MN 55435. Tel: 952/936-7887; Fax: 952/988-8283; Web site: http://www.btree.com. Martin Hahn, Pres. and CEO; Dennis Hykes, CFO; Jaffer Hussain, VP-Mktg.; Prabha Gopinath, VP-Engrg.; Maureen McHenry, VP-Op.; Lisa Christie, VP-Bus. Devel.; Jay LaFrance, VP-Sls. TestQuest, formerly B-Tree Systems, provides embedded systems verification and testing—including the detection of defects in the tiny computers embedded in pacemakers. Manufacturers of embedded and PC-based products in the medical, consumer electronics, portable devices, POS, defense, and industrial control markets use TestQuest's non-intrusive test automation systems (such as the Validor Pro), its services, and its expertise to automate testing of software-based products. TestQuest's solutions help companies meet market demand for fail-proof functionality and reliability, comply with regulatory and other standards, and meet aggressive time-to-market objectives. 75 employees. Founded in 1983. In June 2000 B-Tree Systems changed its name to TestQuest to reflect the company's new focus on providing functional testing systems for information appliances, which are digital consumer electronics that provide access to the Internet. Examples of these devices are Internet gaming consoles, NetTVs, Internet smart handheld devices, Web terminals, e-mail terminals, and screenphones. Independent analyst IDC estimated that 28 million information appliances would be shipped in 2000. "These companies all make extremely complex products that require a high degree of user interaction," said CEO Hahn. "Add to that some incredible time-to-market pressures, where a week delay can make or break the company. Our legacy of expertise in functional testing puts us in a unique position to help these companies quickly identify interoperability and operational errors that would otherwise be found through labor-intensive manual testing or, worse yet, by an unhappy customer." SIC 7372.

Tharaldson Enterprises Inc. 1202 Westrac Dr., Fargo, ND 58103. Tel: 701/235-1060; Fax: 701/235-0948; Web site: http://www.tharaldson.com. Gary Tharaldson, Pres.; Rick Larson, VP-Devel. Annual revenue $247.2 million. Tharaldson Enterprises is the largest independent hotel/motel developer in the United States, with more than 325 properties in 27 states. Tharaldson manages all 325 hotels. Tharaldson is currently the nation's largest franchisee of Marriott Hotels and Choice Hotels International. 11,178 employees (675 in Minnesota; 9,572 part-time). Founded in 1982. SIC 7011.

Theisen Vending Inc. 3800 Nicollet Ave. S., Minneapolis, MN 55409. Tel: 612/827-5588; Fax: 612/827-7543. Thomas Theisen, Pres.; Michael Rugemer, Gen. Mgr.; Dale Lund, Op. Mgr. Theisen Vending provides vending, vending area services, kiddie rides, music, and games; and distributes bubble gum and bubble gum machines. Offices: International Falls and Grand Rapids, Minn. 60 employees (all in Minnesota). Founded in 1960. SIC 5962.

Thiele Technologies Inc. 7225 Bush Lake Rd., Edina, MN 55439. Tel: 952/835-2290; Fax: 952/835-5032; Web site: http://www.thieleengineering.com. Dr. Peter N.Y. Pan, Pres. and CEO. Thiele Technologies manufactures packaging machinery, including cartoners, casepackers, sleevers, placers, liquid and dry fillers, and special assembly machinery. 280 employees. Thiele Technologies manufactures packaging machinery at its Fergus Falls plant. with 98 employees. Founded in 1950. SIC 3565.

Thin Film Technology Corporation 1980 Commerce Dr., North Mankato, MN 56003. Tel: 507/625-8445; Fax: 507/625-3523; Web site: http://www.thin-film.com. H. Inoue, CEO and CFO; Michael Liu, Dir.-Sls./Mktg. Thin Film Technology Corp. is a manufacturer of electronic components, precision resistors, delay lines, surface-mount RCs, and surface-mount delay lines. 115 employees. Founded in 1982. In March 2000 the company divided $1.25 million in profits among its 115 employees—the largest cash distribution in company history. In August, based on its revenue growth from 1995 to 1999, the company was named to Deloitte & Touche's Minnesota Technology Fast 50. SIC 3679. No. 42 Minnesota Technology Fast 50.

Thomas Engineering Company 7024 Northland Dr., Brooklyn Park, MN 55428. Tel: 763/533-1501; Fax: 763/533-8091; Web site: http://www.thomasengineering.com. William J. Thomas, Chm.; Peter H. Voth, VChm. and CEO; Mark Erickson, Pres. and COO; Kent Mishler, Dir.-Mktg.; Tim Aberwild, VP; Sandra Reitsma, Dir.-Hum. Res./Admin.; Mike Gloudemons, Dir.-Prototype Div. Annual revenue $24 million. Thomas Engineering manufactures precision metal stampings for various industries. 140 employees (134 in Minnesota). Founded in 1962. SIC 3469.

Thompson Enterprises Inc. 401 W. 84th St., Bloomington, MN 55420. Tel: 952/703-8920; Fax: 952/703-8921; Web site: http://www.budgetpower.com. Scott Thompson, Chm., Pres., and CEO; Mike Greengard, CFO. Annual revenue $25 million. Thompson Enterprises is a holding company that owns Budget Power (six retail stores that sell plumbing, electrical, lighting, kitchens, and decorative products. 72 employees. Founded in 1929. SIC 5063.

Jeane Thorne Inc. 336 N. Robert St., St. Paul, MN 55101. Tel: 651/298-0400; Fax: 651/298-0448; Web site: http://www.jeanethorne.com. Mary Schmitz, CEO. Jeane Thorne Inc. is a full-service office-support, staffing, and training firm serving businesses and organizations in the Twin Cities: Mankato, Minn.; and Fargo, N.D. 658 employees. Founded in 1969. In May 2000 the company was presented a Crystal Clarion Award by the Twin Cities Chapter of the Association for Women in Communications for outstanding Web design. At the October 2000 American Staffing Association National Advertising Awards, the company was given Top Awards of Excellence in the categories of Newsletter, Web site, and Community Involvement. (Its annual charity golf tournament had raised $225,000 for St. Joseph's Home for Children in Minneapolis.) SIC 7363.

Thorson Inc. 4101 Bemidji Ave. N., Bemidji, MN 56601. Tel: 218/751-5413; Fax: 218/751-5462. W.T. Thorson, Pres. Thorson is a road construction company, specializing in highway construction, serving northwestern Minnesota. 150 employees (100 in Minnesota). Founded in 1967. SIC 1611.

Thrifty White Stores 10700 Highway 55 W., Plymouth, MN 55441. Tel: 763/513-4300; Fax: 763/513-4383. Mark R. Basco, SVP-Fin./Admin./MIS; Robert J. Narveson, Pres. and CEO; Gary Boehler, VP-Pharmacy/Health Care Svs.; Tim Erdle, VP-Mktg.; Jeff Lindoo, VP-Long Term Care; David Rueter, VP-Personnel. Annual revenue $124 million. Thrifty Drug Stores & White Drug Enterprises, dba Thrifty White Stores, operates conventional drugstores with pharmacies; and pharmacies in physician clinics and grocery stores. Thrifty also provides prescription services to several thousand nursing homes; and support services to independent pharmacy operators. 1,174 employees (709 in Minnesota; 565 part-time). Founded in 1957. SIC 5912. No. 99 CRM Private 100.

The Thymes Ltd. 420 N. Fifth St., Minneapolis, MN 55401. Tel: 612/338-4471; Fax: 612/338-3853. Leslie Ross, CEO. The Thymes Ltd. is a manufacturer of luxury scented bath and body products. 60 employees. Founded in 1982. SIC 2844.

Tiffany Fine Woods N37895 U.S. Highways 53 and 121, Whitehall, WI 54773. Tel: 715/538-4285; Fax: 715/538-4505. Jerome Tiffany, Pres. Tiffany Fine Woods produces ties, lumber, dimension, glued-up panels, kiln-dried lumber, hardwood components. 90 employees. Founded in 1973. SIC 2421.

The Tile Shop Inc. 14000 Carlson Pkwy., Plymouth, MN 55441. Tel: 763/541-1444; Fax: 763/541-1411; Web site: http://www.thetileshop.com. Bob Rucker, CEO; Rod Sill, COO; David Slough, Gen. Mgr.; Leigh Behrman, Cont. The Tile Shop is an importer, wholesaler, retailer, designer, and fabricator of ceramic, porcelain, and stone products. Store locations include: Bloomington, Roseville, Brooklyn Park, and Plymouth, Minn.; Milwaukee; Kansas City, Mo.; Detroit; Cincinnati; St. Louis; Indianapolis; and Chicago. 310 employees (80 in Minnesota; 8 part-time). Founded in 1984. SIC 1743, 3253, 5211.

Tiller Corporation 10633 89th Ave. N., P.O. Box 1480, Maple Grove, MN 55311. Tel: 763/425-4191; Fax: 763/425-7153; Web site: http://www.tillercorp.com. Gary B. Sauer, Pres.; Gaylen Ghylin, EVP; Thomas J. Hogan, VP-Admin. Tiller Corp.—also known as Barton Sand & Gravel Co., Commercial Asphalt Co., and Barton Enterprises Inc.—is a road construction materials supplier, specializing in construction sand, gravel, and hot-mix asphalt. 250 employees (all in Minnesota). Founded in 1960. SIC 1442, 2951.

Timberweld Manufacturing 1643 24th St., Billings, MT 59102. Tel: 406/652-3600; Fax: 406/652-3668. Joe Hucke, Pres. Timberweld manufactures and transports laminated structural wood beams and roof systems. 70 employees (1 in Minnesota; 2 part-time). Founded in 1956. SIC 2439.

The Tire Guys P.O. Box 23509, Billings, MT 59104. Tel: 406/245-4006; Fax: 406/245-0257. Chuck Patrick, Pres.; Earl Springer, VP; Trent Fuhrman, Treas.; Warren Patrick, Sec. Annual revenue $41 million. The Tire Guys (dba TIRE-RAMA) distributes tires, tubes, and auto accessories. 277 employees (50 part-time). Founded in 1977. SIC 5014, 5531.

Tiro Industries Inc. 2700 E. 28th St., Minneapolis, MN 55406. Tel: 612/721-6591; Fax: 612/722-1464. Robert O. Vaa, Pres.; Wallace R. Hlavac, EVP. Tiro Industries offers contract packaging and private labeling of cosmetics and chemical specialties to customers ranging from Fortune 50 companies to small salon chains. Its services include concept development, R&D, manufacturing, packaging, warehousing, and shipping. Products include a full range of hair- and skin-care items, plus over-the-counter drugs for both professional salons and retail customers. The company has three manufacturing sites and four warehouses in the Twin Cities, and also operates a 300,000-square-foot manufacturing facility in HaiFeng, China. 3,150 employees (650 in Minnesota). Founded in 1970. In December 1999 Tiro completed the purchase of a 25-acre, 475,000-square-foot manufacturing facility in Fridley, Minn., from The Lamaur Corp. (OTCBB: LMAR) for $13.25 million in cash plus the assumption of certain capital leases. In a related outsourcing agreement, Tiro agreed to manufacture products for, and lease space to, Lamaur. SIC 2844.

Toltz, King, Duvall, Anderson & Associates 444 Cedar St., St. Paul, MN 55101. Tel: 651/292-4400; Fax: 651/292-0083. Darrel H. Berkowitz, Chm. and CEO; Richard N. Sobiech, Pres.; Robert A. Boyer, SVP. TKDA is a consulting engineering and architectural firm providing professional design services to industrial, commercial, institutional, and governmental clients throughout the Midwest. 192 employees (7 part-time). Founded in 1910. SIC 8711, 8712.

Toolkraft Inc. 7500 Commerce Ln., Fridley, MN 55432. Tel: 763/571-7480; Fax: 763/571-9025. Roger Zbikowski, VP; Mark Opsahl, Sls. Mgr.; Margaret Loyo, Fin. Mgr.; Edward Keyport, Program Mgr.; Larry Kranz, Mfg. Mgr. Toolkraft manufactures butterfly valves, flow-selector valves, precision tools, precision production CNC machining, and experimental and prototype machining. 52 employees. Founded in 1965. SIC 3494, 3544.

Torrance Casting Inc. 3131 Commerce St., La Crosse, WI 54603. Tel: 608/781-0600; Fax: 608/781-2333. William A. Torrance, Pres.; Mary K. Affeldt, Sec. and Treas. Annual revenue $6.8 million. Torrance Casting produces gray, ductile, and ni-hard iron castings and provides powder coating services for industries throughout the country. 76 employees (10 in Minnesota; 2 part-time). Founded in 1876. SIC 3321.

Total Solutions Group Inc. 1101 E. 78th St., Suite 100, Bloomington, MN 55420. Tel: 952/831-8320; Fax: 952/831-0509; Web site: http://www.tsg-usa.com. Horace Allen, Founder and Ptnr.; Jon Mrkonich, Founder and Ptnr.; Rick Ross, Ptnr.; Jeff Vance, Ptnr. Total Solutions Group (TSG) provides computer sales, integration, and training. TSG is IBM's exclusive trainer in the Upper Midwest. A company-sponsored program, TSG University, provides free computer training to economically disadvantaged people seeking marketable job skills. 65 employees. Founded in 1993. In June 2000 TSG sold its e-business consulting practice to netASPx, a Herndon, Va.-based e-business application service provider. SIC 5045, 7371.

Town Pump Inc. 600 S. Main, Butte, MT 59701. Tel: 406/497-6700; Fax: 406/723-9533. Thomas F. Kenneally, Pres.; Daniel J. Kenneally, Gen. Mgr.; James M. Kenneally, Dir.-Supply/Distrib.; Bill Hohler, Purch. Mgr.-Stores; Lee Terry, Op. Mgr.-Stores; Cathy McDonald, Op. Mgr.-Motels. Town Pump operates 65 convenience stores in Montana. It also engages in real estate, trucking, petroleum wholesaling, and runs eight motels in Montana. 1,550 employees. Founded in 1952. SIC 6719.

Tradehome Shoe Stores Inc. 429 Prior Ave. N., St. Paul, MN 55104. Tel: 651/646-1345; Fax: 651/646-2705. Donald A. Mains, Co-owner, Chm., and CEO; Harold J. Smith, Co-owner and VChm.; Pat Teal, Pres. and COO. Tradehome Shoe Stores operates full-service family shoe stores in smaller communities in Iowa, Minnesota, Nebraska, North Dakota, South Dakota, Michigan, Kansas, Wyoming, Colorado, and Wisconsin. Despite offers from competitors willing to pay a premium price, Mains and Smith sold the chain at book value to nine key executives in February 1999. 250 employees (150 in Minnesota). Founded in 1921. SIC 5661.

Trail King Industries Inc. 300 E. Norway Ave., Mitchell, SD 57301. Tel: 605/996-6482; Fax: 605/996-4727; Web site: http://www.trailking.com. Jerry Thomsen, Pres.; Charles Noel, VP-Fin.; Lennie Stulc, VP-Mfg. Op.; Steven J. Ford, Sec. and Treas. Annual revenue $108.7 million. Trail King Industries manufactures a complete line of equipment trailers (from 5,000- to 1 million-lb. capacity). Trail King's dealer network includes all 50 states and Canada. 770 employees (2 in Minnesota; 10 part-time). Founded in 1974. SIC 3715.

Tran Electronics Company Inc. 82 Second Ave. S.E., New Brighton, MN 55112. Tel: 651/636-6286; Fax: 651/631-2755. Hoa V. Tran, Pres.; Hoang C. Tran, VP; Dzung C. Tran, VP-Op. Tran Electronics Co. is an electronics contract manufacturer that provides such electronic assembly services as prototype, quick turn, and long term. Capabilities include surface-mount technology, PCMCIA, B&A (ball grid array), fine pitch (12 mils), double-sided, and through-hole technology. The company has a 20,000-square-foot facility equipped with Fuji and Zevatech equipment. 80 employees. Founded in 1979. SIC 3679.

Treasure Island Resort & Casino P.O. Box 75, Red Wing, MN 55066. Tel: 800/222-7077; Fax: 612/385-2560; Web site: http://www.treasureislandcasino.com. Dr. Neil Cornelius, Gen. Mgr.; Darrell Campbell, Tribal Council Treas.; Kevin Shepard, Support Svs. Dir.; Gloria Mistek, Fin. Dir.; Armin Prasch, Hospitality Dir.; Joel Ingram, Info. Sys. Dir.; Barry Joannides, Casino Op. Dir.; Audrey Kohnen, Tribal Council Pres.; Nick Kootsikas, Sls./Mktg. Dir.; Lu Taylor, Tribal Council Sec.; Doreen Hagen, Asst. Sec./Treas. Tribal Council; Deb White, Security Dir.; Noah White Jr., Tribal Council VP; Don Whitebear, Hum. Res. Dir. Treasure Island is an Indian gaming casino and bingo hall operated by the Mdewakanton Dakota community. Located on the banks of the Mississippi River in southeastern Minnesota, Treasure Island offers nationally top-rated blackjack on 64 tables; a mix of more than 2,400 slots; a 250-room Caribbean-themed hotel featuring a tropical pool; a New Horizon child care facility; a 137-slip marina and RV park; and nationally recognized entertainment. It is the largest employer in Goodhue County. 1,515 employees (1,217 in Minnesota; 277 part-time). Founded in 1984. In May 2000 the Prairie Island Indian Community filed suit against the operators of Mirage Resorts in Las Vegas for using the name "Treasure Island" for one of its casinos. The tribe was seeking damages of up to $250 million. SIC 7993, 7999.

Trend Enterprises Inc. 300 Ninth Ave. S.W., New Brighton, MN 55112. Tel: 651/631-2850; Fax: 651/582-3500. Kay Fredericks, Pres. and CEO. Annual revenue $30 million. Trend Enterprises is a designer and publisher of children's educational materials for home and school (preschool to eighth grade). Among the 1,600 products it creates for 43 countries: display materials and decorative cutouts, flash cards and games, stickers, awards, and related items. 151 employees (146 in Minnesota; 3 part-time). Founded in 1968. SIC 2731, 2759.

Tri-Mart Corporation 4603 Domain Dr., Menomonie, WI 54751. Tel: 715/235-2151; Fax: 715/235-1643. Dan Uetz, Pres.; Richard Heitkamp, VP and Dir.-Op. Annual revenue $32 million. Tri-Mart Corp. is a wholesale distributor of snacks, refreshments, tobacco, and grocery items. 77 employees (9 part-time). Founded in 1975. SIC 5149, 5194.

TriMin Systems Inc. 3030 Centre Pointe Dr., Suite 100, Roseville, MN 55113. Tel: 651/636-7667; Fax: 651/636-9932. William W. Metzger, Owner and Pres.; William P. Mori, VP and Sec.; Paul J. Halvorson, Dir.-Mktg. TriMin Systems Inc. provides technological support to manufacturing companies and government organizations through the sales, service, and support of IBM hardware, MAPICS, and government software and services. 83 employees. Founded in 1986. SIC 7371, 7372.

Trollhagen 2232 100th Ave., Dresser, WI 54009. Tel: 715/755-2955; Fax: 715/294-4091. James Rochford, Pres. Trollhagen is a ski resort with a year-round restaurant and a 600-seat convention center. 75 employees (300 part-time). Founded in 1950. SIC 5812, 7011.

Tru-Part Manufacturing Corporation 200 Lothenbach Ave., West St. Paul, MN 55118. Tel: 651/455-6681; Fax: 651/450-8810. Tom Laird, Pres. and CEO; L.W. Templeton, VP and Gen. Mgr.; Buddy Howell, VP-Materials Mgmt.; Mike Spear, VP-Sls.; Tom Griep, VP-Fin. and CFO. Tru-Part Manufacturing is a wholesale distributor of all makes of agricultural tractor and implement parts and components. Primary customers are retail farm equipment dealers and repair shops. Tru-Part services its more than 10,000 accounts from distribution centers in St. Paul; Dallas; Nashville, Tenn.; Richmond, Va.; and Sacramento, Calif. 311 employees (125 in Minnesota). Founded in 1937. SIC 5083.

Truman Farmers Elevator Company 233 W. Ciro, Truman, MN 56088. Tel: 507/776-2831; Fax: 507/776-2871. Allen Brudelie, Pres.; Brian Hendrickson, Sec.; Jeffrey Hoppe, VP. Truman Farmers Elevator Co. is a farmer-owned farm supply cooperative with two John Deere implement dealerships, a feed mill and grain elevator, two fertilizer plants, a lumberyard, a plumbing and heating department, and a convenience store. Other facility locations: Fairmont, Grenada, and Lewisville, Minn. 179 employees (96 part-time). Founded in 1903. SIC 2873, 5083, 5171, 5211, 5411.

Tuohy Furniture Corporation 42 St. Alban Place, Chatfield, MN 55923. Tel: 507/867-4280; Fax: 507/867-4303. F. Mike Tuohy, Chm. and CEO; Daniel J. Tuohy, Pres. and COO; Michael P. Tuohy, VP; Gregory Eichton, Treas. Annual revenue $28 million. Tuohy Furniture manufactures solid-wood executive office furniture and contract furniture. It also deals in forest products. 250 employees (200 in Minnesota). Founded in 1952. SIC 2521, 2531.

Turkey Store Company 34 N. Seventh St., Barron, WI 54812. Tel: 715/537-3131; Fax: 715/537-9446. Jerry Jerome, CEO; Mike Nelms, Pres.; Gregg Gleichert, EVP; Raj Kaul, EVP-Revenue; Dick Pajula, VP-Fin. Turkey Store Co. is a vertically integrated producer, processor, and marketer of fresh turkey products, principally under the brand name The Turkey Store. The company now includes two processing facilities, one hatchery, three feed mills, over 60 breeder and grow-out farms and support facilities. 2,700 employees (600 in Minnesota). Founded in 1945. In January 2000 the company was one of 51 companies nominated for the 1999 Wisconsin Manufacturer of the Year Award. SIC 2015.

Tursso Companies Inc. 223 Plato Blvd. E., St. Paul, MN 55107. Tel: 651/222-8445; Fax: 651/225-6790. Dennis J. Tursso, Chm. and CEO; Bruce Rankin, Pres.; Cary Stewart, Cont. Annual revenue $20 million. Tursso Cos. is a holding company. Divisions include Printing Specialties, Blackbourn Systems, Fast Packaging, Graphics Resources Center, Product Engineering Inc., and Multi-Graphics. Tursso has 40,000-square-foot plants in St. Paul and in Fort Dodge, Iowa. 150 employees (110 in Minnesota). Founded in 1970. SIC 2741, 2752, 2759.

Turtle Mountain Corporation-A Pemstar Company 380 Oak Grove Pkwy., Suite 116, Vadnais Heights, MN 55127. Tel: 651/481-1427; Fax: 651/481-7253; Web site: http://www.turtlemtn.com. John E. Miller, Pres.; Robert F. Wilmot, VP; Patricia A. Miller, Cont.; Jeanne Lovick, Purch. Mgr.; Michael J. Miller, Dir.-MIS/Materials; Michael Kelly, Sls./Mktg. Turtle Mountain Corp. is an ISO 9002-registered, full-service contract manufacturer of printed circuit assemblies, power supplies, cable and wire harnesses, and complete electronic assemblies. 275 employees (15 in Minnesota). Founded in 1974. Purchased by Pemstar Company in August. SIC 3672.

Twin City Co-ops Federal Credit Union 2680 Arthur St., Roseville, MN 55113. Tel: 651/215-3450; Fax: 651/215-3576; Web site: http://www.tcuconnect.com. John G. Gisler, Pres. and CEO; Jim Chamberlain, VP-Tech./Facilities; Louis Doering, VP-Bus. Devel./Training/Staff Devel.; Kris Rasmussen, VP-Hum. Res./Mktg.; Mike Schrader, VP-Member Svs.; Dan Stoltz, VP-Fin. Twin City Co-ops is a federal credit union that provides financial cooperative banking. 147 employees (13 part-time). The company was voted Best Bank in City Pages' 1999 "Best Of" feature. SIC 6111.

Twin City Die Castings Company 1070 33rd Ave. S.E., Minneapolis, MN 55414. Tel: 612/645-3611; Fax: 612/645-0724. James D. Harmon, Chm.; Steven J. Harmon, Pres.; Douglas D. Harmon, VP-Fin. Annual revenue $40 million. Twin City Die Castings is a custom manufacturer of zinc and aluminum die castings machined complete. It has plants in Minneapolis; in Watertown, S.D.; and in Monticello, Minn. 325 employees (190 in Minnesota; 2 part-time). Founded in 1919. In 2000 the company built a $2.5 million plant in Monticello as its first venture into magnesium parts, which were growing in demand because of their strength and light weight. SIC 3356, 3363.

Twin City Fan Companies Ltd. 5959 Trenton Ln. N., Plymouth, MN 55442. Tel: 763/551-7600; Fax: 763/551-7601; Web site: http://www.tcf.com. Charles Barry, Chm. and CEO; Zika Srejovic, VChm.; Michael Barry, Pres. and COO. Annual revenue $104 million. Twin City Fan Cos., Ltd. (dba Twin City Fan & Blower, TC Axial, Aerovent, TC Ventco, Clarage, etc.) manufactures centrifugal and axial fans. It has four plants in South Dakota—in Brookings (opened in 1984), Mitchell (1988), Aberdeen (1993), and Elkton (1998)—and one in Birmingham, Ala. (1997). 900 employees (150 in Minnesota; 35 part-time). Founded in 1974. In April 2000 the company signed a manufacturing cooperation agreement with ZVVZ Co., Milevsko, Czech Republic, to manufacture certain Twin City Fan products. The agreement allows Twin City Fan to supply its equipment to European markets. SIC 3564.

Twin City Wire—MFI P.O. Box 21068, Eagan, MN 55121. Tel: 651/454-8835; Fax: 651/454-7073. Eugene Lentsch, Chm. and Pres.; James A. Fischer, VP; Gregory J. Lentsch, Sec.; David Lentsch, VP and Treas. Twin City Wire—MFI (formerly Minnesota Fence & Iron Works Inc.) performs metal fabrication and wire cloth weaving. 75 employees (5 part-time). Founded in 1869. SIC 3446, 3496.

UFE Inc. 1850 S. Greeley St., P.O. Box 7, Stillwater, MN 55082. Tel: 651/351-4100; Fax: 651/351-4101. Orville D. Johnson, Chm.; Martin N. Kellogg, Pres. and CEO; Roger L. King, VP-Admin. and CFO; Lelan Jamison, Injection Molding; Keith Leary, Mold Mfg.; Robert Sirany, Prod. Engrg.; Thomas Wollisch, Contract Mfg. Annual revenue $80 million. UFE is a professional engineering and precision contract manufacturing services supplier of product design services, injection molds, molded precision mechanical components, and finished assemblies. Markets served: automotive, health care, and technology industries. Production systems employ project management, computer-assisted manufacturing, automation, and statistical process capability technologies. Toolmaking plants in Minnesota and Singapore; production plants in Mexico, Minnesota, Texas, Wisconsin, and Singapore. 780 employees (150 in Minnesota). Founded in 1953. SIC 3089.

UMC Inc. 22510 W. Highway 55, Hamel, MN 55340. Tel: 763/478-6609; Fax: 763/478-6483. Terrance W. Tomann, CEO; Don Tomann, VP. Annual revenue $9 million. UMC is an ISO 9002 certified company, dedicated to providing precision machined parts and assemblies for the medical and aerospace industries. UMC's capabilities include CNC Turning, CNC Milling, Wire DM, and Swiss Turning. 90 employees (all in Minnesota). Founded in 1968. SIC 3599.

USLink Inc. 30925 Second St., P.O. Box 327, Pequot Lakes, MN 56472. Tel: 218/568-4000; Web site: http://www.uslink.com. USLink is a local and long-distance carrier and reseller that provides facilities-based local service, resale local service, Internet, long-distance, voicemail, TI, PRI, 800 lines, and travel cards to the metro area, greater Minnesota, and North Dakota. 178 employees. Founded in 1985. SIC 4813.

U.S. Transformer Inc. 1000 Syndicate St., P.O. Box 98, Jordan, MN 55352. Tel: 952/492-2720; Fax: 952/492-2796. Bruce Nygren, Pres.; K. Kampshoff, CEO. U.S. Transformer remanufactures, rewinds, and repairs electrical power substation transformers from 1KVA to 300 MVA. 120 employees (50 in Minnesota). Founded in 1973. SIC 3612.

Uni-Select USA 2525 Fairview Ave. N., Roseville, MN 55113. Tel: 651/633-8111; Fax: 651/633-0533. Gary Kremer, Pres. Annual revenue $62.8 million. Uni-Select USA distributes motor vehicle supplies and new parts. 91 employees (37 in Minnesota). Founded in 1979. SIC 5013.

Unimax Systems Corporation 430 First Ave. N., Suite 790, Minneapolis, MN 55401. Tel: 612/341-0946; Fax: 612/338-5436; Web site: http://www.unimax.com. Margaret Loftus, Acting CEO; Andrew Hunkins, Pres. and Chief Tech. Officer; John Murphy, CFO; Janet Jaszewski, Mktg. Mgr. Unimax Systems Corp. designs and develops configuration management software for multivendor telecommunications systems: PBX systems, voicemail systems, and the emerging computer telephony industry. Unimax's 2nd Nature architecture is used to create software products that interoperate in a heterogeneous telecommunications environment. The company's partners include many of the largest telecommunications with manufacturers worldwide, including Octel, Intercom, and Philips. 50 employees. In August 2000 Unimax announced that Avaya Communication (formerly the Enterprise Networks Group of Lucent Technologies) was planning to include Mailbox Manager software in shipments of its Intuity AUDIX MAP 40 and 100 voice and fax message servers. Based on its revenue growth from 1995 to 1999, the company was named to Deloitte & Touche's Minnesota Technology Fast 50. SIC 7372. No. 21 Minnesota Technology Fast 50.

United Auto Supply 625 S. Third St., La Crosse, WI 54601. Tel: 608/784-9198; Fax: 608/784-4760. Richard Beirne, Pres. and CEO; Greg Marnach, VP. United Auto Supply offers wholesale and retail auto parts and equipment through 10 stores and one automotive machine shop. 93 employees (4 in Minnesota; 6 part-time). Founded in 1958. SIC 5013.

United Gear and Assembly 1700 Livingstone Rd., Hudson, WI 54016. Tel: 715/386-5867; Fax: 715/386-6473; Web site: http://www.ugaco.com. Eugene S. Ziemba, Pres.; Mike Wodark, CFO; Markus Bieber, Dir.-Sls./Mktg. Annual revenue $20 million. United Gear and Assembly is a world-class manufacturer of gears, shafts, and related assemblies. The company has in-house heat-treating capabilities with available commercial capacity. 200 employees (30 in Minnesota). SIC 3714.

United Hardware Distributing Co. 5005 Nathan Ln., Plymouth, MN 55442. Tel: 763/559-1800; Fax: 763/557-2799; Web site: http://www.unitedhardware.com. Steven Draeger, Chm.; Wayne Cole, VChm.;

David A. Heider, Pres. and CEO; Robert Branton, VP-Sls.; Eugene Nimz, VP-Admin. Support; John Nitsche, VP-Fin. and CFO; Bradley Therrien, VP-Mdsg.; Dennis Swanson, Sec.; Keith Kock, VP-Retail Op. Annual revenue $155 million. United Hardware, a cooperative, is a wholesale distributor of hardware and allied lines to independent hardware stores, home centers, and lumberyards. The company is owned by approximately 475 Hardware Hank dealers. Non-shareholders operate as Trustworthy Hardware stores or Golden Rule Lumber Centers. United Hardware's distribution center is located in Milbank, S.D. 345 employees. Founded in 1945. SIC 5072. No. 16 CRM Cooperatives/Mutuals 20.

United Market Services Company 14500 Burnhaven Dr., Suite 141, Burnsville, MN 55337. Tel: 952/435-7788; Fax: 952/435-6797. Dean Bachelor, CEO; Mike Blair, Cont. United Market Services Co. is the nation's largest livestock marketing company. Its Stockyards Division owns and operates public livestock markets at Sioux Falls, S.D.; Sioux City, Iowa; Omaha, Neb.; St. Joseph, Mo.; and Milwaukee. Founded in 1989. SIC 5154.

United Properties 3500 W. 80th St., Suite 200, Bloomington, MN 55431. Tel: 952/831-1000; Fax: 952/893-8804; Web site: http://www.uproperties.com. Boyd B. Stofer, Pres. and CEO; Jeff Eaton, SVP; Gary Jackson, SVP; Larry Pobuda, SVP; Frank Dutke, SVP; Paul Hawkins, VP and Corp. Cont.; Mike Ohmes, VP-Brokerage Svs. United Properties is a full-service commercial real estate company with 23 million square feet of office, industrial, retail, and multifamily properties under management. The company specializes in diverse real estate services, including brokerage, property management, corporate real estate services, facilities management, construction management, development services, and investment services. 342 employees (296 in Minnesota). Founded in 1937. Formerly owned by The Northland Co. (E.H. Hamm family), the company was sold in 1999 to the Pohlad Cos. (Carl R. Pohlad family). SIC 6519, 6531.

United States Distilled Products Company 1607 S. 12th St., Princeton, MN 55371. Tel: 763/389-4903; Fax: 763/389-2549. Duane Maas, Pres.; Brad Johnson, VP. United States Distilled Products Co. formulates and bottles distilled products. 300 employees (50 part-time). Founded in 1981. SIC 2085.

United Sugars Corporation 7801 E. Bush Lake Rd., Suite 100, Bloomington, MN 55439. Tel: 952/896-0131; Fax: 952/896-0400. Thomas M. McKenna, Pres.; Catherine Maruska, SVP-Admin./Logistics; Richard Saylor, VP-Fin.; Dirk Swart, VP-Industrial Sls.; Brad Wiersum, VP-Sls./Mktg., Consumer Products; Paul Wengronowitz, Corp. Cont. United Sugars Corp., a grower-owned cooperative, is the sales and marketing arm of American Crystal Sugar, Moorhead, Minn.; Southern Minnesota Sugar Beet Cooperative, Renville, Minn.; and Minn-Dak Farmers Cooperative, Wahpeton, N.D. United has sales offices in Illinois, Connecticut, and California. It markets more than 20 percent of the entire domestic sugar supply. Reported revenue is allocated back to the owner cooperatives based on their production percentages for the current growing season. 100 employees (80 in Minnesota). Founded in 1994. SIC 5149.

Universal Cooperatives Inc. 1300 Corporate Center Curve, Eagan, MN 55122. Tel: 651/239-1000; Fax: 651/239-1009; Web site: http://www.ucoop.com. George Winstead, Chm.; Terrence Bohman, Pres. and CEO. Annual revenue $264 million (earnings $3.2 million). Universal Cooperatives manufactures, purchases, and distributes agricultural and farm supplies through the regional farm-supply cooperatives in the United States, Canada, Australia, New Zealand, and Europe. 750 employees (170 in Minnesota). Founded in 1972. July 31, 2000: Fiscal-year earnings nearly tripled, from $1.1 million to $3.2 million, due to improved results from key business areas and expansion with international partnerships. SIC 2298, 2879, 3011, 3523, 5083, 5191. No. 11 CRM Cooperatives/Mutuals 20.

Universal Hospital Services Inc. 1250 Northland Plaza, 3800 W. 80th St., Bloomington, MN 55431. Tel: 952/893-3200; Fax: 952/893-0704; Web site: http://www.uhs.com. David E. Dovenberg, Pres. and CEO; Andrew Amicon, VP-Disposable Sls./Alt. Care; Gerald Brandt, VP-Fin.; Robert Braun, SVP-Sls./Mktg.; Randy Engen, VP-Sls., East; John Gappa, SVP and CFO; Michael Johnson, VP-Admin.; Gary Preston, VP-Nat'l Accounts/Mktg.; Jeffrey Singer, VP-Purch./Logistics; Judy Slater, VP-Sls., West. Annual revenue $79.3 million (loss $5.1 million). Universal Hospital Services (UHS) provides movable medical equipment to more than 4,800 hospitals and alternate-care providers through a national network of 57 district offices and seven regional service centers. The 90,000 medical devices offered by UHS fall into four categories: critical care, monitoring, newborn care, and respiratory therapy. In February 1998 the company, which was then publicly traded, was acquired by J.W. Childs Equity Partners L.P. and certain members of UHS management for $133 million. 516 employees (125 in Minnesota; 31 part-time). Founded in 1939. Dec. 31, 1999: Annual rental revenue increased by 28.6 percent ($61.7 million to $79.3 million), while total revenue increased 32.9 percent ($69.4 million to $92.2 million) compared to the same period in 1998. Adjusted EBITDA increased to $35.9 million (38.9 percent of total revenue) from $30.1 million (43.4 percent of total revenue). The decline in EBITDA margin reflects price discounts associated with the several new and extended group contracts, and higher costs primarily related to integration of acquired companies and Y2K compliance. June 30, 2000: For the first six months of 2000, rental revenue grew 16.4 percent (from $39.4 million in 1999 to $45.8 million in 2000), while total revenue grew 14.4 percent. Year-to-date real growth, after giving effect to the Vital Choice acquisition, was 12.9 percent for rental revenue and 11.1 percent for total revenue. EBITDA was $20.8 million for the first half, versus $18.2 million last year. Sept. 30: For third quarter, real growth for the company, after giving effect to the Vital Choice acquisition, was 21.5 percent for rental revenue and 18.9 percent for total revenue. SIC 7352.

Universal Pensions Inc. 431 Golf Course Dr. N., P.O. Box 979, Brainerd, MN 56401. Tel: 218/829-4781; Fax: 218/825-5652; Web site: http://www.universal-pensions.com. Arnold S. Johnson, CEO; Thomas G. Anderson, Pres.; Steven Benson, VP-Sls.; David M. Lauer, VP; Kevin Clark, VP; Pamela S. O'Rourke, VP and Gen. Counsel; Scott Pearson, VP-Plan Svs.; Cynthia J. Roggenkamp, VP-Mktg.; Todd A. Headlee, Chief Info. Ofcr. Annual revenue $35 million. Universal Pensions Inc. (UPI) is the premier provider of retirement plan expertise, third party record keeping, and business solutions to the financial services industry. Headquarter in Brainerd, Minn., UPI combines leading edge technologies, retirement plan expertise (ERISA) and 25 years of industry experience to provide both stock and custom solutions needed by financial organizations to maintain compliance and build market share in the retirement plans market. 400 employees (380 in Minnesota; 15 part-time). Founded in 1975. In April 2000 UPI signed an agreement with leading Internet banking provider Digital Insight Corp. (Nasdaq: DGIN) to integrate UPI's IRA Service Center into Digital Insight's recently announced Web portal, AXIS eCommerce. The new IRA capability was to allow AXIS clients to use UPI's complete online IRA sales and service solution that includes electronic IRA forms for traditional, Roth, and eEducation IRAs; retirement planning and distribution calculators; and an education component. In October U.S. Bank selected Universal Pensions as the acquirer of a portion of the bank's Master Retirement Program. U.S. Bank was to continue to serve as trustee, with UPI assuming the processing services and providing supplemental support (training, 1-800 consulting services, reference resources, and compliance audits). SIC 7389.

Up North Plastics Inc. 9480 Jamaica Ave. S., P.O. Box 159, Cottage Grove, MN 55016. Tel: 651/734-6200; Fax: 651/734-6300. Ken Hull, Gen. Mgr. Up North Plastics manufactures polyethylene film. 250 employees (all in Minnesota). Founded in 1981. SIC 3081.

Upper Midwest Industries Inc. 2940 Weeks Ave. S.E., Minneapolis, MN 55414. Tel: 612/378-1071; Fax: 612/378-3249. David R. Carlsen, Chm. and CEO; Mark J. Olson, Div. Pres.; David J. Shusterich, Div. Pres.; Brian C. Beich, CFO; Mark R. Engel, Div. Pres.; Jeffrey E. Spethmann, Gen. Mgr. Annual revenue $42 million. Upper Midwest Industries is the parent APG Cash Drawer in Fridley, Minn. (Mark Olson, Pres.) of Atlas Manufacturing in Minneapolis (Mark Engel, Pres.); Spantek Division in Hopkins, Minn. and Coastal Expanded Metal, Inc. in Greensboro, NC. (Dave Shusterich, Pres.); and Blow Molded Specialities Inc. in Foley, MN (Jeff Spethmann, Gen Mgr.). The company is engaged in the fabrication of precision sheet metal, the manufacture of cash drawers and other point-of-sale equipment, the fabrication of precision sheet metal, the manufacture of expanded metal mesh, and the molding of industrial blow molded plastics. 350 employees (335 in Minnesota). Founded in 1981. In April 2000 a Hennepin County jury issued an advisory verdict against the company in favor of former CEO Craig Swanson in the amount of at least $2.5 million for the loss of his job in 1997. Judge John Sommerville must decide whether to accept or reject the advisory jury verdict in final judgement. As of September, the court had not made its final judgement. If judgement is against Upper Midwest Industries, the company plans an appeal. SIC 3089, 3444, 3449, 3579.

Upsher-Smith Laboratories Inc. 14905 23rd Ave. N., Plymouth, MN 55447. Tel: 763/473-4412; Fax: 763/476-4026. Kenneth L. Evenstad, Chm. and CEO; Paul Kralovec, VP-Fin.; Ian Troup, Pres. and COO. Upsher-Smith is a family-owned company that manufactures and markets finished pharmaceutical dosage forms—including the anti-arrhythmic medication Pacerone, the first bio-equivalent alternative brand for Wyeth-Ayerst's widely prescribed Cordarone. The company, known for its quality, value, and innovation, prides itself on providing affordable alternatives to existing pharmaceutical products. 283 employees (10 part-time). Founded in 1919. In November 1999 Upsher-Smith was recognized by the Financial Times Global Pharmaceutical Awards as having one of the top four 1998 product launches in the world. In less than a year, its Pacerone product had captured a 50 percent market share and more than doubled Upsher-Smith's revenue. In May 2000 the company was selected by the Minnesota Chapter of the Society of Financial Service Professionals, from more than 100 nominations, for a Minnesota American Business Ethics Award. The company received FDA approval to market NIACOR (NIACIN Tablets, USP), 500 mg immediate-release, as an adjunct to diet for the reduction of elevated total and LDL cholesterol levels in patients with primary hypercholesterolemia. In June Upsher-Smith announced plans for a 17,300-square-foot addition to its corporate headquarters. The new facility was to provide much-needed manufacturing space. SIC 2834.

PVT

Urban Retreat 1609 W. Lake St., Minneapolis, MN 55408. Tel: 612/827-5595. Thomas Schmidt, CEO; Jeffrey Lillemoe, Pres.; Jon Chartes Phau, Dir.-Styling/Color Depts. Annual revenue $2.9 million. Urban Retreat is a full-service hair salon and day spa specializing in upscale services and unique retail. Owned by Tom Schmidt & Associates Inc. 62 employees (all in Minnesota; 18 part-time). Founded in 1974. SIC 7231. No. 48 CityBusiness Fastest-growing Private Companies.

Valdak Corporation 1149 36th Ave. S., Grand Forks, ND 58201. Tel: 701/746-8371; Fax: 701/780-9286. Norman R. Dufault, Pres.; Monica Musich, Pres.; Kathy Cummins, VP; M. Schmidt, VP. Annual revenue $10 million. Valdak operates retail convenience stores and carwashes. 120 employees. Founded in 1956. SIC 5999.

Valley Craft Inc. 2001 S. Highway 61, Lake City, MN 55041. Tel: 651/345-3386; Fax: 651/345-3606; Web site: http://www.valleycraft.com. Roger Hollman, Gen. Mgr.; Dan Johnson, Sls./Mktg. Mgr.; Glenn Dwelle, Mfg. Engrg. Mgr. Annual revenue $17 million. Valley Craft manufactures materials-handling equipment, furniture, and OEM products. Owned by Liberty Diversified Industries, Minneapolis. 180 employees (all in Minnesota; 4 part-time). Founded in 1950. SIC 3449, 3599.

Valley Forest Resources Inc. 48985 State Highway 38, Marcell, MN 56657. Tel: 218/832-3611; Fax: 218/832-3610. Robert M. Linsmayer, Pres.; James A. Luzum, Treas.; Wendell Freeberg, VP and Sec. Valley Forest Resources manufactures aspen furniture-grade KD lumber; pallet lumber and cants; pallet cut-stock; aspen fiber pellets for fuel, cat litter, cattle feed, horse bedding, research, and zoo animals; and "ultra-dri" incinerable absorbent. Affiliated with Villaume Industries Inc., Eagan, Minn. 65 employees. Founded in 1952. SIC 2048, 2421, 2448.

Valley Oldsmobile-Pontiac-GMC 7500 W 145th St., Apple Valley, MN 55124. Tel: 952/432-9500; Fax: 952/953-2186. Bernie Wagnild, Pres.; Jim Paul, VP and Gen. Mgr. Valley Olds is a dealer of new and used vehicles including Oldsmobile, Pontiac, and GMC. 91 employees (all in Minnesota). Founded in 1985. SIC 5511.

Van Dyke Supply Company Inc. P.O. Box 278, Woonsocket, SD 57385. Tel: 605/796-4425; Fax: 605/796-4085. Jim Cabela, Pres. Annual revenue $16.5 million. Van Dyke Supply Co. Inc. is a mail-order company for taxidermy and antique furniture restoration supplies. 200 employees (15 in Minnesota). Founded in 1948. SIC 3299.

Vanity Inc. P.O. Box 547, Fargo, ND 58107. Tel: 701/237-3330; Fax: 701/235-6789. Jim McLeod, Pres.; Rick Olson, EVP; Collette Bottrell, EVP. Vanity operates junior clothing stores. 1,200 employees (300 in Minnesota; 600 part-time). Founded in 1966. SIC 5621.

Versa Companies 867 Forest St., St. Paul, MN 55106. Tel: 651/778-3300; Fax: 651/778-1321; Web site: http://www.versaco.com. John W. Moffat, Chm. and Pres.; Floyd Anderson, Pres.-Versa Iron and Machine; Philip Bear, Pres.-Versa Die Cast; Kevin Johnsrud, CFO and Pres.-Versa Electronics. Versa Cos. (formerly Northern Malleable Iron Co.) owns Northern Iron Corp., which produces ductile, malleable, gray, and tempered iron castings; Northern Machining Corp., which provides numerically controlled precision machining; and Versa Die Cast Inc. (formerly Rosemount Die Castings Corp.), which produces aluminum die castings. 200 employees. Founded in 1906. SIC 3321, 3364, 3365, 3599.

Ver-Sa-Til Associates Inc. 18400 W. 77th St., Chanhassen, MN 55317. Tel: 952/949-2400; Fax: 952/949-9072. Darrell Tamosuinas, Pres. and CEO; Bill Hickey, Mktg. Mgr. Ver-Sa-til Associates manufactures precision machine parts and assemblies. 100 employees (all in Minnesota). Founded in 1966. SIC 3599.

Viking Acoustical 21480 Heath Ave., Lakeville, MN 55044. Tel: 952/469-3405; Fax: 952/469-4503. Bret Starkweather, CEO; James Thompson, VP. Viking Acoustical manufactures office furniture, acoustical enclosures, office seating, and ergonomic accessories. 74 employees (63 in Minnesota). Founded in 1974. SIC 2522, 2541.

Viking Automatic Sprinkler Company 1301 L'Orient St., St. Paul, MN 55117. Tel: 651/558-3300; Fax: 651/558-3310. Ronald L. Harris, Pres.; Brian Wetterlind, VP-Purch. Mgr.; Lester Steichen, VP-Svc. Mgr.; Quintin Rubald, CFO. Viking Automatic Sprinkler assembles, designs, installs, services, and inspects fire protection sprinkler systems in commercial and industrial buildings. It is the largest fire-protection company in the Upper Midwest. Owned since 1946 by the APi Group, Roseville, Minn. 650 employees. Founded in 1924. SIC 1711, 3569.

Viking Collection Service 7500 Office Ridge Cir., Suite 100, Eden Prairie, MN 55344. Tel: 952/944-7575; Fax: 952/944-0556. Gene Kloeckner, CEO; Donald Corll, Pres. Viking Collection Service is a credit-card collection service. 90 employees (1 part-time). Founded in 1973. SIC 7322.

Viking Drill & Tool Inc. 355 State St., P.O. Box 65278 (55165), St. Paul, MN 55107. Tel: 651/227-8911; Fax: 651/227-1793; Web site: http://www.viking-norsemen.com. J.L. Knight, Chm., Pres., and CEO; Lou Bloch, VP-Sls./Mktg.; Dennis Jungemann, VP-Engrg.; Mary Lou Linder, VP-Hum. Res.; Anita Meyers, VP and Cont.; Denny Nyhus, VP-Mfg. Annual revenue $29.2 million. Viking Drill & Tool manufactures twist drills. Brand names include Viking, Norseman, and Ultra-Cut. 230 employees (229 in Minnesota; 22 part-time). Founded in 1952. SIC 3545.

Viking Engineering & Development Inc. 5750 Main St. N.E., Fridley, MN 55432. Tel: 763/571-2400; Fax: 763/586-1319; Web site: http://www.vikingeng.com. Donald Hewitt, Chm.; Dean Bodem, Pres.; Lawton Cain, VP-Sls./Mktg.; Barbara Wenner, VP-Op.; John Engelbert, VP-Fin. Viking Engineering designs and manufactures automatic nailing machines and related equipment for the wooden pallet and forest products industries. Viking is an ESOP company. 100 employees (82 in Minnesota). Founded in 1975. SIC 3559.

Viking Materials Inc. 3225 Como Ave. S.E., Minneapolis, MN 55414. Tel: 612/623-8060; Fax: 612/623-9070; Web site: http://www.vikingmaterials.com. Allen Applegate, Chm. and CEO; Craig Sauer, Pres. and COO; Doug Lilyquist, VP and CFO. Annual revenue $92 million. Viking Materials Inc. is a steel service center, distributing flat rolled carbon steel. Viking also has a branch in Franklin Park, Ill. 150 employees (90 in Minnesota). Founded in 1973. SIC 5051.

Villaume Industries Inc. 2926 Lone Oak Circle, Eagan, MN 55121. Tel: 651/454-3610; Fax: 651/454-8556; Web site: http://www.villaume.com. J. Nicholas Linsmayer, Pres. and CEO; Issac Ganz, VP; C.J. McMahon, VP; James A. Luzum, Cont. and Treas. Villaume manufactures housing components, including roof and floor trusses, and industrial wood products (boxes, crates, pallets, and specialty items). 140 employees (all in Minnesota). Founded in 1882. SIC 2439, 2448, 2449.

Viromed Laboratories Inc. 6101 Blue Circle Dr., Eden Prairie, MN 55343. Tel: 952/931-0077; Fax: 952/939-4215; Web site: http://www.viromed.com. Bonita L. Baskin, Ph.D., CEO; Bob Fogerson, COO; Dean Enrooth, VP-Bus. Devel.; William Smith, CFO; Neal T. Wetherall, Ph.D., Scientific Dir. Viromed Laboratories is a state-of-the-art medical reference laboratory offering specialized testing services for the clinical, tissue bank, medical device, biotech, pharmaceutical, and chemical germicide industries. 350 employees (280 in Minnesota; 40 part-time). Founded in 1982. SIC 8071.

Harvey Vogel Manufacturing Co. 425 Weir Dr., Woodbury, MN 55125. Tel: 651/739-7373; Fax: 651/739-8666; Web site: http://www.harveyvogel.com. H. Charles Vogel Jr., Chm. and CEO; William Birmingham, VP-Fin.; Bob Verhey, VP-Op. Annual revenue $16 million. Harvey Vogel Manufacturing Co. produces short- to medium- and long-run metal stampings, and provides subassembly and final assembly. 135 employees (114 in Minnesota). Founded in 1942. SIC 3469.

Vomela Specialty Company Inc. 274 E. Fillmore, St. Paul, MN 55107. Tel: 651/228-2200; Fax: 651/228-2295. Thomas L. Auth, Chm.; David DeGree, Pres.; Sharon Schmidt, VP; Jim Cline, VP; Joe Hendershot, Sls. Dir. Vomela Specialty has three main divisions: Image Graphics, which uses both traditional and high-tech digital systems to make color graphics for fleet use, buses, institutions, graphic designers, ad agencies, event marketers, architects, and others; OEM Graphics, which makes identification graphics for sports and leisure products such as motor homes, travel trailers, and snowmobiles; and Engineering Services, which provides a wide range of custom converting for specialized industrial services. One of the country's largest manufacturers of 3M Scotchprint Graphics, Vomela has two plants in St. Paul and sales offices around the country. 175 employees. Founded in 1947. In October 2000 the company acquired Trenmark, a La Miranda, Calif.-based graphics firm. SIC 2671, 2675.

Von Ruden Manufacturing Inc. 1008 N.E. First St., P.O. Box 699, Buffalo, MN 55313. Tel: 763/682-3122; Fax: 763/682-3954. Algerone L. (Al) Anderson, Pres. and CEO. Von Ruden designs, markets, fabricates, assembles, and tests drive components. The company manufactures fluid-power products (hydraulic motors, brakes, and planetary gear boxes), and also mechanical products (right-angle-bevel gearboxes, parallel shaft reducers, and bearing blocks). The company also custom designs, tests, and manufactures piece parts and assemblies. 74 employees. Founded in 1946. SIC 3566, 3594.

PVT

W&G Transport 7700 23rd Ave. S., Minneapolis, MN 55450. Tel: 612/726-9178; Fax: 612/794-9475; Web site: http://www.wgtransport.com. David Gorman, Pres.; George Wessin, Sec.; Robert Book, CFO and Treas. W&G Transport is an on-call courier that handles air express. 850 employees (350 in Minnesota; 50 part-time). Founded in 1973. SIC 4513.

WR Medical Electronics Company 123 N. Second St., Stillwater, MN 55082. Tel: 651/430-1200; Fax: 651/439-9733. Patrick J. Anderson, Pres.; James Nelson, VP-Mktg.; Paul J. Anderson, VP-Res./Devel. WR Medical Electronics Co. is a manufacturer of specialty medical devices. 50 employees (all in Minnesota; 5 part-time). Founded in 1962. SIC 3845, 3999.

Wagers Business Systems Inc. 1955 University Ave. W., St. Paul, MN 55104. Tel: 651/644-3830; Fax: 651/644-2315. Ron Stainer, Pres.; Gerald Burns, VP; Jon Christine, VP-Bus. Imaging Solutions; Tim Condon, Cont. Wagers is a retailer of office copiers, fax machines, computers, furniture, and supplies. 104 employees. Founded in 1903. SIC 5021, 5044, 5045, 5112.

Walbon & Company 4230 Pine Bend Trail, Rosemount, MN 55068. Tel: 651/437-2011; Fax: 651/437-2087. Tom D. Walbon, Pres.; Darby R. Walbon, VP; Richard I. Walbon, Shop Foreman; Thom Sheridan, Op. Dir.; Skip Phillips, Southern Sls. Mgr.; Kathy Baggenstoss, Office Mgr.; Glenn Kasel, Safety Supervisor. Annual revenue $12 million. Walbon & Co. performs for-hire trucking. 145 employees (56 in Minnesota; 30 part-time). Founded in 1976. SIC 4213.

Wall Drug Store Inc. 510 Main St., P.O. Box 401, Wall, SD 57790. Tel: 605/279-2175; Fax: 605/279-2699. Ted Hustead, Pres.; Rick

Hustead, Chm. Wall Drug Store is a pharmacy, souvenir shop, and restaurant complex selling clothing, boots, jewelry, original art, books, and related items. 250 employees (150 part-time). Founded in 1931. SIC 5812, 5912, 5947.

W.W. Wallwork Inc. P.O. Box 1819, 900 35th St. N.W., Fargo, ND 58107. Tel: 701/476-7000; Fax: 701/282-6314; Web site: http://www.wallworktrucks.com. W.W. Wallwork III, Pres.; Cim Drewicke, Treas. Annual revenue $72 million. W.W. Wallwork Inc. is a retail/wholesale Sterling Ford and Kenworth truck and trailer dealership, providing sales, financing, leasing, parts, and service. Wallwork Inc. includes Wallwork Truck Centers and Wallwork Financial, which leases out medium- and heavy-duty trucks. Affiliates include Valley Imports, Wallwork Rent a Car, which sells Mercedes Benz, Audi, Porsche, and Volkswagen vehicles; and The Budget Lot, a used car lot. W.W. Wallwork is the oldest dealership in Fargo and the oldest Ford dealership in the Red River Valley. 125 employees (20 in Minnesota; 30 part-time). Founded in 1921. Recently moved to 900 35th St. NW in Fargo. SIC 5012.

Walman Optical Company 801 12th Ave. N., Minneapolis, MN 55411. Tel: 612/520-6000; Fax: 612/520-6069. Robert Morrow, Chm.; Charles R. Patterson, CEO; Martin Bassett, Pres. and COO; James Grootegoed, VP and Sec.; Charles Pillsbury, VP and Treas. Annual revenue $120 million. Walman Optical manufactures ophthalmic products, distributes instruments, grinds lenses, manufactures and distributes contact lenses, and has some proprietary procedures for plastic eyeglass lenses. Walman Optical is one of the nation's 100 largest employee-owned companies. 650 employees (200 in Minnesota). Founded in 1915. SIC 3851. No. 87 CRM Private 100.

Walser Automotive Group Inc. 3948 W. 50th St., Suite 211, Edina, MN 55424. Tel: 952/929-3535; Fax: 952/929-5252; Web site: http://www.walser.com. Robert J. Walser, Chm.; Paul Walser, Pres. and CEO; Andrew Walser, VP; Barbara Jerich, Gen. Counsel; Kirk Kleckner, Sec. and Treas.. Annual revenue $520 million. Walser Automotive Group is an automobile dealership group representing 13 franchises that includes leasing, body shop, financing, warranty and insurance activities. 1,000 employees (all in Minnesota). Founded in 1956. The January 2000 announcement by the Best Buy Co. to develop a new headquarters campus in Richfield, Minn., disappointed and concerned Walser Automotive Group. This proposal involves the removal of two of Walser's dealerships (a seven-acre site), 68 homeowners, several apartments, and other long-time businesses in the community. The company was promoting an alternative proposal that would redevelop a portion of this area into a new retail, restaurant, and auto-mall concept. In August Walser was continuing to resist the plan, filing suit against the city of Richfield and the Richfield Housing and Redevelopment Authority alleging that city officials violated Minnesota's tax-increment financing statute when they designated Richfield properties as blighted. Meanwhile, in October Walser announced that its Apple Valley, Minn., dealership was moving to Burnsville, Minn., although a new or relocating Walser store was expected to open in Apple Valley in the near future. SIC 5511, 7515. No. 26 CRM Private 100.

Walters Brothers Lumber Manufacturing Inc. P.O. Box 70, Radisson, WI 54867. Tel: 715/945-2217; Fax: 715/945-2878. William Walters, Pres. and CEO; Timothy Walters, EVP. Annual revenue $7.5 million. Walters Brothers Lumber manufactures wooden pallets and SAWS-grade lumber. 67 employees (4 part-time). Founded in 1930. SIC 2421, 2448.

Walter's Publishing 215 Fifth Ave. S.E., Waseca, MN 56093. Tel: 507/835-3691; Fax: 507/835-3217. Wayne Dankert, Pres. Walter's Publishing prints personalized and customized cookbooks and does other short-run publishing. 75 employees. Founded in 1946. SIC 2731, 2752.

WAM!NET Inc. 655 Lone Oak Dr., Eagan, MN 55121. Tel: 651/256-5100. Edward J. Driscoll III, Chm., CEO, and Treas.; Will Sullivan, Pres.; Terri Zimmerman, CFO; Allen L. Witters, Chief Tech. Officer; James R. Clancey, Chief Sls./Mktg. Officer; David T. Ottinger, SVP-Engrg./Op.; Richard G. Marklund, SVP-Int'l; John R. Kauffman, VP-Strategic Mktg./Communications; Gary C. Jarder, VP and Gen. Mgr.-Medical Svs.; Brent L. Bauer, VP-Corp. Mktg.; Keith E. Elzia, VP-Sls.; David A. Townsend, Managing Dir.-Wam!Net U.K.; Mark Marlow, Dir.-Fin.; Charles A. Cannada, Dir.; Robert L. Hoffman, Dir.; Curtis G. Gray, Dir.; K. William Grothe Jr., Dir. Annual revenue $24.8 million (loss $145.1 million). WAM!NET provides a managed, high-speed digital delivery network service that integrates the company's industry-specific work flow applications with commercially available computer and telephony technologies. The company, an affiliate of World Com Inc., offers an "Industry Smart" service designed to provide its subscribers with a turnkey single source solution for the transportation and management of information with a simple "pay by the megabyte" pricing plan requiring no capital investment. 459 employees. Founded in 1994. In December 1999 WAM!NET and the Heidelberger Druckmaschinen AG signed a global agreement for co-sales, co-marketing, and technical exchange. The partnership was to further facilitate both companies' printing and publishing customers in the adoption and utilization of a digital workflow. In January 2000 Winstar Communications (Nasdaq: WCII), New York, agreed to invest up to $100 million in WAM!NET. In turn, WAM!NET was to purchase Winstar's wireless-network facilities over 20 years for $250 million. In March WAM!NET agreed to host Group W Network Service's globalcaptions.com application on its global business-to-business e-services network. On March 15, the company filed a registration statement with the SEC relating to a proposed initial public offering of common stock, withproceeds from the offering to be used for working capital; to repay bank debt; for the expansion of the company's network, hosting, and storage infrastructure; and for possible acquisitions. Merrill Lynch & Co. and Goldman, Sachs & Co. were joint lead managers for the $115 million offering, one of the largest IPOs ever in the Twin Cities. In April, at the National Association of Broadcasters event in Las Vegas, the company announced the immediate availability of new e-services specifically tailored to the timed-base (moving) media creation needs of the film and broadcast industry. Ed Driscoll won the 2000 Minnesota and Dakotas Ernst & Young Entrepreneur of the Year Award in the e-Software & Services category. In May WAMNET.COM, a new industry portal, enabled corporations and their business partners—including advertising agencies, Web site developers, and print production professionals—to collaborate digitally in the creation, distribution, management, and storage of digital content. In July WAM!NET received approval to sell on the General Services Administration (GSA) Schedule for Electronic Commerce Services, launching the company's formal effort to market and sell its e-services to the government marketplace. Two significant initiatives—soon-to-be available ROD! Lite, an Internet version of the WAM!NET rendering service Render On Demand, and a program to develop WAM!NET ROD! Service Bureau, a new network of resellers—that would make its rendering services more accessible to small, medium-size, and large firms involved in the creation, production, and distribution of feature films, television content, advertising, and animation designs. In August, at Seybold San Francisco 2000, WAM!NET announced the commercial availability of WAM!NET WorkSpace, a new online service for collaborative workgroups (corporate clients, advertising agencies, Web site developers, and print production professionals) who create, manage, share, publish, distribute, and store digital media; and WAMNET.COM, the company's new industry portal that provides corporations and their business partners with easy access to the applications and services needed to digitally produce and distribute digital content. In October the company was selected by the General Services Administration to host a new e-commerce platform for government surplus auctions. WAM!NET, along with prime contractor Electronic Data Systems (NYSE: EDS) and principal partners Raytheon Co. (NYSE: RTNB) and WorldCom (Nasdaq: WCOM), was awarded a $6.9 billion Navy and Marine Corps intranet contract, the largest Federal information technology contract ever awarded. The contract was for the creation of a global networked platform to provide voice, video, and data services to the Navy and Marine Corps. Universal Music Group, the world's leading music company, agreed to use WAM!NET's wide-area networking and digital proofing services to reduce the time it takes to distribute packaging artwork and marketing materials worldwide for new music releases. SIC 7379.

Wanner Engineering Inc. 1204 Chestnut Ave., Minneapolis, MN 55403. Tel: 612/332-5681; Fax: 612/332-6937. William F. Wanner Jr., CEO; Payton Hage, Pres.; Joe Greene, CFO; Al Powers, VP-Engrg.; James M. Binger, Sec. Wanner Engineering manufactures Hydra-Cell and StanCor Pumps. Its affiliations include Duo Plastics Farmington, Minn. (Paul Silvernagel); Wanner International, Surrey, England (Dennis Heath). 72 employees (68 in Minnesota). Founded in 1973. SIC 3561.

Ware Manufacturing Company 4300 Quebec Ave. N., New Hope, MN 55428. Tel: 763/533-1551; Fax: 763/533-0439; Web site: http://www.ware.thomasregister.com. Christopher Vollrath, Pres. and CEO; Jan Wojtysiak, Cont. Ware Manufacturing Co. is engaged in sheet metal stamping and wire forming. 106 employees. Founded in 1946. SIC 3469, 3496.

Warner Manufacturing Company 13435 Industrial Park Blvd., Plymouth, MN 55441. Tel: 763/559-4740; Fax: 763/559-1364. Guy Warner, Chm.; Jerry Ranallo, Pres.; Marie Borgen, Treas.; Paul Allee, VP-Mfg.; Douglas Malchow, VP-Product Devel.; Gary Mueller, VP-Sls./Mktg. Warner manufactures and distributes tools and equipment used in home repair and decorating, including drywall and tile installation tools. 138 employees (all in Minnesota). Founded in 1927. SIC 2499, 3089, 3469.

Warren Companies P.O. Box 1128, Sioux Falls, SD 57101. Tel: 605/336-1830; Fax: 605/336-0368. Greg Bannon, Sls. Mgr.-Builders Express; Karel Van Langen, Sls. Mgr.-Warren Comm.; Jim Sexton, Sls. Mgr.-Warren Distrib. Warren Cos. consists of three operating companies: Warren Communications, which sells cellular phones to dealers; Warren Distribution, which sells closed-circuit surveillance system; and Builders Express, which provides appliances and cabinets to building contractors. Other locations: Plymouth, Minn.; Sacramento, Calif. 101 employees (23 in Minnesota). Founded in 1947. SIC 4812, 7382.

Washington Companies P.O. Box 16630, Missoula, MT 59808. Tel: 406/523-1300; Fax: 406/523-1399. Dennis Washington, Chm. and CEO; Mike Haight, Pres. Annual revenue $743 million. Washington Cos. operates in several industries: rail services, copper mining, marine and highway transportation, environmental remediation, machinery sales, and construction. 4,285 employees. SIC 6719.

Waste Management 12448 Pennsylvania Ave. S., Savage, MN 55378. Tel: 952/736-8088. Waste Management is a solid-waste collection and recycling service. 90 employees (all in Minnesota; 10 part-time). Founded in 1961. SIC 4953.

Watertown Monument Works Inc. 1007 Fifth St. S.E., P.O. Box 130, Watertown, SD 57201. Tel: 605/886-6942; Fax: 605/886-6943. Fremont G. Forsberg, Chm.; Gregg A. Forsberg, Pres., CEO, and Treas.; Dexter Forsberg, Sec.; Susanne Grist, VP and Mktg. Dir.; Janet Nagel, Cont. Watertown Monument Works produces granite memorials, countertops, and furniture. 73 employees. Founded in 1882. SIC 3281.

Watertown Public Opinion Company Inc. 120 N.W. Third Ave., Watertown, SD 57201. Tel: 605/886-6901; Fax: 605/886-4280; Web site: http://www.thepublicopinion.com. Steven W. Lowrie, Pres. and Publisher. Annual revenue $5.8 million. Watertown Public Opinion Co. is engaged in commercial printing, the publishing of a daily newspaper, a weekly shopper, magazines, travel brochures, and a web page. 88 employees (12 in Minnesota). Founded in 1887. SIC 2711, 2752.

Watkins Inc. 150 Liberty St., Winona, MN 55987. Tel: 507/457-3300; Fax: 507/452-6723. Irwin L. Jacobs, Owner and CEO; Mark E. Jacobs, Pres.; Martha J. Meehan, VP-Mktg.; Stephen B. Nett, VP-Fin. and CFO; James Yenish, VP-Op. Watkins manufactures and distributes consumer products. Distribution is through catalogs and a direct sales organization of more than 70,000 independent dealers and distributors in the United States and Canada. 445 employees (325 in Minnesota; 75 part-time). Founded in 1868. SIC 2048, 2087, 5149.

Waymar Industries Inc. 14400 Southcross Dr. W., Burnsville, MN 55306. Tel: 952/435-7100; Fax: 952/435-2900; Web site: http://www.waymar.com. Dick Koehring, CEO; Bob Haugen, EVP; JoAnne Stahlecker, Treas. and Sec.; Bill Ziegler, Dir.-Sls./Mktg. Waymar Industries manufactures restaurant, school, military, government, cafeteria, and fast-food seating. 92 employees (all in Minnesota; 3 part-time). Founded in 1961. SIC 2531.

Wayne Transports Inc. 3180 E. 117th St., Inver Grove Heights, MN 55077. Tel: 651/437-6422; Fax: 651/438-2618. Wayne Siemers, Owner; Curtis Mark Siemers, Pres.; Carl D. Vedders, VP; Joseph A. Eschenbacher, VP-Admin.; Clifford A. Guggisberg, VP-Sls./Mktg.; Michael W. Siemers, Sec. and Treas. Wayne Transports provides transportation services handling petroleum, chemicals, compressed gases, and dry food commodities, in bulk. 300 employees (225 in Minnesota). Founded in 1950. SIC 4789.

Weather-Rite Inc. 616 N. Fifth St., Minneapolis, MN 55401. Tel: 612/338-1401; Fax: 612/338-6783. Bruce Triden, Pres. Weather-Rite constructs air heating, make-up air ventilation, cooling, and energy-recovery equipment for commercial and industrial facilities. Weather-Rite constructs systems for the enameling of magnet wire. 110 employees (all in Minnesota). Founded in 1957. SIC 3433.

Weather Shield Manufacturing Inc. One Weather Shield Plaza, P.O. Box 309, Medford, WI 54451. Tel: 715/748-2100; Fax: 715/748-6999. Edward Lee Schield, Founder and CEO; Mark Schield, VP; Kevin Schield, VP. Weather Shield Manufacturing Inc. is the nation's third-largest manufacturer of windows and doors. It operates plants in Ladysmith, Greenwood, and Medford, Wis.; and in Logan, Utah. Weather Shield is one of the most aggressive marketers in the construction products industry. 2,300 employees. Founded in 1953. SIC 2431.

Webster Industries Inc. County Highway U, P.O. Box 297, Bangor, WI 54614. Tel: 608/486-2341; Fax: 608/486-4513. Paul D. Webster, Pres.; Kevin Boling, VP-Mfg.; P. Byron Hawkins, VP-Mktg.; John Sapaula, VP-Millwork Sls.; Joseph Ostervich, VP-Fin. and Sec.; Shon O. Doyle, Treas.; Stan Thomas, VP-Tie Sls. Webster Industries manufactures hardwood lumber, millwork products, and railroad ties. 400 employees. SIC 2426.

Weigh-Tronix Inc. 1000 Armstrong Dr., Fairmont, MN 56031. Tel: 507/238-4461; Fax: 507/238-4195; Web site: http://www.wtxweb.com. David Castle, Pres.; Gene Tonne, Op. Mgr.; John Hughes, VP-Industrial; Dave Cone, Dir.-Dillon Force Measurement; Jim Rather, VP-Mktg.; Bob Seidel, Dir.-Agricultural Sls.; Leon Lammers, Chief Engineer. Annual revenue $370 million. Weigh-Tronix designs and manufactures electronic weighing equipment. Weigh-Tronix North America's three operating divisions are Industrial group (truck scales, industrial products), Force Measurement group (devices for product-line testing applications), and Agricultural group (livestock scales and farm weigh bar kits). Other Weigh-Tronix businesses include Salter Weigh-Tronix, a U.K. company that manufactures, sells, and services electronic and mechanical weighing systems; and Salter Housewares, the U.K. market leader in household scales. Weigh-Tronix was publicly traded until the August 1991 acquisition by former 57 percent owner Staveley Industries; then bought back in May 1998 by Weigh-Tronix LLC. 4,375 employees.

Founded in 1971. In June 2000 the company acquired 4,000-employee Avery Berkel, the chief manufacturer of retail and industrial weighing systems and slicers in the United Kingdom, with operating companies in the United Kingdom, France, Germany, India, Italy, Malaysia, South Africa, Spain, and the United States. The combined company is now the world's second-largest manufacturer of industrial and food weighing products. SIC 3596. No. 79 CRM Private 100.

Weinbrenner Shoe Company Inc. 108 S. Polk St., Merrill, WI 54452. Tel: 715/536-5521; Fax: 715/536-1172; Web site: http://www.weinbrennerusa.com. Lance Nienow, Pres. and CEO; Richard Olson, VP-Credit Admin.; David Gisselman, VP-Fin. Weinbrenner Shoe Co. constructs men's and women's outdoor, safety, uniform, and work footwear under the brand names Thorogood, Thorogard, Mainstream, Wood N-Stream, and Softtrails as well as private label footwear. 375 employees (6 part-time). Founded in 1892. SIC 3143.

Weis Builders Inc. 8009 34th Ave. S., Bloomington, MN 55425. Tel: 952/858-9999; Fax: 952/858-9884; Web: http://www.weisbuilders.com. Jay Weis, Pres.; Erik Weis, EVP; Joe Weis, Chair; Ron Kreinbring, VP-Rochester Office; Brad Folkert, VP-Salt Lake City Office; Peter Desai, VP-Chicago Office; Tom Hartwell, VP-Bus. Devel. Annual revenue $290 million. Weis Builders provides general contracting, construction management, and pre-construction services for nonresidential buildings. Weis has regional offices in Chicago; Rochester, Minn.; Wichita, Kan.; and Salt Lake City. The company serves the following market segments: assisted living, health care, hospitality, commercial/industrial, multi-unit residential, and retail. 340 employees (220 in Minnesota). Founded in 1939. SIC 1542, 8741. No. 47 CRM Private 100.

Carl Weissman & Sons Inc. 59405 Third St., P.O. Box 1609, Great Falls, MT 59403. Tel: 406/761-4848; Fax: 406/791-6731. Jerrold A. Weissman, Pres. and CEO; Thomas Howard, Sec.; A. Schandelson, Treas.; Nadyne B. Weissman, VP-Personnel; Dennis Campbell, EVP. Weissman & Sons is in the hardware, automotive, and steel parts business. 170 employees (3 part-time). Founded in 1915. SIC 5072.

Wells Concrete Products Company P.O. Box 308, 835 Highway 109 N.E., Wells, MN 56097. Tel: 507/553-3138; Fax: 507/553-6089; Web site: http://www.wellsconcrete.com. Leo A. Nesius, Dir.; David Buesing, Pres. and Gen. Mgr.; David A. Nesius, Sec.; Spencer Kubat, VP; Robert Drum, VP; Gary Bielke, VP; Gregg Jacobson, VP; Kim Sorenson, Treas.; Jeffry Stumpf, Dir. Annual revenue $24 million. Wells Concrete Products manufactures and erects prestressed concrete double tees and structural building components, insulated sandwich wall panels, architectural precast wall panels, prestressed bridge beams, ready-mixed concrete, and precast concrete hog slats. The company has one subsidiary: Concrete Inc. in Grand Forks, N.D.(Bob Sween). 240 employees (all in Minnesota; 50 part-time). Founded in 1951. SIC 3272, 3273.

Welsh Companies Inc. 8200 Normandale Blvd., Suite 200, Bloomington, MN 55437. Tel: 952/897-7700; Fax: 952/897-7704. Dennis J. Doyle, CEO; Robert Angleson, Pres.; Scott Frederiksen, SVP; Jean Kane, EVP; William Krake, Pres.-Welsh Construction; Ken Pipes, Pres.-Genesis; Ben Pounds, SVP; Robert Pounds, SVP and Dir.-Property Mgmt. Svs.; Pete Rand, SVP; Bill Ritter, SVP; Dennis Heieic, VP and CFO. Annual revenue $125 million. Welsh is a provider of comprehensive real estate services: property management, leasing, tenant representation, design and construction, development, facility management, financing, investment sales, and corporate consultation. Welsh maintains offices in downtown Minneapolis and downtown St. Paul. 400 employees. Founded in 1978. In December 1999 Investcorp International, New York, bought a significant minority stake to help Welsh Cos. expand into Midwestern and Florida markets. SIC 6512, 6531. No. 90 CRM Private 100.

Wenck Associates Inc. 1800 Pioneer Creek Center, Maple Plain, MN 55359. Tel: 763/479-4200; Fax: 763/479-4242. Norman Wenck, Pres. Wenck Associates resolves environmental problems for businesses by providing a full range of engineering consulting services: air-quality, investigation, and cleanup design for site contamination; and landfill design, wastewater treatment, tank management, industrial environmental compliance, storm-water management, and general civil and chemical engineering. Offices include two in the Twin Cities; Duluth, Minn.; Virginia, Minn.; Brainerd, Minn.; Singapore; and Jordan. Work is carried out throughout the United States and in the Pacific Rim. 93 employees (87 in Minnesota). Founded in 1985. SIC 8711, 8734.

Wendell's Inc. 6601 Industry Ave., P.O. Box 458, Ramsey, MN 55303. Tel: 763/576-8200; Fax: 763/576-0995. Lawerence T. Cody, Pres. and CEO; Teri Magaard, VP-Fin.; Ken Zieska, VP-Mfg. Annual revenue $5 million. Wendell's manufactures commemorative coins and key tags; badges; rubber, steel, and pre-inked stamps; and die engraving. 54 employees (all in Minnesota). Founded in 1882. SIC 3479, 3953, 3999.

Wenger Corporation 555 Park Dr., Owatonna, MN 55060. Tel: 507/455-4100; Fax: 507/455-4258. Jerry A. Wenger, Owner and Chm.; Tim Covey, Pres.; Kenneth Pizel, VP and CFO; Phil Martin, Sec.; Brian Paulson, Asst. Sec. Wenger manufactures and sells products and equipment for music education and the performing arts. Included are items such as stages, platforms, acoustical reflectors, music practice rooms, cabinets, chairs, stands, outdoor performing arts centers, and a wide variety of custom-designed products for these markets. 450 employees (460 in Minnesota; 10 part-time). Founded in 1946. SIC 2541, 3999.

Wenk Foods Inc. 318 S. Highland Ave., Madison, SD 57042. Tel: 605/256-4569; Fax: 605/256-3204. William B. Wenk Jr., Pres. Wenk Foods produces frozen eggs, dried egg solids, and frozen processed geese. 100 employees. Founded in 1919. SIC 2015.

West Central Steel Inc. P.O. Box 1178, Willmar, MN 56201. Tel: 320/235-4070; Fax: 320/235-1816; Web site: http://www.wcsteel.com. Delbert Allinder, Chm.; Jeff Pattison, Pres. and CEO; Jeff Allinder, VP-Sls.; Barb Zwagerman, VP-Purch.; Dave Runke, VP-Op. West Central Steel is a steel service center specializing in preproduction component part manufacturing with distribution throughout the Upper Midwest. 79 employees. Founded in 1961. SIC 5051.

Western Bank 663 University Ave. W., P.O. Box 64689 (55164), St. Paul, MN 55104. Tel: 651/290-8100; Fax: 651/290-8118; Web site: http://www.western-bank.com. A. William Sands Jr., Chm.; Stephen C. Erdall, Pres. and CEO; James J. Kuhn, SVP; Mark H. Luhmann, SVP-Commercial; Christine A. Dressel, VP-Mktg./Hum. Res.; Vicki R. Grant, VP-Retail; Fizal M. Kassim, VP-Brokerage. Annual revenue $17.3 million (earnings $4.9 million). Western Bank is an independent, full-service community bank dedicated to the specialized needs of small businesses. Western has $220 million in assets and six locations in the Twin Cities metro area. 97 employees (all in Minnesota; 16 part-time). Founded in 1915. In August 2000 the company was named one of the Great Places to Work among small to medium-size employers by CityBusiness newspaper. SIC 6022.

Western Graphics Inc. 530 Wheeler, St. Paul, MN 55104. Tel: 651/603-6400; Fax: 651/603-6401; Web site: http://www.western-graphics.com. Robert Keran, CEO; Timothy R. Keran, Pres.; Neal Johnson, VP-Mfg. Annual revenue $8 million. Western Graphics provides customized services that facilitate the on-time delivery of corporate print on demand documents in the one- to four-color, short- to medium-run-length markets. 80 employees (all in Minnesota; 7 part-time). Founded in 1960. SIC 2752.

Western National Insurance Group 5350 W. 78th St., P.O. Box 1463 (55440), Edina, MN 55439. Tel: 952/835-5350; Fax: 952/921-3159. George E. Klouda, Chm. and acting Pres./CEO; Eugene G. Miller, EVP and Agency Dir.; Kenneth T. Stover, EVP and Personal Lines Mgr.; Cynthia Sue Mitchell, SVP, Sec., and Fin. Dir.; Paul R. Nelson, EVP and Commercial Lines Mgr.; Robert L. Hansen, SVP and Claims Mgr.; Dennis R. Ballinger, VP and Work. Comp. Claims Mgr.; Aaron A. Toltzman, VP and Chief Engr.; Tim Lewis, VP and Mgr.-Sys./Programming; David J. Saelens, VP and Asst. Claims Mgr.; John A. Tollefsrud, Asst. VP and Fin. Mgr.; Wayne H. Kahler, Treas. and Statistician; Virginia K. Latocki, Asst. Sec. and Hum. Res. Dir.; Mary S. Manley, Asst. VP and Res./Devel. Mgr.; Mark W. Lapham, VP and Gen. Counsel. Annual revenue $166 million. Western National Insurance Group, a $235.5 million-asset, mutually owned insurance company and stock company subsidiary, is the largest independent agency carrier writing auto insurance in Minnesota. Although it writes 85 percent of its business in Minnesota, it is licensed in 20 states and maintains an office in Seattle. It writes the usual property and casualty lines. 385 employees. Founded in 1901. SIC 6331. No. 15 CRM Cooperatives/Mutuals 20.

Western Petroleum Company 9531 W. 78th St., Eden Prairie, MN 55344. Tel: 952/941-9090; Fax: 952/941-7470; Web site: http://www.westernpetro.com. James W. Emison, CEO; Richard S. Neville, SVP-Mktg.; Christine Hays, VP and Cont.; Arvid Larson, VP-Credit Services. Annual revenue $337 million. Western Petroleum is a marketer of petroleum products. 52 employees. Founded in 1969. SIC 5172. No. 37 CRM Private 100.

Westin Nielsen Corporation 4301 White Bear Pkwy., White Bear Lake, MN 55110. Tel: 651/426-4625; Fax: 651/426-5810; Web site: http://www.westinnielsen.com. William J. Nielsen, Pres. Westin Nielsen Corp. is a manufacturer of wood seating for office, health care, and institutional facilities. 55 employees (all in Minnesota). Founded in 1956. SIC 2521.

Westling Manufacturing Company 1700 12th St. S., Princeton, MN 55371. Tel: 763/389-4440; Fax: 763/332-7130. John Westling, Pres.; Jack Giese, EVP. Westling Manufacturing Co. makes electrical automotive parts, water pumps, clutches, alternators, starters, and assemblies. Founded in 1940. SIC 3714.

Wettstein's 215 N. Third St., La Crosse, WI 54603. Tel: 608/784-6868; Fax: 608/785-1176. John Wettstein, Pres.; Ralph Wettstein, VP; Dan Wettstein, Sls. Mgr. Wettstein's designs, builds, and repairs electronic computerized equipment used in various manufacturing businesses. Wettstein's is also involved in electrical contracting and the retail sale of electronics and appliances. It has a residential lighting showroom and sales, services and support computers for businesses. 160 employees (8 in Minnesota). Founded in 1951. SIC 1731, 5064, 5722, 5731.

Wheeler Manufacturing Company Inc. 107 Main Ave., Lemmon, SD 57638. Tel: 605/374-3848; Fax: 605/374-3655. Bradford J. Wheeler, Pres.; Rob L. Wheeler, VP; Shirley Peters, Sec.; Bob B. Wheeler, Treas. Wheeler Manufacturing Co. produces a wide variety of jewelry. 140 employees. Founded in 1946. SIC 3911, 3961, 3999.

WhereForce 14700 28th Ave. N., Plymouth, MN 55447. Tel: 763/559-5100; Fax: 763/551-4319. Kenneth Searl, Owner and Pres.; Ronald Meinhardt, VP and CFO. WhereForce, formerly Kennsco, provides computer sales, leasing, maintenance, and repair services. It has 22 locations in Minnesota, Florida, Illinois, Iowa, Kansas, Louisiana, Michigan, Missouri, Texas, and Pennsylvania. 150 employees (75 in Minnesota). Founded in 1975. SIC 5045, 7378.

Whirl-Air Flow Corporation 1515 Central Ave. N.E., Minneapolis, MN 55413. Tel: 612/781-3461; Fax: 612/781-3466. E.T. Mueller, Chm. and Pres. Whirl-Air Flow Corp. manufactures foundry equipment and supplies. It also provides fabricating and machining for various special heavy-duty metal products, and designs and manufactures pneumatic conveying systems. 75 employees (74 in Minnesota; 4 part-time). Founded in 1946. SIC 3535, 3537, 3559, 3589.

Whitaker Buick Jeep Company 1225 University Ave., St. Paul, MN 55104. Tel: 651/645-7781; Fax: 651/645-1702; Web site: http://www.whitakerbuickjeep.com. W. Whitaker, Chm.; C.S. Whitaker, VP; S.W. Whitaker, VP; Cindy Rogers, VP; David Kramer, Gen. Mgr.. Whitaker Buick Jeep Company is a Buick and Jeep motor vehicle dealership. 75 employees (all in Minnesota; 10 part-time). Founded in 1954. SIC 5511.

Whitebirch Inc. 9252 Breezy Point Dr., Breezy Point, MN 56472. Tel: 218/562-4204; Fax: 218/562-4930; Web site: http://www.breezypt.com. Robert B. Spizzo, Pres. and CEO; Joyce Bzoskie, VP and Treas.; Dave Graudahl, Gen. Mgr.; Renee Norwood, Dir.-Mktg.; Bonnie Tweed, Convention Coordinator. Annual revenue $15 million. Whitebirch owns Breezy Point Resort and leisure/recreational development on adjoining 3,000 acres (including vacation ownership). The resort has two 18-hole golf courses, as well as a hockey complex to house boys' and girls' hockey camps and figure skating camps. 370 employees (all in Minnesota; 200 part-time). Founded in 1972. SIC 7041.

Wieser Concrete Products Inc. W3716, U.S. Highway 10, Maiden Rock, WI 54750. Tel: 715/647-2311; Fax: 715/647-5181. Joseph H. Wieser, Founder; Phil Miller, Sls. Mgr.; Daniel J. Wieser, Sec.; Andrew G. Wieser, Pres.; Mark A. Wieser, EVP. Wieser Concrete Products manufactures, sells, transports, and installs precast concrete products, such as septic tanks, dry wells, storm/sanitary sewer manholes, steps, highway median barriers, specialty boxes, slatted floors, manure storage, bunker silos, feed bunks, livestock housing, hog fencing, hog feeders, and retaining walls. 95 employees (5 part-time). Founded in 1965. SIC 3272.

Wilbrecht Electronics Inc. 1400 Energy Park Dr., Suite 18, St. Paul, MN 55108. Tel: 651/659-0919; Fax: 651/659-9204. J.K. Wilbrecht, Pres. Wilbrecht manufactures electronic components for medical, OEM, and military markets. Wilbrecht has operations in Cary, Il.; and Huron, S.D. 135 employees (15 in Minnesota). Founded in 1956. SIC 3676, 3679.

Wild Wings Highway 61 S., P.O. Box 100, Lake City, MN 55041. Tel: 651/345-3663; Fax: 651/345-2981. William Webster III, CEO; Randall D. Eggenberger, Pres. Wild Wings is a publisher, wholesaler, direct marketer, and retailer of limited edition wildlife and sporting art prints. Wild Wings also sells original paintings and sporting-related home decorations and gifts. The company has 12 corporate-owned and 11 franchised retail locations around the country. 175 employees (140 in Minnesota; 75 part-time). Founded in 1967. SIC 2721.

Williams Steel & Hardware First and 28th Avenue, Minneapolis, MN 55411. Tel: 612/588-9800; Fax: 612/588-9875. W.R. Winter Jr., Pres.; J. Ocenasek, CEO; J. Hess, VP-Sls.; R. Champa, VP-Op. Williams Steel & Hardware is an industrial wholesaler and steel supplier for the Upper Midwest. 162 employees (140 in Minnesota). Founded in 1860. SIC 5051.

Williston Industrial Supply P.O. Box 2477, Williston, ND 58801. Tel: 701/572-2135; Fax: 701/572-0664. J.R. Scheele, Pres.; Chuck Moline, VP. Williston Industrial Supply provides oil and gas equipment. 75 employees. Founded in 1967. SIC 3599.

Willmar Poultry Company Inc. P.O. Box 753, Willmar, MN 56201. Tel: 320/235-8850; Fax: 320/235-8869. Theodore Huisinga, Pres.; Rayburn Norling, EVP; Ronald Hanson, CFO. Willmar Poultry is a turkey hatchery and a distributor of agricultural supplies. 380 employees. Founded in 1945. SIC 0254, 5191.

The Wilson Center P.O. Box 917, Faribault, MN 55021. Tel: 507/334-5561. Janine Sahagian, MSW, CEO and Hosp. Admin.; Kevin Mahoney, Pres.; Brad Haugen, VP-Fin.; Sean Canney, VP-Community Svs. The Wilson Center provides treatment and learning programs for children, adolescents, and adults with psychiatric disorders. Facilities include The Wilson Center Psychiatric Facility, The Wilson Academy, Cannon Valley Mental Health Clinic, and Whipple Heights School. 210 employees. Founded in 1971. SIC 8069, 8093.

Wilson Tool International Inc. 12912 Farnham, White Bear Lake, MN 55110. Tel: 651/426-1384; Fax: 651/426-9134. Kenneth J. Wilson, Owner and Chm. Wilson Tool manufactures punches and dies. Wilson Tool also has a manufacturing plant in Swindon, England. 495 employees (420 in Minnesota). Founded in 1966. SIC 3544, 3599.

Winco Inc. 225 S. Cordova Ave., Le Center, MN 56057. Tel: 507/357-6821; Fax: 507/357-4857; Web site: http://www.wincogen.com. Ralph Call, CEO; Steven Fraley, COO; Sandra Grieves, Personnel Admin. Annual revenue $25 million. Winco manufactures Winco and Dyna Brand generators. Its product line consists of portable generator sets, mobile diesels, light towers, PTOs, two-bearing generators, and standby power systems, for residential and commercial markets, including industrial, agricultural, consumer, OEM, government, and international. 101 employees (100 in Minnesota). Founded in 1927. SIC 3621.

Wincraft Inc. 1124 W. Fifth St., Winona, MN 55987. Tel: 507/454-5510; Fax: 507/454-6403. Richard J. Pope, Chm., Pres., and CEO. Wincraft manufactures and sells promotional and spirit products to schools, industry, and organizations. Products include buttons, pompons, key tags, pennants, bumper strips, seat cushions, sponges, ribbons, flags, banners, windsocks, pencils, erasers, and decals. Wincraft is also licensed for selling professional sports and NCAA items. 450 employees (400 in Minnesota). Founded in 1961. SIC 2399, 3089, 3961, 3993, 3999.

Windings Inc. 208 N. Valley St., New Ulm, MN 56073. Tel: 507/359-2034; Fax: 507/354-5383; Web site: http://www.windings.com. R.D. Ryberg, Pres.; J. Flatau, Mgr.-Tech. Sls.; J. Kauffman, Mgr.-Engrg.; S.A. Ward, Mgr.-Op. Annual revenue $7.4 million. Windings is a manufacturer of custom stator windings for the motor industry. 100 employees (all in Minnesota; 25 part-time). Founded in 1965. SIC 3621.

Winona Inc. 1200 Storr's Pond Rd., P.O. Box 5400, Winona, MN 55987. Tel: 507/454-3240; Fax: 507/454-6058. Pat Woodworth, Chm., Pres., and CEO; Lynda Carothers, VP; Shirley Benedict, VP. Winona Inc. operates retail apparel stores. 100 employees (50 in Minnesota). Founded in 1977. SIC 5651.

Winona ORC Industries Inc. 1053 E. Mark St., Winona, MN 55987. Tel: 507/452-1855; Fax: 507/452-1857. Geralyn Sharp, Chair; Bill Harris, Exec. Dir.; Sue Hovell, Treas.; Eric Johnsrad, Sec. Annual revenue $3.3 million. Winona ORC Industries produces plastic blister and skin packaging and performs machining operations. 300 employees (275 in Minnesota; 100 part-time). Founded in 1973. SIC 2393, 2399.

Winslow Printing Company 1225 Seventh St. N., Minneapolis, MN 55411. Tel: 612/522-3868; Fax: 612/522-0025. Chuck Winslow, CEO; Robert Garnaas, Pres.; Diana Sanford, Purch. Mgr. Winslow Printing Co. is in the commercial printing business serving both the web and sheetfed market. 110 employees. SIC 2759.

Winthrop & Weinstine P.A. 3200 Minnesota World Trade Center, 30 E. Seventh St., St. Paul, MN 55101. Tel: 651/290-8400; Fax: 651/292-9347; Web site: http://www.winthrop.com. Sherman Winthrop, Chm.; Hart Kuller, Pres. Winthrop & Weinstine P.A. is a law firm practicing primarily in the areas of general corporate, antitrust, administrative, banking, environmental, legislative and regulatory, securities, taxation, and real estate law; probate and estate planning; and commercial and business litigation. Offices are in St. Paul and Minneapolis. 186 employees (27 part-time). Founded in 1979. In March 2000 a federal appeals court overturned a $133 million verdict that the firm had been awarded in an antitrust case against Brunswick Corp. In July the firm won a $30 million settlement for various U.S. small boat manufacturers against Brunswick in a companion case. SIC 8111.

Wipaire Inc. 8520 River Rd., Inver Grove Heights, MN 55076. Tel: 651/451-1205; Fax: 651/451-1786. Bob Wiplinger, Owner and Chm.; Bob Nelson, Pres.; Chris Schmidt, Cont. Wipaire manufactures floats for airplanes. It also performs other aircraft-related services—modification sales, painting, upholstery, servicing, and maintenance. Its major client is Cessna Aircraft Company. 87 employees. SIC 3728.

Wizmo Inc. 7615 Golden Triangle Dr., Eden Prairie, MN 55344. Tel: 952/914-2200; Fax: 952/829-9615; Web site: http://www.wizmo.com. Jim Kopp, CEO; Denny Davies, VP-Planning; Jeff Dekko, Pres./Gen. Mgr.-Application Svs.; Ray Kang, VP-Product Mktg.; Dave Kregness, VP-Sls.; Carrie Maurer, VP-Op.; Dennis McFadden, CFO; Tyler Middleton, VP-Bus. Devel.; Jeff Morin, VP-Web Services; Tim Pawlenty, VP-Corp. Devel.; Brian Provost, VP-Sls.; Jim Stover, VP-Op.; Howard Witherspoon, VP-Mktg. Annual revenue $8.1 million. Wizmo provides e-business consulting, development, and management services to small- and midsize businesses. Wizmo has two divisions. Wizmo Professional Services provides people to consult, develop, implement, and manage client IT and Web infrastructures. Wizmo Application Services serves a desktop of applications over the Internet and from a centrally managed facility. Wizmo Inc. was formed in 1999 by the merger of Professional Computer Services and Burlwood Media Group. 119 employees. Founded in 1993. In July and August 2000, Wizmo closed on $35 million in private financing with partners in Hewlett-Packard, Novell, Sandler Capital Management, and Wheatley Partners. In October Wizmo announced a reseller agreement with Talisma Corp., full-service providers of powerful and easy-to-use electronic customer relationship management (eCRM) solutions, under which Wizmo Professional Services was to market the entire line of Talisma products and services, designed to manage customer Web site interactions for companies of any size. SIC 7373.

Wolkerstorfer Company Inc. 348 First St. S.W., New Brighton, MN 55112. Tel: 651/636-0720; Fax: 651/636-8372. Joseph A. Wolkerstorfer, Pres.; William Wolkerstorfer, EVP; Kenton Wolkerstorfer, EVP. Wolkerstorfer Co. is engaged in metal plating, metal finishing, and painting. 50 employees (all in Minnesota). Founded in 1885. SIC 3471, 3479.

Wood Design Inc. 908 S.W. 15th St., Forest Lake, MN 55025. Tel: 651/464-6190; Fax: 651/464-6191. Gregory P. Swirtz, Chm. and Pres.; Marty Kaye, SVP, Sec., and Treas. Wood Design manufactures wood products, particularly awards, desk items of all kinds, store fixtures, and millwork. Sales are nationwide to the award and recognition industry. Wood Designs also machines small wooden parts on a job shop basis. 67 employees (all in Minnesota). Founded in 1936. SIC 2499.

Woodcraft Industries Inc. 525 Lincoln Ave. S.E., St. Cloud, MN 56304. Tel: 320/252-1503; Fax: 320/252-1504. John Fitzpatrick, Pres. and CFO. Annual revenue $140 million. Woodcraft Industries has five plants that manufacture hardwood and engineered wood components for kitchen cabinet and furniture manufacturers. Majority-owned since February 1996 by Goldner Hawn Johnson & Morrison Inc., a Minneapolis investment company. 1,500 employees (900 in Minnesota). Founded in 1945. SIC 2426. No. 85 CRM Private 100.

Woodland Container Corporation P.O. Box 110, Aitkin, MN 56431. Tel: 218/927-3721; Fax: 218/927-7014; Web site: http://www.woodland-container.com. Richard Jordan, CEO; Donna Price, VP-Sls./Mktg. Annual revenue $20 million. Woodland Container makes wood and plywood shipping containers, skids, pallets, and wood reels. The company has plants in Minnesota, Wisconsin, Iowa, and North Carolina. 180 employees (106 in Minnesota; 5 part-time). Founded in 1986. SIC 2441, 2448, 2449.

Workstations International Inc. 5980 Golden Hills Dr., Golden Valley, MN 55416. Tel: 763/512-3200. David Gigerich, CEO. Workstations International specializes in providing enterprise-wide communications services implemented on a fixed-price, fixed-time-frame basis. 75 employees. Founded in 1994. SIC 7379.

World Aerospace Corporation 8625 Monticello Ln. N., Maple Grove, MN 55369. Tel: 763/424-8999; Fax: 763/424-1419. IE Phelps II, Pres.; I.E. Phelps, Chm. and CEO; Kimberly Campbell, Asst. Sec. Annual revenue $14 million. World Aerospace Corp. operates a full-line precision machining facility, manufacturing parts and components for jet engines, aircraft, and the space program. Products have both commercial and defense applications. 53 employees (all in Minnesota). Founded in 1946. SIC 3724, 3728.

World Data Products Inc. 121 Cheshire Ln., Minnetonka, MN 55305. Tel: 952/476-9000; Fax: 612/404-5247. Marc Ashton, CEO. Annual revenue $57 million. World Data Products is dealer in a new and refurbished computers. 83 employees. Founded in 1987. SIC 5045. No. 22 CityBusiness Fastest-growing Private Companies.

Wrico Stamping Company 2727 Niagara Ln., Plymouth, MN 55447. Tel: 763/559-2288; Fax: 763/553-7976. Keith Griffiths, Pres. Wrico Stamping Co. manufactures metal stampings. Held by Griffiths Corp., also of Plymouth. 525 employees. Founded in 1966. SIC 3469.

Wright-Hennepin Co-op Electric Assn. P.O. Box 330, Rockford, MN 55373. Tel: 763/477-3000; Fax: 763/477-3054. Alvin E. Heinz, Chm.; Mark Vogt, Pres. and CEO; Dale Jans, Treas. and Sec.; Chris Lantto, VChm. Wright-Hennepin Co-op Electric is a utility engaged in the distribution of electric service. 144 employees (all in Minnesota; 21 part-time). Founded in 1937. SIC 4911.

wwwrrr Inc. 800 Washington Ave. N., Suite 670, Minneapolis, MN 55401. Tel: 612/279-1200; Fax: 612/279-1300; Web site: http://www.wwwrrr.net. Dale LaFrenz, Chm.; Paul Gullickson, Pres. and CEO; Joanne Chabot, VP-Op.; Emily Child, VP-Mktg.; Peter Esposito, VP-Sls.; Rhys Larson, VP-Bus. Devel.; Jean Sharp, VP-Product Devel.; Karl Sowa, VP-Enterprise Devel. wwwrrr (pronounced "whir")—which stands for World Wide Web reading, 'riting, 'rithmetic—is an online training, communication, and education company formed in response to national concerns over the Internet's place in education. wwwrrr offers a line of products that enables teachers, students, and parents to use the Internet more effectively—with online technology that transforms the Web into a friendly, useful environment for learning and is the critical link between school and home. Co-founders Dale LaFrenz and Paul Gullickson are former senior executives from the Minnesota Educational Computing Corp. (MECC), the leading developer, publisher, and distributor of interactive, learning software for use by children in schools and homes. 140 employees. Founded in 1999. Year 2000 opened with wwwrrr conducting a pilot program with 25 schools in the Minneapolis Public School System that it expected to roll out to school districts nationwide in second quarter. In January Chicago-based North American Funds made the first major institutional investment in the company. In March wwwrrr and BridgeCom.com Inc.created an alliance to provide equity of access to all parents, students, and teachers who are members of wwwrrr@myschool, no computer needed. Other product alliances: ETA, HowStuffWorks.com, and the National Institute on Media and the Family. In May wwwrrr launched VersaTiles Online, its premiere interactive, Internet-based math product available for students grades 1-8; in June, InternetBasics: Fundamentals for Teachers, the first in a series of online training products designed to train teachers how to use the Internet; and Family Fun, a group of products that focuses on exciting, entertaining, interactive activities for the entire family. In August the company was named one of the CityBusiness Great Places To Work. In October wwwrrr formed a strategic partnership with Net Nanny Software International Inc. (CDNX: NNS, OTCBB: NNSWF), Bellevue, Wash. SIC 8299.

Wyo-Ben Inc. 550 S. 24th W., Suite 201, Billings, MT 59102. Tel: 406/652-6351; Fax: 406/656-0748. David S. Brown, Pres.; Harry R. Funk, VP-Mktg.; Robert W. Stichman, VP-Sls.; Douglas A. Buckingham, VP-Fin. and Treas.; Richard K. Brown, VP-Resources. Annual revenue $21.1 million. Wyo-Ben is engaged in the mining of bentonite (clay). 101 employees. Founded in 1952. SIC 1459.

Wyoming Machine Inc. 30680 Forest Blvd., P.O. Box 180, Stacy, MN 55079. Tel: 651/462-4156; Fax: 651/462-5238. Thomas H. Tapani, Pres.; Wayne L. Williams, VP and Gen. Mgr.; Betty L. Tapani, Sec.; Traci L. Tapani, VP-Sls.; Lori A. Tapani, VP-Op. Wyoming Machine provides precision sheet metal fabrication and laser cutting services. 80 employees (all in Minnesota). Founded in 1974. SIC 3444, 3449.

X-Cel Optical Company 806 S. Benton Dr., P.O. Box 420, Sauk Rapids, MN 56379. Tel: 320/251-8404; Fax: 320/251-0511. J. Doescher Sr., Chm. and Pres. X-Cel is a manufacturer of ophthalmic lens blanks. 230 employees. Founded in 1958. SIC 3851.

Xerxes Corporation 7901 Xerxes Ave. S., Suite 201, Bloomington, MN 55431. Tel: 952/887-1890; Fax: 952/887-1870. Al Dorris, Pres. and CEO. Xerxes manufactures fiberglass corrosion-resistant products such as tanks, fume scrubbers, ducts, pipe, stacks, and fans. The company consists of the Underground Storage Tank and Heil Process Equipment businesses. 435 employees. Founded in 1969. SIC 2821, 3089, 3443.

Yaggy Colby Associates 717 Third Ave. S.E., Rochester, MN 55904. Tel: 507/288-6464; Fax: 507/288-5058; Web site: http://www.yaggy.com. Ronald V. Yaggy, Chm.; Donald R. Borcherding, Pres.; Robert L. Ellis, COO; Christopher W. Colby, EVP; Ronald L. Fiscus, VP; Scott S. Samuelson, CFO; Jose L. Rivas, Sec.; Dale R. Allen, Dir.; Mike Fritz, Dir. Annual revenue $7 million. Yaggy Colby Associates provides engineering, architecture, surveying, planning, and landscape architecture. 92 employees (70 in Minnesota). Founded in 1970. 30-year anniversary in 2000. SIC 8711.

Yamamoto Moss 252 First Ave. N., Minneapolis, MN 55401. Tel: 612/375-0180. Shelly Regan, Pres. Annual revenue $11.7 million. Yamamoto Moss is a strategic corporate- and brand-identity firm. 90 employees (91 in Minnesota; 2 part-time). Founded in 1979. In February 2000 Wells Fargo & Co. hired the firm to develop the brand identity for its newly merged Wells Fargo Funds division, thereby more than doubling the business that Moss previously had with Norwest Corp. and Wells Fargo. In July the firm formed an alliance with Strategic Horizons LLP to market and perform "experience audits" for companies seeking to build brands through staging customer experiences. SIC 7311. No. 27 CityBusiness Fastest-growing Private Companies.

Yankton Area Adjustment Training Center Inc. 909 W. 23rd St., Yankton, SD 57078. Tel: 605/665-2518; Fax: 605/665-0206. Clarence N. Carson, Exec. Dir.; John Lane, Sec.; Dan Gergen, Pres. Yankton Area Adjustment is a vocational employment training program for persons with disabilities. It produces pallets, trellises, grade stakes, and cherry pitters; and provides chair caning, aluminum can recycling, assembly work, collating, and subcontracting. 86 employees. Founded in 1974. SIC 8331.

Yellowstone Electric Company P.O. Box 2018, Billings, MT 59103. Tel: 406/252-3407; Fax: 406/252-8965; Web site: http://www.yellowstoneelectric.com. Richard D. Zier, Pres.; Ronald Smith, Sec. and Treas.; Gary Becker, VP. Annual revenue $9.6 million. Yellowstone Electric Co. does electrical contracting, teledata (copper and fiber cabling, networking, and equipment), thermographic scanning, and special systems. 60 employees. Founded in 1937. SIC 1731.

Young America Corporation 717 Faxon Rd., Young America, MN 55397. Tel: 952/467-1100; Fax: 952/467-3895; Web site: http://www.young-america.com. Charles D. Weil, CEO; Robert A. Harrington, VP-Bus. Devel./Account Mgmt.; Roger D. Andersen, VP and CFO; Michael Larson, VP-Consumer Affairs; Barbara Spiess, VP-Hum. Res.; Mary Lynne Perushek, VP and CIO. Young America provides consumer interaction processing services to more than 150 Fortune 500 companies. The company specializes in high-volume, complex, and time-sensitive programs that often involve custom-designed processes, toll-free consumer services, and database management. The company has branches in Chanhassen, Glencoe, and Mankato, Minn.; and in Oklahoma City. 1,400 employees. Founded in 1972. In November 1997, the company was sold to BT (Bankers Trust) Capital Partners Inc., New York, with the participation of the Ontario Teacher's Plan Board and members of Young America management in a deal valued at more than $100 million. In January 2000 the company the assets of SourceOne Worldwide LLC, located in Denver, Colorado. In May Young America and planet U (www.planetu.com), the online promotions network for the consumer goods industry, announced an online sampling partnership. U-pons Internet Sampling was to offer household-level targeted product samples—along with site placement, dynamic intelligent targeting, secure home delivery, customer service, and actionable data on consumer preferences and demographics. SIC 7389. No. 45 CRM Private 100.

Ziegler Inc. 901 W. 94th St., Bloomington, MN 55420. Tel: 952/888-4121; Fax: 952/887-5885; Web site: http://www.zieglerinc.com. Leonard C. Hoeft, Chm.; William L. Hoeft, Pres. and CEO; S.K. Erickson, EVP-Fin. and Sec./Treas.; R.M. Lervick, EVP-Sls.; A.E. Pearson, VP-Product Support; D.R. Shellenberger, VP-Industrial Devel.; M.R. Allen, Cont. and VP-Admin. Annual revenue $340 million (estimated by Fact Book). Ziegler Inc. is the Minnesota dealer for Caterpillar construction and aggregate/paving products equipment and diesel engines, and for aerial lift equipment. 966 employees. Founded in 1914. SIC 5082. No. 36 CRM Private 100.

Zip Sort Inc. 277 12th Ave. N., Minneapolis, MN 55401. Tel: 612/341-2633; Fax: 612/341-0337. Dana Rhoads, Pres. Zip Sort specializes in the presorting of first- and third-class mail and the application of barcodes to same. A letter shop does commercial and laser printing, inserting, binding, folding, mailing, and labeling. Other locations: Duluth and St. Cloud, Minn.; and locations in four Wisconsin cities: Milwaukee, Madison, Green Bay, and Wausau. 400 employees (250 in Minnesota; 30 part-time). Founded in 1987. SIC 2752.

ZoneTrader.com 5980 Golden Hills Dr., Golden Valley, MN 55416. Tel: 763/512-3200; Fax: 763/512-3219. David Gigerich, Founder, Chm., and CEO; Ruth Bruch, Pres. and COO; Ellen Perl, SVP-Mktg.; Richard A. Smith, SVP and CFO. ZoneTrader.com, formerly Workstations International, is a traditional and online seller of refurbished computer hardware. 60 employees. Founded in 1994. The company received two rounds of venture capital financing: $16.5 million late in 1999 and $47 million in March 2000. In April David Gigerich was named one of 25 finalists in the 2000 Minnesota and Dakotas Entrepreneur of the Year Awards by Ernst & Young. The awards were presented during a gala celebration on June 21. In July the company was named one of Forbes Magazine's "Best of the Web" in the publication's first annual Best of the Web: B2B Guide. The company formed an alliance with Peregrine Systems Inc., San Diego, to help companies better manage their capital assets. Peregrine also made an equity investment in ZoneTrader. In September the company acquired a leading U.S. auction company, National Industrial Services Inc. (NISI), St. Louis. Since it was founded in 1981, NISI had executed more than 900 auctions and sold more than $1 billion in assets for its customers worldwide, recently generating more than $30 million in annual auction revenue. Key clients: Delphi Automotive, Tyco Electronics, and Cooper Industries. SIC 5045.

NOTES

NOTES

NOTES

NOTES

NOTES

NOTES

NOTES

NOTES

NOTES

NOTES

NOTES

NOTES

NONPROFIT COMPANIES

Entries include 232 organizations with 50 or more employees
Each organization is headquartered in the Ninth Federal Reserve District

INCLUDES

CONTACT INFORMATION
DESCRIPTION
OFFICERS
BOARD MEMBERS
REVENUE
EXPENSES
CONTRIBUTIONS
NUMBER OF MINNESOTA EMPLOYEES
YEAR FOUNDED
SIC CODE
RANKINGS
RECENT INFORMATION
(information provided where available)

Information is updated annually by each organization through a questionnaire
(There was no charge for inclusion)

A Plus Home Care Inc.
8932 Old Cedar Ave. S., Bloomington, MN 55425
Tel: 952/854-7760 Fax: 952/854-7842
Web site: http://www.aplushomecare.org
Donna Robb, Pres. and CEO
Deanna Robb, VP
Annual Revenue: $2.5 million.
A Plus Home Care Inc. provides personal care services to the disabled community in their homes, to allow them to live independently.
265 employees.
Founded in 1988. SIC 8082, 8322.

AAA Minneapolis
5400 Auto Club Way, Bloomington, MN 55416
Tel: 952/927-2600 Fax: 952/927-2559
Martha Head, Chm.
Steven Frank, Pres. and CEO
Lee Q. Heutmaker, Treas.
Thomas E. Hyland, Sec.
AAA Minneapolis is a motoring, travel, and financial services organization serving 153,000 members in Hennepin County. It provides insurance, travel agency, and motor vehicle license services to AAA members and nonmembers. Member core services include emergency road service, auto travel, and travel agency services. AAA Minneapolis has eight offices in Hennepin County.
240 employees.
Founded in 1902. SIC 4724, 6331.

Ability Building Center
1911 14th St. N.W., P.O. Box 6938, Rochester, MN 55903
Tel: 507/281-6262 Fax: 507/281-6270
Wallace W. Bigelow, Exec. Dir.
Steve Hill, Asst. Dir.
Ability Building Center provides employment, training, and job placement for persons with a disability. A production area does contract manufacturing and packaging, commercial sewing, mailing services, and sign making.
510 employees.
Founded in 1956. SIC 8331.

ABLE Inc.
137 E. Main St., Caledonia, MN 55921
Tel: 507/724-2486 Fax: 507/724-2495
Celia Fluekiger, Interim Exec. Dir.
ABLE Inc., formerly known as Houston County Group Homes Inc., provides services to people with developmental disabilities and related conditions.
250 employees.
Founded in 1979. SIC 8361.

AccessAbility Inc.
360 Hoover St. N.E., Minneapolis, MN 55413
Tel: 612/331-5958 Fax: 612/331-2448
Bonita Hammel, Pres.
David King, VP
AccessAbility Inc. provides businesses with access to the skills of people with disabilities by providing document destruction, packaging and assembly, and mailing services to business and industry in the Twin Cities Metro area. In addition, people with disabilites are placed in jobs in the community either individually or in work crews.
70 employees.
Founded in 1948. SIC 8331.

Accessible Space Inc.
2550 University Ave. W., Suite 330N, St. Paul, MN 55114
Tel: 651/645-7271 Fax: 651/645-0541
Web site: http://www.accessiblespace.org
Stephen Vander Schaaf, Pres. and CEO
Lynda Adams, Dir.-Contract Admin.
Matthew Crellin, Dir.-Real Estate
Bradley A. Fuller, Gen. Counsel
Robert Hogan, Nevada Program Dir.
Shauna Johnson, Dir.-Hum. Res.
Marjorie A. Lee, Dir.-Finance
David Piltz, Dir.-Research
Jennifer Samaha, Dir.-Programs
Annual Revenue: $21.5 million.
Annual Expenses: $20.3 million.
Contributions: 28.5 percent of revenue.
Accessible Space, Inc. (ASI) provides community-based health care services and outpatient rehabilitation care to adults with severe mobility impairments and brain injuries. ASI also develops and provides accessible, affordable housing for low income people with physical disabilities. The majority of ASI's services are based in Minnesota, but ASI also operates in Arizona, California, Idaho, Montana, Nevada, North Dakota, South Dakota, Tennessee, Texas, Virginia and Washington. New services are underway in five otherstates and cooperative ventures with nonprofit organizations have been initiated in Hawaii, Florida, Massachusetts, Mississippi, Nebraska and Oregon.
600 employees.
Founded in 1978. SIC 8361.
No. 86 CRM Nonprofit 100.

Aitkin Community Hospital Inc.
301 Minnesota Ave. S., Aitkin, MN 56431
Tel: 218/927-2121 Fax: 218/927-6360
Debra K. Boardman, CEO
Kathy Falk, Dir.-Ancillary Svs.
Pauline Long, Dir.-Nursing
Stephen Witt, Dir.-Finance
Sharon Thompson, Dir.
Aitkin Community Hospital Inc. does business as Riverwood Healthcare Center.
310 employees.
Founded in 1948. SIC 8062.

Albert Lea Medical Center—Mayo Health System
404 Fountain St., Albert Lea, MN 56007
Tel: 507/373-2384 Fax: 507/377-6327
Dr. Ronald A. Harmon, Vice Chair and CEO
Scott Rafferty, CFO
Tonia Lauer, Dir.-Hum. Res.
Annual Revenue: $58.5 million.
Annual Expenses: $54 million.
Contributions: 0.2 percent of revenue.
Albert Lea Medical Center—Mayo Health System provides a wide variety of health care management services for other health care providers.
950 employees.
Founded in 1981. SIC 8742.
No. 37 CRM Nonprofit 100.

Allina Health System
5601 Smetana Dr., Minnetonka, MN 55343
Tel: 952/992-2000 Fax: 952/992-3550
Web site: http://www.allina.com
William W. George, Chair
Judith Shank, M.D., Vice Chair
Gordon M. Sprenger, Pres. and CEO
David Strand, System VP-Market Network Pres.
Robert K. Spinner, Pres.-Allina Hosp./Sys. VP
Richard S. Blair, Treas.
Michael W. Howe, Ph.D., SVP-Hum. Res.
David Jones, SVP-Admin.
William MacNally, System VP-Info. Op.
Jan Malcolm, System VP-Community Affairs
Mark G. Mishek, SVP-Legal, Gen. Counsel, Sec.
Julianne Morath, System VP-Quality
David B. Pryor, M.D., SVP, Info. Ofcr.
Karen Vigil, COO-Medica
Nancy DeZellar Walsh, VP-Operations
Annual Revenue: $2.68 billion.

Annual Expenses: $2.68 billion.
Allina Health System is a nonprofit, integrated health care organization serving communities throughout Minnesota, western Wisconsin, and eastern North and South Dakota. Allina Health System includes two divisions: a health plan division and a care-delivery division, as well as the Allina Health System Foundation. Medica, the health plan division, has more than 1 million members. Its provider network includes 10,000 physicians and other health professionals. Allina Hospitals & Clinics, the care-delivery division, is comprised of 11 owned hospitals, six managed hospitals, six owned or managed nursing homes, home care and hospice services, medical transportation, and other health-related services. Allina Medical Clinic, a part of Allina Hospitals & Clinics, serves 45 communities and employs more than 600 physicians and providers. Allina also maintains consumer Web sites, www.allina.com and www.medformation.com.
22,546 employees.
Founded in 1994. SIC 8011.
No. 3 CRM Nonprofit 100.
No. 6 CRM Employer 100.
Recent: *In December 1999 plans to develop a $15 million outpatient clinic in Burnsville, Minn., with HealthSystem Minnesota were halted indefinitely due to the capital constraints of both organizations. Abbott Northwestern was ranked one of the best places in America to have orthopedic surgery, according to a study by Baltimore-based HCIA Inc., the national's largest health care data company. Dec. 31: Continued inflationary pressures on the cost of health care resulted in a net operating loss at Medica for the year of $13.2 million—a comparable improvement over 1998 of more than $17 million. For the third-consecutive year, Medica moved closer to renewed profitability by substantially reducing its operating loss from the $18.8 million loss reported in 1998 and $23.9 million in 1997. Medica's improved 1999 operating line was achieved along with 100 percent payment of its physician reimbursement withhold. (The amount of payment returned to physicians in 1998 was 60 percent.) In January 2000 Allina Medical Clinic's Smokers Helpline (ASH) was testing a new approach using physicians as the initial contact with addicted smokers. In February the testing of a new heart failure therapy began at United Hospital when the first patient in the country received an implanted biventricular pacemaker as part of a national study. In June McKesson HBOC Inc. (NYSE: MCK) agreed to provide its Clinical Reference Systems (CRS) patient education information on www.medformation.com. Phillips Eye Institute's Vision Rehabilitation Center was the first in the Twin Cities to offer NuVision, a breakthrough in optical video technology. "This new device allows people with severely impaired vision to use their remaining vision effectively and become more independent," said Kate Grathwol, program coordinator of Phillips' Vision Rehabilitation Center. The device combines magnification and image enhancement in a personal display using two small LCD screens positioned directly in front of a patient's eyes. On June 30, during remarks closing a three-day National Patient Safety Symposium in Dallas, CEO Sprenger challenged the leadership of the health care industry to make patient safety a board-level priority and adopt full disclosure policies in their organizations' strategic plans. Mercy and Unity Hospitals acquired a powerful new diagnostic tool enabling physicians to see real-time images of the electrical activity within a patient's heart, and thereby pinpoint the location of normal and abnormal heartbeats—information vital to treating arrhythmias. On July 28, United Hospital opened the $25 million John Nasseff Heart Hospital, a state-of-the-art facility combining the healing powers of high touch and ground-breaking technology, dedicated solely to the diagnosis and treatment of heart disease. In October Allina.com was named "Best of the Best" in health care provider Web sites by Modern Healthcare magazine and the CSC (Computer Sciences Corp.) Healthcare Group. A resource found in Allina.com is Medformation.com, the regional health care Web portal designed by Allina Health System and HealthOnline Inc. Many of the special features cited in the award are found on Medformation.com. The Institute for Safe Medication Practices nationally recognized Allina Health System with two medication safety awards. Allina Hospitals & Clinics won the two awards for their entry of a medication safety orientation program and a patient safety culture assessment. Medica signed a letter of intent to develop 32 acres in Hopkins, Minn. (currently the site of a Supervalu warehouse), for its new 900-employee, 300,000-square-foot corporate headquarters.*

Alternatives for People with Autism
5624 73rd Ave. N., Brooklyn Park, MN 55429
Tel: 763/560-5330 Fax: 763/566-5652
John Makepeace, Exec. Dir.
63 employees.
Founded in 1980. SIC 8331.

American Baptist Homes of the Midwest Foundation
11985 Technology Dr., Eden Prairie, MN 55344
Tel: 952/941-3175
Jim McCaul, Co-pres.
Judy Lysne, Co-pres.
Annual Revenue: $0.8 million.
Annual Expenses: $0.1 million.
Contributions: 92.3 percent of revenue.
185 employees (183 in Minnesota).
SIC 8361.

American Cancer Society Midwest Division Inc.
3316 W. 66th St., Edina, MN 55435
Tel: 952/925-2772 Fax: 952/925-6333
Web site: http://www.cancer.org
James M. Smith, CEO-Midwest Div.
Jari Allen, CFO-Midwest Div.
Tom Burns, VP-North Central Region
Jo Carlson, VP-South Region
Jon Carlson, VP-Income Devel.
Laurie Fitz, Evaluation/Planning
Dave Grams, VP-Southeast Region
Howard Heino, VP-Operations
Russ Hinz, VP-Programs
Steve Holtorf, VP-Finance
Judy Ireland, VP-Central Reg.
John Klika, VP-East Region
Jan Klimiades, VP-West Region
William McCracken, COO-Midwest Div.
Rich Smith, VP-Hum. Res.
Maribeth Swenty, VP-Northeast Region
Linda Montet, VP-Mktg./Comm.
Jim Wallace, VP-South Central Region
Annual Revenue: $50.9 million.
Annual Expenses: $47.2 million.
Contributions: 91.9 percent of revenue.
The American Cancer Society is the nationwide community-based voluntary health organization dedicated to eliminating cancer as a major health problem by preventing cancer, saving lives, and diminishing suffering from cancer through research, education, advocacy, and service.
465 employees.
Founded in 1998. SIC 8733.
No. 47 CRM Nonprofit 100.

American Heart Association-Minnesota Affiliate Inc.
4701 W. 77th St., Edina, MN 55435
Tel: 952/835-3300 Fax: 952/835-5828
Web site: http://www.americanheart.org
Robert L. Burfeind, Chm.
Brooks S. Edwards, M.D., Pres.
William J. "Chip" Sugrue, EVP
Patrick Stieg, SVP
Fredrick C. Moors, Dir.-Major/Planned Gifts
American Heart Association Inc.-Minnesota Affiliate raises funds for study and prevention of heart disease and stroke. Approximately 25 percent of total public support is distributed to support national programs and research through the American Heart Association, National Center, Dallas, Texas.
52 employees.
Founded in 1947. SIC 8733.

American Red Cross-Minneapolis Area Chapter
1201 West River Pkwy., Minneapolis, MN 55454
Tel: 612/871-7676 Fax: 612/872-3200
Web site: http://www.mplsredcross.org
Marian S. Adcock, CEO
Jon Eisele, Board Chair

Paul Brown, Treas.
Bonnie Sipkins, Sec.
Annual Revenue: $7.7 million.
Annual Expenses: $5.4 million.
Contributions: 79.5 percent of revenue.
American Red Cross-Minneapolis Area Chapter provides humanitarian assistance in emergencies and health education services to all people. They rely heavily on the volunteer community to develop and deliver programs and services. They are a member of the 145-society International Red Cross movement.
62 employees.
Founded in 1915. SIC 8299, 8322.

American Refugee Committee
2344 Nicollet Ave. S., Suite 350, Minneapolis, MN 55404
Tel: 612/872-7060 Fax: 612/872-4309
Anthony J. Kozlowski, Pres. and CEO
Joe Bock, Deputy Exec. Dir.
Karen Johnson Elshazly, Dir.-Int'l Programs
Greg Fields, Dir.-Devel.
James Mace, Dir.-Finance
Colleen Striegel, Dir.-Hum. Res./Admin.
Annual Revenue: $21.7 million.
Annual Expenses: $20.7 million.
Contributions: 75.3 percent of revenue.
The American Refugee Committee (ARC) provides primary health care, self-help training, and related services to more than 1 million refugees, most of them women and children, in 12 countries. Through the use of volunteer specialists and staff, ARC works to ensure the survival, health, and well-being of refugees, enabling them to rebuild self-sufficient, productive lives of dignity and purpose. ARC operations in Kosovo, Montenegro, Macedonia, Serbia, Sierra Leone, Liberia, Bosnia, Croatia, Rwanda, Sudan, Guinea, and Thailand are served by regional offices in Split, Croatia; Nairobi, Kenya; and Bangkok, Thailand. The organization's employees are mostly refugee and local workers who are supervised and trained by 50 ARC volunteer expatriate specialists.
600 employees.
Founded in 1978. SIC 8399.
No. 84 CRM Nonprofit 100.

Animal Humane Society of Hennepin County
845 Meadow Ln. N., Golden Valley, MN 55422
Tel: 763/522-4325 Fax: 763/522-0933
Alan T. Stensrud, Exec. Dir.
Judy Dworkin, Dir.-Pub. Rel.
Rick Gabrielson, Fund Devel./Gambling Mgr.
Fontaine Hebb, Dir.-Fund Devel.
Mike Petersdorf, Asst. to Exec. Dir.
Rick Riley, Dir.-Facilities/Grounds
Scott Line, Dir.-Education Svs.
The Animal Humane Society of Hennepin County offers educational and therapeutic programs for people; as well as humane, shelter, and adoption services for animals. In 1996, the Animal Humane Society placed 11,270 of the 22,622 animals received. The Animal Humane Society presented over 1,500 programs (including 500 school visits) during 1996 with over 71,000 individuals participating. Staff and volunteers, accompanied by shelter animals, made more than 570 visits to health care facilities. The humane investigation department received over 2,900 reports of cruelty, neglect and animal abuse, and investigated 985 cases of alleged cruelty to animals.
62 employees.
Founded in 1891. SIC 8699.

Arrowhead Economic Opportunity Agency Inc.
702 Third Ave. S., Virginia, MN 55792
Tel: 800/662-5711
Web site: http://aeoa.org
Steve Raukker, Chair
Harlan Tardy, Exec. Dir.
Paul Carlson, Asst. Exec. Dir.
Annual Revenue: $19.8 million.
Annual Expenses: $19.5 million.
Contributions: 76.2 percent of revenue.
Arrowhead Economic Opportunity Agency provides programs and services for those with limited resources.
435 employees.
No. 90 CRM Nonprofit 100.

Aspen Medical Group
1020 W. Bandana Blvd., St. Paul, MN 55108
Tel: 651/641-7000 Fax: 651/642-9441
Peggy Naas, M.D., Chair
Thomas Holets, CEO
Britt Rooney, COO
David Anderson, Dir.-Hum. Res.
Annual Revenue: $101.5 million.
Annual Expenses: $101.4 million.
Aspen Medical Group is a multispecialty medical group practice.
850 employees.
Founded in 1974. SIC 8011.
No. 20 CRM Nonprofit 100.

Assumption Home Inc.
715 N. First St., Cold Spring, MN 56320
Tel: 320/685-3693
Assumption Home Inc. is a long-term care facility for seniors.
106 employees.
Founded in 1963. SIC 8361.

Augsburg College
731 21st Ave. S., Minneapolis, MN 55454
Tel: 612/330-1026 Fax: 612/330-1330
William Frame, Pres.
Marie McNeff, VP-Academic Affairs
Rick Thoni, VP-Enrollment Mgmt.
Ida Simon, VP-Devel.
Paul Carlson, VP-Finance
Annual Revenue: $46.9 million.
Annual Expenses: $43.2 million.
Contributions: 14.2 percent of revenue.
Augsburg College is a four-year, liberal arts college of the Evangelical Lutheran Church in America. Augsburg offers Bachelor of Arts, Bachelor of Music, and Bachelor of Science degrees. Through its Weekend College and traditional undergraduate program, Augsburg also offers master's degrees in leadership, education-leadership, and social work.
623 employees.
Founded in 1869. SIC 8221.
No. 51 CRM Nonprofit 100.

Augsburg Fortress, Publishers
100 S. Fifth St., P.O. Box 1209, Minneapolis, MN 55440
Tel: 612/330-3300 Fax: 612/330-3455
Marvin L. Roloff, Pres. and CEO
Charles C. Halberg, EVP and COO
Kenneth G. Hartwell, SVP and Chief Mktg. Ofcr.
Bruce Keil, VP-Operations
George W. Poehlman, VP-Finance
Sandra Middendorf, VP-Hum. Res.
Annual Revenue: $56.2 million.
Augsburg Fortress, Publishers is the publishing house of the Evangelical Lutheran Church in America. Products include Fortress Press academic books, Augsburg Books, general books, Friar Tuck clergy shirts, church bulletins, music, video products, ecclesiastical arts, and other resources for congregations of the ELCA and for ecumenical denominations. The company has operations in Minnesota, Alberta, Ontario, Puerto Rico, Ohio, Nebraska, Washington, Texas, California, Pennsylvania, Illinois, and New York.
335 employees.
Founded in 1988. SIC 2731.
No. 39 CRM Nonprofit 100.

Augustana Care Corporation
1007 E. 14th St., Minneapolis, MN 55404
Tel: 612/333-1551 Fax: 612/333-7323
Timothy H. Tucker, CEO
Craig Kittelson, CFO
Gerry Berglin, Admin.-Augustana Home of Mpls.

Steven Fritzke, Administrator-Chapel View
Chesley Strom, Corp. Dir.-Devel.
Maggie Grein, Administrator-Home Health
Jackie Nelson, Admin.-Augustana Home Hastings
Kristy Hoepner, Dir.-Augustana Therapy Svc.
Annual Revenue: $34.8 million.
Annual Expenses: $33.3 million.
Contributions: 2.3 percent of revenue.
Augustana Care Corp. is the parent company of Augustana Care Foundation, Augustana Care Services, Augustana Home Health Care Services, Augustana Home of Hastings, and Augustana Chapel View Homes Inc. It was organized to provide health care, housing alternatives, and community services for the elderly. The Augustana Care Foundation manages investments exclusively for the benefit of the charitable purposes of the Augustana Care Corp.
Augustana Care Services provides operational managment for all affiliates. Augustana Home Health Care Services provides home health care to clients on its campuses in the metropolitan area. Augustana Chapel View Homes Inc. owns and operates three licensed nursing facilities and two senior apartment complexes. The organization, as a whole, serves 1,134 residents and provides 300 skilled home health care visits each month, assisted by 448 volunteers.
675 employees.
Founded in 1896. SIC 8051.
No. 60 CRM Nonprofit 100.

Laura Baker Services Association
211 Oak St., P.O. Box 611, Northfield, MN 55057
Tel: 507/645-8866 Fax: 507/645-8869
Web site: http://www.lbsa.com
Sandra R. Gerdes, Exec. Dir.
Paul D. Hermanson, CFO
Deb Carlson, Dir.-Oak St. Svs.
Doug Fitzgerald, Dir.-Community Rel.
Bonita Martinson, Dir.-Community Svs.
Annual Revenue: $3.2 million.
Annual Expenses: $3 million.
Contributions: 0.5 percent of revenue.
Laura Baker Services Association provides residential, educational, and vocational services to people with developmental disabilities. Residents at 211 Oak St. (ICF-MR status) specialize in crisis and transitional services for people with Prader Willi Syndrome.
150 employees.
Founded in 1897. SIC 8211.

Banner Health System
4310 17th Ave. S.W., Fargo, ND 58106
Tel: 701/277-7500 Fax: 701/277-7636
Web site: http://www.bannerhealth.com
Wilford A. Cardon, Chm.
Peter S. Fine, Pres. and CEO
Dave Bixby, EVP, Gen. Counsel, Asst. Sec.
Craig Broman, EVP and CEO-Banner Health West
Ron Bunnell, EVP, CFO, Treas.
Jim Crews, CEO-Arizona Div.
Chuck Welliver, EVP and CEO-Banner Health Ariz
Lynn Bruchhof, SVP-Innovation/Learning
Deborah H. Dahl, SVP-Tech./Materials
Don A. Evans, SVP and COO-Banner Health Ariz
Donald W. Legreid, SVP-Legal/Risk Affairs
Thomas M. Mingen, SVP-Acquisitions/Devel.
Eric M. Monson, SVP-Biotech/Govt. Policy
Dale L. Schultz, SVP-Bus. Health/Risk Mgmt.
Gerri L. Twomey, SVP-People Resources
Douglas Vang, SVP and COO-Banner Health West
Michael S. Warden, SVP and Chief Info. Ofcr.
Shirley A. Schenck, Corp. Sec.
Annual Revenue: $3.89 billion.
Banner Health Systems, formerly Fargo, ND based Lutheran Health Systems, operates hospitals, nursing homes, and other health care services in Alaska, Arizona, California, Colorado, Iowa, Kansas, Minnesota, Nebraska, Nevada, New Mexico, North Dakota, Oregon, South Dakota, and Wyoming. The organization owns, leases, and manages hospitals, nursing homes, home care organizations, and durable medical equipment distributors; and contracts with physicians and clinics to manage health care services for the communities it serves.
24,500 employees.
Founded in 1938. SIC 8051, 8062.
Recent: *In December 1998 the governing boards for Lutheran Health Systems, Fargo, and Samaritan Health System, Phoenix, approved a letter of intent to merge the two not-for-profit health care systems. On Sept. 1, 1999, Samaritan and LHS completed legal transactions creating Banner Health System. In October 2000 the board of directors appointed Peter S. Fine as president and CEO, effective Nov. 13, to replace the retiring Steven Orr. Fine had been EVP/COO of Aurora Health Care in Milwaukee.*

Bear Creek Services Inc.
620 First St. S.W., Rochester, MN 55902
Tel: 507/288-7195
Frank J. Anderson Jr., Exec. Dir.
Annual Revenue: $3.3 million.
Annual Expenses: $3.3 million.
Contributions: 1.1 percent of revenue.
Bear Creek Services Inc. provides residential and support services for adults with developmental disabilities. Financial support comes from the Bear Creek Services Foundation.
131 employees.
Founded in 1976. SIC 8361.

Benedictine Health System
503 E. Third St., Suite 400, Duluth, MN 55805
Tel: 218/720-2370 Fax: 218/720-2373
Web site: http://www.bhshealth.org
Barry J. Halm, Pres. and CEO
Ben Aune, EVP-Strategic Mgmt.
Tom Bila, Pres.-Ben. Health Sys. Fdn.
Lynnette Bouta, EVP-Mission Integration
Tom Crook, VP-Fin. Svs.
Christine Hogan-Newgren, VP-Corp. Compliance/Int. Audit
Janis Kivela Hooey, Communications Mgr.
Marge Johnson, COO-Acute Care Svs. Div.
Dennis Kamstra, EVP-Corp. Devel.
Donald Leiverman, SVP-Acute Care Svs.
Pamela Lindemoen, EVP-Corp. Services
Robert Norman, EVP and CFO
Sr. Claudia Riehl, Dir.-Mission Integration
Dale Thompson, COO-Long Term Care/Housing
Annual Revenue: $227.2 million.
Annual Expenses: $213.8 million.
Contributions: 0.5 percent of revenue.
Benedictine Health System (BHS) is a Catholic mission-directed and values-based organization with corporate offices in Duluth, Cambridge and New Brighton, Minn. BHS, sponsored by the Benedictine Sisters of St. Scholastica Monastery-Duluth, owns and/or manages more than 60 healthcare facilities in nine states.
3,139 employees.
Founded in 1985. SIC 8062.
No. 13 CRM Nonprofit 100.
No. 89 CRM Employer 100.
Recent: *In March 2000 Benedictine Health Dimensions was looking into a plan to build a new, 80-bed nursing home in under-bedded Osseo, Minn.—where the Osseo Health Care Center was being shut down. Effective July 1, the Long Term Care Foundation contracted with the Benedictine Health System Long Term Care & Housing Services Division to provide management for Ashley Crossing Rehabilitation & Nursing Center, a 132-bed nursing facility with subacute care and rehabilitation, Alzheimer's and respite care. Ashley Crossing is located in Charleston, S.C. Mary Washington Health Center, a 60-bed long-term facility in Colonial Beach, Va., became a Benedictine Health System Associate Organization on July 20. The Mary Washington Senior Living Community, a subsidiary of the Living Services*

Foundation of Minnesota, purchased the Center on July 20 from MediCorp Health System. The Living Services Foundation contracted with BHS to manage the Center.

Bethel College & Seminary

3900 Bethel Dr., Arden Hills, MN 55112
Tel: 651/638-6400 Fax: 651/638-6001
Dr. George K. Brushaber, Pres.
James Barnes, Provost
John Bergeson, CFO
Leland Eliason, EVP and Dean-Seminary
James R. Thomann, EVP-Admin./Finance
Ronald R. Harris, VP-Devel.
Judith A. Moseman, VP-Student Life
Annual Revenue: $59.6 million.
Annual Expenses: $58.2 million.
Contributions: 10.8 percent of revenue.
Bethel College & Seminary is a Christian liberal arts college enrolling more than 1,900 students. It offers more than 50 academic majors—plus master's degrees in education, psychology, and organizational leadership. Bethel also offers PACE, an accelerated program for students over 25 who are continuing their education. The student body represents a wide range of national and international cultures and more than 40 church denominations. Bethel also operates a graduate theological seminary with campuses in St. Paul and San Diego.
550 employees.
Founded in 1871. SIC 8221.
No. 34 CRM Nonprofit 100.

Bethesda Homes

901 S.E. Willmar Ave., Willmar, MN 56201
Tel: 320/235-9532 Fax: 320/235-7909
Web site: http://www.bethesdwillmar.com
Douglas Dewane, Exec. Administrator
Bethesda Homes provides nursing care and related housing services for residents.
420 employees.
Founded in 1897. SIC 8059.

Black Hills Workshop & Training Center Inc.

3603 Range Rd., P.O. Box 2104, Rapid City, SD 57709
Tel: 605/343-4550 Fax: 605/343-0879
Web site: http://www.bhws.com
John Howard, Chm.
Dennis E. Popp, Pres. and CEO
Black Hills Workshop provides rehabilitation, residential, and job-placement services to adults with disabilities. We also provide businesses with a workforce skilled in the areas of light manufacturing, assembly, packaging, and mailing. Through BH Services, a division of Black Hills Workshop, we fulfill contracts with government agencies in the areas of custodial service, supply store operations, commissary operations, and food service. Additionally, Dakota Laser Tech is a Black Hills Workshop company, providing quality remanufactured laser printer cartridges to businesses, government offices and individuals in western South Dakota.
300 employees (60 part-time).
Founded in 1958. SIC 3999, 7349, 7389.

The Blake School

110 Blake Rd., Hopkins, MN 55343
Tel: 952/988-3400 Fax: 952/988-3455
John Gulla, Head-School and Pres.
Kathyrn Knapp, Upper School Dir.
Margaret Jadin, Dir.-Business/Finance
Jane Howard, Devel. Dir.
Elizabeth Passi, Lower School Dir.
Adaline Shinkle, Dir.-Admissions
Beth Hower, Lower School Dir.
Charles Seel, Upper School Academic Coord.
Annual Revenue: $25.8 million.
Annual Expenses: $20 million.
Contributions: 21.4 percent of revenue.
The Blake School is a pre-K through 12, nonsectarian, independent, coeducational, college-preparatory day school with campuses in Hopkins, Minneapolis, and Wayzata, Minn., and an enrollment of 1,245 students.
296 employees.
Founded in 1900. SIC 8211.
No. 75 CRM Nonprofit 100.
Recent: *In October 2000 the school officially embarked on a $50 million campaign, one of the largest campaigns ever mounted by an independent pre-K through 12 school in the United States. To date, Blake had received pledges and payments of $31 million from dozens of the school's closest friends and benefactors. It was entering the public part of its campaign, to raise the additional $19 million.*

Blue Cross and Blue Shield of Minnesota

3535 Blue Cross Rd., P.O. Box 64560, Eagan, MN 55164
Tel: 651/456-8000 Fax: 651/456-1570
Mark Banks, M.D., Pres. and CEO
Deborah Madson, VP-Gov't Program/COO-Blue Plus
William Gold, M.D., CMO and VP-Health Mgmt.
Roger W. Kleppe, VP-Hum. Res./Quality Mgmt.
Michael Morrow, VP-Planning/Bus. Devel.
Nancy Nelson, VP and Chief Actuary
Richard P. Neuner, Chief Mktg. Officer, VP-Sales
Richard Niemiec, SVP-Corp. Affairs
John N. Ounjian, CIO and SVP-Info. Systems
Timothy Peterson, CFO and VP-Fin.
Colleen Reitan, SVP-Network Mgmt./Gov't Bus.
Annual Revenue: $2.88 billion.
Annual Expenses: $2.91 billion.
Blue Cross and Blue Shield of Minnesota (BCBSM) is the state's first and largest health coverage carrier. As a nonprofit health service corporation authorized to conduct business under Minnesota statutes, BCBSM is regulated by the Minnesota Department of Commerce. Net enrollment in BCBSM and its nonprofit affiliates, including Blue Plus (the HMO unit), totals more than 1.7 million. BCBS also administers the federal Medicare programs, and serves as the writing carrier for the Minnesota Comprehensive Health Association. The company also offers a variety of other employee benefits services through several for-profit subsidiaries, including pharmaceutical benefits manager Pharmacy Gold. Aware Integrated Inc. is the holding company for BCBSM.
3,137 employees.
Founded in 1933. SIC 6324.
No. 2 CRM Nonprofit 100.
No. 71 CRM Employer 100.
Recent: *When he succeeded Andy Czajkowski as CEO in December 1999, Banks became the only physician leading a Minnesota health plan. In February 2000 A.M. Best Co. affirmed the A (Excellent) rating of BCBSM—reflecting the company's strong market presence, continued enrollment growth, sound financial condition, and advanced operational capabilities. Offsetting factors included a regulatory constraint on capital, competitive conditions in the Minneapolis/St.Paul metropolitan market, and sustained underwriting performance pressure. Blue Plus reached an agreement with Lutheran Social Service (LSS) regarding the inclusion of LSS clinics in Blue Plus' referral network for mental health services. The state Appeals Court ruled that BCBSM should control its $469 million share of the state's 1998 settlement with the big tobacco companies. [In March, arguing that the court went beyond its constitutional authority, the Minnesota Commissioner of Commerce asked the Minnesota Supreme Court to review that decision.] BCBSM intended to invest all excess surplus in health improvement initiatives. In March BCBSM and FirePond Inc., a leader in e-business sales and marketing solutions, released Blue Edge, an interactive selling tool for insurance agents who sell Blue Cross products. Blue Edge was designed to simplify the process of buying insurance, to reduce costs, and to allow efficient comparison-shopping. In August BCBSM reported that Minnesota seniors enrolled in a BCBSM Medicare supplement or select plan saved $6.7 million dollars in prescription drug costs in 1999 through a no-cost prescription drug feature called Rx Advantage. In September BCBSM announced an agreement with ican Inc. giving health professionals access to a high-technology resource with timely, reliable information about infectious diseases and infection control. In October Minnesota Attorney General Mike Hatch filed a lawsuit against BCBSM accusing it of engaging in a "pattern of misconduct" in denying medically necessary health care treatment recommended by physicians for Minnesota children and young adults suffering from mental illness, eating disorders, and chemical dependency. The lawsuit alleged that BCBSM was routinely attempting to sidestep its coverage obliga-*

tions by inappropriately shifting the cost of caring for such children to taxpayers and/or families, including instructing parents to have their children suffer "legal consequences" or to make "use of the juvenile justice system" instead of providing the care covered by the policy. "It's difficult for me to hear the false charges brought forward in the attorney general's lawsuit," Banks responded. "The six illustrations described in the complaint are not typical cases. More than 90 percent of requests to Blue Cross for mental health treatment are covered in accord with the recommendation of the treating practitioner. From January through September 2000, alone, Blue Cross paid out more than $67 million in mental health and chemical dependency benefits for our members. Nearly one-third—$21 million—of those benefits was for mental health and chemical dependency treatment for children. The attorney general suggests that the medical review process employed by Blue Cross is inherently suspect. Yet, the legislature has specifically endorsed the concept of utilization review and peer review with the enactment of comprehensive legislation." BCBSM was awarded the health plan industry's highest honor in the Managed Care Achievements in Tobacco Control category, for an innovative policy that helps smokers quit. The American Association of Health Plans (AAHP) created a "Special Recognition" award level for the policy, which covers physician office visits to treat tobacco use and addiction. BCBSM affiliate Care Delivery Management Inc. launched ExpertChoice, an injury care management program offered to workers' compensation and automobile insurers.

Board of Social Ministry

3490 Lexington Ave. N., Shoreview, MN 55126
Tel: 651/766-4300 Fax: 651/766-4310
Robert D. Armitage, CEO
Kenneth Borle, VP-Finance
Thomas Goeritz, VP-Delivery Systems
Katherine Kopp, VP-Growth/Development
Douglas Newman, VP-Fdn. for Elderly
Annual Revenue: $64.5 million.
Annual Expenses: $64.5 million.
Contributions: 1.3 percent of revenue.
The Board of Social Ministry provides programs that include nonprofit nursing homes, boarding care homes, and senior housing, home care services, rehabilitation services, management services, and consulting.
4,106 employees.
Founded in 1923. SIC 8059, 8082, 8361.
No. 30 CRM Nonprofit 100.
No. 47 CRM Employer 100.

Boy Scouts of America, Indianhead Council

393 Marshall Ave., St. Paul, MN 55102
Tel: 651/224-1891 Fax: 651/224-7239
Web site: http://www.indianhead.org
John R. Andrews, CEO
John W. Maddox, CFO
Annual Revenue: $6.3 million.
Annual Expenses: $6.5 million.
Contributions: 45.7 percent of revenue.
Indianhead Scouting/BSA provides young men (ages 6 through 20) and young women (ages 14 through 20) with programs that facilitate meaningful contact and communication between youth, parents, caring adults and community organizations. The programs offer fun, interesting and age-appropriate activities that help instill traditional values, build character, inspire community service and develop leadership skills.
66 employees.
Founded in 1910. SIC 8641.

Breck School

123 Ottawa Ave. N., Golden Valley, MN 55422
Tel: 763/381-8100
Web site: http://www.breckschool.org
Samuel A. Salas, Headmaster
Wendy Engelman, Business Mgr.
Nancy Speer, Dir.-Devel.
Richard P. Lewis III, Dir.-Middle School
Michael Weiszel, Dir.-Admissions
Barbara F. Stock, Dir.-Upper School
Margaret Bailey, Dir.-Lower School
Annual Revenue: $21.1 million.
Annual Expenses: $15.2 million.
Contributions: 26.3 percent of revenue.
284 employees.
Founded in 1886. SIC 8211.
No. 87 CRM Nonprofit 100.

C

Carleton College

One N. College St., Northfield, MN 55057
Tel: 507/646-4000 Fax: 507/663-4204
Web site: http://www.carleton.edu
Stephen R. Lewis Jr., Pres.
Elizabeth McKinsey, Dean of College
Carol Campbell, VP and Treas.
Barbara Johnson, VP and Treas.
Mark Kronholm, VP-External Relations
Stephen Kelly, Dean of Budget/Planning
Annual Revenue: $181.3 million.
Annual Expenses: $78.5 million.
Contributions: 12.8 percent of revenue.
Carleton College is a four-year, private, liberal arts college that offers a bachelor of arts degree. Carleton has an enrollment of 1,700 on campus, 200 off campus.
650 employees.
Founded in 1866. SIC 8221.
No. 15 CRM Nonprofit 100.
Recent: *President Clinton gave commencement address in June, 2000.*

Catholic Charities of the Archdiocese of St. Paul & Minneapolis

1200 Second Ave. S., Minneapolis, MN 55403
Tel: 612/664-8500 Fax: 612/664-8555
Web site: http://www.ccspm.org
Fr. Larry J. Snyder, VP
Carol Hood, Asst. Dir.-Central Svs.
Mary Ann Sullivan, Asst. Dir.-Family Svs.
Nancy Windyk, Communications Dir.
Morgan Rasmussen, Asst. Dir.-Devel.
Michael Coty, Asst. Dir.-Housing Svs.
Connie Skillingstad, Asst. Dir.-Children's Svs.
Stephanie Burroughs, Dir.-Diversity/Employee Devel.
Annual Revenue: $30.4 million.
Annual Expenses: $31.2 million.
Contributions: 44 percent of revenue.
Catholic Charities of the Archdiocese of St. Paul and Minneapolis provides human services and advocacy for people throughout the 12-county greater metropolitan area—with an emphasis on the poor, the homeless, children, and other vulnerable populations. The agency operates more than 75 programs in 50 locations, which are available to the entire community without regard to religious affiliation. Catholic Charities traces its beginnings as an organized lay ministry to 1869. In 1977 four archdiocesan social service agencies, Catholic Welfare Services of Minneapolis, Catholic Social Services of St. Paul, St. Joseph's Home for Children, and Seton Center were consolidated into one corporate structure.
600 employees.
Founded in 1869. SIC 8322.
No. 66 CRM Nonprofit 100.

Catholic Charities of the Diocese of St. Cloud

1730 Seventh Ave. S., St. Cloud, MN 56301
Tel: 320/252-0412 Fax: 320/240-6892
Steven P. Bresnahan, Exec. Dir.
Annual Revenue: $17.4 million.
Annual Expenses: $15.7 million.
Contributions: 36 percent of revenue.
Catholic Charities of the Diocese of St. Cloud provides a diverse range of social services to people in central Minnesota. Services are provided in a pri-

mary area of 16 counties and a secondary area of 14 counties. The organization operates 32 programs organized into four functional service areas: housing, aging, community, and residential. Catholic Charities is governed by a 25-member operating board.
547 employees.
Founded in 1955. SIC 8322.

Catholic Eldercare Inc.

817 Main St. N.E., Minneapolis, MN 55413
Tel: 612/379-1370 Fax: 612/379-2486
Mary Broderick, Pres. and CEO
Michael J. Shasky, CFO
Kim King, Administrator
Annual Revenue: $10.5 million.
Annual Expenses: $10.4 million.
Catholic Eldercare Inc. provides nursing home care to 150 residents. The organization also provides adult day care to 39 people per day, home health services to 250 people in their homes, and assisted living units are provided to 52 residents.
290 employees.
Founded in 1980. SIC 8051.

Cedar Valley Services Inc.

2111 Fourth St. N.W., Austin, MN 55912
Tel: 507/433-2303 Fax: 507/433-8880
Jim Mueller, Dir.
Cedar Valley Services Inc. provides employment for people with disabilities.
201 employees.
Founded in 1960. SIC 8322.

Center for Alcohol and Drug Treatment

400 Torrey Building, Duluth, MN 55802
Tel: 218/722-4996 Fax: 218/722-2232
Gary P. Olson, Exec. Dir.
Annual Revenue: $2.8 million.
Annual Expenses: $2.4 million.
Contributions: 3.3 percent of revenue.
Center for Alcohol and Drug Treatment provides rehabilitative services for people who are chemically dependent. The Center operates the Marty Mann Halfway House for Women, Howard Friese Halfway House for Men, the Duluth Detoxification Center, and outpatient treatment programs in Duluth and Cloquet.
65 employees.
Founded in 1961. SIC 8093.

CentraCare Health System

1406 N. Sixth Ave., St. Cloud, MN 56303
Tel: 320/255-5661
Al Kremers, Chm.
John R. Frobenius, Co-pres.
Terence R. Pladson, Co-pres.
Annual Revenue: $260.3 million.
Annual Expenses: $262.7 million.
CentraCare is a regional health care delivery system composed of St. Cloud Hospital and more than 100 primary- and specialty-care physicians. The corporation was formed in June 1995 by St. Cloud Hospital and CentraCare Clinic, formerly the St. Cloud Clinic of Internal Medicine. It offers a full range of hospital, clinic, and nursing services.
4,091 employees.
Founded in 1995. SIC 8062.
No. 11 CRM Nonprofit 100.
No. 39 CRM Employer 100.
Recent: *In December 1999 St. Cloud Hospital was one of only five Minnesota hospitals to be ranked in the 100 Top Hospitals in the United States by HCIA-Sachs, the country's largest health care data company. In April 2000 an expanded relationship made CentraCare Health System the sixth member of Life Link III, a mobile intensive care service offering helicopter, ground, and airplane ambulance transport services throughout the region. St. Cloud Hospital and Children's Hospitals and Clinics agreed to develop an outpatient pediatric chemotherapy service in St. Cloud beginning in 2001. Fitch IBCA assigned its 'A' rating to the city of St. Cloud's $168 million health care revenue bonds, series 2000, issued on behalf of St. Cloud Hospital (SCH) and CentraCare Health System (CH). The rating reflects SCH's dominant market share, excellent physician relations, favorable reimbursement environment, and the strong liquidity of CH, the consolidated entity. SCH enjoys a 91 percent market share in its primary service area, as the next-largest hospital within 50 miles of SCH has only 55 staffed beds. This strong market position provides a favorable setting for managed care and physician relationships. This is evidenced by the fact that SCH is profitable on its managed care business and that the Clinic, which employs 108 of CH's 132 employed physicians, has never experienced an annual average loss per physician in its five years of existence. Key credit concerns include the decline in CH's operating margin and its high debt burden. CH's operating margin dropped from 3.9 percent in fiscal 1998 to a negative 0.9 percent in fiscal 1999—due to a one-time write-down of goodwill associated with the acquisition of physician practices, the impact of the Balanced Budget Act of 1997, and the provision of additional, more costly health care services. In May, for the second-consecutive year, St. Cloud Hospital was ranked one of the nation's 100 Top Cardiovascular Hospitals by HCIA-Sachs. St. Cloud Hospital was one of only two Minnesota health care facilities to make the list, the other being SMDC Health System in Duluth. In addition to performing advanced cardiovascular surgery (nearly 4,000 open-heart surgeries to date), the Central Minnesota Heart Center at St. Cloud Hospital provides the latest in diagnostic and interventional cardiology procedures, as well as an extensive cardiology outreach program.*

Central Minnesota Mental Health Center

1321 N. 13th St., St. Cloud, MN 56303
Tel: 320/252-5010 Fax: 320/252-0908
Central Minnesota Mental Health Center reintegrates emotionally disabled people, alcoholics, and substance abusers into the community. The organization also supports reduction and maintenance programs for patients and the community.
80 employees.
Founded in 1963. SIC 8093.

Child Care Resource and Referral Inc.

126 Woodlake Drive S.E., Rochester, MN 55904
Tel: 507/287-2020 Fax: 507/287-2411
Patrick Gannon, Exec. Dir.
Ronald Luck, Finance Dir.
Jeremy Wahlstrom, Research/Education Dir.
Annette Kirchhoff, CACFP Dir.
D. Provo, Head Start Dir.
Carma Bjornson, Family Resource Dir.
Donna Dickison, Child Care Resistance Leader
Becky Pautz, Hum. Res. Mgr.
Child Care Resource and Referral Inc. (CCRR) is dedicated to serving young children, parents, child care professionals, and employers in southeastern Minnesota. The staff and board of directors include parents, child care professionals, and concerned volunteers who are experienced in many areas of child care, parenting, and advocacy for children. CCRR is committed to supporting family cohesion through promoting the quality of existing child care, coordinating child care needs and resources, and facilitating the creation of new programs to meet the expanding needs of children, parents, child care professionals, and employers.
148 employees.
Founded in 1972. SIC 8351.

Children's Home Society of Minnesota

1605 Eustis St., Lauderdale, MN 55108
Tel: 651/646-7771 Fax: 651/646-8676
Web site: http://www.chsm.com
Donna Walgren King, Pres. and CEO
Jacqueline Olafson, VP, Childcare Crisis Nursery
Martha Gerkey, VP-Adoption
Jerald Jackson, VP-Devel.
Annual Revenue: $17.9 million.
Annual Expenses: $16.7 million.
Contributions: 24.2 percent of revenue.
Children's Home Society of Minnesota is a statewide, voluntary, nonsectarian, child-focused agency providing lifelong adoption services, child care and child abuse/neglect prevention. More than 2,000 volunteers assist 440 paid staff in building safe, loving families and helping children thrive.
440 employees.
Founded in 1889. SIC 8322.

No. 100 CRM Nonprofit 100.

Children's Hospitals and Clinics

2525 Chicago Ave. S., Minneapolis, MN 55404
Tel: 612/813-6100 Fax: 612/813-6699
Brock D. Nelson, CEO
Walter Chesley, VP-Hum. Res.
Terril Hart, M.D., VP-Medical Affairs
Phillip M. Kibort, M.D., VP-System Advancement
Jerry Massmann, VP-Finance
Julianne Morath, COO and VP-Care Delivery
Cheryl Olson, VP-Patient Care/Nursing
Annual Revenue: $241.6 million.
Annual Expenses: $236.4 million.
Contributions: 3.4 percent of revenue.
Children's Hospitals and Clinics was formed by the June 14, 1994, merger of Minneapolis Children's Medical Center (founded in 1973) and Children's Hospital of St. Paul (founded in 1924). Children's Hospitals and Clinics includes 268 staffed beds at its hospitals Children's- Minneapolis and Children's-St. Paul; day surgery, diagnostics and rehabilitation/developmental services at Children's West in Minnetonka; rehabilitation/developmental services at Children's-Roseville; pediatric specialty clinics at Children's Clinics-Woodwinds in Woodbury; Children's-Ridges, the pediatric unit at Fairview Ridges Hospital in Burnsville; and Children's-St. Francis, the pediatric unit at St. Francis Regional Medical Center in Shakopee. In addition to general pediatric clinics at Children's-St. Paul and Children's-Minneapolis, Children's offers services at 34 specialty clinics.
3,107 employees.
Founded in 1924. SIC 8069.
No. 12 CRM Nonprofit 100.
No. 63 CRM Employer 100.
Recent: *In January 2000, six months before opening the first and only hospital in the southeast Twin Cities metro area, Woodwinds Health Campus kicked off a hiring blitz. Nearly 400 positions were available throughout the hospital. (Woodwinds Health Campus is a collaboration between HealthEast Care System and Children's Clinics.) In April Children's and St. Cloud Hospital agreed to develop an outpatient pediatric chemotherapy service in St. Cloud beginning in 2001. Children's Hospitals and Clinics of Minnesota was featured on the cover of the July 17 issue of US News and World Report in an article that highlights Children's nationally recognized "patient safety" (medical error reduction) plan. Editors were seeking to profile a health care organization that was addressing patient safety issues in a thoughtful, committed, and long-term way. In April, Children's and St. Cloud Hospital agreed to develop an outpatient pediatric chemotherapy service in St. Cloud in 2001. Children's opened Children's-Clinics at Woodwinds, providing specialty care including developmental and rehabilitation services. In 2000, Children's opened its fourth operating room at Children's West, a day surgery and diagnostic center in Minnetonka.*

Children's Theatre Company & School

2400 Third Ave. S., Minneapolis, MN 55404
Tel: 612/874-0500 Fax: 612/874-8119
Peter C. Brosius, Artistic Dir.
John A. Haynes, Exec. Dir.
Jim Tinsley, Production Mgr.
Anni Gunderson, Dir.-Mktg.
Laura Breeze, Dir.-Devel.
Children's Theatre Company & School, is a repertory theater presenting approximately 450 performances annually to upwards of 400,000 people. The Children's Theatre is dedicated to presenting original work for children and their families. It also produces a national tour visiting as many as 20 states annually. The Children's Theatre is the largest theater in North America for children and their families.
200 employees.
Founded in 1965. SIC 7922.

Chosen Valley Care Center Inc.

1102 Liberty St., Chatfield, MN 55012
Tel: 507/867-4220 Fax: 612/867-4812
George Gensen, Exec. Dir.
Chosen Valley Care Center Inc. is a 86-bed skilled nursing facility for the elderly.
125 employees.
Founded in 1976. SIC 8051.

Citizens' Scholarship Foundation of America Inc.

1505 Riverview Rd., P.O. Box 297, St. Peter, MN 56082
Tel: 507/931-1682 Fax: 507/931-9168
Dr. William C. Nelsen, Pres.
Fred P. Vogel, EVP-Finance/Admin.
H. Stuart Johnson, VP-Scholarship Mgmt. Svs.
Marilyn E. Rundell, VP-Scholarship Mgmt. Svs.
Alan Spillers, VP-Devel.
Linda Mahoney, VP-Dollars for Scholars
Dan Jorgensen, VP-Communications
David Bach, VP-Scholar Shop
Annual Revenue: $102.9 million.
Annual Expenses: $88.9 million.
Contributions: 87.2 percent of revenue.
Citizens' Scholarship Foundation of America Inc. (CSFA) is the nation's largest private sector scholarship and educational support organization. Through its programs—Dollars for Scholars, Scholarship Management Services, and ScholarShop—CSFA is expanding educational opportunities for students throughout the country. CSFA's programs provide financial assistance, as well as academic support, for students pursuing post-secondary education.
138 employees.
Founded in 1958. SIC 6732.
No. 19 CRM Nonprofit 100.
Recent: *In December 1999 the organization was ranked by Smart Money (the personal finance magazine of the Wall Street Journal) as the nation's No. 1 most-efficient educational nonprofit; and, for the third-consecutive year, one of the overall top 10 most-efficient nonprofits in all categories. CSFA devotes 93.9 percent of expenditures to programs and just 2.5 percent to fund-raising. In April 2000 CSFA and Sallie Mae, the nation's largest provider of funds for education loans, announced a five-year sponsorship that was to lead to increased financial support to students throughout the nation. In November CSFA announced details of a new grant from the U.S. Department of Education. Students from low-income urban and rural areas will have increased access to postsecondary educational opportunities through the implementation of the Community Scholarship Mobilization Program. CSFA will use the grant money to establish an endowment fund and use the interest from the endowment to start new Dollars for Scholars chapters in high poverty areas and provide scholarships for students from low-income families.*

The City Inc.

1315 - 12th Ave. N., Minneapolis, MN 55411
Tel: 612/377-7559 Fax: 612/377-6719
Web site: http://www.thecityinc.org
Ralph Weinberge, Chm.
Lawrence H. Borom, Pres.
The City Inc. is a multiservice agency providing education, family, and social services to troubled inner-city youths and their families.
75 employees.
Founded in 1967. SIC 8322.

Client Community Services Inc.

1930 Knollwood Dr., P.O. Box 23, Worthington, MN 56187
Tel: 507/376-3171 Fax: 507/376-3165
Martin D. Rickers, Exec. Dir.
Cindy Burrell, ICF/MR Administrator
Mary Peterson, CLA Dir.
Colette Leopold, SILS Dir.
Jane Feller, Iowa Svs. Dir.
Ray Frazee, Business Mgr.
Kathy Thurston, R.N.
Annual Revenue: $4.3 million.
Annual Expenses: $4.3 million.
Contributions: 7.5 percent of revenue.
Client Community Services provides educational, residential, and related support services to disabled individuals.
185 employees.
Founded in 1955. SIC 8331.

College of St. Benedict
37 College Ave. S., St. Joseph, MN 56374
Tel: 320/363-5407 Fax: 320/363-5136
Mary E. Lyons, Pres.
Dr. Clark Hendley, Provost
Miriam Ardolf, OSB, VP-Finance/Admissions
Charles Villette, Dean, Dir.-BUC
Gilbert Hayes, Exec. Dir.-Inst. Mktg.
Kathleen Allen, VP-Student Devel.
Rita Knuesel, Dean of College
Barbara Carlson, VP-Institutional Advancement
David Hoffman, VP-Devel./Alumnae Relations
Mary Milbert, Dean of Admissions
Susan Gergen, Dir.-Alumnae/Parent Relations
Annual Revenue: $50.2 million.
Annual Expenses: $46 million.
Contributions: 11 percent of revenue.
The College of St. Benedict (CSB) is a Catholic liberal arts college for women. It offers more than 40 majors and pre-professional programs in partnership with St. John's University for men. CSB's enrollment for the 1996-97 school year was 1,893.
427 employees.
Founded in 1913. SIC 8221.
No. 49 CRM Nonprofit 100.

The College of St. Catherine
2004 Randolph Ave., St. Paul, MN 55105
Tel: 651/690-6000 Fax: 651/690-6024
Web site: http://www.stkate.edu
Andrea Lee, Pres.
Mary Margaret Smith, Dean and VP
Mary Des Roches, VP-Fin./Business Op., Treas.
William S. Halloran, VP-Finance
Colleen Hegranes, VP-Student Affairs
Randi Yoder, VP-Institutional Advancement
Cal Mosley-Ryan, Asst. to Pres.-Admissions
Annual Revenue: $52.1 million.
Annual Expenses: $49.9 million.
Contributions: 9.4 percent of revenue.
The College of St. Catherine, the largest Catholic college for women in the country, offers bachelor's, master's, and associate degrees in liberal arts and sciences, health care, and professional studies. Total enrollment is 4,373, consisting of 2,546 undergraduate and 805 graduate students on the St. Paul campus, and 929 undergraduate and 93 graduate students on the Minneapolis campus.
926 employees.
Founded in 1905. SIC 8221.
No. 46 CRM Nonprofit 100.
Recent: *In August 2000 the school created an information systems undergraduate program and added three specialty areas to its Master of Arts in Organizational Leadership: health care, information services and technology, and strategic management.*

College of St. Scholastica
1200 Kenwood Ave., Duluth, MN 55811
Tel: 218/723-6000 Fax: 218/723-6290
Web site: http://www.css.edu
Larry Goodwin, Pres.
Cecelia Taylor, VP-Acad. Affairs/Dean-Faculty
Mary Cahoon, SVP
Patrick Flattery, VP-Finance and Treas.
Chandra Mehrotra, Dean of Graduate Studies
Richard Davis, VP-Institutional Advancement
Brian Dalton, VP-Enrollment Mgmt.
Steve Lyons, VP-Student Life
Annual Revenue: $37.3 million.
Annual Expenses: $34 million.
Contributions: 20.7 percent of revenue.
The college offers bachelor of arts, master of arts, and master of education degrees. Its enrollment exceeds 2,000.
375 employees.
Founded in 1912. SIC 8221.
No. 56 CRM Nonprofit 100.

CommonBond Communities
328 W. Kellogg St., St. Paul, MN 55102
Tel: 651/291-1750 Fax: 651/291-1003
Web site: http://www.commonbond.org
Joseph Errigo Jr., Pres.
Joseph L. Holmberg, SVP and COO
Scott Beckman, VP-Advantage Svs.
Ann Ruff, VP-Devel.
Annual Revenue: $5.6 million.
Annual Expenses: $4.2 million.
Contributions: 47.5 percent of revenue.
CommonBond Communities provides affordable housing for people with low incomes and helps residents connect with services that support their success. More than 4,500 people live in 3,000 CommonBond housing units.
154 employees.
Founded in 1971. SIC 8661.

Communication Service for the Deaf
102 N. Krohn Pl., Sioux Falls, SD 57103
Tel: 605/367-5760 Fax: 605/367-5958
Web site: http://www.c-s-d.org
Benjamin J. Soukup, CEO
Communication Service for the Deaf (CSD) provides direct assistance to deaf and hard-of-hearing individuals in four basic areas: communication, social services, independent living, and community outreach and education. Through education, counseling, training, advocacy, communication assistance, and equipment distribution, CSD provides the deaf with the opportunity for self-actualization, professional growth, and independence.
1,500 employees.
Founded in 1975. SIC 8322.

Community Involvement Programs
1600 Broadway St. N.E., Suite 1, Minneapolis, MN 55413-2617
Tel: 612/362-4400 Fax: 612/362-4479
Web site: http://www.cipmn.org
John Everett, Exec. Dir.
Gary Leier, Dir.-Finance
Lisa Clark, Dir.-Hum. Res.
Community Involvement Programs is a social service agency providing residential, day training, employment, and other services for adults with developmental disabilities and/or mental illness.
250 employees.
Founded in 1971. SIC 8361.

Community Memorial Hospital Association
512 Skyline Boulevard, Cloquet, MN 55720
Tel: 218/879-4641 Fax: 218/879-9167
Web site: http://www.cloquethospital.com
James Carroll, Administrator
Betty Forsberg, Pres.
Sherman Liimatainen, VP
Dr. James Rogers, Sec.
Del Prevost, Treas.
Annual Revenue: $14.8 million.
Annual Expenses: $14.7 million.
Contributions: 0.8 percent of revenue.
Community Memorial Hospital Association provides health care and nursing home care to people in the Cloquet community and the surrounding area.
270 employees.
Founded in 1958. SIC 8059.

Community-University Health Care Ctr/Variety Children's Clinic
2001 Bloomington Ave. S., Minneapolis, MN 55404
Tel: 612/627-4774 Fax: 612/627-4205
Amos Deinard, M.D., Exec. Dir.
Susan Ferron, M.D., Medical Dir.
Community University Health Center/Variety Children's Clinic, a subsidiary of the University of Minnesota, is a neighborhood based, primary health care center. It provides primary medical, dental, and mental health care to a medically and socially high risk, culturally diverse population of children and adults. The clinic uses the Fairview-University Medical Center facilities for inpatient and subspecialty care.

135 employees.
Founded in 1966. SIC 8011, 8021.

Concordia College—Moorhead
901 S. Eighth St., Moorhead, MN 56562
Tel: 218/299-4000 Fax: 218/299-3947
Rev. Thomas W. Thomsen, Pres.
Clyde E. Allen Jr., Treas. and VP-Business Affairs
Morris L. Lanning, VP-Student Aff./Dean-Students
Elizabeth Danielson, VP-Acad. Affairs/Dean-College
Lindsay Rhodenbaugh, VP-Admissions/Financial Aid
Linda Brown, VP-Devel.
Tracey Moorhead, Asst. to Pres.
Annual Revenue: $76 million.
Annual Expenses: $64.1 million.
Contributions: 14 percent of revenue.
Concordia College—Moorhead is a private liberal arts college of the Evangelical Church in America, accredited by the North Central Association of Colleges and Schools and various other accrediting agencies. The college offers 52 professional and 24 teaching majors and offers bachelor of arts and bachelor of music degrees.
730 employees.
Founded in 1891. SIC 8221.
No. 28 CRM Nonprofit 100.

Concordia University—St. Paul
275 N. Syndicate St., St. Paul, MN 55104
Tel: 651/641-8278 Fax: 651/659-0207
Web site: http://www.csp.edu
Dr. Robert Holst, Pres.
Dr. Kay Madson, EVP
Michael Flynn, VP-Advancement
Dr. Eric LaMott, VP-Info. Technology
Thomas Ries, VP-Finance/Operations
Dr. Carl Schoenbeck, VP-Academic Affairs
Dr. Philip C. Tesch, VP-Student Affairs
Roberta Kaufman, Dean
Alan Winegarden, Dean
Robert DeWerff, Dean
Annual Revenue: $24.8 million.
Annual Expenses: $24.1 million.
Contributions: 17.3 percent of revenue.
Concordia University is affiliated with the Lutheran Church—Missouri Synod. Located in the Midway district of St. Paul, Concordia awards the bachelor of arts degree in major subject fields of the liberal arts and in school-age child care, and a bachelor of business administration degree. The university also offers baccalaureate programs for directors of Christian education, Christian outreach, and parish music; early childhood education, secondary education, and middle school licensure; and pre-seminary studies. Majors in organizational management/communication and marketing management, and certificates in finance, nonprofit management, and applied creativity and innovation are available through a degree completion program for the adult learner. A master of arts in education degree, consisting of five distinct programs, and a master of arts degree in organizational management through the Concordia School of Accelerated Learning also are offered.
204 employees.
Founded in 1893. SIC 8221.
No. 78 CRM Nonprofit 100.

Courage Center
3915 Golden Valley Rd., Golden Valley, MN 55422
Tel: 763/588-0811 Fax: 763/520-0577
Web site: http://freenet.msp.mn.us/ip/health/courage_center/
Eric Stevens, Exec. Dir.
Lawrence Johnson, Assoc. Exec. Dir.-Fin.
Mark Moilanen, Assoc. Exec. Dir.-Programs
Todd Johnson, Assoc. Exec. Dir.-Admin./H.R.
Don Taylor, Assoc. Exec. Dir.-Devel.
Mary Schoessler, Dir.-Communications
Courage Center provides rehabilitation, enrichment, vocational, independent living, and educational services. Primary programs include medical therapies, transitional residential and vocational services, camping, sports, and recreation. Courage Center owns and operates Courage Center, Golden Valley; Courage St. Croix, Stillwater, Minn.; Camp Courage, near Maple Lake, Minn.; and Courage North, Lake George, Minn.
495 employees.
Founded in 1928. SIC 8322, 8331.
No. 71 CRM Nonprofit 100.

Covenant Manor
5800 St. Croix Ave. N., Golden Valley, MN 55422
Tel: 763/546-6125 Fax: 763/546-8529
Web site: http://www.covenantretirement.com
Paula Sparling, Health Care Admin.
Jean Bean, Dir.-Nursing
Tom Freudenstein, Dir.-Marketing
Gary Gardeen, Campus Administrator
Covenant Manor is a fully accredited continuing-care retirement community with 300 residents and multiple levels of care. Fully equipped apartments of various sizes provide independent living at Covenant Manor for active older adults. All residents have contracts assuring them lifetime care. The 13-acre campus includes 130 independent living units at Covenant Manor, 16 units of assisted living at Heritage House, 108 skilled nursing beds at Colonial Acres Health Care Center, an adult day-care program, and a wide range of rehabilitation services. 123 additional independent living units will be ready for occupancy in early 2001.
200 employees.
Founded in 1886. SIC 8051.

Crest View Corporation
4444 Reservoir Blvd. N.E., Columbia Heights, MN 55421
Tel: 763/782-1611 Fax: 763/782-0857
Shirley Barnes, CEO
Annual Revenue: $7.6 million.
Annual Expenses: $7.5 million.
Contributions: 0.5 percent of revenue.
Crest View Corp. consists of a 122-bed skilled nursing home, an outpatient physical therapy clinic, a home health agency, 77 independent apartments, 64 assisted-living suites, 40 apartments for seniors on low incomes, and management services. Crest View is accredited by the Lutheran Church Missouri Synod and affiliated with the Evangelical Lutheran Church of America.
160 employees.
Founded in 1952. SIC 8051, 8361.

Dakota's Communities Inc.
680 O'Neill Dr., Eagan, MN 55121
Tel: 651/688-8808 Fax: 651/688-8892
Kathleen LeMay, Pres. and CEO
Georgette Peterson, CFO
Annual Revenue: $13.3 million.
Annual Expenses: $12.6 million.
Contributions: 4.7 percent of revenue.
Dakota's Communities provides residential services, respite care, and in-home services to people with disabilities and to their families. The organization owns and operates 26 homes throughout the Twin Cities and greater metropolitan area, serving 189 people. Dakota's Communities also provides administrative assistance to Dakota's Adults Inc., a related nonprofit corporation, through a management agreement.
500 employees.
Founded in 1972. SIC 8322.

Delta Dental Plan of Minnesota
3560 Delta Dental Dr., P.O. Box 330, Eagan, MN 55122
Tel: 651/406-5900 Fax: 651/406-5933
Web site: http://www.mn.deltadental.org
Michael F. Walsh, Pres. and CEO
Gary Ballman, SVP-Operations
Dominic DiFalco, SVP-Info. Technology

NON

Dani Fjelstad, SVP-Finance
Nancy McMorran, SVP-Professional Services
Mark Moksnes, SVP-Marketing
Annual Revenue: $414.1 million.
Annual Expenses: $406.3 million.
Delta Dental Plan of Minnesota offers comprehensive dental care insurance programs for groups with five or more employees. Delta Dental is the Upper Midwest's largest provider of dental benefits, currently serving more than 2.3 million members enrolled in more than 8,700 purchasing groups.
400 employees.
Founded in 1969. SIC 6324.
No. 7 CRM Nonprofit 100.
Recent: *Dec. 31, 1999: The company's 26.5 percent annual-revenue increase, from $326.7 million in 1998 to $414.1 million, was its most significant growth in six years. Delta credited its efforts to introduce new service options to members, including providing wider access to oral health care and maintaining high customer-service standards. In 1999 customer service processed more than 3.7 million claims, 94.7 percent within 15 days, with an accuracy rate of 98.8 percent. In April 2000 Delta Dental Plan introduced its new international network for emergency dental treatment. Through an exclusive partnership with Europ Assistance, the world's leading supplier of assistance and related insurance services, Delta Dental Plan of Minnesota members and their eligible dependents can receive emergency dental treatment while traveling or working abroad. In July the Iron Range Resources and Rehabilitation Board approved a proposal from Delta Dental to open a 100-employee customer service center on the Iron Range (in Gilbert, Minn.) to be operational by early October. In August the company reported that costs for dental care in Minnesota experienced a 10 percent surge in 1999, compared to 7 percent to 8 percent nationwide. The tight labor market here was leading to an increase in professional salaries, which make up more than 50 percent of a clinic's operating expenses. In November Delta Dental Plan of Minnesota was assigned an ``AA-" counterparty and financial strength rating by Standard & Poor's (S&P), the highest such rating awarded to any Delta Dental plan in the United States. It was also awarded S&P's Security Circle Icon, reserved for a company regarded as "having financial security characteristics that outweigh any vulnerabilities, and highly likely to have the ability to meet financial commitments." The S&P CreditWire announcement noted the following as support for this excellent rating: very strong market position; positive and highly innovative investment strategies; strong capital adequacy; excellent earnings; strong investments and liquidity; consistent significant growth; and consistent strong profitability. CEO Walsh commented: "This rating demonstrates that the innovations we have implemented, such as our PRIME reimbursement system, commitment to superior service, operational efficiency, and product flexibility, are having a positive impact for Delta and our customers."*

East Side Neighborhood Service
1929 Second St. N.E., Minneapolis, MN 55418
Tel: 612/781-6011 Fax: 612/781-9257
William J. Laden, Exec. Dir.
Susan McCauley, Asst. Dir.
Thomas Spurrier, CFO
Annual Revenue: $6.4 million.
Annual Expenses: $0 million.
Contributions: 50 percent of revenue.
East Side Neighborhood Service Inc., provides neighborhood social services, child development services, family violence services, employment services, family care centers, and camp facilities for Twin Cities metropolitan area residents. East Side operates two day care centers for children, a resident camp for young people, an adult day care center, a senior community center, and two nurseries. Additional services include, senior transportation, a senior foodshelf, and numerous programs for youth and families.
120 employees.
Founded in 1915. SIC 8351, 8399.

Education Minnesota
41 Sherburne Ave., St. Paul, MN 55103
Tel: 651/227-9541 Fax: 651/292-4802
Web site: http://www.educationminnesota.org
Sandra Peterson, Co-pres.
Judy Schaubach, Co-pres.
Jeanne Thomas, EVP
Larry Wicks, Exec. Dir.
Education Minnesota is a new organization of 65,000 educators working for excellence in education for all students. An affiliate of the National Education Association, the organization is dedicated to providing high-quality teaching and learning opportunities throughout the state. Its field offices provide professional development training for educators, as well as support on a wide variety of issues; the government relations department advocates strong public policy that supports public schools; the negotiations department provides training in bargaining, as well as research on public education employee contracts and school finance. Education Minnesota was created by the Sept. 1, 1998, merger of the Minnesota Education Association (founded in 1861) with the Minnesota Federation of Teachers.
152 employees.
Founded in 1998. SIC 8631.

Elim Care Inc.
7485 Office Ridge Circle, Eden Prairie, MN 55344
Tel: 952/259-4500 Fax: 952/259-4499
Web site: http://www.elimcare.org
Robert Dahl, Pres. and CEO
Daniel Fair, VP-Business Development
Linda Letich, Exec. Nursing Consultant
Ron Sanford, VP-Operations
Kathy Youngquist, VP-Finance
Annual Revenue: $31.3 million.
Elim Care Inc. heads a family of nonprofit corporations governed by the North Central District Association of the Evangelical Free Church of America. Foremost among them is Elim Homes Inc., which provides nursing facility services in the Spirit of Christ to the elderly, the handicapped, and others with special needs. Other Elim Care organizations: Elim Care Foundation, Elim Preferred Services Inc., Redeemer Residence Inc. (a division of Elim Homes), Elim Shores Inc., New Harmony Care Center, and Guardian Angels Elim Home Care Inc.
800 employees.
SIC 8051.
No. 63 CRM Nonprofit 100.
Recent: *In June 2000 Elim Homes acquired Pro Rehab, a Medicare-certified rehabilitation agency.*

Ely-Bloomenson Community Hospital & Nursing Home
328 W. Conan St., Ely, MN 55731
Tel: 218/365-3271 Fax: 218/365-3064
Larry Ravenberg, Administrator
Scott Kellerman, Dir.-Finance
Eve Olsen, Dir.-Nursing Svs.
Ely-Bloomenson Community Hospital & Nursing Home provides hospital and nursing home services for the Ely community and surrounding area.
230 employees.
Founded in 1956. SIC 8059, 8062.

The Evangelical Lutheran Good Samaritan Society
4800 W. 57th St., P.O. Box 5038, Sioux Falls, SD 57117
Tel: 605/362-3100 Fax: 605/362-3356
Web site: http://www.good-sam.com
Judith A. Ryan, Ph.D., Pres. and CEO
Dave Horazdovsky, VP-Operations and COO
Dean Mertz, VP-Hum. Res.
Dan Holdhusen, VP, CFO, and Treas.
Rusty Williams, VP and Chief Information Ofcr.
Jim Beddow, VP-Learning
William S. Kubat, VP-Care Management
Rev. Greg Wilcox, VP-Mission Effectiveness
Annual Revenue: $689.7 million.
Annual Expenses: $667 million.

Contributions: 1.5 percent of revenue.
The Evangelical Lutheran Good Samaritan Society is the largest nonprofit long-term care provider in the United States. The organization operates 240 long-term care facilities in 25 states, serving approximately 27,500 residents. Services include nursing home care, assisted living, independent living, adult day care, Alzheimer's and dementia units, and home health care.
23,250 employees.
Founded in 1922. SIC 8051, 8059.
No. 30 CRM Employer 100.

Eventide

1405 Seventh St. S., Moorhead, MN 56560
Tel: 218/233-7508 Fax: 218/233-3602
Helen M. Frampton, Pres.
Sandi Petterson, VP-Residential Care
Mary Wittenberg, CFO
Eventide is a 195-bed skilled nursing home serving Clay County, Minn., and Cass County, N.D.
183 employees.
Founded in 1951. SIC 8051.

Fairview

2450 Riverside Ave., Minneapolis, MN 55454
Tel: 612/672-6300 Fax: 612/672-6303
Web site: http://www.fairview.org
Rodney Burwell, Chm.
David R. Page, Pres. and CEO
William K. Maxwell, EVP and COO
James M. Fox, SVP and CFO
Gary Strong, SVP and Chief Info. Ofcr.
Paul Torgerson, SVP, CAO, Gen. Counsel
Fairview is a regionally integrated health care system of hospitals, nursing homes, senior housing facilities, clinics, ambulatory care programs, and affiliated physicians. The hospitals include Fairview Southdale Hospital, Fairview Ridges Hospital, Fairview-University Medical Center (formerly Fairview Riverside Medical Center and University of Minnesota Hospital & Clinic), Fairview Lakes Regional Medical Center, Fairview Northland Regional Hospital, Fairview University Medical Center-Mesabi, and Fairview Red Wing Hospital. Before the merger, Fairview owned 37 primary care clinics, 23 Institutes for Athletic Medicine, seven home care facilities, 10 orthopedic laboratory locations, 20 retail pharmacies, nine Fairview counseling centers, four skilled nursing facilities, and 14 senior housing facilities. The affiliated Fairview Foundation raises and distributes funds for programs that benefit Fairview patients, their families, and the communities Fairview serves.
18,250 employees.
Founded in 1906. SIC 8062.
No. 5 CRM Nonprofit 100.
No. 8 CRM Employer 100.
Recent: *In May 2000 Fairview Southdale Hospital's plan to increase capacity was approved 4-1 by the Edina City Council. The $55 million, two-phase project will add eight operating rooms, a heart and vascular center, a skyway to cross France Avenue, and a 1,000-car parking ramp. In October Fairview Southdale received an award from the National Patient Safety Foundation for improving patient safety.The award recognized Fairview Southdale's work in reducing errors associated with the drug heparin, a commonly used anticoagulant used by patients who have had a stroke, heart problems, or blood clots. The model to reduce intravenous heparin errors in its cardiac care patients accounted for a 64 percent decrease in heparin errors hospital-wide.*

Family & Children's Service

414 S. Eighth St., Minneapolis, MN 55404
Tel: 612/339-9101 Fax: 612/339-9150
Terrence Steeno, Pres.
Mary Greenman, SVP-Programs
Dan Campion, VP-Operations
Annual Revenue: $5 million.
Annual Expenses: $5.1 million.
Contributions: 74.4 percent of revenue.

Family & Children's Service supports, strengthens, and enriches the lives of families, children, and individuals who are struggling from the effects of violence, abuse, mental illness, poverty, changes in family structure, discrimination, stress, and chemical dependence. Available programs include: mental health counseling; family violence counseling; youth diversion; lesbian and gay counseling; education groups and classes related to self-esteem, parenting, and family change; PRIDE, which helps women get and stay out of prostitution; financial counseling; a homemaking service that aids independent living; and public policy advocacy, which seeks legislative and policy changes related to families and children.
110 employees.
Founded in 1878. SIC 8322.

Family Service Inc.

166 E. Fourth St., Suite 200, St. Paul, MN 55101
Tel: 651/222-0311 Fax: 651/222-8920
Web site: http://www.familyinc.org
Ron Reed, Pres.
Annual Revenue: $3.8 million.
Annual Expenses: $3.6 million.
Contributions: 51.2 percent of revenue.
Family Service Inc. is a social service agency whose mission is to help improve the quality of individual, family, and community life.
107 employees.
Founded in 1892. SIC 8322.

First Care Medical Services

900 S. Hilligoss Blvd. E., Fosston, MN 56542
Tel: 218/435-1133 Fax: 218/435-1134
Patricia Wangler, CEO
First Care Medical Services provides hospital, nursing home, home health care, and ambulance service.
255 employees.
Founded in 1947. SIC 8059, 8062.

First Plan of Minnesota

409 17th Ave., Two Harbors, MN 55616
Tel: 218/834-7207 Fax: 218/834-6215
Anthony H. Solem, Pres. and CEO
Timothy A. Miller, Treas. and Dir.-Finance
Julie Stone, VP and COO
Douglas Hiza, M.D., VP and Chief Medical Ofcr.
Nancy Ojard, Dir.-Provider/Pub. Rel.
Kathy McNamara, Senior Dir.-Clinical Operation
Roger McDannold, Dir.-Pharmacy Svs.
Cheryl Macheledt, Dir.-Small Group Marketing
Annual Revenue: $30.5 million.
Annual Expenses: $30.2 million.
First Plan of Minnesota, formerly Community Health Center Inc., provides a continuum of compassionate, cost-effective, high-quality health care. The 14,000-member First Plan HMO is Minnesota's first health maintenance organization (with more than 55 years of service). First Plan also operates three primary care clinics, three pharmacies, two ambulance services, and a home health service.
225 employees.
Founded in 1944. SIC 8062.
No. 65 CRM Nonprofit 100.

Fraser Ltd.

2902 S. University Dr., Fargo, ND 58103
Tel: 701/232-3301 Fax: 701/237-5775
Web site: http://www.fraserltd.org
Sandra Leyland, Exec. Dir.
Howard Vegoe, Board Pres.
David Laske, Board Treas.
Fraser provides services, education and training so people with disabilities can be valued and dignified as members of the community. The Independent Living Services Division provides living alternatives to people with special needs, including Individualized basis to reach and maintain the greatest possible degree of independence. Other support includes Day Services, Support

Services (case management, family support, medial/nursing support), Food Services, Adaptive Equipment Exchange, and Fraser Child Care Center.
130 employees.
Founded in 1893. SIC 8361.

Freeport West Inc.

2222 Park Ave., Minneapolis, MN 55409
Tel: 612/824-3040 Fax: 612/824-0379
Robert E. Smith, Exec. Dir.
Freeport West Inc. works through four programs in Hennepin County to help young people suffering from problems due to neglect, abuse, and institutionalization. Programs help homeless children, "hard to place children", developmentally delayed children, and in-the-home assistance to families of abused children.
68 employees.
Founded in 1970. SIC 8322.

Gillette Children's Specialty Healthcare

200 E. University Ave., St. Paul, MN 55101
Tel: 651/291-2848 Fax: 651/229-3833
Web site: http://www.gillettechildrens.org
Margaret E. Perryman, CEO
John (Jack) Rolig, Chm.
James Gage, M.D., Medical Dir.
Jon Galloway, VP-Devel.
Mary Martin, VP-Hum. Res.
Christine Milbrath, VP-Patient Svs.
John Tomlin, VP-Finance
Kathryn Wardrop, VP-Marketing
John Barrett, Media Relations Specialist
Annual Revenue: $37.4 million.
Annual Expenses: $36.1 million.
Gillette Children's Specialty Healthcare cares for infants, children, and adolescents who have brain or spinal cord injuries, cerebral palsy, craniofacial anomalies, epilepsy, scoliosis or other complex orthopedic problems, spina bifida, or conditions that require the use of a ventilator for breathing.
507 employees.
Founded in 1897. SIC 8069.
No. 55 CRM Nonprofit 100.

Girl Scout Council of Greater Minneapolis

5601 Brooklyn Blvd., Brooklyn Center, MN 55429
Tel: 763/535-4602 Fax: 763/535-7524
Web site: http://www.girlscoutsmpls.org
Lauren P. Weck, CEO
Peggy Erickson, Asst. Exec. Dir.
Catherine Benson, Dir.-Marketing/Communications
Jennifer Kahlow, Dir.-Devel.
David Sussman, Dir.-Admin.
Girl Scout Council of Greater Minneapolis is a dynamic and contemporary organization that prepares girls to be self-sufficient and confident in a changing society. Through an informal, educational program, girls from ages 5-17 learn, have fun, gain self-esteem, and contribute to their communities. In this uniquely all-girl experience, service is provided by skilled staff and trained volunteers. The volunteer structure is innovative and emphasizes adult education and training. Service is provided from offices in Brooklyn Center, Minneapolis, and Burnsville.
60 employees.
Founded in 1914. SIC 8641.

Girl Scout Council of St. Croix Valley

400 S. Robert St., St. Paul, MN 55107
Tel: 651/227-8835 Fax: 651/227-7533
Web site: http://www.girlscoutscv.org
Mary Lee Hoffman, CEO
Kathy May, Pres.
Dan Ursin, CFO
Roberta Allan, VP-Advancement
Susan Olsen, Dir.-Hum. Res.
Annual Revenue: $7.8 million.
Annual Expenses: $4.1 million.
Contributions: 47.8 percent of revenue.
The Girl Scout Council of St. Croix Valley helps more than 20,300 girls grow strong through varied program opportunities like GirlSports, Physicians of Tomorrow mentoring, troops and groups, and Adventures events for 6th through 12th grade girls. In Girl Scouts, girls aged 5-17 build character and skills for success in the real world. With the support of 6,700 committed adult volunteers, they discover the fun, friendship, and power of girls together. The council serves 11 counties in eastern Minnesota and western Wisconsin.
60 employees.
Founded in 1963. SIC 8641.

Gold Cross Ambulance Service

501 Sixth Ave. N.W., Rochester, MN 55901
Tel: 800/933-6296 Fax: 507/288-9004
Web site: http://www.mayo.edu/mmt
John Panicek, Pres.
Stephen Gudgell, Transportation Admin.
Paul Anderson, VP and COO
354 employees.
SIC 4119.

Goodwill Industries Inc./Easter Seals Minnesota

2543 Como Ave., Lauderdale, MN 55108
Tel: 651/646-2591 Fax: 651/649-0302
Web site: http://www.goodwilleasterseals.org
Michael Wirth-Davis, Pres. and CEO
Mark Vanney, CFO
Kelly Matter, VP-Program Svs.
Deborah Ferry, VP-Retail Services
Kay Cady, VP-Communications/Devel.
Annual Revenue: $8.8 million.
Annual Expenses: $8.8 million.
Contributions: 47.9 percent of revenue.
Goodwill Industries Inc./Easter Seals Minnesota is dedicated to serving the community and assisting people with barriers to education, employment, and independence. The organization funds its services partly by selling donated goods in 14 retail stores. Goodwill Industries was founded in 1919 at Central Park Methodist Church by the Reverend Herbert Burgstahler and St. Paul community leaders. It became affiliated with the National Easter Seal Society in 1984. In 1999 the organization helped more than 7,500 people with disabilities or disadvantages achieve their employment, education, or independent-living goals.
380 employees.
Founded in 1919. SIC 8322.
Recent: *In August 2000 the organization acquired three properties in St. Paul to develop a new, larger headquarters.*

Billy Graham Evangelistic Association

1300 Harmon Pl., Minneapolis, MN 55403
Tel: 612/338-0500 Fax: 612/338-6809
Web site: http://www.graham-assn.org
John R. Corts, Pres. and COO
Joel B. Aarsvold, VP-Finance and Sec.
Annual Revenue: $129.3 million.
Annual Expenses: $94.6 million.
Contributions: 79.2 percent of revenue.
The purpose of the Billy Graham Evangelistic Association is to transmit the Gospel of the Lord Jesus Christ by any and all means—including public evangelistic meetings; radio and television; tracts, books, and other publications; Schools of Evangelism; and training programs. The Association broadcasts evangelistic messages during one-hour televison programs (four times per year, two programs each time) on 200 stations. A weekly radio program, "Hour of Decision," is broadcast on 600 stations. The organization also produces evangelistic films and videos for showing in churches; publishes a monthly magazine; and conducts Schools of Evangelism for nearly 3,000 pastors. Bible training seminars for laypeople are conducted at a training

center in North Carolina.
650 employees.
Founded in 1950. SIC 4833.
No. 17 CRM Nonprofit 100.

Grandview Christian Home
800 Second Ave. N.W., Cambridge, MN 55008
Tel: 763/689-1474
Greg Carlson, Exec. Dir.
Grandview Christian Home provides healthcare and retirement services to senior citizens including: transportation, long term care, adult day care, respite, and nutrition.
280 employees.
Founded in 1959. SIC 8052.

Greater Minneapolis Day Care Association
1628 Elliot Ave. S., Minneapolis, MN 55404
Tel: 612/341-1177 Fax: 612/341-4356
Sharon T. Henry, Exec. Dir.
Laurie Possin, Assoc. Dir.
Cassondra Thaddies, Assoc. Dir.
Annual Revenue: $10.3 million.
Annual Expenses: $9.5 million.
Contributions: 97.2 percent of revenue.
The Greater Minneapolis Day Care Association's (GMDCA) is committed to the healthy development of all children. GMDCA promotes quality, affordable, and accessible child care in Hennepin County. GMDCA trains child care providers, makes child care referrals to families, and advocates for young children at the state and local level. GMDCA provides sliding fee subsidies for low income parents with funding from the State of Minnesota, Hennepin County (Federal Child Care Block grant funds), and the City of Minneapolis. GMDCA also administers the City of Minneapolis renovation funding for child care programs and is a vendor for Minneapolis School District school readiness funds to enable "at-risk" children to receive early education and services in child care programs.
45 employees.
Founded in 1968. SIC 8351.

Gustavus Adolphus College
800 W. College Ave., St. Peter, MN 56082
Tel: 507/933-8000 Fax: 507/933-7041
Web site: http://www.gustavus.edu
Axel D. Steuer, Pres.
Henry Toutain, Dean of Students
Elizabeth Baer, VP-Academic Affairs
Dennis Johnson, VP-College Relations
Brenda J. Peterson, VP-Institutional Advancement
Owen Sammelson, VP-Admin.
Kenneth Westphal, VP-Finance and Treas.
Mark Anderson, Assoc. VP-Devel.
Annual Revenue: $77.2 million.
Annual Expenses: $60.1 million.
Contributions: 25.5 percent of revenue.
Gustavus Adolphus, founded by Swedish Lutheran immigrants in 1862 and named for Swedish King Gustav II Adolf, is the oldest Lutheran college in Minnesota. It is a residential liberal arts college of nearly 2,500 that grants undergraduate degrees in 65 majors. Fully accredited, Gustavus hosts a local chapter of Phi Beta Kappa and is internationally known for its annual Nobel Conference.
595 employees.
Founded in 1862. SIC 8221.
No. 26 CRM Nonprofit 100.
Recent: *In January 2000 Gustavus was on of five private liberal arts institutions in the nation to receive a $150,000 John S. and James L. Knight Foundation Presidential Leadership Grant. The unsolicited award recognizes President Steuer's leadership.*

Guthrie Theater Foundation
725 Vineland Pl., Minneapolis, MN 55403
Tel: 612/347-1100 Fax: 612/347-1188
Joe Dowling, Artistic Dir.
David Hawkanson, Managing Dir.
Thomas Proehl, Gen. Mgr.
Steve Bader, Controller
Trisha Kirk, Dir.-Marketing
Dianne Brennan, Devel. Dir.
Annual Revenue: $14.9 million.
Annual Expenses: $12.8 million.
Contributions: 26.5 percent of revenue.
The Guthrie Theater is a resident professional theater company.
150 employees.
Founded in 1963. SIC 7922.
Recent: *In January 2000 the 50-member Guthrie board voted unanimously to approve the historic Mississippi Mill River District as the preferred site for the institution's new three-theater facility. Site negotiations with the Minneapolis Community Development Agency (MCDA) were to begin immediately. In February a bonding bill was submitted in the Minnesota Senate and the House of Representatives requesting $25 million in state financing to support the new facility. The Guthrie planned to raise an additional $50 million from private sources including individuals, corporations, and foundations.*

Hamline University
1536 Hewitt Ave., St. Paul, MN 55104
Tel: 651/523-2800 Fax: 651/523-2956
Web site: http://www.hamline.edu
Larry G. Osnes, Vice Chair
Patti Andreini Arnold, VP-Finance and Treas.
Sally Dufault, Asst. Sec.
Jerry M. Greiner, Provost
Dan Loritz, VP-University Relations
Harry Pontiff, Chief Info. Ofcr.
Annual Revenue: $52.9 million.
Annual Expenses: $51.2 million.
Contributions: 16.1 percent of revenue.
Hamline University is Minnesota's first university, serving a diverse student body of more than 3,300 degree-seeking students and 8,000 professionals in continuing education. Since 1854, it has been a pioneer in preparing people to make the world a better place. Today, Hamline continues its tradition of pioneering new ways of serving the world through its degrees at the bachelor's, master's, and doctorate levels, in four schools: the College of Liberal Arts; the School of Law; a Graduate School of Education; and a Graduate School of Public Administration and Management. Hamline also offers master's degrees in liberal studies and fine arts in writing through its Graduate Liberal Studies Program. Hamline University is affiliated with the United Methodist Church's global network of universities and colleges.
500 employees.
Founded in 1854. SIC 8221.
No. 44 CRM Nonprofit 100.
Recent: *In April 2000 the Hamline University School of Law maintained its sixth-place ranking among law schools for its alternative dispute resolution program.*

Hazelden Foundation
P.O. Box 11, Center City, MN 55012
Tel: 651/213-4000 Fax: 651/257-5101
Web site: http://www.hazelden.org
Jerry W. Spicer, Pres.
Peter Bell, EVP-New Ventures Devel.
Clay Garner, EVP-Information/Educ. Svs.
Gary Hestness, EVP-Devel./Alumni Relations
Jane Nakken, EVP-Board and Comm. Relations
Patricia Owen, EVP-Research
Michael Schiks, EVP-Recovery Services
Bruce Ziegler, EVP-Corp. Mktg. Comm.
Annual Revenue: $68.6 million.
Annual Expenses: $59 million.
Contributions: 8.2 percent of revenue.
Hazelden provides high-quality, affordable rehabilitation for chemically

NON

dependent men, women, older adults, young people, and their families. Hazelden is also the nation's largest provider of educational materials related to chemical dependency.
1,004 employees.
Founded in 1949. SIC 8322, 8361.
No. 29 CRM Nonprofit 100.
Recent: *In November 1999, after a nine-month trial in a joint venture, Hazelden acquired DLCAS.com, an Internet-based distance-learning resource specializing in addiction studies. (Hazelden concluded that, in a field demanding both in working hours and emotional commitment, professionals would support a one-stop online resource that kept them up-to-date on constantly evolving certification and recertification requirements and gave them the courses they needed to fulfill them.) In March 2000 Hazelden and Transitions Bookplace Inc. of Chicago, the country's most renowned bookseller devoted to personal growth and spirituality, joined forces in a historic partnership that was to both produce new books and reinvent important out-of-print titles. The Hazelden Foundation also announced plans to offer both public and private schools, K-12, a customized package of online resources on alcohol, other drugs, and violence prevention through a new Web-based affiliate program titled Educational Partners. In April Hazelden published the first autobiography of Bill W., co-founder of Alcoholics Anonymous; in May, a new book by noted clinical psychotherapist and author Earl Hipp called Understanding The Human Volcano: What Teens Can Do About Violence. In June Hazelden and Transitions Bookplace Inc. of Chicago, the country's most renowned bookseller devoted to personal growth and spirituality, partnered to produce new books and reinvent important out-of-print titles. The partners were to produce a number of original titles in 2000, including "Why Normal Isn't 'Healthy,'" by Dr. Bowen White. The Hazelden Transitions Bookplace (http://www.htbookplace.org), a joint venture of Hazelden Foundation's Information and Education Services Division and the nationally recognized Chicagoland bookseller Transitions Bookplace, opened in June with 450 authors and experts plus 1 million regular online visitors. In July Hazelden announced plans to publish a book based on "Alcohol: Cradle to Grave," Pulitzer Prize-winning journalist Eric Newhouse's year-long investigation into the far-reaching problems of alcohol abuse. In August the Hazelden Foundation was invited to do a signal poster presentation at the 11th World Conference on Tobacco or Health in Chicago. Entitled "Clinical Smoking Cessation Applications in the Recovery Community," the poster addresses the need for a tobacco-cessation component in treatment plans in the recovery community, citing the high instance (90 percent) of tobacco use among recovering chemical dependant adults, and offers a modified 12-step model as an important opportunity to effect institutional change. Hazelden published three new books: Dangerous Drugs, from the Hazelden Foundation's Information and Educational Services is a comprehensive, authoritative guide that covers the full range of drugs of abuse (from cough syrup and household cleansers to herbal remedies and prescription drugs to heroin and methamphetamine); Twin Souls: Finding Your True Spiritual Partner, uncovers the secrets behind our deepest desires for soul union with our one true beloved, and reveals how this fulfillment of the heart's deepest longing is a crucial event in the soul's inexorable evolution toward reunion with God; and Love First, which demonstrates structured intervention techniques that provide families with loving yet effective ways to motivate an alcoholic or addict to accept help. DLCAS.com won approval from the huge National Association of Social Workers (NASW), opening up distance learning to NASW's more than 155,000 members, many of whom are required orelect to seek certification in one or more addiction-related disciplines. DLCAS.com would also receive approval from the prestigious California Board of Behaviorial Sciences, the credentialing board for all California licensed professional counselors and licensed marriage and family therapists, and from the National Board of Certified Counselors. In September Hazelden announced the availability of a new program to all public and private schools K-12: a customized package of online resources on alcohol, other drugs, and violence prevention through a new, no-cost, Web-based affiliate program titled Educational Partners. Hazelden sold the movie rights for its 1997 bestseller "Times Square Rabbi: Finding Hope in Lost Kids' Lives," Yehudah Fine's first hand account of his work from 1985 to 1994 with children caught in the harsh street subculture of Times Square. In November Hazelden received Time Inc Health's prestigious FREDDIE Award for "Gambling: It's Not About The Money," a dramatic and educational documentary that highlights the experience, strength, and hope of a diverse group of recovering gamblers, interviews with two gambling experts, and mind-boggling statistics about gambling addiction in America. Hazelden's www.dlcas.com won approval from American Psychological Association, opening up distance learning to APA's over 159,000 members, many required or elect to seek certification in one or more addiction-related disciplines.*

NON

HealthEast

559 Capitol Blvd., St. Paul, MN 55103
Tel: 651/232-2300 Fax: 651/232-2315
Web site: http://www.healtheast.org
Timothy H. Hanson, Pres. and CEO
Scott Batulis, VP-Bethesda Hospital/Sr. Care
Robert Beck, M.D., VP-Medical Affairs
Doug Cropper, VP-Admin., St. Joseph
Gary French, Group VP-Market Development
Robert D. Gill, VP and CFO
Roger Green, VP-Strategic Planning
Scott Hinrichs, VP-Spiritual Care
William Knutson, VP-Care Systems/Specialty Svs.
Martin Paul, VP-Quality/Risk Mgmt.
Ann Schrader, Group VP-Care Delivery Svs.
Stephen Sprint, VP-Hum. Res.
Annual Revenue: $402.8 million.
Annual Expenses: $396 million.
HealthEast Care System is a community-focused, nonprofit health care system that provides a full spectrum of family health services. Services include hospitals, physician clinics, senior care centers, rehabilitation facilities, hospice, home care, medical equipment and services, outpatient surgery centers and a variety of other health facilities and programs. HealthEast has more than 1,100 physicians on staff. Locally owned and operated, HealthEast is the largest health care provider in the Twin Cities' east metro area.
6,575 employees.
Founded in 1986. SIC 8062.
No. 8 CRM Nonprofit 100.
No. 24 CRM Employer 100.
Recent: *In August 2000, the Woodwinds Health Campus' new hospital began receiving patients. Built in a unique woodland/wetlands setting, the hospital was designed according to healing environment and patient-centered concepts, and features emergency, surgery, outpatient and maternity care services. Also in August, HealthEast's St. Joseph's, St. John's and Bethesda Rehabilitation Hospitals received top marks from the national Joint Commission on Accreditation of Healthcare Organizations—the highest of any East Metro health care organization. HealthEast opened its newest assisted-living facility, Residence in South St. Paul, in August. In spring, the Natural Care Center, a collaboration with Northwestern Health Sciences University, opened at Woodwinds Health Campus. It features chiropractic, naturopathy, acupuncture, and other complementary therapies. The center is the first of its kind in the United States to be part of a medical campus. Earlier in the year, HealthEast and its Foundation opened The Pillars, the first hospice residence in the East Metro. HealthEast also recently opened its Breast Care Center. Located at St. John's Hospital, the Center is designed to provide treatment, care coordination, support, and resources in a single, healing environment. In January 2000 Healtheast was recognized in a national survey as one of the 20 best-governed health care systems in the United States.*

HealthPartners

8100 34th Ave. S., P.O. Box 1309 (Mpls., 55440), Bloomington, MN 55425
Tel: 952/883-6000 Fax: 952/883-5310
Web site: http://www.healthpartners.com
George C. Halvorson, Pres. and CEO
Mary K. Brainerd, EVP and COO
David Abrams, VP and Chief Hum. Res. Ofcr.
Scott Aebischer, VP-Network Mgmt./Devel.
Craig Amundson, D.D.S., COO-Dental Op./Dental Dir.
Babette Apland, VP-Contracted Svs.
Kathy Cooney, SVP-Finance and CFO
Anne Darney, SVP-Underwriting (Subsid. Op.)
James Dixon, VP-Reg'l Hospital Partnerships
David Dziuk, VP-Finance and Cont.
Kirby J. Erickson, EVP and CAO
Susan Freeman, M.D., EVP-Medical Affairs
Terry Finzen, Pres./CEO-Regions Hospital
David D. Gregg, M.D., VP, Medical Ofcr.-Health Init.
George Isham, Medical Dir., Chief Health Ofc
Jill Sammon Larson, Senior Dir.-Gov't Relations

Tammie Lindquist, VP-Health Care Analysis/Rptg.
Nancy McClure, SVP-Medical Group/Clinics
Judy Meath, VP-Physician Support Svs.
Carl Patow, Exec. Dir.-Medical Education
Brian Rank, Medical Dir.-Med. Group
Maureen Reed, Medical Dir.-Contracted Care
Katie Sayre, VP-Admin. Svs.
Doug Smith, VP-Sales
Tobi Tanzer, VP-Corp. Integrity/Compliance
Theodore E. (Ted) Wise, SVP-Cons. Choice/Member Hea
Annual Revenue: $1.49 billion.
Annual Expenses: $1.48 billion.
Contributions: 1.5 percent of revenue.
HealthPartners is a consumer-governed family of nonprofit Minnesota health care organizations focused on improving the health of its members and the community. HealthPartners and its related organizations provide health care services, insurance, and HMO coverage to nearly 660,000 members. More than 9,000 employees staff the various HealthPartners organizations. The HealthPartners family includes the HealthPartners and Ramsey clinics, HealthPartners Medical Group, HealthPartners Dental Group, Regions Hospital, Regions Hospital Foundation, HealthPartners Research Foundation, HealthPartners Institute for Medical Education, Central Minnesota Group Health, Group Health Inc., HealthPartners Administrators, and Midwest Assurance Co.
9,000 employees.
Founded in 1957. SIC 8011, 8021.
No. 4 CRM Nonprofit 100.
No. 14 CRM Employer 100.
Recent: *Sept. 30, 1999: Consolidated net income on a GAAP basis was $3.6 million for the nine months, versus a net loss of $5.6 million for full-year 1998. In February 2000 Standard & Poor's affirmed its triple-'B'-plus counterparty credit and financial strength ratings on HealthPartners Inc.: outlook stable. Rating factors: As one of three leading Minnesota HMOs, HealthPartners has a very strong market position, with a diversified managed care delivery system that serves 792,000 members throughout Minnesota including the Twin Cities region, its primary service area. Although enrollment has grown modestly, total membership was expected to drop to 655,000 in early 2000 primarily because of the loss of an administrative services-only contract with Buyer's Health Care Action Group. Although Standard & Poor's was expecting the competitive market environment and certain greater-than-expected medical cost trends to continue to pose challenges to HealthPartners' ability to return to historical profitability levels, it did expect improved profitability in 2000 due to premium-rate increases and cost-containment initiatives. In 2000 the organization launched the HealthPartners Restaurant Network: 25 restaurants at 125 Twin Cities locations that carry FDA-certified "low-fat" menu items and receive free nutrition consulting services. In June, after a year of consumer meetings, intense market research, focus groups, and discussions with physicians, employers, brokers, and health care consultants—and in response to the state and national debate about the future of health care—the HealthPartners board of directors made 10 very specific commitments to the community and to HealthPartners members, including:1) No Secrets, No Surprises: Consumers are concerned that secret coverage rules will result in their care not being covered by their plan. All care guidelines, benefit definitions, and quality and safety screening approaches that affect health care coverage will now be made available to consumers. Everything will be on the Internet. 2) No Interference with Doctors: No plan approval process will be needed for more than 9,500 medical procedures. Doctors can order tests, make specialty referrals and admit patients to hospitals without needing any plan approval. 3) Wider Range of Choices for patients, members and employers: HealthPartners will now offer a much wider range of benefit and care network options. For the first time, individuals will be able to make choices about their level of health benefits and their personal preference in clinics and physicians. In August American Express Financial Advisors Inc., one of the founders of the Buyers Health Care Action Group, left the coalition to join HealthPartners. HealthPartners was honored with the Dannon Institute Award for Excellence in Community Nutrition. Regions Hospital and the National Hockey League's Minnesota Wild formed a partnership that was to recognize Regions Hospital as the preferred health care provider of the Minnesota Wild and the Xcel Energy Center during Minnesota Wild hockey games. In September HealthPartners again achieved high quality rankings in the HealthPlan Employer Data and Information Set, which is a standardized set of performance measures used to compare health plans and drive quality improvement in the market, by scoring significantly better than the average of all plans across the county in virtually every measure. In October HealthPartners agreed to advertise in the Twin Cities on America Online and AOL's other brands. HealthPartners planned to give members direct access to a broader network of behavioral health providers beginning Jan. 1, 2001. The new approach for behavioral care featured direct access, no prior approval, and no case management for routine behavioral health services within a broader behavioral health network that combines all three of the existing large behavioral care systems, HealthPartners, Allina, and Park Nicollet, into one large network. Members could choose from more than 20 new clinic systems—many with multiple clinic sites—and nearly 40 additional individual practitioners, including psychiatrists and a number of specialists in culturally diverse services. HealthPartners' consumer-elected board of directors approved plans for Partners for Better Health 2005, a set of 35 new, measurable three- to five-year health improvement goals for the organization's membership. Some of these goals included: Reduce the incidence of diabetes among members with high risk by 25 percent; Decrease the risk of heart attacks among patients with diabetes by 25 percent; Decrease by 30 percent the incidence of leg amputations, blindness, and end-stage renal disease among patients with diabetes by reducing modifiable risks; Increase by 50 percent the number of patients with atherosclerotic cardiovascular disease who have all their modifiable risk factors in control; Increase by 50 percent the number of patients at risk for depressionwho are identified, diagnosed and who receive appropriate treatment; Reduce by 50 percent the number of attempted suicides and suicides among HealthPartners members diagnosed with depression.*

Hennepin Faculty Associates

600 HFA Building, 914 S. Eighth St., Minneapolis, MN 55404
Tel: 612/347-5000 Fax: 612/347-6053
Melvin P. Bubrick, M.D., Pres.
Lawrence Fosbury, SVP-Finance/Operations
Donald Jacobs, M.D., SVP-Medical Affairs
Joseph Clinton, M.D., Sec.
Michael K. Popkin, M.D., Treas.
Annual Revenue: $85.3 million.
Annual Expenses: $84.5 million.
Contributions: 16.4 percent of revenue.
Hennepin Faculty Associates is an academic group practice of approximately 260 physicians practicing in over 32 specialties at Hennepin County Medical Center and various other hospitals and clinics throughout the Twin Cities. HFA's mission is focused on patient care, teaching, and research.
702 employees.
Founded in 1983. SIC 8069.
No. 23 CRM Nonprofit 100.

Hiawatha Homes Inc.

1820 Valkyrie Dr. N.W., Rochester, MN 55901
Tel: 507/289-7222 Fax: 507/289-8007
Douglas Butler, Exec. Dir.
Hiawatha Homes Inc. manages five community-based residential facilities, and in-home program, and personal care attendant services in Olmstead County.
235 employees.
Founded in 1976. SIC 8361.

Hiawatha Valley Mental Health Center Inc.

P.O. Box 619, Winona, MN 55987
Tel: 507/454-4341 Fax: 507/453-6267
Ellen Kittleson, Exec. Dir.
Hiawatha Valley Mental Health Center Inc. provides community mental health services and children' s mental health services, including outpatient services, day treatment, chemical dependency assessment and treatment, community support programs for the chronically mentally ill, and a residential treatment program.
90 employees.
Founded in 1965. SIC 8011.

HIRED

1200 Plymouth Ave. N., Minneapolis, MN 55411
Tel: 612/529-3342 Fax: 612/529-7131
Web site: http://www.hired.org
Jane Samargia, Exec. Dir.

Andrea Comstock, JOB LINK Dir.
Laura Vitelli, Devel. Dir.
Annual Revenue: $4.6 million.
Annual Expenses: $4.5 million.
Contributions: 93.7 percent of revenue.
HIRED manages programs which assist unemployed and disadvantaged adults and youth to prepare for and secure careers and jobs leading to economic self-sufficiency. JOB LINK is a computer-based job development system which electronically gathers and distributes job vacancy listings to over 40 community and nonprofit organizations assisting job seekers throughout the Twin Cities area. More than 4,000 employers list positions and electronic posting of vacancies is available. The JOB LINK database also offers workforce and employment trend analysis.
88 employees.
Founded in 1968. SIC 8331.

Homeward Bound Inc.

8401 Wayzata Blvd., Suite 300, Golden Valley, MN 55426
Tel: 952/525-3186 Fax: 952/525-4084
Donna Wain-Erickson, Exec. Dir.
Michael C. House, Dir.-Finance/Property
Nancy Brady, R.N., Dir.-Operations/Nursing
Annual Revenue: $9.1 million.
Annual Expenses: $9.2 million.
Contributions: 0.3 percent of revenue.
Homeward Bound Inc. provides residential and support services for 100 children and adults with severe and complex disabilities.
280 employees.
Founded in 1973. SIC 8059.

Human Development Center

1401 E. First St., Duluth, MN 55805
Tel: 218/728-4491 Fax: 218/728-4404
Glenn Anderson, Exec. Dir.
Human Development Center provides mental health services for individuals, group family therapy, day treatment, psychiatric and psychological education, medication management, and consultation education.
115 employees.
Founded in 1938. SIC 8063.

Human Service Agency—ATCO Enterprises

P.O. Box 1030, 123 19th St. N.E., Watertown, SD 57201
Tel: 605/886-0123
Charles Sherman, CEO
Human Service Agency—ATCO Enterprises manufactures pallets, bridging, deck boards, shutters,and staking; and does light assembling.
150 employees.
Founded in 1963. SIC 2448, 2499.

Human Services Inc. in Washington County, Minnesota

7066 Stillwater Blvd. N., Oakdale, MN 55128
Tel: 651/777-5222 Fax: 651/251-5111
Web site: http://www.hsicares.org
Robert T. Butler, CEO
Robert L. McDonough, Senior Division Dir.
Mark S. Kuppe, Division Dir.
Scott Craven, Division Dir.
Linda Chabot, Finance Dir.
Annual Revenue: $10.7 million.
Annual Expenses: $10 million.
Contributions: 80 percent of revenue.
Human Services Inc. provides mental health, chemical dependency, domestic/sexual abuse, aging/handicapped, and transportation programs and services primarily in Washington County, Minnesota.
300 employees.
Founded in 1969. SIC 8322.

Humphrey Institute of Public Affairs

University of Minnesota, 301 19th Ave. S., Minneapolis, MN 55455
Tel: 612/625-0669 Fax: 612/625-6351
Web site: http://www.hhh.umn.edu
John Brandl, Dean
The Humphrey Institute of Public Affairs, the University of Minnesota's graduate school of public affairs, prepares individuals for public service and designs more effective public policies and institutions. The institute offers four graduate degree programs, which had 215 students enrolled in fall 2000, and is home to 15 research and outreach centers and programs.
189 employees.
Founded in 1979. SIC 8221.

Immanuel-St. Joseph's Hospital of Mankato Inc.

1025 Marsh St., Mankato, MN 56001
Tel: 507/625-4031 Fax: 507/345-2926
Jerome A. Crest, EVP
Gary L. Grovdahl, VP
Annette J. McBeth, VP
Thomas Tiggelaar, Controller
Annual Revenue: $76.7 million.
Annual Expenses: $66.6 million.
Contributions: 0.8 percent of revenue.
Immanuel-St. Joseph's Hospital of Mankato is a general acute-care hospital offering inpatient and outpatient services, home health care, and hospice services to south-central Minnesota.
880 employees.
Founded in 1968. SIC 8062.
No. 27 CRM Nonprofit 100.

Indian Health Board of Minneapolis

1315 E. 24th St., Minneapolis, MN 55404
Tel: 612/721-9800 Fax: 612/721-2904
Yvonne Bushyhead, Exec. Dir.
Lydia Caros, M.D., Chief of Staff
Phyllis Johnson, Comptroller
Indian Health Board of Minneapolis is a comprehensive community health center that provides medical, dental, and mental health services to the Indian community.
70 employees.
Founded in 1971. SIC 8011.

Indianhead Enterprises

1426 Indianhead Dr., Menomonie, WI 54751
Tel: 715/232-6460 Fax: 715/232-6463
Dean Seston, Pres.
Renee Surdick, Administrator
Indianhead Enterprises is a custom packaging and assembly house that also does dry-blend packaging of powder products, and specializing in rehabilitation facilities.
100 employees.
Founded in 1981. SIC 7389.

International Falls Memorial Hospital Association

1400 Highway 71, International Falls, MN 56649
Tel: 218/283-4481 Fax: 218/283-3433
James Lund, Administrator
International Falls Memorial Hospital Association is a general short term acute care facility.
140 employees.
Founded in 1945. SIC 8062.

Itasca Medical Center

126 First Ave. S.E., Grand Rapids, MN 55744
Tel: 218/326-3401
Annual Revenue: $25 million.
Annual Expenses: $22.6 million.
Contributions: 0.1 percent of revenue.
Itasca Medical Center operates an acute-care hospital and a 35-bed skilled

nursing unit.
400 employees.
No. 77 CRM Nonprofit 100.

Jewish Family & Children's Service

13100 Wayzata Blvd., Suite 400, Minnetonka, MN 55305
Tel: 952/546-0616 Fax: 952/593-1778
Jeremy Waldman, Exec. Dir.
Mari Forbush, Assoc. Exec. Dir.
Larry Greenbaum, Dir.-Jewish Vocational Svc.
Annual Revenue: $4.8 million.
Annual Expenses: $5 million.
Contributions: 58.6 percent of revenue.
Jewish Family & Children's Service is a human service agency.
120 employees.
Founded in 1910. SIC 8322.

Lake Region Healthcare Corporation

712 S. Cascade, P.O. Box 728, Fergus Falls, MN 56538
Tel: 218/736-8000 Fax: 218/736-8723
Edward J. Mehl, Administrator and CEO
Ed Strand, CFO and Asst. Administrator
Annual Revenue: $33.3 million.
Annual Expenses: $30.3 million.
Contributions: 0.1 percent of revenue.
Lake Region Healthcare Corp. provides health care services. Its facilities include 100 acute-care beds (including a psychiatric unit) and 44 skilled nursing home beds. Lake Region also provides outpatient services, including a home health agency.
610 employees.
Founded in 1951. SIC 8062.
No. 62 CRM Nonprofit 100.

Lakestate Industries Inc.

1831 N. 21st St., P.O. Box 279, Escanaba, MI 49829
Tel: 906/786-9212 Fax: 906/789-6004
Jennifer Mclearen, Pres. and Exec. Dir.
Tom Harris, VP
Kevin Negri, Sec. and Treas.
Lakestate Industries is engaged in vocational rehabilitation services. Recycling and manufacturing of surveying stakes are among its operations.
96 employees.
Founded in 1972. SIC 2449.

Lakewood Health System

401 E. Prairie Ave., Staples, MN 56479
Timothy Rice, Pres.
Annual Revenue: $18.1 million.
Annual Expenses: $17.9 million.
Contributions: 0.2 percent of revenue.
Lakewood Health System is a district hospital, nursing home, and health clinic.
450 employees.
No. 97 CRM Nonprofit 100.

LifeLink III

2124 University Ave. W., St. Paul, MN 55114
Tel: 651/917-5200 Fax: 651/917-5231
Andrew Kirchoff, Pres. and CEO
Chris Gross, Dir.-Finance
Marty Young, Dir.-Operations
LifeLink III provides critical-care air and ground medical transport by helicopter, fixed wing, and ground ambulances.
170 employees.
Founded in 1985.

Lifetrack Resources

709 University Ave. W., St. Paul, MN 55104
Tel: 651/227-8471 Fax: 651/227-0621
Web site: http://www.lifetrackresources.org
John Mohr, Pres.
Rudy Brynolfson, VP-Fin./Admin.
Cynthia Toppin, VP-Rehab Therapies
Therese Anderson, VP-Devel.
Barbara Grossman, VP-Employment Resources
Annual Revenue: $8.3 million.
Annual Expenses: $7.9 million.
Contributions: 19.7 percent of revenue.
Lifetrack Resources provides outcome-based rehabilitation and employment services to children and adults who have disabilities and people who are disadvantaged. Employment services include community employment, center-based employment, and welfare-to-work programs. Rehabilitation therapy services include occupational and physical therapy, audiology, speech-language therapy, medical social services, and a therapeutic preschool program. Lifetrack Resources was founded as St. Paul Rehabilitation Center in 1948.
160 employees.
Founded in 1948. SIC 8331.

Lifeworks Services

1120 Centre Pointe Dr., Suite 100, Mendota Heights, MN 55120
Tel: 651/454-2732 Fax: 651/454-3174
Web site: http://www.lifeworks.org
Judy Lysne, Pres.
Annual Revenue: $10.3 million.
Annual Expenses: $10.5 million.
Contributions: 1.9 percent of revenue.
Lifeworks Services is an employment resource matching business needs with the skills and interests of people with disabilities. Lifeworks, a private nonprofit organization, works with 125 businesses in the Twin Cities and Mankato areas.
200 employees.
Founded in 1965. SIC 8331.

Lutheran Memorial Homes

P.O. Box 480, Twin Valley, MN 56584
Tel: 218/584-5181 Fax: 218/584-5304
Dwight Fuglie, Exec. Dir.
Lutheran Memorial Homes provides long-term care services to the elderly. The organization operates three nursing facilities and two low income elderly apartments and provides respite care, adult day care, senior meals, and other services.
247 employees.
Founded in 1969. SIC 8051, 8059.

Lutheran Retirement Home of Southern Minnesota Inc.

400 N. Fourth Ave. E., Truman, MN 56088
Tel: 507/776-2031 Fax: 507/776-2034
Rodney Dahlberg, Exec. Dir.
Lutheran Retirement Home of Southern Minnesota Inc. is a nursing home.
93 employees.
Founded in 1963. SIC 8051.

Lutheran Social Service of Minnesota

2485 Como Ave., St. Paul, MN 55108
Tel: 651/642-5990 Fax: 651/969-2360
Web site: http://www.lssmn.org
Mark A. Peterson, Pres. and CEO
Mary Kurth, VP-Finance and CFO
Joyce Norals, VP-Hum. Res.
Mark Stutrud, VP-Children/Family Services
Jeri Nelsen, VP-Community/Congregational

Paul Tillquist, VP-Devel./Communication
Bob York, VP-Disabilities Svs.
Annual Revenue: $50.1 million.
Annual Expenses: $49.3 million.
Contributions: 14.9 percent of revenue.
Lutheran Social Service of Minnesota provides a broad range of human services, including: mental health counseling in over 65 communities; programs that help strengthen families; outreach to at-risk children and youth; services for children and adults with disabilities; independent options for older persons; housing and advocacy; adoption and pregnancy counseling; refugee services; chaplaincy ministry; and congregational services.
2,035 employees.
Founded in 1865. SIC 8322.
No. 50 CRM Nonprofit 100.
Recent: *In February 2000 Blue Plus, the HMO unit of Blue Cross and Blue Shield of Minnesota, reached an agreement with Lutheran Social Service (LSS) regarding the inclusion of LSS clinics in Blue Plus' referral network for mental health services.*

Macalester College
1600 Grand Ave., St. Paul, MN 55105
Tel: 651/696-6000 Fax: 651/696-6500
Web site: http://www.macalester.edu
Michael S. McPherson, Ph.D., Pres.
Craig Aase, VP-Admin. and Treas.
Dan Hornbach, Provost
Richard A. Ammons, VP-College Advancement
Joel Clemmer, VP-Library/Info. Services
Laurie Hamre, Dean of Students
Lorne T. Robinson, Dean-Admissions/Financial Aid
William Shain, Dean of Admissions
Annual Revenue: $91.8 million.
Annual Expenses: $69.2 million.
Contributions: 11.2 percent of revenue.
Macalester College is a four-year, national, residential, liberal arts college. The student body includes 11 percent American minorities and 12 percent international students from 68 countries. Total enrollment is 1,794.
600 employees.
Founded in 1874. SIC 8221.
No. 22 CRM Nonprofit 100.
Recent: *Macalester was named one of the 10 Great Places to Work in Minnesota in the August 2000 issue of Corporate Report magazine.*

Mankato Rehabilitation Center Inc. (MRCI)
15 Map Dr., P.O. Box 328, Mankato, MN 56001
Tel: 507/386-5600 Fax: 507/345-5991
William R. Bickett, Exec. Dir.
Pamela Year, Program Dir.
Lyle Holland, Production Mgr.
Daniel Fogal, Mktg. Mgr.
Annual Revenue: $15.4 million.
Annual Expenses: $15 million.
Contributions: 46.1 percent of revenue.
Mankato Rehabilitation Center Inc. (MRCI) provides vocational rehabilitation and therapeutic services to people with disabilities to enhance their self-reliance, afford them opportunities to make choices, and help them occupy the most integrated environment possible. MRCI Industrial Operations provides contract packaging and assembly plus microfilming services.
268 employees.
Founded in 1953. SIC 8331.

Mayo Foundation
200 First St. S.W., Rochester, MN 55905
Tel: 507/284-2511 Fax: 507/284-8713
Web site: http://www.mayo.edu
Michael Wood, M.D., Pres. and CEO
Richard M. Weinshilboum, M.D., VP
Hugh C. Smith, M.D., Chair, Mayo Rochester Board
Leo F. Black, M.D., Chair, Mayo Jacksonville Board
Michael B. O'Sullivan, M.D., Chair, Mayo Scottsdale Board
Annual Revenue: $3.52 billion.
Annual Expenses: $3.41 billion.
Contributions: 3 percent of revenue.
Mayo Foundation provides comprehensive medical care and education in clinical medicine and medical sciences, and also conducts extensive programs in medical research. Mayo Foundation includes Rochester Methodist Hospital, Saint Marys Hospital of Rochester, St. Luke's Health Systems Inc. (Florida), Mayo Clinic Jacksonville, a new hospital in Phoenix, Mayo Clinic Scottsdale, and various other not-for-profit subsidiaries; Mayo Group Practices, a not-for-profit holding company for most of Mayo Foundation's taxable entities; and two for-profit subsidiaries, Mayo Medical Laboratories (analyzes lab tests for clients around the world) and Mayo Medical Ventures (publishes medical books, newsletters, and computerized medical information).
33,876 employees.
Founded in 1919. SIC 8062.
No. 1 CRM Nonprofit 100.
No. 5 CRM Employer 100.
Recent: *In December 1999 Mayo Clinic created a joint venture with a San Francisco-based group of private investors to launch a second consumer-health Web site that was to include an interactive service through which customers can ask personal questions. In August 2000 the Mayo Clinic said that it was planning to exit the HMO business by the end of 2001. Mayo Health Plan, with 8,800 members (one of the smallest HMOs in Minnesota), experienced a $1.6 million loss in 1999 and was projecting another loss for 2000. In October six leading medical research centers from across the country, including Mayo Clinic, were conducting a peanut allergy study to determine if an investigational drug could lessen the severity of an allergic reaction in sufferers.*

Memorial Blood Centers of Minnesota Inc.
2304 Park Ave., Minneapolis, MN 55404
Tel: 612/871-3300 Fax: 612/871-1359
Web site: http://www.mbcm.org
Jerry Haarmann, CEO
Margaret Hanson, Dir.
Scott Caswell, Dir.-Patient Advocacy
Kathryn Jensen, Mgr.
Donald Schlueter, Dir.-Finance
Jed Gorlin, Medical Dir.
Sally Frones, Dir.-Trans.
Memorial Blood Centers of Minnesota (MBCsM) ensures a safe and sufficient supply of blood and components. More than 82,000 units of blood were received at the MBCsM's two centers, Memorial Blood Center of Minneapolis and Arrowhead Regional Blood Center in Duluth, during the fiscal year ended May 31, 1996. MBCsM also provides a wide range of testing and processing procedures.
231 employees.
Founded in 1948. SIC 8071.

Merrick Companies Inc.
1636 Gervais Ave., Suite 14, Maplewood, MN 55109
Tel: 651/770-6200 Fax: 651/770-7512
Kevin Martineau, CEO
Merrick Cos. Inc. provides training and rehabilitation service for persons with developmental disabilities in Ramsey County. Services include job development, community training, and behavior management and modification.
115 employees.
Founded in 1964. SIC 8331.

Mid-Minnesota Legal Assistance
430 First Ave. N., Suite 300, Minneapolis, MN 55401
Tel: 612/332-1441 Fax: 612/334-5755
Jeremy Lane, Exec. Dir. and Sec.
Roger Cobb, Agency Administrator
Luther Granquist, Managing Attorney
Timothy Thompson, Litigation Dir.
Abigail Turner, Litigation Dir.
Mid-Minnesota Legal Assistance Inc., which includes the Legal Aid Society of

Minneapolis, St. Cloud Area Legal Services, and Western Minnesota Legal Services is an eight-office, 61-attorney program providing free legal representation to low-income, elderly, or disabled clients. Funding sources include the Older Americans Act, the State of Minnesota, Hennepin County, the City of Minneapolis, the United Way, foundations, local law firms and corporations, etc. Mid-Minnesota Legal Assistance enjoys good rapport with, and strong support from, the organized bar. The Legal Aid Society of Minneapolis was founded in 1913.
130 employees.
Founded in 1981. SIC 8111.

Midwest Special Services Inc.
900 Ocean St., St. Paul, MN 55106
Tel: 651/778-1000 Fax: 651/772-4352
Web site: http://www.mwsservices.org
Lyth J. Hartz, Pres.
Annual Revenue: $6 million.
Annual Expenses: $6 million.
Contributions: 4.2 percent of revenue.
Midwest Special Services Inc. provides businesses with contract packaging and assemby services—specializing in blister packaging, shrinkwrapping, and hand assembly. Midwest's Employment Program provides job training and placement services for adults with disabilities. The Developmental Achievement Center Program assists adults with severe disabilities to become as independent as possible in daily life skills.
121 employees.
Founded in 1949. SIC 8331.
Recent: *Working towards QS 9000 certification.*

Mille Lacs Hospital and Home
200 N. Elm St., Onamia, MN 56359
Tel: 320/532-3154 Fax: 320/532-3111
Randy Farrow, Administrator and CEO
Patrick Dunleavy, Treas. and CFO
Barb Burandt, Division Dir.
Kathy Johnson, Division Dir.
Annual Revenue: $13.9 million.
Annual Expenses: $12.6 million.
Contributions: 3.2 percent of revenue.
Mille Lacs Hospital and Home provides hospital nursing home and physician clinic services to its patients.
225 employees.
Founded in 1956. SIC 8059.
Recent: *A $12 million, five-year building project in progress.*

Miller-Dwan Medical Center
502 E. Second St., Duluth, MN 55805
Tel: 218/727-8762 Fax: 218/720-1496
Web site: http://www.miller-dwan.com
William H. Palmer, Pres. and CEO
Daniel L. Svendsen, SVP-Finance and CFO
Michael Lang, VP-Mktg./Community Relations
Joseph Leek, M.D., VP-Medical Affairs
Maureen C. Mahoney, VP-Patient Care Svs.
Pat Rood, VP
Annual Revenue: $54.4 million.
Annual Expenses: $54.9 million.
Miller-Dwan Medical Center is a specialized health care facility serving northeastern Minnesota, northwestern Wisconsin, and the Upper Peninsula of Michigan. Miller-Dwan provides innovative care in areas such as radiation oncology, general surgery, pediatric surgery, urology, plastic and reconstructive surgery, laser surgery, chemical dependency, intensive care, employee assistance, inpatient and outpatient mental health and rehabilitation. The center also operates the region's premier burn-care center, for both serious and minor burns.
800 employees.
Founded in 1934. SIC 8062.
No. 43 CRM Nonprofit 100.

Minneapolis College of Art and Design
2501 Stevens Ave. S., Minneapolis, MN 55404
Tel: 612/874-3700 Fax: 612/874-3711
Web site: http://www.mcad.edu
John S. Slorp, Pres.
Andre Nasset, VP and Dean-Academic Affairs
Pamela Newsome-Prochniak, VP-Personnel/Admin.
Jim Hoseth, Treas.
Annual Revenue: $14.7 million.
Annual Expenses: $12.9 million.
Contributions: 12.9 percent of revenue.
The Minneapolis College of Art and Design (MCAD) is an independent, accredited institution offering a four-year curriculum integrating 14 professional BFA degree majors in Fine Arts, Media Arts, and Desgn; a four-year BS degree program in Visualization; and a two-year MFA degree program in Visual Studies. The campus is one of the finest art college facilities in the country.
145 employees.
Founded in 1886. SIC 8221.
Recent: *In December 1999 Witcher Construction Co., Eden Prairie, Minn., began construction on the 28,200-square-foot first phase of a campus expansion, which was scheduled for September 2000 completion.*

Minneapolis Federation for Jewish Service
5901 S. Cedar Lake Rd., St. Louis Park, MN 55416
Tel: 952/593-2600 Fax: 952/593-2544
Norman Fishman, Camp Dir.
Josh Gruber, Planning and Budget Dir.
Hayim Herring, Identity/Continuity
Sandra T. Hokanson, CFO
Annual Revenue: $22.1 million.
Annual Expenses: $15.6 million.
Contributions: 72.8 percent of revenue.
Minneapolis Federation for Jewish Service is the central fund-raising, allocating, planning, and coordinating agency for the Minneapolis Jewish community. Its mission: to meet local human services needs in Minneapolis, Israel, and the rest of the world. Minneapolis beneficiaries include Community Housing and Service Corp., Hillel Foundation, Jewish Community Center, Jewish Community Relations Council/ADL, Jewish Family and Children's Service, Minneapolis Jewish Day School, Talmud Torah, and Torah Academy.
40 employees.
Founded in 1930. SIC 7389.
No. 83 CRM Nonprofit 100.

Minneapolis Institute of Arts
2400 Third Ave. S., Minneapolis, MN 55404
Tel: 612/870-3046 Fax: 612/870-3004
Web site: http://www.artsmia.org
Evan M. Maurer, Dir. and Pres.
Patricia Grazzini, Assoc. Dir. and COO
John Easley, Dir.-Devel./External Affairs
Denise May, Asst. Sec.
Annual Revenue: $39 million.
Annual Expenses: $27.4 million.
Contributions: 50.3 percent of revenue.
A cultural highlight of the Twin Cities, The Minneapolis Institute of Arts is internationally renowned as one of the great American art museums. In a beautiful landmark structure near downtown Minneapolis, the museum houses a world-class collection of nearly 100,000 objects, representing artistic traditions and treasures spanning 5,000 years. The Institute offers free general admission and welcomes visitors of all ages to enjoy the wonder and beauty of art.
203 employees.
Founded in 1915. SIC 8412.
No. 53 CRM Nonprofit 100.

Minneapolis Medical Research Foundation
914 S. Eighth St., Minneapolis, MN 55404
Tel: 612/347-5165 Fax: 612/337-7189
Chun Chao, Dir.-Research Labs
John Larson, Dir.-Devel.
Alfred Pheley, Dir.-Clinical Epidemiology
Annual Revenue: $15.6 million.
Annual Expenses: $15 million.
Contributions: 84.4 percent of revenue.

Minneapolis Urban League

2000 Plymouth Ave. N., Minneapolis, MN 55411
Tel: 612/302-3100 Fax: 612/521-1444
Gary Suddeth, Exec. Dir.
Minneapolis Urban League provides services to help African American and other minority group members to achieve their full potential. Services include employment, housing and urban affairs, economic/community development, law, and consumer affairs programs.
97 employees.
Founded in 1925. SIC 8399.

The Minnesota Daily Inc.

2301 University Ave. S.E., Minneapolis, MN 55414
Tel: 612/627-4080 Fax: 612/627-4159
Web site: http://www.daily.umn.edu
Kevin Nicholson, Pres.
Sam Rosen, Business Mgr.
Julia Grant, Editor-in-chief
Jennifer Thoen-Swenson, Devel. Dir.
Heather Pahl, Controller
Annual Revenue: $2.5 million.
Annual Expenses: $2.4 million.
The Minnesota Daily Inc. is the student newspaper of the Minneapolis campus of the University of Minnesota.
200 employees.
Founded in 1900. SIC 2711.

Minnesota Diversified Industries Inc.

1700 Wynne Ave., St. Paul, MN 55108
Tel: 651/646-2711 Fax: 651/646-4215
Web site: http://www.mdi.org
Lloyd G. Bratland, Pres. and CEO
Brian T. Gilson, Pres.-Gov. Svs.
Charles E. Baker, VP-Property/Hum. Res.
Betsy Jaros, VP-Devel./Communications
Annual Revenue: $6.5 million.
Annual Expenses: $6.9 million.
Contributions: 14.3 percent of revenue.
Minnesota Diversified Industries (MDI) provides contract packaging and assembly, specializing in high-volume, high-speed production. MDI offers career opportunities for individuals with disabilities, or disadvantages that are barriers to employment.
800 employees (all in Minnesota).
Founded in 1964. SIC 7218, 8331.
Recent: *In August 2000 MDI had to lay off 200 full-time employees in Hibbing (160) and Grand Rapids (40) because of the loss of a contract with the U.S. Postal Service for plastic mail trays.*

Minnesota Masonic Home Care Center

11501 Masonic Home Dr., Bloomington, MN 55437
Tel: 952/948-7000 Fax: 952/948-6210
Edward A. Martini Jr., Pres. and CEO
Michael Hanson, CFO
Barbara Gunderson, Administrator
Annual Revenue: $23.7 million.
Annual Expenses: $23.8 million.
Contributions: 16.7 percent of revenue.
Minnesota Masonic Home Care Center provides programs and services for older adults.
550 employees.
Founded in 1906. SIC 8059.
No. 81 CRM Nonprofit 100.

Minnesota Odd Fellows Home Inc. /Three Links Apartment

815 Forest Ave., Northfield, MN 55057
Tel: 507/645-6611
Carlton Sather, Exec. Dir.
Minnesota Odd Fellows Home Inc. /Three Links Apartment is a 120-bed skilled nursing home. Three Links Apartment is a 84-unit apartment complex for the elderly and handicapped.
105 employees.
Founded in 1891. SIC 8051, 8361.

Minnesota Orchestral Association

1111 Nicollet Mall, Minneapolis, MN 55403
Tel: 612/371-5600 Fax: 612/371-5661
Web site: http://www.mnorch.org
David J. Hyslop, Pres.
E. Benton Gill, VP and Chief Admin. Ofcr.
Paul Stephenson, CFO
Robert R. Neu, VP and Gen. Mgr.
Mary Ellen Kuhi, VP and Dir.-Devel.
Louise Ruhr, VP-Marketing
Karl Reichert, Dir.-Public Affairs
Asadour A. Santourian, Dir.-Artistic Planning
Eiji Oue, Music Dir.
Annual Revenue: $37.7 million.
Annual Expenses: $27.8 million.
Contributions: 51.1 percent of revenue.
Minnesota Orchestral Association owns and operates the Minnesota Orchestra (formerly Minneapolis Symphony Orchestra) and Orchestra Hall. The orchestra performs throughout the Twin Cities, the United States, and abroad.
175 employees.
Founded in 1903. SIC 7929.
No. 54 CRM Nonprofit 100.

Minnesota Public Radio

45 E. Seventh St., St. Paul, MN 55101
Tel: 651/290-1500 Fax: 651/290-1243
Web site: http://www.mpr.org
William H. Kling, Pres.
Thomas J. Kigin, EVP-Admin. and Gen. Counsel
Don Creighton, SVP-Technology
Will Haddeland, SVP-Public Affairs
Anne B. Hovland, SVP-Devel.
Jon McTaggart, SVP-New Media
Deborah Chernick, CFO
Annual Revenue: $31.1 million.
Annual Expenses: $26.3 million.
Contributions: 76.6 percent of revenue.
The mission of Minnesota Public Radio is to enrich the mind and nourish the spirit through radio, related technology, and services; to enhance the lives and expand the perspectives of its audiences, and thereby assist them in strengthening their communities. MPR operates a network of 30 public radio stations in the Minnesota region which, in conjunction with MPR's network production center, produces, acquires and broadcasts two fulltime radio program services (a news & information service and a classical music service). In addition, MPR produces and acquires radio programming for distribution to public radio stations throughout the United States, including "A Prairie Home Companion" with Garrison Keillor, "Marketplace," and "Saint Paul Sunday."
266 employees.
Founded in 1967. SIC 4832.
No. 64 CRM Nonprofit 100.
Recent: *In January 2000 MPR filed a motion to dismiss a lawsuit filed by the state of Minnesota against MPR on the basis that it was clear from the state's complaint that MPR had broken no laws and, in fact, had acted ethically and responsibly in its list-exchange practices. The complaint, brought by the state's attorney general, alleged that MPR made misrepresentations to its members about donor-list exchanges, including such matters as whether the members could expect that their addresses would be exchanged with their names, how many times MPR intended to exchange member names with other organizations, and whether the exchanges would be for fundraising. [Settlement reached in August when MPR agreed to make several minor clarifications to the information it provides to its members]. In April MPR acquired Marketplace Productions, the 11-year-old nonprofit producer of Marketplace, public radio's only national series about business, the global economy, and finance. Marketplace Productions is based at the University of Southern California in Los Angeles. American RadioWorks, the documentary collaboration between MPR and National Public Radio, won two first-place national awards. In June MPR and Public Radio International entered a distribution agreement for the daily business program Marketplace and other programs; which also resolved PRI's concerns about the Marketplace Productions deal. In July MPR chose Hammel Green and Abrahamson, Minneapolis, to design its new home, the site for which had not yet been*

determined. In August, with financial support from Audible Inc., a New Jersey-based provider of Internet-delivered audio and mobile playback, the Technology Desk segments for Marketplace made their debut.

Minnesota Valley Action Council Inc.

410 Jackson, Mankato, MN 56001
Tel: 507/345-6822 Fax: 507/345-2414
Web site: http://www.mnvac.org
John T. Woodwick, Exec. Dir.
John Baerg, Pres.
LaVern Franke, Sec.
Nancy Haag, Dir.-Community Svs.
Tom Kopp, Housing Svs. Dir.
Steve Pierce, VP
Lynn Ruiz, Support Svs. Dir.
Clete Schroepfer, Treas.
Lynn Van Dam, Admin. Svs. Dir.
Annual Revenue: $14.1 million.
Annual Expenses: $13.9 million.
Contributions: 95.5 percent of revenue.
Minnesota Valley Action Council (MVAC) is a private, nonprofit organization incorporated in Minnesota to use federal, state, and local resources to provide assistance wherever needed. Its service area includes the nine counties of south-central Minnesota. The board of directors is made up of 45 members from all nine counties—18 representatives of the low-income population it serves, 18 elected public officials, and nine representatives of private organizations.
176 employees.
SIC 8322.

Minnesota Visiting Nurse Agency

2021 E. Hennepin Ave., Minneapolis, MN 55413
Tel: 612/617-4600 Fax: 612/617-4782
Mary Ann Blade, CEO
Brian Hicks, CFO
Wendy Bauman, Dir.-Corp. Health
Mary Fleming, Dir.-Home Health
Jeff Poferl, Dir.-Hum. Res.
Nancy Reed, Dir.-Family Health
Annual Revenue: $8.5 million.
Annual Expenses: $7.9 million.
Contributions: 11.7 percent of revenue.
Minnesota Visiting Nurse home visiting activities include skilled nursing, home health aide, homemaker, and IV therapy for the care of the ill and disabled; and community services such as home visits to women and children, and services to women's shelters.
220 employees.
Founded in 1902. SIC 8082.

Mitchell Area Adjustment Training Center

804 N. Mentzer, Mitchell, SD 57301
Tel: 605/996-2032 Fax: 605/996-0972
Daryl Kilstrom, Exec. Dir.
Keith Smith, Vocational Sup.
Tim Smith, Pres. of Board
Annual Revenue: $4.6 million.
Annual Expenses: $4.6 million.
Contributions: 18.1 percent of revenue.
Mitchell Area Adjustment Training Center manufactures wood products and fishing tackle. They also provide comprehensive human services for people with developmental disabilities.
135 employees.
Founded in 1959. SIC 2448, 2499.

Mother of Mercy Nursing Home

Box 676, Albany, MN 56307
Tel: 320/845-2195 Fax: 320/845-7092
Bob Wikan, Administrator
Mother of Mercy Nursing Home operates an 84-bed nursing home and 30 market-rate apartments.
110 employees.
Founded in 1966. SIC 8059.

Mounds Park Academy

2051 E. Larpenteur Ave., Maplewood, MN 55109
Tel: 651/777-2555 Fax: 651/777-8633
Robert Kreischer, Dir.
Annual Revenue: $8.6 million.
Annual Expenses: $7.8 million.
Contributions: 12.6 percent of revenue.
Mounds Park Academy is an independent kindergarten through 12th grade school.
115 employees.
Founded in 1982. SIC 8211.

Mount Olivet Rolling Acres Inc.

P.O. Box 220, Victoria, MN 55386
Tel: 952/474-5974 Fax: 952/474-3652
Rev. Paul Youngdahl, Chm.
Wayne Larson, Exec. Dir.
Steven Anderson, Program Dir.
Barb Coyle, Nursing Dir.
Joan Oslund, Program Dir.
Bruce Torgerson, Program Dir.
Annual Revenue: $7.6 million.
Annual Expenses: $7.3 million.
Contributions: 2.7 percent of revenue.
Mount Olivet Rolling Acres Inc. provides residence and many other services for mentally handicapped individuals. It provides homes for handicapped individuals that are integrated into the larger community, as well as outside services for individuals living independently and with families.
260 employees.
Founded in 1965. SIC 8361.

National Marrow Donor Program

3433 Broadway St. N.E., Suite 400, Minneapolis, MN 55413
Tel: 612/627-5800 Fax: 612/627-5899
Web site: http://www.marrow.org
Jeffrey Chell, M.D., CEO
Patricia A. Coppo, COO
Gordon Bryan, CFO
Dennis Confer, M.D., Chief Medical Officer
Chatchada Karanes, M.D., Medical Dir.
R.D. Brown, Dir.-Donor Svs.
Janet Hegland, Dir.-Research/Science
Robert Pinderhughes, Dir.-Comm./Education
Devan Shephard, Dir.-Info. Systems
Michael Spiro, Admin.-Navy Programs
Pam Weisdorf, Dir.-Patient Advocacy
Annual Revenue: $96 million.
Annual Expenses: $87.2 million.
Contributions: 46.2 percent of revenue.
The National Marrow Donor Program (NMDP) is a diverse registry of volunteer marrow donors that facilitates marrow and blood stem cell transplants for patients with life-threatening blood diseases who do not have matching donors in their families. The NMPD receives funding from the Health Resources and Services Administration, the Office of Naval Research, and The Marrow Foundation. The NMDP network is made up of 96 donor centers,117 transplant centers, and 114 collection centers. NMDP has relationships with more than 19 countries in Europe, Asia, South America, the Middle East, and Australia. The NMDP began search operations on Sept. 1, 1987, with fewer than 10,000 volunteer donors listed in the registry. The first transplant facilitated by the NMDP took place in December 1987. The NMDP has provided donors for more than 8,657 transplants since its inception. Currently, the NMDP facilitates more than 130 transplants each month.
211 employees.
Founded in 1987. SIC 8099, 8641.
No. 21 CRM Nonprofit 100.

National Multiple Sclerosis Society/Minnesota Chapter

200 12th Ave. S., Minneapolis, MN 55415
Tel: 612/335-7900 Fax: 612/335-7997
Web site: http://www.mnms.org
Maureen Reeder, Pres.
Lee Hoffman, Gaming Mgr.
Annual Revenue: $5.7 million.
Annual Expenses: $5.1 million.
Contributions: 80.6 percent of revenue.
The National Multiple Sclerosis Society/Minnesota Chapter provides programs and services that enhance the quality of life for persons who have multiple sclerosis, funds research to find the cause of and cure for multiple sclerosis, and advocates accessibility for all persons with disabilities.
258 employees (190 part-time).
Founded in 1954. SIC 8399.

Nexus

3140 Harbor Ln., Suite 100, Plymouth, MN 55447
Tel: 763/551-8640 Fax: 763/553-1637
Web site: http://www.nexustreatment.org
James D'Angelo, CEO
Alan Nordby, CFO
Patricia Nott, VP-Hum. Res.
Pat Rookey, VP-Clinical Operations
Annual Revenue: $26.6 million.
Annual Expenses: $25.6 million.
Nexus is a nationally recognized, nonprofit family of treatment programs designed to help behaviorally and emotionally disturbed children and adolescents, many of whom have engaged in harmful sexual behaviors.
425 employees.
Founded in 1975.
No. 72 CRM Nonprofit 100.

North Country Health Services

1100 W. 38th St., Bemidji, MN 56601
Tel: 218/751-5430 Fax: 218/759-5880
Barb Smith, Chair
Paul Miller, Pres.
John Skjerven, EVP
Vic Hagstrom, VP-Finance
Pat Kelly, VP-Devel.
Joe Dahlby, VP-Nursing
Annual Revenue: $50.5 million.
Annual Expenses: $44.1 million.
Contributions: 0.5 percent of revenue.
North Country Health Services oversees North Country Regional Hospital and North Country Nursing and Rehabilitation Services.
780 employees.
Founded in 1898. SIC 8062.
No. 48 CRM Nonprofit 100.

North Memorial Health Care

3300 Oakdale Ave. N., Robbinsdale, MN 55422
Tel: 763/520-5200 Fax: 763/520-5006
Web site: http://www.northmemorial.com
Scott R. Anderson, Pres. and CEO
David W. Cress, COO
Patrick J. Boran, CFO
Annual Revenue: $298.1 million.
Annual Expenses: $292 million.
Contributions: 0.2 percent of revenue.
North Memorial Health Care is a full-service, not-for-profit hospital with 518 licensed beds and 650 staff physicians. North Memorial provides highly specialized trauma and emergency services, coronary care, oncology services, open-heart surgery, and maternity and neonatal care, as well as general medical, surgical, obstetric, pediatric, and rehabilitative services. North Memorial has its own medical transportation division, which owns and operates ambulance services throughout Minnesota and western Wisconsin, and provides air-care service to Hennepin County Medical Center. North Memorial also owns several primary-care and specialty clinics in the metro area, and participates in joint ventures with other health care providers.
4,454 employees (4,000 in Minnesota).
Founded in 1954. SIC 8062.
No. 10 CRM Nonprofit 100.
No. 51 CRM Employer 100.
Recent: *In February 2000 North Memorial was named the Environmental Protection Agency's "2000 ENERGY STAR Buildings Healthcare Partner of the Year" in recognition of its energy-efficient lighting, heating, cooling, and ventilating equipment. In April North Medical Transportation Services, having successfully met a "gold standard" determined by the ambulance industry, once again received a full three-year accreditation from the Commission on Accreditation of Ambulance Services. At that time, only 75 of the 33,000 U.S. ambulance services had received accreditation. In June North Memorial Medical Center's Heart Center implemented a new program, the first of its kind in the Midwest, called "single-unit stay for cardiac surgery patients." Patients are admitted to one of the 16 beds in the new Cardiovascular ICU and, other than for the surgery itself, remain in the same room until they are discharged. The goal is to keep patients in the same environment for their entire stay, receiving care from the same team of caregivers.*

Northwest Medical Center

120 La Bree Ave. S., Thief River Falls, MN 56701
Tel: 218/681-4240 Fax: 218/683-4511
Web site: http://www.nwmc.org
Richard A. Spyhalski, CEO
Daniel Olson, COO
Annual Revenue: $19.7 million.
Annual Expenses: $18.5 million.
Contributions: 0.1 percent of revenue.
Northwest Medical Center is a community health care organization that consists of a 99-bed acute-care hospital, a 90-bed nursing home, and a mental health unit.
368 employees (87 part-time).
SIC 8062.
No. 91 CRM Nonprofit 100.

Northwestern Health Sciences University

2501 W. 84th St., Bloomington, MN 55431
Tel: 952/888-4777 Fax: 952/888-6713
Web site: http://www.nwchiro.edu
John F. Allenburg, Pres.
Charles E. Sawyer, D.C., SVP
James E. McDonald, Ph.D., VP-Administrative Affairs
Larry Kuusisto, Ph.D., VP-Educational Resources
Stephen T. Bolles, VP-Institutional Advancement
Annual Revenue: $16.4 million.
Annual Expenses: $14.6 million.
Contributions: 3.9 percent of revenue.
The college awards a D.C., Doctor of Chiropractic, degree. Enrollment in fall 1997 was 796.
257 employees.
Founded in 1941. SIC 8221.

Northwestern College & Radio

3003 Snelling Ave. N., Roseville, MN 55113
Tel: 651/631-5100 Fax: 651/631-5269
Web site: http://www.nwc.edu
Dr. Donald O. Ericksen, Chancellor
Dr. David E. Erickson, VP-Coll. Admin., interim Pres.
Dr. Harold A. Miller, VP-Academic Affairs
Wayne A. Pederson, EVP-Broadcasting
Douglas R. Schroeder, VP-Fin. and CFO
Joseph L. Smith, VP-Devel.
Annual Revenue: $35.2 million.
Annual Expenses: $33.7 million.
Contributions: 26.9 percent of revenue.
Northwestern College is a fully-accredited Christian college of the Bible, the arts and sciences, and professional education. It has an enrollment of 2,059 and offers 44 bachelor's degree programs and three associate degree programs, leading to AS, AASB, AAB, BA, and BS degrees. Northwestern also owns and operates a network of 14 Christian radio stations and provides programming to stations nationwide via its Skylight Satellite Network.
542 employees.
Founded in 1902. SIC 8221.
No. 59 CRM Nonprofit 100.

Northwood Children's Home Society Inc.
714 W. College St., Duluth, MN 55811
Tel: 218/724-8815 Fax: 218/724-0251
James F. Yeager, Pres.
Mary R. Rose, Finance Dir.
Richard Wolleat, VP
Northwood Children's Home Society Inc. provides residential, day, and in-home treatment services to children and families of children with mental, emotional, and behavioral disturbances.
172 employees.
Founded in 1883. SIC 8361.

Occupational Development Center Inc.
Highway 32 S., P.O. Box 730, Thief River Falls, MN 56701
Tel: 218/681-4949 Fax: 218/681-7635
Peter J. Lavalier, CEO
Annual Revenue: $5.8 million.
Annual Expenses: $5.4 million.
Contributions: 1.6 percent of revenue.
Occupational Development Center Inc. provides vocational rehabilitation services to individuals with disabilities in both a community and workshop setting in northern Minnesota.
250 employees.
Founded in 1971. SIC 8331.

Olmsted Medical Center
210 Ninth St. S.E., Rochester, MN 55904
Richard Geier, Pres. and Physician
Noel Petersen, Medical Dir.
Annual Revenue: $56.5 million.
Annual Expenses: $53.8 million.
Contributions: 0.2 percent of revenue.
Olmsted Medical Center is an integrated health care system that includes a 77-bed hospital.
770 employees.
No. 38 CRM Nonprofit 100.

Open Door Center
209 S.E. Second St., Valley City, ND 58072
Tel: 701/845-1124 Fax: 701/845-1175
Mary Simonson, Exec. Dir.
Open Door Center manufactures plaques and trophies and provides rehabilitation services for people with disabilities.
200 employees.
Founded in 1957. SIC 3499.

Opportunity Partners Inc.
5500 Opportunity Court, Minnetonka, MN 55343
Tel: 952/938-5511 Fax: 952/930-4279
Web site: http://www.opportunities.org
Jon H. Thompson, Pres.
Bruce Bester, VP-Finance
Chris Burns, VP-Mktg./Comm.
Paul Jaeger, VP-Residential Svs.
Bridget Kohl, VP-Hum. Res.
Carolyn Nelson, VP-Resource Devel.
John Thompson, VP-Production
Tim Vicchiollo, VP-Programs
R. Atwood, MIS Mgr.
Annual Revenue: $16.4 million.
Annual Expenses: $16 million.
Contributions: 4.1 percent of revenue.
Opportunity Partners Inc., formerly known as Opportunity Workshop, provides opportunities in which adults with developmental disabilities, brain injuries, and other special needs can seek dignity, satisfaction, and the achievement of their highest potential. These opportunities include vocational, residential, and personal development programs.
327 employees.
Founded in 1953. SIC 8331.

Ordway Center for the Performing Arts
345 Washington St., St. Paul, MN 55102
Tel: 651/282-3000 Fax: 651/224-5319
Web site: http://www.ordway.org
C.S. Mondelli, Chm.
Kevin McCollum, Pres. and CEO
Christine Sagstetter, VP and CFO
Robert Alwine, Dir.-Programming
Lorraine LeBlanc, Dir.-Devel.
Mary McColl, Dir.-Operations
Lynn VonEschen, Dir.-Sales/Marketing
Annual Revenue: $26 million.
Annual Expenses: $19.8 million.
Contributions: 35.8 percent of revenue.
Ordway Center for the Performing Arts presents a full season of Broadway touring theater, internationally acclaimed theater ensembles, dance, and music. The Ordway's education programs reach more than 50,000 students each year. The Ordway is also the principal venue of the Saint Paul Chamber Orchestra, the Minnesota Opera, the Schubert Club, and the St. Paul series of the Minnesota Orchestra.
260 employees.
Founded in 1982. SIC 6512.
No. 74 CRM Nonprofit 100.
Recent: *In January 2000 the organization officially changed its name from Ordway Music Theatre to the more encompassing Ordway Center for the Performing Arts.*

PPL Industries
509 Washington Ave. S, Minneapolis, MN 55415
Tel: 612/332-0664 Fax: 612/332-4291
Douglas Jewett, Dir.-Operations
Susan Gunder, Career Devel.
Annual Revenue: $2.2 million.
PPL Industries is a labor-intensive job shop. The PPL mission is to employ adults who have not had the opportunity to experience full-time, steady employment in mainstream industries.
200 employees.
Founded in 1982. SIC 8331.

Parents in Community Action Inc.
Administrative Office, 700 Humbolt Ave. N., Minneapolis, MN 55411
Tel: 612/374-8309 Fax: 612/374-8311
Web site: http://www.picaheadstart.org
Alyce M. Dillon, Exec. Dir.
Annual Revenue: $18.5 million.
Annual Expenses: $16.8 million.
Contributions: 99.4 percent of revenue.
Parents in Community Action (PICA) provides a comprehensive child development program for low-income children (aged 3 to 5) and their families. Services include education, nutrition, social services, parent involvement, health (physical, mental, and dental), disability services, and transportation.
279 employees.
Founded in 1969. SIC 8322.
No. 96 CRM Nonprofit 100.
Recent: *At Oct. 31, 2000, the organization had 2,413 families enrolled.*

Park Nicollet Health Services
6500 Excelsior Blvd., St. Louis Park, MN 55426
Tel: 952/993-9900 Fax: 952/993-5936
Web site: http://www.parknicollet.com
David K. Wessner, Pres. and CEO

Benjamin Chaska, M.D., EVP, Chief Medical Officer
Richard Freese, M.D., SVP-Park Nicollet Clinic
A. Stuart Hanson, M.D., Pres.-Park Nicollet Institute
John Herman, EVP, Chief Admin. Officer
Michael Johnson, Pres.-Park Nicollet Foundation
Duane F. Speigle, VP-Real Estate/Support Svs.
Paul J. Tolzmann, M.D., Medical Dir.
James Toscano, EVP-Institute
Annual Revenue: $574.3 million.
Annual Expenses: $569.1 million.
Contributions: 2.2 percent of revenue.
Park Nicollet Health Services, formerly HealthSystem Minnesota, is a non-profit, integrated-care system that includes Methodist Hospital, Park Nicollet Clinic (20 locations), the Park Nicollet Foundation, and Park Nicollet Institute. The system's combination of resources serves the interests of patients and the community by providing quality health care, establishing innovative programs to measure and improve health care, and minimizing costs through joint planning to avoid duplication of services and technology. The organization's 426-bed hospital is served by 530 employed physicians and another 650 affiliated ones.
6,640 employees.
Founded in 1993. SIC 8062.
No. 6 CRM Nonprofit 100.
No. 25 CRM Employer 100.
Recent: *In November 1999 the organization projected losses of $14.6 million for 1999 and $27.2 million for 2000. In response, it was developing a restructuring plan, including program cutbacks in some areas and the addition of more volume to Park Nicollet Clinics, that could improve operations by as much as $25 million. In December the organization laid off 138 employees and eliminated 213 empty positions. Plans to develop a $15 million outpatient clinic in Burnsville, Minn., with Allina Health System were halted indefinitely due to capital constraints at both organizations. A January 2000 agreement to become a participating provider in the Bloomington, Minn.-based Araz Group health insurance network was expected to increase clinic volume by 2,000 to 4,000 patients annually. In March Park Nicollet Clinic and Methodist Hospital received the 2000 American Medical Group Association Acclaim Award, which recognizes improvement efforts led by physician-directed organizations. In June the organization announced a name change, from HealthSystem Minnesota to Park Nicollet Health Services, to build on the strong reputation of its clinics and to increase consumer awareness of the organization.*

People Incorporated

317 York Ave., St. Paul, MN 55101
Tel: 651/774-0011 Fax: 651/774-0606
Timothy Burkett, Exec. Dir.
Mary Kay McJilton, Dir.-Op.
Lynn Lindsay, Dir.-Fin. Op.
People Incorporated provides a variety of programs which assist in meeting the needs of people who are unable to live independently in the community because of physical, mental, and/or emotional handicaps. People Inc. provides services to adults in the areas of mental health, developmental disabilities, physical disabilities, epilepsy, chemical dependency, and services to persons who are deaf and hard of hearing. All programs focus on enabling people to attain and maintain the highest functioning level of which they are capable. Each program is specialized to meet the individual needs of those it serves.
225 employees.
Founded in 1969. SIC 8051.

People Serving People

400 S. Tenth St., Minneapolis, MN 55404
Tel: 612/333-1221 Fax: 612/333-7608
Web site: http://www.peopleservingpeople.org
Mary Crowley, Exec. Dir.
Jim Stillman, Business Mgr.
Dan Goodermont, Client Support Mgr.
Annette Rodriguez, Organizational Resources Mgr.
Brice Scott, Facilities Mgr.
Mike Seiler, Food Svs. Mgr.
Annual Revenue: $4.2 million.
Annual Expenses: $3.2 million.
People Serving People operates a family emergency shelter in Hennepin County, housing up to 400 men, women, and children per night. PSP also offers children's programs and on-site services provided in collaboration with more than 30 community agencies.
49 employees.
Founded in 1982. SIC 8361.

The Phoenix Residence Inc.

135 Colorado St. E., St. Paul, MN 55107
Tel: 651/227-7655 Fax: 651/227-6847
Darlene M. Scott, Pres.
Mary B. Thirsten, VP-Operations
Pam R. Connolly, VP-Financial Svs.
Jody Docken, VP-Residential Svs.
Annual Revenue: $6 million.
Annual Expenses: $6.2 million.
Contributions: 0.2 percent of revenue.
The Phoenix Residence Inc. provides residential and programmatic services to approximately 87 developmentally disabled adults through eight locations.
230 employees.
Founded in 1974. SIC 8361.

Pillsbury Neighborhood Services

1200 37th Ave. N., Minneapolis, MN 55412
Tel: 612/302-3400 Fax: 612/302-3490
Anthony Wagner, Pres.
Yvonne Olsen, VP
Steven Oates, Exec. Dir.
Annual Revenue: $9.6 million.
Annual Expenses: $8.9 million.
Contributions: 93.2 percent of revenue.
Pillsbury Neighborhood Services (PNS) is a not-for-profit human resource and economic development organization serving Minneapolis' inner city neighborhoods.
175 employees.
Founded in 1879. SIC 8322.
Recent: *In 1998, PNS earned the distinction as the first non-profit charity to receive the commitment to quality award from the Minnesota Council on Quality. Staff members were recognized for their commitment to self-assessment as a catalyst for improvement and as a way to promote management excellence.*

Planned Parenthood of Minnesota/South Dakota

1965 Ford Pkwy., St. Paul, MN 55116
Tel: 651/698-2401 Fax: 651/698-2405
Thomas P. Webber, Pres.
Annual Revenue: $12.2 million.
Annual Expenses: $11.4 million.
Contributions: 42.2 percent of revenue.
Planned Parenthood of Minnesota/South Dakota (PPM/SD) operates a network of clinics in Minnesota and South Dakota. The agency also sponsors a training program for women's health care nurse practitioners. PPM/SD conducts significant community and professional education programs, as well as public policy and advocacy activities.
250 employees.
Founded in 1928. SIC 8093.
Recent: *In March 2000 President Thomas P. Webber announced his resignation after 29 years of service.*

Polinsky Medical Rehabilitation Center Inc.

530 E. Second St., Duluth, MN 55805
Tel: 218/725-5300 Fax: 218/727-1167
Ann Bussey, Dir.
Marcia Hermann Courtney, Clinical Pediatric Mgr.
Bill Singpiel, Clinical Musculo-Skeletal Mgr.
Teri Hallbach, Clinical Rehab Mgr.
Polinsky Medical Rehabilitation Center provides comprehensive medical rehabilitation services to children and adults in the Lake Superior region.
170 employees.
Founded in 1950. SIC 8093.

Prairie Public Broadcasting Inc.

207 N. Fifth St., Box 3240, Fargo, ND 58108

Tel: 701/241-6900 Fax: 701/239-7650
Mary Anne Alhadeff, Pres. and CEO
Mark Lande, Controller
Annual Revenue: $6 million.
Annual Expenses: $5.7 million.
Contributions: 77 percent of revenue.
Prairie Public Broadcasting Inc. is a public and educational broadcasting network with seven TV stations and seven radio stations.
131 employees.
Founded in 1959. SIC 4832, 4833.

PreferredOne
6105 Golden Hills Dr., Golden Valley, MN 55416
Tel: 763/847-4000 Fax: 763/847-4010
Web site: http://www.preferredone.com
Marcus Merz, Pres. and CEO
Dave Olsen, EVP and COO
Diana Vance-Bryan, VP and Gen. Counsel
Annual Revenue: $52.2 million.
PreferredOne is a hospital/physician joint venture engaged in health plan administration, managed care, HMO, PPO, and TPA activities.
270 employees.
Founded in 1984. SIC 6324.
No. 45 CRM Nonprofit 100.
Recent: *In June 2000 the Minnesota Health Data Institute and MedServe Link Inc. expanded their eligibility service with the addition of PreferredOne. This contract gave health care providers in Minnesota additional access to PreferredOne's administrative information through the MedNet Central Query Service, an electronic network exchange service offered by MHDI and hosted by MedServe.*

Presbyterian Homes & Services Inc.
3220 Lake Johanna Blvd., Arden Hills, MN 55112
Tel: 651/631-6100 Fax: 651/631-6108
Daniel A. Lindh, Pres. and CEO
Mark T. Meyer, CFO
Becky Conway, Dir.-Home Care
Phil Hanson, Dir.-Hum. Res.
Angela Swetland, Dir.-Housing/Assisted Living
Walt Zimmerman, Dir.-Care Center Operations
Annual Revenue: $84.9 million.
Annual Expenses: $61.9 million.
Contributions: 29.2 percent of revenue.
Presbyterian Homes of Minnesota provides a variety of support services for senior adults, including housing, assisted living, short-term and long-term nursing care, home health care, adult day care, companion/PT, and occupational therapy. The organization has operations in Arden Hills, Roseville, Spring Park (on Lake Minnetonka), Bloomington, Little Canada, Oakdale, and Minnetonka, Minn. It is affiliated with four nursing homes: Presbyterian Homes of Arden Hills, Presbyterian Homes of Roseville, Presbyterian Homes of Bloomington, and Presbyterian Homes on Lake Minnetonka.
1,813 employees.
Founded in 1953. SIC 8082, 8361.
No. 24 CRM Nonprofit 100.
No. 96 CRM Employer 100.

Pride Inc.
1929 N. Washington St., Bismarck, ND 58501
Tel: 701/258-7838 Fax: 701/258-7911
Chuck Bisnett, Pres.
Pride Inc. provides vocational development, counseling, training, residential living, and supported employment for adults who are mentally or physically disabled.
240 employees.
Founded in 1976. SIC 8331.

Professional Association of Treatment Homes
2324 University Ave. W., Suite 101, St. Paul, MN 55114
Tel: 651/641-0455 Fax: 651/641-0452
Timothy D. Plant, CEO
Brian Brommel, CFO
Todd Henry, N. Minnesota Dir.
William Metcalf, North Dakota Dir.
Nancy Anderson, S. Minnesota Dir.
Teri Zywicki-Nelson, Wisconsin Dir.
Annual Revenue: $16.6 million.
Annual Expenses: $16.4 million.
Contributions: 0.3 percent of revenue.
Professional Association of Treatment Homes (PATH) is a private treatment foster care agency with offices in 23 cities in Minnesota, North Dakota, and Wisconsin. PATH serves children, youth, and their families whose special needs require the services of foster parents who are trained, supervised, and supported by agency staff. Services include: Treatment Foster Care, Foster Adoption Services, Respite Foster Care, Medical Foster Care, Adoption Services, Intensive Treatment Foster Care, Group Family Treatment Foster Care, and education through the PATH Foster Care Education Institute.
149 employees.
Founded in 1972. SIC 8361.

Project for Pride in Living Inc.
2516 Chicago Ave. S., Minneapolis, MN 55404
Tel: 612/874-8511 Fax: 612/874-6444
Web site: http://www.ppl-inc.org
Jim Scheibel, Exec. Dir.
Barb McCormick, VP-Housing/Devel.
Susan Baldwin, VP-Human Svs./Admin.
Steve Studt, VP-Finance/Business Op.
Annual Revenue: $10.7 million.
Annual Expenses: $12 million.
Contributions: 45.8 percent of revenue.
Project for Pride in Living (PPL) helps low- and moderate-income people become self-sufficient by addressing their job, housing and neighborhood needs. During the last 28 years, PPL has grown from a volunteer group focused on improving inner-city houses to a 501(c)3 nonprofit organization with the capacity to impact lives, buildings, blocks and communities. Strong and integrated programs address people's barriers to self-sufficiency in a comprehensive way. Today PPL offers more than 200 job training opportunities, houses over 500 families, and works to improve the academic achievement and social development of more than 500 children annually.
100 employees.
Founded in 1972. SIC 8322.
Recent: *Past Executive Director Steve Cramer left to lead the Minneapolis Community Development Agency in 1999. Jim Scheibel, former St. Paul mayor and senior executive at the Corporation for National Service, is now the executive director.*

Public Radio International Inc.
100 N. Sixth St., Suite 900A, Minneapolis, MN 55403
Tel: 612/338-5000 Fax: 612/330-9222
Web site: http://www.pri.org
Stephen Salyer, Pres. and CEO
Bruce Theriault, COO
Bob Ferante, Exec. Producer
Melinda Ward, SVP, Dir.-Programming
Lee Sheehy, SVP-Corp. Affairs
Eleanor Harris, SVP-Marketing
Timothy Engel, VP and CFO
Douglas Eichten, VP-Marketing
Annual Revenue: $19.6 million.
Annual Expenses: $19.4 million.
Contributions: 44.2 percent of revenue.
Public Radio International (PRI), formerly American Public Radio, is a public radio network that acquires, develops, funds, and distributes public radio programming from station-based, independent, and international producers. PRI has more than 600 affiliate stations throughout the United States, Puerto Rico, and Guam. The network emphasizes programming in four general areas: news and information, comedy/variety, classical music, and contemporary music.
46 employees.
Founded in 1983. SIC 4832, 7922.
No. 93 CRM Nonprofit 100.

NON

Ramsey Action Programs Inc.

450 N. Syndicate St., St. Paul, MN 55104
Tel: 651/645-6445 Fax: 651/645-2253
Dale Anderson, Exec. Dir.
Mary Lou Clowes, Dir.-Family Svs.
Karen Schechter, Dir.-Hum. Res./Devel.
Roberta Schmitz, Dir.-Data Processing
Christine Hale, Dir.-Operations
Morris Manning, Dir.-Head Start
Alice Davis, Dir.-Independent Living
Rafael A. Esparza, Affirmative Action Officer
Rebecca Kropelnicki, Public Relations
Annual Revenue: $20.4 million.
Annual Expenses: $20.8 million.
Contributions: 85.7 percent of revenue.
Ramsey Action Programs (RAP) provides community-action, information, referral, and advocacy programs in Ramsey and Washington counties. Programs include services for seniors, energy-assistance programs to assist low-income households, and a Head Start program for at-risk children and their parents. RAP Fare For All is an affordable food package for Minnesota, Wisconsin, Iowa, and North and South Dakota.
355 employees.
Founded in 1964. SIC 8322.
No. 88 CRM Nonprofit 100.

Range Center Inc.

1001 N.W. Eighth Ave., P.O. Box 629, Chisholm, MN 55719
Tel: 218/254-3347 Fax: 218/254-7343
Shelley A. Robinson, Exec. Dir.
Jim Zahorsky, CFO
Range Center Inc. provides vocational and residential services to adults with mental retardation and related conditions. Services are located in Chisholm, Hibbing, Eveleth, and International Falls, Minnesota.
175 employees.
Founded in 1963. SIC 8331, 8361.

Range Mental Health Center Inc.

624 S. 13th St., Virginia, MN 55792
Tel: 218/749-2881 Fax: 218/749-3806
Gordon Hoelscher, CEO
Mary Midtling, CFO
Rosalyn Barker, Health Info. Dir.
Craig Stevens, Dir.-Clinical Services
Alan Abraham, Dir.-Chemical Dep. Svs.
Annual Revenue: $6.2 million.
Annual Expenses: $5.6 million.
Contributions: 14.6 percent of revenue.
Range Mental Health Center Inc. provides comprhensive programs for the treatment of mental illnesses, psychological disorders, chemical dependency, and associated disorders for all age groups and special populations. The RMHC has three offices in Virginia, three in Hibbing, and one in Ely.
140 employees.
Founded in 1961. SIC 8063.

Regina Medical Center

1175 Nininger Rd., Hastings, MN 55033
Tel: 651/480-4100 Fax: 651/438-3570
Lynn W. Olson, CEO
Douglas Montgomery, VP-Finance
Annual Revenue: $25.3 million.
Annual Expenses: $24.6 million.
Contributions: 0.4 percent of revenue.
Regina Medical Center includes a 57-bed, acute-care hospital; a 61-bed skilled nursing facility; a 75-bed residential retirement center; and a clinic (Regina Medical Group).
549 employees.
Founded in 1953. SIC 8011, 8051, 8052.
No. 76 CRM Nonprofit 100.

Resource Inc.

1900 Chicago Ave., Minneapolis, MN 55404
Tel: 612/871-2402 Fax: 612/752-8001
Web site: http://www.RESOURCE-MN-ORG
Robert Berlute, Pres.
Deborah Atterberry, VP
Annual Revenue: $13 million.
Annual Expenses: $12.5 million.
Contributions: 12.8 percent of revenue.
Resource Inc. provides rehabilitation, education, and placement of people who have a disability, are disadvantaged, or are in transition, and helps them achieve greater social and economic independence.
240 employees.
Founded in 1960. SIC 8322.

Resources for Child Caring Inc.

450 N. Syndicate St., Suite 5, St. Paul, MN 55104
Tel: 651/641-0305 Fax: 651/645-0990
Carol Rhode, Exec. Dir.
William H. Mackie, Dir.-Finance/Admin.
Eileen Nelson, Dir.-Education/Publishing
Terry Stuhr, Dir.-Devel.
Annual Revenue: $7.2 million.
Annual Expenses: $7.3 million.
Contributions: 5 percent of revenue.
Resources for Child Caring (RCC) is dedicated to improving the quality of child care and early-education services for all professionals caring for children. A combination of services enables RCC to help thousands each year with issues related to the care of children, including individualized assistance for parents in finding child care; training and education for child care and early education professionals; financial assistance for families and child-care providers; publication and distribution of books, tapes, and cassettes through Redleaf Press; employer consultation and employee service programs for businesses; and community development and advocacy efforts for children. Funding for services comes from user fees, product sales, government programs, and private contributions.
64 employees.
Founded in 1972. SIC 8351.

Ridgeview Medical Center

500 S. Maple St., Waconia, MN 55387
Tel: 952/442-2191 Fax: 952/442-6543
Robert Stevens, Pres. and CEO
John Prondzinski, VP
Pat Michaelson, VP
Bernard J. Buckland III, Dir.-Surgical Services
Annual Revenue: $55.5 million.
Annual Expenses: $53 million.
Ridgeview Medical Center is a full-service, acute-care hospital providing comprehensive medical services to the western and southwestern metro area. Medical staff includes nearly 200 physicians in 34 diverse areas of specialization, including urology, neurology, oncology, otolaryngology, orthopedics, obstetrics, cardiology, and emergency medicine. In addition to primary services, Ridgeview offers a variety of outpatient programs, including home care, occupational health, and sports medicine. Ridgeview also owns six clinics and a multi-specialty medical plaza.
950 employees.
Founded in 1959.
No. 41 CRM Nonprofit 100.
Recent: *In January 2000, after having been run by the city of Waconia since 1959, Ridgeview became an independent nonprofit hospital, a status that allows it to more quickly make the business moves necessary to be competitive in the marketplace. In September Ridgeview became the first organization to offer its employees the innovative, consumer-driven health care plan from Definity Health (www.definityhealth.com). Said CEO Stevens, "With Definity Health, we will improve the delivery of our health benefit by allowing our employees to personally define how their health and wellness needs are met. And we'll do this without gatekeepers and other restrictions that are so common among health plans today."*

Rise Inc.

8406 Sunset Rd. N.E., Spring Lake Park, MN 55432
Tel: 952/786-8334 Fax: 952/786-0008
John Barrett, Pres.
Jack Grunewald, Chair
Thomas Ebert, Treas.
Judi Nevonen, Sec.
Rise Inc. plans, develops, and provides customized employment, affordable housing, and supported living services for men and women with disabilities. Rise supports people with disabilities in attaining their personal measure of vocational achievement, self-sufficiency, and belonging in their communities through creative, responsive, and individualized program services.
125 employees.
Founded in 1971. SIC 8331, 8361.

Riverfront Inc.

3000 South Ave., La Crosse, WI 54601
Tel: 608/784-9450 Fax: 608/784-5345
Dr. Susan Quinn, Board Pres.
Marcia Jagodzinske, Exec. Dir.
Don Brueggen, Finance Dir.
Jean Ruppert, Hum. Res. Dir.
Audra Martine, Lifestyle Dir.
LuAnn Aschenbrenner Jackson, Program Dir.
Pam Solberg, Devel. Dir.
Karen Sepich, Employment Svs.
Jennifer Felty, Buffalo County Program Dir.
Annual Revenue: $5.7 million.
Annual Expenses: $5.6 million.
Contributions: 1.9 percent of revenue.
Riverfront is a rehabilitation agency that deals in subcontracting services (janitorial, clerical, packaging, mail service, salvage, and assembly). The company also provides independent living, day services, and job placement services for people with disabilities in western Wisconsin.
200 employees.
Founded in 1977. SIC 8331.

Riverview Healthcare Association

323 S. Minnesota St., Crookston, MN 56716
Tel: 218/281-9200 Fax: 218/281-9222
Thomas C. Lenertz, Pres.
Jeanine Amon, VP and COO
Joy Johnson, VP
Gary Frisk, Dir.-Finance and CFO
Ardie Carlstrom, Dir.-Nursing
Carrie Peterson, Dir.-Senior Svs./Hillcrest
Layton Anderson, Dir.-Hum. Res.
Gerald Lindsay, Mgr.-Pharmacy
Jeffrey Hoffman, Mgr.-Physical Therapy
Annual Revenue: $19.1 million.
Annual Expenses: $18.3 million.
Contributions: 1.8 percent of revenue.
Riverview Healthcare Association includes Riverview Hospital, Riverview Adult Day Care, Riverview Nursing Home, Hillcrest Nursing Home, Glenmore Recovery Center (chemical dependency), and Riverview Home Care/Hospice.
400 employees.
Founded in 1898. SIC 8062.
No. 94 CRM Nonprofit 100.

St. David's Child Development and Family Services

3395 Plymouth Rd., Minnetonka, MN 55305
Tel: 952/939-0396 Fax: 952/939-9266
Eric Stevens, Exec. Dir.
Joe McHugh, Board Pres.
Nancy Moore Smith, Assoc. Dir.
Kathryn Lange, Dir.-Admin.
St. David's Child Development and Family Services is a large, comprehensive provider of early childhood educational and social services for children and families. Its programs include programs that integrate "typical" preschool children with children with special needs, offer specialized services to families in crisis and extreme stress, provide families of children with physical, mental, and behavorial disabilities respite either in their own homes or "in-center," and serve infants and toddlers with special needs.
400 employees.
Founded in 1961. SIC 8322.

St. Elizabeth Hospital of Wabasha Inc.

1200 Fifth Grant Blvd. W., Wabasha, MN 55981
Tel: 651/565-4531 Fax: 651/565-2482
Thomas Crowley, Pres.
John K. Wolfe, CFO
Rita Fox, VP-Long Term Care
Joni Lommen, VP-Clinical Services
St. Elizabeth Hospital of Wabasha Inc. provides nursing home care, nursing services, laboratory, radiology, and other related hospital functions.
275 employees.
Founded in 1955. SIC 8059, 8062.

St. Francis Medical Center

415 Oak St., Breckenridge, MN 56520
Tel: 218/643-7516
David Nelson, CEO
Bill Satrom, CFO
Mary Helland, VP-Nursing
Carol Grant, Dir.-Hum. Res.
Tim Walker, Dir.-Pharmacy
Annual Revenue: $16.3 million.
Annual Expenses: $14.1 million.
Contributions: 0.3 percent of revenue.
408 employees.
SIC 8011.

St. Gabriel's Hospital

815 Second St. S.E., Little Falls, MN 56345
Tel: 320/632-5441
Larry Schulz, Pres. and CEO
Larry Novakoske, CFO
Mary Bobertz, VP-Patient Care
Cory Glad, VP-Long Term Care
Tom Mach, Dir.-Pharmacy
Mark Ziebarth, Dir.-Mental Health
Annual Revenue: $21.6 million.
Annual Expenses: $21.1 million.
Contributions: 0 percent of revenue.
416 employees.
SIC 8062.
No. 85 CRM Nonprofit 100.

St. John's University

President's Office, Collegeville, MN 56321
Tel: 320/363-2011 Fax: 320/363-2115
Dietrich Reinhart, Pres.
Gar Kellom, VP-Student Affairs
Neil Thorburn, Provost
Warren Janzen, VP-Admin. Svs.
Rob Culligan, VP-Institutional Advancement
Annual Revenue: $59.4 million.
Annual Expenses: $45.8 million.
Contributions: 18.1 percent of revenue.
St. John's University is a private, residential liberal arts college for men, operated by the monks of Saint John's Abbey. St. John's has an enrollment of 1,840. A coordinated academic program with the College of St. Benedict, a nearby women's college with 1,975 women students, provides a coeducational experience for all students. Offers B.A., B.S., M.A. in theology, M.A. in liturgical studies, M.A. in liturgical music, M.A. in pastoral ministry, M.A. in divinity.
440 employees.

Founded in 1857. SIC 8221.
No. 35 CRM Nonprofit 100.

St. Joseph's Area Health Services

600 Pleasant Ave., Park Rapids, MN 56470
Tel: 218/732-3311
David Hove, Pres. and CEO
Brent Schmidt, CFO
Kathy Sundsrud, VP
Babs Debes, Acute/Integrated Div. Dir.
Kathy Kleen, AMB/Comm. Care Div. Dir.
Annual Revenue: $18 million.
Annual Expenses: $16.8 million.
Contributions: 1.6 percent of revenue.
250 employees.
SIC 8062.
No. 99 CRM Nonprofit 100.

St. Joseph's Medical Center

523 N. Third St., Brainerd, MN 56401
Tel: 218/829-2861 Fax: 218/828-3103
Thomas K. Prusak, Pres.
Sister Lynnette Bouta, VP-Operational Svs.
Bonnie Groneberg, VP-Patient Svs.
William Wrigley, VP and CFO
Barb Andersen, Dir.-Devel.
Sister Vivian Arts, Dir.-Mission Effectiveness
Nicholas Bernier, Dir.-Medical Affairs
Annual Revenue: $59.4 million.
Annual Expenses: $52.3 million.
Contributions: 0 percent of revenue.
St. Joseph's Medical Center, a 162-bed, regional, acute-care hospital, was created and organized to own, maintain, operate, and conduct facilities for health care, education, care for the aged, and social services in accordance with the charitable works tradition of the Roman Catholic Church. St. Joseph's has 60 active medical staff; 32 consulting, inpatient and outpatient mental health, and chemical dependency services; and 20 medical specialties.
728 employees.
Founded in 1902. SIC 8062.
No. 36 CRM Nonprofit 100.

St. Luke's Hospital of Duluth

915 E. First St., Duluth, MN 55805
Tel: 218/726-5555 Fax: 218/726-3090
John Strange, Pres. and CEO
Dennis Empey, CFO
Sandra Barkley, VP-Clinics
Tana Casper, VP-Patient Operations
Ron Franzen, VP-Support Svs.
Jo Ann Hoag, VP-Network Devel.
Lee Wuethrich, Controller
Annual Revenue: $117.1 million.
Annual Expenses: $124.5 million.
Contributions: 0.3 percent of revenue.
St. Luke's Hospital of Duluth is a regional neurosurgery center, an ACS Level II trauma center, and a regional vascular institute providing open heart surgery, limb replantation, and neurosurgery; lithotripsy and MRI; general medicine and surgery; and in-home services.
1,370 employees.
Founded in 1881. SIC 8062.
No. 18 CRM Nonprofit 100.

St. Luke's Lutheran Care Center

1219 S. Ramsey, Blue Earth, MN 56013
Tel: 507/526-2184 Fax: 507/526-7427
Web site: stlukes@bevcomm.net
Robert Lake, Administrator
Annual Revenue: $6 million.
Annual Expenses: $6.2 million.
Contributions: 2.3 percent of revenue.
St. Luke's Lutheran Care Center is a long term care facility with emphasis on rehabilitation services. Other services include an Alzheimer's unit, adult day-care, and a child care facility. Apartments are also available for low income elderly. A new market-rate apartment complex was recently added, as well as board and lodging facilities.
250 employees.
Founded in 1963. SIC 8051.

St. Mary's/Duluth Clinic Health System

407 E. Third St., Duluth, MN 55805
Tel: 218/726-4000 Fax: 218/725-3030
Peter E. Person, M.D., CEO
Mary Johnson, SVP-Patient Care Op.
Tom Klassen, SVP-Corp. Svs.
Pam Lindemoen, SVP-Op./Support
Sister Verda Clare Eichner, VP-Nursing-SMMC
Mark J. Huber, VP-SMMC
Hugh Reinier, M.D., VP-SMMC
James Abelsen, Admin.-Legal Svs.
Thomas E. Russ, M.D., Sec.
James Seitz, Treas.
Sister Kathleen Hofer, Board Chair
Annual Revenue: $392 million.
St. Mary's/Duluth Clinic Health System is a regional health care system with locations in 21 communities in Minnesota, Wisconsin, and Michigan.
5,115 employees.
SIC 8062.
No. 9 CRM Nonprofit 100.
No. 42 CRM Employer 100.

St. Mary's Home

1925 Norfolk Ave., St. Paul, MN 55116
Tel: 651/696-8400 Fax: 651/696-8404
Barbara Christen, CEO
Damodar Persaud, CFO
Sandra Vogel, Acting Dir.-Nursing
St. Mary's Home provides services to the elderly and handicapped, including home meal service, adult day care, and senior housing.
225 employees.
Founded in 1938. SIC 8082, 8322.

Saint Mary's University of Minnesota

700 Terrace Heights, Winona, MN 55987
Tel: 507/452-4430 Fax: 507/457-1633
Web site: http://www.smumn.edu
Louis DeThomasis, Pres.
Dr. Jeffrey Highland, VP-Academic Affairs
Anthony Piscitiello, EVP-Admissions
Sharyn Goo, VP-Student Devel.
Cynthia Marek, VP-Financial Affairs
Dr. Mary C. Fox, VP-University Relations
Loras Sieve, VP-Corp./Community Relations
Ann Merchlewitz, VP and Counsel to Pres.
Tim Burchill, VP-Metancia
James Bedtke, VP-Graduate and Special Progr.
Annual Revenue: $44.8 million.
Annual Expenses: $41.6 million.
Contributions: 18.6 percent of revenue.
Saint Mary's University is an undergraduate, residential, coeducational, Catholic liberal arts university administered by the Christian Brothers. Founded as an academy and junior college by Bishop Patrick R. Heffron, the university now offers the following degrees: B.A., B.S., B.F.A., M.A., M.S., M.Ed., and Ed.D. The School of Graduate Programs and the School of Special Studies are nontraditional programs administered from the Twin Cities Campus. They offer 18 master's degree programs, four baccalaureate-completion programs, four post-master's certificate programs, a doctoral program in education, and a range of graduate-level continuing education courses to full-time working professionals who attend graduate school part time.
584 employees.
Founded in 1912. SIC 8221.
No. 52 CRM Nonprofit 100.

St. Olaf College

1520 St. Olaf Ave., Northfield, MN 55057

Tel: 507/646-3004 Fax: 507/646-3549
Web site: http://www.stolaf.edu/
Chris Thomforde, Pres.
James Pence, SVP and Dean of College
Alan J. Norton, VP and Treas.
Greg Kneser, Interim Dean of Student Life
Barbara Lundberg, VP-Admissions
Annual Revenue: $78.9 million.
Annual Expenses: $66.4 million.
Contributions: 22.6 percent of revenue.
St. Olaf College, founded by Norwegian immigrants, is an undergraduate residential liberal arts institution with nearly 3,000 students. It is affiliated with the Evangelical Lutheran Church in America.
779 employees.
Founded in 1874. SIC 8221.
No. 25 CRM Nonprofit 100.

St. Olaf Hospital Association

1000 First Dr. N., Austin, MN 55912
Tel: 507/437-4551 Fax: 507/434-1432
T.J. Johnson, Pres.
R. Graber, COO
F. Bogott, Medical Dir.
Donald Brezicka, EVP
David Pilot, CFO
Annual Revenue: $55.3 million.
Annual Expenses: $51.2 million.
Contributions: 1.5 percent of revenue.
St. Olaf Hospital Association was formerly known as Austin Medical Center.
620 employees.
Founded in 1896. SIC 8062.
No. 42 CRM Nonprofit 100.

St. Paul Academy and Summit School

1712 Randolph St., St. Paul, MN 55105
Tel: 651/698-2451 Fax: 651/698-6787
Web site: http://www.spa.edu
Pamela J. Clarke, Head-School
Tom Hobert, Lower School Principal
Michael Mongeau, Middle School Principal
Henry Horne, Upper School Principal
Jennifer Halcrow, Dir.-Devel.
Melanie Spewock, Dir.-Summer/Extended Programs
Barbara Egan, Dir.-Finance/Operations
Annual Revenue: $20.3 million.
Annual Expenses: $13.2 million.
Contributions: 36.2 percent of revenue.
St. Paul Academy and Summit School is a K-12 independent day school.
164 employees.
Founded in 1900. SIC 8211.
No. 89 CRM Nonprofit 100.
Recent: *During the 2000-2001 school year, the organization was celebrating: its 100th anniversary; the implementation of a 6-8 middle school program in a new facility on its Randolph campus; and the successful completion of a $27 million capital campaign.*

The St. Paul Chamber Orchestra Society

The Hamm Building, 408 Saint Peter St., #500, St. Paul, MN 55102
Tel: 651/292-3248 Fax: 651/292-3281
Web site: http://www.stpaulchamberorchestra.org
Bruce Coppock, Pres. and Managing Dir.
John Huss, Board Chair
Barry Kempton, VP and Gen. Mgr.
Jon E. Limbacher, VP and Dir.-Devel.
Julia Kirchhausen, Dir.-Mktg./Sls./Pub. Rel.
Beth Villaume, Dir.-Fin./Admin.
Annual Revenue: $14.3 million.
Annual Expenses: $9.4 million.
Contributions: 45.5 percent of revenue.
The St. Paul Chamber Orchestra is the only full-time professional chamber orchestra in America. Under the leadership of Music Director Hugh Wolff, the chamber orchestra performs more than 150 concerts in the metro region and reaches thousands more through touring, national radio broadcasts, and recordings. The orchestra's 32 full-time musicians play a 38-week season. The official home of The Saint Paul Chamber Orchestra is The Ordway Center for the Performing Arts in St. Paul.
73 employees.
Founded in 1959. SIC 7929.

St. Therese Home Inc.

8000 Bass Lake Rd., New Hope, MN 55428
Tel: 763/531-5000 Fax: 763/531-5004
Sister Bernice Ebner, Pres. and CEO
David Bredenberg, Administrator
Jay Pizinger, Dir.-Finance
Winifred Kramer, Dir.-Residence
Annual Revenue: $18 million.
Annual Expenses: $17.5 million.
Contributions: 1.1 percent of revenue.
St. Therese Home Inc., Minnesota's seventh-largest nursing home, is a Catholic-sponsored, long-term care, continuum-of-care organization with a 302-bed nursing home and 220-unit apartment complex in New Hope. A number of services are provided for the elderly throughout the area.
565 employees.
Founded in 1968. SIC 8051.
No. 98 CRM Nonprofit 100.

The Salvation Army Minneapolis Program Fund

2300 Freeway Blvd., Brooklyn Center, MN 55430
Tel: 763/566-2040 Fax: 763/566-8954
David E. Grindle, Lt. Colonel-Div. Commander
Robert Thomson, Major-Divisional Sec.
Robert Doliber, Captain-Div. Financial Sec.
The Salvation Army Minneapolis Program Fund is a charitable religious organization.
150 employees.
Founded in 1865.

Sauer Memorial Home

1635 Service Dr., Winona, MN 55987
Tel: 507/454-5540 Fax: 507/454-1647
Ken Bittner, Administrator
Sauer Memorial Home is a nursing home providing care for the elderly and for the infirmed over age 16.
130 employees.
Founded in 1955. SIC 8051.

Science Museum of Minnesota

30 E. 10th St., St. Paul, MN 55101
Tel: 651/221-9488 Fax: 651/221-4777
James Peterson, Pres.
Judson Dayton, Chm.
Duane Kocik, VP-Finance/Admin.
Kathleen Wilson, VP-External Relations
Ronald Lawrenz, Head-Science Div.
David Chittenden, VP-Education Programs
Michael Day, Omnitheater Dir.
Paul Maurer, Dir.-Exhibits Division
Teresa Sterns, Project Mgr.
Annual Revenue: $36.8 million.
Annual Expenses: $22.1 million.
Contributions: 59.4 percent of revenue.
The Science Museum of Minnesota provides hands-on scientific learning programs for children and produces scientific and educational films. The museum receives more than 700,000 visitors a year.
533 employees.
Founded in 1907. SIC 8412.
No. 58 CRM Nonprofit 100.

Second Harvest St. Paul Food Bank

1140 Gervais Ave., Maplewood, MN 55109
Tel: 651/484-5117 Fax: 651/484-1064
Richard F. Goebel, Exec. Dir.
Pat Johnson, VP-Admin.
Cindy Kaczmarek, VP-Marketing

Jaci Stipe, VP-Food Bank Programs
Daniel Allen, VP-Finance
Rob Haarsager, VP-Operations
Annual Revenue: $27.9 million.
Annual Expenses: $27 million.
Contributions: 97 percent of revenue.
Second Harvest St. Paul Food Bank provides food to food shelves and on-site meal facilities, and distributes commodities to low-income families. Its mission is to feed people who lack sufficient resources by providing nutritious food through a network of food distribution organizations. As the largest food bank in Minnesota, Second Harvest distributes more than 19 million pounds of food annually. Second Harvest ensures that all contributions are used efficiently and effectively to feed hungry people in our communities.
57 employees.
Founded in 1974. SIC 8399.
No. 70 CRM Nonprofit 100.
Recent: *In November 2000 Second Harvest St. Paul Food Bank, in partnership with the American Culinary Federation's St. Paul chapter, held a fundraising event: "Chefs Reveal ... a Recipe to Fight Hunger," featuring keynote speaker St. Paul Mayor Norm Coleman.*

Sholom Community Alliance
3620 Phillips Pkwy., St. Louis Park, MN 55426
Tel: 952/935-6311 Fax: 952/935-4837
Bruce Kahn, Exec. Dir.
Michael Klein, COO
Joanie Keller, CFO
Annual Revenue: $28.3 million.
Annual Expenses: $29.3 million.
Contributions: 1.4 percent of revenue.
Sholom Community Alliance is made up of Sholom Home East, Sholom Home West, Knollwood Place, Menorah Plaza, and Menorah West. Through the alliance, a full continuum of care is offered to seniors, including independent/assisted living and varying levels of nursing and dementia care.
700 employees.
Founded in 1995. SIC 8059.
No. 69 CRM Nonprofit 100.

Sioux Vocational Services Inc.
4100 S. Western, Sioux Falls, SD 57105
Tel: 605/336-7100 Fax: 605/338-0259
Anna Rieck Mosena, Acting EVP
Jeff Nichols, VP-Finance
Sioux Vocational Services Inc. is an adjustment training center which provides residential facilities and services, community employment support and job training, sheltered work opportunities, and living training. Vocational skill training is provided in a variety of real production and manufacturing settings. The agency subcontracts with industry for light assembly, operates a custodial services business, recycles paper, and manages a large-scale food services operation.
310 employees.
Founded in 1966. SIC 2448, 2499.

Stratis Health
2901 Metro Dr., Suite 400, Bloomington, MN 55425
Tel: 952/854-3306 Fax: 952/853-8503
David Ziegenhagen, CEO
Sharon Farsht, Dir.-Marketing/Communications
Stratis Health, formerly known as Foundation for Health Care Evaluation, enhances the delivery of quality health care through education, training, research, and cooperative efforts with health care providers. As a contractor with the Health Care Financing Administration and the Department of Defense, it provides quality-improvement and oversight services for Medicare in Minnesota and CHAMPUS nationally. In addition, Stratis Health engages in applied research and health care data analysis.
56 employees.
Founded in 1969. SIC 8733.

Theatre Live!
36 S. Ninth St., Minneapolis, MN 55402
Tel: 612/339-0075
Annual Revenue: $24.5 million.
Annual Expenses: $24.5 million.
Contributions: 0.6 percent of revenue.
Theatre Live! is a performing arts presenter.
5 employees.
No. 79 CRM Nonprofit 100.

Trico Opportunities Inc.
137 N. Hooper St., Kingsford, MI 49801
Tel: 906/774-5718 Fax: 906/774-5746
Albert St. Peter, Exec. Dir.
TRICO Opportunities Inc. is a comprehensive vocational rehabilitation center for the disabled providing all services from assessments to employment as well as private rehab cases for insurance firms. TRICO also manufactures pallets, skids, and shipping containers and does commercial sewing of filter and sand bags as well as other items.
125 employees.
Founded in 1968. SIC 2393.

Twin Cities Public Television Inc.
172 E. Fourth St., St. Paul, MN 55101
Tel: 651/222-1717 Fax: 651/229-1282
Web site: http://www.tpt.org
Ellie Crosby, Chair
James Pagliarini, Pres. and CEO
Glenn Fisher, VP-Devel.
Bill Hanley, EVP-TPT Content
Michael Perelstein, VP and Gen. Counsel
Diane Thompson, Asst. Sec.
Annual Revenue: $23.9 million.
Annual Expenses: $23.1 million.
Contributions: 84.7 percent of revenue.
Twin Cities Public Television (TPT) is a nonprofit community licensee operating KTCA/Channel 2 and KTCI/Channel 17, which are affiliated with PBS. The stations also produce national and local programming, prepare outreach and educational materials, and provide production and teleconferencing services to local clients.
169 employees.
Founded in 1955. SIC 4833.
No. 80 CRM Nonprofit 100.
Recent: *In April 2000 Twin Cities Public Television announced plans to: a) expand its programming by broadcasting 24 hours on Channel 2; and b) increase its programming for kids by providing a new block of PBS children's shows weekdays from 5-7 p.m. on Channel 17. In addition, the nonprofit PBS affiliate simplified its identity under the single name Twin Cities Public Television, or TPT. Beginning on May 1, there was a new on-air look to accompany the simplified name. "This new name is an easier way to identify all the services that we provide to the community—some on the TV screen, some off the screen," said CEO Pagliarini. "We want people to understand that we are a multimedia and community organization." In July Tom Holter, executive director of programming, was named 2000 Programmer of the Year by the Public Television Programmers Association.*

UCare Minnesota
2550 University Ave. W., Suite 201S, St. Paul, MN 55114
Tel: 651/647-2630 Fax: 651/603-0650

Web site: http://www.ucare.org
Nancy Feldman, CEO
Terry Chism, VP-Hum. Res.
Mick Finn, VP-Operations
Mark Hudson, VP and CFO
Ghita Worcester, VP-Pub. Affairs/Devel.
Annual Revenue: $189.7 million.
Annual Expenses: $188.9 million.
UCare Minnesota is a health maintenance organization that was certified in Minnesota in 1989. Currently the state's fourth-largest HMO, it was created to serve people who receive public assistance. UCare provides managed health care services to more than 80,000 members, including 65,000 state public program members and 15,000 Medicare Plus Choice enrollees. UCare Minnesota's network includes 464 primary care clinics, 125 hospitals, and more than 10,000 specialty providers in 73 counties across the state. Members also have access to more than 1,500 dentists, 2,000 mental health providers, 400 chiropractors, and 800 pharmacies.
240 employees.
Founded in 1985. SIC 8099.
No. 14 CRM Nonprofit 100.
Recent: *In August 2000 the organization was named one of the Great Places to Work among small to medium-size employers by CityBusiness newspaper. In September the organization said that, while other Minnesota HMOs were dropping their Medicare plans, UCare was anticipating 20,000 enrollees in its own Medicare+Choice HMOs by January 2001. In October @bovehealth, San Jose, Calif., contracted to provide its Abovehealth Web suite of Internet-based products and services to UCare.*

United Theological Seminary of the Twin Cities

3000 Fifth St. N.W., New Brighton, MN 55112
Tel: 651/633-4311 Fax: 651/633-4315
Web site: http://www.unitedseminary-mn.org
Wilson Yates, Pres.
Jonathan Morgan, VP-Devel./Stewardship
Richard D. Weis, Dean of Seminary
Annual Revenue: $4.3 million.
Annual Expenses: $2.5 million.
United Theological Seminary is an ecumenical graduate theological school whose mission includes preparation of men and women for effective ordained and lay leadership in the church and society. Master of Divinity, M.A. in Theology and the Arts, M.A. in Women's Studies, M.A. in Religion and Theology, M.A. in Religious Leadership, and a Diploma in Indian Ministries are offered.
53 employees.
Founded in 1960. SIC 8221, 8299.

United Way of Minneapolis Area

404 S. Eighth St., Minneapolis, MN 55404
Tel: 612/340-7400 Fax: 612/340-7675
Web site: http://www.unitedwayminneapolis.org
James C. Colville, Pres. and CEO
Terri Barreiro, Senior Dir.-Community Svs.
Michael Thompson, Senior Dir.-Resource Devel.
James R. Boyle, Mktg. Dir.
Annual Revenue: $62.9 million.
Annual Expenses: $57 million.
Contributions: 94.3 percent of revenue.
United Way of Minneapolis Area is an independent local organization founded and governed by local volunteers to help people in the five-county west metro area. United Way works to strengthen families, nurture children and youth, and support older people; to increase self-sufficiency; to respect diversity and end discrimination; and to promote health and healing among people living in Anoka, Carver, Dakota, Hennepin, and Scott counties. Related resources: First Call for Help (651/291-0211).
106 employees.
Founded in 1917. SIC 8322.
No. 31 CRM Nonprofit 100.
Recent: *In 1999 United Way Minneapolis raised $60.2 million to support local health and human services. In March 2000 the organization announced $53.5 million in funding for 2000. In August the organization announced $154,430 in grants to assist funded agencies in enhancing technological capabilities and increasing capacity to serve people in need. The grants were part of United Way's $3.5 million, three-year commitment called the "Service Through Technology Initiative."*

United Way of the St. Paul Area Inc.

166 E. Fourth St., St. Paul, MN 55101
Tel: 651/291-8300 Fax: 651/291-8353
Web site: http://www.uwmsp.org
Lauren A. Segal, Pres.
David Fielding, Chief Admin. Ofcr.
Bill Rodriguez, VP-Marketing
Barbara McGaughey, VP-Community Resources
Tim Deutch, VP-Resource Devel.
Annual Revenue: $30.3 million.
Annual Expenses: $24 million.
Contributions: 91.7 percent of revenue.
The United Way of the St. Paul Area Inc. meets people's health and human service needs by providing support for quality programs, public-private initiatives, and volunteerism. The organization supports 218 programs at 80 health and human services agencies.
68 employees.
Founded in 1920. SIC 8322.
No. 67 CRM Nonprofit 100.

University Affiliated Family Physicians

2550 University Ave. W., Suite 201, St. Paul, MN 55114
Tel: 651/627-4301 Fax: 651/645-1327
Carl Anderson, CEO
Annual Revenue: $30.1 million.
Annual Expenses: $30 million.
270 employees.
SIC 8011.
No. 68 CRM Nonprofit 100.
Recent: *In December 1999 University Affiliated Family Physicians' (UAFP) sole corporate membership in UCare Minnesota was terminated.*

University of St. Thomas

2115 Summit Ave., St. Paul, MN 55105
Tel: 651/962-5000 Fax: 651/962-6110
Web site: http://www.stthomas.edu
Rev. Dennis Dease, Pres.
Dr. Judith Dwyer, Exec. Dir., Sec.
Quentin J. Hietpas, SVP-External Affairs
Terrence O'Connor, VP-Fin./Admin.
Dr. Ralph Pearson, VP-Academic Affairs
Rev. Phillip Rask, VP-School of Divinity
Gregory Roberts, VP-Student Affairs
Dr. Michael Sullivan, VP-Business Affairs
L. Thomas Kelly, Editor-CD
Annual Revenue: $174.7 million.
Annual Expenses: $156.4 million.
Contributions: 15.8 percent of revenue.
The University of St. Thomas, with 10,995 students, is the largest independent college or university in Minnesota. A Catholic, comprehensive university, St. Thomas is governed by a 42-member board that is chaired by the Most Reverend Harry Flynn, archbishop of St. Paul and Minneapolis. St. Thomas has campuses in St. Paul, Minneapolis, and Owatonna, and also offers classes in Anoka, Bloomington, Chaska, Rochester, and Woodbury. It offers 80 undergraduate majors, one education specialist, 28 master's and five doctoral programs. Part of the school's total revenue is from "nonoperational activities," which include capital gains on endowment investments and permanently restricted gifts.
1,803 employees.
Founded in 1885. SIC 8221.
No. 16 CRM Nonprofit 100.
Recent: *In February 2000 Richard Schulze, founder and CEO of Best Buy Co. Inc., and his wife, Sandra, gave St. Thomas $50 million, the largest donation ever reported by a Minnesota college. In September the university outlined plans for a merger of its Graduate School of Business with the 12-year-old William C. Norris Institute, to jointly pursue their common ideals of economic development through entrepreneurship.*

Volunteers of America Care Facilities
5905 Golden Valley Rd., Golden Valley, MN 55422
Tel: 763/546-3242
Web site: http://www.voa.org
Ronald Patterson, Pres.
Craig Abbott, Exec. Dir.
Dana Olson, Exec. Dir.
Deborah Perry, Asst. Sec.
Jim Rogers, Pres.
Angeline Sewall, Exec. Dir.
Jackie Fitzgerald, Rehab. Dir.
Nancy Gavin, Asst. Treas.
Annual Revenue: $55.9 million.
Annual Expenses: $56.7 million.
Contributions: 0.1 percent of revenue.
No. 40 CRM Nonprofit 100.

Volunteers of America of Minnesota
5905 Golden Valley Rd., Suite 110, Golden Valley, MN 55422
Tel: 763/546-3242 Fax: 763/546-2774
Web site: http://www.voamn.org
Michael W. Weber, Pres. and CEO
Barbara A. King, Chair
Jean Greener, Dir.-Senior Resources
Carolyn Hawkins, Dir.-Support Serv. for Seniors
Darlene Leiding, Dir.-Schools
William Nelson, Dir.-Correctional Svs.
Nadine Reiser, Dir.-Senior Nutrition
Michael Thiem, Dir.-Adult Special Svs.
Michael Warden, Dir.-Finance/Admin.
Larry Weight, Dir.-Clinical Svs.
Verlyn Wenndt, Dir.-Children's Svs.
Beth Zemek, Dir.-Support Serv. for Seniors
Annual Revenue: $17.6 million.
Annual Expenses: $17.1 million.
Contributions: 92.2 percent of revenue.
Volunteers of America (VoAm) of Minnesota is a nonprofit social service organization that provides social services within the state of Minnesota. Services are provided to children and their families, school students, homeless women and children, adults with special needs, youth and adult ex-offenders and senior citizens. The organization has over 5,000 volunteers participating every year.
563 employees.
Founded in 1896. SIC 8322.

Voyageur Outward Bound School
111 Third Ave. S., Suite 120, Mill Place, Minneapolis, MN 55401
Tel: 612/338-0131 Fax: 612/338-3540
Melissa Lindsay, Exec. Dir.
Zeb Gray, School Dir.
Leslie Cook, Devel. Dir.
Michelle Mathiesen, Finance Dir.
Elizabeth Westfall, Marketing Dir.
Karl Simer, Group Expeditions Director
Steve McGaughey, Admissions Director
Voyageur Outward Bound School's mission is to develop effective citizenship through the delivery of safe, adventure-based, educational courses and programs, designed to inspire self-esteem, self-reliance, concern for others and care for the environment.
225 employees.
Founded in 1964. SIC 8299.

Walker Art Center
725 Vineland Pl., Minneapolis, MN 55403
Tel: 612/375-7600 Fax: 612/375-7618
Web site: http://www.walkerart.org
Kathy Halbreich, Dir.
David M. Galligan, Treas.
Richard Flood, Chief Curator
Katharine Deshaw, Devel. Dir.
Mary Polta, Finance Dir.
Annual Revenue: $23.2 million.
Annual Expenses: $15.4 million.
Contributions: 29.6 percent of revenue.
Walker Art Center is known for its major exhibitions of 20th-century art; for its presentation of vanguard music, dance, theater, film, and video; and for its innovative education programs and visionary new media initiatives. Many of the Walker's exhibitions travel to major museums around the world. Artists and performers, invited to participate in artist-in-residence activities, are frequently commissioned to create works that premiere in Minneapolis. The Minneapolis Sculpture Garden, a project of the Walker and the Minneapolis Park and Recreation Board, is adjacent to the museum. The Walker's permanent collection of more than 9,000 pieces represents important artistic currents of the 20th century, in styles ranging from figurative to abstract.
150 employees.
Founded in 1879. SIC 8412.
No. 82 CRM Nonprofit 100.

Walker Methodist
3737 Bryant Ave. S., Minneapolis, MN 55409
Tel: 612/827-5931 Fax: 612/827-8458
Web site: http://www.walkermeth.org
Norma L. Larson, Chair
Janet A. Lindbo, Pres. and CEO
Ken Ward, SVP
James A. Blaha, CFO
Bob Manske, VP-Quality Improvement
Keith Tussing, VP-Walker Methodist Foundation
Annual Revenue: $50.3 million.
Annual Expenses: $50.8 million.
Contributions: 0.6 percent of revenue.
Walker Methodist Inc. has been serving seniors since 1945. It owns and operates nine housing facilities, five health care communities, and one stand-alone, assisted living facility in Minnesota, California, and Nebraska. Services include skilled nursing care, independent and subsidized senior living, assisted living, rehabilitation, home health care, and adult day care. Walker's for-profit subsidiary, Walker Management & Development, offers marketing, development, and management services for providers of senior housing and health care. Walker Methodist Inc. is the parent to Walker Senior Services Inc., Walker Methodist Foundation, and Walker Management and Development Inc.
1,400 employees.
Founded in 1945. SIC 8059, 8361.
No. 33 CRM Nonprofit 100.

Waseca Medical Center-Mayo Health System
100 Fifth Ave. N.W., Waseca, MN 56093
Tel: 507/835-1210 Fax: 507/837-4280
Michael Milbrath, EVP
Mavis Wheelock, Purchasing Mgr.
Genise Boettcher, Admin. Asst.
Waseca Medical Center is a rural hospital and physician clinic. It also serves as a teaching facility for residents in Family Practice from the University of Minnesota .
125 employees.
Founded in 1989. SIC 8062.

Weiner Memorial Medical Center
300 S. Bruce St., Marshall, MN 56258
Tel: 507/532-9661 Fax: 507/537-9053
Richard Slieter, CEO
Jerry Boerboom, CFO
Annual Revenue: $19.7 million.
Annual Expenses: $18.5 million.
Contributions: 0.7 percent of revenue.
Weiner Memorial Medical Center provides health care services to the sick and injured through a combination of emergency inpatient and outpatient methods, long-term care (nursing homes), home care, and wellness programs.
350 employees.
Founded in 1946. SIC 8062.
No. 92 CRM Nonprofit 100.

West Central Industries Inc.
1300 S.W. 22nd St., P.O. Box 813, Willmar, MN 56201
Tel: 320/235-5310 Fax: 320/235-5376
Web site: http://www.wctservices.org
Gary Nielsen, Exec. Dir.
Louise Jacobs, Accounting Dir.
Sandy Peters, Program Svs. Dir.
Robert Johnson, Production Dir.
Annual Revenue: $5.3 million.
Annual Expenses: $4.8 million.
West Central Industries Inc. provides job development and placement for persons with disabilities, as well as training and support services, at employer locations. These program services are designed to assist persons in developing career goals, adjusting to work situations and ultimately entering into gainful employment within the community. West Central Industries provided specialized services to 805 people in 1998.
250 employees.
Founded in 1962. SIC 8331.

White Community Hospital Corporation
5211 Highway 110, Aurora, MN 55705
Tel: 218/229-2211 Fax: 218/229-2042
Larry Ravenberg, Administrator
Cynthia Loe, Dir.-Nursing
Paula Schaefbauer, CFO, Asst. Administrator
Peggy Reznicek, Nursing Home Superviser
White Community Hospital Corp. is a 16-bed hospital and 69-bed skilled nursing facility.
130 employees.
Founded in 1959. SIC 8062.

Amherst H. Wilder Foundation
919 Lafond Ave., St. Paul, MN 55104
Tel: 651/642-4000 Fax: 651/642-2050
Thomas W. Kingston, Pres. and CEO
Elizabeth M. Kiernat, Chm.
Bryan Barry, Dir.-Svs. to Organizations
Craig Binger, VP-Admin./Mgmt. Support Svs.
Claudia Dengler, VP-Svs. (Child, Elder, Fam.)
Paul Mattessich, Dir.-Wilder Research Center
Annual Revenue: $61.3 million.
Annual Expenses: $55.4 million.
Contributions: 21.2 percent of revenue.
The Amherst H. Wilder Foundation is an endowed social service organization that serves people and organizations in the greater St. Paul metropolitan area. The foundation operates 105 programs and projects. The Amherst H. Wilder Foundation originated with the establishment of three trusts in 1903, 1904, and 1905 resulting from the wills of Amherst Holcomb Wilder, Fanny Spencer Wilder (his wife), and Cornelia Day Wilder Appleby (their daughter). The major portion of the Wilder estate was willed by the family to "relieve, aid, and assist the poor, sick, needy people of the city of St. Paul."
1,033 employees.
Founded in 1910. SIC 8322.
No. 32 CRM Nonprofit 100.

William Mitchell College of Law
875 Summit Ave., St. Paul, MN 55105
Tel: 651/227-9171 Fax: 651/290-6414
Web site: http://www.mitchell.edu
Harry J. Haynsworth, Pres. and Dean
David Wheaton, VP-Admin./Finance
James Brooks, Dean of Students
Gayle Keller McJunkin, VP-Institutional Advancement
Michael Steenson, Assoc. Dean-Academic Affairs
Susan Banovetz, Dir.-Alumni Relations
Ann Bateson, Dir.-Library
Annual Revenue: $19 million.
Annual Expenses: $17.2 million.
Contributions: 12.8 percent of revenue.
William Mitchell College of Law provides legal education for students pursuing a J.D. degree. It offers full-time, part-time, day, and evening enrollment options. The law school evolved from six predecessor schools. The earliest was the St. Paul College of Law, founded in 1900. William Mitchell has 139 regular full-time and part-time employees, 450 temporary part-time employees (student workers and adjunct faculty), and 1,000 students.
139 employees.
Founded in 1900. SIC 8221.
No. 95 CRM Nonprofit 100.

Winona Health
855 Mankato Ave., P.O. Box 5600, Winona, MN 55987
Tel: 507/454-3650 Fax: 507/457-4413
Web site: http://www.winonahealth.org
Patrick Booth, Pres.
William Fenske, VP-Finance
Rand Gettler, VP-Operations
Mary Reeck, VP-Patient Care
Annual Revenue: $34.3 million.
Annual Expenses: $32.5 million.
Contributions: 0.7 percent of revenue.
Winona Community Memorial Hospital is a 99-bed, acute-care, short-term hospital with an attached 104-bed, long-term-care unit and a detached 141-bed long term care facility.
850 employees.
Founded in 1894. SIC 8062.
No. 61 CRM Nonprofit 100.

Woodland Centers
1125 Sixth St. S.E., P.O. Box 787, Willmar, MN 56201
Tel: 320/235-4613 Fax: 320/231-9140
Eugene Bonynge, Exec. Dir.
Woodland Centers is a diversified mental health organization that serves six counties: Chippewa, Kandiyohi, Lac qui Parle, Meeker, Renville, and Swift. Services include outpatient, crisis/emergency, prevention and education, day treatment, halfway house, detoxification, sexual assault, elderly day care, adolescent day treatment, speech and hearing, community support, and a shelter house for battered women.
200 employees.
Founded in 1958. SIC 8322.

YMCA of Greater St. Paul
476 Robert St. N., St. Paul, MN 55101
Tel: 651/292-4100 Fax: 651/292-4148
Thomas R. Brinsko, Pres. and CEO
Darrell Silverness, Exec. Dir.
Kathy Cheng, VP-Finance
Scott Goyer, SVP
Deanna Sande, VP-Hum. Res.
John Duntley, VP-Camping
Annual Revenue: $26.6 million.
Annual Expenses: $22.3 million.
Contributions: 15.1 percent of revenue.
The YMCA of Greater St. Paul practices Christian values by providing oppor-

tunities for everyone to build strong kids, strong families, and strong communities. YMCA programs guide youth, enrich families, enhance health, and promote intercultural understanding. The YMCA is a nonprofit, charitable, United Way-affiliated agency. It serves people through nine community facilities, three resident camps, eight day camps, and 27 child-care sites.
408 employees.
Founded in 1856. SIC 8322.
No. 73 CRM Nonprofit 100.

YMCA of Metropolitan Minneapolis

30 S. Ninth St., Minneapolis, MN 55402
Tel: 612/371-8700 Fax: 612/371-8716
Harold Mezile, Pres.
Thomas Sisler, Exec. Dir.
Sandy Stooke, SVP
Patricia Lynch, SVP
Tim Chisholm, VP
Carolyn Creager, VP
Rosemary O'Meara, VP
Carol Schmidt, VP
Casey J. Scott, VP
Philip Nyvall, Dir.-Facilities
Annual Revenue: $37.3 million.
Annual Expenses: $31.2 million.
Contributions: 16.3 percent of revenue.
The Metropolitan Minneapolis YMCA is one of the largest YMCAs in the United States. Through its 15 branches, it conducts some 130 programs dedicated to responding to human needs and interests. Major program areas of the association include health enhancement, camping, family life, international, group work, leadership development, youth outreach, student work, and youth sports.
1,800 employees.
Founded in 1866. SIC 8322.
No. 57 CRM Nonprofit 100.

YWCA of Minneapolis

1130 Nicollet Ave., Minneapolis, MN 55403
Tel: 612/332-0501 Fax: 612/332-0500
Web site: http://www.ywca-minneapolis.org
Nancy Hite, CEO
Kathy Purcell, CFO
Pamela Diedrich, Dir.-Health/Fitness
Sue Duoos, Dir.-Health/Fitness
Kimberly Reeve, Dir.-Devel.
Valerie Watson, Dir.-Hum. Res.
Katie Williams, Dir.-Children's Center
Joyce Yamamoto, Dir.-Social Justice Programs
Annual Revenue: $10.8 million.
Annual Expenses: $6.9 million.
Contributions: 57.3 percent of revenue.
The mission of the YWCA of Minneapolis is to empower women and girls and to eliminate racism. We strengthen the lives of women and girls by: promoting economic independence and wellness; providing leadership for social justice; nurturing and mentoring children and youth to achieve their fullest potential; modeling respect for different cultures; and leading women and men together to build a strong, healthy and diverse Minneapolis community. Our programs of social action, health and fitness, early childhood education, ENCOREplus Women's Wellness and girls and youth, serve more than 15,000 individuals each year.
400 employees.
Founded in 1891. SIC 8322.
Recent: *Opened the new Midtown YWCA, located at 2121 East Lake Street. This $21.4 million facility significantly increases the services the YWCA provides to South Minneapolis Communities.*

Zumbro Valley Mental Health Center Inc.

315 Elton Hills Dr. N.W., Rochester, MN 55901
Tel: 507/281-6240 Fax: 507/281-6253
Dale Goodfriend, Interim Exec. Dir.
James Pagel, Pres.
Lawrence Dose, Controller
Marjorie Smith, M.D., VP
Zumbro Valley Mental Health Center Inc. provides a complete range of mental health services including chemical dependency treatment, detoxification services, day treatment, residential treatment, and medication management.
140 employees.
Founded in 1965. SIC 8069.

NOTES

NOTES

NOTES

NOTES

NOTES

NOTES

NOTES

NOTES

NOTES

NOTES

NOTES

NOTES

REGIONAL COMPANIES

735 companies headquartered elsewhere with major local subsidiaries, divisions, or facilities located in the Ninth Federal Reserve District

All operations have at least 50 employees

INCLUDES

CONTACT INFORMATION

DESCRIPTION

PARENT AND ITS LOCATION

LOCAL OFFICER NAMES AND TITLES

LOCAL REVENUE

NUMBER OF MINNESOTA EMPLOYEES

RANKINGS

RECENT INFORMATION

Note: above information provided where available

Information is updated annually by each company via questionnaire
(There is no charge for inclusion)

ABM 760 Harding St. N.E., Minneapolis, MN 55413. Tel: 612/378-0646; Fax: 612/378-9308. Phil Halper, Asst. Mgr.; Dan W. MacDonald, Gen. Mgr.; Jeff Southard, Branch Mgr. ABM (American Building Maintenance) performs building-maintenance activities. 1,400 employees (600 part-time). SIC 7349. Founded in 1909. Owned by ABM Industries Inc. (NYSE: ABM), San Francisco.

ABN AMRO Mortgage 7803 Glenroy Rd., Suite 200, Bloomington, MN 55439. Tel: 952/831-6644; Fax: 952/831-2671. Mark E. Heigl, Pres.; Tom Birch, EVP-Op. ABN AMRO Mortgage, formerly Heigl Mortgage and Financial Corp., is a residential mortgage banker dealing in first and second mortgages, and contracts for deed. It has a branch office in Rochester . Acquired in November 1996. 55 employees (in Minnesota; 1 part-time). SIC 6162. Founded in 1983. Heigl Mortgage officially changed its name to ABN AMRO Mortgage on April 2, 2000. "Being a part of ABN AMRO Mortgage Group Inc. allows us to offer our customers several enhancements, including a high-speed, high-tech system for processing and approving loans," said EVP Birch. Division of ABN AMRO Mortgage Group Inc., a member of ABN AMRO North America Inc., Chicago, which is ultimately owned by ABN-AMRO Holding N.V., Amsterdam.

ADT Security Services Inc. 2561 Territorial Rd., St. Paul, MN 55114. Tel: 651/917-0000; Fax: 651/917-1907. David Lockwood, District Gen. Mgr.; Dave Adams, Service Mgr.; Dave Hirt, Service Mgr.; John Snyder, Research Mgr.; Lee Stover, Commercial Sls. Mgr.; Cathy White, Admin. Mgr. ADT Security Services furnishes security devices and services for commercial and residential use. 100 employees. SIC 7382. Founded in 1874. Division of ADT Inc., Boca Raton, Fla.; subsidiary of ADT Group plc, London. No. 88 CRM Foreign-Owned 100.

AT&T AT&T Tower, 901 Marquette Ave., Minneapolis, MN 55402. Tel: 612/376-5000; Fax: 612/376-5425; Web site: http://www.att.com. Larry M. Newman, Regional VP. AT&T operates the world's largest communications network and serves more than 90 million business and consumer customers. AT&T provides long-distance, wireless, and online services. It also offers local telephone service in selected cities and states. The AT&T Tower in downtown Minneapolis is area headquarters for the Upper Midwest. 2,965 employees (in Minnesota). SIC 3661, 4813, 7373. Founded in 1885. Division of AT&T Corp. (NYSE: T), New York.

Aberdeen News Company P.O. Box 4430, Aberdeen, SD 57402. Tel: 605/225-4100; Fax: 605/229-7532; Web site: http://www.aberdeennews.com. Adrian Pratt, Pres. and Publisher; Jay Kusler, CFO; Cindy Eikamp, Editor. Annual revenue $9 million. Aberdeen News Company publishes a morning daily and Sunday newspaper, Aberdeen American News, and a weekly farm tabloid, Farm Forum. It also has commercial printing facilities. 124 employees (38 part-time). SIC 2711. Founded in 1885. Owned by Knight Ridder Inc. (NYSE: KRI), San Jose, Calif.

Accenture 333 S. Seventh St., Minneapolis, MN 55402. Tel: 612/277-0000; Fax: 612/277-1010; Web site: http://www.ac.com. Mike Badower, Location Lend Ptnr. Accenture, formerly Andersen Consulting, is a leading global management and technology consulting organization whose mission is to help its clients create their future. The organization works with clients from a wide range of industries to link their people, processes, and technologies to their strategies. In August 1999 the company consolidated its two downtown Minneapolis offices into eight floors of the former Metropolitan Centre Tower. 1,200 employees (in Minnesota). SIC 8742. Founded in 1988. In December 1999 Andersen Consulting formed AC Ventures to generate superior economic return by investing in new electronic businesses. In February 2000, the company announced the creation of a global network of 17 Launch Centres, which are production studios that help initially funded startups and spin-offs mature into successful operations. In October the parent announced a change its corporate name from Andersen Consulting to Accenture, effective Jan. 1, 2001. The move was related to the arbitrator's decision that freed the Chicago-based firm from former parent Andersen Worldwide. An August 2000 arbitrator's ruling finalized the split between Andersen Consulting and Andersen Worldwide. Andersen Consulting had to relinquish the esteemend Andersen name and pay $1 billion to its sister company from a disputed revenue-sharing arrangement; but it did not have to pay a $14 billion breakup fee. The Minneapolis operation is a business unit of Accenture, Chicago.

Advance Circuits Inc. 6442 City West Pkwy., Eden Prairie, MN 55344. Tel: 952/988-8700; Fax: 952/988-8740. Benoit Pouliquen, Pres.; David Koebele, Fin. Dir.; Jon P. Kerrick, VP-Engrg.; Jack Kimball, VP-Mktg.; Mike Maxson, Gen. Mgr.-Specialty Div.; Vernon Renner, VP-Materials; Brian Carufel, Gen. Mgr.-Commercial Div.; Carlton Moffett, Dir.-Quality; Bob Zimmer, Dir.-Info. Tech.; Rick Rodgers, Dir.-Hum. Res. Advance Circuits is a supplier of printed circuits for use in telecommunication and computer applications. Its principal commercial customers are manufacturers and assemblers of personal computers, mainframe computers, and peripherals; and cellular telecommunications, office automation, and industrial controls. These manufacturers are developing more complex electronic components; as a consequence, they increasingly require high-volume production of the types of sophisticated, high-technology printed circuits the company produces. The company maintains five production facilities in the Twin Cities area—in Hopkins, Minnetonka, Roseville, Buffalo, and St. Louis Park—and another, Johnson Matthey Semiconductor Packages Inc., in Chippewa Falls, Wis. Advance Circuits, a former publicly traded company, was acquired in August 1995 for $171 million in stock by Johnson Matthey plc. In July 1999 Johnson Matthey agreed to sell its Minnesota plants to AlliedSignal Inc. (the buyers of Honeywell) as part of a larger deal. 1,800 employees. SIC 3672. Founded in 1967. Honeywell International Inc. agreed in October 2000 to be sold. To be owned by General Electric Co. (NYSE: GE), Fairfield, Conn.

Advanstar Communications Inc. 131 W. First St., Duluth, MN 55802. Tel: 218/723-9200; Fax: 218/723-9635; Web site: http://www.advanstar.com. Robert Krakoff, Chm. and CEO; Adele Hartwick, Treas. and Cont. Advanstar Communications publishes specialized business magazines and professional journals. Advanstar also produces several industry newsletters, trade show and meeting publications, and information videotapes. It also manages and operates national and international expositions and conferences for business, professional, and consumer audiences. Advanstar Marketing Services sells database, reference, and marketing products, including direct-mail lists, CD-ROMs, classified advertising, and other data-search services. 310 employees. SIC 2721. Founded in 1904. An operation of Advanstar Communications Inc., Boston.

Advertising Unlimited Inc. 1000 Highway 4 S., P.O. Box 8000, Sleepy Eye, MN 56085. Tel: 507/794-8000; Fax: 507/794-8100. Gary W. Date, Pres.; Gary S. Haley, EVP-Sls. Advertising Unlimited manufactures specialty advertising products and worship bulletins. Formerly a publicly traded company. After becoming a wholly owned subsidiary of R.L. Polk & Co. in 1987, it was again sold in August 1999. 850 employees. SIC 2721, 2752, 2759, 3993. Founded in 1961. Now owned by Norwood Promotional Products Inc. (Nasdaq: NPPI), Austin, Texas.

Aetna/US Health Care 11100 Wayzata Blvd., Minnetonka, MN 55305. Tel: 612/594-6250; Fax: 612/399-2511. Patty Fauro, Ofcr. Aetna's Minneapolis location is a regional operations center serving Aetna HMOs in Chicago and Cleveland. The company also has locations elsewhere in Minnesota that offer managed care services, insurance products, and asset-accumulation and investment services. 650 employees. SIC 6411. Parent is Aetna Inc. (NYSE: AET), Hartford, Conn.

Ag Processing Inc. 800 Diagonal St., Dawson, MN 56232. Tel: 320/769-4386; Fax: 320/769-2668. Scott Quick, Mgr.; Lee Gunderson, Op. Mgr. Ag Processing processes soybean meal and soybean oil, crude. 70 employees (in Minnesota). SIC 2075. Founded in 1951. Division of Ag Processing Inc., Omaha, Neb.

Aggregate Industries North Central Region 2915 Waters Rd., Suite 105, Eagan, MN 55121. Tel: 651/683-0600; Fax: 651/683-8108; Web site: http://www.aggregate.com. Jonathan J. Wilmshurst, Pres. Annual revenue $180 million. Aggregate Industries North Central Region, formerly Camas Minnesota Inc., manufactures construction and industrial aggregates, including sand, gravel, crushed stone, mineral filler, concrete block, and ready-mix concrete. It also manufactures and sells concrete masonry units and keystone retaining wall systems. Aggregate Industries includes the operations formerly known as Shiely Co. 1,090 employees (in Minnesota; 10 part-time). SIC 1422, 1442, 3271, 3272. Founded in 1914. Affiliated with Aggregate Industries Inc., Bethesda, Md., which is owned by Aggregate Industries plc, Leicestershire, U.K. No. 16 CRM Foreign-Owned 100.

Ajilon 3800 W. 80th St., Suite 1130, Bloomington, MN 55431. Tel: 952/893-6650; Fax: 952/893-6651; Web site: http://www.ajilon.com. Ajilon is a computer consulting firm offering mainframe client server, networking and Internet, intranet, programmers, administration and project management. The company specializes in staff augmentation, project outsourcing, staff outsourcing, and century-date changes. 148 employees. SIC 7379. Owned by Ajilon, Towson, Md.

Alcoa Extrusions 2300 Alumax Rd., Yankton, SD 57078. Tel: 605/665-6063; Fax: 605/665-5107. Dave Abbott, Gen. Mgr. Alcoa Extrusions manufactures custom-extruded aluminum, electrostatic paint, and other fabrication. 500 employees. SIC 3334, 3341. Founded in 1979. The former Alumax Extrusions is now owned by ALCOA, the Aluminum Co. of America (NYSE: AA), Pittsburgh.

Allianz Life Insurance Company of North America 1750 Hennepin Ave., Minneapolis, MN 55403. Tel: 763/765-6500; Fax: 763/765-6657; Web site: http://www.allianzlife.com. Lowell C. Anderson, Chm.; Robert W. MacDonald, CEO; Mark Zesbaugh, EVP and CFO; Suzanne Pepin, VP and Sec. Annual revenue $1.54 billion. Allianz Life Insurance Co. offers a variety of individual and mass-marketed life, annuity, and health insurance products in all states except New York, where it sells reinsurance only and markets directly through its wholly owned subsidiary Preferred Life Insurance Co. of New York. Previously known as North American Life and Casualty Co., the Minnesota operations were consolidated with Dallas-based Fidelity Union Life Insurance Co. in July 1993. 1,316 employees (in Minnesota). SIC 6311, 6321. Founded in 1896. In February 2000, in response to a growing demand for multi-manager annuity products, Allianz Life added a number of additional investment options from AIM Advisors Inc., Fred Alger Management Inc., and Allianz of America Inc. to Valuemark fund options. In May Allianz Life and sister company Life USA Holding Inc., which parent Allianz had acquired in October 1999, broke ground for their new corporate headquarters in Golden Valley, Minn., at the junction of Interstate 394 and Highway 100. When completed (in late summer of 2001), the initial 421,000-square-foot facility was to house 1,300 employees. Allianz introduced USAllianz Rewards, a premium bonus variable annuity designed to encourage savers to become investors. Owned by Allianz of America Inc., a majority-owned subsidiary of Allianz AG Holding, Munich, Germany. No. 11 CRM Foreign-Owned 100.

Allied Security Inc. 430 First Ave. N., Suite 280, Minneapolis, MN 55401. Tel: 612/288-0585; Fax: 612/288-0724. Tony Simmons, District Mgr.; John Tetzlaff, Sec. Allied Security provides security personnel, investigative services, facility-management services, and loss-prevention consulting. 225 employees. SIC 7381. Founded in 1957. Branch office of Allied Security Inc., Pittsburgh.

Allied Vaughn 7951 Computer Ave., Bloomington, MN 55435. Tel: 952/832-3200; Fax: 952/832-3147. E. David Willette, Chm. and CEO; Donald J. Drapeau, Pres. and COO; M. Charles Reinhart, Sec. and CFO. Allied Vaughn serves corporate and institutional markets with high-volume videotape duplication and compact-disc replication. The company operates 12 videotape duplication facilities throughout the United States, and a compact-disc replication facility in California. Related services include video compression, graphic design, and print for media packaging, fulfillment, and direct mail; international format conversion and translation services; and rental of audio and video equipment. In March 1999 Vaughn was acquired for $65 million in cash and debt assumption. 852 employees (161 in Minnesota; 110 part-time). SIC 7819. Founded in 1943. Owned through Twin Acquisition Corp., an indirect subsidiary of Allied Digital Technologies Corp., Hauppauge, N.Y.

AmClyde Engineered Products Inc. 240 E. Plato Blvd., St. Paul, MN 55107. Tel: 651/293-4646; Fax: 651/293-4648. Richard J. Juelich, Pres.; Terrie J. Thompson, SVP; Roger Baumhover, CFO and VP-Fin.; Pierre C. Delago, VP-Engrg.; Dennis H. Kalmon, VP-Project Mgmt.; Wayne Long, VP-Products; John Perron, VP-Admin.; Jim Twyman, Dir.-Quality Mgmt. AmClyde designs and manufactures large revolving cranes, derricks, mooring systems, large hoists, capstans, and other specialty mechanical systems—for maneuvering the heaviest loads in the offshore oil markets, for shipyards, for material handling, and for U.S. government installations. The company also provides consulting and engineering services. The company has been recognized in the Guinness Book of Records as the supplier of the largest revolving cranes in the world. A combination of the assets of the Marine & Energy division of American Hoist and the Clyde Iron division of AMCA International, AmClyde was taken private in a management-led leveraged buyout in 1989. In October 1997 AmClyde was one of three closely held makers of drilling-rig equipment to be acquired in a $55 million stock deal. 435 employees (174 in Minnesota). SIC 3531, 3536, 8711. Founded in 1882. Now owned by Halter Marine Group Inc., Gulfport, Miss.

American Bottling 270 Bridgepoint Dr. S., South St. Paul, MN 55075. Tel: 651/552-3400; Fax: 651/645-0247. Scott Palmer, VP-Op. and Sls. Mgr.; Ron Berge, VP-Mktg. American Bottling distributes 260 brands of soft drinks—including Royal Crown Cola, Diet Rite, Diet RC, Sunkist, Canada Dry, A&W Root Beer, A&W Cream Soda, Country Springs Water, NeHi, Tahitian Treat, Big Red, Naya Spring Water, Mistic, Dr. Wells, and Quench. Former names: Royal Crown Beverage Co.; Mid-Continent Bottlers Inc. 160 employees. SIC 2086. Founded in 1934. Now owned by American Bottling, Des Moines, Iowa.

American City Business Journals Inc. 527 Marquette Ave., Suite 300, Minneapolis, MN 55402. Tel: 612/288-2100; Fax: 612/288-2121; Web site: http://www.corpreport.com/ventures. Lisa Bormaster, Publisher; Beth Ewen, Exec. Editor; Janice Meyer, Dir.-Bus./Hum. Res.; Maureen Tubbs, Dir.-Mktg.; Jonathan Hankin, Art Dir.-Ventures; Tom Smith, Research Dir. and Editor-Fact Book. In Minneapolis, American City Business Journals (ACBJ) publishes CityBusiness and Ventures.

CityBusiness delivers breaking news and information to more than 142,000 readers each week. Ventures magazine is the monthly guidebook to help Twin Cities entrepreneurs grow their companies. Other periodicals include the Fact Book, an annual directory of statistical and contact research on Minnesota business; and Employment Weekly, an employee recruitment paper of the Twin Cities. 64 employees (in Minnesota). SIC 2711, 2721, 2731. Founded in 1976. In May 2000 Paul Duncan, then editor of Ventures, was named Minnesota Small Business Journalist of the Year by the U.S. Small Business Administration. In November the company discontinued its monthly magazine, Corporate Report, by merging its resources, news coverage, and special events into CityBusiness and Ventures. American City Business Journals Inc., Charlotte, N.C., is a unit of Advance Publications Inc., Staten Island, N.Y.

American Excelsior Company 831 Pioneer Ave., P.O. Box 391, Rice Lake, WI 54868. Tel: 715/234-6861; Fax: 715/234-6823. Tim Prunty, Mgr. American Excelsior produces bulk excelsior (from wood and paper), evaporated cooler pads, soil erosion-control blankets, packaging, and nest and chick pads. 125 employees. SIC 2429. Founded in 1888. Employee-owned. Home office is American Excelsior Co., Arlington, Texas.

American Express Financial Advisors 108 AXP Financial Center, Minneapolis, MN 55474. Tel: 612/671-3131; Fax: 612/671-5112; Web site: http://www.americanexpress.com/advisors/. David R. Hubers, Chm.; Jim Cracchiolo, Pres. and CEO; Peter Anderson, Chief Investment Strategist; Ward Armstrong, SVP, Pres./CEO-A.E. Retirement Services; Mark Carter, SVP and Chief Mktg. Ofcr.; Pam Moret, SVP-Products Group; Barry Murphy, SVP-U.S. Retail Group; Becky Roloff, SVP-Advice/Information; Steve Roszell, SVP-Institutional Group; Stuart Sedlacek, SVP and CFO. Annual revenue $5.6 billion (earnings $935 million; assets $286 billion). American Express Financial Advisors (AEFA) is the nation's leading financial planning company. It emphasizes long-term planning. Its 2.2 million clients tend to be advisor-receptive, rather than transaction-oriented. Products and services to implement these plans include mutual funds, annuities, certificates, income protection plans, life insurance, limited partnerships, long-term care insurance, medical insurance, qualified retirement plans, securities services, and unit investment trusts. 8,160 employees (in Minnesota; 347 part-time). SIC 6211. Founded in 1894. Dec. 31, 1999: AEFA reported record 1999 earnings of $935 million, up 14 percent from 1998. Also disclosed in the earnings report: Without admitting wrongdoing, AEFA agreed to pay $215 million to 2 million customers to settle several class-action claims about the way it sold life insurance policies and annuities. In January 2000 two women in New Jersey filed charges against AEFA raising the same allegations of sex discrimination as charges filed by four women in Minnesota in October 1999. In March AEFA's veteran advisors were given the choice of associating with the firm as employees or as independent franchisees. The Association of Financial Planning Professionals was organized as an independent voice for financial advisors affiliated with AEFA. AEFA announced that its new corporate headquarters building was to be named the American Express Financial Center. [The building, located at 707 Second Ave. S., officially opened on April 25.] A second new downtown building under construction, the company's Client Service Center, on Third Avenue South at 10th Street, will open early in 2002. The Financial Center will be 30 stories tall and will house 4,000 of the company's nearly 8,000 employees located downtown. Seeking to grow its financial advisor base to 20,000 by 2008, AEFA rolled out an innovative program that offers its financial advisors choices from three different career tracks, including the first franchise option offered by a major financial services company. The three new American Express career tracks are: 1) Employees of American Express. This option is designed for advisors who value stability and corporate support, and want the benefits of being employees of American Express Financial Advisors. They receive salary (also known as a "forgivable draw" within the industry), as well as the opportunity to earn commissions and benefits. Advisors who choose this option will also receive other features, including back office support and help with all licensing, technology, training, marketing, and practice management. 2) Independent contractors/franchisees using the American Express name. This option is designed for advisors who want more autonomy to build and manage their businesses with the benefit and support of the American Express brand. These advisors have access to corporate product experts, research, and advanced professional development and must pay for most desired services. They will also have an ownership stake in their practice. 3) Independent contractors affiliated with Securities America, a broker-dealer owned by American Express. This option was designed for advisors who desire the most flexibility in running their practices. They are independent representatives affiliated with Securities America, operating under their own business names. They do not use the American Express brand name. In April AEFA launched the American Express Mortgage Center (http://www.americanexpress.com/mortgages)—an online mortgage supermarket that offers access to hundreds of mortgage products and financial tools. AEFA and Wells Fargo & Co. (NYSE: WFC) formed a strategic alliance to distribute investment and annuity products through their extensive retail financial networks. In addition, American Express Life Insurance Co. issued two new annuities: the Wells Fargo Advantage Variable Annuity and the Wells Fargo Advantage Builder Variable Annuity. Just after a mini-collapse of the high-tech market, AEFA launched the AXP Innovations Fund to investors. AXP Innovations invests in 50 to 90 small-, mid-, and large-cap stocks in technology, media, and telecommunications. In May AEFA invested $1 million in the Golden Gopher Growth Fund at the University of Minnesota's Carlson School of Management—one of the five largest student-run mutual funds in the country. In June the company launched the American Express Investment Management Account Platinum Card, for American Express customers with a combined minimum balance of $100,000 in their American Express Brokerage and/or American Express Centurion Bank accounts. AEFA launchedthree new mutual funds: AXP European Equity, which focuses on large-cap European stocks out of its London office; AXP Focus 20, a blend of about 20 to 50 mid- and large-cap growth stocks; and AXP Growth Dimensions, which focuses on fast-growing large companies while maintaining some mid-cap exposure. A third-party launch, through Omaha-based Securities America, was also planned. In a major reorganization into four divisions by parent American Express, AEFA was to become part of the global financial services group, along with the international charge card business. This grouping would give AEFA a platform for growth. In a related move, CEO and 36-year veteran David Hubers announced plans to retire. In September AEFA entered into a strategic alliance with Comerica Securities. The two companies will build and distribute annuities through more than 300 Comerica bank branches. As part of its Value Package, American Enterprise Life, a division of AEFA, was providing all Comerica banks with annuity products, training for Comerica investment consultants, financial planning software, and marketing support and training. AEFA and FleetBoston Financial formed a strategic alliance to build and distribute investment and annuity products through their retail financial networks. In October American Express Retirement Servicesrolled out a new Web feature enabling retirement plan participants to change their PIN (personal identification number) online. American Express held an open house to lend its support to Count Me In for Women's Economic Independence, a new national organization to create economic and business opportunities for women. The former IDS Financial Services has been owned since January 1984 by American Express Co. (NYSE: AXP), New York. No. 17 CRM Employer 100.

American Family Insurance Group 6131 Blue Circle Dr., Eden Prairie, MN 55344. Tel: 952/933-4884; Fax: 952/935-3803. Peter B. Walton, VP-Sls., Northwest Region. American Family's Northwest Regional Office is part of the fourth-largest mutual auto insurance company in the United States. The multiline insurer provides a wide variety of products for individuals and businesses. In addition to 677 employees, American Family has 459 agents in the region. 677 employees. SIC 6311, 6321, 6331, 6351. Founded in 1927. Owned by American Family Mutual Insurance Co., Madison, Wis.

American National Can Company 150 26th Ave. S.E., Minneapolis, MN 55414. Tel: 612/378-3333; Fax: 612/378-3380. Chuck Dergren, Mgr. American National Can Co. manufactures flexible packaging at its Minneapolis plant. Other local plants: 3600 Alabama Ave. S., St. Louis Park (flexible packaging); 139 Eva St., St. Paul (aluminum beer beverage containers). 185 employees. SIC 3089. Founded in 1906. Owned by American National Can Co. (NYSE: CAN), Chicago.

American National Can Company 139 Eva St., St. Paul, MN 55107. Tel: 651/227-7211; Fax: 651/227-8300. Al Albright, Plant Mgr. American National Can Co. manufactures aluminum beer beverage containers at its Eva Street plant. 122 employees. SIC 3411. Owned by American National Can Co. (NYSE: CAN), Chicago.

American National Can Company 3600 Alabama Ave. S., St. Louis Park, MN 55416. Tel: 952/929-0364. Todd Appel, Op. Mgr. American National Can Co. manufactures flexible packaging at its St. Louis Park plant. 75 employees. SIC 3089. Owned by American National Can Co. (NYSE: CAN), Chicago.

American Paging Inc. 2980 Commers Dr., Suite 100, Eagan, MN 55121. Tel: 612/623-3100; Fax: 612/623-4413; Web site: http://www.americanpaging.com. Terrence T. Sullivan, Pres. and CEO; Dennis M. Beste, VP-Fin., CFO, and Treas.; James F. Kelly, VP-Sls./Mktg./Field Op.; George H. Orr, VP-Hum. Res.; Larry A. Piumbroeck, VP-Bus. Devel. American Paging provides one-way wireless messaging services through 38 sales-and-service operating centers in 14 states and the District of Columbia. Operations are concentrated in Florida, the Mid-Atlantic, and the Midwest. As of Sept. 30, 1997, the company was serving 792,800 customers in 21 states and the District of Columbia. The total population of the area served is 76 million. Formed as a subsidiary of Telephone and Data Systems Inc. In February 1998 its 81.9 percent owner agreed to acquire the remainder of American Paging, then publicly traded. 735 employees. SIC 3663. Founded in 1980. Owned since March 1998 by Telephone and Data Systems Inc. (ASE: TDS), Chicago.

Americraft Carton Inc. 403 Fillmore Ave. E., St. Paul, MN 55107. Tel: 651/227-6655; Fax: 651/227-4713. Rick Johnson, Chm.; Jack McLaughlin, Pres.; Paul Hile, Gen. Mgr. Americraft Carton designs and manufactures folding cartons, and does lithographing. Formerly known as Kaplan Paper Box Co. 100 employees (in Minnesota). SIC 2657, 2752, 2759. Founded in 1907. Owned by Americraft Carton Inc., Kansas City, Mo.

Amerisource Corporation 6810 Shady Oak Rd., Eden Prairie, MN 55344. Tel: 952/941-9550; Fax: 952/941-9556. Phil Gibson, VP and Gen. Mgr.; Dennis Lindell, VP-Purch.; Dave Lambert, VP-Data Processing. Amerisource Corp., Minneapolis Division is involved in the trade of drugs, proprietaries, and sundries. Formerly Brown Drug Co. 165 employees. SIC 5122. Subsidiary of Amerisource Health Corp. (NYSE: AAS), Malvern, Pa.

Amesbury Group 1111 W. Algonquin, Sioux Falls, SD 57104. Tel: 605/336-1403; Fax: 605/336-1416. Cherrie Haugen, Plant Mgr. Amesbury Group manufactures sash balances for windows. In October 1998 this operation (known then as J.W. Window Components Inc.) was sold by Walter Industries Inc., Tampa, Fla., to its current owner. 130 employees. SIC 3321. Founded in 1946. The Massachusetts-based Amesbury Group is owned by Laird plc, London.

Amesbury Group Inc., Plastic Profiles Division 105 W. Washington St., P.O. Box 456, Cannon Falls, MN 55009. Tel: 507/263-3983; Fax: 507/263-3399. Rick Zeien, Op. Mgr.; Marilyn Petersen, Accounting Mgr.; Kyle Kragenbring, Dir.-Sls./Mktg. Amesbury Group Inc., Plastic Profiles Division manufactures custom profile extrusions used primarily in the fenestration industry, but with many other industrial applications. 93 employees. SIC 3089. Founded in 1978. The Massachusetts-based Amesbury Group is owned by Laird plc, London. No. 93 CRM Foreign-Owned 100.

Anacomp 2520 Pilot Knob Rd., Suite 300, Mendota Heights, MN 55120. Tel: 651/683-1000. Mark Jones, Center Mgr. Anacomp specializes in mirofiche and laser printing geared to mailing services for businesses. Previously known as First Image. 90 employees. SIC 2759, 3861. Now owned by Anacomp Inc. (Nasdaq: ANCO), Indianapolis.

Anagram International Inc. 7700 Anagram Dr., Eden Prairie, MN 55344. Tel: 952/949-5600; Fax: 952/949-5609; Web site: http://www.anagramintl.com. Garry Kieves, Founder and Pres. Anagram International is engaged in the production and worldwide sale of metallic balloons and other products made of synthetic materials to master distributors and mass merchants for resale to novelty, gift, and industrial markets. Anagram's product line includes over 1,700 different types of metallic balloons and other related gift, party, and toy products. It maintains sales offices and distribution facilities in London, Frankfurt, Madrid, Toronto, Paris, Tokyo, Sydney, and Mexico City. 500 employees (in Minnesota). SIC 3944. Founded in 1976. Acquired in September 1998 by Amscan Holdings Inc., Elmsford, N.Y.

Anchor Hocking Plastics 900 Apollo Rd., Eagan, MN 55121. Tel: 651/229-5400; Fax: 651/229-5473. Frederic L. Contino, Pres.; Dave Broadbent, Cont.; Frank Biller, VP-Sls. Anchor Hocking Plastics, formerly Plastics Inc., is the leading manufacturer of upscale plastic serveware for the food service and party goods industries. The company pioneered the market for upscale plastic tableware and drinkware in the early 1950s, supplying the airlines industry with the first disposable injection-molded plastic plates. During the 1970s, Plastics Inc. expanded into the food service and catering industries, which represent the majority of its current customer base. The company also serves restaurants, hotels, and schools. In September 1998 the company was sold by Newell Co. (NYSE: NWL) to its current parent. 450 employees. SIC 3082, 3089. Founded in 1938. Now a stand-alone division of Home Products International Inc. (Nasdaq: HPII), Chicago.

Arthur Andersen LLP 45 S. Seventh St., Minneapolis, MN 55402. Tel: 612/332-1111; Fax: 612/334-4700; Web site: http://www.arthurandersen.com. Steven L. Polacek, Office Managing Ptnr.; William V. Byars Jr., Ptnr.-Head of Business Consulting; Douglas C. Neve, Ptnr.-Head of Audit; Michael C. Stokke, Ptnr.-Head of Tax; Charles F. Berkowitz, Business Devel. Mgr. Arthur Andersen is a multidisciplinary professional services organization that offers assurance and business advisory services, business consulting, economic and financial consulting, and tax, legal, and business advisory services. It has 354 member firms in 76 countries. 406 employees. SIC 8721, 8742. Founded in 1940. An August 2000 arbitrator's ruling that broke up Andersen Worldwide and Andersen Consulting awarded Andersen Worldwide $1 billion from its sister company from a disputed revenue-sharing arrangement. Business unit of Andersen Worldwide, Chicago.

Ansul/Tyco Suppression Systems One Stanton St., Marinette, WI 54143. Tel: 715/735-7411; Fax: 715/732-3800. Jay Thomas, Op. Mgr. Ansul/Tyco Suppression Systems, formerly known as Ansul Tank Manufacturing, makes ASME- and DOT-certified pressure vessels, and does some sheet metal fabrication. 75 employees. SIC 3356, 3399. Founded in 1971. Subsidiary of Grinnell Corp., which is owned by Tyco International Ltd. (NYSE: TYC), Exeter, N.H.

The Antioch Company P.O. Box 767, St. Cloud, MN 56302. Tel: 320/251-3822; Fax: 320/251-6997. Lee Morgan, Chm. and CEO; Chandra Attiken, VP; Ole Dam, VP; Barry Hoskins, VP; Cheryl Lightle, VP and Sec.; Tom Rogers, VP; Robert Hill, Treas.; Dorris Daniel, Asst. Sec. Annual revenue

$201 million. The Antioch Co., formerly known as Webway Inc., manufactures and distributes photo albums and scrapbook products. 766 employees (374 in Minnesota; 31 part-time). SIC 2782. Founded in 1926. Owned by The Antioch Co., Yellow Springs, Ohio.

Aon Risk Services Inc. of Minnesota 8500 Normandale Lake Blvd., Suite 1200, Bloomington, MN 55437. Tel: 952/656-8000; Fax: 952/656-8001. Michael Prins, Pres. Aon Risk Services provides insurance brokerage services (with emphasis on property/casualty), employee benefits consulting, and risk management services for industry. Formerly known as Rollins Hudig Hall. 200 employees (in Minnesota). SIC 6411. Founded in 1979. Its Briarcliff Manor, N.Y.-based parent was acquired in July 1992 by Aon Corp., Chicago.

Apartment Search Inc. 7200 France Ave. S., Suite 237, Edina, MN 55435. Tel: 952/830-0509; Fax: 952/830-9019. Bill Deters, Pres.; John Appert, EVP; Andy White, SVP-Op.; Pat Hovland, VP; Richard K. Hughes, CFO; William D. Frishberg, Gen. Counsel. Apartment Search is a free national apartment locator service with 11 locations in the Twin Cities area, plus offices in Detroit; Baltimore; Washington, D.C.; and Kansas City, Missouri, for a total of 28 stores. Revenue comes from landlords who use the service to find new tenants. The company also does market research. In April 1999 the Times Mirror Co., Los Angeles, sold Apartment Search to a Denver real estate firm. 281 employees (114 in Minnesota). SIC 6531. Founded in 1965. Now owned by AGL Capital Investments, Denver.

Applied Coating Technology Inc. 2411 Pilot Knob Rd., Mendota Heights, MN 55120. Tel: 651/454-7777; Fax: 651/454-6132. Alfred J. Johnson, Gen. Mgr.; Michael T. Meagher, Asst. Gen. Mgr. Annual revenue $24 million. Applied Coating performs industrial spray-painting, powder painting, electrodeposition painting, chromate conversion, anodizing, silkscreening, and miscellaneous finishing processes for a wide range of industries including automotive, computer, aerospace/instrumentation, fitness, and the military. 360 employees (in Minnesota). SIC 3471, 3479. Founded in 1963. In January 2000 the company was acquired, although the purchase had no effect on employees or products. Division of Valmont Industries Inc. (Nasdaq: VALM), Valley (Omaha), Neb.

Apria Healthcare 131 Cheshire Ln., Suite 500, Minnetonka, MN 55305. Tel: 952/926-9808. Michael McKinney, Ofcr. Apria Healthcare provides respiratory therapy, home infusion, and home medical equipment. 235 employees. SIC 8082. Founded in 1985. Owned by Apria Healthcare Group Inc. (NYSE: AHG), Costa Mesa, Calif.

Aptus Inc. 21750 Cedar Ave. S., P.O. Box 550, Lakeville, MN 55044. Tel: 952/469-3475; Fax: 952/469-5091. Aptus specializes in hazardous-waste management, transportation, and disposal; laboratory analytical services; and site remediation. Plants in Minnesota, Kansas, New Jersey, Louisiana, Texas, Tennessee, California, and Utah. Previously known as National Electric Inc. 1,800 employees (50 in Minnesota). SIC 4953, 8734. Founded in 1980. Owned by Rollins Environmental Services Inc., Wilmington, Del.

Arcadia Financial Ltd. 6533 Flying Cloud Dr., Eden Prairie, MN 55344. Tel: 952/914-3620; Fax: 952/944-2819; Web site: http://www.arcadiafinancial.com. Warren Kantor, Chm.; Robert A. Marshall, Pres. and COO; Scott H. Anderson, VChm.-Credit/Collections; Cortes DeRussy, EVP-Originations; Duane E. White, EVP-Corporate Svs.; John A. Witham, EVP and CFO; Brian S. Anderson, SVP and Cont.; James D. Atkinson III, SVP, Chief Legal Ofcr., and Sec.; Steven R. Bednar, SVP-Info. Sys.; James F. Connaughton, SVP-Risk Mgmt.; Jerry Gutierrez, SVP-Remarketing; Mike Oleson, SVP-Collections, Central Region; Jeanne M. Adam, SVP-Quality Assurance; Richard S. Deal, VP-Hum. Res.; David C. Ellis, VP-Collections, Eastern Region; Scott R. Fjellman, VP-Securitization/Investor Rel.; Ronald J. Groves, VP-Info. Resources Mgmt.; Robert A. Hunter, VP-Loan Origination, Eastern Region; Randolph D. Matzke, VP-Special Collections; John L. McCloy, VP-Collections, Western Region; Scott G. McKoin, VP-Loan Origination, Western Region; Michael J. Sherman, VP and Treas.; Randall S. Smathers, VP-Loan Origination, Central Region; Teri Peulen, VP-Loan Servicing; Daniel D. Hill, VP-Senior Corp. Counsel; Bradley R. Krogman, VP-Collections, Central Region. Annual revenue $140.6 million (loss $92.5 million includes special pretax charge of $115.1 million). Arcadia Financial is a Minneapolis-based consumer financial services company specializing in purchasing, selling, and servicing retail installment contracts for new and used automobiles originated in 45 states. The company is the nation's largest independent provider of automobile financing. 1,200 employees (450 in Minnesota). SIC 6153. Founded in 1992. In January 2000 Arcadia announced that it was anticipating a loss for fourth quarter 1999 resulting primarily from Arcadia's decision not to complete a securitization transaction during the quarter (instead, selling loans to Associates Financial Services Co. Inc.), and an expected reduction to Arcadia's gain on sale revenue for the quarter unrelated to the absence of a fourth-quarter securitization transaction. As a result of a merger concluded in April, Arcadia became a wholly owned subsidiary of The Associates—receiving for each share of Arcadia common stock $4.90 in cash, plus a residual value obligation that was to participate in cash flows in excess of agreed-upon amounts released from Arcadia's existing securitization transactions. About 250 employees at corporate headquarters were told that their jobs were to be eliminated (due to redundancy) when their new owner folded Arcadia into its other auto-lending subsidiary, TranSouth Financial Corp. Meanwhile, the outlook for the "B" senior unsecured debt of Arcadia remained on RatingAlert Positive by Fitch IBCA. In May Arcadis commenced a tender offer for both tranches of its 11 1/2% Senior Notes Due 2007. Arcadia was also seeking consents to certain proposed amendments to the documents under which the Notes were issued—to eliminate the reporting requirements and certain restrictive covenants contained in those documents, thereby affording Arcadia additional financial and operational flexibility. In June Arcadia priced its 11 1/2% Senior Notes Due 2007: The purchase price for each $1,000 principal amount of the notes purchased in the offer was to be $1,122.57 plus accrued but unpaid interest to, but excluding, the date of payment—which includes a consent payment in an amount equal to 2 percent of the principal amount. Owned by Associates First Capital Corp. (NYSE: AFS), Dallas.

Arden International Kitchens LLC 21150 Hamburg Ave., Lakeville, MN 55044. Tel: 952/469-2000; Fax: 952/985-5822. Tim Opel, Chm. and CEO. Arden International Kitchens produces and markets frozen prepared food for the food service industry. The company markets three premium-quality brands: the Arden line of home-style entrees; the Charitto's line of Mexican entrees, components, and sauces; and the Ardenelli line of Italian entrees, components, and sauces. The company also produces custom-packed prepared foods for national and regional restaurant chains, and private-label products for regional food distributors. 160 employees (in Minnesota). SIC 2038. Founded in 1977. Owned since 1994 by Schreiber Foods Inc., Green Bay, Wis.

Armour-Freeborn Foods 517 Adams Ave., Albert Lea, MN 56007. Tel: 507/373-4739; Fax: 507/373-8421. Jon M. Hedlund, VP and Gen. Mgr. Armour-Freeborn Foods is a manufacturer of specialty dried animal feed products and dried edible products. 73 employees. SIC 2023. Founded in 1958. Acquired in January 1993 by ConAgra Inc. (NYSE: CAG), Omaha, Neb.

Armour Swift-Eckrich 115 N. Broadway, Wells, MN 56097. Tel: 507/553-6351; Fax: 507/553-6297. Gregg Tucholke, Plant Mgr. Armour Swift-Eckrich operates a poultry and meat further-processing operation in Wells. 141 employees. SIC 0253, 2015. Founded in 1957. Armour Swift-Eckrich, Downers Grove, Ill., is owned by ConAgra Inc. (NYSE: CAG), Omaha, Neb.

Arteka Corporation 15195 Martin Dr., Eden Prairie, MN 55344. Tel: 952/934-2000; Fax: 952/934-2247. Scott Shanesy, Branch Mgr.; Donna Robling, Dir. Annual revenue $8.8 million. Arteka is a landscape, irrigation, and landscape management contractor. 120 employees (in Minnesota; 95 part-time). SIC 0781. Founded in 1974. Owned by ServiceMaster Corp. (SVM: NYSE), Downers Grove, Ill.

Artesyn Technologies 7575 Market Place Dr., Eden Prairie, MN 55344. Tel: 952/941-1100; Fax: 952/829-1837; Web site: http://www.zytec.com. Ervin F. Kamm Jr., Pres. and CEO; Max Davis, VP-Mfg.; Josef J. Matz, Managing Dir.-Zytec GmbH; John B. Rogers, VP-Fin. and Treas.; John M. Steel, VP-Mktg./Sls.; N. Charles Wussow, VP-Engrg.; Sherman Winthrop, Sec.; Thomas J. Kent, VP and Gen. Mgr.-Svs./Logistics. Artesyn Technologies is a designer and manufacturer of custom electronic power supplies for original-equipment manufacturers in the computer and other electronic equipment industries. It also repairs power supplies and related products manufactured by itself and other companies. The company's products and related services are sold in North America and Europe. In December 1997 the publicly traded Zytec Corp. was acquired by Computer Products Inc. in a pooling-of-interests deal valued at $360 million. 544 employees. SIC 3679. Founded in 1983. With the completion of their merger, the two companies began conducting business as Artesyn Technologies, Boca Raton, Fla.

Asarco Inc. P.O. Box 1230, East Helena, MT 59635. Tel: 406/227-7100; Fax: 406/227-8897. John Shaw, Mgr. Asarco is a custom lead smelter. 275 employees. SIC 3339. Founded in 1888. Division of Asarco Inc. (NYSE: AR), New York.

Associated Bank Minnesota 1801 Riverside Ave., Minneapolis, MN 55458. Tel: 612/341-3505; Fax: 612/341-3576; Web site: http://www.riversidebank.com. David E. Cleveland, Chm. and CEO; John Crinklaw, Pres.; Bruce E. Nystrom, SVP and Mgr.-Plymouth; David Richards, SVP; Gwen N. Stanley, SVP and CFO; Michael Zenk, SVP; Leanne Baldwin, VP and Mgr.-Cedar Riverside; Roger D. Hamilton, VP and Mgr.-Northland Park; Paul T. Lilienthal, VP and Mgr.-LaSalle Plaza; John Olcott, VP; Chris Young, VP. Associated Bank Minnesota is the combination of two former independent banks, Riverside Bank and Bank Windsor, with $575 million in combined assets. Associated provides financing for small to mid-sized businesses. It operates five full-service branches with locations in Plymouth, Bloomington, Brooklyn Park, downtown Minneapolis, and the Cedar-Riverside area. In September 1999 Riverside co-owners Cleveland, 65 (35 percent), and his silent partner Tom Redmond Sr. (65 percent) sold the bank for $89.1 million in stock. 138 employees. SIC 6022. Founded in 1973. On Aug. 31, 1999, Riverside Bank was acquired by Associated Banc-Corp. In January 2000 Riverside agreed to merge with another recent Associated acquisition, Bank Windsor, Minneapolis, to become Associated Bank Minnesota. In June SVP Kate Barr, widely thought to be Cleveland's successor, left after 20 years to pursue personal interests. Owned by Associated Banc-Corp. (Nasdaq: ASBC), Green Bay, Wis.

The Athletic Fitters Inc. 7630 Executive Dr., Eden Prairie, MN 55344. Tel: 952/934-8166; Fax: 952/934-7609. Paul J. Taunton, Pres. and Owner. The Athletic Fitters operates 97 retail outlets in 17 states throughout the Midwest that specialize in athletic footwear and apparel. In February 1998 founder Paul J. Taunton agreed to sell his company for more than $30 million to the owners of the 2,300-store Foot Locker chain. 1,300 employees. SIC 2329, 5661. Founded in 1980. To be owned by Woolworth Corp. (NYSE: Z), New York.

Atlantis Plastic Inc. 2111 Third Ave., Mankato, MN 56001. Tel: 507/625-3011; Fax: 507/388-2087; Web site: http://www.atlantisplastics.com. Corky Carr, Plant Mgr. Atlantis Plastic extrudes and converts LDPE polyethylene film. 180 employees (176 in Minnesota). SIC 3089. Founded in 1959. Owned by Atlantis Plastic Inc. (ASE: AZ), Coconut Grove, Fla.

Auto Owners Insurance Company 2539 E. County Rd. E, White Bear Lake, MN 55110. Tel: 651/777-8172; Fax: 651/777-9177; Web site: http://www.autoowners.com. Dale Schnur, Regional VP. Annual revenue $159 million. Auto Owners Insurance Co. sells insurance services through independent agencies. The company had a 1999 surplus of $2.9 billion. 135 employees (130 in Minnesota). SIC 6321. Founded in 1916. Owned by Auto-Owners Insurance, Lansing, Mich.

Avaya Inc. 1650 W. 82nd St., Suite 500, Bloomington, MN 55431. Tel: 800/288-4312; Fax: 612/703-2822; Web site: http://www.lucent.com. Dan Gorski, VP-Area Sls.; Mark Pelletier, VP-Area Svs. Avaya Inc., formerly the Enterprise Networks Group of Lucent Technologies, is the No. 1 provider of business communications systems in the United States and the No. 1 provider of structured cabling systems in the world. Avaya also maintains more than 8 million voice mailboxes in the United States, and is the market leader in the sale of call center systems. 500 employees. SIC 1731. Founded in 1869. Owned by Avaya Inc., Basking Ridge, N.J.

Aveda Corporation 4000 Pheasant Ridge Dr., Blaine, MN 55449. Tel: 763/783-4000; Fax: 763/783-4110; Web: http://www.aveda.com. Horst Rechelbacher, Chm. and CEO; Peter Rechelbacher, Co-pres.; Nicole Rechelbacher, Co-pres.; Tom Petrillo, SVP-Sls./Distrib. Mgmt.; Bob Salem, SVP-Global Mktg./Int'l; Shivnath Tandon, SVP; Jim Pavlakis, VP-Bus. Op.; Prakash Purohit, VP-Tech. Affairs; Charles Weaver, VP-Fin. Aveda Corp. is a manufacturer of hair, skin, makeup, plant Pure-Fume and lifestyle products created from pure flower and plant ingredients. Aveda searches worldwide for ingredients derived from flowers and plants that are organically grown, without the use of petrochemical pesticides. The corporation is committed to creating products and services beneficial to the consumer and the environment. Aveda products are sold in 30,000 professional salons, and in spas, educational institutes, health care facilities, certain department stores, and 130 Aveda Environmental Lifestyle Stores. Predominantly marketed in the United States, Aveda products are available in certain international markets, including the United Kingdom, Australia, and Italy. In November 1997 the privately held Aveda agreed to be acquired for $300 million. 500 employees (400 in Minnesota; 50 part-time). SIC 2844, 7231. Founded in 1978. Owned by The Estee Lauder Cos. Inc. (NYSE: EL), New York.

BBDO Minneapolis 900 Brotherhood Bldg., 625 Fourth Ave. S., Minneapolis, MN 55415. Tel: 612/338-8401; Fax: 612/338-2136. Robert Thacker, Pres. and CEO; Denny Haley, EVP and Exec. Creative Dir.; Nancy Rice, SVP and Group Creative Dir.; Wes Crawford, SVP, Mgmt. Supervisor, and COO. Annual revenue $11.1 million. BBDO Minneapolis is a full-service advertising agency. Major clients include Hormel Foods, Minneapolis Dodge Dealers Association, Buffets Inc., Jennie-O Foods, Dain Rauscher and TCF National Bank. 65 employees. SIC 7311. Founded in 1930. Owned by Omnicom Group Inc., New York.

BGK Finishing Systems 4131 Pheasant Ridge Dr. N.E., Blaine, MN 55449. Tel: 763/784-0466; Fax: 763/784-1362; Web site: http://www.itwbgk.com. Mark Rekucki, Gen. Mgr.; Randy Allen, Op. Mgr.; John Conlon, Sls./Mktg. Mgr.; Jim Nelson, Engrg. Mgr.; Jim Sweeney, Cont. BGK Finishing Systems manufactures and custom-designs infrared curing ovens and material-handling systems. 75 employees (73 in Minnesota). SIC 3567. Founded in 1980. Acquired in 1990 by Illinois Tool Works Inc. (NYSE: ITW), Glenview, Ill.

BP Amoco Oil Company P.O. Box 5000, Mandan, ND 58554. Tel: 701/667-2473; Fax: 701/667-2419. Dan Porter, Refinery Mgr. BP Amoco Oil manufactures three grades of gasoline, two grades of heating oil, two grades of diesel fuel, two grades of jet fuel, residual fuel, and propane. 225 employees. SIC 2911. Founded in 1954. Subsidiary of BP Amoco plc (LON), London.

BRW Group Inc. 700 Third St. S., Minneapolis, MN 55415. Tel: 612/370-0700; Fax: 612/370-1378. Richard Wolsfeld, Pres. BRW's services include civil and structural engineering, site design, utilities design, landscape architectural design, environmental analysis, transportation and traffic engineering, Intelligent Transportation Systems, cultural resources, and Geographic Information Systems. The former Bennett-Ringrose-Wolsfed-Jarvis-Gardner was acquired by Dames & Moore Group in 1996 and URS in 1999. 714 employees (231 in Minnesota). SIC 0781, 4789, 8711, 8712, 8748. Founded in 1956. Owned by URS Corp. (NYSE: URS), San Francisco.

BT Corporate Express 5400 Nathan Ln. N., Plymouth, MN 55442. Tel: 763/553-9500; Fax: 763/553-1075. Sharon Re, Div. Pres. BT Office Products, formerly known as Business Essentials Inc., sells commercial office and computer supplies, and furniture. 161 employees (in Minnesota). SIC 5112. Founded in 1978. Owned by publicly traded BT Office Products International Inc., Buffalo Grove, Ill.

Badger Equipment Company Inc. Airport Industrial Park, P.O. Box 798, Winona, MN 55987. Tel: 507/454-1563; Fax: 507/454-3326; Web site: http://www.badgerequipment.com. Richard Haydysch, Pres.; Sharon Kazemba, Cont. Annual revenue $27 million. Badger Equipment Co. manufactures hydraulic rough-terrain cranes, telescoping-boom excavators, railroad maintenance-of-way cranes, wheel-mounted excavators, sheet/coil/rail/panel lifters, and custom fabricated and welded components. 115 employees (110 in Minnesota; 1 part-time). SIC 3531, 3535. Founded in 1946. Owned by Avis Industrial Corp., Upland, Ind.

Baldor Electric Company 12955 Highway 55, Plymouth, MN 55441. Tel: 763/557-9250; Fax: 763/557-9255. Richard Rebella, Gen. Mgr.; Marty Engebretson, Hum. Res. Mgr. Baldor Electric manufactures electric drives for industrial use. 80 employees (in Minnesota; 16 part-time). SIC 3621. Founded in 1983. Owned by Baldor Electric Co., Fort Smith, Ark.

Baldwin Filters 1901 Hastings Dr., P.O. Box 1019, Yankton, SD 57078. Tel: 605/665-1115; Fax: 605/665-1118. Sam Neuman, Plant Mgr. Baldwin manufactures automotive air and oil filters. Formerly Hastings Filters Inc. 170 employees. SIC 3714. Founded in 1984. Baldwin Filters, Kearney, Neb., is a division of Clarcor Inc. (NYSE: CLC), Rockford, Ill.

Bally's U.S. Swim & Fitness 67 Minnesota Ave., Little Canada, MN 55117. Tel: 651/766-9474. Bally's U.S. Swim & Fitness operates eight Twin Cities clubs that specialize in individual fitness and health programs. 700 employees. SIC 7997. Founded in 1983. Subsidiary of Bally Entertainment Corp., Chicago, which agreed in June 1996 to be acquired by Hilton Hotels Corp. (NYSE: HLT), Beverly Hills, Calif.

Bankers Systems Inc. 6815 Saukview Dr., P.O. Box 1457, St. Cloud, MN 56302. Tel: 320/251-3060; Fax: 320/251-0655. Robert E. White, Pres. and CEO. Bankers Systems Inc. (BSI) provides products, services, and software solutions to meet the changing regulatory and technology needs of the financial services industry. BSI provides transaction and disclosure documents and automation in a variety of media, including PC-based software, electronic, web, and pre-printed forms for lending and new accounts. Its technical support and education business holds more than 400 seminars a year around the country, and provides telephone consulting and other compliance-related support services. Sold in 1994 to an investor group led by Goldner Hawn Johnson & Morrison Inc., Minneapolis, in conjunction with BancBoston Capital Inc., Boston, and BSI management. In July 1999 the company agreed to be acquired for $190 million by Wolters Kluwer, Amsterdam. 850 employees (750 in Minnesota). SIC 7379. Founded in 1952. In December 1999 Bankers Systems unveiled a prototype version of its new ARTA Deposit Documentation System—its third software system designed exclusively for the advanced, 32-bit Microsoft Windows environment. An agreement was struck with Eden Prairie, Minn.-based SuperSolutions Corp. to integrate Bankers Systems' electronic documents into Daybreak-The Big Picture loan-portfolio management software. In February 2000 the company launched a new brand to leverage its position as the leading provider of compliance solutions for financial institutions and their legal counsel. The new brand—Expere—represents the knowledge and experience that's embedded into the company's compliance solutions. In March the U.S. Department of Commerce's Patent and Trademark Office granted the company U.S. Patent #6,006,242 for a document assembly process used in the development of some of its software applications. In April Bankers Systems and the Independent Community Bankers of America announced an educational partnership to bring training and implementation guidance to thousands of community banks on the new financial privacy regulations. As part of their efforts, the two groups were co-sponsoring a live satellite broadcast to 78 cities on May 24. In June Bankers Systems launched PrivacyHeadquarters.com, the most comprehensive portal site dedicated to privacy issues in the financial services industry. Customers were soon able to generate tailored privacy documents on PrivacyHeadquarters.com using docCreator, BSI's newest online innovation. In August BSI and Blauser Technologies, a provider of MICR encoding printing technology for small- to medium-sized financial institutions, formed an alliance to interface Blauser's in-house MICR printing capabilities with Bankers Systems' ARTA Lending software application. In August BSI agreed to provide IRA services to FOLIOfn Inc., one of the most talked about new players in online investing. (Kiplinger's Personal Finance called the company's new way of investing "as revolutionary as former Vanguard chief John Bogle's introduction of index funds 25 years ago.") Now part of CCH Inc., Riverwoods, Ill., a subsidiary of Wolters Kluwer N.V., Amsterdam. No. 21 CRM Foreign-Owned 100.

Banta Catalog 655 N. Fairview Ave., St. Paul, MN 55104. Tel: 651/645-4422; Fax: 651/645-7537. William J. Helper, Pres.; Carol A. Swanson, Mktg. Mgr. Banta Catalog in St. Paul, formerly McGill/Jensen Inc., specializes in quality, cost-effective catalog production services, including printing, digital pre-press, demographic binding, inkjet imaging, database management, and distribution services. Its facilities can also produce a wide variety of commercial printing projects. 400 employees (in Minnesota). SIC 2752, 2759. Founded in 1848. Subsidiary of Banta Corp. (NYSE: BN), Menasha, Wis.

Banta Catalog Group 7401 Kilmer Ln., Maple Grove, MN 55369. Tel: 763/315-8100; Fax: 763/315-8177; Web site: http://www.banta.com. William Hepler, Pres.; Dave Johannes, Plant Mgr. Banta Catalog in Maple Grove specializes in printing, personalization, and mailing catalogs. Formerly called The Printer. 400 employees. SIC 2721, 2741. Founded in 1985. Subsidiary of Banta Corp. (NYSE: BN), Menasha, Wis.

Banta Digital—Minneapolis 18790 W. 78th St., Chanhassen, MN 55317. Tel: 952/937-5005; Fax: 952/937-5034; Web site: http://www.banta.com/digital/overview. David Peterson, Gen. Mgr.; Scott Rosenlund, Bus. Devel. Mgr.; Preston Walklet, Pres.; Len Sands, Sls. Mgr. Annual revenue $16 million. Banta Digital—Minneapolis provides complete graphic arts pre-press services, both electronic and conventional. It is one of six operating units in the $50 million-revenue Banta Digital Group, which has evolved into multimedia, electronic printing, digital photography, creative design services, digital transmission networking, database creation, and customized media packages in preparation for the time when there will be less printed material. 100 employees (in Minnesota). SIC 2796. Founded in 1990. Subsidiary of Banta Corp. (NYSE: BN), Menasha, Wis.

Banta Direct Marketing Group 18780 W. 78th St., Chanhassen, MN 55317. Tel: 952/937-9764; Fax: 952/937-6968. Jim Cartwright, Pres.; John Olin, VP and Gen. Mgr. Banta Direct Marketing Group/The Press specializes in full-color printing of folded flat sheeted work; and catalogs, brochures, calendars, folders, inserts, and direct-mail materials on coated stock. It utilizes half- and full-size web presses and half-size sheetfed presses to produce high-quality printed materials. 320 employees (in Minnesota). SIC 2752, 2759. Founded in 1979. Subsidiary of Banta Corp. (NYSE: BN), Menasha, Wis.

Banta Information Services Group 7000 Washington Ave. S., Eden Prairie, MN 55344. Tel: 952/826-3500; Fax: 952/941-2154. Dan Thornton, VP and Gen. Mgr.; Jeff Folk, VP-Op.; Cyd Perszyk, Dir.-Mktg. Banta Information Services Group, formerly Viking Press, specializes in one- and two-color heat-set signature work. It also offers complete binding services, on-demand printing, disk duplication, CD-ROM replication, and complete turnkey packaging services that are used by several Fortune 500 companies. 300 employees (in Minnesota). SIC 2731, 2752, 2759. Founded in 1962. Subsidiary of Banta Corp. (NYSE: BN), Menasha, Wis.

Banta—L.P. 100 Banta Rd., Long Prairie, MN 56347. Tel: 320/732-2121; Fax: 320/732-6345. Mark Deterding, EVP-Mfg. Banta—L.P., formerly Hart Press, prints magazines and catalogs. 625 employees (in Minnesota). SIC 2721, 2752, 2754, 2759. Founded in 1920. Subsidiary of Banta Corp. (NYSE: BN), Menasha, Wis.

Barko Hydraulics LLC One Banks Ave., Superior, WI 54880. Tel: 715/392-5641; Fax: 715/392-3931; Web site: http://www.barko.com. William C. Hanson, Pres.; Dennis P. Healy, VP-Sls./Mktg. Barko Hydraulics manufactures hydraulic knuckle-boom loaders for the forest products, scrap, and waste-management markets. 150 employees. SIC 3531, 3537. Founded in 1946. Owned by Pettibone Corp., Lisle, Ill.

Bay State Milling Company 55 Franklin St., P.O. Box 188 (55987), Winona, MN 55987. Tel: 507/452-1770; Fax: 507/452-1776. Mark Norton, VP-Prod. Bay State Milling produces wheat flour and rye flour. 102 employees (90 in Minnesota; 9 part-time). SIC 2041. Founded in 1899. Division of Bay State Milling Co., Quincy, Mass.

Beckman Coulter Inc. 1000 Lake Hazeltine Dr., Chaska, MN 55318. Tel: 952/448-4848; Fax: 952/448-1664. Debra Baxter, Hum. Res. Mgr.; Mike Ronningen, Mgr.-Quality Assurance; Richard Creager, Dir.-Res./Devel., Site Mgr.; Mike Renard, Dir.-ACCESS Business/Program Mgmt.; Paul Lundeen, Cont.; Keith Ward, Dir.-Mfg.; Colleen Theuerkauf, Mgr.-Info. Sys. Beckman Coulter Inc. manufactures in vitro immunodiagnostic systems for allergies, infectious diseases, immunology, hormones, and serum proteins. Formerly known as Kallestad Diagnostics and, until May 1997, as Sanofi Diagnostics Pasteur. 425 employees (25 part-time). SIC 2835. Founded in 1969. Now owned by Beckman Instruments Inc. (NYSE: BEC), Fullerton, Calif.

Behr Inc. 47920 Fifth St., P.O. Box 10, Canton, SD 57013. Tel: 605/987-2701; Fax: 605/987-2485. Tony Rado, Plant Mgr. Behr, formerly Heat Transfer Corp., manufactures oil coolers, condensers, evaporators, and charged air coolers for the agriculture and truck markets. 250 employees. SIC 3443, 3585, 3629. Founded in 1976. Subsidiary of Behr GmbH, Stuttgart, Germany.

Belae Brands 1000 Valley Park Dr., Shakopee, MN 55379. Tel: 952/496-4700; Fax: 952/496-4703. Richard C. Greig, VP-Op. Support; Gregg Barette, Senior Dir.-Logistics. Belae Brands distributes home fragrances, toiletries, and health care products. Brand names include Vitabath, Women's Personal Care, Claire Burke (home fragrances), and Kid Care (children's toiletries). Company was known as Minnetonka Corp. until acquired by Tsumura International in August 1989. In December 1998 it was sold in a deal reportedly worth $20 million. 225 employees (100 in Minnesota). SIC 2844. Founded in 1964. Owned by Belae Brands Inc., Phoenix.

Benada Aluminum of Minnesota Inc. 415 Royalston Ave. N., Minneapolis, MN 55405. Tel: 612/375-9197; Fax: 612/375-0063. Frank Bomberg, Gen. Mgr. Benada Aluminum of Minnesota manufactures residential storm products, aluminum storm windows, solid-core storm doors, and replacement prime windows. 50 employees. SIC 3442. Founded in 1957. Owned by Friedkin Industries, Boca Raton, Fla.

Benchmark Electronics 4065 Theurer Blvd., Winona, MN 55987. Tel: 507/452-8932; Fax: 507/453-4608. Chris Nawrocki, Pres. and CEO; Paul Deering, CFO; Doug Darbo, Sls./Mktg. Mgr. Benchmark Electronics, formerly EMD Associates Inc., is an electrical and mechanical design engineering firm. A full-service electronics manufacturing services industry (EMSI) provider, the company offers design services, prototype engineering, materials procurement, assembly, and test services. It has experience with printed circuit-board assemblies in leaded, surface mount, fine pitch, COB, MCM-L, and BGA technologies. Its three manufacturing facilities in Winona, Minn., are ISO 9001-certified. 900 employees. SIC 3679. Founded in 1974. EMD agreed in March 1996 to be acquired for $51 million in cash and stock by Benchmark Electronics Inc. (ASE: BHE), Angleton, Texas.

Bepex Corp. 333 Taft St. N.E., Minneapolis, MN 55413. Tel: 612/331-4370; Fax: 612/627-1458. Gordon Ettie, Pres. Bepex manufactures powder-processing systems. 45 employees. SIC 3559. Subsidiary of Hosokawa Micron Corp., Osaka, Japan.

Berkley Risk Administrators Company LLC 920 Second Ave. S., Suite 700, Minneapolis, MN 55402. Tel: 612/376-4200; Fax: 612/376-4299; Web site: http://www.bracontheweb.com. Mark C. Tansey, Pres. and CEO; Kenneth Hopkins, COO; Kim Brenckman, SVP-Sls.; Leland P. Johnson, SVP-Claims; Doug Pfeifer, SVP; Nancy Young, SVP-Info. Sys.; Steve Davis, CFO; Michael Elsenpeter, VP; Patricia J. Fish, VP-Hum.

Res./Admin.; Fred Mauck, VP. Annual revenue $50 million. Berkley Risk Administrators Co.(BRAC) was recently formed by the merger of Berkley Risk Services LLC and Berkley Administrators. BRAC offers a full range of risk management services including underwriting, reinsurance placement, loss control, claims adjusting, and employee benefit third-party administration. Other services include GAAP and financial accounting, regulatory relations and compliance, captive formation and management, program management, and management of self-funded plans and retention pools. BRAC has 40 offices in 17 states. 650 employees (330 in Minnesota; 29 part-time). SIC 6331. Founded in 1973. Owned by W.R. Berkley Corp. (Nasdaq: BKLY), Greenwich, Conn.

Bernafon-Maico Inc. 9675 W. 76th St., Eden Prairie, MN 55344. Tel: 952/941-4200; Fax: 952/903-4200. Peter Van Nest, Pres.; Pete Marcaccini, Cont.; Susan Scott, VP-Sls./Mktg.; Wayne Morris, VP-Prod. Bernafon Maico manufactures and distributes audiometers (hearing test equipment) and custom-designed, computer programmed hearing aids. 75 employees. SIC 3825, 3842. Founded in 1937. Owned by Oticon Holding, Somerset, N.J., a division of Oticon Holding A/S, Denmark. No. 99 CRM Foreign-Owned 100.

Best Inc. 1751 W. County Rd. B, Suite 300, Roseville, MN 55113. Tel: 651/631-9445; Fax: 651/631-9551. William J. Benzick, Chm.; Perry Rynders, Group Pres.; Susan Ayres, VP-Health Care; Patti O'Brien, VP-Mktg./Health Care; Willie Pouncy, VP-Corrections; Jan Degalla/Wright, VP-Campus/Bus. Dining. Best Inc. is in the food-service and vending management and consultation business—serving penal institutions, schools, private industry, medical and long-term care facilities, and residential treatment facilities. The company also caters for groups and special functions. The privately held company was acquired in August 1997. 2,000 employees. SIC 5812, 5962. Founded in 1975. Now owned by Fine Host Corp., Greenwich, Conn.

Beverly Health and Rehab 7100 Northland Circle, Suite 410, Brooklyn Park, MN 55428. Tel: 763/535-6936; Fax: 763/535-7014. Beverly Health and Rehab is the regional headquarters for Beverly's operations in Minnesota, Nebraska, South Dakota, and Wisconsin. The company provides specialized health care services such as those normally found in long-term care facilities. 4,100 employees (1,689 part-time). SIC 8051, 8059. Founded in 1982. Owned by Beverly Enterprises Inc. (NYSE: BEV), Fort Smith, Ark.

Bill Communications—Human Performance Group 50 S. Ninth St., Minneapolis, MN 55402. Tel: 612/333-0471; Fax: 612/333-6526; Web site: http://www.trainingsupersite.com. Bryan Powell, Div. VP. Annual revenue $30 million. Bill Communications, formerly Lakewood Publications, is a leading provider of information products and services in the training and lifelong learning markets. The company publishes Training, Online Learning, Potentials, and Presentations magazines; and Technology for Learning, and Creative Training Techniques newsletters. It also holds five separate learning conferences. 96 employees (in Minnesota; 8 part-time). SIC 2721. Founded in 1960. Acquired in 1995 by Bill Communications Inc., a unit of VNU-USA Inc., New York, which is owned by VNU BV, Haarlem, Netherlands. No. 91 CRM Foreign-Owned 100.

The Billings Gazette 401 N. Broadway, P.O. Box 36300, Billings, MT 59107. Tel: 406/657-1200; Fax: 406/657-1207. G. Bruce Whittenberg, Publisher. The Billings Gazette publishes a daily newspaper. 278 employees (59 part-time). SIC 2711. Founded in 1885. Owned by Lee Enterprises Inc. (NYSE: LEE), Davenport, Iowa.

Bismarck Tribune Company 707 E. Front Ave., Bismarck, ND 58501. Tel: 701/223-2500; Fax: 701/224-1412. Kevin Mowbray, Publisher. Bismarck Tribune publishes a daily and Sunday newspaper with a circulation of more than 31,000. 150 employees. SIC 2711. Founded in 1873. Owned by Lee Enterprises Inc. (NYSE: LEE), Davenport, Iowa.

E.W. Blanch Company 3500 W. 80th St., Bloomington, MN 55431. Tel: 952/886-8000; Fax: 952/886-8001; Web site: http://www.ewb.com. Chris L. Walker, Pres. and COO; Derek Wortman, SVP; Kevin Campion Jr., EVP; Brian Engel, SVP; Linda Johnson, EVP. E.W. Blanch provides customized risk management services to clients worldwide. These services include reinsurance intermediary services, resinsurance risk management services, wholesale insurance services, and international reinsurance services. 293 employees (in Minnesota). SIC 6411. In November 2000, after announcing an expense realignment program under which it planned to divest noncore assets and lower operating costs, the parent began exploring strategic alternatives that could lead to a business combination or sale of the company. Owned by E.W. Blanch Holdings Inc. (NYSE: EWB), Dallas.

Blandin Paper Company 115 S.W. First St., Grand Rapids, MN 55744. Tel: 218/327-6200; Fax: 218/327-6212. Kevin Lyden, Pres. and CEO; Raimo Malkki, SVP-Op.; John Ward, SVP-Tech./Purch./Env.; Edward Zabinski, VP-Org. Devel./Pub. Affairs; John McCoy, Mgr.-Forestry. Blandin Paper manufactures publication grades of lightweight coated printing paper for use in magazines and catalogs. The seventh-largest of 13 U.S. lightweight papermakers, Blandin can produce 500,000 tons of coated paper annually. Blandin Paper is recognized as the forest industry's environmental leader. 900 employees. SIC 2621. Founded in 1901. In November 1999 Blandin sold its steam and electric cogeneration facility to Allete (formerly Minnesota Power), a Duluth, Minn.-based diversified services company. Minnesota Power was to operate the existing facilities, add new boiler equipment to serve Blandin's future steam needs, and continue providing supplemental electric service. "This sale will allow us to concentrate our efforts on serving our customers by making world-class paper," explained CEO Lyden. Now the sole U.S. operation of UPM-Kymmene Corp., Helsinki, Finland. No. 17 CRM Foreign-Owned 100.

Blount Inc. 474 Birch, P.O. Box 199, Prentice, WI 54556. Tel: 715/428-2111; Fax: 715/428-2156. Dennis J. Kolodze, Gen. Op. Mgr. Blount, formerly Omark Industries, manufactures equipment for forest and industrial applications. 300 employees. SIC 3537. Founded in 1945. Owned by Blount International Inc. (NYSE: BLT), Montgomery, Ala.

Bobcat Company D250 E. Beaton Dr., P.O. Box 6000, West Fargo, ND 58078-6000. Tel: 701/241-8700; Fax: 701/241-8704; Web site: http://www.bobcat.com. Charles Hoge, Pres.; Mike Vig, VP-Op.; Carman P. Lynnes, VP and Gen. Mgr.-Attachments; James E. Smith, VP-Quality; Mack Thomas, VP and Gen. Counsel; Greg Schmalz, VP-Hum. Res.; Bruce Collins, VP-Planning; Doug Freitag, VP-Sls./Mktg. Bobcat Company, formerly known as Melroe Company, manufactures Bobcat and brand skid-steer loaders, compact hydraulic excavators, compact track loaders, and dozens of other attachments for the construction, rental, industrial, agricultural, and municipal markets. The company was started by E.G. Melroe in Gwinner, N.D., as an agricultural implement manufacturer. 2,200 employees. SIC 3523, 3531. Founded in 1947. Since 1995 Bobcat Co. has been a business unit of Ingersoll-Rand Co. (NYSE: IR), Woodcliff Lake, N.J.

Boise Cascade Corporation White Paper Division, 400 Second St., International Falls, MN 56649. Tel: 218/285-5011; Fax: 218/285-5210. Miles Hewitt, Regional Mgr.-Minnesota Op. Boise Cascade's White Paper Division supplies pulpwood from the company's 305,000-acre commercial forest, and procures additional wood from other private and public lands. Products include white paper, form bond, and release papers. 1,150 employees. SIC 2611. Founded in 1910. Owned by Boise Cascade Corp. (NYSE: BCC), Boise, Idaho.

Boise Cascade Office Products 7500 Meridian Circle N., Maple Grove, MN 55369. Tel: 763/615-5100. Bruce Moss, Gen. Mgr. Annual revenue $80 million. Boise Cascade is an office supply company that offers computer hardware and software and specializes in furniture design and business incentives. 180 employees (in Minnesota). SIC 5112. Founded in 1992. Owned by Boise Cascade Corp. (NYSE: BCC), Boise, Idaho.

Oscar J. Boldt Construction Company 1001 Tall Pine Ln., P.O. Box 287, Cloquet, MN 55720. Tel: 218/879-1293; Fax: 218/879-5290. Ronald J. Hanson, VP-MN Office (Cloquet). Annual revenue $71 million. Oscar J. Boldt Construction is a general construction contractor specializing in construction management, machinery erection and rigging, Ceco metal buildings, and rental of cranes and equipment. 350 employees (in Minnesota; 110 part-time). SIC 1541, 1542, 1629, 1771, 1791. Founded in 1889. Oct. 4, 2000: Oscar C. Boldt, Chairman, is inducted into the Paper Industry International Hall of Fame in Appleton, WI. Division of Oscar J. Boldt Construction Co., Appleton, Wis.

Boston Scientific SciMed One SciMed Pl., Maple Grove, MN 55311. Tel: 763/494-1700; Fax: 763/494-2540. Michael Berman, Pres.; Mark Stautberg, VP-Sls.; Paul Bucuman, VP-Sls./Mktg. Boston Scientific SciMed, formerly SciMed Life Systems Inc., develops, manufactures, and markets disposable medical devices, principally coronary and peripheral angioplasty products, for nonsurgical treatment of cardiovascular disease. 2,100 employees (in Minnesota). SIC 3841. Founded in 1972. In March 2000 the FDA gave marketing approval for the NIR with SOX over-the-wire coronary stent system for the treatment of coronary artery disease. In July the company's parent announced plans to close two manufacturing facilities in Plymouth, Minn., and move 741 jobs out of the state as part of a company-wide consolidation. SciMed Life Systems was acquired in February 1995 by Boston Scientific Corp. (NYSE: BSX), Natick, Mass.

Bozell Kamstra Butler Square, 100 N. Sixth St., Suite 800A, Minneapolis, MN 55403. Tel: 612/371-7500; Fax: 612/371-5555; Web site: http://www.bozellkamstra.com. Ron Anderson, Chm.; Dean A. Buresh, Pres.; Bill Coontz, Ptnr. and Gen. Mgr.; Jack Stanton, Ptnr. and Dir.-Strategic Planning; Connie McCaffrey, Ptnr. and Dir.-Public Relations; Glen Jacobs, Exec. Creative Dir.; Claire Canavah, VP-Fin./Admin.; David Dasenbrock, Ptnr.-in-charge, Media; Bob Kay, Ptnr. and Creative Dir.; Christine Neff, Dir.-Media. Bozell Kamstra is a business branding marketing communications agency that provides its clients with a full range of integrated services including advertising, public relations, market research, database marketing, interactive communications, and strategic planning. It has offices in Minneapolis; Austin and Dallas, Texas; Boston; Pittsburgh; Ft. Lauderdale, Fla.; and New York. Clients include Deluxe Corp., Hurd Millwork Co., Canon Inc., General Mills Inc., Ceridian Corp., Billy Graham Evangelical Assoc., Dow Styrofoam, Wagner Spray-Tech, and Blue Cross and Blue Shield of Minnesota. 300 employees (65 in Minnesota). SIC 7311. Founded in 1963. In April 2000 Bozell and Origin Communications Inc., Colorado Springs, Colo.—an advertising, public relations, and marketing firm servicing technology and new economy companies, as well as business-to-business and business-to-consumer firms—formed a strategic alliance to work with emerging companies from start-up through the IPO stage and beyond. In August Campbell Mithun landed the $17 million-to-$20 million ad account of Tony's Pizza (Schwan's Sales Enterprises), which had been represented by Bozell for nearly 20 years. The agency started making up for the loss immediately, by winning Blue Cross and Blue Shield of Minnesota's $2 million ad account. In November 1996 Kamstra Communications Inc. agreed to become a unit of Bozell, Jacobs, Kenyon & Eckhardt, New York, which was acquired in December 1997 by True North Communications Inc. (NYSE: TNO), Chicago.

Bozeman Daily Chronicle P.O. Box 1188, Bozeman, MT 59771. Tel: 406/587-4491; Fax: 406/587-7995; Web site: http://www.gomontana.com. Rick Weaver, Publisher. Bozeman Daily Chronicle publishes a daily newspaper. 117 employees (10 part-time). SIC 2711. Founded in 1911. Owned by Pioneer Newspapers, Seattle.

Brach-Brock Confections 1000 W. Fifth St., Winona, MN 55987. Tel: 507/452-3433; Fax: 507/452-2001. OPEN, Gen. Mgr. Brach-Brock Confections manufactures confectioneries. Products include Amazin' Fruit gummi bears, which it produces under a contract manufacturing agreement with Hershey Chocolate USA. A new $7 million high-speed candy production machine was installed in 1993. Formerly Schuler Chocolates Inc. 150 employees (in Minnesota). SIC 2064. Founded in 1907. Owned by Brock Candy Co., Chattanooga, Tenn.

Brainerd Daily Dispatch 506 James St., P.O. Box 974, Brainerd, MN 56401. Tel: 218/829-4705; Fax: 218/829-7735; Web site: http://www.brainerddispatch.com. Terry McCollough, Publisher. Annual revenue $7.4 million. Brainerd Daily Dispatch publishes a daily newspaper with 15,000 circulation, and the Bunyanland Shopper with 13,500 circulation. It also does commercial printing. Owned from 1931-84 by the McCollough family; from 1984-95 by Stauffer Communications Inc., Topeka, Kan. 100 employees (in Minnesota; 49 part-time). SIC 2711. Founded in 1881. Purchased in 1995 by Morris Communications Corp., Augusta, Ga.

Brookfield Properties Inc. 4340 Multifoods Tower, 33 S. Sixth St., Minneapolis, MN 55402. Tel: 612/372-1500; Fax: 612/372-1510; Web site: http://www.brookfield.ca/index2.htm. Harold R. Brandt, Pres.-Midwest U.S. Group; Thomas Clairmont, VP-Op.; Murray Brown, VP-Cont. U.S.; Jeffrey Essen, VP-Office Mktg.; Robin Keyworth, VP-Retail Leasing/Mktg.; Frank Halm, VP and Regional Counsel. Brookfield Properties is involved in development, ownership, and management of prime commercial and retail properties. Among its local interests are City Center, Gaviidae Common, Multifoods Tower, and Dain Rauscher Plaza—all in Minneapolis. Former names include BCE Development Properties Inc., Brookfield LePage Management; and Brookfield Management Services LLC. 150 employees. SIC 6512. Founded in 1986. Owned by Brookfield Properties Corp. (NYSE: BPO.N), Toronto. No. 72 CRM Foreign-Owned 100.

Brown Printing Company 2300 Brown Ave., P.O. Box 1549, Waseca, MN 56093. Tel: 507/835-2410; Fax: 507/835-0238. Dan Nitz, Pres. and CEO; W.V. Guthrie, SVP-Sls./Mktg.; Harry Popiel, VP-Hum. Res.; Thomas G. Williams, VP and Gen. Mgr.-Waseca Div. Brown Printing Co. is a nationally recognized, full-service, high-volume printer serving America's finest magazine, catalog, and retail insert publishers. Brown prints nearly 500 magazine titles for more than 100 publishers, and more than 250 catalogs for direct marketers. Brown operates manufacturing facilities in eight U.S. locations. 1,100 employees (in Minnesota). SIC 2721, 2752. Founded in 1957. Brown is a wholly owned subsidiary of Gruner + Jahr AG & Co., Hamburg, Germany, which is owned by Bertelsmann AG, Gutersloh, Germany. No. 13 CRM Foreign-Owned 100.

Browning-Ferris Industries of Minnesota Inc. 9813 Flying Cloud Dr., Eden Prairie, MN 55347. Tel: 952/941-8394; Fax: 952/946-5266. Edward Bond, District Mgr. Browning-Ferris Industries of Minnesota Inc. provides solid-waste collection and disposal services to commercial, industrial, and residential customers throughout the seven-county Twin Cities metro area. 70 employees. SIC 4953. Founded in 1974. Owned by Browning-Ferris Industries Inc. (NYSE: BFI), Houston.

Buhler Inc. 1100 Xenium Ln. N., P.O. Box 9497 (55440), Plymouth, MN 55441. Tel: 763/847-9900; Fax: 763/540-9246; Web site: http://www.buhlerusa.com. Eric Von Euw, Pres.; Urs Emch, VP and CFO; Mike Hendley, Group VP; Albert Soder, Group VP; Urs Keller, Group VP. Buhler Inc. designs, manufactures, and sells food processing plants, die casting machines, and bulk-conveying equipment. Food industry segments served include milling, pasta, chocolate, brewing, malting, feed, and oils. Buhler also operates a research center, with manufacturing and warehouse facilities, in Minneapolis. 285 employees. SIC 3535, 3542, 3556, 3559, 5084. Founded in 1957. North American headquarters of Buhler International Ltd., Uzwil, Switzerland. No. 51 CRM Foreign-Owned 100.

The Burlington Northern and Santa Fe Railway Company 80 44th Ave. N.E., Columbia Heights, MN 55421. Tel: 763/782-3146; Fax: 763/782-3019. Joseph Spier, Hum. Res. Mgr. The Burlington Northern and Santa Fe Railway Co. is a rail freight transportation company. The company was formerly headquartered in St. Paul. 2,500 employees (in Minnesota). SIC 4011. In April 2000 retired employee William Purdy, a harsh critic of the railroad's safety practices, won the right to publish company salary information that had accidentally fallen into his hands. A U.S. Circuit Court of Appeals panel lifted a stay blocking Purdy from posting about 800 names and salaries (but not Social Security numbers) on his Web site. In July Canadian National Railway Co. (TSE: CNR)(NYSE: CNI) and Burlington Northern Santa Fe Corp. formally scrapped what would have been the largest rail merger in North American history. The boards of the two railroads voted to end an agreement to combine the two companies into one transcontinental system running from Halifax, Nova Scotia, to the Mexican border and to the Alaskan frontier. Executives of the two railroads said that the decision by the Surface Transportation Board to hold up all mergers for 15 months while guidelines were issued made going ahead with the plan too risky. Owned by Burlington Northern Santa Fe (NYSE: BNI), Fort Worth, Texas. No. 72 CRM Employer 100.

Bush Brothers & Company 600 S. Highway St., P.O. Box 384, Augusta, WI 54722. Tel: 715/286-2211; Fax: 715/286-1179. Joe Breid, Plant Mgr. Bush Brothers produces baked beans and other bean products. 100 employees. SIC 2033. Founded in 1908. Division of Bush Brothers & Co., Dandridge (Knoxville), Tenn.

C

CAE Vanguard Inc. 3500 W. 80th St., Suite 100, Bloomington, MN 55431. Tel: 612/896-3915; Fax: 612/896-3913. Glenn Frederick, Pres. CAE Vanguard provides axle supply, rebuilding, and reconditioning services to North American railways. 200 employees. SIC 3462. Subsidiary of CAE Inc., Toronto. No. 64 CRM Foreign-Owned 100.

CB Richard Ellis 7760 France Ave. S., Suite 770, Bloomington, MN 55435. Tel: 952/924-4600; Fax: 952/831-8023; Web site: http://www.cbrichardellis.com. Matt Nicoll, Managing Dir.; Whitney E. Peyton, Senior Managing Dir. CB Richard Ellis provides a full range of commercial real estate services. Transaction Services provides traditional transaction services. Asset Services provides leasing/marketing, physical property management, asset management, and financial management to owners. Corporate Advisory Services provides strategic planning, acquisition, disposition, turnkey build-out, and related services. Facilities Management provides a broad range of site services for corporate clients. The firm also has an office in St. Paul, in the Piper Jaffray Plaza, 651/222-4600; and in downtown Minneapolis, at 901 Marquette Avenue, 612/672-0448. In May 1998 the similar-sized parents of CB Commercial Real Estate Group and Richard Ellis International merged in a deal worth between $100 million and $150 million—creating a combined company of $1.2 billion in revenue on an international platform. 250 employees (in Minnesota). SIC 6531. Founded in 1974. Parent now known as CB Richard Ellis, Los Angeles.

CCL Label 1209 W. Bailey, Sioux Falls, SD 57104. Tel: 605/336-7940; Fax: 605/331-6284. Jim Slichter, Gen. Mgr.; Colleen Stratton, Hum. Res. Annual revenue $60 million. CCL Label manufactures pressure-sensitive labels and commercial printed products. 420 employees (2 in Minnesota; 2 part-time). SIC 2752, 2759. Founded in 1947. Owned by CCL Industries Inc., Willowdale, Ontario.

CF AirFreight 750 S. Plaza Dr., Suite 101, Mendota Heights, MN 55120. Tel: 651/686-0105; Fax: 651/686-0125; Web site: http://www.flightmasters.com. Richard McCrady Sr., Pres.; Richard McCrady Jr., COO; Mike Epperson, EVP. Annual revenue $20 million. CF AirFreight, formerly FirstAir and Flightmasters/Seamasters, is a nonasset-based air freight forwarder with sophisticated technology infrastructure and management expertise in the growing expedited freight sector. 101 employees (65 in Minnesota). SIC 4731. Founded in 1986. In June 2000 one of the country's largest national LTL transportation and logistics providers purchased the company, intending to make it an aggressive player in the forwarding market with a projected revenue run-rate of $50 million by the end of the first year. Now a wholly owned subsidiary of Consolidated Freightways Corp. (Nasdaq: CFWY), Menlo Park, Calif.

CN Imaging 11201 Hampshire Ave. S., Bloomington, MN 55438. Tel: 952/829-5444; Fax: 952/829-7544. Jean R. Stiegemeier, CEO; George Moore, Pres.; Jim Butala, VP-Fin.; J.R. Robert, National Sls. Dir.; Bernd Tischer, VP-Int'l Sls.; John DeHaan, Dir.-Customer Svc.; Paul Norman, Dir.-Engrg. CN Imaging, formerly Lucht Inc., is a leading supplier of printers, lab automation systems, and digital portrait imaging systems for professional photographic labs. Its product line includes package printers, automated film transports, lab automation software, cutting and packaging equipment, portrait cameras, and electronic imaging systems. Sales offices: California, Connecticut, Georgia, Texas, and Washington. Once privately held, the company was acquired by NorthWestern Corp. (NYSE: NOR), Sioux Falls, S.D., in December 1992, then sold again in November 1998. 160 employees. SIC 5043. Founded in 1972. Owned by Sienna Imaging Inc., Englewood, Colo.

CNH Global 3401 First Ave. N., Fargo, ND 58102. Tel: 701/293-4400; Fax: 701/293-4550. Jennifer Shaul, Mgr.-Info. Svs. CNH manufactures and distributes agricultural and industrial tractors. Former names include Case Corp., Steiger Tractor. 700 employees. SIC 3523, 3531, 5083, 6141. Founded in 1969. In July 2000 immediate parent CNH Global announced a global consolidation that was to include the closing, by 2001, of Fargo's Concord plant, which produced air seeders. Owned by the company created by the November 1999 merger of Case Corp. and Amsterdam-based New Holland, CNH Global (NYSE: CNH), Racine, Wis.

CNH Global P.O. Box 249, Benson, MN 56215. Tel: 320/843-3333; Fax: 320/843-2467; Web site: http://www.teamtyler.com. Irvin E. Aal, Pres.; William Luzum, VP-Fin. CNH Global makes fertilizer- and chemical-handling equipment and related equipment, including electronically controlled precision fertilizer- and chemical-placement machines, for agriculture and industry—most notably, the Tyler Flex Air VR. The company also manufactures self-propelled agricultural machines. Its market is predominantly North America, but sales are growing in parts of Europe and Latin America. Formerly known as Tyler Industries Inc., then as Case Tyler. 350 employees (50 part-time). SIC 3523. Founded in 1958. Acquired in March 1998 by the company created by the November 1999 merger of Case Corp. and Amsterdam-based New Holland, CNH Global (NYSE: CNH), Racine, Wis.

CP Softsoap Enterprises Inc. 134 Columbia Court, Chaska, MN 55318. Tel: 952/448-1700; Fax: 952/448-1500. Joe Wipkewics, Gen. Mgr.; Kathy Winkler, Treas. and Cont. CP Softsoap Enterprises manufactures and distributes health and beauty products and household consumer products. 180 employees (in Minnesota). SIC 2841. Founded in 1987. Subsidiary of Colgate-Palmolive Co., New York.

CR Chicago P.O. Box 567, Springfield, SD 57062. Tel: 605/369-2222; Fax: 605/369-5598. Stephen Suttle, Plant Mgr.; Darold Haberman, Facilities Mgr.; Wade Dangler, Product Engrg.; Ted Wechsler, Continuous Improvement Mgr.; C. Waage, Prod. Mgr.; Maxine Namminga, Cont.; Dick Schwartzmyer, Quality Control Mgr.; Natalie Vollmer, Hum. Res. Mgr. CR Industries Springfield Division manufactures fluid sealing devices. 200 employees. SIC 3053. Founded in 1974. CR Industries Inc., Elgin, Ill., owned by SKF Aktiebolaget, Goteborg, Sweden.

CSC Consulting 5500 Wayzata Blvd., Suite 1100, Golden Valley, MN 55416. Tel: 763/593-1122; Fax: 763/593-1135. Steve Chelstrom, Location Mgr.; Tom Pribyl, Practice Mgr.-Health Care/Ins.; Phil Feldman, Practice Mgr.-Mfg./Distrib.; Dave Scouler, Practice Mgr.-Divers. Industr.; Stuart Nelson, Practice Mgr.-Public Sec./Fin. CSC Consulting combines industry expertise with technology capabilities to help clients solve business problems. CSC serves a wide range of industries and state and local governments. The firm provides services in three broad areas: management consulting, system integration, and technology support. Specialized areas of expertise range from business process redesign and information technology transformation to large-scale system integration and custom application development. 180 employees. SIC 7371, 7372, 7373. Founded in 1975. In August 1999 CSC was awarded the Community Builder Award for its work in creating the Management Information Network System for the Minneapolis Community Development Agency (MCDA). Subsidiary of Computer Sciences Corp. (NYSE: CSC), El Segundo, Calif.

CTC Distribution Direct 6300 Shingle Creek Pkwy., Suite 600, Brooklyn Center, MN 55430. Tel: 763/560-6000; Fax: 763/549-5960; Web site: http://www.shipctc.com. John Clark, CEO; Bruce Lohn, COO. CTC Distribution Direct manages, transports, and arranges the delivery of parcels from catalog retailers and other direct-marketers to the residences of individual consumers throughout the United States. It has offices in Wisconsin, Virginia, Pennsylvania, Arizona, Colorado, Tennessee, and Connecticut. A joint venture with USCO Distribution Services Inc. enables shippers of small parcels to benefit from CTC's parcel consolidation and zone skipping and from USCO's order fulfillment and product inventory storage. 1,100 employees (200 in Minnesota). SIC 4731. Founded in 1982. In February 2000 the company was acquired by the nation's leadingdistributor of catalogs, magazines, books, and direct mail. The resulting enterprise, with $800 million in gross sales, was to help catalogers, e-retailers, publishers and direct marketers deliver their products on time and more efficiently. Owned by R.R. Donnelley Logistics Services (http://www.donnelleylogistics.com), a business unit of R.R. Donnelley & Sons Co. (NYSE: DNY), Chicago.

Campbell Mithun Piper Jaffray Tower, 222 Ninth St. S., Minneapolis, MN 55402. Tel: 612/347-1000; Fax: 612/347-1515. William D. Dunlap, Chm.; David Tree, VChm.; Howard Liszt, CEO; Les Mouser, Pres. and COO; Peter Bach, CFO; Karen Christine (K.C.) Foley, EVP and Dir.-Hum. Res.; John Hurst, EVP and Chief Creative Ofcr.; Don Kvam, EVP, Mgmt. Supv.-Packaged Goods/Special; Ginny Vonckx, EVP, Mgmt. Supv.-Retail 2000; Steve Wehrenberg, EVP, Mgmt. Supv.-Technology/Services; Bob Safford, SVP and Dir.-Integrated Mktg. Svs.; Paula Baldwin, VP and Dir.-Pub. Rel.; Lori Marinucci, Dir.-New Business. Annual revenue $100 million (estimated by Fact Book; $960 million in capitalized billings, up 6.2 percent). Campbell Mithun (CM) is the nation's 22nd-largest marketing communications agency and a member of the world's third-largest organization of advertising agencies. CM is composed of three groups—packaged goods and special segments, retail 2000, and technology and services—each with its own account and creative department leaders. CM clients include Andersen Corp., Borden, Celestial Seasonings, Commerce Bancshares, DowBrands, E&J Gallo, Exide, Frigidaire, GMAC-RFC, General Mills, Honeywell, Interstate Bakeries Corp., Kimberly-Clark, Lamaur, Land O'Lakes, Novartis, Ocean Spray, Overhead Door, Penske Auto Centers, Pfizer, Recovery Engineering, Tony's Pizza Service, Toro, U.S. Bancorp Piper Jaffray, UnitedHealth Group, ValueVision International Inc., and VHA Inc. Pro bono clients include American Academy of Dermatology, Boys & Girls Club, National Easter Seals Society, and Operation Smile. CM maintains field offices in Troy, Mich. (Detroit); Irvine, Calif.; Seattle, and New York. Subsidiary and specialty operations include Cash Plus Inc., KidCom (a kid-targeted marketing unit), CM Health (a direct-to-consumer health and wellness unit), and CM Integrated Communications Group (CM Interactive & Direct, CM Promotion Marketing, CM Public Relations, and CM Video & Film). 600 employees. SIC 7311. Founded in 1933. In December 1999 Cleveland-based KeyCorp (NYSE: KEY), one of the nation's largest financial services companies, selected Campbell Mithun as agency of record for its national advertising account. In January 2000 CM Health picked up the $15 million account of HoMedics, Commerce Township, Mich.; and became the marketing agency for the National Hockey League's Minnesota Wild, which was preparing for its inaugural season in 2000-2001. In March CM merged with international design consultancy Pedersen Gesk, Minneapolis and Toronto, a leader in brand identity and package development for consumer brands in the food, household, personal-care, pharmaceutical, and automotive industries. In May CM picked up a $10 million account for the Jose Ole line of frozen Mexican foods from Specialty Brands [it would launch its first campaign in October], and advanced to the finals of the $100 million H&R Block account—in reviews conducted by the same agency search consultancy. [CM won the H&R Block account in June.] In June the agency split itself into three groups—packaged goods and special segments, retail 2000, and technology and services—in an effort to diversify its technology client base and maintain the integrity of its traditional packaged goods advertising expertise. The agency also returned to its original Campbell Mithun name after 12 years as Campbell Mithun Esty. CM's Lloyd's Barbeque campaign was named national Outdoor Media Plan of the Year by the Outdoor Advertising Association of America. Verio, a Chicago-based Internet service provider, chose CM to create advertising for its $20 million account. After the hiring of a new CEO, Kmart Corp., Troy, Mich., put its $100 million promotion and brand-positioning account, handled for the past five years by CM, up for review. [CM lost the account in September.] In August CM landed the $17 million-to-$20 million ad account of Tony's Pizza (Schwan's Sales Enterprises), which had been represented by Bozell Kamstra for nearly 20 years. In October, following the U S West-Qwest merger, CM's Cash Plus media placement unit laid off 12 employees. In November Burger King Corp. culled its list of advertising agencies in its agency review to three: Campbell Mithun (Minneapolis), Grey Worldwide (New York), and McCann-Erickson (New York). Each of the three finalists for the $400 million account was asked back for a follow-up presentation before corporate and franchise representatives. CM is owned 25 percent by management; 75 percent by The Interpublic Group of Cos. (NYSE: IPG), New York.

Campbell Soup Company P.O. Box 817, Worthington, MN 56187. Tel: 507/376-3131. J. Patrick McCloud, Plant Mgr. Campbell Soup Co.'s Worthington plant packs heat-processed poultry products, under the Swanson label, and processes poultry for soup. 495 employees. SIC 2015. Founded in 1955. Division of Campbell Soup Co. (NYSE: CPB), Camden, N.J.

Campus Card—ICollege 700 22nd Ave. S., Brookings, SD 57006. Tel: 605/697-6311; Fax: 605/697-6304; Web site: http://www.special-teams.com. Don Drew, Materials Mgr. Campus Card—ICollege offers all-campus, single-card electronic access control and management systems. Its offerings—which integrate online system architecture, industry-standard hardware, and the Novell Network operating system—include campuswide features that accept magnetic stripe, bar code, proximity, and smart card technologies. Applications include activities, card production, copier, debit card access, door access, food/dining services with meal plan and debit account management, kiosk, laundry, retail transaction management, and snack vending. Major markets: colleges and universities, health care, and business and industry. More than a dozen regional AEST offices serve 200 accounts throughout North America. Owned at one time by American Express Co. 49 employees (1 in Minnesota; 6 part-time). SIC 3572, 3577, 7372. Founded in 1985. Now owned by privately held College Enterprises Inc., Canoga Park, Calif.

Canadian Pacific Railway (Soo Line) 501 Marquette Bldg., 501 Marquette Ave., Minneapolis, MN 55402. Tel: 612/347-8000; Fax: 612/347-8350; Web site: http://www.cpr.ca. Fern B. Albers, Corp. Sec.; Terry Bagaus, Area Mgr.-Op.; Cathryn S. Frankenberg, Asst. VP-Labor Rel./Hum. Res. (U.S.); Michael S. Hanson, Area Mgr.-Engrg.; James Johnson, Area Mgr.-Mechanical; Timothy Mulcahy, Legal Svs.; Peter M. McNamee, Asst. VP-U.S. Accounts; John C. Miller, Cont.; Mark Nordling, Dir.-Comm'l Devel.; David P. Simpson, Dir.-Interline Bus. Mgmt. Annual revenue $538 million. Canadian Pacific Railway (CPR), formerly known as Soo Line Railroad Co., operates more than 16,000 miles internationally. Operations in Minnesota and six adjacent states comprise the former Soo Line territory. CPR has extensive administrative, freight, and maintenance facilities in the Twin Cities. Soo Line routes date from the 1850s. 3,000 employees (1,200 in Minnesota). SIC 4011. Founded in 1984. All of the outstanding common stock of the Soo Line is owned by Canadian Pacific Railway, Calgary, Alberta. No. 3 CRM Foreign-Owned 100.

Cannon Equipment Company 15100 Business Pkwy., Rosemount, MN 55006. Tel: 651/322-6300; Fax: 651/322-1756. Ronald L. Rosa, Pres. Cannon Equipment manufactures point-of-purchase displays, distribution and material-handling carts, automated load-handling machinery, and conveying systems. It also has a plant in Cannon Falls, Minn. 450 employees. SIC 3496, 3589. Founded in 1972. Subsidiary of IMI plc, Birmingham, U.K. No. 37 CRM Foreign-Owned 100.

Carleton Corporation 7275 Flying Cloud Dr., Eden Prairie, MN 55344. Tel: 952/238-4000; Fax: 952/238-4028; Web site: http://www.carleton-pureview.com. Robert D. Gordon, Chm., Pres., and CEO; David Batt, EVP-Sls./Bus. Devel.; Alexander F. Collier, VP-Research/Devel.; David M. Haggerty, VP-Professional Svs.; Travis M. Richardson, VP-Mktg.; Steve Timjon, VP and CFO; Eugene E. Waara Jr., VP-Sls. Annual revenue $5.6 million. Carleton Corp. provides customer data-management solutions for customer relationship management and related analytical applications. Carleton PureView enables organizations to integrate and deliver customer data from across the enterprise for use in decision support systems and new front-office applications. PureViewAEs Active Customer Data Management architecture provides the full range of customer data transformation, integration, and cleansing capabilities in an integrated, cost-effective solution. With PureView, organizations benefit by delivering their sales and marketing applications faster with higher-quality customer data. 66 employees. SIC 3577, 7372. Founded in 1979. In November 1999 Carleton announced a definitive merger agreement to be acquired for $2.45 per share ($8.7 million in the aggregate). The deal was completed on Jan. 21, 2000. Wholly owned subsidiary of Oracle Corp., Redwood Shores, Calif.

Carmichael Lynch Spong 800 Hennepin Ave., Minneapolis, MN 55403. Tel: 612/334-6000; Fax: 612/334-6256. Jack Supple, Managing Ptnr., Chm., Chief Creative Ofc; Leland T. Lynch, Managing Ptnr. and CEO; John Colasanti, Managing Ptnr. and Pres.; Charlie Anderson, Managing Ptnr. and CFO; Doug Spong, Managing Ptnr.-CLS Pub. Rel.; Cheryl Jean Claude, Senior Ptnr. and Media Dir.; Tom Gunderson, Senior Ptnr. and Interactive Dir. Annual revenue $32 million (estimated by Fact Book; $225 million in capitalized billings, up 22.9 percent). Carmichael Lynch Spong (CLS) is a full-service, fully integrated advertising agency—the third-largest public relations firm in the Twin Cities. A leader in national consumer and business-to-business advertising, the firm offers advertising, public relations, design, direct marketing, research, and account planning services. Accounts include: Korbel Champagne, Harley-Davidson Motor Co., Volvo GM Heavy Trucks, Norwest Bank, Minnesota Department of Tourism, Normark Corp., Polaris, First Alert, A.T. Cross, and Schwinn Cycling and Fitness. 275 employees. SIC 7311. Founded in 1962. In December 1999 the firm landed the $20 million ezgov.com account, its first online client. Carmichael Lynch Spong PR, a 40-employee business unit that generates $5 million in annual fee income, was named one of five finalists for best mid-size agency of the year by the trade journal PRWeek. In April 2000 American icon A.T. Cross (Amex: ATX), one of the world's leading manufacturers and marketers of high-quality writing instruments since 1846, named Carmichael Lynch as its advertising agency of record. June client acquisitions: Trane division of American Standard (B2B advertising in the air-conditioning industry); BabyCenter.com, a parenting Internet site (print advertising); Capella University, Minneapolis; and ZapMedia, Atlanta-based manufacturer of the Zap Station box that, when connected to a home stereo system, offers access to the Internet, TV, and movies. In August CLS opened an office in Denver, to service its White Wave Inc. (soy products) account and to seek additional business in the area. The company was named one of the Great Places to Work among small to medium-sized employers by CityBusiness newspaper. CLS landed the ad account for guitar manufacturer Gibson USA. In October the firm unveiled a new interactive division to be led by Tom Gunderson. At The Show 2000 in Minneapolis, the agency won Best of Show (for a Harley-Davidson motorcycle print ad) and took home the most awards, a total of 66. Carmichael Lynch Spong was acquired in April 1998 for $30 million by The Interpublic Group of Cos. The Interpublic Group of Cos. (NYSE: IPG), New York.

Caterpillar Paving Products Inc. 9401 85th Ave. N., Brooklyn Park, MN 55445. Tel: 763/425-4100; Fax: 763/493-1304. Richard A. Cooper, Pres.; Richard E. Lueders, CFO. Caterpillar Paving Products manufactures compaction equipment, asphalt pavers, milling machines, reclaimers, and stabilizers for the North American construction industry. Besides its Brooklyn Park plant, the division has other Minnesota facilities in Champlin and New Ulm. 700 employees (in Minnesota). SIC 3531. Founded in 1988. In September 2000 the company laid off 45 New Ulm employees, half of its work force there, due to decreased demand for road paving equipment. Wholly owned subsidiary of Caterpillar Inc. (NYSE: CAT), Peoria, Ill.

Celestica Corp. 3054 37th St. N.W., Rochester, MN 55901. Tel: 507/536-3000; ; Web site: http://www.celestica.com. Gary Moore, Gen. Mgr.-Celestica Rochester. Celestica Corp. provides electronics manufacturing services to industry-leading computer, telecommunications, and networking OEMs (original equipment manufacturers). 700 employees (in Minnesota). SIC 3679. In August 2000 the company contracted to lease a build-to-suit office and manufacturing facility in northwest Rochester that is being constructed by M. A. Mortenson Co., Golden Valley, Minn., a leading design-build contractor. Anticipated to be completed by midyear 2001, the facility will consist of 200,000 square feet of office warehouse and manufacturing space. Owned by Celestica Corp., Toronto. No. 24 CRM Foreign-Owned 100.

The Celotex Corporation 200 S. Main St., L'Anse, MI 49946. Tel: 906/524-6101; Fax: 906/524-6613. C.N. Abbott, Plant Mgr. Celotex manufactures mineral-fiber ceiling tiles. 200 employees (1 in Minnesota). SIC 2952, 3296. Founded in 1959. Owned by Jim Walter Corp., Tampa, Fla.

Centron DPL Company 6455 City West Pkwy., Eden Prairie, MN 55344. Tel: 952/829-2800; Fax: 952/829-2861. Richard (Rick) Soskin, Pres. and CEO; Warren Pillsbury, VP-Mktg./Sls.; Roger Weingarth, VP-Customer Op.; Dale Mahaffy, VP-Fin.; Fred Johnson, VP-Hum. Res. Centron offers products and services (both financial and technical) for building corporate data networks. It offers new and used network equipment; leasing; purchase of used equipment; and network design, installation, and support. Specialties include SNA, local-area, and wide-area network technologies. It has 17 locations in the United States and Canada, and four more in Europe. Minnesota clients include Wells Fargo, G&K Services Inc., and American Express Financial Advisors. 345 employees. SIC 7377. Founded in 1976. Owned by GATX Capital Corp. (NYSE: GMT), San Francisco.

Certainteed Corporation 3303 E. Fourth Ave., Shakopee, MN 55379. Tel: 952/445-6450; Fax: 952/496-3850. Richard Gross, Plant Mgr., Dir.-DS Felt; Shambhu Nath, Felt Mill Supt.; Joseph A. McCue, Regional Sls. Mgr.-Roofing; Roland Doerr, Dry Felt Account Mgr. Certainteed manufactures paper pulp, dry felt, and residential roofing. 350 employees. SIC 2952. Founded in 1973. Certainteed Corp., Valley Forge, Pa., owned by Saint-Gobain Corp., Paris. No. 42 CRM Foreign-Owned 100.

Champion International Corporation 100 E. Sartell St., P.O. Box 338, Sartell, MN 56377. Tel: 320/240-7100; Fax: 320/240-7505. Serge Sorokin, VP and Op. Mgr.; Mike Sullivan, Dir.-Public Affairs; Brian Corrigan, Purch./Prod. Svs. Mgr.; Robert W. Clark, Cont.; Everett O'Neil, SCA Line Mgr.; Mark A. Lombardi, Mfg. Support Mgr.; Jack MacBrayne, Pulp Line Mgr.; Bob Kane, Tech. Mgr.; Randy Dittmann, Coated Line Mgr. Champion International manufactures publication paper for magazines and catalogs at its Sartell facility . 605 employees. SIC 2621. Founded in 1905. In June 2000 the fourth owner of the plant, International Paper Co., made its first visit to Sartell. It assured workers that reducing the work force wasn't an option that it was considering. In February 2000 then-owner Champion International Corp., Stamford, Conn., was acquired by UPM-Kymmene Corp., Helsinki, Finland. No. 30 CRM Foreign-Owned 100.

Champps Entertainment Inc. 153 E. Lake St., Wayzata, MN 55391. Tel: 952/449-4841; Fax: 952/449-4963. K.C. Moylan, SVP-Op. Champps Entertainment is a national chain that owns and operates 24 casual theme restaurant/bars, including three in Minnesota, under the name Champps Americana. Those three are located in Richfield (790 W. 66th St., 612/861-3333); Eden Prairie (8010 Glen Ln., 952/942-3331); and Minnetonka (1641 Plymouth Rd., 952/546-3333). Champps also has restaurants in operation through franchise relationships, including seven more in the Twin Cities-area and one in Sioux Falls, S.D. The restaurants feature large portions of burgers, pasta, salads, sandwiches, ribs, pizzas, seafood, chicken, and a variety of other dishes, while providing entertainment options including music and large-screen televisions. Once locally based and publicly traded. 420 employees (in Minnesota). SIC 5812, 5813. Founded in 1990. In June 2000 parent Champps Entertainment acquired two franchised Champps Americana restaurants, in Minnetonka ($6.65 million in revenue), and Eden Prairie ($6.55 million), that had been owned or controlled by Dean Vlahos, a former executive and director of the company. The purchase price for each of the restaurants was $5,675,000. Champps Entertainment Inc., Englewood, Colo., is owned by Compass Group plc, Chertsey, Surrey, U.K. No. 39 CRM Foreign-Owned 100.

Chart Applied Technologies 3505 County Rd. 42 W., Burnsville, MN 55306. Tel: 952/882-5000; Fax: 952/882-5172; Web site: http://www.mve-inc.com. John M. Kucharik, Pres. and CEO; Donald P. Anderson, SVP-Sls./Mktg.; John J. Pint Jr., SVP-Special Projects; Spencer B. Kempf, VP-Sourcing; Paul L. Plooster, VP and Gen. Mgr.-Restaurant/Bulk Oil; Phil D. Preuninger, VP and Gen. Mgr.-CAIRE; Lewis Shender, VP and Gen. Counsel; Ron J. Stark, VP-Int'l. Chart Applied Technologies, formerly MVE (Minnesota Valley Engineering), manufactures vacuum-insulated containment vessels and equipment for storing, transporting, and using cryogenic liquids. These engineered products serve worldwide customers in the industrial gas, restaurant, medical, agricultural, and liquid natural gas alternative fuel industries. Chart's products include a wide range of standard cryogenic storage tanks, specialty tanks, transportation equipment, medical respiratory products (including liquid oxygen systems), equipment for producing carbonated beverages, and equipment used to store and transport biological matter and other temperature-sensitive substances. Its plants operate in Burnsville and New Prague, Minn.; in Georgia; and internationally in Australia, the Czech Republic, and China. Chart is one of five companies in the world that are licensed to build machines for DryWash cleaning, an environmentally friendly process for the dry-cleaning industry. Pursuant to its April 1999 acquisition, for $245.2 million in cash, MVE changed its name to Chart Applied Technologies. 1,500 employees. SIC 3443, 3559, 3821, 3841. Founded in 1963. In May 2000 Applied Technologies agreed to design and produce a new liquid natural gas (LNG) fueling station to be built for the city of San Diego by Applied LNG Technologies (ALT), a privately held company headquartered in Amarillo, Texas. The station was initially to supply LNG to 60 LNG-powered refuse trucks and eventually be expanded in capacity to support a three-times-larger fleet. VP Barr said, "By eliminating dangerous emissions from diesel fuel, Chart is helping the city of San Diego improve their air quality." Now owned by Chart Industries Inc. (NYSE: CTI), Eastlake, Ohio.

Chemrex Inc. 889 S. Valley Park Dr., Shakopee, MN 55372. Tel: 952/496-6000; Fax: 952/496-6062. Reinhard Rutz, Pres. and CEO; Jim Hansen, CFO. Chemrex manufactures specialty chemical products for the construction industry. Formerly Rexnord Chemical Products. 700 employees. SIC 2891, 2899. Founded in 1966. Now a subsidiary of SKW Alloys Inc., Niagara Falls, N.Y.; a subsidiary of SKW Trostberg A.G., Trostberg, Germany. No. 24 CRM Foreign-Owned 100.

Chiquita Processed Foods 150 W. First St., New Richmond, WI 54017. Tel: 715/246-2241; Fax: 715/243-7330. Fritz C. Friday, Chm. and CEO; Roger E. Wert, Pres. and COO. Chiquita Processed Foods processes vegetables in eight plants in Wisconsin. It also participates in a vegetable canning joint venture in China. In October 1997 Friday Canning's parent announced that recent acquisitions Owatonna Canning (see separate entry), Stokely USA Inc., and American Fine Foods would be combined with Friday Canning to create a $400 million business. 500 employees. SIC 2033. Founded in 1925. Owned by Chiquita Brands International Inc. (NYSE: CQB), Cincinnati.

Chubb Group of Insurance Companies 200 S. Sixth St., 1000 Pillsbury Center, Minneapolis, MN 55402. Tel: 612/373-7300; Fax: 612/373-7436; Web site: http://www.chubb.com. Lee Topps, VP. Chubb Group is a multinational provider of personal and commercial insurance products worldwide. Chubb operates through independent agents and brokers supported by over 100 field offices around the world. Formerly the Great Northern Insurance Co. 80 employees. SIC 6331, 6411. Founded in 1960. Owned by Chubb & Son Inc.; subsidiary of The Chubb Corp. (NYSE: CB), Warren, N.J.

CIGNA Behavioral Health 11095 Viking Dr., Suite 350, Eden Prairie, MN 55344. Tel: 952/996-2000; Fax: 952/996-2579. Keith Dixon, Ph.D., Pres. and CEO; Susan Feltus, Legal Counsel; Alan Goodell Holmes, Dir.-National Care Center; Ann McClanathan, EVP and Chief Mktg. Ofcr.; Zachary Meyer, SVP-Employer Svs. Div.; Steve Osterkamp, VP-Sls./Mktg.; Tom Rogstad, VP-Info. Sys.; Vicki Rothenberger, Ph.D., SVP-Health Plan Svs. Div.; David Whitehouse, VP-Corp. Medical Dir.; Chuie Yuen, M.D., Nat'l Medical Dir. CIGNA Behavioral Health is a managed health care company specializing in mental health, substance abuse services, and employee assistance programs. Formerly MCC Behavioral Care. 450 employees. SIC 8093. Founded in 1974. In August 2000 CIGNA Behavioral Health announced plans to introduce a new e-commerce tool that allows behavioral health providers to submit claims over the Internet without using a clearinghouse or purchasing an expensive computer-billing package. In September a CIGNA Behavioral Health Small Company Product that offers Work/Life and Employee Assistance Program (EAP) services to employers with fewer than 200 workers was introduced. The services help employees manage a wide range of issues, such as childcare and eldercare, personal and legal problems, or issues related to work or family. Purchased in January 1989 by CIGNA Corp. (NYSE: CI), Philadelphia.

CIGNA Health Care 1155 Centre Pointe Dr., Suite 1, Mendota Heights, MN 55120. Tel: 651/454-7500. Bobijean Quinlan, Regional Claim Dir./Office Mgr. CIGNA Health Care offers insurance services. 110 employees. SIC 6411. Subsidiary of CIGNA Corp. (NYSE: CI), Philadelphia.

Cinch NuLine 8821 Science Center Dr., New Hope, MN 55428. Tel: 763/537-1010; Fax: 763/537-9614. Jim Abraham, Op. Mgr. Cinch NuLine is a machining support center for the Cinch Connector Divisions. 73 employees. SIC 3643, 3679. Founded in 1956. Owned through Labinal Components and Systems Inc., Lombard, Ill., by Labinal S.A., Montigny-le-Bretonneux, France.

Citizens Communications Company of Minnesota 2378 Wilshire Blvd., Mound, MN 55364. Tel: 952/491-5564; Fax: 952/491-5560. Richard M. Shelton, VP and Gen. Mgr.-MN; John J. Lass, VP and Gen. Mgr.-Central Region. Citizens Utilities Co. of Minnesota provides telecommunications products and services to 128,000 customers in 115 Minnesota communities. In May 1999 GTE Corp., awaiting approval of a $65.1 billion merger with Bell Atlantic Corp., agreed to sell all of its 137,000 Minnesota lines to Citizens Utilities Co. 150 employees (in Minnesota). SIC 4813. Founded in 1968. Now owned by Citizens Communications, Stamford, Conn.

City Pages Inc. 401 N. Third St., Suite 550, Minneapolis, MN 55401. Tel: 612/375-1015; Fax: 612/372-3737; Web site: http://www.citypages.com. Mark Bartel, Publisher; Tom Finkel, Editor; Beth Hawkins, Managing Editor. Annual revenue $9 million. City Pages is a weekly alternative newspaper. 62 employees (61 in Minnesota). SIC 2711. Founded in 1979. In January 2000, after three years of ownership, Stern Publishing, New York, sold its newspaper holdings. Leading equity partner in the deal: New York and San Francisco money management firm Weiss, Peck & Greer. Now part of a stable of alternative newspapers run by new company Village Voice Media Inc., New York.

Clariant Masterbatches Division 9101 International Pkwy., New Hope, MN 55428. Tel: 763/535-4511; Fax: 763/535-0822. Steve Snow, Site Mgr. Clariant Masterbatches, formerly ReedSpectrum, specializes in color and additive concentrates for all engineered thermoplastic applications. Formerly known as Charles B. Edwards & Co. Inc.; more recently as Spectrum Colors Inc. 90 employees. SIC 3087. Founded in 1948. Owned by Clariant Corp., Charlotte, N.C.; a division of Clariant International Ltd., Muttenz, Switzerland. No. 94 CRM Foreign-Owned 100.

Clear Channel 7900 Xerxes Ave. S., Suite 102, Bloomington, MN 55431. Tel: 952/820-4200; Fax: 952/820-4269. Mick Anselmo, EVP-Minneapolis; Dan Seeman, Dir.-Mktg., Twin Cities and Mgr.-KQQL; Scott Fransen, SVP-Sls.; Scott Fransen, Dir.-Sls. and Mgr.-KTCZ; Dan Seeman, SVP-Mktg./Op.; Shelly Malecha Wilkes, Sls. Mgr. and Mgr.-WRQC. Clear Channel, formerly Chancellor Media Corp., owns and operates two AM and five FM radio stations in the Twin Cities market—including KFAN-AM (sports radio), KFXN-AM, KEEY-FM (K102), KDWB-FM, KTCZ-FM, WLOL-FM, and KQQL-FM (oldies). The stations have a combined 30 percent of listenership. 258 employees. SIC 4832. Founded in 1968. Owned by AMFM Inc. (NYSE: AFM), Dallas.

Cloplay Building Products 320 10th Ave. N., Baldwin, WI 54002. Tel: 715/684-3223; Fax: 715/684-7230. Mike Kurkland, Plant Mgr. Clopay Building Products manufactures overhead garage doors of all types. 371 employees. SIC 2431. Acquired by Clopay Corp., Cincinnati, a subsidiary of Griffon Corp. (NYSE: GFF), Jericho, N.Y.

Coldwell Banker Burnet 7550 France Ave. S., Suite 300, Edina, MN 55435. Tel: 952/844-6400; Fax: 952/844-6444; Web site: http://www.burnet.com. Ralph W. Burnet, Chm. and Pres.-NRT Title; Joe Reis Jr., CEO; Robin Peterson, Pres.; Bradley Bixby, CFO; Nancy Seabold, Pres.-Burnet Title; Mary Baymler, Pres.-Burnet Home Loans; Leonard MacKinnon, VP-Mktg./Corp. Communications; Tom Rehman, VP-Sls. Admin.; Monty Smith, Pres.-Burnet Relocation; Doug Ayers, Pres.-Prudential Burnet Realty; Mike Shogren, VP-Corp. Devel.; Cheryl Brady, VP-Burnet Insurance; David Carter, VP and Regional Sls. Mgr.; Al Iverson, VP and Regional Sls. Mgr.; Donald Maietta, VP and Regional Sls. Mgr.; Peter Rizzo, VP and Regional Sls. Mgr.; Matthew Baker, VP and Sls. Mgr.; Susan Balestri, VP-Info. Tech.; Gary Meier, Cont. Coldwell Banker Burnet operates a 67-office real estate company that is Minnesota's largest. Burnet also provides title insurance, abstract updating, real estate closing, and commercial and new construction title services through Burnet Title; mortgage lending services through Burnet Home Loans, a joint venture of Burnet and TCF Bank; corporate relocation services through Burnet Relocation Management; insurance through Burnet Insurance; residential property management services through Burnet Property Management; and home repair and manintenance through Burnet Home Care. In February 1998 co-owners Ralph Burnet and Dar Reedy sold Burnet to national real estate franchisor Cendant Corp. (Coldwell Banker, Century 21, ERA). 3,875 employees. SIC 6531. Founded in 1973. In 1999 Burnet closed 32,375 transaction sides, the most of any realtor in the metro area. (Edina Realty, with 31,377, was a close second.) In March 2000 the Minneapolis Lakes office was awarded Coldwell Banker's Number One Office in Closed Revenue Units (home sales) for 1999, besting 23,000 other offices in 23 countries by closing 2,641 real estate transactions. Owned by Cendant joint venture NRT Inc., Parsippany, N.J.

Cole Sewell Corporation 2288 University Ave. W., St. Paul, MN 55114. Tel: 651/605-4600. James Booy, Pres.; Dave Wamre, VP-Mfg.; John Greening, VP-Sls.; Louis Floden, VP-Fin.; Betsy Lumbard, VP-Purch. Cole Sewell manufactures aluminum doors and windows. The family-owned business agreed in November 1997 to a merger. 300 employees (45 in Minnesota). SIC 3442. Founded in 1923. Now owned by Pella Corp., Pella, Iowa.

Coleman Powermate Compressors 118 W. Rock St., P.O. Box 206, Springfield, MN 56087. Tel: 507/723-6211; Fax: 507/723-5013. David Stearns, Pres. Coleman Powermate Compressors makes air compressors and related accessories. Formerly Sanborn Manufacturing Co., until acquired in 1994. 340 employees. SIC 3563. Founded in 1963. Coleman Powermate Inc., Omaha, Neb., reports to the Coleman Co. Inc., Golden, Colo., which is ultimately owned by MacAndrews & Forbes Holdings Inc., New York.

Colle & McVoy Inc. 8500 Normandale Lake Blvd., Suite 2400, Bloomington, MN 55437. Tel: 952/897-7500; Fax: 952/897-7583; Web site: http://www.collemcvoy.com. Jim Bergeson, CEO; Phil Johnson, Pres.; Jon Anderson, EVP; Jim Heinz, EVP; John Jarvis, SVP and Chief Creative Officer. Annual revenue $28 million (estimated by Fact Book; $192.1 million in capitalized billings, up 31.9 percent). Colle & McVoy (CMI) is an integrated marketing communications firm offering services that include advertising, public relations, direct marketing, creative, media analysis and purchase, market research, and sales promotion. CMI is a partner firm in the International Federation of Advertising Agencies. Major clients: DeKalb Genetics, Pfizer Animal Health, 3M, Caterpillar, Novartis, Winnebago, Associated Banks, LaCrosse Footwear, and Weather Shield Windows & Doors. In March 1999 the firm merged with MDC—which paid $19 million for an 80 percent interest in CMI, with CMI management owning the remaining 20 percent 312 employees (in Minnesota). SIC 7311. Founded in 1935. In August 2000 the firm acquired $8.5 million-revenue, 35-employee Mackenzie Marketing, Minneapolis, which specializes in strategic marketing solutions for Fortune 500 companies such as American Express and Chase Manhattan. In September webADTV.com Inc., a subsidiary of iNTELEFILM Corp. (Nasdaq:FILM), announced that iNTELESource.org, the premiere digital video archiving and retrieval service designed specifically for global advertising agencies, had entered into an agreement with Colle & McVoy. CMI bought five-employee Minneapolis shop Sandcastle Group, known for its expertise in mature-markets advertising. The deal added American Express Retirement Services, Medica, the Minnesota Department of Health and the recently landed SAGEport.com, a senior-friendly Internet service provider, to its roster. Majority-owned by MDC Communications Corp. (Nasdaq: MDCA), Toronto. No. 47 CRM Foreign-Owned 100.

Colorhouse Inc. 13010 County Rd. 6, Plymouth, MN 55441. Tel: 763/553-0100; Fax: 763/550-3600; Web site: http://www.colorhouse.com. William Klocke, Pres. Annual revenue $22 million. Colorhouse is a client-focused, leading-edge company of graphics professionals. The largest full-service prepress company in the Minneapolis area, it offers the following pre-press and digital services: scanning, color separations, packaging, offset printing, data storage and retrieval, image retouching, electronic page assembly, proofing, flexo platemaking, and electronic file transfer. 140 employees. SIC 2752. Founded in 1965. Acquired in February 1999 by Mail-Well Inc. (NYSE: MWL), Englewood, Colo.

Columbia Forest Products 606 Wilderness Dr., Mellen, WI 54546. Tel: 715/274-2311; Fax: 715/274-2433. Larry Carlson, Plant Mgr. Columbia Forest Products' Mellen operations produce veneer. 250 employees. SIC 2435. Division of Columbia Forest Products, Portland, Ore.

Columbia Gear Corporation P.O. Box 1000, Avon, MN 56310. Tel: 320/356-7301; Fax: 320/356-2131. Dana Lynch, Pres. Columbia Gear Corp. manufactures gears and related power-transmission components. 270 employees (265 in Minnesota). SIC 3566. Founded in 1954. Owned by Vesper Corp., Bala Cynwyd, Pa.

Comdisco Network Services 5468 Feltl Rd., Minnetonka, MN 55343. Tel: 952/931-9966; Fax: 952/931-9965; Web site: http://www.netforcemti.com. Jerry L. Ford, VP and COO. Comdisco Network Services is a professional computer network services firm committed to building and maintaining networks to meet business objectives. Its full range of products and services assess, design, implement, and manage enterprise-wide area networks for clients nationally and internationally. The company has offices in Chicago; Cleveland; Washington, D.C.; and Des Moines, Iowa. Former names: MTI Group International Inc.; NetforceMTI. 85 employees. SIC 7373. Founded in 1990. Acquired in October 1995 by Comdisco Inc. (NYSE: CDO), Rosemont, Ill.

Commercial Intertech 1532 93rd Ln. N.E., P.O. Box 49220, Blaine, MN 55434. Tel: 763/780-2550; Fax: 763/780-2565. Paul Johnson, Gen. Mgr. Commercial Intertech's Blaine operations, formerly Cylinder City, manufacture, repair, and service hydraulic cylinders. 100 employees. SIC 3593. Owned by Commercial Intertech Corp. (NYSE: TEC), Youngstown, Ohio.

Commercial Intertech Oildyne 5520 N. Highway 161, New Hope, MN 55428. Tel: 763/533-1600; Fax: 763/535-6483. Van Manusco, Pres. Commercial Intertech Oildyne manufactures hydraulic pumps, pressure switches, and power units. 250 employees. SIC 3494, 3561, 3599. Founded in 1971. Owned by Commercial Intertech Corp. (NYSE: TEC), Youngstown, Ohio.

The Company Store Inc. 455 Park Plaza Dr., La Crosse, WI 54601. Tel: 608/785-1400; Fax: 608/791-5790. Jeff Potts, Pres.; Pat Kelly, VP-Customer Satisfaction. The Company Store manufactures down comforters, pillows, all-cotton bedroom accessories, and down outerwear—selling primarily through mail order. The company also has four retail stores in Wisconsin. 750 employees. SIC 5712, 5719, 5961. Founded in 1911. Parent is catalog company Hanover Direct Inc. (ASE: HNV), Weehawken, N.J.

Compuware Corporation 3600 W. 80th St., Suite 400, Bloomington, MN 55431. Tel: 952/896-0700; Fax: 952/835-7890. Andy Trestrail, Branch Mgr. Annual revenue $46 million. Compuware provides computer systems and programming services to users of mainframe, midrange, and personal computers in a variety of industries. Formerly the publicly traded Technalysis Corp. 450 employees (in Minnesota; 25 part-time). SIC 7371, 7374. Founded in 1968. Owned since May 1996 by Compuware Corp. (Nasdaq: CPWR), Farmington Hills, Mich.

Conseco Finance Corporation 1100 Landmark Towers, 345 Saint Peter St., St. Paul, MN 55102. Tel: 651/293-3400; Fax: 651/293-5746; Web site: http://www.gtfc.com. Bruce A. Crittenden, Pres. and CEO; Gregory D. Aplin, EVP and Pres.-Manufactured Housing Div.; Jerry W. Britton, EVP and Pres.-Commercial Lending Div.; Richard G. Evans, EVP; Edward Finn, EVP and CFO; Jack F. Brandom III, SVP-Manufactured Housing; James R. Breakey, SVP and Chief Info. Ofcr.; Barbara J. Didrikson, SVP-Hum. Res.; Joel H. Gottesman, SVP, Gen. Counsel, Sec.; Joseph E. Huguelet III, SVP and Pres.-Green Tree Agency; Phyllis A. Knight, SVP and Treas.; Michael L. Newell, SVP and Pres.-Consumer Fin. Div.; Brent H. Peterson, SVP; Mark A. Shepherd, SVP-Mortgage/Retail Svs.; Jeffrey A. Vanthournout, SVP and Pres.-Equipment Fin. Div.; Scott Young, SVP and Cont.; Lyle D. Zeller, SVP; Gary V. Busch, VP; Timothy J. Bauer, VP; Timothy Coss, VP; John A. Dolphin, VP and Dir.-Investor Rel.; John F. Durnien, VP; Paul C. Erwin, VP; Thomas B. Garfinkel, VP; Carolyn A. Gerhard, VP; Christopher A. Gouskos, VP; James A. Imsdahl, VP; William M. Jones, VP; Alden W. Lange, VP; Barry E. Lawson, VP; Thomas A. Marchetti, VP; George E. McMackin, VP; Larry E. Peacock, VP; James W. Pope, VP; Randy Shannon, VP; Daniel J. Sullivan, VP; Gary L. Wetherholt, VP; Teddy L. White, VP; Kathryn G. Angles, Asst. VP; Cheryl Collins, Asst. VP and Asst. Cont.; David A. Jaroszek, Asst. VP; Charles S. Salmon, Asst. VP; Ruth R. Stiers, Asst. VP; Jeffrey Surratt, Asst. VP; Gary D. Warner, Asst. VP; Todd G. Woodard, Asst. VP; Timothy R. Jacobson, Asst. Treas. Conseco Finance Corp. (the former Green Tree Financial Corp.) originates, pools, sells, and services conditional sales contracts for new and previously owned manufactured homes, home improvements, and consumer and equipment products—marine products, motorcycles, snowmobiles, and recreational trailers (such as horse, boat, and snowmobile trailers). In addition the company services manufactured-home loans originated by other lenders. The company also markets credit life and homeowners insurance to its customers. Conseco aggregates and securitizes its conventional manufactured home, home improvement, and other contracts, and sells the securities through public offerings and private placements. Conseco retains the servicing on all contracts. The company serves all 50 states through 160 locations. In October 1998 insurer Conseco Inc. acquired Green Tree Financial Corp. in a stock swap valued at $6 billion. 7,000 employees (1,200 in Minnesota). SIC 6141, 6162, 6163. Founded in 1975. In December 1999 Conseco Finance decided to forgo a suburban site and consolidate its Twin Cities operations in downtown St. Paul. As a result, 700 metro-area Conseco employees in Bloomington and Eagan, Minn., were to be added to the 1,400 workers already there. Dec. 31: In a fourth-quarter accounting change, the unit stopped reporting its future estimated profits up front and began tallying actual profits. In addition, the parent company slowed the unit's lending in order to gain the favor of debt-rating agencies.

These actions contributed to a 38 percent drop in parent earnings for the quarter, and were expected to lead to even lower 2000 earnings. In March parent Conseco announced that it was exploring the sale of its $46 billion (managed receivables) consumer finance subsidiary, saying "We believe the time is right for Conseco to expand its role as theleading pure play company in the insurance and investment industry focused on middle American consumers." Fitch IBCA revised its ratings on the `BBB+' counterparty and 'F2' commercial paper of Conseco Finance after the announcement. The long-term counterparty rating was lowered to `BBB' and the `F2' commercial paper rating was affirmed (RatingAlert Negative). At April's end, the parent company's CEO and CFO both stepped down and a buyout firm moved to take control. In May Wall Street investment bank Lehman Brothers signed a nonbinding letter of intent to acquire 72 percent of Conseco Finance for $750 million. When that deal fell through, in June, A.M. Best issued 14 separate downgrades on Conseco's insurance units. The parent company hired a new chairman and CEO, Gary Wendt, who said he would consider all options before deciding what to do with Conseco Finance. Analysts were saying that his only option in the prevailing market might be to shut the business down. In July Conseco Finance Corp. subsidiary sold substantially all of its $400 million Bankcard (Visa/Mastercard) portfolio to Wells Fargo Financial Bank, the credit card subsidiary of Norwest Financial, part of Wells Fargo & Co. However, the sale of the entire unit seemed unlikely after the receipt of three separate bids of only $3 billion. (The parent was seeking as much as $4.6 billion.) In another matter, an arbitrator ruled that the company should pay $20.1 million to South Carolina customers for its practice of not telling them that they could choose their own lawyers and insurance companies when getting loans. At month's end, Conseco Finance's parent announced a restructuring plan that was to cut 2,000 jobs, including 400 in the Twin Cities, by the end of the year. Analysts called the move a vote of confidence for the unit. In November the unit reached an agreement with Menard Inc. to renew its private-label credit card program. Privately held Menards, based in Eau Claire, Wis., is the nation's third-largest home center retailer, with 150 stores in the Upper Midwest. Conseco Finance is a subsidiary of Conseco Inc. (NYSE: CNC), Carmel, Ind.

Consolidated Freightways P.O. Box 8, Circle Pines, MN 55014. Tel: 763/780-3801; Fax: 763/780-7354. Michael Bauer, Div. Mgr. Consolidated Freightways is engaged in over-the-road trucking. It has another terminal at 3701 85th Ave. N.E., Blaine, MN 55439 (612/780-3820). 580 employees (528 in Minnesota). SIC 4213. Owned by Consolidated Freightways Corp. (Nasdaq: CFWY), Menlo Park, Calif.

Consolidated Container Corp. 109 27th Ave. N.E., Minneapolis, MN 55418. Tel: 612/781-0923; Fax: 612/781-0967; Web site: http://www.consolidatedcontainer.com. J. Phillip Dworsky, Gen. Mgr.; Jim Heien, Op. Mgr.; Gene Kuppenbender, Sls. Mgr.; Al Stevenson, Purch. Mgr.; Carl Wagleske, Env. Dir. Annual revenue $20 million. Consolidated Container Corp. is a manufacturer, recycler, and distributor of industrial containers for food, chemical, paint, oil, and environmental industries in the Midwest and western United States. It has plants in downtown and northeast Minneapolis, and a factory in Kansas City, Mo. 130 employees (110 in Minnesota). SIC 3089. Founded in 1905. Former parent was PalEx Inc. of Houston, which was acquired by IFCO Systems in March 2000. In March 1998 the company became one of four container-management firms acquired by IFCO Systems (Nasdaq: IFCO), Amsterdam.

Container Graphics Corporation 4841 White Bear Pkwy., White Bear Lake, MN 55110. Tel: 651/653-1400; Fax: 651/653-9951. Robert R. Manning, Gen. Mgr.; Richard Klick, Sls. Mgr. Container Graphics specializes in graphic design for packaging, flexographic platemaking, and steel rule die making. 90 employees. SIC 3544. Founded in 1959. Owned by Container Graphics Corp., Cary, N.C.

Conwed Plastics 2810 Weeks Ave. S.E., Minneapolis, MN 55414. Tel: 612/623-1700; Fax: 612/623-2501; Web site: http://www.conwedplastics.com. J.H. Rosenberger, Pres.; Gordon Riddles, VP-Global Sls.; Gabriel Cuellar, VP-Global Mktg./Product Devel.; Chris Hatzenbuhler, CFO; Kathleen McCarthy, Hum. Res. Mgr. Conwed Plastics manufactures and markets lightweight specialty netting. Conwed supplies a broad range of extruded, oriented, and cross-laid scrim netting—as well as open-mesh rigid tubes—that improve the performance of its customers' products in the agricultural, construction, home furnishings, packaging, industrial, and other markets around the world. It has manufacturing facilities in Minneapolis and in Athens, Ga.; and a converting, distribution, and sales facility in Belgium. 350 employees (200 in Minnesota). SIC 3089. Founded in 1966. In September 2000 the company announced that, for the second time in three years, it was expanding its production facilities to meet the growing demand for its netting products. The new 90,000-square-foot manufacturing plant was to be built in Genk, Belgium. Owned by Leucadia National Corp. (NYSE: LUK), New York.

Corporate Express 1233 W. County Rd. E, Arden Hills, MN 55112. Tel: 651/636-2250; Fax: 651/638-8855; Web site: http://www.corporateexpress.com. Richard Toppin, Pres.-MN Div. Annual revenue $128 million. Corporate Express of Arden Hills is a distributor of office products, office furniture, educational products, and related services to midsize to large companies. 430 employees (400 in Minnesota). SIC 5943. Founded in 1851. A subsidiary of Corporate Express Inc., Broomfield, Colo., which was acquired in October 1999 by Buhrmann NV (AEX: BUHR), Amsterdam. No. 38 CRM Foreign-Owned 100.

Corporate Express Document & Print Management 150 W. 81st St., Bloomington, MN 55420. Tel: 952/881-6676; Fax: 952/881-5419. David Gray, Div. Sls. Mgr.; Pete Beal, Div. Plant Mgr. Corporate Express Document & Print Management (CEDPM) manufactures and sells business forms, direct mail, labels, and computer supplies. 85 employees (in Minnesota). SIC 2672, 2759, 2761. Founded in 1958. CEDPM was acquired in 1998 by Corporate Express Inc., Broomfield, Colo., which, in turn, was acquired in October 1999 by Buhrmann NV (AEX: BUHR), Amsterdam. No. 96 CRM Foreign-Owned 100.

Cray Inc. 655 Lone Oak Dr., Eagan, MN 55121. Tel: 651/683-7133; Fax: 651/683-5599. James Rottsolk, Pres. and CEO; Rene Copeland, VP-Sls./Mktg.; Dave Kiefer, VP-Hardware Devel.; Brian Koblenz, VP-Software Devel.; Steve Conway, Dir.-Corp. Communications. Annual revenue $200 million. Cray provides the leading supercomputing tools and services to help solve customers' most challenging problems. The company designs, manufactures, markets, and supports high-performance computing systems used primarily for physical simulation in such disciplines as weather forecasting, aircraft and automotive design, nuclear research, geophysical research, and seismic analysis. 200 employees (in Minnesota). SIC 3571. Founded in 2000. In November 2000 Cray's products were named "Best Supercomputers" for 2000 by the readership of Scientific Computing & Instrumentation magazine. The award recognized the entire family of currently available Cray products, including the Cray SV1 and Cray T3E.systems. Owned by the former Tera Computer, which was renamed Cray Inc., Seattle.

Crenlo Inc. 1600 Fourth Ave. N.W., Rochester, MN 55901. Tel: 507/289-3371; Fax: 507/287-3405. Randy Frederick, Pres.; Gary P. Ellis, VP-Sls./Mktg. Annual revenue $128 million. Crenlo is a manufacturer of frames, cabinets, and components for the computer and telecommunications industries—as well as Emcor electronic enclosures, NEMA electrical enclosures, and vehicle cabs for the agricultural and construction equipment markets. 1,100 employees (in Minnesota). SIC 3499, 3629. Founded in 1951. In June 2000 Crenlo broke ground on a new 236,000 square-foot manuacturing facility in Florence, S.C. to meet the new-business needs in that part of the country. The new facility is expected to be operational in early 2001. Now part of Dover Diversified group, Waukesha, Wis., a unit of Dover Corp. (NYSE: DOV), New York.

Crown Cork & Seal Company Inc. 174 Chestnut St., Mankato, MN 56001. Tel: 507/625-5081; Fax: 507/625-5075. David Pierce, Plant Mgr. Crown Cork & Seal Co., Mankato, manufactures aluminum tops for beer and soft drink cans. Formerly known as Continental Can Co. Inc. 130 employees (in Minnesota). SIC 3411. Founded in 1942. Owned by Crown Cork & Seal Co. Inc. (NYSE: CCK), Philadelphia.

Crown Cork & Seal Company Inc. 1701 Fourth St. N.W., P.O. Box 38, Faribault, MN 55021. Tel: 507/334-3981; Fax: 507/334-5320. Jim Zahn, Plant Mgr. Crown Cork & Seal Co., Faribault, manufactures sanitary cans and aerosol cans. 250 employees. SIC 3411, 3441. Founded in 1968. Division of Crown Cork & Seal Co. Inc. (NYSE: CCK), Philadelphia.

Crown Cork & Seal Company Inc. 8415 220th St. W., Lakeville, MN 55044. Tel: 952/469-5491; Fax: 952/461-3977. Tom Lundin, Plant Mgr. Crown Cork & Seal Co., Lakeville, manufactures aluminum beverage containers. 100 employees (in Minnesota). SIC 3411. Owned by Crown Cork & Seal Co. Inc. (NYSE: CCK), Philadelphia.

Crown Simplimatic 907 S.W. 15th St., Forest Lake, MN 55025. Tel: 651/464-4000; Fax: 651/434-4126. Terry Paul, Gen. Mgr.; Derek Roberts, Product Sls. Mgr. Crown Simplimatic manufactures palletizing and de-palletizing equipment, conveying rinsers, combines, and other equipment for the food, beverage, and other packaging lines. Merged with Simplimatic Engineering Co., Lynchburg, Va., in July 1991. 400 employees (110 in Minnesota). SIC 3559. Founded in 1963. Owned through Simplimatic by Crown Cork & Seal Co. Inc. (NYSE: CCK), Philadelphia.

Culligan Store Solutions 1030 Lone Oak Rd., Suite 110, Eagan, MN 55121. Tel: 651/681-9000; Fax: 651/688-0616; Web site: http://www.culligan.com. Paula M. Nelson, VP-Sls.; Dennis Doheny, Gen. Mgr.; Carl Werner, Cont. Annual revenue $10.9 million. Culligan Store Solutions develops, manufactures, markets, distributes, operates, and services equipment that processes ordinary tap water into high-quality drinking water at the point of sale. The company's principal product line consists of the Culligan Fresh Drinking Water System, a self-serve purification and dispensing system for use in supermarkets and other retail locations. As of June 2000, the company had installed systems in 46 states, Canada, and Mexico. In addition, the company develops and markets a line of reusable plastic containers for sale with its dispensing systems and to other wholesale customers. Once publicly traded as Harmony Brook Inc. Owned since March 1998 by Culligan International Co., a subsidiary of U.S. Filter Corp. In March 1999 U.S. Filter was, in turn, acquired. 57 employees (31 in Minnesota). SIC 3589. Founded in 1989. Now owned by Vivendi, Paris.

Curly's Foods Inc. 5775 Wayzata Blvd., St. Louis Park, MN 55416. Tel: 952/546-3516; Fax: 952/546-3258. Neil Feinberg, Co-founder and Pres. Annual revenue $110 million. Curly's Foods is a producer and distributor of specialty meat products, including pork ribs and roasts. It processes meats at its plant in Sioux City, Iowa, and distributes to restaurants throughout the United States and the Far East. Curly's was sold on June 1, 1997. 370 employees. SIC 2011, 2013. Founded in 1987. Now owned by Smithfield Foods Inc. (Nasdaq: SFDS), Smithfield, Va.

Curtis 1000 Inc. 707 W. County Rd. E, Shoreview, MN 55126. Tel: 651/483-6651; Fax: 651/483-9036. Terry Bergeson, Div. Mgr.; Mark Gorski, Prod. Mgr.; T.W. Bergeson, Admin. Mgr. Curtis 1000 manufactures and distributes business forms, envelopes, and stationery. 182 employees. SIC 2752, 2761. Founded in 1882. Subsidiary of American Business Products Inc. (NYSE: ABP), Atlanta.

Custom Coils Inc. 109 S. Iowa St., P.O. Box 348, Alcester, SD 57001. Tel: 605/934-2460; Fax: 605/934-2440. Irvin Sterner, Pres. Annual revenue $4.6 million. Custom Coils Inc. is a manufacturer of electronic components, including transformers and inductors. 85 employees (6 part-time). SIC 3677. Founded in 1967. Acquired in October 1998. Now a wholly owned subsidiary of James Electronics Inc., Chicago.

Cybex 151 24th Ave. N.W., Owatonna, MN 55060. Tel: 507/455-0217; Fax: 507/455-3446. Fred Mather, Plant Mgr. Cybex designs and manufactures CYBEX biomechanically correct variable-resistance strength and fitness machines for the institutional market. The former Eagle Performance Systems Inc. was acquired in 1983. 380 employees. SIC 3949. Founded in 1978. Owned by Cybex International Inc., Ronconcoma, N.Y.

Cypress Semiconductor Minnesota 2401 E. 86th St., Bloomington, MN 55425. Tel: 952/851-5200; Fax: 952/851-5199. Peter Mitchell, Site Dir.; James Weir, VP-Fin. Cypress Semiconductor is a leader in the design, development, and manufacture of a broad line of high-performance digital integrated circuits that are fabricated using its proprietary 0.8- and 1.2-micron CMOS and BiCMOS technologies. Product offerings include RISC microprocessors and peripherals, PLDs (programmable logic devices), static RAMs (rapid-access memories), PROMs (programmable read-only memories), logic devices, high-speed ECL (emitter-coupled logic) devices, and high-speed multichip modules. 400 employees. SIC 3674. Founded in 1991. In March 2000 Cypress contracted for renovation of its Fab 3 in Bloomington, Minn.—a $150 million conversion from 6-inch wafer processing to 8-inch. At full buildout, the conversion was to increase the wafer output of the site by 70 percent. In August Cypress brought Fab 4C online to help meet the growing demands of the company's customers in the Internet, wide-area networking (WAN), and wireless communications markets. Construction at Cypress's Bloomington facility had been initiated in January 2000 and had produced its first silicon wafers in July 2000. Fab 4C will be ramped to full capacity by late 2001, effectively doubling the total capacity of the Minnesota operation. Owned by Cypress Semiconductor Corp. (NYSE: CY), San Jose, Calif.

Cytec Fiberite Inc. 501 W. Third St., Winona, MN 55987. Tel: 507/454-3611; Fax: 507/452-8195. Melvin Johnson, Business Mgr. Cytec Fiberite manufactures specialty thermoset molding compounds and ablative and carbon/carbon materials. Formerly ICI Fiberite. 300 employees. SIC 2295, 3087. Founded in 1948. Parent company Cytec Industries, West Paterson, N.J., is now owned by Rogers Corp. (Amex: ROG), Rogers, Conn.

DBL Labs Inc. 30840 Joseph St., P.O. Box 280, St. Joseph, MN 56374. Tel: 320/363-7211; Fax: 800/888-9624. Roy Hinkemeyer, VP and Gen. Mgr. Annual revenue $20 million. DBL Labs produces prescription and nonprescription eyewear in plastic, polycarbonate, and glass materials. The company is a wholesale ophthalmic laboratory serving opticians, optometrists, and ophthalmologists. 148 employees (in Minnesota). SIC 3851. Founded in 1979. Owned by Omega Optical, Dallas, a division of Essilor International, Paris. No. 77 CRM Foreign-Owned 100.

DDS Inc. 1700 IDS Center, 80 S. Eighth St., Minneapolis, MN 55402. Tel: 612/332-5200; Fax: 612/332-4539. Kevin Kennefick, CEO. DDS (Dynamic Data Solutions), an SAP Logo Partner, provides computer consulting, training, and change-management services. Much of the company's business comes from educating corporate clients in the use of integrated software products, such as those of German firm SAP. Clients include Eli Lilly, BASF, Owens Corning, and Purina at home; Rolls Royce, LSI Semiconductor, and Petroleas de Venezuela abroad. In December 1997 the company was acquired for an industry-estimated $60 million. 255 employees (100 in Minnesota). SIC 7371. Founded in 1987. Owned by PSINet Consulting Solutions (Nasdaq: MMWW), Ashburn, Va.

D&K Healthcare Resources Inc. 800 N. Third St., Minneapolis, MN 55401. Tel: 612/339-7401; Fax: 612/347-9714; Web site: http://www.dkwd.com. Brian G. Landry, VP and Gen. Mgr. D&K Healthcare Resources is a wholesale distributor of prescription pharmaceuticals, proprietary drugs, health and beauty aids, drug sundries, and some general merchandise—to hospitals, clinics, chain and independent pharmacies, mass merchandisers, and other retail outlets. The company also develops and distributes computerized management systems for the pharmacy and medical professions. A subsidiary, Viking Computer Services, also operates in Minneapolis. 51 employees. SIC 5122, 7372. Founded in 1933. Acquired in March 1995 by Healthcare Resources Inc., now known as D&K Wholesale Drug Inc. (Nasdaq: DKWD), St. Louis.

DaimlerChrysler Corporation 13005 Highway 55, Plymouth, MN 55441. Tel: 763/553-2565; Fax: 763/553-2576. Richard A. Haynes, Mpls. Parts Distrib. Center Mgr.; Steve L. Skallerud, Sls. Zone Mgr. DaimlerChrysler Corp. operates two divisions at its Plymouth office. The Minneapolis Parts Distribution Center is a regional distributor for DaimlerChrysler automotive replacement parts. The DaimlerChrysler Sales and Service Zone Office specializes in vehicle distribution, program management, dealer management customer relations, and warranty work. 130 employees (in Minnesota). SIC 5013. Founded in 1965. Since the November 1998 merger between Chrysler Corp. and Daimler-Benz Aktiengesellschaft, this operation has been owned through DaimlerChrysler Corp., Auburn Hills, Mich., by DaimlerChrysler AG, Stuttgart, Germany. No. 82 CRM Foreign-Owned 100.

Dana Corporation/Gresen Hydraulics Division 600 Hoover St. N.E., Minneapolis, MN 55413. Tel: 612/623-1960; Fax: 612/623-1537. Gregory Kern, Plant Mgr. Dana Corp. manufactures control valves, hydraulic components, hydraulic pumps, filters, and pump gears at its Gresen plant in Minneapolis. In July 1999 parent Dana Corp. announced its intent to sell its worldwide, $135 million-revenue Gresen operations, a solid performer, to focus on core business. 350 employees. SIC 3494, 3561, 3569, 3594. Founded in 1945. Until then, this operation is owned by Dana Corp. (NYSE: DCN), Toledo, Ohio.

Dana Corporation 15905 Highway 55, Plymouth, MN 55447. Tel: 763/559-0989; Fax: 763/559-6215. Joe Sober, Plant Mgr. Dana Corp.'s Plymouth operations manufacture gears and axles for off-road equipment. 300 employees. SIC 3566. Founded in 1955. Division of Dana Corp. (NYSE: DCN), Toledo, Ohio.

W.S. Darley & Company 200 E. Walnut St., P.O. Box 577, Chippewa Falls, WI 54729. Tel: 715/726-2650; Fax: 715/726-2656; Web site: http://www.wsdarley.com. William J. Darley, CEO; Paul Darley, Pres. and COO; Peter Darley, VP and COO; Jeffrey S. Darley, VP and COO. W.S. Darley & Co. is a manufacturer of centrifugal fire pumps and fire apparatus. 135 employees. SIC 3561, 3713. Founded in 1908. Owned by W.S. Darley & Co., Melrose Park, Ill.

Dataforms Inc. 316 Lake Hazeltine Dr., Chaska, MN 55318. Tel: 952/448-7503; Fax: 952/448-3552. Doug Hammerseng, VP-Sls., MN; Randy Gillitzer, Prod. Mgr. Dataforms does business-forms printing, warehousing, and distribution. 53 employees (in Minnesota). SIC 2761. Founded in 1921. Owned by The Reynolds and Reynolds Co. (NYSE: REY), Dayton, Ohio.

Datamyte Division, Rockwell Automation 14960 Minnetonka Industrial Blvd., Minnetonka, MN 55345. Tel: 952/935-7704; Fax: 952/935-0018. Robert Remley, VP and Gen. Mgr. Datamyte manufactures data-collection systems for the improvement of quality and productivity. The company's products include roving hand-held and fixed-station systems for collection of SPC attribute and variable data and for SPC analysis software. 130 employees (125 in Minnesota). SIC 3823. Founded in 1965. Owned by Rockwell, Milwaukee, Wis.

DataWorks 600 S. Highway 169, Suite 2000, St. Louis Park, MN 55426. Tel: 952/544-7077; Fax: 952/544-8253. Robert Brandel, Pres.; Phil Moen, VP-Sls. DataWorks authors, publishes, and markets software business systems for make-to-order job shop and custom manufacturers, and provides software consulting and application assistance. Minneapolis is the company's Vista and Vantage software headquarters. 120 employees. SIC 7372, 7379. Founded in 1974. Owned by DataWorks Corp., San Diego.

Dayco Products 4079 Pepin Ave., Red Wing, MN 55066. Tel: 651/388-0771; Fax: 651/388-8429. Lowell Peterson, Plant Mgr. Dayco manufactures industrial and automotive rubber and power transmission belts, V-belts, and synchronous belts. Formerly known as Pirelli Power Transmission Corp. 250 employees (in Minnesota). SIC 3052, 3061. Acquired in June 1993 by Dayco Products Inc., Miamisburg, Ohio; subsidiary of Mark IV Industries Inc. (NYSE: IV), Amherst, N.Y.

Decision One Corporation 6636 Cedar Ave. S., Richfield, MN 55423. Tel: 612/851-4100; Fax: 612/851-4164. Decision One Corp., formerly Bell Atlantic Business Systems Services, offers independent computer maintenance, workstation, and related services to business. 225 employees. SIC 7378, 7379. Founded in 1990. Acquired in February 1996 by Decision One Corp., Frazer (Philadelphia), Pa.

John Deere Company 2001 W. 94th St., Bloomington, MN 55431. Tel: 952/887-6200; Fax: 952/887-6385. C.T. Sherrill, Sls. Branch Mgr. John Deere Co. distributes farm equipment, parts, and consumer products. 241 employees (145 in Minnesota). SIC 3523. Founded in 1958. Division of Deere & Co. (NYSE: DE), Moline, Ill.

Del Monte Foods USA P.O. Box 407, Sleepy Eye, MN 56085. Tel: 507/794-2151; Fax: 507/794-3335. J.R. Knetsch, Area Mgr. Del Monte processes canned peas and corn. 470 employees (400 part-time). SIC 2033. Founded in 1929. Owned by Del Monte Foods Inc., San Francisco.

Deloitte & Touche LLP 400 One Financial Plaza, 120 S. Sixth St., Minneapolis, MN 55402. Tel: 612/397-4000; Fax: 612/692-4155; Web site: http://www.us.deloitte.com. Jonathan F. Eisele, Office Managing Ptnr. Deloitte & Touche provides assurance and advisory, tax, and management consulting services through 30,000 people in more than 100 U.S. cities. Deloitte & Touche is part of Deloitte Touche Tohmatsu, with more than 90,000 people in over 130 countries. 700 employees (in Minnesota). SIC 8721, 8742. Founded in 1895. In December 1999 Deloitte & Touche was named to Fortune magazine's list of "100 Best Companies to Work For in America" for the third-consecutive year. Owned by Deloitte & Touche, Wilton, Conn.

Deltak LLC 13330 12th Ave. N., P.O. Box 9496 (55440), Plymouth, MN 55441. Tel: 763/544-3371; Fax: 763/544-9353; Web site: http://www.deltak.com. G.J. Obermiller, Pres.; Monte E. Ness, VP-Gas Turbine; Tike C. Wong, VP-Specialty Boiler Sys.; Michael H. Hackner, VP-Fin./Admin.; Kevin J. Zahler, VP-China Op.; Theo Goudsmit, VP-Int'l Bus. Deltak designs, manufactures, and installs steam generation and heat recovery systems for power-generating and industrial customers worldwide. Since its establishment in 1972, Deltak has constructed more than 1,000 individually designed systems for domestic and international markets including waste-to-energy conversion, petrochemical process plants, gas turbine cogeneration and combined-cycle plants, alternative-fuel steam plants, and retrofit and upgraded small to medium-sized power plants. 377 employees (372 in Minnesota; 7 part-time). SIC 3443, 3569. Founded in 1972. Acquired in 1998 by Global Energy Equipment Group, Tulsa, Okla.

Destron Fearing Corporation 490 Villaume Ave., South St. Paul, MN 55075. Tel: 651/455-1621; Fax: 651/455-0413; Web site: http://www.destronfearing.com. Randolph K. Geissler, CEO; Thomas J. Patin, Gen. Counsel; James Santelli, CFO and VP-Op.; William J. Battista, VP-Fearing Div.; Ezequiel M. Mejia, Dir.-Engrg., Chief Tech. Ofcr. Annual revenue $18.5 million (earnings $3.5 million). Destron Fearing Corp. manufactures and markets electronic and visual identification devices for companion animals, livestock, laboratory animals, fish, and wildlife. Destron was incorporated in Canada in 1984 to develop, manufacture, and market a line of meat-grading instruments and meat plant data collection hardware and software. In 1987 Destron acquired the assets of Identification Devices Inc. (IDI), a Colorado manufacturer of radio frequency identification products. In 1988 Destron/IDI divested itself of the meat-grading and data collection products. In November 1993 Destron/IDI acquired Fearing Manufacturing Co. Inc., a manufacturer of visual identification devices. In August 1994 the company's name was changed to Destron Fearing Corp. 65 employees (60 in Minnesota). SIC 3663, 3999. Founded in 1984. In January 2000 the company filed a patent application for a new-generation implantable animal identification microchip with a significantly increased read range. "This is a real breakthrough in our implantable microchip technology," said Zeke Mejia, chief technology officer. "Tests show that in our large antenna scanner applications, such as our fish identification program, the read range increase is as much as 50 percent. We have been able to accomplish this without increasing the size of the microchip that is used in our implantable markets." In February the company entered into a three-year agreement with Triumph Pork Group LLC to become the exclusive supplier of electronic identification devices and information systems for Triumph's groundbreaking project to establish a farm-to-table pork production system involving specific genetic lines and certified production protocols with trace-back capability. Both the patented bar coded Duflex/Infecta-Guard ear tag system and the patented electronic microchip ear tag system (e.Tag) were approved for Canada's National Cattle Identification Program. In March Destron Fearing signed a letter of intent to be acquired by Applied Digital Solutions Inc. (Nasdaq: ADSX), an e-business solutions provider offering Internet, telecom, LAN, and software services to a wide variety of businesses throughout North America. Under the agreement, Destron Fearing would be merged into Digital Angel.net Inc., a subsidiary of Applied Digital Solutions. Destron Fearing's CEO, Randolph K. Geissler, would become CEO of Digital Angel.net Inc. Later in March, the company entered into an agreement with Temple Tag Ltd., the largest feedlot tag company in the United States, to supply Destron's patented electronic ear tag (e.Tag) to the cattle market. Applied Digital shareholders approved the deal on Sept. 5, Destron's on Sept. 8. Digital Angel.net received a follow-up order from Schering-Plough (NYSE: SGP), distributor of Digital Angel.net microchips for the U.S. companion animal market. Destron Fearing is now part of Digital Angel.net Inc., a subsidiary of Applied Digital Solutions Inc. (Nasdaq: ADSX), Palm Beach, Fla.

Detector Electronics Corporation 6901 W. 110th St., Bloomington, MN 55438. Tel: 952/941-5665; Fax: 952/829-8750. Gerald Slocum, Pres.; Jim Vogel, VP-Sls./Mkyg.; Denis Regan, CFO. Annual revenue $50 million. Detector Electronics designs, manufactures, and markets explosion-proof flame, smoke, and gas detection systems primarily for the protection of hazardous industrial processes in the petroleum, petrochemical, and munitions industries. 250 employees. SIC 3822, 3823. Founded in 1973. Acquired in 1988 by Williams plc, Derby, U.K. No. 54 CRM Foreign-Owned 100.

DeZurik 250 Riverside Ave. N., Sartell, MN 56377. Tel: 320/259-2000; Fax: 320/259-2227. John Kokula, VP-Fin.; Wayne Robbins, VP-Mktg./Res./Devel. and acting Pres. DeZurik is a worldwide manufacturer of industrial valves and process-control equipment. 1,000 employees (600 in Minnesota). SIC 3494. Founded in 1925. Was a unit of General Signal until that company was acquired in 1998 by SPX Corp. (NYSE: SPW), Muskegon, Mich.

Diamond Products Company 310 E. Fifth, St. Paul, MN 55101. Tel: 651/292-2900; Fax: 651/292-2909. Ron Peterson, Plant Mgr.; Robert Wood, Hum. Res. Dir. Diamond Products' St. Paul Manufacturing Center fills shampoos, hair sprays, hair rinses, and deodorants with liquids and aerosol. 270 employees (in Minnesota). SIC 2844. Founded in 1970. In March 2000 Boston-based Gillette Co. agreed to sell its White Rain hair-care products line in a deal that included its St. Paul manufacturing center. Acquired in April 2000 by Diamond Products Co., Tampa, Fla.

Diamond Vogel North Inc. 2100 Second St. N., Minneapolis, MN 55411. Tel: 612/521-4707; Fax: 612/521-8386. Randy Porter, Div. Gen. Mgr.; Drew Vogel, Pres. and CEO; Harold Pals, Sec. and Treas. Annual revenue $16 million. Diamond Vogel North (dba Diamond Vogel Paints) specializes in paints and coatings. 73 employees (in Minnesota; 2 part-time). SIC 2851. Founded in 1935. Owned by Vogel, Orange City, Iowa.

DiaSorin Inc. 1990 Industrial Blvd., P.O. Box 285, Stillwater, MN 55082. Tel: 651/439-9710; Fax: 651/351-5919; Web site: http://www.INC-STAR.com. Stephen P. Gouze, Pres. and CEO; Elaine Jacklin, VP and CFO; Keith Bevers, Dir.-Sls.; Gordon McFarlane, Ph.D., Dir.-Res./Devel.; Gary Tremain, Dir.-Mktg. Annual revenue $48 million. DiaSorin manufactures and markets more than 200 products used by hospitals, clinical reference laboratories, and medical researchers worldwide. They include immunodiagnostic products, particularly for bone and mineral metabolism, endrocrinology, infectious, blood virus, proteins, and autoimmune diseases. Once publicly traded as Incstar Corp. 163 employees (90 in Minnesota). SIC 2835, 8071. Founded in 1975. Sold again in October 2000 by then-owner American Standard Inc. (NYSE: ASD), Piscataway, N.J. Now owned by a group led by Snia SpA, Turin, Italy. No. 45 CRM Foreign-Owned 100.

Disetronic Medical Systems Inc. 5201 East River Rd., Suite 312, Fridley, MN 55421. Tel: 763/795-5300; Fax: 763/795-5300; Web site: http://www.disetronic-usa.com. Patrick DeHaes, M.D., Pres. and CEO; Jim Myers, VP; Jeffrey P. Shields, CFO. Annual revenue $36.8 million. Disetronic Medical Systems designs, manufactures, and distributes micro-dose pumps for medical applications. The world leader in insulin pump therapy for the treatment of diabetes, Disetronic is one of the fastest-growing medical device companies in Minnesota. In June 1999 the FDA approved Disetronic's Dahedi 25 insulin pump for sale following successful conclusion of its 510(k) registration process. The Dahedi 25, which was already on sale in Germany and the Netherlands, is two-thirds the size of standard insulin pumps and weighs 20 percent less. 90 employees (48 in Minnesota; 6 part-time). SIC 3841. Founded in 1991. In April 2000 the Disetronic Group received approval for the development of an innovative insulin delivery system with integrated monitoring of blood sugar for diabetics. The goal of the ADICOL project (Advanced Insulin Infusion with a Control Loop) was to develop a kind of artificial pancreas to the prototype stage, so that the daily insulin dosage can be administered practically, automatically, and exactly in the required amounts. In May the company announced U.S. availability of the Dahedi Insulin Pump. A June agreement with Humana Inc. subsidiary Employers Health Insurance Company (EHI) made Disetronic the preferred supplier of insulin pumps to EHI members. In August the company introduced the D-TRON insulin pump, a sophisticated, versatile pump that people can customize to accommodate their own unique insulin needs. In September the Disetronic Group concluded a far-reaching cooperation agreement with U.S. company TheraSense to market and distribute the innovative FreeStyle blood glucose monitor. Under the terms of the agreement, Disetronic was to become the exclusive representative for marketing and distributing FreeStyle in Germany, Scandinavia, Holland, Austria, and Switzerland; and was to market and distribute FreeStyle to its own customers in the United States on a nonexclusive basis. Owned by Disetronic Holding, Burgdorf, Switzerland. No. 94 CRM Foreign-Owned 100.

Doane Pet Care 145 N. First St., P.O. Box 190, Perham, MN 56573. Tel: 218/346-7500; Fax: 218/346-7502. Gary Ebeling, Gen. Mgr. Doane Pet Care manufactures Tuffy's pet foods and Heinz dry cat food and dry dog food. Former company names include Heinz Pet Products and Windy Hill Pet Foods. 250 employees. SIC 2047. Owned by Doane Products Co., Joplin, Mo.

Doboy Division of SIG Pack Inc. 869 S. Knowles Ave., New Richmond, WI 54017. Tel: 715/246-6511; Fax: 715/246-6539. William Heilhecker, Pres.; Julie Foss, CFO; John Bowerman, Dir.-Sls.; Dan Erikstrup, Dir.-Hum. Res.; Merle Greer, Dir.-Customer Svc.; Mark Hanson, Dir.-Op.; John Wedel, Dir.-Engrg. Annual revenue $55 million. Doboy Division designs, engineers, and manufactures packaging machinery for wrapping and sealing products in flexible film materials, with applications in the chemicals, agri-products, candy, auto parts, baked goods, hardware, beverages, frozen food, pharmaceuticals, and other industries. The company has a subsidiary, SIG Pack Eagle Corp., in Oakland, Calif. Raymond Automation and SIG Service Inc. were merged into the former Doboy Packaging Machinery Inc. on Jan. 1, 1996. 403 employees (9 part-time). SIC 3565. Founded in 1940. In May 2000 Doboy selected SolidWorks Corp., a leading provider of affordable, easy-to-use 3D CAD software for the mainstream market, as the standard solid-modeling solution for development of its packaging equipment. Doboy was to use 50 seats of SolidWorks for designing and manufacturing flexible packaging equipment for bag closure, tray forming, and carton closing, as well as horizontal wrapping and feeding. Owned through SIG Holding USA Inc., New Richmond, Wis., by Schweizeriche Industrie-Gesellschaft, or SIG Holding AG, Neuhausen/Rheinfall, Switzerland.

The F. Dohmen Co. 2001 Kennedy St. N.E., Minneapolis, MN 55413. Tel: 612/331-6550; Fax: 612/378-1549. Jeff Rehovsky, Div. VP; Allan Lueck, Accounting Mgr. F. Dohmen, formerly known as Northwestern Drug Company, is a wholesale distributor of pharmaceuticals, health aids, sundries, pharmacy computers with company-developed software and programs, and voluntary buying group Merit Plus. Its merger partner is a pioneer in the area of cost-containment through electronic data interchange among manufacturers, distributors, and marketplace providers of pharmaceuticals. 70 employees (69 in Minnesota). SIC 5122. Founded in 1918. In September 1992 it merged with and became a subsidiary of The F. Dohmen Co., Germantown, Wis.

Duke-Weeks Realty Corporation 1550 Utica Ave. S., Suite 120, St. Louis Park, MN 55416. Tel: 952/543-2900; Fax: 952/542-9297; Web site: http://www.dukereit.com. James Gray, VP and Gen. Mgr.-Mpls.; Robb Johnson, VP and Gen. Mgr.-Mpls. Industrial. Duke-Weeks is the Twin Cities-area office of a fully integrated real estate company that owns interests in a diversified portfolio of office, industrial, and retail properties throughout the United States. A $250 million merger with R.L. Johnson in 1997 gave the company its first local properties. 727 employees (52 in Minnesota; 23 part-time). SIC 6531. Founded in 1972. In December 1999 the company announced its purchase of two office/showroom facilities in the Twin Cities' competitive southwest submarket: 111,245-square-foot Edenvale Executive Center and 52,828-square-foot Valley Gate North, both in the heart of the Golden Triangle of technology business parks. In March 2000 the Twin Cities Industrial business unit was honored by its parent as "sales team of the year" for executing more than 1.9 million square feet in new leases and renewals; constructing more than 807,000 square feet in new development; obtaining more than 968,800 square feet in new acquisitions; and obtaining a 40 percent growth in its Twin Cities asset base. Owned by Duke-Weeks Realty Corp. (NYSE: DRE), Indianapolis.

Duluth, Missabe & Iron Range Railway Company Missabe Building, Duluth, MN 55802. Tel: 218/723-2115; Fax: 218/723-2127. A.N. Ojard, Gen. Mgr.; R.E. Adams, Mgr.-Admin. Duluth, Missabe & Iron Range Railway is a railway company that primarily transports iron ore and taconite. 725 employees (in Minnesota). SIC 4011. Founded in 1884. Owned by Transtar Inc., Monroeville, Pa.

Duluth News-Tribune 424 W. First St., P.O. Box 169000, Duluth, MN 55816. Tel: 218/723-5281; Fax: 218/723-5339; Web site: http://www.duluthnews.com. Mary Jacobus, Pres. and Publisher; David Holwerk, Editor; Merry Wallin, Advertising Dir.; Don Wyatt, Managing Editor; Jerome Ferson, Op. Dir.; Curt Peterson, Circulation Dir.; Alan Scherer, CFO. Annual revenue $26 million. Duluth News-Tribune is publisher of a morning and Sunday newspaper circulating in a 24,900-square-mile area that includes northeastern Minnesota, northwestern Wisconsin, Upper Michigan, and Thunder Bay, Ontario. 305 employees (293 in Minnesota; 65 part-time). SIC 2711. Founded in 1869. Owned by Knight Ridder Inc. (NYSE: KRI), San Jose, Calif.

Duluth, Winnipeg & Pacific Railway Company 3192 S. Pokegama Rd., Superior, WI 54880. Tel: 218/726-9200; Fax: 218/726-9298. Ken Haugen, Supt. Duluth, Winnipeg & Pacific Railway is a transportation company. 175 employees. SIC 4011. Founded in 1909. In July 2000 Canadian National Railway Co. (TSE: CNR)(NYSE: CNI) and Burlington Northern Santa Fe Corp. (NYSE:BNI) formally scrapped what would have been the largest rail merger in North American history. The boards of the two railroads voted to end an agreement to combine the two companies into one transcontinental system running from Halifax, Nova Scotia, to the Mexican border and to the Alaskan frontier. Executives of the two railroads said that the decision by the Surface Transportation Board to hold up all mergers for 15 months while guidelines were issued made going ahead with the plan too risky. Owned by Canadian National Railway Co. (NYSE: CNI), Montreal.

Duro Bag Manufacturing Company P.O. Box 247, 486 County Rd. A, Hudson, WI 54016. Tel: 715/386-9386; Fax: 715/386-6253; Web site: http://www.durobag.com. Paul Frye, Gen. Mgr. Annual revenue $25 million. Duro Bag Manufacturing is a converter of paper bags for grocery stores, retail stores, and food service. 85 employees. SIC 2674. Founded in 1976. Owned by Duro Bag Manufacturing Co., Ludlow, Ky.

EFJohnson Division 438 Gateway Blvd., Burnsville, MN 55337. Tel: 952/882-5500; Fax: 952/882-5656; Web site: http://www.transcrypt.com. Jeff Fuller, CEO; David L. Hattey, SVP and Gen. Mgr.-Design/Sourcing; Ed Osborn, SVP-Mktg.; Eric Baumann, VP-Sls.; Joel Young, VP-Engrg.; Mike Wallace, VP-Op. EFJohnson Division, the third-largest manufacturer of land mobile radios in the United States, designs, manufactures, and markets trunked and conventional radio systems, stationary land mobile radio transmitters/receivers, and mobile and portable radios for public safety, public service, business, and industry. Brand names include Multi-Net radio trunking systems; and Viking, Avenger, and Summit radio products. In July 1997 the former E.F. Johnson Radio Systems was acquired for $25.4 million in cash, stock, and debt. 500 employees. SIC 3663. Founded in 1923. In December 1999 EFJohnson received an order from the Bureau of Land Management for $1.1 million for APCO 25 digital radios and repeaters for use in Colorado, Montana, New Mexico, Nevada, Oregon, and Utah. Clay County, Fla., placed an order with EFJohnson for $1.3 million to provide a microwave system to be used in connection with the public safety radio system currently being installed. In January 2000 EFJohnson's parent announced the sale and leaseback of the Waseca, Minn., facility for $2.75 million. In February parent Transcrypt International formed three new business units at its EF Johnson subsidiary: The new State, Local and Commercial Business Unit was to be focused on marketing, sales, and turnkey delivery of high-level public safety and commercial private wireless communications networks; the new Federal Business Unit was to be focused on sales of EF Johnson's digital APCO Project 25 products to federal agencies; and the new Value Added Services and OEM Business Unit was being formed to consolidate EF Johnson's OEM production services and engineering design and support services. In September the company was awarded a contract by the city of Eden Prairie, Minn., for the upgrade of its municipal radio system. EFJohnson reached a significant milestone with its primary contractor to supply a Conventional Mutual Aid System for Minnesota Metro. The contractor accepted EFJohnson's system after extensive factory acceptance testing at EFJohnson's Operations Center located in Waseca. This initial multimillion-dollar subcontract was a portion of a public safety communications contract expected to be worth as much as $60 million when completed. The system interconnects six agencies in a nine-county area to respond to public safety situations with quicker response times and more efficient direction and use of resources. Now owned by Transcrypt International Inc., Lincoln, Neb.

EPC Loudon 1020 E. Maple, Mora, MN 55051. Tel: 320/679-3232; Fax: 320/679-2323. Bradley Kraft, Pres.; Bruce Grant, Pres.-Customer Sls. EPC Loudon, the former Engineered Polymers Corp., is a custom molder of thermoplastic, injection, and structural foam. 460 employees. SIC 3089. Founded in 1960. Acquired in March 1996 for $87 million by Cookson Specialty Molding Group, Latham, N.Y.; subsidiary of Cookson Group plc, London. No. 35 CRM Foreign-Owned 100.

Earth Tech 3033 Campus Dr., Suite 175, Plymouth, MN 55441. Tel: 763/551-1001; Fax: 763/551-2499. J. Michael Valentine, VP. Annual revenue $7 million. Earth Tech is an environmental services company that specializes in air quality, environmental assessment/investigations, regulatory compliance, industrial hygiene, health/safety, construction management oversight, remediation, and asbestos. 56 employees (in Minnesota; 2 part-time). SIC 8711. Founded in 1979. Owned by Tyco International Ltd. (NYSE: TYC), Exeter, N.H.

Earthgrains Taystee Bread 415 S. Mill St., Fergus Falls, MN 56537. Tel: 218/736-7571; Fax: 218/736-2537. Hugh Warner, Gen. Mgr. Earthgrains Taystee Bread, Fergus Falls, produces and distributes wholesale bakery products. Formerly known as Metz Baking Co. 200 employees. SIC 2051. Founded in 1975. Owned by Earthgrains Taystee Bread, Sioux City, Iowa; an operation of Specialty Foods Corp., Deerfield, Ill.

Earthgrains Taystee Bread 2745 Long Lake Rd., Roseville, MN 55113. Tel: 651/636-8400; Fax: 651/628-5234. Parnell Murphy, Gen. Mgr. and VP-Northern Region. Earthgrains Taystee Bread, Roseville, produces and distributes wholesale bakery products under the Taystee, Di-Italiano, Autumn Grain, Master, and Mickey Cake brand names. It also operates 24 retail outlet stores and restaurants in Minnesota in conjunction with its sister company in Fergus Falls. Formerly known as Metz Baking Co. 600 employees (500 in Minnesota). SIC 2051. Founded in 1926. Owned by Earthgrains Taystee Bread, Sioux City, Iowa; an operation of Specialty Foods Corp., Deerfield, Ill.

Earthgrains Taystee Bread 334 Fifth Ave. S., La Crosse, WI 54601. Tel: 608/782-8488. Bill Adler, Gen. Mgr.; John Truesdell, Cont.; Ken Novak, Sls. Mgr.; Robert Shaw, Prod. Mgr. Earthgrains Taystee Bread, La Crosse, produces crouton products for retail and institutional markets. Formerly known as Metz Baking Co. 85 employees. SIC 2051. Owned by Earthgrains Taystee Bread, Sioux City, Iowa; an operation of Specialty Foods Corp., Deerfield, Ill.

Earthgrains Taystee Bread 2800 E. U.S. Highway 16, P.O. Box 838, Sioux Falls, SD 57101. Tel: 605/336-2035. Bob Haertel, Gen. Mgr.; Jeff Merideth, Gen. Sls. Mgr.; Kevin Neuheisel, Prod. Supt.; Lyle Van Peursem, Cont. Earthgrains Taystee Bread, Sioux Falls, produces and distributes wholesale bakery products. Formerly known as Metz Baking Co. 290 employees. SIC 2051. Founded in 1926. Owned by Earthgrains Taystee Bread, Sioux City, Iowa; an operation of Specialty Foods Corp., Deerfield, Ill.

East Side Beverage Company 1260 Grey Fox Rd., Arden Hills, MN 55112. Tel: 651/482-1133; Fax: 651/482-9810. East Side Beverage is a beverage distributor. It handles the Miller and Miller-owned Leinenkugel brands in the Twin Cities, as well as acting as a major distributor for St. Paul's two remaining breweries, Minnesota Brewing Co. and Summit Brewing Co. SIC 5181. Owned by J.J. Taylor Cos. Inc., Florida.

Eaton Corporation Hydraulics Division, 15151 Highway 5, Eden Prairie, MN 55344. Tel: 952/937-9800; Fax: 952/937-7130. Eaton's Hydraulics Division manufactures low-speed, high-torque hydraulic motors; hydrostatic power steering; piston pumps and motors; gear pumps and motors; cylinders; and hydraulic valves. Eden Prairie facility opened in 1965. 700 employees. SIC 3492, 3561, 3569, 3594. Founded in 1911. Division of Eaton Corp. (NYSE: ETN), Cleveland.

EcoWater Systems Inc. P.O. Box 64420, Woodbury, MN 55164. Tel: 651/739-5330; Fax: 651/739-4547; Web site: http://www.ecowater.com. Donald Brockley, Pres. and Gen. Mgr.; John Onken, Cont.; Russ Paterson, Dir.-Mktg.; Al Dennis, Dir.-Sls.; Judy Pretto, Mgr.-Communications; Dave Kell, Dir.-Hum. Res. EcoWater Systems manufactures water-treatment products and drinking-water systems. Plants in Toronto, London, and Brussels report to Woodbury, where the company has a 430,000-square-foot plant. Brand names include Ecowater, North Star, Sears Kenmore, and General Electric. Present plant opened in 1967. Formerly known as Ecodyne Corp./The Lindsay Co. 450 employees (in Minnesota). SIC 7389. Founded in 1925. Owned by The Marmon Group, Chicago.

EESCO United Electric Company 601 Lakeview Point, New Brighton, MN 55112. Tel: 651/582-3900; Fax: 651/582-3999. Rob Olson, District Mgr.; Jim Mulvey, Op. Mgr.; Tom Reu, Sls. Mgr.; Bob Annoni, Sls. Mgr.; Jim Lasota, Tech. Products. EESCO United Electric Co. is a distributor of electrical and electronic products. 158 employees. SIC 5063. Founded in 1915. Owned through WESCO Distribution Inc., Pittsburgh, by WESCO Distribution Inc., Pittsburgh.

Ehlert Publishing Group Inc. 6420 Sycamore Ln., Maple Grove, MN 55369. Tel: 763/383-4400. Stephen M. Hedlund, Pres.; Dick Hendricks, SVP and Group Publisher; Morris Woolery, VP-Prod. Annual revenue $30 million. Ehlert Publishing Group, a special-interest consumer and trade magazine publishing and communications company, is the leading American powersports media company. Titles include: ATV Magazine, Rider, American Rider, Touring Rider, Archery Business, Bowhunting World, 3-D and Target Archery, Snowmobile, Snow Goer, Snow Week, Snowmobile Business, Watercraft Business, PWC Magazine, Watercraft World, Snow Goer TV, and Big East Snowmobile Show. Ehlert was acquired in March 1997 by a California specialty-magazine publishing company run by former Twin Cities media executive Stephen Adams. 65 employees (in Minnesota). SIC 2721. Founded in 1976. In January 2000 the company acquired Thunder Press Inc., the Scotts Valley, Calif.-based publisher of two motorcycle magazines: Thunder Press; and Asphalt Angels (for women). In March Ehlert announced that WomanRider, a new magazine targeting women motorcycle enthusiasts, was set to debut in July with 40,000 free copies being sent to an acquired list of women motorcycle owners. Executives were hoping to make it a paid quarterly. In September Ehlert announced a partnership with Rivals.com, a leading online network of sportsteam and affinity channels and the Internet's No. 1 sports news site in stickiness. Ehlert launched five Web sites devoted to a wide range of enthusiast sports and containing content provided in part by the company's 15 print publications. The fives sites are SnowmobileNews.com, ATVnews.com, WatercraftNews.com, MotorcycleReport.com, and BowhuntingWorld.com. Owned by Affinity Group Inc., Ventura, Calif.

Election Systems 601 28th Ave. S., P.O. Box 548, Waite Park, MN 56387. Tel: 320/252-9268; Fax: 320/253-9822; Web site: http://www.essvote.com. Bill Welsh, Pres.; Lee Storbeck, VP-Sls. Election Systems specializes in election software and systems. 50 employees (in Minnesota; 10 part-time). SIC 7372. Founded in 1974. Owned by Election Systems & Software, Omaha, Neb.

Electric Machinery Company Inc. 800 Central Ave., Minneapolis, MN 55413. Tel: 612/378-8000; Fax: 612/378-8050. Michael Vucelic, Pres. and CEO; Jim Holdredge, VP, COO, and Gen. Mgr.; Daniel Peterson, Dir.-Sls./Mktg.; Lynette Dubbels, Dir.-Admin. Svs.; Azad Mesrobian, Gen. Mgr.-Engrg./Mfg.; Ronald Wuollet, CFO, Cont., and Treas. Annual revenue $35 million. Electric Machinery Co. manufactures, sells, and services synchronous and induction motors, synchronous generators, turbogenerators, and variable-speed systems for utilities, refineries, and the pulp and paper and petroleum industries. 235 employees. SIC 3545, 3621. Founded in 1891. Acquired in March 1999 from Dresser-Rand by Ideal Electric, Mansfield, Ohio.

Electrosonic 10320 Bren Rd. E., Minnetonka, MN 55343. Tel: 952/931-7500; Fax: 952/938-9311; Web site: http://www.electrosonic.com. Kyle Carpenter, Pres. and CEO. Electrosonic designs, manufactures, and installs videowalls, automated display control systems, and business communications systems for retailers nationwide. 75 employees (55 in Minnesota). SIC 3669, 3699. Founded in 1972. Operating as an independent subsidiary of The Mercantile Group, Helsinki, Finland. No. 99 CRM Foreign-Owned 100.

Eller Media Company 3225 Spring Street N.E., Minneapolis, MN 55413. Tel: 612/869-1900; Fax: 612/869-7082; Web site: http://www.ellermedia.com. Lee Ann Mulker, Div. Pres.; Dave Sturzl, Sls. Mgr. Eller Media provides billboards in the Twin Cities 13-county metro area. Eller also provides outdoor advertising space in 42 markets throughout the world. These are the operations of the former Naegele Outdoor Advertising Inc. 60 employees. SIC 3993. Founded in 1937. Now owned by Clear Channel Communications Inc. (NYSE: CCU), San Antonio.

Emerson Motion Control 12005 Technology Dr., Eden Prairie, MN 55343. Tel: 952/995-8000; Fax: 952/995-8011. Tim Erhart, Pres. Emerson Motion Control supplies positioning systems for the industrial market. 130 employees (116 in Minnesota). SIC 5065. Founded in 1980. Owned by Emerson Electric Co. (NYSE: EMR), St. Louis.

Entegee Engineering Technical Group 2955 Xenium Ln. N., Suite 30, Plymouth, MN 55441. Tel: 763/577-9000; Fax: 763/577-9010. Tom Hentges, SVP. Entegee Engineering Technical Group, formerly known as Advance/Possis Technical Services, provides contract technical personnel, CAD services, engineers, designers, drafters, and computer specialists to the engineering industry. The company's Engineering Services Division in St. Paul offers outsourcing design, drafting, and analysis CAD services. Advance Technical Services Inc. acquired Possis Technical Services Division in September 1991 and was, in turn, acquired in 1996. Its current name took effect on June 29, 1998. 700 employees. SIC 8711. Founded in 1976. Owned by Modis Professional Services, Jacksonville, Fla.

Entex Information Services Inc. 1000 Boone Ave. N., Golden Valley, MN 55427. Tel: 763/797-0068; Fax: 763/797-9608. Gary Campbell, Gen. Mgr. Entex Information Services is a value-added reseller of network computing products, services, and support. Known prior to an August 1993 management/employee buyout as JWP Information Services. 206 employees (in Minnesota). SIC 5045. Founded in 1980. Owned by Entex Information Services Inc., Rye Brook, N.Y.

Ernst & Young LLP 1400 Pillsbury Center, Minneapolis, MN 55402. Tel: 612/343-1000; Fax: 612/339-1726; Web site: http://www.ey.com. Jo Marie Dancik, Midwest Area Managing Ptnr.; James Dalbey, Office Dir.-Hum. Res.; Thomas P. Knudsen, Audit Svs. Mng. Ptnr.; James Henderson, Tax Managing Ptnr. Ernst & Young LLP is a diversified professional services firm specializing in accounting, auditing, corporate and individual tax planning, and management consulting services. The firm also offers resident expertise in financial services, health care, manufacturing/high technology, insurance, retail, and entrepreneurial services, as well as customized services in corporate finance, online security, risk management, the valuation of intangibiles and e-business acceleration. First Minnesota facility established in 1918. 361 employees (in Minnesota). SIC 8721. Founded in 1894. In February 2000 the firm introduced its newest Internet-based service, Ernie Online Tax Advisor for corporate tax professionals. Owned by Ernst & Young LLP, New York.

Eselco Inc. 725 E. Portage Ave., Sault Ste. Marie, MI 49783. Tel: 906/632-2221; Fax: 906/632-8444; Web site: http://www.eselco.com. Thomas S. Nurnberger, Chm.; William R. Gregory, Pres. and CEO; Donald Sawruk, EVP and COO; David R. Hubbard, VP-Fin.; James L. Beedy, VP-Engrg.; Steven L. Boeckman, VP and Treas.; Ernest H. Maas, VP-Engrg.; David H. Jirikovic, Asst. VP-Op.; Paul A. Schemanski, Asst. VP-Info. Sys.; Donald C. Wilson, Sec. Eselco Inc. is a holding company with three subsidiaries. Edison Sault Electric Co. is an electric operating utility engaged primarily in the generation, purchase, transmission, and distribution of electric energy. The company has a service area of 2,000 square miles in the eastern portion of Michigan's Upper Peninsula. The utility serves more than 21,000 residential, commercial, and industrial customers. Northern Tree Service Inc.

was formed in 1990 to provide tree-trimming services to both Edison Sault Electric Co. and outside parties. ESEG Inc. began operations in December 1997 when it purchased a 138-KV submarine circuit from Consumers Energy Co. for lease to Edison Sault. Eselco and Wisconsin Energy Corp. merged in June 1998. 88 employees. SIC 0783, 4911. Founded in 1892. Eselco is a wholly owned subsidiary of Wisconsin Energy Corp. (NYSE: WEC), Milwaukee.

Eurest Dining Services/Canteen Vending Services/Chartwells 1091 Pierce Butler Rt., St. Paul, MN 55104. Tel: 651/488-0515; Fax: 651/488-8014; Web site: http://www.compass_usa.com. William Gorman, District Mgr.-Eurest/Chartwells; Vic Kline, District Mgr.-Canteen; Michael Garbel, Regional Sls. Dir. Eurest Dining Services/Canteen Vending Services/Chartwells is a retailer of dining and vending services via corporate and dining centers. 150 employees. SIC 5962. Founded in 1956. Owned by The Compass Group plc, London. No. 72 CRM Foreign-Owned 100.

Eveleth Mines LLC P.O. Box 180, Eveleth, MN 55734. Tel: 218/744-7805; Fax: 218/744-7866. John H. Senseman, CFO; Chuck Williams, VP; Rick Maki, VP; Howard Hilshorst, Pres. Annual revenue $140 million. Eveleth Mines LLC, operating as EVTAC Mining, mines and processes taconite. Annual production is 4.2 million tons. Owned and managed prior to 1996 by Oglebay Norton Co. In February 1999 the plant revealed plans to cut production and lay off up to 150 workers in spring 1999 in response to dipping demand for iron ore. As the year progressed, labor talks were put on hold pending discussions about a job-saving acquisition by Minnesota Iron & Steel Co., Nashwauk, Minn. That company was exploring the possibility of developing a $1.2 billion facility on the Iron Range to fabricate steel from mined ore. 480 employees (in Minnesota). SIC 1011. Founded in 1965. Now owned jointly by A-K Steel Co., Middletown, Ohio; Rouge Steel Co., Dearborn, Mich.; and Stelco Inc., Hamilton, Ontario. No. 33 CRM Foreign-Owned 100.

Everen Securities 80 S. Eighth St., Suite 3400, Minneapolis, MN 55402. Tel: 612/332-1212; Fax: 612/332-4071. George McGough, CEO; Bob Torkelson, Branch Mgr.-Minneapolis; Mike Krempotich, Branch Mgr.-St. Paul; Karl Groth, Branch Mgr.-Wayzata; Stewart Mason, Mgr. and Dir.-Corp. Fin. Everen Securities underwrites and distributes corporate securities and municipal bonds; and stock, bond, option, mutual-fund, insurance, and tax-incentive investments. The company specializes in primary markets and over-the-counter issues. The company has four offices in the Twin Cities area: Minneapolis, St. Paul, Wayzata, and Bloomington. Former names: Craig-Hallum; Principal Financial Securities. 112 employees (1 part-time). SIC 6211. Founded in 1950. Now owned by Everen Securities Inc., Chicago.

Everest Medical Corporation 13755 First Ave. N., Plymouth, MN 55441. Tel: 763/473-6262; Fax: 763/473-6465; Web site: http://www.everestmedical.com. Chris M. Smith, Pres. and CEO; Steven M. Blakemore, VP-Op./Engrg.; Michael E. Geraghty, VP-Sls./Mktg.; Thomas F. Murphy, VP-Fin./Admin.; David J. Parins, VP-Tech. Annual revenue $12.6 million (earnings $4.6 million). Everest Medical Corp. designs, develops, manufactures, and markets disposable bipolar electrosurgical instruments and related medical devices for the minimally invasive surgery market. 110 employees (106 in Minnesota). SIC 3845. Founded in 1983. In December 1999 the company's new QuadripolarCutting Forceps was recognized as one the Society of Laparoendoscopic Surgeons "New Products of the Year" at the Eighth International Meeting of Laparoendoscopic Surgeons Meeting held in New York. The instrument utilizes a new proprietary electrosurgical technology called quadripolarity, which the company believed to represent the next generation of electrosurgery for precise laparoscopic surgery. On Feb. 23, 2000, Everest agreed to be acquired by a Welsh medical products maker in a cash merger valued at $51.6 million. The $4.85 per share price was a 32 percent premium on Everest's Feb. 22 closing stock price. The buyer gained not only Everest's bipolar radio frequency instrumentation, an area not covered, but also access to Everest's independent direct sales force in the United States. In March Gyrus Group commenced a tender offer for all outstanding shares of common and preferred stock of Everest Medical as part of its proposed acquisition. The per share offer price was $4.85 per share in cash, with an aggregate purchase price of $51.6 million. In April the shareholders of Gyrus voted in favor of the acquisition. On April 14, Gyrus Group successfully completed its tender offer—acquiring 94 percent of the total number of shares of Everest Medical common and preferred stock. In August, based on its revenue growth from 1995 to 1999, the company was named to Deloitte & Touche's Minnesota Technology Fast 50. Owned by Gyrus Group plc, U.K. No. 87 CRM Foreign-Owned 100. No. 41 Minnesota Technology Fast 50.

Executone Communication Systems 30 W. Water St., St. Paul, MN 55107. Tel: 651/292-0102; Fax: 651/292-0144; Web site: http://www.executone-MN.com. Executone sells Ericsson, Activevoice, and Centigram along with its own brand of telephone system. 62 employees. SIC 1731. Founded in 1954. Owned by Executone Information Systems Inc. (Nasdaq: XTON), Milford, Conn.

Express Messenger Systems Inc. 2280 Terminal Rd., Roseville, MN 55113. Tel: 651/628-3200; Fax: 651/628-3235; Web site: http://www.ex.mess.com. David Callaway, CEO; Kevin Farmer, VP; Rick Locarni, VP; Kevin Comstock, Ofcr.; Amy Compton Schumacher, Gen. Mgr.-Admin., Mpls. Annual revenue $50 million. Express Messenger Systems is a courier company specializing in urgent delivery service, inter-office mail delivery, and scheduled mail and air courier services for the seven-county metro area. 450 employees (135 in Minnesota). SIC 4215, 4513. Founded in 1976. Express Messenger Systems Inc., Phoenix, is owned by Citigroup Inc., New York, and Air Canada, Saint-Laurent, Quebec. No. 54 CRM Foreign-Owned 100.

Express Scripts Inc. dba Diversified Pharmaceutical Services 6625 W. 78th St., Bloomington, MN 55439. Tel: 952/820-7000; Fax: 952/896-6944. Brad Hewitt, Pres. and CEO; David Moules, SVP-Group Sls. Dept.; Shawn Patterson, SVP-Mktg.; Kurt Briggs, SVP-Managed Sls. Care; Ann Tobin, Gen. Counsel; Chris Pearson, VP-Info. Sys.; Paul Ethridge, VP-Hum. Res. Express Scripts, dba Diversified Pharmaceutical Services (DPS), is one of the leading pharmaceutical benefits managers in the United States, with 300 clients and 30 million individuals covered under plans it administers. DPS has pioneered several benefits innovations, including the first point-of-sale prescription drug card plan; and the first drug outcomes management program, which correlates medical interventions with treatment results. DPS is consistently rated first in customer service by HMOs and employers. Purchased from United HealthCare Corp., Minnetonka, Minn., in May 1994 for $2.3 billion by SmithKline Beecham. 1,000 employees. SIC 6324. Founded in 1976. Now a subsidiary of Express Scripts Inc.(Nasdaq: ESRX), Maryland Heights, Mo.

Express Scripts/ValueRx 4700 Nathan Ln. N., Plymouth, MN 55442. Tel: 763/837-5260; Fax: 763/837-7138; Web site: http://www.valuerx.com. Barrett A. Toan, Pres. and CEO; Stuart L. Bascomb, EVP; Thomas M. Boudreau, SVP, Gen. Counsel, Sec.; Patrick Byrne, SVP-Plymouth Site Op.; Robert W. (Joe) Davis, SVP and Chief Info. Sys. Ofcr.; Linda Logsdon, SVP-Health Mgmt. Svs.; David A. Lowenberg, SVP-Site Op./Service Delivery; George Paz, SVP and CFO. Express Scripts/ValueRx is a pharmacy benefit management company. It manages more than $4 billion in drug expenditures a year through integrated retail and mail service programs. Express Scripts/ValueRx provides medication management services to managed care organizations, Blue Cross and Blue Shield plans, carriers, and third-party administrators and provides a spectrum of cost management and science-based clinical programs. In February 1998, after one year of ownership, Columbia/HCA Healthcare Corp., Nashville, Tenn., agreed to sell ValueRx for $445 million in cash. 1,500 employees (in Minnesota). SIC 6324. Founded in 1987. In May 2000 two futurists speaking at a forum on the pharmaceutical landscape co-sponsored by the Buyers Health Care Action Group (BHCAG) of Minneapolis-St. Paul and Express Scripts predicted that health care consumers soon may see some new but familiar names along side those of their doctors, hospitals, and health plans—names like Schwab, Fidelity, and Visa, from a financial services industry poised for entry into the health care market. In August Express Scripts and the American Cancer Society jointly announced that Express Scripts had agreed to be the premier sponsor of the charity's third annual celebrity golf tournament, which raises money for the fight against breast cancer. Owned by Express Scripts Inc.(Nasdaq: ESRX), Maryland Heights, Mo.

Extendicare Health Facilities Inc. 5801 Duluth St., Suite 360, Golden Valley, MN 55422. Tel: 763/593-0887; Fax: 763/593-1052. Loren Colman, Asst. VP. Extendicare Health Facilities is a subacute long-term care facility with assisted living. 1,500 employees. SIC 8059. Owned through Extendicare Health, Milwaukee, by Extendicare Inc., Markham, Ontario. No. 9 CRM Foreign-Owned 100.

ExxonMobil Refining & Supply P.O. Box 1163, Billings, MT 59103. Tel: 406/657-5380; Fax: 406/657-5374. Steve Cope, Refinery Mgr. ExxonMobil operates a petroleum refinery in Billings, MT. 250 employees. SIC 2911. Founded in 1949. Owned by ExxonMobil (NYSE: XON), Irving, Texas.

FSMC Inc., Financial Services Management Corp. 451 Lakeview St., Lake Lillian, MN 56253. Tel: 320/664-4161; Fax: 320/664-4144; Web site: http://www.fsmcweb.com. Paul Forstrom, Pres.; Jeff Berghuis, EVP; Peggy Ebnet, VP-Forms Mgmt.; Holly Eisch, VP; Sharri Esham, VP-Hum. Res. FSMC Inc. markets high-volume check-processing applications for 250 corporations, one federal agency, and 24 state agencies. The former First State Marketing Corp. was acquired by Minneapolis-based Travelers Express Inc. in January 1997. 150 employees (in Minnesota; 82 part-time). SIC 6099. Founded in 1983. Travelers Express, in turn, is owned by Viad Corp. (NYSE: VVI), Phoenix.

Fair, Isaac and Company Inc. 4295 Lexington Ave. N., Arden Hills, MN 55126. Tel: 651/482-8593; Fax: 651/481-8077; Web site: http://www.fairissac.com. Tom Grudnowski, Pres. and CEO; Eric Educale, EVP-Sls.; John Woldrich, EVP and COO; Marc Pautsch, Software Devel. Fair, Isaac and Co., formerly DynaMark Inc., provides database management and data processing services for direct marketers. The company has developed and managed marketing databases for financial services providers, insurers, retailers, catalogers, publishers, fund-raisers, and advertising agencies. The company's services include database development and management, consulting, modeling and analytics, list processing, data enhancement, and postal optimization. Fair, Isaac also offers data analysis, predictive models, and automated solutions to help businesses make more profitable decisions. Clients include U.S. Bancorp, Wells Fargo & Co., Banc One Corp., and Chase Manhattan Corp. 1,500 employees (500 in Minnesota). SIC 7374. Founded in 1985. Subsidiary of Fair, Isaac and Company Inc. (NYSE: FIC), San Rafael, Calif.

Fairmont Tamper 415 N. Main St., Fairmont, MN 56031. Tel: 507/235-3361; Fax: 507/235-7370. G. Robert Newman, Div. Pres. Fairmont Tamper manufactures railway maintenance-of-way equipment and hydraulic tools. 400 employees. SIC 3743. Founded in 1909. In 1979 merged with Harsco Corp. (NYSE: HSC), Camp Hill, Pa.

Fallon Worldwide 901 Marquette Ave., Suite 3200, Minneapolis, MN 55402. Tel: 612/321-2345; Fax: 612/321-2606; Web site: http://www.fallon.com. Patrick Fallon, Chm.; Eric Block, Gen. Mgr.-Mpls.; Joe Duffy, Chm.-Duffy Design/Interactive; Irving D. Fish, COO; Mark Goldstein, Chief Mktg. Ofcr.; David Lubars, Co-pres./Exec. Creative Dir.-Mpls.; Bob Moore, Creative Dir.; Staney Rostad, CFO-Mpls.; Fred Senn, Ptnr. and Group Dir.-Mpls.; Mark Sitley, Dir.-Broadcast Prod.; Bill Westbrook, Pres.-Int'l; Rob White, Co-pres.-Mpls. Annual revenue $75 million (estimated by Fact Book; $645.6 million in capitalized billings, up 27.4 percent). Fallon is a full-service advertising agency. Its integrated approach to marketing includes aspects such as package design, public relations, and direct mail in addition to traditional advertising campaigns. Minneapolis client list: BMW of North America, Brunswick Corp., Camp Heartland, Children's Defense Fund, Citibank, Drugstore.com, EDS, Holiday Inn Worldwide, IBP, The John Nuveen Co., Lee Co., LifeMinders.com, Long John Silver's, Navistar Int'l, Nikon Inc., Nordstrom, Public Broadcasting Service, Qualcomm, Ralston Purina, Sports Illustrated, Starbucks Coffee Co., Timex Corp., and United Airlines. The agency also operates full-service offices in New York and London. 681 employees (518 in Minnesota). SIC 7311. Founded in 1981. In February 2000 the firm decided to join Europe's largest agency, Publicis Group, in a partnership that was to allow Fallon to establish a worldwide branding network for the Internet age and to fuel its aggressive worldwide expansion plans while still retaining its name, leadership, and culture. The firm landed the $15 million ad account of the Public Broadcasting Service. In March Fallon was awarded the $40 million advertising account of Long John Silver's, the world's largest quick-service seafood restaurant. In August Fallon won Citibank's $120 million-to-$150 million U.S. consumer business, including retail banking and credit cards, boosting Fallon's annual client spending to $725 million. Owned by holding company Publicis Group, Paris. No. 28 CRM Foreign-Owned 100.

Farmland Foods Inc. P.O. Box 1059, Albert Lea, MN 56007. Tel: 507/377-4200; Fax: 507/377-4171. Ray Roberts, Gen. Mgr. Farmland Foods produces and sells processed pork to the Upper Midwest and Southwestern markets under the Farmstead brand name. Former names: Cornbelt Meats; Seaboard Farms of Minnesota Inc. 300 employees (in Minnesota). SIC 2011. Founded in 1982. Now operated by Farmland Industries Inc., Kansas City, Mo.

Federal Cartridge Company 900 Ehlen Dr., Anoka, MN 55303. Tel: 763/323-2300; Fax: 763/323-2506; Web site: http://www.federal-cartridge.com. Federal Cartridge Co. manufactures rifle, pistol, and shotgun ammunition in Anoka, Minn., and clay targets at a plant in Richmond, Indiana. In response to limited expansion opportunities in the sporting-ammunition industry, Federal has positioned itself as a supplier of high-tech products such as the Tungsten-Iron shotshell introduced in 1997. Sold by Pentair Inc. (NYSE: PNR) in 1997. 900 employees (in Minnesota). SIC 3482. Founded in 1922. Now owned by Blount International Inc. (NYSE: BLT), Montgomery, Ala.

Federal Foam Technologies Inc. 1800 Como Ave., St. Paul, MN 55108. Tel: 651/645-4550; Fax: 651/645-4665. Mel Lefkowitz, Chm.; Bill Jwanouskos, VP-Admin. and CFO; Jay Markstrom, VP; Wyman Smith, VP; Greg Windsperger, VP. Annual revenue $30 million. Federal Foam Technologies (FFT) manufactures foam products for the trucking, agriculture, construction-vehicle, marine, bedding, furniture, packaging, and military-packing markets. The company also sells foam and fiber materials to the upholstery, bedding, and crafts industries. Formerly known as Airtex Industries Inc. 200 employees (25 in Minnesota). SIC 3069. Founded in 1946. Owned by Federal International Inc., St. Louis.

Federal—Mogul P.O. Box 456, 520 N. Eighth St., Lake City, MN 55041. Tel: 651/345-4541; Fax: 651/345-3570. David D. Krohn, Pres. Federal—Mogul operates cast iron and aluminum foundries that support a machining center for the manufacture of cast iron pistons, aluminum and bi-metal pistons, cast iron cylinder sleeves, and miscellaneous engine parts.

Former names: JPI Transportation Products Inc.; AE Piston Products Heavy Duty; AE Goetze—Lake City. 530 employees (400 in Minnesota). SIC 3321, 3365, 3541, 3592. Founded in 1868. In October 1999 the Powertrain Systems facility in Lake City, Minn., was recommended for the prestigious ISO 14001 registration to the Environmental Management System by Underwriters Laboratory. The plant has identified recycling projects to achieve savings in energy and water usage and to reduce the risk of pollution from its activities. In March 2000 the Lake City manufacturing facility received top ranking from John Deere's Achieving Excellence Award Program. Lake City supplies 100 percent of the machined cylinder liner requirements to John Deere engine plants located in Dubuque, Iowa, and Torreon, Mexico. The facility also supplies OE Service pistons and liners to several John Deere locations. Owned by Federal—Mogul Corp., Southfield, Mich.

Ferche Millwork Inc. P.O. Box 39, Rice, MN 56367. Tel: 320/393-2288; Fax: 320/393-2545. Gerald Grider, Pres.; Alan Ferche, VP; Ken Luovigson, Treas.; Charlie Meyer, Sls. Ferche Millwork manufactures more than 300 standard moulding profiles, hardwood moulding, and veneer door jambs. 215 employees (200 in Minnesota). SIC 2431. Founded in 1958. Acquired in 1988 by RAF Industries Inc., Elkins Park, Pa.

Feterl Mfg. Company 411 W. Center Ave., Salem, SD 57058. Tel: 605/425-2206; Fax: 605/425-2183; Web site: http://www.feterl.com. Keith Paulsen, Sls. Mgr.; Randy Bauer, Gen. Mgr. Feterl Mfg. manufactures grain-handling equipment, portable hay feeders, OEM component parts, and service bodies. 160 employees. SIC 3523. Founded in 1965. Owned by United Dominion Industries Ltd. (NYSE: UDI), Charlotte, N.C.

Filmtec Corporation 7200 Ohms Ln., Edina, MN 55439. Tel: 952/897-4200; Fax: 952/897-4201. Ian Barbour, Pres.; Upen Bharwada, VP-Res./Devel.; Doug Goring, VP-Op. Annual revenue $90 million. Filmtec manufactures spiral elements for reverse osmosis. The company also produces thin-film composite and ultra-filtration membranes. 360 employees (in Minnesota). SIC 3821. Founded in 1977. Part of the Liquid Separations Business Unit of The Dow Chemical Co. (NYSE: DOW), Midland, Mich.

Fingerhut Cos. Inc. 4400 Baker Rd., Minnetonka, MN 55343. Tel: 952/932-3100; Fax: 952/932-3181; Web site: http://www.fingerhut.com. John D. Buck, Pres. and COO (Office of the Principals); Michael P. Sherman, Pres. and CMO (Office of the Principals); Richard L. Tate, EVP and Pres.-Fingerhut Catalog; Gary Bledsoe, SVP and Chief Info. Ofcr.; Brenda L. Boehler, SVP-Mdsg.; Thomas J. Bozlinski, SVP-Op./Info. Systems Oper.; Megan M. Kavanaugh, SVP-Advertising/Promotions; Michael A. Murray, SVP-Distribution; Paul Bona, Pres.-Figi's Inc.; John S. Christiansen, VP-E-commerce Op.; Laura J. Dale, VP-Hum. Res.; John F. Damrow, VP-Mdsg.; Connie Waters Doepke, VP-Mdsg.; Eric T. Helgeland, VP-Mktg./Bus. Devel.; John Q. Hunsicker, VP and COO, E-commerce; Robert C. Kieffer, VP, Assoc. Gen. Counsel, Asst. Sec.; Steven E. Leighton, VP-Mktg. Svs.; Beth S. Logsdon, VP-Mdsg. Op.; Jacqueline L. Marshik, VP-Bus. Process Improvement; Daniel E. Minton, VP-Purch. Risk Mgmt., Gen. Auditor; Rachel O'Brien, VP-Customer Svs./Telemktg.; Rafael F. Saldana, VP and Gen. Mgr.-Hispanic Business. Fingerhut Cos. Inc. is a direct-to-customer marketing company that sells a broad range of products and services primarily through catalogs, the Internet, and direct marketing. Fingerhut's core competency is the development and use of a proprietary database to provide credit, target offers, and build lifetime relationships with customers. Using its sophisticated proprietary management information systems, the company maintains data on more than 30 million customer households. The nation's second-largest consumer catalog marketer, Fingerhut sells such general merchandise as electronics, housewares, home textiles, jewelry, and furniture using revolving charge. In October 1996 Fingerhut created a separate, publicly traded company from its 83 percent owned financial services business, Metris Cos. Inc. In February 1999 Fingerhut was acquired by Federated Dept. Stores Inc., the owner of Bloomingdale's and Macy's in a cash-and-debt transaction valued at $1.7 billion. 12,000 employees (6,200 in Minnesota). SIC 5961. Founded in 1948. Over the 1999 holiday season, Fingerhut's distribution centers experienced a 50 percent increase in volume over the previous year. The St. Cloud facility experienced an 80 percent increase, and office workers were asked to help pack boxes at the St. Cloud warehouse. The increase was attributed to fulfillment of online orders both from Fingerhut's own Web sites and from others that it services. Fingerhut's Web site traffic increased 10 times over the previous year. Over the month of December, Fingerhut shipped over 6 million packages. In January 2000 Fingerhut acquired a 28 percent equity interest (and an option to increase its stake to a majority interest) in Empire Direct, a Hispanic direct-marketing company. In March Fingerhut partnered with Digital Island Inc. (Nasdaq: ISLD), a leading global e-Business Delivery Network, to increase the online sales of consumer goods. The company acquired the Brownstone Studio and Lew Magram catalogs, both of which sell women's apparel and accessories. In April the U.S. Postal Service recognized Fingerhut and its VP and general manager of Hispanic business, Rafael Saldana, with its Industry Excellence Award for Multi-Cultural Marketing. In May, to accommodate rapid growth, the company was proceeding to consolidate its e-commerce offices (250 to 300 marketing, direct merchandise support, information systems, and creative employees) into 79,000 square feet of a new Edina office building. Fingerhut mailed its Chicago-area customers a full Spanish-language catalog featuring Chicago Cubs star Sammy Sosa on the cover. In July, after warning investors of rising credit-card account delinquencies at Fingerhut, the parent dedicated more management resources to Fingerhut by creating a new "office of the principals." Federated said that it may have to take charges of up to $400 million to resolve the credit delinquency situation. In August the company launched "Fingerhut en Espanol," a Spanish-language Web site located at www.fingerhut.com/espanol. In October Federated announced a significant downsizing of its Fingerhut core catalog operations in order to increase its earnings and cash flow. the restructuring was to eliminate 550 positions, some by the end of October and the remainder in January 2001. Reductions in staffing, across all functional areas, amounted to 24 percent of the 2,300 positions at Fingerhut's headquarters in Minnetonka, its data center in Plymouth, Minn., and its e-commerce operation in Edina, Minn. (Fingerhut's St. Cloud, Minn., distribution center was only slightly affected.) This restructuring was expected to save $40 million annually in overhead expenses, starting in 2001. Now a wholly owned subsidiary of Federated Department Stores Inc. (NYSE: FD), Cincinnati. No. 28 CRM Employer 100.

Fireside Corner 2700 Fairview Ave. N., Roseville, MN 55113. Tel: 651/633-1042; Fax: 651/633-8884. Kirk Sorenson, Pres. Fireside Corner sells and installs fireplaces, including brick mantels, for retail and wholesale markets. The company has another location in Burnsville, Minn. 130 employees (in Minnesota). SIC 3251. Founded in 1951. Owned by Allied Fireside Inc., Madison, Wis.

First Health Strategies 11301 W. Lake Park Dr., Milwaukee, WI 53224. Tel: 414/577-2140; Fax: 414/577-1655. Steven Duckette, VP-Sls. First Health utilizes leading-edge technology to provide the industry's most advanced health care administration system, which integrates claims administration, utilization review, medical case management, data analysis, provider networks, pharmacy benefit management, workers' compensation and disability services, stop-loss insurance products, and outsourcing services for HMOs and other health care providers. Once the publicly traded Employee Benefit Plans Inc. 250 employees. SIC 6321, 6411. Founded in 1974. Since October 1995, owned through First Health Strategies, Salt Lake City, by First Data Corp. (NYSE: FDC), Atlanta.

First Student Inc. 1530 Brewster St., St. Paul, MN 55108. Tel: 651/645-5665; Fax: 651/645-5857. Jeffrey Pearson, Regional VP. First Student, formerly Ryder Student Transportation Services, operates a school bus transportation system in several Twin Cities suburbs. The largest student-transportation provider in the state, its 11 facilities stretch from Stillwater to Burnsville to Minnetonka. First Student also offers charter tours. In July 1999 then-parent Ryder System Inc. sold its school bus business, including this operation, to Britain's largest bus operator. 1,600 employees (in Minnesota; 1,300 part-time). SIC 4142, 4151. In fall 2000 thousands of Minnesota schoolchildren saw a new name on the buses they board for school, as First Student Inc. replaced Ryder Student Transportation as the name of the bus operator. Owned by FirstGroup plc, London. No. 7 CRM Foreign-Owned 100.

Firstar Bank of Minnesota 101 E. Fifth St., 14th Floor, St. Paul, MN 55101. Tel: 651/292-3958; Fax: 651/292-3964; Web site: http://www.firstar.com. James Clifford, Chm. and Pres. Firstar Bank of Minnesota, whose more than 30 Twin Cities-area offices and $3 billion in assets represent an 8.5 percent metro market share, is the fifth-largest bank in Minnesota. Its services include retail and business banking, mortgage, trust, credit cards, insurance, and investment. In November 1998 Firstar's parent was sold to Star Banc Corp., Cincinnati, in a deal worth $7.2 billion. Star Banc took both Firstar's name and its Milwaukee headquarters. 978 employees (in Minnesota; 267 part-time). SIC 6021. Founded in 1991. In October 2000 parent Firstar Corp. (NYSE: FSR) announced a definitive agreement to merge with U.S. Bancorp (NYSE: USB) sometime in the first quarter of 2001 through an exchange of shares valued at $21.2 billion. After the closing, the combined companies were to operate under the U.S. Bancorp name from corporate headquarters in Minneapolis. Until the close of that transaction, this operation is owned by Firstar Corp. (NYSE: FSR), Milwaukee.

Fiskars Inc. Power Sentry Division 3555 Holly Ln., Suite 30, Plymouth, MN 55447. Tel: 763/557-0107; Fax: 763/557-9993. Tim Walsh, Gen. Mgr. Fiskars Power Sentry Division is a manufacturer of multiple-outlet power strips and surge protectors for PCs and home entertainment equipment. Plant locations: Wheaton and Fergus Falls, Minn. The privately held Power Sentry Inc. was acquired in August 1995. 200 employees (25 in Minnesota). SIC 3643. Founded in 1990. Owned through Fiskars Inc., Madison, Wis., by Fiskars Oy AB, Helsinki, Finland. No. 64 CRM Foreign-Owned 100.

Flame Metals Processing Corp. 7317 W. Lake, St. Louis Park, MN 55426. Tel: 952/929-7815; Fax: 952/925-0572. L. Michael McGurk, Pres. and COO; Dennis J. Stevermer, VP and CFO. Annual revenue $9 million (earnings $0.2 million). Flame Metals Processing and its subsidiary generate 100 percent of parent Milastar's consolidated net sales, which flow from the sale of a variety of subcontract services to industrial customers. These special services include metallurgical-related processing involving the heating and cooling of metal products under controlled conditions in order to restructure the molecular property of such products to achieve specified characteristics. Flame Metals' customer list includes more than 800 manufacturers. The customer furnishes all direct materials and components processed for its account. These parts are then heat treated, primarily to achieve a certain hardness or surface finish, to prepare the metal parts for their designated use. 70 employees (in Minnesota). SIC 3398. Founded in 1974. April 30, 2000: Sales of $9.002 million for fiscal 2000 were down 1.3 percent from 1999, primarily attributable to changes in the economy that resulted in higher sales in the New England area being more than offset by lower sales in the Midwest. After-tax profit of $202,000/$0.07 was $260,000 less than 1999, primarily due to lower sales in the Midwest that resulted in reduced operating income. Owned by Milastar Corp., West Palm Beach, Fla.

Fleming Companies P.O. Box 1957, 1637 St. James St., La Crosse, WI 54601. Tel: 608/785-1330; Fax: 608/782-6884. Robert Stauth, CEO. Fleming Companies is a complete-line wholesale grocery company serving stores in Wisconsin, Iowa, Minnesota, Illinois, Nebraska, South Dakota, and Upper Michigan. Primary customers are independent retailers under IGA franchise. Formerly known as Gateway Foods Inc. 1,010 employees. SIC 5141. Founded in 1956. In January 2000 Atlanta-based NDC Health Information Services agreed to provide Rainbow Foods with the industry's first Internet-based prescription price analysis tool, NDC Prescription Price Analyzer, a tool that enhances trend analyses and supports evaluation of competitive pricing, potential markets, and managed care contracts for profitability. Owned by Fleming Cos. Inc. (NYSE: FLM), Oklahoma City.

Fleming Companies Inc., dba Rainbow Foods 800 Excelsior Blvd., Hopkins, MN 55343. Tel: 952/945-2900; Fax: 952/945-3946. Pat Liska, Pres. Fleming Cos., dba Rainbow Foods, operates a chain of 43 supermarkets in the Twin Cities area that command about one-third of the highly competitive local retail grocery market. Successor to the family business Applebaum's Food Markets Inc. 5,340 employees (5,040 in Minnesota; 4,186 part-time). SIC 5411. Founded in 1983. In January 2000 Tom Farello, president of Rainbow Foods, left after three years with the company to take a job at a larger chain. While at Rainbow, Farello brought in more general merchandise and unveiled the Easy Save loyalty card. In February Rainbow decided to close underperforming stores in Minnetonka and Austin, Minn., and to move its accounting function from the Twin Cities to the Omaha, Neb., office that serves other Fleming chains. In April Rainbow's parent hired Morgan Stanley Dean Witter to explore strategic alternatives for its conventional supermarket chains—alternatives that could include a sale. Fleming had decided to focus on distributing to mass merchandise retailers like SuperTarget and Big Kmart that feature food sections. The community was concerned whether new owners would honor workers' seniority and maintain an organized labor force or, perhaps, resort to temporary and part-time workers. In July executives from Fleming were meeting to consider bids they had received for Rainbow. Albertson's Inc. and Safeway Inc. were reportedly two of the suitors. In September Rainbow agreed to pay a $175,000 fine for violating federal child labor laws. Minors at its 37 Twin Cities stores were working beyond permitted hours and performing restricted hazardous tasks. Fleming completed the strategic evaluation of its company-owned conventional retail stores (such as Rainbow). Improved sales and earnings had made the chain too valuable to sell, so Fleming decided to continue to operate 38 of the 43 Rainbow Foods stores. Two stores were to be converted to Fleming's value retail (everyday-low-price) format, and three other stores were to be sold. The continuing improvement in performance at Rainbow was delivering positive same-store-sales gains in a very competitive market. "The physical plants are in great shape and we expect to remain a strong competitor in this market," said Fleming CEO Mark Hansen. "There are additional plans to gain efficiencies in distribution and strengthen market effectiveness with the addition of value retail enhancements." The Minneapolis distribution division was to be dedicated to supplying the Rainbow operation, significantly improving productivity and profitability with the higher throughput of reduced SKUs and advanced distribution techniques. Additionally, a new Rainbow in Inver Grove Heights, Minn., was set for a fall opening. Owned through Fleming's La Crosse, Wis., a division of Fleming Cos. Inc. (NYSE: FLM), Oklahoma City.

Fleming Companies of Minneapolis 3501 Marshall St. N.E., Minneapolis, MN 55418. Tel: 612/781-8051; Fax: 612/782-4405. Mike Carey, Operative Group Pres. Fleming Companies of Minneapolis is a wholesale warehouse distribution center. It purchases and warehouses dry and perishable goods for its retail customers, which include Rainbow Foods, Jubilee Foods, Festival Foods, IGA, and other independent food stores. 1,000 employees. SIC 5141. Owned through the La Crosse, Wis., division of Fleming Cos. Inc. (NYSE: FLM), Oklahoma City.

Food Producers International 10505 Wayzata Blvd., Minnetonka, MN 55305. Tel: 952/544-2763; Fax: 952/544-4186. Peter Rosenberg, Managing Dir. Food Producers International manufactures chocolate and fruit products for the major foodservice, dairy, baking, and catering companies throughout the United States. FPI distributes in 51 countries internationally. Products include hot chocolate drink base concentrate and dispensers, fruit-flavored beverage concentrates, cheese sauces, ice cream toppings, and assorted Mexican food products. Its main registered brand name is Jubilee. 130 employees. SIC 2022, 2037, 2066. Founded in 1945. Owned through Hunt-Wesson Inc., Fullerton, Calif., by ConAgra Inc. (NYSE: CAG), Omaha, Neb.

Ford Motor Company Twin Cities Assembly Plant, 966 S. Mississippi River Blvd., St. Paul, MN 55116. Tel: 651/699-1321; Fax: 651/696-0512. Ernesto Gonzalez, Dir.-Mfg. Ford's Twin Cities Assembly Plant assembles Ranger pickup trucks. In 1992 Ford effected a $96 million conversion and hired 246 additional employees to upgrade the Ranger mid-size pickup line. 1,957 employees (in Minnesota). SIC 3711. Founded in 1924. In January 2000 the parent company announced that its employees, including 1,800 local UAW/Ford workers from the St. Paul Assembly Plant, were to receive a record-average $8,000 in profit sharing for 1999. Production at the St. Paul plant jumped by 23 percent from January (18,320) to March (22,584). Although sales of Ford Ranger trucks nationwide were down in April for the second straight month, the plant was picking up the slack from a previous consolidation of production from three plants down to two (the other making Rangers is in Edison, N.J.). In June a report called the plant the most efficient truck assembly plant in North America, with a speed rating of 18.97 hours per vehicle. In August employees at Ford's Twin Cities assembly plant returned to work early to help speed delivery of replacement tires to local dealers and customers. The plant was in the first week of a two-week shutdown scheduled to free up 15" tires from vehicle production to customers affected by the Firestone recall. In September Ford extended the temporary shutdown another week. The plant was reopened Sept. 18. The lost production of some 23,500 Ford Ranger pickups (at the St. Paul and Edison plants) was to be made up. In October Ford workers were able to obtain home computers free or at a reduced cost, as part of a company program aimed at increasing employees' computer skills. Part of the Ford Motor Co. (NYSE: F), Dearborn, Mich. No. 95 CRM Employer 100.

Fortis Financial Group 500 Bielenberg Dr., P.O. Box 64271 (55164), Woodbury, MN 55125. Tel: 651/738-4496; Fax: 651/738-4024; Web site: http://www.ffg.us.fortis.com. Dean C. Kopperud, Pres. and CEO; Roger Arnold, SVP-Sls. (Retail); Peggy Ettestad, SVP-Op.; Karen Dobbins, SVP-Hum. Res./Devel.; Dickson Lewis, SVP-Distribution/Mktg.; Jon Nicholson, SVP-Custom Solutions Group; Rhonda Schwartz, SVP and Gen. Counsel; Melinda Urion, SVP and CFO; Walter White, SVP-Fortis Investors; Pat Leone, Nat'l VP -Practice Management; Gene Muenchau, Nat'l VP-Variable Annuities/Mutual Funds; Gene Wolfe, Nat'l VP-Variable Life Insurance. Annual revenue $1.32 billion. Fortis Financial Group (FFG) is a financial services company. Its core products include variable annuities, variable universal life, and mutual funds. The FFG mission is to develop, distribute, and support financial tools that are simple to buy, simple to sell, and result in the best solution for the customer. FFG includes Fortis Advisers Inc., fund managers since 1949; Fortis Investors Inc., principal underwriter, a member of NASD and SIPC; and Fortis Benefits Insurance Co. and Fortis Insurance Co., IMSA members and issuers of FFG products. 880 employees (in Minnesota). SIC 6211. Founded in 1949. In October 1999 Fortis introduced the Income Preferred Variable Annuity (VA), its first move into the living benefit market. The product does not force annuitization, but it does guarantee protection from market downturns. In January 2000 Fortis, the innovator of no-load variable universal life (VUL), introduced the next generation of VUL with multiple sales applications. (The original Wall Street Series VUL ignited record-breaking sales, making June-December far and away the best seven months in FFG history.) Fortis Financial Group received a 1999 national DALBAR key honors award for providing consistently good service to its variable annuity customers. In May FFG added AIM, Federated, and MFS to its list of subadvisers—increasing investment options and expanding its investment styles. FFG and Quantum Alliance of Omaha announced a strategic alliance. Quantum Alliance is an organization that supports professional advisors—such as CPAs, estate-planning attorneys, and financial advisers—in providing wealth-design and estate-planning strategies and services to their clients. In July Fortis announced that its new management team had turned its funds into some of the industry's top performers. In 1997 Fortis funds were at near-bottom positions and greatly underperforming their stock-fund peers. At the end of 1999 Fortis funds were experiencing triple-digit returns, earning five-star ratings, and being placed on the Wall Street Journal's quarterly top 10 mutual funds lists. Enhancements to Fortis' Income Preferred VA included a new nine-year step-up provision allowing investors to take withdrawals based on the contract value if higher than the investment amount. FFG is owned through Fortis Inc., New York, by Fortis AMEV and Fortis AG, Utrecht, Netherlands. No. 20 CRM Foreign-Owned 100.

Fortis Information Technology 500 Bielenberg Dr., P.O. Box 64271 (55164), Woodbury, MN 55125. Tel: 651/738-4000; Fax: 651/738-4024; Web site: http://www.us.fortis.com. Jim Jungbauer, Div. VP; Tom Dodd, Chief Info. Tech. Ofcr. Fortis Information Technology provides IT support for the Fortis companies across the U.S. 1,500 employees (350 in Minnesota; 10 part-time). SIC 7374. Founded in 1985. Owned through Fortis Inc., New York, by Fortis AMEV and Fortis AG, Utrecht, Netherlands. No. 9 CRM Foreign-Owned 100.

Forward Technology Industries Inc. 13500 County Rd. 6, Plymouth, MN 55441. Tel: 763/559-1785; Fax: 763/559-3929; Web site: http://www.forwardtech.com. Ronald D. Barg, Pres. and CEO; Peter Davis, VP-Int'l Mktg.; Wayne Mouser, VP-Sls.; Randy Honeck, Mgr.-Engrg.; John Bloomgren, VP-Mfg.; Peter Hobert, VP-Sls.; Carol Wilkie, Mgr.-Mktg. Admin. Forward Technology Industries is a custom manufacturer of plastics assembly equipment and precision cleaning systems, and halogen lampmaking equipment. 165 employees. SIC 3559. Founded in 1965. Owned by Forward Technology Industries plc, London. No. 70 CRM Foreign-Owned 100.

Frigidaire Home Products Freezer 701 33rd Ave. N., St. Cloud, MN 56303. Tel: 320/253-1212; Fax: 320/252-7090. Kyle Chown, VP and Gen. Mgr. Frigidaire Home Products Freezer manufactures a full line of home freezers for major retail outlets and national distribution. 1,775 employees. SIC 3632. Founded in 1945. Division of White Consolidated Industries Inc., Cleveland; a subsidiary of Electrolux AB, Stockholm. No. 6 CRM Foreign-Owned 100.

Frontier Communications Inc. of Minnesota 14450 Burnhaven Dr., Burnsville, MN 55306. Tel: 952/435-3133. Jeff McGehee, VP-Midwest. Frontier Communications Inc. of Minnesota offers local telephone service to 45 communities in Minnesota. It also sells and rents telephones and offers services such as voice mail and custom calling. 350 employees. SIC 4813. Founded in 1991. Owned by Frontier Corp., Rochester, N.Y., which agreed in March 1999 to be acquired by Global Crossing Ltd. (Nasdaq: GBLXF), Hamilton, Bermuda. No. 42 CRM Foreign-Owned 100.

GAF Materials Corporation 50 Lowry Ave. N., Minneapolis, MN 55411. Tel: 612/520-8740; Fax: 612/520-8772. Phil Bennett, Plant Mgr.; David Paulson, Sls. Mgr. GAF Materials Corp. manufactures roofing products. 130 employees (125 in Minnesota). SIC 2952. Founded in 1937. Owned by GAF Corp., Wayne, N.J.

GE Capital Commercial Finance 8500 Normandale Lake Blvd., Suite 810, Bloomington, MN 55437. Tel: 952/897-5660. Robin J. Engelson, SVP. GE Capital offers creatively structured debt and equity facilities providing working capital and long-term financing for corporate acquisitions, recapitalizations, and restructuring. Transactions range in size from $5 million to $500 million. Particular services include: revolving credit lines, term debt, asset securitization facilities, acquisition financing, letter of credit facilities, capital expenditure lines, preferred and common equity, subordinated debt, debtor-in-possession facilities, and plan of reorganization facilities. SIC 6141. All GE Capital Services businesses owned by General Electric Capital Corp., Stamford, Conn.; division of General Electric Co. (NYSE: GE), Fairfield, Conn.

GE Capital Fleet Services 3 Capital Dr., Eden Prairie, MN 55344. Tel: 952/828-1000; Fax: 952/828-2737; Web site: http://www.gefleet.com. Richard F. (Rick) Smith, Pres. and CEO; Tamotsu Adachi, Pres./CEO-Japan; Rich Bacon, SVP-North American Sls.; Michael Bock, Pres./CEO-Australia; Daniel F. Farrar, Pres./CEO-Europe; Rich Neff, Pres./Gen. Mgr.-Small Fleet Svs.; Scott Parker, SVP-Global Fin.; Marian Powell, SVP, E-commerce; Bob Williams, SVP-North American Op. Annual revenue $1.6 billion. GE Capital Fleet Services is the largest corporate auto leasing and fleet management company in the world. The global fleet management company has worldwide assets of $9 billion and more than 1 million vehicles covered under lease, management. Known as Gelco Corp. until purchased by GE in 1987. 3,700 employees (1,000 in Minnesota). SIC 7359, 7513, 7515. Founded in 1957. By November 1999, just five months after its initial launch, GE Capital Fleet Services' Web ordering application, located within gefleet.com, was averaging more than $3 million a day in online vehicle-ordering transactions. The number of transactions was expected to nearly triple over the next six months. Expanding its commitment to e-commerce initiatives for the fleet industry, GE Capital Fleet launched the first phase of its online, driver-based vehicle-ordering application in December. In January 2000 online titling, licensing and registration renewal services were being tested at Departments of Motor Vehicles throughout 20 states. Dealer Services launched GE ASAP (Application, Submittal, and Approval Process), an online tool designed to help commercial dealers expedite transactions and reduce administrative and processing times. In February GE Capital Fleet acquired the $400 million-asset corporate and utility fleet leasing portfolio of Bank of America Leasing and Capital Group, consisting of 26,000 commercial trucks and cars nationwide. In May the company launched an enhancement to Your Office @ Fleet: an online Web-based reporting tool designed to help fleet managers quickly utilize fleet data to audit their bill and eliminate unnecessary expenditures. In June parent General Electric was named "E-Business Of The Year" in a survey conducted by InternetWeek, the leading Internet/IT publication. Said GE Capital Fleet CEO Smith, "This year alone, our automated fleet management system, Your Office @ Fleet, will help eliminate more than 600,000 pages of mailed invoices and reports to our customers. The online functionality is driving our customers' productivity to unprecedented levels." GE Capital Fleet won The Data Warehousing Institute's coveted Best Practices in Data Warehousing Award in the category "The Warehouse and the Web." The company also won DM Review magazine's World Class Solutions Award in the category of "Business Solutions and Analytic Applications." In November the company signed an agreement with U.K.-based Minorplanet Systems plc to begin offering Minorplanet's Vehicle Management Information (VMI) systems, which utilize global positioning satellite technology. Owned by General Electric Capital Corp., Stamford, Conn., which is a division of General Electric Co. (NYSE: GE), Fairfield, Conn.

REG

GE Capital Information Technology Solutions—U.S. 605 Waterford Park, 605 N. Highway 169, Plymouth, MN 55441. Tel: 763/551-2176; Fax: 763/551-2185; Web site: http://www.gecits.ge.com. Perry Monych, Pres./CEO-North America; Steve Stringer, Pres./COO-U.S. Op.; Frank Kuhar, SVP and CFO; Sallie Howell, VP and Chief Info. Ofcr.; Dick Johnston, EVP-Products; Jeremy Bupp, EVP-Life Cycle; Bill Bancroft, EVP-Tech. Solutions; Steve Mihm, VP-Prod. Mgmt.; Mike Muehlberg, VP-Distribution; Jared Sour, VP-Purch.; Chuck Devine, SVP-Hum. Res.; Gordon Schroeder, VP-Hum. Res.; Anne Knapp, VP-Integration; Greg Meunier, VP-Quality; Margaret Gilbert, VP and Gen. Mgr.-Software Sls. GE Capital Information Technology Solutions (GECITS) is the largest global, vendor-independent supplier of comprehensive, fully integrated information technology solutions, with 150 locations in 15 countries throughout North America, Europe, Latin America, and Asia. 857 employees (79 in Minnesota). SIC 7373, 7374. Founded in 1968. In July 1996 what was then AmeriData Technologies was acquired by the GE Capital Technology Management Services Division of General Electric Capital Corp., Stamford, Conn., a division of General Electric Co. (NYSE: GE), Fairfield, Conn.

GMAC-RFC 8400 Normandale Lake Blvd., Suite 600, Bloomington, MN 55437. Tel: 952/832-7000; Fax: 952/832-7585. Bruce Paradis, Pres. and Managing Dir.; Gregory Schultz, Managing Dir.; Dave Olson, CFO and Managing Dir.; Lorna Gleason, Managing Dir.; John Wright, Area Mgr.-GMAC. GMAC-RFC (General Motors Acceptance Corp. and Residential Funding Corp.) is a residential mortgage company operating in the secondary mortgage market—buying packaged loans from, and providing interim funding to, mortgage originators. The company is America's largest private-label issuer of mortgage-backed securities and a leading warehouse lender. The company leverages its strengths in securitization, lending, and investment to offer a broad portfolio of innovative capital solutions. The company operates in the United States, Europe, Latin America, and Japan. 2,070 employees (990 in Minnesota; 150 part-time). SIC 6141, 6162. Founded in 1982. In December 1999 GMAC-RFC added a fifth shelf, Residential Asset Mortgage Products (RAMP), to allow the company to issue a wider variety of mortgage-backed and asset-backed securities (MBS and ABS), providing investors with access to a more diversified array of products. In February 2000 RFC Commercial collaborated with Prudential Mortgage Capital Co. and Heller Financial Inc. on a $957 million commercial mortgage-backed securitization. The collateral included 234 fixed-rate loans on 241 multi-family and commercial properties. Fitch Investor Service and Moody's Investor's Service both gave the transaction high marks. In March GMAC-RFC announced the closing of a $105 million securitization issued off the company's new Residential Asset Mortgage Products (RAMP) shelf. GMAC closed a $426 million, high-loan-to-value (HLTV) securitization, its first HLTV issuance of the year. GMAC and Olympia Capital ASA have signed an agreement calling for joint development of a distressed consumer asset business in Europe. The two companies planned to invest more than $200 million in the new business—initially expanding into Germany, Austria, and Ireland; and eventually into the rest of Europe. In April Homecomings Financial was awarded the top-servicer designation by ratings agency Fitch IBCA. In May GMAC-RFC announced the closing of a new $304 million warehouse lending credit facility. The company was to serve as credit and collateral agent for Provident Funding Associates L.P, a Burlingame, Calif.-based lender and thesingle borrower in the transaction. GMAC announced the closing of a $225 million warehouse line of credit for Atlanta-based HomeBanc Mortgage Corp., which recently separated from First Tennessee National Corp. In June the company introduced the GMAC Venture Capital Fund, which was to invest in businesses with mortgage technologies or products designed to improve the company's core mortgage-related businesses. The initial investments were in HomeAdvisor Technologies Inc. and Basis100 Inc. (Toronto), companies that could revolutionize the way homes are bought and sold by shortening the mortgage-closing process and reducing consumer costs. Homecomings Financial introduced an Internet-based automated underwriting system that allows mortgage brokers to submit loan applications and receive underwriting decisions online and at the point of sale. The new Assetwise Direct system processes applications and provides responses in less than 30 seconds. GMAC-RFC closed a $600 million HLTV home equity loan securitization, the largest HLTV transaction in the company's history. In July GMAC was assigned the top master servicer designation by international rating agency Fitch, marking the first time a company had received the highest distinction possible. The RMS1 rating reflected GMAC-RFC's continued commitment to building strong servicing capabilities in support of its diverse product lines. In August GMAC announced the creation of its Asia business unit with the appointments of Senri Sasahara and Jari Jison as Japan business development director and Asia business development director, respectively. GMAC formed a strategic alliance with Mortgage Lenders Network USA, a wholesale lender of subprime mortgages, to extend credit in exchange for the delivery of mortgages. In September GMAC-RFC issued a record-breaking $2.5 billion in asset-backed securities (ABS), marking the largest issuance month in the company's history. The company entered into a definitive agreement with Enhance Financial Services to purchase a 46 percent interest in C-BASS (Credit-Based Asset Servicing and Securitization), a leading servicer and securitizer of delinquent residential mortgages. GMAC Institutional Capital announced a $500 million acquisition of adjustable-rate mortgage-backed securities (MBS). In October Residential Funding Corp. announced a new program establishing revolving lines of credit to qualified Mexican businesses through GMAC-RFC's affiliate, GMAC Trade Finance Inc., in order to provide financing for purchases of U.S. exports. GMAC Residential Funding announced a new loan program, Home Solution 107, that enables first-time borrowers to qualify for more house and leverage home equity with less out-of-pocket expense. GMAC-RFC is a subsidiary of General Motors Acceptance Corp., a unit of General Motors Corp. (NYSE: GM), Detroit.

GN ReSound 5600 Rowland Rd., Suite 250, Minnetonka, MN 55343. Tel: 952/930-0416; Fax: 952/930-0516. Carsten Trads, CEO; Donald Dahlquist, Dir.-Hum. Res.; David J. Smriga, Industry/Pub. Rel. GN ReSound, formerly GN Danavox, manufactures and distributes custom in-the-ear and behind-the-ear hearing instruments; and provides educational seminars for hearing professionals. The company is the fourth-largest hearing instrument manufacturer, and the only manufacturer of software-based digital hearing instrument technology in the world. In March 1999 the company began the domestic rollout of Danalogic, a next-generation hearing aid with digital technology, priced at $2,000 to $2,500 retail. In September the parent of GN Danavox acquired ReSound Corp., Redwood City, Calif., and merged it into this operation. The merged company was then renamed GN ReSound. 215 employees. SIC 3842. Founded in 1970. In April 2000 GN ReSound's parent agreed to acquire U.S.-based Beltone Electronics Corp., one of the world's largest manufacturers of hearing instruments. Established in 1940 and headquartered in Chicago, Beltone has maintained a unique approach to hearing instrument sales through its exclusive national distribution network and its strong investment in direct-to-consumer brand advertising. Besides improving GN ReSound's position in the U.S. market, this acquisition makes GN ReSound the market leader in Japan and strengthens its market position in the Netherlands, Spain, Canada, Germany, France, and the UK. GN ReSound North America was to continue to operate out of its Minnesota headquarters, and Beltone out of its Chicago headquarters. In June U.S. and European antitrust authorities approved the deal, making the acquisition final as of June 7. In August the company was making plans to consolidate its former GN Danavox (Minnetonka) and ReSound (Eagan, Minn.) operations into a single 120,000-square-foot facility in Bloomington, Minn., by January 2001. Owned by GN Great Nordic Ltd., Copenhagen. No. 61 CRM Foreign-Owned 100.

GSI Lumonics 8401 Jefferson Hwy., Maple Grove, MN 55369. Tel: 763/315-1780; Fax: 763/315-1770; Web site: http://www.gsilumonics.com. Cathy Olson, Gen. Mgr.; Michael A. Del Busso, Prod. Mgr.; Dan Pederson, Sls. Support Mgr. GSI Lumonics designs and manufactures standard and custom industrial-laser systems for cutting, drilling, heat-treating, and welding. Formerly Laserdyne Corp. In 1999 the company purchased 17 acres in Maple Grove and built a 101,000-square-foot, expandable, company-owned facility there. 120 employees. SIC 3699. Founded in 1981. Owned by Lumonics Inc., which merged with General Scanning Inc. in March 1999 to create GSI Lumonics Inc., Kanata, Ontario. No. 86 CRM Foreign-Owned 100.

Gage Marketing Services 2 Carlson Pkwy., Suite 400, Plymouth, MN 55441. Tel: 763/745-1000; Fax: 763/338-6855. Bob Carmichael, Pres.; Ralph Bartolotta, SVP-Sls./Mktg.; Gary Russol, SVP-Op.; Peggy Prideauy, VP-Hum. Res. Gage Marketing Services carries out visual merchandising and point-of-purchase displays in retail stores for manufacturing clients. PIMMS is an acronym for its former name, Professional Inventory Management & Merchandising Services. In April 1999 the company agreed to be acquired. 7,300 employees (7,000 part-time). SIC 7311, 7319. Founded in 1988. Now owned by AHL Services Inc. (Nasdaq: AHLS), Atlanta.

Game Financial Corporation 13705 First Ave. N., P.O. Box 26008 (55426), Plymouth, MN 55441. Tel: 763/476-8500; Fax: 763/476-8402; Web site: http://www.gamecash.com. Andrew A. Sherwin, Pres.; Michael Barcelow, VP-Nat'l Sls.; Deanna Fredericks-Moose, VP-Op.; Jeffrey L. Ringer, VP and CFO; Mary Thielke, Cont.; Cynthia Davies, Hum. Res. Dir. Game Financial Corp. provides cash access services, principally credit card cash advance, check cashing, and ATM services for casino customers. The company adds promotional programs and other value-added customer retention services to the cash access transaction through its proprietary PC-based systems. Once publicly traded. Merged with Travelers Express Co. of St. Louis Park, Minn., in December 1997. 340 employees (80 in Minnesota; 60 part-time). SIC 6099, 7389. Founded in 1990. In April 2000 Game Financial received new contracts to provide its GameCash cash access services to the new Cliff Castle Casino in Camp Verde, Ariz.; Seminole Coconut Creek Casino in Coconut Creek, Fla.; and the Royal Star Casino in Miami, Fla. Also announced were the signings of contracts for expanded GameCash services at the Majestic Star Casino in Gary, Ind.; Seminole Brighton Casino in Brighton, Fla.; and Win River Casino in Redding, Calif. Game Financial also received its first international contract—to provide cash access services at the Divi Carina Bay Casino in St. Croix, U.S. Virgin Islands. May brought a contract at Beau Rivage Resort in Biloxi, Miss. Travelers Express is a subsidiary of Viad Corp. (NYSE: VVI), Phoenix.

Gannett Offset-Minneapolis 8775 Zachary Ln. N., Maple Grove, MN 55369. Tel: 763/315-7700; Fax: 763/315-1494; Web site: http://www.mplsoffset.com. Mike Lake, Pres. and CEO; Linda Cundiff, Cont.; Ron Lustig, Op. Mgr.; Gary Stang, Sls. Mgr.; Warren Weise, Mktg./Comm. Dir. Gannett Offset-Minneapolis, formerly Printed Media Cos., is a full-service commercial printer with four-color web and sheetfed operations. Complete digital graphics, bindery, inside/outside inkjet addressing, complete mailing and fulfillment departments, printer of USA Today. 220 employees. SIC 2759. Founded in 1976. Acquired in May 1997 by Gannett Offset, a division of Gannett Co. Inc. (NYSE: GCI), Arlington, Va.

Gateway Inc. 610 Gateway Dr., North Sioux City, SD 57049. Tel: 605/232-2000; Fax: 605/232-2023; Web site: http://www.gateway.com. Theodore W. Waitt, Chm. and CEO; Richard D. Snyder, Pres. and COO; Robert N. Beck, SVP-Hum. Res.; James P. Collas, SVP-Global Products; William M. Elliott, SVP, Gen. Counsel, Sec.; David J. McKittrick, SVP, CFO, and Treas.; Robert M. Spears, SVP-Americas; James A. Taylor, Ph.D., SVP-Global Mktg.; Joseph J. Burke, VP-Market Devel.; Robert J. Cheng, VP-Europe/Middle East/Africa; Bernard F. Ebert, VP-Op., Americas Group; John d'Auguste, VP-General Sls., Americas; John D. Heubusch, VP-Gov't Rel.; Michael D. Hammond, VP-Asia/Pacific; Timothy J. Hayes, VP-Customer Support, Americas; William G. Shea, VP-Major Accounts, Americas. Gateway, formerly Gateway 2000, develops, markets, sells, and supports a complete line of IBM-compatible desktop and notebook PCs. Its desktop product line includes systems based on Intel's Pentium processor. Products are sold mainly by telemarketing. In 1998 Gateway moved its headquarters to the West Coast because it was having trouble recruiting the highly skilled people it needed in North Sioux City. 6,200 employees. SIC 3571, 3575. Founded in 1985. In January 2000 Gateway delivered Intel's new mobile-processor technology across its Solo line of notebook computers. Gateway's manufacturing plants and the several divisions remaining in South Dakota, including its largest division, Gateway Direct, now report to Gateway Inc. (Nasdaq: GATE), San Diego.

Gehl Company 915 S.W. Seventh St., Madison, SD 57042. Tel: 605/256-6622; Fax: 605/256-3048. Francis Janous, Plant Mgr. Gehl Co.'s Madison plant manufactures skid-steer loaders, one of the fastest-growing segments of the light construction equipment industry. In August 1999 the parent company's board of directors approved a 41,000-square-foot expansion project at the Madison facility. 205 employees. SIC 3523, 3531, 3537. Founded in 1973. Division of Gehl Co., West Bend, Wis.

General Dynamics Information Systems 8800 Queen Ave. S., Bloomington, MN 55431. Tel: 952/921-6700; Fax: 952/921-6869; Web site: http://www.gd-is.com. James E. Juntilla, Pres. General Dynamics Information Systems is a market leader in providing mission-critical processing, information management systems and systems integration. Core competencies include applying commercial off-the-shelf solutions to enhance performance and lower the cost of airborne, ground, sea, and space-based platforms. Specific applications include C41 and intelligence systems that provide integrated information solutions. The company has delivered more than 10,000 airborne computers to the U.S. Navy since 1976, and is now supplying mission-critical computer systems for the U.S. Air Force's F-15 and B-2 aircraft. General Dynamics Information Systems' ultra high-speed processors have logged more than 800,000 hours of operation on 20 satellites. The company has other operations in Arlington, Va.; Colorado Springs and Denver, Colo.; Dayton, Ohio; Lexington, Mass.; and Sacramento, Calif. The Bloomington headquarters operation was known as Computing Devices International (CDI), a division of Ceridian Corp., also of Bloomington, until acquired Dec. 31, 1997, for $600 million in cash. 880 employees (650 in Minnesota; 30 part-time). SIC 7373. Founded in 1957. In 1999 General Dynamics Information Systems was selected as the overall system engineering and integration partner for the Final Analysis FAISAT system, and was awarded the role of prime contractor for the ground segment. In July 2000 Final Analysis, Lanham, Md., selected the General Dynamics/L-3 Communications team to provide the communications payload for the FAISAT global wireless data system being developed by Final Analysis. General Dynamics Information Systems was to provide the overall system engineering and integration for the FAISAT system and also serve as prime contractor for the ground segment. In August General Dynamics received the James S. Cogswell Award for Outstanding Industrial Security Achievement for 2000. Now owned by General Dynamics Corp. (NYSE: GD), Falls Church, Va.

General Motors Corporation Service Parts Division, 7600 Metro Blvd., Edina, MN 55439. Tel: 952/830-4300; Fax: 952/830-4439. Timothy R O'Neil, Mgr. General Motors Corp.'s Service Parts Division wholesales parts and equipment for GM automobiles. 160 employees. SIC 5013. Founded in 1966. Owned by General Motors Corp. (NYSE: GM), Detroit.

Georgia Pacific Corporation P.O. Box 16267, Duluth, MN 55816. Tel: 218/727-6891; Fax: 218/727-3935. Darryl E. Coons, Hardboard Mgr. Georgia Pacific Corp. manufactures hardboard at its plant in Duluth. In March 1999 the parent company closed its 70-employee pulp and paper products plant in Bemidji, Minn., citing changing market conditions and the age and size of the mill. 350 employees. SIC 2493, 2499. Founded in 1945. Wholly owned subsidiary of Georgia-Pacific Corp. (NYSE: GP), Atlanta.

Giddings & Lewis Castings 1610 15th St., Menominee, MI 49858. Tel: 906/863-9944; Fax: 906/863-1193; Web site: http://www.giddings.com/cast. John A. MacIntyre, VP and Gen. Mgr. Giddings & Lewis Castings manufactures gray iron and ductile iron castings from 500 pounds to 70,000 pounds. The company also does castings in flask, flaskless, and pit molding. 130 employees. SIC 3321. Founded in 1958. Owned by Giddings & Lewis Inc., Fond du Lac, Wis.; a subsidiary of Thyssen Krupp, Dusseldorf, Germany.

Globe Building Materials Inc. 50 Bridge St., P.O. Box 707, Cornell, WI 54732. Tel: 715/239-6424; Fax: 715/239-6366. James Coach, Plant Engr.; Rocky Ewer, Plant Chemist/Safety Dir.; Robert Paulsen, Traffic Mgr./Prod. Scheduler; Alice Sime, Plant Cont.; Joseph Savage, Plant Mgr. Globe Building Materials/Cornell manufactures roofing felt. 110 employees. SIC 2621. Founded in 1974. Plant owned by Clegg Industries, New York.

Globe Building Materials Inc. 1120 E. Seventh St., St. Paul, MN 55106. Tel: 651/776-2793; Fax: 651/776-0640. Ervin Erickson, Plant Mgr.; Vickie Ericksen, Hum. Res. Dir. Globe Building Materials/St. Paul manufactures asphalt-based roofing products. 96 employees (91 in Minnesota). SIC 2952. Plant owned by Clegg Industries, New York.

Golden Valley Microwave Foods Inc. 7450 Metro Blvd., Edina, MN 55439. Tel: 952/835-6900; Fax: 952/835-9635. John S. McKeon, Pres.; D. Faye Martin, VP-Hum. Res. Golden Valley Microwave Foods (GVMF) is a worldwide leader in the development and marketing of foods produced specifically for microwave ovens. GVMF is the manufacturer of ACT II, the world's leading microwave popcorn. Its products are distributed through vending machines, mass-merchandise outlets, and grocery stores. GVMF is recognized as an industry leader for marketing and language-specific packaging. 645 employees (in Minnesota). SIC 2038, 2099. Founded in 1978. In May 2000 the company received the Governor's International Trade Award from Jesse Ventura. Since 1991, GVMF has been a unit of ConAgra Inc. (NYSE: CAG), Omaha, Neb.

Gourmet Award Foods Midwest 2050 Elm St., St. Paul, MN 55114. Tel: 651/752-6300; Fax: 651/752-6350. Douglas Rotchadl, Div. Pres. Gourmet Award Foods Midwest distributes specialty and natural foods to grocery stores in the five-state area. 215 employees. SIC 5149. Founded in 1960. Owned through Tree of Life Inc., St. Augustine, Fla., by Koninklijke Wessanen N.V., Amstelveen, Netherlands. No. 61 CRM Foreign-Owned 100.

Gourmet Express Inc. 5748 Olson Memorial Hwy., Golden Valley, MN 55422. Tel: 952/922-3463; Fax: 952/545-1002. Robert Lapkin, CEO. Gourmet Express is a restaurant-delivery service providing restaurant-prepared food to homes and businesses from more than 80 restaurants throughout the Twin Cities. 56 employees. SIC 7389. Founded in 1992. In January 2000 the company was acquired by an investment group led by Ford Smith, founder of Petsmart Inc. and Food.com then combined with 15 others to form Internet company Easytoget.com, Dallas.

W.W. Grainger 2450 Annapolis, New Hope, MN 55428. Tel: 763/531-7600; Fax: 763/531-0335. Kevin Eisen, Mgr.; Daniel J. Zdon, Sls. Mgr.; Dale Ewasiuk, Purch. Mgr. W.W. Grainger is a distributor of machine tools and industrial supplies. Former names: Satterlee Co.; Bossert Industrial Supply Inc. 425 employees. SIC 5084, 5085. Founded in 1897. Owned by W.W. Grainger Inc. (NYSE: GWW), Lincolnshire, Ill.

Grand Forks Herald Inc. P.O. Box 6008, Grand Forks, ND 58206. Tel: 701/780-1100; Fax: 701/780-1123; Web site: http://www.gfherald.com. Michael Maidenberg, Pres. and Publisher; Mike Jacobs, VP and Editor. Grand Forks Herald publishes a daily and Sunday newspaper; and Agweek, a weekly agricultural magazine. 225 employees. SIC 2711. Founded in 1879. Owned by Knight Ridder Inc. (NYSE: KRI), San Jose, Calif.

Grant Thornton LLP 500 Pillsbury Center North, 200 S. Sixth St., Minneapolis, MN 55402. Tel: 612/332-0001; Fax: 612/332-8361; Web site: http://www.gt.com. Thomas C. Walters, Managing Ptnr.; Ben Horak, Nat'l VP; Steve M. Ray, Consulting Ptnr.-in-charge; James W. Ravell, Exempts Ptnr.-in-charge; Stacy D. Rubsam, Tax Ptnr.-in-charge; Todd F. Taggart, Construction Ptnr.-in-charge; E. Brad Wilson, Quality Assurance Partner. Grant Thornton LLP is an accounting and consulting firm that provides audit, tax, and management consulting services to manufacturing, distribution, construction, and other companies. 145 employees (in Minnesota). SIC 8721. Founded in 1924. Office of Grant Thornton LLP, Chicago.

Great Falls Tribune Company 205 River Dr. S., Great Falls, MT 59405. Tel: 406/791-1435; Fax: 406/791-1431. E. Pat Thompson Frantz, Pres. and Publisher; Debbie Kinsinger, Cont.; Paul Dahms, Circulation Dir.; Alan Bublitz, Prod. Dir.; Ann Snortland, Mktg. Devel. Dir.; Jim Strauss, Exec. Editor. Great Falls Tribune Co. publishes a daily newspaper. 180 employees. SIC 2711. Owned by Gannett Co. Inc. (NYSE: GCI), Arlington, Va.

Grede Foundries Inc. 801 S. Carpenter Ave., Kingsford, MI 49802. Tel: 906/774-7250; Fax: 906/779-0228. Randy Priem, Works Mgr.; Jeff Bianco, Factory Mgr. Annual revenue $53 million. Grede Foundries produces gray iron castings for hydraulics, construction, farm equipment, and engine markets. 525 employees. SIC 3321. Founded in 1947. Owned by Grede Foundries Inc., Milwaukee.

Green Bay Packaging Inc. 555 87th Ln. N.W., Coon Rapids, MN 55433. Tel: 763/786-7446; Fax: 763/786-5101; Web site: http://www.gbpc.com. Erwin Hess, Gen. Mgr.; Pete Nelson, Prod. Mgr.; John Towle, Sls. Mgr.; Pat LeRoy, Div. Cont. Green Bay Packaging Twin Town Division manufactures corrugated shipping containers and related corrugated products. 121 employees (in Minnesota). SIC 2653. Founded in 1948. Owned by Green Bay Packaging Inc., Green Bay, Wis.

Greif Bros. Corporation 2750 W. 145th St., Rosemount, MN 55068. Tel: 651/423-2216; Fax: 651/423-1978. Harley Sasse, VP. Greif Bros.' Norco Division manufactures paper bags. 135 employees. SIC 2449, 2655, 3089. Founded in 1960. Division of Greif Bros. Corp. (Nasdaq: GBC-OA), Delaware, Ohio.

Guidant Corporation Cardiac Rhythm Management Group 4100 Hamline Ave. N., Arden Hills, MN 55112. Tel: 651/638-4000; Fax: 651/582-4166; Web site: http://www.guidant.com. Fred McCoy, Pres. and CEO; Sam Cleary, VP-Mktg.; Barbara Reindl, VP-Hum. Res.; Richard Vogel, VP-Fin.; Jay Warren, VP-Res./Devel.; Dale DeVries, VP-Regulatory Affairs; Ralph Hall, Corp. Counsel; Randy Doyle, VP-Mfg. Annual revenue $1.05 billion. Guidant's Cardiac Rhythm Management (CRM) Group manufactures and markets heart pacemaker systems, AICD automatic implantable cardioverter defibrillators, defibrillation and pacing lead systems, device programmers, and related products. 3,000 employees (2,500 in Minnesota). SIC 3842. Founded in 1972. In January 2000 the company announced the European market release of the next generation in pacemaker devices: the PULSAR MAX II blended-sensor pacemaker system and the DISCOVERY II single-sensor system, the world's first pacemaker systems with a combination of features to manage abnormal heart rates in the heart's upper chambers and to provide unmatched stored electrogram quality. Later in the month, Guidant received FDA approval to market the world's smallest physiologically shaped dual-chamber implantable defibrillator the VENTAK PRIZM AICD Automatic Implantable Cardioverter Defibrillator system. In February A. Jay Graf, president and CEO of CRM, was named to parent Guidant Corp.'s newly created, three-person office of the president. He was replaced here by Fred McCoy, then president of Guidant's Japan/Asia-Pacific operations. In March the FDA approved the DISCOVERY II single sensor pacemaker for market release in the United States. In July Guidant announced the worldwide market release of the ZOOM Programming System, used by physicians and other clinicians to analyze data from Guidant cardiac rhythm management devices such as the VENTAK PRIZM implantable defibrillator and the PULSAR MAX pacemaker. In August Guidant received earlier-than-expected FDA approval to market its VENTAK PRIZM 2 system, the world's smallest, thinnest dual-chamber pacemaker/defibrillator; and the VENTAK PRIZM HE system, a new high-output, dual-chamber defibrillation system for patients with high defibrillation thresholds. The HE product was the only one in the industry to provide both a size and output advantage. In September Guidant announced the first implants of the VENTAK PRIZM 2 AICD. Owned by Guidant Corp. (NYSE: GDT), Indianapolis. No. 79 CRM Employer 100.

HDR Engineering Inc. 5401 Gamble Dr., Suite 300, St. Louis Park, MN 55416. Tel: 952/591-5400; Fax: 952/399-4918. Richard R. Bell, Pres.; David D. Costello, SVP and Dept. Mgr.-Mpls.; Edward J. DLaForest, VP; Charles N. Gonderinger, VP; Jeff Holcomb, VP; George M. Waldow, VP. HDR Engineering is an environmental services company specializing in air quality, water resources, hydrology/drainage, wetlands, riparian engineering, site assessment/remediation, EAW/EIS, noise impacts, and monitoring. 57 employees (in Minnesota). SIC 8711. Founded in 1917. Owned by HDR Inc., Omaha, Neb.

Hagen Systems Inc. 6438 City West Pkwy., Eden Prairie, MN 55344. Tel: 952/944-6865; Fax: 952/946-8513; Web site: http://www.hagensys.com. Richard J. Hagen, CEO; Steven R. Peterson, Pres.; Ron Purdes, VP-PMS Team; Dave Reinhart, VP-Tech. Svs.; Robert Bierwagen, VP-Tech.; Robert M. Hanson, VP-Fin.; Gerald Walsh, VP-Market Devel.; Bill Donais, VP-Programming; David Janke, VP-Strategic Accounts. Annual revenue $18 million. Hagen Systems develops, markets, and supports business information processing systems exclusively for the printing industry. 120 employees. SIC 7373. Founded in 1965. In April 2000 the company was acquired by a national Internet company, mirroring a trend in the industry. Owned by printCafe Inc., Pittsburgh.

Hair by Stewart P.O. Box 5026, Sioux Falls, SD 57117. Tel: 605/336-7080; Fax: 605/330-8209. Vito Cowalchuk, COO. Hair by Stewart operates beauty shops, beauty schools (including the Stewart School of Hair Styling, Brooklyn Park, Minnesota), hair salons, and distribution and manufacturing facilities. 600 employees. SIC 7231. Founded in 1950. Owned by Opal Concepts, Anaheim, Calif.

Hanson Pipe & Products Inc.—North Central Region 6055 W. 150th St., Apple Valley, MN 55124. Tel: 952/432-6050; Fax: 952/432-6234. Jim Kitzmiller, Pres.; Gregory P. Corrow, Pres.-North Central Region. Annual revenue $74 million. Hanson Pipe & Products' North Central Region operations, formerly known as North Star Concrete, manufacture precast concrete products. In October 1998 the company's Apple Valley-based parent Condux Corp., the fifth-largest concrete pipe producer in the United States, agreed to be acquired by a U.S. building materials subsidiary for $77.1 million. 685 employees (500 in Minnesota). SIC 3272, 3273. Founded in 1888. Ultimate parent is Hanson plc (NYSE: HAW), London. No. 27 CRM Foreign-Owned 100.

Harley-Davidson Motor Company Tomahawk Plant, 426 E. Somo Ave., Tomahawk, WI 54487. Tel: 715/453-0516; Fax: 715/453-3924. Steve Phillips, Plant Mgr. Harley-Davidson's Tomahawk Plant manufactures, paints, and assembles plastic and fiberglass components for motorcycles. 550 employees. SIC 3751. Founded in 1946. Division of Harley-Davidson Inc. (NYSE: HDI), Milwaukee.

The Hartford 3800 W. 80th St., Suite 600, Bloomington, MN 55431. Tel: 952/844-3300; Fax: 952/893-0053. R.B. Veselick, Gen. Mgr.-Mpls. Regional Office; John Wolff, Regional Mgr.-Group Sls.; Patrick O'Rourke, Regional Dir.-Benefit Mgmt. Svs. The Hartford, formerly the Hartford Insurance Group, provides property, casualty, life, and group insurance products to personal and commercial clients. 200 employees. SIC 6311, 6331. Member of the ITT Hartford Group Inc., Hartford, Conn.; subsidiary of ITT Industries (NYSE: IIN), New York.

Health Systems Integration Inc. Riverview Office Tower, Suite 700, 8009 34th Ave. S., Bloomington, MN 55425. Tel: 952/851-9696; Fax: 952/858-7900. Health Systems Integration provides hardware, software, installation, and support services to a wide variety of companies in the managed-care industry, including, in the Twin Cities, HealthPartners and Northwestern National Life. Products include Managed Care Administration

System, Practice Management System, Automated Medical Record, Data Reporting System, and Web-enabled applications for enterprise-wide data exchange. 335 employees. SIC 7377, 7379. Founded in 1977. Owned by Compucare, Reston, Va.

Heat-N-Glo, a division of Hearth Technologies Inc. 20802 Kensington Blvd., Lakeville, MN 55044. Tel: 952/985-6000; Fax: 952/985-6001; Web site: http://www.heatng-lo.com. Ron Shimek, Pres.; Brad Determan, SVP-Op.; Dan Shimek, Pres.-Hearth Technologies Inc.; Gerry Shimek, Cont.; Steve Shimek, VP-Sls. Heat-N-Glo manufactures wood-burning gas and electric fireplaces, distributing those products throughout the United States and Canada. A holder of more than 15 industry patents, the company is best known for developing the industry's first direct-vent gas fireplace. The company is one of the top two players in the nation in the $600 million annual market for fireplaces and fireplace products. In October 1999 the company moved to its present headquarters from Savage, Minn. 600 employees (in Minnesota). SIC 3429. Founded in 1975. In fall 1999 the company introduced a $150 million national brand-awareness campaign aimed at people building or remodeling homes, which make up half the company's business. The rest comes directly from builders. Owned by HON Industries Inc. (Nasdaq: HONI), Muscatine, Iowa.

Herberger's Division 600 W. St. Germain, P.O. Box H120, St. Cloud, MN 56302. Tel: 320/251-5351; Fax: 320/654-7075. Max Jones, Pres.; John B. Brownson, EVP; James Scully, Treas. The Herberger's Division operates 40 department stores in Minnesota, Wisconsin, North Dakota, South Dakota, Nebraska, Montana, Iowa, Colorado, and Wyoming. The former G.R. Herberger's Inc. was based in St. Cloud and employee-owned from 1972 until November 1996, when it agreed to be acquired in a stock deal valued at $160 million by Saks (formerly Proffitts) Inc. 4,000 employees (2,300 in Minnesota). SIC 5311. Founded in 1927. Herberger's Division, now based in Milwaukee, is a member of Saks Inc. (NYSE: SKS), New York.

Herff Jones/Photo Division 12221 Riverwood Dr., Burnsville, MN 55337. Tel: 952/890-2200; Fax: 952/890-6735. Roger Neitzke, Mgr. Herff Jones/Photo Division processes student school photographs and provides photo processing services to professional photographers. It has a local sales office in Golden Valley, Minn. 185 employees. SIC 7221. Founded in 1955. Owned by Herff Jones Inc., Indianapolis.

Herff Jones/Photography Division 135 Rice St., Lewiston, MN 55952. Tel: 507/523-2101; Fax: 507/523-2005. Pete Boynton, VP and Gen. Mgr. Herff Jones/Photography Division photographs and processes school student pictures, and does photofinishing for professional photographers. 400 employees (100 part-time). SIC 7221, 7384. Founded in 1955. Division of Herff Jones Inc., Indianapolis.

Heritage Exhibits Inc. 375 Rivertown Dr., Woodbury, MN 55125. Tel: 651/578-3600; Fax: 651/578-3663; Web site: http://www.heritageexhibits.com. Joel Turunen, Pres.; Loren Willis, Cont. Annual revenue $15 million. Heritage Exhibits designs and fabricates custom trade show exhibits. 90 employees (83 in Minnesota). SIC 2541, 2542, 3993. Founded in 1963. Owned by Heritage Display Holding Corp., Washington, D.C.

Hibbing Taconite Company County Road 5, P.O. Box 589, Hibbing, MN 55746. Tel: 218/262-6800; Fax: 218/262-6877. L.G. Dykers, Gen. Mgr.; N.J. MacLeod, Asst. Gen. Mgr. Hibbing Taconite mines iron ore and produces iron ore pellets. Ownership structure: Bethlehem Steel 70.3 percent; Cleveland-Cliffs Inc. 15 percent; Stelco 14.7 percent. In September 1999 employees represented by the International United Steelworkers of America ratified a new five-year labor agreement by a positive margin. 830 employees (in Minnesota). SIC 1011. Founded in 1973. Owned by Bethlehem Steel Corp. (NYSE: BS), Bethlehem, Pa.

Hiniker Company P.O. Box 3407, Mankato, MN 56001. Tel: 507/625-6621; Fax: 507/625-5883. V.J. Tomlonovic, CEO; R.D. McNea, CFO. Annual revenue $17 million. Hiniker Co. manufactures agricultural implements and attachments (including electronic monitoring and control devices), and makes water-treatment systems for home, office, industrial, and municipal markets. It also makes salt and sand spreaders for ice and snow control and snowplows for one ton and smaller trucks. 150 employees (in Minnesota). SIC 3523, 3713. Founded in 1969. Owned by Coster Co., Chicago.

Hinshaw & Culbertson 222 S. Ninth St., Suite 1300, Minneapolis, MN 55402. Tel: 612/333-3434; Fax: 612/334-8888; Web site: http://www.hinshawculbertson.com. Kevin P. Staunton, Recruiting Ptnr.; Ann Marie O'Hara-Frykman, Office Mgr. Annual revenue $100 million. Hinshaw & Culbertson is a law firm. Core competencies include: alternative dispute resolution, commercial litigation, corporate law (mergers and acquisitions), financial institutions (regulatory and government transactions, bond and finance), government practice, health care services (corporate), insurance coverage, intellectual property, labor and employment-counseling compliance and labor negotiations, labor and employment litigation, nonprofit orgazinations, producs liability, professional liability, real estate (construction, development, engineers), school and municipal law, securities litigation, tax, and white-collar crime and compliance. In May 1997 Hinshaw & Culbertson acquired Popham, Haik, Schnobrich & Kaufman Ltd., as an entry into the Twin Cities market. 70 employees (in Minnesota). SIC 8111. Founded in 1934. Owned by Hinshaw & Culbertson, Chicago.

Holm Industries Inc. P.O. Box 187, New Ulm, MN 56073. Tel: 507/354-3191; Fax: 507/354-3193. T.C. Zitzmann, Div. Mgr.; F.R. Drill, Materials Buyer; W.R. Kormann, Maintenance Mgr. Holm Industries Inc. New Ulm Division manufactures refrigerator and freezer gaskets, door gaskets, weatherstripping, and window gaskets. 167 employees. SIC 3089. Founded in 1959. Subsidiary of Standard Products Co. (NYSE: SPD), Cleveland.

Holnam—Trident Plant 4070 Trident Rd., Three Forks, MT 59752. Tel: 406/285-3241; Fax: 406/285-3100. Ralph Denoski, Plant Mgr. Holnam manufactures and sells Portland cement and masonry cement at its Trident plant. 100 employees. SIC 3241. Founded in 1908. Holnam Inc., Dundee, Mich., is owned by Holderbank Financiere Glaris S.A., Jona, Switzerland.

Homestake Mining Company 630 E. Summit St., Lead, SD 57754. Tel: 605/584-4600; Fax: 605/584-4625. Bruce Bried, Gen. Mgr. Homestake Mining is a gold mining company. 356 employees. SIC 1041, 1044. Founded in 1876. Division of Homestake Mining Co. (NYSE: HM), San Francisco.

Honeywell 2701 Fourth Ave. S., Minneapolis, MN 55408. Tel: 612/951-1000; Fax: 612/951-8494; Web: http://www.honeywell.com/yourhome. J. Kevin Gilligan, Pres.-Solutions/Svs. Bus.; Albrecht Weiss, Pres.-Products Business; Dana Badgerow, VP-Global Op./Customer Access. Honeywell retains the headquarters of its Home and Building Control division in the Twin Cities. The division designs, develops, manufactures, markets, and maintains control systems that provide automation, energy management, environmental control, and security for buildings and homes, as well as thermostats, gas valves, and other heating/cooling controls for industrial process and manufacturing automation. 13,750 employees (2,400 in Minnesota). Parent Honeywell International still maintains about 8,000 employees in the state. SIC 3812, 3822, 3823. Founded in 1927. Sept. 30, 1999: Nine-month results for the division included revenue of $2.6 billion and operating profit of $267.8 million. In November 1999 Honeywell announced plans to cut as many as 220 jobs from Home and Building Control. A voluntary layoff package was being offered. Having received clearance from the European Commission, AlliedSignal and Honeywell completed their merger on Dec. 1, after the close of trading on the New York Stock Exchange. Based on AlliedSignal's closing price of $60.75, and including $1.5 billion of assumed debt, the total value of the deal was $16.08 billion. In January 2000 Home and Building Control was awarded a $6.34 million contract by the U.S. Air Force to upgrade base housing and several major maintenance facilities at the Luke Air Force Base near Phoenix—home to the U.S. Air Force's F-16 jet fighter training center. In February Home and Building Control was awarded $18.1 million in Energy Savings Performance Contracts by the U.S. Army Engineering and Support Center, Huntsville, Ala., to design and install high-efficiency boiler and building control systems for 116 buildings at the Fort Dix U.S. Army Reserve Installation near Wrightstown in southern New Jersey. In March the parent announced that it was planning to concolidate its 120-employee, Columbia, Md.-based Microelectronics Technology Center into the Solid-State Electronic Center in Plymouth. In May Honeywell launched a "connected home" project in Orlando, Fla.; Dallas; and Riverside/Palm Springs, Calif. (national rollout planned for fourth quarter). The project connects climate control, home security, appliances, and more in a single computerized system that homeowners can direct via the Internet. The company said that the Home Controller was the top-of-the-line product in a category that could generate $250 million to $550 million in revenue by 2004. In June Honeywell introduced the Superstat, a device designed to save utilities and residential customers money while reducing demand for electricity during peak periods year-round. The Superstat, jointly developed by Honeywell and Comverge Technologies (Nasdaq: DSSI), is a state-of-the-art, programmable thermostat with a built-in wireless radio frequency (RF) communication module. In October Honeywell announced the availability of the Honeywell WebPAD Internet Appliance, the first-ever wireless, portable tool for high-speed connection to the Internet and centralized home control applications. The WebPAD allows a user to surf the Internet, send and receive e-mail, and enter information via a wireless touch screen display. The first wireless Internet appliance of its kind in production, the WebPAD is based on National Semiconductor's Geode WebPAD reference platform. Honeywell then introduced the Enviracaire Elite whole-house air-quality system, a powerful solution to many of the air-quality problems homeowners face. Honeywell was one of the 14founding members of a new industry alliance, Internet Home Alliance, dedicated to enhancing consumers' understanding, appreciation, and adoption of the Internet lifestyle. On Oct. 22, Honeywell International agreed to be sold to General Electric Co. for $55 a share, or $45 billion, in a deal expected to be completed in early 2001. Immediately, there was speculation that Home and Building Control would eventually be sold or spun off by GE in favor of other, faster-growing divisions. GE, however, was upbeat about the unit, and even committed to continuing Honeywell's community-giving program in Minnesota. Honeywell Laboratories won a NIST Advanced Technology Program award to share in initial development costs for an intelligent home automation system, Independent Lifestyle Assistant, whose objective is to enable the elderly to live and function safely at home. Honeywell's Minneapolis operation will then be a subsidiary of General Electric Co. (NYSE: GE), Fairfield, Conn. No. 22 CRM Employer 100.

House of Print 322 Benzel Ave., Madelia, MN 56062. Tel: 507/642-3298; Fax: 507/642-3192. Dave McClellan, Gen. Mgr. House of Print is a commercial printer. 130 employees. SIC 2759. Founded in 1963. Owned by Ogden Newspapers Inc., Wheeling, W.Va.

Hubbard Feeds Inc. 424 N. River Front Dr., Mankato, MN 56001. Tel: 507/388-9400; Fax: 507/388-9453. Richard P. Confer, Pres. Hubbard manufactures animal feed. Hubbard Milling, the former parent, was acquired from the Confer family in 1997 for a reported $160 million. 1,200 employees (400 in Minnesota). SIC 2041, 2048. Founded in 1878. Now owned by Ridley Canada Ltd., Winnipeg, Manitoba. No. 11 CRM Foreign-Owned 100.

Hubbard Scientific Inc. 1120 Halbleib Rd., Chippewa Falls, WI 54729. Tel: 715/723-4427; Fax: 715/723-8021; Web site: http://www.amep.com. Thomas Halbleib, Plant Mgr. Hubbard Scientific is a manufacturer and distributor of educational materials for grades K-12. 65 employees. SIC 2759. Founded in 1968. Subsidiary of American Educational Products (Nasdaq: AMEP), Boulder, Colo.

Hudson Foods 702 13th St., Albert Lea, MN 56007. Tel: 507/377-2526; Fax: 507/377-6692. Ken Hakes, Gen. Mgr. Hudson Foods is a food processor for Schweigert and other food producers. 360 employees. SIC 2013. Founded in 1989. Purchased from Land O'Lakes in 1989 by Hudson Foods Inc. (NYSE: HFI), Rogers, Ark.

Hunt-Wesson Inc. 104 River Rd. W., Menomonie, WI 54751. Tel: 715/235-5575; Fax: 715/232-0356. William Butsic, Plant Mgr.; Michael Scharlau, Plant Engr.; Curt Boraas, Hum. Rel. Mgr.; Theresa Meyers, Purch. Hunt-Wesson manufactures and packages nonfat dry milk, hot cocoa mix, refrigerated cupped snacks (pudding and gels), and other food-manufacturing ingredients. The company, then known as Orville Redenbacher/Swiss Miss, was acquired in August 1990 from Beatrice Cos. Inc. 550 employees. SIC 2023. Founded in 1946. Now a division of Hunt-Wesson Inc., Fullerton, Calif., which is owned by ConAgra Inc. (NYSE: CAG), Omaha, Neb.

Huntsman Packaging 1701 First Ave., P.O. Box 189, Chippewa Falls, WI 54729. Tel: 715/723-4456; Fax: 715/723-1015. Dennis Schoch, Plant Mgr. Huntsman Packaging manufactures extruded polyethylene film (blown and cast). 176 employees. SIC 3081. Founded in 1948. Owned by Huntsman Corp., Salt Lake City.

Hurd Millwork Company 575 S. Whelen Ave., Medford, WI 54451. Tel: 715/748-2011; Fax: 715/748-6043. Kenneth Hallgren, Pres. Hurd Millwork manufactures wood windows, patio doors, and aluminum clad wood windows and patio doors at plants in Medford and Merrill, Wis. 1,000 employees. SIC 2431. Founded in 1919. Owned by Harlyn Industries Inc., N.Y.; a division of UIS Inc., New York.

Hutchinson Wil-Rich Mfg. Company P.O. Box 1030, Wahpeton, ND 58074. Tel: 701/642-2621; Fax: 701/642-3372. Ron Werner, Pres. Hutchinson Wil-Rich manufactures farm-tillage and chemicals-application equipment. 200 employees (33 in Minnesota). SIC 3523. Founded in 1964. Owned by TIC United Corp., Dallas.

Hypro Corporation 375 Fifth Ave. N.W., New Brighton, MN 55112. Tel: 651/766-6300; Fax: 651/766-6605. Donald L. Jorgensen, Pres. and CEO; Robert A. Lamp, VP-Bus. Devel.; David C. Wipson, VP, COO-Agricultural/Pressure Products; Lee E. Marks, VP-Op.; Steven C. Panasuk, VP-Product Devel.; Dennis R. Wierzbicki, VP and COO-Sherwood Marine/Industrial; Stephen M. Dickhaus, VP-Fin. Annual revenue $80 million. Hypro manufactures pumps and pumping accessories for high-pressure cleaning; and for industrial and agricultural spraying applications. Pump types include piston, plunger, roller, centrifugal, diaphragm, and the FoamPro System for the fire protection market. 260 employees (255 in Minnesota; 5 part-time). SIC 3561. Founded in 1947. Owned by Wisconsin Energy Corp. (NYSE: WEC), Milwaukee.

IBM Corporation Highway 52 and Northwest 37th Street, Rochester, MN 55901. Tel: 507/253-4011; Fax: 507/253-3290; Web site: http://www.as400.ibm.com. Walt Ling, VP; Martha Morris, VP-Server Group. IBM Corp.-Rochester is the principal hardware and software development and manufacturing facility for IBM's AS/400 family of business computing systems and is a major development location for the IBM RS/6000. Rochester is also the principal manufacturing facility for IBM's RS/6000 family of computing systems. IBM Rochester is also the corporation's sole source supplier of glass disk substrates used in IBM's hard disk drives. 7,200 employees (in Minnesota). SIC 3571, 3674. Founded in 1956. In October 1999 the unit's continued sluggish sales (third-quarter revenue from Rochester had declined 30 percent) contributed to a companywide profit warning. In November the parent company announced pending layoffs at the Server Group's U.S. workforce. In December it confirmed that 3 percent of staff would be laid off, including an unspecified number in Rochester (thought to be between 100 and 150). In February 2000 Celestica Inc. acquired IBM's electronic card assembly operations in Rochester, plus related businesses in Italy, for $500 million. About 500 full-time workers were expected to transfer to Celestica. In March FTL Systems, Rochester, Minn., a leading developer of software that simulates how computer hardware systems will function in real-world environments, announced that its Auriga family of products was performing twice as fast on new IBM RS/6000 workstations compared with previous RS/6000 models. IBM's new RS/6000 44P Model 270 and 44P Model 170 are the world's first UNIX workstations to contain copper-based microprocessors. (Copper can increase microprocessor performance substantially compared with chips that use traditional aluminum wire.) In May IBM officials announced that a change in technology (IBM was switching from aluminum in its computer discs to glass) would mean fewer workers would be needed to manufacture those discs, necessitating a July layoff of 170 workers. The company also introduced a new line of AS/400 servers, developed and manufactured in Rochester. Division of IBM Corp. (NYSE: IBM), Armonk, N.Y.

REG

IBM Corporation 650 Third Ave. S., Minneapolis, MN 55402. Tel: 612/397-2000; Fax: 612/397-6490. John Overbeck, VP-Product Mktg.; Diane Brink, VP-Direct Mktg. IBM Corp.'s marketing and service organization in Minnesota sells and services IBM's entire line of products for customers throughout Minnesota and the Midwest. 700 employees. SIC 5045. Division of IBM Corp. (NYSE: IBM), Armonk, N.Y.

IMI Cornelius Inc. One Cornelius Pl., Anoka, MN 55303. Tel: 763/421-6120; Fax: 763/427-4522. Richard Barkley, Pres.; Charles Fleming, EVP-Op.; David Storey, EVP-Cust. Svc.; Robert Nicholson, EVP-Fin.; William May, COO. IMI Cornelius is the world's leading producer of beverage-dispensing equipment. 600 employees (in Minnesota). SIC 2599, 3581, 3589. Founded in 1937. In May 2000 IMI Cornelius formed an alliance with Microban Products Co., Huntersville, N.C., a leading provider of antibacterial-technology, to produce the first ice machine with antimicrobial product protection for the international commercial market. In September 350 union workers rejected a contract proposal and went on strike. The chief complaint: Double-digit increases in health insurance premiums have been wiping out workers' pay raises over the past few years. On Oct. 8, the month-long strike was prolonged when workers rejected a second contract proposal. Talks then stalled, although the union agreed to have a mediator at subsequent meetings. Owned by IMI plc, Birmingham, U.K. No. 23 CRM Foreign-Owned 100.

ING ReliaStar 20 Washington Ave. S., Minneapolis, MN 55401. Tel: 612/372-5432; Fax: 612/372-1192; Web site: http://www.reliastar.com. John G. Turner, FSA, Chm. and CEO; Robert C. Salipante, Pres. and COO; Wayne R. Huneke, Senior EVP; Kenneth U. Kuk, EVP-Worksite Fin. Svs.; William R. Merriam, EVP-Reinsurance Group; Richard R. Crowl, SVP, Gen. Counsel, and Sec.; Dewey Ingham, SVP-Hum. Res.; Mark S. Jordahl, SVP and Chief Investment Ofcr.; James R. Miller, SVP, CFO, and Treas.; Randall L. Ciccati, Pres./CEO-PriveVest Financial Services; James G. Cochran, Pres.-ReliaStar Employer Financial Svs.; Scott H. DeLong, VP-Corp. Devel.; Michael J. Dubes, Pres./CEO-Northern Life; James R. Gelder, Pres./CEO-Security-Connecticut Life; Paul H. Gulstrand, VP-ReliaStar Employee Benefits; Mark L. Lipson, Chm./CEO-Northstar Investment Mgmt.; Judith H. Lissick, VP-ReliaStar Financial Lifeline; Susan W.A. Mead, VP-Strategic Mktg./ Planning; Blake W. Mohr, VP-ReliaStar Retirement Plans; Jeff A. Montgomery, Pres./CEO-Washington Square Securities; Holly Morris, VP and Chief Info. Ofcr.; Brian H. Myres, Pres.-ReliaStar Bank; Chris D. Schreier, VP and Cont.; Winifred S. Smith, VP-Corp. Properties; John H.P. Wheat, Pres./CEO-Successful Money Mgmt. Seminar. Annual revenue $3.03 billion (earnings $253.6 million). ING ReliaStar specializes in the life and health insurance and annuity business. Through its subsidiaries, including ReliaStar Life, the company offers individual life insurance and annuities, employee benefits, retirement contracts, bank products, trust services, life and health re-insurance, and mutual funds. The company operates in four business segments: individual insurance, employee benefits, life and health reinsurance, and 403(b) annuities. Founded in 1885 as Northwestern National Life, the company adopted a dual stock and mutual structure in 1927. In 1989 the company converted to a completely shareholder-owned company, with The NWNL Cos. succeeding Northwestern National Life as the parent organization. In 1995 NWNL changed its name to ReliaStar. In 2000 ReliaStar was acquired by ING Groep N.V., Amsterdam. 3,800 employees. SIC 6211, 6411. Founded in 1988. In February 2000 ReliaStar and Lexington Global Asset Managers Inc. (Nasdaq: LGAM) signed a definitive agreement for ReliaStar to acquire the $3.6 billion-asset, New Jersey-based asset management and mutual fund company in a stock-and-cash transaction. [At July closing, the deal was valued at $51 million.] "This acquisition enhances our product line and internal asset management capabilities, adds assets, and provides economies of scale," said CEO Turner. "Adding Lexington to our existing Pilgrim mutual fund operation supports our stepped-up focus on gathering and managing assets." He added, "Lexington has significant international equity management capabilities, which is something we don't have inside Pilgrim at this point." With Lexington, ReliaStar grew to $20 billion in assets under management and gained 13 fund families, for a total of 45 funds. In March ReliaStar was the first financial services company to receive permission from the OCC to organize and operate a national bank under the provisions of the Financial Services Modernization Act of 1999. ReliaStar National Trust Co. was to be a "national trust bank," limited to fiduciary powers. In April ReliaStar announced the launch of a new Internet marketing initiative, IHateFinancialPlanning.com, geared to consumers who dislike financial planning and want both simplicity and choice in their buying experience. The new business was to target the estimated 17.6 million Americans who use the Internet and who find saving, investing, and retirement planning to be a frustrating and intimidating experience. On May 1, the board reached a definitive agreement for ReliaStar to be sold to ING Group, a global financial institution active in insurance, banking, and asset management in more than 60 countries, with almost 90,000 employees. With this agreement, ING advanced its strategy of substantially expanding its presence in the United States. The agreement valued ReliaStar at $54 per share, or $5.1 billion (a 25.6 percent premium to the prevailing stock price), plus $1 billion in debt. [Deal close Sept. 1.] ReliaStar was to continue its operations as part of ING Americas under the name ING ReliaStar, and retain current management. CEO Turner was to become a member of Executive Committee ING Americas and vice chairman of the Americas region. He was also to manage ING's mutual fund business, the assets of which had been increased by 12-fold with the acquisition. President Salipante was named president and CEO of the U.S. life insurance operations. Turner said that the pressure over time to fund more technology and to buy national marketing for the ReliaStar brand would soon have caused trouble for a company ReliaSar's size. In addition, Wall Street had soured on the company after operating difficulties in 1999. Because there was little redundancy among operating lines, ING was able to promise no job cuts, which was one of the reasons that ING was seen as the best fit among several suitors in terms of shareholders, customers, employees, and the community at large. In light of the announcement, A.M. Best Co. affirmed the A+ (Superior) financial strength ratings of ReliaStar Life Insurance Co. and its operating life and health insurance affiliates, Northern Life Insurance Co. and ReliaStar Life Insurance Co. of New York. The A (Excellent) financial strength rating of Security-Connecticut Life Insurance Co., a ReliaStar Life affiliate, was also affirmed. Standard & Poor's put its ReliaStar ratings on "CreditWatch with positive implications," expecting to raise them at the deal's conclusion. As part of the sale agreement, 3,800 employees were able to prematurely exercise all of their stock options (collective gross value: $453 million). Integration teams with participation by representatives from each of ReliaStar and ING were charged to capture best practices for each business or functional area. [In July ING Group had reached an agreement to purchase the financial services and international business segments of Aetna, a transaction that would give the combined operations greater scale, a broader product portfolio, and enhanced revenue-generating synergies, such as significant additional cross-selling opportunities.] In August KnowHow Inc., a premier provider of Web-based sales training, agreed to help develop a new online education site for ReliaStar Life Insurance Co. (The site features customized curricula study areas for independent agents and employees.) ING ReliaStar is part of ING Americas, a division of ING Groep N.V., Amsterdam. No. 13 CRM Public 200. No. 2 CRM Foreign-Owned 100.

ITT Industries Cannon 8081 Wallace Rd., Eden Prairie, MN 55344. Tel: 952/934-4400; Fax: 952/934-9121. R.L. Haueter, Pres. ITT Schadow Inc. designs, manufactures, and markets electronic components and systems (including electromechanical switches, conductive rubber switchpads, multifunction grips, and panel assemblies) for the instrumentation, communications, EDP, industrial, and agricultural markets. 150 employees. SIC 3679. Founded in 1978. Owned by ITT Industries (NYSE: IIN), New York.

ITW Heartland 1601 36th Ave., Alexandria, MN 56308. Tel: 320/762-8138; Fax: 320/763-5645. Keith A. Anderson, VP and Gen. Mgr. ITW Heartland machines small quantities of spare parts, and designs and manufactures packaging machines and assembly machines. 140 employees. SIC 3546, 3565. Founded in 1976. Owned by Illinois Tool Works Inc. (NYSE: ITW), Glenview, Ill.

ITW Irathane Systems Inc. P.O. Box 276, Hibbing, MN 55746. Tel: 218/262-5211; Fax: 218/263-9731. Kent R. Salo, National Sls. Mgr.; Chuck Brown, Cont. ITW Irathane Systems is a polyurethane and coatings manufacturing company that sells abrasive products for the mining and aggregate/sand-and-gravel industries. 65 employees (30 in Minnesota). SIC 2851. Founded in 1957. Subsidiary of Illinois Tool Works Inc. (NYSE: ITW), Glenview, Ill.

Ike International Corporation 500 E. Maple St., Stanley, WI 54768. Tel: 715/644-5777; Fax: 715/644-5786. Kuni Igarashi, EVP. Ike International produces commercial hardwood veneer and lumber. 135 employees (2 part-time). SIC 2435. Founded in 1987. Owned by Ike Trading Co. Ltd., Beaverton, Ore.; which is owned by Ikeuchi Industry Co. Ltd., Sapporo, Japan.

Ikon Office Solutions-Minnesota 2740 W. 80th St., Bloomington, MN 55431. Tel: 952/888-8000; Fax: 952/885-3666; Web site: http://www.ikon.com. Robert W. Burton, Pres.; Timothy J. Battis, VP-Sls. Ikon Office Solutions provides copier and facsimile systems (Canon), services, and supplies in the Twin Cities; Duluth, Rochester, St. Cloud, Willmar, Brainerd, Mankato, and Marshall, Minn.; and La Crosse, Wis. D.C. Hey Co. combined with CDP, IOS, and American Photocopy on Oct. 1, 1997, to form Ikon Office Solutions-Minnesota. 700 employees (in Minnesota). SIC 5044. Founded in 1946. Owned by Ikon Office Solutions Inc. (NYSE: IKN), Valley Forge, Pa.

In Home Health Inc. 601 Carlson Pkwy., Suite 500, Minnetonka, MN 55305. Tel: 952/449-7500; Fax: 952/449-7599. C. Michael Ford, Chm. and interim Pres./CEO; Robert J. Hoffman Jr., CFO, Treas., and Sec.; Cathy A. Nielsen, VP-Clinical Svs.; Lisa F. Weber, VP-Op. In Home Health Inc. provides comprehensive health care, including skilled nursing, infusion therapy, hospice, rehabilitation, and personal care, to clients of all ages in their own homes. Begun in a single office in 1984, In Home Health has grown to 38 offices and four pharmacies in 19 geographic markets in 14 states. In Home Health entered into a strategic partnership with, and was later acquired by, ManorCare Health Services, a leading provider of long-term care and post-acute services. This partnership allows In Home Health and ManorCare to provide a broad continuum of quality, cost-effective, and outcome-oriented post-acute services to clients and payors. 2,300 employees (1,600 part-time). SIC 8082. Founded in 1983. On May 31, the company's largest stockholder, a subsidiary of Manor Care Inc. (NYSE: MNR), wrote to demand that In Home call a special meeting of its shareholders to consider three proposals by Manor Care: to remove all members of In Home's board of directors other than C. Michael Ford and Eugene Terry; to fix the number of members of the board at six; and to elect to the board four individuals who are officers and employees of Manor Care or its subsidiaries. (Manor Care owned 2,250,000 shares of In Home's common stock, constituting 41 percent of In Home's outstanding shares of common stock; and 200,000 shares of In Home's Series A Preferred Stock, which was convertible at $6.00 per share into 3,333,333 shares of In Home common stock.) In Home's board authorized the company to hire the investment banking firm of Houlihan, Lokey Howard & Zukin to advise and assist the board in evaluating and responding to Manor Care's interest in the company and in exploring possible strategic alternatives to maximize shareholder value. On June 28 and 29, a subsidiary of Manor Care purchased 1,146,735 additional shares of In Home Health common stock, increasing Manor Care's holdings to a total of 3,396,735 shares, or 61.4 percent of the outstanding shares. In July, after three directors resigned, the board appointed Manor Care officers to two of the vacancies and announced its intent to add two more Manor Care officers in the near future. As a result, Manor Care withdrew its demand for a special meeting. Manor Care then offered to acquire the remaining 38.6 percent not already owned for $3.375 a share ($7.2 million), a 3.8 percent premium over the prevailing price. TOLEDO, Ohio and MINNETONKA, Minn., Sept. 13 /PRNewswire/ —Manor Care, Inc. (NYSE: HCR) and In Home Health, Inc. (Nasdaq: IHHI) announced today that they have signed an Agreement and Plan of Merger according to which Manor Care will acquire all the outstanding IHHI shares that it does not already own. The transaction, which is structured as a cash merger, was approved by IHHI's Board of Directors, acting upon the unanimous recommendation of a special committee of the Board comprising IHHI Board members who are not affiliated with Manor Care. The special committee reached its decision working with its financial advisor, Houlihan Lokey Howard & Zukin Financial Advisors, Inc., which rendered an opinion that the consideration to be received by shareholders in the merger is fair to the holders of common sharesof IHHI from a financial point of view. Pursuant to the merger, shareholders, other than Manor Care and its affiliates, will receive $3.70 for each share of IHHI common stock, which is a premium of 88 percent over the closing price on May 31, 2000, the day before IHHI made public Manor Care's intentions with regard to the company. Consummation of the merger is subject to several conditions specified in the merger agreement. If such conditions are satisfied and the merger is completed, Manor Care will own all of the issued and outstanding shares ofIHHI following the merger. IHHI intends to call and hold a special meeting ofits shareholders to vote upon the merger agreement as soon as practicable. Manor Care and its affiliates currently own approximately 61.3 percent ofIHHI's 5.54 million common shares and 100 percent of IHHI's preferred shares outstanding. Each share of preferred stock is entitled to cast 16.67 votesper share. Manor Care's preferred stock shares combined with its common shares give it the right to cast approximately 75.8 percent of the votes entitled to be cast at the special meeting of shareholders. Owned by Manor Care Inc. (NYSE: MNR), Gaithersburg, Md. No. 93 CRM Public 200.

Inacom Information Systems 10300 Valley View Rd., Suite 101, Eden Prairie, MN 55344. Tel: 952/946-1200; Fax: 952/946-8823; Web site: http://www.inacom.com. James D. Leslie, District Dir. Inacom Information Systems is a personal-computer reseller, specializing in advanced technologies such as local-area networks and UNIX-based systems. It offers design, acquisition, implementation, and outsourcing services, as well as technical support and training. Formerly OPM Information Systems. 200 employees (in Minnesota). SIC 5734. Founded in 1975. In June 1998 OPM was acquired by Inacom Corp. (Nasdaq: INAC), Omaha, Neb.

Inacom Professional Services 10 Second St. N.E., Minneapolis, MN 55413. Tel: 612/378-4400; Fax: 612/378-4401. Steve Hysjulien, Area Principal; Jonathan Secrest, Dir.-Bus. Devel./Mktg.; Greg Thompson, Sls. Mgr. Inacom Professional Services provides mission-critical business networking services—including analysis, design, consulting, implementation, and support—with the latest technological advances. Known prior to March 1996 as DCC Inc., then as Perigee Communications Inc., the company was acquired in December 1996 in a stock deal estimated at $13.8 million. 110 employees. SIC 7373. Founded in 1988. Now owned by Inacom Corp. (Nasdaq: INAC), Omaha, Neb.

Industrial Fabrics Corporation 7160 Northland Circle, Brooklyn Park, MN 55428. Tel: 763/535-3220; Fax: 763/535-6040. Rolf Muehlenhaus, Pres. Industrial Fabrics Corp. manufactures and distributes industrial textiles, including fabrics for filtration, screen printing, and other industrial specialty applications. 100 employees (in Minnesota). SIC 2241. Founded in 1962. Owned by United Silk Mills Ltd., New York.

Information Advantage 7905 Golden Triangle Dr., Eden Prairie, MN 55344. Tel: 952/833-3700; Fax: 952/833-3701; Web site: http://www.infoadvan.com. Richard L. Tanler, Chm.; Larry J. Ford, Pres. and CEO; William Retterath, VP-Fin./Admin. Information Advantage is recognized as the leading provider of business intelligence (BI) solutions under the name of DecisionSuite, which includes integrated query, enterprise reporting, and OLAP for data warehouses/data marts. All products are Web-enabled, and architected using three-tier server-based technology with thin-client desktops. In addition Eureka! applies the same visualization, navigation, agent, delivery, and search principles popularized by Internet portals like Yahoo! and AOL, but does so for corporate intranets—so that people can get information within the organization as easily as they can on the Web. In August 1999 the then-publicly traded Information Advantage was acquired by Sterling Software, one of the 20 largest independent software companies in the world. The offer price, valued at $163 million, represented a 58 percent premium over the 30-day trailing average of Information Advantage's shares. Sterling, in turn, was acquired in April 2000. 500 employees (325 in Minnesota). SIC 7371. Founded in 1990. In December 1999 the company released EUREKA: Portal 2.0. e.Intelligence, a company that is extending business intelligence to include demand planning applications, joined Information Advantage's EUREKA:Partners program. Information Advantage and Verity Inc. (Nasdaq: VRTY), a leading provider of enterprise and Internet knowledge retrieval solutions, announced a partnership agreement to integrate Verity's comprehensive search and retrieval technology into EUREKA:Portal 2.0. In January 2000 SSDS Inc., a leading information technology engineering firm specializing in complex network and system development and implementation, joined the EUREKA:Partners program. The EUREKA:Partners program expanded to include content providers. A partnership with iSyndicate was to enable users of EUREKA:Portal to receive personalized, syndicated content through a single user interface. In February Kelly Services (Nasdaq: KELYA, KELYB), a leading global provider of staffing services, selected EUREKA:Portal, EUREKA:Reporter, and EUREKA:Analyst for its data warehousing initiative. At month's end, SAP Productivity Suite, a complete end-to-end solution for data access, reporting, and analysis for SAP R/3, the industry's leading ERP software application, was launched. In March PEMEX, Mexico's largest company and one of the largest oil companies in the world, chose Information Advantage's EUREKA:Suite technology to provide intuitive, Web-based reporting and analysis. In April INNOLOG (Innovative Logistics Techniques Inc.), McLean, Va., announced plans to integrate the MyEureka!business intelligence portal into the Transaction Engine of its AssetIQ solutions suite. Now owned by Computer Associates International Inc. (NYSE: CA), Islandia, N.Y.

Inland Ispat Mining Company P.O. Box 1, Virginia, MN 55792. Tel: 218/749-5910; Fax: 218/749-5256. Inland Ispat Mining Co. produces iron ore fluxed pellets at the Minorca Mine. The Minorca plant typically produces about 2.7 million tons of taconite pellets annually, which are used as one of the raw materials for steel. 372 employees. SIC 1011. Founded in 1974. Subsidiary of Ispat International N.V., London. No. 41 CRM Foreign-Owned 100.

Inland Paperboard And Packaging Inc. 3900 Highway 101, Shakopee, MN 55379. Tel: 952/445-4201; Fax: 952/445-5633. Steve Nerison, Gen. Mgr.; Richard Carlson, Prod. Mgr. Annual revenue $38 million. Inland Paperboard and Packaging produces and sells corrugated containers. 130 employees (in Minnesota). SIC 2653. Founded in 1960. Inland Container Corp., Indianapolis, owned by Temple-Inland Inc. (NYSE: TIN), Diboll, Texas.

Integrated Logistic Solutions 200 South Owasfo Blvd. East, St. Paul, MN 55117. Tel: 651/482-7400; Fax: 651/486-2571. Larry A. Carlson, Chm. and SVP-Mktg.; Michael J. Lindseth, Pres. and CEO; Kim B. Erickson, VP-Fin. and CFO. Integrated Logistic Solutions is a national distributor of specialty and standard fasteners to the industrial market. It offers an extensive fastener product line and a wide range of value-added services: inventory management programs; electronic data interchange with customers' manufacturing and purchasing departments; custom packaging; bar coding; just-in-time delivery to customers' assembly lines; and electronic billing. The company distributes 18,000 different fasteners to 7,400 original-equipment manufacturers, other industrial manufacturers, industrial distributors, assemblers, and subassemblers. Integrated Logistic Solutions is ISO 9002-certified. 398 employees. SIC 5072. Founded in 1972. Now owned by Park-Ohio Industries Inc. (Nasdaq: PKOH), Euclid, Ohio.

Interim Healthcare Inc. 5131 Edina Industrial Blvd., Edina, MN 55439. Tel: 952/832-9434. Teresa Dock, Ofcr. Annual revenue $17 million. Interim Healthcare is a home health care organization providing registered nurses, licenses practical nurses, home health aides, homemaker services, physical therapy, and occupational therapy. 350 employees. SIC 8082. Founded in 1968. Owned by Spherion (NYSE: SFN), Fort Lauderdale, Fla.

Interlogix Inc. 2266 N. Second St., North St. Paul, MN 55109. Tel: 651/777-2690; Fax: 651/779-4802; Web site: http://www.ititechnologies.com. Thomas L. Auth, Chm.; Ken Boyda, Pres. and CEO; Joe Hurst, SVP; Charles E. Briskey, SVP and Treas.; Charles A. Durant, VP, Gen. Counsel, and Sec.; Jack A. Reichert, VP-Fin.; Reed G. Grothe, VP-Sls.; Gerald U. Klasen, VP-Int'l/Commercial Sls.; Duane Paulson, VP-Mktg.; Brian Seemann, VP-Engrg. Interlogix, formerly ITI Technologies Inc. (Nasdaq: ITII), is the leading designer and manufacturer of wireless security systems. It also manufactures a line of integrated intrusion alarm, access control, and fire protection hardwire security systems; a line of access control systems; and related security equipment. On May 2, 2000, ITI merged with SLC Technologies Inc., Portland, Ore., to create Interlogix. 450 employees (in Minnesota). SIC 3669, 7382. Founded in 1992. In November 1999 Interactive Technologies entered into an agreement with Gradiente Electronica S.A. of Sao Paulo, Brazil, under which Gradiente was to assemble and distribute ITI's popular Simon security system in Brazil. In February 2000 ITI and SLC Technologies Inc. reported that they had satisfied several conditions to the closing of their merger. SLC had received a supplemental ruling from the Internal Revenue Service relating to SLC's 1997 spin-off from its former parent. Receipt of this ruling was a key part of a condition to closing of the merger. The companies also reported that the 30-day waiting period after the filing of reports under the Hart-Scott-Rodino Act had also expired. Finally, the companies reported that SLC had entered into a $325,000,000 credit agreement to refinance the debt of the combined companies after the merger and to finance the cash election provided for in the merger agreement. In March MainStreet Networks and Interactive Technologies Inc. announced a strategic relationship to deliver a broad range of enhanced monitoring solutions. Interactive Technologies announced an agreement with Microsoft Corp. (Nasdaq: MSFT) and other leading companies to join the Universal Plug and Play (UPnP) Forum furthering the companies' shared objective of establishing industry-leading standards for home systems networking. In May the SLC Technologies merger was completed following approval of the merger by ITI's shareholders. Concurrent with the closing of the merger, the name of the combined company was changed to Interlogix Inc. New CEO Boyda said, "Interlogix will be a technology leader with broad product offerings, integrated technological capabilities, and global presence necessary to lead the $10 billion industry that we currently serve. We intend to build upon the broad framework of ITI and SLC to expand product applications beyond conventional industry boundaries by bringing new product offerings in the key growth areas of digital communications, Web-enabled connectivity, and RFID asset tracking." In May Interlogix announced the results of the cash election in connection with the recently closed merger. Existing shareholders had the right to elect to receive from Interlogix $36.50 in cash at closing for each share of stock held, subject to the limitation that no more than 50 percent of the total number of shares of common stock issued and outstanding immediately prior to the closing be exchanged for cash. The transfer agent reported that a total of 7,868,027 shares of stock were exchanged for cash, which is greater than 50 percent of the 8,536,592 shares of common stock outstanding immediately prior to the closing. Consequently, the shares eligible to be exchanged were to be reduced on a pro rata basis. Interlogix acquired the assets and rights to technology of the video transmission product line from 8x8 Inc. d/b/a Netergy Networks (Nasdaq: NTRG). (The 8x8 product line allows for the transmission of security video and audio signals over standard phone lines or high-speed ISDN lines.) In August the company agreed with Tracking Technologies Inc., Minneapolis, to co-brand Security Pro Identi Mark, a product developed from new security technology that readily identifies the owner of stolen property. Owned by Interlogix Inc. (Nasdaq: ILXI), Portland, Ore. No. 86 CRM Public 200.

Intermedia Communications 1270 Northland Dr., Suite 125, Mendota Heights, MN 55120. Tel: 651/468-3840; Web site: http://www.intermedia.com. Dave Ruberg, Ofcr. Intermedia Communications is a telecommunications company that provides Internet, frame relay, Web hosting, private lines, long-distance, T-1, and NNI services. 150 employees. SIC 4813. Founded in 1986. Owned by Intermedia Communications Inc. (Nasdaq: ICIX), Tampa, Fla.

International Dairy Queen Inc. 7505 Metro Blvd., P.O. Box 39286, Edina, MN 55439. Tel: 952/830-0200; Fax: 952/830-0270. Michael P. Sullivan, Chm.; Charles W. (Chuck) Mooty, Pres. and CEO; Edward A. Watson, EVP and COO; David M. Bond, Sec., Asst. Treas., Cont.; Mark S. Broin, VP-Info. Svs.; George H. Fougeron, VP-Franchise Op.; Stephen M. Frances, VP-Franchise Devel./Lease Mgmt.; Michael J. Leary, VP-Purch./Distrib.; Glenn S. Lindsey, VP-Res./Devel.; Srinivasa B. Murthy, VP-Admin. Svs.; Signe M. Pagel, VP-Hum. Res./Meeting/Travel Svs.; Gary H. See, VP-Mktg./Consumer Res.; William C. Zucco, VP-Law and Gen. Counsel. International Dairy Queen Inc. (IDQ) develops, licenses, and services more than 5,700 Dairy Queen stores in the United States, Canada, and other countries. The stores feature hamburgers, hot dogs, various dairy desserts, and beverages. More than 420 Orange Julius stores (featuring blended drinks and other snack items) are found throughout the United States, Canada, and other countries. More than 60 Karmelkorn Shoppes (featuring popcorn and other treat items) are serviced by IDQ. In addition, more than 170 Treat Center stores (offering Dairy Queen treats, Orange Julius drinks, and/or Karmelkorn products) are found throughout the United States and Canada. In October 1997 IDQ agreed to be acquired by Berkshire Hathaway for $585 million. 1,980 employees. SIC 5812. Founded in 1962. In March 2000 American Dairy Queen Corp. introduced the S'more Galore Royal Treat dessert and three new Blizzard Flavor Treat products. In May, in the dispute between IDQ and its franchisees, the court gave final approval to a class-action settlement, ending litigation that was started by a group of franchisees in April 1994. The settlement called for a commitment from IDQ of nearly $5 million annually during the next six years to the franchise system's national advertising fund; and of more than $6 million to the Dairy Queen Operators' Cooperative, to provide for the continued availability of alternative sources of food products and supplies for the Dairy Queen system's stores. (IDQ denied any wrongdoing or liability related to this lawsuit.) In June the fastest market growth in the history of the Dairy Queen franchise system throughout the world resulted in the Minor Food Group, Dairy Queen licensee for Thailand, opening its 100th store. The 100th store was the first one outside the United States to include the new international design featuring a new logo, altered color scheme, and new "eatertainment" design. Owned since January 1998 by Berkshire Hathaway Inc. (NYSE: BRK), Omaha, Neb.

International Decision Systems 60 S. Sixth St., Suite 2300, Minneapolis, MN 55402. Tel: 612/338-2585; Fax: 612/337-5967; Web site: http://www.decisionsys.com. Richard Borchers, Chm.; James Meinen, Pres.; Karen Manthei, Cont. International Decision Systems, formerly Decision Systems Inc., develops, markets, and supports application software products for the equipment and vehicle leasing industry. It is the largest software company in this market, with offices in Minneapolis, Sydney, Singapore, and London. The products include systems for lease pricing, sales tracking, forecasting and budgeting, and asset management; a financial accounting system for lessees; and a lease vs. buy evaluation program. The company currently serves more than 300 independent, bank-related, and captive leasing companies throughout the United States, Canada, Australia, the Pacific Rim, Latin America, Europe, and Africa. 330 employees. SIC 7374, 7379. Founded in 1974. In June 2000 the company announced plans to move from Dain Rauscher Plaza into five floors of the IDS Center in May 2002. (The planned move of American Express Financial Advisors was going to leave 45 percent of the IDS Center vacant.) In September the company agreed to merge with CFS Group plc, a provider of wholesale floor plan and leasing software. The holding company for the merged entities was to be renamed IDS Group plc, U.K. No. 37 Minnesota Technology Fast 50.

International Home Foods Store Brands 21340 Hayes Ave., P.O. Box 430, Lakeville, MN 55044. Tel: 952/469-4981; Fax: 952/469-5550. Glen S. Bolander, Pres. and CEO; Michael J. Cannon, VP-Sls.; Thomas L. Traub, VP-Hum. Res.; Stephen Vuolo, VP-Mktg. International Home Foods Store Brands manufactures and markets a variety of food and snack products under the company's own brand name and through private-label or store brands. These products include fruit snacks, ready-to-eat cereals, granola bars, fruit-filled cereal bars, and pie crusts. In addition, the company provides contract manufactured products for other companies. The company's strategy is to develop high-quality products that are sold at lower prices than comparable brand-name items. In March 1998 publiicly traded Grist Mill Inc., as the company was then known, signed a definitive agreement to be acquired in a transaction valued at $105 million, a 20 percent premium to the prevailing stock price. 650 employees (600 in Minnesota). SIC 2041, 2043, 2099. Founded in 1917. A business unit of International Home Foods Inc., Parsippany, N.J.

Interstate Brands Corporation 8090 Excelsior Blvd., Hopkins, MN 55343. Tel: 763/533-2221. Dave Erno, Gen. Mgr. Interstate Brands Corp. is a distribution center for baked goods (Wonder Bread and Hostess Cake products). 300 employees. SIC 5145. Former owner Continental Baking Co. Inc., St. Louis, was acquired from Ralston Purina Co. in 1995 by Interstate Brands Corp., which is held by IBC Holdings Corp., Kansas City, Mo.

Interstate Brands Corporation P.O. Box 1848, Minot, ND 58702. Tel: 701/852-2531; Fax: 701/838-2788. Mike Connell, Plant Mgr. Interstate Brands manufactures bakery products. 250 employees. SIC 2051. Founded in 1936. Owned by Interstate Brands Corp., which is held by IBC Holdings Corp., Kansas City, Mo.

Interstate Lumber Company 113 S. Main St., Stillwater, MN 55082. Tel: 651/439-4330; Fax: 651/439-4339. Scott Kolva, Regional Mgr. Interstate Lumber Co. is a retail lumber business with 12 locations serving the professional builder. 231 employees (211 in Minnesota; 15 part-time). SIC 5211. Founded in 1899. Owned by Erb Lumber, Birmingham, Mich.

Intertec Publishing Agribusiness Division 7900 International Dr., Suite 300, Bloomington, MN 55425. Tel: 952/851-9329; Fax: 952/851-4701. Bob Moraczewski, SVP and Gen. Mgr.; Debbie Weinhold, Mgr.-Hum. Res.; Ron Sorensen, Publisher; Wayne Bollum, Publisher; Mike Gonitzke, Publisher; Greg Frey, Senior Business Mgr. Intertec Publishing Agribusiness Division produces nine national and regional agricultural publications: Soybean Digest; Beef; National Hog Farmer; Farm Industry News; Hay and Forage Grower; Delta Farm Press; Southeast Farm Press; Southwest Farm Press; and California/Arizona Farm Press. 102 employees (53 in Minnesota; 3 part-time). SIC 2759. Founded in 1882. Owned by PRIMEDIA Intertec Publishing Corp., Overland Park, Kan.; a division of PRIMEDIA Inc. (NYSE: PRM), New York.

Intervet Inc. P.O. Box 775, Worthington, MN 56187. Tel: 507/372-7726; Fax: 507/372-2480. Intervet performs research, development, and production of veterinary vaccines for all major livestock and pets worldwide. Previous owners: Pharmacia & Upjohn (until January 1997); Bayer Corp. (until Aug. 2000). 54 employees (52 in Minnesota; 2 part-time). SIC 2836. Founded in 1983. Owned through the Intervet veterinary business unit of Akzo Nobel NV (Nasdaq: AKZOY), Arnhem, Netherlands.

REG

Iron Mountain 9715 James Ave. S., Bloomington, MN 55431. Tel: 952/888-3852; Fax: 952/888-8445. Michael Rabin, VP. Iron Mountain provides 7.1 million cubic feet of facilities for off-site record storage, climate-controlled vault storage, and destruction of secure documents for its 2,000 corporate clients in the financial, insurance, health care, high-technology, and consumer-products industries, as well as government agencies and universities. The company also provides electronic vaulting—the automatic, remote copying and storing of critical computer data over high-speed communications lines. The former Mohawk Business Record Storage Inc. agreed in October 1996 to be acquired by America's largest records-management company. 140 employees (in Minnesota). SIC 4225. Founded in 1975. Now owned by Iron Mountain Inc., Boston.

Irresistible Ink Inc. 1313 Fairgrounds Rd., Two Harbors, MN 55616. Tel: 888/448-6077. David Knoll, COO; Rob Hughes, VP-Op. Annual revenue $7 million. Irresistible Ink provides personalized direct-mail services. 225 employees (in Minnesota; 175 part-time). SIC 7331. Founded in 1992. Owned by Hallmark Cards Inc., Kansas City, Mo.

Ivex 21925 Industrial Blvd., Rogers, MN 55374. Tel: 763/428-8340; Fax: 763/428-2754. Calvin S. Krupa, Chm., Pres., and CEO; Bradley C. Yopp, Dir.-Fin./Admin.; Greg Nelson, Gen. Mgr. Ivex, formerly Ultra Pac Inc., manufactures quality, high-value containers for the food packaging industry. The containers, which are made in a variety of clear and colored plastic, are made primarily from polyethylene terephthalate (PETE), the world's most widely recycled plastic material. The company's product line is dominated by containers designed for the bakery, deli, and fresh produce markets. In March 1998 the publicly traded Ultra Pac agreed to be acquired for $63.6 million in cash. 169 employees (465 in Minnesota). SIC 3089. Founded in 1987. Now an independent business unit of Ivex Packaging Corp. (NYSE: IXX), Lincolnshire, Ill.

Johnson Truck Bodies/Division Johnson Welding 215 E. Allen St., P.O. Box 480, Rice Lake, WI 54868. Tel: 715/234-7071; Fax: 715/234-4628; Web site: http://www.johnsontruckbodies.com. E.A. Ricci, Pres.; Richard Nichols, VP-Prod.; Ronald Ricci, VP-Sls. Johnson Truck Bodies manufactures specialized fiberglass, refrigerated truck bodies and trailers, ranging from 7 feet to 36 feet long, for a wide range of markets, including dairy, meat, frozen foods, keg beer, live poultry, vending products, ice, flowers, and bedding plants. Family-owned since 1932, Johnson Truck Bodies was acquired in May 1999. 475 employees. SIC 3713, 3715. Founded in 1932. Now owned by Carlisle Cos. Inc. (NYSE: CSL), Syracuse, N.Y.

Jordan Millwork Company 611 W. Algonquin, Sioux Falls, SD 57104. Tel: 605/336-1910; Fax: 605/335-1324. Dennis Brunick, Gen. Mgr.; Larry Meyer, Mktg. Projects Mgr. Jordan Millwork is a wholesale distributor of windows, doors, door units, mouldings, cabinets, hardwood lumber, steel shelving, and building materials. The company has other locations in Omaha, Neb.; Fargo, N.D.; and Des Moines, Iowa. 59 employees. SIC 2431, 2434. Founded in 1887. Jordan Millwork is a division of Jeld-Wen Inc., Klamath Falls, Ore.

The Journal 303 N. Minnesota St., P.O. Box 487, New Ulm, MN 56073. Tel: 507/359-2911; Fax: 507/359-7362; Web site: http://www.oweb.com/newulm. Bruce H. Fenske, Publisher. The Journal is a 10,100-circulation daily newspaper. The company also publishes a weekly shopper, The Retailer, on Tuesdays. 55 employees (in Minnesota). SIC 2711. Founded in 1898. Owned by Ogden Newspapers Inc., Wheeling, W.Va.

KARE 11 8811 Olson Memorial Hwy., Golden Valley, MN 55427. Tel: 763/546-1111; Fax: 763/546-8590; Web site: http://www.kare11.com. John Remes, Pres. and Gen. Mgr.; Tom Lindner, VP and News Dir.; Kiki Rosatti, Community Affairs; Sue Reimer, Hum. Res. KARE 11 is a television station and affiliated with the NBC network. 230 employees (45 part-time). SIC 4833. Founded in 1952. In March 2000 two major broadcast industry organizations, the National Press Photographers Association and the Radio and Television News Directors Association, cited KARE with multiple awards. In October "Whatever," a KARE 11 weekly magazine show for teenagers, received the Iris Award from the National Association of Television Programming Executives. Owned by Gannett Co. Inc. (NYSE: GCI), Arlington, Va.

KDLH-TV 425 W. Superior St., Duluth, MN 55802. Tel: 218/733-0303; Fax: 218/727-7515; Web site: http://www.kdlh.com. Gil Buettner, Gen. Mgr.; Thom Prtiz, Gen. Sls. Mgr.; Nancy Roche, Mktg./Promotions Dir.; Rob Heuerling, News Dir.; Terry Van Dell, Chief Engineer; John Carlson, Dir.-Creative Svs.; Brad Mickelson, Business Mgr. KDLH-TV is a television broadcasting station. 65 employees (in Minnesota; 8 part-time). SIC 4833. Founded in 1954. Owned by Benedek, Chicago.

KPMG LLP 4200 Norwest Center, 90 S. Seventh St., Minneapolis, MN 55402. Tel: 612/305-5000; Fax: 612/305-5039; Web site: http://www.us.kpmg.com. Dave L. Jahnke, Managing Ptnr. KPMG is an international accounting firm that delivers assurance, tax and consulting services to clients in five lines of business: financial services; manufacturing; retail and distribution; health care; information, communications, and entertainment; and public services. 475 employees (in Minnesota). SIC 8721, 8742. Founded in 1904. Office of KPMG LLP, New York.

KSFY Television 300 North Dakota Ave., Sioux Falls, SD 57104. Tel: 605/336-1300; Fax: 605/336-7936; Web site: http://www.ksfy.com. Marilyn Brink, Business Mgr.; Jack Hansen, Gen. Mgr.; Marjorie Hokenuted, Op. Mgr.; Tom Claycomb, News Dir. KSFY Television is involved in television broadcasting. 76 employees (5 part-time). SIC 4833. Founded in 1960. Owned by RayCom Media, Montgomery, Ala.

Kato Engineering P.O. Box 8447, Mankato, MN 56002. Tel: 507/625-4011; Fax: 507/345-2798. Ronald Orcutt, Gen. Mgr.; Les Altenberg, Cont. Annual revenue $75 million. Kato Engineering manufactures rotating electrical equipment, including generators, motor generator sets, and related controls. This former unit of Rockwell International Corp.'s Rockwell Automation business unit was sold in April 1998. Purchased by Emerson Electric from Caterpillar in 1999. 463 employees (459 in Minnesota). SIC 3511, 3621. Founded in 1926. Now owned by Emerson Electric Co. (NYSE: EMR), St. Louis.

Keane Inc. 6700 France Ave. S., Suite 300, Edina, MN 55435. Tel: 952/915-6393; Fax: 952/915-5101; Web site: http://www.keane.com. Chris Mason, Managing Dir.; Tim Jensen, Solutions Dir.; Kirk Douglas, Dir.-Svc. Delivery. Annual revenue $67 million. Keane Inc. is a $1 billion technology services provider that plans, builds, and maintains information systems. Keane's Twin Cities office has grown to be one of the largest providers of information technology services in the area. Services provided to Keane's Minnesota clients include e-strategy and e-solutions, program and project management, applications outsourcing, business process redesign, custom systems development, and software evaluation, selection, and implementation. 700 employees. SIC 7371. Founded in 1983. In October 2000 Keane opened an Advanced Development Center in Rochester, Minn., that delivers off-site development and management capabilities, including emerging software technologies, to Keane's Global 2000 clients. Branch offices of Keane Inc. (ASE: KEA), Boston.

Kewill/JobBoss Software 7701 York Ave. S, Edina, MN 55435. Tel: 800/777-4337; Fax: 952/831-2811; Web site: http://www.kewill.com; www.jobboss.com. Al Peterson, CEO-Kewill ERP/JobBoss; John Moroney, VP-Sls. Kewill/JobBoss Software is one of three operating divisions of Kewill Systems plc, the specialist in supply-chain management software and services. It is the leading provider of ERP systems to the SME sector (Benchmark Research) with more than 10,000 installations worldwide. The company's products comprise complete solutions for job shop, batch, make-to-order, make-to-contract, discrete, and repetitive manufacturers. Its products are known for their rare combination of functional breadth and depth coupled with ease of use and rapid implementation cycles. In February 1999 JobBoss Software Inc.'s sale, for $18.4 million, enhanced its distribution and service capabilities. 135 employees (in Minnesota; 2 part-time). SIC 7372. Founded in 1985. In December 1999 the company announced the availability of JobBoss Enterprise Edition (JBE) running on Microsoft SQL Server 7.0—which allows SME manufacturers to manage a large volume of data for many concurrent users with greater ease-of-use and provides compatibility with the latest SQL database technology. In April 2000 the company announced OfficeBOSS 2.0, enabling owners and managers to access online a detailed weekly shop status report that will provide vital statistics for their businesses, and to create trend analysis reports. In August Kewill received ISO 9001 and TickIT certifications at its Foster City and Minneapolis offices for the design, development, and order fulfillment of business management/enterprise resource planning (ERP) software for small and medium-size enterprises, as well as support services including product maintenance, enhancements, customizations, and phone support. In October JobBoss shop management software won the American Machinist Excellence in Manufacturing Technology Achievement Award in the User Friendliness category. Owned through Kewill ERP Inc., Foster City, Calif., by Kewill Systems plc, Walton on Thames, Surrey, U.K. No. 81 CRM Foreign-Owned 100.

Kleen Brite Laboratories 4404 Anderson Dr., Eau Claire, WI 54703. Tel: 715/836-8660. D. James Manno, CEO. Kleen Brite Laboratories manufactures household cleaning products and laundry detergents. The former Trico Solutions Inc. and Jennico Inc. was acquired in May 1999. 100 employees. SIC 2841, 2842. Founded in 1962. Now owned by Kleen Brite Laboratories Inc., Rochester, N.Y.

Knapp Woodworking Inc. 16430 Highway 65 N., Ham Lake, MN 55304. Tel: 763/434-9528; Fax: 763/434-9893. Philip S. Walter, SVP and Gen. Mgr.; Randy Craig, Plant Mgr. Knapp Woodworking is a cabinet manufacturer. In December 1998 Knapp was acquired. 150 employees (in Minnesota). SIC 2434. Founded in 1965. Now owned by American Woodmark Corp. (Nasdaq: AMWD), Winchester, Va.

Knox Lumber Company 2905 Lexington Ave. S., Eagan, MN 55121. Tel: 651/452-9100; Fax: 651/452-9183. Karl Gunivent, Group Sls. Dir. Knox Lumber Co. is a specialty retailer of lumber, hardware, plumbing products, tools, kitchen and bath products, and related building products at five Minnesota stores. 1,200 employees (in Minnesota). SIC 5211. Founded in 1961. Knox is owned by Payless Cashways (NYSE: PCS), Kansas City, Mo.

Koch Petroleum Group P.O. Box 64596, St. Paul, MN 55164. Tel: 651/437-0700; Fax: 651/438-1219. Jeff Wilkes, VP-MN Op. Koch Petroleum produces gasoline, fuel oil, jet fuel and other energy products. A leading producer of petroleum products, Koch converts 12 million gallons of crude oil into gasoline and other transportation fuels each day at its Pine Bend refinery. A network of 537 miles of pipeline delivers the products throughout Minnesota and the upper Midwest. Koch also maintains a dedicated jet fuel pipeline to Minneapolis-St. Paul International Airport. The company prides itself on its environmental record and on its programs for health, safety and the community. 750 employees (in Minnesota). SIC 2819, 2911. Founded in 1955. In January 1999, a 10-member federal jury affirmed Koch Petroleum Group's actions and integrity with its verdict in a court case involving an ex-employee who had brought a whistle-blower lawsuit. In March 2000, Koch settled with the EPA and the Department of Justice over gasoline leaks discovered in 1997. The U.S. District Court fined Koch $6 million for violations of the Oil Pollution and Clean Water acts. The company was also ordered to pay $2 million in remediation to the Dakota County Park System. In April the city of Hastings and Koch Petroleum Group unveiled a joint initiative to develop a bike trail and a community park (Koch Riverfront Park) on 43 acres of Mississippi riverfront land donated to the city by Koch. In May more than 350 volunteers removed invasive exotic plants and replace them with native plants along the banks of the Mississippi River—part of an innovative partnership with Koch Petroleum Group to improve and manage one of the Twin Cities' highest-quality unprotected natural areas. The volunteers hope to restore ecological integrity to Koch's Pine Bend Bluffs Natural Area by the end of 2001. Koch and the Minnesota Center for Environmental Advocacy were in the process of creating a Web site (separate from Koch's corporate homepage) that will keep the public up to date on Koch's progress in cleaning up its refining facility. Launch was scheduled for fall 2000. In July the U.S. EPA announced an agreement in principle with Koch that outlined how Koch was to set the pace for U.S. refineries in reducing emissions. The agency characterized the agreement as a "major step in fulfilling the promise of the Clean Air Act."

Koch was the first refining company to reach agreement with the EPA. In fall 2000, Koch will launch a new Web site which will provide information on Koch's environmental performance at its Pine Bend refinery. Owned by Koch Industries, Wichita, Kan.

Koehler & Dramm Inc. 2407 E. Hennepin Ave., Minneapolis, MN 55413. Tel: 612/331-4141; Fax: 612/331-5066. Timmothy Deucker, Pres.; Lee Spence, Treas./Fin. Ofcr. Koehler & Dramm is a wholesale florist specializing in cut flowers, floral supplies, and live plants for flower shops. It also runs a state-licensed school for floral design. 145 employees (120 in Minnesota). SIC 5193. Founded in 1955. In November 1997 the company was one of three floral distribution companies that agreed to be acquired by USA Floral Products, Washington, D.C.

Kolberg-Pioneer Inc. P.O. Box 20, Yankton, SD 57078. Tel: 605/665-9311; Fax: 605/665-2623. Jerry Deel, Pres. Kolberg-Pioneer Inc. designs, manufactures, and markets several well-known lines of aggregate processing equipment. Kolberg materials-handling equipment: conveyors, pug mills, screens, sand-classification equipment, blenders, and chemical-processing equipment. Pioneer rock-crushing equipment: portable crushing plants; primary crushers; intermediate, secondary, and tertiary crushers; vibrating screens; feeders; and asphalt-recycling equipment. In December 1997 Astec Industries acquired substantially all of the assets of the Construction Equipment Division of Portec Inc. and renamed it Kolberg-Pioneer. 300 employees. SIC 3531, 3532. Founded in 1965. Owned by Astec Industries Inc. (Nasdaq: ASTE), Chattanooga, Tenn.

Kolpak/River Falls Division 715 Saint Croix St., P.O. Box 137, River Falls, WI 54022. Tel: 715/425-6741; Fax: 715/425-1958. Tom Byrne, Dir.-Op.; Gregory Leier, Cont.; David Anderson, Hum. Res. Kolpak is a manufacturer of insulated modular panels that are primarily used in walk-in coolers, freezers, and insulated warehouses. 210 employees. SIC 3585. Founded in 1956. Acquired in December 1995 by Manitowoc Cos. (NYSE: MTW), Manitowoc, Wis.

Kraft Foods 2525 Bridge St., Box 309, New Ulm, MN 56073. Tel: 507/354-4131; Fax: 507/359-7881. Joe Luetmer, Plant Mgr. Kraft's New Ulm Plant manufactures processed cheese. Brand names include Velveeta, Kraft Singles, and Handi-Snacks. One of Kraft's biggest Velveeta producers, the plant produces 67 million pounds per year—or 5 percent of the total U.S. production of processed cheese. 900 employees. SIC 2022. Founded in 1955. A part of Kraft Foodservice Inc., Deerfield, Ill.; a division of Kraft Foods Inc., Northfield, Ill.; owned by Philip Morris Cos. Inc. (NYSE: MO), New York.

Kraft Foods 1000 E. Kraft Dr., Melrose, MN 56352. Tel: 320/256-7461; Fax: 320/256-4088. Kraft's Melrose Plant manufactures natural cheese. 200 employees. SIC 2022. Founded in 1968. A part of Kraft Foodservice Inc., Deerfield, Ill.; a division of Kraft Foods Inc., Northfield, Ill.; owned by Philip Morris Cos. Inc. (NYSE: MO), New York.

Kwik File LLC 500 73rd Ave. N.E., Fridley, MN 55432. Tel: 763/572-1980; Fax: 763/572-0168. Paul Simons, Pres.; Dan Gray, Dir.-Mktg.; Cheryl Bumstead-Johnson, Gen. Mgr.; Todd Nelson, VP-Sls. Kwik File manufactures specialized office furniture. 70 employees (in Minnesota). SIC 2522. Founded in 1965. Acquired in December 1995 by Mayline Co., Sheboygan, Wis.

LaBounty Manufacturing 1538 Highway 2, Two Harbors, MN 55616. Tel: 218/834-2123; Fax: 218/834-3879. Dennis Bishop, Pres. LaBounty Manufacturing manufactures hydraulic excavator attachments, grapples, steel-cutting shears, and concrete pulverizers. 156 employees. SIC 3531. Founded in 1972. In November 2000 the plant shut down for a week, idling 106 employees, because of weak demand for its products. Acquired in January 1992 by Stanley Hydraulic Tools, Milwaukie, Ore., a division of The Stanley Works (NYSE: SWK), New Britain, Conn.

The Lacek Group Worldwide 10 S. Fifth St., 11th Floor, Minneapolis, MN 55402. Tel: 612/359-3700. Michelle Bottomley, Managing Dir. (New York); Bill Baker, Gen. Mgr.; Peter Brennan, EVP; Chris Hoffman, VP-Hum. Res.; Dan Knudsen, Group VP; Henry Moreno, Group VP; Jeff Patrias, SVP-Int'l; Bruce Samuel, VP-Fin./Admin.; Cathy Sanders, Managing Dir.-South Pacific; Mark Weninger, SVP and Chief Creative Officer. The Lacek Group is a full-service loyalty marketing agency. Subsidiaries include Lacek Travel Services (the former World Class Travel) and technology company Lacek Systems and Software. The company has offices in Atlanta; Seoul, South Korea; Singapore; London; and Sydney, Australia. Clients include Delta Air Lines, MCI, Time Warner Cable, Hyatt Hotels, and Federal Express. 145 employees. SIC 8742. Founded in 1993. In 1999 founder Mark Lacek left the company to start MilePoint.com. In August 2000 the company was sold by Electronic Data Systems Corp. to OgilvyOne Worldwide, New York.

La Crosse Tribune 401 N. Third St., La Crosse, WI 54601. Tel: 608/782-9710; Fax: 608/782-8540; Web site: http://www.lacrossetribune.com. James Santori, Publisher. La Crosse Tribune publishes a daily newspaper. This facility opened in 1973. 185 employees (9 in Minnesota; 50 part-time). SIC 2711. Founded in 1904. Owned by Lee Enterprises Inc. (NYSE: LEE), Davenport, Iowa.

Lafarge Dakota Inc. 684 15th Ave. S.W., P.O. Box 757, Valley City, ND 58072. Tel: 701/845-2421; Fax: 701/845-1849. Martin A. Warborg, Pres. Lafarge Dakota is a wholesale distributor of cement and fly-ash. Known prior to 1993 as Beyers Cement Inc. 60 employees. SIC 5039. Founded in 1962. Owned by Lafarge Corp., Reston, Va.; a subsidiary of Lafarge Coppee S.A., Boulogne, France.

Lagerquist Corporation 1801 West River Rd. N., P.O. Box 58239, Minneapolis, MN 55458. Tel: 612/588-7844; Fax: 612/588-8221. Jerry L. Philpot, Pres.; Juanita Kauffman, Sec. Lagerquist Corp. furnishes, installs, and maintains passenger and freight elevators, escalators, and dumbwaiters throughout Minnesota, Wisconsin, North Dakota, South Dakota, Montana, and Wyoming. 160 employees. SIC 3534. Founded in 1882. Owned by Thyssen Elevator, New York.

Lake Superior Paper Industries 100 N. Central Ave., Duluth, MN 55807. Tel: 218/628-5100; Fax: 218/628-0310. Pat Moore, Mill Mgr. Lake Superior Paper Industries (LSPI) is a paper mill that manufactures supercalendered paper. In May 1995 joint owners Minnesota Power Inc. (NYSE: MPL), Duluth, and Pentair Inc. (NYSE: PNR), Roseville, Minn., divested their interests in LSPI. 340 employees. SIC 2621. Founded in 1986. In February 2000 then-owner Consolidated Papers Inc. (NYSE: CDP), Wisconsin Rapids, Wis., was acquired by Stora Enso Oyj, Helsinki, Finland. No. 54 CRM Foreign-Owned 100.

Lakeside Foods Inc. 1055 W. Broadway, Plainview, MN 55964. Tel: 507/534-3141; Fax: 507/534-3005. William Arendt, Gen. Mgr.; Bruce Jacobson, Gen. Mgr.-Contract Op. Lakeside Foods cans and freezes vegetables—peas, corn, lima beans, beets, and carrots—for private-label companies, mostly in the United States. It also does business in Europe and Southeast Asia. 225 employees (in Minnesota; 100 part-time). SIC 2033, 2037. Founded in 1929. Division of Lakeside Foods Inc., Manitowoc, Wis.

Lamb Weston/RDO Frozen P.O. Box 552, Park Rapids, MN 56470. Tel: 218/732-7252; Fax: 218/732-2175. R.D. Offutt, Pres.; Richard Bogaard, Dir.-Op.; Dave Larson, Plant Mgr.; Dan Riordan, Mgr.-Tech. Svs.; Tim Kohrs, Maintenance Mgr.; Andy Roach, Purch. Mgr.; Julie Larson, Hum. Res. Mgr.; Mic Ryan, Prod. Mgr. Annual revenue $150 million. Lamb Weston/RDO Frozen manufactures french fries, potato puffs, hash browns, and other potato products. The company markets and distributes same under the Lamb-Weston name, per a September 1992 distribution agreement. 500 employees. SIC 2038. Founded in 1981. This operation is a joint venture between R.D. Offutt Co. and Lamb-Weston Inc., which is owned by ConAgra Inc. (NYSE: CAG), Omaha, Neb.

Laminate Systems 230 N. Front St., P.O. Box 1448 (54603), La Crosse, WI 54601. Tel: 608/784-6070; Fax: 608/784-7753. Michael Vallance, VP-Tech.; Rick Kinsley, Dir.-Hum. Res. Laminate Systems manufactures industrial plastic laminates for electrical, electronic, and fabrication applications. 300 employees. SIC 2821. Founded in 1945. Former parent Honeywell International Inc. (AlliedSignal) agreed in October 2000 to be sold. To be owned by General Electric Co. (NYSE: GE), Fairfield, Conn.

Land O'Lakes Fluid Dairy Division 1200 W. Russell St., P.O. Box 479, Sioux Falls, SD 57101. Tel: 605/336-1958; Fax: 605/336-7206. Land O'Lakes' Sioux Falls operation, formerly Lakeside Dairy Co. Inc., is part of Land O'Lakes Fluid Dairy Division—which includes four fluid dairy plants located in Woodbury (Twin Cities area) and Thief River Falls, Minn.; Bismarck, N.D.; and Sioux Falls, S.D., as well as a new extended-shelf-life (ESL) dairy and cultured plant located in Richland Center, Wis. The dairy division markets a full line of fluid milk, yogurt, creams, sour cream, and cottage cheese, 85 percent of which is sold under the Land O' Lakes brand name. Land O'Lakes is the long-term agent for supplying the raw milk requirements of the plants. 185 employees (7 in Minnesota). SIC 2023, 2026. Founded in 1917. In May 2000 Dean Foods acquired Land O'Lakes Upper Midwest fluid milk operations. In addition, Land O'Lakes and Dean Foods each hold a 50 percent interest in a new, independent entity having the U.S. rights to develop, market, and license Land O' Lakes brand cream, half and half, sour cream, and extended-shelf-life products, including the successful GRIP'N GO single-serve milk. No significant changes were anticipated in plant operations, employment, or the positioning of the Land O' Lakes brand name. Owned by Dean Foods Co. (NYSE: DF), Franklin Park, Ill.

W.A. Lang Co. 800 LaSalle Ave., Suite 2100, Minneapolis, MN 55402. Tel: 612/371-9000; Fax: 612/371-0804; Web site: http://www.walang-co.com. Gary K. Wefel, Pres. and CEO; James B. Rechtiene, EVP; Scott Carlson, VP; Robert J. Kranz, VP and CFO. Annual revenue $24 million. W.A. Lang Co. is a full-service brokerage that supplies advice and assistance to commercial and individual clients to manage various risk exposures. Products offered include group employee benefits programs, workers' compensation and property/casualty insurance, and surety bonding. Clients include Lutheran Brotherhood, HealthEast, and Minneapolis Public Schools. 80 employees. SIC 6411. Founded in 1909. In December 1999 the company agreed to be sold to Acordia Inc., a privately held insurance brokerage firm with an office in Edina, Minn. That office was merged into Lang. The 13 Lang shareholders chose Acordia because of its entrepreneurial management style. [Deal closed in January 2000.] Owned by Acordia Inc., Indianapolis.

Jacob Leinenkugel Brewing Company Inc. 1-3 Jefferson Ave., P.O. Box 368, Chippewa Falls, WI 54729. Tel: 715/723-5558; Fax: 715/723-7158; Web site: http://www.leinie.com. Thomas J. Leinenkugel, Pres. and Treas.; William G. Schmus, VP; Michael Jones, Sec. Jacob Leinenkugel Brewing Company Inc. is a fifth-generation family brewer that produces several brands of handcrafted beers—Original Premium, Light, Berry Weiss—which are marketed in 27 states. In 1994 the company completed a $3.5 million expansion, its second in three years, which boosted production from 160,000 barrels to 250,000 barrels a year. 105 employees. SIC 2082. Founded in 1867. Acquired in 1988 by Miller Brewing Co., Milwaukee; subsidiary of Philip Morris Cos. Inc. (NYSE: MO), New York.

Lester Building Systems 1111 Second Ave S., Lester Prairie, MN 55354. Tel: 320/395-2531; Fax: 320/395-2969; Web site: http://www.lesterbuildings.com. Marc Hafer, Pres.; John Hill, VP-Sls.; Bob Schwade, VP-Hum. Res.; Robert Cline, Div. Engrg. Mgr.; Kermit Bantz, VP, Mfg. Mgr.; Tony Nuss, Div. JIT Mgr.; Larry Lembrich, VP and Gen. Mgr.-Lester's of Minnesota; Erling Anderson, Div. Cont.; Craig Loger, Dir.-Mktg./Product Devel. Lester Building Systems is involved in the engineering, fabrication, marketing, and construction of commercial, industrial, and agricultural buildings. 400 employees (300 in Minnesota). SIC 2439, 2452, 2499, 3448. Founded in 1947. Owned by Butler Manufacturing Co. (Nasdaq: BTRY), Kansas City, Mo.

Lewis Engineering Company 4201 Norex Dr., Chaska, MN 55318. Tel: 952/368-3000; Fax: 952/448-7000. John G. Lewis, Pres.; Thomas H. Lewis, Sls. Mgr.; Lyle Marquis, Purch. Mgr. Lewis Engineering is involved in structural and specialty steel fabrication. 125 employees (in Minnesota). SIC 3441. Founded in 1969. On Aug. 15, 1997, Lewis Engineering was acquired by The D.S. Brown Co., North Baltimore, Ohio.

Lexington Standard Corporation 20805 Eaton Ave. S., Farmington, MN 55024. Tel: 651/463-8990; Fax: 651/463-7379; Web site: http://www.lightpoles.com. Richard D. Hanson, Chm. and Pres.; Bryce Kilene, VP and Fin. Mgr.; Gary P. King, VP and Dir.-Mfg.; Thomas Segar, VP and Sls. Mgr. Lexington Standard manufactures tapered aluminum light poles and flagpole shafts. 130 employees. SIC 3648. Founded in 1973. In January 2000 the privately held company was sold. Owned by Valmont Industries Inc. (Nasdaq: VALM), Valley (Omaha), Neb.

Life Fitness-Consumer Division 14150 Sunfish Lake Blvd., Ramsey, MN 55303. Tel: 847/288-3300; Fax: 847/288-3703. Gerald Dettinger, Pres. Life Fitness is the global leader in designing and manufacturing a full line of reliable, high-quality fitness equipment for commercial and consumer use. Its cardiovascular and strength training products, including the renowned Lifecycle exercise bike, are used in health, fitness, and wellness facilities, as well as in homes, worldwide. 1,200 employees. SIC 3949. In October 2000 the company introduced two new total-body elliptical cross-trainers for home use, the Life Fitness X-Series Cross-Trainers. "Our success in this category makes us thrilled to present our third generation of cross-trainers," said President Dettinger. "Life Fitness is continually refining our tremendously popular elliptical equipment to provide the optimum workout right at home, and these new machines represent the latest in elliptical innovation." Owned by Brunswick Corp., Lake Forest, Ill.

Lionite Hardboard P.O. Box 138, Phillips, WI 54555. Tel: 715/339-2111; Fax: 715/339-2120. Don Olson, Plant Mgr. Lionite Hardboard produces tempered, standard, and perforated prefinished wall panels and tile board. 87 employees. SIC 2499. Founded in 1958. Print operation since 1964. Subsidiary of Georgia-Pacific Corp. (NYSE: GP), Atlanta.

Load King Division Rose and Elm Street, Elk Point, SD 57025. Tel: 605/356-3301; Fax: 605/356-3268. Ron Markwood, Pres.; Parris Erickson, Chief Engineer. Load King Division manufactures tagalong, low-bed, bottom-dump, end-dump, and side dump trailers. 109 employees. SIC 3715, 5082. Founded in 1957. Owned by CMI Corp. (NYSE: CMX), Oklahoma City.

Lockheed Martin Naval Electronics & Surveillance Systems 3333 Pilot Knob Rd., P.O. Box 64525 (55164), Eagan, MN 55121. Tel: 651/456-2222; Fax: 651/456-2736. John C. McNellis, Pres. Naval Electronics & Surveillance Systems (NE&SS) provides surface-ship and submarine combat systems, antisubmarine warfare and ocean surveillance systems, missile launching systems, radar and sensor systems, ship systems integration services, and other advanced systems and services to customers worldwide. NE&SS has an operation in Akron, Ohio. 2,300 employees (1,600 in Minnesota). SIC 3577, 3669. Founded in 1945. In June 2000 the company was given the Minnesota American Business Ethics Award for 2000 by the Minnesota Chapters of the Society of Financial Services Professionals. Until May 1995 these operations were part of Unisys Corp. Acquired along with then-owner Loral Corp. in April 1996 by the integration business area of Lockheed Martin Corp. (NYSE: LMT), Bethesda, Md.

Longview Fibre Company 5851 E. River Rd., Fridley, MN 55432. Tel: 763/571-4700; Fax: 763/571-4854. H.K. Broxey, Div. VP-Sls.; Mike Guilday, Sls. Mgr.; Lynne Nowak, Plant Mgr. Longview Fibre's Central Container Division manufactures corrugated shipping containers. 150 employees. SIC 2653. Founded in 1961. Division of Longview Fibre Co. (NYSE: LFB), Longview, Wash.

REG

Louisiana-Pacific Corporation P.O. Box 389, Deer Lodge, MT 59722. Tel: 406/846-1600; Fax: 406/846-3714. Ed Newman, Plant Mgr. Louisiana-Pacific Northern Division operates a sawmill and finger joint operation in Deer Lodge. 190 employees. SIC 2421. Division of Columbia Forest Products, Portland, Ore.

Lund International Holdings Inc. 911 Lund Blvd., Anoka, MN 55303. Tel: 763/576-4200; Fax: 763/576-4297; Web site: http://www.lundinternational.com. Lund International Holdings is a leading designer, manufacturer, and marketer of a broad line of appearance accessories for new and used light trucks, vans, and sport utility vehicles. These products include exterior sun visors, cab and rooftop spoilers, tonneau covers, hood and fender shields, grille inserts, rear valances, running boards, fender extensions, headlight covers, and tail-light covers. The company moved its headquarters from Anoka to Duluth, Ga., in October 2000. 77 employees (in Minnesota). SIC 3714. Founded in 1987. In April 2000 the company announced that part of its restructuring plan would be to outsource the fiberglass production at its Anoka, Minn., facility. The Anoka facility was to continue to be the headquarters for the Light Truck Division—including the division's sales, marketing, administrative, and engineering functions—as well as a distribution center with light packaging and assembly operations. Outsourcing this production affected 70 hourly employees of the 220 employees currently at the Anoka facility. In October Lund announced the relocation of its corporate headquarters from Anoka, Minn., to Duluth, Ga. Further, as part of its restructuring, it was planning to close its Anoka distribution center and relocate it to an existing warehouse in Lawrenceville, Ga. The company was in the process of outsourcing the fiberglass production from the Anoka facility as well. After the sale of the Anoka facility, the 77 employees to be retained in the Twin Cities—mostly in sales, marketing, and resarch—would be moving to leased office space nearby. Owned by Lund International Holdings Inc. (Nasdaq: LUND), Duluth, Ga. No. 72 CRM Public 200.

Lundgren Brothers Construction Inc. 935 E. Wayzata Blvd., Wayzata, MN 55391. Tel: 952/473-1231; Fax: 952/473-7401. Peter Pflaum, Pres. and CEO. Lundgren Brothers Constuction is a general contractor of single-family luxury homes, a developer of real estate, and a remodeler. 100 employees. SIC 1521. Founded in 1970. In April 1999 the company was acquired by U.S. Home Corp. (NYSE: UH), Houston.

M-tron Industries Inc. 100 Douglas Ave., P.O. Box 630, Yankton, SD 57078. Tel: 605/665-9321; Fax: 605/665-1709. Martin J. Kiousis, Chm. and Pres. M-tron Industries manufactures quartz crystals, clock oscillators, and custom hybrid circuits. 180 employees. SIC 3679. Founded in 1965. Owned by Lynch Corp. (ASE: LGL), Greenwich, Conn.

MBI Publishing Company 729 Prospect Ave., P.O. Box 1, Osceola, WI 54020. Tel: 715/294-3345; Fax: 715/294-4448; Web site: http://www.motorbooks.com. Tim Parker, Pres. and CEO; Michael Hesny, VP-Trade Sls.; Carl Fazio, VP and CFO. Annual revenue $34.5 million. MBI Publishing Co. is a publisher, wholesaler, and mail-order retailer of automotive books and videos and aviation, military, farm, and hobby publications. Formerly Motorbooks International. 105 employees (14 part-time). SIC 2731. Founded in 1975. Owned by Flagship Partners, New York.

ME International 3901 University Ave. N.E., Columbia Heights, MN 55421. Tel: 763/788-1651; Fax: 763/788-2874. Timothy Wieland, Pres.; Mark Garton, Admin. Dir.; John Sellars, VP-Mktg., N. America; Art Reith, VP-Mktg./Int'l; Andy Fulton, VP-New Product Devel.; Ray Nieman, Dir.-Hum. Res. ME International makes industrial-carbon and alloy-steel castings, principally for the mineral processing industry. 400 employees (275 in Minnesota). SIC 3325, 3532. Founded in 1917. In June 2000, after 143 workers ratified a five-year contract, the plant initially took back only 65 to 70 workers because of decreased demand for steel castings and the loss of business to foreign competitors. Owned by GS Industries, Charlotte, N.C.

MRM/Elgin Corporation 902 Stokke Parkway Dr., Menomonie, WI 54751. Tel: 715/235-5583; Fax: 715/235-0512. Joseph M. Cozzoli, Chm.; Frank J. Cozzoli, Pres. MRM/Elgin Corp. manufactures packaging machinery for the food and chemical industries. 55 employees. SIC 3565. Founded in 1983. Division of Cozzoli Machine Co., Plainfield, N.J.

MacDermid ColorSpan Inc. 6900 Shady Oak Rd., Eden Prairie, MN 55344. Tel: 800/477-7714; Fax: 952/944-9330; Web site: http://www.colorspan.com. J. Rastetter, EVP and Gen. Mgr.; P. Hursh, VP-Sls./Mktg.; R. DiCenzo, VP-Op. MacDermid ColorSpan manufactures wide-format inkjet printers for signmaking and photo-realistic reproductions. 280 employees. SIC 3577. Founded in 1985. In July 2000 ColorSpan Corp., Kilborn Photo Products Inc., and SuppliesByAir—then the Digital Graphics Business Unit of VirtualFund.com Inc. (Nasdaq: VFND), formerly LaserMaster Technologies Inc.—were acquired by MacDermid for $50 million. Owned by MacDermid Graphic Arts Inc., a division of MacDermid Inc. (NYSE: MRD), Waterbury, Conn.

Madison Marquette Realty Services 11100 Wayzata Blvd., Suite 601, Minnetonka, MN 55305. Tel: 952/852-5188; ; Web site: http://www.madisonmarquette.com. Gregory Karlen, Principal; Michael F. Kelly, Managing Dir. Madison Marquette Realty Services, Madison Marquette's property management division, manages more than 20 million square feet of retail and mixed-use properties nationwide. In addition to its Minnetonka headquarters, it also has offices in San Francisco, Los Angeles, and Irvine, Calif.; and Washington, D.C. Its development focus is on "lifestyle retail," or high-end shopping centers that include upscale retailers and use not only new construction, but also obsolete urban structures such as vacant department stores. Owners of its properties include The Irvine Co., UBS, CIGNA, Lend Lease, Ward Realty LLC, and Madison Marquette. 415 employees (180 in Minnesota). SIC 6531. Founded in 1991. In October 2000 three company-managed properties received the International Council of Shopping Centers' MAXI Award for exceptional shopping center marketing programs. Most of what was formerly Marquette Partners was acquired in January 1995 by Madison Realty Partners, Cincinnati.

Magnetic Data Technologies 6754 Shady Oak Rd., Eden Prairie, MN 55344. Tel: 952/942-4500; Fax: 952/941-7228. John Duffy, Plant Mgr.; Kirk Cramer, New Products Dir. Magnetic Data is an ISO 9000-registered company that offers total computer depot support to OEMs, self-maintainers, third- and fourth-party maintainers, and system integrators. Services offered include depot repair and parts, logistics/inventory management, training, contract manufacturing, and end-of-life manufacturing programs. The company has affiliate operations in California and Belgium. 200 employees. SIC 7378. Founded in 1982. Owned by Delta Bravo Inc., Santa Barbara, Calif.

Mammoth Inc. 101 W. 82nd St., Chaska, MN 55318. Tel: 952/361-2711; Fax: 952/361-2700; Web site: http://www.mammoth-inc.com. David J. Huntley, Pres.; William Haugh, Gen. Mgr.; John Kasel, Plant Mgr.; Roberta Mellen, Mgr.-Hum. Res.; Del Richter, VP-Fin. Mammoth manufactures custom, packaged, rooftop heating, ventilating and air conditioning equipment for industrial, commercial and institutional use. Mammoth also manufactures a full line of water source heat pump products for commercial and institutional buildings. 360 employees (330 in Minnesota). SIC 3443, 3585. Founded in 1933. Mammoth announced plans to expand on a global scale in 2001 with the introduction of Shandong Sanlian Mammoth Air Conditioning Co. Ltd., which will begin manufacturing Water Source Heat Pumps in Jinan, China. Initially, the factory will supply the Chinese HVAC market with WSHPs from 2 to 100 kW for commercial and residential use, high-efficiency units from 4 to 20 kW and unts from 4 to 20 kW for geothermal applications. The company plans to introduce additional products and increase distribution. Owned by Nortek Inc. (NYSE: NTK), Providence, R.I.

Management Graphics Inc. 1401 E. 79th St., Bloomington, MN 55425. Tel: 952/854-1220; Fax: 952/851-6159. James Teter, Gen. Mgr.; Tom Flavin, VP-Sls./Mktg.; Robert Helsing, VP-Fin.; Richard Lundell, VP-Mfg. Management Graphics Inc. (MGI) manufactures computer graphics systems, software, and equipment used in the production of high-resolution film recorders—and color image servers with Adobe postscript level 2—for the print industry. The company's hardware has been used in movies such as "The Matrix," "Terminator 2," and "Antz." In August 1999 the privately held Management Graphics was acquired in a stock-for-stock merger valued at $30.1 million. 70 employees. SIC 3577. Founded in 1981. Now owned by Electronics For Imaging Inc. (Nasdaq: EFII), San Mateo, Calif.

Manistique Papers Inc. 453 S. Mackinac St., P.O. Box 309, Manistique, MI 49854. Tel: 906/341-2175; Fax: 906/341-5635. Joseph Kruger II, Chm. and CEO; R.O. Cyrenne, COO; George Bunze, VP-Fin., CFO, and Treas.. Manistique Papers manufactures and sells newsprint and groundwood specialties. 152 employees. SIC 2621. Founded in 1917. Division of Kruger Inc., Montreal.

Mankato Free Press Company 418 S. Second St., Mankato, MN 56001. Tel: 507/625-4451; Fax: 507/388-4355. Samuel R. Gett Jr., Publisher. Mankato Free Press publishes the Mankato Free Press and an agricultural weekly, The Land. 120 employees (in Minnesota). SIC 2711. Founded in 1887. Wholly owned division of Ottaway Newspapers Inc., Campbell Hall, N.Y.; owned by Dow Jones & Co. Inc. (NYSE: DJ), New York.

Manufacturers' Services Ltd. 4300 Round Lake Rd., Arden Hills, MN 55112. Tel: 651/604-2400. Margit Elo, VP-Central U.S. Op. Mfg. Svs. Annual revenue $200 million. Manufacturers' Services is a full-service contract electronics manufacturer offering Total Cost of Ownership solutions for OEMs in the computer, electronics, and telecommunications industries. The company offers design, engineering, prototyping, assembly, logistics, and distribution services. Among the customers who rely on this site's advanced turnkey operations: AT&T, U.S. Robotics, Unisys, Computer Network Technology Corp., and Rockwell, ADC. Known as NCR Comten until 1991 purchase by AT&T Global Information Solutions. Sold again in January 1995. 600 employees (625 in Minnesota; 25 part-time). SIC 3577. Founded in 1994. Now owned by Manufacturers' Services Ltd. of Boston, Concord.

Marathon Ashland Petroleum 459 Third St., P.O. Box 9, St. Paul Park, MN 55071. Tel: 651/459-9771; Fax: 651/458-6406. James M. Nelson, Plant Mgr. Marathon Ashland Petroleum does crude oil refining. 275 employees (in Minnesota). SIC 2911. Founded in 1939. Owned by a joint venture between USX-Marathon Group, Pittsburgh, and Ashland Inc. (Nasdaq: ASND), Ashland, Ky.

MarchFIRST 1600 Utica Ave. S., Suite 900, St. Louis Park, MN 55416. Tel: 763/546-4000; Fax: 763/546-7000; Web site: http://www.marchfirst.com. Bob Bernard, CEO; Rob Sloat, Office Managing Ptnr.; Erica McLean, Dir.-Corp. Recruiting. Annual revenue $16 million. MarchFIRST is the world's largest, most comprehensive Internet professional services company with 9,400 eployees in 14 countries teamed to deliver strategy, brand building and technology solutions for today's leading edge companies. Clients include Land O'Lakes, Regis Corp., and Parametric Technologies Corp. provides innovative information-system solutions that deliver a competitive edge to its clients. Services include project management, enterprise consulting, software implementation, technology tools, education, and custom programming, designed for middle-market manufacturing, distribution, and financial services companies. Whiteman Hart has a satellite office in Milwaukee. Former names: North Central Consulting; SSA North Central. 171 employees (in Minnesota). SIC 7374. Founded in 1993. Owned since July 1998 by Whittman-Hart Inc. (Nasdaq: WHIT), Chicago.

Marigold Foods Inc. 2929 University Ave. S.E., P.O. Box 9481 (55440), Minneapolis, MN 55414. Tel: 612/331-3775; Fax: 612/378-8398. James B. Green, Pres. and CEO; Larry Gergens, EVP; Greg Kurr, VP-Sls.; Rachel Kyllo, VP-Mktg.; Peter Park, VP-Res./Devel.; Bob Williams, VP-Mfg.; Christopher Thorpe, Dir.-Fin. Svs.; Cindy Trousdale, Dir.-Bus. Svs. Marigold Foods manufactures and distributes fluid-milk and cultured products, ice cream and frozen desserts (Kemps), and novelty products—from five locations in Minnesota and one outstate plant—to more than 600 retail grocery stores in Minnesota, Wisconsin, North Dakota, South Dakota, Iowa, Illinois, Michigan, and Nebraska. 1,500 employees (1,100 in Minnesota). SIC 2022, 2024, 2026. Founded in 1913. In March 2000 the company agreed to acquire the family-owned Oak Grove Dairy, Norwood Young America, Minn., from Geo. Benz & Sons Inc., St. Paul. In April Marigold reached a licensing agreement with rights holders for the diet and cookbook, "Sugar Busters: Cut Sugar to Trim Fat," and added a line of no-sugar-added Sugar Busters ice cream to its Kemp's lines. Marigold Foods is a division of Wessanen, St. Augustine, Fla., a wholly owned subsidiary of Koninklijke Wessanen N.V., Amstelveen, Netherlands. No. 13 CRM Foreign-Owned 100.

Marketwatch.com Inc. 123 N. Third St., Minneapolis, MN 55401. Tel: 612/338-0048; Web site: http://www.cbs.marketwatch.com. Jamie Thingelstad, CTO; Scott Kinney, EVP-Licensing. Marketwatch.com is a leading interactive financial media company. Marketwatch.com provides fast, relevant, and accurate information via the Internet, television, and radio to help people make and save money. The company operates two Internet Web sites: www.cbs.marketwatch.com and www.bigcharts.com. Other locations include New York; Washington, D.C.; Los Angeles; Chicago; Boston; Detroit; Atlanta; Dallas and Austin, Texas; Tokyo; Hong Kong; and London. 90 employees (in Minnesota). SIC 7374, 7375. Owned by Marketwatch.com Inc. (Nasdaq: MKTW), San Francisco.

Marriott Lodging Group 30 S. Seventh St., Minneapolis, MN 55402. Tel: 612/349-4000; Fax: 612/332-7165. Tom Chase, Area Mgr.-Marriott City Center; Quinn Nordman, Gen. Mgr.-Fairfield Inn Airport; El Neklawy Hassan, Gen. Mgr.-Marriott Southwest; Mary Hargens, Gen. Mgr.-Courtyard Mendota Hts.; Teri Butler, Gen. Mgr.-Courtyard Eden Prairie; Steve Niemi, Gen. Mgr.-Res. Inn Eden Prairie; Michelle Steffens, Gen. Mgr.-Res. Inn Eagan; Joel Danko, Gen. Mgr.-Res. Inn Roseville; Jarod Endersbe, Gen. Mgr.-Fairfield Inn Roseville; Tod Oswald, Gen. Mgr.-Marriott Airport; April Hargen, Gen. Mgr.-Fairfield Inn Coon Rapids; Preston Lougheed, Gen. Mgr.-Fairfield Inn Eden Prairie; Chris Engle, Gen. Mgr.-Fairfield Inn Burnsville; Patrick Bissen, Gen. Mgr.-TownePlace Suites Eden Prairie; Bob Doran, Gen. Mgr.-Res. Inn/Courtyard Mall of Am.; Ben Graves, Gen. Mgr.-Res. Inn Downtown Mpls.; Jeff Hayes, Gen. Mgr.-Springhill & TownePlace Suites. Marriott Lodging Group provides accommodations for the business and leisure traveler at: full-service hotel Marriott (City Center, Minneapolis Airport, and Southwest); moderate-priced hotel Courtyard by Marriott (Mendota Heights, Eden Prairie, Mall of America); extended-stay hotel Residence Inn (Eagan, Roseville, Minneapolis, Mall of America, and Eden Prairie); and economy hotel Fairfield Inn by Marriott (Mall of America, Roseville, Coon Rapids, Eden Prairie, and Burnsville); lower- to moderate-priced suites SpringHill Suites (Eagan); and moderate-priced, extended-stay suites TownePlace Suites (Eden Prairie). 1,350 employees. SIC 7011. Founded in 1994. Division of Marriott International Inc. (NYSE: MAR), Washington, D.C.

Marshall Publishing Company 508 W. Main St., P.O. Box 411, Marshall, MN 56258. Tel: 507/537-1551; Fax: 507/537-1557; Web site: http://www.oweb.com/independent. Russ Labat, Gen. Mgr.; Dana Yost, Editor; Connie Nuese, Advertising Dir. Marshall Publishing Co. publishes the 9,000-circulation newspaper, The Marshall Independent, on Mondays through Saturdays. 75 employees (in Minnesota). SIC 2711, 2752. Founded in 1873. Owned by Ogden Newspapers Inc., Wheeling, W.Va.

Martin/Williams Inc. 60 S. Sixth St., Suite 2800, Minneapolis, MN 55402. Tel: 612/340-0800; Fax: 612/342-9700; Web site: http://www.martinwilliams.com. David D. Floren, Chm.; Tim Frojd, VChm.; Tom F. Weyl, VChm.; Steve Collins, Pres.; Mike Gray, EVP; Tom Kelly, EVP and Exec. Creative Dir.; Dan Woodbury, EVP; Jo-Anne Ebensteiner, SVP and Creative Dir.-iGroup; John Karlson, SVP-Strategic Devel.; Gregg Sampson, SVP and Managing Dir.-iGroup. Annual revenue $44 million ($310 million in capitalized billings, up 6.9 percent). Martin/Williams Inc. (M/W) is a full-service marketing company. Operating units include Creo International, international and cross-cultural communications; FAME, retail image management; Karwoski & Courage, public relations; and Martin/Williams Advertising, a full-service advertising agency; and [i]Group integrated services. Current M/W clients include: U.S. Bancorp, 3M Co., Marvin Windows, Rubbermaid, Lincoln Finance, Powertel, Novartis, Cargill, and Target Corp. (including Target Stores). 334 employees (20 part-time). SIC 7311. Founded in 1947. In March 2000 the firm lost long-time client Northern States Power Co. ($2.1 million in billings) to Denver-based McClain Finlon Advertising, the agency of NSP's merger partner, New Century Energies. In April it gained the Victory Motorcycle portion of Polaris Industries Inc.'s ad business ($2 million to $3 million); in May, the ad account for Internet agribusiness marketplace Rooster.com ($5 million to $8 million). In August the firm gave its interactive services division a boost by transferring two veteran branding strategists from its traditional agency to the [i]Group. It also added the account of $3.4 billion-revenue Steelcase, a Grand Rapids, Mich.-based manufacturer of office furniture. In September M/W's pitch to land the $50 million U.S. Navy account was rejected. In October catalog and retail merchandiser L.L. Bean, trying to become more appealing to younger consumers, named M/W to handle its $15 million to $20 million account. At The Show 2000 in Minneapolis, the firm took home 46 honors, second-most in the competition (to Carmichael Lynch). In November M/W beat three larger agencies for the $10 million to $15 million account of Donato's Pizza, which is owned by McDonald's Corp. Owned by Omnicom Group Inc., New York.

Massachusetts Mutual Life Insurance Company 333 S. Seventh St., 2200 Metropolitan Centre, Minneapolis, MN 55402. Tel: 612/333-1413; Fax: 612/333-9041. Peter Schulte, Gen. Agent. Massachusetts Mutual Life is a provider of life insurance, disability insurance, and equity products. 50 employees (45 in Minnesota; 5 part-time). SIC 6311. Founded in 1887. Owned by Massachusetts Mutual Life Insurance Co., Springfield, Mass.

Maurices Inc. 105 W. Superior St., Duluth, MN 55802. Tel: 218/727-8431; Fax: 218/720-2102. Roland Brenninkmeyer, Pres. and CEO; Lisa Rhodes, EVP and Gen. Mdsg. Mgr. Maurices operates more than 400 women's and men's apparel stores nationwide. 4,096 employees. SIC 5621. Founded in 1931. Owned by ARG (American Retail Group), New York.

McCain Foods Inc. East Highway 212, P.O. Box 100, Clark, SD 57225. Tel: 605/532-3651; Fax: 605/532-5583. Dave Musser, Plant Mgr.; Oren Holmstrom, Personnel Mgr. McCain Foods processes potatoes into frozen french fries. 130 employees. SIC 2037. Founded in 1969. Owned through McCain Foods USA, Rosemont, Ill., by McCain Foods Ltd., Florenceville, New Brunswick.

McCloud USA 5100 S. McCloud Ln., Irene, SD 57108. Tel: 605/263-3301; Fax: 605/263-3995. James H. Jibben, Chm.; Thomas W. Hertz, CEO; Craig A. Anderson, Pres.; Timothy Dupic, Sec. McCloud USA is a competitive local exchange carrier (CLEC) specializing in the design, construction, and operation of broadband telecommunications systems for communities in South Dakota and the surrounding states. The company operates 18 exchanges in southeastern South Dakota, four of which were built in 1997, incorporating more than 2,240 miles of copper plant, 300 miles of coaxial cable, and 10,000 fiber miles of fiber optic lines. The company's main growth strategy is to continue to expand and build new systems in South Dakota, Minnesota, Iowa, and Nebraska. Dakota Telecommunications provides a full range of bundled telecommunications products and services to its customers, including switched local dial tone and enhanced services, network access services, long-distance telephone services, operator-assisted calling services, telecommunications equipment sale and leasing services, cable television services, data networking services, Internet access and related services, and local-area network and wide-area network (LAN/WAN) services. Its customer base includes 6,100 local service access lines; 5,500 cable television subscribers; 6,600 Internet users; and more than 2,000 active LAN/WAN business customers located primarily in South Dakota, northwestern Iowa, and southwestern Minnesota. The company and its predecessors have been engaged in the telecommunications business since 1902. 175 employees. SIC 4813. Founded in 1997. Acquired March 5, 1999, by McLeodUSA Inc. (Nasdaq: MCLD), Cedar Rapids, Iowa.

McCracken Brooks Maier 110 Cheshire Ln., Suite 110, Minnetonka, MN 55305. Tel: 952/249-8600; Fax: 952/249-8790; Web site: http://www.mbmusa.com. Mark J. Lenss, CEO; Matt Maier, Pres. McCracken Brooks Maier is a full-service promotional marketing agency. The company creates a measurable change in sales force, trade, and consumer behavior while building brand equity through integrating promotion, direct marketing, and promotional advertising. Major clients: Pillsbury, Cost Cutters, MilkPEP, Tony's Pizza Service, E*Trade, and Washington Mutual. 85 employees. SIC 7311. Founded in 1986. Owned by Bozell, Jacobs, Kenyon & Eckhardt, New York, which was acquired in December 1997 by True North Communications Inc. (NYSE: TNO), Chicago.

McGarvey Superior Coffee Inc. 350 73rd Ave N.E., Suite 15, Fridley, MN 55432. Tel: 763/572-2506; Fax: 763/789-1552. Roger Foxx, Regional Sls. Mgr. McGarvey Coffee primarily imports, roasts, and sells coffee to the food service industry (hotels, restaurants, and hospitals). It also sells gourmet coffees to specialty gourmet stores. The company markets its coffee, allied food products, and coffee-brewing equipment throughout 10 Upper Midwest states. 80 employees. SIC 2095. Founded in 1922. Acquired in February 1991 by Superior Coffee and Foods, Bensenville, Ill.; division of Sara Lee Corp. (NYSE: SLE), Chicago.

McGraw-Hill Healthcare Information Group 4530 W. 77th St., Edina, MN 55435. Tel: 952/835-3222; Fax: 952/835-3460. M. James Dougherty, Group VP; Gary Gyss, VP and Publisher; Stephen J. Rose, VP-Mktg. Annual revenue $40 million. McGraw-Hill Healthcare Information Group consists of two subgroups: Clinical Publications and Technology Publications. Clinical Publications publishes three monthly medical journals: Postgraduate Medicine, Hospital Practice, and The Physician and Sportsmedicine. Technology Publications publishes two medical technology journals: Healthcare Informatics and e.MD. The Healthcare Information Group also publishes a variety of customized products via the Healthcare Information Programs division for both subgroups. 95 employees (in Minnesota). SIC 2721, 2741. Founded in 1947. Owned by The McGraw-Hill Cos. Inc. (NYSE: MHP), New York.

McKechnie Plastic Components/North America 7309 W. 27th St., St. Louis Park, MN 55426. Tel: 952/929-3312; Fax: 952/929-8404. Brian Evenson, Pres.; Mark Schaefer, VP-Bus. Devel. McKechnie Plastic Components Minneapolis is a custom injection molder of thermoplastic resins to close tolerance. Operating 165 injection presses and processing 14.5 million pounds of material annually, it serves technology-driven companies in medical, aerospace/government, business electronics, automotive, power tools, fluid-handling, and industrial-products markets. Additional operations are in Staples, Minn., and Easley, S.C. A registered contract manufacturer of Class III medical devices, the company is GMP-, ISO 9002-, EN46002-, and QS 9000-certified. Formerly known as McCourtney Plastics Inc. 520 employees (250 in Minnesota). SIC 3089. Founded in 1958. Purchased in 1988, renamed in 1992 by McKechnie plc, Walsall, U.K. No. 32 CRM Foreign-Owned 100.

McKessonHBOC Extended Care Division 8121 10th Ave. N., Golden Valley, MN 55427. Tel: 763/595-6000; Fax: 763/595-6566. Gary Keeler, Pres.; Gail Beske, VP-Fin./Reimbursement; Brian Denny, VP-Sls., Western Region; Jim Kohler, VP-Sls., Southern Region; Carol Muratore, VP-Sls., Northern Region; Jim Reinstatler, VP-Info. Svs.; Jean Seratin, VP-Mktg.; Dan Zipes, VP-Logistics. Annual revenue $485.4 million. McKessonHBOC Extended Care Division, formerly Red Line HealthCare Corp., sells medical supplies and services for the long-term care industry nationwide. Its Red Line Medical Supply and Medi Mart divisions operate out of 11 warehouse service centers. In September 1998 Novartis of Basel, Switzerland, agreed to sell Red Line HealthCare for $230 million in cash and assumed debt. 802 employees (350 in Minnesota). SIC 5047. In June 2000 the division acquired the assets of Gatti Medical Supply Inc., Indiana, Pa., a supplier of long-term-care medical supplies to customers in western Pennsylvania; in July, certain assets of Med 90 Inc., St. Louis, another supplier of long-term-care medical supplies. In August McKesson signed up to be the exclusive distributor of Qualigen Inc.'s proprietary, point-of-care blood testing system, the FastPack System. In October McKessonHBOC MedManagement agreed to provide pharmacy management and consulting services to Los Angeles-based AIDS Healthcare Foundation (AHF), the largest community-based HIV/AIDS medical provider in the nation, for its clinic-based, state-of-the-art pharmacy program, the AHF Pharmacy. The company is now a unit of McKessonHBOC Medical Group. Ultimate parent: McKesson HBOC Inc. (NYSE: MCK), San Francisco.

McLean Midwest 11611 Business Park Blvd. N., Champlin, MN 55316. Tel: 763/323-8200; Fax: 763/576-3200. John G. Mogler, Pres.; Michael L. Wilber, VP-Mfg.; Cindy Day, Cont. and Treas.; John O. Buyse, VP-Sls. McLean Midwest manufactures air conditioners and heat exchangers for the electronics and machine-tool industries. 120 employees. SIC 3564, 3585, 3625. Founded in 1975. A subsidiary of Zero Corp. (NYSE: ZRO), Los Angeles.

McLeodUSA 5929 Baker Rd., Suite 470, Minnetonka, MN 55345. Tel: 952/930-4400; Fax: 952/630-4455; Web site: http://www.mcleodusa.com. Clark McLeod, Chm.; Richard Lumpkin, VChm.; Stephen Gray, Pres. and COO; Michael Brown, GVP-Chief Service Ofcr.; Arthur Christoffersen, GVP-Publishing Svs.; Blake Fisher, GVP-Chief Planning/Devel. Ofcr.; Gregg Hammann, GVP-Bus. Devel.; Robert Hatch, GVP-Western Region; David Lunemann, GVP-Central Region; Randall Rings, GVP and Chief Legal Ofcr.; Albert Ruffalo, GVP-Chief People Devel. Ofcr.; Steven Shirar, GVP and Chief Sls. Ofcr.; Donna Stoner, GVP-Eastern Region; J. Lyle Patrick, CFO; Joseph Ceryanec, VP-Fin., Cont., and Treas.; Bryce Nemitz, VP-Communications/Investor Rel.; Roy Wilkens, Chief Tech. Ofcr. McLeodUSA is a facilities-based competitive provider of local and long-distance telecommunications services. McLeodUSA is a significant player in the Twin Cities local business telephone market, where its market share is in the mid-teens. In January 1999 the Minnetonka operation formerly known as Ovation Communications agreed to be acquired for $402.5 million. The high price (100 times cash flow) was commanded by its position as a successful competitor of dominant local company U S West. 331 employees (in Minnesota). SIC 4813. Founded in 1997. In late October, McLeodUSA signed a local telephone contract with rival Qwest. In exchange for $600 million over three years, the interconnection agreement will allow McLeodUSA to acquire local business telephone customers in competition with Qwest without first having to build its own telephone network. Now a part of McLeodUSA Inc. (Nasdaq: MCLD), Cedar Rapids, Iowa.

McLoone Metal Graphics Inc. 75 Summer St., P.O. Box 1117, La Crosse, WI 54602. Tel: 608/784-1260; Fax: 608/782-3711; Web site: http://www.mcloone.com. Judy A. Stauffer, Gen. Mgr. Annual revenue $13.6 million. McLoone Metal Graphics Inc. produces nameplates and labels. 160 employees (5 part-time). SIC 2759, 3993. Founded in 1954. Subsidiary of JSJ Corp., Grand Haven, Mich.

McNeilus Truck & Manufacturing Inc. P.O. Box 70, Dodge Center, MN 55927. Tel: 507/374-6321; Fax: 507/374-2359. Garwin B. McNeilus, Chm. and CEO; Denzil McNeilus, Pres. McNeilus manufactures ready-mix concrete mixers and related parts, and mounts mixers on truck chassis. The company also sells truck/mixer packages through eight company-owned branch facilities with 70 sales representatives. McNeilus Financial, a wholly owned subsidiary, also makes garbage trucks and provides full leasing services to the garbage industry. In December 1997 the company agreed to be acquired for $250 million. In July 1999 its new parent announced plans to invest more than $8.3 million to expand McNeilus' Dodge Center manufacturing facility. 700 employees. SIC 3443, 3531, 3713. Founded in 1970. In October 2000 the company unveiled its newest front-loading refuse truck body at the Solid Waste Association of North America trade show in Cincinnati. The Atlantic Series, designed with numerous features popular with refuse companies in the eastern United States, increases daily productivity and offers greater durability. A key packer element on the Atlantic is a new high-performance telescopic cylinder. Lighter and easier to maintain, it features an induction-hardened rod that is chrome plated for longer life. The cylinder and rod reduce return flow and a new seal improves leakage control. Now owned by Oshkosh Truck Corp. (Nasdaq: OTRKB), Oshkosh, Wis.

McQuay International 13600 Industrial Park Blvd., Plymouth, MN 55441. Tel: 763/553-5330; Fax: 763/553-5177. Gerry Boehrs, Pres. and COO; A. Grundei, VP and Cont.; B. Myer, VP-Quality Assurance. McQuay International manufactures and markets a full line of McQuay and AAF commercial and industrial HVAC equipment; also BarryBlower commercial fans. McQuayService is the company's service arm to the industry. McQuay has U.S. operations in Auburn, N.Y.; Faribault, Fridley, and Owatonna, Minn.; Scottsboro, Ala.; and Staunton, Va. International operations are located in Rome; Cramlington, U.K.; Jarkarta, Indonesia; Pons, France; Shah Alam, Malaysia; and Shenzhen, PRC. 3,000 employees (1,000 in Minnesota). SIC 3585. Founded in 1933. In July 2000 McQuay increased production of Vision customized indoor air handlers at its facility in Faribault and at a plant it was purchasing in Owatonna, Minn. (where the first air handlers were produced in October). Because of this expansion, the company was planning to hire 200 additional employees. In August the company agreed to pay $194,000 to settle a sexual harassment lawsuit brought by three female workers at the Auburn, N.Y., plant. One of two divisions of AAF-McQuay Inc. (formerly SnyderGeneral Corp.), Baltimore, which was acquired in May 1994 by OYL Industries Bhd., Malaysia. No. 3 CRM Foreign-Owned 100.

Mead Paper Division—Michigan Operations P.O. Box 757, Escanaba, MI 49829. Tel: 906/786-1660; Fax: 906/789-3221. Gary L. Butryn, VP-Op.; Keith Van Scotter, VP-Michigan Op.; Al Larson, Dir.-Mfg. Op.; M.A. Forneti, Dir.-Pulping, Utilities; Amy Deiter, Cont.; G.W. Brown, VP-Prod. Tech.; G.A. Van Drese, Dir.-Maintenance/Devel. Mead Paper manufacturers coated and carbonless paper. 1,339 employees. SIC 2621. Founded in 1918. Owned by The Mead Corp. (NYSE: MEA), Dayton, Ohio.

Medallion Kitchens of Minnesota Inc. 180 Industrial Blvd., Waconia, MN 55387. Tel: 763/442-5171; Fax: 763/442-4998. Stan Bandur, Pres.; Thomas E. Cook, EVP and Gen. Mgr.; Larry Stokes, EVP-Sls./Mktg.; Ken Pfarr, VP-Mfg. Annual revenue $72 million. Medallion Kitchens manufactures kitchen cabinets, selling them nationally through independent distributors and retail home-center chains. Medallion operates plants in Waconia, Minn. and Salem, Oregon. 555 employees (450 in Minnesota). SIC 2434, 2541. Founded in 1969. Owned by Elkay Manufacturing Co., Oak Brook, Ill.

Menasha Corporation 8085 220th St. W., Lakeville, MN 55044. Tel: 952/469-4451; Fax: 952/469-1068. John Sondergard, Gen. Mgr.; Bob Jagodzinski, Field Sls./Product Mgr.; Cheryl Morgan, Customer Svc. Mgr. Menasha Corp. manufactures corrugated shipping containers and displays. 185 employees. SIC 2653. Founded in 1969. Division of Menasha Corp., Neenah, Wis.

Menasha Packaging 7301 Northland Dr., Brooklyn Park, MN 55428. Tel: 763/424-6606; Fax: 763/424-9838. Kim E. Dresselhaus, Gen. Mgr. Menasha Packaging, formerly North Star Containers, manufactures corrugated boxes and displays. 130 employees (in Minnesota). SIC 2653. Founded in 1849. Purchased in October 1990 by Menasha Corp., Neenah, Wis.

Mentor Corporation 1601 West River Rd. N., Minneapolis, MN 55411. Tel: 612/588-4685; Fax: 612/287-4201. Paul J. DiCicco, VP and Gen. Mgr.-Urology Op. Mentor Urology develops, manufactures, and markets medical and surgical devices for the specialty of urology, and products for hospital and home health care. 310 employees (in Minnesota). SIC 3069, 3842. Founded in 1969. Owned by Mentor Corp. (Nasdaq: MNTR), Santa Barbara, Calif.

Mercury Minnesota Inc. 901 Hulet Ave., P.O. Box 188, Faribault, MN 55021. Tel: 507/334-5513; Fax: 507/334-0111. Gordy Adameck, VP and Gen. Mgr. Mercury Minnesota makes business-machine frames and parts. The company is also a precision sheet metal and steel tubing manufacturer, principally for computer companies. 180 employees. SIC 3469. Founded in 1957. Owned by Mercury Aircraft Inc., Hammondsport, N.Y.

Merillat Industries Inc. 21755 Cedar Ave. S., P.O. Box 1076, Lakeville, MN 55044. Tel: 952/985-7300. Peter Palpant, Plant Mgr. Merillat Industries manufactures kitchen cabinets and bathroom vanities. 300 employees. SIC 2434, 2493. Founded in 1978. Owned by Merillat Industries, Adrian, Mich.; subsidiary of Masco Corp. (NYSE: MAS), Taylor, Mich.

Metallurgical Inc. 900 E. Hennepin Ave., Minneapolis, MN 55414. Tel: 612/378-1500; Fax: 612/378-0462. John Wielgosz, Pres. Metallurgical Inc. does commercial heat treating. 93 employees. SIC 3398. Founded in 1951. In June 2000 the company was one of three units sold by Thermo Terratech, Waltham, Mass., for $17 million. Now owned by Lindberg Corp. (Nasdaq: LIND), Rosemont, Ill.

Micron Electronics Inc. 2359 Walnut St., Roseville, MN 55113. Tel: 800/438-3343; Fax: 800/362-1205; Web site: http://www.micronpc.com. Joseph Daltoso, Chm., Pres., and CEO. Micron Electronics operates a local call center offering sales and technical support for Micron high-performance personal computer systems and related IBM-compatible hardware products. These products are direct-marketed to business, government, colleges, and the general public. Former public company Zeos International Ltd. was acquired in April 1995. 350 employees (in Minnesota). SIC 5065. Founded in 1981. Owned by Micron Technology Inc. (NYSE: MU), Boise, Idaho.

Midland National Life Insurance Company One Midland Plaza, Sioux Falls, SD 57193. Tel: 605/373-8558; Fax: 605/335-3621; Web site: http://www.mnlife.com. Michael M. Masterson, Chm., Pres., and CEO; John J. Craig, EVP and COO; E. John Fromelt, SVP and Chief Investment Ofcr.; Stephen P. Horvat, SVP; Donald J. Iverson, SVP and Actuary; Thomas M. Meyer, SVP and CFO; Steven C. Palmitier, SVP and Chief Mktg. Ofcr.; Jack L. Briggs, VP, Sec., and Gen. Counsel; Robert W. Buchanan, VP-New Business; Gary W. Helder, VP-Policy Admin. Annual revenue $681 million. Midland National Life is a cost-efficient provider of life insurance and annuity products. 510 employees (8 in Minnesota; 4 part-time). SIC 6311. Founded in 1906. Owned by Sammons Enterprises Inc., Dallas.

Midwest Coca-Cola Bottling Company 2750 Eagandale Blvd., Eagan, MN 55121. Tel: 651/454-5460; Fax: 651/681-3517. Jeff Laschen, VP and Gen. Mgr.; Christine Mackin, VP-Sls./Mktg.; Kevin Morris, Dir.-Corp. Affairs; Brad Wilson, Cont. Midwest Coca-Cola Bottling Co. is a soft drink bottler. 1,300 employees (1,000 in Minnesota). SIC 2086.

Founded in 1919. In June 2000 Teamsters Local 792 held mediated talks with the company after voting to reject a contract offer. Later in the month, those talks resulted in a new three-year agreement. Wholly owned subsidiary of Coca-Cola Enterprises Inc. (NYSE: CCE), Atlanta.

Midwest Electric Products Inc. Highway 22 North, P.O. Box 910, Mankato, MN 56002. Tel: 507/345-2500; Fax: 507/345-2529. William F. Austen, Pres. and Gen. Mgr.; Anne Cooney, Plant Mgr.; Fred Bull, Mktg./Sls. Mgr.; Arden Kraft, Fin. Mgr.; Heather Ludwig, Hum. Res. Mgr.; Bill Childs, Quality Leader; Frank Kurtz, EHS Leader. Midwest Electric Products manufactures weather-tight enclosures and electrical service-entrance equipment. 250 employees (50 part-time). SIC 3612, 3613, 3629, 3643, 3699. Founded in 1946. Owned by General Electric Co. (NYSE: GE), Fairfield, Conn.

Mid-West Spring Manufacturing Company 100 South Owasso Blvd. W., St. Paul, MN 55117. Tel: 651/483-5476; Fax: 651/483-6006. Mark Woda, Gen. Mgr.; Susan O'Kasick, Op. Mgr. Mid-West Spring manufactures springs, wire forms, and stampings for large and small machinery. 70 employees (68 in Minnesota; 2 part-time). SIC 3469, 3493, 3495. Founded in 1928. Owned by Mid-West Spring Manufacturing, Romeoville, Ill.

Milbank Insurance Company 107 Flynn, P.O. Box 2M, Milbank, SD 57253. Tel: 605/432-5551; Fax: 605/432-6536; Web site: http://www.stayto.com. Robert Moone, Pres.; Russel M. Fischer, VP; John R. Lowther, Sec.; James E. Duemey, Investment Ofcr. Milbank Insurance is licensed in 25 states. Its major line of business is private passenger auto liability. It is a member of State Automobiles Insurance Companies, a large insurance group with surplus in excess of $100 million. Milbank also sells fire and property casualty insurance through independent insurance agents in Minnesota, South Dakota, North Dakota, and Utah. 142 employees (12 in Minnesota). SIC 6331. Founded in 1892. Acquired in July 1993 by State Automobile Mutual Insurance Co., Columbus, Ohio.

The Mining Journal 249 W. Washington Ave., P.O. Box 430, Marquette, MI 49855. Tel: 906/228-2500; Fax: 906/228-5556. James A. Reeves, Publisher and Gen. Mgr. The Mining Journal is in the newspaper publishing business. 102 employees. SIC 2711. Founded in 1846. Division of Ogden Newspapers Inc., Wheeling, W.Va.

Minncomm Paging 610 Ottawa Ave. N., Golden Valley, MN 55422. Tel: 763/522-3344; Fax: 763/522-3029. Steven K. Miorana, Gen. Mgr. Minncomm Paging is the largest provider of paging services in the Twin Cities area. 70 employees. SIC 4812. Founded in 1970. Wholly owned by Ameritech Mobile Communications Inc., Schaumburg, Ill., subsidiary of Ameritech Corp., Chicago, which was acquired in 1999 by SBC Communications Inc. (NYSE: SBC), San Antonio.

Minnesota Ore Operations/U.S. Steel Box 417, Mountain Iron, MN 55768. Tel: 218/749-7300; Fax: 218/749-7293. J.E. (Jim) Swearingen, Gen. Mgr.; John E. Skube, Mgr.-Employee Rel. Minnesota Ore Operations (Minntac) mines and processes iron ore, including taconite. Minntac, North America's largest taconite plant, annually produces 16.4 million tons of taconite pellets, which are used as raw material to make steel. Its operations cover nearly 40,000 acres, including a mine that stretches 12 miles along the Mesabi Range. 1,650 employees. SIC 1011, 3312. Founded in 1901. In November 2000 the U.S. Steel Group idled one of five agglomerator lines at its Minntac operations. The line, which represents about 12 percent of Minntac's annual output, is the same one that was idled in October 1998 and remained down for one year. GM Swearingen said, "The agglomerator shutdown at Minntac is expected to last at least through the end of this year. Unfortunately, this may result in substantial layoffs." U.S. Steel Group President Paul J. Wilhelm added, "The need to close the line can once again be attributed primarily to staggering volumes of steel imports, which are on pace this year to match the record levels of 1998. It has become all too clear to the steel industry that the import crisis is far from being over." However, United Steelworkers of America union members approved a company-union agreement that prevented the layoff of 140 Minntac steelworkers through the end of the year. Minntac is owned through the U.S. Steel Group (NYSE: X) by USX Corp. (NYSE: MRO), Pittsburgh.

Minot Daily News P.O. Box 1150, Minot, ND 58702. Tel: 701/857-1900; Fax: 701/857-1961. Steven Baker, Publisher. Minot Daily News publishes a daily newspaper. 134 employees. SIC 2711. Founded in 1884. Owned by Ogden Newspapers Inc., Wheeling, W.Va.

Miracle-Ear Inc. 5000 Cheshire Ln. N., Plymouth, MN 55446. Tel: 763/268-4000; Fax: 76/326-8429. Glenn Hemmerle, Pres.; Tim Kuehn, VP-Fin.; Margaret McDonald, VP-Brand Mgmt.; Anthony Scarfone, Corp. Counsel. Miracle-Ear Inc., formerly Dahlberg Inc., manufactures and markets hearing aids under the Miracle-Ear brand name, including accessory products and replacement parts. It also markets audiometers and hearing aid batteries. The company has 1,000 U.S. stores (160 company-owned, the rest franchised), covering all 50 states. Many of its franchises are located in Sears and Montgomery Ward stores. Acquired in July 1993 for $139 million by Bausch & Lomb Inc. (NYSE: BOL), which subsequently put Dahlberg up for sale in May 1999, citing a desire to focus on its eye-related businesses. When it made Dahlberg its entry into the U.S. market in September 1999, Amplifon became the world's largest hearing-care retailer. 488 employees (in Minnesota). SIC 3842. Founded in 1948. In February 2000, continuing to focus on its retail hearing aid business, Miracle-Ear agreed to sell its Canadian manufacturing subsidiary, 88-employee Dahlberg Sciences Ltd., to the William Demant Holding Group of Denmark. Owned by Amplifon SpA, Milan. No. 17 CRM Foreign-Owned 100.

The Missoulian 500 S. Higgins, P.O. Box 8029, Missoula, MT 59807. Tel: 406/523-5200; Fax: 406/523-5221. Jim Bell, Publisher. The Missoulian is a daily-newspaper publishing company. 200 employees. SIC 2711. Founded in 1873. Owned by Lee Enterprises Inc. (NYSE: LEE), Davenport, Iowa.

Modine Airsystems 2475 Doswell, St. Paul, MN 55108. Tel: 651/646-9631; Fax: 651/646-5867. Dana Henjum, Plant Mgr.; Robert L. Linstroth, Mgr.-Engrg. Modine Airsystems constructs heating, ventilating, air-handling, and evaporation cooling equipment. Formerly Industrial Airsystems. 70 employees. SIC 3433, 3585. Founded in 1976. Now owned by Modine Manufacturing Co. (Nasdaq: MODI), Racine, Wis.

Montana Tunnels Mining Inc. P.O. Box 176, Jefferson City, MT 59638. Tel: 406/933-8314; Fax: 406/933-8373. Roland Erickson, Gen. Mgr.; Jim Chiotti, Mine Cont. Montana Tunnels Mining is a gold, silver, zinc, and lead mining operation. 265 employees. SIC 1031, 1041, 1044. Founded in 1987. Subsidiary of Pegasus Gold Corp., Spokane, Wash.; U.S. headquarters for Pegasus Gold Inc. (ASE: PGU), Vancouver, British Columbia.

Moore North America Publications Group 100 Washington Ave. S., Suite 1000, Minneapolis, MN 55401. Tel: 612/661-1000; Fax: 612/661-1195; Web site: http://www.mgservices.com. Roger Bowman, Dir.-Op.; Andy Boyle, VP-Sls.; Barri Klingaman, Dir.-Digital Publishing Svs. Moore North American Publications Group publishes directories, price books, and catalogs; and manages data for clients nationwide. It provides print and digital services using a blend of production technologies as well as a unique and comprehensive distribution system. Moore has three printing plants and 20 field offices in the United States. 410 employees (200 in Minnesota). SIC 2752, 7374. Founded in 1890. Owned through Moore North America Inc., Bannockburn, Ill., by Moore Corp. Ltd., Toronto. No. 48 CRM Foreign-Owned 100.

Moorhead Machinery & Boiler Company 3477 University Ave. N.E., Minneapolis, MN 55418. Tel: 612/789-3541; Fax: 612/789-3540. Jon A. Schmoeckel, Pres.; Michael J. Toyli, VP and Cont. Moorhead Machinery & Boiler is a contractor that performs boiler erection, repair, and maintenance, and heavy-plate fabrication. 175 employees. SIC 3443. Founded in 1917. Owned by Park Corp., Cleveland.

John Morrell & Company 1400 N. Weber Ave., P.O. Box 5266, Sioux Falls, SD 57117. Tel: 605/338-8200; Fax: 605/330-3167. S.M. Crim, SVP and Plant Mgr. Morrell's Sioux Falls Plant is the largest full-line processing plant in the United States. The facility slaughters hogs; renders and packages lard and shortening; and manufactures smoked meat, sliced bacon, sausage, and canned meats. 2,600 employees. SIC 2011, 2013. Founded in 1911. Owned by Smithfield Foods Inc. (Nasdaq: SFDS), Smithfield, Va.

Motor Coach Industries Inc. 552 W. Stutsman St., Pembina, ND 58271. Tel: 204/287-4360; Fax: 204/475-3003. Doug Ferrif, Plant Mgr. Motor Coach Industries manufactures intercity buses. 600 employees. SIC 3713. Founded in 1962. Owned by MCI Communications Inc., which was acquired in September 1998 by WorldCom Inc. (Nasdaq: WCOM), Jackson, Miss.

REG

Mrs. Smith Bakeries Inc., Foodservice Group 145 N. Jonathan Blvd., Chaska, MN 55318. Tel: 952/448-4493; Fax: 952/448-4095. John Staphs, Pres. Mrs. Smith Bakeries Inc., Foodservice Group, formerly known as Pies Inc., produces an extended variety of frozen pies, which are sold through the food service and in-store bakery industries. 300 employees. SIC 2051. Founded in 1919. Acquired in August 1991 by Flowers Industries Inc. (NYSE: FLO), Thomasville, Ga.

Multi-Clean Inc. 600 Cardigan Rd., Shoreview, MN 55126. Tel: 651/481-1900; Fax: 651/481-9987. Jerome Rau, CEO; Thomas Nolan, VP-Fin.; Gregory Rau, VP-Sls.; Gary Palmer, VP-Engrg. Multi-Clean manufactures cleaning chemical equipment. 50 employees. SIC 3699. Subsidiary of Hako-Werke GmbH & Co., Bad Oldesloe, Germany.

Murphy Oil USA Inc. 2407 Stinson Ave., P.O. Box 2066, Superior, WI 54880. Tel: 715/398-3533; Fax: 715/398-8209. J.P. Kowitz, Refinery Mgr. Murphy Oil Superior Refinery operates an oil refinery. 140 employees (15 in Minnesota). SIC 2911. Founded in 1950. Subsidiary of Murphy Oil Corp. (NYSE: MUR), El Dorado, Ark.

Mustang Manufacturing Company 1605 County Rd. 45 N., Owatonna, MN 55060. Tel: 507/451-7112; Fax: 507/451-8209. Donald A. Kalkman, Chm.; Bruce M. Collins, Pres.; Brian C. Clark, VP-Engrg.; Robert E. Tighe, VP-Fin.; Terry Kanitz, VP-Mfg. Mustang Manufacturing specializes in the manufacture and distribution of skid steer loaders and attachments. Purchased from Brunel Holdings plc in October 1998. 150 employees. SIC 3531. Founded in 1987. Owned by Gehl Co., West Bend, Wis.

NCS Pearson 11000 Prairie Lakes Dr., Eden Prairie, MN 55344. Tel: 952/829-3000; Fax: 952/829-3167; Web site: http://www.ncs.com. David W. Smith, CEO; Robert C. Bowen, VP, Pres.-K-12 Internet Program; Michael C. Brewer, VP and Gen. Counsel; J. McNamara (Mac) Curtis, VP, Pres.-Gov't Solutions; Simon Garneau, VP, Pres.-Data Management Solutions; Clive M. Hay-Smith, VP, Pres.-Int'l; Robert C. Hickcox, VP and Chief Info. Ofcr.; Gary L. Martini, VP-Hum. Res.; Michael A. Morache, VP, Pres.-Education Software/Svs.; Jeffrey W. Taylor, VP and CFO; Adrienne Teissier Tietz, VP-Corp. Devel.; John W. Fenton Jr., Sec. and Treas. Annual revenue $629.5 million (earnings $42.9 million). NCS Pearson, formerly National Computer Systems, is a growing global provider of information services providing software, services, and systems for the collection, management, and interpretation of data. NCS serves important segments of education, testing assessment, and complex data management markets. Education represents 75 percent of NCS' revenue; Data Management, the remaining 25 percent. 5,000 employees. SIC 3577, 7372, 7374. Founded in 1962. In March 2000 NCS signed nearly $7.8 million worth of software licensing and professional services contracts to serve more than 428,000 students and 623 school buildings. School districts included: California's Sacramento Unified, Colton County Joint, and Fresno Unified; Michigan's Grand Rapids Public Schools; Minnesota's Anoka-Hennepin School District; Missouri's St. Louis Public Schools; Nebraska's Omaha Public Schools; and Virginia's Fairfax County. The Fresno Unified School District in Fresno, Calif., licensed two of NCS' e-learning systems, the NovaNET online comprehensive courseware and Educational Structures online lesson-planning resource. NCS began delivery of CompTIA certification exams. In April the company was awarded a major contract with the Texas Education Agency for statewide assessment and testing services related to the Texas Assessment of Academic Skills (TAAS) tests, the largest state testing program in the United States—a total projected value exceeding $233 million over the next five years. The regents of the University of California selected NCS to develop and maintain a Web-based system to collect and report data on California high school students who may be eligible for admission to the University of California system under the Eligibility in the Local Context (ELC) program. The initial three-year contract was valued at up to $3 million. NCS was selected to provide independent auditing services for the United Kingdom's Interim Carrier Pre-Selection (ICPS) process. In May CEO Gullotti announced plans to retire by June 1, 2001. "It was always my intention to remain at this wonderful company for at least 10 years," he said. "My plans were sidetracked, however, when I recently dealt with a health condition." In July Student Financial Assistance (SFA) of the U.S. Department of Education awarded NCS the renewal of the Public Inquiry Contract, which was expected to exceed $100 million in value over five and one-half years. NCS was to establish and operate a comprehensive Customer Relationship Management center. NCS also agreed to develop, host, and maintain customer service Web sites to provide public access to general information and answers to frequently asked questions about SFA—such as inquiries about federal student financial aid programs, defaulted student loans, and other post-secondary education matters—from students, parents, school officials, and members of Congress. The Free Application for Federal Student Aid Web site, www.fafsa.ed.gov, received an E-Gov 2000 Pioneer Award. Late in the month, NCS acknowledged that it had incorrectly graded the math portion of two versions of Minnesota's Basic Standards Test, resulting in failing grades for 8,000 high school students. On July 31, NCS entered into a definitive agreement to be acquired by Pearson plc in a transaction valued at $2.5 billion. The $73 per share cash price was a 25.6 percent premium over the recent closing price. NCS was to become part of $2.7 billion Pearson Education, the world's leading educational publisher (Addison Wesley Longman, Simon & Schuster). [Deal closed in September.] July 29: Six-month revenue was $379.1 million, up 29 percent; earnings also grew 29 percent, to $25.5 million. In August NCS' Mexican subsidiary signed a $10 million-plus multiyear contract extension to its service agreement with Mexico's telephone carriers. The Federal Deposit Insurance Corp. (FDIC) selected NCS to operate its centralized call center in Washington, D.C., a contract worth $3 million over five years. NCS signed an agreement with Timecruiser Computing Corp. to license state-of-the-art Internet-based communication and collaboration tools to be seamlessly integrated into NCS' K-12 next-generation solutions suite. In September NCS launched TeacherCONNECTxp software, which dramat-

ically enhances teacher access to critical student and classroom information. With the acquisition officially completed, the company changed its name to NCS Pearson. VUE contracted with Cisco Systems to begin delivery of Cisco Career Certifications exams. Part of Pearson Education, a division of Pearson plc (LON), London. No. 43 CRM Public 200. No. 1 CRM Foreign-Owned 100.

Nabisco Brands Inc. 730 Stinson Blvd., Minneapolis, MN 55413. Tel: 612/331-4325; Fax: 612/378-2504. John Strotbeck, Plant Mgr. Nabisco Minneapolis Hot Cereal Plant manufactures Cream of Wheat and Cream of Rice hot cereals. 100 employees (120 in Minnesota; 20 part-time). SIC 2043. Founded in 1927. Nabisco Foods Co., Parsippany, N.J., owned by RJR Nabisco Holdings Corp. (NYSE: RN), New York.

Napa Auto Parts 7400 W. 27th St., St. Louis Park, MN 55426. Tel: 952/929-1635; Fax: 952/924-1208. Ted Webber, Gen. Mgr. Annual revenue $96 million. Napa Auto Parts retails and distributes auto parts. 310 employees (305 in Minnesota; 20 part-time). SIC 5013, 5531. Founded in 1925. Division of Genuine Parts Co. (NYSE: GPC), Atlanta.

National Car Rental System Inc. 7700 France Ave. S., Edina, MN 55435. Tel: 952/830-2121; Fax: 952/830-2548; Web site: http://www.nationalcar.com. Jeffrey J. Parell, Pres. and COO; Erv Zinter, EVP and CFO; Bob Dimmick, VP-Mktg./Advertising; Jim Wood, VP-Sls.; Cathy Barthel, Regional VP-Sls., Midwest; Jill Doran, Regional VP-Sls., Northeast. National Car Rental System Inc., which does business as National Car Rental/Interrent, is the country's fourth-largest automobile rental firm, operating a fleet of 100,000 vehicles out of more than 3,000 locations worldwide. It also works with partners in Latin America, Europe, Japan, and the Caribbean. In February 1997 NCR Acquisition Corp., the Lobeck-led investment group that had owned the company since 1995, sold National to billionaire businessman and sports owner H. Wayne Huizenga for $2.3 billion. In July 1999, in a joint announcement with Governor Ventura, AutoNation said that it was planning to make Minnesota the headquarters home of its North American Rental Group spin-off. That did not happen. 200 employees (in Minnesota). SIC 7514. Founded in 1947. In January 2000 parent ANC announced plans to eliminate 400 of the 600 Edina jobs, in stages, over nine months. National is owned by AutoNation Inc.'s January 2000 spinoff ANC Rental Corp. (NYSE: ANR), Fort Lauderdale, Fla.

National Surface Cleaning Inc. 4358 Round Lake Rd. W., Arden Hills, MN 55112. Tel: 651/636-6829; Fax: 651/636-8483. Darryl Schimeck, Pres.; Rob King, Gen. Mgr.; Jim Swanson, Business Devel. Mgr.; Dana Sawrey, Mgr.-HVAC Cleaning Div. National Surface Cleaning provides environmental remediation services such as ventilation-system cleaning, asbestos control, and lead abatement. Its patented commercial building ventilation system cleaning and decontamination services serve the growing indoor air quality industry. 110 employees. SIC 1799. Founded in 1986. Owned by NSC Corp., Methuen, Mass.

Navigant International—Twin Cities 7401 Metro Blvd., Suite 350, Edina, MN 55439. Tel: 952/831-8300; Fax: 952/831-7071; Web site: http://www.navigant.com. Scott G. Kellar, VP-Sls.; Bonita B. Boisner, VP. Annual revenue $75 million (in volume). Navigant International is a business travel management company serving corporations nationwide. Former names: TravelCorp, World Travel & Incentives. 110 employees. SIC 4724. Founded in 1974. Acquired in June 1998 by Navigant International (Nasdaq: FLYR), Englewood, Colo.

Neiman Marcus 505 Nicollet Mall, Minneapolis, MN 55402. Tel: 612/339-2600; Fax: 612/339-9113. Beth Pine, VP and Gen. Mgr. Neiman Marcus (Minneapolis) is one of 30 apparel and fine goods specialty stores with total sales of $1.6 billion. 200 employees. SIC 5311. Founded in 1991. Neiman-Marcus Co., Dallas, owned by Harcourt General (NYSE: H), Chestnut Hill, Mass.

NetDirect Corporation International 3100 W. Lake St., Suite 400, Minneapolis, MN 55416. Tel: 612/915-1122; Fax: 612/915-1133; Web site: http://www.netdirect.com. James D. Ross, Chm.; Gregory A. Appelhof, Pres. and CEO; Jeffrey Maynard, SVP; John Harvatine, CFO; William Brinkman, VP-Bus. Devel.; Pete Rockers, VP-E-business Devel. NetDirect Corp. International—formerly Virtual Technology Corp. and, before that, Network Storage Corp.—is an online retailer of computer hardware and software products. The company was acquired in late 2000 in a reverse merger. 60 employees. SIC 7379. In November 1999 the company changed its name from Virtual Technology Corp. (OTC Bulletin Board: VTCO) to NetDirect Corp. International, to reflect the company's rapid expansion into the global business-to-business and consumer e-commerce markets. A new Web site was launched offering a better way to purchase technology products—including, faster, easier navigation, extensive product information, superior search capabilities, and an increased focus on providing products and services that meet customers' individual needs. In December NetDirect backed away from plans to acquire 24store.com, a struggling Scandinavian e-commerce firm. The company did, however, close on its acquisition of the operating assets of Tech Squared Inc. for a cash purchase price of $3.3 million. The sale included Tech Squared's DTP Direct, Net Direct, and distribution operations, along with various trade and Internet domain names. Compositech Ltd. (Nasdaq: CTEK), Hauppauge, N.Y., developer of high-tech laminates for the printed circuit board industry, agreed to acquire NetDirect in a reverse-merger exchange of common stock worth $157 million. In January 2000 the company acquired http://www.downloadstore.com—along with access to more than 193,000 business customers and consumers and relationships with Internet portals Juno, Prodigy, and Xoom—from Softdisk LLC, for $725,000 in cash and restricted stock. In February the company signed a definitive agreement to acquire privately held, $25 million-revenue HardwareStreet.com of Reno, Nev., a business-to-business e-commerce portal with an established Affinity Partner program that reaches 100 million businesses and consumers. [April's volatile market caused NetDirect's board not to proceed with the acquisition.] In March NetDirect's board of directors voted to terminate a previous letter of intent to merge with Compositech. NetDirect moved its 128 Minnesota-based employees to a new 45,000-square-foot, state-of-the-art facility in Eden Prairie, consolidating four separate offices at various locations throughout Minnesota. In April NetDirect and the University of Minnesota launched a new, secure e-commerce Internet site for University purchasing departments, students, staff, and faculty. In May Netdirect and Wizmo, a commerce service provider (CSP) targeting small- and medium-sized businesses, partnered to launch a private-label e-commerce Community Techmart Web site. In June the company filed documents with the SEC saying that if it "cannot reduce its cash expenditures and raise additional capital, it may be unable to continue [its] operations." NetDirect then announced an agreement to merge with online retailer BuyItNow Inc. of New Jersey, a merger designed to allow the combined companies to compete more effectively in business-to-business and business-to-consumer sales of technology-related products and services. In a reverse merger, BuyItNow was to be the surviving company. Expected to close by July 31, 2000, the deal was still pending well into August. The merger effort was in trouble unless both sides could raise more capital and NetDirect was able to extricate itself from several contracts that its potential partner didn't want. Owned by BuyItNow Inc., Tulsa, Okla. No. 107 CRM Public 200.

Newport Minnesota 5480 Nathan Ln. N., Plymouth, MN 55442. Tel: 763/593-0722; Fax: 763/593-0712. Jim Meyer, Gen. Mgr.; Dave Cermak, Mgr.-Op.; Kevin Duffy, Bus. Devel. Mgr.; Theresa Gade, Mgr.-Hum. Res.; Pat Mathiesen, Materials Mgr.; Bob Snyder, Mgr.-Engrg. Newport Minnesota manufactures the BBIM series of automated systems for Ball-Bond inspection and measurement; the NE-Series of high-precision positioning stages; MikroPro and MikroSkop inspection and metrology systems; and the PSM-1000, a unique probe-station microscope used for emission microscopy. Formerly known as MikroPrecision Instruments. 73 employees (in Minnesota). SIC 3823. Founded in 1984. Since a January 1996 acquisition, it has been a subsidiary of Newport Corp. (Nasdaq: NEWP), Irvine, Calif.

Nichols-Homeshield/Amsco Division 311 W. Coleman St., Rice Lake, WI 54868. Tel: 715/234-9061; Fax: 715/234-7799. J.W. Gulliford, VP and Gen. Mgr.; M.E. Hermann, Op. Mgr.; Herb Seeger, Cont. Nichols-Homeshield manufactures screens, doors, and combination windows. 250 employees. SIC 3442. Founded in 1972. Nichols-Homeshield Inc., Davenport, Iowa, division of Quanex Corp. (NYSE: NX), Houston.

Nilfisk-Advance Inc. 14600 21st Ave. N., Plymouth, MN 55447. Tel: 763/473-1693. Rudi Gutmann, Pres./CEO-Nilfisk-Advance Inc.; Jack Cooney, Pres.-Advance Machine; Joseph Grewe, SVP-Op.; Hroar Toppenberg, CFO; Curt Olson, VP-Sls. Nilfisk-Advance Inc., formerly Advance Machine Co., manufactures floor-maintenance equipment for the commercial/industrial market worldwide. 650 employees. SIC 3589. Founded in 1910. In June 1994 Advance merged with Nilfisk A/S, which was later renamed Nilfisk-Advance A/S, Copenhagen. No. 29 CRM Foreign-Owned 100.

Niro Inc. 1600 O'Keefe Rd., Hudson, WI 54016. Tel: 715/386-9371; Fax: 715/386-9376. Steve Kaplan, Pres.; Ron Matzek, VP; Christian Svensgaard, VP. Annual revenue $40 million. Niro Hudson engineers, designs, and manufactures spray driers, membrane filtration systems, and complete processing and powder-handling systems. 220 employees (48 in Minnesota). SIC 3556. Founded in 1979. Owned by Gea, Bochum, Germany.

The North American Coal Corporation—Land Office 2000 Schafer St., Suite D, Bismarck, ND 58501-1204. Tel: 701/258-2200; Fax: 701/258-0672. James Melchior, Land Mgr. North American Coal's Land Office surface-mines lignite coal, which is sold under long-term contracts to energy-conversion facilities. 611 employees. SIC 1221. Founded in 1957. The North American Coal Corp., Dallas, is owned by Nacco Industries Inc. (NYSE: NC), Mayfield Heights, Ohio.

Northern Castings Corporation, an Intermet Company P.O. Box 98, Hibbing, MN 55746. Tel: 218/263-8871; Fax: 218/263-5039. Kevin Pilon, Plant Mgr. Northern Castings manufactures ductile iron castings. 110 employees. SIC 3321. Founded in 1973. Reports through the Detroit division to Intermet Corp. (Nasdaq: INMT), Troy, Mich.

Northern Hardwoods Highway M-26, P.O. Box 189, South Range, MI 49963. Tel: 906/487-6400; Fax: 906/487-6417. Bill Check, Gen. Mgr.; Michael Lorence, Sls. Mgr.; Sylvia Stephens, Admin. Mgr.; Toivo Salo, Op. Mgr. Northern Hardwoods does forest-products manufacturing; hardwood log, lumber, and dimension products manufacturing; and land management. 175 employees (15 part-time). SIC 2421, 2426, 2429. Owned by Rossi American Hardwoods, Cromwell, Conn.

Northern Sun 126 LaGrange, P.O. Box 74, Red Wing, MN 55066. Tel: 651/388-7111; Fax: 651/388-9488. David Turner, Plant Mgr.; Michelle Vandevoorde, Mdsg. Mgr. Northern Sun, a division of ADM, is a sunflower and flax processor. 70 employees. SIC 2076. Owned by Archer Daniels Midland Co. (NYSE: ADM), Decatur, Ill.

Northfield Freezing Systems 1719 Cannon Rd., P.O. Box 98, Northfield, MN 55057. Tel: 507/645-9546; Fax: 507/645-6148. Bill Capp, Pres. Northfield Freezing Systems designs, installs, and supports inline systems for cooling, chilling, and freezing food. Key products include LTS spiral freezers, coolers, proofers, and dehydrators for the food processing industry. The company operates production facilities inNorthfield, Minn.; Smithville, Ohio; Norwich, England; and Auckland, New Zealand. More than 1,800 Northfield systems—some the largest of their kind—have been installed around the world. 240 employees. SIC 3585. Founded in 1967. In February 2000 then-owner York International (NYSE: YRK) agreed to sell its Northfield Freezing Systems Group for $40 million in cash. Now owned by York International Corp. (NYSE: YRK), York, Pa.

Northland Insurance Companies 1295 Northland Dr., Mendota Heights, MN 55120. Tel: 651/688-4100; Fax: 651/688-4280. Gene G. Gopon, Chm.; Randall D. Jones, CEO; David L. Pickard, Pres./COO-Personal Div.; Gregory K. Erickson, SVP-Info. Sys.; Daniel J. Zaborsky, EVP and Chief Admin. Ofcr.; Allen J. Stendahl, SVP-Professional Svs. Northland Insurance is the largest operating subsidiary of Jupiter Holdings Inc., which specializes in niche property, casualty, and specialty insurance products through several A+ rated subsidiaries. Jupiter had net written premiums of $388 million in 1997. Its insurers are based in Minnesota, Illinois, and Arizona. In accordance with the personal and investment objectives of largest stockholder E.H. Hamm and family, The Northland Co., Bloomington, Minn., divested its insurance operations in 1998. 510 employees. SIC 6331. Founded in 1948. Acquired in December 1998 by Associates First Capital Corp. (NYSE: AFS), Dallas.

Northrop Grumman Dakota Manufacturing Plant P.O. Box 519, New Town, ND 58763. Tel: 701/627-4714; Fax: 701/627-3585. Terrance L. Wilber, Plant Mgr. Northrop Grumman Dakota is involved in electronic assembly and testing of: individual assemblies, circuit cards (printed), harnesses, subsystems, and systems. Northrop operates its own facility within the boundaries of the Fort Berthold Indian Reservation. 80 employees. SIC 3679. Founded in 1970. A unit of the El Segundo, Calif.-based Air Combat Systems business area of the Integrated Systems and Aerostructures Sector of Northrop Grumman Corp. (NYSE: NOC), Los Angeles.

Northstar Auto Auction Inc. 4908 Valley Industrial Blvd. N., Shakopee, MN 55379. Tel: 952/445-5544; Fax: 952/445-6773; Web site: http://www.aotauto.com. Jerry Aman, Gen. Mgr.; Greg Choat, Business Mgr.; Sue Samuelson, Sls. Mgr.; Brett Stanley, Op. Mgr.; Jeff Starn, Hum. Res. Mgr.; Rod Dubbe, Fleet/Lease Mgr.; Mike O'Brien, Reconditioning Mgr. Northstar Auto Auction is a wholesale dealer-vehicle auction company. 265 employees (in Minnesota; 122 part-time). SIC 5012. Founded in 1971. Owned by Tyco International Ltd. (NYSE: TYC), Exeter, N.H.

Northstar Computer Forms Inc. 7130 Northland Circle N., Brooklyn Park, MN 55428. Tel: 800/765-6787; Fax: 612/535-5671; Web site: http://www.nscf.com. Kenneth E. Overstreet, Pres.; Mary Ann Morin, CFO and Sec.; Don Dearborn, VP; Stanley Klarenbeek, VP. Annual revenue $46.3 million (earnings $2.7 million). Northstar Computer Forms Inc. designs, manufactures, and markets custom business forms and financial forms with an emphasis on MICR (magnetic ink character recognition) printing. Customers include financial institutions and processors of MICR-encoded documents. The three business segments sell their products nationally through distributors and through direct marketing to the nation's 200 largest banks. Products include official checks, money orders, teller cash tickets, control documents, and cut-sheet forms. 500 employees (250 in Minnesota). SIC 2761. Founded in 1964. In February 2000 the company agreed to be acquired for $42 million, or $14 a share (a 40 percent premium). The company was to operate as a stand-alone subsidiary, with no management or employment changes expected. [Deal completed in June.] April

30: A temporary softness in its bank forms business segment caused a 6.9 percent decrease in second-quarter sales. In October, Group President Overstreet was appointed to the parent company's board of directors. Now a subsidiary of Ennis Business Forms Inc. (NYSE: EBF), Ennis (Dallas), Texas.

Northwest Athletic Club 5525 Cedar Lake Rd., St. Louis Park, MN 55416. Tel: 952/546-5474; Fax: 952/546-7944; Web site: http://www.wellbridge.com. Ric Zimmerman, Regional Mgr. Annual revenue $60 million. Northwest Athletic Clubs, consists of 12 health clubs in the Twin Cities, featuring state-of-the-art fitness equipment and accommodations. All clubs offer a variety of group fitness classes, tennis racquetball, personal training, league play, acquatics, running trails, massage, and snack bars. The Blast! Kids fitness centers provide activities and fun for children under age 12. 1,700 employees (in Minnesota). SIC 7991, 7997. Founded in 1969. In November 1999, in what could become a model for future expansion, Northwest Athletic partnered with the city of Maple Grove, Minn., to open a 71,000-square-foot, $12 million club there by fall 2000. Owned since March 1997 by health care chain Wellbridge, Denver.

Northwood Panelboard Company Rural Route 1, P.O. Box 2650, Solway, MN 56678. Tel: 218/751-2023; Fax: 218/751-2075. Bruce Grebe, VP-OSB Op.; John Oschwald, Plant Mgr. Annual revenue $82.2 million. Northwood Panelboard produces oriented structural board. 144 employees. SIC 2493. Founded in 1980. Joint-venture partnership between Mead Panelboard Inc., Dayton, Ohio; and Norbord Industries Inc., Toronto. No. 78 CRM Foreign-Owned 100.

Novartis Nutrition Corporation P.O. Box 370, Minneapolis, MN 55440. Tel: 612/925-2100; Fax: 612/593-2087. Michael Valentino, Pres. and CEO; John A. Fontana, EVP; David M. Hurley, EVP. Novartis Nutrition manufactures nutritional products, food, and beverage items for health care, institutional, and retail markets. Formerly Sandoz Nutrition Corp. 700 employees. SIC 2099. Founded in 1932. Now owned by the company created by the December 1996 merger of Sandoz Ltd. and Ciba-Geigy Ltd., Novartis AG, Basel, Switzerland. No. 24 CRM Foreign-Owned 100.

Novartis Seeds Inc. 7500 Olson Memorial Hwy., P.O. Box 959, Golden Valley, MN 55427. Tel: 763/593-7333; Fax: 763/593-7154; Web site: http://www.nk.com. Edward Shonsey, Pres. and CEO; Jon Fobes, VP-Research; Jerry Hoeh, CFO; Albin Hubscher, VP-Sls.; Edward Resler, Corp. Counsel; Dan Lehmann, VP-Supply Mgmt.; Mike Scott, Dir.-Corp. Communications. Novartis Seeds Inc. consists of four U.S. seed companies. One of them, Syngenta Seeds Field Crops (the former Northrup King & Co.), is a leading worldwide researcher and North American producer and marketer of corn, soybean, alfalfa, sorghum, sunflower, and wheat seed—which it sells in the U.S., Canada, and Mexico. 800 employees. SIC 5191. Founded in 1884. In December 1999 Pioneer Hi-Bred International accused the company of infringing a new Pioneer patent for altering the DNA of corn plants to yield more ears of corn. Syngenta Seeds and Diversa Corp., San Diego, announced the formation of a joint venture to pursue opportunities in the fields of animal feeds and agricultural product processing. This operation was among the businesses spun off in December 1999 by Novartis AG to create Syngenta AG, Basel, Switzerland. No. 22 CRM Foreign-Owned 100.

Oak Valley Farms 705 20th Ave. S.W., Watertown, SD 57201. Tel: 605/886-8025; Fax: 605/882-2895. Arthur Milgrim, VP; Leo Rubin, Pres.; Bruce Utain, Treas. Annual revenue $38 million. Oak Valley Farms does processing and cooking of turkey products. 310 employees. SIC 2015. Founded in 1972. Owned by El Jay Poultry Corp., Voorhees, N.J.

Oasis Market 2020 Silver Bell Rd., Suite 23, Eagan, MN 55122. Tel: 651/452-9161; Fax: 651/452-9233. Scott Stevens, Pres.; Johnny Gill, VP-Op./Mktg. Oasis Market operates 78 Oasis Market convenience stores in the Twin Cities metropolitan area. 700 employees. SIC 5399, 5541. Founded in 1994. Owned by Roundtree Capital Corp., Santa Barbara, Calif.

Office Depot Inc. 1105 Xenium Ln. N., Plymouth, MN 55441. Tel: 763/797-9400. Bill Seering, Senior Op. Mgr.; Bill Seering, Regional Sls. Dir. Office Depot is an office supply company that also offers computers, express printing, design services, software, pagers and furniture. 360 employees. SIC 5112. Founded in 1995. In September 1999 the company opened a new store in City Center, in downtown Minneapolis. The 24,000-square-foot store, which occupies space formerly occupied by Montgomery Ward, became Office Depot's 10th store in Minnesota. Owned by Office Depot Inc. (NYSE: ODP), Delray Beach, Fla.

Old Republic Title Insurance Group 400 Second Ave. S., Minneapolis, MN 55401. Tel: 612/371-1111; Fax: 612/371-1191; Web site: http://www.oldrepublictitle.com. R.A. Cecchettini, Pres. and CEO; C.G. Gregory, EVP-Fin. Annual revenue $597.1 million. Old Republic National issues policies and abstracts of title, and offers title insurance, escrow, and closing services to real estate purchasers and investors. Formerly Title Insurance Co. of Minnesota. 2,934 employees (255 in Minnesota; 268 part-time). SIC 6361. Founded in 1907. Owned by Old Republic International Corp. (NYSE: ORI), Chicago.

Onan Corporation 1400 73rd Ave. N.E., Fridley, MN 55432. Tel: 763/574-5000; Fax: 763/574-5298. Ron L. Moore, VP and Gen. Mgr. Onan Corp., also known as Cummins Power Generation/Americas Division and as Cummins Onan, manufactures power generation systems, portable and stationary generator sets and related controls, gasoline engines, AC generators, and power supplies. 1,656 employees (1,631 in Minnesota). SIC 3519, 3621. Founded in 1920. In July 2000 the company kicked off the recreational vehicle (RV) model year with a new product lineup, including another industryfirst for RV electric power. The Onan Marquis Platinum—the first ultra-quiet, sequential-port, electronic fuel-injection (EFI) gasoline RV generator—offers improved combustion, lower emissions, and a new level of electronic microprocessor sophistication never before achieved in an air-cooled RV gasoline genset. The new Onan product lineup also included the Marquis Gold and Emerald Advantage, each fitted, like their Platinum counterpart, with advanced microprocessor hardware and circuitry for optimal ease in maintenance and serviceability. Owned by Cummins Engine Co. Inc. (NYSE: CUM), Columbus, Ind.

1 Potato 2 Inc. 7000 Bass Lake Rd., Suite 200, Crystal, MN 55428. Tel: 763/537-3833; Fax: 763/537-4241; Web site: http://www.1potato2.com. William G. Norton, Pres.; Laurie J. Mikkola, VP-Products/Mktg.; Teresa J. Dery, VP-Fin./Legal. 1 Potato 2 is a 29-store, quick-service franchisor that has capitalized on a 20-year trend toward healthy eating. Its stores serve baked potato entrees with a variety of toppings, fresh-cut fries, potato skins, country skillet combos, gourmet wraps, baked potato soup, salads, beverages, and desserts. 1 Potato 2 began operations in a storefront near the University of Minnesota campus. Its first mall store opened in Burnsville Center in April 1980. Today, all locations are in major regional shopping centers. In November 1999 the company was sold to a leading franchisor of quick-service restaurants. 55 employees. SIC 5812. Founded in 1977. Now owned by Wrapsters Inc. (OTC BB: WRAP), Phoenix.

REG

Otto Bock Health Care 3000 Xenium Ln. N., Plymouth, MN 55441. Tel: 763/553-9464; Fax: 763/519-6153. Bill Clover, EVP-Technical Devel.; Brad Ruhl, EVP-Sls.; Rick Suddendorf, VP-Nat'l Accounts; Sara Hakanson, Dir.-Mktg. Otto Bock Health Care is a leading international prosthetic and orthotic medical equipment manufacturer. 100 employees (in Minnesota). SIC 3842. U.S. headquarters of parent Otto Bock Orthopadische Industrie, Duderstadt, Germany. No. 88 CRM Foreign-Owned 100.

Owatonna Canning Company 900 N. Cedar Ave., P.O. Box 447, Owatonna, MN 55060. Tel: 507/455-7511. Stephens J. Lange, Chm.; Chadwick S. Lange, Pres.; Jerome F. Erck, VP. Owatonna Canning, the largest private-label vegetable canner in Minnesota, operates a canning facility for asparagus, peas, corn, pumpkin, green beans, and wax beans. Goodhue Canning Co., a 125 (seasonal)-employee division in Kenyon, Minn., produces canned cream-style corn. In October 1997 the Owatonna Canning group of companies was acquired for $50 million in stock. 125 employees. SIC 2033. Founded in 1921. Owned by Chiquita Brands International Inc. (NYSE: CQB), Cincinnati.

PCL Construction Services Inc. 12200 Nicollet Ave. S., Burnsville, MN 55337. Tel: 952/882-9600; Fax: 952/882-9900; Web site: http://www.pcl.com. Fred Auch, VP and District Mgr.; Colin Terras, Op. Mgr.; Terry Brickman, Mgr.-Special Projects; Bruce Lowell, Admin. Mgr.; Dan Ilten, Dir.-Design/Construction Svs.; Jim Mortenson, Construction Mgr.; Brad Hendrickson, Chief Estimator. Annual revenue $162.8 million. PCL Construction Services Inc. is one of Minnesota's largest and most diversified construction firms. PCL provides general construction, construction management, and design-build services for commercial, institutional, industrial, and health care projects. PCL also has a Special Projects Division that specializes in interiors, renovations, and remodeling. 2,500 employees (200 in Minnesota). SIC 1541, 1542, 8741. Founded in 1906. In June 1999 PCL started work on the $117 million American Express Client Service Center in downtown Minneapolis—a 1,240,952-square-foot building slated for completion in June 2002. In November 2000 the firm completed the 200-room second phase of the hotel for Mystic Lake Casino and Hotel, Prior Lake, Minn. PCL then continued its work there, building a 460-seat addition to the casino's buffet area. Owned by PCL Enterprises Inc., Denver.

PM Windom 2850 Highway 60 E., P.O. Box 279, Windom, MN 56101. Tel: 507/831-2761; Fax: 507/831-4669. James Bever, Plant Mgr.; Darlene Wood, Cont.; Tom Hodkin, Plant Engr. PM Windom, formerly Caldwell Packing Co., operates a meat-packing plant. 160 employees (in Minnesota). SIC 2011. Founded in 1946. Owned by Beef Specialists of Iowa Inc., Hartley, Iowa.

PSINet Consulting Solutions 2550 University Ave. W., Suite 180 S., St. Paul, MN 55114. Tel: 651/642-2100; Web site: http://www.psinetcs.com. John Scanlon, Ofcr. Annual revenue $44.5 million. PSINet, a computer consulting firm, is a full-service provider of a spectrum of applications and services that enables clients to expand their information technology (IT). 228 employees. SIC 7372. Owned by PSINet Consulting Solutions (Nasdaq: MMWW), Ashburn, Va.

Pac One 9000 Science Center Dr., New Hope, MN 55428. Tel: 763/533-3012; Fax: 763/533-2183. Allen Barnes, Pres. Pac One is a flexible-packaging company that specializes in candy and food packaging. 100 employees (in Minnesota). SIC 7389. Founded in 1989. Owned by Pac One, Atlanta.

Pace Dairy Foods Company 2700 Valley High Dr. N.W., Rochester, MN 55901. Tel: 507/288-6315; Fax: 507/288-6856. Jim Lehman, Gen. Mgr. Pace Dairy Foods engages in the cutting and packaging of natural cheese, as well as the production and packaging of processed cheese. 374 employees. SIC 2022. Founded in 1970. Owned by The Kroger Co. (NYSE: KR), Cincinnati.

Packaging Corp. of America 1821 N.E. Marshall St., Minneapolis, MN 55418. Tel: 612/789-3511; Fax: 612/782-2571. Brett Sweeney, Gen. Mgr.; Brian Pascavis, Prod. Mgr. Packaging Corp. of America (PCA) manufactures corrugated shipping containers and displays at its Minneapolis location. It also operates plants in Golden Valley and Fridley, Minn. Former names: Tenneco Packaging; Northwestern Corrugated Box Co. 103 employees. SIC 2653. Founded in 1929. Newest owner went public in October 1999 as Packaging Corp. of America (NYSE: PKG), Lake Forest, Ill.

Packaging Corp. of America 4300 Olson Memorial Hwy., Golden Valley, MN 55422. Tel: 763/521-3611; Fax: 763/520-9032. Cully Exsted, Gen. Mgr.; Ken Gierl, Prod. Mgr.; Pete Gareri, Sls. Mgr. Packaging Corp. of America (PCA) produces corrugated containers at its Golden Valley location. Formerly owned by Tenneco Inc. (NYSE: TEN). 85 employees. SIC 2653. Founded in 1959. Its newest owner went public in January 2000 as Packaging Corp. of America (NYSE: PKG), Lake Forest, Ill.

PACTIV Corporation 1500 W. River St., Chippewa Falls, WI 54729. Tel: 715/723-9145; Fax: 715/723-0733. George Allen, Plant Mgr. PACTIV Corp. manufactures miscellaneous plastic products, including food service products and building materials. Formerly Amoco Foam Products Co. 327 employees. SIC 3089. Founded in 1967. Division of Tenneco Inc. (NYSE: TEN), Greenwich, Conn.

Parker-Hannifin Corporation 8145 Lewis Rd., Golden Valley, MN 55427. Tel: 763/544-7781; Fax: 763/544-3418. Robert W. Bond, Gen. Mgr. Parker-Hannifin Corporation Quick Coupling Division manufactures quick-action couplings for fluid system conductors. Minneapolis plant is division headquarters, with additional plants located in Wisconsin and Nebraska. 130 employees (114 in Minnesota). SIC 3492. Founded in 1969. Owned by Parker Hannifin Corp. (NYSE: PH), Cleveland.

Partek Forest Inc. 103 N. 12th St., P.O. Box 401, Gladstone, MI 49837. Tel: 906/428-4800; Fax: 906/428-3922. Kimmo Lannenpaa, Pres.; Bert Jonsson, Mgr.-Product Support; Robert J. Wood, Sec. and Treas.; Tim Lee, Sls./Mktg. Mgr. Partek Forest manufactures forestry and underground mining equipment. Former names: Gafner Machine Inc., Valmet Gafner Inc., Sisu Logging USA Inc. 105 employees. SIC 3531, 3532, 3559. Founded in 1946. Now owned by Partek Corp., Helsinki, Finland.

Pearl Baths Inc. 9224 73rd Ave. N., Brooklyn Park, MN 55428. Tel: 763/424-3335; Fax: 763/424-9808. Rob Larson, Gen. Mgr.; Brian McConnell, Plant Mgr.; Ron Crowell, National Sls. Mgr. Pearl Baths manufactures whirlpool bathtubs. 95 employees. SIC 3089. Founded in 1978. Acquired in 1994 by Maax Corp., St. Marie, Quebec. No. 92 CRM Foreign-Owned 100.

Pecos River-Aon Consulting 7600 Executive Dr., Eden Prairie, MN 55344. Tel: 952/975-2100; Fax: 952/975-2199. Larry Wilson, Founder and VChm.; Steve Geiger, Pres.; Dick Krahl, EVP and CFO; A.G. (Buzz) Bainbridge, SVP-Sls.; Audie Dunham, SVP-Mktg.; Carol Clark, VP-Delivery. Pecos River Division of Aon Consulting, formerly Pecos River Learning Centers, help companies institute profound, lasting changes in attitude and performance for individuals, teams, and organizations by boosting teamwork, creativity, and quality. It has 16 partner learning sites in 12 states (including one in Chaska, Minnesota) and two Canadian provinces. 90 employees. SIC 8742. Founded in 1985. Acquired in 1996 by Aon Corp., Chicago.

Pennant Foods 4075 Norex Drive, Chaska, MN 55318. Tel: 952/368-3131 Rex Bell, Plant Mgr. Pennant Foods produces frozen bread dough, English muffins, frozen dinner rolls, cookies, and partially baked products. 107 employees. SIC 2045. Founded in 1968. Pennant, formerly Van den Bergh Foods Co., is based in Lisle, Ill., and has been owned since December 1997 by Leon's Bakery Inc., North Haven, Conn.

Pentax Vision Inc. 11545 Encore Circle, P.O. Box 2300, Hopkins, MN 55343. Tel: 952/945-2700; Fax: 952/935-0350. Mike Jacobson, Pres.; Mark Nesbitt, VP. Pentax Vision Inc. is the largest supplier of stock anti-reflective coated eyeglass lenses in North America. It also serves the optical community with custom anti-reflective coated lenses. 100 employees. SIC 3851, 5043. Founded in 1985. Owned by Asahi Optical Co. Ltd., Tokyo. No. 88 CRM Foreign-Owned 100.

Pepsi-Cola Bottling Company of Minneapolis-St. Paul Inc. 1300 E. Cliff Rd., Burnsville, MN 55337. Tel: 952/890-8940; Fax: 952/895-1403. Phil Faxlanger, Plant Mgr. Pepsi-Cola Bottling Company of Minneapolis-St. Paul bottles, cans, and distributes Pepsi, 7-Up, Dr. Pepper, and Squirt products in the seven-county metro area. 520 employees. SIC 2086. Founded in 1986. In January 2000 four former employees filed a lawsuit accusing the company of race discrimination and a hostile work environment. In June more than 400 production workers, delivery workers, salespeople, loaders, and vending machine technicians represented by Teamsters Local 792 rejected a company offer and went on strike. Disputed issues included pensions, health insurance, wages, and the loss of bargaining-unit work. The plant continued to operate, using nonunion and replacement workers. On Aug. 24, a tentative agreement was reached. Union officials lauded the deal for its significant improvements in pension benefits, some improvement in wages, and concessions on some work rules issues. On Aug. 28, the deal was approved by Pepsi workers by a 257-114 margin. Owned by Pepsi Bottling Group, Somers, N.Y., a subsidiary of Pepsico Inc. (NYSE: PEPCO), Purchase, N.Y.

Phillips & Temro Industries Inc. 9700 W. 74th St., Eden Prairie, MN 55344. Tel: 952/941-9700; Fax: 952/941-2285. Bill Rose, Pres. Phillips & Temro Industries manufactures cold-weather starting products, including engine heaters, cords, diesel fuel heaters, and starting fluid systems for cars, trucks, and industrial applications. 185 employees. SIC 3694. Founded in 1945. Owned by Thyssen Krupp, Dusseldorf, Germany. No. 67 CRM Foreign-Owned 100.

Pillsbury Pillsbury Center, 200 S. Sixth St., Minneapolis, MN 55402. Tel: 612/330-4966; Fax: 612/330-5200; Web site: http://www.pillsbury.com. John N. Lilly, CEO; Robert E. Briggs, SVP and CFO; Lou de Olejo, SVP-Hum. Res./Corp. Affairs; Chris Killingstad, SVP, Gen. Mgr.-Frozen/Pillsbury Canada; Peter Robinson, SVP, Gen. Mgr.-Refrigerated/Shelf Stable; John R. Speirs, SVP-Strategic Brand Devel.; S. Paul Oliver, Pres.-Pillsbury Bakeries; Lucio Rizzi, Pres.-Pillsbury International; William Birtcil, VP-Corp. Affairs. Annual revenue $6.08 billion (loss $141 million). Pillsbury is a North American-based subsidiary of Diageo plc. It produces a range of grocery items, frozen foods, and refrigerated dough products for international consumer markets. The company is also a major supplier of baking and other food products to the food service and commercial baking industries. Pillsbury's portfolio of leading brands includes Pillsbury, Green Giant, Old El Paso, Progresso, Hungry Jack, Totino's, and Haagen-Dazs. 16,750 employees (2,180 in Minnesota). SIC 2041, 2099. Founded in 1869. Dec. 31, 1999: Pillsbury's operating margin slid from 13.8 percent to 13.2 percent in the first half of fiscal 2000, a difficult period for food companies. Despite a 15 percent increase in advertising, Pillsbury's sales increased only 5 percent, and that primarily in low-margin products. In January 2000 Progresso expanded its line of soups with the addition of four new flavors: vegetarian vegetable with barley, creamy cheddar chicken, southwestern-style corn chowder, and roasted potato garlic. In February the Pillsbury Bakeries & Foodservice unit (PB&FS) agreed to acquire Kerry's DCA Bakery business in the United States and Canada for $100 million. The $102 million-revenue, 330-employee DCA Bakery manufactures and sells a variety of bakery mixes, fillings, icings, and glazes to the bakery business. In an effort to cut costs, the company was not going to consider pay raises for its 6,000 salaried employees this year. In March Pillsbury joined Land O'Lakes and General Mills Inc. (NYSE: GIS), who had formed an innovative supply chain alliance to engage in joint purchasing and refrigerated distribution activities. The alliance was expected to generate purchasing synergies and improved customer service for both companies and was to utilize new Web-based technologies from Nistevo.com. At month's end, in the face of falling margins and stiff competition in the food industry, Pillsbury announced changes designed to improve volume and profit performance by bringing innovation to the marketplace more quickly. The changes, which included a strategic focus on the company's dough-based business and the announcement of an innovative new sales operation, were accompanied by the elimination of 750 positions (278 locally). Pillsbury also announced an alliance with Dallas-based CrossMark Inc., one of only four national food brokers, to represent all Pillsbury brands at most regional customers, as well as provide complete retail store coverage for all customers. In May Pillsbury announced plans to cease production at its McMinnville, Ore., plant, idling 95 workers. June 30: Pillsbury's sales dropped slightly, from $6.14 billion in 1999 to $6.08 billion in 2000, but the company narrowed its fiscal 2000 loss to $141 million from $230 million. In spite of consistently strong earnings before interest and taxes, Pillsbury had experienced a five-year string of net losses due to significant intercompany debt as a subsidiary of Diageo. During the summer, there was intense speculation that Pillsbury would succoumb to ongoing consolidation in the food manufacturing industry. On July 17, General Mills (NYSE: GIS), Golden Valley, Minn., agreed to acquire Pillsbury in a half-stock, half-debt deal valued at $10.5 billion, based on General Mills' stock price of $38 before a deal became widely anticipated. The deal, expected to become final by the end of the year, was likely to result in job losses at both companies. In October, consistent with a previously announced intention to sell certain assets in conjunction with the proposed acquisition of Pillsbury by General Mills, Pillsbury announced an offering to sell its Pillsbury- and Martha White-branded U.S. retail Dessert and Baking Mix business, and its Hungry Jack Potato and Hungry Jack shelf-stable breakfast businesses, which contributed more than $500 million in sales in the past fiscal year. Founded in 1869, Pillsbury was acquired in December 1988 by Grand Metropolitan plc, which is now known as Diageo plc, London. No. 67 CRM Employer 100.

Pinkerton's Security Service 3400 W. 66th St., Edina, MN 55435. Tel: 952/285-1900; Fax: 952/285-1744. C.J. Fox, District Mgr. Pinkerton's offers security services. 450 employees. SIC 7381. Founded in 1850. Owned by Pinkerton's Inc. (NYSE: PKT), Encino, Calif.

Pitney Bowes Inc. 10025 Valley View Rd., Suite 160, Eden Prairie, MN 55344. Tel: 800/322-8000; Fax: 952/944-8739; Web site: http://www.pitneybowes.com. Paul Murphy, District Dir. Pitney Bowes performs mailing, shipping, inserting, addressing, labeling, and folding services. 50 employees (in Minnesota). SIC 7334. Owned by Pitney Bowes Inc. (NYSE: PBI), Stamford, Conn.

Plainwell Tissue 1200 Forest St., Eau Claire, WI 54703. Tel: 715/834-3461; Fax: 715/833-3140. Donald Winrich, Pres.; Denis Faltynski, Plant Mgr. Annual revenue $129.2 million. Plainwell Tissue's Consumer Products Division manufactures and converts bathroom tissue, facial tissue, napkins, and paper towels for the private-label market. Formerly owned by Pope & Talbot Inc., Portland, Ore. 345 employees. SIC 2676. Founded in 1882. Dec. 31, 1999: For the year the Consumer Products Division reported net sales of $129.2 million, a decrease of 6.5 percent compared with 1998, on a proforma basis. The division's EBITDA before corporate overhead was $14.0 million, down from $21.1 million in 1998. Although tons sold declined from 1998, the largest factors contributing to the decline in EBITDA were increased raw material costs and a reduction in net realized selling prices (net sales divided by tons sold). "Last year was challenging for Plainwell, especially in the consumer products market," said William L. New, parent chairman and CEO. "Although we successfully improved our manufacturing processes and lowered production costs, significant increases in fiber costs during the second half of the year and the continuing price pressures driven by excess market capacity resulted in a less than satisfactory performance in 1999." Division of Plainwell Inc., Plainwell, Mich.

Platinum Technology 7760 France Ave. S., Suite 810, Bloomington, MN 55435. Duane Cologne, VP. Platinum Technology provides enterprise-scale data-warehousing and decision-support software products (Beacon, Synergy) for large and medium-sized organizations. 60 employees (40 in Minnesota). SIC 7372. Founded in 1987. Acquired in February 1996 by Platinum Technology Inc., Oakbrook Terrace, Ill.

Post-Bulletin Company LLC 18 First Ave. S.E., Rochester, MN 55904. Tel: 507/285-7600; Fax: 507/285-7666; Web site: http://www.postbulletin.com. William C. Boyne, Publisher; Jon Losness, Editor and Gen. Mgr. Post-Bulletin Co. is a printer and a distributor of daily newspapers. 255 employees (in Minnesota; 21 part-time). SIC 2711. Founded in 1925. Subsidiary of Small Newspaper Group, Kankakee, Ill.

Potlatch Corporation 207 Avenue C, Box 510, Cloquet, MN 55720. Tel: 218/879-0404; Fax: 218/879-0417; Web site: http://www.potlatch-corp.com. Philip Baker, VP-MN Pulp/Paper Div.; Anna M. Haney, VP-Mfg., Brainerd; John Hanson, VP-Sls./Mktg.; Barbara A. Rehar, VP-Mfg., Cloquet; Ronald Salisbury, Gen. Mgr.-Wood Products Div., MN. Annual revenue $1.6 billion. Potlatch's mills in Cloquet and Brainerd produce free-sheet coated printing papers for art prints, books, high-quality advertising, and corporate publications such as annual reports, product catalogs, and capability brochures. Potlatch also operates oriented strand board plants in Bemidji (218/751-1708); Cook (218/666-5246); and Grand Rapids (218/327-3650). The three facilities have a combined annual capacity of 1.1 billion square feet. Potlatch also operates a lumbermill in Bemidji (218/751-6144). 6,400 employees (2,500 in Minnesota). SIC 2493, 2621. Founded in 1898. In March 2000 the parent company announced that its first-quarter 2000 earnings would be well below the consensus of analysts' estimates. The company attributed the anticipated shortfall primarily to the performance of its Minnesota Pulp and Paper Division, where the new pulp mill at Cloquet had encountered some startup difficulties during the quarter that resulted in lower-than-expected production and higher costs. The company noted that the problems had been resolved. In addition, the division was experiencing lower-than-expected realizations due to an unfavorable sales mix. Potlatch CEO L. Pendleton Siegel expressed his disappointment, but added, "These setbacks, which are now fully resolved, should have no impact on the pulp mill's long-term contribution to earnings and shareholder value." In May Potlatch and Minnesota Power Inc. (NYSE: MPL) agreed to install a 24-megawatt turbine generator at the Potlatch facility in Cloquet. Minnesota Power's nonregulated electric business was to own the turbine generator, with Potlatch operating and maintaining the unit. Through a process called cogeneration, steam used for industrial processes was to be used to produce electricity, achieving energy efficiency greater than 80 percent—more than twice the efficiency of traditional power sources. An environmentally friendly mix of wood wastes and natural gas was to fuel the process. In November the parent company announced curtailments at its coated printing paper mill in Brainerd, Minn., and its oriented strand board plant in Cook, Minn. The Brainerd paper mill was to curtail production during the weeks of Nov. 20 and Dec. 18, 2000, to control inventories and respond to seasonally weak markets and increased import pressures. The company's Cloquet pulp and paper mill was to continue to operate. The company also planned to curtail production at its Cook oriented strand board (OSB) plant from Dec. 11, 2000, to Jan. 10, 2001, to complete the final stages of a major modernization and expansion that was to increase OSB production from 250 million to 435 million square feet annually (on 3/8" basis). Division of Potlatch Corp. (NYSE: PCH), Spokane, Wash. No. 79 CRM Employer 100.

Pratt & Whitney Cenco Inc. 2930 Anthony Ln., Minneapolis, MN 55418. Tel: 612/781-6557; Fax: 612/781-3525; Web site: http://www.pwcenco.com. Erik Schindler, Pres.; Jane Haatvedt, Dir.-Hum. Res.; Don Drewry, Dir.-Sls./Mktg.; Ron Severson, Cont. Annual revenue $26 million. Pratt & Whitney Cenco manufactures ground support equipment for aircraft. 126 employees. SIC 3728. Founded in 1958. Division of Pratt & Whitney, Hartford, Conn.

Precision Optics Inc. 6925 Saukview Dr., P.O. Box 1288, St. Cloud, MN 56302. Tel: 320/251-8591; Fax: 800/535-1165. Roy Hinkemeyer, VP and Gen. Mgr. Precision Optics produces prescription eyewear in plastic, polycarbonate, and glass materials. The company is a wholesale ophthalmic laboratory serving opticians, optometrists, and ophthalmologists. 128 employees (in Minnesota). SIC 3851. Founded in 1960. Owned by Omega Optical, Dallas, a division of Essilor International, Paris. No. 85 CRM Foreign-Owned 100.

Precision Twist Drill Company 1176 Coon St., Rhinelander, WI 54501. Tel: 715/369-3700; Fax: 715/369-4763. Terry Goldbach, Hum. Res. Mgr.; Don Wiese, Purch. Agt.; William Collier Jr., VP-Op.; Charles Lundborg, Engrg. Precision manufactures twist drills and cutting tools. 446 employees. SIC 3541, 3545. Founded in 1972. Owned through Sandvik Inc., Fair Lawn, N.J., by Sandvik AB, Sandviken, Sweden.

PremiumWear Inc. 5500 Feltl Rd., Minnetonka, MN 55343. Tel: 952/979-1700; Fax: 952/979-1717; Web site: http://www.premiumwear.com. David E. Berg, Pres. and CEO; James S. Bury, VP-Fin. and Asst. Sec.; Cynthia L. Boeddeker, VP-Op.; Timothy C. Klouda, Pres.-Klouda-Lenz Promotional Products; Dennis G. Lenz, EVP-Klouda-Lenz Promotional Products; James Murphy, Gen. Mgr.-Golf Division. Annual revenue $47 million (earnings $1.4 million). PremiumWear Inc. is an apparel wholesaler of the Munsingwear brand (formerly Munsingwear Inc.) to the Advertising Specialty Industry (ASI), and Promotional Products Advertising Industry (PPAI) markets under an exclusive license. In addition, the company markets its Page & Tuttle apparel to golf pro shops and resorts and to ASI/PPAI marketplaces. 200 employees (65 in Minnesota). SIC 2321, 2325, 5136. Founded in 1923. In December 1999 the company's stock listing moved from the NYSE to the Nasdaq National Market. In January 2000 PremiumWear began directly contracting with its independent sales agents representing the company's Page & Tuttle line of apparel to resort and golf pro shops. (Since Page & Tuttle's startup two years previous, PremiumWear had contracted with Wingert & Associates to represent the line through that firm's sales agents located across the U.S.) In February PremiumWear was named the exclusive representative for CROAKIES eyewear retainer products—and for SOFTSPIKES Inc. products (customizable MagneSport magnetic golf bracelets, DriStix golf bag raincovers)—to the advertising specialty industry. In April the company extended its licensing agreement with Perry Ellis International Inc., for use of the Munsingwear brand for woven shirts, through 2006 with a renewal option through 2010. In May PremiumWear purchased the Pickering and Lady Pickering brands, well-recognized names in golf apparel for nearly 30 years, from Philadelphia-based Kimberton Co.—with plans to market men's and women's golf apparel under the Pickering brands to golf and resort shops. The company signed license agreements with Field & Stream Licenses Co., Plymouth, Minn., to design and market—under the Field & Stream license—a line of men's, women's, and children's sportswear as well as pants and shorts, headwear, rainwear, and sport and tote bags for the corporate, promotional products market. On May 30, PremiumWear and New England Business Service Inc. (NYSE: NEB) announced a definitive agreement under which NEBS will acquire all outstanding shares of PremiumWear stock for $13.50 per share, payable in cash. The price, a 36.7 percent premium to PremiumWear's prevailing stock price, plus the assumption of $2.2 million in existing PremiumWear debt, placed the deal's value at $40 million. New England Business Service (NEBS) supplies a wide variety of business products and services to 2.5 million small businesses in the United States, Canada, France, and the United Kingdom. In accordance with the terms of the agreement, a subsidiary of NEBS was to commence a tender offer for all of the outstanding shares of PremiumWear no later than June 9, 2000. At least a majority of the outstanding PremiumWear shares had to be validly tendered and not withdrawn. The transaction was expected to be consummated in early July. PremiumWear was to remain in Minnetonka and operate as a wholly owned subsidiary; no job losses were expected. For PremiumWear, NEBS offers access to financial and technological resources that should provide additional growth opportunities, improve efficiencies, and enhance customer service. In June PremiumWear licensed from Jockey International Inc. exclusive rights to market men's and women's knit and woven shirts, sweaters, pants, shorts, outerwear, windshirts, and headwear bearing the Jockey brand to the corporate/advertising specialty market in the United States and Canada—with shipping to start in the first quarter of 2001 and last for seven years, including renewal periods. On June 27, the Federal Trade Commission granted early termination of all waiting periods under the Hart-Scott-Rodino Antitrust Improvements Act applicable to New England Business Service's proposal to acquire the outstanding public shares of PremiumWear. The merger was completed in July and PremiumWear Inc. stock was de-listed from Nasdaq at that time. Owned by New England Business Service Inc. (NYSE: NEB), Groton, Mass. No. 114 CRM Public 200.

PricewaterhouseCoopers LLP 650 Third Ave. S., Suite 1300, Minneapolis, MN 55402. Tel: 612/596-6000; ; Web site: http://www.pwcglobal.com. Mark Chronister, Mpls. Managing Ptnr.; Lee Gremillion, Ptnr.; Keith A. Peterson, Managing Dir. PricewaterhouseCoopers (PwC), the world's largest professional services organization, helps its clients build value, manage risk, and improve their performance. The company provides a full range of business advisory services to leading global, national, and local companies and to public institutions. Services include audit, accounting, and tax advice; management, information technology, and human resource consulting; financial advisory services such as mergers and acquisitions, business recovery, project finance, and litigation support; and business process outsourcing services. The Edina office (4620 W. 77th St., Edina 55435; 952/835-4884), formerly Cytrol Inc., provides management consulting services to the financial services industry in the areas of information technology and strategic and organizational change. The firm offers full life-cycle information systems development services including strategic planning, requirements analysis, package search and evaluation, systems integration, process and data design, and project management. On July 1, 1998, PwC was created by the merger of two firms—PriceWaterhouse and Coopers & Lybrand—each with historical roots going back some 150 years. 540 employees (in Minnesota). SIC 7372, 7373, 7379, 8721, 8742. Founded in 1962. In October 2000 Lisa Naatz, a former senior manager in PwC's Minneapolis office, won a $1.625 million sex-discrimination suit against the firm after being passed over for promotion. Offices of PricewaterhouseCoopers LLP, New York.

PrimeNet Marketing Services Inc. 2250 Pilot Knob Rd., P.O. Box 21800, Mendota Heights, MN 55120. Tel: 651/405-4000; Fax: 651/405-4100. Mark J. Keefe, Pres.; Sam Anderson, VP-Fin./Admin.; Chuck Alsdurf, VP-Sls./Bus. Devel.; Frank Powell, VP-Info. Svs. PrimeNet Marketing Services, formerly PrimeNet DataSystems, is a provider of database marketing services for medium-sized and large consumer and business-to-business marketers. These services include database design and management, computer processing and programming for list maintenance and enhancement, mail processing, list brokerage, inbound inquiry/order management, and product/literature fullfillment. 100 employees. SIC 7331, 7374. Founded in 1962. In May 2000 Sun Country Airlines, Mendota Heights, Minn., signed an agreement with PrimeNet for printing, mailing, and analytical services. In August the company assumed ownership of operations for Journal Sentinel Direct's Milwaukee lettershop and production facility. Acquired in January 1994 by Journal Communications Inc., Milwaukee.

Primera Foods Corporation 612 S. Eighth St., Cameron, WI 54822. Tel: 715/458-4075; Fax: 715/458-4078. Michael Shevi, Chm.; Jon E. Luikart, Pres. and CEO. Annual revenue $42 million. Primera Foods is a leading producer and wholesale distributor of dried food ingredients including dried egg products and dried vegetables. The company markets its products to consumer food companies for use as an ingredient in the preparation of both ready-to-eat foods such as baked goods, salad dressings, and ready-to-prepare foods such as cake mixes and pastas. The company is a diversified processor, packager, and distributor of food products and ingredients for consumer food companies. 147 employees (68 in Minnesota). SIC 2034, 2099. Founded in 1989. In January 2000 the U.S. Environmental Protection Agency(EPA) Region 5 reached a settlement with Primera that resolved an administrative action filed by the EPA against Primera for an alleged 1998 violation of the federal law requiring the immediate reporting of any release of hazardous chemicals (namely 1,680 pounds of anhydrous ammonia). Primera agreed to pay a $14,000 fine and to complete environmental projects that were to cost $101,126. In February Primera acquired a 105,000-square-foot food manufacturing facility that had been idle since its closure by Jerome Foods (The Turkey Store) in 1996. Primera was expected to invest $10 million in the Altura facility and equipment to prepare the plant for production activity. In June Primera Foods was recognized as theSupplier of the Year by the Agriculture and Marketing Service group (AMS) of the United States Department of Agriculture. At the award presentation, Primera Foods was lauded for developing special relationships with small, minority-owned businesses to create growth opportunities for these organizations; and for 100 percent on-time, error-free deliveries.In January 28 2000, Primera Foods acquired Innovative Food Processors Inc. and Zumbro Inc. Both companies are specialty food ingredient processors located in southern Minnesota. Owned by Cham Foods (Israel Ltd.).

PrimeSource Corporation 2420 Long Lake Rd. N., Roseville, MN 55113. Tel: 651/452-9320; Fax: 651/634-9325. E.W. (Ted) Padley, VP; Rick Guy, Dir.-Op.; James Menne, Dir.-Bus. Devel.; Kevin Loecken, Sls. Mgr.; Jeff Nylund, Gen. Mgr.-Roseville branch. PrimeSource Corp., formerly known as PrimeSource/T.K. Gray, is a distributor and value-added reseller of desktop publishing and graphic arts equipment and supplies to the five-state printing industry. In November 1996, PrimeSource bought four branches of VGC Corp. in Minnesota, Iowa, Nebraska, and Wisconsin, to form PrimeSource Corp. With the acquistion of Bell Olson Graphics business from Bell Industries in Sept 1998, the number of branches is now 32. 113 employees (in Minnesota). SIC 5045. Subsidiary of PrimeSource Corp. (Nasdaq: PSRC), Pennsauken, N.J.

Proex Photo Systems 7101 Ohms Ln., Edina, MN 55439. Tel: 952/893-1915; Fax: 952/893-9444. Bruce Thompson, Pres.; Jann Olsten, VP. Proex Photo Systems provides film developing and portraiture services in the Twin Cities, St. Cloud, and Rochester, Minn. 500 employees. SIC 7384. Founded in 1981. Owned by Wolf Camera Inc., Atlanta.

Prometric 2601 W. 88th St., Bloomington, MN 55431. Tel: 952/896-7000; Fax: 952/820-5064. Kam Talebi, Cont. Prometric is a pioneer and the global leader in delivering and administering computer-based certification and assessment testing programs. Its network of 740 testing centers in 70 countries on six continents is the largest of its type in the world. Prometric annually delivers thousands of exams on behalf of industry-leading companies, professional associations, and government agencies. Its elaborate testing procedures protect against theft by encrypting the software so that it cannot be read before the test is given. Clients include Microsoft Corp., Lotus Development Corp., Novell Inc., the Federal Aviation Administration, and the U.S. Environmental Protection Agency. The former Drake Prometric was acquired by Sylvan Learning Systems (Nasdaq: SYLN) in 1995. 300 employees (in Minnesota). SIC 8748. Founded in 1990. In March 2000 Sylvan Learning Systems sold Prometric for $775 million. Now owned by The Thomson Corp. (LON: TOC), Stamford, Conn.

Prospect Foundry Inc. 1225 Winter St. N.E., Minneapolis, MN 55413. Tel: 612/331-9282; Fax: 612/331-4122; Web site: http://www.prospectfoundry.com. Joseph A. Dougherty, Pres. Prospect Foundry produces gray iron, ductile iron castings, and austempered ductile iron. 230 employees (in Minnesota). SIC 3321. Founded in 1936. Owned by Atchison Casting Corp. (NYSE: FDY), Atchison, Kan.

Protein Design Labs 3955 Annapolis Ln. N., Plymouth, MN 55447. Tel: 763/551-1778; Fax: 763/551-1780. Peter Grassam, VP-Mfg. and Gen. Mgr. Protein Design Labs (PDL) develops human and humanized antibodies to prevent or treat a variety of viral and immune-mediated diseases and certain cancers and cardiovascular conditions. Four potential drug compounds are in human clinical trials. 247 employees (84 in Minnesota). SIC 8731. Founded in 1991. Owned by Protein Design Labs, Fremont, Calif.

Prudential Insurance Company of America 13001 County Rd. 10, P.O. Box 1143 (55440), Plymouth, MN 55442. Tel: 763/553-6000; Fax: 763/557-4084. Kirsten Cecil, VP and Insurance Op. Ofcr.; John B. Miller, VP-Mpls. Customer Svc. The Prudential, the largest insurance company in North America, provides a wide variety of insurance and financial products. It maintains a second major Minnesota site at 3033 Campus Dr., Plymouth. 3,400 employees (in Minnesota). SIC 6141, 6211, 6311, 6321, 6331. Founded in 1952. Owned by The Prudential Insurance Co. of America, Newark, N.J. No. 53 CRM Employer 100.

Publishing Business Systems 2611 Hamline Ave. N., Roseville, MN 55113. Tel: 651/639-0662. Steve Smith, Ofcr. Publishing Business Systems is the developer of the MediaPlus line of software products for the publishing industry. The company has developed utilities for advertising management, circulation management, insert management, list match, insight, and preprint inventory. 92 employees. SIC 7372. Founded in 1972. Owned by Publishing Business Systems, Barrington, Ill.

Pulte Homes of Minnesota 1355 Mendota Heights Rd., Suite 300, Mendota Heights, MN 55120. Tel: 651/452-5200; Fax: 651/452-5727; Web site: http://www.pulte.com. Thomas J. Standke, Pres. Annual revenue $87 million. Pulte Homes of Minnesota builds and sells single-family, detached and attached housing. 65 employees (in Minnesota). SIC 1521, 1522. Founded in 1956. Owned by PHM Corp., Bloomfield Hills, Mich.

PUR Water Filtration Products 9300 N. 75th Ave., Brooklyn Park, MN 55428. Tel: 763/315-5500; Fax: 763/315-5505; Web site: http://www.purwater.com. Charles F. Karpinske, VP and CFO; Richard D. Hembree, VP-Engrg.; Dan Seebart, VP-Mfg.; Jeffrey Dekko, VP-Mktg.; Barry B. Van Lerberghe, VP-Sls. PUR Water Filtration Products, formerly Recovery Engineering Inc., designs, develops, manufactures, and markets small-scale drinking water treatment systems. The company's product line includes a line of self-monitoring water filters for household use; a rugged line of portable drinking water systems for outdoor enthusiasts and international travelers; and an energy-efficient line of desalinators for sailors and military personnel. In September 1999 Recovery Engineering agreed to be sold to Procter & Gamble through a cash tender offer, at a price of $35.25 per share—a total enterprise value of $265 million. 380 employees (375 in Minnesota). SIC 3589. Founded in 1986. In January 2000 the company said that PUR Ultimate faucet-mountwater filters significantly reduce levels of the contaminant methyl tertiary butyl ether (MTBE) from drinking water, according to recent testing by an independent laboratory. The tests found that the PUR Ultimate filters removed 95 percent of MTBE, a widely used fuel additive that has been detected in ground water in 49 states. In June the company advised consumers of a potential problem with the carbon packs for its Stop Top carbon cartridge—an accessory that is sold with the Voyageur, Scout, and Explorer models, all designed for outdoor water purification. Company-sponsored testing had revealed variations in the grade of carbon used in the Stop Top—variations that could interfere with the purifier's ability to fully eliminate viruses in outdoor (untreated) water. New carbon packs were to be available within a few weeks. Water-filter maker KX Industries, Orange, Conn., accused the company of infringing a patent for a process used to produce composite materials that can be used as filters. When residents served by the Seelyville, Ind., water system experienced problems with their drinking water—including sediment, taste, and smell—PUR Water Purification Products donated 1,200 water filtration units to residents. Now owned by The Procter & Gamble Co. (NYSE: PG), Cincinnati.

Purina Mills Inc. 3901 Hiawatha Ave. S., Minneapolis, MN 55406. Tel: 612/721-0738; Fax: 612/721-0717. Lee Engelbart, Gen. Mgr. Purina Mills manufactures animal feeds and animal health products. 90 employees. SIC 2048. Founded in 1894. Owned by Purina Mills Inc., St. Louis.

QLogic 6321 Bury Dr., Suite 13, Eden Prairie, MN 55346. Tel: 952/932-4000; Fax: 952/932-4037; Web site: http://www.ancor.com. Kenneth E. Hendrickson, Chm. and CEO; Calvin G. Nelson, Pres.; Steven E. Snyder, VP, CFO, and Sec.; Max Davis, VP-Op.; Rob Davis, VP-Advanced Product Planning; Carla Kennedy, VP-Mktg.; Paul N. Pasqua, VP-Worldwide Sls.; Thomas Raeuchle, VP-Engrg. Annual revenue $13 million (loss $8.7 million). QLogic, formerly Ancor Communications Inc., develops Fibre Channel switch and switch management products for storage area networks (SANs), flexible "any to any" infrastructures that link multiple servers to multiple storage devices. 116 employees. SIC 3577. Founded in 1986. In December 1999 the company, them knoen as Ancor Communications, announced an agreement with Intel Corp. (Nasdaq: INTC), Santa Clara, Calif., to develop and market switches based on the new InfiniBand* architecture. In a related transaction, Intel made a $14.8 million investment in the company to purchase 280,000 newly issued, unregistered shares of Ancor common stock (a 1 percent stake). Ancor shares rose 37 percent on the news to an all-time high of $85.88. The deal was not meant to replace Ancor's storage area network (SAN) strategy, but rather to provide another potential source of revenue down the road. According to the Wall Street Journal, Ancor stock, which ended the year at $67.88, was Nasdaq's second-best performing stock of 1999. In January 2000 a preannouncement of poor fourth-quarter results cut Ancor's stock to $43.50. Ancor's SANbox Fibre Channel Director was named a finalist for 1999 Product of the Year by the I/O Technologies Forum & Expo Awards. In March Ancor announced software support for the new Jiro Technology Developer's Release introduced by Sun Microsystems Inc. Forbes ASAP, a regular supplement of Forbes Magazine, rated Ancor the 10th-best "ramping" technology company in the world, citing Ancor's successful switch from the LAN to storage networking markets, intense sales tactics, and impressive technology, including the industry's first 64-port Fibre Channel switch, the SANbox-64. Bell Microproducts agreed to integrate and distribute Ancor's SANbox-8 and SANbox-16 Fibre Channel switches in North America, South America, and Europe. Under an April OEM agreement with EMC Corp.—the world's leading provider of enterprise storage systems, software, and services—Ancor was to provide its SANbox 16-port Fibre Channel switches for use in EMC's Enterprise Storage Network. In May Anacomp Inc. (Nasdaq: ANCO), a leading provider of document-management solutions, announced that its Field Service business unit were to provide maintenance and support for Ancor's SANbox family of switches. Ancor and Datalink Corp. (Nasdaq: DTLK) formed a partnership to deliver data-intensive SANs. On May 8, QLogic Corp. (Nasdaq: QLGC), a leading supplier of Fibre Channel connectivity solutions, entered into an agreement to acquire Ancor. Under the terms of the agreement, which were unanimously approved by the boards of directors of both companies, QLogic was to exchange 0.5275 shares of common stock for each share of Ancor common stock (a 69 percent premium to the closing market price for Ancor stock as of Friday, May 5). Upon the closing of the merger, Ken Hendrickson, Ancor's CEO, was to be nominated to become a member of the QLogic board of directors. Based on the closing market price for QLogic of $99.94 as of Friday, May 5, the transaction value was $1.7 billion. [QLogic stock fell to $74.75 on May 8 and $61.94 on May 9, as the market anticipated problems between QLogic and partner Brocade Communications Systems Inc., an Ancor competitor.] Completion of the proposed transaction, which was subject to approval of the shareholders of both companies and appropriate regulatory clearances, was expected in the third calendar quarter. The acquisition of Ancor was to extend QLogic's extensive portfolio of products based on Fibre Channel technology. (Ancor's SANbox family is recognized as one of the broadest lines of Fibre Channel switches in the industry, delivering the hardware and fabric management software essential for SAN infrastructures.) The two companies were expected to leverage key customer relationships to produce synergistic Fibre Channel solutions for the rapidly growing SAN marketplace. Ancor's operations would remain in Minnesota, and its 150-employee work force could even expand. Goldman, Sachs & Co. acted as financial advisor to Ancor for this transaction. Ancor displayed its entire family of SANbox Fibre Channel switches, including its 64-port SANbox Director, at the Networld + Interop Show in Las Vegas. In June SANbox switches were selected for Sun Microsystem's StorEdge T3 arrays, the industry's most scalable network storage solution. ACAL Electronics, a leading distributor of SAN) throughout Europe, the Middle East, and Africa, agreed to distribute Ancor's SANbox switch product line. QLogic and Ancor announced that the Federal Trade Commission and the Department of Justice granted early termination of the Hart-Scott-Rodino waiting period for QLogic's acquisition of Ancor. In July Ancor signed an OEM agreement with Hewlett-Packard Co. to provide SANbox 8- and 16-port switches for HP's enhanced next-generation enterprise storage portfolio. Ancor was acquired in August 2000 by QLogic Corp. (Nasdaq: QLGC), Aliso Viejo, Calif. No. 170 CRM Public 200. No. 44 Minnesota Technology Fast 50.

Quebecor World Saint Cloud Inc. 660 Mayhew Lake Rd. N.E., P.O. Box 1007 (56302), St. Cloud, MN 56304. Tel: 320/654-2400; Fax: 320/252-1894. George Wilkes, Plant Mgr. Annual revenue $75 million. Quebecor Printing St. Cloud Inc. is the only remaining Minnesota plant belonging to North America's second-largest commercial printer. 550 employees (in Minnesota; 25 part-time). SIC 2759. Founded in 1949. In April 2000 Quebecor's 500-employee St. Paul plant was closed due to company realignment. Formerly owned by Maxwell Communication Corp. plc; now owned by Quebecor Inc., Montreal. No. 31 CRM Foreign-Owned 100.

Quest Diagnostics 600 W. County Rd. D, Interstate Corporate Centre, New Brighton, MN 55112. Tel: 651/635-1500; Fax: 651/635-1507. Carlton Burgess, Bus. Dir. Quest Diagnostics is a comprehensive clinical laboratory providing services to referring physicians, hospitals, and other organizations. Previous owner SmithKline Beecham plc sold the company in August 1999. 170 employees (in Minnesota). SIC 8071. Founded in 1952. Now owned by Quest Diagnostics Inc. (NYSE: DGX), Teterboro, N.J.

Qwest 200 S. Fifth St., Minneapolis, MN 55402. Tel: 800/879-4357; ; Web site: http://www.uswest.com. Jim Smiley, VP-MN. Qwest, formerly U S West, provides a full range of telecommunications services, including local services, wireless, PCS, data networking, directory, and information services, to 14 Western and Midwestern states including Minnesota. U S West serves 2.2 million business and residential telephone lines in the Twin Cities, Duluth, Rochester, St. Cloud, and many smaller towns throughout Minnesota. 7,000 employees (in Minnesota). SIC 4813. Founded in 1878. In June 2000 the Minnesota Public Utilities Commission gave its approval to the $57 billion acquisition of U S West by Qwest Communications International Inc., the broadband Internet communications company. U S West and Winstar Communications were awarded a $60 million, multiyear contract to provide government agencies in the cities and surrounding metropolitan area of Minneapolis and St. Paul with standard voice services (Centrex, Business Line, PBX Access Trunks, Key System Access, Private Line, and ISDN services), switched data service, and dedicated transmission service offerings at competitive rates. On June 30, Qwest completed its merger with U S West. The companies closed the transaction in 49 weeks, faster than any other large merger in the communications industry. Government officials at the federal and state levels gave fast-track approval to the merger, which was the first combination of old and new economy communications companies. In August, while contemplating companywide adminstrative cuts of up to 4,000, Qwest was still going forward with the hiring of up to 500 customer service workers in Minnesota. In September, in a competitive move aimed at the two Twin Cities cable companies that were also offering high-speed cable modem services (Time Warner Cable and AT&T Broadband), Qwest more than doubled the speed of its entry-level DSL Internet access services without increasing the cost. The next day the new parent company announced 11,000 job cuts (15 percent), including 330 to 350 jobs in Minnesota, primarily in middle management. In late October, Qwest signed a local telephone contract with rival McLeodUSA Inc., Cedar Rapids, Iowa. The interconnection agreement will generate $600 million in voice and data revenue for Qwest over three years. Division of Qwest Communications International Inc. (NYSE: Q), Denver. No. 22 CRM Employer 100.

RBC Dain Rauscher Wessels Dain Rauscher Plaza, 60 S. Sixth St., Minneapolis, MN 55402. Tel: 612/371-2711; Fax: 612/371-7933; Web site: http://www.dainrauscher.com. Irving Weiser, Chm., Pres., and CEO; John C. Appel, VChm., CEO-Insight Investment Management; Peter M. Grant, Pres.-DRW/Equity Capital Markets; Ronald A. Tschetter, Senior EVP and Pres.-Private Client Grou; John Adams, Senior Mng. Dir., Dir-Equity Research (D; Joseph Ali Jr., Senior Mng. Dir., Dir.-Equity Trading; Daniel Collins, SVP and Cont.; Chris Crosby, VP, Dir.-Internet/InfoNET; B.J. French, SVP and Dir.-Corp. Communications; Peder Furuseth, SVP and Dir.-Mktg.; Charles Grose, SVP and Dir.-Upper Midwest Region; Linda Henderson, SVP, Dir.-Fixed Income Research/Strategy; John Hickey, Managing Dir.-Dain Correspondent Svs.; Larry Holtz, SVP and Dir.-Taxable Fixed Income (FICM); David Jennings, SVP, Dir.-Municipal Fixed Income (FICM); Mike Kavanagh, SVP and Dir.-Correspondent Svs.; Karl Leaverton, SVP and Dir.-Western Region (PCG); Wade Massad, Senior Mng. Dir.-Syndicate/Corp. Svs.; Ted Mortonson, Senior Mng. Dir.-Institutional Equity; David Parrin, SVP and CFO; Richard J. Pedersen, Managing Dir.-Taxable Fixed Income (FICM; Paula Phillippe, EVP, Dir.-Hum. Res./Communications; Carla Smith, SVP, Sec., and Gen. Counsel; David Sogge, SVP and Dir.-Rocky Mountain (PCG); Nikki Sorum, SVP, Dir.-Strategic Plng./Corp. Devel.; Doug Strachan, SVP and Chief Info. Ofcr.; John Taft, CEO-Voyageur Asset Mgmt.; Robert Vanosky, EVP and Dir.-Public Fin. (FICM); Michelle White, SVP and Dir.-Op.; Dan Wilhite, EVP and Dir.-Southwest (PCG). Annual revenue $944.2 million (earnings $66.6 million). RBC Dain Rauscher Wessels—formerly named Dain Rauscher Corp., Interra Financial Inc., and Inter-Regional Financial Group Inc.—is the parent company of Dain Rauscher Inc. (formerly Dain Bosworth Inc. and Rauscher Pierce Refsnes Inc.), a regional securities firm; and RPR Correspondent Clearing, a unit that supports correspondent firms with securities clearing, trade settlement, and technology services. Until they were combined, Dain Bosworth (founded in 1909) served the Midwest, Rocky Mountain, and Pacific Northwest regions of the United States through 64 offices in 18 states; and Rauscher Pierce Refsnes, based in Dallas, served the Southwest with 26 offices in nine states. 3,700 employees. SIC 6211. Founded in 1973. In December 1999 securities regulators ordered Dain Rauscher Inc. to pay $16.5 million, including $7.1 million in punitive damages, to crosstown competitor Kinnard Investments Inc. for luring away about 20 Kinnard brokers and assistants during 1997 and 1998. Dec. 31: Record 1999 net income of $66.6 million was fueled by increased corporate finance activity and favorable markets. Dain Rauscher Wessels (DRW) doubled its revenue. In January 2000 Dain decided to appeal the Kinnard ruling, even though it had been made in an industry-designed arbitration forum. [In August the Hennepin County District Court would confirm the award.] Meanwhile, Dain said that it was planning to begin online trading in the summer of 2000. In February Dain Rauscher Wessels signed a strategic partnership and cooperative agreement with Israeli investment bank Tamir Fishman & Co. In March an article published by CommScan Analytics, a market data provider that tracks initial public offerings, said that, among investment banks that managed a minimum of 20 IPOs in 1999, DRW ranked first in aftermarket performance, with an average appreciation of 549 percent.

Wessels analyst Stephen Sigmond was named one of Institutional Investor magazine's Home-Run Hitters for his early call on VeriSign—a stock that rose 1,200 percent during 1999. In April Comerica Bank and Dain Rauscher Inc.joined forces, making Comerica's personal trust services, estate planning, and income tax management available to Dain Rauscher clients in the United States; and expanding Comerica's sales force with Dain Rauscher investment executives marketing Comerica's fiduciary services to its clients. Dain agreed to pay $12.9 million to federal and local governments as part of an industry-wide settlement regarding municipal bond-market abuses known as "yield burning." Dain lost a $360,000 arbitration award to rival U.S. Bancorp Piper Jaffray over the 1998 departure of top stockbrokers from Piper's Duluth office. In May Dain Rauscher Wessels (DRW) opened an institutional equity sales office in Paris. In September DRW opened a corporate finance office in Atlanta. Dain Rauscher and Stockwalk.com Group Inc. (Nasdaq: STOK) settled the NASD arbitration case filed against Dain Rauscher by John G. Kinnard and Co., a Minneapolis brokerage firm now part ofStockwalk.com Group Inc. As part of the settlement, Dain Rauscher paid Stockwalk.com $13.3 million. [In December 1999, an NASD arbitration panel awarded Kinnard $16.6 million; with interest, the award had grown to $17.2 million.] On Sept. 28, $300 billion-asset Royal Bank of Canada agreed to acquire Dain Rauscher. The transaction was to provide Royal Bank with established U.S. capabilities in full-service retail brokerage and investment banking—as well as a solid platform for future U.S. acquisitions—and give the newly named RBC Dain Rauscher Wessels greater critical mass to compete in an increasingly capital-intensive business. As a result of the merger, each share of Dain Rauscher common stock was to be converted into the right to receive US$95.00 in cash (an 18.9 percent premium over the previous day's close). The transaction was valued at US$1.456 billion. The merger—which was subject to regulatory approval, approval from the stockholders of Dain Rauscher, and other customary closing conditions—was expected to be completed by the end of the year, leaving the Twin Cities without a major independent stock-trading firm. Because of no overlap between Royal Bank's operations and Dain's U.S. territory, no job losses were expected. Sept. 30: Strong levels of equity trading and higher interest rates contributed to a 37 percent increase in third-quarter net income. In October Dain agreed to acquire $6 billion-asset Voyageur Asset Management, the money management arm of Dougherty Financial Group, Minneapolis. Merging Voyageur with Insight Investment Management would create a $13 billion firm—ranking 125th in industry league tables for assets under management—that manages bond, equity, and money market portfolios. At month's end, Dain Rauscher entered into an agreement with ABN AMRO Inc., an investment banking, advisory, and brokerage firm, to acquire its Chicago-based private client brokerage office. As part of the transaction, 41 employees, including 24 registered investment executives, were to join Dain Rauscher's downtown Chicago office, doubling its size. RBC Dain Rauscher Wessels is to be owned by Royal Bank of Canada (TSE, NYSE: RY), Toronto. No. 37 CRM Public 200. No. 6 CRM Performance 100.

RCM Technologies 80 S. Eighth St., Minnetonka, MN 55305. Tel: 952/229-9300; ; Web site: http://www.sysg.com. Vincent Freese, VP and Gen. Mgr.-Msn; Steve Blatnik, VP-Tech.; Joe Golemo, VP-Bus. Devel.; Julie Decker, Staffing Mgr.; Ruth Moe, Hum. Res. Mgr.; Steve Levey, Cont.; Brenda Nemastil, Lawson Software Practice Mgr.; Marie Pratlutsky, Office Mgr. RCM Technologies, part of which was formerly Systems Group Inc., provides business, technology, and resource solutions and contractual staffing in information technology and professional engineering to customers in corporate and government sectors in the Twin Cities area. RCM is a Lawson Star Partner, authorized to sell and implement Lawson Software's complete range of software products for the AS/400, UNIX, and Windows NT markets; an IBM Business Partner; and a Microsoft Certified Solutions Provider. In 1998, just after finding itself one of eight Minnesota firms to be ranked in the Inc. magazine list of America's 500 fastest-growing private companies (No. 93), Systems Group agreed to be acquired. 380 employees. SIC 7371, 7374. Founded in 1993. Owned since September 1998 by RCM Technologies Inc. (Nasdaq: RCMT), Fairfield, N.J.

RSM McGladrey Inc. 3600 W. 80th St., Suite 500, Bloomington, MN 55431. Tel: 952/921-7700; Fax: 952/921-7702; Web site: http://www.rsmmcgladrey.com. Mark Scally, Chm. and CEO; Tom Rotherham, Pres. and COO; Michael Bohning, EVP-E-business Consulting; Audian Dunham, EVP-Consulting; Pat Murphy, EVP-Tax Svs.; Pat Tabor, EVP-Int'l Svs.; Bob Jensen, SVP-Mergers/Transitions; Kathy Kenny, SVP-People; Mike Kirley, SVP-Economic Units; Doug Opheim, SVP-Fin.; Duane Tyler, SVP-Growth. RSM McGladrey Inc. is one of the nation's largest tax and business consulting firms serving midsized businesses. In addition to tax planning and compliance work, the firm offers consulting services in the following areas: financial management, human resources, information technology, operations, and strategic planning. RSM McGladrey serves clients from more than 60 offices nationwide, including Minnesota offices in St. Paul, Bloomington, Rochester, and Duluth. Other offices in the Upper Midwest include three in Wisconsin and three in South Dakota. RSM McGladrey serves its clients' audit and attest needs through a professional relationship with McGladrey & Pullen LLP. In June Block agreed to acquire the nonauditing business of the former McGladrey & Pullen for $240 million in cash plus the assumption of $50 million in pension liabilities, in what was the first combination between a major financial services company and a top-10 accounting firm. The new parent was planning to increase Minnesota employment by 50 percent in five years, as RSM McGladrey's overall business triples in size. 3,380 employees (600 in Minnesota). SIC 8721, 8742. Founded in 1908. In February 2000 RSM's Integrated Technology Solutions Group and All Systems Go established joint venture e.Vantage! to strengthen the technology infrastructure practice of both firms. RSM agreed to acquire TOBACK Technology Group, with offices in Phoenix and Denver, making it the largest U.S. dealer of Great Plains, a major provider of mid-market ERP software. TOBACK was to join RSM's Integrated Technology Solutions group's Rocky Mountain division. In April RSM and the University of Chicago Graduate School of Business introduced an intensive educational program to groom high-level business advisors who can deliver strategic advice to the firm's clients. In July RSM expanded its service offerings to include investment advisory services. In August RSM merged with Rudolph, Palitz LLC, Blue Bell, Pa.; and acquired the non-attest (non-CPA) business of Mullen & Co. LLP, Burlington, Mass. In September it merged with Wallace Sanders & Co., Dallas. In October RSM agreed to acquire the tax, accounting, and consulting business of Edward Isaacs & Co. LLP, with offices in New York City and White Plains, N.Y. In November insurance carriers Jefferson Pilot Financial, Pacific Life Insurance Co., and National Life Insurance Co. agreed to provide life insurance solutions to RSM McGladrey clients under terms of a strategic alliance. Owned by what is now the sixth-largest accounting firm in the country, H&R Block Inc. (NYSE: HRB), Kansas City, Mo.

Brad Ragan Tire & Service/Winona 5110 Service Dr., Winona, MN 55987. Tel: 507/454-5181; Fax: 507/454-5186. Tom Taylor, Branch Mgr. Brad Ragan Inc. produces fabricated rubber tires and retreads. 70 employees (in Minnesota; 2 part-time). SIC 7534. Owned by The Goodyear Tire and Rubber Co. (NYSE: GT), Akron, Ohio.

Rainforest Cafe Inc. 720 S. Fifth St., Hopkins, MN 55343. Tel: 952/945-5400; Fax: 952/945-5492; Web site: http://www.rainforestcafe.com. Lyle Berman, Chm. and CEO; Charles Robinson, SVP-Op.; Steven W. Schussler, SVP-Devel.; Ercu Ucan, SVP-Retail; Stephen Cohen, VP-Real Estate and General Counsel; Robert Hahn, VP and CFO; Jack Malisow, VP-Mktg. Annual revenue $262.7 million (earnings $5.7 million). Rainforest Cafe Inc. owns and operates large, high-volume, themed restaurant/retail facilities under the name "Rainforest Cafe—A Wild Place to Shop and Eat." The cafes are designed to provide a visually and aurally stimulating and entertaining rain forest environment. Each Rainforest Cafe consists of a dining area and a Retail Village. The restaurant offers a full menu and generous portions. The Retail Village features apparel and gifts with the Rainforest Cafe logo and eight proprietary animal characters, as well as other items reflecting the rain forest theme. At the end of October 1999, the company had 27 domestic locations (including Mall of America, Bloomington, Minn.) and 10 international locations. 6,800 employees. SIC 5812. Founded in 1994. In December 1999 Lakes Gaming Inc. (Nasdaq: LACO) and Rainforest Cafe announced plans to merge. Upon completion of the merger, Rainforest was to become a wholly owned subsidiary of Lakes, but continue to be run as a separate operating entity. In January 2000 tThe company received an unsolicited proposal to pursue discussions for the acquisition of Rainforest Cafe by a publicly held company. The proposal would involve the purchase of Rainforest Cafe for $125 million, 50 percent in cash and 50 percent in stock of the third party. Later in the month, Lakes and Rainforest mutually agreed to terminate their merger. In February the company signed a joint venture agreement to open the first location in Japan, at the Ikspiari complex at the Tokyo Disney Resort. Rainforest then signed a definitive merger agreement to be acquired by Landry's Seafood Restaurants, Houston, for $125 million in a combination of common stock (65 percent) and cash (35 percent). (Landry's is the second-largest and fastest-growing casual-dining seafood restaurant chain in the Unites States.) In March 1 the plaintiffs in the two purported class action lawsuits filed on Dec. 23, 1999, and Jan. 13, 2000, amended their original complaints to allege, among other things, that the directors breached their fiduciary duties in connection with their consideration of the merger with Landry's. Six percent shareholder Heartland Value Fund filed a class-action lawsuit, alleging disabling conflicts of interest on the Rainforest board; 11 percent shareholder the State of Wisconsin Investment Board launched a proxy fight, citing the ridiculously low price that had been agreed to. On March 31, the company projected sales for fiscal 2000 to be in the range of $255 to $265 million based upon the disappointing first-quarter sales for most of the company's mall locations. Operating net income for the year would be in the range of $2 million to $4 million or 10 cents to 15 cents per share—or 75 percent below analyst consensusestimates. In April Institutional Shareholder Services (ISS), the nation's leading proxy voting advisory firm, recommended that shareholders vote for the proposed merger. ISS stated, "We believe that, absent a higher offer, the Landry's offer represents the best alternative to shareholders. The structure of the merger consideration also allows shareholders to receive stock in the combined entity, which willallow shareholders to participate in any potential synergies that may be generated." In a further blow to suing shareholders, a Hennepin County judge refused a request to speed up evidence gathering. However, Proxy Monitor Inc., a New York-based advisory firm, urged shareholders to vote against the merger. The Minnesota State Board of Investment opposed the sale. The company postponed a shareholders' vote 16 hours before it was to take place, citing misinformation circulated by a dissident shareholder but also giving it time to solicit the additional proxies needed to pass the deal. However, on April 26, Landry's canceled the proposed merger, citing Rainforest's inability to obtain their shareholders' approval. (Although the majority of voting shareholders voted in favor of the merger, Minnesota law requires an affirmative vote by an absolute majority of all shareholders.) According to Landry's CEO Tilman J. Fertitta, "Due to an extremely aggressive campaign by the State of Wisconsin Investment Board urging Rainforest shareholders to vote against the merger, it was apparent that Rainforest would not obtain the requisite votes necessary to allow for consummation of the merger by the scheduled meeting of shareholders." The Wisconsin Investment Board said that its next step would be to effect a change in the makeup of Rainforest's current six-person board: Lyle Berman, three other company insiders, and two executives from Wilsons (originally Bermans) The Leather Experts. Meanwhile, Rainforest's newest international location opened at the Liang Court in Singapore. In May, a week after the merger breakup, Kenneth Brimmer announced his resignation as president—although he remained a consultant and company director. Rainforest stock hit a 52-week low of $2.75 on May 2, and analysts weren't expecting any new offers. The board of directors adopted a Shareholder Rights Plan and declared a dividend of one right on each outstanding share of the company's common stock to shareholders of record on May 24, 2000. The 10-year plan was designed to ensure the fair treatment of shareholders in connection with any potential takeover of the company and to guard against partial tender offers, open market accumulations, and other abusive tactics to gain control of the company. (The Wisconsin Investment Board would have preferred a shorter time period.) A new restaurant was opened May 11 at Opry Mills in Nashville, Tenn.—the 29th domestic location and 40th location overall. The Wisconsin Investment Board formally proposed that the board be restructured to consist of a majority of independent directors. The June opening of its location in San Francisco at Fisherman's Wharf marked the company's 30th domestic location and 41st location worldwide. Rainforest took a charge during the quarter of $102 million for asset impairment and a store closing. July brought the grand opening of its newest international location at the Ikspiari complex at the Tokyo Disney Resort in Japan, the company's 12th international location and its fourth icon unit in a Walt Disney Resort complex. In August the company abandoned its intentions to expand in malls, opting instead for larger restaurants at tourist locations. In addition, some current mall locations, including Aventura Mall in Miami, were to be closed. In September Rainforest announced plans to close its store in the Trafford Center mall located in Manchester, England. Eleven other international locations, including one in London at Piccadilly Circus, were to remain open. Rainforest was also planning to close its store at The Source Mall in Westbury, N.Y., citing high operating costs as the reason. To help boost repeat business, Rainforest created a loyalty program called Safari Club. On Sept. 26, Landry's Seafood Restaurants Inc. (NYSE: LNY), a 4.5 percent shareholder of Rainforest, entered into a definitive agreement to acquire all outstanding shares of Rainforest Cafe for $3.25 per share in cash, which represents a 60 percent premium over the previous day's closing stock price of $2.03. Both companies' boards approved the merger agreement. However, the merger agreement did not restrict the Rainforest Cafe board from accepting a higher offer. Landry's was to commence the transaction with a cash tender offer for 100 percent, but not less than a majority, of the outstanding Rainforest Cafe common shares. U.S. Bancorp Piper Jaffray delivered its opinion that the tender offer price in the amount of $3.25 was fair, from a financial point of view, to Rainforest Cafe stockholders. The transaction was valued at $74.4 million based on 22.9 million outstanding shares of Rainforest common stock. "Given the current challenges faced by Rainforest Cafe, most significantly the trend of continued declines in same-store sales, we view this offer to purchase Rainforest Cafe shares for cash as an alternative that mitigates a future full of uncertainties for Rainforest Cafe shareholders," CEO Berman stated. "The performance of the Rainforest Cafe business, particularly at the top line, has continued to erode and has continued to fall short of management's expectations. Very simply, as salescontinue to decline, many of the units are approaching levels where cash flow is negative and costly exit strategies must be assessed. Furthermore, as sales decline, the ability to leverage marketing and general and administrative efforts turns from a positive to a negative scenario. Absent a successful turnaround effort, our analysis indicates that it may be necessary to close as many as 20 stores." The State of Wisconsin Investment Board (SWIB), Rainforest's largest single institutional investor and a vocal opponent of Landry's earlier offer (which was $50 million higher), was shocked, calling the new offer "an outrage to shareholders." Landry's and Rainforest had structured their new deal so that Rainforest could terminate the agreement upon the receipt of a superior proposal. Tilman J. Fertitta, CEO of Landry's, responded, "I invite SWIB, or anyone else for that matter, to top our offer." A Landry's SEC filing indicated that it planned to lay off half of Rainforest's 100 corporate employees and move half of the remainder to Houston. Rainforest's change-of-control provision that was implemented in summer was to provide $9.8 million in lump-sum payments to employees, including a total of $1.5 million to Berman, Schussler, and Ucan. In October SWIB asked Rainforest to redeem or amend its poison pill takeover defense, which SWIB felt was inhibiting the actions of existing shareholders to ward off the Landry's offer. Citing the absence of any other offers, the Rainforest Cafe board declined. An hour-long meeting between Rainforest executives and SWIB officials did not change the investment board's opposition to the deal. Meanwhile, MJE Securities L.P. announced that it would tender its Rainforest Cafe shareholdings into Landry's $3.25 cash tender offer. When SWIB asked for a 30-day delay of the transaction, Rainforest responded that "a request to delay the transaction would not be in the best interest of our shareholders." Central Florida Investments (David Siegel) also requested a delay in order to put together its own bid. Landry's still believed that all conditions to the successful completion of its pending tender offer for Rainforest would be satisfied by Oct. 27, 2000, subject to Rainforest shareholders tendering the majority of their shares. As of Oct. 25, no competing offers had been received. Berman noted, "Shareholders who wish to receive prompt payment for their shares following the closing of the offer need to tender by the October 27 deadline." According to Siegel, Central Florida's interest was being stymied by the terms of Rainforest's required confidentiality agreement. On Oct. 27, Landry's finally acquired Rainforest. Landry's, which had offered jobs in Houston to a handful of corporate employees, was planning to eventually close down Rainforest's 100-employee Hopkins headquarters. Acquired by Landry's Seafood Restaurants Inc. (NYSE: LNY), Houston.

Randstad Northland Plaza, Suite 1155, 3800 W. 80th St., Bloomington, MN 55431. Tel: 952/897-5222; Fax: 952/893-7550; Web site: http://www.accustaff.com. James Ginther Sr., Pres.-MN Region; Pamela Pech, Regional Mgr. Annual revenue $17 million. Randstad, formerly AccuStaff, specializes in permanent and temporary office staffing and computer software training. Minnesota operations include branches in Minneapolis, St. Paul, Bloomington, Plymouth, Brooklyn Center, and Eagan. 140 employees (in Minnesota). SIC 7363. Founded in 1967. Owned through Randstad N.A., Atlanta, by Randstad Holding nv, Diemen, Netherlands. No. 79 CRM Foreign-Owned 100.

Rapp Collins Worldwide 901 Marquette Ave., 17th Floor, Minneapolis, MN 55402. Tel: 612/373-3000; Fax: 612/373-3135; Web site: http://www.rcwmpls.com. Patrick Furey, Pres.; Julie Moore, SVP; John Moody, SVP and Creative Dir.; Bruce Edwards, SVP and Creative Dir.; Brian Schwen, Cont. Rapp Collins Worldwide is a marketing services network dedicated to helping clients build and manage a more profitable customer base. Founded in 1965, Rapp Collins Worldwide now has 54 offices in 30 countries, five of which are in North America — Chicago, Dallas, New York, Toronto, and Minneapolis. Formerly U.S. Communications Corp. 63 employees (in Minnesota). SIC 7311. Founded in 1975. By July 2000, after just seven months under new president Furey, the firm had landed accounts totaling $2 million in revenue from three new clients (Genmar Holdings, MainStreet Networks, and Dain Rauscher). Owned by Omnicom Group Inc., New York.

Reinsurance Alternatives Inc. 7900 Xerxes Ave. S., Suite 2030, Bloomington, MN 55431. Tel: 952/832-3366; Fax: 952/832-3379. Richard E. Swager, Chm. and CEO; Christopher J. Williams, Pres. Reinsurance Alternatives is an insurance broker. SIC 6411. Owned by Willis Corroon Group plc, London.

Reliant Energy Minnegasco 800 LaSalle Ave., Floor 11, P.O. Box 59038, Minneapolis, MN 55459. Tel: 612/321-4664; Fax: 612/321-4873; Web site: http://www.minnegasco.com. Gary M. Cerny, Pres. and COO; Daniel O. Hagen, VP-Fin./Admin.; N. Jean Krause, VP-Hum. Res.; Steven J. Holmstoen, SVP-Delivery Svs.; Phillip R. Hammond, VP-Supply Mgmt./Regulatory Svs.; Andrea Newman, VP-Retail Svs.; Dan Hagen, VP and CFO. Annual revenue $671.4 million. Reliant Energy Minnegasco is Minnesota's largest natural gas utility, serving 650,000 residential, commercial, and industrial customers in 240 communities. The company also provides nonregulated services to customers through its Home Service Plus Business. In a name change effected during 1999, Minnegasco became Reliant Energy Minnegasco. 1,460 employees (in Minnesota; 73 part-time). SIC 4924. Founded in 1870. In March 2000 Minnegasco's parent said it was looking at strategic alternatives for the slow-growth regulated utility, including a potential sale. But by June, Reliant had changed its mind about selling Minnegasco and its other natural gas operations. In October MinnegascoHome Service Plus joined with Dunwoody Institute to offer a Home Appliance Technician Program designed for women. Part of Reliant Energy Delivery Group, a unit of Reliant Energy Inc. (NYSE: REI), Houston.

Reptron Manufacturing Services-Hibbing 3125 14th Ave. E., Hibbing, MN 55746. Tel: 218/263-8971; Fax: 218/263-8970. Bonnie Fena, Pres.; Steve Johnson, VP-Engrg./Tech. Svs.; Charles Crep, VP-Op.; Jake A. Dungan, VP-Fin./Admin.; Bill Baltus, Quality Mgr.; Craig Bronniche, Resource Planning Mgr.; Jo Ann Bujarski, MIS Mgr.; Debbie Clement, Accounting Mgr.; Nancee Majkich, Hum. Res. Mgr.; Lynn Nichols, Mfg. Mgr.; Deborah Thompson, Corp. Purchasing Mgr.; Michael Walsh, Mktg. Mgr. Annual revenue $170 million. Reptron Manufacturing Services-Hibbing, formerly Hibbing Electronics, performs high-complexity subcontract assembly of electronic circuit boards, and final product integration, for low- to medium-volume customers. Hibbing Electronics' parent was acquired by merger on June 1, 1998. 609 employees (in Minnesota; 50 part-time). SIC 3579, 8711. Founded in 1974. Company is now part of Reptron Electronics, Inc., Tampa, Fla., a division of Reptron Electronics Inc. (Nasdaq: REPT), Tampa, Fla.

Resistance Technology Inc. 1260 Red Fox Rd., Arden Hills, MN 55112. Tel: 651/636-9770; Fax: 651/636-8944. Mark S. Gorder, Pres. and CEO; S.M. Binnix, VP-Electronics SBU; G.H. Broecker, VP-Fin.; D.L. Gonsior, VP-Medical Infusion SBU; M.P. Geraci, VP-Hearing Health SBU. Annual revenue $42 million. Resistance Technology Inc. (RTI) manufactures micro-miniature electronic and medical products for the electronics and medical industries. 382 employees (239 in Minnesota; 20 part-time). SIC 3674. Founded in 1977. In March 2000 RTI signed a strategic alliance with Medtronic Inc.(NYSE: MDT) and its Tempe, Ariz.-based Microelectronics Center. The agreement established RTI as the exclusive outlet for Microelectronics Center's integrated circuits (ICs) for the hearing health market, while making Medtronic's Microelectronics Center the exclusive provider of development services as well as manufacturer of custom BiCMOS and CMOS integrated circuits for RTI. In April RTI agreed to purchase all of the issued and outstanding shares of Lectret Precision Pte. Ltd., Singapore, for $3 million in cash. Lectret Precision is an established manufacturer of professional audio devices and accessories for the professional audio, military, and radio communications markets. RTI was acquired in October 1993 for $22.3 million by Selas Corp. of America (ASE: SLS), Dresher, Pa.

Rexam Flexible Packaging 8235 220th St. W., Lakeville, MN 55044. Tel: 952/469-5461; Fax: 952/469-5337. David M. Timmons, Gen. Mgr.; Dennis G. Leisten, Dir.-Sls./Mktg. Annual revenue $50 million. Rexam Flexible Packaging manufactures food and medical packaging films, flame-retardant films, and industrial packaging materials, as well as construction and agricultural films. Formerly Startex Corp. 130 employees. SIC 2673, 3089. Founded in 1963. Now owned by Rexam plc, London. No. 82 CRM Foreign-Owned 100.

Ribi ImmunoChem Research Inc. 553 Old Corvallis Rd., Hamilton, MT 59840. Tel: 406/363-6214; Fax: 406/363-6129; Web site: http://www.ribi.com. Robert E. Ivy, Chm., Pres., and CEO; John L. Cantrell, Ph.D., EVP; Vern D. Child, VP-Fin. and Treas.; Gary T. Elliott, Pharm.D., Ph.D., VP-Pharmaceutical Devel.; Ronald H. Kullick, R.Ph., J.D., VP, Legal Counsel, and Sec.; Charles E. Richardson, Ph.D., VP-Pharmaceutical Discovery; Kenneth B. Von Eschen, Ph.D., VP-Clinical/Regulatory Affairs. Ribi Immunochem Research develops biopharmaceutical products designed to stimulate an immune response in humans and animals in order to prevent or treat malignant, infectious, and other diseases. The company is engaged in the research, development, production, and marketing of these products, some of which are under investigation by other companies for use as adjuvants. The company also engages in activities related to its research and development projects, such as the custom formulation and sale of research products, and contract research. In October 1999 Corixa Corp., a research and development biotechnology company, acquired all outstanding shares of Ribi in a merger valued at $56.3 million. 85 employees. SIC 2836. Founded in 1981. Now owned by Corixa Corp. (Nasdaq: CRXA), Seattle.

Ridgedale Center 12401 Wayzata Blvd., Minnetonka, MN 55345. Tel: 952/541-4864; Fax: 952/540-0154. F. Scott Ball, VP and Regional Mgr.; Jill Noack, VP and Gen. Mgr. Ridgedale Center operates a regional shopping mall. 60 employees. SIC 6512. Founded in 1974. A joint venture partnership of Cigna Investment Group Inc., Bloomfield, Conn.; Ivanhoe, Inc., Montreal; and The Rouse Co. (NYSE: RSE), Columbia, Md.

Risk Management Alternatives Inc. 1500 Commerce Dr., Mendota Heights, MN 55120. Tel: 651/688-5000; Fax: 651/688-5440. Dennis Cunningham, CEO; Jack L. Hurley, EVP; Patrick McGuire, COO; David Lanari, VP-MIS; Joseph Dudek, VP-Sls./Mktg. Risk Management specializes in credit-reporting and collection services. The privately held Associated Bureaus was sold on June 30, 1997. 322 employees (15 part-time). SIC 7322, 7323. Founded in 1928. Now owned by Risk Management Alternatives Inc., Atlanta.

Ritrama Duramark Companies Inc. 800 Kasota Ave. S.E., Minneapolis, MN 55414. Tel: 612/378-2277; Fax: 612/378-9327. Daryl Hanzal, Pres.; Don Pierce, VP-Fin. Annual revenue $60 million. Ritrama Duramark Cos. manufactures graphic arts supplies and pressure-sensitive films. 160 employees. SIC 2672. Founded in 1962. Owned by Ritrama S.p.A., Milan. No. 70 CRM Foreign-Owned 100.

Ritz Camera 1201 W. Broadway, Minneapolis, MN 55411. Tel: 612/521-2224; Fax: 612/521-3417. Ritz Camera Centers has 48 retail stores in the Midwest. Company stores carry brand-name cameras and accessories, and offer on-site photofinishing. Formerly Black Photo (USA) Inc. 450 employees. SIC 7384. Owned by Ritz Camera Centers Inc., Beltsville, Md.

Riverwood International First Street Southwest, P.O. Box 190, Crosby, MN 56441. Tel: 218/546-2100; Fax: 218/546-2104; Web site: http://www.riverwood.com. Greg Mangan, Gen. Mgr.; Kenneth Campbell, Sls. Mgr.; Lynda Everson-Bitner, Hum. Res. Mgr; Ralph Hoff, Materials Mgr. Riverwood International designs and manufactures packaging machinery for the beverage market. Its Minnesota Automation Placers division designs and manufactures couponers. 120 employees. SIC 3565. Founded in 1979. Owned through Riverwood International Corp., Atlanta, by CD&R (Clayton, Dublier & Rice) Inc., New York.

Road Rescue Inc. 1133 Rankin St., St. Paul, MN 55116. Tel: 651/699-5588; Fax: 651/699-9899. Norbert Conzemius, CEO; Charles D. Drake, Pres.; Don Zahm, VP-Op.; Thomas Thaller, Cont. Annual revenue $22 million. Road Rescue is a market leader producing specialty vehicles such as ambulances, rescue trucks and other emergency vehicles. In January 1998 the company was sold. Its new owners retained Road Rescue's West End facilities, management, and workers. 140 employees (138 in Minnesota; 2 part-time). SIC 3711. Founded in 1976. Owned by Spartan Motors Inc. (Nasdaq: SPAR), Charlotte, Mich.

RoadRunner Transportation Inc. 2395 Capp Rd., St. Paul, MN 55114. Tel: 651/644-8444; Fax: 651/659-6416. James Isaacson, Pres. and CEO; Doris Isaacson, Sec. RoadRunner Transportation is an on-call interstate courier that also offers overnight distribution and local trucking. The majority of its operations are in the Minneapolis-St. Paul area, but it also operates in Denver, and in Dallas, San Antonio, and Austin, Texas. Acquired in May 1997 for a combination of cash and stock totaling $14 million. 200 employees. SIC 4215. Founded in 1979. Owned by Dynamex Inc., Dallas.

Robbins Inc. 445 Greenwood St., Ishpeming, MI 49849. Tel: 906/486-4455; Fax: 906/486-9449. James H. Stoehr, Pres. and CEO. Robbins produces hardwood dimension lumber, flooring mills, and recreational flooring products. 110 employees. SIC 2426. Founded in 1977. Owned by Robbins Inc., Cincinnati.

Rock-Tenn Company 2250 Wabash Ave., St. Paul, MN 55114. Tel: 651/641-4938; Fax: 651/641-4791. Jack Greenshields, Gen. Mgr.-St. Paul Mill; Tom Garland, Gen. Mgr.-St. Paul Folding Carton; Tom Troskey, Mgr.-Paper Recycling. Rock-Tenn's St. Paul plant manufactures recycled paperboard, recycled corrugated medium, and folding cartons. While known as Waldorf Corp., the company was privately held during the period from a 1985 leveraged buyout until December 1996, when then-owner Eugene U. Frey sold the company for $410 million. 750 employees. SIC 2621, 2631, 2657. Founded in 1886. Owned by Rock-Tenn Co. (Nasdaq: RKTN), Atlanta.

RocketChips Inc. 7901 Xerxes Ave. S., Suite 316, Bloomington, MN 55431. Tel: 952/948-0000; Fax: 952/948-0044; Web site: http://www.rocketchips.com. Raymond Johnson, Pres. and CEO; Robert M. Keller, VP-Bus. Devel.; Tim Hemken, VP-Sls./Mktg. RocketChips is a leading supplier of multigigabit serial transceiver ICs and intellectual property cores enabling high-bandwidth silicon connectivity solutions for wired and wireless communications. Specializing in physical layer serializer/deserializer technology for data communications, RocketChips provides CMOS-standard products and IP solutions for Gigabit Ethernet, Fibre Channel, Serial Backplane, InfiniBand, XAUI, and Bluetooth. The fab-less semiconductor company has additional design centers in Ames, Iowa, and Austin, Texas. 70 employees (25 in Minnesota). SIC 3674. Founded in 1997. In November 2000 the company was acquired in a stock deal valued at $216 million. Now owned by Xilinx Inc. (Nasdaq: XLNX), San Jose, Calif.

Rockwell Automation/Allen-Bradley 6950 Washington Ave. S., Eden Prairie, MN 55344. Tel: 952/942-3600; Fax: 952/942-3636; Web site: http://www.electro-craft.com. Dan Coriesback, Dir.-Electro-Craft; Dale Kersten, Purch. Mgr. Rockwell Automation/Allen-Bradley, formerly Electro-Craft, manufactures servomotors, controls, AC motors, and gear motors. Formerly Reliance Motion Control. 250 employees. SIC 3621. Founded in 1960. Owned by Rockwell, Milwaukee, Wis.

Rorke Data Inc. 9700 W. 76th St., Eden Prairie, MN 55344. Tel: 952/829-0300; Fax: 952/829-0988; Web site: http://www.rorke.com. Herb Rorke, Pres. and CEO; Joe Swanson, VP-Sls.; Joe Rorke, VP-Mktg.; Tim Hanscom, VP-Supply Div.; Paul Norr, VP-Fin. Rorke Data is a full digital storage solutions provider with expertise in RAID subsystems, high-performance magnetic drives, tape and optical libraries, Unix NT and Mac environments, high-bandwidth networks, digital asset and document management, and engineering and maintenance services. Together with its European subsidiary, 50-employee Rorke Data Europe, located in Emmen, Netherlands, the company comprises six divisions: Audio/Video, Prepress, Imaging, Document Management, Digital Media Supplies, and Engineering and Installation Services. Products and services include high-end computer disk storage systems; stand-alone paperless office workstations for scanning documents; printer ribbons, optical disks, computer tape, and printers; and on-site computer services and maintenance. 135 employees (85 in Minnesota). SIC 5045. Founded in 1985. A December 1999 partnership agreement with FAST Multimedia U.S. was to allow multiple users of the 601 non-linear editing system and Rorke's StudioNet-FC to concurrently share the same footage from a Storage Area Network (SAN) system. (Most post-production facilities feel that collaboration among users on a single project adds creativity and speed.) In February 2000 Rorke said that it was in receipt of a letter of intent for the strategic acquisition of its data storage and systems business in both the U.S. and Europe. FLEXSTOR.net Inc., a new company spun off by Rorke in 1999, was not part of the acquisition. In March Rorke Data U.S. and its software development team at Rorke Data Europe in Emmen, The Netherlands, introduced the company's new PostScript LanguageLevel 3-compatible RIP option for Rorke's PageComposer file conversion application. In April Rorke entered into a strategic partnership with Media 100 (Nasdaq: MDEA), the pioneer and market leader of streaming media production tools for the Internet. Emulex Corp. (Nasdaq:EMLX), an industry leader in fibre channel products and technology, partnered with Rorke to demonstrate a wide range of video applications at the National Association of Broadcasters convention. In August Konica Medical Imaging agreed to feature Rorke's storage libraries, including its AIT technology, as the primary archive product for the NetStar PACs solution. In September Rorke's StudioNet-FC high-bandwidth Fibre Channel work group solution was chosen for use by Northern Oklahoma College and by LES FILMS DU SOLEIL.Media 100 Inc. (Nasdaq: MDEA), the leading provider of software, systems, and services for streaming media on the Internet, selected Rorke Data to develop a sophisticated, powerful storage area network solution to manage the exploding demand for streaming media encoding and hosting services. Rorke Data was chosen by Broadway Sound, a division of Broadway Video Inc., for the installation of a Storage Area Network (SAN) for its New York-based audio post-production facility. Rorke began shipping an optional PageComposer module that enables scatterproofing of TIFF/IT-P1 and Scitex NewCT/NewLW files on any digital proofer at any resolution. Rorke introduced a new line of NT servers developed specifically for the high-bandwidth requirements of the prepress and publishing markets. To be owned by Bell Microproducts Inc. (Nasdaq: BELM), San Jose, Calif.

Rosemount Inc. 12001 Technology Dr., Eden Prairie, MN 55344. Tel: 952/941-5560; Fax: 952/828-7777. Robert J. Bateman, CEO. Rosemount designs and manufactures measurement, pressure, temperature, flow, and level instrumentation, serving industrial process-control markets. 1,857 employees (125 part-time). SIC 3823, 5049. Founded in 1956. In March 2000 Rosemount filed a patent-infringement complaint against Ohmart/VEGA Corp.—regarding a patent related to technology useful in measuring the height of fluids in a tank. In May Rosemount and SAAB Marine Electronics AB of Sweden signed a cross-license agreement for use of their respective patents covering tank-level measurement using electromagnetic signals. SAAB's patent relates to tank-level measurement through a stilling well in a tank. Rosemount's patent relates to a two-wire, process control, loop-powered tank-level measurement transmitter. Owned since 1976 by Emerson Electric Co. (NYSE: EMR), St. Louis.

Rosemount Inc. 8200 Market Blvd., Chanhassen, MN 55317. Tel: 952/941-5560; Fax: 952/949-7001. Rick Green, VP. Rosemount's Measurement Division manufactures pressure and temperature transmitters for industrial use. 1,200 employees. SIC 3823, 5049. Founded in 1992. Owned by Emerson Electric Co. (NYSE: EMR), St. Louis.

Joseph T. Ryerson & Son Inc. 1605 N. Highway 169, P.O. Box 619 (55440), Plymouth, MN 55441. Tel: 763/544-4401; Fax: 763/544-2816. John Rich, Gen. Mgr. Joseph T. Ryerson & Son sells steel, alloys, aluminum, and plastics. 140 employees. SIC 5051. Founded in 1842. Owned through Ryerson Tull, Chicago, by Ispat International N.V., London. No. 79 CRM Foreign-Owned 100.

SCI Systems Inc. 222 Disk Dr., Rapid City, SD 57701. Tel: 605/394-6200; Fax: 605/394-6287. David Marler, VP-Op.; Bob Phillips, Mktg. Mgr. SCI Systems manufactures leading computer technology, printed circuit boards, and box-build assemblies. 1,100 employees. SIC 3672. Founded in 1969. Owned by SCI Systems Inc. (NYSE: SCI), Huntsville, Ala.

SDRC Metaphase Technology Division 4233 Lexington Ave. N., Suite 3290, Arden Hills, MN 55126. Tel: 651/482-4219; Fax: 651/482-2215; Web site: http://www.sdrc.com. Ron Schmitz, Ofcr. Annual revenue $135.8 million. SDRC Metaphase Technology is a division of a leading global provider of e-business collaborative solutions for the product lifecycle. Its products in the areas of Product Knowledge Management (PKM), Collaborative Product Commerce, and e-Design Automation—when coupled with process engineering and consulting services—facilitate innovation through collaboration, enabling industry leaders to optimize product development early in the design process, increase productivity, and significantly improve time-to-market. Metaphase, the industry-leading enterprise PKM solution, provides a comprehensive approach to the management and control of product information, configuration, release management, and work flow. 350 employees (in Minnesota). SIC 7372. Founded in 1992. Owned by Structural Dynamics Research Corp. (Nasdaq: SDRC), Milford, Ohio.

SL Montevideo Technology Inc. 2002 Black Oak Ave., Montevideo, MN 56265. Tel: 320/269-6562; Fax: 320/269-7662. Alan Pelan, Pres.; Marv Dehne, Purch. Agt.; Ron E. Intilia, VP-Sls./Mktg.; Tim Forde, VP-Fin. SL Montevideo Technology manufactures avionics components, precision windings, aircraft instrument meter movements, AC and DC servo motors, and brushless DC systems. 270 employees. SIC 3621, 3679. Owned by SL Industries Inc. (NYSE: SL), Mt. Laurel, N.J.

SPL Integrated Solutions 525 N. Washington Ave., Minneapolis, MN 55401. Tel: 612/333-1271; Fax: 612/333-0225; Web site: http://www.splis.com. Larry Golen, Pres.; Phil Dalen, EVP-Sls./Mktg.; Kevin Powers, VP; Vicki Strahan, Regional Sls. Mgr. SPL Integrated Solutions, formerly Caribiner International and, before that, Blumberg Communications, provides communications and presentation technologies to business, industry, government, medical, education, and television markets. Services include audio and video sales and consulting; rental and staging of audiovisual, video, sound, and lighting systems; creative services; design and installation of presentation products; and maintenance and repair. 300 employees (55 in Minnesota). SIC 1799. Founded in 1963. Now owned through Total Audio Visual Services, Atlanta, by Production Resources Group, Mt. Vernon, N.Y.

SPM 9300 52nd Ave. N., New Hope, MN 55428. Tel: 763/537-8587; Fax: 763/537-9228. Mike Noggle, CEO; Larry Noggle, EVP. SPM is a custom thermoplastic injection molder of precision components for industry. The company has complete tooling facilities. Branch offices are located in El Paso, Texas, and Hickory, N.C. 175 employees. SIC 3089. Founded in 1966. Acquired in May 1994 by Dynacast Inc., Yorktown Heights, N.Y., whose ultmate parent is Coats Viyella plc, London. In July 2000 Dynacast agreed to sell the company to United Plastics Group, Westmont, Ill.

SPX Corporation 655 Eisenhower Dr., Owatonna, MN 55060. Tel: 507/455-7000; Fax: 507/455-7106; Web site: http://www.spx.com. Mike Macrellis, Dir.-Op., Eisenhower Dr. SPX Corporation manufactures special high-tech diagnostic tools and equipment designed and engineered for the automotive maintenance market—equipment for the maintenance of trucks, crawler tractors, and farm tractors. Globally, SPX has operations in the United Kingdom, Germany, Australia, and Japan. Formerly Owatonna Tool Co. 1,000 employees. SIC 3421, 3429, 3544, 3569, 3825. Founded in 1925. Division of SPX Corp. (NYSE: SPW), Muskegon, Mich.

SPX Power Team 2121 W. Bridge St., Owatonna, MN 55060. Tel: 507/455-7100; Fax: 507/455-7130. Brian S. Behm, Pres. SPX Power Team produces a high-quality line of high-pressure hydraulic products, workholding components, maintenance tools and equipment, and test devices. 450 employees. SIC 3429. Founded in 1985. Division of SPX Corp. (NYSE: SPW), Muskegon, Mich.

St. Cloud Times 3000 Seventh St. N., P.O. Box 768, St. Cloud, MN 56302. Tel: 320/255-8700; Fax: 320/255-8775. Sonja Sorensen Craig, Pres. and Publisher; Susan Ihne, Exec. Editor; Tove Hicks-Klund, Advertising Dir.; Geary Yaeger, Circulation Dir.; Barb Rosenberger, Acting Prod. Dir.; Berni Hollinger, Cont.; Mark Milam, Dir.-Hum. Res. The St. Cloud Times is involved in newspaper publishing and commercial printing. The newspaper's weekday circulation is 28,740; Sunday circulation is 38,400. On Sept. 27, 1999, the St. Cloud Times converted to a morning newspaper. 245 employees (in Minnesota; 100 part-time). SIC 2711. Founded in 1861. Subsidiary of Gannett Co. Inc. (NYSE: GCI), Arlington, Va.

St. Paul Pioneer Press 345 Cedar St., St. Paul, MN 55101. Tel: 651/222-5011; Fax: 651/228-5416; Web site: http://www.pioneerplanet.com. Rick Sadowski, Publisher and Pres.; Walker Lundy, SVP and Editor; Vicki S. Gowler, Managing Editor; Marj Ranes, SVP-Sls./Mktg.; Bruce K. Bryant, VP and CFO. St. Paul Pioneer Press publishes the St. Paul Pioneer Press, daily and Sunday and Home Seller biweekly (a real estate publication), and maintains two Web sites (http://www.pioneer-press.com and http://www.twincities.com). Average circulation is 208,062 daily and 262,144 Sunday. As of early 2000, the Saint Paul Pioneer Press was the fifth-fastest-growing newspaper in the country. 980 employees (in Minnesota; 345 part-time). SIC 2711. Founded in 1849. March 26, 2000: For the six months, the paper's weekday circulation rose 2.2 percent over the previous year, to 208,062, according to the Audit Bureau of Circulation. Sunday circulation increased 0.6 percent in the paper's primary market, but dropped 0.4 percent overall. In April the Pioneer Press was awarded journalism's highest honor—the Pulitzer Prize. Pioneer Press reporter George Dohrmann's stories about the largest case of academic fraud in the history of the NCAA won the 2000 Pulitzer Prize for beat reporting. This was the newspaper's third Pulitzer, but its first in the beat reporting category. (In 1986 and 1988 the paper won the Pulitzer for feature writing.) Owned by Northwest Publications Inc., a subsidiary of Knight Ridder Inc. (NYSE: KRI), San Jose, Calif.

Saks Fifth Avenue 655 Nicollet Mall, Minneapolis, MN 55402. Tel: 612/333-7200; Fax: 612/333-8481. Maureen McNally, Gen. Mgr.; Jeffrey Gernand, Asst. Gen. Mgr.-Op.; Kevin Foley, Asst. Gen. Mgr.-Op. Saks Fifth Avenue is a specialty store featuring men's and women's apparel and accessories. 200 employees (in Minnesota). SIC 5611, 5621, 5632. Founded in 1989. Saks Fifth Avenue, New York, is owned by the former Proffitt's Inc., which, in 1998, merged into Saks Inc. (NYSE: SKS), New York.

Sam's Club 1300 E. Mendota Rd., Inver Grove Heights, MN 55077. Tel: 651/451-1482; Fax: 651/451-1193. Hoss Stamper, Gen. Mgr. Sam's Club is a wholesaler of goods and supplies to businesses and club members. It has nine Minnesota locations. 120 employees. SIC 5099. Founded in 1983. Division of Wal-Mart Stores Inc. (NYSE: WMT), Bentonville, Ark.

Sathers One Sather Plaza, P.O. Box 28, Round Lake, MN 56167. Tel: 507/945-8181; Fax: 507/945-8343. Dick Boyce, CEO; Steve Kaplan, COO and CFO; Steve Luitjens, VP-Sls.; Brooks Gruemmer, Sec. Sathers manufactures candies; processes nuts; and distributes cookies, candies, and nuts at the retail and wholesale level. Distribution is nationwide, by a company-owned fleet of trucks, from plants in Round Lake, Minn.; Chattanooga, Tenn.; and Pittston, Pa. In August 1996 the privately held Sathers was acquired by Favorite Brands International Inc., Lincolnshire, Ill. In September 1999 Favorite Brands itself was acquired. 1,200 employees (500 in Minnesota; 50 part-time). SIC 2052, 2064, 2068, 2099, 5149. Founded in 1936. Now Sathers is a division of Nabisco Foods Co., Parsippany, N.J., which is owned by RJR Nabisco Holdings Corp. (NYSE: RN), New York.

Sauer-Sundstrand Electrohydraulics Division 3500 Annapolis Ln. N., Plymouth, MN 55447. Tel: 763/509-2000; Fax: 763/559-5769; Web site: http://www.sauer.com. Tim Kramer, Dir.-Op.; David Gawthrop, Mgr.-Admin. Sauer-Sundstrand Electrohydraulics Div. manufactures electrohydraulic control systems for mobile applications. 205 employees. SIC 3679. Division of Sauer-Sundstrand Co., Ames, Iowa; subsidiary of Sauer-Sundstrand GMBH, Neumuenster, Germany. No. 63 CRM Foreign-Owned 100.

Saunatec Inc. 575 E. Cokato St., Cokato, MN 55321. Tel: 320/286-5584; Fax: 320/286-6100; Web site: http://www.finnleo.com. Keith Raisanen, Pres. Saunatec is a manufacturer and distributor of sauna and steambath products. 130 employees (65 in Minnesota). SIC 3634. Owned by Saunatec plc, Hanko, Finland. No. 82 CRM Foreign-Owned 100.

Scherping Systems 801 Kingsley St., Winsted, MN 55395. Tel: 320/485-4401; Fax: 320/485-2666. Virgil Scherping, Chm.; Rodney Scherping, Pres. Scherping Systems does stainless steel fabrication—storage tanks, process tanks, and process controls. The company also makes installation piping. 140 employees. SIC 3443. Founded in 1968. In August 1996 the company was acquired by Carlisle Cos. Inc. (NYSE: CSL), Syracuse, N.Y.

Schult Homes HBOS Mfg. LP 201 Industrial Dr., P.O. Box 399, Redwood Falls, MN 56283. Tel: 507/637-3555; Fax: 507/637-5167. James Toth, Gen. Mgr.; Dennis Moore, Sls. Mgr.; Joel Buller, Services Mgr.; Doug Frayseth, Purch. Mgr. Annual revenue $33 million. Schult Homes manufactures factory-built housing. 195 employees (in Minnesota). SIC 2451. Founded in 1974. Division of Oakwood Homes (NYSE OH), Greensboro, N.C.

Schwing America Inc. 5900 Centerville Rd., White Bear, MN 55127. Tel: 651/429-0999; Fax: 651/429-3464. Thomas M. Anderson, Pres.; Bradley E. Wucherpfennig, COO and CFO. Schwing America makes concrete pumps, slurry pumps, transit mixers, and booms for fire fighting. Facility opened in 1979. 468 employees. SIC 3531, 3561. Founded in 1972. Owned by Friedrich Wilh. Schwing GmbH, Herne, Germany. No. 34 CRM Foreign-Owned 100.

Seagate Technology Inc. Recording Head Operations (RHO), One Disc Dr., Bloomington, MN 55435. Tel: 952/844-8000; Fax: 952/844-7008; Web site: http://www.seagate.com. Seagate RHO designs, develops, and manufactures recording heads, which are miniature electromagnets that "fly" micro-inches above the discs in a hard drive, reading and writing data. These heads, currently about the size of a flake of pepper, are produced using semiconductor-like manufacturing processes and equipment. Seagate acquired Imprimis Technology, a subsidiary of Control Data Corp., in 1989. 4,200 employees. SIC 3577. In March 2000 parent Seagate Technology Inc. (NYSE: SEG) reached an agreement with Veritas Software Corp. and an investor group to be taken private in a deal worth $17.5 billion. A division of Seagate Technology Inc. (NYSE: SEG), Scotts Valley, Calif.

Seagate Technology Inc. Product & Technology Development Center, 1280 Disc Dr., Shakopee, MN 55379. Tel: 952/806-8000; Fax: 952/844-5703; Web site: http://www.seagate.com. This operation designs and develops products for Seagate's core business, data storage. Worldwide demand for storage doubles every nine months, creating a storage market opportunity estimated to reach $100 billion by 2002. The Product and Technology Development Center has developed such leading-edge technology as the Fibre Channel interface and the 10,000-RPM Cheetah disc drive (of which 5 million have been shipped in three years). Enterprise drives designed in Shakopee are used in such high-volume, data-intensive applications as motion picture special effects, airline reservation systems, and ATM transactions. 1,200 employees (in Minnesota). SIC 3572. Founded in 1988. A division of Seagate Technology Inc. (NYSE: SEG), Scotts Valley, Calif.

Sealy of Minnesota Inc. 825 Transfer Rd., St. Paul, MN 55114. Tel: 651/645-8143; Fax: 651/645-1255; Web site: http://www.sealy.com. Zan Uicino, Plant Mgr.; M. Kwaitkowski, Sls. Mgr.; W. Dusek, Cont. Sealy of Minnesota manufactures mattresses and box springs. 125 employees. SIC 2515. Founded in 1970. Subsidiary of Sealy Corp. Inc., Cleveland.

Secure Computing Corporation 2675 Long Lake Road, Roseville, MN 55113. Tel: 408/918-6100; Fax: 408/918-6101; Web site: http://www.securecomputing.com. John McNulty, Pres. and CEO; Tom Haigh, VP and Chief Technologist; Timothy P. McGurran, CFO and VP-Op.; Reinhold Linstaedt, VP-Int'l Op.; Carr Biggerstaff, VP-Bus. Dev./Mktg./Planning; David Peatrowsky, VP-Sls., America. Annual revenue $27.1 million. Secure Computing is one of the largest network security companies in the world. The company provides enterprise, network and e-commerce security solutions to a worldwide partner and customer base in financial services, telecom, aerospace, manufacturing, high-tech, service providers and government agencies. The business was spun out of Honeywell Inc., Minneapolis, in July 1989. In November 1995 an initial public offering raised $32.7 million. In February 1998 Secure moved its corporate headquarters from Roseville to the West Coast. 247 employees (in Minnesota). SIC 7379. Founded in 1989. Parent is Secure Computing Corp. (Nasdaq: SCUR), San Jose, Calif.

Seneca Foods Corporation 1217 Third Ave. S.E., Rochester, MN 55904. Tel: 507/280-4500; Fax: 507/280-4579. M.H. Haney, Pres.-Vegetable Div.; Brian Thiel, Plant Mgr. Seneca Foods produces canned and frozen vegetables—including peas, carrots, lima beans, corn, beets, and potatoes. Brand names include Seneca, Libby, and Aunt Nellie's Farm Kitchen. 560 employees (210 in Minnesota; 350 part-time). SIC 2033. Founded in 1949. Owned through Seneca Foods Corp., Janesville, Wis., a division of Seneca Foods Corp. (OTC: SENEA), Pittsford, N.Y.

Serving Software Group, HBO & Company 2700 N. Snelling Ave., Fourth Floor, Roseville, MN 55112. Tel: 651/698-5900; Fax: 651/697-5910. Dave Del Turo, VP-Res./Devel. and Gen. Mgr. Serving Software develops, markets, and supports computer software systems for scheduling and information management in hospitals and related medical facilities. The systems are designed to automate certain data management at the departmental level and hospital-wide—thereby increasing productivity, reducing operating costs, enhancing user revenue opportunities, and improving quality assurance, report accuracy, and patient care. Software products include Pathways Healthcare Scheduling, Surgi-Server 2000, and Onmi-Server 2000. 190 employees (180 in Minnesota; 2 part-time). SIC 7371. Founded in 1984. Owned since May 1994 by HBO & Co. (Nasdaq: HBOC), Atlanta.

Shakopee Valley Printing 5101 Valley Industrial Blvd. S., P.O. Box 359, Shakopee, MN 55379. Tel: 952/445-5800; Fax: 952/445-5805. Mike Theis, Pres. Shakopee Valley Printing (SVP) prints newspapers, shoppers, catalogs, inserts, and other publications (heatset and non-heatset). It operates a complete bindery and does mailing in-house. In August 1995 SVP merged into American Color Graphics, Brentwood, Tenn. 415 employees (414 in Minnesota; 28 part-time). SIC 2711, 2731, 2741, 2752. Founded in 1861. American Color Graphics is owned by Morgan Stanley Group Inc. (NYSE: MS), New York.

Shandwick International 8400 Normandale Lake Blvd., Suite 500, Bloomington, MN 55437. Tel: 952/832-5000; Fax: 952/831-8241; Web site: http://www.shandwick.com. David L. Mona, Chm.; Sara Gavin, Managing Dir.; Chris Malecek, EVP; Jorg Pierach, EVP; Bob Rumpza, EVP; Jeanne Carpenter, SVP-Mktg./Business Devel.; Kelly Digrado, SVP-Fin./Admin.; Susan Eilertsen, SVP; Cathryn I. Kennedy, SVP; Dave Kuhn, SVP; Heidi Libera, SVP-Prospera Design; Nancy Longley, SVP; Steve Mercer, SVP; Eric Pehle, SVP; Barbara Young, SVP; Mary Milla, VP; Walter Parker, SVP; Bruce Benidt, Chief Learning Ofcr. Annual revenue $19.6 million. The Twin Cities office of Shandwick International is the largest public relations office in the North Central region of the United States. The firm is a full-service public relations and marketing communications firm. Shandwick's practice specialties include consumer brand and lifestage marketing, financial services, home products, technology, agribusiness, environmental, corporate communications, public affairs, business-to-business, investor relations, and health care. The firm also offers graphic design through Prospera. Weber Shandwick is a world leader in global reputation management with offices located in all major financial, business and media centers around the world. Key clients: Northwest Airlines, The Coca-Cola Co., Mall of America, Medtronic, Qwest, Best Buy, Hallmark, 3M, eFunds Corp., Wells Fargo Bank Minneapolis, Hormel Foods Co., Deluxe Corp., Novartis, and Personnel Decisions International. The Minneapolis office is the former Mona Meyer McGrath & Gavin. 230 employees. SIC 8743. Founded in 1986. In May 2000 the Twin Cities office won two Creativity in Public Relations Awards (CIPRAs), for programs executed on behalf of U S West (now Qwest) and 3M. Shandwick Worldwide is owned by The Interpublic Group of Cos. (NYSE: IPG), New York.

Shaw Contract Flooring 151 Cheshire Ln., Suite 500, Plymouth, MN 55441. Tel: 763/475-5200; Fax: 763/475-5220. D.David Vita, Pres. Shaw Contract Flooring is a flooring contractor (carpet, resilient flooring, ceramic). 110 employees. SIC 1752, 5023. Founded in 1920. Division of Shaw Industries Inc. (NYSE: SHX), Dalton, Ga.

Siemens 7225 Northland Dr., Brooklyn Park, MN 55428. Tel: 763/536-4100; Fax: 763/536-4018. Siemens provides control systems to electric utilities worldwide. Part of Control Data Corp./Ceridian Corp. until acquired in March 1993. Formerly known as Empros Power Systems Control Division. 406 employees. SIC 7373. Founded in 1847. Owned through Siemens Energy Automation Inc., Atlanta, by Siemens AG, Munich, Germany. No. 40 CRM Foreign-Owned 100.

Sifco Custom Machining Company 2430 Winnetka Ave. N., Golden Valley, MN 55427. Tel: 763/544-3511; Fax: 763/544-2206. Marty Gonior, Pres.-Mpls.; Roger Harma, Dir.-Sls./Mktg.; Dave Lane, Mgr.-Mfg. Annual revenue $9.2 million. Sifco Custom Machining Co. does precision machining, repair, and modification of jet engine components. 74 employees (in Minnesota). SIC 3599, 3724. Founded in 1956. Owned by Sifco Industries Inc., Cleveland.

Silent Knight LLC 7550 Meridian Circle, Maple Grove, MN 55369. Tel: 763/493-6400; Fax: 763/493-6475. John Ellis, Pres.; Barry Stahl, VP-Sls./Mktg. Silent Knight manufactures high-technology intrusion detectors, fire detectors, and access-control systems for commercial, institutional, and residential settings. Products are distributed by an exclusive network of authorized dealers, as well as by security equipment distribution facilities. Waycrosse Inc., the private investment arm of the Cargill and MacMillan families (owners of Cargill Inc., Wayzata, Minn.), sold the company in August 1999 in order to gain more liquidity and diversify its investments. 120 employees. SIC 3669. Founded in 1966. Now owned by Pittway Corp. (NYSE: PRY), Chicago.

Silgan Containers Corporation 12130 Lynn Ave. S., Savage, MN 55378. Tel: 952/890-2120; Fax: 952/890-5456. Jack Bohnert, Plant Mgr. Silgan manufactures metal food containers at its Savage plant. Known as American National Can Co. until purchased Aug. 1, 1995. 156 employees. SIC 3411. Owned through Silgan Containers Corp., Woodland Hills, Calif., by Silgan Corp. (Nasdaq: SLGN), Stamford, Conn.

Silgan Containers Mfg. Corporation 755 N. Prior, St. Paul, MN 55104. Tel: 651/643-3200; Fax: 651/644-3406. Jack Unmuth, Plant Mgr. Annual revenue $38 million. Silgan Containers Corp. manufactures metal food containers and ends at its North Prior plant. 151 employees (in Minnesota). SIC 3411. Founded in 1936. Owned through Silgan Containers Corp., Woodland Hills, Calif., by Silgan Corp. (Nasdaq: SLGN), Stamford, Conn.

Silicon Graphics Inc. 655 Lone Oak Dr., Eagan, MN 55121. Tel: 651/452-6650; Fax: 651/683-7198. Irene M. Qualters, Pres. and COO; Gary D. Ball, VP-Gov't; Michael Booth, VP-Applications/Software; Rene G. Copeland, VP-Customer Rel.; Gary Geissler, VP-Engrg., Chippewa Falls; Karalyn Harrington, VP-Hum. Res.; Yoshikazu Hori, VP and Chm.-Cray Research Japan; Steven E. Snyder, Cont.; Debbie Sparkman, VP-Mfg.; John L. Sullivan, Gen. Counsel and Sec.; Patrick C. Tullo, Chief Info. Ofcr.; Anthony A. Vacca, VP-Tech. Silicon Graphics' regional operations here were formerly owned by Cray Research, a publicly traded company acquired in February 1996 for $736 million in cash and stock. Silicon Graphics operates software development, marketing support, and administrative facilities in the Minneapolis area. 870 employees (350 in Minnesota). SIC 3571, 7373. Founded in 1972. In March 2000 the Cray vector supercomputer business (500 of Silicon Graphics' 1,370 employees regionally) was sold to Seattle-based Tera Computer (renamed Cray Inc.) for cash, stock, and notes amounting to about $100 million. The remaining Cray Research operations are still owned by Silicon Graphics Inc. (NYSE: SGI), Mountain View, Calif.

J.R. Simplot Inc. 3630 Gateway Dr., Grand Forks, ND 58203. Tel: 701/746-6431; Fax: 701/780-7882. Arlin Hagen, Plant Mgr. J.R. Simplot processes frozen potato products. 538 employees. SIC 2037. Founded in 1966. Division of J.R. Simplot Co., Boise, Idaho.

Simpson Electric Company P.O. Box 99, Lac du Flambeau, WI 54538. Tel: 715/588-3311; Fax: 715/588-3326; Web site: http://www.simpsonelectric.com. Thomas Maulson, Chm.; Edward Herter, Pres. and CEO; Donald Anderson, VP. Simpson Electric manufactures electrical measuring instruments and electronic test equipment. 219 employees (2 part-time). SIC 3825. Division of Simpson Electric Co., Elgin, Ill.

SIMS Deltec Inc. 1265 Grey Fox Rd., Arden Hills, MN 55112. Tel: 651/633-2556; Fax: 651/628-7135. James Stitt, Pres.; Betty Potasnak, VP-Hum. Res.; Karen Linnard, VP-Fin. Annual revenue $150 million. SIMS Deltec (Deltec) develops, manufactures, and markets implantable venous access systems (PORT-A-CATH) and computerized ambulatory drug delivery (CADD) pumps, which facilitate the intravenous delivery of medications. These products are used in chemotherapy; pain-management therapies; antibiotic therapies, including treatments related to AIDS; and total parenteral nutrition, for patients who are unable to digest food. Principal markets are hospitals and alternative-care settings worldwide. The company was acquired in July 1994 from previous parent Pharmacia AB of Sweden. 452 employees. SIC 3823, 3841. Founded in 1986. In December 1999 the company signed an agreement to become the exclusive distributor for two pole-mounted infusion pumps manufactured by SIGMA International, Medina, N.Y. In January 2000 Deltec introduced the P.A.S. PORT Elite implantable access system, a new peripherally inserted central venous access system for delivery of chemotherapeutic drugs, antibiotics, pain medications, nutritional solutions, and other intravenous therapies. In February the company was awarded a contract by Child Health Corp. of America to provide ambulatory infusion and telecommunication products to CHCA members serving the alternate-site market. In March Deltecannounced a new line of Winged Infusion Set needle systems for accessing implantable ports for infusion therapy. The new PORT-A-CATH Winged Infusion Sets are non-coring, non-siliconized, natural rubber latex-free to reduce potential allergic reactions and include TOTM-plasticized tubing allowing compatibility with a wider variety of medications. In May Consorta Catholic Resource Partners awarded Deltec a contract to provide ambulatory pain management products to all Consorta facilities (more than 400 acute-care and long-term care facilities in 35 states). In July Deltec announced the availability of a new line of PICC (peripherally inserted central catheter) and Midline catheters. The new CliniCath PolyFlow catheters are made of polyurethane, which allows a small outer diameter for less vessel trauma and a large inner diameter providing optimal flow rates for a wide variety of short- and long-term I.V. infusion therapies. Polyurethane catheters are also firm when outside the body for ease of insertion, and soft at body temperature to minimize stenosis, erosion, and vessel damage. In August Deltec announced availability of a new plastic central venous access system for cost-effective delivery of chemotherapeutic drugs, antibiotics, pain medications, nutritional solutions, and other intravenous therapies. In October the company launched the CADD-Prizm PCS II ambulatory infusion pump, a pain-control system for patients in the hospital setting. Deltec was awarded a 4.5-year contract with Novation to provide ambulatory infusion pumps and accessories to University HealthSystem Consortium hospital members and affiliates. SIMS Deltec is an operating company of the Smiths Industries Medical Systems (SIMS) group, Keene, N.H.; owned by Smiths Industries plc, London. No. 36 CRM Foreign-Owned 100.

Sims Security 1751 W. County Rd. B, Roseville, MN 55113. Tel: 651/631-1981; Fax: 651/644-0567. Sims Security provides a full range of security services to businesses in office buildings, retail centers, industrial complexes, construction sites, residential facilities, and others. Additionally, the company provides special-event personnel, serving the Hubert H. Humphrey Metrodome, the University of Minnesota-Twin Cities, Williams Arena, and numerous other event venues. 1,300 employees. SIC 7381. Founded in 1958. Subsidiary of Borg-Warner Protective Securities Corp. Parsippany, N.J.; owned by Borg-Warner Security Corp. (NYSE: BOR), Chicago.

Sioux Falls Newspapers Inc./Argus Leader P.O. Box 5034, Sioux Falls, SD 57117. Tel: 605/331-2200; Fax: 605/331-2260. Arnold Garson, Pres. and Publisher. Sioux Falls Newspapers publishes a daily newspaper, The Argus Leader, with circulations of 52,500 daily and 76,000 Sunday. It also publishes a total market-coverage product, Shopping Leader. 300 employees. SIC 2711, 2741, 2759. Founded in 1881. Owned by Gannett Co. Inc. (NYSE: GCI), Arlington, Va.

Smurfit—Stone Container
50 37th Ave. N.E., Columbia Heights, MN 55421. Tel: 763/789-2485; Fax: 763/782-4260. Bill Kotrba, Gen. Mgr.; Robert Giefer, Sls. Mgr.; Dave Mortensen, Prod. Mgr.; Dick Voit, Cont. Smurfit—Stone Container/Minneapolis manufactures corrugated shipping containers. 164 employees (160 in Minnesota). SIC 2675. Founded in 1955.

100 E. Benson Rd., Sioux Falls, SD 57104. Tel: 605/336-0975; Fax: 605/336-6839. Larry Stauffacher, Gen. Mgr.; John Monahan, Plant Mgr.; Ed Anstine, Sls. Mgr.; Tim Ruppert, Cont. Smurfit—Stone Container/Sioux Falls manufactures corrugated shipping containers. 159 employees. SIC 2653. Founded in 1954.

3075 Long Lake Rd., Roseville, MN 55113. Tel: 651/636-1220; Fax: 651/636-3201. David W. Halper, Gen. Mgr.-Corrugated Container. Smurfit—Stone Container/St. Paul manufactures corrugated cartons. 320 employees. SIC 2653, 2671. Founded in 1976.

One Superior Way, Ontonagon, MI 49953. Tel: 906/884-7100; Fax: 906/884-7154; Web site: http://www.ontonagonmill.com. Ron Howard, Gen. Mgr. Smurfit—Stone Container/Ontonagon manufactures corrugating medium. 263 employees. SIC 2653. Founded in 1925.

655 41st Ave. N., St. Cloud, MN 56303. Tel: 320/252-3660; Fax: 320/252-7742. Bill Kotrba, Gen. Mgr.; Gary Griggs, Sls. Mgr.; Larry Corbin, Plant Mgr.; Anne Oberman, Cont. Smurfit—Stone Container/St. Cloud manufactures corrugated shipping containers. 188 employees. SIC 2653. Founded in 1960.

1050 N. Kent St., St. Paul, MN 55117. Tel: 651/488-2551; Fax: 651/487-4473. Walter D. Clapp, Gen. Mgr. Smurfit—Stone Container/St. Paul manufactures folding cartons. 150 employees. SIC 2657. Founded in 1950.

All divisions owned by Smurfit—Stone Container Corp. (Nasdaq: SSCC), Chicago. No. 72 CRM Foreign-Owned 100.

Snappy Air Distribution Products 1011 11th Ave. S.E., Detroit Lakes, MN 56501. Tel: 218/847-9258; Fax: 218/847-6322. Paul Schornack, Pres. Snappy Air Distribution Products Division manufactures galvanized warm-air fittings for the heating and air-conditioning industry. 210 employees. SIC 3444, 3541. Founded in 1954. Owned by Standex International Corp. (NYSE: SXI), Salem, N.H.

Snyder Drug Stores Inc. 14525 Highway 7, Minnetonka, MN 55345. Tel: 952/935-5441; Fax: 952/936-2512. Gordon Barker, CEO; Howard Watkins, GVP-Store Op.; John Greer, SVP-Admin.; Barb Miller, SVP-Op.; Bill Wilson, SVP-Mktg.; Jerry Edwards, VP-Pharmacy; Philip D. Perkins, VP-Mktg.; John H. Stubstad, VP-Info. Svs.; William White, VP and CFO. Snyder's operates 63 company-owned and 80 independent drug stores in six states centered in the Twin Cities area. In May 1999 Snyder Drug Stores agreed to be acquired by a $544 million-revenue, Canada-based company—one with substantial drug store chain holdings throughout Canada, but making its first foray into the United States. Snyder's was to retain its corporate name, its Minnesota headquarters, and its 1,600 Minnesota employees. A definitive agreement was signed in July. After regulatory approval, the deal closed Oct. 12. 1,600 employees (in Minnesota). SIC 5912. Founded in 1928. In March 2000 Snyder acquired Delano Snyder Drug Store, Delano, Minn. In May Snyder joined the redtagbiz.com Internet business-to-business wholesale marketplace. In August Snyder acquired Seymour Pharmacy, St. Paul, and combined it with a Snyder's store in nearby Hillcrest Center. Now owned by The Katz Group, Edmonton, Alberta. No. 91 CRM Employer 100. No. 7 CRM Foreign-Owned 100.

Sodexho Marriott Services 2 Appletree Square, Suite 245, Bloomington, MN 55425. Tel: 952/851-9317; Fax: 952/851-9304. Russ Kaegebein, VP-Op. Sodexho Marriott provides management services to companies that operate executive dining rooms, restaurants, and cafeterias. 450 employees (in Minnesota). SIC 8741. Founded in 1927. Division of Sodexho Marriott Services (NYSE: SDH), Washington, D.C.

Soft Link Inc. 2375 Ariel St. N., Maplewood, MN 55109. Tel: 651/776-7963; ; Web site: http://www.softlinkinc.com. Gretchen Artig-Swomley, CEO; Kellie Gunn, VP-Hum. Res.; Susan Griffith, VP-Sls.; Michelle Meer, Cont. Annual revenue $32.4 million. Soft Link is an international full-service software consulting firm specializing in human resources, financial, manufacturing, and student administration applications. Industry partnerships include PeopleSoft, Ultimate Software, Sun-NetScape Alliance, Siebel Systems Inc., Concur Technologies, Seagate Software, Lawson Software and Global Knowledge Network-OnDemand. 175 employees. SIC 7379. Founded in 1992. Wholly owned subsidiary of Interliant Inc. (Nasdaq: INIT), Purchase, N.Y.

Solvay Pharmaceuticals Inc. 210 Main St. W., Baudette, MN 56623. Tel: 218/634-3500; Fax: 218/634-3540; Web site: http://www.solvay.com. Kevin Miodonski, Gen. Mgr.; Joseph Brucianni, Dir.-QX/QC. Solvay Pharmaceuticals Inc. of Baudette, Minn., is a research-based pharmaceuticals company active in the therapeutic areas of cardiology, women's health, gastroenterology, and mental health. 225 employees. SIC 2834, 2836, 2879. Founded in 1935. Solvay Pharmaceuticals Inc., Marietta, Ga., is a member of the worldwide Solvay Group of chemical and pharmaceutical companies, owned by Solvay S.A., Brussels. No. 58 CRM Foreign-Owned 100.

Spartech Corporation 480 Industrial Rd., Mankato, MN 56001. Tel: 507/345-4691; Fax: 507/345-4693. Ray Washington, Plant Mgr. Spartech Corp. extrudes rigid plastic sheeting and roll stock for food packaging, agriculture, manufacturing, and the medical and recreation industries. Primary materials used: styrene and PET. 100 employees. SIC 3081. Founded in 1964. Subsidiary of Spartech Corp. (NYSE: SEH), Clayton, Mo.

Spherion Inc. 7900 Xerxes Ave. S., Bloomington, MN 55431. Tel: 952/832-5220; Fax: 952/832-5320; Web site: http://www.spherion.com. Sharon Wienandt, Group VP; Julia Zimmer, Integration Dir.; Mike Weiner, Managing Dir.; Mary McKay, Recruiter; Nadine Friederichs, Implementations Mgr. Annual revenue $30.3 million. Spherion is a human capital management organization that builds talent, technology, and outsourcing solutions to enhance workforce performance. Its business groups include technology (business and infrastructure solutions), human capital consulting (Saratoga Institute, talent solutions), assessment, executive search, professional recruiting, legal, staffing, and outsourcing (business processes, workforce management). A St. Louis Park-based Spherion unit is a computer consulting firm that provides end-to-end e-business solutions, information technology (IT) systems integration, and eSQSM performance to clients such as Jostens and Lutheran Brotherhood. 300 employees. SIC 7363. Owned by Spherion (NYSE: SFN), Fort Lauderdale, Fla.

Sprint Corporation 3800 W. 80th St., Suite 300, Bloomington, MN 55431. Tel: 952/896-3500; Fax: 952/896-3528. James P. Holt, Regional Dir.; Maureen Fahey, Branch Mgr.; Don Libby, Branch Mgr.; Michael Newman, Branch Customer Support Mgr.; Mike Walter, Branch Customer Support Mgr. Sprint's Bloomington operation offers long-distance telephone systems to national and mid-market clients. 80 employees. SIC 4813. Owned by Sprint Corp. (NYSE: FON), Westwood, Kan.

Sprint Corporation 166 W. Third St., Winona, MN 55987. Tel: 507/454-8386; Fax: 507/453-4392. Don Walz, Dir.-Winona Op. Center. Sprint's Winona operation, known as Hospitality Market Group, establishes phone systems for hotels, motels, colleges, and universities nationwide. 365 employees (in Minnesota). SIC 4813. Founded in 1899. Owned by Sprint Corp. (NYSE: FON), Westwood, Kan.

Sprint/United Telephone—Minnesota 343 E. 82nd St., Chaska, MN 55318. Tel: 952/448-8121; Fax: 952/221-0264. Victor E. Dobras, Dir.-Gov't/Public Affairs; Patrick Stutzman, Dir.-Op. Sprint/United Telephone—Minnesota provides telephone service to 81 communities in Minnesota (more than 137,000 access lines). It offers a full range of telephone services to residential and business customers. 300 employees (in Minnesota). SIC 4813. Owned by Sprint Corp. (NYSE: FON), Westwood, Kan.

Standard Register Company 5775 Wayzata Blvd., Minneapolis, MN 55416. Tel: 612/591-1404; Fax: 612/591-7713; Web site: http://www.stdreg.com. T.A. Dobratz, Regional Sls. Mgr. Standard Register produces business forms, forms-handling equipment, pressure-sensitive labels, data systems, check-protecting equipment, encoding equipment, financial equipment, print on demand solutions, and forms automation. District sales offices are located in St. Paul and Minneapolis; printing and distribution facilities in Eagan, Minn. Communicolor, the direct-response marketing division, is located in Bloomington, Minn. 83 employees (in Minnesota). SIC 2761, 7331, 7374. Founded in 1912. Division of The Standard Register Co. (NYSE: SR), Dayton, Ohio.

The Star Tribune Company 425 Portland Ave. S., Minneapolis, MN 55488. Tel: 612/673-4000; Fax: 612/673-7122; Web site: http://www.startribune.com/company. John R. Schueler, Publisher and Pres.; Tim McGuire, Editor and SVP; Susan Albright, Ed.-Editorial Pages; Steve Alexander, VP-Circulation; Craig Eiter, SVP-Fin.; Pam Fine, Managing Editor; Steve Hanson, VP and Chief Info. Ofcr.; Tom Hardie, VP-Mfg.; Pamela D. Henson, SVP-Mktg./Sls. Div.; Patricia L. (Patty) Jones, SVP-Admin.; Nancy Koo, VP-Hum. Res.; Randy Lebedoff, VP-Gen. Counsel; Franklin J. Parisi, SVP and Chief Comm. Officer; Paul Reese, SVP-Op.; Nick Rogosienski, VP-Interactive Media. The Star Tribune Co., an information and communications company serving the Twin Cities area of Minneapolis and St. Paul is a subsidiary of The McClatchy Company of Sacremento, Calif. Star Tribune produces the Star Tribune newspaper, the 16th-largest daily metropolitan newspaper in the nation (daily circulation 410,564 for the six-month period ended Sept. 30, 2000) and the 12th-largest metropolitan Sunday newspaper (circulation 674,346). The company also produces a variety of niche print, direct marketing, and electronic services products, including startribune.com. Star Tribune originated in 1935 when John Cowles acquired The Minneapolis Star. In March 1998 Star Tribune parent Cowles Media Co., Minneapolis, was sold for $1.4 billion. 2,436 employees (in Minnesota; 610 part-time). SIC 2711, 2721. Founded in 1867. In November 1999 startribune.com added a retail shopping center to its network. In January 2000 startribune.com was again selected as one of the nation's three best newspaper-sponsored online services by Editor & Publisher Interactive. In April Star Tribune announced plans to begin offering Post-it Notes advertising to its marketer customers. While most newspapers offering Post-it Notes advertising require their carriers to affix the Post-it Notes to their newspapers, Star Tribune was installing labeling equipment at its production facility that applies the Post-it Notes in the upper left-hand corner of the newspaper. In June dbusiness.com (http://www.dbusiness.com), the nation's leading local business-to-business news, content, and e-commerce destination, began providing breaking local business news to startribune.com's new "emerging-company news" channel under a new co-branded alliance. Publisher Schueler stepped away from a campaign for a new Minnesota Twins ballpark in downtown Minneapolis so as not to damage the newspaper's credibility. On Aug. 28, startribune.com set a new single-day record for page views per day: more than 1 million. Sept. 30: The Star Tribune achieved its fifth-consecutive circulation increase according to numbers released by the Audit Bureau of Circulation. Six-month results show Star Tribune circulation up 0.1 percent on both Sunday and daily (Thurs.-Sat.) compared to the same period last year. Owned by McClatchy Newspapers Inc. (NYSE: MNI), Sacramento, Calif. No. 77 CRM Employer 100.

Starmark Inc. 700 E. 48th St. N., Sioux Falls, SD 57104. Tel: 605/335-8600; Fax: 605/336-5566. Bob Goucher, Pres.; Emery Lee, Dir.-Fin.; Doug Chadwick, National Sls. Mgr. Starmark manufactures wood cabinets for kitchens, baths, and other rooms in single- and multifamily dwellings. The company has three plants: Starmark, for medium-priced products; Encore, for low-priced products; and a Lynchburg, Va., location that manufactures for both price ranges. 559 employees. SIC 2434. Founded in 1978. Owned by Masco Corp. (NYSE: MAS), Taylor, Mich.

State Farm Mutual Automobile Insurance Company 8500 State Farm Way, Woodbury, MN 55125. Tel: 651/578-4000; Fax: 651/578-4835. Doug Thompson, Regional VP; Donita Stuart, VP-Op. State Farm Mutual Automobile Insurance Co. provides insurance services through agents and brokers. 1,432 employees (in Minnesota). SIC 6311, 6331. In June 2000 State Farm announced plans to return $13.4 million in premium paid by its Minnesota auto insurance policyholders—as part of a $1 billion policyholder dividends program approved by the State Farm board of directors. Owned by State Farm Mutual Automobile Insurance Co., Bloomington, Ill.

Stearns Inc. 1100 Stearns Dr., Sauk Rapids, MN 56379. Tel: 320/252-1642; Fax: 320/252-4425. David G. Cook, Pres.; Paul Ebnet, VP-Sls./Mktg.; Mike Krmpotich, VP-Fin.; Joel Lindmeier, VP-Mfg. Annual revenue $72 million. Stearns manufactures recreational and industrial water safety products and outdoor products. Formerly SMCA Inc. 700 employees (in Minnesota). SIC 3089. Founded in 1948. Owned by K2 Inc. (NYSE: KTO), Los Angeles.

Stella Foods 14449 S.D. Highway 109, Big Stone City, SD 57216. Tel: 605/862-8131; Fax: 605/862-8413. Russ Thielke, Gen. Mgr. Stella Foods operates an age-processing plant for Italian cheese. 270 employees. SIC 2022. Founded in 1962. Subsidiary of Stella Foods, Green Bay, Wis.

Sterner Lighting Systems Inc. 7575 Corporate Way, Eden Prairie, MN 55344. Tel: 952/906-7300; Fax: 952/906-7338; Web site: http://www.sternerlighting.com. Mike Naylor, Gen. Mgr.; Joe Schermann, Mktg. Comm. Mgr. Sterner Lighting Systems designs, manufactures, both standard and custom-designed outdoor and indoor lighting equipment. It also designs, manufactures, precision custom floodlighting. 250 employees. SIC 3646. Founded in 1961. Now owned by Hubbell Lighting, Inc. (NYSE: HUBA), Orange, Conn.

StorageTek 7600 Boone Ave. N., Brooklyn Park, MN 55428. Tel: 763/424-4888; Fax: 763/424-1733; Web site: http://www.storagetek.com. Joan Wrabetz, Gen. Mgr.; Greg Dahl, VP-Sls./Mktg.; Robert Munsey, VP-Hum. Res.; Bill Way, Dir.-Bus. Devel.; Erik Norlander, Dir.-Channel Mktg.; Mark Schrandt, Dir.-Engrg. StorageTek provides network storage. The company's strategy is to provide "Open Intelligent and Integrated" programs that combine storage products, storage management software, and storage services. The former publicly traded Network Systems Corp. was acquired in March 1995 for $170 million in stock. 250 employees (in Minnesota). SIC 3577. Founded in 1974. In October 2000 the company's Colorado parent sued Cisco Systems Inc., San Jose, Calif., alleging alleging that recent Cisco acquisition and StorageTek competitor NuSpeed Internet Systems, Maple Grove, Minn., had unfairly targeted StorageTek for recruiting purposes. Now a division of Storage Technology Corp. (NYSE: STK), Louisville, Colo.

Stork Twin City Testing 662 Cromwell Ave., St. Paul, MN 55114. Tel: 651/645-3601; Fax: 651/659-7348. James Haney, Pres.; Gregg Jandro, VP-MN District. Stork Twin City Testing provides independent scientific and engineering analysis of the environment—in addition to construction and products—from 28 offices in Minnesota, Iowa, Wisconsin, North Dakota, South Dakota, Nebraska, Illinois, Kansas, and Missouri. Formerly known as Twin City Testing Corp. 1,000 employees. SIC 8711, 8731, 8734. Founded in 1938. Acquired in May 1995 by Maxim Technologies Inc., Dallas.

Strongwell, Chatfield Division 1610 Highway 52 S., Chatfield, MN 55923. Tel: 507/867-3479; Fax: 507/867-4031; Web site: http://www.strongwell.com. Jeff Tickle, Gen. Mgr.; Sue Hollermann, Div. Cont. Annual revenue $24 million. Strongwell manufactures fiber-reinforced composite materials. 192 employees (in Minnesota). SIC 3089. Founded in 1972. Division of Strongwell, Bristol, Va.

Strout Plastics Division 9611 James Ave. S., Bloomington, MN 55431. Tel: 952/881-8673; Fax: 952/881-3031; Web site: http://www.stroutplastics.com. Thomas S. Everett, VP and Gen. Mgr.; Paul Kirst, CFO; Thomas P. O'Malley, National Sls. Mgr. Annual revenue $20 million. Strout Plastics manufactures flexible packaging, printed and plain plastic bags, construction film, tubing, and related products. 150 employees (in Minnesota). SIC 3081, 3089. Founded in 1961. Owned by Jim Pattison Group, Vancouver, British Columbia. No. 72 CRM Foreign-Owned 100.

Sulzer Spine-Tech 7375 Bush Lake Rd., Edina, MN 55439. Tel: 952/832-5600; Fax: 952/830-3688. Paul R. Lunsford, Pres.; Don Kennedy, VP-Mktg.; Dan Mans, VP-Clinical/Regulation; Steve Griffith, VP-Research; Ross Longhini, VP-Product Devel.; Mike McCormick, VP-Sls.; Denny Thalhuber, VP-Fin.; Paul Owen, VP-Hum. Res.; Matt Murokski, VP-Op. Sulzer Spine-Tech designs, develops, manufactures, and sells implants and instruments for the surgical treatment of degenerative disc disease and other spinal conditions. The company's principal products are hollow, threaded cylindrical devices, made of a titanium alloy, that are surgically implanted in the disc space between two or three vertebrae to stablize the spine and facilitate a fusion. The company completed its initial public offering in June 1995. Publicly traded Spine-Tech Inc. agreed in December 1997 to a $595 million cash merger. 279 employees. SIC 3841, 3845. Founded in 1988. Business unit of Sulzer Orthopedics, a division of Sulzer Ltd., Winterthur, Switzerland. No. 53 CRM Foreign-Owned 100.

Sun Newspapers 10917 Valley View Rd., Eden Prairie, MN 55377. Tel: 952/829-0797; Fax: 952/392-6868; Web site: http://www.mnsun.com. Frank Chilinski, Pres. and Publisher; Yvonne Klinnert, Exec. Editor; Richard Hendrickson, CFO; Pam Dahl, Hum. Res. Sun Newspapers is a newspaper publisher. Sun-Sailor, Sun-Current, and Sun-Post are among the total of 30 community weeklies it publishes in the Twin Cities area. The company publishes the Stillwater Gazette. Headquartered in Eden Prairie, the company also has publishing offices in Bloomington, Minnetonka, Burnsville, Robbinsdale, Osseo, Delano, and St. Michael, Minn. In July 1998 Minnesota Sun Publications was acquired by two newspaper veterans who had just formed Lionheart Newspapers. In December 1998 Minnesota Sun became Sun Newspapers. 250 employees (in Minnesota). SIC 2711. Owned by Lionheart Newspapers Inc., Fort Worth, Texas.

Sungard Securities Systems Inc. 601 Second Ave. S., Hopkins, MN 55343. Tel: 952/935-3300; Fax: 952/936-8888; Web site: http://www.sungardss.com. Conde Cristobel, COO-SDS; Greg Pond, Group CEO-Securities/Treasury; Leo Belanger, Pres.-SSS; Joseph Slattery, VP-Fin. and CFO-SFS; Gus Kirn, VP-Op./Cust. Svc.-SSS; Joyce LaMere, VP-Hum. Res., SFS; Colleen S. Nelsen, VP-Mktg., SSS; Richard Kohout, VP-Sys./Tech.; Herb Hesch, VP-Sys. Devel. Sungard Securities Systems provides investment accounting and portfolio management computer services and software to the financial services industry, principally bank capital markets treasury departments. 175 employees (150 in Minnesota). SIC 7389. Founded in 1968. Subsidiary of Sungard Data Systems Inc. (NYSE: SDS), Wayne, Pa.

Super Mom's Kitchen 625 Second St., St. Paul Park, MN 55071. Tel: 651/459-2253; Fax: 651/459-0804. Peter W. Nowicki, Bakery Op. Mgr.; Thomas W. Haertl, Commissary Op. Mgr.; Douglas Muchow, Gen. Mgr. Super Mom's Kitchen services 160 SuperAmerica stores in Minnesota with bakery goods and sandwiches. 230 employees. SIC 2051, 5145, 5812. Founded in 1981. Division of SuperAmerica Inc., Bloomington, Minn.; owned by a joint venture between USX-Marathon Group, Pittsburgh, and Ashland Inc. (Nasdaq: ASND), Ashland, Ky.

Superior Products 510 W. County Rd. D, New Brighton, MN 55112. Tel: 651/636-1110; Fax: 651/636-3671. Patrick J. Peyton, CEO; Robert Kurek, Pres. and COO; James Cox, EVP-Sls.; Steve Tuomie, VP and CFO. Superior Products is a wholesale distributor of bar and restaurant equipment and supplies. A leader in catalog marketing, the company serves its customer base of 160,000 foodservice operators from a nationwide network of facilities: Anaheim and San Jose, Calif.; Orlando, Fla.; Hartford, Conn.; Reno, Nev.; Charlotte, N.C.; Boston, Baltimore, St. Louis, Dallas, Atlanta, Chicago, Fort Worth, and Philadelphia. 260 employees. SIC 5046. Founded in 1937. Now owned by U.S. Foodservice (NYSE: UFS), Columbia, Md.

Sweets Group 4530 W. 77th St., Suite 350, Edina, MN 55435. Tel: 952/832-7887; Fax: 952/832-7908. Peggy Hausler, District Mgr. Sweets Group is a publisher of construction product information catalogs. 200 employees (2 in Minnesota). SIC 2731. Founded in 1906. Owned by The McGraw-Hill Cos. Inc. (NYSE: MHP), New York.

Swift & Company Highway 60 Northeast, P.O. Box 369, Worthington, MN 56187. Tel: 507/372-2121; Fax: 507/372-4611. Gerald Wachter, Plant Mgr. Swift & Co. of Worthington, formerly Sipco Monfort Pork Division, is a fresh-meat company that slaughters pork. 1,600 employees (in Minnesota). SIC 2011. Founded in 1982. Swift & Co., Greeley, Colo., is owned by ConAgra Inc. (NYSE: CAG), Omaha, Neb.

Syntegra (USA) Inc. 4201 Lexington Ave. N., Arden Hills, MN 55126. Tel: 651/415-2999; Fax: 651/415-4891; Web site: http://www.syntegra.com. James E. Ousley, Chm.; Michael G. Eleftheriou, Pres.-System Integration Svs.; David Folsom, Pres.-eBusiness solutions. Annual revenue $1 billion. Syntegra (USA), the former Control Data Systems, is a global eBusiness systems integration company dedicated to helping organizations develop the enterprise integration systems required to create, transmit, access, and manage business information. The company is focused on the architecture, implementation, and lifetime support of electronic commerce, product design, and product information solutions. In September 1997 Control Data Systems was acquired by New York investment firm Welsh, Carson, Anderson & Stowe for $288.7 million. On June 30, 1999, the company was again sold, this time for $340 million, in a deal that joined Control Data's expertise on the Internet and e-commerce side to its new parent's expertise on the network and communication side. 900 employees (in Minnesota). SIC 7373. Founded in 1992. In 1999 Syntegra processed more than 250 million e-mail messages for large, multinational corporations, delivering 98.2 percent of those messages to destinations around the world in less than a minute. In March 2000 the company previewed Keep-Tabs, the first complete, Web-based, platform-independent service that combines technical capabilities with legal support services to help companies and employees protect themselves against the increasing problems and liability associated with e-mail misuse. Syntegra designed the system driving a new e-mail service for the 5.5 million residents of Taiwan's two largest cities, Taipei and Kaoshiung. Syntegra and Voice & Data Systems Inc., a provider of networked unified messaging systems, announced the availability of unified messaging solutions and managed services that increase productivity by giving business users far greater control over the flood of messages they receive every day. In April Keep-Tabs was introduced as the first e-mail reporting and tracking service to help organizations address the problem of office e-mail abuse. (The U.S. Department of Justice was offered free use of Keep-Tabs to assist in the analysis and investigation of White House e-mail usage.) Syntegra also released Directory Sentinel, the first software package on the market to protect directory content from unauthorized access; and Web Personal Assistant, which provides access to full-service e-mail, shared and private folders, directory services, message filters, and password update capabilities for users. Syntegra's new Directory Sentinel security software package won a Best of Show Award at EMA 2000, the Electronic Messaging Association's annual conference and exposition. In May customers of Syntegra's worldwide messaging solutions were protected from the latest e-mail virus threat, the ILOVEYOU virus, within moments of its recognition. In August Syntegra signed an agreement with America's Second Harvest, the nation's largest domestic hunger relief organization, to host e-mailboxes and provide e-mail virus protection services for more than 200 food banks and food-rescue organizations across the United States and Puerto Rico. Lightning Rod Software Inc. (Nasdaq: LROD), a leading provider of real-time customer interaction solutions for e-businesses, agreed to allow Syntegra to sell the LROD Interaction Manager product suite to its customers. In October a worldwide partnership with Baltimore Technologies (Nasdaq: BALT; London: BLM), a worldwide leader in eSecurity solutions, made Syntegra an official integrator of Baltimore's award-winning Public Key Infrastructure technology and full-strength cryptography tools, which enable customers to conduct trusted, authenticated e-business. Owned since Sept. 1, 1999, by Syntegra, the global consulting and information systems business of British Telecommunications plc, London. No. 17 CRM Foreign-Owned 100.

Sysco Food Services of Minnesota Inc. 2400 County Rd. J, Mounds View, MN 55112. Tel: 612/757-9000; Fax: 612/785-7385. Philip J. Seipp, Pres. and CEO; Timothy K. Hogan, EVP; Debra A. Hamernick, SVP; Ann Marie Walenta, Dir.-Fin. Sysco Food Services is a wholesale foodservice distributor to the institutional market. Former names: New York Tea; Continental Minnesota. 660 employees (645 in Minnesota). SIC 5141. Founded in 1882. Owned by Sysco Corp. (NYSE: SYY), Houston.

TCR Corporation 1600 67th Ave. N., P.O. Box 29068, Brooklyn Center, MN 55430. Tel: 763/560-2200; Fax: 763/561-0949. John Funk, Pres. TCR Corp. manufactures metal component parts by cold forging and machining. Products include externally threaded specialty fastening devices for the automotive, heavy vehicle, marine, and industrial markets. 200 employees (in Minnesota). SIC 3499. Founded in 1963. Owned by TransTechnology Corp. (NYSE: TT), Liberty Corner, N.Y.

TKI Consulting 1000 Shelard Pkwy., Suite 360, St. Louis Park, MN 55426. Tel: 952/545-0980. Cindy Neis, Pres. TKI Consulting is an IT consulting firm specializing in e-commerce, Internet, and client server business solutions. TKI provides full lifecycle software development services to mid-sized companies in Minnesota and nationally. TKI serves as a Microsoft Certified Solutions Provider, Consulting Partner for Progress, WebSpeed, Actuate, and CorVu, and as a complementary service provider for QAD. In August 1999 the company entered into a definitive agreement to sell its assets for $7.2 million. 75 employees (in Minnesota). SIC 7371, 7379. Founded in 1994. Now operating as a wholly owned subsidiary of Hall, Kinion & Associates Inc. (Nasdaq: HAKI), San Francisco.

TL Systems Corporation 8700 Wyoming Ave. N, Brooklyn Park, MN 55445. Tel: 763/424-4700; Fax: 763/493-6711; Web site: http://www.bosch.de/vmtl/etl_indx.htm. Don DeMorett, Pres.; John Kirk, VP-Liq. Pharm.; Jack Lysfjord, VP-Tech.; Tom McDaniel, VP-Op.; Karen Angst, Dir.-Hum. Res.; Stefan Tolle, VP-Dry Pharm.; Jack Tsahalis, Cont. TL Systems manufactures materials-handling and packaging machinery for the pharmaceutical and related industries. 170 employees (150 in Minnesota). SIC 3565, 3569. Founded in 1970. Acquired in 1995 by Robert Bosch Corp., Broadview, Ill. Bosch is owned by Robert Bosch GmbH, Stuttgart, Germany. No. 69 CRM Foreign-Owned 100.

TMP Worldwide Olympic Financial Center, 7825 Washington Ave. S., #800, Eden Prairie, MN 55439. Tel: 952/903-4600; Fax: 952/903-4680; Web site: http://www.tmp.com. Peri Bergh, VP and Gen. Mgr.; Myles Bergh, Dir.-Interactive; Beckey Mowers, Sls. Mgr.; Carrie Young, Dir.-Client Svs.; Nickey Larson, Dir.-Client Svs. TMP Worldwide's Eden Prairie office is part of the largest Yellow Pages, recruitment, and interactive advertising agency in the world. 77 employees (in Minnesota). SIC 7311. Founded in 1967. Subsidiary of TMP Worldwide Inc., New York.

TRW 2604 Highway 20 N., Jamestown, ND 58401. Tel: 701/252-6250; Fax: 701/251-1046. James A. Boyd, Business Devel. Mgr. TRW's Jamestown operations manufacture commercial aerospace products, including cargo systems and aerostructures. 500 employees. SIC 3728. Founded in 1970. Owned by Lucas Varity (U.K.), Solihull, U.K.

TRW Automotive Electronics Body Control Systems 5676 Industrial Park Rd., Winona, MN 55987. Tel: 507/457-3750; Fax: 507/454-7115. Richard Angell, Dir.-Hum. Res.; Greg Hagen, Dir.-Op.; Lynn Honsey, Gen. Mgr.; Gordon Spaete, VP-Engrg./Quality; Terry Westkey, Dir.-Program Mgmt. TRW-Body Control Systems is a custom contract manufacturer of mechanical, electromechanical, and electronic assemblies and subassemblies. 1,864 employees (1,346 in Minnesota). SIC 3469, 3569, 3679. Founded in 1948. Owned by TRW Inc. (NYSE: TRW), Cleveland.

Telespectrum Worldwide Inc. 2001 W. Lincoln Ave., Fergus Falls, MN 56537. Tel: 218/739-4000; Fax: 218/736-3900. Pete Talbott, CEO; Jim Carroll, Pres. Telespectrum Worldwide, formerly Telnet Systems, provides outbound telemarketing services—including sales, sales-lead generation, market research, and fundraising—for medium- to large-size businesses, from locations in Fergus Falls, Duluth, and Bemidji, Minn. 650 employees (in Minnesota; 110 part-time). SIC 7389, 7389. Founded in 1986. Acquired in April 1997 by Telespectrum Worldwide Inc., King of Prussia, Pa.

Temple Inland Mortgage Corporation 3001 Metro Dr., Suite 400, Bloomington, MN 55425. Tel: 952/204-2600; Fax: 952/204-2516. Richard M. Hebl, SVP; Jeffrey Lipes, SVP-National Lending; Lawrence Spera, SVP-Secondary Mktg.; Mike Woodfin, SVP and Mgr.-ITS; Douglas M. Wynn, SVP and CFO; Deanne S. Heise, VP and Cont. Temple Inland Mortgage Corporation originates, acquires, sells, and services single-unit residential mortgage loans. Knutson originates more than $1 billion in residential mortgages annually, and it services $7.5 billion. 329 employees (206 in Minnesota). SIC 6162. Founded in 1954. Acquired in June 1997 by Temple-Inland Mortgage Corp., Austin, Texas, sub. Guaranty Federal Bank fsb, sub. Temple-Inland Inc. (NYSE: TIN), Diboll, Texas.

REG

Tension Envelope Corporation 5401 Smetana Dr., Minnetonka, MN 55343. Tel: 952/935-3131; Fax: 952/935-0233. Henk Boon Jr., Gen. Mgr. Tension Envelope manufactures all types of business, specialty, and packaging envelopes. 110 employees. SIC 2677. Founded in 1929. Division of Tension Envelope Corp., Kansas City, Mo.

Tetra Rex Inc. 451 Industrial Blvd., Minneapolis, MN 55413. Tel: 612/362-8500; Fax: 612/623-4212. Karl Theis, Pres. Tetra Rex is in the carton business. The company defines the carton specifications, manufactures equipment to fill and distribute the carton, and retains overall responsibility for the system's profitability. Previous names: Lincomatic Industries, Haskon/Hercules, Liquipak International Inc., Tetra Pak EquipUS Inc., and Tetra Rex Packaging Systems Inc. 220 employees (137 in Minnesota). SIC 3565. Founded in 1965. Owned through Alfa Laval Inc., Rosemont, Ill., by Tetra Laval Group, Lund, Sweden. No. 59 CRM Foreign-Owned 100.

Thermo King Corporation 314 W. 90th St., Bloomington, MN 55420. Tel: 952/887-2200; Fax: 952/887-2615. John (Sean) Kinsella, Pres. Thermo King manufactures transport refrigeration, air conditioning, and heating equipment for trailers, trucks, sea-going containers, buses, and rail cars. Minneapolis corporate headquarters is one of 15 plants serving 400 dealers worldwide. Other locations include Nebraska, Georgia, Alabama, and Puerto Rico; Brazil, Ireland, Spain, Germany, Denmark, Belgium, the Czech Republic, Hong Kong, and China. In September 1997 Westinghouse agreed to sell Thermo King for $2.56 billion. 5,000 employees. SIC 3433, 3585.

Founded in 1937. In February 2000 the company agreed to acquire a majority stake (expected to be more than 60 percent) in Tokyo-based Zexel Corp.'s wholly owned refrigeration equipment subsidiary. In addition to the Japanese market, Thermo King was hoping to expand into Southeast Asia and China. The new owner is Ingersoll-Rand Co. (NYSE: IR), Woodcliff Lake, N.J.

Thermo Sentron Inc. 501 90th Ave. N.W., Coon Rapids, MN 55433. Tel: 763/783-2589; Fax: 763/783-2680; Web site: http://www.thermo.com/subsid/tsr.html. Lewis J. Ribich, Pres. and CEO; Theo Melas-Kyriazi, CFO; Anne Pol, SVP-Hum. Res.; Daniel Walsh, VP-Fin.; Seth H. Hoogasian, Gen. Counsel; Kenneth J. Apicerno, Treas.; Sandra L. Lambert, Sec. Annual revenue $107.8 million (earnings $6.4 million). Thermo Sentron Inc., formerly Ramsey Technology Inc., designs, develops, manufactures, and sells high-speed precision weighing and inspection equipment for industrial production and packaging lines. The company's products are used to ensure that packaged goods contain the designated quantity of materials, to monitor inventories, to optimize production processes, and to certify quantities of goods in connection with the transfer of title. The company serves the packaged goods and bulk materials market. 200 employees (in Minnesota). SIC 3532, 3596, 3625, 3629. Founded in 1995. In January 2000 74.2 percent shareholder Thermedics Inc. (Amex: TMD), announced plans to make a cash tender offer for any and all of the outstanding shares of Thermo Sentron common stock at $15.50 per share. This action was part of a major reorganization plan under which ultimate parent Thermo Electron Corp. was spinning in, spinning off, and selling various businesses to focus solely on its core measurement and detection instruments business. In March, when Thermedics' ownership exceeded 90 percent (98.6 percent), it was able to acquire all remaining outstanding shares of Thermo Sentron common stock through a "short-form" merger—which does not require Thermo Sentron board or shareholder approval. This occurred on April 4. Owned by Thermo Electron Corp. (NYSE: TMO), Waltham, Mass. No. 88 CRM Public 200.

REG

Thermoform Plastics Inc. 4221 Otter Lake Rd., White Bear Lake, MN 55110. Tel: 651/426-7319; Fax: 651/426-8420. Dan Sweet, EVP; Chuck Dudas, Purch. Annual revenue $65 million. Thermoform Plastics manufactures single-sheet, twin-sheet, and pressure-form medium- and heavy-gauge, extruded sheet plastic (up to 120-inch by 168-inch) covers and enclosures for recreational, agricultural, and industrial markets; and medical material-handling trays and pallets. 425 employees (230 in Minnesota). SIC 3089. Founded in 1965. Owned by Wilbert Inc., Broadview, Ill.

Thermotech/Division of Menasha Corporation 1202 S. Fifth St., Hopkins, MN 55343. Tel: 952/933-9400; Fax: 952/933-9412; Web site: http://www.thermotech.com. John Bonham, Div. Pres. Annual revenue $70 million. Thermotech is a molder of custom thermoplastic and thermoset injection-molded plastic parts. 617 employees (421 in Minnesota). SIC 3089. Founded in 1952. Owned by Menasha Corp., Neenah, Wis.

Thomas & Betts Corporation Highway 63 North, Hager City, WI 54014. Tel: 715/792-2811; Fax: 715/792-5322. Jeff Boigenzahn, Plant Mgr. Thomas & Betts Corp. manufactures steel transmission poles for high-voltage power lines. 195 employees (80 in Minnesota). SIC 3441. Founded in 1920. Owned by Thomas & Betts Corp. (NYSE: TNB), Memphis, Tenn.

Ticona Celstran Inc. 4610 Theurer Blvd., Winona, MN 55987. Tel: 507/454-4150; Fax: 507/457-4040; Web site: http://www.polymercomposites.com. E. Dean Wendler, Site Mgr.; Paul D. Zakashefski, Product Mgr.; Randy Skarlupka, Tech. Mgr.; Beth Ede, Hum. Res. Mgr. Ticona Celstran, formerly Polymer Composites, manufactures long-fiber reinforced thermoplastics with a primary focus on metal replacement. The company has licensees in Japan and a European operation in Kelsterbach, Germany. 80 employees (in Minnesota). SIC 3087. Founded in 1981. Owned through Hoechst Celanese Corp., Somerville, N.J., by Hoechst AG, Frankfurt, Germany. No. 97 CRM Foreign-Owned 100.

Timber Lodge Steakhouse Inc. 4021 Vernon Ave. S., St. Louis Park, MN 55416. Tel: 952/929-9353; Fax: 952/929-5658. Dermot F. Rowland, Chm., CEO, and Sec.; Peter S. Bedzyk, Pres. and COO. Timber Lodge Steakhouse Inc. operates steakhouse restaurants in the Twin Cities, Owatonna, and Duluth, Minn.; Sioux Falls, S.D.; Fargo, N.D.; Green Bay and Madison, Wis.; Arizona; Utah; and Niagara Falls, N.Y. Once publicly traded. 1,750 employees (780 in Minnesota; 900 part-time). SIC 5812. Founded in 1989. The company was planning to have 26 locations in seven states by year-end 2000. The four newest locations were in Owatonna, Minn.; Stillwater, Minn.; Maple Grove, Minn.; and Fargo, N.D. "We're experiencing some rapid growth right now, jumping from 22 to 26 restaurants in less than three months," said President Bedzyk in October. "We're opening three new restaurants in Minnesota this fall, bringing our total here to 15. Plus, we found ourselves with a great opportunity in Fargo that we didn't want to pass up. This will be our first restaurant in North Dakota." Owned since September 1998 by Santa Barbara Restaurant Group, Santa Barbara, Calif.

Timber Products Michigan M-28 East, P.O. Box 338, Munising, MI 49862. Tel: 906/452-6221; Fax: 906/452-6361. James Ellisor, Cont.; Bruce Strand, Hum. Res. Mgr.; Mike Larsen, Op. Mgr. Timber Products Michigan produces hardwood lumber and hardwood rotary face veneer. 290 employees. SIC 2411, 2429, 2435. Founded in 1961. Owned by The Timber Products Group, Springfield, Ore.

Time Warner Cable 801 Plymouth Ave. N., Minneapolis, MN 55411. Tel: 612/522-5200; Fax: 612/521-7626. David Auger, Div. Pres.; Mark Hammerstrom, VP-Mktg./Sls.; Matt Haviland, VP-Engrg./Tech. Svs.; Monica Jeffries, VP-Fin.; Bob Lindberg, VP-Admin.; Kim Roden, VP-Public Affairs/Customer Serv.; Roger Werner, VP-Ad Sls. Time Warner Cable, formerly Paragon Cable, supplies information, entertainment, and educational cable television services to 200,000 customers in Minneapolis, several southern and western suburbs, and other areas throughout Minnesota. 450 employees (in Minnesota; 20 part-time). SIC 4841. Founded in 1980. In October 1999 the company announced plans for a $28 million upgrade, to begin in second quarter 2000, that was to bring high-speed Internet service ("RoadRunner Service"), more TV channels, digital TV, better pictures, and increased system reliability to its Minneapolis cable TV subscribers. In November Time Warner Cable reduced subscriber fees for its RoadRunner High Speed Online Internet service, including a $39.95 monthly rate for all subscribers. The Minnesota division also added new services for online customers, including a package to support home networking. Division of Time Warner Inc. (NYSE: TWX), New York.

Timesavers Inc. 5270 Hanson Court, Crystal, MN 55429. Tel: 763/537-3611; Fax: 763/537-9247. Raymond S. Vold, Pres. Annual revenue $62 million. Timesavers manufactures wide-belt sanding and coated abrasive machining systems, metal deburring and finishing machines. 445 employees (240 in Minnesota). SIC 3541, 3553, 3714. Founded in 1946. Owned by CRL Industries Inc., Bannockburn, Ill.

Toshiba America Business Solutions Inc. 901 N. Foster, Mitchell, SD 57301. Tel: 605/996-7731; Fax: 605/995-2039. F. Nishimura., VP and Gen. Mgr.; Dave Trounes, VP-Mfg./Admin.; M. Cunnigham, Dir.-Sls./Mktg.; N. Sorensen, Div. Cont.; M. Kimura, Tech. Dir. Toshiba America Business Solutions manufactures toner powders. 154 employees (5 in Minnesota). SIC 2865. Founded in 1986. Toshiba America Business Soltions Inc., Irvine, Calif., owned by Toshiba Corp., Tokyo.

Tousley Ford Inc. 1493 E. County Rd. E, White Bear Lake, MN 55110. Tel: 651/484-7231; Fax: 651/484-9128. Tom Bennett, Pres.; Ron Glassman, VP. Tousley Ford is Minnesota's largest Ford dealer. It has built its reputation on a "one price, no haggling" sales approach and a salaried sales staff. Acquired in September 1998 by the most aggressive buyer of auto dealers in the nation. 325 employees. SIC 5511. Founded in 1956. Now owned by AutoNation Inc. (NYSE: AN), Fort Lauderdale, Fla.

Towers Perrin 8300 Norman Center Dr., Suite 600, Bloomington, MN 55437. Tel: 952/897-3300; Fax: 952/835-1437; Web site: http://www.towers.com. John Naylor, Mpls. Office Mgr.; John Lynch, CEO. Towers Perrin, an international management consulting firm, helps organizations manage their investment in people—advising them on human resource management, employee benefits, risk management, compensation, and communication. It also consults on overall strategy and organizational effectiveness. It has offices in over 70 cities worldwide. 125 employees (in Minnesota). SIC 8741, 8742. Founded in 1977. Owned by the partners of the firm Towers Perrin, New York.

The Trane Company 3600 Pammel Creek Rd., La Crosse, WI 54601. Tel: 608/787-2000; Fax: 608/787-2552; Web site: http://www.trane.com. James H. Schultz, EVP-NACG; John Suzukida, SVP-Mktg./Strategy, NACG; Fred Kautz, VP-Sls./Mktg., NACG; Tom Mikulina, VP-Industry Rel., NACG. The Trane Co. is a worldwide manufacturer of heating, ventilating, air conditioning, and building-management equipment and systems. The 73-employee Trane Co. Asset Management Services is a White Bear Lake, Minn., unit of Trane Co. 14,000 employees (180 in Minnesota). SIC 3433, 3564, 3585. Founded in 1913. Owned by American Standard Inc. (NYSE: ASD), Piscataway, N.J.

TranScape 10800 Lyndale Ave. S., Suite 300, Bloomington, MN 55420. Tel: 952/885-7287; Fax: 952/885-7220; Web site: http://www.pbtranscape.com. Stephen M. Smith, Pres. TranScape is a logistics software company. The company provides multiplatform software solutions, which enable companies to better manage every stage of the order fulfillment process. The company's software and integration services enable any size company to share critical shipping information among supplier, vendor, and every level of management. 235 employees (100 in Minnesota; 12 part-time). SIC 4731. Division of Pitney Bowes Inc. (NYSE: PBI), Stamford, Conn.

Transx Ltd. 2929 Lone Oak Circle, Eagan, MN 55121. Tel: 651/454-9666; Fax: 651/454-7753; Web site: http://www.transx.ca. Thomas Slaird, COO; Mike Udermann, VP-Sls./Mktg.; Randy Busse, Terminal Mgr. Transx is a truckload carrier operating vans and heaters primarily east of the Mississippi River. The company also serves less-than-truckload shippers in Minnesota to all points in Canada. 70 employees (60 in Minnesota). SIC 4212, 4213. Founded in 1964. Subsidiary of Transx, Winnipeg, Manitoba.

Travelers Express Company Inc. 1550 Utica Ave. S., St. Louis Park, MN 55416. Tel: 952/591-3000; Fax: 952/591-3121; Web site: http://www.travelersexpress.com. Philip W. Milne, Pres. and CEO; Anthony Ryan, VP and CFO. Travelers Express is an issuer of money orders for both the retail and financial markets, and a major processor of share drafts and official checks for financial institutions. The company markets the DELTA automated dispensing system for money order agents. It also has a "pay in person" utility bill payment service called BuyPay; and an International Money Transfer product, Moneygram, that operates in 120 countries. Travelers Express annually processes 1 billion payment transactions valued at $120 billion. It serves 5,000 financial institutions and 65,000 retail locations. 1,850 employees (1,100 in Minnesota). SIC 6099. Founded in 1940. In May 2000 Mercantile Bancorp. Inc., St. Louis, a recent acquisition of Firstar Corp., Milwaukee, converted its official check and money order service to Travelers Express. In July ACE Cash Express Inc. (Nasdaq: AACE), the nation's largest check-cashing chain and a significant provider of related retail financial services, signed a new wire transfer agreement with Travelers. Under the new seven-year deal, ACE was to exclusively offer Travelers Express' MoneyGram wire transfer services in exchange for a $12.5 million incentive payment. In November the Harris Teeter grocery chain started offering both Travelers Express money orders and MoneyGram money transfers in its 153 stores in six states.Travelers is owned by the former Dial Corp, now called Viad Corp. (NYSE: VVI), Phoenix.

Triangle Services Corporation of Minnesota 2609 Aldrich Ave. S., Minneapolis, MN 55408. Tel: 612/872-9000; Fax: 612/872-9707. Michael Spahn, Regional VP; Brian Westphal, Bus. Devel. Mgr. Triangle Services provides building-maintenance services. Subsidiaries include Viking Security, a Full Service Security Officer group. 165 employees (in Minnesota; 29 part-time). SIC 7349, 7381. Founded in 1952. Owned by Triangle Maintenance Corp., Valley Stream, N.Y.

Trussbilt Inc. 2112 Old Highway 8, New Brighton, MN 55112. Tel: 651/633-6100; Fax: 651/633-7100. Steven Wolgamot, Pres. Annual revenue $27 million. Trussbilt manufactures detention and commercial hollow metal doors and frames at its St. Paul headquarters and two manufacturing plants in Huron, South Dakota. Acquired by current owner in February 1997. 250 employees (40 in Minnesota). SIC 3442. Founded in 1926. Owned by United Dominion Industries Ltd. (NYSE: UDI), Charlotte, N.C.

Truth Hardware 700 W. Bridge St., Owatonna, MN 55060. Tel: 507/451-5620; Fax: 507/451-5655. Brian Ennis, Pres. Truth Hardware is a window hardware manufacturer. 1,100 employees (856 in Minnesota). SIC 3429. Founded in 1914. Owned by FKI Industries plc, Halifax, U.K. No. 13 CRM Foreign-Owned 100.

Turck Inc. 3000 Campus Dr., Plymouth, MN 55441. Tel: 763/553-9224; Fax: 763/553-0708; Web site: http://www.turck.com. William A. Schneider, Pres. and CEO; Lawrence G. Worth, Dir.-Hum. Res.; Jeffrey C. Ursell, VP-Sls./Mktg.; William Eaton, Chief Engineer; William E. Christianson, VP-Fin.; Hans J. Ziesch, VP-Mfg.; Tom Collen, Dir.-Bus. Unit, Cordsets; Robb Black, Dir.-Bus. Unit, Sensors; Bradley V. Larson, Dir.-Bus. Unit, Intrinsic Safety; Sondra M. Weber, Strategic Bus. Mgr. (e-commerce). Turck manufactures and markets proximity sensors and connector products that sense metallic and nonmetallic materials for manufacturing automation applications. These advanced sensing solutions help manufacturers improve their automated processes, products, and profits. In 1998 the company started up a joint venture, Interlink BT, focusing on factory networks. 336 employees (335 in Minnesota). SIC 3625. Founded in 1976. Subsidiary of Hans Turck GmbH & Co. KG, Muelheim, Germany. No. 46 CRM Foreign-Owned 100.

Twin Cities Newspaper Service 220 Fillmore Ave. E., St. Paul, MN 55107. Tel: 651/222-8298; Fax: 651/222-2594. Scott Frantzen, VP; Jim Olichwier, Circulation Op. Mgr. Twin Cities Newspaper Service is an on-call courier that delivers periodicals, movie film, and newspapers throughout much of Minnesota and western Wisconsin. It is operated by the St. Paul Pioneer Press. 65 employees (62 in Minnesota; 33 part-time). SIC 4215. Owned by Knight Ridder Inc. (NYSE: KRI), San Jose, Calif.

Twin City Optical Company Inc. 5205 Highway 169 N., Plymouth, MN 55442. Tel: 763/551-2000; Fax: 763/551-2020. Gary L. Threlkeld, Pres.; LeRoy Greenfield, VP. Twin City Optical is a wholesale eyeglass fabricator and a buying group. Owned by private investment firm The Churchill Cos., Minneapolis, until aquired in April 1998. 340 employees (108 in Minnesota). SIC 3827, 5048. Founded in 1910. Now owned by Essilor International, Paris. No. 44 CRM Foreign-Owned 100.

Tyco Plastics and Adhesives 1401 W. 94th St., Bloomington, MN 55431. Tel: 952/884-7281; Fax: 952/885-9355; Web site: http://www.carlisle-plastics.com. Steve McDonough, Pres.-Tyco Plastics Group; Dave Bubar, Corp. Cont.-Carlisle Plastics; Dave Riffay, VP-Retail Sls.; Bill Weber, VP-Institution Sls.; Rick Franzen, VP-Mktg. Tyco Plastics and Adhesives manufactures and sells consumer trash bags and plastic sheeting products for consumer and commercial uses. Once known as Carlisle Plastics and, before that, as Poly-Tech Inc. (a publicly traded company). 950 employees (240 in Minnesota). SIC 2673. Founded in 1959. Now owned by Tyco International Ltd. (NYSE: TYC), Exeter, N.H.

Tyco Plastics Inc. 1800 N. M Ave., Sioux Falls, SD 57104. Tel: 605/334-0334; Fax: 605/334-1227. Tyco Plastics Inc. manufactures a wide variety of polyethylene film products. Product lines include noncommercial and commercial products ranging from liners for trash cans to packaging film and custom bags. The company and its subsidiaries market a wide range of plastic bags and plastic packaging products nationally—to consumers, to institutions, and to industry. Once known as Carlisle Plastics and, before that, as American Western Corp. (a publicly traded company). 350 employees. SIC 2673. Founded in 1983. Now owned by Tyco International Ltd. (NYSE: TYC), Exeter, N.H.

Tyson Seafood Group-Duluth 3931 W. First St., P.O. Box 16147, Duluth, MN 55816. Tel: 218/628-0365; Fax: 218/628-3564. Roland Chambers, Gen. Mgr. Tyson Seafood Group-Duluth produces Louis Kemp brand crab, lobster, and scallop products for both retail and food service sales. Sold to Oscar Mayer Inc., Madison, Wis., in 1987. 200 employees. SIC 2091. Founded in 1985. Acquired in 1992 by Tyson Foods Inc. (Nasdaq: TYSNA), Springdale, Ark.

REG

USFilter Control Systems 1239 Willow Lake Blvd., Vadnais Heights, MN 55110. Tel: 651/766-2700; Fax: 651/766-2701; Web site: http://www.controlsystems.usfilter.com. Duane Schlicht, VP and Gen. Mgr.; Dave Lee, VP-Sls./Mktg.; Tom Luedtke, VP and Cont.; Jon Ragnow, VP-Op.; Gregg Beckman, Dir.-Engrg.; Tom Coakley, Dir.-Education/Communications; Mike Schmitz, Dir.-Info. Sys. Annual revenue $55 million. USFilter Control Systems manufactures liquid-level, pressure, and flow sensors and controls for pumping, valves, and liquid-handling automation equipment (including data communication devices). The privately held Consolidated Electric Co. was purchased in January 1997 by USFilter Corp. In March 1999 USFilter was, in turn, acquired. 280 employees (220 in Minnesota). SIC 3823. Founded in 1922. Now owned by Vivendi, Paris. No. 52 CRM Foreign-Owned 100.

USFilter/Johnson Screens 1950 Old Highway 8 N.W., P.O. Box 64118 (55164), New Brighton, MN 55112. Tel: 651/636-3900; Fax: 651/638-3132; Web site: http://www.johnsonscreens.com. John Heeney, Pres.; Steve Uban, VP and Gen. Mgr. Annual revenue $75 million. USFilter/Johnson Screens is a world leader in the engineering and manufacture of liquid/solid separation products, water/wastewater process systems, and surface-preparation systems. Environmental products relate to drinking water, wastewater, and groundwater monitoring/remediation. It is the world's largest water well and industrial profile wire screen manufacturer. It also manufactures wedgewire, looped wore screens, wire mesh, and wire cloth porducts. The company operates in coal and mineral mining, hydrocarbon processing, food processing, oil and gas production, and groundwater. In 1904 Edward E. Johnson, St. Paul, invented the continuous-slot screen. USFilter Corp. acquired the company in 1996 from Wheelabrator Technologies Inc. In March 1999 USFilter was, in turn, acquired. 240 employees (200 in Minnesota). SIC 3496, 3532, 3533. Founded in 1904. Now owned through Vivendi Water North America, Palm Desert, Calif., by Vivendi, Paris. No. 57 CRM Foreign-Owned 100.

US Food Service 9605 54th Ave. N., Plymouth, MN 55442. Tel: 763/559-9494. David Leonhardi, Gen. Sls. Mgr.; Lisa Osier, Head Buyer. US Food Service, formerly Olfisco, is a distributor of specialty foods to supermarkets and restaurants. 50 employees (in Minnesota). SIC 5141, 5149. Founded in 1910. Owned by Rykoff-Sexton Inc. (NYSE: RYK), Lisle, Ill.

U.S. Office Products 2050 Old Highway 8, New Brighton, MN 55112. Tel: 651/639-4700; Fax: 651/639-4747; Web site: http://www.usop.com. Randy Danielson, District Pres. Annual revenue $47 million. U.S. Office Products is an office supply company that also sells office furniture, computer supplies, coffee and beverages, and advertising specialities. 150 employees (in Minnesota). SIC 5112. Founded in 1963. Owned by U.S. Office Products Co. (Nasdaq: OFIS), Washington, D.C.

USG Interiors Inc. 35 Arch St., Cloquet, MN 55720. Tel: 218/878-4000. Chris Lawson, Plant Mgr. USG Interiors makes ceiling tile and synthetic mineral fiber. 450 employees. SIC 2823, 5033. In January 2000 employees voted 261 to 140 against joining the Teamsters Local 346, culminating a contentious process that had begun six months earlier. Management promised to address concerns raised during the unionization effort. Owned by USG Corp. (NYSE: USG), Chicago.

USX Corporation—Minnesota 444 Cedar, Piper Jaffray Suite 1600, St. Paul, MN 55101. Tel: 952/887-6100; Fax: 952/887-6114. Robert C. Hardman, Regional VP. Annual revenue $1.6 billion. USX Minnesota performs store operations, merchandising, warehousing, administration, engineering, maintenance, training, franchising, and security. 5,778 employees (4,132 in Minnesota; 1,646 part-time). SIC 5399, 5411, 5531, 5541. Founded in 1960. Owned by a joint venture between USX-Marathon Group, Pittsburgh, and Ashland Inc. (Nasdaq: ASND), Ashland, Ky.

Ultimate Electronics/Audio King Regional Office 3501 Highway 100 S., St. Louis Park, MN 55416. Tel: 952/920-0505; Fax: 952/920-0940. Randel S. Carlock, Chm.; Samuel F. Nichols, SVP-Mktg., Audio King Inc.; Robert E. Thiner, SVP-Fin., CFO, and Treas.; M. Phillip Ward, SVP-Sls.-Audio King Inc.; Audrey M. Brick, VP and CFO-Audio King Inc.; Steve Gusa, VP-Mgmt. Devel./Trng., Audio King Inc.; Michael L. Sell, VP-FasTrak Electronic Repair; Stuart L. Finney, Sec. Ultimate Electronics/Audio King manages the operations of both wholly owned subsidiary Audio King Inc. and Audio King Inc.'s subsidiary, Specialty Home Electronics Repair Inc. Audio King is a retail sales and service organization for audio and video equipment. It has 11 specialty stores—eight in Minnesota, one in Sioux Falls, S.D., and one each in Des Moines and Cedar Rapids, Iowa. The company's Audio Video Environments division operates a design showroom in Edina, which offers custom design and installation of home entertainment systems. The subsidiary, Specialty Home Electronics Repair, operates an independent service center under the name Fast Trak Electronic Repair Service. 370 employees. SIC 5731, 7699. Founded in 1985. Merged in June 1997 with Ultimate Electronics Inc. (Nasdaq: ULTE), Denver.

Union Pacific Railroad Company 206 Eaton St., St. Paul, MN 55107. Tel: 651/552-3909; Fax: 651/552-3914. O.W. Cromwell, Supt.-Transportation Svs.; L.E. Bradley, Dir.-Quality Transportation; J.R. Panning, Senior Mgr.-Terminal Op. Union Pacific Railroad Co. provides railroad line-operating, switching, and terminal services. The former Chicago & Northwestern Railway Co. merged in October 1995 with Union Pacific. 495 employees (in Minnesota). SIC 4011, 4013. Owned by Union Pacific Railroad Co. (NYSE: UNP), Omaha, Neb.

Uni-Patch 1313 W. Grant Blvd., Wabasha, MN 55981. Tel: 651/565-2601; Fax: 651/565-3971. Brian Wolfe, Pres.; Dianne Schjolberg, Dir.-Hum. Res.; Tim Kretschmer, VP-Sls./Mktg.; Larry Duppong, Plant Mgr.; Ronald Schurhammer, Cont. Annual revenue $19 million. Uni-Patch manufactures TENS (transcutaneous electrical nerve stimulation) devices and electromedical supplies. 250 employees (146 in Minnesota; 50 part-time). SIC 3841. Founded in 1978. Owned by Ludlow Technical Products, Chicopee, Mass., a subsidiary of Tyco International Ltd. (NYSE: TYC), Exeter, N.H.

Unisource Worldwide 6610 W. Broadway, P.O. Box 100 (55440), Brooklyn Park, MN 55428. Tel: 763/536-5600; Fax: 763/536-5640; Web site: http://www.unisourcelink.com. R.W. Turnquist, Market Area Dir.; Keith LeBlanc, EVP. Unisource Worldwide is a wholesale distributor of printing papers, specialty grades, envelopes, stationery, and related products to customers across the Upper Midwest. In addition, it is the leading marketer and distributor of supply systems (disposable paper and plastic products, packaging equipment and supplies, and sanitary maintenance products) in the Minneapolis marketplace. 275 employees (in Minnesota). SIC 5111, 5112. Founded in 1923. In August 2000 the company broke ground on a 380,000-square-foot facility at Crosstown North Business Center in Brooklyn Park. Expected to open next spring, the facility was to consolidate the 275 Unisource employees from three Twin Cities locations. Unisource Worldwide Inc., Exton, Pa., was acquired in June 1999 by Georgia-Pacific Corp. (NYSE: GP), Atlanta.

Unisys Corporation 2276 Highcrest Dr., Roseville, MN 55113. Tel: 651/635-7777; Fax: 651/635-5938; Web site: http://www.unisys.com. James Commander, VP-Central Devel. Laboratory; Hal Becker, Dir.-Eagan Service Center. Unisys' Computer Systems Group is the Unisys technology business Unisys CSG has extensive experience in designing and developing technology for high-volume transaction processing; and in integrating diverse technologies into heterogeneous enterprise environments. Unisys Marketing & Customer Services, 3199 Pilot Knob Rd., Eagan, MN 55121 (612/687-2200) is the local marketing, customer service, and data processing center. 2,150 employees (in Minnesota). SIC 3577. Founded in 1986. In October 2000 the parent company announced plans to use early-retirement packages to cut up to 1,500 jobs, or 8.3 percent of its U.S. workforce, in the face of double-digit earnings declines in the past three quarters. Division of Unisys Corp. (NYSE: UIS), Blue Bell, Pa. No. 88 CRM Employer 100.

United Building Centers 125 W. Fifth St., Winona, MN 55987. Tel: 507/452-2361; Fax: 507/457-6780. Dale Kukowski, Pres.; Dave Binius, VP; Douglas Johnson, VP; John Lochner, VP; Tom Larson, VP. United Building Centers deals in retail building materials through 130 stores in thirteen states. It also wholesales trusses, millwork, and other building materials through twelve Timber Roots locations. 2,800 employees (650 in Minnesota). SIC 5211. Founded in 1855. Owned by Lanoga Corp., Redmond, Wash.

United Defense L.P., Armament Systems Division 4800 N.E. East River Rd., Fridley, MN 55421. Tel: 763/571-9201; Fax: 763/572-3300; Web site: http://www.uniteddefense.com. Frederick M. Strader, VP and Gen. Mgr.; Jeff Van Keuren, Mgr.-Public Affairs. Annual revenue $484 million. United Defense L.P. Armament Systems Division designs and manufactures defense equipment at a 135-acre plant in Fridley. A member of Team Crusader—developers of the Army's new self-propelled, 155-mm howitzer—the company is recognized for outstanding research and development, industry-leading engineering and system integration skills, and proven logistics support capabilities. Previously owned by FMC Corp. 1,420 employees (1,900 in Minnesota). SIC 3489. Founded in 1907. In December 1999 the company was awarded a $22 million licensed co-production contract by Kia Heavy Industries Corp. (KHI), Republic of Korea, for three Mk 45 Mod 4, 5-inch/62-Caliber Lightweight Gun Systems. In June 2000 Crusader successfully completed a major milestone in its design refinement that brought the weight down from 55 to 40 tons while still maintaining its survivability, lethality, and overall force effectiveness. The program was scheduled to move immediately into preliminary, then detailed design. In August United Defense awarded two contracts for continued development of a Long Range Land Attack Projectile (LRLAP) for the Advanced Gun System (AGS). Receiving Demonstration Phase awards were the Missiles Systems unit of Raytheon Co. in Tucson, Ariz., and Science Applications International Corp. in McLean, Va. Division of United Defense L.P., Arlington, Va.

United Parcel Service Inc. 3312 Broadway St. N.E., Minneapolis, MN 55413. Tel: 612/379-6668; Fax: 612/379-6622; Web site: http://www.ups.com. Ed Gill, COO. Annual revenue $600 million. United Parcel Service Inc. (UPS) is a provider of air courier and parcel delivery services worldwide. It has major hubs in both Eagan, Minn., and Minneapolis. 3,640 employees (5,440 in Minnesota; 1,800 part-time). SIC 4513. Founded in 1907. In November 1999 the Minnesota Chamber of Commerce awarded United Parcel Service the 1999 business Spirit of MinnesotaAward for business—in recognition of UPS' exemplary ideals and contributions to the community. In December Forbes magazine named the parent its company of the year, for being "the missing link in the burgeoning world of e-commerce." Owned by United Parcel Service of America Inc. (NYSE: UPS), Atlanta. No. 33 CRM Employer 100.

United Stationers 7509 Boone Ave. N., Brooklyn Park, MN 55428. Tel: 763/424-9600; Fax: 763/424-4373; Web site: http://www.unitedstationers.com. Neal Bailey, Area Mgr. United Stationers is a warehouse and distribution center. It has a second facility at 1720 Alexander Rd., Eagan, MN, 55121. 200 employees (in Minnesota). SIC 5112. Owned by United Stationers Inc. (Nasdaq: USTR), Des Plaines, Ill.

United Steel Products Company 703 Rogers Dr., P.O. Box 80, Montgomery, MN 56069. Tel: 507/364-7333; Fax: 507/364-8762. Robert Brunson, COO; Daniel Caudill, VP-Sls./Mktg.; Lexia Bosch, Cont. United Steel Products is a national manufacturer of wood-to-wood and wood-to-concrete metal lumber connectors—such as joist supports, wall bracing, bridging, truss plates, and shelf and pole brackets—plus custom construction hardware and engineered products. Privately held United Steel was acquired in June 1998. 500 employees (250 in Minnesota). SIC 3441. Founded in 1954. Now owned by Gibraltar Steel Corp. (Nasdaq: ROCK), Buffalo, N.Y.

United Television Inc. 11358 Viking Dr., Eden Prairie, MN 55344. Tel: 952/944-9999; Fax: 952/942-0286; Web site: http://www.kmsp.com. Stuart Z. Swartz, VP and Gen. Mgr.; Scott Frantzen, VP-Circulation. United Television Inc. runs broadcasting company KMSP Channel 9. United Television is a subsidiary of Chris Craft Inc., which owns 11 television stations—making it the fourth-largest television company in the United States. 156 employees (in Minnesota; 39 part-time). SIC 4833. Founded in 1955. Owned by United Television Inc., Los Angeles.

Universal Circuits Inc. 8860 Zachary Ln. N., Maple Grove, MN 55369. Tel: 763/682-0019; Fax: 763/682-3956. Kevin Barfknecht, Gen. Mgr. Universal Circuits manufactures printed wiring and printed boards. 125 employees. SIC 3672, 3679. Founded in 1969. Owned by Dielectric, Menomonee Falls, Wis.

Universal International Inc. 5000 Winnetka Ave. N., New Hope, MN 55428. Tel: 763/533-1169; Fax: 763/533-1158. Richard Ennen, Pres. and CEO; Robert R. Langer, COO-Only Deals; Dennis Hill, CFO. Universal International acquires closeout merchandise from company overstocks, business liquidations, and other sources and sells the merchandise through its wholesale and retail operations. In 1991 the company formed a wholly owned retail-store subsidiary, Only Deals Inc. The company currently owns 51 retail-store locations. In December 1994 Universal acquired a 40.5 percent interest in Odds-N-Ends, a closeout retailer based in Buffalo, New York. Odds-N-Ends owns and operates 22 retail stores offering closeout merchandise in New York state. 958 employees. SIC 5023, 5099, 5199, 5331. Founded in 1956. Acquired in September 1998 by 99 Cents Only Stores (NYSE: NDN), City of Commerce, Calif.

Upper Peninsula Power Company 600 Lakeshore Dr., P.O. Box 130, Houghton, MI 49931. Tel: 800/562-7680; Fax: 906/483-4510. Clarence R. Fisher, Pres. and CEO; Lynwood Hart, VP-Admin. Annual revenue $60.1 million. Upper Peninsula Power Co. (UPPCO), is an electric utility that serves approximately 47,500 customers in 10 of the 15 counties in Michigan's Upper Peninsula. The company's service area covers 4,460 square miles and has a population of 130,000. UPEN and WPS Resources merged on Sept. 29, 1998. 172 employees. SIC 4911. Founded in 1947. Owned by WPS Resources Corp. (NYSE: WPS), Green Bay, Wis.

REG

Valleyfair One Valleyfair Dr., Shakopee, MN 55379. Tel: 952/445-7600; Fax: 952/445-1539. Walter Wittmer, VP and Gen. Mgr.; Alan Schwartz, VP-Fin.; Linnea Stromberg-Wise, VP-Mktg.; Mark Freyberg, VP-Park Op. Valleyfair operates an amusement park. 1,300 employees (1,225 part-time). SIC 7996. Founded in 1976. Owned by CedarFair L.P. (NYSE: FUN), Sandusky, Ohio.

Varitronic Systems Inc. 6835 Winnetka Circle, Brooklyn Park, MN 55428. Tel: 763/536-6400; Fax: 763/536-0769. David C. Grey, Gen. Mgr. Varitronics develops, manufactures, and markets supply-consuming labeling, signage, and presentation systems that enhance the quality, professionalism, and effectiveness of a wide range of communications. Since 1983, the foundation of the company's business has been the sale of electronic lettering systems for a variety of applications, including labels, charts, name badges, and architectural and engineering drawings. In fiscal 1989 the company added the PosterPrinter product line. The PosterPrinter enlarges standard-sized originals to poster- or banner-sized documents. In fiscal 1993 the company introduced the EasyStep 4000 Label and Sign Maker for the industrial labeling and signage market. The company also offers a broad line of consumable supplies and accessories that are used with its products. In the United States, Varitronics markets its products through 295 independent dealerships; district offices of Lanier Worldwide Inc.; branch offices of Gestetner Corporation; and private-label distributors. Internationally, products are sold in 35 countries through 65 independent distributors. Once publicly traded. 235 employees. SIC 3953. Founded in 1983. Since 1996 Varitonics has been a decentralized subsidiary of W.H. Brady Co. (Nasdaq: BRCOA), Milwaukee.

Ventura Foods LLC 919 14th St., Albert Lea, MN 56007. Tel: 507/373-2431; Fax: 507/373-7069. Aaron Summers, VP-Midwest; Douglas Kallemeyn, Plant Mgr. Ventura Foods manufactures, packages, and distributes margarine, salad dressings, syrups, preserves, sauces, mayonnaise, olives, and other food items. Other plants are in Chicago; Omaha, Neb.; Philadelphia; Portland and Salem, Ore.; Waukesha, Wis.; City of Industry and Los Angeles, Calif.; St. Joseph, Mo.; Saginaw, Texas; and Atlanta. In June 1996 Harvest States Cooperatives, St. Paul, agreed to merge its Holsum Foods division based in Waukesha, Wis., with Wilsey Foods Inc., City of Industry, Calif., forming Ventura Foods. 150 employees. SIC 2079. Founded in 1965. In June 2000 U.S. Environmental Protection Agency (EPA) Region 5 filed an administrative complaint against Ventura Foods for violation of laws on the reporting of a hazardous chemical release, as well as failure to maintain required hazardous chemical records. EPA proposed a $302,528 fine. (EPA alleged that on Aug. 30, 1998, the company failed to promptly report the release of an estimated 1,000 lb to 1,500 lbs. of ammonia into the air.) In November the company agreed to pay a $34,554 fine and complete environmental projects costing $128,905, for a total settlement of $163,459. Wilsey Foods is owned by Mitsui & Co. Ltd., Tokyo. No. 72 CRM Foreign-Owned 100.

Vincent Metal Goods, a division of Rio Algom Inc. 455 85th Ave. N.W., Coon Rapids, MN 55433. Tel: 763/717-9000; Fax: 763/717-7176; Web site: http://www.vincentmetalgoods.com. Harrison P. Jones, Pres. and CEO; Michael H. Goldberg, EVP and COO; Michael Reichenbacher, SVP-Eastern Division; David O. Cagle, VP-Fin./Admin.; Terry Becker, SVP-Western Div. Annual revenue $1.1 billion. Vincent Metal Goods is a full-line metal service center that distributes and processes aluminum, stainless steel, brass, copper, and carbon steel at 50 U.S. locations. 2,000 employees (275 in Minnesota). SIC 5051, 6719. Founded in 1936. A metals distribution division of Rio Algom Ltd., Toronto. No. 5 CRM Foreign-Owned 100.

Virchow, Krause & Company LLP 7900 Xerxes Ave. S., Suite 2300, Bloomington, MN 55431. Tel: 952/835-1344; Fax: 952/835-5845. Jerry Brown, Ptnr.-in-charge, MN Region; Dana W. House, Managing Ptnr.; David Zuelke, Ofcr. Virchow, Krause & Co. LLP is an accounting firm that provides accounting, tax, and audit services; retirement planning; computer consulting; and medical services. In October 1999 House, Nezerka & Froelich P.A. merged with Virchow, Krause to create the 18th-largest accounting firm in the country. Locally, Virchow, Krause's 25-employee office in the TCF Tower was folded into House, Nezerka's 56-employee Bloomington office. 81 employees (in Minnesota). SIC 8721. Founded in 1977. In August 2000, while the firm's downtown office was being remodeled, employees painted houses owned by Opportunity Partners, which helps those who have suffered brain injuries. Regional office of Virchow, Krause & Co. LLP, Madison, Wis.

Vision World Inc. 2277 W. Highway 36, Roseville, MN 55113. Tel: 651/633-7736; Fax: 651/633-7629; Web site: http://www.visionworld.com. Russell Trenholme, Pres. and CEO; Paul Ramaker, COO; Takako Trenholme, Sec. and Treas.; Daron Johnson, Cont.; Susan Peterson, VP-Bus.s Devel. Vision World is a retailer of optical goods—including glasses, contact lenses, and sunglasses—at 38 locations in Minnesota, Wisconsin, North Dakota, and Iowa. Its central production lab and optician training center are located in Roseville. The company also provides eye exams through independent doctors of optometry. In July 1998 the company was sold to Vision Twenty-One Inc., Largo, Fla., for $18.3 million in cash. In July 1999 it was sold again, so that Vision Twenty-One could focus on the high-growth laser eye-surgery market. Russell Trenholme and his wife Takako, founders of the company, continue to manage Vision World. 400 employees (335 in Minnesota; 100 part-time). SIC 5995. Founded in 1977. Now owned by the 351-store national chain Eye Care Centers of America Inc., San Antonio.

VISTAinfo Real Estate Solutions 100 Washington Ave. S., Suite 1000, Minneapolis, MN 55401. Tel: 612/661-1000; Fax: 612/661-1704; Web site: http://www.mdms.com. Thomas Gregorich, Pres.; Lori Brostrom, VP-Mktg.; Bob Dolan, VP-Fin.; Howard Latham, VP-Sls. Annual revenue $100 million. VISTAinfo Real Estate Solutions develops real estate solutions for multiple-listing services (MLS), brokers, and agents nationwide. Its MLS information systems include Internet/intranet access to listing, tax, statistical data, property photo, and mapping information (CyberHomes, RE/Xplorer). It also provides software to improve agent and broker productivity, office management, and listings presentations; and printed materials such as MLS catalogs and advertising tabloids. These services support the dayto-day sales efforts of more than 350,000 residential real estate brokers and agents, their boards, and associations—the largest user base of any MLS vendor. 543 employees (120 in Minnesota). SIC 7374. Founded in 1963. In December 1999 the company, then called Moore Data Management Services, was sold by then-owner Moore Corp. Ltd., Toronto, for $50 million in cash and debt. Now owned by VISTAinfo (Nasdaq: VINF), San Diego.

Visy Paper Menominee 144 First St., P.O. Box 310, Menominee, MI 49858. Tel: 906/863-5595; Fax: 906/864-3325. W. Roger Smith, VP and Gen. Mgr.; Gary Byrd, CEO; Dick Brown, Deputy CEO. Visy Paper Menominee manufactures linerboard and media for the corrugated box industry. Secondary products include machine-glazed tissue and wax paper. Formerly known as Menominee Paper Co. 280 employees. SIC 2621, 2631. Founded in 1973. Now owned by Visy Industries Inc., Conyers, Ga.

Vital Signs Minnesota Inc. 12250 Nicollet Ave. S., Burnsville, MN 55337. Tel: 952/894-7523; Fax: 952/894-0546. Susan Brunsvold, VP and Gen. Mgr. Vital Signs Minnesota manufactures disposable medical products and laparoscopic surgical products. Known as Biomedical Dynamics Corp. until acquired in April 1992. 79 employees. SIC 3841. Founded in 1980. Owned by Vital Signs Inc. (Nasdaq: VITL), Totowa, N.J.

WCCO 11th On the Mall, 90 S. 11th St., Minneapolis, MN 55403. Tel: 612/339-4444; Fax: 612/330-2411. Jan McDaniel, VP and Gen. Mgr.; Kathy Mohn, Dir.-Sls.; Gregory M. Keck, Dir.-Engrg./Op. WCCO operates a television broadcasting station owned by the CBS network. 250 employees. SIC 4833. Founded in 1949. In April 2000 a complaint of sexual harassment against female technicians at WCCO-TV and five other CBS stations that had been filed in 1996 was granted class-action status. [The EEOC had previously determined that CBS had denied its female technicians equal opportunities.] CBS denied allegations that it condoned a hostile, discriminatory workplace. In October CBS agreed to pay $8 million to 221 technicians (25 here), and to change certain employment practices, in order to avoid protracted litigation. Owned by CBS Corp., New York.

WCCO Radio 830 AM 625 Second Ave. S., Minneapolis, MN 55402. Tel: 612/370-0611; Fax: 612/370-0159; Web site: http://www.wcco.com. Brian Whittemore, Gen. Mgr.; Allen Eitzel, Gen. Sls. Mgr.; Chuck Dickemann, Op. Mgr. WCCO Radio 830 is a 50,000-watt AM radio station affiliated with the CBS network. 73 employees. SIC 4832. Founded in 1924. In October 2000 Don Shelby, anchor for WCCO 4 News at 6:00 and 10:00 p.m., was named WCCO-AM's afternoon drive host. The show airs weekdays from 3:00-5:00 p.m. In addition, WCCO 4 News at 5 began simulcasting on WCCO-AM 830, followed by a half-hour news show with the WCCO Radio News Team. Owned by CBS Corp., New York.

WFTC-TV, Fox 29 1701 Broadway St. N.E., Minneapolis, MN 55413. Tel: 612/379-2929; Fax: 612/379-2900; Web site: http://www.fox29.com. Steve Spenslove, VP and Gen. Mgr. WFTC-TV, Fox 29 is the Twin Cities Fox television network affiliate. 50 employees. SIC 4833. Owned by Clear Channel Communications Inc. (NYSE: CCU), San Antonio.

WRR Environmental Services Company Inc. 5200 State Road 93, Eau Claire, WI 54701. Tel: 715/834-9624; Fax: 715/836-8785; Web site: http://www.wrres.com. James L. Hager, Pres. and CEO; J. Lee, VP-Quality Control; Bruce Heath, SVP; Don Reali, CFO, Sec., and Treas.; John M. Prock, VP-Sls./Mktg.; Brian K. Schneider, VP and Plant Mgr.; Steven P. Stokke, VP-Op. Support; Eric G. Gunderson, VP-Laboratory Op. WRR Environmental Services Company Inc. provides remediation, solvent recycling, incineration, lab packs, training/consulting services, transportation, fuel blending, laboratory services, parts washers, custom chemical processing, and emergency response. 100 employees (1 in Minnesota). SIC 1629, 4953, 7389, 8744. Founded in 1970. Owned by The Ziegler Co. Inc., West Bend, Wis.

Wagner Spray Tech Corporation 1770 Fernbrook Ln., Plymouth, MN 55447. Tel: 763/553-7000; Fax: 763/553-7288. Sean C. James, Pres.; Thomas B. Craig, VP-Fin. Wagner Spray Tech manufactures electric and gas airless paint-spray equipment for professional users and homeowners, and painting and decorating products for homeowners. 300 employees. SIC 3563. Founded in 1970. Wholly owned through Wagner U.S. Holdings Inc. by Wagner International AG, Altstaetten, Switzerland. No. 48 CRM Foreign-Owned 100.

Warner Industrial Supply Inc. 2211 E. Hennepin Ave., Minneapolis, MN 55413. Tel: 612/378-7300; Fax: 612/623-9038; Web site: http://www.warnerindustrialsupply.com. Jim Zechmann, Pres.; Joe Morgan, VP-Purch.; Ron Johnson, VP-Mktg.; Kevin Milbery, VP-Sls.; Teresa Nelson, VP-Hearing Tech. Annual revenue $49 million. Warner Industrial Supply is an ISO 9002-certified wholesale distributor of industrial supplies—including cutting tools, abrasives, air tools, paint and finishing, and clean room supplies. It has branches in Bismarck, N.D.; Watertown, S.D.; Moline, Ill.; Eau Claire and Madison, Wis.; Billings and Missoula, Mont.; Spokane, Wash.; Grand Rapids, Mich.; and Denver. Under the name Warner Technologies, the company also serves hearing-aid manufacturers, dispensers, and audiologists. 135 employees (90 in Minnesota; 5 part-time). SIC 5085. Founded in 1875. Warner was acquired in April 1999. Now a wholly owned subsidiary of Cameron & Barkley Inc., Charleston, S.C.

Waste Management 10050 Naples St. N.E., Blaine, MN 55449. Tel: 763/784-8349; Fax: 763/783-5477. Waste Management is an environmental services company offering waste transportation and disposal, recycling transportation and processing, and waste stream evaluations and consulting 240 employees (in Minnesota). SIC 4953. Founded in 1984. Owner Waste Management Inc., Oak Brook, Ill., was acquired in 1998 by USA Waste Services Inc., Houston.

Waterous Company 125 Hardman Ave. S., South St. Paul, MN 55075. Tel: 651/450-5000; Fax: 651/450-5090; Web site: http://www.waterousco.com. Donald J. Haugen, Pres. Annual revenue $100 million. Waterous manufactures waterworks hydrants, valves, and fire truck pumps. 385 employees (in Minnesota). SIC 3561. Founded in 1886. Subsidiary of American Cast Iron Pipe Co., Birmingham, Ala.

Wausau-Mosinee Paper Corporation 515 W. Davenport St., Rhinelander, WI 54501. Tel: 715/369-4100; Fax: 715/369-4450. San Orr, Chm.; Thomas Howatt, Pres. and CEO; Stuart R. Carlson, SVP; Albert Davis, VP and Gen. Mgr. Wausau-Mosinee Paper produces technical specialty and coated papers and torula yeast. Formerly known as Rhinelander Paper Co. 600 employees. SIC 2099, 2621, 2672. Founded in 1903. Owned by Wausau-Mosinee Paper Corp. (NYSE: WMO), Wausau, Wis.

Wells Fargo & Company Wells Fargo Center, Sixth Street and Marquette, Minneapolis, MN 55479. Tel: 612/667-1234; Fax: 612/667-7680; Web site: http://www.norwest.com. James R. Campbell, EVP-MN Banking Group; John E. Ganoe, EVP-Mergers/Acquisitions; Cynthia J. Gray, EVP-Mktg.; Diane Palmer Lilly, EVP; Michael Newburg, SVP-Corp. Tax; Paula S. Roe, SVP-Compensation; K.C. Kidder, VP-Risk Mgmt.; Laura Groschen, Cash-Based Bus. Segment; Tim King, Norwest Insurance; Jerry E. Gray, Wells Fargo SBA Funding; Jerome Fons, Wells Fargo Fleet Leasing Svs.; Rick Ferris, U.S. Corporate Banking; Lennie Kaufman, Shareowner Svs.; Brian Bartlett, Corp. Trust; Jay Kiedrowski, Institutional Investments Group; John McCune, Institutional Brokerage; Marty McKinley, Wells Fargo Business Credit Inc.; Jim Renner, Wells Fargo Equipment Fin.; George Still, Norwest Equity Ptnrs.; Peter Glanville, Lowry Hill; Bob Mersky, Peregrine Capital; Dr. Sung Won Sohn, Wells Fargo Chief Economist; J. Thomas Wittlund, Correspondent Banking. Wells Fargo & Co., formerly Norwest Corp., is a diversified financial services company with $234 billion in assets, providing banking, insurance, investments, mortgage and consumer finance from about 5,300 stores and the Internet (wellsfargo.com) across North America and internationally. In the Midwest, Wells Fargo Banks offer financial services through 376 banking stores in Minnesota, Montana, North Dakota, South Dakota, Wisconsin and Michigan, Wells Fargo Online Banking, Wells Fargo's 24-hour telephone banking service, and Wells Fargo ATMs. Mortgage, investments, insurance and other financial services are available through other Wells Fargo subsidiaries. 21,146 employees (14,097 in Minnesota). SIC 6712. Founded in 1929. In December 1999 Norwest Mortgage (now Wells Fargo Home Mortgage) agreed to acquire the headquarters campus of Honeywell Inc. in south Minneapolis. Plans were made to consolidate 2,500 employees there—from six other leased locations in the Twin Cities area—by June 2002. In May 2000 Wells Fargo and Norwest launched the online Wells Fargo Resource Center for Small Business Owners. In June Wells Fargo pulled some relocation information for home buyers from its Web site after being accused of redlining. Wells Fargo's trust operations division was consolidating into Minneapolis, a decision that added 100 new jobs immediately (from California) and would eventually add 80 more (from Utah, Alaska, Colorado, and Michigan). Wells Fargo became a title sponsor of the Wells Fargo Family Farm at the Minnesota Zoo, which opened in June. The Norwest name in Minnesota was officially changed to Wells Fargo on July 8. In July the company was negotiating to lease the retail levels of the Minnesota World Trade Center, St. Paul, for new branch space and drive-in teller windows. Wells Fargo agreed to a five-year sponsorship of the expansion Minnesota Wild of the National Hockey League. In August Wells Fargo opened a wealth planning center in Minneapolis to cater to the investment needs of clients with $5 million or more. Wells Fargo Minnesota was named one of the 10 Great Places to Work in Minnesota in the August issue of Corporate Report magazine. Division of Wells Fargo & Co. (NYSE: WFC), San Francisco. No. 10 CRM Employer 100.

West Group 610 Opperman Dr., Eagan, MN 55123. Tel: 651/687-7000; Fax: 651/687-5581; Web site: http://www.westgroup.com. Dwight D. Opperman, Chm. Emeritus; Brian H. Hall, CEO; Michael Wilens, Pres.; Dennis Beckingham, EVP and CFO; Andrew Prozes, EVP and COO-WESTLAW; James Greenawalt, SVP-Hum. Res.; Ruth Stanoch, VP-Communications. West Group provides business and legal information to a worldwide market. Products include more than 1,000 print publications and more than 400 CD-ROM titles, including federal and state statutes and rules, law school publications, legal practice guides, and secondary resources such as American Law Reports and American Jurisprudence. Online services include West's Legal Directory (www.wld.com), a legal directory of nearly 1 million legal professionals; and WESTLAW, a computer-assisted legal research service with more than 9,000 databases. 8,000 employees (5,729 in Minnesota). SIC 2731. Founded in 1876. In January 2000 West Group announced the formation of the WestWorks Team: bringing together Microsoft, IBM, and Elite.com to create a product that integrates legal research, document assembly, document management, case management, time and billing, client management, calendars, and dockets in a seamless, Web-centric desktop. In March West Group announced Westnew, the new name for Westlaw News & Business. Westnews features Dow Jones Interactive, a premier business intelligence service offered by Factiva, a Dow Jones & Reuters Co., for legal researchers who need comprehensive news and business information in addition to case law and regulatory materials. In April West Group and Northern Light Technology Inc. (http://www.NorthernLight.com), a leading Internet search engine, announced an agreement to create the most comprehensive, accurate, and organized legal Web search engine in the world. Legal professionals would soon have access to more than 13,000 Westlaw databases of legal information and Northern Light's Web database of more than 220 million Web pages in a single, integrated search. In June Law Office Computing magazine named Westlaw its Reader's Choice Award winner in the online Legal Research category. In July CareThere.com selected West's Lawoffice.com as the exclusive provider of its Legal Advisor directory. West introduced Legal Marketplace on Lawoffice.com, a searchable directory of individuals and businesses that provide services and products frequently used by lawyers, legal professionals, and law firms. Lawoffice.com and Internet Broadcasting Systems (IBS) (http://www.ibsys.com), the company leading the convergence of local television and the Internet, announced that Lawoffice.com had agreed to become the exclusive provider of legal information and resources across IBS' network of local TV Web channels. In August the company announced plans to plug into WorldCom's (Nasdaq: WCOM) nationwide Enterprise DSL (digitalsubscriber line) service to introduce its new WestWorks practice management suite for law firms, set to launch later in the year in Miami, Houston, and San Francisco. In September West Group was named Best of the Best by the Master Printers of America in its Best Workplace in America competition. West Group announced Westlaw Anywhere, which provides fast, convenient access to Westlaw content through wireless handheld computers such as the Palm VIIx handheld with Palm.Net service. In addition Westlaw Anywhere provides the ability to download eBooks from West Group's online store to a variety of personal digital assistants. West and eRoom Technology, a leading provider of digital workplaces for the extended enterprise, announced FirmSite WorkSpace—Powered by eRoom, a new extranet offering for the legal market. FirmSite WorkSpace is a comprehensive, flexible, secure online extranet where law firms can manage cases and collaborate electronically with their legal teams, clients, and co-counsel. Parent company Thomson strengthened its commitment to Minnesota by selecting West Group's Eagan site as the headquarters for Thomson Legal & Regulatory. In October New2USA.com selected Lawoffice.com as the exclusive provider of its lawyer directory and legal information. In November bizjournals.com, the Internet subsidiary of American City Business Journals Inc., Charlotte, N.C., selected Lawoffice.com as the exclusive provider of its lawyer directory and legal information. West Group and the National Bar Association donated a gift of Westlaw access to the United Nations for use by the International Criminal Tribunals for Rwanda and for the former Yugoslavia. West Group, consisting of the former West Publishing (acquired in 1997) and Thomson Legal Publishing companies, is a division of the Thomson Financial & Professional Publishing Group, which is owned by The Thomson Corp. (LON: TOC), Stamford, Conn. No. 35 CRM Employer 100.

Westfalia.surge LLC 20903 W. Gale Ave., Galesville, WI 54630. Tel: 608/582-2221; Fax: 608/582-2581. Ralph Rottier, Gen. Mgr. Westfalia.surge LLC Dairy Systems Division manufactures and markets dairy-farm equipment. Formerly owned by Babson Bros. Co. 200 employees (10 in Minnesota; 10 part-time). SIC 3523, 5083. Founded in 1943. Now owned by Westfalia Landtechnik, Oelde, Germany.

Weston Engraving Company 2626 Second St. N.E., Minneapolis, MN 55418. Tel: 612/789-8514; Fax: 612/789-5424. Jim Moen, Pres. Weston Engraving is in the business of laser color separations and electronic imaging. 101 employees. SIC 2752, 2796. Founded in 1915. Owned by Schawk Inc. (NYSE: SGK), Des Plaines, Ill.

Weyerhaeuser Company 1900 Eighth St. N.E., Austin, MN 55912. Tel: 507/433-3467; Fax: 507/437-0803. Ivan Winship, Cont.; Teri Cirillo, Hum. Res. Mgr.; Dan Hawkins, Quality Mgr.; Dave Rae, Op. Mgr.; Kathy Borland, Customer Svc. Team Leader. Weyerhaeuser Co.'s Austin Plant manufactures corrugated shipping containers. 140 employees. SIC 2653. Founded in 1954. Owned by Weyerhaeuser Co. (NYSE: WY), Federal Way, Wash.

Weyerhaeuser Paper Company 1699 W. Ninth St., White Bear Lake, MN 55110. Tel: 651/426-0345; Fax: 651/426-6203. Andy Schippers, Gen. Mgr. Weyerhaeuser Paper Co.'s White Bear Lake Plant makes corrugated shipping containers for industrial use across a five-state area. The company has another plant in Austin, Minn., and a sales office in Minneapolis. 130 employees (in Minnesota). SIC 2653. Founded in 1954. Owned by Weyerhaeuser Co. (NYSE: WY), Federal Way, Wash.

Willamette Industries Inc. 2425 Terminal Rd., Roseville, MN 55113. Tel: 651/633-8220; Fax: 651/633-0306. Gary Schiltz, Gen. Mgr. Willamette Industries St. Paul Corrugated manufactures 640 million square feet of corrugated containers per year in its 260,000-square-foot plant. It was acquired by Willamette for $12.8 million from Boise Cascade Corp.—part of a larger deal that included 11 corrugated manufacturing plants east of the Mississippi River. 140 employees (in Minnesota). SIC 2653. Founded in 1963. Acquired in July 1992 by Willamette Industries Inc. (NYSE: WLL), Portland, Ore.

Willmar Cookie and Nut Company dba Gurley's Foods P.O. Box 88, 118 E. Highway 12, Willmar, MN 56201. Tel: 320/235-0600; Fax: 320/235-0659. Mike Mickelson, Pres.; Tom Taunton, National Sls. Mgr. Willmar Cookie and Nut Co., dba Gurley's Foods, bakes cookies, makes candy, and roasts and packages a variety of nuts under the Gurley's brand name. Products are available nationwide in retail stores and through catalog sales. 140 employees (in Minnesota). SIC 2052, 2068. Founded in 1953. Owned by Consolidated Biscuit, McComb, Ohio.

Wilson Learning Worldwide 7500 Flying Cloud Dr., Eden Prairie, MN 55344. Tel: 952/944-2880; Fax: 952/828-8835; Web site: http://www.wilsonlearning.com. Dave Wondra, VP-Hum. Res.; Donald R. Kielley, CEO; Gayle Kirkeby, VP-Nat'l Account Sls.; Linda Mantel, VP-Agency Sls.; Kathe Grooms, VP-Int'l; Mik Lucas, VP-Market Devel.; Carol Lenhart, CFO. Wilson Learning Worldwide is a leader in human resource development for organizations throughout the United States and 50 business capitals worldwide. The company provides flexible, integrated learning systems that support business strategy and individual growth. Wilson Learning programs and services address leadership effectiveness, sales, team collaboration, innovation, customer satisfaction, and change management. The company also offers a full spectrum of measurement and assessment tools, multimedia reinforcement, and customized consulting. 300 employees (100 in Minnesota). SIC 8742. Founded in 1965. Wilson Learning Worldwide is owned by Wilson Learning Worldwide Inc., Tokyo. No. 48 CRM Foreign-Owned 100.

Winona Daily News 601 Franklin St., Winona, MN 55987. Tel: 507/454-6500; Fax: 507/454-1440. George Althoff, Publisher. Winona Daily News publishes a daily morning newspaper and a shopper, and offers commercial printing services, target marketing, and online products. 69 employees (25 part-time). SIC 2711, 2759. Founded in 1855. Owned by Lee Enterprises Inc. (NYSE: LEE), Davenport, Iowa.

The Winona Group Inc. 8040 Old Cedar Ave. S., Bloomington, MN 55425. Tel: 952/881-5400; Fax: 952/881-0763; Web site: http://www.winonaresearch.com. Simon Chadwick, CEO; Diane Frederick, CEO; Bruce Lervoog, EVP; Karen Siwek, CFO. The Winona Group is a unique group of businesses dedicated to enhancing understanding of consumer behavior, improving customer relationships and leveraging communications between companies and their target markets. Winona Group companies in Phoenix, Minneapolis, Chicago, and Salt Lake City offer marketing consulting, modeling, full-service marketing research, tracking, performance measurement, and call-center solutions. 61 employees. SIC 8732. Founded in 1953. Owned by WPP Group plc, London.

Wirsbo Company 5925 148th St. W., Apple Valley, MN 55124. Tel: 612/891-2000; Fax: 612/891-2008. Frank Bailor, Pres. and Managing Dir.; Jim Bjork, Gen. Mgr.; John Harmon, CFO and Fin. Mgr.; Randy Knapp, Engrg. Mgr.; Joe Pauley, Sls. Mgr.; Greg Lange, Hum. Res. Mgr.; Bob Balcerzak, Op. Mgr. Wirsbo Co. manufactures plastic piping for under-floor radiant heating systems and plumbing systems. The company offers six complete lines of PEX tubing for hydronic radiant floor, radiant ceiling, plumbing, and snow-melt systems. It has a second office in Regina, Saskatchewan. Originally founded in 1620 in Virsbo, Sweden. 190 employees. SIC 3084. Founded in 1984. Owned by OY Uponor AB, Espoo, Finland. No. 66 CRM Foreign-Owned 100.

Wisconsin Public Service Corporation P.O. Box 160, Rhinelander, WI 54501. Tel: 800/450-7260; Fax: 715/369-7153. V.B. Davis, Mgr.-Rhinelander District; D.M. Loy, Mgr.-Rhinelander District. Wisconsin Public Service Corp. is an investor-owned gas and electric utility. 60 employees. SIC 4939. Founded in 1883. Division of WPS Resources Corp. (NYSE: WPS), Green Bay, Wis.

Witcher Construction Company 9855 W. 78th St., Suite 270, Eden Prairie, MN 55344. Tel: 952/830-9000; Fax: 952/830-1365; Web site: http://www.witcherconstruction.com. Kenneth A. Styrlund, Pres.; David Burtness, VP; Douglas Loeffler, VP; Scott Sharp, VP. Annual revenue $83 million. Witcher Construction Co. is a general contracting/construction management firm, specializing in commercial and institutional construction. Representative projects include new and renovated retail, religious, hospitality, cultural, educational, health care, office, and housing facilities. The company works primarily in Minnesota but has completed major projects in more than 25 states. Witcher can perform its own contracting operations in the disciplines of light demolition, concrete, masonry, and carpentry. 200 employees (in Minnesota). SIC 1540, 1541, 1542. Founded in 1945. In August 2000 Witcher was contracted for the $7 million project to build a 32,700-square-foot addition to Frontier Hall, a residence hall on the University of Minnesota campus. In September 2000, the company completed construction on the 28,200-square-foot first phase of an expansion on the campus of Minneapolis College of Art & Design, Minneapolis. Owned by Dunn Industries Inc., Kansas City, Mo.

Woods/Du-Al 1000 W. Cherokee St., Sioux Falls, SD 57104. Tel: 605/336-3860; Fax: 605/336-6750. Shawn Cleary, Op. Mgr.; Dustin Williams, Mfg. Mgr. Woods manufactures hydraulic front-end loaders, backhoes, and trenchers for light- to medium-duty industrial and construction tractors; hydraulic front-end loaders for farm tractors; manure spreaders; and other farm materials-handling equipment. Formerly known as Du-Al Manufacturing Co. 105 employees (2 in Minnesota). SIC 3523. Founded in 1945. Owned by Woods Equipment Co., Oregon, Ill.

WorldCom 5500 Wayzata Blvd., Suite 400, Golden Valley, MN 55416. Tel: 763/591-0705; ; Web site: http://www.wcom.com. Bernard Ebbers, Ofcr. WorldCom is a telecommunications company that provides high-speed data including frame relay, PVT line, and ATM; DSL, Internet, local, long-distance, and paging services statewide. 450 employees. SIC 4813. Founded in 1975. Owned by WorldCom Inc. (Nasdaq: WCOM), Jackson, Miss.

XPEDX 2850 Anthony Ln. S., St. Anthony, MN 55418. Tel: 763/781-6611; Fax: 763/781-0641. Patrick Hennessy, VP and Gen. Mgr. XPEDX is a distributor of fine paper, graphic supplies, and industrial products to printers nationwide. Former names: Leslie Paper; ResourceNet International. 150 employees (in Minnesota). SIC 5111. Founded in 1894. Owned by International Paper Co. (NYSE: IP), Purchase, N.Y.

Xerox of the Upper Midwest 3500 W. 80th St., Bloomington, MN 55431. Tel: 952/921-1300; Fax: 952/921-1438. Chris Bernish, Mgr.-Sls. Op.; Kevin Groff, VP and Gen Mgr.; Paul Knapp, Mgr.-Tech. CPS; Kelly Brand, Mktg. Mgr. Annual revenue $284 million. Xerox sells, services, and administers copiers, duplicators, professional workstations and networking equipment, laser printing equipment, and facsimile equipment. 569 employees (335 in Minnesota). SIC 3572, 3579. Founded in 1959. Division of Xerox Corp. (NYSE: XRX), Stamford, Conn.

XIOtech Corp. 6455 Flying Cloud Dr., Eden Prairie, MN 55344. Tel: 952/828-5980; Fax: 952/828-5990; Web site: http://www.xiotech.com. XIOtech Corp. designs, manufactures, and markets high-performance, application-driven storage solutions. The award-winning XIOtech MAGNITUDE's software-based architecture provides more than 3TB of high-performance, centralized storage that can be accessed continuously by multiple heterogeneous servers. The MAGNITUDE, a Storage Area Network (SAN) in a Box, is the only storage subsystem to offer server clustering and a true zero-backup window. XIOtech sells and services its products directly to major corporations worldwide and through reseller relationships and OEM partnerships within the storage industry. SIC 3572. Founded in 1995. The company was acquired in January 2000 for $360 million in Seagate common stock. In October the Internal Revenue Service (IRS)Statistics of Income Division chose the XIOtech MAGNITUDE SAN server to provide continuous access to more than two terabytes of image files that are created for Exempt Form 990 Tax Returns. Now a wholly owned subsidiary of Seagate Technology Inc. (NYSE: SEG), Scotts Valley, Calif.

Z

Carl Zeiss IMT Corporation 7008 Northland Dr., Brooklyn Park, MN 55428. Tel: 763/533-9990; Fax: 763/533-4903. Gregory Lee, Pres. and CEO; Chris Grow, Dir.-Mktg.; Bill Bell, VP-Sls.; Joseph Schesnthane, Dir.-Prod. Carl Zeiss IMT (Industrial Measuring Technology) manufactures precision measuring systems for dimensional inspection and quality control. The former public company Numerex Corp. was acquired in October 1989. 220 employees (115 in Minnesota). SIC 3559. Founded in 1977. In July 2000 the company received the first Ford Motor Co. Q1 Award granted to a coordinate measure machine (CMM) manufacturing company. A division of Carl Zeiss Inc., Oberkochen, Germany. No. 59 CRM Foreign-Owned 100.

Zero Max Inc. 13200 Sixth Ave. N., Plymouth, MN 55441. Tel: 763/546-4300; Fax: 763/546-8260. Stan Vogel, Chm.; Lyle Gerads, Pres. Annual revenue $13.5 million. Zero Max manufactures adjustable-speed drives, couplings, right-angle gear boxes, and linear actuators. 80 employees (in Minnesota). SIC 3566, 3568. Founded in 1949. Owned by Miki Pulley Co. Ltd., Kawasaki, Japan. No. 97 CRM Foreign-Owned 100.

WHO'S WHO

539 BUSINESS LEADERS IN THE UPPER MIDWEST

INCLUDES

NAME

TITLE

CONTACT INFORMATION

BIRTH DATE AND PLACE

SPOUSE AND CHILDREN

EDUCATION

CAREER HISTORY AND ACTIVITIES

AWARDS, ACTIVITIES, MEMBERSHIPS

(above information provided where supplied)

Information is updated annually by each individual via questionnaire
(There was no charge for inclusion)

David H. Abramson Nat'l Managing Ptnr.-Fin. Svs., Grant Thornton LLP, 500 Pillsbury Center, Minneapolis, MN 55402. Tel: 612/332-0001. **B:** Jun. 19, 1941, St. Paul. **M:** Joyce, 1964. **C:** Michelle, Laura, Jeffrey, Dan. **E:** U. of MN, BS; U. of Michigan, MBA. **Career Hist.:** Arthur Young, New York, 1964-66; Grant Thornton, 1966-present: 1966, joined Minneapolis office; 1972-present, Mng. Ptnr., Minneapolis office; 1982-1998, N.W. Area Mng. Ptnr.; 1988-90, Natl. Mng. Dir.-Client Svs.; 1999-present National Managing Partner of Financial Services. **Career Act.:** Pres., Dir., MN Soc. of CPAs; Division Chair, Greater Mpls. United Way; Dir., past Chair, Greater Mpls. Chamber of Commerce; Treasurer and Founding Member Great North; Co-Chair, St. Louis Park Bi-Centennial Commission; Mem.-Ethics Committee, Hennepin County Bar Assn.; Fin. Advisory and Long Range Planning Ctees., St. Louis Park School District; past Mem.-Ruling Council, American Institute of CPAs; Chairman, MN Cooperation for Job Creation. **Dec./Awd.:** Accountant of the Year, Rho (U. of MN) Chapter of Beta Alpha Psi, 1984; SuperCPA Year 2000. **Act./Mem.:** Pres./Trustee, Temple Israel.

Linda L. Ahlers Pres.-Department Store Div., Target Corp., 777 Nicollet Mall, Minneapolis, MN 55402. Tel: 612/370-6948. **E:** BA-Retailing, U. of Wisconsin. **Career Hist.:** H.C. Prange Dept. Stores of WI, 1972-77; Dayton Hudson Corp., now Target Corp.: Senior Buyer, Target, 1977-89; SVP-Mdse./Planning/Control, 1989-95; EVP-Mdsg., Dept. Store Div., 1995-96; Pres., Dept. Store Div., 1996-present. **Career Act.:** Dir., Guthrie Theater; MN Comm. of 200, MN Women's Economic Roundtable. **Act./Mem.:** Mem., Mount Olivet Church.

Patrick D. Alexander Chair, CEO, Cold Spring Granite Co., 202 S. Third Ave., Cold Spring, MN 56320. Tel: 320/685-3621. Email: csginfo@coldspringgranite.com **B:** Oct. 25, 1947, St. Cloud, Minn. **M:** Mary Catherine. **C:** Heidi, Holly. **E:** St. Edward's U., BBA, 1970. **Career Hist.:** Chair, Pres., CEO, Cold Spring Granite Co., 1983-present. **Career Act.:** Dir., First National Bank (Cold Spring); 1990 Pres., Building Stone Institute; Pres., Sec., National Building Granite Quarriers Assn. **Act./Mem.:** Minneapolis Athletic Club, Minnesota Business Partnership, World Presidents Organization, Lafayette Country Club, United Way.

Anthony Lee Andersen Dir., retired Chair, H.B. Fuller Co., 2424 Territorial Rd., St. Paul, MN 55114. Tel: 651/236-4316. **B:** Dec. 10, 1935, Minneapolis. **C:** Amy. **E:** Macalester Coll., BS-Bus. Admin., 1957. **Career Hist.:** H.B. Fuller Co., 1957-present: Field Sls./NE, 1957-60; Field Sls./NY, 1960-63; Product Mgr./Hot Melt, 1963-65; Mktg. Mgr., 1965-67; EVP-U.S. Op., 1967-71; Dir., 1967-present; Pres., 1971-1992; CEO, 1974-1994; Chair, 1992-99. **Career Act.:** Dir. (for-profit companies), H.B. Fuller Co., Minnesota Mutual Life Insurance Co., ECM Publishers Inc.; Dir. (non-profit organizations), The Amherst H. Wilder Fdn., U. of MN Carlson School of Management Bd. of Overseers, Elmer L. and Eleanor J. Andersen Fdn., MN Council of Fdns., MN Center for Corporate Responsibility, MN Costa Rica Fdn., Hill Reference Library, Honorary Counsul of Costa Rica to MN. **Dec./Awd.:** 1989 Executive of the Year, Corporate Report Minnesota. **Act./Mem.:** Minnesota Club, St. Paul Rotary Club, St. Paul-Minneapolis Ctee. on Foreign Relations, Town & Country Club, Mt. Massive Lakes.

Elmer L. Andersen retired Chair/CEO, H.B. Fuller Co., 2400 Energy Park Dr., St. Paul, MN 55108. Tel: 651/645-3401. **B:** Jun. 17, 1909, Chicago. **M:** Eleanor, 1932. **C:** Anthony, Julian, Emily. **E:** U. of MN, BBA. **Career Hist.:** State Sen., 1949-58; Gov. of MN, 1961-63; Chair, H.B. Fuller Company, 1941-61 and 1963-92; President, H.B. Fuller Company, 1941-60 and 1966-71; Publisher, Princeton Union-Eagle, Mille Lacs County Times, Elk River Star News. **Career Act.:** Chair, U. of MN Fdn.; Fellow, Pierpont Morgan Library; Pres., Charles A. Lindbergh Mem. Fund; past Pres., Adhesive Assn. of America; past Chair, MN Constitutional Study Ctee.; past Regent, Chair, U. of MN; past Dir., First Trust Co., MN Mutual Life Ins. Co., George A. Hormel & Co., Natl. Assn. of Manufacturers. **Dec./Awd.:** U. of MN Outstanding Achievement Award; Order of the Lion, Finland; Award of Merit, Izaak Walton League; Silver Beaver, Silver Antelope Awards, Boy Scouts; Minneapolis Jr. Chamber Conservation Award; AAA Service to Motoring Award; Alpha Kappa Psi Award, Twin Cities Alumni Chapter; Taconite Award, American Inst. of Mining Engineers of America—MN Chapter, 1976; National Phi Kappa Phi Award, U. of MN, 1977; MN Bus. Hall of Fame Award, 1977; St. Paul Chamber's Great Living Saint Paulite Award, 1980; Dist. MN and Rotarian, R.I. Dist. Conf., 1980. **Act./Mem.:** past Pres., MN Historical Soc. Exec. Council; Dir., past Pres., Voyageurs National Park Assn., American Antiquarian Soc.; past Pres., St. Paul Rotary Club; past Dist. Gov., Rotary Intl.; past Pres., Child Welfare League of America; past Mem., MN Higher Education Coordinating Commission; past Mem., National Parks Centennial Commission; past Dir., Minneapolis Soc. of Fine Arts, MN Orchestral Assn., Assn. of Governing Bds. of Colleges and Universities, MN Judicial Planning Ctee.; past Chair-Exec. Ctee., Council on Foundations; Dir., MN Center for Book Arts; Chair, CEO, ECM Publishers Inc. (Princeton, MN); Regent, Candidate Advisory Commission; Co-Chm., Ctee. on Environmental Trust Fund.

Bradbury H. Anderson Pres., COO, Best Buy Co. Inc., 7075 Flying Cloud Dr., P.O. Box 9312 (55440), Eden Prairie, MN 55344. Tel: 612/947-2000. **Career Hist.:** Best Buy Co., 1973-present: Retail Sales, Store Mgr., Sls. Mgr., 1973-86; EVP-Mktg., 1986-95; Pres., COO, 1995-present. **Career Act.:** Dir., Best Buy Co., Junior Achievement (Colorado Springs).

David W. Anderson Founder, Chair, Famous Dave's of America Inc., 7657 Anagram Dr., Eden Prairie, MN 55344-7310. Tel: 612/833-9300. **E:** Harvard U., John F. Kennedy School of Gov't, Masters-Public Admin., 1986. **Career Hist.:** Grand Casinos Inc., Co-Founder, 1989; Rainforest Cafe Inc., Co-Founder, 1994; Famous Dave's Inc., Founder, 1994. **Career Act.:** Participant, National Task Force-"The Problems Of Minorities In Small Business" (1977), Bureau Of Indian Affairs' National Task Force on Reservation Gaming (1983), Wisconsin's Council on Minority Business Development (1983); Mem., Wisconsin Council Of Tourism (1984); Dir., Rainforest Cafe Inc. (1995). **Dec./Awd.:** Bush Leadership Fellow, 1985; Famous Dave's BBQ named "Best BBQ Sauce In America, Mild Tomato Sauce Division" at American Royal International Contest, 1995; Famous Dave's BBQ Shack named "Best Barbecue Joint" in Twin Cities by MPLS.ST. PAUL magazine, 1995; Famous Dave's named One of America's "Hottest Concepts" by Nations Restaurant News, 1997. **Act./Mem.:** Mem., Choctaw/Chippewa Indian Tribes; Enrolled Mem., Lac Courte Oreilles Lake Superior Band Of Ojibwa.

Gordon B. Anderson CEO, Gordy's Inc., 1131 Oxford St., Worthington, MN 56187. Tel: 612/559-7871. **B:** Aug. 7, 1927, Minneapolis. **M:** Doris, 1995. **C:** Tom, Bruce, Janet, Kurt, Scott, Krista. **E:** U. of MN. **Career Hist.:** Meat Dept. Mgr., A & P Stores, 1946-54; Meat Dept. Mgr., Super Valu Stores Inc., 1954-58. **Dec./Awd.:** Minnesota Grocer of the Year, 1995.

Harold E. Anderson Pres., Anderson Trucking Service Inc., 203 N. Cooper Ave., St. Cloud, MN 56302. Tel: 320/255-7400. **B:** Sep. 2, 1916, Cokato, Minn. **M:** Jeanette, 1944. **C:** Rollie, Barb (Fanslau), Jim. **Career Hist.:** Truck Driver, Cold Spring Granite Co., 1935-41; Pilot, U.S. Army Corps, 1942-45; Truck Fleet Mgr., Cold Spring Granite Co., 1946-55; Pres., Anderson Trucking Service Inc., 1955-present. **Career Act.:** Past Trustee/VChair, Calvary Baptist Church; Dir., Interstate Carriers Conf.; past Dir., St. Cloud Area Chamber of Commerce; past Trustee, past Bd. of Governors, Bethel Coll. and Seminary Fdn.; VP-at-large, American Trucking Association; Dir., Citizens Savings Bank (past); Past President's Council, Trinity Evangelical Divinity School. **Dec./Awd.:** Air Medal and Distinguished

Flying Cross, U.S. Army Air Corps; President's Award, MN Motor Transport Assn. 1984; Founder's Award, American Truck Historical Soc. 1985; Fifty Year Award, American Trucking Assn. 1986; Minnesota and Dakotas Entrepreneur of the Year (Transportation/Distribution category), Ernst & Young LLP, 1998; Bethel College and Seminary-Arnold T. Wicklund Award1993; St. Cloud Area Chamber-Chairperson's Award 1995; Truckload Carriers Assoc.-Past Chairman's Award 1998; St. Cloud Area Chamber-Entrepreneurial Success Award 1998; Minnesota Trucking Assoc.-Lifetime Achievement Award 1999; Minnesota Transportation Alliance-Minnesota Transp. Advocate Award 2000. **Act./Mem.:** St. Cloud Airport Advisory Bd.; Exec. Comm., American Trucking Assoc.; Board of Dir., Truckload Carriers Conf.; Board of Dir., Specialized Carriers and Rigging Assoc.; Board of Dir. SC & RA Foundation; Board of Dir., Minnesota Trucking Assoc.; Board of Dir., Central MN Transportation Alliance; Board of Dir., Harold Anderson Entrepreneurial Center.

Lee R. Anderson Chair, CEO, APi Group, 2366 Rose Place, Roseville, MN 55113. Tel: 651/636-4320. Email: Enirkath@aol.com **B:** Jun. 22, 1939, Minneapolis. **M:** Penny Pilney, 1965. **C:** Andy, Katharine. **E:** U.S. Military Academy at West Point, BS-Civil Engrg., 1961. **Career Hist.:** Chair and CEO, APi Group Inc., 1964-present; Chair, Intl. Bancorp., 1980-present; Chair and CEO, APi Supply Co., 1985-present. **Career Act.:** Dir., Pan-O-Gold Bakeries. **Dec./Awd.:** L.B. Hartz Professional Achievement Award, Moorhead State U., 1990. **Act./Mem.:** Minikahda Club; Minneapolis Club; Braden Lodge Masons; Osman Shrine; 1988 Commodore, Minneapolis Aquatennial.

Lowell C. Anderson Chair, Pres., CEO, Allianz Life Insurance Co. of North America, 1750 Hennepin Ave., Minneapolis, MN 55403. Tel: 612/347-6500. **B:** May 20, 1937, Minneapolis. **M:** Madeleine. **C:** Elizabeth Hellman, William Anderson, Katherine Carpenter. **E:** BBA, Macalester College, 1963. **Career Hist.:** CT General Life Insurance Co., agent/manager, 1963-69; North American Life & Casualty Co. (now Allianz Life): St. Paul Branch Mgr.; Chair, Pres., CEO, 1988-present. **Career Act.:** Trustee, U. of St. Thomas; Exec. Bd. Mem./Chair-Mktg. Ctee., National Boy Scouts of America; past Chair, YMCA of Minneapolis; past Pres., Viking Council-BSA; Dir., NALAC Financial Plans, Preferred Life Insurance Co. of New York, YMCA of Metropolitan Minneapolis, Minnesota Historical Society, St. Jude Medical Inc. **Dec./Awd.:** Viking Council, BSA: Silver Eagle Award, Silver Beaver Award; Paul Harris Fellow (Rotary); CLU - Chartered Life Underwriter. **Act./Mem.:** Investment Ctee., United Way of Minneapolis; Minikahda Club; Minneapolis Club.

Marge Anderson Former CEO, Mille Lacs Band/Ojibwe Indians, 43678 Henry Davis Dr., Onamia, MN 56359. Tel: 320/532-4181. **B:** Apr. 1932, Vineland, Minn. **M:** Merlin, 1954. **E:** Onamia High School, 1952; Honorary doctorate of law, Hamline U., 1998. **Career Hist.:** District Rep., Mille Lacs Band Tribal Council, 1976-1987; Sec./Treas., Mille Lacs Band, 1987-1991; Chief Executives, Mille Lacs Band, 1991-2000. **Career Act.:** Mille Lacs Band representative at a coffee with President Clinton, February 1996; named president of the 33-member Midwest Alliance of Sovereign Tribes (MAST), January 1997; two terms as Minneapolis Area Regional VP for the National Congress of American Indians; Minnesota Chippewa Tribe's Education, Chair MN Chippewa Tribe Housing Corporation 1996-2000, and Economic Development, and Legislative subcommittees; VP MN Chippewa Tribe; Dir. Federal Home Loan Bank, 1997-present; MN Housing Finance Board Member 2000-present. **Dec./Awd.:** Indian Child Advocate of the Year, 1994; Lifetime Achievement Award, Native American Finance Officers Association, 1994; September Woman of Distinction, Mpls.St.Paul magazine/KARE-TV, 1995; Distinguished Achievement Award, U. of MN College of Education and Human Development, 1996; Tribal Leader of the Year, Minnesota American Indian Chamber of Commerce, 1996; profiled on CBS-TV's "Sunday Morning with Charles Osgood," November 1996; Excellence in Leadership award, Intl. Gaming Business Expo, 1997; Tribal Leader of the Year, National Congress of American Indians, 1997; Susan B. Anthony Award, MN Center for Women in Gov't, 1999; Wendell Chino Humanitarian Award, Nat'l Indian Gaming Ass'n, 2000.

Scott R. Anderson Pres., CEO, North Memorial Health Care, 3300 Oakdale Ave. N., Robbinsdale, MN 55422. Tel: 612/520-5001. **B:** Mar. 25, 1940, Fargo, N.D. **C:** Scott, Kelly, Kara, Matt.. **E:** U. of N. Dak., BS, BA, 1962; U. of Iowa, MA, 1964. **Career Hist.:** North Memorial, 1964-present: VP, 1964-81; Pres. and CEO, 1981-present. **Career Act.:** Dir., Courage Center, Empi Inc., Healthcare Education and Research Fdn., Medical Alley Assn., Minnesota Hospital and Healthcare Partnership, Telident Inc. **Act./Mem.:** Golden Valley Country Club; Adjunct Faculty, U. of Iowa, Concordia College.

David L. Andreas Chair, CEO, National City Bancorp., 651 Nicollet Mall, Minneapolis, MN 55402. Tel: 612/904-8500. **B:** Mar. 1, 1949, St. Paul. **M:** Debra, 1985. **E:** Denver U., BA, 1971; Mankato State U., MA, 1976. **Career Hist.:** Credit Mgmt. Trainee, First Interstate Bank, 1976-77; National City Bank of Minneapolis: Comm. Loan Officer, 1977-80; Dir., 1980-1994; Chair, 1991-1994; CEO, 1994-present; National City Bancorporation, 1980-present: VP, 1980-85; SVP, 1985-87; Chair, CEO, 1987-present. **Career Act.:** Pres., CEO, National City Bank of Minneapolis; Chair, CEO, National City Bancorporation. **Act./Mem.:** Exec., Ctee.-Children's HeartLink; Minneapolis Club; Member, Mankato State U., College of Business Advisory Council, Minneapolis College of Art & Design (Chair-Board of Trustees); Dir., Minnesota Center for Corporate Responsibility; Trustee, Breck School.

Lowell W. Andreas Dir., National City Bancorp., 651 Nicollet Mall, Minneapolis, MN 55402. Tel: 612/904-8500. **B:** Feb. 24, 1922, Lisbon, Iowa. **M:** Nadine B. **C:** Pamela Stisser, David. **E:** Wheaton College, Wheaton, IL, 1939-41; U. of IA, Iowa City, IA, 1941-42. **Career Hist.:** Adjustor, Pilgrim Mutual Ins. Co., 1946-47; Dir., VP, Sec., Treas., Honeymead Products Co., 1947-53; Dir., Pres., Interoceanic Industries Inc., 1953-64; Dir., Pres., Honeymead Trading Corp., 1960-67; VP, Farmers Union Grain Terminal Assn., 1960-67; Pres., Honeymead Products Co., 1960-67; Archer Daniels Midland Co.: EVP, 1968-69; Pres., 1969-72; Dir., Mem.-Exec. Ctee., Fin./Mgmt. Ctee., Audit Ctee., 1968-1997; Dir., National City Bancorporation, 1983-1996.

John C. Appel VChair, CFO, Dain Rauscher Corp., Dain Bosworth Plaza, 60 S. Sixth St., Minneapolis, MN 55402. Tel: 612/371-2748. Email: jcappel@interrafin.com **E:** Bachelor's-Accounting, U. of Michigan; MBA, Harvard School of Business. **Career Hist.:** Partner, Deloitte Haskins & Sells (now Deloitte & Touche), 1982-86; Dain Rauscher Corp., 1986-present: SVP and CFO (1986), EVP (1990), Pres./COO-Dain Bosworth (1994), VChm. and CFO (1997), Pres.-Fixed Income Capital Markets Group (2000). **Career Act.:** Mem., Dain Bosworth Exec. Ctee., Dain Rauscher Corp. Exec. Ctee., Dain Rauscher Corp. Sr. Exec. Group, Dain Rauscher Corp. Bd. of Directors; Mem., NYSE regional firms ctee., United Way of the Mpls. Area; Dir., Smith Breeden Associates, MN Orchestral Assn., MN Zoo (Chair).

George Aristides CEO, Graco Inc., 4050 Olson Memorial Hwy., P.O. Box 1441 (55440), Golden Valley, MN 55422. Tel: 612/623-6607. **B:** Jan. 3, 1936. **M:** Diana. **E:** McMaster U., Toronto, Registered Indl. Accountant, 1966. **Career Hist.:** Accountant, Olympic Airways, 1960-62; Group Controller, Carlson Companies, 1962-73; Graco Inc., 1973-present: Corporate Controller, 1973-85; VP, 1980; VP-Mfg. Op. and Cont., 1985-93; EVP, Indl./Automotive Div., Mfg./Distrib./Eurafrican Op., 1993; Pres., COO, 1993-95; CEO, 1996-present. **Career Act.:** Dir., Graco Inc.; Registered Industrial Accountants; MA Retail Institute; MN Executive Program. **Act./Mem.:** Minnesota Business Partnership, Wayzata Country Club.

Robert D. Armitage CEO, Board of Social Ministry, 3490 Lexington Ave N., Shoreview, MN 55126. Tel: 651/766-4300. **B:** May 14, 1942, Neillsville, Wis. **M:** Kathleen M., 1966. **C:** Dale, Daniel. **E:** U. of Hawaii, MSW, 1967. **Career Hist.:** Social Work Department Director, Moose Lake State Hospital, 1967-70; VP of Operations, National Health Enterprises,

1970-74; VP and Dir. of Operations, Gold Medallion Corporation, 1974-78; Admin., Mt. Sinai Green Tree Health Care Center Inc., 1978-81; CEO, Ebenezer Social Ministries, 1997-1999; Pres./CEO Board of Social Ministry, 1982-present.

Scott D. Augustine, M.D. Chair, CEO, Augustine Medical Inc., 10393 W. 70th St., Eden Prairie, MN 55344. Tel: 612/947-1200. **B:** Jan. 22, 1954, New Britain, Conn. **M:** Sue Dykins, 1978. **C:** Ryan, Brent, Garrett. **E:** BA, U. of MN, 1975; MD, U. of MN School of Medicine, 1979. **Career Hist.:** Founder, Mgr., Sandstone Lighthouse Co., 1971-79; Medical Officer, U.S. Navy, 1980-87; Staff Anesthesiologist, Mercy Hospital (San Diego), 1984-87; Staff Anesthesiologist, Research Medical Center (Kansas City, MO), 1987-89; Asst. Professor of Anesthesiology, U. of MN, 1989-93; Founder, Chair, CEO, Augustine Medical, 1987-present. **Career Act.:** Mem., American Soc. of Anesthesiologists, American Medical Assn., MN Soc. of Anesthesiologists, Intl. Anesthesia Research Soc.; Dir., Center for Biomedical Engrg.-U. of MN, MN High Tech Council, American Soc. of Post Anesthesia Nurses Fdn.; holds patents on Bair Hugger Patient Warming System and Augustine Intubation Guide. **Dec./Awd.:** Outstanding Achievement in a Health Care Product, Medical Alley, 1992; MN Entrepreneur of the Year, 1992.

William F. Austin Chair, Pres., CEO, Starkey Laboratories Inc., 6700 Washington Ave. S., Eden Prairie, MN 55344. Tel: 612/941-6401. **B:** Feb. 25, 1942, Springfield, Mo. **C:** Gregory, Alexandria. **E:** Oregon State U. **Career Hist.:** Mgr., South Dakota Hearing Center, 1961; Owner, Professional Hearing Aid Service, 1962-70; Pres., Starkey Laboratories Inc., 1970-present. **Career Act.:** Dir., Hearing Industries Assn., Dir., USA-USSR Connect; Dir., International Hearing Fdn.. **Dec./Awd.:** Recognition Award, Intl. Hearing Fdn.; Sponsor Award, World Games for the Deaf; Founder, Bob Hope Cultural Center, Gene Autry Western Museum; Peace Corps "Leader of the Peace" Award; Outstanding Business Leader Award, Northwood Institute; "Entrepreneur of the Year" Award, Inc. magazine. **Act./Mem.:** Calhoun Beach Club; Palm Springs Senior Center; Palm Springs Youth Center; Desert Museum; Sonance; Sponsor, Better Hearing Institute, Thalians Mental Health Org.; Diamonds of the Desert; City of Hope; Child Help USA; Big Horn Institute Fdn.

Thomas L. Auth Chair, CEO, ITI Technologies Inc., 2266 N. Second St., North St. Paul, MN 55109. Tel: 651/777-2690. **B:** Jan. 21, 1945, Durand, Wis. **M:** Sharon, 1966. **E:** BS-Accounting, U. of Wisc.-Eau Claire, 1967; MBA, U. of Minn., 1969. **Career Hist.:** CPA, Deloitte & Touche; Pres., ITI Technologies, 1981-present. **Career Act.:** Owner, Chair, CEO, Vomela Specialty Co.; Dir., ITI Technologies Inc., Ergodyne Inc., E.H. Publishing Inc., Compu-Shop Inc.; past Dir., Security Industry Association. **Dec./Awd.:** St. Paul Small Businessman of the Year, 1985. **Act./Mem.:** North Oaks Country Club.

B

Harold O. (Hal) Bakke Chair, Pres., Christian Brothers Inc., 1001 State St., Warroad, MN 56763. Tel: 218/386-1111. **B:** Dec. 22, 1932, Minneapolis. **M:** Joan Ellenson, 1964. **C:** Chad, Kim. **E:** St. Olaf Coll.; U. of MN; American Institute of the Air. **Career Hist.:** Radio Announcer, Account Exec., KWAD Radio, 1954-59; Radio Announcer, Account Exec., KRAD Radio, 1959-61; Mgr., KRAD Radio, 1962-63; Mgr., KRWB Radio, 1964-70; Founder, Pres., Christian Brothers Inc., 1964-present. **Career Act.:** Dir., Christian Brothers Inc.. **Dec./Awd.:** Distinguished Service Award, Lions Club, 1988. **Act./Mem.:** Lions Club; Warroad City Council, 1987-94.

Earl E. Bakken Founder, Dir. Emeritus, Medtronic Inc., 7000 Central Ave. N.E., Fridley, MN 55432. Tel: 612/514-3000. **B:** Jan. 10, 1924, Minneapolis. **M:** Doris Bakken, 1982. **C:** Wendy, Jeff, Brad, Pam. **E:** BS-Electrical Engrg., U. of Minn., 1948. **Career Hist.:** United States Air Force, 1942-46; Medtronic, 1949-present: Co-Founder; Partner, 1949-57; Chair, CEO, 1957-76; Senior Chair, 1976-1989; Dir., 1989-94; Consultant, 1994-present. **Career Act.:** Pres., Board of Directors, North Hawaii Community Hospital; Chair, Board of Directors, Archaeus Project; Chair, Board of Directors, The Bakken (A Library and Museum of Electricity in Life); Vice Chair, Pavek Museum of Broadcasting; Board of Members, Children's Heart Fund; Honorary Board of Trustees, Science Museum of Minnesota; past Mem., Medical Alley; President, Five Mountain Medical Community; Director Emeritus, Board of Directors, Medtronic Inc.; Vice Chairman, Board of Directors, Friends of the Future, Hawaii. **Dec./Awd.:** MN Bus. Hall of Fame, 1978; U. of MN Outstanding Achievement Award, 1981; Centennial Medal, Institute of Electrical and Electronics Engineers, 1984; NASPE's Distinguished Service Award, 1985; Centennial Medal, St. Thomas College, 1986; Governor's Award for Medical Leadership, Minnesota Medical Alley Assn., 1988; Achievement Award, Leadership in the Business Application of Science and Technology, Science Museum of MN, 1988; Honorary Dr. of Science, Tulane U., 1988 and U. of MN, 1988; Outstanding MN/Year, MN Broadcasters Assn., 1988; Officer in the Order of Orange-Nassau, 1989; Lifetime Achievement Award, Entrepreneur of the Year, 1991 and 1993, MN Entrepreneur's Club; Eli Lilly Award in Medical and Biological Engineering, IEEE, 1994; MN Inventors Hall of Fame, 1995; Special Service Award, Richard Smart Big Island Community Achievement, Waimea, Hawaii, 1995; Heart Ball Honoree, American Heart Assn., 1996; Lifetime Achievement Award, MN High Technology Council, 1996; Creative Achievment Award, American Creativity Assn., 1996; Gold Medal, the European Society of Cardiology, June 1999; NASPE Pioneering Award for Contributions to the Fields of Cardiac Packing and Electrophysiology, June 1999; Living Treasure of Hawaii Award, Honpa Hongwanji Mission of Hawaii; Special Award Cardiostim, Anniversary for Engineers and Industry Founders, June 1998; Association for the Advancement of Medical Instrumentation (AAMI) Foundation Laufman-Greatbatch Prize, 1998; Texas Heart Institute Innovator Award, 1998. **Act./Mem.:** Fellow, Bakken Society, Institute of Electrical and Electronic Engineers, Instrument Society of America. Mem., American Antiquarian Soc., Assn. for the Advancement of Medical Instrumentation, National Academy of Engineering Associate Member, North American Society of Pacing and Electrophysiology Inc.; Honorary Fellow, American College of Cardiology, International College of Surgeons.

Mark Banks, M.D. Pres., CEO, Blue Cross and Blue Shield of Minnesota, RiverPark Office Building, 3400 Yankee Dr., Eagan, MN 55121. Tel: 651/456-8438. **E:** BA-Biology (Magna Cum Laude, Phi Beta Kappa, Sigma Xi), Carleton College, 1971; M.D., U. of MN Medical School, 1976; Internal Medicine Residency, U. of MN Hospitals, 1979. Academic Positions: Clinical Asst. Professor of Medicine, U. of MN School of Medicine; Adjunct Asst. Professor, U. of MN School of Pharmacy. Certifications: License to Practice Medicine, MN State Bd. of Medical Examiners, 1977-present; Diplomate, Natl. Bd. of Medical Examiners, 1977; Diplomate, American Bd. of Internal Medicine, 1979; Qualified Reviewer, Natl. Ctee. for Quality Assurance, 1991. **Career Hist.:** Private Practice (Internal Medicine), 1979-85; Medical Advisor, Fdn. for Health Care Evaluation (Minneapolis), 1981-85; Medical Dir., Coordinated Health Care (St. Paul), 1985-87; Medical Dir. for Quality Improvement, BCBSM, 1985-86; Assoc. Medical Dir., Center for Quality Health Care-Blue Cross and Blue Shield Assn. (Chicago), 1989-90; VP and Medical Dir., Blue Plus, 1986-92; SVP-BCBSM and COO-Blue Plus, 1992-93; Gp. VP-BCBSM and Pres./CEO-Blue Plus, 1993-1998; Pres., COO, BCBSM, 1998-99; Pres., CEO, BCBSM, 1999-present. **Career Act.:** Chair/Mem.-Steering Ctee., Technical Advisory Gp.-Health Plan Comparison Project-MN Coalition on Health; Mem.-Quality and Data Ctee., MN Medical Assn.; Clinical Advisory Panel, Voluntary Healthcare Information Project-Healthcare Education & Research Fdn.; Dir., Fdn. for Health Care Evaluation (MN PRO); Myocardial Infarction Task Force, MN Clinical Comparison and Assessment Project; Exec. Ctee., Itasca Heart Project (Grand Rapids, MN); Market Information Task Force, MN Coalition on Health; Steering Ctee., AIDS Education Program-MN Chamber of Commerce. Professional Affiliations: American College of Physicians, American Medical Assn., MN Medical Assn., Hennepin County Medical Soc., Soc. of General Internal Medicine, American

Academy of Medical Dirs., American Public Health Assn., Soc. for Medical Decision Making, Ordway Music Theatre, United Way of the St. Paul Area. **Dec./Awd.:** Governor's Award for Excellence in Health Promotion Programs from the MN Dept. of Health (for Itasca Heart Project).

William P. Bartkowski Chair, CEO, Bluefire Partners, 1300 Fifth Street Towers, 150 S. Fifth St., Minneapolis, MN 55402. Tel: 612/344-1012. Email: bartkowski@nhbpr.com **B:** Oct. 3, 1951, Bismarck, N.D. **M:** Colette Bauer, 1978. **C:** Sarah Kay. **E:** U. of Mary, BA English, 1974; St. Thomas School of Theology (Denver), MA Theology, 1975; North Dakota State U., MA-English, 1979; Colombia Pacific, Ph.D.-Adult Ed., 1984. **Career Hist.:** North Dakota State U., college lecturer in English, Counselor, 1976-80; Nativity Parish, Dir.-Religious Education, 1980-82; Fargo Catholic Diocese, Dir., Religious Education, 1982-84; Metropolitan Financial Corporation, 1984-95: Dir.-Corp. Communications, 1984-86; AVP, 1986-88; VP, 1988-89; SVP-Corp. Relations, 1989-90; EVP, Chief Admin. Officer, 1990-94; Neuger Henry Bartkowski, Partner and Managing Director, 1995-present. **Career Act.:** Chair, Board of Regents, U. of Mary (Bismarck), 1992-present; Dir. and past Chair, Minnesota League of Savings and Community Bankers; past Dir., National Investor Relations Institute; Dir., Catholic Spirit, Indianhead Council, Boy Scouts of America. **Dec./Awd.:** Eagle Scout, University of Mary Alumni Recognition Award, Distinguished Toastmaster Award. **Act./Mem.:** University of Mary Presidents Club, Minneapolis Club, Lafayette Club, St. Bartholomew's Catholic Church (Wayzata).

Paul Baszucki Chair, Norstan Inc., 605 N. Highway 169, 12th Floor, Plymouth, MN 55441. Tel: 612/420-1210. **B:** May 15, 1940, Saskatchewan. **M:** Helen Beleyowski, 1961. **C:** Greg, Todd, Cindy, David. **E:** U. of Saskatchewan, Bach. of Commerce, 1962; McGill U., Chartered Accountant, 1964. **Career Hist.:** Norstan Communications: VP, 1973-78; Pres., 1978-83; Norstan Inc.: Pres., 1984-1988; VChair, CEO, 1988-95; Co-Chair, CEO, 1995-1997; Chair of the Board, 1997-present; also currently Chair, Norstan Network Services Inc., Norstan Canada Inc., Norstan Network Services of New Hampshire Inc.; Chair and Pres. of Norstan Financial Services Inc. **Career Act.:** Dir., Washington Scientific Industries Inc., G&K Services Inc., Norstan Inc.. **Dec./Awd.:** Annual Bishops Award, Catholic Charities, 1984; Jewish Christian Brotherhood Award, 1996. **Act./Mem.:** United Way volunteer; Minneapolis Club; Wayzata Country Club.

Ronald O. Baukol EVP-Intl. Op., 3M Co., 3M Center, Bldg. 220-14E-14, Maplewood, MN 55144. Tel: 651/733-1110. Email: robaukol@mmm.com **B:** Aug. 11, 1937, Chicago. **M:** Gay, 1959. **C:** David, Andrew, Kathlyn. **E:** BS-Chem. Engrg., Iowa St. U., 1959; MS-Chem. Engrg., M.I.T., 1960. **Career Hist.:** Non-3M (on leave): White House Fellow, Office of Communications, Washington, D.C., 1970-71; Dir., Office of Regional Liaison-E.P.A., Washington, D.C., 1971-72; 3M: New Product Devel. Engr., Medical Products Div. Lab., 1966-68; New Product Devel. Supv., Medical Products Div. Lab., 1968-70; Mgr., New Health Care Enterprises, Medical Products Div., 1972-74; Dept. Mgr., New Health Care Enterprises, Medical Products Div., 1974-77; Dept. Mgr., Diagnostics, Medical Products Div., 1977-79; Dept. Mgr., Dental Products, Health Care Products/Services Group, 1979-82; Gen. Mgr., Riker Laboratories Inc., 1982-84; VP/Gen. Mgr.-Riker Laboratories Inc. and Chair-3M Human Relations Advisory Committee, 1984-86; Mng. Dir./Chief Exec., 3M U.K. plc, 1986-88; Chair/CEO-3M U.K. plc and Mng. Dir.-3M Ireland, 1988-89; Group VP, Pharmaceutical/Dental Products, 1989-90; Group VP, Medical Products, 1990-91; VP, Asia-Pacific, 1991-94; VP, Asia-Pacific/Canada/Latin America, 1994-95; EVP, International Operations, 1995-present; Dir., 1996-present. **Career Act.:** Past Dir./VChair/Chair, St. Paul Chapter-American Red Cross; past Dir., Alumni Assn.-Iowa St. U., Pharmaceutical Mfrs. Assn., Children's Health Care Fdn.; past trustee, MN Medical Fdn., The Children's Hospital Inc.; past Mem., British Institute of Mgmt.; Dir., Graco Inc., The Toro Co., past Dir. Minnesota Meeting; Gov., ISU Fdn.-Iowa St. U.; Trustee and Vice Chair, U.S. Council for Intl. Business; Mem., Intl. Programs Advisory Council, Carlson School of Management, U. of Minn.; Dir., Great North Alliance.

John R. Beardsley Chair, CEO, Padilla Speer Beardsley Inc., 224 Franklin Ave. W., Minneapolis, MN 55404. Tel: 612/872-3710. Email: jbeardsley@psbpr.com **B:** Jan. 10, 1937, Minneapolis. **M:** Sharon, 1960. **C:** Elizabeth, Alison, Leslie. **E:** Augustana College, English and Philosophy, 1961. **Career Hist.:** News Ed., *Daily Argus Leader,* 1961-64; City Ed., *Worthington Daily Globe,* 1964; Correspondent, News Ed., Associated Press, 1965-68; Mgr. of Communications, Pillsbury Co., 1968; Mgr. of Communications Projects, Dayton Hudson, 1969; Padilla & Speer Inc., 1970-87: Acct. Exec., 1970; VP, 1972; SVP, 1978; CEO, 1983; Chair, CEO, Padilla Speer Beardsley Inc., 1987. **Career Act.:** Mem., Minneapolis Athletic Club, Counselors Acad.-Public Relations Soc. of America, Twin Cities Chapter-Natl. Investor Relations Institute; Mem., past Pres., MN Chapter-Public Relations Soc. of America; President in 1995, Public Relations Society of America. **Act./Mem.:** Bd., American Red Cross North Central Blood Services Region.

Jane G. Belau Chair, Pres., Belau Consulting Group, 916 Fourth St. S.W., Rochester, MN 55902. Tel: 507/288-1978. Email: jbrr@millcomm.com **B:** Oct. 21, 1934, Fertile, Minn. **M:** Dr. Paul G. Belau, 1957. **C:** Steven, Matthew, Nancy. **E:** Concordia College (Moorhead, MN); Fairview, R.N., 1956; U of MN. **Career Hist.:** private consultant to industry, state and federal governments, universities, and foundations, 1968-78; Consultant, U.S. Dept. of Health, Educ. & Welfare; Commissioner, MN State Corrections Authority, 1974-75; Consultant, McKnight Fdn., 1974-78; Control Data Corp., 1978-1990: VP-Strategic Programs, 1979-81; VP-Bus. Devel./Human Svs., 1981-82; VP-MN Industry, Academic and Govt. Affairs, 1982-84; VP-Support Svs. U.S.S.A., 1984; VP-State Mktg. and Govt. Affairs, 1984-1990; Chair and Pres., Belau Consulting Group, present; Consultant to Ceridian Corporation. **Career Act.:** Minnesota Regent Candidate Advisory Council; Minnesota Commission on Reform and Efficiency (CORE); Minnesota Milestones Commission; Current Dir., MN High-Tech Council, MN Private College Council, MN 4-H Fdn. Bd. of Trustees, U of MN Graduate School Bd. of Advisors; Natl. Advisory Council, St. John's U.; past Pres., Dir., Rochester Area Economic Development Inc.; past Dir, Olmsted Community Hospital Bd., Natl. Lutheran Academy; past U.S. Chamber of Commerce Committee on Nation's Health Care; President's Council, College of St. Catherine; past Dir., Rochester Area Chamber of Commerce, Group Health Assn. of America, Courage Center; Founding Dir., Vinland Natl. Center, MN Women's Economic Roundtable; past Mem., Commission on MN Future, MN Cable Comm. Bd., State Health Coordinating Council Bd., MN Ombudsman Ctee.; Founder, past Pres., Natl. Conference on Devel. Disabilities; past Chair, Natl. Advisory Council on Devel. Disabilities and MN Governor Council; Delegate, White Conference on Aging; Chair, Public Salaries Commission, 1995; Chair and member, Rochester City Charter Commission, 1997-present; Chairman, Olmsted County Planning and Zoning Commission; member, Board of Directors American Electronics Association. **Dec./Awd.:** Outstanding Leadership Award, Intl. Assn. of Women Executives, 1980; Woman of the Year, Business and Professional Women, 1974; Natl. Cable Television Assn. Award, 1976; Leadership Award, Courage Center; National Developmental Disabilities Assn. Appreciation Award, 1982 Who's Who in American Women; Who's Who in Finance and Industry; Who's Who in Media and Communications; Minnesota Community Television Lifetime Service Award, 1995; the Athena Award, 1999. **Act./Mem.:** Rotary International, Antique Arts Club.

T. Geron (Jerry) Bell Pres., Minnesota Twins Baseball Club Inc., 34 Kirby Puckett Place, Minneapolis, MN 55415. Tel: 612/375-1366. **M:** Phyllis. **Career Hist.:** Asst. Executive Dir., Metropolitan Sports Facilities Commission, 1977-87; Pres., Minnesota Twins, 1987-present. **Career Act.:** Dir., Minneapolis Downtown Council; Mem., Minneapolis Chamber of Commerce Communications Ctee.; Dir., Greater Convention and Visitors Assn.; Mem., Executive Ctee. of the Mpls./St. Paul Final Four Organizing Ctee. **Act./Mem.:** Dir., Twins Community Fund; Mem., North St. Paul/Maplewood School Board.

Melanie Benjamin CEO, Mille Lacs Band/Ojibwe Indians, HCR 67, Box 194, Onamia, MN 56359. Tel: 320/532-4181. **E:** BA. **Career Hist.:** Mmgt. Consultant; Bus. Dev. Specialist; College Instructor; Band's Commissioner of Administration, 1989-97, which included serving as SVP of Admin. and Finance at Grand Casino Hinckley; Asst. Teacher, Band's Nay Ah Shing Schools library; Acting Site Mgr. for the Mille Lacs Indian Gaming Assoc.; Minnesota Family Investment Program Case Worker; Kathio Township Supervisor. **Career Act.:** Dir., Bemidji State University Alumni Board; Dir., Woodlands National Bank Board of Directors; Citizen for the Minnesota Governor's Roundtable for Sustainable Development; Secretary for the National Indian Gaming Assoc.; Treas. of the Minnesota Indian Gaming Association.

Duane Benson Exec. Dir., Minnesota Business Partnership Inc., 4050 IDS Center, 80 S. Eighth St., Minneapolis, MN 55402. Tel: 612/370-0840. Email: mbp@mn.uswest.net **B:** Aug. 5, 1945, Belmond, Iowa. **M:** Melissa. **C:** Brooke, Jess. **E:** Hamline U. **Career Hist.:** State Senator District #31, 1980, 1982, 1986, 1990, and 1992; Senate Republican Leader, 1987-92. **Career Act.:** Mem. Senate Ctees., Government and Operations, Health Care, Rules and Administration, Taxes, and Tax Laws. **Act./Mem.:** Lions Club, Minnesota Cattleman's Assn.; Minnesota Corn Growers Assn.; Minnesota Zoo Board; NFL Alumni Association; Dir., HMN Financial Inc.

N.L. Bentson Chair, Midcontinent Media Inc., 7900 Xerxes Ave. S., Suite 1100, Bloomington, MN 55431. Tel: 612/844-2600. **B:** Jun. 17, 1921, St. Paul. **M:** Nancy, 1946. **C:** two. **E:** BS-Geology, BA-Petroleum Engrg., U. of MN, 1943. **Career Hist.:** Pres., WMIN Broadcasting Co. (Minneapolis/St. Paul), 1949-52; Midcontinent Broadcasting Co./Midcontinent Media Inc.: EVP, 1952-86; Pres., 1986-88; Chair/Pres./CEO, 1988-95; Chair/CEO, 1995-96, Chair, 1996-present. **Career Act.:** Participated in early development of FM radio stations by coordinating successful efforts of Twin Cities stations to establish the multiplexed FM antenna complex atop the IDS building; past Dir., FM Broadcasters Assn., MN Broadcasters (Pres.), Mutual Broadcasters Affiliates, Natl. Assn. of Broadcasters (two terms); past mem., Natl. Cable Television Cooperative; Officer/Dir., MN Advertising Club, Mount Zion Temple, Pavek Museum of Broadcasting, U. of MN Hospital, Variety Club Children's Hospital, Variety Club of the Northwest. **Dec./Awd.:** Presidential Citation, Variety Clubs Intl., 1982; Eddie Ruben Golden Heart Award, 1988; Pioneer of the Year, MN Broadcasters Assn., 1990; Humanitarian Award, Variety Club Assn., 1993. **Act./Mem.:** Donor, Pediatric Cardiology Dept. Chair, U. of MN; Mem., Chamber of Commerce, Decathlon Club, Dunkers, Mpls. Club, MN Press Club, Oakridge Country Club.

Lyle Berman Chair, CEO, Lakes Gaming Inc., 130 Cheshire Ln., Minnetonka, MN 55305. Tel: 612/449-7001. **B:** Aug. 6, 1941, Minneapolis. **M:** Janis. **C:** Julie, Bradley, Amy, Jessie. **E:** U. of Minn., BS, 1964. **Career Hist.:** VP-Store Operations, Berman's Specialty Stores Inc.; Pres., CEO, Bermans Specialty Stores Inc., 1978-88; Consultant, Wilsons Suede and Leather, 1989; Chair, Berman Consulting Corp., 1989-1998; Chair, Grand Casinos Inc.; Lakes Gaming Inc., Chair and CEO. **Career Act.:** Dir., G-III Apparel Group Ltd., New Horizon Kids Quest Inc., Wilsons The Leather Experts; Chair & CEO, Rainforest Cafe Inc.; Fanball Inc. **Dec./Awd.:** B'nai B'rith Great American Traditions Award, 1995; Gaming Executive of the Year, Casino Journal magazine, 1996.

Michael Berman Pres., SCIMED Life Systems Inc./Boston Scientific Corp., One SCIMED Place, Maple Grove, MN 55311. Tel: 612/494-2729. Email: bermanm@bsci.com **B:** Oct. 28, 1957, Ithaca, N.Y. **M:** Judy, 1981. **C:** Oren, Noah. **E:** Cornell U.: BS, 1979; MBA, 1986. **Career Hist.:** SCIMED, 1986-present: Product Mgr., Dir.-Mktg., VP-Sls./Mktg., Pres. (since July 1995). **Act./Mem.:** Board, Minneapolis Jewish Day School; Corporate Chair, Juvenile Diabetes Walk for the Cure; Co-chair, Campaign for the Bio-Medical Engineering Institute.

William F. Bieber Chair, Acrometal Cos. Inc., 2600 Niagara Ln. N., Plymouth, MN 55447. Tel: 612/553-7700. **B:** Poughkeepsie, N.Y. **M:** Kathleen, 1969. **C:** Christine, James, Kerri. **E:** U. of MI, BS; Harvard Graduate School, Smaller-Company Mgmt. Program. **Career Hist.:** Various mgmt. positions, Acrometal Family of Companies., 1964-present. **Career Act.:** Chair: Acrometal Family of Companies; Dir., Weather Rite Inc., Hammer Residences Inc., Quast Transfer, TCF Bank Minnesota; Trustee, Dunwoody Institute. **Act./Mem.:** Minneapolis Club; World Presidents Organization; United Way; Intl. Wire Assn.; Metropolitan Breakfast Club; MN State Squash Rackets Assn.; MN Executives Organization.

James Henry Binger private investor, 4522 IDS Center, 80 S. Eighth St., Minneapolis, MN 55402. Tel: 612/341-3500. **B:** May 16, 1916, Minneapolis. **M:** Virginia McKnight, 1939. **C:** James M., Cynthia (Boynton). **E:** Yale U., AB, Econ., 1938; U. of MN Law School, 1941. **Career Hist.:** Private Law Practice, 1941-43; Honeywell, 1943-78; Private Investor, 1978-present. **Career Act.:** Owner, Chair, Jujamcyn Theaters Corporation; Mem. Exec. Ctee., League of American Theaters; Dir., The Guthrie Theater; Retired Dir., Northwest Airlines; Retired Dir., 3M Company; Retired Director, Honeywell; Mem., Business Council; Chair, International Peace Academy; Gov., Dir., Atlantic Institute of Foreign Affairs; Owner, Chair, Tartan Farms Corporation; Former Chair, Calder Race Course; Former Chair, Tropical Park Inc.; Retired Dir., The McKnight Fdn.; Mem., Advisory Ctee. on Trade Negotiations; Retired Dir., Chase Manhattan Bank.

John A. (Gus) Blanchard III Chair, Pres., CEO, Deluxe Corp., 3680 Victoria St. N., P.O. Box 64235 (55164), Shoreview, MN 55126. Tel: 651/483-7234. **B:** 1942, Laurel, Miss. **M:** Mary, 1968. **C:** Kate, Anne. **E:** Princeton U., BA, 1965; MIT's Sloan School of Management, MS, 1978. **Career Hist.:** Various positions to SVP, AT&T, 1965-1990; CEO, Harbridge Merchant Services, 1991-93; EVP, General Instrument Corp., 1994-1995; Pres. and CEO, Deluxe Corp., 1995-present, Chair, May 1996-present. **Career Act.:** Chair, Deluxe Corp.; Dir.; ADC Telecommunications; Wells Fargo & Co. **Act./Mem.:** Dir. Minnesota Opera Co.; Board of Advisors, Carlson School of Management, University of Minnesota.

Michael J. Bleck Chair, CEO, Oppenheimer Wolff & Donnelly, 45 S. Seventh St., Suite 3400, Minneapolis, MN 55402. Tel: 612/360-7726. Email: mbleck@owdlaw.com **B:** Apr. 8, 1950, Michigan City, Ind. **M:** Laurie Zenner, 1990. **C:** Andrew, Erica, Jack, Paul. **E:** BA, DePauw U., 1972; JD, Indiana U., School of Law, 1975. **Career Hist.:** Law Clerk to Judge Roy L. Stephenson, U.S. Court of Appeals for the Eighth Circuit, 1975-77; Oppenheimer Wolff & Donnelly, 1977-present: Associate, 1977; Partner, 1983; Chair/CEO, 1995. **Career Act.:** Chair-Business Litigation Dept. and Mem.-Policy Ctee., Oppenheimer Wolff & Donnelly; Mem., Am. Bar Assn. (Securities Litigation Committee), Hennepin County Bar Assn. (Litigation Section), MN State Bar Assn. (Court Rules Committee), Defense Research Inst. (Professional Liability Ctee. and Accountants Liability Subctee.). **Dec./Awd.:** Magna Cum Laude, Indiana U. School of Law, 1975. **Act./Mem.:** Minnesota Meeting Board of Directors; Capital City Partnership Board of Directors.

Charles N. Blitzer Pres., CEO, MGI Pharma Inc., 6300 W. Old Shakopee Rd., Suite 110, Bloomington, MN 55438-2684. Tel: 612/935-7335. **B:** Mar. 27, 1941, Toledo, Ohio. **M:** Debra Lenn. **C:** Sandra, Lynn. **E:** BS-Pharmacy, U. of Toledo (OH), 1965; JD-Law, American U., Washington (D.C.) College of Law, 1970; MBA, Rockhurst College (Kansas City, MO), 1984. **Career Hist.:** Senior Associate, Sughrue, Rothwell, Mion, Zinn & Macpeak (Washington, D.C.), 1970-73; VP, Corp. Counsel, INTERx Research Corp. (Lawrence, KS), 1973-77; Marion Laboratories Inc./Marion Merrell Dow Inc. (Kansas City, MO), 1977-91: General and Patent Counsel, 1977-80; Dir.-Licensing, 1980-84; VP-Licensing, 1984-89; Corp. VP-Licensing and Business Devel., 1989-91; Pres., CEO, Oncologix Inc. (Gaithersburg, MD), 1992-96; Pres., CEO, MGI Pharma Inc., April 1996-present. **Career Act.:** Mem., State Bars of Ohio, Kansas, Virginia, Washington, D.C.; Mem., U.S.

Federal Court System, U.S. Patent Bar, Licensing Exec. Soc., American Bar Assn., Patent Bar Assn.; speaker, panelist for several major biotechnology conferences. **Dec./Awd.:** President's Award, Marion Laboratories, 1984; Advisor to Michael Milken regarding foundation for funding cancer research; Runner-up, Entrepreneur of the Year for Metropolitan Washington, D.C., Entrepreneur and Inc. magazines, 1994; Finalist- "Fast 50" Contest, Minneapolis (years 1998, 1999). **Act./Mem.:** American Bar Assn.

David L. Boehnen EVP, Supervalu Inc., 11840 Valley View Rd., P.O. Box 990 (55440), Eden Prairie, MN 55344. Tel: 612/828-4151. **B:** Mitchell, SD. **M:** Shari. **C:** three. **E:** Cornell University Law School, J.D. with honors; Notre Dame University, A.B. **Career Hist.:** Partner, Dorsey & Whitney, 1971-89; VP Admin., Supercomputer Systems, Inc., 1990-91. **Career Act.:** Dir. ATS Medical, Inc.; Board of Trustees, Minneapolis Institute of Arts; Advisory Council of the University of Notre Dame's Art and Letters; former Dir. of Catholic Charities of the Archdioceses of St. Paul and Minneapolis; former member and chair, Law Advisory Council of Cornell University.

Terrence Bohman Pres., CEO, Universal Cooperatives Inc., 1300 Corporate Center Curve, Eagan, MN 55121-1233. Tel: 612/854-0800. Email: terryb@ucoop.com **B:** Jan. 20, 1958, Park Rapids, Minn. **M:** Jane, 1988. **E:** Bachelor of Agricultural Business Admin., U. of MN, 1981. **Career Hist.:** Universal Cooperatives Inc.: Dir.-Fin., 1986-88; CFO, 1988-89; CFO and VP-Intl., 1989-96; Pres. and CEO, 1996-present. **Career Act.:** Dir., Agricultural Cooperative Development Intl.; Dir., MSI.

Glen S. Bolander Pres., CEO, Int'l Home Food Store Brands, P.O. Box 430, Lakeville, MN 55044. Tel: 612/469-4981. Email: Glen_Bolander@Grist-Mill.com **B:** Sep. 24, 1946, New York. **M:** Diana, 1969. **C:** Lori. **E:** Southwestern College, AS-Chem., 1967; San Diego State U., BA-Chem., 1969; CA State U.-Hayward, MBA, 1978. **Career Hist.:** Naval Flight Officer, USNR, 1969-72; Technical Sls. Rep., Pfizer Chemicals Div., 1972-78; Food Broker, Bradford Co., 1978-80; Pres., Contract Mfg. Svs., 1980-82; Grist Mill Co. (now Int'l Home Food Store Brands): VP, 1982-85; EVP, 1985-87; Pres., 1987-present; COO, 1988-93; CEO, 1993-present. **Career Act.:** Dir., Grist Mill Co., Private Label Manufacturers Assn., 1995-1998. **Act./Mem.:** Institute of Food Technologists; American Mgmt. Assn.; Brackett's Crossing Country Club.

William J. Bolton EVP, Pres./COO-Retail Food Cos., Supervalu Inc., 11840 Valley View Rd., P.O. Box 990 (55440), Eden Prairie, MN 55344. Tel: 612/828-4051. **E:** B.S., Food Mktg., Western Mich. U. **Career Hist.:** Pres., Jewel Food Stores; Chair and CEO, Bruno's Inc.; EVP, Pres., COO, Retail Food Cos., Supervalu Inc., 1997-present.

Gerry E. Boschwitz Pres., CEO, Home Valu, 5401 East River Rd., Fridley, MN 55421. Tel: 612/571-2636. **B:** Sep. 14, 1958, Oshkosh, Wis. **M:** Janet, 1993. **C:** David, Benjamin, Michael. **E:** BS, Carleton College. **Career Hist.:** Home Valu, 1981-present. **Act./Mem.:** Young Pres. Organization, TwinWest Chamber, Lafayette Club, Minneapolis Federation for Jewish Services.

Donald L. Bottemiller Pres., Homecrest Industries Inc., Box 350, Wadena, MN 56482. Tel: 218/631-1000. **B:** Jul. 14, 1939, Minneapolis. **M:** Nancy Bloomfield, 1965. **C:** Sharon, Mark. **E:** St. Olaf Coll., BA; St. Louis U.. **Career Hist.:** Prod. Control Coordinator, Control Data, 1964-66; Homecrest Industries, 1966-present: Engr., 1966-73; VP, Gen. Mgr., 1973-75; Pres., 1975-present. **Career Act.:** Chairman, Northern Great Plains Institute for Rural Development; Dir., TRI County Hospital, American Furniture Manufacturers Assn.; Pres., Wadena Area Concert Assn. **Act./Mem.:** Immanual Lutheran Church; Wadena Lions Club.

Pete Boynton VP, Gen. Mgr., Herff Jones-Photography Division, P.O. Box 100, Lewiston, MN 55952. Tel: 507/523-2101. **B:** Dec. 12, 1943, Winona, Minn. **M:** Lenora, 1970. **C:** Carolyn, Lance, Holly, Jason, Jena. **E:** U. of MN, BS, 1966. **Career Hist.:** Herff Jones-Photography Div. (formerly Camera Art), 1959-present, working in photography, sales, personnel, production, and operations..

James W. Bracke, Ph.D. Pres., CEO, Lifecore Biomedical Inc., 3515 Lyman Blvd., Chaska, MN 55318. Tel: 612/368-4300. **B:** Apr. 4, 1947, St. Paul. **M:** Carol, 1971. **C:** Christopher, Emily. **E:** Mankato State U., B.A. Biology, 1969; M.A. Biology, 1973; U. of IA, Ph.D.-Microbiology, 1977; NIH Post-Doctoral Fellow, U. of MN School of Dentistry, 1977-78. **Career Hist.:** Instructor, U. of MN School of Dentistry, 1978; Senior Research Microbiologist, 3M Central Research Laboratories, 1978-81. Lifecore Biomedical Inc.: Senior Research Scientist, 1981; VP and Technical Dir., 1981-83; Dir., 1982-present; Pres./CEO, 1983-present. **Career Act.:** Dir., Lifecore Biomedical Inc., College of Veterinary Medicine U. of MN, Biotechnology Advisory Council Mankato State U.; Chair, Raptor Center. **Dec./Awd.:** National Research Service Postdoctoral Fellowship Award, 1977; National Institute of Dental Research Fellowship Award, 1977; Mankato State U. Distinguished Alumnus of the Year, 1985; Adjunct Professor, U. of MN School of Dentistry.

J.S. (Jack) Braun Founder, Chair, Braun Intertec Corp., 8000 Town Line Ave. S., P.O. Box 39108, Bloomington, MN 55439. Tel: 612/946-6000. **B:** Jan. 19, 1933, St. Cloud, Minn. **M:** Priscilla W., 1958. **C:** Philip M., Stephen J., Elizabeth Braun Fransen. **E:** MS-Civil Engrg., U. of MN Institute of Technology, 1957. **Career Hist.:** Founded Braun Intertec in 1957. **Career Act.:** Dir., Northstar Computer Forms Inc., Community Bank Group; Advisory Board, University of Minnesota College of Architecture. **Act./Mem.:** Edina Rotary, Mpls. Golf Club, Skylight Club.

Wayne Brunetti Pres., CEO, Xcel Energy Inc., 414 Nicollet Mall, Minneapolis, MN 55401. Tel: 612/330-5500. **B:** Oct. 14, 1942, Cleveland, OH. **M:** Mollie Brunetti. **C:** Kelly Rose, Drew. **E:** Univ. of Florida, B.S. in accounting. **Career Hist.:** Florida Power and Light, 1964-91; Founder and CEO, Mgmt. Systems Intl. 1991-94; started as Pres. and COO, now Chairman, Pres. and CEO; Public Service of Colorado, 1994-present; slated to be President and CEO of Xcel Energy Inc. after planned merger of NSP and New Century.

Dr. George K. Brushaber Pres., Bethel College & Seminary, 3900 Bethel Dr., Arden Hills, MN 55112. Tel: 651/638-6400. **B:** Dec. 15, 1938, Milwaukee. **M:** Darleen, 1962. **C:** Deanna, Donald. **E:** AB, Wheaton College, 1959; MA-Philosophy of Religion, Wheaton Graduate School, 1961; M.Div., Gordon Divinity School, 1963 (Summa Cum Laude); Ph.D.-Epistemology/Metaphysics, Boston U., 1967; graduate studies at U. of Chicago, U. of WI. **Career Hist.:** Teaching Fellow, Wheaton College, 1960-61; Adjunct Prof. of Ethics, Curriculum Consultant in Liberal Arts, MA College of Pharmacy, 1968-72; Dir.-Admissions/Records, Assoc. Prof. of Philosophy of Religion, Gordon-Conwell Theological Seminary, 1965-72; Assoc. Prof. of Philosophy, Dept. Chair, Dir.-Pre-Theological Studies, Dir.-Fdn./Grant Support, Dir.-Evening Div./Extension Centers, Gordon College, 1962-72; VP/Academic Dean, Prof. of Philosophy/Religious Studies, Westmont College, 1972-75; Bethel College and Seminary: VP, Dean of College, 1975-82; Pres., 1982-present. **Career Act.:** Mem.-Edit. Staff, Bulletin of Evangelical Theological Soc., 1959-61; Editor, Chair, Gordon Review, 1965-70; Staff mem., Religious and Theological Abstracts, 1967-70; Fdg. Editor, Chair-

Trustees, Christian Scholar's Review, 1970-78; Edit. Dir., Christian U. Press, 1975-83; Chair-Bd. of Sr. Editors, Christianity Today; Board Mem., MN Seminary Consortium; Dir., Christian College Assn.; Chair, Scripture Press Ministry; Dir., Cook Communications, Int'l; Dir., MN Private College Council.

Melvin P. Bubrick, M.D. Pres., Hennepin Faculty Associates, 600 HFA Building, 914 S. Eighth St., Minneapolis, MN 55404. Tel: 612/347-7674. Email: melvin.bubrick@co.hennepin.mn.us **B:** Jun. 2, 1944, Chicago. **M:** Barbara, 1969. **C:** Jerome, Ellen, Dena. **E:** U. of IL, A.B., 1964, M.D., 1968; U. of WI, internship, 1968-69; Hennepin County General Hospital, residency in surgery, 1969-74; American Cancer Society Fellow in Colon and Rectal Surgery, U. of MN, 1974-75. **Career Hist.:** Staff Surgeon, Hennepin County Medical Center, 1975-80; Staff Surgeon, Park Nicollet Medical Center, 1980-87; Assistant Chief of Surgery, HCMC, 1980-88; Chief of Surgery, HCMC, 1988-94; Pres., Hennepin Faculty Associates, 1995-present. **Career Act.:** Member of 15 medical and surgical societies. **Act./Mem.:** Dir., Minneapolis Medical Research Fdn.

Robert C. Buhrmaster Chair, Pres., CEO, Jostens Inc., 5501 Norman Center Dr., Bloomington, MN 55437. Tel: 612/830-3300. **B:** Aug. 28, 1947, Schenectady, N.Y. **M:** Maureen. **C:** Kate, Sarah. **E:** Rensselaer Polytechnic Institute, Bachelor's degree, Mechanical Engrg., 1969; Dartmouth College, MBA, 1974. **Career Hist.:** Various positions, Corning Inc., 1974-1993; Pres. and COO, Jostens Inc., 1993-94; CEO, Jostens Inc., 1994-present; Chair, Jostens, February, 1998-present. **Career Act.:** Dir., The Toro Co., Jostens Inc.; Pres., The Viking Council-Boy Scouts of America; Director, National Alliance of Business. **Dec./Awd.:** MAEF Hero, MN Academic Excellence Fdn., 1996. **Act./Mem.:** Minikahda Country Club.

John J. Burke retired VChair, The Montana Power Co., 40 E. Broadway, Butte, MT 59701. Tel: 406/494-2965. Email: jjburke@in-tch.com **B:** Jul. 25, 1928, Butte, Mont. **M:** Nancy Calvert, 1952. **C:** Cheryl, Mary, Kathleen, John, Elisabeth. **E:** U. of MT, BS-Business, BA-Law, JD-Law. **Career Hist.:** Partner, Weir, Gough, Booth & Burke, 1954-59; Montana Power Company, 1960-95: Attorney, 1960-67; VP, 1967-78; EVP, 1979-84; VChair, 1984-1993. **Career Act.:** Trustee, Carroll College, MT State Historical Soc., Burton K. Wheeler Center, U. of MT Fdn., 1984-90; Dir., Lazard Funds Inc., Montana Power (1980-95), Pacific Steel & Recycling, Sletten Construction Company; U. of MT-Bus. Advisory Ctee., U. of MT-Alumni Assn.. **Act./Mem.:** Butte Rotary Club; B.P.O.E.; Butte Country Club; MT Club; 116 Inc. (Washington D.C.); Holy Spirit Catholic Church; Silver Bow Bar Assn.; State of MT Bar Assn.; American Bar Assn.; ButteSilver Bow Transportation Advisory Ctee., MT State Highway Commission; Governor's Task Force.

Paul B. Burke Chair, Pres., CEO, BMC Industries Inc., One Meridian Crossings, Suite 850, Minneapolis, MN 55423. Tel: 612/851-6000. **B:** Mar. 3,1956, Detroit. **M:** Shannon L. Egan, 1978. **C:** Kelly, Clayton, Cassandra. **E:** Yale U., BA-History, 1978; U. of Michigan, J.D., 1981. **Career Hist.:** Assoc. Attorney, Oppenheimer, Wolff & Donnelly, 1981-83; Assoc., Gen. Counsel, BMC Industries Inc., 1983-85; VP, Sec., & Gen. Counsel, BMC Industries Inc., 1985-87; VP/Plant Mgr., Vison-Ease Lens, Ft. Lauderdale Op., 1987-89; Pres., Vision-Ease Lens, 1989-91; Pres. & COO, BMC Industries Inc., 1991; Pres. & CEO, 1991-95; Chair, Pres., CEO, 1995-present. **Career Act.:** Dir., BMC Industries Inc., Donaldson Co. Inc., Minnesota Orchestral Assn., United Way of the St. Paul Area; Mem., Society for Information Display, Vision Industry Council of America. **Act./Mem.:** Decathlon Athletic Club, Minneapolis Club, Young Presidents' Org., Somerset C.C.

Ralph W. Burnet Chair, CEO, Coldwell Banker Burnet, 7550 France Ave. S., Edina, MN 55435. Tel: 612/844-6450. **B:** Oct. 1, 1945, Pittsburgh. **M:** Peggy, 1966. **C:** Kimberly, Stephanie, Ryan. **E:** St. Lawrence U., 1963-65. **Career Hist.:** Founder Chair, Burnet Financial Group (formerly Burnet Realty Inc.), 1973-present. Sold to Merrill Lynch in 1982, purchased back in 1990. Eastern Region Pres., Merrill Lynch, 1983-88. **Career Act.:** Trustee, Breck School; Pres., Walker Art Center; Dir., Piper Jaffray Companies Inc., Greater Minneapolis Chamber of Commerce; Mem., Fannie Mae Natl. Advisory Council, 1996-98. **Dec./Awd.:** Entrepreneur of the Year (Master Category) 1994; Service to Humanity Award, United Hospital, 1995. **Act./Mem.:** Mem., Woodhill Country Club, Minneapolis Club, The Honors Course, Somerset Country Club; United Way; Virginia Piper Cancer Center; past Chair, Minnesota Leadership Council.

Winslow H. Buxton Chair, CEO, Pentair Inc., Wells Fargo Center, 90 S. Seventh St., 36th floor, Minneapolis, MN 55402. Tel: 651/636-7920. **B:** Apr. 19, 1939, Coral Gables, Fla. **M:** Linda, 1958. **C:** Winslow III, Krisell, Gregory. **E:** U. of WA, BS, Chemical Engrg., 1961. **Career Hist.:** Mill Manager, Boise Cascade Corp., 1968-72; Chief Engineer, Willamett Industries, 1972-78; VP, Pulp and Paper, Smurfit Newsprint Co., 1978-86; Pres., and CEO, Pentair Inc., 1987-2000, Chairman and CEO 2000-present.. **Career Act.:** Dir., Bemis Co. Inc.; Chair, Pentair Inc.; Dir., The Toro Co.; Dir., Willamette Industries Inc. **Act./Mem.:** Indianhead Council BSA (Pres.), Minneapolis Club, North Oaks Golf Club, White Bear Racquet Club; Layfayette Club.

William J. Cadogan Chair, Pres., CEO, ADC Telecommunications Inc., P.O. Box 1101, Bloomington, MN 55440. Tel: 612/938-8080. **B:** Jun. 29, 1948, Boston. **M:** Barbara Needham. **C:** Melissa, William, Brett, Elyse. **E:** Northeastern U., Boston, MA, BA-Electrical Engrg.; Wharton School of Business/U. of PA, MBA. **Career Hist.:** District Op. Mgr., National Sls. Mgr., AT&T, 1971-86; Gen. Mgr., Intelsat, 1986-87; SVP, ADC Telecommunications Inc., 1987-90; Pres. & COO, ADC, 1990-91; Pres., CEO, ADC, 1991-94; Chair, Pres., CEO 1994-present. **Career Act.:** Dir., ADC Telecommunications Inc., Banta Corp., Pentair Inc.; Chair, Telecommunications Industry Assn.; Bd. of Governors, Electronic Industry Assn.; Dir., Greater Mpls. Chamber of Commerce. **Act./Mem.:** Dir., Junior Achievment of Minnesota; United Way.

James R. Campbell Chair/CEO-Wells Fargo Bank Minnesota N.A., Wells Fargo & Co., Sixth and Marquette, MAC N9305, Minneapolis, MN 55479. Tel: 612/667-9141. Email: james.r.campbell@norwest.com **B:** May 24, 1942, Rochester, Minn. **M:** Carmen, 1964. **C:** Peter I., Kathryn A.. **E:** U. of MN, BA-Bus., 1964. **Career Hist.:** Northwestern National Bank Minneapolis, 1964-79: Trainee, 1964-66; Asst. Cashier and Comm. Lending Officer, 1966-69; AVP-Comm. Loans, 1969-71; VP-Lease Northwest, 1971-72; Pres., Dir.-Lease Northwest, 1972-76; SVP, Mgr.-National Accts., 1976-79; Pres., Dir., U.S. National Bank-Omaha, 1979-82; Reg. Pres., Region V, Norwest Bancorp., 1982; VChair, U.S. National Bank-Omaha, 1982-83, Chair, CEO, 1983-84; Norwest Bank-Minneapolis, 1984-88: Pres., Dir., 1984-86; Pres., CEO, Dir., 1986-88; Pres., CEO, Dir., Norwest Bank MN, 1988-96; EVP, Norwest Corp. (Wells Fargo & Co.), 1988; Chair, Dir., NBM. Currently: Group EVP, Wells Fargo & Company and Chairman and CEO Wells Fargo Bank Minnesota, N.A. **Career Act.:** Mem., MN Executive Organization, The Financial Services Roundtable; Dir., Allianz Life Insurance Co. of North America, Abbott-Northwestern Hospital, Wells Fargo Bank MN, U. of MN Fdn., Viking Council-Boy Scouts of America; Mem., Carlson School of Management Board of Overseers, Minneapolis Institute of Arts; Mem.-Steering Ctee., United Way of Minneapolis, Board Member and Member of Executive Council. **Dec./Awd.:** Outstanding Achievement Award, U. of MN, 1996. Recipient of the 1999 University of Minnesota Regents Award. **Act./Mem.:** Minikahda Country Club; Minneapolis Club, Spring Hill Golf Club, Bay Colony Golf Club.

Randel S. Carlock Chair, Ultimate Electronics/Audio King, 3501 Highway 100 S., St. Louis Park, MN 55416. Tel: 612/920-0505. **M:** Cheryl. **C:** Sydney, Lily, Grace. **E:** U. of MN, BS, 1970; MA, 1976; MBA, 1983; Ph.D., 1991. **Career Hist.:** Executive, Dayton Hudson Corp., 1971-76; Pres. and CEO, Audio King Inc., 1976-90; Prof., U. of St. Thomas Graduate School of Business, 1990-present; Chair, Audio King, 1990-present. **Career Act.:** Opus Endowed Prof./Dir., Center for Family Enterprise—U. of St. Thomas; Dir., GrowBiz International, Audio King Inc.; Education Dir., St. Paul Inner City Business Development Project. **Dec./Awd.:** Price-Babson Fellowship for Entrepreneurial Education, 1991; Academy of Management Innovation Award, 1993; Audio Video International Retailer of the Year; Edwin M. Appel Prize for Teaching Entrepreneurship, 1994; Outstanding Entrepreneurship Teaching Award, Coleman Fdn., 1995. **Act./Mem.:** Academy of Management; Family Firm Institute; Family Bus. Network (Switzerland).

David R. Carlsen Chair, CEO, Upper Midwest Industries Inc., 2940 Weeks Ave. S.E., Minneapolis, MN 55414. Tel: 612/378-1071. Email: davidcarlsen@worldnet.att.com **B:** Dec. 30, 1953, Fort Leonard Wood, Mo. **M:** Kathleen Quast, 1977. **C:** Samuel, Charlotte. **E:** U. of MN, BA, 1975; JD, Georgetown U., 1979. **Career Hist.:** Attorney, Carlsen, Greiner & Law, 1979-83; Attorney, David. R. Carlsen P.A., 1983-85; Upper Midwest Industries Inc., 1985-present: Sec. and Gen. Counsel, 1985-90; Chair and CEO, 1990-present. **Act./Mem.:** Chair of Board, MN Chamber of Commerce; Board Mem., YMCA of Metro. Mpls. Viking Council Boy Scouts; Mem., Minikahda Club.

Robert W. Carlson Jr. Chair, Quadion Corp., 3630 Wooddale Ave., St. Louis Park, MN 55416. Tel: 612/927-1410. **B:** Oct. 14, 1947, Kalamazoo, Mich. **M:** Virginia D., 1984. **C:** Dana Marie, Robert William III. **E:** Northern State College, Aberdeen, SD. **Career Hist.:** Sales Trainee, Cleveland Sales Rep., Minnesota Rubber, 1969-75; Pres., Tool Products Company, 1975-77; MN Rubber, Quadion Corp.: CEO 1977-94; Chair 1977-present. **Career Act.:** Chair (1997), Dunwoody Bd. of Trustees; Dir., Davanni's Pizza, Woody's Grille. **Dec./Awd.:** First Honorary Degree from Dunwoody. **Act./Mem.:** Interlachen Country Club; United Way, Metropolitan Breakfast Club.

Emmett D. Carson Pres., CEO, The Minneapolis Foundation, 821 Marquette Ave. S., Suite A200, Minneapolis, MN 55402. Tel: 612/672-3838. **B:** Chicago, Ill. **E:** B.A., Economics, Morehouse College, 1980; M.P.A., Public and International Affairs, Princeton University, 1983; Ph.D., Public and International Affairs, Princeton University, 1985. **Career Hist.:** Congressional Research Service, 1985-86; Adjunct Lecturer, U of Md., 1987-89; Project Dir., Joint Ctr. for Political and Economic Studies, 1986-89; Program Officer, The Ford Foundation, 1989-94; Pres. and CEO, The Minneapolis Fdn., 1994-present. **Career Act.:** Bd. of Dir., BlueCross BlueShield of Minn., 2000-present; Dir., Council on Foundations, 1999-present; Board of Governors, Center for the Study of Philanthropy, 1995-1997, 2000-present; Overseer, Carlson School of Mgmt., 1998-present; **Dec./Awd.:** E.B. Williams Economics and Business Award, 1981; National Economic Assn. Dissertation Award, 1986; Joint Ctr. for Political and Economic Studies' Superior Performance Award, 1988; CityBusiness 40 Under 40 Award, 1995; The Nonprofit Times Top 50 List of Power and Influence, 1998; Lead Presenter, First White House Conference on Philanthropy, 2000; Ninth James Joseph Lecturer, Assoc. of Black Fnd. Exec., 2000. **Act./Mem.:** Bd. of Trustees, KTCA/KTCI TV, 1995-1999; Bd. of Governors, Eleven Who Care, KARE-11 TV, 1995-present; Advistory Ctee., NYU School of Law, Philanthropy and Law Ctr., 1997-present; Editorial Advisory Bd., Tufts U., Tufts Nonprofits Series on Civil Society, 1998-present; Advisory Ctee., Urban Institute Ctr. on Nonprofit and Philanthropy, 1998-present; Bd. of Overseers, Carlson School of Mgmt., U of MN, 1998-present; Bd. of Dir., Council on Fdns., 1999-present.

John W. Castro Pres., CEO, Merrill Corp., One Merrill Circle, St. Paul, MN 55108. Tel: 651/649-1211. Email: John.Castro@merrillcorp.com **B:** Jul. 20, 1948, Oak Park, Ill. **M:** Linnea. **C:** Joseph, Lisa, Brian, Kristine, Alexandra, Samantha. **E:** college, 3 yrs. **Career Hist.:** Typesetter, Production Mgr., VP-Op., Adwest Corp., 1970-78; Merrill Corp., 1978-present: Prod. Mgr., 1978-79; VP-Prod., 1979-81; Pres., 1981-present; CEO, 1984-present.. **Career Act.:** Dir., United Way of St. Paul, BMC Industries Inc., Merrill Corp. **Act./Mem.:** Young Presidents Organization, United Way.

Richard J. Cathcart EVP, Pentair Inc., 1500 County Rd. B2 W., Suite 400, Waters Edge Plaza, Roseville, MN 55113. Tel: 651/636-7920. **B:** Sep. 28, 1944, Port Angeles, Wash. **M:** Kathy, 1968. **C:** Kelly, Tara, Ryan, Michael, Ashley. **E:** U.S. Air Force Academy, B.S.-Engrg., 1967. **Career Hist.:** USAF, Capt., Pilot, 1968-74; VP/Gen. Mgr.-Building Controls, Honeywell Inc., 1975-95; EVP-Corp. Devel./Water Products Group, Pentair Inc., 1995-present. **Career Act.:** Dir., Fairview Hospital and Healthcare Svs., Fairview Physicians Associates, Urban Coalition.

R.A. Cecchettini Pres., CEO, Old Republic National Title Insurance Group, 400 Second Ave. S., Minneapolis, MN 55401. Tel: 612/371-1144. Email: rac@oldrepnatl.com **B:** Oct. 29, 1933, Sacramento, Calif. **M:** Nan Wille, 1999. **E:** BA, U. of California-Berkeley, 1955. **Career Hist.:** Title Ins. and Trust, 1958-72; SVP, Pioneer National Title (New York), 1972-76; SVP, Pioneer National Title (Chicago), 1976-81; Old Republic Title, 1981-present: SVP to Pres./CEO. **Career Act.:** Past Pres., American Land Title Assn. **Act./Mem.:** North Central Morgan Assn., American Morgan Horse Assn.

Gary M. Cerny Pres., COO, Reliant Energy Minnegasco, 800 LaSalle Ave., Floor 11, P.O. Box 59038, Minneapolis, MN 55402. Tel: 612/372-4664. **B:** Oct. 8, 1955, Houston. **E:** Sam Houston St. U., BS-Physics/Math, 1978; Texas A&M, Masters of Engrg., 1979. **Career Hist.:** Lab Instructor, Sam Houston St. U., 1976-78; Research Graduate, Texas A&M, 1978-79; Entex, 1980-98; Minnegasco (Reliant Energy Minnegasco), Pres., COO, 1998-present. **Career Act.:** Dir., Greater Mpls. Chamber of Commerce. **Dec./Awd.:** Keynote Speaker for Dale Carnegie Annual Meeting; Outstanding Presenter, Leadership Houston Class VI; Outstanding Outreach Volunteer for Gladney Auxiliary; Outstanding Volunteer for MADD; President's Marketing Award; President's Safety Award.

Tom Chase Gen. Mgr.-Marriott City Center; Market Mgr.-Midwest, Marriott Lodging Group, Mpls. Marriott City Center, 30 S. Seventh St., Minneapolis, MN 55402. Tel: 612/349-4000. **B:** Dec. 23, 1950, Grand Rapids, Minn. **M:** Lynn, 1971. **C:** Tim, Joe. **E:** U. of MN. **Career Hist.:** Marriott: 1974-present; General Manager, 1983-present. **Career Act.:** Pres., Minnesota Hotel & Lodging Assn.; Dir., Greater Minneapolis Convention and Visitors Bureau. **Dec./Awd.:** Regional General Manager of the Year, 1995; Minnesota's Lodging Most Valuable Volunteer 1999. **Act./Mem.:** Mem. Boy Scouts of America.

Leeann Chin Chair, Founder, Leeann Chin Inc., Suite 120, 3600 W. 80th St., Bloomington, MN 55431. Tel: 612/896-3606. **B:** Feb. 13, 1933, Canton, China. **M:** widowed. **C:** Laura, Katie, Jean, Bill, Linda. **E:** High school. **Career Hist.:** Seamstress, 1957-71; Cooking teacher, 1971; Cooking teacher and caterer, 1971-1980; Restaurant owner, 1980-present.. **Career Act.:** Minnesota Meeting, Greater Minneapolis Chamber of Commerce, P.A.C.E.R., St. Paul Downtown Council, Indianhead Council of Boy Scouts, Committee of 100; Lowertown Redevelopment Board Member, Vikings Advisory Board, MLB Twins Board. **Dec./Awd.:** MN Business Hall of Fame, 1986; Business Owner of the Year, National Assn. of Women Business Owners, 1988; MN Woman of Distinction, 1988; MN Entreprenuer of the Year, MN Entreprenuers Club, 1993; Small Business Administration Regional Award, 1996. **Act./Mem.:** NAWBO; Committee of 100; Organizations of Chinese Americans, IACP.

Kyle Chown VP, Gen. Mgr., Frigidaire Co. Freezer Products, 701 33rd Ave. N., St. Cloud, MN 56303. Tel: 320/253-1212. **M:** Marsha, 1976. **C:** Nate, Alison. **E:** U. of Northern Iowa, BA-Business Mgmt. **Career Hist.:** Square D. Co., 1977-91; Operations mgr., 1988-90; Mgr. Mfg. Engrg. and Svs., 1990-91. Frigidaire Co., 1991-present: Plant manager-laundry products, Jefferson, Iowa, 1991-92; Plant manager-laundry products, Webster City, Jefferson, Iowa, 1992-93; VP/Gen. Mgr.-freezer products, St. Cloud, 1995-present.

Anton J. Christianson Chair, Cherry Tree Investments Inc., Centennial Lakes Office Park, 7601 France Ave. S., Suite 225, Edina, MN 55435. Tel: 612/893-9012. **B:** May 12, 1952, Elbow Lake, Minn. **M:** Paige, 1984. **C:** Kathleen, Nicholas, Lucas, William, Robert, Andrew. **E:** BS-Acctg., St. John's U. (Collegeville, MN), 1974; MBA, Harvard Bus. School, 1978. **Career Hist.:** Consultant, Arthur Andersen & Co., 1974-76; VP, Norwest Growth Fund, 1978-80; Fdr., Mng. Ptnr., Cherry Tree Investments Inc., 1980-present. **Career Act.:** Dir., Fourth Shift Corp., Transport America, Dolan Media Co., Capella Education, Peoples Publishing, AmeriPride Svs. Inc., Greenspring Cos., FIC-Fair Isaac and Company. **Dec./Awd.:** Entrepreneur of the Year (sponsored by Ernst & Young): Supporter; 1995 Finalist. **Act./Mem.:** National Venture Capital Assn.; MN Venture Capital Assn.; St. Bartholomew's Church (Wayzata, MN).

Barbara Mitchell Christie CEO, Mikara Corp., 3109 Louisiana Ave. N., New Hope, MN 55427. Tel: 612/546-9500. **B:** May 29, 1923, Chippewa Falls, Wis. **M:** Richard E. Christie, 1980. **C:** B. Alan Brown, Gloria Hassett. **E:** U. of MN; Northwestern U. **Career Hist.:** Owned and operated a chain of seven beauty salons in the Chicago, IL, area; Tech. Sls. Rep., Helene Curtis Industries; Asst. Sec., VP, Dir., National Beauty, 1970-79; Pres., Dir., National Beauty (now known as Mikara Corporation), 1979-present.. **Career Act.:** Mem., Fashion Group of Minneapolis.. **Dec./Awd.:** Honorary Chairman Gala Boys and Girls Club; Honorary Minnesota Cosmotology Association, 1998. **Act./Mem.:** Women's Board, Boys and Girls Club of Minneapolis; Lafayette Club; 19th Century Club (Oak Park, IL); Wayzata Country Club; Minneapolis Club.

Michael V. Ciresi Chair, Ptnr., Robins, Kaplan, Miller & Ciresi LLP, 2800 LaSalle Plaza, 800 LaSalle Ave., Minneapolis, MN 55402. Tel: 612/349-8500. **B:** Apr. 18, 1946, St. Paul. **M:** Ann Barcelow, 1992. **C:** Adam, Dominic. **E:** BA, U. of St. Thomas, 1968; JD, U. of MN, 1971. **Career Hist.:** Robins, Kaplan, Miller & Ciresi, 1971-present: Ptnr., 1971-present; Chair, 1995-present. Admissions: MN Supreme Court, 1971; U.S. District Court of Appeals, 1971; U.S. District Court, District of MN, 1974; U.S. Supreme Court, 1981; U.S. Court of Appeals, Second Circuit, 1986; U.S. Court of Appeals, Ninth Circuit, 1987; U.S. Court of Appeals, Tenth Circuit, 1990; State of New York Supreme Court, 1995; U.S. Court of Appeals, Federal Circuit, 1998; U. S. Court of Appeals, Fifth Circuit, 1999. **Career Act.:** Mem., MN State Bar Assn., American Bar Assn., Hennepin County Bar Assn., Inner Circle of Advocates, Intl. Bar Assn., Ramsey County Bar Assn., Assn. of Trial Lawyers of America, American Board of Trial Advocates, MN Trial Lawyers; Dir., Trial Lawyers for Public Justice, Ordway Music Theatre; Trustee, U. of St. Thomas; Mem.-Advisory Bd., Centre of Advanced Litigation at Nottingham (England) Law School; Dir., National Assn. for Public Interest Law; declared for 2000 U.S. Senate race as Democrat. **Dec./Awd.:** "Ten of the Nation's Top Trial Lawyers," National Law Journal, 1989, 1993; "The Best Lawyers in America," 1989-90, 1991-92, 1993-94, 1995-96, 1997-98; "Product Liability Lawyer of the Year," Australian National Consumer Law Assn., 1989; Marquis Who's Who in the World and Who's Who in American Law; One of "The 100 Most Influential Lawyers in America," National Law Journal, 1997; "Lawyer of the Year," MN Law and Politics, 1997; "1998 Trial Lawyer of the Year Award," Trial Lawyers for Public Justice Fdn.; "Lifetime Achievement Award," MN Trial Lawyers, 1998; "Distinguished Alumnus Award," U. of St. Thomas, 1999; "Outstanding Achievement Award," U. of MN, 1999; "100 most influential lawyers," National Law Journal, 2000. **Act./Mem.:** Dir., The Guthrie Theater; Dir., Ordway Music Theater.

James F. Clifford Chair, Pres., Firstar Bank, 101 E. Fifth St., St. Paul, MN 55101. Tel: 651/292-3955. **B:** Oct. 23, 1955, St. Paul. **M:** Mary. **C:** Theresa, James, Michael. **E:** U. of St. Thomas. **Career Hist.:** First Bank, Norwest Bank, Irving Trust Co., Firstar Bank (1990), Chm. and Pres. **Act./Mem.:** Dir., Business Economics Education Fdn., Childrens Theater Co., Capital City Partnership, Culture Inc.

Christopher E. Clouser CEO, Minnesota Twins Baseball Club Inc., 34 Kirby Puckett Place, Minneapolis, MN 55415. Tel: 612/726-2331. **B:** 1952, St. Louis, Mo. **M:** Patsy. **C:** Todd, Bradley. **E:** U. of MO. **Career Hist.:** Exec. Asst. to U.S. Senator Thomas F. Eagleton, 1973-81; VP-Pub. Affairs/Comm., Hallmark Cards Inc., 1981-85; VP-Corp. Relations/Admin., U.S. Sprint Comm. Co. and VP-Corp. Relations, United Telecom, 1988-91; Northwest Airlines Corp.: SVP-Corp. Comm./Advertising, then SVP-Admin., 1991-99; CEO, Minnesota Twins, 2000-present. **Career Act.:** Dir., Delta Beverage Group, Mesaba Holdings Inc., Marquette Bancshares Inc., past Dir., Muscular Dystrophy Assn., Epilepsy Fdn. of America, Children's HeartLink, Greater Mpls. Chamber of Commerce. **Dec./Awd.:** Prism Award and President's Award, Public Relations Society of America; Gold Quill Award, Intl. Assn. of Business Communicators; one of nation's 40 most successful young business leaders, BusinessWeek magazine, 1988.

Dan Coborn Chair, Coborn's Inc., 1445 E. Highway 23, St. Cloud, MN 56304. Tel: 320/252-4222. **B:** Jul. 25, 1930, St. Cloud, Minn. **M:** Mabel Hansen, 1952. **E:** St. John's U., Economics, 1952. **Career Hist.:** Chair, Coborn's Inc., 1954-present. **Career Act.:** Past Dir./Chair, MN Grocers Assn., Sauk Rapids/Rice School; past Dir., National Grocers Assn., MN Chamber of Commerce, St. Benedicts College, St. Cloud Hospital, Centra Care, Wells Fargo Central MN, Central MN Boy Scouts; Board of Trustees MnSCU; Board Member, FMI. **Dec./Awd.:** Sauk Rapids Citizen of the Year, 1989; MN Grocer of the Year, 1988; 1998 Entrepeneur of the Year ; Paul Newman/George Magainze "Most Generous Company Top 10." **Act./Mem.:** St. Cloud Country Club, St. Cloud Exchange Club.

Daniel E. Cohen Chair, CEO, CNS Inc., 4400 W. 78th St., Bloomington, MN 55435. Tel: 612/820-6696. Email: dan_cohen@cnxs.com **B:** Jun. 5, 1952, Philadelphia, Pa. **M:** Ellen, 1975. **C:** Jason, David, Mike, Whitney. **E:** BS (high distinction), Penn State, 1973; MD, Temple Medical School, 1977; internship, Hennepin County Medical Center; residency (neurology), U. of MN Hospitals. **Career Hist.:** Clinical instructor (neurology), U. of MN Hospitals; neurological consultant, St. Paul Ramsey Hospital; Chair and CEO, CNS Inc., 1982 (inception)-present. **Career Act.:** Dir., Interactive Learning Group.

Melvin S. Cohen Chair, National Presto Industries Inc., 3925 N. Hastings Way, Eau Claire, WI 54703. Tel: 715/839-2121. **B:** Jan. 16, 1918, Minneapolis. **M:** Eileen Phillips, 1947. **C:** Amy, Mary-Jo. **E:** U. of MN, BS-Law, 1939, JD, 1941. **Career Hist.:** Attorney, 1941-42; National Presto Industries Inc., 1944-present: Attorney, 1944-50; Treas., 1950-51; VP-Admin., Treas., 1951-54; EVP, 1954-60; Pres., 1960-75; CEO, 1975-94; Chair, 1975-present. **Career Act.:** Dir., Century Metalcraft Corp. (Los Angeles), Guardian Service Security Systems (Los Angeles), Presto Mfg. Company (Jackson, MS), Johnson Printing (Eau Claire, WI), United Truck Leasing Inc. (Minneapolis), Red Wing Truck Rental Inc., Lawrence Motors Inc. (Red Wing, MN), Red Wing Transportation Corp., World Aerospace Corp., Master Corp. TX (Abilene, TX), Jackson Sales & Storage Company, Presto Parts & Service Corp.-Mineola NY-Los Angeles-Atlanta, National Presto Industries Export Corp., Presto International Ltd. (Hong Kong), Canton Mfg. Company, National Automatic Pipeline Operators Inc., First WI National Bank-Eau Claire; VP, Dir., National Pipeline Company (Cleveland); Pres., Trustee, Presto Fdn. (Eau Claire); Mem., Advisory Commissions for Aluminum Industry and Internal Combustion Engine Industry, NPA. **Act./Mem.:** Eau Claire Country Club.

Richard Cohen VChair, Norstan Inc., 605 N. Highway 169, Plymouth, MN 55441. Tel: 612/420-1100. **B:** May 15, 1944, Fort Monmouth, N.J. **M:** Diane, 1966. **C:** Matt, Nick & Tom. **E:** U of PA, B.S.E., 1966. **Career Hist.:** Norstan Inc., 1971-present. **Act./Mem.:** Oakridge Country Club, Minneapolis Club, United Way, Temple Israel, Beth El Synagogue..

Mark A. Cohn Chair, CEO, Damark International Inc., 7101 Winnetka Ave. N., Brooklyn Park, MN 55428. Tel: 612/531-0066. **B:** Mar. 22, 1957, New York. **M:** Claudia. **C:** Ashley, Jesse, Tyler. **E:** State U. of New York, College of New Paltz, 1976 -79.. **Career Hist.:** CEO, Damark International Inc., 1986-present. **Career Act.:** Pres., Children's Grand Prix of Minnesota Inc.; Streamline Svs., Children's Cancer Research Fund, Children's Hospitals and Clinics; past Dir., Children's Home Society of MN; United Way-1993 Leaders in Giving, 1994 Retail Pacesetter Division Chair. **Dec./Awd.:** "America's Smartest Young Entrepreneurs-40 Who Made Their Mark," Fortune magazine, 1994; America's Fastest Growing Companies-#35, Fortune magazine, 1993; Fastest Growing Companies-#6, Inc. magazine, 1991; Selected for Inaugural Birthing of Giants Program, Inc./YEO/MIT, 1991; Entrepreneur of the Year, Ernst & Young and Inc. magazine, 1990; Entrepreneur of the Year, Merrill Lynch-Minnesota Regional Retail/Wholesale category, 1990; Direct Marketer of the Year Award, Midwest Direct Marketing Association, 1990.

Arthur D. Collins Jr. Pres., COO, Medtronic Inc., 7000 Central Ave. N.E., Fridley, MN 55432. Tel: 612/574-4000. **B:** 1947, Lakewood, Ohio. **M:** Anne. **C:** Elizabeth, Emily. **E:** Bachelor's, Milami (OH) U., 1969; MBA, Wharton School-U. of PA. **Career Hist.:** Officer, U.S. Navy, 1969-73; Consultant, Booz, Allen & Hamilton, 1974-78; Corp. VP, Abbott Laboratories, 1978-92; Medtronic Inc.: Corp. EVP, Pres.-Medtronic Intl., 1992-94; COO, 1994-96; Pres., COO, 1996-present. **Career Act.:** Dir., Medtronic Inc., U.S. Bancorp, Walker Art Center, Tennant Co., Cargill. **Act./Mem.:** United Way, Minneapolis Club, Minikahda Club.

William J. Collins CEO, AgriBank fcb, 375 Jackson St., P.O. Box 64949 (55164), St. Paul, MN 55164. Tel: 651/282-8800.

James C. Colville Pres., United Way of Minneapolis Area, 404 S. Eighth St., Minneapolis, MN 55404. Tel: 612/340-7400. **B:** Gulfport, Miss. **M:** Sarah. **C:** Teryll, Scott, Brandt. **E:** Texas Christian U., BBA. **Career Hist.:** Sls., Leonards Department Store, 1961-63; Assoc., J.C. Penney Company, 1963-64; Campaign Director and various positions, United Way of Fort Worth, 1964-72; Campaign Dir., United Way of Houston, 1972-78; Pres., United Way of Mineapolis area, 1978-present. **Career Act.:** St. Olaf College Board of Regents, Hunger Related Events (sponsors Taste of the NFL); Dir., Plymouth Music Series of MN, The Mentoring Partnership.

Thomas G. Colwell Chair, Colwell Industries Inc., 123 N. Third St., Minneapolis, MN 55401. Tel: 612/340-0365. **B:** Aug. 27, 1930, Minneapolis. **M:** Phyllis Daugherty, 1952. **C:** Felton, Carolyn. **E:** Carleton College, BA-Govt. and Intl. Relations, 1952. **Career Hist.:** Founder, Litho Supply Depot Inc., 1952; Gen. Mgr., Colight Inc., 1954-58; Gen. Mgr.-Color Card Div., Colwell Press Inc., 1958-63; Gen. Mgr., Colwell Press, 1963-66; Pres., Colwell Press, 1966-78; Chair, Pres., Colwell/General Inc. and Colwell Industries Inc., 1966-81; Chair, Pres., Colwell Industries Inc., 1982-96, Chair, 1996-present. **Career Act.:** Carleton College Trustee. **Act./Mem.:** Mem., World Presidents Org.; Chief Exec. Org., Minikahda Club, Minneapolis Club, Woodhill Country Club; past Pres., MN International Center; past Chair, World Affairs Center, U. of MN; past Dir., MN Orchestra Assn., Chief Execs. Organization; past Pres., Minneapolis City League Golf Assn.; Part Dir., The Blake School; Past Dir., Minneapolis College of Art and Design.

James Commander VP, Gen. Mgr., Unisys Corp., 2276 Highcrest Dr., P.O. Box 64942 (55164), Roseville, MN 55113. Tel: 651/635-6551. Email: james.commander@unisys.com **B:** Apr. 18, 1942, San Diego, Calif. **M:** Donna, 1962. **C:** Lance, Michelle. **Career Hist.:** U.S. Air Force; Control Data Corp.; Unisys Computer Systems.

Richard P. Confer Pres., Hubbard Milling Co., 424 N. Front St., Mankato, MN 56001. Tel: 507/625-1882. **B:** Mankato, Minn. **E:** Westminster College (Fulton, Missouri), BA-Economics, 1974. **Career Hist.:** Hubbard Milling: various positions, 1966-present.

Ed Conlin Owner, The Conlin Cos. (The Business Management Services), 4900 IDS Center, Minneapolis, MN 55402. Tel: 612/375-0084. **B:** Feb. 14, 1924, Williston, N.D. **M:** Joann, 1953. **C:** Joseph, Mary, Kathleen, Patrick, Kelly, Maureen, Michelle. **E:** U.S. Military Academy (West Point, NY), BS, 1946; Harvard Business School, OPM, 1979. **Career Hist.:** U.S. Army, 1st Lt. Infantry, 1946-50; Conlin Cos., Owner, 1950-present; Analytics Investment Advisors, VP, 1997-present. **Career Act.:** ND Jr. Chamber Of Commerce, Pres., 1952; Missouri Valley Family YMCA, Founder/First Pres., 1963; National Council YMCA 1973-76; Heartview Fdn. (Mandan, ND), Founder/First Pres., 1963-80; YMCA Annual Campaign, General Chair, 1989; YMCA of Minneapolis, General Board Of Directors, 1988-97; Harvard Business School Club of MN, VP, 1989. **Dec./Awd.:** Sertome Club Service to Mankind Award, 1967. **Act./Mem.:** Rotary, Exchange Club, Harvard Club of NY, Minikahda Club, Minneapolis Club, Woodhill Country Club, Vintage Club (Indian Wells, CA).

David G. Cook Pres., Stearns Inc., P.O. Box 1498, St. Cloud, MN 56302. Tel: 320/252-1642. **B:** Jun. 5, 1938, Austin, Minn. **M:** Lucile, 1961. **C:** Barb, Dave, Craig, Cathy. **E:** U. of MN, BS-Bus. Admin., 1964. **Career Hist.:** VP-Range Prods., Litton Industries, 1966-79; Pres., CEO, Stearns Inc., 1979-present; VP-KA Inc. 1990-present; Pres., Stearns 1990-present.. **Career Act.:** Dir., Stearns-Canada; Dir. Michaels of Oregon. **Dec./Awd.:** Executive of the Year, Anthony Industries, 1991. **Act./Mem.:** St. Cloud Chamber of Commerce; Celebration Lutheran Church; Mem., American Sport Fishing Assn., National Marine Manufacturers Assn..

Richard A. Coonrod Pres., CEO, Coonrod Agriproduction Corp., 5720 Smetana Dr., Suite 300, Minnetonka, MN 55343. Tel: 612/939-3940. **B:** Mar. 30, 1931, Mahaska, Kan. **M:** Phyllis, 1960. **C:** Amy, Wade, Paul. **E:** KS State U., BS-Milling Science, 1953.. **Career Hist.:** Pillsbury Company, 1957; VP, Gen. Mgr.-Commodity Merchandising, Pillsbury, 1957-77; VP, Gen. Mgr.; Group VP, Gen. Mgr., Agri-Products Div., Pillsbury, 1977-79; EVP, Pillsbury, 1979-85; Pres., Agri-Prods. Group, 1981-85; Pres., CEO, Agri Industries (Des Moines, IA), 1985-86; Pres., CEO, Coonrod Agriproduction Corp., 1985-present; Pres., CEO, St. Louis Ship (St. Louis, MO) 1988-92; General Ptnr., The Food Fund, 1990-present; Chm. Exec Network (FOOD) Glencoe Capital. **Career Act.:** Dir., Mem.-Exec. Ctee., Millers National Federation; Dir., Natl. Grain and Feed Assn., Urban Coalition League of Minneapolis, Norwest Bank Minnesota, Portland Foods (Portland, OR), Zapata-Haynie (Hammond, LA), Benson Quinn Co. (Mpls.), Orange-co Inc. (Bartow, FL), Xerxes Corp. (Mpls.); Dir., Michael Foods; Packaged Ice Dir; Precision Foods-Dir.; Stratetic Equipment Dir. **Act./Mem.:** Interlachen Country Club; Minneapolis Club.

Richard A. Cooper Pres., Caterpillar Paving Products Inc., 9401 85th Ave. N., Brooklyn Park, MN 55445. Tel: 612/493-1301. Email: cat-paver@aol.com **B:** Jul. 22, 1950, Minneapolis. **M:** Pamela, 1972. **C:** Molly, Cara. **E:** BA, U. of MN, 1972; MBA, Portland St. U., 1981. **Career Hist.:** Raygo-Wagner, Raygo Inc., 1973-87; Caterpillar Paving Products Inc., 1988-present: Dir.-Mfg., 1988-91; Gen. Mgr.-MN Op., 1991-96; Pres., 1996-present. **Career Act.:** Dir., Construction Industry Mfrs. Assn.; Exec. Committee, American Road and Transportation Builders Assoc.

William A. Cooper Chair, CEO, TCF Financial Corp., 801 Marquette Ave., Minneapolis, MN 55402. Tel: 612/370-7206. **B:** Jul. 3, 1943, Detroit. **M:** Sharron, 1971. **C:** William Jr., Christine, Bob, Brian, Kelley, Ashley, Lauren. **E:** Wayne State U., BS-Accounting/Economics, 1967; CPA, 1969. **Career Hist.:** Sr. Auditor, Touche Ross & Co. (Detroit), 1967-71; SVP, Cont., Michigan Natl. Corp., 1971-78; EVP, then Pres., Huntington Bank of Columbus, 1978-84; Pres., COO, American Savings of Miami, 1984-85; Chm., CEO, TCF Financial Corp., 1985-present. **Career Act.:** Dir., TCF Financial Corp., MN Business Partnership, Center of the American Experiment, Kids First Scholarship Fund of MN, Inc. Providence Academy; MN Republican Congressional Ctee., American Institute of CPAs, MN Executives' Organization, Chief Executives' Organization. **Act./Mem.:** Mem., Minneapolis Club, Wayzata Country Club.; Spring Hill Country Club.

Clarence C. Cornell Chair, ABC Bus Cos. Inc., 1506 30th St. N.W., Faribault, MN 55021. Tel: 507/334-1871. **B:** Feb. 25, 1930, Faribault, Minn. **M:** Mary Ann. **C:** Ron, Dane, Debra (Stanton), Roxanne. **E:** High school. **Career Hist.:** Operator, intercity buses in Iowa and Nebraska; Owner/Operator, Faribault Bus Service, 1958-72; Founder, Chair, CEO, ABC Bus Cos. (sales and service, family business), 1972-present. **Dec./Awd.:** Finalist-Entrepreneur of the Year Award, 1996. **Act./Mem.:** Numerous civic and social organizations.

John R. Corts Pres., COO, Billy Graham Evangelistic Association, 1300 Harmon Place, Minneapolis, MN 55403. Tel: 612/335-1394. Email: jcorts@graham-assn.org **B:** Jan. 26, 1936, Hammond, Ind. **M:** Jo-Ann, 1956. **C:** Alicia. **E:** Trinity College, BA, 1956.. **Career Hist.:** Ordained to ministry by Gospel Tabernacle Church, St. Petersburg, Florida, 1957; Pastor, Christian Fellowship Church, 1957-58; Registrar, Trinity College, 1957; Pastor, First Evangelical Baptist Church, 1958-62; Executive Dir. of Youth for Christ, 1962-64; Crusade Assoc., Billy Graham Evangelistic Assn., 1964-80; Pastor, Idlewild Baptist Church, 1980-83; Billy Graham Evangelistic Assn., 1983-present.

Gary E. Costley Chair, Pres., CEO, International Multifoods Corp., 110 Cheshire Ln., Suite 300, Minnetonka, MN 55305. Tel: 612/594-3300. Email: gcostley@multifoods.com **B:** Oct. 26, 1943, Caldwell, Idaho. **M:** Cheryl Zesiger. **C:** Angela (Harris), Chad. **E:** Oregon State U.: Bachelor's (1964) in animal science; Master's (1966) and Ph.D. (1970) in nutrition, with minors in physiology and biochemistry. **Career Hist.:** Kellogg Co., 1970-94: Dir.-Nutrition, VP-Public Affairs, VP and Asst. to Pres. LaMoth, SVP-Corp. Devel., EVP and Pres.-Kellogg U.S. (1986), EVP and Chair-Kellogg USA/Mrs. Smith's Frozen Foods (1988), EVP and Area Dir.-Kellogg North America (1992); Dean-Babcock School of Mgmt., Wake Forest U., 1995-97; Chair, Pres., CEO, Multifoods, 1997-present. **Career Act.:** Dir., Pharmacopeia Inc. (Princeton, NJ), Candlewood Hotel Co. Inc. (Wichita, KS), ecfood.com (Santa Clara, CA). **Act./Mem.:** United Way volunteer, 1999; Wayzata Country Club.

Jerome A. Crest EVP, Immanuel-St. Joseph's Hospital of Mankato Inc., 1025 Marsh St., Mankato, MN 56001. Tel: 507/625-4031. **E:** U. of MN, BSB-Business Admin., 1963; U. of MN, Master's Degree-Hospital/Health Care Admin., 1968. **Career Hist.:** Charles T. Miller Hospital: Admin. Resident, 1967-68, Asst. Admin., 1968-72; United Hospitals Inc., Assoc. Admin., 1972-74; Douglas County Hospital, Admin., 1974-83; Lakes Area Health Svs., EVP, 1980-83; West Central Linen Service, CEO, 1981-83; Immanuel-St. Joseph's Hospital, Pres., 1984-96; Immanuel St. Joseph's-Mayo Health System, EVP, 1996-present. **Career Act.:** American College of Healthcare Executives, Fellow, 1992-95; U. of MN: Program in Hospital/Health Care Admin., Alumni Assn., Sec.-Editor, 1973-76, Member, Alumni Institute Planning Ctee., 1991, Preceptor, Independent Study Program, 1975-78, Preceptor, Masters Program, 1990-present; MN Hospital Assn.: Chair-Elect, 1983, Chair, 1984-85, Dir., 1978-87; Min-Dak Health Systems Agency Inc., Dir., 1980-84; MN Dept. of Health, Executive Ctee., Statewide Community Health Svs. Advisory Ctee., 1979-83; United Way: Dir., 1985-91, Drive Chair, 1987; Mankato Heart Health/Health Promotion Council, Board Of Directors, 1986-91; Mankato Lutheran Home, Board Of Directors, 1984-87; Mankato YMCA: Dir., 1984-91, Pres., 1989; Valley Industrial Development Corp.: Dir., 1989-present, Chair, 1992; Mankato School District 77, Citizens Advisory Ctee. On Facility Needs, Chair, 1990. **Dec./Awd.:** Mankato Area Chamber of Commerce Business Hall Of Fame Award, 1998.

John Crinklaw Pres., Associated Bank-Minnesota, 740 Marquette Ave., Minneapolis, MN 55402. Tel: 612/338-2150. **B:** Nov. 22, 1941, Minneapolis. **M:** Shirley, 1965. **C:** Dawn, Diana. **E:** BS-Bus. Admin., U. of MN, 1964. **Career Hist.:** EVP, National City Bank, 22 years; Pres., CEO, Bank Windsor, 1992-1999. 1999 President, Associated Bank-Minnesota. **Career Act.:** Dir., VChair-Membership, Greater Mpls. Chamber of Commerce; Chair-Mgmt. Ctee., MN Bankers Assn.; past Pres.-MN Chapter, Robert Morris Assn.; past Dir., Downtown YMCA. **Act./Mem.:** Div. Chair, United Way, 1998; Wayzata Country Club, Minneapolis Club.

Terry M. Cummings Chair, Bremer Financial Corp., 445 Minnesota St., Suite 2000, St. Paul, MN 55101. Tel: 651/227-7621. **E:** Accounting degree, College of St. Thomas, 1962. **Career Hist.:** Bremer Financial Services Inc.: Pres., 1982-98; Pres./CEO-Bremer Financial Corp., 1988-98; Chm. 1998-present. **Career Act.:** Dir., Bremer Financial Services Inc., Bremer Financial Corp.

Michael R. Cunningham Dir., Gray, Plant, Mooty, Mooty & Bennett P.A., 3400 City Center, 33 S. Sixth St., Minneapolis, MN 55402. Tel: 612/343-2800. **B:** Oct. 13, 1944, Winterset, Iowa. **M:** Jean, 1974. **C:** Katie, Peter, Steven, William. **E:** BBA, U. of IA, 1967; JD, U. of IA College of Law, 1970. **Career Hist.:** Judicial Clerkship, Chief Judge of U.S. District Court/MN (Edward J. Devitt), 1970-71; Gray, Plant, Mooty, Mooty & Bennett, 1971-present: Chair and Mng. Officer, 1987-2000.

Steven O. Curry Pres., CEO, Knutson Construction Co., 5500 Wayzata Blvd., Suite 300, Golden Valley, MN 55416. Tel: 612/546-1400. **B:** Edina, Minn. **E:** Notre Dame, BBA; U of MN, MBA.. **Career Hist.:** First Bank System, 1976-84; Varitronic Systems Inc., 1984-86; Knutson Construction Company, 1986-present.. **Dec./Awd.:** United Hospital Foundation, AGC, United Way, Youth Hockey Coach. **Act./Mem.:** U of M Alumni Club; Notre Dame Alumni Club; Member-Interlachen Country Club.

Thomas A. Cusick VChair, COO-TCF Financial Corp., TCF Financial Corp., 801 Marquette Ave., Minneapolis, MN 55402. Tel: 612/661-6561. **B:** Dec. 19, 1944, Detroit. **M:** Charlene, 1974. **C:** Kevin, Theresa, Kelly. **E:** U. of Detroit, BBA, 1971; Stonier Grad. School of Banking/Rutgers U.. **Career Hist.:** Various positions, ending as Div. SVP, Michigan National Corp., 1976-1984; EVP, American Savings Bank (Miami), 1984-85; TCF Financial Corp., 1985-present. **Career Act.:** Dir., TCF Financial Corp., Damark Intl. Inc.; past Trustee, College of St. Benedict.. **Act./Mem.:** Minneapolis Club, Wayzata Country Club.

Christopher T. Dahl Chair, Pres., CEO, iNTELEFILM, 5501 Excelsior Blvd., Minneapolis, MN 55416. Tel: 612/925-8840. Email: cdahl@intelefilm.com **B:** Sep. 27, 1943, Louisville, Ky. **C:** Chris Jr., Cortland. **E:** B.A., U. of MN, 1967. **Career Hist.:** Account Exec., Alberto-Culver, 1968-69; Founder, Community Airwaves Corp., 1986-2000; Founder, Children's Broadcasting Corp., 1990-97; Pres. and Chair, Harmony Holdings Inc., 1997-

present. Chair and CEO 1997 to present iNTELEFILM. **Career Act.:** Mem., World Presidents' Organization, MN Executives Organization, National Assn. of Broadcasters, American Film Institute, National Bison Assn. **Dec./Awd.:** Alumni of Notable Achievement, U of Minn., 1997. Entrepreneur of the Year-Chamber of Commerce, 1995. **Act./Mem.:** Dir., Assn. of Publicly Traded Cos.; Nation Co-Chair, Recording Artists, Actors, and Athletes Against Drunken Driving. Interlachen Country Club, Minneapolis Club.

Burton F. Dahlberg Chair-Operations Ctee., Kraus-Anderson Inc., 523 S. Eighth St., Minneapolis, MN 55404-1030. Tel: 612/881-8166. **B:** Dec. 14, 1932, Ashland, Wis. **M:** Sandra, 1985. **C:** Michael, Andrea, David. **E:** U. of MN, BA-Bus. and Econ., 1960. **Career Hist.:** Oneida Realty, 1963; real estate analyst, Control Data Corp., 1965; real estate manager, Kraus-Anderson, 1968-84; Pres., COO, Kraus-Anderson Realty and Kraus-Anderson Inc., 1984-2000; Chm.-Operations Ctee., 2000-present. **Act./Mem.:** Mem. and past pres. Minneapolis Building Owners and Mgrs. Assn.; member and past dir., National Assn. of Office and Industrial Parks, Institute of Real Estate Mgmt., Bloomington Chamber of Commerce, Decathlon Athletic Club; past regional dir., International Council of Shopping Centers; dir., Minnesota Taxpayers Assn.; Pres., MN Thoroughbred Assn.; Dir., MN Chamber of Commerce, Minneapolis Chamber of Commerce.

H. David Dalquist Chair, Northland Aluminum Products Inc., 5005 Highway 7, St. Louis Park, MN 55416. Tel: 612/924-8534. **B:** May 25, 1918, Minneapolis. **M:** Dorothy M., 1945. **C:** Corrine D. (Lynch), H. David III, Linda Ruth (Jeffrey), Susan D. (Brust). **E:** U. of MN, BS-Chem. and Business Admin., 1942. **Career Hist.:** Northland Aluminum Prods. Inc., 1946-present: Founder, Pres., 1946-1985; Chair, 1985-present. **Career Act.:** Dir., Northland Aluminum Prods. Inc., Great Lakes Cruising Club, Minneapolis Heart Institute, Lake Superior Center. **Dec./Awd.:** Entrepreneurs Hall of Fame, New England Housewives Club, 1987; Fifty-fifth Laureate, MN Business Hall of Fame, 1987. **Act./Mem.:** Lafayette Country Club; Madeline Island Yacht Club; U. of MN Alumni Club; Royal Roundtable of Sweden, America.

H. David Dalquist III Pres., CEO, Northland Aluminum Products Inc., 5005 Highway 7, St. Louis Park, MN 55416. Tel: 612/920-2888. **B:** Feb. 4, 1949, Minneapolis. **M:** Martha, 1976. **C:** Jennifer, Michelle. **E:** U. of MN Inst. of Tech., BS-Mech. Engrg.; U. of MN College of Bus. Admin., BS-Bus. Admin. **Career Hist.:** Northland Aluminum Products, 1972-present: Mfg. Engr., 1972-74; VP-Admin., 1974-76; VP-Sls./Admin., 1976-77; EVP, 1977-82; Pres., 1982-90; Pres. and CEO, 1990-present.

John H. Dasburg Pres., CEO, Northwest Airlines Corp., 5101 Northwest Dr., Eagan, MN 55111. Tel: 612/726-2111. **B:** Jan. 7, 1943, New York. **M:** Mary Lou. **C:** two. **E:** U. of Florida, BSIE, 1966; MBA, 1971; JD 1973. **Career Hist.:** Marriott Corp., 1984-89; EVP-Admin., Northwest Airlines, 1989-90; Pres., CEO, Northwest Airlines, 1990-present. **Career Act.:** Dir., Northwest Airlines Corp., The St. Paul Companies Inc., U. of Florida Fdn., Minneapolis Institute of Arts; Mayo Fdn., Guthrie Theater. **Dec./Awd.:** Gordon Grand Fellow, Yale U.; White House Fellows, Appointed by President Bush; "Man of the Year," Travel Agent Magazine, 1994.

Mark E. Davis Pres., Davisco International Inc., 704 N. Main St., P.O. Box 69, Le Sueur, MN 56058. Tel: 507/665-8811. **B:** Mar. 19, 1941, Frost, Minn. **M:** Mary, 1962. **C:** Mitchell, Martin, Matthew, Julie, Jon. **E:** Mankato State College, B.A. **Career Hist.:** Has been in a family dairy and food industry business since 1960. **Career Act.:** American Dairy Products Institute; Pres., National Independent Dairy Assn.; past Pres., North Central Cheese Industries Assn., International Dairy Foods Assn., National Cheese Industry B.O.D. **Dec./Awd.:** 2000 Award of Merit from American Dairy Products Institute; Outstanding Alumnus-Minnesota State University 2000.

Robert Dayton CEO, Okabena Co., 5140 Norwest Center, 90 S. Seventh St., Minneapolis, MN 55416. Tel: 612/339-7151. **B:** Apr. 2, 1942, Minneapolis. **M:** Joan, 1964. **C:** three grown sons. **E:** BA, Yale U., 1964; PMD, Harvard Business School, 1972. **Career Hist.:** EVP, Dayton Hudson Department Stores, 1974-77; CEO, Harold Corp., 1977-91; CEO, Okabena Co., 1993-present. **Career Act.:** Dir., First American Funds. **Act./Mem.:** Mem.-Steering Ctee., Mpls. Convention Center Completion Project; Chair-Leadership Council, Mentoring Partnership of Minnesota; Dir., past Chair, Mpls. United Way; past Pres., Mpls. Club, Woodhill Country Club; Dir., National Mentoring Partnership, Minneapolis United Way; Board of Overseers, U of MN Carlson School of Mgmt.; Dir. Center for Corporate Responsibility; Dir. Great North.

Rev. Dennis Dease Pres., University of St. Thomas, 2115 Summit Ave., St. Paul, MN 55105. Tel: 651/962-6500. Email: djdease@stthomas.edu **B:** May 12, 1943, Minneapolis. **E:** St. Paul Seminary, BA, 1965, M.Div. 1973; U. of St. Thomas, MA, 1972; Catholic U. of America, Ph.D., 1978. **Career Hist.:** Counselor, St. John Vianney Seminary, 1971-74; Faculty, U. of St. Thomas, 1974-79; Faculty, St. Paul Seminary, 1979-85; Pastor, Basilica of St. Mary, 1985-91; Pres., U. of St. Thomas, 1991-present.. **Career Act.:** Mem., Domestic Policy Ctee., United States Catholic Conference; Dir., Allianz Life Ins. Co. of North America, Packaging Inc., Premier Banks; Trustee, U. of St. Thomas; Dir., MN Private College Council; Research Fdn. and Fund (Chair, 1996-97), Minnesota Meeting; Chair, Board of Dir. Assn. of Catholic Colleges and Universities; Dir., Natl. Catholic Educ. Assoc. **Dec./Awd.:** Harriet P. Burns Award, College of St. Thomas Professional Psychology faculty, 1990.

Arlene M. DeCandia CEO, Riverwood Metro Business Resort, 10990 95th St. N.E., Monticello, MN 55362. Tel: 612/441-6833. **B:** Oct. 24, 1946, Hoboken, N.J. **M:** Sven Arne Wasberg, 1994. **C:** Daniel, Tanja, Sarenja. **E:** U. of MN, B.S. Scientific/Tech. Communications, 1977. **Career Hist.:** Founder, owner, Riverwood Metro Business Resort, 1979-present; Founder, owner, Timothy's Restaurant, 1992-present.. **Career Act.:** Board Mem., First American Bank of St. Cloud, National Assn. of Women Business Owners, MN Women's Economic Roundtable. **Dec./Awd.:** Finalist, Entrepreneur of the Year, Twin West Chamber of Commerce, 1985, 1992; Finalist, Woman of Enterprise, Avon Products, Inc. and SBA; Finalist, Entrepreneur of the Year, Ernst & Young and Merrill-Lynch; Recipient, Woman Business Owner of the Year, National Assn. of Woman Business Owners; Recipient, Minnesota's Small Business Person of the Year, SBA, 1993; State designee, Blue Chip Enterprise Initiative, 1994.

Robert A. Degenhardt CEO, The Ellerbe Becket Co., 800 LaSalle Ave., Minneapolis, MN 55402. Tel: 612/376-2546. Email: bob_degenhardt@ellerbebecket.com **B:** May 29, 1943, Kearney, Neb. **M:** Elizabeth S. Scholl 1999. **C:** Barry, Christopher, Kathleen. **E:** U. of Nebraska BSME, 1965; MSME, 1968.. **Career Hist.:** U.S. Army, Project Engr., 1968-70; Sundstrand Aviation, Project Engr., 1970-74; DFSD Architects and Engrs., Dir. of Engrg., 1974-77; The Durrant Group, VP and Dir. of Mechanical Engrg., 1977-80; Ellerbe Associates Inc., VP and Dir. of Mechanical Engrg., 1980-82; VP and Dir. of Op., 1982-1985; Senior VP and Dir. of Washington, D.C. office, 1985-89; The Ellerbe Becket Co., Pres. and COO, 1989-94; Pres. and CEO, 1994-1998; CEO, 1998-present. **Career Act.:** Executive Ctee., American Consulting Engineers Council Design Professionals Coalition; Mem., American Institute of Architects Large Firm Roundtable, Construction Industry Roundtable; MN Center for Corporate Responsibility; Past Dir., Consulting Engineers Council of MN; past Chair, MN Chapter American Society of Heating, Refrigerating, and Air Conditioning Engineers (ASHRAE), HVAC Advisory Ctee.-U. of MN Continuing Education in Engrg. and Science; Mem., Penn State U. Consortium for Advancement of Building Sciences. **Act./Mem.:** United Way Key Account Exec.

Theodore Deikel Pres., CEO, Chair, Boom Buy Inc., 7587 Equitable Dr., Eden Prairie, MN 55344. Tel: 612/936-5408. **B:** Oct. 5, 1935, Minneapolis. **C:** Eve M. Deikel, Laura D., Daniel A., Andrew J.. **E:** U. of MN, 1958-61. **Career Hist.:** U.S. Marine Corps, 1954-57; self-employed, direct mail business, 1961-63; Fingerhut Corp., 1963-83: Pres., 1974, Pres., CEO, 1975, Chair, Pres., CEO, 1978; Chair, CEO, Pickwick International Inc. and The Musicland Group, 1979-83; American Can Company (now Primerica), 1979-83: SVP, 1979-81, EVP 1981-83; Chair, CEO, CVN Companies, 1983-89. Chair, CEO, Fingerhut Companies Inc., 1989-99. **Career Act.:** Past Dir., Metris Cos. Inc., Minnesota Orchestral Assn., Methodist Hospital Fdn., Methodist Hospital, Guthrie Theater, Mt. Sinai Hospital; past Trustee, Blake School; Dir., Fingerhut Cos. Inc., National Retail Federation, MN Business Partnership, International Special Olympics; past Mem., National Advisory Ctee., Hubert H. Humphrey Cancer Research Center, Boston U. Medical Center, MN Governor's Loaned Executive Program (L.E.A.P.), MN Commission on Education for Economic Growth, MN Business Partnership Inc., fundraising campaign for (FLIR) Forward Looking Intrared Radar system purchased for the MN State Patrol; Founder, Take A Taxi On Us Program, 1979-present. **Dec./Awd.:** Commendations by Pres. Jimmy Carter, Mayor Al Hofstede, Gov. Albert Quie; Human Relations Award, Music and Performing Arts Div. of Anti-Defamation League, 1981; Direct Mktr. of the Year, Midwest Direct Mktg. Assn., 1987; DreamMaker Award, Children's Cancer Research Fund, 1992; Others Award, Salvation Army, 1993; Executive of the Year, Corporate Report Minnesota magazine, 1994; Lifetime Achievement Award, Hennepin Country Mothers Against Drunk Drivers, 1996; Entrepreneur of the Year, 1999, Ernst & Young; 1998 Ellis Island Medal of Honor Recipient. **Act./Mem.:** Minneapolis Club.

Patrick Delaney Attorney, Lindquist & Vennum PLLP, 4200 IDS Center, 80 S. Eighth St., Minneapolis, MN 55402. Tel: 612/371-3211. **B:** Aug. 12, 1942. **M:** Kitty, 1966. **C:** Kevin, Patrick, Monica. **E:** BA, St. John's U./U. of St. Thomas, 1964; JD, U. of MN, 1967. **Career Hist.:** Delaney & Solum, 1972-84; Lindquist & Vennum, 1984-present. **Career Act.:** Director and Secretary, Community First Bankshares Inc.; Secretary, Cardia, Inc.; Director and Secretary; CNS, Inc., Director and Secretary; Banner Engineering Corp.; Chair, Securities Regulation Advisory Committee (MN Commerce Dept.) 1993 to 1996.

WHO

Livio D. DeSimone Chair, CEO, 3M Co., 3M Center, 220-14W-05, Maplewood, MN 55144. Tel: 651/733-1110. **B:** Jul. 16, 1936, Montreal. **E:** McGill U. (Montreal), Bachelor of Chem. Engrg., 1957.. **Career Hist.:** 3M Company, 1957-present: Process Engr., 3M Canada, 1957-61; Abrasives, St. Paul, 1961-63; 3M Australia, 1963-64; 3M Brazil, 1965-71; Managing Dir., 3M Brazil, 1971-75; Gen. Mgr., BS&CP Div., 1975; Area VP, Latin America, 1975-79; VP-Abrasives, Adhesives, Bldg. Svs. and Chem. Group, 1979-81; EVP-Life Sciences Sector, 1981-84; EVP-Industrial and Consumer Sector, 1984-87; EVP-Industrial and Electronic Sector and Corporate Svs., 1987-89; EVP-Information and Imaging Technologies Sector and Corporate Svs., 1989-90; Chair, CEO, 1991-present. **Career Act.:** Dir., 3M Fdn., Cargill Inc., Dayton Hudson Corp., Junior Achievement Inc., Vulcan Materials Company, General Mills Inc., National Legal Center for the Public Interest, The Conference Board of Canada; Trustee, U of MN Fdn., Board of Trustees, The Conference Board; Chair, World Business Council for Sustainable Development; Mem., The Business Council, The Business Roundtable, MN Business Partnership, U.S.-Japan Business Council, U.S. Chamber of Commerce, Alliance for Global Sustainability, Metropolitan Economic Devel. Assn., Singapore Economic Devel. Board International Advisory Council, Council on Competitiveness; Department Chair, The Prince of Wales Business Leaders Forum; Indianhead Council, Boy Scouts of America; Ex Officio Mem., International Chamber of Commerce. **Dec./Awd.:** Executive of the Year, Corporate Report MN, 1998; S. Bayard Colgate Award, Junior Achievement Inc., 1999.

Louis DeThomasis, F.S.C. Pres., St. Mary's University of Minnesota, 700 Terrace Heights, Winona, MN 55987. Tel: 507/457-1503. **B:** Oct. 6, 1940, Brooklyn, N.Y. **E:** Georgetown U., School of Foreign Service, 1963; The Union Institute, Ph.D., 1982. **Career Hist.:** Metro Graphics Inc., Pres. and CEO, 1964-68; LaSalle Academy (Rhode Island), Faculty, 1969-71; LaSalle Military Academy (New York), Assoc. Headmaster to Chief Operating Officer, 1971-73; The Christian Brothers, VP of Fin. to Chief Financial Officer, 1973-76; LaSalle Military Academy, Pres. and CEO, 1976-84; St. Mary's U., 1984-present.. **Career Act.:** Dir: The Galaxy Funds, Boston; the MN Private College Council; St. Mary's College of California; Chirstian Brothers, U. of Memphis; The National Fdn. for Independent Higher Education. **Dec./Awd.:** Doctor of Laws, Honoris Causa, Benedictine U., 1989; Knighthood, The Order of the Holy Sepulchre of Jerusalem, 1989; Founders' Collegium, Pontifical North American College, Rome, 1994; Pro Ecclesia Et Pontiface Medal, Rome 1998.

Mark D. Dixon Administrator, Abbott Northwestern Hospital, 800 E. 28th St., Minneapolis, MN 55407. Tel: 612/863-4201. Email: dixon@allina.com **B:** Oct. 16, 1955, Minneapolis. **M:** Susan, 1978. **E:** BS-Pharmacy, U. of MN, 1978; Master's-Hospital/Health Care Admin., U. of MN, 1984. **Career Hist.:** Abbott Northwestern Hospital: Asst. Admin. to Operations VP, 1984-97; Admin., 1997-present. **Career Act.:** Dir., Greater Mpls. Chamber of Commerce, Axis Healthcare, WestHealth Inc., Abbott Northwestern, Physician Hospital Org.-Abbott Northwestern, Sister Kenny Institute; past Chair, Lifelink III.

Janet M. Dolan Pres., CEO, Tennant Co., 701 N. Lilac Dr., P.O. Box 1452 (55440), Golden Valley, MN 55422. Tel: 612/540-1290. **B:** Nov. 25, 1949, Benson, Minn. **M:** William G. Moore, 1977. **C:** Jack, Bob. **E:** College of St. Catherine, BA, 1971; William Mitchell College of Law, JD, 1976. **Career Hist.:** So. MN Regional Legal Svs., Staff Attorney, 1978-80; MN Lawyers' Professional Responsibility Board: Asst. Dir., 1980-81; First Asst. Dir., 1981-85; Tennant Co.: Assoc. Gen. Counsel, 1986-87; Gen. Counsel and Sec., 1988-90; VP, Gen. Counsel, and Sec., 1990-94; Head of Floor Coatings Div., 1993-96; Head of Field Op., 1994-96; SVP and Gen. Counsel, 1994-96; EVP, 1996-98; Pres. and COO, 1998-99; Pres. and CEO, 1999-present. **Career Act.:** Dir., Donaldson Co., United Way of Minneapolis; Trustee, William Mitchell College of Law. **Act./Mem.:** College of St. Catherine Alumna Assn.

James E. Donaghy Chair, Sheldahl Inc., 1150 Sheldahl Rd., Northfield, MN 55057. Tel: 507/663-8660. Email: james.donaghy@sheldahl.com **B:** Aug. 28, 1934, Pittsburgh. **M:** Anne Bailey, 1958. **C:** Julia Western, Stephen Bruce, Thomas Gregory. **E:** Harvard, AB, 1956; MIT, MS, 1958. **Career Hist.:** DuPont Co.: Dir., Electronic Materials; Dir., Berg Electronics; Dir., Planning and Devel. for Electronics Group, 1958-1988. **Career Act.:** Dir., Sheldahl Inc., Hutchinson Technology Inc.; Chair-IPC International, 1998. **Act./Mem.:** Dir., William Mitchell College of Law.

Larry Dorn CEO, Dorn & Co. Inc., 216 E. Washington, Fergus Falls, MN 56537. Tel: 218/739-5236. Email: dornco@prtel.com **B:** Feb. 9, 1942, Fergus Falls, Minn. **M:** Jeanette, 1963. **C:** Jennifer, Matthew. **E:** St. Cloud State, BA-Business Administration, 1964. **Career Hist.:** Pres., Dorn & Co. Inc. 1968-present. **Career Act.:** Trustee, Securities Industry Institute, Wharton School; Pres. Lake Region Hospital Board of Trustees; Pres., Lake Region Hospital Fdn.; **Dec./Awd.:** Outstanding Broker Award, Registered Representative Magazine, 1993; Distinguished Alumni Award, St. Cloud State U., 1994; Broker Hall of Fame, Research Magazine, 1996. **Act./Mem.:** Kiwanis Club, Twin City Bond Club, International Assn. of Financial Planners, Securities Industry Assn., Institute trustee.

James E. Doubles Chair, Pres., CEO, TSI Inc., 500 Cardigan Rd., P.O. Box 64394 (55164), Shoreview, MN 55126. Tel: 651/490-2719. **B:** Mar. 21, 1941, Muskegon, Mich. **M:** Virginia, 1964. **C:** Amy, Matthew. **E:** B.S., U.S. Naval Academy, 1964; M.B.A., U. of St. Thomas, 1992. **Career Hist.:** VP-Sls./Mktg., Smith Meter Div., Geosource Inc., 1982-84; VP-Sls./Mktg. C-E Inalco, 1984-85; VP-Mktg./Strategic Planning, TSI Inc., 1985-89; EVP and COO, TSI Inc., 1989-92; Pres. and COO, TSI Inc., 1992-97; Pres. and CEO, TSI Inc., 1997-present. **Career Act.:** Mem., Instrument Society of America, American Mgmt. Assn., American Electronics Assn.

Richard A. Downs CEO, Tony Downs Foods Co., 400 Armstrong Blvd., St. James, MN 56081. Tel: 507/375-3111. **B:** Worthington, Minn. **M:** Jane Marquardt, 1968. **C:** Matthew, Jennifer, Elizabeth, Anthony, Lucas, Alexander. **Career Hist.:** Op. Mgr., Butterfield Foods, 1970-73; Pres., Wadco Foods, 1973-78; Pres., Butterfield Foods, 1978-81; Chair, Tony Downs Foods Company, 1981-present. **Career Act.:** Dir., MN Poultry Industry; Chair, Butterfield Foods Co.

Dennis J. Doyle CEO, Welsh Cos. Inc., 8200 Normandale Blvd., Suite 200, Bloomington, MN 55437. Tel: 612/897-7700. Email: ddoyle@welshco.com **B:** Jun. 8, 1952, St. Louis. **M:** Megan, 1983. **C:** Nathan, Devin. **E:** U. of MT, 1970-74 (football scholarship). **Career Hist.:** Welsh Cos., 1978-present: Co-founder with George Welsh (retired); CEO, Welsch Cos. Inc.; Chair, Corporate Living. **Career Act.:** Mem., NAIOP; American Church Mortgage Co., Rottlund Homes, Gresser Concrete. **Dec./Awd.:** Small Business Person of the Year, Eden Prairie Chamber of Commerce, 1990; Entrepreneur of the Year real estate finalist, Ernst & Young/Merrill Lynch, 1990 and 1991. **Act./Mem.:** Teen Challenge. Olympic Hills.

Andrew S. Duff Pres./CEO-U.S. Bancorp Piper Jaffray Inc.; Vice Chair U.S. Bank, U.S. Bancorp, 222 S. Ninth St., Piper Jaffray Tower, Minneapolis, MN 55402. Tel: 612/342-6000. **B:** Dec. 19, 1957. **M:** Lucia Scott. **C:** Meredith K., Walter D. **E:** BA-Economics, Tufts U., 1980; Advanced Exec. Prog. at the J.L. Kellogg Graduate School of Mgmt. **Career Hist.:** Piper Jaffray (now U.S. Bancorp Piper Jaffray Inc.), 1980-present: Pres., 1996-present. **Career Act.:** Mem., Dir.-Mgmt. Ctee., U.S. Bancorp Piper Jaffray Inc. **Act./Mem.:** Dir., Walker Art Center; Trustee, Minneapolis Fdn.; Member of the SIA Regional Firms Committee; has served as a member of the New York Stock Exchange Regional Firms Advisory Committee.

William D. Dunlap Jr. Chair, Campbell Mithun, 222 S. Ninth St., Minneapolis, MN 55402. Tel: 612/347-1312. **B:** Apr. 8, 1938, Austin, Minn. **M:** Lois Mary, 1961. **C:** Kristin, Leslie, Brenda. **E:** Carleton College, BA, 1960. **Career Hist.:** Dir.-New Products, Procter & Gamble (Cincinnati, OH), 1960-69; Asst. Postmaster Gen., U.S. Govt. (Washington, D.C.), 1971-75; Pres., MCA Advertising (New York, NY), 1976-81; Campbel Mithun Inc.: Pres., 1981-83; Chair, CEO, 1983-94; Chair, 1994-present. **Act./Mem.:** Minneapolis Club; United Way; Greater Minneapolis Chamber of Commerce; American Assn. of Advertising Agencies; Dir., Hazelden Fdn.

Joseph T. Dunsmore Chair, Pres., CEO, Digi International Inc., 11001 Bren Rd. E., Minnetonka, MN 55343. Tel: 952/912-3444. **E:** University of Northern Iowa, B.A.; Florida Institute of Technology, M.B.A. **Career Hist.:** Various marketing positions, AT&T Paradyne Corp.; VP of New Business Units at U.S. Robotics and VP of Prod. Mgmt. and Marketing; CEO, NetFax, Inc.; VP of Access, Lucent Technologies, Inc.

Mark U. Edwards Jr. Pres., St. Olaf College, 1520 St. Olaf Ave., Northfield, MN 55057. Tel: 507/646-3000. Email: edwards@stolaf.edu **B:** Jun. 2, 1946, Oakland, Calif. **M:** Linda Johnson, 1968. **C:** Teon, Elizabeth. **E:** Stanford U., BA, 1968; MA, 1969; Ph.D., 1974. **Career Hist.:** Wellesley College, Asst. Prof., 1974-80; Purdue U., Prof., 1980-87; Harvard U., 1987-94: Prof., 1987-94; Acting Dean of the Divinity School, 1990-91; ELK Software Devel. Corp., VP, 1986-present; Pres., St. Olaf College, 1994. **Career Act.:** MN Private College Council, Associated Colleges of the Midwest; Mem., National Assn. of Independent Colleges and U., Norwegian American Historical Assn.; Holden Board Mem.; Dir., Kare 11. **Dec./Awd.:** Knight First Class, Norwegian Government, 1996. **Act./Mem.:** St. Olaf College Board of Regents, 1994-present; Holden Village Board, Chelan, Wash., 1993-present; LECNA Board, July 1998; Minnesota Private College Fund-Public Policy Ctee, July 1998; Minnesota Private College Fund-Pres. Ctee. and Board of Dirs., 1994-present; Kare 11 Bd. of Dirs., 1997-present; NAICU Policy Analysis, 1996-present; NAICU Presidents 1994-present; Harvard Visiting Ctee., 1996-present; ACM Presidents, 1994-present; ELCA Presidents, 1994-present; NAHA, St. Olaf College; Elk Software Development Corp. Founder and VP, 1985-present.

Gerald L. Egan retired Chair/Pres./CEO, The Egan Cos., 7100 Medicine Lake Rd., New Hope, MN 55427. Tel: 612/544-4131. **B:** Mar. 10, 1931, Minneapolis. **M:** Mary. **C:** Pam (Blahna), Diane (Slayton), Dave, Tom, Denise, Elizabeth, Joseph. **E:** High school, Dunwoody Institute. **Career Hist.:** U.S.A.F., 1951-55; Egan & Sons Company, 1955-present: Apprentice Plumber, 1955-60; Journeyman, Master Plumber, Estimator, 1960-70; Pres., 1970-87; The Egan Companies: Pres., CEO, 1987-92; Chair, Pres., CEO, 1992-2000. **Career Act.:** past Pres., Twin Cities Piping Ind. Assn., Sheet Metal and Roofing Contractors Assn.; Mem., Labor Users Contractors Assn., Regional Congress of Construction Employees; 1986 Chair, YMCA Minneapolis Metro Sustaining Membership Pres., Mechanical Contractors Assn. America (MCAA); Dir., Dunwoody Institute. **Dec./Awd.:** Outstanding Service, YMCA, 1973; Service Award, YMCA, 1972-79; Distinguished Service Award, MN Mechanical Contractors Assn., 1987; Outstanding Contractor, Sheet Metal and Roofing Contractors Assn., 1990 Entrepreneur Award, Dunwoody Institute, 1990. **Act./Mem.:** YMCA; Minneapolis Country Club; Colliers Reserve C.C., Naples.

John J. Egart Pres., CEO, First Team Sports Inc., 1201 Lund Blvd., Anoka, MN 55303. Tel: 612/576-3500. **B:** Mar. 9, 1950, Evanston, Ill. **M:** Patricia, 1975. **E:** BA, U. of Notre Dame. **Career Hist.:** Sls. Rep., Parker Bros. Games, 1972-76; Sls./Promo Rep-Upper Midwest, Converse, 1976-83; Sales Rep., Adidas, 1983-87. **Career Act.:** Dir., First Team Sports Inc., Kelly Russell Studios Inc.

Steven C. Eggimann Managing Ptnr., Meagher & Geer PLLP, 4200 Multifoods Tower, 33 S. Sixth St., Minneapolis, MN 55402. Tel: 612/338-0661. **B:** Jan. 31, 1948, Ames, Iowa. **M:** Dianne J. Van Tasell, 1980. **E:** U. of Iowa: BA, 1970; JD, 1973. **Career Hist.:** Clerk to the Honorable K. David Harris, Justice of the Iowa Supreme Court, 1973-74; Clerk to the Honorable David Leslie, Judge of District Court, Hennepin Co. (MN), 1974-75. Federal Bar Admissions: U.S. District Court, District of MN, 1975; Eighth Circuit Court of Appeals, Seventh Circuit Court of Appeals, Eastern and Western Districts of WI, Eastern District of MI, all 1987; State: IA, 1973, MN, 1975, WI, 1986. Qualified neutral mediator and arbitrator, MN Supreme Court; lecturer on trial practice and insurance law; two-term managing partner, manager of Commercial Litigation Practice, Meagher & Geer; "AV" rating from Martindale-Hubbell. **Career Act.:** Mem., Defense Research Institute, MN Defense Lawyers Assn., Hennepin County Bar Assn. (Committee on Professional Conduct), MN State Bar Assn., American Bar Assn.

John R. (Jack) Eickhoff EVP, CFO, Ceridian Corp., 3311 E. Old Shakopee Rd., Minneapolis, MN 55425. Tel: 612/853-8100. **B:** Apr. 17, 1940, St. Cloud, Minn. **M:** Rita. **E:** BA, St. Cloud St. U. **Career Hist.:** E5, Ft. Leonard Wood (MO)/Ft. Ord (CA), U.S. Army, 1959-60; Ceridian Corp., 1963-present: Various accounting and financial planning assignments, 1963-82; VP-Corp. Svs., 1983; VP (Cont.)-Fin. Plans and Controls, Commercial Credit, 1983; VP (Cont.)-Fin. Plans and Controls, Fin. and Business Svs., 1985; VP (Cont.)-Fin. Plans and Controls, Intl., 1985; VP (Cont.)-Fin. Plans and Controls, Computer Systems and Svs. Group, 1986; VP (Cont.)-Fin. Plans and Controls, Computer Products Group, 1988; VP and Corp. Cont., 1989;

CFO, 1993; EVP and CFO, 1995. **Career Act.:** Trustee, Boys and Girls Club of Mpls.; Mem. Emeritus-Board of Overseers, Carlson School of Mgmt. (U. of MN); Mem., Financial Executives Institute (both Natl. and Twin Cities Chapter), Ceridian Corp. Retirement Ctee.

Jonathan F. Eisele Office Managing Ptnr., Deloitte & Touche LLP, 400 One Financial Plaza, 120 S. Sixth St., Minneapolis, MN 55402. **E:** B.B.A., U. of Iowa; Executive Education, Columbia U. **Career Act.:** Board Mem., Minn. Business Partnership; Board Mem., Minneapolis Downtown Council. **Act./Mem.:** Chair, Minneapolis Area Red Cross; Dir., Minn. Orchestral Assn; Professional Advisory Council Mem., Accounting Dept. of the U. of Iowa; Bd. of Trustees, Colonial Church.

Richard P. Ekstrand Pres., CEO, Rural Cellular Corp., 3905 Dakota St. S.W., P.O. Box 2000, Alexandria, MN 56308. Tel: 320/762-2000. **B:** Aug. 13, 1949, Alexandria, Minn. **M:** Tamara, 1972. **C:** Dacia, Bria, Joshua. **E:** Augsburg Coll., B.B.A. **Career Hist.:** United Telephone Co. and State of MN, Mgr.; Lowry Telephone Co. Inc., VP, 1984-present; R.P. Ekstrand Management Svs. Corp., Owner; Rural Cellular Corp., Pres., CEO, 1991-present; RCC Paging Inc. (KEYPAGE), Pres. **Career Act.:** Pres., Dir., Chair-Board of Governors; Dir., Lowry Telephone Co. Inc., Cellular 2000 Inc., Rural Cellular Assn., CTIA; past Pres., Assn. of MN Telephone Utilities; Dir., past Pres., MN Telephone Assn., MN Telecommunications Assn., Switch 2000 Inc.; Dir., Cellular Telecommunications Industry Assn. **Dec./Awd.:** Celli Award, GTE, 1997; Minnesota and Dakotas Entrepreneur of the Year (Entertainment/Communications category), Ernst & Young LLP, 1998.

Joel A. Elftmann Chair, FSI International Inc., 322 Lake Hazeltine Dr., Chaska, MN 55318. Tel: 612/448-8009. Email: jelftmann@fsi-intl.com **B:** Jan. 19, 1940, Minneapolis. **M:** Mary Ann, 1959. **E:** Dunwoody Institute, 1960; Harvard OPM program, 1981. **Career Hist.:** FSI International: COO, 1973-78; 1973-77 VP and Gen. Mgr., 1977-83 Pres. CEO, Chairman P3-9/CEO, Chair; Pres., 1978-83; Chair, CEO, 1983-88; Chair, 1988-90; Chair, CEO 1991; 1991-99 Pres., CEO, Chairman; 2000 Chairman.. **Career Act.:** Chair, FSI International Inc.; Dir., m-FSI Ltd., Metron Technology, SEMI/SEMATECH, MN Orchestral Assn., Institute for Ecumenical & Cultural Research, Veeco Instruments Inc.; Trustee, Dunwoody Industrial Institute; Dir. Emeritus, Semiconductor Equipment Materials International. **Act./Mem.:** Hazeltine National Golf Club, United Way Contact Executive.

Sidney W. (Chip) Emery Pres., CEO, MTS Systems Corp., 14000 Technology Dr., Eden Prairie, MN 55344. Tel: 612/937-4000. **E:** U.S. Naval Academy, BS, 1968; Stanford U., MS, Ph.D., 1973. **Career Hist.:** Has run major units of large companies, most recently, Honeywell Inc. (Brussels, Belgium), VP For Western/Southern Europe; MTS, Pres., CEO, 1998-present.

James W. Emison CEO, Western Petroleum Co., 9531 W. 78th St., Eden Prairie, MN 55344. Tel: 612/941-9090. **B:** Sep. 21, 1930, Indianapolis. **M:** Jane Bale Larson, 1983. **C:** Catherine, Elizabeth, Thomas, William. **E:** DePauw U., BA-History and English Lit., 1952. **Career Hist.:** U.S. Marine Corps, 1952-54; Gen. Mgr., C & C Oil Company Inc., 1954-60; Pres., May Petroleum Company, 1960-61; Sls. Mgr., Oskey Bros. Petroleum Corp., 1961-65; VP, Newfoundland Refining Company Ltd., 1965-69; VP, Oskey Gasoline & Oil Co., 1969-76; Pres., CEO, Western Petroleum Co., 1976-present. **Career Act.:** Dir., Hydrocarbon Trading and Transport Company Inc., Community Bank Group, Inc., Western International Trading Company; Ptnr., Bellwood Partners, VChair DePauw U., Board of Trustees, 1996-1997. **Act./Mem.:** Mem., National Petroleum Council, American Petroleum Institute; Pres., DePauw U. Alumni Assn., 1980-82; Trustee, DePauw U., 1982-present; Governor, Marine Corps Assn. Board of Governors, 1981-84; Trustee, U.S. Marine Corps Command and Staff College Fdn., 1984-96; Dir., Assn. of Governing Boards of Universities and Colleges Board of Dir., 1994-present; The Minikahda Club, Decathlon Club, Army Navy Club, Monterey Peninsula Country Club, Headwaters Country Club, Park Rapids, MN, Ballybunion Golf Club, Ireland, Tralee Golf Club, Ireland, FaithLegg Golf Club, Ireland; Woodhill Country Club, Spring Hill Golf Club.

Karol D. Emmerich Pres., The Emmerich Foundation, 7302 Claredon Dr., Edina, MN 55439. Tel: 612/941-9280. **B:** Nov. 21, 1948, St. Louis. **M:** Richard Emmerich, 1969. **C:** James Andrew. **E:** Northwestern U., BA-Math., 1969; Stanford U., MBA, 1971. **Career Hist.:** Natl. Div. Loan Officer, Bank of America, 1971-72; Dayton Hudson Corp., 1972-93: Fin. Analyst, 1972-83; Sr. Fin. Analyst, 1973-74; Mgr.-Short Term Financing, 1974-76; Asst. Treas., 1976-79; Treas., 1979-80; VP, Treas., 1980-89; VP, Treas. and Chief Acctg. Officer, 1989- 93; Pres., The Emmerich Foundation, 1993-present. **Career Act.:** Advisory Board, Slumberland; Executive Fellow at U. of St. Thomas Graduate School of Business; Mem., Minnesota Women's Economic Roundtable. **Act./Mem.:** Dir., Women's Opportunity Fund, Opportunity International; Royal Treasure; Adv. Board, WomenVenture.

Susan E. Engel Chair, CEO, Department 56 Inc., One Village Place, 6436 City West Pkwy., Eden Prairie, MN 55344. Tel: 612/944-5600. **B:** Oct. 21, 1946, New York. **M:** Arthur Eisenberg. **E:** Cornell U., B.S., 1968; Harvard Business School, MBA, 1976. **Career Hist.:** Ptnr.-in-charge/U.S. Eastern Region, Booz, Allen & Hamilton, 1977-91; Pres., CEO, Champion Products Inc., 1991-93; Consultant to retail and consumer goods companies, 1993-94; Pres., COO, Department 56, 1994-95; Pres., CEO 1995-present; Chairwoman and CEO 1997-present. **Career Act.:** Dir., Wells Fargo & Co., SuperValu Inc., Guthrie Theater, St. Paul Chamber Orchestra; Board of Overseers at the Carlson School of Management, U. of MN **Act./Mem.:** Presidents Council of Cornell Women, Cornell University; Minneapolis League of Women Voters.

John D. Erickson EVP-Fin. and CFO, Otter Tail Power Co., 215 S. Cascade St., P.O. Box 496, Fergus Falls, MN 56537. Tel: 218/739-8200. **B:** Moorhead, MN. **E:** North Dakota University, B.S. agricultural econ.; CPA **Career Hist.:** Joined Otter Tail Power in 1980-Analyst, Dir. Market Strategies; VP, CFO, Treas. **Act./Mem.:** Member of the American Institute of Public Accountants; Member of the North Dakota Society of Public Accountants; Fergus Falls Area United Way board of directors; church committees.

Kirby J. Erickson EVP, CAO, HealthPartners, 8100 34th Ave. S., P.O. Box 1039, Bloomington, MN 55425. Tel: 612/883-6698. **B:** Mar. 30, 1940, Dodgeville, Wis. **M:** Katie White. **E:** Superior (WI) High School, 1958; BS, ND State U., 1962; Master of Hospital and Health Care Admin., U. of MN, 1965. **Career Hist.:** More than 25 years of leadership experience in health care management, including: Regional VP, Aetna Health Plans; Exec. Dir., MedCenters Health Plan; COO, Physicians Health Plan; SVP-Regional Op., Fairview Community Hospitals; EVP-Admin./Health, HealthPartners. **Career Act.:** Chair, Dir., MCHA (MN Comprehensive Health Assn.); Mem., MN Council of HMOs (Pres.-elect), American College of Healthcare Executives; Clinical Faculty-Graduate Program, U. of MN.

Jack W. Eugster Chair, Pres., CEO, Musicland Stores Corp., 10400 Yellow Circle Dr., Minnetonka, MN 55343. Tel: 612/931-8005. **B:** Oct. 7, 1945, Mound, Minn. **M:** Carol Marie. **C:** Nicholas, Wilson, Wendi, Kelly. **E:** Carleton College, BA, 1967: Stanford U., MBA, 1969. **Career Hist.:** Merchandising Mgr., Target Stores, 1969-72; EVP, Dir., The Gap Stores Inc., 1972-80; EVP, Pickwick International, 1980; Chair, Pres., CEO, Musicland Group Inc., 1981-present. **Career Act.:** Donaldson Co. Inc., ShopKo Stores Inc.; past Pres., Dir., National Assn. of Recording Merchandisers (1981-1988, and 1998); Dir., past Chair, Country Music Assn. (1985-1991); Trustee, Carleton College; Board of Overseers, Carlson School of Mgmt./U. of MN; Dir. Emeritus, Children's Home Society of MN; Pres., MN Business

Partnership. **Dec./Awd.:** Human Relations Award for Music and Video Division of the Anti-Defamation League, 1996; Video Hall of Fame, 1998. **Act./Mem.:** United Way, Youth Basketball Coach, Wayzata Country Club, Minneapolis Club, Spring Hill Golf Club.

Brian Evenson Pres., McKechnie Plastic Components/North America, 7309 W. 27th St., St. Louis Park, MN 55426. Tel: 612/929-3312. **B:** Jul. 29, 1963, Madison, Minn. **M:** Mary, 1986. **E:** BS-Accounting, Moorhead St. U., 1986. **Career Hist.:** Cost Accountant, Modern Controls Inc., 1986-88; Cont., Datamyte/Div. Allen-Bradley, 1988-93; Gen. Mgr., Jet Edge Inc., 1993-94; McKechnie Plastic Components, 1994-present: VP and Cont., 1994-96; Pres., 1996-present. **Career Act.:** Mem., Society of Plastic Engineers, American Mgmt. Assn.

Max Fallek Pres., American Institute of Small Business, 7515 Wayzata Blvd., St. Louis Park, MN 55426. Tel: 612/545-7001. **B:** Feb. 4, 1930, Albany, N.Y. **M:** Lillian Hieb. **C:** David, Susan. **E:** NY U., BA; U. of IA, MBA-Mktg.. **Career Hist.:** Dir. of Mktg., Tescom Corp., 1960-75; Pres., Quantum Labs, 1977-86, Fallek and Associates, 1975-present; Pres., American Institute of Small Business, 1985-present. **Career Act.:** Mem., Natl. Advisory Council—U.S. Small Business Admin., Minneapolis Federation Jewish Services, Small Business Directors Assn., Intl. Council for Small Business; Representative, White House Council for Small Business, Midwest Regional Council to U.S. Small Business Admin.; Co-Chair, NAACP Public Relations Ctee. 92nd Annual Convention; Board of Trustees, Temple Israel; Delegate, 1995 White House Conference for Small Business.

William F. Farley Chair, Pres., CEO, Kinnard Investments Inc., Kinnard Financial Center, 920 Second Ave. S., Minneapolis, MN 55402. Tel: 612/370-2956. Email: bfarley@jqkinnard.com **B:** Mar. 12, 1944, Sacramento, Calif. **M:** Kathleen G., 1971. **C:** Ellen, Amy. **E:** Stanford U.: AB (Econ. and Math), 1966; MBA (Finance, top 10%), 1969. **Career Hist.:** Citicorp/Citibank: various positions ending as VP in Europe (1966-81); Alexander & Alexander Svs.: SVP, CFO (1981-84); First Bank System: Pres.-First Bank Minneapolis (1984-88); Headrick & Farley, Ptnr. (1988-90); US Bank: VChair (1990-96); Kinnard Investments Inc.: Chair, Pres., CEO (1997-2000); Kinnard was acquired by Stockwalk.com Group Inc. in 2000. **Career Act.:** Dir., C.M. Russell Museum (Great Falls, MT); Mem., Abbott Northwestern Hospital. **Act./Mem.:** Minneapolis Club, Woodhill Country Club, Spring Hill Golf Club.

John J. Fauth Founder, Chairman, Pres., CEO, Churchill Capital Inc., 2400 Lincoln Centre, Minneapolis, MN 55418. Tel: 612/673-6633. **E:** Georgetown University, B.S. Business, Finance, 1967. Graduate studies at New York University. **Career Hist.:** VP and Senior Credit Officer, 1967-80; EVP and COO, Waterways Transportation, Inc. 1980-82; Founder, Chairman, Pres. and CEO, The Churchill Companies/Churchill Industries, 1982. **Career Act.:** Chair, Board of Visitors, Georgetown University School of Business Admin.; Dir. Georgetown University; Dir. John G. Kinnard & Co. Investment Securities; Dir. Children's Health CAre, 1994-97; Chair, Worthington Bancshares, 1987-92. **Act./Mem.:** Woodhill Country Club; Minikahada Country Club; Minneapolis Club; Spring Hill Golf Club; Larchmont Yacht Club (NY); The Links (NY).

David E. Feinberg Chair, CEO, EMC Corp., 875 Montreal Way, St. Paul, MN 55102. Tel: 651/215-7600. Email: defein@emcp.com **B:** Jul. 17, 1922, Minneapolis. **C:** Susan Feinberg Hughes, Donald E. Feinberg. **E:** U. of MN, BSME. **Career Hist.:** U.S. Air Conditioning Corp., 1948-1960: Pres., 1956-60; EMC Corp., 1961-present: VP, 1961-67; Pres., 1968-87; CEO, 1987-present. **Career Act.:** Dir., Paradigm Publishing Inc., Digital Excellence Inc. **Act./Mem.:** United Way Volunteer; Board, Sholom Home Fdn., Board United Jewish Fund and Council (St. Paul).

Nancy Feldman CEO, UCare Minnesota, 2550 University Ave. W., Suite 201-S, St. Paul, MN 55114. Tel: 651/603-5368. Email: nfeldman@ucare.org **B:** Jul. 6, 1946, Green Bay, Wis. **M:** Bob Feldman, 1968. **C:** Sara. **E:** U. of WI-Madison, B.A., 1969; MS, 1974. **Career Hist.:** Mgmt. analyst, Federal Home Loan Bank Board, 1971-72; Supervisor, EPSDT Program/MN Dept. of Human Svs., 1974-80; Health Care Programs/MN Dept. of Human Svs., 1980-84; Team Leader, Hum. Res. Budget/MN Dept. of Fin., 1984-87; Asst. Commissioner, MN Dept. of Health, 1987-91; Team Leader, CORE Program/MN Dept. of Admin., 1991-93; Dir., State Public Programs/Allina Health System, 1993-95; CEO, UCare MN, 1995-present. **Career Act.:** Chair, MN Council of Health Plans; Chair, Volunteers of America National Svs.; Mem., Women's Health Leadership Trust; Vice Chair, Center for Victims of Torture; Dir., Healthcare Education and Research Fdn.; Children's Defense Fund Advisory Board; member, Healthy Learning Board. **Dec./Awd.:** Women's Health Leadership Trust Member of the Year, 2000; CityBusiness Great Places to Work Award to UCare, 2000.

John E. Feltl Pres., R.J. Steichen & Co., 120 S. Sixth St., Suite 100, Minneapolis, MN 55402. Tel: 612/341-6200. **B:** Jul. 5, 1939, Minneapolis. **M:** Mary Joanne, 1963. **C:** two. **E:** St. Mary's College; U. of MN. **Career Hist.:** Lowe Bros. Paint (Cleveland), 1962-70; R.J. Steichen, 1970-present: Registered Rep., 1970-86; Owner, 1986-present. **Career Act.:** Pres., Business Men's Forum.

Daniel L. Fesler Chair, Lampert Yards Inc., 1850 Como Ave., P.O. Box 64076 (55164), St. Paul, MN 55108. Tel: 651/645-8155. **B:** Nov. 6, 1925, Minneapolis, Minn. **M:** Ester, 1989. **C:** Daniel, Timothy, Terry, Jeffrey, Colleen, Kim. **E:** Shattuck School, 1943; U. of Minn., 1949. **Career Hist.:** Lampert Yards, 1949-present. **Career Act.:** Dir., Liberty State Bank. **Act./Mem.:** Mem., St. Paul Rotary Club.

Norman E. Fey Chair, Pres., Fey Industries Inc., 200 Fourth Ave. W., Edgerton, MN 56128. Tel: 507/442-4311. **B:** Nov. 22, 1942, Artesia, Calif. **M:** Ethelyn, 1964. **C:** Michelle, Michael, Matthew. **E:** Cerritos College. **Career Hist.:** VP, Fey Industries, 1965-81; Chair, Pres., 1981-present. **Career Act.:** Pres., Specialty Advertising Assn. Upper Midwest, Edgerton Devel. Corp., Edgerton Chamber of Commerce. **Act./Mem.:** First Presbyterian Church.

Alan R. Fine SVP Investment Banking, Mesirow Financial, 5775 Wayzata Blvd., Suite 700, St. Louis Park, MN 55416. Tel: 952/582-2900. Email: afine@mesirowfinancial.com **E:** B.A., M.B.A., C.P.A. **Career Hist.:** Pres. Fine Enterprises, Inc.; CFO, Artistic Finishes; Accountant/Mgmt. Consultant, Lurie, Besikof & Lapidus; Mgmt. Consultant, Arthur Andersen & Company. **Career Act.:** Director of Entrepreneurial Studies, Carlson School of Management, U of M. Author: Empower Your Self: A Framework for Personal Success. **Dec./Awd.:** Sons of the American Revolution Award, 1980; Undergraduate Teacher of the Year, Carlson School of Management, 1997-98, 1998-99.

Richard Merrill Fink Chair, G&K Services Inc., 5995 Opus Parkway, Suite 500, Minnetonka, MN 55343. Tel: 612/912-5500. **B:** 1930, Minneapolis. **M:** Beverly, 1988. **C:** Susan, David. **E:** U. of MN, 1952; Oxford U., Rhodes Scholar; Harvard U., 1961.. **Career Hist.:** Prof.-Political Science, U. of WI-Madison; G & K Services Inc., 1964-present. **Career Act.:** Past Chair, Board of Dir., Uniform and Textile Services Assn.; Dir., Textile Rental Svs. Assn., G&K Svs. Inc. **Act./Mem.:** United Way; Mpls. Federation for Jewish Service: Oak Ridge Country Club.

Quentin E. Finkelson Chair, Pres., CEO, Nortech Systems Inc., 641 E. Lake St., Suite 206, Wayzata, MN 55391. Tel: 612/473-4102. **B:** Oct. 30, St. Paul. **M:** widower. **C:** Ann, Matt. **E:** Hamline, B.A., 1956. **Career Hist.:** 3M, 1956-75; Kusan Inc., 1975-80; Pako Corp., 1980-88; Nortech Systems, 1988-present. **Career Act.:**. **Dec./Awd.:** Outstanding Young Man of the Year, 1966; National Defense Executive Reserve, 1968. **Act./Mem.:** Pool & Yacht Inc., Wayzata Country Club, Minneapolis Athletic Club.

Paul D. Finkelstein Pres., CEO, Regis Corp., 7201 Metro Blvd., Edina, MN 55439. Tel: 612/947-7777. **B:** Aug. 26, 1942, New York. **M:** Barbara. **C:** Michael, Brad. **E:** U. of PA, Wharton School, BS; Harvard Business School, MBA. **Career Hist.:** Glemby International, 1966-81; Seligman & Latz (S&L), 1981-84; Turner Hall Corp., CEO, 1984-87; Regis, 1987-present. **Career Act.:** Dir., Regis Corp., Eagle Supply Group Inc. **Act./Mem.:** World Presidents Organization, Chief Executives Organization.

Michael B. Fiterman Pres., CEO, Liberty Diversified Industries Inc., 5600 N. Highway 169, New Hope, MN 55428. Tel: 612/536-6600. **B:** 1948, Minneapolis. **E:** U. of MN, BS, Business. **Career Hist.:** Liberty Diversified Industries: 1970-present; CEO, 1985-present. **Career Act.:** Dir., Minneapolis United Way; Dir., Fibre Box Assn. **Act./Mem.:** World Presidents Organization, MN Executives Oragnization, and MN Business Partnership.

WHO

Silas B. Foot III Pres., S.B. Foot Tanning Co., Bench Street, Red Wing, MN 55066. Tel: 651/388-4731. **B:** Feb. 13, 1947, Red Wing, Minn. **M:** Joan Esselen, 1970. **C:** Eleanor, Margaret, Christopher. **E:** Princeton U., BA, 1969; U. of MI, JD, 1975. **Career Hist.:** Pres., S.B. Foot Tanning Company, 1981-present. **Career Act.:** Dir., Goodhue County National Bank, Red Wing Shoe Company Inc., Fairview Red Wing Health Services, Footwear Industries of America; Dir. past Chair, Leather Industries of America; Trustee, Red Wing Family YMCA. **Act./Mem.:** Kiwanis, Red Wing Country Club.

Richard Forschler Ptnr., Faegre & Benson, 2200 Norwest Center, Minneapolis, MN 55402. Tel: 612/336-3385. Email: rforschl@faegre.com **B:** Apr. 8, 1951, La Crosse, Wis. **M:** Kari Breen, 1986. **C:** Katherine, Zachary, David, Emma, Sarah. **E:** BA, U. of MN, 1974; JD, Georgetown U. Law Center, 1977. **Career Hist.:** Attorney, Larkin Hoffman Daly & Lindgren, 1977-88; Ptnr., Faegre & Benson, 1988-present. **Career Act.:** First VChair, VChair-Public Policy, Dir., Greater Mpls. Chamber of Commerce; Chair, Hennepin Avenue Advisory Ctee.; Deputy, MN Business Partnership; Board of Dir., Minnesota Taxpayer's Assn.; Board of Directors, Citizens' League.

Wayne M. Fortun Pres., CEO, COO, Hutchinson Technology Inc., 40 W. Highland Park, Hutchinson, MN 55350. Tel: 320/587-3797. **B:** Mar. 2, 1949, Litchfield, Minn. **M:** Terry. **Career Hist.:** Hutchinson Technology Inc., 1975-present: various engrg. and mktg. positions, including Op. Mgr. and VP-Op., 1975-83; Dir., 1983; Pres. and COO, 1983; CEO, 1996. **Career Act.:** Dir., MN Council for Quality, Intl. Disk Drive Eqt. and Matls. Assn. (IDEMA), G&K Services, Excelsior-Henderson Motorcycle Mfg. Co.

J. Leonard Frame Pres., FluiDyne Engineering Corp. dba Phoenix Solutions Co., 5900 Olson Memorial Hwy., Golden Valley, MN 55422. Tel: 612/544-2721. **B:** May 24, 1924, Castle Rock, Minn. **M:** Dorothy Gadde, 1944. **C:** Peggy, Susan, Douglas, Julie, Jennifer. **E:** U. of MN, BS-Aeronautical Engrg., 1943. **Career Hist.:** Flight Test Engr., Bell Aircraft Corp., 1943-44; Flight Test Engr., Natl. Advisory Ctee. for Aeronautics, 1944-45; Rocket Test Engr., Bell Aircraft Corp., 1946-47; Admin. Scientist, U. of MN, 1947-52; Pres., FluiDyne Engrg. Corp., 1952-present. **Career Act.:** Assoc. Fellow, American Institute for Aeronautics and Astronautics; Mem., American Mgmt. Assn., Presidents Assn.; Dir., MOCON. **Dec./Awd.:** Outstanding Achievement Award, U. of MN Institute of Technology. **Act./Mem.:** U. of MN Institute of Technology Alumni Assn.; Valley Community Presbyterian Church; Apollo Club; Minneapolis Athletic Club.

William Frame Pres., Augsburg College, 2211 Riverside Ave., Minneapolis, MN 55454. Tel: 612/330-1000. Email: frame@augsburg.edu **B:** May 31, 1938, Philadelphia. **M:** Anne Lewis, 1993. **C:** Samuel, Kelly, Kate, Kathy, Paul, Mark, Carol. **E:** U. of Hawaii, Bachelor's Degree, 1962, Master's Degree, 1964; U. of WA, Ph.D., 1969. **Career Hist.:** Kenyon College, Faculty, 1967-82; First National Bank of Chicago, Sr. Corp. Banker, 1981-89; Tonka Corp., VP/ Treas., 1989-92; Pacific Lutheran U., CFO, 1993-97; Augsburg College, President, 1997-present. **Career Act.:** Richard R. Green Institute For Teaching & Learning, Chair; MN Meeting, Dir.; Dir. Dart Transit Inc.; Dir., Associated Colleges of the Twin Cities; Minnesota Private Colleges. **Act./Mem.:** Minneapolis Club; Central Lutheran Church; Torske Klubben (honorary).

Peter L. Frechette Pres., CEO, Patterson Dental Co., 1031 Mendota Heights Rd., St. Paul, MN 55120. Tel: 651/686-1600. Email: pete_frechette@pattersondental.com **B:** 1938, Janesville, Wis. **E:** U. of WI, BS, 1960. Northwestern U., MBA, 1980. **Career Hist.:** Pres., Scientific Prod. Div.-American Hospital Supply Co., 1975-82; Pres., Patterson Dental Co., 1982-present. **Career Act.:** Dir., American Dental Trade Assn., Patterson Dental Co.

Kay Fredericks Pres., CEO, TREND enterprises, Inc., 300 Ninth Ave. S.W., New Brighton, MN 55112. **B:** May 9, 1943, Litchfield, Minn. **M:** Richard Cisek, 1999. **E:** B.S., St. Cloud State U., 1965. **Career Hist.:** Pres. and CEO, TREND enterprises Inc., present. **Career Act.:** Founding Mem., Dir., Ctee. of 200, 1982-present; Dir., Employer's Assn. Inc., 1984-98; Advisory Council Mem., Federal Reserve Bank of Mpls., 1991-93; Trustee, Hamline U., 1988-present; Exec. Ctee., Hamline U.,1991-96; Chair, U of Life Ctee., Hamline U., 1998-present; Fellow, International Business Fellows, 1987, Pres., Upper Midwest Chapter, 1988-93; Dir., Norris Education Innovations, 1996-1999.; Dir., Minn. Chamber, 1987-91; Mem., Minn. Women's Economic Roundtable, 1991-present; Mem., Minn. National Assn. of Women Business Owners, 1979-present; Dir., Northeast State Bank, 1998-present. **Dec./Awd.:** Who's Who in U.S. Executives, 1989, 1990; Who's Who in Manufacturing, 1990; Phi Kappa Phi Honor Society, 1990-present; Small Business of the Week, Star Tribune, 1991; Business Owner of the Year Award, Minn. Chapter of NAWBO, 1991; Distinguished Alumni Award, St. Cloud State U., 1991; Spurgeon Award, Indianhead Council, Boy Scouts of America, 1992; Silver Beaver Award, Indianhead Council, Boy Scouts of America, 1993; Lifetime Achievement Award, NAWBO, 1997; Golden Apple Award, Educational Dealers and Suppliers Assn., 1998; Finalist, Minnesota and Dakotas' Entrepreneur of the Year, Ernst & Young, 1998; Champion of Eagles Award, Boy Scouts of America, 1999; Emerging Marketing Executive Award, Women and Business, 2000. **Act./Mem.:** Founder, Boosters Club, Minnesota Academic Excellence Fdn., 1997; Chair Advisory Bd., Carlson School of Mgmt., U. of MN, 1993-present; Advantage Minn., 1991-98; various positions, Indianhead Council, Boy Scouts of America, 1986-present; Mem., St. Paul Rotary, 1987-96.

James P. Fritz CEO, Fritz Co. Inc., 1912 Hastings Ave., Newport, MN 55055. Tel: 651/459-9751. **B:** 1937. **M:** Barbara. **C:** Elizabeth, Victoria, Barbara. **E:** College of St. Thomas. **Career Hist.:** Fritz Co. Inc., 1962-present: various positions, 1962-82; Pres., CEO, 1982-present. **Act./Mem.:** Dir., Divine Redeemer Hospital.

John R. Frobenius Co-Pres.-CentraCare, CEO-St. Cloud Hospital, CentraCare, 1406 Sixth Ave. N., St. Cloud, MN 56303. Tel: 320/255-5661. **B:** Jan. 25, 1942, Muscatine, Iowa. **M:** Nancy, 1994. **E:** U. of NE, BA, 1963; U. of MN, MHA, 1969. **Career Hist.:** Assoc. admin., Stormont Vail Hospital (Topeka, KS), 1969-73; EVP, St. Luke's Regional Medical Center (Boise, ID), 1973-85; Pres., CEO, St. Cloud Hospital, 1985-present; Co-Pres., CentraCare, 1995-present. **Career Act.:** Mem.-Region Three Coordinating Board, MN Health Care Commission; Trustee, past Dir., MN Hospital and Healthcare Partnership; MHHP Delegate, American Hospital Assn.; Dir., past Chair, Voluntary Hospitals of America-North Central; past Dir., past Chair, MN Conference of Catholic Health Facilities; past Mem.-Acute Care Ctee., Catholic Health Assn.; Mem., American College of Hospital Administrators; past clinical preceptor and faculty mem., Independent Study Program-Hospital and Health Care Admin., U. of MN. **Dec./Awd.:** Distinguished Service Award, MN Hospital and Healthcare Partnership, 1995; "25 Outstanding Health Care Administrators," MN Physician, 1995. **Act./Mem.:** Board Mem., St. Cloud Area Chamber of Commerce, First American Bank-St. Cloud; Former Board Mem., St. Cloud Area United Way.

James D. Gabbert Chair, CEO, Gabberts Furniture & Design Studio, 3501 W. 69th St., Edina, MN 55435. Tel: 612/927-1514. **B:** Sep. 15, 1952, Minneapolis. **M:** Barbara, 1981. **C:** Michael, Mari, Julia, Allison. **E:** Colorado College, BA, 1975. **Career Hist.:** Buyer, Dept. Mgr., Gabberts, 1976-78; Founder, Pres., Games by James, 1978-83; Gabberts Furniture & Design Studio, 1980-present: Pres., COO, 1980-87; Chair, Pres., CEO, 1988-95; Chair, CEO, 1995-present. **Career Act.:** Dir., National Home Furnishings Assn.; Co-Chair, Home Furnishings Council. **Dec./Awd.:** 1990 NHFA, Retailer of the Year; ARTS Academy of Achievement Award, 1993, 1998; B'nai B'rith Great American Traditions Award, 1998. **Act./Mem.:** Rotary; United Way; Minikahda Country Club; Flagship Athletic Club.

Edwin C. (Skip) Gage Chair, CEO, Gage Marketing Group LLC, 10000 Highway 55, Plymouth, MN 55441. Tel: 612/595-3800. **B:** Nov. 1, 1940, Evanston, Ill. **M:** Barbara Carlson, 1965. **C:** Geoff, Scott, Christine, Richard. **E:** Northwestern U., BS-Bus. Admin. 1963; Northwestern U., MS-Journalism/Advertising, 1965; Exec. Mgmt. Program, U. of MN. **Career Hist.:** Acct. Exec., Foote, Cone & Belding, Chicago, 1965-68; Premium Corp. of America, 1968-77: Dir.-Mktg./Devel., 1968-70; VP-Direct Mktg./Consumer Products, 1970-75; EVP, 1975-77; Carlson Cos. Inc., 1977-1991: Pres., Carlson Mktg. Group, 1977-84; EVP, Carlson Cos. Inc., 1983-84; Pres. & COO, Carlson Cos., 1984-89; Pres., CEO, Carlson Cos., 1989-1991; VChair, Carlson Holdings Inc., 1991-92; Founder, Chair, CEO, Gage Marketing Group, 1992-present. **Career Act.:** Dir., Gage Marketing Group LLC, Carlson Holdings Inc., Carlson Cos. Inc., Carlson Real Estate Co., SUPERVALU Inc., Kellogg Graduate School of Mgmt.-Northwestern U.; Mem., AHL Svs. Inc., Carlson School of Mgmt. Board of Overseers, U of MN **Dec./Awd.:** Walter Smart Award, Northwestern U., 1962; Northwestern Men's Outstanding Sr. Athlete Award, 1963; Entrepreneur of the Year, 1999, Ernst & Young. **Act./Mem.:** MN Executives Organization; Woodhill Country Club; Wayzata Country Club; Northwestern Tennis Patrons.

Michael J. Galvin Jr. Attorney, Briggs and Morgan P.A., 2400 IDS Center, Minneapolis, MN 55402. Tel: 651/223-6600. **B:** Jul. 8, 1930, Winona, Minn. **M:** Frances Culligan Galvin, 1957. **C:** Sean, Kevin, Kathleen, Nora, Mary, Margaret, Patricia. **E:** U. of St. Thomas, BA, 1952; U. of MN, LLB, 1957. **Career Hist.:** Briggs & Morgan, 1957-present. **Career Act.:** Ramsey County Bar Assn., Pres., 1984; MN State Bar Assn. Labor & Employment Law Section, Chair, 1985; MN State Bar Assn., Board of Governors, 1985-87, 1990-96, Treas., 1990-92, Pres.-Elect, 1993-94, Pres., 1994-95; MN Volunteer Attorney Program, Pres., 1993-94; Trustee College of St. Catherine, Chair St. Paul Area Chamber of Commerce 1998-99. **Dec./Awd.:** Who's Who in America, 47th Edition; Best Lawyers in America, 1987-present; Alumni of the Year, University of St. Thomas 1983; Great Living Saint Paulite; St. Paul Area Chamber of Commerce, 2000. **Act./Mem.:** Minnesota Club; St. Paul Winter Carnival; Town & Country Club.

Thomas H. Garrett III self-employed, 4200 IDS Center, 80 S. Eighth St., Minneapolis, MN 55402. Tel: 612/371-3211. **B:** Feb. 3, 1945, St. Paul. **M:** Linda, 1981. **C:** Karen, Tina, Charlie. **E:** BS, U. of MN, 1967; JD, U. of MN, 1970. **Career Hist.:** Lindquist & Vennum, 1970-96; Self-employed Business Consultant, 1996-present. **Career Act.:** Dir., St. Jude Medical Inc., Check Technology Corp., Lifecore Biomedical Inc., Kovex Corp. **Act./Mem.:** Pres., Somerset Country Club, 1994-96; Co-Chair, HCBA Diversity Ctee., 1994-96.

Sara Gavin Managing Dir., CEO, Shandwick, 8400 Normandale Lake Blvd., Suite 500, Bloomington, MN 55437. Tel: 612/841-6174. Email: sgavin@shandwick.com **B:** Oct. 9, 1955, San Antonio. **M:** Thomas, 1980. **C:** Benjamin, Erin, Ryan, Anne. **E:** BA-History/Poli. Sci. (Phi Beta Kappa), College of St. Catherine; graduate courses, U. of MN MBA program. **Career Hist.:** Public relations: MN Board on Aging, Doremus & Co.; VP, Hill and Knowlton (Twin Cities office), 1980-83; Managing Dir., Shandwick (founded as Mona Meyer McGrath & Gavin), 1983-present. **Career Act.:** Trustee, executive committee, College of St. Catherine; past Dir., Ceres Communications, MN Private College Council, Citizens League; Mem., Public Relations Society of America; trustee MN Public Radio; Board Member, Minnesota Meeting; past board Pres. MN Women's Economic Roundtable. **Dec./Awd.:** One of MN's 40 Under 40, CityBusiness, 1995; Silver Anvil Award, PRSA, 1998. **Act./Mem.:** Town and Country Club, St. Paul.

Thomas L. Gegax Morgan Tire and Auto Body, Tires Plus, 600 W. Travelers Trail, Burnsville, MN 55337. Tel: 612/894-2700. **B:** Oct. 4, 1946, Connersville, Ind. **C:** Trent, Chris. **E:** Indiana U., BS, 1968. **Career Hist.:** Shell Oil Co., 1968-76: Analyst/Recruiter, 1968-70; Sls., 1970-73; Sls. Mgr., 1973-76. Tires Plus Group (now Team Tires Plus), 1976-present: Founder and Head Coach. **Career Act.:** Dir., EarthSave International, Deepak Chopra's Worldwide Enterprises, Better Business Bureau, American Cancer Society; Author, "Winning in the Game of Life." **Dec./Awd.:** Retail/Wholesale Entrepreneur of the Year, 1995; Tire Dealer of the Year, Modern Tire Dealer magazine, 1998. **Act./Mem.:** American Heart Assn., Board of Directors.

William W. George Chair, CEO, Medtronic Inc., 7000 Central Ave. N.E., Fridley, MN 55432. Tel: 612/574-3108. **B:** Sep. 14, 1942, Muskegon, Mich. **M:** Penny. **C:** Jeff, Jon. **E:** Georgia Institute of Technology, BS Industrial Engrg. (high honors), 1964; Harvard Business School, MBA (high distinction), 1966. **Career Hist.:** Special Asst. to Sec. of the Navy and Asst. to Asst. Sec. of Defense, 1966-69; Pres., Litton Microwave Cooking Products; Pres., Space and Aviation Systems, Industrial Automation and Control, European operations, Honeywell Inc., 11 years; Medtronic Inc.: Pres., COO, 1989-91; Pres., CEO, 1991-96; CEO, Chair, 1996-present. **Career Act.:** Dir., Medtronic Inc., Valspar Corp., Target Corp., Imation, Allina Health System (Chair), Food and Drug Law Institute; Chair, Health Industry Manufacturers Assn., MN Thunder Soccer, United Way of Minneapolis.

Dec./Awd.: Gold Award in hospital supply and medical technology industry-large capitalization companies, The Wall Street Transcript, 1994; Alumni Achievement Award, Harvard U. Graduate School of Business, 1997; Renaissance Award, College of St. Benedict, 2000.

Larry D. Geske Chair, Pres., CEO, Energy West Inc., P.O. Box 2229, Great Falls, MT 59403. Tel: 406/791-7501. **B:** Jan. 14, 1939, Niles, Kan. **M:** Sandra, 1961. **C:** Michael, Matthew. **E:** KS State U., BS-Mech. Engrg.; U. of MT, MBA (honors), 1988.. **Career Hist.:** Student Engr., Gas Service Company, 1960; Field Engr., Northern Illinois Gas Company, 1960-69; Sr. Consultant, Stone & Webster Mgmt. Consultants Inc., 1969-75; EVP, Great Falls Gas Company, 1975-78; Pres., CEO, Energy West, 1979-present. **Career Act.:** Dir., Chair, Small Utility Coordinating, Council American Gas Assn.; Pres., Great Falls Dodgers; past Chair, Great Falls Area Chamber of Commerce, Great Falls Capital Corp.; past Dir.-Exec. Ctee., First Interstate Bank; past Dir., Midwest Gas Assn.; past Pres., Great Falls Credit Bureau. **Dec./Awd.:** Kansas State U., Alumni Fellow, February 1997. **Act./Mem.:** Rotary Program Chair; Boy Scouts Exec. Board; past Devel. Chair, K-M Scout Ranch, Neighborhood Housing Svs.; Pres., United Way; past Dir., Northern Rocky Mountain Easter Seal Society; Dir., Montana Ambassadors; Chair, Vision 2000 Great Falls, Chair, Great Falls Downtown Revitalization; Past Dir., Montanta Community Fdn..

Tom R. Gessner Chair, CEO, Al Johnson Construction Co., 2626 E. 82nd St., Suite 300, Bloomington, MN 55425. Tel: 612/831-8151. **B:** Jun. 1, 1937, Grand Rapids, Minn. **M:** Pat, 1969. **C:** Karin, Susan, Mike. **E:** Dartmouth College, BA-Math., 1959; Stanford U., MSCE, 1961. **Career Hist.:** Al Johnson Construction Company, 1961-present: Office Engr., 1961-62; Project Engr., 1962-64; Project Mgr., 1964-66; Project Sponsor, 1966-68; EVP, 1968-71; Pres., 1971-83; Chair, Pres., 1983-present. **Career Act.:** Pres., Beavers (Heavy Construction Group), 1987; Mem., American Society for Testing and Materials, American Society of Civil Engineers..

Stan Geyer CEO, Entegris Inc., 3500 Lyman Blvd., Chaska, MN 55318. Tel: 612/448-8154. Email: stan_geyer@fluoroware.com **B:** Dec. 5, 1948, Munich. **M:** Beverly L., 1970. **C:** Christian, Annie. **E:** U. of CO-Boulder, BS. **Career Hist.:** Fluoroware Inc. (now Entegris Inc.), Mktg. Mgr.; VP-Mktg.; EVP; Pres., COO; CEO. **Career Act.:** Dir., Fluoroware, Wallestad Fdn., Search Ministries. **Dec./Awd.:** State Amateur Ski Champion (Alpine), 1966; U. of CO Ski Team, 1967-69. **Act./Mem.:** Christ Presbyterian Church, Edina Country Club.

John E. (Jack) Gherty Pres., CEO, Land O'Lakes Inc., 4001 Lexington Ave. N., Arden Hills, MN 55112. Tel: 651/481-2505. Email: jgher@landolakes.com **B:** Jan. 31, 1944, New Richmond, Wis. **M:** Anne, 1979. **E:** U. of WI-Madison, BBA, 1965; JD, 1968; MA, 1970. **Career Hist.:** Land O' Lakes Inc., 1970-present; Pres. and CEO, 1989-present. **Career Act.:** Chm., CF Industries (Rosemont, Ill.); Dir., Recovery Engineering Inc., National Council of Farmer Cooperatives, MN Business Partnership Board, National 4-H Fdn. **Act./Mem.:** Board of Visitors, U of WI, Law School.

E. Peter Gillette Jr. retired Pres.-Piper Trust Co., VChair-Piper Capital Mgmt., U.S. Bancorp, 222 S. Ninth St., Piper Jaffray Tower, Minneapolis, MN 55402. Tel: 612/342-1840. **B:** Jul. 26, 1934, Minneapolis. **M:** Scotty, 1961. **C:** Julie Gillette Johns, Anne Gillette Clevelend, Rebecca Gillette. **E:** Princeton U., AB, 1956; William Mitchell College of Law, LLB, 1963; Stonier Graduate School of Banking (honors), 1969; Harvard Business School/Advanced Mgmt. Program, 1973. **Career Hist.:** Norwest Corp., 1959-85: Pres./CEO-Norwest Bank of Minneapolis, 1980-81; Corp. VChair, 1981-85; Sr. Investment Banker, Piper Jaffray Inc., 1986-90; Commissioner, MN Dept. of Trade/Economic Devel., 1991-95; Pres., Piper Trust Co., 1995-present. **Career Act.:** Dir., Hormel Foods Corp., Piper Capital Mgmt. Co., The Resource Cos.; Trustee, Lakewood Cemetery; past Trustee, Princeton U., Macalester College, Blake School; Major (ret.), USMCR; past Dir., Dayton Hudson Corp., Norwest Corp.; Original Mem., Metropolitan Council, MN Business Partnership. **Dec./Awd.:** Outstanding Young Man of the Year, Mpls. Jr. Chamber of Commerce, 1970; Leadership Fellow, Bush Fdn., 1971. **Act./Mem.:** Mem., Minneapolis Club, Minikahda Club, Princeton Club (New York City); past Pres., United Way of Mpls.

Tony Goddard Acting Pres., Greater Minneapolis Chamber of Commerce, 81 S. Ninth St., Suite 200, Minneapolis, MN 55402. Tel: 612/370-9132. **B:** Oct. 5, 1949, Camrose, Alberta. **M:** Susan McGuire. **C:** Nora, Ann. **E:** U. of MN, BA-Urban Studies, MA-Geography. **Career Hist.:** Dept. of Planning/Economic Devel., Mayor's Office, City of St. Paul; Pres., St. Cloud Area Economic Devel. Partnership; Greater Minneapolis Chamber Of Commerce (GMCC): VP-Economic Devel., Jan.-Aug. 1998, Acting Pres., Aug. 1998-present. **Career Act.:** Adjunct Faculty Member, St. Cloud State U. (Geography) and St. Cloud Technical College (Supervisor Mgmt. degree program); co-authored book examining Twin Cities urban development; serves on the boards of several state and local organizations in economic development, technology assistance, workforce and training, and the arts.

Donald W. Goldfus retired Chair/CEO, Apogee Enterprises Inc., 7900 Xerxes Ave. S., Bloomington, MN 55431. Tel: 612/835-1874. **B:** Feb. 17, 1934, Minneapolis. **M:** Therese, 1959. **C:** Karen, Brian. **E:** U. of MN. **Career Hist.:** Editor, Sporting Goods Journal, 1958-59; Sls. Mgr., Harmon Glass, 1959-67; EVP, Harmon Glass Company, 1967-82; EVP, Apogee Enterprises, 1982-84; Pres., CEO, Apogee Enterprises, 1984-1998, Chair, 1988-99. **Career Act.:** Dir., Apogee Enterprises (1964-present); Chair-Advisory Board, U. of MN Leukemia Research Fund; Dir., past Pres., National Glass Assn.; Dir., G&K Services Inc., Lifetouch Inc. **Dec./Awd.:** Man of the Year, Sls. and Mktg. Execs. of Minneapolis; Glass Dealer of the Year, National Glass Assn. **Act./Mem.:** Lake Harriet Masonic Lodge; Bearpath Country Club.

Larry Goodwin Pres., CEO, College of St. Scholastica, 1200 Kenwood Ave., Duluth, MN 55811. Tel: 218/723-6033. Email: 1goodwin@css.edu **B:** Jun. 12, 1946, Washington, D.C. **M:** Kim, 1988. **C:** Caitlin, Celia. **E:** U. of Chicago, Ph.D., 1976; U. of Chicago, M.A., 1973; Bellarmine College, B.A., 1968. **Career Hist.:** Pres., College of St. Scholastica, 1998-present; VP, Academic Affairs and Dean of Faculty, College of St. Scholastica, 1993-1998; Dean of Faculty, College of St. Scholastica, 1987-1998; Acting Assoc. Academic Dean, College of St. Catherine, 1985-1987; Chair, Dept. of Theology, College of St. Catherine, 1980-1983. **Career Act.:** Campus Coordinator, Assn. of American Colleges' project, "Strong Foundations for General Education;" Editorial Consultant, The Journal of Religion; Pres., Upper Midwest Region of the American Academy of Religion. **Dec./Awd.:** Faculty Award, College of St. Catherine, 1980; Teacher of the Year, College of St. Catherine, 1976; College Valedictorian, Bellarmine College, 1968. **Act./Mem.:** United Way Review Panel; Duluth Superior Symphony Orchestra (ex-officio); Chair, Leadership Duluth Ethics Session.

Sam Grabarski Pres., CEO, Minneapolis Downtown Council, 81 S. Ninth St., Suite 260, Minneapolis, MN 55402. Tel: 612/338-3807. **E:** B. Mus. Ed., Ill. Wesleyan U., 1969; M.M., The Julliard School, 1972; Ed.D., U of IL, 1979. **Career Hist.:** Exec. Dir., Minnesota State Arts Board, 1984-96; Pres. and CEO, Minneapolis Downtown Council, 1996-present. **Career Act.:** Chair, Minn. Governor's Residence Council; Mem., Bds. of Greater Mpls. Chamber of Commerca & Greater Mpls. Convention & Visitors Assn.; Mem., MN Public Radio Advisory Ctee.; Mem., MN Chamber of Commerce Transportation Ctee.; State Coordinator, International Downtown Assn. **Dec./Awd.:** Distinguished Svc. Award, Iowa Governor Terry Branstad, 1984; Distinguished Svc. Commendation, Minn. Governor Arne Carlson, 1996. **Act./Mem.:** Mem., Minneapolis Club, Mendakota Country Club.

A. Jay Graf Pres., CEO, Guidant Corp./CPI, 4100 Hamline Ave. N., Arden Hills, MN 55112. Tel: 651/582-4000. **B:** Chicago. **M:** Mary Ann, 1970. **C:** Andrew, Allison. **E:** Boston U., BS, 1970; Indiana U., MBA, 1976. **Career Hist.:** Eli Lilly and Co., 1976-90; Guidant/CPI Corp. (formerly Cardiac Pacemakers Inc.), 1990-present: Pres. and COO, 1990-92; Pres. and CEO, 1992-2000; Guidant Group Chairman 2000-present. **Career Act.:** Dir., ATS Medical Inc.; Board of overseers U of MN Business School; Board Member Indiana University Healthcare Academy.

Ronald J. Graham Pres., Better Business Bureau of Minnesota, 2706 Gannon Rd., St. Paul, MN 55116. Tel: 651/699-0011. **B:** May 2, 1935, Minneapolis, Minn. **M:** Lemmie. **C:** Greg, Glory, Grant, Ginger, Gretchen, Garrick. **E:** Augsburg College, 1959; B.A., Business, Metropolitan State U., 1975. **Career Hist.:** Minneapolis Better Business Bureau, 1959-75; VP, Better Business Bureau of Minn., 1975-79; Pres., Better Business Bureau of Minn., 1979-1998.

Jerry E. Gray Pres.-Wells Fargo SBA Lending, Wells Fargo & Co., 1455 W. Lake St., # 306, MAC N9338-030, Minneapolis, MN 55408. Tel: 612/667-5393. Email: jerryegray@norwest.com **M:** yes. **C:** one daughter. **E:** BS, U. of Arizona; MBA-Finance, UCLA. **Career Hist.:** (Wells Fargo & Co.), 1992-2000: Mrg. with Cash Magmt/SVP, Financial Institutions Div.; EVP, Reg. Mgr. Twin Cities Business Bankingest Bank MN (responsible for 15 locations serving small businesses and middle-market companies; also responsible for financial institutions div., serving insurance companies and broker/dealers; and the commercial real estate group); present: president, national SBA leading which originates small business administration (SBA) loans across the nation. **Career Act.:** MacPhail Center for the Arts. **Act./Mem.:** Orono youth softball program.

Vincent J. Graziano Pres., Co-CEO, Northern Technologies International Corp., 6680 N. Highway 49, Lino Lakes, MN 55014. Tel: 651/784-1250. **B:** Apr. 7, 1933, Providence, R.I. **E:** U. of RI, BS-Elec. Engrg.; Lehigh U., MS-Indl. Engrg. **Career Hist.:** Engr., Bell Telephone Labs, 1961-62; Engr., Western Electric Co., 1962-66; Mgmt. Consultant, Peat, Marwick, Mitchell, 1966-76; VP, Northern Instruments Corp., 1976-79; Pres., Northern Technologies International Corp. (fka Northern Instruments Corp.), 1979-present.. **Dec./Awd.:** Small Business Exporter of the Year, for the state of Minnesota, 1989.

Frederick M. Green Chair, Pres., CEO, Ault Inc., 7300 Boone Ave. N., Brooklyn Park, MN 55428. Tel: 612/493-1900. Email: fmg@aultinc.com **B:** Apr. 14, 1943, Birmingham, Ala. **M:** Toni D. Green, 1985. **C:** Frederick D., Katrina A.. **E:** U of MN, BS-Mechanical Engrg., 1967; College of St. Thomas, MBA, 1977. **Career Hist.:** Technician, 3M, 1967; Engr., Honeywell, 1967-70; Engr., Plant Mgr., Dir.-Mfg., Control Data, 1970-80; EVP, Pres., CEO, Ault Inc., 1980-present. **Career Act.:** past Chair, MN High Tech. Council; Dir., Communications Systems Inc. **Act./Mem.:** Dir., United Way, 1992-94, Washburn Child Guidance Center, MN Diversified Industries Inc.; Mem., Minneapolis Club.

Jeffrey W. Green Chair, Hutchinson Technology Inc., 40 W. Highland Park, Hutchinson, MN 55350. Tel: 605/330-1608. **B:** Aug. 4, 1940, Brooklyn, N.Y. **M:** Sandra J. Stewart, 1961. **C:** Edward, Richard, Susan. **Career Hist.:** Engr., M.J. Green Company, 1960-61; Engr., Griffin Engrg., 1961-62; Engr., Strom Engrg., 1962-65; Hutchinson Technology Inc., 1965-present: VP, Pres., 1965-85; CEO, 1985-96; Chair, 1985-present. **Career Act.:** Dir., Hutchinson Technology Inc., MN Chamber of Commerce, Medwave Inc. and Contimed Inc; South Dakota Chamber of Commerce and Industry. **Dec./Awd.:** MN Quality Award for Hutchinson Technology, 1992; honorary degree, South Dakota School of Mines and Technology, 1996. **Act./Mem.:** MN Chamber of Commerce, Industry and Commerce Assn. of South Dakota.

Richard C. Greig VP-Op. Support, Belae Brands Inc., 1000 Valley Park Dr., Shakopee, MN 55379. Tel: 612/496-4609. **B:** Apr. 7, 1946, Omaha, Neb. **M:** Janice, 1968. **C:** one boy, one girl. **E:** BS-Business Admin., U. of MN, 1985. **Career Hist.:** Mgr.-Forecasting/Inv. Ctrl., Gould Inc. (St. Paul), 1972-79; Mgr.-Production/Distribution, Amway Corp. (Ada, Michigan), 1980-84; VP-Op., Quintessence Inc. (Chicago), 1984-91; SVP-Op., Tsumura Intl. Inc., 1991-1999; VP Operation Support, 1999-present. **Career Act.:** Dir., Tsumura Intl. Inc. **Dec./Awd.:** Award of Excellence, Tsumura Intl. Inc., 1995. **Act./Mem.:** Past Pres., Twin Cities Chapter of APICS; Dir., Shakopee Chamber of Commerce.

John F. (Jack) Grundhofer Chair, Pres., CEO, U.S. Bancorp, 601 Second Ave. S., Minneapolis, MN 55402. Tel: 612/973-0401. **B:** Jan. 1, 1939, Los Angeles. **M:** Beverly. **C:** Karen, Kathy. **E:** Loyola U., Los Angeles, BA-Economics,1960; USC, MBA-Finance, 1964.. **Career Hist.:** Union Bank (Los Angeles), 1960-72; Reg. VP, Union Bank, 1972-78; EVP, Wells Fargo Bank N.A. (Los Angeles), 1978-86; VChair and Senior Executive Officer, Wells Fargo Bank N.A. (Los Angeles), 1986-1990; Chair, Pres., CEO, First Bank System Inc., 1990-1997; Pres., CEO, U.S. Bancorp, 1997-1999. **Career Act.:** Dir., Minnesota Mutual Life Insurance Company; Dir., Irvine Apartment Communities Inc.; Rocky Mountain BankCard System Inc.; Dir., Donaldson Company; Mem., MEDA (Metro. Economic Devel. Assn.) Advisory Board, Bankers Roundtable, USC School of Business Admin.'s CEO Board, MN Business Partnership; Mem., MN Meeting; Horatio Alger Board. **Dec./Awd.:** Horatio Alger Award, 1997.

Joan Grzywinski Pres., District Mgr.-St. Paul/South Metro Mpls. District, Wells Fargo & Co., Wells Fargo, 55 E. Fifth St., St. Paul, MN 55101. Tel: 612/205-8555. **B:** Mar. 10, 1945, St. Paul. **M:** Robert F., 1965. **C:** Andrea Grzywinski Honda, Rebecca Grzywinski Martin. **E:** BS, U. of MN, 1965. **Career Hist.:** Registered Dental Hygienist (incl. St. Paul School District Public Health), 1965-80; Norwest Corp. (Wells Fargo & Co.): Mgmt. Trainee, 1981; Hum. Res.-Employee Relations Specialist, 1982; Commercial Loan Officer/Business Banker, Norwest Bank East St. Paul, 1983; VP-Private Banking, Norwest Bank St. Paul, 1985; Securities Sls. Rep., 1987; VP/Mgr.-Private Banking, Norwest Bank St. Paul, 1988; VP/Mgr.-Private Banking/Consumer Banking, Norwest Bank St. Paul, 1991; Pres. and Managing Officer, Norwest Bank N.A., 1992; Pres./District Mgr.-St. Paul/South Metro Mpls. District, 1995. **Career Act.:** St. Paul Area Chamber of Commerce; Commissioner (Mayoral appointee), Chair, St. Paul Port Authority; Dir., Mem.-Finance Ctee., HealthEast; Past Chair, SPACC Board of Directors, 1999; Chair of SPACC Foundation, chair of SPACC nominating committee. **Act./Mem.:** Dir., Chair-1997 Spurgeon Awards, IndianHead Council-Boy Scouts of America; Board of Advisors, Phalen Corridor Initiative; Advisory Council, Local Initiatives Service Corp. (LISC); Dir., St. Paul Progress, St. Paul Public Schools Fdn., League of Women Voters; past Dir., Ramsey County Historical Society, MN Museum of American Art.

Kenneth Francis Gudorf Pres., CEO, Agio Capital Partners I L.P., First Bank Place, Suite 4600, 601 Second Ave. S., Minneapolis, MN 55402. Tel: 612/935-8161. **B:** Mar. 3, 1939, Minster, Ohio. **M:** Evelyn, 1961. **C:** Eric, Craig, Caroline. **E:** U. of Dayton, AB, 1961; U. of MI, MBA, 1967. **Career Hist.:** Gulf Oil Corp.: Eastern Hemisphere-Dep. Treas., 1970-74; Fin. Rep. (Washington, D.C.), 1974-76; VP-Planning, 1976-78; Sr. Dir.-Mergers, Acquisitions and Divestments, 1978-81; Diversified Energies Inc., SVP, CFO, 1981-1985; VP, CFO, Carlson Companies Inc., 1985-89; Pres., KFG Ventures, 1989-91; VChair, Gage Marketing Inc., Pres., Gage Investments, 1992-95; Pres. and CEO, Agio Capital Mgmt. LLC, 1995-present. **Career Act.:** Pres.-Fin. Execs. Institute; MN Council for Economic Education; State of MN Investment Advisory Council; Presidents Club-U. of Dayton; Sister Kenny Institute; KTCA/Channel 2; Dir., Gage Mktg. Inc.; BOD, 1997; National Flood Svs., 1997; Electro Source, 1997; Engineered Products, 1998; Endres Processing, 1998; Altier Technologies 2000; Rourke Publishing 2000; Biovance 1998. **Act./Mem.:** Minneapolis Club; Interlachen Golf and Country Club.

WHO

Esperanza Guerrero-Anderson Pres., CEO, Milestone Growth Fund Inc., 401 Second Ave. S., Suite 1032, Minneapolis, MN 55401. Tel: 612/338-0090. Email: milestone7@aol.com **B:** Dec. 22, 1944, Managua, Nicaragua. **M:** Larry Anderson, 1990. **C:** Katie, Liz, Chris. **E:** Universidad Centramericana, Nicaragua, 1966; M.A., U. of Minn, 1973; Executive Mgmt. Program, Yale U., 1989; Reflective Leadership Program on Public Policy, U of Minn., 1987. **Career Hist.:** Central Bank of Nicaragua; First Bank of Minneapolis; Mgmt. Consultant, Touche Ross; Pres. and CEO, Metropolitan Economic Devel. Assn. **Career Act.:** Dir., National City Bancorp.; Dir., Greak Lakes Higher Education Corp; Dir., Milestone Growth Fund. **Dec./Awd.:** U.S. Small Business Admin. Minority Advocate of the Year, 1998; Bush Fdn. Fellowship, 1989; regional winner, "Hispanic Businesswoman of the Year Award", U.S. Hispanic Chamber of Commerce, 1992; Regional Ernst and Young Entrepreneur of the Year, Supporter of Entrepreneurship category, 1996; CityBusiness, Top 25 Most Influential Women, 1999. **Act./Mem.:** Community Bd., Center for the American Experiment; Bd., Walker Art Ctr.; Bd., Guthrie Theater; Bd., Minnesota Ctr. for Corporate Responsibility.

Kathy Halbreich Dir., Walker Art Center, Vineland Place, Minneapolis, MN 55403. Tel: 612/375-7600. **E:** BA (Visual Arts, Literature), Bennington (VT) College, 1971. **Career Hist.:** Dir.-Albert and Vera List Visual Arts Center, MIT (Cambridge, MA), 1976-86; Independent Curatorial Consultant, 1986-88; Curator of Contemporary Art, Museum of Fine Arts (Boston), 1988-90; Dir., Walker Art Center, 1991-present. **Career Act.:** Commissioner, Kwangju Biennale (Korea), 1995; Mem., Documenta 10 Intl. Ctee. (Kassel, Germany), 1993-94; Dir., Piper Jaffray Cos. Inc., 1994-present; Dir., The Andy Warhol Fdn. for the Visual Arts Inc., 1992-present; Trustee, Twin Cities Public Television, 1992-present; Mem., Assn. of Art Museum Directors, 1991-present.

James T. Hale EVP, Sec., Gen. Counsel, Target Corp., 777 Nicollet Mall, Minneapolis, MN 55402. Tel: 612/370-6948. **B:** May 14, 1940, Minneapolis. **M:** Sharon, 1960. **C:** David, Eric, Kristin. **E:** Dartmouth, BA, 1962; U. of MN Law School, LLB, 1965. **Career Hist.:** Law Clerk, Supreme Court U.S., 1965-66; Attorney, Faegre & Benson, 1966-79; VP-Corporate Growth, General Mills, 1979-80; VP-Fin. and Control, General Mills, 1981; SVP, Gen. Counsel, Corp. Sec., Dayton Hudson Corp., now Target Corp., 1981-present.. **Career Act.:** MN Board of Continuing Legal Education; Exec. Ctee., The Fund for Legal Aid Society; Dir., Ordway Center for the Performing Arts.

Roger L. Hale Pres., CEO, Tennant Co., 701 N. Lilac Dr., Golden Valley, MN 55422. Tel: 612/540-1212. **B:** Dec. 13, 1934, Plainfield, N.J. **M:** Nor Hall, 1989. **C:** Jocelyn J., Leslie A., Nina E., Deirdre McCarrell. **E:** Brown U., BA, 1956; Harvard Business School, MBA, 1961. **Career Hist.:** Tennant Co., 1961-present: Asst. to Pres., 1963-68; VP, Dir.-Systems and Corp. Devel., 1968-72; VP-Intl., 1972-75; Pres., COO, 1975-76; Pres., CEO, 1976-1998; Chair, CEO 1998-present. **Career Act.:** past Dir. Dayton Hudson Corp., Donaldson Corp., St. Paul Cos., Valspar; Dir., Tennant Co., U.S. Bank Corp.; Mem., MN Business Partnership; Chair, Public Radio International. **Dec./Awd.:** Executive of the Year, Corporate Report Minnesota, 1989; CEO of the Year Bronze Award, Small Mfg., CFO Magazine, 1991; Special Recognition Award for Community Service, City of Minneapolis, 1993; One of five "Outstanding Minnesota Directors," Minnesota Business Monthly, 1996. **Act./Mem.:** Minneapolis Club, Harvard Business School Club of Twin Cities.

Thomas W. Haley Chair, Innovex Inc., 5540 Pioneer Creek Dr., Maple Plain, MN 55359-9003. Tel: 612/938-4155. **B:** Oct. 23, 1936, Bird Island, Minn. **M:** Mary E. Curtin, 1994. **C:** Sheila Marie. **E:** U. of MN, Fin., 1964. **Career Hist.:** Innovex: Chair, CEO, 1972-1999; Chair, 2000-present. **Act./Mem.:** Minneapolis Golf Club.

Brian H. Hall CEO, West Group, 610 Opperman Dr., Eagan, MN 55123. Tel: 651/687-7000. **B:** Aug. 22, 1947, Buffalo, N.Y. **M:** Linda T., 1969. **C:** Bryce, Corey. **E:** BS, The Defiance College (Ohio), 1971; MBA, Rochester (NY) Institute of Technology, 1978. **Career Hist.:** Sls./mktg. positions, Cooperative Publishing (Rochester, NY), 1971; Shepard's McGraw-Hill (Colorado Springs, CO): Dir.-Sls./Mktg., 1981-85; Pres., 1985-95; concurrent executive responsibilities at Cyma/McGraw-Hill (Tempe, AZ), 1988-95, and Aardvark/McGraw-Hill (Milwaukee), 1988-95; Pres., CEO, Thomson Legal Publishing/West Group, 1995-present. **Career Act.:** Past Dir., BankOne (Colorado Springs), Colorado Springs Chamber of Commerce, Colorado Springs Symphony, Penrose/St. Francis Hospital. **Dec./Awd.:** Appointed by Gov. Roy Romer to serve on the Colorado Commission on Higher Education, 1989. **Act./Mem.:** Genessee Valley Club (Rochester, NY), El Paso Club (Colorado Springs), Country Club of CO (Colorado Springs), Bearpath Country Club.

Barry J. Halm Pres., Benedictine Health System, 503 E. Third St., Suite 400, Duluth, MN 55805. Tel: 218/720-2370. Email: bhalm@bhshealth.com **B:** Aug. 30, 1950, Moorhead, Minn. **M:** Cleo. **C:** Tyler, Valerie, Cassie. **E:** ND St. School Of Science, Assoc. Of Science Degree-Business Admin., 1971; Moorhead St. U., BA-Business Admin./Finance, 1973; Concordia College, Certificate of Hospital Admin., 1973; U. of MN, Hospital Admin./Health Facilities Mgmt. courses, 1975; California Coast U., MBA Program. **Career Hist.:** Western ND Health Systems Agency (Bismarck, ND), Exec. Dir./Staff Dir., 1976-80; St. Joseph's Hospital (Minot, ND), Dir.-Shared Svs., Admin.-Kenmare Community Hospital, 1980-81; Mercy Medical Center (Williston, ND), Pres., CEO, 1981-88; Catholic Health Corp. (Omaha NE), VP-Op. Svs., 1981-88; United Medical Center-Pres./CEO, United Health Systems (Moline, IL), Pres./CEO, 1988-92; Team Consulting Group (Rock Island, IL), Pres./CEO, 1992-93; Benedictine Health System, Pres./COO, 1993-97, Pres./CEO, 1997-present. **Career Act.:** Regent (1997-01), American College Of Healthcare Executives; Dir., MN Hospital & Healthcare Partnership, Living Services Fdn.; Member, Academy For Catholic Healthcare Leadership, American Mgmt. Assn., American Academy Of Medical Administrators. **Dec./Awd.:** Distinguished Alumni Award, Moorhead St. U., 1998; Outstanding Jaycee, ND, 1975.

Phil Halper Div. Mgr., American Building Maintenance, 760 Harding St. N.E., Minneapolis, MN 55413. Tel: 612/378-0646. **Career Act.:** B.O.M.A., Building Owners and Managers of St. Paul.

George C. Halvorson Pres., CEO, HealthPartners, 8100 34th Ave. S., Bloomington, MN 55425. Tel: 612/883-6000. **B:** Jan. 28, 1947, Fargo, N.D. **M:** Mary, 1986. **C:** Jonathon, Seth, Charles, Michael. **E:** Concordia College; graduate studies, U of MN, U of Nebraska, U. of St. Thomas. **Career Hist.:** Pres., Health Accord; Pres., Senior Health Plan; SVP, Blue Cross Blue Shield; Exec. Dir., HMO MN; Pres. and CEO, HealthPartners. **Career Act.:** Dir., HealthPartners, KTCA/Channel 2, Alliance of Community Health Plans, Boy Scouts Indianhead Council, MN Business Partnership, American Assn. of Health Plans, St. Paul Academy, American Diabetes Assn., International Federation of Health Plans, Commonwealth Fund Advisory Board.

Alan J. Hamel Pres., Gaughan Cos., 199 N.W. Coon Rapids Blvd., Coon Rapids, MN 55433. Tel: 612/786-6320. **B:** May 28, 1947, Marquette, Mich. **M:** divorced. **C:** Alison, Ann Marie. **E:** U. of WI: BA, 1969; MA, 1971. **Career Hist.:** City Planning Dir., City of Coon Rapids, 1971-77; Gaughan

WHO

Cos., 1977-present: VP-Devel., 1977-87; Pres., 1987-present. **Career Act.:** Ptnr., various real estate ventures; Dir., Sec., MN Multi-Housing Assn.; Chair, First Circle Medical Inc., Anoka County Business Assistance Network, City of Coon Rapids Budget Evaluation Commission, Anoka-Ramsey Community College Advisory Board; Mem., Metropolitan Council Housing Ctee., YMCA Steering Ctee., Church Building Ctee., Boy Scout ctees.; Jr. Achievement Consultant; Dir., Quality Sterilization Services Inc.; Dir., North Metro Convention Bureau. **Dec./Awd.:** Govt. Service Award, MN Builders Assn.; Economic Developer of the Year Award, MIDA; Reggie Award of Excellence, Mpls. Builders Assn.; Outstanding Grad., U. of WI Geography Dept., 1969. **Act./Mem.:** Coon Rapids Rotary.

W. Kirk Hankins Chair, Pres., CEO, CFO, Winland Electronics Inc., 1950 Excel Dr., P.O. Box 473, Mankato, MN 56001. Tel: 507/625-7231. **B:** Feb. 16, 1928, Minneapolis. **M:** Joyce. **C:** Susan, Kristine, Katherine, Kirk P., Terrance, Kimberly. **E:** U.S.C., BS, MA. **Career Hist.:** Corp. Cont., Mgr.-Admin., Global Marine Inc., 1970-74; Div. Cont., Western Precipitation Div. of Joy Mfg., 1974-76; CEO, Owner, mgmt. consulting firm, 1976-83; Chair, Pres., CEO, Winland Electronics Inc., 1983-present. **Career Act.:** Dir., Playtronics. **Act./Mem.:** Natl. Assn. of Accountants; American Acctg. Assn.

S. Albert D. Hanser Chair, Hanrow Financial Group Ltd., 5960 Golden Hills Dr., Minneapolis, MN 55416. Tel: 612/417-4203. Email: albert@astrocorp.com **B:** May 30, 1937, St. Louis. **M:** Sally Dodge, 1961. **C:** Elise Kingman, Laura Thatcher, Wendy Huml, S. Albert III. **E:** Brown U., BA, 1959; Wharton School. **Career Hist.:** Ptnr., Smith Moore, 1959-67; SVP, Dain Bosworth, 1967-79; Chair, Resource Companies, 1979-83; Chair, FBS Merchant Banking Group, 1983-89; Chair, Hanrow Financial Group Ltd. (Merchant Banking Partnership), 1989-present; Chair, Astrocom Corp., 1992-present; Chair, Prevention First Inc., 1997-present. **Career Act.:** Trustee, past Chair, U. of MN Hospitals; Board of Advisors, Brown U.; past Dir., United Way, MN Public Teaching Hospital Assn. (M.A.P.T.H.), Interstate Medical Clinic (Red Wing); past Trustee, Blake Schools; Dir., Astrocom, Hawkins Chemical Inc., E-Z Gard, Premis Corp., Prevention First Inc., Fairview University Medical Center; Fairview Health System. **Act./Mem.:** Woodhill Country Club; Minneapolis Club; Lafayette Club; MN Alumni Club; Citizens League, United Way.

Timothy H. Hanson Pres., HealthEast, 559 Capitol Blvd., St. Paul, MN 55103. Tel: 651/232-2300. **B:** Nov. 26, 1946, Grand Forks, N.D. **M:** Jane, 1966. **C:** Amy, Kathryn. **E:** U. of ND, BS, BA, 1971; U. of MN, MHA, 1973. **Career Hist.:** medic, U.S. Army, 1966-68; Inhalation Therapy Technician, Deaconess Hospital, 1968-71. Bethesda Hospital, 1972-86: Admin./VP, 1982-86. HealthEast: COO, 1986-89; Pres. and CEO, 1989-present.. **Career Act.:** Chair, MN Hospital and Healthcare Partnership, United Way of the St. Paul Area; Mem., Governers Taks Force on Violence as a Public Health Problem; Dir., MN Business Partnership; Dir. Capital City Partnership. **Act./Mem.:** United Way, Red Cross, Boy Scouts, St. Paul Chamber.

Roe H. Hatlen Chair, CEO, Buffets Inc., 1460 Buffet Way, Eagan, MN 55121. Tel: 612/942-9760. **B:** 1943. **M:** Beverly Thompson. **E:** Pacific Lutheran U., BA, Accounting, 1965; U. of Oregon, MBA, Accounting and Business Statistics, 1965. **Career Hist.:** CPA, Herziner Porter Addison & Blind; Chief Financial Officer, International King's Table Inc.; Chief Financial Officer, Pizza Ventures Inc.; CEO, Buffets Inc., 1983-present. **Career Act.:** Dir., Buffets Inc., Minnesota Life College. **Dec./Awd.:** Distinguished Alumnus, Pacific Lutheran U., 1995; Master Entrepreneur of the Year-Minnesota, 1993.

David A. Heider Pres., CEO, United Hardware Distributing Co., 5005 Nathan Ln., Plymouth, MN 55442. Tel: 612/559-1800. **B:** Mar. 30, 1941, Oconomowoc, Wis. **M:** Ann M. Heider, 1966. **C:** Daniel, Kathryn. **E:** Swarthmore College, BA, 1964; Harvard U, MBA, 1966.. **Career Hist.:** Instructor, Harvard Business School, 1966-69; Admin., Harvard Medical School, 1969-72; Pres., Gambles Continental Bank, 1972-76; VP, Gamble-Skogmo Inc., 1976-1980; VP, Merrimac Associates Inc., 1980-83; EVP, Sullivan Associates Inc., 1983-89; Pres., Shelburne Mgmt. Company Inc., 1989-91; Pres., CEO, United Hardware Distributing Company, 1991-present. **Career Act.:** Dir., International Hardware Distributors Assn.; Chair, Distribution America Inc.; Chair, Distribution Services LLC; Dir., Plymouth Trading Co. LLC.

Michael J. Helgeson CEO, Gold'n Plump Poultry, 4150 S. Second St., St. Cloud, MN 56301. Tel: 320/251-3570. Email: mhelgeson@goldnplump.com **B:** May 21, 1952, St. Cloud, Minn. **M:** Karel, 1974. **C:** Paul, Erik. **E:** Gustavus Adolphus College, BA, Business, 1974; U. of St. Thomas, MBA, 1987; Stanford Executive Program. **Career Hist.:** Jack Frost/Gold'n Plump Poultry, 1974-present: Project Mgr.; Elevator and Purchasing Mgr.; Personnel Mgr.; New Products Mgr.; Pres., North Bay Fish and Seafood; EVP, CEO Gold'n Plump. **Career Act.:** Dir., National Chicken Council, MN Business Partnership; MN Chamber of Commerce.

Randy Hendricks Senior Ptnr., Head-Gov't Treasury group, Andersen Consulting, 333 S. Seventh St., Minneapolis, MN 55402. Tel: 612/277-5976.

Peter S. Hendrixson Managing Ptnr., Dorsey & Whitney LLP, Pillsbury Center South, 220 S. Sixth St., Minneapolis, MN 55402. Tel: 612/340-2600. **B:** April 9, 1947, Wilmington, Delaware. **M:** Carolyn Ford Hendrixson. **C:** Julie, Brad. **E:** Northwestern University, B.A., 1969; Harvard University, J.D 1972, magna cum laude. **Career Hist.:** Dorsey & Whitney LLP, 1973; Chair Trial Dept. 1989-93; Chair Trial & Administrative Group, 1994; Management Committee, 1994; Managing Partner, 2000-present. **Dec./Awd.:** Editor, officer Harvard Law Review 1970-72; Treasurer Fraser for Mayor Campaign; Board of Governor-Children's Theatre, Mpls. 1987-92; Board Dir. LaCreche Early Childhood Center 1990-98; Children's Home Society, St. Paul 1990; Guthrie Theatre, 1995; various positions Mayflower Cong. Church; Chair Anti-Trust Law Section, 1992-93.

Bruce E. Hendry Chair, CEO, MBC Holding Co., 882 W. Seventh St., St. Paul, MN 55102. Tel: 651/228-9173. **B:** Dec. 13, 1942, San Diego. **M:** Sharon, 1970. **C:** Amy, Jill. **E:** BS, U. of MN School of Business. **Career Hist.:** Chair, Pres., Erie Lackawanna Railroad; Chair, CEO, Kaiser Steel Corp.; Chair-Creditors Ctee., First Republic Bank; Chair, CEO, Minnesota Brewing Co., now MBC Holding Co. **Career Act.:** Board of Overseers, Carlson School of Mgmt., U of MN; Chair-Scholarship Ctee., Alpha Kappa Psi.

Jay A. Herman Pres., CEO, Check Technology Corp., 12500 Whitewater Dr., Minnetonka, MN 55343. Tel: 612/939-9000. **Career Hist.:** General Mills Inc.; Gelco Corp., 1979-88: VP-Admin. Svs., Dir.-Planning/Budget-Fleet Leasing Div., VP/CFO-International Div.; Check Technology Corp., 1988-present: EVP/CFO; Pres. since 1989.

John H. Herrell Chief Admin. Ofcr., Mayo Foundation, 200 First St. S.W., Rochester, MN 55905. Tel: 507/284-2193. **B:** Jan. 2, 1941, Rochester, Minn. **M:** Roberta Kay McGillicuddy. **C:** Lisa Anne Herrell, Suzanne Hanley Herrell, Molly Herrell Labrum. **E:** U. of VA, BA, 1963; Harvard, MBA, 1965. **Career Hist.:** Commercial Credit Analysis and Commercial Loan Officer, Harris Trust and Savings Bank, 1965-68; Financial Analysis and Planning Section, Mayo Clinic, 1968-83; Research Svs. Section, Mayo Clinic, 1978-82; Planning Section, Mayo Clinic, 1980-89; Admin., Div. of Thoracic Diseases and Internal Medicine, 1972-77; Chair, Financial Svs. Div., 1984-89; VChair-Admin., Mayo Clinic, 1990-92; Asst. Treas., Mayo Fdn., 1982-83; Treas./CFO, Mayo Fdn., 1984-92; Chair-Investment Ctee., 1984-present; VP and Chief Administrative Officer, Mayo Fdn., 1993-present. **Career Act.:** past Chair, Kahler Corp.,1981-96; Mem. Valuation Ctee. Palmer Organization Venture Capital Funds; Chair, State of MN Investment Advisory Council, 1981-82; Mem. Advisory Board, Protection Mutual Insurance Company-North Central Region, 1987-93; Adjunct Prof. of Business Admin. College of St. Thomas-1986; Mem. Advisory Board, First Trust National Assn., 1992-96; Dir., Universal Health Services Inc. 1994 - present. **Act./Mem.:** Pres., Rochester Golf & Country Club, 1976-77; Phi Beta Kappa, 1963; Loch Lomond Golf Club (Luss, Scotland); Old Baldy Club (Saratoga, Wyoming).

Brad Hewitt Pres., CEO, Diversified Pharmaceutical Services Inc., 6625 W. 78th St. Suite 100, P.O. Box 390842, Bloomington, MN 55439-0842. Tel: 612/820-7000. Email: brad.l.hewitt@diversified.com **B:** Jun. 10, 1060, Minneapolis. **M:** Susan, 1985. **C:** Matthew, Melissa. **E:** Bachelor's-Math/Econ. (with honors), U. of WI-River Falls, 1982; Fellow, Life Mgmt. Institute, 1984; Executive Mgmt. Program, Harvard Graduate School of Business. **Career Hist.:** Park Security Officer, Bloomington Police Dept. (F.T. summer); MN Mutual Life, 1982-86, Actuarial Dept.: Assoc. Case Underwriter, Group Case Underwriter, Supv.-Group Case Underwriting, Mgr.-Group Case Underwriting; United HealthCare Corp., 1986-95: Underwriting Consultant, Regional Underwriting Consultant, Senior Underwriter, Dir.-Group Underwriting; Diversified Pharmaceutical Services Inc., 1993-present: CFO, 1993, EVP and COO, 1995, Pres. and CEO, 1997. **Career Act.:** Past Dir., MN Health Care Reinsurance Assn.; past Mem.-Actuarial Ctee., MCHA. **Act./Mem.:** Executive Advisor, Jr. Achievement; Teacher, St. Michael's Adult Education; skiing, camping, biking, reading, tennis.

Miles Hewitt Regional Mgr.-Minnesota Op., Boise Cascade Corp., 400 Second St., International Falls, MN 56649. **B:** Dec. 9, 1958, Niagra Falls, N.Y. **M:** Lorna, 1984. **E:** B.S., Pulp & Paper Science, 1982; B.S. Chemical Engrg., 1982. **Career Hist.:** Process Engr., Production Engr., Pulp Mill Day Supervisor, Pulp Mill Superintendent, Mill Mgr., Regional Mgr., Boise Cascade. **Career Act.:** Dir., Pulp & Paper Fdn.

Karen L. Himle SVP-Corp./Gov't Affairs, The St. Paul Cos. Inc., 385 Washington St., St. Paul, MN 55102. Tel: 651/310-8553. Email: karen.himle@ stpaul.com **B:** Jan. 9, 1956, Chicago. **M:** John 1986. **C:** Lauren, Kirsten. **E:** B.S., cum laude, U. of Nebraska, 1976; J.D., College of Law, U. of Nebraska, 1980. **Career Hist.:** Staff, Gov. Charles Thone of Nebraska, 1979-82; Regional Gov't. Relations Coordinator, Peoples Natural Gas Co., 1982-85; The St. Paul Cos., 1985-present: Sr. Gov't. Affairs Officer; VP-Corp. Affairs; SVP-Corporate and Gov't Affairs (1997). Oversees government affairs, public relations, communications, media relations, corporate mktg., and advertising for U.S. and international operations; oversees company's $10 million charitable giving program. **Career Act.:** 1997 Chair, St. Paul Area Chamber of Commerce; 1997 St. Paul Chair, WAMSO Symphony Ball; Humphrey Institute Advisory Board; Mem., American Bar Assn., Public Relations Society of America; Dir., The Guthrie Theater Board of Trustees; Dir., Minnesota Chamber of Commerce, Board of Directors Minneapolis Club Board of Governors, St. Paul Foundation. **Act./Mem.:** Normandale Lutheran Church.

Gregory T. Hitchcock Chair, Pres., CEO, Hitchcock Industries Inc., 8701 Harriet Ave. S., Bloomington, MN 55420. Tel: 612/881-1000. Email: gthitchcock@hitchcock-ind.com **B:** Jun. 8, 1947, Minneapolis. **C:** Carleton Gregory, Jonathan Todd. **E:** U. of MN. **Career Hist.:** Engr., Hitchcock Industries Inc., 1965-70; VP, Routson-Hitchcock Motors Inc., 1970-71; Pres., Todd Chevrolet Inc., 1971-75; Hitchcock Industries Inc.: Corp. Sec., 1976-78; VP, 1979-80; EVP, 1981-86; Chair, 1987-present; Chair, Pres., CEO, 1998-present; VChair, Watkins Pattern Co., 1987-1998, Chair and CEO 1998-present . **Career Act.:** Boys and Girls Clubs of America Inc. **Act./Mem.:** Interlachen Country Club; Edina Country Club.

William A. Hodder retired Chair/CEO, Donaldson Co. Inc., 1400 W. 94th St., Bloomington, MN 55431. Tel: 612/887-3006. **B:** May 6, 1931, Lincoln, Neb. **M:** Suzanne, 1954. **C:** Kent, Laurie, Susan, Mark, Beth. **E:** U. of NE, BA; Harvard U., PMD 1. **Career Hist.:** Mktg., IBM Corp., 1954-66; VP-Organizational Planning and Devel., Dayton's, 1966-68; Pres., Target Stores, 1968-73; Dayton Hudson Corp., 1969; SVP, Dayton Hudson Corp., 1970; Pres., Donaldson Company Inc. 1973-80; Pres., CEO., Donaldson Company Inc., 1982-1984; Chair, Pres., CEO, Donaldson Company Inc., 1984-94; Chair, CEO, Donaldson Company Inc., 1994-96 (retired). **Career Act.:** Dir., Norwest Corp., Tennant Company, ReliaStar Financial Corp., SUPERVALU Inc., Cowles Media, Musicland Stores Corp.; Mem., Board of Overseers, U. of MN Carlson School of Mgmt.; Mem., Chief Execs. Organization Inc.. **Act./Mem.:** Harvard Bus. School Club of MN; MN Execs. Organization.

William L. Hoeft Pres., CEO, Ziegler Inc., 901 W. 94th St., Bloomington, MN 55420. Tel: 612/888-4121. **B:** Apr. 26, 1957, Minneapolis. **M:** Anastasia, 1980. **C:** Andreas, William, Alexandra, Michael. **E:** St. Olaf College, B.A., Religion, 1979. **Career Hist.:** Ziegler Inc., 1974-present; Barlow Rand South Africa, 1981-82.. **Career Act.:** Pres., Parish Council, St. Mary's Greek Orthodox Church; Ziegler Inc., Generation II Locomotives, ZTR Control Systems, Amgems, MN Methane, National Cooling Co., St. Olaf Board of Regents, Board of Trustees Hellenic College/Holy Cross Greek Orthodox School of Theology; Board, Children's Hospital Foundation Board. **Act./Mem.:** Minneapolis Club, Minikahda Club, MN. Horse and Hunt Club, Young Presidents Organization, Edina Country Club, Sons of the American Revolution; Tournament Players Club.

Sister Kathleen Hofer Pres., St. Mary's Medical Center, 407 E. Third St., Duluth, MN 55805. Tel: 218/726-4493. Email: khofer@ssmcdu-luth.com **B:** Jul. 6, 1933, Grand Forks, N.D. **E:** College of St. Scholastica, BA, 1963; George Washington U., MBA, 1967. **Career Hist.:** St. Mary's Hospital, Duluth, Asst. and Dir., Medical Record Dept., 1964-65; College of St. Scholastica, 1967-76: Chair, Department of Medical Record Adminstration, 1967-71; Chair, Division of Health Sciences, 1971-76. Benedictine Sisters Benevolent Assn., St. Scholastica Priory, Treas., 1976-81; St. Mary's Medical Center, Pres. and CEO, 1982-1996, Chair, 1997-present; Pres., Benedictine Health System, 1986-87 and 1990-93; Chair, CEO, 1993-1997; St. Mary's/Duluth Clinic Health System, Active Board Chair, 1997-present; St. Scholastica Monastery, Prioress, 1999 to present. **Career Act.:** Past Trustee, Catholic Health Corp., College of St. Scholastica, Blue Cross Blue Shield of MN; past Dir., Minnesota Power, United Way of Greater Duluth, Duluth Area Chamber of Commerce; Advisory Board of Dir., First Bank Duluth; past Pres., American Medical Record Assn., MN Medical Record Assn.; Allied Health Grant Review Consultant for Department of Health, Education, and Welfare, 1976-77; Chair, Duluth Graduate Medical Education Council; Dir., MN Hospital and Healthcare Partnership; Co-chair, Duluth Local Initiatives Support Corp. (LISC) Advisory Ctee. **Dec./Awd.:** Presidential Alumni Award, College of St. Scholastica, 1996; Heart of MN Award, Health Care Auxilary of MN, 1995; Sister Ann Edward Scanlon Award (Outstanding Service to Community), Alumni Association of College of St. Scholastica, 1991; Business Person of the Year, School of Business and Economics, U. of Minnesota-Duluth, 1996.

G.L. Hoffman Chair, Pres., CEO, Sec., Insignia Systems Inc., 5025 Cheshire Ln. N., Plymouth, MN 55446. Tel: 612/930-8200. **B:** Dec. 31, 1949, Abilene, Kan. **M:** Susan, 1978. **C:** Gavin, Marin. **E:** US Air Force Academy, BS, 1971. **Career Hist.:** VP, Conklin Company; Co-founder, Chm., Varitronic Systems, 1982-90; Chm., Pres., CEO, Insignia Systems Inc..

George T. Holden Chair, Holden Graphic Services, 607 Washington Ave. N., Minneapolis, MN 55401. Tel: 612/339-0241. **B:** Jul. 31, 1945, Minneapolis. **M:** divorced. **C:** Libby, Tricia, Allie. **E:** Northwestern U., BS-Bus. Admin.; Harvard Graduate School of Business Admin., MBA. **Career Hist.:** Asst. to Sls. Mgr., Holden Business Forms Co., summer 1964, 1967-68; Auditor, Main LaFrentz & Co., 1968-70; Brand Asst., Procter and Gamble

Co., 1970-71; Mktg. Mgr., Holden Business Forms Co., 1972-73; Chair, Holden Graphic Services, 1973-present. **Career Act.:** past Chair, International Business Forms Industries Inc.; Dir., Bolger Printing/Publishing, past dir. Jones-Harrison Fdn. and director, Walker Methodist Inc., present director Security Life Insurance Co., Harvard Business School Club of MN, Greater Minneapolis Chamber of Commerce; past president of Hennepin Church Board of Trustees and Foundation Board. **Act./Mem.:** Past Trustee, Boys' and Girls' Clubs of Minneapolis; past Pres., Harvard Business School Club of MN; Mem., Masonic Lodge, Zuhrah Temple, Minikahda Club, Minneapolis Club, Hennepin Avenue Methodist Church.

Thomas E. Holloran Prof., University of St. Thomas/Graduate School of Business, 1000 LaSalle, Suite 343, Minneapolis, MN 55403. Tel: 612/962-4243. **B:** Sep. 27, 1929, Minneapolis. **M:** Patricia, 1954. **C:** Mary Harley, Anne Holloran. **E:** U. of MN Law School, JD, 1955. **Career Hist.:** Attorney, Fredrikson & Byron; EVP, Medtronic Inc., 1967-73; Pres., Medtronic Inc., 1973-75; Chair, Pres., CEO, Inter-Regional Financial Group, 1976-85; Prof., Graduate School of Business, U. of St. Thomas, 1985-present. **Career Act.:** Dir.: Flexsteel Industries Inc., Medtronic Inc., MTS Systems Corp., ADC Telecommunications Inc., Malt-O-Meal Co., National City Bancorporation. **Act./Mem.:** Minneapolis-St. Paul Metro. Airports Commission: VChair, 1974-82, Chair, 1989-91; Trustee, College of St. Thomas, 1978-88; Dir., Bush Fdn. 1980-2000; Chair Bush Fdn., 1991-96; past Pres., U. of MN Alumni Assn.; Governing Ctee., Minneapolis Club, 1987-89; past Chair, MN Project on Corp. Responsibility.

Gary S. Holmes Pres., Owner, CSM Corp., 2575 University Ave. W., Suite 150, St. Paul, MN 55114. Tel: 651/646-1717. **M:** Mary. **C:** Max, Jake, Kip. **E:** Mankato, U of MN, B.A. business and finance. **Career Hist.:** Pres. and Owner, CSM Corp. 1976-present. **Career Act.:** Owner and Dir., Century Bank; Major shareholder of Tri-West Building Corp.; International Council of Shopping Centers; National Apartment Association; Minnesota Shopping Center Association; Minnesota Multi-Housing Association; Minnesota Housing Association; National Association of Industrial and Office Parks. **Dec./Awd.:** Marriott 2000 Developer of the Year Award; John F. Cade Award for Distinguished Entrepreneur of the Year-University of St. Thomas; NAIOP Award of Excellence. **Act./Mem.:** Dir. and Founder of Minneapolis Heart Institute; Board member Abbot Northwestern Hospital; Children's Cancer Research Fund; U of MN Carlson School of Bus. Mentorship Prog.; Town & Country Club; Wayzata Country Club; Lafayette Country Club.

James J. Horvath Pres., CEO, American Crystal Sugar Co., 101 N. Third St., Moorhead, MN 56560. Tel: 218/236-4400. **B:** Jul. 19, 1945, Milwaukee, Wis. **M:** Carol Ann 1968. **C:** Bradley and Brian. **E:** B.S., MBA University of Wisconsin-Milwaukee. **Career Hist.:** Pres. CEO American Crystal, 1998 - present; CFO 1985 - 98; Miller Brewing Co., 1969-85. **Career Act.:** Board of Dir., United Sugars Corp.; Midwest Agri-Commodities; The Sugar Assn. Trustee, United States Beet Sugar Assn.

Robert F. Hosch Chair, CEO, Harris Contracting, 909 Montreal Circle, St. Paul, MN 55102. Tel: 651/602-6601. **B:** Aug. 27, 1944, St. Paul. **M:** Mary Ellen, 1968. **C:** Greg, Angela. **E:** Trade School; Extension courses from U. of MN; College of St. Thomas. **Career Hist.:** Harris Mechanical Contracting Company: Pipefitter Foreman, 1968-69; Estimator/Fab. Shop Coor., 1969-72; Chief Estimator, 1972-75; VP-Op., 1975-77; VP, Gen. Mgr., 1977-83; Chair, Pres., 1983-present; Chair and CEO, 1997. **Career Act.:** Mem., Plumbing Comm., MCAA; Ctee. Chair, St. Paul Jaycees; Chair, MCAA Labor Estimating Ctee.; Mem., Mechanical Contractors Assn. of America; Past Chair, Harris-Waldinger Corp.; Past Dir., Associated General Contractors of MN. **Dec./Awd.:** First Place, St. Paul Pipefitter Apprentice Contest, 1966; First Place, MN Apprentice Contest, 1966; Third Place, Natl. Apprentice Contest, 1966. **Act./Mem.:** Eagan Rotary; Dir., Westend Fishing and Hunting Club; Mem., Bonita Bay Country Club; Member Pool and Yacht Club.

James Joseph Howard III Chair, Pres., CEO, Xcel Energy Inc., 414 Nicollet Mall, Minneapolis, MN 55401. Tel: 612/330-7707. **B:** Jul. 1, 1935, Pittsburgh. **M:** Donna, 1955. **C:** James J. IV, Catherine A., Christine A., William F.. **E:** U. of Pittsburgh, BBA, 1957; MIT, MS, 1970. **Career Hist.:** Sloan Fellow, MIT, 1969; VP, Gen. Mgr., Bell Telephone of PA, 1976-78; WI Telephone Company, 1978-83: VP-Op., 1978-79; EVP, COO, 1979-81; Pres., 1981-83; Chair, CEO, 1983; COO, Ameritech, 1983-87; Northern States Power Co., now Xcel Energy Inc.: Dir., Pres., CEO, 1987-92; Chair, CEO, 1988-94; Chair, Pres., CEO, 1994-present. **Career Act.:** Board of Trustees, U. of St. Thomas; 1991 Chair, Greater Minneapolis Chamber of Commerce; Dir., Honeywell Inc., Ecolab Inc., Walgreens, MN Business Partnership, ReliaStar Financial Corp., Northern States Power Company, Federal Reserve Bank of Minneapolis, U. of Pittsburgh/Joseph M. Katz Grad. School of Business, MCCR, Edison Electric Institute; Chair, Nuclear Energy Institute, 1996-1998. **Act./Mem.:** 1994 Chair, United Way of Minneapolis; Dir., Danny Thompson Memorial Leukemia Fdn.

Stanley S. Hubbard Chair, Pres., CEO, Hubbard Broadcasting Inc., 3415 University Ave., St. Paul, MN 55114. Tel: 651/642-4200. **B:** May 28, 1933, St. Paul. **M:** Karen Holmen, 1959. **C:** Kathryn (Rominski), Stanley E. II, Virginia (Morris), Robert W., Julia (Coyte). **E:** U. of MN, BA, 1955. **Career Hist.:** Hubbard Broadcasting, 1951-present: various positions, 1951-56; Mgr., Radio, 1956-64; VP, Gen. Mgr., 1964-67; Pres., Gen. Mgr., 1967-83; Chair, Pres., CEO 1983-present; Pres., CEO, United States Satellite Broadcasting, 1981-95; Chair, USSB, 1995-1999. **Career Act.:** Past Dir., U.S. Satellite Broadcasting Company Inc., American Friends of Jamaica, Assn. for Maximum Service Television, past Broadcast Pioneers Library, past Fingerhut Companies Inc., Hubbard Fdn., MN Business Partnership, U. of MN Fdn. Board of Trustees, U. of St. Thomas Board of Trustees, Metropolitan Airports Public Fdn. Advisory Bd.; Chair, St. Croix Valley Youth Center; Mem., International Radio and Television Society, Royal Television Society of London, Society of Professional Journalists, Society of Satellite Professionals, World Presidents Organization. **Dec./Awd.:** Inductee, Hunkpapa Sioux Tribe, 1959; Spurgeon Award/Boy Scouts of America, 1985; International Humanitarian Award, American Friends of Jamaica, 1989; *Broadcasting & Cable Magazine*, (first) Hall of Fame, 1991; Mitchell Charnley Award, Northwest Broadcast News Assn., 1991; Society of Satellite Professionals International Hall of Fame, 1992; Silver Satellite Award, American Women In Radio & Television (AWRT), 1994; SBCA's Arthur C. Clarke Award, 1994; Children's Cancer Research Fund DreamMaker Award, 1994; National Assn. of Broadcasters' Distinguished Service Award, 1995; Broadcast Cable & Financial mgmt.'s Avatar Award, 1995; American Jewish Ctee. Human Rights Award, 1995; Mpls./St. Paul Chapter, Alzheimer's Assn. Community Leadership Award, 1995; MN High Tech. Council Most Innovative Product Award, 1995; Honorary Doctor of Humanities, Hamline U. (St. Paul), 1995; U. of Nebraska Journalism Innovator Award, 1996; U. of St. Thomas MN Family Business Award, 1996; Distinguished Alumnus of the Year, Breck School, 1996; IRTS Fdn. Award, 1996; MN & The Dakotas Entrepreneur of the Year, 1996; U.S. Hockey Hall of Fame Heritage Award, 1996; U. of MN M Club Lifetime Achievement Award, 1996; *Dealerscope* magazine 1996 Hall of Fame; Broadcasters' Fdn. Golden Mike Award, 1997; Academy of Achievement's Golden Plate Award 1997; Minnesota Broadcasters Assn. Pioneer Broadcaster Award 1998; St. Croix Valley Sports Hall of Fame 2000; RTNDA John S. Hogan Distinguished Service Award, 2000. **Act./Mem.:** Town and Country Club; Minneapolis Club; St. Petersburg Yacht Club; St. Croix Sailing Club; St. Croix Yacht Club; Ocean Reef Club; Key Largo Anglers Club; Somerset Country Club; Minnesota Club; Lauderdale Yacht Club; Lyford Cay Club; New York Yacht Club.

David R. Hubers Chair, American Express Financial Advisors, IDS Tower 10, Minneapolis, MN 55440. Tel: 612/671-2812. **B:** Jan. 28, 1943, Pease, Minn. **M:** Shirley A. Hubers, 1964. **C:** Stephanie, Lisa, Christa. **E:** U of MN, BSB Accounting, 1965; U of MN, MBA Finance, 1970. **Career Hist.:** Various positions, American Express Financial Advisors (formerly IDS Financial Services), 1965-present; Pres., CEO, 1993-2000; Chm., 2000-present. **Career Act.:** Dir., Carlson School of Mgmt., MN Business Partnership, Fairview Hospitals (including Chair, Fairview Hospitals Hum. Res. Ctee.), United Way; Board Mem. Investment Co. Institute (ICI); Board Mem. RTW Inc.; Executive Ctee. United Way. **Dec./Awd.:** CFA, Institute of Chartered

Financial Analysts, 1977; Outstanding Alumni Lifetime Achievement Award, Carlson School of Management, U of MN 1998. **Act./Mem.:** United Way, North Oaks Country Club, Whitefish Golf Club, Minneapolis Club; Spring Hill Golf Club.

Thomas G. Hudson Pres., CEO, Chair, Computer Network Technology Corp., 605 N. Highway 169, Plymouth, MN 55441. Tel: 612/797-6000. Email: tom_hudson@cnt.com **B:** Apr. 2, 1946, New York. **M:** Regina, 1968. **C:** Thomas, Matthew, Ann, Gina. **E:** BS-Electrical Engrg., Notre Dame, 1968; MBA-Finance, NYU, 1974; AMP, Harvard Grad School, 1990. **Career Hist.:** VP/Gen. Mgr.-Services Sector, IBM Corp., 1968-93; SVP/Gen. Mgr., McGraw-Hill, 1993-96; Pres./CEO, Computer Network Technology, 1996-present. **Career Act.:** Dir., CNT; past Dir., Seer Technologies, FTI Technologies. **Act./Mem.:** United Way Sponsor Exec., Minnetonka Country Club, Sorin Society (ND).

Russell Huffer Chair, Pres., CEO, Apogee Enterprises Inc., 7900 Xerxes Ave. S., Suite 1800, Bloomington, MN 55431. Tel: 612/835-1874. **B:** May 21, 1949, Greenville, Ohio. **M:** Margaret, 1971. **C:** Jill, Anne, Michael. **E:** USAF Academy, BS, 1971; Troy State U., MS, 1977. **Career Hist.:** USAF Captain, 1971-78; Guardian Industries, Manufacturing Mgr., 1980-86; Viracon, VP/GM, 1986-96; Glass Technologies, Pres., 1996-98; Apogee Enterprises Inc., Pres./CEO, 1998-present; Pres./CEO Chmn. 1999-present. **Career Act.:** Past Pres., SIGMA (Glass Industry) Assn.; Dir., Hutchinson Technology Inc. Member, Board of Advisors-University of St. Thomas Graduate School of Business. **Dec./Awd.:** Three Patents (U.S.) Thin Film Optical Coatings. **Act./Mem.:** Owatonna Youth Hockey Assn.

Margery G. Hughes Pres., COO, Allianz Life Insurance Co. of North America, 300 S. Highway 169, Suite 95, St. Louis Park, MN 55426. Tel: 612/546-7386. **C:** Alexis, 19. **E:** BA-Communications, U. of IA, 1971. **Career Hist.:** Communications Specialist, the Freshwater Fdn. (Navarre, MN), 1976-79; Independent Consultant, 1979-82 and 1984-87; Account Exec., VP, Padilla Speer Beardsley (Minneapolis), 1982-84 and 1987-90; EVP/COO, Life USA (now part of Allianz Life Insurance Co. of North America), 1990-96; Pres./COO, 1996-present. **Career Act.:** Bd. of Trustees, Washburn Child Guidance Center; has served: Leadership Mpls., The Playwright's Center, Minneapolis Society for the Blind, Washburn Child Guidance Center, Medical Alley, Mayoral Task Force on Children, Hmong Folk Art.

Shirley Hughes SVP-Hum. Res., Ceridian Corp., 3311 E. Old Shakopee Rd., Minneapolis, MN 55425. Tel: 612/853-8100. **B:** Dec. 6, 1945, Minneapolis. **E:** Coe College, BA, Political Science, 1967; U. of WI, Masters Program, Urban Affairs. **Career Hist.:** Control Data Corp., Admin.-Corporate Equal Opportunity Planning to Dir.-Hum. Res., Scientific Information Svs., 1969-87; Imprimis Inc., Dir.-Hum. Res. Programs/Data Storage Products to VP-Hum. Res., 1987-89; Seagate Technology, VP-Hum. Res., 1989-90; Ceridian Corp., VP-Hum. Res./Info. Svs., 1991-92; VP-Hum. Res., 1992-94; Mercy Health Svs., VP-Hum. Res., 1994-98; Ceridian Corp., SVP, Hum. Res., 1998-present. **Career Act.:** Dir., Natl. Assoc. of Manufacturers; Dir., Greater Minneapolis Convention and Visitors Association; Dir., Minnesota Dollars for Scholars; Dir., Big Brothers, Big Sisters of Greater Minneapolis; Dir., The Friends of the Minneapolis Public Library; Member, MN Women's Economic Roundtable. **Dec./Awd.:** Named One Of 100 Top Black Professional Women by Dollars And Sense Magazine, 1988. **Act./Mem.:** Dir./past Pres., The Friends Of The Minneapolis Public Library; Dir., Senior Resources (Minneapolis), Leadership Detroit, Mercy High School (Farmington Hills, MI); Partner, Cornerstone School (Detroit); Minneapolis Urban League.

Wayne R. Huneke SVP, ReliaStar Financial Corp., 20 Washington Ave. S., Minneapolis, MN 55401. Tel: 612/372-5432. **B:** Jun. 10, 1951, Council Bluffs, Iowa. **M:** Marilyn. **C:** Thomas, Sara. **E:** BBA-Accounting (with Distinction), U. of IA, 1973; Tuck Exec. Program, Dartmouth College, 1993. **Career Hist.:** Coopers and Lybrand (Mpls.), 1973-86: Staff Accountant, 1973-75; Senior Accountant, 1975-78; Audit Mgr., 1978-86; ReliaStar Financial Corp., 1986-present: Asst. VP, Asst. Cont., 1986-87; Asst. VP, Asst. Cont., Asst. Treas., 1987-89; 2VP, Treas., CAO, 1989-90; VP, Treas., CAO, 1990-94; SVP, CFO, Treas., 1994-1997, SVP 1997-99; SEVP, 1999 - present. **Career Act.:** CPA, 1974; Mem., American Institute of CPAs, 1975; Mem., MN Society of CPAs, 1975; Fellow, Life Mgmt. Institute (FLMI), 1978; Mem., ReliaStar Council, 1991; Dir., ReliaStar Life Insurance Co., 1995. **Act./Mem.:** Mem., American Council of Life Insurance-Ctee. on GAAP Fin. Reporting; Dir., Business Economics Education Fdn.; past Mem., AICPA Insurance Companies Ctee.; past Mem., New Agency Ctee., Monitoring Panel, United Way.

Richard R. Hylland Pres., COO, NorthWestern Corp., 125 S. Dakota Ave., Sioux Falls, SD 57104. **B:** May 14, 1960, Madison, S.D. **M:** Traci K. Hylland, 1985. **C:** Jamie, Matt. **E:** B.S., Accounting, U of S.D., 1982. **Career Hist.:** Mgr., Arthur Andersen & Co., 1987-89; Cont., NPS, 1989; Cont. and Asst. Treas., NPS, 1989-90; Cont. and Treas., NPS, 1990-91; VP-Fin. and Treas., NPS, 1991-93; VP-Fin./Corp. Devel./Treas., NPS, 1993-94; VP-Fin./Corp. Devel., NPS, 1994-95; VP-Strategic Devel, NPS, 1995; EVP-Strategic Devel., NPS, 1995-96; EVP, NPS, 1996-98; Pres. and COO, NGC, 1994-98; Pres. and COO, NOR, 1998-present; VChair, NGC, 1998-present. **Career Act.:** Dir., NorthWestern Corp., 1998-present; VChair, NorthWestern Growth Corp. 1998-present; VChair, NorthWestern Services; VChair, Blue Dot Services Inc.; VChair, Cornerstone Propane; VChair, Expanets Inc.; VChair, Grant Inc.; VChair, NorthWestern Networks Inc.; VChair, NorthWestern Systems Inc.; VChair, Syn, Inc.; Chair, Franklin Industries; Dir. LodgeNet Entertainment; Dir. MDC Communications. **Dec./Awd.:** Outstanding Senior of USD Business School, 1982. **Act./Mem.:** Mem., Young Presidents Organization; Financial Executives Institute; Edison Electric Institute; American Gas Assoc.; American Institute of CPAs; Colorado Society of CPAs; South Dakota Society of CPAs; United Way (Sioux Empire) Corporate Gifts Campaigner; Sioux Council Boy Scouts of America-Board of Trustees; Salvation Army-Trustee; Minnehaha Country Club.

David J. Hyslop Pres., Minnesota Orchestral Association, 1111 Nicollet Mall, Minneapolis, MN 55403. Tel: 612/371-5600. **B:** Jun. 27, 1942, Schenectady, N.Y. **M:** Sally Fefercorn. **C:** Alexander, Kristopher. **E:** Ithaca College, School of Music, Music Education degree, 1965. **Career Hist.:** Elementary and Vocal Music Supervisor of the Elmira Heights New York music system and Gen. Mgr. of the Elmira Symphony and Choral Society, 1965-66; Martha Baird Rockefeller grant awardee, 1966-67; Admin. Asst., Minnesota Orchestra, 1967-68; Assistant Managing Dir., Minnesota Orchestra, 1969-72; Gen. Mgr., Oregon Symphony Orchestra, 1972-78; Executive Dir., St. Louis Symphony Orchestra Society, 1978-89; Pres., St. Louis Symphony Society, 1989-91; Pres. of the Minnesota Orchestral Assn., 1991-present. **Career Act.:** Dir., American Symphony Orchestra League; Chair, Nominating Ctee., American Symphony Orchestra League; Mem., American Symphony Orchestra League Mgmt. Fellowship program ctee.; Honorary Advisory Council Member, Oregon Symphony 100th Anniversary; guest lecturer, U. of Cincinnati, U. of MN, Ithaca College; Mem., NEA Music Creation and Presentation Panel. **Dec./Awd.:** David J. Hyslop permanently endowed 3rd Trumpet Chair, St. Louis Symphony Orchestra, 1991. **Act./Mem.:** Minneapolis Club; Mem., Fine Arts and Library Committee.

Ann Rockler Jackson CEO, Rockler Cos. Inc., 4365 Willow Dr., Medina, MN 55340. Tel: 612/478-8201. **B:** Feb. 2, 1950, Minneapolis. **M:** Robert P. Jackson III. **C:** Elizabeth, Alex. **E:** U. of MN, BA; working on Master's Degree. **Career Hist.:** CEO, Rockler Cos. Inc., dba Rockler Woodworking and Hardware, publisher of Woodworker's Journal magazine.

Career Act.: Mem., Undergraduate Advisory Board-Carlson School of Mgmt., U. of MN; World Presidents Organization, Board of Trustees-MN Magazine Publishers Association. **Dec./Awd.:** Midwest Direct Mktg. Assn. Long Term Achievement Award, 1996. **Act./Mem.:** WPO, Ctee. of 200, NAWBO.

Eric H. Jackson SVP, The Scoular Co., Minnesota Building, Suite 1120, 46 E. Fourth St., St. Paul, MN 55101. **B:** Sep. 29, 1957, Cambridge, Mass. **M:** Jerilyn, 1985. **C:** Rachel, Alex. **E:** Bachelors in Agricultural Economics, U. of IL, 1983. **Career Hist.:** Pillsbury, 1983-88: trainee, mdser, senior trader, mgr. of mkt. development; IPC, 1988 to 1998: VP, SVP, Pres., CEO; The Scoular Co., 1998-2000 SVP. **Career Act.:** Dir., American Fats & Oils Assn.; member of numerous trade associations. **Act./Mem.:** National Advocate, U. of IL Fdn.; VP, St. Paul Lutheran Church (Stillwater, MN); Den Leader, Boy Scouts of America.

Irwin L. Jacobs Chair, Genmar Holdings Inc., 100 S. Fifth St., Suite 2400, Minneapolis, MN 55402. Tel: 612/339-7600. **B:** Jul. 15, 1941, Minneapolis. **M:** Alexandra, 1962. **Career Hist.:** Pres., Jacobs Management Corp.; Chair, Watkins Inc.; Chair, Genmar Industries Inc., Jacobs Trading Co., Genmar Holdings Inc.; Chair, Operation Bass Inc. **Career Act.:** Dir., Genmar Holdings Inc., IPI Inc., IMR General Inc. **Act./Mem.:** Minneapolis Club; Oak Ridge Country Club; Lafayette Club.

Mary Jacobus Pres., Publisher, Duluth News-Tribune, 424 W. First St., Duluth, MN 55816. Tel: 218/723-5240. Email: mjacobus@duluthnews.com **M:** Dean. **C:** Kelly, Kimberly, Bill. **E:** LeMoyne College (Syracuse, NY). **Career Hist.:** Long Beach Press-Telegram, Advertising/Circulation, 1981-89; Escondido Times Advocate, Sls./Mktg. Dir., 1989-95; Colorado Springs Gazette, VP-Sales/Mktg., 1995-98; Duluth News-Tribune, Pres./Publisher, 1998-present. **Act./Mem.:** Dir., Duluth Area Chamber Of Commerce, Duluth-Superior Symphony Orchestra.

Robert I. Janssen Principal Owner, Chair, CEO, Padco Inc., 2220 Elm St. S.E., Minneapolis, MN 55414. Tel: 612/378-7270. **B:** Jan. 30, 1921, St. Paul. **E:** U. of MN, 1946-47. **Career Hist.:** Industrial Engr., American Hoist and Derrick, 1947-52; Industrial Engr., Johnson Hydraulic Equipment, 1952-54; Industrial Engr. and Asst. to VP-Manufacturing, Gould National Batteries Inc., 1954-63; Founder, Chair, Pres., CEO, Plas-Tech Inc., 1963-65; Founder, Padco Cos. Inc. (Padco Inc., Padco Ltd., Padco Gmbh, Padco S.A., Padco San Jose S.A.) 1965-present. **Act./Mem.:** Mem., Toronto Curling, Cricket, and Figure Skating Club; Lieutenant Commander, Navy Supply Corps., U.S. Naval Reserve (retired); Founder of the National Paint-a-Thon Fdn.

Larry E. Jodsaas Chair, CEO, PolarFab, 2800 E. Old Shakopee Rd., Bloomington, MN 55425. Tel: 612/853-3179. **B:** May 11, 1935, Lisbon, N.D. **M:** Patricia, 1990. **C:** Sherry, Rick, Kimberly, Adam, Carmel, Con. **E:** U of ND, BSEE, 1962. **Career Hist.:** Control Data Corp., 1962-88, engineer to president, computer systems; VTC Inc. (now PolarFab), 1988-present, Chair, CEO. **Career Act.:** Dir., PolarFab, Paralon, Wells Fargo Bloomington, PeopleNet Inc., Normandale Fdn., the Minnesota-Dakotas Chapter of the Alzheimer's Assn. **Dec./Awd.:** Special Achievement Award, MN High Technology Council, 1997. **Act./Mem.:** United Way, Bearpath.

Eldon Johnson Pres., CEO, Dakota Electric Association, 4300 220th St. W., Farmington, MN 55024. Tel: 651/463-7134. **B:** May 3, 1943, Thief River Falls, Minn. **M:** Penny, 1964. **C:** Lana (dec.), Troy. **E:** Electrical Technology, North Dakota State College of Science, 1964. **Career Hist.:** Dakota Electric Assn. (30 yrs.): Engineering, 18 yrs.; Asst. Gen. Mgr., 3 yrs.; Pres./CEO, 9 yrs. **Career Act.:** Chair, Dakota Energy Alternatives Inc.; Chair-Manager Advisory Ctee., Cooperative Power; Mem., Statewide Competition Planning Ctee., IEEE; past Mem. (9 yrs.), Eagan (MN) Economic Devel. Commission; various regional and national task forces. **Act./Mem.:** Chamber of Commerce, Mount Calvary Lutheran Church, St. Paul Area United Way; Travis Tritt's Country Club.

Jerry E. Johnson Pres., CEO, DataCard Group, 11111 Bren Rd. W., Minnetonka, MN 55343. Tel: 612/933-1223. **B:** Jun. 8, 1956, Moorhead, Minn. **M:** Vicky, 1976. **C:** Russ, Derek, Tracy, Amy. **E:** BSEE (Cum Laude), U. of ND; MBA-Management, Stanford U. (Sloan Program). **Career Hist.:** Prior to 1986: Universal Electric, now owned by Magnetek; and Brown-Boveri Corp., now Asea Brown Boveri, a Swiss company specializing in power generation products worldwide; Onan, 1986-99: progressively responsible positions ending as VP and Gen. Mgr.; Pres., CEO, DataCard Group, June 1999-present. **Career Act.:** Mem.-Engrg. Advisory Council, U. of ND. **Dec./Awd.:** Bush Fellowship Award, 1988. **Act./Mem.:** United Way, Junior Achievement.

Joel W. Johnson Chair, Pres., CEO, Hormel Foods Corp., One Hormel Place, Austin, MN 55912. Tel: 507/437-5219. **B:** Jul. 14, 1943, Staten Island, N.Y. **M:** Elizabeth Bates, 1967. **C:** Katherine, Geoffrey, Peter. **E:** Hamilton College, BA-Economics, 1965; Harvard U., MBA, 1967. **Career Hist.:** Sls., General Foods, 1967-68; Captain, U.S. Army, 1968-71; various positions, General Foods, 1971-86: Asst. Product Mgr.-Log Cabin, 1971; Assoc. Product Mgr.-Log Cabin, 1971-73; Product Mgr.-Tang, 1973; Sr. Product Mgr.-Tang, 1973-76; Product Grp. Mgr.-Maxwell House, 1976-78; Mgr. Strategic Planning, 1978-79; Catagory Mgr., 1979-83; Mktg. & Devel. Mgr.-Maxwell House Brand and Div., 1983-86. Various positions, Oscar Mayer (subsid. of General Foods), 1986-91: VP-Consumer Products Div., 1986; SVP-Mktg. and Mktg. & Sls., 1986-90; EVP, Mktg. & Sls., 1990-91; EVP & Gen. Mgr., Oscar Mayer Foods and all subsidiaries, 1991. Hormel, 1991-present: EVP-Sls. & Mktg., 1991; Pres., 1992-93; COO, 1993; CEO, 1993-present; Chair, 1995-present. **Career Act.:** Dir., Hormel Foods Corp., The Hormel Fdn., American Meat Institute, Ecolab Inc., Grocery Manufacturers of America, Hamilton College, Meredith Corp.; Mem., Carlson School of Mgmt. Board of Overseers. **Dec./Awd.:** Bronze Star, Vietnam, 1969. **Act./Mem.:** Austin Rotary Club, Austin Country Club.

WHO

John D. Johnson Pres., CEO, Cenex Harvest States Cooperatives, 5500 Cenex Dr., Inver Grove Heights, MN 55077. Tel: 651/646-9433. **B:** Rhame, N.D. **M:** Shirley. **E:** Black Hills State U., BA, 1970. **Career Hist.:** Harvest States Cooperatives, 1976-present: feed consultant-GTA Feeds Div., Regional Sls. Mgr., Dir.-Sls./Mktg., Gen. Mgr., Group VP-Farm Mktg./Supply, Pres. and CEO, 1995-98; Pres., Gen. Mgr., CEO, Cenex Harvest States Cooperatives, 1998-present. **Career Act.:** Chair, National Council Farmers Cooperatives (NCFC) Trade and Credit Ctee., Ventura Foods; Dir. NCFC; Advisory Board, International Trade, Co-Bank; Board Mem., Sparta Foods and United Harvest. **Dec./Awd.:** Distinguished Alumni, Black Hill State U., 1996. **Act./Mem.:** Dellwood Hills Country Club; Council Member, St. Andrews Lutheran Church.

Lloyd P. Johnson retired Chair, Wells Fargo & Co., 4900 IDS Center, 800 S. Eighth St., Minneapolis, MN 55479. Tel: 612/667-0033. **B:** May 1, 1930, Minneapolis. **M:** Rosalind Gesner, 1954. **C:** Russell L., Marcia J. (Campbell), Paul C.. **E:** Carleton College, BA, 1952; Stanford Graduate School of Business, MBA, 1954. **Career Hist.:** Security Pacific National Bank, 1956-84: Trainee, 1956-57; Regional VP, San Diego Div.; Regional VP-Western Region, 1964-67; EVP, Chief Admin.-Central and Northern CA, 1972-76; EVP, Mem.-Mgmt. Ctee., 1976-78; VChair.-Bank/Corp., Mem.-Chief Exec. Office, 1978-84; Chair, Pres., CEO, Norwest Corp., 1985-88; Chair, CEO, 1989-93; Chair, 1993-1995. **Career Act.:** Dir., Wells Fargo & Co., Cargill Inc., Musicland Stores Corp., The Valmont Cos.; Trustee, Minneapolis Institute of Arts; VChair-Board of Trustees, Carleton College; Member Emeritus, U. of MN Curtis L. Carlson School of Mgmt. Board of Overseers; Trustee, Minnesota Mutual Life Insurance Co.; Mem.-Advisory Board, Minnegasco. **Dec./Awd.:** Executive of the Year, Corporate Report Minnesota, 1991. **Act./Mem.:** Minneapolis Club, Woodhill Country Club.

S.A. (Tony) Johnson Pres., CEO, Hidden Creek Industries, 4508 IDS Center, Minneapolis, MN 55402. Tel: 612/332-2335. **B:** May 14, 1940, Bremerton, Wash. **M:** Carolyn, 1968. **C:** Marni, Ron. **E:** U. of WA, BSME, 1962; Stanford U., MBA, 1964. **Career Hist.:** Cummins Engine Company: Field Sls. Rep., Automotive Sls. Mgr., Dir.-Mkt. Support, Div. Mgr.-West, VP/Gen. Mgr.-Cummins Asia Pacific, VP-Automotive Mktg., VP-North American Bus., 1964-81; Pres., CEO, Onan Corp., 1981-85; Pentair Inc.: EVP, COO, 1985-86; Pres., COO, 1986-89; Pres., CEO, Hidden Creek Industries, 1989-present. **Career Act.:** Manufacturers Alliance; Chair, Dura Automotive Systems Inc., Chair, Tower Automotive Inc.; Chair, J.L. French Automotive Castings; Chair, Heavy Duty Holdings; Chair, Automotive Performance Industries; Chair, Saleen Performance Inc.; Mem.-Stanford GSB Board of Advisors. **Act./Mem.:** Mem., Lafayette Club, Minneapolis Club; Dir., Jr. Achievement of the Upper Midwest.

James W. Jungels Chair, Pres., CEO, Polar Corp., 1015 W. Saint Germain St., Suite 420, St. Cloud, MN 56301. Tel: 320/746-2255. Email: polarcorp@cloudnet.com **B:** 1941, Cold Spring, Minn. **M:** Sharon, 1962. **C:** Sherry and Julie. **Career Hist.:** Cold Spring Granite Co.; Polar Corp., 1978-present. **Career Act.:** Chair, Dir., Tank Conference of Truck Trailer Manufacturers Assn.

Donald F. Kajans COO, Little Six Inc., 2400 Mystic Lake Blvd., Prior Lake, MN 55372. Tel: 612/445-9000. **E:** U. of AZ; CPA. **Career Hist.:** Cont., Caesar's Casino Hotel (Reno, NV); CFO, VP, Peppermill Casino Hotel (Reno, NV); COO, Little Six Inc. (dba Mystic Lake Casino Hotel).

Ervin F. Kamm Jr. Pres., CEO, Paper, Calmenson & Co., Highways 280 and 36, P.O. Box 64432 (55164), Roseville, MN 55113. **B:** Oct. 28, 1939, Superior, Wis. **M:** Jenny, 1962. **C:** Ken, Kris, Kerri. **E:** U.S. Military Academy-West Point, BS-Engrg. Science, 1962. **Career Hist.:** Dir.-Military Programs, Control Data, 1970-74; Pres., CEO, Delano Granite Inc., 1974-76; COO, Van Dale Inc., 1976-79; Pres., CEO, Despatch Industries, 1979-84; Pres., CEO, Gate City Steel, 1984-85; Pres., CEO, Plato Wicat Systems, 1985-87; Pres., COO, Norstan Inc., 1988-95; Pres., CEO, Digi International, 1995-97; Zytec (Artesyn Technologies): Pres.-Zytec Power Conversion, 1997; Pres. and COO, 1997-98; Pres., CEO, Paper, Calmenson & Co., 1999-present. **Career Act.:** Dir., Micromedics Inc., The Fortunate Fdn., Walker Methodist Foundation, Northland College, BridgeCom. **Dec./Awd.:** U.S. Army: Bronze Star, Meritorious Service Medal, Air Medal, Army Commendation Medal, Purple Heart, 1962-70. **Act./Mem.:** Wayzata Country Club; MN Executive Assn.; World's Presidents Organization.

Elliot S. Kaplan Ptnr., Robins, Kaplan, Miller & Ciresi LLP, 2800 LaSalle Plaza, 800 LaSalle Ave., Minneapolis, MN 55402. Tel: 612/349-8500. **B:** Nov. 28, 1936, St. Paul. **M:** Eloise, 1986. **C:** Jane Kirshbaum, Cindy Kaplan, Peter Kaplan, Jed Stillman, Scott Stillman. **E:** BA, U. of MN School of Business Admin., 1957; JD, U. of MN Law School, also 1961. **Career Hist.:** Ptnr., Chair-Executive Board (1987-95), Robins, Kaplan, Miller & Ciresi. **Career Act.:** Dir., Best Buy Co., inforUSA Inc., Franklin Corp., Past President and member of Board of Trustees Temple Israel, St. Paul Chamber Orchestra, Oak Park Home for Children (Pres., 1973-75), Union of American Hebrew Congregations, Board of Directors Minneapolis Institute of Arts, Chairman of U. of M Law School/Capital Campaign, Co-Chair of Minneapolis Federation for Jewish Service Capital Campaign. **Dec./Awd.:** Best Lawyer in America (1985-2000); Best Lawyers in Minnesota. **Act./Mem.:** Mpls. Club, Colliers Reserve Country Club, United Way, Mpls. Art Institute, Walker Art Center, KTCA, other civic organizations.

David B. Kaysen Pres., CEO, Rehabilicare Inc., 1811 Old Highway 8, New Brighton, MN 55112. Tel: 651/631-0590. Email: davek@rehabilicare.com **B:** Aug. 20, 1949, St. Paul. **M:** Nancy, 1971. **C:** Sean, Gavin. **E:** U. of MN, BS Science/Business Admin., 1972. **Career Hist.:** American Hospital Supply, 1974-86; VP-Mktg., Redline Healthcare, 1986-88; Pres., CEO, Surgidyne, 1988-89; VP-Sls./Mktg., Lectec, 1989-90; VP-Emeritus, Lectec, 1990-92; Pres., CEO, Rehabilicare, 1992-present. **Career Act.:** Dir., Rehabilicare Inc., Surgidyne Inc., CFR Corp.

Michael F. Kelly Managing Dir., Madison Marquette Realty Services Ltd., 11100 Wayzata Blvd., Minnetonka, MN 55305. Tel: 612/333-6515. **B:** Oct. 10, 1930, Cloquet, Minn. **M:** Peggy, 1957. **C:** Michele (Herring), Michael Jr., Mary Anne (Loncar). **E:** U. of Notre Dame, BS-Fin., 1952; U. of MI Law School, LLB, 1957. **Career Hist.:** Atty., Allied Prod. Corp. (Detroit, MI), 1957-58; Atty., The J.L. Hudson Company (Detroit, MI), 1958-65; Mgr.-R.E. and Ins., Asst. Gen. Counsel, The J.L. Hudson Company, 1966-68; Dir.-R.E., Asst. Sec., The J.L. Hudson Company, 1968-69; VP-R.E. (Southfield, MI), The J.L. Hudson Company, 1969-71; VP-Devel., Dayton Hudson Properties, 1971-72; SVP-R.E. and Construction, Dayton Hudson Properties, 1972-75; SVP-Op./Devel., Dayton Hudson Properties, 1975-77; Pres., Dayton Hudson Properties, 1977-80; Pres., Principal, The Center Companies, 1980-89; Chair, Principal, TCC Properties Group, Inc. 1989-90; Chair, Principal, Marquette Partners Inc., 1990-94; Managing Dir., Madison Marquette Realty Services, 1995-present. **Career Act.:** past Pres., Civitan Club (Detroit); past Pres., past Trustee, Urban Land Institute; past Trustee, ICSC; Mem., Bar Assn. (MN, MI, Detroit, Hennepin County); Pres., Edina Foundation; Mem., Real Estate Bd. (MI, Detroit). **Act./Mem.:** Interlachen Country Club; Minneapolis Club; Rotary Club (Minneapolis); United Way; Captiva Island Yacht Club (Florida); Edina Fdn.

David Kidwell Dean, Carlson School of Management, University of Minnesota, 271 19th Ave. S., Room 230, Mgmt./Econ. Bldg., Minneapolis, MN 55455. Tel: 612/625-9336. Email: dkidwell@csom.umn.edu **B:** Nov. 24, 1940, Eugene, Ore. **M:** Jillinda, 1987. **E:** B.S.E., California State U. at San Diego, 1964; M.B.A., California State U. at San Diego, 1970; Ph.D., U. of Oregon, 1975. **Career Hist.:** Construction Sls. Engr., Bethlehem Steel Corp., 1964-68; Consulting staff, Coopers & Lybrand, 1970-71; Asst. Prof. of Mgmt., Purdue U., 1974-79; Chair of Mgmt., Texas Tech U. College of Business Admin., 1979-81; Prof of Fin., U. of Tennessee College of Business Admin., 1981-85; Prof. of Banking, Tulane U., 1985-88; Dean and Prof., U. of Conn. School of Business Admin., 1988-91; Dean and Prof., U. of MN, 1991-present. **Career Act.:** Chair, President's Ctee. to Evaluate Performance of SVP for Fin. and Op., 1994; Mem., Pres. Outreach Council, 1992-98; Chair, University Community Campaign Drive, 1993-94; Mem., East Asia Strategy Ctee., 1995-98; Mem., RCM Steering Ctee., 1996-98; Mem., EVP and Provost's Advisory Ctee., 1998-present; Mem., Pres. Ctee. of the University of Minn. Fdn. **Dec./Awd.:** Pres., Beta Gamma Sigma, National Business Academic Honor Society, Calif. State U., 1969-70; Ayers Fellow, Stonier Graduate School of Banking, American Banker's Assn., 1976; Alumni Fdn. Outstanding Undergraduate Teaching Award, Krannert Graduate School of Mgmt., Purdue U., 1978; Teacher of Honor Roll, A.B. Freeman School of Business, 1985, 1986, 1987; Dir., Eastern Fin. Assn., 1987-90; Best Article of the Year, U. of Conn., 1991. **Act./Mem.:** Dir., Schwan's Sls. Enterprises, 1999-present; Sec. and Treas., Internal Assn. for Mgmt. Education, 1999-present; Trustee, Minn. Life Insurance Co., 1994-present; Advisory Bd. of Dir., Minnegasco, 1992-99; Bd. of Advisors, Stonier Graduate School of Banking, 1989-present.

Robert A. Kierlin Chair, Pres., Fastenal Co., 2001 Theurer Blvd., P.O. Box 978, Winona, MN 55987. Tel: 507/454-5374. **B:** Jun. 1, 1939, Winona, Minn. **M:** Mary Burrichter. **C:** Lara, Monique. **E:** Graduated from Winona Cotter High School in the late 1950s, as did the other founders. U. of MN, Bachelor of Mechanical Engrg., 1962; MBA, 1964. **Career Hist.:** Peace Corps Volunteer, 2 yrs; IBM-Rochester, 7 yrs. **Career Act.:** Dir., Fastenal Co.; Mem., Minnesota State Senate. **Act./Mem.:** Dir., Cotter High School, Cotter Schools Inc., Hiawatha Education Fdn., Vanguard Technologies.

Barbara A. King Pres., Landscape Structures Inc., 601 Seventh St. S., Delano, MN 55328. Tel: 612/972-3391. **M:** Steven. **E:** BS, IA State U., 1968. **Career Hist.:** Food Stylist, The Pillsbury Co., 1968-71 and Barbara Thornton Associates, 1971-73; Landscape Structures Inc., 1973-present. **Career Act.:** Chair, Volunteers of America; Dir., MN Safety Council; Pres., MN Chapter-Natl. Assn. of Women Business Owners (NAWBO); Trustee, Northwestern Mutual Life Insurance. **Dec./Awd.:** Entrepreneur of the Year, 1992; Blue Chip Incentive, 1993; Outstanding Business Woman of the Year, Athena Fdn., 1993; Small Business Person of the Year (MN and Region), 1994; MN Woman Business Owner of the Year, Nat'l Assn. of Woman Business Owners, 2000.

Reatha Clark King VP-General Mills Inc.; Exec. Dir.-General Mills Fdn., General Mills Inc., One General Mills Blvd., P.O. Box 1113 (55440), Golden Valley, MN 55426. Tel: 612/540-7890. **B:** Apr. 11, 1938, Pavo, Ga. **M:** Dr. N. Judge King, 1961. **C:** N. Judge III, M.D.; Scott. **E:** BS-Chemistry/Math, Clark College (Atlanta); Master's and Doctorate in Chemistry, U. of Chicago; MBA, Columbia U. **Career Hist.:** Research Chemist, National Bureau of Standards (Washington, D.C.); Prof. of Chemistry, Assoc. Dean, York College/City U. of New York; Pres., Metropolitan State U., (Twin Cities), 11 years; General Mills: Pres./Exec. Dir.-General Mills Fdn., 1988-present. **Career Act.:** Bds: Council on Fdns., Exxon Mobil Corp., MN Mutual Life Insurance Co., H.B. Fuller Co., Wells Fargo & Co.; Clark Atlanta University Dir.; Mem., Exec. Leadership Council (Washington, D.C.); Delegate, 1997 President's Summit for America's Future; Mem.-Advisory Ctee. for Gov. Jesse Ventura; University of Chicago Life Trustee; Delta Sigma Theta Sorority; Links, Inc. **Dec./Awd.:** King has received numerous honors and awards, including 13 honorary doctorate degrees. She is well known as a pioneer in social change and an outstanding leader in the fields of education, business, and philanthropy.

Thomas W. Kingston Pres., Amherst H. Wilder Foundation, 919 Lafond Ave., St. Paul, MN 55104. Tel: 651/642-4000. **B:** Apr. 1, 1945, Stevens Point, Wis. **M:** Mary, 1979. **E:** St. Mary's College, BA; U. of St. Thomas, Masters in Teaching; U. of MN, MBA, 1983. **Career Hist.:** Cretin High School, Teacher, 1967-70; New Connection Programs, Co-founder and CEO, 1970-80; Wilder Fdn.: Special Asst. to the Pres., 1980; SVP-Direct Care Svs., 1985; Pres., CEO, 1990-present. **Career Act.:** MN Fdn., the Forum for Nonprofit Leadership, Saint Paul Tomorrow, Twin Cities Family Housing Fund, Model Cities, Saint Paul Chamber of Commerce (Executive Board), Neighborhood Devel. Center, Capital City Partnership, St. Paul-Ramsey County Children's Initiative, The Minnesota Fdn., President's Advisory Council for Common Bond Communities.

Arlen T. Kitsis Pres., CEO, Shari Candies Inc., 5780 Lincoln Dr., Suite 124, Edina, MN 55436. Tel: 612/935-2266. **B:** Jan. 16, 1935, Mankato, Minn. **M:** Tybelle Scherling, 1956. **C:** Steven, Mindy, Edward. **E:** A.A., U. of MN, 1956. **Career Hist.:** Shari Candies Inc., 1956-present: VP-Sls., 1956-66; EVP, 1966-76; Owner/Pres., 1984-present; Pres.-Confectionery Div., CFS Continental (Chicago), 1976-84. **Career Act.:** Past Bus. Chair Chapter American Cancer Society; past Mem.-Exec. Ctee., City of Hope; Mem., Mankato Chamber of Commerce, National Candy Wholesalers Assn. **Dec./Awd.:** Golter Award, City of Hope, 1976; U. of MN, College of Liberal Arts, Alumnus of Notable Achievement, 1997. **Act./Mem.:** Past Trustee, B'nai Emet Synagogue; Mem., Golden Valley Country Club, Oak Ridge Country Club (Mpls.), B'nai B'rith (past Pres), Shriners.

Robert C. Klas Sr. Chair, TapeMark Co., 150 E. Marie Ave., West St. Paul, MN 55118. Tel: 651/455-1611. **B:** Feb. 26, 1928, Wabasha, Minn. **M:** Alexandra Boardman, 1950. **C:** Frances, Margaret, Robert, Elizabeth, Thomas, Christine. **E:** Hamline U., BA, 1952. **Career Hist.:** TapeMark Company, 1952-present; Chair, WTC Industries Inc., 1995, Chair, CEO, 1996-present. **Career Act.:** . **Dec./Awd.:** MN Small Businessman of the Year, 1967; St. Paul Small Business Person of the Year, 1987. **Act./Mem.:** Southview Country Club; Dir., TapeMark Charity Pro-Am; Hamline U. Distinguished Achievement Alumnus, 1990.

William H. Kling Pres., Minnesota Public Radio Inc., 45 E. Seventh St., St. Paul, MN 55101. Tel: 651/290-1500. **E:** St. John's U., B.A. Economics, 1964; Boston U., post graduate study, 1964-66. **Career Hist.:** Greenspring Co. (a for-profit company) and Minnesota Public Radio (a non-profit company) share a common parent, Minnesota Communications Group (a nonprofit parent support organization). Greenspring has two operating subsidiaries: Minnesota Monthly Publications, and The MNN Radio Networks. Kling is Pres. and CEO of Greenspring, and Chair of each of the operating subsidiaries. Kling is also Pres. of Minnesota Public Radio, which also owns the nonprofit Fitzgerald Theater Co. **Career Act.:** Dir., Greenspring Co., The St. Paul Cos. Inc., Irwin Financial (Columbus, IN), and several fund boards of the Capital Group American Funds mutual-funds family.

Richard L. Knowlton Chair, The Hormel Foundation, 301 N. Main St., Austin, MN 55912. Tel: 507/437-5357. **B:** Jun. 9, 1932, Austin, Minn. **M:** Nancy, 1954. **C:** Scott, Kimberly, Claudia, David, Julie. **E:** U. of CO, BA 1954. **Career Hist.:** Hormel Foods Corp., 1948-1995: Laborer, summer work, 1948; Sls., 1951; Slsmn., 1954; Merchandise Mgr., 1956-59; Sls. Mgr.-Midwest Div., 1959-64; Sls. Mgr.-Austin Plant, 1964-67; Gen. Sls. Mgr., 1967-69; Gen. Mgr.-Austin Plant, 1969-74; VP-Op., 1974-75; GVP-Op., 1975-79; Pres., COO, 1979-81; Chair, Pres., CEO, 1981-92; Chair, CEO, 1992-93; Chair, 1993-1995. **Career Act.:** Dir., The Hormel Fdn. (Chair), First Bank Austin (1979-93), American Meat Institute (past Chair), ReliaStar, formerly Northwestern National Life Insurance Company (1988-present), Perth Corp. (1996-present), Mayo Fdn. (1988-present), Austin YMCA, Rotary Club (member), U. of CO Fdn. (1989-present), MN Business Partnership, Grocery Manufacturers of America (1991-94), First Bank System (1992-1999), Supervalu Inc. (1995-present), Horatio Alger Assn., (1995-present) Pres. and CEO (April 1998). **Dec./Awd.:** Outstanding Crisis Manager of the Year, Carnegie-Mellon, 1987; Hall of Fame, U. of CO, 1989; William H. Albers Award, Food Marketing Institute, 1989; Man of Achievement Award, Anti-Defamation League, 1990; Honorary American FFA Degree, FAA, 1991; Honorary Mem., Mayo Alumni Assn., Horatio Alger Award, 1992, elected Pres. and CEO 1998; Distinguished Business Service Award, U. of CO, College of Business, 1995; Herbert Hoover Award, National Assoc. of Wholesale Grocers, 1994; Wall Street Transcript named Outstanding CEO Food Processing and Commodity categories seven times, 1986-1993. **Act./Mem.:** Crane Chapel; Masons; Rotary; YMCA; Austin Country Club; Vintage Club.

David A. Koch Chair, Graco Inc., 88 11th Ave. N.E., Minneapolis, MN 55413. Tel: 612/623-6600. **B:** Jun. 17, 1930, Boston. **M:** Barbara, 1956. **C:** Leil, C. Kaylin, Elizabeth Ann, Stephen D.. **E:** U. of Notre Dame; College of St. Thomas, BA. **Career Hist.:** Investment Counselor, Kalman & Co., 1954-56; Graco Inc., 1956-present: various capacities, 1956-62; Pres., CEO, 1962-84; Chair, CEO, 1984-95; Chair, 1996-present. **Career Act.:** Dir., SurModics Corp., MN Center for Corporate Responsibility, Center of the American Experiment; Trustee, U. of St. Thomas; Exec. Council, MN Historical Society. **Dec./Awd.:** Uncommon Citizen Award, Greater Minneapolis Chamber of Commerce, 1986; Distinguished Service Award, United Way, 1982; Outstanding Philanthropist of the Year, MN Chapter of National Society of Fund Raising Excellence, 1982; Distinguished Alumnus Award, College of St. Thomas, 1981; Distinguished Corporate Citizen, MN Center for Corporate Responsibility, 1997. **Act./Mem.:** Junior Achievement of the Upper Midwest.

Judi Koch Pres., A-Plus Demonstrations Inc., 970 Raymond Ave., G50, St. Paul, MN 55114. Tel: 651/645-1358. Email: APlusDemos@aol.com **B:** Mar. 5, 1937, Red Wing, Minn. **M:** Arthur, 1957. **C:** Kimberly, David. **E:** U. of MN. **Career Hist.:** Mktg. Rep., Greetings Unltd., 1970-75; Pres., A-Plus Demonstrations, 1975-present. **Career Act.:** Past mem., Advisory Bd., First Bank Minneapolis-St. Anthony Falls Branch; Donaldson's St. Paul Advisory Comm.; Dir., National Association Demonstration Co., Children's Cancer Research Fund. **Act./Mem.:** Southview Country Club; Children's Hospital Assn. of St. Paul; Children's Cancer Research Fund; United Way; Indianhead Council Boy Scouts of America; Dir., FMSA.

Dean C. Kopperud CEO, Fortis Financial Group, 500 Bielenberg Dr., Woodbury, MN 55125. Tel: 651/738-4251. **E:** U. of St. Thomas, 1977. **Career Hist.:** Paine Webber, Northwestern National Life, Integrated Resources, Fortis.

Donald L. Kotula Pres., CEO, Northern Tool & Equipment Co., 2800 Southcross Dr. W., P.O. Box 1219, Burnsville, MN 55337. Tel: 612/894-9510. Email: donk@northern-online.com **B:** Oct. 1, 1945, Hibbing, Minn. **M:** Judy, 1991. **C:** Ryan, Wade, Josie. **E:** UMD, Business & Fin., 1969. **Career Hist.:** Accountant, Montgomery Wards, 1970-71; Accountant and Budget Analyst, NWA Inc., 1972-74; General Accounting, Control Data, 1974-75; Heavy equipment sls. and purch., Ziegler, 1975-80; Pres., CEO, Northern Hydraulics Inc. (now Northern Tool & Equipment Co.), 1980-present. **Dec./Awd.:** Nomination for Small Business of the Year, Burnsville 1986; Sponsor YMCA; Business Person of the Year, Bursnville Chamber, 1996. **Act./Mem.:** Burnsville Chamber of Commerce; Greater MN Chamber of Commerce.

Calvin S. Krupa Chair, Pres., CEO, Ultra Pac Inc., 21925 Industrial Blvd., Rogers, MN 55374. Tel: 612/428-8340. **B:** Feb. 20, 1947, Little Falls, Minn. **M:** Nancy, 1972. **C:** Jenny, Katie. **E:** U of MN, Agribusiness, 1968. **Career Hist.:** Traffic Mgr., Pillsbury Company; Pres., Custom Thermoform, 1974-84; VP-Mktg., Innovation Plastics, 1984-87; Pres., CEO, Ultra Pac Inc., 1987-present. **Career Act.:** Chamber of Commerce, SPI. **Dec./Awd.:** Finalist, Emerging Growth Entrepreneur, 1991; Winner, Emerging Growth Entrepreneur, 1992; Governors Award for Entrepreneurs, 1992. **Act./Mem.:** Rogers Chamber of Commerce; S.P.I.

William G. Kuban Pres., Kurt Manufacturing Co., 5280 Main St. N.E., Fridley, MN 55421. Tel: 612/572-1500. **B:** 1930. **Career Hist.:** Kurt Manufacturing Company, 1953-present.

John M. Kucharik Pres., CEO, Chart Applied Technologies, 3505 County Rd. 42, Burnsville, MN 55306. Tel: 612/882-5000. Email: jkucharik@mve-inc.com **B:** Apr. 28, 1950. **M:** Gail (Papa) Kucharik, 1994. **C:** Arran, Caitlin. **E:** Colgate U., BA-Liberal Arts, 1972. **Career Hist.:** Tioga Casting Facilities, Asst. to VP-Op., 1973-79; Ingersoll-Rand Co., Plant Mgr., 1979-82; Gleason Corp., Foundry Div. Mgr., 1982-84, Dir.-Machine Shop Op., 1984-86, Dir., Gen. Mgr., 1986-89, VP-Mfg., 1989-90; ENBI Corp., Pres./CEO, 1990-93; Alliance Metal Stamping, VP/Gen. Mgr., 1993; General Signal Corp., VP/Gen. Mgr., 1993-95, Pres., 1995-97; MVE Holdings Inc. (now Chart Applied Technologies), Pres./CEO, 1997-present. **Career Act.:** Board of Govenors, Compressed Gas Assn.; Dir., Hydraulic Institute. **Act./Mem.:** United Way (Rochester, NY).

Hart Kuller Pres., Winthrop & Weinstine P.A., 3200 Minn. World Trade Center, 30 E. Seventh St., St. Paul, MN 55101. Tel: 651/290-8400. Email: hk@email.winthrop.com **B:** Dec. 5, 1951, St. Paul. **M:** Susan, 1973. **C:** two. **E:** Northwestern U., BA-Econ., 1973; U. of MN Law School, JD, 1976. **Act./Mem.:** Mem., Board of Dir., Science Museum of Minnesota; Mem., Board of Dir., Common Bond Communities.

Myron D. Kunin Chair, Regis Corp., 7201 Metro Blvd., Edina, MN 55439. Tel: 612/947-7000. **B:** Sep. 29, 1928, Minneapolis. **M:** Anita, 1951. **C:** Timothy, William, David, Andrew. **E:** U. of MN, BA, 1949. **Career Hist.:** Regis Corp., 1950-present: Dir., 1954-present; VP, 1954-65; Pres., 1965-87; Chair, CEO, 1983-95; Chair, 1995-present. **Career Act.:** Dir., Nortech Systems Inc., 1990-present; Regis Corp., Minneapolis Institute of Arts (Accessions and other ctees.). **Act./Mem.:** Past Chair of the Board of Trustees and Life Trustee of the Minneapolis Institute of Arts. Member of the Accessions Ctee. of the Minneapolis Institute of Arts; Paintings Council, Decorative Arts Council.

William La Macchia Jr. Pres., CEO, Sun Country Airlines, 2520 Pilot Knob Rd., Suite 250, Mendota Heights, MN 55120. Tel: 651/681-3928. Email: blamacchiajr@suncountry.com **B:** May 6, 1966, Kenosha, Wis. **E:** B.S., Business Admin., Marquette U., 1988. **Career Hist.:** Asst. Dir. Leisure Mktg., The Mirage Casino-Hotel, 1990-91; Dir., Hotel Sls. and Mktg., Golden Nugget Hotel & Casino, 1991-97; Pres. and CEO, Sun Country Airlines, 1997-present. **Act./Mem.:** Board Mem., MacCall Youth Fdn., Las Vegas, N.V.

John J. Labosky Pres., CEO, Capital City Partnership, 2490 Minnesota World Trade Ctr, 30 E. Seventh St., St. Paul, MN 55101. Tel: 651/291-5600. Email: ccp@usinternet.com **B:** Aug. 24, 1948, Johnstown, Pa. **M:** Julie J. Labosky, 1992. **C:** Jason, Joseph, Andrew, Daniel, Megan. **E:** Penn State U., BS-Architectural Engrg., 1971; Oxford U. (England, U.K.), Legal Studies in Residence, 1977; U. of Detroit/School of Law, Juris Doctor, 1978. **Career Hist.:** U.S. Army Corps of Engrs., Captain, Smith, Hinchman & Grylls (Detroit, MI), 1972-82: Project Designer, Project Mgr., Div. Discipline Head, Assoc.; Ellerbe Becket Inc. (Minneapolis), 1982-88: VP, Studio Dir., SVP, Div. Dir., Pres., CEO; Minneapolis Downtown Council, 1988-96: Pres., CEO; Capital City Partnership, 1996-present, Pres., CEO. **Career Act.:** Dir., Metropolitan Economic Devel. Assn., Public Art/St. Paul, Capital River Council, Presbyterian Homes Fdn.; Capital City Partnership. **Dec./Awd.:** Distinguished ROTC Military Grad., 1971; Michigan Society of Prof. Engrs., Young Engineer of the Year Award, 1980; PA State U., Outstanding Engrg. Alumnus Award, 1986; Registered Professional Architectural Engr. 1976; Admitted to Michigan and Federal Bar in 1978. **Act./Mem.:** Minneapolis Club, Interlachen Country Club, NSPE, NSAE, ABA.

Frederick W. Lang Chair, CEO, Analysts International Corp., 7615 Metro Blvd., Edina, MN 55435. Tel: 612/835-2330. **B:** Sep. 26, 1924, Minneapolis. **M:** Katherine Frost, 1957. **C:** Frederick C., Katherine. **E:** U. of MN, BSEE, BBA. **Career Hist.:** Joined Engrg. Research Assoc. in 1952; helped develop the FAA's air traffic control system while at the Univac division of Remington Rand Corp.; Founder, Chair, and CEO of Analysts International Corp. since 1966. **Career Act.:** Dir., Analysts International Corp. **Act./Mem.:** Lafayette Country Club, Audubon Country Club.

Joseph E. Laptewicz Jr. Chair and CEO, Empi Inc., 599 Cardigan Rd., St. Paul, MN 55126. Tel: 651/415-7451. **B:** Mar. 20, 1949, Hudson, Mass. **M:** Maria, 1970. **E:** Worcester Polytechnic Institute, BS-Chemical Engrg., 1971; Cornell U., MS-Chemical Engrg., 1972; U. of New Haven, MBA-Mktg./Fin., 1978. **Career Hist.:** Pfizer Inc., 1972-94: Chemical Div., Central Research Div., Hospital Products Group (Southport, NC and Groton, CT); VP/Gen. Mgr.-Schneider U.S. Stent Div. (Plymouth, MN), 1990-91; EVP-Schneider (USA) Inc.: 1991-92; Pres., CEO, 1992-94; Empi Inc.: Pres., CEO, 1994-99; Chm., CEO, 1999-present. **Career Act.:** Mem., American Institute of Chemical Engrs., American Society for Artificial Internal

Organs; Dir., Angiodynamics Inc.; Dir., Advanced Neuromodulation Systems Inc. **Dec./Awd.:** Holds 11 patents on biomedical products or processes. **Act./Mem.:** past Dir., Plymouth Civic League; Key Acct. Exec., Mpls. United Way; W.P.I. Alumni Fund; Cypress Landing Golf Club.

Richard G. Lareau Ptnr., Oppenheimer Wolff & Donnelly, 45 S. Seventh St., Minneapolis, MN 55401. Tel: 612/607-7262. **B:** Jun. 11, 1928, Woonsocket, R.I. **M:** Thelma, 1970. **C:** Alan. **E:** BA, St. Michael's College, 1949 (Magna Cum Laude); JD, U. of MN School of Law, 1952 (Order of the Coif). **Career Hist.:** 1952-56, Judge Advocate General's Dept. of Air Force; 1956-present, Oppenheimer Wolff & Donnelly: Ptnr., 1960; past Chair, Mem.-Policy Ctee. **Career Act.:** Mem., American Bar Assn. (Section of Business Law), Hennepin County Bar Assn. (Securities Law Section, MN State Bar Assn. (Business Law Section-past Chair), Center for Public Resources (Franchise Panel, Panel of Distinguished Neutrals), American Arbitration Assn. (Panel, Financial Industry Advisory Ctee.); Dir., Ceridian Corp., Merrill Corp., Nash Finch Co., Norris Education Innovations Inc., Northern Technologies International Corp., MN Institute for Talented Youth, The Fund for the Legal Aid Society, MN Cooperation Office for Small Business and Job Creation; Trustee, Mesabi Trust; Mem., Ins. Laws Ctee. for Recodification of MN Ins. Laws; past Chair-Ctee. on Officers and Directors, Advisory Task Force on MN Corporate Law; Mem.-Policy Committee, MN Project for Corporate Social Responsibility (past Chair); frequent lecturer.

Kenneth R. Larson Pres., CEO, Slumberland Inc., 3060 Centerville Rd., Little Canada, MN 55117. Tel: 651/482-7500. **B:** St. Paul. **M:** Barbara. **C:** five adult children. **Career Hist.:** Owner/Pres./CEO, Slumberland, 33 years. **Career Act.:** Past Dir., HealthEast; past Chair, Evangelical Free Church of America (EFCA); Chair, 1995 MN Prayer Breakfast; past Dir., Free Church Ministers and Missionaries Retirement Fund; past Trustee, Bethel College & Seminary Fdn.; Dir., Evangelical Council for Financial Accountability, Northwestern College. **Dec./Awd.:** Layman of the Year, EFCA, 1988; Retailer of the Year, National Home Furnishings Assn., 1995; Retailer of the Year, GERS (the nation's largest home furnishings software system); Alumni of the Year, Minnehaha Academy, 1996; Minnesota and Dakotas Entrepreneur of the Year (Retail/Wholesale category), Ernst & Young LLP, 1998; First Annual Integrity Award, Better Business Bureau 2000. **Act./Mem.:** White Bear Yacht Club.

Norma L. Larson Chair, Walker Methodist Inc., 3737 Bryant Ave. S., Minneapolis, MN 55409. Tel: 612/827-8389. **M:** widowed. **C:** two. **E:** Sparta (WI) High School; St, Catherine's College (St. Paul); Ancker Hospital School of Nursing (St. Paul). **Career Hist.:** Medical Asst. for Internist and Obstetrician/Gynecologist. **Career Act.:** VP, Community Education Advisory Council (S. St. Paul, MN); St. Croix Valley Girl Scout Council; Dir., Emma Norton Residence, health One Corp., Home Health Plus; Pres., United Hospital Auxiliary; Chair, PEO-MN State Chapter, Cottey College Scholarship Ctee.; Chair, United Hospital Annual Campaign (3 years); Co-chair-Raines Renovation Campaign, Walker Methodist; past Chair, Metro Hospital Trustee Council; Dir., Diabetes House Inc., United Hospital (past Chair), United Hospital Fdn. (VChair), Walker Methodist (Chair; Interim Pres./CEO, 1997), Walker Development Inc. (Chair), Westwood Ridge Senior Housing (Chair), Allina Health System. **Act./Mem.:** United Methodist denomination: Volunteer for State, National, World Bodies and Pres.-MN's Council of Fin./Admin.; Mem., First United Methodist Church (S. St. Paul), South St. Paul Study Club; PEO, Chapter H.

Richard Lawson Chair, EVP-Internet Products, Lawson Software, 380 St. Peter St., St. Paul, MN 55102. Tel: 651/767-7000. **M:** Pat. **C:** Lance, Rick. **E:** BS, Oklahoma Christian U.; MS-Computer Science, Purdue U. **Career Hist.:** Founding Ptnr., Chair, EVP-Internet Products, Lawson Software. **Career Act.:** Speaker, Forbes CEO Forum; featured in Computerworld, PC Week, Information Week, BusinessWeek. **Dec./Awd.:** Entrepreneur of the Year, Twin Cities Business Monthly, 1996.

William Lawson Sr. Pres., CEO, Lawson Software, 380 St. Peter St., St. Paul, MN 55102. Tel: 651/767-7000. Email: william.b.lawson@lawson.com **B:** 1942, Wichita, Kan. **M:** Ruth. **C:** Billy, 36; Gary, 35; Darren, 33; Damon, 32; Gregory, 30—all employed at Lawson. **E:** Wichita State U., BS-Business Admin., 1969. **Career Hist.:** Systems Analyst, Analysts International Corp., 1969-75; Lawson Assoc. Inc./Lawson Software: COO, 1975-96; Pres., CEO, 1996-present.

Douglas W. Leatherdale Chair, CEO, The St. Paul Cos. Inc., 385 Washington St., St. Paul, MN 55102. Tel: 651/310-7230. **B:** Dec. 6, 1936, Morden, Manitoba. **M:** Louise, 1988. **C:** Mary Jo, Christopher, Tim, Tom. **E:** United College, BA, 1957. **Career Hist.:** Investment Analyst Officer, Great West Life Assurance Co. (Winnipeg, Manitoba, Canada), 1957-68; Assoc. Executive Sec., Board of Pensions, Lutheran Church of America, (Minneapolis, MN), 1968-72; EVP, VP, The St. Paul Investment Mgmt. Co. (Sub. of The St. Paul Companies Inc.), 1972-77; The St. Paul Cos. Inc.: VP-Fin., 1974-81; SVP-Fin., 1981-82; EVP, 1982-89; Pres., COO, 1989; Chair, CEO, 1990; Board of Dir., St. Paul Cos., John Nuveen Co. **Career Act.:** Dir., The St. Paul Cos. Inc., UnitedHealth Group, Northern States Power Co., U. of MN Fdn.; Exec. Ctee., The International Insurance Society; Trustee, Carleton College; past Chair, Minnesota Insurance Federation, American Insurance Assn.; Mem., Carlson School of Mgmt. Board of Overseers. **Dec./Awd.:** Humanity Award, National Conference of Christians and Jews, 1996; Service to Humanity Award, United Hospital Fdn., 1996; MAEF Hero, MN Academic Excellence Fdn., 1996; Int'l Insurance Award, Int'l Insurance Council, 1999; Board of Dir., Minnesota Orchestral Assn.; Board of Dir., Saint Paul Riverfront Corp.; Board of Dir., Ordway Music Theatre. **Act./Mem.:** Twin Cities Society of Security Analysts; Financial Executives Institute; MN Meeting; Brian Coyle Leadership Award from the Human Rights Campaign Fund; Great Living Saint Paulite Award, 1997; Insurance Industry Charitable Fund honoree, 1999.

Sheila T. Leatherman SVP, UnitedHealth Group, 300 Opus Center, 9900 Bren Rd., P.O. Box 1459 (55440), Minnetonka, MN 55343. Tel: 612/936-1300. **M:** Jim Leatherman. **C:** Erica, Laura. **E:** BA, Tulane U.; MS, U. of AK. **Career Act.:** Founder, Pres., Center for Health Care Policy and Evaluation; Adjunct Professor, School of Public Health, U of North Carolina; Senior Assoc., Judge Institute of Mgmt. Studies, Cambridge U. (England); Mem.-Ctee., International Society for Quality of Care; Mem., President Clinton's Advisory Commission on Consumer Protection and Quality in the Health Care Industry (named 3/97); Invited by the Nuffield Trust to conduct a year-long evaluation of the National Health Service in the United Kingdom from 10/97-10/98; Mem., Health Advisory Board, Institute of Medicine. **Dec./Awd.:** Fellow, Assoc. of Health Services Research, 1996; Distinguished Fellow, Darwin College, U. of Cambridge.

John W. Lettmann Pres., CEO, Malt-O-Meal Co., 2600 IDS Tower, 80 S. Eighth St., Minneapolis, MN 55402. Tel: 612/338-8551. **B:** Jul. 5, 1942, St. Louis. **M:** Vicky, 1968. **C:** Susan, Jason, Michael. **E:** U. of KS, BS, 1964; Indiana U., MBA, 1968. **Career Hist.:** Senior Auditor, General Mills Inc., 1964-66; Product Mgmt., General Mills Inc., 1968-71; Malt-O-Meal Company, VP-Mktg.Sls., 1975-85; Pres., CEO Malt-O-Meal Company, 1985-present. **Career Act.:** Dir., Blue Cross Blue Shield, Horton Manufacturing Company, American Mgmt. Assn., Liberty Mutual Insurance Advisory Board. **Act./Mem.:** Minneapolis Athletic Club; Interlachen Country Club.

Joseph C. Levesque Chair, Pres., CEO, Aetrium Inc., 2350 Helen St., North St. Paul, MN 55109. Tel: 651/770-2000. **B:** Dec. 9, 1944, North Attleboro, Mass. **M:** Christine, 1993. **C:** Jacob, Michelle, Renee. **Career Hist.:** RCA Corp., Mgr.; Data General, Engrg. Process Mgr.; Micro Component Technology Inc.: VP-Sls./Mktg., VP-Op., SVP, EVP; Aetrium Inc.: Pres. and CEO. **Career Act.:** Dir., Arden Fasteners, TSI Inc. **Dec./Awd.:** Entrepreneur of the Year Award, 1994; Deubener Award, 1995.

Merle D. Lewis Chair, CEO, NorthWestern Corp., 125 S. Dakota Ave., Suite 1100, Sioux Falls, SD 57104. Tel: 605/978-2900. **B:** Nov. 21, 1947, Madison, S.D. **M:** Barbara Kay Minnaert, 1969. **C:** Eric James, Robin Renee, Amy Lynne. **E:** Dakota State College, 1970, BS; U. of SD School of Law, 1973, JD; U. of MI, The Executive Course, 1993. **Career Hist.:** John Morrell & Co., 1967-70; USD Postal Service, 1971-73; Private Law Practice (Mitchell, SD), 1973-75; Northwestern, 1975-present: Corp. Attorney, 1975-85; Asst. Corp. Sec., 1982-93; Asst. VP-Corp. Svs., 1985-87; VP-Corp. Svs., 1987-92; EVP-Corp. Svs., 1992-93; EVP, 1993-94; Pres., CEO, 1994-1997; Chair, Pres., CEO, 1997-1998; Chair and CEO, 1998-present. **Career Act.:** Dir., NorthWestern Corp., Cornerstone Propane Partners, South Dakota Rural Enterprise Inc., Sioux Falls Chamber of Commerce; South Dakota Symphony Orchestra; Midwest Energy Assn.; past Dir., SD Water Congress, James River Water Devel. District; past Mayor, City of Huron; past City Commissioner, City of Huron; past SD Army National Guard and U.S. Army Reserve (Lt. Col, ret.). **Dec./Awd.:** Who's Who in American Colleges and Universities, 1968-69; "Top 25" Local Presidents, U.S. Jaycees, 1979; Outstanding Young Citizen, SD Jaycees, 1980; Outstanding Young Americans, 1981; Eyes on You, 1993; Jaycees International Senator, Jaycees International; Northwestern Corporation-2000 Fortune's Most Admired Company; 2000 Forbes Platinum 400. **Act./Mem.:** Mem., South Dakota Bar Assn., American Legion, B.P.O. Elks-No. 444, Sioux Falls Chamber of Commerce, Minnhaha Country Club, Huron Masonic Lodge #26 AF & AM, Kappa Sigma Iota, Gloria Dei Lutheran Church.

Stephen R. Lewis Jr. Pres., Carleton College, One N. College St., Northfield, MN 55057. Tel: 507/646-4305. **B:** Feb. 11, 1939, Englewood, N.J. **M:** Judith Frost Lewis, 1996. **C:** Virginia, Deborah, Mark. **E:** Williams College, BA, 1960; Stanford U., MA, 1962 and Ph.D., 1963. **Career Hist.:** Research Adviser, Pakistan Institute of Devel. Economics, 1963-65; Asst. Prof., Harvard U., 1965-66; Williams College, 1966-87 (Provost, 1968-71, 1973-77; Prof. of Economics 1973-87); Economic Adviser, Government of Kenya, 1971-73; Economic Consultant, Government of Botswana, 1975-present; Pres. and Prof. of Economics, Carleton College, 1987-present. **Career Act.:** Trustee, Carnegie Endowment for International Peace; Executive Ctee., Indianhead Council-Boy Scouts of America; Mem., Council on Foreign Relations. **Dec./Awd.:** Presidential Order of Meritorious Service, Botswana, 1982; LL.D., Williams College, 1987; LH.D. Doshisha U., 1993; Distinguished Eagle Scout Award, 1993. **Act./Mem.:** Minneapolis Club, Minnesota Club.

WHO

Diane Palmer Lilly VP-Corp. Affairs, Wells Fargo & Co., Norwest Center (55479), MAC # N9305-171, Minneapolis, MN 55402. Tel: 612/667-8308. **B:** Minneapolis. **M:** David Lilly Jr. **C:** Irene G. **E:** Newton College of the Sacred Heart, Newton, MA, BA-English Literature. **Career Hist.:** Federal Reserve Bank of Minneapolis, 1969-78: Dir.-Research/Admin., 1972-75; Dir.-Research/Data Svs., 1975-77; Special Asst. to Pres., 1977-78; Federal Govt. Relations Officer, Norwest Corp., 1978-81; VP-Govt. Relations, Norwest Corp., 1981-87; VP-Corp. Affairs, Norwest Corp. (Wells Fargo & Co.), 1987-present; Pres., Norwest Fdn., 1987-98. **Career Act.:** Mem., MN Women's Economic Roundtable; Board Member, Twin Cities Public Television; VChair, Minneapolis Institute of Arts; Past Dir., MN Council Fdns.past Dir., Hennepin Center for the Arts, Guthrie Theater, MN Private College Council, MN Citizens for the Arts; past Pres., Guthrie Theater Supporting Cast; past Trustee, YWCA; past Mem., Political Effectiveness Ctee.-MN Business Partnership, Govt. Relations Ctee.-American Bankers Assn.; past Chair, Legislative Liaison Advisory Ctee.-American Bankers Assn., United Way's Downtown Gen. Business Div. Campaign; past Participant, Leadership Minneapolis; past Dir., Planned Parenthood of MN; Dir., Fund and Research Fdn., United Way of Minneapolis Community Resources Ctee., MN Council on Fdns., Minneapolis Chamber of Commerce Business Action Resource Council; Mem., Allocation Panel of Minnesota State Arts Board. **Dec./Awd.:** Angelus Award, 2000-Academy of the Holy Angels. **Act./Mem.:** Minikahda Club, Minneapolis Club.

Daniel A. Lindh Pres., CEO, Presbyterian Homes of Minnesota Inc., 3220 Lake Johanna Blvd., Arden Hills, MN 55112. Tel: 651/631-6100. **B:** Oct. 19, 1953, St. Paul. **M:** 1980. **C:** Jordan, Cory, Grant. **E:** Bethel College, B.A., 1975; U. Of MN, Nursing Home Admin., 1978, U. Of St. Thomas, MBA, 1981. **Career Hist.:** Presbyterian Homes, Accounting to CEO, 1976-present. **Career Act.:** Dir., MN Assn. of Homes for the Aging, Service Corp. (Chair), American Assn. of Homes for the Aging (Mem.-House Of Delegates), American Assn. of Homes and Service for the Aging (Mem.-Managed Care Ctee.), Valley Senior Services Alliance, Care Partners (Treas.), Calvary Church (Chair). **Act./Mem.:** Downtown St. Paul Kiwanis Club.

Robert M. Linsmayer Chair, Villaume Industries Inc., 2926 Lone Oak Circle, Eagan, MN 55121. Tel: 651/454-3610. **B:** Jun. 2, 1922, Minneapolis. **M:** Christine Meyerding, 1944. **C:** Nicholas, Christopher. **E:** U. of MN, BSME, 1944; Carnegie Mellon, MS, 1946. **Career Hist.:** Engr., General Electric, 1947-48; Engr., U.S. Air Force, Wright Field, 1948-51; Villaume Industries, 1951-present: Op. Mgr., 1951-58; Pres., 1958-89; Chair, 1990-present; Chair, Valley Forest Resources Inc. (Marcell, MN), 1987. **Act./Mem.:** Rotary Club, Minnesota Club, Encampment Forest Assn., Southview Country Club.

Howard P. Liszt CEO, Campbell Mithun, Piper Jaffray Tower, 222 S. Ninth St., Minneapolis, MN 55402. Tel: 612/347-1000. **B:** Aug. 12, 1946, Minneapolis. **M:** Roberta, 1971. **C:** Andrew, Daniel. **E:** U. of MN: BA, 1968; MBA, 1970. **Career Hist.:** Product Mgmt., Green Giant Co., 1971-76; Campbell Mithun Esty, 1976-present: Gen. Mgr., 1984; Pres., COO, 1994; CEO, January 1995. **Career Act.:** Founding Dir., MN Children's Museum; Mem., American Cancer Society, Greater Minneapolis Chamber of Commerce, Blake Schools; Dir., Coleman Natural Products, Zomax Optical Media, National Easter Seals, Boys and Girls Clubs, MN Business Partnership, American Assn. of Advertising Agencies; Senior Fellow, U. of MN School of Journalism/Mass Communications (2000-). **Act./Mem.:** Minneapolis Club, Oak Ridge Country Club.

Philip F. Litchfield Chair, CEO, Applied Coating Technology, 2411 Pilot Knob Rd., Mendota Heights, MN 55120. Tel: 651/454-7777. **B:** Minneapolis. **M:** Margaret Shields. **E:** U. of MN Institute of Technology. **Career Act.:** Mem., Society of Mfg. Engrs., Twin City Society of Metal Finishers, MN Assn. of Commerce and Industry. Act.Mem.: Rotary; Hazeltine National Golf Club.

Brian Luborsky Chair, CEO, Premier Salons International, 6800 France Ave. S., Suite 300, Edina, MN 55435. Tel: 612/924-7200. **B:** May 19, 1957, Windsor, Ontario. **M:** Victoria, 1994. **C:** Alexa. **E:** Commerce Degree; Chartered Accountant. **Career Hist.:** C.A, Coopers & Lybrand; Chair, and Owner of Premier. **Dec./Awd.:** Canada's Fastest Growing Company, Profit Magazine, 1996. **Act./Mem.:** Badminton & Raquet Club, Toronto.

Robert B. Ludlow Pres., Bedford Industries Inc., 1659 Rowe Ave., P.O. Box 39, Worthington, MN 56187. Tel: 507/376-4136. Email: bedford@bedfordind.com **B:** Jun. 30, 1929, Wausau, Wis. **M:** Patricia Snyder, 1954. **C:** Peter J., Sarah Milbrandt. **E:** U. of MN, BS, 1954. **Career Hist.:** Asst. Sales Mgr., Raven Industries Inc. (Sioux Falls, SD), 1957-64; Sls. Mgr., Griffolyn Co. (Houston, TX), 1964-66; Founder, CEO, Bedford Industries Inc. (Worthington, MN), 1966-present; Founder, CEO, Bedford Plastics Inc., (Sioux Falls, SD), 1981-88; Founder, CEO, Bedford Transportation Ltd.

(Worthington, MN), 1988-present. **Career Act.:** Mem., District 518 School Bd., Worthington Regional Hospital Board, Worthington Chamber of Commerce Board, Gov. Board Worthington Kiwanis Club, Worthington YMCA Board.

Russell T. (Tres) Lund III Pres., Lunds Inc., 1450 Lake St. W., Minneapolis, MN 55408. Tel: 612/825-4433. **E:** U. of MT. **Career Hist.:** Third-generation family member responsible for running the Lund family's grocery operations and other business interests.

Edward L. Lundstrom Pres., CEO, Sheldahl Inc., 1150 Sheldahl Rd., Northfield, MN 55057. Tel: 507/663-8420. Email: ed.lundstrom@sheldahl.com **B:** Jun. 13, 1950. **M:** Anne. **E:** B.A., Accounting, U. of Minn.; graduate, Minn. Management Institute. **Career Hist.:** Corporate Tax Mgr., Corporate Cont., VP and Treas., Pres.-Sheldahl Symbolic Displays Inc., VP, Gen. Mgr.-Northfield Circuit Division, Sheldahl, 1976-89; VP-Mktg./Sls, Sheldahl, 1989-95; EVP, 1995-97; President, Sheldahl, 1997-present. **Career Act.:** Mem., Ford Supplier Council.

James W. Lupient Owner, Pres., Lupient Automotive Group, 750 Pennsylvania Ave. S., Golden Valley, MN 55426. Tel: 612/544-6666. **B:** Nov. 14, 1934, Aberdeen, S.D. **M:** Barbara. **C:** Michael, Richard, Sandra, Jeffrey, Jennifer. **Career Hist.:** Auto Sls. Dealership Mgmt., 1952-69; Owner, CEO, Lupient Automotive Group, 1969-present; CEO, Midwest Mgmt., Midwest Automalls; Chair, Hayden Murphy. **Career Act.:** Dir., Chair-Advert. Ctee., MN Better Business Bureau; Member, Greater Minneapolis Chamber of Commerce; Dir., Firstar Bank-Shelard, Dir., North Memorial Medical Center; Mem.-Steering Ctee., Mpls. Convention Center Completion Project. **Dec./Awd.:** Time Magazine Quality Dealer of the Year Award, 1990; Sports Illustrated American Dealer of the Year, 1992; Top Foreign Car Sales Award, 1992. **Act./Mem.:** Interlachen Country Club.

Leland T. Lynch Managing Ptnr., Chair, CEO, Carmichael Lynch Spong, 800 Hennepin Ave., Minneapolis, MN 55403. Tel: 612/334-6000. **B:** 1945. **Career Hist.:** Co-Founder, Carmichael Lynch, 1962. **Career Act.:** Chair, Minneapolis Downtown Council. **Act./Mem.:** Dir., Planned Parenthood of Minnesota; Dir., Minn. Public Radio.

Dr. Mary E. Lyons Pres., College of Saint Benedict, 37 S. College Ave., St. Joseph, MN 56374. Tel: 320/363-5011. Email: mlyons@csbsju.edu **B:** Oct. 4, 1947, Sebastopol, Calif. **C:** Timothy. **E:** Sonoma State College, BA-English, 1971; San Jose State, MA-English, 1976; U. of CA-Berkeley, doctorate in rhetoric, 1983. **Career Hist.:** Franciscan School of Theology, Graduate Theological Union, Berkeley, CA, 1984-90; Pres., California Maritime Academy, Vallejo, CA, 1990-96; Pres., College of St. Benedict, 1996-present. **Career Act.:** Naval Reserve Assn.; Armed Services Ctee., Captain, U.S. Naval Reserve; Wells Fargo Bank Community Board; Mem., Minnesota Women's Forum, St. Cloud Chamber of Commerce Exec. Dialogue Group, Women's College Coalition Executive Board; Trustee, Graduate Theological Union, Berkeley, Ca. **Dec./Awd.:** Educator of the Year Award, National Defense Transportation Assn., 1996; Medallion for scholarly achievement and community service, U. of San Francisco, 1993; Distinguished Alumna, Sonoma State College, 1992; Newhall Research Fellowship, Graduate Theological Union, 1988/89; Thomas More-Jacques Maritain Institute Fellowship, 1981. **Act./Mem.:** St. Cloud Country Club, Minneapolis Club.

Reid V. MacDonald Pres., CEO, Faribault Foods Inc., 1000 Baker Bldg., Minneapolis, MN 55402. Tel: 612/333-6461. **B:** Jun. 7, 1947, San Francisco. **M:** Ann Reppert, 1982. **C:** Maria, Catherine, Laura, Vandever. **E:** Stanford U., BA, 1970; U. of MN Law School, JD, 1976. **Career Hist.:** Faribault Foods Inc., 1973-present: VP, 1973-77; Pres., 1977-present; CEO, 1984-present. **Career Act.:** past Dir., Minnesota Dance Theatre, Walker Art Center; Dir., KTCA, Varitronics, Young President's Organization.

Robert W. MacDonald Chair, CEO, Allianz Life Insurance Co. of North America, 300 S. County Rd. 169, St. Louis Park, MN 55426. Tel: 612/546-7386. **B:** Feb. 11, 1943, Rochester, N.Y. **C:** Ryan, Brandy, Piper, Colin, Braden, Bo. **E:** Loyola U.; BS, Law, from Western State College of Law, 1972. **Career Hist.:** Regional Agency Mgr., Jefferson Standard Life, 1970-75; VP, State Mutual Life, 1975-77; President and CEO, ITT Life, 1977-87; Chair and CEO, LifeUSA (now part of Allianz Life Insurance Co. of North America), 1987-present. **Career Act.:** Dir., Life USA Holding Inc., Arthritis Fdn. of MN, Viking Council-Boy Scouts of America. **Dec./Awd.:** MN Entrepreneur of the Year (Emerging Companies category), 1992; Minnesota and Dakotas Entrepreneur of the Year (Service category), Ernst & Young LLP, 1998. **Act./Mem.:** Honorary Mem., Wayzata Country Club.

John C. MacFarlane Chair, Pres., CEO, Otter Tail Power Co., 215 S. Cascade St., Fergus Falls, MN 56537. Tel: 218/736-5411. **B:** Nov. 8, 1939, Hallock, Minn. **M:** Eunice Axvig, 1963. **C:** Charles, James, William. **E:** U. of ND, BS-Electrical Engrg, 1961. **Career Hist.:** Otter Tail Power Company: Staff Engr.; Division Engr.; District Mgr.; VP-Planning and Control; EVP; Pres.; Pres., CEO; Chair, Pres., CEO. **Career Act.:** Dir., Otter Tail Power Company, Norwest Bank, Pioneer Mutual Life Insurance Company, Fergus Falls Port Authority, U. of ND Alumni Assn., U. of ND Energy Research Center, The Village Family Service. **Dec./Awd.:** ND Governors Leadership Award, 1977; JCI Senate, Jaycees, 1975; Energy Champion, Energy and Environmental Research Center, 1990; Friend of Small Business Award, U.S. SBA; Sioux Award, U. of ND, 1996; Honorary doctorate from UMD. **Act./Mem.:** Rotary; Masons; Salvation Army.

Harvey B. Mackay Chair, Mackay Envelope Co., 2100 Elm St. S.E., Minneapolis, MN 55414. Tel: 612/331-9311. **B:** Oct. 24, 1932, St. Paul. **M:** Carol Ann, 1960. **C:** David, Miriam, Joanne. **E:** U. of MN, BA, 1954; Stanford Business School, Advanced Mgmt. Program, 1968. **Career Hist.:** Sls., Quality Park Envelope Co., 1954-59; Pres., Mackay Envelope Co. (which he founded), 1959-84; Chair, CEO, 1984-2000 (when he sold it to current management). **Career Act.:** Author of Swim with the Sharks Without Being Eaten Alive, Beware the Naked Man Who Offers You His Shirt, The Harvey Mackay Rolodex Network Builder, Sharkproof, Dig Your Well Before You're Thirsty, and Pushing the Envelope: All the Way to the Top; Syndicated Columnist for United Feature Syndicate; Dir., Sundance Institute, MN Orchestral Assn., Twin Cities Business Monthly magazine, The Leadership Institute-Graduate School of Business-U. of S. Calif.; Mem., Twin Cities Communications Council; past Chair, American Cancer Society, Greater Minneapolis Chamber of Commerce Domed Stadium Task Force, Fundraising Campaign-U. of MN Concert Band, 1984 Minnesota Twins Ticket Buyout, Wack Attack sales campaign for 1993 U. of MN football season tickets; Co-Chair, 1992 Minnesota Super Bowl Task Force; past Pres., Envelope Mfrs. Assn. of America, Greater Minneapolis Chamber of Commerce, U. of MN "M" Club, U. of MN Alumni Assn., Young Presidents' Organization of Twin Cities; past Dir., Atwood Richards, Chief Executives Organization, Board of Overseers of U. of MN School of Mgmt., Industry Square Devel. Corp., Temple Israel, Mount Sinai Hospital, Minneapolis Downtown Council, Guthrie Theatre, United Way; Leader of MN businessmen's trade delegation to China. **Dec./Awd.:** Honorary Doctor of Laws Degree, Iowa Wesleyan College, 1981;

Volunteer of the Year, National Society of Fundraising Execs., 1982; Citizen of the Month, MN Governors Award, 1984; Distinguished Community Citizen, March of Dimes, 1985; MN Entrepreneur of the Year, 1988; MN Business Hall of Fame Award, 1988; Alumni Service Award, U of MN, 1988; Sls./Mktg. Executives International Award, 1989; Lifetime Achievement Award, U. of MN M Club, 1992; voted one of top five speakers in world, Toastmasters International, 1993.. **Act./Mem.:** Mem., MN Execs. Organization, Oak Ridge Country Club, Minneapolis Club, U. of MN Alumni Assn., Stanford Alumni Assn., Chief Executive Organization; past Head Coach, Minneapolis Dunkers Club.

Whitney MacMillan retired Chair/CEO, Cargill Inc., 15407 McGinty Rd., Box 9300 (55440), Minnetonka, MN 55345. Tel: 612/475-7575. **B:** Sep. 25, 1929. **M:** Elizabeth. **C:** Betsy. **E:** Yale U. **Career Hist.:** Cargill Inc., 1951-present: Merchandising, 1951-59; VP-Grain Div., 1959-62; Asst. to VP, 1962-68; GVP, 1968-71; EVP 1971-75; Pres., 1975-76; CEO, 1976-77; Chair, CEO, 1977-present. **Career Act.:** Trustee, Mayo Fdn.; Dir., Deluxe Corp. **Dec./Awd.:** Executive of the Year, *Corporate Report Minnesota*, 1993.

William C. Marcil Pres., CEO, Publisher, Forum Communications Company, 101 N. Fifth St., Fargo, ND 58102. Tel: 701/235-7311. **B:** Mar. 9, 1936, Rollette, N.D. **M:** Jane Black, 1960. **C:** Debora, William Jr.. **E:** U. of ND, BA, 1958. **Career Hist.:** Ad. Sls., Classified Ad. Mgr., Promotion Dir., Prod. Mgr., Asst. to Publisher, *The Fargo Forum,* 1961-69; Pres., Publisher, 1969-present. **Career Act.:** past Chair, American Newspaper Publisher Assn.; past Pres., ND Professional Chapter-Delta Sigma Chi, Jr. Achievement Board, Fargo Chamber of Commerce, ND State U. Devel. Fdn., GNDA, State Chamber of Commerce; past Dir., ND Newspaper Assn., Blue Cross, Blue Shield of ND, United Way of Fargo-Moorhead, Moorhead State U. Devel. Fdn., ANPA Fdn.; past Mem., Audit Ctee. of Associated Press, Postal Ctee. of American Newspaper Publishers Assn.; Dir., First Bank of ND, The Neuropsychiatric Inst., ND St. U. Devel. Fdn., ND State Chamber of Commerce, Chmn, North Central Region-Boy Scouts of America, Western States Life Ins. Company; Dir.,Past Chairman of the Board, U.S. Chamber of Commerce. Mem., Inland Daily Press Assn., ND Newspaper Assn., MN Newspaper Assn., National Assn. of Broadcasters, American Newspapers Publishers Assn., Sigma Delta Chi; Board of Advisors, U. of ND Journalism School. **Dec./Awd.:** Greater North Dakota Award, State Chamber of Commerce; Sioux Award, U. of ND, L.B. Hartz Award, Honorary Doctorate, North Dakota State University. **Act./Mem.:** Rotary Club; Fargo ND Country Club; Metropolitan Club, Washington DC; Gainey Ranch Golf Club, Scottsdale, AZ.

Ron Marshall Pres., CEO, Nash Finch Co., 7600 France Ave. S., P.O. Box 355 (55440), Edina, MN 55435. **M:** Nancy. **C:** Katy, Susie. **E:** B.S., Wright State U., 1976; C.P.A., 1997. **Career Hist.:** Mgr. of Internal Auditing, Jack Eckerd Corp., 1979-86; VP and CFO, NBI's The Office Place, 1986-88; VP and CFO, Barnes & Noble Bookstores Inc., 1988-91; SVP and CFO, Dart Group Corp., 1991-94; EVP and CFO, Pathmark Stores Inc., 1994-98; Pres. and CEO, Nash Finch Co., 1998-present. **Career Act.:** Dir., Food Marketing Institute.

Siri S. Marshall SVP, Gen. Counsel, General Mills Inc., One General Mills Blvd., P.O. Box 1113 (55440), Golden Valley, MN 55426. Tel: 612/540-2311. **B:** Jul. 7, 1948, Meriden, Conn. **M:** Bob. **C:** Serin. **E:** Bachelor's (with honors), Harvard U., 1970; JD, Yale Law School, 1974. **Career Hist.:** Avon Products Inc., 1979-94: Attorney-U.S. Legal Dept., VP-Legal Affairs/Worldwide Govt. Affairs, Corp. Sec., SVP and Gen. Counsel; General Mills, 1994-present: SVP Corporate Affairs and Gen. Counsel. **Career Act.:** Dir., American Arbitration Assn., and JAFRA ; Mem., Chief Legal Officers Roundtable, Assn. of General Counsel; Mem.-Exec. Ctee., CPR Institute for Dispute Resolution; Trustee, Mpls. Institute of Arts; past Mem., New York Stock Exchange Legal Advisory Ctee. **Act./Mem.:** United Way Legal Division Chair.

Frank R. Marvin VChair, Marvin Lumber & Cedar Co., Highway 11, P.O. Box 100, Warroad, MN 56763. Tel: 218/386-1430. **B:** Oct. 28, 1941, Warroad, Minn. **M:** Margaret Johnston, 1966. **C:** Virginia, Daniel, Paul, William, Catherine, Sarah. **E:** St. Cloud State U. **Career Hist.:** Sls. Rep., PPG Industries, 1965-69. **Career Act.:** Past Pres., Warroad Area Chamber of Commerce; Dir., Warroad Laker Hockey Assn.; Dir., Pres., National Wood Window & Door Assn. (NWWDA). **Act./Mem.:** Sr. Warden, St. Peter's Episcopal Church; Mem., Northwestern MN Mfg. Assn., Chamber of Commerce-Warroad; Dir., Warroad Boy Scouts Troop #151; Northern Lights Council.

John W. (Jake) Marvin COO, Marvin Lumber & Cedar Co., Highway 11, P.O. Box 100, Warroad, MN 56763. Tel: 218/386-1430. **B:** Warroad, Minn. **M:** Katherine. **C:** John, Brooke, Mark, James and Desiree. **E:** BA, Parsons College; JD, U. of Houston. **Career Hist.:** Marvin Windows, 1974-2000: CEO. **Career Act.:** Dir., Exec. Ctee., MN Business Partnership; Dir., U.S. Satellite Broadcasting Co. Inc., Northwest Minnesota Manufacturers Assn., Marvin Windows and Doors. Director, Window and Door Manufacturers Association.

William S. Marvin Chair, CEO, Marvin Lumber & Cedar Co., Highway 11, P.O. Box 100, Warroad, MN 56763. Tel: 218/386-1430. **B:** Aug. 25, 1917, Warroad, Minn. **M:** Margaret W., 1940. **C:** Frank, Peggy, Jake, George, Susan, Bob. **E:** U. of MN, BS-Agronomy and Ag. Economics. **Career Hist.:** Mortgage Trainee, General Mills, 1939; CEO, Marvin Windows/Marvin Lumber & Cedar Company, 1939-89. **Career Act.:** Dir., American National Bank of St. Paul; Charter Mem., Northwest Manufacturers Assn.; past Dir., Mem., National Wood Window and Door Assn. **Dec./Awd.:** MN Business Hall of Fame and Greater MN Award, MN Chamber of Commerce; Distinguished Personal Service Award, National Wood Window and Door Assn. Outstanding Achievement Award, College of Agriculture U. of MN, 1992. **Act./Mem.:** St. Peter's Episcopal Church; Mem., past Pres., Warroad Chamber of Commerce.

Melvin L. Masters Chair, Pres., CEO, Virtual Fund Inc., 7100 Shady Oak Rd., Eden Prairie, MN 55344. Tel: 612/941-8687. **B:** Oklahoma City. **M:** Jessica. **C:** Max, Matt. **E:** "Bailed out of college in favor of self-employment." **Career Hist.:** Self-employed, 1970-84; Intran Corp., Consultant, 1984-85; Virtual Fund, Inc., CEO, 1985-present. **Career Act.:** Dir., Virtual Fund, Inc., GOAT Industries Inc., TimeMasters Inc., X. Works Inc.

Ronald A. Matricaria Chair, Pres., CEO, St. Jude Medical Inc., One Lillehei Plaza, Little Canada, MN 55117. Tel: 651/481-7601. **B:** Nov. 2, 1942, Derby, Conn. **M:** Lucille, 1968. **C:** Lee, Ronald Jr., Andrew. **E:** Massachusetts College of Pharmacy, B.S., 1966. **Career Hist.:** Eli Lilly and Company Inc.: EVP and Pres. of North American Op., Pharmaceutical Div.; Pres., Medical Devices and Diagnostics Div.; Pres. and CEO, Cardiac Pacemakers Inc.; Pres. and CEO, St. Jude Medical Inc., 1993-present; Chair and CEO, St. Jude Medical Inc., 1995-present. **Career Act.:** Dir., St. Jude Medical Inc., Centocor Inc., Ceridian Inc. **Act./Mem.:** Kappa Psi.

Donald D. Maurer past Chair/CEO, Empi Inc., 599 Cardigan Rd., St. Paul, MN 55126. Tel: 651/415-9000. Email: maure006@gold.tc.umn.edu **B:** Jul. 17, 1936, Lead, S.D. **M:** Judith, 1967. **C:** Daniel, Joseph. **E:** M.S.O.E., AAS; SD State, BSEE; IA State U., MSBME. **Career Hist.:** Prod. Engr., Control Data Inc., 1965-66; Dir.-Research Neuro., Medtronics Inc., 1966-77; Dir.-Rehab Engrg., Courage Center, 1977-79; Empi Inc., 1977-present: Chair, 1977-79; Chair, CEO, 1979-93; Chair, Pres., CEO, 1993-94; Chair, CSO, 1994-99. **Career Act.:** Chair, Dir., Medical Alley; Dir., Empi Inc., American Lung Assn., Angeion Corp.; Trustee, Minneapolis College of Art and Design; Mem., Board of Regents-M.S.O.E.; Institute of Electrical and Electronics Engrs., Neuroelectric Society, Electrostatic Society of America, American Congress of Rehab. Medicine, American Assn. of Medical Instrumentation,

International Pain Society, American Pain Society; holds 37 U.S. patents; has published 15 scientific papers; Certified Clinical Engr. **Dec./Awd.:** Medical Alley Outstanding Achievement Award; Outstanding Alumnus Award, M.S.O.E., 1990; Entrepreneur of the Year, MN Regional High Tech/Medical.

Evan M. Maurer Dir., Pres., Minneapolis Institute of Arts, 2400 Third Ave. S., Minneapolis, MN 55404. Tel: 612/870-3222. **B:** Aug. 14, 1944, Newark, N.J. **M:** Naomi E., 1968. **C:** Noah, Aaron. **E:** Amherst College, B.A., 1966; U. of MN, M.A. 1968; U. of PA, Ph.D., 1974. **Career Hist.:** Asst. to the Dir., Curator, Minneapolis Institute of Arts, 1971-73; Curator of African, Oceanic, and Modern Art, Minneapolis Institute of Arts, 1973; Curator, Dept. of Africa, Oceania, and the Americas, The Art Institute of Chicago, 1973-81; Dir., The U. of MI Museum of Art, Prof., Dept. of the History of Art, Assoc. Prof., School of Art, 1981-88. **Career Act.:** Chair, National Advisory Ctee. on Education, American Assn. of Museums; Planning Advisory Panel for the Museum and Visual Arts Program, National Endowment for the Arts; National Application Reviewer, Institute of Museum Svs.; Assn. of Art Museum Directors (Trustee 1994-present, Pres. 1993-94, VP 1991-93); Chair, Assn. of Art Museum Directors Education Ctee.; National Grant Review Ctee., American Council of Learned Societies. **Dec./Awd.:** Honorary doctroate of fine arts, MCAD 1999; Honorary doctroate of humane letters, St. John's University, 1998; Honorary doctroate of humanities, Amhearst College, 1996. **Act./Mem.:** Minneapolis Club.

William K. Maxwell EVP, COO, Fairview, 2450 Riverside Ave., Minneapolis, MN 55454. Tel: 612/672-6300. **B:** Apr. 12, 1945, Shawnee Mission, Kan. **M:** Leftta. **C:** Stacy, Brian. **E:** Kansas St. U., B.S.-Business Admin., 1968; U. of MN, MHA, 1974; U. of St. Thomas, MBA, 1983. **Career Hist.:** Fairview Health System, VP/Administrator, SVP, EVP, 1978-present. Currently EVP and COO. **Career Act.:** Past Chair, MN Hospital Assn.; Dir., MN Colon & Rectal Fdn., PreferredOne Mgmt. Co., Fairview Hospital & Healthcare Svs., Fairview Clinics, Fairview Red Wing Health Svs., University Medical Center-Mesabi; Mem., American College Of Healthcare Executives; Assoc. Mem., Medical Group Mgmt. Assoc.; Preceptor, U. of MN-MHA Program.

Wally McCarthy Owner, CEO, The McCarthy Group, 1900 W. 78th St., Richfield, MN 55423. Tel: 612/869-1414. **B:** Jun. 26, 1923, Rush City, Minn. **M:** Judy, 1990. **C:** Julie, Candi, Tom, Melanie, Jason. **E:** St. Paul Park High School, Academy of Accountancy. **Career Hist.:** Wally McCarthy's Oldsmobile Inc., 1963; Wally McCarthy's Pontiac-GMC Trucks-Hyundai Inc., 1984; McCarthy's Oldsmobile-GMC Trucks Inc., 1988; Wally McCarthy's Cadillac Inc., 1991; Wally McCarthy's Chevrolet-Cadillac, LLC, 1997. **Career Act.:** Mem., Oldsmobile Board of Governance, Delco Electronics Advisory Board, National Oldsmobile Golf Scamble Board; Pres., Richfield/Bloomington Advertising Board, Greater Metropolitan Oldsmobile Dealer Assn., Cadillac Dealer Council. **Dec./Awd.:** Hall of Fame of Richfield; B'Nai B'rith International Humanitarian Award; U. of MN Bernie Beirman Hall of Fame Award. **Act./Mem.:** National Kidney Fdn. Board; MN Multiple Sclerosis Society Board; Chamber of Commerce; Osman Temple Shrine; ZURAH Temple Shrine; U. of MN Wheels Club; Board of Childrens Heart Fund; Community Leadership Award/Alzheimers Assn.; Interlachen; Mendakota Country Club.

Kevin McCollum Pres., CEO, Ordway Center for the Performing Arts, 345 Washington St., St. Paul, MN 55102. Tel: 651/282-3000. **B:** Mar. 1, 1962, Honolulu. **M:** Lynnette, 1997. **E:** Conservatory of Music, U. of Cincinnati, Bachelors; Peter Stark Motion Picture Producing Program; U. of Southern CA, Masters. **Career Hist.:** Assoc. Producer, St. Louis MUNY; Executive Producer, Tri-State Center of the Arts (Pine Plains, NY); Co-Founder, Ptnr., Booking Office (New York); Pres., CEO, Ordway Music Theatre, now Ordway Center for the Performing Arts; Executive Producer of the film "Jeffrey"; Producer of Broadway musical "Rent". **Dec./Awd.:** Robert Whitehead Producing Award, New York; Tony Award, Best Musical "RENT," 1996; Ten Outstanding Young Americans, 1998. **Act./Mem.:** Independent Feature Film Project North; Minnesota Jaycees.

Fred McCoy Pres., CEO, Guidant Corp. Cardiac Rhythm Management Group, 4100 Hamline Ave. N., Arden Hills, MN 55112. Tel: 651/582-4000. **B:** Feb. 19, 1957, Charlotte, NC. **M:** Mary, 1994. **C:** Georgia, Conrad, Rachel. **E:** University of North Carolina, B.S., 1979; Northwestern University, M.M., 1981. **Career Hist.:** Eli Lilly and Company,1981-88; Hybritech Inc., 1988-91; Cardiac Pacemakers, Inc., 1991-94; VP Sls., Guidant Corp., 1994-96; Pres. Guidant Corp. Asia Pacific Operations, 1997-2000. **Career Act.:** Member-Kellogg Alumni Advisory Board; Past Chair, American Chamber of Commerce in Japan, Subcommittee on Medical Equipment and Supplies; St. Andrews Presbyterian College Trustee.

Jan McDaniel VP, Gen. Mgr., WCCO-TV, 11th On the Mall, Minneapolis, MN 55403. Tel: 612/330-2600. Email: jmcdanie@wcco.com **B:** Jun. 27, 1951, St. Louis. **M:** Russ, 1979. **E:** BA-Journalism, U. of MO, 1973. **Career Hist.:** Exec. Editor, WEEI-AM Radio (Boston); CBS News: radio news writer/editor/producer, 1975-76; News Assignment Mgr.-Washington Bureau, 1976-84; Washington Bureau Chief, Chronicle Broadcasting Co. (KRON-TV San Francisco, WOWT-TV Omaha NE, KAKE-TV Wichita KS), 1984-88; News Dir., KAKE-TV, 1988-90; VP-News/Operations, KAKE-TV, 1990-91; Pres. and Gen. Mgr., KAKE-TV and KS Television Network, 1991-96; VP and Gen. Mgr., WCCO-TV, 1996-present. **Career Act.:** Dir., VChair-Community Leadership, Greater Minneapolis Chamber of Commerce; Mem.-Twin Cities Chapter, Young Presidents Org.; Dir., YWCA of Minneapolis, Downtown Council; Mem.-U. of MN Journalism Center Advisory Board. **Act./Mem.:** United Way 1998 Campaign Cabinet; Twin Cities Communications Council.

Burton J. McGlynn Chair, McGlynn Bakeries Inc., 7350 Commerce Ln., Fridley, MN 55432. Tel: 612/574-2222. **B:** Nov. 16, 1923, Minneapolis. **M:** Rosalynn J. McGlynn. **C:** Michael, Timothy, Daniel, Molly, Thomas. **E:** High School. **Career Hist.:** Chair, McGlynn Bakeries, 1946-present. **Career Act.:** Board of Governors, American Bakers Assn.; Board of Trustees, American Institute of Baking, College of St. Catherine; Dir. Catholic Community Fdn. (St. Paul). **Dec./Awd.:** Honorary Degree, St. Mary's U. (Winona, MN), 1995; Alumni Entrepreneur Award, Dunwoody Institute (Mpls.), 1999. **Act./Mem.:** Interlachen Country Club, Captiva Island Yacht Club, Sanctuary Golf Club (Sanibel, FL), Layayette Country Club.

Michael J. McGlynn CEO, McGlynn Bakeries Inc., 7350 Commerce Ln., Minneapolis, MN 55432. Tel: 612/574-2222. **B:** Jun. 10, 1950, Minneapolis. **M:** Julie, 1983. **C:** Jenny, Elissa, Betsy, Emily. **E:** U. of CO, BS-Business, 1972. **Career Hist.:** McGlynn Bakeries: VP, 1972-80; Pres., 1981-92; VP, Gen. Mgr. Foodservice, Grand Metropolitan/Pillsbury, 1992-93; CEO, McGlynn Bakeries, 1993-present. **Career Act.:** Trustee, Dunwoody Institute; Director, Red Wing Shoe Co. **Act./Mem.:** Interlachen Country Club, Minneapolis Club, United Way, Country Club of Naples.

Thomas J. McGough Sr. Pres., CEO, McGough Cos., 2737 N. Fairview Ave., Roseville, MN 55113. Tel: 651/633-5050. **B:** Feb. 6, 1934, St. Paul, Minn. **M:** Jean 1958. **C:** Colleen, Thomas, Mary Jean, Ann Margaret, Michael. **E:** College of St. Thomas, U. of MN. **Career Hist.:** various positions, VP, McGough Construction 1956-1996; McGough Cos., 1996-present.

William W. McGuire, M.D. Chair, Pres., CEO, UnitedHealth Group, 300 Opus Center, 9900 Bren Rd., P.O. Box 1459 (55440), Minnetonka, MN 55343. Tel: 612/936-1300. **B:** Apr. 15, 1948, Troy, N.Y. **M:** Nadine M. **E:** U. of TX, B.A., 1970; U. of TX Medical Branch, M.D., 1974.

Career Hist.: Dir. Critical Care Svs., St. Francis Hospital, 1983-85; Medical Dir., CostGuard Insurance Company, 1984-86; VP-Health Systems, Peak Health Care Inc., 1985-86; Pres., CEO, Peak Health Plan, 1986-88; EVP, United HealthCare Corp., 1988-89; EVP, COO, United HealthCare Corp., 1989; Pres., COO, United HealthCare Corp., 1989-91; Pres., CEO, United HealthCare Corp., 1991; Chair, Pres., CEO, United HealthCare Corp., now UnitedHealth Group, 1991-present. **Career Act.:** past Chair, Colorado Fdn. of Medical Care; Dir., United HealthCare Corp., MN Meeting, MN Business Partnership, MN Orchestral Assn.; past Dir., Nexagen Inc. (Boulder, CO); Trustee, Advisor, American Board of Internal Medicine; Mem., Institute of Medicine; National Cancer Policy Board. **Dec./Awd.:** Parker B. Francis Fdn. Fellowship, 1978-80.

Gary T. McIlroy, M.D. Chair, CEO, Health Risk Management Inc., 10900 Hampshire Ave. S., Bloomington, MN 55438. Tel: 612/829-3500. **B:** Jul. 26, 1940, Minot, N.D. **M:** Marlene Travis, 1962. **E:** George Washington U., BS; UCLA, MD, 1967. **Career Hist.:** VP, Meidinger Health Risk Mgmt.; VP, Damon Corp.; Pres. and co-founder, Midwest Laboratory Assn.; Pres., Upper Mississippi Pathologists, P.A.; Chair and CEO, Health Risk Mgmt. Inc. 1977-present.

J. David McIntosh EVP, The Toro Co., 8111 Lyndale Ave. S., Bloomington, MN 55420. Tel: 612/888-8801. **B:** 1944, Cedar Rapids, Iowa. **M:** Jennifer. **E:** BBA, IA St. U., 1967. **Career Hist.:** Hum. Res. positions at Dayton Hudson Corp., The Gap Stores, and National Tea Co.; The Toro Co., 1975-present: various, including VP and Gen. Mgr.-Consumer Div.; in 1996, named to three-member Office of the Pres., with responsibility for sales, marketing, service, and product development of core businesses and in 1998 promoted to EVP. **Act./Mem.:** Board of Dir./Sec.-The Johnson Institute Foundation.

Edward J. McIntyre VP, CFO, Xcel Energy Inc., 414 Nicollet Mall, Minneapolis, MN 55401. Tel: 612/330-7712. **B:** Jan. 29, 1951, Grand Forks, N.D. **M:** Peggy. **C:** Patrick, Brian, Andrew. **E:** Minot State U., BA Business Admin., 1973. **Career Hist.:** Accountant, Northern States Power Co., 1973; Revenue Requirements, NSP Co., 1975; Dir.-Gas supply, NSP Co., 1983; VP, NSP Gas Utility, 1985; Pres./CEO, NSP (Wisconsin) Eau Claire, 1985-93; VP, CFO, Northern States Power Co., now Xcel Energy Inc., 1993-present. **Career Act.:** The Greater Minneapolis Metropolitan Housing Corp., Junior Achievment, Como Zoo and Conservatory Society. **Act./Mem.:** Financial Executive Institute.

Garwin B. McNeilus Chair, CEO, McNeilus Truck & Manufacturing Inc., Highway 14 East, Dodge Center, MN 55927. Tel: 507/374-6321. **B:** Jul. 18, 1938. **M:** Marilee, 1959. **C:** Denzil, Brandon, Laura. **E:** Oak Park Academy (12th grade). **Career Hist.:** Owner, ready-mix plants, 1964-70; Owner, McNeilus Truck & Mfg. Inc., 1970-present.

Michael S. McPherson Pres., Macalester College, 62 Macalester St., St. Paul, MN 55105. Tel: 651/696-6207. Email: mcpherson@macalester.edu **B:** Jun. 6, 1947. **M:** Margaret. **C:** Steven, Sean. **E:** U. of Chicago: BA (Mathematics), 1967; MA (Economics), 1970; Ph.D. (Economics), 1974. **Career Hist.:** Economics Instructor, U. of IL-Chicago Circle, 1971-74; Visiting Fellow-Econ. Dept., Princeton U., 1977-78; Study Dir.-Ctee. on Continuity in Academic Research Performance, National Research Council-National Academy of Sciences, 1979; Asst. Prof. of Economics, Williams College, 1974-81; Mem.-School of Social Science/Institute for Advanced Study, Princeton, 1981-82; Assoc. Prof. of Economics, Williams College, 1981-84; Senior Fellow, The Brookings Inst., 1984-86; Prof. of Economics, Williams College, 1984-96; Chair-Economics Dept., Williams College, 1986-90 and 1993-94; Chair-Political Economy Program, Williams College, 1992-93; Co-Dir., Williams Project on the Economics of Higher Education, 1989-present; Dean of the Faculty, Williams College, 1994-96; Pres., Macalester College, 1996-present. **Career Act.:** McPherson has written widely on topics in ethics and economics and in the economics of higher education. He served as one of the founding editors of the journal Economics and Philosophy and has co-authored four recent books—Keeping College Affordable: Government and Educational Opportunity (1991); Paying the Piper: Productivity, Incentives and Financing in American Higher Education (1993); Economic Analysis and Moral Philosophy (1996); and The Student Aid Game: Meeting Need and Rewarding Talent in American Higher Education (fall, 1998). Recent professional service (since 1991) includes: Mem., National Academy of Sciences Ctee. on Postsecondary Education and Training for the Workplace, 1991-93; Mem.-Advisory Panel for the Office of Planning/Budget/Evaluation, U.S. Dept. of Education, 1992-93; Chair-Advisory Panel for the Survey of Doctorate Recipients, National Academy of Sciences, 1992-94; Mem., Advisory Panel for the National Science Fdn. Report on Science and Engrg. Education Indicators; Mem., Governing Council of the International Consortium for Social and Political Research, 1994-96; Chair-Economics Advisory Panel, Council of Research Libraries, 1994-1996; Trustee, College Board, 1997-2000. **Dec./Awd.:** Grants: National Endowment for the Humanities, National Science Fdn., Mellon Fdn., Spencer Fdn., Ford Fdn.; American Council of Learned Societies Study Fellowship, 1977-78.

Alvin E. McQuinn Chair, CEO, Ag-Chem Equipment Co. Inc., 5720 Smetana Dr., Minnetonka, MN 55343. Tel: 612/933-9006. **B:** Oct. 22, 1931, Butler, Mo. **M:** Mary Agnes Starr, 1954. **C:** Anne, Susan (Arndt), Mary Margaret (Jetland), Charles. **E:** U. of MO, BS-Agriculture, 1954. **Career Hist.:** Pilot U.S. Army, 1955-58, Army Reserve, 1958-64, fertilizer materials sales in MN, 1958-63; Pres., Ag-Chem Equipment Co. Inc., 1963-76; Chair, Pres., CEO, Ag-Chem Equipment Co. Inc., 1976-1997; Chair, CEO, Ag-Chem Equipment Co. Inc., 1976-present. **Career Act.:** Pres., CEO, and Dir., Lor Al Products, Inc., Ag-Chem Sales Co. Inc. Ag-Chem Equipment Canada Ltd., and Ag-Chem International Inc.; Chair and CEO, Ag-Chem Manufacturing Co. Inc.; Supervisory Dir., Ag-Chem Europe B.V.; Dir.,The Fertilizer Institute; Mem., Board of Advisors U. of St. Thomas Graduate School of Business. **Dec./Awd.:** MN Business Hall of Fame, 1988; National Fertilizer Solutions Assn., Man-of-the-Year Award, 1989; Merit Award for Outstanding Achievment and Meritorious Service in Agriculture, Alumni Assn. U. of MO-Columbia, 1993; John F. Cade Award, U. of St. Thomas Center for Entrepreneurship, 1996; Entrepreneur of the Year/Master Category/Minnesota and the Dakotas, 1997; Agricultural Retailers Association Lifetime Member Award, 1997. **Act./Mem.:** Interlachen Country Club, Mount Olivet Lutheran Church.

Edward J. Mehl CEO, Administrator, Lake Region Healthcare Corp., 712 S. Cascade, P.O. Box 728, Fergus Falls, MN 56538. Tel: 218/736-8000. **B:** Aug. 21, 1945, Breckenridge, Minn. **M:** divorced. **C:** Jeffrey, Christopher, Joseph, Jacqueline. **E:** North Dakota State College of Science, AS, 1963-65; Moorhead State U., BA, 1967; U. of MN, Masters-Hospital Admin., 1980. **Career Hist.:** St. Francis Hospital, Laborer, 1961-67. Lake Region Healthcare Corp., 1967-present: Business Office Mgr./Cont., 1967-74; Asst. Admin./Dir. of Finance, 1974-81; CEO, 1981-present.

Kendrick B. Melrose Chair, CEO, The Toro Co., 8111 Lyndale Ave. S., Bloomington, MN 55420. Tel: 612/887-5901. Email: Ken.Melrose@toro.com **B:** Jul. 31, 1940, Orlando, Fla. **M:** Julie, 1994. **C:** Robert, Velia, Kendra, Taylor. **E:** Princeton U.; Sloan School of Mgmt.; MIT: U. of Chicago, BA, 1962; SM, 1965; MBA, 1967. **Career Hist.:** Dir.-Corp. Planning, Bayfield Technologies, 1969-70; Mktg. Mgr., The Pillsbury Companies, 1967-69; Toro Company, 1970-present: Dir.-Mktg., Consumer Products Div., 1970-73; Pres., Toro Game Time, 1973-76; GVP-Outdoor Power Equipment, 1976-80; EVP, 1980-81; Pres., 1981-83; Pres., CEO, 1983-87; Chair, CEO, 1987-present. **Career Act.:** Dir., The Toro Company, Valspar Corp., Donaldson Company Inc., Surmodics Inc., Jostens Inc., Outdoor Power Equipment Institute Inc., The Guthrie Theater Fdn.; past Dir. and Pres., The Children's Theatre; Trustee, Breck School. **Dec./Awd.:** U.S. patent; Sloan School Businessman of the Year. **Act./Mem.:** United Way; Author of the book, "Making the Grass Greener on Your Side," 1995.

Donald R. Mengedoth Chair, Community First Bankshares Inc., Community First Towers, 520 Main Ave., Fargo, ND 58124. Tel: 701/298-5701. **B:** Aug. 10, 1944, Naperville, Ill. **M:** Stacy Halverson, 1992. **C:** Paul, Daniel, Mary. **E:** Marquette U., BS, 1968; Marquette Grad. School, MBA, 1973. **Career Hist.:** VP-Op., First Bank-Milwaukee, 1970-73; SVP-Consumer Div., First Bank Milwaukee, 1973-79; VP-Op., First Bank System Inc., 1979-82; SVP, First Bank System Inc., 1982-85; Mng. Dir., ND Region, First Bank System Inc., 1985-87; Community First Bankshares Inc.: Pres., CEO, 1987-2000; Chm., 1993-2000; Chair, Community First Bankshares, Inc., 1987-present. **Career Act.:** Dir., Shanley Grow Endowment, Community First Bankshares Inc., Treasure Enterprises Inc., Northern Wildlife Park; past Dir., Pres., Tyme Corp.; past Dir., WI Automated Clearing House; Chair, Dir., Plus System Inc.; VChair, Government Relations Council; Pres., American Bankers Association; past Chair, Legislative Ctee., ND Bankers Association. **Dec./Awd.:** Man of the Year, Sales & Marketing Executives (Fargo Chapter), 1991; Executive of the Year, Red River Chapter-International, 1995; Entrepreneur of the Year, Minnesota and Dakotas Ernst & Young, 1996; Association of Administrative Professionals; Greater North Dakotan Award 2000; North Dakota National Leadership Award of Excellence, 2000. **Act./Mem.:** past United Way Co-Chair; United Way Advisory Ctee.; Fargo Country Club; Shanley Grow; past Dir., VChair, Red River Zoological Society.

Gary S. Mertz Pres., Business Information Technologies Inc., 4640 W. 77th St., Suite 262, Edina, MN 55435. Tel: 612/820-0255. Email: garym94@aol.com **B:** Jul. 30, 1947, Rochester, Minn. **M:** Betsy, 1970. **E:** BA-Math. **Career Hist.:** Various sales, marketing, management, and executive positions, Control Data, 20 years; Datamap: VP-Sls./Mktg., Pres., COO, 1990-93; CEO, 1993-95; Pres., Business Information Technologies Inc., 1995-present.

Marlene A. Messin Pres., Owner, Plastic Products Co. Inc., 30355 Akerson St., Lindstrom, MN 55045. Tel: 651/257-5980. **B:** Oct. 6, 1935, St. Paul. **M:** Frank, 1982. **C:** four children, five stepchildren. **Career Hist.:** Bookkeeper, Jeans Implement, 1953-57; Credit Mgr.'s Sec., Great Plains Supply Company, 1960-62; Bookkeeper, Plastic Products Company Inc., 1962-75; Pres., Plastic Products Company Inc., 1975-present; Owner, Treas., Gustaf's Fine Gifts, Gustaf's World of Christmas, and Gustaf's Dept. 56 (Lindstrom, MN). **Act./Mem.:** American Swedish Institute; Smithsonian; Science Museum of MN; MN Historical Society; Southview Country Club; Chisago County Historical Society; Lindstrom Historical Society.

James S. Meyer COO, United Parcel Service Inc., 3312 Broadway St. N.E., Minneapolis, MN 55413. Tel: 612/379-6666. **B:** Feb. 17, 1944, Fond du Lac, Wis. **M:** Arlene, 1967. **C:** Kellie Ann, Matthew. **E:** UW-Oshkosh, BS. **Career Hist.:** United Parcel Service: various positions, 1969-present.

Harold Mezile Pres., CEO, The YMCA of Metropolitan Minneapolis, 30 S. Ninth St., Minneapolis, MN 55402. Tel: 612/371-8713. **B:** May 14, 1944, Kansas City, Mo. **M:** Peggye. **C:** Rheyna, Elana. **E:** U. of MO, B.A. Social Work, 1966; M.S. Social Work, 1968. **Career Hist.:** Armco Steel; Kansas City Model Cities Health Center,1968-73; Exec. Dir., Linwood Branch of Greater Kansas City YMCA, 1973-81; Dir.-Op., Greater Kansas City YMCA, 1981-85; Sr. Field Consultant, YMCA of the USA, 1985-88; Pres., CEO, Greater Baltimore YMCA, 1988-94; CEO, YMCA of Metropolitan Minneapolis, 1995-present. **Career Act.:** National YMCA Black Svs. Conference; National YMCA Hum. Res. Task Force; National Public Policy Conference, National Urban Symposium. **Dec./Awd.:** Distinguished Citizen Award, Fullwood Fdn., 1992; Heritage Award, YMCA East Field Black Services Conference, 1994; Mayor's Outstanding Service Award (Baltimore), 1994. **Act./Mem.:** VChair, Minneapolis Community Technical College Fdn.; Mem., New Workforce Policy Council, Rotary Club, Youth Trust Board (Delegate-President's Summit).

Joseph P. Micatrotto Ptnr., Pres., CEO, Buca Inc., 1300 Nicollet Mall, Minneapolis, MN 55403. Tel: 612/288-2382. **B:** July 11, 1951, Cleveland, Ohio. **M:** Connie. **C:** Joseph, Justin. **E:** Miami University, B.S. Business Administration/Hotel Restaurant Mgmt., 1973; M.B.A. 1975. **Career Hist.:** Developed Hall's Waffles, a three-store chain in southern Ohio; Steak & Ale Restaurants Corp.; Pres. and CEO Chi-Chi's; Pres., CEO, COO, Panda Mgmt. Company, Inc.; Chairman, CEO, and Pres. of Buca di Beppo, 1996-present. **Career Act.:** Dir. National Restaurant Association; Pres. and Co-founder, American Beverage Institute.

Ernest S. Micek retired Chair, Cargill Inc., 15615 McGinty Rd. W., Wayzata, MN 55391. Tel: 612/742-7575. **B:** Feb. 18, 1936, Arcadia, Wis. **M:** Sally, 1959. **E:** U. of WI, Chemical Engrg., 1959; Minnesota Exec. Program, 1980; Harvard Agricultural Course, 1987. **Career Hist.:** Cargill, 1959-2000: Pres., CEO, 1995-99; Chair, 1995-2000; Retired 2000. **Career Act.:** Dir., Cargill Inc., Schneider National (Green Bay), U.S. Chamber of Commerce; Dir., Treas., Chair-Audit Ctee., United Way of Minneapolis Area; Mem., Carlson School of Mgmt. Board of Overseers, Visiting Ctee.-U. of MI, President's Export Council; Chair-Industrial Liaison Council, U. of WI; Trustee, U. of St. Thomas; Chair, Emergency Ctee. for American Trade (ECAT); APEC business advisory council member; UW Alumni Research Foundation Trustee. **Dec./Awd.:** Engrg. Achievement, U. of WI, 1991; Ellis Island Medal of Honor, 1997; Hon. Doctorate of Science, S.D. School of Mine & Technology; Annual Service Award, Consumers for World Trade, 1999; Coya Knutson Humanitarian Award, 1999; Hon. Doctorate of Science, UW.

James H. Michael Chair, ENStar Inc., 7450 Flying Cloud Dr., Eden Prairie, MN 55344-3720. Tel: 612/546-7500. **B:** Jul. 29, 1920, Minneapolis. **C:** Jeffrey, Janette, Jennifer, Roxanne, Rosemary. **E:** U. of MN, BS; U. of MN, LLB. **Career Hist.:** Chair, Michael/Curry Companies Inc. (Suite 300, 5500 Wayzata Blvd., Minneapolis, MN 55416; 612/546-1400), present; Chair, Michael Foods Inc. (324 Park National Bank Building, 5353 Wayzata Blvd., Minneapolis, MN 55416; 612/546-1500), present; Chair, Michael Development (609 Park National Bank Building, 5353 Wayzata Blvd., Minneapolis, MN 55416; 612/542-1473), present. **Career Act.:** Dir., North Star Universal Inc. **Act./Mem.:** Town and Country Club; Minneapolis Club; Minneapolis Athletic Club.

Jeffrey J. Michael Pres., CEO, Corstar Holding, Inc., 7450 Flying Cloud Dr., Eden Prairie, MN 55344. Tel: 612/941-3200. **B:** Jul. 18, 1956, Minneapolis. **M:** Deanne. **C:** Lauren. **E:** Northwestern U., B.A. Economics, 1978; Kellogg Graduate School of Mgmt., M.M.-Fin./Mgmt. Policy, 1982. **Career Hist.:** North Star Universal, Inc. Pres. and CEO 1990-1997; ENStar Inc. Pres. and CEO, 1997-1999; Corstar Holdings, Inc. Pres. and CEO-present. **Career Act.:** Dir., Michael Foods Inc., CorVel Corp.

John B. Miller VP-Minneapolis Customer Svc., Prudential Insurance Co. of America, 3033 Campus Dr., Plymouth, MN 55441. Tel: 612/557-4000. **B:** Feb. 27, 1960, Minneapolis. **M:** Debbie, 1984. **C:** Christopher, Elizabeth. **E:** U. of MN, 1982. **Career Hist.:** VP, Minneapolis Customer Service Office, Prudential, 1998-present; VP, Minneapolis Service Op., Prudential, 1997; Dir., West Geographic Service, American Express, 1997; Process Owner, Insurance, New Business and Underwriting, American Express, 1997; Operations Leader, American Express, 1994-1997. **Career Act.:** Minority Interchange Member.

Tom Miller Pres., REM Inc., 6921 York Ave. S., Edina, MN 55435. Tel: 612/925-5067. Email: tmiller@reminc.com **B:** Mar. 23, 1948, Minneapolis. **M:** Kathy, 1972. **C:** Jennifer, Robb. **E:** BA (Psychology/Sociology), St. Cloud State U., 1970; MA (Urban/Regional Studies), Mankato State U., 1975; MS (Special Ed./Mental Retardation), Mankato State U., 1982; Ph.D. (Business Admin./Special Ed.), Columbia Pacific U., 1984. **Career Hist.:** City of Wayzata, 1971-72; REM, 1972-present.

WHO

Career Act.: Mem., past Pres. ARRM, Assn. for Residential Resources in MN; Licensed Real Estate Broker; Licensed Nursing Home Admin.; past Council member, City of Pine Springs; past member U of M Board of Nursing Foundation, past board member workabilities, past board member-ANCHOR-American Network of Community Options and Resources. **Dec./Awd.:** Entrepreneur of the Year finalist, master division, REM Inc. **Act./Mem.:** Dir.,Pres., Edina ABC Fdn.; Dir., St. Cloud State U. Alumni Fdn.; Boardmember; Dir., Mem. and past Pres., Edina Country Club.

Jonathan S. Miner Chair, Team Coach, The Miner Group International, 3430 Winnetka Ave., New Hope, MN 55427. Tel: 612/504-6151. **B:** Nov. 18, 1940, Grand Rapids, Minn. **C:** Mark, Jay. **E:** Bachelors degree, Macalester, 1962; postgraduate studies, William Mitchell College of Law; American Institute Banking. **Career Hist.:** Mello Smello and The Miner Group International, 1980-present. **Career Act.:** Dir., Miner Group, EZ GARD, Big Picture, Judy Garland Birthplace & Children's Museum. **Dec./Awd.:** Tag & Label Plant of the Year, 1995-96; Prestigious Benny award for GE Electric annual report, Printing Industry of America Inc., 1995, 1996. **Act./Mem.:** Dir., Pacer, Masonic Cancer Fund, USA Values for Children, Mission Nutrition; active, Make-A-Wish, Boy Scouts; Mem., USA Values, U.S. Golf Assn., Masonic Lodge, Osman Shrine Temple.

T. Scott Mitchell Pres., COO, Mackay Envelope Corp., 2100 Elm St. S.E., Minneapolis, MN 55414. Tel: 612/331-9311. Email: mitchell@mackay.com **B:** Feb. 1, 1949, Duluth, Minn. **M:** Doreen, 1982. **C:** Michael Carlos, Drew, Ted, Nathan, Lauren, David. **E:** Dartmouth College, BA-English/Education (cum laude), 1971. **Career Hist.:** Sls., Mgmt., IBM Corp., 1973-85; Moore Data Mgmt. Svs: VP, 1985-86; Divisional Pres., 1986-93; Pres., COO, Mackay Envelope Corp., 1993-present. **Career Act.:** Dir., Envelope Mfrs. Assn. **Dec./Awd.:** Honorary Doctor of Humane Letters Degree, Iowa Wesleyan College, 1994. **Act./Mem.:** Mem., MN Dunkers; Contact Exec., United Way.

Thomas Moberly Pres., CEO, G&K Services Inc., 5995 Opus Parkway, Suite 500, Minnetonka, MN 55343. Tel: 612/912-5500. **B:** Jun. 16, 1948, Minneapolis. **M:** Yvonne, 1974. **C:** Amy, Chris, Jennifer. **E:** U. of MN (3 years). **Career Hist.:** G&K Services Inc.: Gen. Mgr., 1980-85; Regional VP, 1985-93; EVP, 1993-97; Pres., 1997-present; CEO, 1999. **Act./Mem.:** Olympic Hills Country Club.

Thomas O. Moe Chair, Dorsey & Whitney LLP, 220 S. Sixth St., Minneapolis, MN 55402. Tel: 612/340-2843. Email: moe.tom@dorseylaw.com **B:** Jun. 3, 1938, Des Moines, Iowa. **M:** Karen Marie, 1969. **C:** Laura, Mark, Mike, Jamie, Jennie, Jackie, Tom II. **E:** U. of MN, BA, Economics, 1960; JD, 1963 (order of Coif). **Career Hist.:** Dorsey & Whitney, LLP: Assoc., 1963-68; Ptnr., 1969-89; Chair, Mng. Ptnr., 1989 to 1999; Chairman 1999 to present. Interim Athletic Director, U of MN 1999 to present. **Career Act.:** Dir., Cargill Fdn., Gopher News Co., Dir., Personnel Decisions Int'l, U. of MN Intercollegiate Athletic Advisory Board, Dir., MN Meeting. **Dec./Awd.:** Lawyer of Year 2000 (Law and Politics). **Act./Mem.:** Past United Way, VChair-Professional Div.; Dir., Interlachen Country Club; Board of Governors, Minneapolis Club; Dir., U of MN Alumni Assoc.

David L. Mona Chair, Shandwick, 8400 Normandale Lake Blvd., #500, Bloomington, MN 55437. Tel: 612/832-5000. Email: dmona@shandwick.com **B:** Jun. 4, 1943, Minneapolis. **M:** Linda, 1968. **C:** Erik, Kirk. **E:** U. of MN, BA-Journalism, 1965. **Career Hist.:** Reporter, WCCO-TV, 1962-65; Staff Writer, Minneapolis Tribune, 1965-69; Mgr.-Media Relations, Lutheran Brotherhood, 1969-70; Dir., Corp. Public Relations, International Multifoods, 1970-78; VP-Communications, The Toro Company, 1978-81; Mona, Meyer, McGrath & Gavin, 1981-present (company now called Shandwick). **Career Act.:** Dir., Methodist Hospital, Thunderbird Hotel and Convention Center, Wedgewood Golf, MN Council of Growing Companies, MN Medical Fdn.; 2000 Chair, Greater Minneapolis Chamber of Commerce; Exec. Ctee., MN Super Bowl Host Ctee.; Mem., Public Relations Society of America; Mem. Governor's Commission on Future of Canterbury Downs; Chair, "Vote Yes for Edina Kids" School Board Referendum; Dir., Minnesota Vikings Children's Fund; Minnesota Chair, 1996 Olympic Torch Run; 1997-98 Chair, The Council of Growing Companies (Washington, D.C.). **Dec./Awd.:** Small-Business Person of the Year, Bloomington (MN); Inc. magazine, Inc. 500, 1987, 1988; Award of Excellence, U. of MN School of Journalism Mass Communications, 1993; Award of Excellence, Minnesota Daily Alumni Assn., 1993. **Act./Mem.:** Mem, past Dir., U. of MN Alumni Assn.; Mem., past Dir. Twin Cities Dunkers; Mem., Interlachen Country Club; Co-host, WCCO Radio Sports Huddle; Owner Field of Dreams, Mall of America, Ridgedale and Galleria.

William T. Monahan Chair, CEO, Imation Corp., One Imation Place, Oakdale, MN 55128. Tel: 651/704-4000. **B:** 1947, Scranton, Pa. **E:** BS-Econ., St. Peter's College; MBA, Rutgers U. **Career Hist.:** 3M Co., 1972-96, numerous management positions, including: Group VP-Telecom/Visual Systems; Division VP-Data Storage Products; Sr. Mng. Dir.-3M Italy; Group VP-Electro/Communication Systems (Austin, TX); named, finally, to lead development and creation of 3M spin-off Imation, its structure, and management team; Imation Corp.-Chairman, Pres. and CEO 1996-present. **Career Act.:** Board Member-Capital City Partnership; Board Member-United Way of Minneapolis/St. Paul; Board Member-Hutchingson Technology Inc.; Board of Overseers-U of M Carlson School of Mgmt.; Board of Advisors-University of St. Thomas Graduate School of Business.

Perry Monych Pres., CEO, General Electric Capital I.T. Solutions, 5121 Winnetka Ave. N., Minneapolis, MN 55428. Tel: 612/557-2549. Email: perry.monych@gecits.ge.com **B:** Oct. 10, 1954, Kamboops, B.C. **M:** Diane, 1977. **C:** Gordon, Heather. **E:** U. of British Columbia, BS, 1984; Harvard Business School, MBA, 1986. **Career Hist.:** GE Hamilton: VP-Finance and Planning,1988-93; Pres., 1993-96; Pres. and CEO, GE Capital I.T. Solutions, 1996-present. **Career Act.:** Co-chair of GE Capital TMS Diversity Council. **Dec./Awd.:** GE Capital Pinnacle Winner, 1995, 2996, 1997. **Act./Mem.:** United Way, Minneapolis Golf Club, Y.P.O.

Cornell L. Moore Ptnr., Dorsey & Whitney LLP, Pillsbury Center South, 220 S. Sixth St., Minneapolis, MN 55402. Tel: 612/340-6331. Email: moore.cornell@dorseylaw.com **B:** Sep. 18, 1939, Tignall, Ga. **M:** Wenda Weekes Moore. **C:** Lynne, Jonathon, Meredith. **E:** Bachelor's degree socioeconomics, 1961, VA Union U.; JD, 1964, Howard U. School of Law;. **Career Hist.:** Trust officer, Crocker Bank, 1964-66; regional counsel, Cont. of the Currency, 1966-68; legal officer, Northwestern National Bank, 1968-70; EVP, Shelter Mortgage Co., 1970-74; Senior Assoc., Robins, Davis and Lyons, 1974-78; family-owned financial services and real estate firm, Leverette Weekes, 1978-87; SVP and General Counsel, Miller & Schroeder Financial Inc., 1987-95; law firm partner, Dorsey & Whitney, 1995-present. **Career Act.:** Dir., Greater Minneapolis Metropolitan Housing Corp., William Mitchell College of Law, United Negro College Fund, Dunwoody Industrial Institute, Virginia Union U., Johnson C. Smith U. (Charlotte, NC), MN Better Business Bureau; Greater Minneapolis Convention & Visitors Association; Co-Chair, Penumbra Theater-70th Anniversary; Mem.-Steering Ctee., Minneapolis Convention Center Completion Project; Chairman, Minneapolis Public Housing Authority; Trustee, Howard University Advisory Board; Lundstrom Center for Performing Arts; Marquette Bank-Golden Valley; Co-chair, Capital Campaign; AAFS. **Dec./Awd.:** MN Arthritis Man of the Year, 1997; Sigma Pi Phi Man of the Year, 1994; Commodore, Minneapolis Aquatennial, 1998. **Act./Mem.:** Minneapolis Club, Calhoun Beach Club, Two Rivers Country Club & Marina (Williamsburg, Virginia), Sigma Pi Phi Fraternity, Omega Psi Phi Fraternity; Delegal Creek Marina, Skidaway Island, GA.

John W. Mooty retired Chair, International Dairy Queen Inc., 7505 Metro Blvd., Bloomington, MN 55439. Tel: 612/830-0200. **B:** Nov. 27, 1922, Adrian, Minn. **M:** Jane N. Mooty, 1972. **C:** David N., Bruce W., Charles W.,. **E:** U. of MN, BSL 1943, LLB 1944. **Career Hist.:** Gray, Plant, Mooty, Mooty &

Bennett, P.A.: Principal, 1945-present, Managing Ptnr., 1970-90; International Dairy Queen Inc.: Dir., 1970-present, Chair, 1976-present.. **Career Act.:** Officer or Dir.: Bureau of Engraving Inc.; Rio Verde Svs. Inc.; Culligan Soft Water Service Company; Riverway Company; Member: Hennepin County Bar Assn., Minnesota Bar Assn., American Bar Assn. **Dec./Awd.:** Alumni Service Award, U. of MN, 1985; Outstanding Achievement Award, U. of MN, 1990; Gray, Plant, Mooty, Mooty, & Bennett Fdn. Professorship in Honor of John W. Mooty established at the U. of MN Law School in 1990. **Act./Mem.:** Member/Past Pres.: U. of MN Alumni Assn.; Minneapolis Rotary Club; Citizens League of Minneapolis. Member: Lafayette Club; Minneapolis Club; Minikahda Club; Rio Verde Country Club; Tonto Verde Country Club.

John L. Morrison Principal, Goldner Hawn Johnson & Morrison Inc., 5250 Norwest Center, 90 S. Seventh St., Minneapolis, MN 55402. **B:** Apr. 6, 1945, Minneapolis. **M:** Christine, 1967. **C:** Kelly, Jeb. **E:** B.A., Yale University, 1967; M.B.A., Harvard Business School, 1971. **Career Hist.:** VP, Kidder Peabody, 1971-75; EVP and Chair, Consumer Products, Pillsbury Co., 1976-89; Mng. Dir., Goldner Hawn Johnson & Morrison Inc., 1989-present. **Career Act.:** Dir., Andersen Windows, Woodcraft Industries, CSI Industries, Am. Engineered Components, Cityforest Inc. **Act./Mem.:** Bd. Mem., Minneapolis Institute of Arts, YMCA, Spring HIll Golf Club.

M.A. Mortenson Jr. Chair, CEO, M.A. Mortenson Co., 700 N. Meadow Ln., Golden Valley, MN 55422. Tel: 612/522-2100. **B:** 1936. **M:** Alice, 1964. **C:** David, Mark, Christopher, Mathias. **E:** U. of CO, BS, 1958. **Career Hist.:** M.A. Mortenson Company, 1960-present. **Dec./Awd.:** Distinguished Engrg. Alumni Award, U. of CO, College of Engrg., 1992. **Act./Mem.:** Westminster Presbyterian Church.

Miranda Moss Principal, Yamamoto Moss Inc., 252 First Ave. N., Minneapolis, MN 55401. **E:** Maryland Institute College of Art, B.A.; Graduate work at the American University in Washington D.C., MCAD, U of M, and College of St. Catherine. **Career Hist.:** Instructor, MCAD. **Career Act.:** Advisory Board, Design Mgmt. Institute; Carlson School of Business Advising Council for Communications. **Dec./Awd.:** Entrepreneur of the Year, National Association of Women Business Owners.

Robert E. Murphy CEO, Japs-Olson Co., 7500 Excelsior Blvd., St. Louis Park, MN 55426. Tel: 612/522-4461. **B:** Sep. 19, 1931, Frederic, Wis. **M:** Judy, 1958. **C:** Patrick, Kathleen, Marjorie, Monica, Bridget, Michael. **Career Hist.:** Japs Olson Company, 1965-present. **Career Act.:** Past Chair, Printing Industry of MN; Chair, Government Affairs Ctee. Printing Industries of America, PIM Environmental Task Force and Government Affairs; Graphic Arts Show Company; The Environmental Group; Board of Dir., Printing Industries of America; Chair, Printing Industries of America. **Dec./Awd.:** 1991 PIM Graphic Arts Leader of the Year; 1993, Printing Impressions/RIT Hall of Fame; 1994, Walter A. Soderstrom Society; Ash Kahn Society; Lewis Lifetime Memorial. 2000, Graphic Arts Leader of the Americas. **Act./Mem.:** Minneapolis Club; 6 O'Clock Club; Skylight Club.

Lynn A. Nagorske Pres., TCF Financial Corp., 801 Marquette Ave., Suite 302, Minneapolis, MN 55402. Tel: 612/661-6557. **B:** Jul. 21, 1956, Windom, Minn. **M:** Pamela, 1977. **C:** Rebecca, Megan. **E:** BS-Accounting, Mankato State U., 1977; CPA. **Career Hist.:** KPMG Peat Marwick (Minneapolis), 1977-86, ending as Sr. Mgr.-Audit Dept.; TCF, 1986-present: SVP and Cont. (1986), Treas. and CFO (1987), EVP (1988), Pres. and COO (1993), and Dir. (1995), and Pres./CEO-TCF Bank Minnesota (1996). **Career Act.:** Trustee and Treas., Science Museum of MN; Mem., American Institute of CPAs, Young Presidents Organization. **Act./Mem.:** Minneapolis Club.

Mahendra Nath CEO, Nath Cos. Inc., 900 E. 79th St., Suite 300, Bloomington, MN 55420. Tel: 612/853-1400. **B:** Jun. 11, 1940. **M:** Asha. **C:** Shalini, Deepak. **E:** B.S., Mechanical Engineering, Dehli U., 1961; M.S., Industrial Engineering, U. of Minn., 1965. **Career Hist.:** Group Mgr.-Industrial Engineering, Sperry Corp., 1965-85; Pres. and CEO, Nath Cos., 1985-present. **Dec./Awd.:** "Family Business of the Year Award," U. of St. Thomas, 1997; "Outstanding Marketing Executive of the Year Award," Minnesota DECA, 1998; Entrepreneur of the Year, 1999, Ernst & Young. **Act./Mem.:** Mem., Rotary Club of Bloomington; Dir., North Hennepin Community College Fdn.; Trustee, Hindu Society of Minn.

William C. Nelsen Pres., Citizens' Scholarship Foundation of America Inc., 1505 Riverview Rd., P.O. Box 297, St. Peter, MN 56082. Tel: 507/931-1682. Email: prescsfa@aol.com **B:** Oct. 18, 1941, Omaha, Neb. **M:** Margaret R., 1981. **C:** Bill, Shawna, Sarah. **E:** Midland Lutheran, B.A., 1963; Columbia U., M.A. in Religion and Ethics, 1966; U. of PA, Ph.D. in Political Science, 1971. **Career Hist.:** VP, Dean, St. Olaf College, 1974-80; Program Exec., Danforth Fdn., 1970-73; Pres., Augustana College (SD), 1980-86; Pres., Citizens' Scholarship Foundation of America, 1986-present. **Career Act.:** Dir., First National Bank-St. Peter; past Dir., National Council of Independent Colleges; Mem. Connect America Council, Points of Light Fdn.; Board Mem. Council for Aid to Education; Board Chair, U.S. Dream Academy. **Dec./Awd.:** Fulbright Scholar; Honorary Doctorate, Midland Lutheran College; Danforth Graduate Fellow; Charter Member, Athletic Hall of Fame, Midland Lutheran College; Woodrow Wilson Fellow. **Act./Mem.:** Pres., Shoreland Country Club; Chair Endowment Ctee., Trinity Lutheran Church; Mem., Rotary Club.

Brock D. Nelson CEO, Children's Health Care, 2525 Chicago Ave. S., Minneapolis, MN 55404. Tel: 612/813-6112. **B:** Mar. 23, 1951, Fargo, N.D. **M:** Martha, 1973. **C:** Thor, Haakon, Kolbjorn, Berit. **E:** St. Olaf College, BA, 1973; U. of MN, Master of Hospital Admin., 1976. **Career Hist.:** St. Luke's Regional Medical Center, Boise, Idaho, Admin. Resident, 1975-76. United Hospital, 1976-83: Admin. Asst., 1976-77; Asst. VP, 1977-80; VP, 1980-83; Pres., 1983-94; Children's Health Care, CEO, 1994-present. **Career Act.:** Chair-Elect, MN Hospital and Healthcare Partnership; Dir., National Assn. of Children's Hospitals, St. Paul Regional Red Cross, Voluntary Hospitals of America-Upper Midwest. **Dec./Awd.:** Healthcare Forum, Emerging Leader, 1989. **Act./Mem.:** White Bear Yacht Club, The Minneapolis Club, The Minnesota Club.

Curtis C. Nelson Pres./CEO-Carlson Hospitality Worldwide, Carlson Cos. Inc., Carlson Parkway, Box 59159 (55459), Minnetonka, MN 55305. Tel: 612/449-1000. **E:** B.S. Hospitality Mgmt., Cornell U.; M.B.A., Carlson School of Mgmt., U. of Minn. **Career Hist.:** Carlson Hospitality Worldwide, 1989-present. **Career Act.:** Dir., United Way of Minneapolis.

Glen D. Nelson, M.D. VChair, Medtronic Inc., 7000 Central Ave. N.E., Fridley, MN 55432. Tel: 612/514-3144. **B:** Mar. 28, 1937, Minneapolis. **M:** Marilyn, 1961. **C:** Diana, Curtis, Wendy, Juliet. **E:** Harvard U., AB, 1959; U. of MN, M.D., 1963. **Career Hist.:** VChair, Medtronic Inc., 1986-present; Chair, CEO, American MedCenters Inc., 1984-86; Chair, Pres., and CEO, Park Nicollet Medical Center, 1975-86. **Career Act.:** Charter Mem., American Academy of Medical Dirs.; Fellow, American College of Surgeons; Dir., Medtronic Inc., Carlson Holdings, ReliaStar Financial Corp., St. Paul Companies; Mem., Hennepin County Medical Assn., MN State Medical Assn., American College of Surgeons, American College of Physician Executives, Jackson Hole Group, American Medical Assn.; past Dir., Walker Art Center;

past Regent, St. John's U.; past trustee, Blake Schools; past Chair, Greater Minneapolis Chamber of Commerce. **Act./Mem.:** Special Gifts Ctee., Harvard Capital Campaign; Harvard U. Resources Ctee.; Board of Overseers, Carlson School of Mgmt.

James W. Nelson EVP, L.J. Melody & Co., P.O. Box 1385, Minneapolis, MN 55440. Tel: 612/336-4200. **B:** Jan. 8, 1942, Minneapolis. **M:** Lorna K. Nelson, 1997. **C:** Lucy, Tom, Libby, Mandee, Lucas. **E:** Princeton U.; U. of MN, BA-History, 1964; U. of MN Law School. **Career Hist.:** Eberhardt Company, 1965-present: Pres., 1976-90; CEO and Chair, 1990-1999; currently EVP of L.J. Melody & Co., acquirer of Eberhardt Co.. **Career Act.:** Trustee, Lakewood Cemetery Assn.; Dir., Williams Steel and Hardware Supply; Pres., Mortgage Bankers Assn. of America, 1990-91; Chair, Fannie Mae-Federal National Mortgage Assn., National Advisory Council, 1993; past Pres., MN Mortgage Bankers Assn.; past Commissioner, Edina Housing and Redevelopment Authority; former Advisory Trustee, Metro YWCA; past Dir., Exec. Ctee., Courage Center. **Dec./Awd.:** Mortgage Bankers Legion, 1979; Certified Mortgage Banker, 1979; Counselor of Real Estate (CRE), 1985; Ronald McRoberts Exemplary Service Award, 1994. **Act./Mem.:** Minikahda Club; Spring Hill Golf Club; Minneapolis Club; Young Presidents Organization.

Marilyn C. Nelson Chair, Pres., CEO, Carlson Cos. Inc., P.O. Box 59159, Minnetonka, MN 55459. Tel: 612/449-1272. Email: mnelson@carlson.com **B:** Aug. 19, 1939, Minneapolis. **M:** Glen David Nelson, 1961. **C:** Diana, Curtis, Wendy. **E:** Smith College, BA-Intl. Econ.; Graduate School, Political Science and Economics (Geneva, Switzerland). **Career Hist.:** Security Analyst, Paine-Webber-Jackson & Curtis, 1961-63; Owner, Chair, Citizen's State Bank of Waterville, Citizen's State Bank of Montgomery, 1975-94; SVP-Carlson Holdings, 1988-91; VChair, 1991-99; COO, 1997-98; Pres., CEO, 1998-present; Chair, 1999-present. **Career Act.:** Dir., U.S. National Tourism Organization; past Pres., Minneapolis United Way; Co-Founder, Dir., MN Women's Economic Roundtable; Dir., Carlson Companies (Chair-Exec. Ctee.), Exxon Corp., U S West Corp., Bretton Woods Ctee. International Advisory Council; Chair, Minnesota Super Bowl Task Force; Founder, MN Midsummer Music Festival; Dir., Center for International Leadership; National First VChair, Travel Industry Assn. of America. **Dec./Awd.:** Honorary Doctorate, College of St. Catherine, Gustavus Adolphus College; United Way Award for Outstanding Achievement, 1975, 1978-82; Carlson Companies, YWCA Leader Lunch Annual Recognition for Community Women, 1979-82; Volunteer of the Year Award, Jr. League of Minneapolis; Downtown Council of Minneapolis and the Greater Minneapolis Chamber of Commerce Salutes Marilyn Nelson, Patron of the Arts; Congressional Award for Initiative and Service in the Community (Scandinavia Today); MN Citizen of the Month, Gov. Rudy Perpich; Independence Award, Vinland National Center; Royal Order of the North Star First Class; The Order of the White Rose, Officer First Class; WCCO Good Neighbor Award, State of MN Certificate of Commendation for Scandinavia Today; MN's Swede of the Year, Swedish Community-Svenskarnas Dag Ctee.; Woman of the Year, The MN Women's Yearbook Advisory Board; Career Achievement Award, Sls. and Mktg. Exec. of Minneapolis, 1983; "Marilyn Nelson Day"; Distinguished Service Award, City of Minneapolis; Outstanding Business Leader, Northwood U., 1995; National Caring Award, Caring Institute, 1995; "Woman of the Year", Roundtable for Women in Foodservice, 1995; "Most Powerful Women in Travel," Travel Agent magazine, 1997; "Person of the Year," Travel Agent magazine, 1998; Honorary Doctor of Business Admin. Hospitality Mgmt. from Johnson & Wales U., Providence, RI, 1998; ranked seventh on Fortune magazine's inaugural list of the 50 Most Powerful Women in American Business (Oct. 1998); Executive of the Year, Corporate Report MN, 1999; Service Above Self Award, Rotary Club of Downtown Minneapolis, 1999; Medalist, Smith College, 2000; Most Powerful Woman in Travel, Travel Agent magazine, 2000. **Act./Mem.:** past Chair, Scandinavia Today-MN, 1980-83; past Dir., Jr. Achievement, KTCA Channel 2, MN Congressional Awards (1980-83), Wamso (MN) Opera Companies, Greater Minneapolis Girl Scout Council; Campaign Chair, United Way of Minneapolis; Mem., Ctee. of 200, Woodhill Country Club, Northwest Tennis Club, Minneapolis Club, Hennepin County Medical Society Auxiliary Inc., MN Meeting, Jr. League of Minneapolis, Smith College Alumni Assn., Smith Club of MN.

William G. Ness Chair, Arctic Cat Inc., P.O. Box 810, Thief River Falls, MN 56701. Tel: 218/681-8558. Email: wgacat@aol.com **B:** May 22, 1938, Fosston, Minn. **M:** Henrietta, 1960. **C:** Gregory, Teresa, Jon, Jeffrey, Rachel. **E:** U. of ND-Grand Forks, BS-Electrical Engrg., 1960; U. of MN, Exec. Program, 1971-72. **Career Hist.:** Electrical Engr., Remington Rand Univac, 1960-61; Dir.-Engrg., Dow Key Company, 1961-66; Arctic Enterprises: Dir.-Engrg., 1966-76; EVP, 1976-81; Arctic Cat Inc.: Pres., CEO, 1982-85; Chair, 1985-present. **Career Act.:** Dir., Northern State Bank (Thief River Falls), Northern Woodwork Inc. (Thief River Falls), Itasca-Bemidji Inc. (Bemidji), May Corp. (Mpls.). **Dec./Awd.:** 1973 Boss of the Year, Thief River Falls Jaycees; President's Award, Thief River Falls Chamber of Commerce, 1985; Snowmobile Hall of Fame, 1996. **Act./Mem.:** Ducks Unlimited; Catholic Church; Sno-Drifters.

Ann K. Newhall EVP, COO, Rural Cellular Corp., 3905 Dakota St. S.W., P.O. Box 2000, Alexandria, MN 56308. Tel: 320/762-2000. **B:** March 23, 1951, Fairmont, MN. **M:** Richard Schleuss. **C:** Amanda, Ben. **E:** St. Olaf College, B.A.; U of M Law School, J.D. with honors. **Career Hist.:** Joined Moss & Barnett law firm in 1977 and was a shareholder from 1980-99; served as a member of the Board of Dir. from 1995-99; served as Pres./COO from 1997-99; joined Rural Cellular in Feb. 1999 as SVP and Gen. Counsel; served as member of the Board of Directors from Aug. 1999-present and as EVP and COO from Aug. 2000 to present.

Richard D. Newland Pres., CEO, Connexus Energy, 14601 Ramsey Blvd., Ramsey, MN 55303. Tel: 612/323-2600. **B:** Feb. 14, 1947, Medford, Ore. **M:** Carol, 1968. **C:** Rick, Scott. **E:** U. of Oregon, BS-Business Admin., 1974; U. of St. Thomas, MBA, 1995. **Career Hist.:** Gen. Mgr., Lane Electrical Cooperative (Eugene, Oregon), 1977-81; Communications Mgr., WPPSS (Richland, Washington), 1981-83; Utilities Mgr., Ketchikan (Alaska) Public Utilities, 1983-85; Gen. Mgr., Chugach (Alaska) Electrical Co-op, 1985-88; Pres., CEO, Connexus Energy, 1988-present.

Kathleen Picotte Newman Pres., Larkin, Hoffman, Daly & Lindgren Ltd., 1500 Norwest Financial Center, 7900 Xerxes Ave. S., Bloomington, MN 55431. Tel: 612/896-3283. **B:** Oct. 26, 1948, Newport, R.I. **M:** David P. Newman, 1984. **C:** Tina Picotte, Matthew Newman. **E:** BA-Economics, Hamline U., 1978; JD, William Mitchell College of Law, 1981. **Career Hist.:** Jack S. Jaycox law Offices Ltd., 1981-83; Larkin, Hoffman, Daly & Lindgren, 1983-present. **Career Act.:** Larkin, Hoffman Strategic Planning Ctee., Hennepin County Legal Ethics Ctee.; Co-Chair, Family Law Section, Hennepin County Bar Assn.; Pres., Larkin, Hoffman, Daly & Lindgren Ltd. **Dec./Awd.:** Best Lawyers in America, 1993-94, 1995-96, 1997-1998; MN Leading Attorney, 1993-present. **Act./Mem.:** Hennepin County Bar Assn., American Bar Assn.

Larry M. Newman Regional VP-Sls., AT&T, AT&T Tower, 901 Marquette Ave., Minneapolis, MN 55402. Tel: 612/376-5401. **B:** Jun. 11, 1950, Omaha, Neb. **M:** Roberta S., 1976. **C:** Jerad, Randy. **E:** U of MO, BS, Mktg., 1972; Advanced Mgmt. Program-AT&T, 1990; Harvard U. Strategic Mgmt. and Mktg. Program, 1995. **Career Hist.:** Northwestern Bell, 1976-82: Market Mgr., 1976-77; Sls. Mgr., 1978-79; District Mktg. Mgr., 1980-81; Division Mktg. Mgr., 1982; American Bell, Branch Mgr., 1983-85; AT&T, Div. Mgr., Product Mktg., 1986-89; Call Interactive, COO, 1989-92; AT&T, Regional VP, 1992-present.. **Career Act.:** Dir., 1997 Chair, Greater Minneapolis Chamber of Commerce; Trustee, William Mitchell College of Law. **Act./Mem.:** Golden Valley Country Club, Minneapolis Club.

Dieter H. Nickel Chair, Pres., Church Mutual Insurance, 3000 Schuster Ln., Merrill, WI 54452. Tel: 715/536-5577. **B:** Jul. 27, 1936, Minneapolis. **M:** Pamela, 1961. **C:** Theodore, Karl, Nickel, Kathy, Lyn, Riegelman. **E:** Valparaiso U.: BA-Political Science, 1958; JD, 1960. **Career Hist.:** U.S. Marine Corps Reserve, 1960-66; Practicing Attorney, Nienow and Nickel Attorneys, 1961-67; Practicing Attorney, Schmitt, Nienow, Nickel and Nolan Law Firm, 1968-71; Church Mutual Insurance Co., 1971-present: Pres., 1971-present; Chair, 1979-present. **Career Act.:** Dir., Church Service Corp., Merrill Federal Savings and Loan Assn., Alliance of American Insurers (Chair,1988-89); Mem., American Bar Assn., State Bar of WI, Lincoln County Bar Assn., Valparaiso U. Advisory Board, Merrill Area Development Corp.; past D.A., Lincoln Co. (WI); past Chair, Lincoln County Republican Party; past Pres., Merrill Area Lions Club; past Dir., M&I First American National Bank (Wausau, WI). **Dec./Awd.:** Distinguished Service Award, Merrill Jaycees, 1970; Merrill-On-The-Move Civic Award, 1981. **Act./Mem.:** Mem./Sec., Merrill Fire and Police Commission; Mem., Great Speakers Forum Ctee., Alliance of American Insurers-Investment Ctee.; Dir., Lutheran Music Program; past Chair (5-term), Re-Election Ctee. for Sheehan Donoghue for WI State Assembly.

Laurence J. Niederhofer Dir., Apogee Enterprises Inc., 7900 Xerxes Ave. S., Bloomington, MN 55431. Tel: 715/842-4006. **B:** Jul. 15, 1932, Minneapolis. **M:** Shirley, 1958. **C:** Renee, James, Anne. **E:** College of St. Thomas, BA, 1958. **Career Hist.:** CPA, Sevenich & Company, 1957-61; Cont., Apogee Enterprises Inc., 1961-68; Wausau Metals Corp.: Pres., 1968-80; CEO, 1980-91; CEO, Window Fabrication Div. of Apogee Enterprises Inc., 1991-93; VChair, Apogee Enterprises Inc., 1983-93. **Career Act.:** Dir., Apogee Enterprises, 1964-present. **Dec./Awd.:** 20-year leadership award presented by Apogee Enterprises Inc., 1981. **Act./Mem.:** past Dir., Wausau Area Chamber of Commerce; past VP, Architectural Aluminum Assn.; Dir., M&I First American National Bank (Wausau); past Chair, Wausau Area Jr. Achievement; Past Pres., United Way; Chair, Community Health Care Inc.

Richard (Dick) Niemiec SVP-Corp. Affairs/Affiliate Op., Blue Cross and Blue Shield of Minnesota, 3535 Blue Cross Rd., P.O. Box 64560, Eagan, MN 55164. Tel: 651/456-1515. Email: dniemiec@bcbsmn.com **B:** Sep. 3, 1943, Chicago. **M:** Joan, 1968. **C:** Sara, Randy, Jessica. **E:** Bachelor's-Math, Beloit (WI) College, 1965; Master's-Statistics, U. of Missouri, 1967. **Career Hist.:** Sr. Systems Analyst, Honeywell, 1969-73; Blue Cross and Blue Shield of Minnesota/Blue Plus, affiliate HMO, 1973-present: Mrg.-Technical Svs., 1973-75; Mgr.-Actuarial Research, 1975-82; SVP-Corp. Affairs, 1982-present. **Career Act.:** Mem., American Academy of Actuaries, MN HealthCare Commission (1992-1997), MN Small Group Reinsurance Assn. Board (1992-present), MN Risk Adjustment Assn. Bd. (1994-1997), American Red Cross National Biomedical Board (1998 to present) American Red Cross Regional Blood Services; Board (Chair, 1994-present), Walk-In Counseling Center Board (1983-present, past Pres.); Smoke-Free 2000 Coalition 1986-1995 (past Pres.); MN Higher Education Board (1991-94); MN Community College Board (past Pres., 1984-92), MN Legislative Task Force on Education Organization (1989-1990); Kobe College Foundation Board (1992 to present). **Dec./Awd.:** Teaching Excellence Certificate, Metropolitan State University, 1981; Clara Barton Award for Meritorious Volunteer Leadership, American Red Cross, 2000. **Act./Mem.:** United Way, Friends of Scouting; Distinguished Alumni Award, Beloit College, 1996; Spurgeon Award-Outstanding Role Model for Youth, Indianhead Council, Boy Scouts of America, 2000.

Lance Nienow Pres., CEO, Weinbrenner Shoe Co. Inc., 108 S. Polk St., Merrill, WI 54452. Tel: 715/536-5521. **B:** Oct. 20, 1943, Merrill, Wis. **C:** Nicole, Carrie. **E:** U. of WI: BS, 1965; MA, 1967. **Career Hist.:** Pres., CEO, Weinbrenner Shoe Co., 28 years.

Dan Nitz Pres., CEO, Brown Printing Co., 2300 Brown Ave., P.O. Box 1549, Waseca, MN 56093. Tel: 507/835-2410. **B:** Jun. 17, 1946, Janesville, Wis. **M:** Linda, 1967. **C:** Marnie, Mandy. **E:** U. of WI: BSME (Mechanical Engrg.), 1969; MBA, 1979. **Career Hist.:** 10 years with Procter & Gamble; 20 years with Brown Printing.

John C. Noble Chair, CEO, Northwestern Travel Management, 7250 Metro Blvd., Minneapolis, MN 55439. Tel: 612/921-3700. Email: reefkeys@aol.com **B:** Sep. 27, 1930, Evanston, Ill. **M:** Linda, 1991. **C:** Peter, Clifford, John P., Jack. **E:** Brown U. (Providence, RI); U. of MN, business degree. **Career Hist.:** Account Supervisor, Campbell-Mithun Advertising, 1957-71; Chair, Northwestern Travel Service (dba Northwestern Travel Management/Mainline Travel/Northwestern Incentive Services/Dayton's Travel), 1971-present. **Career Act.:** Mem., Travel Agent Advisory Board, Alamo Rent a Car, Assn. of Corporate Travel Executives, American Society of Travel Agents; past Pres., Upper Midwest Chapter of American Society of Travel Agents, Ritz-Carlton Hotel Travel Advisory Board; Chair, Woodside Travel Trust, 1989-2000.. **Dec./Awd.:** Certificate of Commendation for participation in MS 150 Bike Tour, 1990; Certificate of Completion, Colorado Outward Bound Course, 1990. **Act./Mem.:** Minneapolis Club; Woodhill Country Club; Ocean Reef Club.

Jeffrey Noddle Pres., COO, Supervalu Inc., 11840 Valley View Rd., P.O. Box 990 (55440), Eden Prairie, MN 55344. Tel: 612/828-4000. **B:** Jun. 2, 1946, Omaha, Neb. **M:** Linda, 1968. **C:** Julie, Stacey. **E:** BA-Business Admin., U. of IA, 1969; American Mgmt. Assn. Executive Course, 1975; Levinson Inst., 1978; Wharton School Executive Advanced Mgmt. Program, 1990. **Career Hist.:** Retail positions, Supermarkets Interstate (div. J.C. Penney Co.), 5 years; Supervalu Inc. (1976-present): Dir.-Retail Op., Dir.-Mdsg., VP-Mktg., JM Jones (Champaign, IL), 1976-82; Div. Pres. (Fargo, ND; Miami), 1982-85; Corp. VP-Mdsg., 1985-88; SVP-Mktg., 1988-92; EVP, 1992-present; Pres./COO-Wholesale Food Cos., 1995-2000; 2000-present, Pres. and COO of SuperValue, Inc. **Career Act.:** Industry ECR Exec. Ctee.; Exec. Board, Sarah W. Stedman Center for Nutritional Studies/ Duke Medical Center; Board of Dir., IGA USA and National Grocers Assn.; Board of Gov. Food Distributor International; Board of Dir., BICCGeneral. **Act./Mem.:** United Way Campaign of Minneapolis; Board of Directors, Boys and Girls Club of the Twin Cities.

Lowell Noteboom Pres., Leonard, Street and Deinard, 150 S. Fifth St., Suite 2300, Minneapolis, MN 55402. Tel: 612/335-1573. Email: ljn1573@email.leonard.com **B:** Aug. 22, 1942, Viborg, S.D. **M:** Sonja, 1964. **C:** Todd, Dana, Andrea. **E:** BA, Augustana College, 1964; JD, U. of Denver College of Law, 1967. **Career Hist.:** Leonard, Street and Deinard, 1971-present: Attorney, 1971; Pres., 1993. **Career Act.:** Founding Chair, Construction Law Dept. (Leonard, Street and Deinard); past Dir., MacPhail Center for the Arts (Chair in 1993 & 1994); Dir., St. Paul Chamber Orchestra; Trustee, National Guild of Community Schools of the Arts. **Dec./Awd.:** Certified Trial Specialist.

Jay Novak SVP, Stockwalk.com Group Inc., 5500 Wayzata Blvd., Suite 800, Golden Valley, MN 55416. Tel: 763/543-4904. Email: jnovak@mjk-sales.com **B:** May 30, 1950, Milwaukee. **M:** Jennifer, 1974. **C:** Amanda, Nicholas, Joseph. **E:** U. of WI, B.A.-Journalism, 1972; U. of MN, Masters in Journalism, 1976. **Career Hist.:** Reporter and Editor, Worthington Daily Globe, 1976-81; Editor, Commercial West, 1981-83; Editor and Assoc. Publisher, Corporate Report Minnesota, 1983-90 (also editor CityBusiness newspaper, 1989); Dir.-Communications, Boschwitz reelection campaign, 1990; Dir.-Communications, General Mills Inc., 1990-93; Editor, Twin Cities Business Monthly, 1993-95; Commissioner, MN Dept. of Trade and Economic Devel., 1995-99; SVP, Miller, Johnson & Kuehn (now Stockwalk.com Group Inc.), 1999-present. **Career Act.:** Chair, MN Public Facilities Authority, Urban Initiatives Board, Minn. Agricultural and Economic Devel., MN Job Skills Partnership, MN Export Finance Authority; Dir. and Mem., MN Housing Finance Authority, MN World Trade Center, Advantage

MN; Dir., Canada-MN Business Council, MN Technology Inc.; Dir., MN Turnaround Mgmt. Assn., Greater Minneapolis Convention and Visitors Assn.; International Technology Consultants; Mem., Legislative Council on Competitiveness, Legislative Commission on Corporate Subsidiaries, U. of MN Carlson School International Advisory Board, Governor's Workforce Devel. Council, Six O'Clock Club, Twin Cities Discussion Group, The Collaborative, Dakota County Economic Devel. Partnership, Association for Corporate Growth. **Dec./Awd.:** Harrison Salisbury Annual Achievement Award, U. of MN Daily Alumni Assn.; U. of MN College of Liberal Arts, "Alumnus of Notable Achievement".

Daniel W. O'Brien Chair, Maple Island Inc., 2497 Seventh Ave. E., North St. Paul, MN 55109. Tel: 651/773-2671. Email: dwo@maple-island.com **B:** Jan. 6, 1926, St. Paul. **M:** Sarah Stoltze, 1952. **C:** Bridget, D. William, Kevin, Timothy. **E:** U. of MN, BSL, JD, 1949. **Career Hist.:** Attorney, 1949-65; Pres., F.H. Stoltze Land & Lumber Company, 1964-present; Counsel, Doherty Rumble & Butler, 1965-1999; Pres., Maple Island Inc., 1968-1996. **Career Act.:** past Dir., Villaume Industries, Evercolor Inc.; Mem., MN Execs. Organization, World Business Council, Chief Executives Organization.

James E. O'Brien Chair, CEO (retired), Moss & Barnett, 4800 Norwest Center, 90 S. Seventh St., Minneapolis, MN 55402. Tel: 612/347-0273. Email: OBrienJ@moss-barnett.com **B:** Jun. 10, 1937, Minneapolis. **M:** Patricia, 1958. **C:** Daniel, Martin. **E:** BA, U. of Alaska, 1962; JD (cum laude, Law Review 1963-65, Senior Editor 1965, Order of the Coif), U. of MN, 1965. **Career Hist.:** Russian Linguist, U.S. Air Force Security Service; Moss & Barnett: has been employed there as an attorney since 1965 and has held all officer positions. **Career Act.:** Mem., American Bar Assn., MN State Bar Assn., Hennepin County Bar Assn.; has taught various business law courses at U. of MN; has lectured on corporate, tax, and securities law involving the purchase and sale of a business. **Dec./Awd.:** Selected by peers as Leading Minnesota Attorney in Publicly Held Corporation Law, Securities and Venture Finance Law, and Small and Privately Held Business Law, 1994-99; Elected Chair of Unilaw, an association of law firms across the U.S. **Act./Mem.:** Past Dir., and Chair, Opportunity Partners Inc.; Dir., Fund for the Legal Aid Society; Mem. and Dir., Mpls. Kiwanis Club (past Trustee/Pres., Mpls. Kiwanis Fdn.).

Gary Olen Chair, The Sportsman's Guide Inc., 411 Farwell Ave., South St. Paul, MN 55075. Tel: 651/451-3030. **B:** Mar. 29, 1942, Milwaukee. **C:** Wendy, Jeff. **E:** Marquette U. high school. **Career Hist.:** Trainee, Supervisor, Mgr., Rebuyer, J.C. Penney Catalog Div., 1960-67; Merchandise Mgr., C&H Distributors, 1967-70; Merchandise Dir., Fidelity Products, 1970-77; The Sportsman's Guide: EVP, Pres. and CEO,1977-2000; Chm., 2000-present. **Career Act.:** Dir., The Sportsman's Guide. **Act./Mem.:** Direct Mail Mktg. Assn.; National Sporting Goods Assn.; NRA.

Dale R. Olseth Chair, CEO, SurModics Inc., 9924 W. 74th St., Eden Prairie, MN 55344. Tel: 612/829-2700. **B:** Oct. 5, 1930, St. James, Minn. **M:** Nancy; 1960. **C:** Cheryl, Karen, Jon, David. **E:** U. of MN, BA-Business Admin., 1952; Amos Tuck School of Business Admin., Dartmouth College, MBA, 1956. **Career Hist.:** Supv. of Budgets, Cummins Engine Company, 1956-58; Merchandise Mgr., Foley Mfg. Company, 1958-61; VP, Dir., Dain, Kalman & Quail, 1961-71; Pres., CEO, Tonka Corp., 1971-76; Pres., CEO, Medtronic Inc., 1976-86; Chair, CEO, Pres. SurModics Inc., 1986-present; Chair and CEO, SurModics, Inc. 1998-present. **Career Act.:** Dir., Graco Inc., Toro Company, U. of MN Alumni Assn., U. of MN Fdn.; U of MN Gateway Corporation; past Gen. Chair, and Pres., United Way of Minneapolis; Dir., past Pres., Jr. Achievement of Minneapolis; Past Chair, U. of MN Fdn.; VChair, Greater MN Corp.; past Board of Regents, St. Olaf College; past Chair, Health Industry Mfrs. of America; Dir. and Past Chair, MN Orchestral Assn.; Dir., Carlson School of Mgmt.; past Chair, Twin City Public Television; past vice chair, Sister Kenny Institute; Past Board Methodist Hospital; past board member Minneapolis Club; past board member YMCA; past board member MN Business Partnership; past board member STEP-State of Minnesota. **Dec./Awd.:** Regents Award, U. of MN, 1989; Distinguished Service Award, United Way of Minneapolis, 1985; Outstanding Philanthropist of the Year (MN chapter); Service Above Self Award, Rotary Intl. **Act./Mem.:** United Way of Minneapolis, Interlachen Country Club, Minneapolis Club.

David C. Olson Pres., Minnesota Chamber of Commerce, 30 E. Seventh St., Suite 1700, St. Paul, MN 55101. Tel: 651/292-4650. **B:** July 25, 1956, Minneapolis. **M:** Carolyn, 1983. **C:** Erik, Nick. **E:** B.A., St. Olaf College, 1978; M.S., Mankato State U., 1981; Graduate, U.S. Chamber of Commerce Institute of Organization Mgmt., 1985. **Career Hist.:** Asst. to Mpls. City Clerk, 1978-1979; Program Mgr., Energy Council and Transportation Council, Greater Mpls. Chamber of Commerce, 1979-1981; Group Mgr.-Economic Devel., Greater Mpls. Chamber of Commerce, 1981-1982; Exec. Dir., Burnsville Chamber of Commerce, 1982-1985; Pres., TwinWest Chamber of Commerce, 1985-1990; VP-Op. and Devel., Minnesota Chamber of Commerce, 1990-1991; Pres., Minn. Chamber of Commerce, 1991-present. **Career Act.:** Chair, U.S. Chamber of Commerce Institute for Organization Mgmt.; Mem., Governor's Workforce Devel. Council; Mem., U.S. Chamber of Commerce Ctee.; Dir., Minn. Chamber of Commerce; Mem., Workers' Compensation Advisory Council; Member, Supreme Court Jury Task Force. **Dec./Awd.:** CityBusiness 40 Under 40, 1996.

Dwight D. Opperman Chair, Key Investment Inc., 601 Second Ave. S., Suite 5200, Minneapolis, MN 55402. Tel: 612/370-1721. **B:** Jun. 26, 1923, Perry, Iowa. **M:** Jeanice, 1942 (deceased). **C:** Vance K., Fane W.. **E:** Drake U., LLB, JD, 1951. **Career Hist.:** West Publishing Co., 1951-1996: Editor, 1951-60; Asst. Editorial Counsel, 1960-64; Mgr.-Reporters and Digest Dept., 1964-65; VP, 1965-68; Asst. to Pres., 1967-68; Pres., 1968-93; CEO, 1978-96; Chair, 1993-96; Chair Emeritus, 1996-1997; Key Investment Inc.: Chair, 1996-present. **Career Act.:** VP, Dir., Exec. Ctee., American Judicature Society; Trustee, Founder, Chair, Supreme Court Hist. Society; Trustee, United Way of St. Paul, James J. Hill Reference Lib., Drake U.; Mem., National Advisory Ctee., National Institute for Citizen Education in the Law; past Pres., MN Club; Drake Board of Governors; Drake Task Force; Dir., Institute of Judicial Admin., Minnesota DARE, Brennan Center for Justice, MN Chapter Federal Bar Assn., National Legal Center for Public Interest, New York U Law School, National Center for State Courts; member American Law Institute. **Dec./Awd.:** Distinguished Service Award, Drake U. National Alumni Assn., 1974; Centennial Award, Drake U. National Alumni Assn., 1981; Herbert Harley Award, American Judicature Society, 1984; Outstanding Alumni Award, Drake U., 1988; Justice Award, American Judicature Society, 1992; Wickersham Award, Library of Congress, 1993; Lifetime Achievement Award, MN State Bar Assn., 1997; Benefactor ($50 million donation), Drake U. (Des Moines, IA), 1996 LLD Drake 1998. **Act./Mem.:** American Bar Assn., Federal Bar Assn., MN Club, American Law Institute, Fellows of the American Bar Fdn., Minneapolis Club.

Vance K. Opperman Pres., CEO, Key Investment Inc., 601 Second Ave. S., Minneapolis, MN 55402. Tel: 612/333-6700. **B:** Jan. 8, 1943, Des Moines, Iowa. **M:** Darin. **C:** Grant, Hayley, Nathaniel, Cassandra, Chaney, Vanessa. **E:** J.D., U. of MN, 1969. **Career Hist.:** Assoc., Doherty Rumble & Butler, 1969-74; Ptnr., Doherty Rumble & Butler, 1974-78; Founder and Ptnr., Opperman Heins & Paquin, 1978-93; Pres., West Publishing, 1993-96; Chair, Gen. Counsel, MN Journal of Law & Politics, 1996-present; Pres., CEO, Key Investment Inc., 1997-present. **Career Act.:** Dir., Thomson Corp., Metropolitan Economic Devel. Assn. (MEDA). **Dec./Awd.:** 1996 Entrepreneur of the Year, MN High Technology Council.

Donald G. Oren Pres., CEO, Dart Transit Co., 800 Lone Oak Rd., P.O. Box 64110 (55164), Eagan, MN 55121. Tel: 651/688-2000. **B:** May 13, 1931, St. Paul. **M:** Beverly, 1957. **C:** David, Daniel, Bradley, Angela. **E:** Augsburg College, BA, 1953; U. of MN, MBA, 1956. **Career Hist.:** Dart Transit Co., 1953-present: Marketing and operations positions; CEO and Pres. **Career Act.:** North Park University, Board of Trustees (1995-2000); Augsburg College, Board of Regents (1982-1994); Minnesota Trucking Assn., Board of Dir. (1998-2000). **Dec./Awd.:** Minnesota Trucking Association President's Award, 1983; St. Paul Chamber of Commerce Small Business Person Award, 1997.

Steven R. Orr Chair, Pres., CEO, Banner Health System, 4310 17th Ave. S.W., P.O. Box 6200, Fargo, ND 58106. Tel: 701/277-7500. **E:** BA, Macalester College, 1969; MHA, U. of MN, 1973. **Career Hist.:** Coord. master's studies programs in hospital and health care admin., U. of MN, 1974-76; VP, Fairview Community Hospitals (Mpls.), 1976-81; COO-Mid Atlantic Health Group, Admin.-Monmouth Medical Center (Long Branch, NJ), 1981-83; VP, The Planning Decisions Group (Chicago), 1983-85; Principal, Peat Marwick Main & Co. (Mpls.), 1985-88; Pres./CEO, Lutheran Health Systems (Fargo, ND), 1988-94; Chair/Pres./CEO, LHS Inc./Lutheran Health Systems (now Banner Health System), 1994-present. **Career Act.:** Dir., Healthcare Forum, Premier, American Excess Insurance Ltd.; Mem./Delegate/Chair-Elect of the Gov. Council of the Section for Health Care Systems, American Hospital Assn.; Preceptor, U. of MN Graduate Program in Hospital Admin.

Greg Ortale Pres., CEO, Greater Mpls. Convention and Visitors Assn., 4000 Multifoods Tower, 33 S. Sixth St., Minneapolis, MN 55402. **B:** Dec. 29, 1948. **M:** yes. **C:** two adult children. **E:** BA-Poli.Sci./History, Drake U. (Des Moines, IA). **Career Hist.:** Dir.-Sls., Des Moines Convention Bureau, 1972; Dir., Flint (MI) Area Convention & Tourist Council; Michigan Travel Commission, 1975; Sr. Mgr.-Business Devel. Div., Greater Des Moines Chamber of Commerce Federation, 1977; Gen. Mgr., Greater Houston Convention and Visitors Council, 1979 (EVP and Gen. Mgr., 1984); Pres., CEO, Greater Mpls. Convention and Visitors Assn., 1987-present. **Career Act.:** International Assn. of Convention & Visitor Bureaus: Chair, (1999-2000), Mem., American Society of Assn. Execs., MN Society of Assn. Execs.; Dir., Minneapolis Downtown Council, Metropolitan Public Airports Fdn.; Texas Travel Industry Congress, National Association of Black Meeting Planners.

Roger O'Shaughnessy Pres., Cardinal IG Co., 12301 Whitewater Dr., Suite 250, Hopkins, MN 55343. Tel: 612/935-1722. **B:** Jan. 15, 1943, San Francisco. **M:** 1964. **E:** U. of MN. **Career Hist.:** Cardinal IG, 1966-present: VP, 1966-67; Pres., 1967-present.

Larry G. Osnes Pres., Hamline University, 1536 Hewitt Ave., St. Paul, MN 55104. Tel: 651/523-2202. Email: presoffice@gw.hamline.edu **B:** Oct. 30, 1941, Scottsbluff, Neb. **M:** Susan, 1962. **C:** Justin. **E:** Anderson College, BA, 1963; Wayne State U., MA, 1965; U. of Cincinnati, Ph.D., 1970. **Career Hist.:** Anderson College, 1970-83: Dir. of American Studies, 1970-75; Chair, Dept. of History, Philosophy, and Government, 1975-76; Dir., Center of Public Service, 1973-77; Dean, Academic Devel., 1975-78; Asst. Corp. Sec. and Dean of Academic Devel. & Public Affairs, 1978-83. MN Private College Council, Pres., 1983-88; Hamline U., Pres., 1988-present. **Career Act.:** American Council on Education, National Assn. of Schools and Colleges of the United Methodist Church, Associated Colleges of the Twin Cities, Educational and Institutional Insurance Administrators Inc. **Act./Mem.:** Hazelden.

Gregg A. Ostrander Pres., CEO, Michael Foods Inc., 324 Park Natl. Bank Building, 5353 Wayzata Blvd., St. Louis Park, MN 55416. Tel: 612/546-1500. **B:** Feb. 20, 1953, Cincinnati. **M:** Kristin, 1979. **C:** David, Joseph, Gregory. **E:** U. of WI-Madison, BA, 1975; MS, 1981. **Career Hist.:** Beatrice Foods, 1975-85: Product Mgmt., 1975-83; Dir. of Mktg., 1983-85. Armour Swift-Eckrich, 1985-93: VP Mktg., 1984-86; SVP Mktg., 1986-90. Pres., Swift-Eckrich Prepared Foods, 1990-93. Michael Foods, COO, 1993; President/CEO, 1994-present. **Career Act.:** Dir., Michael Foods Inc., Arctic Cat Inc.; Celestial Seasonings Inc.

James E. Ousley Chair, Syntegra (USA) Inc., 4201 Lexington Ave. N., Arden Hills, MN 55126. Tel: 651/415-4481. Email: james.e.ousley@cdc.com **B:** Jan. 20, 1946, Burbank, Calif. **M:** Peggy, 1995. **C:** James Jr., Nicholas. **E:** U of NE, B.S., Business Admin., 1968; Harvard International Business School, 1986. **Career Hist.:** Control Data Corp.: 1968-92: Sls. Rep., 1968; Sls. Rep.-Data Svs., U.S. Mktg., 1971; Sr. Consultant, Industry Mktg., 1973; District Sls. Mgr., U.S. Mktg., 1976; Regional Sls. Mgr., EDP Sls., U.S. Mktg., 1979; G. M., Industry Mktg., 1981; Regional VP, U.S. Mktg., 1982; VP, Peripheral Products Company, 1984; Pres., Peripheral Components International, 1986; VP and G.M., Components Business Unit, 1987; VP, Worldwide Sales and Svs.,1988-89; Pres. Computer Products Group,1989; Control Data Systems/Syntegra (USA) Inc.: Pres. and CEO, 1992; Chm., 2000. **Career Act.:** Dir., Control Data Systems Inc., MN Business Partnership, ActivCard; Bell Micro.

Gregory R. Palen Pres., CEO, Spectro Alloys Corp., 550 Vandalia St., St. Paul, MN 55114. Tel: 651/642-2546. **B:** Sep. 8, 1955. **M:** Peg, 1980. **C:** Luke, David, Kate. **E:** St. Johns U., BA; U. of MN, MBA. **Career Hist.:** VP, HT Inc.; Service Mgr., Palen/Kimball; Pres., Palen/Kimball; presently CEO, Palen/Kimball, Spectro Alloys Corp. **Career Act.:** Dir., Claremont Institute, North Central Life, Palen/Kimball Co., Polaris Inc., Spectro Alloys Corp., Valspar Corp.; Board of Regents, St. John's U; Opus Northwest LLC. **Act./Mem.:** St. Odilia Church, North Oaks Country Club, Young Presidents Organization.

William H. Palmer Pres., CEO, Miller-Dwan Medical Center, 502 E. Second St., Duluth, MN 55805. Tel: 218/727-8762. **B:** 1939, Rockford, Ill. **M:** Saundra, 1962. **E:** Rockford College, MS, 1966; U. of MN, Master's Hospital Admin., 1968. **Career Hist.:** Fairview Hospital, 1967-1975; Pres., Miller-Dwan Medical Center, 1975-present. **Career Act.:** Pres., Chair, Duluth Superior Symphony, Woodland Hills Treatment Home, Distnet Hospital Assn., Miller-Dwan Fdn.; Dir., Northland Fdn., MN Hospital Assn., Northern Lakes Healthcare Consortium, Duluth Graduate Medical Education Council; Chairman, MN Safety Council Board. **Act./Mem.:** Northland Country Club, Kitchi Gammi Club.

Anita M. Pampusch Pres., Bush Foundation, First National Bank Bldg., St. Paul, MN 55101. Tel: 651/227-0891. **B:** Aug. 28, 1938, St. Paul. **E:** College of St. Catherine, BA, Math, 1962; U. of Notre Dame, MA-Philosophy, 1970, Ph.D., 1972. **Career Hist.:** St. Joseph's Academy, Math and Science Teacher, 1962-66. College of St. Catherine, 1970-present: Philosophy Prof., 1970-76; Assoc. Academic Dean, 1977-79; VP and Academic Dean, 1979-84; Pres., 1984-97; Pres., The Bush Fdn., 1997-present; Dir., U. of Notre Dame; Dir., William Mitchell College of Law; Dir. Council of Independent Colleges. **Career Act.:** Dir., The St. Paul Companies Inc., Assn. of American Colleges and Universities, the Allina Fdn.; Dir., The Bush Fdn. (Trustee, 1996 Chair), MN Meeting, MN Historical Society, St. Paul Area Chamber of Commerce, MN Women's Forum; Governing Board, Minneapolis Club; past Dir., St. Paul Academy/Summit School, St. Paul United Way, St. Paul Athletic Club, National Council of Christians and Jews, Children's Theatre, J.J. Hill Reference Library, Derham Hall High School; Executive Ctee., Chair, Women's College Coalition. **Dec./Awd.:** Leadership Award in Education, YWCA, 1987; Otto Bremer So. St. Paul Hall of

Excellence, 1987; Doctor of Humane Letters, Honoris Causa: College of St. Mary's of Omaha, 1990, Concordia College, 1997, College of Our Lady of the Elms (Springfield, MA),1997; Macalester College, 1999; MN Alumni Award of the Year, U. of Notre Dame, 1990; Lumen Vitae Award, College of St. Benedict, 1997. **Act./Mem.:** Minneapolis Club, Minnesota Club; University Club.

Jeffrey J. Parell Pres.-North American Group, AutoNation Inc., 7700 France Ave. S., Edina, MN 55435. Tel: 612/830-2121. **B:** Nov. 29, 1954, Chicago. **M:** Linda. **C:** two. **E:** BA, Western IL U., 1977. **Career Hist.:** Div. VP-Central Op., Hertz Car Rental, 1977-87; National Car Rental Systems (AutoNation): Regional Mgr.-Op., 1978; EVP-Op., 1995; Pres. and COO, 1997-98; Pres.-North American Rental Group 1998-present. **Act./Mem.:** Interlachen Country Club.

Gerald A. Paulsen CEO, Jerry's Enterprises Inc., 5101 Vernon Ave. S., Edina, MN 55436. Tel: 612/929-2685. **B:** May 1, 1923, Minneapolis. **M:** Shirley, 1947. **C:** Charlotte, LuAnn, Cheryl. **E:** U. of MN, BA. **Act./Mem.:** Rotary.

Eric H. Paulson Pres., CEO, Navarre Corp., 7400 49th Ave. N., New Hope, MN 55428. Tel: 612/535-8333. **B:** Apr. 24, 1945, South Bend, Ind. **M:** Karen. **C:** Janel Olson, Natalie Ogg, Ann Nugent, Joshua Wright, Mike Winter, Jill Winter. **E:** U. of Southern WI. **Career Hist.:** Sls. Mgr., National Tape and Record, 197-70. Producer, SRO Production, 1970-72. National Sls. Mgr., Transcontinental Music, 1972-74; SVP and Gen. Mgr., Pickwick International, 1974-83. Chair and CEO, Navarre Corp., 1983-present. **Career Act.:** Dir., Navarre Corp., River Road Productions, River Road Records, Digital Entertainment, Lakefront Entertainment; Chair, Net Radio; Dir., Net Radio; Dir., NARM; Board of Gov., Lafayette County Clev. **Dec./Awd.:** Purple Heart, Vietnam, 1965; Branch Manager of the Year, Pickwick International, 1976; Entrepreneur of the Year Runner-up, 1989, 1995. **Act./Mem.:** Layfayette Country Club, Calhoun Beach Club, Children's Cancer Research Institute; Dir., NARM.

Luigino F. (Jeno) Paulucci Chair, Luigino's Inc., 525 Lake Ave. S., Duluth, MN 55802. Tel: 218/723-5555. **B:** Jul. 7, 1918, Aurora, Minn. **M:** Lois Mae Trepanier, 1947. **C:** Michael J., Cynthia J., Gina J. **E:** Hibbing (MN) Jr. College, 1936-37. **Career Hist.:** City Markets (Hibbing), 1932-33; MN Market (Hibbing), 1933-35; Hancock-Nelson Co. (St. Paul), 1935-43. Founder, Bean Sprouts Growers Assn., 1944-47; Founder and Pres., Chun King Corp. (Duluth), 1947-67; Etor Realty Co. (Duluth). Chair, Co-founder, R.J. Reynolds Foods Inc., now Nabisco Reynolds, New York; 1967-71; Chair, Dir., Jeno's Inc. (Duluth), 1968-85; Jeno F. Paulucci Enterprises (now Paulucci International Ltd.), 1967-present. JFP Gray Process Ltd. (Duluth), 1967-present; Central Produce and Equipment Inc. (Sanford, Florida), 1967-present; Founder and Chair, J.F.P. & Associates Inc. (Heathrow, Florida), 1969-present; Chair, Luigino's Pasta and Steak House Inc. (Sanford, Florida), 1988-present; Luigino's Inc. (Duluth): Founder, 1990; CEO, 1990-2000; Chair, 1990-present; Founder, Self Serve Centers Inc., 2000. **Career Act.:** Founder, Chair, Publisher, Attenzione magazine, 1979-82; Founder, Developer, Heathrow (FL) planned community, 1982; Dir., National Frozen Food Assn., Children's Home Society, Florida Central Academy; past Chair, Dir., Cornelius Co., 1969-82; Founder, Pres., N.E. MN Org. for Economic Education, 1960; Mem., Governor's Business Advisory Council, National Council-USO, U.S. Office of Emergency Planning; Founder, Chair, Jeno & Lois Paulucci Family Fdn.; Trustee, Missouri Valley College; Chair, Co-Founder, National Italian-American Fdn.; Founder, Chair, National Italian-American Fdn.'s International Board of Dir. (Washington, D.C.); Chair, Central Produce & Equipment Co.; Owner, Republic Banks of MN. **Dec./Awd.:** Decorated Order of Merit, Italy; Duluth Hall of Fame, 1962; Horatio Alger Award,1965; Outstanding Italian-American, 1965,1979; MN Salesman of the Year, Minneapolis Sls. Exec. Club, 1967; Outstanding Industrialist award, Governor of Florida, 1967; MN of the Year, MN Broadcasters Assn., 1967; Distinguished Citizen Award, MN Chapter-Public Rel. Society of America, 1967; Rizzuto medal, U.S. UNICO National, 1968; D.B.A. (hon.) Missouri Valley College, 1970; Duluth Employer of the Year, 1972; Employer of the Year, MN Governor's Council on Employment of the Handicapped, 1972; U.S. Employer of the Year, President's Council on Employment of the Handicapped-NAM, 1972; Svenskamas Dag Honorary Swede of the year, 1973; LL.D. College St. Scholastica, 1974; I Numero Uno award, Italy, 1978; U.S. Employer of the Year, WI Rehabilitation Assn., 1979; LL.D., Potomac School of Law, 1979; National Citation, National Rehabilitation Assn., 1980; Man of the Year, National Italian Org. for Charities, 1980; Lehman-La Guardia Civic Achievement Award, New York, 1984; D.B.A. (hon.), Johnson & Wales College, 1984; Mem., MN Business Hall of Fame; America's Free Enterprise Legend Award, 1992; Presbyterian Church Outstanding Marketing Executive of the Year, MN Association of DECA (Distributive Education Clubs of America), 1993; Guelielmo Marconi Award, National Order, Sons of Italy in America, 1995; Frozen Food Hall of Fame, 1997. **Act./Mem.:** Presbyterian Church.

Ronald J. Peltier Pres., CEO, Homeservices.com, 6800 France Ave. S., Suite 600, Edina, MN 55435. Tel: 612/928-5710. **B:** Mar. 18, 1949, St. Paul. **M:** Arlie, 1970. **C:** Jean Paul, Janee. **E:** U. of MN, BA, 1971; College of St. Thomas, MBA, 1974. **Career Hist.:** Edina Realty (now Homeservices.com): Sls., 1977-79; Branch Mgr., 1979-1980; Regional Mgr., 1980-83; Gen. Mgr., 1983-1992; Pres. and CEO, 1992-present. **Career Act.:** NAR Task Force; Dir., MN Club, Reliance Relocation; Chm., Realty Alliance. **Dec./Awd.:** Sponsor, Pine Tree Apple Classic Tennis Tournament for Children's Hospital Cancer Research ; Sponsor, Pass It On; Sponsor, Edina Realty Fdn. **Act./Mem.:** Rotary; "M" Club, Church activities, community coach and volunteer; Dir., Fairview Fdn.; Dir., Augsburg College.

Richard W. Perkins Pres., Dir., Perkins Capital Management Inc., 730 E. Lake St., Wayzata, MN 55391. Tel: 612/473-8367. **B:** Dec. 29, 1930, La Crosse, Wis. **C:** Richard C., Daniel S., Pamela L. **E:** U. of WI-Madison: BBA, 1955; MBA, 1957; American Institute of Banking Certificate, 1958; Chartered Financial Analyst Designation, 1966; Financial Analysts Federation Fellow, 1974; Institute of Chartered Financial Analysts Certificates of Achievement, 1986-94. **Career Hist.:** Research Dir., First Federal Savings and Loan Assn. (Chicago), 1956-57; Investment Analyst, Mgr., Investment Trust Svs. Dept.-American National Bank and Trust Co. (Chicago), 1957-58; Asst. Endowment Fund Mgr., Mayo Fdn. (Rochester, MN), 1958-65; Pension Fund Mgr., Standard Oil Co. of Ohio (Cleveland), 1965-66; Piper Jaffray Inc. (Mpls.), 1966-84: VP, 1966-78; SVP-International Dept., 1978-84; Pres., Dir., and Senior Portfolio Mgr., Perkins Capital Mgmt. Inc., 1985-present. **Career Act.:** Pres., Dir., Perkins Fdn., Perkins and Partners Inc.; Ptnr., Quest Venture Partners; Dir., Bio-Vascular Inc., Intellifilm Corp., CNS Inc., Duke Financial Group, PW Eagle, Inc., Lifecore Biomedical Inc., LSC Inc., Nortech Systems Inc., PureChoice Inc., Quantech Ltd., Vital Images Inc., Harmony Holdings Inc., American Oats Inc., TeleDigital Devel. Inc., Paper Warehouse, Inc. **Dec./Awd.:** Outstanding Director Award, 1996; Norskedahlen "Man of the Year," 1995. **Act./Mem.:** Minneapolis Club, Wayzata Country Club, City of London (England) Club.

Lawrence Perlman retired Chair/CEO, Ceridian Corp., 8100 34th Ave. S., Bloomington, MN 55425. Tel: 612/853-5283. **B:** Apr. 8, 1938, St. Paul. **M:** Linda Peterson, 1997. **C:** David, Sara. **E:** Carleton College, B.A., 1960; Harvard Law School, J.D., 1963. **Career Hist.:** Practicing Attorney 1963-1975, 1978-1980; EVP, Medtronic Inc., 1975-1978; Control Data Corp., 1980-1992; VP, Gen. Counsel and Sec., Pres. and COO, Commercial Credit Co.; Pres. and CEO, Imprimis Technology Inc.; Chair, Pres., and CEO, Ceridian 1992-1999. **Career Act.:** Advisor on work force training and development to U.S. Secretary of Labor; governing board of the Business Roundtable and chair of its Working Group on Workforce Training and Development; Dir., Ceridian Corp. (Chair), Carlson Cos. Inc., Seagate Technology Inc., The Valspar Corp.; Walker Art Center (former chair and president); MN Public Radio, Center for the American Experiment; Trustee, Carleton College; Chair, Minneapolis Police Chief Search Advisory Ctee., 1995; Mem., Governor of Minnesota's Glass Ceiling Task Force, 1995; Regent, U. of MN, 1993-95; Mem., Advisory Bd., U. of Minn. Center for

Labor Policy; Advisory Bd., J.L. Kellogg Graduate School of Mgmt. at Northwestern U.; Mem., Twenty-first Century Workforce Commission; Bd. of Trustees, Washburn Child Guidance Center. **Dec./Awd.:** Employer of the Year, National Employee Svs. and Recreation Assn., 1992; Women and Corporations that Make a Difference Award, The International Women's Forum, 1994; one of four recipients of the "Breaking the Glass Ceiling" Award, presented by Women Executives in State Government, 1995; Technology Leadership Award, MN High Technology Council, 1996; Chairman's Award, MN High Technology Council, 1997; Spirit of Minnesota Award, MN Chamber of Commerce, 1999; Executive of the Year, Corporate Report MN, 2000.

Margaret E. Perryman Pres., CEO, Gillette Children's Specialty Healthcare, 200 E. University Ave., St. Paul, MN 55101. Tel: 651/229-3839. **B:** Mar. 15, Sheridan, Wyo. **E:** U. of St. Thomas, MBA, 1978. **Career Hist.:** VP-Admin., Minneapolis Children's Medical Center, 1985-87; Pres. and CEO, Gillette Children's Specialty Healthcare, 1987-present. **Career Act.:** Dir., Gillette Children's Specialty Healthcare, Vinland Center, National Assn. of Children's Hospitals; Chair, Audubon Center of Northwoods. **Dec./Awd.:** Carroll College Alumni Hall of Fame, 1998. **Act./Mem.:** American College of Healthcare Executives, Health Leadership Trust, United Way of St. Paul, Audubon Center of North Woods, Church Finance Ctee., Board of Trustees-Carroll College.

Peter E. Person CEO, St. Mary's/Duluth Clinic Health System, 400 E. Third St., Duluth, MN 55805. Tel: 218/725-3183. Email: pperson@smdc.org **B:** Nov. 27, 1951, Sleepy Eye, Minn. **M:** Carol, 1976. **C:** Anna, Nicholas. **E:** BA, U. of MN (Morris), 1973; MD, U. of MN Medical School (Minneapolis), 1978; Residency in Internal Medicine, Mayo Clinic (Rochester, MN), 1978-81; MBA Program, U. of St. Thomas (St. Paul), MBA, 1999. **Career Hist.:** Duluth Clinic: Staff Physician-Section of General Internal Medicine, 1981-present; Board VP, 1993-95; Pres., CEO, 1995-present; CEO, St. Mary's/Duluth Clinic Health System, 1997-present. **Career Act.:** Clinical Asst. Prof., U. of MN-Duluth School of Medicine (1983-present); Dir., Division of Business and Occupational Medicine (1985-91); Dir., Duluth Clinic (1988-93, 1994-present); Chair-Compensation Ctee., Duluth Clinic (1990-95); Chair-Transition to Capitation Ctee. (1993-94); Chair, Physician Surgeons Liability Insurance Co. (1995-present); Dir., Wells Fargo Bank Duluth (1995-present); Dir., Itasca Medical Center, Grand Rapids, MN (1997-present); Chair Duluth Graduate Medical Education Committee (2000-present). **Dec./Awd.:** Diplomat, American Bd. of Internal Medicine, 1981; Fellow, American College of Physicians, 1989. **Act./Mem.:** MN Medical Assn., Lake Superior Medical Assn., American College of Physicians, Mayo Alumni Assn., Medical Group Mgmt. Assn., American College of Physician Executives.

Arthur M. Peterson Pres., CEO, Kampgrounds of America, Transwestern III Building, P.O. Box 30558, Billings, MT 59114. Tel: 406/248-7444. **B:** Oct. 16, 1934, Centerville, S.D. **M:** Carol, 1957. **C:** Curtis, Bryan, Kristin. **E:** L.A.C.C. **Career Hist.:** Various jobs, from Mgmt. Trainee to District Mgr., S.H. Kress & Co., 1952-69; National Merchandise Mgr., Kampgrounds of America, 1969-72; VP, KOA, 1972-78; EVP, COO, KOA, 1978-80; Pres., CEO, KOA, 1980-present. **Career Act.:** Chair, Dir., Sir Speedy Inc., West Advertising. **Act./Mem.:** Mem., Yellowstone Country Club, Billings Rotary, Petroleum Club, Hilands Country Club, Recreation Roundtable; Chair, National Rural Tourism Fdn.

David H. Peterson Chair, Pres., CEO-NRG Energy Inc., NRG Energy Inc., 1221 Nicollet Mall, Suite 700, Minneapolis, MN 55403. Tel: 612/373-5300. Email: david.peterson@NRGenergy.com **B:** May 1, 1941, Fergus Falls, Minn. **M:** Betty, 1960. **C:** Richard, Randall, Suzanne. **E:** U. of ND, BSE-Mechanical Engrg.; Stanford U. Graduate School of Business, Exec. Program. **Career Hist.:** Northern States Power Co., various positions, 1964-present: Pres., NRG Energy Inc. (wholly owned subsidiary of Northern States Power Co.),1989-present; Chair, Pres., and CEO, NRG Energy Inc., 1994-present. **Career Act.:** Mem., President's National Coal Council, Electric Generation Assn.; Chair, MIBRAG (Netherlands), Gladstone Joint Venture Management Ctee. (Australia), Bolivian Power Co. (Bolivia); past Dir., Western Coal Transportation Assn.; past Exec. Ctee., Montana Coal Council; past Chair, Electric Power Research Institute Ctee.; Mgmt. Ctee., Loy Yang Power, Australia. **Dec./Awd.:** Elected to Who's Who Registry of Global Business Leaders.

Mark A. Peterson Pres., CEO, Lutheran Social Service of Minnesota, 2485 Como Ave., St. Paul, MN 55108. Tel: 651/642-5990. Email: mpeterso@lss.usa.com **B:** May 1, 1945, Traverse City, Mich. **M:** Mary, 1966. **C:** Sara, Nate. **E:** St. Olaf College, BA, 1966; Lutheran School of Theology at Gettysburg, M.Div., 1970; U. of PA School of Social Work, MSW, 1972. **Career Hist.:** Lutheran Social Services of IL, Area Director, 1972-74; Lutheran Social Services of MI, VP, 1974-86; Lutheran Social Service of MN, 1987-present, Pres. **Career Act.:** Behavioral Healthcare Providers (Fairview).

Wallace R. Pettit Pres., Polka Dot Dairy Inc./Tom Thumb Food Markets, 110 E. 17th St., Hastings, MN 55033. Tel: 651/437-9023. **B:** Nov. 22, 1930, Loretto, Minn. **M:** Penny, 1954. **C:** Brenda Fahey, Bruce, Dana, Dawn Wigness, Patrick, Joel. **E:** 10th grade. **Career Hist.:** Route Driver, Dairy Home, 1946-57; Co-owner and Route Driver, Polka Dot Dairy, 1957-73; CEO and Pres., Polka Dot Dairy and Tom Thumb, 1973-present. **Dec./Awd.:** MN Grocer of the Year, 1996.

Patrick J. Peyton Chair, CEO, Despatch Industries Inc., 65 St. Anthony Parkway, Minneapolis, MN 55418. Tel: 612/781-5465. Email: ppeyton600@aol **B:** Aug. 4, 1959, Philadelphia. **M:** Melanie, 1981. **C:** Jessica, Matthew, Katherine, Kelsey. **E:** BS-Accounting/Business, Regis U. (Denver), 1981; CPA. **Career Hist.:** 1987-89: Arthur Andersen & Co. (Washington, D.C.); 1989-93: CFO-Gordon P. Getty Family and Trust (San Francisco/Washington, D.C.), CEO, Grove Press Inc. (New York);1993-94: Pres., Patrick J. Peyton & Associates; Chair/CEO, Superior Products Mfg. Co. (St. Paul) 1994-1999 Despatch Industries (Minneapolis), Ransco Industries (Oxnard, CA). **Career Act.:** Dir., Superior Products Mfg. Co., Despatch Industries, Ransco Industries, Grove Press, Weidenfeld & Nicolson (London), Delta Oil & Gas (Tyler, TX), Consortium to Serve Homeless Families (Washington, D.C.). **Act./Mem.:** Interlachen Country Club (Edina, MN), AICPA, DCICPA; Associate Cabinet Member-Holy Family Catholic High School, Minneapolis.

Addison L. Piper Chair, U.S. Bancorp Piper Jaffray, U.S. Bancorp Center, 800 Nicollet Mall, Minneapolis, MN 55402. Tel: 612/342-6060. **B:** Oct. 10, 1946, Minneapolis. **M:** Cynthia, 1979. **C:** Gretchen Piper, Tad Piper, William Piper, Betsy LaBelle, Toby LaBelle. **E:** Williams College, BA-Econ., 1968; Stanford U., MBA, 1972. **Career Hist.:** Mktg. Consultant, Earl Savage & Co., 1968-69; Piper Jaffray, 1969-present: Capital Mkt. Dept., 1969-70; Asst. Syndicate Mgr., 1972-73; VP, Dir.-Trading, 1973-77; VP, Dir.-Sls., 1977-79; EVP, Dir.-Mktg., 1979-83; CEO, Chair-Mgmt. Ctee., 1983-87; Chair, CEO, 1988-1999; 2000-present Chairman. **Career Act.:** Dir., Allina Health System; Minnesota Business Partnership; Minnesota Public Radio; St. Martin's Church Foundation; Regent of St. Olaf College; former Chairman of Abbott Northwestern Hospital; Minnesota Communications Group; former VChair Minneapolis Downtown Council and Board of Governors of the Securities Industry Association, former chair of the NYSE Regional Firms Advisory Group Committee; former Director of Greenspring Corp.; former Trustee of Woodhill Country Club, Guthrie Theatre, Washburn Child Guidance Center and the Stanford University Business School Trust. Served as warden at St. Martins By-The-Lake Church. **Act./Mem.:** Past Finance Chair, Sen. David Durenberger Finance Ctee.; Minneapolis Club, Woodhill Country Club, Country Club of the Rockies; Ventana Country Club.

Delbert L. Ploen Chair, Pres., CEO, Quali-Tech Inc., 318 Lake Hazeltine Dr., Chaska, MN 55318. Tel: 612/448-5151. **B:** May 1, 1933, Miles, Iowa. **M:** Kay, 1991. **C:** Jeffrey, Mark, Kye, Cory, Jennifer, Timothy. **E:** IA State College, BS-Forestry, 1955. **Career Hist.:** Asst. Mgr., Stabilized Vitamins (Clinton, IA), 1960-61; Mgr., Stabilized Vitamins Div. of CSC, 1961-62; Prod. Supv., Stabilized Vitamins Div. of CSC (Peoria, IL), 1962-63; Quality Control, CSC Feed Blending Plant (Terre Haute, IN), 1964-67; Founder, Quali Tech Inc., 1967; Pres., Quali Tech Inc., 1969-present. **Career Act.:** Dir. (1980-88), Chair (1986-87), National Feed Ingredients Assn.; past Pres., Northwest Feed Mfrs. Assn.; Chair, Ridgeview Hospital Fdn. (1991-92); Pres., Rotary (1993-94); Co-chair Auburn Manor Funding Campaign (1996-99). **Dec./Awd.:** Chaska Chamber of Commerce "Spirit of Chaska" Award 1998 for outstanding public service. **Act./Mem.:** Mem., past Dir., past Treas., past Pres., Chaska Rotary Club; Mem., past Dir., Chaska Chamber of Commerce; Mem., Hazeltine National Golf Club, Chaska Chamber Exec. Club; Dir., Ridgeview Hospital Fdn., Southwest Corridor Transportation Coalition, Carver-Scott Educational Cooperative, Christmas in May Chaska; United Way Key Account Executive; Co-Chair Auburn Manor Fund Drive; Ridgeview Hospital Board Member.

Carl R. Pohlad Pres., Marquette Bancshares Inc., 3800 Dain Rauscher Plaza, 60 S. Sixth St., Minneapolis, MN 55402. Tel: 612/661-3800. Email: carl.pohlad@marquette.com **B:** Aug. 23, 1915, West Des Moines, Iowa. **M:** Eloise O'Rourke, 1947. **C:** James O'Rourke, Robert Carl, William Michael. **E:** Gonzaga U. (Spokane, WA), Honorary Doctor of Laws. **Career Hist.:** Pres., Marquette Bancshares Inc. **Career Act.:** Owner, Minnesota Twins Inc.; Chair, Mesaba Holdings Inc.; past Dir., Carlson Companies; past Chair, Continental Airlines Holdings Inc.; Dir., HealthSystem MN, Boy's and Girl's Club of Minneapolis, Hugh O'Brien Youth Fdn.; past Pres., Minneapolis Chamber of Commerce; Board of Counselors, Freeman Center for International Economic Policy, Humphrey Institute of Public Affairs; Mem.-Advisory Council, Johns Hopkins Dept. of Orthopaedic Surgery. **Dec./Awd.:** Horatio Alger Assn. Award, 1989; Lifetime Achievement Award, Entrepreneur of the Year, 1995; Ellis Island Medal of Honor, 1990. **Act./Mem.:** Interlachen Country Club; Minikahda Country Club; Minneapolis Club; Minneapolis Athletic Club.

Robert M. Price Pres., PSV Inc., 14579 Grand Ave. S., Suite 100, Burnsville, MN 55306. Tel: 612/898-1171. **B:** Sep. 26, 1930, New Bern, N.C. **M:** Mary, 1952. **C:** E. Delice (Meland), Mary (Hubbard), Carrie (Walkiewicz). **E:** Duke U., BS-Math. (Magna Cum Laude), 1952; Georgia Institute of Technology, MS-Applied Math., 1958. **Career Hist.:** Mathematician, Lawrence Radiation Labs., 1953-54; Research Engr., Convair/Div. of Gen. Dynamica (San Diego), 1954-56; Research Mathematician, GA Institute of Technology, 1956-58; Mathematician, Standard Oil of CA (San Francisco), 1958-61; Control Data, 1961-90: Mathematical Staff Specialist, 1961; Mgr.-Applications Svs., 1961; Dir.-International Op., 1963; Gen. Sls. Mgr.-International Op., 1966; Gen. Sls. Mgr.-EDP Sls., 1966; VP-Sls., 1967; VP-Systems and Data Svs. Mktg., 1969; VP, Group Exec.-Svs., 1970; SVP, Group Exec.-Svs., 1972; Pres.-Systems/Svs., 1973; Pres.-Systems/Svs./Mktg., 1975; Pres.-Computer Co., 1977; Pres., COO, 1980; Chair, Pres., CEO, 1986-88; Chair, CEO, 1988-90 (retired); Chair, CEO, International Multifoods Inc., 1996-1997; Pres., PSV Inc., 1990-present. **Career Act.:** Dir., International Multifoods Inc., Public Service Company of New Mexico Inc., Tupperware Corp., Fourth Shift Corp., Affinity Technology Group Inc., Datalink Corporation; Senior Advisor and Board of Visitors, Fuqua School of Business/Duke U.; Mem., The Governor's Business Executives for Education (New Mexico); Mem.-Advisory Board, Center for International Leadership; Fellow, The International Academy of Mgmt.; Chair, National Center for Social Entrepreneurs; Co-Chair, Professional Development Ctee. of NM Goals 2000 Panel. **Dec./Awd.:** Distinguished Alumnus, Duke University, 1998. **Act./Mem.:** Fellow, International Academy of Mgmt.; Phi Beta Kappa; Sigma Xi; Omicron Delta Kappa; past Dir., United Way of Minneapolis Area; Minneapolis Club, Interlachen Country Club.

John R. Prichard COO, McGlynn Bakeries Inc., 7350 Commerce Ln., Fridley, MN 55432. Tel: 612/574-2222. **B:** Aug. 13, 1955, Siren, Wis. **M:** Patricia, 1977. **E:** BS, St. Cloud State U., 1977; Licensed CPA, 1979. **Career Hist.:** Staff Accountant, Arthur Andersen & Co., 1977-80; McGlynn Bakeries Inc., 1980-present: Cont., 1980-82; VP and Cont., 1982-86; CFO, 1986-92; COO, 1992-present. **Career Act.:** Dir., McGlynn Bakeries Inc.; Trustee Twin Cities Bakery Driver Pension Fund. **Act./Mem.:** Mem., Treas., Maple Grove Evangelical Free Church; Mem., Wayzata Country Club.

David C. Prosser Dir., RTW Inc., 8500 Normandale Lake Blvd., P.O. Box 39327, Bloomington, MN 55437. Tel: 612/893-0403. **B:** Oct. 21, 1924, Minneapolis. **M:** Margaret, 1948. **C:** Daniel, Pamela, Polly, Thomas, John. **E:** BS-Mechanical Engrg., U. of MN, 1947. **Career Hist.:** Mgmt. and engrg. position, 3M Co., 1947-65; Pres., Vocational Personnel Services Inc., 1965-83; Chair, Pres., CEO, RTW Inc., 1983-97; Chiar RTW 1997-present. Director 1999 to present.

Gregory J. Pulles VChair, Gen. Counsel, Sec., TCF Financial Corp., 801 Marquette Ave., Suite 302, Minneapolis, MN 55402. Tel: 612/661-6500. **B:** Minneapolis. **M:** Michelle. **C:** Carla, Dan, Samantha, Matthew, Patrick, Melanie, Kate. **E:** Magna cum laude graduate of U. of MN and U. of MN Law School; Mem., Order of the Coif. **Career Hist.:** Mackall, Crounse & Moore, 1973-85 (Ptnr., 1977); TCF, 1985-present: EVP/Gen. Counsel (1985) and Sec. (1989) and VChair (1993). **Career Act.:** Mem., Hennepin County Bar Assn., MN Bar Assn.; Dir., MN League of Savings and Community Bankers (Gen. Counsel, 1982-85; Chair, 1996); Trustee, Washburn Child Guidance Center (Chair-Board of Trustees, 1996), Academy of the Holy Angels; Ascension School, Legatus. **Act./Mem.:** Wayzata Country Club.

Gary B. Rappaport Chair, CEO, Venturian Corp., 11111 Excelsior Blvd., Hopkins, MN 55343. Tel: 612/931-2400. Email: garyr@venturian.com **B:** Apr. 27, 1937, Minneapolis. **M:** Susan Heller, 1961. **C:** Debra, Melissa. **E:** Wharton School of Fin. and Commerce, U. of PA, BS-Econ. **Career Hist.:** Napco Industries, 1959-1984; Asst. to Pres., 1959-61; VP, 1961-64; EVP, 1964-65; Pres., 1965-74; Chair, CEO, 1974-84; Chair, Venturian Corp., 1984-present. **Career Act.:** past Dir., Lamaur Inc.; past Mem., Twin Cities Chapter, Young Presidents Organization (Chap. Chair 1981), MN Exec. Organization. **Act./Mem.:** past Chair-Bd. of Governors, Mt. Sinai Hospital; Trustee, Metropolitan-Mt. Sinai Fdn.; past Dir., past Campaign Chair, Minneapolis Federation for Jewish Service; past Co-Chair Keystone Div., United Way; past Dir., Children's Theater Company, Minneapolis Fdn.; Mem., Temple Israel congregation; past Dir., Junior Achievement.

Gerald A. Rauenhorst Founding Chair, Opus group of cos., 10350 Bren Road West, P.O. Box 59110 (55459), Minnetonka, MN 55343. Tel: 612/936-4400. **B:** Dec. 8, 1927, Minneapolis. **M:** Henrietta Schmoll, 1950. **C:** Judith, Mark, Neil, Joseph, Michael, Susan, Amy. **E:** College of St. Thomas, BA, 1948; Marquette U., BCE, 1951. **Career Hist.:** Pres. and Founder, Rauenhorst Corp. (now Opus Corp.), 1953-99: Founding Chair-Opus Corp., 1982-99; Founding Chair-Opus LLC, Chair/CEO-Opus National LLC, 1997-99. **Career Act.:** Dir., Trustee, U. of St. Thomas, Marquette U.; Treas., Trustee, Mem.-Devel. Ctee., Papal Fdn.; Dir. Emeritus, Catholic Community Fdn. **Dec./Awd.:** Alumnus of the Year, Marquette U., 1969; Honorary Doctor of Law, U. of St. Thomas, 1971; Alumnus of the Year, U. of St. Thomas, 1978; Outstanding Engineer of the Year, Marquette U., 1973; MN Business Hall of Fame, 1980; Exec. of the Year, 1983; Engr. of the 1960's, MN Society of Professional Engrs., 1989; John F. Cade Award for entrepreneurial attributes, U. of St. Thomas, 1992; NAIOP Developer of the

Year, 1992; Ranked fourth largest industrial developer in year 2000 by National Real Estate Investor; Ernst & Young Lifetime Achievement Award, 1997;. **Act./Mem.:** Sierra International; Interlachen Country Club; Minneapolis Club; Naples Yacht Club; Port Royal Club; Royal Poinciana Club.

Shelly Regan Pres., Yamamoto Moss, 251 First Ave. N., Minneapolis, MN 55401. Tel: 612/375-0180. Email: sregan@yamamoto-moss.com **E:** BA-Journalism/Speech (cum laude), Marquette U. (Milwaukee), 1976. **Career Hist.:** Publications Editor, Blue Cross Blue Shield United of WI (Milwaukee), 1978-81; Public Relations Mgr., The Pillsbury Co. (Minneapolis), 1981-83; Corp. Communications Dir., Dyco Petroleum Corp. (Minneapolis), 1983-86; Public Relations Dir., Minnegasco Inc. (Minneapolis), 1986-87; Greater Minneapolis Chamber of Commerce, 1987-98: VP-Communications/Mktg. (1987); EVP (1990); Pres. (1994); Pres., Yamamoto Moss, 1998-present. **Career Act.:** Dir., Girl Scout Council of Greater Minneapolis; Board of Trustees, College of St. Benedict; Mem., MN Women's Economic Roundtable. **Act./Mem.:** Minneapolis Club.

Dietrich Reinhart CEO, St. John's University, President's Office, Collegeville, MN 56321. Tel: 320/363-2011. **B:** Minneapolis. **E:** St. John's; Brown U. BA; Ph.D.

George S. Richards Pres., COO, Damark International Inc., 7101 Winnetka Ave. N., Brooklyn Park, MN 55428. Tel: 612/531-0066. **B:** Apr. 30, 1964, Philadelphia. **M:** Martha, 1989. **C:** Olivia. **E:** The Wharton School, University of Pennsylvania: BS, Economics, 1986; MBA, 1987. **Career Hist.:** McKinsey & Co., Engagement Mgr., 1987-90; Sears, Roebuck & Co., Dir.-Strategic Planning/Mktg., 1990-93; McKinsey & Company, Senior Engagement Mgr., 1993-94; Montgomery Ward Direct, VP, 1994-95; Damark International Inc., Pres., COO, SVP, 1995-present.

Phillip C. Richards Chair, North Star Resource Group, 2222 Park Ave., Minneapolis, MN 55404. Tel: 612/872-1300. **B:** Oct. 18, 1940, Easton, Pa. **M:** Susan, 1962. **E:** Temple U. (wrestling scholarship): BA, 1962 (Sword Award); Law School, 1963. **Career Hist.:** Head-Group Pension Contract Dept., Penn Mutual, 1962-65; Brokerage Sales, Hartford Insurance, 1965-67; Asst. Superintendent of Agencies, MN Mutual Life Insurance Co., 1967-69; North Star Resource Group, 1969-present: Chair, CEO. **Career Act.:** Exec. Bd., Ariz. Council for Quality; Dir., General Agents and Managers Assn. (GAMA); Arbitrator, Dir., MN Better Business Bureau; Sec., Better Business Bureau; Adjunct Prof., U of MN. Carlson School. **Dec./Awd.:** National Mgmt. Award, GAMA, 1973-present (every year); Master Agency Builder Award, 1987-present (every year).

Dale Riley Operations, Kowalski's, 1261 Grand Ave., St. Paul, MN 55105. Tel: 651/698-3366. **B:** Oct. 25, 1949, Detroit. **M:** Janet, 1972. **C:** Allison. **E:** BBA, U. of MN, 1971. **Career Hist.:** Byerly's, 1971-97: Part-time, full-time (1971), various mgmt. positions, Gen. Mgr. (1978), responsible for opening stores (1987), Dir.-Retail Op. (1989), VP-Retail Op. (1990), COO (1994), Pres. and COO (Dec. 1995); EVP, COO, Lund Food Holdings Inc., 1997-99 (overseeing both Lunds Food Stores and Byerly's); Head of Drug Stores, Supervalu Inc., 1999-2000; Head of Operations, Kowalski's, 2000-present. **Career Act.:** Guest Lecturer: The Carlson School of Mgmt.-U. of MN, U. of St. Thomas Grad. School of Business; Dir., WomenVenture; Mem.-Board of Advisors, The Retail Food Industry Center (U. of MN); Mem.-Retail Advisory Bd., Supervalu Inc. **Dec./Awd.:** March of Dimes Distinguished Volunteer Service Award, 1996/1997; Corporate Volunteer of the Year, Lupus Fdn. of America Inc., 1999. **Act./Mem.:** March of Dimes: Mem.-Campaign Ctee.; Chair-WalkAmerica, 1995-97; Dir., March of Dimes Birth Defects Fdn.

Jeannine M. Rivet CEO-Health Care Svs., UnitedHealth Group, 300 Opus Center, 9900 Bren Rd., P.O. Box 1459 (55440), Minnetonka, MN 55343. Tel: 612/936-7213. Email: jrivet@uhc.com **B:** Jun. 1, 1948, Rhode Island. **M:** Warren Herreid II. **E:** Diploma R.N., (Providence) Rhode Island Hospital School of Nursing, 1968; BS-Nursing, Boston College, 1972; MPH-Public Health, Boston U., 1981. **Career Hist.:** (Providence) Rhode Island Group Health Assn.: Pediatric Nurse, 1975-76; Pediatric Supv., 1976-77; Asst. Dir.-Health Center Admin., 1977-82; Assoc. Dir.-Health Center Admin., 1982; Dir.-Clinical Svs., Group Health Assn. Inc. (Washington, D.C.), 1982-85; SVP, Peak Health Plan Ltd. (Colorado Springs), 1985-89; VP-Group Op., The Prudential Ins. Co. of America (Boston), 1989-90; United HealthCare Corp., now UnitedHealth Group: VP-Health Svc. Op., 1990-93; SVP-Health Plan Op., 1993-94; EVP, COO-Health Plan Div., 1994-98; CEO-Health Plan Div., 1998-present. **Career Act.:** Mentor, Menttium 100; Mem., American Mgmt. Assn., Mem.-Policy Advisory Comm., American Assn. of Health Plans. **Dec./Awd.:** 50 Most Powerful Women (inaugural list), Fortune magazine, 1998.

Lucio Rizzi Pres.-Pillsbury International, Pillsbury, 200 S. Sixth St., Minneapolis, MN 55402. Tel: 612/330-4427. **B:** 1941, Bologna, Italy. **M:** Madeleine. **E:** Law and business degrees, Bologna U., 1964; MBA, Padua U., 1966. **Career Hist.:** Brand mgr., Gerber Baby Foods–CPC Italy, 1966; international trainee, CPC France, CPC Brussels, 1971; mktg. and mgmt., CPC–Middle East, Europe, and Latin America, 1972-88; executive SVP, CPC–Europe, 1988-94; Pres., Pillsbury International, 1994-present. **Act./Mem.:** Tennis, diving.

Orem O. Robbins Chair, Security American Financial Enterprises Inc., 10901 Red Circle Dr., Minnetonka, MN 55343. Tel: 612/544-2121. **B:** Feb. 5, 1915, Minneapolis. **M:** Annette D. Scherer, 1992. **C:** Ford, Ross, Gail Tomei, Cynthia Rothbard. **E:** U. of MN, BBA, 1936; William Mitchell College of Law, BSL, 1946, JD, 1948. **Career Hist.:** Service Rep., N.W. Bell Telephone, 1936-41; U.S. Army, 1941-46; Commercial Rep., N.W. Bell, 1946-48; Dep. Dir.-Savings Bond Div., U.S. Treasury, 1948-49; Agent, Connecticut General Life Insurance Company, 1949-56; Founder, Chair, Security Life Insurance Company of America, 1956-present; Chair, SAFE, 1972-present. **Career Act.:** Founder, Chair, Security Life Insurance Company of America; past Pres., Life Insurance Leaders of MN, Chartered Life Underwriters-Minneapolis Chapter; Fellow, Life Mgmt. Institute; Mem., MN State Bar Assn. **Dec./Awd.:** Legion of Merit, U.S. Army, 1966. **Act./Mem.:** Masons; Past Commander Downtown Post American Legion; past Pres., Life Dir., Family and Children's Service-United Way; past Pres., MN Dept. Reserve Officers Assn.; past Chair, Methodist Hospital; National Eagle Scout Assn.; Minneapolis Club; Naples Yacht Club; Hole in the Wall Golf Club; Delta Sigma Pi; Beta Gamma Sigma; Skylight Club; Assn. of U.S. Army; Past Chair and Life Trustee, Hamline U.

John H. Roe Chair, Bemis Co. Inc., 222 S. Ninth St., Suite 2300, Minneapolis, MN 55402. Tel: 612/376-3000. **B:** Dec. 12, 1939, St. Paul. **M:** Sandra, 1962. **C:** three. **E:** Williams College, BA, 1962; Harvard Business School, MBA, 1964. **Career Hist.:** Bemis, 1964-present: sales and manufacturing positions in Massachusetts, Indiana, and California; VP-Op., 1976-82; EVP, 1982-87; COO, 1987-90; CEO, 1990-96; Chair, CEO, 1996-2000, Chairman, 2000. **Career Act.:** Dir., Bemis Co., Andersen Corp. **Act./Mem.:** Trustee, Science Museum of Minnesota, Carlton College.

David L. Rogers Pres., COO, Wilsons The Leather Experts, 7401 Boone Ave. N., Brooklyn Park, MN 55428. Tel: 612/391-4426. **B:** Dec. 8, 1942, Columbus, Ohio. **M:** Diane. **C:** Melissa, Brian. **E:** OH State U., B.S. Accounting, MBA. **Career Hist.:** Pickwick/Musicland, 1977-80; Wilsons, 1980-present. **Career Act.:** Dir., Rainforest Cafe Inc., Grand Casinos Inc., AICAA, MnCPA, OhCPA, Wilsons The Leather Experts. **Dec./Awd.:** Beta Alpha Psi-Honorary. **Act./Mem.:** United Way, Wayzata Country Club, Lafayette Country Club, Grey Oaks Country Club, Wooddale Church.

Daniel C. Rohr EVP-Commercial/Business Banking, U.S. Bancorp, U.S. Bank Pl., 601 Second Ave., P.O. Box 522 (55480), Minneapolis, MN 55402. Tel: 612/973-0405. **B:** Apr. 9, 1946, Chicago, Ill. **C:** Becky, Dave, Jim, Bob. **E:** B.A., St. Ambrose College; M.B.A., U. of Notre Dame. **Career Hist.:** Continental Bank of Chicago, 1971-88; EVP and Chief Credit Officer, Columbia Savings and Loan Assn., 1988-90; Vice Chairman and manager of Large Corporate Banking and Mgr.-commercial and business banking group, U.S. Bancorp, 1990-present. **Career Act.:** Mem., Greater Minneapolis Chamber of Commerce, Robert Morris Assn. **Act./Mem.:** Past Chair, Minnesota Zoo, MacPhail Center for the Arts.

Arthur J. Rolnick SVP, Dir.-Research, Federal Reserve Bank Minneapolis, 90 Hennepin Ave., P.O. Box 291, Minneapolis, MN 55480-0291. Tel: 612/340-2350. Email: ajr@res.mpls.frb.fed.us **E:** Wayne State U.: Bachelor's-Math., Master's-Economics; U. of MN, Doctorate-Economics. **Career Hist.:** Visiting Prof.: Boston College, U. of MN; Adjunct Prof., U. of MN, 1997; Minneapolis Fed, 1970-present. **Career Act.:** Mem., Federal Open Market Ctee., MN's Council of Economic Advisers, Minneapolis Star Tribune's Board of Economists; past Pres., MN Economic Assn.; Co-author of annual report essays arguing for: ending the economic war among the states; reforming the nation's deposit insurance system; and using fixed exchange rates.

Rev. Marvin L Roloff Pres., CEO, Augsburg Fortress, Publishers, 100 S. Fifth St., P.O. Box 1209, Minneapolis, MN 55402. Tel: 612/330-3301. Email: roloffm@augsburg-fortress.org **B:** Mar. 5, 1934, Waverly, Iowa. **M:** Shirley, 1959. **C:** Reed, Ross, Robyn. **E:** Wartburg College, B.A.; Wartburg Theological Seminary, B.D.; Princeton Theological Seminary, th.M. **Career Hist.:** Augsburg Fortress Publishers, 1965-1995: VP-Customer Resources/Relationships; Pres., CEO, 1996-present. **Career Act.:** President, Protestant Church-owned Publishers' Association 1998-2000. **Dec./Awd.:** Honorary Doctor of Divinity degree, Wartburg Theological Seminary, Dubuque, IA, 1997.

Richard M. Rompala Chair, Pres., CEO, The Valspar Corp., 1101 Third St. S., Minneapolis, MN 55415. Tel: 612/332-7371. **B:** Dec. 13, 1946, Pittsburgh. **M:** Jean, 1970. **C:** Mike, Matt. **E:** Columbia U., BA-Chemistry and BS-Chemical Engrg., 1969; Harvard U., MBA, 1975. **Career Hist.:** SVP, Mueller Brass Co.; VP, Group VP, PPG Industries, 1985-94; Pres., Valspar Corp., 1994-95; Pres., CEO, Valspar Corp., 1995-present; Chair 1997-present. **Career Act.:** Dir., The Valspar Corp., Minneapolis YMCA, Carlson School Advisory Board, Olin Corporation, Reliastar, National Paint and Coatings Association. **Act./Mem.:** Minneapolis Club, Minikahda Country Club, Laurel Valley Golf Club.

Thomas J. Rosen Pres., CEO, Rosen's Diversified Inc., 1120 Lake Ave., Fairmont, MN 56031. Tel: 507/238-4201. **B:** Jun. 26, 1948, Fairmont, Minn. **M:** Julie, 1982. **C:** Wade, Karin, Reid. **E:** BS-Business Admin., Morningside College, 1970. **Career Hist.:** Sls., Marion Laboratories, 1970-73; Rosen's Inc., 1973-present: Sls., 1973-82; Gen, Mgr., 1982-91; Pres., CEO, 1991-present. **Career Act.:** Dir., Morningside College; Mem., MN Business Partnership, Fairmont Economic Devel. Board. **Dec./Awd.:** Athletic Hall of Fame, Morningside College. **Act./Mem.:** Junior High boys basketball coach, Rotary, Interlachen Country Club.

Steven G. Rothmeier Chair, CEO, Great Northern Capital, 332 Minnesota St., Suite W-1099, St. Paul, MN 55101. Tel: 651/222-6130. **B:** Oct. 4, 1946, Mankato, Minn. **E:** U. of Notre Dame, BA-Business Admin., 1968; U. of Chicago, MBA, 1972. **Career Hist.:** NWA Inc., 1973-89: Corp. Fin. Analyst, 1973; Mgr.-Economic Analysis, 1973-78; Dir.-Economic Plng., 1978; VP-Fin., Treas., CFO, 1978-82; EVP, Treas., Dir., 1982-83; EVP-Fin./Admin., Treas., Dir., 1983; Pres., COO, 1983-84; Pres., CEO, 1985-86; Chair, CEO, 1986-89; Pres., IAI Capital Group, 1989-93; Chair, Alliant Techsystems, 1990-94; Chair, CEO, Great Northern Capital, 1993-present. **Career Act.:** Dir., Honeywell Inc., E.W. Blanch Holdings, Department 56, Inc., Precision Castparts Corp., Waste Management Inc.; American Council on Germany; Trustee, U. of Chicago; St. Agnes Fdn.; Catholic Views Broadcast Inc. MN. **Dec./Awd.:** Army Commendation Medal and Bronze Star Medal, U.S. Army, 1968, 1971. **Act./Mem.:** Governor, Minnesota Club; Mem., Minneapolis Club.

David H. Rotter Pres., CEO, The Rottlund Co. Inc., 2681 Long Lake Rd., Roseville, MN 55113. Tel: 651/638-0500. **B:** Sep. 9, 1946, St. Paul. **C:** two. **Career Hist.:** The Rottlund Co.: VP, 1973-1990; Pres., 1990-present. **Career Act.:** Dir., The Rottlund Co. Inc., Housing Software Corp.; past Dir., Twin Cities Builders Assn. **Dec./Awd.:** 1992 Entrepreneur of the Year. **Act./Mem.:** Minneapolis Board of Realtors.

Don L. Russell Chair, CEO, Cloverdale Foods Co., P.O. Box 667, Mandan, ND 58554. Tel: 701/663-9511. **B:** Feb. 28, 1943, Mandan, N.D. **M:** Evelyn, 1963. **C:** Catherine, Thomas, Scott, Steven, Craig. **E:** ND State U., Bus. Econ., 1965. **Career Hist.:** Sls. Rep., Midwest Motor Express, 1966-69; Pres., Speedy's Tire Center Inc., 1969-81; Cloverdale Foods Company: EVP, 1972-74; Pres., 1974-1999. **Career Act.:** Pres., Missouri River Royalty Corp. (1984-present); Gen. Partner, Rainbow Gas (1986-present); VP, Sec., Rainbow Energy Mktg. Inc. (1994-present); past Dir., Mandan Chamber of Commerce, 1st Southwest Bank; past Chair, Speedy's Tire Center Inc. of Aberdeen, Director, Cloverdale Foods Company 1972-present. **Act./Mem.:** Elks, Eagles.

Edwin L. Russell Chair, Pres., CEO, ALLETE, 30 W. Superior St., Duluth, MN 55802. Tel: 218/723-3915. Email: erussell@mnpower.com **B:** Feb. 15, 1945, New York. **M:** Lisa, 1972. **C:** Bobby, Amanda. **E:** Bowdoin College, International Government; Harvard U. Graduate School of Business Admin., MBA. **Career Hist.:** Intelligence officer, U.S. Army, 1967-69; senior associate, McKinsey & Co., 1971-74; mgr., FMC Corp., 1974-77; director of corporate business planning, FMC, 1977-78; managing dir., FMC Food Machinery Europe N.V., 1978-81; VP-Corp. Devel., Stanadyne Inc., 1981-89; VP-Corp. Devel., Group VP, J.M. Huber Corp., 1989-95; Minnesota Power Inc. (now ALLETE): Pres., 1996; Chair, CEO, Pres., 1996-present. **Career Act.:** Dir., ALLETE, United Way of Greater Duluth, The Great Lakes Acquarium, Edison Electric Institute, Tennant Co.; Minnesota Public Radio, Watch Hill Yacht Club. **Act./Mem.:** Rotary Club of Duluth, Harvard Business School Club of MN, Northland Country Club, Misquamicut Country Club, Union Club.

Alan K. Ruvelson Chair, Pres., First Midwest Ventures Inc./First Midwest Financial L.L.C., 1600 University Ave. W., Suite 214, St. Paul, MN 55104. Tel: 651/649-3588. **B:** Sep. 5, 1915, St. Paul. **M:** Louise Loidoldt, 1966. **C:** Judith, Alan Jr., Connie, Richard. **E:** U. of MN, BBA, 1936. **Career Hist.:** VP, Phil G. Ruvelson Inc., 1936-59; Pres., First Midwest Corp., 1959-86; Pres., First Midwest Ventures Inc., 1986-present; Special General Partner of Saint Paul Growth Ventures Fund, 1990-present; Pres., Chair, First Midwest Financial L.L.C., 1995-present. **Career Act.:** past Pres., National Assn. of Small Business Investment Companies, MN Assn. of Commerce and Industry; past Mem., Governor's Advisory Ctee. on Economic Devel. under four governors; Mem.-Exec. Ctee., Business Industry Political Action Ctee. of MN; past Mem., Lawyers Professional Responsibility Board; past Trustee, St. Thomas Academy, MN Business Hall of Fame; past Dir., Fdn. for MN Progress, Comserv Corp., American Arbitration, Dicomed Corp., Applied

Spectrum Technologies Inc., Sign Consultants Inc.; past Dir., HEI Inc., National Acquisition Corp.; past Mem., Advisory Ctee. of the U of MN Early-Stage Technology Devel. Fund; Mem., Technology Evaluation Council at U. of MN; Advisory Board, Convergent Capital, 1998-present. **Dec./Awd.:** Hames Memorial Alumni Award, St. Thomas Academy, 1979; Inductee, MN Business Hall of Fame, 1980; Cross of Merit with Silver Star, Knights of Holy Sepulcare of Jerusalem, 1983; Financial Services Advocate to Small Business for the State of MN, SBA, 1985; national Supporter Entrepreneur of the Year, 1994; President's Medal of Honor, College of St. Catherine, 1989; Diakona Award for Distinguished Service, College of St. Benedict, 1997; Opus Sancti Thomae Award, St. Thomas Academy, 1997. **Act./Mem.:** past National Pres., Dir., U. of MN Alumni Assn.; past Pres., U. of MN Alumni Club; past Trustee, Visitation Convent, St. Catherine's College, College of St. Benedict, St. Mary's Hospital, St. Thomas Academy; Past Mem., Lay Advisory Bd.-St. Mary's Hospital; Town and Country Club; Dir., Marian Center Fdn.

James R. Ryan CEO, Ryan Cos. U.S. Inc., 700 International Centre, 900 Second Ave. S., Minneapolis, MN 55402. Tel: 612/336-1200. **B:** Aug. 12, 1942, Hibbing, Minn. **M:** Colleen. **E:** Notre Dame, bus. degree, 1964. **Career Hist.:** Ryan Construction (now Ryan Cos. U.S.), 1960-present: Project Mgr., 1960-68; Construction Mgr., 1968-78; Pres., 1978-1997; CEO, 1990-present. **Career Act.:** Dir., Amicus, Lake Minnetonka Sailing School, School of Architecture-Notre Dame; Co-chair, Parents' Council-St. Mary's, Notre Dame. **Act./Mem.:** Contact Executive, United Way; Trustee, Minneapolis Fdn.

Robert L. Ryan SVP, CFO, Medtronic Inc., 7000 Central Ave. N.E., Fridley, MN 55432. Tel: 612/574-4000. **B:** Apr. 15, 1943, Detroit. **M:** Sharon. **C:** Lesley, Eric. **E:** BS-Electrical Engrg., Wayne State U. (Detroit), 1966; MS-Electrical Engrg., Cornell U., 1968; MBA, Harvard Business School, 1970. **Career Hist.:** Mgmt. Consultant, McKinsey & Co. (New York), 1970-75; VP, Citicorp, 1975-82 (responsible for Citibank's relationships with all companies in the broadcasting and cable television industries); Union Texas Petroleum Corp. (Houston), 1982-93: Treas. (1982), Cont. (1983), VP and CFO (1984); SVP and CFO, Medtronic Inc., 1993-present. **Career Act.:** Dir., TECO (Tampa Electric Co.) Energy Inc., Interra Financial Inc., Abbott Northwestern Hospital, United HealthCare Corp.

William S. Sadler Pres., Treas., Dotronix Inc., 160 First St. S.E., New Brighton, MN 55112. Tel: 651/633-1742. **B:** Mar. 29, 1926, St. Louis. **M:** Dorothy, 1954. **C:** Jill Diane, William R., Kurt T.. **E:** U. of MN, BSB. **Career Hist.:** Dir. Eng., KSTP-TV-AM, 1953-60; Pres., CEO, Ball-Miratel, 1960-76; Pres., CEO, Audiotronics Display, 1976-1980; Pres., CEO, Dotronix Inc., 1980-present. **Dec./Awd.:** St. Paul Business Person of the Year, 1988; Commemorative Medal, Russian People for Service in U.S. Merchant Marine WWII by Pres. Boris Yeltsin, 1993. **Act./Mem.:** Founder, Charter Mem., Academy of Teleision Arts and Sciences, San Francisco Chapter, 1949.

Rick Sadowski Publisher, Pres., St. Paul Pioneer Press, 345 Cedar St., St. Paul, MN 55101. Tel: 651/228-5404. Email: rsadowski@pioneerpress.com **B:** Mar. 26, 1947, Springfield, Mass. **M:** Mary, 1982. **C:** Andrew. **E:** FL State U., 1970. **Career Hist.:** *Miami Herald*: 1970-1979; *Long Beach Press-Telegram*: Circulation Dir., 1979-1980; VP, 1980-1987; Fort Wayne Newspapers: VP, 1987; Pres., CEO, 1988; *Press-Telegram*: Pres., Publisher, 1992; *St. Paul Pioneer Press* : Pres., Publisher, 1997-present. **Career Act.:** Mem., MN Business Partnership; Dir., Capital City Partnership; Board of Dir., Inland Daily Press Assn., U of MN School of Journalism National Advisory Board.

Robert C. Salipante Pres., COO, ReliaStar Financial Corp., 20 Washington Ave. S., Minneapolis, MN 55401. Tel: 612/342-3599. Email: bob.salipante@reliastar.com **B:** May 19, 1956, Laconia, N.H. **M:** Cathie. **E:** BA-Economics (with high distinction, Phi Beta Kappa), U. of MI, 1978; MS-Mgmt., M.I.T./Sloan School of Mgmt., 1981. **Career Hist.:** Ameritrust Co. N.A., 1978-92: various positions, 1978-86; SVP-Mgmt. Information Systems, 1986-88; EVP-Banking Services Group, 1988-92; ReliaStar Financial Corp., 1992-present: SVP and CFO, 1992-94; SVP-Strategic Mktg./Technology, 1994-96; SVP-Individual Div./Technology, 1996; SVP-Personal Financial Svs., 1996-99; President and COO, 1999-present. **Career Act.:** Dir., Northern Life Insurance Co., ReliaStar United Services Life, ReliaStar Life Insurance Co., ReliaStar Fdn., Washington Square Securities Inc., Deluxe Corp., MN Diversified Industries Inc. (VChm., 2000), Security-Connecticut Life Insurance Co.; Northern Life Insurance Co.; Reliastar Bank; past Mem.-Advisory Board, Summit Partners Venture Capital Fund; United Way of Minneapolis (Mem., Mktg. and Resource Devel. Ctee.; past Mem., Investment Ctee.). **Dec./Awd.:** James B. Angell Scholar, U. of MI; Osterweil Prize in economics, U. of MI; Brooks Prize for best thesis, Sloan School of Mgmt. **Act./Mem.:** Running, bicycling, climbing.

Curtis A. Sampson Chair, Pres., CEO, Communications Systems Inc., 213 Main St. S., Hector, MN 55342. Tel: 320/848-6231. **B:** Jul. 6, 1933, Hector, Minn. **M:** Marian, 1954. **C:** Paul, Randall, Russell, Susan (Puchalski). **E:** U. of MN, BBA, 1955. **Career Hist.:** Auditor, Peat, Marwick, Mitchell & Company, 1954-55; Cont., MN Central Tel Co, 1955-65; EVP, Treas., CFO, North American Comm. Corp., 1965-70; Chair, CEO, Communications Systems Inc., 1970-present; Chair, CEO, Hector Communications Corp., 1990-present; Pres, Alliance Telecommunications; Chair, Pres., Hector Communications Corp., 1994-present. **Career Act.:** Pres., United States Telecommunications Suppliers Assn., 1984-85; Dir., United States Telecommunications Suppliers Assn., Hands Inc., Fidelity State Bank (Hector), Rural Telephone Bank, Canterbury Park Holding Corp., Dir., Sec., Hector Industries Corp.; VP, Dir., National Rural Telecom Assn.; past Pres., Kiwanis, Chamber of Commerce; past VChair, School Board, Renville County Republican Party; past Mem., State Central Ctee.; Mem.-Board of Regents, Augsburg College (St. Paul); Mem.-Board of Overseers, Carlson School of Mgmt, National Exchange Carrier Assn.; Trustee, U of Minn. Fdn. **Dec./Awd.:** Small Businessman of Year—MN, Fidelity State Bank, 1978; Outstanding Achievement Award, U. of MN, 1996. **Act./Mem.:** Masons; Kiwanis; Church Choir, First Evangelical Lutheran Church; Oakdale Country Club; Hector Athletic Club.

Arend J. Sandbulte retired Chair/CEO, ALLETE, 30 W. Superior St., Duluth, MN 55802. Tel: 218/723-3965. **B:** Dec. 9, 1933, Sioux Center, Iowa. **M:** Verna, 1953. **C:** Ruth, Gregory, Kristin, Rachel. **E:** IA State U., BS-Electrical Engrg., 1959; U. of MN, MBA, 1966. **Career Hist.:** Rate Engr., NSP, 1959-64; Minnesota Power Inc. (now ALLETE), 1964-present: Rate Engr., 1964; Financial Asst., 1965; Dir.-Budgets, Research, 1966-72; Asst. VP-Budgets and Corp. Planning, 1972-74; VP-Corp. Planning, 1974-76; VP-Fin., CFO, 1976-78; SVP-Fin., Admin., CFO, 1978-80; EVP, CFO, 1980-83; EVP, CFO COO, 1983-84; Pres., COO, 1984-88; Pres., CEO, 1988-89; Chair, Pres., CEO, 1989-98. **Career Act.:** Pres., Assn. of Edison Illuminating Companies; Chair, College of St. Scholastica Capital Campaign; Chair, Lake Superior Center; Mem., College of St. Scholastica Investment Ctee.; Dir., Advantage MN; Mem., Edison Electric Institute, Florida Council of 100, IA State U. Electrical Engrg. Advisory Board, IA State U. Fdn. Board of Governors, IA State U. Fdn. Investment Ctee., MN Business Partnership Inc., ALLETE, MN Private College Council, North Central Electric Assn., Norwest Bank Minnesota North-Duluth Community Board, Public Utilities Reports, St. Mary Land & Exploration Company, U.S. West Communications Minnesota State Executive Board, Utech Venture Capital Corp. **Dec./Awd.:** Boss of the Year, Duluth Jaycees, 1974; Nikola Tesla Award, 1975; CEO of the Year Bronze Award, Financial World, 1990, 1993, 1994; Professional Achievement Citation in Engineering Award, IA State U., 1991. **Act./Mem.:** Engineers Club of Northern MN; Institute for Electrical & Electronic Engineers; Kitchi Gammi Club; Minneapolis Club; Northland Country Club; Elder and past trustee of Glen Avon Presbyterian Church.

Stephen W. Sanger Chair, CEO, General Mills Inc., One General Mills Blvd., Golden Valley, MN 55426. Tel: 763/764-2311. **B:** Apr. 10, 1946, Cincinnati. **M:** Karen. **C:** two. **E:** DePauw U., Bachelor's-History, 1968; U. of MI, MBA, 1970. **Career Hist.:** Various mktg. and sls. positions with Proctor & Gamble, 1970-73; various positions General Mills, 1974-present; Pres.-Big G cereal div.; Pres.-Yoplait USA; Gen. Mgr.-New Business Devel.; Pres., General Mills, 1993-95; Chair and CEO, General Mills, 1995-present. **Career Act.:** Dir., General Mills Inc., Target Corp., Donaldson Co., Grocery Mfrs. of America, and Catalyst National Campaign to Prevent Teen Pregnancy; President of the Guthrie Theater; Trustee, Ctee. for Economic Devel., The Conference Board; Mem., The Business Council, The Business Roundtable; Chair, MN Business Partnership.

Mark Sathe Pres., Founder, Sathe & Associates Executive Search, The Sathe Building, 5821 Cedar Lake Rd., Minneapolis, MN 55416. Tel: 612/546-2100. **B:** Dec. 31, 1947, Jackson, Minn. **M:** Ginny, 1974. **C:** Katie, Jono. **E:** St. Cloud State U., BA-Industrial Psychology/Business, 1971; U. of St. Thomas, Post-Graduate work. **Career Hist.:** Pres. Sathe & Associates Executive Search, 1974-present. **Career Act.:** Dir., Greater Minneapolis Chamber of Commerce, Methodist Hospital Fdn., Twin West Chamber of Commerce; past Pres., MN Assn. of Personnel Consultants; Delegate, White House Conference on Small Business; Dir., SLP Rotary Foundation; Founder Minnesota Academy for the Blind, Founder of Sathe and Associates Executive Search; Dir., Sunset Ridge Business Park. **Dec./Awd.:** Entrepreneur of the Year, Twin West Chamber; MN Business Hall of Fame nominee; St. Cloud State Distinguished Alumni; Who's Who in American Executives, U.S. Registry; Keystone Award (firm); Vanguard, Women in Communications; Rotary Paul Harris Fellow; Distinguished Service Award, MN Assn. of Personnel Consultants; WCCO Good Neighbor. **Act./Mem.:** Dir., Izatys, Methodist Hospital Fdn., Rotary Fdn. St. Louis Park, MN Academy for the Blind, MN Boys Choir; past Community Chair, Special Olympics; past Pres., Sunset Ridge Business Park, Business Booster Club, Insurance National Search; Mem., Golden Valley Country Club; Elected delegate to White House Conference on Small Business for 1995; Delegate, State Senate, 1996; Viking Boy Scout Council Golf Tournament Chair; Health Care Consumer Advisory Board.

WHO

John A. Satorius Pres., Fredrikson & Byron, 1100 International Centre, 900 Second Ave. S., Minneapolis, MN 55402. Tel: 612/347-7000. **B:** Aug. 20, 1946, Berwyn, Ill. **M:** Linda, 1968. **C:** Katherine, Joseph. **E:** U. of VA, BA, 1968; Harvard Law School, JD, 1975; Harvard, Ph.D., 1977. **Career Hist.:** Attorney, Fredrikson & Byron, 1975-present; Chair-Corporate Practice Group, 1994-1996; Pres., Fredrikson & Byron, 1997-present. **Career Act.:** Dir., Belevin Foundation, Minnesota Land Trust.

R.F. Saunders Chair, CEO, Dakco Distributors Inc., P.O. Box 5009, 101 E. Central Ave., Minot, ND 58702. Tel: 701/857-1140. **B:** Oct. 3, 1919, Minot, N.D. **M:** Beulah, 1944. **E:** Minot State College, Minot, ND; U. of MN, Bach. of Pharmacy, 1943. **Career Hist.:** Saunders Bros. Wholesale Drug, (name changed) Dakco Distributors Inc. (holding company for Dakota Drug, Nodak Distributors, Northland Sports, and Micro Data Systems), 1947-present. **Career Act.:** Mem., past Pres., Wholesalers and Mfrs. Assn. of ND; Dir., Norwest Bank Corp. of Minot, ND; past Dir., National Sporting Goods Wholesale Assn.; Special Advisor, National Federation of Independent Business; Advisor, National Security Council. **Dec./Awd.:** Paul Harris Fellow, Rotary Fdn.-Rotary International, 1983. **Act./Mem.:** Mem., past Pres., Minot Rotary Club; Mem., past Board of Elders, First Presbyterian Church; past Pres., Alumni Assn. of State U. of Minot; past Dir., Minot Chamber of Commerce; past Mem.-Advisory Board, ND Game and Fish Dept.; Mem.-Board of Regents, State U. of Minot; Mem.-Alumni Advisory Board, NDSU College of Pharmacy (Fargo, ND); Mem., Minot Tennis Club; Minot Gun Club.

Thomas K. Scallen Pres., CEO, International Broadcasting Corp., 4701 IDS Center, Minneapolis, MN 55402. Tel: 612/333-5100. **B:** Aug. 14, 1926, Minneapolis. **M:** Bille Jo Scallen, 1990. **C:** Tommy, Sheila, Eileen, Patrick, Maureen, Timothy. **E:** U. of Denver, BA, 1949, JD, 1950. **Career Hist.:** International Broadcasting Corp., Pres., 1976-92; Chair, 1992. **Career Act.:** Chair, CEO, Century Park Pictures Corp., 1992. **Act./Mem.:** Minneapolis Club; Edina Country Club; Minnesota Club; Friars Club-New York; MN Execs. Organization; World Presidents Organization; Lafayette Club; California Yacht Club.

Peter Scherer Pres., CEO, Scherer Bros. Lumber Co., 9110 83rd Ave. N., Brooklyn Park, MN 55445. Tel: 612/627-0871. Email: pscherer@schererbros.com **B:** Sep. 18, 1963, Minneapolis. **M:** Geri, 1986. **C:** Laura, Sam, Ben. **E:** BBA-Finance, U. of Notre Dame, 1986. **Career Hist.:** Commercial Real Estate, American National Bank, 1986-89; various positions, Scherer Bros. Lumber Co., 1989-present. **Career Act.:** Scherer Bros. Lumber Co. (1992-present); Mem., National Lumber and Building Material Dealers Assn. **Act./Mem.:** Young Presidents Org., Mpls. Club; TwinWest Chamber-PAC Board; Minneapolis Fdn.

Thomas W. Schini Chair, Pres., CEO, First Federal Capital Corp., 605 State St., P.O. Box 1868, La Crosse, WI 54602. Tel: 608/784-8000. **B:** Oct. 1, 1935, La Crosse, Wis. **M:** Lorna. **E:** BBA-Business, U. of WI, 1959. **Career Hist.:** First Federal Savings Bank, 1959-present (currently Chair, Pres., CEO); First Federal Capital Corp., 1989-present (currently Chair, Pres., CEO). **Career Act.:** Dir., TYME Corp., Advisory Bd., Viterbo College (La Crosse); past Chair, WI League of Financial Institutions; past Pres., La Crosse Area United Way; Past Dir., FHLB Chicago. **Act./Mem.:** Rotary; La Crosse Country Club.

Guy Schoenecker Pres., CEO, BI "Your Business Improvement Company", 7630 E. Bush Lake Rd., Edina, MN 55439. Tel: 612/835-4800. **B:** Eden Valley, Minn. **M:** Barbara. **C:** Lisa, Larry, Paul, Bob, Sue, Dave, Shelley. **E:** U. of St. Thomas, BA; U. of MN Law School, BSL. **Career Hist.:** Founder, BI, a trade name of Schoeneckers, Inc. **Dec./Awd.:** MN Business Hall of Fame; 1st Entrepreneur Award; MN Quality Award, 1994; Malcolm Baldrige National Quality Award 1999; Honorary Doctor of Law degree from University of St. Thomas.

Brad J. Schreier Pres., COO, Taylor Corp., 1725 Roe Crest Dr., Mankato, MN 56001. Tel: 507/625-2828. Email: bjschreier@taylorcorp.com **B:** Aug. 19, 1951, Currie, Minn. **M:** Marge, 1971. **C:** Ryan, Kyle. **E:** Mankato State U., BS, 1973. **Career Hist.:** Carlson Craft, 1971-80: Pressman, 1971-72; Prod. Foreman, 1972-73; Prod. Supv., 1973-74; Outside Sls. Rep., 1974-75; Office Supv., 1975-76; Office Mgr., 1977-78; Sls. Mgr., 1978-80; VP-Sls./Mktg., Taylor Corp., 1980-85; Pres., Taylor Corp., 1985-present. **Career Act.:** Pres., Mankato Area United Way; Treas., Mankato Area YMCA; Dir., Chair Immanuel St. Joseph's Hospital, 1990; Pres., International Thermographers Assn.; Chair, Mankato Area Catholic Schools Board, Holy Rosary Parish Council; Dir., Mankato Area Jaycees; Pres., Mankato Royals, Baseball Boosters; Dir., Pres., Mankato Youth Basketball Assn.; Board of Regents, St. John's U., 1998-present. **Dec./Awd.:** Book of Golden Deeds Award, Exchange Club, 1994; 1999 Distinguished Alumni Achievement Award from Minnesota State University, Mankato. **Act./Mem.:** Mem., Parish Council-Holy Rosary Parish, Jaycees, United Way Campaign and Board, YMCA Capital Campaign, Mankato Area Catholic Schools Capital Campaign Ctee. Chair; Capital Campaign Steering Committee for Minnesota State University and for Bethany Lutheran College.

John A. Schuchart Chair, MDU Resources Group Inc., P.O. Box 5650, Bismarck, ND 58506. Tel: 701/222-7900. **B:** Nov. 13, 1929, Omaha, Neb. **M:** Joyce Schock, 1950. **C:** Deborah Kelley, Susan Felton. **E:** U. of NE, BS-Bus., 1950; Stanford U. Grad. School of Business, Exec. Program, 1968. **Career Hist.:** various positions in accounting, finance, and mgmt., including Mgr.-Accounting, Admin. Mgr., Asst. Sec., Northern Natural Gas Company (Omaha, NE), 1950-71; VP, Treas., CFO, Intermountain Gas Company (Boise, ID), 1972-75; MDU Resources Group Inc., 1976-present: VP, Treas., CFO, 1976-78; Pres., COO, 1978-80; Pres., CEO, 1980-83; Chair, Pres., CEO, 1983-92; Chair, CEO, 1992-94; Chair, 1983-present. **Career Act.:** Dir., MDU Resources Group

Inc.; Ex-officio, Knife River Corp., WBI Holdings, Inc.; Board of Regents, U. of Mary; Past Mem., Industry Sector Advisory Ctee. on Energy for Trade Policy Matters, U.S. Dept. of Commerce; Trustee, YMCA, ND Chapter of the Nature Conservatory; Mem., American Gas Assn., Edison Electric Institute, Financial Execs. Institute; Mem.-Business Advisory Board, MT State U.-Billings. **Dec./Awd.:** Order of Accounting Merit (1968) and Award of Merit (1978), American Gas Assn.; Scroll and Merit Award Key, Administrative Mgmt. Society, 1972; U. of NE-Omaha, Citation for Alumnus Achievement Award 1987,Distinguished Achievement Award, 1989; 19th Annual CEO of the Year Bronze Award; Financial World, 1993; 1994 Communication and Leadership Award Toastmasters.

John R. Schueler Pres., Publisher, Star Tribune, 425 Portland Ave. S., Minneapolis, MN 55488. Tel: 612/673-4767. Email: john.schueler@startribune.com **B:** Jun. 28, 1949, Grosse Point, Mich. **C:** Tracie, Lindsey. **E:** B.B.A., Western Mich. U., 1971; Sr. Executive Program, Stanford Graduate School of Business, 1997. **Career Hist.:** Detroit Free Press, 1971; Dir.-Sls., Atlanta Journal and Constitution, 1979-82; VP-Consumer Mktg. and Circulation, Miami Herald, 1984-89; Pres., New England Newspapers and publisher Fall River Herald/News, 1989-91; Pres. and COO, Orange County Register, 1991-98; Pres. and Publisher, Star Tribune, 1998-present. **Career Act.:** Chair, Orange County Business Council; Chair, Vital Link Advisors; Dir., United Way of Minneapolis.

James H. Schultz EVP-North American Commercial Group, The Trane Co., 3600 Pammel Creek Rd., La Crosse, WI 54601. Tel: 608/787-3250. Email: jschultz@trane.com **B:** Oct. 20, 1948, Sioux City, Iowa. **M:** Debbie, 1970. **C:** Chris, Jenny. **E:** BS-Industrial Engrg., IA State, 1970. **Career Hist.:** Trane, 1970-present: Sls. mgmt.-several product areas, 1970-79; Mgr.-Applied Products Mktg., Commercial Air Conditioning Div., 1979-81; VP-Op., Trane Thermal (Conshohocken, PA), 1981-83; VP, Gen. Mgr.-Applied Unitary-Refrigeration Systems Div., 1983-87; VP and Gen. Mgr.-Commercial Systems Div., 1987-88; EVP, Commercial Systems Group (now North American Commercial Group), 1988-present; also VP, Group Exec., American Standard Cos. **Career Act.:** Dir., First Bank of WI, Lutheran Hospital of La Crosse, WI Mfrs. & Commerce; Chair, Air Conditioning and Refrigeration Institute (ARI).

Richard M. Schulze Founder, Chair, CEO, Best Buy Co. Inc., 7075 Flying Cloud Dr., P.O. Box 9312 (55440), Eden Prairie, MN 55344. Tel: 612/947-2456. **B:** Jan. 2, 1941, St. Paul. **M:** Sandra, 1962. **C:** Susan, Debra, Nancy, Rick. **Career Hist.:** VP, Northern States Distributing, 1960-66; Best Buy Co. Inc.: Founder, Pres., 1966-92; Founder, Chair, CEO, 1992-present. **Career Act.:** Dir., Pentair Inc., Best Buy Co. Inc.; Bd. of Overseers, Carlson School of Mgmt.; Bd. of Trustees, Advisory Bd.-Science/Technology Center, U. of St. Thomas. **Dec./Awd.:** Consumer Electronics Hall of Fame, 1990; Retailer of the Year, Consumer Electronics and Audio-Video International (fourth consecutive year), 1990; Richard M. Schulze day, Governor Arne Carlson, November 9, 1991; Torch of Liberty Award, B'nai B'rith Anti-Defamation League, 1991; Executive of the Year, Corporate Report Minnesota, 1992; Mem., Institute of American Entrepreneurs, 1992; finalist, National Entrepreneur of the Year, 1992. CES Daily News: Man of the Year, 1993; Retailer of the Year, 1994; Lifetime Achievement Award, 1995. Specialty Discounter of the Year, Discount Store News, 1994; International Entrepreneur of the Year, U. of MO-Kansas City, 1994; Computerworld Smithsonian Award Nomination, 1995; #1 Pentium Processor Retailer in the World, Intel Corp., 1995; honorary doctor of laws degree, U. of St. Thomas, 1998; 100 best CEOs (No. 9), Chief Executive magazine, 1999; Red Wagon, America's Promise, 1999; Corporate Leader of the Year, Juvenile Diabetes Fdn. MN Chapter, 1999; National Entrepreneur of the Year, Ernst & Young, 1999; inaugural Robert C. McDermond Medal, Robert C. McDermond Center for Management and Entrepreneurship, 2000.

Allan L. Schuman Pres., CEO, Ecolab Inc., Ecolab Center, St. Paul, MN 55102. Tel: 651/293-2864. **B:** May 24, 1934, New York. **M:** Judi, 1961. **C:** Robert, Michael. **E:** NY U., BS-Mktg. and Mgmt. Harvard, Wharton, and U. of Chicago, mgmt. seminars. **Career Hist.:** Ecolab, 1957-present: Pres. and COO, 1992-95; Pres. and CEO, 1995-present. **Career Act.:** Dir., Ecolab Inc., Henkel-Ecolab GmbH, Culinary Institute of America Corp., Ordway Music Theatre, Hazelden Fdn., Soap and Detergent Assn., Guthrie Theater; Board of Overseers, Carlson School of Mgmt. **Act./Mem.:** Flagship Athletic Club; Olympic Hills Club.

Steven A. Schumeister Managing Ptnr., Robins, Kaplan, Miller & Ciresi LLP, 2800 LaSalle Plaza, 800 LaSalle Ave., Minneapolis, MN 55402. Tel: 612/349-8500. Email: SASchumeister@robins.com **B:** Mar. 19, 1950, St. Paul, Minn. **M:** Judith, 1983. **C:** Stacey, Andrew. **E:** B.A., U. of Minn., 1972; J.D., William Mitchell College of Law, 1976. **Career Hist.:** Mng. Ptnr., Robins, Kaplan, Miller & Ciresi. **Career Act.:** Member, Guthrie Business Council; Director, Legal Rights Center.

Alfred Schwan Chair, CEO, Schwan's Sales Enterprises Inc., 115 W. College Dr., Marshall, MN 56258. Tel: 507/532-3274. **M:** Doris.

Lauren A. Segal Pres., United Way of the Saint Paul Area Inc., 166 E. Fourth St., St. Paul, MN 55101. Tel: 651/291-8300. **M:** Rich Grigos. **E:** Guilford College, B.S. Management. **Career Hist.:** United Way Of America: Mgr. Trainee, 1980-81; Campaign Div. Dir. (Worcester, MA), 1981-83; Campaign Dir. (Kalamazoo, MI), 1983-86; Pres. (Somerset County, NJ), 1987-94; Pres. (St. Paul), 1994-present. **Career Act.:** Human Svs. Council, 1994-present; Greater St. Paul Tomorrow Board, 1994-present; Twin Cities One-To-One Board, 1995-present; Children's Initiative Governance Board, 1994-96; Rotary Club of St. Paul, 1994-present; MN Women's Economic Roundtable, 1996-present; Pres., United Way Of MN, 1997; Ramsey County Welfare Reform Task Force, Ctee. Mem., 1997-98. **Dec./Awd.:** CityBusiness "40 Under 40" Award, 1995. **Act./Mem.:** Chair, Summitt Hill House Tour, 1998-2000.

Andrew C. Selden Attorney, Briggs and Morgan P.A., 2400 IDS Center, Minneapolis, MN 55402. Tel: 612/334-8485. Email: Seland@email.briggs.com **B:** Jan. 19, 1947, Orange, N.J. **E:** BA, Carleton College, 1968; JD (magna cum laude), U. of MN, 1971. **Career Hist.:** Practice areas: franchise, antitrust, intellectual property law. **Career Act.:** Past Chair-Forum on Franchising, American Bar Assn. (1985-89); Chair, Better Business Bureau of MN Inc. (1995-97); Reporter, Uniform Franchise and Business Opportunities Act, National Conference of Commissioners on Uniform State Laws. **Dec./Awd.:** J.D., Magna cum laude, U. of MN, 1971; Order of the Coif, U. of MN, 1971. **Act./Mem.:** Pres., MN Assn. of Railroad Passengers.

Robert L. Senkler Chair, Pres., CEO, Minnesota Life, Minnesota Mutual Life Center, 400 N. Robert St., St. Paul, MN 55101. Tel: 651/665-3500. **B:** Sep. 23, 1952, St. Paul. **M:** Pam, 1975. **C:** Christopher, Richard. **E:** U. of MN-Duluth, BA-Math, 1974; Fellow, Society of Actuaries, 1979. **Career Hist.:** MN Mutual Life Insurance Company, 1974-present: Individual Actuarial Dept., 1974; Actuarial Analyst, 1974; Actuarial Asst., 1977; Senior Actuarial Asst., 1978; Asst. Actuary, 1979; Assoc. Actuary, 1982; Actuary, 1983; Second VP-Individiual Actuarial, 1984; VP and Actuary, 1987; Chair, Pres., CEO, 1994-present. **Career Act.:** Chm., Insurance Federation of MN; Mem., Carlson School of Mgmt. Board of Overseers; Dir., MN Business Partnership, MN Orchestra, Capital City Partnership, Wilder Fdn., Health East, American Council of Life Insurance. **Act./Mem.:** White Bear Lake Tennis Club, White Bear Yacht Club, Minnesota Club.

Stephen G. Shank Chair, CEO, Capella Education Co., 330 Second Ave. S., Suite 550, Minneapolis, MN 55401. Tel: 612/339-7665. Email: sshank@minn.net **B:** Dec. 6, 1943, Tulsa, Okla. **M:** Judith, 1966. **C:** Susan, Mary. **E:** BA, U. of IA, 1965; MA, Fletcher School/Tufts U., 1966; JD, Harvard Law School, 1972. **Career Hist.:** Attorney, Dorsey & Whitney, 1972-74; Gen. Counsel, Tonka Corp., 1974-78; Chair, CEO, Tonka Corp., 1979-91; Chair, CEO, Founder, Learning Ventures International, 1992-present. **Career Act.:** Dir., National Computer Systems, Polaris Industries. **Dec./Awd.:** Wall Street Transcript Gold Award, Top Toy and Hobby Industries CEO, 1981; Wall Street Transcript Gold Award, Top Leisure Industries CEO, 1989.

Michael E. Shannon retired Chair, Ecolab Inc., Ecolab Center, St. Paul, MN 55102. Tel: 651/293-2396. **M:** Laura. **E:** U. of Notre Dame, 1958; MBA, Stanford U., 1960. **Career Hist.:** Various domestic and international financial positions, Gulf Oil Corp., 1962-75; Treas., then EVP and CFO, Republic Steel Corp. (Cleveland), 1975-84; Ecolab Inc.: EVP and CFO, 1984-92; CFO and CAO, 1992-present; Dir., 1991-present; Vice Chair, 1992-96; Chair, 1996-99. **Career Act.:** Dir., Ecolab Inc., Apogee Enterprises Inc., MN Mutual Life Insurance Co., National Assn. of Mfrs., MN Public Radio; Chair, MN Orchestral Assn.; Mem- Advisory Council for Grad. Studies/Research, U. of Notre Dame; Mem., former Chapter Dir., Financial Executives Institute.

Raghu Sharma Founder, Chair, Pres., Multi-Tech Systems Inc., 2205 Woodale Dr., Mounds View, MN 55112. Tel: 612/785-3500. Email: rsharma@multitech.com **B:** Mar. 28, 1938, District Montgomery, Pakistan. **M:** Patricia, 1981. **C:** Janel, Matthew, Adrienne. **E:** U. of MN, Ph.D.-Electrical Engrg., 1969. **Career Hist.:** Multitech Systems Inc., Founder, Pres., and Chair, 1970-present. **Act./Mem.:** TIA.

Jeffrey F. Shaw Pres., Briggs and Morgan P.A., 2400 IDS Center, Minneapolis, MN 55402. Tel: 612/223-6565. Email: shajef@email.briggs.com **B:** Jun. 27, 1947, Minneapolis. **M:** Catherine. **C:** Kristin. **E:** U. of MN: BA, 1969; JD, 1974. **Career Hist.:** Attorney, Federal Trade Commission (Washington, D.C.), 1974-77; Briggs and Morgan P.A., 1977-present. **Career Act.:** Dir., Briggs and Morgan P.A.

Christina L. Shea SVP, Pres. GMI New Ventures, General Mills Inc., One General Mills Blvd., P.O. Box 1113 (55440), Golden Valley, MN 55426. Tel: 612/540-2311. **B:** Apr. 10, 1953. **M:** Hank. **C:** Tate, Rob, H.J., Claire. **E:** Boston College, Bachelor's Degree; Amos Tuck School of Business, MBA. **Career Hist.:** General Mills: Asst. Product Mgr., 1978-80, Product Mgr., 1980-83, Mktg. Dir., 1983-87, VP-New Business Devel., 1987-92, VP, Gen. Mgr.1992-94, Pres.-Betty Crocker Products Div., 1994-98, SVP-Betty Crocker Div., 1998-99; SVP, GMI New Ventures. **Career Act.:** Board Member: Amos Tuck Business School, Walker Art Center.

Michael R. Sill Chair, Road Machinery & Supplies Co., 5633 W. Highway 13, Savage, MN 55378. Tel: 612/895-7014. **B:** Nov. 3, 1931, Duluth, Minn. **M:** Barbara B., 1959. **C:** Debra S. Williams, Michael M., Patricia J., Douglas C.. **E:** U. of MN, BS-Bus., 1955. **Career Hist.:** Road Machinery & Supplies Co., 1956-present: VP, 1956-64; Pres., 1964-82; Chair, CEO, 1982-1996; Chair 1997-present. **Career Act.:** Dir., Road Machinery & Supplies Co.; past Pres., Associated Equipment Distributors. **Act./Mem.:** Wayzata Country Club; Chief Execs. Organization; World Presidents Organization; Spring Hill Country Club.

Gerald W. Simonson Pres., Omnetics Connector Corp., 7260 Commerce Circle E., Fridley, MN 55432. Tel: 612/572-0656. **B:** Jul. 19, 1930, Vermilion Lake Towns, Minn. **C:** Michael L., Bruce B., Karen M., Philip E. **E:** BA, Macalester College, 1952. **Career Hist.:** Auditor, Price Waterhouse & Co., 1955-61; Pres., Community Investment Enterprises Inc., 1962-79; Venture Capital investor, 1979-present; Pres., Omnetics Connector Corp., 1991-present. **Career Act.:** Dir., Chromaline Corp., Excorp, Broadview Media Inc.

James D. Smiley Minnesota VP and Gen. Man., Qwest, 200 S. Fifth St., Rm. 390, Minneapolis, MN 55402. Tel: 612/663-6913. Email: jsmiley@uswest.com **B:** Apr. 8, 1949, Bozeman, Mont. **M:** Rhonda, 1975. **C:** Derek, Shannon. **E:** BA-Communications, Washington State U., 1971. **Career Hist.:** Pacific NW Bell (Seattle), 1971; Mountain Bell (Cheyenne, WY), 1973; Mountain Bell (Denver), 1975; AT&T (Basking Ridge, NJ), 1978; Mountain Bell (Denver), 1981; U S West (Washington, D.C.), 1984; U S West (Denver), 1986; U S West (Sioux Falls, SD), 1989; U S West (Washington, D.C.), 1993; U S West (Minnesota), now Qwest, 1996. **Career Act.:** Board of Dir., United Way of Minneapolis Area; Chair, United Negro College Fund, 1998; Mem., MN Business Partnership; Board of Dir., MEDA; Board of Dir., MN High Technology Assoc.; Board of Dir., Capital City Partnership.

Richard F. (Rick) Smith Pres., CEO, GE Capital Fleet Services, 3 Capital Dr., Eden Prairie, MN 55344. Tel: 612/828-2099. **E:** Graduate, Purdue U. **Career Hist.:** GE, 1982-present: Positions in mktg., sls., product mgmt., gen. mgmt., GE Plastics/Polymerland; Pres., CEO, GE Capital Modular Space, 1994-95; Pres., CEO, GE Capital Fleet Svs., 1996-present.

Sung Won Sohn EVP, Chief Economist, Wells Fargo & Co., Norwest Center, Sixth and Marquette, Minneapolis, MN 55479. Tel: 612/667-7498. **B:** Nov. 11, 1944, Seoul, Korea. **M:** Yoon-Sun Sohn, 1994. **C:** Anne Marie, Rebecca Jill, Andrew Lee. **E:** U. of FL, BA, 1965; Wayne State U., MA, 1968; U. of Pittsburgh, Ph.D., 1972; Harvard Business School, PMD, 1978. **Career Hist.:** Tenured Prof., Slippery Rock State College, 1969-73; Adjunct Prof. of Finance, Bethel College, 1979-82; Sr. Economist, President's Council of Economic Advisors, The White House, 1973-74; VP, Northwestern National Bank (Minneapolis), 1974-77; SVP, Norwest Bank (Minneapolis), 1977-84; SVP, Norwest Corp. (Wells Fargo & Co.), 1984-present. **Career Act.:** Dir., Ministers Mutual Life Insurance Company, MN Wellspring, American Heart Assn., American Refugee Ctee., Bethel College Fdn., Children's Theatre Company & School, Girl Scouts of MN. **Dec./Awd.:** Honorary Citizenships of Duluth, MN and Helena, MT; voted Distinguished Prof. of the School by students at Slippery Rock State College; National Science Fdn. Grants for teaching and research in computer applications to social sciences. **Act./Mem.:** Harvard Business School; National Assn. of Business Economists; Western Economic Assn.; Atlantic Economic Assn.; Southern Economic Assn.

Richard (Rick) Soskin Pres., CEO, Centron DPL Co., 6455 City West Pkwy., Eden Prairie, MN 55344. Tel: 612/829-2800. **B:** Jan. 3, 1956, St. Louis Park, Minn. **M:** Stephanie. **E:** Duke U., U. of MN Law School AB, JD. **Career Hist.:** Centron DPL Company: General Counsel, 1986; CFO, 1988; Pres., CEO, 1991. **Act./Mem.:** Dir., MN Golf Assn., Western Golf Assn.; Mem., Young Presidents Organization; Chair, Joan Soskin Memorial Diabetes Classic.

D. Dean Spatz Chair, Pres., CEO, Osmonics Inc., 5951 Clearwater Dr., Minnetonka, MN 55343. Tel: 612/933-2277. **B:** Mar. 20, 1944, Montclair, N.J. **M:** Ruth Carol, 1968. **C:** Mark, Sharon. **E:** Dartmouth College, AB, 1966; BS-Engrg., 1967; MS-Engrg., Thayer School of Engrg., 1968. **Career Hist.:** Research Assoc., Thayer School of Engrg., Dartmouth College, 1965-68; Mgr. of Engrg., Water and Filter Div., Ecological Sciences Corp., 1968-69; Founder, CEO and Chair, Osmonics Inc., 1969-present. **Career Act.:** Registered Professional Chem. Engr.; Chm., Freshwater Society (Minn.), MN

High Technology Council; Dir., Sigma Aldrich Corp.; Dir., Structural Instrumentation Inc.; Dir., Water Quality Assn.; Dir., Embion. **Dec./Awd.:** Putnam Food Award, 1975; Chemical Equipment Energy Award, *Chemical Equipment* magazine, 1982; Vaaler Award, *Chemical Processing* magazine, 1984; MN 1991 Entrepreneur of the Year, *Inc.* magazine; "200 Best Small Companies in America," *Forbes* magazine, 1991/1994/1995; Filtration & Separation's Product Achievement Awards, 1999. **Act./Mem.:** Mem., American Institute of Chemical Engrs., American Chemical Society, American Water Works Assn., ASTM, American Desalting Assn., International Desalting Assn., Freshwater Fdn., World Presidents Organization, North American Membrane Society, International Society of Beverage Technologists.

William H. Spell Pres., PW Eagle Inc., 222 S. Ninth St., #2880, Piper Jaffray Tower, Minneapolis, MN 55402. Tel: 612/371-9650. **B:** Mar. 21, 1957, Minneapolis, MN. **M:** Tiki, 1984. **C:** Nichole, Harry. **E:** B.S., U of MN ., 1979; M.B.A., U of Minn., 1981. **Career Hist.:** VP and Dir.-Corp. Fin., John G. Kinnard & Co., 1981-88; CEO, Eagle Pacific Industries (now PW Eagle Inc.), 1992-present; Spell Capital Ptnrs., 1998-present. **Career Act.:** Dir., PW Eagle Inc., iNTELEFILM Corp. **Dec./Awd.:** 40 Under 40 Award, CityBusiness. **Act./Mem.:** Mem., Young Presidents Organization, Minneapolis Club.

Jerry W. Spicer Pres., CEO, Hazelden Foundation, P.O. Box 11, Center City, MN 55012. Tel: 651/213-4100. Email: jspicer@hazelden.org **B:** May 22, 1948, Thermopolis, Wyo. **M:** Cheryl, 1968. **C:** Brian, Margaret. **E:** U. of WY, ma; U. of MN mha; Capella University, abd. **Career Hist.:** Prof. of Sociology, Peninsula College, 1982-85; Dir. of Research, Manitoba, Healthcare Commission, 1985-88; various positions, Hazelden, 1978-present. **Career Act.:** Dir., St. Croix Hospital, American College of Addiction Treatment Admin.; The Executive Ctee. **Dec./Awd.:** Special Recognition Award, Executive Office of the President, 1998; Top 100 Healthcare Leaders. **Act./Mem.:** Mem., Minnesota Quality Council; American College of Healthcare Executives, the Executive Ctee.; City Mayor.

Gordon M. Sprenger Pres., CEO, Allina Health System, 5601 Smetana Dr., Minnetonka, MN 55440. Tel: 612/992-3990. Email: gsprenger@allina.com **B:** Apr. 30, 1937, Albert Lea, Minn. **M:** Dee. **C:** Mike, Kris, Angie. **E:** St. Olaf College, BA-Economics, 1959; U. of MN, Master-Hospital Admin., 1961. **Career Hist.:** Asst. Admin., St. Luke's Hospital, Milwaukee, 1964-67; Northwestern Hospital, Asst. Admin. 1967-68, Admin. 1968-71; Abbott Northwestern Hospital, 1971-1992: EVP, 1971-75, Pres./CEO, 1975-88; CEO 1988-92; Pres./CEO, LifeSpan Inc., 1982-92; CEO, HealthSpan Health Systems Corp., 1992-94; Allina Health System, 1994-present: Exec. Officer, 1994-99; Pres. and CEO, 1999-present. **Career Act.:** past Chair, American Hospital Assn. Board of Trustees; Mem., Board of Consultants Hospital Research & Devel. Insititute; Dir., Medtronic Inc., The St. Paul Companies, St. Olaf College, Bush Fdn.; Mem., Board of Overseers Carlson School of Mgmt.; past Chair, Voluntary Hospitals of America; past Trustee, Intermountain Healthcare; Mem. Exec. Ctee., MN Business Partnership.. **Dec./Awd.:** U. of MN Sabra Hamilton Award, 1961; St. Olaf College Blue Key Award, 1961; St. Olaf College Distinguished Alumnus Award, 1982; distinguished service award, MN Hospital Assn., 1989; U. of MN Alumni Assn., Captain's Chair Award, 1991; U. of MN Outstanding Achievement Award, 1998. **Act./Mem.:** Co-Chair, Phillips Neighborhood Partnership; St. Olaf College Baord of Trustees.

James R. Steele Chair, Pres., CEO, Dynamic Air Inc., 1125 Wolters Blvd., St. Paul, MN 55110. Tel: 651/486-3000. **B:** Jun. 27, 1941, St. Paul. **M:** Carolyn Ehrler, 1963. **C:** Gregory, Karen, Mike, Jean. **E:** U. of MN; St. Paul Tech. Vocational. **Career Hist.:** Draftsman, Pioneering Engrg., 1962-63; VP-Engrg., Whirl Air Flow, 1963-69; Pres., Dynamic Air Inc., 1969-present. **Career Act.:** Mem., American Foundryman's Society, American Ceramic Society. **Act./Mem.:** American Foundryman's Society.

James P. Stephenson Chair-Mgmt. Ctee., Faegre & Benson, 2200 Norwest Center, Minneapolis, MN 55402. Tel: 612/336-3000. Email: jstephen@faegre.com **B:** Dec. 22, 1943, Windom, Minn. **M:** Janis, 1968. **C:** Anne, Elliot, Caroline. **E:** U.S. Military Academy, B.S., 1965; Harvard Law School, J.D., 1973. **Career Hist.:** Faegre & Benson, 1973-present: Partner, 1981-present; Chair, 1997-present.

Gary H. Stern Pres., Federal Reserve Bank Minneapolis, P.O. Box 291, Minneapolis, MN 55480. Tel: 612/204-5000. **B:** Nov. 3, 1944, San Luis Obispo, Calif. **M:** Mary K., 1969. **C:** Matthew, Meredith. **E:** AB-Economics, Washington U. (St. Louis), 1967; Rice U. (Houston): MA-Economics, 1970; Ph.D.-Economics, 1972. **Career Hist.:** Federal Reserve Bank of New York, 1970-77: Economist, 1970-72; Chief-Business Conditions Div., 1972-73; Mgr.-Domestic Research Dept., 1973-77; VP/Economist, Loeb Rhoades Hornblower & Co., 1977-78; Sr. Economist/Account Mgr., A. Gary Shilling & Co. Inc., 1978-81; Federal Reserve Bank of Minneapolis, 1983-present: SVP, Dir.-Research, 1982-85; CFO, 1983-85; Pres., March 1985-present. **Career Act.:** past Adjunct Faculty Mem.: Columbia U., NYU, Washington U., CUNY, Rutgers U., Pace U.; Trustee, National Council on Economic Education, Educational Testing Service, Minneapolis College of Art and Design; Dir., MN Meeting, Northwest Area Fdn.; Overseer, Carlson School of Mgmt.; past Dir., Blue Cross Blue Shield of MN (Chm. 1990-93), Minneapolis-St. Paul Public Television.

Axel D. Steuer Pres., Gustavus Adolphus College, 800 W. College Ave., St. Peter, MN 56082. Tel: 507/933-7538. Email: asteuer@gac.edu **B:** Mar. 7, 1943, Kotzenau, Germany. **M:** Loreli Olson Steuer, 1970. **E:** Occidental College, AB, 1965; Harvard U., MA, 1967; Harvard Divinty School, STB, 1969; U. of PA, Ph.D., 1974. **Career Hist.:** Asst. to Dean of Students, U. of PA, 1970-72; Lecturer, Haverford College, Swarthmore College, Princeton U., 1972-74; Asst. Prof., Haverford College, 1974-76; Occidental College, 1976-91: Prof. of Religion, Chair, 1976-86; Assoc. Dean of Faculty, 1987; Exec. Asst. to Pres., 1987-91; Pres., Gustavus Adolphus College, 1991-present. **Career Act.:** MN Campus Compact, Gustavus Adolphus College, MN Private College Council, Lutheran Educational Conference of North America, MN Intercollegiate Athletic Conference, Swedish Council of America, Society for Values in Higher Education, American Academy of Religion; NAICU, Minnesota Public Radio. **Dec./Awd.:** Royal Order of the Polar Star, conferred by His Majesty King Carl XVI Gustaf of Sweden, 1996.

Eric Stevens Exec. Dir., Courage Center, 3915 Golden Valley Rd., Golden Valley, MN 55422. **B:** Mar. 8, 1947, Bronx, N.Y. **M:** Caroline, 1970. **C:** Jessica Stevens. **E:** Queens College of the City University of New York, B.A. 1967; Stanford MBA, 1968; Central Washington State, M.Ed.; Leadership Institute of Seattle, M. Applied Behavioral Science. **Career Hist.:** Exec. Dir., St. David's Child Develop. 1979-99; Exec. Dir., Courage Center 1999-present.

Boyd B. Stofer Pres., CEO, ONCOR International, 3500 W. 80th St., Bloomington, MN 55431. Tel: 612/831-1000. Email: bstofer@uproperties.com **B:** Sep. 18, 1949, Lakewood, Ohio. **M:** Cherie. **E:** Cornell U., 1971; MBA, Harvard Graduate School of Business, 1975. **Career Hist.:** Pres., CEO, United Properties (ONCOR International), 21 years. **Career Act.:** Dir., past Pres.-MN Chapter, National Assn. of Industrial and Office Parks (NAIOP); Full Mem., Urban Land Institute. **Dec./Awd.:** Real Estate Entrepreneur of the Year finalist, Merrill Lynch/Ernst & Young/Inc. magazine, 1992 and 1993; Outstanding Service as Dir., NAIOP, 1994; President's Award, MN Chapter-NAIOP, 1999. **Act./Mem.:** Dir., Boys and Girls Clubs of the Twin Cities; St. Paul Capital City Partnership; U of W; MNREJ Editorial Advisory Board.

Gordon F. Stofer Managing Ptnr., Cherry Tree Investments Inc., 7601 France Ave. S., Edina, MN 55435. Tel: 612/893-9012. **B:** Mar. 15, 1947, Cleveland. **M:** Debbie, 1987. **C:** Gordy, Brett, Scott, Teddy, Jimmy. **E:** BSIE, Cornell U., 1969; MBA, Harvard Business School, 1975. **Career Hist.:** Asst.

to Cont., Maine National Bank, 1972-73; Mktg. Mgr., Honeywell Inc., 1975-77; VP, Norwest Growth Fund, 1977-80; Founder, Mng. Ptnr., Cherry Tree Investments Inc., 1980-present; Founder, managing partner, Cherry Tree & Co., 1997-present. **Career Act.:** Dir., Verdant Corp., Insignia Systems Inc., Coda Music Technology Inc., VEE Corp. (Sesame Street Live). **Dec./Awd.:** Entrepreneur of the Year Finalist, Ernst & Young, 1995; Outstanding Director of the Year, Twin Cities Business Monthly and National Assn. of Corporate Directors, 1997. **Act./Mem.:** MN Venture Capital Assn.; National Venture Capital Assn.; Mt. Olivet Church (Board of Life and Growth, Usher); Children's Cancer Research Fund (Benefactor).

Karl F. Storrie Pres., CEO, Dura Automotive Systems Inc., 4508 IDS Center, Minneapolis, MN 55402. Tel: 612/332-2335. **B:** Aug. 10, 1937. **M:** Sally. **C:** Stephanie, Scot, Sara. **E:** U. of Southern CA, BS. **Career Hist.:** Group Pres. and Division Pres., Coltec Industries, 1981-91; Pres. and CEO, Dura Automotive Systems, 1991-present. **Career Act.:** Dir., Argo Tech Corp.; Mem., Society of Automotive Engrs., Manufacturers Alliance (Presidents Council); Society of Manufacturing Engrs.; National Assn. of Manufacturing Engrs. **Act./Mem.:** Oakland Hills Country Club.

Frederick M. Strader VP, Gen. Mgr., United Defense L.P./Armament Systems Division, 4800 East River Rd., Fridley, MN 55421. Tel: 612/572-6504. **B:** 1953, Richland Center, Wis. **M:** Betty. **C:** Jay, Courtney, Kent, Blake. **E:** Ripon College, BA; Wharton School at the U. of PA, MBA. **Career Hist.:** Four years active duty in the U.S. Army; FMC Corp., 1980-present: Gen.l Mgr., FMC/Agricultural Machinery Div., 1992-94; Gen. Mgr., Armament Systems Div., 1994-present.

David Strand COO, Allina Health System, 5601 Smetana Dr., Minnetonka, MN 55343. Tel: 612/992-3952. **E:** BA, Gustavus Adolphus College, 1978; law degree, U. of MN, 1981. **Career Hist.:** Popham Haik Schnobrich & Kaufman: Partner and Chair-National Health Care Practice Group; Medica: SVP/Gen. Counsel-Medica Health Plans and CEO-Medica Self-Insured; Allina: System VP-Market/Network Mgmt., Pres.-Medica Health Plans. **Career Act.:** Founder, Medica (now Allina) Fdn.; Chair, MN Health Care Coalition on Violence, Dir. MN Council of Health Plans; Dir., Allina Fdn. **Dec./Awd.:** Up and Comers, Modern Health Care Magazine, 1995; 40 Under 40, CityBusiness, 1995; Intl. Emerging Leaders in Healthcare Award, Healthcare Forum, 1997. **Act./Mem.:** Mem., Board of Dir., MN Public Radio; Mem., Board of Dir., MN Communications Group; Mem., Board of Dir., Gustavus Adolphus College.

John Strange Pres., CEO, St. Luke's Hospital of Duluth, 915 E. First St., Duluth, MN 55805. Tel: 218/726-5555. **B:** Nov. 22, 1949, Milwaukee. **M:** Mackey, 1975. **C:** Katie, Amber. **E:** U. of WI-Stevens Point, BS, 1972; Cardinal Stritch College, MS, 1985. **Career Hist.:** Senior Accountant, Pepsi Cola Bottling Group, 1976-78; Cont., VP-Finance, Memorial Hospital, 1978-91; EVP, Memorial Hospital, 1991-92; VP-Finance, CFO, St. Luke's Hospital, 1992-95; Pres., CEO, St. Luke's Hospital, 1995-present. **Career Act.:** Chair, Duluth Graduate Medical Education Council Inc.; Mem., Lakeview Hospital Board, Boy Scout Executive Council; Light House for the Blind Board Member. **Act./Mem.:** Rotary; Dir., Lake View Hospital.

Ralph Strangis Mem., Kaplan, Strangis and Kaplan P.A., 90 S. Seventh St., Suite 5500, Minneapolis, MN 55402. Tel: 612/375-1138. Email: rs@kskpa.com **B:** Jun. 22, 1936, Minneapolis. **M:** Grace, 1992. **C:** Ralph Jr., Paul, Jason, Anthea. **E:** U. of MN: BSL, 1958; JD, 1960. **Career Hist.:** Mem., Kaplan, Strangis and Kaplan P.A., 1978-present. **Career Act.:** Damark International Inc., TCF Financial Corp., Miller Waste Mills Inc. **Dec./Awd.:** Twin Cities Business Monthly Outstanding Dir., 1997. **Act./Mem.:** Trustee, Treas., Chair-Audit/Fin. Ctee., The Minneapolis Institute of Arts; Mem., Minikahda Country Club.

Albert P.L. Stroucken Chair, Pres., CEO, H.B. Fuller Co., P.O. Box 64683, St. Paul, MN 55164. **M:** Gerda. **C:** Michael, Chris. **Career Hist.:** Bayer AG (Leverkusen, Germany), 1969-98: rotational international job assignments culminating in EVP and Pres.-Industrial Chemicals Div., Bayer Corp. U.S.; then Gen. Mgr.-Inorganics Div.; H.B. Fuller Co.: Pres., CEO, 1998-present; Chm., 1999-present.

Marion Melvin Stuckey Chair, CEO, Fourth Shift Corp., 2 Meridian Crossings, Minneapolis, MN 55423. Tel: 612/851-1500. Email: mstuckey@fs.com **B:** 1938, Oran, Mo. **M:** Lee, 1962. **C:** Kimberly, Cristen. **E:** BS-Southern Methodist U., 1961. **Career Hist.:** Gen. Mgr., IBM Corp.; Pres.-Peripherals Div., Control Data Corp.; Chair, CEO, Fourth Shift Corp. **Career Act.:** Author of book DEMASS; has explained DEMASS concepts on television and at national business convetions; author of feature articles for news periodicals such as Industry Week; On various boards of public and private companies. **Dec./Awd.:** Entrepreneur of the Year, MN Software Assn., 1993; Fifty R&D Stars to Watch, Industry Week, 1993. **Act./Mem.:** Alliance of Chief Executives.

Brian F. Sullivan Chair, CEO, Recovery Engineering Inc., 9300 N. 75th Ave., Minneapolis, MN 55428. Tel: 612/315-5500. **B:** 1961, Charlottesville, Va. **M:** Mia, 1993. **C:**. **E:** Bachelor's-Economics (Magna Cum Laude), Harvard U.; John Harvard U. scholarship; internships with member of British parliament and two members of the U.S. Congress. **Career Hist.:** Chairman, CEO, Co-Founder, Recovery Engrg. Inc., 1986. **Career Act.:** Dir., Claremont (CA) Institute of Political Philosophy, North Central Life Insurance Co. (St. Paul). **Dec./Awd.:** Entrepreneur of the Year finalist, Ernst & Young, 2000. **Act./Mem.:** United Way: Founder and chair of ctee. to enhance participation of local entrepreneurs; four-year member of Campaign Cabinet; Dir., MN Orchestral Assn.

Michael P. Sullivan Chair, International Dairy Queen Inc., Box 39286, Edina, MN 55439. Tel: 612/830-0308. **B:** Dec. 5, 1934, Minneapolis. **M:** Marilyn Emmer, 1964. **C:** Katherine A., Michael P., Maureen E., Bridget M., Daniel W., Thomas F.. **E:** Marquette U., BS, 1956; U. of MN, JD, 1962. **Career Hist.:** U.S. Navy and Naval Reserve, 1956-61; Ptnr., Assoc., Gray Plant Law Firm, 1962-77; Mng. Ptnr., Gray, Plant, Mooty, Mooty & Bennett P.A., 1977-87; International Dairy Queen Inc.: Pres., CEO, 1987-2000; Chm., 2000-present. **Career Act.:** Mem., American Bar Assn.; past Mem., ABA, House of Delegates; past Mem. MN State Bar Assn. Board of Govenors, 1976 State Convention Chair; past Chair Client Security Fund; past Chair, CLE Div., MN Bar Assn.; Mem. past Pres., Hennepin County Bar Assn.; past Dir., Hennepin County Bar Fdn.; Mem., past Pres., National Conference of Commissioners on Uniform State Laws; past Mem., Metropolitan Transit Commission Panel of Examiners; past Special Counsel, MN Attorney General; past Trustee, Lawyers Public Affairs Commission; Fellow, American Bar Fdn.; past Mem., Supreme Court Advisory Ctee. on Rules of Board on Judicial Standards; CLE Lecturer; Dir., Valspar Corp., International Dairy Queen, Allianz Life Insurance Co. of North America, Opus Corp.; Mem., American Law Institute; Past Pres., Canada/Minnesota Business Council. **Dec./Awd.:** Medal of Honor, College of St. Catherine, 1995. **Act./Mem.:** Our Lady of Grace Parish; Citizen's League; Dir., Pres., U. of MN Law School Alumni Assn. and Board of Visitors; Past Chair, St. Mary's Jr. College; Dir., Past Pres., Legal Aid Society of Minneapolis, Central MN Legal Services Corp.; past Trustee, College of St. Catherine; Mem., past Chair, The Fund for the Legal Aid Society; Dir., Greater Minneapolis YMCA (Chair of the Board), U. of MN Alumni Assn., St. Paul Seminary; Board of Governors, Children's Miracle Network; Campaign Chair, MN Independent School Fund (1991-92); Dir., American Arbitration Assn.; MN Business Partnership; past Dir., Fairview Health Systems; Dir. Visitation Convent School; Board of Regents, St. John's University.

William J. Sweasy Chair, Red Wing Shoe Co. Inc., Riverfront Centre, 314 Main St., Red Wing, MN 55066. Tel: 651/388-8211. Email: bsweasy@redwing.com **B:** Red Wing, Minn. **M:** Carol. **E:** BS, U. of MN.

Thomas E. Sween Chair, CEO, E.A. Sween Co., 16101 W. 78th St., Eden Prairie, MN 55344. Tel: 612/949-1421. Email: tsween@pclink.com **B:** Sep. 12, 1948, Minneapolis. **M:** Jeanne, 1990. **C:** Tasha Rae, Thomas Hans, Drew. **E:** U. of Denver, BSBA, 1970. **Career Hist.:** Sls. Mgr., Mastercraft Kitchens, 1969-70; Promotional Sls., Stewart Sandwiches, 1970-71; District Mgr., Stewart Sandwiches, 1971-72; Div. Mgr., Stewart Sandwiches, 1972-74; Pres., Stewart Sandwiches, 1974-80; Pres., E.A. Sween Company DELI EXPRESS, 1980-86; Chair, Pres., E.A. Sween Co. DELI EXPRESS, 1987-1998; Chairman/CEO, E.A. Sween Co. Deli Express, 1999-present. **Career Act.:** Mem.-Exec. Ctee., Young Presidents Organization; Trustee, Breck School; Dir., Robertson Inc.; member, World Presidents Organization. **Act./Mem.:** Flagship Athletic Club; Lafayette Club; Bearpath Golf & Country Club.

Glen A. Taylor Chair, CEO, Taylor Corp., 1725 Roe Crest Dr., North Mankato, MN 56003. Tel: 507/625-2828. **B:** Apr. 20, 1941, Springfield, Minn. **M:** Bonnie, 1999. **C:** Terri, Jean, Taylor Moor, Jeff, Kendahl, Darik. **E:** Mankato State U., BS, 1962; Harvard Graduate School of Business, Smaller-Co. Mgmt. Program. **Career Hist.:** various positions, Carlson Wedding Service and Carlson Craft, 1960-74; Chair, CEO, Taylor Corp., 1975-present; MN State Senator, 1980-89; MN Senate Minority Leader, 1984-86; Owner, MN Timberwolves, MN Lynx. **Career Act.:** Dir., Imation; Dir., Schwan's; Dir., Angeion Corp.; past Pres., YMCA; Dir., Chamber of Commerce, Mankato State U. Fdn.; past Pres., Mankato Jaycees; Campaign Chair, United Way. **Dec./Awd.:** Mankato Area Distinguished Service Award; Mankato State U. Distinguished Alumni Award; Outstanding Chapter Pres., MN Jaycees; listed in Jaycees Outstanding Young Men of America; Book of Golden Deeds Award; MN State U. System, Distinguished Service Award; Phi Kappa Phi Honor Society; 1987 Executive of the Year Corporate Report MN; 1987 Laureate; 1987 MCFR Friend of the Family MN Council on Family Relations; Youth Leadership Award (first honoree), Camp Fire Boys and Girls/MN Council, 1995; MN Business Hall of Fame; Honorary Doctor of Laws from Mankato State U.; Sales Exec. of the Year, Sales & Marketing Executives of Minneapolis/St. Paul, 1999. **Act./Mem.:** Young Presidents Organization; World Presidents Organization.

Maurice R. Taylor II Chair, CEO, MEDgenesis Inc., 5182 W. 72nd St., Edina, MN 55439. Tel: 612/979-3600. **Career Hist.:** Chronimed Inc.: Co-Founder, 1985, Chair/CEO, 1985-present. **Career Act.:** Chairman Chronimed Inc., Chairman, Whittier Institute For Diabetes, Chairman, Clinical Network Inc., Chairman, Linguistic Technologies Inc., Dir. MN Zoo.

Doug Thompson Regional VP, State Farm Mutual Automobile Insurance Co., 8500 State Farm Way, Woodbury, MN 55125. Tel: 651/578-4001. **B:** Jul. 11, 1942, Rushford, Minn. **M:** Lynn, 1968. **E:** Winona St. U.: BA, BS, post-graduate work. **Career Hist.:** State Farm Mutual Automobile Insurance Co., 1970-present: Agent, 1970-73; Field Agency Mgmt., 1973-85; Deputy Regional VP, 1985-90; Regional VP, 1991-present. **Career Act.:** Dir., St. Paul Chamber of Commerce, Minneapolis Chamber of Commerce, Neighborhood Housing Svs.; Mem.-Exec. Ctee., Insurance Federation of MN; Mem., American Society of CLUs, National Assn. of Life Underwriters. **Act./Mem.:** Incarnation Lutheran Church; North Oaks Country Club.

Mary M. Tjosvold, Ph.D. CEO, Mary T Inc., 1555 118th Lane N.W., Coon Rapids, MN 55448. Tel: 612/754-2505. Email: maryt@skypoint.com **B:** Apr. 22, 1943, Appleton, Wis. **E:** U. of MN: BS-Math. Education, 1964; Special Ed. Certificate, 1974; MA-Educational Admin., 1975; Ph.D.-Educational Admin., 1975; Owner/Pres. Mgmt. (OPM) Program, Harvard Business School, 1985-87. **Career Hist.:** Math. Teacher (Illinois, Minnesota), 1964-73; Founder, CEO, Mary T. Inc., 1976-present. **Career Act.:** Developer, Ptnr., CEO, Camilia Rose Convalescent Center and Group Home, Six Acres Townhomes, Mary T. Inc. Mgmt. Co., Margaret Place Apartments for Seniors, Outreach Group Homes, ABLECARE Home Services, Mary T. Associates Inc. Group Homes, Margaret Place Catered Living (DeMar, Shingle Creek, Eagle), Villas of Caroline, Villas of Palm, and Villas of Prescott, ETC By Design; advocate, speaker, co-author (with brother Dean Tjosvold) on mgmt., productive conflict, and team based organization; Chair, MN Joint Conference Planning Ctee., 1984-87; Sec., Harvard OPM Alumni Assn.; Dir., Northeast State Bank; Mem., Coon Rapids Economic Devel. Commission; Board member, American Refugee Ctee.; Mem.-U. of MN BioMedical Ethics Center Community Advisory Board; Mem.-Community Advisory Board-Leonard Street and Demard. Board Member: Advisory Committee Rasmussen Center for Cardiovascular Disease Prevention. **Dec./Awd.:** Bush Fellowship, 1985. **Act./Mem.:** Dir., Anoka County Assn. for Retarded Citizens, U. of MN Alumni Society, National Conference Christians and Jews, U. of MN Bio-Medical Ethics Center; Mem., MN Assn. for Retarded Citizens, National Assn. for Retarded Citizens, MN and Hennepin County Women's Political Caucus, American Qualified Mental Retardation Professionals Assn., American Assn. on Mental Deficiency/State of MN (Pres., 1984), City of Coon Rapids Year 2000 Task Force; Organizer, Women's Education Action Group, MN Women for Educational Equality; Founder, Dir., Minn-We (nonprofit org. to support women in business).

Marlene O. Travis Pres., COO, Health Risk Management Inc., 10900 Hampshire Ave. S., Bloomington, MN 55438. Tel: 612/829-3500. **B:** Jul. 31, 1939, Edmonton, Alberta. **M:** Gary McIlroy, M.D., 1962. **C:** Jennifer, Montgomery. **E:** Undergraduate upper-level coursework: political science, business admin., mass communications at Metropolitan U., St. Cloud State U., Santa Monica Community College, Rochester Junior College; post-graduate business education at Aresty Inst./Entrepreneurial Center of The Wharton School/U. of PA; TQM at Harvard School of Public Health; Ctee. of 200 co-faculty: Stanford, Harvard. **Career Hist.:** Pres., Co-founder, Dir., Health Risk Mgmt. Inc., 1977-present; Chair, CEO, Health Resource Management Ltd.; Chair, CEO, Institute for Healthcare Quality; Pres., Travis-McIlroy Fdn. **Career Act.:** Community Leadership (Brainerd and Crow Wing County, MN): Founder/Incorporator, Mid-MN Women's Center; Dir., Greater Minneapolis Chamber of Commerce; Founder, Crow Wing County Sexual Assault Svs.; Chair, Crow Wing County Attorney's Task Force on Sexual Assault. Affiliations: American Biographical Institute, American Managed Care & Review Assn., Canadian College of Health Care Execs., Medical Alley (2VCh.), MN Coalition on Health Care Mkt. Reform, MN Chamber of Commerce, National Assn. of Corporate Directors, National Assn. of Employers on Health Care Action, National Employee Benefits Institute, National Women's Health Network, Self-Insured Inst. of America, Society for Medical Decision Making, WA Business Group on Health, Ctee. of 200; Dir., Greater Minneapolis Chamber of Commerce. **Dec./Awd.:** Recognized by: International Directory of Distinguished Leadership, International Who's Who of Intellectuals, Who's Who in Finance, Who's Who in the Midwest, Who's Who in the World, Who's Who Registry of Global Business Leaders, World's Who's Who of Women. **Act./Mem.:** AACW, C-200, Mem., United Way Keystone.

Ronald A. Tschetter Pres.-Private Client Group, Dain Rauscher Corp., Dain Rauscher Plaza, 60 S. Sixth St., Minneapolis, MN 55402. Tel: 612/371-2899. **B:** Oct. 4, 1941, Huron, SD. **M:** Nancy 1965. **C:** John, Jeff. **E:** B.A., Bethel College. **Career Hist.:** Investment Executive, Dain Bosworth, 1973-82; Regional Dir., Dain Bosworth, 1982-1991; Pres., Dain Bosworth (now Dain Rauscher Corp.) Private Client Group, 1991-present. **Career Act.:** Mem., NYSE Regional Firms Ctee.; SIA, Sls. and Mktg. Committee. **Dec./Awd.:** Bethel College Alumni of the Year, 1993. **Act./Mem.:** Mem./Chair, National Peace Corps Assn.; Bd. of Regents, Bethel College and Seminary; Dir., Courage Center; Dir., Minn. Private College Council.

Timothy H. Tucker CEO, Augustana Care Corp., 1007 E. 14th St., Minneapolis, MN 55404. Tel: 612/333-1551. **B:** May 5, 1951, Minneapolis. **M:** Patricia, 1979. **C:** Jennifer, Richard. **E:** BA, U. of MN. **Career Hist.:** Augustana Care Corp., 1983-present. **Career Act.:** Dir., East Downtown

Council, Elliot Park Neighborhood Inc., U. of MN Special Projects Fdn., Care Choice; Mem., American College of Health Care Admin., MN Gerontological Society, MN Assn. of Homes for the Aging; Friends of the U. of MN Dept. of Art. **Dec./Awd.:** Alumni of Notable Achievement, 1997, U of M.

Kathy H. Tunheim Pres., CEO, Tunheim Group Inc., 8009 34th Ave. S., Suite 1100, Bloomington, MN 55425. Tel: 612/851-1605. **E:** B.A., Political Science and econ., U of MN. **Career Hist.:** Asst. Press Sec., Senator Wendell Anderson; Mktg. Communications Mgr., NCR Comten; VP-Corp. Public Relations, Honeywell Inc.; Pres. and CEO, Tunheim Group. **Career Act.:** Dir. Bush Foundation, Nobel Peace Prize Forum, and the United Way of Minneapolis Area; serves as a trustee on the boards of The Minneapolis Foundation and the Science Museum of Minnesota; Chair of the Exec. Committee and Board of Regents for Augsburg College; Member of the Arthur W. Page Society, Council of Public Relations Firms, and Public Relations Society of America; Advisory Board of the School of Journalism and Mass Communication with the U of M. **Act./Mem.:** Dir., Bush Fdn., Nobel Peace Prize Forum, United Way of Mpls. Area; Trustee, Mpls. Fdn. and Science Museum of Minn.; Chair Executive Ctee., Augsburg College; Mem., Arthur W. Page Soc., Council of Public Relations Firms, Public Relations Society of America.

F. Mike Tuohy Chair, CEO, Owner, Tuohy Furniture Corp., 42 St. Albans Place, Chatfield, MN 55923. Tel: 507/867-4280. **B:** Mar. 27, 1936, Rochester, Minn. **M:** Gina, 1999. **C:** Tori, Dan, Katy, Michael. **E:** Loras College (Dubuque, IA). **Career Hist.:** Co-Founder, Tuohy Church Furniture, 1955; Tuohy Furniture Corp., 1970; Tuohy Forest Corp., 1977. **Career Act.:** past Dir. Advisory Board, Federal Reserve Bank-Ninth District; VP, Past Pres., Business Institutional Furniture Manufacturers Assn., Regional MN Technology; MN Sustainable Devel. Initiative; Pres. Chatfield Economic Devel. Assn., Fillmore County Planning Commission; Dir., F&M Bank. **Dec./Awd.:** MN Pollution Control Agency, Certificates of Commendation, 1995; Eagle Scout/Silver Beaver Awards, Boy Scouts of America; Paul Harris Fellow, Rotary. **Act./Mem.:** Rotary Club, Gamehaven Fdn. (Boy Scouts); Chosen Valley Golf and Country Club; Rochester Golf and Country Club.

WHO

John G. Turner Chair, CEO, ReliaStar Financial Corp., 20 Washington Ave. S., Minneapolis, MN 55401. Tel: 612/372-5305. **B:** Oct. 3, 1939, Springfield, Mass. **M:** Leslie Corrigan, 1962. **C:** Jeff, Marcie, James, Andrew. **E:** BA-Math., Amherst College, 1961; Society of Actuaries Fellowship, 1967; Harvard Business School-Advanced Mgmt. Program, 1980. **Career Hist.:** Actuarial Student, Monarch Life (Springfield, MA), 1961; Northwestern National Life Insurance Company/The NWNL Companies Inc./ReliaStar Financial Corp., 1967-present: Asst. Actuary, 1967-72; 2VP, Group Actuary, 1972-75; VP, Group Div., 1975-78; SVP-Group Div., 1978-79; SVP, Chief Actuary, 1979-81; EVP, Chief Actuary, 1981; Sr. EVP, 1982; Pres., 1983-86; Pres., COO, 1986-91; Pres., CEO, 1991-93; Chair, CEO, 1993-present. **Career Act.:** Chair, ReliaStar Financial Corp., ReliaStar Life, ReliaStar United Svs. Life, ReliaStar Bankers Security Life, Northern Life, Northstar Investment Mgmt. Corp., Insurance Federation of MN, Retirement Security Steering Ctee., American Council of Life Insurance; Dir., ShopKo Stores Inc., Health Insurance Assn. of America, Life & Health Insurance Medical Research Fund, Greater Minneapolis Metropolitan Housing Corp., MN Center for Corporate Responsibility, United Way of Minneapolis Area, MN Private College Council Fund and Research Fdn., Carlson School of Mgmt. (U. of MN), Minneapolis Club; VChair, Hamline U. Board of Trustees. **Dec./Awd.:** Insurance Industry-CEO of the Year, Wall Street Transcript, 1996. **Act./Mem.:** Mem.-Investment Ctee., Allina Health System; United Way of Minneapolis; United States Golf Assn.

Ronald L. Turner Chair, Pres., CEO, Ceridian Corporation, 3311 E. Old Shakopee Rd., Bloomington, MN 55425. Tel: 612/853-8100. **B:** Sep. 4, 1946, Brownsville, Tenn. **M:** Catherine. **E:** BS-Aerospace Engrg., U. of TN; MS-Engrg., U. of FL; MS-Mgmt., M.I.T. (Sloan Fellow). **Career Hist.:** U.S. Air Force Systems Command, 1968-73; Martin Marietta Corp., 1973-87: Advanced Systems Mgr., Mktg. Mgr., Systems Engr. (1973), Deputy Dir.-Advanced Programs, Martin Marietta Aerospace (1977), Dir.-Strategic Planning, Corp. (1979), Pres., Martin Marietta Aggregates (1980), VP-Business Devel., Martin Marietta Aerospace (1983), VP-Electronic Systems Div., Orlando Aerospace (1984), VP-Tactical Interdiction Systems Div., Orlando Aerospace (1986); Pres., CEO, GEC-Marconi Electronic Systems Corp., 1987-93; Ceridian Corp., 1993-present: Pres./CEO, Computing Devices International (1993); EVP-Op. (1997); Pres., COO (1998); Chm., Pres., and CEO (2000). **Career Act.:** Vice Chairman, Electronic Industries Assn.; Dir., Electronic Industries Assn. Govt. Div. (Past Chair), Director Ceridian Corp., BTG Inc., FLIR Systems; past Chair-Board of Governors, MN High Technology Council, MN Federal Govt. Contractor's Council; past Pres.-Board of Governors, M.I.T. Society of Sloan Fellows; VP, National Security Industrial Assn.; Board of Directors: Minnesota Meeting, Minnesota Business Partnership; Member, The Business Roundtable.

Christopher A. Twomey Pres., CEO, Arctic Cat Inc., 601 Brooks Ave. S., Thief River Falls, MN 56701. Tel: 218/681-8558. **B:** May 25, 1948, Grand Forks, N.D. **M:** Darla. **C:** Jeffrey, Kammile. **E:** U. of ND, Grand Forks, BA, 1971; completed graduate course work, 1977. **Career Hist.:** Occupational Devel. Center, 1973-75 and Exec. Dir., 1977-83; Arctic Cat Inc.: Dir.-Corp. Admin., 1983-86; Pres./CEO, 1986-present. **Career Act.:** Dir., Arctic Cat Inc.; Chair, International Snowmobile Manufacturers Association (ISMA). **Act./Mem.:** Thief River Falls Rotary Club.

Robert J. Ulrich Chair, CEO, Target Corp., 777 Nicollet Mall, Minneapolis, MN 55402. **B:** 1944. **E:** U. of MN, 1967. **Career Hist.:** Began working for Dayton Hudson Corp., now Target Corp., in 1967; CEO of Target Stores before succeeding Ken Macke as Chair/CEO of the entire corporation in April 1994. **Career Act.:** Dir., Dayton Hudson Corp., Minneapolis Institute of Art, National Retail Federation; Advisory Board Mem., Metropolitan Economic Devel. Assn.; Mem., MN Business Partnership and Business Roundtable, Business Ctee. for the Arts.

Daryle Uphoff Managing Ptnr., Lindquist & Vennum PLLP, 4200 IDS Center, 80 S. Eighth St., Minneapolis, MN 55402. Tel: 612/371-3211. **B:** Jan. 21, 1943, Minonk, Ill. **M:** Lucy Savage, 1982. **C:** Jeanne, John. **E:** BA, Trinity College (CT), 1965; JD, U. of IL, 1971. **Career Hist.:** Lindquist & Vennum, 1971-present. **Act./Mem.:** Lafayette Club.

William G. Van Dyke Chair, Pres., CEO, Donaldson Co. Inc., 1400 W. 94th St., P.O. Box 1299 (55440), Bloomington, MN 55431. Tel: 612/887-3131. Email: dcivandyke@aol.com **B:** Jun. 30, 1945, Minneapolis. **M:** Karin. **E:** U. of MN: BA-Economics, 1967; MBA, 1976. **Career Hist.:** Financial Cont., Torit Corp., 1972-77; VP and CFO, Northland Aluminum Co., 1977-78; Donaldson Co. Inc., 1979-present: Corp. Cont.; VP and Cont.; VP and CFO; VP and Gen. Mgr.-Industrial Group; Pres. and COO; Chair, Pres., and CEO. **Career Act.:** Dir., Donaldson Co. Inc., Graco Inc.; Mem., MN Business Partnership; Board of Overseers, Carlson School of Mgmt., U. of MN. **Act./Mem.:** Mem., Minneapolis Club, Interlachen Country Club.

James F. Van Houten Pres., CEO, MSI Insurance Cos., P.O. Box 64035 (55164), Arden Hills, MN 55110. Tel: 651/631-7004. **B:** Jan. 13, 1942, Fullerton, Calif. **M:** Dr. Mary Ann Nelson. **C:** Kimberly Riley, Lori Van Houten. **E:** BA, English Literature, St. Mary's U. (San Antonio, Texas); MBA, IL State. **Career Hist.:** VP-Profit Center Gen. Mgr.; VP-Corp. Life & Health Mktg., Wausau Insurance Companies, 1974-84; VP-Mktg./Business Planning, Country Companies Insurance Group, 1984-89; Pres., CEO, MSI Insurance Companies, 1989-present. **Career Act.:** Former Chair, Insurance Federation of MN; Mem.-Exec. Ctee., National Cooperative Business Assn., Cooperative Devel. Fdn.; Pres., MN Assn. of Mutual Insurance Companies; Dir., MN Business Partnership; Treas. and Mem.-Exec. Ctee., Center of the American Experiment, Cooperative Development Fdn., Arrowhead Council-Boy Scouts of America; Mem.-Graduate Faculty, Carlson School of Business; Dir.-Strategy Mgmt. Research Center, U. of MN; Mem.-Board of Advisors, MN Assn. of Scholars. **Dec./Awd.:** Outstanding MBA Award, IL State U., 1989; Life Member, Sigma Iota Epsilon, National Honor Society, 1988; CPCU (Chartered Property Casualty Underwriter) and CLU (Chartered Life Underwriter). **Act./Mem.:** Mem. Advisory Ctee.; Chair, MN No Show Ball Ctee.; CARE; MN Assn. of Scholars.

Daryl R. (Sid) Verdoorn Pres., CEO, C.H. Robinson Co., 8100 Mitchell Rd., Suite 200, Eden Prairie, MN 55344. Tel: 612/937-8500. Email: verdsid@chrobinson.com **B:** Feb. 11, 1939, Albert Lea, Minn. **M:** Carol, 1959. **C:** Jay, Jeff, Jim. **E:** Central College, Pella, IA. **Career Hist.:** C.H. Robinson Company: Sales (Minneapolis), 1963-66; Branch Mgr., San Francisco, 1966-71; Personnel Dir., 1971-75; VP, 1975-77; Pres., 1977-present. **Career Act.:** Dir./Officer, Produce Marketing Assn.; Dir., United Fresh Fruit Assn. **Dec./Awd.:** Entrepreneur of the Year finalist, Ernst & Young, 2000. **Act./Mem.:** Lafayette Country Club.

Jack M. Vilett Pres., Northland Electric Supply Co., 521 S. 10th St., P.O. Box 1275 (55440), Minneapolis, MN 55404. Tel: 612/341-6100. **M:** Mary Mueller, 1968. **C:** Jason, Betsy. **Career Act.:** Chair, National Assn. Electrical Distributors, Young Exec. Program; National Assn. Wholesalers Young Exec. Program. **Act./Mem.:** Mem., Board of Govenors, National Assn. of Electrical Distributors; MN Family Business Council; Minikahda Country Club; NAED (Trade Assoc.) Finance/Operations Ctee..

Manuel A. (Manny) Villafana Chair, CEO, ATS Medical Inc., 3905 Annapolis Ln., Plymouth, MN 55447. Tel: 612/553-7736. **B:** Aug. 30, 1940, Bronx, N.Y. **M:** Elizabeth, 1984. **C:** Michael, Ann Marie, Jude; twins Elisa Beverly and Manuela Elizabeth. **E:** Cardinal Hayes High School, 1958. **Career Hist.:** Latin America Sls. Mng. Dir., Medtronic Inc., 1967-71; Chair, Founder, Cardiac Pacemakers Inc., 1971-76; Chair, Founder, St. Jude Medical Inc., 1976-82; Co-Founder, Chair, GV Medical Inc., 1983-87; Founder, Chair, CEO, ATS Medical Inc., 1987-present. **Career Act.:** Co-Founder, Dir., Lillehei Surgical Society; Co-Founder MN New Venture Collaborative. **Dec./Awd.:** Laureate, MN Business Hall of Fame, 1983; Entrepreneur of the Year, 1989, 1990; Hispanic of the Year, 1990; National Master Entrepreneur, Inc. magazine, 1990; National Hall of Fame, Boys and Girls Club, 1993; Cardinal Hayes Hall of Fame, 1994. **Act./Mem.:** Dir., Kips Bay Boys and Girls Club.

Raymond S. Vold Pres., Timesavers Inc., 5270 Hanson Court N., Crystal, MN 55429. Tel: 612/537-3611. Email: timesvr@aol.com **B:** Jun. 14, 1933, Osseo, Wis. **M:** Rachel, 1955. **C:** Michael, Patricia, Susan. **E:** WI State College, BS-Math., BS-Econ., 1959.. **Career Hist.:** Cost Account Cont., Domain Industries, 1959-68; Timesavers Inc., 1968-present: Cont., 1968-70; VP, Treas., 1970-77; EVP, 1977-82; Pres., CEO, Timesavers Inc., Abrasive Engrg. and Manufacturing Company, 1983-present; Mng. Dir., Timesavers International B.V. (Goes, The Netherlands), 1996-present. **Career Act.:** Dir., Timesavers Inc., Abrasive Engrg. and Manufacturing, International Woodworking Show, Wood Machinery Mfrs. of America; past Pres., Twin-West Chamber of Commerce. **Dec./Awd.:** Ralph B. Baldwin Award of Excellence, Wood Machinery Manufacturers of America, 1994. **Act./Mem.:** Golden Valley Country Club; House of Hope Lutheran Church; Twin-West Chamber of Commerce.

Momchilo Vucenich Managing Dir., U.S. Bancorp, 222 S. Ninth St., Piper Jaffray Tower, Minneapolis, MN 55402. Tel: 612/921-7968. **B:** Feb. 22, 1945. **M:** Shirley Fjone Vucenich, 1965. **C:** Todd, Rodney. **E:** U. of MN, BA (cum laude), 1971. **Career Hist.:** Investment Executive, Paine Webber, 1973-77; 1st VP, Piper Jaffray, 1977-84; Chair and CEO, IRI Securities, 1984-86; President and CEO, Craig Hallum, 1986-93; Managing Dir., Piper Jaffray, 1993-present. **Career Act.:** Dir., Craig Hallum, 1986-93; Dir., IRI Securities, 1983-86; Dir., Hamilton Investments, 1992-93; Piper Capital, 1994. **Act./Mem.:** Minneapolis Club, United Way.

Robert R. Waller, M.D. past Pres./CEO, Mayo Foundation, 200 First St. S.W., Rochester, MN 55905. Tel: 507/284-2511. **B:** Feb. 19, 1937, New York. **M:** Sarah Pickens. **C:** three. **E:** Duke U., 1958; U. of TN, 1963; U. of Jacksonville, Hon. Dr. Humane Letters, 1991. **Career Hist.:** Consultant in Ophthalmology, Mayo Clinic, 1970-present; Prof. of Ophthalmology, Mayo Medical School, 1980; Pres. and CEO, Mayo Fdn., 1988-98. **Career Act.:** Dir., Hormel Foods Corp., Malcolm Baldrige National Quality Award Fdn., Institute for Healthcare Improvement; Healthcare Leadership Council.

Winston Roger Wallin Chair Emeritus, Medtronic Inc., 2550 Metropolitan Centre, 333 S. Seventh St., Minneapolis, MN 55402. Tel: 612/338-0477. **B:** Mar. 6, 1926, Minneapolis. **M:** Maxine Houghton, 1949. **C:** Rebecca, Brooks, Lance, Bradford. **E:** U. of MN, BBA, 1948. **Career Hist.:** U.S. Navy, 1943-45; Pillsbury Company, 1948-85: Mgr.-Grain Procurement, 1965-71; VP-Commodity Op., 1971-76; EVP, 1976; Pres., COO, 1977-84; VChair, 1984-85; Pres., Medtronic 1985-89; Chair, CEO, Medtronic Inc., 1985-91; Chair, 1986-96; Chair Emeritus, 1996-present. **Career Act.:** Dir., McGlynn Bakeries, Galagen Inc., Integ Inc., Pillsbury, Supervalu, Cargill, Bemis Co., Medtronic, SooLine RR, First Bank Minneapolis, Minneapolis Art Institute; Board of Trustees, Carleton College, Minneapolis Fdn.; Board of Overseers, U. of MN; Chair, Caux Round Table (Caux, Switzerland). **Dec./Awd.:** Outstanding Achievement Award, U. of MN, 1992; 1995 Chairman's Award, Health Industry Mfrs. Assn., 1995; Honorary Dr. of Laws Degree, U. of MN, 1995; Edgar M. Carlson Award, 1997; Chairman's Award, MN High Technology Council, 1997; Honorary Doctorate of Laws Degree, Carleton College, 1999; Service Above Self, Rotary Club, 2000. **Act./Mem.:** Minneapolis Club; Minikahda Club; The Boulders, Carefree Az.; Donor, $10 million scholarship program to Mpls. schools.

Richard A. Walter Chair, CEO, Scicom Data Services Ltd., 10101 Bren Rd. E., Minnetonka, MN 55343. Tel: 612/933-4200. **B:** Nov. 24, 1936, Minneapolis. **M:** Colleen, 1961. **C:** Beth, Steve, Mike, Kathy. **E:** U. of MN, BSB; William Mitchell College, JD. **Career Hist.:** Mktg. Rep., IBM, 1962-65; Principal, Anderson, Kasdan, O'Brien & Walter, 1965-68; Scicom Data Svs., 1968-present.

Donald C. Wegmiller Pres., CEO, HealthCare Compensation Strategies, 608 Second Ave. S., Suite 370, Minneapolis, MN 55402. Tel: 612/337-1115. Email: dwegmill@mcghealth.com **B:** Sep. 25, 1938, Cloquet, Minn. **M:** Janet, 1958. **C:** Katherine, Mark, Dean. **E:** U of MN-Duluth and U of MN, BA, 1960; Mast.-Hospital Admin., 1962. **Career Hist.:** Career Hist.:

Admin. Resident, Fairview Hospital, 1962-62; Asst. Admin., Fairview Hospital, 1962-65; Asst. Admin., Fairview-Southdale Hospital, 1965-66; Admin., Fairview-Southdale Hospital 1966-76; SVP, Health Central System, 1976-78; Pres., Health Central Inc., 1978-80; Pres., Health Central Corp., 1980-87; Pres., HealthOne Corp., 1987-93; Pres., Health Care Compensation Strategies,1993-present.. **Career Act.:** Chair, Trustee, American Hospital Assn.; Gov., American Healthcare Systems; Dir., Possis Medical Inc. ALLETE (formerly known as Minnesota Power); JLJ Medical Devices International, LLC; Fellow, American College of Healthcare Execs.; Clinical Faculty, U. of MN, U. of MI, Duke; Trustee, National Ctee. for Qual. Health Care; Advisory Board Mem., Health Mgmt. Quarterly magazine; U.S. Delegate, King's Fund International Hospital Federation—25th Congress in Helsinki, 1987; Mem., National Advisory Council on Social Security; Special Consultant to U.S. State Dept. on project to develop a new health care delivery system in Russia, 1995. **Dec./Awd.:** 1st Hudgen's Mem. Award as Outstanding Young Hospital Admin. in the U.S. ACHA, 1969; Outstanding Young Man of 1970; Minneapolis Jr. Chamber of Commerce; B'nai B'rith 5th Annual National Healthcare Award, 1987; Selected One of Five Outstanding Directors of 1999 by Twin Cities Business Monthly and National Association of Corporate Directors, 1999. **Act./Mem.:** Mem., Chair-Board of Education, Richfield School Dist.; past Pres., Greater Edina Chamber of Commerce, Minneapolis Jr. Chamber of Commerce; Dir., MN Business Partnership, Council of Hospital Corps., MN Center on Corp. Responsiblity; past Chair Board of Mgmt., Southdale YMCA; Dir., Trustee, St. Scholastica College; past Dir., Richfield Bank & Trust Company, past Dir., G.D. Searle and Co., McKesson HBOC; InPhynet Medical Management, Inc., LifeRate Systems, Health Providers Insurance Co., International Clinical Laboratories, Inc., SelectCare, Medical Graphics; Staff Assistant to the President for President Richard Nixon (1971-74), President Gerald Ford (1974-76), and President Reagan (1981-88); Hazeltine National Golf Club; TPC Twin Cities.

Charles D. Weil Pres., CEO, Young America Corp., 717 Faxon Rd., Young America, MN 55397. Tel: 612/467-1100. Email: chuckw@young-america.com **B:** May 16, 1944, Chicago. **M:** Wendy, 1977. **C:** Will, Luke. **E:** Dartmouth College: BA-Economics; MBA, Amos Tuck Graduate School of Business. **Career Hist.:** General Mills Inc., 1968-87 (Pres., Yoplait USA, 1984-87); Pres.-Friskies Petcare Group, Nestle USA, 1987-91; Pres., COO, ConAgra Frozen Foods, 1991-93; Pres., CEO, Young America Corp., 1993-present. **Career Act.:** Mem., PMAA, DMA. **Act./Mem.:** Wayzata Country Club.

Irving Weiser Chair, Pres., CEO, Dain Rauscher Corp., Dain Rauscher Plaza, 18C9, 60 S. Sixth St., Minneapolis, MN 55402. Tel: 612/371-2703. Email: IWeiser@dainrauscher.com **B:** Dec. 4, 1947, Munich. **M:** Marjorie, 1970. **C:** Jennifer, Dana. **E:** State U. of NY-Buffalo, BA, 1969; Brooklyn Law School, JD, 1973. **Career Hist.:** Assoc., Dorsey & Whitney, 1973-78; Ptnr., Dorsey & Whitney, 1979-85; Inter-Regional Financial Group Inc. (now Dain Rauscher Corp.): Pres., 1985-89, Pres., CEO, 1990-94; Chair, Pres., CEO,1995-present. **Career Act.:** Dir., Dain Rauscher Corp., Dain Bosworth Inc., Rauscher Pierce Refsnes Inc., Securities Industry Association (VChair, 1996; Chair-Elect, 1997), The Guthrie Theater Fdn.(Pres., 1995-97), Minneapolis Institute of Arts; Mem., MN Business Partnership, Board of Overseers-Carlson School of Mgmt. (U. of MN), Cabinet-United Way of Minneapolis. **Act./Mem.:** Young Presidents Organization (North America Region and International Chapter), United Way of Minneapolis Area; Minneapolis Club.

Jerrold A. Weissman Pres., CEO, Carl Weissman & Sons, P.O. Box 1609, Great Falls, MT 59403. Tel: 406/761-4848. **B:** Jun. 25, 1936, Great Falls, Mont. **M:** Nadyne, 1968. **C:** Aaron, Leila. **E:** U. of Miami, AB, 1958; Graduate Studies-History, Economics. **Career Hist.:** various positions, Carl Weissman & Sons Inc., 1950-present; CEO, Chair, Northwest Steel Company, 1962-81; Pres., National General Supply Company, 1978-present; Pres., Carl Weissman & Sons Inc., 1987-present. **Career Act.:** past Dir., N.A.S.P.D., Rocky Mountain Chapter of I.S.I.S.. **Act./Mem.:** Masons, Scottish Rite; Meadowlark Country Club; Great Falls Symphony Assn.; AIPAC.

W. Hall Wendel Jr. Chair, CEO, Polaris Industries Inc., 1225 Highway 169 N., Plymouth, MN 55441. Tel: 763/542-0500. Email: nlbrand@mailhost.polarisind.com **B:** Jan. 17, 1943, Washington, D.C. **M:** Deborah, 1967. **C:** Amy. **E:** U.S. Naval Academy, BS, 1966; Harvard U., MBA, 1972. **Career Hist.:** Lieutenant, U.S. Navy, 1966-1972; Asst. to the Pres., 1972-74; Sls. Admin., E-Z-Go Golf Carts, division of Textron Inc., 1973-74; National Sls. Mgr., E-Z-Go Golf Carts, 1974-77; VP-Sls.Mktg., Polaris E-Z-Go, 1977-80; Pres, Polaris E-Z-Go, 1980-81; Chair, CEO, Polaris Industries Inc., 1981-present. **Career Act.:** The Wendel Fdn.; past Mem., Young President's Organization, American Business Conference, Walker Art Center.

Donald C. Wildman Chair, Scoville Press Inc., 14505 27th Ave. N., Plymouth, MN 55447. Tel: 763/553-1400. **B:** Sep. 25, 1932, Oak Park, Ill. **M:** Nina, 1972. **C:** Russell, Pamela, Donald, Mark, Susan. **E:** Carnegie Tech., BS-Printing Mgmt., 1954. **Career Hist.:** Slsman., Jensen Printing Co., 1956-73; Slsman., Alden Press, 1973-74; Pres., Scoville Press, 1974-92; Chm., Scoville Press, 1992-present. **Career Act.:** Dir., Printing Industry of MN. **Act./Mem.:** Lafayette Club.

William D. Wilkening Pres., Paragon (now part of Time Warner), 115 First Ave. E., Shakopee, MN 55379. **B:** Oct. 30, 1932, Welcome, Minn. **M:** Donna, 1963. **C:** Daniel, Mark. **E:** U. of WI Graduate School of Banking. **Career Hist.:** Fourth Northwestern Bank, 1952-67: Bookkeeper, Teller, Pers./Op. Mgr., Cashier, VP and Cashier; Northwestern Southwest, 1967-74: Cashier, VP, SVP; VP, Norwest Corp., 1974-76; Pres., Norwest Bank MetroWest, 1977-85; Pres., Norwest Bloomington, 1984-88; Pres./CEO Citizens Independent Bank, 1988-2000. **Career Act.:** Mem., Independent Bankers of MN, MN Bankers Assn.. **Act./Mem.:** Interlachen Country Club, United Way, Normandale Lutheran Church, Twin West Chamber of Commerce, Minnesota Chamber of Commerce, St. Louis Park Rotary.

E. David Willette CEO, Vaughn Communications Inc., 5050 W. 78th St., Edina, MN 55435. Tel: 612/832-3200. **B:** Aug. 20, 1935, Chippewa Falls, Wis. **M:** Kaye, 1961. **C:** Melissa, Lindsay, Lisabeth. **E:** College of St. Thomas, BA, 1957; Notre Dame, BSME, 1959. **Career Hist.:** Engr., Consolidated Thermoplastics, 1958-60; VP, Applied Research and Devel. Corp.; 1960-66; Division Gen. Mgr., Amoco Chemicals Corp., 1966-71; Pres., CEO, Vaughn Communications Inc., 1971-95; Chair, CEO, Vaughn Communications Inc., 1995-present. **Career Act.:** Mem., MN Film Board (Chair, 1992-94); Pres., MN Executives' Organization; Founding Dir., American Video Duplication Assn.; past Chair, MN Young Presidents Org. **Act./Mem.:** Wayzata Yacht Club, Minnetonka Yacht Club, Woodhill Country Club.

Leslie A. Willig Chair, Photo Control Corp., 4800 Quebec Ave. N., New Hope, MN 55428. Tel: 612/537-3601. **B:** Jan. 29, 1926, Fort Wayne, Ind. **C:** Constance Hansen, Diana Osborne, Larry, Rosanne Johnson, Laura Wells. **E:** Purdue U., BNS&T, BS; U. of Louisville, MA; U. of IA, Ph.D. **Career Hist.:** Asst. Dean of Men, Instructor of Indust. Mgmt., U. of IA, 1954-56; Assoc. Prof. of Psychology, Asst. Dir., Purdue U., (Fort Wayne Campus) 1956-60; Academic Dean, EVP, Tri-State U., 1960-70; Business Broker (Fort Wayne, IN), 1970-present; Chair, CEO, Pres., Photo Control Corp., 1974-1997; Chair, 1997-present. **Career Act.:** past Dir., VP, Bankers Investment Corp.; Dir., Sec., North Snow Bay Inc.; past National Pres., Naval Reserve Assn.; past Chair, International Science Fair Council; Co-founder, Dir., Science Education Fdn. of Indiana; Mem., American Psychological Assn., Midwestern Psychological Assn., Naval Reserve Assn. **Dec./Awd.:** Distinguished Public Service Award, U.S. Navy, 1973. **Act./Mem.:** past Mem., Fort Wayne (IN), Angola (IN) Rotary Clubs; Fourth Degree Member, Knights of Columbus; Mem., VFW, American Legion, Summit Club, Fort Wayne (IN).

Gary L. Wilson Chair, Northwest Airlines Corp., 5101 Northwest Dr., Eagan, MN 55111. Tel: 612/726-2111. **B:** Jan. 16, 1940, Alliance, Ohio. **M:** Barbera Thornhill, 1992. **C:** Christopher, Derek, Gary. **E:** Duke U., 1962; MBA, Wharton Graduate School of Finance and Commerce. **Career Hist.:** EVP, Dir., Trans-Philippines Investment Corp.; EVP, CFO, Marriott Corp.; EVP, CFO, Walt Disney Co., 1985-1990; Co-Chair, Northwest Airlines Corp., 1990-1996; Chair, 1997-present. **Career Act.:** Dir., Northwest Airlines Corp., Walt Disney Co., National Collegiate Athletic Assn. Fdn., CB Richard Ellis; Board of Vis., Fuqua School of Business; Past Chair, American Hotel and Motel Assn.; Board of Trustees, Duke U.; Board of Overseers, The Wharton School.

Harold K. Wilson Pres., CEO, Sico Inc., 7525 Cahill Rd., Edina, MN 55439. Tel: 612/941-1700. **B:** Jun. 12, 1940, Minneapolis. **M:** Jeanne Wilson, 1990. **C:** Mary, Christopher, Leilani, Jocelyn, Sarah. **E:** U. of MN, 1958-62. **Career Hist.:** Sico Inc., 1959-present: Dir., 1962; Regl. Sls. Mgr., 1963-64; Purch. Mgr., 1964-68; VP-International Sls., 1969-72; EVP, 1973-77; Pres., 1977-present, CEO, 1991-present;. **Career Act.:** Dir., Nippon-Sico (Japan), Sico-Asia (Singapore), Council of Independent Mgrs., MN Employers Assn.; Chair, Sico Europe; CEO, Dir., Sico South Pacific Ltd. (Australia); Mem., American Hotel Assn., MN World Trade Assn., World Presidents Organization, U.S. Chamber of Commerce, Norex Forum Group; past Mem., Young Presidents Org. Past Director Council of Independent Managers. **Act./Mem.:** past Pres., New Prague Rotary Club; past Dir., Edina Rotary Club, Edina Hockey Assn.; Theta Delta Chi Fraternity; Triumph Car Club; National Genealogical Society; Past Pres., Cedar Lake Improvement Assn.

Robert C. Wingrove Chair, Rehabilicare Inc., 1811 Old Highway 8, New Brighton, MN 55112. Tel: 651/631-0590. **B:** Sep. 11, 1932, Warsaw, Pa. **M:** Linda A. Wingrove, 1972. **C:** Mary, Robert L., Joanna, Jennifer, Reed. **E:** U. of MN, B.E.E., 1961. **Career Hist.:** U.S. Air Force, 1952-56; Research Dir., Dir.-Advanced Products, Medtronic, 1958-1972; Founder, VP-R&D, Pres., Chair, Medical Devices Inc., 1972-present.

Linda Hall Whitman Pres.-Ceridian Performance Ptnrs., Ceridian Corp., 8100 34th Ave. S., Bloomington, MN 55425. Tel: 612/853-5254. Email: linda.h.whitman@ceridian.com **E:** B.S., Special Education, U. of Mich., 1969; M.A., Psychology/Education, U. of Mich., 1970; M.S.W., Social Work, U of Minn., 1975; Ph.D., Educational Administration, U of Minn., 1980. **Career Hist.:** Dir.-Customer Svc./Traffic/Distribution, Honeywell Inc., 1985-86; Dir.-Mktg./HVAC Commerical Controls, Honeywell Inc., 1986-90; Dir.-Home Systems, Honeywell Inc., 1991-93; VP-Consumer Business Group, Honeywell Inc., 1993-95; VP-Business Integration, Ceridian Performance Partners, 1995-96; Pres., Ceridian Performance Partners, 1996-present. **Career Act.:** Dir., MTS Systems Corp., Science Museum of MN, MN Visiting Nurse Assn., Federal Reserve Bank of Minneapolis; Mem., MN Women's Economic Roundtable, Committee of 200. **Dec./Awd.:** Phi Beta Kappa, Phi Kappa Phi, James B. Angell Scholar, 1969; YWCA Women's Leadership Recognition, 1984; Lund Managerial Excellence Award nominee, 1986; Minnesota-Russi Women's Leadership Program, 1993. **Act./Mem.:** Wayzata Community Church Celebration Singers, 1996-present; Menttium, 1994-present; Mentor Connection, 1994-present; Committee of 200, 1998-present; Minnesota Women's Economic Roundtable, 1995-present.

Robert J. Wood Pres., RisComp Industries Inc., 2905 Northwest Blvd., Suite 30, Plymouth, MN 55441. Tel: 612/553-2220. **B:** Jan. 9, 1940, Duluth, Minn. **M:** Marlys, 1960. **E:** BA, U. of TX, 1962; 4-yr. Cert. Transportation, U. of Chicago, 1967; MMBA, St. Thomas College. **Career Hist.:** Accounting Mgr., Rand Corp. (2 yrs.); Transportation Mgr., Chun-King Corp. (2 yrs.); CBM/RisComp Industries (25 yrs.). **Career Act.:** Mem., BSCA, NAPEO. **Act./Mem.:** Rotary.

Kenneth B. Woodrow VChair, Target Corp., 33 S. Sixth St., Minneapolis, MN 55402. Tel: 612/304-6073. **E:** B.A., Economics, Yale U., 1966; M.B.A., Finance, Harvard Business School, 1970. **Career Hist.:** SVP-Distribution, Target Stores, 1982-85; SVP-Admin., Target Stores, 1985-89; EVP-Admin./Distribution, Target Stores, 1989-93; VChair, Target Stores, 1993-94; Pres., Target Stores, 1994-99, VChm., Target Corp., 1999-present.

Pat Woodworth Chair, Pres., CEO, Winona Inc., 1200 Storr's Pond Rd., P.O. Box 400, Winona, MN 55987. Tel: 507/454-3240. **B:** Jun. 15, 1944, Norfolk, Va. **M:** Rowena, 1968. **E:** Dartmouth College, BA, 1966. **Career Hist.:** Helicopter Pilot, USMC, 1966-71; Plant Mgr., Winona Knitting Mills Inc., 1973-77; Pres., Winona Knits Inc./Winona Inc., 1977-present. **Career Act.:** past Pres., Winona Chamber of Commerce; Historical Society; Convention and Visitors Bureau.

Michael W. Wright Chair, Pres., CEO, Supervalu Inc., P.O. Box 990 (55440), Eden Prairie, MN 55344. Tel: 612/828-4048. **B:** Jun. 13, 1938, Minneapolis. **M:** Judy. **C:** Michael, Jennifer, Molly, Julie, Adam. **E:** U. of MN, BA, 1961; LLB, 1963. **Career Hist.:** Ptnr., Dorsey & Whitney, 1963-77; EVP, Supervalu Inc., 1977-78; Pres., COO, 1978-81; Pres., CEO, 1981-82; Chair, Pres., CEO, 1982-present. **Career Act.:** Dir., Supervalu Inc., Honeywell Inc., Wells Fargo & Co., Musicland Stores Corp., Cargill Inc., Food Distributors International, The Food Business Forum (CIES), Infection Control Advisory Network, Center of the American Experiment; Chair, Food Mktg. Institute (FMI); past Chair, Federal Reserve Bank of Minneapolis, MN Business Partnership. **Dec./Awd.:** Executive of the Year, Corporate Report MN, 1997; Outstanding Leadership Award, MN Grocers Assn., 1998; Horatio Alger Award, 1999. **Act./Mem.:** Mem., American Bar Assn., Minneapolis Club, Woodhill Country Club; Trustee, Carlson School of Mgmt., St. Thomas Academy; Spring Hill Country Club.

Rodney A. Young Chair, Pres., CEO, Lectec Corp., 10701 Red Circle Dr., Minnetonka, MN 55343. Tel: 612/933-2291. **B:** Feb. 15, 1955, St. Louis, Mo. **M:** Carla, 1987. **E:** B.S., Business Admin., Northeast Missouri State U., 1977. **Career Hist.:** Pharmaceutical Sls., UpJohn Co.; Medical Products Sls./Mktg., 3M Co; Div. VP/Gen. Mgr., Baxter International. **Career Act.:** Dir., Possis Medical; Dir., Dental Dental of Minn.

Larry Zavadil Pres., CEO, American Business Forms Inc., 31 E. Minnesota Ave., P.O. Box 218, Glenwood, MN 56334. Tel: 320/634-5471. Email: lzavadil@americanabf.com **B:** Jan. 4, 1949, Glenwood, Minn. **M:** Diane Marie, 1970. **C:** Jessica, Joshua, Justin. **E:** BA, U. of MN, 1973. **Career Hist.:** Ptnr., Mr. Z's Pizza & Branstock Productions (6 mos.); Sls./Mgmt., National Cash Register/NCR (7+ yrs.); Pres./CEO, American Business Forms (20+ yrs.). **Career Act.:** School Board Rep.: Glenwood Public Schools (1976-93), Minnewaska Area Schools (1993-98); Lector/Usher/Greeter, Sacred Heart Catholic Church (1976-2000). **Dec./Awd.:** Inc. 500, 1986; SBA Award, 1988; Distributor of the Year Award, 1995; Number One Distributor in the Industry, AFL&S and DMIA (1998, 1999). **Act./Mem.:** DMIA, IBFI, ASI, SAAUM, XPLOR, WBSA.

Ronald N. Zebeck Pres., CEO, Metris Cos. Inc., 600 S. Highway 169, Suite 1800, St. Louis Park, MN 55426. Tel: 612/525-5020. **B:** 1955, Baltimore. **M:** Rita, 1981. **C:** Jillian, Jordan. **E:** BS-Bus. Admin./Mktg., Towson State U. **Career Hist.:** Citicorp, 1977-86; Dir.-Mktg., Advanta Corp., 1986-91; Mng. Dir.-GM Card Op., General Motors, 1991-94; Pres. and CEO, Metris Cos., 1994-present. **Career Act.:** Dir., MasterCard International Global Board, MasterCard International U.S. Board, Integon Corp.; Mem.-President's Council, Donnelly Mktg.; Mem.-Financial Svs. Council, Direct Mail Assn. **Dec./Awd.:** Top 100 Marketers, Advertising Age, 1992; Silver Anvil, PRSA, 1993; Leader in the Bank Card Business, American Banker, 1997; Executive of the Year, Credit Card Mgmt., 1993; Top 100 Marketers, Advertising Age, 1993; Leader of the Bankcard Business, American Banker, 1993; Direct Marketer of the Year, Midwest Direct Marketing Assn., 1999; Minnesoa and Dakotas Entrepreneur of the Year, Ernst & Young, 2000. **Act./Mem.:** Wayzata Country Club, Burl Oaks Golf Club.

Charles A. Zelle Pres., CEO, Jefferson Partners L.P., 2100 E. 26th St., Minneapolis, MN 55404. Tel: 612/332-8745. Email: czelle@jeffersonlines.com **B:** Aug. 18, 1955, Minneapolis. **M:** Julie Brooks, 1990. **C:** Charlotte, Nicholas. **E:** BA, Bates College, 1977; MBA, Yale mgmt. School, 1983. **Career Hist.:** Mgr.-Industry Affairs, American Bus Assn., 1977-79; Senior Assoc., Merrill Lynch Capital Markets, 1983-86; Pres., Jefferson Real Estate Group, 1986-89; Pres., Jefferson Lines, 1990-present. **Career Act.:** VChair, American Bus Assn.; Chair, Greater Minneapolis Convention and Visitors Assn. **Act./Mem.:** Sec., Guthrie Theater Fdn.; Trustee, St. Paul Academy and Summit School; Dir., St. Paul Riverfront Corp.; Past Pres., Minneapolis Club.

Richard A. Zona VChair-Fin., U.S. Bancorp, 601 Second Ave. S., P.O. Box 522 (55480), Minneapolis, MN 55402. Tel: 612/973-0407. **E:** BS/BA, Roosevelt U. (Chicago); CPA. **Career Hist.:** Ernst & Whinney (Minneapolis): National Dir. of National Financial Svs.; First Bank System Inc./U.S. Bancorp: development and execution of acquisition strategy since 1991; EVP and CFO, 1989-91; VChair and CFO, 1991-96; VChair-Finance, 1996-present. **Career Act.:** Dir., Jostens Inc., MN Opera; Mem., American Institute of CPAs, MN Society of CPAs.

Stan Zylstra Chair, Land O'Lakes Inc., 4001 Lexington Ave. N., Arden Hills, MN 55112. Tel: 651/481-2503. **B:** Dec. 18, 1943, Hull, Iowa. **M:** Ruth, 1964. **C:** Rachel, Carl. **E:** Northwestern College, BA, 1965; U of SD, MA, 1969. **Career Hist.:** Math teacher, Counselor, Boyden-Hull School, 1965-73; Farmer, Hull, IA, 1970-present. **Career Act.:** Chair, Land O'Lakes Inc. **Act./Mem.:** Mem., Kiwanis, Reformed Church in America.

SALARY CHARTS

SALARY CHARTS OF COMPANIES' HIGHEST PAID OFFICERS

INCLUDES

TITLE

A BREAKDOWN OF ANNUAL COMPENSATION

Note on Stock Options:

Options directly link pay to performance, and their popularity is on the rise.
Options only take on value to the extent the company's stock price rises above the option's exercise price. This makes it difficult to determine an option's present value.

The SEC now requires companies to disclose hypothetical evaluations of their option grants. Most companies use a complex formula that takes into account scenarios with both 5 percent and 10 percent stock appreciation rates.

Another approved methodology is the Black-Scholes pricing model. Finally, some smaller companies leave the evaluating to the reader...in which case we use the option's value at fiscal year end. Because the latter methods result in only a single evaluation number, some entries in the 10 percent column will be blank.

Information was gathered from companies' fiscal 99-00 proxy statements.
All proxy footnotes have been eliminated.

SALARY INDEX

	Salary ($)	Bonus ($)	Restricted Stock ($)	Options @5% ($)	Options @10% ($)	Other ($)
ACI Telecentrics Inc.						**FISCAL YEAR 1999**
Rick N. Diamond CEO	157,836	12,138				16,706
Gary B. Cohen President	157,836	12,138				14,325
Dana A. Olson COO	140,000	12,138				
Lois J. Dirksen VP-Sales	101,308	12,138				
ADC Telecommunications Inc.						**FISCAL YEAR 1999**
William J. Cadogan Chairman, President, and CEO	683,462	412,768		4,721,315		63,779
Lynn J. Davis SVP, Pres.-Broadband Connectivity Group	334,269	381,343		3,403,001		56,902
Robert E. Switz SVP and CFO	300,231	192,466		538,110		9,639
APA Optics Inc.						**FISCAL YEAR 2000**
Anil K. Jain Chairman, President, and Treasurer	136,463					
ASV Inc.						**FISCAL YEAR 1999**
Gary D. Lemke President	150,000					
ATS Medical Inc.						**FISCAL YEAR 1999**
Manuel A. (Manny) Villafana Chairman and CEO	243,013	25,516		68,392	173,319	
Richard W. Kramp President and COO	198,726	20,866		68,392	173,319	2,500
Russell W. Felkey EVP-Regulatory Affairs	176,400	18,522		68,392	173,319	2,500
John H. Jungbauer VP-Finance and CFO	140,001	14,700		810,330	2,053,537	2,500
Frank R. Santiago VP-Sales/Marketing	138,602	12,474		68,392	173,319	2,254
Aero Systems Engineering Inc.						**FISCAL YEAR 1999**
Donald Kamis VP-Wind Tunnel/Automotive Programs	105,290					3,817
Charles H. Loux * President and CEO	40,385					8,075
Aetrium Inc.						**FISCAL YEAR 1999**
Joseph C. Levesque Chairman, President, and CEO	174,314	38,190				2,051
Douglas L. Hemer Group VP	145,439	31,841				1,912
Stephen P. Weisbrod VP-Corporate Technology	131,269	28,814				1,593
Daniel M. Koch VP-Worldwide Sales	121,654	21,444		39,111	86,425	1,791
Ag-Chem Equipment Company Inc.						**FISCAL YEAR 1999**
Alvin E. McQuinn Chairman and CEO	337,700					

* Compensation for partial year only

	Salary ($)	Bonus ($)	Restricted Stock ($)	Options @5% ($)	Options @10% ($)	Other ($)
Donald D. Pottinger President	204,000			842		
John C. Retherford SVP and CFO	153,000			842		
Mary M. Jetland SVP-Advanced Technology/Manufacturing	127,500			842		
Allete						**FISCAL YEAR 1999**
Edwin L. Russell Chairman, President, and CEO	475,939	744,110		188,813		266,873
Robert D. Edwards EVP and Pres.-MP Electric	276,308	234,199		93,795		137,595
James P. Hallett EVP and Pres./CEO-ADESA	271,908	276,210		87,849		299,070
John E. Fuller EVP and Pres./CEO-AFC	254,923	265,980		105,285		116,211
John A. Cirello EVP and Pres./CEO-MP Water Resources	240,538	212,320		82,248		113,720
Alliant Techsystems						**FISCAL YEAR 2000**
Paul David Miller Chairman and CEO	600,000	800,000		2,883,089	7,306,313	60,168
Scott S. Meyers VP and CFO	272,504	302,000		2,424,782	6,144,873	29,847
Paul A. Ross Senior Group VP-Aerospace	246,672	275,000		627,401	1,589,957	17,971
Nicholas G. Vlahakis Group VP-Conventional Munitions	216,674	220,000		517,875	1,312,397	11,090
American Medical Systems Holdings Inc.						**FISCAL YEAR 1999**
Lawrence W. Getlin VP-Regulatory/Medical Affairs/Quality	170,000	9,690		157,224	398,436	11,618
Douglas W. Kohrs President and CEO	155,192	20,000		471,671	1,195,307	
Janet L. Dick VP-Human Resources	134,000	16,344		157,224	398,436	6,555
Gregory J. Melsen VP-Finance and CFO	124,496	15,192		157,224	398,436	15,939
Brian A. Millberg VP-Manufacturing/Operations	117,500	6,120		157,224	398,436	4,500
Analysts International Corporation						**FISCAL YEAR 2000**
Frederick W. Lang Chairman and CEO	376,000			291,498	738,749	6,542
Michael J. LaVelle President and COO	260,000			503,692	1,276,475	1,980
Sarah P. Spiess EVP	259,000			120,855	306,286	2,250
Thomas R. Mahler Secretary and General Counsel	196,000			89,020	225,606	1,440
Marti R. Charpentier VP-Finance and Treasurer	152,000			127,341	322,722	779
Apogee Enterprises Inc.						**FISCAL YEAR 2000**
Russell Huffer Chairman, President, and CEO	416,154			569,145	1,442,335	26,463

* Compensation for partial year only

SALARY INDEX

	Salary ($)	Bonus ($)	Restricted Stock ($)	Options @5% ($)	Options @10% ($)	Other ($)
Joseph T. Deckman EVP-Glass Service	272,731	96,026	192,052	142,286	360,584	266,415
Larry D. Stordahl EVP-Glass Technologies	229,558			142,286	360,584	5,857
Appliance Recycling Centers of America Inc.						**FISCAL YEAR 1999**
Edward R. Cameron Chairman, President, and CEO	150,000	10,000		13,280		
Arctic Cat Inc.						**FISCAL YEAR 2000**
Christopher A. Twomey President and CEO	292,000	233,880		300,248		5,368
Timothy C. Delmore CFO and Secretary	159,000	78,012		131,359		5,001
Mark E. Blackwell VP-Marketing	157,000	77,030		131,359		4,987
Ronald G. Ray VP-Manufacturing	150,000	81,072		93,828		4,938
Ole E. Tweet VP-New Product Development	140,000	76,267		93,828		4,938
Astrocom Corporation						**FISCAL YEAR 1999**
Ronald B. Thomas President, CEO, Secretary, and Treasurer	115,504					
August Technology Corporation						**FISCAL YEAR 1999**
Thomas C. Verburgt Chief Technical Officer	114,000	50,400				
Jeff L. O'Dell President and CEO	109,000	52,200				
Mark R. Harless Chief Engineer	105,000	50,400				
Thomas C. Velin CFO	103,000	50,300		21,708	50,590	
David L. Klenk COO	85,000	40,800		57,889	134,908	
Ault Inc.						**FISCAL YEAR 2000**
Frederick M. Green Chairman, President, and CEO	263,651			166,781	392,921	2,691
Gregory L. Harris VP-Marketing	140,298			83,390	196,461	2,022
Donald R. Henry VP, CFO, and Asst. Secretary	126,521			55,421	140,449	1,521
Hokung C. Choi VP-Far East Operations	115,712			18,874	46,816	2,023
BMC Industries Inc.						**FISCAL YEAR 1999**
Paul B. Burke Chairman and CEO	400,000		50,000	999,000		217,331
Jon A. Dobson VP-Human Resources, Gen. Counsel, Sec.	112,923		4,837	103,350		31,763
BNCCORP Inc.						**FISCAL YEAR 1999**
Tracy J. Scott Chairman and CEO	200,000					6,398

* Compensation for partial year only

	Salary ($)	Bonus ($)	Restricted Stock ($)	Options @5% ($)	Options @10% ($)	Other ($)
Gregory K. Cleveland President and COO	175,000					6,398
Brad J. Scott EVP-Finance, BNC North Dakota	120,000	48,234				5,198
James D. LaBreche Pres.-BNC Minnesota	119,359		46,250			116
David J. Sorum Pres.-BNC National Bank, Fargo branch	100,000		59,125			198
Ballistic Recovery Systems Inc.						**FISCAL YEAR 1999**
Mark B. Thomas President, CEO, and CFO	88,218					
Bemis Company Inc.						**FISCAL YEAR 1999**
John H. Roe Chairman	700,000	874,650	24,331	836,266	2,122,884	13,645
Jeffrey H. Curler President and CEO	500,000	542,063	14,897	512,898	1,299,693	5,737
Thomas L. Sall VP-Operations	375,000	365,203	9,310	320,573	812,338	9,851
Scott W. Johnson SVP, General Counsel, and Secretary	325,000	298,594	6,455	222,257	563,204	5,192
Benjamin R. Field III SVP, Treasurer, and CFO	325,000	298,594	32,275	1,031,937	2,730,339	13,402
Best Buy Company Inc.						**FISCAL YEAR 2000**
Richard M. Schulze Founder, Chairman, and CEO	1,000,000	1,550,792		3,446,000	8,734,000	24,890
Bradbury H. Anderson President and COO	730,000	679,247		2,133,000	5,407,000	10,590
Allen U. Lenzmeier EVP and CFO	525,000	423,366		1,231,000	3,119,000	8,590
Wade R. Fenn EVP-Marketing	525,000	423,366		1,231,000	3,119,000	3,590
Michael P. Keskey SVP-Sales	337,080	230,006		739,000	1,872,000	3,590
BigSky Transportation Company						**FISCAL YEAR 1999**
Kim B. Champney President and CEO	95,000	7,791				25,435
Bio-Vascular Inc.						**FISCAL YEAR 1999**
M. Karen Gilles President and CEO	200,000	32,000	80,110	87,393	216,718	
James F. Pfau Pres.-Jerneen Micro Medical	132,000	30,000				
David A. Buche VP-Marketing/Sales	120,000	18,000				
Connie L. Magnuson VP-Finance, CFO, and Secretary	120,000	19,200				
B. Nicholas Oray VP-Research/Development	120,000	12,000				18,501
Black Hills Corporation						**FISCAL YEAR 1999**
Daniel P. Landguth Chairman and CEO	262,600	127,350		103,635		

* Compensation for partial year only

	Salary ($)	Bonus ($)	Restricted Stock ($)	Options @5% ($)	Options @10% ($)	Other ($)
Everett E. Hoyt Pres./COO-Regulated Business Group	169,100	53,100		35,280		
Gary R. Fish Pres./COO-Non-Regulated Business Group	142,300	61,250		46,305		
Thomas M. Ohlmacher VP-Power Supply	126,500	35,700		35,280		
James M. Mattern SVP-Administration, Asst. to the CEO	116,200	37,800		35,280		
Broadview Media Inc.						FISCAL YEAR 2000
Phillip A. Staden President and CEO	165,384	19,180				3,834
Michael D. Smith VP-Programming	120,000	22,772				1,525
Nancy L. Reid VP-Sales/Marketing	97,620	7,000				2,218
Buca Inc.						FISCAL YEAR 1999
Joseph P. Micatrotto Chairman, President, and CEO	309,615	100,000		406,147	1,049,791	
Greg A. Gadel CFO, Treasurer, and Secretary	143,544	70,000		64,129	235,389	
Leonard A. Ghilani COO	137,461	75,800		64,129	235,389	
CNS Inc.						FISCAL YEAR 1999
Marti Morfitt President and COO	275,000	90,889		106,126	268,944	90
Daniel E. Cohen Chairman and CEO	253,750	83,864				135
John J. Keppeler VP-Woldwide Sales	167,515	41,718		31,838	80,683	81
Teri P. Osgood VP-U.S. Marketing	158,487	31,428		26,532	67,237	81
Carol J. Watzke VP-Consumer Strategy	155,963	30,927		26,532	67,237	207
Canterbury Park Holding Corporation						FISCAL YEAR 1999
Randall D. Sampson President, General Manager, and CFO	85,054	5,600		21,654	47,849	4,381
Ceridian Corporation						FISCAL YEAR 1999
Ronald L. Turner Chairman, President, and CEO	466,654	318,267		6,280,313	15,850,313	4,800
John R. Eickhoff EVP and CFO	344,992	203,691		439,622	1,109,522	4,800
Stephen B. Morris EVP and Pres.-Arbitron	329,992	218,090		879,244	2,219,044	4,800
Tony G. Holcombe EVP and Pres.-Ceridian Employer Services	318,124	249,487		1,566,338	3,953,138	
Check Technology Corporation						FISCAL YEAR 1999
Jay A. Herman President and CEO	209,751	45,000		81,584	200,218	4,800
Peter J. Wood VP-Engineering	119,104	5,000		54,389	133,479	2,000

SAL

* Compensation for partial year only

	Salary ($)	Bonus ($)	Restricted Stock ($)	Options @5% ($)	Options @10% ($)	Other ($)
ChoiceTel Communications Inc.						**FISCAL YEAR 1999**
Jeffrey R. Paletz President	108,375					
Christopher & Banks Corporation						**FISCAL YEAR 2000**
William J. Prange Chairman and CEO	339,583	727,829				20,705
Joseph E. Pennington President and COO	214,583	558,002				7,704
Ralph C. Neal EVP-Store Operations	193,750	485,219				5,508
Kathryn R. Gangstee SVP-General Merchandise Manager	125,000	225,600				2,902
Andrew K. Moller SVP and CFO	116,667	266,871		214,015	542,546	2,246
The Chromaline Corporation						**FISCAL YEAR 1999**
Claude Piguet VP-Operations	86,000	11,720		25,328	35,077	3,842
Chronimed Inc.						**FISCAL YEAR 2000**
Henry F. (Hank) Blissenbach Chairman and CEO	232,200	60,000				4,025
Perry L. Anderson SVP-Retail Pharmacy	162,500	99,900				5,020
Patrick L. Taffe Chief Information Officer	160,000	76,800				4,167
Gregory H. Keane CFO and Treasurer	146,600	80,000				2,911
Shawn L. Featherston VP-Human Resources	130,000	55,000				
CIMA LABS Inc.						**FISCAL YEAR 1999**
John M. Siebert President and CEO	259,393	55,000		53,063	134,472	10,413
John Hontz COO	158,798	46,750		53,063	134,472	1,543
Ciprico Inc.						**FISCAL YEAR 1999**
Robert H. Kill Chairman, President, and CEO	175,000	88,268		60,302	140,529	4,229
Stephen R. Hansen VP-Product Development/Operations	104,756	36,275	8,125	23,000	50,825	2,372
Communications Systems Inc.						**FISCAL YEAR 1999**
Curtis A. Sampson Chairman and CEO	202,913	50,000		31,849	92,371	13,712
Jeffrey K. Berg EVP and Pres.-Suttle Apparatus Corp.	125,867	31,250		41,691	92,126	9,957
Thomas J. Lapping Pres./CEO-JDL Technologies Inc.	101,351	50,000		28,001	61,875	7,291
Community First Bankshares Inc.						**FISCAL YEAR 1999**
Donald R. Mengedoth Chairman	524,720	227,500		738,165	1,870,655	30,529
Ronald K. Strand Vice Chairman and COO	354,226	110,500		492,110	1,247,103	20,758

* Compensation for partial year only

SALARY INDEX

	Salary ($)	Bonus ($)	Restricted Stock ($)	Options @5% ($)	Options @10% ($)	Other ($)
Mark A. Anderson President and CEO	349,058	110,500		492,110	1,247,103	20,630
David A. Lee Vice Chairman-Regional Banking	236,977	73,125		184,541	467,664	13,691
Gary A. Knutson Pres.-Eastern Region/Utah/California	199,714	43,875		123,028	311,776	11,663
Computer Network Technology Corporation						**FISCAL YEAR 1999**
Thomas G. Hudson Chairman, President, and CEO	330,000	11,880		4,134,375	10,434,375	36,689
Nick V. Ganio VP-Worldwide Sales/Marketing/Services	192,500	239,335		413,438	1,043,438	21,209
Gregory T. Barnum VP-Finance, CFO, and Secretary	190,000	4,560		1,240,313	3,130,313	5,024
William C. Collette VP-Advanced Technology and CTO	165,000	29,012		620,156	1,565,156	7,311
Peter Dixon VP-Worldwide Business Development	150,000	48,281				9,856
CorVu Corporation						**FISCAL YEAR 1999**
Justin MacIntosh Chairman, President, and CEO	412,000					
Alan Missroon VP-Marketing	124,500			39,741		
David Carlson CFO	100,000			178,763		
CyberOptics Corporation						**FISCAL YEAR 1999**
Steven M. Quist President	208,462	32,000		478,488	761,912	2,180
Steven K. Case Chairman	179,230	28,800		599,852	756,940	17,918
Michael D. Wetle VP and Gen. Mgr.-Semiconductor Group	159,701	34,609		416,907	663,855	62,089
Bruce E. Batten VP-Global Sales/Customer Engineering	130,577	24,375		138,969	221,285	4,200
William J. Farmer VP and Gen. Mgr.-OEM Sensors	123,446	11,900				9,633
Daktronics Inc.						**FISCAL YEAR 2000**
Dr. Aelred J. Kurtenbach Chairman and CEO	225,385	62,500		36,638	105,155	1,531
James B. Morgan President and COO	181,217	50,000		103,139	261,374	1,577
Frank J. Kurtenbach VP-Sales	118,389	31,250		38,677	98,015	1,584
Paul J. Weinand Treasurer and CFO	113,350	33,170		25,785	65,343	1,573
Damark International Inc.						**FISCAL YEAR 1999**
Mark A. Cohn Chairman and CEO	475,000	712,500				
George S. Richards President and COO	325,000	487,500		323,743	515,506	1,440
Stephen P. Letak EVP and CFO	250,000	337,500				695

* Compensation for partial year only

SALARY INDEX

	Salary ($)	Bonus ($)	Restricted Stock ($)	Options @5% ($)	Options @10% ($)	Other ($)
Michael D. Moroz VP-Operations, ClickShip Direct	250,000	337,500				1,440
Rodney C. Merry SVP and CIO-Provell	200,000	270,000				1,440
Datakey Inc.						**FISCAL YEAR 1999**
Carl P. Boecher President and CEO	133,893	9,180				5,649
Alan G. Shuler VP and CFO	112,046	3,469				3,769
Michael L. Sorensen VP and Gen. Mgr.-Electronic Products	109,177	3,791				5,817
Datalink Corporation						**FISCAL YEAR 1999**
Greg R. Meland President and CEO	250,000					14,000
Scott D. Robinson Chief Technology Officer	129,996					45,253
Daniel J. Kinsella CFO	114,231			472,850	1,198,295	36,110
Stephen M. Howe VP-Sales	90,000					110,882
Michael J. Jaeb VP-Operations/Administration	75,724			118,507	300,321	22,431
Deluxe Corporation						**FISCAL YEAR 1999**
John A. (Gus) Blanchard III Chairman, President, and CEO	680,000	680,000		4,181,167	10,595,897	159,266
Lawrence J. Mosner Vice Chairman	440,000	440,000		1,808,072	4,582,010	51,517
Thomas W. VanHimbergen EVP and CFO	325,000	243,750		1,130,045	2,863,756	59,114
Ronald E. Eilers SVP and Gen. Mgr.-Paper Payment Systems	302,333	146,858		759,267	1,904,793	35,348
Department 56 Inc.						**FISCAL YEAR 1999**
Susan E. Engel Chairman and CEO	543,046			976,576	2,464,692	69,838
David W. Dewey EVP-Overseas Operations	322,639			488,288	1,232,346	35,632
David H. Weiser SVP-Legal/Hum. Res., Gen. Counsel, Sec.	206,594			206,583	521,377	26,731
Percy C. (Tom) Tomlinson Jr. * EVP and CFO	67,392	20,000		2,110,534	5,326,582	473
Developed Technology Resource Inc.						**FISCAL YEAR 1999**
John P. Hupp President and CEO	110,000					3,300
Diametrics Medical Inc.						**FISCAL YEAR 1999**
David T. Giddings Chairman, President, and CEO	300,000	292,000		369,790	1,525,121	
Roy S. Johnson EVP and Pres./Mng. Dir.-DML	177,169	108,722		110,937	457,536	49,675
Laurence L. Betterley SVP-Finance and CFO	175,000	94,063		92,448	381,280	

* Compensation for partial year only

SAL

SALARY INDEX

	Salary ($)	Bonus ($)	Restricted Stock ($)	Options @5% ($)	Options @10% ($)	Other ($)
James R. Miller SVP-Sales/Marketing/Commercial Devel.	175,000	87,500		92,448	381,280	
Digi International Inc.						**FISCAL YEAR 1999**
Douglas J. Glader EVP and Gen. Mgr.-MiLAN Technology	193,242	147,288		352,867	894,233	1,675
S. (Kris) Krishnan SVP-Finance/Admin./Accounting and CFO	122,019	108,000		458,203	1,161,177	995
Digital Biometrics Inc.						**FISCAL YEAR 1999**
James C. Granger Chairman	197,918	100,000				4,995
John J. Metil President and interim CEO	162,917	82,500				5,000
Michel R. Halbouty VP-Operations	136,666	84,151				
Barry A. Fisher VP-Sales/Marketing/Business Development	126,249	75,000				5,000
Digital River Inc.						**FISCAL YEAR 1999**
Joel A. Ronning CEO	225,000	112,500				1,000
Perry W. Steiner President	200,000	100,000		1,848,656	4,665,656	
Jay A. Kerutis EVP-Software/Digital Commerce Services	171,124	87,850		3,682,547	9,294,047	
Robert E. Strawman CFO and Treasurer	120,000	50,000		246,488	622,088	
Donaldson Company Inc.						**FISCAL YEAR 2000**
William G. Van Dyke Chairman, President, and CEO	593,846	738,000		1,021,042	2,588,264	407,935
James R. Giertz SVP-Commercial/Industrial	259,539	208,075		559,718	1,373,390	142,376
Nickolas Priadka SVP-OEM Engine Systems/Parts	239,077	142,070		325,864	826,042	127,676
William M. Cook SVP-International	228,077	227,095	249,219	311,381	789,329	160,924
Lowell F. Schwab SVP-Operations	222,846	188,474	179,438	304,140	770,972	124,621
Dotronix Inc.						**FISCAL YEAR 2000**
William S. Sadler President and Treasurer	180,000					2,991
Dura Automotive Systems Inc.						**FISCAL YEAR 1999**
Karl F. Storrie President and CEO	500,000	800,000		1,496,769	3,793,107	61,220
Joe A. Bubenzer SVP	259,000	275,000		534,560	1,354,681	6,802
Milton D. Kniss VP	250,000	275,000		534,560	1,354,681	6,949
Jurgen von Heyden * VP	204,157	429,000				
John J. Knappenberger VP	200,000	210,000		534,560	1,354,681	7,264

* Compensation for partial year only

SAL

SALARY INDEX

	Salary ($)	Bonus ($)	Restricted Stock ($)	Options @5% ($)	Options @10% ($)	Other ($)
E.mergent Inc. — FISCAL YEAR 1999						
James Hansen Chairman, CEO, and Treasurer	84,000	46,500				
Robin Sheeley * CTO and Pres.-Acoustic Communication	56,250	26,500				
Ecolab Inc. — FISCAL YEAR 1999						
Allan L. Schuman Chairman, President, and CEO	750,000	1,200,000	520,000	6,275,391	15,837,891	139,167
John P. Spooner EVP-International Group	375,000	223,600	123,200	510,817	1,289,204	18,103
James L. McCarty Senior EVP-Institutional Group	365,000	205,500	160,000	627,539	1,583,789	17,115
Richard L. Marcantonio EVP-Industrial Group	350,000	200,200	128,000	514,582	1,298,707	16,506
Electro-Sensors Inc. — FISCAL YEAR 1999						
Bradley D. Slye Chairman and President	147,612					4,428
Endocardial Solutions Inc. — FISCAL YEAR 1999						
James W. Bullock President and CEO	230,384	65,673		400,920	1,016,011	
Michael D. Dale VP-Sales/Marketing	175,000	15,000		430,636	1,091,315	138,631
Richard J. Omilanowicz VP-Manufacturing	145,653	20,180		53,456	135,468	
Frank J. Callaghan VP-Research/Development	144,523	17,180		53,456	135,468	
Graydon E. Beatty Chief Technical Officer	133,076	10,875				
Energy West Inc. — FISCAL YEAR 1999						
Larry D. Geske Chairman, President, and CEO	114,967	9,518		11,800		39,389
Edward J. Bernica EVP, CFO, and COO	97,760	8,092				18,413
Tim A. Good VP and Mgr.-Energy Mktg./Wholesale	92,057	10,520				14,834
John C. Allen VP-Human Resources, Corp. Counsel, Sec.	84,625	20,788		5,900		15,724
Entegris Inc. — FISCAL YEAR 1999						
Stan Geyer CEO	250,000	64,000				16,000
James E. Dauwalter President and COO	230,000	64,000				16,000
Daniel R. Quernemoen Chairman	196,517					16,000
John D. Villas CFO	133,269	41,200				13,313
FSF Financial Corporation — FISCAL YEAR 1999						
Donald A. Glas CEO	182,000	38,000		97,922	248,153	32,110

* Compensation for partial year only

	Salary ($)	Bonus ($)	Restricted Stock ($)	Options @5% ($)	Options @10% ($)	Other ($)
George B. Loban President	182,000	38,000		97,922	248,153	32,110
Richard H. Burgart CFO and Secretary	128,750	27,000		66,809	169,307	31,173
FSI International Inc.						**FISCAL YEAR 1999**
Joel A. Elftmann Chairman	315,000			90,180	229,485	91,595
Dr. Benjamin J. Sloan EVP and Pres.-Microlithography Division	240,000			67,635	172,113	65,187
Benno G. Sand EVP, Bus. Dev. and Investor Relations	220,000	43,000		67,635	172,113	78,817
Luke R. Komarek VP and General Counsel	140,000	38,000		56,362	143,428	30,523
Famous Dave's of America Inc.						**FISCAL YEAR 1999**
Martin J. O'Dowd President and CEO	121,154					
Fargo Electronics Inc.						**FISCAL YEAR 1999**
Gary R. Holland President and CEO	271,876					15,090
I. Tony Haugen VP-Manufacturing/Operations	168,000	6,150	1,000			
Gary A. Lenz VP-Research/Development	150,000					1,000
Jeffrey D. Upin VP-Administration and General Counsel	98,000	10,511				1,000
Fastenal Company						**FISCAL YEAR 1999**
Willard D. Oberton VP and COO	193,083	30,841				
Robert A. Kierlin Chairman, President, and CEO	117,000					
Daniel L. Florness Treasurer, CFO, and CAO	92,916	24,492				
FieldWorks Inc.						**FISCAL YEAR 1999**
Gary J. Beeman Vice Chairman, VP-Info. Tech.	140,000					5,484
Robert C. Szymborski VP-Business Development	140,000					8,392
David C. Malmberg * Chairman	53,436			71,245	166,025	63
First Federal Capital Corporation						**FISCAL YEAR 1999**
Thomas W. Schini Chairman and CEO	350,000	175,224				21,134
Bradford R. Price EVP and Secretary	169,433	67,940				9,097
Jack C. Rusch President and COO	169,433	67,940				10,009
Joseph M. Konradt SVP	158,333	63,500				8,667
Robert P. Abell SVP	125,800	37,800				8,763

* Compensation for partial year only

	Salary ($)	Bonus ($)	Restricted Stock ($)	Options @5% ($)	Options @10% ($)	Other ($)
First Team Sports Inc.						**FISCAL YEAR 2000**
John J. Egart President and CEO	140,592	70,000		55,343	128,974	17,378
Kent A. Brunner VP-Finance and CFO	102,564	45,000		53,435	124,515	12,677
Fourth Shift Corporation						**FISCAL YEAR 1999**
Marion Melvin Stuckey Chairman and CEO	305,000					18,333
Jimmie H. Caldwell President and COO	230,000					18,333
David G. Latzke VP and CFO	165,000					3,333
H.B. Fuller Company						**FISCAL YEAR 1999**
Albert P.L. Stroucken Chairman, President, and CEO	621,000	497,674		894,267	2,266,249	4,800
Lars T. Carlson SVP-Manufacturing Integration	269,342	120,866		178,859	453,264	4,786
Alan R. Longstreet SVP-Global Strategic Business Units	263,322	155,455		268,288	679,895	54,817
Peter Koxholt Pres./Gen. Mgr.-Europe	230,218	130,598	42,500	194,457	492,792	
G&K Services Inc.						**FISCAL YEAR 2000**
Thomas Moberly President and CEO	395,000			311,303	788,904	44,817
Richard M. Fink Chairman	367,538			307,853	780,160	96,470
Jeffrey L. Wright CFO, Treasurer, and Secretary	176,539		80,672	197,477	500,445	10,670
Robert G. Wood EVP and Pres.-Canadian Rental Operation	149,004		150,007	237,306	601,379	32,339
GalaGen Inc.						**FISCAL YEAR 1999**
Henry J. Cardello President and CEO	240,000			464,831	1,177,975	2,108
Robert A. Hoerr Chairman and Chief Technology Officer	200,000			135,605	343,651	9,704
Michael E. Cady VP-Manufacturing	120,000			14,150	35,859	1,914
Eileen F. BostwickPh.D. VP-Science/Research	110,000			16,508	41,836	1,744
General Mills Inc.						**FISCAL YEAR 2000**
Stephen W. Sanger Chairman and CEO	696,150	1,264,600	316,138	17,174,914	43,624,873	104,659
Raymond G. Viault Vice Chairman	533,334	753,825		6,022,689	15,297,838	61,088
Stephen R. Demeritt Vice Chairman	459,569	646,500	161,557	4,825,663	12,257,348	477,738
James A. Lawrence EVP and CFO	425,000	478,800	119,730	3,618,589	9,191,340	37,291
Siri S. Marshall SVP-Corporate Affairs, General Counsel	315,522	307,000	913,351	2,492,245	6,330,389	33,934

* Compensation for partial year only

SALARY INDEX

	Salary ($)	Bonus ($)	Restricted Stock ($)	Options @5% ($)	Options @10% ($)	Other ($)
GeoResources Inc.						**FISCAL YEAR 1999**
Jeffrey P. Vickers President	76,307					1,820
Glacier Bancorp Inc.						**FISCAL YEAR 1999**
Michael J. Blodnick President and CEO	168,040	40,000		85,946	217,042	24,352
William L. Bouchee Pres.-First Security Bank	132,020	22,831		85,946	217,042	23,730
James H. Strosahl EVP, CFO, and Sec./Treas.	108,000	30,000		85,946	217,042	20,929
Graco Inc.						**FISCAL YEAR 1999**
George Aristides CEO	406,876	182,001		369,200		4,800
Dale D. Johnson President and COO	160,287	76,234		92,300		4,800
Robert M. Mattison VP, General Counsel, and Secretary	150,639	75,281		46,150		4,800
Charles L. Rescorla VP-Manufacturing/Distribution	150,262	91,141		69,225		4,800
Great Plains Software Inc.						**FISCAL YEAR 2000**
Douglas J. Burgum Chairman, President, and CEO	336,000	2,272				2,500
Darren C. Laybourn VP-Global Development	209,667	975		268,852	681,325	
Jeffrey A. Young * EVP-Global Operations	186,667	20,648				
Jodi A. Uecker-Rust COO	184,333	700		268,852	681,325	
Tami L. Reller * CFO	171,375	800				3,112
Grow Biz International Inc.						**FISCAL YEAR 1999**
Charles V. Kanan VP-Operations, Play it Again Sports	142,000	26,625		23,400	51,800	7,713
HEI Inc.						**FISCAL YEAR 1999**
Donald R. Reynolds President	138,788					
Anthony J. Fant * Chairman and CEO	75,293					216
HF Financial Corporation						**FISCAL YEAR 2000**
Curtis L. Hage Chairman, President, and CEO	218,927	60,884				10,131
Gene F. Uher EVP and COO	148,000	41,159				9,049
Brent E. Johnson SVP, CFO, and Treasurer	104,833	19,195				5,995
Mark S. Sivertson SVP and Trust Officer	102,000	23,256				5,835
Michael H. Zimmerman SVP and Senior Retail Lending Officer	99,050	18,136				5,589

* Compensation for partial year only

	Salary ($)	Bonus ($)	Restricted Stock ($)	Options @5% ($)	Options @10% ($)	Other ($)
HMN Financial Inc.						**FISCAL YEAR 1999**
Michael McNeil President	180,000	50				16,271
Hawkins Chemical Inc.						**FISCAL YEAR 1999**
John R. Hawkins Chairman and CEO	146,560	173,400				34,500
Kurt R. Norman President	111,788	149,000				34,500
Health Outcomes Management Inc.						**FISCAL YEAR 2000**
Peter J. Zugschwert Chairman and interim Pres./CEO	34,700					61,550
Health Risk Management Inc.						**FISCAL YEAR 1999**
Gary T. McIlroy Chairman and CEO	278,000			27,600	61,100	33,845
Marlene O. Travis President, COO, and Secretary	250,000			27,600	61,100	30,868
Thomas P. Clark EVP-Acquisitions/Business Development	200,000		15,000			46,654
Adele M. Kimpell EVP-Operations	171,420					4,290
Hector Communications Corporation						**FISCAL YEAR 1999**
Curtis A. Sampson Chairman and CEO	154,615	35,000		14,985	43,394	13,668
Steven H. Sjogren President and COO	114,554	20,000		28,181	62,272	11,229
HickoryTech Corporation						**FISCAL YEAR 1999**
Robert D. Alton Chairman, President, and CEO	241,972	223,657		198,750	504,375	84,600
Jon L. Anderson VP, Pres.-Communications Products Sector	135,000	46,421		49,688	126,094	6,667
Bruce H. Malmgren VP, Pres.-Billing/Data Services Sector	135,000	131,384		24,844	63,047	1,349
David A. Christensen VP, CFO, Treasurer, and Secretary	131,000	85,899		56,313	142,906	19,104
F. Ernest Lombard VP, Pres.-Communications Services Sector	125,000	78,205		49,688	126,094	2,495
HomeServices.com Inc.						**FISCAL YEAR 1999**
Ronald J. Peltier President and CEO	350,000	200,000		8,958,500	22,714,500	140,705
Jack W. Frost Pres./CEO-J.C. Nichols	255,750	100,000		943,000	2,391,000	141,517
Arne M. Rovick Vice Chairman, Gen. Counsel-Edina Realty	255,750	100,000		282,900	717,300	141,517
R. Michael Knapp Pres./CEO-Iowa Realty	230,166	200,000		943,000	2,391,000	142,392
Joseph J. Valenti Pres./CEO-CBS Home	179,025	144,900		471,500	1,195,500	5,000
Hormel Foods Corporation						**FISCAL YEAR 1999**
Joel W. Johnson Chairman, President, and CEO	610,600	1,065,600		1,800,604	4,563,084	3,378,148

* Compensation for partial year only

	Salary ($)	Bonus ($)	Restricted Stock ($)	Options @5% ($)	Options @10% ($)	Other ($)
Gary J. Ray EVP-Refrigerated Foods	252,700	488,400		600,201	1,521,028	1,687,174
Eric A. Brown Group VP-Prepared Foods	191,200	344,100		300,101	760,514	1,125,892
Hutchinson Technology Inc.						**FISCAL YEAR 1999**
Wayne M. Fortun President and CEO	495,684			559,050	1,416,450	9,600
Jeffrey W. Green Chairman	225,014					9,600
John A. Ingleman VP, CFO, and Secretary	223,283			212,253	537,779	9,600
Richard J. Penn VP-Sales/Marketing	221,551			212,253	537,779	9,738
Beatrice A. Graczyk COO and VP-Operations	218,956			212,253	537,779	10,430
Hypertension Diagnostics Inc.						**FISCAL YEAR 1999**
Greg H. Guettler President	132,423	25,200				
Charles F. Chesney EVP, Chief Tech. Officer, Secretary	111,646	20,160				
James S. Murphy SVP-Finance/Administration and CFO	107,905	20,020				
IPI Inc.						**FISCAL YEAR 1999**
Robert J. Sutter Chairman	206,900	17,650				3,160
David C. Oswald President and CEO	98,000	41,950				2,215
Thomas C. Johnson VP-Marketing	86,500	27,650				2,172
David M. Engel VP-Finance and CFO	72,000	32,850				1,873
Image Sensing Systems Inc.						**FISCAL YEAR 1999**
William L. Russell Chairman, President, and CEO	144,585	26,250				2,165
Image Systems Corporation						**FISCAL YEAR 2000**
Dean Scheff President	90,000					
Imation Corporation						**FISCAL YEAR 1999**
William T. Monahan Chairman, President, and CEO	530,040	568,823		642,600		53,934
Robert L. Edwards SVP, CFO, and CAO	290,000	280,550		302,400		51,485
Steven D. Ladwig SVP and Pres.-Data Storage/Info. Mgmt.	280,000	306,225		302,400		20,683
John L. Sullivan VP, General Counsel, and Secretary	240,000	137,034		189,000		25,835
David H. Wenck VP-Int'l Operations and Pres.-DSS	210,000	194,729		189,000		25,336

* Compensation for partial year only

	Salary ($)	Bonus ($)	Restricted Stock ($)	Options @5% ($)	Options @10% ($)	Other ($)
Industrial Rubber Products Inc.						**FISCAL YEAR 1999**
Daniel O. Burkes Chairman and CEO	274,846					5,700
Christopher M. Liesmaki EVP and COO	103,869		8,800			2,809
John Kokotovich VP, CFO, and Secretary	103,869		8,800			2,923
Infinite Graphics Inc.						**FISCAL YEAR 2000**
Clifford F. Stritch Jr. Chairman, CEO, and CFO	145,134	45,200				5,410
Innovex Inc.						**FISCAL YEAR 1999**
Thomas W. Haley Chairman	182,311			325,467	824,798	7,154
William P. Murnane President and CEO	174,990	37,100		325,467	824,798	5,555
Allan J. Chan SVP-Sales/Marketing	169,999	22,525		289,304	733,153	5,592
Timothy S. McIntee SVP-Corporate	169,998	28,832		253,141	641,509	5,180
Venkatraman B. (Ven) Rao VP-Research/Development	110,000	19,292		245,175	621,320	1,629
Insignia Systems Inc.						**FISCAL YEAR 1999**
Scott Drill President and CEO	200,000					396
G.L. Hoffman Chairman and Secretary	160,000					6,290
Gary Vars EVP and General Mgr.-POPS Division	144,000					666
John R. Whisnant VP-Finance	112,500					6,234
International Multifoods Corporation						**FISCAL YEAR 2000**
Gary E. Costley Chairman, President, and CEO	677,500	290,000	21,038	273,567	693,278	32,055
Robert S. Wright SVP, Pres.-U.S. Foodservice/Operations	330,000	178,400	5,259	95,749	242,647	13,608
Frank W. Bonvino VP, General Counsel, and Secretary	263,750	88,800		82,070	207,983	11,922
IntraNet Solutions Inc.						**FISCAL YEAR 2000**
Robert F. Olson Chairman and CEO	199,533	6,250				4,146
Vernon J. Hanzlik President	145,833	55,394		2,249,910	3,582,607	1,654
Gregg A. Waldon CFO, Secretary, and Treasurer	125,000	38,000		1,335,694	2,126,869	6,704
K-tel International Inc.						**FISCAL YEAR 2000**
Philip Kives CEO				5,433,000	13,769,000	
LaCrosse Footwear Inc.						**FISCAL YEAR 1999**
George W. Schneider Chairman	170,000					12,638

* Compensation for partial year only

	Salary ($)	Bonus ($)	Restricted Stock ($)	Options @5% ($)	Options @10% ($)	Other ($)
George W. Schneider Chairman	170,000					12,638
Joseph P. Schneider EVP, interim Pres./CEO-Danner	152,650	44,580		18,985	48,111	3,200
Joseph P. Schneider EVP, interim Pres./CEO-Danner	152,650	44,580		18,985	48,111	3,200
Robert J. Sullivan VP-Finance/Administration and CFO	107,870	20,226		27,121	68,730	2,951
Robert J. Sullivan VP-Finance/Administration and CFO	107,870	20,226		27,121	68,730	2,951
Lakes Gaming Inc.						**FISCAL YEAR 1999**
Timothy J. Cope EVP, CFO, and Secretary	150,000	23,520		1,053,399	2,669,519	4,432
Joseph Galvin Chief Administrative Officer	150,000	24,080		1,124,149	2,848,814	3,043
Lyle Berman Chairman and CEO	100,000	72,800		2,633,496	6,673,797	3,859
Lectec Corporation						**FISCAL YEAR 1999**
Rodney A. Young Chairman, President, and CEO	200,000			79,756	169,058	2,358
Jane M. Nichols VP-Marketing/New Business Development	117,300			18,890	40,040	1,173
Daniel M. McWhorter VP-Research/Development	111,200			31,958	100,669	2,577
John D. LeGray VP-Quality Assurance/Regulatory Affairs	98,400			18,890	40,040	2,460
Legal Research Center Inc.						**FISCAL YEAR 1999**
Christopher R. Ljungkull Co-chairman, CEO, and CFO	84,000	42,000				
James R. Seidl President	84,000	68,039				
Lifecore Biomedical Inc.						**FISCAL YEAR 2000**
James W. Bracke President and CEO	290,158	29,315		876,522	2,221,279	
Dennis J. Allingham EVP and CFO	184,645	18,655		438,261	1,110,639	
Brian J. Kane VP-Marketing/New Business Development	147,717	14,924		131,478	333,192	
Colleen M. Olson VP-Administrative Operations	132,948	13,432		219,130	555,320	
LodgeNet Entertainment Corporation						**FISCAL YEAR 1999**
Scott C. Petersen Chairman, President, and CEO	320,000	193,280				26,735
John M. O'Haugherty SVP and COO	170,000	74,779				15,510
David M. Bankers SVP and Chief Technology Officer	160,000	71,430				15,595
Jeffrey T. Weisner SVP and CFO	150,000	62,044				19,355

* Compensation for partial year only

	Salary ($)	Bonus ($)	Restricted Stock ($)	Options @5% ($)	Options @10% ($)	Other ($)
MBC Holding Company						**FISCAL YEAR 1999**
John J. (Jack) Lee President and CEO	122,972					
MDU Resources Group Inc.						**FISCAL YEAR 1999**
Martin A. White President and CEO	323,077	203,960	229,063			4,872
Ronald D. Tipton CEO-Montana-Dakota Utilities Co.	235,508	70,327	114,532			4,863
Douglas C. Kane EVP, CAO, Chief Development Officer	210,220	79,146	114,532			5,100
Warren L. Robinson EVP, Treasurer, and CFO	172,396	86,591	91,625			4,872
Lester H. Loble II VP, General Counsel, and Secretary	150,750	55,355	68,719			10,264
MGI Pharma Inc.						**FISCAL YEAR 1999**
Charles N. Blitzer President and CEO	325,000	135,000		485,428	1,230,170	93,599
William C. Brown CFO and Secretary	144,146	42,000		199,674	506,013	22,699
Leon O. (Lonnie) Moulder Jr.* EVP	54,404	60,000		377,337	956,245	19,000
MTS Systems Corporation						**FISCAL YEAR 1999**
Sidney W. (Chip) Emery Jr. Chairman, President, and CEO	302,081			470,233		10,564
Keith D. Zell EVP	199,593	10,745		314,295		10,564
Mauro G. Togneri VP-Sensors Division	165,338	20,675		132,971		10,564
Steven M. Cohoon VP-Vehicle Dynamics Group	148,329	66,437		209,127		10,564
Marten Transport Ltd.						**FISCAL YEAR 1999**
Randolph L. Marten Chairman and President	300,000	60,000				9,188
Robert G. Smith COO and VP-Operations	165,600	33,120				2,647
Timothy P. Nash VP-Sales	165,600	33,120				3,840
Darrell D. Rubel EVP, CFO, Treasurer, and Asst. Secretary	142,000	26,000				82,408
Franklin J. Foster VP-Finance	124,200	24,840				1,240
MedAmicus Inc.						**FISCAL YEAR 1999**
James D. Hartman President and CEO	130,000					668
Christina M. Temperante VP, Gen. Mgr.-Fiber Optic Division	120,000					633
Medi-Ject Corporation						**FISCAL YEAR 1999**
Franklin Pass Chairman, President, and CEO	216,300					16,545

* Compensation for partial year only

	Salary ($)	Bonus ($)	Restricted Stock ($)	Options @5% ($)	Options @10% ($)	Other ($)
Peter Sadowski EVP and Chief Technical Officer	118,300			6,600	16,740	
Lawrence M. Christian * VP-Finance/Administration and CFO	68,538			23,100	58,380	
MEDTOX Scientific Inc.						**FISCAL YEAR 1999**
Harry G. McCoy Chairman and President	200,000			64,462	163,359	
Richard J. Braun CEO	200,000			128,923	326,717	11,910
Medtronic Inc.						**FISCAL YEAR 2000**
William W. George Chairman and CEO	870,000	698,582		8,408,199	21,308,028	49,683
Arthur D. Collins Jr. President and COO	760,000	647,782		5,803,398	14,706,951	43,581
Glen D. Nelson, M.D. Vice Chairman	575,000		57,550	5,754,343	14,582,634	48,235
Robert L. Ryan SVP and CFO	420,000			3,426,959	8,684,589	27,947
Stephen H. Mahle SVP and Pres.-Cardiac Rhythm Mgmt.	370,000	289,988		2,198,653	5,571,817	28,834
Mesaba Holdings Inc.						**FISCAL YEAR 2000**
John S. Fredericksen VP-Administration and General Counsel	163,076	123,600		98,253	222,904	5,455
Scott L. Durgin VP-Customer Service	119,855	79,240		70,451	159,825	1,798
Paul F. Foley President and CEO	103,912	312,500		494,329	1,121,464	9,826
Metris Companies Inc.						**FISCAL YEAR 1999**
Ronald N. Zebeck Chairman and CEO	681,827	1,280,676	4,092,689	3,553,792		487,823
David D. Wesselink Vice Chairman	300,000	470,250	78,375	761,792		485,607
Douglas L. Scaliti Pres./COO-Enhancement Services	217,987	342,421	34,242	516,756		155,189
Joseph A. Hoffman EVP-Consumer Credit Cd. Mktg./Operations	206,538	399,107	27,009	269,421		141,738
Patrick J. Fox EVP-Business Development	192,404	350,000	50,000	249,634		139,025
Michael Foods Inc.						**FISCAL YEAR 1999**
Gregg A. Ostrander Chairman, President, and CEO	506,000	416,980		676,137	1,713,507	7,604
Jeffrey M. Shapiro EVP and Secretary	270,000	230,658		227,226	575,847	7,337
John D. Reedy EVP, CFO, and Treasurer	260,000	217,055		258,616	655,397	7,295
Bill L. Goucher Pres.-M.G. Waldbaum Co.	230,000	170,471		167,300	423,979	7,167
Norman A. Rodriguez Pres.-Crystal Farms	203,000	187,875		137,338	348,045	7,461

* Compensation for partial year only

	Salary ($)	Bonus ($)	Restricted Stock ($)	Options @5% ($)	Options @10% ($)	Other ($)
Micro Component Technology Inc.						**FISCAL YEAR 1999**
Roger E. Gower Chairman, President, CEO, and Secretary	252,500					13,512
Dennis L. Nelson EVP-Sales/Marketing	197,297					2,281
Jeffrey S. Mathiesen VP and CFO	113,077					1,590
Lawrence J. Brezinski * VP-Engineering	99,423					
3M Company						**FISCAL YEAR 1999**
Livio D. DeSimone Chairman and CEO	1,047,600	947,502	774,698	2,969,011		1,587,774
Ronald O. Baukol EVP-International Operations	521,700	423,918	129,447	936,879		602,465
John W. Benson EVP-Health Care Markets	437,700	332,339	48,137	917,200		171,716
Minntech Corporation						**FISCAL YEAR 2000**
Barbara A. Wrigley EVP-Corp. Development, General Counsel	211,864			50,705	128,495	10,961
Paul E. Helms SVP-Operations	195,805			60,846	154,194	10,142
MOCON Inc.						**FISCAL YEAR 1999**
Robert L. Demorest Chairman and CEO	155,790	50,847				1,920
Daniel W. Mayer EVP	131,364	42,874				1,814
Musicland Stores Corporation						**FISCAL YEAR 1999**
Jack W. Eugster Chairman, President, and CEO	650,000	780,000				445,234
Gilbert L. Wachsman Vice Chairman	460,375	368,300				66,388
Keith A. Benson Vice Chairman and CFO	358,804	287,043				192,389
Jonathan T.M. Reckford * Pres.-Stores	209,231	272,000	307,500	644,617	1,633,586	98,490
NRG Energy Inc.						**FISCAL YEAR 1999**
David H. Peterson Chairman, President, and CEO	367,992	192,970				195,327
Craig A. Mataczynski SVP-North America	246,250	150,000				35,490
Ronald J. Will SVP-Europe	214,160	107,341				70,512
James J. Bender VP, General Counsel, Secretary	213,746	100,000				32,429
Leonard A. Bluhm EVP and CFO	194,590	72,150				68,568
NU-Telecom Inc.						**FISCAL YEAR 1999**
Bill Otis President	125,000	15,625				8,227

SAL

* Compensation for partial year only

	Salary ($)	Bonus ($)	Restricted Stock ($)	Options @5% ($)	Options @10% ($)	Other ($)
Nash Finch Company						**FISCAL YEAR 1999**
Ron Marshall Jr. President and CEO	498,629					46,780
William A. Merrigan SVP-Distribution/Logistics	219,397					149,140
Bruce A. Cross SVP-Business Transformation	204,630					54,020
Norman R. Soland SVP, General Counsel, and Secretary	204,630			25,646	57,398	4,634
National City Bancorporation						**FISCAL YEAR 1999**
Robert L. Olson Pres./CEO-Diversified Business Credit	310,000	606,811				4,800
David L. Andreas President and CEO	271,656	80,736				20,450
Thomas J. Freed Secretary and CFO	127,450	25,133				3,823
National Presto Industries Inc.						**FISCAL YEAR 1999**
Melvin S. Cohen Chairman	107,200	23,525				
Maryjo Cohen President and CEO	64,000	206,000				3,200
Richard F. Anderl VP-Engineering	45,000	85,000				2,500
James F. Bartl EVP, Secretary, Resident Counsel	44,600	180,400				3,200
Donald E. Hoeschen VP-Sales	41,370	124,000				3,157
Navarre Corporation						**FISCAL YEAR 2000**
Eric H. Paulson Chairman, President, and CEO	325,950			162,315	358,675	
Charles E. Cheney Vice Chairman, CFO, and Chm./CEO-D.E.	232,500			162,315	358,675	9,346
Net4Music Inc.						**FISCAL YEAR 1999**
John W. Paulson Chairman and CEO	148,100	22,215				
Mark E. Dunn SVP-Product Development	115,900	20,862				
Barbara Sima Remley CFO, Secretary, and Treasurer	105,000	18,000				
Glenna A. Dibrell VP-Marketing/Sales	105,000	18,000				
Net Perceptions Inc.						**FISCAL YEAR 1999**
Steven J. Snyder President and CEO	150,000	40,000				
Nanci Andersen VP-Customer Solutions	130,000	21,850		210,680	533,904	
Thomas M. Donnelly CFO and Secretary	125,000	40,000		269,638	683,318	

* Compensation for partial year only

	Salary ($)	Bonus ($)	Restricted Stock ($)	Options @5% ($)	Options @10% ($)	Other ($)
NetRadio Corporation						**FISCAL YEAR 1999**
Michael P. Wise * VP, CFO, and Secretary	98,558	29,400		69,000	152,500	
Norstan Inc.						**FISCAL YEAR 2000**
Paul Baszucki Chairman	363,262		50,000	360,534	913,662	13,941
Peter E. Stilson EVP-Communication Solutions	174,615		10,000	252,112	638,901	5,635
Roger D. Van Beusekom EVP-Financial Services	156,869	49,549	10,000	144,194	365,415	6,387
Michael E. Laughlin * EVP-Communication Services	154,519		10,000	216,139	547,739	5,549
Michael J. Theisen * EVP-Convergent Services	144,711	17,980	10,000	144,194	365,415	5,952
Nortech Systems Inc.						**FISCAL YEAR 1999**
Quentin E. Finkelson Chairman, President, and CEO	150,320					
Gregory D. Tweed EVP and COO	127,722					
Garry M. Anderly SVP-Finance, Treasurer	105,248					
Northern Technologies International Corporation						**FISCAL YEAR 1999**
Donald A. Kubik VP and Chief Technology Officer	200,000					4,667
Constance M. Fason VP-Domestic Marketing/Sales	108,000					2,520
Northwest Airlines Corporation						**FISCAL YEAR 1999**
John H. Dasburg President and CEO	500,000	1,049,750	2,002,500			98,461
Richard H. Anderson EVP and COO	432,599	285,391		2,302,076		79,483
Douglas M. Steenland EVP and Chief Corporate Officer	432,599	285,390		2,302,076		53,784
Mickey P. Foret EVP-Finance, CFO, Pres.-Northwest Cargo	400,000	253,680				180,733
J. Timothy Griffin EVP-Marketing/Distribution	371,390	237,825		993,302		5,016
NorthWestern Corporation						**FISCAL YEAR 1999**
Merle D. Lewis Chairman and CEO	627,167	783,733		2,203,456	5,561,869	125,357
Richard R. Hylland President and COO	416,542	666,211		1,120,635	2,828,658	54,038
Daniel K. Newell SVP-Finance and CFO	278,917	561,532		557,479	1,407,164	16,524
Walter A. (Trey) Bradley III VP and Chief Information Officer	249,875	120,396		323,143	815,664	16,127
Michael J. Hanson Pres./CEO-Northwestern Public Service	245,583	293,117		95,439	240,903	11,107

* Compensation for partial year only

SALARY INDEX

	Salary ($)	Bonus ($)	Restricted Stock ($)	Options @5% ($)	Options @10% ($)	Other ($)
Oakridge Holdings Inc.						**FISCAL YEAR 2000**
Robert C. Harvey Chairman and CEO	112,500	10,000				4,248
Robert B. Gregor VP and Secretary	91,350					420
Marie Leshyn CEO-Cemetery	84,140	42,377				9,200
OneLink Communications Inc.						**FISCAL YEAR 1999**
Paul F. Lidsky President and CEO	175,000	87,500				7,678
Kirk C. Danzl Chief Technology Officer	97,667	50,000				572
Gregory H. Mohn VP-Business Development	96,667	50,000				545
Ontrack Data International Inc.						**FISCAL YEAR 1999**
Gary S. Stevens SVP-Engineering	212,000	16,000				4,200
Michael W. Rogers Chairman and CEO	201,000	95,000				4,200
Thomas P. Skiba VP and CFO	143,000	63,000		53,110	134,592	3,700
John M. Bujan VP, General Counsel, and Secretary	142,000	72,000		70,814	179,455	3,700
Optical Sensors Inc.						**FISCAL YEAR 1999**
Paulita M. LaPlante President and CEO	186,923					
Victor Kimball VP-Strategic Planning/Product Devel.	125,767					
Wesley G. Peterson VP-Finance, CFO, and Secretary	104,980					
Orphan Medical Inc.						**FISCAL YEAR 1999**
William Houghton COO	200,000			124,521	315,561	2,260
John Howell Bullion Chairman and CEO	175,000	1,875				264
Dayton T. Reardan VP-Regulatory Affairs	146,667			24,212	61,359	155
Patti A. Engel VP-Marketing/Sales	111,344	45,704		78,492	198,915	118
Timothy McGrath * CFO	33,750	68,943		178,048	451,208	15
Osmonics Inc.						**FISCAL YEAR 1999**
D. Dean Spatz Chairman and CEO	290,000			17,360		9,866
Edward J. Fierko President and COO	150,000			83,378		78,074
Roger S. Miller SVP-Corporate Sales/Marketing	130,000			41,689		7,949

* Compensation for partial year only

	Salary ($)	Bonus ($)	Restricted Stock ($)	Options @5% ($)	Options @10% ($)	Other ($)
Otter Tail Power Company						**FISCAL YEAR 1999**
John C. MacFarlane Chairman, President, and CEO	337,389	51,511		145,080		13,093
Douglas L. Kjellerup VP and COO-Energy Delivery	157,629	78,939		44,640		8,207
Ward L. Uggerud VP, COO-Energy Supply	151,629	46,105		44,640		5,931
John D. Erickson EVP, CEO and Treas.	135,963	26,131		44,640		7,175
Rodney C.H. Scheel VP-Delivery Systems	108,681	22,694		16,740		5,877
PPT Vision Inc.						**FISCAL YEAR 1999**
Joseph C. Christenson President and CEO	156,000			31,550	73,526	2,000
Arye Malek VP-Marketing	116,865			15,775	36,763	2,000
Thomas R. Northenscold Gen. Mgr.-Vision Systems Division	115,667			23,663	55,144	2,000
Larry G. Paulson Chief Technology Officer	100,565			15,775	36,763	2,000
PW Eagle Inc.						**FISCAL YEAR 1999**
William H. Spell CEO	145,700	280,000	70,000	22,011	55,780	7,404
James K. Rash * President	68,368	86,576	103,313	162,432	411,633	11,871
Larry I. Fleming * SVP	53,172	46,207	105,000	148,576	376,522	10,845
Paper Warehouse Inc.						**FISCAL YEAR 2000**
Yale T. Dolginow Chairman, President, and CEO	285,000					27,405
Cheryl W. Newell VP and CFO	139,000					1,342
Steven R. Anderson VP and Chief Information Officer	135,000					53
Steven P. Durst VP-Merchandising	114,400					1,023
Patterson Dental Company						**FISCAL YEAR 2000**
Peter L. Frechette Chairman, President, and CEO	332,784	259,586				1,600
James W. Wiltz VP, Pres.-Patterson Dental Supply, Inc.	202,800	121,680				1,600
R. Stephen Armstrong * EVP, CFO, and Treasurer	166,666	99,231		540,219	1,369,022	
R. Reed Saunders Pres.-Colwell Systems	162,240	36,910	3,164			12,083
Gary D. Johnson VP-Sales	162,240	77,875				14,727
Pemstar Inc.						**FISCAL YEAR 2000**
Steve V. Petracca EVP-Business Development	182,948			660,339	1,673,429	5,192

* Compensation for partial year only

	Salary ($)	Bonus ($)	Restricted Stock ($)	Options @5% ($)	Options @10% ($)	Other ($)
Allen J. Berning Chairman and CEO	156,346			679,206	1,721,242	4,656
William B. Leary EVP-Rochester Site Operations	126,154			424,504	1,075,776	2,360
Hargopal (Paul) Singh EVP-International Operations	126,154			424,504	1,075,776	2,360
David L. Sippel EVP-Engineering Services and CTO	126,154			424,504	1,075,776	2,390
Pentair Inc.						**FISCAL YEAR 1999**
Winslow H. Buxton Chairman	718,000	174,546		2,217,876	5,620,532	557,487
Joseph R. Collins Vice Chairman	400,000	400,000	45,898	996,798	2,526,082	159,574
Randall J. Hogan President and CEO	312,500	312,500	21,313	622,999	1,578,801	12,658
Richard J. Cathcart EVP, Pres.-Water/Fluid Technologies	310,000	296,608	24,211	622,999	1,578,801	161,051
Photo Control Corporation						**FISCAL YEAR 1999**
John R. (Jack) Helmen President and CEO	120,000	23,000				
Curtis R. Jackels VP-Finance	97,000	16,000				28,357
PLATO Learning Inc.						**FISCAL YEAR 1999**
William R. Roach Chairman and CEO	225,000			615,723	980,435	12,480
John Murray President, COO, and acting CFO	175,000	100,000		307,862	490,218	
G. Thomas Ahern SVP-PLATO Education Sales/Marketing	140,000	48,733		241,891	385,171	
Wellesley R. (Rob) Foshay VP-Instructional Dsgn./Cognitive Lrng.	140,000			153,930	245,111	
David H. LePage VP-PLATO Support Services/Distribution	130,000			179,588	285,963	
Polaris Industries Inc.						**FISCAL YEAR 1999**
Thomas C. Tiller President and CEO	418,273	836,545	789,063	992,474	2,515,125	15,769
W. Hall Wendel Jr. Chairman	240,000	240,000	290,375	396,990	1,006,050	25,875
Jeffrey A. Bjorkman VP-Operations	148,654	150,000	78,906	107,187	271,633	15,789
Michael W. Malone VP-Finance, CFO, and Secretary	140,000	125,000	51,131	69,473	176,059	13,981
Possis Medical Inc.						**FISCAL YEAR 1999**
Robert G. Dutcher President and CEO	167,250	88,000		109,673	277,933	6,398
T.V. Rao VP and Gen. Mgr.-AngioJet	140,462	47,300		91,394	231,611	
Irving R. Colacci VP-Legal/Human Res., Gen. Counsel, Sec.	104,904	36,900		73,115	185,288	3,747
James D. Gustafson VP-Quality Systems, Reg./Clin. Affairs	102,482	36,700		73,115	185,288	3,674

* Compensation for partial year only

SALARY INDEX

	Salary ($)	Bonus ($)	Restricted Stock ($)	Options @5% ($)	Options @10% ($)	Other ($)
Printware Inc. — FISCAL YEAR 1999						
Daniel A. Baker President and CEO	143,000			143,467	363,572	982
Thomas W. Petschauer EVP and CFO	116,018			58,959	149,413	870
Timothy S. Murphy VP-Marketing/Sales	107,630			27,514	69,726	759
RDO Equipment Company — FISCAL YEAR 2000						
Thomas K. Espel CFO	190,000	40,000				
Larry E. Scott SVP-Southwest Construction Equipment	160,000	47,334				
Paul T. Horn Office of the Chairman and President	150,000					
Kenneth J. Horner Jr. EVP-Construction Equipment Division	147,308	60,000				
Jack Summerville* SVP-South Central Construction Equipment	106,731	115,500		109,270	276,913	
RSI Systems Inc. — FISCAL YEAR 1999						
Marti D. Miller VP-Engineering	129,969					
James D. Hanzlik CFO	102,625					4,800
RTW Inc. — FISCAL YEAR 1999						
Carl B. Lehmann Chairman, President, and CEO	416,000			283,003	717,184	56,789
Jeffrey B. Murphy CFO, Secretary, and Treasurer	250,000	100,000				2,400
Anthony J. Rotondi COO	200,000	20,000				2,400
Raven Industries Inc. — FISCAL YEAR 2000						
Ronald M. Moquist President and CEO	175,300			19,685	43,499	25,126
Gary L. Conradi VP-Administrative Services	105,600	6,336		11,811	26,099	31,370
Thomas Iacarella VP-Finance, Secretary/Treasurer	105,000	7,476		11,811	26,099	23,203
Regis Corporation — FISCAL YEAR 2000						
Myron D. Kunin Chairman	636,721			311,302	788,902	29,289
Paul D. Finkelstein President and CEO	520,000	208,000		3,687,806	9,345,625	80,221
Christopher A. Fox EVP-Real Estate	270,500	108,200		633,793	1,606,157	37,443
Mary F. Andert EVP-Merchandising/Marketing	250,000	100,000		1,157,480	2,933,282	36,500
Gordon B. Nelson SVP-Fashion/Education	250,000	100,000		633,793	1,606,157	25,500

* Compensation for partial year only

	Salary ($)	Bonus ($)	Restricted Stock ($)	Options @5% ($)	Options @10% ($)	Other ($)
Rehabilicare Inc.						**FISCAL YEAR 2000**
David B. Kaysen President and CEO	300,357			29,010	64,104	9,496
W. Glen Winchell VP-Finance and CFO	162,462			19,340	42,736	3,354
William J. Sweeney VP-Sales/Marketing	147,846			14,505	32,052	3,015
Wayne K. Chrystal VP-Operations	114,231			9,670	21,368	1,725
Research Inc.						**FISCAL YEAR 1999**
Claude C. Johnson President and CEO	158,941	40,500		25,176	55,633	8,226
Bruce E. Bailey VP-Drying Division	107,065	55,863		14,919	32,968	5,758
David G. Brady VP-Assembly Automation Division	106,331	6,813		14,919	32,968	6,188
Retek Inc.						**FISCAL YEAR 1999**
John Buchanan Chairman and CEO	250,000	106,250		4,222,084	10,699,590	
Gordon Masson President	200,000	66,700		2,959,421	7,499,753	
John L. Goedert SVP-Research/Development	190,000	81,288		2,773,268	7,028,006	
David A.J. Bagley VP-Product Strategy/Marketing	170,000	49,610		1,689,682	4,281,987	
Victor Holysh VP-Services	150,000	35,683		1,217,029	3,084,191	
Rimage Corporation						**FISCAL YEAR 1999**
Bernard P. Aldrich President and CEO	206,000	100,700		94,334	239,061	17,500
David J. Suden Chief Technology Officer	186,000	100,630		94,334	239,061	17,250
Kenneth J. Klinck VP-Sales/Marketing	165,020	35,574		47,167	119,531	3,773
C.H. Robinson Worldwide Inc.						**FISCAL YEAR 1999**
Daryl R. (Sid) Verdoorn Chairman and CEO	182,786	345,000		237,604	602,136	8,800
Barry W. Butzow SVP	102,399	345,000		316,806	802,848	8,800
Gregory D. Goven SVP	101,500	335,000		316,806	802,848	13,600
John P. Wiehoff President	91,500	215,000		316,806	802,848	13,600
Joseph J. Mulvehill VP-International	89,514	210,000		126,722	321,139	13,600
Rochester Medical Corporation						**FISCAL YEAR 1999**
Anthony J. Conway Chairman, President, and CEO	134,750	40,132		102,824	260,577	
Brian J. Wierzbinski EVP, CFO, and Treasurer	124,385	37,012		68,550	173,718	

* Compensation for partial year only

	Salary ($)	Bonus ($)	Restricted Stock ($)	Options @5% ($)	Options @10% ($)	Other ($)
Philip J. Conway VP-Operations	108,837	24,488		68,550	173,718	
Richard D. Fryar VP-Research/Developement	108,837	24,488		68,550	173,718	
The Rottlund Company Inc.						**FISCAL YEAR 2000**
David H. Rotter President	250,000	129,522				
Bernard J. Rotter VP	250,000	129,522				
Todd M. Stutz EVP	140,000	262,610				
John J. Dierbeck III EVP	117,500	55,509				
Rural Cellular Corporation						**FISCAL YEAR 1999**
Richard P. Ekstrand President and CEO	362,000	274,938		165,085	418,357	5,000
Wesley E. Schultz EVP and CFO	254,000	162,398		82,542	209,179	5,000
Ann K. Newhall * EVP and COO	224,100	151,050		688,514	1,744,829	4,412
Scott G. Donlea VP-Market Development	144,000	56,033				3,778
David J. DelZoppo VP-Finance/Accounting	105,000	39,223				2,063
SAC Technologies Inc.						**FISCAL YEAR 1999**
Barry M. Wendt Chairman and CEO	128,440					4,873
Benedict A. Wittig Secretary and Dir.-Systems Software	107,147					5,299
Gary E. Wendt CFO	100,274					5,299
St. Jude Medical Inc.						**FISCAL YEAR 1999**
Ronald A. Matricaria Chairman	500,481	513,172				106,68
Terry L. Shepard President and CEO	418,019	384,832		4,770,200		47,849
Daniel J. Starks Pres.-CRMD	346,875	201,621		486,923		30,964
John C. Heinmiller VP-Finance, CFO	247,404	129,887		378,718		30,945
Kevin T. O'Malley VP and General Counsel	221,692	116,388		378,718		51,625
Robert Cohen VP-Business/Technology Development	215,000	90,300		378,718		4,010
The St. Paul Companies Inc.						**FISCAL YEAR 1999**
Douglas W. Leatherdale Chairman and CEO	940,385	2,287,500	935,812	1,231,155		88,770
Paul J. Liska EVP and CFO	640,385	791,250		656,616		59,231
James F. Duffy Chm./CEO-St. Paul Re	438,462	250,000	37,342	328,308		235,085

* Compensation for partial year only

	Salary ($)	Bonus ($)	Restricted Stock ($)	Options @5% ($)	Options @10% ($)	Other ($)
Steven W. Lilienthal Pres.-U.S. Operations	382,693	300,000	482,812	328,308		111,246
Select Comfort Corporation						**FISCAL YEAR 1999**
Ronald E. Mayle SVP-Retail	202,615			524,722	1,330,071	13,077
Gregory T. Kliner SVP-Operations	183,197			120,122	304,498	2,139
James C. Raabe CFO	141,520			263,621	668,340	2,139
James D. Gaboury VP-Direct Sales	134,003	12,500		125,776	319,076	2,139
Patrick A. Hopf Chairman				185,115	469,445	
Semitool Inc.						**FISCAL YEAR 1999**
Timothy C. Dodkin SVP, Managing Dir.-Semitool Europe	310,000					10,188
Fabio Gualandris President and CEO	265,008	60,000		41,271	104,589	
William A. Freeman SVP-Finance and CFO	180,007	40,000		41,271	104,589	5,000
Gregory L. Perkins VP-Operations	160,006					5,000
Raymon F. Thompson Chairman	150,006					4,971
Sheldahl Inc.						**FISCAL YEAR 1999**
Edward L. Lundstrom President and CEO	200,176			241,731	612,595	3,687
James Havener VP-Micro Products Business Unit	175,001					3,500
Gregory D. Closser VP-Materials/Flexible Interconnect	137,345					2,581
ShowCase Corporation						**FISCAL YEAR 2000**
Kenneth H. Holec President and CEO	228,000	48,500				6,029
Patrick Dauga EVP-Worldwide Field Operations	183,067	59,377				45,262
Jonathan P. Otterstatter EVP-Technology	156,250	16,500				7,632
Kevin R. Potrzeba VP-Sales	145,000	58,512				8,919
Theresa Z. O'Neil * VP-Marketing	66,667	2,133		243,697	617,575	2,053
SpectraSCIENCE Inc.						**FISCAL YEAR 1999**
Chester E. Sievert Jr. Chairman, President, and CEO	135,000	44,000		258,045	653,937	11,300
The Sportsman's Guide Inc.						**FISCAL YEAR 1999**
Gary Olen Chairman	270,931			165,777	420,111	
Gregory R. Binkley Pres., CEO, Pres./CEO-GuideOutdoors.com	185,947			41,444	105,028	

* Compensation for partial year only

	Salary ($)	Bonus ($)	Restricted Stock ($)	Options @5% ($)	Options @10% ($)	Other ($)
Charles B. Lingen SVP-Finance, CFO, and Treasurer	141,795			31,083	78,771	
John M. Casler SVP	138,114			31,083	78,771	
Barry W. Benecke SVP-Creative Services	131,726			29,011	73,519	
Stockwalk.com Group Inc.						**FISCAL YEAR 2000**
Eldon C. Miller Chairman and CEO	300,000	206,960		32,182	69,206	18,362
David B. Johnson EVP	300,000	848,347		59,894	128,800	10,023
Paul R. Kuehn President	150,000	283,689		28,606	61,516	7,362
Stanley D. Rahm SVP	150,000	188,625		17,879	38,448	17,157
Robert J. Vosburgh * CEO-Online Brokerage Solutions	108,333	99,593		671,961	1,559,242	
Stratasys Inc.						**FISCAL YEAR 1999**
S. Scott Crump Chairman and CEO	136,500	25,000		7,880	31,900	
Thomas W. Stenoien CFO and Secretary	94,431	32,500		5,280	13,680	
Supervalu Inc.						**FISCAL YEAR 2000**
Michael W. Wright Chairman and CEO	931,505	1,583,559	801,279			116,943
Jeffrey Noddle Pres./COO, interim Pres./COO-Retail Food	489,955	489,955	320,334	780,615	1,978,233	8,578
David L. Boehnen EVP	361,971	361,971	217,961	650,513	1,648,527	14,244
Pamela K. Knous EVP and CFO	350,000	350,000	173,876	650,513	1,648,527	2,305
Surgidyne Inc.						**FISCAL YEAR 1999**
Charles B. McNeil EVP and Treasurer	43,284					4,800
TCF Financial Corporation						**FISCAL YEAR 1999**
William A. Cooper Chairman and CEO	700,000	1,050,000				85,818
Thomas A. Cusick Vice Chairman and COO	360,000	540,000				26,586
Lynn A. Nagorske President	304,000	456,000				17,855
Gregory J. Pulles Vice Chairman, Gen. Counsel, Secretary	264,000	396,000				16,899
Target Corporation						**FISCAL YEAR 2000**
Robert J. Ulrich Chairman and CEO, Chm./CEO-Target Stores	1,027,874	3,500,000				5,272,328
Gregg W. Steinhafel Pres.-Target Stores	726,375	1,205,143		4,402,276	11,156,232	1,905,727

* Compensation for partial year only

SALARY INDEX

	Salary ($)	Bonus ($)	Restricted Stock ($)	Options @5% ($)	Options @10% ($)	Other ($)
Techne Corporation — FISCAL YEAR 2000						
Thomas E. Oland Chairman, President, CEO, and Treasurer	210,000					20,141
Monica Tsang, Ph.D. VP-Research	180,000	36,000		13,429	31,296	
Thomas C. Detwiler VP-Scientific/Regulatory Affairs	165,000	33,000		11,394	26,553	20,141
Timothy M. Heaney VP, Secretary, General Counsel	117,123	35,000		646,272	1,506,088	
Marcel Veronneau VP-Hematology Operations	110,000	22,000		7,737	18,031	15,732
Tennant Company — FISCAL YEAR 1999						
Janet M. Dolan President and CEO	327,500	38,415	35,000	2,011,622	5,079,300	203,557
James H. Moar COO	268,763	13,939	27,520	545,118	1,381,437	9,072
Thomas J. Vander Bie SVP-N.A. Commercial Sales	210,964	86,664	21,120	195,876	489,983	86,079
Keith D. Payden VP and Chief Information Officer	191,330	44,667	19,120	203,700	509,460	144,657
John T. Pain III VP and Treasurer	178,200	7,770	17,840	239,527	607,009	23,325
The Toro Company — FISCAL YEAR 1999						
Kendrick B. Melrose Chairman and CEO	597,503	1,190,530	167,845	414,190		478,974
J. David McIntosh EVP-Professional Business/International	302,500	427,981		136,640		129,887
Stephen P. Wolfe VP-Finance, Treasurer, and CFO	237,333	340,933	50,009	112,728		99,848
Karen M. Meyer VP-Administration	227,670	327,852	47,946	108,458		97,057
J. Lawrence McIntyre VP, Secretary, and General Counsel	211,227	291,744	44,497	91,378		78,927
Touch America Inc. — FISCAL YEAR 1999						
Robert P. Gannon Chairman, President, and CEO	408,600	263,671		1,499,589		141,054
Jerrold P. Pederson Vice Chairman and CFO	200,022	112,915		1,000,048		66,400
Richard F. Cromer EVP and COO-Energy Supply	198,288	117,187		314,538		123,888
John D. Haffey EVP and COO-Energy Services Division	195,190	115,356		314,538		109,400
Michael J. Meldahl EVP and COO-Technology	194,616	177,165	438,750	908,871		27,585
Tower Automotive Inc. — FISCAL YEAR 1999						
Dugald K. Campbell President and CEO	531,690	248,400		1,392,215	3,528,147	18,783
Anthony A. Barone VP and CFO	254,443	137,500		605,311	1,533,977	17,117
Tom G. Pitser VP	247,482	96,000		484,249	1,227,182	17,040

* Compensation for partial year only

	Salary ($)	Bonus ($)	Restricted Stock ($)	Options @5% ($)	Options @10% ($)	Other ($)
Jim Arnold VP	210,319			181,593	460,193	9,598
Transport Corporation of America Inc.						**FISCAL YEAR 1999**
Robert J. Meyers President, CEO, COO, and CIO	254,167	50,000				1,600
Larry E. Johnson VP-Marketing	109,808			6,285	13,889	1,600
Keith R. Klein * CFO	75,766	20,000		77,704	171,706	
Tricord Systems Inc.						**FISCAL YEAR 1999**
John J. Mitcham Chairman and Co-CEO	240,000					4,500
Alexander H. Frey SVP and Chief Technical Officer	160,000					1,000
Charles E. (Ed) Pearsall VP-Engineering	150,000					1,000
U.S. Bancorp						**FISCAL YEAR 1999**
John F. (Jack) Grundhofer Chairman, President, and CEO	895,003	750,000		35,484,400	89,930,800	239,442
Gary T. Duim Vice Chairman	450,015	325,000		3,034,850	7,691,450	31,529
Richard A. Zona Vice Chairman	450,015	325,000		3,501,750	8,874,750	40,202
Andrew S. Duff VChair-Wealth Mgmt.; Pres.-Piper Jaffray	202,500	1,645,000		6,069,700	15,382,900	49,772
United Financial Corporation						**FISCAL YEAR 1999**
Kevin P. Clark SVP and Secretary	105,000	35,000				8,400
Steve L. Feurt SVP and Chief Credit Officer	89,250	29,750				6,000
UnitedHealth Group						**FISCAL YEAR 1999**
William W. McGuire Chairman and CEO	1,588,461	2,978,365		53,412,807	135,358,539	205,342
Stephen J. Hemsley President and COO	747,116	1,167,368		25,907,314	65,654,221	43,232
Jeannine M. Rivet CEO-United HealthCare	442,831	442,831		2,518,696	6,382,869	21,008
R. Channing Wheeler CEO-Uniprise	420,192	475,000		3,501,525	8,873,552	12,100
Arnold H. Kaplan CFO	405,715	400,000		2,271,096	5,755,402	26,311
United Shipping & Technology Inc.						**FISCAL YEAR 2000**
Peter C. Lytle Chairman and CEO	215,929	105,000				
Timothy G. Becker CFO	215,929	175,000				
Urologix Inc.						**FISCAL YEAR 2000**
Michael M. Selzer Jr. President and CEO	217,692	73,773		70,184	177,861	

* Compensation for partial year only

	Salary ($)	Bonus ($)	Restricted Stock ($)	Options @5% ($)	Options @10% ($)	Other ($)
Ronald A. Blasewitz * SVP and COO	130,769	19,362		490,538	1,243,119	
David J. Talen * VP-Urologix International	121,090	33,444		72,022	174,845	7,277
Christopher R. Geyen VP and CFO	114,230	22,132		154,507	311,005	
Uroplasty Inc.						**FISCAL YEAR 2000**
Daniel G. Holman President and CEO	179,945	17,255				23,294
Susan Hartjes-Doherty VP-Operations/Regulatory Affairs, Sec.	123,745	11,275				
The Valspar Corporation						**FISCAL YEAR 1999**
Richard M. Rompala Chairman, President, and CEO	586,923		873,342	1,210,550	3,067,900	75,031
Rolf Engh SVP, General Counsel, and Secretary	262,500	103,766	102,218	385,175	976,150	35,060
Paul C. Reyelts SVP and CFO	262,500		304,500	385,175	976,150	33,408
William L. Mansfield SVP-Packaging/Industrial Coatings	254,654		323,410	385,175	976,150	31,493
Steven L. Erdahl SVP-Operations	244,308		302,942	385,175	976,150	30,808
ValueVision International Inc.						**FISCAL YEAR 2000**
Gene McCaffery Chairman and CEO	541,667	678,000		2,550,954	6,464,618	
Steve Jackel Pres.-ValueVision, TV Home Shopping	197,115	44,231		1,617,588	3,769,668	
Vascular Solutions Inc.						**FISCAL YEAR 1999**
Howard Root CEO	140,000	28,000		754,674	1,912,491	2,046
Michael Nagel VP-Sales/Marketing	130,000	25,000		183,166	464,178	7,697
Charmaine Sutton VP-Regulatory Affairs	110,000	20,000		58,173	147,422	250
James Quackenbush * VP-Manufacturing	88,000	20,000		99,051	251,015	3,760
Venturian Corporation						**FISCAL YEAR 1999**
Gary B. Rappaport Chairman and CEO	125,000					4,856
Charles B. Langevin Pres.-Napco International	125,000					2,500
Don M. House Jr. President and COO	120,000	50,000				
Verdant Brands Inc.						**FISCAL YEAR 1999**
Scott A. Glatstein VP and Gen. Mgr.-Retail Brands Division	150,000					4,800
Volker G. Oakey EVP and Chief Technology Officer	125,825					
Steve Hartmeier VP-Commercial Products Division	114,800					

* Compensation for partial year only

	Salary ($)	Bonus ($)	Restricted Stock ($)	Options @5% ($)	Options @10% ($)	Other ($)
Vicom Inc.						**FISCAL YEAR 1999**
James L. Mandel CEO	133,117					
Steven M. Bell President	108,392					
Video Update Inc.						**FISCAL YEAR 2000**
Daniel A. Potter Chairman and CEO	360,000	138,546		84,888	215,136	28,820
John M. Bedard President	240,000	159,186		47,160	119,520	21,032
Michael P. Gebauer * CFO	134,333	130,776		42,444	107,568	10,504
Daniel C. Howard COO	128,400			42,444	107,568	12,252
Michael G. Schifsky SVP	116,167			5,659	14,342	15,020
VirtualFund.com Inc.						**FISCAL YEAR 1999**
Melvin L. Masters Chairman, President, and CEO	175,000					9,494
Robert J. Wenzel COO	175,000					
Danny J. Vatland Chief Technical Officer	175,000					
Stephen Fisher Senior Strategist-B2BXchange Inc.	150,000	155,750		129,988	608,156	
Timothy N. Thurn Treasurer	100,000			117,919	298,819	
Vital Images Inc.						**FISCAL YEAR 1999**
Douglas M. Pihl Chairman	120,000					
Vincent J. Argiro Chief Technology Officer and Founder	120,000	26,766		79,377	190,122	6,265
Gregory S. Furness VP-Finance, CFO, Treasurer, Secretary	120,000	26,766		79,377	190,122	
Jay D. Miller VP-Business Development and Gen. Mgr.	120,000	26,766		79,377	190,122	
Steven P. Canakes VP-Sales	120,000	26,766		79,377	190,122	
Albert Emola * President and CEO				467,757	1,120,360	
WSI Industries Inc.						**FISCAL YEAR 1999**
Michael J. Pudil President and CEO	194,602			69,200	175,300	2,292
Waters Instruments Inc.						**FISCAL YEAR 2000**
Jerry W. Grabowski President and CEO	177,150	80,791				4,719
Gregg J. Anshus CFO and Treasurer	86,615	15,508				1,894

* Compensation for partial year only

SAL

	Salary ($)	Bonus ($)	Restricted Stock ($)	Options @5% ($)	Options @10% ($)	Other ($)
Wells Financial Corporation						**FISCAL YEAR 1999**
Lawrence H. Kruse President and CEO	111,909	1,824				36,641
Wilsons The Leather Experts						**FISCAL YEAR 2000**
Joel N. Waller Chairman and CEO	410,461	340,000				20,806
David L. Rogers President and COO	410,461	340,000				19,516
John Fowler SVP and General Merchandise Mgr.	300,000	180,000		388,980		105,007
John Serino EVP-Store Sales	262,692	159,000				17,693
Lisa Stanley VP-Marketing	250,000	130,000				13,789
Winland Electronics Inc.						**FISCAL YEAR 1999**
W. Kirk Hankins Chairman and CEO	142,000	15,787				3,333
Lorin E. Krueger President and COO	120,000	15,787				3,333
Winter Sports Inc.						**FISCAL YEAR 2000**
Michael J. Collins President and CEO	105,309					
Xcel Energy Inc.						**FISCAL YEAR 1999**
James J. Howard III Chairman	730,000	233,346	335,800	2,433,187	6,166,174	51,250
Wayne Brunetti President and CEO	590,000	228,802		564,980		41,984
Edward J. McIntyre VP and CFO	375,000	92,200	101,250	707,501	1,792,946	10,646
Paul E. Anders Jr. VP and Chief Information Officer	296,000	231,100	79,920	465,390	1,179,390	9,730
Gary R. Johnson VP and General Counsel	260,000	71,300	70,200	408,780	1,035,929	11,951
Zamba Corporation						**FISCAL YEAR 1999**
Paul D. Edelhertz Chairman	229,327	1,000				72
Todd X. Fitzwater VP	228,375	1,000				72
Peter D. Marton * EVP and COO	178,125	1,000		817,563	2,071,865	60
Michael H. Carrel VP and CFO	152,885	42,500				2,390
Zomax Inc.						**FISCAL YEAR 1999**
James T. Anderson Chairman and CEO	400,000	2,677,416				
Michelle S. Bedard EVP-Sales/Marketing	300,000	719,354				
Anthony Angelini President and COO	225,000	809,273				
James E. Flaherty CFO and Secretary	175,000	367,206				

* Compensation for partial year only

GEOGRAPHIC
(ZIP CODE)
INDEX

THIS SECTION IS A GEOGRAPHIC INDEX OF COMPANIES PROFILED

Primary sort is by zip code

Within each zip code, companies are listed alphabetically

A page reference is included to locate the company's profile

Michigan

Wisconsin

Minnesota

GEOGRAPHIC INDEX

GEOGRAPHIC INDEX

GEOGRAPHIC INDEX

GEO

GEO

584	North Country Health Services	Bemidji	56601
535	Thorson Inc.	Bemidji	56601
533	TEAM Industries Inc.Industries Inc.	Bagley	56621
676	Solvay Pharmaceuticals Inc.	Baudette	56623
424	Anderson Fabrics Inc.	Blackduck	56630
508	Palace Bingo-Casino-Hotel	Cass Lake	56633
515	Rajala Cos.	Deer River	56636
618	Boise Cascade Corp.	International Falls	56649
578	International Falls Memorial Hospital	International Falls	56649
540	Valley Forest Resources Inc.	Marcell	56657
515	Red Lake Gaming Enterprises Inc.	Red Lake	56671
661	Northwood Panelboard Co.	Solway	56678
136	Arctic Cat Inc.	Thief River Falls	56701
470	Hydra Mac International	Thief River Falls	56701
472	Independent Machine Service Minnesota	Thief River Falls	56701
504	Northern Pride Inc.	Thief River Falls	56701
584	Northwest Medical Center	Thief River Falls	56701
585	Occupational Development Center Inc.	Thief River Falls	56701
517	River Road Casino and Bingo	Thief River Falls	56701
446	Dahlgren & Co. Inc.	Crookston	56716
449	Dee Inc.	Crookston	56716
589	Riverview Healthcare Association	Crookston	56716
469	Homark Co. Inc., The	Red Lake Falls	56750
503	Nordic Fiberglass Inc.	Warren	56762
489	Marvin Lumber & Cedar Co.	Warroad	56763
524	Seven Clans	Warroad	56763
511	Polman Transfer Inc.	Wadena	56842

South Dakota

421	Alkota Cleaning Systems Inc.	Alcester	57001
627	Custom Coils Inc.	Alcester	57001
487	Luverne Truck Equipment Inc.	Brandon	57005
507	Pace Manufacturing Inc.	Brandon	57005
621	Campus Card—ICollege	Brookings	57006
447	Dakota, Minnesota & Eastern Railroad	Brookings	57006
173	Daktronics Inc.	Brookings	57006
457	Falcon Plastics Inc.	Brookings	57006
481	Larson Manufacturing Co. Inc.	Brookings	57006
617	Behr Inc.	Canton	57013
525	Sioux Valley Southwestern Electric Co.	Colman	57017
532	T&R Electric Supply Co. Inc.	Colman	57017
418	Aaladin Industries Inc.	Elk Point	57025
652	Load King Division	Elk Point	57025
453	East River Electric Power Cooperative	Madison	57042
639	Gehl Co.	Madison	57042
519	Rosco Manufacturing Co.	Madison	57042
544	Wenk Foods Inc.	Madison	57042
639	Gateway Inc.	North Sioux City	57049
470	IBP Inc.	Dakota Dunes	57049
635	Feterl Mfg. Co.	Salem	57058
621	CR Chicago	Springfield	57062
611	Alcoa Extrusions	Yankton	57078
616	Baldwin Filters	Yankton	57078
439	Cimpls Inc.	Yankton	57078
650	Kolberg-Pioneer Inc.	Yankton	57078
652	M-tron Industries Inc.	Yankton	57078
500	Morgen Manufacturing Co.	Yankton	57078
525	Shur-Co	Yankton	57078
548	Yankton Area Adjustment Training	Yankton	57078
446	Dakota Industries Inc.	Sioux Falls	57101
631	Earthgrains Taystee Bread	Sioux Falls	57101
453	Egger Steel Co.	Sioux Falls	57101
651	Land O'Lakes Fluid Dairy Division	Sioux Falls	57101
525	Sioux Falls Construction Co.	Sioux Falls	57101
543	Warren Cos.	Sioux Falls	57101
226	HF Financial Corp.	Sioux Falls	57102
522	Schoeneman Bros. Co.	Sioux Falls	57102
426	Austad Golf Stores	Sioux Falls	57103
570	Communication Service for the Deaf	Sioux Falls	57103
519	Ronning Enterprises	Sioux Falls	57103
613	Amesbury Group	Sioux Falls	57104
620	CCL Label	Sioux Falls	57104
437	Carlson (Henry) Co.	Sioux Falls	57104
441	Component Manufacturing Co.	Sioux Falls	57104
648	Jordan Millwork Co.	Sioux Falls	57104
649	KSFY Television	Sioux Falls	57104
301	NorthWestern Corp.	Sioux Falls	57104
675	Smurfit—Stone Container	Sioux Falls	57104
677	Starmark Inc.	Sioux Falls	57104
532	Sweetman Construction Concrete Matls.	Sioux Falls	57104
682	Tyco Plastics Inc.	Sioux Falls	57104
687	Woods/Du-Al	Sioux Falls	57104
483	Lewis Drugs Inc.	Sioux Falls	57105
592	Sioux Falls Vocational Services Inc.	Sioux Falls	57105
525	Sioux Falls Shopping News Inc.	Sioux Falls	57105
527	Sonstegard Foods Co.	Sioux Falls	57105
461	Gage Brothers Concrete Products Inc.	Sioux Falls	57106
170	Credit Store Inc., The	Sioux Falls	57107
262	LodgeNet Entertainment Corp.	Sioux Falls	57107
508	Pam Oil Inc.	Sioux Falls	57107
523	Schulte (Terry) Automative Inc.	Sioux Falls	57107
523	Sencore Inc.	Sioux Falls	57107
654	McCloud USA	Irene	57108
454	Electronic Systems Inc.	Sioux Falls	57117
572	Evangelical Lutheran Good Samaritan Soc.	Sioux Falls	57117
456	Everist (L.G.) Inc.	Sioux Falls	57117

North Dakota

Montana

STANDARD INDUSTRIAL CLASSIFICATION
(SIC CODE)

AN INDEX ARRANGED BY SIC CODE

SIC codes were developed to classify establishments by type of business

SIC codes promote the uniformity and comparability of statistical data collected by federal and state agencies, trade associations, and private research organizations

SEARCH

PRODUCT GROUPS

ALPHABETICALLY WITHIN CATEGORIES

BY PAGE REFERENCE

The abbreviation *nec* at the end of some product group descriptions stands for not elsewhere classified

Codes are based on the 1987 revision of the Standard Industrial Classification Manual

MAJOR GROUP 01

Agricultural Production—Crops

MAJOR GROUP 02

Agricultural Production—Livestock and Animal Specialties

MAJOR GROUP 07

Agricultural Services

MAJOR GROUP 10

Metal Mining

MAJOR GROUP 12

Coal Mining

MAJOR GROUP 13

Oil and Gas Extraction

MAJOR GROUP 14

Mining and Quarrying of Nonmetallic Minerals, Except Fuels

MAJOR GROUP 15

Building Construction—General Contractors and Operative Builders

MAJOR GROUP 16

Heavy Construction Other Than Building Construction—Contractors

MAJOR GROUP 17

Construction—Special Trade Contractors

MAJOR GROUP 20

Food and Kindred Products

MAJOR GROUP 22

Textile Mill Products

MAJOR GROUP 23

Apparel and Other Finished Products Made From Fabrics and Similar Materials

MAJOR GROUP 24

Lumber and Wood Products, Except Furniture

MAJOR GROUP 25

Furniture and Fixtures

MAJOR GROUP 26

Paper and Allied Products

MAJOR GROUP 27

Printing, Publishing, and Allied Industries

MAJOR GROUP 28

Chemicals and Allied Products

MAJOR GROUP 29

Petroleum Refining and Related Industries

MAJOR GROUP 30

Rubber and Miscellaneous Plastics Products

MAJOR GROUP 31

Leather and Leather Products

MAJOR GROUP 32

Stone, Clay, Glass, and Concrete Products

MAJOR GROUP 33

Primary Metal Industries

MAJOR GROUP 34

Fabricated Metal Products, Except Machinery and Transportation Equipment

MAJOR GROUP 35

Industrial and Commercial Machinery and Computer Equipment

MAJOR GROUP 36

Electronic and Other Electrical Equipment and Components, Except Computer Eqt.

MAJOR GROUP 37

Transportation Equipment

MAJOR GROUP 38

Measuring, Analyzing, Controlling Instruments; Photographic, Medical, Optical

MAJOR GROUP 39

Miscellaneous Manufacturing Industries

MAJOR GROUP 40

Railroad Transportation

MAJOR GROUP 41

Local and Suburban Transit and Interurban Highway Passenger Transportation

MAJOR GROUP 42

Motor Freight Transportation and Warehousing

MAJOR GROUP 44

Water Transportation

MAJOR GROUP 45

Transportation by Air

MAJOR GROUP 46

Pipelines, Except Natural Gas

MAJOR GROUP 47

Transportation Services

MAJOR GROUP 48

Communications

MAJOR GROUP 49

Electric, Gas, and Sanitary Services

MAJOR GROUP 50

Wholesale Trade Durable Goods

MAJOR GROUP 51

Wholesale Trade—Nondurable Goods

MAJOR GROUP 52

Building Materials, Hardware, Garden Supply, and Mobile Home Dealers

MAJOR GROUP 53

General Merchandise Stores

MAJOR GROUP 54

Food Stores

MAJOR GROUP 55

Automotive Dealers and Gasoline Service Stations

MAJOR GROUP 56

Apparel and Accessory Stores

MAJOR GROUP 57

Home Furniture, Furnishings, and Equipment Stores

MAJOR GROUP 58

Eating and Drinking Places

MAJOR GROUP 59

Miscellaneous Retail

MAJOR GROUP 60

Depository Institutions

MAJOR GROUP 61

Nondepository Credit Institutions

MAJOR GROUP 62

Security and Commodity Brokers, Dealers, Exchanges, and Services

MAJOR GROUP 63

Insurance Carriers

MAJOR GROUP 64

Insurance Agents, Brokers, and Service

MAJOR GROUP 65

Real Estate

MAJOR GROUP 67

Holding and Other Investment Offices

MAJOR GROUP 70

Hotels, Rooming Houses, Camps, and Other Lodging Places

SIC

MAJOR GROUP 72

Personal Services

MAJOR GROUP 73

Business Services

MAJOR GROUP 75

Automotive Repair, Services, and Parking

MAJOR GROUP 76

Miscellaneous Repair Services

MAJOR GROUP 78

Motion Pictures

MAJOR GROUP 79

Amusement and Recreation Services

MAJOR GROUP 80

Health Services

MAJOR GROUP 81

Legal Services

MAJOR GROUP 82

Educational Services

8211 Elementary and secondary schools

8221 Colleges and universities, nec

8231 Libraries

8243 Data processing schools

8244 Business and secretarial schools

8299 Schools and educational services, nec

MAJOR GROUP 83

Social Services

8322 Individual and family social services

8331 Job training and related services

8351 Child day care services

8361 Residential care

8399 Social services, nec

MAJOR GROUP 84

Museums, Art Galleries, and Botanical and Zoological Gardens

8412 Museums and art galleries

MAJOR GROUP 86

Membership Organizations

8621 Professional organizations

8631 Labor organizations

8641 Civic and social associations

8661 Religious organizations

8699 Membership organizations, nec

MAJOR GROUP 87

Engineering, Accounting, Research, Management, and Related Services

8711 Engineering services

FACT BOOK INDEX

THIS INDEX PROVIDES AN ALPHABETICAL GUIDE

PEOPLE AND COMPANIES ARE LISTED

IN A SINGLE INDEX

ALPHABETICALLY IN WORD-BY-WORD ORDER

INITIALISMS PRECEDE WORDS

PEOPLE PRECEDE COMPANIES

REFERENCES

PUBLIC COMPANIES

PRIVATE COMPANIES

NONPROFIT COMPANIES

REGIONAL OPERATIONS

WHO'S WHO EXECUTIVES

CROSS-REFERENCES

SUBSIDIARIES, DIVISIONS, AFFILIATES

PARENT COMPANIES

ALTERNATE COMPANY NAMES

FORMER COMPANY NAMES

A page reference is included to locate the company's profile

FACT BOOK INDEX

IND

FACT BOOK INDEX

B

C

IND

D

IND

E

IND

F

G

I

J

K

L

IND

M

FACT BOOK INDEX

N

IND

P

Q

R

S

IND

U

V

W